A DICTIONARY OF
CHRISTIAN BIOGRAPHY

AND LITERATURE TO THE END OF THE SIXTH CENTURY A.D.,
WITH AN ACCOUNT OF THE PRINCIPAL SECTS AND HERESIES

EDITED BY

HENRY WACE, D.D.

AND

WILLIAM C. PIERCY, M.A.

PEABODY, MASSACHUSETTS 01961-3473

A DICTIONARY OF CHRISTIAN BIOGRAPHY

Hendrickson Publishers, Inc. edition

ISBN: 1-56563-057-2

reprinted from the edition originally titled
A Dictionary of Christian Biography and Literature,
published by John Murray, London, 1911

First Printing — January 1994

Printed in the United States of America

PREFACE

THIS volume is designed to render to a wider circle, alike of clergy and of laity, the service which, as is generally admitted, has been rendered to the learned world by *The Dictionary of Christian Biography, Literature, Sects, and Doctrines*, published under the editorship of Dr. Wace and the late Dr. Wm. Smith, about twenty years ago, in four large volumes. That work covered the whole of the first eight centuries of the Christian era, and was planned on a very comprehensive scale. It aimed at giving an account, not merely of names of importance, but of all names, however small, concerned in the Christian literature of those eight centuries ; and to illustrate its extent and minuteness, it may be enough to mention that no fewer than 596 Johns are recorded in due order in its columns. The surviving Editor may be pardoned for expressing his satisfaction that the work is now recognized, abroad as well as at home, as a valuable work of reference, being constantly quoted alike in the great Protestant *Cyclopaedia* of Herzog, in its third edition now happily complete, and in the *Patrology* of the learned Roman Catholic Professor at Munich, Dr. Bardenhewer. To the generous band of great English scholars to whose unstinted labours the chief excellences of that work are due, and too many of whom have now passed away, it is, or it would have been, a welcome satisfaction to find it described in the *Patrology* of that scholar as "very useful, relatively complete and generally reliable." *

But that work was mainly adapted to the use of men of learning, and was unsuited, both by its size and expense, and by the very wideness of its range, for the use of ordinary readers, or even for the clergy in general. In the first place, the last two centuries of the period which it covered, although of immense interest in the history of the Church, as including the origins of the Teutonic civilization of Europe, have not an equal interest with the first six as exhibiting primitive Christianity in its purer forms. With the one important exception of John of Damascus, the Fathers of the Church, so called, alike in East and West, fall within the first six centuries, and in the West the series is closed by St. Gregory the Great, who died in the year 604. English divines accordingly, since the days of Bp. Jewel, have, like Bp. Cosin, appealed to the first six centuries of the Church as exhibiting, in doctrine as well as in practice, subject to Holy Scripture, the standards of primitive Christianity. Those six centuries, consequently, have a special interest for all Christian students, and part-

* Edition of 1908, published in English at Freiburg im Breisgau, and at St. Louis, Mo., U.S.A., translated from the second German edition by Dr. T. J. Shahan, Professor of Church History in the Catholic University of America, p. 11.

icularly for those of our own Church, and deserve accordingly some special treatment. It was thought, therefore, that a Dictionary of Christian Biography which confined itself to this formative and authoritative period of the Church's history would be of special interest and service, not only to the clergy, but also to the Christian laity and to students for Holy Orders.

But the limitation of such a work to this period at once disembarrassed our pages of the mass of Teutonic, and sometimes almost pagan, names with which, after the settlement of the barbarians in Europe, we were overwhelmed; and thus of itself rendered it possible to bring the work into much narrower compass. Moreover, a mass of insignificant names, which the principles of scholarly completeness obliged us to introduce into the larger Dictionary, were not needed for the wider circle now in contemplation. They were useful and necessary for purposes of learned reference, but they cast no light on the course and meaning of Church history for ordinary readers. We have had to exercise a discretion (which may sometimes seem to have been arbitrary) in selecting, for instance, from the 596 Johns just mentioned those which were the most valuable for such readers as we had in view; and for the manner in which we have exercised that discretion we must trust ourselves to the indulgent judgment of our readers. The publisher gave us generous limits; but it seemed to him and to ourselves indispensable for the general usefulness of the Dictionary that it should be restricted to one volume; and we were thus, with respect to the minor names, obliged to omit many which, though of some interest, seemed to be such as could be best dispensed with.

By omissions of this nature we have secured an object which will, we are sure, be felt to be of inestimable value. We have been able to retain, with no material abbreviation, the admirable articles on the great characters of early Church history and literature which were contributed, with an unselfish devotion which can never be sufficiently acknowledged, by the great scholars who have been the glory of the last generation or two of English Church scholarship, and some of whom are happily still among us. To mention only some of the great contributors who have passed away, such articles as those of Bp. Westcott on Clement of Alexandria and Origen, Bp. Lightfoot on Eusebius, Archbp. Benson on St. Cyprian, Dr. Bright on St. Athanasius and kindred subjects, Dr. Salmon on varied subjects of the first importance, Bp. Stubbs on early English history, and some by the learned Professor Lipsius of Jena, have a permanent value, as the appreciations of great characters and moments of Church history and literature by scholars and divines who have never been surpassed, and will hardly be equalled again, in English sacred learning. We deemed it one of the greatest services which such a work as this could render that it should make accessible to the wide circle in question these unique masterpieces of patristic and historical study. It has therefore been one of our first objects to avoid, as far as possible, any abbreviation of the body of these articles. We have occasionally ventured on slight verbal condensation in secondary passages, and we have omitted some purely technical discussions of textual points and of editions. But in the main the reader is here placed in possession, within the compass of a moderate volume, of what will probably be allowed to be at once the most valuable and the most interesting series of monographs, on the chief characters and incidents of early Church history, ever contributed to a single undertaking by a band of Christian scholars. We feel it no more than a duty to pay this tribute of gratitude and admiration to the great divines, to whose devotion and learning all that is permanently valuable in these pages is due, and we are confident that their monographs, thus rendered generally available, will prove a permanent possession of the highest value to English students of Church history.

We must further offer the expression of our cordial gratitude to several living scholars, who have contributed new articles of similar importance to the present volume, in place of some in the original edition which the lapse of time or other circumstances had rendered less valuable than the rest. In particular, our warmest thanks are due to Dr. Robertson, the present Bp. of Exeter, who has substituted for the sketch of St. Augustine contributed to the original edition by an eminent French scholar, M. de Pressensé, a study of that great Father, similar in its thoroughness to the other great monographs just mentioned. We are also deeply indebted to the generosity of Chancellor Lias for fresh studies of such important subjects as Arius and Monophysitism ; and a valuable account of the Nestorian Church has been very kindly contributed by the Rev. W. A. Wigram, who, as head of the Archbishop of Canterbury's Assyrian Mission, possesses unique qualifications for dealing with the subject. We have to thank also the eminent learning of Dr. A. J. Mason for an article on Gaudentius of Brescia, who was unaccountably omitted from the larger work, and whose name has of late acquired new interest. The gratitude of the Editors, is also specially due to Dr. Knowling and Dr. Gee, of Durham University, for their assistance in some cases in which articles required to be supplemented or corrected by the most recent learning.

In all cases where the writers of the original articles are still living they were afforded the opportunity, if they desired it, of revising their work and bringing it up to date, and of checking the condensations : though the Editors and not the writers must take the responsibility for the latter and also, in most cases, for bibliographical additions. The Editors desire gratefully to record their appreciation of the assistance thus readily and kindly rendered by most of the original writers who are still spared to us, and, as an example, we are glad to thank the Rev. E. B. Birks for his very thorough revision of his article on the *Epistle to Diognetus*.

Cross-references are inserted, where needed, on the principle adopted in *Murray's Illustrated Bible Dictionary* (to which this is intended to be a companion volume in size, appearance, and price)—namely, the name of the article to which a cross-reference is intended is printed in capitals within brackets, but without the brackets when it occurs in the ordinary course of the text.

In the headings of articles the numbers in brackets after names which are common to more than one person are retained as in the large edition, to facilitate reference to that edition when desired, and also to indicate that there were other persons of the same name.

It was not consistent with the limits of the work to retain in all cases the minute bibliography sometimes furnished in the larger edition. But, on the other hand, an endeavour has been made to give references, at the end of articles, to recent publications of importance on each subject; and in this endeavour the Editors must express their great indebtedness to the valuable *Patrology* of Professor Bardenhewer, already referred to, and to the admirable third edition of Herzog and Hauck's Protestant *Cyclopaedia*, and occasionally to the parallel Roman Catholic Cyclopaedia of Wetzer and Welte, edited by Cardinal Hergenröther. It may be permissible, in referring to these auxiliary sources, to express a deep satisfaction at the increasing co-operation, in friendly learning, of Protestant and Roman Catholic scholars, and to indulge the hope that it is an earnest of the gradual growth of a better understanding between those two great schools of thought and life.

The Editors cannot conclude without paying a final tribute of honour and gratitude to the generous and devoted scholar whose accurate labours were indispensable to the original work, as is acknowledged often in its Prefaces, and who rendered invaluable assistance in the first stage of the preparation of the present volume—the Rev. Charles Hole, late Lecturer for many years in Ecclesiastical History in King's College, London. Dr. Wace hoped to have had the happiness of having his own name associated with that of his old teacher, friend, and colleague on the title-page of this volume, and he laments that death has deprived him of this privilege. He cannot, however, sufficiently express his sense of obligation to his colleague, Mr. Piercy, for the ability, skill, and generous labour without which the production of the work would have been impossible.

LIST OF WRITERS

Initials	
A.H.D.A.	The Right Hon. A. H. Dyke Acland, LL.D. Hon. Fellow of Balliol College, Oxford.
M.F.A.	The late Rev. M. F. Argles, M.A. Formerly Principal of St. Stephen's House, Oxford.
C.J.B.	Rev. C. J. Ball, M.A. Lecturer in Assyriology, Oxford; Rector of Blechingdon.
J.B—y.	The late Rev. J. Barmby, B.D. Formerly Principal of Bishop Hatfield's Hall, Durham, and Rector of Pilkington.
S.A.B.	S. A. Bennett, Esq., B.A. Of Lincoln's Inn.
E.W.B.	The late Most Rev. E. W. Benson, D.D. Formerly Archbishop of Canterbury.
E.B.B.	Rev. E. B. Birks, M.A. Vicar of Kellington; formerly Fellow of Trinity College, Cambridge.
C.W.B.	The late Rev. C. W. Boase, M.A. Formerly Fellow of Exeter College, Oxford.
W.B.	The late Rev. Canon W. Bright, D.D. Formerly Regius Professor of Ecclesiastical History, Oxford.
T.R.B.	The late Right Hon. T. R. Buchanan, M.A., M.P. Fellow of All Souls' College, Oxford.
D.B.	The late Rev. D. Butler, M.A. Formerly Rector of Thwing, Yorkshire.
J.G.C.	The late Rev. J. G. Cazenove, D.D. Formerly Provost of Cumbrae College, N.B.
M.B.C.	Rev. M. B. Cowell, M.A. Vicar of Ash Bocking.
F.D.	F. H. Blackburne Daniel, Esq. Of Lincoln's Inn.
G.W.D.	The Ven. G. W. Daniell, M.A. Archdeacon of Kingston-on-Thames.
T.W.D.	The late Rev. T. W. Davids. Upton.
L.D.	Rev. L. Davidson, M.A. Rector of Stanton St. John, Oxford.
J.Ll.D.	Rev. J. Ll. Davies, D.Litt. Formerly Fellow of Trinity College, Cambridge.
C.D.	Rev. C. Deedes, M.A. Prebendary of Chichester.
W.P.D.	The late Rev. W. P. Dickson, D.D. Formerly Professor of Divinity, Glasgow.
E.S.Ff.	The late Rev. E. S. Ffoulkes, M.A. Formerly Fellow of Jesus College, Oxford, and Vicar of St. Mary's.
A.P.F.	The late Right Rev. A. P. Forbes, D.C.L. Formerly Bishop of Brechin.
W.H.F.	The Very Rev. and Hon. W. H. Fremantle, D.D. Dean of Ripon.
J.M.F.	The late Rev. J. M. Fuller, M.A. Formerly Fellow of St. John's College, Cambridge.

INITIALS	
J.G.	REV. J. GAMMACK. M.A. Rector of St. James's, Hartford, Connecticut, U.S.A.
H.G.	REV. H. GEE, D.D. Master of University College, Durham.
C.G.	The RIGHT REV. C. GORE, D.D. Bishop of Birmingham.
J.Gw.	REV. J. GWYNN, D.D., D.C.L. Regius Professor of Divinity, T.C.D.
A.W.H.	The late REV. A. W. HADDAN, B.D. Formerly Fellow of Trinity College, Oxford.
T.R.H.	The late REV. T. R. HALCOMB, M.A. Formerly Fellow of Lincoln College, Oxford.
C.H.	The late REV. C. HOLE, B.A. Formerly Rector of Loxbear, and Lecturer in Ecclesiastical History in King's College, London.
H.S.H.	REV. CANON H. SCOTT HOLLAND, D.D. Regius Professor of Divinity, Oxford.
H.	The late REV. F. J. A. HORT, D.D. Formerly Fellow of Emmanuel College, Cambridge.
D.R.J.	The late REV. D. R. JONES. Oxford.
R.J.K.	REV. CANON R. J. KNOWLING, D.D. Professor of Divinity, Durham.
J.J.L.	REV. CHANCELLOR J. J. LIAS, M.A. Chancellor of Llandaff Cathedral.
L.	The RIGHT REV. J. B. LIGHTFOOT, D.D. Formerly Bishop of Durham.
R.A.L.	The late R. A. LIPSIUS, D.D. Formerly Professor of Divinity, University of Jena.
W.L.	REV. W. LOCK, D.D. Ireland Professor of Exegesis, Oxford; Warden of Keble College.
J.H.L.	The late REV. J. H. LUPTON, M.A. Formerly Fellow of St. John's College, Cambridge.
G.F.M.	The late REV. G. F. MACLEAR, D.D. Formerly Warden of St. Augustine's College, Canterbury.
A.C.M.	A. C. MADAN, ESQ., M.A. Senior Student of Christ Church, Oxford.
S.M.	The late REV. S. MANSEL, M.A. Formerly Fellow of Trinity College, Cambridge.
A.J.M.	REV. A. J. MASON, D.D. Master of Pembroke College, Cambridge, and Canon of Canterbury.
W.M.	The late REV. W. MILLIGAN, D.D. Formerly Professor of Divinity, Aberdeen.
G.H.M.	The late REV. G. H. MOBERLY, M.A. Formerly Fellow of Corpus Christi College, Oxford.
T.D.C.M.	The late REV. T. D. C. MORSE. Formerly Rector of Drayton, Nuneaton.
H.G.C.M.	The RIGHT REV. H. G. C. MOULE, D.D. Bishop of Durham.
J.R.M.	J. R. MOZLEY, ESQ., M.A. Formerly Fellow of King's College, Cambridge.
F.P.	The RIGHT REV. F. PAGET, D.D. Bishop of Oxford.
H.W.P.	The late REV. H. W. PHILLOTT, M.A. Formerly Rector of Staunton-on-Wye.
W.C.P.	REV. W. C. PIERCY, M.A. Dean and Chaplain of Whitelands College, S.W.
E.H.P.	The late REV. E. H. PLUMPTRE, D.D. Formerly Dean of Wells.
P.O.	The late REV. P. ONSLOW, B.A. Formerly Rector of Upper Sapey.
J.R.	The late REV. CANON J. RAINE, M.A. Formerly Fellow of Durham University.

Initials	
H.R.R.	The late Rev. H. R. Reynolds, D.D. Formerly Principal of Cheshunt College.
A.R.	The Right Rev. A. Robertson, D.D. Bishop of Exeter.
G.S.	The late Rev. G. Salmon, D.D. Formerly Regius Professor of Divinity and Provost of Trinity College, Dublin.
P.S.	The late Rev. P. Schaff. Bible House, New York.
W.M.S.	The Ven. W. M. Sinclair, D.D. Formerly Archdeacon of London.
I.G.S.	Rev. I. G. Smith, LL.D. Formerly Fellow of Brasenose College, Oxford.
R.P.S.	The late Very Rev. R. P. Smith, D.D. Formerly Dean of Canterbury.
G.T.S.	The late Rev. G. T. Stokes, M.A. Formerly Professor of Ecclesiastical History, Trinity College, Dublin.
S.	The late Right Rev. W. Stubbs, D.D. Formerly Bishop of Oxford.
E.S.T.	The Right Rev. E. S. Talbot, D.D. Bishop of Winchester.
R.St.J.T.	The late Rev. R. St. J. Tyrwhitt. Formerly Student of Christchurch, Oxford.
E.V.	The late Rev. Canon E. Venables. Formerly Precentor of Lincoln Cathedral.
H.W.	The Very Rev. H. Wace, D.D. Dean of Canterbury.
M.A.W.	Mrs. Humprhy Ward. Stocks House, Tring.
H.W.W.	The Ven. H. W. Watkins, D.D. Prof. of Hebrew, Durham University, and Archdeacon of Durham.
W. or B.F.W.	The late Right Rev. B. F. Westcott, D.D. Formerly Bishop of Durham.
W.A.W.	Rev. W. A. Wigram, M.A. Archbishop of Canterbury's Mission to Assyria.
H.A.W.	Rev. H. A. Wilson, M.A. Fellow of Magdalen College, Oxford.
J.W.	The Right Rev. J. Wordsworth, D.D. Bishop of Salisbury.
E.M.Y.	The late Rev. E. M. Young, M.A. Formerly Headmaster of Sherborne School.

DICTIONARY OF CHRISTIAN BIOGRAPHY

A

Abercius ('Αβέρκιος, 'Αουίρκιος, 'Αουέρκιος, etc.; Lat. Avircius, or Avercius; on the form and origin, see Ramsay, *Expositor*, ix. (3rd ser.), pp. 268, 394, and Zahn, art. "Avercius," *Realencyclopädie für protest. Theol. und Kirche*, Hauck). The *Life* of the saint, described as bp. of Hierapolis in Phrygia in the time of M. Aurelius and L. Verus, as given by Symeon Metaphrastes and in the Bollandist *Acta Sanctorum*, Oct. 22, is full of worthless and fantastic tales. But the epitaph which the Acts incorporate, placed, according to the story, on the altar brought from Rome by the demon whom the saint had driven out of the emperor's daughter, is of great value, and the discovery of some of the actual fragments of the inscription may well be called "a romance of archaeology." For this rediscovery our thanks are due to the rich labours of Prof. Ramsay. The fact that Abercius was described as bp. of Hier*a*polis at the time mentioned above had contributed to hesitation as to the genuineness of the epitaph. But Ramsay (*Bulletin de correspondance hellénique*, Juillet 1882) pointed out that Hier*a*polis had been frequently confounded with Hier*o*polis; and he also published in the same journal a metrical and early Christian epitaph of a certain Alexander (A.D. 216), discovered at Hier*o*polis, and evidently copied from the epitaph of Abercius, as given in his *Life*. As to the copying, there can be no doubt, for the third line of the epitaph of Alexander, son of Antonius, will not scan, owing to the substitution of his name for that of Abercius (Lightfoot, *Apost. Fathers*[2], i. p. 479; Headlam in *Authority and Archaeology*, pp. 307 ff., 1899). Ramsay's attention being drawn to the earlier epitaph, he collected various topographical notices in the *Life* of the saint, which pointed to Hier*o*polis, near Synnada (not Hier*a*polis on the Maeander), and he further established the case for the former by finding, in 1883, in the bath-room at some hot springs near Hier*o*polis, a small portion of the epitaph of Abercius himself on the fragment of an altar-shaped tomb; the hot springs in their position *near* the city exactly correspond with the position of the hot springs described in the *Life*. We have thus fortunately a threefold help in reconstructing the text of the whole epitaph—(1) the text in the *Life*; (2) the rediscovered fragments in the stone; (3) the epitaph on the tomb of Alexander.

There is much to be said for the identification of Abercius with the Avircius Marcellus (Eus. *H. E.* v. 16) to whom the extracts of the anonymous writer against Montanus are dedicated. We cannot be sure as to the date of these extracts, but there is reason to place them towards the close of the reign of Commodus, 180-192, and the epitaph of Abercius must at least have been earlier than 216, the date of the epitaph of Alexander. But the writer of the extracts addresses the person to whom he dedicates his work as a person of authority, although he does not style him a bishop (but see Lightfoot, *u.s.* p. 483), who had urged him a very long time ago to write on the subject. Avircius Marcellus might therefore have well flourished in the reign of M. Aurelius, and might have visited Rome at the time mentioned in the legend, A.D. 163. Further, in the extracts mention is made by the writer of one Zoticus of Otrous, his "fellow-presbyter," and Otrous was in the neighbourhood of this Hieropolis (for the identification, see further Lightfoot and Zahn, *u.s.*; Headlam, *u.s.*; Ramsay, *Expositor*, ix. (3rd ser.), p. 394). Against the attempt of Ficker to prove that the epitaph was heathen, *Sitzungsberichte d. Berl. Akad.* 1895, pp. 87-112, and that of Harnack, *Texte und Untersuchungen*, xii. 4*b*, p. 21, to class it as partly heathen and partly Christian, see Zahn, *u.s.*, and further in *Neue Kirchliche Zeitschrift*, 1895, pp. 863-886; also the criticism of Ramsay, quoted by Headlam, *u.s.* Both external and internal evidence are in favour of a Christian origin, and we have in this epitaph what Ramsay describes, *C. R. E.* pp. 437 ff., as "a testimony, brief, clear, emphatic, of the truth for which Avircius had contended—the one great figure on the Catholic side produced by the Phrygian church during this period," a man whose wide experience of men and cities might in itself have well marked him out as such a champion. The faithful, *i.e.* the sacred writings, the Sacraments of Holy Baptism and Holy Communion, the miraculous birth of our Lord (the most probable reference of παρθένος ἁγνή), His omnipresent and omniscient energy, the fellowship of the members of the church, not only in Rome but elsewhere—all these (together with the mixed cup, wine and water; the prayer for the departed; the symbolic ΙΧΘΥΣ, one of its earliest instances) have a place in the picture of early Christian usage and belief gained from this one epitaph; however widely Abercius travelled, to the far East or West, the same picture, he assures us, met his gaze. We thus recover an instructive and enduring monument of Christian life in the 2nd cent., all the more remarkable because it is presented to us, not in any systematic form, but as the natural and simple expression of a pure and devout soul. For full literature, see Zahn, *u.s.*; for the development of the legend from the facts mentioned in the epitaph, and for the reconstruction of the text by Lightfoot and Ramsay, see three articles by the latter in *Expositor*, ix. (3rd ser.), also Ramsay's *Cities and Bishoprics of Phrygia*, ii. 722. In addition to literature above, cf. art. by Lightfoot in *Expositor*, i. (3rd ser.), pp. 3 ff.; and Farrar, *Lives of the Fathers*, i. pp. 10 ff. Prof. V. Bartlet discusses Harnack's hypothesis in the *Critical Review*, April 1896, and regards it as at present holding the field; though he finds Harnack's elimination of any reference to Paul the Apostle in the inscription quite unintelligible. Even Schmiedel (*Encycl. Bibl.* ii. 1778) refers unhesitatingly to the inscription as Christian. See further Dr. Swete's art. *J. T. S.* July 1907, p. 502, on Avircius and prayers for the departed.

The following is a translation of the epitaph: "Citizen of a chosen city I have made this (tomb) in my lifetime, that I may have here *before the eyes of men* (φανερῶς *v.l.* καιρῷ) a resting-place for my body—Avircius by name, a disciple of the pure Shepherd, who on the mountains and plains feedeth the flocks of His sheep, who hath eyes large and beholding all things. For He was my Teacher, teaching me (διδάσκων, so Ramsay, omitted by Zahn) the faithful writings; who sent me to Rome to behold the *King* (βασιλῆαν, so Ramsay, but Lightfoot βασίληαν, Zahn, βασιλῆ ἀναθρῆσαι), and to see the Queen in golden robes and golden sandals, and there, too, I saw a people bearing a shining seal (a reference to Baptism). And I saw the plain of Syria and all its cities, even Nisibis, having crossed the Euphrates, and everywhere I had fellow-worshippers (συνομήθεις, so Lightfoot and Ramsay; συνοδίτην, Zahn, referring to Paul). With Paul in my hands *I followed* (i.e. the writings of Paul, Ramsay; but Lightfoot and Di Rossi apparently 'with Paul as my comrade'; whilst Zahn conjectures ἔποχον, or rather ἐπ' ὀχῶν instead of ἑπόμην), while Faith everywhere led the way, and everywhere placed before me food, the Fish from the fountain, mighty, pure, which a spotless Virgin grasped (Ramsay refers to the Virgin Mary, but see also Lightfoot and Farrar). And this she (*i.e.* Faith) gave to the friends to eat continually, having excellent wine, giving the mixed cup with bread. These words, I, Avircius, standing by, bade to be thus written; I was in fact in my seventy-second year. On seeing this let every one who thinks with him (*i.e.* who is also an anti-Montanist, so Ramsay; Lightfoot and Farrar simply 'fellow-Christian') pray for him (*i.e.* Avircius). But no one shall place another in my tomb, but if so, he shall pay 2000 gold pieces to the Romans, and 1000 gold pieces to my excellent fatherland *Hierapolis*" (so Ramsay, *vide Expositor*, ix. 3rd ser. p. 271, for a justification of this reading). [R.J.K.]

Abgar. [THADDAEUS.]

Acacius (2), bp. of Caesarea, from a personal defect known as ὁ μονόφθαλμος, the pupil and biographer of Eusebius the church historian. He succeeded his master as bishop, A.D. 340 (Socr. *H. E.* ii. 4; Soz. *H. E.* iii. 2). He is chiefly known to us as the bitter and uncompromising adversary of Cyril of Jerusalem, and as the leader of an intriguing band of ambitious prelates. The events of his life show Acacius to have been a man of great intellectual ability but unscrupulous. After the death of Eusebius of Nicomedia, *c.* 342, he became the head of the courtly Arian party, and is thought by some to be the person styled by Greg. Naz. (*Orat.* xxi. 21) "the tongue of the Arians," George of Cappadocia being "the hand." He assisted in consecrating Cyril, A.D. 351, and in accordance with the 7th Nicene Canon claimed a right of priority for the metropolitical see of Caesarea over that of Jerusalem. This Cyril refused to yield. Acacius, supported by the Palestinian bishops, deposed Cyril on frivolous grounds, and expelled him from Jerusalem, A.D. 358. [CYRIL OF JERUSALEM.] (Soz. iv. 25; Theod. ii. 26.)

Acacius attended the council of Antioch, A.D. 341 (Soz. iii. 5), when in the presence of the emperor Constantius "the Golden Basilica" was dedicated by a band of ninety bishops, and he subscribed the ambiguous creeds then drawn up from which the term Homoousion and all mention of "substance" were carefully excluded. With other bishops of the Eusebian party he was deposed at the council of Sardica, A.D. 347. They refused to submit to the sentence, and withdrew to Philippopolis, where they held a council of their own, deposing their deposers, including Pope Julius and Hosius of Cordova (Theod. ii. 26; Socr. ii. 16; Soz. iii. 14; Labb. *Conc.* ii. 625-699). According to Jerome (*Vir. Ill.* 98), his influence with the emperor Constantius was considerable enough to nominate Felix (the antipope) to the see of Rome at the fall of Liberius, A.D. 357. Acacius took a leading place among the intriguing prelates, who succeeded in splitting into two the oecumenical council which Constantius had proposed to summon, and thus nullifying its authority. While the Western bishops were assembling at Rimini, A.D. 359, he and his brethren of the East gathered at Seleucia, where he headed a turbulent party, called after him Acacians. After the majority had confirmed the semi-Arian creed of Antioch ("Creed of the Dedication"), Acacius brought forward a Confession (preserved by Athanasius, *de Synod*, § 29; Socr. ii. 40; Soz. iv. 22) rejecting the terms Homoousion and Homoiousion "as alien from Scripture," and anathematizing the term "Anomoeon," but distinctly confessing the "likeness" of the Son to the Father. This formula the semi-Arian majority rejected, and becoming exasperated by the disingenuousness of Acacius, who interpreted the "likeness of the Son to the Father" as "likeness in will alone," ὅμοιον κατὰ τὴν βούλησιν μόνον, and refused to be judged by his own published writings (Socr. and Soz. *l.c.*), they proceeded to depose him and his adherents. Acacius and the other deposed prelates flew to Constantinople and laid their complaints before the emperor. The adroit Acacius soon gained the ear of the weak Constantius, and finding that the favour he had shown to the bold blasphemies of Aetius had to some degree compromised him with his royal patron, he had no scruple in throwing over his former friend. A new council was speedily called at Constantinople, of which Acacius was the soul (Philostorg. iv. 12). Mainly through his intrigues the Council was brought to accept the Confession of Rimini, by which, in Jerome's strong words, "the whole world groaned and wondered to find itself Arian" (*Dial. adv. Luc.* 19). To complete their triumph, he and

Eudoxius of Antioch, then bp. of Constantinople, put forth their whole influence to bring the edicts of the Nicene council, and all mention of the Homoousion, into disuse and oblivion (Soz. iv. 26). On his return to the East in 361 Acacius and his party consecrated new bishops to the vacant sees, MELETIUS being placed in the see of Antioch. When the imperial throne was filled by the orthodox Jovian, Acacius with his friends found it convenient to change their views, and in 363 they voluntarily accepted the Nicene Symbol (Socr. iii. 25). On the accession of the Arian Valens in 364 Acacius once more went over to the more powerful side, making common cause with the Arian Eudoxius (Socr. iv. 2). But he found no favour with the council of Macedonian bishops at Lampsacus, and his deposition at Seleucia was confirmed. According to Baronius, he died A.D. 366.

Acacius enriched with parchments the library at Caesarea founded by Pamphilus (Hieron. *Ep. ad. Marcellam,* 141). He wrote on Ecclesiastes, six books of *σύμμικτα ζητήματα* and other treatises; a considerable fragment of his Ἀντιλογία against Marcellus of Ancyra is preserved by Epiphanius (*Haer.* 72, 6-9). His *Life* of Eusebius Pamphili has unhappily perished. See Fabricius, *B. G.* vii. p. 336, ix. pp. 254, 256 (ed. Harless); Tillemont, *Mem. eccl.* vi. (*passim*); Rivington (Luke), *Dublin Review,* 1894, i. 358-380; Hefele, *Konz. Gesch.* Bd. i. [E.V.]

Acacius (4), bp. of Beroea, in Syria, *c.* A.D. 379-436. He was apparently a Syrian by birth, and in his early youth adopted the ascetic life in the monastery of Gindarus near Antioch, then governed by Asterius (Theod. *Vit. Patr.* c. 2). Not much is known with certainty of this period of his life. He appears, however, to have been prominent as a champion of the orthodox faith against the Arians, from whom he suffered (Baluz. *Nov. Collect. Conc.* p. 746), and it is specially mentioned that he did great service in bringing the hermit Julianus Sabbas from his retirement to Antioch to confront this party, who had falsely claimed his support (Theod. *Vit. Patr.* 2, *H. E.* iv. 24). We find him in Rome, probably as a deputy from the churches of Syria when the Apollinarian heresy was treated before pope Damasus (Baluz. *Conc.* 763). After the return of Eusebius of Samosata from exile, A.D. 378, Acacius was consecrated to the see of Beroea (the modern Aleppo) by that prelate (Theod. *H. E.* v. 4). As bishop he did not relax the strictness of his asceticism, and like Ambrose (August. *Confess.* vi. 3), throwing the doors of his house open to every comer, he invited all the world to witness the purity and simplicity of his life (Soz. *H. E.* vii. 28). He attended the council of Constantinople in 381 (Theod. v. 8). The same year, on the death of Meletius, taking a prominent part in the consecration of Flavian to the bishopric of Antioch [FLAVIANUS], thus perpetuating the Eustathian schism, he incurred displeasure both in East and West, and was cut off from communion with the church of Rome (Soz. vii. 11). The council of Capua at the close of 391 or 392 received Acacius again into communion, together with the prelates of Flavian's party (Ambros. *Ep.* 9; Labb. *Conc.* ii. 1072); while Flavian himself, through the exertions of Acacius, received letters of communion not only from Rome, but also from Theophilus of Alexandria and the Egyptian bishops. The whole merit of this success was ascribed by the bishops of the East to "their father" Acacius (Socr. vi. 9; Soz. viii. 3; Theod. v. 23; Labb. *Conc.* iii. p. 391; Pallad. p. 39). Acacius was one of the most implacable of the enemies of CHRYSOSTOM. He bore part in the infamous "Synod of the Oak," A.D. 403; took the lead in the Synod of 404, after Chrysostom's return from exile; and joined in urging Arcadius to depose him (Pallad. p. 82). He added acts of open violence to his urgency with the timid emperor, until he had gained his end in the final expulsion of the saint, June 20, 404. Nor was his hostility even now satiated. Acacius sent to Rome one Patronus, with letters accusing Chrysostom of being the author of the conflagration of his own church. The pope treated the accusation with deserved contempt, and Acacius was a second time suspended from communion with Rome (Pallad. p. 35), which he did not regain till 414, and then chiefly through Alexander of Antioch. The letter sent to the pope by Acacius, with those of Alexander, was received with haughty condescension, and an answer was returned readmitting the aged prelate on his complying with certain conditions (*Conc.* ii. 1266-8). His communion with Alexander was fully restored, and we find the two prelates uniting in ordaining Diogenes, a "bigamus" (Theod. *Ep.* 110). Acacius's enmity to Chrysostom's memory seems however to have been unquenched; and on the succession of Theodotus of Antioch, A.D. 421, he took the opportunity of writing to Atticus of Constantinople to apologize for the new bishop's having, in defiance of his better judgment, yielded to popular clamour and placed Chrysostom's name on the diptychs (Theod. v. 34; Niceph. xiv. 26, 27). On the rise of the Nestorian controversy Acacius endeavoured to act the part of a peacemaker, for which his age of more than 100 years, and the popular reverence which had gained for him the title of "the father and master of all bishops," well qualified him. With the view of healing the breach between Cyril of Alexandria and Nestorius, he wrote a pacificatory reply to a violent letter of the former (A.D. 430). In the general council which followed at Ephesus, A.D. 431, he entrusted his proxy to Paul of Emesa. The influence of the aged Acacius was powerful at court. Theodosius wrote to him in most reverential terms beseeching him to give his endeavours and prayers for the restoration of unity to the distracted church. Acacius was also appealed to by Pope Sixtus III. for the same object (Baluz. *Conc.* pp. 721, 754, 757; Labb. *Conc.* iii. 1087).

Acacius disapproved of Cyril's anathemas of Nestorius, which appeared to him to savour of Apollinarianism; but he spent his last days in promoting peace between the rival parties, taking part in the synod held at the emperor's instance in his own city of Beroea, A.D. 432, by John of Antioch, and doing all in his power, both by personal influence and by letters to Cyril and to the

Roman bp. Coelestinus to bring about an agreement. He ultimately succeeded in establishing friendly communion between John and Cyril. He saw the peace of the church re-established, and died full of days and honour, aged, it is said, more than 110 years, A.D. 436.

Three letters are still extant out of the large number that he wrote, especially on the Nestorian controversy: two to Alexander of Hierapolis, Baluzius, *Nov. Collect. Concil.* c. xli. p. 746, c. lv. p. 757; and one to Cyril, *ib.* c. xxii. p. 440; Labbe, *Conc.* vol. iii. p. 382 (Cave, *Hist. Lit.* i. 417; Tillemont, *Mem. eccl.* vol. xiv.; Hefele, *Konz. Gesch.* Bd. ii.). [E.V.]

Acacius (7), patriarch of Constantinople, A.D. 471-489. Acacius was originally at the head of an orphanage at Constantinople, which he administered with conspicuous success (Suidas, *s.v.* Ἀκάκιος). His abilities attracted the notice of the emperor Leo, over whom he obtained great influence by the arts of an accomplished courtier (Suidas, *l.c.*). On the death of Gennadius (471) he was chosen bp. of Constantinople, and soon found himself involved in controversies, which lasted throughout his patriarchate, and ended in a schism of thirty-five years' duration between the churches of the East and West. On the one side he laboured to restore unity to Eastern Christendom, which was distracted by the varieties of opinion to which the Eutychian debates had given rise; and on the other to aggrandize the authority of his see by asserting its independence of Rome, and extending its influence over Alexandria and Antioch. In both respects he appears to have acted more in the spirit of a statesman than of a theologian; and in this relation the personal traits of liberality, courtliness, and ostentation, noticed by Suidas (*l.c.*), are not without importance.

The first important measures of Acacius carried with them enthusiastic popular support and earned for him the praise of pope Simplicius. In conjunction with a Stylite monk, Daniel, he placed himself at the head of the opposition to the emperor Basiliscus, who, after usurping the empire of the East, had issued an encyclic letter in condemnation of the council of Chalcedon, and taken Timotheus Aelurus, the Monophysite patriarch of Alexandria, under his protection, A.D. 476. The resistance was completely successful. In the meantime Zeno, the fugitive emperor, reclaimed the throne which he had lost; and Basiliscus, after abject and vain concessions to the ecclesiastical power, was given up to him (as it is said) by Acacius, after he had taken sanctuary in his church, A.D. 477 (Evagr. *H. E.* iii. 4 ff.; Theod. Lect. i. 30 ff.; Theophan. *Chron.* pp. 104 ff.; Procop. *B. V.* i. 7, p. 195). At this period the relations between Zeno, Acacius, and Simplicius appear to have been amicable, if not cordial. They were agreed on the necessity of taking vigorous measures to affirm the decrees of the council of Chalcedon, and for a time acted in concert (Simplic. *Epp.* 5, 6). Before long a serious difference arose, when Acacius, in 479, consecrated a bishop of Antioch (Theophan. *Chron.* p. 110), and thus exceeded the proper limits of his jurisdiction. However, Simplicius admitted the appointment on the plea of necessity, while he protested against the precedent (Simplic. *Epp.* 14, 15). Three years later (482), on the death of the patriarch of Alexandria, the appointment of his successor gave occasion to a graver dispute. The Monophysites chose Petrus Mongus as patriarch, who had already been conspicuous among them; on the other side the Catholics put forward Johannes Talaia. Both aspirants lay open to grave objections. Mongus was, or at least had been, unorthodox; Talaia was bound by a solemn promise to the Emperor not to seek or (as it appears) accept the patriarchate (Liberat. c. 17; Evagr. *H. E.* iii. 12). Talaia at once sought and obtained the support of Simplicius, and slighted Acacius. Mongus represented to Acacius that he was able, if confirmed in his post, to heal the divisions by which the Alexandrine church was rent. Acacius and Zeno readily listened to the promises of Mongus, and in spite of the vehement opposition of Simplicius, received the envoys whom he sent to discuss the terms of reunion. Shortly afterwards the Henoticon (An Instrument of Union) was drawn up, in which the creed of Nicaea, as completed at Constantinople, was affirmed to be the one necessary and final definition of faith; and though an anathema was pronounced against Eutyches, no express judgment was pronounced upon the doctrine of the two Natures (Evagr. *H. E.* iii. 14). Mongus accepted the Henoticon, and was confirmed in his see. Talaia retired to Rome (482-483), and Simplicius wrote again to Acacius, charging him in the strongest language to check the progress of heresy elsewhere and at Alexandria (Simplic. *Epp.* 18, 19). The letters were without effect, and Simplicius died soon afterwards. His successor, Felix III. (II.), espoused the cause of Talaia with zeal, and despatched two bishops, Vitalis and Misenus, to Constantinople with letters to Zeno and Acacius, demanding that the latter should repair to Rome to answer the charges brought against him by Talaia (Felix, *Epp.* 1, 2). The mission utterly failed. Vitalis and Misenus were induced to communicate publicly with Acacius and the representatives of Mongus, and returned dishonoured to Italy (484). On their arrival at Rome a synod was held. They were themselves deposed and excommunicated; a new anathema was issued against Mongus, and Acacius was irrevocably excommunicated for his connexion with Mongus, for exceeding the limits of his jurisdiction, and for refusing to answer at Rome the accusations of Talaia (Evagr. *H. E.* iii. 21; Felix, *Ep.* 6); but no direct heretical opinion was proved or urged against him. Felix communicated the sentence to Acacius, and at the same time wrote to Zeno, and to the church at Constantinople, charging every one, under pain of excommunication, to separate from the deposed patriarch (*Epp.* 9, 10, 12). Once again the envoy of the pope was seduced from his allegiance, and on his return to Rome fell under ecclesiastical censure (Felix, *Ep.* 11). For the rest, the threats of Felix produced no practical effect. The Eastern Christians, with very few exceptions, remained in communion with Acacius; Talaia acknowledged the hopelessness of his cause by accepting the bishopric of Nola; and Zeno and Acacius took active measures to obtain the general acceptance of the Henoticon. Under these circumstances the condemnation of Acacius, which had been made in the name of the Pope, was repeated in the name of the council of Chalcedon, and the schism was complete * (485). Acacius took no heed of the sentence up to his death in 489, which was followed by that of Mongus in 490, and of Zeno in 491. Fravitas (Flavitas, Flavianus), his successor, during a very short patriarchate, entered on negotiations with Felix, which led to no result. The policy of Acacius broke down when he was no longer able to animate it. In the course of a few years all for which he had laboured was undone. The Henoticon failed to restore unity to the East, and in 519 the emperor Justin submitted to pope Hormisdas, and the condemnation of Acacius was recognized by the Constantinopolitan church.

Tillemont has given a detailed history of the whole controversy, up to the death of Fravitas, in his *Mémoires*, vol. xvi., but with a natural bias towards the Roman side. The original documents, exclusive of the histories of Evagrius, Theophanes, and Liberatus, are for the most part collected in the 58th volume of Migne's *Patrologia*. See also Hefele, *Konz. Gesch.* Bd. ii. [W.]

Acephali (from ἀ and κεφαλή, those without a head or leader) is a term applied :—(1) To the bishops of the oecumenical council of Ephesus in 431, who refused to follow either St. Cyril or John of Antioch—the leaders of the two parties in the Nestorian controversy. (2) To a radical branch of Monophysites, who rejected not only the oecumenical council of Chalcedon in 451, but also the *Henoticon* of the emperor Zeno, issued in 482 to the Christians of Egypt, to unite the orthodox and the Monophysites. Peter Mongus, the Monophysite patriarch of Alexandria, subscribed this compromise [ACACIUS (7)]; for this reason many of his party, especially among the monks, separated from him, and were called *Acephali*. They were condemned, under Justinian, by a synod of Constantinople, 536, as schismatics, who sinned against the churches, the pope, and the emperor. Cf. Mansi, *Conc.* tom. viii. p. 891 sqq.; Harduin, *Conc.* tom. ii. 1203 sqq.; Walch, *Ketzerhistorie*, vol. vii.; Hefele, *Conciliengeschichte*, vol. ii. pp. 549, 744. (3) To the *clerici vagi*, i.e. clergymen belonging to no diocese (as in Isid. Hispal. *de Offic. Eccl.*, the so-called Egbert's *Excerpts*, 160, and repeatedly in Carlovingian Councils: see Du Cange) [*D. C. A.* art. VAGI CLERICI]. (4) It is said to be used sometimes for αὐτοκέφαλοι. [*D. C. A.* art. AUTOCEPHALI.] [P.S.]

Adamantius (1). [ORIGEN.]

Aerius, 'Αέριος, founder of the heretical sect of the **Aerians**, *c.* 355, still living when Epiphanius wrote against heresies, 374-376. He was the early friend and fellow-disciple of EUSTATHIUS OF SEBASTE in Pontus. While they were living an ascetic life together, the bishopric of Sebaste became vacant. Each of the friends was a candidate for the office. The choice fell on Eustathius. This was never forgiven by Aerius. Eustathius endeavoured to soften his friend's disappointment by at once ordaining Aerius presbyter, and setting him over the hospital established at Sebaste (ξενοδοχεῖον, or πτωχοτροφεῖον). But all his attempts were fruitless. Aerius threw up his charge, deserted the hospital, and openly published grave accusations against his bishop. The rupture with Eustathius widened into a rupture with the church. Aerius and his numerous followers openly separated from their fellow-Christians, and professed ἀποταξία, or the renunciation of all worldly goods. They were consequently denied not only admission to the churches, but even access to the towns and villages, and they were compelled to sojourn in the fields, or in caves and ravines, and hold their religious assemblies in the open air exposed to the severity of Armenian winters.

Our knowledge of Aerius is from Epiphanius (*Haer.* 75). Augustine, *de Haeresibus*, c. 53, merely epitomises Epiphanius. Aerius went so fearlessly to the root of much that the church was beginning to cling to, that we cannot feel much surprise at the vehemence of Epiphanius with regard to his teaching.

Epiphanius asserts that he went beyond Arius in his impieties, specifying four counts. (1) The first, with which the name of Aerius has been chiefly identified in modern times, is the assertion of the equality of bishops and presbyters, μία τάξις, μία τιμή, ἓν ἀξίωμα. (2) Aerius also ridiculed the observance of Easter as a relic of Jewish superstition. (3) Prayers and offerings for the dead he regarded as pernicious. If they availed for the departed, no one need trouble himself to live holily: he would only have to provide, by bribes or otherwise, a multitude of prayers and offerings for him, and his salvation was secure. (4) All set fasts he condemned. A Christian man should fast when he felt it to be for his soul's good: appointed days of fasting were relics of Jewish bondage. Philaster, whose unconfirmed authority is very small, confounds the Aerians with the ENCRATITES, and asserts that they practised abstinence from food and rejected marriage (Philast. *Haer.* 72). Consult Schröckh, *Christliche Kirch. Gesch.* vol. vi. pp. 226-234; Walch, *Ketzerhist.* vol. iii. pp. 221 seq.; Neander, *Ch. Hist.* vol. iii. pp. 461-563 (Clark's trans.); Herzog. *Realencycl.* vol. i. 165; Tillemont, *Hist. eccl.* vol. ix. pp. 87 seq. [E. V.]

Aetius ('Αέτιος), the founder and head of the strictest sect of Arianism, upon whom, on account of the boldness of his reasonings on the nature of God, was affixed the surname of "the ungodly," ἄθεος (Soz. iii. 15). He was the first to carry out the doctrines of Arius to their legitimate issue, and in opposition both to Homoousians and Homoiousians maintained that the Son was *unlike*, ἀνόμοιος, the Father, from which his followers took the name of ANOMOEANS. They were also known as Eunomians, from his amanuensis EUNOMIUS, the principal apologist of the party; and

* This appears to be the best explanation of the "double excommunication" of Acacius. Cf. Tillemont, *Mémoires*, xvi. n. 25, pp. 764 f.

as Heterusiasts and Exukontians, as affirming that the Son was ἐξ ἑτέρας οὐσίας from the Father, and created ἐξ οὐκ ὄντων.

The events of his singularly vagrant and chequered career are related from very different points of view by the Eunomian Philostorgius, and the orthodox writers Socrates, Sozomen, Theodoret, and Gregory Nyssen. We must regard Aetius as a bold and unprincipled adventurer, endowed with an indomitable love of disputation, which led him into incessant arguments on the nature of the Godhead, the person of our Lord, and other transcendental subjects, not only with the orthodox but with the less pronounced Arians. He was born at Antioch. His father, dying insolvent, left Aetius, then a child, and his mother in extreme destitution (Philost. *H. E.* iii. 15; cf. Valesius's notes; Suidas, *sub. voc.* Ἀέτιος). According to Gregory Nyssen, he became the slave of a woman named Ampelis; and having obtained his freedom in some disgraceful manner, became a travelling tinker, and afterwards a goldsmith. Having been convicted of substituting copper for gold in an ornament entrusted to him for repair, he gave up his trade, and attaching himself to an itinerant quack, picked up some knowledge of medicine. He met with a ready dupe in an Armenian, whose large fees placed Aetius above the reach of want. He now began to take rank as a regular and recognized practitioner at Antioch (Greg. Nys. *adv. Eunom.* lib. i. vol. ii. p. 293). Philostorgius merely tells us that he devoted himself to the study of philosophy and dialectics, and became the pupil of Paulinus the Arian bishop, recently removed from Tyre to Antioch, *c.* 323 (Philost. iii. 15). Aetius attached himself to the Aristotelian form of philosophy, and with him, Milman remarks (*Hist. of Christianity*, vol. ii. p. 443), the strife between Aristotelianism and Platonism among theologians seems to have begun. His chief study was the Categories of Aristotle, the scope of which, according to Socrates (*H. E.* ii. 35), he entirely misconceived, drawing from them sophistical arguments repudiating the prevailing Platonic mode of argument used by Origen and Clemens Alex. On the death of Paulinus his protector, *c.* 324, he was banished to Anazarbus in Cilicia, where he gained his livelihood by his trade. Here his dialectic skill charmed a grammarian, who instructed him more fully, receiving repayment by his menial services. Aetius tried his polemic powers against his benefactor, whom he put to public shame by the confutation of his interpretation of Scripture. On the ignominious dismissal which naturally followed, Athanasius, the Arian bishop of the place, opened his doors to the outcast, and read the Gospels with him. Aetius also read St. Paul's Epistles at Tarsus with Antonius, who, like Athanasius, was a disciple of Lucian, Arius's master. On Antonius's elevation to the episcopate, Aetius returned to Antioch, where he studied the prophets, particularly Ezekiel, with Leontius, afterwards bishop of that see, also a pupil of Lucian. A storm of unpopularity soon drove him from Antioch to Cilicia; but having been defeated in argument by one of the Borborian Gnostics, he betook himself to Alexandria, where he soon recovered his character as an invincible adversary by vanquishing the Manichean leader Aphthonius. Aphthonius, according to Philostorgius (*H. E.* iii. 15), only survived his defeat seven days. Here Aetius took up his former professions, studying medicine and working as a goldsmith.

On the return of St. Athanasius to Alexandria in 349, Aetius retired to Antioch, of which his former teacher Leontius was now bishop. By him Aetius was ordained deacon, *c.* 350 (Philost. iii. 17; Socr. *H. E.* ii. 35; Athan. *de Synod.* § 38, Oxf. trans. p. 137; Suidas, *s.v.*). His ordination was protested against by Flavian and Diodorus, and he was inhibited from the exercise of his ministry (Theod. *H. E.* ii. 24). Epiphanius erroneously asserts that he was admitted to the diaconate by George of Cappadocia, the intruding bp. of Alexandria (Epiph. *Haeres.* lxxvi. 1). Aetius now developed more fully his Anomoean tenets, and he exerted all his influence to induce the Arian party to refuse communion with the orthodox. He also began to withdraw himself from the less pronounced Arians (Socr. *H. E.* ii. 359). This schism in the Arian party was still further developed at the first council of Sirmium, A.D. 351, where he attacked the respectable semi-Arian (Homoiousian) bishops, Basil of Ancyra and Eustathius of Sebaste (Philost. *H. E.* iii. 16), reducing them to silence. Exasperated by his discomfiture, Basil denounced Aetius to Gallus. His life was spared at the intercession of bp. Leontius; and being subsequently introduced to Gallus by Theophilus Blemmys, he was sent by him to his brother Julian to win him back from the paganism into which he was lapsing. Gallus also appointed him his religious teacher (Philost. *H. E.* iii. 27; Greg. Nys. *u.s.* p. 294).

The fall of Gallus in 354 caused a change in the fortunes of Aetius, who returned to Alexandria in 356 to support the waning cause of Arianism. The see of Athanasius was then occupied by George of Cappadocia, under whom Aetius served as a deacon, and when nominated to the episcopate by two Arian bishops, Serras and Secundus, he refused to be consecrated by them on the ground that they had held communion with the Homoousian party (Philost. iii. 19). Here he was joined by his renowned pupil and secretary Eunomius (Greg. Nys. *u.s.* p. 299; Socr. *H. E.* ii. 22; Philost. *H. E.* iii. 20). Greater troubles were now at hand for Aetius. Basil of Ancyra denounced him to the civil power for his supposed complicity in the treasonable designs of Gallus, and he was banished to Pepuza in Phrygia. The influence of Ursacius and Valens procured his recall; but he was soon driven again into exile. The hard irreverence of Aetius, and the determination with which he pushed conclusions from the principles of Arius, shocked the more religious among the Arian party, and forced the bishops to use all measures to crush him. His doctrines were also becoming alarmingly prevalent. "Nearly the whole of Antioch had suffered from the shipwreck of Aetius, and there was danger lest the whole (once more) should be submerged" (Letter of George, bp. of Laodicea, ap. Soz. *H. E.* vi. 13). A synod was therefore appointed for Nicomedia in Bithynia. A violent earthquake and the intrigues of the court brought about its division into two synods. The West met at Ariminum; the East at Seleucia in Isauria, A.D. 359. The latter separated without any definite conclusion. "The Arians, semi-Arians, and Anomoeans, mingled in tumultuous strife, and hurled anathemas at one another" (Milman, *Hist. Christ.* iii. c. 8). Whatever triumph was gained rested with the opponents of the Aetians, who appealed to the emperor and the court, and a second general council was summoned to meet at Constantinople (Athan. *de Synod.* § 10, 12). Of this council Acacius was the leading spirit, but a split occurred among the Anomoean followers of Aetius. The party triumphed, but its founder was sent into banishment, first to Mopsuestia, then to Amblada in Pisidia. Here he gained the goodwill of the savage inhabitants by his prayers having, as they supposed, averted a pestilence (Theod. ii. 23; Soz. iv. 23, 24; Philost. iv. 12; Greg. Nys. *u.s.* p. 301).

The death of Constantius, A.D. 361, put an end to Aetius's exile. Julian recalled all the banished bishops and invited Aetius to his court (*Ep. Juliani*, 31, p. 52, ed. Boisson; Soz. v. 5), and at the instance of Eudoxius (Philost. ix. 4) presented him with an estate in the island of Lesbos. The ecclesiastical censure was taken off Aetius by Euzoius, the Arian bp. of Antioch (*ib.* vii. 5), who, with the bishop of his party, compiled a defence of his doctrines (*ib.* viii. 2). According to Epiphanius (*Haer. u.s.*), he was consecrated bishop at Constantinople, though not to any particular see; and he and Eunomius consecrated bishops for his own party (Philost. viii. 2). On the death of Jovian, A.D. 364, Valens shewed special favour to Eudoxius, between whom and Aetius and Eunomius a schism had arisen. Aetius in disgust retired to his farm in Lesbos (*ib.* ix. 4). The revolt of Procopius once more endangered his life. He was accused to the governor, whom Procopius had placed in the island, of favouring the cause of Valens, A.D. 365-366 (*ib.* ix. 6). Aetius returned to Constantinople. He was the author of several letters to Constantius and others, filled with subtle disquisition on the nature of the Deity (Socr. ii. 35), and of 300 heretical propositions, of which Epiphanius has preserved 47 (*Haer.* lxxvi. § 10), with a refutation of each. Hefele, *Konz. Gesch.* Bd. i. [E.V.]

Africanus, Julius ('Αφρικανός), a Christian writer at the beginning of the 3rd cent. A great part of his life was passed at Emmaus in Palestine—not, however, the Emmaus of St. Luke (xxiv. 16), as assumed by the ancient authorities (Soz. *H. E.* v. 21; Hieron. *in libro de Locis Hebraicis*, *s.v.* 'Εμμαοῦς, ii. p. 439; et *in Epitaph. Paulae*, iv. p. 673); but, as Reland has shewn in his *Palaestina*, pp. 427, 758 (see also Smith's *Dict. of Geogr. s.v.* Emmaus), the Emmaus in the plain (1 Macc. iii. 40), 22 Roman miles (=176 stadia) from Jerusalem. He may have been born A.D. 170 or a little earlier, and died A.D. 240 or a little later. There seems to be no ancient authority for dating his death A.D. 232.

Africanus ranks with Clement and Origen as among the most learned of the ante-Nicene fathers (Socr. *H. E.* ii. 35; Hieron. *Ep. ad Magnum*, 83, vol. iv. p. 656). His great work, a comparative view of sacred and profane history from the creation of the world, demanded extensive reading; and the fragments that remain refer to the works of a considerable number of historical writers. His only work now extant in a complete state is his letter to Origen referred to by many authors (Eus. *H. E.* vi. 31; Hieron. *de Vir. Ill.* c. 63; Photius, Cod. 34; Suidas, *s.v.* 'Αφρικανός; Niceph. Call. *H. E.* v. 21, and others). The correspondence originated in a discussion between Origen and a certain Bassus, at which Africanus was present, and in which Origen appealed to the authority of that part of the Book of Daniel which contains the story of Susanna. Africanus afterwards wrote a short letter to Origen urging several objections to the authenticity of this part of the book; among others, that the style is different from that of the genuine book, that this section is not in the book as received by the Jews, and that it contains a play on Gk. words which shews that, unlike other O.T. books, it was originally written in Gk. and not in Heb. Origen replied at greater length. That Africanus had any intimate knowledge of Heb. must not be regarded as proved by this letter. The date of the correspondence is limited by the facts that Origen writes from Nicomedia, having previously visited Palestine, and refers to his labours in a comparison of the Gk. and Heb. text, indicating that he had already published the Hexapla. These conditions are best satisfied by a date *c.* 238.

Not less celebrated is the letter of Africanus to Aristides on the discrepancy in our Saviour's genealogies as given by St. Matthew and St. Luke. A considerable portion of this has been preserved by Eusebius (*H. E.* i. 7), and Routh (*Rel. Sac.* ii. 228) has published this together with a fragment not previously edited. A compressed version of the letter is given also in Eusebii ad Stephanum, *Quaest.* iv. (Mai, *Script. Vet. Nov. Coll.* vol. i.). Africanus begins by rejecting a previous explanation that the genealogies are fictitious lists, designed to establish our Lord's claim to be both king and priest by tracing His descent in one Gospel from Solomon, in the other from Nathan, who was assumed to be Nathan the prophet. Africanus argues the necessity of maintaining the literal truth of the Gospel narrative, and against drawing dogmatic consequences from any statements not founded on historical fact. He then gives his own explanation, founded on the levirate law of the Jews, and professing to be traditionally derived from the Desposyni (or descendants of the kindred of our Lord), who dwelt near the villages of Nazareth and Cochaba. According to this view Matthew gives the natural, Luke the legal, descent of our Lord. Matthan, it is said, of the house of Solomon, and Melchi of the house of Nathan, married the same woman, whose name is given as Estha. Heli the son of Melchi (the names Matthat and Levi found in our present copies of St. Luke are omitted by Africanus) having died childless, his uterine brother Jacob, Matthan's son, took his wife and raised up seed to him; so that the offspring Joseph was legally Heli's son as stated by St. Luke, but naturally Jacob's son as stated by St. Matthew. For a critical examination and defence of this solution, which is adopted by St.

Augustine (*Retract.* lib. ii. c. vii.), see Mill, *On the Mythical Interpretation of the Gospels*, p. 201.

The great work of Africanus was his "accurately laboured" (Eus. *H. E.* vi. 31) treatise on chronology, in five books. As a whole it is lost, but we can form a good idea of its general character from the still remaining *Chronicon* of Eusebius, which was based upon it, and which undoubtedly incorporates much of it. Eusebius himself, p. 132, mentions Africanus among his authorities for Jewish history, subsequent to O.T. times. Several fragments of the work of Africanus can be identified by express quotations, either by Eusebius in his *Praeparatio* and *Demonstratio Evangelii*, or by other writers, in particular by Georgius Syncellus in his *Chronographia.* These have been collected by Gallandi (*Bibl. Vet. Pat.* vol. ii.), and more fully by Routh (*Rel. Sac.* vol. ii.).

Christian Apologists had been forced to engage in chronological discussions, to remove the heathen contempt of Christianity as a novelty, by demonstrating the great antiquity of the Jewish system, out of which the Christian sprang. Thus Tatian (*Or. ad Graec.* c. 39), Theophilus of Antioch (*ad. Autol.* iii. 21), Clement of Alexandria (*Stromata*, i. 21), discuss the question of the antiquity of Moses, and, following Josephus (*cont. Apion.* i. 16), arrive at the conclusion that Moses was a contemporary of Inachus, and that the Exodus took place 393 years before the coming of Danaus to Argos. Africanus set himself to make a complete synopsis of sacred and profane history from the Creation, and to establish a synchronism between the two. He concludes that Moses and Ogyges were contemporaries. He thinks a connexion between the Ogygian deluge and the plagues of Egypt likely; and confirms his conclusions by deducing from Polemo, Apion, and Ptolemaeus Mendesius, that Moses was a contemporary of Inachus, whose son, Phoroneus, reigned at Argos in the time of Ogyges. Africanus follows the LXX: he counts 2262 years to the Deluge; he does not recognize the second Cainan; he places the Exodus A.M. 3707. In computing the years of the Judges he is blamed by Eusebius for lengthening the chronology by adding, without authority, 30 years for the elders after Joshua, 40 for anarchy after Samson, and 25 years of peace. He thus makes 740 years between the Exodus and Solomon. Our Lord's birth he places A.M. 5500, and two years before our common computation of Anno Domini. But he allows only one year for our Lord's public ministry, and thus dates the Crucifixion A.M. 5531. He calculates the commencement of the 70 weeks from the 20th year of Artaxerxes: from this to the death of our Lord he counts only 475 years, contending that the 70 weeks of Daniel are to be understood as 490 lunar years of 354 days each, equivalent to 475 Julian years.

Another interesting passage in the χρονικά is one in which he treats of the darkness at the Crucifixion, and shews, in opposition to the Syrian historian Thallus, that it was miraculous, and that an eclipse of the sun could not have taken place at the full moon. Lastly, we may notice his statement that there were still in his time remains of Jacob's terebinth at Shechem, Gen. xxxv. 4, held in honour; and that Jacob's tent had been preserved in Edessa until struck by lightning in the reign of the emperor Antoninus (Elagabalus?). Africanus probably had personally visited Edessa, whose king, Abgarus, he elsewhere mentions.

The work in all probability concluded with the Doxology, which St. Basil has cited (*de Spir. Sanct.* § 73, iii. 61) in justification of the form of doxology σὺν Ἁγίῳ Πνεύματι.

It remains to speak of another work, the κεστοί, expressly ascribed to Africanus by Eusebius (*H. E.* vi. 31), Photius (*l.c.*), Suidas (*l.c.*), and Syncellus (p. 359), perhaps (as Scaliger suggests) quoting the *Chronica* of Eusebius. According to this authority, the work consisted of nine books; and it is probably owing to errors of transcribers that we now find Photius enumerating 14 and Suidas 24. The work seems to have received the fanciful name of *Cesti*, or variegated girdles, from the miscellaneous character of its contents, which embraced the subjects of geography, natural history, medicine, agriculture, the art of war, etc. The portions that remain have suffered mutilation and addition by different copyists. The external evidence for ascribing the *Cesti* and *Chronology* to the same author is too strong to be easily set aside, and is not without some internal confirmation. Thus the author of the *Cesti* was better acquainted with Syria than with Libya; for he mentions the abundance of a certain kind of serpent in Syria, and gives its Syrian name (*Vet. Math.* p. 290), but when he gives a Libyan word (*Geopon.* p. 226) he does so on second-hand testimony. And he was a Christian, for he asserts (*Geopon.* p. 178) that wine may be kept from spoiling by writing on the vessels "the divine words, Taste and see that the Lord is gracious." The unlikelihood of Africanus having written such a work becomes less if we look upon him not as an ecclesiastic, but as a Christian philosopher, pursuing his former studies after his conversion, and entering in his note-books many things more in accordance with the spirit of his own age than with that of ours. Cf. Harnack on Julius Africanus Sextus in Herzog, 3rd ed. The last edition of the *Chronography* is in Gelzer, *Sex. Jul. Afr.* (2 vols. Leipzig, 1880-1898); see also Spitta (Halle, 1877) on the letter to Aristides, Harnack, *Lit.* i. 507-513 and ii. 1, pp. 124 sqq. [G.S.]

Agapetus, bp. of Rome, was, we are told, a Roman by birth, the son of Gordianus a priest (Anast. quoted by Clinton, *Fasti Romani*, p. 763; Jaffé, *Regesta Pontificum*, p. 73). He was already an old man when, six days after the death of Johannes II., he was elected pope in June 535. He began by formally reversing an act of Bonifacius II., one of his own immediate predecessors, fulminating anathemas against the deceased antipope Dioscorus, A.D. 530 (Anast. vol. i. p. 100).

We next find him entering Constantinople on Feb. 19, 536 (Clint. *F. R.* p. 765), sent thither by Theodahad to avert, if possible, the war with which he was threatened by the emperor Justinian in revenge for the murder of his queen Amalasontha: and we are told that he succeeded in the objects of his mission (Anast. vol. i. p. 102), which must refer to other objects, for he certainly failed to avert the war; Justinian had already incurred such expense as to be unwilling to turn back (Liberat. quoted by Baronius, *Annales Ecclesiastici*, vii. p. 314), and as a matter of fact Belisarius took Rome within the year. In 535 Anthimus, who was suspected of Monothelitism, had been appointed patriarch of Constantinople by the influence of Theodora. Agapetus, on his first arrival, refused to receive Anthimus unless he could prove himself orthodox, and then only as bp. of Trebizond. for he was averse to the practice of translating bishops. At the same time he boldly accused Justinian himself of Monophysitism; who was fain to satisfy him by signing a "libellus fidei" and professing himself a true Catholic. But the emperor insisted upon his communicating with Anthimus, and even threatened him with expulsion from the city if he refused. Agapetus replied with spirit that he thought he was visiting an orthodox prince, and not a second Diocletian. Then the emperor confronted him with Anthimus, who was easily convicted by Agapetus. Anthimus was formally deposed, and Mennas substituted; and this was done without a council, by the single authority of the pope Agapetus; Justinian of course allowing it, in spite of the remonstrances of Theodora (Anast. vol. i. p. 102; Theophanes, *Chronogr.* p. 184). Agapetus followed up his victory by denouncing the other heretics who had collected at Constantinople under the patronage of Theodora. He received petitions against them from the Eastern bishops, and from the "monks" in Constantinople, as the Archimandrite coenobites were beginning to be called (Baronius, vii. p. 322). He died on April 21, 536 (Clint. *F. R.* p. 765). His body was taken to Rome and buried in St. Peter's basilica, Sept. 17. Five of his letters remain: (1) July 18, 535, to Caesarius, bp. of Arles, about a dispute of the latter with bp. Contumeliosus (Mansi, viii. p. 856). (2) Same date, to same, "De augendis alimoniis pauperum" (*ib.* 855). (3) Sept. 9, 535, Reply to a letter from African bishops to his predecessor Johannes (*ib.* 848). (4) Same date, reply to Reparatus, bp. of Carthage, who had congratulated him on his accession (*ib.* 850). (5) March 13, 536, to Peter, bp. of Jerusalem, announcing the deposition of Anthimus and consecration of Mennas (*ib.* 921). Hefele, *Konz. Gesch.* Bd. ii. [G.H.M.]

Agatha, a virgin martyred at Catana in Sicily under Decius, Feb. 5, 251, according to her *Acta*; but under Diocletian according to the Martyrol. and Aldhelm (*de Virgin.* 22); mentioned by Pope Damasus A.D. 366 (*Carm.* v.), and by Venantius Fortunatus *c.* 580; inserted in the Canon of the Mass by Gregory the Great according to Aldhelm (*u.s.*, and see also S. Greg. M. *Dial.* iii. 30); and commemorated in a homily by Methodius, *c.* 900. Her name is in the Carthag. Calendar of *c.* 450; in Ruinart, p. 695; and in the black-letter calendar in our Prayer-book. Churches at Rome were dedicated to her by pope Symmachus *c.* 500; by Ricimer A.D. 460, enriched with her relics by Gregory the Great; and by Gregory II. in 726. She is the patroness of Malta (Butler's *Lives of Saints*). See also the homily against *Peril of Idolatry*, p. iii. [A.W.H.]

Agnes, M. a virgin, 12 or 13 years old, beheaded at Rome under Diocletian, celebrated by Ambrose (*de Offic.* i. 41; *de Virg. ad Marcell.* i. 2), Jerome (*Ep.* 97 *ad demetriad.*), Augustine (*Serm.* 273, 286, and 354), Sulp. Sever. (*Dial.* ii. 14), Prudentius (περὶ Στεφάνων, xiv.), Venant. Fortunatus (*Poem.* vii. iii. 35), Aldhelm (*de Virgin.*); and by her *Acta* in Syriac in Assemani, *Act. Mart.* ii. 148 seq.; besides *Acta* falsely attributed to St. Ambrose, a doubtful homily of St. Maxim. Taurin., and some verses questionably assigned to pope Damasus. Her name is in the Carthag. Cal. of *c.* 450, Jan. 21; in Ruinart, p. 695. A church at Rome, in her honour, said to have been built under Constantine the Great, was repaired by Pope Honorius, A.D. 625-638, and another was built at Rome by Innocent X. (Assemani, *Act. Mart.* ii. 154, 155). See also *Act. SS.* Jan. 21, on which day her name stands in the black-letter calendar of our Prayer-book. Baeda and Usuard place it on Jan. 23; the *Menolog.* and *Menaea* on July 5. [A.W.H.]

Agnoëtae (from ἀγνοέω, *to be ignorant of*), a name applied to two sects who denied the omniscience either of God the Father, or of God the Son in His state of humiliation.

I. The first were a sect of the Arians, and called from Eunomius and Theophronius "*Eunomio-Theophronians*" (Socr. *H. E.* v. 24). Their leader, Theophronius, of Cappadocia, who flourished about 370, maintained that God knew things past by memory and things future only by uncertain prescience. Sozomen (*H. E.* vii. 17) writes of him: "Having given some attention to the writings of Aristotle, he composed an appendix to them, entitled *Exercises of the Mind.* But he afterwards engaged in many unprofitable disputations, and soon ceased to confine himself to the doctrines of his master. [EUNOMIUS.] Under the assumption of being deeply versed in the terms of Scripture, he attempted to prove that though God is acquainted with the present, the past, and the future, *his knowledge on these subjects is not the same in degree, and is subject to some kind of mutation.* As this hypothesis appeared positively absurd to the Eunomians, they excommunicated him from their church; and he constituted himself the leader of a new sect, called after his own name, 'Theophronians.'"

II. Better known are the *Agnoëtae* or *Themistiani*, in the Monophysite controversy in 6th cent. Themistius, deacon of Alexandria, representing a small branch of the Monophysite Severians, taught, after the death of Severus, that the human soul (not the Divine nature) of Christ was like us in all things, even in the limitation of knowledge, and was ignorant of many things, especially the day of judgment, which the Father alone knew (Mark xiii. 32, cf. John xi. 34). Most Monophysites rejected this view, as inconsistent with their theory of one nature in Christ, which implied also a unity of knowledge, and they called the followers of Themistius *Agnoëtae.* The orthodox, who might from the Chalcedonian dogma of the two natures in Christ have inferred two kinds of knowledge, a perfect Divine and an imperfect human admitting of growth (Luke ii. 52), nevertheless rejected the view of the Agnoëtae, as making too wide a rupture between the two natures, and generally understood the famous passage in Mark of the *official* ignorance only, inasmuch as Christ did not choose to reveal to His disciples the day of judgment, and thus *appeared* ignorant for a wise purpose (κατ' οἰκονομίαν). His inquiry concerning Lazarus was explained from reference to the Jews and the intention to increase the effect of the miracle. Eulogius, Patriarch of Alexandria, wrote against the Agnoëtae a treatise on the absolute knowledge of Christ, of which Photius has preserved large extracts. Sophronius, patriarch of Jerusalem, anathematized Themistius. Agnoëtism was revived by the Adoptionists in the 8th cent. Felix of Urgel maintained the limitation of the knowledge of Christ according to His human nature, and appealed to Mark xiii. 32. Gallandi, *Bibl. Patr.* xii. p. 634; Mansi, *Conc.* xi. 502; Leont. Byz. *de Sectis, Actio X.* c. iii.; Photius, *Cod.* 230 (ed. Bekk. p. 284); Baronius, *Annal.* ad A.D. 535; Walch. *Hist. der Ketzereien*, viii. 644-684; Baur, *Lehre v. der Dreieinigkeit*, etc., ii. pp. 87 ff; Dorner, *Entwicklungsgeschichte*, etc., ii. pp. 172 f; cf. *D. C. B.* (4 vol. ed.) art. PERSON OF CHRIST. [P.S.]

Alaric (Teut. prob. = Athalaric, *noble ruler*), general and king (398) of the Goths, the most civilized and merciful of the barbarian chiefs who ravaged the Roman Empire.

Alaric first appears among the Gothic army who assisted Theodosius in opposing Eugenius, 394. He led the revolt of his nation against Arcadius, ravaged the provinces south of the Danube, and invaded Greece 395. Athens capitulated, and afterwards Corinth, Argos, and Sparta. Under the title of Master-General of Eastern Illyricum, 398, he became the ally of Arcadius and secretly planned the invasion of Italy. In the winter of 402 he crossed the Alps, was defeated by Stilicho at Pollentia on Easter Day 403, and driven from Italy. In 404 he exchanged the prefecture of Eastern for that of Western Illyricum, and the service of Arcadius for that of Honorius, and, after the incursion and annihilation of Radagaisus and his Sclavonian hordes in 405, he was subsidized for his supposed services to the empire by the payment of 4,000 pounds of gold. Stilicho's ruin and death in 408, the subsequent massacre of the Goths settled in Italy, and Honorius's impolitic refusal of Alaric's equitable terms, caused the second invasion of Italy, and the first siege of Rome, which ended in a capitulation. At the second siege in 409, preceded by the capture of Ostia, the city was surrendered unconditionally, and Alaric set up Attalus as emperor, in opposition to Honorius, who remained at Ravenna. At the close of the third siege, in 410 (Aug. 24), the city was in the hands of the Goths for six days, during three of which the sack was continued. Alaric died at Consentia late in 410.

The effect of Alaric's conquests on the cause of Christianity, and on the spiritual position of Rome in Western Christendom, is well traced by Dean Milman (*Lat. Christ.* i. 110-140). Alaric and his Goths had embraced Christianity probably from the teaching of Ulfilas, the Arian bishop, who died in 388 (Mosheim, ed. Stubbs, i. 233). This age witnessed the last efforts of Paganism to assert itself as the ancient and national religion, and Rome was its last stronghold. Pagans and Christians had retorted upon each other the charge that the calamities of the empire were due to the desertion of the old or new system of faith respectively, and the truth or falsehood of either was generally staked upon the issue. The almost miraculous discomfiture of the heathen Radagaisus by Stilicho, in spite of his vow to sacrifice the noblest senators of Rome on the altars of the gods which delighted in human blood, was accepted as an ill omen by those at Rome who hoped for a public restoration of Paganism (Gibbon, iv. 47-49, ed. Smith; Milman, *Lat. Christ.* i. 122). Rome, impregnable while Stilicho, her Christian defender, lived, could submit only to the approach of Alaric, "a Christian and a soldier, the leader of a disciplined army, who understood the laws of war, and respected the sanctity of treaties." In the first siege of Rome both pagan and Christian historians relate the strange proposal to relieve the city by the magical arts of some Etruscan diviners, who were believed to have power to call down lightning from heaven, and direct it against Alaric's camp. That pope Innocent assented to this public ceremony rests only on the authority of the heathen Zosimus (v. 41). It is questioned whether this idolatrous rite actually took place. Alaric perhaps imagined that he was furthering the Divine purpose in besieging Rome. Sozomen (*Hist. Eccl.* ix. c. 7) mentions as a current story that a certain monk, on urging the king, then on his march through Italy, to spare the city, received the reply that he was not acting of his own accord, but that some one was persistently forcing him on and urging him to sack Rome.

The shock felt through the world at the news of the capture of Rome in Alaric's third siege, 410, was disproportioned to the real magnitude of the calamity: contrast the exaggerated language of St. Jerome, *Ep. ad Principiam*, with Orosius, l. vii. c. 39, and St. Augustine, *de Civ. Dei*, ii. 2 (a work written between 413 and 426 with the express object of refuting the Pagan arguments from the sack of Rome), and his tract, *de Excidio Urbis* (*Opp.* t. vi. 622-628, ed. Bened.). The book in which Zosimus related the fall of Rome has been lost, so that we have to gather information from Christian sources; but it is plain that the destruction and loss was chiefly on the side of Paganism, and that little escaped which did not shelter itself under the protection of Christianity. "The heathens fled to the churches, the only places of refuge. . . . There alone rapacity and lust and cruelty were arrested and stood abashed" (Milman, p. 133). The property of the churches and the persons of Christian virgins were generally respected. The pagan inhabitants of Rome were scattered over Africa, Egypt, Syria, and the East, and were encountered alike by St. Jerome at Bethlehem and by St. Augustine at Carthage. Innocent I. was absent at Ravenna during the siege of Rome. On his return heathen temples were converted into Christian churches; "with Paganism expired the venerable titles of the religion, the great High Priests and Flamens, the Auspices and Augurs. On the pontifical throne sat the bp. of Rome, who would soon possess the substance of the imperial power" (*ib.* p. 139). Alaric was also instrumental in driving Paganism from Greece. Zosimus (v. 7) asserts that on his approach to Athens its walls were seen to be guarded by Minerva and Achilles. Gibbon says that "the invasion of the Goths, instead of vindicating the honour, contributed, at least accidentally, to extirpate the last remains of Paganism" (vol. iv. p. 37).

The conquests of Alaric, though achieved at an age when the Church boasted many eminent saints and writers, afford far fewer materials for the martyrologist and hagiologist than those of Attila. Alaric, though an Arian, is nowhere recorded to have persecuted the Catholics whom war had placed in his power. Jornandes and Isidore of Seville, Gothic historians, and Orosius, a Spanish Catholic, are equally silent on this point. The following facts of personal history have been preserved. In the sack of Rome Marcella, an aged matron, was thrown on the ground and cruelly beaten (Hieron. *Ep. ad Princip.*); a nameless lady, who persistently repelled her capturer, was conducted by him to the sanctuary of the Vatican; and an aged virgin, to whose charge some sacred vessels had been entrusted, through her bold constancy preserved them intact. At the plunder of Nola in Campania, St. Paulinus its bishop is said to have prayed, "Lord, let me not suffer torture either for gold or silver, since Thou knowest where are all my riches" (Fleury, *Eccl. Hist.* ed. Newman, bk. xxii. c. 21). Proba, widow of the prefect Petronius, retired to Africa with her daughter Laeta and her granddaughter Demetrias (Hieron. *Ep.* cxxx. t. i. p. 969, ed. Vallars.), and spent her large fortune in relieving the captives and exiles. (See Tillemont, *Mém. ecclés.* t. xiii. pp. 620-635.) Valuable contributions to the history of Alaric not already mentioned are Sigonius, *Opp.* t. i. par. 1, pp. 347 sqq. ed. Argellati; Aschbach, *Gesch. der Westgothen.* [C.D.]

Albanus, M. The protomartyr of Britain was martyred probably at Verulamium, and according to either the "conjecture" or the "knowledge" (*conjicimus* or *cognoscimus*) of Gildas, in the time of Diocletian, and if so, A.D. 304, but according to another legend, which, however, still speaks of Diocletian, in 286 (*Anglo-Sax. Chron.*, *Lib. Landav.*). Eusebius (*H. E.* viii. 13, and *de Mart. Palaest.* xiii. 10, 11), Lactantius (*de Mort. Persecut.* xv. xvi.), and Sozomen (i. 6) deny that there was any persecution during the time of Constantius in "the Gauls," which term included Britain. Possibly, however, Constantius may have been compelled to allow one or two martyrdoms. It is certain that 125 years after the latest date assigned to Alban's martyrdom, 144 after the earliest, viz. A.D. 429 (Prosper, *Chron.*), Germanus visited his relics in Britain, presumably at Verulamium (Constant. in *V. S. Germani*, written A.D. 473-492). Gildas mentions him in 560 (his statement, however, about the persecution is of no value, being simply a transference of Eusebius's words to Britain, to which Eusebius himself says they did not apply), and Venantius Fortunatus (*Poem.* viii. iv. 155) *c.* 580. Bede, in 731, copies Constantius and certain *Acta* otherwise unknown. And the subsequent foundation of Offa in 793 only serves to identify the place with the tradition. The British *Life* discovered by the St. Albans monk Unwona in the 10th cent., according to Matthew Paris, in *VV. Abb. S. Alban.*, is apparently a myth; and the *Life* by William of St. Albans (12th cent.) is of the ordinary nature and value of lives of the kind and date. But the testimony of Germanus, in Constantius's *Life* of him, seems sufficient proof that a tradition of the martyrdom of somebody named Albanus existed at Verulamium a century and something more after the supposed date of that martyrdom. His martyrdom with many fabulous details is related in Bede (i. 7). W. Bright, *Chapters of Early Ch. Hist.* (1897), p. 6. [A.W.H.]

Albion, king of the Langobardi, or Lombards, and founder of the kingdom subject to that people in Italy, was the son of that Audoin under whom the Lombards emerge from obscurity to occupy Pannonia, invited by the Emperor of Constantinople, in accordance with the usual Byzantine policy, as a check to the Gepidae. In the wars with the latter nation Alboin first appears. The confused accounts of them which Procopius preserves exhibit the tribe and their prince as rude and ferocious barbarians, and Alboin was a fit leader of such a tribe (Paul. Diac. i. 27, ii. 28). That he was personally a Christian, though an Arian, is proved by a letter from a Gallic bishop to his first wife, a Gallic princess, which deplores, not his heathenism, but his heresy (Sirmond. *Conc. Gall.* i.). Succeeding his father, Alboin accomplished, by the aid of the Avars, the destruction of the Gepidae (see Gibbon, c. xlv.). The conquest of Italy followed. Alboin's invading army was heterogeneous. Besides 20,000 Saxons accompanied by their families, who recrossed the Alps after the conquest, Muratori has deduced (*Antich. It.* i. diss. 1) from Italian topography the presence of the Bavarians, and Paul. (ii. 26) adds distinctly the names of several other tribes. The number of the army is unknown, but was considerable, as it was a migration of the whole tribe, and it largely changed the character and arrangements of population in Italy. Alboin left Pannonia in April 568; the passes were unguarded, and he learnt from his own success the need of securing his rear and the frontier of his future kingdom, and entrusted the defence and government of Venetia Prima, his first conquest, to Gisulf his nephew, with the title of duke and the command of those whom he should himself select among the most eminent of the "Farae" or nobles (Paul. ii. ix.). From this point the conquest was rapid. In Liguria (the western half of north Italy), Genoa, with some cities of the Riviera, alone escaped. Pavia held out for three years: perhaps its siege was not very vigorously pressed, for we know that a great part of Alboin's force was detached in flying squadrons which ravaged the country southwards all through Tuscany and Aemilia, to so great a distance that Paul mentions Rome and Ravenna as almost the only places which escaped. The death of Alboin followed the fall of Pavia. The story of his death is like that of his early life in the picture which it gives of a thoroughly barbaric society, where the skull of an enemy is used as a drinking-cup, and the men hold their banquets apart from the women (Gibbon, c. 45). Paul. avouches that the cup was to be seen in his own day. The chief authority for the life of Alboin, Paulus Diaconus, lived towards the end of the 8th cent., in the last days of the Lombard monarchy. [E.S.T.]

Alexander, St., archbp. of Alexandria, appears to have come to that see in 313, after the short episcopate of Achillas. He was an elderly man, of a kindly and attractive disposition; "gentle and quiet," as Rufinus says (i. 1), but also capable of acting with vigour and persistency. Accusations were laid against him by the malcontent Meletian faction, "before the emperor," Constantine (Athan. *Apol. c. Ar.* 11; ad *Ep. Aeg.* 23), but apparently without result. He was involved in a controversy with one Crescentius as to the proper time for keeping Easter (Epiph. *Haer.* 70, 9). But in 319 he was called upon to confront a far more formidable adversary. [ARIUS.] Arius was the parish priest, as he may be described, of the church of Baukalis, the oldest and the most important of the churches of Alexandria, situated "in the head of the mercantile part of the city" (Neale, *Hist. Alex.* i. 116), a man whose personal abilities enhanced the influence of his official position; he had been a possible successor at the last vacancy of the "Evangelical Throne," and may have consequently entertained unfriendly feelings towards its actual occupant. But it would be unreasonable to ascribe his opinions to private resentment. Doubtless the habits of his mind (Bright, *Hist. Ch.* p. 11) prepared him to adopt and carry out to their consequences, with a peculiar boldness of logic, such views as he now began to disseminate in Alexandrian society: that the Son of God could not be co-eternal with His Father; that He must be regarded as external to the Divine essence, and only a creature. The bishop tried at first to check this heresy by remonstrance at an interview, but with no real success. Agitation increasing, Alexander summoned a conference of his clergy; free discussion was allowed; and, according to Sozomen, Alexander seemed to waver between the Arian and anti-Arian positions. Ultimately he asserted in strong terms the co-equality of the Son; whereupon Arius criticized his language as savouring of the Sabellian error [SABELLIUS] which had "confounded the Persons." The movement increased, and Alexander himself was charged with irresolution or even with some inclination towards the new errors. It was then, apparently, that Colluthus, one of the city presbyters, went so far as to separate from his bishop's communion, and, on the plea of the necessities of the crisis, "ordained" some of his followers as clergy. (See Valesius on Theod. i. 4, and Neale, i. 116). Alexander's next step was to write to Arius and his supporters, including two bishops, five priests, and six deacons, exhorting them to renounce their "impiety"; and the majority of the clergy of Alexandria and the Mareotis, at his request, subscribed his letter. The exhortation failing, the archbishop brought the case formally before the synod of his suffragans, who numbered nearly 100. The Arians were summoned to appear: they stated their opinions; the Son, they held, was not eternal, but was created by the impersonal "Word," or Wisdom of the Father; foreign, therefore, to the Father's essence, imperfectly cognizant of Him, and, in fact, called into existence to be His instrument in the creation of man. "And can He then," asked one of the bishops, "change from good to evil, as Satan did?" They did not shrink from answering, "Since He is a creature, such a change is not impossible"; and the council instantly pronounced them to be "anathema." Such was the excommunication of Arius, apparently in 320. It was as far as possible from arresting the great movement of rationalistic thought (for this, in truth, was the character of Arianism) which had now so determinedly set in. The new opinions became extraordinarily popular; Alexandrian society was flooded with colloquial irreverence. But Arius ere long found that he could not maintain his position in the city when under the ban of the archbishop; it may be that Alexander had power actually to banish him; and he repaired to Palestine, where, as he expected, he found that his representations of the case made a favourable impression on several bishops, including Eusebius of Caesarea. Some wrote in his favour to Alexander, who, on his part, was most indefatigable in writing to various bishops in order to prevent them from being deceived by Arius; Epiphanius tells us that seventy such letters were preserved in his time (*Haer.* 69. 4). Of these, some were sufficiently effectual in Palestine to constrain Arius to seek an abode at Nicomedia. He had secured the support of the bishop of the city, the able but unprincipled Eusebius (Theod. i. 5; Athan. *de Syn.* 17); and he now wrote (Athan. *de Syn.* 16) in the name of "the presbyters and deacons" who had been excommunicated, to Alexander, giving a statement of their views, and professing that they had been learned from Alexander himself; the fact being, probably, as Möhler thinks, that Alexander had formerly used vague language in an anti-Sabellian direction. Eusebius now repeatedly urged Alexander to readmit Arius to communion; and the other bishops of Bithynia, in synod (Soz. i. 15), authorized their chief to send circular letters in his favour to various prelates. A Cilician bishop, Athanasius of Anazarbus, wrote to Alexander, openly declaring that Christ was "one of the hundred sheep"; George, an Alexandrian presbyter, then staying at Antioch, had the boldness to write to his bishop to the effect that the Son once "was not," just as Isaiah "was not," before he was born to Amoz (Athan. *de Syn.* 17), for which he was deposed by Alexander from the priesthood. Arius now returned into Palestine, and three bishops of that country, one of whom was Eusebius of Caesarea, permitted him to hold religious assemblies within their dioceses. This permission naturally gave great offence to Alexander. He had hitherto written only to individual bishops, but he now * drew up (perhaps with the help of his secretary and "archdeacon," Athanasius) his famous encyclic to all his fellow-ministers, i.e. to the whole Christian episcopate, giving an account of the opinions for which the Egyptian synod had excommunicated the original Arians, adducing Scriptural texts in refutation, and warning his brethren against the intrigues of Eusebius (Socr. i. 6). This letter, which he caused his

* A comparatively late date for this encyclic appears necessary, on account of its allusions to Eusebius. (See Neale, *Hist. Alex.* i. 127.) Some identify the encyclic with the Tome.

clergy to sign, probably preceded the "Tome" or confession of faith which he referred to as having been signed by some bishops, when he wrote to Alexander, bp. of Byzantium, the long and elaborate letter preserved by Theod. i. 4; in which, while using some language which in strictness must be called inaccurate, he gives an exposition of texts which became watchwords of the orthodox in the struggle (A.D. 323).

Another correspondent now appears on the scene. Eusebius of Nicomedia, who had a strong influence over the emperor Constantine, persuaded the latter to write, or to adopt and sign, a letter to Alexander and Arius, in which the controversy was treated as a logomachy (Eus. *Vit. Con.* ii. 64 seq.; Socr. i. 7). The imperial epistle was entrusted to a prelate of very high position, Hosius of Cordova, who can have had but little sympathy with the tone assumed by the Emperor. The council held at Alexandria on his arrival decided one point very unequivocally: the ordinations performed by Colluthus were pronounced absolutely null (Athan. *Apol.* 76). Peace was impossible on the basis of indifferentism, and Constantine summoned a general assembly of bishops to meet at Nicaea, in June 325. [*D. C. A.*, art. NICAEA, COUNCIL OF.] The Arians were condemned, and the Nicene Creed, in its original form, was drawn up.

The story told by Epiphanius, of severities used by Alexander towards the Meletians [MELETIUS], and of a consequent petition addressed by them to Constantine, appears to be one of several misstatements which he adopted from some Meletian sources. Athanasius tells us expressly that Alexander died within five months after the reception of the Meletians into church communion in the council of Nicaea (*Apol. c. Ari.* 59), and this, if strictly reckoned from the close of the council, would place his death in Jan. 326. It cannot be dated later than April 18 in that year. See further, ATHANASIUS.

Athanasius mentions a circumstance of Alexander's local administration which furnished a precedent, on one occasion, for himself. Alexander was building the church of St. Theonas at Alexandria, on a larger scale than any of the existing churches, and used it, for convenience' sake, before it was completed (*Ap. ad Const.* 15). He is also said by tradition to have never read the Gospels in a sitting posture, and to have never eaten on fast days while the sun was in the sky (Bolland. *Act. SS.*, Feb. 26). Two short fragments of a letter addressed by him to a bishop named Aeglon, against the Arians, are quoted in the works of Maximus the Confessor (in the Monothelite controversy), vol. ii. p. 152. A trans. of his extant writings is in the *Ante-Nicene Lib.* (T. & T. Clark). [W.B.]

Alexander, St., bp. of Byzantium, as the city was then called (Theod. *Hist.* i. 19) for about 23 years, his consecration being variously dated from A.D. 313 to 317. He was already 73 years old at the time (Socr. *Hist.* ii. 6; Soz. *Hist.* iii. 3). He is highly praised by Gregory of Nazianzum (*Or.* 27), and by Epiphanius (*adv. Haer.* lxix. 10). Theodoret calls him an "apostolic" bishop (*Hist.* i. 3, cf. *Phil.* 12). In the commencement of the Arian troubles the co-operation of Alexander was specially requested by his namesake of Alexandria (Theod. i. 4); and he was present at the council of Nicaea (Soz. ii. 29). When Constantine, induced by the Eusebians (Athan. *Ep. ad Serap.*; Rufinus, *Hist.* i.), and deceived by the equivocations of Arius (Socr. i. 37), commanded that Arius should be received to communion, Alexander, though threatened by the Eusebians with deposition and banishment, persisted in his refusal to admit the archheretic to communion, and shut himself up in the church of Irene for prayer in this extremity. Alexander did not long survive Arius (Socr. ii. 6; Theod. i. 19). On his deathbed he is said to have designated Paulus as his successor, and warned his clergy against the speciousness of Macedonius. [I.G.S.]

Alexander, bp. of Hierapolis Euphratensis and metropolitan in the patriarchate of Antioch; the uncompromising opponent of Cyril of Alexandria, and the resolute advocate of Nestorius in the controversies that followed the council of Ephesus, A.D. 431. His dignity as metropolitan gave him a leading place in the opposition of which the patriarch John of Antioch was the head, and his influence was confirmed by personal character. He may have commenced his episcopate as early as A.D. 404, when with uncompromising zeal he erased from the diptychs of one of his churches the name of Julian, a man famous for sanctity, but accused of Apollinarianism (Baluz. *Nov. Coll. Conc.* p. 867).

Alexander arrived at the council of Ephesus in company with his brother metropolitan Alexander of Apamea on or about June 20, 431. As soon as the Alexanders discovered Cyril's intention to open the council before John of Antioch's arrival they, on June 21, united with the other bishops of the East in signing a formal act demanding delay (Labbe, *Concil.* iii. 552, 660, 662; Baluz. 697, 699). The council heeded them not, opened their sittings the next day, June 22, and soon did the work for which they had been summoned, the condemnation of Nestorius. When John at last arrived, June 27, Alexander joined in the counter-council held by him and the prelates of his party in his inn, and signed the acts which cancelled the proceedings of the former council, deposing Cyril and Memnon, bp. of Ephesus, and declaring Cyril's anathemas heretical. As a necessary consequence Alexander was included in the sentence against John, and cut off from communion with Cyril's party (Labbe, iii. 764; Baluz. 507). Later he joined the council held by John at Tarsus, which pronounced a fresh sentence of deposition on Cyril (Baluz. 840, 843, 874); also that at Antioch in the middle of December, ratifying the former acts and declaring adherence to the Nicene faith. A meeting was held at Antioch early in 432, attended by Alexander, when six alternative articles were drawn up, one of which it was hoped Cyril would accept, and so afford a basis of reconciliation (*ib.* 764). One declared a resolution to be content with the Nicene Creed and to reject *all* the documents that had caused the controversy. Another council was summoned at Beroea. Four more articles were added to the six, and the whole were despatched to Cyril. Cyril was well content to express his adherence to the Nicene Creed, but felt it unreasonable that he should be required to abandon all he had written on the Nestorian controversy (Labbe, iii. 114, 1151, 1157, iv. 666; Baluz. 786). Cyril's reply was accepted by Acacius and John of Antioch, and other bishops now sincerely anxious for peace, but not by Alexander or Theodoret (Baluz. 757, 782). The former renewed his charge of Apollinarianism and refused to sign the deposition of Nestorius (*ib.* 762-763). This defection of Acacius of Beroea and John of Antioch was received with indignant sorrow by Alexander. It was the first breach in the hitherto compact opposition, and led to its gradual dissolution, leaving Alexander almost without supporters. In a vehement letter to Andrew of Samosata, he bitterly complained of Acacius's fickleness and protested that he would rather fly to the desert, resign his bishopric, and cut off his right hand than recognize Cyril as a Catholic until he had recanted his errors (*ib.* 764-765). The month of April, 433, saw the reconciliation of John and the majority of the Oriental bishops with Cyril fully established (Labbe, iv. 659; Cyril, *Ep.* 31, 42, 44). Alexander was informed of this in a private letter from John, beseeching him no longer to hinder the peace of the church. Alexander's indignation now knew no bounds. He wrote in furious terms to Andrew and Theodoret (Baluz. 799, 800). His language became more and more extravagant, "exile, violent death, the beasts, the fire, the precipice, were to be chosen before communion with a heretic" (*ib.* 768, 775, 799, 800, 809, 810), and he even "made a vow to avoid the sight, hearing, or even the remembrance of all who in their hearts turned back again to Egypt" (*ib.* 865). Alexander's contumacy had been regarded as depriving him of his functions as metropolitan. John, as patriarch, stepped in, A.D. 434, and ordained bishops in the Euphratensian province. This act, of very doubtful legality, excited serious displeasure, and was appealed against by Alexander and six of his suffragans (*ib.* 831-833, 865)

The end was now near at hand. Pulcheria and Theodosius had been carefully informed of the obstinate refusal of Alexander and the few left to support him to communicate with those whose orthodoxy had been recognized by the church. John had obtained imperial rescripts decreeing the expulsion and banishment of all bishops who still refused to communicate with him (*ib.* 876). This rescript was executed in the case of other recusants; Alexander still remained. John expressed great unwillingness to take any steps towards the deprivation of his former friend. He commissioned Theodoret to use his influence with him. But Theodoret had again to report the impossibility of softening his inflexibility. John now, A.D. 435, felt he could not offer any further resistance to the imperial decrees. But no compulsion was needed: Alexander obeyed the order with calmness, and even with joy at laying aside the burdens and anxieties of the episcopate. He went forth in utter poverty, not taking with him a single penny of his episcopal revenue, or a book or paper belonging to the church. His sole outfit consisted of some necessary documents, and the funds contributed by friends for the hire of vehicles (*ib.* 868, 881, 882). The banishment of their beloved and revered bishop overwhelmed the people of Hierapolis with grief. Fear of the civil authorities deterred them from any open manifestation, but they closed the churches, shut themselves up in their houses, and wept in private. In exile at the mines of Phamuthin in Egypt, Alexander died, sternly adhering to his anathemas of Cyril to the last (Tillemont, *Mém. Ecclés.* xiv. xv.; Labbe, *Concil.* vol. iii.; Baluz. *Nov. Collect.*) [E.V.]

Alexander, bp. of Jerusalem, was an early friend and fellow scholar of Origen at Alexandria, where they studied together under Pantaenus and Clemens Alex. (Eus. *H. E.* vi. 14). He was bishop of a city in Cappadocia (*ib.* vi. 11); or, according to Valesius (*Not. ad Euseb.*) and Tillemont (*Mém. eccl.* iii. p. 183), of Flaviopolis in Cilicia. He became a confessor in the persecution of Severus, A.D. 204, and was thrown into prison, where he continued some years. He was still a prisoner at the commencement of Caracalla's reign, A.D. 211, when he sent a letter by the hand of Clemens to congratulate the church of Antioch on the appointment of Asclepiades as their bishop in the room of Serapion (Eus. vi. 11). The next year he was released from prison, and, in fulfilment of a vow, visited Jerusalem, where he was chosen coadjutor to the aged bp. Narcissus. This being the first occasion of the translation of a bishop, as well as of the appointment of a coadjutor bishop, and in apparent violation of the canons of the church, it was deemed essential to obtain the sanction of the whole episcopate of Palestine. A synod was summoned at Jerusalem, and the assembled bishops gave their unanimous consent to the step, A.D. 213 (Hieron. *de Script. Eccl.*; Vales. *Not. in Euseb.* vi. 11; Socr. vii. 36; Bingham, *Origines,* bk. ii. § 4). On the death of Narcissus, Alexander succeeded as sole bishop. His chief claim to celebrity rests on the library he formed at Jerusalem, and on the boldness with which he supported Origen against his bishop, Demetrius of Alexandria. [ORIGEN.] The friendship of Alexander and Origen was warm and lasting; and the latter bears testimony to the remarkable gentleness and sweetness of character manifested in all Alexander's public instructions (Orig. *Homil. I. in Lib. Reg.* No. 1). Alexander was again thrown into prison at Caesarea in the Decian persecution, where he died A.D. 251 (Eus. *H. E.* vi. 46; Hieron. *Script. Eccl.*). Eusebius has preserved some fragments of Alexander's letters: to the Antinoites, *H. E.* vi. 11, to the church of Antioch, *ib.*; to Origen, *H. E.* vi. 14, and to Demetrius, *H. E.* vi. 19. These have been published by Galland, *Biblioth. Vet. Patrum,* vol. ii. pp. 201 seq. Clemens Alex. dedicated his *Canon Ecclesiasticus* to him (Eus. vi. 13). [E.V.]

Alexander I., bp. of Rome, is stated by all the authorities to have been the successor of Evaristus. Eusebius (*H. E.* iv. 4) makes him succeed in A.D. 109, in his Chronicle, A.D. 111 (f. 89). He assigns him in both works a reign of ten years. He has been confused with a martyr of the same name, who is mentioned in a fragment of an inscription. [G.H.M.]

Alogians, or **Alogi** (from ἀ privative and Λόγος, *deniers of the Logos*, or at least of the strongest witness for the Logos; not from ἄλογοι, *unreasonable*), a heretical sect of disputed existence in the latter half of 2nd cent. (*c.* 170). Epiphanius invented the term (*Haeres.* l. 1, *adv. Al.* c. 3), to characterize their rejection of the Divine Word preached by John (ἐπεὶ οὖν τὸν Λόγον οὐ δέχονται τὸν παρὰ Ἰωάννου κεκηρυγμένον, Ἄλογοι κληθήσονται). He traces their origin to Theodotus of Byzantium (*Haer.* liv. c. 1). According to his representation they denied, in ardent opposition to the Gnosticism of Cerinthus on the one hand, and to the Montanists on the other, that Jesus Christ was the eternal Logos, as taught in John i. 1-14; and rejected the Fourth Gospel and the Apocalypse as productions of Cerinthus.* Heinichen supposes that the Alogi rejected only the Apocalypse and not the Fourth Gospel; but this is directly contradicted by Epiphanius (l. c. 3; cf. *Haer.* l. iv. 1). That they attributed these books to Cerinthus, the Docetist and enemy of St. John, shows their utter want of critical judgment. They tried to refute the Gospel of St. John by the Synoptic Gospels, but with very poor arguments. In opposition to the Montanists, they also denied the continuance of the spiritual gifts in the church. It is not clear from Epiphanius whether the Alogi rejected only St. John's doctrines of the Logos, or also the divinity of Christ in any form. He calls them in his violent way (l. c. 3) ἀλλότριοι παντάπασιν τοῦ κηρύγματος τῆς ἀληθείας; and says of their heresy (*Haer.* liv. c. 1) that it denied the Gospel of St. John and the God-Word taught therein (τὸν ἐν αὐτῷ ἐν ἀρχῇ ὄντα θεὸν λόγον). Yet he clearly distinguishes them from the Ebionites; and their opposition to Cerinthus implies that they believed in the real humanity of Christ. Dorner (*Hist. of Christology*, i. p. 503, German ed.) thinks it probable that they allowed no distinctions in the Godhead, and thought that the divinity of the Father dwelt in the man Jesus. But this would identify them with the Patripassians. Lardner (*Works*, iv. 190, viii. 627) doubts the existence of this sect, because of the absence of other data, and the tendency of Epiphanius to multiply and exaggerate heresies. But the testimony of Epiphanius is essentially sustained by Irenaeus, who mentions persons who rejected both the Gospel of St. John and the prophetic Spirit (*simul et evangelium et propheticum repellunt Spiritum: adv. Haer.* iii. c. 11, § 9).

Epiphanius, *Haer.* 50, and esp. 54; M. Merkel, *Historisch-kritische Aufklärung der Streitigkeit der Aloger über die Apokalypsis* (Frankf. and Leipz. 1782); F. A. Heinichen, *de Alogis, Theodotianis atque Artemonitis* (Leipz. 1829); Neander, *Kirchengesch.* i. ii. pp. 906, 1003; Dorner, *op. cit.* vol. ii. pp. 500-503; Harnack, *Literatur*, ii. 1; Zahn, *Neutest. Kanon.* i. 220, ii. 967. [P.S.]

Ambrosiaster, or **Pseudo-Ambrosius,** a name generally employed to denote the unknown author of the *Commentaria in* xiii *Epistolas beati Pauli*, formerly ascribed to St. Ambrose and usually printed along with his works. The commentary itself contains no definite indication of its authorship. An incidental remark, however, on 1 Tim. iii. 15, "Ecclesia . . . cujus hodie rector est Damasus," shows that it was written during the pontificate of Damasus (366-384). It has been suggested that this clause may be an interpolation; but such an interpolation seems difficult to account for. Other marks, negative and positive, point to the same period. The text used is not the Vulgate, but a prior form of the Latin version. The ecclesiastical authors to whom he refers—Tertullian, Cyprian, Victorinus—belong to an earlier date. Among the heresies which he mentions he applies himself more especially to those of the 4th cent.—*e.g.* those of Arius, Novatian, Photinus—while the absence of allusion to later forms of error points the same way. He speaks of the Marcionites as on the verge of extinction ("quamvis pene defecerint," *in Ep. ad Timoth.* I. iv. 1). The date thus indicated would be the latter half of the 4th cent.; although, in that case, it is certainly somewhat surprising that Jerome in his treatise *de Scriptoribus Ecclesiasticis* should not mention any other Latin commentator on the Pauline Epistles than Victorinus.

It was the generally received opinion in the Middle Ages that our author was Ambrose, bp. of Milan; but this belief, which Erasmus was among the first to question, is now universally admitted to rest on no sufficient grounds, though opinions differ much as to the probable author. From certain expressions which appear favourable to Pelagianism the work has been assigned by some to Julian of Aeclanum; but, as Richard Simon has naïvely remarked, "if the writer does not always appear orthodox to those who profess to follow the doctrine of St. Augustine, it must be taken into account that he wrote before that Father had published his opinions." The expressions in question were probably employed without reference to the Pelagian controversy, and previous to its emergence, and are, moreover, accompanied by others entirely incompatible with a Pelagian authorship (*e.g.* the statement *in Ep. ad Rom.* v. 12, "Manifestum est in Adam omnes peccasse quasi in massâ").

The only positive statement as to the authorship is contained in the following passage of Augustine, *Contra duas Epistolas Pelagianorum*, lib. iv. c. 7: "Nam et sic sanctus Hilarius intellexit quod scriptum est, in quo omnes peccaverunt: ait enim, 'In quo, id est in Adam omnes peccaverunt.' Deinde addidit: 'Manifestum est in Adam omnes peccasse quasi in massâ; ipse enim per peccatum corruptus, quos genuit omnes nati sunt sub peccato.' Haec scribens Hilarius sine ambiguitate commonuit, quomodo intelligendum esset, in quo omnes peccaverunt." As the words cited are found in this commentary, it may be reasonably assumed that the statement applies to it, and that Augustine reckoned Hilarius its author. Of the persons of that name, Augustine elsewhere mentions only Hilarius the Sardinian, deacon of the Roman church, sent by pope Liberius in 354 to the emperor Constantius after the synod

* This, it may be remarked, is an argument against the criticism of the Tübingen school, which would bring the composition of the Gospel of St. John down to the middle of the 2nd cent.; for Cerinthus was a contemporary of the apostle. Had the Alogi had any idea of the recent origin of St. John, they would have made much account of it.

of Arles. By many modern scholars Hilary the deacon has been accepted as the author of the work. But Petavius and others have objected that Augustine was not likely to apply the epithet *sanctus* to one whom he must have known to be guilty of schism. There can be little doubt that, whoever was the author, the work no longer retains its original form. The well-meaning zeal of copyists appears to have freely inserted comments from various sources, such as Augustine, Chrysostom, Jerome, the commentary which is printed at the end of the works of Jerome and is usually ascribed to Pelagius. These circumstances sufficiently account for the various forms of the text in MSS., and for the discrepancies and inequalities of treatment in several parts.

There is, moreover, a marked affinity between this commentary and certain portions of the *Quaestiones Veteris et Novi Testamenti* usually printed with the works of St. Augustine. The similarity of ideas and, in various cases, identity of language can only be explained by supposing either that they have had a common author, or that the writer of the one work has borrowed largely from the other. The note of time in the *Quaestiones*—300 years after the destruction of Jerusalem—and some references to contemporary events suit the period of Damasus, and have induced many to ascribe this work also to Hilary the deacon. But the authorship of both remains uncertain, and probably the *Quaestiones* was composed subsequently to the commentary.

The commentary on the Pauline Epistles, notwithstanding its inequalities of treatment, is of great value, and is well characterized by Sixtus Senensis as "brief in words, but weighty in matter"; and, although the writer is frequently controversial, he speedily returns to the proper work of exegesis. In consequence of his use of the old Latin version and frequent reference to various readings, his work affords important materials for textual criticism.

The commentary on the Epistle to the Hebrews, which accompanies the others in some editions, but is omitted by the Benedictine editors, is a compilation from various Patristic sources, principally from Chrysostom. Cf. H. B. Swete, *Theod. Mops. Comm.* (1880), vol. i. p. lxxviii., vol. ii. p. 351.

The commentary was issued separately at Cologne in 1530 and 1532. Cf. *A Study of Ambrosiaster* by A. Souter (Camb. Univ. Press); *Text and Studies*, vol. vii. No. 4. [W.P.D.]

Ambrosius (1) ('Αμβρόσιος) of Alexandria, a deacon according to Jerome (*de Vir. Ill.* 56), the disciple and friend of Origen, died *c.* 250.

It is not certain whether Ambrose was a Christian by birth; but he was of a noble and wealthy family (Orig. *Exhort. ad. Mart.* 14 f. 49; Hieron. *l.c.*), and probably occupied some office under the Imperial Government (Epiph. *Haer.* 64, 3: cf. Orig. *ib.* c. 36). Endowed with an active and critical mind, he at first neglected the simple teaching of the Gospel for the more philosophic systems of heresy (Orig. *in Johann.* tom. v.). However, when he met Origen he recognized his true teacher, and embraced the orthodox faith (Epiph. *l.c.*). From that time to his death Ambrose devoted his whole energy to encouraging his great master in his labours on Holy Scripture, and used his fortune to further them (Eus. *H. E.* vi. 23).

Ambrose left no writings of his own except some letters, but it is evident that he exercised a powerful influence upon Origen, who called him his "taskmaster," ἐργοδιώκτης (*in Johann.* tom. v.), and it may have been through his zeal in "collation" (Orig. *Ep.* l.) that Origen undertook his critical labours. Through mistaken devotion, Ambrose indiscreetly permitted the publication of some unrevised treatises of Origen which were intended only for his own use (Hieron. *Ep.* 84, 10). [B.F.W.]

Ambrosius (2), "a chief man of Greece," and a "senator," "who became a Christian," and, according to the title of the Syriac translation, wrote the "Address to the Greeks" (Λόγος πρὸς Ἕλληνας), which is published with the works of Justin Martyr (Cureton, *Spicil. Syr.* pp. xi. 61). There is no other trace of this tradition, nor ground for identifying him with Ambrose of Alexandria. [B.F.W.]

Ambrosius, St., bp. of Milan (A.D. 374-397). The chief materials for his life are his own works, which include an important collection of letters. Another source is a *Life* by Paulinus, his *notarius* or secretary, who had been with him at his death and wrote at the suggestion of St. Augustine. This *Life* is full of prodigies, and adds hardly anything to what we learn from the works. The letters have been reduced to a chronological order with great care by the Benedictine editors of St. Ambrose, who have also digested the various particulars into a useful biography.

Ambrose's father, who bore the same name, was a Roman of the highest rank, and at the time of St. Ambrose's birth was prefect of the Galliae, a province which included Britain and Spain, and constituted one of the four great praetorian prefectures of the empire. The only datum for determining the year of Ambrose's birth is a passage in one of his letters in which he happens to mention that he is fifty-three years old, and at the same time contrasts the quiet of Campania with the commotions by which he was himself surrounded (*Ep.* lix. 3). There are two periods to which this description would apply, A.D. 387 or 393. If we assume, as seems most probable, that Ambrose was fifty-three years old in 393, we shall place his birth in 340.

After receiving a liberal education at Rome, Ambrose devoted himself to the profession of the law, which was then the usual path to the highest civil offices (see Gibbon, c. xvii.). He practised at the court of the praetorian prefect of Italy, Probus, who appointed him "consular" * magistrate of the provinces of Liguria and Aemilia. He made an admirable magistrate, and became known to the people of Milan, where he held his court, as a high-minded, conscientious, and religious man. Whilst he was discharging his office, Auxentius, whom the Arian party had foisted into the see of Milan, died. The Catholic party had now grown stronger, and a vehement strife

* The empire was divided into 116 provinces, of which 3 were governed by *pro-consuls*, 37 by *consulars*, 5 by *correctors*, and 71 by *presidents* (Gibbon, *u.s.*).

arose as to the appointment of a successor to Auxentius. The consular came down to the church to keep the peace and was addressing the people in his character as a civil magistrate, when a cry (which tradition asserts to have been that of a child) was heard, "Ambrose for bishop!" In a moment it struck the whole multitude as a solution in which both parties might acquiesce without the sense of defeat, and a unanimous shout arose, "We will have Ambrose for bishop!" It was a singular choice, even for those rougher and more tumultuous times, for Ambrose was not yet so much as baptized. But he was an earnest Christian in his belief, and had only been kept from seeking baptism by a religious awe, of which there were then many examples. Such an one naturally shrank from being made bishop. With undoubted sincerity, he resisted this popular nomination. He was, he says, *raptus a tribunalibus ad sacerdotium* *de Officiis*, i. 4). He was baptized, passed summarily through the intermediate ecclesiastical stages, and on the eighth day was consecrated bp. of Milan. This was in the year 374 (a year after the death of Athanasius, and before the death of Valentinian I.), Ambrose being thirty-four years of age. The *vox populi* was never more thoroughly justified. The foundation of his excellence was laid in a singular and unsullied purity of character. In the see of Milan Ambrose had found precisely his place, and he laboured indefatigably as its bishop for twenty-three years till his death.

One of his first cares after his ordination was to divest himself of the charge of private property. As a member of a wealthy family he appears to have possessed both money and lands. What he did not give away to the poor or the church or reserve as an income for his sister, he placed entirely under the management of a dearly loved brother named Satyrus. He was thus free to devote his whole energies to the work of his calling. His writings enable us to follow him in both his ordinary and his extraordinary occupations. He was wont to "celebrate the sacrifice" every day (*Ep.* xx. 15). Every Lord's Day he preached in the Basilica. His extant works consist mainly of addresses and expositions which had been first spoken in the church and were afterwards revised for publication. They bear traces of this mode of composition in their simplicity and naturalness, and also in their popular character and undigested form. Ambrose had to begin, as he ingenuously declares, to learn and to teach at the same time (*de Officiis*, lib. i. cap. i. 4). In doctrine he followed reverently what was of best repute in the church in his time, carefully guarding his own and his people's orthodoxy from all heresy, and urging, but with wholesome, if not always consistent, qualifications, the ascetic religious perfection which the best Christians were then pursuing. The sacred books, for which he had a profound reverence, were to him—what pastoral and didactic theology has always tended to make them—verbal materials for edification, which was to be extracted from them by any and every kind of interpretation to which their letter could be subjected. His writings, therefore, or sermons, are chiefly of interest with reference to the history and character of their author; but they are lively and ingenuous, full of good practical advice, and interspersed with gnomic sentences of much felicity.

One of the secrets of Ambrose's influence over the people was his admission of them into all his interests and cares. He had nothing private from the congregation in the Basilica. The sister Marcellina and the brothers Satyrus and Ambrose (this was the order of their ages) were united together by a remarkable affection. The three loved one another too devotedly to think of marrying. Marcellina became early a consecrated virgin, but continued to feel the keenest and tenderest concern in her brothers' lives. When Ambrose became a bishop, Satyrus appears to have given up an important appointment in order to come and live with his brother and take every secular care off his hands. These domestic virtues of Marcellina and Satyrus we learn from sermons of Ambrose. His discourses on virginity became famous, and attracted virgins from distant parts to receive consecration at his hands. These discourses, in the third year after his ordination, he digested into three books, *de Virginibus*, which were addressed in their new form to his sister, and which contain, besides much praise of Marcellina, the address made to her at her consecration by the bp. of Rome. A year or two later occurred the death of Satyrus, in the flower of his age. In the depth of his grief Ambrose pronounced a funeral discourse upon his brother (*de Excessu Satyri*), which was followed seven days after by a sermon upon the hope of a future life (*de Fide Res.*).

The bp. of Milan, exercising the authority of a patriarchate, and presiding over a city which was frequently the residence of the emperor, was a great dignitary. But we cannot fail to recognize the high reputation which Ambrose had won for himself personally and in a surprisingly short period, when we observe the deference paid to him by the emperors of his time. He was certainly fortunate in the sovereigns with whom he had to do. The youths Gratian and Valentinian II., and the great Theodosius, were singularly virtuous and religious princes. Gratian was a boy of sixteen when the death of his father placed him on the throne, and in the year 377, the third of Ambrose's episcopate, he was two years older. In that year he was preparing to go to the assistance of his uncle Valens against the barbarian invaders by whom he was hard pressed; and desiring to be fortified against the arguments of the Arians whom Valens was favouring at Constantinople, he wrote to Ambrose, and asked him to furnish him with a controversial treatise in support of the orthodox faith. Ambrose complied with the pious youth's request by writing two books *de Fide*. In the following year Gratian wrote a letter, preserved with those of Ambrose, in which he requests another copy of that work, together with an additional argument upon the divinity of the Holy Spirit. In this letter he calls Ambrose *parens*. Ambrose amplified his former treatise by adding three books to the two he had already composed. This work *de Fide* was reckoned an important defence of the orthodox faith. The work *de Spiritu Sancto*, in three books, was written in the year 381.

The successes of the Goths which attended the defeat and death of Valens were the occasion of frightful calamities to the empire. From Illyricum and Thrace, especially, an immense number of captives were carried off by the barbarians, in ransoming whom the whole available resources of the church were exhausted by Ambrose; and when everything else had been taken, he did not scruple to break up and sell the sacramental vessels. He himself relates this fact with pride (*de Off.* lib. ii. 136, 138). We now see Ambrose zealous in the general affairs of the church, and the leading ecclesiastic of his time. Presiding in the council of Aquileia, 381, he questioned the two Arianizing prelates who were put on their trial before it. Several letters addressed to the emperor at this time in the name of the council of Aquileia or of the Italian episcopate on the general government of the church are preserved amongst Ambrose's letters (*Epp.* ix.-xii.). When Acholius died—the bp. of Thessalonica by whom Theodosius had been baptized—his death was formally announced to Ambrose by the clergy and people of his diocese; and we have two letters in reply, one written to the church and the other to Anysius the new bishop. The next two letters of the collection (xvii., xviii.) are addressed to the emperor Valentinian, after the death of Gratian, to exhort him not to comply with a request of Symmachus, prefect of the city, that he would replace the altar of Victory in the Senate House, and restore the funds for certain heathen ceremonies. Ambrose, whose influence was invoked by the bp. of Rome, protested strongly against any such concessions to paganism; and Victory, as it was said, favoured in the result her enemy more than her champion.

The struggle between Ambrose and Justina, the mother of Valentinian II., which afterwards reached such a height at Milan, had been begun with a preliminary trial of strength about the appointment of a bishop at Sirmium. But when the usurpation of Maximus occurred (A.D. 383), and had been stained by the violent death of Gratian, Justina in her alarm had recourse to the great Catholic bishop, and persuaded him to go on an embassy to Maximus, to beg him to leave Italy untouched. Maximus had Theodosius to deal with behind the boy-emperor and his mother; and his first act, when Gaul had fallen into his hands, was to send to Theodosius and propose to him, instead of war, the partition of the empire. Theodosius was constrained by motives of policy to assent to the proposal; and Ambrose had the comfort of returning to Milan with the announcement that the new emperor would refrain from passing the boundary of the Alps. Allusions are made to this embassy in a letter of Ambrose (*Ep.* xxiv. 7) in which he reports the less successful issue of a later appeal to Maximus.

One of the chief glories of Ambrose is that St. Augustine ascribed to him his conversion, and sought Christian baptism at his hands. The circumstances of his intercourse with St. Ambrose (A.D. 383-387) are related by St. Augustine in his *Confessions*. He tells us of the singularly eminent position of St. Ambrose (vi. 3), of his reputation for eloquence (vi. 13), of the difficulty of getting an opportunity of conversing with him on account of his many engagements, and his habit of reading to himself when company was present (v. 3), and of his method of expounding the Old Testament by finding under the letter a spiritual or mystical sense (vi. 4).

It was during this period, in the years 385-6, that Ambrose defended the churches of Milan so stoutly against the intrusion of Arian worship. Justina, who patronized the languishing Arian party, was bent on obtaining one of the churches at Milan for the use of her friends. Ambrose was not likely to make the concession. How in this matter he resisted the violent efforts of Justina, and the authority of her son (at this time fifteen years of age), is described at length by Ambrose himself in letters to his sister Marcellina and to Valentinian, and in a sermon preached at the crisis of the struggle (*Epp.* xx. xxi., and the *Sermo de Basilicis Tradendis* which follows them). There appear to have been two churches at Milan, the one without, the other within, the walls. The former, as of less importance, was first asked for. This being refused, some persons of the court came to Ambrose, and begged him to concede—probably for partial use only—the newer and larger basilica, and to exert his influence to prevent any popular disturbance. For it is important to observe that throughout the struggle the people were on the Catholic side. Ambrose replied loftily that the temple of God could not be surrendered by His priest. The next day, which was Sunday, as Ambrose was officiating in the principal basilica, news came that police-agents had been sent from the palace, who were hanging on the Portian basilica the curtains which marked a building as claimed for the imperial treasury. A part of the multitude hastened thither; Ambrose remained to perform Mass. Then he heard that the people had seized on a certain Arian presbyter, whom they met on the way. Ambrose began to pray with bitter tears that the cause of the church might not be stained with blood; and sent presbyters and deacons, who succeeded in rescuing the prisoner unhurt. Justina, in her irritation, treated the rich men of the city as responsible for a tumult, and threw many of them into prison. The imperial authority was being dangerously strained. Politic officials came to Ambrose and entreated him to give way to the sovereign rights of the emperor; Ambrose replied that the emperor had no rights over what belonged to God. A body of troops was sent to take possession of the basilica, and there was great fear of blood being shed; but after mutual appeals between their officers and Ambrose, the soldiers withdrew, and Ambrose remained all day in the church. At night he went home, and on coming out the next morning he found that the church (the Portian) was surrounded by soldiers. But the soldiers were in awe of Ambrose, and, learning that he had threatened them with excommunication, they began to crowd in, protesting that they came to pray and not to fight. Ambrose took the lesson for the day as the subject of a sermon, and whilst he was preaching he was told that the imperial curtains were taken down. The emperor was worsted by the bishop, and was naturally angry. He sent a secretary to reproach Ambrose, and ask if he meant to make himself a tyrant. Soldiers continued to surround the church, and Ambrose remained there singing psalms with the faithful. The next day the soldiers were withdrawn, and the merchants who had been imprisoned were released. The struggle was over; but Ambrose heard that the emperor had said bitterly to the soldiers, "If Ambrose orders you, you will give me up in chains." He records another saying, which drew from him a retort of characteristic felicity. The court chamberlain sent him a message: "Whilst I am alive, shall you despise Valentinian? I will take off your head." Ambrose answered: "May God grant you to fulfil what you threaten; for then my fate will be that of a bishop, your act will be that of a eunuch."

In the course of the following year the attempts of the Arian party, and of the emperor as at this time governed by that party, were renewed. Ambrose was asked to hold a discussion with Auxentius, an Arian bishop, before chosen judges in the presence of the court, or else to withdraw from Milan. He consulted such bishops and presbyters as were within reach, and in their name wrote a letter to the emperor (*Ep.* xxi.), declining the discussion. An alarm was spread amongst the people that he was going to be taken away from Milan, and for some days, by night and by day, he was surrounded and watched by an immense concourse of his friends. He preached them a sermon (*de Basilicis Tradendis*), assuring them of his steadfastness, and encouraging them to confidence, and at the same time gave them hymns composed by himself to sing—hymns in honour of the Trinity—by which their fervour was greatly stimulated. Again the court party found themselves worsted, and gave way.

The singing of hymns, by which this remarkable occupation of the basilica was characterized, is described by St. Augustine as extremely moving (*Conf.* vi. 7), and is said by him to have been an imitation of Eastern customs, and to have been followed generally throughout the church. Paulinus also observes that at this time "antiphons, hymns, and vigils began to be performed in the church of Milan, and had spread thence amongst all the churches of the West" (*Vita*, 13). The reputation of St. Ambrose as a composer of hymns was such that many certainly not his have been attributed to him, and amongst them the *Te Deum*. The Benedictine edition gives twelve hymns, which there is some good authority for ascribing to Ambrose, the best known of which are those beginning *Aeterne rerum conditor*, *Deus creator omnium*, *Veni redemptor gentium*, and *O lux beata Trinitas*. They have a brightness and felicity which have reasonably made them favourites in the church to the present day.

We must take into account the state of mind brought about in the bishop and his flock by that protracted vigil in the basilica, when we read of the miracles into which their triumph over heresy blazed forth. We have a narrative from St. Ambrose's own pen, in a letter to Marcellina (*Ep.* xxii.), of the wonderful discovery of the remains of two martyrs, and of the cures wrought by them. A basilica was to be dedicated, and Ambrose was longing to find some relics of martyrs. A presage suddenly struck him. (This "presagium" is called a vision by St. Augustine, *Conf.* lx. 7, *de Civ. Dei*, xxii. 8.) He caused the ground to be opened in the church that was consecrated by the remains of St. Felix and St. Nabor. Two bodies were found, of wonderful size (*ut prisca aetas ferebat*), the heads severed from the shoulders, the tomb stained with blood. This discovery, so precious to a church "barren of martyrs," was welcomed with the wildest enthusiasm. Old men began to remember that they had heard formerly the names of these martyrs—Gervasius and Protasius—and had read the title on their grave. Miracles crowded thick upon one another. They were mostly cures of demoniacs, and of sickly persons; but one blind man received his sight. Ambrose himself, for once, eagerly and positively affirms the reality of the cure; and Augustine, who generally held that the age of miracles was past, also bears witness to the common acceptance of the fact at Milan. Gibbon has some excuse for his note, "I should recommend this miracle to our divines, if it did not prove the worship of relics, as well as the Nicene Creed." The Arians, as we learn from Ambrose and Paulinus, made light of the healing of demoniacs, and were sceptical about the blind man's history. The martyrs' bones were carried into the "Ambrosian" Basilica (now the church of St. Ambrogio), and deposited beneath the altar in a place which Ambrose had designed for his own remains.

The memory of this conflict did not restrain Justina and her son from asking help shortly after of Ambrose. It was evident that Maximus was preparing to invade Italy; and as Ambrose had apparently been successful in his former embassy, he was charged with another conciliatory appeal to the same ruler. The magnanimous bishop consented to go, but he was unfavourably received, and having given great offence by abstaining from communion with the bishops who were about Maximus, he was summarily ordered to return home. He reports the failure of his mission in a letter to Valentinian (*Ep.* xxiv.). It is worthy of remark that the punishment of heresy by death was so hateful to Ambrose that he declined communion with bishops who had been accomplices in it ("qui aliquos, devios licet a fide, ad necem petebant," *ib.* 12). These bishops had prevailed on Maximus to put to death Priscillian—the first time that heresy was so punished. [PRISCILLIANUS.]

Maximus was not diverted from his project. He crossed the Alps, and Justina, with her son, fled to Theodosius. It was not long before the vigour and ability of Theodosius triumphed over Maximus, who perished in the conflict he had provoked. Ambrose, who withdrew from Milan when Maximus came to occupy it, appears to have been near Theodosius in the hour of victory, and used his influence with him in favour of moderation and clemency, which the emperor, according to his usual habit, displayed in an eminent degree (*Ep.* **xl.**

32). But Ambrose unhappily prevailed upon Theodosius to abandon a course which his stricter sense of his duty as a ruler had prompted him to take. In some obscure place in the East the Christians had been guilty of outrages, from which it had often been their lot to suffer. With the support of their bishop, they had demolished a Jewish synagogue and a meeting-house of certain Gnostic heretics. Theodosius, hearing of this violence, had ordered that the bishop should rebuild the synagogue at his own expense, and that the rioters, who were chiefly monks, should be punished at the discretion of the local governor. This order naturally affronted the party spirit of the Christians. Ambrose could not bear that his fellow-believers should be thus humiliated. He wrote a letter to the emperor (who was at Milan, Ambrose being for the moment at Aquileia), entreating him most earnestly to revoke the order. With much that Ambrose says we can sympathize; but he lays down a principle fruitful in disastrous issues: *Cedat oportet censura* (the functions of the civil ruler) *devotioni* (*Ep.* xl. 11). Shortly after, he had the opportunity of preaching before the emperor at Milan. In a letter to his sister he gives the sermon at length, with its conclusion, addressed directly to the emperor, and begging of him the pardon of those who had been caught in a sin. When he came down from the pulpit, Theodosius said to him, *De nobis proposuisti.* "Only with a view to your advantage," replied Ambrose. "In truth," continued the emperor, "the order that the bishop should rebuild the synagogue was too hard. But that is amended. The monks commit many crimes." Then he remained silent for a while. At last Ambrose said, "Enable me to offer the sacrifice for thee with a clear conscience." The emperor sat down and nodded, but Ambrose would not be satisfied without extracting a solemn engagement that no further proceedings should be taken in the matter. After this he went up to the altar; "but I should not have gone," adds Ambrose, "unless he had given me his full promise" (*Ep.* xli. 28).

About two years later (A.D. 390) the lamentable massacre at Thessalonica gave occasion for a very grand act of spiritual discipline. The commander of the garrison at Thessalonica and several of his officers had been brutally murdered by a mob in that city. The indignation of the emperor was extreme; and after appearing to yield to gentler counsels, he sent orders, which were executed by an indiscriminate slaughter of at least 7,000 persons in Thessalonica. Ambrose protested against this in the name of God and of the church. He had always acted on the principle that "nothing was more dangerous before God or base amongst men than for a priest not to speak out his convictions freely," and his lofty disinterestedness (*non pro meis commodis faciebam*, Ep. lvii. 4) gave him great power over a religious and magnanimous mind like that of Theodosius. Ambrose now wrote him a letter (Ep. li.), which Gibbon most unjustly calls "a miserable rhapsody on a noble subject," but which most readers will feel to be worthy of its high purpose. With many protestations of respect and sympathy Ambrose urges his Emperor to a genuine repentance for the dreadful deed to which in an access of passion he had given his sanction. He intimates that he could not celebrate the Eucharist in the presence of one so stained with blood. Gibbon represents the behaviour of Ambrose as marked by a prelatical pomposity, of which there is no trace whatever in the only documents on which we can rely. In his own letter the bishop is most considerate and tender, though evidently resolute. He and Paulinus record simply that the emperor performed public penance, stripping himself of his royal insignia, and praying for pardon with groans and tears; and that he never passed a day afterwards without grieving for his error (Paulinus, 24; Amb. *de Ob. Theod.* 34).

In the course of the following year (391), Theodosius having returned to the East, the weak authority of Valentinian II. was overthrown by Arbogastes and his puppet Eugenius, and the unfortunate youth perished by the same fate as his brother. He was in Gaul at the time of his death, and Ambrose was at that moment crossing the Alps to visit him there, partly by the desire of the Italian magistrates, who wished Valentinian to return to Italy, and partly at the request of the emperor himself, who was anxious to be baptized by him. In the next year (392) a funeral oration was delivered at Milan by Ambrose (*de Obitu Valentiniani*), in which he praises the piety as well as the many virtues of the departed. It appears that under the influence of Theodosius, Valentinian had learnt to regard Ambrose with the same reverence as his brother had done before him (Letter to Theodosius, *Ep.* liii. 2). He had died unbaptized; but Ambrose assures his sorrowing sisters that his desire was equivalent to the act of baptism, and that he had been washed in his piety as the martyrs in their blood (*de Ob. Val.* 51-53).

Eugenius held the sovereign power in the West for two or three years, and made friendly overtures to the great Italian prelate. But Ambrose for a time returned no answer; and when Eugenius came to Milan, he retired from that city. Shortly after this withdrawal, he wrote a respectful letter to Eugenius, explaining that the reason why he had refused to hold intercourse with him was that he had given permission, though himself a Christian, that the altar of Victory should be restored—the boon which Symmachus had begged for in vain being yielded to the power of Arbogastes.

When the military genius and vigour of Theodosius had gained one more brilliant triumph by the rapid overthrow of Arbogastes and Eugenius, Ambrose, who had returned to Milan (Aug. A.D. 394), received there a letter from Theodosius requesting him to offer a public thanksgiving for his victory. Ambrose replies (*Ep.* lxi.) with enthusiastic congratulations. But the happiness thus secured did not last long. In the following year the great Theodosius died at Milan (Jan. 395), asking for Ambrose with his last breath (*de Obitu Theod.* 35). The bishop had the satisfaction of paying a cordial tribute to his memory in the funeral oration he delivered over his remains.

Ambrose himself had only two more years

to live. The time was filled with busy labours of exposition, correspondence, and episcopal government; and, according to Paulinus, with various prodigies. Unhappily this biographer spoils with his childish miracles what is still a touching account of the good bishop's death. It became known that his strength was failing, and the count Stilicho, saying that the death of such a man threatened death to Italy itself, induced a number of the chief men of the city to go to him, and entreat him to pray to God that his life might be spared. Ambrose replied, "I have not so lived amongst you, that I should be ashamed to live; and I do not fear to die, because we have a good Lord." * For some hours before his death he lay with his hands crossed, praying; as Paulinus could see by the movement of his lips, though he heard no voice. When the last moment was at hand, Honoratus, the bp. of Vercellae, who was lying down in another room, thought he heard himself thrice called, and came to Ambrose, and offered him the Body of the Lord; immediately after receiving which he breathed his last breath—a man, Paulinus says well, who for the fear of God had never feared to speak the truth to kings or any powers. He died on Good Friday night, 397, and was buried in the Ambrosian Basilica, in the presence of a multitude of every rank and age, including even Jews and pagans.

By the weight of his character St. Ambrose gave a powerful support to the tendencies which he favoured. He held without misgivings that the church was the organ of God in the world, and that secular government had the choice of being either hostile or subservient to the Divine authority ruling in the church. To passages already quoted which express this conviction may be added a remark let fall by Ambrose at the council of Aquileia, "Sacerdotes de laicis judicare debent, non laici de sacerdotibus" (*Gesta Conc. Aqu.* 51). He was of strict Athanasian orthodoxy as against heresy of every colour. His views of the work of Christ in the Incarnation, the Passion, and the Resurrection, have in a marked degree the broad and universal character which belongs to the higher patristic theology on this subject. (For example, speaking of the resurrection of Christ, he says, "Resurrexit in eo mundus, resurrexit in eo coelum, resurrexit in eo terra," *de Fide Res.* 102.) With regard to religion and religious practices, he is emphatic in insisting that the worship of the heart is all-important ("Deo enim velle pro facto est," *de Fide Res.* 115; "Deus non sanguine sed pietate placatur," *ib.* 98; "Non pecuniam Deus sed fidem quaerit," *de Poen.* ii. ix.); but at the same time his language concerning the two Sacraments is often undeniably that of materializing theology. Attempts have been made, chiefly on this account, to call in question the Ambrosian authorship of the treatises *de Mysteriis* and *de Sacramentis*; but their expressions are supported by others to be found in undoubted works of Ambrose. He praises his brother Satyrus for having tied a portion of the consecrated elements in a napkin round his neck when he was shipwrecked, and adds, that having found the benefit of "the heavenly mystery" in this form, he was eager to receive it into his mouth—"quam majus putabat fusum in viscera, quod tantum sibi tectum orario profuisset!" (*de Exc. Sat.* 43, 46). He argues for the daily reception of the Eucharist from the prayer, Give us this day our daily bread (*de Sacr.* v. 25). His frequent strong recommendations of virginity are based, not on a theory of self-denial, but rather on one of detachment from the cares of the world and the troubles inseparable from matrimony and parentage. According to him, marriage is the more painful state, as well as the less favourable to spiritual devotion. Nevertheless, he did not expect or desire a large number to embrace the life which he so highly eulogized. "Dicet aliquis: Ergo dissuades nuptias? ego vero suadeo, et eos damno qui dissuadere consuerunt. . . . Paucarum quippe hoc munus [virginity] est, illud omnium" (*de Virginibus*, I. vii.). He and his sister used to press Satyrus to marry, but Satyrus put it off through family affection—"ne a fratribus divelleretur" (*de Exc. Sat.* §§ 53, 59). Fasting is commended, not as self-torture pleasing to God, but as the means of making the body more wholesome and stronger. A keen sense of the restraints and temptations and annoyances which reside in the flesh is expressed in Ambrose's remarkable language concerning death. It is a great point with him that death is altogether to be desired. He argues this point very fully in the address *de Fide Resurrectionis* and in the essay *de Bono Mortis*. There are three kinds of death, he says—the death *of* sin, death *to* sin, and the death of the body (*de B. M.* § 3). This last is the emancipation of the soul from the body. He appeals to the arguments of philosophers and to the analogies of nature, as well as to Scripture, to shew not only that such a deliverance may be hoped for, but that it must be a thing to be desired by all. The terrors of the future state almost entirely disappear. He admits now and then that punishment must be looked for by the wicked; but he affirms that even to the wicked death is a gain (*de B. M.* § 28). There are two reasons why the foolish fear death: one because they regard it as destruction; "altera, quod poenas reformident, poetarum scilicet fabulis territi, latratus Cerberi, et Cocyti fluminis tristem voraginem, etc., etc. Haec plena sunt fabularum, nec tamen negaverim poenas esse post mortem" (*ib.* 33). "Qui infideles sunt, descendunt in infernum viventes; etsi nobiscum videntur vivere sed in inferno sunt" (*ib.* 56).

The see of Milan was in no way dependent upon that of Rome; but Ambrose always delighted to pay respect to the bp. of Rome, as representing more than any other the unity of the church. His feeling towards Rome is expressed in the apology with which he defends the custom of washing the feet in baptism—a custom which prevailed at Milan but not at Rome. "In omnibus cupio sequi Ecclesiam Romanam; sed tamen et nos homines sensum habemus; ideo quod alibi rectius servatur, et nos rectius custodimus. Ipsum sequimur apostolum Petrum, . . . qui

* St. Augustine was wont to express his peculiar admiration of this saying, with its *elimata ac librata verba* (Possidius, *Vit. Aug.* c. xxvii.).

sacredos fuit Ecclesiae Romanae" (*de Sacramentis*, III. §§ 5, 6).

As a writer, St. Ambrose left a multitude of works behind him, which show competent learning, a familiar acquaintance with Plato, Cicero, Vergil, and other classics, and much intellectual liveliness and industry. Their want of originality did not hinder them from obtaining for their author, through their popular and practical qualities, a distinguished reputation as a sound and edifying teacher. He is often mentioned with respect by his contemporaries, St. Jerome and St. Augustine (see especially the latter, *de Doctrinâ Christianâ*, iv. 46, 48, 50). He came to be joined with them and Gregory the Great as one of the four Latin doctors of the church. His writings may be classified under three heads, as (1) Expository, (2) Doctrinal or Didactic, and (3) Occasional.

(1) The first class contains a long list of expositions, delivered first as sermons, of many books of Scripture. They begin with the *Hexaemeron*, or commentary on the Creation. Of this work St. Jerome says, "Nuper S. Ambrosius sic Hexaemeron illius [Origenus] compilavit, ut magis Hippolyti sententias Basiliique sequeretur" (*Ep.* 41). It is in a great part a literal translation from St. Basil. St. Augustine was interested by the method of interpretation in which Ambrose followed Basil, Origen, and Philo Judaeus, finding a spiritual or mystical meaning latent under the natural or historical. The *Hexaemeron* (6 books) is followed by *de Paradiso, de Cain et Abel* (2), *de Noe et Arcâ, de Abraham* (2), *de Isaac et Animâ, de Bono Mortis, de Fugâ Saeculi, de Jacob et Beatâ Vitâ* (2), *de Joseph Patriarchâ, de Benedictionibus Patriarcharum, de Eliâ et Jejunio, de Nabuthe Jezraelitâ, de Tobiâ, de Interpellatione Job et David* (4), *Apologia Prophetae David, Apol. altera ib., Enarrationes in Psalmos* (12), *Expositio in Ps. cxviii., Expositio Evang. secundum Lucam* (10).

(2) The second class contains *de Officiis Ministrorum* (3 books), *de Virginibus* (3), *de Viduis, de Virginitate, Exhortatio Virginitatis, de Lapsu Virginis Consecratae, de Mysteriis, de Sacramentis* (6), *de Poenitentiâ* (2), *de Fide* (5), *de Spiritu Sancto* (3), *de Incarnationis Dominicae Sacramento.* Of these the books *de Officiis*, addressed to the clergy (imitated from Cicero), and those *de Fide*, mentioned above, are the most important.

(3) The occasional writings, which are biographically the most valuable, are the discourses *de Excessu Fratris sui Satyri* (2), *de Obitu Valentiniani Consolatio, de Obitu Theodosii Oratio*, and the *Epistles*, ninety-one in number, with the *Gesta Concilii Aquileiensis* inserted amongst them.

Various ecclesiastical writings have been attributed to Ambrose, which critical examination has determined to be spurious. [AMBROSIASTER.] Most of these are given in the Benedictine edition; in that of Migne there is an additional appendix, containing some other compositions which have borne Ambrose's name, but are either manifestly spurious or have no sufficient title to be considered genuine. Some of his genuine works appear to have been lost, especially one, mentioned with high praise by St. Augustine (*Ep.* xxxi. 8), against those who alleged that our Lord had learnt from Plato.

Of the connexion of St. Ambrose with the liturgical arrangement which bears his name, we know nothing more than what has been quoted above from Paulinus. [See *D. C. A.*, arts. LITURGIES; AMBROSIAN MUSIC.]

There are three principal editions of Ambrose's works—that of Erasmus, the Roman, and the Benedictine. Erasmus's ed. was pub. at Basle, by Froben, in 1527. He divided the works into four tomes, with the titles, (1) *Ethica*, (2) *Polemica*, (3) *Orationes, Epistolae, et Conciones*, (4) *Explanationes Vet. et Novi Testamenti.* The great Roman edition was the work of many years' labour, undertaken by the desire of popes Pius IV. and Pius V., and begun by a monk who afterwards became pope with the name of Sixtus V. It was pub. in 5 vols. at Rome, in the years 1580-1-2-5. This edition superseded all others, until the publication of the excellent work of the Benedictines (du Frische and Le Nourry) at Paris, A.D. 1686 and 1690. A small revised ed. of the *de Officiis* and the *Hexaemeron* has been printed in the *Bibliotheca Pat. Eccl. Latin. Selecta* (Tauchnitz, Leipz.). Some of his works are reprinted in the Vienna *Corpus Ser. Eccl. Lat.*; and in the 10th vol. of the *Nic. and Post-Nic. Fathers* are English trans. of select works. An elaborate *Life* of St. Ambrose by Baronius, extracted from his *Annales*, is prefixed to the Roman edition; but improved upon by the more critical investigations of the Benedictine editors, who have laid the basis for all subsequent Lives. (Cf. Th. Forshaw, *Ambrose, Bp. of Milan*, 1884; a *Life* by the duc de Broglie in *Les Saints*, 1899 (Paris). A cheap popular *Life* by R. Thornton is pub. by S.P.C.K. in their *Fathers for Eng. Readers.*) [J.LL.D.]

Ammon (or **Amon**), St., the founder of the celebrated settlement of coenobites and hermits on and near Mons Nitria (Ruf. *de Mon.* 30); he is often styled the "father of Egyptian monasticism." He was contemporary with St. Anthony, and filled the same place in Lower Egypt as Anthony in the Thebaid. Being left an orphan by his parents, wealthy people near Alexandria, he was forced by his uncle to marry. But on the wedding day he persuaded his bride to take a vow of celibacy, and for eighteen years they lived together as brother and sister: afterwards with her consent he withdrew to Nitria, and from that time only visited his wife twice a year (Pall. *Hist. Laus.* 8). A great multitude of zealous disciples soon gathered round him; so that Palladius not many years later found about five thousand monks, some living quite alone, some with one or more companions; while six hundred "advanced in holiness" (τελέιοι) dwelt apart from the rest in more complete isolation (*ib.*). Several miracles are related of Ammon (Socr. *Hist.* iv. 23; Soz. *Hist.* i. 14; Niceph. *Hist.* viii. 41). [I.G.S.]

Ammonius, a disciple of Pambo, and one of the most celebrated of the monks of Nitria. Being of unusual stature, he and his brothers DIOSCORUS, Eusebius, and Euthymius were called the Tall Brothers (Soz. *Hist.* viii. 12). Ammonius himself was distinguished by the epithet παρωτής (Niceph. *Hist.* xi. 37), in consequence of having cut off one of his ears to escape being made a bishop (Pall. *Hist. Laus.* 12). In his youth he accompanied St. Athanasius to Rome (Socr. *Hist.* iv. 23; Pall. 12). He was a learned man, and could repeat, it is said, the O. and N. T. by heart, as well as passages from Origen and other Fathers (Pall. 12). He was banished to Diocaesarea in the persecution under Valens (*ib.* 117). After being for some time high in favour with Theophilus of Alexandria, he and his brothers were accused by him of Origenism. Sozomen (viii. 12) and Nicephorus (xiii. 10) ascribe the accusation to personal animosity on the part of Theophilus. Socrates (vi. 7) explains the accusation as an attempt to divert from himself the odium which he had incurred as an Origenist. Jerome considers the accusation merited (*Ep. ad Alex.*). Driven from Egypt, the brothers took refuge first in Palestine (Niceph. xiii. 11) and afterwards at Constantinople, where they were well received by Chrysostom (viii. 13). There they were protected also by the favour of the Empress Eudoxia (Soz. viii. 13), and even satisfied Epiphanius of Salamis, who came to Constantinople at the instigation of Theophilus to convict them of heresy (viii. 15). At the synod "ad Quercum," held on the arrival of Theophilus, they were persuaded to submit to him, Ammonius being ill at the time. He died shortly afterwards. Perhaps this Ammonius is the author of the *Institutiones Asceticae*, of which 22 chapters are extant (Lambec. *Biblioth. Vindob.* iv. 155). [I.G.S.]

Ammonius Saccas. Next to nothing is known of this philosopher. That he obtained his name of Saccas (= σακκοφόρος) from having been a porter in his youth is affirmed by Suidas (under *Origenes*) and Ammianus Marcellinus (xxii. 528). He was a native of Alexandria; Porphyry asserts that he was born of Christian parents, and returned to the heathen religion. Eusebius (*H. E.* vi. 19, 7) denies this, but perhaps confounds him with another Ammonius, the author of a Diatessaron, still extant. That the founder of the Alexandrian school of philosophy (for such Ammonius Saccas was) should have been at the same time a Christian, though not impossible, seems hardly likely. Moreover, the Ammonius of Eusebius wrote books; whereas, according to both Longinus and Porphyry, Ammonius Saccas wrote none. Plotinus is said to have been most strongly impressed with his first hearing of Ammonius, and to have cried out, "This is the man I was looking for!" (τοῦτον ἐζήτουν), after which he remained his constant friend till the death of the elder philosopher. Among other disciples of Ammonius were Herennius, the celebrated Longinus, Heracles the Christian, Olympius, Antonius, a heathen called Origen, and also the famous Christian of that name. It is possible, however, that the Christians, Origen and Heracles, may have been the disciples of that Ammonius whom Eusebius confounds with Ammonius Saccas, and who was himself a Christian; but this cannot be certainly known. We may guess something concerning the philosophy of Ammonius Saccas from the fact that Plotinus was his pupil. Hierocles (*ap.* Photius) affirms that his aim was to reconcile the philosophies of Plato and Aristotle, hence he appears to have combined mysticism and eclecticism. Nemesius, a bishop and a neo-Platonist of the close of the 4th cent., cites two passages, one of which he declares to contain the views of Numenius and Ammonius, the other he attributes to Ammonius alone. They concern the nature of the soul and its relation to the body; but they appear to have been merely the traditional views of Ammonius, not any actual written words of his. The life and philosophy of Ammonius have been discussed by Vacherot, *Hist. de l'Ecole d'Alex.* i. 342; Jules Simon, *Hist. de l'Ecole d'Alex.* i. 204; Dehaut in his historical essay on the life and teaching of our philosopher; and Zeller in his *Philosophie der Griechen*, who also mentions other writers on Ammonius. [J.R.M.]

Amphilochius (1), archbp. of Iconium. Of this great Catholic leader, who was regarded by his contemporaries as the foremost man in the Eastern church after his friends Basil of Caesarea and Gregory of Nazianzus, very scanty information remains. The works ascribed to him are mostly spurious; and the *Life* (Migne, *Patr. Gk.* xxxix. p. 14) is a later fiction. Various references to the writings of Basil and Gregory contain nearly all that is known of him and his family. Amphilochius appears to have been a first cousin of Gregory Nazianzen. The language of Basil (*Ep.* 161) might imply that he was born and lived in Basil's own town Caesarea. Gregory expresses regret that he did not see much of Amphilochius during his earlier years (*Ep.* 13). Their intimate friendship commenced at a later date. Amphilochius, like many other eminent Christian fathers, was educated for the bar. The letters of his cousin imply that he carried on his profession at Constantinople.

It is not improbable that trouble in regard to money matters about 369 weaned Amphilochius from his worldly pursuits and turned his thoughts inward. He had abandoned his profession, and was then living in retirement at Ozizala, devoting himself apparently to religious exercises and to the care of his aged father. His cousin Gregory appears to have been mainly instrumental in bringing about this change. At least he says with honest pride, that "together with the pure Thecla"* he has "sent Amphilochius to God" (*Op.* ii. p. 1068). And now his closer friendship with Basil and Gregory begins. Ozizala was situated not far from Nazianzus, for Gregory's correspondence implies that they were near neighbours. A letter of Basil, apparently belonging to this period, is in the name of one Heraclidas, who, like Amphilochius, had renounced the profession of the bar and devoted himself to a religious life. Heraclidas, lodged in a large hospital (πτωχοτροφεῖον) recently erected by Basil near Caesarea, and enjoying the constant instructions of the bishop, urges Amphilochius to obtain leave from his father to visit Caesarea and profit by the teaching and example of the same instructor (*Ep.* 150). This letter was written in the year 372 or 373 (see Garnier's Basil. *Op.* iii. p. cxxxiv.). The

* This seems to be the same Thecla with whom Gregory elsewhere corresponds, and not the monastery of St. Thecla, whither Gregory retired.

invitation to Caesarea appears to have been promptly accepted, and was fraught with immediate consequences. It does not appear that at that time Amphilochius was even ordained; yet at the very beginning of the year 374 we find him occupying the important see of Iconium. Amphilochius can hardly have been then more than about 35 years of age. A few months before Faustinus, bp. of Iconium, had died, and the Iconians applied to the bp. of Caesarea to recommend them a successor (Basil. *Ep.* 138). It is impossible not to connect this application to Basil with the ultimate appointment of Amphilochius.

From this time forward till his death, about five years afterwards, Basil holds close intercourse with Amphilochius, receiving from him frequent visits. The first took place soon after his consecration, about Easter 374, and was somewhat protracted, his ministrations on this occasion making a deep impression on the people of Caesarea (*Ep.* 163, 176).

It was probably in another visit in 374 (see Garnier, *Op.* iii. p. cxl.) that Amphilochius urged Basil to clear up all doubt as to his doctrine of the Holy Spirit by writing a treatise on the subject. This was the occasion of Basil's extant work, *de Spiritu Sancto* (see § 1), which, when completed, was dedicated to the petitioner himself and sent to him engrossed on vellum (*Ep.* 231). During this and the following year Basil likewise addresses to Amphilochius his three *Canonical Letters* (*Ep.* 188, 199, 217), to solve some questions relating to ecclesiastical order, which the bp. of Iconium had propounded to him. At this same period also we find Amphilochius arranging the ecclesiastical affairs of Isauria (*Ep.* 190), Lycaonia (*Ep.* 200), and Lycia (*Ep.* 218), under the direction of Basil. He is also invited by Basil to assist in the administration of his own diocese of Caesarea, which has become too great a burden for him, prostrated as he now is by a succession of maladies (*Ep.* 200, 201). The affectionate confidence which the great man reposes in his younger friend is a powerful testimony to the character and influence of Amphilochius.

After the death of Basil, the slender thread by which we trace the career of Amphilochius is taken up in the correspondence of Gregory. Gregory writes with equal affection and esteem, and with more tenderness than Basil. He has been ill, and he speaks of Amphilochius as having helped to work his cure. Sleeping and waking, he has him ever in his mind. He mentions the many letters which he has received from Amphilochius (*μυριάκις γράφων*), and which have called forth harmonies from his soul, as the plectrum strikes music out of the lyre (*Ep.* 171). The last of Gregory's letters to Amphilochius (*Ep.* 184) seems to have been written about the year 383. Not long before (A.D. 381) Amphilochius had been present with his friend at the council of Constantinople, and had subscribed to the creed there sanctioned, as chief pastor of the Lycaonian church, at the head of twelve other bishops (Labb. *Conc.* ii. p. 1135, ed. Coleti). At this council a metropolitan authority was confirmed to, rather than conferred on, his see of Iconium; for we find it occupying this position even before his election to the episcopate. During this sojourn at Constantinople he signs his name as first witness to Gregory's will (Greg. *Op.* ii. p. 204), in which the testator leaves directions to restore to his most reverend son the bp. Amphilochius the purchase-money of an estate at Canotala (*ib.* p. 203). It was probably on this occasion also that Amphilochius fell in with Jerome and read to him a book which he had written on the Holy Spirit (Hieron. *de Vir. Ill.* 133) as Jerome is known to have paid a visit to Gregory Nazianzen at this time (Hieron. *Op.* xi. 65 seq., ed. Vallarsi).

About two years later must be placed the well-known incident in which the zeal of Amphilochius against the Arians appears (Theod. *H. E.* v. 16).* Obtaining an audience of Theodosius, he saluted the emperor himself with the usual marks of respect, but paid no attention to his son Arcadius, who had recently (*νεωστί*) been created Augustus and was present at the interview. Theodosius, indignant at this slight, demanded an explanation. "Sire," said the bishop, "any disrespect shewn to your son arouses your displeasure. Be assured, therefore, that the Lord of the universe abhorreth those who are ungrateful towards His Son, their Saviour and Benefactor." The emperor, adds Theodoret, immediately issued an edict prohibiting the meetings of the heretics. As Arcadius was created Augustus in the beginning of the year 383 (Clinton, *Fast. Rom.* i. p. 504), and as Theodosius issued his edict against the Eunomians, Arians, Macedonians, and Apollinarians in Sept. of that year (*ib.* p. 507), the date is accurately ascertained (see Tillem. *Mém. eccl.* vi. pp. 627 seq., 802). In 383 also we find Amphilochius taking energetic measures against heretics of a different stamp. He presided over a synod of 25 bishops assembled at Sida in Pamphylia, in which the Messalians were condemned, and his energy seems to have instigated the religious crusade which led to the extirpation of this heresy (Photius, *Bibl.* 52; Theod. *E. H.* iv. 10; cf. Labb. *Conc.* ii. 1209, ed. Coleti).

The date of Amphilochius's death is uncertain. When Jerome wrote the work quoted above, he was still living (A.D. 392); and two years later (A.D. 394) his name occurs among the bishops present at a synod held at Constantinople, when the new basilica of St. Peter and St. Paul was dedicated (Labb. *Conc.* ii. 1378, ed. Coleti). On the other hand, he is not mentioned in connexion with the troubles of St. Chrysostom (A.D. 403 seq.); and it is a fairly safe assumption that he was no longer living. Despite the martyrologies, he probably died in middle life. His day is Nov. 23 in both Greek and Latin calendars.

The works ascribed to Amphilochius (*Iambi ad Seleucum*, *Homilies*, etc.) seem to be mostly spurious, with the exception of an *Epistola Synodica* (Migne, p. 94), on the Macedonian heresy. Its object is to explain why the Nicene fathers did not dwell on the doctrine of the Spirit, and to justify the ordinary form

* Sozomen (vii. 6) tells the story, but without the name of the bishop. He describes him as "an old man, a priest of an obscure city, simple and inexperienced in affairs." This description is as unlike Amphilochius as it could possibly be.

of the doxology. It is entitled Ἀμφιλοχίῳ Βασίλειος in one MS., but was certainly not written by Basil, who indeed is mentioned in it.

Of his ability as a theologian and a writer the extant fragments are a wholly inadequate criterion; but his reputation with his contemporaries and with the later church leaves very little ground for doubt. His contemporary Jerome, an eminently competent judge, speaks of the Cappadocian triad, Basil, Gregory, and Amphilochius, as writers "who cram [*refarciunt*] their books with the lessons and sentences of the philosophers to such an extent that you cannot tell which you ought to admire most in them, their secular erudition or their Scriptural knowledge" (*Ep.* 70, i. p. 429).

Of his character his intimate friends are the best witnesses. The trust reposed in him by Basil and Gregory appears throughout their correspondence. The former more especially praises his love of learning and patient investigation, addressing him as his "brother Amphilochius, his dear friend most honoured of all" (*de Spir. Sanct.* § 1); while the latter speaks of him as "the blameless high-priest, the loud herald of truth, his pride" (*Carm.* ii. p. 1068). He seems to have united the genial sympathy which endears the friend, and the administrative energy which constitutes the ruler, with intellectual abilities and acquirements of no mean order. [L.]

Amphilochius (2), bp. of Sida in Pamphylia. Like his more famous namesake of Iconium, he appears as an antagonist of the Messalians. He was urged, as one of the Pamphylian metropolitans, to take measures against them in encyclical letters written by two successive bps. of Constantinople, Atticus and Sisinnius (Phot. *Bibl.* 52), and seems to have prosecuted the matter with zeal. He brought forward the subject at the council of Ephesus (A.D. 431) in conjunction with Valerianus; and in consequence of their representations the council confirmed the decrees of former synods against these heretics (Labbe, *Conc.* iii. 1331 seq., ed. Coleti). At this same council we find him assenting to Cyril's letter, and subscribing in very strong language to the condemnation and deposition of Nestorius (*ib.* pp. 1012, 1046, 1077, 1133). His conduct, later, was marked by great vacillation, if not insincerity. It is sometimes stated that he was present at the "Robbers' Synod" (A.D. 449), and there committed himself to the policy of Dioscorus and the heresy of Eutyches (Le Quien, *Oriens Christ.* i. 998); but his name does not appear in the list of bishops assembled there (Labbe, *Conc.* iv. 889 seq.). At the council of Chalcedon, however (A.D. 451), he shewed great tenderness for Dioscorus, and here his career of tergiversation began. He tried to defer the second citation of Dioscorus (iv. 1260); and when after three citations Dioscorus did not appear, he consented to his condemnation, though with evident reluctance (iv. 1310, 1337). At a later session, too, he subscribed his assent to the epistle of pope Leo (iv. 1358, 1366; and we find his name also appended to the canons of the council (iv. 1715). Thus he committed himself fully to the principles of this council, and to the reversal of the proceedings of *Latrocinium*. But a few years later (A.D. 458), when the emperor Leo wrote to the bishops to elicit their opinions, Amphilochius stated, in reply, that, while he disapproved the appointment of Timotheus Aelurus, he did not acknowledge the authority of the council of Chalcedon (Evagr. *H. E.* ii. 10). Yet, as if this were not enough, we are told that he shortly afterwards assented and subscribed to its decrees (Eulogius in Phot. *Bibl.* 230). [L.]

Anastasia. [CHRYSOGONUS.]

Anastasius (1), a presbyter of Antioch, the confidential friend and counsellor of Nestorius, the archbp. of Constantinople. Theophanes styles him the "syncellus," or confidential secretary of Nestorius, who never took any step without consulting him and being guided by his opinions. Nestorius having commenced a persecution against the Quartodecimans of Asia in 428, two presbyters, Antonius and Jacobus, were dispatched to carry his designs into effect. They were furnished with letters commendatory from Anastasius and Photius, bearing witness to the soundness of their faith. The two emissaries of the archbp. of Constantinople did not restrict themselves to their ostensible object, to set the Asiatics right as to the keeping of Easter, but endeavoured to tamper with their faith. At Philadelphia they persuaded some simple-minded clergy to sign a creed of doubtful orthodoxy, attributed to Theodore of Mopsuestia. This was strongly opposed by Charisius, the oeconomus of the church, who charged Jacobus with unsoundness in the faith. His opposition aroused the indignation of Anastasius and Photius, who dispatched fresh letters, reasserting the orthodoxy of Jacobus, and requiring the deprivation of Charisius (Labbe, *Conc.* iii. 1202 seq.; Socr. vii. 29).

It was in a sermon preached by Anastasius at Constantinople that the fatal words were uttered that destroyed the peace of the church for so many years. "Let no one call Mary Θεοτόκος. She was but a human being. It is impossible for God to be born of a human being." These words, eagerly caught up by the enemies of Nestorius, caused much excitement among clergy and laity, which was greatly increased when the archbishop by supporting and defending Anastasius adopted the language as his own (Socr. *H. E.* vii. 32; Evagr. *H. E.* i. 2). [NESTORIUS.] In 430, when Cyril had sent a deputation to Constantinople with an address to the emperor, Anastasius seems to have attempted to bring about an accommodation between him and Nestorius (Cyril, *Ep.* viii.; Mercator, vol. ii. p. 49). We find him after the deposition of Nestorius still maintaining his cause and animating his party at Constantinople (Lupus, *Ep.* 144).

Tillemont identifies him with the Anastasius who in 434 wrote to Helladius, bp. of Tarsus, when he and the Oriental bishops were refusing to recognize Proclus as bp. of Constantinople, bearing witness to his orthodoxy, and urging them to receive him into communion (Baluz. § 144). [E.V.]

Anastasius I., bp. of Rome, was consecrated A.D. 398 ("Honorio IV. et Eutychiano coss."

Prosp. Aq. *Chron.*), and died in April, 402 (Anast. Bibl. vol. i. p. 62). According to Anastasius Bibliothecarius, he put an end to an unseemly strife between the priests and deacons of his church, by enacting that priests as well as deacons should stand bowed ("curvi starent") at the reading of the Gospels. Jerome calls him a "vir insignis," taken from the evil to come, *i.e.* dying before the sack of Rome by Goths, A.D. 410. One letter by Anastasius is extant. Rufinus wrote to him shortly after his consecration (not later than A.D. 400, Constant. *Epp. Pont. Rom.* p. 714) to defend himself against the charge of complicity in the heresy ascribed to Origen. Anastasius replied (see Constant. *l.c.*) in a tone which, dealing leniently with Rufinus, explicitly condemned Origen. Nine other letters are referred to :—(1-5) To Paulinus, bp. of Nola (Paul. Nol. *Ep.* 20). (6) To Anysius. bp. of Thessalonica, giving him jurisdiction over Illyria ; referred to by Innocent I., in his first letter (Constant.). (7) To Johannes, bp. of Jerusalem. (8) To African bishops who had sent him an embassy to complain of the low state of their clergy. (9) Contra Rufinum, an epistle sent ad Orientem (Hieron. *Apol.* lib. 3). [G.H.M.]

Anastasius II., bp. of Rome, succeeded Gelasius I. in Nov. 496 (Clinton's *Fasti Romani*, pp. 536, 713). The month after his accession Clovis was baptized, and the new Pope wrote congratulating him on his conversion. Anastasius has left a name of ill-odour in the Western church ; attributable to his having taken a different line from his predecessors with regard to the Eastern church. Felix III. had excommunicated Acacius of Constantinople, professedly on account of his communicating with heretics, but really because Zeno's *Henoticon*, which he had sanctioned, gave the church of Constantinople a primacy in the East which the see of Rome could not tolerate. Gelasius I. had followed closely in the steps of Felix. But Anastasius, in the year of his accession, sent two bishops, Germanus of Capua and Cresconius of Todi, (Baronius) to Constantinople, with a proposal that Acacius's name, instead of being expunged from the roll of patriarchs of Constantinople as Gelasius had proposed, should be left upon the diptychs, and no more be said upon the subject. This proposal, in the very spirit of the Henoticon, gave lasting offence to the Western church, and it excites no surprise that he was charged with communicating secretly with Photinus, a deacon of Thessalonica who held with Acacius ; and of wishing to heal the breach between the East and West —for so it seems best to interpret the words of Anastasius Bibliothecarius—"voluit revocare Acacium" (vol. i. p. 83).

Anastasius died in Nov. 498. He was still remembered as the traitor who would have reversed the excommunication of Acacius ; and Dante finds him suffering in hell the punishment of one whom "Fotino" seduced from the right way (Dante, *Inf.* xi. 8, 9).

Two epistles by him are extant : one informing the emperor Anastasius of his accession (Mansi, viii. p. 188) ; the other to Clovis as above (*ib.* p. 193). [G.H.M.]

Anastasius Sinaita ('Αναστάσιος Σιναίτης). Three of this name are mentioned by ecclesiastical writers, among whom some confusion exists. Two were patriarchs of Antioch, and it has been reasonably questioned whether they were ever monks of Mount Sinai, and whether the title "Sinaita" has not been given to them from a confusion with the one who really was so, and who falls outside our period (see Smith's *D. C. B. in loc.*).

(1) Bp. of Antioch, succeeded Domnus III. A.D. 559 (Clinton, *Fasti Romani*). He is praised by Evagrius (*H. E.* iv. 40) for his theological learning, strictness of life, and well-balanced character. He resolutely opposed Justinian's edict in favour of the Aphthartodocetae, and encouraged the monastic bodies of Syria against it, A.D. 563 (Evagr. iv. 39, 40). Justinian threatened him with deposition and exile, but his death in 565 hindered his design, which was carried into effect by his nephew Justin II., A.D. 570. Fresh charges were brought against Anastasius of profuse expenditure of the funds of his see, and of intemperate language and action in reference to the consecration of John, bp. of Alexandria, by John, bp. of Constantinople, in the lifetime of the previous bp. Eutychius (Evagr. v. 1 ; Valesius's *notes*, *ib.* ; Theoph. *Chron.* ; Clinton, *Fast. Rom.*). He was succeeded by Gregory, on whose death, in the middle of 593 (Clinton), he was restored to his episcopate. This was chiefly due to the influence of Gregory the Great with the emperor Maurice and his son Theodosius (Evagr. vi. 24 ; Greg. Mag. *Ep.* i. 25, 27, Ind. ix.). Gregory wrote him a congratulatory letter on his return to Antioch (*Ep.* iv. 37 ; Ind. xiv.) ; and several epistles of his are preserved relating to the claim the bp. of Constantinople was then making to the title of "universal bishop" (*Ep.* iv. 36, Ind. xiii. ; vi. 24, 31, Ind. xv.). Anastasius defended the orthodox view of the Procession of the Holy Ghost (Baron. *Annal. Eccl.* 593), and died at the close of 598 (Clinton, *Fast. Rom.*). Five sermons, "de Orthodoxa Fide," and five others, printed in a Latin version by Migne and others, are ascribed by some to this Anastasius. Oudin, Dupin, and others refer them more probably to a later Anastasius. For a catalogue and description of the works assigned to him, either existing or lost, see Fabricius, *Bibl. Graec.* vol. ix. pp. 332-336, and Migne.

(**2**) Followed the preceding as bp. of Antioch in the beginning of 599. A letter of Gregory the Great to him (*Ep.* vii. 48, Ind. ii.) acknowledges one announcing his appointment and declaring his adherence to the orthodox faith. Gregory had written to him before 597 (*Ep.* vii. 3, Ind. i.), exhorting him to constancy under the persecutions of heretics. He translated Gregory's *de Curâ Pastorali* into Greek (*ib.* x. 22, Ind. v.). His death occurred in an insurrection of the Jews, Sept. 610 (Clinton, *F. R.*). Nicephorus (*H. E.* xviii. 44) confounds him with (1). [E.V.]

Anatolius, bp. of Constantinople, 449 A.D., through the influence of Dioscorus of Alexandria with Theodosius II., after the deposition of Flavian by the "Robber Council," having previously been the "apocrisiarius" or representative of Dioscorus at Constantinople (Zon. *Ann.* iii.). After his consecration, being under suspicion of Eutychianism (Leo, *Epp. ad. Theod.* 33 *ad Pulch.* 35), he publicly condemned the heresies both of Eutyches and Nestorius, signing the letters of Cyril against Nestorius and of Leo against Eutyches (Leo, *Epp.* 40, 41, 48). In conjunction with Leo of Rome, according to Zonaras (*Ann.* iii.), he requested the emperor Marcian to summon a general council against Dioscorus and the Eutychians; but the imperial letter directing Anatolius to make preparations for the council at Chalcedon speaks only of Leo (Labbe, *Conc. Max. Tom.* iv.). In this council Anatolius presided in conjunction with the Roman legates (Labbe, *Conc. Max.* iv.; Evagr. *H. E.* ii. 4, 18; Niceph. *H. E.* xv. 18). By the famous 28th canon, passed at the conclusion of the council, equal dignity was ascribed to Constantinople with Rome (Labbe, iv. 796; Evagr. ii. 18). Hence arose the controversy between Anatolius and the Roman pontiff. Leo complained to Marcian (*Ep.* 54) and to Pulcheria (*Ep.* 55) that Anatolius had outstepped his jurisdiction, by consecrating Maximus to the see of Antioch; and he remonstrated with Anatolius (*Ep.* 53). After the council of Chalcedon some Egyptian bishops wrote to Anatolius, earnestly asking his assistance against Timotheus, who was usurping the episcopal throne at Alexandria (Labbe, *Conc. Max.* iv. iii. 23, p. 897). Anatolius wrote strongly to the emperor Leo against Timotheus (Labbe, iii. 26, p. 905). The circular of the emperor requesting the advice of Anatolius on the turbulent state of Alexandria is given by Evagrius (*H. E.* ii. 9), and by Nicephorus (*H. E.* xv. 18). The crowning of Leo on his accession by Anatolius is said (Gibbon, iii. 313) to be the first instance of the kind on record (Theoph. *Chron.* 95 *Par.*). [I.G.S.]

Anatolius, bp. of Laodicea in Syria Prima (Eus. *H. E.* vii. 32). He had been famous at Alexandria for proficiency in the liberal arts, while his reputation for practical wisdom was so great that when the suburb of Brucheium was besieged by the Romans during the revolt of Aemilianus, A.D. 262, the command of the place was assigned to him. Provisions having failed, and his proposition of making terms with the besiegers having been indignantly rejected, Anatolius obtained leave to relieve the garrison of all idle mouths, and by a clever deception marched out all the Christians, and the greater part of the rest, many disguised as women. Having passed over to Palestine, he was ordained by Theotecnus, bp. of Caesarea, as bishop-coadjutor, with the right of succession. But going to Antioch to attend the synod against Paul of Samosata, on his way through Laodicea, which had just lost its bishop, his old friend Eusebius, he was detained and made bishop in his room, A.D. 269.

Eusebius speaks of him as not having written much, but enough to show at once his eloquence and manifold learning. He specially mentions a work on the Paschal question, published in a Latin version by Bucherius (*Doct. Temp.*, Antv. 1634). Some fragments of his mathematical works were pub. at Paris, 1543, and by Fabricius (*Bibl. Graec.* iii. 462; Hieron. *Sc. Eccl.* c. 73). For an Eng. trans. of his extant works see *Ante-Nicene Lib.* (T. & T. Clark). [E.V.]

Ancyra, Seven Martyrs of, female victims of Diocletian's persecution, 304. They were unmarried, about 70 years old, and notable for piety and good works. When the persecution was determined upon, Theotecnus, a magician, a philosopher and pervert from Christianity, was dispatched as governor to Galatia to root out Christianity. Among the earliest victims were the seven virgins, Tecusa, Alexandra, Faina, Claudia, Euphrasia, Matrona, Julitta. Theotecnus called upon them to offer incense, and upon their refusal condemned them to the public brothel, from which they escaped scatheless on account of their age, and by the ingenuity of Tecusa their leader. He then ordered them to officiate as priestesses of Diana and Minerva in washing their statues according to the annual custom of Ancyra. They were accordingly carried naked through the streets to a neighbouring lake, where garlands and white garments were offered them in which to fulfil his commands. Upon their refusal Theotecnus ordered them to be drowned in the lake, with heavy stones tied round their necks lest their bodies should be recovered and buried by their fellow-Christians. Many legends have gathered round the story. The acts of the seven virgins and of St. THEODOTUS (a tavern-keeper of Ancyra martyred for rescuing and burying the bodies) are recorded in Gk. in a Vatican MS., purporting to have been written by an eye-witness named Nilus. They are found in Gk. and Lat. in Boll. *Acta SS.* May 18; cf. also Ruinart, *Acta Sincera*, p. 336; Ceillier, iii. 15. [G.T.S.]

Andreas of Caesarea. [ARETHAS.]

Andreas Samosatensis, bp. of Samosata at the time of the council of Ephesus, A.D. 431. Sickness prevented his attending the council (Labbe, *Conc.* iii. 506), but he took a leading part in the controversies between Cyril and the Oriental bishops that succeeded it. Without identifying himself with the erroneous teaching ascribed to Nestorius, he shewed himself his zealous defender, and remained firm to him when his cause had been deserted by almost all. For his zeal in the defence of an heresiarch he is styled by Anastasius Sinaita ὁ δράκων. The reputation of Andreas for learning and controversial skill caused John of Antioch to select him, together with his attached friend Theodoret, to answer Cyril's anathemas against Nestorius (Labbe, iii. 1150; Liberatus, c. iv. p. 16). Cyril replied and wrote in defence of his anathemas, which called forth a second treatise from Andreas (Labbe, iii. 827). In 453 Andreas accompanied Alexander and Theodoret to the council summoned at Antioch by Aristolaus the tribune, in compliance with the commands of Theodosius, to consult how the breach with Cyril might be healed (*ib.* 764). On the amicable reception by Acacius and John of Cyril's letter written in answer to the rescript of this council, Andreas fully sympathized with his aged metropolitan Alexander's distress and indignation. Andreas deplored the recognition of Cyril's orthodoxy by so many bishops, and desired to bury himself in some solitude where he might weep (*ib.* 784, 785,

796, 797). This was before he had see Cyril's letter. On perusing Cyril's own statement his opinions changed. What Cyril had written was orthodox. No prejudice against him ought to prevent his acknowledging it. The peace of the church was superior to all private feelings. His alteration of sentiments exasperated Alexander, who refused to see or speak to his former friend (*ib.* 810, 811). Andreas deeply felt this alienation of one he so much venerated, but it could not lead him to retrace his steps. He used his utmost endeavours in vain to persuade Alexander to attend the council at Zeugma, which acknowledged the orthodoxy of Cyril's letter (*ib.* 805).

His death must have occurred before 451, when Rufinus was bp. of Samosata. Theodoret speaks of Andreas with much affection and esteem, praising his humility and readiness to help the distressed (Theod. *Ep.* xxiv. p. 918). His own letters give us a high idea of his sound, practical wisdom, readiness to confess an error, and firmness in maintaining what he believed right. [E.V.]

Anicetus, bp. of Rome, stated in Eusebius's *History* (iv. 11) and by Irenaeus (*Adv. omn. Haer.* iii. 3, 3) to have succeeded Pius. As to the date of his pontificate, see Lightfoot's elaborate discussion in *Apost. Fathers* (part i. vol. i. pp. 201-345). As Polycarp visited him at Rome, and as Polycarp's death has been fixed by recent criticism in 155, Lightfoot says that "the latest possible date for the accession of Anicetus is 154," and if he sat for eleven years, as is said, his death would be in 165. Anastasius Bibliothecarius singles him out as the pope who prescribed the tonsure for the clergy (Anast. vol. i. p. 13); and a forged letter upon this subject is given by Isidorus Mercator (Constant. p. 75). But the single reliable fact recorded of him has reference to the early Paschal controversy (Eus. *H. E.* iv. 24). He, like his four predecessors, did not allow the Jewish or Quartodeciman usage within their own church, but communicated as freely as before with other churches which did allow it. Polycarp visited Rome, hoping to persuade Anicetus to adopt the Quartodeciman practice. But Anicetus was firm, even against the age and saintliness of Polycarp. As a mark of personal respect, he allowed him to celebrate the Eucharist in Rome; but they parted without agreement, though with mutual cordiality. We are told that Anicetus was buried in the Calixtine cemetery on April 20. [G.H.M.]

Anomoeans (from ἀνόμοιος, *dissimilar*), one of the appellations of the radical Arians who, in opposition to the Athanasian or Nicene doctrine of the consubstantiality (ὁμοουσία) and the semi-Arian view of the *likeness* (ὁμοιουσία) of the Son to the Father, taught that the Son was dissimilar, and of a different substance (ἑτεροούσιος). [ARIANISM.] [P.S.]

Anonomastus (Iren. 56: cf. 54). [VALENTINUS; EPIPHANES.] [H.]

Anthimus, bp. of Tyana, a contemporary of St. Basil bp. of Caesarea in Cappodocia (Basil. *Ep.* 58). In 372 he joined in subscribing a circular letter addressed by the Oriental bishops to those of Italy and Gaul (*Ep.* 92). But dissensions broke out between them. (1) When the civil province of Cappadocia was divided and Tyana became the capital of the second division, Anthimus, insisting that the ecclesiastical arrangements should follow the civil, claimed metropolitan rights over several of Basil's suffragans. Herein he was assisted by the disaffection which prevailed in Basil's province. He was even bold enough to attack Basil on a journey, and plunder a train of mules laden with supplies of money and provisions for the bp. of Caesarea. Basil, thinking to establish an invincible outpost against his aggressive antagonist, consecrated his friend Gregory bp. of Sasima, a town not far from Tyana and one over which Anthimus claimed metropolitan rights. So long as Gregory remained there, he staunchly resisted alike the enticements and the menaces of Anthimus; but he soon resigned the see which he had unwillingly occupied. [GREGORY NAZIANZEN.] A peace was patched up between Basil and Anthimus, apparently by the intercession of Gregory. This happened in the year 372 (Greg. Naz. *Or.* xliii. i. pp. 813 seq.; *Ep.* 47, 48, 49, 50, ii. pp. 42 seq.; *Carm.* ii. pp. 696 seq.). (2) A certain Faustus had applied to Basil to consecrate him to an Armenian see; but as he did not produce the proper authority, the consecration was deferred. Faustus immediately applied to Anthimus, who at once complied with his request, thus setting canonical rules at defiance (Basil, *Ep.* 120, 121, 122). A reconciliation, however, seems to have been effected, as Basil afterwards spoke of Anthimus in very friendly terms (*Ep.* 210, τὸν ὁμόψυχον ἡμῶν). Except in connexion with Basil and Gregory, nothing is known of this prelate. (See Tillemont, *Mém. eccl.* ix. pp. 174 seq., 196 seq.; Garnier, Vit. Bas. *Op.* iii. pp. cxi. seq., pp. cxxiii. seq.) [L.]

Anthropolatrae (Ἀνθρωπολάτραι), a nickname given by the Apollinarians (*c.* A.D. 371) to the Catholics, on the assumption that the union of "perfect God" with "perfect Man" necessarily involved two Persons in Christ, and therefore that the Catholic exposition of the doctrine implied the worship of a *man*: an inference assumed to be avoided by the special Apollinarian dogma. See APOLLINARIS (the Younger). The nickname in question is mentioned by St. Greg. Naz. *Orat.* li., who retorts that in truth, if any one is to be called by a name of the kind, the Apollinarian ought to be called "σαρκολάτρης." [A.W.H.]

Anthropomorphitae (*Anthropomorphism*), (ἄνθρωπος, *man*, and μορφή, *form*). Terms applied to those who ascribe to God human shape and form. We must distinguish two kinds of anthropomorphism, a doctrinal and a symbolical. The former is heretical, the latter Scriptural, and necessarily arises from the imperfection of human language and human knowledge of God. The one takes the Scripture passages which speak of God's arm, hand, eye, ear, mouth, etc., literally; the other understands and uses them figuratively. Anthropomorphism is always connected with anthropopathism (from ἄνθρωπος and πάθος, *passion*), which ascribes to God human passions and affections, such as wrath, anger, envy, jealousy, pity, repentance. The latter, however, does not necessarily imply the former. All forms of idolatry, especially those of Greece and Rome, are essentially anthropomorphic and anthropopathic. The classical divinities are in character simply deified men and women. The Christian, Jewish, and Mohammedan religions teach that God is a Spirit, and thus elevate him above the reach of materialistic and sensual conceptions and representations. But within the Christian church anthropomorphism appeared from time to time as an isolated opinion or as the tenet of a party. Tertullian is often charged with it, because he ascribed to God a body (*Adv. Prax.* c. 7: "Quis enim negabit, Deum corpus esse, etsi Deus spiritus est? Spiritus enim corpus sui generis in effigie"). But he probably identified corporeality with substantiality, and hence he maintained that everything real had a body of some kind (*de Carne Chr.* c. 11: "Omne quod est, corpus est sui generis, nihil est incorporale, nisi quod non est"). The pseudo-Clementine Homilies (xvii. 2 seq.) teach that God, in order to be an object of love, must be the highest beauty, and consequently have a body, since there is no beauty without form; nor could we pray to a God Who was mere spirit. (Cf. Baur, *Vorlesungen über die Dogmengeschichte*, vol. i. p. 412.) In the middle of the 4th cent. *Audius*, or *Audaeus*, of Syria, a bold censor of the luxury and vices of the clergy, and an irregularly consecrated bishop, founded a strictly ascetic sect, which were called *Audians* or *Anthropomorphites*, and maintained themselves, in spite of repeated persecution, till the close of the 5th cent. He started from a literal interpretation of Gen. i. 28, and reasoned from the nature of man to the nature of God, Whose image he was (Epiphanius, *Haer.* 70; Theod. *H. E.* iv. 9; Walch, *Ketzerhistorie*, iii. 300). During the Origenistic controversies towards the end of the 4th cent., anthropomorphism was held independently by many Egyptian monks in the Scetic desert, who, with Pachomius at their head, were the most violent opponents of the spiritualistic theology of Origen, and were likewise called Anthropomorphites; they felt the need of material conceptions in their prayers and ascetic exercises. Theophilus of Alexandria, formerly an admirer of Origen, became his bitter opponent, and expelled the Origenists from Egypt, but nevertheless he rejected the Anthropomorphism of the anti-Origenistic monks (*Ep. Pastr.* for 399). In the present century Anthropomorphism has been revived by the Mormons, who conceive God as an intelligent material being, with body, members, and passions, and unable to occupy two distinct places at once. [P.S.]

Antidikomarianitae (Ἀντιδικομαριανῖται = Adversaries of Mary: Epiph. *Haer.* lxxxix.). The name given to those in Arabia in the latter part of the 4th cent. who (in opposition to the Κολλυριδιάνιδες) maintained the novel supposition advanced at that time by Bonosus of Sadica, and by Helvidius, that "our Lord's brethren" were children borne by the Blessed Virgin to Joseph after our Lord's birth. The controversy arose out of the then prevailing reverence for virginity, which in its extreme form had led certain women, originally from Thrace, but dwelling in Arabia, to celebrate an idolatrous festival in honour of the Virgin, by taking certain cakes (κολλύριδες) about in chariots, and then solemnly offering them to her and consuming them, in imitation of the Lord's Supper, or (more probably) of the pagan worship of Ceres. The reaction from this superstition led to the existence of the sect spoken of in this article, which, contemporaneously with the controversy carried on by St. Jerome and by others against Helvidius and BONOSUS, the literary supporters of the hypothesis, was led to endeavour to cut away all pretence for the Collyridian superstition by adopting their view and so denying its very groundwork. The controversy itself is discussed in Smith's *D. B.* (4 vols. 1893) under BROTHERS and JAMES, and in Murray's *Illus. B. D.* (1908) under JAMES. For its literary history, see under HELVIDIUS, HIERONYMUS. [A.W.H.]

Antiochus (1), bp. of Ptolemais, *c.* A.D. 401. To display his oratorical powers in a wider field he left Ptolemais and settled at Constantinople, where his fine voice and appropriate action, together with the eloquent and perspicuous character of his discourses, soon attracted large auditories, by whom, like his great contemporary John, he was surnamed "The Golden-mouthed." Having amassed considerable wealth, he returned to his deserted see, where he employed his leisure in composing a long treatise "against avarice." He took a zealous part in the proceedings against Chrysostom, and is reckoned by Palladius among his bitterest enemies. He died in the reign of Arcadius, before A.D. 408, and, according to Nicephorus, his end, like that of all the enemies of Chrysostom, was miserable. A homily on *The Cure of the Blind Man* is also mentioned. With the exception of a sentence quoted by Theodoret, *Dial.* 2, and a longer fragment given in the *Catena on St. John*, xix. p. 443, his works have perished (Socr. vi. 11; Soz. viii. 10; Niceph. xiii. 26; Gennadius in *Catalog.*; Pallad. *Dialog.* p. 49; Fabr. *Bibl. Gk.* ix. 259). [E.V.]

Antipopes, claimants to the popedom in opposition to the lawful popes. There were seven such during the first six centuries, some owing their elevation to the existence of conflicting parties at Rome, others intruded into the see by the civil power. A fuller account of them, with the authorities, is given under their respective names—viz. NOVATIANUS; FELIX; URSINUS (or Ursicinus); EULALIUS; LAURENTIUS; DIOSCORUS; VIGILIUS. [J. B—Y.]

Antoninus, Pius, emperor, A.D. 138-161. The character of this prince as loving righteousness and mercy, choosing rather, in his own noble words, "to save the life of one citizen than to slay a thousand foes," shewed itself, as in other things, so also in his treatment of the Christians of the empire. Hadrian had checked the tendency to persecution by imposing severe penalties on false accusers (Just. Mart. *Apol.* i. c. 68). In some way or other, Antoninus was led to adopt a policy which was even more favourable to them (Xiphilin. *Epit. Dion. Cass.* 1, 70, p. 1173). Melito, writing his *Apologia* to Marcus Aurelius (Eus. *H. E.* iv. 26), speaks of edicts which Antoninus had issued, forbidding any new and violent measures against the Christians. A more memorable proof of his tolerance is found, if the document be genuine, in the decree addressed to the general assembly of the proconsular province of Asia, at a time when the Christian church was exposed to outrages of all kinds (πρὸς τὸ κοινὸν τῆς Ἀσίας). It speaks in admiring terms of the innocence of the Christians, declares the charges against them to be unproved, bids men admire the steadfastness and faith with which they met the earthquakes and other calamities that drove others to despair, ascribes the persecution to the jealousy which men felt against those who were truer worshippers of God than themselves. Unfortunately, however, the weight of both textual and internal evidence preponderates against the genuineness of the edict as it stands, but some modern authorities are disposed to regard it as an interpolated form of a real edict of similar character. See, *e.g.*, Renan, *L'Eglise Chrétienne,* p. 302. In any case it is natural to connect the more lenient policy, which there is no doubt that Antoninus adopted, with the memorable *Apologia* which Justin addressed to him. Confining ourselves to its bearing on the character of the emperor, we note (1) that there had been at least the threat of persecution even unto death (c. 68); (2) that it is written throughout in a tone of manifest respect as to men not unworthy of the epithets that were attached to their names ("Pius" to Antoninus, "philosopher" to Verissimus and Lucius); (3) that the mere fact of the dedication and, apparently, presentation of such an address implies a tolerance which had not been often found in preceding emperors; (4) that even the forged document, if it be such, shews a certain verisimilitude in the ascription of such a document to him. See Champagny, *Les Antonines* (Paris), and Aubé, *Hist. des Persécut.* (Paris, 1875), pp. 297-341. [E.H.P.]

Antonius, St. (Abbas), termed by Athanasius "the founder of asceticism" and his life a "model for monks" (Praef. *Vit. St. Ant.*). We have a tolerably complete, but probably interpolated, biography of him by Athanasius, derived in part from his own recollections, in part from others who had known him, as well as frequent mention of him by the ecclesiastical historians; and we shall here treat Anthony as a historic character, despite the recent assumption that he is "a myth" (see, *e.g.*, Gwatkin's *Arian Controversy*, 1891, and cf. F. W. Farrar, *Contemp. Rev.* 1887, pp. 617-627).

Anthony was born *c.* A.D. 250 at Coma, on the borders of Upper Egypt (Soz. *Hist.* i. 13). By his parents, who were wealthy Christians. he was trained in pious habits (Athan. *Vit. St. Ant.*; Aug. *de Doct. in Prol.*). Six months after the death of his parents, being then 18 years of age, he chanced to hear in church the words "If thou wilt be perfect," etc., and resolved to obey the precept literally, reserving only a small portion for his sister. Returning into the church he heard, "Take no thought for the morrow." On this he resolved to commend her to the care of some devout woman, and gave away all his property to the poor (Athan. cf. Soz. i. 13).

At that time cells of Anchorites (μοναστηρία) were very rare in Egypt, and none far from the habitations of men. Anthony retired by degrees farther and farther from his native village, fixing his abode first in a tomb, afterwards in a ruined castle near the Nile. Here he remained some 20 years, shut up for months at a time with only bread and water (the bread of the country is said to be good for keeping), and issuing forth only to instruct the multitudes who flocked to see and hear him; at other times communication was prevented by a huge stone at the entrance. During the persecution of Maximinus (A.D. 311), in which their bishop had fallen, he went to comfort the Christians of Alexandria; and though the presence of monks at these trials was forbidden as encouraging the martyrs in their disobedience to the emperor's edict, he persisted in appearing in court. When the storm had ceased he withdrew, though now an old man, to a more complete isolation than ever, near the Red Sea; and here, to save his disciples the trouble of bringing him food, he made a small field of wheat, which he cultivated with his own hands, working also at making mats. From time to time he revisited his former disciples in the Thebaid, always, however, declining to preside over a convent. About A.D. 335 he revisited Alexandria, at the urgent request of Athanasius, to preach against the Arians (Theod. *Hist.* iv. 27), and there was followed by crowds as "the man of God." But he soon returned to the congenial seclusion of his cell, and there died, at the great age of 105, in the presence of the two disciples, Amathas and Macarius, who had ministered to his wants during the last 15 years. To them he bequeathed his hair-shirt; and the rest of his worldly goods, his two woollen tunics and the rough cloak on which he slept, to bp. Serapion and St. Athanasius (Athan. *Vit. St. Ant.*).

The fame of Anthony spread rapidly through Christendom; and the effect of his example in inducing Christians, especially in the East, to embrace the monastic life is described by his biographers as incalculable. In the next century he began to be venerated as a saint by the Greek church, and in the ninth by the Latin. St. Jerome says he was the author of seven Epistles to certain Eastern monasteries, which have been translated from the Egyptian into the Greek (Hieron. *de Script.* 88), but whether these are the same as those now extant in Latin is doubtful (cf. Erdinger's ed. of them (Innsbruck, 1871). Though by all accounts far from being a learned man (Soz. *Hist.* i. 13; Niceph. *Hist.* vii. 40; Athan. *Vit. St. Ant.*), his discourses are evidence that he was not altogether illiterate. His influence was great at the court of the emperor. Constantine the Great and his sons wrote to him as a father (Athan.), and when Athanasius was contending with the Meletians, Anthony wrote from his cell to the emperor in behalf of his friend (Soz. ii. 31). His austerities were great; as a rule he fasted till sunset, and sometimes for four days together. Of sleep he was equally sparing. His coarse rough shirt is said to have lasted him for a lifetime; and his only ablutions seem to have been involuntary in wading occasionally through a river. Yet he lived to an unusual age, robust, and in full possession of his faculties to the last. He was not morose to others; only to heretics was he austere and repulsive, refusing to hold any intercourse with them even for a moment. He was careful always, though so universally revered, not to arrogate to himself priestly functions, shewing, even in his old age, a marked and studious deference even to the youngest deacons.

Anthony was evidently a man, not merely of strong determination, but of ability, and the discourses, if indeed they are his, which his disciples record as addressed to themselves and to the pagan philosophers who disputed with him, shew that if he read little he thought much. He met objections against the doctrines of the Incarnation and the Resurrection as mysterious by the retort that the pagan mythology, whether in its grossness as apprehended by the vulgar or as the mystical system of philosophers, was equally above reason. From their dialectical subtleties he appealed to facts, to a Christian's contempt of death and triumph over temptation; and contrasted the decay of pagan oracles and magic with the growth of Christianity in spite of persecutions. He taught that prayer to be perfect must be ecstatic (Cass. *Coll.* ix. 31). Mingled with sound and practical advice are strange stories of his visions, in which he describes himself as engaged continually in deadly conflict with evil spirits.

Beyond these encounters and powers of exorcism it is not clear how far and in what manner Anthony believed himself able to work miracles. It would indeed be strange if so lonely an existence did not breed many involuntary and unconscious illusions; still more strange if those whose eyes were dazzled by the almost more than human self-abnegation of the great eremite had not exaggerated this aspect of his story. Among the many in whom the marvellous experiences of Anthony awoke a longing to renounce the world was Augustine himself (Aug. *Conf.* viii. 6, 12). A. Verger, *Vie de St. Antoine le Grand* (Tours, 1898). [I.G.S.]

Aphraat (*Aphrahat*, *Farhad*, "the Sage of Persia"). Little is known of the life of this writer, who was the principal theologian of the Persian (*i.e.* Eastern or Nestorian) church in the 4th cent. He was born late in the 3rd cent., and was certainly a monk, and probably a bishop of his church. Tradition says that he resided at the monastery of Mar Mattai, near Mosul, and was bishop in that province. Either at his baptism or consecration he adopted the name Jacob (ܝܥܩܘܒ) in addition to his own, and for this reason his works have sometimes been attributed to better-known namesakes.

In the year 344 he presided over a council of the church of his province (Adiabene), and the synodal letter is included in his works (*Homily* xiv.). Sapor's persecution was then raging in the country, but is known to have been, for local reasons, less severe in this district than elsewhere. The time and manner of his death are not known.

Works.—These consist of a collection of 22 *Homilies*, written at the request of a friend (a monk) to give an exposition of the Christian faith. Their importance consists in the picture that they give of the current teaching of an independent church, already organized under its own primate, outside the Roman empire. The language is Syriac, the quotations from the O.T. are taken from the *Peshitta*, but in the N.T. he quotes the Gospels from the *Diatessaron*. Some of his interpretations (e.g. *Hom.* xv.) shew signs of Jewish or "Talmudical" teaching.

Doctrine.—As a theologian, Aphraat is strikingly independent and remote from the controversies of his day in the Roman empire. Writing 20 years after the council of Nicaea, he expresses himself in a way impossible for any one who had heard of the Arian controversy, whatever his sympathies in it; with him we are back in the indefiniteness of an earlier age, when an orthodox writer might use on one page the language of psilanthropism (*Hom.* xvii.) and on another confess both the Trinity and the Divinity of Christ (vi. ll.). This is consistent with the fact that the "church of the East" was so isolated that it was never asked to accept the Nicene Creed till the year 410; and apparently used, till that date, the formula that Aphraat gives (*Hom.* i.). See NESTORIAN CHURCH.

A curious feature in Aphraat's teaching is the use of expressions that plainly suggest that he regarded the Holy Spirit as the female element in the Godhead (xviii. 10). It is a thought strange to us, but not necessarily unorthodox, and natural to a mind of Semitic cast, that used a word for "spirit" that is feminine; its absence from Greek and Latin theology may account in part for the enthronement of another figure as Queen of Heaven. Aphraat's whole teaching has the ascetic cast natural to a 4th-cent. Oriental monk. The celibates (xviii.) are emphatically the aristocracy of the church, the professors of the higher life, who alone can attain to true communion with God. Any one who doubts his own capacity for the keeping of a vow of virginity, which apparently was often taken at the time of baptism, is advised to marry before that rite, a fall subsequent to it being a heinous sin (vii. 10). Nevertheless, all are warned that open abandonment of the resolution and avowed marriage is better than secret incontinence.

Broadly, Aphraat shews us the existence of an independent Oriental theology, which, however, was not allowed to develop on its own lines, but was assimilated to Greek standards a few generations later. This was a distinct loss to the fullness of Christian thought, and a misfortune to the Syriac church itself, in that it soon shewed itself unable to think on Greek lines, so that schisms resulted that endure to this day. Parisot, *Patrol. Syriac. Aphraatis Demonstrationes*; Labourt. *Christianisme dans l'empire perse*; Burkitt, *Early Eastern Christianity*. [W.A.W.]

Aphthartodocetae (from ἄφθαρτος, *incorruptible*, and δοκέω, *to think*), a sect of the MONOPHYSITES, which arose in the 6th cent. They were also called *Phantasiastae*, because they appeared to acknowledge only a *seeming* body of Christ, and to border on Docetism; and *Julianists*, from their leader Julian, bp. of

Halicarnassus, and his contemporary Xenajas of Hierapolis. They argued, from the commingling (σύγχυσις) of the two natures of Christ, that the body of our Lord, from the very beginning, became partaker of the incorruptibility of the Logos, and was subject to corruptibility merely κατ' οἰκονομίαν. They appealed in proof especially to Christ's walking on the sea during His earthly life. Their opponents among the Monophysites, the *Severians* (from Severus, patriarch of Antioch), maintained that the body of Christ *before* the Resurrection was corruptible, and were hence called *Phthartolatrae* (Φθαρτολάτραι, from φθαρτός and λάτρεια), or *Corrupticolae*, i.e. Worshippers of the Corruptible. Both parties admitted the incorruptibility of Christ's body *after* the Resurrection. The word φθορά was generally taken in the sense of corruptibility, but sometimes in the sense of mere frailty. This whole question is rather one of scholastic subtlety, though not wholly idle, and may be solved in this way: that the body of Christ, before the Resurrection, was similar in its constitution to the body of Adam before the Fall, containing the germ or possibility of immortality and incorruptibility, but subject to the influence of the elements, and was actually put to death by external violence, but through the indwelling power of the sinless Spirit was preserved from corruption and raised again to an imperishable life, when—to use an ingenious distinction of St. Augustine—the *immortalitas minor* became *immortalitas major*, or the *posse non mori* a *non posse mori*.

The Aphthartodocetae were subdivided into *Ktistolatrae*, or, from their founder, *Gajanitae*, who taught that the body of Christ was *created* (κτιστόν), and *Aktistetae*, who asserted that the body of Christ, although in itself created, yet by its union with the eternal Logos became *increate*, and therefore incorruptible. The most consistent Monophysite in this direction was the rhetorician Stephanus Niobes (about 550), who declared that every attempt to distinguish between the divine and the human in Christ was improper and useless, since they had become absolutely one in him. An abbot of Edessa, Bar Sudaili, extended this principle even to the creation, which he thought would at last be wholly absorbed in God.

Cf. the dissertations of Gieseler, *Monophysitarum variae de Christi Persona Opiniones*, 1835 and 1838; the remarks of Dorner, *History of Christology*, ii. 159 ff. (German ed.); Ebrard, *Church and Doctrine History*, i. 268; and Schaff, *Church History*, iii. 766 ff. [P.S.]

Apion. The name is properly Egyptian (see Procop. *Pers.* i. 8; Ross. *Inscr.* fasc. 2, p. 62) and derived from the god Apis, after the analogy of Anubion, Serapion, etc.

(1) The son of Poseidonius (Justin (?) *Coh, ad Gent.* § 9; Africanus in Eus. *Pr. Ev.* x. 10. p. 490), a grammarian of Alexandria in the 1st cent. His literary triumphs and critical labours on Homer do not fall within our scope, but his conflict with Jews and Jewish Christians entitles him to a place here.

(i) His hostility to Judaism was deep, persistent, and unscrupulous (Joseph. *c. Ap.* ii. 1-13; Clem. *Hom.* iv. 24, v. 2, πάνυ Ἰουδαίους δι' ἀπεχθείας ἔχοντα, v. 27, 29, ὁ ἀλόγως μισῶν τὸ Ἰουδαίων κ.τ.λ.; Clem. *Strom.* i. 21), as the direct extracts preserved by Josephus from his writings clearly prove. These attacks were contained in two works especially: in his *Egyptian History* (Αἰγυπτιακά), and in a separate treatise *Against the Jews* (κατὰ Ἰουδαίων βίβλος, Justin. (?) *l.c.*; Africanus, *l.c.*). Josephus exposes the ignorance, mendacity, and self-contradictions of Apion.

(ii) It is not surprising that the spent wave of this antagonism should have overflowed on Judaic Christianity. Whether Apion actually came in contact with any members of the new brotherhood is more than questionable. His early date (for he flourished in the reigns of Tiberius, Caius, and Claudius) renders this improbable. But in the writings of the Petro-Clementine cycle he holds a prominent place as an antagonist of the Gospel. In the Clementine *Homilies* he appears in company with Anubion and Athenodorus among the satellites of Simon Magus, the arch-enemy of St. Peter and St. Peter's faith. The Clementine *Recognitions* contain nothing corresponding to the disputes of Clement and Apion in the 4th, 5th, and 6th books of the *Homilies*; but at the close of this work (x. 52), as at the close of the *Homilies*, he is introduced as a subsidiary character in the plot. See the treatises on these writings by Schliemann, Uhlhorn, Hilgenfeld, Lehmann, and others.

(2) A Christian author about the end of 2nd cent., who wrote on the *Hexaemeron* (Eus. *H. E.* v. 27; Hieron. *Vir. Ill.* 49). [L.]

Apolinaris, or Apolinarius Claudius. Ἀπολινάριος: so spelt in the most ancient Gk. MSS.; Latin writers generally use the form Apollinaris), bp. of Hierapolis, in Phrygia A.D. 171 and onwards (Eus. *Chron.*); one of the most active and esteemed Christian writers of the day, he is praised by Photius for his style (Phot. *Cod.* 14). Jerome enumerates him among the ecclesiastical writers who were acquainted with heathen literature, and who made use of this knowledge in the refutation of heresy (*Ep. ad Magnum*, iv. 83, p. 656. Cf. Theod. *Haer. Fab. Compend.* iii. 2).

Only a few fragments of his works have been preserved. Eusebius (*H. E.* iv. 27) gives the following list of those which had fallen into his hands; and his list is repeated by St. Jerome (*de Vir. Ill.* c. 26) and Nicephorus (*H. E.* iv. 11). (1) An apology addressed to Marcus Aurelius, probably written after A.D. 174, since it is likely that it contained the reference to the miracle of the Thundering Legion elsewhere quoted by Eusebius from Apolinaris (*H. E.* v. 5). (2) Five books πρὸς Ἕλληνας, written according to Nicephorus in the form of a dialogue. (3) Two books περὶ ἀληθείας. (4) Two books πρὸς Ἰουδαίους: these are not mentioned by St. Jerome, and the reference to them is absent from some copies of Eusebius. (5) Writings against the Phrygian heresy, published when Montanus was first propounding his heresy; *i.e.* according to the *Chronicon* of Eusebius, *c.* 172. These writings, which were probably in the form of letters, are appealed to by Serapion, bp. of Antioch (Eus. *H. E.* v. 19); and Eusebius elsewhere (v. 16) describes Apolinaris as raised up as a strong and irresistible weapon against Montanism. The situation of his see sufficiently accounts for the prominent part taken by Apolinaris in this controversy. We are told indeed by an anonymous writer who probably wrote at the end of the 9th cent. (Auctor, *Libelli Synodici* apud Labbe et Cossart, i. 599) that Apolinaris on this occasion assembled twenty-six other bishops in council, and excommunicated Montanus and Maximilla, as well as the shoemaker Theodotus. Besides the works mentioned by Eusebius, who does not give his list as a complete one, Theodoret (*Haer. Fab.* ii. 21) mentions (6) that Apolinaris wrote against the Encratites of the school of Severus (*πρὸς τοὺς Σεουηριανοὺς Ἐγκρατίτας*). (7) Photius (*Cod.* 14) mentions having read Apolinaris's work *πρὸς Ἕλληνας καὶ περὶ ἀληθείας καὶ περὶ εὐσεβείας.* (8) In the preface to the Alexandrian Chronicle a work *περὶ τοῦ πάσχα* is attributed to Apolinaris, from which two extracts are furnished which have given rise to much controversy; the main point being whether (if the fragments are genuine) Apolinaris wrote on the side of the practice of the Roman church, or on that of the Quartodecimans of Asia Minor. In support of the former view is urged the similarity of the language of these fragments with that of Clement of Alexandria and of Hippolytus, who advocated the Western practice; and also the fact that Apolinaris is not claimed as a Quartodeciman by Polycrates, bp. of Ephesus, in his letter to Victor of Rome. On the other side it is urged that Apolinaris speaks of his antagonists as "some who raise contention through ignorance," language which would rather convey the impression that Apolinaris was writing against the opinions of some small sect than that he was combating the belief of the whole church of Asia Minor to which he belonged; and it is further urged that if Apolinaris had been the first to defend in the East the practice which ultimately prevailed, it is incredible that neither Eusebius nor any early writer mentions this early champion of the Catholic practice. Socrates the historian (*H. E.* iii. 7) names Apolinaris, together with Irenaeus, Clement, and Serapion, as holding the doctrine that our Lord when He became man had a human soul (*ἔμψυχον τὸν ἐνανθρωπήσαντα*).

Apolinaris had been set down as a Chiliast on St. Jerome's authority (*de Vir. Ill.* c. 18), but Routh (*Rel. Sac.* i. 174) has given good reason for thinking that the Apollinaris intended is the younger Apollinaris, of Laodicea; since Jerome speaks of Irenaeus and Apollinaris as the first and the last of the Greek Millenarians (lib. xi. *Comm. in Ezech.* c. 36, iii. 952), and also states that Apollinaris answered Dionysius of Alexandria (*Prooem.* in lib. xviii. *Comm. Esaiae* iii. 478).

The Martyrologies commemorate the death of Apollinaris on Feb. 7. Of the year or of the place and manner of his death nothing is known; but that it was before the end of the 2nd cent. may be inferred from the language in which he is described in the letter of Serapion written about that time (*Κλαυδίου Ἀπολιναρίου τοῦ μακαριωτάτου γενομένου ἐν Ἱεραπόλει τῆς Ἀσίας ἐπισκόπου*). [G.S.]

Apollinarianism, Apollinarians, Apollinarists. [APOLLINARIS THE YOUNGER.]

Apollinaris, St. and Mart., first bp. or archbp. of Ravenna, perhaps from 50-78. According to the Life written by Agnellus in 9th cent. (*Liber Pontificalis,* ap. Muratori, *Rer. It. Script.* ii. part i.), St. Apollinaris was a native of Antioch, well instructed in Gk. and Lat. literature, who followed St. Peter to Rome, and was sent by him to Ravenna. On his way he healed the son of Irenaeus who was blind, and did other miracles. At Ravenna he baptized in the river Bidens, and raised the daughter of the patrician Rufus to life; imprisoned by the heathen near the capitol, he was there fed by angels. Afterwards, being expelled from the city, he preached in Dalmatia, Pannonia, Thrace, and Corinth. After three years he returned, suffered new persecutions, and did new miracles, destroying a statue and temple of Apollo by his prayers. He was martyred under Vespasian, after an episcopate of over 28 years.

Other lives, such as that in the *Acta Sanctorum,* are more full of miracles, but do not add anything else of importance. The day of his death is agreed upon as July 23; the year may have been 78. From a sermon of St. Peter Chrysologus in 5th cent. (No. 128, pp. 552 seq. ed. Migne), it appears that St. Apollinaris was the only bp. of Ravenna who suffered martyrdom, and that he, strictly speaking, can only be called a confessor. He did not die, it would seem, a violent death, though it may have been hastened by the persecutions he underwent. Probably, like his successor Aderitus, he died in the port-town Classis, where he was buried. A new church, still existing, was built about the same time as that of St. Vitale, and into this his body was translated by St. Maximianus *c.* 552. The mosaic over the apse seems to realize the words of St. Peter Chrysologus (*u.s.*), "Ecce vivit, ecce ut bonus pastor suo medius assistit in grege." As early as 575 it was the custom to take solemn oaths upon his relics (St. Greg. Magn. *Ep.* vi. 61). His body was taken to Ravenna in 1515 for safety, but restored in 1655 (see authorities in *Acta Sanctor.* for July 23). This most interesting basilica, with the vacant monastery adjoining, is now the only remnant of the town of Classis. [J.W.]

Apollinaris (or, according to Greek orthography, *Apollinarius*) **the Elder,** of Alexandria, was born about the beginning of the 4th cent. After teaching grammar for some time at Berytus in Phoenicea, he removed, A.D. 335, to Laodicea, of which church he was made presbyter. Here he married and had a son, afterwards the bp. of Laodicea. [APOLLINARIS THE YOUNGER.] Both father and son were on intimate terms with the heathen sophists Libanius and Epiphanius of Petra, frequenting the lecture-room of the latter, on which account they were admonished and, upon their venturing to sit out the recitation of a hymn to Bacchus, excommunicated by Theodotus, bp. of Laodicea, but restored upon their subsequent repentance (Socr. *Eccl. Hist.* iii. 16; Soz. vi. 25).

The elder Apollinaris is chiefly noted for

his literary labours. When the edict of Julian, A.D. 362, forbade the Christians to read Greek literature, he undertook with the aid of his son to supply the void by reconstructing the Scriptures on the classical models. Thus the whole Biblical history down to Saul's accession was turned into 24 books of Homeric hexameters, each superscribed, like those of the *Iliad*, by a letter of the alphabet. Lyrics, tragedies, and comedies, after the manner of Pindar, Euripides, and Menander, followed. Even the Gospels and Epistles were adapted to the form of Socratic disputation. Two works alone remain as samples of their indomitable zeal: a tragedy entitled *Christus Patiens*, in 2601 lines, which has been edited among the works of Gregory Nazianzen; and a version of the Psalms, in Homeric hexameters. The most that can be said of this Psalter is that it is better than the tragedy, and that as a whole it fully bears out the reputation of the poet (Basil. *Ep.* 273, 406) that he was never at a loss for an expression. Socrates, who is more trustworthy than Sozomen (v. 18), ascribes the O.T. poems to the father (iii. 16), and adds that the son as the greater rhetorician devoted his energies to converting the Gospels and Epistles into Platonic dialogues. He likewise mentions a treatise on grammar compiled by the elder Apollinaris, χριστιανικῷ τύπῳ. For different opinions as to the authorship of father and son, cf. Vossius, *de Hist. Graec.* ii. 18; *de Poet. Graec.* c. 9; Duport, Praef. ad *Metaph. Psalm.* (Lond. 1674).

The *Metaphrasis Psalmorum* was published at Paris 1552; by Sylburg, at Heidelberg, 1596; and subsequently in various collections of the Fathers. The latest edition is that in Migne's *Patr. Gk.* xxiii. [E.M.Y.]

Apollinaris the Younger, bp. of Laodicea, flourished in the latter half of the 4th cent., and was at first highly esteemed, even by Athanasius and Basil, for his classical culture, piety, and adhesion to the Nicene Creed during the Arian controversy, until he introduced a Christological heresy which is called after him, and which in some respects prepared the way for Monophysitism. He assisted his father in rewriting the Christian Scriptures in imitation of the style of Homer, Menander, etc., mentioned in the preceding article. He also wrote in defence of Christianity against Julian and Porphyry; of orthodoxy against the Manicheans, Arians, Marcellus, Eunomius, and other heretics; Biblical commentaries, and other works, of which only fragments remain. Jerome enjoyed his instruction, A.D. 374. He did not secede from the communion of the church and begin to form a sect of his own till 375. He died about 392. After his death his followers, who were not numerous, were divided into two parties, the Polemians and Valentinians. His doctrine was condemned by a synod of Alexandria (not naming him), by two synods at Rome under Damasus (377 and 378), and by the second oecumenical council (381). Imperial decrees prohibited the public worship of the Apollinarists (388, 397, 428), until during the 5th cent. they were absorbed partly by the orthodox, partly by the Monophysites. But the peculiar Christology of Apollinaris has reappeared from time to time, in a modified shape, as an isolated theological opinion.

Apollinaris was the first to apply the results of the Nicene controversy to Christology proper, and to call the attention of the church to the psychical and pneumatic element in the humanity of Christ; but in his zeal for the true deity of Christ, and fear of a double personality, he fell into the error of a partial denial of His true Humanity. Adopting the psychological trichotomy of Plato (σῶμα, ψυχή, πνεῦμα), for which he quoted I. Thess. v. 23 and Gal. v. 17, he attributed to Christ a human body (σῶμα) and a human soul (the ψυχὴ ἄλογος, the *anima animans* which man has in common with the animal), but not a rational spirit (νοῦς, πνεῦμα, ψυχὴ λογική, *anima rationalis*), and put in the place of the latter the divine Logos. In opposition to the idea of a mere connexion of the Logos with the man Jesus, he wished to secure an organic unity of the two, and so a true incarnation; but he sought this at the expense of the most important constituent of man. He reached only a θεὸς σαρκοφόρος, as Nestorianism only an ἄνθρωπος θεοφόρος, instead of the proper θεάνθρωπος. He appealed to the fact that the Scripture says, "the Word was made *flesh*"—not *spirit*; "God was manifest in the *flesh*," etc. To which Gregory Nazianzen justly replied that in these passages the term σάρξ was used by synecdoche for the whole human nature. In this way Apollinaris established so close a connexion of the Logos with human flesh, that all the divine attributes were transferred to the human nature, and all the human attributes to the divine, and the two merged in *one* nature in Christ. Hence he could speak of a crucifixion of the Logos, and a worship of His flesh. He made Christ a middle being between God and man, in Whom, as it were, one part divine and two parts human were fused in the unity of a new nature. He even ventured to adduce created analogies of mixtures in nature. Christ, said he, is οὔτε ἄνθρωπος ὅλος, οὔτε θεός, ἀλλὰ θεοῦ καὶ ἀνθρώπου μίξις. On the other hand, he regarded the orthodox view of a union of full humanity with a full divinity in one person—of two wholes in one whole—as an absurdity, in a similar category with the mythological figure of the Minotaur. But the Apollinarian idea of the union of the Logos with a truncated human nature might be itself more justly compared with this monster. Starting from the Nicene *homoousion* as to the Logos, but denying the completeness of Christ's humanity, he met Arianism half-way, which likewise put the divine Logos in the place of the human spirit in Christ. But he strongly asserted Christ's unchangeableness, while Arians taught His changeableness (τρεπτότης).

The faith of the church revolted against such a mutilated and stunted humanity of Christ, which necessarily involved also a merely partial redemption. The incarnation is an assumption of the entire human nature, sin only excluded. The ἐνσάρκωσις is ἐνανθρώπησις. To be a full and complete Redeemer, Christ must be a perfect man (τέλειος ἄνθρωπος). The spirit or rational soul is the most important element in man, the seat of intelligence and freedom, and needs redemption as well as the soul and the body; for sin has corrupted all the faculties.

Athanasius, the two Gregories, Basil, and Epiphanius combated the Apollinarian error, but were unprepared to answer duly its main point, that two integral persons cannot form one person. The later orthodox doctrine surmounted this difficulty by teaching the impersonality of the human nature of Christ, and by making the personality of Christ to reside wholly in the Logos.

Apollinarianism opened the long line of Christological controversies, which resulted in the Chalcedonian symbol.

LITERATURE.—Of the writings of Apollinaris, περὶ σαρκώσεως, περὶ πίστεως, περὶ ἀναστάσεως, κατὰ κεφάλειον, and other polemical and exegetical works and epistles, only fragments remain in the answers of Gregory of Nyssa and Theodoret, in Leontius Byzant. in the Catenae, and in Angelo Mai's *Nova Bibliotheca Patrum*, tom. vii. (Rom. 1854) pt. ii. pp. 82-91. Against Apollinaris are directed Athanasius's *Contra Apollinarium*, or rather περὶ σαρκώσεως τοῦ Κυρίου ἡμῶν Ἰ. Χ. (*Opera*, ed. Bened. tom. i. pt. ii. pp. 921-955), written about 372 without naming Apollinaris; Gregory of Nyssa, Λόγος, ἀντιῤῥητικὸς πρὸς τὰ Ἀπολλιναρίου, first edited by Zaccagni, Rom. 1698, and then by Gallandi, *Bibl. Vet. Patr.* vi. 517-577; Basilius M., *Ep.* 265 (*Opera*, ed. Ben. t. iii. pt. ii. 591 sqq.); Epiph. *Haer.* lxxvii.; Theod. *Fabulae Haer.* iv. 8, v. 9. Of the later literature, cf. especially Petavius, *de Incarnatione Verbi*, i. c. 6; Dorner, *History of Christology*, i. 974-1080; Neander, *History*, i. 334-338; Schaff, *History of the Christian Church*, iii. 708-714; Harnack, *Dogmengesch.* (1909), ii. 324-334; Thomasius, *Dogmengesch.* (1889), 314 f.; Schwane, *Dogmengesch.* (1895), 277-283; G. Voisin, *L'Apollinarisme* (Paris, 1901). [P.S.]

Apollonius, M. [COMMODUS.]

Apollonius of Ephesus, so called on the doubtful authority of the writer of *Praedestinatus*, ed. by Sirmond, who styles him bp. of Ephesus, but the silence of Eusebius and all other earlier testimony makes it difficult to lay much stress on this statement. He wrote a work in five books against the Cataphrygian or Montanist heresy. Fragments of the first three books are extant in Eusebius (*H. E.* v. 18), and contain much that is curious and valuable with regard to the lives and characters of Montanus, the prophetesses Priscilla and Maximilla, and their followers. Jerome also devotes an article to Apollonius. *Vir. Illust.* c. 50, in which he calls him ἀνὴρ ἐλλογιμώτατος, the author of a μέγα καὶ ἐπίσημον τεῦχος, and quotes him as stating that Montanus and his prophetesses hanged themselves. The book professes to be written 40 years after the commencement of Montanus's pretensions to prophesy. Taking for the rise of Montanism the date given in the *Chronicon* of Eusebius (A.D. 172), this would give about A.D. 210 for the date of this work. Eusebius mentions also that Apollonius cites the Revelation of St. John, that he relates the raising to life of a dead man at Ephesus by the same John, and that he makes mention of the tradition quoted also by Clement of Alexandria (*Strom.* vi. 5 *sub finem*) from the Apocryphal "Preaching of Peter" that our Lord commanded His apostles not to leave Jerusalem for twelve years after His ascension. This work of Apollonius was thought sufficiently important by Tertullian to demand an answer; bk. vii. of his lost work, *de Ecstasi*, was devoted to a refutation of his assertions (Hieron. *de Vir. Ill.* c. 50). Tillemont, *Hist. Eccl.* ii. 426; Bonwetsch. *Gesch. des Montanismus* (Erlanger, 1881). [E.V.]

Apollonius of Tyana. The life of this philosopher is related by Philostratus, but the entire fabulousness of his story is obvious. The prodigies, anachronisms, and geographical blunders, and entire absence of other authority are fatal to it (see H. Conybeare in the *Guardian*, June 21, 1893, and Apollon. *Apology, Acts*, etc, Lond. 1894). Philostratus indeed claims the authority of "the records of cities and temples, and Apollonius's epistles to the Eleans, Delphians, Indians, and Egyptians"; but the cities and temples are nameless.

What, then, can we really be said to know of Apollonius of Tyana? That he was born at Tyana and educated at Aegae, that he professed Pythagoreanism, and that he was celebrated in his day for what were considered magical arts, are the only facts that rest on altogether unexceptionable authority. The account of his opposition to the Stoic Euphrates may perhaps also be taken as authentic. His reputation as a magician is confirmed by the double authority of Moeragenes and Lucian (*Pseudomantis*, c. 5). Yet there are also reasons for believing that he was more than a mere magician, and even a philosopher of some considerable insight. Eusebius (*Praep. Ev.* p. 150 *b*) quotes a passage from his book *On Sacrifices* (with the reservation "Apollonius is *said* to write as follows"), which if really his is certainly remarkable. All later authorities base their accounts on the Life by Philostratus; except Origen, who quotes Moeragenes. Hierocles mentions Maximus of Aegae and Damis, but probably only knew of them through Philostratus. We now come to the collection of letters still extant which are attributed to Apollonius. Prof. Jowett (in the *D. of G. and R. Biogr.*) thinks that part may be genuine; but Kayser and Zeller reject them summarily, and most writers on Apollonius barely mention them. Zeller even says that they are obviously composed to suit the Life by Philostratus. We do not think that this opinion can be held by any one who attentively compares the letters with the biography; and we think it probable that the letters, whether genuine or not, were composed before the work of Philostratus, and hence form our earliest and best authority respecting Apollonius.

The question arises, Had Philostratus in the biography any idea of attacking Christianity by setting up a rival to Christ? Hierocles, at the end of the 3rd cent., was the first person who actually applied the work of Philostratus to this purpose, as is said expressly by Eusebius, who replied to him. The Deists of the 18th cent., both in France and England, used them thus; but whereas Hierocles would admit the miracles *both* of Christ and of Apollonius,

Voltaire and Lord Herbert had an equal disbelief in both. Naturally, none of these writers held that Philostratus wrote in direct imitation of the Gospels, as it would have marred their point to do so. But equally naturally the orthodox writers, beginning with Huet, bp. of Avranches, and coming down through Paley to our own day, have considered Philostratus a direct though concealed antagonist of Christianity. This view has been opposed in Germany by Meiners, Neander, Buhle, and Jacobs, and in England by Watson (*Contemp. Rev.* Feb. 1867). Baur took an intermediate view in his *Apollonius von Tyana und Christus*, Tübingen, 1832), which in its main outline will we think commend itself as by far the most probable account. According to this view Philostratus wrote with no strictly polemical reference to Christianity, but, in the eclectic spirit of his time, strove to accommodate Christianity to the heathen religion. We are disposed to believe, without attributing to Philostratus any formal design of opposing or assimilating Christianity, that he was strongly influenced by its ideas and history.

The central aim of his biography is to set forth, not merely wise precepts in the abstract, but an example of supreme wisdom for humanity to imitate. It is not implied by this that Philostratus considered Apollonius as entirely and necessarily unique among men; but it is implied that he considered him as more than a mere teacher of doctrine, as a pattern to men in his own person, as one in whom wisdom and truth were incorporate. He wished men to honour Apollonius himself, and not merely to study or believe certain truths delivered by Apollonius. This cannot, we think, be doubted by any one who reflects on the whole tone of the book. Apollonius is called "divine"; his disciples stand in an altogether different relation to him from that in which the disciples of Socrates stand to Socrates; they do not argue with him as equals with an equal; they follow him, listen to him, are rebuked by him. His miracles, again, do not result from his being in possession of any secret communicable to other men, but arise from his own nature and wisdom. Such a character must remind us, however different in some respects, of the Christ of the Gospels. But was any character like this, or approaching to this, drawn by any heathen writer before Christ? We think not. Philosophy and magic, the search after knowledge and the search after power, were familiar to men who had never heard of Christianity; but this ideal is different from either, and from both of them united. Those who affirm that Philostratus never thought of the Christian history in his work, say that he intended Apollonius as a rival to Pythagoras. But by whom was Pythagoras portrayed as this superhuman ideal? Not certainly by any writer of the centuries before Christ. Even Plutarch (*Numa*, c. viii.) does not set him up as an ideal exemplar. Is it possible that the age of Caracalla and Severus, so eclectic, so traditional, so unoriginal, can of its own mere motion have gone off into this new and unheard-of line?—unheard-of, that is, unless, as we must, we suppose it to have been borrowed from Christianity. The Christians were not then by any means an unknown sect; so well known were they that Alexander Severus (with a singular parallelism to the supposed conduct of Philostratus) placed Christ with Abraham, Orpheus, and Apollonius himself, among his household gods. Secondly, the resemblance to the Gospel histories is in particular instances very broad indeed. The miraculous birth of Proteus, and the circumstances attending it; the healing of demoniacal possessions (was the idea of such possessions in any way familiar to the Greeks?); the raising of the dead; the appearance of Apollonius to two of his disciples after his deliverance from Domitian; his ascent to heaven, and appearance after his death,—these are points of similarity that cannot be evaded: and, taken together with the central idea of the book, they seem to imply that Philostratus consciously borrowed from the Gospels. It should be noticed that the very striking resemblances between the biography of Apollonius and the Gospels are resemblances in externals; the inner spirit is entirely different: in the one we find the self-contained philosophic spirit, striking even amid all the rhetoric and tawdry marvels with which Philostratus has dressed it; in the other, the spirit of the insufficiency of self.

Those who wish to examine the whole question respecting Apollonius should consult Baur, *op. cit.*; Kayser's *Philostratus*; Zeller's *Philosophie der Griechen*; and the writers noticed above. [J.R.M.]

Apostolic Fathers. *Definition of the Term.*—The adjective *Apostolicus* (ἀποστολικός) is used to denote either morally or doctrinally accordance with the Apostles, or historically connexion with the Apostles. In this latter sense it is especially applied to churches founded directly by Apostles, or to persons associated with and taught by Apostles. The former are *Apostolicae ecclesiae*; the latter *Apostolici viri*, or *Apostolici* simply. See especially Tertull. *de Praescr.* 32, "ut primus ille episcopus aliquem ex apostolis vel apostolicis viris, qui tamen cum apostolis perseveravit, habuerit auctorem et antecessorem. Hoc enim modo ecclesiae apostolicae census suos deferunt sicut Smyrnaeorum ecclesia Polycarpum ab Joanne collocatum refert, sicut Romanorum Clementem a Petro ordinatum itidem," with the whole context. Cf. also *de Praescr.* 20, 21; *adv. Marc.* i. 21, v. 2; *de Carn. Chr.* 2; *de Pudic.* 21. Hence among the Evangelists, while St. Matthew and St. John are *Apostoli*, St. Mark and St. Luke are *Apostolici* (*adv. Marc.* iv. 2). In accordance with this usage the term *Apostolic Fathers* is confined to those who are known, or may reasonably be presumed, to have associated with and derived their teaching directly from some Apostle. In its widest range it will include Barnabas, Hermas, Clemens, Ignatius, Polycarp, Papias, and the writer of the epistle to Diognetus. Some of these fail to satisfy the conditions which alone entitle to a place among the works of the Apostolic Fathers. Thus the "Shepherd" of Hermas has been placed in this category, because it was supposed to have been written by the person of this name mentioned by St. Paul (Rom. xvi.

14; see Origen *ad loc. Op.* iv. 683); but a more authentic tradition ascribes it to the brother of Pius, who was bp. of Rome a little before the middle of 2nd cent. (*Canon. Murat.* p. 58, ed. Tregelles; see pseudo-Tertull. *Poem. adv. Marc.* iii. 294, in Tertull. *Op.* ii. 792, ed. Oehler). Thus again the claim of Papias to be considered an Apostolic Father rests on the supposition that he was a disciple of St. John the Evangelist, as Irenaeus apparently imagines (*Haer.* v. 33, § 4); but Eusebius says that Irenaeus was mistaken, and that the teacher of Papias was not the Apostle St. John, but the presbyter of the same name (*H. E.* iii. 39). Again, there is some uncertainty about the *Epistle to Diognetus.* Its claim is founded on an expression which occurs in § 11, and which has been interpreted literally as implying that the writer was a personal disciple of one or other of the Apostles. But *in the first place* the context shews that this literal interpretation is out of place, and the passage must be explained as follows: "I do not make any strange statements nor indulge in unreasonable questionings, but having learnt my lessons from the Apostles (lit. having become a disciple of Apostles), I stand forward as a teacher of the nations"; and *secondly*, this is no part of the *Ep. to Diognetus* proper (§§ 1-10), but belongs to a later writing, which has been accidentally attached to the Epistle, owing to the loss of some leaves in the MS. This latter fact is conclusive. If therefore the Epistle has any title to a place among the Apostolic Fathers, it must be established by internal evidence; and though the internal character suggests an early date, perhaps as early as about A.D. 117 (see Westcott, *Canon*, p. 79), yet there is no hint of any historical connexion between the writer and the Apostles. Lastly, the so-called Ep. of Barnabas occupies an unique position. If the writer had been the companion of St. Paul who bore that name, then he would more properly be styled, not an "apostolic man," as he is designated by Clement of Alexandria (*Strom.* ii. 20, p. 489, ὁ ἀποστολικὸς Βαρνάβας), but an "apostle," as the same Clement elsewhere styles him (*Strom.* ii. 6, p. 445; ii. 7, p. 447), in accordance with St. Luke's language (Acts xiv. 14). But if the writer be not the Apostle Barnabas, then we have no evidence of any personal relations with the Apostles, though such is not impossible, as the Epistle must have been written at some date between the age of Vespasian and that of Nerva. Three names remain, Clement, Ignatius, and Polycarp, about which there is no reasonable ground for hesitation.

All the genuine writings of these three Apostolic Fathers are epistolary in form, modelled more or less after the pattern of the Canonical Epistles, especially those of St. Paul, and called forth by pressing temporary needs. In no case is any literary motive prominent. A famous teacher writes in the name of the community over which he presides to quell the dissensions of a distant but friendly church. An aged disciple on his way to martyrdom pours out a few parting words of exhortation to the Christian brotherhoods with whom he is brought in contact during his journey. A bishop of a leading church, having occasion to send a parcel to another brotherhood at a distance, takes the opportunity of writing, in answer to their solicitations, a few plain words of advice and instruction. Such is the simple account of the letters of Clement, Ignatius, and Polycarp respectively.

The same form is preserved in the Ep. of Barnabas and the letter to Diognetus. But the spirit is somewhat different. They are rather treatises clothed in an epistolary dress, the aim of the one being polemical, of the other apologetic. Herein they resemble *Hebrews* more than the Epp. of St. Paul.

"The Apostolic Fathers," says de Pressensé, "are not great writers, but great characters" (*Trois Premiers Siècles*, ii. 384). Their style is loose; there is a want of arrangement in the topics, and an absence of system in their teaching. On the one hand they present a marked contrast to the depth and clearness of conception with which the several N.T. writers place before us different aspects of the Gospel, and by which their title to a special inspiration is established. On the other, they lack the scientific spirit which distinguished the Fathers of the 4th and 5th cents., and which enabled them to formulate the doctrines of the faith as a bulwark against unbridled speculation. But though they are deficient in distinctness of conception and power of exposition, "this inferiority" to the later Fathers "is amply compensated by a certain naïveté and simplicity which forms the charm of their letters. If they have not the precision of the scientific spirit, they are free from its narrowness." There is a breadth of moral sympathy, an earnest sense of personal responsibility, a fervour of Christian devotion, which is the noblest testimony to the influence of the Gospel on characters obviously very diverse, and which will always command for their writings a respect to which their literary merits could lay no claim. The gentleness and serenity of Clement, whose whole spirit is absorbed in contemplating the harmonies of nature and of grace; the fiery zeal of Ignatius, in whom the one overmastering desire of martyrdom has crushed all human passion; the unbroken constancy of Polycarp, whose protracted life is spent in maintaining the faith once delivered to the saints,—these are lessons which can never become antiquated or lose their value.

Their Relation to the Apostolic Teaching and to the Canonical Scriptures.—Of the respective provinces of the Apostolic Fathers, we may say that Clement co-ordinates the different elements of Christian teaching as left by the Apostles; and Ignatius consolidates the structure of ecclesiastical polity, as sketched out by them; while for Polycarp, whose active career was just beginning as theirs ended, and who lived on for more than half a century after their deaths, was reserved the task of handing down unimpaired to a later generation the Apostolic doctrine and order thus co-ordinated and consolidated by his elder contemporaries—a task for which he was eminently fitted by his passive and receptive character.

The writings of these three Fathers lie well

within the main stream of Catholic teaching. They are the proper link between the Canonical Scriptures and the church Fathers of the succeeding ages. They recognize all the different elements of the Apostolic teaching, though combining them in different proportions. "They prove that Christianity was Catholic from the very first, uniting a variety of forms in one faith. They shew that the great facts of the Gospel narrative, and the substance of the Apostolic letters, formed the basis and moulded the expression of the common creed" (Westcott, *Canon*, p. 55).

But when we turn to the other writings for which a place among the Apostolic Fathers has been claimed, the case is different. Though the writers are all apparently within the pale of the church, yet there is a tendency to that one-sided exaggeration—either in the direction of Judaisms or the opposite—which stands on the very verge of heresy. In the Ep. of Barnabas and in the letter to Diognetus, the repulsion from Judaism is so violent, that one step further would have carried the writers into Gnostic or Marcionite dualism. On the other hand, in the *Shepherd* of Hermas, and possibly in the *Expositions* of Papias (for in this instance the inferences drawn from a few scanty fragments must be precarious), the sympathy with the Old Dispensation is unduly strong, and the distinctive features of the Gospel are darkened by the shadow of the Law thus projected upon them. In Clement, Ignatius, and Polycarp, both extremes are avoided.

For the relation of these writers to the Canonical Scriptures the reader is referred to the thorough investigation in Westcott's *Hist. of the Canon*, pp. 19-55. It will be sufficient here to state the more important results: (1) The Apostolic Fathers do not, as a rule, quote by name the canonical writings of the N.T. But (2), though (with exceptions) the books of the N.T. are not quoted by name, fragments of most of the canonical Epistles lie embedded in the writings of these Fathers, whose language is thoroughly leavened with the Apostolic diction. In like manner the facts of the Gospel history are referred to, and the words of our Lord given, though for the most part not as direct quotations. For (3) there is no decisive evidence that these Fathers recognized a Canon of the N.T., as a distinctly defined body of writings; though Barnabas once introduces our Lord's words as recorded in Matt. xx. 16, xxii. 14, with the usual formula of Scriptural citation, "As it is written (ὡς γέγραπται)." But (4), on the other hand, they assign a special and pre-eminent authority to the Apostles which they distinctly disclaim for themselves. This is the case with Clement (§§ 5, 7) and Ignatius (Rom. 4), speaking of St. Peter and St. Paul; and with Polycarp (§ 3), speaking of St. Paul —the only Apostles that are mentioned by name in these writings. (5) Lastly, though the language of the Canonical Gospels is frequently not quoted word for word, yet there is no distinct allusion to any apocryphal narrative. [L.]

The standard work on the Apostolic Fathers is by the writer of the above article, the late bp. Lightfoot. His work on the principal subject, in five 8vo volumes, includes Clement, Ignatius, Polycarp. But after his death a single vol. was pub. containing revised texts of all the Apostolic Fathers, with short introductions and Eng. translations.

Apostolici, one of the names adopted by an ascetic sect in Phrygia, Cilicia, and Pamphylia. Their leading principle seems to have been the rejection of private property. They are also said to have resembled Tatian, the Encratites, and the "Cathari" (Novatianists), in that they refused to admit offenders to communion, and condemned marriage. They appealed chiefly to the apocryphal *Acts of Andrew* and *of Thomas*. They entitled themselves *Apotactici*, i.e. "Renuntiants." What little is recorded about them, beyond the name, we owe to Epiphanius (*Haer.* lxi. 506-513), who apparently knew them only by vague oral report. Their place in his treatise would naturally assign them to the 3rd cent.; and they evidently had not ceased to exist in the 4th. "Encratites, Saccophori, and Apotactites," described together as "an offshoot of the Marcionites," are associated with Novatianists by Basil in a letter answering queries from Amphilochius of Iconium (cxcix. can. 47; cf. clxxxviii. can. 1), written in 375, when Epiphanius had begun and not completed his work. A law of Theodosius against the Manicheans in 381 (*Cod. Theod.* XVI. v. 7; cf. 11 an. 383) alleges that some of these heretics endeavoured to evade the existing severe legislation by calling themselves "Encratites, Apotactites, Hydroparastatae, or Saccophori." Any true historical connexion, however, between the Apostolici and either the Marcionists or the Manicheans is highly improbable. [H.]

Apphianus, or **Appianus,** or **Amphianus,** M., a son of rich parents at "Pagae" (probably Araxas) in Lycia, educated in the schools of Berytus, who being not twenty years old interrupted the governor at Caesarea when sacrificing, by an exhortation to desist from idolatry, and was, after horrible tortures —*e.g.* by his feet being wrapped in a *tunica molesta* of flax steeped in oil and set on fire— finally martyred by drowning, April 11, 306 (Eus. *de Mart. Palaest.* iv.; Syriac *Acta*, in Assemani, *Act. Mart.* ii. 189 seq.). [A.W.H.]

Aquila (Ἀκύλας), the author of a translation of the O.T. into Greek, which was held in much esteem by the Jews and was reproduced by Origen in the third column of the Hexapla, seems to have belonged to the earlier half of 2nd cent. Little is known regarding his personal history beyond the fact that he was, like the Aquila associated with St. Paul, a native of Pontus, and probably, according to the more definite tradition, of Sinope. We learn also from Irenaeus, in whom we find the earliest mention of him (*adv. Haer.* iii. 24), that he was a proselyte to the Jewish faith—a statement confirmed by Eusebius (*Demonst. Evang.* vii. 1: προσήλυτος δὲ ὁ Ἀκύλας ἦν οὐ φύσει Ἰουδαῖος), Jerome (*Ep. ad Pammach. Opp.* iv. 2, p. 255), and other Fathers, as well as by the Jerusalem Talmud (*Megill.* f. 71, c. 3; *Kiddush.* f. 59, c. 1, where there can be little doubt that the Akilas referred to is to be identified with Aquila).

From this circumstance he is frequently called "Aquila the proselyte."

The object of Aquila was to furnish a translation on which the Jews could rely as a more accurate rendering of the Hebrew than that of the Septuagint, which not only was in many instances loose and incorrect from the first, but had also in the course of four centuries undergone change and corruption. With this view he made his version strictly literal, striving to provide a Greek equivalent for every Hebrew word and particle, in frequent disregard of the rules of grammar and of idiom, and with the result of often rendering his meaning hardly intelligible to those who were not acquainted with Hebrew (as in Job xxx. 1, καὶ νῦν ἐγέλασαν ἐπ' ἐμοὶ βραχεῖς παρ' ἐμὲ ταῖς ἡμέρας Ps. xlix. 21, ὑπέλαβες ἐσόμενος ἔσομαι ὅμοιός σοι Ps. cxlix. 6, καὶ μάχαιρα στομάτων ἐν χερσὶν αὐτῶν). He carefully endeavoured even to reproduce Hebrew etymologies in Greek, and for that purpose freely coined new forms (as in Ps. xxi. 13, δυνάσταιΒασὰν διεδημα τίσαντό με Ps. cxviii. 10, μὴ ἀγνοηματίσῃς με). Origen accordingly characterizes him as δουλεύων τῇ Εβραϊκῇ λέξει (*Ep. ad Afric.*), and the fragments of the version which have been preserved amply bear out the truth of the description. But the excessively literal character of the work, while impairing its value as a translation for those who were not Jews, renders it all the more valuable as a witness to the state of the Hebrew text from which it was made. (As to the nature and value of the version, see Smith's *D. B.* iii. 1622.)

Several scholars of eminence have recently maintained that Aquila is to be identified not only with the Akilas of the Talmud, but also with Onkelos, whose name is associated with the well-known Targum on the Pentateuch; holding that the latter is merely an altered form of the name, and that the. Chaldee version came to receive what is now its ordinary designation from its being drawn up on the model, or after the manner, of that of Aquila. The arguments in support of this view, which appear to have great weight, are set forth with much clearness and force by Mr. Deutsch in his article on "Versions, Ancient, (Targum)," in Smith's *D. B.* iii. 1642-1645.

The fragments of the version of Aquila—first collected by Morinus for the Sixtine edition of the Septuagint, Rome, 1587, and subsequently by Drusius, in his *Veterum interp. Graec. in V. T. Fragmenta*, Arnb. 1622—are more fully given in the edition of the Hexapla by Montfaucon, Paris 1714, and its abridgment by Bahrdt, 1769-1770. A most complete and valuable edition is that by Mr. Frederick Field: Oxf. 1867-1870 (see Field, *Hexapla* [1875], xvi-xxvii). The chief questions connected with Aquila are discussed by Montfaucon, and by Hody (*de Bibliorum Textibus Originalibus*, Oxf. 1705). [W.P.D.]

Archelaus, supposed bp. of Carchar (perhaps Carrhoe Harrom in Mesopotamia). A work is attributed to him called *Acta Disputationis Archel. Ep. Mesop. et Manetis haeresiarchae.* It is extant in a Latin translation from a Greek text, but some think the Greek is derived from a Syriac original. The author was probably (cf. Phot. *Cod.* 85) a certain Hegemonius. The disputation and Archelaus himself seem to be fictitious; but the work affords valuable information respecting the Manichean system (cf. Bardenhewer, 1908, pp. 208-269). [H.W.]

Arethas, bp. of Caesarea in Cappadocia, and **Andreas**, an earlier archbp. of the same see, are so intimately associated as commentators on the Book of Revelation, and so little known otherwise, that they may most fitly be noticed together. We have no direct information regarding either, beyond the bare fact of their common connexion with the see of Caesarea. The dates at which they flourished can only be inferred approximately, and somewhat vaguely, from incidental notices of persons or of events in their writings. The question has been most fully discussed by Rettig (*Die Zeugnisse des Andreas und Arethas . . .* in the *Theol. Studien und Kritiken* for 1831, pp. 734 seq.); and his conclusions have been very generally accepted. He has shewn by enumerating the succession of bishops in Caesarea that the last 30 or 40 years of the 5th cent. may be assigned to Andreas and Arethas; and the absence of any reference to later events favours the belief that the work was prepared towards the close of the 5th, or in the earlier part of the 6th, cent.

The commentary of Andreas on the Apocalypse (entitled Ἑρμηνεία εἰς τὴν Ἀποκάλυψιν) seems to have been the earliest systematic exposition of the book in the Greek church. The statement of R. Simon, Fabricius, Rosenmüller, and others, that the work belongs to the class of Catenae, is not borne out either by its form or by the language of the Preface, which simply means that he made use of the materials which he found in the early writers whom he names, and occasionally quoted their expressions (παρ' ὧν ἡμεῖς πολλὰς λαβόντες ἀφορμάς . . . καθὼς ἔν τισι τόποις χρήσεις τούτων παρεθέμεθα). He wrote, in compliance with the urgent request of persons who had a greater opinion of his judgment than he had himself, "to unfold the meaning of the Apocalypse, and to make the suitable application of its predictions to the times that followed it" (ἀναπτύξαι τὴν . . . Ἀποκάλυψιν, καὶ τοῖς μετὰ τὴν αὐτῆς ὀπτασίαν χρόνοις ἐφαρμόσαι τὰ προφητευθέντα). His method rests on the distinction of a threefold sense in Scripture—the literal or outward historical (τὸ γράμμα καὶ ἡ κατ' αἴσθησιν ἱστορία), the tropological or moral (ἡ τροπολογία ἐξ αἰσθητῶν ἐπὶ τὰ νοητὰ ὁδηγοῦσα τὸν ἀναγινώσκοντα), and the mystical or speculative (ἡ τῶν μελλόντων καὶ ὑψηλοτέρων ἀναγωγὴ καὶ θεωρία); the expositor of the Revelation is chiefly concerned with the latter. He divided the text into twenty-four λόγοι corresponding to the four-and-twenty elders, and 72 κεφάλαια, according to the threefold distinction of body, soul, and spirit ($24 \times 3 = 72$). The exposition contains not a little that is of value, but it is full of the fanciful interpretations to which the method gave rise. The paucity of MSS. of the Apocalypse renders the text which accompanies the commentary of great importance to criticism; and Bengel was of opinion that the work of Andreas, by directing fresh attention to the book, contributed in no small degree to its more frequent use and transcription. An interesting passage in the Preface, where the writer mentions Papias among the other Fathers whose testimony to the inspiration of the book rendered it superfluous to enlarge on that point, has been much discussed.

The work of Arethas, again, professes to be a compilation. It is no mere reproduction of the work of his predecessor, although it incorporates a large portion of the contents of that work, occasionally abridging or modifying the language of Andreas, and often specifying with more precision the sources of his quotations. But it contains much derived from other sources, or contributed by Arethas himself.

The commentary of Andreas was first printed in the form of an imperfect and inaccurate Latin version by Peltanus in 1574. The Greek text was first edited by Sylburg from a collation of three MSS. in 1596, along with a reprint of the Latin version. It has been several times reissued in connexion with the works of Chrysostom. The Greek text of Arethas is presented in its fullest and best form by Cramer (in his *Catenae Gk. Patrum in N. T.*, Oxf. 1840); whose valuable additions, furnished chiefly by the Codex Baroccianus, exhibit the text in a shape so different from that previously printed as to make the latter often appear a mere abridgment. [W.P.D.]

Arinthaeus, a general under Valens, with whom St. Basil corresponds, and from whom he seeks protection for a friend in difficulty (*Ep.* 179). On his death Basil writes a letter of consolation to his widow, in which he dwells on his remarkable endowments, his striking personal beauty and strength, as well as his lofty character and renown. Like many others in that age, Arinthaeus, though a devout Christian and a protector of the Church, deferred his baptism till at the point of death (*Ep.* 269). He was consul in the year 372, and must have died before Basil (A.D. 379). If the story told by Theodoret (*H. E.* iv. 30) be true, that he was present and seconded the rebuke administered to Valens by the general Trajan in 378 for his persecution of the Catholics, his death cannot have preceded his friend's by many months. For his military achievements see Tillemont, *Empereurs*, v. 100. [L.]

Aristides, of Athens; mentioned by Eusebius as having presented to the emperor Hadrian an Apology for the Christians (*Hist. Eccl.* iv. c. 3). Jerome also (*de Vir. Ill.* c. 20, and *Ep.* 83, *ad Magnum*) mentions him as an Athenian philosopher and a disciple of Christ; and says that his Apology, containing the principles of the faith, was well known. But it was lost until, in 1878, the Mechitarists published part of an Armenian translation, the genuineness of which was vindicated by Harnack in *Texte und Untersuch.* i. 1, 2. But in 1891 J. Rendel Harris and J. Armitage Robinson (now Dean of Westminster) published in *Texts and Studies*, I. i., a complete Syrian translation from the Codex Sinait. Syr. 16, and shewed that the greater part of the Apology was found in Greek in the legend of *Barlaam and Josaphat*. These texts have been carefully discussed, especially by Seeberg (in Zahn's *Forschungen*, V. p. 159, and in an edition published at Erlangen 1894), and it is not yet agreed whether the Syrian or the Greek represents the original. It seems clear that the Apology was presented, not to Hadrian, but to Antoninus Pius. The main subject of the Apology, which, in the legend, is supposed to be addressed by Barlaam to Josaphat, is that the Christians alone possess the true knowledge of God. The emperor is invited to consider the conceptions of God among the various races of mankind, Barbarians and Greeks, Jews and Christians; it is then shewn how the Christians express their belief in their lives, and an attractive sketch of Christian life is given. The Apology has points of contact with the *Preaching of Peter*, with the *Shepherd*, with the Didaché, with Justin Martyr, and particularly with the *Ep. to Diognetus*. Mention is made of the Incarnation of the Son of God through a Hebrew maiden and of Christ's return to judgment. The Apology is thus of an interesting and original character. Two other fragments exist in Armenian which are ascribed to Aristides, a homily on the cry of the Robber and the answer of the Crucified, and a passage from "a letter to all philosophers," but their genuineness is doubtful, and F. C. Conybeare, in the *Guardian*, 1894 (July 18), has shewn that in the 5th and 7th cents. literary frauds were often connected with the name of Aristides and other names of old Christian literature. [H.W.]

Aristion, one of the "elders" from whom PAPIAS professed to have derived traditional information (Eus. *H. E.* iii. 39), and described by him as a personal follower of our Lord. Beyond this, there is no trustworthy information about him. The Roman Martyrology (p. 102, Ven. 1630), apparently referring to the description just quoted, states on the authority of Papias that he was one of the seventy-two disciples of Christ. It commemorates his martyrdom at Salamis in Cyprus on Feb. 22, the same day as that of Papias at Pergamus. Cotelerius conjectures that he may be the Aristo who is given as the first bp. of Smyrna (*Apost. Const.* vii. 45; Harnack, *Altchr. Lit.* i. 64; Conybeare, in *Expositor*, 1893). [G.S.]

Aristo Pellaeus, the supposed author of a lost dialogue between Papiscus and Jason, quoted, without his name, by Origen (*cont. Celsus*, iv. 52) and referred to by Eusebius (*Hist. Eccl.* iv. c. 6, pp. 145, 146); by Moses Chorenensis, in a history of Armenia (bk. ii. c. 57); and by Maximus, in his notes on the work *de Mystica Theol.*, ascribed to Dionysius the Areopagite (c. i. p. 17, ed. Corderii) in these words, "I have also read the expression 'seven heavens' in the dialogue of Papiscus and Jason, composed by Aristo of Pella, which Clemens of Alexandria in the 6th book of his Hypotyposes says was written by St. Luke." This testimony is the only one connecting the name of Aristo with the dialogue, and though doubt has been thrown on its trustworthiness by its strange assertion that Clement attributed the work to St. Luke, Maximus is far less likely to be in error when simply giving the name of an author than when repeating another's words. Jason, a Jewish Christian, argues so conclusively that the Messianic prophecies are fulfilled in our Lord that his opponent, the Jew Papiscus, begs to be baptized.

We cannot fix the date of this dialogue, except that it must have been written before the time of Celsus, *i.e.* before the middle of the 2nd cent.; and, if Aristo be its author, we see from Eusebius (*l.c.*) that he lived after the destruction of Jerusalem. It is referred to in a pseudo-Cyprianic Ep. Hartd. *Opp. Cypr.* iii. p. 119. If Maximus's information be correct, Clement's belief that St. Luke was the writer of the Dialogue shews at least that it must have been commonly assigned to a very early date (Routh, *Rel. Sac.* i. 91-109; Harnack, *Alt. Chr. Lit.* i. 92 95-97). [S.M.]

Arius (Ἀρειος) the heresiarch was born in Africa—the locality is disputed—in A.D. 256. In his early days he was a pupil of Lucian of Antioch, a celebrated Christian teacher, and a martyr for the faith. By some Arius is said to have derived his heresy from Lucian (see LUCIANUS, 12). This statement is made in a letter written by Alexander, bp. of Alexandria, to bp. Alexander of Constantinople. The object of the letter is to complain of the errors Arius was then diffusing. The writer says of Lucian that he lived for many years out of communion with three bishops (Theod. *Eccl. Hist.* i. 4). But the charge is somewhat vague in itself; it is unsupported by other authority, and Alexander's language, like that of most controversialists in past days, is not a little violent. Moreover, Lucian is not stated, even by Alexander himself, to have fallen into the heresy afterwards promulgated by Arius, but is accused generally —rather *ad invidiam*, it would seem—of heretical tendencies. The question of the exact nature of the relation between the Father and the Son had been raised some 50 years before the Nicene controversy arose. But the discussion of it at that time had been insufficient and unsatisfying. So far as the earlier controversy could be said to have been decided, it was decided in favour of the opinions afterwards held by Arius. But so unsatisfactory was that settlement that the reopening of the question sooner or later was practically unavoidable, especially in an atmosphere so intellectual as that of Alexandria. The reason of the deposition of PAUL OF SAMOSATA in A.D. 269 was his agreement with those who had used the word ὁμοούσιος to express the relation of the Father and the Son. The expression was at that time thought to have a Sabellian tendency, though, as events shewed, this was on account of its scope not having been satisfactorily defined. In the discussion which then arose on the question, Dionysius, bp. of Alexandria, had used much the same language as Arius afterwards held, and a correspondence is extant in which Dionysius of Rome blames his brother of Alexandria for using such language. Dionysius of Alexandria withdrew, or perhaps rather explained (see Athan. *de Decret. Syn. Nic.* c. 25), the expressions complained of, and posterity has been inclined to blame him for vacillation. Whether this accusation be just or not, it is quite clear that the position in which a question of such supreme importance was left by the action of Dionysius could only postpone the controversy, and that its resumption was therefore only a question of time. For the synod of Antioch which condemned Paul of Samosata had expressed its disapproval of the word ὁμοούσιος in one sense. The bp. (Alexander) of Alexandria (*c.* 320) undertook its defence in another.

The character of Arius has been severely assailed by his opponents. Alexander, bp. of Alexandria, in a letter to Alexander of Constantinople, describes it in very unfavourable terms. But in those days it was customary to mingle personal attacks with religious controversies. Arius appears to have been a man of ascetic character, pure morals, and decided convictions. It has been stated that his action was largely the result of jealousy on account of his having been a candidate for the patriarchal throne of Alexandria, when Alexander was elected to it. But the best early authorities are doubtful on the point. He had no doubt a disproportionate number of female supporters, but there seems no ground for the insinuation of Alexander of Alexandria, in the above-mentioned letter, that these women were of loose morals. There appears, however, more foundation for the charge that Arius allowed the songs or odes contained in the book called *Thaleia*—which he wrote after his first condemnation, in order to popularize his doctrine—to be set to tunes which had gross and infamous associations. Nor can he be acquitted of something like a personal canvass of the Christian population in and around Alexandria in order to further his views.

The patriarch of Alexandria has also been the subject of adverse criticism for his action against his subordinate. He too, like his predecessor Dionysius, has been charged with vacillation in his treatment of Arius. Yet it is difficult to see how he could have acted otherwise than he did. The question, as we have seen, had been left unsettled two generations previously, or, if in any sense it could be said to have been settled, it had been settled in favour of the opponents of the Homoousion. Therefore Alexander allowed the controversy to go on until he felt that it was becoming dangerous to the peace of the church. Then he called a council of bishops (about 100 in number), and sought their advice. They decided against Arius. Alexander then delayed no longer. He acted with resolution as well as promptitude, deposed Arius from his office, and repelled both him and his supporters from communion. Then he wrote (the letters are extant) to Alexander of Constantinople and Eusebius of Nicomedia (where the emperor was then residing), detailing the errors into which Arius had fallen, and complaining of the danger to the Christian church arising from his heresy. It is clear, from Arius's own letter (also extant) to Eusebius of Nicomedia, that Alexander's charges against Arius were in no way unfair. The question, as the event has shewn, was a vital one, and plainly called for an authoritative decision. Arius taught: (1) that the Logos and the Father were not of the same οὐσία (essence); (2) that the Son was a created being (κτίσμα or ποίημα); and (3) that though He was the creator of the worlds, and must therefore have existed before them and before all time, there was—Arius refused to use such terms as χρόνος or αἰών—when He did not exist. The subsequent controversy shews that the absence of the words χρόνος or αἰών was a mere evasion, and that when defending himself he argued in just the same manner as though he *had* used those words. Moreover, he asserted that the Logos had an ἀρχή (beginning); yet not only Athanasius, but Origen before him, had taught that the relation of the Son to the Father had no beginning, and that, to use Dorner's words (*Person of Christ*, ii. 115), "the generation of the Son is an eternally completed, and yet an eternally continued, act"; *i.e.* the Father has, from all eternity, been communicating His Being to the Son, and is doing so still.

Arius was obviously perplexed by this doctrine, for he complains of it in his letter to the Nicomedian Eusebius, who, like himself (see above), had studied under Lucian, in the words, ἀειγεννής ἐστιν; ἀγεννητογενής ἐστιν. It is unquestionably to be lamented that so much stress should have been laid in the controversy on words which, when used, not popularly, but in metaphysical discussions, had a tendency to confound the eternal generation of the Son with the purely physical process of the generation of men and animals. The latter is a single act, performed at a definite moment in time. The former is a mysterious, eternal process, for ever going on. Had the defenders of the Nicene doctrine made more general use of the term *communication of Being*, or *Essence*, they would have made it clearer that they were referring to a continual and unchangeable relation between the First and Second Persons in the Trinity, which bore a very slight analogy indeed to the process which calls inferior creatures into existence. Moreover, Arius contended that the Son was unchangeable (ἄτρεπτος). But what he thus gave with the one hand he appears to have taken away with the other. For so far as we can understand his language—on a subject which even Athanasius seems to have admitted to have been beyond his power thoroughly to comprehend—he taught that the Logos was changeable in Essence, but not in Will. The best authorities consider that he was driven to this concession by the force of circumstances. [See art. ARIUS, FOLLOWERS OF.] He was doubtless confirmed in his attitude by his fear of falling into Sabellianism [SABELLIUS], which practically represented the Logos as a sensuous emanation of the Godhead for the purpose of carrying out the work of salvation, or else as a purely subjective human conception of certain aspects of the Divine Being—not as an eternal distinction subsisting objectively in the Godhead itself. Arius, while opposing the Sabellian view, was unable to see that his own view had a dangerous tendency to bring back Gnosticism, with its long catalogue of aeons. MACEDONIUS, who had to a certain extent imbibed the opinions of Arius, certainly regarded the Son and the Spirit in much the same light in which the Gnostic teachers regarded their aeons. Yet Arius undoubtedly derived some support from the dangerous language of Origen, who had ventured to represent the Logos as a δεύτερος (or δευτερεύων) θεός. Origen (see his *de Principiis*, I. ii. 6, 12) had also made use of expressions which favoured Arius's statement that the Logos was of a different substance to the Father, and that He owed His existence to the Father's will. But it is not sufficiently remembered that the speculations of Origen should be regarded as pioneer work in theology, and that they were often hazarded in order to stimulate further inquiry rather than to enable men to dispense with it. This explains why, in the Arian, as well as other controversies, the great authority of Origen is so frequently invoked by both sides.

The Christian church had by this time become so powerful a force in the Roman world that Constantine, now sole emperor, found himself unable to keep aloof from the controversy. He was the less able to do so in that he had himself been brought up under Christian influences. [CONSTANTINE.] He therefore sent the venerable Hosius, bp. of Cordova, a man who had suffered cruelly on behalf of his faith, on a mission to Egypt, with instructions to put an end, if possible, to the controversy. But as it continued to rage, Constantine took a step hitherto unprecedented in Roman history. Republican Rome of course had her free institutions, and the Christian church had been accustomed to determine matters of faith and practice in her local assemblies. But anything like a council of delegates, summoned from all parts of the empire, had been hitherto unknown. Such an assembly Constantine determined to call together. All the secular dioceses into which the empire had been for some time divided, Britain only excepted, sent one or more representatives to the council. The majority of the bishops came from the East, but there was, nevertheless, an imposing display of men of various races and languages. Sylvester of Rome, himself too aged to be present, sent two presbyters as his delegates. The object of the council, it must be remembered, was not to pronounce what the church *ought to* believe, but to ascertain as far as possible *what had been taught from the beginning*. It was indeed a remarkable gathering. There was not only as good a representation of race and nationality as was possible under the circumstances, but the ability and intellect of the church were also well represented. There was Eusebius of Nicomedia, the astute politician and man of the world. There was also the renowned Eusebius of Caesarea, a sound theologian, and perhaps the most well-informed, careful, impartial, and trustworthy ecclesiastical historian the church has ever possessed. Alexander, patriarch of Alexandria, was also a man of mark. And, young as he was, the great Athanasius was already a host in himself, from his clearness of insight into the deepest mysteries of our religion. And beside these there were men present who manifested the power of faith—the brave "confessors," as they were called, whose faces and limbs bore evident traces of the sufferings they had undergone for their Master. Nor could any one object that it was a packed assembly. The emperor did his best to secure an honest selection and an honest decision.

The council met (325) at Nicaea, in Bithynia,

a town of some importance, on the Sea of Marmora, near Constantinople. The number of bishops present is variously stated at from 250 to 318. But the latter number, as typified by the number of Abraham's servants when he rescued Lot, was generally accepted before the council of Constantinople. No Acts of the council are extant. In the writings of two men of note who were present, Athanasius, then a young deacon of about 28 years old, and the already celebrated and learned Eusebius of Caesarea, we have accounts of what happened. Moreover, well-informed and honest, if sometimes more or less inaccurate, historians have studied and handed down documents of great value, bearing on the proceedings. Constantine himself was present at the council. At first he refused to take part in its deliberations, or even to take a seat until invited. But he afterwards departed from that humble attitude, if some of our authorities are to be trusted, and when he found difficulties arising, did his best to remove them by joining in the discussions. At the outset he administered a well-merited rebuke to the bishops for the spirit in which many of them had come to the council. Producing a number of recriminatory letters from those who were present, he called for a brazier, and burnt them all before the assembly, begging the bishops to lay aside their personal animosities, and to devote themselves whole-heartedly to setting forth the truth. The question next arose, in what form the universal belief of the church from the beginning should be expressed. This, of course, was the *crux* of the whole situation. Hitherto particular churches had their own forms of creed (*πίστις*) for use at baptisms and in catechetical instruction. There was no substantial difference between them, consisting as they did of a confession of faith in the Trinity, as well as a summary of the main facts recorded in the gospels. But now a dogmatic formula for Christendom had to be drawn up, a task full of difficulty and even of danger. Some few of the bishops, we learn, apparently under the leadership of Eusebius of Nicomedia, presented a document so frankly Arian that it was at once torn to pieces by those present, and Arius was excommunicated by all but Theonas and Secundus. Then, as it seems, the famous scholar and ecclesiastical historian Eusebius of Caesarea intervened, and produced a Palestinian Creed, which he said he had received from "the bishops before him." He adds that "no one present could gainsay" the orthodoxy of this creed. This statement must, however, be taken with some limitations. The Palestinian Creed could only, if accepted, have been accepted as a basis for discussion. It was not ultimately adopted in the shape in which it was propounded, but underwent considerable alteration. The sentence *γεννηθέντα ἐκ τοῦ Πατρός μονογενῆ* was made definitely *τούτεστιν ἐκ τῆς οὐσίας τοῦ Πατρός*. Further on, the words *ὁμοούσιον τῷ Πατρί* were added after the words "begotten, not made." And the word *ἐνανθρωπήσαντα*, which means rather more than "made man," and implies an intimate association of the Godhead with the Manhood, was added after "was Incarnate" (*i.e.* made flesh—*σαρκωθέντα*—a phrase which was felt to be insufficient and even misleading by itself). The anathema which was also added embraces those who deny that the Son and the Father were of one *οὐσία* or *ὑπόστασις*, as well as those who say that there was a time when the Son did not exist, or that He was created from nothing, or that He was liable to change or alteration. At this stage of the controversy the words *οὐσία* (essence) and *ὑπόστασις* (substance) were used as synonymous. It will be seen [art. ARIUS, FOLLOWERS OF] that Basil and the Gregories afterwards wrung from Athanasius a concession on this point. Athanasius had warmly attacked Arius for asserting that there were three hypostases in the Trinity. But at the later date it was agreed that the word *οὐσία* might be used to denote what was *common* to all three Persons, and *ὑπόστασις* to denote the *distinctions* (which we call *Persons*) between them. For the present, however, any distinction between *οὐσία* and *ὑπόστασις* was considered heretical. The council then broke up, after having addressed a letter to the churches in and around Alexandria. Constantine issued a circular letter to the same effect. Arius, Theonas, and Secundus were deposed and banished, while three other bishops, who had displayed leanings toward Arius, namely Eusebius of Nicomedia, Theognis of Nicaea itself, and Maris of Chalcedon, a city on the Asiatic shore opposite Constantinople, were unwilling signatories of the document, but affixed their signatures in deference to the emperor's wishes. Eusebius of Caesarea describes himself, in a letter to some Arians who had accused him of tergiversation, as having demurred to the changes in the creed which he had himself presented, but as having finally accepted them in the interests of peace (Theod. *H. E.* i. 12, from Athan. *de Decret. Syn. Nic.*).

That the apparent unanimity of the council (Secundus and Theonas of Lower Egypt being the only dissentients) covered a considerable amount of divergent opinion is indisputable. Doubts of the wisdom of employing a term which had been rejected at an important council as savouring of Sabellianism weighed on the minds of many who had submitted. Eusebius of Caesarea has been charged by many later writers as having coquetted with Arianism. But his moderate attitude throughout the period which followed proves that his objections to the decision, which he allowed his love of peace to overrule, were more owing to the dread of possible consequences than to the decision in itself. Though a man of ability, learning, and honesty, he was timorous withal, and desirous to stand well with the powers that be. And his allusion to the proceedings at Nicaea in the letter just mentioned shews that his apprehensions were not altogether unreasonable. For he remarks how it was elicited after considerable discussion at the council that the term *ὁμοούσιον* was not intended to signify that the Son formed an actual *portion* (*μέρος*) of the Father. That would have been Sabellianism pure and simple, a danger against which it was necessary to guard. And much of the dissension to which the adoption of the creed of Nicaea led was due to this very natural apprehension. But Eusebius emphatically condemned the language of Arius, and there is no reason whatever to suspect his sincerity in so doing. On the other hand, Athanasius was convinced—and the event proves that he was right—that unless the Essence of the Son was definitely understood to be the same as that of the Father, it would inevitably follow that the Son would at best be no more than the highest of a series of Gnostic aeons. As to Eusebius of Nicomedia, it is clear that Constantine found some reason to suspect his sincerity, as well as that of Theognis and Maris, for he soon after included them in the sentence pronounced on Arius. Philostorgius says that Secundus and Theonas predicted that this would happen when they themselves had been sentenced to banishment. Possibly expressions fell from them in the heat of argument which led Constantine to the conclusion that their submission was not genuine.

It must be confessed that the Nicene settlement, though necessary in itself and satisfactory in the end, was at least premature. The controversy recommenced as soon as the decrees were promulgated. When Alexander died at Alexandria in 327, the election of Athanasius in his place was only secured in the face of violent opposition from the Arianizing faction. Soon after, Eusebius of Nicomedia was reinstated in his see, after having written a diplomatic letter to the emperor. Arius, who had taken refuge in Palestine, was also soon permitted to return, after having made a somewhat disingenuous recantation. So astute a politician as the Nicomedian Eusebius was not long before he regained his influence with the emperor, and then began a series of intrigues which led to a complete reversal of the position of the contending parties. Eustathius of Antioch, one of the staunchest adherents of Athanasius, was the first victim. The question of heterodoxy was skilfully kept in the background, and a number of false and odious personal charges were trumped up against him by men and women of abandoned lives. If Theodoret is to be trusted, one of the women aforesaid, when seized by a serious illness, retracted her accusation in a remarkably sensational manner. But the other historians (Socrates and Sozomen) are reticent about the nature of the charges, and only tell us that Eustathius had been unfortunate enough to get involved in a controversy with Eusebius Pamphili (of Caesarea). Eustathius was at once ejected from his see, and was regarded by the emperor as having been the cause of the riot his expulsion excited among the people, with whom Eustathius was a favourite. Marcellus of Ancyra was the next victim. He had all along been the friend and champion of Athanasius. But unfortunately he was not at home in the thorny paths of metaphysical theology, and found it impossible to defend the Nicene decisions without falling into Sabellianism. There was no need, therefore, for the Arianizers to bring personal charges against him. Accordingly few, if any such, were brought. He was charged, and quite fairly, with Sabellianism. On this point Eusebius Pamphili came safely to the front, and wrote strongly against Marcellus, while the latter sturdily defended himself. The actual condemnation of Marcellus was deferred till 336, and in the meantime Eusebius of Nicomedia had commenced proceedings against the only rival he really dreaded, Athanasius himself. He had, as we have seen, contrived the restoration of Arius to the emperor's favour by inducing the latter to write an insincere retractation, and when the emperor, deceived by this manœuvre, laid his commands on Athanasius to readmit Arius to communion, Athanasius, naturally, pleaded reasons of conscience against doing so. Then the storm burst forth in all its fulness. The accusations of treason against the emperor and the insinuations that the patriarch wished to set up an empire of his own against or above the supreme authority of the divine Augustus had certainly some effect on the mind of Constantine. Charges were made of sacrilege, tyranny, magic, mutilation, murder, of immorality (as some allege), and, worst of all in the emperor's eyes, of raising funds for treasonable objects. They were investigated (if the scenes of violence and passion which took place can be termed an investigation) at a synod of 150 bishops at Tyre (335).

The triumphant vindication of himself by Athanasius at that council, the dramatic scenes with which that vindication, according to some historians, was accompanied, and the equally dramatic appeal from his accusers to Constantine himself in the streets of Constantinople (which all the accounts describe as having taken place), belong rather to the history of Athanasius than of Arius. [Athanasius.] Suffice it to say that the bold and decisive action, backed by innocence, of the great archbishop only succeeded in deferring his fall. The synod of Tyre had already issued a condemnation while he was on his way to Constantinople in order to appeal to the emperor. The emperor, for the moment, was struck and touched by the appeal and by the commanding personality of Athanasius. But Eusebius proved ultimately to be master of the situation. With consummate dexterity the wily tactician, with the aid of Theognis and Maris, his old associates, as well as of the arch-intriguers Ursacius and Valens, of whom we shall hear so much in the next article, contrived that the old charges of ecclesiastical offences should be dropped, and that fresh charges of interference with the secular affairs of the empire should be substituted for them. Accordingly, Athanasius was now charged with detaining the corn which was ordered to be sent from Egypt to Constantinople. The artifice succeeded. Constantine was weary of the strife. His only object had been the settlement of the question. The shape which that settlement took was to him a secondary matter. He had, as he himself tells us (see his letters to Alexander and Arius in the *Life of Constantine* by Eusebius Pamphili), a strong objection to idle and word-splitting discussions, private or public, and considered them unnecessary and unprofitable. The measures he had been persuaded to take at Nicaea had not produced the effect which he had expected from them. So, like other despots in a similar position, he turned fiercely on those who had induced him to adopt them. That it was Athanasius who had advocated the measures which had so palpably failed needed no demonstration. So he was exiled to Trier (Trèves), after a number of leading bishops had been assembled at Constantinople to try him, and Alexander of Constantinople was ordered to receive Arius back into church communion. But God had otherwise ordained. Alexander was in dire perplexity. He dared not disobey the command, neither dare he obey it. In his extremity he asked the prayers of the orthodox that either he or Arius might be removed from the world before the latter was admitted to communion. The prayer was, we must admit, a strange one. But even Gibbon records the incident as a fact, though he makes it the occasion for one of his characteristic gibes at Christianity and Christians. Meanwhile, as the historian Socrates tells us, Arius was ordered to appear before the emperor, and asked whether he was willing to sign the Nicene decrees. He replied, without hesitation, that he was ready to do so. Asked whether he would confirm his signature by an oath, he agreed to do this also. This last fact Socrates declares (*H. E.* i. 38) that he had verified by an inspection of the imperial archives. The very day before the one appointed for his readmission to communion, Arius died suddenly, and in a most remarkable manner. Whether his death can be described as a miracle or not may be disputed. It seems preferable to attribute it to natural causes. But that the event was one of the numerous occasions in history when we are compelled to recognize a Divine interposition can hardly be doubted. The extraordinary occurrence made a vast impression throughout Christendom. The heresiarch had only been able to obtain the decree for readmission to communion by a feigned adherence to the Nicene symbol. His position was, therefore, in the eyes of Christendom one of gross and palpable deception—nothing less than an act of glaring and defiant impiety. Socrates tells us that in his time, a century afterwards, the place where he died was still pointed out. Athanasius himself describes the incident (*de Morte Arii*). There are therefore few facts in history more fully attested. The tragic death of Arius, followed as it was a year later by that of Constantine himself, led to a temporary lull in the controversy. The sequel will be found in the next article.

Bibliography.—(1) *Ancient.* The writings of Athanasius generally, especially his *de Incarnatione Verbi Dei* and *de Decretis Synodi Nicenae*; the *Vita Constantini* of Eusebius Pamphili; and the ecclesiastical histories of Socrates, Sozomen, and Theodoret. Of these the first is the best, though the documents cited at length by Theodoret are valuable. English translations of these authors, save of quite recent date, are by no means implicitly to be trusted, especially as to metaphysical terms. The ecclesiastical history of Philostorgius, which would give us the Arian point of view, is unfortunately only known to us through a hostile epitome by Photius, patriarch of Constantinople in 9th cent.

(2) Of comparatively modern works the church histories of Neander and Gieseler contain very valuable information, as does also Dorner's learned and impartial treatise *On the Person of Christ.* Bp. Martensen's *History of Christian Dogmatics* is also valuable; Gibbon's *Decline and Fall* is useful in giving us the secular view of the period. Bp. Kaye's *Council of Nicaea* will be found worth reading. De Broglie's *L'Eglise et l'Empire romain au IVe siècle* is full of information. Newman's *Arians of the Fourth Century* is marred by some prejudices and prepossessions. Dean Stanley's account of the Nicene council in his *Eastern Church* will be found more picturesque than accurate. Prof. Gwatkin's *Studies of Arianism* is, as its title implies, rather a series of sketches than a detailed history, but contains a vast amount of original research, illuminated by flashes of insight into the characters and motives of the principal actors in the controversy, and gives an exhaustive bibliography. His *Arian Controversy* is a brief summary for popular use. There is a valuable article in *Texts and Studies,* vol. vii. (1901), by Mr. Bethune Baker on "The Meaning of Homoousios in the Constantinopolitan Creed." His *Introduction to the Early Hist. of Christian Doctrine* (1903) will be found useful, as will the art. "Arianism" in Hastings's *Encycl. of Religion and Ethics,* i. (1908). Harnack, *Hist. of Dogma* (Eng. trans. 1894-1899), gives the modern German view. [J.J.L.]

Arius, Followers of. After the deaths of Arius and Constantine we enter on a tangled web of controversy which lasted from A.D. 336 to 381, when the question was finally decided by the acceptance of the Nicene Creed at the council of Constantinople. This period of confusion is due to the change of conditions under which the contest was carried on. For a time the division of the empire between three Augusti contributed an additional element of uncertainty to the conflict. Yet when the deaths of the younger Constantine and his brother Constans left the whole empire for eleven years in the hands of Constantius, matters were scarcely less involved. Constantius, though by no means devoid of ability, as his success in maintaining his undivided authority against such rebellions as those of Magnentius and Vetranio proves, was far inferior to his father in clearness of vision and breadth of aim. The great Constantine himself was not altogether inaccessible to flattery and family influences. His sister Constantia is credited with having prevailed upon him to allow Eusebius of Nicomedia and Arius to return from exile. But her influence was still more strongly felt in the next reign, and after the death of the astute and able Eusebius of Nicomedia, mere intriguers, such as Ursacius and Valens, and even the worthless eunuchs about the court, were able to persuade the emperor into unreasonable and tortuous courses, of which jealousy of the great Athanasius formed in reality the secret motive. Amid all the distractions of the time, three main stages may be marked in the progress of the controversy. The first consisted of the six years between the death of Constantine and the council of Sardica (343). During this period the attitude of all the various parties save those who adhered to the Nicene symbol is most perplexing, and the changes of opinion most bewildering. Court intrigue occupies a prominent place in the history. Yet it gradually became clear, as far as the march of opinion was concerned, that the West was irrevocably attached to the views of Athanasius, while in the East opinion was divided and variable, and the court influence grew more decisive on the progress of events in proportion as the power of Constantius increased. The second period was that between the councils of Sardica and Ariminum (Rimini, in Italy) in 359, during which opinion was gradually settling down into three distinct forms, which may be roughly described as the orthodox, the semi-Arian, and the Arian view. The last period, that between 359 and 381, is that during which Homoeanism and Anomoeanism (see below) became gradually discredited, while Homoiousians and orthodox approximated by degrees, until the final victory of the Nicene symbol at Constantinople. The ferment of opinion may be gauged by the fact that the historian Socrates gives no less than *ten* forms of creed—*eleven* if we count that presented at Nicaea by Eusebius of Caesarea—which were produced at various councils in hope of settling the controversy. But the Nicenes remained firmly attached to the creed of Nicaea, while their opponents were divided into three groups—the Anomoeans, or Arians proper, who taught the *unlikeness* of the nature of the Son to that of the Father; the Homoeans, who believed the Son's nature to bear only a general resemblance to that of the Father; and the Homoiousians, who believed in the *similarity* (but not the identity) of the *essence* of the Son to that of the Father. These last are also called semi-Arians.

The first important step in the history of the controversy after the death of Arius was the return of Athanasius to his diocese (337) permitted by Constantine II., in whose division of the empire Egypt lay. But he was not suffered to remain long unmolested. In 340 Constantine II. died, and Eusebius of Nicomedia, the ablest of Athanasius's antagonists, contrived to get himself removed to Constantinople after the death of the bishop, Alexander. His proximity to the emperor secured to him the leading influence in affairs ecclesiastical. The orthodox party had elected Paul as their bishop, but Eusebius contrived to get this election annulled, and to secure the vacant post for himself. He "left no stone unturned," as the historian Socrates puts it, to overthrow one whom he had long regarded as a rival. A council was assembled at Antioch (338-339), in which the old charges were revived against Athanasius, and which confirmed his sentence of deposition from his see. Athanasius was expelled in the spring of 339; and after a *third* Eusebius (afterwards bp. of Emesa), a man of principle and character, had declined to take his place, one Gregory was appointed, who speedily became unpopular in consequence of his violence and cruelty. Eusebius Pamphili of Caesarea, who would undoubtedly, had he survived, have been a moderating force, died about this time, and was succeeded by Acacius, who played a prominent part in the subsequent proceedings, but lacked the special knowledge of Church history, as well as the experience and judgment, of his celebrated predecessor. Athanasius fled to Rome, and thus brought its bishop Julius on the scene. Julius acted with spirit and discretion. He summoned a synod of 50 bishops of the West, who annulled the deposition of Athanasius, and acquitted him of all the charges against him. He further transmitted to Antioch a strong remonstrance against the inconsistency and unfairness of the proceedings at the council held there. The Eastern bishops, however, were not to be deterred from their course by his representations. At the council held at the dedication (*encaenia*) of a church at Antioch in 341, the sentence on Athanasius was confirmed, and after the rejection of a creed of distinctly Arian tendencies, a new creed, either composed by Lucian the Martyr or by his disciple Asterius, was brought forward as a substitute for the symbol of Nicaea. It rejected the expression ὁμοούσιον, but it as emphatically rejected Arianism by declaring the Son to be unchangeable and unalterable, and by adding that He was "the Image of the essence, the power, the will, and the glory of the Father." But Eusebius had not thrown over the symbol of Nicaea for such a halting substitute as this. On the other hand, Athanasius did not fail to point out that the language of the creed of Lucian was not more that of Scripture than was the language of the creed of Nicaea. The court party, whose object was simply to produce a formula which would, as they thought, meet the emperor's views by putting a stop to controversy, endeavoured to force another creed on the council, but in vain. This additional creed was a compromise pure and simple, enshrining no truth, although in form corresponding as nearly to the Nicene formula as possible. Its supporters then put the document into the hands of Constans, emperor of the West, who had demanded the assembling of another general council. The West had been roused by the proceedings at Antioch, and Constantius, now engaged in a war with Persia, dared not refuse. The able leader of the dissentients, however, Eusebius of Nicomedia, was now dead, and the leadership had fallen into the hands of Ursacius and Valens, who were mere opportunists. To their dismay and that of their party, it was settled that the council should be held at Sardica, in Dacia, just within the limits of the Western empire. Thither, in 343, the deputies repaired. But the courtiers perceived that there was no chance whatever of forcing their views upon a phalanx consisting, as it is now thought, of about 100 Western bishops devoted to the decisions of Nicaea. So they left Sardica in haste, and betook themselves to Philippopolis, a city just across the Eastern border. There, after declaring that the decrees of one council cannot be revised by another, they began inconsistently to revise the decrees of former councils, and to hurl charges against the venerated Fathers of the West, Hosius and Julius. The Westerns at Sardica, meanwhile, had once more acquitted Athanasius and his allies, and had rejected the Eastern formulae, as leaning to the Gnostic doctrine of successive emanations from the source of all being. The proceedings at Philippopolis and the outrageous conduct of Stephen, then patriarch of Antioch, gave offence even in the East, and the decision of the Western bishops to hold no communion with their Eastern brethren while the existing state of things lasted produced a reaction. Another council was held at Antioch, and a new and more conciliatory creed, usually called μακρόστιχος, from its exceeding length, was substituted for the Lucianic document. As Constans pressed for the restoration of Athanasius, and Constantius had the war with Persia still on hand, the latter gave way, the more readily because Gregory the intruder was now dead (345). Constantius summoned Athanasius to his presence, and after a friendly interview dismissed him, and wrote three letters, one to the bishops and clergy in Egypt, one to the laity, and one to the governors of provinces, explaining that it was his will that Athanasius should be allowed to return in peace to his flock. But when he demanded of Athanasius that he should allow the use of one church to the Arians in Alexandria, the latter preferred a request in his turn that the same thing should be done in cities where the Arians were in possession—a request which Constantius did not deem it prudent to grant. Athanasius therefore, unfettered by conditions, returned (346) to Alexandria, and the people, wearied of Arian violence and cruelty, received him with the warmest demonstrations of joy.

Peace was thus restored for the moment, but it endured only so long as Constantius was occupied with foreign war and intestine strife. It is noteworthy that the restless intriguers, URSACIUS and Valens, found it prudent just at present to repair to Rome and make friends with Julius and the West. Socrates (*H. E.* ii. 37) remarks on their disposition to identify themselves with the strongest side. But permanent peace was impossible until the questions at issue had been fully threshed out. As soon as Constans (350) was dead, and Magnentius, the usurper, defeated and slain (353), the strife recommenced. For ten years Athanasius had remained undisturbed at Alexandria, but premonitory signs of the eruption which was soon to burst forth had long been discernible. On the one hand the Easterns were beginning to substitute the semi-Arian doctrine of the *likeness* (ὁμοιούσιος) of the Son to the Father for the vaguer conception of the more moderate Arians of the earlier period. On the other hand, the *un*likeness of the Son to the Father was more boldly and defiantly pressed by the holders of that doctrine, and by degrees a sect, which almost reduced Christ to the level of a mere man, appeared on the scene. The chief exponents of this doctrine were AETIUS and EUZOIUS. The Anomoeans now began to separate themselves more definitely from the orthodox. All this was not without its effect on Constantius, whose sole object, like that of most politicians, was to avoid dissensions. When the tide turned, Ursacius and Valens were ready, as usual, with suggestions. But he could not at once take the steps they urged. New wars confronted him, and the attitude of the West was decidedly disquieting. The Western church had found a new champion in Hilary of Poictiers (Hilarius Pictavensis), whose ability, learning, and high character were recognized by his own contemporaries. Constantius shewed his sense of his abilities by exiling him, as well as Liberius, bp. of Rome, who had succeeded Julius (355). Early in 356 the imperial troops burst into the cathedral at Alexandria to seize ATHANASIUS, who was at prayer with his flock. It was night, and Athanasius almost miraculously escaped in the tumult, and remained secreted for some time. From his undiscovered retreat he issued numerous letters and treatises, by which he kept up the courage of his adherents. His Arian successor, one George, did not venture to set foot in Alexandria till a year after the departure of Athanasius, and his atrocious cruelties soon made him hated as well as feared by the populace.

Meanwhile the court intriguers resumed their activity. Sirmium, in Slavonia, between the Save and the Drave, now takes the place of Antioch in the matter of creed-making. A creed had already been issued thence in 351 against Sabellianism. In the latter part of 357 the emperor was in residence there, and Ursacius and Valens naturally took the opportunity of renewing their mischievous activity. A second creed was promulgated there, in which the difference between the Father and the Son was strongly insisted upon; the Father and the Son were declared to be two Persons (πρόσωπα), and the use of the words οὐσία and ὑπόστασις, as applied to God's nature, was condemned, as not warranted by Scripture. The intriguers no doubt imagined that, as the supporters of the Nicene formula were in exile, they could give no further trouble, and that the line of least resistance would be to come to an arrangement with the Arian (Anomoean) party. But events proved them utterly wrong. The result was just the opposite: to convert the moderates into a distinctly semi-Arian party, laying especial stress on the *likeness* of the Son's essence (ὁμοιούσιον) to that of the Father, instead of minimizing the likeness, as the Homoeans had done. The Homoiousians thus began to lean to the orthodox side, while the Homoeans inclined more and more to those who denied even the likeness of the Son's essence to that of the Father. Hilary now (359) intervened with his *de Synodis*, in which he reviewed the action of previous councils, and defended the Nicene Creed, yet in such a way as he thought best calculated to win back the semi-Arians (or Homoiousians) to the orthodox camp. This treatise marks the stage in the controversy in which semi-Arianism began definitely to separate itself from its doubtful allies, and to draw towards union with the orthodox party. Hilary, it may be added, admits the force of some semi-Arian objections to the word ὁμοούσιον, and suggests certain express limitations of its meaning. Two other creeds of considerable length, one of them provided with innumerable anathemas, were drawn up at Sirmium. The last of these, commonly known as the *dated* creed (359), was ridiculed by Athanasius for its pompous opening, and for its assumption that the Catholic faith had, at the date given, been proclaimed for the first time. It is clear, he adds, from their own confession, that theirs is a new faith, not the old one.

We now enter upon the last stage of the controversy. It is marked by the first attempt to make a distinction between οὐσία and ὑπόστασις —terms which had hitherto been regarded as synonymous—and to use the former as indicating the nature which is *common* to beings of the same order, while the latter was used to express the *diversities* between these possessors of a common nature. The word οὐσία was used to indicate the Divine Nature, while ὑπόστασις was henceforth used by the Greeks of the *Persons* in the Trinity. (It should, however, be observed that *substantia* remained the Latin equivalent of οὐσια.) The first to press this use of language was Basil of Ancyra, at a council he had called to protest against the proceedings at Sirmium. He defends the new use of the word ὑπόστασις in an able minute he issued, criticizing the proceedings at Sirmium, by pointing out that a word was needed—and it must be neither οὐσία nor ἀρχή—to denote the underlying and definitely existing (ὑπαρχούσας) distinctions (ἰδιότητας) of the Persons (προσώπων); and he acutely remarks that if οὐσία was a term not to be found in Scripture, the Godhead was indicated there by the words ὁ ὤν. In the end, this new and more careful use of words completely revolutionized the situation. Henceforth the semi-Arians as a body not only laboured for an understanding with the orthodox, but also drew still more markedly apart from the Homoeans and Anomoeans. The calling of a new council in the same year at Rimini (Ariminum) in Italy brought these new tendencies very plainly to light. Constantius, finding it impossible to lay down a common basis for action between the East and the West, commanded the Eastern bishops to meet at Seleucia in Cilicia, a mountain fortress near the sea. Sozomen tells us that the reason for calling this council was the growing influence of Anomoeanism through the influence of Aetius. The Western bishops, who numbered more than 200, had no scruples in the matter. They boldly deposed Ursacius and Valens, who had been sent to bring them to submission, and as boldly reaffirmed the Nicene symbol, and they sent a deputation of 20 bishops to the emperor to defend their action. He was, however, (or pretended to be) too busy to see them. The Easterns were still inclined to hesitate. The semi-Arian majority desired to accept the Nicene Creed, with the omission of the obnoxious ὁμοούσιον. The Homoeans, under the leadership of Acacius of Caesarea in Cappadocia, condemned the expressions ὁμοούσιον and ὁμοιούσιον, but anathematized the expression ἀνόμοιον. "The Acacian [Homoean] party" (Socr. *H. E.* ii. 40) "affirmed that the Son was like the Father as respected His will only, and not in His substance or essence." And they tendered yet another creed in accordance with these views, which the council rejected, and deposed those who had tendered it. Among those who were present at this council were men so diverse as the hated tyrant George of Alexandria, and Hilary of Poictiers, still exiled from his diocese. Meanwhile, Ursacius and Valens were engaged in the congenial task of endeavouring to persuade the deputies from Ariminum to sign yet another creed at Niké in Thrace, in the hope, if some authorities are to be trusted, of making the world believe, from the similarity of names, that it was the renowned document promulgated at the Nicene council. But this was surely an impossibility. The Nicene symbol was far too well known to the Christian world. Athanasius now intervened from his retreat, and wrote his famous treatise *de Synodis*, in which he reviewed the creeds and acts of the various councils. But he assumed no *non-possumus* attitude. He had even seemed inclined, for a moment, to admit the orthodoxy of the expression ὁμοιούσιον. But in this treatise he points out (c. 41) that though brass is like gold, tin like iron, and the dog like the wolf, yet they are of *different* natures, and no one could call the wolf the offspring of the dog. Nevertheless, he still endeavours to bridge over the gulf between himself and the semi-Arians.

These two councils were the final turning-point of the controversy. It had clearly appeared that, whenever the Nicene definitions had been rejected, Anomoeanism, which was Arianism in a more definite philosophical shape, came once more to the front, and this fact was increasingly seen to point to the Nicene symbol as the only safe way out of the difficulty. Henceforth the secular authority might retard, but it could not prevent, the victory of Athanasius and his followers. From this moment (see Socr. *H. E.* ii. 22) the Western churches definitely renounced communion with those of the East. The episode of Meletius of Antioch (not to be confounded with Meletius of Egypt) shewed plainly which way events were tending. He had been elected patriarch of Antioch by the Homoean party. But in his inaugural speech he frankly confessed his Nicene leanings, and when a busy archdeacon rushed up and closed his mouth, he continued by gestures to affirm what he had previously affirmed by his voice. Meletius was promptly banished, but before the year (361) was over Constantius was dead. The action of his successor Julian, who had renounced Christianity, gave a still further impulse to the policy of conciliation. As between heathenism and Christianity, impartiality cannot certainly be predicated of him. But he was impartial enough in his hostility to Christians of all shades of opinion. This threw them, for the time, into one another's arms. True, when the external pressure was removed, the suspicions and jealousies, as is commonly the case, broke out afresh. But none the less had an impulse been given towards union which henceforth never ceased to be felt. The oppressor George had been expelled from Alexandria by a rising of the populace as early as 358. In 361, on his return to Alexandria, he was seized and murdered by his exasperated flock. The edict of Julian (361) permitting the return of the exiles left the way open to Athanasius to rejoin his people. He at once (362) summoned a council, in which Macedonianism [MACEDONIUS], an offshoot from Arianism which applied the same line of argument to the Holy Spirit which had previously been applied to the Son, was condemned as well as Arianism. But Athanasius was wise and liberal enough to make overtures to the semi-Arians. Three men almost worthy to stand on a level with Athanasius himself had appeared among the Eastern bishops—men who were capable of negotiating on equal terms with that great and prescient theologian. These were BASIL, afterwards bp. of Caesarea in Cappadocia, his brother GREGORY, bp. of Nyssa, and the brilliant orator, poet, and thinker GREGORY OF NAZIANZUS, who was the intimate friend of both. These men had some opinions in common with the less extreme members of the semi-Arian party, and were therefore quite ready to resume the work of conciliation which, as we have seen, had been attempted by Basil of Ancyra. Athanasius, on his part, was ready to accept the distinction mentioned above between *οὐσία* and *ὑπόστασις*, which had not been recognized at Nicaea. Before the death of Jovian (364), Acacius of Caesarea, who cannot be acquitted of being an unworthy intriguer or at best a time-server, came forward to make his peace by accepting the Nicene formula. On the death of Jovian the empire was divided between Valentinian and Valens, the former taking the West, the latter the East, under his charge. Valentinian, as a man unacquainted with theology, was naturally influenced by the general opinion in the West, which had remained decisively Nicene. Valens as naturally fell under the influence of the Eastern bishops, and the time was not yet ripe for their acceptance of the Nicene decision. The Anomoeans were still a powerful party, and so determined were they to enforce their views that they persecuted not only the orthodox but the semi-Arians and Macedonians. When the semi-Arians, with the permission of Valentinian, held a council at Lampsacus in 364, its decisions were set aside by Valens, whose hand had already been heavy on the Homoousians, and who now exiled the semi-Arian bishops. Four years later he dealt equally harshly with the Macedonians, who were terrified into imploring the help of the orthodox West, and endeavoured to secure it by promising Liberius that they would receive the Nicene Creed. But the latter replied in a letter in which he declared that the faith depended on the acceptance of the words hypostasis (in the sense in which it is used in the Nicene formula) and homoöusios. On the other hand, the dissensions which broke out between EUDOXIUS, patriarch of Antioch and afterwards of Constantinople and his Arian (or Anomoean) allies, drove both him and Valens into the arms of the Homoeans, in whose possession most of the churches were. But the affairs of the empire fell into confusion in the incompetent hands of Valens, and the influence of the Arian and Homoean parties was steadily waning. Athanasius died in 373, after a noteworthy attempt to cast his shield over his faithful supporter and friend Marcellus. The result was that Marcellus was acquitted, but his school disappeared with him (he died in 371), and the way lay clear for the conciliatory action of the three great Eastern leaders already mentioned. There was no theologian in Christendom who could withstand them. Among their opponents no concert reigned, but only confusion; their ascendancy was founded on court intrigue and imperial violence. Sozomen (*H. E.* vi. 6) tells us how Valentinian, while he stedfastly clung to orthodoxy, studiously refrained from harassing those opposed to it, and notes with disapproval the different course taken by Valens. The cause of genuine, practical Christianity suffered seriously under these divisions, intrigues, and acts of violence, and men of earnest and even indifferent minds were longing for peace. When Theodosius succeeded Valens in 379 (Valentinian was already dead) there was no force strong enough among the heretical factions to resist the coalition between the semi-Arians and the Nicenes. The West was united in support of the latter, the strength and patience of the divided East were exhausted. A council of 150 bishops—all Easterns—assembled at Constantinople, and the weary 56 years of conflict and confusion terminated in the acceptance of the symbol * which, in the East and West, is repeated whenever Christians who profess the Catholic faith meet for communion with one another and their Lord. Arianism had no moral strength with which to resist persecution. But it still lingered among the Goths for some centuries. They were not an educated race, and Ulphilas, who converted them to Christianity, was a missionary rather than a theologian. And so it came to pass in the end that, so far as this vital doctrine of the Christian faith is concerned, "they all escaped safe to land."

The bibliography of this period is much the same as has been given in art. ARIUS, only that the *Life of Constantine*, by Eusebius Pamphili, is of course no longer available. The *de Synodis* of Athanasius passes in review the various councils and their creeds, from the Encaenia at Antioch to the councils of Ariminum and Seleucia. Various monographs connected with the history of this period will be found mentioned by Prof. Gwatkin in his *Studies of Arianism*, if the student wishes to go more deeply into the subject than is possible here. [J.J.L.]

Arnobius, an eminent Latin apologist for Christianity. The records of his life are meagre and somewhat uncertain; consisting in a few brief notices by St. Jerome, and another by Trithemius, aided by his own few incidental allusions to himself.

The outbreak of the last great persecution (303-313) found Arnobius a professor of rhetoric at Sicca, in Africa. His reputation was high, and his pupils numerous and distinguished; among them was LACTANTIUS. Arnobius was a sincere pagan; versed in schemes of philosophy; but none the less an unhesitating and even abject idolator. He was, moreover, active as a lecturer in attacks upon Christianity. The sight, however, of

* It ends, however, as far as the council of Nicaea is concerned, with the words, "And I believe in the Holy Ghost."

the martyrdoms which followed the edict of Nicomedia appears speedily to have touched him; and a dream or vision (says St. Jerome) warned him to submit to Christ. He presented himself to the church at Sicca; but "they were afraid of him," and demanded from their late enemy some hostage for sincerity. The result was the composition of the *Disputations against the Pagans*; whether in their present form or not. He was thereupon baptized, and (according to Trithemius) attained the rank of presbyter. Of his subsequent history we know nothing. Some doubt attaches to the *exact date* of the conversion of Arnobius and publication of his treatise. On the whole the evidence points to some date between 303 and 313 (Hieron. *de Scr. Eccl.* c. 79; id. *in Chronicon Eusebii;* Trithemius, *de Scr. Eccl.* p. 10 *a*).

The *title* of Arnobius's work usually appears as *Disputationes adversus Gentes*; occasionally, *adv. Nationes.* It is divided into seven books of unequal length. The first two are devoted to the defence of Christianity, the remainder to the exposure of paganism.

Of *God*, he speaks in the noblest and fullest language of adoration. His existence is assumed (i. 33) as a postulate in the argument. He is the First Cause; the Father and Lord of things; foundation of all; author of only good; unborn; omnipresent; infinite, incorporeal; passionless; shrouded in light; to be known only as the Ineffable (see especially i. 31). Arnobius hesitates, however, over the details of creation; thinking apparently that alike the human soul and the lower animals—insects and reptiles—are the work of some intermediate creator (ii. 36, 47).

Of the *Lord Jesus Christ* he uses the most glowing language. As a *man* He is the supreme philosopher and teacher, both of nature and religion. But He is also God: "Deus re certâ: Deus, homo tamen natus; Deus interiorum potentiarum; Deus sublimis; radice ex intimâ; ab incognitis regnis; sospitator, ab omnium principe missus"; His *pontificium* is to give salvation to the soul; He is the only path to light; His followers alone are saved; He is stronger than fate. Some doubt may, perhaps, be thrown over the extent of these ascriptions of deity by the vague language with which Arnobius speaks of the gods (see below). But with every deduction they are magnificent, and at least lie in the direction of the fullest orthodoxy. The allusions to the incarnation, life, and death of the Redeemer are numerous. The first is somewhat vaguely described as the assumption of a *man* to the *self*, the God; its motive was the presentation of the God to human senses, and the general performance of Christ's mission. His resurrection and the subsequent appearances are insisted upon; it is asserted (apparently) that He still appears to the faithful. To the Second Advent there is at most only a doubtful allusion (i. 39). (See generally, i. 36, 65; ii. 60.)

On the origin of the *Soul* he is far more speculative than is his wont. Its sin, imperfection, and inborn infirmity (he holds) forbid the belief that it comes direct from the Supreme Cause. It cannot for the like reasons be immortal (*i.e.* absolutely and *per se*); it outlives the body, but depends wholly on the gift of God for eternal duration. After death there awaits the evil a second death, a Gehenna of unquenchable fire, in which gradually they are consumed and annihilated (see especially ii. 15-54). The resurrection of the flesh is emphatically asserted, but in somewhat obscure terms (ii. 13).

Of the existence of *gods* he speaks with much ambiguity. The actual objects of heathen worship he concludes from the nature of their mythology and ritual to be real but evil beings. But he nowhere denies that there exist also *dii boni*; only he views them (if existent) as mere reflexes of the Supreme Nature, and as in no sense distinct objects of worship and prayer. In worshipping the Supreme (he argues), we worship by implication—if to be worshipped they are—such gods as are gods indeed.

On the nature and efficacy of *prayer* he uses perplexing language. His belief apparently is that in the present life all externals are fixed by an immovable destiny (vii. 10); that prayer is useful only as a means of divine communion; but he yet describes the prayers of the Christian church as petitions for peace and pardon for all classes of mankind; the emperor, the magistrate, the armies, etc. (iv. 36). Prayer is regarded as (in some sense not specified) efficacious for the dead (*l.c.*). Arnobius asserts the "freedom of the will"; God calls man "non vi sed gratiâ" (ii. 64).

In the latter books his arguments against heathen sacrifices are so managed as logically to exclude altogether the sacrifices both of the Jewish temple and of the Cross. Of idol-worship and incense he speaks in terms which prove that he can have known nothing of images, or incense, or a local presence, in the *conventicula* of the Christians.

Of the *Holy Scriptures* Arnobius appears to have known very little. He makes some acute remarks (i. 58) on the rude style of the evangelists, but only one text (I. Cor. iii. 19) is quoted *verbatim*; and even this is introduced as *illud vulgatum* (ii. 6). He records apocryphal miracles as evangelical (i. 46, 53); he knows nothing of any promise of temporal happiness (ii. 76); he confuses the Pharisees with the Sadducees (iii. 12). Of the O.T. he was apparently quite ignorant. In one passage (iii. 10) he even seems to speak of it with disrespect; though the passage has been explained of the Rabbinical books. In many places he shews by implication a total ignorance of the national election and the ritual of the Jews (to whom he scarcely alludes at all), and of the Scriptural prophecies and chronology. These phenomena are, of course, in great measure accounted for by the alleged circumstances of the composition of the work. They render more remarkable the faintness of the tinge of Gnosticism in its pages. Obviously the authority of Arnobius on points of Christian doctrine is reduced almost *ad nihilum* by these indications; and we can hardly wonder that in the 5th cent. his treatise was banished by pope Gelasius to the index of apocryphal works.

Critical opinions on the merits of Arnobius have been very various. St. Jerome's verdict varies between praises of his *libri luculentissimi* and censure of his defects as *inaequalis, nimius, confusus*, in style, method, and doctrine. Dr. Woodham (in his edition of Tertullian's *Apology*, preliminary Essays, ed. 1850) protests against the obscurity and neglect which have attended his name; holds that his "peculiar position and character invest his sentiments and reasoning with very singular interest and value"; pronounces him to be in some respects "the keenest of the apologists," and to be remarkably apposite to the popular arguments of modern times (pp. 21, 29, 52, 53).

To the whole of this verdict we subscribe. Arnobius presents as a *man* a mind and character combining much ardour with much common sense. His sincerity is eminently manifest. He has apprehended to a degree nowhere and never common the great fact of human ignorance. As a *writer*, he appears as the practised and facile, but not very fanciful, rhetorician of his time and country; and is even a master and model of that peculiar style of a declining age which consists in a subtle *medium* between the dictions of poetry and of prose.

As a storehouse of old Latinity and of allusions to points of antiquity—to heathen mythology and ceremonial; to law, education, and amusements—his work is of the greatest interest and importance.

The following *editions* of Arnobius may be mentioned:—1816, Leipz., J. C. Orellius (excellent for a full and learned commentary); Halle, 1844, ed. G. F. Hildebrand; Paris, 1844, Migne's *Patr. Lat.*; Reifferscheid, Vienna, 1875 (*Corpus Script. Eccl. Lat.* iv.). For an Eng. trans. see *Ante-Nicene Lib.* (T. &. T. Clark). [H.C.G.M.]

Arnobius, Junior, a presbyter, or possibly bp., of Gaul; presumed, from internal evidence of his writings, to have lived at least as late as A.D. 460.

The only external notices seem to be those of Venerable Bede, who praises his *Commentary on the Psalms*, and of Alcuin, who favourably alludes to his *Altercation with Serapion* in a letter addressed to Flavius Merius, and in the sixth book of his treatise *Contra Felicem Urgelitanum.* The internal evidence is based upon the *Commentarium in Psalmos*, the Notes on some passages of the Gospels, and the *Altercatio cum Serapione.* The *Commentary* and *Altercation* may both be found in the *Bibliotheca Patrum Maxima* (tom. viii.), Lyons, 1677; but the contents render it very difficult to believe that the same person was author of both.

The *Commentary on the Psalms* is avowed by its author, who dedicates it to Leontius, bp. of Arles, and to Rusticus, bp. of Narbonne. The comments are devout, practical, and pointed, but brief and uncritical, interpreting everything as referring to Christ and the church. They are, however, accused of a semi-Pelagian tendency; and a very learned writer, whose *Hist. Eccl.* appeared *c.* 1686, Natalis Alexander, invites special attention to remarks of Arnobius upon Pss. l. ciii. cviii. and cxxvi. (in the Heb.; in A.V., li. civ. etc.). But Nat. Alexander was a Jansenist; and anti-Jansenist writers, such as the Bollandists, might maintain that the majority were capable of an orthodox interpretation. It must, however, be allowed that the author of the Commentary is anti-Augustinian; as on Ps. cviii. (cix.) 16, 17, he speaks of the *heresy*, "quae dicit Deum aliquos praedestinâsse ad benedictionem, alios ad maledictionem."

The *Altercatio cum Serapione* is a dialogue, represented as having been held between Arnobius and Serapion. Serapion by turns plays the part of a Sabellian, an Arian, and a Pelagian, and is gradually driven from each position. Considerable learning is displayed and a clear apprehension of the points at issue, combined with much real ingenuity of argument. The circumstance of Arnobius being the chief speaker does not of course prove that the authorship is his, any more than the position of Socrates in certain of the Platonic dialogues would prove that Socrates wrote them. Moreover, just as we cannot make Socrates responsible for all that Plato has put into his mouth, so neither can Arnobius *junior* be justly credited with the tenets here ascribed to him by some unknown author. Both the style and tone of the *Altercation* seem different from that of the *Commentary*; and though there is in both works a consentient rejection of the errors condemned in the first four general councils, yet it is hardly possible that an author of semi-Pelagian leanings, who had stigmatized predestinarian doctrine as a heresy, should declare, as Arnobius is made to do towards the conclusion of the *Altercatio cum Serapione*, that he "accepts and defends the *dicta* of St. Augustine concerning Pelagianism, as if they were the most hallowed writings of the Apostles."

The Notes on some passages of the Gospels, which seem really to belong to Arnobius *junior*, are given in the edition of his works by Laurence de la Barre (Paris, 1639). But for a new view of the authorship of these works see G. Morin in *Revue Bénédictine* (1903). He thinks that the author of the *Adnotationes*, the *Altercatio*, and the *Predestinatus* is probably an Illyrian, who lived in Rome. Of the events of our author's life we are wholly ignorant. [J.G.C.]

Arsacius, the intruding archbp. of Constantinople, after the violent expulsion of Chrysostom (A.D. 404). He was the brother of Nectarius, Chrysostom's predecessor, and had served as archpresbyter under Chrysostom (Photius C. 59). In earlier life his brother had selected him for the bishopric of Tarsus, and had attributed his refusal to an ambitious design of becoming his successor at Constantinople. On this, Palladius asserts, he swore voluntarily that he would never accept the see of Constantinople (Pallad. c. xi.). After he had passed his 80th year, the success of the base intrigue of Eudoxia and Theophilus against Chrysostom opened an unexpected way for his elevation to the archiepiscopal throne. Eudoxia and the party now triumphant wanted for their new archbishop a facile tool, under whose authority they might shelter the violence of their proceedings. Such an instrument they had in Arsacius. Moreover, his hostility to Chrysostom had been sufficiently testified at the synod of the Oak, when he appeared as a witness against him and vehemently pressed his condemnation. He was consecrated archbishop on June 27, 404. Chrysostom, on hearing of it, denounced him "as a spiritual adulterer, and a wolf in sheep's clothing" (*Ep.* cxxv.). The diocese soon made it plain that they regarded the new archbishop as an intruder. The churches once so thronged became empty; with the exception of a few officials, the dependants of the court party, and the expectants of royal favour, the people of Constantinople refused to attend any religious assembly at which he might be expected to be present. Deserting the sacred edifices, they gathered in the outskirts of the city, and in the open air. Arsacius appealed to the emperor Arcadius, by whose orders, or rather those of Eudoxia, soldiers were sent to disperse the suburban assemblies. Those who had taken a leading part in them were apprehended and tortured, and a fierce persecution commenced of the adherents of Chrysostom. [OLYMPIAS (2)]. We learn from Sozomen (*H. E.* viii. 23) that Arsacius was not personally responsible for these cruel deeds; but he lacked strength of character to offer any decided opposition to the proceedings of his clergy. They did what they pleased, and Arsacius bore the blame. His position became intolerable. In vain all the bishops and clergy who, embracing Chrysostom's cause, had refused to recognize him were driven out of the East (Nov. 18, 404). This only spread the evil more widely. The whole Western episcopate refused to acknowledge him, and pope Innocent, who had warmly espoused Chrysostom's interests, wrote to the clergy and laity of Constantinople strongly condemning the intrusion of Arsacius, and exhorting them to persevere in their adhesion to their true archbishop (Soz. *H. E.* vi. 22, 26). It is no cause for surprise that Arsacius's episcopate was a brief one, and that a feeble character worn out by old age should have soon given way before a storm of opposition so universal. He died Nov. 11, 405 (Socr. *H. E.* vi. 19; Soz. *H. E.* viii. 23, 26; Phot. *C.* 59; Pallad. *Dial.* c. xi.; Chrys. *Ep.* cxxv.). [E.V.]

Arsenius, called "the Great," one of the most famous of the monks of Egypt. He was of high Roman family; born probably in 354. He was deeply read in Greek literature. About 383, Theodosius the Great being desirous of finding a suitable instructor for his sons Arcadius and Honorius, the elder of whom was then about six years old, Arsenius was recommended to him, it is said, by the Roman bishop, and in this way came into the service of the best of the Christian Caesars. The time that Arsenius spent at the court came to an end when he was forty years old, in 394. A thoughtful and high-souled Roman Christian living under the ascendancy of Rufinus might not unnaturally be impelled towards monastic seclusion by sheer disgust and despair as to the prospects of so-called Christian society. He gave up his charge, in obedience, as he said, to a voice which bade him "fly from men, if he would be safe."

Arsenius, arriving at the monastic wilderness of Scetis, begged the clergy there to put him in the way of salvation by making him a monk. They took him to abbot John Colobus (the Dwarfish), who invited them to a meal: Arsenius was kept standing while they sat; a biscuit was flung at him, which he ate in a kneeling posture. "*He* will make a monk," said John; and Arsenius stayed with him until he had learned enough of the monastic life from John's teaching, and then established himself as a hermit in Scetis, where he continued forty years. His love of solitude became intense; the inward voice had seemed to bid him "be silent, be quiet," if he would keep innocency. One visitor he even drove away with stones; he discouraged the visits of Theophilus the archbp.; and when a high-born Roman lady visited him during one of his occasional sojourns outside the desert, her request to be remembered in his prayers was met by the brusque expression of a hope that he might be able to forget her. Whenever he came into a church he hid himself behind a pillar; he even shrank at times from his brother hermits, remarking that the ten thousands of angels had but one will, but men had many. But with all his sternness, which was coupled with more than the usual monastic austerities, Arsenius could be cordial, and even tender. His humility was worthy of a follower of Anthony. He was heard to cry aloud in his cell, "Forsake me not, O God! I have done no good in Thy sight, but, in Thy goodness, grant me to make a beginning." A very famous saying of his referred to faults of the tongue: "Often have I been sorry for having spoken—never for having been silent." The *Exhortation to Monks*, ascribed to him (Combefis, *Gr. Patr. Auctarium*, i. 301; Galland, *Biblioth.* vii. 427), exhibits the results of deep spiritual experience. It warns the monk not to forget that his great work is not the cleansing of the outer life, but of the inner man: spiritual sins, not carnal only, have to be conquered; many a good action has, through the tempter's sublety, become the door to unexpected evil; many who have thought their battle with sin accomplished have relapsed through the perilous hearing of other men's sin: "we must keep guard all round."

In 434 Arsenius left Scetis, driven forth by an irruption of the Mazici. He stayed at Troe, near Memphis, until 444; then spent three years at the little island (not the city) of Canopus; returned to Troe for the two remaining years of his long monastic life. The Greek church honours him as "our Father, Arsenius the Great," on May 8; the Latin, on July 19. [W.B.]

Artemon, Artemonites, belong to that class of ante-Nicene Monarchians, or Antitrinitarians, who saw in Christ a mere man filled with divine power. Of Artemon, or Artemas, we know very little. He taught in Rome at the end of the 2nd and beginning of the 3rd cent., and was excommunicated by pope Zephyrinus (202-217), who, as we learn from the *Philosophumena* of Hippolytus, favoured the opposite error of Patripassianism. He declared the doctrine of the divinity of Christ to be an innovation dating from the time of Zephyrinus, the successor of Victor, and a relapse into heathen polytheism. He asserted that Christ was a mere man, but born of a virgin, and superior in virtue to the prophets. The Artemonites were charged with placing Euclid above Christ, and abandoning the Scriptures for dialectics and mathematics. This indicates a critical or sceptical turn of mind. The views of Artemon were afterwards more fully developed by Paul of Samosata, who is sometimes counted with the Artemonites. The sources of our fragmentary information are Eusebius, *Hist. Eccl.* v. 28; Epiphanius, *Haer.* lxv. 1, 4; Theodoret, *Haer. Fab.* ii. 4; Photius, *Biblioth.* 48. Cf. Schleiermacher's essay on the Sabellian and Athanasian conceptions of the Trinity (*Works*, vol. ii.), and Dorner's *Entwicklungsgeschichte der L. v. d. Person Christi*, 2nd ed. i. 508 ff. [P.S.]

Asterius (1), a bp. of Arabia (called bp. of Petra, *Tomus ad Antioch.* § 10). He accompanied the Eusebians to the council of Sardica, but separated himself from them along with bp. Arius or Macarius (who by some confusion is also called bp. of Petra), complaining of the violent treatment to which the deputies had been subjected, with the view of driving them into supporting the Eusebian faction (Theod. ii. 8). The Eusebians soon had their revenge, and the two bishops were banished to Upper Libya, where they endured much suffering (Athan. *Hist. Arian.* § 18; *Apol.* § 48). On the promulgation of the edict of Julian, recalling all the banished bishops, Asterius returned, and (A.D. 362) took part in the important council summoned by the newly restored Athanasius at Alexandria, for the purpose of promoting union between the orthodox and those who, without embracing the errors of Arius, had held communion with the Arian party. One of the chief subjects that came before this synod was the unhappy schism at Antioch between the Eustathians and the Meletians. [LUCIFERUS (1); MELETIUS; PAULINUS (6).] On the singular fact that the name of Asterius, together with that of Eusebius of Vercelli, is found among those to whom this letter is addressed, as well as among those by whom it was written, of which it is difficult to give a satisfactory explanation, cf. Tillemont, *Mém.* viii. p. 707; Baronius, *Ann.* sub. ann. 362, § 219. [E.V.]

Asterius (2), bp. of Amasea in Pontus, a contemporary of St. Chrysostom. He himself tells us that his teacher was a certain Scythian (*i.e.* Goth), who, having been sold in his youth to a citizen of Antioch, a schoolmaster, had made marvellous progress under his owner's instructions, and won himself a great name among Greeks and Romans (Phot. *Bibl.* 271, p. 1500). Beyond this not a single incident in his life is recorded. His date, however, is fixed by allusions to contemporary events in his Homilies. He speaks of the apostasy of Julian as having happened within his memory (Aster. *Or.* 3, p. 56, ed. Combefis); and in his sermon on the Festival of the Calends (*Or.* 4, p. 76) he mentions the consulate and fall of Eutropius as an event of the preceding year. This sermon therefore must have been delivered on New Year's Day, 400. Elsewhere he spoke of himself as a man of very advanced age (Phot. *Amphil.* 125 [312]).

The extant works of Asterius consist almost solely of sermons or homilies. Of these we possess twenty-two perfect; twelve on various subjects included in the edition of Combefis (Paris, 1648); eight on the Psalms, of which one is found among the works of St. Chrysostom, and the remaining seven were published by Cotelier, *Mon. Eccl. Graec.* ii. (Paris, 1688); and two again on other subjects, which are published among the works of Gregory Nyssen, but must be assigned to Asterius on the authority of Photius. Besides these Photius (*Bibl.* 271) gives extracts from several others. In addition to these homilies, a *Life* of his predecessor, St. Basil of Amasea, printed in the *Acta Sanctorum*, April 26, is ascribed to him. A complete collection of his works will be found in Migne's *Patr. Gk.* xl.; a complete list in Fabric. *Bibl. Gk.* ix. 513 seq. ed. Harles. An account of their contents is given by Tillemont, x. 409 seq.

Asterius was a student of Demosthenes (*Or.* 11, p. 207), and himself no mean orator. His best sermons (for they are somewhat uneven) display no inconsiderable skill in rhetoric, great power of expression, and great earnestness of moral conviction; and some passages are even strikingly eloquent. His orthodoxy was unquestioned. Photius (*Amphil. l.c.*) contrasts him with his Arian namesake, as stanch in the faith, devoting himself to the care of his flock, and setting an example of a virtuous and godly life. His authority was quoted with great respect in later ages, more especially during the Iconoclastic controversy at the second council of Nicaea, when with a play on his name he was referred to as "a bright star (*astrum*) illumining the minds of all" (Labbe, *Conc.* viii. 1385, 1387, ed. Coleti). Bardenhewer (1908) refers to a *Syllogehistorica* on Asterius by V. de Buck in *Acta SS.* Oct. (Paris, 1883), xiii. 330-332. [L.]

Athanasius, St., archbp. of Alexandria. The life of Athanasius divides itself naturally into seven sections, respectively terminated by (1) his consecration; (2) his first exile; (3) his second exile; (4) his second return; (5) his third exile; (6) his fourth exile; (7) his death.

(1) He was born at Alexandria, and had but scanty private means (*Apol. c. Ar.* 51; Socr. iv. 13). We must date his birth *c.* 296; not earlier, because he had no personal remembrance of the persecution under Maximian in 303 (*Hist. Ar.* 64), and was comparatively a young man when consecrated bishop, soon after the Nicene council; not later, because he received some theological instruction from persons who suffered in the persecution under Maximian II. in 311 (*de Incarn.* 56), and the first two of his treatises appear to have been written before 319. There can be no reason to doubt that Athanasius became an inmate of bp. Alexander's house, as his companion and secretary (Soz. ii. 17). The position involved great advantages. The place held by Alexander as "successor of St. Mark," and occupant of "the Evangelical throne," was second in the Christian hierarchy: we may call the bps. of Alexandria in the 4th cent., for convenience' sake, archbishops or patriarchs, although the former name was then very rarely applied to them, and the latter not at all, and they were frequently designated, though not in contradistinction to all other prelates, by the title of Papas (pope), or "dear father."

Their power throughout the churches of Egypt, Libya, and Pentapolis was, by ancient custom, which the Nicene council afterwards confirmed, almost monarchical, extending over about a hundred bishops, who revered their judgments as the decisions of the see of Rome were revered in Italy. One experience of a different kind, most fruitful in its consequences, was Athanasius's acquaintance with the great hermit Anthony. He tells us, in his *Life of Anthony*, that he often saw him; and although that reading of the conclusion of the preface, which makes him say that "he himself for some time attended on him, and poured water on his hands," may be considered doubtful, yet we know that he was afterwards spoken of as "the ascetic," and that when, years later, he took shelter in the cells of the monks of Egypt, he found himself perfectly at home. He contracted an admiration for monasticism, which will not surprise those who remember that the spiritual intensity of the Christian life had found a most emphatic, though a one-sided expression, in the lives of men who fled, like Anthony, from a society at once tainted and brutalized beyond all modern conception. [ANTONIUS.]

The two essays of Athanasius, *Against the Gentiles* and *On the Incarnation*, which form one complete work addressed to a convert from heathenism, cannot be dated later than the end of 318; for they make no reference to the Arian controversy which broke out in 319. Dorner, in his work *On the Person of Christ*, has given a *résumé* of their argument on the threefold subject of God, man, and the Incarnate Word; and Möhler calls the book on the Incarnation "the first attempt that had been made to present Christianity and the chief circumstances of the life of Jesus Christ under a scientific aspect. By the sure tact of his noble and Christian nature, everything is referred to the Person of the Redeemer: everything rests upon Him: He appears throughout." The young author seems to have been ordained deacon about this time, and placed in the position of chief among the Alexandrian deacons. Among the clergy who joined the archbishop in calling on Arius to retract, and who afterwards assented to his deposition, was the young archdeacon of Alexandria (see the *Benedictine Athanasius*, i. 396 seq.). In this spirit he attended Alexander to the Nicene council in 325.

In that assembly he is represented by Gregory of Nazianzum (*Orat.* 21) as "foremost among those who were in attendance on bishops," and as "doing his utmost to stay the plague." His writings may assure us of the argument which he would maintain: that the real Divinity of the Saviour was (i) asserted in many places of Scripture, (ii) involved in the notion of His unique Sonship, (iii) required by the Divine economy of redemption, and (iv) attested by the immemorial consciousness of the church. And although, as he himself informs us, the council would willingly have confined themselves to purely Scriptural terms (*de Decr.* 19) if their legitimate sense could have been *bonâ fide* admitted; although too he was far from imagining that any form or expression of human thought would *adequately* represent a Divine mystery; yet his convictions went thoroughly with the adoption of the term "Homoousion" or "coessential," explained, as it was, in a sense which made it simply equivalent to "truly Son of God," and proposed as a test of adherence to the Scriptural Christology. And if we are to understand his mind at the close of the council, we must say that he regarded its proceedings as something done, in fact, "for the rightful honour of Jesus." Nothing was to him more certain than that Jesus was, in the full force of the words, God Incarnate; that Arianism was essentially a denial, and the "Homoousion" the now authenticated symbol, of His claim on men's absolute devotion; and that it was infinitely worth while to go through any amount of work or suffering in defence of such a truth, and in the cause of such a Master.

More work was near at hand, and suffering was not far off. A solemn and touching incident of Alexander's last moments is connected with the history of Athanasius, who was then absent from Alexandria. The dying man, while his clergy stood around him, called for Athanasius. One of those present, also bearing that name, answered, but was not noticed by the archbishop, who again repeated the name, and added, "You think to escape—but it cannot be." Some time appears to have elapsed between his death and the assembling of the Egyptian bishops to consecrate a successor. An encyclical letter of these same Egyptian prelates proclaimed to all Christendom, some years later, that a majority of them had elected Athanasius in the presence, and amid the applause, of the whole Alexandrian laity, who for nights and days persevered in demanding him as "the good, pious, *ascetic* Christian," who would prove a "genuine bishop," and prayed aloud to Christ for the fulfilment of their desire (*Apol. c. Ar.* 6). It was granted; and then, in the words of Gregory, "by the suffrages of the whole people, and not by those vile methods, afterwards prevalent, of force and bloodshed, but in a manner apostolic and spiritual, was Athanasius elevated to the throne of Mark," some time after the beginning of May in 326, and very probably on June 8.

(2) *From his Consecration* (326) *to his First Exile* (336).—At the outset of his archiepiscopate is to be placed the organization of the church in Ethiopia or Abyssinia by his consecration of Frumentius as bp. of Axum. [EDESIUS.] Another event of these comparatively quiet times was Athanasius's visitation of the Thebaid, a region where much trouble was being caused by the Arians, and by the Meletians, who resisted his earnest efforts to repress their separatist tendency.

Now began the troubles from which the Arians never suffered Athanasius to rest till the last hour of his life. It was probably in 330 that he had his first severe experience of their hatred. After the Nicene council, Constantine had become a zealot for orthodoxy, and Eusebius of Nicomedia had been exiled. But Eusebius had procured his recall by orthodox professions; it may have been by his means that Arius himself was recalled, perhaps in Nov. 330. Eusebius now entered into a league with the Meletians of Egypt, of whom a bishop named John Arcaph was the head. "He *bought* them," says Athanasius, "by large promises, and arranged that they should help him on any emergency" by that machinery of false accusation which they had already employed against three archbishops. The charges were not to be theological: to attack Athanasius's teaching would be to declare against the Nicene doctrine, and this was a step on which Eusebius could not venture. He began by writing to Athanasius in behalf of Arius, and urging that, as a man whose opinions had been seriously misrepresented, he ought in justice to be received to church communion. Athanasius's answer shews the ground on which he took his stand. "It cannot be right to admit persons to communion who invented a heresy contrary to the truth, and were anathematized by the oecumenical council." It is probable that (as Fleury thinks, though Tillemont and Neander date it much later) we should refer to this period the visit of Anthony to Alexandria (*Vit. Ant.* 69), when he confounded the Arians' report that he "agreed with them." This would be a great support to Athanasius. But Eusebius had recourse to Constantine, who thereupon wrote, commanding Athanasius to admit into the church "all who desired it," on pain of being removed from his see by sheer State power. This gave him an opportunity of laying before Constantine his own views of his duty. "There could be no fellowship," he wrote, "between the Catholic church of Christ and the heresy that was fighting against Him." Not long afterwards, in compliance with instructions from Eusebius, three Meletians, Ision, Eudaemon, and Callinicus, appeared before the emperor at Nicomedia with a charge against Athanasius that he had assumed the powers of the government by taxing Egypt to provide linen vestments for the church of Alexandria. But two of Athanasius's priests, happening to be at court, at once refuted this calumny; and Constantine wrote to Athanasius, condemning his accusers, and summoning him to Nicomedia. Eusebius, however, persuaded the accusers to meet him on his arrival with a bolder charge: "he had sent a purse of gold to Philumenus, a rebel." This, being easily overthrown, was at once followed up by the famous story of the broken chalice. A certain Ischyras, a layman pretending to the character of a presbyter, officiated at a little hamlet called "the Peace of Sacontarurum," in the Mareotis; Athanasius, being informed of this while on a visitation tour, sent a priest named Macarius, with the actual pastor of the district, to summon Ischyras before him, but found him ill. Ischyras, on recovering, attached himself to the Meletians, who, resolving to use him as a tool, made him declare that Macarius had found him in church "offering the oblations," had thrown down the holy table, broken the chalice, and burnt the church books; of which sacrilege Athanasius was to share the responsibility. But Athanasius was able to prove before Constantine at Nicomedia, early in 332, that, point by point, it was a falsehood. About mid-Lent he returned home with a letter from Constantine reprobating his enemies and praising him as "a man of God"; whereupon Ischyras came to him, asking to be received into the church, and piteously protesting that the Meletians had set him on to assert a falsehood. But he was not admitted to communion; and the story was ere long revived in an aggravated form—Athanasius himself being now called the perpetrator of the outrage (*Apol.* 62, 64, 28, 74, 17, 65, 68).

A darker plot followed. John Arcaph persuaded a Meletian bishop, named Arsenius, to go into hiding. A rumour was then spread that he had been murdered, and dismembered for purposes of magic, by Athanasius, in proof of which the Meletians exhibited a dead man's hand (*Apol.* 63, 42; Socr. i. 27; Soz. ii. 25; Theod. i. 30). The emperor was persuaded to think it a case for inquiry. Athanasius received a summons to appear at Antioch and stand his trial. At first he disdained to take any steps, but afterwards sent a deacon to search for the missing Arsenius. The deacon ascertained that Arsenius was concealed in a monastery at Ptemencyrcis, on the eastern side of the Nile. Before he could arrive there the superior sent off Arsenius, but was himself arrested by the deacon, and obliged to confess "that Arsenius was alive." At Tyre Arsenius was discovered. Constantine stopped the proceedings at Antioch on hearing of this exposure, and sent Athanasius a letter, to be read frequently in public, in which the Meletians were warned that any fresh offences would be dealt with by the emperor in person, and according to the civil law (*Apol.* 9, 68).

The slandered archbishop had now a breathing-time. Arcaph himself "came into the church," announced to Constantine his reconciliation with Athanasius, and received a gracious reply; while Arsenius sent to his "blessed pope" a formal renunciation of schism, and a promise of canonical obedience (*Apol.* 66, 17, 70, 69, 8, 27).

But the faction had not repented. Eusebius persuaded Constantine that such grave scandals as the recent charges ought to be examined in a council; and that Caesarea would be the fitting place. There a council met in 334 (see Tillemont, *Ath.* a. 15; cf. *Festal. Epp.* index, for A.D. 334). Athanasius, expecting no justice from a synod held under such circumstances, persisted, Sozomen says (ii. 25), "for thirty months" in his refusal to attend. Being at last peremptorily ordered by Constantine to attend a council which was to meet at Tyre, he obeyed, in the summer of 335, and was attended by about fifty of his suffragans. Athanasius saw at once that his enemies were dominant; the presiding bishop, Flacillus of Antioch, was one of an Arian succession. Some of the charges Athanasius at once confuted; as to others he demanded time. Incredible as it may seem, the dead man's hand was again exhibited. Athanasius led forward a man with downcast face, closely muffled; then, bidding him raise his head, looked round and asked, "Is not this Arsenius?" The identity was undeniable. He drew from behind the cloak first one hand, and then, after a pause, the other; and remarked with triumphant irony, "I suppose no one thinks that God has given to any man more hands than two." The case of the broken chalice now remained; it was resolved to send a commission of inquiry to the Mareotis. Ischyras accompanied the commissioners, as "a sharer in lodging, board, and wine-cup"; they opened their court in the Mareotis. It appeared in evidence that no books had been burned, and that Ischyras had been too ill to officiate on the day of the alleged sacrilege. An inquiry of such an *ex parte* character called forth indignant protests from the Alexandrian and Mareotic clergy, one of the documents bearing the date Sept. 7, 335. The commissioners, disregarding remonstrance, returned to Tyre (*Apol.* 27, 73-76, 17, 15).

Athanasius, regarding the proceedings of the council of Tyre as already vitiated (*Apol.* 82), resolved, without waiting for the judgment of such an assembly, "to make a bold and dangerous experiment, whether the throne was inaccessible to the voice of truth." Attended by five of his suffragans, he took the first vessel for Constantinople, and suddenly presented himself in the middle of the road when the emperor was riding into the city. Constantine, on learning who he was, and what was his errand, tried to pass him by in silence; but Athanasius firmly stood his ground. "Either summon a lawful council, or give me opportunity of meeting my accusers in your presence." The request was conceded. The bishops of the council, after receiving their commissioners' report, had by a majority condemned Athanasius, and then pronounced Arius orthodox on the ground of a doctrinal statement made five years earlier, when they were startled by an imperial letter expressing suspicion of their motives, and summoning them to Constantinople. Many of them, in alarm, fled homewards; but the two Eusebii, Theognis, Patrophilus, Valens, and Ursacius repaired to court, and, saying nothing of "the chalice," or the report of the commission, presented a new charge, like the former quasi-political ones—that Athanasius had talked of distressing Constantinople by preventing the sailing of Alexandrian cornships. "How could I, a private person, and poor, do anything of the kind?" asked Athanasius. Eusebius of Nicomedia answered by affirming with an oath that Athanasius was rich and powerful, and able to do anything. The emperor cut short Athanasius's defence with a show of indignation; and, perhaps not from real belief in the charge, but by way of getting rid of the case and silencing the archbishop's enemies in his own interest, banished him to the distant city of Trier or Trèves, the seat of government of his eldest son Constantine, who received the exile with much kindness, in Feb. 336.

(3) *From his First Exile* (336) *to his Second* (340).—His life at Trèves, including nearly two years and a half, was an interval of rest, much needed and doubtless invigorating, between the storms of the past and those of the future. He had now to "stand and wait"—a new experience for him. He was "abundantly supplied with all necessaries" (Constantine II. in *Apol.* 87); he had the friendship of Maximin, the orthodox bp. of Trèves, afterwards canonized; he had with him some Egyptian "brethren," and kept up a correspondence with his friends at home, although at the risk of having his letters seized.

For more than a year Constantine's death produced no change in Athanasius's position; but at length, on June 17, 338, Constantine II., who in the partition of the empire had a certain precedency over his brothers Constantius and Constans, the sovereigns of the East and of Italy, wrote from Trèves to the Catholics of Alexandria, announcing that he had resolved, in fulfilment of an intention of his father, to send back Athanasius, of whose character he expressed high admiration (*Apol.* 87). In this he appears to have presumed his brother's consent, and to have then taken Athanasius with him to Viminacium, an important town of Moesia Superior, on the high-road to Constantinople. Here the three emperors had a meeting, and all concurred in the restoration of Athanasius, who, after passing through Constantinople, saw Constantius a second time, at a farther point on his homeward journey, at Caesarea in Cappadocia (*Apol. ad Const.* 5; *Hist. Ar.* 8). His arrival at Alexandria, in Nov. 338, was hailed by popular rejoicing: the churches resounded with thanksgivings, and the clergy "thought it the happiest day of their lives." But his enemies bestirred themselves, and "did not shrink from long journeys" in order to press on the emperors new charges against him—that he had misappropriated the corn granted by the late emperor for charitable purposes in Egypt and Libya, and that the day of his return had been signalized by bloodshed. Constantius wrote to him in anger, assuming the truth of the former charge; but Athanasius was successful in disproving both. However, Constantius—who was so soon to be "his scourge and torment" (Hooker, v. 42, 2)—fell more and more under the influence of his great enemy Eusebius, now transferred from Nicomedia to the see of Constantinople, which had been forcibly vacated by the second expulsion of the orthodox Paul. The Eusebians now resumed a project which had been found impracticable while Constantine lived; this was to place on "the Evangelical throne" an Arian named Pistus, who had been a priest under Alexander, had been deposed by him for adhering to Arius, and had been consecrated, as it seems (*Apol.* 24), by a notorious Arian bishop named Secundus. It was argued that Athanasius had offended against all ecclesiastical principles by resuming his see in defiance of the Tyrian sentence, and by virtue of mere secular authority. The charge did not come well from a party which had leaned so much on the court and the State; but it must be allowed that Athanasius's return had given some colour to the objection, although he doubtless held that the assembly at Tyre had forfeited all moral right to be respected as a council. By way of harassing Athanasius, the Eusebians, apparently about this time, made Ischyras a bishop, after obtaining an order in the name of the emperor that a church should be built for him—an order which failed to procure him a congregation (*Apol.* 12, 85).

The Eusebians now applied to the West in behalf of their nominee Pistus. Three clergy appeared as their envoys before Julius, bp. of

Rome; on the other hand, Athanasius sent to Rome presbyters to state his case, and an encyclic—the invaluable document which has furnished us with so much information—from "the holy synod assembled at Alexandria out of Egypt, Thebais, Libya, and Pentapolis," composed, says Athanasius, of nearly 100 prelates. At Rome his envoys gave such evidence respecting Pistus as to cause the senior of the Eusebian envoys to decamp by night in spite of an indisposition. His companions asked Julius to convoke a council, and to act, if he pleased, as judge. He accordingly invited both parties to a council, to be held where Athanasius should choose. Thus matters stood about the end of 339.

Early in 340 a new announcement disquieted the Alexandrian church. It was notified in a formal edict of the prefect that not Pistus, but a Cappadocian named Gregory, was coming from the court to be installed as bishop (*Encycl.* 2). This, says Athanasius, was considered an unheard-of wrong. The churches were more thronged than ever; the people, in great excitement, and with passionate outcries, called the magistrates and the whole city to witness that this attack on their legitimate bishop proceeded from the mere wantonness of Arian hatred. Gregory, they knew, was an Arian, and therefore acceptable to the Eusebian party: he was a fellow-countryman of Philagrius. Philagrius attacked the church of St. Quirinus, and encouraged a mob of the lowest townspeople and of savage peasants to perpetrate atrocious cruelties and profanations. Athanasius was residing in the precincts of the church of St. Theonas: he knew that he was specially aimed at, and, in hope of preventing further outrage, he withdrew from the city to a place of concealment in the neighbourhood, where he busied himself in preparing an encyclic to give an account of these horrors. This was on March 19. Four days later Gregory is said to have "entered the city as bishop." Athanasius, after hastily completing and dispatching his encyclic, sailed for Rome in the Easter season of 340, some weeks after Constantine II. had been slain during his invasion of Italy.

(4) *From his Second Exile* (340) *to his Second Return* (346).—After Julius had welcomed Athanasius, he sent two presbyters, Elpidius and Philoxenus, in the early summer of 340, to repeat his invitation to the Eusebian prelates, to fix definitely the next December as the time of the proposed council, and Rome as the place. Athanasius received much kindness from the emperor's aunt, Eutropion, and from many others (*Ap. ad Const.* 417; cf. *Fest. Ep.* 13). He had with him two Egyptian monks. Their presence in the city, and Athanasius's enthusiasm for Anthony and other types of monastic saintliness, made a strong impression on the Roman church society, and abated the prejudices there existing against the very name of monk, and the disgust at a rude and strange exterior. In fact, Athanasius's three years (340-343) at Rome had two great historic results. (*a*) The Latin church, which became his "scholar" as well as his "loyal partisan," was confirmed by the spell of his master-mind "in its adhesion to orthodoxy, although it did not imbibe from him the theological spirit"; and (*b*) when Gibbon says that "Athanasius introduced into Rome the knowledge and practice of the monastic life," he records the origination of a vast European movement, and represents the great Alexandrian exile as the spiritual ancestor of Benedict, of Bernard, and of the countless founders and reformers of "religious" communities in the West.

Meantime Elpidius and Philoxenus had discharged their errand. The Eusebians at Antioch, finding that Athanasius was at Rome, and that the council to which they were invited would be a free ecclesiastical assembly, detained the Roman legates beyond the time specified, and then dismissed them with the excuse that Constantius was occupied with his Persian war. At the same time they stimulated Philagrius and Gregory to new severities. Orthodox bishops were scourged and imprisoned; Potammon never recovered from his stripes; Sarapammon, another confessor-bishop, was exiled (*Hist. Ar.* 12). The letters of Alexandrians to Athanasius, consolatory as proofs of their affection, gave mournful accounts of torture and robbery, of hatred towards himself shewn in persecution of his aunt, of countenance shewn to Gregory by the "duke" Balacius; and some of these troubles were in his mind when, early in 341, he wrote "from Rome" his Festal Letter for the year. That year had begun without any such settlement of his case as had been hoped for at Rome. December had passed, and no council could be held, for the Eusebians had not arrived. January came, and at last the legates returned, the unwilling bearers of a letter so offensive that Julius "resolved to keep it to himself, in the hope that some Eusebians" would even yet arrive (*Apol.* 24) and render the public reading of it unnecessary. No one came. On the contrary, the Eusebians resolved to take advantage of the approaching dedication of a new cathedral at Antioch, "the Golden Church," in order to hold a council there. Accordingly, ninety-seven bishops, many of whom were rather negatively than positively heterodox, assembled on this occasion, apparently in Aug. 341. Constantius was present. The sentence passed against Athanasius at Tyre was affirmed; several canons were passed; and three creeds were framed, in language partly vague and general, partly all but reaching the Nicene standard (cf. Newman, *Arians*, c. 4, s. 1; cf. *Athan. Treatises*, i. 105 seq.). This business necessarily lasted some time; and no information as to this council had reached Rome when, in Nov. 341, Athanasius having now been waiting at Rome for eighteen months (*Apol.* 29), Julius assembled the long-delayed council, consisting of more than fifty bishops, in the church of the presbyter Vito. Athanasius's case was fully examined; Athanasius was formally pronounced innocent; his right to brotherly treatment and church communion—admitted from the first by the Roman bishop—was solemnly recognized by the Italian council. The year 342 is not eventful in his history. Constans had shewn himself friendly to Athanasius, who at his request had sent him from Alexandria some bound copies of the Scriptures (*Ap. ad Const.* 4).

Narcissus, Maris, and two other prelates appeared before Constans at Trèves, spoke in support of the decisions against Athanasius, and presented a creed which might, at first sight, appear all but to confess the "Homoousion." But Constans, doubtless swayed by bp. Maximin, who would not admit the Eastern envoys to communion, dismissed them from his presence (Athan. *de Syn.* 25 ; Soz. iii. 10 ; Hil. *Fragm.* iii. 27).

Athanasius remained at Rome until the summer of 343, when, "in the fourth year" from his arrival, he received a letter from Constans, by which he was ordered to meet him at Milan (*Ap. ad Const.* 3, 4). Surprised at the summons, he inquired as to its probable cause, and learned that some bishops had been urging Constans to propose to Constantius the assembling of a new council, at which East and West might be represented. On arriving at the great capital of Northern Italy, which was to be so memorably associated with the struggle between the church and Arianism, he was admitted, with Protasius, bp. of Milan, behind the veil of the audience-chamber, and received with "much kindness" by Constans, who told him that he had already written to his brother, "requesting that a council might be held." Athanasius left Milan immediately afterwards, being desired by Constans to come into Gaul, in order to meet Hosius, the venerated bp. of Cordova, and accompany him to the council, which both sovereigns had now agreed to assemble on the frontier line of their empires, at the Moesian city of Sardica. And there, about the end of 343, some 170 prelates met, a small majority being Westerns.

It soon appeared that united action was impossible. The majority, ignoring the councils of Tyre and Antioch, and treating the whole case as open, could not but regard Athanasius as innocent, or, at least, as not yet proved guilty; and he "joined them in celebrating the Divine mysteries" (Hil. *Fragm.* iii. 14). The Eusebian minority, on reaching Sardica, had simply announced their arrival, and then shut themselves up in the lodgings provided for them at the palace, and refused to join their brethren until the persons whom they denounced as convicted men should be deprived of seats in the council. The answer was, that the council was prepared to go into all the cases which could be submitted to it: each party would be free to implead the other. The Eusebian bishops, although urged to confront their adversaries, withdrew from Sardica and established themselves as a council at Philippopolis within the Eastern empire, renewed the sentences against Athanasius, put forth new ones against Julius, Hosius, and others, drew up an encyclic, and adopted a creed (*Apol.* 36, 45, 48 ; *Hist. Ar.* 15, 16, 44 ; Hil. *de Syn.* 34 ; *Fragm.* 3). The prelates at Sardica proceeded with their inquiry, recognized the innocence of Athanasius, and excommunicated eleven Eusebian bishops, as men who "separated the Son from the Father, and so merited separation from the Catholic church." They enacted several canons, including the famous one providing for a reference, in certain circumstances, to "Julius, bp. of Rome," in "honour of Peter's memory," so that he might make arrangements for the rehearing of a prelate's cause. It need hardly be added that they would have no creed but the Nicene. They wrote letters of sympathy to the suffragans of Athanasius and the churchmen of Alexandria, urging the faithful "to contend earnestly for the sound faith and the innocence of Athanasius."

The bold line taken at Sardica provoked the advisers of Constantius to fresh severities; and the Alexandrian magistrates received orders to behead Athanasius, or certain of his clergy expressly named, if they should come near the city. Athanasius, still kept under the emperor's ban, had gone from Sardica to Naissus, and thence, at the invitation of Constans, to Aquileia. There, in company with the bp. Fortunatian, he was admitted to more than one audience; and whenever Constans mentioned Constantius, he replied in terms respectful towards the latter. Constans peremptorily, and even with a threat of civil war, urged his brother to reinstate Athanasius (Socr. ii. 22). The death of Gregory, about Feb. 345 (*Hist. Ar.* 21), gave Constantius an occasion for yielding the point. He therefore wrote to Athanasius, affecting to be solicitous of the Western emperor's assent to an act of his own free clemency. He wrote two other letters (*Apol.* 51 ; *Hist. Ar.* 22), and employed six "counts" to write encouragingly to the exile; and Athanasius, after receiving these letters at Aquileia, made up his mind, at last, to act on those assurances; but not until Constantius could tell Constans that he had been "expecting Athanasius for a year." Invited by Constans to Trèves, Athanasius made a diversion on his journey in order to see Rome again; it was some six years since he had been cordially welcomed by Julius, who now poured forth his generous heart in a letter of congratulation for the Alexandrian church, one of the most beautiful documents in the whole Athanasian series. Julius dwelt on the well-tried worth of Athanasius, on his own happiness in gaining such a friend, on the steady faith which the Alexandrians had exhibited, on the rapture with which they would celebrate his return; and concluded by invoking for his "beloved brethren" the blessings "which eye had not seen, nor ear heard." * Athanasius travelled northward about midsummer; visited Constans, passed through Hadrianople (*Hist. Ar.* 18), proceeded to Antioch, and saw Constantius for the third time (*Ap. ad Const.* 5). The reception was gracious: the emperor valued himself on his impassive demeanour (Ammian. xvi. 10). Athanasius, without vilifying his enemies, firmly desired leave to confront them (*Ap. ad Const. l.c.* ; *Hist. Ar.* 22, 44). "No," said Constantius, "God knows, I will never again credit such accusations; and all records of past charges shall be erased." This latter promise he at once fulfilled, by orders sent to the authorities in Egypt; and he wrote letters in favour of the archbishop to the clergy of Egypt and the laity of Alexandria. One thing he asked, that Athanasius would allow the Alexandrian Arians a single church. Athanasius promptly replied that he would do so, if a church might be granted at Antioch to

* *Apol.* 55. Socrates (ii. 23) inserts eulogistic phrases which Athanasius's text does not give.

the "Eustathian" body, which held aloof from the crypto-Arian bp. Leontius, and whose services, held in a house, he had been attending. The emperor would have agreed to this, but his advisers stood in the way.*

From Antioch Athanasius proceeded to Jerusalem, where an orthodox council met to do him honour, and to congratulate his church. And now he had but to return home and enjoy the welcome which that church was eager to give. This he did, according to the Festal Index, on Oct. 21 (Paophi 24), 346. We see in Gregory Nazianzen's panegyric a picture of the vast mass of population, distributed into its several classes, and streaming forth, "like another Nile," to meet him at some distance from Alexandria; the faces gazing from every eminence at the well-known form, the ears strained to catch his accents, the voices rising in emulous plaudits, the hands clapping, the air fragrant with incense, the city festal with banquets and blazing with illuminations—all that made this return of Athanasius in after-times the standard for any splendid popular display.

(5) *From his Second Return* (346) *to his Third Exile* (356).—His 19th Festal Letter, for 347, begins with a thanksgiving for having been "brought from distant lands." The Egyptian prelates, in council, received the decrees of Sardica. More than 400 bishops of different countries, including Britain, were now in communion with Athanasius; he had a multitude of their "letters of peace" to answer. Many persons in Egypt who had sided with the Arians came by night to him with their excuses: it was a time "of deep and wondrous peace" (*Hist. Ar.* 25), which lasted for a few years. Valens and Ursacius had already, it seems, anathematized Arianism before a council at Milan; but they deemed it expedient to do more. In 347 they appeared at Rome, and presented to Julius a humble apologetic letter, having already written in a different strain to Athanasius, announcing that they were "at peace with him." † He believed at the time that they were sincere; they afterwards ascribed their act to fear of Constans (*Hist. Ar.* 29). This motive, if it existed, was ere long removed; the revolt of Magnentius brought Constans to an ignominious death at the foot of the Pyrenees, in Feb. 350. This tragedy was a severe shock to Athanasius. He received, indeed, letters from Constantius, assuring him of continued favour, and encouraging him to pursue his episcopal work. The Alexandrian authorities were also commanded to suppress any "plotting against Athanasius." Thereupon in presence of high state officers, including the bearers of these letters, Athanasius desired his people, assembled in church, "to pray for the safety of the most religious Constantius Augustus." The response was at once made, "O Christ, help Constantius!" (*Ap. ad Const.* 9, 10, 23; *Hist. Ar.* 24, 51). He had leisure for writing *On the Nicene Definition of Faith* * and *On the Opinions of Dionysius*, his great predecessor in the 3rd cent., whose language, employed in controversy with Sabellianism, had been unfairly quoted in support of Arianism.† [DIONYSIUS.] He also brought out, at this time, what is called his *Apology against the Arians*, although he afterwards made additions to it.‡ It may have been about this time that he chose the blind scholar Didymus, already renowned for vast and varied learning, to preside over the "Catechetical School." [DIDYMUS.] When Magnentius sent envoys to Constantius, one of them visited Alexandria; and Athanasius, in speaking to him of Constans, burst into tears. He at first had some apprehension of danger from Magnentius; but it was soon evident that his real danger was from the Arianizing advisers of Constantius. Valens and Ursacius, having now recanted their recantation, were ready to weave new plots; and Liberius, the new bp. of Rome, was plied with letters against him, which were outweighed, in the judgment of a Roman synod, by an encyclic of eighty Egyptian prelates; and Rome remained faithful to his cause. (See Liberius's letter to Constantius, Hil. *Fragm.* 5. Another letter, in which Liberius is made to say that he had put Athanasius out of his communion for refusing to come to Rome when summoned, is justly regarded as a forgery.) This was in 352; and Athanasius, in May 353, thought it well to send 5 bishops (Soz. iv. 9, and *Fragm. Maff.*), one being his friend Serapion of Thmuis, and 3 presbyters, to disabuse Constantius of bad impressions as to his conduct. Five days later, May 23, Montanus, a "silentiary" or palace chamberlain, arrived with an imperial letter forbidding him to send envoys, but granting a request for himself to go to Milan. Athanasius, detecting an attempt to decoy him, replied that as he had never made such a request, he could not think it right to use a permission granted under a misconception; but that if the emperor sent him a definite order, he would set forth at once (*Ap. ad Const.* 19-21). Montanus departed; and the next news that Athanasius received from Europe was such as to make him forget all personal danger. The Western usurper had been finally overthrown in August; and Constantius, having gone to Arles for the

* See Socr. ii. 23, Soz. iii. 20. They were called after bp. Eustathius (*Hist. Ar.* 4), deposed by Arians in 330. For Leontius, see *de Fuga*, 26; Theod. ii. 24; Hooker, v. 42, 9. Many of the orthodox continued to worship in his churches (*e.g.* Flavian and Diodore). Constantius's absolute dependence on his advisers is scornfully noted in *Hist. Ar.* 69, 70.

† See Newman's note, *Hist. Tracts*, p. 86 (*Apol.* 19): cf. *Apol.* 2; *Hist. Ar.* 26, 44. As Westerns, they naturally treated the bp. of Rome with much greater deference than the bp. of Alexandria; and even in their statement to Julius they betray their distrust of Athanasius. That they should retract, from motives of policy, was for them no unnatural course: cf. Hil. *Fragm.* i. 20.

* In this treatise he guards the Catholic sense of the title "Son," gives some account of the council's proceedings, and defends the language adopted by it, adducing ante-Nicene authorities. (He upholds Origen's orthodoxy.)

† He urged that Dionysius had been speaking simply of Christ's *Manhood* (see Liddon's *Bamp. Lect.* p. 425).

‡ In the Bollandist Life (*Act. SS.*, May 2), the *Apology against Arians* is called the Syllogus, or collection of documents, etc., framed about 342, and afterwards appended to the *Arian History* "ad Monachos." The old name of *Second Apology* is, at all events, clearly misapplied.

winter, was induced by the Arians to hold there, instead of at Aquileia, the council which Liberius and many Italian bishops had requested him to assemble.* The event was disastrous: Vincent, the Roman legate, was induced to join with other prelates in condemning Athanasius; but Paulinus of Trèves had inherited Maximin's steadfastness, and preferred exile to the betrayal of a just cause.

In the Lent of 354 the Alexandrian churches were so crowded that some persons suffered severely, and the people urged Athanasius to allow the Easter services to be held in a large church which was still unfinished, called the Caesarean. The case was peculiar (*Ap. ad Const.* 15; Epiph. *Haer.* 69, 2): the church was being built on ground belonging to the emperor; to use it prematurely, without his leave, might be deemed a civil offence; to use it before dedication, an ecclesiastical impropriety. Athanasius tried to persuade the people to put up with the existing inconvenience: they answered, they would rather keep Easter in the open country. Under these circumstances he gave way. The Arianizers were habitually courtiers, and ready, on occasion, to be formalists likewise; and this using of the undedicated imperial church was one of several charges now urged at court against their adversary, and dealt with in his *Apology to Constantius*; the others being that he had stimulated Constans to quarrel with his brother, had corresponded with Magnentius, and that he had not come to Italy on receiving the letter brought by Montanus. A letter which Athanasius wrote before the Easter of this year, or perhaps of 355, is particularly interesting; he seeks to recall Dracontius, a monk who had been elected to a bishopric, and had weakly fled from his new duties. The earnestness, good sense, and affectionateness of this letter are very characteristic of Athanasius. He dwells repeatedly on the parable of the Talents, reminds Dracontius of solemn obligations, and warns him against imagining the monastic life to be the one sphere of Christian self-denial.† The calm contemplation of fast-approaching trials, which would make a severe demand on Christian men's endurance, shews a "discernment" of the "signs" of 354-5 in Athanasius.

For, in the spring of 355, he would hear of the success of Constantius in terrorizing the great majority of a large council at Milan, which had been summoned at the urgent desire of Liberius. A few faithful men, such as Eusebius of Vercelli, Lucifer of Caliaris, Dionysius of Milan, after a momentary weakness, and Maximus of Naples, who was suffering at the time from illness, alone refused to condemn Athanasius (*Hist. Ar.* 32-34); and in standing out against the incurable tyrannousness of Caesarism, as thus exhibited, must have felt themselves to be contending both for civil justice and for Nicene orthodoxy.

That some *coup d'état* was meditated against Athanasius must have been evident, not only from the emperor's passionate eagerness to have him condemned, and from the really brutal persecution which began to rage throughout the empire against those who adhered to his communion (*Hist. Ar.* 31), but from the appearance at Alexandria, in July or Aug. 355, of an imperial notary, named Diogenes, who, though he brought no express orders, and had no interview with Athanasius, used every effort to get him out of the city. Failing in this, he departed in Dec.; and on Jan. 5, 356, Syrianus, a general, with another notary named Hilarius, entered Alexandria. The Arian party exulted in their approaching triumph; Athanasius asked Syrianus if he had brought any letter from the Emperor. He said he had not. The archbishop referred him to the guarantee of security which he had himself received; and the presbyters, the laity, and the majority of all the inhabitants supported him in demanding that no change should be made without a new imperial letter —the rather that they themselves were preparing to send a deputation to Constantius. The prefect of Egypt and the provost of Alexandria were present at this interview; and Syrianus, at last, promised "by the life of the emperor" that he would comply with the demand. This was on Jan. 18; and for more than three weeks all was quiet. But about midnight on Thursday, Feb. 8, when Athanasius was at a night-long vigil service in St. Theonas's church, preparatory to the Friday service, Syrianus, with Hilarius, and Gorgonius, the head of the police force, beset the church with a large body of soldiers. "I sat down," says Athanasius, "on my throne" (which would be at the extreme end of the church), "and desired the deacon to read the Psalm" (our 136th), "and the people to respond, *For His mercy endureth for ever*, and then all to depart home." This majestic "act of faith" was hardly finished, when the doors were forced, and the soldiers rushed in with a fierce shout, clashing their arms, discharging their arrows, and brandishing their swords in the light of the church lamps. Some of the people in the nave had already departed, others were trampled down or mortally injured; others cried to the archbishop to escape. "I said I would not do so until they had all got away safe. So I stood up, and called for prayer, and desired all to go out before me . . . and when the greater part had gone, the monks who were there, and certain of the clergy, came up to me and carried me away." And then, he adds, he passed through the mass of his enemies unobserved, thanking God that he had been able to secure in the first instance his people's safety, and afterwards his own. As on a former occasion, he deemed it his duty to accept an opportunity of escape, especially when the sacrifice of his life would have been ruinous to the cause of the church in Egypt (see Augustine, *Ep.* 228, 10); and he therefore concealed himself in the country, "hiding himself," as the *Arian History*, c. 48, employs the prophet's words, "for a little moment, until the indignation should be overpast."

(6) *From his Third to his Fourth Exile* (356-362).—On leaving Alexandria, Athanasius at first thought of appealing in person to Con-

* See Liberius's letter to Hosius in Hil. *Fragm.* 6. The spurious letter referred to above (as to which see de Broglie, *L'Egl. et l'Emp.* 2me part. i. 233) begins "Studens paci," and forms *Fr.* 4.

† "I know of bishops who do, and of monks who do not, fast."

stantius, who could not, he tried to hope, have sanctioned the late outrage. But he was deterred by the news of one woe following upon another (*Ap. ad Const.* 27, 19). Bishops of the West who had refused to disown him were suffering under tyranny, or had been hurried into exile. Among the latter class was the Roman bishop himself, who had manfully spurned both gifts and menaces (Theod. ii. 16); and Hosius, on addressing to Constantius a remonstrance full of pathetic dignity, had been sent for to be detained at Sirmium. Then came news which touched Athanasius more closely. It was given out that one George, a Cappadocian of evil reputation and ruthless temper, was coming to supersede him; and that a vague creed, purporting to be simply Scriptural, but in fact ignoring the Nicene doctrine, was to be proposed for his suffragans' acceptance. This last report set him at once to work on a *Letter to the Egyptian and Libyan Bishops*. But he had soon to hear of a repetition of the sacrileges and brutalities of the days of Gregory. As before, Lent was the time chosen for the arrival of the usurper. Easter brought an increase of trouble in the persecution of prelates, clergy, virgins, widows, the poor, and even ordinary Catholic householders. On the evening of the Sunday after Pentecost, when "the brethren" had met for worship, apart from the Arians, in the precincts of a cemetery, a military commander, named Sebastian, a fierce-tempered Manichean, whose sympathies went with George, came to the spot with more than 3000 soldiers, and found some virgins and others still in prayer after the general congregation had broken up. On their refusal to embrace Arianism, he caused them to be stripped, and beaten or wounded with such severity that some died from the effects, and their corpses were kept without burial. This was followed by the banishment of sixteen bishops, doubtless for rejecting the new-made creed; more than thirty fled, others were scared into an apparent conformity, and the vacated churches were given over to men whose moral disqualifications for any religious office were compensated by their profession of Arianism. Tragical as were these tidings, Athanasius still clung to his purpose of presenting himself before Constantius, until he learned that one imperial letter had denounced him as a fugitive criminal who richly merited death, and another had exhorted the two Ethiopian sovereigns to send Frumentius to Alexandria, that George might instruct him in the knowledge of "the supreme God."

Then it was that Athanasius, accepting the position of a proscribed man who must needs live as a fugitive, "turned back again," as he says, "towards the desert," and sought for welcome and shelter amid the innumerable monastic cells. Anthony had died at the beginning of the year, desiring that a worn-out sheepskin cloak (the monk's usual upper dress), which when new had been the gift of Athanasius, might be returned to him (*Vit. Ant.* 91). As Athanasius appears to have made secret visits to Alexandria, he probably spent some time among the recluses of Lower Egypt, but he also doubtless visited what Villemain calls "the pathless solitudes which surround Upper Egypt, and the monasteries and hermitages of the Thebaid." A veil of mystery was thus drawn over his life; and the interest was heightened by the romantic incidents naturally following from the Government's attempts to track and seize him. When comparatively undisturbed, he would still be full of activities, ecclesiastical and theological. Athanasius made those six years of seclusion available for literary work of the most substantial kind, both controversial and historical. The books which he now began to pour forth were apparently written in cottages or caves, where he sat, like any monk, on a mat of palm-leaves, with a bundle of papyrus beside him, amid the intense light and stillness of the desert (Kingsley's *Hermits*, p. 130, 19). He finished his *Apology to Constantius*, a work which he had for some time in hand, and which he still hoped to be able, in better days, to deliver in the emperor's presence. He met the taunts of "cowardice" directed against him by the Arians with an *Apology for his Flight*. To the same period belong the *Letter to the Monks*, with the *Arian History* (not now extant as a whole), which it introduces (and as to which it is difficult to resist the impression that part of it, at least, was written under Athanasius's supervision, by some friend or secretary); a *Letter to Serapion*, bp. of Thmuis, giving an account of the death of Arius, the details of which he had learned from his presbyter Macarius, while he himself was resident at Trèves; and, above all, the great *Orations* or *Discourses against the Arians*. These last have been described by Montfaucon as "the sources whence arguments have been borrowed by all who have since written in behalf of the Divinity of the Word." The first discourse is occupied with an exposition of the greatness of the question at issue; with proofs of the Son's eternity and uncreatedness, with discussion of objections, and with comments on texts alleged in support of Arianism (*i.e.* Phil. ii. 9, 10; Ps. xlv. 7, 8; Heb i. 4). The second, written after some interval, pursues this line of comment, especially on a text much urged by Arians in the LXX version (Prov. viii. 22). The third explains texts in the Gospels, and in so doing sets forth the Christ of the church, as uniting in Himself true Godhead and true Manhood; and it then passes to the consideration of another Arian statement, that the Sonship was a result of God's mere will. Differing from other writers, Dr. Newman considers the fourth Discourse to be an undigested collection of notes or memoranda on several heresies, principally that which was imputed to his friend Marcellus, and to persons connected with him—an imputation which Athanasius, about 360, began to think not undeserved. It may be thought by some who have no bias against the theology of the Discourses that his tenderness towards an old associate is in striking contrast with the exuberance of objurgation bestowed on the Arian "madmen" and "foes of Christ." But not to urge that the 4th cent. had no established rules of controversial politeness, and that the acerbity of Greek disputation and the personalities of Roman society had often too much influence on the tone of Christian argument, one must remember that Athanasius is not attacking all members of the Arian communion, but representatives of it who had been conspicuous, not for heterodoxy alone, but for secularity in its worst form, for unscrupulousness, and for violence. He followed up his Discourses by four *Letters to Serapion* of Thmuis, of which the second briefly repeated the teaching of the Discourses, while the others were directed against a theory then reported to him by Serapion as springing up, and afterwards known as Macedonianism; which, abandoning the Arian position in regard to the Son, strove with singular inconsistency to retain it in regard to the Spirit. Athanasius met this error by contending for "a Trinity real and undivided," in which the Spirit was included with the Father and the Son.

The general aspect of church affairs was very unhopeful. At Constantinople an Arian persecution had again set in. But the defection of Hosius in 357, and Liberius in 358, after hard pressure and cruel usage, from the steadfastness which Athanasius had so much admired, must have wounded him to the heart. Yet he speaks of them with characteristic and most generous tenderness, and with full recognition of the trials under which they had given way (*Hist. Ar.* 45, 41; *Apol.* 89; *de Fugâ,* 5). In 359 the general body of Western bishops, at the council of Ariminum, were partly harassed and partly cheated into adopting an equivocal but really Arian confession, which was also adopted at the beginning of 360 by the legates of the Eastern council of Seleucia. An account of the earlier proceedings of these two councils was drawn up, in the form of a letter, by Athanasius, who, on the ground of a few words in the opening of this *Letter on the Councils of Ariminum and Seleucia,* has been thought by Tillemont and Gibbon to have been present at any rate at the latter place. The treatise is remarkable for his considerateness towards those of the semi-Arians whose objections to the Nicene Creed were rather verbal than real, while the second creed of Sirmium had driven them into open hostility to the Arians properly so-called, which they had expressed in their council of Ancyra in 358. Athanasius, then expressly naming their leader, Basil of Ancyra, welcomes them as brothers who mean essentially what churchmen mean. He will not for the present urge the Homoousion upon them. He is sure that in time they will accept it, as securing that doctrine of Christ's essential Sonship which their own symbol "Homoiousion" could not adequately guard (*de Syn.* 41). But while exhibiting this large-minded patience and forbearance he is careful to contrast the long series of Arian creeds with the one invariable standard of the orthodox; the only refuge from restless variations will be found in a frank adoption of the creed of Nicaea (*ib.* 32; cf. *ad Afros,* 9).

On Nov. 30 the accession of Julian was formally proclaimed at Alexandria. The Pagans, in high exultation, thought that their time was come for taking vengeance on the Arian bishop, whom they had once before tumultuously expelled for oppressive and violent conduct. They rose in irresistible force, threw George into prison, and on Dec. 24 barbarously murdered him. The Arians set up one Lucius in his place; but Julian, as if to shew his supercilious contempt for the disputes of "Galileans," or his detestation of the memory of Constantius, permitted all the bishops whom his predecessor had exiled to return; and Athanasius, taking advantage of this edict, reappeared in Alexandria, to the joy of his people, Feb. 22, 362.

One of his first acts was to hold a council at Alexandria for the settlement of several pressing questions. (*a*) Many bishops deeply regretted their concessions at Ariminum in 359: how were they to be treated? (*b*) It had become urgently necessary to give some advice to Paulinus and his flock at Antioch, with a view to healing the existing schism there. (*c*) A dispute which had arisen as to the word "hypostasis" had to be settled. (4) A correct view as to the Incarnation and the Person of Christ had to be established. The work before the council was that of harmonizing and reconciling. A synodal letter, or "Tome," addressed "to the Antiochenes" (*i.e.* to Paulinus and his flock), and composed by Athanasius, is one of the noblest documents that ever emanated from a council. But it came too late to establish peace at Antioch. Lucifer of Caliaris had taken upon him to consecrate Paulinus as the legitimate bp. of Antioch, and so perpetuated the division which his wiser brethren had hoped to heal.

The pagans of Alexandria had been rebuked by Julian for the murder of George, but he lent a ready ear to their denunciations of Athanasius as a man whose influence would destroy their religion. Julian assured them that he had never intended Athanasius to resume "what is called the episcopal throne"; and peremptorily commanded him to leave Alexandria; the imperial edict was communicated to Athanasius on Oct. 23 (=Paophi 27, *Fest. Ind., Fragm. Maff.*). The faithful gathered around him weeping. "Be of good heart," he said; "it is but a cloud; it will soon pass." He instantly embarked to go up the Nile. But Julian's implied orders were not forgotten; some Government agents pursued his vessel. They met a boat coming down the river, and asked for news of Athanasius. "He is not far off," was the reply. The boat was his own—he himself, perhaps, the speaker (Theod. iii. 9). His facilities of information had given him warning of the peril, and his presence of mind had baffled it. He sailed on towards Alexandria, but concealed himself at Chaereu, the first station from the capital, then proceeded to Memphis, where he wrote his Festal Letter for 363, and then made his way to the Thebaid.

(7) *From his Fourth Exile to his Death* (362-373). It was probably about this time, shortly before Easter, 363, that Athanasius was met, while approaching Hermopolis, by Theodore of Tabenne, the banks of the Nile being thronged by bishops, clergy, and monks. Night apparently favoured this demonstration; Athanasius, having disembarked, mounted an ass which Theodore led, and pursued his way amid a vast body of monks bearing lanterns and torches, and chanting psalms. He stayed some time at Hermopolis and Antinoe, for the purpose of preaching;

then proceeded southwards to Tabenne. At midsummer, according to another narrative, he was at Antinoe, apprehensive of being arrested and put to death, when Theodore and another abbot named Pammon came to see him, and persuaded him to embark with them in Theodore's closely covered boat, in order to conceal himself in Tabenne. Athanasius was in prayer, agitated by the prospect of martyrdom, when Theodore, according to the story, assured him that Julian had at that very hour been slain in his Persian war. The day of Julian's death was June 26, 363.

"The cloud had passed," and Athanasius returned by night to Alexandria. After his arrival, which was kept secret, he received a letter from the new emperor Jovian, desiring him to resume his functions, and to draw up a statement of the Catholic faith. Athanasius at once assembled a council, and framed a synodal letter, in which the Nicene Creed was embodied, its Scripturalness asserted, and the great majority of Churches (including the British) referred to as professing it: Arianism was condemned, semi-Arianism pronounced inadequate, the Homoousion explained as expressive of Christ's real Sonship, the coequality of the Holy Spirit maintained in terms which partly anticipate the language of the Creed of Constantinople. On Sept. 5 Athanasius sailed to Antioch, bearing this letter. He was most graciously received, while the rival bp. Lucius and his companions were rebuffed with some humour and some impatience by the blunt soldier-prince, who, however, during his brief reign, shewed himself as tolerant as he was orthodox. The general prospects of the church must now have seemed brighter than at any time since 330. Liberius was known to have made a full declaration of orthodoxy; and many Western bishops, responding to the appeals of Eusebius and Hilary of Poictiers, had eagerly renounced the Ariminian Creed and professed the Nicene. But the local troubles of Antioch were distressing; and Athanasius, seeing no other solution, recognized their bishop Paulinus as the true head of the Antiochene church, on his appending to his signature of the Tome a full and orthodox declaration, which, according to Epiphanius (*Haer.* 77, 20), Athanasius himself had framed.

Having written his Festal Letter for 364 at Antioch, Athanasius reached home, apparently, on Feb. 13, a few days before Jovian's death. Valentinian I. succeeded, and soon afterwards assigned the East to his brother Valens. The Alexandrian church was not at first a sufferer by this change of monarchs; and 364-365 may be the probable date for the publication of the *Life of Anthony*, which Athanasius addressed "to the monks abroad," *i.e.* those in Italy and Gaul. But, ere long, his troubles to some extent reappeared. According to the Egyptian documents, it was the spring of 365 when Valens issued an order for the expulsion of all bishops who, having been expelled under Constantius, had been recalled under Julian, and thereby announced that he meant to follow the Arian policy of Constantius. On May 5 this order reached Alexandria, and caused a popular ferment, only quieted on June 8 by the prefect's promise to refer the case of Athanasius to the emperor. If we may combine his statement with Sozomen's (who, however, places these events in a subsequent year), we should suppose that the prefect was but biding his time; and on the night of Oct. 5, Athanasius, having doubtless been forewarned, left his abode in the precinct of St. Dionysius's church, and took refuge in a country house near the New River. For four months the archbishop's concealment lasted, until an imperial notary came to the country house with a great multitude, and led Athanasius back into his church, Feb. 1 (Mechir 7), 366. His quiet was not again seriously disturbed, and Athanasius was free to devote himself to his proper work, whether of writing or of administration. His Festal Letter for 367 contained a list of the books of Scripture which, so far as regards the New Testament, agrees precisely with our own (see, too, *de Decr.* 18). The canonical books are described as "the fountains of salvation, through which alone" (a mode of speaking very usual with Athanasius) "is the teaching of religion transmitted"; a second class of books is mentioned, as "read" in church for religious edification; the name "apocryphal" is reserved for a third class to which heretics have assigned a fictitious dignity (Westcott, *On the Canon*, pp. 487, 520). To this period has been assigned the comment on doctrinal texts which is called a treatise *On the Incarnation and against the Arians*; but its entire genuineness may be reasonably doubted. In or about 369 he held a council at Alexandria, in order to receive letters from a Roman council held under Damasus, the successor of Liberius, and also from other Western prelates, excommunicating Ursacius and Valens, and enforcing the authority of the Nicene Creed. Hereupon Athanasius, in a synodal letter addressed *To the Africans*, i.e. to those of the Carthaginian territory, contrasts the "ten or more" synodical formulas of Arianism with the Nicene Creed, gives some account of its formation, and exposes the futile attempt of its present adversaries to claim authority for the later, as distinct from the earlier, proceedings of the Ariminian council. It appears that on Sept. 22, 369, Athanasius, who had in May 368 begun to rebuild the Caesarean church, laid the foundations of another church, afterwards called by his own name (*Fest. Ind.*). We find him excommunicating a cruel and licentious governor in Libya, and signifying the act by circular letters. One of these was sent to Basil, who had just become exarch, or archbp., of Caesarea in Cappadocia, and had received, perhaps at that time, from Athanasius, a formal notification of the proceedings of the council of 362 (*Ep.* 204). Basil immediately announced to his own people the sentence pronounced in Egypt; the strong sense of church unity made such a step both regular and natural, and he wrote to assure Athanasius that the offender would be regarded by the faithful at Caesarea as utterly alien from Christian fellowship (*Ep.* 60). This led to a correspondence, carried on actively in 371. Basil, who had troubles of all kinds weighing upon his spirit, sought aid in regard to one of them—the unhappy schism of Antioch (*Ep.*

66). He wanted Athanasius to promote the recognition by the Westerns of Meletius as rightful bp. of Antioch, and to induce Paulinus to negotiate. In the autumn Basil wrote again (*Ep.* 69), and the tone which he adopts towards Athanasius is very remarkable. He calls him the foremost person (literally, the *summit*) of the whole church, the man of "truly grand and apostolic soul, who from boyhood had been an athlete in the cause of religion"—"a spiritual father," whom he longed earnestly to see, and whose conversation would amply compensate for all the sufferings of a lifetime (*Ep.* 69, 80, 82). But although Athanasius consented to act as a medium between Basil and the Westerns (*Ep.* 90), he could not take any direct part in favour of Meletius, whose rival's position he had unequivocally recognized. Nothing came of the application.

Athanasius was far from tolerating, in these latter years of his life, any theories which seemed definitely heterodox respecting what may be called the human side of the Incarnation. If, in his *Letter to Adelphius*, he condemned a certain class of Arians, and vindicated against their cavils the adoration paid to Christ's Manhood, that is, to His one Person Incarnate; if, in his *Letter to Maximus*, he denounced those who spoke of the man Christ as simply a saint with whom the Word had become associated; he was also, in his *Letter to Epictetus*, bp. of Corinth—a tract called forth by a communication from Epictetus—most earnest against some who, while "glorying in the Nicene confession, represented Christ's body as not truly human, but formed out of the essence of Godhead. This was, in fact, the second proposition of the heresy called Apollinarian; the first being that which had attracted the attention of the council of 362, and had been disclaimed by those whom the council could examine—as to the non-existence, in Christ, of a rational soul, the Word being supposed to supply its place. These views had grown out of an unbalanced eagerness to exalt the Saviour's dignity: but the great upholders of Nicene faith saw that they were incompatible with His Manhood and His Headship, that they virtually brought back Docetism, and that one of them, at any rate, involved a debased conception of Deity. In the next year, 372, he combated both these propositions with "the keenness and richness of thought which distinguish his writings generally" (see Newman, *Church of the Fathers*, p. 162; *Praef. ed. Benson*, ii. 7) in two books entitled *Against Apollinaris*. These books are remarkable for the masterly distinctness with which the one Christ is set forth as "perfect God and perfect Man" (i. 16): if words occur in ii. 10 which seem at first sight to favour Monothelitism, the context shews their meaning to be that the Divine will in Christ was dominant over the human; if in the next chapter the phrase "God suffered through the flesh" is called unscriptural, the whole argument shews that he is contending against the passibility of the Saviour's Godhead. Inexact as might be some of his phrases, the general purport of his teaching on this great subject is unmistakable; it is, as he says in *Orat.* iii. 41, that Christ was "very God in the flesh, and very Flesh in the Word." In truth, these later treatises, like the great Discourses, exclude by anticipation both the forms of heresy, in reference to the Person and Natures of Christ, which troubled the church in the next three centuries (see especially i. 11, ii. 10). Athanasius, in the fruits of his work, was "in truth the Immortal" (*Christ. Remembr.* xxxvii. 206): he was continually "planting trees under which men of a later age might sit." It might indeed be said that he "waxed old in his work" (Ecclus. xi. 20).

But the time of work for him came to an end in the spring of 373. The discussions about the year of his death may be considered as practically closed; the Festal Index, although its chronology is sometimes faulty, may be considered as confirming the date of 373, given in the Maffeian Fragment, supported by other ancient authorities, and accepted by various writers. The exact day, we may believe, was Thursday, May 2, on which day of the month Athanasius is venerated in the Western church. He had sat on the Alexandrian throne, as his great successor Cyril says in a letter to the monks of Egypt, "forty-six complete years"; had he lived a few weeks longer, the years of his episcopate would have been forty-seven. Having recommended Peter, one of his presbyters, for election in his place, he died tranquilly in his own house, "after many struggles," as Rufinus says (ii. 3), "and after his endurance had won many a crown," amid troubles which Tillemont ventures to call a continual martyrdom.

Such was the career of Athanasius the Great, as he began to be called in the next generation. Four points, perhaps, ought especially to dwell in our remembrance: (*a*) the deep religiousness which illuminated all his studies and controversies by a sense of his relations as a Christian to his Redeemer; (*b*) the persistency, so remarkable in one whose natural temperament was acutely sensitive; (*c*) the combination of gifts, "firmness with discretion and discrimination," as Newman expresses it, which enabled him, while never turning aside from his great object, to be, as Gregory Nazianzen applies the apostolic phrase, "all things to all men"; and in close connexion with this, (*d*) the affectionateness which made him so tender as a friend, and so active as a peacemaker—which won for him such enthusiastic loyalty, and endowed the great theologian and church ruler with the powers peculiar to a truly lovable man. That he was not flawless, that his words could be somewhat too sharp in controversy, or somewhat unreal in addressing a despot, that he was not always charitable in his interpretation of his adversaries' conduct, or that his casuistry, on one occasion, seems to have lacked the healthy severity of St. Augustine's—this may be, and has been, admitted; but it is not extravagant to pronounce his name the greatest in the church's post-apostolic history.

In 1698 appeared the great Benedictine ed. of his works, enriched by the Life from the pen of Montfaucon, who in 1707 published, in one of the volumes of his *Nova Patrum et Scriptorum Graecorum Collectio*, additional remains collected by his industry. The work on the "Titles of the Psalms" was edited by Nic. Antonelli at Rome, in 1746; and in 1777 appeared at Padua an ed. in 4 vols. fol., combining the labours of previous editors.

A few English translations of some of Athanasius's works had appeared before the publication of any part of the "Library of the Fathers." But the volume of *Historical Tracts of St. Athanasius*, and the two volumes of *Treatises in Controversy with the Arians*, published in that series at Oxford in 1843-1844, under Dr. Newman's editorship, must (whatever exceptions may be taken to a few passages in the notes) be always ranked among the richest treasures of English Patristic literature. These translations have been reprinted and revised in what is now the best collection in English of Athanasius's chief works, with a very valuable introduction, life, and illustrative notes by Dr. A. Robertson, bp. of Exeter, in the *Post-Nicene Fathers*, ed. by Dr. Schaff and Dr. Wace. The *Orations against Arius*, with an account of the life of Athanasius by W. Bright, are pub. by the Clarendon Press, as also his *Historical Writings* according to the Benedictine text, with intro. by W. Bright. A cheap popular Life of Athanasius by R. W. Bush is pub. by S.P.C.K. in their *Fathers for Eng. Readers*; and a cheap trans. of the *Orations* in "A. and M. Theol. Lib." (Griffith). [W.B.]

Athanasius (1), bp. of Anagastus in Cilicia Secunda and metropolitan, a disciple of St. Lucian of Antioch (Philost. *H. E.* iii. 15), reckoned by Arius, in his letter to Eusebius Nicom., among the bishops who coincided with him in doctrine (Theod. *H. E.* i. 5). The great Athanasius (*de Synod.* p. 886) accuses him of having, previous to the council of Nicaea, written blasphemies equal to those of Arius, of which he gives a specimen. He is said by Le Quien, on the authority of the *Lib. Synod. Graec.*, to have supported Arius at the council of Nicaea. Philostorgius (*H. E.* iii. 15) tells us that when Aetius was expelled from his master's house, after his unlucky victory in argument, Athanasius received him and read the Gospels with him. [E.V.]

Athanasius (2), an Arian bp. who succeeded Philip in the see of Scythopolis, *c.* 372. He is charged by Epiphanius with pushing his Arian tenets to the most audacious impiety, asserting that the Son and Holy Spirit were creatures, and had nothing in common with the Divine nature (Epiph. *Haer.* lxxiii. c. 37, p. 885). [E.V.]

Athanasius (3), bp. of Perrha, a see dependent on the Syrian Hierapolis; present at the council of Ephesus, 431, supporting Cyril of Alexandria. Grave accusations, brought against him by his clergy, led him to resign his see. Through the intervention on his behalf of Proclus of Constantinople and Cyril of Alexandria, Domnus II., patriarch of Antioch, summoned a council to consider the matter. Athanasius, refusing to appear, was unanimously condemned by default and deposed from his bishopric, to which Sabinianus was consecrated. After "the Robber Synod" of Ephesus, A.D. 449, had made Dioscorus of Alexandria the temporary ruler of the Eastern church, Sabinianus was in his turn deposed, and Athanasius reinstated at Perrha. Sabinianus appealed to the council of Chalcedon, A.D. 451, where both he and his rival signed as bp. of Perrha. His case was fully heard, and it was determined that the original charges against him should be investigated by Maximus at Antioch. We are in complete ignorance of the issue of this investigation. (Labbe, *Conc*, iv. 717-754; Liberatus Diac. in *Breviario*. Labbe, v. 762; Cave, *Hist. Lit.* i. 479; Christ. Lupus, ii.) [E.V.]

Athanasius (4), bp. of Ancyra in N. Galatia (A.D. 360-369). His father, who bore the same name, was a man of high family and great learning, and had held important offices in the State (ἐθνῶν καὶ πόλεων ἀρχὰς διευθύναντος); but was reputed harsh and unfatherly to his children. This rumour, reaching St. Basil's ears, led him to write a friendly remonstrance, and hence arose a correspondence of which one letter is preserved (*Ep.* 24). The son Athanasius was raised to the see of Ancyra by the Arian Acacius of Caesarea, through whose influence his predecessor Basilius had been deposed at a synod held at Constantinople A.D. 360 (Soz. iv. 25; Philost. v. 1). But notwithstanding this inauspicious beginning, he gave unquestionable proofs of his orthodoxy by taking an active part in the Synod of Tyana (A.D. 367), at which the Nicene symbol was accepted (Soz. vi. 12). By St. Basil he is commended as "a bulwark of orthodoxy" (*Ep.* 25), and Gregory Nyssen praises him as "valuing the truth above everything" (*c. Eunom.* i. ii. 292). Owing to some misunderstanding, however, Athanasius had spoken in very severe terms of St. Basil, misled, as Basil conjectures, by the fact that some heretical writings had been fathered upon him; and the bp. of Caesarea sends an affectionate letter of remonstrance (*Ep.* 25), in which he speaks of Athanasius in the highest terms. At his death Basil writes a letter of condolence to the church of Ancyra, on the loss of one who was truly "a pillar and foundation of the church" (*Ep.* 29). This seems to have happened A.D. 368 or 369 (see Garnier, Basil. *Op.* iii. p. lxxvii. seq.). [L.]

Athenagoras.—I. *Life.*—There is scarcely one catalogue of the ancient writers of the church wherein we find mention of Athenagoras or his works. He is not noticed by Eusebius, Jerome, Photius, or Suidas. But in a fragment of the book of Methodius, bp. of Tyre (3rd cent.), *de Resurrectione Animarum* against Origen, there is an unmistakable quotation from the *Apology* (c. 24, p. 27 B) with the name of Athenagoras appended. This fragment is given by Epiphanius (*Haer.* 64, c. 21) and Photius (*Cod.* 224, 234). Scanty as this information is, it yet assures us of the existence of the *Apology* in the 3rd cent. and its ascription to Athenagoras. Much more is told us by Philippus Sidetes, deacon of Chrysostom (5th cent.), in a fragment preserved by Nicephorus Callistus (Dodwell, *Diss. in Irenaeum*, 429) to this effect: "Athenagoras was the first head of the school at Alexandria, flourishing in the times of Hadrian and Antoninus, to whom also he addressed his *Apology for the Christians*; a man who embraced Christianity while wearing the garb of a philosopher, and presiding over the academic school. He, before Celsus, was bent on writing against the Christians; and, studying the divine Scriptures in order to carry on the contest with the greater accuracy, was thus himself caught by the all-holy Spirit, so that, like the great Paul, from a persecutor he became a teacher of the faith which he persecuted." Philippus says, continues Nicephorus, "that Clemens, the writer of the *Stromata*, was his pupil, and Pantaenus the pupil of Clemens." But Philippus's statement about Pantaenus is not true, according to Clemens and Eusebius; his character as an historian is severely criticized, and his book pronounced valueless by Socrates Scholasticus (*Hist. Eccl.* vii. 27) and Photius (*Cod.* 35, p. 7, Bekker); and his assertion that the *Apology* was addressed to Hadrian and Antoninus is contradicted by its very inscription. Nevertheless, as he was a pupil of Rhodon (head of the school in the reign of Theodosius the Great) he may be supposed to have had some facts as the groundwork of what he has said. The only other source of information about Athenagoras is the inscription of his *Apology* with such internal evidence as may be gathered from his works themselves. The inscription runs thus: "The embassy (πρεσβεία) of Athenagoras of Athens, a Christian philosopher, concerning Christians, to the emperors Marcus Aurelius, Antoninus, and Lucius Aurelius Commodus, Armeniaci, Sarmatici, and, greatest of all, philosophers." Without at present considering the peculiar difficulties involved in this inscription (of which below), we learn from it in general that Athenagoras was an Athenian and a philosopher, which character and profession he evidently retained after his conversion. His connexion with Athens (probably his birth there) and profession of philosophy are thus substantiated; and the manner in which he became converted to Christianity may very well have been as described by Philippus, whose account that he was head of the Academics is probably but an exaggeration of the fact that he had belonged to that sect. That he was ever leader of the Catechetical school of Alexandria cannot be definitely proved. In the *Commentatio* of Clarisse, § 8, is the acute conjecture that the treatise *de Resurrectione* was written at Alexandria rather than Athens, from c. 12, p. 52 A, where the builder of a house is represented as making stalls for his *camels*; and on a supposed Alexandrian tinge in the philosophy of Athenagoras *vide* Brucker (*Hist. Crit. Philosophiae*, iii. 405 seq.). Of his death nothing is known, the idea that he was martyred apparently arising from a confusion between him and Athenogenes. That the *Apology* was really intended to be seen and read by the emperors is obvious; how it reached them is less clear; we are hardly entitled to assert that it was in any formal or public manner delivered to them by Athenagoras himself, an idea which may be due to the title it bears, of Πρεσβεία, or "Embassy." Πρεσβεία, however, according to Stephanus (*Thesaur. Ling. Graec.* iii. col. 543), is occasionally used for an apology, intercession, or deprecation.

II. *Genuine Works.*—These are, (1) the *Apology*; (2) the *Treatise on the Resurrection of the Dead.*

(1) *Apology. Genuineness.*—The testimonies to this work are the inscription which it bears, and the quotation by Methodius given above. Some indeed have supposed that when Jerome speaks of an apology delivered by Justin Martyr to Marcus Antoninus Verus and Lucius Aurelius Commodus, he refers (since these obtained the empire after Justin's death) to the *Apology* of Athenagoras and attributes it to Justin; but it appears that he intends Marcus Aurelius and Lucius Verus (Mosheim, *Dissert. ad Hist. Eccles. pertinent.* i. 279), to whom Justin's *Lesser Apology* was given (*vid. Prolegomena* to Maranus's *Justin*, pt. iii. c. 8, § 4, pp. 93 sqq.). Attempts to prove the work in question to be that of Justin (*vid.* Le Moyne, *Varia sacra*, ii. 171), or of a later author (*vid.* Semler, *Introduction* to Baumgarten's *Theolog. Streitigkeiten*, ii. 70 note) have alike failed. There is nothing whatever in the writings of Athenagoras unsuitable to their assigned age; and Athenagoras's name was not sufficiently known to have been selected for the author of a supposititious book.

Date.—This is a difficult question; some have taken the Commodus of the inscription for Lucius Aelius Aurelius Verus (d. 169), son-in-law and brother of Marcus Antoninus. But Lucius Aelius Aurelius Commodus, Antoninus's son and successor, must be intended; for Verus dropped the name of Commodus after obtaining a share in the government, and could never have been called Sarmaticus; for Sarmatia was not conquered till after his death. Mommsen, following Tentzel, but without MS. authority, would read Γερμανικοῖς for Ἀρμενιακοῖς. As little right had Commodus to the title of "philosopher." Athenagoras may have only intended to include the son in the honours of the father. At all events, the illustration (at c. 18, p. 17 D) of the Divine government, taken from that of the two emperors, father and son, seems conclusive. We have also allusions to the profound peace of the empire, appropriate only between A.D. 176, when Avidius Crassus's insurrection was crushed, and A.D. 178, when the outbreak of the Marcomannic wars occurred. The *Apology* cannot well have been of later date than A.D. 177, since in that year arose the fearful persecution of the Christians of Vienne and Lyons, upon the accusations brought by their slaves; whereas in c. 35, p. 38 B, Athenagoras declares that no slaves of Christians had ever charged their masters with the crimes popularly imputed to them; nor is there any allusion whatever to this persecution, which would hardly have been passed over in silence. We therefore conclude that the *Apology* was written between the end of A.D. 176 and that of A.D. 177.

Analysis.—The *Apology* consists of categorical answers to the three charges usually brought against the Christians, of (*a*) atheism, (*b*) incest, and (*c*) cannibalism. (*a*) They worship one God, and can give a reason why. The philosophers have held like views; Polytheism and its worship are absurd, modern, and the work of demons. (*b*) Incest is most contrary to their pure and even ascetic life. (*c*) They are even more humane than the heathen, condemning abortion, infanticide, and gladiatorial games as murder.

(2) *Treatise on the Resurrection. Genuine-*

ness and Date.—There is no independent external evidence for the authorship of this work; but there is no reason whatever to doubt that, as its inscription informs us, it is from the pen of Athenagoras. It closely agrees with the *Apology* in style and thought, and all that has been said above of the internal evidence for the genuineness of the former work applies equally to this. That such a treatise was in Athenagoras's mind when he wrote the *Apology* appears from the words near its close, c. 36, p. 39 C, "let the argument upon the Resurrection stand over"; from which words we may not unfairly gather that the *Treatise on the Resurrection* shortly followed the former work. This is the only clue to its date which we possess. From the closing sentences of c. 23 (p. 66 C) it seems that it was intended as a lecture. "We have not made it our aim to leave nothing unsaid that our subject contained, but summarily to point out to those who came together what view ought to be taken in regard to the Resurrection" must allude not merely to a few friends who might happen to be present when the book was read, but to a regular audience. From a reference, c. 1, p. 41 B, to an occasional mode for arranging his arguments, it may be supposed that Athenagoras was in the habit of delivering public lectures upon Christianity. The arrangement, too, and peculiar opening of the treatise decidedly favour the view that it was a lecture, somewhat enlarged or modified for publication.

Analysis.—The work consists of two parts: (i) The removal of the objections (1) that God wants the power (2) or the will to raise the dead. (1) He does not want the power to do it, either through ignorance or weakness—as Athenagoras proves from the works of creation; defending his positions against the philosophic objections, that the bodies of men after dissolution come to form part of other bodies; and that things broken cannot be restored to their former state. (2) God wants not the will to raise the dead—for it is neither unjust to the raised men, nor to other beings; nor unworthy of Him—which is shewn from the works of creation. (ii) Arguments for the Resurrection. (1) The final cause of man's creation, to be a perpetual beholder of the Divine wisdom. (2) Man's nature, which requires perpetuity of existence in order to attain the true end of rational life. (3) The necessity of the Divine judgment upon men in body and soul, (*a*) from the Providence, (*b*) from the justice of God. (4) The ultimate end of man's being, not attainable on earth.

III. *Athenagoras as a Writer.*—To most of the apologists Athenagoras is decidedly superior. Elegant, free from superfluity of language, forcible in style, he rises occasionally into great power of description, and his reasoning is remarkable for clearness and cogency; *e.g.* his answer to the heathen argument, that not the idols, but the gods represented, are really honoured. His treatment of the Resurrection is for the most part admirable. Even where the defective science of the day led him into error, *e.g.* in answering the question, apparently so difficult, as to the assimilation of the materials of one human body into another the line taken is one that shews no little thought and ability; and his whole writings indicate a philosophic mind, which amply justifies the title given to him in the inscription of his two works.

His style, however, is not unfrequently somewhat obscured by difficult elliptic or parenthetical passages, and anacolutha (for examples of which see the *Apology*, c. 1, p. 2 C; c. 20, p. 19 B; c. 22, p. 23 B; and *de Resurr.* c. 18, p. 60 D). Among his peculiar words and phrases, Clarisse notices his use of ἄγειν in the sense of *ducere*, to think, and τὰ ἐπισυμβεβηκότα Θεῷ for the attributes of God.

IV. *His Philosophy.*—Mosheim represents Athenagoras as having been the first of the Eclectics. It is far more true to say that he shared in the eclecticism which then pervaded all philosophy. That he had been a Platonist appears, on the whole, from his continual reference to Plato and the thoroughly Platonic view which on many points pervades his works. We easily recognize this view in his language about matter and the souls, angels, natures sensible and intelligible, and the contemplation of God as the end of man's being; and also in that referring to the Son of God as the Logos and Creator (except that this is not at all peculiar to Athenagoras), more especially in his calling the Word "idea (or archetype) and energy" in the work of Creation. He also appears to allude slightly to the doctrine of reminiscences (*de Resurr.* c. 14, p. 55 A). The Platonism of Athenagoras was modified, however, by the prevailing eclecticism (cf. *e.g.* the Peripatetic doctrine of the mean, so alien to Plato, *Resurr.* c. 21, p. 64 B), and still more, of course, by his reception of Christianity, which necessitated the abandonment of such views as the unoriginated nature of the soul. With all this agrees excellently so much of Philippus Sidetes's account as connects Athenagoras with the Academics; whose Platonism was precisely such as is here described. Allusions to the other philosophers are abundant; *e.g.* to Aristotle and the Peripatetics, *Apol.* c. 6, p. 7 A; c. 16, p. 15 D; to the Stoics, *ib.* c. 6, p. 7 B; to the Cyrenaics and Epicureans, *Resurr.* c. 19, p. 62 B. We see from *Apol.* c. 7, p. 8 A, that he regarded the Gentile philosophers as possessing some measure of Divine light in their minds, but unable thereby to come to the full knowledge of God, because this could only be obtained by revelation, which they never sought.

V. *Theology, etc.*—Athenagoras's proof of the Divine unity rests on the propositions, expressed or implied, that God is perfect, self-existent, uncompounded; the Creator, Sustainer, and Ruler of the universe. Were there more gods than one, they could not co-exist and co-work as a community of beings similar to each other, in the same sphere; for things self-existent and eternal cannot be like a number of creatures formed all on one pattern, but must be eternally distinct and unlike. They could not be parts of one whole, for God has no parts. There could be no place for another God in connexion with this universe, for the Creator is over and around His own works. Another God, confined to some other universe of his own, could not concern us; and so would be but a finite being.

The Son of God.—In God, since He is an

eternal, rational Mind, there dwelt from eternity the "*Logos*" ("Reason," "Expression," or "Word") as His Son, and in the Son dwelt the Father. To bring matter into existence, and afterwards give it form and order, the Divine Word "came forth" (*i.e.* the eternal Son assumed, towards the finite, the office and relation of "the Word" or Manifestor of God), to be the Archetype and Effectuating Power of creation (*Apol.* c. 10, p. 10 D). His Incarnation is only indirectly mentioned, in the supposition at c. 21, p. 21 D (*ib.*), of God assuming flesh according to divine dispensation.

The Holy Ghost is said to be the Spirit Who spoke by the prophets, and an Emanation from God (*Apol.* c. 10, p. 10 D), flowing forth and returning as a ray from the sun. It has hence been much disputed whether Athenagoras believed the Blessed Spirit to be a distinct Person, or not. His expressions greatly resemble those used by some whom Justin condemns for their denial of the personality of the Son: "They say that this virtue is indivisible and inseparable from the Father, as the sunlight on earth is indivisible and inseparable from the sun in the heavens" (*Dial. c. Tryph.* c. 128, p. 358 B). But it must be remembered that the apologists present the *actings* and *offices* of the three Blessed Persons of the Godhead in creation, etc., rather than Their eternal *subsistence*; and of necessity do this in a form intelligible to a heathen mind, yet so as not to be confounded with polytheism. It is not doubted that Athenagoras held the personality of the Father, but with "God the Father, and God the Son" (*Apol.* c. 10, p. 11 A) he joins as third, the Holy Spirit; so also c. 12, p. 62 D, and again c. 24, p. 26 D. That two Divine Persons and an impersonal emanation should be thus enumerated together by so philosophic a writer as Athenagoras is not conceivable. The angels, too—indubitably personal beings—are mentioned as holding a place after the Trinity, in Christian theology (c. 10); and it is worthy of notice that, in the passage cited above from Justin, angels as well as the Word are described by the persons whom that writer is condemning as temporary appearances; as if it were the Sadducees, or some similar Jewish sect, of which he is speaking. We are, therefore, decidedly of opinion that the personality of the Holy Spirit is held by Athenagoras; cf. however, Clarisse.

Man he holds to be composed of body and soul, the latter immortal, with spiritual powers of its own (*Apol.* c. 27, p. 31 A); but assigns the rational judgment not to the soul alone, but to the whole compound being, man; perhaps implying that in the actings and expression of thought both the mind and the bodily organs share. Hence he shews that the soul without the body is imperfect; that only when embodied can man be justly judged, or render to God perfect service, in a heavenly life. The sin and misery of man are described, in the Platonic manner, as entanglement with matter (*Apol.* c. 27, p. 30 C), and missing the true aim of his existence (*Resurr.* c. 25, p. 68 B); which is said to be the state of the majority, a prevalence of evil which he connects with the influence of the demons, *i.e.* of fallen angels, or their offspring by human wives, a view common with the apologists. The evil angels he regards as having fallen by misuse of free will, as did also man; cf. *Apol.* c. 25, p. 29 B. Of infants he remarks (*Resurr.* 614, p. 55 D) that they need no judgment, inasmuch as they have done neither good nor evil. The nature of the scheme of redemption is not treated of by Athenagoras.

VI. *Was Athenagoras a Montanist?*—This idea was suggested by Tillemont, who founds it upon two points in the opinions of Athenagoras, his account of prophecy, and his absolute condemnation of second marriages. In the *Apology*, c. 9, p. 9 D, Athenagoras's view of inspiration is thus given: "who" (*i.e.* the prophets) "rapt in mind out of themselves by the impulse of the Spirit of God, uttered the things with which they were inspired; the Spirit using them as if a flute player were breathing into his flute." With this has been compared the language of Montanus (Epiphanius Panar. *Haer.* 48, c. 4, p. 405), where the prophet is said to be as a lyre, the Spirit like the plectrum. So Tertullian, *Against Marcion*, c. 22. Yet similar language is found in Justin (*Dial. c. Tryph.* c. 115, p. 343 A); and Athenagoras may only mean that the prophet was carried beyond himself by the Holy Spirit, and that the words uttered were not his own. The severe condemnation of second marriage, in the works of Athenagoras, is doubtless a point of contact with the Montanists; but the same view is very common with the Greek Fathers (*vid.* Hefele's *Beiträge*, vol. i. lect. 2). Moreover, of the authority and office of the Paraclete, in the sense attributed to Montanus, there is no trace in the writings of Athenagoras.

VII. *Quotations of Scripture, Early Writers, etc.*—The inspiration of Scripture is strongly stated by Athenagoras, e.g. *Apol.* c. 9, p. 9 D. He is seldom careful to quote exactly, so that it is not always certain what version is employed; probably the Septuagint throughout. From the N.T. he often quotes or borrows phrases, without mentioning whence they come. It is treated as authoritative amongst Christians; its maxims being used shewing their discipline and practice (*vid.* Lardner, *Credibility*; Clarisse, *Athenag.* § 55).

It has been disputed whether Athenagoras refers to other Christian writers, especially the *Apology* of Justin Martyr, which some consider him to have made the foundation of his own. Certainly the resemblance between them seems too great to be the result of accident alone. Both Justin and Athenagoras urged that Christians were unconvicted of any crime, that the mere name does not deserve punishment, and that they were no more Atheists than the poets and the philosophers; and both, in a similar manner, shew the unworthiness of sacrificial worship. They give very much the same view of the Christian way of life; and both lay great stress on chastity, and on the confining of marriage to its sole end, the begetting of children. Nearly the same account of the fall of the angels is found in both: the same books are quoted, often the same passages; by both the very same phrases are occasionally employed. This correspondence is especially seen between the exordium of Justin's first *Apology* and that of Athenagoras. Hence Clarisse infers (*Comm. in Athenag.* § 57) that Athenagoras intended to rearrange and epitomize the work of his predecessor. In the treatise *On the Resurrection*, c. 8, p. 48 c, is an apparent imitation of Tatian, *Or. ad Graec.* c. 6, p. 146 B.

VIII. *Editions.*—A good ed. of Athenagoras is that of Otto (Jena, 1857); its text is based on the three earliest MSS. (viz. the Cod. Paris. CDLI., Cod. Paris. CLXXIV., and Cod. Argentoratensis), with which the rest have been collated, some for the first time; the most recent is by E. Schwartz, Leipz. 1891 (*Texte und Untersuchungen*, iv. 2). There is an Eng. trans. in the *Ante-Nicene Fathers*.

IX. *Spurious Works.*—From a careless expression of Gesner, in reference to the books of Antoninus, Περὶ τῶν εἰς ἑαυτόν, a notion arose of the existence, amongst Gesner's books, of a work by Athenagoras with the above title; an idea which, though wholly erroneous, was entertained by Scultatus, and at one time by Tentzel, with some others.

About the close of the 16th cent. there appeared a French romance, entitled *Du vray et parfait Amour*, purporting to be a work of Athenagoras, trans. by M. Fumée, Seigneur de S. Geuillac. Its many anachronisms and whole character prove it, however, the work of some later author, probably Fumée himself. Certainly no Greek original has ever been produced.

The following may be consulted: Clarisse, *Comm. in Athen.*; Hefele, *Beiträge*; Möhler, *Patrol.*; J. Donaldson, *Hist. Christ. Lit.*; L. Arnould, *de Apol. Athen.* (Paris, 1898). [S.M.]

Atticus, archbp. of Constantinople, succeeding Arsacius in March 406. He died Oct. 10, 426. Born at Sebaste in Armenia, he early embraced a monastic life, and received his education from some Macedonian monks near that place. Removing to Constantinople, he adopted the orthodox faith, was ordained presbyter, and soon became known as a rising man. He proved himself one of Chrysostom's most bitter adversaries. If not, as Palladius asserts (c. xi.), the architect of the whole cabal, he certainly took a very leading part in carrying it into execution. The organization of the synod of the Oak owed much to his practical skill (Phot. Cod. 59). The expulsion of Chrysostom took place June 10, 404. His successor, the aged Arsacius, died Nov. 5, 405. Four months of intrigue ended in the selection of Atticus.

Vigorous measures were at once adopted by Atticus in conjunction with the other members of the triumvirate to which the Eastern church had been subjected, Theophilus of Alexandria, and Porphyry of Antioch, to crush the adherents of Chrysostom. An imperial rescript was obtained imposing the severest penalties on all who dared to reject the communion of the patriarchs. A large number of the bishops of the East persevered in the refusal, and suffered a cruel persecution; while even the inferior clergy and laity were compelled to keep themselves in concealment, or to fly the country. The small minority of Eastern bishops who for peace's sake deserted Chrysostom's cause were made to feel the guilt of having once supported it, being compelled to leave their sees and take other dioceses in the inhospitable regions of Thrace, where they might be more under Atticus's eye and hand (Socr. vii. 36; Niceph. xiii. 30; Pallad. c. xx.).

Unity seemed hardly nearer when the death of Chrysostom (Sept. 14, 407) removed the original ground of the schism. A large proportion of the Christian population of Constantinople still refused communion with the usurper, and continued to hold their religious assemblies, more numerously attended than the churches, in the open air in the suburbs of the city (Niceph. xiv. 23, 27), until Chrysostom's name took its place on the registers and in the public prayers of the church of Constantinople.

Atticus's endeavours were vigorously directed to the maintenance and enlargement of the authority of the see of Constantinople. He obtained a rescript from Theodosius subjecting to it the whole of Illyria and the "Provincia Orientalis." This gave great offence to pope Boniface and the emperor Honorius, and the decree was never put into execution. Another rescript declaring his right to decide on and approve of the election of all the bishops of the province was more effectual. Silvanus was named by him bp. of Philippolis, and afterwards removed to Troas. He asserted the right to ordain in Bithynia, and put it in practice at Nicaea, A.D. 425, a year before he died (Socr. vii. 25, 28, 37).

He also displayed great vigour in combating and repressing heresy. He wrote to the bishops of Pamphylia and to Amphilochius of Iconium, calling on them to drive out the Messalians (Phot. c. 52). The zeal and energy he displayed against the Pelagians are highly commended by pope Celestine, who goes so far as to style him "a true successor of St. Chrysostom" (Labbe, *Conc.* iii. 353, 361, 365, 1073; cf. S. Prosper. p. 549; S. Leo. *Ep.* cvi.; Theod. *Ep.* cv.). His writings were quoted as those of an orthodox teacher by the councils of Ephesus and Chalcedon (Labbe, iii. 518, iv. 831).

Atticus was more an actor than a writer; and of what he did publish little remains. A treatise *On Virginity*, combating by anticipation the errors of Nestorius, addressed to Pulcheria and her sisters, is mentioned by Marcellinus, *Chron.* sub ann. 416, and Gennadius, *de Scrip. Eccl.* c. 52.

Socrates, who is a partial witness, attributes to him a sweet and winning disposition which caused him to be regarded with much affection. Those who thought with him found in him a warm friend and supporter. Towards his theological adversaries he at first shewed great severity, and after they submitted, changed his behaviour and won them by gentleness (Socr. vii. 41; Soz. viii. 27). [E.V.]

Attila, king and general of the Huns. For the facts of his life and his personal and moral characteristics see *D. of G. and R. Biogr.* It comes within our scope only to note his influence upon Christendom; though, throughout, it is difficult to separate legend from history. The rapid series of events between the Hunnish attack on the Eastern empire in 441 and the battle of Châlons in 451 has been compared to a deluge of rain which sweeps a district and leaves no further trace than the débris which the torrent has washed down. But in Eastern Europe, though Attila's kingdom was dismembered at his death, the great body of the Huns, who had followed him from the wilds of Central Asia, settled permanently in the wide plains of the Lower Danube; while, viewed as a special instrument of Providence, "a Messiah of grief and ruin," whose mission it was to chastise the sins of Christians, the "*scourge* (or rather *flail*) *of God*" had an abiding influence over Western Christendom, and the virtues and merits of the saints who thwarted him by bold resistance or prudent submission shone forth the brighter, the darker became the picture of the oppressor.

Portents in sky and earth announced to the inhabitants of Gaul that the year 450 was the opening of a terrible epoch (Idat. *Chron.* ann. 450). Servatius, bp. of Tongres, visiting Rome to consult St. Peter and St. Paul, was informed that Gaul would be entirely devastated by the Huns, but that he himself would die in peace before the devastation came (Paul. Diac. ap. Bouquet, *Rec.* i. p. 649). Attila, strengthened by an alliance with Genseric, king of the Vandals (Jorn. *Reb. Get.* 36), had two pretexts for his attack—his claim to the hand of Honoria, and the vindication of the rights of an elder son of a Frank prince against his brother, whom Aetius had given possession of their paternal territory (Prisc. *Exc. Leg.* p. 40). Theodoric, king of the Goths, whose alliance was sought by both Attila and Valentinian, inclined to the side of order, and the Hun, who now took the *rôle* of chastising his rebellious subjects, the Visigoths, marched with five, or perhaps seven, hundred thousand warriors, including many Franks, Burgundians, and Thuringians (Sid. Apoll. *Paneg. Avit.* v. 324), to the banks of the Rhine, which he crossed near Coblenz. He installed himself at Trèves, the Roman metropolis of Gaul, which was pillaged. After one fruitless attempt, he entered Metz on Easter Eve, April 8, slaughtered indiscriminately priests and people, except the bishop, and reduced the city to ashes, all the churches perishing except the oratory of St. Stephen (Paul. Diac. ap. Bouquet, *Rec.* i. p. 650). Rheims, deserted by its inhabitants, was easily reduced, and a Hun struck off the head of its bishop, Nicacius, while he was precenting the words "Quicken me according to Thy word" (Ps. cxix. 25) (Frodoard. *Martyr. Remens.* p. 113). Tongres, Arras, Laon, and Saint-Quentin also fell. The inhabitants of Paris had resolved on flight, but the city was saved by the resolution and devotion of St. Geneviève (Genovefa), the maiden of Nanterre who was warned in a vision that Paris would be spared (*Act. SS. Boll.* Jan. i. 143-147). Attila did not wish to wage war against Christianity, though doubtless some of his followers were stimulated by polemical rancour; he fought against Rome, not its church. Nor did he intend to give up Gaul to indiscriminate pillage; he hoped to crush the Visigoths first, and then to cope separately with Aetius and the Roman forces. About April 10 he left Metz for Orleans. Anianus (St. Agnan), bp. of Orleans, hastened to Arles to apprise Aetius of their danger, but Orleans was only relieved by the influence of the senator Avitus of Clermont, who secured the help of Theodoric, when the gates had actually been opened to the Huns and pillage was beginning (*Vita S. Aniani*, in Bouquet, *Rec.* i. 645). Attila retreated precipitately towards Châlons-sur-Marne, in the *Campi Catalaunici.* Near Troyes he was met by its bishop, Lupus (St. Loup), at whose intercession Attila spared the defenceless inhabitants of Champagne, carrying Lupus with him as a hostage to the banks of the Rhine. For the subsequent military movements and the battle of Châlons, see Thierry, *Hist. d'Attila*, pp. 172-188, 428-437, and art. "Attila" in the *Nouv. Biog. Gén.* In the spring of 452 Attila penetrated into Italy by the passes of the Julian Alps (Prosp. Aquit. *Chron.*), Aetius having sent Valentinian for safety to Rome. Attila received his first check at the walls of Aquileia; but after three months' resistance he observed some storks preparing to leave their nests with their young (Jorn. *Reb. Get.* 42), and, taking this as a favourable omen, redoubled the vigour of his siege, and a century afterwards Jornandes (*ib.*) could scarcely trace the ruins of Aquileia. Milan and Pavia were sacked, and probably also Verona, Mantua, Brescia, Bergamo, and Cremona. An embassy, sent by the people and senate of Rome, to endeavour to obtain Attila's peaceful evacuation of Italy, met the invaders on the Mincio, near Mantua and Vergil's farm. At its head were two illustrious senators and the eloquent Leo the Great, who had been bp. of Rome since 440. His appearance in pontifical robes awoke in Attila some feeling akin to awe, and he retired as before a power superior to his own. Soon after he died from the bursting of a blood-vessel, though not without suspicion of foul play. Cf. Leo I.

Undoubtedly the great and distinguishing feature of the war in the eyes of 5th-cent. Christians would be the threefold repulse of Attila, "*the scourge of God*"; from Orleans by St. Agnan, from Troyes by St. Loup, and, above all, from Rome by St. Leo; so signal a triumph was it of the church's spiritual weapons over the hosts who were held to symbolize the powers of darkness and of Antichrist. It was the final and conclusive answer to the few heathen who still referred all the misfortunes of the empire to the desertion of the ancient polytheism. For a discussion of the various national legends that have clustered around Attila, "the hammer of the world," see *D. C. B.* (4-vol. ed.), *s.v.* The leading authorities for his life are in Gibbon's *Roman Empire* (ed. Smith), iv. 191 (notes). See also his Life by Am. Thierry, 1855. [C.D.]

Augustinus, Aurelius.

A. Early Life.—§§ 1, 2, Name, Materials for biography; § 3. Early life; § 4. Manicheism; § 5. Philosophical period; § 6. Conversion; § 7. Early Christian life: (*a*) as layman, (*b*) as presbyter.

B. Episcopate.—§ 8. Donatism: (*a*) Origin, (*b*) Early history, (*c*) Augustine and the schism; § 9. Paganism and the *de Civitate Dei*; § 10. Pelagianism: (*a*) Origin, (*b*) Zosimus and Julian, (*c*) The semi-Pelagians, (*d*) Doctrinal issues; § 11. Augustine and Greek Christendom; § 12. Augustine and the hierarchy: (*a*) Church authority and episcopate, (*b*) Equality of episcopate, (*c*) Rome and the episcopate: Case of Apiarius, (*d*) Rome and doctrinal authority, (*e*) Ultimate authority; § 13. Death and character.

C. Influence.—§ 14. Writings; § 15. Asceticism and the "Rule": The Church and property; § 16. Intellectual influence: (*a*) Philosophic Theism, (*b*) Ecclesiasticism, (*c*) Predestinarianism; § 17. Bibliography.

A. Early Life.—§ 1. *Name.*—Orosius, *Hist. adv. Pagan.* I. 4; Prosper, *Car. de Ingrat.* i. 3, and *Chron.* ad ann. 430; Claudian Mamert. *de Stat. An.* ii. 10; Bede, *Vit. St. Cuthb.*, give the name as above. The name Aurelius is not given by Possidius, nor is it ever used by Augustine himself nor by any of his correspondents. But the Benedictine editors find it in the earliest MS. titles of his works, and it is probably authentic.

§ 2. *Materials for Biography.*—These are exceptionally ample. For his first thirty-three years we have, in the *Confessions*, the most perfect of religious autobiographies (see below, § 8, *ad init.*). The word "Confessions" *includes* not only the idea of self-accusation, but also that of thanksgiving (see IX. vi. *confiteor tibi dona tua*, and the use of *confiteor* in the Vulgate Psalter). For his career as a Christian and a bishop, we possess an admirably simple and graphic life by his pupil and friend Possidius, bp. of Calamis. The writings and correspondence of Augustine himself copiously supplement the narrative. The Benedictine editors have worked up the whole of the material into a very accurate biography in eight books. It fills 513 columns of the *Patr. Lat.*, and leaves little to be added by others. (See below, § 17.)

§ 3. *Birth and Early Years* (354-373).—Augustine was born at Thagaste in Numidia Proconsularis, on Nov. 13, 354 (for evidence as to this date, see Bened. *Life* in *Patr. Lat.* I. 118). His father Patricius, a jovial, sensual, passionate man, and till near the end of his life a heathen, was one of the *curiales* of the town, but without large means. His mother Monnica was a Christian by parentage, conviction, and character. Augustine acknowledged (*de Vit. Beat.* i. 6) that he owed his all to her; conversely we can trace to her anxious care for her son's spiritual well-being a distinct deepening of her own character (see *Conf.* II. iii. *sub fin.*; IX. viii. ix.). From his mother he received the elements of Christian teaching, and, as he tells us, a devotion to the very name of Jesus Christ which his later spiritual wanderings never wholly extinguished, and which forbade him to find satisfaction in any writings which lacked it (*Conf.* III. iv. 3). As a child he had a severe illness, and demanded baptism. His mother had agreed to allow it; but when he recovered, in accordance with the then prevailing dread of post-baptismal sin, she put off his baptism to riper years. Augustine was one of several children (we read of his brother Navigius, *Conf.* IX. xi., *de Beat. Vit.* i. 6; a sister, *Ep.* 211[4]; nieces, Possid. xxvi.; nephew Patricius and nieces, *Serm.* 356[3], see Bened. *Life,* I. i. 4). He early shewed signs of pre-eminent ability, and his parents, both of whom entertained the ordinary parental ambitions, found means to send him to school at the neighbouring town of Madaura. Here, though he found the study of Greek distasteful, he made good progress; in fact it became clear that he was ripe for the higher schools of Carthage, and he was withdrawn from Madaura. The difficulty of providing the means for his studies at the more expensive and distant capital kept him at home for a year (369-370). He laments bitterly the company he kept and the habits into which he fell at this period. The boyish freak of robbing a pear-tree with his companions weighed heavily on his mind in later years (*Conf.* II. iv. ix.). He tells us, however, with shame, that in order not to be outdone by his companions he boasted of licentious acts which he had not committed. This may modify our natural inferences from the self-accusing language of the *Confessions*.

At last, aided by their wealthy and benevolent neighbour Romanianus, his parents were able to send him to Carthage. Here, at the age of sixteen, Augustine began his "university" life, as a student of Rhetoric. Again he speaks with an agony of remorse of his life as a student. It is certain that he contracted an irregular union, and in 372 he became the father of a son, Adeodatus. But he remained faithful to his mistress until the very eve of his conversion, and watched over his son's education and character. Eventually father and son were baptized together (see below, § 6; also cf. *Conf.* VI. xv. 25). We must infer that his life was on the whole above the average level of student life in Carthage. He tells us that the "best set" among them were given to brutal horse-play, directed especially against shy freshmen; but although he associated with these "eversores," he took no part in their wild doings.

In 371 his father had died, but, aided once more by the kindness of Romanianus, Monnica was able still to keep her son at Carthage. Ambition for social success, and for a future career at the bar, rather than any deeper motive, led him to pursue his studies with ardour. But in his nineteenth year, while reading Cicero's *Hortensius*, he became deeply impressed with the supreme value of Wisdom, as contrasted with the vain hopes and fleeting opinions of the world. From this time onward he is a restless seeker after Truth (*Conf.* III. iv.). His first impulse was toward the Scriptures, but their simplicity repelled him; "they seemed to me to be far inferior to the dignity of Tully."

§ 4. *Manicheism* (373-383).—A baffled inquirer, he was attracted by the Manichean system, which appears to have been actively pushed in Africa at this period. This is not the place for a description of Manicheism. From Augustine's many allusions to its tenets, it appears to have been a strange medley of dualism and materialism, asceticism and licence, theosophy and rationalism, freethought and superstition. What specially attracted Augustine appears to have been the high moral pretensions of the sect, their criticism of Scripture difficulties, and their explanation of the origin of evil by the assumption of an independent evil principle. For nine years (373-382, *Conf.* IV. i., *de Util. Cred.* 2) Augustine was an ardent Manichean. He brought over his friends Alypius and Honoratus, and his patron Romanianus, to the same convictions, and delighted in controversy with Catholics. He remained an "auditor" only. The "electi" were bound to strict continence, and Augustine was increasingly conscious of the chasm between his ideal and his practice. "Make me chaste, but not yet," was his prayer during this period of his life (*Conf.* VIII. vii.). Augustine completed his studies, and returned to Thagaste as a teacher of grammar. His mother, overwhelmed with horror at his new opinions, refused to receive him at home. At first, therefore, he lived with Romanianus. Monnica's prayers were answered by a consoling dream (*Conf.* III. xi.) and a friend, a bishop, himself a convert from Manicheism, whom she entreated to argue with her son, while wisely refusing her request, dismissed her with the words, "It cannot be that the son of those tears of yours should be lost." She accepted the words as a voice from Heaven, and received Augustine into her household. The death of a dear friend—Augustine was a man of warm friendships (*Conf.* IV. ix.)—moved him to leave Thagaste, and return, as a teacher of Rhetoric, to Carthage. Here he studied zealously, devoting attention to the "liberal arts," astronomy, and other subjects, and lived a life of cultivated society and successful literary effort. He tells us of a prize poem which won a crown in the theatre from the proconsul Vindicianus, a wise old physician who convinced him (but see *Conf.* VII. vi.) of the futility of astrology (*Conf.* IV. iii.; this apparently occurred at Carthage). About this time he wrote a work in two or three books, *de Pulcro et Apto*, which he inscribed to Hierius, a professor of Rhetoric at Rome, whom he had come to admire by reputation. These books he did not preserve; they appear to have been his first. Meanwhile, he began to be less satisfied with the Manichean view of existence; these misgivings were intensified by disillusion in regard to the morals of the *electi* (*de Moribus Man.* 68 sqq.). But his Manichean friends urged him to await the arrival at Carthage of Faustus, a "bishop" of the sect, who enjoyed a reputation for brilliant ability and learning, and who could be trusted to resolve all his doubts. But when the great Faustus appeared, Augustine soon discovered him to be a very ordinary person, "of charming manner and pleasant address, who said just what the others used to say, but in a much more agreeable style" (*Conf.* V. iii. 6). When, after his addresses to the crowd, Augustine laid before him some of his doubts, his mediocrity was transparent. "He knew that he did not know, and was not ashamed to confess the fact . . . and for this I liked him all the better." But he liked the system all the less; and without formally separating from the Manicheans, he adopted an "academic" suspense of judgment in regard to the opinions he had hitherto adopted; henceforth he held them provisionally, pending the discovery of something better (*de Vit. Beat.* i. 4).

§ 5. *Rome. Philosophy* (383-386).—Mainly in disgust at the rough and disorderly students of Carthage (*Conf.* V. viii.), Augustine now migrated to Rome. With bitter self-reproach he tells us of the deceit by means of which he left his mother, who had followed him to Carthage, behind (*Conf.* V. viii.). At Rome, his host was a Manichean, Alypius and other Manichean friends surrounded him, and in a severe illness he received the greatest kindness from them all. But the students of Rome disappointed Augustine. They were less rude, but also less honest, than those of Carthage, especially in the matter of payment of their fees (*Conf.* V. xi.). Presently (about the summer of 384) Symmachus, the *Praefectus Urbi*, was commissioned by the Milanese to find them a professor of Rhetoric. Augustine, by the aid of his Manichean friends, obtained the post, and travelled, at the public expense, to Milan. Here he was attracted by the eloquence of Ambrose, then at the height of his fame, and soon made his acquaintance. "I began to love him, not at first as a teacher of the truth, which I despaired of finding in Thy Church, but as a fellow-creature who was kind to me." Contemptuous of the subject-matter of his sermons, Augustine listened to them as an interested professional critic. "I cared not to understand what he said, but only to hear how he said it." But it was impossible to keep form and substance wholly apart, and by degrees he began to realize that the case for Catholic Christianity was not wholly beneath discussion. This was especially the case with regard to the O.T., a principal target for Manichean ridicule. The allegorical method of exegesis by which Ambrose explained every difficulty struck away the substratum of literalism upon which Manichean objections were based. "For while I read those Scriptures in the letter, I was slain in the spirit." But though one main foundation of his Manicheism was thus giving way, the materialistic presuppositions remained. "Had I been able to conceive of a spiritual substance, all their devices would have been broken, but this as yet I found impossible." He remained in a state of suspense; his philosophic position was that of the "New Academy," one of pure negation. However, pending further light, he resumed the position he had occupied in boyhood of a catechumen in the Catholic church (*Conf.* V. xiv.). Alypius, who was in legal practice, had accompanied him to Milan, and presently their friend Nebridius joined them. Monnica, probably accompanied by his brother Navigius, soon followed her son to Milan (*Conf.* VI. ix.). The friends appear (*Conf.* VIII. viii.) to have hired a roomy house and garden. Augustine's worldly prospects seemed excellent, a career of official distinction was opening before him (*Conf.* VI. xii.); his mother, hoping that it would lead to his baptism, encouraged him in the selection of a wife. But two years had to pass before the lady was of age (*Conf.* VI. xiii.). Meanwhile his mistress was dismissed (*ib.* xv.), to his and her great grief, and Augustine took another.

Augustine was now thirty years of age. He had almost wholly shaken off Manicheism, and was, as his mother saw, steadily gravitating towards the Catholic church. His successful and interesting work, honourable position, and delightful social surroundings made his lot outwardly enviable. But he pronounces, and apparently with some truth, that at this period he touched his lowest moral level (*Conf.* VI. xvii., VII. i., VIII. v.). At any rate the contrast between his actual life and his habitual idealism was never more painfully realized. His ideal was the philosophic life, and but for his matrimonial plans and his still active ambition, he would probably have joined his friends in founding a small philosophic community with a common purse and household (*Conf.* VI. xiv.; *c. Academ.* II. ii. 4, *de Beat. Vit.* i. 4, ne in philosophiae gremium celeriter advolarem, uxoris honorisque illecebra detinebar). But his enthusiasm burned low (*c. Acad.* II. ii. 5), until it was kindled afresh by his study of the Platonic philosophy. A friend (apparently Theodorus, who became consul in 399—see *Retr.* I. ii. *Displicet autem*, etc., and *Conf.* VII. ix. *immanissimo typho turgidum*) put into his hands (*Conf.* VII. ix., *de Beat. Vit.* i. 4) some translations of the neo-Platonist authors, probably by Victorinus. The effect was rapid and profound. Much Christian truth he found there, but not inward peace: the eternal Word, but not Christ the Word made flesh. But his flagging idealism was braced, he was once for all lifted out of materialism, and his tormenting doubts as to the origin of evil were laid to rest by the conviction that evil has its origin in the will, that evil is but the negation of good, and that good alone has a substantive existence (*Conf.* VII. vii. xiv.). His first impulse was to give up all earthly ties ("omnes illas ancoras," *Vit. Beat.* 4), resign his professorship, and live for philosophy alone. But this he delayed to do, until, after his conversion, a serious lung-attack gave him what was now a welcome excuse (*Conf.* IX. ii., cf. *Solil.* I. i. 1; *c. Acad.* I. i. 3; *de Beat. Vit.* i. 4). Meanwhile he read with care the Epistles of St. Paul, in which he found a provision for the disease of sin, which he had vainly sought in the Platonic books. But his life remained unregenerate, and his distress thickened. He then laid his case before Simplicianus, the spiritual adviser, and eventually the successor, of Ambrose. Simplicianus described to him the conversion of the aged Victorinus, to whose translation of the Platonists he had owed so much (*Conf.* VIII. ii.). Augustine longed to follow the example of his public profession of faith, but the flesh still held him back, like a man heavy with drowsiness who sinks back to sleep though he knows that the hour for rising has struck. So he went on with his usual life.

§ 6. *Conversion* (386-387).—One day a Christian fellow-townsman, Pontitianus, who held an appointment at court, called to visit Alypius. Observing with pleasure a volume of St. Paul's Epistles, he went on to talk to his friends of the wonderful history of the hermit Anthony, whose ascetic life had begun from hearing in church a passage of the gospel (Matt. xix. 21), on which he had promptly acted; he then described the spread of the monastic movement, and informed his astonished hearers that even at Milan there was a monastery in existence. As Pontitianus told his tale, Augustine was filled with self-reproach. Conscience shamed him that after ten years of study he was still carrying a burden which men wearied by no research had already cast aside. When Pontitianus had gone, he poured out his incoherent feelings to the astonished Alypius, and then, followed by his friend, fled into the garden. "Let it be now—let it be now," he said to himself; but the vanities of his life plucked at his clothes and whispered, "Do you think you can live without us?" Then again the continence of the monks and virgins confronted him with the question, "Can you not do as these have done?" Alypius watched him in silence. At last he broke down and, in a torrent of tears, left his friend alone. He threw himself down under a fig-tree, crying passionately, "Lord, how long?—to-morrow and to-morrow!—why not now?" Suddenly he heard a child's voice from the next house repeating, in a sing-song voice, "Take and read" (*tolle, lege*). He tried to think whether the words were used in any kind of children's game; but no, it must be a divine command to open the Bible and read the first verse that he should happen upon. He thought of Anthony and the lesson in church. He ran back to Alypius and opened "the Apostle" at Rom. xii. 13, 14, "Not in rioting and drunkenness, not in chambering and wantonness, not in strife and envying; but put ye on the Lord Jesus Christ, and make not provision for the flesh to fulfil the lusts thereof." "No further would I read, nor was it necessary." The peace of God was in his heart, and the shadows of doubt melted away. He marked the passage and told Alypius, the friends exchanged confidences, and Alypius applied to himself the words, a little further on, "Him that is weak in the faith receive" (Rom. xv. 1). They went in, and filled the heart of Monnica with joy at the news (*Conf.* VIII. viii.). It was now the beginning of the autumn vacation. Augustine decided to resign his chair before the next term, and meanwhile wrote to Ambrose to announce his desire for baptism. His friend Verecundus, who was himself on the eve of conversion, lent his country house at Cassiciacum, near Milan, to Augustine and his party; there they spent the vacation and the months which were to elapse before baptism (winter 386-387). At Cassiciacum he spent a restful, happy time with his mother and brother, his son Adeodatus, Alypius, and his two pupils, Licentius and Trygetius, the former a son of his old patron Romanianus. He wrote several short books here, "in a style which, though already enlisted in Thy service, still breathed, in that time of waiting, the pride of the School" (*Conf.* IX. iv.). These were the three books *contra Academicos*, two *de Ordine*, the *de Beata Vita*, and two books of *Soliloquies*; to this period also belong letters 1-4, of which 3 and 4 are the beginning of his correspondence with Nebridius (*Conf.* IX. iii.). Ambrose had, in answer to his request for advice, recommended him to read Isaiah. But he found the first chapter so hard that he put it aside till he should be more able to enter into its meaning. The Psalms, however, kindled his heart at this time. To him, as to many in most diverse conditions, they seemed to interpret the depths of his soul and the inmost experiences of his life (*Conf.* IX. iv.). But Augustine's main intellectual interest was still philosophical. Except when engaged upon the classics with his pupils, or on fine days in country pursuits ("in rebus rusticis ordinandis," *c. Acad.* I. v. 14; cf. II. iv. 10), the time was spent in discussing the philosophy of religion and life. The abovementioned books, of which those *de Ordine* are perhaps the most characteristic, are, excepting of course the *Soliloquies*, in the form of notes of these discussions. The time to give in his name for baptism was approaching, and the party returned to Milan. Augustine was baptized by Ambrose, along with his heart's friend Alypius, and his son Adeodatus. The church music, which Milan, first of all the Western churches, had recently adopted from the East, struck deep into his soul: "The tide of devotion swelled high within me, and the tears ran down, and there was gladness in those tears."

§ 7. (*a*) *Early Christian Life. Death of Monnica. Return to Africa. Life as a Layman* (387-391).—While waiting for baptism at Milan, Augustine had written a short book, *de Immortalitate Animae*, and the first part, *de Grammatica*, of a work on the "liberal arts": the latter, though included by Possidius in his list of Augustine's literary remains, was early lost by him (*Retr.* I. vi.). After the baptism, Augustine, with Alypius, and Evodius, a fellow-townsman, converted before Augustine himself, who had joined him at Milan, set out for Africa, with the intention of continuing their common life. But at Ostia, Monnica was seized with fever, and died "in the fifty-sixth year of her age, and the thirty-third of mine." Augustine's account of her life and character, and of his conversations with her, shortly before her death, on Eternal Life, forms perhaps the most exquisite and touching part of the *Confessions* (IX. viii.-xiii.). He prayed for her soul, believing that what he prayed for was already performed. "Let none have power to drag her away from Thy protection. . . . For she will not answer that she owes nothing, lest she should be confuted and seized by the crafty accuser; but she will answer that her debt has been forgiven by Him, to Whom none can give back the ransom which He paid on our behalf, though He owed it not." Augustine now remained in Rome till the autumn of 388 ("jam post Maximi tyranni mortem," *c. lit. Petil.* III. 30, cf. *Retr.* I. vii.-ix.). Of his life there, the two books *de Moribus Ecclesiae Catholicae et de Moribus Manichaeorum*, the *de Quantitate Animae*, and the first of his three books *de Libero Arbitrio*, are the monument. From them we gather that he lived with Evodius a life of "abundant leisure," entirely given to the studies begun at Cassiciacum. The book on the morals of the Manicheans, founded on his former converse with them at Rome (see above, § 5), was reserved for completion and publication in Africa (xii. 26). At last Augustine crossed with Alypius to Carthage (*de Civ.* XXII. viii.), and returned to Thagaste. A work composed by him here, *de Magistro* (*Conf.* IX. vi.; *Retr.* I. xii.), is in the form of a dialogue with Adeodatus, and Augustine assures us that the substance of the words was really from the lips of his son at the age of sixteen, *i.e.* not later than 388. The boy died young, full of piety and promise; we do not know the date, but he was present at Monnica's death (*Conf.* IX. xi.), and very probably lived to accompany his father to Africa. At Thagaste Augustine and his friends lived on his paternal estate for nearly three years, a quiet, industrious, and prayerful life. Nebridius (*Ep.* 5) condoles with him for having to give so much time to the *negotia civium*; but evidently there was plenty of leisure for study. We saw above (§ 6) that Augustine's studies were, up to the present, philosophical rather than Biblical. His ordination found him still but little versed in Scripture (*Ep.* 213). His continued correspondence with Nebridius (*Epp.* 5-14) shews the continued predominance of philosophical interest; the same may be said of the writings of the period, *de Genesi adv. Manichaeos, de Musica, de Magistro, de Vera Religione*, and parts of the *Liber de Diversis Quaestionibus LXXXIII*. The *de Musica* was a portion of the above-named unfinished work on the "liberal arts": he wrote it at the request of an African bishop. It is interesting as giving one side of Augustine's view of secular culture, for which he claims, in the spirit of Plato, that if rightly used, it leads up to God, the underlying Truth of all things. The other works of this period are still pervaded with the Manichean controversy. This is the origin of the *de Vera Religione*, one of Augustine's ablest works; years later (about 414) he refers Evodius to it for the theistic argument (*Ep.* 162, 2). There is a difference of opinion as to the exact time at which Augustine sold his father's estate, and as to the monastic or lay character of the life at Thagaste. The Benedictine *Life* (III. ii.-v.), maintaining that Augustine's settlement at Thagaste was strictly monastic, accounts for the fact that he lived on his patrimony by supposing that he did so as a tenant of the purchaser. Of this there is no evidence whatever. The most probable inference from the crucial passage (*Serm.* 355, 2) combined with the statements of Possidius, is briefly as follows:—Augustine and his friends lived at his home in Thagaste, realizing approximately the ideal, formed already at Milan (*Conf.* VI. xiv.), and partially realized at Cassiciacum, of a common life of study and detachment from worldly cares. The *tendency* to a monastic ideal was there, and as time went on, Augustine determined to sell his property, and find a home more suitable for a monastery. Possibly the importunate demands of his fellow-citizens upon his kindness (see above) made Thagaste itself unsuitable. Hand in hand with the question of the place went the question of recruits. Augustine travelled to different places in search of a suitable site—avoiding towns where the see was vacant, for he knew that his growing fame might lead men to think of him. Among other places, he came to Hippo (*Bona*), where he knew of a young official whom he hoped to enlist for his monastery ("juvenis veni ad istam civitatem, quaerebam ubi constituerem monasterium . . . veni ad istam civitatem propter videndum amicum quem putabam lucrari me posse Deo ut nobiscum esset in monasterio." The *monasterium* is clearly prospective). This was probably early in 391. Augustine had come to Hippo intending to stay no time, "with nothing but his clothes"; but as it happened, he entered the church just as Valerius, the aged bishop, was addressing the people on the necessity of choosing a new presbyter. Valerius, by birth a Greek (Possid. v. "homo natura Graecus"), wanted a fluent Latin preacher. Augustine's reputation had come before him. With one accord the people seized Augustine, and presented him to Valerius for ordination. With sincere reluctance and many tears Augustine yielded; Hippo became his home, and the Christian ministry his calling. Knowing of his plans, Valerius gave him a *monasterium* in the episcopal gardens. He had possibly already sold his small estate at Thagaste; if not, he did so now: the proceeds were spent on the poor of that place, and the people of Hippo approved and felt no jealousy (see *Ep.* 126[7], 157[39]). He assembled in his monastery a number of brethren like-minded, each with nothing of his own and all things common; above all, the common aim, "commune nobis ut esset magnum et uberrinum praedium ipse Deus."

(*b*) *Augustine a Presbyter of Hippo* (391-395).—Augustine at the time of his ordination as presbyter (he does not appear to have passed, as Ambrose had formally done, through the diaconate) was a Christian Platonist. His temper was absolutely Christian, his stock of ideas wholly Platonic. He had used the Bible devotionally rather than worked at its theology. Fully conscious of this, he obtained from his bishop a short period of leisure in order to master the minimum of Scriptural knowledge necessary for the discharge of his office (*Ep.* 21). At Easter, 391, he was entrusted with the *traditio symboli.* His addresses to the candidates for baptism on that occasion are still extant (*Serm.* 214-216). He was, in fact, soon full of work. His monastery, the first in Africa (see below, § 15), became a training-school for clergy. Possidius tells us of ten bishops who proceeded from it. Among the earliest were Alypius, who in 394 went to Thagaste, and Evodius, to Uzala. Possidius himself became bp. of Calamus, but appears to have spent much of his time at Hippo, which was only some forty miles away. Moreover, the example of the monastic life spread rapidly (*Ep.* 24, *sub fin.*); before Augustine died, there were at least three monasteries in Hippo alone (*Vit. Ben.* III. v. 4). Of his life as a presbyter we know few details. He corresponds with Aurelius, the new bp. of Carthage, with a view to putting down the disorderly feasts over the tombs of the martyrs (*Epp.* 22, 29; *Conf.* V. ii.). At the end of Aug. 392, he held a public discussion for two days with Fortunatus, a Manichean presbyter, the notes of which remain. Possidius tells us that as the result Fortunatus left Hippo and never returned. In 393 a general council of African bishops met at Hippo, and Augustine preached to them *de Fide et Symbolo* (one of his best-known shorter works); he also mentions (*Retr.* I. 23) a stay at Carthage which must have been of some length, as it was there that he held his epoch-marking discussions of difficulties in the Ep. to the Romans, and at the request of his friends committed the results to writing (see below, § 10). We know that a council was held at Carthage in 394: possibly that may have been the occasion of his presence. The Manichean controversy still claimed his energies. In addition to the public discussions already referred to, he wrote at this time the famous tract *de Utilitate Credendi*; another, *de Duabus Animabus*, a tract against the Manichean Adimantus; and the imperfect work *de Genesi ad Literam*, a work which he abandoned, as he felt his novice-hand unequal to the task (*Retr.* I. xviii.; see below, § 14). A new task, imposed upon him by his official responsibilities, was the controversy with the Donatists (see below, § 8). Early in his presbyterate he wrote to a neighbouring bishop of that sect to remonstrate with him for rebaptizing (*Ep.* 23). He also composed, for popular use, an acrostic song in refutation of the sect (about 394: *Psalmus contra partem Donati*), and a tract, now lost, *contra Epistolam Donati.* To this period, lastly, belong a group of exegetical works which shew a rapid advance in the command of Holy Scripture, the fruit of systematic study: an exposition of the Sermon on the Mount, a commentary on Galatians, some of the *Quaestiones LXXXIII.* (*supra*, § 7 *a*), and the above-mentioned notes on Romans. He began a continuous commentary on the Epistle, but only succeeded in completing the Salutation. The *de Mendacio* (see *Retr.* I. xxvii.) was also written at this period, but its issue was deferred till about 420, when the *contra Mend.* was also published (*Retr.* II. lx.). Generally speaking, the works of this transition period are remarkable for the supersession of the philosophical form of the older works by Biblical, and to a great extent Pauline, categories. The philosophical substratum of Platonism remains, but Augustine is now a Biblical and ecclesiastical theologian. (For a detailed analysis of the ideas distinctive of this and the preceding periods respectively, see the masterly article of Loofs, mentioned at the end of this article, pp. 270-276.) Lastly, it was as a presbyter that he completed his three books *de Libero Arbitrio* (*supra*, § 7 *a*): they were directed against the Manichean theory of the origin of evil (*supra*, § 4), and vindicate the moral responsibility of man against the theory of a physical principle of evil. To the position taken up in these books the Pelagians (*infra*, § 10) appealed, against Augustine's later doctrine of irresistible grace. Augustine has no difficulty in shewing that he had even at this early date refuted them by anticipation. But it was less easy to meet the appeal of the so-called semi-Pelagians (see below, § 10 *d*), who were on the side of the church against Pelagius, but demurred to positions taken up by Augustine later in life. Of personal interest is Augustine's correspondence with the saintly Paulinus of Nola, to whom he sent the books on Free Will. Paulinus had heard of the growing fame of Augustine, and sought his acquaintance by letters addressed to Alypius and to Augustine himself (*Epp.* 24-27, 30-32). Augustine at this period also began to correspond with Jerome (*Ep.* 28); in a letter of about this date he indignantly rejects the theory that the scene at Antioch between SS. Paul and Peter was to be explained *patrocinium mendacii suscipiendo.*

B. EPISCOPATE (from 395).—§ 8. *The Donatist Controversy.* (*a*) *Origin.*—Valerius was old and infirm, and had marked out Augustine as his successor. But he daily feared that some other church might elect him as bishop, and that he would therefore be lost to Hippo. So, with the eager consent of his flock, he took a step then almost without precedent, and, unconsciously breaking the letter of the eighth canon of Nicaea, induced Megalius of Calama, the "primae sedis Episcopus," *i.e.* bishop senior by consecration in Numidia, to consecrate Augustine as his coadjutor with right of succession. Valerius had (Possid. viii.) privately gained the consent of Aurelius, bp. of Carthage; Megalius made some personal objections, which he subsequently withdrew (references in *Vit. Ben.* IV. i. 2). Valerius did not long survive the fulfilment of his hopes and prayers; for nearly thirty-five years Augustine was bp. of Hippo. His episcopate was occupied by grave controversies, and productive of monumental works; but it was not eventful as regards Augustine's personal history. It will be best, therefore, to deal with it, not by annalistic narrative, but by considering in turn the great questions with which Augustine had to deal. We have spoken sufficiently of the Manichean controversy. As a bishop (about 397-400) Augustine wrote against these heretics the tracts *c. Ep. Fundamenti* and *de Agone Christiano.* The *Confessions,* written about this time, give an insight into Augustine's personal experiences of Manicheism (see above, §§ 2, 4). About 400 he refuted, in thirty-three short books, a treatise by his old Manichean friend Faustus; at the end of 404 (*Retr.* II. viii., cf. *Ep.* 29) he held a public discussion with a Manichean named Felix, and as a result penned the short tract *de Natura Boni.* Somewhat later he was brought into controversy with the Manichean "auditor" Secundianus. Of his reply he says, "*omnibus, quae adversus illam pestem scribere potui, facile praepono.*" These are writings drawn out by occasional contact with a controversy which Augustine had outgrown. It was otherwise with the Donatist struggle, which pressed continually upon him for the first twenty years of his episcopate. As we have seen, it claimed some of his energy already as a presbyter. But it may fairly be called the one great question of his earlier episcopate. According to Possidius, the Donatists were at the time of Augustine's ordination a majority among the Christians of the African provinces; at Hippo they were a very large majority, and terrorized the Catholics by exclusive dealing (*c. Duas Lit. Petil.* II. 184). The schism had existed since about 311, when Caecilianus was elected bp. of Carthage. Personal dislike to the election found a pretext for denying its validity. Felix of Aptunga, his consecrator, was alleged to have been a *traditor*—i.e. to have given up the sacred books during persecution. This, it was argued, vitiated his power to give valid Orders. For to communicate with an offender is to take part in his offence; and Felix's offence, *ipso facto,* cut him off from the church. Like Cyprian, the opponents of Caecilianus denied the validity of any sacrament conferred outside the church. These two principles, then, were involved: firstly, the old Cyprianic denial of the *validity of sacraments* conferred by *heretical* (or schismatical) hands; secondly, the nullity of sacraments performed by *unworthy ministers*: "oleum peccatoris non impinguet caput meum" (Ps. cxl. 5, Vulg.). The question at issue, then, was really that of the *essential nature of the church as a holy society* (see Reuter, pp. 236 sqq. note 2). The Catholics, in reply, insist on the fact that the church throughout the world is on their side, and that the Donatists are, by their separation, offenders against the bond of charity which maintains the peace and *unity of the church*: "Una est columba mea, speciosa mea" (Cant. vi. 9).

(*b*) *Earlier History of Donatists.*—It is not necessary here to detail the phases through which the controversy had passed in the nearly three generations which preceded the episcopate of Augustine, nor to unravel the intricate charges and counter-charges which encumber the real principles at issue. The principal landmarks in the question were: (1) The appeal to Constantine, apparently first made by the Donatists, which resulted in the adverse decisions of the councils of Rome (313) and Arles (314). (2) The consecration of Majorinus as bp. of Carthage in opposition to Caecilianus (311). He died in 315, and was succeeded by Donatus, a man of great energy, to whom the schism probably owes its name. (3) Imperial persecution of the Donatists, first by Constantine in 316, and then, after an attempt to bribe the Donatists into submission (340), a ruthless suppression by Constans in 347. This was successful in producing temporary submission, but it intensified the feeling of protest; moreover, the fanatical ferocity of the "Circumcellions," which Constantine's first persecuting edict had evoked, was smouldering in readiness to break out again. (4) Return of the Donatists under Julian. In 361, agreeably to his general policy of the restoration of ecclesiastical exiles, Julian repealed his predecessor's measures against the Donatists, and during his short reign they exercised a violent supremacy in Africa. (5) Optatus and Parmenian. Donatus had died in exile, and was now succeeded by Parmenianus, an able and comparatively moderate man. With him begins the first phase of the *literary debate* between Donatists and Catholics. The opponent of Parmenianus was Optatus of Milevis, who was still living after 384. His work on the Donatist schism is a rich mine of materials for its history. It is to be noted that Parmenianus and Optatus both believe in the visible *unity* of the church. But Parmenianus, insisting on the *holiness* of the church, identifies it with the separatist body in Africa, while Optatus insists upon the *Catholicity* of the church, and upon its *Apostolicity* as tested by communion with the chair of St. Peter and with the seven churches of the Apocalypse. (6) Disintegration of Donatism. This began to be apparent in the

Mauretanian schism of Rogatus, whose followers unchurched the other Donatists, and repudiated the Circumcellions; in the moderate Donatism of Tyconius (the author of a work on exegesis, of which Augustine speaks highly, *de Doctr. Chr.* III. xxx.), who exposed the inconsistencies of the Donatist position, and was consequently excommunicated by Parmenianus; and lastly, in the formidable Maximianist schism of 393, which resulted in the election of a second Donatist bishop, Maximianus, at Carthage, in opposition to Primianus, the successor of Parmenianus. Over 100 bishops sided with Maximianus; a council of 310 Donatist bishops in 394 decided against him. The civil authority was then invoked against the dissidents, who were persecuted with the usual severity.

Meanwhile the council of Hippo in 393 (*supra*, § 7 *b*) had, by judicious reforms and conciliatory provisions, paved the way back to the church for any Donatists who might be disillusioned by the inward breakdown of the sect. But its external position was still imposing. Edicts issued against the Donatists (since 373, *Cod. Theod.* XVI. vi.) by Valentinian and Gratian had had, owing to the state of the empire, but little effect. The edict of Theodosius against heretics (392, *Cod. Theod.* XVI. v.) was not enforced against them; in fact, from some time previous to the death of Theodosius in 395 till 398 the imperial writ did not run in the African provinces.

(*c*) *Augustine and Donatism.* — When Stilicho recovered Africa for Honorius from the usurper Gildo, Augustine had been a bishop seven years. He had preached, corresponded, and written actively against the Donatists, who had heard his sermons and read his tracts in great numbers. Their leaders had realized that they were now opposed by a champion of unexampled power, and endeavoured to keep their publications from falling into his hands. His earliest episcopal work, *contra Partem Donati*, is lost. But in 400 he wrote a reply to an old letter of Parmenianus, and the seven books *de Bapt. c. Donat.* In 401 and 402 he replied to a letter of Petilianus, the Donatist bp. of Cirta, and wrote his letter to the Catholics, *de Unitate Ecclesiae*, an important contribution to the controversy. In 403 the Catholic bishops in synod at Carthage agreed to propose a decisive conference; the Donatists declined, and in 404 the Catholic synod determined to ask for a revival of the imperial laws against the schism. From 405-409 the remedy of force was once more tried, with very partial success. In the latter year the Catholic synod petitioned Honorius to order a conference, and as the Donatists were now understood to agree, Marcellinus, a "tribune," was specially commissioned to arrange for the meeting. At the conference Augustine naturally played the principal part on the Catholic side. Marcellinus closed the proceedings by giving judgment in favour of the Catholics, and in 412 this was followed up by an imperial edict of drastic severity.

During this period Augustine wrote, in addition to twenty-one extant letters on the controversy, and four lost works, the following, which we still have: four books *contra Cresconium*; one *de Unico Baptismo*, the *Breviculus Collationis* (a report of the conference mentioned above), and a book *contra Donatistas post Collationem.* After 412, physical force had to some extent diminished the need for argument. A few more letters—an address to the people at Caesarea (Algiers), a public discussion with Emeritus, on Sept. 20, 418, two books *contra Gaudentium* (a Donatist bishop, *c.* 420)—are the remains of a waning controversy. For a fuller account of the history, and of the contents of some of Augustine's anti-Donatist writings, see art. DONATISM, *D. C. B.* (4-vol. ed.).

It remains to gather up briefly the importance of the controversy in Augustine's life and thought. So far as Donatism fell before argument, its fall was the work of Augustine. But what was the reflex effect of the controversy upon Augustine himself? Augustine was the first Christian writer who made the *church*, as such, the subject of systematic thought. But this was not wholly the result of the Donatist crisis. He fought Donatism in part with arguments which had been current for over two generations of the controversy, and which we find less lucidly formulated in Optatus, partly with conceptions which his own personal history and reflections had impressed upon his mind before he came into the conflict. The utmost that can justly be said —but that much is important—is that the Donatist conflict crystallized ideas which needed a shock of the kind to bring them into clear shape and form. It was beside the purpose to insist, as Cyprian had done, upon the episcopate, which the Donatists possessed, or upon the unity of the church, which they claimed for themselves. The question at issue went behind these points to the spiritual conditions necessary to the *saving* efficacy of means of grace. This exists, argued Augustine, only in the *Catholic* church. The baptism and orders of the Donatists were valid sacramentally, but useless spiritually. In a sense, the Holy Spirit operates in schismatical sacraments, so that a convert to the Catholic church will not be re-baptized or re-ordained. But it is only in the Catholic church that the Spirit operates, *as the Spirit of peace and love.* "Non autem habent Dei caritatem qui ecclesiae non diligunt unitatem; ac per hoc *recte* intelligitur dici *non accipi nisi in Catholica* Spiritus Sanctus" (*de Bapt.* III. xvi.). Augustine formulates with a clearness not found in any previous writer the distinction between what in later times was called the "gratia gratis data," which confers *status* only (the indelible "character" of a "baptizatus" or a priest), without any necessary change in the *moral or spiritual* character; and "gratia gratum faciens," which makes a man not only a member of the visible church, but a real member of Christ, not merely a priest, but a good priest. This distinction was hardly perceived by Cyprian (see Cypr. *Epp.* 65-67, esp. 66: "credere quod indigni . . . sint qui ordinantur quid aliud est quam contendere quod non a Deo. . . . sacerdotes ejus in ecclesia constituantur?"), who regarded a deposed bishop as a mere layman with but "the empty name and shadow" of priesthood. The recognition of the validity of Donatist orders and sacraments was imposed upon Augustine by the settled judgment of the Catholic church, especially of the council of Arles, in 314 (Can. xiii., cf. viii., rejecting the Cyprianic view). But he clearly found it difficult to grasp habitually the distinction between the "*Spiritus Sanctus*," the agent in *every* "valid" sacrament (="gratia gratis data"), and the "*Spiritus caritatis*," which makes the sacrament a means of grace ("gratum faciens") to the *Catholic* recipient. His frequent denials that "the Holy Spirit" could be possessed outside the visible unity of the church relate really to the latter, though there are passages which seem to extend to the former. But on the whole his mind is clear. He distinguishes sharply between *Office* and *Person*; between the sacramental act and its benefit to the soul. The former can exist outside the Catholic church, the latter only within it. In this respect Augustine is an uncompromising assertor of Cyprian's axiom, *extra ecclesiam nulla salus*. But it must be observed that he subordinates the *institutional* to the *spiritual* conception of the church. The Donatists are wrong, because they have broken the bond of *caritas* which unites the Catholic society. It is this, and not the mere fact, necessary though it be, of the episcopal succession, that unites Catholics with the Apostolic churches and through them by an "inconcussa series" with the Apostles themselves. (See below, § 16, *b*, *c*; also Gore, *The Church and the Ministry*, latter part of c. iii.; Hatch, *Organization*, v.; Reuter, pp. 231-283, an able and thorough discussion.)

§ 9. *Augustine and the Heathen. Philosophy of History*.—Augustine tells us (*de Civ. Dei*, XVIII. liii. 2) of an oracle current among the heathen, that the Christian religion would last 365 years, and then come to an end. He reckons that this time expired in the year 399. As a matter of fact, the year in question was marked by a widespread destruction of *pagan* temples throughout the Roman world (*Vit. Bened.* IV. xvi.). In this year apparently the counts Gaudentius and Jovius arrived in Africa to execute an imperial decree for the dismantling of the temples. At Carthage the splendid temple of Dea Coelestis, which had been closed, as it seems, since the law of 391 (*Cod. Th.* XVI. x. 10), and was already overgrown with weeds and bushes, was taken possession of by the Christians. But in 421 it was razed to the ground (Prosper, *de Praed.* III. xxxviii.). In some places images were hidden to preserve them from destruction. Heathen customs, as we gather from a sermon of Augustine (*Serm.* 62, 4), were still secretly observed even by some Christians. A council at Carthage in 401 petitioned the emperor to abolish public feasts and games which were, in spite of a previous imperial prohibition (*Cod. Th. ib.* 17), occasions of heathenish observances. The destruction of a statue of Hercules at Colonia Suffectana (? Sufetula) was the cause of a riot in which sixty Christians lost their lives (*Ep.* 50). In 407-408 a sweeping law, confiscating temples and ordering the destruction of altars, images, etc., was issued (*Cod. Th. ib.* 19, cf. *Vit. Bened.* VI. iv. 2, v. 3). Its promulgation was attended by most serious riots at Calama, where the church was repeatedly wrecked by the heathen (*Ep.* 90, 91, 103, 104). The murder of Stilicho (Sept. 408), and the rumours that the laws against the heathen and the Donatists passed during his life lapsed with his death, caused a further widespread outburst of heathen violence in Africa (cf. *Cod. Th. App.* Sirm. XIV.; Aug. *Ep.* 97). A stringent law, passed apparently at the instance of the provincial council at Carthage, of which Augustine was not a member, ordered rigorous penalties against all the offenders, and against conniving officials. Alarmed by the state of the empire, the ministers of Honorius appear to have relaxed for a time the rigour of the laws against paganism and heresy alike, but at the urgent request of the African bishops they were again strictly enforced. On the whole, Augustine's tone and attitude towards the pagans is dignified and conciliatory (*Epp.* 133, etc.), but he shares in the general responsibility for persecution which must be allotted to the churchmen of this degenerate age.

In 408 and 409 the Goths, under Alaric, had laid siege to Rome, and after long and fruitless negotiations, the city was taken and sacked on Aug. 24, 410. The sack of Rome, in its direct effects, was but an incident in the profound abasement of the empire in the miserable reign of Honorius. But the downfall of the "Eternal City" struck awe into the minds of men who failed to appreciate the material and moral exhaustion which the disaster merely symbolized. Augustine's friend Marcellinus, the imperial officer who had been in charge of the conference with the Donatists, introduced him to a distinguished ("illustris") official, Volusianus, who was kept back from the Christian faith by difficulties relating to the Old Testament, the Incarnation, and the incompatibility of some principles of the Gospel with civil life and the public good (*Epp.* 135-138, cf. 132). The last-named question naturally connected itself with the prevalent heathen explanation of the fall of Rome, as due to the desertion of the old gods and the progress of Christianity. Augustine, unable at the time to discuss this question except in passing (*Ep.* 138[1, 9-16], cf. 136[3]), presently began a more thorough consideration of it. This is his famous treatise *de Civitate Dei*, begun about the end of 412, and not completed until 426. The first two books are addressed to Marcellinus, who was put to death, Sept. 13, 413; with a third book, they were published before 415. In this year, about Lent, he wrote two more (*Ep.* 169[1]) In 416-417, when he was advising Orosius to write his *Historia adversus Paganos*, Augustine had published ten books, and was at work on the eleventh. By 420 he had published fourteen; the eighteenth was finished "nearly thirty years" after the consulate of Theodorus (399), *i.e.* hardly earlier than 426. The work then was continued amid interruptions, and the plan widened out from a refutation of the heathen calumny (*Retr.* II. xliii.) to a comprehensive explanation of the course of human affairs—a religious philosophy of history.

The problem was one of terrible actuality. The ancient world and its civilization were in real truth breaking up, and the end of Rome seemed like a giving way of the solid earth beneath men's feet. Lesser men were moved to write: Orosius, mentioned above, in 417, and Salvian, whose lurid indictment of the sins of the Christian world (*de Gubernatione Dei*) was penned in 451, four years before the sack of Rome by Gaiseric. But it was Augustine who brought the problem under a single master-idea. This idea (which occurs already in *de Catech. Rud.*, written as early as A.D. 400) is that of the two *civitates*, which, after a refutation of paganism as useless alike in this world (I.-V.) and in the next (VI.-X.), are treated of constructively in the remainder of the work, in respect of their origin (XI.-XIV.), history (XV.-XVIII.), and destiny (XIX.-XXII.). The work would have gained by condensation, but as it stands, with all the marks of discontinuous production, it is a priceless legacy of Augustine's most characteristic thoughts (on *Ep.* 102, which illustrates the *de Civ.*, and was written about 409, see below, § 16*a*). By the word *civitas*, commonly rendered "city," Augustine means rather a bond of union, or citizenship (cf. Philipp. iii. 20 Gk., "*duo quaedam genera humanae societatatis*" XIV. i., the "civitas" takes visible form in the shape of a government, but its essential character is in the spirit that animates it). There are then two, and only two, *civitates*, the one heavenly, the other earthly. The *civitas terrena* began with the fall of the angels, was continued by that of man, in the history of the Cainites, of Babel, and of the great world-empires. The *civitas Dei* began with Creation; its earthly realization is traceable in the history of the Sethites, of Noah, Abraham, Israel, of Christ, and of His people. The one is rooted in love of God, *usque ad contemptum sui*; the other in love of self, *usque ad contemptum Dei.* The chief good of the one is the *pax coelestis* (XIX. 13), that of the other, the *pax terrena.* The great empires are, in their genesis, the State is *per se* (*remota justitia*), "latrocinium magnum" (IV. 4). So that, looked upon in the abstract, since there are but two *civitates*, the state is the *civitas diaboli*, the church the *civitas Dei.*

But this conclusion is not, thus baldly stated, that of Augustine. To begin with, his conception of the church (see §§ 8, 16, *b*, *c*) is not consistent. Does he mean the visible church, the *communio externa*, or the *communio sanctorum*, the number of those predestined to life, to which not all belong who are members of the visible church, and to which some belong who are not? Augustine's language on this point is not always uniform. But at the time when he wrote the *de Civitate*, the predestinarian idea was growing upon him, and the two *civitates* tend to coincide with the predestined on the one hand, and, on the other, the rest of mankind. Again, the visible church, even apart from its merely nominal members, is but part of a larger whole, but the empirical shadow of a transcendent reality, the *civitas superna*, which includes angels as well as redeemed humanity (XI. 7). And in its earthly visible existence the church borrows the form of the earthly state (XV. 2). Again, historically, the two *civitates* are mingled together and interpenetrate. Moreover, the church needs the *pax terrena*, and is dependent for it on the *civitas terrena* (XIX. 17, cf. "per jura regum possidentur possessiones," *in Joh. Tr.* VI. 15); practically for all civil purposes the churchman must obey the law. But, on the other hand, the *civitas terrena* cannot attain its chief good, the *pax terrena*, unless heavenly motives are brought to bear; for the social bond of *caritas*, for the elementary requisite of *justitia*, it is dependent upon the *civitas Dei.*

The destiny of the *civitas terrena*, therefore, when at the Judgment the two are finally separated, is the destruction of its social bond; it will cease to be a *civitas* at all. There is, then, if we look at things in their eternal aspect, *only one civitas*, and, applying the ideal to the empirical, the state (*qua* good, *i.e.* if Christian) is in the church. Optatus had said (*de Schism.* III. 3) "Ecclesia in Imperio." Augustine reverses this relation: "Dominus jugo suo *in gremio ecclesiae* toto orbe diffuso omnia terrena regna subjecit." The state is in the church, and is bound to carry out the church's aims. The subject of "Church and State" was not the theme of the book, and it is not easy to extract from it a strictly consistent theory of their relations (see Reuter, pp. 125-150, 380-392). But these relations were the question of the future, and in the *de Civitate* Augustine laid the theoretical foundation for the medieval system (see also below, § 16 *ad fin.*). The modifying ideas alluded to above were not forgotten, but their assertion was the work of the opponents of the medieval hierocracy; and Dante, *de Monarchia*, is practically a reversal of the characteristic doctrine of the *de Civitate Dei*, after that doctrine, tested by being put into practice, has been found to lead to unchristian results. One unchristian corollary of Augustine's doctrine was the persecution of heretics as a duty of the Christian state. In his earlier days Augustine disapproved of this (*contr. Ep. Man.* 1-3; *Ep.* 23, 7; 93, 2, 5, etc.); but the stress of the Donatist controversy changed his mind; in the interest of the doubtful, the weak, the generations to come, he found a sanction for persecution in St. Luke xiv. 23: *Cogite intrare.*

§ 10. *The Pelagian Controversy* (412-430).—Augustine, in his first days as a Christian, held the common view that, while the grace of God is necessary to the *salvation* of man, the first step, the act of faith, by which man *gains access* to grace, is the act of man, and not itself the gift of God (*de Praed.* III. 7). This view is manifest in the *Expos. Propos. in Rom.* 13-18, 55, etc., and traceable in *de Quaest. LXXXIII.*, qu. 68 and 83). He came to see that faith itself is the gift of God, and that the very first step to Godward must be of God's doing, not of our own. This conviction was not due to reaction against Pelagianism; on the contrary, Pelagius himself was roused to contradiction by Augustine's language in his *Confessions*: "Domine da quod jubes" (see *de Don. Persev.* 53). Augustine's change of mind was directly and wholly due to his study of St. Paul (see above, § 7*b*); partly his wrestling with the difficulties of the Ep. to the Romans; but especially his reflection on St. Paul's question (I. Cor. iv. 7), "What hast thou that thou hast not received?"

coupled with Rom. ix. 16. The change may be assigned to the year 396, when, in the first book, he wrote as a bishop (*de Divers. Quaest. ad Simplic.* I.), as he says (*Retr.* II. i. 1), "to solve this question, we laboured in the cause of the freedom of the human will, but *the grace of God won the day*" (cf. *de Don. Pers.* 52, *plenius sapere coepi*). To Simplicianus he says, I. ii. 13: "If it is in man's own power *not* to obey the call, it would be equally correct to say, 'Therefore it is not of God that sheweth mercy, but of man that runs and wills,' because the mercy of Him that calls *does not suffice*, unless the obedience of him who is called results. . . . God shews mercy on no man in vain; but on whom He has mercy, him He calls in such sort as He knows to be fitted for him [*congruere*], so that He does not reject him that calleth." Here we have the essential of the "Augustinian" doctrine of grace, the distinction of the *vocatio congrua* and *vocatio non congrua* ("Illi enim *electi* qui congruenter *vocati*"), formulated more than fifteen years before the Pelagian controversy began (see also Loofs, pp. 279-280, who shews in detail that Augustine's whole later position is virtually contained in *de Div. Quaest. ad Simplician.*). For the details of this controversy, see the church histories; *D. C. B.* (4-vol. ed.), *s.v.*; Bright, Introd. to *Anti-Pelagian Treatises*, and other authorities. (A lucid summary in Gibson, *XXXIX. Articles*, art. ix.) It will suffice here to mention the main outlines.

(*a*) 410-417.—PELAGIUS, offended at a passage in Augustine's *Confessions* (see above), began at Rome (405-409) to express his disapproval of such an insistence upon Divine grace as should undermine human responsibility. Before the siege of Rome (*supra*, § 9) he left with his friend Coelestius for Africa; there Pelagius left Coelestius, and went to Palestine. Coelestius sought ordination at Carthage, and thus attracted additional attention to his doctrines. A council of bishops in 412 condemned him; he went away to Ephesus, and there he was ordained. Subsequently he went to Constantinople and (417) to Rome. Meanwhile, opposed by Jerome in Palestine, Pelagius was found not guilty of heresy by John, bp. of Jerusalem, and by councils at Jerusalem and Diospolis (415). He dispatched to Rome (417) a confession of faith to be submitted to Innocentius: it arrived after that bishop's death. Coelestius shortly afterwards (still in 417) arrived at Rome, and submitted his confession of faith to the new bp. Zosimus. Augustine appears to have been partly aware of the opinions of Pelagius before his arrival in Africa (see *de Gest. Pel.* 46; also probably through Paulinus of Nola, see *de Grat. Christi*, 38), but he appears to have attached little importance to them at the time; and the arrival of Pelagius found him in the very thick of other questions (see above, §§ 8, 9). He alludes to the Pelagian doctrines (without any mention of names) in preaching (*Serm.* 170, 174, 175), but took no part in the proceedings at Carthage in 412. But his friend Marcellinus (*supra*, § 9) pressed him for his opinion upon the questions there discussed, and his first anti-Pelagian writings (A.D. 412, *de Pecc. Meritis et Remiss.* lib. III., and *de Spiritu et Litera*) were addressed to him. In 415 he wrote *de Natura et Gratia*, and probably the tract, in the form of a letter to Eutropius and Paulus, *de Perfectione Justitiae Hominis*, in refutation of the propositions of Coelestius in 412; in 417 he wrote *de Gestis Pelagii*, a discussion of the proceedings in Palestine above referred to. Augustine and the African bishops, who had been represented in Palestine not only by Jerome, but by Orosius, fresh from Hippo, were naturally dismayed at what had happened there. They knew that Pelagius and Coelestius were likely to address themselves to Rome, where they had a strong following (*Ep.* 177, 2). Accordingly councils at Carthage and at Milevis, at the latter of which Augustine was present, wrote to urge Innocentius to support them against the "alleged" decision of the Palestinian councils, either by reclaiming the heretics or by adding the authority of his see to their condemnation. A letter carefully explaining the doctrinal issue was also sent by Aurelius of Carthage, Augustine, Alypius, Possidius, and Evodius (see above, §§ 6, 7). Augustine certainly drew up the latter two (*Epp.* 176, 177), and his inspiration is also manifest in the Carthaginian letter. Innocent, unable to conceal his satisfaction at so important an appeal to his authority (he assumes that the African bishops, though they do not refer to them, are not unacquainted with the "*instituta patrum*," which direct that nothing shall be done in any province of the church without reference to the Apostolic See; *Epp.* 181^1, 182^2; see below, § 12, *c*), responded cordially with a prompt condemnation of Pelagianism, root and branch. Augustine was triumphant. The unfortunate proceedings of Diospolis were more than neutralized. Preaching on Sunday, Sept. 23, 417, he says: "Jam enim de hac causa duo concilia missa sunt ad sedem Apostolicam, inde etiam rescripta venerunt. Causa finita est; utinam aliquando finiatur error" (*Serm.* 131). But the author of the *rescripta* was already dead six months before, and there was need of another council. The cause was not "finished" yet.

(*b*) *Zosimus. Julian* (418-430).—Zosimus, the new bp. of Rome (see *D. C. B.* 4-vol. ed. *s.v.*), was favourably impressed with the confessions of faith submitted by Pelagius and Coelestius, as well as by their deference to his authority. He pronounced them orthodox, and twice wrote indignantly to Aurelius and the Africans for their hasty condemnation of the accused in their absence. He adds that he has admonished Coelestius and others to abstain from curious and unedifying questions. But the original accusers of Pelagius were unmoved. After some correspondence with Zosimus they held a plenary council at Carthage (May 418), in which they passed nine dogmatic canons condemning the characteristic Pelagian theses. Meanwhile, Aurelius had been taking more practical steps. A rescript in the emperor's name (Honorius was here, as in the Donatist question, the passive instrument of his advisers, probably count Valerius, whose ear Aurelius gained—"secuta est clementia nostra judicium sanctitatis tuae," Honorius writes in 419) ordered the banishment of Pelagius, Coelestius, and all their adherents. Zosimus at once came round to the side of the Africans. In a circular letter (*tractoria*) he condemned Coelestius and Pelagianism alike, and required all the bishops of his jurisdiction to signify their adhesion. Thus ended the official support of Pelagius in the West. (On Augustine's view of Zosimus, see Reuter, pp. 312-322, and below, § 12 *d*. On the whole question, see Garnier in *Marii Mercat. opp*. I. p. 19.) Zosimus appears to have imperfectly grasped the points at issue, and in this case, as in that of Apiarius in the same year (*infra*, § 12, *c*), and in that of the metropolitan rights of Arles, he appears to have been in a greater hurry to assert the claims of his see than to ascertain the merits of the question in debate.

The most able advocate of Pelagianism now appears in the person of Julian, bp. of Eclanum in Southern Italy. He refused to sign the *tractoria*, accused Zosimus of changing his front under imperial pressure ("jussionis terrore perculsos," *c. Duas Epp. Pelag*. ii. 3), and appealed to a general council. This appeal came to nothing (*ib*. iv. 34). Julian was deposed by Zosimus, banished by the Government, and took refuge in the East. He is said to have found a friend in Theodore of Mopsuestia. At any rate, in 431 the Westerns secured the condemnation of Pelagianism (without specification of its tenets) along with Nestorianism at the council of Ephesus, on the ground of the kindred nature of the two heresies. This was not without substantial reason. The two heresies rest upon the same fundamental idea of the benefit which the redemptive work of Christ brings to man—viz. moral improvement by perfect teaching and example, rather than atonement for an inherently guilty race (" ut vel sero redamaremus eum," Julian in *Op. Imperf*. I. xciv.). Augustine continued to write against Pelagianism. In 418 he wrote two books, *de Gratia Christi et de Peccato Originali*; in the two following years the two books *de Nuptiis et Concupiscentia*, and four *de Anima ejusque Origine*. These works bore on the *transmission* of original sin, and the difficult collateral question of the origin of the soul, whether by direct creation or *ex traduce*. Tertullian had roundly maintained *tradux animae, tradux peccati*. Pelagius denied both. Augustine cannot decide the question; he half leans to creation, but his theory appears to require the other alternative (see below, § 15). Julian attacked the *de Nuptiis* hotly. Augustine's four books, *contra Duas Epp. Pelagianorum* (420) are in reply to Julian on this as well as on the historical questions; they were followed by six books *contra Julianum* (about 421). Julian replied with vigour, and Augustine at the time of his death had only finished six books of a rejoinder which he intended to be complete (*Opus Imperfectum*).

(*c*) *The semi-Pelagians* (from about 426).—In the combat with Pelagianism, Augustine cannot be said to have changed his views (*supra*, § 10, *sub init*.); but he stated, with increasing clearness and sharper consistency, opinions which he had gathered from his study of St. Paul long before the combat began. These opinions were new to most churchmen, although reaction from the paradoxes of Pelagius, and Augustine's immense authority throughout the Latin church, gained them widespread acceptance. But there were, especially in monastic circles, grave misgivings as to their soundness. The three points to which most serious objection was felt were the doctrines of the total depravity of fallen man, of irresistible grace, and of absolute predestination, *not* on the ground of *foreseen merit*. The Christian, as taught by Augustine, received instruction, baptism, the subsequent *beneficia gratiae* which went to build up the Christian life and train the soul for its eternal home. But the success or failure, the *permanent* value of the whole process, depended upon the crowning *beneficium gratiae*, the *Donum Perseverantiae*, which even at the very moment of death decides whether the soul departs in Christ or falls from Him. This awful gift, which *alone* decides between the saved and the lost, may be withheld from many who have lived as good and sincere Christians: it may be granted to those whose lives have been far from Christ. Its giving or withholding depends upon the Divine predestination only; God's foreknowledge of those who will " persevere " is but His own foreknowledge of what He Himself will give or withhold. Only the foreknown *in this sense* are called with *vocatio congrua*. If these doctrines were true, if free will was by itself entirely powerless to accept the Divine call or to reject the *vocatio congrua*, if man's salvation at bottom depended simply and solely upon the Divine predestination, what appeal was possible to the conscience of the wicked (*correptio*)? Was not preaching deprived of its *raison d'être*?

This was the view of John Cassian, the father of Western monachism, and of Vincent and other monks of Lerins on the southern coast of Gaul. These " semi-Pelagians," who may with equal justice be called " semi-Augustinians," were *not a sect outside the church, but a party of dissentient Catholics*. Excepting the above-mentioned points and certain obvious corollaries, such as the doctrine of " particular " redemption, they accepted the entire Augustinian position. The controversy, which is in reality insoluble, lasted long after Augustine's death. Temporarily laid to rest at Orange (where a modified Augustinianism was adopted by a small council in 529), it burst out again in the Gottschalk troubles in the 9th cent., it ranged the Scotists against the Thomists in the 13th, the Arminians against the Calvinists, the Jesuits against the Jansenists in the 17th. Intellectually it is a case of an " antinomy," in which from obvious truths we are led by irresistible logic to incompatible conclusions. Morally, our *crux* is to insist on human *responsibility* while excluding human *merit*. The religious instinct of deep and genuine self-accusation is not easy to combine with the unreserved acknowledgment that we have no power of ourselves to help ourselves. We must, with Cassian, appeal to free will from the pulpit, but Augustine is with us in the secret sanctuary of prayer.

Augustine's attention was drawn to these difficulties by Hilary and Prosper of Aquitaine, the latter the most active, and indeed bitter, opponent of the *Ingrati*, as he calls Cassian and his friends. The works *de Gratia et Libero*

Arbitrio and *de Correptione et Gratia* (426-427) relate to the moral issues of the question, while the *de Praedest. Sanctorum* and *de Dono Perseverantiae* (428, 9) are in direct controversy with the "brethren" of Southern Gaul.

(*d*) *The Doctrinal Issues.*—Pelagianism split upon the rock of infant baptism. Had this practice not become general by the time when Pelagius arose, Augustine would have had to combat him by arguments which churchmen at large would have found difficulty in following. As it was, to the question, "Why"—if Adam's sin directly affected himself only, and extended to his descendants *non propagine sed exemplo*—"why, then, are infants baptized?" Pelagius had no satisfactory reply. His answer, that the unbaptized infant is excluded, not from eternal life, but only from the kingdom of heaven, was a relic of Millenniarism with which the Eastern church had even less sympathy than the West. Pelagius allowed that man can do no good thing without the grace of God. But his conception of grace was loose and shallow; practically it went back to the general providence of God, which supplies our temporal and spiritual wants alike. His assertion that a sinless life was not only possible, but was actually lived by many of the holy men of the Bible, was in direct conflict with the promptings of a deep religious sense (*de Nat. et Grat.* xxxvi. 42). His conception of the *beneficium Christi* (*supra, b, c*) was shallow and unsatisfying. Pelagius was an ardent churchman, a strict ascetic, and a believer in sacramental grace. The earlier church had reflected but little on the questions raised by him. "Unde factum est ut de gratia Dei quid sentirent breviter *ac transeuntes attingerent.*" Free will equipped with sacraments, the Christian religion a "New Law," predestination founded upon prescience, fairly represent the implicit pre-Augustinian view of the Christian life and its relation to the mystery of Divine election. Augustine pressed Pelagius with the implications of sacramental grace. If free will is as complete as Pelagius believed, sacraments are in reality superfluous as means of grace. If sacramental grace is as real as Pelagius admitted it to be, then man depends for his salvation not upon his own free will, but upon the gift of God. Augustine, assuming the church doctrine of sacramental grace, gave it a deeper meaning and a wider context, and brought it into close relation with the almost forgotten Pauline categories of sin, faith, justification, and the *gratia Christi* (see Reuter, pp. 40-45). It was formerly thought (by Baur and others) that Augustine's antagonism to Pelagius was dictated by his conception of the church and the sacraments, especially of baptism. This we have seen to be incorrect. As a matter of fact, Pelagius was, as the proceedings at Diospolis shew, hard to convict of heresy on merely ecclesiastical grounds. The theological principles which Augustine brought to the analysis of ecclesiastical practice, and to the refutation of Pelagianism, he had learned from St. Paul at first hand. Pelagius appealed to the naïve language of churchmen before him, who as Augustine says, "Pelagianis nondum litigantibus *securius* loquebantur." Augustine shewed that the accord was superficial, and that if Pelagius were right, the church and the positive religion of Christ had only a relative value. Moreover, it was impossible for the Pelagians to argue out their case without exposing themselves to an array of damaging quotations from recognized Fathers of the church (*c. Julian.* I. II.). And it is impossible to deny that Augustine, in the points at issue with the semi-Pelagians, was following out the strict logical consequences of the elementary truths which Pelagius and Julian denied. He admits frankly, in this as in some other questions, that he had changed his mind, *plenius sapere coepi*, but he again and again protests that he is merely defending the doctrine which *nunquam Ecclesia Christi non habuit* (i.e. predestination, *de Don. Persev.* xiv. 36, etc.).

This is certainly sincere, but also certainly incorrect, so far as concerns the *formal assertion* of absolute predestination, irresistible grace, and total depravity. And it must further be noted that the doctrine of predestination is, logically at least, as subversive of the worth of church and sacraments as is the Pelagian doctrine of human nature (see below, § 16, *c*). Probably neither Augustine nor the Pelagians were conscious of the full consequences of their position—the naturalism of the one and the transcendentalism of the other were alike tempered by common church teaching. But the ecclesiastical instinct has generally been (in spite of the rapier-thrusts of a Pascal) to seek some illogical *via media* between the Augustinian and the semi-Pelagian (itself an illogical) position. Instinct in such a matter is perhaps a safer guide than logic. But it is important to bear in mind that *in rejecting Pelagianism* the whole church, Augustinian and semi-Pelagian alike, were as one. [PELAGIANISM.]

§ 11. *Augustine and Greek Christendom.*—The last sentence may seem questionable so far as the Greek-speaking churches were concerned. But we must remember that Coelestius found no welcome at Constantinople, that Augustine not only wrote (*Ep.* 179) to bp. John of Jerusalem to warn him of Pelagius's errors, but also quotes John's arguments as decisive against Pelagianism (*Ep.* 186[36], *de Gest. Pel.* 37 seq., "*sanctus* Johannes"), and that Pelagianism was formally condemned at the council of Ephesus. But Augustine is somewhat biased in his review of the proceedings in Palestine by the assumption, which it never occurred to him to question, of the absolute doctrinal homogeneity of the East and West. Accordingly he explains the acquittal of Pelagius by the difficulty of language, and by the evasive answers of Pelagius, without allowing for the strangeness to Greek theology of the very categories of the question at issue. The catholicity of the church, he argues against the Donatists, is to be tested by communion, not only with the apostolic see of Rome, but with the other apostolic churches, and with Jerusalem, the common source of all (*ad Don. Post Collat.* xxix. 50; *de Unit.* x. xi.; *Ep.* 52[3]). In Augustine's time the first symptoms of the coming rift between the Greek and Latin churches had indeed appeared, but few realized their meaning. Augustine certainly did not. He meets the arguments of Julian, who claimed the Greek Fathers for his side, by an appeal to the Greek text of Chrysostom. On the other hand, he does not, even in the *de Trinitate* (written 400-416: "juvenis inchoavi senex edidi"), spontaneously build much upon Greek theology. The Nicene Creed, which he accepted of course *ex animo*, is but seldom referred to in that work; of the "Constantinopolitan" Creed he shews no knowledge. The *de Trinitate* is Western in the texture of its thought, true to the original sense of the ὁμοούσιον, a formula imposed on the Eastern church at Nicaea by Western influences (see the present writer's *Prolegomena* to Athanasius in *Nic. Lib.* IV. p. xxxii., etc.) in the interest *of the Divine Unity*. Augustine paves the way, by his insistence on the doctrine of the One Personal God, for the scholastic doctrine of the *Una Res*, the specifically Western product of Trinitarian theology. The same holds good of Christology. At Chalcedon, Leo's tome, which shews the profound influence of Augustine, carried the day in the teeth of the dominant tone of Greek Christology; and it is interesting to find Theodoret, who of all Greek churchmen had most reason to welcome the result, quoting Ambrose and Augustine as authorities in his dogmatic Dialogues—an exception to the general indifference of the East to Latin theologians. Another exception, due in part to independent controversial reasons, is the protest of Leontius and the "Scythic monks," under Justinian, against the "semi-Pelagianism" of Faustus of Reii; Leontius shews some knowledge, direct or second-hand, of Augustine (Loofs's *Leontius*, pp. 231 ff.). Augustine's influence, then, on Greek Christianity has been very slight. But although he has powerfully contributed to the divergence in thought and feeling of Latin Christianity from Greek, he is personally unconscious of any such tendency. Of his own knowledge of Greek he speaks slightingly; Gibbon (c. xxiii.[28]) and others take him strictly at his word, but Reuter (pp. 179, etc.) shews that we must rate it somewhat more highly than Augustine himself does.

§ 12. *Augustine and the Constitution of the Church. The Roman See.*—Augustine's view of the relation of the church to the civil power (see above, § 9) prepared the way for the medieval system. But in Augustine's hands the theory lacked elements indispensable for its practical application. Not only did his conception of the church hover between the transcendental spiritual ideal and the empirical, tangible organization, but his conception of the organization of the visible church itself lacked that practical precision without which the church could assert no effective claim to control the secular arm. To the authority of the church he surrendered himself with passionate affection. "I should not believe in the Gospel," he wrote in the early days of his episcopate, "did not the authority of the Catholic church compel me" (*c. Ep. Fund.* 6, in A.D. 397). But this was the *immanent* authority which the church by her life, creed, and worship exercised upon his soul, rather than her official decisions. These, again, he accepted with all his heart. But what was the ultimate *organ* of the church's authority? Where was its centre? What was the final standard of appeal? To these questions it is hard to obtain from Augustine a definite answer. Augustine was not an ecclesiastical statesman. His interest was above all in personal religion, and *therefore*, in a secondary degree, in doctrine and discipline. Although he takes for granted the Cyprianic view of the episcopal office, he does not insist upon it with special emphasis; he emphasises, on the other hand, in a marked manner, the universal priesthood of Christians. His insistence on the indelible character of the priestly ordination is not in the interest of "sacerdotalism," but as against the spiritual value of valid but schismatical orders (*supra*, § 8, *c*). He accepts the authority of Nicaea (the only strictly general council known to him), but as to the authority of other councils his language is ambiguous. He disallows Julian's appeal to a general council on the ground that "the cause is finished" by "a competent judgment of bishops" (*c. Jul.* III. 5). But in another passage (*supra*, § 10, *a, fin.*) he is understood to say, "the cause is finished" by two African councils, *plus* "rescripts from the apostolic see." What is his real view of the supreme organ of church authority?

(*a*) The Apostles in their lifetime were the leaders, "*principes*" (Ps. lxvii.[26] Vulg.; see *Enarr.* in loc.), and "*patres*" (Ps. xliv.[17] and *Enarr.*); now that they are gone, we have their *filii* in their place, the *bishops*, who are *principes super omnem terram*. The Apostles still live on in the bishops, who are accordingly the vehicle of the supreme authority of the church. The Donatist bishops cannot claim this status (*Ep.* 53[3], etc.), because they are out of communion with the apostolic churches. Hence (*b*) the *unity and continuity of the episcopate* are essential to its Apostolic rank. *In* this unity even *mali praepositi* are authoritative, "non enim sua sunt quae dicunt, sed Dei, qui *in cathedra unitatis doctrinam posuit veritatis*" (*Ep.* 105[16]). This is the old Cyprianic doctrine, which Augustine, like Cyprian, finds in the symbolic foundation of the Church upon Peter, who *represents the whole body*. All bishops are equal; there is no *Episcopus episcoporum* (*de Bapt.* III. 5, VI. 9, quoting Cyprian). But as Peter *represented* his co-equal colleagues, the Apostles, so his successors in the Roman see represent their co-equal colleagues the bishops (cf. *ad Classic.* in *Ep.* 250, *ad fin.* . . . ".n concilio nostro agere cupio, et *si opus fuerit* [1]ad Sedem Apost. scribere, ut . . . quid sequi debeamus *communi omnium* auctoritate . . . firmetur"). All bishops alike hold the *cathedra unitatis*, all alike trace their succession to one or other of the Apostles. This is more easily traceable in some cases (*i.e.* the churches *quibus Apostoli scripserunt*) than in others, but most obvious in the Roman see, whose bishops, from the *sedes* (i.e. episcopate, *c. Ep. Fund.* 5; cf. "*primae sedis* episcopus," *supra*, § 8, *init.*) of Peter himself, have followed one another in a succession known to all (*Psalm c. Donat.* sub fin., *Ep.* 53[3]). The *successio sacerdotum* at Rome and the *successiones episcoporum* generally (*de Util. Cred.* xvii. 35) are, to Augustine, *co-ordinate* and convertible ideas. Even with regard to the authority of councils, there is no real finality. Earlier councils are subject to correction by later (*de Bapt.* II. iii. 4). This is the position of Julius I. (see below, § 16, and the present writer's *Roman Claims to Supremacy*, iii. *fin.*).

(*c*) *The Episcopate and the Roman See.*—The Roman see was *Apostolica sedes*, not exclusively (*c. Faust.* xi. x.; *de Doct. Christ.* II. viii. 12), but conspicuously. This implied a pre-eminence of rank, at any rate over sees not "Apostolic" (*Ep.* 43[4], "Rom. ecclesiae, in qua semper *Apostolicae Cathedrae viguit principatus*"; *c. Jul.* I. iv. 13, *prior loco*; *c. Duas Epp. Pel.* I. i. 2 [to pope Bonifatius], "quamvis *ipse in ea* [sc. communi specula pastorali] *praeemineas celsiore fastigio*," and *ib.* 1, "qui non alta sapis *quamvis altius praesideas*"). But in none of the passages where this is fully recognized is any *definite authority* assigned to the "apostolic see." Peter was first of the Apostles, superior to any bishop (even to Cyprian, *de Bapt.* III. i.-2); but he is simply the representative of the Apostles, nor does Augustine ascribe to him authority over the others (see *Serm.* 46[30]), and the same applies to his estimate of Peter's successors.

Augustine's own instinct towards Rome is one of unbounded respect. Towards the end of his life (about 423) he had to remove, for obvious unfitness, Antonius, the bishop of the newly-created see of Fussala, a daughter-church of Hippo (*Ep.* 209). Antonius, like Apiarius (of whom presently), and possibly encouraged, like others (*ib.*[8]), by his example, decided to try his fortune at Rome. He obtained from the senior bp. of Numidia a favourable verdict and an introduction to Bonifatius, who was, *prima facie*, inclined to take up his cause, and wrote to that effect. But Bonifatius died (422), and his successor Coelestinus had to deal with the case. Rumours reached Fussala that he would insist on the restoration of Antonius, and that the Government would support him by military force. Augustine, in fear lest the people of Fussala should go back *en masse* to the Donatists, writes to Coelestinus to entreat his support. He entreats him by the memory of St. Peter, "who warned the *praepositi* of Christian peoples not to domineer over their brethren" (*ib.* 9). The case is an interesting one, but it loses some of its importance in view of the fact that the African church was then still bound by voluntary promise, pending inquiry into the genuineness of an alleged Nicene canon to that effect, to allow appeals to Rome by bishops. The promise arose out of the famous case of Apiarius. This presbyter was deposed by Augustine's friend and pupil Urbanus, bp. of Sicca, and appealed to Zosimus, bp. of Rome. Zosimus had hastily taken his side and ordered his restoration. Urbanus refused, both on the merits of the case, which he knew and Zosimus did not, and also on the ground that Zosimus had no right to interfere. This was the real question at issue. Zosimus first wrote (418), basing his right to interfere on the canons of Nicaea. As the African bishops found no such provision in their copy of the canons, they postponed the matter for further verification of the true text, promising meanwhile (*paulisper*) to act (without prejudice) on the assumption that the alleged canon was genuine. In reply, Zosimus sent three legates—Faustinus, bp. of Potentia in Picenum, and the presbyters Philip and Asellus—to Carthage, with written and oral instructions. The written instructions (*commonitorium*) comprised four points (Bruns *Canones*, I. 197): (1) the right of the Roman See to receive appeals from bishops (see *Can. Sard.* Lat. 3, 4); (2) bishops not to go over the sea to court (*i.e.* from Africa) "*importune*" (*ib.* 8); (3) presbyters and deacons excommunicated by their bishop to have an appeal to *finitimi episcopi* (*ib.* 17); (4) Urbanus to be excommunicated, "or even cited to Rome." Of these points, (2) betrays the soreness of Zosimus at the way in which Aurelius had forced his hand (*supra*, § 10, *b*); (4) hangs upon (1); (3) is necessary in order to bring the case of Apiarius, *who was not a bishop*, somehow under the scope of the pretended Nicene canon relating to (1); the case of Apiarius would become a factor in that of Urbanus, which Zosimus would, by stretching the right of receiving appeals to a right of *evocatio*, claim to deal with under (1). A reference to the Sardican canons will shew how flimsy a foundation they offer for the claims founded upon them. But what is important to observe is that Zosimus, like Innocentius (*supra*, § 10, *a*), bases his right to interfere simply upon canonical authority. On neither side is there any notion of jurisdiction inherent in the Roman see prior to ecclesiastical legislation. If the alleged canon was genuinely Nicene, it established the jurisdiction; if not, the jurisdiction fell to the ground.

When Faustinus and his colleagues reached Africa, Zosimus had been succeeded by Bonifatius. They were received by the plenary council of the African provinces at Carthage (419). Alypius and Augustine were there, and joined in the proceedings (Bruns, pp. 155 ff.). The council cut short the verbal instructions of Faustinus (*ib.* p. 197), and insisted upon hearing the *commonitorium*. When it was read, and the canon on episcopal appeals was quoted, Alypius undertook the invidious duty of pointing out that the Latin and the Greek copies of the Nicene canons accessible at Carthage contained no such canon. He suggested that both sides should obtain authentic copies from the bps. of Constantinople, Alexandria, and Antioch. Meanwhile, the copies above referred to should be placed on the minutes; but the alleged canon should be observed *donec integra exemplaria veniant*. Augustine proposed a like action with regard to (3); the proposals were unanimously carried, and accepted, though with no good grace, by Faustinus. The council wrote to Bonifatius intimating their action (Bruns, pp. 196 f.), stating how they had dealt with Apiarius, and complaining with dignity and firmness of the insolence of Faustinus, which, they add, they believe and hope they will not, under the new Roman bishop, be called upon to suffer. The signatures include those of Augustine and Alypius. Six years later (425) an African council (Bruns, p. 200) receive Faustinus once again. Coelestinus, now bp. of Rome, writes that "he has been rejoiced by the coming of Apiarius," and with Faustinus, Apiarius once more reappears at Carthage. But not only did the culprit finally and ignominiously break down before the council: the replies from the Eastern churches had come in, with authentic copies of the Nicene canons; and the canons put forward by Zosimus and his successors were not there. [It must be noted that, although Gratus of Carthage was possibly present at Sardica in 343 (see *Nicene Lib.* vol. 4, Athanasius, p. 147), the African church knew nothing of the canons passed there. They only knew Sardica by repute as an "Arian" synod, and friendly to the Donatists (*Ep.* 44[6]; *c. Crescon.* IV. xliv. 52). The canons of Sardica had not passed into the generally accepted rules of the church.] The council press the ignominious exposure, which makes a clean sweep of papal jurisdiction in Africa, with a firm but respectful hand. They are content to ask Coelestinus to observe the canons, not to receive appellants, not to send legates *tanquam a latere*, and, above all, not to inflict Faustinus upon them any more. The Roman chancery did not learn from this painful experience not to tamper with the canons (see the present writer's *Roman Claims to Supremacy*, iv., S.P.C.K. 1896), but the incident is decisive as to the mind of the African church. Though Reuter, in his scrupulous desire to be fair, minimizes the part taken by Augustine in the case (pp. 306 seq.), there is nothing to shew that in this matter he was in other than perfect accord with Aurelius and the African bishops. On the contrary, he says, late in his life, of clergy who merely evade his own rigorous diocesan rule: "interpellet contra me mille concilia, *naviget* contra me *quo voluerit*, adjuvabit me Deus ut ubi ego episcopus sum, ille clericus esse non possit." This tone implies that the Apiarius case is now matter of history (*Serm.* 156[1]). But Reuter is probably right in his view that Augustine's interest in constitutional questions was small compared to his concern for doctrine.

(*d*) *The Roman See and the Final Doctrinal Authority.*—Augustine shews no jealousy of the power and prestige of the Roman see. On the contrary, he regarded it as, in a special degree, the depository of apostolic tradition. What degree of dogmatic authority did this imply? The principal data for answering this question are connected with the Pelagian controversy (*supra*, § 10, *a*, *b*). Innocentius certainly reads into the letters of the Africans (Aug. *Epp.* 175-177, see 181-183) a hyper-Sardican attitude towards his chair of which they were innocent. But it is clear that the Africans attach the greatest importance to his approbation of their decision, only they do not treat the doctrinal issue as at all doubtful or subject to papal decision; on the contrary, in the private letter (*Ep.* 177[3, 6-9]) which Augustine sends to ensure that Innocentius shall not lack full information on the merits of the case, he takes for granted that the *ecclesiastica et apostolica veritas* is already certain. He assumes (with probable historical correctness) that the African church owes its original tradition to Rome (*ib.*[19]); but both have their source ("ex eodem capite") in the Apostolic tradition itself (see Reuter, pp. 307-311). Augustine refers to Innocentius's reply in a letter to Paulinus of Nola (*Ep.* 186). He treats it not as a doctrinal *decision*, but as a splendid confirmation of a doctrine *already* certain (see Reuter, p. 311). As a result, the Pelagians have definitely lost their case: "causa finita est." Augustine uses this phrase twice: once (§ 10, *a*, *fin.*) with reference to the African councils and the reply of Innocentius; once (see beginning of this section) in 421 of the condemnation of Pelagianism by the *judicium episcoporum*. With the latter passage we must compare *Ep.* 190[22] (written in 418), where the "adjutorium Salvatoris qui suam tuetur ecclesiam" is connected with the "conciliorum episcoporum vigilantia," not with the action of popes Innocentius and Zosimus. At a much later date (426), reviewing the controversy as a whole, he speaks of the whole cause as having been dealt with *conciliis episcopalibus*; the letters of the Roman bishops are not dignified with separate mention (*Ep.* 214[5]). On the whole, these utterances are homogeneous. The prominence, if any, assigned to the *rescripta* over the *concilia* in *Serm.* 131, 10 (*supra*, § 10, *a*, *fin.*) is relative to a passing phase of the question. Its sense is, moreover, wholly altered in the utterance invented for Augustine by some Roman Catholic apologists: *Roma locuta est, et causa finita est.* It occurred to no one in those days to put any bishop, even of an apostolic see, above a council, although there are signs at Rome of a tendency to work the Sardican canons in that direction. Augustine experienced, as we have seen, a signal, and to him especially galling, papal blunder in the action of Zosimus with reference to the Pelagians. The brunt of the correspondence with Zosimus at this painful crisis apparently fell upon Aurelius and the bishops of his province (Afri. *c. Duas Epp. Pel.* II. iii. 5), rather than upon Numidia, Augustine's own province. Augustine, as compared with the African bishops, distinctly minimizes the indictment. Zosimus had pronounced the *libellus* of Coelestius *catholic.* Augustine explains this favourably, as referring not to his doctrine, but to his profession of submission to correction; "voluntas emendationis, non falsitas dogmatis approbata est." The action of Zosimus was well meant, even if too lenient (*lenius actum est.* See also *de Pecc. Orig.* vi. 7, vii. 8). The letter of the *Afri*, which was stern and menacing in tone ("*Constituimus* . . . per venerabilem . . . Innocentium . . . prolatam *manere sententiam*," Prosp. *adv. Coll.* v. 15) put an end to all hopes of compromise. Zosimus, however (*c. Duas Epp.*, *u.s.*), "never by a word, in the whole course of the proceedings," denied original sin. His *faith* was consistent throughout. Coelestius deceived him for a time, but *illam sedem usque ad finem fallere non potuit* (*de Pecc. Orig.* xxi. 24). "The Roman church, where he was so well known, he could not deceive permanently" (*ib.* viii. 9). But there had been danger. "Supposing—which God forbid!—the Roman church had gone back upon the sentence of Innocentius and approved the *dogmata* condemned by him, then it would be necessary rather [*potius*] to brand *the Roman clergy* with the note of '*praevaricatio.*'" Even in contemplating the repellent possibility that the action of Rome had been worse than he will allow, Augustine evidently shrinks from pushing the conclusion to its full consequences to the extent of censuring Zosimus by name. "Rather" he would brand "the Roman clergy" *in confuso.* But this reserve must not be misconstrued as an anticipation of later Roman infallibilism; not even St. Peter was strictly infallible in Augustine's eyes (refs. in Reuter, pp. 326 ff.), much less his successors', none of whom "Petri apostolatui conferendus est" (*de Bapt.* VI. ii. 3).

(*e*) *Conclusion.*—Augustine has no consistent theory of the ultimate organ of church authority, whether legislative, disciplinary, or dogmatic. This authority resides in the Episcopate, its content is the *catholica veritas*, and in practical matters the *consuetudo* or *traditio.* These are to be interpreted by the bishops acting in concert—especially in councils. The "regional" council is subordinate to the "plenary," the plenary council of the province to that of the whole church (*de Bapt.* V. xvii., VII., liii.; *Ep.* 43, 9; *de Bapt.* II. iii. 4); while of the latter, the earlier are subject to amendment by later councils. Even, then, with regard to the authority of councils there is no real finality; Augustine sees, like Julius of Rome in 340 (see the writer's *Roman Claims to Supremacy*, iii. *ad fin.*), no remedy but the revision of earlier councils by later. Clearly we have here no complete system of thought. Augustine falls back on the *sensus catholicus*, a real and valuable criterion, but not easy to bring within a logical definition. The church is infallible, but he cannot point to an absolutely infallible organ of her authority. By his very vagueness on this point, Augustine practically paved the way for the future centralization of infallible authority in the papacy (on the whole question, see Reuter, pp. 329-355; and below, § 16, *b*).

§ 13. *Death and Character.*—Augustine died on Aug 28, 430. Clouds were thickening over his country and church. The Vandals, invited by the error, too late discovered, of Augustine's friend count Bonifatius (see *Ep.* 220), welcomed by the fierce Moors and the persecuted Donatists, had swept Numidia and Africa. Carthage, Cirta, and Hippo alone remained untaken (Possid. xxviii.). Bonifatius, routed by Gaiseric, was besieged by him in Hippo itself. Augustine had exhorted all bishops, so long as they had any flocks to minister to, to remain at their posts (*Ep.* 228; Possid. xxx.); but many, whose dioceses were swept away, took refuge, like Possidius himself, at Hippo. Up to the time of his death, during three months of the siege, Augustine was working at his unfinished refutation of Julian. He prayed, so he told his friends at table, that God would either see fit to deliver the city, or fortify His servants to bear His will, or at any rate would take him out of this world to Himself. In the third month he was attacked by fever. Now, as on other marked occasions (Possid. xxix.), his prayer was heard. He healed a sick man who came to him as he lay upon his death-bed. He had a copy of the Penitential Psalms written out, and fixed to the wall opposite his bed. For ten days, at his special request, he was left alone, except when the physician came or food was brought. He spent his whole time in prayer, and died in the presence of his praying friends, in a green old age, with hearing, sight, and all his bodily faculties unimpaired. The Sacrifice was offered and he was buried. He left no will, nor any personal property. His books he had given to the church to be kept for ever; fortunately, they survived when Hippo was destroyed by the Vandals; his writings, says Possidius, "will for ever keep his character fresh in the minds of his readers, yet not even they will supply, to those who knew him, the place of his voice and his presence. For he was one who fulfilled the word of St. James: 'So speak ye, *and so do.*'" He had lived 76 years, and nearly 40 in the ranks of the clergy. Till his last illness he had preached regularly. His arbitration was greatly in request, on the part both of churchmen and non-churchmen. He gladly aided all, taking opportunity when he could to speak to them for the good of their souls. For criminals, he would intercede with discrimination and tact, and rarely without success. He attended councils whenever he could, and in these, as in the ordination of bishops and clergy, he was conspicuously conscientious. In dress and furniture he followed a just mean between luxury and shabbiness; his table was spare, his diet mainly vegetarian, though meat was there for visitors or for *infirmiores.* Wine he always drank. His spoons were silver, but his other vessels wood, earthenware, or marble. His hospitality never failed: his meals were made enjoyable, not by feasting and carousing, but by reading or conversation. Ill-natured gossip he sternly repressed. He had this motto conspicuously displayed:

Quisquis amat dictis absentem rodere vitam,
Hanc mensam indignam noverit esse sibi.

He sharply rebuked even bishops for breaches of this excellent rule. He freely spent upon the poor both the income of his see and the alms of the faithful. To ill-natured grumblings about the wealth of his see, he replied that he would gladly resign all the episcopal estates, if the people would support him and his brethren wholly by their offerings. "Sed nunquam id laici suscipere voluerunt." The whole management of the property of the see was entrusted to the more capable clergy in rotation, subject only to an annual report to himself. He would never increase the estate by purchase, but he accepted bequests. Only he refused them if he thought they entailed hardship upon the natural heirs. He felt but little interest in such affairs—his part was that of Mary, not that of Martha. Even building he left to his clergy, only interfering if the plans seemed extravagant. If the annual accounts shewed a deficit, he would announce to the Christian people that he had nothing left to spend on the poor. Sometimes he would have church plate melted to relieve the poor or ransom prisoners. His clergy lived with him, and no one who joined them was permitted to retain any property of his own. If one of them swore at table, one of the regulation number of cups of wine (these were strictly limited, even for visitors) was cut off by way of fine. Women, even near relatives, were excluded.

He never would speak to them *solus cum solis*. He was prompt in visiting the fatherless and widows in their affliction, and the sick. But he would never visit the *feminarum monasteria* except under urgent necessity. In regard to death, he was fond of quoting the dying Ambrose, who replied to his friend's entreaty that he would ask God for a respite of life: "I have not so lived as to be ashamed to remain with you; but neither do I fear to die, for we have a gracious God." To this artless picture, drawn by Possidius, it seems impertinent to add supplementary touches. Possidius, as Loofs has excellently remarked, shews himself saturated by the consciousness that he is erecting a lasting memorial to a great historical personage.

Without doubt Augustine is the most commanding religious personality of the early church. No Christian writer since the apostolic age has bequeathed to us so deep an insight into the working of a character penetrated with the love of God, none has struck deeper into the heart of religion in man.

C. INFLUENCE.—§ 14. *Retractations and Other Writings*.—Shortly before his last illness (Possid. xxviii.) he went over all his writings, noting points, especially in the earlier books, which he would wish amended. The result is his two books of *Retractationes*, which, from the chronological order, and the mention of the circumstances which elicited the several writings, places the literary history of St. Augustine on an exceptionally sure footing. He enumerates, characterizes, and identifies by the first words, two hundred and thirty-two books. His letters and sermons he mentions collectively, but he did not live to reconsider them in detail. Possidius includes most of them in the *indiculus* of Augustine's works appended to the Life; but it is not always easy to identify them by the titles he employs. Some of the letters, however, are counted as "books" in the *Retractations*, while the books *de Unitate Ecclesiae, de Bono Viduitatis ad Julianum*, and *de Perfectione Justitiae* are passed over (being reckoned as letters) in the *Retractations*. The *Sermons* are not chronologically arranged in the Bened. ed.; some are duplicate recensions of the same discourse. Augustine preached extempore, but with careful preparation (*de Cat. Rud.* 2, 3); his words were taken down by shorthand, or else dictated by himself. On one occasion we read (Possid. xv.) that he abandoned his prepared matter and spoke on another subject, with the result of the conversion of a Manichean who happened to be present. His homilies (*tractatus*) on St. John, and on the "Epistle of John to the Parthians" (*i.e.* 1 John), belong to the ripest period of his theological power, about 416; these and the somewhat later *Enarrationes in Psalmos* are his most important exegetical works.

Many of his works have been already mentioned in connexion with the occasion of their production. For a full list of other writings, see *D. C. B.* (4-vol. ed.), *s.v.*, and the art. of Loofs referred to below. But one or two of special importance must be briefly characterized. He accomplished by 415 the task, his first attempt at which had failed, of a commentary on Genesis *ad literam* (*Retr.* II. xxiv.; cf. I. xviii., and *supra*, § 7, *b*). But even now, he claims to have reached only problematical results. The *de Catechizandis Rudibus* (*c.* 400) gives a syllabus of the course for catechumens, with hints as to effective method in their instruction. It is full of wisdom, and suggestive to all engaged in teaching. The *de Spiritu et Litera* (*supra*, § 10) was supplemented (*c.* 413) by the book *de Fide et Operibus*, in which he deals with the obligations of the Christian life, insisting that faith cannot save us without charity. Here occurs the often quoted reference to the Lord's Prayer as the *quotidiana medela* for sins not demanding public penance (xxvi. 48), nor even fraternal rebuke (*correptio*, Matt. xviii. 15, cl. *Serm.* 352). The *Encheiridion* (*c.* 421) is Augustine's most complete attempt at a brief summary of Christian doctrine. Nominally it is based on the triple scheme of Fides, Spes, Charitas. But the latter two are very briefly treated at the end; practically the whole comes under the head of Fides, and is an exposition of the Creed and its corollaries. It should be compared with the much earlier tract *de Fide et Symbolo* (*supra*, § 7, *b*). On the *de Trinitate*, see above, § 11. The last work to be specially mentioned is the *de Doctrina Christiana* (written in 397 as far as III. xxv.), which contains Augustine's principles of Scriptural exposition, and a discussion of the exegetical "rule" of Tyconius. Bk. iv. (added in 426) is on the method and spirit in which the sense of Scripture should be taught. It supplements the more special "pedagogics" of the *de Catech. Rudibus*.

Of Augustine as a writer, Gibbon says: "His style, though sometimes animated by the eloquence of passion, is usually clouded by false and affected rhetoric." This verdict would gain in justice if the words "usually" and "sometimes" were transposed. Augustine had indeed learned and taught rhetoric to some purpose; but tried by Aristotle's criterion—the revelation of character—Augustine stands far above the category of rhetorical writers. He rarely or never spends words upon mere effect. He is always intent upon bringing home to his hearers or readers things which he feels to be momentously real. He handles subjects of intimate and vital interest to the human spirit. And whether he is right or wrong, his deep feeling cannot fail to kindle the hearts of those who read him.

§ 15. *Asceticism. Estimate of Poverty and Riches*.—Among the attractions which Manicheism had for Augustine in his youth, the strict continency supposed to prevail among the *perfecti* (*supra*, § 4) had been prominent. His whole early experience had led him to regard sexual temptation as the great ordeal of life. Disillusioned with the *perfecti*, he was fired with the ideals of Catholic monasticism (§ 6), and one of his earliest resolves at the time of his conversion was to forswear for ever even lawful marriage. The whole drift of Christian feeling at that period was in this direction. The influence of Ambrose, the horror of representative churchmen at the anti-monastic tenets of Jovinian and Vigilantius, the low tone even of nominally Christian society in an age of degenerate civilization, all tended to fix in him the conviction, exemplified in his last letter to count Bonifatius, that practically the one escape from an immoral life was in the vow of monastic continence. He is aware of the difficulties of the questions raised, and endeavours to face them in his books *de Bono Conjugali*, *de Virginitate* (401, against Jovinian), and *de Continentia*. He is specially anxious not to depreciate marriage; but in his attempt to explain the transmission of original sin, not merely by the fact "that the human embryo grows from the very first in a soil positively sinful," but by the assumption that the mode of ordinary human generation is inevitably sinful, he fairly lays himself open to the charge of doing so (*de Nupt.* II. 15; *Enchir.* xii. 34; *de Civ.* XIV. xvi.-xxi.). The orthodox theology of original sin has by common consent dropped this element of the Augustinian theory, which shifts the fundamental Christian condemnation of sensuality from the basis of moral insight to that of semi-Manichean dualism. But Julian was wrong in setting it down wholly to Augustine's Manichean past. This may at most account for a bias, which neither his subsequent philosophical studies nor the atmosphere of the church were likely to eradicate. Augustine only exaggerates an instinct not dominant, but really present (Matt. xix. 12; I. Cor. vii. 1, 26) in the Christian religion from the first, strengthened by the influences of the times, especially that of the Christian Platonism, and by the end of the 4th cent. elevated to unassailable supremacy. In that cent. the influx of heathen society into the church threatened her distinctive character as a holy society. The monastic ideal of life, with its corollary of a double standard of Christian morality—baleful as the latter was in its effects—was probably the church's *then* only possible response to the challenge of a momentous peril. Augustine introduced monachism into North Africa, and its spread there was rapid. In Hippo it was compulsory for the clergy. At first, Augustine permitted a "secular" clergy, but toward the end of his life the permission was revoked. With celibacy went the common life and the obligation of absolute personal poverty. We saw above (§ 7, *a*) how Augustine had followed, early in his Christian career, the example of Anthony. He took the communism of Acts iv. 32 as the normal ideal of Christian life (*Enarr. in Ps.* cxxxi. 5), and his community was modelled upon it (*supra*, § 13). At the same time, in the book *de Opere Monachorum* (*c.* 400), he insists that monks must work, and not idly rely upon the alms of the faithful. He shews an almost prophetic appreciation of monastic abuses (cf. what he says of the Euchites, *de Haer.* lvii.). He regards poverty as a *consilium* (*de Bono Conj.* xxiii. 30, *Ep.* 157[29]), not a *praeceptum*. Worldly possessions are allowed to the good as well as to the evil, "et a malis habetur et a bonis; *tanto melius habetur quanto* minus amatur" (*Ep.* 153[26], cf. *de Civ.* XVIII. liv.). The Pelagians, who naturally insisted on human effort as a condition of salvation, took a severer view of wealth than did Augustine (*Epp.* 157, 186[32], *divites baptizatos*, sqq.). He combats them on Biblical grounds: Dives and Lazarus, the rich Abraham, the rich young man, the camel and the needle's eye, St. Paul's charge to the rich in this world; but his treatment of the question is not constructively built on first principles. He perceives that it is the *spirit*, not the *mere fact* of riches or poverty that is all-important; even a rich man may be poor in spirit and ready to suffer not only the loss of all, but martyrdom itself, for Christ's sake (see *Serm.* 50[5], 14; *Ep.* 157,[29, 34, 36], etc.; *de Virg.* 14). Yet riches—and this is the reflection towards which he gravitates—are, as a matter of experience, a great hindrance; the rich are as a rule the chief offenders "difficile est ut non plura peccata contrahant" (*in Psalm.* cxxxii. 4), therefore "abstineamus nos, fratres, a possessione rei privatae . . . fac locum domino" (*ib.* cxxxi.[6]); the counsel of poverty is the safe course. Augustine bases this on the temptation to misuse of wealth; this would tend to place the man who uses his wealth well and wisely, overcoming temptation, in God's service, higher than him who evades the trial. But the drift of church feeling was too strong for this thought to prevail. Augustine and Pelagius were agreed that monks *as a class* must rank above "secular" Christians; widely removed as Augustine was from the Pelagian idea of merit, yet practically he often subordinates the importance of the inward to the outward, of character to works. But monks must live, and, as we have seen, Augustine would have them work. To "take no thought for the morrow" means to seek first the Kingdom of God; not improvidence or laziness, but singleness of aim is the note of the Christian life (*in Serm. in Mont.* II. 56).

Augustine had occasion (*Ep.* 211) to address a long letter to his nuns, giving directions for the abatement of evils incidental to the common life, and for the regulation of their prayers, food, costume, and other details. This letter, a model of good sense and right-mindedness, is the basis of the "Regula" for monks printed among his works. This Rule is therefore an *adaptation* of Augustine's actual counsels, but can hardly be from his own hand. It has been much valued by monastic reformers, and was the basis of the rules of St. Norbet, of St. Dominic (1216), and of the different communities of "canons regular" and friars which have borne the title of "Augustinian" (from 1244).

It will be noticed that Augustine's theory of property is vitiated by the assumption that Acts iv. 32 implies a permanent condemnation of private property. This was even more conspicuously the case with St. Ambrose, who speaks very strongly of the duty of Christians to treat their possessions as the property of the poor. Augustine, in a passage not wholly consistent with some referred to above, speaks similarly of the private property of Christians as the common property of all; to treat it otherwise is *damnabilis usurpatio* (*Ep.* 105[35]). This "Christian communism," it may be remarked in passing, differs from that of Proudhon ("la propriété c'est le vol") as the *duty to give* differs from the *right to take*. In one point Augustine takes the opposite view to Ambrose, namely, in the theory of church property. Ambrose, in his resistance to the action of the empress Justina, who attempted to transfer the church at Milan to the Arian bishop, anticipated the medieval theory of the absolute right of the church to ecclesiastical property, a right with which the emperor, who is *intra ecclesiam*, may not presume to tamper. This agrees perfectly with principles laid down by Augustine in the *de Civitate Dei* (*supra*, § 9: *imperium in ecclesia*, etc.). But Augustine, defending the action of Honorius (or his ministers) in transferring to the Catholics the church property of the Donatists, strongly maintains that all rights to property are created by the State. The church's external power and property are hers by *indirect* Divine right, *i.e.* because they are conferred on her by the *ordinatissima potestas* of the sovereign power (*Ep.* 105[5, 6]). "Per jura regum possidentur possessiones" (*in Joh. Tr.* vi. 25); the Donatist objects to state interference with religion, but "Noli dicere Quid mihi et Regi! Quid tibi *et possessioni*?" (*ib.* 15). As one side of Augustine's theory of the church prepares the way for the Gregorian system (§ 9), so here we have that conception of Apostolic poverty consistently applied to church property, which underlies so much medieval reaction against the Gregorian system from Arnold of Brescia onwards.

§ 16. *Intellectual Influence on Christian Posterity.*—The diverse influences which met in Augustine, held together rather than fused into unison by the strength of his superb personality, parted in after-times into often conflicting streams. It has been said with truth (Loofs) that three primary elements determine Augustine's complex realm of ideas: his neo-Platonist philosophical training (*supra*, § 5), his profound Biblical studies (§§ 7, *b*, 10, *init.*), and his position as an officer of the church. In combinations which we can in part analyse, these elements, given the Augustine of A.D. 387, go to constitute Augustine as he became—the greatest of the Latin doctors, the pioneer of modern Christianity—in his threefold significance for the church of all time. Augustine is (*a*) the prince of theists, (*b*) the incomparable type of reasoned devotion to the Catholic church, and (*c*) the founder of the theology of sin and grace.

(*a*) *Theistic Transcendentalism.*—The passion of theism was the core of his personal religion. His was an experimental theism, a theism of the heart. The often quoted words, "Tu Domine fecisti nos ad te, et inquietum est cor nostrum donec requiescat in te" (*Conf.* I. i.), sum up his inmost personal experience. This is, above all, what Augustine found in the Psalms, which were his introduction to the deeper study of Scripture (*supra*, § 6). "Mihi autem adhaerere Deo bonum est" (Ps. lxxii. 28, Vulg.) is the immovable centre upon which his whole religion and theology turns. But his theism was also speculative and metaphysical, and intimately bound up with the philosophical framework of his theology. God, though not beyond our apprehension ("ex minima quidem parte, sed tamen sine dubitatione," *c. Ep. Fund.* 5), is beyond our knowledge; "ego sum qui sum *quae mens potest capere*?" (*in Joh. Tr.* viii. 8). To be, to be good, to be one, are correlative attributes; they belong to God alone. All things that exist, do so by "participation" of God (*in Joh. Tr.* xxxix. 8—the Platonic doctrine of μέθεξις); but by comparison with God they are non-existent (*Enarr. in Ps.* xxxviii. 22, cxxxiv. 4). Real being is *incommutable* being, which belongs to God only. *Reality*, then, *can only be found out of time*: "ut ergo et tu sis, transcende tempus" (*in Joh. Tr.* xxxviii. 10); anything mutable is not really existent—it is in process, has been, is to be, but is not *in being*: "praesens quaero, nihil stat" (*ib.*). Absolute good is therefore the only reality, namely, God. Absolute evil is the non-existent. All created existence, so far as it has reality ("Deus fecit hominem, *substantiam* [*i.e.* aliquid esse] fecit," *Enarr. in Ps.* lxviii. 5), is good ("in quantum *sumus, boni sumus*," *de Doctr.* I. 35). There is no "*natura* tenebrarum," no *evil substance* (*Conf.* IV. xv. 24). Sin has its roots in the *evil will*; it is negative ("non est substantia," Ps. lxviii. 3, Vulg.); the evil will consists in "inordinate moveri, *bona inferiora superioribus praeponendo*" (*de Gen. ad lit.* xi. 17); sin is therefore an *inclinatio in nihilum*; yet the sinner "non penitus perit, sed in infimis ordinatur" (*Enarr. in Ps.* viii. 19)—even Satan, in that he exists, has something of the good, though he is worse than the worst we know. "In quantum mali sumus, in tantum etiam *minus sumus*" (*de Doctr.*, *u.s.*). It is easy to see that this idealism, taken by itself, tends to lower the importance of everything that takes place in time, of everything empirical and historical, in comparison with the transcendent being and unchangeable will of God, in which nothing "takes place," but all is eternally, immovably real. In Augustine this idealism did not stand alone; but under all his passionate appreciation of the church and the historical elements of Christianity there is in the background, as a limiting influence, the appeal to the view of things *sub specie aeterni*; and the drift of his theological reflection strengthened this element in his view of ultimate problems.

From this point of view we can partly understand Augustine's famous conception of the *universality of the Christian Religion.* This he insists on in his letter to Deogratias (*Ep.* 102) *contra Paganos.* At all times, he writes, since the world began, the same faith has been revealed to men, at one time more obscurely, at another more plainly, as the circumstances altered; but what we now call the Christian religion is but the clearest revelation of a religion as old as the world. Never has its offer of salvation been withheld from those who were worthy of it (see references, Reuter, p. 91 *n*), even though they may not be (like Job, etc.) mentioned in the sacred record. Such men, who followed His commands (however unconsciously), were *implicit* believers in Christ. The changing (and therefore semi-real) form represents the one constant reality, the saving grace of God, *revealed* through the passion and resurrection of Christ (*Ep.* 189[15]).

(*b*) *Catholic Churchmanship.*—Of this we have already spoken (§ 8). Augustine was not the first to formulate belief in the Holy Catholic Church; but no one before him had reflected so deeply, or expressed himself with such inimitable tenderness and devotion, on the church as the nurse and home of the Christian life, and the saving virtue of her means of grace. The church to him is the society of the saints, the Kingdom of God on earth. With the whole drift of contemporary churchmanship, asceticism, miracles, relics, the incipient cultus of saints (he believes in their *intercession*, but strongly dissuades from "placing our hope" in them: "*noli facere*"; if we pray to God alone, we shall be the *more* likely to benefit by their intercession: "non solum tibi non succensebunt; sed tunc amabunt, tunc magis favebunt"; but Augustine is evidently correcting a known tendency to invocation, *Serm.* 46[17]), he is in entire sympathy. It is unnecessary to multiply examples of what every page of his writings abundantly illustrates. But it must be noted that his interest throughout is in the spiritual life rather than in the external system; the latter is but the means to the former. Augustine, first of all extant Christian writers, identifies the Kingdom of God (so far as it exists on earth; its full realization, in common with all Christian antiquity, he reserves for the end) with the Catholic church: but not in respect of its government or organization. It is the Kingdom of Christ in so far as Christ reigns in His saints and they (even on earth, in a sense) reign with Him. From this point of view, we may trace the negative influence of Augustine's idealism (*supra, a*) upon his view of the church. We saw above (§ 15, *e*) his inability to complete his theory of church authority by the essential feature of an infallible organ of authority. Councils are authoritative, but earlier councils are subject to later ones, there is no *final* expression of *absolute positive* truth (of course there is *relative* truth; the church will never rehabilitate Arianism nor Pelagianism *inferiora superioribus praeponendo*, see above, *a*). Truth is, ideally, perceived by the reason (*de Util. Cred.* 34); infallibility is an *ideal* attribute of the church, its realization now is subject to the semi-reality which is the condition of all things on earth. She has *catholica veritas*, but never as *ultimate* truth that man can explicitly grasp. To the church, as to the individual, it may be said, "ut et tu sis, transcende tempus." Ideally, authority is but the "door" to reason; authority is for the babes, the *stulti*, who are not the type of mature Christian growth. The *intelligendi vivacitas* is for the *paucissimi*, the *credendi simplicitas* is safest for the *turba* (*c. Ep. Fund.* 5). But Augustine does not press these thoughts to their full issue. "Alia est ratio verum tacendi, alia verum dicendi necessitas . . . *ne pejores faciamus eos qui non intelligunt dum volumus eos qui intelligunt facere doctiores*" (*de Dono Persev.* 40). Practically they operate negatively, by leaving in the vague the question of an infallible organ of authority, while the positive conception of the church is left unaffected. In the sphere of transcendent reality, the decrees of councils may be provisional only; but in practice *any* authoritative decision is final, even the appeal to a general council (*supra,* § 10, *b*, Julian) may be ignored, "causa finita est" (*supra*, 15, *d*). Medieval ecclesiasticism accepted Augustine's homage to the external fabric of the church, and concerned itself little with his metaphysical conception of Reality (see references to Gregory VII., in Reuter, pp. 499 seq.).

(*c*) *Influence of his Doctrine of Grace.*—Augustine's conception of the church, little as it was modified in practice by his transcendental theory of "Being" taken by itself, was more seriously affected by his predestinarian doctrine, which his transcendentalism certainly tended to reinforce. Augustine had first found salvation in the Catholic church (*c. Ep. Fund.* 6) in self-surrender to the authority of Christ (*c. Acad.* III. 43: "mihi autem certum est nusquam prorsus ab auctoritate Christi discedere," etc.). His whole religious thought, founded upon his experience of the Catholic church, turned upon Christ as its fountain-head and centre (see the passages collected by Reuter, pp. 19-25). His whole being, and that of the church, was owing to the grace of Christ ("gratia Dei *per* Christum, *propter* Christum," etc.); the *gratia Christi* is the central idea of his theology. We saw above (§ 10) by what steps he was led, from the inward recognition of the sovereignty of grace in his personal life, to the logical conclusion that salvation depends upon the Divine will irrespective of merit or of anything which takes place on earth. Membership of the church, a holy life, use of the means of grace, may be indispensable to the predestined; but they are in no sense *conditions* of predestination, which is absolute. They depend on it, not it on them. Even the historical work of Christ is secondary to the Divine purpose to save some and "pass over" the rest of mankind. Hence, on the one hand, the doctrine of particular redemption (for *none* perish for whom Christ died, *Ep.* 169[4], while those predestined *ad interitum* are "*non* ad vitam aeternam sui sanguinis pretio comparati"—*in Joh. Tr.* xlvii. 11, 4), on the other hand, a tendency to make the atonement not an *efficient* cause of redemption but a proof (to the elect) of God's love: "*ut ostenderet* Deus dilectionem suam," etc. (*de Catech. Rud.* 4; cf. *Ep.* 177[15]: "gratia Dei quae *revelata est* per passionem et resurrectionem Christi"). The number of the predestined is irrevocably fixed, and this *certus numerus* constitute the church as it will be in the perfect Kingdom of God. The church on earth, viewed as it is in God's sight, in its true "being," consists of the elect and of them alone. The old Catholic axiom *extra ecclesiam nulla salus* thus acquires a new and unlooked-for meaning: out of the *number of the elect* there is no salvation. This is the Augustinian doctrine of the *communion of saints*, which stands in contrast with the *externa communio* or visible church as the invisible reality with the semi-real phenomenon. The distinction is not quite identical with the familiar distinction of wheat and tares, nominal and real Christians; for even real Christians have no certainty that they are "elect." The *donum perseverantiae*, which is as absolutely unmerited as that of faith, and is, in fact, the turning-point of the whole predestinarian scheme, may fail them (*supra*, § 10, *c*). In that case they are, after all, vessels of wrath; while again it may be vouchsafed to others who are now but nominal Christians, or not even that. When Augustine identifies the church with the Kingdom of

God, it is really of the *communio sanctorum* that he is thinking. The logical incompatibility of the predestinarian and the Catholic view of the church is obvious, and Augustine never effected their reconciliation. The obvious reconciliation, upon which he often appears to fall back, is that although the church contains many who are not "elect," it yet contains *all* the elect. But this is to assume that the Divine election is absolutely bound to external means, which Augustine does not really hold. On the contrary, his conception of the universality of the One Religion of Christ (*supra, a*, sub fin.) brings in Job, the Sibyl, and doubtless many others "qui secundem Deum vixerunt eique placuerunt, pertinentes ad spiritalem Hierusalem" (*de Civ.* XVIII. xlvii.). Again, there are the unjustly excommunicated, who have nothing of the character of schismatics: "hos coronat in occulto Pater," etc. (*de Vera Relig.* ii. cf. *de Bapt.* I. 26, *Epp.* 78. 3, 250, *fragm. ad. fin.*). But practically Augustine passes to and fro between the thought of the *numerus praedestinatorum* and that of the visible church without being careful to distinguish them, and he freely applies to the latter the exalted and ideal prerogatives which are theoretically proper to the former.

To this side of Augustine's teaching applies the remark of Gibbon, that "the rigid system of Christianity which he framed or restored has been entertained with public applause and secret reluctance by the Latin church." In fact, as the ecclesiastical side of Augustine's thought supplied the inspiration for the medieval theocracy, so his predestinarian idea of the church furnished the theological foundation for most of the medieval counter-movements, especially those of Marsilius, of Wyclif, and of Hus; and the Zwinglian idea of an invisible church is little more than an isolation of this doctrine from the Catholic context which surrounded it in Augustine's own theology.

§ 17. *Select Bibliography.* (1) *History of Publication.*—Augustine's *Retractationes*, coupled with the *Indiculus* of Possidius, give a practically complete list of his authentic works and of the occasions of their composition and publication. During his lifetime they were widely multiplied in Latin Christendom (Possid. vii.); the *Emendatiora Exempla*, revised by himself, and bequeathed to the church of Hippo, were preserved through the disasters which overtook the town (*ib.* xviii.). The history of the study and literary influence of Augustine in after-times must be read in the histories of Christian doctrine. For the 11th cent. we have a useful investigation by Mirbt (pupil of Reuter), *Die Stellung Augustins in der Publizistik des Gregorianischen Kirchenstreits* (Leipz. 1888). The history of manuscript transmission may be read in the prefatory notes to the several treatises in the Benedictine ed., and in the *Prolegomena* to the instalments of Augustine's works that have so far been published in the Vienna *Corpus Script. Eccles. Latinorum.* The list of editions since the first by Amerbach (Basel, 1506) may be found in the article by Loofs (*infra*). The standard ed. is that by the Benedictines of St. Maur (see Kukula and Rottmanner in *Hist. Phil. Transactions of the Vienna Academy*, 1890-1892, and Tassin, *Hist. lit. de la Congrég. de S. Maur.*, Brux. 1770), completed in 1690. The edition was by several hands, and was attacked fiercely by the opponents of Jansenism. This was perhaps inevitable in the attempt to make Augustine speak for himself. The principal points of attack were the *Preface*, by Mabillon, *to the Tenth Volume*, which its author revised under pressure, and the *Index*. The latter is a marvel of completeness, and many of its articles are in substance theological treatises. The *Vita*, mainly by Vaillant, is largely indebted to the contemporary work of Tillemont, the thirteenth vol. of whose *Mémoires*, a *Life* of St. Augustine, in 1075 pp., appeared after his death (1698). The Bened. ed. was reprinted at Venice, 1729-1735. The eleven vols. in folio were replaced in the next reprints (Venice, 1756-1769, Bassano, 1797-1807) by eighteen in quarto. The Paris reprint of Gaume (1836-1839) and that of Migne (in the *Patr. Lat.*, vols. 32-46) return to the arrangement of eleven vols.; but in Migne some of the vols. are subdivided, and a twelfth of supplementary matter (*Patr. Lat.* 47) is added. This edition is better printed than many of the series, and is the most convenient for reference. Its text should be superseded by that of the Vienna Corpus; but at present only a portion of Augustine's works have appeared in this series (*Confessions, de Civ. Dei, Letters*, 1–133, *Speculum*, several exegetical works, anti-Manichean treatises, various anti-Pelagian works, and a vol. containing *de Fid. et Symb.*, the *Retractationes*, and other works (1900); also the excerpts of Eugippius, an edition important for the light thrown by it on the text of Augustine).

(2) *Editions of Separate Works.*—We have a good edition of the *de Civitate Dei*, by Dombart (Trübner, 1863), and a more recent one of bks. xi. and xii., with intro., literal trans., and notes by Rev. H. Gee (Bell, 5*s.*), who has also ed. *In Joannis Evang. Tract.* xxiv.-xxvii. and lxvii.-lxxix. (1*s.* 6*d.* each, Bell), with trans. by Canon H. Brown; a number of smaller tracts, and the *de Trinitate* in the SS. Patr. Opusc. Selecta, by H. Hurter, S.J. (Innsbruck, Wagner); *Anti-Pelagian Treatises*, with valuable Introduction by Dr. Bright (Clarendon Press, 1880); *de Catechiz. Rud.*, by Krüger (in his *Quellenschriften*, 4, Frieburg, 1891); *Confessions*, by Pusey (Oxf. 1838), and Gaume (Paris, 1836, 12mo). The new ed. of *Tract. in Joh.* lxvii.-lxxix., by H. F. Stewart (Camb. 1900), has a translation and some admirably digested introductory matter.

(3) *Translations.*—The translations in the Oxford *Library of the Fathers*, and in Clark's series (Edin. 1866-1872), are incorporated and supplied with useful introductory matter in the *Post-Nicene Library* (ser. 1), ed. by Dr. Philip Schaff (Buffalo, 1886-8). *Three Anti-Pelagian Treatises*, by Woods and Johnston (D. Nutt, 1887). The *Confessions*, bks. i.-ix., are translated by Dr. Charles Bigg (Methuen, 1897, with a most interesting Introduction). The extracts in this article follow this translation. Another ed. by Temple Scott, with intro. by Mrs. Meynell, is pub. by Mowbray (7*s.* 6*d.* net.), and follows Dr. Pusey's trans. Dr. Hutchings trans. and ed. the *Con-*

fessions (Longmans, 2s. 6d.). *Preaching and Teaching acc. to S. Aug.* is a new trans. of the *de Doct. Christ.* bk. iv., and *de Rudibus Catech.* with 3 intro. essays by Rev. W. J. V. Baker and C. Bickersteth and a preface by Bp. Gore (Mowbray, 2s. 6d.).

(4) *Biographies.*—In addition to that of Possidius, and those of the Benedictines and Tillemont mentioned above, see Remy Ceillier, *Auteurs Sacrés*, vols. 11 and 12; *Acta Sanctorum*: Aug. vol. 6; Poujoulat, *Hist. de Saint Aug.* (Paris, 1843); Böhringer, *Aur. Aug.* (2 ed., Stuttg. 1878); Naville, *St. Aug.: Etude sur le développement de sa pensée*, etc. (Geneva, 1872); Bindemann, *der h. Aug.* (3 vols., Berlin, 1844-1869); Harnack, *Augustin's Confessionem* (Giessen, 1888). The greater Church Histories, and works on Christian literature, deal fully with Augustine. A brochure, *S. Augustine and African Church Divisions* by the Rev. W. J. Sparrow Simpson, was pub. by Longmans in 1910. Of articles in Dictionaries, etc., we may mention those of de Pressensé, in *D. C. B.* (4-vol. ed.), which gives a very useful list of the contents of the several vols. of his works in the great Benedictine edition, and Loofs, in Herzog-Hauck's *Real-Encyclopädie* (Leipz. 1897), an article worthy of the writer's high reputation, and much used in the present article.

(5) *Doctrinal and General.*—For older literature, see the references to fuller bibliographies at the end. The *Augustinische Studien* of Hermann Reuter (Gotha, 1887), so frequently quoted above, are beyond comparison for thoroughness and impartiality, and indispensable. The histories of doctrine should be consulted. Harnack's treatment of Augustine (in his *Dogmengeschichte*, vol. 3) is among the most sympathetic and powerful portions of that work; the writer's instinctive appreciation of a great religious personality is nowhere more apparent than here. Loofs's *Leitfaden* is also most useful. Mozley, *The Augustinian Doctrine of Predestination* (3rd. ed. 1883); Nourrisson, *La Philosophie de St. Augustin* (Paris, 1886, 2 vols.); Bright, *Lessons from the Lives of Three Great Fathers* (ed. 2, Oxf. 1891); Cunningham, *St. Austin* (Hulsean Lectures, 1886); Bigg, *Christian Platonists of Alexandria* (Bampton Lectures, 1886; comparison of Aug. with Origen, etc.); Robertson, *Regnum Dei* (Bampton Lectures, No. 5); Dorner, *Augustinus* (Berlin, 1873); Gibb and Montgomery's ed. of the *Confessions* in the *Camb. Patristic Texts*, 1908, a valuable critical ed. with Introduction.

The above list is a mere selection. For more complete bibliography see Loofs (*u.s.*); Bardenhewer's *Patrology*, Dr. Shahan's trans. 1908, pub. by Herder, Freiburg i/B. and St. Louis, Mo.; Potthast, *Bibliotheca Hist. Medii Aevi* (ed. 2, 1896), vol. ii. p. 1187; Chevallier, *Répertoire des sources historiques*; de Pressensé (*u.s.*); *Nicene and post-Nicene Libr.*, ser. 1, vol. i. A short popular *Life* of St. Augustine is pub. in their *Fathers for Eng. Readers*, by S.P.C.K., who also pub. an Eng. trans. of the *Treatise on the City of God*, by F. R. M. Hitchcock. Cheap trans. of the *Confessions* and the *City of God* (2 vols.) are in *A. and M. Theol. Lib.* (Griffith). [A.R., 1901.]

Augustinus, St., archbp. of Canterbury. The materials for the life of the first archbp. of Canterbury are almost entirely comprised in the first and second books of Bede's *Ecclesiastical History*, with some additional points in Gocelin's *Life of St. Augustine*, Thorn's *Chronicles of St. Augustine's Abbey*; a few letters of Gregory the Great; the Lives of Gregory the Great by Paul the Deacon and John the Deacon.

His mission to England was due to the circumstance of Gregory the Great, a monk in the monastery of St. Andrew, on the Caelian Mount at Rome, one day passing through the market-place of the city, and noticing three boys exposed for sale who told him they were Angles from Deira, a province of King Ella. By a playful interpretation of the word he was reminded of *angels*, delivered from *wrath*, with songs of *hallelujah*. Years passed away and the idea ripened into a mission to Britain headed by Augustine the abbot of St. Andrew's.

In the summer of A.D. 596 they set out, traversed the north of Italy, and reached the neighbourhood of Aix, in Provence, and the north of France. They crossed the English Channel and landed at Ebbe's Fleet, in the Isle of Thanet and kingdom of Kent.

King Ethelbert received the missionaries in a friendly spirit, either in the open space near Ebbe's Fleet, or, according to another account, under an ancient oak in the middle of the island. To make a deeper impression on the monarch's mind, Augustine came up from the shore in solemn procession, preceded by a verger carrying a large silver cross, and followed by one bearing aloft on a board, painted and gilded, a representation of the Saviour. Then came the rest of the brethren and the choir, headed by Honorius and the deacon Peter, chanting a solemn litany for the eternal welfare of themselves and the people amongst whom they had come. Ethelbert listened attentively to Augustine's address, delivered through interpreters, and then, in a manner at once politic and courteous, replied that the promises of the strangers were fair, but the tidings they announced were new and full of a meaning he did not understand. He could not give his assent to them and leave the customs of his people, but he promised the strangers kindness and hospitality, together with liberty to celebrate their services, and undertook that none of his subjects who might be so disposed should be prohibited from espousing their religion. Augustine and his companions again formed a procession, and crossing the ferry to Richborough, advanced to Canterbury, chanting one of the solemn litanies learnt from Gregory, and took up their abode in the Stable-gate, near the present church of St. Alphege, till the king should finally make up his mind.

Thus admitted into the city, the missionaries commended their message by their self-devotion and pure and chaste living. Before long they were allowed to worship in the church of St. Martin, which Ethelbert's Christian queen Bertha, a Gallic princess with bp. Liudhard for her chaplain, had been accustomed to attend, and they were thus encouraged to carry on their labours with renewed zeal. At last Ethelbert avowed himself ready to accept Christianity, and was baptized on Whitsunday, June 2, 597, probably at St. Martin's church.

The conversion of their chief was, as is illustrated again and again in the history of medieval missions, the signal for the baptism of the tribe. At the next assembly, therefore, of the *Witan*, the matter was formally referred to the authorities of the kingdom, and they decided to follow the example of Ethelbert. Accordingly, on Dec. 25, 597, upwards of 10,000 received baptism in the waters of the Swale, at the mouth of the Medway, and thus sealed their acceptance of the new faith.

Thus successful in the immediate object of the mission, Augustine repaired to France, and was consecrated the first archbp. of Canterbury by Virgilius, the metropolitan of Arles. On his return he took up his abode in the wooden palace of Ethelbert, who retired to Reculver, and this, with an old British or Roman church hard by, became the nucleus of Augustine's cathedral. Another proof of the king's kindness was soon displayed. To the west of Canterbury, and midway between it and the church of St. Martin, was a building, once a British church, but now used as a Saxon temple. This Ethelbert, instead of destroying, made over to the archbishop, who dedicated it to St. Pancras, in memory, probably, of the young Roman martyr on the tombs of whose family the monastery on the Caelian Mount at Rome had been built. Round this building now rose another monastery, at the head of which Augustine placed one of his companions, Peter, as its first abbot.

Before, however, these arrangements were completed, he sent Peter and Laurence to inform Gregory of the success of the mission.

Gregory was overjoyed at the receipt of the intelligence, and after an interval sent over a reinforcement of fresh labourers for the mission, amongst whom were Mellitus, Paulinus, and Justus. They brought ecclesiastical vestments, sacred vessels, some relics of apostles and martyrs, a present of books, and the pall of a metropolitan for Augustine himself, who was thus made independent of the bishops of France. In a lengthened epistle Gregory sketched out the course which the archbishop was to take in developing his work. London was to be his metropolitan see, and he was to consecrate twelve bishops as suffragans. Moreover, whenever Christianity had extended to York, he was to place there also a metropolitan with a like number of bishops under him. As to the British bishops, they were all entrusted to his care, "that the unlearned might be instructed, the weak strengthened by persuasion, the perverse corrected with authority." Augustine, thereupon, invited the British clergy to a conference on the confines of Wessex, near the Severn, under an oak, long after known as *Augustine's oak*. Prepared to make considerable concessions, he yet felt that three points did not admit of being sacrificed. He proposed that the British church should (1) conform to the Roman usage in the celebration of Easter; and (2) the rite of baptism; and (3) that they should aid him in evangelizing the heathen Saxons. The discussion was long and fruitless. At last the archbishop proposed that an appeal should be made to the Divine judgment. A blind Saxon was introduced, whom the British clergy were unable to cure. Augustine supplicated aid from above, and the man, we are told, forthwith recovered his sight.

Convinced but unwilling to alter their old customs, the vanquished party proposed another meeting. Seven British bishops met on this occasion, together with Dinoth, abbot of the great monastery of Bangor in Flintshire. Before the synod assembled, they proposed to ask the advice of an aged hermit whether they ought to change the traditions of their fathers. "Yes," replied the old man, "if the new-comer be a man of God?" "But how," they asked, "are we to know whether he be a man of God?" "The Lord hath said," was the reply, "'Take My yoke upon you and learn of Me, for I am meek and lowly.' Now if this Augustine is meek and lowly, be assured that he beareth the yoke of Christ." "Nay, but how are we to know this?" they asked again. "If he rises to meet you when ye approach," answered the hermit, "hear and follow him; but if he despise you, and fails to rise up from his place, let him also be despised by you." The synod met, and Augustine remained seated when they approached. It was enough. It was deemed clear that he had not the Spirit of Christ, and no efforts of the archbishop could induce the British clergy to yield to any of his demands. Thereupon Augustine broke up the conference with an angry threat that, if the British clergy would not accept peace with their brethren, they must look for war with their foes, and if they would not proclaim the way of life to the Saxons, they would suffer deadly vengeance at their hands. Thus, unsuccessful, Augustine returned to Canterbury, and there relaxed none of his efforts to evangelize the Saxon tribes. As all Kent had espoused the Faith, it was deemed advisable to erect a second bishopric at Rochester. Over it Augustine placed his companion Justus, and Ethelbert caused a cathedral to be built, which was named after St. Andrew, in memory of the monastery dedicated to that Apostle on the Caelian Hill at Rome, whence the missionaries had started. At the same time, through the connexion of the same monarch with the king of Essex, who was his nephew, Christianity found its way into the adjacent kingdom, and the archbishop was able to place Mellitus in the see of London, where Ethelbert built a church, dedicated to St. Paul.

This was the limit of Augustine's success. It fell, indeed, far short of Gregory's grand design; but this had been formed on a very imperfect acquaintance with the condition of the island, the strong natural prejudices of the British Christians, and the relations which subsisted between the different Anglo-Saxon kingdoms. On Mar. 12, 604, Gregory died, and two months afterwards according to some authorities, or a year after according to others, Augustine followed his patron and benefactor, and was buried in the cemetery which he himself had consecrated, beside the Roman road that ran over St. Martin's Hill from Richborough to Canterbury.

The most important modern authorities for the life of the first archbp. of Canterbury are Montalambert, *Monks of the West*, iii.;

Hook, *Archbishops of Canterbury*, i.; Stanley, *Memorials of Canterbury*, 4th ed. 1865; Milman, *Hist. of Latin Christianity*, ii. 4th ed. 1867; A. J. Mason, *The Mission of St. Aug. to Eng.*, 1897; Bp. Browne, *Aug. and his Companions*, 1895; Gasquet, *Missions of St. Aug.*; Bp. Collins, *Beginnings of Eng. Christianity*. [G.F.M.]

Aurelian, A.D. 270-275. The few facts which connect the name of this emperor with the history of the Christian church are as follows:—(1) he is said (Vopiscus, c. 20) to have reproached the Roman senate for not consulting the Sibylline books, as their fathers would have done, at a time of danger and perplexity. "It would seem," he said, "as if you were holding your meetings in a church of the Christians instead of in the temple of all the gods." The words clearly imply a half-formed suspicion that the decline of the old faith was caused by the progress of the new. The decree of Gallienus recognising Christianity as a *religio licita* had apparently stimulated church building. (2) Startled by the rapid progress of Christianity, Aurelian is said to have resolved towards the close of his reign on active measures for its repression. The edict of Gallienus was to be rescinded. A thrill of fear pervaded the Christian population of the empire. The emperor was surrounded by counsellors who urged on him a policy of persecution, but his death hindered the execution of his plans. (3) In the interval we find him connected, singularly enough, with the action of the church in a case of heresy. Paul of Samosata had been chosen as bp. of Antioch in A.D. 260. A synod of bishops including Firmilianus of the Cappadocian Caesarea, Gregory Thaumaturgus, and others, had condemned his teaching; but on receiving promises of amendment had left him in possession of the see. Another (A.D. 270) deposed him, and Domnus was appointed in his place. Paul refused to submit and kept possession of the episcopal residence. Such was the position of affairs at Antioch when Aurelian, having conquered Zenobia, became master of the city. The orthodox bishops appealed to the emperor to settle whose the property was, and he adjudged it to belong to those to whom the bishops in Italy and in Rome had addressed their epistles (Eus. *H. E.* viii. 27-30). [E.H.P.]

Aurelius, Marcus, emperor, A.D. 161-180. The policy adopted by Marcus Aurelius towards the Christian church cannot be separated from the education which led him to embrace Stoicism, and the long training which he had, after he had attracted the notice of Hadrian and been adopted by Antoninus Pius, in the art of ruling. In the former he had learnt, as he records with thankfulness, from his master Diognetus (*Medit.* i. 6), the temper of incredulity as to alleged marvels, like those of seers and diviners. Under HADRIAN and ANTONINUS PIUS he had acquiesced, at least, in a policy of toleration, checking false accusations, requiring from the accusers proof of some other crime than the mere profession of Christianity. It is, therefore, startling to find that he takes his place in the list of persecutors along with Nero and Domitian and Decius. The annals of martyrdom place in his reign the deaths of Justin Martyr at Rome (A.D. 166), of Polycarp at Smyrna (A.D. 167), of Blandina and Pothinus and the other sufferers at Lyons (A.D. 177). The last-named year seems indeed to have witnessed an outburst of popular fury against the new sect, and this could not have been allowed to rage without the emperor's sanction, even if there were no special edicts like those of which Melito speaks (Eus. *H. E.* iv. 26) directly authorizing new measures of repression. It was accordingly an era of Apologies; Justin had led the way under Antoninus Pius, and the second treatise that bears his name was probably written just before his own martyrdom under Aurelius. To the years 177 and 178 are assigned those which were written by Melito, Tatian, Athenagoras, Apollinaris, and Theophilus, perhaps also that of Miltiades. The causes of this increased rigour are not difficult to trace. (1) The upward progress of Christianity brought its teachers into rivalry with the Stoic philosophers who up to this time, partly for good and partly for evil, had occupied the position of spiritual directors in the families in which there was any effort to rise out of the general debasement. They now found themselves brought into contact with men of a purer morality and a nobler fortitude than their own, and with a strange mysterious power which enabled them to succeed where others failed. Just in proportion, therefore, as the emperor was true to his Stoicism was he likely to be embittered against their rivals. (2) A trace of this bitterness is found in his own *Meditations* (xi. 3). Just as Epictetus (Arrian, *Epict.* iv. 7) had spoken of the "counterfeit apathy" which was the offspring not of true wisdom, but "of madness or habit like that of the Galileans," so the emperor contrasts the calm considerate preference of death to life, which he admired, with the "mere obstinacy (παράταξις) of the Christians." "The wise man," he says, "should meet death σεμνῶς καὶ ἀτραγῴδως." The last word has, there seems reason to believe, a special significance. Justin, towards the close of his second Apology, presented to this emperor, had expressed a wish that some one would stand up, as on some lofty rostrum, and "cry out with a *tragic voice*, Shame, shame on you who ascribe to innocent men the things which ye do openly yourselves. . . . Repent ye, be converted to the ways of purity and wisdom (Μετάθεσθε, σωφρονίσθητε)." If we believe that his acts were in harmony with his words or that what he wrote had come under the emperor's eye, it is natural to see in the words in which the latter speaks so scornfully of the "tragic airs" of the Christians a reference to what had burst so rudely upon his serene tranquillity. (3) The period was one of ever-increasing calamities. The earthquakes which had alarmed Asia under Antoninus were but the prelude to more serious convulsions. The Tiber rose to an unprecedented height and swept away the public granaries. This was followed by a famine, and that by a pestilence, which spread from Egypt and Ethiopia westward. Everywhere on the frontiers there were murmurs of insurrection or invasion. The year 166 was long known as the "annus calamitosus," and it was in that year that the persecution broke out and that Justin suffered. These calamities roused the superstition of the great mass of the people, and a wild fanaticism succeeded to an epicurean atheism. The gods were wroth, and what had roused their anger but the presence of those who denied them? "*Christianos ad leones*" seemed the remedy for every disaster. The gods might accept that as a piacular offering. On the other hand, the Christians saw in them signs of the coming judgment, and of the end of the world; and now in apocalyptic utterances, now in Sibylline books, uttered, half exultantly, their predictions of the impending woe (cf. Tertull. *ad Scap.* c. 3). All this, of course, increased the irritation against them to the white heat of frenzy (Milman's *Hist. of Christianity*, bk. ii. c. 7). They not only provoked the gods, and refused to join in sacrifices to appease them, but triumphed in their fellow-citizens' miseries.

Two apparent exceptions to this policy of repression have to be noticed. (1) One edition of the edict πρὸς τὸ κοινὸν της 'Ασίας, though ascribed by Eusebius (*H. E.* iv. 13) to Antoninus Pius, purports, as given by him, to come from Aurelius. But the edict is unquestionably spurious, and merely shows the wish of some Christians, at a later stage in the conflict, to claim the authority of the philosopher in favour of his brethren. (2) There is the decree mentioned by Eusebius (*H. E.* v. 5) on the authority of Tertullian (*Apol.* c. 5, *ad Scap.* c. 4, p. 208) and appended to Justin's first Apology, which purports to be addressed to the Senate, informing them how, when he and his army were in danger of perishing for want of water in the country of the Marcomanni, the Christians in his army had prayed to their God, and refreshing rain had fallen for them, and a destroying hail on their enemies, and bidding them therefore to refrain from all accusations against Christians as such, and ordering all who so accused them to be burnt alive. (Cf. THUNDERING LEGION in *D. C. B.* 4-vol. ed.) The decree is manifestly spurious. An interesting monograph, *M. Aurelius Antoninus als Freund und Zeitgenosse des Rabbis Jehudas ben Nasi*, by Dr. A. Bodek (Leipz. 1868), may be noticed as maintaining that this emperor is identical with the Antoninus ben Ahasuerus, who is mentioned in the Talmud as on terms of intimacy with one of the leading Jewish teachers of the time. If this be accepted, it suggests another possible element in his scorn of Christianity. G. H. Rendal, *Marcus Aurelius Antoninus, to Himself*, Eng. trans. with valuable Intro. (Lond. 1898). [E.H.P.]

Ausonius, Decimus Magnus, a native of Bordeaux, was the son of Julius Ausonius, a physician of Cossium (*Bazas*), in Aquitania (Aus. *Idyll.* ii. 2). His poems, which are singularly communicative as to his private history, display him to us in riper years both as student and courtier, professor and prefect, poet and consul. At the age of 30 he was promoted to the chair of rhetoric in his native city, and not long after was invited to court by the then Christian emperor Valentinian I., who appointed him tutor to his son Gratian (*Praef. ad Syagr.* 15-26). Ausonius was held in high regard by the emperor and his sons and accompanied the former in his expedition, against the Alemanni. It was no doubt during the residence of the court at Trèves at this time that he composed his *Mosella.* From Valentinian he obtained the title of Comes and the office of Quaestor, and on the accession of Gratian became successively Prefect of Latium, Libya, and Gaul, and finally, A.D. 379, was raised to the consulship (*Praef. ad Syagr.* 35, etc.; *Epigr.* ii. iii., *de fast.*). After the death of Gratian, A.D. 383, although he seems to have enjoyed the favour of Theodosius (*Praef. ad Theodos.*), it is probable that he returned to the neighbourhood of his native city and spent the remainder of his life in studious retirement (*Ep.* xxiv.). His correspondence with Paulinus of Nola evidently belongs to these later years. The date of his death is unknown, but he was certainly alive in A.D. 388, as he rejoices in the victory of Theodosius over the murderer of Gratian at Aquileia (*Clar. Urb.* vii.).

The question of the poet's religion has always been a matter of dispute. Voss, Cave, Heindrich, Muratori, etc., maintain that he was a pagan, while Jos. Scaliger, Fabricius, Funccius, and later M. Ampère, uphold the contrary view. Without assenting to the extreme opinion of Trithemius, who even makes him out to have held the see of Bordeaux, we may safely pronounce in favour of his Christianity. The negative view rests purely upon assumptions, such as that a Christian would not have been guilty of the grossness with which some of his poems are stained, nor have been on such intimate terms with prominent heathens (Symmach. *Epp. ad Auson.* passim), nor have alluded so constantly to pagan rites and mythology without some expression of disbelief. On the other hand, he was not only appointed tutor to the Christian son of a Christian emperor, whom he seems at any rate to have instructed in the Christian doctrine of prayer (*Grat. Act.* 43); but certain of his poems testify distinctly to his Christianity in language that is only to be set aside by assuming the poems themselves to be spurious. Such are (1) the first of his idylls, entitled *Versus Paschales*, and commencing *Sancta salutiferi redeunt solemnia Christi*, the genuineness of which is proved by a short prose address to the reader connecting it with the next idyll, the *Epicedion*, inscribed to his father. (2) The *Ephemeris*, an account of the author's mode of spending his day, which contains not merely an allusion to the chapel in which his morning devotions were performed (I. 7), but a distinct confession of faith, in the form of a prayer to the first two Persons of the Trinity. (3) The letters of the poet to his friend and former pupil St. Paulinus of Nola, when the latter had forsaken the service of the pagan Muses for the life of a Christian recluse. This correspondence, so far from being evidence that he was a heathen (see Cave, etc.), displays him to us rather as a Christian by conviction, still clinging to the pagan associations of his youth, and incapable of understanding a truth which had revealed itself to his friend, that Christianity was not merely a creed but a life. The letters are a beautiful instance of wounded but not embittered affection on the one side, and of an attachment almost filial tempered by firm religious principle on the other. Paulinus nowhere chides Ausonius for his paganism; on the contrary, he assumes his Christianity (Paulin. *Ep.* ii. 18, 19), and this is still further confirmed by a casual passage in one of the poet's letters to Paulinus, in which he speaks of the necessity of returning to Bordeaux in order to keep Easter (*Ep.* viii. 9). Ausonius was not a Christian in the same sense as Paulinus; he was one who hovered on the borderland which separated the new from the old religion: not ashamed, it is true, to pen obscenities beneath the eye and at the challenge of his patron, yet in the quiet of his oratory feeling after the God of the Christians; convinced apparently of the dogma of the Trinity, yet so little penetrated by its awful mystery as to give it a haphazard place in a string of frivolous triplets composed at the dinner-table (*Gryph. Tern.* 87): keenly alive to natural beauty, and susceptible of the tenderest affection, he yet fell short of appreciating in his disciple the more perfect beauty of holiness, and the entire abnegation of self for the love of a divine master. Probably his later Christianity would have disowned his own youthful productions.

The works of Ausonius comprise: *Epigrammaton Liber,* a collection of 150 epigrams on all manner of subjects, political, moral, satirical, amatory; many of which for terseness and power of sarcasm are only surpassed by those of Martial. *Ephemeris* (see above). *Parentalia,* a series of tributes to the memory of those of his family and kindred who had died before him, many of which are full of pathos. The *Mosella* is a poem in praise of his favourite river. The *Epistolae* are, on the whole, the most interesting, because the most heartfelt, of the works of Ausonius; they number 25, addressed to various friends. Those to St. Paulinus of Nola prove that the poet was capable of earnestness when his heart was stirred.

The works of Ausonius are published in Migne's *Patr. Lat.* vol. xix. There is a complete ed. by R. Peiper (Leipz. 1886); H. de la V. de Mirmont, *Mosella,* with trans. (Bordeaux, 1889); also *de Mosella* (Paris, 1892); Dill, *Roman Society* (Lond. 1898). [E.M.Y.]

Avitus, Alcimus Ecdicius, archbp. of Vienne in Narbonian Gaul; born about the middle of 5th cent. His father belonged to a family of senatorial rank. His mother, Audentia, was, in all probability, a sister of M. Maecilius Avitus, emperor of the West, A.D. 456. The mother of Sidonius Apollinaris the poet, who, in a letter to Alcimus Avitus, speaks of their near relationship and the identity of their youthful pursuits, seems to have been another sister of the same illustrious family (Sidon. Apoll. *Ep.* iii. 1, 61). A student's life attracted Avitus more than did wealth and rank, and at an early age he bestowed his patrimony upon the poor and retired into the seclusion of a monastery close to the walls of his native city. Here he gained so high a reputation for piety and learning that in 490 A.D., upon the death of his father, he was elected to succeed him in the archbishopric. The fame of Avitus rests partly upon his poetry and partly upon the important part he was called to play in the controversies of his time. In 499 Vienne was captured by Gundobald, king of the Burgundians, who was at war with Clovis, king of the Franks; and Avitus, as metropolitan of S. and E. Gaul, took the lead in a conference between the Catholic and Arian bishops held in presence of Gundobald at Sardiniacum near Lyons (Greg. Turon., ii. 34). The king was convinced by the earnest entreaties and powerful reasoning of Avitus, who addressed several extant letters to him, but could never be induced to recant his errors publicly. His successor Sigismund was converted by Avitus from Arianism.

Avitus published treatises in confutation of the Nestorian, Eutychian, and Sabellian heresies; he also wrote against the Pelagian errors of Faustus, abbot of Lerins, and converted many Jews who had settled in his diocese (Venant. Fortun. l. v. c. 5).

From a letter of pope Hormisdas to Avitus (*Ep.* x.) we gather that he was made vicar apostolic in Gaul by that pontiff; and in A.D. 517 he presided in this capacity at the council of Epaune (Concilium Epaonense) for the restitution of ecclesiastical discipline in Narbonian Gaul. But his influence seems to have extended far beyond the limits of his own diocese, as is shewn by his correspondence with several historical personages at Rome, *e.g.* Faustus, Symmachus, Vitalianus, etc. He appears also to have exerted himself to terminate the dispute between the churches of Rome and Constantinople which arose out of the excommunication of ACACIUS; that this was accomplished before his death we gather from his letters (*Epp.* iii, vii.).

Avitus died Feb. 5, 523, and was buried in the monastery of St. Peter and St. Paul at Vienne, where the greater part of his youth had been spent.

The extant works of St. Avitus are as follows: A poem in five books on subjects drawn from Genesis and Exodus: *de Origine Mundi; de Peccato Originali; de Sententia Dei; de Diluvio; de Transitu Maris Rubri,* this is dedicated to his brother Apollinaris, and consists of 2611 hexameter lines. The first three books might almost have suggested the idea of Milton's *Paradise Lost,* to which they bear a curious and in many points interesting analogy. A collection of 91 letters, several of historical interest, especially that addressed to Clovis (*Ep.* xli.) upon his baptism. A homily, *de Festo Rogationum,* from which the religious observance of Rogation days took its origin. [MAMERTUS.] A second homily representing the Rogation of the third day, which was discovered in the library of the Grande Chartreuse, and first published in 1717 by Dom Marten (*Thesaur. Anecd.* p. 47). A homily preached on the occasion of the dedication of a church erected by Maximus, bp. of Geneva. Seventy-two short fragments of homilies, sermons, etc. The *Collatio Episcoporum contra Arianos coram Gundobaldo rege,* first published in d'Achery's *Spicilegium,* 1655 ff. (tom. iii. p. 304, ed. Paris, 1725). These remains contain much that is valuable with reference to the history, doctrine, and discipline of the church in the 5th cent. The works of Avitus are contained in Migne's *Patrologia*, vol. lix. *Oeuvres*, ed. N. Chevallier (Lyons, 1890). [E.M.Y.]

B

Babylas (1), bp. of Antioch from A.D. 237 or 238 until his martyrdom, A.D. 250 or 251, under Decius, either by death in prison for the faith (Eus. *H. E.* vi. 39), or by direct violence (St. Chrys. *de St. Bab. c. Gentes*, tom. i.); other authorities—Epiphanius (*de Mens.* xviii.), Sozomen (v. 19), Theodoret (*H. E.* iii. 6)—simply calling him martyr, while St. Jerome (*de Scriptt. Eccl.* liv. lxii.) gives both accounts in different places. The *Acta* of Babylas (*Acta SS.* Jan. 24), place his martyrdom under Numerian, by a confusion (according to Baronius's conjecture, *ad ann.* 253, § 126) with one Numerius, who was an active officer in the Decian persecution (Tillemont, *M. E.* iii. 729). The great act of his life was the compelling the emperor Philip, when at Antioch shortly after the murder of Gordian, to place himself in the ranks of the penitents, and undergo penance, before he was admitted to church privileges (κατέχει λόγος, according to Eus. *H. E.* vi. 34, but asserted without qualification by St. Chrysostom, as above, while the *V. St. Chrys.* in *Acta SS.* Sept. tom. iv. 439, transfers the story, against all probability, to Decius, and assigns it as the cause of St. Babylas's martyrdom). But his fame has arisen principally from the triumph of his relics after his death over another emperor, viz. Julian the Apostate, A.D. 362. The oracle of Apollo at Daphne, it seems, was rendered dumb by the near vicinity of St. Babylas's tomb and church, to which his body had been translated by Gallus, A.D. 351. And Julian in consequence, when at Antioch, ordered the Christians to remove his shrine (λάρνακα), or rather (according to Amm. Marcell. xxii.), to take away all the bodies buried in that locality. A crowded procession of Christians, accordingly, excited to a pitch of savage enthusiasm characteristic of the Antiochenes, bore his relics to a church in Antioch, the whole city turning out to meet them, and the bearers and their train tumultuously chanting psalms the whole way, especially those which denounce idolatry. On the same night, by a coincidence which Julian strove to explain away by referring it to Christian malice or to the neglect of the heathen priests, the temple of Apollo was struck by lightning and burned, with the great idol of Apollo itself. Whereupon Julian in revenge both punished the priests and closed the great church at Antioch (Julian Imp. *Misopog. Opp.* ii. 97 (Paris, 1630); St. Chrys. *Hom. de St. Bab. c. Gent.* and *Hom. de St. Bab.*; Theod. *de Cur. Graec. Affect.* x. and *H. E.* iii. 6, 7; Socr. iii. 13; Soz. v. 19, 20; Rufin. x. 35; Amm. Marcell. xxii. pp. 225, 226). St. Chrysostom also quotes a lamentable oration of the heathen sophist Libanius upon the event. The relics of St. Babylas were subsequently removed once more to a church built for them on the other side of the Orontes (St. Chrys. *Hom. de St. Bab.*; Soz. vii. 10). [A.W.H.]

Bachiarius, a monk, early in the 5th cent., author of two short treatises printed in the *Biblioth. Vet. Patr.* of Galland, vol. ix. and the *Patrologia* of Migne, vol. xx. He is commemorated by Gennadius (c. 24), who attributes to him several works, only one of which he acknowledges to have read—viz. the *Libellus de Fide Apologeticus*, to satisfy the bp. of Rome of his orthodoxy, who regarded him with suspicion on account of his being a native of a country tainted with heresy. What this country was there is nothing in his *Libellus* to determine. Bachiarius's profession of faith is thoroughly orthodox in all leading points. Its date is fixed approximately at about the middle of the 5th cent., by his denial of the tenets of Origen regarding the soul and the resurrection life, and those of Helvidius on the perpetual virginity of the Virgin (§ 3, 4), and by his omission of the Son when speaking of the procession of the Holy Ghost. This confession is an interesting document, and will repay perusal. It was first printed by Muratori (*Anecd. Latin.* ii. 939). He also wrote *ad Januarium Liber de Reparatione Lapsi* in behalf of a monk whom Januarius had expelled from the monastery of which he was the head for immorality with a nun. He rebukes Januarius and his monks for refusing to receive the monk again on his penitence.

Bachiarius has been confused by Cave, Bale, and others with Mochta, a disciple of St. Patrick. Tillemont, xvi. 473-476; Cave, *Hist. Lit.* i. 429. [E.V.]

Bardaisan (*Bardesanes*). A Syrian theologian, commonly reckoned among Gnostics. Born at Edessa A.D. 155, and died there A.D. 222-223. His theology as known to us is doubtless a mere fraction of his actual theology. His reception of the Pentateuch, which he seemed to contradict, is expressly attested, and there is no reason to suppose that he rejected the ordinary faith of Christians as founded on the Gospels and the writings of the apostles, except on isolated points. The more startling peculiarities of which we hear belong for the most part to an outer region of speculation, which it may easily have seemed possible to combine with Christianity, more especially with the undeveloped Christianity of Syria in the 3rd cent. The local colour is everywhere prominent. In passing over to the new faith, Bardaisan could not shake off the ancient glamour of the stars, or abjure the Semitic love of clothing thoughts in mythological forms. Scarcely anything survives of his writings, for a Dialogue concerning Fate, extant in Syriac under the title "Book of the Laws of the Countries," is by his disciple Philip. The 56 Hymns of Ephrem Syrus against Heresies are intended to refute the doctrines of Marcion, Bardaisan, and Mani, but Ephrem's criticism is harsh and unintelligent. On the whole, whatever might have come to Bardaisan through Valentinianism might as easily have come to him directly from the traditions of his race, and both alternatives are admissible. It is on any supposition a singular fact that the remains of his theology disclose no traces of the deeper thoughts which moved the Gnostic leaders. That he held a doctrinal position intermediate between them and the church is consistent with the circumstances of his life, but is not supported by any internal evidence. On this, as on many other points, we can only deplore our ignorance about a person of singular interest.—(From H. in *D. C. B.* 4-vol. ed.; cf. Bardenhewer, p. 78.)

Barnabas, Epistle of.—I. *Authenticity.*—Is this epistle the production of the Barnabas so often associated with St. Paul; or has it been falsely connected with his name? The question is one of deep interest, bearing on the historical and critical spirit of the early Christian church.

It is admitted on all sides that the *external evidence* is decidedly in favour of the idea that the epistle is authentic. Clement of Alexandria bears witness to it as the work of "Barnabas the apostle"—"Barnabas who was one of the seventy disciples and the fellow-labourer of Paul"—"Barnabas who also preached the Gospel along with the apostle according to the dispensation of the Gentiles" (*Strom.* ii. 7, 35; ii. 20, 116; v. 10, 64. Cf. also ii. 6, 31; ii. 15, 67; ii. 18, 84; v. 8, 52). The same may be said of Origen, who speaks of it as "the Catholic Ep. of Barnabas" (*c. Cels.* i. 63). Eusebius disputes its canonicity, but is hardly less decided in favour of its authenticity. It is included by him at one time among the disputed, at another among the spurious books; yet there is no reason to doubt that when, in both passages, he calls it the Ep. of Barnabas, he understands not an unknown person of that name but the Barnabas of Scripture (vi. 14, iii. 25). Jerome must be understood to refer to it when he tells us of an Ep. read among the apocryphal books, and written by Barnabas of Cyprus, who was ordained along with Paul the Apostle of the Gentiles (*de Vir. Ill.* c. vi.). In the *Stichometria* of Nicephorus, in the 5th cent., it is enumerated among the uncanonical books; and, at the close of that cent., a similar place is assigned to it by Anastasius Sinaita. Since it is, moreover, found in Codex ℵ attached to the books of N.T., there is no doubt the early Christian church considered it authentic. That she refused to allow its canonicity is little to the purpose. The very fact that many thought it entitled to a place in the canon is a conclusive proof of the opinion that had been formed of its authorship. The early Church drew a line between apostles and companions of apostles; and, although writings of the latter, such as the Gospels of St. Mark and St. Luke, and the Ep. to the Hebrews, were received into the canon, the connexion between the writers of these books and one or other of the apostles was believed to be such that the authority of the latter could be transferred to the former. Such a transference would be more difficult in the case of Barnabas, because, although associated at one time with St. Paul in his labours, the two had differed in opinion and separated.

It is on *internal evidence* that many distinguished critics have denied its authenticity. That there is great force in some at least of the arguments adduced by them from this source it is impossible to deny, yet they do not seem so irresistible as to forbid renewed consideration. They have been summed up by Hefele (*Patr. Apost.* p. 14), and succeeding writers have added little to his statement. Of his eight arguments, five may be at once rejected: The first, that the words of Augustine regarding the Apocrypha of Andrew and John, *si illorum essent recepta essent ab ecclesia*, show that our epistle would have been placed in the canon had it been deemed authentic; for Andrew and John were apostles, Barnabas was not. The second, that Barnabas had died before the destruction of Jerusalem, while the epistle bears clear marks of not having been written until after that date; for this idea is no just inference from the texts referred to, Col. iv. 10, 1 Pet. v. 13, 2 Tim. iii. (iv. ?) 11, and the authority of a monk of the 6th or 9th cent. is not to be relied on. The third, that the apostles chosen by our Lord are described in c. v. as ὑπὲρ πᾶσαν ἁμαρτίαν ἀνομώτεροι; for these words are simply introduced to magnify the grace of Christ in calling not the righteous but sinners to repentance. It was an undoubted fact that the Saviour had associated with publicans and sinners, and Barnabas may mean no more than that out of that class were the apostles chosen. He may even have had the career of Saul previous to his call to the apostleship mainly in view. The fourth argument of Hefele, that the epistle betrays in c. x. so much ignorance of the habits of various animals, is not valid; for natural history was then but little known. The fifth argument of the same writer to be set aside is that Barnabas, who had travelled in Asia Minor, and lived at Antioch in Syria, could not have asserted in c. ix. that the Syrians were circumcised, when we know from Josephus (*contr. Ap.* i. 22; *Antiq.* viii. 10, 3) that they were not; for, however frequently this statement has been repeated, Josephus says nothing of the kind. What he says is, that a remark of Herodotus, to the effect that the Syrians who live in Palestine are circumcised, proves that historian's acquaintance with the Jews, because the Jews were the only inhabitants of Palestine by whom that rite was practised, and it must have been of them, therefore, that he was speaking, and he quotes Herodotus, and without any word of dissent, as saying that the Syrians about the rivers Thermodon and Parthenius, that is in the northern parts of Syria, did submit to circumcision. He may thus be even said to confirm the statement of our epistle.

The three remaining arguments of Hefele are more important.

(1) That the many trifling allegories of cc. v.-xi. are unworthy of one who was named the "Son of Consolation." It is true that it is difficult to conceive how such a one could find in the numeral letters of the Greek version of the O.T. an indication of the will of Him Who had given that Testament in Hebrew to His ancient people. Yet, after all, is it not the time rather than the writer that is here in fault? It is unfair to take as our standard of judgment the principles of interpretation just now prevailing. We must transfer ourselves into the early Christian age, and remember the spirit of interpretation that then prevailed. We must call to mind the allegorical explanations of both Jewish and heathen schools, whose influence passed largely into the Christian church. Above all, we must think of the estimation in which the epistle was held for centuries, *e.g.* by Clement and Origen; that some would have assigned it a place in the canon; and that, even by those who denied

it that place, it was regarded as a most useful and edifying work. In judging, therefore, of the ability of our author, we must turn from the form to the substance of his argument, from the shell in which he encloses his kernel of truth to that truth itself. When we do so his epistle will appear in no small degree worthy of approbation. It exhibits a high appreciation of many of the cardinal truths of Christianity, of the incarnation and death of Christ, of the practical aims of the Gospel, of the freedom and spirituality of Christian living; while the general conception of the relation of the N. T. to the Old, although in some respects grievously at fault, embodies the important principle that the Old is but the shadow of the New, and that "the testimony of Jesus is the spirit of prophecy." Throughout the epistle there are many sentences of great beauty and warmth of Christian feeling, and the description of the rebuilding of the spiritual temple in c. xvi. is most eloquent.

(2) Against its authenticity are urged, next, the numerous mistakes committed by the writer in cc. vii. viii. with regard to the rites and ceremonies of Judaism, mistakes to all appearance inconsistent with the idea that he could be a Jew, a Levite, who had lived long in Jerusalem, and must have been acquainted with the ceremonial institutions of the Jews. It is impossible not to feel the great force of the objection, or even to complain of one who, upon this ground alone, should reject the authorship of Barnabas. Let it only be remembered that these mistakes are almost equally inexplicable on the supposition that the author was not Barnabas. If such rites were not actually practised, whence did he learn their supposed existence? It is out of the question to think that they were a mere fancy of his own. And how came the great Fathers whose names have been already mentioned, how came the church at large, to value the epistle as it did if in the mention of them we have nothing but absurdity and error? We are hardly less puzzled to account for such inaccuracies if the writer was an Alexandrian Christian of heathen origin than if he were a Jew and a Levite.

(3) The third and last important argument adduced by Hefele is founded upon the unjust notions with regard to Judaism which are presented in our epistle. They are correctly so described. But it is not so clear that they might not have been entertained by one who, educated in the school of St. Paul and animated by a high sense of the spirituality and universality of the Christian faith, would be easily led, in the heat of the Judaic controversies of his day, to depreciate a system which was threatening to overthrow the distinctiveness and power of the Gospel of Christ.

To these arguments recent writers have added that the strong anti-Judaistic tendency of the epistle is inconsistent with its ascription to Barnabas, inasmuch as he erred in too great attachment to the Jewish party (Gal. ii. 13). But the incident thus referred to reveals no such trait in the character of Barnabas. His conduct on that occasion was a momentary weakness by which the best may be overtaken; and it rather shews us that his position on the side of the freer party had been previously a decided one, "insomuch that *even* Barnabas was carried away by their dissimulation." The incident may also have made him in time to come ashamed of his weakness, firmer and more determined than before.

To sum up the evidence, it seems to the present writer that its balance favours its composition by Barnabas more than critics have been generally willing to allow. The bearing of the external evidence upon this result is unquestionable; and, where we have such evidence, it is a sound principle that nothing but the strongest internal evidence should be permitted to overcome it. The traditions of the early church with regard to historical facts do not appear to have been so loose as is often alleged. It is difficult also to imagine how a generally accepted and firmly held tradition could arise without some really good foundation.

Finally, we are too prone to forget that the substance of Christian truth may be held by others in connexion with misapprehensions, imperfections, misinterpretations, of Scripture, absurd and foolish views, in connexion with which it would be wholly impossible for us to hold it. The authorship of Barnabas is rejected by, among others, Neander, Ullman, Hug, Baur, Hefele, Winer, Hilgenfeld, Donaldson, Westcott, Mühler, while it is maintained by Gieseler, Credner, Guericke, Bleek, Möhler, and, though with hesitation, De Wette. [The weighty judgment of bp. Lightfoot must now (1911) be added to the list in favour, and will generally be considered as decisive: see *Apost. Fathers*, pt. i. vol. ii. pp. 503-512.]

II. *The Date of the Epistle.*—External evidence does not help us here. We are thrown wholly upon the internal. Two limits are allowed by all, the destruction of Jerusalem on the one hand, and the time of Clement of Alexandria on the other—that is, from A.D. 70 to the last years of the 2nd cent. Between these two limits the most various dates have been assigned to it; the general opinion, however, being that it is not to be placed earlier than towards the close of the 1st, nor later than early in the 2nd cent. Most probably it was written only a very few years after the destruction of Jerusalem.

III. *Object of the Epistle, and Line of Argument pursued in it.*—Two points are especially insisted on by the writer: first, that Judaism, in its outward and fleshly form, had never been commended by the Almighty to man, had never been the expression of God's covenant; secondly, that that covenant had never belonged to the Jews at all.

In carrying out his argument upon the first point, the writer everywhere proceeds on the idea that the worship which God requires, which alone corresponds to His nature, and which therefore can alone please Him, is spiritual, not a worship of rites and ceremonies, of places and seasons, but a worship of the heart and life. It is not by sacrifices and oblations that we approach God, Who will have no offerings thus made by man * (c. ii.); it is not by keeping sabbaths that we honour

* The reading of Codex ℵ is to be preferred to that of the Latin, *ἵνα ὁ καινὸς . . . μὴ ἀνθρωποίητον ἔχῃ τὴν προσφοράν*. For the sense cf. Matt. xv. 9.

Him (c. xv.); nor is it in any temple made with hands that He is to be found (c. xvi.). The true helpers of our faith are not such things, but fear, patience, long-suffering, continence; and the "way of light" is found wholly in the exhibition of moral and spiritual virtues (c. xix.). But how was it possible to reconcile with such an idea the facts of history? Judaism had had, in time past, and still had, an actual existence. Its fasts and sacrifices, its sabbaths and temple, seemed to have been ordained by God Himself. How could it be pleaded that these things were not the expression of God's covenant, were not to be always binding and honoured? It is to the manner in which such questions are answered that the peculiar interest in our epistle belongs. They are not answered as they would have been by St. Paul. The Apostle of the Gentiles recognized the value of Judaism and of all the institutions of the law as a great preparatory discipline for the coming of the Messiah, as "a schoolmaster to bring us unto Christ." There is nothing of this kind in the argument of Barnabas. Judaism has in it nothing preparatory, nothing disciplinary, in the sense of training men for higher truths. It has two aspects—the one outward and carnal, the other inward and spiritual. The first was never intended by God; they who satisfy themselves with it are rather deceived by "an evil angel." The second is Christianity itself, Christianity before Christ (c. ix. and *passim*). This view of the matter is made good partly by shewing that, side by side with the institutions of Israel, there were many passages of the Prophets in which God even condemned in strong language the outward ceremony, whether sacrifice, or fasting, or circumcision, or the temple worship (cc. ii. iii. ix. xvi.); that these things, in their formal meaning, were positively rejected by Him; and that the most important of them all, circumcision, was fully as much a heathen as a divine rite (c. ix.). This line of argument, however, is not that upon which the writer mainly depends. His chief trust is in the γνῶσις, that deeper, that typical and allegorical, method of interpreting Scripture which proceeded upon the principle that the letter was a mere shell, and had never been intended to be understood literally. By the application of this principle the whole actual history of Israel loses its validity as history, and we see as the true meaning of its facts nothing but Christ, His cross, His covenant, and the spiritual life to which He summons His disciples. It is unnecessary to give illustrations. What is said of Moses, that he spoke ἐν πνεύματι, is evidently to be applied to the whole O. T. The literal meaning is nowhere what was really intended. The Almighty had always had a deeper meaning in what was said. He had been always thinking, not of Judaism, but of Christ and Christianity. The conclusion, therefore, could not be mistaken; Judaism in its outward and carnal form had never been the expression of God's covenant. To whom, then, does God's covenant belong? It is indeed a legitimate conclusion from the previous argument that the Jews cannot claim the covenant as theirs. By the importance they always attached, and still attach, to outward rites they prove that they have never entered into the mind of God; that they are the miserable victims of the wiles of Satan (cc. iv. ix. xvi.). But the same thing is shewn both by Scripture and by fact—by Scripture, for in the cases of the children of Rebekah, and of the blessing of Ephraim and Manasseh, we learn that the last shall be first and the first last (c. xiii.); by fact, for when Moses broke the two tables of stone on his way down from the mount, the covenant which was at that moment about to be bestowed upon Israel was dissolved and transferred to Christians (c. xiv.).

This line of argument clearly indicates what was the special object of the epistle, the special danger against which it was designed to guard. It was no mere Judaizing tendency that was threatening the readers for whom it was intended. It was a tendency to lapse into Judaism itself. The argument of those who were endeavouring to seduce them was, "The covenant is ours" (c. iv.).* These men, as appears from the tenor of the whole chapter, must have been Jews, and their statement could have no other meaning than that Judaism, as the Jews understood and lived it, was God's covenant, that it was to be preferred to Christianity, and that the observance of its rites and ceremonies was the true divine life to which men ought to be called. Yet Christians were shewing a disposition to listen to such teaching, and many of them were running the serious risk of being shattered against the Jewish law (c. iii.).† With this the errors of a coarsely Judaistic life naturally connected themselves, together with those many sins of the "evil way" in which, when we take the details given of them in c. xx., we can hardly fail to recognize the old features of Pharisaism. In short, those to whom Barnabas writes are in danger of falling away from Christian faith altogether; or, if not in actual danger of this, they have to contend with those who are striving to bring about such a result, who are exalting the ancient oeconomy, boasting of Israel's nearness to God, and praising the legal offerings and fastings of the O.T. as the true way by which the Almighty is to be approached. It is the spirit of a Pharisaic self-righteousness in the strictest sense of the words, not of a Judaizing Christianity, that is before us. Here is at once an explanation of all the most peculiar phenomena of our epistle, of its polemical zeal pointed so directly against Judaism that, as Weizäcker has observed, it might seem to

* The ὡς ἤδη δεδικαιωμένοι of c. iv. has led Hilgenfeld (*die Apost. Väter*, p. 38) to think of those who were turning the grace of God into lasciviousness. But the whole passage leads rather to the thought of a proud Judaic self-righteousness, "the temple of the Lord, the temple of the Lord are we."

† Ἵνα μὴ προσερχώμεθα ὡς ἐπηλύται τῷ ἐκείνων νόμῳ. So Hilgenfeld reads, *Nov. Test. extra Canonem*; but Codex ℵ, ἵνα μὴ προσρησσώμεθα ὡς ἐπίλυτῳ τῷ ἐκείνων νόμῳ. The passage is almost unintelligible. Weizäcker proposes to read ἐπιλύτῳ; and to render by means of 2 Pet. i. 20, which is utterly untenable. Might we suggest that ἐπίλυτοι may here be used in the sense of "set loose," the figure being that of persons or things loosened from their true foundations or securities, and then dashed against a wall, or perhaps against the beach, and thus destroyed?

be directed as much against Jews as against Judaizers *; of its effort to shew that the whole O. T. *cultus* had its meaning only in Christ; of its denial of all value to outward Judaism; of its aim to prove that the inward meaning of that ancient faith was really Christian; of its exclusion of Jews, as such, from all part in God's covenant; and of its dwelling precisely upon those doctrines of the Christian faith which were the greatest stumbling-block to the Jewish mind, and those graces of the Christian life to the importance of which it had most need to be awakened.

IV. *Authorities for the Text.*—These consist of MSS. of the Greek text, of the old Latin version, and of citations in early Christian writings. The MSS. are tolerably numerous, but the fact that, except the Sinaiticus (א), which deserves separate mention, they all lack exactly the same portion of the epistle, the first five and a half chapters, seems to shew that they had been taken from a common source and cannot be reckoned as independent witnesses. Since the discovery of Codex א by Tischendorf a new era in the construction of the text has begun. Besides bringing to light the portion previously wanting, valuable readings were suggested by it throughout, and it is now our chief authority for the text. The old Latin version is of high value. The MS. from which it is taken is probably as old as the 8th cent., but the translation itself is supposed by Müller to have been made from a text older even than that of Codex א. It wants the last 4 chapters of the epistle. Citations in early Christian writings are extensive.

Editions and Literature.—Valuable editions are those of Hefele, 1855 (4th ed.); Dressel, 1863; Hilgenfeld, 1866; and Müller, 1869. Dressel was the first to make use of Codex א, but of all these editors Müller seems to have constructed his text upon the most thoroughly scientific principles. The literature is very extensive. Notices of the Epistle will be found in the writings of Dorner, Baur, Schwegler, Ritschl, Lechler, Reuss, and others. The following monographs are especially worthy of notice; Hefele, *Das Sendschreiben des Apostels Barnabas aufs neue untersucht, übersetzt und erklärt* (Tübingen, 1840); Hilgenfeld in his *Die Apostolischen Väter* (Halle, 1853); Weizäcker, *Zur Kritik des Barnabasbriefes aus dem Codex Sinaiticus* (Tübingen, 1863); J. G. Müller's *Erklärung des Barnabasbriefes, Ein Anhang zu de Wette's Exegetischem Handbuch zum neuen Testament* (Leipz. 1869), contains general *prolegomena* to the epistle, a critically constructed text, and an elaborate commentary, together with careful *Excursus* on all the most important difficulties. W. Cunningham, *A Dissertation on the Ep. of B.* (Lond. 1877). A trans. of the epistle is contained in the vol. of the *Apost. Fathers* in the *Ante-Nicene Christian Lib.* (T. & T. Clark, 10s. 6*d*.). The *ed. princeps* by archbp. Ussher (Oxf. 1642) has been reprinted by the Clarendon Press with a dissertation by J. H. Backhouse. The best text for English scholars is given in Lightfoot, *Apostolic Fathers*, ed. by bp. Harmer (Lond. 1891), pp. 237-242. [W.M.]

Barsumas (the Eutychian), an archimandrite of a Syrian monastery, who warmly espoused the cause of Eutyches. When, in 448, Eutyches was denounced before the local synod of Constantinople, Barsumas, who was resident in the city, raised a violent opposition to the Eastern bishops. The next year, 449, at the "Robbers' Synod" of Ephesus, Theodosius II. summoned Barsumas as the representative of the malcontent monastic party, and granted him a seat and vote among the bishops. He was the first monk allowed to act as a judge at a general council. Barsumas brought with him a turbulent band of 1000 monks to coerce the assembly, and took a prominent part in the disorderly proceedings, vociferously expressing his joy on the acquittal of Eutyches and joining in the assault on the aged Flavian by the monks and soldiers. The injuries inflicted were so serious that the venerable patriarch died three days afterwards. When with great effrontery Barsumas presented himself at the council of Chalcedon, 451, an outcry was raised against him as "the murderer of the blessed Flavian." He actively propagated Eutychian doctrines in Syria and died 458. His disciple, Samuel, carried Eutychianism into Armenia. He is regarded among the Jacobites as a saint and worker of miracles (Assemani, *Bibl. Orient.* ii. 4; Labbe, iv. 105 seq.; Liberatus, c. 12; Tillemont, xv.; Schröckh, xvii. 451 seq.). [E.V.]

Barsumas (the Nestorian), bp. of Nisibis and metropolitan, 435-489, who, after the suppression of Nestorianism within the empire, engaged successfully in its propagation in Eastern Asia, especially in Persia. Banished from Edessa by Rabulas, after his desertion of his former friends, Barsumas proved the chief strength and wisdom of the fugitive church. In 435 he became bp. of Nisibis, where, in conjunction with Maanes, bp. of Hardaschir, he established a theological school of deserved celebrity, over which Narses presided for fifty years. Barsumas had the skill to secure for his church the powerful support of the Persian king Pherozes (Firuz), who ascended the throne in the year 462. He worked upon his enmity to the Roman power to obtain his patronage for a development of doctrine which had been formally condemned by the emperor and his assembled bishops, representing to him that the king of Persia could never securely reckon on the allegiance of his subjects so long as they held the same religious faith with his enemies. Pherozes admitted the force of this argument, and Nestorianism became the only form of Christianity tolerated in Persia. Barsumas died in 489, in which year the emperor Zeno broke up the theological seminary at Edessa on account of its Nestorianism, with the result that it flourished still more at Nisibis. Missionaries went out from it in great multitudes, and Nestorianism became the recognized form of Christianity in Eastern Asia. The Malabar Christians are the lineal descendants of their missions. Assemanni, *Bibl. Or*, iii. 1, 16-70; Wigram, *Hist. of Assyrian Ch.* c. viii. [NESTORIAN CHURCH.] [E.V.]

Basilides (Βασιλείδης), the founder of one of the semi-Christian sects, commonly called Gnostic, which sprang up in the early part of the 2nd cent.

I. *Biography.*—He called himself a disciple

* *L.c.* pp. 5, 15.

of one Glaucías, alleged to be an interpreter (ἑρμηνέα) of St. Peter (Clem. *Strom.* vii. p. 898). He taught at Alexandria (Iren. p. 100 Mass.; followed by Eus. *H. E.* iv. 7; Epiph. *Haer.* xxiv. 1, p. 68 C; cf. xxiii. 1, p. 62 B; Theod. *Haer. Fab.* i. 2): Hippolytus (*Haer.* vii. 27, p. 244) in general terms mentions Egypt. Indeed Epiphanius enumerates various places in Egypt visited by Basilides; but subsequently allows it to appear that his knowledge of the districts where Basilidians existed in his own time was his only evidence. If the Alexandrian Gnostic is the Basilides quoted in the *Acts of the Disputation of Archelaus and Mani* (c. 55, in Routh, *Rell. Sac.* v. 196; see later, p. 276), he was reported to have preached in Persia. Nothing more is known of his life. According to Epiphanius (62 B, 68 D, 69 A), he had been a fellow-disciple of Menander with Saturnilus at Antioch in Syria; but this is evidently an arbitrary extension of Irenaeus's remarks on the order of doctrines to personal relations. If the view of the doctrines of Basilides taken in this article is correct, they afford no good grounds for supposing him to have had a Syrian education. Gnostic ideas derived originally from Syria were sufficiently current at Alexandria, and the foundation of what is distinctive in his thoughts is Greek.

Several independent authorities indicate the reign of Hadrian (A.D. 117-138) as the time when Basilides flourished. To prove that the heretical sects were "later than the Catholic church," Clement of Alexandria (*l.c.*) marks out early Christian history into different periods: he assigns Christ's own teaching to the reigns of Augustus and Tiberius; that of the apostles, of St. Paul at least, ends, he says, in the time of Nero; whereas "the authors of the sects arose later, about the times of the emperor Hadrian (κάτω δὲ περὶ τοὺς κ.τ.λ. γεγόνασι), and continued quite as late as the age of the elder Antoninus." He gives as examples Basilides, Valentinus, and (if the text is sound) Marcion, taking occasion by the way to throw doubts on the claims set up for the two former as having been instructed by younger contemporaries of St. Peter and St. Paul respectively, by pointing out that about half a century lay between the death of Nero and the accession of Hadrian. Again Eusebius (*l.c.*) places Saturnilus and Basilides under Hadrian. Yet his language about Carpocrates a few lines further on suggests a doubt whether he had any better evidence than a fallacious inference from their order in Irenaeus. He was acquainted with the refutation of Basilides by Agrippa Castor; but it is not clear, as is sometimes assumed, that he meant to assign both writers to the same reign. His chronicle (Armenian) at the year 17 of Hadrian (A.D. 133) has the note "The heresiarch Basilides appeared at these times"; which Jerome, as usual, expresses rather more definitely. A similar statement without the year is repeated by Jerome, *de Vir. Ill.* 21, where an old corrupt reading (*mortuus* for *moratus*) led some of the earlier critics to suppose they had found a limit for the date of Basilides's death. Theodoret (*l.c.*) evidently follows Eusebius. Earliest of all, but vaguest, is the testimony of Justin Martyr. Writing in or soon after A.D. 145, he refers briefly (*Ap.* i. 26) to the founders of heretical sects, naming first the earliest, Simon and Menander, followers of whom were still alive; and then apparently the latest, Marcion, himself still alive. The probable inference that the other great heresiarchs, including Basilides, were by this time dead receives some confirmation from a passage in his *Dialogue against Trypho* (c. 35), a later but probably not much later book, where the "Marcians," Valentinians, Basilidians, Saturnilians, "and others," are enumerated, apparently in inverse chronological order: the growth of distinct and recognized sects implies at least the lapse of some time since the promulgation of their several creeds. It seems therefore impossible to place Basilides later than Hadrian's time; and, in the absence of any evidence to the contrary, we may trust the Alexandrian Clement's statement that his peculiar teaching began at no earlier date.

II. *Writings.*—According to Agrippa Castor (Eus. *H. E. l.c.*), Basilides wrote "twenty-four books (βιβλία) on the Gospel." These are no doubt the *Exegetica*, from the twenty-third of which Clement gives an extract (*Strom.* iv. §§ 83 ff., pp. 599 f.). The same work is doubtless intended by the "treatises" (*tractatuum*), the thirteenth book of which is cited in the *Acta Archelai*, if the same Basilides is referred to. The authorship of an actual Gospel, of the "apocryphal" class, is likewise attributed to Basilides on plausible grounds. The word "taken in hand" (ἐπεχείρησαν) in Luke i. 1 gives Origen occasion to distinguish between the four evangelists, who wrote by inspiration, and other writers who "took in hand" to produce Gospels. He mentions some of these, and proceeds "Basilides had even the audacity" (ἤδη δὲ ἐτόλμησεν, more than ἐπεχείρησεν) "to write a Gospel according to Basilides"; that is, he went beyond other fabricators of Gospels by affixing his own name (*Hom. in Luc.* i.). This passage is freely translated, though without mention of Origen's name, by Ambrose (*Exp. in Luc.* i. 1); and is probably Jerome's authority in an enumeration of the chief apocryphal Gospels (*Com. in Matt. praef.* t. vii. p. 3); for among the six others which he mentions the four named by Origen recur, including that of the Twelve Apostles, otherwise unknown (cf. Hieron. *Dial. cont. Pelag.* iii. 2, t. ii. p. 782). Yet no trace of a Gospel by Basilides exists elsewhere; and it seems most probable either that Origen misunderstood the nature of the *Exegetica*, or that they were sometimes known under the other name (cf. Hilgenfeld, *Clem. Rec. u. Hom.* 123 ff.).

An interesting question remains, in what relation the *Exegetica* stand to the exposition of doctrine which fills eight long chapters of Hippolytus. Basilides (or the Basilidians), we are told (vii. 27), defined the Gospel as "the knowledge of supermundane things" (ἡ τῶν ὑπερκοσμίων γνῶσις), and the idea of the progress of "the Gospel" through the different orders of beings plays a leading part in the Basilidian doctrine (cc. 25 ff.). But there is not the slightest reason to think that the "Gospel" here spoken of was a substitute for the Gospel in a historical sense, any more than in St. Paul's writings. Indeed several passages (p. 238, l. 28 ff.; 239, 42, 58; 240, 79 ff. of Miller), with their allusions to Rom. v. 14, viii. 19, 22, 23; I. Cor. ii. 13; II. Cor. xii. 4; Eph. i. 21, iii. 3, 5, 10, prove that the writer was throughout thinking of St. Paul's "*mystery* of the Gospel." Hippolytus states distinctly that the Basilidian account of "all things concerning the Saviour" subsequent to "the birth of Jesus" agreed with that given in "the Gospels." It may therefore be reasonably conjectured that his exposition, if founded on a work of Basilides himself (see § III.), is a summary of the opening book or books of the *Exegetica*, describing that part of the redemptive process, or of the preparation for it, which was above and antecedent to the phenomenal life of Jesus. The comments on the Gospel itself, probably containing much ethical matter, as we may gather from Clement, would have little attraction for Hippolytus.

The certain fragments of the *Exegetica* have been collected by Grabe (*Spicil. Patr.* ii. 35-43), followed by Massuet and Stieren in their editions of Irenaeus; but he passes over much in Clement which assuredly has no other origin. A single sentence quoted in Origen's commentary on Romans, and given further on (p. 275), is probably from the same source. In an obscure and brief fragment preserved in a Catena on Job (Venet. 1587, p. 345), Origen implies the existence of Odes by Basilides and Valentinus. No other writings of Basilides are mentioned.

III. *Authenticity of the Hippolytean Extracts.*—In endeavouring to form a clear conception of the work and doctrine of Basilides, we are met at the outset by a serious difficulty. The different accounts were never easy to harmonize, and some of the best critics of the first half of the 19th cent. considered them to refer to two different systems of doctrine. But till 1851 their fragmentary nature suggested that the apparent incongruities might conceivably be due only to the defects of our knowledge, and seemed to invite reconstructive boldness on the part of the historian. The publication of Hippolytus's *Refutation of all Heresies* in 1851 placed the whole question on a new footing. Hardly any one has ventured to maintain the possibility of reconciling its ample statements about Basilides with the reports of Irenaeus and Epiphanius. Which account then most deserves our confidence?

Before attempting to answer this question it is well to enumerate the authorities. They are Agrippa Castor as cited by Eusebius, Clement of Alexandria, Irenaeus, the anonymous supplement to Tertullian, *de Praescriptione*, the *Refutation* of Hippolytus, Epiphanius, Philaster, and Theodoret, and possibly the *Acta Archelai*, besides a few scattered notices which may be neglected here. This ample list shrinks, however, into small dimensions at the touch of criticism. Theodoret's chapter is a disguised compilation from previous Greek writers. The researches of Lipsius have proved that Epiphanius followed partly Irenaeus, partly the lost Compendium of Hippolytus, this same work being also the common source of the Latin authors pseudo-Tertullian and Philaster. Our ultimate authorities therefore are Irenaeus (or the unknown author from whom he took this section of his work), the Compendium of Hippolytus (represented by Epiphanius [part], Philaster, and pseudo-Tertullian), Clement and the *Refutation* of Hippolytus, together with a short statement by Agrippa Castor, and probably a passing reference and quotation in the *Acts of Archelaus*.

It is now generally allowed that the notices of Clement afford the surest criterion by which to test other authorities. Not only does his whole tone imply exact personal knowledge, but he quotes a long passage directly from the *Exegetica*. Is then his account, taken as a whole, consistent with other accounts? And does it agree best with the reports of Irenaeus and Hippolytus in his younger days, or with the elaborate picture drawn by Hippolytus at a later time? This second question has received opposite answers from recent critics. A majority have given the preference to Hippolytus; while Hilgenfeld (who three years before, in his earliest book, the treatise *On the Clementine Homilies and Recognitions*, pp. 125-149, had described the Basilidian system from the then known records, endeavouring with perverse ingenuity to shew their virtual consistency with each other) has prided himself on not being dazzled by the new authority, whom he holds to be in effect describing not Basilides but a late development of his sect; and Lipsius takes the same view.

It should be observed at the outset that the testimony of Clement is not quite so homogeneous as is generally assumed. Six times he criticises doctrines of "Basilides" himself; eight times he employs the ambiguous plural (οἱ ἀπὸ Β., οἱ ἀμφὶ τὸν Β.). Are we to suppose a distinction here, or is the verbal difference accidental? Both views might be maintained. The quotation from the *Exegetica* (*Strom.* iv. pp. 599 f.) is a piece of moral argument on Providence, wholly free from the technical terms of Gnostic mythology. In the succeeding discussion Clement eventually uses plurals (εἰ . . . τις αὐτῶν λέγοι—πέπτωκεν ἡ ὑπόθεσις αὐτοῖς—ὡς φάναι, apparently a misreading for ὥς φασιν—ὡς αὐτοὶ λέγουσιν), which might equally imply that he employs both forms indifferently, or that he distinguishes Basilides from his followers within the limits of a single subject. The other references to "Basilides" are likewise of a distinctly ethical character, while several of the passages containing the plural name abound in technical language. Yet the distinction is not absolute on either side. "Basilides" furnishes the terms "the Ogdoad," "the election," "supermundane"; while such subjects as the nature of faith, the relation of the passions to the animal soul, and the meaning of Christ's saying about eunuchs, occur in the other group, though they remind us rather of Basilides himself. In the last passage, moreover (*Strom.* iii. pp. 508 ff.), the ambiguous plural (οἱ ἀπὸ Β. φασὶ—λέγουσι—'ξηγοῦνται—φασὶ *bis*) is applied to a quotation intended to shame by contrast the immoral Basilidians of Clement's own time; and a similar quotation from Basilides's son Isidore immediately follows; the authors of the two quotations being designated as "the forefathers of their (the late Basilidians') doctrines." It is hard to believe that mere anonymous disciples, though of an earlier date, would be appealed to in this manner, or would take precedence of the master's own son. On the whole, there can be no reasonable doubt that all the doctrinal statements in Clement concern Basilides himself, when not distinctly otherwise expressed, and depend on direct knowledge of the *Exegetica*. With good reason therefore they may be assumed as a trustworthy basis for the whole investigation. The most doubtful instances are the passages cited presently on the Baptism and (in the *Exc. Theod.*) on the descent of the Minister (διάκονος), *i.e.* the Holy Spirit.

The range of possible contact between the quotations and reports of Clement and any of the other authorities is not large. His extant writings contain nothing like an attempt to describe the Basilidian System. The *Stromates*, which furnish the quotations from Basilides, expressly limit themselves to moral and practical questions (ὁ ἠθικὸς λόγος); and reserve for a future work, *i.e.* the lost *Hypotyposes*, the exposition of the higher doctrine (τῆς κατὰ τὴν ἐποπτικὴν θεωρίαν γνώσεως,—τὴν τῷ ὄντι γνωστικὴν φυσιολογίαν) belonging to the department of knowledge which the Stoics called Physics, beginning with the Creation and leading up to Theology proper (*Strom.* i. p. 324; iv. pp. 563 f., 637; vi. pp. 735 f., 827; vii. 829, 902; cf. Bunsen, *Anal. Antenic.* i. 159 ff.). Now it is precisely to this latter department that the bulk of Gnostic speculation would belong, and especially such theories as Hippolytus ascribes to Basilides; and moreover Clement distinctly promises that in the course of that loftier investigation he will "set forth in detail the doctrines of the heretics (τῶν ἑτεροδόξων), and endeavour to refute them to the best of his power" (iv. § 3, p. 564). We have therefore no right to expect in the *Stromates* any cosmological or even theological matter respecting Basilides except such as may accidentally adhere to the ethical statements, the subjects treated of in the various books "against all heresies" being formally excluded by Clement. His sphere being thus distinct from theirs, the marked coincidences of language that we do find between him and Hippolytus afford a strong presumption that, if the one account is authentic, the other is so likewise. Within the narrow limits of Clement's information we meet with the phrases "primitive medley and confusion" (σύγχυσις), and on the other hand "separation" (differentiation) and restoration (σοφία φυλοκρινητική, ἀποκαταστατική); with a division of the universe into stages (διαστήματα), and prominence given to the sphere of "super-mundane" things; with an "Ogdoad" and an "Archon"; all of these terms being conspicuous and essential in the Hippolytean representation. Above all, we hear of the amazement of the Archon on receiving "the utterance of the ministering Spirit" or "Minister" (διάκονος, cf. *Ecl. Theod.* p. 972) as being that fear of the Lord which is called the beginning of wisdom (*Strom.* ii. p. 448); the utterance itself being implied to be a Gospel (εὐηγγελισμένον); while Hippolytus describes the same passage as interpreted of the amazement of the Great Archon on receiving "the Gospel," a revelation of things unknown, through his Son, who had received it from a "power" within the Holy Spirit (vii. 26). The coincidences are thus proportionately great, and there are no contradictions to balance them: so that it would require strong evidence to rebut the conclusion that Clement and Hippolytus had the same materials before them. Such evidence does not exist. The coincidences between Clement and the Irenaean tradition are limited to the widely spread "Ogdoad" and a single disputable use of the word "Archon," and there is no similarity of doctrines to make up for the absence of verbal identity. The only tangible argument against the view that Hippolytus describes the original system of Basilides is its Greek rather than Oriental character, which is assumed to be incompatible with the fundamental thoughts of a great Gnostic leader. We shall have other opportunities of inquiring how far the evidence supports this wide generalization as to Gnosticism at large. As regards Basilides personally, the only grounds for expecting from him an Oriental type of doctrine are the quotation in the *Acts of Archelaus*, which will be discussed further on, and the tradition of his connexion with Saturnilus of Antioch, which we have already seen to be founded on a misconception. The fragmentary notices and extracts in Clement, admitted on all hands to be authentic, are steeped in Greek philosophy; so that the Greek spirit of the Hippolytean representation is in fact an additional evidence for its faithfulness.

It may yet be asked, Did Hippolytus consult the work of Basilides himself, or did he depend on an intermediate reporter? His own language, though not absolutely decisive, favours the former alternative. On the one hand it may be urged that he makes no mention of a book, that occasionally he quotes by the words "they say," "according to them," and that his exposition is immediately preceded by the remark, "Let us then see how openly both Basilides and [his son] Isidore (Β. ὁμοῦ καὶ Ἰ.) and the whole band of them not merely calumniate Matthias [from whom they professed to have received records of Christ's secret teaching], but also the Saviour Himself" (c. 20). Against these indications may be set the ten places where Basilides is referred to singly, and the very numerous quotations by the words "he says." It is true that Greek usage permits the occasional use of the singular even when no one writer or book is intended. But in this case the most natural translation is borne out by some of the language quoted. The first person singular (ὅταν δὲ λέγω, φησίν, τό Ἦν, οὐχ ὅτι ἦν λέγω, ἀλλ' ἵνα σημάνω τοῦτο ὅπερ βούλομαι δεῖξαι, λέγω, φησίν, ὅτι ἦν ὅλως οὐδέν· . . . καὶ οὐ δέχομαι, φησὶν κ.τ.λ.) proves the book in Hippolytus's hands to have been written by an original speculator; yet this very quotation is immediately followed by a comment on it with the third person plural which here at least can mean no more than that Hippolytus held the Basilidians of his own day responsible for the doctrines of his author. The freshness and power of the whole section, wherever we touch the actual words of the author, strongly confirm the impression that he was no other than Basilides himself. Thus we are led independently to the conclusion suggested by the correspondence with the information of Clement, whom we know to have drawn from the fountain-head, the *Exegetica.* The fancy that the book used by Hippolytus was itself the Traditions of Matthias has nothing to recommend it. The whole form is unlike that which analogy would lead us to expect in such a production. If it was quoted as an authority in the *Exegetica*, the language of Hippolytus is justified. Nor is there anything in this inconsistent with the fact vouched for by Clement (*Strom.* vii. p. 898) that Basilides claimed to have been taught by Glaucias, an "interpreter" of St. Peter.

We shall therefore assume that the eight chapters of Hippolytus (vii. 20-27) represent faithfully though imperfectly the contents of part at least of the *Exegetica* of Basilides; and proceed to describe his doctrine on their authority, using likewise the testimony of Clement wherever it is available.

IV. *Doctrine.*—Basilides asserts the beginning of all things to have been pure nothing. He uses every device of language to express absolute nonentity. He will not allow the primitive nothing to be called even "unspeākable": that, he says, would be naming it, and it is above every name that is named (20). Nothing then being in existence, "not-being God" (or Deity, *οὐκ ὢν θεός*: the article is omitted here) willed to make a not-being world out of not-being things. Once more great pains are taken to obviate the notion that "willing" implied any mental attribute whatever. Also the world so made was not the extended and differentiated world to which we gave the name, but "a single seed containing within itself all the *seed-mass* of the world," the aggregate of the seeds of all its forms and substances, as the mustard seed contains the branches and leaves of the tree, or the peahen's egg the brilliant colour of the full-grown peacock (21). This was the one origin of all future growths; their seeds lay stored up by the will of the not-being God in the single world-seed, as in the new-born babe its future teeth and the resemblances to its father which are thereafter to appear. Its own origin too from God was not a *putting-forth* (*προβολή*), as a spider puts forth its web from itself. (By this assertion, on which Hippolytus dwells with emphasis, every notion of "emanation" is expressly repudiated.) Nor was there an antecedent matter, like the brass or wood wrought by a mortal man. The words "Let there be light, and there was light" convey the whole truth. The light came into being out of nothing but the voice of the Speaker; "and the Speaker was not, and that which came into being was not."

What then was the first stage of growth of the seed? It had within itself "a tripartite sonship, in all things consubstantial with the not-being God." Part of the sonship was subtle of substance (*λεπτομερές*), part coarse of substance (*παχυμερές*), part needing purification (*ἀποκαθάρσεως δεόμενον*). Simultaneously with the first beginning of the seed the subtle sonship burst through (*διέσφυξεν*) and mounted swiftly up "like a wing or a thought" (Odyss. vii. 36) till it reached the not-being God; "for toward Him for His exceeding beauty and grace (*ὡραιότητος*) every kind of nature yearns (*ὀρέγεται*), each in its own way." The coarse sonship could not mount up of itself, but it took to itself as a wing the Holy Spirit, each bearing up the other with mutual benefit, even as neither a bird can soar without wing, nor a wing without a bird. But when it came near the blessed and unutterable place of the subtle sonship and the not-being God, it could take the Holy Spirit no further, as not being consubstantial or of the same nature with itself. There, then, retaining and emitting downwards the fragrance of the sonship like a vessel that has once held ointment, the Holy Spirit remained, as a firmament dividing things above the world from "the world" itself below (22).

The third sonship continued still within the heap of the seed-mass. But out of the heap burst forth into being the Great Archon, "the head of the world, a beauty and greatness and power that cannot be uttered." He too raised himself aloft till he reached the firmament which he supposed to be the upward end of all things. Then he became wiser and every way better than all other cosmical things except the sonship left below, which he knew not to be far better than himself. So he turned to create the world in its several parts. But first he "made to himself and begat out of the things below a son far better and wiser than himself," for thus the not-being God had willed from the first; and smitten with wonder at his son's beauty, he set him at his right hand. "This is what they call the Ogdoad, where the Great Archon is sitting." Then all the heavenly or ethereal creation (apparently included in the Ogdoad), as far down as the moon, was made by the Great Archon, inspired by his wiser son (23). Again another Archon arose out of the seed-mass, inferior to the first Archon, but superior to all else below except the sonship; and he likewise made to himself a son wiser than himself, and became the creator and governor of the aerial world. This region is called the Hebdomad. On the other hand, in the heap and seed-mass, constituting our own (the terrestrial) stage, "those things that come to pass come to pass according to nature, as having been previously uttered by Him Who hath planned the fitting time and form and manner of utterance of the things that were to be uttered (*ὡς φθάσαντα λεχθῆναι ὑπὸ τοῦ τὰ μέλλοντα λέγεσθαι ὅτε δεῖ καὶ οἷα δεῖ καὶ ὡς δεῖ λελογισμένου*): and these things have no one to rule over them, or exercise care for them, or create them: for sufficient for them is that plan (*λογισμός*) which the not-being One planned when He was making" [the seed-mass] (24).

Such is the original cosmogony as conceived by Basilides, and it supplies the base for his view of the Gospel, as well as of the interval before the coming of the Gospel into the world. When the whole world had been finished, and the things above the world, and nothing was lacking, there remained in the seed-mass the third sonship, which had been left behind to do good and receive good in the seed; and it was needful that the sonship thus left behind should be revealed (Rom. viii. 19) and restored up yonder above the Limitary Spirit to join the subtle and imitative sonship and the not-being One, as it is written, "And the creation itself groaneth together and travaileth together, expecting the revelation of the sons of God." Now we the spiritual, he said, are sons left behind here to order and to inform and to correct and to perfect the souls whose nature it is to abide in this stage. Till Moses, then, from Adam sin reigned, as it is written; for the Great Archon reigned, he whose end reaches to the firmament, supposing himself to be God alone, and to have nothing above him, for all things remained guarded in secret silence; this is the mystery which was not made known to the former generations. But in those times the Great Archon, the Ogdoad, was king and lord, as it appeared, of all things: and moreover, the Hebdomad was king and lord of this stage; and the Ogdoad is unutterable, but the Hebdomad utterable. This, the Archon of the Hebdomad, is he who spoke to Moses and said, "I am the God of Abraham and Isaac and Jacob, and the name of God did I not make known to them" (for so, says Hippolytus, they will have it read), that is, of the unutterable God who is Archon of the Ogdoad. All the prophets, therefore, that were before the Saviour, spoke from that source (ἐκεῖθεν).

This short interpretation of the times before Christ, which has evidently suffered in the process of condensation by Hippolytus, carries us at once to the Gospel itself. "Because therefore it was needful that we the children of God should be revealed, concerning whom the creation groaned and travailed, expecting the revelation, the Gospel came into the world, and passed through every principality and power and lordship, and every name that is named." There was still no downward coming from above, no departure of the ascended sonship from its place; but "from below from the formlessness of the heap the powers penetrated (διήκουσιν) up to the sonship" (*i.e.* probably throughout the scale the power of each stage penetrated to the stage immediately above), and so thoughts (νοήματα) were caught from above as naphtha catches fire at a distance without contact. Thus the power within the Holy Spirit "conveyed the thoughts of the sonship, as they flowed and drifted (ῥέοντα καὶ φερόμενα) to the son of the Great Archon" (25); and he in turn instructed the Great Archon himself, by whose side he was sitting. Then first the Great Archon learned that he was not God of the universe, but had himself come into being, and had above him yet higher beings; he discovered with amazement his own past ignorance, and confessed his sin in having magnified himself. This fear of his, said Basilides, was that fear of the Lord which is the beginning of wisdom (wisdom to "separate and discern and perfect and restore," Clem. *Strom.* ii. 448 f.). From him and the Ogdoad the Gospel had next to pass to the Hebdomad. Its Archon's son received the light from the son of the Great Archon, he became himself enlightened, and declared the Gospel to the Archon of the Hebdomad, and he too feared and confessed, and all that was in the Hebdomad received the light (26).

It remained only that the formlessness of our own region should be enlightened, and that the hidden mystery should be revealed to the third sonship left behind in the formlessness, as to "one born out of due time" (οἱονεὶ ἐκτρώματι, I. Cor. xv. 8). The light came down from the Hebdomad upon Jesus the Son of Mary. That this descent of the light was represented as taking place at the Annunciation, and not merely at the Baptism, is clearly implied in the express reference to the words of the angel in Luke i. 35, "A Holy Spirit shall come upon thee," which are explained to mean "that [? spirit] which passed from the sonship through the Limitary Spirit to the Ogdoad and the Hebdomad till it reached Mary" (the interpretation of the following words, "And a power of the Most High shall overshadow thee," appears to be hopelessly corrupt). On the other hand, when it is described as a result of the descent of the light from the Hebdomad "upon Jesus the Son of Mary," that He "was enlightened, being kindled in union with the light (συνεξαφθεὶς τῷ φωτὶ) that shone on Him," the allusion to the traditional light at the Baptism can hardly be questioned; more especially when we read in Clement's *Excerpta* (p. 972) that the Basilidians interpreted the dove to be "the Minister," *i.e.* (see pp. 270, 276) the revealing "power" within the Holy Spirit (26).

From the Nativity Hippolytus's exposition passes on at once to its purpose in the future and the final consummation. The world holds together as it is now, we learn, until all the sonship that has been left behind, to give benefits to the souls in formlessness and to receive benefits by obtaining distinct form, follows Jesus and mounts up and is purified and becomes most subtle, so that it can mount by itself like the first sonship; "for it has all its power naturally established in union (συνεστηριγμένην) with the light that shone down from above" (26). When every sonship has arrived above the Limitary Spirit, "then the creation shall find mercy, for till now it groans and is tormented and awaits the revelation of the sons of God, that all the men of the sonship may ascend from hence" (27). When this has come to pass, God will bring upon the whole world the Great Ignorance, that everything may remain according to nature, and that nothing may desire aught that is contrary to nature. Thus all the souls of this stage, whose nature it is to continue immortal in this stage alone, will remain without knowledge of anything higher and better than this, lest they suffer torment by craving for things impossible, like a fish desiring to feed with the sheep on the mountains, for such a desire would have been to them destruction. All things are indestructible while they abide in their place, but destructible if they aim at overleaping the bounds of Nature. Thus the Great Ignorance will overtake even the Archon of the Hebdomad, that grief and pain and sighing may depart from him: yea, it will overtake the Great Archon of the Ogdoad, and all the creations subject to him, that nothing may in any respect crave for aught that is against nature or may suffer pain. "And in this wise shall be the Restoration, all things according to nature having been founded in the seed of the universe in the beginning, and being restored at their due seasons. And that each thing has its due seasons is sufficiently proved by the Saviour's words, 'My hour is not yet come,' and by the beholding of the star by the Magi; for even He Himself was subject to the 'genesis' [nativity] of the periodic return (ἀποκαταστάσεως, here used in the limited astrological sense, though above as 'restoration' generally) of stars and hours, as foreordained [προλελογισμένος: cf. c. 24, s. f.; x. 14] in the great heap." "He," adds Hippolytus, evidently meaning our Lord, "is [in the Basilidian view] the inner spiritual man in the natural [psychical] man; that is, a sonship leaving its soul here, not a mortal soul, but one remaining in its present place according to nature, just as the first sonship up above hath left the Limitary Holy Spirit in a fitting place; He having at that time been clothed with a soul of His own" (27).

These last two remarks, on the subjection to seasons and on the ultimate abandonment of the immortal but earth-bound soul by the ascending sonship or spiritual man, taking place first in the Saviour and then in the other "sons of God," belong in strictness to an earlier part of the scheme; but they may have been placed here by Basilides himself, to explain the strange consummation of the Great Ignorance. The principle receives perhaps a better illustration from what purports to be an exposition of the Basilidian view of the Gospel, with which Hippolytus concludes his report. "According to them," he says, "the Gospel is the knowledge of things above the world, which knowledge the Great Archon understood not: when then it was shewn to him that there exists the Holy Spirit, that is the Limitary Spirit, and the sonship and a God Who is the author (αἴτιος) of all these things, even the not-being One, he rejoiced at what was told him, and was exceeding glad: this is according to them the Gospel." Here Hippolytus evidently takes too generally the special form under which Basilides represented the Gospel as made known to the Great Archon. Nor, when he proceeds to say that "Jesus according to them was born in the manner that we have previously mentioned," is it clear that Basilides gave a different account of the Nativity itself from that accepted by the church, because he gave a peculiar interpretation to the angel's words. "After the Nativity already made known," adds Hippolytus, "all incidents concerning the Saviour came to pass according to them [the Basilidians] as they are described in the Gospels." But all this is only introductory to the setting forth of the primary principle. "These things" (apparently the incidents of our Lord's life) "are come to pass that Jesus might become the first fruits of the sorting of the things confused" (τῆς φυλοκρινήσεως τῶν συγκεχυμένων). For since the world is divided into the Ogdoad and the Hebdomad and this stage in which we dwell, where is the formlessness, "it was necessary that the things confused should be sorted by the division of Jesus. That therefore suffered which was His bodily part, which was of the formlessness, and it was restored into the formlessness; and that rose up which was His psychical part, which was of the Hebdomad, and it was restored into the Hebdomad; and he raised up that which belonged to the summit where sits the Great Archon (τῆς ἀκρωρείας τοῦ μ. ἄ.), and it abode beside the Great Archon: and He bore up on high that which was of the Limitary Spirit, and it abode in the Limitary Spirit; and the third sonship, which had been left behind in [the heap] to give and receive benefits, through Him was purified and mounted up to the blessed sonship, passing through them all." "Thus Jesus is become the first fruits of the sorting; and the Passion has come to pass for no other purpose than this [reading γέγονεν ἢ ὑπέρ for γέγονεν ὑπό], that the things confused might be sorted." For the whole sonship left behind in the formlessness must needs be sorted in the same manner as Jesus Himself hath been sorted. Thus, as Hippolytus remarks a little earlier, the whole theory consists of the confusion of a seed-mass, and of the sorting and restoration into their proper places of things so confused (27).

Clement's contributions to our knowledge of Basilides refer chiefly, as has been said, to the ethical side of his doctrine. Here "Faith" evidently played a considerable part. In itself it was defined by "them of Basilides" (οἱ ἀπὸ B.) as "an assent of the soul to any of the things which do not excite sensation, because they are not present" (*Strom.* ii. p. 448); the phrase being little more than a vague rendering of Heb. xi. 1, in philosophical language. From another unfortunately corrupt passage (v. p. 645) it would appear that Basilides accumulated forms of dignity in celebration of faith. But the eulogies were in vain, Clement intimates, because they abstained from setting forth faith as the "rational assent of a soul possessing free will." They left faith a matter of "nature," not of responsible choice. So again, while contrasting the honour shewn by the Basilidians to faith with its disparagement in comparison with "knowledge" by the Valentinians, he accuses them (οἱ ἀμφὶ τὸν B.) of regarding it as "natural," and referring it to "the election" while they apparently considered it to "discover doctrines without demonstration by an intellective apprehension" (τὰ μαθήματα ἀναποδείκτως εὑρίσκουσαν καταλήψει νοητικῇ). He adds that according to them (οἱ ἀπὸ B.) there is at once a faith and an election of special character (οἰκείαν) in each "stage" (διάστημα), the mundane faith of every nature follows in accordance with its supermundane election, and for each (? being or stage) the [Divine] gift of his (or its) faith corresponds with his (or its) hope (ii. 433 f.). What "hope" was intended is not explained: probably it is the range of legitimate hope, the limits of faculty accessible to the beings inhabiting this or that "stage." It is hardly likely that Clement would have censured unreservedly what appears here as the leading principle of Basilides, the Divine resignment of a limited sphere of action to each order of being, and the Divine bestowal of proportionally limited powers of apprehending God upon the several orders, though it is true that Clement himself specially cherished the thought of an upward progress from one height of being to another, as part of the Divine salvation (*Strom.* vii. p. 835, etc.). Doubtless Basilides pushed election so far as to sever a portion of mankind from the rest, as alone entitled by Divine decree to receive the higher enlightenment. In this sense it must have been that he called "the election a stranger to the world, as being by nature supermundane"; while Clement maintained that no man can by nature be a stranger to the world (iv. p. 639). It is hardly necessary to point out how closely the limitation of spheres agrees with the doctrine on which the Great Ignorance is founded, and the supermundane election with that of the Third Sonship.

The same rigid adhesion to the conception of natural fixity, and inability to accept Christian beliefs, which transcend it, led Basilides (ὁ B.) to confine the remission of sins to those which are committed involuntarily and in ignorance; as though, says Clement (*Strom.* iv. p. 634), it were a man and not God that bestowed the gift. A like fatalistic view of Providence is implied in the language held by Basilides (in the 23rd book of his *Exegetica*, as quoted by Clement, *Strom.* iv. pp. 599-603) in reference to the sufferings of Christian martyrs. In this instance we have the benefit of verbal extracts, though unfortunately their sense is in parts obscure. So far as they go, they do not bear out the allegations of Agrippa Castor (ap. Eus. *H. E.* iv. 7, § 7) that Basilides taught that the partaking of food offered to idols, and the heedless (ἀπαραφυλάκτως) abjuration of the faith in time of persecution was a thing indifferent; and of Origen (*Com. in Matt.* iii. 856 Ru.), that he depreciated the martyrs, and treated lightly the sacrificing to heathen deities. The impression seems to have arisen partly from a misunderstanding of the purpose of his argument, partly from the actual doctrine and practices of later Basilidians; but it may also have had some justification in incidental words which have not been preserved. Basilides is evidently contesting the assumption, probably urged in controversy against his conception of the justice of Providence, that the sufferers in "what are called tribulations" (ἐν ταῖς λεγομέναις θλίψεσιν) are to be regarded as innocent, simply because they suffer for their Christianity. He suggests that some are in fact undergoing punishment for previous unknown sins, while "by the goodness of Him Who brings events to pass" (τοῦ περιάγοντος) they are allowed the comfort of suffering as Christians, "not subject to the rebuke as the adulterer or the murderer" (apparently with reference to 1 Pet. iii. 17, iv. 15, 16, 19); and if there be any who suffers without previous sin, it will not be "by the design of an [adverse] power" (κατ' ἐπιβουλὴν δυνάμεως), but as suffers the babe who appears to have committed no sin. The next quotation attempts at some length an exposition of this comparison with the babe. The obvious distinction is drawn between sin committed in act (ἐνεργῶς) and the capacity for sin (τὸ ἁμαρτητικόν); the infant is said to receive a benefit when it is subjected to suffering, "gaining" many hardships (πολλὰ κέρδαινον δύσκολα). So it is, he says, with the suffering of a perfect man, for his not having sinned must not be set down to himself; though he has done no evil, he must have willed evil; "for I will say anything rather than call Providence (τὸ προνοῦν) evil." He did not shrink, Clement says, and the language seems too conclusive, from applying his principle even to the Lord. "If, leaving all these arguments, you go on to press me with certain persons, saying, for instance, 'Such an one sinned therefore, for such an one suffered,' if you will allow me I will say, 'He did not sin, but he is like the suffering babe'; but if you force the argument with greater violence, I will say that any man whom you may choose to name is a man, and that God is righteous; for 'no one,' as it has been said, 'is clear of defilement'" (ῥύπου). He likewise brought in the notion of sin in a past stage of existence suffering its penalty here, "the elect soul" suffering "honourably (ἐπιτίμως) through martyrdom, and the soul of another kind being cleansed by an appropriate punishment." To this doctrine of metempsychosis (τὰς ἐνσωματώσεις) "the Basilidians" (οἱ ἀπὸ B.) are likewise said to have referred the language of the Lord about requital to the third and fourth generations (*Exc. Theod.* 976); Origen states that Basilides himself interpreted Rom. vii. 9 in this sense, "The Apostle said, 'I lived without a law once,' that is, before I came into this body, I lived in such a form of body as was not under a law, that of a beast namely, or a bird" (*Com. in Rom.* iv. 549, Ru.); and elsewhere (*Com. in Matt. l.c.*) Origen complains that he deprived men of a salutary fear by teaching that transmigrations are the only punishments after death. What more Basilides taught about Providence as exemplified in martyrdoms is not easily brought together from Clement's rather confused account. He said that one part of what is called the will of God (*i.e.* evidently His own mind towards lower beings, not what He would have their mind to be) is to love (or rather perhaps be satisfied with, ἠγαπηκέναι) all things because all things preserve a relation to the universe (λόγον ἀποσῴζουσι πρὸς τὸ πᾶν ἅπαντα), and another to despise nothing, and a third to hate no single thing (601). In the same spirit pain and fear were described as natural accidents of things (ἐπισυμβαίνει τοῖς πράγμασιν), as rust of iron (603). In another sentence (602) Providence seems to be spoken of as set in motion by the Archon; by which perhaps was meant (see Hipp. c. 24, cited above, p. 272 A) that the Archon was the unconscious agent who carried into execution (within his own "stage") the long dormant original counsels of the not-being God. The view of the harmony of the universe just referred to finds expression, with a reminiscence of a famous sentence of Plato (*Tim.* 31 B), in a saying (*Strom.* v. p. 690) that Moses "set up one temple of God and an only-begotten world" (μονογενῆ τε κόσμον: cf. Plut. ii. 423 A, ἕνα τοῦτον [τὸν κόσμον] εἶναι μονογενῆ τῷ θεῷ καὶ ἀγαπητόν).

We have a curious piece of psychological theory in the account of the passions attributed to the Basilidians (οἱ ἀμφὶ τὸν B.). They are accustomed, Clement says (*Strom.* ii. p. 488), to call the passions Appendages (προσαρτήματα), stating that these are certain spirits which have a substantial existence (κατ οὐσίαν ὑπάρχειν), having been appended (or "attached," or "adherent," various kinds of close external contact being expressed by προσηρτημένα, cf. M. Aur. xii. 3, with Gataker's note, and also Tertullian's *ceteris appendicibus, sensibus et affectibus, Adv. Marc.* i. 25, cited by Gieseler) to the rational soul in a certain primitive turmoil and confusion, and that again other bastard and alien natures of spirits grow upon these (προσεπιφύεσθαι ταύταις), as of a wolf, an ape, a lion, a goat, whose characteristics (ιδιώματα), becoming perceptible in the region of the soul (φανταζόμενα περὶ τὴν ψυχήν), assimilate the desires of the son to the animals; for they imitate the actions of those whose characteristics they wear, and not only acquire intimacy (προσοικειοῦνται) with the impulses and impressions of the irrational animals, but even imitate (ζηλοῦσι) the movements and beauties of plants, because they likewise wear the characteristics of plants appended to them; and [the passions] have also characteristics of habit [derived from stones], as the hardness of adamant (cf. p. 487 med.). In the absence of the context it is impossible to determine the precise meaning and origin of this singular theory. It was probably connected with the doctrine of metempsychosis, which seemed to find support in Plato's *Timaeus* 42, 90 f.), and was cherished by some neo-Pythagoreans later in the 2nd cent. (cf. Zeller, *Philos. d. Gr.* v. 198 f.); while the plurality of souls is derided by Clement as making the body a Trojan horse, with apparent reference (as Saumaise points out, on Simplic. *Epict.* 164) to a similar criticism of Plato in the *Theaetetus* (184 D). And again Plutarch (*de Comm. Not.* 45, p. 1084) ridicules the Stoics (*i.e.* apparently Chrysippus) for a "strange and outlandish" notion that all virtues and vices, arts and memories, impressions *and passions and impulses* and assents (he adds further down even "acts," ἐνεργείας, such as "walking, dancing, supposing, addressing, reviling") are not merely "bodies" (of course in the familiar Stoic sense) but living creatures or animals (ζῷα), crowded apparently round the central point within the heart where "the ruling principle" (τὸ ἡγεμονικόν) is located: by this "swarm," he says, of hostile animals they turn each one of us into "a paddock or a stable, or a *Trojan horse.*" Such a theory might seem to Basilides an easy deduction from his fatalistic doctrine of Providence, and of the consequent immutability of all natures.

The only specimen which we have of the practical ethics of Basilides is of a favourable kind, though grossly misunderstood and misapplied by Epiphanius (i. 211 f.). Reciting the views of different heretics on Marriage, Clement (*Strom.* iii. 508 ff.) mentions first its approval by the Valentinians, and then gives specimens of the teaching of Basilides (οἱ ἀπὸ B.) and his son Isidore, by way of rebuke to the immorality of the later Basilidians, before proceeding to the sects which favoured licence, and to those which treated marriage as unholy. He first reports the exposition of Matt. xix. 11 f. (or a similar evangelic passage), in which there is nothing specially to note except the interpretation of the last class of eunuchs as those who remain in celibacy to avoid the distracting cares of providing a livelihood. He goes on to the paraphrase of I. Cor. vii. 9, interposing in the midst an illustrative sentence from Isidore, and transcribes the language used about the class above mentioned. "But suppose a young man either poor or (?) depressed [κατηφής seems at least less unlikely than κατωφερής], and in accordance with the word [in the Gospel] unwilling to marry, let him not separate from his brother; let him say 'I have entered into the holy place [τὰ ἅγια, probably the communion of the church], nothing can befall me'; but if he have a suspicion [? self-distrust, ὑπονοίαν ἔχῃ], let him say, 'Brother, lay thy hand on me, that I may sin not,' and he shall receive help both to mind and to senses (νοητὴν καὶ αἰσθητήν); let him only have the will to carry out completely what is good, and he shall succeed. But sometimes we say with the lips, 'We will not sin,' while our thoughts are turned towards sinning: such an one abstains by reason of fear from doing what he wills, lest the punishment be reckoned to his account. But the estate of mankind has only certain things at once necessary and natural, clothing being necessary and natural, but τὸ τῶν ἀφροδισίων natural, yet not necessary" (cf. Plut. *Mor.* 989).

Although we have no evidence that Basilides, like some others, regarded our Lord's Baptism as the time when a Divine being first was joined to Jesus of Nazareth, it seems clear that he attached some unusual significance to the event. "They of Basilides (οἱ ἀπὸ B.)," says Clement (*Strom.* i. 146, p. 408), "celebrate the day of His Baptism by a preliminary night-service of [Scripture] readings (προδιανυκτερεύοντες ἀναγνώσεσι); and they say that the 'fifteenth year of Tiberius Caesar' (Luke iii. 1) is (or means) the fifteenth day of the [Egyptian] month Tybi, while some [make the day] the eleventh of the same month." Again it is briefly stated in the *Excerpta* (16, p. 972) that the dove of the Baptism is said by the Basilidians (οἱ ἀπὸ B.) to be the Minister (ὁ διάκονος). And the same association is implied in what Clement urges elsewhere (*Strom.* ii. p. 449): "If ignorance belongs to the class of good things, why is it brought to an end by amazement [*i.e.* the amazement of the Archon], and [so] *the Minister* that they speak of [αὐτοῖς] is superfluous, and the Proclamation, *and the Baptism*: if ignorance had not previously existed, the Minister would not have descended, nor would amazement have seized the Archon, as they themselves say." This language, taken in conjunction with passages already cited from Hippolytus (c. 26), implies that Basilides regarded the Baptism as the occasion when Jesus received "the Gospel" by a Divine illumination. The supposed descent of "Christ" for union with "Jesus," though constantly assumed by Hilgenfeld, is as destitute of ancient attestation as it is inconsistent with the tenor of Basilidian doctrine recorded by Clement, to say nothing of Hippolytus. It has been argued from Clement's language by Gieseler (in the Halle *A.L.Z.* for 1823, i. 836 f.; cf. *K.G.* i. 1. 186), that the Basilidians were the first to celebrate our Lord's Baptism. The early history of the Epiphany is too obscure to allow a definite conclusion on this point; but the statement about the Basilidian services of the preceding night receives some illustration from a passage of Epiphanius, lately published from the Venice MS. ii. 483 Dind.: iii. 632 Oehler), in which we hear of the night before the Epiphany as spent in singing and flute-playing in a heathen temple at Alexandria: so that probably the Basilidian rite was a modification of an old local custom. According to Agrippa Castor (Eus. *l.c.*) Basilides "in Pythagorean fashion" prescribed a silence of five years to his disciples.

The same author, we hear, stated that Basilides "named as prophets to himself Barcabbas and Barcoph, providing himself likewise with certain other [? prophets] who had no existence, and that he bestowed upon them barbarous appellations to strike amazement into those who have an awe of such things." The alleged prophecies apparently belonged to the apocryphal Zoroastrian literature popular with various Gnostics.

From Hippolytus we hear nothing about these prophecies, which will meet us again presently with reference to Basilides's son Isidore, but he tells us (*Haer.* vii. 20) that, according to Basilides and Isidore, Matthias spoke to them mystical doctrines (λόγους ἀποκρύφους) which he heard in private teaching from the Saviour: and in like manner Clement (*Strom.* vii. 900) speaks of the sect of Basilides as boasting that they took to themselves the glory of Matthias. Origen also (*Hom. in Luc.* i. t. iii. p. 933) and after him Eusebius refer to a "Gospel" of or according to Matthias (*H. E.* iii. 25, 6). The true name was apparently the *Traditions of Matthias*: three interesting and by no means heretical extracts are given by Clement (*Strom.* ii. 452; iii. 523 [copied by Eusebius, *H. E.* iii. 29. 4]; vii. 882). In the last extract the responsibility laid on "the elect" for the sin of a neighbour recalls a passage already cited (p. 275 B) from Basilides.

It remains only to notice an apparent reference to Basilides, which has played a considerable part in modern expositions of his doctrine. Near the end of the anonymous *Acts of the Disputation between Archelaus and Mani*, written towards the close of the 3rd cent. or a little later, Archelaus disputes the originality of Mani's teaching, on the ground that it took rise a long time before with "a certain barbarian" (c. 55, in Routh, *Rell. Sac.* v. 196 ff.). "There was also," he says, "a preacher among the Persians, a certain Basilides of great [or 'greater,' *antiuqior*] antiquity, not long after the times of our Apostles, who being himself also a crafty man, and perceiving that at that time everything was preoccupied, decided to maintain that dualism which was likewise in favour with Scythianus," named shortly before (c. 51, p. 186) as a contemporary of the Apostles, who had introduced dualism from a Pythagorean source. "Finally, as he had no assertion to make of his own, he adopted the sayings of others" (the last words are corrupt, but this must be nearly the sense). "And all his books contain things difficult and rugged." The writer then cites the beginning of the thirteenth book of his treatises (*tractatuum*), in which it was said that "the saving word" (the Gospel) by means of the parable of the rich man and the poor man pointed out the source from which nature (or a nature) without a root and without a place germinated and extended itself over things (*rebus supervenientem, unde pullulaverit*). He breaks off a few words later and adds that after some 500 lines Basilides invites his reader to abandon idle and curious elaborateness (*varietate*), and to investigate rather the studies and opinions of barbarians on good and evil. Certain of them, Basilides states, said that there are two beginnings of all things, light and darkness; and he subjoins some particulars of doctrine of a Persian cast. Only one set of views, however, is mentioned, and the Acts end abruptly here in the two known MSS. of the Latin version in which alone this part of them is extant.

It is generally assumed that we have here unimpeachable evidence for the strict dualism of Basilides. It seems certain that the writer of the Acts held his Basilides responsible for the barbarian opinions quoted, which are clearly dualistic, and he had the whole book before him. Yet his language on this point is loose, as if he were not sure of his ground; and the quotation which he gives by no means bears him out: while it is quite conceivable that he may have had some acquaintance with dualistic Basilidians of a later day, such as certainly existed, and have thus given a wrong interpretation to genuine words of their master (cf. Uhlhorn, 52 f.). It assuredly requires considerable straining to draw the brief interpretation given of the parable to a Manichean position, and there is nothing to shew that the author of it himself adopted the first set of "barbarian" opinions which he reported. Indeed the description of evil (for evil doubtless is intended) as a *supervenient* nature, *without root* and without place, reads almost as if it were directed against Persian doctrine, and may be fairly interpreted by Basilides's comparison of pain and fear to the rust of iron as natural accidents (ἐπισυμβαίνει). The identity of the Basilides of the Acts with the Alexandrian has been denied by Gieseler with some shew of reason. It is at least strange that our Basilides should be described simply as a "preacher among the Persians," a character in which he is otherwise unknown; and all the more since he has been previously mentioned with Marcion and Valentinus as a heretic of familiar name (c. 38, p. 138). On the other hand, it has been justly urged that the two passages are addressed to different persons. The correspondence is likewise remarkable between the "treatises" in at least thirteen books, with an interpretation of a parable among their contents, and the "twenty-four books on the Gospel" mentioned by Agrippa Castor, called *Exegetica* by Clement. Thus the evidence for the identity of the two writers may on the whole be treated as preponderating. But the ambiguity of interpretation remains; and it would be impossible to rank Basilides confidently among dualists, even if the passage in the Acts stood alone: much more to use it as a standard by which to force a dualistic interpretation upon other clearer statements of his doctrine.

Gnosticism was throughout eclectic, and Basilides superadded an eclecticism of his own. Antecedent Gnosticism, Greek philosophy, and the Christian faith and Scriptures all exercised a powerful and immediate influence over his mind. It is evident at a glance that his system is far removed from any known form of Syrian or original Gnosticism. Like that of Valentinus, it has been remoulded in a Greek spirit, but much more completely. Historical records fail us almost entirely as to the personal relations of the great heresiarchs; yet internal evidence furnishes some indications which it can hardly be rash to trust. Ancient writers usually name Basilides before Valentinus; but there is little doubt that they were at least approximately contemporaries, and it is not unlikely that Valentinus was best known personally from his sojourn at Rome, which was probably (Lipsius, *Quellen d. ält. Ketzergeschichte*, 256) the last of the recorded stages of his life. There is at all events no serious chronological difficulty in supposing that the Valentinian system was the starting-point from which Basilides proceeded to construct by contrast his own theory, and this is the view which a comparison of doctrines suggests. In no point, unless it be the retention of the widely spread term *archon*, is Basilides nearer than Valentinus to the older Gnosticism, while several leading Gnostic forms or ideas which he discards or even repudiates are held fast by Valentinus. Such are descent from above (see a passage at the end of c. 22, and p. 272 B, above), putting forth or pullulation (imperfect renderings of προβολή, see p. 271 B), syzygies of male and female powers, and the deposition of faith to a lower level than knowledge. Further, the unique name given by Basilides to the Holy Spirit, "the Limitary (μεθόριον) Spirit," together with the place assigned to it, can hardly be anything else than a transformation of the strange Valentinian "Limit" (ὅρος), which in like manner divides the Pleroma from the lower world; though, in conformity with the unifying purpose of Basilides, the Limitary Spirit is conceived as connecting as well as parting the two worlds (cf. Baur in *Theol. Jahrb.* for 1856, 156 f.). The same softening of oppositions which retain much of their force even with Valentinus shews itself in other instances, as of matter and spirit, creation and redemption, the Jewish age and the Christian age, the earthly and the heavenly elements in the Person of our Lord. The strongest impulse in this direction probably came from Christian ideas and the power of a true though disguised Christian faith. But Greek speculative Stoicism tended likewise to break down the inherited dualism, while at the same time its own inherent limitations brought faith into captivity. An antecedent matter was expressly repudiated, the words of Gen. i. 3 eagerly appropriated, and a Divine counsel represented as foreordaining all future growths and processes; yet the chaotic nullity out of which the developed universe was to spring was attributed with equal boldness to its Maker: Creator and creation were not confused, but they melted away in the distance together. Nature was accepted not only as prescribing the conditions of the lower life, but as practically the supreme and permanent arbiter of destiny. Thus though faith regained its rights, it remained an energy of the understanding, confined to those who had the requisite inborn capacity; while the dealings of God with man were shut up within the lines of mechanical justice. The majestic and, so to speak, pathetic view bounded by the large Basilidian horizon was well fitted to inspire dreams of a high and comprehensive theology, but the very fidelity with which Basilides strove to cling to reality must have soon brought to light the incompetence of his teaching to solve any of the great problems. Its true office consisted in supplying one of the indispensable antecedents to the Alexandrian Catholicism which arose two generations later.

V. *Refutations.*—Notwithstanding the wide and lasting fame of Basilides as a typical heresiarch, no treatise is recorded as written specially in confutation of his teaching except that of Agrippa Castor. He had of course a place in the various works against all heresies; but, as we have seen, the doctrines described and criticized in several of them belong not to him but to a sect of almost wholly different character. Hippolytus, who in later years became acquainted with the *Exegetica*, contented himself with detecting imaginary plagiarisms from Aristotle (vii. 14-20). Even Origen, who likewise seems to have known the work (if we may judge by the quotation on metempsychosis given at p. 275, and by a complaint of "long-winded fabling," *aut Basilidis longam fabulositatem: Com. in Matt.* xxiv. 23, p. 864 Ru.), shews in the few casual remarks in his extant writings little real understanding even of Basilides's errors. On the other hand, Clement's candid intelligence enables him to detect the latent flaws of principle in the Basilidian theory without mocking at such of the superficial details as he has occasion to mention. Hilgenfeld, writing (1848) on the pseudo-Clementine literature, made a singular attempt to shew that in one early recension of the materials of part of the *Recognitions* Simon was made to utter Basilidian doctrine, to be refuted by St. Peter, the traces of which had been partly effaced by his becoming the mouthpiece of other Gnostics in later recensions. Ritschl took the same view in the first ed. of his *Entstehung d. altkath. Kirche* (1850, pp. 169-174); but the whole speculation vanishes in his far maturer second ed. of 1857. The theory lacks even plausibility. The only resemblances between this part of the *Recognitions* and either the true or the spurious Basilidianism are common to various forms of religious belief; and not a single distinctive feature of either Basilidian system occurs in the *Recognitions*. A brief but sufficient reply is given in Uhlhorn's *Hom. u. Recog. d. Clem. Rom.* 1854, pp. 286 ff.

VI. *Isodorus*.—In the passage already noticed (*Haer.* vii. 20) Hippolytus couples with Basilides "his true child and disciple" Isidore. He is there referring to the use which they made of the *Traditions of Matthias*; but in the next sentence he treats them as jointly responsible for the doctrines which he recites. Our only other authority respecting Isidore is Clement (copied by Theodoret), who calls him in like manner "at once son and disciple" of Basilides (*Strom.* vi. 767). In this place he gives three extracts from the first and second books of Isidore's *Expositions* (Ἐξηγητικά) *of the Prophet Parchor*. They are all parts of a plea, like so many put forward after the example of Josephus *against Apion*, that the higher thoughts of heathen philosophers and mythologers were derived from a Jewish source. The last reference given is to Pherecydes, who had probably a peculiar interest for Isidore as the earliest promulgator of the doctrine of metempsychosis known to tradition (cf. Zeller, *Philos. d. Griechen*, i. 55 f. ed. 3). His allegation that Pherecydes followed "the prophecy of Ham" has been perversely urged as a sign that he set up the prophets of a hated race against the prophets of Israel. The truth is rather that the identification of Zoroaster with Ham or Ham's son, whatever may have been its origin, rendered it easy to claim for the apocryphal Zoroastrian books a quasi-biblical sanctity as proceeding from a son of Noah, and that Isidore gladly accepted the theory as evidence for his argument. "The prophets" from whom "some of the philosophers" appropriated a wisdom not their own can be no other than the Jewish prophets. Again Clement quotes his book *On an Adherent Soul* (Περὶ προσφυοῦς ψυχῆς) in correction of his preceding quotation from Basilides on the passions as "appendages" (*Strom.* ii. 488). If the eight lines transcribed are a fair sample of the treatise, Isidore would certainly appear to have argued here against his father's teaching. He insists on the unity (μονομερής) of the soul, and maintains that bad men will find "no common excuse" in the violence of the "appendages" for pleading that their evil acts were involuntary: our duty is, he says, "by overcoming the inferior creation within us (τῆς ἐλάττονος ἐν ἡμῖν κτίσεως) through the reasoning faculty (τῷ λογιστικῷ), to shew ourselves to have the mastery." A third passage from Isidore's *Ethics* (*Strom.* iii. 510) is intercalated into his father's argument on I. Cor. vii. 9, to the same purport but in a coarser strain. Its apparent difficulty arises partly from a corrupt reading (ἀντέχου μαχίμης γυναικός, where γαμετῆς must doubtless be substituted for μαχίμης, ἀντέχου meaning not "resist," which would be ἀντέχε, as in the preceding line, but "have recourse to"); partly from the assumption that the following words ὅταν δὲ κ.τ.λ. are likewise by Isidore, whereas the sense shews them to be a continuation of the exposition of Basilides himself.

Basilides had to all appearance no eminent disciple except his own son. In this respect the contrast between him and Valentinus is remarkable. A succession of brilliant followers carried forward and developed the Valentinian doctrine. It is a singular testimony to the impression created at the outset by Basilides and his system that he remained for centuries one of the *eponymi* of heresy; his name is oftener repeated, for instance, in the writings of Origen, than that of any other dreaded of the ante-Nicene church except Marcion, Valentinus, and afterwards Mani. But the original teaching, for all its impressiveness, had no vitality. The Basilidianism which did survive, and that, as far as the evidence goes, only locally, was, as we have seen, a poor and corrupt remnant, adulterated with the very elements which the founder had strenuously rejected.

VII. *The Spurious Basilidian System*.—In briefly sketching this degenerate Basilidianism it will seldom be needful to distinguish the authorities, which are fundamentally two, Irenaeus (101 f.) and the lost early treatise of Hippolytus; both having much in common, and both being interwoven together in the report of Epiphanius (pp. 68-75). The other relics of the Hippolytean Compendium are the accounts of Philaster (32), and the supplement to Tertullian (4). At the head of this theology stood the Unbegotten (neuter in Epiph.), the Only Father. From Him was born or put forth Nûs, and from Nûs Logos, from Logos Phronesis, from Phronesis Sophia and Dynamis, from Sophia and Dynamis principalities, powers, and angels. This first set of angels first made the first heaven, and then gave birth to a second set of angels who made a second heaven, and so on till 365 heavens had been made by 365 generations of angels, each heaven being apparently ruled by an Archon to whom a name was given, and these names being used in magic arts. The angels of the lowest or visible heaven made the earth and man. They were the authors of the prophecies; and the Law in particular was given by their Archon, the God of the Jews. He being more petulant and wilful than the other angels (ἰταμώτερον καὶ αὐθαδέστερον), in his desire to secure empire for his people, provoked the rebellion of the other angels and their respective peoples. Then the Unbegotten and Innominable Father, seeing what discord prevailed among men and among angels, and how the Jews were perishing, sent His Firstborn Nûs, Who is Christ, to deliver those Who believed on Him from the power of the makers of the world. "He," the Basilidians said, "is our salvation, even He Who came and revealed to us alone this truth." He accordingly appeared on earth and performed mighty works; but His appearance was only in outward show, and He did not really take flesh. It was Simon of Cyrene that was crucified; for Jesus exchanged forms with him on the way, and then, standing unseen opposite in Simon's form, mocked those who did the deed. But He Himself ascended into heaven, passing through all the powers, till He was restored to the presence of His own Father. The two fullest accounts, those of Irenaeus and Epiphanius, add by way of appendix another particular of the antecedent mythology; a short notice on the same subject being likewise inserted parenthetically by Hippolytus

(vii. 26, p. 240: cf. Uhlhorn, *D. Basilid. Syst.* 65 f.). The supreme power and source of being above all principalities and powers and angels (such is evidently the reference of Epiphanius's αὐτῶν: Irenaeus substitutes "heavens," which in this connexion comes to much the same thing) is Abrasax, the Greek letters of whose name added together as numerals make up 365, the number of the heavens; whence, they apparently said, the year has 365 days, and the human body 365 members. This supreme Power they called "the Cause" and "the First Archetype," while they treated as a last or weakest product (*Hysterema*, a Valentinian term, contrasted with *Pleroma*) this present world as the work of the last Archon (Epiph. 74 A). It is evident from these particulars that Abrasax was the name of the first of the 365 Archons, and accordingly stood below Sophia and Dynamis and their progenitors; but his position is not expressly stated, so that the writer of the supplement to Tertullian had some excuse for confusing him with "the Supreme God."

On these doctrines various precepts are said to have been founded. The most distinctive is the discouragement of martyrdom, which was made to rest on several grounds. To confess the Crucified was called a token of being still in bondage to the makers of the body (nay, he that denied the Crucified was pronounced to be free from the dominion of those angels, and to know the economy of the Unbegotten Father); but it was condemned especially as a vain and ignorant honour paid not to Christ, Who neither suffered nor was crucified, but to Simon of Cyrene; and further, a public confession before men was stigmatized as a giving of that which is holy to the dogs and a casting of pearls before swine. This last precept is but one expression of the secrecy which the Basilidians diligently cultivated, following naturally on the supposed possession of a hidden knowledge. They evaded our Lord's words, "Him that denieth Me before men," etc., by pleading, "We are the men, and all others are swine and dogs." He who had learned their lore and known all angels and their powers was said to become invisible and incomprehensible to all angels and powers, even as also Caulacau was (the sentence in which Irenaeus, our sole authority here, first introduces *Caulacau*, a name not peculiar to the Basilidians, is unfortunately corrupt). And as the Son was unknown to all, so also, the tradition ran, must members of their community be known to none; but while they know all and pass through the midst of all, remain invisible and unknown to all, observing the maxim, "Do thou know all, but let no one know thee." Accordingly they must be ready to utter denials and unwilling to suffer for the Name, since [to outward appearance] they resembled all. It naturally followed that their mysteries were to be carefully guarded, and disclosed to "only one out of 1000 and two out of 10,000." When Philaster (doubtless after Hippolytus) tells us in his first sentence about Basilides that he was "called by many a heresiarch, because he violated the laws of Christian truth by making an outward show and discourse (*proponendo et loquendo*) concerning the Law and the Prophets and the Apostles, but believing otherwise," the reference is probably to this contrast between the outward conformity of the sect and their secret doctrines and practices. The Basilidians considered themselves to be no longer Jews, but to have become more than Christians (such seems to be the sense of the obscure phrase Χριστιανοὺς δὲ μηκέτι γεγενῆσθαι, for the *nondum* of the translator of Irenaeus can hardly be right). Repudiation of martyrdom was naturally accompanied by indiscriminate use of things offered to idols. Nay, the principle of indifference is said to have been carried so far as to sanction promiscuous immorality. In this and other respects our accounts may possibly contain exaggerations; but Clement's already cited complaint of the flagrant degeneracy in his time from the high standard set up by Basilides himself is unsuspicious evidence, and a libertine code of ethics would find an easy justification in such maxims as are imputed to the Basilidians. It is hardly necessary to add that they expected the salvation of the soul alone, insisting on the natural corruptibility of the body. They indulged in magic and invocations, "and all other curious arts." A wrong reading taken from the inferior MSS. of Irenaeus has added the further statement that they used "images"; and this single spurious word is often cited in corroboration of the popular belief that the numerous ancient gems on which grotesque mythological combinations are accompanied by the mystic name ΑΒΡΑΣΑΞ were of Basilidian origin. It is shewn in *D. C. B.* (4-vol. ed.), art. ABRASAX, where Lardner (*Hist. of Heretics*, ii. 14-28) should have been named with Beausobre, that there is no tangible evidence for attributing any known gems to Basilidianism or any other form of Gnosticism, and that in all probability the Basilidians and the heathen engravers of gems alike borrowed the name from some Semitic mythology.

Imperfect and distorted as the picture may be, such was doubtless in substance the creed of Basilidians not half a century after Basilides had written. Were the name absent from the records of his system and theirs, no one would have suspected any relationship between them, much less imagined that they belonged respectively to master and to disciples. Outward mechanism and inward principles are alike full of contrasts; no attempts of critics to trace correspondences between the mythological personages, and to explain them by supposed condensations or mutilations, have attained even plausibility. Two misunderstandings have been specially misleading. Abrasax, the chief or Archon of the first set of angels, has been confounded with "the Unbegotten Father," and the God of the Jews, the Archon of the lowest heaven, has been assumed to be the only Archon recognized by the later Basilidians, though Epiphanius (69 B.C.) distinctly implies that each of the 365 heavens had its Archon. The mere name "Archon" is common to most forms of Gnosticism. So again, because Clement tells us that Righteousness and her daughter Peace abide in substantive being within the Ogdoad, "the Unbegotten Father" and the five grades or forms of creative mind which intervene between Him and the creator-angels are added in to make up an Ogdoad, though none is recorded as acknowledged by the disciples: a combination so arbitrary and so incongruous needs no refutation. On the other hand, those five abstract names have an air of true Basilidian Hellenism, and the two systems possess at least one negative feature in common, the absence of syzygies and of all imagery connected directly with sex. On their ethical side the connexion is discerned with less difficulty. The contempt for martyrdom, which was perhaps the most notorious characteristic of the Basilidians, would find a ready excuse in their master's speculative paradox about martyrs, even if he did not discourage martyrdom himself. The silence of five years which he imposed on novices might easily degenerate into the perilous dissimulation of a secret sect, while their exclusiveness would be nourished by his doctrine of the Election; and the same doctrine might further after a while receive an antinomian interpretation. The nature of the contrast of principle in the theological part of the two creeds suggests how so great a change may have arisen. The system of Basilides was a high-pitched philosophical speculation, entirely unfitted to exercise popular influence, and transporting its adherents to a region remote from the sympathies of men imbued with the old Gnostic phantasies, while it was too artificial a compound to attract heathens or Catholic Christians. The power of mind and character which the remains of his writings disclose might easily gather round him in the first instance a crowd who, though they could enter into portions only of his teaching, might remain detached from other Gnostics, and yet in their theology relapse into "the broad highway of vulgar Gnosticism" (Baur in the Tübingen *Theol. Jahrb.* for 1856, pp. 158 f.), and make for themselves out of its elements, whether fortuitously or by the skill of some now forgotten leader, a new mythological combination. In this manner evolution from below might once more give place to emanation from above, Docetism might again sever heaven and earth, and a loose practical dualism (of the profounder speculative dualism of the East there is no trace) might supersede all that Basilides had taught as to the painful processes by which sonship attains its perfection. The composite character of the secondary Basilidianism may be seen at a glance in the combination of the five Greek abstractions preparatory to creation with the Semitic hosts of creative angels bearing barbaric names. Basilidianism seems to have stood alone in appropriating Abrasax; but Caulacau plays a part in more than one system, and the functions of the angels recur in various forms of Gnosticism, and especially in that derived from Saturnilus. Saturnilus likewise affords a parallel in the character assigned to the God of the Jew as an angel, and partly in the reason assigned for the Saviour's mission; while the Antitactae of Clement recall the resistance to the God of the Jews inculcated by the Basilidians. Other "Basilidian" features appear in the *Pistis Sophia*, viz. many barbaric names of angels (with 365 Archons, p. 364), and elaborate collocations of heavens, and a numerical image taken from Deut. xxxii. 30 (p. 354). The Basilidian Simon of Cyrene is apparently unique.

VIII. *History of the Basilidian Sect.*—There is no evidence that the sect extended itself beyond Egypt; but there it survived for a long time. Epiphanius (about 375) mentions the Prosopite, Athribite, Saite, and "Alexandriopolite" (read Andropolite) nomes or cantons, and also Alexandria itself, as the places in which it still throve in his time, and which he accordingly inferred to have been visited by Basilides (68 c). All these places lie on the western side of the Delta, between Memphis and the sea. Nearer the end of cent. iv. Jerome often refers to Basilides in connexion with the hybrid Priscillianism of Spain, and the mystic names in which its votaries delighted. According to Sulpicius Severus (*Chron.* ii. 46) this heresy took its rise in "the East and Egypt"; but, he adds, it is not easy to say "what the beginnings were out of which it there grew" (*quibus ibi initiis coaluerit*). He states, however, that it was first brought to Spain by Marcus, a native of Memphis. This fact explains how the name of Basilides and some dregs of his disciples' doctrines or practices found their way to so distant a land as Spain, and at the same time illustrates the probable hybrid origin of the secondary Basilidianism itself.

IX. *Literature.*—Basilides of course occupies a prominent place in every treatise on Gnosticism, such as those of Neander (including the *Church History*), Baur (the same), Lipsius, and Möller (*Geschichte der Kosmologie in der Christlichen Kirche*). Two reviews by Gieseler (*Halle A. L. Z.* for 1823, pp. 335-338; *Studien u. Kritiken* for 1830, pp. 395ff.) contain valuable matter. The best monograph founded on the whole evidence is that of Uhlhorn (*Das Basilidianische System*, Göttingen, 1855), with which should be read an essay by Baur (*Theol. Jahrb.* for 1856, pp. 121-162); Jacobi's monograph (*Basilidis Philosophi Gnostici Sententius*, etc., Berlin 1852) being also good. Able expositions of the view that the true doctrine of Basilides is not represented in the larger work of Hippolytus *Against all Heresies* will be found in a paper by Hilgenfeld, to which Baur's article in reply is appended (pp. 86-121), with scattered notices in other articles of his (especially in his *Zeitschrift* for 1862, pp. 452 ff.); and in Lipsius's *Gnosticismus.* Three articles by Gundert (*Zeitschrift f. d. Luth. Theol.* for 1855, 209 ff., and 1856, 37 ff., 443 ff.) are of less importance. The lecture on Basilides in Dr. Mansel's posthumous book on *The Gnostic Heresies* is able and independent and makes full use of the best German criticisms, but underrates the influence of Stoical conceptions on Basilides, and exaggerates that of Platonism; and after the example of Baur's *Christliche Gnosis* in respect of Gnosticism generally, though starting from an opposite point of view, it suffers from an effort to find in Basilides a precursor of Hegel. Cf. Harnack, *Gesch. Alt. Chr. Lit.* 1893, pp. 157-161; Th. Zahn, *Gesch. des N. T. Kanon* (1888-1889), i. 763-774; J. Kennedy, "Buddhist Gnosticism: the System of Basilides" (Lond. 1902, *Journal of the Royal Asiatic Society*). [H.]

Basiliscus, martyr, bp. of Comana, martyred with Lucianus at Nicomedia under Maximin, A.D. 312 (Pallad. *Dial. de V. St. Chrys.* xi., misreading, however, Maximian for Maximin). St. Chrysostom, when exiled, was received upon his journey in a "martyrium," built some five or six miles out of Comana in memory of Basiliscus, and there died and was buried (Theod. *H. E.* v. 30; Soz. viii. 28; Pallad. as above; Niceph. xiii. 37). Basiliscus is said to have been shod with iron shoes, red hot, and then beheaded and thrown into the river (*Menol.* in Baron. May 22). [A.W.H.]

Basilius of Ancyra (Βασίλειος, also called **Basilas**, Socr. ii. 42), a native of Ancyra, originally a physician (Hieron. *de Vir. Ill.* 89; Suidas, *s.v.*), and subsequently bp. of that city, A.D. 336-360, one of the most respectable prelates of the semi-Arian party, whose essential orthodoxy was acknowledged by Athanasius himself, the differences between them being regarded as those of language only (Athan. *de Synod.* tom. i. pp. 915, 619, ed. Morell, Paris, 1627). He was a man of learning, of intellectual power, and dialectical skill, and maintained an unwavering consistency which drew upon him the hostility of the shifty Acacians and their time-serving leader. The jealousy of Acacius was also excited by the unbounded influence Basil at one time exercised over the weak mind of Constantius, and his untiring animosity worked Basil's overthrow. On the deposition of Marcellus, the aged bp. of Ancyra, by the Eusebian party, on the charge of Sabellianism, at a synod meeting at Constantinople, A.D. 336, Basil was chosen bishop in his room. He enjoyed the see undisturbed for eleven years; but in 347, the council of Sardica, after the withdrawal of the Eusebians to Philippopolis, reinstated Marcellus, and excommunicated Basil as "a wolf who had invaded the fold" (Socr. ii. 20). Three years later, A.D. 350, the Eusebians were again in the ascendant, through the powerful patronage of Constantius, and Basil was replaced in his see by the express order of the emperor (Socr. ii. 26). Basil speedily obtained a strong hold over Constantius, who consulted him on all ecclesiastical matters, and did nothing without his cognizance. He and George of Laodicea were now the recognized leaders of the semi-Arian party (Epiph. *Haer.* lxxiii. 1). The next year, A.D. 351, Basil took the chief part in the proceedings of the council that met at Sirmium, where Constantius was residing, to depose Photinus the pupil of Marcellus, who was developing his master's views into direct Sabellianism (*ib.* lxxi. lxxiii.; Socr. ii. 30). Shortly after this we find him attacking with equal vigour a heresy of an exactly opposite character, disputing with Aetius, the Anomoean, in conjunction with Eustathius of Sebaste, another leader of the semi-Arian party. The issue of the controversy is variously reported, according to the proclivities of the historians. Philostorgius (*H. E.* iii. 16) asserts that Basil and Eustathius were worsted by their antagonist; orthodox writers assign them the victory (Greg. Nys. *in Eunom.* lib. i. pp. 289, 296). Basil's representations of the abominable character of Aetius's doctrines so exasperated Gallus against him that he issued an order for his execution; but on having personal intercourse with him pronounced him maligned, and took him as his theological tutor. [AETIUS.] Basil's influence increased, and just before Easter, A.D. 358, when a number of bishops had assembled at Ancyra for the dedication of a new church that Basil had built, Basil received letters from George of Laodicea speaking with great alarm of the spread of Anomoean doctrines, and entreating him to avail himself of the opportunity to obtain a synodical condemnation of Aetius and Eunomius. Other bishops were accordingly summoned, and eighteen anathemas were drawn up. Basil himself, with Eustathius and Eleusius, were deputed to communicate these anathemas to Constantius at Sirmium. The deputies were received with much consideration by the emperor, who ratified their synodical decrees and gave his authority for their publication. Basil availed himself of his influence over Constantius to induce him to summon a general council for the final settlement of the questions that had been so long distracting the church. It was ultimately decided to divide the council into two, and Ariminum was selected for the West, and Seleucia in Isauria for the East. The Eastern council met, Sept. 27, 359. Basil did not arrive till the third day. He was soon made aware that his influence with the emperor had been undermined by his Acacian rivals, and that his power was gone. When he reproved Constantius for unduly favouring them, the emperor bid him hold his peace, and charged him with being himself the cause of the dissensions that were agitating the church (Theod. ii. 27). At another synod convened at Constantinople under the immediate superintendence of Constantius, Acacius found himself master of the situation and deposed whom he would. Basil was one of the first to fall. No doctrinal errors were charged against him. He was condemned on frivolous and unproved grounds, together with Cyril of Jerusalem, Eustathius of Sebaste, and other leading prelates. Banishment followed deposition. Basil was exiled to Illyria (Soz. iv. 24; Philost. v. 1). On the accession of Jovian, A.D. 363, he joined the other deposed bishops in petitioning that emperor to expel the Anomoeans and restore the rightful bishops; but Basil seems to have died in exile (Socr. iii. 25).

Athanasius speaks of his having written περὶ πίστεως (Athan. *de Synod. u.s.*). Ittigius (*de Haer.* p. 453) defends him from the charge of Arianism. Jerome identifies him, but unjustly, with the Macedonian party (Tillemont, vol. vi. *passim*). [E.V.]

Basilius of Ancyra, a presbyter who became a martyr under Julian A.D. 362. During the reign of Constantius he had been an uncompromising opponent of Arianism. He was more than once apprehended by the provincial governors, but recovered his liberty. The Arian council under Eudoxius at Constantinople in 360 forbade him to hold any ecclesiastical assembly. The zeal of Basil was still further quickened by the attempts of Julian to suppress Christianity. Sozomen tells us that he visited the whole of the adjacent district, entreating the Christians everywhere to be constant to the faith and not to pollute themselves with sacrifices to idols (Soz. *H. E.* v. 11). He was apprehended and put to the torture. On the arrival of Julian at Ancyra, Basil was presented to him, and after having reproached the emperor with his apostasy was further tortured. Basil's constancy remained unshaken, and after a second interview with Julian, in which he treated the emperor with the greatest contumely, he suffered death by red-hot irons on June 29 (Soz. *H. E.* v. 11; Ruinart, *Act. Sinc. Martyr.* pp. 559 seq.; Tillemont, vii. 375 seq.). [E.V.]

Basilius, bp. of Caesarea in Cappadocia, commonly called **Basil the Great,** the strenuous champion of orthodoxy in the East, the restorer of union to the divided Oriental church, and the promoter of unity between the East and the West, was born at Caesarea (originally called Mazaca), the capital of Cappadocia, towards the end of 329. His parents were members of noble and wealthy families, and Christians by descent. His grandparents on both sides had suffered during the Maximinian persecution, his maternal grandfather losing both property and life. Macrina, his paternal grandmother, and her husband, were compelled to leave their home in Pontus, of which country they were natives, and to take refuge among the woods and mountains of that province, where they are reported to have passed seven years (Greg. Naz. *Or.* xx. p. 319). [MACRINA.] His father, whose name was also Basil, was an advocate and teacher of rhetoric whose learning and eloquence had brought him a very large practice. Gregory Nazianzen speaks of this elder Basil in terms of the highest commendation as one who was regarded by the whole of Pontus as "the common instructor of virtue" (*Or.* xx. p. 324). The elder Basil and Emmelia had ten children, five of each sex, of whom a daughter, Macrina, was the eldest. Basil the Great was the eldest son; two others, Gregory Nyssen and Peter, attained the episcopate. Naucratius the second son died a layman. Four of the daughters were well and honourably married. Macrina, the eldest, embraced a life of devotion, and exercised a very powerful influence over Basil and the other members of the family. [MACRINA, (2).] Basil was indebted for the care of his earliest years to his grandmother Macrina, who brought him up at her country house, not far from Neocaesarea in the province of Pontus (Bas. *Ep.* 210, § 1). The date of Basil's baptism is uncertain, but, according to the prevalent custom, it was almost certainly deferred until he reached man's estate. For the completion of his education, Basil was sent by his father first to his native city of Caesarea (Greg. Naz. *Or.* xx. p. 325). From Caesarea he passed to Constantinople (Bas. *Epp.* 335-359; Liban. *Vita*, p. 15), and thence to Athens, where he studied during the years 351-355, chiefly under the Sophists Himerius and Prohaeresius. His acquaintance with his fellow-student and inseparable companion Gregory Nazianzen, previously begun at Caesarea, speedily ripened at Athens into an ardent friendship, which subsisted with hardly any interruption through the greater part of their lives. Athens also afforded Basil the opportunity of familiar intercourse with a fellow-student whose name was destined to become unhappily famous, the nephew of the emperor Constantius, Julian. The future emperor conceived a warm attachment for the young Cappadocian, with whom—as the latter reminds him when the relations between them had so sadly changed—he not only studied the best models of literature, but also carefully read the sacred Scriptures (*Epp.* 40, 41; Greg. Naz. *Orat.* iv. *adv. Julian*, pp. 121 seq.). Basil remained at Athens till the middle or end of 355, when with extreme reluctance he left for his native city. By this time his father was dead. His mother, Emmelia, was residing at the village of Annesi, near Neocaesarea. Basil's Athenian reputation had preceded him, and he was received with much honour by the people of Caesarea, where he consented to settle as a teacher of rhetoric (Greg. Naz. *Or.* xx. p. 334). He practised the profession of a rhetorician with great celebrity for a considerable period (Rufin. ii. 9), but the warnings and counsels of Macrina guarded him from the seductions of the world, and eventually induced him to abandon it altogether and devote himself to a religious life (Greg. Nys. *u.s.*). Basil, in a letter to Eustathius of Sebaste, describes himself at this period as one awaked out of a deep sleep, and in the marvellous light of Gospel truth discerning the folly of that wisdom of this world in the study of which nearly all his youth had vanished. His first care was to reform his life. Finding, by reading the Gospels, that nothing tended so much toward perfection as to sell all that he had and free himself from worldly cares, and feeling himself too weak to stand alone in such an enterprise, he desired earnestly to find some brother who might give him his aid (*Ep.* 223). No sooner did his determination become known that he was beset by the remonstrances of his friends entreating him, some to continue the profession of rhetoric, some to become an advocate. But his choice was made, and his resolution was inflexible. Basil's baptism may be placed at this epoch. He was probably baptized by Dianius, bp. of Caesarea, by whom not long afterwards he was admitted to the order of reader (*de Spir. Sancto*, c. xxix. 71). Basil's determination in favour of a life of devotion would be strengthened by the death of his next brother, Naucratius, who had embraced the life of a solitary, and about this period was drowned while engaged in works of mercy (Greg. Nys. *de Vit. S. Macr.* p. 182). About A.D. 357, when still under thirty, Basil left Caesarea to seek the most celebrated ascetics upon whose life he might model his own; visiting Alexandria and Upper Egypt, Palestine, Coelesyria, and Mesopotamia. He records his admiration of the abstinence and endurance of the ascetics whom he met, their mastery over hunger and sleep, their indifference to cold and nakedness, as well as his desire to imitate them (*Ep.* 223, § 2). The year 358 saw Basil again at Caesarea resolved on the immediate carrying out of his purpose of retiring from the world, finally selecting for his retreat a spot near Neocaesarea, close to the village of Annesi, where his father's estates lay, and where he had passed his childhood under the care of his grandmother Macrina. To Annesi his mother Emmelia and his sister Macrina had retired after the death of the elder Basil, and were living a semi-monastic life. Basil's future home was only divided from Annesi by the river Iris, by which and the gorges of the mountain torrents a tract of level ground was completely insulated. A wooded mountain rose behind. There was only one approach to it, and of that he was master. The natural beauties of the spot, with its ravines, precipices, dashing torrents, and waterfalls, the purity of the air and the coolness of the breezes, the abundance of flowers and multitude of singing birds ravished him, and he declared it to be more beautiful than Calypso's island (*Ep.* 14). His glowing description attracted Gregory for a lengthy visit to study the Scriptures with him (*Ep.* 9), together with the commentaries of Origen and other early expositors. At this time they also compiled their collection of the "Beauties of Origen," or "Philocalia" (Socr. iv. 26; Soz. vi. 17; Greg. Naz. *Ep.* 87). In this secluded spot Basil passed five years, an epoch of no small importance in the history of the church, inasmuch as it saw the origin under Basil's influence of the monastic system in the coenobitic form. Eustathius of Sebaste had already introduced monachism into Asia Minor, but monastic communities were a novelty in the Christian world, and of these Basil is justly considered the founder. His rule, like that of St. Benedict in later times, united active industry with regular devotional exercises, and by the labour of his monks over wide desert tracts, hopeless sterility gave place to golden harvests and abundant vintages. Not the day only but the night also was divided into definite portions, the intervals being filled with prayers, hymns, and alternate psalmody. The day began and closed with a psalm of confession. The food of his monks was limited to one meal a day of bread, water, and herbs, and he allowed sleep only till midnight, when all rose for prayer (*Ep.* 2, 207). On his retirement to Pontus, Basil devoted all his worldly possessions to the service of the poor, retaining them, however, in his own hands, and by degrees divesting himself of them as occasion required. His life was one of the most rigid asceticism. He had but one outer and one inner garment; he slept in a hair shirt, his bed was the ground; he took little sleep, no bath; the sun was his fire, his food bread and water, his drink the running stream (Greg. Naz. *Or.* xx. p. 358; Greg. Nys. *de Basil.* p. 490). The severe bodily austerities he practised emaciated his frame and ruined his already feeble health, sowing the seeds of the maladies to which in later years he was a martyr. His friend describes him as "without a wife, without property, without flesh, and almost without blood" (Greg. Naz. *Or.* xix. p. 311). Basil's reputation for sanctity collected large numbers about him. He repeatedly made missionary journeys through Pontus; his preaching resulting in the founding of many coenobitic industrial communities and monasteries for both sexes, and in the restoration of the purity of the orthodox faith (Rufin. ix. 9; Soz. vi. 17; Greg. Nys. *de Basil.* p. 488). Throughout Pontus and Cappadocia Basil was the means of the erection of numerous hospitals for the poor, houses of refuge for virgins, orphanages, and other homes of beneficence. His monasteries had as their inmates children he had taken charge of, married persons who had mutually agreed to live asunder, slaves with the consent of their masters, and solitaries convinced of the danger of living alone (Basil, *Regulae*, 10, 12, 15).

After two years thus spent Basil was summoned from his solitude in 359 to accompany Basil of Ancyra and Eustathius of Sebaste, who had been delegated by the council of Seleucia to communicate the conclusions of that assembly to Constantius at Constantinople. Basil seems from his youth and natural timidity to have avoided taking any part in the discussions of the council that followed, 360, in which the Anomoeans were condemned, the more orthodox semi-Arians deposed, and the Acacians triumphed. But when Constantius endeavoured to force those present to sign the creed of Ariminum, Basil left the city and returned to Cappadocia (Greg. Nys. *in Eunom.* pp. 310, 312; Philost. iv. 12). Not long after his return George of Laodicea arrived at Caesarea as an emissary of Constantius, bringing with him that creed for signature. To Basil's intense grief, bp. Dianius, a gentle, undecided man, who valued peace above orthodoxy, was persuaded to sign. Basil felt it impossible any longer to hold communion with his bishop, and fled to Nazianzus to find consolation in the society of his dear friend Gregory (*Ep.* 8, 51). He denied with indignation the report that he had anathematized his bishop, and when two years afterwards (362) DIANIUS was stricken for death and entreated Basil to return and comfort his last hours, he at once went to him, and the aged bishop died in his arms.

The choice of Dianius's successor gave rise to violent dissensions at Caesarea. At last the populace, wearied with the indecision, chose Eusebius, a man of high position and eminent piety, but as yet unbaptized. They forcibly conveyed him to the church where the provincial bishops were assembled, and compelled the unwilling prelates first to baptize and then to consecrate him. Eusebius was bp. at Caesarea for 8 years (Greg. Naz. *Or.* xix. 308, 309).

Shortly before the death of Dianius, Julian had ascended the throne (Dec. 11, 361), and desired to surround himself with the associates of his early days (Greg. Naz. *Or.* iv. 120). Among the first whom he invited was his fellow-student at Athens, Basil. Basil at first held out hopes of accepting his old friend's invitation; but he delayed his journey, and Julian's declared apostasy soon gave him sufficient cause to relinquish it altogether. The next year Julian displayed his irritation. Receiving intelligence that the people of Caesarea, so far from apostatizing with him and building new pagan temples, had pulled down the only one still standing (Greg. Naz. *Or.* iii. 91, xix. 309; Socr. v. 4), he expunged Caesarea from the catalogue of cities, made it take its old name of Mazaca, imposed heavy payments, compelled the clergy to serve in the police force, and put to death two young men of high rank who had taken part in the demolition of the temple. Approaching Caesarea, he dispatched a minatory letter to Basil demanding a thousand pounds of gold for the expenses of his Persian expedition, or threatening to rase the city to the ground. Basil, in his dauntless reply, upbraids the emperor for apostasy against God and the church, the nurse and mother of all, and for his folly in demanding so vast a sum from him, the poorest of the poor. The death of Julian (June 26, 363) delivered Basil from this imminent peril.

One of the first acts of bp. Eusebius was to compel the reluctant Basil to be ordained priest, that the bishop might avail himself of Basil's theological knowledge and intellectual powers to compensate for his own deficiencies. At first he employed him very largely. But when he found himself completely eclipsed he became jealous of Basil's popularity and treated him with a marked coldness, amounting almost to insolence, which awoke the hostility of the Christians of Caesarea, whose idol Basil was. A schism was imminent, but Basil, refusing to strengthen the heretical party by creating divisions among the orthodox, retired with his friend Gregory to Pontus, where he devoted himself to the care of the monasteries he had founded (Greg. Naz. *Or.* xx. pp. 336, 337; Soz. vi. 15).

Basil had passed about three years in his Pontic seclusion when, in 365, the blind zeal of the emperor Valens for the spread of Arianism brought him back to Caesarea. As soon as it was known that Valens was approaching that city, the popular voice demanded the recall of Basil as the only bulwark against the attack on the true faith and its adherents meditated by the emperor. Gregory acted the part of a wise mediator, and Basil's return to the bishop was effected (Greg. Naz. *Ep.* 19, 20, 169; *Or.* xx. p. 339). Treating Eusebius with the honour due to his position and his age, Basil now proved himself, in the words of Gregory, the staff of his age, the support of his faith; at home the most faithful of his friends; abroad the most efficient of his ministers (*ib.* 340).

The first designs of Valens against Caesarea were interrupted by the news of the revolt of Procopius (Amm. Marc. 26, 27). He left Asia to quell the insurrection which threatened his throne. Basil availed himself of the breathing-time thus granted in organizing the resistance of the orthodox against the Eunomians or Anomoeans, who were actively propagating their pernicious doctrines through Asia Minor; and in uniting the Cappadocians in loyal devotion to the truth. The year 368 afforded Basil occasion of displaying his large and universal charity. The whole of Cappadocia was desolated by drought and famine, the visitation pressing specially on Caesarea. Basil devoted his whole energies to helping the poor sufferers. He sold the property he had inherited at the recent death of his mother, and raised a large subscription in the city. He gave his own personal ministrations to the wretched, and while he fed their bodies he was careful to nourish their souls with the bread of life (Greg. Naz. *Or.* xx. 340-342; Greg. Nys. *in Eunom.* i. 306).

Eusebius died towards the middle of 370 in Basil's arms (Greg. Naz. *Or.* xix. 310, xx. 342). Basil persuaded himself, not altogether unwarrantably, that the cause of orthodoxy in Asia Minor was involved in his succeeding Eusebius. Disappointed of the assistance anticipated from the younger Gregory, Basil betook himself to his father, the aged bp. of Nazianzus of the same name. The momentous importance of the juncture was more evident to the elder man. Orthodoxy was at stake in Basil's election. "The Holy Spirit must triumph" (Greg. Naz. *Or.* xx. 342). Using his son as his scribe, he dictated a letter to the clergy, monks, magistrates, and people of Caesarea, calling on them to choose Basil; another to the electing prelates, exhorting them not to allow Basil's weakness of health to counterbalance his marked pre-eminence in spiritual gifts and in learning (Greg. Naz. *Ep.* 22, 23). No orthodox prelate had at that time a deservedly greater influence than Eusebius of Samosata. Gregory wrote to him and persuaded him to visit Caesarea and undertake the direction of this difficult business (Bas. *Ep.* 47). On his arrival, Eusebius found the city divided into two opposite factions. All the best of the people, together with the clergy and the monks, warmly advocated Basil's election, which was vigorously opposed by other classes. The influence and tact of Eusebius overcame all obstacles. The people warmly espoused Basil's cause; the bishops were compelled to give way, and the triumph of the orthodox cause was consummated by the arrival of the venerable Gregory, who, on learning that one vote was wanting for the canonical election of Basil, while his son was still hesitating full of scruples and refused to quit Nazianzus, left his bed for a litter, had himself carried to Caesarea at the risk of expiring on the way, and with his own hands consecrated the newly elected prelate, and placed him on his episcopal throne (Greg. Naz. *Ep.* 29, p. 793, *Or.* xix. 311, xx. 343). Basil's election filled the orthodox everywhere with joy. Athanasius, the veteran champion of the faith, congratulated Cappadocia on possessing a bishop whom every province might envy (Ath. *ad. Pallad.* p. 953, *ad Joann. et Ant.* p. 951). At Constantinople it was received with far different feelings. Valens regarded it as a serious check to his designs for the triumph of Arianism. Basil was not an opponent to be despised. He must be bent to the emperor's will or got rid of. As bp. of Caesarea his power extended far beyond the limits of the city itself. He was metropolitan of Cappadocia, and exarch of Pontus. In the latter capacity his authority, more or less defied, extended over more than half Asia Minor, and embraced as many as eleven provinces. Ancyra, Neocaesarea, Tyana, with other metropolitan sees, acknowledged him as their ecclesiastical superior.

Basil's first disappointment in his episcopate arose from his inability to induce his dear friend Gregory to join him as his coadjutor in the government of his province and exarchate. He consented at last for a while, but soon withdrew. Difficulties soon thickened round the new exarch. The bishops who had opposed his election and refused to take part in his consecration, now exchanged their open hostility for secret opposition. While professing outward union, they withheld their support in everything. They treated Basil with marked slight and shewed a complete want of sympathy in all his plans (*Ep.* 98). He complains of this to Eusebius of Samosata (*Epp.* 48, 141, 282). This disloyal behaviour caused him despondency and repeated attacks of illness. He overcame all his opponents in a few years by firmness and kindness, but their action had greatly increased the difficulties of the commencement of his episcopate.

Basil had been bishop little more than twelve months when he was brought into open collision with the emperor Valens, who was traversing Asia Minor with the fixed resolve of exterminating the orthodox faith and establishing Arianism. No part of Basil's history is better known, and in none do we more clearly discern the strength and weakness of his character. "The memorable interview with St. Basil," writes Dean Milman, "as it is related by the Catholic party, displays, if the weakness, certainly the patience and toleration of the sovereign—if the uncompromising firmness of the prelate, some of that leaven of pride with which he is taunted by St. Jerome" (*Hist. of Christianity*, iii. 45). Valens had never relinquished the designs which had been interrupted by the revolt of Procopius, and he was now approaching Caesarea determined to reduce to submission the chief champion of orthodoxy in the East. His progress hitherto had been one of uniform victory. The Catholics had everywhere fallen before him. Bithynia had resisted and had become the scene of horrible tragedies. The fickle Galatia had yielded without a struggle. The fate of Cappadocia depended on Basil. His house, as the emperor drew near, was besieged by ladies of rank, high personages of state, even by bishops, who entreated him to bow before the storm and appease the emperor by a temporary submission. Their expostulations were rejected with indignant disdain. A band of Arian bishops headed by Euippius, an aged bishop of Galatia and an old friend of Basil's, preceded Valens's arrival with the hope of overawing their opponents by their numbers and unanimity. Basil took the initiative, and with prompt decision separated himself from their communion (Bas. *Epp.* 68, 128, 244, 251). Members of the emperor's household indulged in the most violent menaces against the archbishop. One of the most insolent of these was the eunuch Demosthenes, the superintendent of the kitchen. Basil met his threats with quiet irony, and was next confronted by Modestus, the prefect of the Praetorium, commissioned by the emperor to offer Basil the choice between deposition or communion with the Arians. This violent and unscrupulous imperial favourite accosted Basil with the grossest insolence. He refused him the title of bishop; he threatened confiscation, exile, tortures, death. But such menaces, Basil replied, were powerless on one whose sole wealth was a ragged cloak and a few books, to whom the whole earth was a home, or rather a place of pilgrimage, whose feeble body could endure no tortures beyond the first stroke, and to whom death would be a mercy, as it would the sooner transport him to the God to Whom he lived. Modestus expressed his astonishment at hearing such unusual language (Greg. Naz. *Or.* xx. 351; Soz. vi. 16). "That is," replied Basil, "because you have never before fallen in with a true bishop." Modestus, finding his menaces useless, changed his tone. He counselled prudence. Basil should avoid irritating the emperor, and submit to his requirements, as all the other prelates of Asia had done. If he would only yield he promised him the friendship of Valens, and whatever favours he might desire for his friends. Why should he sacrifice all his power for the sake of a few doctrines? (Theod. iv. 19). But flattery had as little power as threats over Basil's iron will. The prefect was at his wit's end. Valens was expected on the morrow. Modestus was unwilling to meet the emperor with a report of failure. The aspect of a court of justice with its official state and band of ministers prepared to execute its sentence might inspire awe. But judicial terrors were equally futile (Greg. Nys. *in Eunom.* p. 315). Modestus, utterly foiled, had to announce to his master that all his attempts to obtain submission had been fruitless. "Violence would be the only course to adopt with one over whom threats and blandishments were equally powerless" (Greg. Naz. *Or.* xx. p. 350). Such Christian intrepidity was not without effect on the feeble, impressionable mind of Valens. He refused to sanction any harsh measures against the archbishop, and moderated his demands to the admission of Arians to Basil's communion. But here too Basil was equally inflexible. To bring matters to a decided issue, the emperor presented himself in the chief church of Caesarea on the Epiphany, A.D. 372, after the service had commenced. He found the church flooded with "a sea" of worshippers whose chanted psalms pealed forth like thunder, uninterrupted by the entrance of the emperor and his train. Basil was at the altar celebrating the Eucharistic sacrifice, standing, according to the primitive custom, behind the altar with his face to the assembled people, supported on either hand by the semicircle of his attendant clergy. "The unearthly majesty of the scene," the rapt devotion of the archbishop, erect like a column before the holy table, the reverent order of the immense throng, "more like that of angels than of men," overpowered the weak and excitable Valens, and he almost fainted away. When the time came for making his offering, and the ministers were hesitating whether they should receive an oblation from the hand of a heretic, his limbs failed him, and but for the aid of one of the clergy he would have fallen. Basil, it would seem, pitying his enemy's weakness, accepted the gift from his trembling hand (*ib.* p. 351). The next day Valens again visited the church, and listened with reverence to Basil's preaching, and made his offerings, which were not now rejected. The sermon over, Basil admitted the emperor within the sacred veil, and discoursed on the orthodox faith. He was rudely interrupted by the cook Demosthenes, who was guilty of a gross solecism. Basil smiled and said, "We have, it seems, a Demosthenes who cannot speak

Greek; he had better attend to his sauces than meddle with theology." The retort amused the emperor, who retired so well pleased with his theological opponent that he made him a grant of lands for the poor-house Basil was erecting (Theod. iv. 19; Greg. Naz. *Or.* xx. 351; Bas. *Ep.* 94). The vacillating mind of Valens was always influenced by the latest and most imperious advisers, and when Basil remained firm in his refusal to admit them to his communion, the Arians about the emperor had little difficulty in persuading him that he was compromising the faith by permitting Basil to remain, and that his banishment was necessary for the peace of the East. The emperor, yielding to their importunity, ordered Basil to leave the city. Basil at once made his simple preparations for departure, ordering one of his attendants to take his tablets and follow him. He was to start at night to avoid the risk of popular disturbance. The chariot was at his door, and his friends, Gregory among them, were bewailing so great a calamity, when his journey was arrested by the sudden and alarming illness of Galates, the only son of Valen and Dominica. The empress attributed her child's danger to the Divine displeasure at the treatment of Basil. The emperor, in abject alarm, sent the chief military officials of the court, Terentius and Arinthaeus, who were known to be his friends, to entreat Basil to come and pray over the sick child. Galates was as yet unbaptized. On receiving a promise that the child should receive that sacrament at the hands of a Catholic bishop and be instructed in the orthodox faith, Basil consented. He prayed over the boy, and the malady was alleviated. On his retiring, the Arians again got round the feeble prince, reminded him of a promise he had made to Eudoxius, by whom he himself had been baptized, and the child received baptism from the hands of an Arian prelate. He grew immediately worse, and died the same night (Greg. Naz. *Or.* xx. 352, 364; Theod. iv. 19; Socr. iv. 26; Soz. iv. 16; Eph. Syr. *apud* Coteler. *Monum. Eccl. Graec.* iii. 63; Rufin. xi. 9). Once more Valens yielded to pressure from the unwearied enemies of Basil. Again Basil's exile was determined on, but the pens with which Valens was preparing to sign the decree refused to write, and split in his agitated hand, and the supposed miracle arrested the execution of the sentence. Valens left Caesarea, and Basil remained master of the situation (Theod. iv. 19; Ephr. Syr. *u.s.* p. 65). Before long his old enemy Modestus, attacked by a severe malady, presented himself as a suppliant to Basil, and attributing his cure to the intercessions of the saint, became his fast friend. So great was Basil's influence with the prefect that persons came from a distance to secure his intercession with him. We have as many as six letters from Basil to Modestus in favour of different individuals (Bas. *Epp.* 104, 110, 111, 279, 280, 281; Greg. Naz. *Or.* xx. pp. 352, 353).

The issue of these unsuccessful assaults was to place Basil in a position of inviolability, and to leave him leisure for administering his diocese and exarchate, which much needed his firm and unflinching hand. His visitation disclosed many irregularities which he sternly repressed. The chorepiscopi had admitted men to the lower orders who had no intention of proceeding to the priesthood, or even to the diaconate, but merely to gain immunity from military service (*Ep.* 54). Many of his suffragans were guilty of simony in receiving a fee for ordination (*Ep.* 55). Men were raised to the episcopate from motives of personal interest and to gratify private friends (*Ep.* 290). The perilous custom of unmarried priests having females (συνείσακται, *subintroductae*) residing with them as "spiritual sisters" called for reproof (*Ep.* 55). A fanatic deacon, Glycerius, who had collected a band of professed virgins, whom he forcibly carried off by night and who wandered about the country dancing and singing to the scandal of the faithful, caused him much trouble (*Epp.* 169, 170, 171). To heal the fountain-head, Basil made himself as far as possible master of episcopal elections, and steadily refused to admit any he deemed unworthy of the office. So high became the reputation of his clergy that other bishops sent to him for presbyters to become their coadjutors and successors (*Ep.* 81). Marriage with a deceased wife's sister he denounced as prohibited by the laws both of Scripture and nature (*Ep.* 160). Feeble as was his health, his activity was unceasing. He visited every part of his exarchate, and maintained a constant intercourse by letter with confidential friends, who kept him informed of all that passed and were ready to carry out his instructions. He pushed his episcopal activity to the very frontiers of Armenia. In 372 he made an expedition by the express command of Valens, obtained by the urgency of his fast friend count Terentius, to strengthen the episcopate in that country by appointing fresh bishops and infusing fresh life into existing ones (*Ep.* 99). He was very diligent in preaching, not only at Caesarea and other cities, but in country villages. The details of public worship occupied his attention. Even while a presbyter he arranged forms of prayer (εὐχῶν διατάξεις), probably a liturgy, for the church of Caesarea (Greg. Naz. *Or.* xx. 340). He established nocturnal services, in which the psalms were chanted by alternate choirs, which, as a novelty, gave great offence to the clergy of Neocaesarea (*Ep.* 207). These incessant labours were carried out by one who, naturally of a weak constitution, had so enfeebled himself by austerities that "when called well, he was weaker than persons who are given over" (*Ep.* 136). His chief malady, a disease of the liver, caused him repeated and protracted sufferings, often hindering him travelling, the least motion bringing on a relapse (*Ep.* 202). The severity of winter often kept him a prisoner to his house and often even to his room (*Ep.* 27). A letter from Eusebius of Samosata arrived when he had been 50 days ill of a fever. "He was eager to fly straight to Syria, but he was unequal to turning in his bed. He hoped for relief from the hot springs" (*Ep.* 138). He suffered "sickness upon sickness, so that his shell must certainly fail unless God's mercy extricate him from evils beyond man's cure" (*Ep.* 136). At 45 he calls himself an old man. The next year he had lost all his teeth. Three years before his death all remaining hope of life had left him (*Ep.* 198). He died, prematurely aged, at 50. Seldom did a spirit of so indomitable activity reside in so feeble a frame, and, triumphing over weakness, make it the instrument of such vigorous work for Christ and His church.

In 372 a harassing dispute with Anthimus, bp. of Tyana, touching ecclesiastical jurisdiction, led to the chief personal sorrow of Basil's life, the estrangement of the friend of his youth, Gregory of Nazianzus. The circumstances were these. Towards the close of 371 Valens determined to divide Cappadocia into two provinces. Podandus, a miserable little town at the foot of mount Taurus, was at first named as the chief city of the new province, to which a portion of the executive was to be removed. The inhabitants of Caesarea entreated Basil to go to Constantinople and petition for the rescinding of the edict. His weak health prevented this, but he wrote to Sophronius, a native of Caesarea in a high position at court, and to Aburgius, a man of influence there, begging them to use all their power to alter the emperor's decision. They could not prevent the division of the province, but did obtain the substitution of Tyana for Podandus (*Epp.* 74-76). Anthimus thereupon insisted that the ecclesiastical division should follow the civil, and claimed metropolitan rights over several of Basil's suffragans. Basil appealed to ancient usage in vain. Anthimus called a council of the bishops who had opposed Basil's election and were ready to exalt his rival. By flattery, intimidation, and even the removal of opponents, Anthimus strengthened his faction. Basil's authority was reduced to a nullity in one-half of his province (Greg. Naz. *Or.* xx. 355; *Epp.* 31, 33; Bas. *Ep.* 259). Basil appealed to his friend Gregory, who replied that he would come to his assistance, though Basil wanted him no more than the sea wanted water. He warned Basil that his difficulties were increased by the suspicions created by his intimacy with Eustathius of Sebaste and his friends, whose reputation for orthodoxy was more than doubtful (Greg. Naz. *Ep.* 25). On Gregory's arrival the two friends started together for the monastery of St. Orestes on mount Taurus, in the second Cappadocia, the property of the see of Caesarea, to collect the produce of the estate. This roused Anthimus's indignation, and despite his advanced age, he occupied the defile, through which the pack-mules had to pass, with his armed retainers. A serious affray resulted, Gregory fighting bravely in his friend's defence (Greg. Naz. *Or.* xx. 356; *Ep.* 31, *Carm.* i. 8). Basil erected several new bishoprics as defensive outposts against his rival. One of these was near St. Orestes at Sasima, a wretched little posting-station and frontier custom-house at the junction of three great roads, hot, dry, and dusty, vociferous with the brawls of muleteers, travellers, and excisemen. Here Basil, disregarding Gregory's delicate temperament, determined to place him as bishop. Gregory's weaker character bowed to Basil's iron will, and he was most reluctantly consecrated. But Anthimus appointed a rival bishop, and Gregory took the earliest opportunity of escaping from the unwelcome position which he could only have maintained at the risk of continual conflict, and even bloodshed. [GREGORY NAZIANZEN; ANTHIMUS.] A peace was ultimately patched up, apparently through the intercession of Gregory and the mediation of Eusebius of Samosata and the senate of Tyana. Anthimus was recognised as metropolitan of the new province, each province preserving its own revenues (Bas. *Epp.* 97, 98, 122). Gregory attributed Basil's action to a high sense of duty, but could never forget that he had sacrificed his friend to that, and the wound inflicted on their mutual attachment was never healed, and even after Basil's death Gregory reproaches him with his unfaithfulness to the laws of friendship. "This lamentable occurrence took place seven years before Basil's death. He had before and after it many trials, many sorrows; but this probably was the greatest of all" (Newman, *Church of the Fathers*, p. 144).

The *Ptochotropheion*, or hospital for the reception and relief of the poor, which Basil had erected in the suburbs of Caesarea, afforded his untiring enemies a pretext for denouncing him to Helias, the new president of the province. This establishment, which was so extensive as to go by the name of the "New Town," ἡ καινὴ πόλις (Greg. Naz. *Or.* xx. p. 359), and subsequently the "Basileiad" after its founder (Soz. vi. 34), included a church, a palace for the bishop, and residences for his clergy and their attendant ministers; *hospices* for the poor, sick, and wayfarers; and workshops for the artisans and labourers whose services were needed, in which the inmates also might learn and practise various trades. There was a special department for lepers, with arrangements for their proper medical treatment, and on these loathsome objects Basil lavished his chief personal ministrations. By such an enormous establishment Basil, it was hinted, was aiming at undue power and infringing on the rights of the civil authorities. But Basil adroitly parried the blow by reminding the governor that apartments were provided in the building for him and his attendants, and suggesting that the glory of so magnificent an architectural work would redound to him (*Ep.* 84).

Far more harassing and more lasting troubles arose to Basil from the double dealing of Eustathius, the unprincipled and time-serving bp. of Sebaste. [EUSTATHIUS OF SEBASTE.] Towards the middle of June 372, the venerable Theodotus, bp. of Nicopolis, a metropolitan of Lesser Armenia, a prelate of high character and unblemished orthodoxy, deservedly respected by Basil, had invited him to a festival at Phargamon near his episcopal see. Meletius of Antioch, then in exile in Armenia, was also to be there. Sebaste was almost on the road between Caesarea and Nicopolis, and Basil, aware of the suspicion entertained by Theodotus of the orthodoxy of Eustathius, determined to stop there on his way, and demand a definite statement of his faith. Many hours were spent on fruitless discussion until, at three in the afternoon of the second day, a substantial agreement appeared to have been attained. To remove all doubt of his orthodoxy, Basil requested Theodotus to draw up a formulary of faith for Eustathius to sign. To his mortification not only was his request refused, but Theodotus plainly intimated that he had now no wish for Basil's visit. While hesitating whether he should still pursue his journey, Basil received letters from his friend Eusebius of Samosata, stating his inability to come and join him. This at once decided him. Without Eusebius's help he felt himself unequal to face the controversies his presence at Nicopolis would evoke, and he returned home sorrowing that his labours for the peace of the church were unavailing (*Epp.* 98, 99). A few months later the sensitive orthodoxy of Theodotus prepared another mortification for Basil. In carrying out the commands of Valens, mentioned above, to supply Armenia with bishops, the counsel and assistance of Theodotus as metropolitan was essential. As a first step towards cordial co-operation, Basil sought a conference with Theodotus at Getasa, the estate of Meletius of Antioch, in whose presence he made him acquainted with what had passed between him and Eustathius at Sebaste, and his acceptance of the orthodox faith. Theodotus replied that Eustathius had denied that he had come to any agreement with Basil. To bring the matter to an issue, Basil again proposed that a confession of faith should be prepared, on his signing which his future communion with Eustathius would depend. This apparently satisfied Theodotus, who invited Basil to visit him and inspect his church, and promised to accompany him on his journey into Armenia. But on Basil's arrival at Nicopolis he spurned him with horror (ἐβδελύξατο) as an excommunicated person, and refused to join him at either morning or evening prayer. Thus deserted by one on whose co-operation he relied, Basil had little heart to prosecute his mission, but he continued his journey to Satala, where he consecrated a bishop, established discipline, and promoted peace among the prelates of the province. Basil well knew how to distinguish between his busy detractors and one like Theodotus animated with zeal for the orthodox faith. Generously overlooking his former rudenesses, he reopened communications with him the following year, and visiting Nicopolis employed his assistance in once more drawing up an elaborate confession of faith embodying the Nicene Creed, for Eustathius to sign (Bas. *Ep.* 125). Eustathius did so in the most formal manner in the presence of witnesses, whose names are appended to the document. But no sooner had this slippery theologian satisfied the requirements of Basil than he threw off the mask, broke his promise to appear at a synodical meeting called by Basil to seal the union between them and their respective adherents, and openly assailed him with the most unscrupulous invectives (*Epp.* 130, 244). He went so far as to hold assemblies in which Basil was charged with heterodox views, especially on the Divinity of the Holy Spirit, and with haughty and overbearing behaviour towards his chorepiscopi and other suffragans. At last Eustathius pushed matters so far as to publish a letter written by Basil twenty-five years before to the heresiarch Apollinaris. It was true that at that time both were laymen, and that it was merely a friendly letter not dealing with theological points, and that Apollinaris had not then developed his heretical views and stood high in the esteem of Athanasius. But its circulation served Eustathius's ends in strengthening the suspicion already existing against Basil as a favourer of false doctrine. The letter as published by Eustathius had been disgracefully garbled, and was indignantly repudiated by Basil. By a most shameful artifice some heretical expressions of Apollinaris, without the author's name, had been appended to Eustathius's own letter accompanying that attributed to Basil, leading to the supposition that they were Basil's own. Basil was overwhelmed with distress at being represented in such false colours to the church, while the ingratitude and treachery of his former friend stung him deeply. He restrained himself, however, from any public expression of his feelings, maintaining a dignified silence for three years (Bas. *Epp.* 128, 130, 224, 225, 226, 244). During this period of intense trial Basil was much comforted in 374 by the appointment of his youthful friend AMPHILOCHIUS to the see of Iconium. But the same year brought a severe blow in the banishment of his intimate and confidential counsellor Eusebius of Samosata. At the end of this period (375) Basil, impelled by the calumnies heaped upon him on every side, broke a silence which he considered no longer safe, as tending to compromise the interests of truth, and published a long letter nominally addressed to Eustathius, but really a document intended for the faithful, in which he briefly reviews the history of his life, describes his former intimacy with Eustathius, and the causes which led to the rupture between them, and defends himself from the charges of impiety and blasphemy so industriously circulated (Bas. *Epp.* 223, 226, 244). It was time indeed that Basil should take some public steps to clear his reputation from the reckless accusations which were showered upon him. He was called a Sabellian, an Apollinarian, a Tritheist, a Macedonian, and his efforts in behalf of orthodoxy in the East were continually thwarted in every direction by the suspicion with which he was regarded. Athanasius, bp. of Ancyra, misled by the heretical writings that had been fathered upon him, spoke in the harshest terms of him (*Ep.* 25). The bishops of the district of Dazimon in Pontus, giving ear to Eustathius's calumnies, separated themselves from his communion, and suspended all intercourse, and were only brought back to their allegiance by a letter of Basil's, written at the instance of all the bishops of Cappadocia, characterized by the most touching humility and affectionateness (*Ep.* 203). The alienation of his relative Atarbius and the church of Neocaesarea, of which he was bishop, was more difficult to redress. To be regarded with suspicion by the church of a place so dear to himself, his residence in youth, and the home of many members of his family, especially his sainted grandmother, Macrina, was peculiarly painful. But the tendency of the leading Neocaesareans was Sabellian, and the emphasis with which he was wont to assert the distinctness of the Three Persons was offensive to them. They took umbrage also at the favour he shewed to monasticism, and the nocturnal services he had established. Basil wrote in terms of affectionate expostulation to them, and took advantage of the existence of his brother Peter's monastic community at Annesi to pay the locality a visit. But as soon as he was known to be in the neighbourhood a strange panic seized the whole city; some fled, some hid themselves: Basil was everywhere denounced as a public enemy. Atarbius abruptly left the synod at Nicopolis on hearing of Basil's approach. Basil returned, mortified and distressed (*Epp.* 126, 204, 207, 210). Besides other charges Basil was widely accused of denying the proper divinity of the Holy Spirit. This charge, which, when made by some Cappadocian monks, had been already sternly reproved by Athanasius (Ath. *ad. Pall.* ii. 763, 764), was revived at a later time on the plea that he had used a form of the doxology open to suspicion, "Glory be to the Father, through the Son, in the Holy Spirit" * (*de Spir. Sanct.* c. 1, vol. iii. p. 3). Self-defence was again reluctantly forced on the victim of calumny. He prayed that he might be deserted by the Holy Ghost for ever if he did not adore Him as equal in substance and in honour (ὁμοούσιον καὶ ὁμότιμον) with the Father and the Son (Greg. Naz. *Or.* xx. 365). Similar charges made at the festival of St. Eupsychius in 374 led Amphilochius to request him to declare his views, which he did in his treatise *de Spiritu Sancto* (§ 1; *Ep.* 231). Maligned, misrepresented, regarded with suspicion, thwarted, opposed on all hands, few champions of the faith have had a heavier burden to bear than Basil. The history of the Eastern church at this period is indeed little more than a history of his trials and sufferings. But his was not a nature to give way before difficulties the most tremendous and failures the most disheartening. The great object he had set before himself was the restoration of orthodoxy to the Eastern church, and the cementing of its disorganized fragments into one compact body capable of withstanding the attacks of hostile powers. This object he pursued with undaunted perseverance, notwithstanding his feeble health, "which might rather be called the languor of a dying man." Cut to the heart by the miserable spectacle which surrounded him, the persecution of the orthodox, the triumphs of false doctrine, the decay of piety, the worldliness of the clergy, the desecration of the episcopate by ambition and covetousness, rival bishops rending asunder the venerable church of Antioch, Christians wasting in mutual strife the strength that should have been spent in combating the common foe, feeling himself utterly insufficient in his isolation to work the reformation he desired, Basil had looked round eagerly for effectual aid and sympathy. He naturally turned first to that "great and apostolic soul who from boyhood had been an athlete in the cause of religion," the great Athanasius (*Epp.* 69, 80, 83). In the year 371 he begged his assistance in healing the unhappy schism of Antioch by inducing the Western Church to recognize Meletius, and persuading Paulinus to withdraw. He called on him to stir up the orthodox of the East by his letters, and cry aloud like Samuel for the churches (*Epp.* 66, 69). In his request about Antioch, Basil "was inviting Athanasius to what was in fact impossible even to the influence and talents of the primate of Egypt; for being committed to one side in the dispute he could not mediate between them. Nothing then came of the application" (J. H. Newman, *Church of the Fathers*, p. 105). Basil had other requests to urge on Athanasius. He was very desirous that a deputation of Western prelates should be sent to help him in combating the Eastern heretics and reuniting the orthodox, whose authority should overawe Valens and secure the recognition of their decrees. He asked also for the summoning of a council of all the West to confirm the decrees of Nicaea, and annul those of Ariminum (*Epp.* 66, 69).

Basil next addressed himself to the Western churches. His first letter in 372 was written to Damasus, bp. of Rome, lamenting the heavy storm under which almost the whole Eastern church was labouring, and entreating of his tender compassion, as the one remedy of its evils, that either he, or persons likeminded with him, would personally visit the East with the view of bringing the churches of God to unity, or at least determining with whom the church of Rome should hold communion (*Ep.* 70). Basil's letters were conveyed to Athanasius and Damasus by Dorotheus, a deacon of Antioch, in communion with Meletius. He returned by way of Alexandria in company with a deacon named Sabinus (afterwards bp. of Piacenza) as bearer of the replies of the Western prelates. These replies were full of expressions of sympathy, but held out no definite prospect of practical help. Something, however, was hoped from the effect of Sabinus's report on his return to the West, as an eye-witness of the lamentable condition of the Eastern church. Sabinus was charged with several letters on his return to Italy. One, bearing the signatures of thirty-two Eastern bishops, including besides Basil, Meletius of Antioch, Eusebius of Samosata, Gregory Nyssen, etc., was addressed to the bishops of Italy and Gaul; another was written in Basil's own name to the bishops of the West generally. There were also private letters to Valerian of Aquileia and others. These letters gave a most distressing picture of the state of the East. "Men had learnt to be theorists instead of theologians. The true shepherds were driven away. Grievous

* Cf. Hooker, *Eccl. Pol.* V. xlii. 12, "Till Arianism had made it a matter of great sharpness and subtilty of wit to be a sound believing Christian, men were not curious what syllables or particles of speech they used. Upon which when St. Basil began to practise the like indifferency, and to conclude public prayers, glorifying sometime the Father *with* the Son and the Holy Ghost, sometime the Father *by* the Son *in* the Spirit, whereas long custom had inured them to the former kind alone, by means whereof the latter was new and strange in their ears; his needless experiment brought afterwards upon him a necessary labour of excusing himself to his friends and maintaining his own act against them, who because the light of his candle too much drowned theirs, were glad to lay hold on so colourable a matter, and exceedingly forward to traduce him as an author of suspicious innovation."

wolves, spoiling the flock, were brought in instead. The houses of prayer were destitute of preachers, the deserts full of mourners. The faithful laity avoided the churches as schools of impiety. Priestly gravity had perished. There was no restraint on sin. Unbelievers laughed, the weak were unsettled. . . . Let them hasten to the succour of their brethren, nor allow the faith to be extinguished in the lands whence it first shone forth" (*Ep.* 93). A Western priest, Sanctissimus, who visited the East towards the end of 372—whether travelling as a private individual or deputed by Damasus is uncertain—again brought assurances of the warm attachment and sincere sympathy of the Italian church; but words, however kind, were ineffectual to heal their wounds, and Basil and his friends again sent a vehement remonstrance, beseeching their Western brethren to make the emperor Valentinian acquainted with their wretched condition, and to depute some of their number to console them in their misery, and sustain the flagging faith of the orthodox (*Epp.* 242, 243). These letters, transmitted by Dorotheus—probably a different person from the former—were no more effectual. The only point gained was that a council—confined, however, to the bishops of Illyria—was summoned in 375 through the instrumentality of Ambrose, by which the consubstantiality of the Three Persons of the Trinity was declared, and a priest named Elpidius dispatched to publish the decrees in Asia and Phrygia. Elpidius was supported by the authority of the emperor Valentinian, who at the same time promulgated a rescript in his own name and that of his brother Valens, who dared not manifest his dissent, forbidding the persecution of the Catholics, and expressing his desire that their doctrines should be everywhere preached (Theod. iv. 8, 9). But the death of Valentinian on Nov. 17, 375, frustrated his good intentions, and the persecution revived with greater vehemence.

The secret of the coldness with which the requests for assistance addressed by the Eastern church were received by the West was partly the suspicion that was entertained of Basil's orthodoxy in consequence of his friendship with Eustathius of Sebaste and other doubtful characters, and the large-heartedness which led him to recognize a real oneness of belief under varying technical formulas, but was principally due to his refusal to recognize the supremacy of the bp. of Rome. His letters were usually addressed to the bishops of the West, and not to the bp. of Rome individually. In all his dealings Basil treats with Damasus as an equal, and asserts the independence of the East. In his eyes the Eastern and Western churches were two sisters with equal prerogatives; one more powerful than the other, and able to render the assistance she needed, but not in any way her superior. This want of deference in his language and behaviour offended not Damasus only, but all who maintained the supremacy of Rome. Jerome accused Basil of pride, and went so far as to assert that there were but three orthodox bishops in the East—Athanasius, Epiphanius, and Paulinus (*ad Pammach.* 38). His appeals proving ineffectual, Basil's tone respecting Damasus and the Western prelates changed. He began to suspect the real cause of the apathy with which his entreaties for aid had been received, and to feel that no relief could be hoped from their "Western superciliousness" (τῆς δυτικῆς ὀφρύος), and that it was in vain to send emissaries to "one who was high and haughty and sat aloft and would not stoop to listen to the truth from men who stood below; since an elated mind, if courted, is sure to become only more contemptuous" (*Epp.* 215, 239). But while his hope of assistance from the West lessened, the need for it increased. The persecution of the orthodox by the Arians grew fiercer. "Polytheism had got possession. A greater and a lesser God were worshipped. All ecclesiastical power, all church ordinances, were in Arian hands. Arians baptized; Arians visited the sick; Arians administered the sacred mysteries. Only one offence was severely punished, a strict observance of the traditions of the Fathers. For that the pious were banished, and driven to deserts. No pity was shewn to the aged. Lamentations filled the city, the country, the roads, the deserts. The houses of prayer were closed; the altars forbidden. The orthodox met for worship in the deserts exposed to wind and rain and snow, or to the scorching sun" (*Epp.* 242, 243). In his dire extremity he once more appealed to the West, now in the language of indignant expostulation. "Why," he asks, "has no writing of consolation come to us, no visitation of the brethren, no other of such attentions as are due to us from the law of love? This is the thirteenth year since the war with the heretics burst upon us. Will you not now at last stretch out a helping hand to the tottering Eastern church, and send some who will raise our minds to the rewards promised by Christ to those who suffer for Him?" (*Ep.* 242). These letters were dispatched in 376. But still no help came. His reproaches were as ineffectual as his entreaties. A letter addressed to the Western bishops the next year (377) proves that matters had not really advanced a single step beyond the first day. We find him still entreating his Western brethren in the most moving terms to grant him the consolation of a visit. "The visitation of the sick is the greatest commandment. But if the Wise and Good Disposer of human affairs forbids that, let them at least write something that may comfort those who are so grievously cast down." He demands of them "an authoritative condemnation of the Arians, of his enemy Eustathius, of Apollinaris, and of Paulinus of Antioch. If they would only condescend to write and inform the Eastern churches who were to be admitted to communion and who not, all might yet be well" (*Ep.* 263). The reply brought back by the faithful Dorotheus overwhelmed him with sorrow. Not a finger was raised by the cold and haughty West to help her afflicted sister. Dorotheus had even heard Basil's beloved friends Meletius and Eusebius of Samosata spoken of by Damasus and Peter of Alexandria as heretics, and ranked among the Arians. What wonder if Dorotheus had waxed warm and used some intemperate language to the prelates? If he had done so, wrote Basil, let it not be reckoned against him, but put down to Basil's account and the untowardness of the times. The deep despondency which had seized Basil is evidenced by his touching words to Peter of Alexandria: "I seem for my sins to prosper in nothing, since the worthiest brethren are found deficient in gentleness and fitness for their office from not acting in accordance with my wishes" (*Ep.* 266).

Foiled in all his repeated demands, a deaf ear turned to his most earnest entreaties, the council he had begged for not summoned, the deputation he had repeatedly solicited unsent, Basil's span of life drew to its end amid blasted hopes and apparently fruitless labours for the unity of the faith. It was not permitted him to live to see the Eastern churches, for the purity of whose faith he had devoted all his powers, restored to peace and unanimity. "He had to fare on as he best might—admiring, courting, but coldly treated by the Latin world, desiring the friendship of Rome, yet wounded by her superciliousness—suspected of heresy by Damasus, and accused by Jerome of pride" (Newman, *Church of the Fathers*, p. 115).

Some gleams of brightness were granted to cheer the last days of this dauntless champion of the faith. The invasion of the Goths in 378 gave Valens weightier cares than the support of a tottering heresy, and brought his persecution of the orthodox to an end on the eve of his last campaign, in which he perished after the fatal rout of Hadrianople (Aug. 9, 378). One of the first acts of the youthful Gratian was to recall the banished orthodox prelates, and Basil had the joy of witnessing the event so earnestly desired in perhaps his latest extant letter, the restoration of his beloved friend Eusebius of Samosata (*Ep.* 268). Basil died in Caesarea, an old man before his time, Jan. 1, 378, in the 50th year of his age. He rallied before his death, and was enabled to ordain with his dying hand some of the most faithful of his disciples. "His death-bed was surrounded by crowds of the citizens, ready," writes his friend Gregory, "to give part of their own life to lengthen that of their bishop." He breathed his last with the words "Into Thy hands I commend my spirit." His funeral was attended by enormous crowds, who thronged to touch the bier or the hem of his funeral garments, or even to catch a distant glimpse of his face. The press was so great that several persons were crushed to death, almost the object of envy because they died with Basil. Even Jews and pagans joined in the general lamentations, and it was with some difficulty that the bearers preserved their sacred burden from being torn to pieces by those who were eager to secure a relic of the departed saint. He was buried in his father's sepulchre, "the chief priest being laid to the priests; the mighty voice to the preachers; the martyr to the martyrs" (Greg. Naz. *Or.* xx. 371, 372). In person he was tall and thin, holding himself very erect. His complexion was dark, his face pale and emaciated with close study and austerities; his forehead projecting, with retiring temples. A quick eye, flashing from under finely arched eyebrows, gave light and animation to his countenance. His speech was slow and deliberate. His manner manifested a reserve and sedateness which some of his contemporaries attributed to pride, others to timidity. Gregory says, "It was the self-possession of his character, and composure and polish, which they called pride," and refers not very convincingly to his habit of embracing lepers as a proof of the absence of superciliousness (*Or.* xx. 360). Basil's pride, indeed, was not the empty arrogance of a weak mind; but a well-grounded confidence in his own powers. His reserve arose partly from natural shyness—he jestingly charges himself with "the want of spirit and sluggishness of the Cappadocians" (*Ep.* 48)—partly from an unwillingness to commit himself with those of whom he was not sure. It is curious to see the dauntless opponent of Modestus and Valens charged with timidity. The heretic Eunomius after his death accused him of being "a coward and a craven skulking from all severer labours," and spoke contemptuously of his "solitary cottage and close-shut doors, and his flustered look and manner when persons entered unexpectedly" (Greg. Nys. *adv. Eunom.* i. p. 318). Philostorgius also speaks of Basil as "from timidity of mind withdrawing from public discussions" (*H. E.* iv. 12). The fact seems to be that Basil was like many who, while shewing intrepid courage when once forced into action, are naturally averse from publicity. He was a great lover of natural beauty, as shewn by his letters. The playful turn of his mind is also seen in many passages of his familiar letters, which sufficiently vindicate him from the charge of austerity of character. In manner he united Oriental gravity with the finished politeness of the Greeks, and sedateness with sweetness; his slightest smile was commendation, and silence was his only rebuke (Greg. Naz. *Or.* xx. 260, 261).

The voice of antiquity is unanimous in its praise of Basil's literary works (Cave, *Hist. Lit.* i. 239). Nor has the estimate of modern critics been less favourable. "The style of Basil," writes Dean Milman, "did no discredit to his Athenian education. In purity and perspicuity he surpasses most of the heathen as well as Christian writers of his age" (*Hist. of Christianity*, iii. 110).

The works of Basil which remain may be classed as: I. Expository, II. Dogmatic, III. Moral, IV. Epistolary, V. Liturgical.

I. *Expository.*—Cassiodorus records that Basil wrote commentaries on almost all the books of Holy Scripture. The greater part of these are lost. Those that remain are—

1. *Hexaemeron.*—Nine Homilies on the Six Days' Work of Creation. This is the most celebrated of all his works.

2. *Seventeen Homilies on the Psalms.*—These were preached *ad populum.* The first, on the Psalms generally, was translated by Rufinus, and is found prefixed to St. Augustine's Commentaries. The only other homilies that have reached us are those on Ps. 7, 14 (two), 28 (two), 29, 32, 33, 37, 44, 45, 48, 59, 61, and 114 (two).

3. *Commentaries on the first Sixteen Chapters of Isaiah*, a continuous work.

II. *Dogmatic.*

1. Five books *against Eunomius.*—Commended by Jerome (*egregii libri*), Gregory Nazianzen, and Photius (ἐξαίρετοι λόγοι).

2. *On the Holy Spirit,* addressed to Amphilochius and written at his request.

3. *On Baptism,* two books.

4. *Homilies.*

III. *Moral* and *Ascetic.*

1. *Homilies,* against envy, drunkenness, anger, on fasting, etc. A very sensible admonition to a young man how to read the books of heathen writers with profit (*Homil.* 24), included among these homilies, has been frequently translated and separately published, among others by abp. Potter, 1694. Several homilies are in honour of local martyrs, St. Julitta, St. Barlaam, St. Mammas, etc.

2. *On true Virginity,* a treatise addressed to Letoius, bp. of Melitene, rejected by Garnier on internal evidence, but generally accepted.

3. *Ascetic Writings,** including—(a) *Prefatory Discourse*; (b) *Discourse on the Renunciation of Worldly Goods*; (c) *On the Ascetical Life*; (d) *On Faith*; (e) *On the Judgment of God,* a prologue to the *Ethics*; (f) *Ethics or Morals,* under 80 heads, compiled from N.T.; (g) *On the Monastic Institutions,* including λόγος ἀσκητικός, and ὑποτύπωσις ἀσκήσεως; (h) *The Greater Monastic Rules,* ὅροι κατὰ πλάτος, 55 in number (in the form of Basil's answers to questions of his monks), with a proem; (i) *The Lesser Rules,* ὅροι κατὰ ἐπιτομήν, 313 in number, in the same form of question and answer; (k) *Animadversions on Delinquent Monks and Nuns,* a very early example of a *Poenitentiale*; (l) *Monastic Constitutions,* ἀσκητικαὶ διατάξεις, in 34 chapters.

IV. *Epistolary.*—In addition to those just mentioned we have a collection of no fewer than 365 letters addressed by Basil to his private and official correspondents, including two attributed to the emperor Julian and twelve to Libanius (cf. F. Loofs, *Eustathius von Sebaste und die Chronologie der Basilianischen Briefe,* Halle, 1897). Excerpts from some Letters of Basil from papyrus MSS. were published by H. Landwehr: Greek MS. from Fayoum, 1884.

V. *Liturgical.*—There is no reason to call in question the universal tradition of the East, that Basil was the composer of a liturgy. Those offices, however, which have come down to us under his name have been so largely interpolated at many different periods, that it is impossible to ascertain the correct text of the liturgy as drawn up by him. There are three chief editions of the Liturgy bearing Basil's name: (1) the Greek or Constantinopolitan, (2) the Syriac, translated into Latin by Masius, (3) the Alexandrian, found in Coptic, Greek, and Arabic, which versions concur in establishing one text. Of these, the Constantinopolitan furnishes the surest materials for ascertaining the genuine form.

The standard edition is the Benedictine, pub. at Paris, 1721-1730, by Julian Garnier, in 3 vols. fol., reprinted by Migne, *Patr. Gk.* vol. 29-32. In Pitra's *Analecta* (Paris, 1888) some *Fragmenta Ascetica* and *Epitimia,* and *in Psalmos* were ascribed to Basil. An English translation of some selected works and letters and useful Prolegomena are given in *Post-Nicene Fathers* (Wace and Schaff) by W. Blomfield Jackson, 1895. A revised text of the treatise *On the Holy Spirit* with notes and intro. is pub. by the Clarendon Press. A cheap popular Life by R. T. Smith is pub. by S.P.C.K. in their *Fathers for Eng. Readers.* [E.V.]

Basilius, the intimate friend of CHRYSOSTOM, with whom he resolved on the adoption of an ascetic life, and whose consecration to the episcopate he secured by a strange deception. His see is unknown, but was probably near Antioch. [E.V.]

Basilius of Cilicia, presbyter of Antioch and bp. of Irenopolis in Cilicia, *c.* 500; the author of an *Ecclesiastical History* in three books, from A.D. 450 to the close of Justin's reign. Photius speaks disparagingly of it (*Cod.* 42). He also wrote a violent book against Joannes Scythopolitanus, and Photius (*Cod.* 107) says its object was to oppose the doctrine of the union of the two natures in Christ. [E.V.]

Basilius, bp. of Seleucia, in Isauria, and metropolitan, succeeded Dexianus, who attended the council at Ephesus, and therefore after 431. He is erroneously identified by Photius with the early friend of Chrysostom, who must have been considerably his senior (Tillemont, xv. p. 340). He is very unfavourably known from the vacillation he displayed with regard to the condemnation of Eutyches. He took a leading part in the council at Constantinople in 448, at which Eutyches was condemned; and the next year, when the fidelity of the acts of the council was called in question, was one of the commission appointed to verify them (Labbe, *Concil.* vol. iv. 182, 230). But at the "Robbers' Synod" held at Ephesus a few months later his courage gave way, and he acquiesced in the rehabilitation of Eutyches, and retracted his obnoxious language. Before long he returned to orthodoxy, and in 450 affixed his signature to the famous *Tome* of pope Leo, on the Incarnation. At the council of Chalcedon, 451, the imperial commissioners proposed his deposition, together with that of other prelates who had aided in restoring Eutyches. But Basil submitted, concurred in the condemnation of Eutyches, and his offence was condoned (*ib.* 553, 604, 787).

His extant works comprise 39 homilies (17 on O.T. and 22 on N.T.), the titles and subjects being given by Fabricius, *Bibl. Graec.* lib. v. c. 19, 10. Four on John xi., published as his, prove to be the work of St. Chrysostom. A *Homily on the Transfiguration* was added to the series in the ed. of the Jesuit Dausqueius, in 1604. A prose work on *The Life and Miracles of St. Thecla* has been attributed to him; but not only does the style differ, and savour of a later age, but we learn from Photius that Basilius wrote St. Thecla's life in verse. Another supposititious work is the *Demonstratio contra Judaeos,* which appears in the Heidelberg ed. of 1596. Basil's homilies shew much oratorical power and skill in the use of figurative language. He does not lose

*** Sozomen informs us that in his day the ascetic writings commonly attributed to Basil were ascribed by some to his, at one time, friend and companion Eustathius of Sebaste.**

sight of perspicuity, but overburdens his style with metaphors. He not unfrequently reminds us of Chrysostom, though greatly his inferior in power. His homilies were first pub. in Gk. by Commelin, Lugd. Bat. 1596, 8vo; and in Latin by Claud. Dausqueius, 1604, 8vo. They are in the *Bibl. Patr.* Colon. v. and Lugd. Bat. viii. 1677. They were also printed at the end of the works of Gregory Thaumaturgus, Paris, 1672, fol. (Phot. *Cod.* 168; Tillemont, *Mém. eccl.* xv. 340, seq. *et passim*; Cave *Hist. Litt.* 441). [E.V.]

Beda, more correctly **Baeda, The Venerable.** [*Note.*—Though not properly coming within the period of this condensed ed., Dr. Stubbs's valuable art. is retained as Bede is the classical historian of the English Church for so much of our proper period.—*Ed.*] Bede was born on the estate given by Ecgfrith, king of Northumbria, to Benedict Biscop for the foundation of his sister monasteries of Wearmouth and Jarrow, probably, however, before the lands were so bestowed; for the Wearmouth estate was given in 674, and the Jarrow one in 682, whilst the birth of Bede seems satisfactorily fixed to 673. The place of his birth is uncertain, for whilst tradition and local history fix it at Jarrow, there is no positive evidence. Nor are the names of his parents preserved. He himself, writing, as may be reasonably concluded, immediately on the completion of his History in 731, describes himself then as in his 59th year; this would fix his birth in 673; but as he lived until 735, and the passage may have been added at any time between 731 and 735, his birth has been sometimes put as late as 677. Mabillon, however, whose arguments are sound and whose conclusion has been generally received, accepts 673. At the age of 7 Bede was handed over by his relations to the care of Benedict Biscop, who had not, in 680, begun the buildings at Jarrow, but had just returned from Rome bringing the arch-chanter John. Bede was educated in one or both of the sister monasteries, and after Benedict's death he passed under the rule of Ceolfrith. At the age of 19 he was ordained deacon by John of Beverley, then bp. of Hexham, and in his 30th year received the priesthood from the same prelate; as John ceased to be bp. of Hexham in 705, and the later date for Bede's birth would place his ordination as priest in 706 at the earliest, this conclusively favours the earlier date; in which case he was ordained deacon in 691 and priest in 702. From his admission to the joint monastery to his death he remained there employed in study and devotional exercises, and there is no evidence that he ever wandered further than to York, which he visited shortly before his death. In the valuable MS. Cotton, Tiberius A. xv. fo. 50, which is not later than the 10th cent., is preserved a letter of pope Sergius to Ceolfrith, desiring him to send to Rome "religiosum famulum Dei N. venerabilis monasterii tui," to assist in the examination of some points of ecclesiastical discipline. This letter was very early believed to refer to Bede; and by the time of William of Malmesbury had begun to be read, "religiosum Dei famulum *Bedam*, venerabilis monasterii tui *presbyterum*"; the name of Bede resting on the authority of William of Malmesbury only, and the word presbyterum on an interlineation in the Cotton MS. as well. If *presbyterum* be authentic, it is a strong argument against the identification of Bede, for he was not ordained priest until 702, and Sergius died in 701; but it is not essential to the sense, rests apparently on an interpolation, and if genuine may be a mistake of the pope. Intercourse between Wearmouth and Rome was nearly continuous at this time, and there is no more likely monk under Ceolfrith's rule than Bede. Some monks of the monastery went to Rome in 701 (Bede, *de Temporum Ratione*, c. 47), and brought a privilege from Sergius on their return (*Hist. Abbat.* c. 12), but Bede was not among them. The invitation was probably meant for Bede, and perhaps the acceptance of it was prevented by the death of Sergius. Whether Bede's studies were mainly at Wearmouth or at Jarrow is not important; as he died and was buried at Jarrow, he probably lived there chiefly, but the two houses were in strict union, and he was equally at home in both. Under the liberal and enlightened ministration of Benedict Biscop and Ceolfrith, he enjoyed advantages perhaps not elsewhere available in Europe, and perfect access to all existing sources of learning in the West. Nowhere else could he acquire at once the Irish, Roman, Gallican, and Canterbury learning; that of the accumulated stores of books which Benedict had bought at Rome and at Vienna; or the disciplinary instruction drawn from the monasteries of the continent as well as from the Irish missionaries. Amongst his friends and instructors were Trumbert, the disciple of St. Chad, and Sidfrid, the fellow-pupil of St. Cuthbert under Boisil and Eata; from these he drew the Irish knowledge of Scripture and discipline. Acca, bp. of Hexham and pupil of St. Wilfrid, furnished him with the special lore of the Roman school, martyrological and other; his monastic learning, strictly Benedictine, came through Benedict Biscop from Lerins and many other continental monasteries; and from Canterbury, with which he was in friendly correspondence, he probably obtained instruction in Greek, in the study of the Scriptures, and other refined learning. His own monastery offered rest and welcome to learned strangers like abbot Adamnan (Bede, *H. E.* v. 21), and Bede lost no opportunity of increasing his stores.

He describes the nature of his studies, the meditation on Scripture, the observance of regular discipline, the care of the daily singing in church, "semper aut discere, aut docere, aut scribere dulce habui." These were the occupations of his youth. After his ordination he devoted himself to selecting from the Fathers passages suitable for illustration and edification, and, as he says modestly, added contributions of his own after the pattern of their comments.

The list of his works given at the conclusion of his History, Bede seems to have arranged in order of relative importance, not of their composition; and most of them afford only very slight indications of the dates of writing. Probably the earliest of his writings are the more elementary ones, on Orthography, the *Ars Metrica* and the *de Natura Rerum*. The

Ars Metrica is dedicated to Cuthbert, a "con-levita," which seems to fix the date of writing before 702 (*Opp.* ed. Giles, vi. 78). The *de Temporibus*, the latest date of which is 702, may have followed almost immediately, and the *de Natura Rerum* has been referred to the same date. The *de Sex aetatibus Saeculi* was written 5 years later to be read to Wilfrid. The whole of the commentaries are later; they are all dedicated to bp. Acca, who succeeded his master Wilfrid in 709. The Commentaries on the Apocalypse, the Catholic Epp., and Acts, came first. Then that on St. Luke; that on Samuel followed, 3 books of it being written before the death of Ceolfrith in 716; that on St. Mark many years after. *De Temporum Ratione* is assignable on internal evidence to 726. Before the History come the Life of Cuthbert and of the abbots of Wearmouth and Jarrow which are referred to in the greater work. The History was completed in 731, after which only the *Ep. ad Egbertum* seems to have been written. The work on which he was employed at the time of his death was the translation of St. John's Gospel.

Bede's attainments were very great. He certainly knew Greek (*H. E.* v. 24) and some Hebrew. He knew Vergil, Ovid, Lucan, Lucretius, Terence, and a host of smaller poets. Homer he quotes once, perhaps at second-hand. He knew nearly all the second-rate poets, using them to illustrate the *Ars Metrica.* The earlier Fathers were, of course, in familiar use. The diversity and extent of his reading is remarkable: grammar, rhetoric, poetry, hagiography, arithmetic, chronology, the holy places, the Paschal controversy, epigrams, hymns, sermons, pastoral admonition and the conduct of penitents; even speculations on natural science, on which he specially quotes Pliny, employed his pen, besides his great works on history and the interpretation of Scripture. On all these points his knowledge was thoroughly up to the learning of the day; his judgment independent and his conclusions sound. He must have had good teachers, a good library, and an insatiable desire for learning. These qualifications fitted him for the remarkable place he holds in literature.

By promoting the foundation of the school of York, he kindled the flame of learning in the West at the moment that it seemed to be expiring both in Ireland and in France. This school transmitted to Alcuin the learning of Bede, and opened the way for culture on the continent, when England was relapsing into barbarism under the terror of the Danes. It is impossible to read the more popular writings of Bede, especially the *Ecclesiastical History*, without seeing that his great knowledge was coupled with the humility and simplicity of the purest type of monasticism. Employed on a theme which, in the prevailing belief of miraculous stories, could scarcely be treated of without incurring the charge of superstition, he is eminently truthful. The wonders he relates on his own account are easily referred to natural causes; and scarcely ever is a reputed miracle recounted without an authority. His gentleness is hardly less marked. He is a monk and politician of the school of Benedict Biscop, not of that of Wilfrid. The soundness and farsightedness of his ecclesiastical views would be remarkable in any age, and especially in a monk. His letter to Egbert contains lessons of wisdom, clear perception of abuses, and distinct recommendation of remedies, which in the neglect of observance of them might serve as a key for the whole later history of the Anglo-Saxon church. It breathes also the purest patriotism and most sincere love of souls. There is scarcely any father whose personal history is so little known, and whose personal character comes out in his writings so clearly as does that of Bede in this letter, and in his wonderful History.

Loved and honoured by all alike, he lived in a period which, at least for Northumbria, was of very varied character. The wise Aldfrid reigned during his youth and early manhood, but many years of disquiet followed his death, and even the accession of his friend Ceolwulf in 731 did not assure him of the end of the evils, the growth of which, since king Aldfrid's death, he had watched with misgivings. His bishops, first John of Beverley, and after the few years of Wilfrid's final restoration, Acca his friend and correspondent, and his abbots, first Ceolfrith and then Huaetbert, were men to whom he could look up and who valued him. His fame, if we may judge from the demand for his works immediately after his death, extended wherever English missionaries or negotiators found their way, and must have been widespread during his life. Nearly every kingdom of England furnished him with materials for his history: a London priest searched the records at Rome for him; abbot Albanus transmitted him details of the history of the Kentish church; bp. Daniel, the patron of Boniface, supplied the West Saxon; the monks of Lastingham, the depositories of the traditions of Cedd and Chad, reported how Mercia was converted; Esi wrote from East Anglia, and Cynibert from Lindsey.

Soon after visiting Egbert at York in 734 his health began to fail; and by Easter, 735, he had become asthmatic. But he laboured to the last, and, like Benedict Biscop, spent the time of unavoidable prostration in listening to the reading and singing of his companions. When he could, he continued the work of translation, and had reached the 9th verse of John vi. on the day he died. As the end approached, he distributed the few little treasures he had been allowed to keep in his chest, a little pepper, incense, and a few articles of linen; then, having completed the sentence he was dictating, he desired to be propped up with his face towards his church. He died repeating the *Gloria Patri.* The day is fixed by the letter of Cuthbert, who details the events of his deathbed to his friend Cuthwin, May 26, 735. He was buried at Jarrow where he died; his relics were in the 11th cent. removed to Durham, and in 1104 were found in the same coffin with those of St. Cuthbert. The story of his epitaph and the tradition of the bestowal of the title of Venerable is too well known and too apocryphal to be repeated here. For the subsequent fate of his remains see CUTHBERT. Alcuin has preserved one of his sayings: "I know that the angels visit the canonical hours and gatherings of the brethren; what if they find not me there among the brethren? Will they not say, Where is Bede: why does he not come with the brethren to the prescribed prayers?" (Alc. *Ep.* 16, ed. Migne).

Of the legendary or fictitious statements about Bede, the following are the most important: his personal acquaintance with Alcuin, which is impossible; his education and sojourn at Cambridge, on which see Giles, *PP. Eccl. Angl.* i. lxx. seq.; his visits to Italy and burial at Genoa or at Rome, which seem to belong to another person of the same name, (*ib.* i. cvi.), and the legendary statements about his title of Venerable (*ib.* i. ci.). For a detailed investigation of these, and the alleged authorities for them, see Gehle's learned monograph, *Disp. Hist. Theol. de Bed. Ven.* (Leyden, 1838), pp. 2-4, 17-21, and for the fallacies as to the date of Bede's death, *ib.* pp. 31 seq.

Bede's own list of his works may be rearranged as follows:

(1) Commentaries on O.T.—viz. Gen. 4 books, derived chiefly from Basil, Ambrose, and Augustine; the Tabernacle, 3 books; Sam. 3 books; the Building of the Temple, 2 books; on Kings, 30 questions dedicated to Nothelm; Prov. 3 books; Canticles, 7 books; on Isa., Dan., the 12 minor prophets, and part of Jer., extracts from Jerome; on Ezra and Neh. 3 books; on the Song of Habakkuk, 1 book; on Tobit, 1; chapters of lessons on the Pentateuch, Josh., and Judges; Kings, Job, Prov. Eccles. Canticles, Isa., Ezra, and Neh.

(2) Commentaries on N.T.: St. Mark, 4 books; St. Luke, 6 books; 2 books of homilies on the Gospels; Acts, 2 books; a book on each Catholic Ep.; 3 books on the Apocalypse, Lessons on the whole N.T. except the Gospels.

(3) Letters: *de Sex Aetatibus; de Mansionibus filiorum Israel; de eo quod ait Esaias "et claudentur, etc."; de Ratione Bissexti; de Aequinoctio.*

(4) Hagiographies: on St. Felix, rendered from the poem of Paulinus; on Anastasius, a revised trans. from the Greek; on St. Cuthbert, in verse and prose; the abbots of Wearmouth and Jarrow; the History of the English Church; the Martyrology.

(5) Hymns and epigrams.

(6) Scientific books: *de Natura Rerum, de Temporibus, de Temporum Ratione.*

(7) Elementary books: on *Orthography, Ars Metrica, Schemato, and Trope.*

Besides these he wrote translations into English, none of which are extant, from the Scriptures; *Retractationes* on the Acts; the Letter to Egbert; and a book on penance is ascribed to him.

Bede's collected works, including many not his, were pub. at Paris, 1544; Basle, 1563; Cologne, 1612, 1688; and by Dr. Giles (Lond. and Oxf.) in 1843; and in Migne's *Patr.* xc.-xcv. [S.]

All study of Bede must henceforth begin with Mr. C. Plummer's monumental edition of the historical writings *Baedae Opera Historica* (Clarendon Press, 1896). It contains the *Historia Ecclesiastica Gentis Anglorum*, the *Historia Abbatum*, the *Ep. ad Egbertum*, and the anonymous *Historia Abbatum*. An excellent introduction presents a critical survey of Bede's works with large references in footnotes to modern authorities. The student should consult the index in vol. ii. 418 for the frequent allusions scattered throughout the two vols. to the various writings of Bede. For the text of works other than historical reference must still be made to Migne's *Patr. Lat.* (vols. 94-95), or to Dr. J. A. Giles's *Patres Ecclesiae Anglicanae* (vols. 1-12). A critical edition of, at all events, the Biblical words of Bede is still a desideratum. Dr. Giles edited some of the smaller treatises 50 years ago, and Mr. Edward Marshall published Bede's Explanation of the Apocalypse in 1878; but with these exceptions few, if any, of his writings have in recent years appeared separately. In the 16th and 17th cents. homilies and other works were frequently printed. Reference may be made on this point to the art. BEDE in the 4-vol. ed. of this DICT. Translations of the historical books were made by Dr. Giles in 1840, Mr. Gidley in 1870, and by Miss A. M. Sellar in 1907. The last named is the most useful for the student. It is a revision of Dr. Giles, and his work is in turn based upon Mr. Stevens (1723). The notes in Mayor and Lumby's ed. of *H. E.* iii. and iv. (Camb. Univ. Press) are learned and important. Reference should also be made to Lives of Bede by Bp. Browne (1879) and Canon H. D. Rawnsley (1904), and to the general treatment of Bede and his times in Dr. Bright's *Chapters from Early English Church Hist.* (pp. 335-338), and Dr. W. Hunt's *History of the English Church* (vol. i. pp. 205-208). A monograph on "Place Names in the English Bede and the Localization of the MSS.," by Thomas Miller, was contributed to *Quellen und Forschungen zur Sprach- und Culturgeschichte der germanischen Völker* (Strassburg, 1896). The important question of the chronological order of Bede's works is discussed by Mr. Plummer, *op. cit.* (i. cxlv.-clix.). [H.G.]

Benedictus of Nursia. St. Benedict, abbot of Monte Cassino ("Abbas Casinensis"), called "patriarch of the monks of the West," lived during the troubled and tumultuous period after the deposition of Augustulus, when most of the countries of Europe were either overrun by Arians or still heathen. There were many monks in southern Europe, but without much organization till Benedict reformed and remodelled the monastic life of Europe (Mab. *Ann.* I. i.). The principal, almost sole, authority for the life of St. Benedict are the Dialogues of Gregory the Great. The genuineness of these has been questioned, but without sufficient cause.

Benedict was born about A.D. 480 at Nursia (Norcia), anciently belonging to the Sabines ("frigida Nursia," Virg.), an episcopal city in the duchy of Spoleto in Umbria. His parents were of the higher class ("liberiori genere," *Praef. Dial.*). A later writer gives their names, Euproprius and Abundantia (Petr. Diac. *de Vir. Ill.* i.). The ruins of the ancestral palace are shewn at Norcia, with a crypt, the reputed birthplace of Benedict (Mab. *Ann.* i. 4). He was sent as a boy to be educated at Rome; but soon, shocked by the immorality of his companions, fled, followed by his nurse (Cyrilla; Petr. D. *de Vir. Ill.* i.), to Ahle (Effide), on the Anio (Teverone), about forty miles from Rome (*Dial.* ii. 1). Thence he retired to a cave at

Sublaqueum (Subiaco), where he lived as a hermit in almost utter isolation for some years, visited only from time to time by a priest of the neighbourhood, Romanus (*Dial.* ii. 1). The cave, the well-known "il Sagro Speco," is shewn about three miles of very steep ascent above the town of Subiaco, and the traditionary spot marked by a monastery, once famous for its library and for the first printing press in Italy, where the youthful anchoret rolled naked in the thorn-bushes to overcome sensual temptations (Mab. *Ann.* i. 8). The fame of his sanctity spreading abroad, Benedict was invited, his youth notwithstanding, by the monks of a neighbouring monastery (at Vicovarro) to preside over them, and very reluctantly consented. Soon, however, their laxity rebelled against his attempts at reformation (he seems thus early to have shewn the organizing faculty for which he became afterwards so remarkable), and he abdicated, after miraculously escaping being poisoned by them (*Dial.* ii. 3). He retired to his cave; and undertook the superintendence of youths, among whom were two who became foremost among his followers, Maurus and Placidus, sons of Roman patricians (*Dial.* ii. 4). Here he founded, it is said, twelve monasteries, each of twelve monks with a "father" at the head of them (*Dial.* ii. 3). Of these only two remain, "Il Sagro Speco" and "Sta. Scholastica"; the rest being in ruins, or merely oratories (Mab. *Ann.* ii. 1). That of "Sta. Scholastica," so named after Benedict's sister, enjoys special privileges, and takes precedence among the Benedictine foundations even of Monte Cassino, as of older date (Alb. Butler, *Lives of the Saints*). Several of the miracles ascribed to Benedict are connected with Subiaco. But, after some time, finding his work continually hindered by the machinations of a dissolute priest, Florentius, he removed, probably *c.* 530 (Mab. *Ann.* iii. 5), with some of his disciples to Monte Cassino (*Dial.* ii. 8), destined to become illustrious as the headquarters of the great Benedictine order, and as a stronghold of learning and liberal arts even in the darkest ages. The mountain, with a town and stream at its base, all of the same name, stands on the borders of what were formerly Latium and Campania, nearer to Naples than Rome, a few miles from the birthplace of the great Dominican, Thomas Aquinas. Some ruins of an old Roman amphitheatre mark the site of the town, near the modern St. Germano; the little stream flows into the Rapido, a tributary of the Garigliano (Liris). The summit of the mountain three miles above the town, and even at the present time inaccessible to carriages, was crowned, before the arrival of Benedict, by a temple of Apollo; frequented even then by the rustics (*Dial.* i. 8), although the existence of a bp. of Cassino is indicated by the list of bishops present at the Roman council, A.D. 484 (Mab. *Ann.* iii. 5). On this precipitous eminence, looking down on the plains washed by the peaceful Liris ("taciturnus amnis," Hor.), and backed by the wild crags of the Abruzzi Benedict set himself with new vigour to carry out his plans of a revival of monasticism. The miraculous intervention of which Gregory hands down the story (*Dial.* ii. 9, 10) is not necessary to explain how the missionary spirit of Benedict and his monks overthrew the image and altar of Apollo, and reared shrines of St. John Evang. and St. Martin, the founder of monasticism in France, within the very walls of the Sun-god's temple —it was customary to reconsecrate, not to destroy, pagan edifices (Greg. M. *Ep.* xi. 76) —where now stands one of the most sumptuous of Italian churches. Here Benedict commenced the monastery destined to a world-wide reputation. Here for 12 years or more he presided over his followers; here he is believed to have composed the Benedictine Rule, in the same year, it is said, in which the schools of Athens were suppressed, and his famous Code was promulgated by Justinian; and from this sequestered spot he sent forth his emissaries not only to Anxur (Terracina, *Dial.* ii. 22), but beyond the borders of Italy to Sicily (Mab. *Ann.* iii. 25). Mabillon considers the narrative in Greek by Gordianus of the Mission of Placidus into Sicily spurious, but the mission itself beyond doubt. Not many years elapsed before this and other similar foundations were richly endowed with lands and other offerings (Greg. M. *Ep.* iii. 3).

It was in the vicinity of Monte Cassino that Benedict confronted and rebuked the ferocious Totila (A.D. 542) at the head of his victorious Ostrogoths (*Dial.* ii. 14, 15), and that he was wont to cheer his solitude by brief and rare interviews with his beloved sister, Scholastica, herself a recluse at no great distance (*ib.* 33). He is said to have been summoned to a synod at Rome (A.D. 531) by Boniface II. (Cave, *Hist. Litt.* on the authority of a codex in *Bibl. Vat.* by Ant. Scrip. Mon. Cas., *Eleg. Abb. Cas.* p. 25). His death is variously computed from 539 (*Schol. Bened.* in Honor. August. iii. 30 ap. *Fabr. Bibl. Eccl.*) to A.D. 543 (Trithem, *de Vir. Ill.* c. 300, ap. Fabr.; cf. Clint. *Fast. Rom.* and Mab. *AA. SS. O.S.B.* Praef.). Some few writers assign a yet later date. His sister (his twin-sister according to Trithemius, but cf. Mab. *Ann.* iii. 14) shortly predeceased him. She is called abbess by Bertharius, Abb. Cas. in the 8th cent. (*ib.*); but probably lived alone (cf. Greg. M. *Dial.* iii. 7, 14), or as one of a sisterhood. The words "ad cellam propriam recessisset" are ambiguous (*Dial.* ii. 34; cf. *Act. Sanct.* Feb. 10).

The character of St. Benedict may be best estimated from his *Regula Monastica*, if, as indeed is reasonable to suppose, it was his composition. In contrast to monastic rules already in existence, chiefly of Eastern origin, it breathes a spirit of mildness and consideration, while by the sanction for the first time given to study it opened the way for those literary pursuits which afterwards developed themselves so largely within convent walls. The account of the great Reformer's tender affection for his sister, and of his withdrawal before opposition at Subiaco, seems to give verisimilitude to the traditionary portraits of him, as of gentle though dignified aspect. His demeanour before Totila, the strict rule under which he kept others as well as himself (*Dial.* ii. 23, etc.), and his severity in repressing the slightest disobedience (24, 28, etc.) testify to his practical insight into character (20), as well as to his zeal and courage. In *Dial.* iii. 161 he is said (like Anthony) to have reproved a hermit who had chained himself to a rock, in these words, "Brother, be bound only by the chain of Christ!" The character of the Benedictine Order, by the specialities which have always distinguished it from other religious orders, attest the sagacious and liberal character of its founder. Fleury thinks he was not ordained, although he preached (*Eccl. Hist.* xxxii. 15). The idea of his being a priest is modern (Mab. *Ann. O.S.B.* v. 122; Murat. *Scr. Ital.* iv. 27).

Some, probably not all, of the remains of St. Benedict were transferred from his shrine at M. Cassino to the Benedictine abbey at Floriacum (Fleury), on the Loire, in the 7th cent. or at a later date (Mab. *Acta,* ii. 339). The question is discussed at length in *AA. SS.* Boll. 21 Mar. iii. 299-301, and in Mab. *AA. SS. O.S.B.* Saec. ii. 337-352.

For his life, see Greg. M. *Dial.* lib. ii. in Migne's *Patr.* lxvi., also in Mabillon's *Acta Sanctorum O.S.B.* Saec. i., in Muratori, *Script. Rer. Italic.* iv., and elsewhere. *Vita S. Benedicti* (in verse), by Marcus Poeta, said to be a disciple of St. Benedict, in Mab. *AA. SS.* Saec. i.; cf. Pauli Diac. *Histor. Langobard.* i. 26; see also *Grégoire le Grand, la vie de St. Benoit,* etc., par Jos. Mege, Par. 1734, 4to; Mab. *Ann. O.S.B.* i. viii., *Acta Sanctorum* (Bolland.), 21 Mar. iii. Bened. Haefteni, *Commentar. in Vit. S. Bened.* For a more complete catalogue of hymns, sermons, etc., on St. Benedict see Potthast *s.v.* Among modern biographies see *Le pitture dello Zingaro nel chiostro di S. Severino in Napoli pubblicate per la prima volta e dilucidate da Stanislao d'Aloe* (Napoli, 1846, 4to); also Tosti *St. Ben.,* historical discourse on his life from the Italian (Lond. 1896), and Essays on Tosti's Life (Lond. 1896). In a new ed. of the English trans. of Montalembert's *Monks of the West* (Lond. 6 vols. 1896) is an introduction by Dom Gasquet on the Rule. A convenient ed. of the Rule, by D. H. Blair, with Eng. translation, was pub. at Lond. and Edin. (2nd. ed.), 1896. [I.G.S.]

Benedictus I., pope, called by the Greeks **Bonosus** (Evagr. Sc. *H. E.* v. 16), son of Boniface, a Roman, was elected successor to John III. on June 3, 574 (Jaffé, *Regesta Pont.*; the dates given by Baronius are erroneous; cf. Clinton, *F. R.* ii. 543, on the causes of discrepancy in the pontifical chronology). During his pontificate Italy was harassed by the invasion of the Lombards. Though they never actually penetrated into the city of Rome, they ravaged the suburbs, violated the cemeteries, and persecuted the Christians. Misery and famine ensued, and Rome was only relieved eventually by a corn fleet from Egypt, dispatched at the pope's request by the emperor Justin. Benedict died in July 578, and was buried on the last day of that month in St Peter's. He was succeeded by Pelagius II. (Anastas. *Liber. Pontif.*; cf. Paul. Diac. *de Gestis Long.* ii. 10, ap. Muratori, i.). According to Ciacconius (*Vitae Pont. Rom.*) his memory was eulogized by Gregory the Great. His restoration of certain lands to the Abbot of San Marco at Spoleto rests on the same authority (Greg. *Op.* ii. 950, ed. Bened.); see generally Baronius, *sub annis* 573-577; Labbe, *Concil.* vol. v.). [T.R.B.]

Bertha (*Bercta*), wife of Ethelbert, king of Kent. She was daughter of Caribert, king of Paris, by his wife Ingoberga (Greg. Turon. iv. 26, ix. 26), and lost her father in 575, her mother in 589. The date of her marriage is unknown, but it was probably after the death of her mother, although Bede speaks of the king receiving her "a parentibus." Ethelbert was still a heathen, and on his marriage it was made a condition that his wife should be allowed to enjoy the exercise of her own religion, and should be attended by a bishop. Liudhard, or Letard, who is called by the Canterbury historians bp. of Senlis (Thorn, ed. Twysden, 1767), was chosen to accompany her, and the remains of the church of St. Martin, at Canterbury, were allotted for Christian worship (Bede, *H. E.* i. 26). It was partly, no doubt, by her influence that Ethelbert was induced to receive the Roman mission and to be baptized. Pope Gregory, in 601, when sending Mellitus to reinforce Augustine's company, addressed a letter to Bertha, in which he compliments her highly on her faith and knowledge of letters, and urges her to make still greater efforts for the spread of Christianity. He also ascribes the conversion of the English mainly to her, and compares her to the empress Helena (St. Greg. *Epp.* xii. 29; Haddan and Stubbs, *Councils,* iii. 17, 18). The date of her death is unknown. She was buried in the porch of St. Martin, in the church of SS. Peter and Paul (Bede, *H. E.* ii. 5). Ethelbert seems to have married again after her death. She was the mother of Eadbald, who succeeded to the throne on Ethelbert's death, and of Ethelburga, who, in 625, was married to Edwin, King of Northumbria. As her son was unbaptized in 616, it is probable that she found considerable difficulty in promoting Christianity in her own family, or else that she died whilst her children were very young. Elmham (ed. Hardwick, p. 110) says she took part in founding the monastery of St. Augustine, at Christmas, 604, but this is merely traditional; and the latest trustworthy trace of her is St. Gregory's letter of 601. [S.]

Beryllus, bp. of Bostra,* in Arabia, known in his day as one of the most learned teachers of the church. He conceived heretical views as to the person of our blessed Lord, to consider which a synod assembled at Bostra, A.D. 244. The bishops unanimously condemned his teaching, and declared that Christ at His Incarnation was endowed with a human soul (Socr. *H. E.* iii. 7), but were unable to convince Beryllus of his error. Origen, however, who, having been recently degraded from Holy Orders and excommunicated at Alexandria, was then residing at Caesarea, had been invited to the synod, and by his intellectual superiority, dialectical skill, and friendly moderation succeeded in proving to Beryllus the unsoundness of his tenets, and in leading him back to the orthodox faith. For this, according to Jerome, he received the thanks of Beryllus in a letter extant in his time. Our only authority as to the tenets of Beryllus is a somewhat obscure passage of Eusebius, *H. E.* vi. 33, and a fragment of Origen's commentary on the Epistle to Titus, found in the

* Socr. *H. E.* iii. 7, erroneously makes Beryllus bp. of Philadelphia.

apology of Pamphilus, Orig. *Opp.* tom. iv. p. 22, ed. Bened., which have led to very opposite conclusions. These may be seen in Dorner, where the whole question is discussed at length. His views were Monarchian, and are identified by Schleiermacher with those of the Patripassians, and by Baur with those of Artemon and the neo-Ebionites. According to Dorner, Beryllus occupies a middle place, forming a connecting link between the Patripassians and Sabellius. The leading ideas of his teaching as developed by Dorner from Eusebius were as follows: (1) there existed a πατρικὴ θεότης in Christ, but not an ἰδία θεότης: (2) Christ had no independent existence in a circumscribed form of being of His own (κατ' ἰδίαν οὐσίας περιγραφήν), before His Incarnation (ἐπιδημία). (3) Subsequently to His Incarnation, He Who had been identified with the πατρικὴ θεότης became a circumscribed Being possessed of an independent existence; the being of God in Christ being a circumscription of the θεότης of the Father, *i.e.* of God Himself. According to Eusebius, *H. E.* vi. 20, Beryllus was the author of epistles and treatises displaying considerable elegance. Hieron. *de Script. Eccl.* No. lx.; Niceph. *H. E.* v. 22; Neander ii. pp. 350 ff.; Gieseler, v. p. 219; Dorner, *Person of Christ*, First Period, Second Epoch, § i. c. 2, div. i. vol. ii. pp. 35-45, Clark's trans.; Schröckh, iv. 38; Mosheim, *de Reb. Christ. ante Constant.* p. 699; Ullman, *Comment. de Beryll. Bost.* (Hamb. 1835); Fock, *Diss. de Christolog. Beryll. Bost.* (1843). [E.V.]

Blandina, martyr, a female slave, reckoned as the chief among the martyrs of Lyons, in that, although weakest in body, she suffered longest and most bravely the most various and prolonged torture. Among other things she was stretched upon a cross and thrown to wild beasts, which, however, refused to touch her; and finally she was tied up in a net and gored to death by a bull. (Eus. *H. E.* v. 1; Eucher. Lugdun. *Hom. inter Hom. Euseb. Emesen.* xi.; Greg. Tur. *de Glor. Martt.* xlix.; Baron. June 2.) [A.W.H.]

Boëthius (Βοέτιος, Procop.), **Anicius Manlius Severinus.*** This honourable name, invested by the church for so many centuries with a halo of sanctity, can hardly be excluded from a Dictionary of Christian Biography, though some criticism in modern times has tended to distinguish the Roman senator, the author of the *Consolatio Philosophiae*, from the writer of certain theological treatises which bear his name, and upon the genuineness of which depends his claim to be enrolled among the martyrs of Christendom. These works, (i.) *de Sancta Trinitate*, (ii.) *Utrum Pater et Filius Substantialiter Praedicentur*, (iii.) *de Duabus Naturalis et una Persona Christi, contra Eutychen et Nestorium*, (iv.) *Fidei Confessio seu brevis Institutio Religionis Christianae*, based upon the Aristotelian Categories, and compiled in great measure from the writings of St. Augustine, being concerned entirely with abstract questions of dogma, offer but little to compare with the *Consolatio*, into which the mind and heart of its author were manifestly thrown; nevertheless Hand (*Encyclopädie, v.* Ersch. u. Gruber, *in voce*) has endeavoured to shew that they are alien in point of philosophy as well as in the method of thought and expression from the undoubted writings of Boëthius. For instance, although philosopher and theologian alike demonstrate the *substantial* as opposed to the *accidental* nature of God, Boëthius (*ad* Arist. *Categ.* c. 4) maintains Aristotle's distinction of substances, whereas the author of the first theological treatise insists upon the substantial *indifference* of the three persons in the Trinity. Again, while Boëthius translates the οὐσία of Aristotle by *substantia*, the author of the third treatise adopts the later rendering *essentia*, while he also follows ecclesiastical writers in his use of the words *substantia* (ὑπόστασις) and *persona* (πρόσωπον). The arguments of Hand have been controverted by Gustave Baur (*de Boëth. Christianae Fidei Assertore*, c. 1), but the theory of a second Boëthius, whom Hand supposes to have been confounded at an early date with the philosopher, so far from being refuted, has suggested the still more plausible conjecture of Obbarius (*Proleg. ad Consol. Phil.* p. xxxvii. Jenae, 1843) that another Severinus was the author of the works in question, and that to this person, and not to the author of the *Consolatio*, belong the honours of martyrdom in defence of the Catholic faith. In support of this conjecture there are the facts: (i.) That no author is known to mention the theological works of Boëthius before Alcuin (*de Proc. Spir. Sancti*, p. 752), who flourished nearly three centuries after his death. (ii.) That although the tradition was current in the Middle Ages, from Paulus Diaconus (8th cent.) downwards, that Boëthius laid down his life in his zeal for the Catholic faith against the Arian invaders of Italy, this is not his own account of his fall from court favour nor is it supported by any contemporary writer. (iii.) That in the epitaph of Gerbertus, bp. of Ravenna, afterwards pope Sylvester II., inscribed upon the monument raised in his honour by Otho III., A.D. 996, no mention is made of martyrdom or of canonization (Migne, *Patr.* vol. 139, p. 287). (iv.) That while the church of Rome knows nothing of St. Boëthius, the festival of St. Severinus has been held on Oct. 23 ever since the 8th cent., in the neighbourhood of Ticinum, where Boëthius is popularly believed to have been executed. The double clue runs throughout the history of Boëthius, as derived from various sources; the same twofold character, half secular, half ecclesiastical, pervades the whole; and hence the unusual number of so-called fables mingled with the best authenticated facts—*e.g.*:—

(1) The wife of Boëthius was unquestionably Rusticiana, the daughter of the senator Symmachus (*Cons. Phil.* ii. 3, 4; Procop. *Goth.* iii. 20), by whom he had two sons, Aurelius Anicius Symmachus and Anicius Manlius Severinus, who were consuls A.D. 522 (*Cons. Phil.* ii. 3, 4); but tradition makes him to have been also the husband of *Elpis*, a Sicilian lady and the authoress of two hymns in the Breviary [ELPIS], and by her to

* The additional name of *Torquatus* does not occur before the 15th cent. Bertius is the only commentator who gives the praenomen *Flavius*.

have had two sons, Patricius and Hypatius, Greek consuls A.D. 500.

(2) According to his own statement, Boëthius was imprisoned (*Cons. Phil.* I. ii. *metr.* 24) at a distance of 500 miles from Rome (*ib.* i. 4); according to other accounts he was simply exiled, a confusion which no doubt arose from the epitaph of the said Elpis, in which she is said (Burm. *Anth. Lat.* tom. ii. epigr. 138) to have followed her husband into banishment.

(3) His fall and death is mixed up by Paulus Diaconus and other writers, who are followed among modern writers by Bähr (*Rom. Lit.* p. 162) and Heyne (*Censar. Ingenii, etc., Boeth.*), with the constrained embassy of pope John to Constantinople on behalf of the Arians of the East, which is said to have resulted in the suspicion of his treachery and finally in his death; whereas Boëthius was put to death, according to others (Anonym. Vales., etc.), before the embassy, or at least before the return of the pope, A.D. 525, and as he himself implies (*Cons. Phil.* i. 4), on suspicion of conspiracy, not against Arianism, but for the restoration of the liberty and power of the senate.

(4) Two distinct accounts exist of his execution, one stating that he was beheaded at Ticinum (Anast. *Vit. Pontif.* in Johanne I.; Aimoin, *Hist. Franc.* ii. 1), where he was imprisoned, according to popular tradition, in a tower still standing at Pavia in 1584 (Tiraboschi, iii. l. 1, c. 4); another relating (Anonym. Vales. p. 36, in Gronov. ed. Amm. Marcell.) that he was confined along with Albinus in the baptistery of a church, and soon afterwards executed "in agro Calventiano," first being tortured by a cord tightly twisted round his forehead, and then beaten to death with a club.

(5) He is claimed by the church as a saint and martyr under the name of Severinus, the friend of St. Benedict (Tritenhem, *ap. Fabric. Bibl. Lat.* iii. 15), and the worker of a miracle at his death (Martianus Rota, vid. Boëth. in usum Delphin.), but of all this his contemporaries knew nothing, and no hint of it appears until three centuries after his death, when he also becomes the author of four dogmatic treatises on the mysteries of the Trinity.

Whether or not this double tradition has grown out of the history of two distinct individuals, there can be little doubt that to obtain a true estimate of the character and writings of Boëthius, the author of the *Consolatio* must be distinguished from Severinus, saint and martyr, or whoever else was the writer of the above-mentioned theological works. It remains for us briefly to notice the most authentic facts of the philosopher's life, and to inquire how far his thoughts were coloured by the contemporaneous influence of Christianity, or exercised an influence in their turn upon the religious thought of the Middle Ages.

Boëthius was born between the years A.D. 470-475, as is inferred from his contemporary Ennodius (*Eucharisma de Vitâ suâ*), who says that he himself was sixteen when Theodoric invaded Italy, A.D. 490. As a wealthy orphan (*Cons. Phil.* ii. 3) Boëthius inherited the patrimony and honours of the Anician family, was brought up under the care of the chief men at Rome (*ib.* ii. 3), and became versed in the erudition of his own country and likewise in that of Greece. In the words of his friend Cassiodorus, "The geometry of Euclid, the music of Pythagoras, the arithmetic of Nicomachus, the mechanics of Archimedes, the astronomy of Ptolemy, the theology of Plato, and the logic of Aristotle," were translated and illustrated for the benefit of the Romans by his indefatigable pen (*Var.* i. *Ep.* 45). Nor was he less distinguished for his virtue. His purse was ever open to the poor of Rome (Procop. *Goth.* I. i.). He exerted his authority and eloquence on behalf of the oppressed provincials (*Cons. Phil.* i. 4). Such conspicuous merit was at first appreciated by Theodoric. He received the title of patrician while still a youth (*ib.* i. 3), became consul A.D. 510, and princeps senatus (Procop. *Goth.* I. i.), was employed in the important station of master of the offices (Anonym. Vales. p. 26), in which post his scientific knowledge and mechanical skill were turned to ample account (Cassiod. *Ep.* i. 10, 45, ii. 40), and reached the summit of his fortune on the day when, supported by his two sons, who had just been inaugurated in the consulship, he pronounced a panegyric upon Theodoric and gratified the populace with a largess (*Cons. Phil.* ii. 3). But a reverse was at hand. The philosopher had exerted himself to rescue the state from the usurpation of ignorance; the senator had opposed his integrity to the tyranny and avarice of the barbarians who did not in general share the moderation of their leader. His expression, "palatini canes" (*ib.* i. 4), shews his uncompromising spirit against their iniquities; and it is not surprising that the courage and sympathy he shewed in pleading the cause of Albinus, a senator who was accused of "hoping the liberty of Rome" (*ib.*), joined to other similar conduct, and misrepresented by his foes, at length poisoned the mind of Theodoric, who seems to have appointed one Decoratus, a man of worthless character, to share and control the power of his favourite (*ib.* iii. 4). As to the existence of any widespread conspiracy to overthrow the Ostrogothic rule there is but very faint evidence, and against this must be set down his own indignant self-justification (*ib.* i. 4). A sentence of confiscation and death was passed upon him by the senate without a trial; he was imprisoned in the Milanese territory, and ultimately executed in one of the ways named above, probably about the 50th year of his age, A.D. 520-524. His father-in-law, Symmachus, was involved in his ruin (Procop. *Goth.* I. i.), and his wife, Rusticiana, reduced to beggary (*ib.* iii. 20). The remorse of Theodoric, which came too late to save "the last of the Romans," is the natural and tragic finish to a story which has too many parallels in history.

It was during his imprisonment that Boëthius composed his *Consolation of Philosophy*, a work described by Gibbon as "a golden volume, not unworthy of the leisure of Plato or Tully." It is a dialogue in prose and verse (a species of composition suggested probably by the medleys of Petronius and Capella) between the author and his visitant, Philosophy, whom he represents as a woman of reverend mien and varying stature, upon the borders of whose vesture were woven the letters Π and Θ, symbolizing no doubt the Platonic division of philosophy into πρακτική and θεωρητική. Those who regard the "Consolation" as the work of a Christian have not unnaturally been perplexed by its total silence as to the distinctive faith of Christianity, and have been forced to suppose it incomplete (Bertius, Lips. 1753), or to interpret it allegorically (Gervais, vid. Schröckh, *Hist. Eccles.* xvi. 118). It breathes a spirit of resignation and hope, but so does the Phaedo. It is based upon a firm belief in Providence, but it is only in his poetic flights that the author's language seems to savour of a belief in a personal God (*Cons. Phil.* iii. *metr.* 9), his faith never elsewhere rising higher than Theism, and occasionally passing into Pantheism (*ib.* iii. 12, *et pass.*). He asserts the efficiency of prayer, but the injunction thereto is drawn from the Timaeus and not from the N.T. (*ib.* iii. 9), while the object of his aspirations is not the στέφανος ζώης or δικαιοσύνης of the Apostle, but the *summum bonum* of the Greek philosopher. He has been thought to betray an acquaintance with the Christian idea of heaven (*ib.* i. 5, iii. 12, iv. 1, v. 1), but his *patria* is the peace of the philosophic mind, not the πολίτευμα ἐν οὐρανῷ ὕπαρχον. In short, the whole work, with the exception of words and phrases which merely imply an acquaintance with Christian writers, might have been written, so far as theology is concerned, by Cicero himself. The works of Boëthius prove his intimate knowledge of Greek literature, and were for centuries the only vehicle by which Greek philosophy penetrated to the West; but his chief work is now of value only as serving, along with the poetry of Claudian and Ausonius, to mark the point of contact between the thought of heathendom and the faith of Christianity. That from the 6th to the 14th cent. its author was invested with a monopoly of philosophic greatness was natural in the utter decay of learning, but it was the excess of darkness which made his light of brightness sufficient to shine across the ages till it paled in the rising splendour of the revival of letters.

His works are: *de Consolatione Philosophiae libri* v.; *in Porphyrii Isagogen a Victorino Translatam Dialogi* ii.; *in eandem a se ipso Latine Translatam libri* v.; *in Categorias Aristotelis libri* ii.; *in Ejusdem Librum περὶ ἑρμηνείας lib.* i.; *Editionis secundae libri* vi.; *Analyticorum Aristotelis Priorum et Posteriorum libri* iv.; *Topicorum Aristotelis libri* viii.; *in Aristotelis Topica libri* viii. (not extant); *Introductio in Syllogismos Categoricos; de Syllogismis Hypotheticis libri* ii.; *de Divisione; de Definitione; de Differentiis Topicis libri* iv.; *in Topica Ciceronis libri* vi.; *Elenchorum Sophisticorum libri* ii.; *de Arithmeticâ libri* ii.; *de Musicâ libri* v.; *de Geometriâ libri* ii.; also two short treatises entitled respectively "*de Rhetoricae Cognatione,*" and "*Locorum Rhetoricorum Distinctio,*" discovered by cardinal Mai in a MS. of the 11th cent. Doubtful works: *de Unitate et Uno; de Bono; de Hebdomadibus;* all of which are dedicated to pope John.

The most complete ed. of his works is in Migne's *Patr. Lat.*, which is a collation of the best edd. The best edd. of the *Consolatio* are those of Theod. Obbarius (Jenae, 1843) and R. Peiper (Leipz. 1871), the latter including the theological works and *prolegomena.* The most interesting trans. is that into Anglo-Saxon by Alfred the Great, edited by W. J. Sedgefield (Lond. 1899). See also G. Boissier, "Le Christianisme de Boëce" in *Journal des savants* (Paris, 1899).

The chief ancient authorities for the life of Boëthius are the epistles of his contemporaries Cassiodorus and Ennodius, and the History of Procopius. The best modern authorities are Hand, in Ersch and Gruber's *Encyclop.*; and for an opposite view of his religious faith, Gustave Baur, *de Boëth. Christianae Fidei Assertore* (Darmst. 1841); Heyne, *Censura Boëth. de Cons. Phil.* (Gotting. 1805), in Opusc. Academ. vi. 142; the "Prologomena de Boëthii vitâ et scriptis" to the ed. of the *Cons. Phil.* by Obbarius; A. Hildebrand, *Boëthius und seine Stelling zum Christenthum* (Regussburg, 1885); and H. F. Stewart, *Boëthius*, an Essay (Edin. 1891). [E.M.Y.]

Bonifacius I., pope and saint, successor of Zosimus, a Roman, son of a priest, Jocundus, has been identified with Boniface the priest, the papal representative at Constantinople during the time of Innocent I. (Baronius *s.a.* 405, § 15, cf. Bianchi-Giovini, *Storia dei Papi*, i. 353). Zosimus died on Dec. 26, 418. On the 28th Boniface was elected bishop in the Church of St. Theodora by a majority of the clergy and people, and consecrated next day in the church of St. Marcellus. Previously, however, a small body of the clergy, contrary to the command of the prefect Symmachus, had shut themselves up in the Lateran, and as soon as the burial of Zosimus took place, proclaimed Eulalius the archdeacon pope. Three bishops (including the bp. of Ostia) assisted at the consecration of Eulalius, nine at that of Boniface. Symmachus reported to the emperor Honorius in favour of Eulalius. Honorius decided accordingly, and ordered Boniface to quit the city, but ultimately pronounced in his favour. This was the third disputed election (see full account, with all the documents, in Baronius *s.a.* 419; Jaffé, *Regesta*). Personally, Boniface is described as an old man at the time of his appointment, which he was unwilling to accept, of mild character, given to good works (Anastasius, *Lib. Pont.*). In the contest against Pelagius, Boniface was an unswerving supporter of orthodoxy and Augustine. [PELAGIUS.] Two letters of the Pelagians had fallen into the pope's hands, in both of which Augustine was calumniated. Boniface sent them promptly by the hands of Alypius to Augustine himself, that he might reply to them. His reply, contained in the "Quatuor libri contra duas Epp. Pelagianorum" (*Opp.* x. 411, Ben. ed.; cf. *Repr.* ii. 61 in vol i.), is addressed to Boniface, and bears testimony to the kindness and condescension of his character. Boniface was strenuous in enforcing the discipline of the church. Thus he insisted that Maximus, bp. of Valence, should be brought to trial for his misdemeanours before the bishops of Gaul (see letter in Labbe, *Conc.* ii. 1584). So also in the case of the vacancy of the see of Lodève he insisted on a rigid adherence to the decrees of the council of Nicaea, that each metropolitan, and in this case the metropolitan of Narbonne, should be supreme within his own province, and that the jurisdiction conferred by his predecessor Zosimus on the bp. of Arles should be of none effect (Labbe, *ib.* 1585). On the significance of this transaction as regards the history of the relation of the pope to the metropolitans, see Gieseler, *Ecc. Hist.* i. § 92 (p. 265, Eng. trans.). Nor was he less strenuous in his assertion of the rights of the Roman see. Following the policy of his predecessors, Siricius and Innocent, he vindicated the supremacy of his patriarchate over the province of Eastern Illyria. The people of Corinth had elected a certain Perigenes bishop, and sent to Rome to ask the pope to ratify the election. Boniface refused to entertain their request until sent through the hands and with the consent of the papal legate, Rufus, archbp. of Thessalonica. The party in Corinth opposed to Perigenes appealed to the Eastern emperor. Theodosius decreed that canonical disputes should be settled by a council of the province with appeal to the bp. of Constantinople. Boniface immediately complained to Honorius that this law infringed the privileges of his see, and Theodosius, on the request of his uncle, annulled it. Proposals, however, had actually been made for the convocation of a provincial council to consider the Corinthian election. To check this tendency to independence, and to defeat the rival claims of Constantinople, Boniface forthwith addressed letters to Rufus, to the bishops of Thessaly, and to the bishops of the entire province. Rufus was exhorted to exercise the authority of the Roman see with all his might; and the bishops were commanded to obey him, though allowed the privilege of addressing complaints concerning him to Rome. "No assembly was to be held without the consent of the papal vicar. Never had it been lawful to reconsider what had once been decided by the Apostolic see" (see documents in Labbe, iv. 1720 sqq.). Among the lesser ordinances attributed to him by Anastasius the most important is that whereby he forbade slaves to be ordained without the consent of their masters. Boniface died on Sept. 4, 422, and was buried, according to the *Martyr. Hieronym.* (ap. Jaffé, *Reg.*), in the cemetery of St. Maximus, according to Anastasius in that of St. Felicitas (cf. Ciacconius, *Vit. Pont.* who gives several epitaphs). He was succeeded by Celestine I. His letters are given by Labbe, vol. iv.; Migne, *Patr.* vol. xx.; Baronius. (Cf. Jaffé, *Regesta* and *App.* pp. 932, 933, where spurious letters and decrees attributed to Boniface are given). [T.R.B.]

Bonifacius II., pope, successor to Felix IV., of Roman birth but Gothic parentage, son of Sigisbald or Sigismund, was elected bp. of Rome on Sept. 17, 530, and consecrated five days later in the basilica of Julius (Jaffé, *Regesta Pont.*). At the same time a rival party in the basilica of Constantine elected and consecrated Dioscorus. The Roman church was saved from schism by the death of Dioscorus a few weeks afterwards; but Boniface carried his enmity beyond the grave, and anathematized his dead rival for simony (cf. Cassiodorus, *Var.* 9, *Ep.* 5). This anathema was subsequently removed by Agapetus I. It has been conjectured (by Baronius, Labbe, Cave, etc.) that the double election was brought about by Athalaric the Gothic king, that he might have an opportunity to intervene after the example of Theodoric, and place a partisan of his own upon the papal throne. [THEODORICUS (3); FELIX III. (cf. Gieseler, *Eccl. Hist.* i. § 115, p. 340, Eng. trans. and reff.).] The pontificate of Boniface is chiefly remarkable for the bold measure proposed and carried by him at a council at St. Peter's, by which he was empowered to nominate his own successor. Accordingly he nominated the deacon Vigilius (subsequently pope, 537), and obtained the consent of the clergy thereto. Shortly afterwards, however, another council met and annulled the previous decree as contrary to the canons. Boniface acknowledged his error and publicly burned the document with his own hands. Some (*e.g.* Bianchi-Giovini, *Storia dei Papi*, ii. 165) have conjectured that Boniface acted throughout as the tool of the unprincipled Vigilius; others (*e.g.* Baronius, Milman, etc.) that the object of Boniface was to prevent for the future the interference of the Gothic king, and that it was the Gothic king that compelled him to rescind the decree. It would have been equally difficult, however, to have brought the clergy and people of Rome to tolerate such a scheme. Of the pontificate of Boniface there is little else to record. A petition was presented to him (in which he is styled "Universal Bishop") by Stephen, archbp. of Larissa, metropolitan of Thessaly, complaining of the encroachments of the patriarch of Constantinople, who had suspended Stephen from his office. The result of the council held is unknown, but there can be little doubt that Boniface followed the policy of his predecessors in this matter and asserted the authority of the Roman see over the whole of the province of Illyria (see documents in Labbe, *Conc.* iv. 1690 seq., also BONIFACIUS I.). He died in Oct. 532, and was buried on the 17th in St. Peter's. He was succeeded by John II. (see generally Anastasius, *Lib. Pont.*; Labbe, *Conc.* iv. 1682 sqq.; Baronius, *sub annis*; Migne, *Patr.* lxv.). [T.R.B.]

Bonosus, the founder of the sect of the Bonosiani, was bp. of Sardica in Illyria at the end of the 4th cent. (Tillemont, x. 754). Bonosus is only known to us as holding the same views with Helvidius with regard to the perpetual virginity of the mother of our Lord, and as to His brethren, whom he affirmed to have been the natural offspring of Joseph and Mary. At the synod of Capua, convened by Valentinian, A.D. 391, to settle the rival claims of Flavian and Evagrius to the see of Antioch, opportunity was taken to lay an accusation against Bonosus. The synod was unwilling to consider the question, and transferred it to Anysius, the bp. of Thessalonica and metropolitan, and his suffragans, who, as a neighbour of Bonosus, might be supposed to be more fully acquainted with the merits of the case (Labbe, ii. 1033). Bonosus was condemned for heretical teaching, deposed, and his church closed against him. Bonosus consulted Ambrose, who recommended patience and submission. This prudent counsel was not followed, and the difference was exaggerated into a schism, which lasted into the 7th cent. Bonosus and his followers were widely accredited with heretical views respecting the conception and person of Christ. Mercator calls him an Ebionite, and a precursor of Nestorius (*Dissert.* i. *de Haeres. Nestor.* § 6, ii. 315). But the Bonosians were more usually charged with Photinianism (Gennadius, *de Eccl. Dogm.* c. 52, "Photiniani qui nunc vocantur Bonosiaci"). Whether these charges were well grounded, or were based on the general unpopularity of the sect, it is impossible to determine. Their baptism was pronounced valid by the 17th canon of the second synod of Arles, A.D. 445, on the ground that, like the Arians, they baptized in the name of the Trinity (Labbe, iv. 1013). But Gregory the Great, in a letter to the Irish bishops (*Ep.* lib. ix. 61), includes them in those whose baptism the church rejected because the name of the Trinity was not invoked (cf. Gennadius, *de Eccl. Dogm.*, *u.s.*). They on their part rebaptized those who joined them. The third council of Orleans, A.D. 538, ordained that they who did so should be arrested by the royal officers and punished. The Bonosians were anathematized by pope Vigilius (*Ep.* xv.; Labbe, v. 333). [E.V.]

Bosphorius, bp. of Colonia in Cappadocia Secunda, a confidential friend and correspondent of Gregory Nazianzen and Basil the Great. His episcopate was prolonged through at least 48 years (Pallad. c. 20, p. 203), and must have commenced in 360. From the letters of Gregory we learn that he and Bosphorius had lived together in youth, laboured together, and grown old together (Greg. *Ep.* 141, 227). He had great influence over the gentler nature of Gregory, who speaks of him with the highest respect, both for the purity of his faith and the sanctity of his life, as well as for his successful exertions in bringing back wanderers to the truth, acknowledging the benefit he had derived, both as hearer and teacher, from him (*Ep.* 164, 225). He persuaded Gregory to remain at Nazianzus after his father's death, and to accept the unwelcome charge of the see of Constantinople. Gregory bitterly complained of his unscrupulous importunity, but yielded (*Ep.* 14, 15). In 383 Bosphorius was accused of unsoundness in the faith—a charge which greatly distressed Gregory, who wrote urgently in his behalf to Theodore of Tyana, Nectarius, and Eutropius (*Ep.* 225, 227, 164). Basil addressed to him a letter denying the charge of having excommunicated his bp. Dianius (*Ep.* li.). He attended the second oecumenical council at Constantinople in 381 (Labbe, ii. 956). Palladius speaks with gratitude of the sympathy shewn by him towards the bishops banished in 406 for adherence to Chrysostom's cause (Pallad. c. 20, p. 203). [E.V.]

Brigida (5), V., abbess of Kildare—Feb. 1, 523. The designation "Fiery Dart" seems peculiarly appropriate for "the Mary of Ireland," who, although her fame on the continent is eclipsed by the greater reputation there of her namesake the widow-saint of Sweden, yet stands forth in history with a very marked individuality, though the histories that have come down to us are mainly devoted to a narrative of the signs and wonders which God wrought by her. As to her Acts, Colgan has published six Lives in his *Trias Thaumaturga*, and the Bollandists five. It is more difficult to trace the historical points in St. Bridget's life than to recount the legendary accretions which testify to a basis of fact, could we but find it after so many centuries. In the legend there is no little beauty, and in almost all we find an undercurrent of true human feeling and deep Christian discernment. (See some of them given at length in Bp. Forbes's *Kal. Scott. Saints*, 288 seq., from Boëce, *Breviary of Aberdeen*, and Colgan's *Tr. Thaum.* For a full and critical account of her life, see Lanigan, *Eccl. Hist. Ir.* i. 68, 335, and chaps. viii. and ix. *passim*; Todd, *Book of Hymns*, i. 65 seq.; O'Hanlon, *Ir. Saints*, ii. 1 seq.; Baring-Gould, *Lives of the Saints*, ii. 14 seq.) Her chief residence was the monastery of Kildare, "cella quercus," which she founded; but affiliated houses of both men and women ("de utroque sexu") were raised all over the country, she being abbess above all other abbesses, and the bishop with her at Kildare being similarly above all bishops in her other monasteries. Montalembert (*Monks of the West*, Edin. ii. 393-395) gives an account of St. Brigida and her monasteries, and places her birth at A.D. 467 and her death at A.D. 525. He says, "There are still 18 parishes in Ireland which bear the name of Kilbride or the Church of Bridget" (*ib.* ii. p. 395, n.). The Irish annals, however, vary as to the date of her death, but the most probable, and resting on highest authority, is A.D. 523 (O'Conor, *Rer. Hib. Scrip.* iv. 13; Bp. Forbes, *Kal. Scott. Saints*, 287). In Scotland the cultus of this saint was very extensive, her dedications being chiefly found in the parts nearest to Ireland and under Irish influence. (For a short list see Bp. Forbes, *Kal. Scott. Saints*, 290-291.) [A.P.F.]

C

Caecilia (1), St., a Roman lady, one of the four principal virgins and martyrs of the Western Church, who is commemorated in both the Latin and Greek churches on Nov. 22, but of whom we have hardly any authentic account.

The veneration paid to her can be traced to a very early period. Her martyrdom and that of her three companions is referred to in nearly all the most ancient Latin breviaries and missals—*e.g.* in the Sacramentary of pope Gregory; the breviary and missal of Milan ascribed to St. Ambrose; the Mozarabic or Spanish liturgy, with proper prayers and prefaces; and a grand office for her feast is contained in the Gallican missal, which is believed to have been in use in Gaul from the 6th cent. down to the time of Charlemagne. Her name appears in the Martyrology attributed to Jerome, in that of Bede, and in all the others, and her martyrdom is placed at Rome. Yet it is very difficult, says Tillemont, to find her true place in the chronology.

The earliest writer who mentions her is Fortunatus, bp. of Poictiers, at the end of the 6th cent., who states that she died in Sicily between A.D. 176 and 180, under the emperor M. Aurelius or Commodus. The Life of St. Caecilia by Symeon Metaphrastes, a hagiographer of the 10th cent., makes her contemporary with Urban, and places her martyrdom at Rome under Alexander Severus, *c.* 230; the Greek menologies place it under Diocletian (284-305). On the other hand, the Roman calendar drawn up at Rome under pope Liberius, *c.* A.D. 352-366, contains no mention of her. This, indeed, is not a complete list of martyrs, but a list of the chief feasts (Rossi, i. 116). Her body must, however, have been there not long after this period; for in the time of pope Symmachus (A.D. 498) there was a church of St. Caecilia at Rome, in which he held a council.

The account of her life and martyrdom by Symeon Metaphrastes, to be found in Surius, is of no authority. The narrative is full of marvels and improbabilities, and the internal evidence alone is quite sufficient to prove its legendary character, though some critics have of late endeavoured to uphold its credibility, and to refer its compilation in its present form to the commencement of the 5th cent. (cf. Ceillier, *Hist. des Auteurs Sacrés*, vol. ii. Paris, 1859, and see below). There can be little doubt that these Acts of St. Caecilia were composed to be read in the church of the saint on the day of her feast. According to the legend, she was born at Rome of a noble family. She resolved, from love to her Lord, to devote herself to Him by a vow of perpetual virginity. Her parents wished her to marry Valerian, a young Roman, who at that time was not a Christian. She went through the marriage ceremonies; but when alone with her young husband, told him of her vow, and Valerian allowed her to keep it. At her entreaty, he sought out the retreat of Urban, and received baptism at his hands. On returning to his spouse, wearing the white robe of a neophyte, he found her praying in her chamber, and an angel of God at her side. In answer to Valerian's prayer, the angel promised that his brother, Tiburtius, should become a Christian, and foretold that both brothers should receive the crown of martyrdom. In A.D. 230 Turcius Almachius, prefect of the city, took advantage of the emperor's absence to give free vent to his hatred of the Christians, and daily put many to death. Valerian and Tiburtius were soon brought before his tribunal. After being scourged, the two brothers were commanded to offer incense to the gods. On refusing, they were condemned to be beheaded and given in charge to Maximus. So moved was he by their exhortations that in the night he and all his family, together with the lictors, believed and were baptized. On the morrow his prisoners were beheaded at the place called Pagus Triopius on the Via Appia at the fourth mile from Rome. When the news reached the prefect that Maximus also had become a Christian, he ordered him to be scourged to death with leaden balls. Soon afterwards he sent his officers to Caecilia and bade her sacrifice to the gods. As she refused, he commanded her to be shut up in her bath, and that the furnace should be heated with wood seven times hotter than it was wont to be. But a heavenly dew falling upon the spouse of Christ refreshed and cooled her body, and preserved her from harm. A day and a night the prefect waited for news of her death. Then he sent one of his soldiers to behead her; but though the sword smote her neck thrice, the executioner could not cut off her head, and he departed, leaving her on the floor of her bath bathed in blood. For three days longer she lived, never ceasing to exhort the people whom she loved to continue steadfast in the Lord, and watching over the distribution of her last alms. Having given her house to the church, she gave up her spirit into the hands of the living God. Urban and his deacons buried her in the cemetery of Calixtus on the Via Appia near the third milestone. Her house he consecrated to God as a church for ever. It is alleged that her body was found at Rome by pope Paschal I. (A.D. 821), in the cemetery of Praetextatus, adjoining that of Calixtus on the Via Appia, and that it was removed by him to the church of St. Caecilia, which he was then rebuilding, and which stands, as is said, on the site of her house, at the extremity of the Trastevere. Here, it is said, her body was again discovered at the end of the 16th cent. in the time of Clement VIII. Baronius has given a long account of the circumstances connected with this pretended discovery, of which he was a witness (*s. ann.* 821).

The legend of this saint has furnished the subject of several remarkable pictures. The oldest representation of her is a rude picture or drawing on the wall of the catacomb called the cemetery of San Lorenzo, of the date probably of the 6th or 7th cent. (See d'Agincourt, plate xi.) In the 13th cent. Cimabue painted an altar-piece, representing different episodes in the life of the saint for the church dedicated to her at Florence. In both these she appears with the martyr's crown. In fact, before the 15th cent. St. Caecilia is seldom depicted with her musical instruments. She has generally the martyr's palm and the crown of red or white roses. When she came to be regarded as the patron saint of musicians is unknown, nor have we any record of her use of instruments of music. The most celebrated representation of St. Caecilia as patroness of this art is the picture by Raphael (*c.* A.D. 1513), now in the gallery of Bologna.

In 1584, in the time of pope Pius V., an academy of music was founded at Rome, and placed under the tutelage of St. Caecilia. Thenceforward she came to be more and more regarded as queen of harmony, and Dryden's well-known ode has rendered her familiar to us in this character.

For a more detailed account, we may refer to the following: *de Vitis Sanctorum*, ed. Surius (Venice, 1581), tom. vi. p. 161, *s.d.* Nov. 22; *Acta Sanctorum*, by the Bollandists, *s.d.* April 14, p. 204; *Baronii Annales s. an.* A.D. 821; Tillemont, vol. iii. pp. 259-689; *S. Caeciliae Acta a Laderchio* (Rome, 1722), 2 vols. 4to, incorporating the work of Bosio, with large additions; *Sacred and Legendary Art*, by Mrs. Jameson, 3rd ed. (Lond. 1857), pp. 583-600; Ceillier, *Histoire des Auteurs*

Sacrés, vol. ii. (Paris, 1859); *S. Cécile*, par Dom. Guéranger (Paris, 1874). [T.D.C.M.]

Here may be added the ingenious explanation, given by bp. Fitzgerald, of how St. Caecilia became regarded as the patron of music. She is described as steeling her heart at her marriage festivities against all the allurements to sensual pleasure, and among these, special mention is made of the "symphonia instrumentorum" to which she refused to hearken; but "organis cantantibus die nuptiarum" she made melody in her heart to God, saying, "May my heart and body be undefiled." The necessities of the pictorial art demanded that each saint should be depicted with an appropriate and distinctive symbol. Bp. Fitzgerald suggests that St. Caecilia was hence represented in early pictures with the organ prominent in her Acts; and that she was thence imagined to be a musician by those who did not understand that she was only represented with an organ as other saints are depicted with the instrument of torture by which they suffered. We may certainly believe that Dryden's "drew an angel down" had its origin in a misunderstanding of pictures. The Acts relate that on her wedding night she told Valerianus that she was under the protection of an angel who would punish him if he did not respect her chastity, and whom he could see for himself if he would be baptized. This no doubt is the angel who appears in pictures of St. Caecilia, and there is no ground for the idea that the angel came down to listen to her music.

Erbes (*Zeitschrift f. Kirchengeschichte*, ix. 1) thinks that the Acts of St. Caecilia are not earlier than the end of the 5th cent. They not only exhibit a use of St. Augustine's work on the Trinity which appeared in A.D. 416, but coincidences in language, as well as in substance, make it probable that the whole story of Caecilia is derived from the story of Martinianus and Maxima told by Victor Vitensis, I. 30. This would bring down the date of the Acts to *c.* A.D. 490. Erbes remarks that the original day of commemoration of St. Caecilia was Sept. 16: Nov. 22 really commemorates the dedication of the church of St. Caecilia, which probably took place under Sixtus III. between 434 and 440. Concerning the neighbourhood of the burial-place of St. Caecilia in the catacombs to that of certain popes, Erbes holds that in the year 236 a suitable burial-place was being prepared for the body of Pontianus, then brought from Sardinia, as well as for that of Anteros who had died in Rome, that the site was furnished by the Caecilian family, and that in order to make room for the two bishops the body of Caecilia was moved to an adjacent side chamber. As to how Caecilia suffered martyrdom we have no authentic information. [G.S.]

Caecilianus (2), first archdeacon, then (A.D. 311) bp., of Carthage. Of importance in connexion with the Donatist controversy. When archdeacon, he resolutely supported his bishop Mensurius in opposing the fanatical craving for martyrdom. The Christianity of N. Africa exhibited an extravagance in this respect which reached its height after Diocletian's persecution. Men courted death that they might be honoured as martyrs and confessors; some, without doubt, in a spirit which commands our respect, but others in a spirit which fostered the supposition that the martyr's cross would wash away for eternity the misery, follies, sins, and crimes of a whole life.

On the death of Mensurius, Caecilian was nominated as his successor. The part he had taken against the would-be martyrs was then brought up against him. The religious world of Carthage divided itself broadly into two sections, the moderate and rigoristic parties, or the supporters and opponents of the principles of Caecilian. At the head of the latter was a devout and wealthy lady named Lucilla, who had been severely rebuked by the archdeacon for superstitious veneration for martyrs' relics. The rigoristic party wished to fill the vacant see with one of their own followers. Caecilian's party hastened matters, and the archdeacon was consecrated by Felix, bp. of Aptunga; whether in the presence of any Numidian bishops or not seems uncertain. Secundus, primate of Numidia and bp. of Tigisis, was presently invited to Carthage by the rigoristic party. He came, attended by 70 bishops, and cited Caecilian before them. Felix of Aptunga was denounced as a "traditor" (*i.e.* one who had delivered up the sacred writings in his possession), and consequently it was claimed that any ordination performed by him was invalid. Caecilian himself was charged with unnecessary and heartless severity to those who had visited the confessors in prison; he was denounced as a "tyrannus" and a "carnifex." He declined to appear before an assembly so prejudiced; but professed his willingness to satisfy them on all personal matters, and offered, if right was on their side, to lay down his episcopal office, and submit to re-ordination. Secundus and the Numidian bishops answered by excommunicating him and his party, and ordaining as bishop the reader Majorinus, a member of Lucilla's household.

The church of N. Africa now became a prey to schism. The party of Caecilian broke off from that of Majorinus, and the Christian world was scandalized by fulminations, excommunications, invectives, charges, and countercharges. Both parties confidently anticipated the support of the state; but Constantine, now emperor of this part of the Roman world, took the side of the Caecilianists. In his largesse to the Christians of the province, and in his edicts favourable to the church there, he expressly stipulated that the party of Majorinus should be excluded: their views were, in his opinion, the "madness" of men of "unsound mind." The rigoristic party appealed to the justice of the emperor, and courted full inquiry to be conducted in Gaul—at a distance, that is, from the spot where passions and convictions were so strong and one-sided. A council met A.D. 313 at Rome, in the Lateran, presided over by Melchiades (Miltiades), bp. of Rome, who had as his assessors the bishops of Cologne, Arles, and seventeen others. Caecilian appeared with ten bishops; Donatus, bp. of Casae Nigrae, in Numidia, headed the party of Majorinus. The personal charges against

Caecilian were examined and dismissed, and his party proclaimed the representatives of the orthodox Catholic church; Donatus himself was declared to have violated the laws of the church, and his followers were to be allowed to retain their dignity and office only on condition of reunion with Caecilian's party. The bitterness of this decision was modified by Caecilian's friendly proposal of compromise; but his advances were rejected, and the cry of injustice raised. It was wrong, the rigorists pleaded, that the opinion of twenty should overrule that of seventy; and they demanded first that imperial commissioners should investigate matters at Carthage itself, and that then a council should be summoned to examine their report, and decide upon its information. Constantine met their wish. Jurists went to Carthage, collected documents, tabulated the statements of witnesses, and laid their report before the bishops assembled (A.D. 314) at Arles. This council, presided over by Marinus, bishop of the see, and composed of about 200 persons, was the most important ecclesiastical assembly the Christian world had yet seen; and its decisions have been of permanent value to the church. As regarded Caecilian personally, the validity of his ordination was confirmed, the charge raised against his consecrator, Felix, being proved baseless; and as regarded the general questions debated—such as traditorship, its proof or disproof; ordination by traditors, when valid or not; baptism and re-baptism—canons of extreme importance were passed. [ARLES, SYNOD OF, in *D. C. A.*]

The temper displayed by the victors was not calculated to soothe the conquered; and an appeal was at once made from the council to the emperor himself. Constantine was irritated; but, after some delay, ordered the discussion of the question before himself personally. This occurred at Milan (A.D. 316). The emperor confirmed the previous decisions of Rome and Arles, and followed up his judgment by laws and edicts confiscating the goods of the party of Majorinus, depriving them of their churches, and threatening to punish their rebellion with death.

From this time the schism in the N. African church lost its purely personal aspect, and became a stern religious contest on questions of discipline. [DONATISM.] Caecilian lived to *c.* A.D. 345. (For authorities, etc., see DONATISM.) [J.M.F.]

Caesarius (2), St., of Nazianzus, physician, son of Gregory bp. of Nazianzus, brother of St. Gregory of the same place, and youngest of the family, born probably *c.* A.D. 330. His death occurred in A.D. 368 or 369. The name is simply a derivative from Caesar, originally adopted in compliment to the reigning family.

Authorities.—The funeral oration by his brother, St. Gregory Nazianzen (the 7th, in some ed. the 10th); two letters addressed by Gregory to Caesarius and one to the *Praeses* Sophronius (numbered 17, 18, 19, or, more commonly, 50, 51, 52), and a few lines in the *Carmen de Vitâ Suâ* of the same. Photius, *Bibliotheca Cod.* 210 (p. 168 ed. Bekker, Berolini, 1824).

Life.—According to the testimony of his brother, Caesarius owed much to the careful training received from his parents. He betook himself to Alexandria, "the workshop of every sort of education," for better instruction in physical science than he could obtain in Palestine. There he behaved as a model student, being very careful in the matter of companionship, and earnest in pursuit of knowledge, more especially of geometry and astronomy. This last-named science he studied, says his panegyrist, in such wise as to gain the good without the evil—a remark readily intelligible to those who are aware how deeply a fatalistic astrology was at that period associated with the study of astronomy.

Refusing a post of honour and emolument at Byzantium, he came home for a time, but returned to the court and was much honoured by Julian. There is a slight, but not perhaps irreconcilable, discrepancy between the funeral oration delivered by Gregory and the letter (17 or 51) which Gregory addressed to his brother. The oration seems to depict Caesarius as from the first spurning all offers of Julian, but the letter severely rebukes Caesarius for becoming a member of the imperial household, and taking charge of the treasury. Such a step is called a scandal in a bishop's son, and a great grief to his mother. Caesarius, however, finally avowed himself a Christian, and broke with Julian. His conduct, together with that of Gregory, caused Julian to exclaim, "Oh happy father! oh unhappy sons!" Under subsequent emperors, more especially under Valens, Caesarius more than regained his former honours, and became a quaestor of Bithynia. A remarkable escape from a terrible earthquake at Nicaea, apparently *c.* A.D. 367 or 368, to which many distinguished men fell victims, induced Caesarius, at his brother's suggestion, to arrange for retirement from worldly cares. He received Baptism, and soon after died.

The Πύσπεις or *Quaestiones* (*sive Dialogi*) *de Rebus Divinis*, attributed to this physician, may be safely ascribed to *some* Caesarius. But the name was not an uncommon one, and some considerations seem to shew that the author was not Caesarius of Nazianzus. Photius treats the supposed authorship as merely a current unexamined tradition, and the book refers to Maximus, who lived subsequently. [J.G.C.]

Caesarius (3), St., sometimes called of Châlons (*Cabillonensis seu Cabellinensis*) from his birthplace Châlons-sur-Saône; but more usually known as Caesarius of Arles (*Arelatensis*) from his see, which he occupied for forty years. He was certainly the foremost ecclesiastic in the Gaul of his own age. The date of his birth lies between A.D. 468 and 470; the date of his death is Aug. 27, 542.

Authorities.—(1) The biography, written by his admiring disciple, St. Cyprian, bp. of Toulon (*Tolonensis*) with the aid of other ecclesiastics (ed. by d'Achery and Mabillon in the *Acta Sanctorum Ord. S. Benedicti*, Venet. 1733, tom. i. p. 636, et sqq., also in the Bollandists' *Acta Sanctorum* under date of Aug. 27). (2) His will, first published by Baronius (*Annal.* tom. vi. ad ann. 508) from archives preserved at Arles; also given by Surius, *l.c.*; a document of some interest for the student of Roman law, but thought by

Brugsch (archives of the Society of Ancient History) to be a forgery of Hincmar of Rheims. (3) Acts of various councils, over all of which Caesarius presided (Labbe, *Concilia*, tom. ii. pp. 995-1098, ed. Parisiis, 1714). (4) The *Regula ad Monachos* and *Regula ad Virgines*, drawn up by him for a monastery and a convent of his own foundation (ed. by Holstenius in his *Codex Regularum*, and by P. de Cointe in his *Annales Ecclesiastici Francorum*). Trithemius, fixing the date of Caesarius much too late, fell into the error of supposing him to be a Benedictine. (5) His sermons. Of these 40 were pubd. at Basle in 1558; 46 in a *Bibliotheca Patrum*, ed. at Leyden in 1677; 14 more in another *Bibl. Patr.* of Gallandi, Venice 1776 (cf. Oudin in *Comment. de Script. Eccles.* vol. i. p. 1339); and 102, formerly ascribed to St. Augustine, are by the Benedictine editors assigned to Caesarius (Appendix to tom. v. of the works of St. Augustine). Others have been separately pubd. by Baluz; but Neander justly remarks that a complete collection of his sermons, conveying so much important information respecting the character of Caesarius and his times, still remains a *desideratum* (*Church Hist.* vol. v. p. 4, note). Cf. also A. Malnory, *St. Césaire, évêque d'Arles* (Paris, 1894); Arnold, *Cesarius von Arelate*, (Leipz. 1894).

Life.—Caesarius was born at Châlons of pious parents. His sister Caesaria afterwards presided over the convent which he founded, and to her he addressed his *Regula ad Virgines*. At the age of thirteen he betook himself to the famous monastery of Lerins (*Lerinum*), where he rapidly became master of all which the learning and discipline of the place could impart. Having injured his health by austerities, he was sent to Arles (*Arelate*) to recruit. There the bp. Eonus, having made his acquaintance, ordained him deacon and then presbyter. For three years he presided over a monastery in Arles; but of this building no vestige is now left.

At the death of Eonus the clergy, citizens, and persons in authority proceeded, as Eonus himself had suggested, to elect Caesarius, sincerely against his own wish, to the vacant see. He was consecrated in A.D. 502, being probably about 33 years of age. In the fulfilment of his new duties he was courageous and unworldly, but yet exhibited great power of kindly adaptation. He took great pains to induce the laity to join in the sacred offices, and encouraged inquiry into points not made clear in his sermons. He also bade them study Holy Scripture at home, and treat the word of God with the same reverence as the sacraments. He was specially zealous in redeeming captives, even selling church ornaments for this purpose.

A notary named Licinianus accused Caesarius to Alaric as one who desired to subjugate the *civitas* of Arles to the Burgundian rule. Caesarius was exiled to Bordeaux, but was speedily, on the discovery of his innocence, allowed to return. He interceded for the life of his calumniator. Later, when Arles was besieged by Theodoric, apparently *c.* A.D. 512, he was again accused of treachery and imprisoned. An interview with the Ostrogothic king at Ravenna in A.D. 513 speedily dispelled these troubles, and the remainder of his episcopate was passed in peace.

The directions of Caesarius for the conduct of monks and nuns have been censured as pedantic and minute. They certainly yielded to the spread of the rising Benedictine rule, but must be judged by their age and in the light of the whole spirit of monasticism.

As the occupant of an important see, the bishop of Arles exercised considerable influence, official as well as personal. Caesarius was liberal in the loan of sermons, and sent suggestions for discourses to priests and even bishops living in Spain, Italy, Gaul, and France (*i.e.* the province known as the Isle of France). The great doctrinal question of his age and country was that of semi-Pelagianism. Caesarius, though evidently a disciple of St. Augustine, displayed in this respect considerable independence of thought. His vigorous denial of anything like predestination to evil has caused a difference in the honour paid to his memory, according as writers incline respectively towards the Jesuit or Jansenist views concerning divine grace.

The most important local council over which Caesarius presided was that of Orange. Its statements on the subject of grace and free agency have been justly eulogized by modern historians (see, *e.g.*, Canon Bright's *Church History*, ch. xi. *ad fin.*). The following propositions are laid down in canon 25: "This also do we believe, in accordance with the Catholic faith, that after grace received through baptism, all the baptized are able and ought, with the aid and co-operation of Christ, to fulfil all duties needful for salvation, provided they are willing to labour faithfully. But that some men have been predestinated to evil by divine power, we not only do not believe, but if there be those who are willing to believe so evil a thing, we say to them with all abhorrence *anathema*. This also do we profess and believe to our soul's health, that in every good work, it is not *we* who begin, and are afterwards assisted by Divine mercy, but that God Himself, with no preceding merits on our part, first inspires within us faith and love." On the express ground that these doctrines are as needful for the laity as for the clergy, certain distinguished laymen (*illustres ac magnifici viri*) were invited to sign these canons. They are accordingly subscribed by 8 laymen, and at least 12 bishops, including Caesarius. [PELAGIANISM.]

As a preacher, Caesarius displayed great knowledge of Holy Scripture, and was eminently practical in his exhortations. Besides reproving ordinary vices of humanity, he had often to contend against lingering pagan superstitions, as auguries, heathen rites on the calends, etc. His sermons on O.T. are not critical, but dwell on its typical aspects.

Some rivalry appears to have existed in the 6th cent. between the sees of Arles and Vienne, but was adjusted by pope Leo, whose adjustment was confirmed by Symmachus. Caesarius was in favour at Rome. A book he wrote against the semi-Pelagians, entitled *de Gratiâ et Libero Arbitrio*, was sanctioned by pope Felix; and the canons passed at Orange were approved by Boniface II. The learned antiquary Thomassin believed him to have been the first Western bishop who received a pall from the pope. Guizot, in his *Civilisation en France*, cites part of one of his sermons as that of a representative man; while Neander has nothing but eulogy for his "unwearied, active, and pious zeal, ready for every sacrifice in the spirit of love," and his moderation on the controversy concerning semi-Pelagianism. This is indeed the great glory of Caesarius. He more than anticipates the famous picture drawn by Chaucer of a teacher, earnest, sincere, and humble, but never sparing reproof where needed. [J.G.C.]

Caesarius (7). Among the works attributed to Chrysostom is a treatise entitled *ad Caesarium Monachum Epistola contra Apollinaristas*. We only possess it in a Latin translation, though a few fragments of the Greek original are found in Anastasius and John Damascene and elsewhere. This tract, the literary history of which is very curious, is of disputed authenticity. If it is genuine, Caesarius had embraced a religious life from his childhood and become a monk; his piety had secured Chrysostom's affection, and at one time he had lived with him. Meeting with some Apollinarists, he purchased a book by Apollinarius which led him eagerly to embrace those views. The intelligence caused great grief to Chrysostom, then in exile at Cucusus, who sent him this letter to refute the Apollinarian heresy. It contains a celebrated passage illlustrating the doctrine of the two distinct natures in the one person of Jesus Christ by reference to the holy Eucharist, in which he speaks of the nature of bread as remaining in that which by the sanctifying grace of God is freed from the appellation of bread and thought worthy to be called the body of the Lord. This passage was adduced in controversy about the year 1548 by Peter Martyr, who deposited a transcript of it in archbp. Cranmer's library. After Cranmer's death this document was lost, and Martyr was accused of having forged it (Perron, *de l'Euchar.* 381-3). His reputation was cleared by the rediscovery by Emeric Bigot, in a Florentine library, of doubtless the very MS. which Martyr, himself a Florentine, had used. Bigot in 1680 printed the epistle with Palladius's Life of Chrysostom. Previous to publication, through the influence of two censors of the Sorbonne, Louis XIV. ordered the leaves containing the letter to be cancelled. For an account of the mutilation see Mendham's *Index of Pope Gregory XVI.* xxxii.-xxxiv. But Bigot having made known his discovery to literary friends, Allix (preface to Anastasius in *Hexaemeron*, 1682) protested against the suppression, and the cancelled leaves were printed by le Moyne, *Varia Sacra*, 1685, by Wake, 1686, and by Basnage, 1687. The Jesuit Harduin published the epistle in 1689, accepting it as Chrysostom's, and vindicating the consistency of its doctrine with that of his church. It is accepted as genuine by Tillemont and Du Pin. The genuineness was first assailed by Le Quien (1712) in the preface to his edition of John of Damascus, and his arguments were adopted and enlarged by Montfaucon. Maffei found a Greek fragment also at Florence, professing to be from Chrysostom, the first sentence of which is identical with one in this letter, but proceeding to illustrate its doctrine by two similes not found in the Latin. The extract was printed by Basnage in Canisius's *Lectiones Antiquae* (Antwerp, 1725), pp. 283-287. The second paragraph may be taken from a different work, but the MS. gives no indication of a change of author. Perhaps the Latin does not represent the whole of the letter. Against the genuineness it is urged that Caesarius is not mentioned elsewhere by Chrysostom, though the letter implies that they had been intimate from youth; that the style (if so little of the Greek allows us to judge) is rugged and abrupt, and the tone more scholastic than is common with Chrysostom; that the earliest Greek author who quotes it as Chrysostom's is of the 7th cent., though we should expect it to have been used in the Eutychian disputes, and quoted in the Acts of the 4th, 5th, and 6th councils. Le Quien also urged that language is used which is not heard of until employed by Cyril of Alexandria in controversy with Nestorius. Montfaucon, however, has produced precedents for much of this language from Athanasius, and has clearly proved that the letter was directed not against Eutychianism, but against Apollinarianism; and with much probability he identifies the work assailed with a work of Apollinarius quoted by Eulogius (ap. Photium, Cod. 230, p. 849). This being so, we are more inclined to accept the letter as written while the Apollinarian disputes were raging than, as Montfaucon conjectures, forged a century or two afterwards for use in the Eutychian controversy, since one of the arguments against its genuineness is that there is no evidence that it ever was so used. On the controversy as to the genuineness, see the authorities referred to by Fabricius, *Bibl. Gr.*, ed. Harles, i. 699; Chrys. iii. 747-760, and xiii. 496, ed. Migne; iii. 736-746, ed. Montfaucon; Tillemont, vii. 629, and xi. 340-343; Routh, *Opuscula*, ii. (479-488). [E.V.]

Cainites. [CARPOCRATES.]

Caius (2), an ecclesiastical writer at the beginning of the 3rd cent., according to late authority, a presbyter of the Roman church. Eusebius mentions but one work of his, to which he refers four times (*H. E.* ii. 25, iii. 28, 31, vi. 20), and from which he gives some short extracts. This was a dialogue purporting to be a report of a disputation held at Rome during the episcopate of Zephyrinus (A.D. 201-219) between Caius and Proclus, a leader of the sect of Montanists. [PROCLUS.]

This dialogue is mentioned by the following writers, who may, however, have only known it from the account given by Eusebius:—Hieron. *de Vir. Ill.* 59; Theod. *Haer. Fab.* ii. 3; iii. 2, where the present text, doubtless by a transcriber's error, reads Patroclus instead of Proclus (Niceph. Call. *H. E.* iv. 12, 20; Photius, *Bibl.* 48). Only the last of these attributes any other work to Caius. Theodoret says that he wrote against Cerinthus, but is probably referring to a part of the dialogue in question.

In the short fragments preserved, Proclus defends the prophesyings of his sect by appealing to the four daughters of Philip, who with their father were buried at Hierapolis; Caius, on the other hand, offers to shew his antagonist at the Vatican and on the Appian Way the tombs of the apostles "who founded this church." That Caius should have conducted a disputation at Rome does not of itself prove that he, any more than Proclus, permanently resided there. Yet the expression cited conveys the impression that he did; and Eusebius was apparently of that opinion, for elsewhere (vi. 20), having mentioned that Caius only counted St. Paul's epistles as thirteen, omitting that to the Hebrews, he adds that even in his own time "some of the Romans" did not ascribe that epistle to the apostle. It is just possible that we are still in possession of the list of genuine apostolic writings which Eusebius (*l.c.*) intimates that Caius gave, in order to rebuke the rashness of his opponents in framing new Scriptures. Muratori attributed to Caius the celebrated fragment on the canon published by him, which concludes with a rejection of Montanist documents. [MURATORIAN FRAGMENT.] But it is difficult to believe that if this were the list referred to by Eusebius, he would not have quoted it more fully. Among the heretical writings rejected by Caius was a book of Revelations (Eus. ii. 25) purporting to be written by a great apostle and ascribed by Caius to Cerinthus, in which the author professes to have been shewn by angels that after the resurrection Christ's kingdom should be earthly, that men should inhabit Jerusalem, should be the slaves of lusts and pleasures, and should spend a thousand years in marriage festivities. The strongest reason for thinking that the book intended is the canonical book of the Revelation is that Dionysius of Alexandria (Eus. *H. E.* vii. 25) asserts that some of his predecessors had maintained that the Apocalypse is the work of Cerinthus, and describes their views in language strongly resembling that of Caius.

There had been much speculation respecting Caius himself (*s.v. D. C. B.* 4-vol. ed.); and Lightfoot, in his *Apostolic Fathers* (Clement of Rome, vol. ii. p. 377), questions his existence. But Dr. Gwynn, of Dublin, pub. in *Hermathena* VI. some fragments of *Capita adv. Caium*, written by Hippolytus, which he had discovered in Cod. Mus. Brit. Orient. 560. These passages shew that he had attacked the Apocalypse of St. John, and treated the book as inconsistent with the Holy Scriptures. Harnack (Herzog.³) thinks it not improbable that he had treated the Apocalypse as a work of Cerinthus; and as he would be at one in this opinion with the Alogi of Asia Minor, a connexion between him and them may be supposed. Nothing more is known with certainty of him (cf. Zahn, *Gesch. des N. T. Kanons*, ii. 985 seq.). [G.S. AND ED.]

Caius (3). Pope from Dec. 17 (16?) A.D. 283 (9 or 10 days after the death of his predecessor Eutychianus), to Apr. 22, A.D. 296, *i.e.* for 12 years 4 months 1 week (*Pontifical*, Bucher, p. 272), but only for 11 years according to Anastasius (c. 24) and to most Latins, and for 15 years according to Eusebius, who speaks of him as a contemporary (*H. E.* vii. 32; Chron. 284). He is probably the same as Caius the deacon, imprisoned with pope Stephen, A.D. 257 (Anastas. c. 24). Just as he was raised to the chair, the stern old Roman Carus died mysteriously in a thunderstorm in the East, and his profligate son Carinus succeeded to the empire at Rome. These events would seem to make a persecution, such as is assigned to this period by various martyr Acts, not in itself improbable, and though the Acts in question are untrustworthy (see Tillemont, iv. 565), we are hardly justified in taking Eusebius for a witness to the contrary, as far as concerns the West. The probability is confirmed by the delay of the funeral of Eutychianus till July 25, 284 (v. Rossi, ii. 378). The persecution is not represented as general, but as aimed at a few obnoxious devotees, and Caius does not appear as leading, accompanying, or inciting them, but only as exercising a fatherly supervision. Probably the persecution continued for some time under Diocletian. The early Pontifical, as well as Anastasius, makes Caius of Dalmatian origin and cousin to this emperor. The Acts of St. Susanna confirm this, but are untrustworthy (Till. iv. 760). Caius is said in the early Pontifical to have avoided persecution by hiding in the crypts. During his latter years the Church must have enjoyed peace. He is said by Anastasius to have established the 6 orders of usher, reader, exorcist, subdeacon, deacon, and presbyter, as preliminary stages necessary before attaining the episcopate, and also to have divided Rome into regions assigned to the deacons. He is said to have sent Protus and Januarius on a mission to Sardinia (*Mart. Rom.* Baron. Oct. 25). He died in peace according to the 6th-cent. Pontifical, and is not called a martyr by any one earlier than Bede and Anastasius. He was succeeded by Marcellinus. A decretal is ascribed to him. From a confusion between the calends of March and of May in the *Mart. Hieron.*, Rabanus assigns his death, and Notker his burial, to Feb. 20 (Rossi, ii. 104). His commemoration on July 1 in the *Mart. Hieron.* is unexplained (*ib.* p. 105). He was the last of the 12 popes buried in the crypt of Sixtus, in the cemetery of Callistus (*ib.* p. 105). He is therefore mentioned again, Aug. 9, at which date a copy of the inscription set up by Sixtus III. was placed in the margin of the ancient martyrology (*ib.* pp. 33-46). [E.B.B.]

Calandio or Calendio (Καλανδίων), succeeded Stephen II. as bp. of Antioch, A.D. 481. He owed his promotion to the episcopate to the emperor Zeno and Acacius, bp. of Constantinople; but the exact circumstances of his appointment are uncertain. There is a large body of evidence (not, however, to be admitted without grave question) that Calandio's election was of the same uncanonical character as that of his predecessor in the see [STEPHEN II.]; and that being at Constantinople on business connected with the church of Antioch at the time of the vacancy of the see, he was chosen bishop, and ordained by Acacius; but the letter of pope Simplicius to Acacius, dated July 15, A.D. 482, conveying his sanction of Calandio's election (Labbe, *Conc.* iv. 1035), suggests a possible confusion between the election of Calandio and of Stephen II.

Calandio commenced his episcopate by excommunicating his theological opponents. He refused communion with all who declined to anathematize **Peter the Fuller.** Timothy the Weasel, and the Encyclic of Basiliscus condemning the decisions of the council of Chalcedon (Evagr. *H. E.* iii. 10; Niceph. *H. E.* xv. 28). He is reported to have endeavoured to counteract the Monophysite bias given to the *Trisagion* by Peter the Fuller in the addition of the words ὁ σταυρωθεὶς δι' ἡμᾶς, by prefixing the clause Χριστὲ Βασιλεῦ (Theod. Lector. p. 556 B.) Calandio translated the remains of Eustathius, the banished bp. of Antioch, with the permission of Zeno, from Philippi in Macedonia, where he had died, to his own city—a tardy recognition of the falsehood of the charges against Eustathius, which had the happy result of reuniting to the church the remains of the party that still called itself by his name (Theod. Lector. p. 577; Theophanes, p. 114). Calandio fell into disfavour and was banished by the Emperor Zeno, at the instigation of Acacius, to the African Oasis, A.D. 485, where, probably, he died. The charge against him was that of having erased from the diptychs the name of Zeno, as the author of the *Henoticon*; and of having favoured Illus and Leontius in their rebellion, A.D. 484. But the real cause of his deposition was the theological animosity of Acacius, whom he had offended by writing a letter to Zeno accusing Peter Mongus of adultery, and of having anathematized the decrees of the council of Chalcedon (Evagr. *H. E.* ii. 16; Liberatus Diaconus, *Breviar.* c. xviii.; Gelasius, *Ep.* xiii. *ad Dardan. Episc.*; Labbe, iv. 1208-1209, xv. *ad Episc. Orient. ib.* 1217). On his deposition, the victorious Peter the Fuller was recalled to occupy the see of Antioch. [E.V.]

Calligonus, eunuch and chamberlain to Valentinian II., insulted Ambrose, A.D. 385 (Ambr. *Ep.* xx. (1), iii. p. 859). He conveyed a message, or reported a saying, of the emperor's, and added, "While I am alive, dost thou contemn Valentinian? I will remove thy head from off thee." Ambrose answered, "God grant thee to fulfil thy threat; for I shall suffer what bishops suffer, and thou wilt do what eunuchs do. And would that God would avert them from the church, that they might turn all their weapons on me." Calligonus was afterwards put to death on a peculiarly infamous charge (Augustine, *contra Julianum,* vi. 14, vol. x. 845). Tillemont (x. 175) supposes that these events were in the mind of Ambrose when he wrote the 6th chapter of his book on Joseph. This is very probable, but the further inference that that book was written two years later seems wholly erroneous. The event that occurred after two years was the usurpation of Maximus. It is possible that Ambrose encountered two eunuchs. Cf. also de Broglie, *l'Église et l'Empire,* vi. 173. [E.B.B.]

Callistus (1) (i. q. formosissimus; later spelt Calistus, but Calixtus first in 11th cent., Bunsen's *Hippolytus,* i. 131, note), the successor of pope Zephyrinus in A.D. 218, said to have been a Roman, and the son of Domitius.

Nothing was known of Callistus, except that the *Martyrologium Romanum* contained a tradition of his martyrdom, till the discovery of the *Philosophumena* in 1850. This work, which first appeared under the name of Origen, but is now ascribed to Hippolytus, almost certainly the contemporary bp. of Portus, gives an account of the life of Callistus which is scarcely credible respecting one of the bishops of Rome, who had before been honoured as a saint and martyr. Accordingly, much controversy has sprung up round the names of Callistus and Hippolytus. If Hippolytus is to be believed, Callistus was an unprincipled adventurer; if Callistus can be defended, grave doubt is thrown upon the veracity of Hippolytus. Bunsen and Wordsworth adopt the former view; Döllinger the latter, in an ingenious treatise translated by Dr. Plummer (T. &. T. Clark, 1876). The story as told by Hippolytus is lifelike and natural, and, however much we may allow for personal rancour, we cannot but believe it to be substantially true.

He tells us that Callistus was originally a slave in the household of a rich Christian called Carpophorus. His master intrusted to his charge a bank in the Piscina Publica, where Callistus induced his fellow-Christians to deposit their savings upon the security of the name of Carpophorus. The bank broke, and Callistus fled, but Carpophorus tracked him to Portus, and found him on board an outward-bound ship. The slave threw himself overboard in despair, but was picked up, and delivered to his master, who brought him back and put him to the *pistrinum,* or mill worked by the lowest slaves, for a punishment. After a time, however, he was set at liberty, and again attempted suicide, and for this purpose raised a riot in a synagogue of the Jews. By them he was brought before Fuscianus, the praefectus urbi, who, in spite of the fact that Carpophorus claimed him as his slave, condemned him, as a disturber of public worship allowed by the Roman laws, to be sent to the mines of Sardinia (*Philosophumena,* ed. Miller, pp. 286, 287).

His supposed desire for death certainly seems an inadequate motive for raising the riot in the Jewish synagogue. Döllinger supposes that, while claiming his debts at the hands of members of the Jewish synagogue, his zeal for religion impelled him to bear witness for Christ, and that thus his exile to Sardinia was a species of martyrdom for Christianity (Döllinger, *Hippolytus u. Kallistus,* p. 119). The date of his exile is proximately fixed, since Fuscianus served the office of praefectus urbi between A.D. 188 and A.D. 193 (Bunsen's *Hippolytus,* i. 138). Some time after, proceeds Hippolytus, Marcia, the Christian mistress of COMMODUS, persuaded the emperor to grant an amnesty to Christians undergoing punishment in Sardinia; and Callistus, at his own entreaty, was released, although his name was not on the list (supplied by the then bp. Victor) of those intended to benefit by Marcia's clemency. Callistus reappeared in Rome, much to the annoyance of Victor, for the outrage on the synagogue was recent and notorious. He therefore sent him to Antium, making him a small monthly allowance (*Philosophumena,* p. 288). Milman dates this *c.* A.D. 190, in the very year of Victor's accession (*Lat. Christ.* i. 55, note).

That Carpophorus's runaway slave should be of such importance that the pope should buy him off with an allowance, and insist upon his residing at a distance, shews that Callistus was already thought to be no ordinary man. He must have resided at Antium for a long time; for Zephyrinus, who did not succeed Victor till A.D. 202, recalled him. The new bishop "gave him the control of the clergy, and set him over the cemetery" (*Phil.* p. 288). This suggests that Callistus had been ordained at Antium; and the words "set him over the cemetery" (εἰς τὸ κοιμητήριον κατέστησεν) have a special interest; for one of the largest catacombs in Rome is known as the Coemeterium Sti. Calixti. That this should have been intrusted to the same man to whom also was given the control of the clergy proves what a high value was set upon this first public burial-place of the Christians in Rome. Thirteen out of the next eighteen popes are said to have been buried here; and the names of seven of the thirteen (Callistus himself being one of the exceptions) have been identified from old inscriptions found in one crypt of this cemetery.

Now (A.D. 202) for the first time Callistus became a power in the Roman church. To Hippolytus, who held a double position in that church [HIPPOLYTUS], he became especially obnoxious. Being set over the Roman clergy, he was over Hippolytus, who was the presbyter of one of the Roman *cardines* or churches; but as a presbyter himself, he was inferior ecclesiastically to one who was also the bp. of Portus. Hippolytus claims to have detected Callistus's double-dealing from the first; but tells us that Callistus, aspiring to be bp. of Rome himself, would break openly with neither party. The question which now divided the church was that of the Monarchia, or how to reconcile the sovereignty of the Father with the Godhead of the Son. Callistus, who had obtained a complete ascendancy over the mind of Zephyrinus, according to Hippolytus an ignorant and venal man, took care to use language now agreeing with the Sabellians, now with Hippolytus. But he personally sided with Sabellius, called Hippolytus a Ditheist, and persuaded Sabellius, who might otherwise have gone right, to coalesce with the Monarchians. His motive, says Hippolytus, was that there might be two parties in the church which he could play off against each other, continuing on friendly terms with both (*Phil.* p. 289).

We find from Tertullian that Zephyrinus began, no doubt under Callistus's influence, the relaxation of discipline which he himself afterwards carried further when he became bishop. Under Zephyrinus the practice first obtained of allowing adulterers to be readmitted after public penance (*de Pudicitiâ*, i. 21; Döllinger, pp. 126-130). Zephyrinus died in A.D. 218, and Callistus was elected bishop instead; and Hippolytus does not scruple to avow that by this act the Roman church had formally committed itself to heresy. He regards his own as the orthodox church, in opposition to what he henceforth considers as only being the Callistian sect (*Phil.* pp. 289, 292). Yet the first act apparently of Callistus as bishop was towards conciliating his rival. He threw off, perhaps actually excommunicated (ἀπέωσε), Sabellius. But he only did this, says Hippolytus, to proclaim a heresy quite as deadly as the other. If he is to be believed, he is right in thus characterizing it. The Father and the Son, Callistianism said, were one; together they made the Spirit, which Spirit took flesh in the womb of the Virgin. Callistus, says Hippolytus indignantly, is as Patripassian as Sabellius, for he makes the Father suffer *with* the Son, if not *as* the Son (*ib.* pp. 289-330).

Hippolytus brings against him several other grave accusations of further relaxing the bonds of church discipline (*ib.* pp. 290, 291)—*e.g.* (1) He relaxed the terms of readmission into the church: accounting no sin so deadly as to be incapable of readmission, and not exacting penance as a necessary preliminary. (2) He relaxed the terms of admission into orders, ordaining even those who had been twice or thrice married; and permitting men already ordained to marry freely. (3) He also relaxed the marriage laws of the church, thereby bringing them into conflict with those of the state; and Hippolytus says that a general immorality was the consequence. Döllinger, however, pertinently observes that Hippolytus does not even hint a charge of personal immorality against Callistus (Döllinger, *Hippolytus und Kallistus*, p. 195). (4) He allowed second baptisms, which perhaps means that a repetition of baptism was substituted for the penance which had been necessary at the readmission of grievous sinners into the church. This is the only accusation which Döllinger meets with a distinct contradiction, on the ground that no such practice was known in the later Roman church (p. 189). Yet it surely is not as inconceivable as it seemed to him that later bishops of Rome might have reversed the acts of their predecessor.

Callistus is said to have died in A.D. 223 (Eus. *H. E.* vi. 20). Tradition tells us that he was scourged in a popular rising, thrown out of a window of his house in Trastevere, and flung into a well. This would account for no epitaph being found to Callistus in the papal crypt of his own cemetery in the catacombs. E. Rolffs, in *Texte und Untersuch.* (1893), xi. 3; P. Battifol, *Le Décret de Callist.* in *Etudes d'Hist. et de Théol.* (Paris, 1902), pp. 69 seq. [G.H.M.]

Caprasius (2), St., presbyter at Lérins (l'Isle de St. Honorat). Having a great desire to become a hermit, he distributed his goods to the poor and with St. Honoratus ultimately fixed on the isle of Lérins, described as a frightful desert where nothing was to be seen but serpents and other venomous creatures. There Honoratus built a monastery, into which he received many monks from the neighbouring countries. It was under the discipline of Caprasius and Honoratus, who are said to have made it the home of saints. Hilarius describes their new monastery as being distinguished for chastity, faith, wisdom, justice, truth. They also built in the island a church, of which Honoratus became minister. Caprasius died *c.* 430, and is commemorated on June 1. (*Acta Sanctorum*, Jun. 1, p. 77; Hilar. Arelat. *de Vita S. Honorati*, cap. ii. *Patr. Lat.* l. p. 1255; Eucherius Lugd. *de Laud. Eremi*, 42, *Patr. Lat.* l. p. 711; Sidonius Apoll. *Carm.* § 384, *Patr. Lat.* lviii. p. 721; Ceillier, *Hist. des Auteurs Sacrés et Ecclés.* t. viii. p. 439.) [C.H.]

Capreolus, bp. of Carthage, known in connexion with the council of Ephesus, A.D. 431. N. Africa at that time being ravaged by the Vandals under Genseric, it was impossible to convene the bishops to appoint representatives from the church of Carthage at the council. The bishop, however, in his zeal for the catholic doctrine, dispatched an elaborate letter in its defence, which is extant, both in Greek and Latin. There is also extant another letter by Capreolus on this controversy, written in answer to inquiries addressed to him from Spain, by Vitalis and Constantius. Both letters are in Migne, vol. liii. p. 843. Also a fragment of the letter which he addressed to Theodosius, who convoked the council, is quoted by Ferrandus in his letter to Pelagius and Anatolius, c. 6, *Patr.* Migne, lxvii. 925. The *Sermo de Tempore Barbarico*, on the Vandal invasion of Africa, usually attributed to St. Augustine, and other sermons in which Augustine describes the Vandal ravages, are considered by Tillemont (xvi. 502) to have been written by Capreolus (Hardouin, i. 1419-1422; Fleury, xxv. 41; Till. xii. 559, xiii. 901, xiv. 376, 399, xvi. 495, 502, 789), but this is doubtful. [D.B.]

Tillemont supposes Capreolus to have succeeded to the see of Carthage shortly before the death of Augustine (430), as the letter convoking the council of Ephesus seems to have been addressed to him and to Augustine (xii. 559). Another object of his letter to Ephesus was to implore the council not to reopen the question of the Pelagian heresy. When his letter was read, Cyril and all the bishops exclaimed, "That is what we all say; that is what we all wish," and they ordered it to be inserted in the Acts of the council (Vinc. Lerin. c. 31; Labbe, *Conc.* iii. 529). He is probably the "priest" in Africa in the time of Aspar, mentioned in the Book of Promises, ascribed to Prosper (i. 4, c. 6).

It is instructive to note the importance that he attaches to the descent of the God-man into Hades. Chaps. 5-12 are taken up with answering the new error. He quotes Ps. xvi. 10; John x. 18; I. Cor. ii. 7, 8; II. Cor. v. 18, 19; Heb. i. 2, 3; Col. ii. 15; Heb. x. 28-30; John xx. 17. He does not quote John xvi. 32, but says (c. 13) that it would be endless to adduce all scripture testimonies. His answer to the argument from Ps. xxii. 1 is drawn from the latter half of the verse (as it is in the LXX and Vulgate, which are not improbably right), "Far from my health are the words of my failings," and based on the mystery of the union of the two natures, "that human condition should know itself" (c. 5).

The death of Capreolus is generally dated *c.* A.D. 435. His burial was commemorated in the calendar of Carthage between July 21 and 30; the note of the day is lost. [E.B.B.]

Caracalla, the nickname of M. Aurelius Severus Antoninus Bassianus, son of Lucius Septimius Severus, born April 4, 188, declared Caesar A.D. 196, three years after his father's accession; succeeded to the empire in conjunction with his brother Geta, Feb. 211, sole emperor after slaying his brother in his mother's arms A.D. 212, in Gaul 213, in Germany and on the Danube 214, at Antioch and Alexandria 215, marched against Parthia 216, killed on the way from Edessa to Carrhae, April 8, 217. His mother, according to contemporary authorities, was Julia, a Syrian woman, whom Severus had married because of certain prophecies. Spartianus, in the time of Constantine, assures us that Julia was his stepmother, and that his mother was Severus's first wife Marcia. This would make his story somewhat less horrible, but compels the historian at the cost of some inconsistency to refer his birth to 174, or earlier.

The principal authorities are Tertullian, addressing Scapula, governor of Africa, in 211; the sober, contemporary, and apparently impartial, narrative of Herodian (bks. vii. viii.); the abridgment, by the very late compiler Xiphilinus, of the 77th book of the contemporary historian Dion Cassius, with which the compiler seems to have incorporated fragments of other works of a like early date; the narrative written for Constantine by Lampridius Spartianus in the *Historia Augusta*; laws, coins, inscriptions (see Clinton), and especially a record in the Digest, bk 1, tit. 5, l. 17, from the 22nd book of Ulpian.

Dion charges him with inheriting all the worst features of the races from which he sprang; on his father's side, the braggart levity of the Gaul and the truculence of the African; on his mother's, the tricksiness of the Syrian. Tertullian (*ad Scap.* c. 4) calls him Antoninus, and informs us that "his father Severus had a regard for Christians; . . . and Antoninus . . . was brought up on Christian milk. And, moreover, Severus knew most illustrious men and most illustrious women to be of this sect, and not only did not hurt, but honoured [*exornavit* or, more probably, *exoneravit*, exonerated] them by the witness he bore them, and withstood the raging populace." It has been inferred that the young prince was not only brought up amid Christian influences, but had a Christian wet-nurse.

We can easily conceive how injurious it must have been for the child to find the Christians in the palace screened, while yet he was taken to see shows of wild beasts where Christians were thrown to them to devour. Spartianus tells us that he was a most charming child, quick at learning, engaging with his prattle, and of a very tender heart. "If he saw condemned criminals thrown to the beasts, he cried, or looked away, which more than won the hearts of the people. At seven years of age, when he heard that a boy that was his playmate had been severely beaten for Jewish superstition, it was a long while before he would look at his own father or the boy's father again, or at the people who had him flogged. By his own intercession he restored their ancient rights to the people of Antioch and Byzantium, who had helped Niger against his father. It was for his cruelty that he took an aversion to Plautianus. But all this was only while he was a boy [*sed haec puer*]." The "Jewish superstition" has been interpreted, with great probability, to mean Christianity. The Plautianus mentioned was, *teste* Herodian, a vile tyrant, all-powerful with Severus, whose daughter Caracalla was compelled to marry, much against his will, in the hope of reforming him from certain low tastes, such as won him the favour of the city populace.

Spartianus tells us that when Caracalla emerged from boyhood, before his accession, he was so changed, so stern, that no one would have known him; whereas his brother Geta, who had been an unpleasing child, was very much improved as he grew up. His narrative, and the abridgment of Dion, afford no clue to the enmity that sprang up between the brothers, and deeper principles seem to have been involved than mere fraternal jealousy. Caracalla's early life was such as to teach him heart-hardening dissimulation; Tertullian, while the brothers yet ruled jointly, urges at once the uncertainty of human life, and the probability that Caracalla would favour the Christians; and it is the fact that his victory coincided with a general and prolonged cessation of a long and cruel persecution.

We cannot tell whether he had any higher motives than a mean malice and uneasy envy in his murder of his brother, and whether the mother, for whose sake he claimed to have done it and whom he would not allow to utter or even listen to a complaint, ever forgave him. The incredible charge of incest was afterwards brought against them. But there is little doubt as to the results of the deed. He did not become a Christian, and the ancient gods of the state were the last to whom he had recourse. He patronised Philostratus, who wrote for his mother and for him the Life of Apollonius of Tyana. He thus fostered one of the chief counterfeits of Christianity. He gathered round him all who professed to read the future, and he worshipped the spirits of the dead. But they could not rid his ears of his brother's dying cry, *μῆτερ, μῆτερ, τεκοῦσα, τεκοῦσα, βοήθει, σφάζομαι.* He continued to court the city populace, and enriched Rome with magnificent baths, which even in ruins are the most superb monuments of refined luxury. But his fits of savagery must have made it hard for him to continue a favourite of the populace. Henceforth he relied mainly on his army, and sought ease of mind in excitement. Both necessities involved expense. Whatever impulse he gave to the corruption of the capital, he himself contentedly shared the roughest privileges of the soldiers. But that alone could not secure their affection. In the first day of his crime he had lavished the wealth his father had been eighteen years in acquiring. New sources of revenue were needed.

It is the method that Caracalla adopted to raise a revenue that gives him his main claim to a place in the catalogue of men whose lives affected the Christian church. His act, as Gibbon has shewn, marked an era in the decline of the empire. But more than that, it affected very greatly the position of Christians in all future persecutions. It is this indeed mainly that enables us to pronounce with certainty that the act was his, and belonged to no earlier date. "All who are in the Roman world," says Ulpian, "have been made citizens of Rome by an institution of the emperor Antoninus." "A most grateful and humane deed!" exclaims Augustine (*de Civ. Dei*, v. 17, vol. vii. 161), and immediately subjoins the proviso that made the boon so equivocal. At a stroke the Roman world was pauperized. Every citizen resident in the capital was entitled to receive every month, at a cheap rate—the indigent quite gratuitously—a certain amount of corn or bread. This was one of the chief drains upon the revenue, and one of the main causes of extortion in the provinces. But Augustus laid a tax on citizens from which aliens were exempt, a tax which made the franchise in many cases a burden to be declined rather than a boon to be coveted, a duty of five per cent. on all bequests. Nerva and Trajan, however, exempted the passage of moderate inheritances from parent to child, or *vice versâ* (Plin. *Paneg.* 37, 38). Caracalla, by raising the provincials to the franchise, did not free them from the tribute they owed before, but imposed this additional burden, which he doubled in amount, and which involved the odious intrusion of the taxgatherer in seasons of domestic bereavement. The act seems to synchronize with a *congiarium* or largess to the populace in A.D. 214. Thenceforward Caracalla's laws, wherever promulgated, seemed to be dated at Rome. Oppressive as were the effects of the act, it seems yet to have been welcomed. It was but fair, thought Augustine, that rustics who had lands should give food to citizens who had none, so long as it was granted as a boon and not extorted as a right.

But besides its effects as a financial measure, Caracalla's act broke down the barriers of society; annulled, as far as any imperial institution could, the proud old sovereign commonwealth, the queen of nations, whose servants and ministers the emperors had ever professed to be; opened the command of armies to unlettered barbarians; removed the bars to the influx of Greek and Syrian and Egyptian corruption into Rome; reduced the subjects to a level, above which only the emperor, the minion of the army, towered supreme.

In earlier times St. Paul's Roman citizenship had stood him in good stead; and in the story of the martyrs in Gaul under M. Aurelius the Roman citizens had been reserved till the emperor's will was known. A boon now so widely diffused could scarcely retain the same value. But we hear no more of Christians being crucified, unless they were slaves, or first reduced to slavery. Unutterably horrible as the tortures devised against them were, they were no longer commonly thrown to the beasts as a show. They suffered by the sword at last, and all their tortures were such as might befall any citizen of Rome who transgressed the mandate of the emperor. [*D. C. A.* PERSECUTION; TORTURE.] Thus martyrdom, instead of the obstinacy of an abject alien superstition, became the bold and cheerful resistance of free citizens to the arbitrary will of one who, when he began to torture, became a barbarous tyrant. [E.B.B.]

Caritas. Charity with her virgin sisters, Faith and Hope, and their mother Wisdom, seem to have been the names of real martyrs. The names were very natural ones for Christians to give to their children. On the Aurelian Way, in the church of St. Pancras, lay Sophia with her three daughters: Sapientia, with her daughters Fides, Spes, and Charitas, as William of Malmesbury calls them; but the Latin names nowhere else occur in this order, the Greek names, when given in full, always do.

Sophia, Pistis, Elpis, Agape, are said to have been a mother and daughters who suffered in September, and whose relics were transferred to the church of St. Silvester. On the other hand, Sapienta, Spes, Fides, Caritas, are said by Ado to have suffered Aug. 1, and were buried on the Appian Way, in the crypt of St. Caecilia. In that crypt has been found the inscription, PISTE SPEI SORORI DULCISSIMAE FECIT. In the same place, if we rightly understand de Rossi, was found AGAPE QVE VXIT ANNIS VGINTI ET SEX IN PACE—Agape, who lived twenty-six years in peace. There is no statement of relationship in the notices of the tombs on the Appian Way. It appears probable that Ado has confounded the widely celebrated martyrs who are said to have suffered in September under Adrian, with the occupants of some Christian tombs in a crypt where there were many celebrations early in August. The Menology gives the ages of Faith, Hope, and Love as 12, 10, and 9. (De Rossi, *Rom. Sott.* i. 180-183, ii. 171 ff., pl. lv. 10; Bede, *Mart.* July 1, Bede, *Mart. Auct.* June 23; Usuard, Aug. 1; *Menol. Basil.* Sept. 16.) [E.B.B.]

Carpocrates (Καρποκράτης, Irenaeus; Καρποκρᾶς, Epiphanius and Philaster, both probably deriving this form from the shorter treatise against heresies by Hippolytus), a Platonic philosopher who taught at Alexandria early in the 2nd cent., and who, incorporating Christian elements into his system, became the founder of a heretical sect mentioned in one of our earliest catalogues of heresies, the list of Hegesippus, preserved by Eusebius (*H. E.* iv. 22). These heretics are the first of whom Irenaeus expressly mentions that they called themselves Gnostics; Hippolytus first speaks of the name as assumed by the Naassenes or Ophites (*Ref.* v. 1). Of all the systems called Gnostic, that of Carpocrates is the one in which the Hellenic element is the most strongly marked, and which contains the least of what is necessarily Jewish or Oriental. He is described as teaching with prominence the doctrine of a single first principle: the name μοναδικὴ γνῶσις, given by Clement of Alexandria (*Strom.* iii. 2) to the doctrine of the school which he founded, is made by Neander to furnish the key to the whole Carpocratian system; but possibly is only intended to contrast with the doctrine of the Valentinian teachers, who thought it necessary to provide the first Being with a consort, in order that emanations from Him might be conceivable. Carpocrates taught that from the one unknown unspeakable God different angels and powers had emanated, and that of these the lowest in the series, far below the unbegotten Father, had been the makers of the world. The privilege of the higher souls was to escape the rule of those who had made the world; even by magical arts to exercise dominion over them, and ultimately, on leaving the world, to pass completely free from them to God Who is above them. Jesus he held to be a mere man naturally born of human parents, having no prerogatives beyond the reach of others to attain. His superiority to ordinary men consisted in this, that His soul, being steadfast and pure, remembered those things which it had seen in the revolution (τῇ περιφορᾷ) in which it had been carried round with the unbegotten God, and therefore power [or a "power"] had been sent from God enabling Him to escape the makers of the world. Though brought up in Jewish customs, He had despised them, and therefore had received powers enabling Him to destroy the passions which are given to men as a punishment. But in this there was nothing special: others might be the equals or the superiors not only of Peter or Paul, but of our Lord Himself. Their souls, too, might remember the truths they had witnessed; if they despised the rulers of the world as much as Jesus did, they would be given the same privileges as He, and higher if they despised them more. Thus the Carpocratians gave honour, but not an exclusive honour, to Christ. They had pictures of Him, derived, it was said, from a likeness taken by Pilate's order; and images, which they crowned and treated with other marks of respect; but this they did also in the cases of Pythagoras, Plato, Aristotle, and other philosophers.

In the opening statement concerning the making of the world, the doctrine ascribed to Carpocrates is almost identical with that ascribed to Saturninus; but in the next paragraph the language is distinctly taken from the myth in Plato's *Phaedrus*, in which human knowledge is made to be but a recollection of what the soul had seen when carried round with the gods in their revolution, and permitted to see the eternal forms of things.

The doctrine of the duty of despising the rulers of the world received among the Carpocratians an interpretation which enabled them to practise immorality without scruple. Things in themselves were indifferent; nothing was in its own nature good or evil, and was only made so by human opinion. The true Gnostic might practise everything—nay, it was his duty to have experience of all. A doctrine concerning the transmigration of souls which was taught by other Gnostic sects, and which harmonized well with Platonic teaching, was adopted by the Carpocratians in the form that a soul which had had its complete experience passed at once out of the dominion of the rulers of the world, and was received up to society with the God above them: those which had not were sent back to finish in other bodies that which was lacking to them; but all ultimately would be saved. But as was also taught by the Basilidians of Irenaeus and by the Ophites, salvation belonged to the soul alone; there would be no resurrection of the body. In conformity with this theory was interpreted the text from the Sermon on the Mount, "Agree with thine adversary quickly." The "adversary" (whom, Epiphanius tells us, they named Abolus, a corruption, doubtless, from the Diabolus of Irenaeus) was one of the world-making angels, whose office it was to conduct the soul to the principal of these angels, "the judge." If he found that there were acts left undone, he delivered it to another angel, "the officer," to shut it up "in prison"—*i.e.* in a body—until it had paid the last farthing. The doctrine that we ought to imitate the freedom with which our Lord despised the rulers of the world raises the question, Did Carpocrates intend to impute immorality to Him? On this point Carpocrates was misunderstood either by Hippolytus or by his own disciples. According to Hippolytus, Carpocrates taught that Jesus surpassed other men in justice and integrity (*σωφροσύνῃ καὶ ἀρετῇ καὶ βίῳ δικαιοσύνης*, Epiphanius), and no doubt our Lord's example might have been cited only in reference to freedom from Jewish ceremonial obligations; yet the version of Irenaeus seems more trustworthy, which does not suggest that the superiority of Jesus consisted in anything but the clearer apprehension of eternal truths which His intellect retained. Carpocrates claimed to be in possession of the true teaching of Christ spoken secretly by Him to His apostles, and communicated by them in tradition to the worthy and faithful; and the apostolic doctrine that men are to be saved by faith and love was used by him to justify an antinomian view of the complete indifference of works. EPIPHANES, the son of Carpocrates by a Cephallenian woman, maintained a licentious theory of communism in all things, women included. The Carpocratians and the Cainites have often been coupled together as the two most immoral of the Gnostic sects, and in practical effects their doctrines may not have been very different; but the Carpocratian theory of the indifference of human actions fell short of the inversion of good and evil which is ascribed to the Cainites. Whereas the latter represented the God of the Jews and Maker of the world as an evil Being who ought to be resisted, the former only spoke of the makers of the world as inferior beings whose restrictions it is true enlightenment to despise; and the arguments of Epiphanes, derived from the equality that reigns in nature, assume that the creation is so far conformed to the will of God that from the laws which pervade it we may infer what is pleasing to the supreme power. Whether immorality were directly taught by Carpocrates himself or not, his followers became proverbial for deliberate licentiousness of life. The Christians thought it likely that the stories current among the heathen of scenes of shameless debauchery in the Christian love-feasts had a real foundation in what took place among the Carpocratians. Philaster, who, apparently through oversight, enumerates the Carpocratians twice, the second time (57) giving them the alternative names of *Floriani* and *Milites*, directly asserts this. His predecessors had suggested it as probable (Clem. Alex. *Strom.* iii. 2; cf. Justin Martyr, *Apol.* 26). Irenaeus counts Carpocratian doctrines and practices as means employed by Satan to discredit the Christian name among the heathen. (See also Eus. *H. E.* iv. 7.)

A more trifling heathen belief about the Christians generally seems to have been true of the Carpocratians, viz. that they knew each other by secret bodily marks (*notaculo corporis*, Minucius Felix, cc. 9, 31); for the Carpocratians marked their disciples by cauterizing them in the back of the lobe of the right ear. It appears from Heracleon (Clem. Alex. p. 995, *Eclog. ex Script. Proph.* xxv.) that this was a baptismal ceremony, intended to represent the "baptism with fire," predicted of our Lord by the Baptist. This confirms the evidence as to the use of at least St. Matthew's Gospel by the Carpocratians furnished by Epiphanius (*Haer.* xxx. p. 138) and by the use made of the Sermon on the Mount. Celsus probably refers to this rite (Origen, v. 64) when he says that Christians gave to certain others of them the opprobrious name *ἀκοῆς καυστήρια*. Origen, however, supposes that I. Tim. iv. 2 is here referred to.

Mention has already been made of the cultivation of magic by the Carpocratians, and their pretension to equal the miraculous powers of our Lord. Hippolytus, in the fourth book of the Refutation, gives us several specimens of wonders exhibited by magicians, not very unlike feats performed by professional conjurors to-day. It was easy for Irenaeus to shew (ii. 32) how very unlike these transient wonders were to be permanent miracles of healing effected by our Lord, and which, as he claimed, continued in the church.

According to Neander, the Carpocratian system sees in the world's history one struggle between the principles of unity and of multiplicity. From one eternal Monad all existence has flowed, and to this it strives to return. But the finite spirits who rule over several portions of the world counteract this universal striving after unity. From them the different popular religions, and in particular the Jewish, have proceeded. Perfection is attained by those souls who, led on by reminiscences of their former condition, soar above all limitation and diversity to the contemplation of the higher unity. They despise the restrictions imposed by the mundane spirits; they regard externals as of no importance, and faith and love as the only essentials; meaning by faith, mystical brooding of the mind absorbed in the original unity. In this way they escape the dominion of the finite mundane spirits; their souls are freed from imprisonment in matter, and they obtain a state of perfect repose (corresponding to the Buddhist Nirwana) when they have completely ascended above the world of appearance.

With respect to the Carpocratians, the primary authorities are Irenaeus (i. 25, ii. 31-34), Clem. Alex. (*Strom.* iii. 2); Tertullian (*de Anima*, 23, 35), who appears to have drawn his information from Irenaeus; Philaster (35) and Pseudo-Tertullian (9), who represent the earlier treatise of Hippolytus; Epiphanius (27), who weaves together the accounts of Hippolytus and of Irenaeus; and Hippolytus, who in his later treatise (vii. 20) merely copies Irenaeus, with some omissions, thereby suggesting that he was not acquainted with the work of Irenaeus when he wrote the earlier treatise. He certainly had at that time other sources of information, for he mentions three or four points not found in Irenaeus—*e.g.* he emphasizes the Carpocratian doctrine of the unity of the first principle, tells of emanations from that principle of angels and powers, gives a different version of the excellence of Jesus, and says that Carpocrates denied the resurrection of the body. It is not impossible that Justin's work on heresies may have furnished some materials for Irenaeus. In any case Irenaeus probably added much of his own, for the pains he has taken with the confutation make it probable that in his time the sect was still active at Rome.

We cannot assign an exact date to Carpocrates; but there are affinities between his system and those of Saturninus and Basilides, which suggest one a little later than Basilides, from whom he may have derived his knowledge of Christianity. Eusebius is probably right in placing him in the reign of Hadrian (*d.* A.D. 138). It suffices merely to mention the invention of the writer known as Praedestinatus (i. 7) that the Carpocratians were condemned in Cyprus by the apostle Barnabas. Matter, in his history of Gnosticism, gives an account of certain supposed Carpocratian inscriptions, since found to be spurious (Gieseler's *Ecc. Hist.* c. ii. § 45, note 16). [G.S.]

Cassianus (2) **Julius,** a heretical teacher who lived towards the end of the 2nd cent., chiefly known to us by references to his writings made on two occasions by Clemens Alexandrinus. In the first passage (*Strom.* i. 21, copied by Eusebius, *Praep. Ev.* x. 12) Clement engages in a chronological inquiry to shew the greatly superior antiquity of Moses to the founders of Grecian philosophy, and he acknowledges himself indebted to the previous investigations made by Tatian in his work addressed to the Greeks, and by Cassian (spelt *Casianus* in the MS. of Clement, but not in those of Eusebius) in the first book of his *Exegetica.* Vallarsi (ii. 865) alters without comment the Cassianus of previous editors into Casianus, in Jerome's Catalogue 33, a place where Jerome is not using Clement directly, but is copying the notice in Eusebius (*H. E.* vi. 13). Jerome adds that he had not himself met the chronological work in question. In the second passage (*Strom.* iii. 13, seq.) Cassian is also named in connexion with Tatian. Clement is, in this section, refuting the doctrines of those Gnostics who, in their view of the essential evil of matter, condemned matrimony and the procreation of children; and after considering some arguments urged by Tatian, says that similar ones had been used by Julius Cassianus whom he describes as the originator of Docetism (ὁ τῆς δοκήσεως ἐξάρχων), a statement which must be received with some modification. [DOCETAE.] He quotes some passages from a treatise by Cassian on Continence (περὶ ἐγκρατείας, ἢ περὶ εὐνουχίας), in which he wholly condemned sexual intercourse, and referred its origin to instigations of our first parents by the serpent, alleging in proof II. Cor. xi. 3. Cassian quoted Is. lvi. 3, Matt. xix. 12, and probably several other passages which are discussed by Clement without express mention that they had been used by Cassian. Cassian also uses certain alleged sayings of our Lord, cited likewise in the so-called second epistle of the Roman Clement to the Corinthians, cap. xii., as well as in the *Excerpta Theodoti,* lxvii. p. 985. Lightfoot notices (*Clement, l.c.*) that Cassian, by the omission of a clause, makes the Encratite aspect of the passage much stronger than it appears in the citation of the Pseudo-Clement. Clemens Alexandrinus makes no complaint of unfairness in the quotation; but while he remarks that the sayings in question are not found in our four Gospels, but only in the Gospel according to the Egyptians, he gives a different explanation far less natural than that of Cassian.

Another specimen of Cassian's arguments in this treatise is preserved in Jerome's Commentary on Gal. vi. 8. Jerome there answers an Encratite argument founded on this text, viz. that he who is united to a woman soweth to the flesh, and therefore shall of the flesh reap corruption. This argument is introduced with words which, according to the common reading, run, "Tatianus qui putativam Christi carnem introducens, omnem conjunctionem masculi ad foeminam immundam arbitratur, tali adversum nos sub occasione praesentis testimonii usus est argumento." There is little doubt that we are to read instead of Tatianus, Cassianus. The Benedictine editor who retains the old reading notes that Cassianus is the reading of two of the oldest MSS., while Vallarsi says that Cassianus was the reading of every MS. he had seen.

The Docetism of Cassian was closely connected with his Encratism, for it was an obvious answer of the orthodox to his doctrine on Continence, that if the birth of children were essentially evil, then our Lord's own birth was evil, and His mother an object of blame. This was met by a denial of the reality of our Lord's body. Cassian also taught that man had not been originally created with a body like ours, but that these fleshly bodies were the "coats of skin" in which the Lord clothed our first parents after the Fall. This notion, probably derived from Valentinus (Iren. I. v. p. 27), had considerable currency. References for it will be found in Huet's *Origeniana*, ii. Qu. 12, viii., and Beausobre, *Manichéisme*, ii. 135).

Theodoret (*Haer. Fab.* i. 8) enumerates among the followers of Valentinus one Cossian, by whom, no doubt, Julius Cassianus is intended; for many greater inaccuracies in the names are in the present text of Theodoret, and Theodoret would have found authority in Clement for classing Cassian with Valentinus.

The coincidences between Tatian and Cassianus seem too close to be accidental, but we have not data to determine their relative priority. If Cassian were really the founder of the sect called Docetae, he must have been some time antecedent to Serapion (Eus. *H. E.* vi. 12). His country may have been Egypt (cf. Harnack, *Gesch. der Alt. Chr. Lit.* pp. 201-204). [DOCETAE; ENCRATITES]. [G.S.]

Cassianus (6), bp. of Autun. The date we assign him will vary according as we attach more weight to the ancient Life of him, which professes to be based on a contemporary record (*Acta SS.* Aug. 5, vol. ii. p. 64), as Ruinart prefers to do, or to a casual statement by Gregory of Tours, who was shewn his tomb (*Glor. Conf.* 74, 75), as do Tillemont and the Bollandists. The Life tells us that he was born of noble parents in Alexandria, and brought up by a bp. Zonis; that he made his house a Christian hospital in the time of Julian, liberated his slaves, and built a church to St. Lawrence at Orta in Egypt, at which place he was made bishop against his will in the time of Jovian, A.D. 363.

The tomb of Cassian was famous. A stain in the form of a cross appeared on it, which is said to have prompted Germanus to hold a conversation with the saint in his tomb. He asked him how he did, and the saint answered that he was at rest. This is told in his Life, and may explain the great eagerness to obtain dust scraped from the stones of his tomb, which was almost bored through in consequence, as testified by Gregory. [E.B.B.]

Cassianus (11) Johannes has been called the founder of Western monachism and of the semi-Pelagian school. More exactly, he was the first to transplant the rules of the Eastern monks into Europe, and the most eminent of the writers who steered a course between Pelagianism and the tenets of St. Augustine. Like St. Chrysostom, St. John Damascene, and others, he is usually designated by his agnomen. His birth is dated between A.D. 350 and 360; his birthplace is not known. Gennadius calls him "Scytha" (Fabric. *Biblioth. Eccles.* s.v.); but this may be merely a corruption from Scetis or Scyathis, where Cassian resided for some time among the monks of Nitria. His parents, of whose piety he speaks gratefully (*Coll.* xxiv. 1), sent him to be educated in a monastery at Bethlehem; and there he would have frequent intercourse with pilgrims from the West. This cannot have been, as some have thought, the monastery of St. Jerome, for that was not then in existence, nor does Cassian ever refer to Jerome as his teacher. Here Cassian became intimate with Germanus, the future companion of his travels. The fame of the Egyptian monks and hermits reached Cassian and his friend in their cells. About A.D. 390 they started, with leave of absence for seven years, to study by personal observation the more austere rules of the "renuntiantes," as they were called, in the Thebaid. At the end of seven years they revisited Bethlehem; and thence returned very soon to the Egyptian deserts (*Coll.* xvii. 31). Thus Cassian collected the materials for his future writings. Besides other voluntary hardships, he speaks of the monks having to fetch water on their shoulders a distance of three or four miles (*Coll.* xxiv. 10). Evidently in his estimation, as in that of his contemporaries generally, the vocation of a solitary is holier than even that of a coenobite.

About A.D. 403 we find Cassian and Germanus at Constantinople, perhaps attracted by the reputation of Chrysostom. By him Cassian was ordained deacon, or, as some think, appointed archdeacon; and in his treatise *de Incarnatione* (vii. 31) he speaks of Chrysostom with affectionate reverence. Cassian and his friend were entrusted with the care of the cathedral treasures; and, after the expulsion of Chrysostom, they were sent by his adherents on an embassy to Rome *c.* A.D. 405 to solicit the intervention of Innocent I. No further mention is made of Germanus; nor is much known of Cassian during the next ten years. Probably he remained at Rome after Chrysostom died, A.D. 407, until the approach of the Goths under Alaric, and thus acquired a personal interest in the Pelagian controversy.

After quitting Rome it has been inferred from a casual expression in the *de Institutis* (iii. 1) that Cassian visited the monks of Mesopotamia; some say that he returned for a time to Egypt or Palestine; and by some he is identified with Cassianus Presbyter. Probably Cassian betook himself from Rome to Massilia (Marseilles). In this neighbourhood he founded two monasteries (one afterwards known as that of St. Victor) for men and women respectively. Tillemont says that the rule was taken from the fourth book of the *de Institutis*; and that many monasteries in that part of Gaul owed their existence to this foundation. As Cassian is addressed in the Epistola Castoris as "abbas," "dominus," and "pater," it is argued, but not with certainty, that he presided over his new monastery. Here he devoted himself to literary labours for many years, and died at a very great age, probably between A.D. 440 and 450.

The *de Institutis Renuntiantium*, in twelve books, was written *c.* 420 at the request of Castor, bp. of Apta Julia, in Gallia Narbonensis (Praef. *Inst.*). Books i.-iv. treat of the monastic rule; the others of its especial hindrances. The former were abridged by Eucherius Lugdunensis. The *Collationes Patrum in Scithico Eremo Commorantium*, in which Cassian records his Egyptian experiences, were evidently intended to complete his previous work; his purpose being to describe in the *de Institutis* the regulations and observances of monachism; in the *Collationes* its interior scope and spirit: in the former he writes of monks, in the latter of hermits. The *Collationes* were commenced for Castor, but after his death *Collat.* i.-x. were inscribed to Leontius, a kinsman of Castor, and Helladius, bishop in that district; xi.-xvii. to Honoratus, abbat of Lerins, and Eucherius, bp. of Lugdunum (Lyons); xviii.-xxiv. to the monks and anchorets of the Stoechades (Hyères). The *Collationes* have been well called a "speculum monasticum": St. Benedict ordered them to be read daily; they were highly approved also by the founders of the Dominicans, Carthusians, and Jesuits. But the orthodoxy of the *Collationes*, especially of iii. and xiii., on the subject of Grace and Freewill, was impugned by St. Augustine and Prosper of Aquitania. [PELAGIANISM.] An attempt was made by Cassiodorus and others to expurgate them. Cassian's last work, *de Incarnatione Christi* (cf. i. 3, v. 2), was directed against the Nestorian heresy, *c.* 429, at the suggestion of Leo, then archdeacon and afterwards pope. Probably Cassian was selected for this controversy as a disciple of Chrysostom, the illustrious predecessor of Nestorius in the see of Constantinople (*Inc.* vii. 31). The treatises *de Spirituali Medicinâ Monachi*, *Theologica Confessio*, and *de Conflictu Virtutum ac Vitiorum* are generally pronounced spurious.

Cassian is remarkable as a link between Eastern and Western Christendom, and as combining in himself the active and the contemplative life. It is difficult to overestimate his influence indirectly on the great monastic system of mediaeval Europe. His writings have always been in esteem with monastic reformers; especially at the revival of learning in the 15th cent. Even his adversary Prosper calls him "insignis ac facundus." Cassian shews a thorough knowledge of the Holy Scriptures; often with a good deal of quaintness in his application of it. His style, if not so rich in poetic eloquence as that of his great opponent, is clear and forcible; and he is practical rather than profound. His good sense manifests itself in his preface to the *Instituta*, where he announces his intention to avoid legendary wonders and to regard his subject on its practical side. He insists continually on the paramount importance of the intention, disclaiming the idea of what is called the "opus operatum"—for instance, on almsgiving (*Inst.* vii. 21), fasting (*Coll.* i. 7), and prayer (ix. 3); and he is incessant in denouncing the especial sins of cloister-life, as pride, ambition, vainglory. The life of a monk, as he portrays it, is no formal and mechanical routine; but a daily and hourly act of self-renunciation (xxiv. 2). On the other hand, he is by no means free from exaggerated reverence for mere asceticism; and, while encouraging the highest aspirations after holiness, allows too much scope to a selfish desire of reward. As a casuist he is for the most part sensible and judicious, *e.g.*, in discriminating between voluntary and involuntary thoughts (i. 17). But he presses obedience so far as to make it unreasonable and fanatical (*Inst.* iv. 27, etc.), and under certain circumstances he sanctions deceit (*Coll.* xvii.).

On the subject of Predestination Cassian, without assenting to Pelagius, protested against what he considered the fatalistic tendency of St. Augustine. In the *Collationes* he merely professes to quote the words of the Egyptian "fathers"; and in the *de Incarnatione* he distinctly attacks Pelagianism as closely allied with the heresy of Nestorius (i. 3, vi. 14). Still, it is certain from the tenor of his writings that Cassian felt a very strong repugnance to any theory which seemed to him to involve an arbitrary limitation of the possibility of being saved. It has been well said that St. Augustine regards man in his natural state as dead, Pelagius as sound and well, Cassian as sick. [PELAGIANISM.]

The best critical ed. of Cassian's works is in the *Corp. Scr. Eccl. Lat.* xiii. xvii., ed. by Petschenig. In Schaff and Wace's *Post-Nicene Library* there is a translation of most of them, with valuable prolegomena and notes by Dr. Gibson, Bp. of Gloucester. [I.G.S.]

Cassiodorus (or rather, **Cassiodorius**) **Magnus Aurelius,** senator, and chief minister to the Ostrogothic princes of Italy, born at Scylacium (Squillace) in Bruttium, 469-470, of a noble, wealthy, and patriotic family. Cassiodorus was brought up under circumstances highly favourable to his education, which included the study of grammar, rhetoric, dialectic, music, arithmetic, geometry, astronomy, mechanics, anatomy, Greek, and the sacred Scriptures. His learning and accomplishments early attracted the notice of Odoacer, the first barbarian ruler of Italy, by whom he was made "comes privatarum," and subsequently "comes sacrarum largitionum" (*Var.* i. 4). After the final defeat of Odoacer by Theodoric at Ravenna, 493, Cassiodorus retired to his patrimonial estate in Bruttium, and secured the wavering allegiance of the provincials to the cause of the new ruler; for this service he was appointed by Theodoric to the official government of Lucania and Bruttium. Happy in the art of ruling to the satisfaction of the governed without neglecting the interests of his master, he was summoned, upon the conclusion of his prefecture, to Ravenna, and advanced successively to the dignities of secretary, quaestor, master of the offices, praetorian prefect, patrician, and consul. Meanwhile he enjoyed an intimacy with the prince, which, reflected as it is in his *Varieties*, has given to that work much of the character and value of a state journal. Illiterate himself, Theodoric employed the eloquent pen of his minister in all public communications, and spent his leisure time in acquiring from him erudition of various kinds (*Var.* ix. 24). It would seem to have been the ambition of Cassiodorus, whose genius for diplomacy was consummate, to bring about a fusion between the Arian conquerors and the conquered Catholic population of Italy, to establish friendly relations with the Eastern empire, and possibly to create at Rome a peaceful centre to which the several barbaric kingdoms which had established themselves in Gaul, Spain, and Africa might be attracted. The progress of Theodoric to the capital, where the schism between pope Symmachus and his rival, Laurentius, was then raging, A.D. 500, was probably planned by him in view of this result (*Var.* xii. 18, 19; cf. Gibbon, *Decl. and Fall*, c. 39); but the temper of Theodoric's declining years must have disappointed the hopes of Cassiodorus, and in 524 he resolved to divest himself of his honours, and to seek shelter in his Calabrian retreat from the storm which proved fatal to his co-senators, Boëthius and Symmachus. After the death of Theodoric, 525, Cassiodorus again became conspicuous as the trusted adviser of his daughter Amalasuntha, widow of Eutaric, who acted as regent for her son Athalaric (*Var.* ix. 25). By his influence the Goths were kept in subjection to the new rule, notwithstanding the Roman proclivities of Amalasuntha as displayed in the education of the young prince. The threatened danger of an invasion by Justinian was likewise averted by the ready aid of his purse and pen (Procop. *B. G.* i. 3). Upon the enforced acceptance by Amalasuntha of Theodatus as co-regent, Cassiodorus again submitted to circumstances (*Var.* x. 6, 7), and wrote letters soliciting the goodwill of the senate and the emperor (x. 1, 2, 3). He was then praetorian prefect and continued to serve under Theodatus after the untimely death of Athalaric and the treacherous murder of Amalasuntha. One is tempted to suspect the nobleness of a character which, no matter how infamous the ruler, could accommodate itself with such singular tact to every change of government; but Cassiodorus was no mere time-server. His writings shew him to have been animated by a truly patriotic spirit; and if he adapted himself skilfully to the varying humours of the court, it was that he might be able to alleviate the misfortunes of his conquered countrymen.

Upon the triumph of Belisarius and the downfall of the Ostrogoths, Cassiodorus, now 70 years of age, withdrew to his native province and founded the monastery of Viviers at the foot of Mount Moscius, which he describes (xii. 15). For 50 years he had laboured to preserve authority from its own excesses, to soften the manners of the Goths and uphold the rights of the Romans; but, weary of the superhuman task, turned to the cloister for repose and freedom. His activity, however, was not satisfied with the ordinary occupations of monastic life. Hence while the summit of the mountain was set apart for the hermits of the community (*monasterium castellense*), there sprang up at its base, beneath his own immediate auspices, a society of coenobites, devoted to the pursuit of learning and science (*monasterium vivariense*). He endowed the monastery with his extensive Roman library (*Div. Lit.* c. 8). The monks were incited by his example to the study of classical and sacred literature, and trained in the careful transcription of manuscripts, in the purchase of which large sums were continually disbursed. Bookbinding, gardening, and medicine were among the pursuits of the less intellectual members of the fraternity (*ib.* 28, 30, 31). Such time as he himself could spare from the composition of sacred or scientific treatises he employed in constructing self-acting lamps, sundials, and water-clocks for the use of the monastery. Nor was the influence of his example confined to his own age, institution, or country; the multiplication of manuscripts became gradually as much a recognized employment of monastic life as prayer or fasting; and for this the statue of Cassiodorus deserves an honourable niche in every library. The date of his death is uncertain. He composed his treatise on orthography in his 93rd year (*de Orthogr. praef.*).

Of his extant writings, the twelve Books of Varieties, consisting principally of letters, edicts, and rescripts, are the only work of real importance; apart, however, from the study of these pages, it is hardly possible to obtain a true knowledge of the Italy of the 6th cent. The very style of the writer, possessing, as it does, a certain elegance, yet continually deviating from pure idiom and good taste, is singularly characteristic of the age which witnessed the last flicker of Roman civilization under the Ostrogothic rule. It is as though the pen of Cicero had been dipped in barbaric ink. The general result is artificial and bizarre; but though his meaning is frequently obscured by his rhetoric, his manner is not as unpleasing as is often asserted. It will be sufficient to enumerate here the other writings of Cassiodorus, a more detailed account of which is given in Smith's *D. of G. and R. Biogr.* (2) *Historiae Ecclesiasticae Tripartitae*, libri xii., being an epitome of the ecclesiastical histories of Sozomen, Socrates, and Theodoretus, as digested and translated by Epiphanius Scholasticus. (3) *Chronicon*, chiefly derived from Eusebius, Jerome, and Prosper. (4) *Computus Paschalis.* (5) *Expositio in Psalmos*, principally borrowed from St. Augustine. (6) *Expositio in Cantica Canticorum*, of doubtful authenticity. (7) *De Institutione Divinarum Literarum*, an interesting work as illustrating the enlightened spirit which animated the monastic life of Viviers. (8) *Complexiones in Epistolas Apostolorum, in Acta, et in Apocalypsin*, first brought to light by the Marquis Scipio Maffei at Florence, in 1721. (9) *De Artibus ac Disciplinis Liberalium Literarum.* (10) *De Oratione et de Octo Partibus Orationis*, of doubtful authenticity. (11) *De Orthographia.* (12) *De Anima.* Of the lost writings of Cassiodorus the most important appears to have been *de Rebus Gestis Gothorum*, libri xii., of which we have the abridgment of Jornandes.

The best ed., together with an appendix containing the commentaries discovered by Maffei, s in Migne's *Patr.* vols. lxix. lxx. [E.M.Y.]

Catharine (Catharina, Catherine, etc.), St., virgin and martyr of Alexandria. Tillemont writes, in the 17th cent., that it would be hard to find a saint more generally reverenced, or one of whom so little was known on credible authority, and adds that no single fact about her is certain (*Mém. eccl.* vii. pp. 447, 761; cf. Papebrocius, as quoted in Baron. *Ann. Eccl.* ed. Theiner, iii. *ad ann.* 307).

The earliest mention of St. Catharine in the Eastern church (v. *Menology of Basil*) under the name of Hικαθαρίνα (possibly a corruption of ἡ καθαρίνη, dim. of καθαρός, pure), is about the end of 9th cent. (Tillem. *u.s.*; Baillet, *Vies des Saints*, tom. viii. Nov. 25); in 13th cent. she appears in the Latin Martyrologies (Baillet, *ib.*), the crusaders having brought her fame to Europe among other marvels from the East. Some time in the 8th or 9th cent. the monks on Mount Sinai disinterred the body, as they were eager to believe, of one of those Christian martyrs whose memory they cherished. Eusebius relates how a lady of Alexandria—he omits her name—was one of the victims of Maximinus early in 4th cent. (*H. E.* xiii. 14). It was easy to identify the corpse as that of the anonymous sufferer, to invent a name for it, and to bridge over the distance between Alexandria and Mount Sinai. Simeon Metaphrastes, a legendist of Constantinople in 10th cent., gives a long account of St. Catharine's martyrdom, with horrible details of her tortures, an exact report of her dispute in public with the philosophers of the city and of the learned oration by which she converted them and the empress Faustina and many of the court, and how her corpse was transported to Mount Sinai by angels (Martin, *Vies des Saints*, tom. iii. pp. 1841, seq.). But the whole story is plainly unhistorical, even apart from the significant fact that there is no external testimony to its authenticity. For in Eusebius the emperor's exasperation is provoked, not, as in the legend, by a refusal to abjure Christianity and to sacrifice to his gods, but by a refusal to gratify his guilty passion; and the punishment inflicted is merely exile, not torture and death. Even Baronius, who suggests emendations to make the legend more probable, hesitates to accept it as historical, while his commentator, with Tillemont and Baillet, abandons altogether the hopeless attempt to reconcile Simeon Metaphrastes with Eusebius.

The martyrdom of St. Catharine is commemorated in the Latin and Greek calendars on Nov. 25; the discovery ("invention") of her body on Mount Sinai on May 13 in the French Martyrology (Baillet, *u.s.*). In England her festival was promoted from the 2nd class (on which field labour, though no other servile work, was permitted) to the 1st class of holydays in 13th cent. (*Conc. Oxon.* A.D. 1222, c. 8; *Conc. Vigorn.* A.D. 1240, c. 54), and retained as a black-letter day at the Reformation. It was left untouched in Germany at the retrenchment of holidays in A.D. 1540. In France it was gradually abolished as a holiday, although the office was retained in 17th cent. (Baillet, *u.s.*). In Europe during the middle ages her name was held in great reverence. Louis IX. of France erected in Paris a costly church in her name; and the famous Maid of Orleans claimed her special favour and tutelage (Martin, *u.s.*). The head of St. Catharine was alleged to be preserved in her church in the Piazza of St. Peter's at Rome. She was regarded generally as the patron saint of schools, probably from the tradition of her learned controversy with the philosophers at Alexandria. A semi-monastic order, the Knights of Mount Sinai or of Jerusalem, instituted in Europe A.D. 1063 in honour of St. Catharine, under the rule of St. Basil, bound themselves by vows to chastity, though not to celibacy (*castità conjugale*), to entertain pilgrims, and in rotation, each for two years, to guard the holy relics. Their dress was a white tunic, and embroidered on it a broken wheel, armed with spikes, in memory of the jagged wheel on which, according to the legend, the saint was racked, and which was miraculously shattered by divine interposition. The order became extinct after the fall of Constantinople; but in the 17th cent. the Basilian monks at Paris gave the badge of the order to any candidates who would take the vow of chastity and of obedience to the rule of St. Basil (Moroni, *Dizion. Eccles.* Reference to Giustiniani, *Hist. Chronol. d. Ordini Equestri*, p. 121; Bonami, *Catalogo d. Ord. Equest.* p. 21).

See Tillem. *Mém. eccl.*; Baronius (Caesar), *Annales Ecclesiastici* (Barri Ducis, 1864, 4to, tom. iii.); Bollandus Joannes, *Les Actes des saints*, etc. (Lyons, Besançon, 1865, 8vo, Nov. 25); *Life of St. Catharine, with its Latin original from the Cotton MSS.*, ed. with Intro., etc., by E. Einenkel (Lond. 1884); *Life and Martyrdom of St. Cath. of Alex.* (Roxburghe Club, No. 90, Lond. 1884). [I.G.S.]

Caulacau. [BASILIDES.]

Celsus (1). Of the personal history of this, the first great polemical adversary of Christianity, we know nothing with certainty; and even Origen, from whom the whole of our knowledge of Celsus is derived, had received the work of Celsus, entitled ἀληθὴς λόγος, or the *True Discourse*, without any hint of the history or date of its author.

But questions far more interesting than personal ones are raised by his attack on Christianity, of which enough has been preserved by Origen in his *contra Celsum* to convey to us a very tolerable idea of its nature. We must be on our guard at once against disparaging it too much, and against thinking too highly of its ability. Origen, indeed, who to all appearance is a very fair antagonist, speaks of it with contempt. But Celsus was not a mere polemical assailant; he was a philosopher on his own account, and held in certain respects by no means unenlightened opinions. He had strong faith in reason. "What evil is it," he asks, "to be learned and to have cultivated the intellect with the best pursuits, to be and to appear wise? What obstacle are these things to the knowledge of God? Do not they rather lead and assist to the attainment of truth?" Nor had that similarity between the human and the animal frame, which the natural science of our own day insists upon, escaped his notice. Hence he deduces that ants "converse, have reason, notions of general truths, speech," etc. (iv. 84), and even that they have knowledge of God. It would be hard, again, to cavil at his ideas of the Divine Nature; he speaks of men "burning with the love of it" (i. 8); he is intolerant of the association of it with anything that is mortal or perishable. He was not free from superstition; he believed in magic, and declared that serpents and eagles were more skilled in it than men (iv. 86). Baur says that "in acuteness, in dialectical aptitude, in many-sided cultivation, at once philosophic and general, Celsus stands behind no opponent of Christianity." Admitting that this panegyric is not groundless, we must add, that in vital insight Celsus was deficient. As an opponent of Christianity, the chief characteristic of Celsus is a strong, narrow, intolerant common sense. To him Christianity is an "exitiabilis superstitio"; he gives credence to every story against it on which he can lay his hands; he dwells with coarse jocularity on the Jewish tradition of Panthera and the Virgin Mary (i. 28, sqq.); he unearths a certain Diagramma, a figure symbolizing the world, and consisting of a circle called Leviathan enclosing ten other circles, apparently used in the rites of some sect more or less approximating to the Christians (vi. 22). He has no idea of regarding Christianity from the inside, and of inquiring into the reason of its influence; he uses jest for argument, and interprets everything in a bad sense. Treating of the flight of Jesus into Egypt, and afterwards (as he alleges) before the betrayal, he asks, "Had God need to fly from His enemies? Does fear belong to God?"

From such instances it is evident that Celsus wholly misapprehended the force of the doctrine that he was attacking. There are cases, indeed, in which he shews himself more acute. He challenges the evidence of Christianity, and asks, "Who saw the dove lighting on the head of Jesus after His baptism?" As to the Resurrection, he makes the remark which has been copied by Renan and others, that it was Mary Magdalene, "a fanatical woman," who was the first witness of the resurrection, according to all the accounts (ii. 55); and remarks on the disbelief invariably given to such accounts as those of the resurrection of Zamolxis, Pythagoras, Orpheus, Protesilaus, Hercules, and Theseus. But the most remarkable portions of his attack are those directed against the general character of Christianity. He dwells on the numerous sects of Christians, all of whom said, "Crede, si salvus fieri velis," and asks how one is to judge between so many? Origen does not deny the fact, but maintains that it is a proof of the importance of that on which they debated, and further that they all set forth Jesus alone as the means of salvation (vi. 11). Celsus accuses the Christians of lawlessness, and of keeping wholly to themselves, and not caring for those outside. He complains vehemently of them as discouraging learning, wisdom, and thought; as rejecting the authority of reason; as being the patrons of sinners, whereas to the heathen mysteries only "the holy and virtuous" were invited. He makes a great point of the opposition between the morality of the Old and New Testaments, in respect of the earthly success which is the crowning happiness of the former, and so strongly reprobated by the latter. Finally, he maintains that no revelation of the Supreme Being can be made; but that, if it could be made, it must be of universal and compelling efficacy; that, however, all that is possible is revelation by an angel or demon, and even that he denies to Judaism or Christianity.

The form of Celsus's work, the ἀληθὴς λόγος, is well known. He begins with a dialogue between a Jew and a Christian, in which the Jew sets forth his objections to Christianity. But he had not any partiality for Judaism. He treats Moses and the Jewish Scriptures with a contempt which amusingly contrasts with the uncritical reverence which he pays to the Galactophagi of Homer, the Druids, and the Getae, whom he terms "wise and ancient nations" (i. 16); and with which he accepts the stories of Linus and Musaeus, though afterwards he rejects those of Perseus and Amphion (i. 64). In one of the most unpleasing passages of his work, he compares Jews and Christians to a set of worms or frogs squabbling in the mud, and saying, "God is, and we are next to Him, and it is for our sake that the whole world is made; and God will come and take us up to heaven, except those who are bad, whom He will burn with fire."

The work of Origen against him is, as a whole, of much controversial merit and philosophical breadth. Origen, indeed, like Celsus, is not free from the superstitions of his time; thus he defends the star whose appearance is told in the second chapter of St. Matthew by a reference to comets, which, he remarks, portend future events, such as wars and pestilences. But, on the whole, there are few works of the ancient Fathers which can be read with more pleasure and profit. F. C. Baur has written an elaborate critique on Celsus in his work on *Christendom and the Christian Church in the First Three Centuries* (Tübingen, 1853). But especially valuable is Prof. Theodor Keim's monograph (Celsus's *Wahres Wort.* Zürich, 1873). Dr. Keim gathers together, and translates, the fragments of Celsus contained in Origen; and adds disquisitions of much interest, both on Celsus himself and on two of his contemporaries, Lucian of Samosata and Minucius Felix. Both Baur and Keim rate Celsus too highly; but the general tendency of Christian writers has naturally been to underrate him. The date of Celsus's treatise is fixed by Keim as A.D. 177, or 178. (Cf. Renan, *Marc-Aurèle*; Pelagaud, *Étude sur Celse* (Lyons, 1828); Aubé, *Histoire des persécutions* (Paris, 1878); Lightfoot, *Apost. Fath.* II. i. pp. 513 ff.) [J.R.M.]

Cerdo (1) (Κέρδων), a Gnostic teacher of the first half of the 2nd cent., principally known as the predecessor of MARCION. Epiphanius (*Haer.* 41) and Philaster (*Haer.* 44) assert him to have been a native of Syria, and Irenaeus (i. 27 and iii. 4) states that he came to Rome in the episcopate of Hyginus. This episcopate lasted four years, and Lipsius (*Chronologie der römischen Bischöfe*) places its termination A.D. 139-141. Bearing in mind the investigations of M. Waddington concerning the year of Polycarp's martyrdom, we prefer the earlier date, if not a still earlier one, and would put Cerdo's arrival at Rome as early as A.D. 135.

According to the account of Irenaeus, Cerdo had not the intention of founding a sect apart from the church. He describes him as more than once coming to the church and making public confession, and so going on, now teaching his doctrine in secret, now again making public confession, now convicted in respect of his evil teaching, and removed, or, as some think, voluntarily withdrawing himself, from the communion of the brethren (ἀφιστάμενος τῆς τῶν ἀδελφῶν συνοδίας). Epiphanius seems inaccurate in giving a heading to a sect of Cerdonians. Preceding writers speak only of Cerdo, not of Cerdonians; and probably his followers were early merged in the school of Marcion, who is said to have joined himself to Cerdo soon after his arrival in Rome.

Apparently Cerdo left no writings, nor is there evidence that those who report his doctrine had any knowledge of it independent of the form it took in the teaching of his Marcionite successors. Consequently we cannot now determine with certainty how much of the teaching of Marcion had been anticipated by Cerdo, or what points of disagreement there were between the teaching of the two. Hippolytus, in his *Refutation* (x. 19), makes no attempt to discriminate between their doctrines. Tertullian, in his work against Marcion, mentions Cerdo four times, but only as Marcion's predecessor. Irenaeus says that Cerdo taught that the God preached by the law and the prophets was not the Father of our Lord; for that the former was known, the latter unknown; the former was just, the latter good. Pseudo-Tertullian's account (*Haer.* 16) may be regarded as representing that in the earlier treatise of Hippolytus, which was also used by Philaster and Epiphanius. Thus we learn that Cerdo introduced two first principles (ἀρχαί) and two gods, the one good, the other evil, the latter the creator of the world. It is an important difference that to the good god is opposed in the account of Irenaeus a just one; in that of Hippolytus, an evil one. In the later work of Hippolytus already cited, Cerdo is said to have taught three principles of the universe, ἀγαθὸν, δίκαιον, ὕλην. Ps.-Tertullian goes on to say that Cerdo rejected the law and the prophets, and renounced the Creator, teaching that Christ was the son of the higher good deity, and that He came not in the substance of flesh but in appearance only, and had not really died or really been born of a virgin; and that Cerdo only acknowledged a resurrection of the soul, denying that of the body. He adds, but without support from the other authorities, that Cerdo received only the Gospel of St. Luke, and that in a mutilated form; that he rejected some of Paul's epistles and portions of others, and completely rejected the Acts and the Apocalypse. There is every appearance that Ps.-Tertullian here transferred to Cerdo what in his authority was stated of Marcion. For a discussion of his other doctrines see MARCION. [G.S.]

Cerinthus, a traditional opponent of St. John. It will probably always remain an open question whether his fundamentally Ebionite sympathies inclined him to accept Jewish rather than Gnostic additions. Modern scholarship has therefore preferred to view his doctrine as a fusing together and incorporating in a single system tenets collected from Jewish, Oriental, and Christian sources; but the nature of that doctrine is sufficiently clear, and its opposition to the instruction of St. John as decided as that of the Nicolaitanes.

Cerinthus was of Egyptian origin, and in religion a Jew. He received his education in the Judaeo-Philonic school of Alexandria. On leaving Egypt he visited Jerusalem, Caesarea, and Antioch. From Palestine he passed into Asia and there developed τῆς αὐτοῦ ἀπωλείας βάραθρον (Epiph. xxviii. 2). Galatia, according to the same authority, was selected as his headquarters, whence he circulated his errors. On one of his journeys he arrived at Ephesus, and met St. John in the public baths. The Apostle, hearing who was there, fled from the place as if for life, crying to those about him: "Let us flee, lest the bath fall in while Cerinthus, the enemy of the truth, is there."

The value of this and other such traditions is confessedly not great—that of the meeting with St. John in the bath is told of "Ebion" as well as of Cerinthus;—but a stratum of fact probably underlies them, and they at least indicate the feeling with which the early "Churchmen" regarded him. Epiphanius, by whom the majority are preserved, derived the principal portion of his statements partly from Irenaeus, and partly, as Lipsius has shewn with high probability, from the now lost earlier work of Hippolytus on heresies.

His doctrines may be collected under the heads of his conception of the Creation, his Christology, and his Eschatology. His opinions upon two of these points, as preserved in existing works, support the usual view, that Cerinthus rather than Simon Magus is to be regarded as the predecessor of Judaeo-Christian Gnosticism.

Unlike Simon Magus and Menander, Cerinthus did not claim a sacred and mystic power. Caius the Presbyter can only assert against him that he pretended to angelic revelations (Eus., Theod.). But his mind, like theirs, brooded over the *co-existence* of good and evil, spirit and matter; and his scheme seems intended to free the "unknown God" and the Christ from the bare imputation of infection through contact with nature and man. Trained as he was in the philosophy of Philo, the Gnosis of Cerinthus did not of necessity compel him to start from *opposition*—in the sense of malignity—of evil to good, matter to spirit. He recognized opposition in the sense of difference between the one active perfect principle of life—God—and that lower imperfect passive existence which was dependent upon God; but this fell far short of malignity. He therefore conceived the material world to have been formed not by "the First God," but by angelic Beings of an inferior grade of Emanation (Epiph.). More precisely still he described the main agent as a certain Power (δύναμις) separate and distinct from the "Principality" (ἡ ὑπὲρ τὰ ὅλα αὐθεντεία, v. Suicer, *Thes.* s.v. αὐθ.) and ignorant of τὸν ὑπὲρ πάντα θεόν. He refused in the spirit of a true Jew to consider the "God of the Jews" identical with that author of the material world who was alleged by Gnostic teachers to be inferior and evil. He preferred to identify him with the Angel who delivered the Law (Epiph. and Philastr.). Neander and Ewald have pointed out that these are legitimate deductions from the teaching of Philo. The conception is evidently that of an age when hereditary and instinctive reverence for the law served as a check upon the system-maker. Cerinthus is a long way from the bolder and more hostile schools of later Gnosticism.

The Christology is of an Ebionite cast and of the same transition character. It must not be assumed that it is but a form of the common Gnostic dualism, the double-personality afterwards elaborated by Basilides and Valentinus. Epiphanius, the chief source of information, is to many a mere uncritical compiler, sometimes following Hippolytus, sometimes Irenaeus. Now it is *Christ* Who is born of Mary and Joseph (Epiph. xxviii. 1), now it is *Jesus* Who is born like other men, born of Joseph and Mary; He differs from others only in being more righteous, more prudent, and more wise; it is not till after baptism, when Jesus has reached manhood, that Christ, "that is to say, the Holy Spirit in the form of a dove," descends upon Jesus from above (ἄνωθεν ἐκ τοῦ ἄνω Θεοῦ· ἀπὸ τῆς ὑπὲρ τὰ ὅλα αὐθεντείας, Iren.), revealing to Him and through Him to those after Him the "unknown Father." If, as Lipsius thinks (p. 119), Irenaeus has here been influenced by the later Gnostic systems, and has altered the original doctrine of Cerinthus as given in Hippolytus, that doctrine would seem to be that he considered "Jesus" and "Christ" titles given indifferently to that One Personality Which was blessed by the descent of the Holy Spirit, the Power on high (ἡ ἄνωθεν δύναμις). This Power enables Jesus to perform miracles, but forsakes Him at His Passion, "flying heavenwards." So, again, it is *Jesus*, according to one passage of Epiphanius, Who dies and rises again, the Christ being spiritual and remaining impassible; according to a second, it is *Christ* Who dies, but is not yet risen, nor shall He rise till the general resurrection. That passage, however, which allows that the human body of Jesus had been raised from the dead separates its author completely from Gnostic successors.

The Chiliastic eschatology of Cerinthus is very clearly stated by Theodoret, Caius, Dionysius (Eus.), and Augustine, but not alluded to by Irenaeus. His silence need perhaps cause no surprise: Irenaeus was himself a Chiliast of the spiritual school, and in his notes upon Cerinthus he is only careful to mention what was peculiar to his system. The conception of Cerinthus was highly coloured. In his "dream" and "phantasy" the Lord shall have an earthly kingdom in which the elect are to enjoy pleasures, feasts, marriages, and sacrifices. Its capital is Jerusalem and its duration 1000 years: thereafter shall ensue the restoration of all things. Cerinthus derived this notion from Jewish sources. His notions of eschatology are radically Jewish: they may have originated, but do not contain, the Valentinian notion of a spiritual marriage between the souls of the elect and the Angels of the Pleroma.

Other peculiar features of his teaching may be noted. He held that if a man died unbaptized, another was to be baptized in his stead and in his name, that at the day of resurrection he might not suffer punishment and be made subject to the ἐξουσία κοσμοποιός (cf.

I. Cor. xv. 29). He had learned at Alexandria to distinguish between the different degrees of inspiration, and attributed to different Angels the dictation severally of the words of Moses and of the Prophets; in this agreeing with Saturninus and the Ophites. He insisted upon a partial observance of the "divine" law, such as circumcision and the ordinances of the sabbath; resembling, in this severance of the genuine from the spurious elements of the law, the school which produced the *Clementina* and the *Book of Baruch*. He did not even scruple (acc. to Epiph.) to call him who gave the law "not good," though the epithet may have been intended to express a charge of ethical narrowness rather than an identification of the Lawgiver with the πονηρός of Marcion. Epiphanius admits that the majority of these opinions rest upon report and oral communication. This, coupled with the evident confusion of the statements recorded, makes it difficult to assign to Cerinthus any certain place in the history of heresy. He can only be regarded generally as a link connecting Judaism and Gnosticism. The traditionary relations of Cerinthus to St. John have probably done more to rescue his name from oblivion than his opinions. In the course of time popular belief asserted that St. John had written his Gospel specially against the errors of Cerinthus, a belief curiously travestied by the counter-assertion that not St. John but Cerinthus himself was the author of both the Gospel and the Apocalypse. It is not difficult to account on subjective grounds for this latter assertion. The Chiliasm of Cerinthus was an exaggeration of language current in the earliest ages of the church; and no work in N.T. reproduced that language so ingenuously as the Apocalypse. The conclusion was easy that Cerinthus had but ascribed the Apocalypse to the Apostle to obtain credit and currency for his own forgery. The "Alogi" argued upon similar grounds against the Fourth Gospel. It did not agree with the Synoptists, and though it disagreed in every possible way with the alleged doctrines of Cerinthus, yet the false-hearted author of the Apocalypse was, they asserted, certainly the writer of the Gospel.

The Cerinthians (known also as Merinthians) do not appear to have long survived. If any are identical with the Ebionites mentioned by Justin (*Dial. c. Tryph.* 48), some gradually diverged from their master in a retrograde direction (Dorner, p. 320); but the majority were engulfed in sects of greater note. One last allusion to them is found in the ecclesiastical rule applied to them by Gennadius Massiliensis: "Ex istis si qui ad nos venerint, non requirendum ab eis utrum baptizati sint an non, sed hoc tantum, si credant in ecclesiae fidem, et baptizentur ecclesiastico baptismate" (*de Eccles. Dogmatibus*, 22; Oehler, i. 348).

The following primary and secondary authorities upon Cerinthus may be mentioned: Irenaeus, *adv. Haer.*; S. Hippolytus, *Refutatio omn. Haeres.* ("Philosophumena"); Theod. *Haeret. Fab. Comp.*; Epiphanius, *Epit. Panar.*, *Haer.*; Philastrius, *de Haeret.*, *Corp. Haeresolog.*; Augustine, *de Haer.* lib. viii.; Pseudo-Tertullian, *Lib. adv. omn. Haeres.* x.; Eus. *Hist. Eccles.*; Neander, *Ch. Hist.*; Ewald, *Gesch. d. Volk. Israel*; Gieseler, *Eccles. Hist.*; Lipsius, *Zur Quellen-Kritik d. Epiphanius*; Dorner, *Die Lehre v. d. Person Christi*; Milman, *Hist. of Christianity*; Robertson, *Hist. of Christ. Ch.*; Westcott, *Canon of N.T.*, p. 243 (ed. 1866); Zahn, *Gesch. der N.T. Canons*, vol. i. 220-262, vol. ii. 973 etc. [J.M.F.]

Christopher, St. (Χριστοφόρος), a martyr of universal fame, baptized by St. Babylas, the martyr-bp. of Antioch, who suffered (*c.* 250) under Decius in Lycia. From early times the untrustworthy character of some of the popular stories of him has been acknowledged. Usuard (A.D. 876) thus commemorated him (July 25) after St. James, according to the common Western use, in his *Martyrologium*: "At Samos in Licia. After he had been scourged with iron rods, and then delivered from the broiling flames by the virtue of Christ, his head was at last severed from his body, which had fallen full of arrow-wounds, and the martyr's witness was complete."

For the legends respecting him (including the very familiar, but quite unauthentic, one of his bearing the Christ-child), see *D. C. B.* (4-vol. ed., *s.v.*), and two simple works written respectively by the late Archd. Allen and W. G. Pearse (S.P.C.K.). [E.B.B.]

Chromatius, bp. of Aquileia, one of the most influential Western prelates of his day, the friend and correspondent of Ambrose, Jerome, Rufinus, and other leading ecclesiastics, and a warm supporter of Chrysostom against his Oriental assailants. He was a native of Aquileia, where he resided under the roof of his widowed mother, together with his brother Eusebius and his unmarried sisters. Jerome, writing *c.* A.D. 374, congratulates the mother on her saintly offspring (Hieron. *Ep.* xliii. [vii.]). He was still a presbyter when he took part in the council held at Aquileia, against the Arians Palladius and Secundianus, A.D. 381 (Ambrose, *Gest. Concil. Aquil.* tom. ii. pp. 834, § 45; 835, § 51; 843, § 76). On the death of Valerian, Chromatius became bishop of his native city. The date is placed by Baronius towards the end of A.D. 388.

It was at his request that St. Ambrose expounded the prophecy of Balaam in an epistolary form (Ambros. *Ep.* lib. i. ep. 50, § 16). To his importunities, together with those of Heliodorus, bp. of Altino, and the liberality with which they both contributed to the expenses, we owe several of Jerome's translations of and commentaries on the books of O.T. (*e.g.* Tobit, Prov., Eccl., Cant., and Chron.). In A.D. 392 he dedicated to Chromatius his two books of Commentaries on Habakkuk (*Prolog. ad Habacc.*), and *c.* 397 yielded to his urgency and undertook the translation of Chronicles (*Praef. in Paralip.*).

Chromatius was also an early friend of Rufinus, who, whilst an inmate of the monastery at Aquileia, received baptism at his hands *c.* A.D. 371 (Rufin. *Apolog. in Hieron.* lib. i. p. 204). When, on the publication of Rufinus's translation of Origen's *de Principiis*, the friendship between Jerome and Rufinus was exchanged for violent animosity, Chromatius maintained his friendship with both, and did his best to reconcile them. Chromatius imposed on Rufinus the task of translating the *Ecclesiastical History* of Eusebius into Latin, together with Origen's Homilies on Joshua (Rufin. *Hist.* p. 15).

In the persecution of Chrysostom, Chromatius warmly embraced his cause. The position he held in the West is shewn by Chrysostom's uniting his name with those of Innocent bp. of Rome and Venerus bp. of Milan in the protest addressed to the Western church (Pallad. c. ii. *ad fin.*). Chromatius sent Chrysostom a letter of sympathy by the hands of the Western deputation (*ib.* c. iv.), and A.D. 406 received from him a letter of grateful thanks (Chrys. *Ep.* clv.). Chromatius also wrote in Chrysostom's behalf to Honorius, who forwarded his letter to his brother Arcadius as an evidence of the sentiments of the Western church (Pallad. c. iii. iv.). He died *c.* 407.

We have under his name 18 homilies on "the Sermon on the Mount," commencing with a *Tractatus Singularis de Octo Beatitudinibus*, followed by 17 fragments of expositions on Matt. iii. 15-17; v.; vi. His interpretation is literal, not allegorical, and his reflections moral rather than spiritual. Galland. *Bibl. Vet. Patr.* viii. c. 15; Migne, *Patr. Lat.* xx. 247 seq.; Tillemont, *Mém. eccl.* xi. pp. 538 seq.; Cave, *Hist. Lit.* i. p. 378. [E.V.]

Chrysippus, one of four brothers, Cappadocians by birth, of whom two others were named Cosmas and Gabriel, as recorded by Cyril of Scythopolis. They left their native country for Jerusalem, that they might be instructed by the celebrated abbat Euthymius. In 455 Chrysippus was made the superior of the monastery of Laura, and subsequently of the church of the Resurrection, by the patriarch Juvenal. He was raised to the presbyterate, and on the elevation of his brother Cosmas, who had held the office, to the see of Scythopolis, was appointed "guardian of the Holy Cross," which he held till his death. Chrysippus was a copious author, and according to Cyril, who praises him as *θαυμαστὸς συγγραφεύς*, "left many works worthy of all acceptation," very few of which are extant. A "laudatio Joannis Baptistae," delivered on the occasion of his festival, is printed in a Latin translation by Combefis (*Biblioth. Concionat.* vii. 108). Fabricius mentions a *Homilia in Deiparam*, printed in the *Auctarium Biblioth. Patr.* (Paris, 1624), vol. ii. p. 424, and a *Laudatio Theodori Martyris*, which appears to be lost. Photius (Cod. 171) records his having read in a writing of Chrysippus a statement relating to the baptism of Gamaliel and Nicodemus by SS. Peter and John, and the martyrdom of the latter, which Chrysippus had derived from a fellow-presbyter, Lucian, to whom it had been revealed in a dream, together with the localities in which their bodies and that of St. Stephen were to be found. This is a very early example of the dreams indicating the position of valuable relics which we meet with so frequently in the middle ages, by which the failing fortunes of a religious house were revived, or the rival attractions of another establishment emulated (Cyrill. Scythop. *Vit. S. Euthym.*; Cave, *Hist. Lit.* i. 444; Combefis, *Bibl. Conc.* i. 8.) [E.V.]

Chrysogonus (1), martyr in the persecution of Diocletian, whose name was inserted in the Canon of the Mass from a very early period, which shews his importance, though little is now known of him. In the *Menology* he is commemorated along with Anastasia, Dec. 22. He was of "great Rome," "a man that feared God," "teacher of the Christians"; "and when persecution was set on foot he was arrested and cast into prison." "Diocletian, staying at Nice, wrote to Rome that all the Christians should die, and that Chrysogonus should be brought bound to Nice, and when he was brought he beheaded him." For Nice we should probably read Nicomedia. In these acts it is easy to trace the effects of the first and second of Diocletian's edicts. Chrysogonus evidently was not one of the traditors, so numerous at Rome under the first edict, Feb. A.D. 303. Hence, when by the second edict, not long after, all the clergy were committed to jail, he exercised great influence from his prison on the faithful, still for the most part unscathed and at large. The question is to what we are to refer the statement about the decree that all Christians should be killed, and that Chrysogonus should be brought to Bithynia. His passion is assigned to Dec. 22. By the third edict, on the great anniversary festival of the emperor on the 21st, the clergy were to sacrifice if they were to be included in the general release of prisoners; if not, torture was to be employed to induce them. But there were no general orders for the arrest of all Christians. The rescript of Trajan was still in force. But the great festival must have brought to light many a recusant. They might not be executed, but if they died under torture it was strictly legal. When, in the spring of A.D. 304, the fourth edict appears, it sets forth no new penalties; it merely interprets the previous decrees in all the grim pregnancy of their meaning: "certis poenis intereant."

It may well be that the constancy of men like Chrysogonus, under their tortures, was among the things that drove Diocletian mad; and that he left word at his hurried departure from Rome (Dec. 22, A.D. 303), "Send him after me." The martyrdom is assigned by several Western authorities to Aquileia or the neighbouring Aquae Gradatae in Friulia. The day to which it is almost universally assigned in the West, from the Calendar of Carthage onwards, is Nov. 24. Anastasia's commemoration in the West is on Dec. 25, and in some of the Hieronymian martyrologies her passion is assigned to Sirmium, which was probably the scene of Diocletian's illness. But Usuard tells that she was transported to the little isle Palmaruola (about lat. 41°, long. 31°) in the Tyrrhene sea. [E.B.B.]

Chrysologus, Petrus, archbp. of Ravenna, A.D. 433-454, said to have been born at Forum Cornelii (Imola), according to Agnellus, in the episcopate of Cornelius, by whom he was brought up (*Serm.* 165), ordained deacon, and made *oeconomus* of the church. The ordinary account of Peter's elevation to the see of Ravenna, which is repeated by successive biographers with ever-increasing definiteness of statement, does too much violence to the facts of history to be worthy of credit. The improbabilities of the story are exposed by Tille mont, and it is stigmatized by Dupin as "a groundless tale related by no credible author." It is, however, given so circumstantially by

Agnellus in his *Liber Pontificalis* that it may contain some distorted elements of truth.

In the 176 sermons of his still extant we look in vain for traces of the golden eloquence to which he owed his surname. They are very short, written in brief simple sentences; his meaning is always clear, and his language natural; but there is nothing in them calculated to touch the heart or move the affections. His fame as a preacher evidently depended more on voice and manner than on matter. His sermons are almost all on subjects from the gospels, usually the parables and miracles, commencing with a course of six on the prodigal son. Many other works ascribed to him, including commentaries on Scripture, and letters against the Arians, have all perished by fire, partly in the siege of Imola, by Theodoric, *c.* A.D. 524; partly in the conflagration of the archbishop's library at Ravenna, *c.* A.D. 700.

Tillemont, xv. 114 seq.; Cave, *Hist. Lit.* i. 432; Migne, *Patr. Lat.* lii. pp. 9-680; Herzog, *Real-Encyc.* ii. 695. [E.V.]

Chrysostom, John (Ἰωάννης Χρυσόστομος). The surname "golden-mouthed," given to the great preacher of Antioch, and bp. of Constantinople, on account of the magnificent brilliancy of his eloquence (cf. PETRUS CHRYSOLOGUS), has entirely superseded his personal name John, which alone is found in contemporary or closely subsequent writers. When the epithet was first applied is unknown. There is no trace of it in his lifetime, but it was in common use before the end of the 5th cent.

Chrysostom was born at Antioch probably A.D. 347. He was of good family; his father Secundus filling the post of "magister militum" (στρατηλάτης), one of the eight men of distinguished rank—*illustres viros* (Veget. *de Re Militari*, ii. 9)—who commanded the imperial armies. His mother, Anthusa, was also a lady of good family (Pallad. p. 40; Socr. vi. 3). Anthusa, while John was an infant, was left a widow at the age of twenty, refused all offers of marriage, and devoted herself to the education of her boy and the care of his property (*de Sacerdot.* lib. i. c. 55). Her unremitting devotion to her maternal duties excited admiration even from the heathen (*Ep. ad Vid. Jun.* i. c. 2, p. 340).

St. Chrysostom's life may be conveniently divided into five epochs: (*a*) His life as a layman at Antioch till his baptism and admission as a reader, A.D. 347-370; (*b*) his ascetic and monastic life, A.D. 370-381; (*c*) his career as deacon, presbyter, and preacher at Antioch, A.D. 381-398; (*d*) his episcopate at Constantinople, A.D. 398-404; (*e*) exile, A.D. 404-407.

(*a*) *Life as a Layman at Antioch.*—The intellectual power manifested at a very early age marked him out as fitted for one of the learned professions. The bar was chosen, and at about 18 years of age he began to attend the lectures of the celebrated sophist Libanius, the intimate friend and correspondent of the emperor Julian, and tutor of Basil the Great, who had come to end his days in his native city of Antioch. The genius and ability of the pupil excited the greatest admiration in his master, who, being asked on his deathbed, *c.* A.D. 395, which of his pupils he thought worthiest to succeed him, replied, "John, if the Christians had not stolen him from us" (Soz. *H. E.* lib. viii. c. 2). When Chrysostom commenced practice as an advocate, his gift of eloquence speedily displayed itself. His speeches were listened to with delight, and were highly praised by Libanius, no mean judge of rhetoric. A brilliant career was opening before the young man, leading to all that men most covet, wealth, fame, high place. But a change, gradual but mighty, came over his spirit, and like another young student of the neighbouring province of Cilicia, "the things that were gain to him he counted loss for Christ." Like Timothy at the knees of Eunice, "from a child" Chrysostom had learnt from his devout mother the things that were "able to make him wise unto salvation," and his soul revolted at the contrast between the purity of the gospel standard and the baseness of the aims and viciousness of the practices prevalent in the profession he had chosen. To accept a fee for making the worse appear the better cause seemed to his generous and guileless soul to be bribed to lie—to take Satan's wages—to sin against his own soul. His disinclination to the life of a lawyer was much increased by the influence of the example of his intimate friend Basil, the companion of his studies and the sharer of all his thoughts and plans. The two friends had agreed to follow the same profession; but when Basil decided on adopting a monastic life, and to follow, in Chrysostom's words, "the true philosophy," Chrysostom was unable at once to resolve to renounce the world, to the attractions of which his ardent nature was by no means insensible, and of which he was in some danger of becoming a slave. He was "a never-failing attendant at the law courts, and passionately enamoured of the theatre" (*de Sacerdot.* lib. i. c. 14, p. 363). His friend Basil's adoption of an ascetic life at first caused an interruption of their intercourse. But life was intolerable separated from his second self. He renewed his intimacy with Basil. The pleasures and pursuits of the world became distasteful to him, and he soon resolved to abandon it altogether, quitting mother and home, and finding some sacred retreat where he and his friend could devote themselves to strict ascetism (*ib.* c. 4). This decisive change—Chrysostom's conversion we should now call it—was greatly promoted by the acquaintance he formed at this period with the mild and holy Meletius, the orthodox and legitimate bp. of Antioch, who had recently returned to his see after one of his many banishments for the faith. Meletius quickly observed the intellectual promise of the young lawyer, and, enamoured of the beauty of his disposition, sought frequent opportunities of intercourse, and in a prophetic spirit declared the greatness of his future career (Pallad. p. 40). Up to this time Chrysostom, though the child of Christian parents, had remained unbaptized, a not unfrequent practice at this epoch. The time for public profession of his faith was now come, and after a probation of three years, Meletius baptized him, and ordained him reader. This was in A.D. 369 or 370, when Chrysostom was about 23 years old (Pallad. p. 41).

(*b*) *Ascetic and Monastic Life.*—Baptism restored the balance which Chrysostom tells us had been so seriously disturbed by Basil's higher religious attainments (*de Sacerdot.* lib. i. c. 3, p. 363). He became in the truest sense "a new man" (Pallad. p. 184). His desire to flee from the world, with his beloved Basil, was established, and only frustrated by the passionate entreaties of his weeping mother that her only child, for whom she had given up all, would not desert her. The whole scene is narrated by Chrysostom in a passage of exquisite simplicity and tenderness (*de Sacerdot.* lib. i. c. 5, pp. 363-365). His affectionate nature could not resist a mother's tears. In spite of Basil's continued urgency, he yielded so far as to remain at home. But if out of filial regard he abstained from deserting his home for a monastery, he would make a monastery of his home. He practised the most rigid asceticism, ate little and seldom, and that of the plainest, slept on the bare ground, and rose frequently for prayer. He rarely left the house, and, to avoid his old habit of slander, kept almost unbroken silence. It is not surprising that his former associates called him morose and unsociable (*ib.* lib. vi. c. 12, p. 431).

Upon some of these associates, however, his influence began to tell. Two of his fellow-pupils under Libanius, MAXIMUS, afterwards bp. of Seleucia, and THEODORUS, bp. of Mopsuestia, adopted the ascetic life under the superintendence of DIODORUS and Carterius, who presided over a monastery in or near Antioch. From Diodorus Chrysostom learnt the clear common-sense mode of interpreting Holy Scripture (repudiating the allegorizing principle), of which he and Theodore became such distinguished representatives. The inability of his friend Theodore to part definitely with the world, and stifle natural instincts, was the occasion of the composition of Chrysostom's earliest extant treatises. Theodore's love for a girl named Hermione led him to leave the ascetic brotherhood and return to secular life. Chrysostom's heart was deeply stirred at this. He regarded it as a sin to be repented of and forsaken if Theodore would not forfeit salvation. He addressed two letters to him full of impassioned eloquence, earnestly calling him to penitence and amendment. His fervid remonstrances succeeded. Theodore gave up his engagement, and finally abandoned the world (*ad Theodorum Lapsum*, Ep. i. ii.; Socr. *H. E.* vi. 3).

We now come to a passage in Chrysostom's life which we must condemn as utterly at variance with truth and honour. Yet we must bear in mind that the moral standpoint of the Fathers was on this point different from our own. It was generally held that the culpability of an act of deception depended upon its purpose, and that if this was good the deception was laudable. Chrysostom himself says, "There is a good deceit such as many have been deceived by, which one ought not even to call a deceit at all," instancing that of Jacob, "which was not a deceit, but an economy" (*Homil.* vi. *in Col.* ii. 8). On this principle, which every healthy conscience now repudiates, Chrysostom proceeded to plan and execute a deliberate fraud to entrap his friend Basil into consecration to the episcopate. Several sees were now vacant in Syria, which it was desirable to fill without delay. A body of prelates met at Antioch for this purpose. Among those suitable for the episcopate, Chrysostom and Basil were pointed out, though they were not yet even deacons. Chrysostom's awful sense of the weight and responsibility of the priestly office, which breathes in every line of his treatise *de Sacerdotio*, and of his own unfitness, made him tremble at the idea of ordination. Basil, on the contrary, he considered to be well qualified, and he was fully resolved that the church should not lose the services of his friend. While, therefore, he pretended acquiescence in his friend's proposition that they should decide alike in the matter, he secretly resolved to avoid the dreaded honour by concealment. When the time of consecration arrived, and Basil was carried before the bishops, and reluctantly forced to accept ordination, Chrysostom was nowhere to be found, and it was represented to Basil that he had been already consecrated. When too late Basil discovered the unfaithfulness to their compact, and upbraided Chrysostom; his complaints were received with laughter and loud expressions of thankfulness at the success of his plot (*de Sacerdot.* lib. i. c. 3, p. 365). [BASILIUS.]

About A.D. 374 Chrysostom carried into effect his resolution of devoting himself to an ascetic life, and left his home for a monastic community on one of the mountain ranges S. of Antioch. As there is no reference in any of his writings to any opposition from his mother, it is probable that her death had left him free. After four years spent in unremitting austerities, he left the society of his kind, and, dwelling in a mountain cavern, practised still more rigid self-discipline (Pallad. p. 41). At the end of two years his health so completely gave way that he was forced to return to his home in Antioch. To these austerities may be attributed that debilitated frame, weakness of digestion, and irritability of temperament, to which his constant physical sufferings and many of his chief difficulties and calamities are not remotely traceable.

(*c*) *A Preacher and Presbyter at Antioch.*—Chrysostom did not return to Antioch to be idle. He was ordained deacon by Meletius A.D. 381, shortly before the latter left to preside over the oecumenical council of Constantinople (Pallad. p. 42). Meletius died during the session of the council, and his successor Flavian raised Chrysostom to the presbyterate early in A.D. 386 (*ib.*). During his five years' diaconate he had gained great popularity by his aptness to teach, and his influence had made itself widely felt at Antioch. While deacon he composed the *de Virginitate*: the *Ep. ad Viduam Juniorem*, addressed to the young widow of Therasius (*c.* 381); its sequel *de non Iterando Conjugio*; and the orations *de Martyre Babyla.* After his ordination he preached his first sermon before the bishop, and a vast crowd was gathered by the fame of his eloquence (*Sermo, cum Presbyt. fuit Ordinatus, de se ac de Episcopo, deque Populi Multitudine*). The succeeding ten years, embracing Chrysostom's life as a presbyter at Antioch, were chiefly devoted to the cultivation of the gift of pulpit eloquence on which his celebrity mainly rests. It was during this period that "the great clerk and godly preacher," as our First Homily terms him, delivered the greater part of the discourses extant, which must be but a very small portion of those preached, for he preached regularly twice a week, on Saturday and Sunday, besides Lent and saints' days, and, as we learn from his homilies on Genesis, sometimes five days in succession (Tillemont, tom. xi. p. 34). Flavian appointed him frequently to preach in the cathedral. Whenever he preached the church was densely thronged, the hearers testifying their delight in loud and noisy applause. This was highly offensive to Chrysostom, who often rebuked their unseemly behaviour (*adv. Arian. de Incomprehen. Dei Natura*, Homil. iii. c. 7, p. 471; Homil. iv. § 6, p. 480). The most remarkable series of homilies, containing his grandest oratorical flights, and evincing most strikingly his power over the minds and passions of men, are the *Homilies on the Statues*, delivered in March and April, A.D. 387, while the fate of Antioch was hanging in awful suspense on the will of the justly offended emperor Theodosius. The demand for a large subsidy to pay a liberal donative to the army had exasperated the citizens. The ominous silence with which the proclamation of the edict was received, Feb. 26, broken only by the wailings of the women, was soon succeeded by mutinous cries, and all the symptoms of a popular outbreak. The passions of the mob were stimulated by those who had nothing to lose and might gain from public disorder. The influence of Flavian might have calmed the tumult, but he was from home. The rabble, swelling in numbers and fury as it rushed through the city, proceeded to acts of open violence. The public baths were ransacked; the praetorium was attacked and the mob with difficulty repulsed, the governor saving himself by flight through a back door, and finally the hall of judgment was stormed. This was the scene of their crowning act of insurrection. The portraits of the emperors, which decorated the walls of the court, were pelted with stones and filth, and torn to shreds, the Augusti themselves were loaded with curses, and the statues of Theodosius and his deceased wife, the excellent Flaccilla, were torn from their pedestals and ignominiously dragged through the streets. Further outrages were only stopped by the appearance of a band of archers dispatched by the prefect. The mutiny quelled, calm reflection set before them the probable consequences of this recent fury. Panic fear, as is usual, succeeded the popular madness. The outbursts of unrestrained passion, to which the emperor was subject, were well known. The insult to his beloved empress would be certain to be keenly resented and terribly avenged. It was only too probable that an edict would be issued for the destruction of Antioch or for the massacre of its inhabitants, foreshadowing that of Thessalonica, which three years later struck horror into the Christian world. Their only hope lay in the intercession of Flavian, who, regardless of his age and the serious illness of his sister, had instantly started for the imperial city, to lay at the emperor's feet the confession of his people and to supplicate for pardon. Day by day, during this terrible suspense, lasting for three weeks, Chrysostom devoted his noblest gifts as a sacred orator to awaken repentance among the dissolute crowds hanging on his impassioned words. Just before Easter Flavian returned with the glad tidings that their crime was pardoned. The homily delivered by Chrysostom on Easter day (the 21st of the series) describes the interview of Flavian with Theodosius, the prelate's moving appeal for clemency, and its immediate effect on the impressionable mind of the emperor, who granted a complete amnesty and urged Flavian's instant return to relieve the Antiochenes from their terrible suspense. One happy result of this crisis was the conversion of a large number of the still heathen population to Christianity (*Homil. de Anna.* I. c. 1, vol. iv. p. 812).

These events occurred in the spring of A.D. 387. For ten years longer Chrysostom continued as a preacher and teacher at Antioch. To this period may be assigned his commentaries on Gen. and Pss., St. Matt. and St. John, Acts, Rom., Cor., Gal., and Eph. Those on Tim. i., ii., Tit., and on the other Epp. of St. Paul, are considered by Tillemont to have been certainly delivered at Constantinople (Till. *Mém. eccl.* tom. xi. pp. 92-97, 370-376).

(*d*) *Episcopate of Constantinople.*—Chrysostom's residence at Antioch ended in A.D. 397. In Sept. the bp. of Constantinople, the amiable and indolent Nectarius, died. The vacant see was one of the most dignified and influential in the church. Public expectation was excited as to his successor. The nomination rested with the emperor Arcadius, but virtually with the prime minister Eutropius. Passing by numerous candidates, he determined to elevate one who had no thought of being a candidate at all, John of Antioch, whose eloquence had impressed him during a recent visit to Antioch on state business. Chrysostom's name was received with delight by the electing prelates, and at once unanimously accepted. The difficulty lay with Chrysostom himself and the people of Antioch. The double danger of a decided "nolo episcopari" on Chrysostom's part and of a public commotion among the Antiochenes was overcome by stratagem. Asterius, the "comes orientis," in accordance with secret instructions from Eutropius, induced Chrysostom to accompany him to a martyr's chapel outside the city walls. There he was apprehended by the officers of the government, and hurried over the 800 miles under military escort from stage to stage, and reached his imperial see a closely guarded prisoner. His remonstrances were unheeded; his inquiries met with obstinate silence. Resistance being useless, Chrysostom felt it more dignified to submit. He was consecrated Feb. 26, 398, by Theophilus, patriarch of Alexandria. The duty was very unwelcome, for Theophilus had left no stone unturned to secure the nomination of Isidore, a presbyter of Alexandria. The ceremony was witnessed by a vast multitude, assembled to listen to the inaugural sermon of one of whose eloquence they had heard so much. This "sermo enthronisticus" is lost (Socr. *H. E.* vi. 2; Soz. *H. E.* viii. 2; Pallad. p. 42).

Constantinople soon learnt the difference between the new bishop and his predecessor. Chrysostom at once disfurnished the episcopal residence, and disposed of the costly plate and rich equipment for the benefit of the poor and the hospitals (Pallad. pp. 46, 47). Instead of banqueting with the laity, he ate the simplest fare in his solitary chamber (*ib.* pp. 101, 102). He studiously avoided the court and association with the great, and even ordinary conversation, except when duty compelled (*ib.* pp. 103, 120-123). Such behaviour could hardly fail to be misrepresented. To the populace, accustomed to the splendour of former bishops, Chrysostom's simplicity appeared unworthy of his lofty station, and he was openly charged with parsimony, moroseness, and pride (Socr. *H. E.* vi. 4; Soz.. *H. E.* viii. 9). Nor was the contrast more acceptable to most of his clergy, whose moral tone was far from elevated. Chrysostom, with uncompromising zeal, attempted to bring them back to simplicity of life and to activity in their calling. He deposed some on charges of homicide and adultery, and repelled others from the Eucharist. He set his face resolutely against the perilous custom of receiving "spiritual sisters" (συνείσακται), which was frequently the source of the grossest immoralities. To obviate the attractions of the Arians who at night and at early dawn gathered large crowds by their antiphonal hymns under porticoes and in the open air, as well as for the benefit of those unable to attend the church in the day, he revived the old custom of nocturnal services with responsive chanting, to the indignation of those clergy to whom ease was dearer than the spiritual improvement of their flocks (Pallad. p. 47; Soz. *H. E.* viii. 8; *Homil. in Acta*, 26, c. 3, p. 212). His disciplinary measures were rendered more unpopular by his lack of a conciliatory manner, coupled with irritability of temper and no small obstinacy (Socr. *H. E.* vi. 3, 21; Soz. *H. E.* viii. 3). He was also too much swayed by his archdeacon, Serapion, a proud, violent man, who is reported to have exclaimed at an assembly of the clergy, "You will never be able, bishop, to master these mutinous priests unless you drive them before you with a single rod" (Pallad. 18, 19; Socr. *H. E.* vi. 4; Soz. viii. 9).

But while his relations with his clergy were becoming increasingly embittered, he stood high in favour with the people, who flocked to his sermons, and drank in greedily his vehement denunciations of the follies and vices of the clergy and aristocracy (Socr. vi. 4, 5). He was no less popular with Arcadius and his empress, the Frankish general's daughter, Eudoxia, who was beginning to supplant the author of her elevation, the eunuch Eutropius, and to make her feeble partner bow to her more powerful will. For a time the bishop and the empress, between whom was afterwards so uncompromising an hostility, vied with one another in expressions of mutual admiration and esteem. Towards the latter part of 398, not long after Chrysostom had taken possession of his see, the relics of some anonymous martyrs were translated by night with great ceremony to the martyry of St. Thomas, on the seashore of Drypia, about nine miles from the city, which the empress had instituted in a fit of religious excitement. So lengthened was the procession and so brilliant the torches, that Chrysostom compares it to a river of fire. The empress herself in royal diadem and purple, attended by nobles and ladies of distinction, walked by the side of the bishop, in the rear of the chest enclosing the sacred bones. It was dawn before the church was reached and Chrysostom began his sermon. It was full of extravagant laudations of Euxodia and of ecstatic expressions of joy, which afterwards formed a ground of accusation against him (*Homil. Dicta Postquam Reliquiae, etc.* vol. xii. pp. 468-473). The next day the emperor with his court visited the shrine, and, laying aside his diadem, reverenced the holy martyrs. After the departure of Arcadius Chrysostom delivered a second enthusiastic homily in praise of his piety and humility (*Homil. Dicta Praesente Imperatore*, ib. pp. 474-480).

At the same period the largeness of Chrysostom's heart and the sincerity of his Christian love were manifested by his care for the spiritual state of the numerous Goths at Constantinople. Some were Catholics, but the majority were Arians. He had portions of the Bible translated into their vernacular, and read by a Gothic presbyter to his countrymen in the church of St. Paul, who afterwards addressed them in their own tongue (*Homil.* 8, vol. xii. pp. 512-526). Chrysostom himself frequently preached to them by an interpreter. He ordained native readers, deacons, and presbyters, and dispatched missionaries to the Gothic tribes who still remained on the banks of the Danube, and consecrated a bishop from among themselves named Unilas (Theod. *H. E.* v. 30; *Ep.* 14, 207). Having learnt that the nomad Scythian tribes on the banks of the Danube were desirous of being instructed in the faith, he at once dispatched missionaries to them, and corresponded with Leontius, bp. of Ancyra, with regard to the selection of able men from his diocese for this work (*ib. H. E.* v. 31). In his zeal for the suppression of pagan idolatry he obtained an imperial edict, A.D. 399, for the destruction of the temples in Phoenicia, which was carried out at the cost of some Christian ladies of Constantinople, who also supplied funds for missionary exertions in that country (*ib.* v. 29). These efforts for the propagation of the faith were very dear to Chrysostom's heart, and even during his exile he superintended and directed them by letter (*Ep.* 53, 54, 123, 126). He endeavoured to crush false doctrine wherever it was making head. Having learnt that the Marcionite heresy was infecting the diocese of Cyrus, he wrote to the then bishop, desiring him to expel it, and offering to help him in putting in force the imperial edicts for that purpose. He thus evidenced, in the words of Theodoret, that, like St. Paul, he bore in his heart "the care of all the churches" (*H. E.* v. 31).

EUTROPIUS fell from power in 399. He had hoped for a subservient bishop; but not only did Chrysostom refuse to countenance his nefarious designs, but denounced his vices from the pulpit with unsparing fidelity. The unhappy man, hurled in a moment from the pinnacle of his greatness, took refuge for a while in the church, but was ultimately beheaded at Chalcedon (Socr. *H. E.* vi. 5; Soz. *H. E.* viii. 7; Philost. *H. E.* xi. 6; Zosimus, v. 18; Chrys. *Hom. in Eutrop.* vol. iii. pp. 454-460; *de Capto Eutrop.* ib. pp. 460-482).

Early in A.D. 400 Gainas, the haughty Goth who had had a large share in the downfall of Eutropius, demanded the surrender of three leading ministers, Aurelianus the consul, Saturninus, and count John the empress's chief favourite. To relieve the emperor of embarrassment, they surrendered themselves. Their lives were in extreme danger. Chrysostom resorted to Gainas's camp, pleaded the cause of the hostages, and endeavoured to persuade the Goth to lessen his extravagant demands to be made consul and commander-in-chief, which would have placed the emperor at his mercy. Gainas had urged his claim for one of the churches of Constantinople for Arian worship, but Chrysostom's eloquence and spiritual authority overpowered him, and he desisted for a time at least in pressing his demand (Soz. *H. E.* viii. 4; Socr. *H. E.* vi. 6; Theod. *H. E.* v. 32, 33; Chrys. *Hom. cum Saturn. et Aurel.* etc., vol. iii. pp. 482-487). The sequel belongs to general history. The emperor, as a last resort, declared Gainas a public enemy; the inhabitants of the city rose against the Goths; a general massacre ensued, and Gainas was forced to flee for safety (Zosim. v. 18-22).

At this epoch the power and popularity of Chrysostom was at its culminating point. We have now to trace its swift and complete decline. The author of his overthrow was the empress Eudoxia. Her shortlived religious zeal had burnt itself out, and when she found Chrysostom too clear-sighted to be imposed upon by an outward show of piety, and too uncompromising to connive at wrong-doing even in the highest places, and that not even her rank as empress could save her and her associates from public censure, her former attachment was changed into the most implacable enmity. Jealousy of Chrysostom's influence over Arcadius contributed to her growing aversion. Chrysostom was now the only obstacle to her obtaining undisputed supremacy over her imbecile husband, and through him over the Eastern world. Means must be found to get rid of this obstacle also. Chrysostom himself afforded the opportunity in his excess of zeal for the purity of the church by overstepping his episcopal jurisdiction, not then so strictly defined as in modern dioceses. Properly speaking, the bp. of Constantinople had no jurisdiction beyond the limits of his own city and diocese. For Constantinople, as a city whose imperial dignity was of modern creation, was not a metropolitan see, but subject ecclesiastically to the metropolitan of Heraclea (otherwise Perinthus), who was exarch of the province of Thrace. The claims of Heraclea becoming antiquated, the prelates of Alexandria, as the first of the Eastern churches, gradually assumed metropolitan rights over Byzantium. But subjection to any other see was soon felt to be inconsistent with the dignity of an imperial city, and by the third canon of the oecumenical council held within its walls, A.D. 381, its bishop was declared second to the bp. of Rome, after him coming the metropolitans of Alexandria and Antioch. But this precedence was simply honorary, and although Nectarius had set the precedent followed by Chrysostom of exercising jurisdiction in the Thracian and Asiatic dioceses, the claim did not receive legal authority until the council of Chalcedon (can. 28). At a conference of bishops held at Constantinople in the spring of A.D. 400, Eusebius of Valentinopolis accused his brother bishop, Antoninus of Ephesus, of selling ordination to bishoprics, melting down the church plate for his own benefit, and other grave offences (Pallad. p. 126). A delegacy was dispatched to Asia to investigate these charges. Many dishonest and vexatious delays occurred, and the accused bishop died before any decision could be arrived at (*ib.* pp. 130-133). The Ephesian clergy and the bishops of the circuit appealed to Chrysostom to make peace. Prompt at the call of duty, Chrysostom, though it was the depth of winter (Jan. 401), and he in very feeble health, proceeded to Ephesus. On his arrival he exercised metropolitical authority, deposing six bishops convicted of simony, and correcting with unsparing hand the venality and licentiousness of the clergy (*ib.* pp. 134-135; Socr. *H. E.* vi. 10; Soz. *H. E.* viii. 6). His excessive severity did not reconcile the reluctant ecclesiastics to the questionable authority upon which he acted. The results of Chrysostom's absence of three months from Constantinople were disastrous. He had entrusted his episcopal authority to Severian, bp. of Gabala, who basely abused his trust to undermine Chrysostom's influence at court. The cabal against Chrysostom was headed by the empress and her favourite ladies, of whose extravagance of attire and attempts to enhance their personal charms, the bishop had spoken with contemptuous ridicule, and among whom the wealthy and licentious widows Marsa, Castricia, and Eugraphia, "who used for the ruin of their souls the property their husbands had gained by extortion" (Pallad. pp. 35, 66), were conspicuous. This cabal received an important accession by the arrival of two bishops from Palestine, Antiochus of Ptolemais and the grey-haired Acacius of Beroea (Pallad. 49). [ACACIUS; ANTIOCHUS.] Serapion, Chrysostom's archdeacon, had kept his master informed of Severian's base proceedings, and had continually urged his speedy return. His return was the signal for the outbreak of open hostilities, which Chrysostom's vehement and unguarded language in the pulpit exasperated. Soon after his return, he chose his text from the history of Elijah, and exclaimed, "Gather together to me those base priests that eat at Jezebel's table, that I may say to them, as Elijah of old, 'How long halt ye between two opinions?'" (*ib.* 74). This allusion was only too clear. He had called the empress Jezebel. The haughty Eudoxia could not brook the insult, and the doom of Chrysostom was sealed. But until the plot was ripe it was necessary to keep up the semblance of friendship, and even of deference, towards one who could still make ecclesiastical authority felt. Some half-heard words of Severian, uttered in annoyance at Serapion's discourtesy, were distorted by the archdeacon into a blasphemous denial of Christ's Divinity (Socr. *H. E.* vi. 10; Soz. *H. E.* viii. 10). The charge was rashly credited by Chrysostom, who, without further inquiry, sentenced him to excommunication and banishment from Constantinople. Chrysostom was still the idol of the common people. The news spread that Severian had insulted their bishop, and Severian's life would have been in danger had he not speedily fled to Chalcedon, and put the Bosphorus between himself and the enraged mob. All the authority of the emperor and the passionate entreaties of the empress, who even placed her infant son on Chrysostom's knees in the church of the Apostles as an irresistible plea for yielding to her petition, were needed to extort forgiveness for Severian. Chrysostom interceded for him with the populace (*Hom. de Recipiendo Severiano*, vol. iii. pp. 492-494), and the semblance of peace was restored (Socr. and Soz. *u.s.*).

The secret intrigues, checked for the time, soon broke out afresh. The allusion to Jezebel was not forgiven by Eudoxia, and Severian was equally implacable. The clergy were eager to rid themselves of one who, in the words of Palladius, "like a lamp burning before sore eyes," was intolerable from the brilliancy of his virtues. All they wanted was a powerful leader.

Such a leader was found in Theophilus, bp. of Alexandria, who had been unwillingly compelled to consecrate Chrysostom. A pretext for his interference was afforded by the hospitality shewn by Chrysostom and his friends to some Egyptian monks, known from their remarkable stature as "the Tall Brethren" [AMMONIUS], whom Theophilus had treated with great injustice and cruelty, nominally because of their Origenistic views, but really because they were privy to his own avarice and other vices (Isid. Pelusiot. *Ep.* i. 142). Chrysostom had received them kindly, and written in their behalf to Theophilus, who replied with an indignant remonstrance against protecting heretics and interfering in the affairs of another diocese. The monks claimed the right of prosecuting their defamers (Pallad. pp. 51-62; Socr. *H. E.* vi. 7, 9; Soz. *H. E.* viii. 12, 13). A personal appeal to Eudoxia secured them this. Theophilus was summoned to appear before a council for the investigation of the whole case of these Nitrian monks, while their calumniators were called upon to substantiate their charges or suffer punishment. Theophilus, however, devised a scheme for turning the tables upon Chrysostom, and transforming the council into one before which Chrysostom himself might be arraigned (Pallad. p. 64). [DIOSCORUS.]

To pave the way for the execution of this plot Theophilus induced Epiphanius, the venerable bp. of Salamis, to visit Constantinople, with the decrees of a council recently held in Cyprus, by which the tenets of Origen which the Nitrian monks were charged with holding were condemned, for Chrysostom's signature (Socr. *H. E.* vi. 10-14; Soz. *H. E.* viii. 14). Epiphanius petulantly declined the honours and hospitality prepared for him until Chrysostom had formally condemned Origen and expelled "the Tall Brethren." Chrysostom replied that he left both to the coming council, and would not prejudge the matter. The relations between the two prelates were further embittered by the ordination of a deacon by Epiphanius in violation of the canons of the church (Socr. *H. E.* vi. 11). No better success attended Epiphanius's attempt to obtain a condemnation of Origen from the bishops then at Constantinople. An interview with the accused monks, at which Epiphanius was obliged to acknowledge that he had not read a page of their writings, and had condemned them on hearsay, seems to have opened his eyes to the real character of Theophilus and the nature of the transaction in which he had become an agent. He refused to take any further share in the designs of Theophilus, and set sail for Cyprus, dying on his voyage or soon after his return (Socr. *H. E.* vi. 12-14; Soz. *H. E.* viii. 14, 15).

Shortly after Epiphanius's departure Theophilus arrived at Constantinople, accompanied by a bodyguard of rough sailors from his own city of Alexandria, laden with costly presents. He received a vociferous welcome from the crews of the Egyptian corn-ships, but the bishops and clergy of the city kept aloof. He refused all communications with Chrysostom, rejected all his offers of hospitality, and, assuming the position of an ecclesiastical superior, not of a defendant about to take his trial, openly declared that he had come to depose Chrysostom for grave offences. The three weeks between his arrival and the commencement of the synod were devoted to ingratiating himself with influential personages and the disaffected clergy, by flattery, sumptuous banquets, and splendid gifts. Arcadius, probably unaware of the plans of the secret cabal, remonstrated with Chrysostom for his delay in proceeding to Theophilus's trial, which Chrysostom justified by his unwillingness to usurp a jurisdiction not legitimately his (Socr. *H. E.* vi. 15; Soz. *H. E.* viii. 16; Pallad. 65, 66; Chrys. *Ep. ad Innocent.* 1). Theophilus had no such scruples. He assumed as patriarch of Alexandria the supremacy over all Eastern bishops, and claimed the right of summoning Chrysostom as a suffragan before his tribunal. Apprehensive of the well-known popularity of Chrysostom with the lower orders, he dared not venture to hold a synod in Constantinople. The place chosen was a suburb of Chalcedon, on the other side of the Bosphorus, known as "the Oak," where was a large church with contiguous buildings for the clergy and monks. Thirty-six bishops, of whom all but seven were Egyptians, Theophilus's suffragans, formed the council. The Asiatic bishops were mainly such as Chrysostom had made his enemies during his recent visitation. None was more hostile than Gerontius of Nicomedia, whom he had deposed. The presidential chair was occupied by the bp. of Heraclea, as metropolitan. To this packed council, the members of which were at the same time "judges, accusers, and witnesses" (Phot. *Cod.* 59, *ad init.*), in the middle of July, A.D. 403, Chrysostom was summoned to answer to a list of charges containing 29 articles drawn up by the archdeacon John. Many of these were contemptibly frivolous, others grossly exaggerated, some entirely false (Pallad. p. 66). They had reference to the administration of his church and the alleged malversation of its funds; to his violent and tyrannical behaviour towards his clergy; to his private habits—"he had private interviews with women"—"he dined gluttonously by himself as a cyclops would eat"; to ritual irregularities—"he robed and unrobed himself on his episcopal throne, and ate a lozenge after celebration" (Pallad. p. 66), and had violated the rule as to fasting communion; to his having ordained unworthy persons; and heretical deductions were drawn from some incautious and enthusiastic expressions in his sermons. A second list of charges under 18 heads was presented by Isaac the monk. In these the accusation of violence and inhospitality was renewed, and he was charged with invading the jurisdiction of other prelates (Phot. *Cod.* 59; Chrys. *Ep.* 125, *ad Cyr.*). The most flagrant charge was that of uttering treasonable words against the empress, comparing her to Jezebel (Pallad. p. 74). This was construed into exciting the people to rebellion, and on this his enemies chiefly relied. The sessions lasted 14 days. Four times was Chrysostom summoned to appear before the self-appointed tribunal. His reply was dignified and unwavering. He refused to present himself before a packed synod of his enemies, to which he was summoned by his own clergy, and he appealed to a lawfully constituted general council. But irregular as the synod was, he expressed his readiness, in the interests of peace, to appear before it, if his avowed enemies, Theophilus, Severianus, Acacius, and Antiochus, were removed from the number of the judges. As this proposal met with no response, Chrysostom summoned a counter-synod of bishops attached to his cause, forty in number, whose letter of remonstrance to Theophilus was treated with contempt. At its twelfth sitting a message from the court urged the packed synod to come to a speedy decision. To this it yielded prompt obedience. By a unanimous vote it condemned Chrysostom as contumacious and deposed him from his bishopric. The charge of uttering treasonable words was left to the civil power, his enemies secretly hoping for a capital sentence (Socr. *H. E.* vi. 15; Soz. *H. E.* viii. 17). The imperial rescript confirming the sentence of deposition, however, simply condemned the bishop to banishment for life. The indignation of the people knew no bounds, when, as the evening wore on, the sentence on their beloved bishop became generally known. A crowd collected round Chrysostom's residence, and kept watch for 3 days and nights at its doors and those of the great church, lest he should be forcibly carried off. A word from him would have raised an insurrection. But the sermons he addressed to the vast multitudes in the cathedral advocated patience and resignation to the Divine Will. On the third day, during the noontide meal, he slipped out unperceived by a side door, and quietly surrendered himself to the imperial officers, by whom he was conducted after dark to the harbour and put on board a vessel which conveyed him to Hieron at the mouth of the Euxine. The victory of his enemies seemed complete. Theophilus entered the city in triumphal state and wreaked vengeance on the bishop's partisans. The people, who had crowded to the churches to pour forth their lamentations, were forcibly dislodged, not without bloodshed. Furious at the loss of their revered teacher, they thronged the approaches to the imperial palace, clamouring for his restoration and demanding that his cause should be heard before a general council. Constantinople was almost in revolt (Socr. *H. E.* vi. 16; Soz. *H. E.* viii. 18; Theod. *H. E.* v. c. 34; Zosim. *Hist.* v. 23; Pallad. p. 15). The following night the city was convulsed by an earthquake, felt with peculiar violence in the bedroom of Eudoxia. The empress fell at Arcadius's feet, and entreated him to avert the wrath of Heaven by revoking Chrysostom's sentence. Messengers were dispatched to discover the exiled prelate, bearing letters couched in terms of the most abject humiliation. The news of Chrysostom's recall caused universal rejoicing. Late as it was, a whole fleet of barques put forth to meet him. The Bosphorus blazed with torches and resounded with songs of triumph (Theod. *H. E.* v. 34). Chrysostom at first halted outside the city, claiming to be acquitted by a general council before resuming his see. The people suspected another plot, and loudly denounced the emperor and empress. Fearing a serious outbreak, Arcadius sent a secretary to desire Chrysostom to enter the walls without delay. As a loyal subject he obeyed. On passing the gates he was borne aloft by the crowd, carried into the church, placed on his episcopal seat, and forced to deliver an extemporaneous address. His triumph was now as complete as that of his enemies a few days before. Theophilus, and some of the leaders of the cabal, lingered on in Constantinople, hoping for a turn in the tide. But they were now the unpopular party, and could hardly shew themselves in the streets without being attacked and ill-treated. The person of Theophilus was no longer safe in Constantinople; while a more formidable danger was to be apprehended if the general council, which Chrysostom prevailed on the emperor to convoke, met and proceeded to inquire into his conduct. On the plea that his diocese could no longer put up with his absence, Theophilus abruptly left the city, and sailed by night for Alexandria (Socr. *H. E.* vi. 17; Soz. *H. E.* viii. 19; Chrys. *Ep. ad Innocent.*). His flight was speedily followed by the assembling of a council of about 60 bishops, which annulled the proceedings at the council of the Oak, and declared Chrysostom still legitimate bp. of Constantinople. This judicial sentence removed all Chrysostom's scruples, and he resumed his episcopal duties (Soz. *H. E.* viii. 19). The first result of the failure of the machinations of Chrysostom's enemies was an apparently complete reconciliation between him and the empress, who seemed entirely to have forgotten her former resentment. But, within two months, circumstances arose which proved the unreality of the friendship, and awakened a still more irreconcilable feud. Eudoxia aspired to semi-divine honours. A column of porphyry was erected in the lesser forum, in front of the church of St. Sophia, bearing aloft her silver statue for the adoration of the people. Its dedication in Sept. 403 was accompanied by boisterous and licentious revelry. The noise of this unseemly merriment penetrated the church and disturbed the sacred services. Chrysostom's holy indignation took fire, and he mounted the ambo and thundered forth a homily, embracing in its fierce invective all who had any share in these profane amusements, above all, the arrogant woman whose ambition was the cause of them. "Herodias," he was reported to Eudoxia to have exclaimed, "is once more maddening; Herodias is once more dancing; once more Herodias demands the head of John on a charger." All her former fury revived, and she demanded of the emperor signal redress. Sacerdotal and imperial authority stood confronted. One or other must yield (Socr. *H. E.* vi. 18; Soz. *H. E.* viii. 20; Theophan. p. 68; Zosim. v. 24). The enemies of Chrysostom were not slow in reappearing. Acacius, Severian, Antiochus, with other members of the old cabal, hastened from their dioceses, and were soon in close conference with their former confederates among the fashionable dames and worldly and frivolous clergy of the city. After repeated deliberations they decided their policy. For months past Chrysostom had been wearying the emperor with demands for a general council. Let such a council be called, care being taken to select its members discreetly, and let this fresh outburst of treasonable language be laid before it, and the result could not be doubtful. Theophilus, too wary to appear again on the scene of his defeat, directed the machinations of the plotters. He put a new and powerful tool in their hands, in the 12th canon of the council of more than doubtful orthodoxy held at Antioch, A.D. 341, pronouncing the *ipso facto* deprivation of any bishop who, after deposition, appealed to the secular arm for restoration. The council met towards the end of 403. On the succeeding Christmas Day the emperor refused to communicate, according to custom, in the cathedral, on the ground of the doubtful legality of Chrysostom's position (Socr., Soz. *u.s.*). This was justly regarded as ominous of Chrysostom's condemnation. Chrysostom, supported by 42 bishops, maintained his usual calm confidence. He continued to preach to his people, and his sermons were characterized by more than common vigour and unction (Pallad. p. 81). The synod determined to submit the decision to the emperor. An adroit demand was made in Chrysostom's favour by Elpidius, the aged bp. of Laodicea, himself a confessor for the faith, that the chief promulgators of the canon of Antioch, Acacius and Antiochus, should subscribe a declaration that they were of the same faith as its original authors, who were mainly Arians. The emperor was amused, and at once agreed to the proposal. The two bishops caught in the trap became livid with rage (ἐπὶ τὸ πελιδνότερον μεταβαλόντες τὴν μορφήν, Pallad. p. 80), but were compelled to promise a compliance, which their astuteness had little difficulty in evading. The synod continued its protracted session. We have no record of any formal decision or sentence. None indeed was necessary; Chrysostom's violation of the Antiochene canon had deposed him: he was no longer bp. of Constantinople. Meanwhile Easter was fast approaching. It would be intolerable if the emperor were a second time shut out from his cathedral on a chief festival of the church. Chrysostom must be at once removed: if possible, quietly; if not, by force. Assured by Antiochus and his companions that Chrysostom had been actually condemned and had ceased to be a bishop, Arcadius was persuaded to order his removal (*ib.* p. 81). An imperial officer was sent to desire the bishop to leave the church immediately. Chrysostom respectfully but firmly refused. "He had received the church from God, and he would not desert it. The emperor might expel him forcibly if he pleased. His violence would be his excuse before God for leaving his post." When the time arrived for the great baptismal function on Easter Eve, when no fewer than 3,000 catechumens were expected, he calmly left his residence, despite the orders of the emperor, and proceeded to the cathedral. The imperial guards, forbidden to use force, dared not interfere. The perplexed emperor summoned Acacius and Antiochus, and reproached them for their advice. They replied that "Chrysostom, being no longer a bishop, was acting illegally in administering the sacraments, and that they would take his deposition on their own heads" (*ib.* p. 82). The emperor, overjoyed at having the responsibility of the bishop's condemnation removed from himself, at once ordered some guards to drag Chrysostom from the cathedral as usurping functions no longer his, and reconduct him to his domestic prison. A vast crowd was assembled in the church of St. Sophia, to keep the vigil of the Resurrection. The sacrament of baptism was being administered to the long files of catechumens. Suddenly the din of arms broke the solemn stillness. A body of soldiers, sword in hand, burst in, and rushed, some to the baptisteries, some up the nave to the sacred bema and altar. The catechumens were driven from the font at the point of the sword. Many were wounded, and, as an eye-witness records, "the waters of regeneration were stained with blood" (*ib.* p. 81). The baptisteries appropriated to the females were invaded by the rude, licentious soldiers, who drove the women, half-dressed, shrieking into the streets. Other soldiers forced open the holy doors, and the sanctuary was profaned by the presence of pagans, some of whom, it was whispered with horror, had dared to gaze on and even to handle the Eucharistic elements. The clergy, clad in their sacred robes, were forcibly ejected, and chased along the dark streets by the brutal soldiery. With holy courage the dispersed catechumens were reassembled by their clergy in the baths of Constantine, which, hastily blessed by the priests, became sacred baptisteries. The candidates were again approaching the laver of regeneration, when they were once more forcibly dispersed by the emissaries of Antiochus. The soldiers, rude barbarians from Thrace, executed their commission with indiscriminating ferocity. The ministering priest received a wound on the head; a blow on the arm caused the deacon to drop the cruet of sacred chrism. The women were plundered of their robes and ornaments; the clergy of their vestments, and the extemporized altar of its holy vessels. The fugitives were maltreated and beaten, and many dragged off to prison. The horrors of that night remained indelibly imprinted on the minds of those who witnessed them, and were spoken of long afterwards with shuddering. Similar scenes were enacted wherever the scattered congregations endeavoured to reunite. For the greater part of Easter week Constantinople was like a city that had been stormed. Private dwellings were invaded to discover clandestine assemblies. The partisans of Chrysostom—the Joannites, as they began to be called—were thrown into prison on the slightest suspicion, and scourged and tortured to compel them to implicate others (Chrys. *Ep. ad Innocent.* ap. Pallad. pp. 17-20; Pallad. pp. 82-88). For two months the timid Arcadius could not be prevailed upon to sign the decree for Chrysostom's banishment, and Chrysostom continued to reside in his palace, which was again guarded by successive detachments of his adherents. His life was twice attempted by assassins (Soz. *H. E.* viii. 21).

(*e*) *Exile.*—At last, on June 5, A.D. 404, Arcadius was persuaded to sign the edict of banishment. Chrysostom, after a final prayer in the cathedral with some of his faithful bishops, prepared with calm submission to yield it prompt obedience. To guard against a popular outbreak, he directed that his horse should be saddled and taken to the great west entrance, and after a tender farewell of his beloved Olympias and her attendant deaconesses, he passed out unobserved at a small postern and surrendered himself to the guard, who conveyed him, with two bishops who refused to desert him, to a vessel which instantly started under cover of night for the Asiatic shore (Pallad. pp. 89-90). He had scarcely left the city when the church he had just quitted took fire; the flames, which are said to have broken out first in the episcopal throne, caught the roof, and the conflagration spread to the senate house and adjacent public buildings (*ib.* pp. 91-92; Socr. *H. E.* vi. 18; Soz. *H. E.* viii. 22; Zosim. v. 24). The suspicion, however unjustly entertained, that this fire was due to Chrysostom's adherents, resolved that the church of their beloved teacher should never be possessed by his enemies, led to a relentless persecution of the Joannites under the semblance of a judicial investigation. Innocent persons of every age and sex were put to the torture, in the vain hope that they would inculpate leading members of their party. The presbyter Tigrius and the young reader Eutropius expired under their torturer's hands. Others barely escaped with their lives, maimed and mutilated (Soz. *H. E.* viii. 22-24). The tender heart of Chrysostom was wrung upon hearing of the sufferings inflicted on his friends, especially upon his dearly loved Olympias. To the charge of incendiarism was added that of contumacious resistance to the emperor's will, in refusing to hold communion with Arsacius and Atticus, who in succession had been thrust into Chrysostom's see. [ARSACIUS; ATTICUS.] This was made a crime punishable with degradation from official rank, fine, and imprisonment. The clergy faithful to Chrysostom were deposed, and banished with every circumstance of brutality. Some did not reach their place of banishment alive. The most persevering endeavours were made to stamp out the adherents of the banished prelate, not only in Constantinople but in Asia Minor and Syria—endeavours which only deepened their attachment to him, and confirmed their resolution never to yield (Theod. *H. E.* v. 34).

All other help failing, the persecuted party appealed to the Western church as represented by its chief bishops. Letters were sent addressed to Innocent, bp. of Rome, Venerius of Milan, and Chromatius of Aquileia, by Chrysostom himself, by the 40 friendly bishops, and by the clergy of Constantinople (Pallad. p. 10). Theophilus and his adherents sent counter-representations (*ib.* p. 9). Innocent, without hesitation, pronounced the synod that had condemned Chrysostom irregular, and annulled his deposition because pronounced in the absence of the accused, and wrote authoritative letters to the chief parties. To Theophilus he addressed sharp reproof, to the Constantinopolitan clergy fatherly sympathy, to Chrysostom himself sympathy and encouragement (*ib.* pp. 23, 24; Soz. *H. E.* viii. 26), and he persuaded Honorius to write a letter to his brother Arcadius, urging the convocation of a general synod. This letter was conveyed to Constantinople by a deputation of Western bishops. But Arcadius was not a free agent. The bishops were not allowed admission to his presence. The letters they bore were wrested from them, the thumb of one of the bishops being broken in the struggle. They were insulted, maltreated, and sent home with every mark of contumely (Pallad. pp. 30-33; Soz. *H. E.* viii. 28).

Chrysostom's place of exile, selected by Eudoxia's hatred, was Cucusus, a lonely mountain village in the Tauric range, on the borders of Cilicia and Lesser Armenia. It had a most inclement climate and was exposed to perpetual inroads from Isaurian marauders. Chrysostom first learnt at Nicaea the place of his future abode. His disappointment was severe, but remonstrance was vain. Refreshing breezes from lake Ascanius invigorated his worn constitution, and helped him to face the long and sultry journey. It was the season when the heat was most oppressive, and his conductors were instructed to push on with the utmost speed, without regard to his strength or comfort. Whatever kind consideration could do to mitigate his sufferings was done by the officers in charge, Anatolius and Theodorus, who gladly executed for him all the duties of personal servants. On July 5 Chrysostom left Nicaea to traverse the scorching plains of Galatia and Cappadocia under a midsummer sun. More dead than alive, he reached Caesarea. The bp. Pharetrius, an unworthy successor of the great Basil and a concealed enemy of Chrysostom (Pallad. p. 77), was greatly troubled at a halt being fixed at Caesarea. His clergy were Joannites almost to a man: if he treated Chrysostom badly, he would offend them; if well, he would incur the more terrible wrath of the empress. So, while sending complimentary messages, he carefully avoided an interview, and used all means to dispatch him from Caesarea as quickly as possible. This was not so easy, for a severe access of his habitual ague-fever had compelled Chrysostom to seek medical aid (*Ep.* 12). He was received with enthusiastic affection by all ranks in the city. His lodging was attacked by a body of fanatical monks, probably the tools of Pharetrius, who threatened to burn it over his head unless he instantly quitted it. Driven out by their fury, Chrysostom, suffering from a fresh attack of fever, found refuge in the country house of a wealthy lady near, named Seleucia. But the threats of Pharetrius prevailed on Seleucia to turn Chrysostom out of doors in the middle of the night, on the pretext that the barbarians were at hand, and that he must seek safety by flight. The dangers of that terrible night, when the fugitives' torches were extinguished for fear of the Isaurians and, his mule having fallen under the weight of his litter, he was taken up for dead and had to be dragged or rather carried along the precipitous mountain tracks, are graphically described in his letters to Olympias (*Epp.* 12, 14). He reached Cucusus towards the end of August. His reception was of a nature to compensate for the fatigues of the way and to mitigate the trials of exile (*Ep.* 14, § 1). He found agreeable occupation in writing and receiving letters, and in social intercourse with congenial friends. Never even as bp. of Constantinople did he exert a wider and more powerful influence. The East was almost governed from a mountain village of Armenia. His advice was sought from all quarters. No important ecclesiastical measure was undertaken without consulting him. In the words of Gibbon, "the three years spent at Cucusus were the most glorious of his life. From that solitude Chrysostom, whose active mind was invigorated by misfortunes, maintained a strict and frequent correspondence with the most distant provinces; exhorted the separate congregations of his faithful adherents to persevere in their allegiance; urged the destruction of the temples of Phoenicia, and the extirpation of heresy in the isle of Cyprus; extended his pastoral care to the missions of Persia and Scythia, and negotiated by his ambassadors with the Roman pontiff and the emperor Honorius." His voluminous correspondence, which all belongs to this period, shews how close a connexion he kept up with the clergy and laity of his former diocese, and how unremitting was his oversight of the interests of his church (Soz. *H. E.* viii. 27). His chief cause of suffering was the variable climate and the length and severity of the winter. In the winter of 405 the intelligence that the Isaurian brigands were intending a *coup de main* on Cucusus drove nearly the whole of the inhabitants from the town. Chrysostom joined the fugitives. The feeble old man with a few faithful companions, including the presbyter Evethius and the aged deaconess Sabiniana, wandered from place to place, often passing the night in forests or ravines, pursued by the terror of the Isaurians, until they reached the mountain fort of Arabissus, some 60 miles from Cucusus, in the castle of which place, "more a prison than a home," he spent a winter of intense suffering, harassed by the fear of famine and pestilence, unable to procure his usual medicines, and deprived of the comfort of his friends' letters, the roads being blocked with snow and beset by the Isaurians who ravaged the whole district with fire and sword (*Epp.* 15, 61, 69, 70, 127, 131). Once he narrowly escaped falling into the hands of the marauders, who made a nocturnal attack, and all but took the town (*Ep.* 135). With the return of spring the Isaurians retired, and Chrysostom was able to descend to Cucusus early in 406. After Arabissus this desolate little town seemed a paradise. His greatest joy was in being nearer his friends and receiving their letters more regularly (*Epp.* 126, 127, 128). A third winter brought its usual hardships, but Chrysostom was now somewhat acclimatized and endured them without a recurrence of illness (*Epp.* 4, 142). His wonderful preservation from dangers hitherto, and the manner in which his feeble health, instead of sinking under the accumulated trials of his banishment, became invigorated, awoke sanguine anticipations, and he now confidently anticipated his return from banishment and his resumption of the care of his diocese (*Epp.* 1, 2, 4). But this was not to be. The unhappy Eudoxia had preceded the victim of her hatred to the grave, but left other equally relentless enemies behind. Stung with disappointment that the rigours of Cucusus had failed to kill him, and that from his mountain banishment he exercised a daily growing influence, they obtained a rescript from Arcadius transferring him first to Arabissus (Pallad. p. 96), and then to the small town of Pityus at the roots of Caucasus on the bleak N.E. shores of the Euxine. This was chosen as the most ungenial and inhospitable spot in the whole empire, and therefore the most certain to rid them quickly of his hated existence, even if, as proved to be the case, the long and toilsome journey had not previously quenched the feeble spark of life. This murderous purpose was plainly evidenced by the selection of two specially ferocious and brutal praetorian guards to convey him there, with instructions to push forward with the most merciless haste, regardless of weather or the health of their prisoner, a hint being privately given that they might expect promotion if he died on the road (*ib.* p. 98). The journey was to be made on foot. Towns where he might enjoy any approach to comfort and have the refreshment of a warm bath were to be avoided. The necessary halts, as few and brief as possible, were to be at squalid villages or in the unsheltered country. All letters were forbidden, the least communication with passers-by punished with brutal blows. In spite of some approach to consideration on the part of one of his guards, the three months' journey between Cucusus and Comana must have been one long slow martyrdom to the fever-stricken old man. His body was almost calcined by the sun, and, to adopt Palladius's forcible image, resembled a ripe apple ready to fall from the tree (*ib.* p. 99). On reaching Comana it was evident that Chrysostom was entirely worn out. But his pitiless guard hurried him through the town without a moment's halt. Five or six miles outside stood a chapel over the tomb of the martyred bishop, Basiliscus. Here they halted for the night. In the morning Chrysostom begged for a brief respite in vain; but he had gone scarcely four miles when a violent attack of fever compelled them to return to the chapel. Chrysostom was supported to the altar, and, clothed in white baptismal robes, he distributed his own clothes to the bystanders, partook of the blessed Eucharist, prayed a last prayer "for present needs," uttered his accustomed doxology, "Glory be to God for all things," and having sealed it with an "Amen," yielded up his soul to his Saviour, Sept. 14, 407, in the 60th year of his age and 10th of his episcopate, 3 years and a quarter of which he had spent in exile. He was buried in the martyry by the side of Basiliscus (*ib.* pp. 99-101). Thirty-one years afterwards (Jan. 27, 438), when Theodosius II. was emperor, and Proclus, formerly a disciple of Chrysostom, was bp. of Constantinople, Chrysostom's body was taken from its grave near Comana and translated with great pomp to his own episcopal city, and deposited hard by the altar in the church of the Holy Apostles, the place of sepulture of the imperial family and of the bishops of Constantinople, the young emperor and his sister Pulcheria assisting at the ceremony, and asking the pardon of Heaven for the grievous wrong inflicted by their parents on the sainted bishop (Socr. *H. E.* vii. 45; Theod. *H. E.* v. 36; Evagr. *H. E.* iv. 31).

The personal appearance of Chrysostom, as described by contemporary writers, though dignified, was not imposing. His stature was diminutive (*σωμάτιον*); his limbs long, and so emaciated by early austerities and habitual self-denial that he compares himself to a spider (*ἀραχνώδης*, *Ep.* 4). His very lofty forehead, furrowed with wrinkles, expanded widely at the summit, his head was bald "like that of Elisha," his eyes deeply set, but keen and piercing; his cheeks pallid and withered; his chin pointed and covered with a short beard. His habits were of the simplest, his personal wants few and easily satisfied. The excessive austerities of his youth had ruined his digestive powers and he was unable to eat food except in the smallest quantities and of the plainest kind. Outward display in dress, equipage, or furniture was most distasteful to him. Enamoured of the cloister, the life of the bishop of the capital of the Eastern world, compelled by his position to associate with persons of the highest rank and magnificence of life, was intolerable. It is not surprising that he was thought morose and ungenial and was unpopular with the upper classes. His strength of will, manly independence, and dauntless courage were united with an inflexibility of purpose, a want of consideration for the weaknesses of others, and an impatience at their inability to accept his high standard, which rendered him harsh and unconciliatory. Intolerant of evil in himself, he had little tolerance for it in other men. His feebleness of stomach produced an irritability of temper, which sometimes led to violent outbursts of anger. He was accused of being arrogant and passionate. He was easily offended and too ready to credit evil of those whom he disliked. Not mixing with the world himself, he was too dependent on the reports of his friends, who, as in the case of Serapion, sometimes abused his confidence to their own purposes. But however austere and reserved to the worldly and luxurious, he was ever loving and genial to his chosen associates. In their company his natural playfulness and amiability was shewn, and perhaps few ever exercised a more powerful influence over the hearts and affections of the holiest and most exalted natures. His character is well summed up by Dr. Newman—"a bright, cheerful, gentle soul," his unrivalled charm "lying in his singleness of purpose, his fixed grasp of his aim, his noble earnestness; he was indeed a man to make both friends and enemies, to inspire affection and kindle resentment; but his friends loved him with a love 'stronger' than 'death,' and his enemies hated him with a hatred more burning than 'hell,' and it was well to be so hated, if he was so beloved."

Chrysostom's extant works are more voluminous than those of any other Father, filling 13 folios in the Benedictine ed. They may be roughly divided into—I. *Treatises*; II. *Expositions of Scripture*, chiefly in the form of Homilies, but partly continuous Commentaries; III. *Homilies*, (*a*) *doctrinal*, (*b*) *occasional*, (*c*) *panegyrical*, (*d*) *general*; IV. *Letters*; V. *Liturgy*.

I. *Treatises*.—The earliest works we have from his pen are his letters *ad Theodorum Lapsum*, i. ii. (see *supra*), written while Chrysostom was still resident at Antioch before A.D. 372. To his early monastic life we may assign the two books *de Compunctione*, addressed respectively to Demetrius and Stelechius. His three books in defence of the monastic life (*adversus Oppugnatores Vitae Monasticae*) were called forth by the decree of Valens enforcing military service and civil functions on monks, A.D. 373. His short treatise, *Comparatio Regis et Monachi*, belongs to the same period. The three books *de Providentiâ*, written to console his friend Stagirius, the subject of an hysterical seizure then identified with demoniacal possession, were probably composed after his return to Antioch, *i.e.* subsequently to 381. Before ordination to the priesthood he composed two letters on the superior happiness of a single life (*ad Viduam Juniorem*) and his treatise on celibacy (*de Virginitate*). His six books *de Sacerdotio*, justly ranked among his ablest, most instructive, and most eloquent writings, are among his earliest, and placed by Socrates (*H.E.* vi. 3) in the first days of his diaconate, *c.* 382. Its maturity of thought and sobriety of tone prevent our fixing this work at a much earlier period. The treatises denouncing the custom for the clergy to have "spiritual sisters" residing under the same roof with them (*contra eos qui subintroductas habent*; *Regulares foeminae viris cohabitare non debent*), incorrectly assigned by Socrates (*ib.*) to his diaconate, were written, Palladius tells us (p. 45), after he became bp. of Constantinople, *c.* 398. To his exile belong the *Nemo laeditur nisi a seipso*, and *Ad eos qui scandalizati sunt ob adversitates*.

II. *Expositions of Scripture*.—It is as an expositor of Scripture that Chrysostom is most deservedly celebrated. His method of dealing with the divine Word is characterized by the sound grammatical and historical principles and the healthy common sense, introduced by his tutor Diodorus, which mark the exegetical school of Antioch. He seeks to discover not what the passage before him may be made to mean, but what it was intended to mean; not what recondite lessons or truths may be forced from it by mystical or allegorical interpretations, but what it was intended to convey;

not what may be introduced into it, but what may be legitimately elicited from it. While regarding Scripture in the strictest sense as the word of God, no sentence of which must be neglected, he is far from ignoring the human element in it, holding that though its writers "spoke as they were moved by the Holy Ghost," they retained their personal individuality; that their natural powers were quickened and illuminated, not superseded by divine inspiration. He regards the Scriptures as a connected whole, and avoiding the erroneous plan of treating texts as isolated *gnomes*, he seeks always to view a passage in relation to its context, and to the general teaching of Scripture. His expository works, being chiefly homiletic, do not give any continuous or systematic exegesis of the text. His primary object was a practical one—the conversion and edification of his hearers—and he frequently disappoints those who, looking for the meaning of a difficult passage, find instead a vehement denunciation of some reigning vice or fashionable folly, or an earnest exhortation to cultivate some Christian grace or virtue (cf. Phot. *Cod.* 174).

We are told by Suidas and Cassiodorus that Chrysostom wrote commentaries on the whole of Holy Scripture, from the beginning to the end. Among those extant are the 67 *Homilies on Genesis*, preached at Antioch; and 8 shorter and slighter, but more florid and rhetorical, sermons on topics from Gen. i. and ii., delivered earlier in the same year. The ninth of these sermons, *de Mutatione Nominum*, does not belong to the series. The only other homilies on the historical books of O.T. are five on the narrative of *Hannah* in I. Samuel, and three on *David and Saul*, assigned by Tillemont to A.D. 387. He delivered homilies on the whole book of *Psalms*, of which we have only those on Ps. iii.-xii., xliii.-xlix., cviii.-cl. (inclusive), collected at an early period with great critical acumen. As early as Photius the gaps indicated already existed. There is a homily on the opening verses of Ps. xli., which belongs to a different series. On *Isaiah* a continuous commentary was composed by Chrysostom, but only the part on cc. i.-viii. 11 is extant. There is a series of six homilies on the opening verses of c. vi., *in Oziam seu de Seraphinis*. The fourth of these belongs to a different series. To these we may add a homily on Is. xlv. 7. The only extant commentary on any part of *Jeremiah* is one "on free will," Jer. x. 23. Chrysostom's general views on prophecy are given in two sermons *de Prophetiarum Obscuritate*, justly ranked by Montfaucon "inter nobilissimas." The *Synopsis Sacrae Scripturae* is an imperfect work, ending with Nahum.

His commentaries on N.T. commence with 90 on *Matthew*, delivered at Antioch. St. Thomas Aquinas is reported to have said that he would rather possess these homilies than be the master of all Paris. There are none on *Mark* or *Luke*; but we have 88 on *St. John's Gospel*, also preached at Antioch. These are more doctrinal than hortatory or practical, being chiefly against the Anomoeans. The 55 homilies on *Acts* are among his feeblest works. The style is inelegant, the language unrefined, and the line of interpretation jejune (Phot. Cod. 174). The secret of their inferiority is that they were written at Constantinople in the midst of the troubles arising from Gainas and the Goths, when he had no time for studied composition; as also were the 24 homilies on *Eph.*, the 15 on *Phil.*, the 12 on *Col.*, the 11 on I. *Thess.*, and the 5 on II. *Thess.*, which hardly reach Chrysostom's highest standard of excellence. On the other hand, the 33 on *Rom.*, which were certainly delivered at Antioch, are among his most elaborate discourses. Nowhere does he shew more argumentative power or greater skill in developing his author's meaning. On I. *Cor.* we have 44 homilies, and 30 on II. *Cor.*, preached at Antioch, of which the former series "have ever been considered by devout men as among the most perfect specimens of his mind and teaching" (Keble). The commentary on *Gal.* is continuous, not in the homiletical form, and a somewhat hasty work. Montfaucon correctly assigns the 18 homilies on I. *Tim.*, the 10 on II. *Tim.*, and the 6 on *Tit.* to his ministry at Antioch. From some marks of negligence the three on *Philemon* have been thought to be extemporaneous addresses taken down by others. The 34 on *Hebrews* were delivered at Constantinople, and pub. from notes by Constantine, a presbyter, after Chrysostom's death.

III. *Homilies*, (*a*) *Doctrinal*.—The chief of these are the 12 delivered against the Anomoean form of Arianism, in the first year of his presbyterate, at Antioch, A.D. 387. "They are," writes Stephens, "among the finest of his productions." Soon after he wrote the 8 against the Jews and Judaizing Christians (*contra Judaeos*).

(*b*) *Occasional*.—Not a few of his grandest flights of Christian oratory were called forth by the events of the stirring times in which he lived. The most remarkable is the series of 21 "On the Statues" (*ad Populum Antiochenum de Statuis*), for the circumstances of which see *supra*. Another class includes orations delivered at Constantinople on the fall of Eutropius, on the insurrection of Gainas, on the troubles connected with Severian, and the noble and pathetic series connected with his own deposition and exile. To these we may add homilies delivered on the great Church festivals.

(*c*) *Panegyrical*.—These deserve careful attention as illustrating "the passionate devotion to the memory of departed saints which was rapidly passing into actual adoration." The earliest is probably that commemorating his venerated spiritual father Meletius, A.D. 386. The others are mostly devoted to the eulogy of the bishops and martyrs of the church of Antioch, St. Ignatius, St. Eustathius, St. Babylas, St. Pelagia, St. Domnina and her two daughters, and others, and were delivered at the *martyria*, or chapels erected over their remains. Chrysostom delivered a homily on the day of the commemoration of the emperor Theodosius, and heaped extravagant laudations on the empress Eudoxia and on Arcadius during his ardent but short-lived friendship with them at the outset of his episcopate.

(*d*) *General*.—Among these we include those belonging to Christian life generally, *e.g.* the 9 *de Poenitentia*, 2 *Catecheses ad Illuminandos*, those *de Continentia, de Perfecta Caritate, de Consolatione Mortis*, and numerous ones on single texts or separate parables.

On his homilies, expository and practical, Chrysostom's fame chiefly rests, and that deservedly. He was in truth "the model of a preacher for a great capital. Clear, rather than profound, his dogmatic is essentially moulded up with his moral teaching. . . . His doctrines flow naturally from his subject or from the passage of Scripture under discussion; his illustrations are copious and happy; his style free and fluent; while he is an unrivalled master in that rapid and forcible application of incidental occurrences which gives such life and reality to eloquence. He is at times, in the highest sense, dramatic in manner" (Milman, *Hist. of Christ.* iii. 9).

IV. *Letters.*—The whole of Chrysostom's extant letters belong to his banishment, written on his road to Cucusus, during his residence there, or in the fortress of Arabissus. The most important are 17 addressed to the deaconess Olympias, who shared his hopes and fears and all his inmost feelings. The whole number is 242, written to every variety of friend—men of rank, ladies, ecclesiastics of every grade, bishops, presbyters, deacons and deaconesses, monks and missionaries, his old friends at Antioch and Constantinople, and his more recent acquaintances at Caesarea and other halting-places on his journey—and including every variety of subject; now addressing reproof, warning, encouragement, or consolation to the members of his flock at Constantinople, or their clergy; now vigorously helping forward the missionary work in Phoenicia, and soliciting funds for pious and beneficent works; now thanking his correspondents for their letters or their gifts; now complaining of their silence; now urging the prosecution of the appeal made in his behalf to Innocent and the Western bishops, and expressing his hope that through the prayers of his friends he would be speedily given to them again; and the whole poured forth with the undoubting confidence of a friend writing to friends of whom he is sure. We have in this correspondence an index to his inner life such as we possess of few great men. The letters are simply inestimable in aiding us to understand and appreciate this great saint. In style, as Photius remarks, they are characterized by his usual brilliancy and clearness, and by great sweetness and persuasive power (Phot. *Cod.* 86).

V. *Liturgical.*—It is impossible to decide how much in the liturgies passing under the name of St. Chrysostom is really of his age. There are very many editions of the liturgy, no two of which, according to Cave (*Hist. Lit.* i. 305), present the same text; and hardly any that do not offer great discrepancies. It would be, of course, a fundamental error to attribute the composition of a liturgy *de novo* to Chrysostom or any of the old Catholic Fathers. When a liturgy is called by the name of any Father, all that is implied is that it was in use in the church to which that Father belonged, and that it may have owed some corrections and improvements to him. The liturgy known in comparatively late times by the name of Chrysostom has been from time immemorial that of the church of Constantinople.

The best and most complete edition of Chrysostom, as of most of the Christian Fathers, is the Benedictine, prepared by the celebrated Bernard de Montfaucon, who devoted to it more than twenty years of incessant toil and of journeys to consult MSS. It was pub. at Paris, in 13 vols. fol. in 1718. The value of this magnificent edition lies more in the historical and critical prefaces, and other literary apparatus, than in the text, which is faulty. It has been reprinted at Venice in 1734 and 1755, and at Paris in 1834-1839. The most practically useful edition is in the *Patrologia* of the Abbé Migne, in 13 vols. 8vo. (Paris, 1863). It is mainly a reprint of the Benedictine ed., but enriched by a judicious use of the best modern commentators. The chief early authorities for the life of Chrysostom, besides his own works, are the *Dialogue* of his contemporary Palladius, bp. of Hellenopolis, which, however valuable for its facts, deserves Gibbon's censure as "a partial and passionate vindication," and the Ecclesiastical Histories of Socrates (lib. vi.), Sozomen (lib. viii.), and Theodoret (lib. v.), the Lexicon of Suidas (*sub voc.* Ἰωάννης), and the letters of Isidorus of Pelusium (ii. *Ep.* 42). The biography by George of Alexandria is utterly worthless, being more an historical romance than a memoir. Of more modern works, it will suffice to name "the moderate Erasmus" (tom. iii. *Ep.* 1150), the "patient and accurate" Tillemont (*Mém. Eccl.* tom. ix.), and the diligent and dull Montfaucon. The brilliant sketch of Gibbon (*Decl. and Fall*, c. xxxii.) must not be omitted. Neander's *Life of St. Chrysostom* is a work of much value, more for the account of Chrysostom's opinions and words than for the actual life. Amadée Thierry's biographical articles in the *Revue des Deux Mondes* describe Chrysostom's fall and exile most graphically, though with the licence of an artist. The most satisfactory biography is by Rev. W. R. W. Stephens (Lond. 1872), to which the foregoing article is largely indebted. Translations of several of his works are contained in the *Post-Nicene Fathers*, edited by Schaff and Wace. S.P.C.K. publishes cheaply St. Chrys. *On the Priesthood*, by T. A. Moxon, and extracts from his writing in *St. Chrysostom's Picture of his Age* and *Picture of the Religion of his Age.* [E.V.]

Claudius (1), A.D. 41-54. The reign of this emperor has special interest in being that to which we must refer the earliest distinct traces of the *origines* of the church of Rome. Even before his accession, the new faith may have found its way there. The "strangers of Rome, Jews and proselytes" (Acts ii. 10), who were at Jerusalem on the day of Pentecost, or some of the "synagogue of the Libertines" (Acts vi. 9), yielding to the arguments of Stephen, may have brought it thither. "Andronicus and Junia or Junias," who were "in Christ" before the conversion of St. Paul (Rom. xvi. 7), and at Rome when that apostle wrote to the church there, may have been among those earlier converts. When Herod Antipas and Herodias came to court the favour of Caligula (Joseph. *Antiq.* xviii. 7) and gain for the former the title of king, they must have had some in their train who had known—perhaps those who had reported to him (Matt. xiv. 1, 2)—the "mighty works" of the prophet of Nazareth. The frequent visits of Herod Agrippa would make events in Judaea common topics at Rome. His presence there when Claudius came to the throne (Joseph. *Antiq.* xix. 4, 5) may reasonably be connected with the indulgence then extended to the Jews by that emperor (*ib.* xix. 5). The decree mentioned in Acts xviii. 2, and by Suetonius (*Claudius*, c. 25), indicates a change of policy, and the account of Suetonius probably tells the cause of the change, "Judaeos impulsore Chresto assidue tumultuantes Româ expulit." * He does not give the date of the expulsion, but it was probably between A.D. 43, when Agrippa left Rome, and A.D. 51, when St. Paul arrived at Corinth, and when the decree is mentioned as recent. The explanation turns upon the interpretation of the words "impulsore Chresto." We know from Tertullian (*Apol.* c. 3) that "Christianus" was commonly pronounced "Chrestianus" by those ignorant of its derivation; and that the name of *Christ* was for long similarly mispronounced we learn from Lactantius ("immutatâ literâ *Chrestum* solent dicere," *Ver. Sap.* iv. 7). It seems legitimate, therefore, to assume that the name "Christ" had been heard in the disputings of Jews and Christians, and that the prefects and Roman population, ignorant of its true significance, conceived it to be the name of some local ringleader in a seditious riot. Many indications in *Acts* and *Romans* imply a considerable growth of the Christian community before the accession of Nero.

It is obvious further, (1) that the expulsion of Christians who had been Jews or proselytes would leave a certain proportion of purely Gentile Christians whom the edict would not touch; and (2) that those who returned would naturally settle, not in the Jewish trans-Tiberine quarter of the city, but in some safer locality, and that thus the church at Rome, at or soon after the death of Claudius, would gradually become more and more free from Jewish or Judaizing influences. (On other points connected with the rise and progress of Christianity at Rome under Claudius see "Aquila and Priscilla," and the "Protomartyr Stephen," in the writer's *Biblical Studies*.) [E.H.P.]

Clemens (1), Flavius, son of Sabinus, brother of the emperor Vespasian, and therefore first cousin to Domitian, whose niece Flavia Domitilla was his wife. Domitian regarded his kinsman with great favour, and placed his two sons, whom he caused to be named after himself and his brother, Vespasianus and Domitianus, under the tuition of Quintilian as his destined successors. Flavius Clemens was consul in A.D. 95, and had only just resigned the office when he and his wife Domitilla were suddenly arrested and convicted on the charge of "atheism," by which there is no reasonable doubt that Christianity is intended. The crime on which they were condemned was, according to Dio Cassius, that of "Judaizing," from which in the popular mind Christianity was hardly distinguishable. The religious charge was regarded by Suetonius as a most trivial one, the object of suspicion rather than of proof—"tenuissima ex suspicione"—but it was strengthened by a neglect of the ordinary usages of Roman social and political life, almost unavoidable by a Christian, which was regarded as a "most contemptible indolence" meriting severe animadversion. Clemens suffered death; his wife Domitilla was banished to an island off the W. coast of Italy. [DOMITIANUS, (1).] Sueton. *Domit.* § 15; Dio Cassius, *Hist.* lxvii. 14; Tillem. tom. ii. p. 124; Merivale, *Romans under the Empire*, vol. vii. c. lxii. p. 383. Lightfoot, *Philippians*, p. 22. [E.V.]

* Dio Cassius (lx. p. 669) speaks of Claudius as not expelling the Jews, but only forbidding them to assemble. Probably this was an earlier measure not found sufficiently effective. The expulsion of the "Mathematici" about the same time (Tacitus, *Ann.* xii. 52) implies a general alarm as to the spread of "Eastern superstitions."

Clemens Romanus. According to common tradition, one of the first, if not the first, bp. of Rome after the apostles, and certainly a leading member of that church towards the end of the 1st cent.

(1) Among the most authentic proofs of the connexion of Clement with the Roman church is the mention of his name in its liturgy. The early Christians on the death of a bishop did not discontinue the mention of his name in their public prayers. Now the Roman Canon of the Mass to this day, next after the names of the apostles, recites the names of Linus, Cletus, Clemens; and there is some evidence that the liturgy contained the same names in the same order as early as the 2nd cent; Probably, then, this commemoration dates from Clement's own time.

(2) An independent proof that Clement held high position in the church of Rome is afforded by the *Shepherd of Hermas*, a work not later than the episcopate of Pius (A.D. 141-156), the writer of which claims to have been contemporary w th Clement. He represents himself as commissioned to write for Clement the book of his *Visions* in order that Clement might send it to foreign cities, that being his function; while Hermas himself was to read the *Vision* at Rome with the elders who presided over the church. Thus Clement is recognized as the organ by which the church of Rome communicated with foreign churches; but the passage does not decide whether or not Clement was superior to other presbyters in the domestic government of the church.

(3) Next in antiquity among the notices of Clement is the general ascription to him of the *Epistle to the Church of Corinth*, commonly known as Clement's first epistle. This is written in the name of the church of Rome, and neither in the address nor in the body of the letter contains Clement's name, yet he seems to have been from the first everywhere recognized as its author. We may not unreasonably infer from the passage just cited from *Hermas* that the letter was even then celebrated. About A.D. 170 it is expressly mentioned by Dionysius, bp. of Corinth, who, acknowledging another letter written from the church of Rome to the church of Corinth by their then bp. Soter, states that their former letter written by Clement was still read from time to time in their Sunday assemblies. Eusebius (*H. E.* iii. 16) speaks of this public reading of Clement's epistle as the ancient

custom of very many churches down to his own time. In the same place (and in *H. E.* iv. 22) he reports that Hegesippus, whose historical work was written in the episcopate next after Soter's, and who had previously visited both Rome and Corinth, gives particulars concerning the epistle of Clement, and concerning the dissensions in the Corinthian church which had given rise to it. The epistle is cited as Clement's by Irenaeus (*adv. Haer.* iii. 3), several times by Clement of Alex., who in one place gives his namesake the title of Apostle (*Strom.* i. 7, iv. 17, v. 12, vi. 8); by Origen (*de Princip.* ii. 3, *in Ezech.* 8, *in Joan.* i. 29); and in fact on this subject the testimony of antiquity is unanimous. A letter which did not bear Clement's name, and which merely purported to come from the church of Rome, could scarcely have been generally known as Clement's, if Clement had not been known at the time as holding the chief position in the church of Rome.

(4) Last among those notices of Clement which may be relied on as historical, we place the statement of Irenaeus (*l.c.*) that Clement was third bp. of Rome after the apostles, his account being that the apostles Peter and Paul, having founded and built up that church, committed the charge of it to Linus; that Linus was succeeded by Anencletus, and he by Clement. This order is adopted by Eusebius, by Jerome in his *Chronicle*, and by Eastern chronologers generally.

A different order of placing these bishops can also, however, lay claim to high antiquity. The ancient catalogue known as the Liberian, because ending with the episcopate of Liberius, gives the order and duration of the first Roman episcopates: Peter 25 years, 1 month, 9 days; Linus 12 years, 4 months, 12 days; Clemens 9 years, 11 months, 12 days; Cletus 6 years, 2 months, 10 days; Anacletus 12 years, 10 months, 3 days: thus Anacletus, who in the earlier list comes before Clement, is replaced by two bishops, Cletus and Anacletus, who come after him; and this account is repeated in other derived catalogues. Irenaeus himself is not consistent in reckoning the Roman bishops. [CERDO.] The order, Peter, Linus, Clemens, is adopted by Augustine (*Ep.* 53 *ad Generosum*) and by Optatus of Milevis (*de Schism. Donatist.* ii. 2). Tertullian (*de Praescrip.* c. 32) states that the church of Rome held Clement to have been ordained by Peter; and Jerome (*Cat. Scr. Ecc.* 15), while adopting the order of Irenaeus, mentions that most Latins then counted Clement to have been second after Peter, and himself seems to adopt this reckoning in his commentary on Isaiah (c. 52). The *Apostolic Constitutions* (vii. 46) represent Linus to have been first ordained by Paul, and afterwards, on the death of Linus, Clement by Peter. Epiphanius (*Haer.* xxvii. 6) suggests that Linus and Cletus held office during the lifetime of Peter and Paul, who, on their necessary absence from Rome for apostolic journeys, commended the charge of the church to others. This solution is adopted by Rufinus in the preface to his translation of the *Recognitions*. Epiphanius has an alternative solution, founded on a conjecture which he tries to support by a reference to a passage in Clement's epistle, viz. that Clement, after having been ordained by Peter, withdrew from his office and did not resume it until after the death of Linus and Cletus. A more modern attempt to reconcile these accounts is Cave's hypothesis that Linus and after him Cletus had been appointed by Paul to preside over a Roman church of Gentile Christians; Clement by Peter over a church of Jewish believers, and that ultimately Clement was bishop over the whole Roman church. Still later it has been argued that the uncertainty of order may mean that during the 1st cent. there was no bishop in the church of Rome, and that the names of three of the leading presbyters have been handed down by some in one order, by others in another. The authorities, however, which differ from the account of Irenaeus, ultimately reduce themselves to two. Perhaps the parent of the rest is the letter of Clement to James [CLEMENTINE LITERATURE] giving an account of Clement's ordination by Peter; for it seems to have been plainly the acceptance of this ordination as historical which inspired the desire to correct a list of bishops which placed Clement at a distance of three from Peter. The other authority is the *Chronicle* of Hippolytus, pub. A.D. 235 (see CHRONICON CANISIANUM in *D. C. B.* 4-vol. ed.), and the memoir of Mommsen there cited), for it has been satisfactorily shewn that the earlier part of the Liberian catalogue is derived from the list of Roman bishops in this work. The confusion of later writers arises from attempts to reconcile conflicting authorities, all of which seemed deserving of confidence: viz. (1) the list of Irenaeus, and probably of Hegesippus, giving merely a succession of Roman bishops; (2) the list of Hippolytus giving a succession in somewhat different order and also the years of the duration of the episcopates; and (3) the letter to James relating the ordination of Clement by Peter. The main question, then, is, which is more entitled to confidence, the order of Irenaeus or of Hippolytus? and we have no hesitation in accepting the former. First, because it is distinctly the more ancient; secondly, because if the earlier tradition had not placed the undistinguished name Cletus before the well-known Clement, no later writer would have reversed its order; thirdly, because of the testimony of the liturgy. Hippolytus being apparently the first scientific chronologer in the Roman church, his authority there naturally ranked very high, and his order of the succession seems to have been generally accepted in the West for a considerable time. Any commemoration, therefore, introduced into the liturgy after his time would have followed his order, Linus, Clemens, Cletus, or, if of very late introduction, would have left out the obscure name Cletus altogether. We conclude, then, that the commemoration in the order, Linus, Cletus, Clemens, had been introduced before the time of Hippolytus, and was by then so firmly established that even the contradictory result arrived at by Hippolytus (because he accepted as historically true the ordination of Clement by Peter as related in the Ep. to James) could not alter it. The *Recognitions* are cited by Origen, the contemporary of Hippolytus; and the account which their preface gives of Clement's ordination seems to have been fully believed by the Roman church. The death of Clement and the consequent accession of Evaristus is dated by Eusebius in his *Chronicle* A.D. 95, and in his *Church History* the third year of Trajan, A.D. 100. According to the chronology of the Liberian Catalogue, the accession of Evaristus is dated A.D. 95. Now no one dates the death of Peter later than the persecution of Nero, A.D. 67. If, therefore, Clement was ordained by Peter, and if we retain the order of Irenaeus, Clement had an episcopate of about 30 years, a length far greater than any tradition suggests. Hippolytus, probably following the then received account of the length of Clement's episcopate, has placed it A.D. 67-76; and, seeing the above difficulty, has filled the space between Clement and Evaristus by transposing Cletus and, as the gap seemed too large to be filled by one episcopate, by counting as distinct the Cletus of the liturgy and the Anacletus of the earlier catalogue. Apparently it was Hippolytus who devised the theory stated in the *Apostolic Constitutions*, that Linus held the bishopric during the lifetime of Peter; for this seems to be the interpretation of the dates assigned in the Liberian Catalogue, Peter 30-55, Linus 55-67. But the whole ground of these speculations is removed if we reject the tale of Clement's ordination by Peter; if for no other reason, on account of the chronological confusion which it causes. Thus we retain the order of Irenaeus, accounting that of Hippolytus as an arbitrary transposition to meet a chronological difficulty. The time that we are thus led to assign to the activity of Clement, viz. the end of Domitian's reign, coincides with that which Eusebius, apparently on the authority of Hegesippus, assigns to Clement's epistle, and with that which an examination of the letter itself suggests (see below).

The result thus arrived at casts great doubt on the identification of the Roman Clement with the Clement named Phil. iv. 3. This identification is unhesitatingly made by Origen (*in Joann.* i. 29) and a host of later writers. Irenaeus also may have had this passage in mind when he speaks of Clement as a hearer of the apostles, though probably he was principally influenced by the work which afterwards grew into the *Recognitions*. But though it is not actually impossible that the Clement who held a leading position in the church of Philippi during Paul's imprisonment might thirty years afterwards have presided over the church of Rome, yet the difference of time and place deprives of all likelihood an identification merely based upon a very common name. Lightfoot has remarked that Tacitus, for instance, mentions five Clements (*Ann.* i. 23, ii. 39, xv. 73; *Hist.* i. 86, iv. 68). Far more plausibly it has been proposed to identify the author of the epistle with another Clement, who was almost certainly at the time a distinguished member of the Roman church. We learn from Suetonius (*Domit.* 15) and from Dio Cassius, lxvii. 14, that in 95, the very year fixed by some for the death of bp. Clement, death or banishment was inflicted by Domitian on several persons addicted to Jewish customs, and amongst them Flavius Clemens, a relation of his own, whose consulship had but just expired, was put to death on a charge of atheism, while his wife Domitilla, also a member of the emperor's family, was banished. The language is such as heathen writers might naturally use to describe a persecution of Christians; but Eusebius (*H. E.* iii. 13) expressly claims one Domitilla, a niece of the consul's, as a sufferer for Christ; and (*Chron.* sub anno 95) cites the heathen historian Bruttius as stating that several Christians suffered martyrdom at this time. If, then, the consul Clement was a Christian martyr, his rank would give him during his life a foremost position in the Roman church. It is natural to think that the writer of the epistle may have been either the consul or a member of his family. Yet if so, the traditions of the Roman church must have been singularly defective. No writer before Rufinus speaks of bp. Clement as a martyr; nor does any ancient writer in any way connect him with the consul. In the *Recognitions* Clement is represented as a relation of the emperor; not, however, of Domitian, but of Tiberius. A fabulous account of Clement's martyrdom, probably of no earlier origin than the 9th cent., tells how Clement was first banished to the Crimea, worked there such miracles as converted the whole district, and was thereupon by Trajan's order cast into the sea with an anchor round his neck, an event followed by new prodigies.

The only genuine work of Clement is the Ep. to the Corinthians already mentioned. Its main object is to restore harmony to the Corinthian church, which had been disturbed by questions apparently concerning discipline rather than doctrine. The bulk of the letter is taken up in enforcing the duties of meekness, humility, submission to lawful authority, and but little attempt is made at the refutation of doctrinal error. Some pains, it is true, are taken to establish the doctrine of the Resurrection; but this subject is not connected by the writer with the disputes, and so much use is made of Paul's Ep. to the Corinthians that we cannot lay much stress on the fact that one of the topics of that epistle is fully treated. The dissensions are said to have been caused by the arrogance of a few self-willed persons who led a revolt against the authority of the presbyters. Their pride probably rested on their possession of spiritual gifts, and perhaps on the chastity which they practised. Though pains are taken to shew the necessity of a distinction of orders, we cannot infer that this was really questioned by the revolters; for the charge against them, that they had unwarrantably deposed from the office of presbyter certain who had filled it blamelessly, implies that the office continued to be recognized by them. But this unauthorized deposition naturally led to a schism, and representations made at Rome by some of the persons ill-treated may have led to the letter of Clement. It is just possible that we can name one of these persons. At the end of the letter a wish is expressed that the messengers of the Roman church, Ephebus and Bito, with Fortunatus also, might be sent back speedily with tidings of restored harmony. The form of expression distinguishing Fortunatus from the Roman delegates favours the supposition that he was a Corinthian, and as Clement urges on those who had been the cause of dissension to withdraw for peace' sake, it is possible that Fortunatus might have so withdrawn and found a welcome at Rome. Another conjecture identifies him with the Fortunatus mentioned in St. Paul's Ep. to the Corinthians.

However precarious this identification may be, internal evidence shews that the epistle is not so far from apostolic times as to make it impossible. None of the apostles are spoken of as living, but the deaths of Peter and Paul, described as men of their own generation, are referred to as then recent, and some of the presbyters appointed by the apostles are spoken of as still surviving. The early date thus indicated is confirmed by the absence of allusion to controversial topics of the 2nd cent., and by the immaturity of doctrinal development on certain points. Thus "bishop" and "presbyter" are, as in N.T., used convertibly, and there is no trace that in the church of Corinth one presbyter had any very pronounced authority over the rest. The deposition of certain presbyters is not spoken of as usurpation of the authority of any single person, but of that of the whole body of presbyters. Again, to the writer the "Scriptures" are the books of the O.T.; these he cites most copiously and uses to enforce his arguments. He expressly mentions St. Paul's Ep. to the Corinthians; and twice reminds his hearers of words of our Lord. The way in which he uses the quotations implies the existence of written records recognized by both parties. Besides these, without any formal citation he makes unmistakable use of other N.T. books, chiefly of Heb., but also of Rom. and other Pauline, including the Pastoral, epistles, Acts, James, and I. Peter. Still, their authority is not appealed to in the same manner as is that of the O.T. It may be mentioned here that Clement's epistle contains the earliest recognition of the Book of Judith. He quotes also from O.T. apocryphal books or interpolations not now extant.

To fix more closely the date of the epistle, the principal fact available is, that in the opening an apology is made that the church of Rome had not been able to give earlier attention to the Corinthian disputes, owing to the sudden and repeated calamities which had befallen it. It is generally agreed that this must refer to the persecution under either Nero or Domitian. A date about midway between these is that to which the phenomena of the epistle would have inclined us; but having to choose between these two we have no hesitation in preferring the latter. The main argument in favour of the earlier date, that the temple service is spoken of as being still offered, is satisfactorily met by the occurrence of a quite similar use of the present tense in Josephus. Indeed the passage, carefully considered, suggests the opposite inference; for Clement would Judaize to an extent of which there is no sign elsewhere in the epistle, if, in case the temple rites were being still celebrated, he were to speak of them as the appointed and acceptable way of serving God. All the other notes of time are difficult to reconcile with a date so close to the apostles as the reign of Nero.

As to whether the writer was a Jew or a Gentile, the arguments are not absolutely decisive; but it seems more conceivable that a Hellenistic Jew resident at Rome could have acquired the knowledge of Roman history and heathen literature exhibited in the epistle, than that one not familiar from his childhood with the O.T. could possess so intimate an acquaintance with it. This consideration, of course, bears on the question whether Flavius Clemens could have written the letter.

The letter does not yield any support to the theory of 1st cent. disputes between a Pauline and an anti-Pauline party in the church. No such disputes appear in the dissensions at Corinth; and at Rome the Gentile and Jewish sections of the church seem in Clement's time to be completely fused. The obligation on Gentiles to observe the Mosaic law does not seem a matter of concern. The whole Christian community is regarded as the inheritor of the promises to the Jewish people. Clement holds both SS. Peter and Paul in the highest (and equal) honour.

The epistle was known until 1875 only through a single MS., the great Alexandrian MS. brought to England in 1628, of which an account is given in all works on the criticism of the N.T. One leaf, containing about the tenth part of the whole letter, has been lost. In this Greek Bible of the 5th cent. the two letters of Clement to the Corinthians are books enumerated among N.T., not with the apostolic epistles, but after the Apocalypse. Hence the ecclesiastical use of Clement's letter had probably not ceased when this MS. was copied. The ep. was first ed. by Patrick Young (Oxf. 1633), and often since, among the most important edd. being Cotelier's in his *Apostolic Fathers* (Paris, 1672); Jacobson's; Hilgenfeld's in his *N.T. extra Canonem Receptum*; Lightfoot's (Camb. 1869, and in his great ed. of the *Apostolic Fathers*, 1890); Tischendorf's (Leipz. 1873); and Gebhardt and Harnack's (Leipz. 1875). A photograph of this portion of the MS. was pub. by Sir. F. Madden in 1856. An Eng. trans. of the ep. (and of those on *Virginity*) is in the *Lib. of Ante-Nicene Fathers*.

An entirely new authority for the text of the epistle was gained by the discovery in the library of the Holy Sepulchre at Fanari, in Constantinople, of a MS. containing an unmutilated text of the two epistles ascribed to Clement.* The new authority was announced, and first used in establishing the text, in a very careful and able ed. of the epp. by Bryennius, metropolitan of Serrae, pub. in Constantinople at the end of 1875. The MS., which is cursive and dated A.D. 1056, is contained in a small octavo volume, 7½ inches by 6, which has, besides the Epp. of Clement, Chrysostom's synopsis of the O.T., the Ep. of Barnabas, the Teaching of the Twelve Apostles (occupying in the MS. less space by one-fourth than the second Ep. of Clement), and a collection of Ignatian epistles. It gives a very good text of the Clementine letters, independent of the Alexandrian MS., but, on the whole, in tolerably close agreement with it, even in passages where the best critics had

*** Still later a Syriac MS. purchased for the University of Cambridge was found to contain a trans. of these two epistles. This has been ed. with notes and a facsimile plate by R. L. Bensley (Camb. Univ. Press).**

suspected error. Besides filling up small lacunae in the text of the older MS., it supplies the contents of the entire leaf which had been lost. This part contains a passage quoted by Basil, but not another quoted by Pseudo-Justin, confirmed in some degree by Irenaeus, which had been referred to this place (see Lightfoot, p. 166). Except for trifling omissions we must have the letter now as complete as it was originally in the Alexandrian MS. For Harnack, on counting the letters in the recovered portion, found that they amounted almost exactly to the average contents of a leaf of the older MS. Lightfoot has pointed out that by a small change in the text of Ps.-Justin, his reference is satisfied by a passage in the newly discovered conclusion of the second epistle. The new portion of the first principally consists of a prayer, possibly founded on the liturgical use of the Roman church. What has been said in the beginning of the letter as to the calamities under which that church had suffered is illustrated by some of the petitions, and prayer is made for their earthly rulers and that they themselves might submit to them, recognizing the honour given them by God, and not opposing His will. Very noticeable in this new part of the letter is the tone of authority used in making an unsolicited interference with the affairs of another church. "If any disobey the words spoken by God through us, let them know that they will entangle themselves in transgression, and no small danger, but we shall be clear from this sin." "You will cause us joy and exultation if, obeying the things written by us through the Holy Spirit, you cut out the lawless passion of your jealousy according to the intercession which we have made for peace and concord in this letter. But we have sent faithful and discreet men who have walked from youth to old age unblameably amongst us, who shall be witnesses between us and you. This have we done that you may know that all our care has been and is that you may speedily be at peace." It remains open for controversy how far the expressions quoted indicate official superiority of the Roman church, or only the writer's conviction of the goodness of their cause. We may add that the epithet applied by Irenaeus to the epistle *ἱκανωτάτη* proves to have been suggested by a phrase in the letter itself, *ἱκανῶς ἐπεστείλαμεν*.

Lightfoot gives references to a succession of writers who have quoted the epistle. Polycarp, though not formally quoting Clement's epistle, gives in several passages clear proof of acquaintance with it. A passage in Ignatius's epistle to Polycarp, c. 5, may also be set down as derived from Clement, but other parallels collected by Hilgenfeld are extremely doubtful. The epistle does not seem to have been translated into Latin, and was consequently little known in the West.

For some of the spurious works ascribed to Clement see CLEMENTINE LITERATURE.

The Second Epistle to the Corinthians.—This letter also formed part of the Alexandrian MS., but its conclusion had been lost by mutilation. We now have it complete in the edition of Bryennius. In the list of contents of the older MS. it is marked as Clement's second epistle, but not expressly described as to the Corinthians. It is so described in the later MS. It is not mentioned by any writer before Eusebius, and the language used by some of them is inconsistent with their having accepted it. Eusebius mentions it as a second letter ascribed to Clement, but not, like the former, used by the older writers, and he only speaks of one as the acknowledged epistle of Clement. The two epistles are placed among the books of the N.T., in the 8th book of the *Apostolic Constitutions*, which probably belongs to the 6th cent. The second epistle is first expressly cited as to the Corinthians by Severus of Antioch early in the same cent. Internal evidence, though adverse to Clementine authorship, assigns to the work a date not later than the 2nd cent., and probably the first half of it. The writer is distinctly a Gentile, and contrasts himself and his readers with the Jewish nation in a manner quite unlike the genuine Clement; and his quotations are not, like Clement's, almost exclusively from O.T.; the gospel history is largely cited, and once under the name of Scripture. Many of the quotations, however, differ from our canonical gospels, and since one of them agrees with a passage referred by Clement of Alexandria to the gospel of the Egyptians, this was probably the source of other quotations also. The epistle would seem from this to be earlier than the close of the 2nd cent., at which time our four gospels were in a position of exclusive authority. The controversies with which the writer deals are those of the early part of the 2nd cent. In language suggested by the Ep. to the Ephesians, the spiritual church is described as created before the sun and moon, as the female of whom Christ is the male, the body of which he is the soul. It seems likely that a work using such language had gained its acceptance with the church before Gnostic theories concerning the Aeons Christus and Ecclesia had brought discredit upon such speculations. The doctrine of the pre-existence of the church is, as Harnack noted, one of several points of contact between this work and the *Shepherd of Hermas*, making it probable that both emanate from the same age and the same circle. We therefore refer the place of composition to Rome, notwithstanding an apparent reference to the Isthmian games which favours a connexion with Corinth. The description of the work as an Ep. to the Corinthians, never strongly supported by external evidence, is disproved by the newly discovered conclusion, whence it clearly appears that the work is, as Dodwell and others had supposed, no epistle, but a homily. It professes, and there seems no reason to doubt it, to have been composed to be publicly read in church, and therefore the writer's position in the church was one which would secure that use of his work. But he does not claim any position of superiority, and the foremost place in ruling and teaching the church is attributed to the body of presbyters. He nowhere claims to be Clement. But it is not strange that an anonymous, but undoubtedly early document of the Roman church should come to be ascribed to the universally acknowledged author of the earliest document of that church; nor that when both had come to be received as Clement's, the second should come to be regarded as, like the first, an epistle to the Corinthians.

The Two Epistles on Virginity.—These are extant only in Syriac, and only in a single MS. purchased at Aleppo *c.* A.D. 1750, for Wetstein. He had commissioned a copy of the Philoxenian version of the N.T. to be bought, and this MS. proved to be only a copy of the well-known Peshito. But the disappointment was compensated by the unexpected discovery of these letters, till then absolutely unknown in the West. After the Ep. to the Hebrews, the last in the Peshitta canon, the scribe adds a doxology, and a note with personal details by which we can date the MS. A.D. 1470, and then proceeds, "We subjoin to the epistles of Paul those epistles of the apostles, which are not found in all the copies," on which follow II. Peter, II., III. John, and Jude, from the Philoxenian version, and then, without any break, these letters, with the titles: "The first epistle of the blessed Clement, the disciple of Peter the apostle," and "The second epistle of the same Clement." The MS. is now preserved in the library of the Seminary of the Remonstrants at Amsterdam. The letters were published, as an appendix to his Greek Testament, by Wetstein, who also defended their authenticity. The last editor is Beelen (Louvain, 1856). The letters, though now only extant in Syriac, are proved by their Graecisms to be a translation from the Greek, and by the existence of a fragment containing an apparently different Syriac translation of one passage in them. This fragment is contained in a MS. bearing the date A.D. 562. The earliest writer who quotes these letters is Epiphanius. In a passage, which until the discovery of the Syriac letters had been felt as perplexing, he describes Clement as "in the encyclical letters which he wrote, and which are read in the holy churches," having taught virginity, and praised Elias and David and Samson, and all the prophets. The letters to the Corinthians cannot be described as encyclical; and the topics specified are not treated of in them, while they are dwelt on in the Syriac letters. St. Jerome, though in his catalogue of ecclesiastical writers he follows Eusebius in mentioning only the two letters to the Corinthians as ascribed to Clement, yet must be understood as referring to the letters on virginity in his treatise against Jovinian where he speaks of Clement as composing almost his entire discourse concerning the purity of virginity. He may have become acquainted with these letters during his residence in Palestine. The presumption against their genuineness, arising from the absence of notice of them by Eusebius and every other writer anterior to Epiphanius, and from the limited circulation which they appear ever to have attained in the church, is absolutely confirmed by internal evidence. Their style and whole colouring are utterly unlike those of the genuine epistle; and the writer is evidently one whose thoughts and language have been moulded by long and early acquaintance with N.T., in the same manner as those of the real Clement are by his acquaintance with the Old. The Gospel of St. John is more than once cited, but not any apocryphal N.T. book. Competent judges have assigned these epistles to the middle of the 2nd cent., but their arguments hardly suffice to exclude a somewhat later date.

The Epistles to James our Lord's Brother.—In the article CLEMENTINE LITERATURE is given an account of the letter to James by Clement, which relates how Peter, in immediate anticipation of death, ordained Clement as his successor, and gave him charge concerning his ministry. After the trans. of this letter by Rufinus, some Latin writer added a second, giving instruction as to the administration of the Eucharist and church discipline. These two letters had considerable currency in the West. In the forged decretals both were much enlarged, and 3 new letters purporting to be Clement's added. James is in the original Clementines the head of the church, but in the later epistle receives instruction and commands from Peter's successor Clement. There must have been yet other letters ascribed to Clement in the East if there be no error in the MS. of Leontius (Mai, *Script. Vet. Nov. Coll.* vii. 84), who cites a passage not elsewhere extant as from the *ninth* letter of Clement. Discourses concerning Providence and the righteous judgment of God are cited by Anastasius of Antioch; and a 13th-cent. writer (*Spicilegium Acherianum*, viii. 382) reports having seen in a Saracen MS. a book of Revelations of Peter, compiled by Clement. The highest, and probably the final, authority on St. Clement of Rome is now the great work of Bp. Lightfoot, forming, in 2 parts, pub. 1890, vol. i. of his ed. of the *Apostolic Fathers*. See also Harnack, *Chronol. der Altchr. Lit.*, 1897, pp. 251 ff., 438 ff.; an ed. by A. Jacobson of Clement's works in 2 vols. in *Apost. Patr.* (Clar. Press); an Eng. trans. of the *Epistle of Clement*, by J. A. F. Gregg (S.P.C.K.). [G.S.]

Clement of Alexandria. i. *Life.*—His full name, Titus Flavius Clemens, is given by Eusebius (*H. E.* vi. 13) and Photius (*Cod.* 111) in the title of the *Stromateis* (Τίτου Φλαυίου Κλήμεντος [Photius adds *πρεσβυτέρου 'Αλεξανδρείας*] *τῶν κατὰ τὴν ἀληθῆ φιλοσοφίαν γνωστικῶν ὑπομνημάτων στρωματεῖς*). The remarkable coincidence of the name with that of the nephew of Vespasian and consul in 95 cannot have been accidental, but we have no direct evidence of Clement's connexion with the imperial Flavian family. Perhaps he was descended from a freedman of the consul; his wide and varied learning indicates that he had received a liberal education, and so far suggests that his parents occupied a good social position. The place of his birth is not certainly known. Epiphanius, the earliest authority on the question, observes that two opinions were held in his time, "some saying that he was an Alexandrian, others that he was an Athenian" (*ὅν φασί τινες 'Αλεξανδρέα ἕτεροι δὲ 'Αθηναῖον*, *Haer.* xxxii. 6). Alexandria was the principal scene of his labours; but there was no apparent reason for connecting him with Athens by mere conjecture. The statement that he was an Athenian must therefore have rested upon some direct tradition. Moreover, in recounting his wanderings he makes Greece the starting-point and Alexandria the goal of his search (*Strom.* I, § 11, p. 322); and in the 2nd cent. Athens was still the centre of the literary and spiritual life of Greece. We may then with reasonable probability conclude that Clement was an Athenian by training if not by origin, and the fact that he was at the head of the catechetical school of Alexandria towards the close of the century fixes the date of his birth *c.* A.D. 150-160. Nothing is recorded of his parentage; but his own language seems to imply that he embraced Christianity by a personal act, as in some sense a convert (*Paed.* i. § 1, p. 97, τὰς παλαιὰς ἀπομνύμενοι δόξας; cf. *Paed.* ii. § 62, p. 206, δάκρυά ἐσμεν . . . οἱ εἰς αὐτὸν πεπιστευκότες), and this is directly affirmed by Eusebius (*Praep. Ev.* ii. 2 f.), though perhaps simply by inference from Clement's words. Such a conversion would not be irreconcilable with the belief that Clement, like Augustine, was of Christian parentage at least on one side; but whether Clement's parents were Christians or heathens it is evident that heathenism attracted him for a time; and though he soon overcame its attractions, his inquisitive spirit did not at once find rest in Christianity. He enumerates six illustrious teachers under whom he studied the "true tradition of the blessed doctrine of the holy apostles." His first teacher in Greece was an Ionian (Athenagoras?); others he heard in Magna Graecia; others in the East; and at last he found in Egypt the true master for whom he had sought (*Strom.* i. § 11, p. 322). There can be no doubt that this master was Pantaenus, to whom he is said to have expressed his obligations in his *Hypotyposes* (Eus. *H. E.* vi. 13, v. 11). Pantaenus was then chief of the catechetical school, and though the accounts of Eusebius and Jerome (Eus. *H. E.* v. 10; Hieron. *de Vir. Ill.* 36, 38) are irreconcilable in their details and chronology, it is certain that on the death or retirement of Pantaenus, Clement succeeded to his office, and it is not unlikely that he had acted as his colleague before. The period during which Clement presided over the catechetical school (*c.* A.D. 190-203) seems to have been the season of his greatest literary activity. He was now a presbyter of the church (*Paed.* i. § 37, p. 120) and had the glory of reckoning Origen among his scholars. On the outbreak of the persecution under Severus (A.D. 202, 203) in which Leonidas, the father of Origen, perished, Clement retired from Alexandria (Eus. *H. E.* vi. 3), never, as it seems, to return. Nothing is directly stated as to the place of his withdrawal. There are some indications of a visit to Syria (Eus. *H. E.* vi. 11, ὃν ἴστε); and, later, we find him in the company of an old pupil, Alexander, afterwards bp. of Jerusalem, and at that time a bp. of Cappadocia, who was in prison for the faith. If therefore Clement had before withdrawn from danger, it was through wisdom and not through fear. Alexander regarded his presence as due to "a special providence" (cf. Eus. *H. E.* vi. 14), and charged him, in most honourable terms, with a letter of congratulation to the church of Antioch on the appointment of Asclepiades to the bishopric of that city, A.D. 311 (Eus. *H. E.* vi. 11). This is the last mention of Clement which has been preserved. The time and the place of his death are alike unknown. Popular opinion reckoned him among the saints of the church; and he was commemorated in the early Western martyrologies on Dec. 4. His name, however, was omitted in the martyrology issued by Clement VIII. after the corrections of Baronius; and Benedict XIV. elaborately defended the omission in a letter to John V. of Portugal, dated 1748. Benedict argued that the teaching of Clement was at least open to suspicion, and that private usage would not entitle him to a place in the calendar (Benedicti XIV. *Opera*, vi. pp. 119 ff. ed. 1842, where the evidence is given in detail; cf. Cognat, *Clément d'Alexandrie*, pp. 451 ff.).

ii. *Works.*—Eusebius, whom Jerome follows closely with some mistakes (*de Vir. Ill.* 38) has given a list of the works of Clement (*H. E.* vi. 13): (1) Στρωματεῖς, libb. viii.; (2) Ὑποτυπώσεις, libb. viii.; (3) Πρὸς Ἕλληνας λόγος προτρεπτικός (*adversus Gentes*, Jerome); (4) Παιδαγωγός, libb. iii.; (5) Τίς ὁ σωζόμενος πλούσιος; (6) Περὶ τοῦ πάσχα; (7) Διαλέξεις περὶ νηστείας; (8) Περὶ καταλαλίας; (9) Προτρεπτικὸς εἰς ὑπομονήν ἢ πρὸς τοὺς νεωστὶ βεβαπτισμένους (omitted by Jerome); (10) Κανὼν ἐκκλησιαστικὸς ἢ πρὸς τοὺς Ἰουδαΐζοντας (*de Canonibus Ecclesiasticis et adversum eos qui Judaeorum sequuntur errorem*, Jerome). Photius (*Bibl.* Codd. 109-111) mentions that he read the first five works on the list, and knew by report 6, 7, 8 (περὶ κακολογίας); 10 (περὶ κανόνων ἐκκλησιαστικῶν); from the variations in the titles and the omission of 9, it is evident that he derived his knowledge of these simply from the secondary Greek version of Jerome's list. Nos. 1, 3, 4, 5 are still preserved almost entire. Of 2 considerable fragments remain; and of 6, 8, 10 a few fragments are preserved in express quotations.

Quotations are also found from a treatise περὶ προνοίας, and from another περὶ ψυχῆς, to which Clement himself refers (*Strom.* iii. 13, p. 516; v. 88, p. 699). Elsewhere Clement speaks of his intention to write *On First Principles* (περὶ ἀρχῶν, *Strom.* iii. 13, p. 516; *id.* 21, p. 520; cf. iv. 2, p. 564); *On Prophecy* (*Strom.* v. 88, p. 699; *id.* iv. 93, p. 605); *Against Heresies* (*Strom.* iv. 92, p. 604); *On the Resurrection* (*Paed.* i. 6, p. 125); *On Marriage* (*Paed.* iii. 8, p. 278). But the references may be partly to sections of his greater works, and partly to designs never carried out (cf. *Strom.* iv. 1-3, pp. 563 f.). No doubt has been raised as to the genuineness of the *Address*, the *Tutor*, and the *Miscellanies*. Internal evidence shews them all the work of one writer (cf. Reinkens, *de Clemente*, cap. ii. § 4), and they have been quoted as Clement's by a continuous succession of Fathers even from the time of Origen (*Comm. in Joh.* ii. 3, p. 52 B; *Strom.*; anonymous). These three principal extant works form a connected series. The first is an exhortation to the heathen to embrace Christianity, based on an exposition of the comparative character of heathenism and Christianity; the second offers a system of training for the new convert, with a view to the regulation of his conduct as a Christian; the third is an introduction to Christian philosophy. The series was further continued in the lost *Outlines* (ὑποτυπώσεις), in which Clement laid the foundation of his philosophic structure in an investigation of the canonical writings. The mutual relations of these writings shew that Clement intended them as a complete system of Christian teaching, corresponding with the "whole economy of the gracious Word, Who first addresses, then trains, and then teaches" (*Paed.* i. 1), bringing to man in due succession conviction, discipline, wisdom. The first three books correspond in a remarkable degree, as has frequently been remarked (Potter, *ad Protrept.* i.), with the stages of the neo-Platonic course, the *Purification* (ἀποκάθαρσις), the *Initiation* (μύησις), and the *Vision* (ἐποπτεία). The fourth book was probably designed to give a solid basis to the truths which were fleeting and unreal in systems of philosophy. Though his style is generally deficient in terseness and elegance, his method desultory, his learning undigested; yet we can still thankfully admire his richness of information, his breadth of reading, his largeness of sympathy, his lofty aspirations, his noble conception of the office and capacities of the Faith.

I. *The Address to the Greeks* (Λόγος προτρεπτικὸς πρὸς Ἕλληνας: cf. *Strom.* vii. § 22, p. 421, ἐν τῷ προτρεπτικῷ ἐπιγραφομένῳ ἡμῖν λόγῳ).—The works of Clement were composed in the order in which they have been mentioned. The *Tutor* contains a reference to the *Address* in the first section (ὁ λόγος ὁπηνίκα μὲν ἐπὶ σωτηρίαν παρεκάλει, προτρεπτικὸς ὄνομα αὐτῷ ἦν: cf. *Strom.* vii. § 22; Pott. p. 841); and, if we can trust the assertion of Eusebius (*H. E.* v. 28), some of Clement's works were composed before the accession of Victor (A.D. 192). Putting these two facts together, we may reasonably suppose the *Address* written *c.* A.D. 190. It was addressed to *Greeks* and not to *Gentiles* generally, as Jerome understood the word ("adversus gentes," *de Vir. Ill.* 38). It deals almost exclusively with Greek mythology and Greek speculation.

Its general aim is to prove the superiority of Christianity to the religions and the philosophies of heathendom, while it satisfies the cravings of humanity to which they bore witness. The gospel is, as Clement shews with consummate eloquence, the New Song more powerful than that of Orpheus or Arion, new and yet older than the creation (c. 1), pure and spiritual as contrasted with the sensuality and idolatry of the pagan rites, clear and substantial as compared with the vague hopes of poets and philosophers (2-9). In such a case, he argues, custom cannot be pleaded against the duty of conversion. Man is born for God, and is bound to obey the call of God, Who through the Word is waiting to make him like unto Himself. The choice is between judgment and grace, between destruction and life: can the issue then be doubtful (10-12)?

It is not difficult to point out errors in taste, fact, and argument throughout Clement's appeal; but it would be perhaps impossible to shew in any earlier work passages equal to those in which he describes the mission of the Word, the Light of men (p. 88), and pictures the true destiny of man (pp. 92 ff.).

II. *The Tutor* (ὁ Παιδαγωγός: cf. Hos. v. 2, quoted in *Paed.* i. 7, p. 129).—The *Tutor* was written before the *Miscellanies*, in which the *Tutor* is described generally (*Strom.* vi. § 1, p. 736)—i.e. *c.* A.D. 190-195. The writer's design was "to prepare from early years, that is from the beginning of elementary instruction (ἐκ κατηχήσεως), a rule of life growing with the increase of faith, and fitting the souls of those just on the verge of manhood with virtue so as to enable them to receive the higher knowledge of philosophy" (εἰς ἐπιστήμης γνωστικῆς παραδοχήν, *Strom. l.c.*).

The main scope of the *Tutor* is therefore practical: the aim is action and not knowledge; but still action as preparatory to knowledge, and resting upon conviction. It is divided into three books. The first gives a general description of the Tutor, Who is the Word Himself (1-3); of the "children" whom He trains, Christian men and women alike (4-6); and of His general method, using both chastisements and love (7-12). The second and third books deal with special precepts designed to meet the actual difficulties of contemporary life and not to offer a theory of morals. It would not be easy to find elsewhere, even in the Roman satirists, an equally vivid and detailed picture of heathen manners. The second book contains general directions as to eating and drinking (1 f.), furniture (3), entertainments (4-8), sleep (9), the relations of men and women (10), the use of jewellery (11 f.). The third book opens with an inquiry into the nature of true beauty (c. 1). This leads to a condemnation of extravagance in dress both in men and in women (2 ff.), of luxurious establishments (4 f.), of the misuse of wealth (6 f.). Frugality and exercise are recommended (8-10); and many minute directions are added—often curiously suggestive in the present times—as to dress and behaviour (11 f.). General instructions from Holy Scripture as to the various duties and offices of life lead up to the prayer to the Tutor—the Word—with which the work closes. Immediately after the *Tutor* are printed in the editions of Clement two short poems, which have been attributed to him. The first, written in an anapaestic measure, is *A Hymn of the Saviour Christ* (ὕμνος τοῦ Σωτῆρος Χριστοῦ), and the second, written in trimeter iambics, is addressed *To the Tutor* (εἰς τὸν Παιδαγωγόν). The first is said to be "Saint Clement's" (τοῦ ἁγίου Κλήμεντος) in those MSS. which contain it; but it may be a work of primitive date, like the *Morning Hymn* which has been preserved in our Communion Office as the *Gloria in Excelsis*. If it were Clement's, and designed to occupy its present place, it is scarcely possible that it would have been omitted in any MS.; while it makes an appropriate and natural addition if taken from some other source. There is no evidence to shew that the second is Clement's work; it is doubtless an effusion of some pious scholar of a later date.

III. *The Miscellanies* (Στρωματεῖς).*—The title, *patchwork* (or rather *bags for holding the bedclothes*, like στρωματόδεσμοι), suggests a true idea of the character of the work. It is designedly unmethodical, a kind of meadow, as Clement describes it, or rather a wooded

* The full title is given at the close of Books i. iii. v.: τῶν κατὰ τὴν ἀληθῆ φιλοσοφίαν γνωστικῶν ὑπομνημάτων στρωματεῖς.

mountain (vii. § 111), studded irregularly with various growths, and so fitted to exercise the ingenuity and labour of those likely to profit by it (vi. § 2, p. 736, Pott.). But yet the book is inspired by one thought. It is an endeavour to claim for the gospel the power of fulfilling all the desires of men and of raising to a supreme unity all the objects of knowledge, in the soul of the true gnostic—the perfect Christian philosopher. The first book, which is mutilated at the beginning, treats in the main of the office and the origin of Greek philosophy in relation to Christianity and Judaism. Clement shews that Greek philosophy was part of the Divine education of men, subordinate to the training of the law and the prophets, but yet really from God (§§ 1-58; 91-100). In his anxiety to establish this cardinal proposition he is not content with shewing that the books of O.T. are older than those of the philosophers (59-65; 101-164; 180-182); but endeavours to prove also that the philosophers borrowed from the Jews (66-90; 165 f.). After this he vindicates the character and explains the general scope of the law—"the philosophy of Moses" (167-179). The main object of the second book lies in the more detailed exposition of the originality and superiority of the moral teaching of revelation as compared with that of Greek philosophy which was in part derived from it (§§ 1 ff.; 20-24; 78-96). The argument includes an examination of the nature of faith (4-19; 25-31), resting on a godly fear and perfected by love (32-55); and of repentance (56-71). He discusses the sense in which human affections are ascribed to God (72-75); and shews that the conception of the ideal Christian is that of a man made like to God (97-126), in accordance with the noblest aspirations of philosophy (127-136). The book closes with a preliminary discussion of marriage. The third book investigates the true doctrine of marriage (§§ 57-60) as against those who indulged in every license on the ground that bodily actions are indifferent (1-11; 25-44); and, on the other hand, those who abstained from marriage from hatred of the Creator (12-24; 45-46). Various passages of Scripture wrongly interpreted by heretics are examined (61-101); and the two main errors are shewn to be inconsistent with Christianity (102-110). The fourth book opens with a very interesting outline of the whole plan of the comprehensive apology for Christianity on which he had entered (§§ 1-3). The work evidently grew under his hands, and he implies that he could hardly expect to accomplish the complete design. He then adds fresh traits to his portrait of the true "gnostic." Self-sacrifice, martyrdom, lie at the root of his nature (8-56; 72-77), virtues within the reach of all states and of both sexes (57-71), though even this required to be guarded against fanaticism and misunderstanding (78-96). Other virtues, as love and endurance, are touched upon (97-119); and then Clement gives a picture of a godly woman (120-131), and of the gnostic, who rises above fear and hope to that perfection which rests in the knowledge and love of God (132-174). In the fifth book Clement, following the outline laid down (iv. 1), discusses faith and hope (§§ 1-18), and then passes to the principle of enigmatic teaching. This, he argues, was followed by heathen and Jewish masters alike (19-26); by Pythagoras (27-31); by Moses, in the ordinances of the tabernacle (32-41); by the Aegyptians (42-44); and by many others (45-56). The principle itself is, he maintains, defensible on intelligible grounds (57-60), and supported by the authority of the apostles (61-67). For in fact the knowledge of God can be gained only through serious effort and by divine help (68-89). This review of the character and sources of the highest knowledge leads Clement back to his characteristic proposition that the Greeks borrowed from the Jews the noblest truths of their own philosophy. The sixth and seventh books are designed, as Clement states (vi. § 1) to shew the character of the Christian philosopher (the gnostic), and so to make it clear that he alone is the true worshipper of God. By way of prelude Clement repeats and enforces (§§ 4-38) what he had said on Greek plagiarisms, yet admitting that the Greeks had some true knowledge of God (39-43), and affirming that the gospel was preached in Hades to those of them who had lived according to their light (44-53), though that was feeble compared with the glory of the gospel (54-70). He then sketches the lineaments of the Christian philosopher, who attains to a perfectly passionless state (71-79) and masters for the service of the faith all forms of knowledge, including various mysteries open to him only (80-114). The reward of this true philosopher is proportioned to his attainments (115-148). These are practically unlimited in range, for Greek philosophy, though a gift of God for the training of the nations, is only a recreation for the Christian philosopher in comparison with the serious objects of his study (149-168). In the seventh book Clement regards the Christian philosopher as the one true worshipper of God (§§ 1-5), striving to become like the Son of God (5-21), even as the heathen conversely made their gods like themselves (22-27). The soul is his temple; prayers and thanksgivings, his sacrifice; truth, the law of his life (28-54). Other traits are added to the portraiture of "the gnostic" (55-88); and Clement then meets the general objection urged against Christianity from the conflict of rival sects (89-92). Heresy, he replies, can be detected by two tests. It is opposed to the testimony of Scripture (93-105); and it is of recent origin (106-108). At the close of the seventh book Clement remarks that he "shall proceed with his argument from a fresh beginning" (τῶν ἑξῆς ἀπ' ἄλλης ἀρχῆς ποιησόμεθα τὸν λόγον). The phrase may mean that he proposes to enter upon a new division of the *Miscellanies*, or that he will now pass to another portion of the great system of writings sketched out in *Strom.* iv. 1-3. In favour of the first opinion it may be urged that Eusebius (*H. E.* vi. 13) and Photius (*Cod.* 109) expressly mention *eight* books of the *Miscellanies*; while on the other hand the words themselves, taken in connexion with vii. 1, point rather to the commencement of a new book. The fragment which bears the title of the eighth book in the one remaining MS. is in fact a piece of a treatise on logic. It may naturally have served as an introduction to the examination of the opinions of Greek philosophers, the interpretation of Scripture, and the refutation of heresies which were the general topics of the second principal member of Clement's plan (iv. 2); but it is not easy to see how it could have formed the close of the *Miscellanies*. It is "a fresh beginning" and nothing more. In the time of Photius (*c.* A.D. 850) the present fragment was reckoned as the eighth book in some copies, and in others the tract, *On the Rich Man that is Saved* (*Bibl.* 111). Still further confusion is indicated by the fact that passages from the *Extracts from the Prophetical Writings* are quoted from "the eighth book of the *Miscellanies*" (Bunsen, *Anal. Ante-Nic.* i. 288 f.), and also from "the eighth book of the *Outlines*" (*id.* 285); while the discussion of prophecy was postponed from the *Miscellanies* to some later opportunity (*Strom.* vii. 1, cf. iv. 2). Perhaps the simplest solution is to suppose that at a very early date the logical introduction to the *Outlines* was separated from the remainder of the work, and added to MSS. of the *Miscellanies*. In this way the opinion would arise that there were 8 books of the *Miscellanies*, and scribes supplied the place of bk. viii. according to their pleasure.

IV. *The Outlines* (Ὑποτυπώσεις) probably grew out of the *Miscellanies*. Several express quotations from the 4th, 5th, 6th, and 7th books of the *Outlines* have been preserved; but the fragments are too few and Clement's method too desultory to allow these to furnish a certain plan of the arrangement of the work. They agree, however, fairly with the summary description of Photius, and probably books i.-iii. contained the general introduction, with notes on the O.T. ("Genesis, Exodus, and the Psalms"); books iv.-vi., notes on the Epp. of St. Paul; books vii. viii., on the Catholic Epp.*

In addition to the detached quotations, there can be no reasonable doubt that the three series of extracts, (a) *The summaries from the expositions of Theodotus and the so-called Western school*, (b) *The selections from the comments on the prophets*, and (c) *The outlines on the Catholic Epistles*, were taken from the *Outlines*. But partly from the method of compilation, partly from the manner in which they have been preserved in a single MS., these fragments, though of the deepest interest, are at present only imperfectly intelligible.

(*a*) The *summaries from Theodotus* (ἐκ τῶν Θεοδότου καὶ τῆς ἀνατολικῆς καλουμένης διδασκαλίας κατὰ τοὺς Οὐαλεντίνου χρόνους ἐπιτομαί) are at once the most corrupt and the most intrinsically difficult of the extracts. It appears as if the compiler set down hastily the passages which contained the interpretations of the school which he wished to collect, without regard to the context, and often in an imperfect form. Sometimes he adds the criticism of Clement (ἡμεῖς δέ, § 8; Ἐμοὶ δέ, § 17; ὁ ἡμέτερος [λόγος], § 33); but generally the Valentinian comment is given without remark (οἱ ἀπὸ Οὐαλεντίνου, §§ 2, 6, 16, 23, 25; οἱ Ουαλεντινιανοί, §§ 21, 24, 37; ὥς φησιν ὁ Θεόδοτος, §§ 22, 26, 30; φησί, §§ 41, 67; φασί, §§ 33, 35; λέγουσιν, § 43). It follows that in some cases it is uncertain whether Clement quotes a Valentinian author by way of exposition, or adopts the opinion which he quotes. The same ambiguity appears to have existed in the original work; and it is easy to see how Photius, rapidly perusing the treatise, may have attributed to Clement doctrines which he simply recited without approval and without examination. Thus, in the fragments which remain, occasion might be given to charge Clement with false opinions on the nature of the Son (§ 19), on the creation of Eve (§ 21), on the two Words (§§ 6, 7, 19), on Fate (§§ 75 ff.), on the Incarnation (§ 1). There is no perceptible order or connexion in the series of extracts. The beginning and end are equally corrupt. Some sections are quite detached (*e.g.* §§ 9, 18, 21, 28, 66, etc.); others give a more or less continuous exposition of some mystery: *e.g.* §§ 10-16 (the nature of spiritual existences); 39-65 (the relations of wisdom, Jesus, the Christ, the demiurge; the material, the animal, the spiritual); 67-86 (birth, fate, baptism).

(*b*) *The prophetic selections* (ἐκ τῶν προφητικῶν ἐκλογαί) are for the most part scarcely less desultory and disconnected than the *Summaries*, but far simpler in style and substance. They commence with remarks on the symbolism of the elements, and mainly of water (§§ 1-8). Then follow fragmentary reflections on discipline (9-11), on knowledge, faith, creation, the new creation (12-24), fire (25 f.), on writing and preaching (27), on traits of the true gnostic (28-37). A long and miscellaneous series of observations, some of them physiological, succeeds (38-50), and the collection closes with a fairly continuous exposition of Ps. xviii. (xix.).

Manuscript.—The *summaries from Theodotus* and the *prophetic selections* are at present found only in *Cod. Flor.* (L.). The text given in the edd. of Clement is most corrupt. The conjectural emendations and Latin trans. of J. Bernays, given by Bunsen in his ed. of the fragments of *The Outlines* (*Anal. Ante-Nic.* i.), are by far our most valuable help for the understanding of the text. Dindorf, in his ed., has overlooked these.

(*c*) The third important fragment of the *Outlines* consists of a Latin version of notes on detached verses of I. Peter, Jude, and I., II. John, with several insertions, probably due in some cases to transpositions in the MS. (*e.g.* I. John ii. 1, hae namque primitivae, virtutes—audita est, Pott. p. 1009, stands properly in connexion with the line of speculation on Jude 9); and in others to a marginal illustration drawn from some other part of the work (*e.g.* Jude 24, cum dicit Daniel—confusus est). Cassiodorus says (*Inst. Div. Litt.* 8) that Clement wrote some remarks on I. Peter i., II. John, and *James*, which were generally subtle, but at times rash; and that he himself translated them into Latin, with such revision as rendered their teaching more safe. It has generally been supposed, in spite of the difference of range (*James* for *Jude*) that these Latin notes

* Bunsen (*Anal. Ante-Nic.* i. pp. 163 f.) arranges the contents of the books very differently. The evidence is slight; but it does not appear from Photius that the Gospels formed the subject of special annotation, and Bunsen makes the third book *Commentarius in Evangelia*.

are the version of Cassiodorus. It seems, however, more probable that the printed notes are mere glosses taken from a *Catena*, and not a substantial work. The *Adumbrationes* were published by de la Bigne in his *Bibliotheca Patrum*, Par. 1575 (and in later editions); but he gives no account of the MS. or MSS. from which the text was taken. Ph. Labbe, however, states (*de Scriptt. Eccles.* 1660, i. p. 230) that he saw an ancient parchment MS., "qui fuit olim Coenobii S. Mariae Montis Dei," which contained these *Adumbrationes*, under that title, together with Didymus's commentary on the Catholic Epistles. De la Bigne then, probably, found the notes of Clement in the "very ancient but somewhat illegible MS." from which he took his text of Didymus, which follows the *Adumbrationes* (*Bibl.* vi. p. 676 n.).

V. The remaining extant work of Clement, *Who is the Rich Man that is Saved?* (τίς ὁ σωζόμενος πλούσιος;) is apparently a popular address based upon Mark x. 17-31. The teaching is simple, eloquent, and just; and the tract closes with the exquisite "story, which is no story" of St. John and the young robber, which Eusebius relates in his *History* (iii. 23).

iii. *Clements' Position and Influence as a Christian Teacher.*—In order to understand Clement rightly, it is necessary to bear in mind that he laboured in a crisis of transition. This gives his writings their peculiar interest in all times of change. The transition was threefold, affecting doctrine, thought, and life. Doctrine was passing from the stage of oral tradition to written definition (1). Thought was passing from the immediate circle of the Christian revelation to the whole domain of human experience (2). Life in its fulness was coming to be apprehended as the object of Christian discipline (3). A few suggestions will be offered upon the first two of these heads. (1) Clement repeatedly affirms that even when he sets forth the deepest mysteries, he is simply reproducing an original unwritten tradition. This had been committed by the Lord to the apostles Peter, James, John, and Paul, and handed down from father to son, till at length he set forth accurately in writing what had been delivered in word (*Strom.* i. § 11, p. 322; cf. vi. 68, p. 774; and fragm. ap. Eus. *H. E.* ii. 1). But this tradition was, as he held it, not an independent source of doctrine, but a guide to the apprehension of doctrine. It was not co-ordinate with Scripture, but interpretative of Scripture (*Strom.* vi. 124 f., pp. 802 f.; *de Div. Sal.* § 5, p. 938). It was the help to the training of the Christian philosopher (ὁ γνωστικός), and not part of the heritage of the simple believer. Tradition in this aspect preserved the clue to the right understanding of the hidden sense, the underlying harmonies, the manifold unity of revelation. More particularly the philosopher was able to obtain through tradition the general principles of interpreting the records of revelation and significant illustrations of their application. In this way the true "gnostic" was saved from the errors of the false "gnostic" or heretic, who interpreted Scripture without regard to "the ecclesiastical rule" (*Strom.* vi. 125, p. 803, κανὼν ἐκκλησιαστικός: ὁ ἐκκλ. κ. *ib.* vi. 165, p. 826; vii. 41, p. 855; cf. ὁ κανὼν τῆς ἀληθείας, *ib.* vi. 124, p. 802; 131, p. 806; vii. 94, p. 890; ὁ κανὼν τῆς ἐκκλησίας, *ib.* i. 96, p. 375; vii. 105, p. 897). The examples of spiritual interpretation which Clement gives in accordance with this traditional "rule" are frequently visionary and puerile (*e.g. Strom.* vi. 133 ff. pp. 807 ff.). But none the less the rule itself witnessed to a vital truth, the continuity and permanent value of the books of Holy Scripture. This truth was an essential part of the inheritance of the Catholic church; and Clement, however faulty in detail, did good service in maintaining it (*id.* vii. 96, p. 891). As yet, however, the contents of the Christian Bible were imperfectly defined. Clement, like the other Fathers who habitually used the Alexandrine O.T., quotes the books of the Apocrypha without distinguishing them in any way from the books of the Hebrew canon, and he appears to regard the current Greek Bible as answering to the Hebrew Scriptures restored by Ezra (*Strom.* i. 124, p. 392; *id.* 148, p. 409). There is the same laxity of usage in Clement with regard to the N.T. He ascribes great weight to the *Ep. of Barnabas* (*Strom.* ii. 31, p. 445; *id.* 116, p. 489); and makes frequent use of the *Preaching of Peter* (*Strom.* i. 182, p. 427, etc.); and quotes the *Gospel acc. to the Hebrews* (*Strom.* ii. 45, p. 453). Eusebius further adds that he wrote notes on the *Revelation of Peter*, which is in fact quoted in the *Extracts from the Prophets* (§§ 41, 48, 49). The text of his quotations is evidently given from memory (*e.g.* Matt. v. 45, vi. 26, etc.). But as the earliest Greek writer who largely and expressly quotes the N.T. (for the Greek fragments of Irenaeus are of comparatively small compass), his evidence as to the primitive form of the apostolic writings is of the highest value. Not unfrequently he is one of a very small group of witnesses who have preserved an original reading (*e.g.* I. Cor. ii. 13, vii. 3, 5, 35, 39, etc.). In other cases his readings, even when presumably wrong, are shewn by other evidence to have been widely spread at a very early date (*e.g.* Matt. vi. 33).

It is impossible here to follow in detail Clement's opinions on special points of doctrine. The contrast which he draws between the gnostic (the philosophic Christian) and the ordinary believer is of more general interest. This contrast underlies the whole plan of his *Miscellanies*, and explains the different aspects in which doctrine, according to his view, might be regarded as an object of faith and as an object of knowledge. Faith is the foundation; knowledge the superstructure (*Strom.* vi. 26, p. 660). By knowledge faith is perfected (*id.* vii. 55, p. 864), for to know is more than to believe (*id.* vi. 109, p. 794). Faith is a summary knowledge of urgent truths: knowledge a sure demonstration of what has been received through faith, being itself reared upon faith through the teaching of the Lord (*id.* vii. 57, p. 865). Thus the gnostic grasps the complete truth of all revelation from the beginning of the world to the end, piercing to the depths of Scripture, of which the believer tastes the surface only (*id.* vi. 78, p. 779; 131, p. 806; vii. 95, p. 891). As a consequence of this intelligent sympathy with the Divine Will, the gnostic becomes in perfect unity in himself (μοναδικός), and as far as possible like God (*id.* iv. 154, p. 633; vii. 13, p. 835). Definite outward observances cease to have any value for one whose whole being is brought into an abiding harmony with that which is eternal: he has no wants, no passions; he rests in the contemplation of God, which is and will be his unfailing blessedness (*id.* vii. 35, p. 851, 84, p. 883; vi. 71, p. 776; vii. 56, p. 865). In this outline it is easy to see the noblest traits of later mysticism; and if some of Clement's statements go beyond subjects which lie within the powers of man, still he bears impressive testimony to two essential truths, that the aim of faith through knowledge perfected by love is the present recovery of the divine likeness; and that formulated doctrine is not an end in itself, but a means whereby we rise through fragmentary propositions to knowledge which is immediate and one.

(2) The character of the gnostic, the ideal Christian, the perfect philosopher, represents the link between man, in his earthly conflict, and God: it represents also the link between man and men. The gnostic fulfils through the gospel the destiny and nature of mankind, and gathers together the fruit of their varied experience. This thought of the Incarnation as the crown and consummation of the whole history of the world is perhaps that which is most characteristic of Clement's office as an interpreter of the faith. It rests upon his view of human nature, of the providential government of God, of the finality of the Christian dispensation. Man, according to Clement, is born for the service of God. His soul (ψυχή) is a gift sent down to him from heaven by God (*Strom.* iv. 169, p. 640), and strains to return thither (*id.* 9, p. 567). For this end there is need of painful training (*Strom.* i. 33, p. 335; vi. 78, p. 779); and the various partial sciences are helps towards the attainment of the true destiny of existence (*Strom.* vi. 80 ff. pp. 780 ff.). The "image" of God which man receives at his birth is slowly completed in the "likeness" of God (*Strom.* ii. 131, p. 499; cf. *Paed.* i. 98, p. 156). The inspiration of the divine breath by which he is distinguished from other creatures (Gen. ii. 7) is fulfilled by the gift of the Holy Spirit to the believer, which that original constitution makes possible (*Strom.* v. 87 f.; p. 698: cf. *Strom.* iv. 150, p. 632). The image of God, Clement says elsewhere, is the Word (Logos), and the true image of the Word is man, that is, the reason in man (*Cohort.* 98, p. 79). It follows necessarily from this view of humanity, as essentially related to God through the Word, that Clement acknowledged a providential purpose in the development of Gentile life. He recognized in the bright side of Gentile speculation many divine elements. These he regarded as partly borrowed from Jewish revelation, and partly derived from reason illuminated by the Word (Λόγος), the final source of reason. Some truths, he says, the Greek philosophers stole and disfigured; some they overlaid with restless and foolish speculations; others they discovered, for they also perhaps had "a spirit of wisdom" (Ex. xxviii. 3) (*Strom.* i. 87, p. 369). He distinctly recognized the office which Greek philosophy fulfilled for the Greeks as a guide to righteousness, and a work of divine providence (*Strom.* i. 176 ff. pp. 425 ff.; 91 ff. pp. 372 ff.). He regarded it as a preparation for justifying faith (*Strom.* i. 99, p. 377; vi. 44, p. 762; *id.* 47 ff. pp. 764 ff.), and in a true sense a dispensation, a covenant (*Strom.* vi. 42, p. 761; *id.* 67, p. 773; *id.* 159, p. 823; i. 28, p. 331).

The training of Jews and of the Greeks was thus in different ways designed to fit men for the final manifestation of the Christ. The systems were partial in their essence, and by human imperfection were made still more so. The various schools of philosophy, Jewish and heathen, are described by Clement under a memorable image, as rending in pieces the one truth like the Bacchants who rent the body of Pentheus, and bore about the fragments in triumph. Each, he says, boasts that the morsel which it has had the good fortune to gain is all the truth. Yet by the rising of the light all things are lightened, and he who again combines the divided parts and unites the exposition (λόγος) in a perfect whole will look upon the truth without peril (*Strom.* i. 57, p. 349).

Towards this great unity of all science and all life Clement himself strove; and by the influence of his writings kept others alive to the import of the magnificent promises in the teaching of St. Paul and St. John. He affirmed, once for all, upon the threshold of the new age, that Christianity is the heir of all past time, and the interpreter of the future. Sixteen centuries have confirmed the truth of his principle, and left its application still fruitful.

Clement of Alexandria's works are in Migne's *Patr. Gk.* vols. viii. ix.; and an ed. of his *Opera ex rec. Guil. Dindorfii* in 4 vols. with Latin notes is pub. by the Clarendon Press. A full enumeration of the MSS. of Clement's works will be found in *D. C. B.* (4-vol. ed.).

Besides the chief Church Histories, the following works are important for the study of Clement: Le Nourry, *Appar. ad Bibliothecam Patrum,* lib. iii. (reprinted in Dindorf's edition); Moehler, *Patrologie,* 1840; Mansel, *The Gnostic Heresies,* lect. xvi.; and the histories of the Alexandrine School, by Guericke, Matter, J. Simon, Vacherot. Interesting summaries of Clement's teaching, besides those in the general works of Lumper, Maréchal, and Schramm, are given by bp. Kaye (*Some Account of the Writings and Opinions of Clement of Alexandria,* Lond. 1835); abbé Freppel (*Clément d'Alexandrie, cours à la Sorbonne,* Paris, 1866); Ch. Bigg (*The Christian Platonists of Alexandria,* Oxf. 1886); F. J. A. Hort (*Six Lectures on the Ante-Nicene Fathers,* Lond. 1895). A cheap popular Life is pub. by S.P.C.K. in their *Fathers for Eng. Readers*; an Eng. trans. of the *Homily on the Rich Man* by P. M. Barnard (S.P.C.K.), text by the same in *Texts and Studies,* vol. v. No. 2 (Camb. Univ. Press), who has also collected Clement's Biblical text for the gospel and Acts (*ib.* vol. v. No. 4). A valuable ed. of the 7th book of the *Miscellanies,* with translation, introduction and notes, was pub. in 1902 at Cambridge by the late Prof. Hort and Prof. J. B. Mayor. Translations of most of his works are contained in the *Ante-Nicene Lib.* vol. ii. (T. & T. Clark). [B.F.W.]

Clementine Literature. Among the spurious writings attributed to Clement of Rome, the chief is one which purported to contain a record made by Clement of discourses of the apostle Peter, together with an account of the circumstances under which Clement came to be Peter's travelling companion, and of other details of Clement's family history. This work assumed a variety of forms. The Ebionitism with which the original work had been strongly coloured was first softened, then removed. Changes were also made with a view to improvement of the story; and as time went on far more interest was felt in the framework of narrative than in the discourses themselves. In the latest forms of the work, several of the discourses are omitted, and the rest greatly abridged. In early times, even when the work was rejected as heretical, it yet seems to have been supposed to rest on a groundwork of fact, and several statements passed into church tradition which appear primarily to rest on its authority. Afterwards, in its orthodox form, it was accepted as a genuine work of Clement and a trustworthy historical authority. On the revival of learning the disposition was to disregard the book as a heretical figment quite worthless to the student of church history. Later it was seen that even if no more than a historical novel composed with a controversial object towards the end of the 2nd cent., such a document must be most valuable in shewing the opinions of the school from which it emanated; and accordingly the Clementine writings play an important part in all modern discussions concerning the history of the early ages of the church.

The work has come down to us in three principal forms. I. *The Homilies* (in the MSS. τὰ Κλημέντια), first printed by Cotelier in his edition of the *Apostolic Fathers* 1672, from one of the Colbertine MSS. in the Paris Library. This manuscript is both corrupt and defective, breaking off in the middle of the 19th of the 20 homilies of which the entire work consists. The complete work was first pub. by Dressel, 1853, from a MS. which he found in the Ottobonian Library in the Vatican. Notes on the homilies by Wieseler, which were intended to have formed part of this publication, only appeared in 1859 as an appendix to Dressel's ed. of the *Epitomes* (see below). The two MSS. mentioned are the only ones now known to exist.

II. *The Recognitions* (ἀναγνώσεις, ἀναγνωρισμοί) bears in the MSS. a great variety of titles, the most common being *Itinerarium S. Clementis* (corresponding probably to περίοδοι Κλημέντος or περίοδοι Πέτρου). The original is lost, but the work is preserved in a translation by Rufinus, of which many MSS. are extant. Rufinus states in his preface that there were then extant two forms differing in many respects. He adds that he had omitted certain passages common to both, one of which he specifies, as being, to say the least, unintelligible to him; and elsewhere expresses his opinion that those passages had been interpolated by heretics. He claims to have aimed at giving rather a literal than an elegant translation; and there seems reason to regard this translation as more faithful than some others by him. We can test his work in the case of fragments of the original preserved by quotation, and, moreover, we have a Syriac trans. of the first three books, which is in the main in fair agreement with the Latin. For one of the most important variations see Lightfoot *On the Galatians*, 4th ed. p. 316. The trans. of Rufinus was first pub. by Sichardus (Basle, 1526). The most important later edd. are by Cotelier in his *Apostolic Fathers* (Paris, 1672) and by Gersdorf (Leipz. 1838). A new ed., founded on a better collation of MSS., is much to be wished for. The Syriac trans., an ed. of which was pub. by de Lagarde, 1861, is preserved in two MSS. in the British Museum. The older of these claims to have been written at Edessa, A.D. 411, and exhibits errors of transcription, which shew that it was taken from a still earlier MS. It contains the books i. ii. and iii. of the *Recognitions* and part of c. i. of book iv., at the end of which is marked "the end of the first discourse of Clemens." Then follow the 10th homily headed "the third against the Gentiles"; the 11th homily headed "the fourth"; the 12th and 13th homilies, the former only as far as c. xxiv., with the heading "from Tripoli in Phoenicia"; and the 14th homily headed "book xiv.," after which is marked "the end of the discourses of Clemens." The other MS. is some four centuries later, and contains only the first three books of the *Recognitions*, the note at the end being "the ninth of Clemens who accompanied Simon Cephas is ended." Eng. trans. of both the *Homilies* and the *Recognitions* are given in the *Ante-Nicene Lib.* (T. & T. Clark).

III. *The Epitome*, first pub. by Turnebus, 1555, is an abridgment of the first form (*i.e.* the *Homilies*), and contains also a continuation of the story, use being made therein of the martyrdom of Clement by Simeon Metaphrastes, and of a tale by Ephraim, bp. of Chersonesus, of a miracle performed at the tomb of Clement. The *Epitome* is given in forms of varying fulness in different MSS. The edition by Dressel (Leipz. 1859), besides giving a fuller version of the *Epitome* as previously pub., contains also a second form considerably different. There must have been at least one other form not now extant, called by Uhlhorn the orthodox Clementines, which retained the discourses, but completely expurgated the heresy contained in them. This is inferred from the citations of the late Greek writers (Nicephorus Callisti, Cedrenus, and Michael Glycas); and the Clementines so amended were so entirely accepted by the later Greek church, that a Scholiast on Eusebius is quite unable to understand the charge of heresy which his author brings against them. In what follows we set aside the *Epitomes* as being manifestly a late form, and confine our attention to the other two forms, viz. the *Homilies* and *Recognitions*, to which, or to their writers, we shall refer as H. and R. Of these the *Homilies* contain all the characteristics of Ebionitism in much the harsher form; but before discussing the doctrine, we will compare the narratives as told in either form. The following is an abstract of the *Recognitions*. The form is that of an autobiography addressed by Clement to James, bp. of Jerusalem. The work divides itself into three portions, probably of different dates.

I. Clement, having stated that he was born

at Rome and from early years a lover of chastity, gives a lively description of the perplexity caused him by his anxiety to solve the problems, what had been the origin and what would be the future of the world, and whether he himself might look forward to a future life. He seeks in vain for knowledge in the schools of the philosophers, finding nothing but disputings, contradiction, and uncertainty. At length a rumour that there had arisen in Judaea a preacher of truth possessed of miraculous power is confirmed by the arrival of Barnabas in Rome, who declares that the Son of God was even then preaching in Judaea, and promising eternal life to His disciples. Barnabas is rudely received by the Roman rabble, and returns to his own country in haste to be present at a Jewish feast. Clement, though desirous to accompany him for further instruction, is detained by the necessity of collecting money due to him; but sails shortly after for Palestine, and after a fifteen days' voyage arrives at Caesarea. There he finds Barnabas again and is introduced by him to Peter, who had arrived at Caesarea on the same day, and who was on the next to hold a discussion with Simon the Samaritan. Peter forthwith frees Clement from his perplexities, by instructing him in the doctrine of the "true prophet." For one who has received the true prophet's credentials there is an end of uncertainty; faith in Him can never be withdrawn, nor can anything which He teaches admit of doubt or question. Clement by Peter's orders committed his teaching to writing, and sent the book to James, to whom Peter had been commanded annually to transmit an account of his doings. We are next told that Simon postponed the appointed discussion with Peter, who uses the interval thus gained to give Clement a continuous exposition of the faith, in which God's dealings are declared from the commencement of the world to the then present time. This section includes an account of a disputation held on the temple steps between the apostles and the various sects of the Jews, viz. the priests, the Sadducees, the Samaritans, the Scribes and Pharisees, and the disciples of John. When the apostles are on the point of success the disputation is broken off by a tumult raised by an unnamed enemy, who is unmistakably Saul, who flings James down the temple steps, leaving him for dead, and disperses the assembly. The disciples fly to Jericho, and the enemy hastens to Damascus, whither he supposes Peter to have fled, in order there to make havoc of the faithful. At Jericho, James hears from Zacchaeus of the mischief being done by Simon at Caesarea, and sends Peter thither to refute him, ordering him to report to him annually, but more particularly every seven years. In the section just described there are some things which do not harmonize with what has gone before. The date of the events related is given as seven years after our Lord's passion, although the previous story implies that Clement's voyage had been made in the very year that ended our Lord's ministry. Also in one place (I. 71) Peter is mentioned in the third person, though he is himself the speaker. These facts prove that the story of Clement has been added on to an older document. It has been conjectured that this document was an Ebionite work Ἀναβαθμοὶ Ἰακώβου, the contents of which, as described by Epiphanius (xxx. 16), well correspond with those of this section, and the title of which might be explained as referring to discourses on the temple steps. But this conjecture encounters the difficulty that the author himself indicates a different source for this part of his work.

We are next introduced to two disciples of Peter, Nicetas and Aquila, who had been disciples of Simon. These give an account of the history of Simon and of his magical powers, stating that Simon supposed himself to perform his wonders by the aid of the soul of a murdered boy, whose likeness was preserved in Simon's bed-chamber. Prepared with this information, Peter enters into a public discussion with Simon which lasts for three days, the main subject in debate being whether the difficulty of reconciling the existence of evil with the goodness and power of the Creator does not force us to believe in the existence of a God different from the Creator of the world. The question of the immortality of the soul is also treated of, and this brings the discussion to a dramatic close. For Peter offers to settle the question by proceeding to Simon's bed-chamber, and interrogating the soul of the murdered boy, whose likeness was there preserved. On finding his secret known to Peter, Simon humbles himself, but retracts his repentance on Peter's acknowledging that he had this knowledge, not by prophetic power, but from associates of Simon. The multitude, however, are filled with indignation, and drive Simon away in disgrace. Simon departs, informing his disciples that divine honours await him at Rome. Peter resolves to follow him among the Gentiles and expose his wickedness; and having remained three months at Caesarea for the establishment of the church, he ordains Zacchaeus as its bishop, and sets out for Tripolis, now the centre of Simon's operations. This brings the third book of the *Recognitions* to a close; and here we are told that Clement sent to James an account in ten books of Peter's discourses, of which the author gives the contents in detail, from which we may conclude that they formed a work really in existence previous to his own composition. These contents can scarcely be described as an abstract of the three books of the *Recognitions*; for though the same topics are more or less touched on, the order and proportion of treatment are different. One of the books is described as treating of the Apostles' disputation at the temple; and therefore it seems needless to look for the original of this part in the *Ascents of James* or elsewhere.

II. On Peter's arrival at Tripolis he finds that Simon, hearing of his coming, had fled by night to Syria. Peter proceeds to instruct the people; and his discourses, containing a polemic against heathenism, occupy the next three books of R. Bk. vi. terminates with the baptism of Clement and the ordination of a bishop, after which Peter sets out for Antioch, having spent 3 months at Tripolis.

III. With bk. vii. the story of Clement's recognition of his family begins. We shall presently discuss how an occasion is skilfully presented for Clement's relating his family history to Peter. That history is as follows: Clement's father, Faustinianus, was a member of the emperor's family, and married by him to a lady of noble birth, named Mattidia. By her he had twin sons, Faustus and Faustinus, and afterwards Clement. When Clement was five years old, Mattidia told her husband that she had seen a vision warning her that unless she and her twin sons speedily left Rome and remained absent for ten years, all must perish miserably. Thereupon the father sent his wife and children with suitable provision of money and attendance to Athens, in order to educate them there. But after her departure no tidings reached Rome, and Faustinianus, having in vain sent others to inquire for them, at length left Clement under guardianship at Rome, and departed himself in search of them. But he too disappeared, and Clement, now aged thirty-two, had never since heard of father, mother, or brothers. The story proceeds to tell how Peter and Clement on their way to Antioch go over to the island of Aradus to see the wonders of a celebrated temple there. While Clement and his party are admiring works of Phidias preserved in the temple, Peter converses with a beggar woman outside, and the story she tells of her life is in such agreement with that previously told him by Clement, that Peter is able to unite mother and son. The vision which she had related had been feigned in order to escape from the incestuous addresses of her husband's brother, without causing family discord by revealing his wickedness. On her voyage to Athens she had been shipwrecked, and cast on shore by the waves, without being able to tell what had become of her children. All now return to the main land, and on telling the story to their companions who had been left behind, Nicetas and Aquila recognize their own story and declare themselves to be the twin sons, who had been saved from the wreck and sold into slavery by their rescuers. Mattidia is baptized. After the baptism Peter and the three brothers, having bathed in the sea, withdraw to a retired place for prayer. An old man in a workman's dress accosts them and undertakes to prove to them that prayer is useless, and that there is neither God nor Providence, but that all things are governed by astrological fate (genesis). A set disputation takes place and occupies bks. viii. ix.; the 3 brothers, being well trained in Grecian philosophy, successively argue on the side of Providence, and discuss the evidence for astrology. The discussion is closed by a dramatic surprise. When all the old man's other difficulties have been solved, he undertakes to produce a conclusive argument from his own experience. His own wife had been born under a horoscope which compelled her to commit adultery, and to end her days by water in foreign travel. And so it turned out. She had been guilty of adultery with a slave, as he had learned on his brother's testimony, and afterwards leaving Rome with her twin sons on account of a pretended vision, had perished miserably by shipwreck. Peter has now the triumph of fully reuniting the family and gaining a victory in the discussion, by shewing the complete falsification of the astrological prediction. From the account given by Rufinus, it would seem that one of the forms of the *Recognitions* known to him closed here; but in the tenth book as we have it, the story is prolonged by discourses intended to bring Faustinianus to a hearty reception of Christianity. After this Simon is again brought on the stage. He has been very successful at Antioch in shewing wonders to the people and stirring up their hatred against Peter. One of Peter's emissaries, in order to drive him to flight, prevails on Cornelius the centurion, who had been sent on public business to Caesarea, to give out that he had been commissioned to seek out and destroy Simon, in accordance with an edict of the emperor for the destruction of sorcerers at Rome and in the provinces. Tidings of this are brought to Simon by a pretended friend, who is in reality a Christian spy. Simon, in alarm, flees to Laodicea, and there meeting Faustinianus, who had come to visit their common friends, Apion (or, as our author spells it, Appion) and Anubion, transforms by his magic the features of Faustinianus into his own, that Faustinianus may be arrested in his stead. But Peter, not being deceived by the transformation, turns it to the greater discomfiture of Simon. For he sends Faustinianus to Antioch, who, pretending to be Simon, whose form he bore, makes a public confession of imposture, and testifies to the divine mission of Peter. After this, when Simon attempts again to get a hearing in Antioch, he is driven away in disgrace. Peter is received then with the greatest honour and baptizes Faustinianus, who has meanwhile recovered his own form.

We turn now to the story as told in the *Homilies*. The opening is identical with that of the *Recognitions*, except for one small variation. Clement, instead of meeting Barnabas in Rome, has been induced by an anonymous Christian teacher to sail for Palestine; but being driven by storms to Alexandria, there encounters Barnabas. It is not easy to say which form is the original. On the one hand, the account that Clement is delayed from following Barnabas by the necessity of collecting money due to him is perfectly in place if the scene is laid at Rome, but not so if Clement is a stranger driven by stress of weather to Alexandria. The author, who elsewhere shews Alexandrian proclivities, may have wished to honour that city by connecting Barnabas with it; or was perhaps unwilling that Peter should be preceded by another apostle at Rome. On the other hand, the rabble which assails Barnabas is in both versions described as a mob of *Greeks*, and the fifteen days' voyage to Palestine corresponds better with Alexandria than with Rome. The narrative proceeds as in R. as far as the end of Peter's disputation with Simon at Caesarea; but both Peter's preliminary instructions to Clement and the disputation itself are different. In H. Peter prepares Clement by teaching him his secret doctrine concerning difficulties likely to be raised by Simon, the true solution of which he could not produce before the multitude. Simon would bring forward texts which seemed to speak of a plurality of Gods, or which imputed imperfection to God, or spoke of Him as changing His purpose or hardening men's hearts and so forth; or, again, which laid crimes to the charge of the just men of the law, Adam and

Noah, Abraham, Jacob, and Moses. In public it would be inexpedient to question the authority of these passages of Scripture, and the difficulty must be met in some other way. But the true solution is that the Scriptures have been corrupted; and all those passages which speak against God are to be rejected as spurious additions. Although this doctrine is represented as strictly esoteric, it is reproduced in the public discussion with Simon which immediately follows. This disputation in H. is very short, the main conflict between Peter and Simon being reserved for a later stage of the story. It is here stated, however, that this disputation at Caesarea lasted three days, although only the subjects treated on the first day are mentioned. We have next a great variation between H. and R. According to H., Simon, vanquished in the disputation, flies to Tyre, and Nicetas, Aquila, and Clement are sent forward by Peter to prepare the way for him. There they meet Apion, and a public disputation on heathen mythology is held between Clement and Apion, the debate going over many of the topics treated of in the tenth book of R. On Peter's arrival at Tyre, Simon flies on to Tripolis, and thence also to Syria on Peter's continuing the pursuit. We have, as in R., discourses delivered to the heathen at Tripolis, and the story of the discovery of Clement's family is in the main told as in R., with differences in detail to be noticed presently. In H., the main disputation between Peter and Simon takes place after the recognitions, and is held at Laodicea, Clement's father (whose name according to H. is Faustus) acting as judge. The last homily contains explanations given by Peter to his company after the flight of Simon; and concludes with an account similar to that in R., of the transformation of Clement's father.

To this analysis must be added an account of the prefatory matter. Neither the Latin nor Syriac version of the *Recognitions* translates any preface; but Rufinus mentions having found in his original a letter of Clement to James, which he does not prefix, because, as he says, it is of later date and he had translated it elsewhere. The remark about later date need not imply any doubt of its genuineness, but merely that the letter, which purports to have been written after the death of Peter, is not rightly prefixed to discourses which claim to have been written some years previously. The letter itself is preserved in the MSS. of the *Homilies*, and gives an account of Peter's ordination of Clement as his successor at Rome, and closes with instructions to Clement to send to James an abstract of Peter's discourses. The work that follows purports to contain an abridgment of discourses already more fully sent to James; and is given the title: "An epitome by Clement of Peter's discourses during his sojournings" (ἐπιδημιῶν κηρυγμάτων). The *Homilies* contain another preface in the form of a letter from Peter himself to James. In this no mention is made of Clement, but Peter himself sends his discourses to James, strictly forbidding their indiscriminate publication, and charging him not to communicate them to any Gentile, nor even to any of the circumcised, except after a long probation, and the later ones only after such an one had been tried and found faithful with regard to the earlier. Subjoined is an oath of secrecy to be taken by those to whom the writings shall be communicated. Examination shews that the letter of Clement cannot belong to the *Homilies*; for its account of Clement's deprecation of the dignity of the episcopate, and of the charges given to him on his admission to it, are in great measure identical with what is related in the 5th homily, in the case of the ordination of Zacchaeus at Caesarea. These are omitted from the story as told in the *Recognitions.* The inference follows that the letter of Clement is the preface to the *Recognitions.* Thus, according to the conclusion we form on other grounds as to the relative priority of the two forms, either R., when prefixing his account of Clement's ordination, transposed matter which the older document had contained in connexion with Zacchaeus, or H., when substituting for the letter of Clement a letter in the name of Peter himself, found in Clement's letter matter which seemed too valuable to be wasted, and therefore worked it into the account of the first ordination related in the story, that of Zacchaeus. The letter of Peter thus remains as the preface either to the *Homilies* or to the earlier form of the work before the name of Clement had been introduced. On the question of relative priority it may be urged that it is more likely that a later writer would remove a preface written in the name of Clement, in order to give his work the higher authority of Peter, than that the converse change should be made; and also that the strong charges to secrecy and to the communication of the work in successive instalments would be accounted for, if we suppose that at the time of the publication of the *Homilies* another version of Peter's discourses had been in circulation, and that the writer was anxious to offer some account why what he produced as the genuine form of the discourses should not have been earlier made known. Respecting this relative priority there has been great diversity of opinion among critics: Baur, Schliemann, Schwegler, and Uhlhorn give the priority to H., Hilgenfeld and Ritschl to R.; Lehmann holds R. to be the original for the first three books, H. in the later part. Lipsius regards both as independent modifications of a common original. Without speaking over-confidently, our own conclusion is, that while neither of the existing documents can claim to be the original form, they are not independent; that H. is the later and in all that relates to Clement's family history has borrowed from R. Probably the original form contained little but discourses, and was probably an esoteric document, in use only among the Ebionites; and the author of R. may have added to it the whole story of Clement's recovery of his parents, at the same time fitting the work for popular use by omitting or softening down the harshest parts of its Ebionitism; and finally, H., a strong Ebionite, may have restored some of the original discourses, retaining the little romance which no doubt had been found to add much to the popularity and attractiveness of the volume. The following are some of the arguments which prove that H. is not an original.

(1) The story of Clement's first recognition of his family is told in exactly the same way in R. book 7, and in H. book 12. Clement, anxious to be permitted to join himself permanently as travelling companion to Peter, reminds him of words used at Caesarea: how Peter had there invited those to travel with him who could do so with piety, that is, without deserting wife, parents, or other relations whom they could not properly leave. Clement states that he is himself one thus untrammelled, and he is thus led to tell the story of his life. These words of Peter, to which both R. and H. refer, are to be found only in R. (iii. 71), not in H. It has been stated that the ordination of Zacchaeus at Caesarea is told fully in H., and only briefly in R. In recompense R. has a long section describing the grief of the disciples at Peter's departure and the consolations which he addressed to them; all this is compressed into a line or two in H. It is matter which any one revising R. would most naturally cut out as unimportant and uninteresting; but we see that it contains words essential in the interests of the story, and can hardly doubt that these words were introduced with a view to the use subsequently made of them. This instance not only shews, as Lehmann admits, that H. is not original in respect of the Caesarean sections, but still more decisively refutes Lehmann's own hypothesis that it was H. who ornamented an originally simpler story with the romance of the recognitions. Either the author of that romance, as is most probable, was also the author of Peter's Caesarean speech, which has little use except as a preparation for what follows; or else, finding that speech in an earlier document, used it as a connecting link to join on his own addition. In either case he must have been fully alive to its importance, and it is quite impossible that he could have left it out from his version of the story. Moreover, of the two writers H. and R., H. is the one infinitely less capable of inventing a romance. Looking at the whole work as a controversial novel, it is apparent all through that H. feels most interest in the controversy, R. in the novel.

(2) Further, in the same section in the passage common to H. and R., Peter sends on Nicetas and Aquila to prepare the way for his coming. He apologizes for parting company with them, and they express grief at the separation, but console themselves that is it only for two days. On their departure Clement says, "I thank God that it was not I whom you sent away, as I should have died of grief." Then follows the request that Peter would accept him as his inseparable companion. This is all consistent as told by R.; for these regrets are expressed on the first occasion that any of the three brothers is removed from personal attendance on Peter. But as H. tells the story, Peter had already sent on Clement, while still unbaptized, together with Nicetas and Aquila, to Tyre, where they hold a disputation with Apion. There is not a word of grief or remonstrance at the separation for more than a week, and it is therefore strange that subsequently there should be so much regret at a two days' parting. It is plain that H. has interpolated the mission to Tyre; but failed to notice that he ought in consistency to have modified some of the next portion of R. which he retained. This disputation with Apion has been alleged as a proof of the priority of H., for Apion is introduced also into R., but only as a silent character; and it is urged that the original form is more likely to be that in which this well-known adversary of Judaism conducts a disputation, than that in which he is but an insignificant companion of Simon. But this argument does not affect the relative priority of H. and R., whatever weight it may have in proving R. not original. Eusebius (iii. 38) mentions a long work ascribed to Clement, and then but recently composed (as he infers from not having seen it quoted by any earlier writer), containing dialogues of Peter and Apion. This description may be intended for the *Homilies*; but may refer to a still earlier work. There are expressions in R. which seem to imply that the writer believed himself to be making an improvement in substituting for Peter as a disputant against heathenism, persons whose early training had been such as to give them better knowledge of heathen mythology and philosophy.

(3) The story of Clement's recognition of his brothers contains plain marks that H. has abridged R. According to R., Nicetas and Aquila, seeing a strange woman return with Peter and Clement, ask for an explanation. Peter then repeats fully the story of the adventures of Clement's mother. Nicetas and Aquila listen in silence until Peter describes the shipwrecked mother searching for her children and crying, "Where are my Faustus and Faustinus?" then, hearing their own names mentioned, they start up in amaze and say, "We suspected at the first that what you were saying might relate to us; but yet as many like things happen in different persons' lives, we kept silence; but when you came to the end and it was entirely manifest that your statements referred to us, then we confessed who we were." H. avoids what seems the needless repetition of an already-told story, and only states in general terms that Peter recounted Mattidia's history; but the amazed starting-up of the brothers, and their words, are the same as in R.; while, as the incident of the mention of their former names is omitted, it is in this version not apparent why the conclusion of Peter's speech brought conviction to their minds. Evidently H., in trying to shorten the narrative by clearing it of repetition, has missed a point in the story.

(4) As told above, in R. the recognition of Clement's father crowns a disputation on astrological fate. In H. the whole story is spoiled. An old man accosts Peter, as in R., and promises to prove from his personal history that all things are ruled by the stars; but nothing turns on this. The recognition takes place in consequence of a chance meeting of Faustinianus with his wife, and has no relation to the subject he undertakes to discuss with Peter. The obvious explanation is, that H. has copied the introduction from R.; but omits the disputation because he has already anticipated it, having put the argument for heathenism into the mouth of the eminent rhetorician Apion, who seemed a fitter char-

acter to conduct the disputation than the unknown Faustinianus. Further H. (xx. 15) and R. (x. 57) both state that the magical transformation of Clement's father takes place on the same day that he had been recognized by his family. This agrees with the story as told by R.; but H. had made five days' disputation intervene between the recognition and the transformation. Thus in the account of each of the three sets of recognitions there is evidence that H. copied either from R. or from a writer who tells the story exactly as R. does; and the former hypothesis is to be preferred because there is no evidence whatever of R.'s non-originality in this part of his task.

(5) We have seen that in H. there are two disputations of Simon with Peter, viz. at Caesarea and at Laodicea. There is decisive proof that in this H. has varied from the original form, which, as R. does, laid the scene of the entire disputation at Caesarea. The indications here, however, point to a borrowing not from R. but from a common original. H. does relate a disputation at Caesarea, but evidently reserves his materials for use further on, giving but a meagre sketch of part of one day's dispute, while he conscientiously follows his authority and relates that the dispute lasted three days. Afterwards at Laodicea the topics brought forward in the earlier discussion are produced as if new. Simon, *e.g.*, expresses the greatest surprise at Peter's manner of disposing of the alleged spurious passages of the Pentateuch, although exactly the same line of argument had been used by Peter on the former occasion. The phenomenon again presents itself (H. xviii. 21) of a reference to former words of Peter which are not to be found in H. itself, but are found in R. ii. 45. Lastly, in the disputation at Laodicea, the office of summoning Peter to the conflict is ascribed to Zacchaeus, in flagrant contradiction of the previous story, according to which Zacchaeus was the leading man of the church at Caesarea before Peter's arrival, and had been left behind as its bishop on Peter's departure. This alone is enough to shew that H. is copying from an original, in which the scene is laid at Caesarea. It may be added that the *Apostolic Constitutions* make mention only of a Caesarean disputation.

(6) It has been stated that the last homily contains private expositions by Peter to his disciples, and these can clearly be proved to be an interpolation. In R., after the disputation on "genesis" in which Clement's father is convinced, the party having returned home and being about to sit down to meat, news comes of the arrival of Apion and Anubion and Faustinianus goes to salute them. In H. the party have retired to rest, and Peter wakes them up in the middle of the night to receive his instructions; yet in the middle of this midnight discourse we have an account, almost verbally agreeing with R., of the news of the arrival of Apion coming just as they were about to sit down to meat, and the consequent departure of Clement's father. The discourse, thus clearly shewn to be an interpolation, contains H.'s doctrine concerning the devil, and is in such close connexion with the preceding homily (which relates how Peter, in his Laodicean disputation, dealt with the problem of the permission of evil in the universe) that this also must be set down as an addition made by H. to the original story. We can see why H. altered the original account of a Caesarean disputation—namely, that he wished to reserve as the climax of his story, the solutions which he put into Peter's mouth of the great controversy of his own day.

(7) In section H. ii. 19-32, which contains the information given by Nicetas and Aquila concerning Simon, there are plain marks that H. is not original. Nicetas, in repeating a conversation with Simon, speaks of himself in the third person: "Nicetas answered," instead of "I answered." In the corresponding section of R., Aquila is the speaker, and the use of the third person is correct. Yet this matter, in which H. is clearly not original, is so different from R., that we conclude that both copied from a common original. One instance in this section, however, deserves to be mentioned as an apparent case of direct copying from R. In H. ii. 22, Simon is represented as teaching that the dead shall not rise, and as rejecting Jerusalem and substituting Mount Gerizim for it; but nowhere else is there a trace of such doctrine being ascribed to Simon; and no controversy on these subjects is reported in the *Homilies*. There is strong reason for suspecting that H. has here blundered in copying R. i. 57, where a Samaritan, whom there is no ground for identifying with Simon, is introduced as teaching these doctrines of the non-resurrection of the dead, and of the sanctity of Mount Gerizim.

We turn to some of the reasons why R. must also be regarded as the retoucher of a previously existing story. The work itself recognizes former records of the things which it relates. In the preface it purports to be an account written after the death of Peter of discourses, some of which had by Peter's command been written down and sent to James during his own lifetime. R. iii. 75 contains an abstract of the contents of ten books of these previously-sent reports. Again, R. v. 36, we are told of the dispatch to James of a further instalment. Everything confirms the conclusion that R. is here using the credit which an existing narrative had gained, in order to obtain acceptance for his own additions to the story. Moreover, as we have seen, there are instances in the first division of the work where H. is clearly not original, and yet has not copied from R.; whence we infer the existence of an independent authority, at least for the earlier portion, employed by both writers. There are places where H. and R. seem to supplement one another, each supplying details omitted by the other; other places where it would seem as if an obscure passage in the common original had been differently understood by each; and in the discourses common to both, there are places where the version presented by H. preserves so much better the sequence of ideas and the cogency of argument that it is scarcely possible to think the form in R. the original (cf. esp. H. ix. 9, 10, R. iv. 15, 16). There are places, again, where both seem to have abridged the common original. Thus R. mentions concerning an early conversation, that none of the women were present. There is no further mention of women in the party until quite late in the story both H. and R. incidentally speak of Peter's wife as being in the company. In may be noted in passing that they do not represent Peter and his wife as living together as married people; but Peter always sleeps in the same room with his disciples. We may conjecture that the original contained a formal account of the women who travelled with Peter, and this is confirmed by St. Jerome, who refers to a work called the circuits of Peter (περίοδοι) as mentioning not only Peter's wife, but his daughter, of whom nothing is said either by H. or R. The work cited by Jerome contained a statement that Peter was bald, which is not found either in H. or R. In like manner we may infer that the original contained a formal account of the appointment of 12 precursors (πρόοδοι) who were to go before Peter to the different cities which he meant to visit. H. several times speaks of the precursors, assuming the office to be known to the reader, but without ever recording its appointment. R. does give an account of its appointment, but one which implies that Peter had come attended by 12 companions, of whom Clement was already one. We have already mentioned inconsistencies in this first section from which we infer, that though the original form of the story mentioned the name of Clement, the introduction containing the account of Clement's journey from Rome is a later addition.

We conclude that the work cited by Jerome is the common original of H. and R.; and a comparison of the matter common to the two shews that both pretty freely modified the original to their own uses. From what has been said concerning H. under No. 7, we infer that the original contained mention both of Clement and of Nicetas and Aquila, and it is likely that Clement was there too represented as the recorder of the discourses. The original must have contained an account of a three days' disputation with Simon held at Caesarea; it also included the polemic against heathenism contained in the Tripolis discourses, as may be inferred both from R. v. 36 and also from a comparison of the two records of these discourses. It is likely that the same work contained the disputation of Peter and Apion referred to by Eusebius, and that H. followed the original in making Apion a speaking character, although he has been involved in confusion in trying to combine this with the additional matter imported by R. We may conjecture too (see R. x. 52) that it also contained a disputation by Anubion on the subject of "genesis." On the other hand, there is no evidence that the original contained anything concerning the recognitions by Clement of the members of his family. In this part of the story R. makes no acknowledgment of previous accounts sent to James; and he shews every sign of originality and of having carefully gone over the old story, skilfully adapting it so as to join on his own additions. It appears from H. ii. 22, 26, that in quite an early part of the history the original introduced Nicetas and Aquila as addressing their fellow-disciple Clement as "dearest brother," and this probably gave R. the hint (see R. viii. 8) of representing them as natural brothers. R. omits these expressions in the place where they are inappropriate. A question may be raised whether the document referred to in R. iii. 75, and which contained an account of the disputation with Simon, was part of the same work as that referred to in v. 36, which contained the disputation against the heathen. We have marked them as probably different. It may be remarked that Peter's daily bath, carefully recorded in the later books, is not mentioned in the three earlier. A question may be raised whether the original did not contain an account of a meeting of Simon and Peter at Rome; and it is not impossible that such an account may have been originally designed by the author; as one or two references to Rome as well as the choice of Clement as the narrator give cause to suspect. But that in any case the design was not executed appears both from the absence of any early reference to a Roman contest between Simon and Peter; and also from the diversity of the accounts given as to the manner of Simon's death, since we may believe that if the document we are considering had related the story, its version would have superseded all others.

Quite a different impression as to relative originality is produced when we compare the doctrine of H. and R., and when we compare their narratives. The doctrine of H. is very peculiar, and, for the most part, consistently carried through the whole work; in R. the deviations from ordinary church teaching are far less striking, yet there are passages in which the ideas of H. can be traced, and which present the appearance of an imperfect expurgation of offensive doctrine. In H., Judaism and Christianity are represented as identical, and it is taught to be enough if a man recognize the authority either of Christ or of Moses; in R. he is required to acknowledge both. On this point, however, H. is not consistent; for in several places he agrees with R. in teaching the absolute necessity of baptism to salvation. H. rejects the rite of sacrifice altogether; according to R. the rite was divinely permitted for a time until the true prophet should come, who was to replace it by baptism as a means of forgiveness of sins. With respect to the authority of O.T. alleged for the rite of sacrifice, and for certain erroneous doctrines, H. rejects the alleged passages as falsified; R. regards them merely as obscure, and liable to be misunderstood by one who reads them without the guidance of tradition. The inspiration of the prophets later than Moses is denied by H. and admitted by R., though quotations from their writings are alike rare in both forms. According to H., the true prophet has presented himself in various incarnations, Adam, who is regarded as being identical with Christ, being the first and Jesus the last; and the history of Adam's sin is rejected as spurious; according to R., Christ has but revealed Himself to and inspired various holy men of old. And, in general, concerning the dignity and work of our Lord, the doctrine of R., though short of orthodox teaching, is far higher than that of H. The history of the fall, as far, at least, as regards the temptation of Eve, is referred to by R. as historical; but concerning Adam there are intimations of an esoteric doctrine not fully explained. H. gives what may be called a physical theory of the injury done by demons. They are represented as having sensual desires, which, being spirits, they can gratify only by incorporation with human bodies. They use therefore the permission which the divine law grants them, of entering into the bodies of men who partake of forbidden food, or who, by worshipping them, subject themselves to their power; and with these the union is so close, that after death, when the demons descend to their natural regions of fire, the souls united to them are forced to accompany them, though grievously tormented by the element in which the demon feels pleasure. The opposition between fire and light is much dwelt on; and again, the water of baptism and other ablutions is represented as having a kind of physical efficacy in quenching the demonic fire. All this doctrine concerning demons shews itself comparatively faintly in R.; yet there seem indications that the doctrine as expounded in H. was contained in the original on which R. worked. It is natural to think that the earlier form is that one of which the doctrine is most peculiar; the later, that in which the divergences from orthodox teaching are smoothed away. Yet it is not always true that originality implies priority; and the application of this principle has caused some of the parts of H. which can be shewn to be the most recent, to be accepted as belonging to the original. For instance, we have seen that the private conversation between Peter and his disciples in the 20th homily bears on the face of it marks of interpolation; yet the clearness and peculiarity of its doctrine have caused it to be set down as belonging to the most ancient part of the work. The same may be said of the section concerning philanthropy at the end of the 12th homily, which, however, is wanting in the Syriac, and may be reasonably set down as one of the most modern parts. For it is an addition made by H. to the story of the recognitions as told by R.; and we have already shewn that in all that relates to the recognitions H. is more recent than R. We arrive at more certain results, if, examining the sections we have named, and for which H. is most responsible, we try to discover his favourite thoughts and forms of expression, and so to recognize the hand of the latest reviser in other parts of the work. Space will not permit such an examination here; but we may notice the fondness of H. for discovering a male and female element in things, and for contrasting things under the names of male and female. The almost total absence of the idea from R. makes it unlikely that it could have had any great prominence in the original document. The idea, however, became very popular in the sect to which H. belonged; and is noticed by a writer of the 10th cent. as a characteristic of some Ebionites then still remaining (see Hilgenfeld, *N.T. Extra Can. Recept.* iii. 156). The germ, however, of the distinction between male and female prophecy, on which H. lays so much stress, was apparently in the original document, which disposed of the testimony borne by our Lord to John the Baptist by the distinction that John was the greatest of the prophets born of *women*, but not on the level of the Son of *Man*. The general result of an attempt to discriminate what belongs to H. and R. respectively, from what they found in their common original, leads to the belief that H., far more nearly than R., represents the doctrinal aspect of the original, from which the teaching of H. differs only by legitimate development.

The Clementines are unmistakably a production of that sect of Ebionites which held the book of Elkesai as sacred. For an account of the sources whence our knowledge of this book is derived, and for the connexion of the sect with Essenism, see ELKESAI in *D. C. B.* (4-vol. ed.). Almost all the doctrines ascribed to them are to be found in the Clementines—*e.g.* the doctrine of successive incarnations of Christ, and in particular the identification of Christ with Adam, the requirement of the obligations of the Mosaic Law, the rejection however of the rite of sacrifice, the rejection of certain passages both of O.T. and N.T., hostility to St. Paul, abstinence from flesh (H. viii. 15, xii. 6, xv. 7), the inculcation of repeated washing, discouragement of virginity, concealment of their sacred books from all but approved persons, form of adjuration by appeal to the seven witnesses, ascription of gigantic stature to the angels (H. viii. 15), permission to dissemble the faith in time of persecution (R. i. 65, x. 55); while again the supposed derivation of the book of Elkesai from the Seres is explained by R. viii. 48, where the Seres are described as a nation by whom all the observances on which the Ebionites laid stress were naturally kept, and who were consequently exempt from the penalties of sickness and premature death which attended their neglect. Ritschl regards the book of Elkesai as an exposition of these doctrines later than the *Homilies*; but we are disposed to look on it as earlier than the work which formed the common basis of H. and R. A recognition of this book is not improbably contained in a passage which is important in reference to the use made by H. and R. of their common original. The date which the book of Elkesai claimed for itself was the third year of Trajan. Whether it actually were so old need not here be inquired, but the fact that it was confessedly no older might seem to put it at a disadvantage in comparison with the Pauline system which it rejected. But its adherents defended their position by their doctrine of pairs—viz. that it has been ever God's method to pair good and evil together, sending forth first the evil, then the countervailing good. Thus Cain was followed by Abel, Ishmael by Isaac, Esau by Jacob, so now, Simon Magus by Peter; and at the end of the world Antichrist will be followed by Christ. The penultimate pair enumerated takes, in the translation of Rufinus, a form scarcely intelligible; but the Syriac shews that the version given by R. did not essentially differ from that of H.; and that the contrasted pairs predicted by Peter are a false gospel sent abroad by a deceiver, and a true gospel secretly disseminated after the destruction of the holy place, for the rectification of the then existing heresies. It seems most probable that we are here to understand the doctrine of Paul and of Elkesai; and it may be noted that the fact, that, in this pair, gospels, not persons, are contrasted, favours the conclusion that Hippolytus was mistaken in supposing Elkesai to be the name of a person. Two other of the contrasted pairs deserve notice : H. contrasts Aaron and Moses, R. the magicians and Moses. Again, H. contrasts John the Baptist and our Saviour, R. the tempter and our Saviour. In both cases the version of H. seems to be the original, since in that the law of the pairs is strictly observed that an elder is followed by a better younger ; and we can understand R.'s motive for alteration if he did not share that absolute horror of the rite of sacrifice which ranked Aaron on the side of evil, or that hostility to John the Baptist which shews itself elsewhere in H., as, for example, in ranking Simon Magus among his disciples. There are passages in R. which would give rise to the suspicion that he held the same doctrines as H., but concealed the expression of them in a book intended for the uninitiated, for though in H. the principle of an esoteric doctrine is strongly asserted, the book seems to have been written at a later period, when concealment had been abandoned. However, the instance last considered is one of several, where R.'s suppression of the doctrinal teaching of his original seems to imply an actual rejection of it.

It remains to speak of that part of the Clementines to which attention has been most strongly directed by modern students of the early history of the church—their assault on St. Paul under the mask of Simon Magus. In the first place it may be remarked that the school hostile to St. Paul which found expression in these Clementines cannot be regarded as the representative or continuation of the body of adversaries with whom he had to contend in his lifetime. Their connexion was with the Essenes, not the Pharisees ; and they themselves claimed no earlier origin than a date later than the destruction of Jerusalem, an event which would seem to have induced many of the Essenes in some sort to accept Christianity. We have seen that a theory was devised to account for the lateness of the period when what professed to be the true gospel opposed to St. Paul's was published. It follows that whatever results can be obtained from the Clementines belong to the history of the 2nd cent., not the first. The name of Paul is mentioned neither by H. nor R. Hostility to him appears in R. in a milder form ; R., plainly following his original, ignores St. Paul's labours among the heathen, and makes St. Peter the apostle of the Gentiles; and in one passage common to H. and R., and therefore probably belonging to the earlier document, a warning is given that the tempter who had contended in vain with our Lord would afterwards send apostles of deceit, and therefore the converts are cautioned against receiving any teacher who had not first compared his doctrine with that of James, lest the devil should send a preacher of error to them, even as he had raised up Simon as an opponent to Peter. It need not be disputed that in this passage, as well as in that concerning the pairs already quoted, Paul is referred to, his preaching being spoken of in the future tense as dramatic propriety required, since the action of the story is laid at a time before his conversion. In both places Paul, if Paul be meant, is expressly distinguished from Simon. In the letter of Peter prefixed to the *Homilies*, we cannot doubt that Paul is assailed as the enemy who taught that the obligations of the Mosaic law were not perpetual, and who unwarrantably represented Peter himself as concurring in teaching which he entirely repudiated. There remains a single passage as the foundation of the Simon-Paulus theory. In the Laodicean disputation which H. makes the climax of his story, a new topic is suddenly introduced (xvii. 13-20), whether the evidence of the senses or that of supernatural vision be more trustworthy ; and it is made to appear that Simon claims to have obtained, by means of a vision of Jesus, knowledge of Him superior to that which Peter had gained during his year of personal converse with Him. In this section phrases are introduced which occur in the notice of the dispute at Antioch, between Peter and Paul, contained in the Ep. to the Galatians. It need not be doubted, then, that in this section of the *Homilies* the arguments nominally directed against Simon are really intended to depreciate the claims of Paul. Since von Cölln and Baur first took notice of the concealed object of this section, speculation in Germany has run wild on the identification of Paul and Simon. The theory in the form now most approved will be found in the article on Simon Magus in Schenkel's *Bibel-Lexikon*. It has been inferred that Simon was in Jewish circles a pseudonym for Paul, and that all related of him is but a parody of the life of Paul. Simon as a historical character almost entirely disappears. Even the story told in the Acts of the Apostles has been held to be but a caricature of the story of Paul's bringing up to Jerusalem the collection he had made, and hoping by this gift of money to bribe the apostles to admit him to equal dignity. In order to account for the author of the Acts admitting into his narrative the section concerning Simon, explanations have been given which certainly have not the advantage in simplicity over that suggested by the work itself—viz. that the author having spent seven days in Philip's house had learned from him interesting particulars of his early evangelical work, which he naturally inserted in his history. The Simon-Paulus theory has been particularly misleading in speculations as to the literary history of the tales concerning Simon. Lipsius, for instance, has set himself to consider in what way the history of Simon could be told, so as best to serve the purpose of a libel on Paul ; and having thus constructed a more ingenious parody of Paul's life than any which documentary evidence shews to have been ever in circulation, he asks us to accept this as the original form of the story of Simon. It becomes necessary, therefore, to point out on how narrow a basis of fact these speculations rest. To R., anti-Pauline though he is, the idea of identifying Simon with St. Paul seems never to have occurred. All through his book Paul is Paul, and Simon Simon. The same may be said of the whole of the *Homilies*, except this Laodicean disputation, which is the part in which the latest writer has taken the greatest liberties with his original. Before any inference can be drawn from this section as to an early identification of Simon and Paul, it must be shewn that it belongs to the original document, and is not an addition of the last reviser only. The object of the latter may be inferred from what he states in the form of a prediction (xvi. 21), that other heretics would arise who should assert the same blasphemies against God as Simon; which we may take as implying that the writer has put into the mouth of Simon doctrines similar to those held by later heretics against whom he had himself to contend. In particular, this Laodicean section is strongly anti-Marcionite; and it is just possible that this section may have been elicited by Marcionite exaggeration of the claims of Paul. But we own, it seems to us far more probable that H. has here preserved a fragment of an earlier document, the full force of which it is even possible he did not himself understand. Further, it is altogether unproved that in this earlier document this particular disputation was directed against Simon. The original work may well have included conflicts of St. Peter with other adversaries, and in another instance we have seen reason to think that H. has made a mistake in transferring to Simon words which in the earlier document referred to another. Again, even if the earlier writer did put Pauline features into his picture of Simon, it no more follows that he identified Simon with St. Paul than that the later writer identified him with Marcion. The action of the story being laid at a date antecedent to St. Paul's conversion, it was a literary necessity that if Pauline pretensions were to be refuted, they must be put into the mouth of another. At the present day history is often written with a view to its bearing on the controversies of our own time; but we do not imagine that a writer doubts Julius Caesar to be a historical character, even though in speaking of him he may have Napoleon Bonaparte in his mind. Now, though the author of the Clementines has put his own words into the mouth both of Simon and Peter, it is manifest that he no more doubted of the historical character of one than of the other. For Simon, his authorities were—(1) the account given in Acts viii. which furnished the conception of Simon as possessed of magical powers; (2) in all probability the account given by Justin Martyr of honours paid to Simon at Rome; and (3) since R. refers to the *writings* of Simon, it can scarcely be doubted that the author used the work ascribed to Simon called the *Great Announcement*, some of the language of which, quoted by Hippolytus, is in the Clementines put into the mouth of Simon. Hence has resulted some little confusion, for the heresy of the *Great Announcement* appears to have been akin to the Valentinian; but what the Clementine author has added of his own is Marcionite.

Quotations from N.T. in the Clementines.—All the four gospels are quoted; for since the publication of the conclusion of the *Homilies* by Dressel, it is impossible to deny that St. John's gospel was employed. Epiphanius tells us that a Hebrew translation of St. John's gospel was in use among the Ebionites. The quotations are principally from St. Matthew, but often with considerable verbal differences from our present text; and there are a few passages quoted which are not found in any of our present gospels. The deviations from the existing text are much smaller in R. than in H., and it may be asserted that R. always conforms to our present gospels in his own added matter. Since it is known that the Ebionites used an Aramaic gospel, which in the main agreed with St. Matthew but with considerable variations, we may conclude that this was the source principally employed by the author of the original. H. seems to have used the same sources as the original; but yet two things must be borne in mind before we assert that variations in H. from our existing texts prove that he had a different text before him: one is the laxity with which he cites the O.T.; the other, the fact that the story demands that Peter should be represented as quoting our Lord's discourses from memory and not from any written source; and the author would naturally feel himself entitled to a certain amount of licence in quotations of such a kind.*

Place and Time of Composition of the Clementine Writings.—The use made of the name of Clement had caused Rome to be accepted as the place of composition by the majority of critics, but the opposite arguments urged by Uhlhorn appear conclusive, and to, at least, the original document an Eastern origin must be assigned. Hippolytus mentions the arrival in Rome of an Elkesaite teacher *c.* A.D. 220, whose doctrines would seem to have been then quite novel at Rome, and not to have taken root there. The scene of the story is all laid in the East, and the writings shew no familiarity with the Roman church. The ranking Clement among the disciples of Peter may be even said to be opposed to the earliest traditions of the Roman church, which placed Clement third from the apostles; but it is quite intelligible that in foreign churches, where the epistle of Clement was habitually publicly read in the same manner as the apostolic epistles, Clement and the apostles might come to be regarded as contemporaries. Clement might naturally be chosen as a typical representative of the Gentile converts by an Ebionite who desired by his example to enforce on the Gentile churches the duty of obedience to the church of the circumcision. For all through it is James of Jerusalem, not Peter, who is represented as the supreme ruler of the churches. The author of the original document habitually used an Aramaic version of N.T.; and there are a few phenomena which make it seem not incredible that the original document itself may have been written in the same language. Uhlhorn's conjecture of Eastern Syria as the place of composition seems not improbable. The *Recognitions* with the prefatory letter relating the ordination of Clement as bp. of Rome may, however, have been a version designed for Roman circulation. The data for fixing the time of composition are but scanty. The *Recognitions* are quoted by Origen (with, however, a division of books differing from the present form) *c.* A.D. 230.

* In one place (xix. 3) H., having quoted some sayings of our Lord, makes the slip of referring to these as "Scripture." It thus clearly appears that the author used written gospels to which he ascribed the authority of Scripture.

This gives the latest limit for the publication of R. We may infer that the chronicle of Hippolytus A.D. 235 recognizes the Ep. of Clement to James, since it counts Peter as first bp. of Rome, and places the episcopate of Clement at a time so early as to make his ordination by Peter possible. [CLEMENS ROMANUS.] It is not unreasonable to date the Ep. of Clement to James at least a quarter of a cent. earlier, in order to allow time for its ideas to gain such complete acceptance at Rome. Irenaeus is ignorant of the episcopate of Peter, but ranks Clement as a contemporary of the apostles. It is likely, therefore, that he knew the work on which the *Recognitions* were founded, but not this later version. As a limit in the other direction we have the use of the name Faustus for one represented as a member of the imperial family, which points to a date later than the reign of Antoninus, whose wife, and whose daughter married to Marcus Aurelius, both bore the name of Faustina. A section (R. ix. 17-29) is identical with a passage quoted by Eusebius, *Praep. Ev.* 6, 10, as from the dialogues of Bardesanes. But the date of Bardesanes himself is uncertain. [BARDESANES.] The date assigned by Eusebius in his chronicle for his activity, A.D. 173, seems to need to be put later, because an authority likely to be better informed, the Chronicle of Edessa, with great particularity assigns for the date of his birth July 11, A.D. 154. Further, the dialogue cited by Eusebius and by R. has been now recovered from the Syriac, and has been published in Cureton's *Spicilegium Syriacum* (1855). From this it appears that the dialogue does not purport to be written by Bardesanes himself, but by a scholar of his, Philippus, who addresses him as father and is addressed by him as son. This forbids us to put the dialogue at a very early period of the life of Bardesanes, and R. may have been the earlier. Merx (*Bardesanes von Edessa*) tries to shew that other sections also in R. were later interpolations from Bardesanes; but his arguments have quite failed to convince us. On the whole, A.D. 200 seems as near an approximation as we can make to the probable date of R. The form H. must be dated later, possibly A.D. 218, the time when, according to Hippolytus, the Elkesaite Alcibiades came from Apamea to Rome. There is little to determine very closely the date of the original document. If we could lay stress on a passage which speaks of there being *one* Caesar (R. v. 19, H. x. 14), we should date it before A.D. 161, when Marcus Aurelius shared the empire with Verus; and though this argument is very far from decisive, there is nothing that actually forbids so early a date, though we could not safely name one much earlier.

The prolegomena of the earlier editors of the Clementines are collected in Migne's *Patrologia*. The most important monographs are von Cölln's article in Ersch and Gruber (1828), Schliemann, *Die Clementinen* (Hamburg, 1844); Hilgenfeld, *Die clementinischen Recognitionen und Homilien* (Jena, 1848); Uhlhorn, *Die Homilien und Recognitionen des Clemens Romanus* (Göttingen, 1854); Lehmann, *Die clementinische Schriften* (Gotha, 1867). In these works will be found references to other sources of information. Baur has treated of the Clementines in several works: the section in *Die christliche Gnosis*, pp. 300-414, may especially be mentioned. Ritschl, *Die Entstehung der altkatholischen Kirche*, enters more largely into the subject of the Clementines in his first ed. See also Lipsius, *Quellenkritik des Epiphanios* and *Die Quellen der Römischen Petrussage*, and an interesting review by Lipsius of Lehmann's work in the *Protestantische Kirchenzeitung* (1869), pp. 477-482. Cf. Lightfoot's *Clement of Rome*, part i. pp. 99 ff. and 406 ff.; and Harnack, *Gesch. der Alt.-Ch. Lit.* p. 212 ff. [G.S.]

Cletus or **Anacletus**, " le même que St. Clet, comme les savants en conviennent " (*L'Art de vérif. les dates*, i. 218). Eusebius calls him Anencletus, and says that he was succeeded in the see of Rome by Clement in the twelfth year of Domitian, having himself sat there twelve years. According to this, his own consecration would have fallen in the first year of Domitian, or A.D. 81; but it is variously dated by others (cf. Gieseler, *E. H.* § 32 with note 4, Eng. tr.). Eusebius indeed nowhere says that he succeeded Linus, or was the second bp. of Rome: yet he places him between Linus, whom he calls the first bishop, and Clement, whom he calls third. Other ancient authorities make Clement the first bishop (see Clinton, *F. R.* ii. 399). Rohrbacher, on the strength of a list attributed to pope Liberius, places Clement after Linus, Cletus after Clement, and another pope named Anencletus after Cletus (*E. H.* iv. 450). This Gieseler calls " the modern Roman view." [But for this question of the succession of the Roman bishops, see Lightfoot, *Clement of Rome*, part i. pp. 201-345; of which Bp. Westcott says (Preface to Lightfoot), " Perhaps it is not too much to say that the question of the order of the first five bps. of Rome is now finally settled."] Three spurious epistles have the name of Anacletus affixed to them in the Pseudo-Isidorian collection (Migne, *Patr.* cxxx. 59 and seq.). [E.S.FF.]

Clovis (in the chroniclers *Chlodovechus*, etc., modern German *Ludwig*, modern French *Louis*), son of Childeric, one of the kings of the Salian Franks, born A.D. 466, succeeded his father in 481 (Greg. Tur. ii. 43). As soon as he reached manhood (486) he attacked Syagrius, " rex Romanorum " (Greg. ii. 23), son of Aegidius, the isolated and independent representative of the Roman power in Gaul (Junghans, pp. 22, 23). Syagrius was defeated, and Clovis advanced his territory from the Somme to the Seine, and afterwards to the Loire (*Gesta Francorum*, 14), was recognized as king by the former subjects of Syagrius (Greg. ii. 27), and transferred his capital from Tournai to Soissons (*Vita S. Remigii*, ap. Bouquet, iii. 377 E). Waitz (ii. 60 *n.*) doubts this (see Junghans, p. 34, *n.* 3). Many wars and conquests followed (Greg. ii. 27).

About A.D. 492 Clovis married the Burgundian princess Clotilda, a Christian and a Catholic, and she is said to have made many attempts to convert her husband from idolatry (Greg. ii. 29; Rückert, *Culturgeschichte*, i. pp. 316, 317; Binding, *Das Burgundisch-Romanische Reich*, Leipz. 1868, pp. 111-114, doubts the value of Clotilda's work; Bornhak, *Geschichte der Franken unter den Merovingern*, Greifswald, 1863, pp. 207, 208, magnifies it). What her entreaties could not effect the crisis of war brought about. During a battle against the Alamanni (whether at Tolbiac or elsewhere, see Bornhak, p. 209, note 2; Waitz, ii. 65, note 2) the Franks were hard pressed, and beginning to yield. Clovis raised his eyes to heaven and invoked the aid of Christ. Forthwith the tide of battle turned, and the Alamanni fled. Remigius, at the instance of Clotilda, called on Clovis to fulfil his vow. "Gladly," replied the king, "but I must first obtain the consent of my own people." His warriors signified their assent in the well-known words, "Gods that die we cast away from us: the god that dies not, whom Remigius preaches, we are prepared to follow." On Christmas Day, 496, Clovis, with his sisters Albofleda, a heathen, and Lantechild, an Arian, was baptized by Remigius at Rheims. "Gently, Sicambrian, bow down thy head, worship what thou hast hitherto destroyed, destroy what thou hast hitherto worshipped," were the apt words of Remigius (Greg. ii. 30, 31; *Vita Rem.* ap. Bouquet). How important this conversion was in the eyes of the Catholic world of the day may be seen from the letters of congratulation addressed to Clovis by Avitus, bp. of Vienne (Bouquet, iv. 49), and by pope Anastasius, who wrote both to the king and to the bishops of Gaul (Thiel, *Ep. Rom. Pont.* pp. 624 and 634). Theodoric, the Ostrogothic king of Italy, was an Arian, though a tolerant one, but Euric, the Visigoth, had proclaimed himself militant and proselytizing (Fauriel, ii. 28); the Burgundian and Vandal princes were also Arian. The majority of the population of Gaul was Catholic, and Clovis was the only Catholic prince. (On the relation of these Arian princes to their Catholic subjects, see Binding, pp. 125 ff.) Whatever may have been his motives, and every variety has been attributed to him, from direct inspiration of the Holy Ghost (Rettberg, *Kirchengeschichte*, i. pp. 274, 275) to the coldest political calculation (Binding, pp. 111-114), Clovis must have been aware that by his conversion to the Catholic faith he would make the majority of his own subjects firm in their allegiance, and the Roman subjects of the Arian princes in the south ill-affected towards their rulers. (An instance of such disaffection may be found in Greg. ii. 36.) Nor can he have been ignorant of the political importance of the aid which he would get from the Catholic priesthood throughout Gaul. From this point, therefore, dates an increase of influence among the Roman population, the foundations were laid of a Roman nobility of office and intellect capable of superseding the old Teutonic no bility of race (Bornhak, pp. 219-221). Thus, whilst from one point of view this was the "first step towards the world-historical union of Teutonic civilization with the Roman church" (Richter, p. 36, note 6), on the other hand, a reaction of Roman civilization against its Teutonic conquerors now set in, and modern Latin France became possible. As an immediate consequence of the conversion, a body of Frankish warriors not yet converted joined Rachnachar (*Vita Rem.* ap. Bouquet, iii. p. 377 C, D). Whether this was also a desertion of Clovis is doubtful (see Junghans, p. 59). The conversion of the nation was not completed till long afterwards (see Waitz, ii. 85, note 1; and Rettberg, pp. 285-287). All questions connected with the conversion of Clovis are fully treated by Rückert, *Culturgeschichte des Deutschen Volkes in der Zeit des Uebergangs aus dem Heidenthum in das Christenthum* (Leipz. 1853-1854).

The next war of Clovis was with Burgundy, A.D. 500. Gundobald, the uncle of Clotilda and murderer of her parents, was defeated at Dijon. Clovis annexed part of the Burgundian dominion, and gave the rest to Godegisel, another brother. Shortly afterwards Gundobald returned, expelled Godegisel, and apparently became reconciled to Clovis, for in 507 the Burgundians helped Clovis in his expedition against the Visigoths. (This alliance is not mentioned by Gregory, but see Binding, p. 194, note 659; and Richter, p. 41, note *e.*) Between 505 and 507 Clovis is said to have been inflicted with tedious illness (*Vita Severini*, Bouquet, iii. 392 B); on his recovery he immediately issued his famous declaration of war against the Visigoths: "Verily it grieves my soul that these Arians should hold a part of Gaul; with God's help let us go and conquer them, and reduce their territory into our hands" (Greg. ii. 37). From Paris Clovis marched through Orleans to Tours, gave strict orders for the protection of the Catholic church and its property (*Ep.* ap. Bouquet, iv. 54), met and defeated the Visigoths at Voullon or Vouglé near Poictiers, and slew king Alaric with his own hand (Richter, p. 40 notes and reff.). The winter of 507-508 Clovis spent at Bordeaux, carried off the Visigothic treasure from Toulouse, and reduced Angoulême and the surrounding territory before his return to Paris, which city henceforward he made his capital (Greg. ii. 38). That the religious element was very powerful in this war (Rückert, i. 324) is evident from the letter of Clovis to the bishops (Bouquet, *l.c.*), from the vain attempts which Alaric had made to confirm the allegiance of his Catholic and Roman subjects (Richter, p. 39, note 2), and from what Cassiodorus (Var. iii. *Ep.* 1-4) tells us of the negotiations before the war. Theodoric the Ostrogoth had proposed an alliance of the Arian German kings for the maintenance of peace; and when the Franks began to pursue their victories in a fresh campaign and laid siege to Arles, Theodoric interfered, sent an army under Ibbas, which defeated the Franks and relieved Arles, and eventually agreed to a peace, by which Provence was annexed by the Ostrogothic power, Septimania adhered to the Visigothic kingdom of Spain, and Clovis's conquest of Aquitaine was acknowledged (Binding, p. 212 and note 731). We do not know whether Clovis joined personally in this Rhone campaign. No mention of it is made by Gregory. It was at Tours, on his return from Bordeaux in 508, that Clovis received a letter from the emperor Anastasius, "conferring upon him the consular dignity, from which time he was habitually called consul and Augustus" ("ab Anastatio Imperatore codicillos de consulatu accepit, et in basilicâ beati Martini tunicâ blateâ indutus est et chlamyde, imponens vertice diadema, . . . et ab eâ die tanquam consul et (al. 'aut') Augustus est vocitatus," Greg. ii. 38). Much discussion has taken place as to the exact meaning of this passage. The name of Clovis does not appear in the consular Fasti, but in the prologue to the Lex Salia he is entitled "proconsul" (Sybel, *Jahrb. d. Alt. in Rheinl.* iv. p. 86). Again, the chlamys and the diadem are the insignia of the patriciate. Hence it has been assumed by many that what was conferred on Clovis was the proconsulate and the patriciate (Valesius, i. 299; Richter, pp. 40, 41; Junghans, pp. 126-128). On the contrary, Waitz (ii. 59-61) and others (*e.g.* Pétigny, ii. 533; and Bornhak, pp. 234, 235), adhering to the exact words of Gregory, maintain that it was the title of consul that was conferred on Clovis. The significance of the event itself is plain. Anastasius saw the value to the empire of the Frankish power as a counterpoise to the Ostrogothic. Clovis willingly accepted any title of honour by which he obtained a quasi-legal title in the eyes of his Roman subjects (cf. Hallam, *Middle Ages*, vol. i. note 3 on c. i.).

The well-known story of the vase of Soissons (Greg. ii. 27) not only shews how ill Clovis brooked the liberty and equality of the other Frankish chiefs, but reveals the most unfavourable side of his character—his deceitfulness. "Dolus," however, if on the right side, is seldom an attribute of blame with the mediaeval chroniclers. The most discreditable deeds of this character attributed to Clovis are the machinations by which he subjected the other Frankish chiefs originally his equals, and brought about the unification of the Frankish empire. Thus he suggested the murder of his father to Sigebert, king of the Ripuarian Franks, and when the deed was done, himself took possession of the kingdom (Greg. ii. 40). King Chararich was first imprisoned, and then put to death (*ib.* 41; cf. c. 27 *clam* feriri, of Syagrius), and likewise king Rachnachar of Cambrai and his two brothers (*ib.* 42).

Early in 511 Clovis summoned a council of 32 bishops to Orleans (see *Decrees* ap. Sirmondi, *Conc. Gall.* i. 177). Before the close of the year he died at the age of 45, and was buried at Paris in the church of the Apostles (afterwards St. Geneviève's) which he and Clotilda had built. He left four sons, Theodoric the eldest (illegitimate); Clodomir, Childebert, and Lothar, by Clotilda.

The only first-class original authority for the reign of Clovis is Gregory of Tours, *Historia Francorum*, ii. 27-43, contained in the collections of Duchesne, vol. i.; and Bouquet, *Recueil des Historiens*, etc., vol. ii. (in the 3rd vol. of Bouquet are extracts from the lives of the saints relating to this reign. On the authority of Gregory see Löbell, *Gregor von Tours und seine Zeit*, pp. 320 ff.; Monod, in the *Bibliothèque de l'Ecole des hautes Etudes*, part viii. (1872); and Wattenbach, *Deutschlands Geschichtsquellen im Mittelalter* (3rd ed. 1873), vol. i. pp. 76-83. The best monograph on the subject of Clovis is Junghans, *Geschichte der Frankischen Könige Childerich und Chlodovech* (Göttingen, 1857). Cf. also G. Kurth, *Hist. Poét. des Méroving.* (Paris 1893); Prou, *La Gaule Méroving.* On the constitution of the kingdom of Clovis and its constitutional history, see Waitz, *Deutsche Verfassungsgeschichte*, ii. pp. 51-71; and G. Richter, *Annalen d. Deutschen Geschichte im Mittelalter*, i. pp. 27-32 (1873). [T.R.B.]

Coelestinus, commonly called **Celestine**, 42nd bp. of Rome, succeeded Boniface I. on Sunday, Sept. 10, 422, without any delay or contest. He was of Roman birth, the son of Priscus. In early life he had visited Milan during the episcopate of St. Ambrose. While deacon to Innocent, he had written a cordial letter to St. Augustine, who returned a suitable reply (Aug. *Ep.* 192). Soon after his accession to the see of Rome, Celestine received a letter from Augustine (*Ep.* 209) on the case of one Antony, bp. of Fussala, 40 miles from Hippo, who had gravely misconducted himself in his office, been compelled by a synod of bishops to leave Fussala, and had afterwards applied to Boniface for restoration. Augustine entreated Celestine not to impose on the people of Fussala, by aid of secular power, a prelate so unworthy. After this, the African bishops resolved no longer to allow appeals to Rome from their country; and when Celestine, apparently in 426, wrote to them in behalf of the priest Apiarius, a general council of Africa sent a reply begging Celestine to observe the Nicene rule (can. 5) and not receive to communion those excommunicated by them. The African church thus claimed its right to decide its own causes. They pointed out that the Nicene council had ordered that all causes should be decided where they arose; nor could anyone "believe that our God will inspire a single individual with justice, and deny it to a large number of bishops sitting in council." That persons should be sent from Rome to decide causes in Africa had been "ordained by no synod"; and they had proved to Celestine's predecessor, by authentic copies of Nicene canons, that such a claim was wholly baseless (*Cod. Can. Eccl. Afric.* ad. fin.; Galland, *Bibl. Patr.* ix. 289).

Celestine was zealous against Pelagianism, and constrained Coelestius, the companion of Pelagius, to leave Italy.

The affairs of eastern Illyricum occupied the attention of Celestine, as of his predecessors. This civil "diocese" was attached, politically, to the eastern empire; but the see of Rome had kept a hold over its churches by committing a sort of vicarial authority to the see of Thessalonica, which was its head. Thus Damasus is said to have made the bps. of Thessalonica his representatives. See Fleury, b. xviii. c. 22. Le Quien, *Or. Christ.* ii. 9, thinks this an over-statement; but at any rate, he observes, Siricius (who succeeded Damasus), and afterwards Innocent, gave a delegated authority to Anysius of Thessalonica. In A.D. 421 a collision took place between the Roman bp. Boniface and Theodosius II., who "claimed the power of transferring to the bp. of Constantinople that superintendence over the bps. of Illyricum" which Rome had entrusted to Thessalonica (Fleury, xxiv. 31). But Theodosius appears to have yielded the point; and Celestine having already "interposed" in behalf of an Illyrian bishop named Felix, who was "in peril of being crushed by factious accusers," afterwards wrote (Cel. *Ep.* 3) to Perigenes of Corinth and eight other prelates of eastern Illyricum, asserting his right, as successor of St. Peter, to a general oversight ("necessitatem de omnibus tractandi"), and directing his "beloved brethren" to refer all causes to his deputy, Rufus of Thessalonica, and not to consecrate bishops, nor hold councils, without the sanction of that bishop. "Dominentur nobis regulae," writes Celestine, "non regulis dominemur; simus subjecti canonibus," etc. But, says Tillemont significantly, "it is difficult to see how he practised this excellent maxim"; for by the sixth Nicene canon the Illyrian bishops would be subject to their several metropolitans and provincial synods (xiv. 150).

Another letter from Celestine (*Ep.* 4) was addressed, July 25, 428, "to the bishops of the provinces of Vienne and Narbonne, for the purpose of correcting several abuses" (Fleury, xxiv. 56). Some bishops, he had learned, "surreptitiously" wore the philosophic "pallium," with a girdle, by way of carrying out Luke xii. 35. "Why not," asks Celestine, "also hold lighted lamps and staves?" The text is to be understood spiritually. This sort of dress, he adds, may be retained by those who dwell apart (monks), but there is no precedent for it in the case of bishops. "We ought to be distinguished from the people, not by dress, but by teaching; not by attire, but by conduct." On other matters he comments. Some refuse to give absolution to penitents even at the hour of death: this is a barbarous "killing of the soul." Some consecrate laymen to the episcopate. Let no one be consecrated until he has gone through all degrees of the ministry: he who would be a teacher must first be a disciple. In the appointment of bishops he said that the wishes of the flock must be respected: Nullus invitis detur episcopus. These words became the recognized expression of a great principle of church law.

With this letter may be compared a short one (*Ep.* 5), written in 429, to urge the Apulian and Calabrian bishops to observe the canons, and not to gratify any popular wish for the consecration of a person who had not served in the ministry. (On this subject of *per saltum* consecrations, see Bingham, ii. 10, 4 seq.)

In the same year (429) Germanus bp. of Auxerre and Lupus of Troyes were sent into Britain to repress Pelagianism. Prosper, in his Chronicle, says that Celestine sent German to guide the Britons to Catholic faith. Constantius of Lyons, the biographer of German, whom Bede follows (*H. E.* i. 17), says that German and Lupus were sent by a large synod of Gallic bishops. (Prosper was then in Gaul, and ere long became Celestine's secretary: Constantius wrote some sixty years later, but with full access to local information.) The accounts may be reasonably harmonized. In German's case there was probably a special commission from Celestine, in addition to that which emanated from the Gallican synod. In this way, apparently, Celestine, as Prosper afterwards wrote in another work (*C. Collatorem*, 21, al. 24), "took pains to keep the Roman island Catholic." It will be natural to consider next Celestine's proceedings in regard to Ireland, which, says Prosper, in the same sentence, he "made Christian." Two years after the expedition of German he consecrated Palladius, and sent him to "the Scots, who believed in Christ," *i.e.* to the Irish, "as their first bishop." Such is Prosper's statement in his Chronicle. Palladius had but little success, and stayed in Ireland but a short time; and there is no sufficient evidence for associating the mission of his great successor, St. Patrick, with Celestine or with the see of Rome. (See Todd's *Life of St. Patrick*, pp. 309 seq., 352, 387, etc.)

We now turn to the part which Celestine took in the great doctrinal controversy raised by Nestorius at Constantinople at the end of 428. Celestine (*Ep.* 13) early in 429 received copies of controversial discourses said to be by Nestorius, and wrote on his own behalf, and on that of other Italian bishops, to Cyril of Alexandria, asking for information. [CYRIL.] Cyril purposely kept silence for a year; and before he wrote, Celestine had received from Nestorius himself, by the hands of a man of high rank, named Antiochus, copies of his discourses, with a letter, in which Nestorius speaks of certain exiled Pelagians resident in Constantinople; and then passes on to the controversy about the Incarnation, and describes his opponents as Apollinarians, etc. He wrote more than once again (Mansi, iv. 1023), and another extant letter resumes the same topic.

Celestine caused the Nestorian discourses to be rendered into Latin; and meanwhile received a letter from Cyril, accompanied by other translations of these documents, made at Alexandria. Thus aided, Celestine formed his own opinion on their theological character, and summoned a synod of bishops at the beginning of Aug. 430. We possess an interesting fragment of his speech on this occasion. "I remember that Ambrose of blessed memory, on the day of the Nativity of our Lord Jesus Christ, made the whole people sing to God with one voice—

> 'Veni, Redemptor gentium,
> Ostende partum Virginis;
> Miretur omne saeculum;
> Talis decet partus Deum'"

(Ambros. *Hymn* 12; in *Brev. Ambros.* first vespers of Nativ.). "Did he say, 'Talis decet partus *hominem*'? So, the meaning of our brother Cyril, in that he calls Mary 'Theotokos,' entirely agrees with 'Talis decet partus Deum.' It was God Whom the Virgin, by her child-bearing, brought forth, through His power Who is full of omnipotence." He proceeded to quote a passage from Hilary, and two shorter ones from Damasus (Mansi, iv. 550; Galland, ix. 304). The council's resolutions were expressed by Celestine in letters to Cyril and to Nestorius. The former (*Ep.* 11) commends Cyril's zeal in a cause which is, in truth, that of "Christ our God"; and concludes by saying that unless Nestorius should, within ten days, condemn his own wicked doctrines by a written profession of the same faith, as to "the birth of Christ our God," which is held by the Roman, by the Alexandrian, by the entire church, provision must be made for the see of Constantinople as if vacant, and Nestorius must be treated as one "separate from our body." This letter was dated Aug. 11, 430. Celestine wrote also to John, bp. of Antioch, Juvenal of Jerusalem, Flavian of Philippi, and Rufus of Thessalonica (*Ep.* 12). His meaning is evident: he is not professing to act as the sole supreme judge and oracle of Christendom, or as the mouthpiece of the Catholic church; he announces his resolution, in concert with the Alexandrian church, to break off all communion with the bp. of Constantinople, unless the latter retracted his heretical sentiments. Another letter was addressed to Nestorius himself (*Ep.* 13): its point is contained in the observation, "You have been warned once, twice—I now give you the third warning, according to the rule of St. Paul: if you wish to retain communion with myself and with the bp. of Alexandria, affirm what he affirms—confess our faith." Celestine also wrote (*Ep.* 14) to the clergy and laity of Constantinople, exhorting the orthodox clergy to endure manfully, and to take example from St. Chrysostom and St. Athanasius.

For the events which followed the council of Rome, see CYRIL. In Nov. 430, when Theodosius had summoned an oecumenical council to meet at Ephesus at the coming Whitsuntide, and before the Roman and Alexandrian resolutions had been communicated to Nestorius, the latter wrote to Celestine that the best solution would be the adoption of the word "Christotokos," although he did not object to "Theotokos," if it were used so as not to imply "a confusion of natures." In the spring of 431 Cyril wrote again to Celestine, asking what should be done if Nestorius—having refused to retract at the summons of Rome and Alexandria—were to retract at the coming synod. Celestine answered, May 7 (*Ep.* 16), in a tone which exhibits him in a more favourable light than his great Alexandrian colleague, "I am anxious for the salvation of him who is perishing, provided that he is willing to own himself sick: if not, let our previous decisions stand." Next day, May 8, Celestine wrote instructions for the three persons whom he was sending to represent him at the council (*Ep.* 17). The substance was, "When you reach Ephesus, consult Cyril in everything, and do what he thinks best. But if the council should be over when you arrive, and Cyril gone to Constantinople (*i.e.* to consecrate a new bishop), you must go thither also, and present to the emperor the letter which you will be charged with for him. If you find matters still unsettled, you will be guided by circumstances as to the course which, in conjunction with Cyril, you should take." On the same day Celestine wrote the most remarkable of his letters, that addressed to the council of Ephesus (*Ep.* 18), which was afterwards read, first in Latin, then in a Greek translation, at the second sitting of the council (see Mansi, iv. 1283). Celestine, citing Matt. xviii. 20, adds, "Christ was present in the company of apostles when they taught what He had taught them. This duty of preaching has been entrusted to all the Lord's priests in common, for by right of inheritance are we bound to undertake this solicitude. Let us act now with a common exertion, that we may preserve what was entrusted to us and has been retained through succession from the apostles (*per apostolicam successionem*) to this very day." Celestine then insists on those recollections of the pastoral epistles which the place of the council's meeting should inspire. "*Idem locus, eadem causa. . . .*" "Let us be unanimous, let us do nothing by strife or vainglory." He reminds them of the words of St. Paul to the "episcopi" of Ephesus, Acts xx. 28. It was on July 10 that the three deputies appeared in the council, Nestorius having been deposed on June 22; the council, as Firmus of Caesarea told the deputies, had "followed in the track" of Celestine's previous decision; but, it must be observed, after a full and independent examination of the evidence. The deputies on the next day heard the "acts" of the first session read, and then affirmed the sentence passed on Nestorius in that session, taking care to dwell on the dignity of the see of St. Peter, while Cyril was not less careful to refer to them as representing "the apostolic chair *and* the council of Western bishops." The council wrote to Celestine as their "fellow-minister" (*Ep.* 20), giving a narrative of events, and saying that they had read and affirmed the sentences formerly pronounced by him against the Pelagian heretics. They evidently regarded him as first in dignity among all bishops, but not as master or ruler of all; they "admire him for his far-reaching solicitude as to the interests of religion." "It is your habit, great as you are, to approve yourself in regard to all things, and to take a personal interest in the defence of the churches."

Nestorius, though sent away from Ephesus, had been allowed to live at his old home near Antioch. Celestine objected strongly to this, and thought that Nestorius ought to be placed where he could have no opportunity of spreading his opinions. The birthplace of the Christian name is beset by a pestilent "disease." As for Nestorius's adherents, he thinks, there are many points for consideration, and that a distinction should be drawn between heresiarchs and their followers. The latter "should have opportunity of recovering their position on repentance." The consecrators of Maximian appeared to him to have passed a too indiscriminating sentence against all Nestorianizing bishops, and Celestine wished to moderate their zeal. He also wrote (*Ep.* 23) to Theodosius, extravagantly lauding his acts in behalf of orthodoxy, speaking highly of Maximian, and hinting that Nestorius ought to be sent into distant exile.

"One of Celestine's last actions," says Tillemont, xiv. 156, "was his defence of the memory of St. Augustine as a teacher, against the semi-Pelagians of Gaul. He wrote to Venerius, bp. of Marseilles, and five other Gallic prelates, urging them not to be silent. When presbyters spoke rashly and contentiously, it was not seemly that bishops should allow their subordinates 'to claim the first place in teaching,' especially when they raised their voices against 'Augustine of holy memory'" (*Ep.* 21). The nine articles on the doctrine of grace appended to this letter are not by Celestine (see note to Oxf. ed. of Fleury, iii. p. 143).

Celestine is described by Socrates (vii. 11) as having treated the Novatianists of Rome with harshness, taken away their churches, and obliged their bishop Rusticola to hold his services in private houses. Celestine died on or about July 26, 432 (Tillemont, xiv. 738), and was succeeded by Sixtus III. Hefele, *Conc. Gesch.* ed. 2, pp. 164 ff. [W.B.]

Coelestius occupies a unique position among the Hibernian Scots, as he taught not the faith, but heresy. The general belief is that he was a native of Ireland, of noble birth, and, in early years, of singular piety. About A.D. 405 he is found attached to Pelagius at Rome, and the names of these two figure largely in the history of the church, till they are finally condemned in the Ephesine council, A.D. 431. Coelestius had for some time studied law, and then become a monk, when his speculations upon the conditions of grace and nature attracted attention, as he affirmed the leading points of what were afterwards known as the Pelagian heresy upon the fall of man and the need of supernatural assistance, in effect denying both. These errors he had partly learned, as he said, from a holy presbyter, Rufinus, of whom nothing else is known. From Rome, on the approach of the Goths, he passed to Sicily, and thence to Carthage; by a council at Carthage, under Aurelius the bishop, his teaching was condemned, A.D. 412, though St. Augustine of Hippo had not yet taken up the controversy against him. He soon after retired to Ephesus, where he obtained the priesthood which he had sought in vain at Carthage. On an appeal to pope Zosimus, A.D. 417, he presented his teaching in such a light as to procure acquittal before the pope, who, however, in the following year saw good reason to condemn him. At Carthage he always met with a determined opposition, and at Constantinople and Rome both the imperial and the ecclesiastical powers were finally arrayed against him. After the condemnation of the doctrines of Pelagius by the oecumenical council at Ephesus, Coelestius passed from sight. His chief opponents were St. Augustine and St. Jerome Mosheim, *Eccl. Hist.* i. cent. v. c. 23 seq.; Gennadius, *de Script. Eccl.* c. 44; Robertson, *Ch. Hist.* i. B. ii. c. 8; O'Conor, *Rer. Hib. Scrip.* iv. 97 n.; Gieseler, i. 2; Dupin, *Hist. Ch.* cent. v. c. 2. [PELAGIUS; ZOSIMUS.] [J.G.]

Coelicolae. The death of Julian (A.D. 363) was followed by a reaction in favour of the Christians and against the Jews. The fierce bitterness of the edicts of Constantine and Constantius was never perhaps renewed, but the decrees of Theodosius the Great (379-395) and his son Honorius (395-423) were sufficiently strong and cruel to make it evident how the Roman emperors were influenced, both theologically and politically. The Christians convinced themselves that a stand must be made more earnestly than ever against any heresy which would seduce their members in the direction of either Judaism or paganism. The possible confusion of Christianity with either was by all means to be avoided. Most especially should this be the case as regarded Judaism. The scandal at Antioch which roused the holy indignation of St. Chrysostom—Christian ladies frequenting the synagogues and observing the Jewish festivals, Christian men bringing their lawsuits by preference before the judges of Israel (Grätz, *Gesch. d. Juden*, iv. 315)—found its reflection in many of the chief centres of the Eastern and Western empires. Hence the effort became more and more strenuous to suppress not only such open approximation of the two religious bodies, but also such sects as indicated, by their forms and doctrines, the intention of presenting a compromise with the truth. St. Augustine (*Op.* ii. *Ep.* xliv. cap. vi. § 13, ed. Migne) wrote to the "Elder" of one of these sects, the *Coelicolae*, inviting him to a conference. Edicts of Theodosius and Honorius denounced the "new doctrine" of the sect, which was said to be marked by "new and unwonted audacity," and to be nothing else than a "new crime of superstition" (*Cod. Theod.* xvi. t. v. viii. x. *Cod. Justin.* i. tit. ix.). Happily there is reason to believe that kinder counsels moderated the severity of such intolerance (Grätz, p. 386 seq.; Levysohn, *Diss. Inauguralis de Jud. sub Caesar Conditione*, pp. 4 seq.).

It is difficult to ascertain precisely the views of the Coelicolae. In one edict they are classed with the Jews and the Samaritans, in a second with the Jews only. But it would be a mistake to consider them simply Jews. The Romans, it is well known, called the Jews worshippers of idols through a mistaken notion that the Jewish use of the word "Heaven" for "God" (Buxtorf, *Lex. Rabb.* s.v. שמים, p. 2440; Jost, *Gesch. d. Judenthums*, i. 303) indicated the worship of some created embodiment of heaven (Vitringa, *de Synag.* i. 229). The Coelicolae proper would therefore be easily included by the Romans under the one general title "Jews." From St. Augustine's letter it would seem that the Coelicolae used a baptism which he counted sacrilege—*i.e.* they probably combined a Christian form of baptism with the Jewish rite of circumcision. Such a compromise would appear most objectionable and dangerous to St. Augustine. If, moreover, as their name may indicate, the Coelicolae openly professed their adhesion to the Jewish worship of the One God and rejected the Christian doctrine of the Trinity, this would be an error for which their abhorrence of pagan forms of idolatry would not compensate.

More than this it seems impossible to ascertain. The Coelicolae of Africa, like their congeners the Θεοσεβεῖς of Phoenicia and Palestine, and the Hypsistarii of Cappadocia, were soon stamped or died out. J. A. Schmid, *Hist. Coelicolarum*; C. G. F. Walch, *Hist. Patriarcharum Jud.* pp. 5-8; Bingham, *Orig. Eccles.* vii. 271; Niedner, *K. G.* p. 321 n. (1866); Hase, *K. G.* p. 121; Hasse-Köhler, *K. G.* i. 103; Herzog, *R. E.* s.v. "Himmelsanbeter." [J.M.F.]

Colluthus (2), presbyter and founder of a sect at Alexandria early in the 4th cent. He claimed (on what grounds it is unknown) to exercise episcopal functions; but the council of Alexandria under Hosius (A.D. 324) decided that he was only a presbyter, from which it was held to follow necessarily that ISCHYRAS and others ordained by him were only laymen (Ath. *Apol. cont. Arian.* 12, 75-77, 80, pp. 106, 152). The passages cited mention also a sect of Colluthians. Bp. Alexander, in a letter preserved by Theodoret (*Ecc. Hist.* i. 4), seems to imply that Colluthus commenced his schismatical proceedings before Arius had separated from the church. A phrase used by Alexander (Χριστεμπορεία) has been understood by Valesius to charge Colluthus with taking money for conferring orders. Valesius also infers that the cause of Colluthus's separation was impatience that Alexander had not taken stronger measures against Arianism. The name Colluthus is the first among those presbyters who subscribed to Alexander's condemnation of Arius (Gelas. Cyzic. ii. 3). These authorities accuse Colluthus of schism, not heresy; as is also indicated by the mildness of the action of the council, which would probably have excommunicated him had he been deeply tainted with erroneous doctrine. Epiphanius mentions in general terms (*Haer.* 69, 728) that Colluthus taught some perverse things, and founded a sect, which was soon dispersed. The first to give Colluthus a separate heading in heretical lists is Philastrius (79), followed by Augustine and later heresiologists. Philastrius charges him with contradicting Is. xlv. 7, by teaching that God did not make evil. Tillemont, vi. 231; Walch, *Hist. der Ketz.* iv. 502; Harnack, *Alt. Chr. Lit.* i. 480. [G.S.]

Collyridians. Under this name Epiphanius (*Haer.* 79) assails certain women who had brought from Thrace into Arabia the practice of performing on certain days rites in honour of the Blessed Virgin, the chief being the offering of a cake (κολλυρίς), and the partaking of it by the worshippers. Epiphanius condemns their conduct because (*a*) women ought not to offer sacrifice, and (*b*) Mary is to be honoured, God only to be worshipped. The name Collyris (or kindred forms) is to be found in the LXX translation of Lev. vii. 12, viii. 26; 2 Sam. vi. 19, xiii. 68; and the word passed thence into the Latin versions. [G.S.]

Columba (1) Columcille, June 9. The life, character, and work of this saint have been exhaustively treated by an Irish and a French author, Reeves and Montalembert. St. Columba was the son of Fedhlimidh, son of Fergus Cennfada, and thus descended from Niall of the Nine Hostages, monarch of Ireland, his great-great-grandfather. Born at Gartan, a wild district in co. Donegal, on Dec. 7, most probably in 521, he was baptized at Tulach-Dubhglaise (now Temple-Douglas, about halfway between Gartan and Letterkenny), under the name, first, of Crimthann (wolf), and then of Colum (dove), to which was afterwards added the suffix *cille*, as some say, from his close attendance at the church of his youthful sojourn, and as others, from the many communities founded and governed by him. His chief instructor was bp. Finnian of Moville (by whom he was ordained deacon). While at Clonard with St. Finnian he was ordained to the priesthood by bp. Etchen of Clonfad, to whom he was sent by St. Finnian for that purpose. Why he was never raised to the episcopate is a matter of speculation: in the Scholia on the *Felire of St. Aengus the Culdee* there is a legend relating how the order of the priesthood was conferred by mistake in place of that of the episcopate (Todd, *St. Patrick,* 70-71; *Book of Obits of C. C. Dublin,* Dubl. 1844, p. liv.; Colgan, *Acta SS.* 306 n[17]). Bp. Lloyd supposes a political reason, and Lanigan thinks he applied only for the office of chorepiscopus. But Dr. Reeves is of opinion that he really shrank from the responsibilities and many obligations of the highest ecclesiastical rank. In and about A.D. 544 we have probably to place the many ecclesiastical and monastic foundations attributed to him in Ireland, his chief favourites being Durrow and Derry. The reasons usually given for his afterwards leaving Ireland are various. But whatever they may have been, he is said to have used his influence to excite a quarrel between the families of the north and south Hy Neill, and the consequence was the battle fought in the barony of Carberry, between Drumcliff and Sligo, on the borders of Ulster and Connaught, A.D. 561, and gained by the Neills of the North, the party of St. Columba. In consequence of St. Columba's participation in this quarrel, a synod was assembled at Teltown in Meath to excommunicate him for his share in shedding Christian blood, and if the sentence of excommunication was not actually pronounced, it was owing to the exertions of St. Brendan of Birr and bp. Finnian of Moville on his behalf. Whether by the charge of the synod of Teltown, that he must win as many souls to Christ by his preaching as lives were lost at Cul-Dreimhne, or through his own feeling of remorse, or his great desire for the conversion of the heathen he left Ireland in 563, being 42 years old, and, traversing the sea in a currach of wickerwork covered with hides, landed with his 12 companions on the small island of I, Hy, I-colmkille, Iova, or Iona, situated about 2 miles off the S.W. extremity of Mull in Argyllshire. There, on the border land between the Picts and Scots, and favoured by both, St. Columba founded his monastery, the centre from which he and his followers evangelized the Picts and taught more carefully the Scots, who were already Christians at least in name. Hy was henceforth his chief abode, but he frequently left it for Scotland, where he founded many churches, penetrating N. even to Inverness, and probably farther, and E. into Buchan, Aberdeenshire, sending his disciples where he himself had not leisure to go. His connexion with Ireland was not broken; and in 575 he attended the synod of Drumceatt, with his cousin king Aidan of Dalriada, whom he had crowned in Iona in 574. From Iona as a centre he established Christianity on a firm basis to the N. of the Tay and Clyde. Unfortunately, valuable as St. Adamnan's *Life of St. Columba* is, it is written rather to extol its subject than to present a picture of the time, and so gives little chronological sequence to the events of the thirty years and upwards of his sojourn in Iona. We gather, however, that in his monastery he was indefatigable in prayer, teaching, study, and transcription of the Scriptures; people came to him from all quarters, some for bodily aid, but most for spiritual needs; and soon smaller societies had to be formed, as at Hinba (one of the Garveloch Islands), Tyree, etc., for the requirements of the monastery. He visited king Bruide at Craig-Phadrick, beside Inverness, and established the monastery of Deer in the N.E. corner of Aberdeenshire, where he left St. Drostan, so that his churches are traced all over the N. of Scotland (*Book of Deer,* pref.). He also frequently visited Ireland on matters connected with his monasteries, the superintendence of which he retained to the last. He manifested the greatest favour for the bards and national poetry of his country, being himself accounted one of the poets of Ireland, and poems attributed to him are preserved and quoted by Dr. Reeves and Montalembert (see also *Misc. Arch. Soc.* 1 seq.). In A.D. 593 he seems to have been visited by sickness, and the angels sent for his soul were stayed but for a time. As the time approached, and the infirmities of age were weighing upon him, he made all preparations for his departure, blessing his monastery, visiting the old scenes, and taking his farewell of even the brute beasts about the monastery. On a Sat. afternoon he was transcribing the 34th Psalm (Ps. xxxiii. E.V.), and coming to the verse, "They who seek the Lord shall want no manner of thing that is good," he said, "Here I must stop—at the end of this page; what follows let Baithen write." He then left his cell to attend vespers, and, returning at their close, lay down on his couch of stone, and gave his last injunctions to Baithen, till the bell at midnight called them to the nocturnal office. St. Columba was the first to enter the oratory, and when the brethren followed with lights they found the saint prostrate before the altar, and he soon passed away, with a sweet smile upon his face, as though he had merely fallen into a gentle sleep. This, according to Dr. Reeves's computation, was early in the morning of Sun. June 9, 597. Ireland justly mourned for one of the best of her sons; Scotland for one of her greatest benefactors. *The Life of St. Columba, written by Adamnan, ninth Abbat of that Monastery*, by W. Reeves, D.D. (Dubl. 1857); a more modern ed. giving Lat. text ed. with intro., notes, glossary, and trans. by Dr. J. T. Fowler (Oxf. Univ. Press); *Les Moines d'Occident*, par le Comte de Montalembert, vol. iii. (Paris, 1868). See also *The Life of St. Columba*, ed. by John Smith, D.D. (Edinb. 1798). In his preface Dr. Reeves gives a full bibliographical account of the Irish and Latin *Acts* and *Life of St. Columba*, with a notice of the MSS., codices, authors, and edd. Cf. Lanigan, *Eccl. Hist. Ir.* ii. 107. [J.G.]

Columba occupies in missionary history the entire generation preceding the arrival of Augustine (A.D. 597). The Celtic apostle of Caledonia died the very year in which the Roman mission set foot in the south of Britain. The first abbat of Iona laboured much longer, in a far wider sphere, and personally with more success, as well as prodigiously more romance, than the first archbp. of Canterbury. [ADAMNAN.] [C.H.]

Columbanus, abbat of Luxeuil and Bobbio, Nov. 21. On this day, in the *Mart. Doneg.* (by Todd and Reeves, 315), is the entry "Columban, abbat, who was in Italy." Thus simply does the Irish calendar refer to an Irishman famous in France, Switzerland, and Italy, the great champion of public morals at a cruel and profligate court, the zealous preacher of the Gospel in lands where it had been all but forgotten, and the pious founder of monasteries. His life, written with great care and minuteness by Jonas, of Susa in Piedmont, a monk of his monastery at Bobbio, in the time of Attala and Eustace, his immediate successors, is now pub. by Mabillon (in *Acta SS. Ord. St. Bened.* tom ii. sec. ii. 2-26), and by Messingham (*Flor. Ins. Sanct.* 219-239), who appends the account of miracles omitted by Jonas, and other additions (*ib.* 239-254), also adding the Rule of St. Columbanus in ten chaps., a short Homily by the saint on the fallaciousness of human life, and some carmina (*ib.* 403-414). The fullest account of his life, works, and writings is in Fleming's *Collectanea Sacra* (fol. Lovan. 1667), which includes Jonas's Life and St. Columbanus's writings. His writings are also in *Bibl. Mag. Vet. Pat.* vol. viii. (Paris, 1644), and *Bibl. Max. Vet. Pat.* vol. xii. (Lyons, 1677). His poems were first printed by Goldastus (*Paraen. Vet.* pars. i. 1604). Wright (*Biog. Brit. Lit.* 157 seq.) gives useful particulars of the editions of his writings.

St. Columbanus was born in Leinster in or about A.D. 543, the year in which Benedict, his great monastic predecessor, died at Monte Cassino. His chief training was in the monastery of Bangor, on the coast of Down, under the eye of St. Comgall, where he accepted the monastic vows and habit. At the age, most probably, of a little over forty, he was seized with a desire to preach the Gospel beyond the limits of Ireland, and with 12 companions crossed over to France, *c.* A.D. 585, making a short visit to Britain as he went. For several years he traversed the country, teaching the faith, but apparently without building any monastery, till, coming to Burgundy at the solicitations of Gontran the king, he took up his abode in a deserted part of the Vosges mountains. He first chose the ruined Roman fort of Anagrates, now Annegray, a hamlet of the commune of Faucogney (Haute-Saône); then, needing a larger foundation, removed, A.D. 590 or 591, to the ruins of the ancient Luxovium, about 8 miles from Annegray, and established his celebrated monastery of Luxeuil, on the confines of Burgundy and Austrasia. But soon he had to erect another monastic establishment at Fontaines, or Fontenay, and divide his monks among these houses. Over each house he placed a superior, who yet was subordinate to himself, and for their management he drew up his well-known Rule, derived no doubt in great measure from his master St. Comgall, and perhaps to some extent from St. Benedict of Monte Cassino. The great principle of this Rule was obedience, absolute and unreserved; and the next was constant and severe labour, to subdue the flesh, exercise the will in daily self-denial, and set an example of industry in cultivation of the soil. The least deviation from the Rule entailed a definite corporal punishment, or a severer form of fast as laid down in the Penitential (see the *Rule* in Messingham, *u.s.*, Fleming, *u.s.*, and *Max Bibl. Vet. Patr.* tom. xii. Lyons, 1677; and on it see Montalembert, *Monks of the West*, ii. 447 seq.; Lanigan, *Eccl. Hist. Ir.* ii. 267-269; Neander, *Gen. Ch. Hist.* v. 36, 37; Ussher, *Eccl. Ant.* c. 17, wks. vi. 484 seq.; Mabillon, *Ann. Bened.* lib. viii. sect. 17). For 20 years in the wooded and all but inaccessible defiles of the Vosges mountains St. Columbanus laboured with his monks, and all classes of men gathered round him, notwithstanding the severe discipline. His own inclination was always to retire into the wood and caves and hold unrestrained communion with God; but besides the claims of his monasteries, Christian zeal and charity drew him forth. He excited against himself strong feeling among the Gallican clergy and in the Burgundian court. A worldly priesthood felt the reproach of his exceeding earnestness and self-denial, and his pure severity was a constant accusation of loss of love and truth in them. Moreover, he carried with him the peculiar rites and usages of his Irish mother-church; the Irish mode of computing Easter, the Irish tonsure, and the "Cursus Scotorum" which he had received from St. Comgall. This gave great offence to the Gallo-Frank clergy, and in 602 he was arraigned before a synod, where he defended himself boldly, pleading that if error there was it was not his, but had been received from his fathers, and he asked but the licence "to live in silence, in peace and in charity, as I have lived for 12 years, beside the bones of my 17 departed brethren." At the same time he wrote to pope Gregory the Great several letters on the subject, as afterwards to pope Boniface IV., but with what immediate result we know not, though the haughty bearing and generally independent tone, in words and letters, of "Columbanus the sinner" were little calculated to propitiate the favour of bishops or popes; while Gregory's very friendly connexion with queen Brunehault would make that pope give little heed to the appeals of the stranger whom she disliked. But he received great opposition from the Burgundian court. Thierry II., called also Theodoric, was under age, and his grandmother Brunehault ruled in violent and arbitrary fashion, and encouraged the young king in every form of vice, that she might retain the control of the kingdom. This open profligacy St. Columbanus reproved by word and writing, and thus incurred the bitterest enmity of the king, and specially of the queen-mother. Gifts and flattery proving in vain, he was first carried prisoner to Besançon, and finally banished from the kingdom, A.D. 610. He departed from Luxeuil after 20 years' labour there, never to return. With his Irish monks he eventually arrived at the Lake of Constance. First he came to Arbon on its W. coast; then, hearing of the ruins of Bregentium, now Bregenz, at its S.E. corner, he went thither with St. Gall and his other monks, and spent three years preaching to the people, and contending with privation and difficulty. When Bregenz was brought under the power of Burgundy, St. Columbanus had again to flee, and leaving St. Gall at Bregenz he himself, with only one disciple, passed S. across the Alps into Lombardy, where he was honourably received by king Agilulf. At Milan he was soon engaged in a controversy with the many Arians of Lombardy, and about this time wrote to the pope Boniface IV. at the suggestion of king Agilulf and his queen Theodelind. Agilulf, in 613, presented Columbanus with a district in the wild gorges of the Apennines, between Genoa and Milan, not far from the Trebbia, and there he built his celebrated monastery of Bobbio, and there, Nov. 21, 615, calmly resigned his spirit. For his life and times, see Lanigan, *Eccl. Hist. Ir.* ii. c. 13; Ussher, *Eccl. Ant.* cc. xv. xvii.; *Ind. Chron.* A.D. 589, 614; Montalembert, *Monks of the West*, ii. bk. vii.; Butler, *Lives of the SS.* xi. 435 seq.; Neander, *Gen. Ch. Hist.* v. 35 seq.; Milman, *Hist. Lat. Christ.* ii. bk. iv. c. 5. In his writings St. Columbanus everywhere shews sound judgment, solid ecclesiastical learning, elegant taste, and deep spiritual discernment, which says much for the man and for the school in which he was educated. This is well pointed out by Moore in his *Hist. of Ireland* (i. p. 267). [J.G.]

It is the great distinction of Columbanus, as Neander has observed, that he set the example at the end of the 6th cent. of that missionary enterprise in remote countries of Europe which was afterwards so largely followed up from England and Ireland, as the names of Cilian, Wilfrid, Willebrord, Boniface, Willibald, Willehad, remind us. Colonies of pious monks journeyed forth under the leadership of able abbats, carrying the light of Christianity through the dangerous wilds of continental heathendom. It was about 12 years before the arrival of the Roman mission in England (A.D. 597), and the same length of time before the death of Columba the apostle of Caledonia, that Columbanus, fired perhaps by the example of this energetic missionary, passed over into Gaul.

Columbanus's foundation of Luxeuil achieved as great a celebrity as his Rule, and a more enduring one. It became the parent of numerous streams of monastic colonies, which spread through both Burgundies, Rauracia (the ancient bishopric of Basel), Neustria, Champagne, Ponthieu, and the Morini. Luxeuil was, in short, as Montalembert expresses it, the monastic capital of Gaul, as well as the first school in Christendom, a nursery of bishops and saints; while Bobbio, although for so brief a period under the government of its founder, became a stronghold of orthodoxy against the Arians, and long remained a school of learning for North Italy.

The works of Columbanus contained in Fleming's *Collectanea Sacra* (Lovanii, 1667) are as follows. *Prose*:—I. *Regula Monastica*, in 10 short chaps. II. *Regula Coenobialis Fratrum, sive Liber de Quotidianis Poenitentiis Monachorum*, in 15 chaps. III. *Sermones sive Instructiones Variae*, 17 discourses, the first being "de Deo Uno et Trino," and the last, "Quod per Viam Humilitatis et Obedientiae Deus quaerendus et sequendus sit." IV. *Liber seu Tractatus de Modo seu Mensura Poenitentiarum*, the second title being *de Poenitentiarum Mensura Taxanda*. It prescribes penances for various sins. V. *Instructio de Octo Vitiis Principalibus*, less than a column in length. The vitia are gula, fornicatio, cupiditas, ira, tristitia, acedia, vana gloria, superbia. VI. Five *Epistolae Aliquot ad Diversos*: (1) "ad Bonifacium IV."; (2) "ad Patres Synodi cujusdam Gallicanae super Quaestione Paschae Congregatae"; (3) "ad Discipulos et Monachos suos"; (4) "ad Bonifacium Papam"; (5) "ad S. Gregorium Papam." These are especially interesting for the information they give on the dispute between the Roman and Irish churches. In reference to (1), see BONIFACIUS IV. The poetical works, *Poemata Quaedam*, occupy about 8 pp. fol., ranging in length from 4 lines to 164. The metres are both classical and medieval. [C.H.]

Comgall, one of the most prominent leaders of monasticism in Ireland, said to have had as many as 3,000 monks under him at one time in Bangor and affiliated houses. He was a native of Mourne, now Magheramorne, in the co. of Antrim, and on the shore of Lough Larne. He was probably born A.D. 517 (Reeves). After teaching for some years he founded in 558 his great monastery at Bangor, in the Ards of Ulster and co. of Down. Hither multitudes flocked from all quarters, and for it and kindred institutions he drew up a Rule which was considered one of the chief ones of Ireland. His most noted disciples at Bangor were Cormac, son of Diarmaid and king of South Leinster, who in his old age abdicated and became a monk, as is related in the *Life of St. Fintan*; and St. Columbanus, abbot of Luxeuil and Bobbio. [COLUMBANUS.] After ruling the monastery of Bangor and its dependencies for "10 days, 3 months and 50 years," as the calendars say, but about 44 years according to computation, St. Comgall died at Bangor on May 10, A.D. 602, aged 85, having received his viaticum from St. Fiachra (Feb. 8) of Congbail. He is justly reckoned among the Fathers of the Irish church. He was buried at Bangor. See further Lanigan, *Eccl. Hist. Ir.* ii. c. 10; Reeves, *Adamnan*, pass. and *Eccl. Ant.* pass.; Ussher, *Eccl. Ant.* cc. 13-17, wks. v. vi., Ind. Chr. A.D. 456, 516; Bp. Forbes, *Kal. Scott. Saints*, 108-110. His dedications in Scotland were at Durris, Kincardineshire, and possibly Dercongal, or Drumcongal, now Holywood, in Galloway (Forbes, *u.s.*). [J.G.]

Commodianus, the author of two Latin poems, *Instructiones adversus Gentium Deos pro Christiana Disciplina*, and *Carmen Apologeticum adversus Judaeos et Gentes*. His *Instructions* are included "inter apocrypha" in a synodal decree of Gelasius (*Concil.* tom. iv.), probably because of certain heterodox statements respecting Antichrist, the Millennium, and the First Resurrection. In what age he lived has been much disputed. Internal evidence in the poem shews that the author lived in days of persecution. The style of the *Instructions* points to the age of Cyprian, with whose works they have more than once been edited. There is an allusion to the Novatian Schism (§ xlvii. ad fin.), and the language of § lii. seems to be aimed against the "Thurificati" and "Libellatici" of the 3rd cent. In § lxvi. 12 a "subdola pax" is mentioned, which Cave refers to the temporary quiet enjoyed by the Christians under Gallienus, after the Decian and before the Aurelian persecution. Other expressions (e.g. *agonia propinqua*, § liii. 10) clearly point to the expectation of fresh suffering. But the most important passage as affecting the date of the poem is one in which the author upbraids the Gentiles for perseverance in unbelief, though Christianity has prevailed for 200 years (§ vi. 2), and this, which, singularly enough, seems to have escaped the notice of the earlier critics, must be held to fix the date of Commodian as approximately A.D. 250. The barbarity of his style, and the peculiarity of certain words (e.g. *Zabulo*, *Zacones*), led Rigault to infer that he was of African extraction. He applies to himself the epithet "Gazaeus," but this probably refers to his dependence upon the treasury of the church (*gazophylacium*) for support, and not to any connexion with Gaza. Originally a heathen (*Instruct. Praef.* 5, § xxvi. 24), he was converted by the perusal of the Scriptures (*Praef.* 6), and if the words "Explicit tractatus sancti Episcopi . . ." discovered on the MS. of the *Carmen Apologeticum* by Pitra, may be taken to refer to the author of the poem, who, from internal evidence, is conclusively proved to have been Commodian, it would seem that he ultimately became a bishop.

His works (a trans. of which is given in the *Ante-Nicene Lib.*), though utterly valueless as literature, are of considerable interest in the history of the Latin language as showing that the change had already commenced which resulted in the formation of the Romance languages.

The *Instructions* are in Migne's *Patr. Lat.* vol. v.; the *Apology* in Pitra's *Spicilegium Solismense*, vol. i. [E.M.Y.]

Commodus, A.D. 180-193. The monstrous vices of this degenerate son of Marcus Aurelius brought at least one counterbalancing advantage. The persecutions of his father's reign ceased for a time in his. The popular feeling against the Christians, though it still continued, was no longer heightened and directed by the action of the Imperial government, and the result was a marked increase of numbers. Many rich and noble, with their households and kindred, professed themselves Christians (Eus. *H. E.* v. 21), even in the emperor's palace, but it is uncertain whether they were officers, freedmen, or slaves (Iren. *adv. Haer.* iv. 30). Marcia, the favourite mistress of the emperor, is said by Dio Cassius (lxxii. 4) or Xiphilinus writing in his name, to have used her influence with Commodus in their favour and to have done them much good service. The strange history of CALLISTUS in the *Refutation of all Heresies* attributed to Hippolytus (ix. 6) throws fresh light on Marcia's connexion with the Christian church at Rome. The epithet by which he describes her as a "God-loving woman" may be, as Dr. Wordsworth suggested, ironical; but it is clear that she was in frequent communication with the officers of the church. Callistus had been brought before Fuscianus, the city prefect, charged with disturbing a synagogue of the Jews, and was sentenced to hard labour in the mines of Sardinia. Marcia sent for Victor, a bishop of the church, asked what Christians were suffering for their faith in Sardinia, and obtained from Commodus an order of release. The order was given to an eunuch, Hyacinthus, who carried it to Sardinia, and obtained the liberation of Callistus and others, alleging his own influence with Marcia as his warrant, though the name of Callistus had not been included in the list. The narrative clearly implies that Hyacinthus was a Christian.

Thus some Christians had, as such, been condemned to exile; and persecutions, though less frequent, had not altogether ceased. One sufferer of the time takes his place in the list of martyrs. Apollonius, a Roman citizen of distinction, perhaps a senator, of high repute for philosophical culture, was accused before Perennius, the prefect of the city, by one of his own slaves. In accordance with an imperial edict sentencing informers, in such cases, to death even when the accused was found guilty, the slave had his legs broken.

Apollonius delivered before the senate an elaborate *Apologia* for his faith. By what Eusebius speaks of as an ancient law (possibly the edict of Trajan) he was beheaded (*H. E.* v. 21). [E.H.P.]

Constans I., the youngest of the three sons of Constantine the Great, was born *c.* 320 and made Caesar in 333; he reigned as Augustus 337-350, when he was killed by the conspiracy of Magnentius. [CONSTANTIUS II.] De Broglie (iii. pp. 58, 59) in his character of him remarks: "As far as we can discriminate between the contradictory estimates of different historians, Constans was of a simple, somewhat coarse, nature, and one without high aims though without malice. As regards the inheritance of his father's qualities, while Constantius seemed to have taken for his share his political knowledge, his military skill, and his eloquence (though reproducing a very faint image of them), Constans had only received great personal courage and a straightforwardness that did him honour. He was, besides, a lover of pleasure: he was suspected of the gravest moral irregularities. . . . He had firm, though certainly unenlightened, faith, and frequently gave proofs of it by distributing largesses to the churches and favours to the Christians" (cf. Eutrop. *Brev.* x. 9, Vict. *Caes.* 41, *Epit.* 41). Zosimus (ii. 42) gives him a worse character than do the others. Libanius in 348 delivered a panegyric on Constans and Constantius, called βασιλικὸς λόγος, vol. iii. ed. Reiske, pp. 272-332. St. Chrysostom in the difficult and probably corrupt passage of his *15th Homily on the Philippians*, p. 363, ed. Gaume, speaks of him as having children and as committing suicide, statements elsewhere unsupported. The most favourable evidence for Constans is the praise of St. Athanasius (*Apol. ad Constantium*, 4 sqq.; cf. the letter of Hosius in *Hist. Arian. ad Monachos*, 44). His conduct with respect to the Arian and Donatist controversies gained him the esteem of Catholics. He was a baptized Christian; his baptism is referred to in *Ap. ad C.* 7. [J.W.]

Constantinus I.—I. A. *Ancient Authorities* (Heathen).—Eutropius, *Breviarium, Hist. Rom.*, end of 9th and beginning of 10th book. This historian was secretary to the emperor, and his short account is therefore valuable. The *Caesares* and the *Epitome*, current under the name of Aurelius Victor, were doubtless the work of different authors. The first, who wrote under Constantius, was a friend of Ammianus, and *praefectus urbi* towards the close of the cent.; the second, who excerpted from the first, lived a generation later, and continued his compilation down to the death of Theodosius the Great. They seem to have used the same sources as Zosimus, whom they supplement. The Panegyrists, as contemporary writers, deserve more attention than has been given them, allowance being made for the defects incident to their style of writing. Those relating to our subject—*Anon. Panegyr. Maximiano et Constantino* (A.D. 307), Eumenii *Constantino in natalibus urb. Trevir.* (310), and *Gratiarum actio Flaviensium nomine* (311), *Anon. de Victoria adv. Maxentium* (313), and Nazarii *Paneg. Constantino* (321)—are all the product of Gallic rhetoricians. The *Scriptores Hist. Augustae* contain several contemporary references to Constantine; those in Julian's *Caesars* are, as might be expected, unfriendly and satirical. The first vol. of the Bonn ed. of the Byzantine historians contains the fragments of Eunapius, Priscus, Dexippus, etc., but these are of little moment, as are the extracts from Praxagoras in Photius, *Cod.* 62. Indirectly it is supposed that we have more of the matter of these earlier writers in Zosimus's ἱστορία νέα, bk. ii. This historian lived probably *c.* 450. He was a bitter enemy of Constantine, whom he accuses of various crimes and cruelties, and blames for the novelties of his policy, shewing a particular dislike of his conversion. He falls into several historical blunders. The part of Ammianus's *Histories* relating to this reign is unfortunately lost. Some remarks on it occur in the part preserved, from which we gather his general agreement with his friend and contemporary Victor. The text of Ammianus, pub. by Gardthausen (Teubner, 1874), may be recommended. He has also given a revised text from the MSS. of the anonymous excerpts generally cited as *Anonymus Valesii*, *Excerpta Valesiana*. They received this name from being first printed by H. Valois, at the end of his ed. of Ammianus. Some of these extracts may be traced word for word in Eutropius and Orosius; hence their author did not live earlier than the 5th cent. Others are valuable as coming from sources elsewhere unrepresented.

(Christian.) The earliest contemporary authority is Lactantius, *de Mortibus Persecutorum*, a tract pub. after the defeat of Maxentius and before Constantine had declared himself the enemy of Licinius—*i.e.* probably 313 or 314. His bitterness is unpleasant, and his language exaggerated and somewhat obscure, but his facts are generally confirmed by other authors, where we can test them. The most important is Eusebius. Three of his works especially treat of Constantine, *Hist. Eccl.* ix. and x., down to 324, and probably pub. before the death of Crispus in 326; *de Vita Constantini*, in four books, with a translation of Constantine's *Oratio ad Sanctorum Coetum* as an appendix, pub. after his death; and, thirdly, τριακονταετηρικὸς, or *Laudes Constantini*, a panegyric at his tricennalia, containing little but rhetoric. To harmonize Eusebius and Zosimus is difficult. Fleury's dictum, "On ne se trompera sur Constantin en croyant tout le mal qu'en dit Eusèbe, et tout le bien qu'en dit Zosime," may be perfectly true, but Zosimus says very little good of him and Eusebius very little harm. Eusebius has great weight as a contemporary and as giving documents, which have not for the most part been seriously challenged; but he is discredited by fulsomeness and bad taste in his later works, and by inconsistencies of tone between them and his history. He announces, however, that he will only recount those actions of the emperor which belong to his religious life (*V. C.* i. 11: μόνα τὰ πρὸς τὸν θεοφιλῆ συντείνοντα βίον), and is open to the criticism of Socrates (*H. E.* i. 1) as τῶν ἐπαίνων τοῦ βασιλέως καὶ τῆς πανηγυρικῆς ὑψηγορίας τῶν λόγων μᾶλλον ὡς ἐν ἐγκωμίῳ φροντίσας ἢ περὶ τοῦ ἀκριβῶς περιλαβεῖν τὰ γενόμενα. We must allow for the natural exultation of Christians over the emperor who had done so much for them and openly professed himself an instrument of Providence for the advancement of Christianity. Neither in the case of Eusebius nor of Zosimus must we push our distrust too far. The best ed. of the historical works of Eusebius is by F. A. Heinichen, repub. and enlarged (Leipz. 1868-1870, 3 vols.).* The laws issued by Constantine (after 312) in the *Theodosian* and *Justinian Codes* are very important contemporary documents. The first are in a purer state, and may be consulted in the excellent ed. of Hänel (Bonn. 1842-1844), or in the older standard folios of Godefroi, with their valuable historical notes. Both codes are arranged chronologically in Migne's *Patrologia, Opera Constantini*, which also contains the Panegyrists and documents relating to the early history of the Donatists.

Socrates, *H. E.* i., and Sozomen, *H. E.* i. and ii. (about a cent. later), give an account of the last period of his reign; Socrates being generally the safer guide. On his relations with Arianism much is found in the treatises and epp. of St. Athanasius, and occasional facts may be gleaned from other Fathers. As a hero of Byzantine history and *ἰσαπόστολος*, Constantine has become clothed in a mist of fiction. Something may be gathered from Joannes Lydus, *de Magistrat. P. R.*, and among the fables of Cedrenus and Zonaras may be found some facts from more trustworthy sources.

B. *Modern Authorities.*—It will be unnecessary to enumerate the well-known writers of church history and the multitude of minor essays on separate points of Constantine's life. As early as 1720 Vogt (*Hist. Lit. Const. Mag.* Hamburg) gave a list of more than 150 authors, ancient and modern, and the number has since infinitely increased. The first critical life of importance is by J. C. F. Manso (*Leben Constantins des Grossen*, Wien, 1819, etc.), but it is hard and one-sided, unchristian, if not antichristian. Jacob Burckhardt largely follows Manso, but is much more interesting and popular (*Die Zeit Constantins des Gr.* Basel, 1853), though not always fair. Some misstatements in it are noticed below. He views the emperor merely as a great politician, and shews much bitterness against Eusebius. Theodore Keim's *Der Uebertritt Const. des Gr.* (Zürich, 1862) is in many points a good refutation of Burckhardt, as well as being a fair statement from one not disposed to be credulous. The first two volumes of *L'Eglise et l'Empire au IVᵉ Siècle*, by A. de Broglie (Paris, 1855, etc.), give the views of a learned Roman Catholic, generally based on original authorities, and this is perhaps the most useful book upon the subject. The section (134) in Dr. P. Schaff's *Gesch. der Alten Kirche* (Leipz. 1867, also trans.) is as good a *short* account of Constantine as can be named. In English we have a short life by a Nonconformist, Mr. Joseph Fletcher (Lond. 1852, 16mo), but no standard work of importance. The brilliant sketch by Dean Stanley in his *Eastern Church* is probably the fairest picture of Constantine in our language. For his relations with Arianism we may refer to Newman's *Arians of the Fourth Cent.* (1st ed. 1833; 3rd ed. 1871); Neale's *Eastern Church, Patriarchate of Alexandria*; Bright's *History of the Church*, A.D. 313-451, 2nd ed. 1869; and Gwatkin's *Arian Controversy*. A simple monograph on Constantine by E. L. Cutts is pub. by S.P.C.K.

* For a careful judgment of Eusebius's Life of Constantine, Heinichen's 23rd Meletema may be consulted (vol. iii. p. 754). Cf. also de Broglie, *L'Eglise et l'Empire*, vol, iii. p. 39.

II. *Life.—Period* i. To 312.—Flavius Valerius Aurelius Constantinus, surnamed Magnus or the Great, was born Feb. 27, probably in 274, at Naïssus (Nissa), in Dardania or Upper Moesia, where his family had for some time been settled. His father, Constantius Chlorus, was still young at the time of his son's birth. He was of a good family, being nephew by the mother's side of the emperor Claudius. A few years later we find him high in favour with Carus, who intended, it was said, to make him Caesar. Constantine's mother Helena, on the other hand, was of mean position, and apparently was married after her son's birth. Constantine was brought up at Drepanum in Cicilia, his mother's birthplace (Procop. *de Aedif. Justin.* v. 2). His father, on becoming Caesar and taking another wife, sent him, when about 16 years old, as a sort of hostage to Diocletian at Nicomedia, who treated him with kindness. His first military service was to accompany that emperor against Achillaeus in 296, and Eusebius saw him as a young and handsome man passing through Palestine into Egypt (*V. C.* i. 19). In 297 he took part in the successful war of Galerius against the Persians; and about this time married Minervina. Constantine continued in the East while his father was fighting in Gaul and Britain. In 303 he was present when the edict of persecution against the Christians was promulgated at Nicomedia and the palace soon after struck by lightning. The concurrence of these two events made a strong impression upon him (*Orat. ad Sanct. Coet.* 25). He also witnessed in 305 the abdication of the two Augusti, Diocletian and Maximian.

A higher destiny awaited him in another part of the empire. His father insisted upon his return, and Galerius at length was persuaded to give permission and the seal necessary for the public posts, ordering him not to start before receiving his last instructions on the morrow. Constantine took flight in the night. He had probably good reasons for his mistrust, and to stop pursuit maimed the public horses at many stations on his road (Zos. ii. 8; Anon. Val. 4; Victor, *Caes.* 21), which lay partly through countries where the persecution was raging. He arrived at Gesoriacum (Boulogne) just in time to accompany his father to Britain on his last expedition against the Picts (Eumen. *in Nat. Urb. Trev.* vii.). Constantius died at York, July 306, in the presence of his sons, after declaring Constantine his successor (*de M. P.* xxiv.). He was almost immediately proclaimed Augustus by the soldiers (Σεβαστὸς πρὸς τῶν στρατοπέδων ἀναγορευθεὶς, Eus. *H. E.* viii. 13). Almost at the same time another claimant of imperial power appeared at Rome in Maxentius, son of the retired Maximian, who now came forward again to assist his son. Constantine's first act was to shew favour to the Christians (*de M. P.* xxiv.), who had been exposed to little of the violence of persecution under the mild rule of Constantius. (*V. C.* i.

13-17. Eusebius seems here to exaggerate. Cf. *Episcopor. partis Majorini preces ad Constantinum*, in *Op. Const.* Migne, col. 747.) Constantine had at once to defend Gaul against the Franks and German tribes, who had risen during the absence of Constantius in Britain (Eumen. *ib.* x.). In 307 Maximian, who had quarrelled with his son, crossed the Alps and allied himself with the Caesar of the West. Constantine received as wife his daughter Fausta, and with her the title of Augustus (*Pan. Max. et Const.* v.). For three years after marriage he found sufficient employment in consolidating his government in the West, and in wars upon the frontier of the Rhine, over which he began to build a bridge at Cologne. The seat of his court was Trèves, which he embellished with many buildings, including several temples and basilicas, and the forum. Meanwhile Galerius was seized with a painful illness, and on April 30, 311, shortly before his death, issued his haughty edict of toleration, the first of the series, to which the names of Constantine and Licinius were also affixed. Constantine remained in the West engaged in wars with the Alemanni and Cherusci, and in restoring the cities of Gaul (cf. Eumen. *Gratiarum actio Flaviensium Nomine*, on the restoration of the schools of Autun). He is said to have interfered by letter on behalf of the Eastern Christians whom Maximinus Daza now began to molest, and this is in itself probable (*de M. P.* xxxvii.). We must remember that there were now four Augusti, Licinius and Maximinus in the East; Maxentius and Constantine in the West. The two latter had for some time acknowledged one another (see below, § VI. *Coins*), and probably by tacit consent the four restricted themselves pretty nearly to the limits which afterwards bounded the four great prefectures. But there was little united action between them, and sole empire was perhaps the secret aim of each. Maxentius now felt himself strong enough to break with Constantine, and declared war against him. The latter determined to take the initative, and crossed the Cottian Alps, by the pass of Mont Genévre, with a force much smaller than that of his opponent. Later historians affirm that the Romans besought him by an embassy to free them from the tyrant (Zon. *Ann.* xiii.; Cedrenus, § 270), and this is probable, for Maxentius, by folly, insolence, and brutality had greatly alienated his subjects. Constantine had allied himself with one of the Eastern Augusti, Licinius, whom he engaged in marriage with his sister Constantia, but had to proceed against the counsels and wishes of his generals and the advice of the augurs (*Pan. de Vict. adv. Maxent.* ii.). After taking Turin, he rested some days at Milan, where he was received in triumph, and gave audience to all who desired it (*ib.* vii.). We may assume that at the same place and time, the spring or summer of 312, occurred also the betrothal of Constantia with Licinius, and the issue of a second edict of toleration to the Christians, that somewhat *hard edict* to which the emperors refer in the more celebrated announcement of 313 (see below § III. B. *Religious Policy*, and cf. Keim, *Uebertritt*, note 11). After taking Verona, Constantine apparently met with little resistance till within a few miles of Rome, though this is not quite consistent with the statement of Lactantius (*de M. P.* xliv.). He had turned the advanced guard of the enemy at Saxa Rubra, close to the Cremera, and then pressed forward along the Flaminian road to the walls of the city itself. With great rashness Maxentius had determined to give battle exactly in front of the Tiber, with the Milvian bridge behind him, about a mile from the gates of Rome. It was Oct. 26, and during the night, according to our earliest authority, Constantine was warned in a dream to draw the monogram of Christ, the ☧, upon the shields of his soldiers, and now, if not before, learnt to invoke the name of Christ to help his arms (*H. E.* ix. 9, 12). For the different accounts of the vision see below, § V. Maxentius, meanwhile, spent the night in sacrifices and divination (Zos. ii. 16, etc.). Next morning the two armies met. That of Maxentius was totally routed, although the praetorians vigorously resisted. The fugitives crowded upon the bridge, and upon the pontoons at its side which Maxentius had devised, according to an almost incredible statement, so as to give way beneath his opponent (Eus. *H. E.* ix. 9; 5, 6; *V. C.* i. 38; Zos. ii. 15). He was himself precipitated into the river, where his body was found the next day. The victor entered Rome in triumph, and was received with great joy (*Pan. de Vict. adv. M.* xix.). He used his victory on the whole with moderation. Eusebius tells us that he set up a statue of himself with a spear terminating in a cross in his right hand, and an inscription to the effect that by this salutary sign (*or* standard) he had restored the Roman senate and people to their ancient glory and freedom (*H. E.* ix. 9; cf. *V. C.* i. 40). He now enlarged and endowed many churches in and near Rome (*V. C.* i. 42), and wrote the letters to Anulinus in behalf of the Catholic church in Africa which led to such important consequences (ap. Eus. *H. E.* x. 5, 7). From these documents it is evident that Constantine had already a strong disposition to favour the Christians, especially the Catholic body. The answers to one of them brought the case of Caecilian and the Donatists to his notice, and involved him in the affairs of the African church. He accepted the title and insignia of Pontifex Maximus, and both were borne by his successors till Gratian (Zos. iv. 36).

Period ii. 312-324. Commencement of the cycle of *Indictions*, Sept. 1, 312. Constantine sole emperor of the West.—Constantine at the age of about 38 was now sole Augustus of the West. Having settled the affairs of Rome, he proceeded early in 313 to meet Licinius at Milan. There the marriage of the latter with Constantia was consummated, and the full edict of toleration, the *Edict of Milan*, was promulgated. The emperors then separated, Licinius to defend himself against Maximinus Daza, Constantine to guard the Rhine. Both were victorious. Licinius soon after became sole master of the East by the death of Maximus at Tarsus (Zos. ii. 17; *de M. P.* xlix.). The latter had followed the edict of Milan, at the behest of the other emperors, by an act of toleration of his own, but of a less full and generous nature. This did not prevent him from taking advantage of the absence of Licinius to invade his territory, who had in consequence to fight Maximinus at Adrianople with a force half as large as that opposed to him. The battle was in many details like that against Maxentius—Licinius was favoured with a mysterious dream, and solemnly put his army under the protection of the God of the Christians, and on the morning of the battle repeated aloud three times with his officers a prayer to the holy and supreme God (*de M. P.* xlvi.). After his victory he entered Nicomedia in triumph, proclaimed the edict of Milan, June 13, and then pursued Maximinus into Cilicia, where he found that last of the persecutors dying a horrible and painful death (*de M. P.* xlix.; Eus. *H. E.* ix. 10, 14). The brothers-in-law were thus raised to an equality of power, and were not likely to remain long at peace. The occasion of their quarrel is obscure. Constantine accused Licinius of fomenting a conspiracy against him. Licinius was defeated and made peace by the cession of Illyricum—*i.e.* of the whole peninsula of which Greece is the extremity. Constantine was not too busy during this campaign to attend to the arrangement of the council of Arles, and to interest himself vehemently in the Donatist disputes. Peace followed for nine years, during which the emperor employed himself with barbarian wars, and with legislation civil and religious, as detailed below. His Decennalia were celebrated at Rome 315, 316, and the triumphal arch dedicated. Two years later his son Crispus, now a young man, and his infant son and nephew Constantine and Licinianus, were raised to the rank of Caesar at Arles (Zos. ii. 20, etc.). His other sons by Fausta were born also in this period, Constantius in 317 and Constans in 323. Licinius meanwhile began to oppress his subjects, especially the Christians. He forbade the synods of bishops, interfered with their worship, and in many cases destroyed their churches (even Julian, *Caes.* p. 315, is unfavourable to Licinius). Constantine was engaged in defending his Danubian frontier from Goths and Sarmatians, and took the Sarmatian king Rausimodes prisoner (Zos. ii. 21). In some of these expeditions he had trespassed across the boundaries of Licinius, and this was the pretext for a quarrel, which was increased by the expostulations of Constantine against the treatment of the Christians, and after some changes of temper on the part of Licinius, an open rupture took place.

The character of the former war was ambiguous. This one was in great measure a religious war or crusade (Eus. *H. E.* x. 9). Before any conflict was fought (it was said) the subjects of Licinius thought they saw the victorious legions of Constantine marching through their streets at midday (*V. C.* ii. 6). The monogram of Christ was now stamped on almost all his coinage (*infra*, § VI.). The labarum became a talisman of victory (*οἱονεί τι νικητικὸν ἀλεξιφάρμακον*, *V. C.* ii. 7). The emperor surrounded himself with Christian priests, and believed himself favoured with visions as he prayed in the tent containing the standard of the cross, and leapt up as if inspired to victory (*ib.* 12). The sentiment of a divine vocation was probably a real one to him, and was fostered by the approbation of the Christians. Licinius, on the very scene of his conflict as a Christian champion with Maximinus, prepared for battle by sacrifice and worship of the gods, against whom he had then fought, and Constantine prepared by prayer and by giving the watchword Θεὸς σωτήρ (*V. C.* ii. 5 and 6; cf. Soz. *H. E.* i. 7 on the perversion of Licinius). The battle of Adrianople, July 3, 323, was a second victory for the Christian arms. Constantine pursued his opponent to Byzantium. Meanwhile Crispus, who had already won his youthful laurels against the Franks, shewed himself most active in command of the fleet, and defeated the admiral Amandus in the Hellespont. This caused Licinius to quit Byzantium for Chalcedon, where he appointed one of his chief officers, Martinianus, as Caesar. Constantine pursued him, and on Sept. 10, after some negotiations, achieved a final victory at Chrysopolis. Licinius, on the entreaty of Constantia, was permitted to retire to Thessalonica; but was not allowed to live above a year longer. Socrates relates that after remaining quiet a short time, "he collected some barbarians, and attempted to repair his defeat" (*H. E.* i. 4; so Zonaras and Niceph. Call.), and Eusebius justifies his execution by the law of war (*V. C.* ii. 19). Zosimus and the heathen historians make it an instance of the emperor's faithlessness (Zos. ii. 28; Victor, *Epit. l.c.*; Eutrop. *Brev.* x. 6), as does also the chronicle of Jerome (ann. 2339, "Licinius Thessalonicae contra jus sacramenti privatus occiditur"). Yet apparently Constantia did not resent the execution of her husband, nor Fausta the death of her father. Constantine was thus master of the whole empire, and his first act was to issue edicts of toleration and favour to the Christians of the East (*V. C.* ii. 24 seq., cited as *Provincialibus Palestinae* and 48 seq. *Prov. Orientis*). He now specially assumed the title of Victor (*νικήτης*) (*V. C.* ii. 19). He had won it by his constant successes against barbarians on the Rhine and Danube and rival emperors from the Tiber to the Bosphorus: his twenty years of empire had brought him from London in the far West to Byzantium, the centre of the Eastern world, and had been years of uninterrupted conquest. He was not unthankful to the Providence which had guided him, nor indisposed to acknowledge that something was due from him in return (*Prov. Pal. V. C.* ii. 28, 29). But his progress had not led him to a victory over himself, or rather his success made him forget his own liability to crime.

Period iii. 324-337. Constantine sole emperor.—The history of the last twelve years of Constantine's reign is of a very different character from that of preceding periods. As sole emperor he loses rather than gains in our estimation. He had no longer a religious cause to fight for nor a dangerous rival to overthrow. The hardness of his character fitted him for a life of strong excitement, but not for the intrigues of an Eastern court and the subtle questions of Eastern theology. His immoderate profusion in building and other expensive operations gained him the name of "spendthrift," and his liberality towards the church was by no means free from the evils that attend prodigal benevolence. But he had no less a providential part to play in the internal history of that church than he had had up to this time in the destruction of her persecutors. As emperor of the West he had been led to interfere in her councils by the African schism, on which his decision was desired by both parties. As monarch also of the East he was brought directly into contact with speculations on points of Christian doctrine which had their origin and home there. He again attempted to realize his idea of unity. Taking as precedent the great council of Western bishops he had summoned at Arles (Aug. 314) in the case of Caecilian, he determined to call together representatives of the whole empire to decide on the doctrines of Arius and the Paschal controversy (see below, § III. 2). To Constantine is due in great measure the holding of the council of Nicaea (June and July, 325). But the success of that great meeting unfortunately filled him with overweening pride. The conclusion of their session fell at the beginning of the 20th year of his reign, and he celebrated the condemnation of Arius as a second triumph (*V. C.* iii. 14). He entertained all the bishops at his table. "The guards," says Eusebius, "kept watch with drawn swords round the vestibule of the palace; the men of God passed through their midst without fear, and entered the inmost parts of the royal dwelling. Some of them reclined by his side, and others were placed on couches on either hand. One might have seemed to picture to oneself an image of Christ's kingdom; the whole thing was more like a dream than a reality" (*ib.* 15). The same writer suggests that the church of the Anastasis, built by Constantine, fulfilled the prophecies about the New Jerusalem (*V. C.* iii. 33). Constantine's interest in the success of the council did not end with its dispersion. He wrote to those concerned in its decrees, strongly enforcing conformity with them. The same feelings led him to compose and deliver theological declamations, and to attempt the conversion of his courtiers. Large crowds attended to listen to the philosophizing prince, who did not spare their faults. But the matter was not one merely of philosophy. It may be, as Burckhardt suggests (p. 454), that he took such opportunities of seriously warning or even denouncing those of his "companions" and "palatines" whose presumption on his favour had become intolerable. The passionate and almost eloquent law of this year, promulgated at Nicomedia, calls upon any one who feels wronged by such officials to declare their grievances freely, and promises personal vengeance on those "who up to this time have deceived us by simulated integrity"; and when Constantine felt himself wronged he did not hesitate to strike (*Cod. Th.* ix. 1, 4 in 325).

After a prolonged sojourn in the East his presence was now required in Rome. He advanced thither by slow stages, arriving about July 8, in time to celebrate the completion of his 20th year of empire, July 25, 326. He left it certainly before the end of Sept.; but in that short space of time all that was tragical in his life seems to have reached its climax. There was much in the city itself to irritate and disturb him. The ancient aristocracy, in the absence of a resident emperor, preserved many of its old heathen traditions. Though he came determined to be tolerant (*Cod. Th.* xv. 1, 3) and desirous of gaining the favour of the senate (*id.* xv. 14; 3, 4), it soon became evident that he was out of harmony with Rome. He would not join in the solemn review of the knights held on July 15, and in their procession and sacrifice to Jupiter Capitolinus; but viewed it contemptuously from the Palatine and ridiculed it to those around him (Zos. ii. 29). Such an action, joined with his Oriental dress and general bearing, seems to have aroused popular indignation against him. Though tempted to revenge himself by force, he was wise enough to refrain. (See esp. de Broglie, *l.c.* ii. c. 5, for the events of this year. He puts together Liban. *Or.* 12, p. 393; *Or.* 15, p. 412, and Chrys. *Or. ad Pop. Antioch.* 21.) But this outburst was followed by far heavier tragedies within his own household. In relating them we have to rely on the vague and inconsistent tales of later writers, those nearest the emperor, Eutropius and Eusebius, being markedly silent. They seem to have originated with divisions, such as easily arose in a family composed of so many different elements. The half-brothers of Constantine, the sons of Constantius and Theodora, naturally took part with their mother's half-sister, Fausta, and her sons. On the other hand, Helena had reason to sympathize with her grandson Crispus, the son of Minervina. Probably it was in connexion with these divisions that Crispus was suddenly arrested and conveyed to an unknown death at Pola in Istria (Amm. Marc. xiv. 11). Niebuhr thought it probable that the accusation of treason against his father, reported by Gregory of Tours (*Hist. Franc.* i. 36), had some foundation of truth. Another, but not an early account, represents Fausta as playing to Crispus the part of Phaedra towards Hippolytus (Zos. ii. 29), and other authors name her as his accuser without specifying the nature of the charge (Vict. *Epit.* 41, Philostorgius, ii. 4. Sozomen, *H. E.* i. 5, implies that the death of Crispus was required of Constantine by others). The young and promising Caesar Licinianus was at the same time unjustifiably put to death (Eutrop. x. 6; Hieron. *Chron. Ann.* 2342). The following satirical distich, attributed to the city prefect Ablavius, was found on the palace doors after the death of Crispus (Sidon. Apollin. *Ep.* v. 8):—

> "Saturni aurea saecla quis requirat?
> Sunt haec gemmea, sed Neroniana."

But he was avenged much more tragically, and at no distant date. (Jerome puts it three years later, the others connect the two events.) Fausta herself was executed in as sudden and as dark a way as Crispus. The complaints of Helena seemed to have aroused her son to this dire act of retribution (Zos. ii. 29; Vict. *Epit.* 41). Later writers represent the empress as guilty of adultery (Philost. ii. 4; Sidon. Apoll. *l.c.*; Greg. Turon. *H. F.* i. 34), and her punishment is said to have been suffocation in the steam of a hot bath.

There cannot, we think, despite the doubts raised by Gibbon, be any real doubt that Crispus and Fausta perished, both probably in 328, by the orders of Constantine, acting as the instrument of family jealousies. The death of Fausta was followed by the execution of many of her friends, presumably those who had taken part against Crispus (Eutrop. x. 4). Popular traditions represent Constantine as tormented by remorse after his delirium of cruelty had passed, and as seeking everywhere the means of expiation; and nothing can be more in harmony with the character of Constantine and of the age than to suppose this. Christian bishops could only urge him to repentance to be followed by baptism. But for reasons which we do not thoroughly know, Constantine put off this important step, and also the baptism of his sons. That he bestowed some possessions on the church at this time, and built or handed over basilicas to it, is very probable. Among the many which claim foundation at his hand we may name the Vatican, which was destroyed to make room for the modern St. Peter's; St. Agnes, which has an inscription referring to his daughter Constantina; and the Lateran, once the palace of Fausta and the seat of the first council about the Donatists, and still the real cathedral of the pope. Probably the pilgrimage of Helena to Palestine in pursuance of a vow, and the "Invention of the Cross," is to be assigned to the time that immediately follows. Constantine gave her every assistance, and authorized her to spend money freely both in alms and buildings (Paulinus of Nola, *Ep.* 11, *ad* Sulpic. Sever.; cf. *V. C.* iii. 47, 3). Possibly he delayed his own Baptism in the hope that he might soon follow her example and be washed in the holy waters of Jordan (*V. C.* iv. 62). He now left Rome never to return, but with the project of founding a new Rome in the East, which should equal if not surpass the old.

The beauty and convenience of the site of Byzantium had long been noticed (cf. Herod. iv. 144); it was the birthplace of Fausta, and its immediate neighbourhood had seen the final defeat of Licinius. The emperor had perhaps already formed the idea of embellishing it and calling it by his own name. He had probably moved a mint thither as early as 325, and used the name (*Constantinopolis*) upon his coins. But now his intention may have been strengthened by his distaste for Rome, and by a superstition that Rome's fall from power was at hand (*Chron. Pasch.* ed. Bonn, p. 517). Other cities had attracted his attention; his final choice was Byzantium. Many stories are told of the ceremonies with which he laid out the plan of the new Rome, enclosing like its prototype the tops of seven hills. De Broglie places the foundation in 328 or 329 (*l.c.* ii. 441). The Christian historians assert that the absence of heathenism from the city was the express desire of the emperor (e.g. *V. C.* iii. 48).

The removal of Sopater perhaps gave room for the power of Helena to reassert itself. She communicated to her son the success of her pilgrimage, and forwarded him certain relics, which he received with great joy. [HELENA.] The death about the same time of his sister Constantia had important consequences. She was much under the influence of Eusebius of Nicomedia, and had in her household an Arian priest, who persuaded her that Arius had been most unjustly treated. She had not courage to speak on the subject herself to her brother, but on her deathbed strongly recommended this priest to him, and he was taken into the imperial family, soon gaining influence over the emperor. The result, it is said, was Constantine's gradual alienation from the Catholics (Socr. i. 25; see de Broglie, c. v., at the end). Meanwhile the building of the new capital went on with great vigour, temples and cities, especially in Greece and Asia Minor, being despoiled to beautify it and to fit it for the residence of a new nobility, some created, and others transferred from Rome. Of the population that gathered into it almost all the pagans and many of the Jews became Christians. The city was solemnly consecrated on May 11, 330, followed by a feast of forty days (Idatius, *fasti*, *Chron. Pasch.* A.D. 330), and the anniversary was long kept as the nativity of Constantinople. It is indeed a very important era, marking the greatest political transformation that the Roman empire underwent. With it were connected the great constitutional changes detailed below, § III. 1, under which grew up the Byzantine spirit with its peculiar character, turbulent, slavish, and unimaginative, but yet capable of endurance tempered with a certain kind of morality.

The years that followed brought Constantine more than ever into the debates of the church. The emperor recalled Arius, but Athanasius, now bp. of Alexandria, refused to receive him. In the middle of his 30th year, 335, Constantine distributed the territories under his dominion between his three sons and two nephews. The eldest, Constantine, received the provinces of his grandfather, Britain, Spain, and Gaul; Constantius, Asia, Syria, and Egypt; Constans, Italy and Africa. Dalmatius, with the title of Caesar, had the large province of Illyricum; and Hannibalian, Armenia and Pontus, with the extraordinary name of *king*. The evidence of coins would lead us to see in this measure a reconciliation of the two branches of the family. The end of Constantine's eventful life was now at hand, and as some of his first military services had been against the Persians, so now he was obliged at its close to prepare for war against that people, though he never actually engaged in it (*V. C.* iv. 57). The labarum had now been for many years the recognized standard of the empire, wherever the emperor was present; and as in the time of the war with Licinius, the monogram of Christ was in these last years largely stamped upon its coins (see § VI.). Constantine made also other preparations for the use of religious service in war, especially of a tent for his own chapel (*V. C.* iv. 56; Socr. i. 18), and he had some time before taught his soldiers, heathen as well as Christian, a common daily prayer, and ordered Sunday to be kept as a holy day (*V. C.* iv. 19 and 20; *L. C.* ix. 10; cf. *Cod. Th.* II. 8, 1, in 321). At Easter 337 he completed and dedicated his great church of the Holy Apostles, in which he desired to be buried. In the week that followed, his health, hitherto extremely good, gave way, and he sought relief in the warm baths at Helenopolis. Feeling his death approaching, he confessed his sins in the church of the martyrs (of the martyr Lucianus ?), and now first received imposition of hands as a catechumen. Then he moved back to the villa Ancyrona, a suburb of Nicomedia (Eutrop. x. 8; Vict. *Caes.* 41), and desired Baptism of the bishops whom he there assembled (*V. C.* iv. 61). He had wished once, he said, to be baptized in Jordan, but God had decided otherwise. He felt that now the blessing he had so long hoped for was offered him. "Let there be no doubt about it," he added, "I have determined once for all, if the Disposer of life and death sees fit to raise me up again to fellowship with His people, to impose upon myself rules of life such as He would approve" (*V. C.* iv. 62, see Heinichen's note). Baptism was administered to him by the Arian prelate Eusebius of Nicomedia (Hieron. *Chron.* ann. 2353). From that moment he laid aside the purple robe, and wore only the white garment of a neophyte. He died on Whitsunday 337, in the 31st year of his reign, dating from July 25, 306.

III. *Religious Policy.*—The great change which makes the reign of Constantine an epoch in church history is the union between church and state, and the introduction of the personal interference of the emperor. The proximate cause of his great influence was the reaction of feeling which took place, when the civil governor, from being a persecutor or an instrument of persecution, became a promoter of Christianity. Something, no doubt, was owing to the teaching of Christian moralists as to submission to the powers that be, and to the general tendency towards a system of official subordination, of which the political constitution of Constantine is the great example. His success in establishing that constitution, without any serious opposition, seems to shew the temper of men's minds at the time, and the absence of individual prominence or independence of thought amongst either followers or opponents. This was true as well of the church as of the state. The great men who have left their mark on church organization and policy had either passed away, like St. Cyprian, or had not yet attained their full powers. The two seeming exceptions are Hosius bp. of Cordova and St. Athanasius. The first had great influence over the emperor, but probably lacked genius, and is but obscurely known to us. Athanasius, though he might have sympathized with some of the wide conceptions of Constantine, never came sufficiently into contact with him to overcome the prejudices raised against him by the courtiers; and the emperor could not really comprehend the importance of the points for which Athanasius was contending. The period, too, of Athanassiu's greatest activity was in the succeeding reign.

Constantine, therefore, was left very much to make his own way, and to be guided by his own principles or impulses. With regard to his religious policy we have an expression of his own, in his letter to Alexander and Arius, which may help us in our judgment of its merits (Eus. *V. C.* ii. 65). Two principles, he said, had guided his actions; the first to unify the belief of all nations with regard to the Divinity into one consistent form, the second to set in order the body of the world which was labouring as it were under a grievous sickness. Such, no doubt, were the real desires of Constantine, but he was too impulsive, too rude in intellect, too credulous of his own strength, to carry them out with patience, wisdom, and justice. We shall arrange the details of this policy under three heads:

(1) *Acts of Toleration.*—During the first period of his reign it is probable that Constantine as well as Constantius Chlorus prevented any violent persecution. His first public act of toleration, of which we have any certain record, was to join together with Licinius in the edict issued by Galerius in 311 (given in *de M. P.* 34 and more diffusely by Eus. *H. E.* viii. 17). The edict acknowledged that persecution had failed, and gave permission to Christians to worship their own God and rebuild their places of meeting, provided they did nothing contrary to good order (contra *disciplinam,* misrendered ἐπιστήμη in Eus.). The death of Galerius followed almost directly, and in the spring or summer of 312 Constantine and Licinius promulgated another edict perhaps not very different from that of Galerius. The text of it is lost. It allowed liberty of worship, but specified certain hard conditions; amongst others that no converts should be made from heathenism; that no sect outside "the body of Christians, the Catholic Church," should be tolerated; that confiscated property should not be restored, except, perhaps, the sites of churches. This edict, issued before the conflict with Maxentius, contrasts strikingly with the much more liberal edict of Milan issued in the spring of 313, which gave free toleration to every religious body. The purport of this edict may be summed up thus: "We have sometime perceived that liberty of worship must not be denied to Christians and to all other men, but whereas in our former edict divers conditions were added, which perhaps have been the cause of the defection of many from that observance, we Constantine and Licinius, Augusti, meeting in Milan, decree that both Christians and all other men soever should have free liberty to choose that form of worship which they consider most suitable to themselves in order that the Divinity may be able to give us and our subjects His accustomed goodwill and favour. We abolish all those conditions entirely. Further for the body of the Christians in particular, all places of meeting which belonged to them, and have since been bought by or granted to others, are to be restored; and an indemnity may be claimed by the buyers or grantees from our treasury; and the same we decree concerning the other corporate property of the Christians. The execution of the law is committed to the civil magistrates, and it is everywhere to be made public." The change of feeling here evinced was more strongly marked in other documents that followed, which more peculiarly expressed the mind of Constantine. The first in order is a letter to Anulinus, proconsul of Africa, giving directions for the execution of the edict, in which the term "Catholic Church" is substituted for that of "body of Christians" (Eus. *H. E.* x. 5, 15). Then follows

another addressed to the same official liberating the clergy "in the Catholic church of which Caecilian is president" from the pressure of public burdens. This concession, at first apparently made to Africa alone, was extended to the whole church in 319 (*C. Th.* xvi. 2, 2). The description of Christianity in the privilege granted to the African church is remarkable "as the religion in which the crowning reverence is observed towards the holiest powers of heaven" (*H. E.* x. 7). The mention of Caecilian and this definition of the Catholic church in the same document was not allowed to pass unchallenged by the Donatists. They presented to Anulinus an appeal, *Libellus Ecclesiae Catholicae criminum Caeciliani*, and a request for a commission of inquiry, both of which he forwarded to the emperor (Aug. *Ep.* 88 (68), 2; Migne, *Const. Mag.* col. 479).

(2) *The Donatist Schism.*—The appeal of the Donatists brought Constantine directly into the heart of church controversies, and was the first occasion of his gradually growing interference. Though his relations with this schism form only an episode in its history, their consequences were important. [DONATISTS.] The results were such a mixture of good and evil as seems inseparable from the union of church and state. The church profited by the development of her system of councils, and a general growth in organization and polity; the emperor gained a nearer insight into the feeling of the church; and the state obtained a most important support. On the other hand must be set the identification of the Catholic with the dominant and worldly church, and the precedent allowed of imperial interference in questions of schism. From the banishment of the Donatists for schism it was no great step to the persecutions of Arians and Catholics for heresy, and not much further to the execution of the Priscillianists by Magnus Maximus.

(3) *The Arian Controversy.*—The relation of the emperor to this great controversy was the result of his last achievement of power. His complete victory over Licinius in 323 brought him into contact with the controversies of his new dominions in the East, just as his victory over Maxentius had led to the Donatist appeals in the West. The first document which connects him with this controversy is a letter to Alexander and Arius (Eus. *V. C.* ii. 64-72; Socr. i. 7 gives only the latter half of it). He expresses his longing for "calm days and careless nights," and exhorts the opponents to reconciliation. The whole had arisen from an unpractical question stirred by Alexander, and from an inconsiderate opinion expressed by Arius. Again and again he insists on the insignificance of the dispute (*ὑπὲρ μικρῶν καὶ λίαν ἐλαχίστων φιλονεικούντων—ὑπὲρ τῶν ἐλαχίστων τούτων ζητήσεων ἀκριβολογεῖσθε*, etc.), shewing in a remarkable manner his own ignorance and self-confidence. This letter was sent by Hosius, but naturally had no effect: though we are ignorant of his proceedings at Alexandria, except that he combated Sabellianism (Socr. iii. 8, p. 394 Migne; Hefele, § 22). Arius seems to have now written a letter of remonstrance, to which Constantine, who was under other influences or in a different mood, replied in an extraordinary letter of violent invective. The detailed history of this time is involved in difficulty, but the expedient of a general council was a natural one both to the emperor and to the church at large. The Meletian schism in Egypt and the Paschal controversy required settlement, and in Constantine's mind the latter was equally important with Arianism. The idea and its execution are ascribed to Constantine without any mention of suggestions from others, except perhaps from Hosius (Sulpic. Sever. *Chron.* ii. 40, "S. Nicaena Synodus auctore illo confecta habebatur"). He sent complimentary letters in every direction, and gave the use of public carriages and litters to the bishops. The year of the council is allowed to be 325, but the day is much debated. Hefele discusses the various dates, and places the solemn opening on June 14 (Councils, § 26). The bishops were arranged round a great hall in the middle of the palace, when Constantine entered to open the proceedings, dressed magnificently, and making a great impression by his stately presence, lofty stature, and gentle and even modest demeanour. This is not the place to trace the course of the discussions that followed. [ARIUS.] Two points are deserving of note—first, the story of his burning the memorials and recriminations of the different parties addressed to him; secondly, his relation to the *ὁμοούσιον*. As to the first, it is said that Constantine brought them into the synod in a sealed packet and threw them into the fire, saying to the bishops: "You cannot be judged by a man like myself: such things as these must wait till the great day of God's judgment," adding, according to Socrates, "Christ has advised us to pardon our brother if we wish to obtain pardon ourselves" (Socr. i. 8, p. 63 Migne; Soz. i. 17). His relation to the *ὁμοούσιον* rests on the Ep. of Eusebius to his own church, in which he gives an account of the synod to his own advantage (Socr. i. 8; Theod. i. 12; Athan. *Decret. Synod. Nic.* 4). He gives the text of the creed which he proposed to the council; and tells us that after it was read no one got up to speak against it, but, on the contrary, the emperor praised it very highly and exhorted everyone to embrace it with the addition only of one word —"consubstantial." He then proceeded to comment on it, declaring that the word implied neither a corporeal substance nor a division of the divine substance between the Father and the Son, but was to be understood in a divine and mysterious sense. Though it is pretty clear that the word *ὁμοούσιος* was in the minds of the orthodox party throughout, they may have hesitated to propose it at first, as its association with Paul of Samosata was provocative of much disputation. Hosius, it may be, suggested to the emperor that the proposition should come from his lips. He must have had some tuition in theological language from an orthodox theologian before he could give the interpretation with which Eusebius credits him. When the creed was finally drawn up, the emperor accepted it as inspired, and with his usual vehemence in the cause of peace proceeded to inflict penalties upon the few who still refused to sign it. He wished even to abolish the name of Arians and to change it into Porphyrians (*Ep. ad Ecclesias*, Migne, p. 506; Socr. i. 9). Later

Eusebius of Nicomedia and Theognis of Nicaea were deposed and banished, as they had not recognized the deposition of Arius, though they had been brought to sign the creed. Constantine indulged particularly in invectives against Eusebius of Nicomedia, accusing him of having stirred up persecution under Licinius, and of deceiving himself at Nicaea (*Ep. ad Nicomedienses c. Eus. et Theognium*, Migne, pp. 519 f., from Gelasius, iii. 2, and the collections of councils). Constantine expressed an immoderate joy at the success of the council, considering it a personal triumph. Eusebius has preserved the letter the emperor then wrote to all the churches (*V. C.* iii. 17-20).

Constantine in his relations to Arianism was obviously the instrument for good as well as for evil. On the one hand, he acted with good intentions, and was able by the superiority of his position to take a wide view of the needs of the church; on the other he was very ignorant, self-confident, credulous, and violent. We know too little of the influences by which he was swayed: how, for instance, Hosius acquired and lost his ascendancy; what Eusebius of Caesarea really did; how Eusebius of Nicomedia obtained influence with the emperor in the last period of his life. We only know that the emperor, in his anxiety above all things for peace, was led to do violent acts of an inconsistent character that made peace impossible; but we must remember that he was living in an age of violent men.

For details of Constantine's relations with heathenism see especially: A. Beugnot, *Hist. de la destruction du Paganisme en Occident*, 2 vols. (Paris, 1835), an important and thoughtful book, unfortunately scarce; and E. Chastel, *Hist. de la destruction du Paganisme dans l'Empire d'Orient* (Paris, 1850)—both crowned by the Academy. Less important is *Der Untergang des Hellenismus und die Entziehung seiner Tempelgüter durch die Christlichen Kaiser*, by Ernst von Lasaulx (München, 1854).

IV. *Character.*—Constantine deserves the name of Great, whether we consider the political or the religious change that he effected, but he belongs to the second, rather than the first, order of great men. Notwithstanding his wide successes, and his tenacious grasp over the empire in which he worked such revolutions, notwithstanding his high sense of his own vocation and the grandeur of some of his conceptions, his personal character does not inspire us with admiration. With many of the impulses of greatness it remained to the last unformed and uncertain, and never lost a tinge of barbarism. He was wanting in the best heathen and Christian virtues; he had little of dignity, cultivation, depth, or tenderness. If we compared him with any great man of modern times it would rather be with Peter of Russia than with Napoleon.

V. *Vision of the* ☧.—The question of the reality of this vision is perhaps the most unsatisfactory of the many problems in the life of Constantine. The almost contemporary account of Lactantius has been already mentioned; *Life*, period i.; from *de M. P.* 44: "Commonitus est in quiete Constantinus ut caeleste signum Dei notaret in scutis atque ita proelium committeret. Fecit ut jussus est et tranversa X littera, summo capite circumflexo, Christum in scutis notat." This took place on the night before the battle of the Milvian bridge. Eusebius's narrative (*V. C.* i. 27-32) contrasts very strikingly with this. He represents Constantine as looking about for some god to whom he should appeal for assistance in his campaign against Maxentius, and as thinking of the god of his father Constantius. He besought him in prayer to reveal himself, and received a sign, which the historian could not distrust on the word and oath of the emperor given to himself many years later. About the middle of the afternoon (for so the words seem to be best interpreted), he saw with his own eyes the trophy of the cross figured in light standing above the sun, and with the letters τούτῳ νίκα attached to it. He and his army were seized with amazement, and he himself was in doubt as to the meaning of the appearance. As he was long considering it night came on, and in sleep Christ appeared to him with the sign that appeared in heaven, and ordered him to make a standard of the same pattern. The next day he gave directions to artificers how to prepare the labarum, which was adorned with gold and precious stones. Eusebius describes it as he afterwards himself saw it. It consisted of a tall spear with a bar crossing it, on the highest point of which was a ☧ encircled with a crown, while a square banner gorgeously embroidered hung from the cross bar, on the upper part of which were the busts of the emperor and his sons. Constantine immediately made inquiries of the priests as to the figure seen in his vision, and determined with good hope to proceed under that protection.

Eusebius nowhere states exactly where or when this took place; his vague expressions seem to place it near the beginning of the campaign. The senate acknowledged an *instinctus divinitatis* and the contemporary panegyrist refers to *divina praecepta* in the campaign with Maxentius.

Another sort of divine encouragement is recorded later by the heathen panegyrist Nazarius in 321, c. 14. "All Gaul," he says, "speaks of the heavenly armies who proclaimed that they were sent to succour the emperor against Maxentius." "Flagrabant verendum nescio quid umbone corusci et caelestium armorum lux terribilis ardebat . . . Haec ipsorum sermocinatio, hoc inter audientes ferebant 'Constantinum petimus, Constantino imus auxilio.'" A distinct incident is added by the late and antagonistic Zosimus, but he tells us nothing of what happened to Constantine, only of a prodigious number of owls which flocked to the walls of Rome when Maxentius crossed the Tiber (ii. 16).

On the Christian side the only independent account of later date seems to be that of Sozomen, i. 3, who afterwards gives the account of Eusebius. "Having determined to make an expedition against Maxentius, he was naturally doubtful of the event of the conflict and of the assistance he should have. While he was in this anxiety he saw in a dream the sign of the cross flashing in the sky, and as he was amazed at the sight, angels of God stood by him and said, 'O Constantine, in this conquer!' It is said too that Christ appeared to him and shewed him the symbol of the cross, and ordered him to make one like it, and to use it in his wars as a mainstay and pledge of victory. Eusebius Pamphili, however," etc. Rufinus also gives both accounts. Later writers repeat one or other of these narratives, adding details of time and place, for which there is no warrant.

That something took place during the campaign with Maxentius which fixed Constantine's mind upon Christ as his protector and upon the cross as his standard, no unprejudiced person can deny. It is equally certain that he believed he had received this intimation by divine favour and as a divine call. Those who give him credit for inventing the whole story out of political considerations totally misapprehend his character. But two questions obviously remain to be discussed: (1) Which account is to be preferred, that of Eusebius or Sozomen? (2) Can we speak of the circumstance as a miracle?

(1) Eusebius's account, being the most striking and resting on the authority of the emperor, has been most popularly received. It is open to obvious difficulties, arising from the silence of contemporaries and the lateness of the testimony. Dr. J. H. Newman, in his *Essay on Ecclesiastical Miracles*, has said perhaps all that can be said for Eusebius. He thinks it probable that the panegyrist of 313 refers to this vision as the adverse omen which he will pass over and not raise unpleasant recollections by repeating (cap. 2)—for the cross would be to Romans generally a sign of dismay, and Constantine (says Eusebius) was at first much distressed in mind with regard to it. The panegyrist also praises Constantine for proceeding "contra haruspicum monita," and asserts "habes profecto aliquod cum illa mente divina, Constantine, secretum, quae, delegata nostri diis minoribus cura, uni se tibi dignetur ostendere?" Optatian also, writing *c.* 326, though he does not mention the vision, speaks of the cross as "caeleste signum." Those modern writers too, who think of a solar halo or parhelion as an explanation, prefer the account of Eusebius. J. A. Fabricius was perhaps the first to offer this explanation (*Exercitatio Critica de Cruce Const. Mag.* in his *Bibliotheca Graeca*, vol. vi.), which is followed by Manso, Milman, Stanley, Heinichen, and others.* The latter in his 24th Meletema gives a useful *résumé* of the literature of the subject. Few historians adopt the alternative, which Schaff accepts, of a providential dream (§ 134). It is difficult in fact to resist the impression that there was some objective sign visible in daylight, such as Eusebius describes, notwithstanding the omission of it by Lactantius.

(2) Can this sign be considered a miracle? The arguments for this conclusion are well put by Newman. He shews that little or nothing is gained by explaining the circumstances as a natural phenomenon or a subjective vision, if once we allow it to be providential; and that *a priori* this seems a fitting juncture for a miracle to have been worked. "It was first a fitting rite of inauguration when Christianity was about to take its place among the powers to whom God has given rule over the earth; next it was an encouragement and direction to Constantine himself and to the Christians who marched with him; but it neither seems to have been intended nor to have operated as a display of divine power to the confusion of infidelity or error" (§ 155). Newman seems to be right in arguing that nothing is gained—in regard to difficulties like this—by transferring the event from the category of miracle to that of special Providence. [J.W.]

* Mr. Whymper has given a good picture of such a phenomenon, observed by him after the fatal accident on the first ascent of the Matterhorn (*Scrambles amongst the Alps*, London, 1871, p. 399).

Constantinus II., the eldest son of Constantine the Great by Fausta, born A.D. 312, was made Caesar in 316 together with Crispus, and his quinquennalia were celebrated by the panegyric of Nazarius in 321. At the death of his father, the empire being redivided, Constantine as the eldest son seems to have claimed Constantinople, but this was overruled, and he was placed over the West. Constantine thus came into contact with St. Athanasius in his exile at Trèves, and at once took him under his protection. [ATHANASIUS.] In 340 Constantine invaded the dominions of Constans and penetrated into Lombardy, where he was killed in a small engagement. His dominions then went to Constans, who thus ruled the entire West. Of his character we know little or nothing. He appears to have been a staunch Catholic, but his attack upon the dominions of his brother Constans does not put his character in a favourable light. His short reign makes him very unimportant. [J.W.]

Constantius I. Flavius Valerius, surnamed **Chlorus** (ὁ Χλωρός, "the pale"), Roman emperor, A.D. 305, 306, father of Constantine the Great, son of Eutropius, of a noble Dardanian family, by Claudia, daughter of Crispus, brother of the emperors Claudius II. and Quintilius. Born *c.* A.D. 250. Distinguished by ability, valour, and virtue, Constantius became governor of Dalmatia under the emperor Carus, who was prevented by death from making him his successor. Diocletian (emperor, A.D. 284-305), to lighten the cares of empire, associated Maximian with himself; and arranged that each emperor should appoint a co-regent caesar. Constantius was thus adopted by Maximian, and Galerius by Diocletian (Mar. 1, A.D. 292). Each being obliged to repudiate his wife and marry the daughter of his adopted father, Constantius separated from Helena, the daughter of an innkeeper, who was not his legal wife but was mother of Constantine the Great, and married Theodora, stepdaughter of Maximian, by whom he had six children. As his share of the empire, Constantius received the provinces Gaul, Spain, and Britain. In A.D. 296 he reunited Britain to the empire, after the rebellion of Carausius, and an independence of ten years. In A.D. 305, after the abdication of Diocletian and Maximian, Galerius and Constantius became Augusti, and ruled together. As the health of Constantius began to fail, he sent for his son Constantine, who was already exceedingly popular, and who was jealously kept by Galerius at his own court. Constantine escaped, and arrived at his father's camp at Gessoriacum (Boulogne-sur-Mer) before embarking on another expedition to Britain. In A.D. 306 Constantius died in the imperial palace at Eboracum (York). He is described as one of the most excellent characters among the later Romans. He took the keenest interest in the welfare of his people, and limited his personal expenses to the verge of affectation, declaring that "his most valued treasure was in the hearts of his people." The Gauls delighted to contrast his gentleness and moderation with the haughty sternness of Galerius. His internal administration was as honourable as his success in war. The Christians always praised his tolerance and impartiality. Theophanes calls him Χριστιανόφρων, a man of Christian principles. He had Christians at his court. Although a pagan, he disapproved of the persecution of Diocletian, and contented himself by closing a few churches and overthrowing some dilapidated buildings, respecting (as the author of the *de Morte Persecutorum* says) *the true temple of God.* Christianity spread in Gaul under his peaceful rule, and at the end of the 4th cent. that province had more than 20 bishops. Eutrop. ix.; Aurel. Vict. *Caes.* 39, etc.; Theoph. pp. 4-8, ed. Paris; Eus. *Vit. Const.* i. 13-21; Lactantius, *de Morte Persecutorum*, 15; Smith, *D. of G. and R. Biog.*; Ceillier, iii. 48, 140, 579. [W.M.S.]

Constantius II., son of Constantius the Great, was the second of the sons of Fausta, born at Sirmium Aug. 6, 317, and emperor 337-361. De Broglie remarks of him (iii. pp. 7, 8), "Of the sons of Constantine he was the one who seemed best to reproduce the qualities of his father. Although very small in stature, and rendered almost deformed by his short and crooked legs, he had the same address as his father in military exercises, the same patience under fatigue, the same sobriety in diet, the same exemplary severity in all that had regard to continence. He put forward also, with the same love for uncontrolled preeminence, the same literary and theological pretensions: he loved to shew off his eloquence and to harangue his courtiers." Victor, *Caes.* 42, speaks well of Constantius: the writer of the *Epitome* credits him with some virtues but speaks of the eunuchs, etc., who surrounded him, and of the adverse influence of his wife Eusebia. Ammianus (xxi. 16) gives an elaborate and balanced character of Constantius which seems to be fair. The Christian writers were naturally not partial to an emperor who leaned so constantly towards Arianism and was such a bitter persecutor of the Nicene faith, and did not scruple to call him Ahab, Pilate, and Judas. St. Athanasius nevertheless addressed him in very complimentary terms in the apology which he composed as late as 356. Constantius was not baptized till his last year, yet interfered in church matters with the most arrogant pretensions.

Period i., 337-350.—*Constantine II., Constans, Constantius II., Augusti.*—On the death of Constantine, Constantius hurried to Constantinople for the funeral of his father. The armies, says Eusebius, declared unanimously that they would have none but his sons to succeed him (*V. C.* iv. 68)—to the exclusion, therefore, of his nephews Dalmatius and Hannibalian. There followed shortly after a general massacre of the family of Constantius Chlorus and Theodora. Many writers, and those of such distinct views as St. Athanasius, Ammianus, and Zosimus as well as Julian, openly charge Constantius with being the author of this great crime, others imply only that he allowed it. Constantine and Constans are in no way implicated in it. A new division of empire followed; for which purpose the brothers met at Sirmium. Speaking generally, Constantine had the west, Constans the centre, and Constantius the East.

From the division of empire between Constans and Constantius we must date the beginnings of separation of the churches. The Eastern church recovered indeed at length from Arian and semi-Arian influences, but the habit of division had been formed and varieties of theological conception became accentuated; then the Roman church grew rapidly in power and independence, having no rival of any pretensions in the West, while in the East the older apostolic sees were gradually subordinated to that of Constantinople, and the whole church was constantly distracted by imperial interference.

Constantius was especially ready to intervene. In 341, in deference to the Dedication Council of Antioch, he forcibly intruded one Gregorius into the see of Alexandria; in 342 he sent his magister equitum, Hermogenes, to drive Paulus from Constantinople, but he did not confirm Macedonius, the rival claimant (Socr. ii. 13). These events took place while St. Athanasius was received with honour at the court of Constans, for whose use he had prepared some books of Holy Scripture (Athan. *Apolog. ad Const.* 4). Constans determined to convoke another oecumenical council, and obtained his brother's concurrence. The place fixed upon was Sardica, on the frontier of the Eastern and Western empires, where about 170 bishops met in 343. Then occurred the first great open rupture between East and West, the minority consisting of Western bishops siding with St. Athanasius, while the Eastern or Eusebian faction seceded to Philippopolis across the border. After the dissolution of the council Constans still attempted to enforce the decrees of Sardica, by requiring of his brother the restoration of Athanasius and Paulus, threatening force if it was refused (Socr. ii. 22; Soz. iii. 20). The shameful plots of the Arian bp. of Antioch, Stephen, against the messengers of Constans were happily discovered, and the faith of Constantius in the party was somewhat shaken (St. Athan. *Hist. Arian. ad mon.* 20; Theod. ii. 9, 10). The pressure of the war with Persia no doubt inclined him to avoid anything like a civil war, and he put a stop to some of the Arian persecutions. Ten months later—after the death of the intruded Gregory—he invited St. Athanasius to return to his see, which Athanasius did in 346, after a curious interview with the emperor at Antioch (see the letters in Socr. ii. 23 from Athan. *Apol. c. Arianos*, 54 f.). Other exiled bishops were likewise restored. In the West, meanwhile, Constans was occupied with the Donatists, whose case had been one of the elements of division at Sardica. He sent a conciliatory mission to Africa, but his bounty was rudely refused by that Donatus who was now at the head of the sect—himself a secret Arian as well as a violent schismatic—with the famous phrase, "Quid est imperatori cum ecclesiâ?" The turbulence of the Circumcellions provoked the so-called "Macarian Persecution"; some of the schismatics were put to death, others committed suicide, others were exiled, and so for a time union seemed to be produced. (Bright, pp. 58-60; Hefele, § 70, *Synod of Carthage.* The history is in Optatus Milev. iii. 1, 2.) Early in the year 350 Constans was put to death, or rather forced to commit suicide, by the partisans of the usurper Magnentius. His death was a great loss to the orthodox party, whose sufferings during the next ten years were most intense.

Period ii., 350-361. *Constantius sole Augustus.*—The usurpation of Magnentius in Gaul seems to have been largely a movement of paganism against Christianity and of the provincial army against the court. It was closely followed by another, that of Vetranio in Illyria. We need not follow the strange history of these civil wars, nor recount in detail how Vetranio was overcome by the eloquence of Constantius in 350, and Magnentius beaten in the bloody battle of Mursa, Sept. 351, that cost the Roman empire 50,000 men. Between these two events Constantius named his cousin, Gallus, caesar and attended the first council of Sirmium. Some time before the battle he must have received the letter from St. Cyril of Jerusalem, describing a cross of light which appeared "on May 7, about the third hour," "above the holy Golgotha and stretching as far as the holy mount of Olives," and seen by the whole city. St. Cyril praises Constantius and reports this marvel as an encouragement to him in his campaign. The genuineness of the letter has however been doubted, especially from the word "consubstantial" appearing in the doxology at the end. At the time of the battle of Mursa Constantius came much under the influence of Valens, the temporizing bishop of the place, who pretended that the victory was revealed to him by an angel, and from this time he appears more distinctly as a persecutor of the Nicene faith, which he endeavoured to crush in the West. His general character also underwent a change for the worse after the unexpected suicide of Magnentius, which put him in sole possession of the empire. It is difficult to say whether he appears to least advantage in the pages of Ammianus or of St. Athanasius. It would take too long to recount the disgraceful proceedings at the council of Arles in 353, where the legates of the new Pope Liberius were misled, or at Milan in 355, when Constantius declared that his own will should serve the Westerns for a canon as it had served the Syrian bishops, and proceeded to banish and imprison no less than 147 of the chief orthodox clergy and laity (*Hist. Ar. ad Mon.* 33, etc.; see De Broglie, iii. p. 263). The most important sufferers were Eusebius of Vercelli, Lucifer of Cagliari, and Dionysius of Milan. Soon after followed the exile of Liberius, and in 355 that of Hosius. All this was intended to lead up to the final overthrow of Athanasius. Early in 356 Syrianus, the duke of Egypt, began the open persecution of the Catholics at Alexandria, and Constantius, when appealed to, confirmed his actions and sent Heraclius to hand over all the churches to the Arians, which was done with great violence and cruelty (*Hist. Ar.* 54). George of Cappadocia was intruded into the see, and Athanasius was forced to hide in the desert. In the same year Hilary of Poictiers was banished to Phrygia.

Meanwhile Constantius had been carrying on a persecution of even greater rigour against the adherents of Magnentius, which is described by Ammianus (xiv. 5), whose history begins at this period. His suspicions were also aroused against his cousin Gallus, whose violence and misgovernment in the East, especially in Antioch, were notorious. The means by which Constantius lured him into his power and then beheaded him are very characteristic (Amm. xiv. 11). At the end of the same year, 355, he determined to make his younger brother, Julian, caesar in his place, putting him over the provinces of Gaul, and marrying him to his sister Helena.

In the church worse things were yet to come: the fall of Hosius, who accepted the creed of the second council of Sirmium, then that of Liberius, the first after torture and severe imprisonment, the second after two years of melancholy exile, both in 357. Of the numerous councils and synods at this time, the most famous and important was that of Rimini in 359, in conjunction with one in the East at Seleucia, when the political bishops succeeded in carrying an equivocal creed approved by the emperor, and omitting the homoousion. Constantius, tired of the long controversy, attempted to enforce unity by imposing the formula of Rimini everywhere, and a number of bishops of various parties were deposed (Soz. iv. 23, 24). In 360 Julian was proclaimed Augustus by his army, and proposed a division of the empire, which Constantius did not accept (Amm. xx. 8). A civil war was impending: Constantius was at first contemptuous, but ere long began to be haunted with fears of death, and caused himself to be baptized by Euzoius, the Arian bp. of Antioch. He expired, after a painful illness, at Mopsucrene at the foot of mount Taurus, Nov. 4, 361 (Socr. ii. 47; Amm. xxi. 15). He was at least three times married: in 352 or 353, after the successful issue of the civil war, to Aurelia Eusebia, a very beautiful, accomplished, and gentle lady, but an Arian, who had great influence with him. She died some time before the usurpation of Julian. Besides his wives, on whom he was accustomed to lean, his chief adviser was the eunuch Eusebius, of whom Ammianus says so sarcastically, "apud quem, si vere dici debet, multum Constantius potuit." He also trusted much to a detestable man the notary Paulus, nicknamed Catena. Another of the same class was Mercurius, called Comes Somniorum. These men, with an army of spies (*curiosi*), organized a reign of terror for three years after the overthrow of Magnentius, especially in Britain, acting particularly on the laws against sacrifice and magic (cf. Liban. *pro Aristophane*, i. p. 430).

Laws in Favour of Christianity.—These will

be found chiefly in the second title of book xvi. of the Theodosian code, headed *de episcopis ecclesiis et clericis*. In 357 the emperor confirmed all the privileges granted to the church of Rome, at that time under the emperor's nominee, Felix, whilst Liberius was in exile. Another rescript of the same year is addressed to Felix, more explicitly guaranteeing the immunity from taxation and forced service. The next law (A.D. 360) refers to the synod of Rimini, and the opinion expressed by various bishops from different parts of Italy, and from Spain and Africa. The last law in the series (in 361) is remarkable, as the heading gives Julian the title of Augustus.

Relations to Heathenism.—The state of things that we have seen in the last years of Constantine continued during his son's reign. There was the same disposition on the part of the empire to put down paganism and the same elements of reaction. In the West, especially in Rome, real heathenism still retained much of its vitality and still swayed the minds of the aristocracy and the populace; in the East the supporters of the old religion were the philosophers and rhetoricians, men more attached to its literary and artistic associations than prepared to defend polytheism as a creed. They were mixed up with another class, the theurgists, practisers of a higher kind of magic which was particularly attractive to Julian.. The following laws from the tenth title of book xvi. of the Theodosian code relate distinctly to heathen sacrifice. Sec. 2, in 341, issued by Constantius, says: "Cesset superstitio, sacrificiorum aboleatur insania," and refers to the law of Constantine noticed above. A year or two later (the date is uncertain and wrongly given in the code), Constantius and Constans ordered the temples in Roman territory to be kept intact for the pleasure of the Roman people, though all "superstition" is to be eradicated; almost at the same time they issued a law to the praetorian prefect inflicting death and confiscation on persons sacrificing. In 353 Constantius forbade the "nocturna sacrificia" permitted by Magnentius: in 356 he and Julian made it capital to sacrifice or worship images. [J.W.]

Cornelius (2), bp. of Rome, successor of Fabianus, said to have been son of Castinus. After the martyrdom of Fabianus in Jan. 250, in the Decian persecution, the see remained vacant for a year and a half. In June, A.D. 251, Cornelius was elected to the vacant post; and, although very reluctantly, he accepted an election almost unanimously made by both orders, during the life of a tyrant who had declared that he would rather see a new pretender to the empire than a new bishop of Rome (Cyprian, *Ep.* lii.). Decius was at that time absent from Rome, prosecuting the Gothic war which ended in his death in the winter of the same year. The persecution of the Christians thus came to an end; but then arose the difficult question of how to treat the *libellatici*, Christians who had bought their life by the acceptance of false certificates of having sacrificed to heathen gods. Cornelius took a line at variance with that of Cyprian and the church of Carthage, which required rigorous penance as the price of readmission, while Rome prescribed milder terms. The difference was kept alive by the discontent of the minority within both the churches. This was represented at Carthage by Novatus, who separated from the church when unable to obtain less harsh terms; in Rome by a man of similar name, Novatian, who was in favour of greater rigour than the church would allow. Novatus crossed the sea to aid Novatian in designs at Rome which must have been directly opposed to his own at Carthage. Mainly by his influence Novatian was consecrated a bishop, and thus constituted the head of a schismatic body in Rome. Eusebius (*Hist. Eccl.* vi. 43) quotes from a letter of bp. Cornelius to bp. Fabius of Antioch, in which he gives an account of his rival, with statistics as to the number of Roman clergy in his day. These were 46 priests, 7 deacons, 7 subdeacons, 42 acolytes, 52 exorcists, 52 readers and ostiarii; 1,500 widows and orphans were provided for by the church.

The Novatianist heresy gave rise to a correspondence between Cyprian and Cornelius. Persecution was revived in Rome by Gallus, and Cornelius, followed by almost the whole church (among whom were many restored libellatics), took refuge at Centumcellae in Etruria. There Cornelius died, and another bishop, Lucius, was at the head of the church when it returned. It is doubtful whether Cornelius died a violent death. Cyprian and Jerome both speak of him as a martyr. He died Sept. 14, 252. His name as a martyr has been found in the Catacombs at some little distance from those of other popes, and in a cemetery apparently devoted almost exclusively to the gens Cornelia, whence De Rossi argues that he probably belonged to that patrician gens (*Roma Sotterranea*, by Northcote and Brownlow, pp. 177-183). [G.H.M.]

Cosmas (1) and **Damianus,** brothers, physicians, "silverless" martyrs. They became types of a class, the ἀνάργυροι, "silverless" martyrs, *i.e.* physicians who took no fees, but went about curing people gratis, and claiming as their reward that those whom they benefited should believe in Christ. They were certainly not earlier than the last quarter of the 3rd cent., and the legends of martyrs of that time, whose fame is known only by popular tradition, seem in many cases to succeed naturally to the place of those heathen myths that were slowest to die. For Hercules, Christopher; for Apollo, Sebastian; for Diana, Ursula; for Proserpine, Agnes. Cosmas and Damian take the place of Aesculapius, in whose story heathenism made the nearest approach to Christianity. The Greeks distinguished three pairs of these brothers. (1) July 1, in the time of Carinus; (2) Oct. 27, Arabs, with their brothers, Anthimus, Leontius, and Euprepius, martyred under Diocletian; (3) Nov. 1, sons of Theodote. (*Menol.*) For the legends connected with them see *D. C. B.* (4-vol. ed.). The names were early inserted in the *Canon of the Mass*. [E.B.B.]

Cosmas (3), surnamed **Indicopleustes** (Indian navigator), a native of Egypt, probably of Alexandria (lib. ii. 114, vi. 264), originally a merchant (lib. ii. 132, iii. 178, xi. 336), who flourished about the middle of the 6th cent. In pursuit of his mercantile business he navigated the Mediterranean, Red Sea, and Persian

Gulf, also visiting India and Ceylon. His travels enabled Cosmas to collect a large store of information respecting not only the countries he visited, but also the more remote lands whose merchants he met. Weary of the world and its gains, he resigned his occupation as a merchant, and, embracing a monastic life, devoted his leisure to authorship, enriching his writings with descriptions of the countries he had visited and with facts he had observed or learned from others. He was no retailer of travellers' wonders, and later researches have proved that his descriptions are as faithful as his philosophy is absurd.

His *Christian Topography* (12 books) is his only work which has survived; the last book is deficient in the Vatican MS. and imperfect in the Medicean. The work was not all published at one time, nor indeed originally planned in its present extent; but gradually grew as book after book was added by him at the request of his friends, or to meet the objections of the opponents of his theory.

The proximate date, A.D. 547, for the earlier books is afforded by the statement (lib. ii. 140) that, when he wrote, 25 years had elapsed since the expedition of Elesbaon, king of the Axiomitae, against the Homeritae, which Pagi *ad ann.* dates A.D. 522. The later works were written about 13 years subsequently. Near the end of lib. x. he speaks of the recent death of Timotheus, patriarch of Alexandria, A.D. 536, and mentions his heretical successor Theodosius, A.D. 537.

The chief design of the *Christian Topography* is "to confute the impious heresy of those who maintain that the earth is a globe, and not a flat oblong table, as is represented in the Scriptures" (Gibbon, *Decline and Fall*, c. xlvii. § i. note i.). The old objections of the Epicureans are revived, and the plane surface is not circular as with Thales, but a parallelogram twice as long as broad, surrounded by the ocean. Its length from E. to W. is 12,000 miles; its breadth from N. to S. 6,000. The parallelogram is symmetrically divided by four gulfs; the Caspian (which joins the Ocean), the Arabian (Red Sea), the Persian, and that of the Romans (Mediterranean). Beyond the ocean, on each side of the interior continent, lies another land, in which is the Garden of Eden. Here men lived till the Deluge, when Noah and his family crossed the intervening flood in the Ark, and peopled the present world. The rivers of Paradise he supposes to run under the sea, Alpheus-like, and to reappear in our earth. The Nile is the Gihon of Eden. The whole area is surrounded by lofty perpendicular walls, from the summit of which the sky stretches from N. to S. in a cylindrical vault, meeting similar vaults at either extremity (lib. iv. 186, 187). Our author divides this huge vaulted chamber into lower, second, and third stories. The dead occupy the nethermost division; the middle compartment is the home of the living; the uppermost, that of the blessed. Heaven is divided from the lower regions by a solid firmament, through which Christ penetrated—and that is the Kingdom of Heaven (lib. iv. 186-188). The vicissitudes of day and night are caused by a mountain of enormous bulk, rising at the N. extremity of the oblong area. Behind this the sun passes in the evening, and reappears on the other side in the morning. The conical shape of the mountain produces the variation in the length of the night; as the sun rises higher above, or sinks down towards the level of the earth. Eclipses are due to the same cause. The round shadow on the moon's disk is cast by the domical summit of the mountain (lib. iv. 188).

The views on cosmography thus propounded, absurd and irrational as they appear to us, were those generally entertained by the Fathers of the church. Pinning their faith on the literal meaning of the words of Scripture according to its traditional interpretation, they deduced a system which had for them all the authority of a divine revelation, any departure from which was regarded as impious and heretical. The arguments by which Cosmas supports his theory are chiefly built on isolated passages of Scripture, as interpreted by the early Fathers. Some, however, are drawn from reason and the nature of the case—*e.g.* the absurdity of the supposition of the existence of antipodean regions, inasmuch as the beings on the other side of the world must drop off, and the rain would fall upwards instead of downwards; while the supposed rotatory motion of the universe is disproved by the disturbance that would be caused to the repose of the blessed in heaven by their being perpetually whirled through space. Cosmas denounces as heretics those who, following the false lights of science, venture to maintain opposite views, and speaks in terms of strongest condemnation of "men who assume the name of Christians, and yet in contempt of Holy Scripture join with the pagans in asserting that the heavens are spherical. Such assertions are among the weapons hurled at the church. Inflamed by pride as if they were wiser than others, they profess to explain the movements of the heavens by geometrical and astronomical calculations" (lib. i. Prolog.). One of his strongest arguments in support of his plan of the universe is drawn from the form of the Tabernacle of Witness, which the words ἅγιον κοσμικόν (Heb. ix. 1) warrant him in considering to have been like Noah's Ark, expressly constructed as an image of the world.

The subjects of the 12 books are: (1) Against those who claim to be Christians, and assert with pagans that the earth is spherical. (2) The Christian hypothesis as to the figure and position of the universe proved from Scripture. (3) The agreement on these points of the O.T. and N.T. (4) A brief recapitulation, and a description of the figure of the universe according to Scripture, and a confutation of the sphere. (5) A description of the Tabernacle and the agreement of the Prophets and Apostles. (6) The magnitude of the sun. (7) The duration of the heavens. (8) Hezekiah's song, and the retrogression of the sun. (9) The course of the stars. (10) *Testimonies of the Fathers*, including 11 citations from the *Festal Epistles of Athanasius*, and other important Patristic fragments. (11) A description of the animals of India, and of the island of Ceylon. (12) Testimonies of heathen writers to the antiquity of Holy Scripture.

Setting aside the absurdities of his cosmographical system, Cosmas is one of the most valuable geographical writers of antiquity. His errors were those of his age, and rest chiefly on his reverence for the traditional interpretation of the Bible. But he was an acute observer and vivid describer, and his good faith is unquestionable. He seems well acquainted with the Indian peninsula, and names several places on its coast. He describes it as the chief seat of the pepper trade, of which he gives a very rational account, and mentions *Mali*, in which Montfaucon recognizes the origin of *Malabar*, as much frequented by traffickers in that spice. He furnishes a detailed account of the island of *Taprobana* (Ceylon), which he calls *Sielidiba*, then the principal centre of trade between China (he calls the Chinese Τζινίτζαι) and the Persian Gulf and Red Sea, where the merchants exchanged their costly wares, and the nations of the East obtained the advantages of commercial intercourse, which rapidly increased and had in his time assumed considerable importance. The connexion between Persia and India was at that time evidenced by the existence of a large number of Christian churches, both on the coast of India and the islands of Socotra and Ceylon, served by priests and deacons ordained by the Persian archbp. of Seleucia and subject to his jurisdiction, which had produced multitudes of faithful martyrs and monks (lib. iii. 179). These congregations appear to be identical with the Malabar Christians of St. Thomas. His 11th book contains a very graphic and faithful description of the more remarkable animal and vegetable productions of India and Ceylon, the rhinoceros, elephant, giraffe, hippopotamus, etc., the cocoa-nut tree, pepper tree, etc.

His remarks on Scripture manifest a not altogether uncommon mixture of credulity and good sense. He mentions that, to the discomfiture of unbelievers, the marks of the chariot wheels of the Egyptians were still visible at Clysma, where the Israelites crossed the Red Sea (v. 194); but he explains the supposed miraculous preservation of the garments of the Israelites (Deut. xxix. 5) as meaning no more than that they lacked nothing, since merchants visited them from adjacent countries with clothing and with the wheat of which the shewbread was made (v. 205). The catholic epistles he plainly relegates to the "Amphilegomena," making the erroneous statement that such was the universal ancient tradition and that no early expositor comments upon them. The Ep. to the Hebrews he ascribes to St. Paul, and asserts that it, as well as the Gospel of St. Matt., was rendered into Gk. by St. Luke or St. Clement. Cosmas preserves a monument of very considerable historical value, consisting of two inscriptions relating to Ptolemy Euergetes, B.C. 247-222, and an unnamed king of the Axumitae, of later date. These were copied by him from the originals at the entrance of the city of Adule, an Aethiopian port on the Red Sea; the former from a wedge-shaped block of basanite or touch-stone, standing behind a white marble chair, dedicated to Mars and ornamented with the figures of Hercules and Mercury, on which the latter inscription was engraved. Notwithstanding the different localities of the inscriptions and the fact that the third person is used in the former, the first in the latter, the two have been carelessly printed continuously and regarded as both relating to the conquests of Ptolemy, who has been thus accredited with fabulous Aethiopian conquests. (So in Fabricius, *Bibl. Graec.* lib. iii. 25; cf. Vincent, *Commerce*, ii. 533-589.) They were first distinguished from each other by Mr. Salt (*Voyages and Travels to India*, etc., 1809, vol. iii. 192; *Travels in Abyssinia*, 1814, p. 412), and are printed with full comments by Böckh (*Corpus Inscript. Graec.* 1848, vol. iii. fasc. ii. 508-514). The inscription relating to Ptolemy describes his conquest of nearly the whole of the empire of the Seleucidae, in Asia, which, says Dean Vincent (*Ancient Commerce*, ii. 531), "was scarcely discovered in history till this monument prompted the inquiry, and was then established on proofs undeniable." Cf. Chishull, *Antiq. Asiat.* p. 76; Niebuhr, *Vermischte Schriften*, p. 401; Letronne, *Matériaux pour l'hist. du Christianisme en Egypte*, etc. (1832), p. 401; Buttmann, *Mus. der Alterthumsw.* ii. 1, p. 105.

A full account of this work is given by Photius (Cod. xxxvi.), under the inappropriate title Ἑρμηνεία εἰς Ὀκτάτευχον, but without the author's name. From this, Fabricius very needlessly questions whether the author was really named Cosmas, or whether that was an appellation coined to suit the subject of the work, like that of Joannes Climacus. Photius censures the homeliness of the style, which he considers hardly to approach mediocrity. But elegance or refinement of diction is not to be expected from a writer, who, in his own words (lib. ii. 124), destitute of literary training and entangled in business, had devoted his whole life to mercantile pursuits, and had to contend against the disadvantages of very infirm health and weak eyesight, incapacitating him for lengthened study. We learn from his own writings that Cosmas also wrote:

(1) A *Cosmographia Universalis*, dedicated to a certain Constantine (lib. i. 113), the loss of which is lamented with tears by Montfaucon.

(2) A work on the motions of the universe and the heavenly bodies, dedicated to the deacon Homologus (lib. i. 114, vii. 274).

(3) Ὑπομνήματα *on the Canticles*, dedicated to Theophilus (lib. vii. 300).

(4) Exposition of the more difficult parts of the Psalms (Du Cange, *Gloss. Graec.* s.v. Ἰνδικοπλευστής; *Bibl. Coislin.* p. 244).

(Montfaucon, *Collect. Nov. Pat. Gk.* (Paris, 1706), vol. ii. 113-346; Gallandi, *Bibl. Vet. Patr.* (Ven. 1765), vol. ix.; Cave, *Hist. Lit.* i. 515; Fabric. *Bibl. Graec.* lib. iii. 25; Vincent, *Commerce*, ii. 505-511, 533-537, 567; Bredow, *Strabo*, ii. 786-797; Thevenot, *Coll. des voyages*, vol. i.; Gosselin, *Géogr. syst. des Grecs*, iii. 274; Mannert, *Einleit. in der Geogr. d. Alten*, 188-192; Charton, *Voyages*, vol. ii.) [E.V.]

Cyprianus (1) Thascius Caecilius. *Name.*—He is styled Thascius Cyprianus by the proconsul (*Vit. Pontii*), and styles himself "Cyprianus qui et Thascius" in the singular heading of *Ep.* 66. He took the name Caecilius, according to Jerome (*Cat. Ill. Vir.* v.), from the presbyter who converted him, and is called Caecilius Cyprianus in the proscription (*Ep.* 66).

Cyprian was an orator, and afterwards even

a teacher of rhetoric ("in tantam gloriam venit eloquentiae ut oratoriam quoque doceret Carthagini," Hieron. *Comm.* Jon. c. 3, and cf. Aug. *Serm.* 312, § 4). It is not quite clear what is meant by Jerome in speaking of him as a former "adsertor idololatriae," and Augustine as "having decorated the crumbling doctrines of demons." His style is very polished, and, as Augustine points out, became more simple and beautiful with time, and (as his critic believed) with the purer taste of Christianity. He edited for Christians the phraseological dictionary of Cicero (see Hartel's praef. *ad fin.*). His systematic habits and powers of business contributed greatly to his success as the first of church organizers. His address was dignified, conciliatory, affectionate; his looks attractive by their grave joyousness. He never assumed the philosopher's pall, which Tertullian his "master" maintained to be the only dress for Christians; he thought its plainness pretentious. Augustine speaks of the tradition of his gentleness, and he never lost the friendship of heathens of high rank (Pont. 14). He was wealthy, his landed property considerable, and his house and gardens beautiful (Pont. *Vit. ad Don.* i. xv. xvi.).

His conversion was then important in the series of men of letters and law who were at this time added to the church, and who so markedly surpass in style and culture their heathen contemporaries. Pearson rightly sets aside the inference of Baronius (from De Dei gratia) that Cyprian was old at his conversion, but that he was so seems to be stated, however obscurely, by Pontius (c. 2, "adhuc rudis fidei et cui nondum forsitan crederetur supergressus vetustatis actatem"). Christian doctrines, especially that of regeneration, had previously excited his wonder, but not his derision (*ad Don.* iii. iv.). He was converted by an aged presbyter, Caecilian. During his catechesis he analysed and conversed with the circle about him on Scripture Lives, devoted himself to chastity, and sold some estates and distributed the proceeds to the poor. He composed, in his *Quod Idola dii non sint*, a Christian assault on Polytheism, freely compiling the 1st and 2nd sections of his tract from Minucius, § 20-27, § 18, § 32, and his 3rd section from Tertullian's *Apology*, § 21-23, with some traces of Tert. *de Anima naturaliter Christiana.* A comparison of this pamphlet with the originals well illustrates his ideal of style. He mainly retains the very language, but erases whatever seemed rugged, ambiguous, or strained. He maintains a historical kernel of mythology, points out the low character of indigenous Roman worship; illustrates the activity of deluding daemons from the scenes at exorcisms, of which, however, he scarcely seems (as Tertullian does) to have been an eye-witness. He contrasts this with the doctrine of Divine unity, which he describes nobly, but illustrates infelicitously. The history of Judaism, its rejection of its Messiah, and the effects which Christianity is producing in the individual and commencing on society bring him to his new standpoint. He is perhaps the first writer who uses the continuous sufferings of believers as evidence of their credibility. This restatement and co-ordination of previous arguments was probably not ineffective, but as yet Cyprian exhibits no conception that Christianity is to be a world-regenerating power. He deliberately excludes providence from history (*Quod Id.* v.).

At the Easter following, the season most observed in Africa for this purpose, he was probably baptized, and to the autumn after we refer the *ad Donatum*, a monologue, a brief Tusculan held in his own villa, on *The Grace of God.* It already exhibits Cyprian not as a spiritual analyst or subtle theologian, but irrefragable in his appeals to the distinctly New Life which has appeared in the world, amid the contemporary degradations—the repudiation of the responsibility of wealth, the disruption of the client-bond, the aspect of the criminal classes, the pauperization of the mass, and the systematic corruption by theatre and arena. For the present, however, withdrawal from the world into Christian circles is the only remedy in which he can hope. "Divine Grace" is an ascertained psychological fact, and this, though as yet narrow in application, is the subject of the treatise.

He soon after sold, for the benefit of the poor, his horti, which some wealthy friends bought up afterwards and presented to him again. Meantime he resided with Caecilian. We can only understand the expression of Pontius (who lived similarly as a deacon with Cyprian), "erat sane illi etiam de nobis contubernium . . . Caeciliani," to mean that he was at that time "of our body," the diaconate. We find other instances of the closeness of this bond. Baronius and Bp. Fell are equally inexcusable in understanding what is said of Caecilian's family and of Job's wife as having any bearing upon the question of Cyprian's celibacy. There is no indication of his having been married. Caecilian at his death commended his family to him, although not as officially curator or tutor, which would have contradicted both Christian and Roman usage.

His Ordination.—His activity while a member of the ordo or concessus of presbyters is noticed, but he was yet a neophyte when he became bishop. The step was justified on the ground of his exceptional character, but the opposition organized by five presbyters was now and always a serious difficulty to him. The Plebes would listen to no refusal, and frustrated an attempt to escape. He subsequently rests his title (*Ep.* 43, *Ep.* 66, *Vit.*) on their suffrages, and on the "judicium Dei," with the *consensus* of his fellow bishops. In ordinary cases he treats the *election* by neighbour bishops as necessary to a valid episcopate (*Ep.* 57, v.; *Ep.* 59, vii.; *Ep.* 66). From this time Cyprian is usually addressed both by others and by the Roman clergy as *Papa*, though the title is not attributed to the bp. of Rome until long after. An earlier instance of the use of the name occurs at Alexandria, but probably the first application of the name is traceable to Carthage. Some time between July 248 and April 249 Cyprian became bishop, a few months before the close of the "thirty years' peace" of the church.

His *Theory of the Episcopal Office* seems to have been his own already, and as it supplies the key to his conception of church government may be stated at once. The episcopate succeeded to the Jewish priesthood * (*Epp.* 8, i.; 69, viii.; 65; 67, i.; *Testim.* iii. 85); the bishop was the instructor (*Ep.* 50, xi.; *Unit.* x.) and the judge (*Ep.* 17, ii.). In this latter capacity he does nothing without the information and advice of presbyters, deacon, and laity. He is the apostle of his flock (*Ep.* 3, iii.; 45; 66, iv.) by direct succession, and the diaconate is the creation of his predecessors. The usual parallel between the three orders of the Christian and Jewish ministry differs entirely from that drawn by Cyprian.

The stress laid on the responsibility of the laity is very great. Though the virtue of the office is transmitted by another channel, it is they who, by the "aspiration of God," address to each bishop his call to enter on that "priesthood" and its grace, and it is their duty to withdraw from his administration if he is a "sinner" (*Ep.* 67). The bishops do not co-opt into or enlarge their own college. Each is elected by his own Plebes. Hence he is the embodiment of it. "The bishop is in the church and the church in the bishop." They have no other representatives in councils; he is naturally their "member." These views appear fully developed in his first epistle, and in the application of texts in his early *Testimonia*; it is incredible that they should have been borrowed from paganism, and unhistorical to connect them with Judaizers. They are (although Cyprian does not dwell on this aspect) not incompatible with a recognition of the priesthood of the laity as full as that of Tertullian. The African episcopate had declined in character during the long peace; many bishops were engaged in trade, agriculture, or usury, some were conspicuously fraudulent or immoral or too ignorant to instruct catechumens and avoid using heretical compositions in public prayers (*de Laps.* 4; *Ep.* 65, iii.; *Auct. de Rebapt.* ix.; Aug. *c. Don.* vii. 45; *Resp. ad Epp.* [Sedatus]). Similarly among the presbyters strange occupations were possible (Tert. *de Idol.* cc. 7-9) and unmarried deacons shared their chambers with spiritual sisters who maintained their chastity to be unimpaired. The effect of the persecution was salutary on this state of things, and was felt to be so. To the eighteen months of "peace" which remained belong his *Epp.* 1-4, and the treatise on the dress of virgins, which answers to his description of his employment as "serving discipline" during that interval. In three of the letters his authority is invoked beyond his diocese, and wears something of a metropolitan aspect. Otherwise it is to be noticed that the African bishops rank by seniority. To these letters Mr. Shepherd has taken objections, which, if valid, would be fatal to the genuineness of much of the Cyprianic correspondence; but a rigorous investigation of those objections is conclusive in favour of the epistles.

De Habitu Virginum.—Many Christian women lived, as a "work of piety," the self-dedicated life of virgins in their own homes. Tertullian had killed the fashion of going unveiled, which some had claimed as symbolic of childlike innocence, yet with the avowed object of rendering their order attractive. Vanity, sentiment, and the sense of security were still mischievous elements, and Cyprian writes mainly against the extravagant fashions, half Roman, half Tyrian, in which the wealthier sisters appeared. His book, though in language drawing largely from Tertullian's treatise of similar title, resembles much more in matter and aim his *Cultus Feminarum.* Cyprian is here so minute and fastidious in his reduction of the violent rhetoric of Tertullian that this might almost pass for a masterly study of writing; and Augustine regards it as a very perfect work, drawing from it illustrations both of the "grand" and of the "temperate" style (Aug. *de Doctrina Christiana,* bk. iv. pp. 78, 86). In estimating the probable influence of this booklet on ascetic life, it is not satisfactory to find that the incentives used are partly low and partly overstrained—the escape from married troubles, espousals with Christ, higher rank in the resurrection; while efficiency in works of charity, the power of purity, self-sacrifice and intercession, are not dwelt upon.

Testimonia ad Quirinum, libb. iii.—These, though not certainly belonging to this time, are more like his work now than afterwards. They are texts compiled for a layman (*filius*). I. in 24 heads on the succession of the Gentile to the Jewish church. II. 30 heads on the Deity, Messiahship, and salvation of Christ. III. 120 on Christian duty. The skill and toil of such a selection are admirable. The importance of the text in elucidation of the Latin versions then afloat is immense, and Hartel is quite dissatisfied with what he has been able to contribute to this object (Hartel, Praefat. *Cyp.* p. xxiii.).

Decian Persecution.—Cyprian's conviction of the need of external chastisements for the worldliness of the church was supported by intimations which he felt to be supernatural. The edict which began to fulfil them in the end of A.D. 249 aimed at effecting its work by the removal of leaders, and at first fixed capital penalties on the bishops only (Rettberg, p. 54; *Ep.* 66, vii.). Monotheism, even when licensed (like Judaism), had an anti-national aspect, and Christianity could not be a *licita religio,* simply because it was not the established worship of any locality or race. In this, and in the fact that torture was applied to procure not (as in other accusations) confession but denial of the charge (*Apol.* ii.; Cyp. *ad Demet.* xii. 11), in the encouragement of delation as to private meetings (*Dig.* xlviii. 4; *Cod.* ix. 8, iv. vi. vii.), and in the power given to magistrates under standing edicts to apply the test of sacrifice at any moment to a neighbourhood or a person, lay the various unfairnesses of which Tertullian and Cyprian complain. Dionysius of Alexandria, and with him Origen, Gregory Thaumaturgus, Maximus of Nola, Babylas of Antioch, Alexander of Jerusalem, Fabian of Rome, were all attacked, the last three martyred. There was no fanaticism of martyrdom as yet. It seemed wrong to expose a successor to instant death, and no bishop was elected for 16 months at Rome. Like the former three, Cyprian placed himself (before the end of Jan.; Lipsius, *Röm. Bisch.*

* The bishop alone is called *sacerdos* throughout the Cyprianic correspondence. The presbyter also answers to the Levitic tribe; each congregation (diocese) to "the congregation of Israel."

Chronol. p. 200) out of reach, and, with the same determination with which he afterwards pronounced that his time was come, refused concealment. The grounds for his retirement, consistently stated by himself, are the necessity of continuing the administration (*Ep.* 12, i. v. vi.), the danger which at Carthage he would have attracted to others (*Epp.* 7, 14), the riots it would have aroused (*Ep.* 43), and the insistence of Tertullus (*Epp.* 12, 14). The Cyprianic epistles of this period, passing between the Roman presbyters, the Carthaginian bishop and certain imprisoned presbyters (Moyses, Maximus), deacons (Rufinus and Nicostratus), laymen, and particularly an imperfectly educated Carthaginian confessor Celerinus (whose ill-spelt letters *Epp.* 21 and 22 are extant), present, when worked out, a tesselated coherence with each other and with slight notices in Eusebius (vi. 43), which is absolutely convincing as to the originality and genuineness of the documents.

The Lapsi.—Five commissioners in each town and the proconsul on circuit (*Epp.* 43, iii.; 10; 56) administered the Decian edict. The sufferings by torture, stifling imprisonments, and even fire (14, 21) were very severe (*Ep.* 22). Women and boys were among the victims. Exile and confiscation were employed. In the first terror there was a large voluntary abjuration of Christianity, whether literally by "the majority of his flock" (*Ep.* 11) may be uncertain, but Cyprian felt himself "seated in the ruins of his house." Scenes of painful vividness are touched in, but these must be passed by. Many of the clergy fell or fled, leaving scarcely enough for the daily duty of the city (*Epp.* 34, iv.; 40; 29), as did many provincial bishops (*Epp.* 11, 59). Different classes of those who conformed were the Thurificati, Sacrificati (the more heinous) (*Ep.* 59), and LIBELLATICI (*q.v.* in *D. C. A.*, as also LIBELLI), whose self-excision was less palpable. Of this class there were some thousands (*Ep.* 24).

Formation of a General Policy.—Cyprian from his retirement guided the policy of the whole West upon the tremendous questions of church communion which now arose. (1) Indifferentism offered the lapsed an easy return by means of indulgences from, or in the names of, martyrs. (2) Puritanism barred all return. The Roman clergy first essayed to deal with the question in conjunction with the clergy of Carthage independently of Cyprian, whose absence they invidiously deplore (*Ep.* viii.). Their letter was returned to them by Cyprian himself, with some caustic remarks on its style (which are singularly incorrect; see Hartel's *Praefatio*, xlviii.) as well as on the irregularity of the step. After this an altered tone, and Novatian's marked style, is discernible in their letters (*Epp.* 30 and ? 36).

The granting of indulgences (not by that name) to lapsed persons, by confessors and martyrs, which had been first questioned and then sharply criticised by Tertullian (*ad Mart.* 1; *de Pudic.* 22), grew very quickly under the influence of some of those clergy who had opposed Cyprian's election. The veneration for sufferers who seemed actually to be the saviours of Christianity was intense, and many heads were turned by the adulatory language of their greatest chiefs (cf. *Ep.* x. 24). Their *libelli* would presently have superseded all other terms of communion.

A strange document (*Ep.* 23) is extant in the form of an absolution to "all the lapsed" from "all the confessors," which the bishops are desired to promulgate. Rioters in some of the provincial towns extorted communion from their presbyters (*Ep.* 27, iii.). At Rome itself the influence of Novatian with the confessors created a tendency to strictness rather than indulgence, and there were no such disorders, but they prevailed elsewhere (*Epp.* 27, 31, 32; *Ep.* 30, iv. 4; 30, vii.). Cyprian at once proposed by separate letters to his clergy and laity (to whom he writes with warm confidence), to various bishops, and to the Roman confessors and clergy (*Epp.* 15, 16, 17, 26), one general course of action: to reserve all cases of lapsed, without regard to the confessors' libelli, until episcopal councils at Rome and Carthage should lay down terms of readmission for the deserving (*Ep.* 20; 55, iv.); then the bishops, with clergy and laity (*Ep.* 17, iv.; *Ep.* 31) assisting, to investigate each case; public acknowledgment to be made, readmission to be by imposition of hands by bishop and clergy. Meantime the acts of the confessors to be recognized (*Ep.* 20, iii.) so far as that persons in danger, who might hold a *libellus*, should be readmitted by any presbyter, or *in extremis* by a deacon (*Epp.* 18, 19). All others to be exhorted to repentance, and commended with prayer to God at their deaths. The grounds he urged were—(1) the wideness of the question, which was too large for individual discretion (*totius orbis*, *Ep.* 19, iii. cf. 30, vi.). (2) That if restored at once the lapsed would have fared better than those who had borne the loss of all for Christ. These principles are developed also in the *de Lapsis*, which, however, is not quite as M. Freppel describes it, "a résumé of the letters," but a résumé of the modified views of Cyprian a little later. In M. Freppel's Sorbonne Lectures (*St. Cyprien*, pp. 195-221) may be studied with profit the Ultramontane representation of this scheme as equivalent to the modern indulgence system, backed by assertions that the Roman church "indicated to Carthage the only course," which Cyprian "fully adopted." All, however, that the Roman clergy had recommended was mere readmission of sick penitents, without any conception of a policy, or of the method by which it could be worked. These are developed step by step in *Epp.* 17, 18, 19, and communicated to the Roman church (*Ep.* 20). In replying through Novatian (*Ep.* 30, see 55 v.) the Roman presbyters re-state and adopt them (cf. *Ep.* 31, vi. 41).

Temper in Carthage.—Through the earlier part of the above section of correspondence is perceptible a reliance on the laity. The clergy do not reply to his letters (*Ep.* 18), they defer to the *libelli*, or use them against him (*Ep.* 27). In *Ep.* 17 he entreats the aid of the laity against them. When the concurrence of the African and Italian episcopate is obtained (*Ep.* 43, iii.), and that of Novatian and the Roman clergy and confessors (*Epp.* 30, 31), assuming a stronger tone (*Ep.* 32) with his own clergy, he requires them to circulate the whole correspondence, which is done (*Ep.* 55.

iv.), and excommunication is announced against any who should allow communion except on the agreed terms.

About Nov. 250, persecution relaxed (possibly owing to the Gothic advance in Thrace), and though it was still unsafe for Cyprian to return, he endeavoured to deal with the distress of sufferers who had lost their all, and to recruit the ranks of the clergy and allay the excitement among the lapsed, by a commission (vicarii) of three bishops, Caldonius, Herculanus, Victor, and two presbyters, Numidicus and Rogatian (*Epp.* 41, 26).

Declaration of Parties.—The excitement on the question of the lapsed is evinced by two classes of stories then afloat as to judgments following on unreconciled offences and on presumptuous communion (*de Lapsis*, 24, 25, 26). Cyprian employed both to urge delay, but they do not emanate from his party of moderation. At Carthage the party of laxity became prominent; at Rome, that of exclusiveness.

(1) *The party of laxity* was composed of confessors, spoiled by flattery (*de Laps.* 20), fashionable *lapsi*, who declined all penance (*Laps.* 30), influential ones, who had forced certain clergy to receive them, but also some clergy who united against Cyprian's policy with the five presbyters who had from the first resisted him. Of these, three were undoubtedly DONATUS, Gordius, Fortunatus (Maran. *Vit. Cyp.* § xvii.; Rettberg, pp. 97–112). That the fourth was Gaius of Didda, or Augendus, is but a guess. The principal in position and ability was the presbyter NOVATUS (Pearson's Jovinus and Maximus, and Pamelius's Repostus and Felix are impossible). That Cyprian's five original opponents still acted against him is shewn by "olim secundum vestra suffragia" (*Ep.* 43, v.), though in 43, ii. he seems only to conjecture their complicity with FELICISSIMUS, whom Novatus had associated with himself as deacon in managing a district called Mons (possibly the Bozra itself) (*Epp.* 52, 59, 36). Cyprian complains of not having been consulted in this appointment, which, owing to the then position of the deacons, gave the party control of considerable funds. All the arrangements hitherto agreed on were disregarded by them, Cyprian's missives unanswered, and his commission of relief treated as an invasion of the diaconal office of Felicissimus, who announced, while other *lapsi* were at once received into communion, that whoever held communications with or accepted aid from the commission would be excluded from communion or relief from the Mons (*Ep.* 43, ii.; *Ep.* 41, where the conjecture *in morte*, or references to *Monte* in Numidia, or to the *Montenses* at Rome, who were Donatists, and were never (anciently) confused with the Novatianists or called Montanistae, are absurd; though Hefele, *Novatianischer Schisma*, ap. Wetzer and Welte, K. Lexik. and *Conciles*, t. ii. p. 232, countenances these confusions). It is with the name of Felicissimus that the lax party is generally connected (*Ep.* 43, iii. v. vii.), and he, with a fellow-deacon Augendus, a renegade bishop Repostus, and certain others, the five presbyters not among them, was presently excommunicated. There is no evidence, nor any contemporary instance, to warrant the belief that Novatus *ordained* Felicissimus deacon (see the MSS. reading *Ep.* 52, "satellitem suum diaconum constituit," which Hartel has unwarrantably departed from), nor is there any such appearance of presbyterian principles in this party, as divines of anti-episcopal churches, Neander, Rettberg, d'Aubigné, Keyser, have freely assumed. The party were in episcopal communion, took part in the episcopal election at Carthage, presently elected a new bishop for themselves, and procured episcopal consecration for him. When Novatus visited Rome, he threw himself into the election then proceeding, and, after opposing the candidate who was chosen, procured episcopal consecration for his nominee there also. Felicissimus too must have been a deacon already, or he could not have involved himself and Novatus in the charge of defrauding the church (*Epp.* 52, i.; 50, i.).

(2) *The Puritan Party.*—The strength of the Puritans, on the other hand, was in Rome. A group of confessors there, of whom the presbyters Moyses and Maximus were the chief, united with Novatian and the clergy in approving Cyprian's proposals. The modification of discipline by martyrs' merits was never countenanced here (*Ep.* 28, ii.); nevertheless, Moyses, before his death (which probably happened on the last day of 250), had condemned the extreme tendencies of Novatian towards the non-reconcilement of penitents (see Valesius's correct interpretation of Eus. vi. 43, and Routh, *R. S.* iii. p. 81). While Cornelius at Rome and Cyprian were moving towards greater leniency than their resolutions had embodied, Novatian, without questioning the hope of salvation for the lapsed, was now for making their exclusion perpetual, and teaching that the purity of the church could not otherwise be maintained.

The earthly conditions of the invisible and visible church had not yet been discussed as the Donatists compelled them to be, and Novatian's growing error, though in the present application it completely severed him from Cyprian and the church, was not in principle different from that which Cyprian (though without producing a schism) held in relation to Baptism. Early in A.D. 251 the Roman confessors were liberated; they lost whatever influence Moyses had exercised on them; they had been drawn towards Novatian, and when Novatus, arriving from Carthage, attached himself to this party, because, though its puritanism was alien to his own practices at home, it was the only opposition existing in the capital which threatened to overthrow the Cyprianic side, they were at once organized into a party to secure the election of a bp. of Rome who would break with Cyprian. The moment for election was given by the absence of Decius and his leading officers on the frontier or in Illyria on account of the base alliance of Priscus with Cniva, and the revolt of Valens. The party of moderation, however, prevailed and secured the election of Cornelius, and consecrated him in spite of himself by 16 bishops * ("vim" *Ep.* 55, vii.).

* Lipsius has shewn conclusively that the consecration of Cornelius was about Mar. 5 (*Chronol. d. römischen Bischöfe*, p. 18); the usual statement that it was in June introduces endless contradictions into

First Council.—Cyprian returned to Carthage after Easter (Mar. 23) from his 14 months' absence (biennium), which seems to have been prolonged by a fear of the "faction" (*Ep.* 43, i.) rekindling persecution (*Ep.* 55, v.) by some demonstration. The bishops of the province met in April for the first council, held in Carthage, for half a century [Agrippinus], but the discussion on the lapsed was postponed by letters from Rome, which Cyprian laid before them, viz. Cornelius's announcement of his election (*Ep.* 45, ii.) and a temperate protest against it from Novatian (45, iv.) (Maran, p. lx. misinterprets this against the sense of Baluze, whom he edits). The protest was soon followed by a mass of charges, which Cyprian declined to submit to the council. This was excellent policy, but at the same time a curious exercise of personal authority in that earliest type of returning freedom—the church council. At the same time he made them dispatch two of their number, Caldonius and Fortunatus, to Rome, to report. Caldonius was instructed to procure attestations of the regularity of the ordination of Cornelius from bishops who had attended it (*Ep.* 44 and cf. 45, i.). Meantime, communications with the Roman church were to be addressed only to the clergy and not to Cornelius. (The statement of Lipsius, p. 204, on *Ep.* 45, v., is too strong.) He was also to lay before the clergy and laity, so as to guard them against clandestine influence, the whole correspondence about Felicissimus (*Epp.* 41, 43, 45, v.). The council, then reverting to its programme, was obliged to dispatch first the question of Felicissimus, since, if he were justified in his reception of the lapsed, no terms of communion need be discussed; but if the main issue went against him they could not on such *ex post facto* ground deal with him disciplinarily. His offence consisted not in his theory, which might conceivably be correct, but in his readmitting people whose cases had been by due notice reserved. Cyprian, to his honour and like a good lawyer, was not present during the trial of his opponent, who was condemned. He does not employ the first person in relating it (*Ep.* 45, v.), as he always does of councils which he attended, and from *Ep.* 48 we must conclude that he was at Hadrumetum at that very time.* The programme of the council was again interrupted still more seriously. Two African bishops fresh from Rome, Stephanus and Pompeius, had brought evidence of the regularity of Cornelius's ordination (*Ep.* 55, vii.) as conclusive as the commissioners could have obtained, and the council had expressed itself as formally satisfied (*Ep.* 45, i.) when four new delegates from Rome (Maximus, not the confessor; Augendus, etc.) announced the consecration of Novatian to the Roman see. This surprise (for fuller details of which see Novatian) was prepared by the party of severity, who were disappointed by the election of Cornelius, stimulated by Evaristus, whom Cyprian regarded as the author of the movement (*Ep.* 50), and directed in their action by Novatus, who, possibly without being a mere adventurer, nor on the other hand at all deserving Neander's characteristic exculpations, had no doctrine of his own to maintain, but came to Rome simply to endeavour to promote a supposed independence by frustrating the arrangements made by the bishops as to the reception or exclusion of the lapsed. At Carthage therefore he belonged to the broad party, at Rome to the narrow.* It is a mistake to suppose that his change of party was unnoted; cf. *Ep.* 52, iii. (4), "damnare nunc audet sacrificantium manus," with *Ep.* 43, iii., "nunc se ad perniciem lapsorum verterunt," *i.e.* by indulgence. It is also a mistake (though Lipsius falls into it, and it is universal with the earlier writers) and introduces confusion into the history to assume that Novatus made several voyages to and fro. If his arrival be fixed soon after Mar. 5, A.D. 251, it will be found to solve the various problems. Their embassy to Carthage, rejected by the council ("expulsi," *Ep.* 50, not *from Africa*, as Pearson), appealed to Cyprian (*Ep.* 44). They were not prepared to find that he had moved towards leniency as much as Novatian to severity from their late common standpoint; and they are told plainly that their position must now be considered as external to the church. Accepting this, they proceed to construct a schismatic episcopal body with wide alliances. Somewhere close to this point the treatise *de Unitate*, or the germ of it, was first delivered in the form of a speech, or a read pamphlet, to the council. We give an outline of it later. Messengers to Cornelius (Primitivus, Mettius, Nicephorus, an acolyte) then convey full accounts of the procedure, and inform him of his general recognition as bishop.† Simultaneously,

the common account, and has obliged even Pearson to resort to unmanageable hypotheses of long recesses in the first council of Carthage and of several journeys of Novatus to Rome.

* This absence of Cyprian from the trial of his opponent solves difficulties otherwise insoluble. Pearson and Tillemont attribute to the council various adjournments, partly to dispose of the long period required by their false date for Cornelius's election, and partly to give room for the visit to Hadrumetum. *Frequenter acto* (*Ep.* 59, xvi.) means *largely attended*, not, as Pearson and Tillemont, *assembled again and again*. Lipsius has ingeniously conjectured, to meet the second difficulty, that the council empowered Cyprian to recognize Cornelius after their dissolution, if he were satisfied. But the council, before breaking up, were abundantly satisfied, and directed him to be acknowledged (*Ep.* 45). So that it is out of the question that *afterwards* Cyprian should have gone to Hadrumetum and suspended its correspondence with Cornelius.

* It may here clear some difficulties in Cyprian's letters which Maran and others have confused, if we observe that Stephen and Pompey left Rome before Novatian's consecration. It is clear from the sensation they produced that the Novatianist embassy brought the *first* news of it. The council could "refute and repel" its charges, because, though they had *not* received (*expectavimus*) their own commissioner's report (as Maran, *V. Cyp.* lxi., erroneously), they had been satisfied by Stephen's. Hence *supervenerunt*, 44 i. (1), means "came on the top of our expectancy," *not* "came after the Novatianist embassy." The council could not, as they did, have excommunicated the embassy at once, if up till then they had only received Cornelius's letters, of which they were seeking ratification.

† There is no reason to suppose with Lipsius (p. 204, n.) that any correspondence is lost, except the synodic epistle about Felicissimus, for *Ep.* 44 says expressly that the details will be given *vivâ voce*.

appeals, which were ultimately successful, were addressed by Cyprian to the Roman confessors to detach themselves from the schism in which they found themselves involved. The original work before the council, the restoration of the lapsed, had been facilitated by the two episodes, which had cleared off the extreme parties on either side. They now listened to Cyprian's treatise on the lapsed; but they inclined to a course even milder than he suggested, while they were less disposed than he to give the "Martyres" any voice in the decisions.* Their encyclical is lost, but the particulars are extricable from his *Letter to Antonian* (*Ep.* 55), which, since it treats only of the restoration of the *libellatici*, not of the lapsed, must be earlier than the second council, A.D. 252, and from the verbal resemblance of *Ep.* 54 (3) to 55 (v.) must be very near the event. We thence gather that they resolved—(1) On an individual examination of the *libellatici*; (2) Episcopal restoration of non-sacrificers after penance (*Ep.* 55, v.); (3) Of sacrificers if penitents at death (55, xiv.); (4) No restoration of those who deferred penance till death (55, xix.). A Roman synod was held in June or July † by 60 bishops of Italy, who accepted these decisions, and excommunicated Novatian. Cornelius announced the facts in *four* (so Tillemont correctly) *Greek* (so Valois correctly) letters to Antioch (Eus. vi. 43), with two (non-extant) of Cyprian. Briefly to sum up the constitutional results of this first council of Carthage: 1. The views of the primate are submitted to those of the council; he admits the change (*Ep.* 55, iii.). 2. The intercession and merits of the martyrs, as affecting the conditions of restoration, are set aside entirely. 3. On the other hand (as against Novatian), no offences are considered to be beyond the regular power of the church to remit. 4 (against Felicissimus). No power except that of the authentic organization can fix terms of communion. It will be at once seen that the free council of bishops had taken position as a Christian institution, exercising supreme governmental functions, and had laid clear lines as to where church authority resided. They further ruled that there could be no subsequent canvassing of the claims of a bishop once ordained. The resolutions were issued in the name of the bishops only.

The Reconciliation of the Novatianist Confessors at Rome.—A second embassy of Novatianists followed the report of the first, in order to press Cyprian home—Primus, Dionysius, Nicostratus, Evaristus, and above all, NOVATUS; to whose leaving Rome Cyprian does not hesitate partly to ascribe his own next success (*Ep.* 52 (2), ii.). Cyprian's letters to the Novatianist confessors are among the most beautiful and skilful in the collection; and Augustine cites no less than three times a passage from the letter on their return as embodying the absolute scriptural answer to puritan separations. It is the *first* exposition of the parable of the Tares, and St. Paul's image of the Great House. Prevailed on by the arguments used to them, and shocked by the consequences of their action, the whole party, with numerous adherents, returned to the Catholic side, and were publicly and magnanimously received, like the leaders of the same sect at Nicaea, and the Donatists at Carthage, and the Arians at Alexandria, without forfeit of dignity (*Epp.* 49, 52, 53, 46, 54, 51). To Cyprian this was more than an occasion of Christian joy. It was the triumph of his theory (*Ep.* 51 *ad fin.*). The *date* of this event may be accurately determined as being *after* the Carthaginian council (since Cyprian does not mention this as sitting, in his letters on the confessors, and he read the account of their recantation to the *church*, *Ep.* 51, not to the *bishops*), but *prior* to the Roman council, or else they would have been excommunicated by it, which they evidently were not; and since Cyprian says they recanted on the departure of Novatus, it was after the second embassy had left Rome.

Treatise on Unity.—The principles of this treatise, read in the council, and sent to the Roman confessors (*Ep.* 54), so shape all Cyprian's policy, that it is best to notice it here. It indicates its date minutely by allusions to the severe party (Novatian's) (iii. ministros, etc., viii. uno in loco, etc., ix. feritas, x. confessor, xi. episcopi nomen, xiii. aemuli), and by the absence of allusion to the lax party (Felicissimus), whose schism must have been noticed in such a paper if the question had not been concluded. In c. v. its original form as an address to bishops is traceable. The first appearance of Cyprian's characteristic error about baptism occurs in c. xi. Its first problem is the existence of schism (as distinct from heresy), "altar against altar," with freedom from corrupt doctrines and lives. The sole security is the ascertainment of the seat of authority and bond of unity. This is indicated by Christ's commission given once to Peter alone, yet again to all the apostles in the same terms. The oneness of the commission and the equality of the commissioned were thus emphasized. The apostleship, continued for ever in the episcopate, is thus universal, yet one: each bishop's authority perfect and independent, yet not forming with the others a mere agglomerate, but being a full tenure on a totality, like that of a shareholder in a joint-stock property. "Episcopatus unus est cujus a singulis in solidum pars tenetur." It is in the above definition, c. iv., that the famous interpolation has been made, which Roman authorities (Mgr. Freppel, late Professor at the Sorbonne, *S. Cyprien et l'Égl. d'Afr.* lect. 12; Prof. Hurter, of Innspruck, *SS. PP. Opuscula*, v. i. p. 72) even now feel it important to retain. The loss of it suggested the endeavour to make up for it by weaving together other texts from Cyprian to prove that this one after all represented his

* *Ep.* 54, iii. 55 v. 3. To postpone the appearance of the *de Lapsis* to Nov., as Pearson does, or to any moment after the council was over, is to attribute to Cyprian a publication quite out of date and recommendations already disposed of. Therefore, if "ultio," c. i. is to be pressed to mean the death of Decius (which is not necessary, in spite of the consensus for it), it only shews that ours is a second ed.

† The old date, Oct., is due to the mistake as to Cornelius's election. Jerome calls this synod "Romana Italica Africana," as if it were one with the Carthaginian Synod (*de Scr. Ecc.* 66, Labbe, i. pp. 865-868), and from this phrase Baronius has imagined three councils.

doctrine—an attempt which would certainly never have been dreamed of if this spurious passage had not seemed to make him so strong a support. Such special pleading is performed with fullest ability by P. Ballerini (A.D. 1756, *de Vi ac Primatu Romm. Pontiff*. xiii. § iii. ed. Westhoff, 1845). The MS. history is to be found fully in Hartel's preface, p. ix. p. xliii. It was rejected by Baluze (p. xiii. p. 397, p. 409, and Latini, *Bib. S.* p. 179 and praef.) and inserted by authority in the editions by Manutius and the Benedictines. The actual origin of the interpolation is partly in marginal glosses (as Latini proved) and partly in an Ep. of Pelagius, ii. (A.D. 854; Pelag. ii. *Ep.* 6; Labbe, vol. vi. p. 627; ed. Ven. 1729), who produces as "terrible testimonies of the Fathers" a passage of Augustine nowhere else found, as well as this one four centuries before it made its way into a manuscript. Its introduction of the primacy of Peter as the centre of unity is a clumsy interruption of the argument and an overthrowal of Cyprian's universal principle of the "copiosum corpus Episcoporum" (*Ep.* 68, iii.; 55, xx.) as the core of the visible unity of the church. The rest of the treatise is the development in beautiful language, and the illustration from nature and scripture, of his principle. Schism is a divine test and prejudicial separation of unbelievers in principle. Lastly, unity in the visible church must mirror the unity of God and the faith, and separations are due, not so much to individual teachings as to a radical selfishness commonly sanctioned in religious, no less than in secular, life.

The Working of the Legislation.—The legislation had been brought out by the clergy—naturally the austerer class; the one which had most inducements not to fall. It was too severe. The approach of the great plague evoked edicts for sacrifice and roused superstitions which renewed the popular feeling against Christians, and led to the magisterial and popular outbreak of A.D. 252, which is too formally called the Persecution of Gallus (*Ep.* 59, viii.), and which supernatural presages, not justified by the event, foreshewed as more cruel than that of Decius (*Epp.* 57, vi.; 58, i.). Of the libellatics some rigorously tried to follow, others openly defied the conciliar enactments (*Epp.* 57; 65, iii.; 68, ii.). Many palliations appeared on examination. A second council of 42 bishops at Carthage, held on May 15, 252 (*Ep.* 59, xiii.), determined to readmit without exception or postponement all who had continued penitent. Their synodic letter (*Ep.* 57), by Cyprian's hand, is a complete answer to his former sterner strain. The motive cause is the necessity of strengthening by communion those who will shortly be called to suffer.* The Novatianists having attracted converts from heathenism and now given up hope of Cyprian, consecrated their legate Maximus to be (anti-) bishop of Carthage.* The lapsed of the lax party, not being penitents, were not admissible on the new conditions; the party had increased to a number reckoned scarcely smaller than the Catholics (*Ep.* 59, xxi. 17), but the milder terms now offered would diminish them. The leaders therefore needed a more positive basis (*Ep.* 59, xv. xvi. [14]), and being taunted as the only unepiscopal body among Christians (*Ep.* 43, v.), procured the adhesion of PRIVATUS, a deposed bishop (*Ep.* 59, xiii.), and consecrated Fortunatus a second anti-bishop in Carthage † by the hands of five bishops.‡ This fact was immensely exaggerated (59, xiv. 11), and Felicissimus sailed to Rome as legate of his new chief, hoping that a recognition might be procured for numbers which would be useful against Novatianism. They reported the unpopularity of Cyprian at Carthage, and threatened to appeal, if rejected, to the Roman laity (*Ep.* 59, ii. iii. xxv.). Cornelius was disconcerted. Cyprian's observations on this, which begin in a half sarcastic tone (*Ep.* 59, ii.), rise to glowing indignation, as he narrates the overwhelming work at this moment entailed on him by the examination in presence of the *plebes* of the returning schismatics and libellatics. The demand for strictness in readmission comes (as usual after times of trial) from the mass.§

The leniency of the bishop and council, the gross mistake of a rival episcopacy, and the popular claim for discipline, rapidly broke up the party (59, xxi.) and reduced its congregation to a handful.

Clerical Appeals under the Same Regulations.—It is not safe to assert that the terms of readmission for clerics were considered separately at the second council, but immediately after it is accepted that lapsed bishops and clerks could never resume orders (*Ep.* 55, ix.).

* *Ep.* 64. The synodic letter of the third council characterizes the ground for readmission accepted by the second council as *necessitate cogente*, and that of the first as *infirmitate urgente*, and blames bp. Therapius for having neglected both. *Ep.* 64, therefore, cannot, with Mr. Shepherd (Letter ii. p. 10, following Lombert ap. Pearson, *Ann. Cyp.* p. 45*b*), be dated before *Ep.* 57, nor (as *Maran*) synchronize with it; for they could not censure the neglect of a rule they were in the act of making; and why should only 42 bishops have issued letter 57, out of 66 who issued *Ep.* 64? Add to which that 64 is written in a peaceful time, such as began with Aemilian Ap. 253. See further Pearson's arguments, of which one is good, one inadequate.

* Not earlier. *Ep.* 52 ii. Novatus has *not yet* made a bishop in Carthage. *Ep.* 59 xi. Maximus is spoken of as sent *nuper* (A.D. 251) consecrated *nunc* (the *Ep.* being subsequent to Id. Mai. A.D. 252). From *Ep.* 55 x. we find they had bishops in many places before Council II. The step, then, had been *delayed in Carthage*, and this must have been because they still had hopes of Cyprian, which, though misplaced, seem to me not unnatural.

† Dean Milman (*Lat. Chr.* vol. i. p. 48) apparently missed the fact that there were two anti-bishops, one of each extreme; and also fell into the error of making Fortunatus a Novatianist.

‡ These were Privatus of Lambaese, condemned by a council of 90 bishops, under Donatus, Cyprian's predecessor; Felix, a pseudo-bishop of Privatus's making; Repostus, a lapsed bishop; Maximus and Jovinus, *Sacrificati*, whom, from their having been condemned by nine bishops, and then by the first council, I conclude to have been bishops.

§ Socrates's (v. 19) statement that this was the occasion on which Poenitentiaries were first appointed to hear private confession, seems counter to the whole spirit of the time. Sozomen (vii. 6) represents the Roman mode of penance much later, when the bishop is himself the fellow penitent and the absolver. This contradiction of his statement that Poenitentiaries were an institution in the West as well as the East shews how little was known of the origin or date of the office.

In *Ep.* 65 Cyprian rests this on the Levitical institution and on his own visions. In *Ep.* 67, vi., however, he speaks of all bishops being agreed on this. In *Ep.* 72, iii., four years later, the principle extends to presbyters and deacons who had taken part in a heresy or schism. And at first sight it presents a singularly contradictory appearance of laxity that only Novatianists and Donatists held the indelibility of orders to be such that their recanting bishops resumed their functions (Optatus, i. p. 27). There are three cases: (1) Therapius, bp. of Bulla, admits Victor, a lapsed presbyter, without due penance. Fidus, bp., reports this to the third council of 67 bishops (A.D. 253), considering that Victor should be re-excommunicated. The council decline to rescind the boon of "God's priest," but censure Therapius, apparently in his place (*Ep.* 64—*objurgare et instruxisse*), for neglecting the terms of the second council without any consultation of the laity. The same letter (*ad Fidum*, 64) contains an important decision as to age of baptism. [FIDUS.] (2) Fortunatus, bp. of Assurae, lapsed, and in his place was elected Epictetus; but the lapsed party (*Ep.* 65, v. iii.) on their return claimed for him the function and emoluments. The ground of order would have been sufficient; but Cyprian, with his characteristic error, urges the vitiation of any church function discharged by an unworthy minister, and recommends individual canvassing, if necessary, to unite the flock under Epictetus. (3) The most important case is that of Basilides and Martial, in A.D. 254, when the Spanish churches of Leon, Astorga, and Merida appeal to Cyprian against the negligent decision of Stephanus, now bp. of Rome, in favour of the restoration of their lapsed bishops. The letter of the Carthaginian council of 37 bishops, A.D. 254 (*Ep.* 67), penned by Cyprian, declares the verdict of the bp. of Rome mistaken and to be disregarded. This letter also insists on the duty of a laity to withdraw from communion with a "sacrilegious" or "sinful" bishop, and marks the universal sense that there resided in a congregation no power to make valid the sacramental acts of a nominee who lacked the note of true orders (*Ep.* 67, iii.; cf. Routh, vol. iii. p. 152).

Practical Organizations and Christian Culture.—(*a*) *Captivity.*—During the session of the council an extensive raid was executed by the Berbers, who, severely ruled as they were without any attempt to civilize them, were beginning that steady advance on Numidia which in a few years replaced the whole range of Ferratus in their possession. In 252 their front line reached from Thubunae on the salt-marsh to the terebinth forests of Tucca, and they deported large numbers of the Christians of no less than eight sees. Several inscriptions relate to this invasion (see *Revue Afric.* vols. iv. vii. viii.). About £800 were subscribed by the 60 bishops and Carthaginian community (*Ep.* 62), and sent to them.

(*b*) *Plague.*—But the great field on which the expanding powers of humanity were gathered up and animated by the church was opened by the great plague which reached Carthage in A.D. 252, having travelled two years from Ethiopia through Egypt. Great physical disturbances had preceded it (*ad Dem.* ii. 1, vii. 5). The eruption and the brain affection which marked the plague of Athens are not recorded of this; nor yet the pulmonary symptoms, which, perhaps, were not developed in the African climate. The other symptoms seem to be identical, and the devastation far more awful, extensive, and enduring. It lasted 20 years; reduced the population of Alexandria by half; destroyed the armies of Valerian before Sapor; kept the Goths off the Thracian border, and for some time killed 5,000 persons daily in Rome (Eutrop. ix. v.; *Hist. Aug.* Galli, v. p. 177; Dionys. *ap. Eus.* vii. 22; Greg. Nys. *Vit. Greg. Thaum.* § 12). The efforts of the Emperors Gallus and Valerian in burying the dead were appreciated, otherwise their efforts were confined to supplications to Saturn and Apollo. (See three types of coins of Gallus in British Museum, and see Cohen, *Médailles Impér.* vol. iv. p. 270; Bandusi, vol. i. p. 58.) Horrible scenes of desertion and spoliation ensued in Carthage as in Athens (*Pontii Vit. Cyp.* and *Cyp. ad Dem.* 10 [8], 11 [9]), when universal physical terror or audacity overpowered all other sentiments. As in Neo-Caesarea and Alexandria so in Carthage, the Christian clergy stood out as the first champions of life, health, and feeling. Cyprian addressed his community in a speech, which it was wished could have been delivered to the city from the rostrum, on the duty and divineness of prayer and help to the persecutors (*Respondere Natalibus* was his watchword), and then proposed and carried a scheme for the systematic care of the city. Filled with his motives and under his influence rich and poor undertook the parts he assigned, raised a large fund, formed a nursing staff and burial staff, and allowed no religious distinction in their ministrations. But their abstinence from religious processions and sacrifices marked the Christians as enemies of God and man, and the "Overseer of the Christians" was demanded by name for a contest with a lion (*Epp.* 59, viii.; 66, 44). The terrible work lasted on till his exile five years later, as we must conclude from Pontius's juxtaposition of the events, with his remark that exile was the reward for "withdrawing from human sight a horror like hell."

(*c*) *Ad Demetrianum.*—Their chief foe was an aged magistrate (sub ipso exitu *Dem.* 25 [22]), not the pro-consul (Pearson), but perhaps one of the five *primores,* formerly an inquirer into the truth of Christianity, in Cyprian's own friendship (i.), now himself an inventor of accusations (c. 2) and tortures, xii. (10). The pamphlet in which Cyprian assails him is much wider in its aim than Tertullian's *ad Scapulam*; both have the remonstrance against the suppression of the one natural worship, the appeal to the demeanour of the now prevalent sect (pars paene major cujusque civitatis), to the effects of exorcism, and the influence through suffering of the Christians. But while Tertullian for once refrains from denunciation, and is almost gentle in his examples of warning, Cyprian's object is wider; he answers the question, "Whence all this political and this physical misery?" The heathen answer attributed it to the divine displeasure at toleration. Cyprian accepts also a certain theory of mundane decrepitude, but bases his real reply on the general dissolution of the bonds of society; an important passage, perhaps the very earliest on slavery (viii. [6]), marks the exact stage reached by the Christian consciousness on this subject. So also the theory of *Resentment* is exhibited in a certain stage of purification, though some of the language would be intolerable now. The eternal conservation of beings for eternal suffering is laid down (xxiv. 21). The most original part of the essay is the development for the first time of the theory of *Probation* (already struck out in his slightly earlier epistle 58 to Thibaris) as grouping the phenomena of humanity. Jerome hastily (*Ep.* 83 *ad Magn.*; Lact. *Inst.* 5, 4) criticizes Cyprian for advancing scriptural proofs to a heathen. But (1) Demetrian already knew something of Christianity; (2) Cyprian does not quote authors' names, as to one familiar; (3) he quotes nothing but *plainly fulfilled* predictions. All which (as well as the classical tone and quotations) fits the case exactly, and answers Rettberg's incompetent conjecture that Demetrian is a fancy figure.

(*d*) *On the Mortality.*—This treatise, or epistle as Augustine calls it (he quotes it no less than six times), presents to the Christians the consolatory primitive view of the topics set threateningly before Demetrian. It is meant to elevate their view of both the persecution and the plague, from which some expected providential exemptions, while others hated it only as an interference with martyrdom; he explains his theory of probation and of predictions as evidencing a divine plan. He cannot reject, but he gives a Christian turn to the general belief in the world's decay; urges organizations for relief of suffering; treats moral causes in society as affecting general and even physical phenomena. In c. xxvi. occurs what seems more than a coincidence with phrases in the Te Deum. In c. xx. he condemns the use of black for mourners.

(*e*) *On Work and Alms.*—A pastoral, which may indeed be connected with the incidents of *Ep.* 62, but more probably has a wider reference to the demands made by the plague and coincident troubles on the exertions and liberality of the Christians. Among circumstances known to us directly it would be more natural to link it to the great speech which Pontius mentions as having been delivered at that time to the community. Here again we find Cyprian working out the new faith into a life-system; philosophically (as in a kind of Tusculan) adjusting moral feeling and practice to the newly gained higher facts about God and Man. See cc. ix. x. xi. practically developing that "loss is gain," and "gain is loss," to those who are within the care of Christ, xvi. Christianity becomes a social element which uplifts the poor; their claims take precedence of family claims; the possession of a family only increases the obligation to Christ's poor.—In xxii. is a bold passage, almost Goethesque, in which Satan apostrophizes Christ on the superior liberality of his own school.—The *doctrine* of the first part i–vii. develops the unfortunate conception (roundly stated in *Ep.* 55, xviii. [14]) of *good works* acting on sins done after baptism, as baptism acts to remit former sin. Neander (*Ch. Hist.* vol. i. p. 391, Bohn) remarks that while this same thought appears in Tertullian (*de Poenit.*), yet no one person can be regarded as the author of it. It is a natural and popular materialistic germ of the doctrines of Rome on penance.

(*f*) *The Exhortation to Confessorship* is a practical manual of Scripture passages, connected by brief remarks, under 13 heads of reflection; compiled at the request of a layman, Fortunatus. Its existence sufficiently indicates the extent of suffering which a persecution developed. A more sober tone as to the perfections of the martyrs is perceptible. The introduction of the seven Maccabees not only as examples, but as a type of unity (*ad Fort.* xi.), dates this as later than *de Unitate*, where every other possible type is accumulated but not this one. The teaching on probation also marks the stage of his thoughts. He computes the world to be near 6,000 years old (*ad Fort.* ii.; cf. Tert. *de V. V.* i.).

(*g*) *On the Lord's Prayer.*—To promote intelligent devotion was his next aim. This treatise is written with precision and with visible delight. The time is clearly shewn by his deductions on unity (xxiv.; cf. *de Unit.* xiv. [12]); on the danger of withholding communion from penitents (*de Or.* xviii.), and on the confessor's temptations to arrogance (xxiv.). Cyprian follows Tertullian freely, not transcribing as before; adopts the African "ne nos patiaris induci" without remark (cf. Aug. *de Dono Persev.* vi. 12), and "fiat in caelo" (*id.* iii. 6); illustrates more fully from Scripture, and uses a different version. His silence probably evinces Tertullian's success in remonstrating against superstitious observances in praying (Tert. *Deor.* xi. xvi.), and he does not, like his "master," hail the "confusion of nations" as a mark of the kingdom; but in his expansion of the symbolism of praying thrice a day we have the earliest use of Trinitas in Latin as a name of Deity (in Tert. *adv. Prax.* 3, it is not exactly this). In A.D. 427 Augustine (*Ep.* ccxv.) used the treatise successfully with the monks of Adrumetum to prove the Pelagian errors contrary to the Cyprianic doctrine. He quotes this short treatise of "*victoriosissimus Cyprianus*" elsewhere 13 times to the same effect. Yet not one term occurs in it which became technical in that controversy—a fact which would alone evince its early date. Mr. Shepherd, however (Fourth Letter to Dr. Maitland, 1853), has undertaken to prove that its writer was acquainted with the work of Chromatius (*d.* A.D. 406) and is more "sacramental" than that author, Gregory Nyssen, or Chrysostom, and than Augustine's doubt as to the application of the "daily bread" allows; he observes that Venantius (6th cent.) does not use it, though his predecessor, Hilary, refers the readers of his commentary to it in preference to commenting himself; having thus satisfied himself of the lateness of the Cyprianic treatise, Mr. Shepherd therefore asperses the genuineness of the great Augustinian works which cite it. A critical comparison with Chromatius would require a minuteness and space here inadmissible, but the result of such investigation leaves no doubt that Cyprian is the middle term between Tertullian and Chromatius. Briefly, Chromatius knows no argument or illustration of Tertullian's which Cyprian has not employed; almost every one of these has in Chromatius (though a most condensed prosaic writer) some additional Cyprianic touch or colour adhering to it. Observe too Chromatius's insertion of the negative, *in his qui necdum crediderunt* (§ iv.), in mistaken elucidation of Cyprian's obscure *in illis credentibus* (§ xvii.) precisely as later MSS. and editors have altered it. As to the Eucharistic language about daily bread, it is admittedly not more strong than in other Cyprianic treatises, nor visibly stronger than Chromatius. The Antiochene Fathers of course are not Eucharistic in this clause, because they followed Origen's interpretation of ἐπιούσιος. Augustine will not strictly limit the petition to the Eucharist (though for singular reasons, *Serm.* 56, 57, 58), but his more analytical, yet more mystical treatment of it is distinctly in a later mood than the simply moral handling of Cyprian. That Venantius does not mention Cyprian in his unfinished treatise surely demands no explanation. His aim is more theological and his language very compressed. But tinges of Cyprian are perceptible in the passages on Sonship; perseverance; reigning with Christ; resistance to God's will, and ourselves being made heavenly to do it; but we may add that Ambrose's omission to comment on vv. 1-5 of c. xi. is inexplicable, except for the existence of some standard treatise, such as is mentioned by Hilary (Mt. V.): "De orationis sacramento necessitate nos commentandi Cyprianus liberavit."

Interval.—Cornelius's exile, with others, to Civita Vecchia, his decease in June 253, as a *martyr*, in the then sense of the word, the short episcopate of Lucius, his exile, speedy return, and death, not later than Mar. 5, A.D. 254 (Cyp. *Epp.* 60, 61, 67, 68), find place in Cyprian's correspondence,* not without some undue exaggerations, as when he compares the reappearance of Lucius to that of John Baptist, as heralding the advent. Not later than this we place the epistle (63) to bp. Caecilius, reproving the omission of wine in the chalice, and distinctly indicating the symbolical importance of a mixed cup; the necessity of a congregation to constitute a sacrament; the irregularity of evening communion. To Sept. 253, and its council of 66 bishops, belongs the condemnation of the postponing for even a few days, on ritual grounds, the administration of the other sacrament to infants. To it belongs the affair of Therapius, as above.

Changed Relations with Rome, and Cyprian's Error of Rebaptism.—In A.D. 254 Easter was on April 23; Stephanus was made bp. of Rome May 12; the Carthaginian council met towards autumn (September ?). It had seemed to Cyprian a token of divine displeasure with the Novatianists that they did not suffer with the church; and their prosperity might have seemed to form Stephen's policy in so anti-puritan a mould, except for his over-indulgence to MARCION, the Novatianist bp. of Arles (*Ep.* 68); but his was rather a policy of general resistance to the spiritual power compacted by Cyprian and Cornelius; a policy of the widest comprehension on the one basis of submissiveness to his see. The cases of Basilides and Martial have been mentioned. Cyprian's tone to him is one of both compassion and dictation (*Ep.* 68), and from his letter to Florentius Pupienus (66) it is plain that others besides Stephen felt, rightly or wrongly, more than aversion to the immense influence of Cyprian. And, although the whole church has decided that Stephen was right in the great controversy which arose, it was long before his character recovered the shock of his impetuous collision with Cyprian, and grew capable of his fictitious crown of martyrdom. The next group of documents belongs to A.D. 255 and 256, and is occupied with the controversy on rebaptism (*Epp.* 69-75, *Sentt. Epp.* lxxxvii.). For though Cyprian objects to that term (*Ep.* 73, i.), catholic doctrine insists on the assertion it involves. Notwithstanding the council of Agrippinus, and the reception of thousands of heretics by rebaptism in the African church (*Ep.* 73, iii.), numbers had been readmitted without it (*Ep.* 73, xxiii.; Aug. says the practice had fallen off). On the other hand, though Stephen appeals to the constant tradition of his church against rebaptizing, this is simply to ignore the action of Callistus (Hippolytus, p. 291, a passage which is against the idea of that author's Novatianism, but which Hefele monstrously wants to apply to Agrippinus [*Hist. des Conciles*, vol. i. p. 87, Paris]). An allusion to Stephen (*Ep.* 69, x.) seems to imply that Stephen stirred the question first. Rettberg considers, after Maran, that his Oriental dispute had already occurred (p. 170). So Hefele. But this is not necessary. Cyprian (*de Un.* xi.) early committed himself to language as strong as he ever used again. The original inquiry is whether the non-heretical Novatianists, baptized as such, can be received to catholic communion. It extended itself (73, iv.), until the cases of Marcionites and even Ophites were debated; Stephen would include, and Cyprian exclude, all. At first the difficulty was only "Is not the exclusive African practice itself a Novatianist mark—being otherwise used only in that sect?" Our briefest method will be first to enumerate the documents, and then to classify their often repeated arguments.

(1) Magnus, a layman, makes the first application, and is replied to by Cyprian with affectionate respect (*Ep.* 69). (2) The bishops of Numidia, who, though without formal vote, had adopted the practice, apply next; the reply is from 33 bishops of Africa, with the presbyters of Carthage (*Ep.* 71). This is Cyprian's *5th Council and 1st on Baptism. Ep.* 70 is their conciliar declaration of the necessity of (re)baptism. (3) A Mauritanian bishop, Quintus, is answered in *Ep.* 71, enclosing *Ep.* 70, now widely circulated (71, iv.), breathing an injured tone as towards Stephen, and indicating that the council had not been unanimous (*Ep.* 71, i., plurimi . . . nescic qua praesumptione quidam). (4) The *de Bono Patientiae* was published about

* On the death of Cornelius and his sepulture, see Mommsen, *Chronog. vom Jahre* 354, p. 631; de Rossi, *Roma Sott.* vol. ii. pp. 66-68; and on the true date of his death, as distinct from his festival, Lipsius, *Chron. d. Pap.* p. 192.

this time, to be, without one word upon the subject matter of the controversy, a calming voice in the rising storm. The *de Zelo et Livore* is generally (and probably) thought to be a very little later in date, and similar in purpose. It is equally reticent on passing events, unless (in vi. 5) there may be an allusion to Novatian. There are a few close verbal resemblances between the two treatises, especially in *de Pat.* xix. (11) and *de Zelo*, iv. and v. (5) Next year, A.D. 256, the *6th Council under Cyprian and 2nd on Baptism*, composed of 71 bishops, Numidian and African,* unanimously reaffirm the opinion in an unconciliatory synodical epistle to Stephen, conscious of the offence they will give, and enclosing *Epp.* 70 and 71. This epistle is mentioned by Jerome, *adv. Lucif.* But Augustine (*Resp. ad Epp.* 15) seems not to have seen it, which is strange. (6) Jubaian, a bp. of Mauritania, forwards to Cyprian a copy of a paper there circulating, with some authority, which recognizes even Marcion's baptism (*Ep.* 73, iv.). It may have been issued by one of those native bishops who dissented (*Sentt. Epp.* 59, 38, and cf. Aug. *Resp. ad Epp.* 52, *con. Donat.* vii. 16, 6). Rettberg agrees with "Constant. *Ep. Pontif.* p. 226," that it was Stephen's letter to the East. Cyprian sent Jubaian a reply so elaborate that, at the final council, he read it aloud as his own best exposition of his views, with Jubaian's convinced answer. Cyprian's letter was accompanied with all the documents sent to Stephen, and a copy of his *Patience.* (7) A deputation of bishops waited on Stephen but were not received (*Ep.* 75, xxv.); the letter which they bore was answered (74, i.) in terms appreciative of the greatness of the question (75, xvii.) but not arguing it, charitable to the separatists, affirming the tradition (75, v.; 73, xiii.), resting on the authority of the see (75, xvii.), and styling Cyprian "a pseudo-Christ, a pseudo-apostle and treacherous worker." It would be unfair not to recognize anxiety under the word "treacherous," while Fabian of Antioch, by dallying with Novatianism, was complicating Stephen's position; and Cyprian's own language as to "favourers of Antichrist" (69, x.) had exposed him to retaliation. Stephen had circulated in the East a paper which awakened "lites et dissensiones per ecclesias totius mundi" (75, xxiv.), declaring he would hold no communion with bishops who used second baptism (*Ep.* 75, xxiv.; 74, viii.; Dionys. Al. ap. Eus. vii. 5).† The natural reply of the metropolitan of Cappadocia was "Thou hast excommunicated thyself." The general history of rebaptism must be read elsewhere, but it was held in Cappadocia, Pamphylia, and other regions of Asia Minor as a practice received from "Christ and from the apostle" (75, xix.), and it had been confirmed by the councils of Synnada and Iconium.‡ Dionysius the Great recommended *forbearance* to Stephen, and to the eminent Roman presbyters Dionysius and Philemon.* (8) Pompey, bp. of Sabrata on the Syrtis, was the next inquirer, asking for Stephen's reply (*Ep.* 74). Cyprian sends it with the antidote, a fine letter, though not moderate, closing with an amendment on the canon of Stephen. Pompey was convinced if he had wavered, and his proxy at the council was presented by his neighbour the bp. of Oea. (9) The 7th council of Carthage, or 3rd on baptism, held Sept. 1, A.D. 256. Eighty-seven bishops of all the three provinces, with presbyters and deacons, met in the presence of a vast laity.† The council opened with the reading of the Jubaian correspondence, and the letter to Stephen (*Sent.* 8), and with a brief speech from Cyprian, large and pacific (Aug. *R. Epp.*). Each bishop then by seniority delivered his opinion, of which we have a verbal report: from some a good argument, from some a text, an antithesis, an analogy, or a fancy: here a rhetorical sentence, there a solecism or an unfinished clause; a simple restatement, a personality, a fanaticism; two of the juniors vote with the majority on the ground of inexperience. But on the whole we must admire the temper and the ability of so large a number of speakers. The council had a great moral effect. It kept Roman influence at bay for a long time. Jerome is mistaken in asserting, in his youthful *contra Luciferianos*, that these Fathers recanted. The custom was not specifically repealed till the synod of Arles, nor for Asia Minor till the first of Constantinople. But, from peculiar circumstances, it was specially accepted in the East, and is the basis now of the rebaptism by the Jacobites, not only of heretics and Nestorians, but of orthodox Christians.‡ Before

* A.D. 312. The relations of Numidia with Carthage seem unsettled (Hefele, *Conciles*, vol. i. p. 170).

† H. Valois is right, I believe, in thinking this a threat. Routh thinks it was actual excommunication, and Lipsius that he excommunicated Cyprian. Several bishops of the seventh council were very early in the Roman calendar for iv. Id. Sep.

‡ Lipsius's reasons (pp. 219, 220) for dating Iconium so late as A.D. 255 are surely quite insufficient. Eusebius (vii. 3) says Cyprian was πρῶτος τῶν τότε to hold rebaptism, which is a most accurate expression. He has already said that it had been held in very populous churches, and has told us of the old council of Agrippinus which declared it. Asia had quietly continued, Africa had mostly dropped the practice, and Cyprian was the first τῶν τότε to revive it. Lipsius is actually driven by his own special pleading to say there were *two* synods of Iconium "which must not be confounded," one named by Firmilian, and one by Dionysius—about the baptism of heretics—at the same place—at a very considerable interval—both making exactly the same declaration.

* Jerome (*Script. Ecc.*) says Dionysius took the strict view. He himself seems (Eus. vii. 9) to say the opposite, and cf. vii. 7.

† I believe this to be a simple and sufficient account of the circumstances of the correspondence, and Mosheim's and Rettberg's little amusement of inventing lost documents is unnecessary. The letter of Stephanus shewn to Pompeius is the same which Firmilian saw. The legation of course presented the synodal letter, which was meant to be final: accordingly Cyprian (in *Sentt. Ep.*) speaks of the question as resting henceforth with individual bishops.

‡ Of the seventh council Mr. Shepherd says, "Wonderful to say, it has a date." So has the second (*Ep.* 59, xlii.). Of another event he remarks, "It would have been far more natural to have said A.D. 180, or some such date." It would have been an excessively interesting use of the Christian era, and Mr. Shepherd has doubtless noted the careful dates of other documents, Tertullian's historical allusions, Augustine's letters. The paucity of dates is, however, singular. It may have some connexion with the African hostility, even to civil usages dependent on heathenism. The Donatists at Carthage,

the winter of 256* Cyprian's messengers to Firmilian returned with (10) his reply, the most enthusiastic letter of the series. We have it in Cyprian's translation from the Greek.† It has points of great interest; compares the bp. of Rome to Judas; shews the antiquity of rebaptism in Asia; touches on their annual synods; the fixed and extempore portions of the liturgy; the quasi-supremacy of Jerusalem; the unity under wide divisions. For arguments to the point it relies on Cyprian's letters.

We will now briefly classify Cyprian's arguments and the answers to them, avoiding the making him responsible for his partisans, whose judgment in council (vii.) differs much from his. Firmilian, on the other hand, summarizes sensibly. Cyprian then urges for rebaptism (A), *Objective grounds.* (*a*) *The unity of the church*, viz. that in the critical point of "church and non-church," schism does not differ from heresy (69, iii.): the representation of sacred acts outside not equivalent to sacred acts within: "one Lord, one faith," there may be, but not "one baptism," for this implies "one church," which the schismatic renounces. (*b*) *Unity of Belief.* In its African form the creed ran, "Dost thou believe the remission of sins and life everlasting *through holy church*?" and was accordingly null at the moment of baptism away from the church. (*c*) *Baptism is a function of holy orders* on account of its remissory virtue in respect of sin (not Tertullian's doctrine [*de Bap.* xvii.]), and holy orders have no being outside the church (73, vii.), so that the whole question of episcopal authority as the bond of unity and divine organization is

A.D. 411, treat the fact that the Acts of the council of Cirta, A.D. 305, commence with the consular date as an evidence against their genuineness. The Catholics reply, that though the Donatists avoid dates, the Catholics use them. But it may be that the Donatists preserve the old puritanic tradition. Cf. Aug. *Brev. Coll. c. Don.* p. 569, 3ii. diei, cap. xv. § 26, 27. (Athanasius's objection to the date in the creed of Sirmio is of another colour.) For an account of the Romanist assaults on it, see Rettberg, pp. 189, 190. Augustine accepted it, when some wished to make it of Donatist origin, on the ground of its containing so much against Donatism.

* Stephen died, and Cyprian was exiled before the winter of 257.

† It is impossible not to recognize Cyprian's style in it; equally impossible not to see the Gk. [A] in some of its compound phrases and coupled epithets (*e.g.* i. magnam voluntatis caritatem in unum convenire; iii. velociter currentes, iv. quoniam sermo . . . distribuatur, etc.). [B] In the literal (sometimes awkward) rendering of words: iv. seniores et praepositi (= presbyteri et epicopi) for πρεσβύτεροι καὶ προεστῶτες; vii. praesident *majores natu*, where Cyprian could not have used presbyteri, and yet age is not to the point; fratribus tam longe positis (μακρὰν κειμένοις); v. inexcusabilem; vi. eos qui Romae sunt; aequaliter quae; vii. *possident* potestatem; x. nec vexari *in aliquo*; quamvis ad imaginem veritatis tamen; xxiii. volentibus vivere; xii. *Nos* etiam *illos quos hi qui.* [C] Instances where the Gk. is not thoroughly mastered: viii. nisi si his episcopis *quibus nunc* minor fuit Paulus (? τῶν νῦν); xii. ut per eos qui *cum* ipsi, etc.; *cum* unmeaning—observe in ix. *patrias* of local persecutions in *Asia Minor.* The remarkable translation of *Eph.* 4, 3, in xxiv. is in the same words as in three other places of Cyprian, and differs from every other known rendering; even the African Nemesianus in this council uses *curantes* instead of *satisagentes.*

involved * (*Ep.* 72, i.), and if external baptism is true, the church has many centres; not one foundation rock, but several (75, xvii.). The separatist teacher surrenders (70, ii.) the animating, unifying Spirit, and cannot through his personal earnestness convey that Spirit to followers by baptizing them † (*Ep.* 69). (*d*) *The imposition of hands on the readmitted separatist* expresses that he has not, but needs to receive, the Holy Ghost; Stephen's party use this rite, and quote the apostles at Samaria as an example. But without that Spirit how could the separatist consecrate even the water or the unction of confirmation? (*Ep.* 70, i.; cf. *Sentt. Epp.* 18; on the significance of this "royal" oil, see Bunsen; and on the Novatianist disuse of it, Routh, vol. iii. pp. 69, 70). Above all, how give the New Birth which, as the essence of the sacrament, is essentially the Spirit's act (*Ep.* 74, v. vi. etc.)? (*e*) *Baptism in the absence of the Spirit is a Judaic, a carnal rite; a defilement;* more than a deceiving semblance, a material pollution (*Ep.* 75, xiii.; 72, i.; 73, xxi.; 69, xvi.; cf. Sedatus, *Sentt. Epp.* 18; Victor Gordub. *Sent.*, whom Augustine criticizes as going to lengths beyond Cyprian; still the frightful expression of *de Unit.* xi. involves all this). The pretender can "neither justify nor sanctify" (69, x.), who but the holy can hallow (69, ii.)? who but the living give life (71, i.)? (*f*) *Christ not present to make up for the unworthiness of the minister.* For if so His Spirit could not be absent (75, xii.), and that He is absent is admitted by the necessity for imposition of hands (*id.* xiii.).

(B) *Subjective Grounds.* (*a*) *Faith of recipient insufficient* (*Epp.* 73, 75, ix.): to be effective must be true; but is deficient in a cardinal point, viz. the remission of sins by the church; even if not false and, as often, blasphemous (73, iv. v; 74). (*b*) *Not secured by the formula.* In the Roman church there was still such absence of rigidity that it was argued that without the Trinal form baptism into Christ's name sufficed (*Ep.* 74, v.). Cyprian however points to the clear words of institution, and appeals to common reason to decide whether one is truly baptized into the Son who denies His Humanity (*Ep.* 73, v.),‡ or treats the God of the O. T. as evil (74, iii.): even if the genuine formula be used, still the rite is no question of words; the absent Christ and Spirit are not bound by them as a spell. (*c*) *Incapable of definition.* It is not the church's part to graduate departures from the faith. Even death in behalf of a heresy cannot restore to the church. If what is universally accepted as *ipso facto* baptism (in blood) is unavailing, how can ordinary extraneous baptism be more (*Ep.* 73, xxi.; *de Unit.* xiv. (12) xix.; or *Dom.* xxiv.)?

(C) *The historical argument* is handled by Cyprian in the most masterly way. (*a*) Usage is not worth considering as more than an apology for ignorance; cannot be matched

* This view becomes "Christus baptizandi potestatem episcopis dedit" in the mouth of one of the bishops (*Sentt. Ep.* 17).

† "Qui non habet quomodo dat?" became a catchword of the Donatists. The reply of the Catholics was "Deum esse datorem" (Optat. p. 103).

‡ The basis of this is Tert. *de Bapt.* xv.

against reason (71, iii. 73); (*b*) is not universal on side of Stephen (*Ep.* 71); (*c*) cannot be inferred from the non-baptism of restored perverts: their case differs from that of heathens, who had (to begin with) been made heretics, not Christians. (*d*) The practice of heretical bodies, which had always recognized any previous baptism, was no example to the church (74, iv.); nor could the Novatianist practice of rebaptism be a warning against it (73, ii.); it was either accidental coincidence or imitation (*simiarum more*), and, if the latter, it was evidence. (*e*) *Casuistic difficulties* upon the necessity of "regeneration within the church" as to the position of unbaptized martyrs (73, xxii.), heretics hitherto readmitted and deceased (xxiv.), cases of rebaptism where baptism had been valid, baptism by a demoniac, are met by Cyprian with a breadth of which St. Augustine (*contra Crescon.* ii. 41) says, in the midst of his refutation, "such simplicity is enough for me."

(D) *Biblical Arguments.*—The familiar ones need no more than enumeration: the one loaf; one cup; the ark; the schismatic (not heretical) gainsaying of Korah; the apostles' baptism of men who had already received the Spirit, a fortiori needed for those who confessedly had not. We may admire the ingenuity with which he treats such passages as Acts ii. 38, in *Ep.* 73, xvii., or Phil. i. 18, in *Ep.* 74, 75, 73, xiv.; but about many Cyprian might fairly be addressed in the words which Optatus (b. iv. p. 96) uses to Parmenian: "You batter the law to such purpose that wherever you find the word Water there you conjure out of it some sense to our disadvantage." He probably originated the application of Ecclus. xxxiv. 25, "Qui baptizatur a *mortuo* quid proficit lavatio ejus," which the Donatists constantly quote against Augustine, and which Augustine answers only by referring *mortuus* to a heathen priest or vicious Christian instead of a heretic. He quotes several times the LXX addition to Prov. ix. 19, "Drink not of the strange font," and Jer. xv. 18, ii. 13, "deceiving waters," "broken cisterns." In some of these applications there is poetical force, as of his favourite "garden enclosed and fountain sealed," and of the doctrines of New Birth and Sonship (*Ep.* 74, v. vi.); in Heresy who was never the Spotless Spouse we can never find a mother (*Ep.* 75). To this Stephen finely answers that she was an unnatural mother indeed (75, xiv.) who exposed her children so soon as they were born, but that the church's part was to seek them and bring them home and rear them for Christ. Dispersed as this system of Cyprian's lies, through his correspondence and tracts, it will be seen that in his mind it was not fragmentary, but logical and coherent. Over the theory promulgated by one of his powers and character, backed by an army of bishops,* moving as one man under him, yet independent enough each to find their own telling arguments (Conc. III.), Stephen's triumph without a council, against remonstrances from the East, and hindered by his own pretentiousness and uncharitableness,* was great. It was deserved also, for Rome represented freedom, comprehensiveness, and safe latitude. She decided upon one grand principle, the same on which Jerome afterwards decided the analogous question of reordination (*adv. Lucif.*). Cyprian's principle was the same which blinded Tertullian (*de Bapt.* xv.); which was extended by the Donatists to make moral defects in the minister debar grace; † which led Knox and Calvin to deny baptism to the infant children of "papists," and the Genevan divines to allow it, on the hope that "the grace which had adopted" the great-grandfathers might not yet be so "wholly extinct that the infants should have lost their right to the common seal" (Hooker, iii. 1, 12). Augustine (*Resp. ad Episcopos*) developed the categorical answer to each separate argument of Cyprian and his bishops, but the true solution was applied at once by Stephen. The grace of baptism is of Christ, not of the human baptizer.‡ He who baptizes does not "give being or add force" to the sacrament. Cyprian's language about "justifying and sanctifying" may well have shocked the church of Rome, and makes Stephen's anger partly intelligible. The child or heathen who learns Christ through the teaching of the heretic cannot be charged with "defect or disorder," in the reception of a sacrament, to which he comes with purest faith, and which it is the will of God to impart to all. Though excluded "from fellowship in holy duties with the visible church," he is still a member of such visible church. (*Ep.* 73, xvi. We must take the fragmentary quotation, 75, i., "Si quis ergo a quacunque haeresi venerit" with the other, "In nomine Christi baptizatus," and cf. Routh, *R. S.* vol. iii. p. 183.) The only real blot which Cyprian struck was the *vulgar explanation* of the laying on of hands at readmission. Upon that hypothesis his own view was justifiable. But the act was not really understood by the intelligent to be the imparting of the Spirit for the first time to those who had it not; it was the renewing by the Spirit, and introducing to communion of a repentant and now enlightened child of God.§ "A son of God" in spite of any theological error, Stephen declares him in the fullest sense to be (*Ep.* 74, vi.; 75, xvii.). The expression seems to have been much cavilled at in Carthage, and is mentioned even in *Ep.* 72, after the second council. And now it ought to

* Some required exorcism (*Sentt.* 7, 8, 31); some declared heretics worse than heathens—a painfully early development.

* Animosus, iracundus; again, audacia, insolentia, inhumanitas are some of the sins charged to him.

† Of the use they made of Cyprian himself see Aug. *contra Crescon.* II. xxiii. 40: "Scripta Cypriani nobis tanquam firmamenta canonicae auctoritatis opponitis." Cf. *Ep.* 93, *ad Vincent.*; *Epp.* 108, 9, *ad Macrob.*

‡ Optatus, b. v. p. 99, well expresses it: "Has res unicuique non ejusdem rei operarius sed credentis fides et *Trinitas* praestat." By implication he answers many of the detailed difficulties, but the great name of Cyprian visibly restrains him. Again, p. 103: "Omnes qui baptizant operarios esse non dominos et sacramenta per se sancta esse non per homines."

§ Besides its use in ordination the imposition of hands had three intentions: (1) Confirmation. (2) Reception of penitents. (3) Exorcism. The 2nd is what Stephen applies here. The 3rd was desired by some extreme partisans.

be noticed that (as the Novatianists saw) Cyprian had a real point of contact with Novatianism. In the instance of Lapse he discovered its fallacy. In the instance of Heresy he fell into it. The visible church, according to him, included the worst moral sinner in expectation of his penitence; it excluded the most virtuous and orthodox baptized Christian who had not been baptized by a catholic minister.* Nevertheless, although the Roman church then took a wider view than Cyprian as to the sonship of man to God, Cyprian was much greater (and this is the true church-moral of this part of his history) upon the possibility and duty of union in diversity. Augustine well draws out the independence of thought and action which Cyprian wished to be maintained without exclusiveness, and tells us (Aug. v. *de Bapt.* 17) how he was never weary of reading the conclusion of the Ep. to Quintus. Every bishop was free to judge for himself, none to be persecuted for his views, and *therefore* every one to be tender of the bonds of peace: "Salvo jure communionis diversa sentire." The unanimity of such early councils and their erroneousness are a remarkable monition. Not packed, not pressed; the question broad; no attack on an individual; only a principle sought; the assembly representative; each bishop the elect of his flock; and all "men of the world," often christianized, generally ordained late in life; converted against their interests by conviction formed in an age of freest discussion; their Chief one in Whom were rarely blended intellectual and political ability, with holiness, sweetness, and self-discipline. The conclusion reached by such an assembly uncharitable, unscriptural, uncatholic, and unanimous. The consolation as strange as the disappointment. The mischief silently and perfectly healed by the simple working of the Christian society. Life corrected the error of thought. Augustine beautifully writes: "It is of no light moment that though the question was agitated among bishops of an age anterior to the faction of Donatus, and although opinions differed without the unity of the colleagues being marred, still this our present use has been settled to be observed throughout the whole Catholic church diffused throughout the world" (*contra Crescon.* i. xxxii. 38). The disappearance of the Cyprianic decisions has its hope for us when we look on bonds seemingly inextricable, and steps as yet irretrievable. It may be noted, as affording some clue to the one-sided decisions, that the laity were silent, though Cyprian seemed pledged to some consultation with them. (See esp. *Ep.* 31 and 19, ii.) It must have been among them that there were in existence and at work those very principles which so soon not only rose to the surface, but overpowered the voices of her bishops for the general good. It was a parliament of officials, provincial governors. That it did not represent church opinion (that, namely, which we now accept as church doctrine), may be inferred—(1) from the absolute unanimity of the 87 utterances; (2) from the strange avowal of two, that, being incompetent to give an opinion, they vote with the majority; (3) from the very important and powerful contemporary work of the "Auctor de Rebaptismate"; (4) from the silent reversal of the decision.

* Thus the extreme of sacerdotalism was a fixed tenet with our own Puritan divines, who held the minister "to be of the substance of the sacrament." Cf. Hooker, *Ec. Pol.* V. lxi. 5; Neander, vol. i. p. 540, Bohn tr.

The Last Persecution.—Of the 31 Numidian bishops who sat in the great council, the next glimpse of church offices shews 9 as convicts * in the mines *metallum Siguense* (? Siga, where there were copper-mines in Mauritania, or Siguita in Numidia itself) and in two other places.† A subdeacon and four acolytes were commissioned by the metropolitan (already himself an exile) and his friend Quirinus to visit them, and supply them with necessaries (*Epp.* 77-79). Cyprian had been apprehended, as perhaps the first African prisoner (*Epp.* 77-78), in Aug. A.D. 257. Valerian's first edict (*Acta Proconsulis,* and *Acta Praef. Augustalis*) had then been issued on the suggestion of Macrianus, a principal patron of the Egyptian "Magi," after a long administration of fairness to the Christians. The "eighth" persecution lasted the Apocalyptic 42 months until his death in 260. (Dion. Al. ap. Pearson, *Ann. Cyp.* p. 59; Eus. vii. 10, v. ii. 70.) On Aug. 2, 257, before the exile of Cyprian, Stephen died. His reputation as a martyr, dating from the 6th cent., is due to a transference to him of incidents from the death of Xystus, of which the singular history is traced by de Rossi, *Roma Sott. Cr.* vol. ii. p. 85, etc. He was succeeded on Aug. 25 by Xystus,‡ whom, not without a stroke at the dead lion, Pontius calls "a good pacific high-priest." No "state enemy" could be treated with more consideration than Cyprian received. Aspasius Paternus, the proconsul, heard him *in secretario,* and without confiscation or personal restraint simply required his retirement to Curubis, a free town, near the sea (*in deserto loco*), lonely, but pleasant, and well supplied (Pontius; cf. Gibbon, vol. ii. 248, Smith's ed.). It was at the same time that the withdrawal of Dionysius was ordered and performed (Eus. vii. 11). On Sept. 14 a dream, related at once to his friends, was found after his martyrdom to have foretold it for that day year. Attended by his deacon, and allowed the presence of friends, and "offering," no doubt, as in his former banishment, "his daily sacrifice," he actively organized relief for more helpless sufferers and subsidized them largely himself.§ After 11 months spent thus, the new proconsul Galerius Maximus, already a dying man, recalled him to his home in Carthage (*horti*). When a rumour arrived that Marcianus,

* Morcelli, *Africa Christiana,* vol. i. p. 21, questions whether the separate Praeses Numidiae was continued long after Septimius, apparently not noticing (Cyp. *Ep.* 77, ii.) that these confessors were tried before the Praeses.

† Pearson supposes a marble-quarry to be their work-place—*tenebrae* and *teter odor fumi* indicate mining and smelting rather.

‡ See these calculations in Lipsius, *Chron. d. Röm. Bisch.* p. 213.

§ Gibbon strangely seems to have understood the words *documentum professionis dedit* (*i.e.* taught how to hold fast our profession) to mean "an account of his behaviour was published for the edification of the Christian world" (*Ep.* 77).

"entrusted with the whole republic" by Valerian, now on his last march to Persia, was determined to carry things to an extremity with Christians, Cyprian was probably the first African who procured a copy of the tremendous rescript, and of the letter which was about to be issued to the Praesides (*Ep.* 80). The proconsul in Cyprian's trial mentions both the extension of capital penalties to presbyters, and the new prohibition of the use of cemeteries for worship. His messenger returned with the full intelligence of sweeping measures before their publication, and with news that Xystus had been beheaded (*Pont. Vit. Cyp.* xii.; *Leon. Sacr.* Muratori, vol. i. p. 391) on Sunday, Aug. 5, in the cemetery of Praetextatus * when actually "teaching" in his episcopal chair, and with him four of the great Roman deacons.† It may be taken as historical fact that on Wed. the 29th of the previous June, Xystus had translated the supposed remains of St. Peter to the cemetery known as Cata Cumbas, on the Appian Way, and those of St. Paul to the Ostian Way. It is possible that this increasing reverence to two malefactors executed two centuries before both shewed the magistrates that the spirit of the sect was becoming more dangerous and determined them to withdraw from Christians the protection which the burial laws hitherto accorded to rites celebrated in connexion with places of sepulture; and further, that this occasioned a withdrawal from the better-known cemetery of Callistus to the more obscure one of Praetextatus (see de Rossi, *Rom. Sott.* vol. ii. p. 41; and Lips. *ll.cc.*), and the death of Xystus in that place. The news of it had scarcely reached Carthage when Galerius, now in residence at Utica, summoned Cyprian thither in honourable form (*Ep.* 81). Having previously refused offers of a retreat, urged on him even by heathens, he now said he was resolved not to die, or utter the dying prophecy with which he apparently expected to be inspired, away from his people. Accordingly, informed of the dispatch before it came, he went into hiding in Carthage, there to await the proconsul's return. On his return, he reappeared and reoccupied his own house.‡ The details of the trial are too numerous to repeat and too remarkable to abridge. They are found not only in the narrative of Pontius, but also in a "Passion of Cyprian," which we have in different forms, and which from its simplicity, provinciality, and minute topography, must be contemporary.§ Cyprian was removed from his home on Aug. 13; the magistrate's broken health prolonged the examination; but the prisoner's rank shielded him from suffering or indignity. Though the language of the judge was stern, the Christians confessed the reluctance with which he gave sentence. In them sense of triumph in the possession of such a martyr is dwelt on with almost as much force as the sense of loss. With a strange mingled feeling, characteristic of the vividness with which in intense moments circumstances are apprehended which would at other times be trivial, they marked how little incidents combined to do him honour. The seat he rested on for the last time happened to be covered with a white cloth, the episcopal emblem. The trees were climbed, as he passed, by many a Zacchaeus. The eve and vigil of his martyrdom were kept by all his flock, watching through the night in the streets before his house, when as yet the only vigil of the Christian year was that which preceded the day of Christ's own Passion. The idea of this parallel took such hold that Augustine carries it to a painful pitch (*Serm.* 309). The two officers between whom Cyprian rode are compared to the two malefactors between whom our Lord went to His Passion. Pontius compares the words of the sentence to the prophecy of Caiaphas. Cyprian received no dying prophecy, nor uttered any, though his time was ample. His words were very few, and no exhortation could have been so eloquent as the "Thanks be to God" with which he answered the judgment: "Our pleasure is that Thascius Cyprianus be executed by the sword."

Personal, Theological, and Political Effectiveness.—To sum up the effect of Cyprian's 13 years' episcopate in briefest terms. Over and above, (1) the *social* impressiveness for the time of a convert with such culture and such mental habits, and of that perfect ἐπιείκεια and πρᾳότης to which Augustine constantly reverts with delight, comes (2) his *Philosophy*. It is usual to expand the fact that he was no philosopher. Nevertheless his writings on Resentment, Patience, Probation, Envy, Self-devotion, are most able essays towards establishing a new Christian basis of Morals, and have a permanent place in the series. (3) *Evidences*. As against both contemporary Judaism and contemporary paganism his collections have a distinct worth. (4) *Interpretation*. He has a free ideal scheme before him (*Ep.* 64), but in detail falls from it, and makes mere riddles of texts. (5) *Organization*. This is the real epigraph of his career. The magnitude of the effect he produced is incomparably greater than that of any other person, not excepting Hildebrand. (*a*) The *Church Council*, a local and doubtful institution before, became through his management a necessary institution and the imperial power of the church, and, with its system of representation by a life-aristocracy popularly elected, and its free discussionary scheme, exercised an important

* After 11 months and 12 (6 ?) days' episcopate. Eusebius, by an error, in which he indulges in other instances, ascribes to him *years* for *months* both in chronicle and history; and Jerome repeats it from him. So in vii. 15 he seems to speak of him as alive after the edict of restoration. See Lipsius, *l.c.*

† *Sic lege* "cum eo diacones quattuor."

‡ Nothing is more self-consistent than the language of *Ep.* 83, or more inconsistent with Gibbon's "recovering that fortitude which his character required."

§ They are entitled *Acta Proconsularia*, and so accepted by Pearson and Gibbon. Aug. *Serm.* 309 seems to quote either this Passio or some earlier document which is now embedded in it. *Ep.* 77, ii. refers to Cyprian's confession "Apud Acta proconsulis" just after it was made. Does Acta mean merely "trial before"? (Cf. Optat. B. iii. p. 68, apud acta locuti sunt.) If it means "official report," how could a Christian report be so styled, or how could a heathen one give the details with such advantage to the prisoners? Dionysius Alex. refers a carping adversary to the record of his own trial before Aemilian, then prefect of Egypt (Eus. vol. i. p. 384, notes on ὑπεμνηματίσθη).

function in the regeneration of liberty. (*b*) *Episcopacy* grew silently into an institution of the Roman empire, strong with the lasting virtues of Roman institutions, and only biding its time for recognition. (6) The *Individual Independence*, as he sketches it, of *elected bishops* preserved, while it remained, a grand democratic strength to what after a time sank to an oligarchic, and under the papacy to an administrative, magistracy. This must again be the key of church governments in states which have not that intimate union with the church which the ideal of a Christian nation requires. We here give references on the subject of this *Independence*, which to the policy of Cyprian's time was so essential (*Ep.* 55, xvii.; actum suum, etc., 72, iv.; quando habet, etc., 73, xxxvi.; nemini praescribentes, etc., 57, vi.; si de collegis, etc., 69, xvii.; statuat. *Sentt. Epp.* Praef. 6). There exists what may be called "resistance to Roman claims"; but Cyprian is totally unconscious of any claims made by the see, and resists Stephen purely as an arrogant individual.

Cultus.—There were two famous basilicas erected, one on the place of his martyrdom (*in agro sexti*), where was the *Mensa Cypriani*, from which Augustine often preached; the other on the shore (Aug. *Conf.* v.; *ad Mappalia*, Aug. vol. vii. App. p. 37; *ad Piscinas*, Victor Vitens. i. v. iv.). In this Monica spent the night of her son's departure for Italy, praying and weeping. In Sulpicius Severus (*Dial.* i. 3) his friend comes hither to pray on his way from Narbonne to Egypt. The adoration reached such a height that Gibbon is charmed to call him "*almost* a local deity." His feast and the gales which blew then were called Cypriani (Procop. *Vand.* i. 20, 21; Greg. Naz. *Or.* 18, ap. Ducange, *s.v.*). There are still on the "brink of the shore" the massive ruins of a church which must be St. Cyprian's. Davis (*Carthage and her Remains*, p. 389) describes them fully, and it is not hard to see how he has misled himself into not recognizing what they are. The relics of Cyprian were given (strange conjunction) by Haroun al Raschid to Charlemagne. The sequel may be seen in Ruinart, *Acta Mm. Cypr.* § 17, and in the epistle of J. de la Haye, prefixed to Pamelius's *Cyprian*, fol. *b*. 3.

Texts.—Of the MSS. and their connexions, and also of the edd., a good account is given by Hartel in his preface; cf. *D. C. B.* (4-vol. ed.). Besides the ed. in *Patr. Lat.* may be mentioned one by D. J. H. Goldhorn (Leipz. 1838), a useful text-book, well emended. But the best ed. now is by J. Hartel (3 vols. 8vo, 1868-1871), in the Vienna *Corpus Scriptt. Eccll. Latt.*, which contains all the works attributed to Cyprian, with the *ad Novatianum, Auctor de Rebaptismate, Pontii Vita*, etc., and Indices. It is a new recension, for which above 40 MSS. have been studied, classified, valued, and reduced to a most clear apparatus criticus, with keen attention to orthography, and almost always a judicious discrimination of the preferable readings; a valuable preface on the principles and history of the text-formation. [E.W.B.]

[The authoritative work on St. Cyprian is by the writer of this art. English trans. of several of Cyprian's works and his Epp. are given in the *Ante-Nicene Lib.* (T. & T. Clark). A simple monograph on his *Life and Times* is pub. in the cheap *A. and M. Theol. Lib.* (Griffith); and an Eng. trans. of his treatise *On the Lord's Prayer* by T. H. Bindley is pub. by S.P.C.K.; the text, with trans., has been ed. by Rev. H. Gee (Bell).]

Cyra. [MARANA.]

Cyriacus (19), 30th patriarch of Constantinople, A.D. 595. He was previously presbyter and steward, οἰκονόμος, of the great church at Constantinople (*Chronicon Paschale*, p. 378). Gregory the Great received the legates bearing the synodal letters which announced his consecration, partly from a desire not to disturb the peace of the church, and partly from the personal respect which he entertained for Cyriac; but in his reply he warned him against the sin of causing divisions in the church, clearly alluding to the use of the term oecumenical bishop (Gregorii *Ep.* lib. vii. 4, *Patr. Lat.* lxxvii. 853). The personal feelings of Gregory towards Cyriac appear most friendly.

Cyriac did not attend to the entreaties of Gregory that he would abstain from using the title, for Gregory wrote afterwards both to him and to the emperor Maurice, declaring that he could not allow his legates to remain in communion with Cyriac as long as he retained it. In the latter of these letters he compares the assumption of the title to the sin of Antichrist, since both exhibit a spirit of lawless pride. "Quisquis se universalem sacerdotem vocat, vel vocari desiderat, in elatione sua Antichristum praecurrit, quia superbiendo se ceteris praeponit" (Greg. *Ep.* 28, 30). In a letter to Anastasius of Antioch, who had written to him to remonstrate against disturbing the peace of the church, Gregory defends his conduct on the ground of the injury which Cyriac had done to all other patriarchs by the assumption of the title, and reminds Anastasius that not only heretics but heresiarchs had before this been patriarchs of Constantinople. He also deprecates the use of the term on more general grounds (*Ep.* 24). In spite of all this Cyriac was firm in his retention of the title, and appears to have summoned, or to have meditated summoning, a council to authorize its use. For in A.D. 599 Gregory wrote to Eusebius of Thessalonica and some other bishops, stating that he had heard they were about to be summoned to a council at Constantinople, and most urgently entreating them to yield neither to force nor to persuasion, but to be steadfast in their refusal to recognize the offensive title (*ib.* lib. ix. 68 in *Patr. Lat.*). Cyriac appears to have shared in that unpopularity of the emperor Maurice which caused his deposition and death (Theophan. *Chron.* p. 242, A.M. 6094; Niceph. Callis. *H. E.* xviii. 40; Theophylact. *Hist.* viii. 9). He still, however, had influence enough to exact from Phocas at his coronation a confession of the orthodox faith and a pledge not to disturb the church (Theoph. *Chron.* p. 243, A.M. 6094). He also nobly resisted the attempt of Phocas to drag the empress Constantia and her daughters from their sanctuary in a church of Constantinople (*ib.* p. 246, A.M. 6098). Perhaps some resentment at this opposition to his will may have induced Phocas to accede more readily to the claims of Boniface III. that Rome should be considered to be the head of all the church, in exclusion of the claims of Constantinople to the oecumenical bishopric (*Vita Bonifacii III.* apud Labbe, *Acta Concil.* t. v. 1615). Cyriac died in 606, and was interred in the church of the Holy Apostles (*Chronicon Paschale,* p. 381). He appears to have been a man of remarkable piety and earnestness, able to win the esteem of all parties. He built a church dedicated to the Θεοτόκος in a street of Constantinople called Diaconissa (Theoph. *Chron.* 233, A.M. 6090; Niceph. Callis. *H. E.* xviii. 42). [P.O.]

Cyrillus (2), Κύριλλος, bp. of Jerusalem, was probably born in Jerusalem or its immediate neighbourhood, *c.* 315. His writings prove that his education was liberal, and embraced a large variety of subjects. Touttée has laboriously collected evidences (c. ii.) of his acquaintance with physics, dialectics, physiology, mythology, etc. That he was a diligent student of Holy Scripture is certain, from the intimate knowledge, at least of the text, shewn in his Catecheses. But he was only acquainted with the LXX. His knowledge of Hebrew was only second-hand, and often incorrect. He was ordained deacon probably by Macarius bp. of Jerusalem, *c.* 335 (Soz. *H. E.* iv. 20, where the text is doubtful), and priest by his successor Maximus, *c.* 345. Maximus, notwithstanding Cyril's youth, entrusted him with the responsible duty of instructing catechumens, and preparing them for baptism. He also allowed him the exceptional privilege, sometimes granted by bishops to presbyters of eminent ability (*e.g.* to Chrysostom by Flavian of Antioch, and to Augustine by Valerius of Hippo), of preaching to the people in full church on the Lord's Day. In his office of catechist, *c.* 347, Cyril delivered the catechetical lectures by which his name is chiefly known (Hieron. *de Vir. Illust.* § 12). These lectures were preached without book on the evenings of the weeks of Lent, in the basilica of the Holy Cross, or *Martyrium,* erected on Calvary by St. Helena. His references to the locality are numerous and interesting (*e.g.* iv. 10-14, x. 19, xiii. 4, 22, 39, xviii. 33). The five mystagogical lectures were addressed during Easter-week at noon to those baptized on Easter-eve in the Anastasis, or church of the Holy Sepulchre.

The episcopate of Maximus terminated at the close of 350 or the beginning of 351, and Cyril was chosen to fill the episcopal chair of Jerusalem. A cloud of doubt and difficulty hangs over his elevation to the episcopate. Jerome can hardly have been mistaken as to the main fact, though theological prejudice and personal dislike may have warped his judgment and caused him to represent the case in the least favourable light. On some leading questions Cyril and Jerome were decidedly opposed. In the great controversy of the day Cyril belonged to the Asiatic party, Jerome to that of Rome. In the Meletian schism at Antioch also they took opposite sides: Cyril supporting Meletius, Jerome being a warm adherent of Paulinus. Jerome asserts (*Chronicon ad ann.* 349) that on the death of Maximus the Arians invaded the church of Jerusalem and promised to appoint Cyril to the vacant throne if he would repudiate his ordination by Maximus; that Cyril consented to the humiliating terms, served some time in the church as a deacon, and was then rewarded with the episcopate by Acacius, the semi-Arian bp. of Caesarea, and according to the seventh Nicene canon metropolitan of Palestine; that Cyril then dishonourably persecuted Heraclius, whom Maximus, on his deathbed, had nominated his successor, and degraded him to the presbyterate. This account is supported by Rufinus (*H. E.* i. 23, "Sacerdotio, confusa jam ordinatione, suscepto"). Socrates and Sozomen, though they say nothing of Cyril's repudiation of his orders, are almost equally unfavourable to his orthodoxy, identifying him with the semi-Arian party of Acacius and Patrophilus. They also introduce a new element of confusion by the statement that the see of Jerusalem was vacant not by death, but by Maximus's deposition and expulsion by the semi-Arians (Socr. ii. 38; Soz. iv. 20; Theophan. *Chronograph.* p. 34). This may safely be rejected. In refutation of Jerome's account, Cyril's advocates triumphantly point to the synodical letter to pope Damasus of the bishops assembled at Constantinople, the year after the second oecumenical synod, A.D. 382, which speaks of Cyril in terms of high eulogy, as a champion of the orthodox faith against Arian heresy, and affirms his canonical election to the see of Jerusalem (Theod. *H. E.* v. 9). But this does not touch the point at issue. Acacius was the metropolitan of Cyril's province. He and his fellow-bishops were, notwithstanding their heretical bias, the legitimate authorities for conferring the episcopate. Cyril's election and consecration was therefore strictly canonical. Besides, the silence of the members of the synod as to facts occurring 30 years before does not disprove them. Whatever might have been Cyril's earlier heretical failings, he was on the orthodox side then (cf. Socr. v. 8, and Soz. vii. 7). His adhesion was valuable, and it would have been as impolitic as it was needless to revive an almost forgotten scandal. Yet Cyril's own writings quite forbid us to follow Jerome's authority in classing him with the Arians, or charging him with heretical tenets. Circumstances might render his orthodoxy equivocal. His early patron, Maximus, was somewhat of a waverer. His friends and associates were semi-Arians, and he was chosen to the episcopate by them, with the hope of his supporting their cause. But no error of doctrine is to be discovered in his writings, though he avoids the test word "homoousion" in his catecheses. He is well characterized by the Duc de Broglie (*l'Eglise et l'Empire,* iii. 402) as "formant l'extrémité de l'aile droite du Semi-arianisme touchant à l'orthodoxie, ou de l'aile gauche de l'orthodoxie touchant au Semi-arianisme," and may be regarded, certainly in the later part of his life, as one of those of whom Athanasius speaks (*de Synod.* 41) as "brothers who mean what we mean, and only differ about the word." The first year of Cyril's episcopate was rendered memorable by the appearance, May 7, 351, of a remarkable parhelion, or other atmospheric phenomenon, over Jerusalem, which was regarded as a miraculous manifestation of the symbol of redemption intended to establish the faith and confute gainsayers, and produced great excitement in the city. The churches were thronged with worshippers, and many Jews and Gentiles were converted to the faith. So important did the phenomenon appear to Cyril that he wrote to the emperor Constantius describing it. This letter has been preserved. Its authenticity has been called in question by Rivet, but the internal evidence from the similarity of style is strong, and it is accepted by Blondel. The occurrence of the word "homoousion" at the close of the letter is, however, suspicious, and leads us to question whether the prayer for the emperor in which it stands is not a later addition (Soz. iv. 5; Philostorg. iii. 26; *Chron. Alex.* p. 678; Theophan. p. 35 A). If Acacius had reckoned on Cyril as a faithful adherent and ready instrument in carrying out his plans, the fallacy of his expectations was very soon shewn. Scarcely had Cyril established himself in his see when a distressing controversy, which became the source of much evil to the church, arose as to the claim to priority of their respective sees (Theod. ii. 25; Soz. iv. 25). Cyril grounded his claim on the apostolical rank of his see, Acacius on the decision of the council of Nice (Can. vii.), which placed the bp. of Aelia—*i.e.* Jerusalem—under the bp. of Caesarea as metropolitan. This contest for pre-eminence was speedily embittered by mutual accusations of heterodoxy (Soz. iv. 25). For two years Acacius continued vainly summoning Cyril to his tribunal, and at last cut the controversy short by deposing him from his see (Soz. *u.s.*, 357 or 358) at a small packed synod of his own adherents. The ostensible grounds were very trivial: contumacy in refusing to appear, and the charge—afterwards brought against Ambrose by the Arians—of having sold some of the church ornaments during a prevailing scarcity to supply the wants of the poor (Socr. ii. 40; Soz. iv. 25; Theod. ii. 26; Epiphan. *Haeres.* lxxiii. §§ 23-27), and also of having held communion with Eustathius and Elpidius after their deposition by the synod of Melitina, in Lesser Armenia (Soz. *u.s.*; Basil. *Ep.* 253 [74]). Cyril was forced to yield. He left his see, not, however, without an appeal to a larger council, the justice of which was allowed by Constantius. This is noted by Socrates (ii. 40) as the first instance of an appeal against the decision of an ecclesiastical synod. On leaving Jerusalem Cyril first retired to Antioch and thence to Tarsus, where he was hospitably received by the bp. Silvanus, one of the best of the semi-Arians, who availed himself of Cyril's powers as a preacher. We find him also here in communion and friendship with other leading members of the same party, Eustathius of Sebaste, Basil of Ancyra, and George of Laodicea (Soz. iv. 25; Philost. iv. 12). The enmity of Acacius pursued his rival. Silvanus was warned against holding communion with one who had been deposed for contumacy and other crimes. But Cyril had gained great popularity at Tarsus by his sermons, the people would not hear of his leaving them, and Silvanus declined to attend to the admonition (Theod. *u.s.*). Nearly two years after his deposition, Sept. 359, Cyril laid his appeal before the council of Seleucia, at which he took his place among the semi-Arians. Acacius vehemently protested against his admission to the council. "If Cyril did not leave the synod, he must." Some of the bishops, in the cause of peace, begged Cyril to yield, at least temporarily, till his appeal had been heard. Cyril refused, and Acacius quitted the council, but soon returned, and took a leading part in the subsequent stormy debates. The semi-Arians who were opposed to Acacius were in the ascendant. Acacius was himself deposed, and Cyril restored (Theod. ii. 26; Socr. ii. 40; Soz. iv. 22; Philost. iv. 12). Acacius and his friends at once started for the capital, where they easily persuaded the weak Constantius to summon a fresh council. Fresh accusations were added to those formerly adduced. The charge of sacrilegiously disposing of the church goods was revived, and the emperor's indignation was excited by hearing that a baptismal robe of gold brocade, presented by his father Constantine to Macarius, which had been sold, had unfortunately found its way into the wardrobe of a theatre, and been recognized on the stage. Acacius's arts prevailed, and Cyril was a second time banished (Socr. ii. 42; Soz. iv. 25; Theod. ii. 27).

On the accession of Julian, 361, Cyril was reinstated, together with all the exiled bishops (Socr. iv. 1; Soz. *u.s.*; Theod. iii. 4; Amm. Marcell. xxii. 5). At Jerusalem Cyril calmly watched the attempts of Julian to rebuild the Temple, and foretold that it must fail (Socr. iii. 20; Rufinus, i. 37).

During the reign of the orthodox Jovian Cyril's episcopate was undisturbed, and the accession of Valens and Valentinian found him in quiet possession of his see, 364. In 366 Acacius died, and Cyril immediately claimed the nomination to the see of Caesarea, and appointed Philomenus. Philomenus was deposed by the Eutychian faction, and another Cyril substituted. He, in return, was deposed by Cyril of Jerusalem, who consecrated his sister's son Gelasius in his room, A.D. 367 (Epiphan. *Haer.* lxxiii. 37). In 367 Cyril was a third time deposed and exiled, with all the prelates recalled by Julian, by the edict of the Arian Valens (Socr. ii. 45; Soz. iv. 30; Epiph. *Haer.* lxvi. 20). His banishment lasted till Valens died and Theodosius succeeded, Jan. 19, 379, when he reoccupied his see, which he retained quietly for the 8 remaining years of his life (Hieron. *Vir. Ill.* c. 112; Socr. v. 3; Soz. vii. 2). On his return he found Jerusalem rent with schisms, infested with almost every form of heresy, and polluted by the most flagrant crimes. To combat these evils he appealed to the council held at Antioch, 379, which dispatched Gregory Nyssen to his aid. But the disease was too deeply seated to admit of an easy or speedy remedy. Gregory departed hopeless of a cure, and in his *Warning against Pilgrimages* drew a dark picture of the depravation of morals in the Holy City (*de Euntibus Hieros.* p. 656). In 381 Cyril was present at the second oecumenical council held at Constantinople, when he took rank with the chief metropolitans, the bps. of Alexandria and Antioch. He there declared his full adhesion to the Nicene faith, and his acceptance of the test word "homoousion" (Socr. iv. 8; Soz. iv. 7).

Cyril died Mar. 18, 386 (Socr. v. 15; Soz. vii. 14; Bolland. Mar. 18, p. 625 B). He was bp. of Jerusalem for 35 years, 16 of which he passed in exile.

His works consist of 18 "Catechetical lectures" addressed to catechumens (*κατηχήσεις φωτιζομένων*), and 5 "Mystagogical lectures" to the newly baptized (*μυσταγωγικαὶ κατηχήσεις πρὸς τοὺς νεοφωτίστους*). These were composed in his youth (*ἃς ἐν τῇ νεότητι συνέταξεν*, Hieron. *de Vir. Ill.* c. 112), *c.* 347, while still a presbyter. The "Catechetical lectures" possess considerable interest as the earliest example extant of a formal system of theology; from their testimony to the canon of Scripture, the teaching of the church on the chief articles of the creed, and on the sacraments; and from the light they throw on the ritual of the 4th cent. The perfect agreement of his teaching, as Dr. Newman remarks (*Lib. of the Fathers*, vol. ii. part i. pp. ix.-x.), as regards the Trinity, with the divines of the Athanasian school, is of great weight in determining the true doctrine of the early church on that fundamental question, and relieves Cyril from all suspicion of heterodoxy. But his Catecheses do not rank high as argumentative or expository work, nor has Cyril any claim to a place among the masters of Christian thought, whose writings form the permanent riches of the church.

All previous editions of his works were surpassed by the Benedictine ed. of A. A. Touttée (Paris, 1720, fol., and Venice, 1761, fol.). The introduction contains very elaborate and exhaustive dissertations on his life, writings, and doctrines. These are reprinted in Migne's *Patrologia*, vol. xxxiii.

The chief modern authorities for Cyril's life and doctrines are Touttée, *u.s.*; Tillem. *Mémoires Ecclés.* vol. viii.; Cave, *Historia Lit.* i. 211, 212; Schröckh, *Kirchengeschichte*, xii. 343 seq.; Newman, preface to the Oxf. trans., *Lib. of the Fathers*, ii. 1. Newman's trans. was carefully revised by Dr. E. H. Gifford in the *Lib. of Nicene and Post-Nicene Fathers* (1894), and furnished with a very important introduction. [E.V.]

Cyrillus (7), St., archbp. of Alexandria. He was a native of Alexandria, and had learned theology under monastic discipline in "the desert." During this period he had been reproved by Isidore of Pelusium, who was for years his venerated monitor, for occupying himself, even in "solitude," with worldly thoughts and interests (Isid. *Ep.* i. 25); and it is evident from his whole career that so strong a will and so vehement a nature could never be thoroughly satisfied with a life of contemplation. After five years' abode in mount Nitria, his uncle, the then archbp. Theophilus, summoned him to Alexandria, where he was ordained, and expounded and preached with great reputation (Neale, *Hist. Alex.* i. 226). Theophilus died Oct. 15, A.D. 412. Cyril was put forward for the vacant chair; and after a tumultuous contest was enthroned, three days after his uncle's death. (See his first Paschal homily.) His episcopate, begun in trouble and discord, seemed at first to forebode nothing better than a course of violent and untempered zeal, as if the fierce spirit of Theophilus were governing his conduct. He shut up the chamber of the Novatianists, took away their "sacred treasure," and deprived their bishop, Theopemptus, of all his property (Socr. vii. 7). He then made an attack upon the large body of Jewish residents. They had provoked him by implacable hostility. One Hierax, a schoolmaster, always foremost in applauding Cyril's sermons, was denounced by the Jews as an encourager of sedition when he was in the theatre at the promulgation of a prefectorial edict. Orestes, the prefect, who hated Cyril as a formidable rival potentate, had Hierax publicly tortured in the theatre. Cyril thereupon tried the effect of menaces on the principal Jews of Alexandria. This only increased their bitterness; they began to organize plots against the Christians; and one night a cry rang through the streets that "Alexander's church was on fire." The Christians rushed to save their sanctuary: the Jews, recognizing each other, as prearranged, by rings made from the bark of palm branches, slew the Christians whom they met. At daybreak Cyril, at the head of an immense crowd, took forcible possession of the synagogues, expelled the Jews from the city and abandoned their property to plunder. Orestes, naturally indignant, complained to the emperor, Theodosius II., then a boy of fourteen. Cyril addressed to the court an account of the Jewish outrages, and, at the suggestion of the people, endeavoured to pacify the prefect. Orestes would not listen. Cyril extended to him, as a form of solemn appeal, the book of the Gospels; it might well have occurred to Orestes that the archbishop had forgotten some of its precepts when he in person led a multitude of Christian zealots to revenge one violence by another. The gifted female philosopher, Hypatia, the boast of Alexandrian paganism, was dragged from her carriage into the great Caesarean church, where her body was torn to pieces. This hideous crime, done in a sacred place and in a sacred season—it was the Lent of 415—brought, as Socrates expresses it (vii. 15), "no small reproach on Cyril and the church of the Alexandrians." Was this foul murder what Gibbon calls it, an "exploit of Cyril's"? Did he take any part in it, or approve it *ex post facto*? It has been said that "Cyril was suspected, even by the orthodox, of complicity in the murder" (Stanley's *Lect. on East. Ch.* 293). Socrates, as sympathizing with the Novatianists, has been considered to do Cyril less than justice; but he does not suggest such a suspicion against him, or against the whole church of Alexandria. He says, fairly, that this church and its chief pastor were to some extent disgraced by such a deed of members of it. As for Damascius's assertion that Cyril really prompted the murder (Suidas, p. 1059), we cannot consider as evidence the statement of a pagan philosopher who lived about 130 years after the event, and was a thorough hater of Christianity. We are justified in regarding it, with Canon Robertson (*Hist. Ch.* i. 401), as "an unsupported calumny"; but, as he adds, "the perpetrators were mostly officers of his church, and had unquestionably derived encouragement from

Cyril's earlier proceedings; and his character deservedly suffered in consequence." The turbulent and furious "parabolani" and others, who shed Hypatia's blood at the foot of the altar, were but "bettering the instruction" which had let them loose upon the synagogues. Cyril's name has paid dearly for the error, and the great doctrinal cause which he upheld so stoutly in after-years has suffered for the faults of his earlier life.

It was but natural that the government should the next year restrain the clergy from political action, especially by restrictions on the number and conduct of the parabolani.

Cyril had inherited his uncle's animosity against John Chrysostom, who, in his opinion, had been canonically deposed; he rejected with bitterness the advice of Atticus of Constantinople to place "John's" name on his church diptychs (*Ep.* p. 204); and it was not until after the memory of that persecuted saint had been rehabilitated at Constantinople as well as at Antioch that the archbp. of Alexandria, urged by Isidore of Pelusium (Isid. i. 370), consented in 417 to follow these precedents. (See Tillemont, xiv. 281.)

We pass over several uneventful years, during which Cyril doubtless occupied himself in ordinary church affairs and in theological literature, and come to the great controversy with which his name is pre-eminently associated. In the end of 428 he became aware of the excitement caused in Constantinople by the preaching of archbp. Nestorius. The line of thought which Nestorius had entered upon (under the influence, as it seems, of Theodore of Mopsuestia) led him to explain away the mystery of the Incarnation by reducing it to a mere association between the Eternal Word and a human Christ. The Alexandrian see had agents at Constantinople, and the denial, by Nestorius and his supporters, of the strict personal oneness between "God the Word" and the Son of Mary—expressed by the formula, "Let no one call Mary Theotokos"—was an event which was certain to excite the vigilant zeal of a prelate like Cyril, opposed, alike by temperament and antecedents, to whatever undermined the mysterious majesty of the Christian faith. Very early in Jan. 429 Cyril dealt with the subject in his Paschal letter or homily, the 17th of the series; in which, while affirming with great vividness and emphasis the reality and permanence of Christ's manhood, he enforced the singleness of his Divine Personality, and applied to His human mother, in two distinct passages, a phrase even stronger than "Theotokos"—*μήτηρ Θεοῦ*. About the end of Apr. 429, when the controversial sermons of Nestorius—exhibiting no little confusion of thought, but clearly indicating a disbelief in what is theologically termed the Personal Union—had reached Egyptian monks, Cyril wrote to all who within his jurisdiction were "practising the solitary life," a long letter, upholding the term "Theotokos" in its true sense, as not meaning "mother of the Godhead," but mother, as regarded the manhood, of Him Who, being in the form of God, assumed the form of a servant, and, being the Lord of Glory, condescended to suffer the death of the cross. If it was true, Cyril argued, that Jesus Christ was God, it was by consequence not less true that His mother was "Theotokos." If she was not rightly so called, her Son was a human individual external to the divine nature, and not in a true sense Emmanuel. This letter cites at length the Nicene Creed in its original form, ignoring the alterations made by the council of Constantinople, and insisting that the creed identified Jesus Christ with the Divine Co-essential Son. Nestorius was much displeased at the reception given to this letter by some official persons at Constantinople. He ordered one Photius to answer it, and encouraged some Alexandrians residing at the imperial city, who had been rebuked by Cyril for gross offences, to prefer complaints against him (Mansi, iv. 1003, 887). On the other hand, Cyril, having also been interrogated by Celestine of Rome as to the genuineness of Nestorius's sermons, wrote his first letter to Nestorius (Cyr. *Ep.* p. 19; Mansi, iv. 883), the point of which was that the prevailing excitement had been caused, not by the letter to the monks of Egypt, but by Nestorius's own refusal to allow to Christ's mother a title which was the symbol of her Son's real Divinity. Cyril also referred to a work *On the Holy and Co-essential Trinity*, which he himself had written in the lifetime of Nestorius's predecessor Atticus, and in which he had used language on the Incarnation which harmonized with his letter to the monks. Nestorius replied very briefly, and in a courteous tone; although he intimated dislike of what he deemed harsh in Cyril's letter (Cyr. *Ep.* p. 21; Mansi, iv. 885). He evidently did not wish to quarrel with the see of Alexandria, although he practised considerable severities on monks of his own city who withstood him to the face. Cyril, too, was not forward to press the controversy to extremes. During the latter part of 429 he was even blamed by some for inactivity. But he may have written at this period, as Garnier thinks, his "Scholia," or "Notes," on the Incarnation of the Only-begotten (Mar. Merc. ii. 216), and in Feb. 430 (probably after hearing how Nestorius had upheld a bishop named Dorotheus in his anathema against the word "Theotokos") he wrote, in synod, a second Ep. to Nestorius—the letter which became a symbolic treatise sanctioned by general councils. (See it in Cyr. *Ep.* p. 22; Mansi, iv. 887; cf. Tillemont, xiv. 338). Nothing can be more definite and luminous than his disclaimer of all Apollinarian notions, which had been imputed by Nestorius to those who confessed the "Theotokos"; his explanation of the idea intended by that phrase; his peremptory exclusion of the theory of a mere association as distinct from a hypostatic or personal union, and his not less emphatic assertion of the distinctness of the natures thus brought together in the one Christ. "Not that the difference of the natures was annulled by the union, but rather that one Godhead and Manhood constituted the one Lord Jesus Christ, by their ineffable concurrence into unity. . . . Thus we confess one Christ and Lord." The answer of Nestorius was characterized by *ignoratio elenchi*, and could not be regarded as a satisfactory statement of belief (Cyr. *Ep.* p. 25;

Mansi, iv. 891). Cyril wrote another letter to some of his own clergy resident at Constantinople; the Nestorian argument from the impassibility of the Godhead he put aside as not to the purpose; and charged Nestorianism with making two Christs and two Sons (Cyr. *Ep.* p. 32; Mansi, iv. 1003). This letter recognizes the proverbial eloquence of "John" Chrysostom, and expresses the writer's desire for peace, if peace could be had without a sacrifice of truth. He disapproved of a draft petition to the emperor, sent him by these clerics, as too vehement. In a similar strain he wrote to a common friend of Nestorius and himself, declaring earnestly that he cared for nothing so much as the faith, and desired that Nestorius might be preserved from the charge of heresy (Cyr. *Ep.* p. 31; Mansi, iv. 899). A long letter "On the Right Faith," which he wrote about the same time to the emperor Theodosius, contained an elaborate survey of former heresies, and of the error now spreading in the church (Cyr. tom. v. par. 2; Mansi, iv. 617). Cyril's keen-eyed speculative orthodoxy did not stand coldly apart from all care for practical religion. He felt the vital importance of his cherished doctrine in its bearings on the Christian life; he urged in this treatise that if the Word were not personally incarnate, *i.e.* if the human Teacher and Sufferer were not really one with the eternal Son of God, the faith of Christian men would be made void, the work of their salvation annihilated, and the cross lose its virtue. For the very principle of Christian redemption lay in this, that it was one and the same "Ego" Who, possessing, by virtue of His incarnation, at once a divine and a human sphere of existence, could be at once the God of mankind and the Saviour Who died for them. In c. 21 he dwells, in pursuance of this idea, on the death of Christ as being a full satisfaction (δῶρον ἀληθῶς ἀντάξιον). This treatise contains an argument on which Cyril was never weary of insisting: it was particularly congenial to the depth and awe, the richness and the tenderness, of his thoughts on the great mystery of incorporation into Christ. From the admitted truth that the flesh of Christ was received in the Eucharist as life-giving, he argued that it must be, in a real sense, the flesh of God. In c. 6 of the treatise, he says that Nestorians would not have erred by dwelling simply on the difference between the natures of "God" and "flesh"—that difference was undeniable; but they went on to assert an individual and separate being for the man Jesus as apart from the Divine Word, and this was the very point of their heresy. In c. 27 he rises to almost Chrysostomic eloquence when he sets forth the superangelic greatness involved in the idea of "the Lord of Glory." Another treatise, in two books, was addressed to the princesses, Pulcheria, the gifted sister of the feeble emperor, Arcadia, and Marina (Cyr. tom. v. par. 2; Mansi, iv. 679 seq.). In bk. i. he argued at length from Scripture for the oneness and Divinity of Christ, for His position as the true object of faith, and for His office as life-giver and atoner; and among the texts he urged were Heb. i. 3, 6, xiii. 8; Tit. ii. 13; I. Cor. ii. 8; II. Cor. viii. 9; Eph. iii. 17; Gal. i. 1; Phil. ii. 6; Matt. xi. 28, xvi. 16, 20; John i. 14, xvii. 3; I. John v. 5 (without the words about the "heavenly witnesses"). He laid great stress on the vastness of the claim advanced by and for Christ in Scripture, and on the unreasonableness of demanding so absolute an obedience if He were not personally Divine. He asked how the death of a mere man could be of such importance for the race? Many a saint had lived and died, but not one by dying had become the saviour of his fellows. He quoted nine passages from earlier writers in support of the term "Theotokos," or of the doctrine which it guarded. In bk. ii. he explained texts relied on by Nestorians, including parts of Heb. ii. and Matt. xxvii. 46, Luke ii. 40, 52, John iv. 22, Mark xii. 32; in the last text seeming to recognize, as he does elsewhere (though sometimes favouring a different view), a limitation of knowledge in Christ's manhood, analogous to His submission, in His human sphere, to pain and want, and consistent with a perpetual omniscience in His Divine consciousness (*ad Regin.* ii. 17). In accordance with the emphatic assertion (ii. 7) of the value imparted to Christ's death by His Divinity, the work concludes with "for all our hope is in Christ, by Whom and with Whom," etc.

In these treatises, if some texts are strained beyond their natural meaning, there is yet a remarkable exhibition of acuteness and fertility of thought, pervaded and quickened by what Dorner calls Cyril's "warm interest" in Christianity as a religion. Probably *c.* Apr. 430 Cyril answered the letter of the Roman bishop, received a year before (*Ep.* p. 26); he informed him that the main body of the faithful of Constantinople (acting on the principle fully recognized in the ancient church, that loyalty to the faith was a higher duty than ecclesiastical subordination) were holding off from the communion of Nestorius, but greatly needed support and countenance; and in very deferential terms asked Celestine to say whether any fellowship could be maintained by orthodox bishops with one who was disseminating heresy (Mansi, iv. 1011). With this letter he sent a series of passages illustrative of what Nestorius held and of what church-writers had taught, translated into Latin "as well as Alexandrians could" perform such a task, and to be shewn by his messenger Posidonius to Celestine, *if* the latter had received anything from Nestorius. One other letter of Cyril's belongs to the summer of 430: he addressed himself to the aged Acacius, bp. of Berrhoea, who communicated the letter to John, patriarch of Antioch, but informed Cyril that many who had come to Syria, fresh from the preaching of Nestorius, were disposed to think him not committed to heresy. It is observable that Cyril tells Acacius that some had been led on by Nestorianism into an express denial that Christ was God (see Mansi, iv. 1053).

We now reach a landmark in the story. On Aug. 11, 430, Celestine, having held a synod which pronounced Nestorius heretical, gave Cyril a stringent commission (see this letter in Mansi, iv. 1017) to "join the authority of the Roman see to his own" in warning Nestorius that unless a written retractation were executed within ten days, giving assurance of his accepting the faith as to "Christ our God," which was held by the churches of Rome and Alexandria, he would be excluded from the communion of those churches, and "provision" would be made by them for the church of Constantinople, *i.e.* by the appointment of an orthodox bishop. Had Cyril been as violent and imperious as he is often said to have been, he would not have deferred by a single day the carrying out of these instructions. But he took time to assemble, at Alexandria, a "council of all Egypt," and then, probably on Mon. Nov. 3, 430, wrote his third Letter to Nestorius (*Ep.* p. 57; Mansi, iv. 1067; Routh, *Scr. Op.* ii. 17), in which he required him to anathematize his errors, and added a long dogmatic exposition of the true sense of the Nicene Creed, with a careful disclaimer of all confusion between Godhead and manhood. To this letter were appended 12 "articles," or "chapters," anathematizing the various points of the Nestorian theory—*e.g.* that Emmanuel is not really God, and Mary not Theotokos; that the Word was not personally joined to flesh; that there was a "connexion" of two persons; that Christ is a "God-bearing man"; that He was a separate individual acted on by the Word, and called "God" along with Him; that His Flesh was not the Word's own; that the Word did not suffer death in the flesh. These propositions were not well calculated to reclaim Nestorius; nor were they, indeed, so worded throughout as to approve themselves to all who essentially agreed with Cyril as to the Personal Deity of Christ, and he was afterwards obliged to put forth explanations of their meaning. Cyril wrote two other letters to the clergy, laity, and monks of Constantinople, urging them to contend, or praising them for having already contended, for that faith in Christ's true Godhead of which "Theotokos" was the recognized expression (Mansi, iv. 1094). Four bishops were sent from Alexandria to bear the synodal documents to Constantinople and deliver the anathemas to Nestorius in his palace, after the conclusion of the Eucharistic service, either on Sun. Nov. 30, 430, or Sun. Dec. 7. Nestorius met the denunciations of the Alexandrian synod by enlisting several Eastern bishops in his cause, including John of Antioch, and Theodoret, who accused Cyril of Apollinarianism; by preaching in an orthodox strain to his own people, and by framing 12 anathemas of his own, some of which betrayed confusion of thought, while some tended directly to confirm the charges against his teaching—*e.g.* he would not allow Emmanuel to be called Very God. Theodoret, whose views on the subject were not as yet clear or consistent, composed a reply to Cyril. Andrew of Samosata, in the name of the "Eastern" bishops properly so called, also entered the lists against the great theologian of Egypt, who answered both his new antagonists in an *Apology* for the 12 articles (Mansi, v. 19), and a Defence of them against Theodoret's objections, the latter addressed to a bishop named Euoptius (Mansi, v. 81). These treatises threw light on the state of mind to which Cyril's anathemas had seemed so offensive. The Easterns, or Andrew speaking in their name, exhibit some remarkable misconceptions of Cyril's meaning—*e.g.* they tax him with denying Christ's flesh to be of real human derivation; but they absolutely disclaim the view which would make Jesus merely a preeminent saint, and they speak of worship being due to the One Son. Theodoret uses much language which is *primâ facie* Nestorian; his objections are pervaded by an *ignoratio elenchi*, and his language is repeatedly illogical and inconsistent; but he and Cyril were essentially nearer in belief than, at the time, they would have admitted (Hooker, v. 53, 4), for Theodoret virtually owns the personal oneness, and explains the phrase "God assumed man" by "He assumed manhood." Both writers speak severely of each other: Theodoret calls Cyril a wolf, and Cyril treats Theodoret as a calumniator. Cyril, in his *Reply to the Easterns* and in his letter to Euoptius, earnestly disclaims both forms of Apollinarianism—the notion of a mindless manhood in Christ, and the notion of a body formed out of Godhead. The latter, he says, is excluded by John i. 14. In the reply (on art. 4) he admits "the language appropriate to each nature." Cyril points out the confusions of thought which had misled Theodoret as to "God" and "Godhead"; insists that the eternal Son, retaining His divine dignity and perfections, condescended to assume the limitations of manhood; and so (*ad Euopt.* 4, as in *ad Regin.* ii. 17, etc.) explains Mark xii. 32, and says, with a touch of devotional tenderness particularly refreshing amid the clash of polemics, "He wept as man, that He might stop thee from weeping. He is said to have been weak as to His manhood, that He might put an end to thy weakness" (*ad Euopt.* 10). He adhered with characteristic definiteness to the point really involved—the question whether Jesus were a human individual (to be viewed ἰδικῶς, as he repeatedly says), or whether He were the Divine Son Himself appearing in human form and occupying, without prejudice to His inalienable and preexistent majesty, a human sphere of existence. In the former case, the Son of Mary must be regarded simply as a very highly favoured saint, and Christianity loses its distinctive power and preciousness; in the latter case, He is a Divine Redeemer, and Christianity is a Gospel worthy of the name. "Let us all acknowledge as Saviour the Word of God, Who remained impassible in the nature of the Godhead, but suffered, as Peter said, in the flesh. For, by a true union, that body which tasted death was His very own. Else, how was 'Christ from the Jews according to the flesh,' and 'God over all, and blessed for ever, amen'? and into Whose death have we been baptized, and by confessing Whose resurrection are we justified? . . . The death of a mere man," etc., "or do we, as is indeed the case, proclaim the death of God Who became man and suffered for us in flesh, and confessing His resurrection, put away the burden of sin?" (*ad Euopt.*) To this same period or the preceding year (429) may be assigned Cyril's five books *Against Nestorius*. In these he comments on passages in Nestorius's sermons, and by all forms of argument and illustration sets forth the question really at stake—Had the Divine Son Himself become incarnate, or had He closely allied Himself to a man?

We must now return to the events of Nov. 430. Before the Egyptian deputies could reach Constantinople, Theodosius II. issued letters to the metropolitans of his empire, summoning them to meet at Ephesus in the Pentecost of 431, with such bishops as each might select, to hold a general council. This resolution, taken at the instance of Nestorius, had the effect of suspending all hostile action on the part of any individual bishop or provincial synod. Theodosius, who was prejudiced against Cyril, wrote sharply to him, censuring his "meddlesomeness" and "rashness," and complaining of his having written separately to the princesses. In compliance with the imperial order, Cyril arrived at Ephesus with 50 bishops, about June 2, 431. For the details of the history of the Ephesine Council, or third oecumenical synod, see art. "Ephesus, Councils of," in *D. C. A.* It is enough here to specify the occasions on which Cyril came prominently forward. A fortnight elapsed before the council was opened: Cyril, like other prelates, employed himself in strengthening the cause he had at heart by earnest addresses. After waiting long for the arrival of John of Antioch and his attendant bishops, Cyril received a cordial letter from his brother patriarch, announcing that he had been travelling incessantly for a month, and hoped to "embrace Cyril" in five or six days more (*Ep.* p. 83). There also arrived two metropolitans, who bore from him a message to the bishops requesting them to proceed with business if he were delayed. The question at once arose—"Should the bishops wait any longer?" It would have been clearly better, even as a matter of policy, to wait a few days for John's arrival. The cause of orthodoxy could never be aided by its being associated with, to say the least, the appearance of unfairness or impatience. But Cyril and his suffragans were probably not at all desirous of John's presence, for they knew he would be hostile to the Cyrilline articles: they encouraged the idea that he was purposely loitering from reluctance to join in measures against Nestorius (an idea which appears to have been unfounded, Evagr. i. 3), and took advantage of the fact that other bishops were weary of waiting, the rather that illness, and even death, had occurred among them. So the council was opened on June 22, 431; and John's message, which evidently referred to a possible delay beyond the six days specified, was unjustifiably quoted to defend a refusal to wait even that period. In this it is impossible to acquit Cyril of blame; and the fault "brought its own punishment in the confusions that ensued" (Neale, *Hist. Alex.* i. 259).

Cyril presided in the assembly; not in virtue of the commission from Celestine to act in his stead—which had been already acted upon in the Alexandrian council of Nov. 430—but as the prelate of highest dignity then present, and as holding the proxy and representing the mind of the Roman bishop, until the Roman legates should arrive (see Tillem. xiv. 393). Cyril called on the council to judge between himself and Nestorius: the main facts were stated by his secretary; when Nestorius refused to appear, Cyril's second letter to him was read, and at Cyril's request the bishops pronounced upon its orthodoxy, declaring it in entire accordance with the faith. His third letter was received merely with a tacit assent, which might be held to extend to the "articles." (The council professed, afterwards, that it had approved Cyril's *epistles*; Mansi, iv. 1237.) After evidence as to Nestorius's opinions and the mind of orthodox Fathers had been laid before the council (great stress being doubtless laid on Nestorius's recent avowal, "I never will admit that a child of two or three months old was God," Mansi, iv. 1181, 1239), his deposition and excommunication were resolved on by the assembled bishops; and Cyril signed the sentence before his brethren in these words: "I, Cyril, bp. of Alexandria, sign, giving my judgment together with the council."

When the patriarch of Antioch, with a few bishops, arrived on June 26 or 27, in vexation at the course taken by the majority, they held a "council" or their own, and "deposed" Cyril, and Memnon, bp. of Ephesus, imputing to the former not only Apollinarianism, but also the heresy of the ultra-Arian rationalist Eunomius. On the other hand, the council of Ephesus, now reinforced by the Roman legates, treated Cyril and Celestine as one in faith, and proceeded to summon John—Cyril being disposed, had not the bp. of Jerusalem prevented it, to move for a sentence of deposition on the patriarch of Antioch, after the first summons (see Mansi, iv. 1311). Cyril repudiated and anathematized the heresies imputed to him, and coupled with them the Pelagian errors and those of Nestorius. John of Antioch, having disowned the council's summons, was excommunicated, with his adherents. Late in July count John, the imperial high treasurer, was sent by Theodosius to Ephesus, with a letter in which Cyril, Memnon, and Nestorius were treated as deposed. Accordingly all three were arrested, and guards slept at Cyril's chamber door. His opponents induced Isidore of Pelusium to write to him, exhorting him to avoid the bad precedents of his uncle's violent conduct, and not to give occasion for the charge of personal animosity (*Ep.* i. 310). Cyril, for his part, spoke, in a letter to three of his suffragans then at Constantinople (*Ep.* p. 91), of infamous falsehoods circulated against him, but detected by count John. He thanked God for having been counted worthy to suffer, for His Name's sake, not only bonds but other indignities. He received from a priest named Alypius a letter describing him in glowing terms as an imitator of Athanasius. While the two rival assemblies of bishops, the council and the "conciliabulum," sent deputies to the court of Theodosius, Cyril wrote an "Explanation" of his "articles," vindicating them against the charge of a confusion between the Godhead and the Manhood, or of teaching inconsistent with the distinct existence of the latter, in the one Divine Person of the Incarnate Lord. Theodosius finally ordered Cyril and his friends to return home, but abstained from condemning the "Eastern" bishops, who on their side complained of his partiality to their opponents.

On Oct. 30, 431, Cyril returned to Alexandria; and shortly afterwards Maximian, a pious and simple-hearted man, who by virtue of an imperial mandate had been consecrated to the see of Constantinople in the room of Nestorius, announced his accession to Cyril, who in his reply compared him to the faithful Eliakim, invested with the stewardship of Hezekiah's household on the deprivation of the unworthy Shebna. This letter contained a statement of orthodox doctrine, and a disclaimer of all ideas of "confusion" or "alteration" in the divine nature of the Word (*Ep.* p. 94 seq.; Mansi, v. 257 seq.). Cyril next began a vindication of his conduct to be laid before the emperor (Mansi, v. 225). Theodosius, hoping for a reconciliation, endeavoured to arrange a meeting between John and Cyril at Nicomedia. Cyril was now disposed to moderation, and resolved to insist only upon the condemnation of Nestorius and the recognition of Maximian. The meeting, it was found, could not take place; but a council at Antioch framed six articles, expressly rejecting those of Cyril, while accepting Athanasius's letter to Epictetus as an exposition of Nicene orthodoxy. Cyril's reply shewed that he had mastered his tendency to vehement and unyielding self-assertion. He wrote to Acacius of Berrhoea, the oldest bp. in Syria, who had forwarded to him the six articles by the hands of the "tribune and notary" Aristolaus. Cyril's letter (preserved, in a Lat. version, in the "Synodicon," Mansi, v. 831) is worth attention: he represented the impossibility of withdrawing what he had written against Nestorius—it would be easy to come to a good understanding about the "articles" of the Alexandrian synod if only the Easterns would accept the deposition of Nestorius. "Those who anathematize them will see that the meaning of the articles is directed solely against his blasphemies." For himself, Cyril disavowed and condemned once more the heresies imputed to him, and asserted the impassibility of the divine nature in Christ, while insisting that He, the Only-begotten Son, Himself "suffered for us in the flesh," according to the words of St. Peter. This letter (referred to by Cyril in subsequent letters, *Ep.* pp. 110, 152, 155) opened the way to his reconciliation with John. The latter, although in his recent council he had bound himself to demand a recantation of the Cyrilline articles, now declared that Cyril had fully cleared himself from all heretical opinions. After a conference with Acacius of Berrhoea, John sent to Alexandria, Paul bp. of Emesa, a man of experience whom they both could trust, to confer with Cyril (see Cyril's letters to Acacius and Donatus, *Ep.* pp. 111, 156). When Paul reached Alexandria, Cyril was laid up with illness (Mansi, v. 987), but, when able, received him, as Paul himself said, kindly and pacifically (Mansi, v. 288). They began their conference: Paul presented to Cyril a confession of faith as exhibiting the mind of John of Antioch (*Ep.* p. 103); it had been originally written at Ephesus by Theodoret (Tillem. xiv. 531). "We confess," so ran this formulary, "our Lord Jesus Christ, the Only-begotten Son of God, to be perfect God and perfect Man, of a reasonable soul and a body, before the ages begotten of the Father according to Godhead, but in the last days Himself the self-same, for us and for our salvation, born of the Virgin Mary according to Manhood; of one essence with the Father as to Godhead, of one essence with us as to Manhood. For there took place an union of two natures; wherefore we confess one Christ, one Son, one Lord. According to this idea of an union without confusion, we confess the Holy Virgin to be Theotokos, because God the Word was incarnate and made Man, and from His very conception united to Himself the temple assumed from her." The formulary, although it dwelt more than Cyril had been wont to do on the double aspect of the Incarnation, was accepted by Cyril as representing Paul's own faith, and he placed a corresponding statement in the hands of Paul. The latter asked whether he would stand by Athanasius's letter to Epictetus. "Certainly; but is your copy of it free of corruption?" Paul produced his copy; Cyril, comparing it with the authentic text, found that it had been tampered with (Mansi, v. 325). After further conversation the two bishops agreed to "forget" the troubles of Ephesus. Paul gave Cyril a letter from John, which, though gentle and dignified in tone, referred to the "articles" in language which annoyed Cyril, and he spoke of the letter as "insulting." Paul soothed him with courteous assurances, but Cyril proceeded to the point which John had ignored—the recognition of the deposition of Nestorius, and the condemnation of his heresy. Paul offered to make such a declaration in John's name, but Cyril promptly and keenly insisted that John himself should make it (*ib.* 313). Just as little could Cyril give way as to the four Nestorianizing metropolitans deposed by the new archbp. of Constantinople: that sentence, he insisted, must stand good (*ib.* 349). Paul then, in writing, satisfied Cyril as to his own orthodoxy, and Cyril allowed him to join in the church-service of Alexandria, even inviting him to preach on Christmas Day, 432, in the great church (*ib.* 293). The bp. of Emesa began with the angelic hymn, proceeded to the prophecy of Emmanuel, and then said, "Thus Mary, Mother of God, brings forth Emmanuel." A characteristic outbreak of orthodox joy interrupted the discourse. The people cried out, "This is the faith! 'Tis God's own gift, O orthodox Cyril! This is what we wanted to hear." Paul then went on to say that a combination of two perfect natures, the Godhead and Manhood, constituted "for us" the one Son, the one Christ, the one Lord. Again the cry arose, "Welcome, orthodox bishop!" Paul resumed his discourse, and explained St. Peter's confession as implying a duality of nature and an unity of person in Christ. On New Year's Day, 433, after alluding to Cyril as a kind-hearted trainer who had smiled upon his performance, he preached at greater length on the unity of the Person and the distinctness of the natures, as being co-ordinate and harmonious truths; and his teaching was heartily endorsed by Cyril, who sent two of his own clergy to accompany him and Aristolaus, the emperor's secretary, who was very zealous for the reunion, to Antioch, with a paper for John to sign, and a letter of communion to be given him when he had signed it. But Cyril considered Maximian also languid in the cause, and he wrote many letters to persons connected with the imperial court, including the "Augusta" Pulcheria, to bring their influence to bear upon John and separate him definitely and finally from Nestorius (Mansi, v. 988). These letters were backed up by presents euphemistically called "blessings" (*eulogiae*), which were employed by Cyril as a matter of course, for he knew but little of delicacy and scrupulosity as to the means to be used in gaining a court to the church's interests. Cyril also assured Theognostus, Charmosynus, and Leontius, his "apocrisiarii" or church agents at Constantinople (*Ep.* p. 152) that this peace with John implied no retractation of his old principles. In the spring of 433 John of Antioch wrote to Cyril, reciting the formulary of reunion, abandoning Nestorius, and condemning Nestorianism (Mansi, v. 290). In another letter John entreated Cyril in a tone of warm friendship to believe that he was "the same that he had known in former days" (*Ep.* p. 154). On Apr. 23 (Pharmuthi 8) Cyril announced this reconciliation in a sermon (Mansi, v. 310, 289), and began his reply to John, "Let the heavens rejoice and the earth be glad" (*Ep.* p. 104; Mansi, v. 301). In this letter (afterwards approved by the council of Chalcedon) he cited the text, "One Lord, one faith, one baptism," as expressing the happiness of the restored peace; and added his usual disclaimers of all opinions inconsistent with the reality of Christ's manhood. He commented on John iii. 13, I. Cor. xv. 47, I. Pet. iv. 1. He also sent to John a copy of the genuine text of Athanasius's letter to Epictetus. John himself became an object of suspicion and animosity to the thoroughgoing Nestorians; and even Theodoret, though he admitted that Cyril's recent language was orthodox, would not abandon Nestorius's cause. In another direction doubts and anxieties were excited by the language now sanctioned by Cyril. Isidore, to whom Cyril had always allowed great freedom of admonitory speech, and who had blamed him for unyieldingness, now expressed a fear that he had made too great concessions (*Ep.* i. 324). Other friends of his were scandalized by his acceptance of the phrase "two natures." Was not this, they began to ask, equivalent to a sanction of Nestorianism? To vindicate his orthodoxy herein, Cyril wrote a long letter to Acacius of Melitene (*Ep.* p. 109; Mansi, v. 309), who had signified to him that some disquietude was felt. He narrated the recent transactions; and after insisting that the formulary was not (as some had represented it) a new creed, but simply a statement called forth by a special emergency (as those who signed it had been accused of rejecting the Nicene faith, and were therefore constrained to clear themselves), he proceeded to exhibit the essential difference between the formulary and the Nestorian error. Nestorius, in fact, asserted two Christs: the formulary confessed one, both divine and human. Then Cyril added that the two natures spoken of in the formulary were indeed separate in mental conception, *i.e.* considered apart from Christ, but that "after their union" in Christ "*the nature of the Son was but one*, as belonging to one, but to One as made man and incarnate." Again, "The nature of the Word is confessedly one, but has become incarnate," for "the Word took the form of a servant," and "in this sense only could a diversity of natures be recognized, for Godhead and Manhood are not the same in natural quality." Thus, in regard to the Incarnation, "the mind sees two things united without confusion, and nowise regards them, when thus united, as separable, but confesses Him Who is from both, God, Son, and Christ, to be one." "Two natures," in Nestorius's mouth, meant two natures existing separately, in One Who was God and in One Who was Man; John of Antioch and his brethren, while admitting that Godhead and Manhood in Christ might be regarded as intrinsically different, yet unequivocally acknowledged His Person to be one. The phrase "one incarnate nature" of God the Word, or "one nature, but that incarnate," had been already (*ad Regin.* i. 9) quoted by Cyril as Athanasian: although it is very doubtful whether the short tract *On the Incarnation of God the Word*, in which it is found, was really written by Athanasius. But, as now used by Cyril in his vindication of the formulary from Nestorianism, it became in after-days a stumbling-block, and was quoted in support of Monophysitism (Hooker, v. 52, 4). Did, then, Cyril in fact hold what was condemned in 451 by the council of Chalcedon? Would he have denied the distinct co-existence of Godhead and Manhood in the one incarnate Saviour? Were the Fathers of Chalcedon wrong when they proclaimed Cyril and Leo to be essentially one in faith? What has been already quoted from the letter to Acacius of Melitene seems to warrant a negative answer to these questions. What Cyril meant by "one nature incarnate" was simply, "*Christ* is one." He was referring to "nature" as existing in Christ's single Divine Personality (cf. *adv. Nest.* ii.; cf. note in Athan. Treatises, *Lib. Fath.* i. 155). When he denounced the idea of the separation of the natures after the union, he was in fact denouncing the idea of a mere connexion or association between a human individual Jesus and the Divine Word. Therefore, when he maintained the nature to be one, he was speaking in a sense quite distinct from the Eutychian heresy, and quite consistent with the theology of Chalcedon. Other letters, written by Cyril under the same circumstances, throw light on his true meaning. Successus, an Isaurian bishop, had asked him whether the phrase "two natures" were admissible (*Ep.* p. 135; Mansi, v. 999). Cyril wrote two letters to him in reply. In the first, after strongly asserting the unity of the Son both before and since the Incarnation, he quoted the "one nature incarnate" as a phrase of the Fathers, and employed the illustration from soul and body, "two natures" being united in one man in order to set forth the combination of Godhead and Manhood in one Christ (cf. his *Scholia de Inc.* 8). There was, he added, neither a conversion of Godhead into flesh nor a change of flesh into Godhead. In other words, Christ's body, though glorified, and existing as God's body, was not deprived of its human reality. In the second letter, replying to objections made by Successus to statements in the first, Cyril fully admitted that Christ "arrayed Himself with our nature," so that in Him both Godhead and Manhood, in Christ, retained their natural distinctness (cf. p. 143), and that the human nature was neither diminished nor subtracted. Further on he repeated the phrase "one nature, but that incarnate," in the sense (as the context shews) of "One Who in His original nature was God, by incarnation becoming man." In another letter he gave, to a priest named Eulogius, a similar account of the phrase, and obviously viewed it as guarding the truth of the Personal Union (*Ep.* p. 133). In another, addressed to a bishop named Valerian (and remarkable for the emphasis with which the Divinity of Christ is exhibited as bearing on His Atonement), the word "nature," in this connexion, is evidently used as synonymous with "person" or hypostasis; and as if specially anxious to exclude all possible misconception, he wrote: "He, being by nature God, became flesh, that is, perfect man. . . . As man He was partaker of our nature." This language agrees with that of his 17th Paschal Homily (Cyr. v. ii. 226). Cf. also his statement in *adv. Nest.* ii. t. vi. 50, that while the divine and the human natures are different things, as all right-thinking men must know, yet after the Incarnation they must not be divided, for there is but one Christ. Again (*ib.* p. 45) that Christ is not twofold is explained by the context to mean that Christ before and since the Incarnation is one and the same Person; and (*ib.* p. 48), the reason for calling Christ's Godhead the φύσις is explained by the consideration that He was originally God, while in the fifth book (*ib.* p. 139) He is said to have given up His body to the laws of its own nature (τῆς ἰδίας φύσεως). In the ninth book, *de S. Trinitate* (dial. quod unus est Christus), he denies all transmutation or confusion of the natures, asserts the distinctness of Godhead and Manhood, adding that "the bush burning yet unconsumed was a type of the non-consumption of the Manhood of Christ in its contact with His Divinity" (cf. *Scholia*, 2, 9).

To return to the history. Maximian, dying in Apr. 434, was succeeded by Proclus, whose glowing sermon on the Incarnation had been among the earliest expressions of orthodox zeal against the Nestorian theory, and who deserves to be remembered as a very signal example of the compatibility of orthodox zeal with charitable tenderness (Socr. vii. 41). Soon after his accession the imperial court resolved to enforce on all Eastern bishops the acceptance of the concordat which had reconciled John of Antioch with Cyril, upon pain of expulsion from their dioceses. The Nestorians, on their side, were indefatigable in circulating the works of Theodore of Mopsuestia, who had formed the theological mind of Nestorius; and Cyril, who was informed of this during a visit to Jerusalem, was stirred to new energy by the evident vitality of the theory which he so earnestly abhorred. He wrote to the "tribune" Aristolaus, and to John of Antioch, complaining that, as he was informed, some bishops were repudiating Nestorianism insincerely or inadequately, and were declaring that its author had been condemned merely for denying the "Theotokos" (Mansi, v. 996, cf. *ib.* 970). He urged that the bishops should anathematize Nestorianism in detail. John wished no new test to be imposed; and Cyril found he had gone too far (*ib.* 969, 972, 996). John was much annoyed at Theodoret's pertinacious refusal to anathematize Nestorius—a refusal in which Theodoret persisted until the eighth session of the council of Chalcedon (*ib.* 997). As the Nestorianizers professed entire adhesion to the Nicene Creed, Cyril drew up an exposition of it (*Ep.* p. 174, Mansi, v. 383, cf. *ib.* 975) addressed to certain "fathers of monks," in which he urged the incompatibility of that "venerable and oecumenical symbol of faith" with the denial of the personal unity of the Saviour. In this tract, a copy of which he sent to Theodosius, he disclaimed, as usual, any "fusion, commixture, or so-called consubstantiation" (συνουσίωσιν) of the Godhead with the flesh. He drew up a short treatise in three books to prove that Mary was Theotokos, that Christ was one and not two, and that while He was impassible as God, He suffered for us in flesh that was His own. This he intended as an antidote to the Nestorian arguments which, as he learned, were rife in Syria (Mansi, v. 995). The name of Theodore of Mopsuestia was at this time a watchword of eager controversy. Proclus of Constantinople, in his "Tome" addressed to the Armenian clergy, in which he spoke of "one incarnate person" (not "nature") of God the Word, had condemned Theodore's opinions without naming him (*ib.* 421): the messengers who carried this document to John of Antioch inserted Theodore's name, without authority from Proclus, as the author of certain passages selected for censure. John and his suffragans accepted the Tome, but declined to condemn Theodore by name. Proclus rejoined that he had never wished them to go beyond a condemnation of the extracts. Cyril, so far from feeling any tenderness towards Theodore, traced Nestorianism to his teaching and to that of Diodore of Tarsus (*ib.* 974) and wrote vigorously in support of this thesis (*ib.* 992). A synodal letter from John and his suffragans, stating their objections to Theodore's name being anathematized on the score of expressions which, they urged, could be taken in a sense accordant with the language of eminent Fathers, drew forth from Cyril a somewhat indignant reply. Theodore, he said (*Ep.* p. 195), had "borne down full sail against the glory of Christ"; it was intolerable that any parallel should be drawn between his language and that of Athanasius or Basil: he insisted that no one should be allowed to preach Theodore's opinions; but he did not urge any condemnation of his memory, and even dwelt on the duty of welcoming all converts from Nestorianism without a word of reproach as to the past. He saw that it would be imprudent to proceed publicly against the memory of a theologian so highly esteemed that the people cried out in some Eastern churches, "We believe as Theodore did," and would rather be "burnt" than disown him; and he wrote to Proclus advising that no further steps should be taken in the matter (*Ep.* p. 199). The remaining events of Cyril's long episcopate may be told briefly. He wrote to Domnus, the successor of John in the see of Antioch (and afterwards unhappily conspicuous in the Eutychian controversy), in behalf of Athanasius sometime bp. of Perrha, who described himself, falsely it appears, as sorely wronged by some of his own clergy (*Ep.* p. 208). In another letter to Domnus, peremptory in style, he took up the cause of another aged bishop named Peter, who professed to have been expelled and plundered of his property on the pretext of a renunciation of his see, which after all had been extorted from him (*Ep.* p. 209). In both these cases Cyril shewed a somewhat impulsive readiness to believe the story of a petitioner, and a somewhat dictatorial temper in regard to the affairs of another patriarchate. He wrote also a work against the Anthropomorphites, whose wild fancies about the Divine nature (as being limited and corporeal) had given such trouble in the days of his predecessor; and in a letter on this subject to Calosirius, bp. of Arsinoe, he added a caution against the false mysticism which insisted on prayer to the exclusion of all labour, and on the "senseless" opinion that the Eucharistic consecration lost its efficacy if the sacrament was reserved until the following day. "Christ's holy Body," wrote Cyril, "is not changed; but the power of consecration and the life-giving grace still remain in it" (*Op.* vi. 365). In the last year of his life he wrote to Leo, then bp. of Rome (to whom, as archdeacon of Rome, he had written in 431 against the ambitious schemes, as he regarded them, of Juvenal bp. of Jerusalem [Leon. *Ep.* 119, 4]) on the right calculation of Easter for A.D. 444, which, according to the Alexandrian cycle of 19 years, he fixed for April 23. In 444, on June 9 or 27, his eventful life ended.

Cyril's character is not, of course, to be judged by the coarse and ferocious invective against his memory, quoted as Theodoret's in the fifth general council (Theod. *Ep.* 180; see Tillem. xiv. 784). If this were indeed the production of Theodoret, the reputation to suffer would assuredly be that writer's. What Cyril was, in his strength and in his weakness—in his high-souled struggle for doctrines which were to him, as to all thoughtful believers in Christ's Divinity, the expressions of essential Christian belief; or in the moments when his old faults of vehemence and impatience reappeared in his conduct—we have already seen. He started in public life, so to speak, with dangerous tendencies to vehemence and imperiousness which were fostered by the bad traditions of his uncle's episcopate and by the ample powers of his see. It would be impossible to maintain that these evils were wholly exhausted by the grave errors which—exaggerations and false imputations set aside—distinguished his conduct in the feud with the Jews and with Orestes; when, although guiltless of the blood of Hypatia, he must have felt that his previous violence had been taken as an encouragement by her fanatical murderers. The old impatience and absolutism were all too prominent at certain points of the Nestorian struggle; although on other occasions, as must be admitted by all fair judges, influences of a softening and chastening character had abated the turbid impetus of his zeal and had taught him to be moderate and patient. "We may," says Dr. Newman (*Hist. Sketches*, iii. 342), "hold St. Cyril a great servant of God, without considering ourselves obliged to defend certain passages of his ecclesiastical career. . . . Cyril's faults were not inconsistent with great and heroic virtues, faith, firmness, intrepidity, fortitude, endurance, perseverance." Those who begin by condemning dogmatic zeal as a fierce and misplaced chivalry for a phantom, will find it most difficult to be just to a man like Cyril. But if his point of view, which was indeed that of many great religious heroes, and eminently of Athanasius, be fully understood and appreciated, it ought not to be difficult to do justice to his memory. The issue raised by Nestorianism was to Cyril a very plain one, involving the very essence of Apostolic Christianity. Whatever ambiguities might be raised by a Nestorian use of the word πρόσωπον, it was clear to Cyril that the new theory amounted to a denial of the Word Incarnate. Nor was it a mere theory of the schools. Its promulgator held the great see of the Eastern capital, involving a central position and strong court influence, and was no mere amiable dreamer or scholastic pedant, whose fancies might die away if left to themselves. He has in modern times been spoken of as "the blameless Nestorius": he was in his own times spoken of as "the incendiary" on account of a zeal against other forms of heresy which impelled him to take strong measures against opponents of his own. This was the enemy against whom Cyril did battle for the doctrine of a real Incarnation and a really Divine Christ. He had to reckon on opposition, not only from Nestorius himself, but from large numbers—a miscellaneous company, including civil functionaries as well as prelates—who accepted the Nestorian theology, or who thought strong language against it uncalled-for and offensive. He might have to encounter the displeasure of an absolute government—he certainly had for some time the prospect of that displeasure, and of all its consequences; he had the burden of ill-health, of ever-present intense anxiety, of roughly expressed censure, of reiterated imputations affecting his own orthodoxy, of misconceptions and suspicions which hardly left him a moment's rest. Whatever faults there were in his conduct of the controversy, this at least must be said—not only by mere eulogists of a canonized saint, but by those who care for the truth of history—that the thought as well as the heart of Christendom has for ages accepted, as the expression of Christian truth, the principle upheld by Cyril against Nestorius. A real and profound question divided the disputants; and that stanza of Charles Wesley's Christmas hymn which begins,

"Christ, by highest heaven adored,"

conveys the Cyrilline or Ephesine answer to that question in a form which exhibits its close connexion with the deepest exigencies of spiritual life. Cyril, as a theological writer, has greater merits than are sometimes allowed by writers defective in a spirit of equity. His style, as Cave admits, may be deficient in elegance and in eloquence; he may be often tedious, and sometimes obscure, although, as Photius says (*Cod.* 136), his *Thesaurus* is remarkable for its lucidity. His comments on Scripture may be charged with excessive mysticism, or with a perpetual tendency to bring forward his favourite theological idea. There may be weak points in his argument—*e.g.* undue pressing of texts, and fallacious inferences, several of which might be cited from the treatise *To the Princesses.* But any one who consults, *e.g.*, the *Thesaurus*, will acknowledge the ability with which Cyril follows up the theological line of Athanasius (see pp. 12, 23, 27, 30, 50), and applies the Athanasian mode of thought to the treatment of Eunomian rationalism (p. 263), and the vividness with which, in this and in other works, he brings out the Catholic interpretation of cardinal texts in N.T. His acquaintance with Greek literature and philosophy is evident from the work against Julian ; but he speaks quite in the tone of Hippolytus's "Little Labyrinth" (Eus. v. 28) when he deprecates an undue reliance on Aristotelian dialectics and *a priori* assumption on mysteries transcending human thought (*Thesaur.* 87, *de recta fide* 16, 17).

Fragments of Cyrilline treatises not otherwise extant are preserved in synodal acts and elsewhere, and other works, as his *Paschal Cycles* and *The Failure of the Synagogue*, are mentioned by Sigebert and Gennadius. The Monophysites used on festivals a "Liturgy of St. Cyril," which is substantially identical with the Gk. "Liturgy of St. Mark" (see Palmer's *Orig. Liturg.* i. 86, and Neale's *Introd. East. Ch.* i. 324), and their traditionary belief, expressed in a passage cited from Abu'lberkat by Renaudot, *Lit. Orient.* i. 171, is that Cyril "completed" St. Mark's Liturgy. "It seems highly probable," says Dr. Neale, quoting this, "that the liturgy of St. Mark came, as we have it now, from the hands of St. Cyril" ; although, as Palmer says, the orthodox Alexandrians preferred to call it by the name of the Evangelist founder of their see. The Coptic Cyrilline Liturgy is of somewhat later date, and more diffuse in character. It seems not improbable that the majestic invocation of the Holy Spirit which is one of the distinctive ornaments of St. Mark's Liturgy, if it was not composed during the Macedonian controversy in the 4th cent., represents to us the lively zeal of the great upholder of the Hypostatic Union for the essential Divinity of the Third Person in the Godhead.

Cyril's works were well edited by John Aubert (1658) in six volumes, an edition not yet superseded ; there is no Benedictine St. Cyril. In 1859 Dr. Payne Smith pub. Cyril's Commentary on St. Luke's Gospel, trans. from a Syriac version. An elaborate edition by P. E. Pusey, M.A., of Christ Church, of the Commentary on the Minor Prophets (2 vols.) and the Commentary on S. John's Gospel (3 vols.) is pub. by the Clarendon Press, as is also the text and trans. with Lat. notes of the *Comm. in Luc.* ed. by R. P. Smith. An important work has recently been published by Dr. Bethune Baker, of Cambridge, entitled *Nestorius and his Teaching, a Fresh Examination of the Evidence*, which adduces much, from new discoveries, in vindication of Nestorius from the heresy attributed to him. See also CHRISTOLOGY, in *D. C. B.* (4-vol. ed.). [W.B.]

Cyrillus (13) of Scythopolis (Bethshan), so called from his birthplace, a hagiologist, fl. *c.* 555. His father, John, was famous for his religious life. Cyril commenced an ascetic career at the age of 16. On leaving his monastery to visit Jerusalem and the holy places, his mother bid him put himself under the instruction of John the Silentiary, by whom he was commended to Leontius, abbat of the monastery of St. Euthymius, who admitted him as a monk in 522. Thence Cyril passed to the Laura of St. Saba, where he commenced his sacred biographies with the Lives of St. Euthymius and St. Saba, deriving his information from the elder monks who had known those saints. He also wrote the Life of St. John the Silentiary and other biographies, affording a valuable picture of the inner life of the Eastern church in the 6th cent. They have been unfortunately largely interpolated by Metaphrastes. The following biographies are attributed to Cyril by Fabricius (*Bibl. Graec.* lib. v. c. 41, x. 155): (1) *S. Joannes Silentiarius* (ap. Surium, May 13) ; (2) *S. Euthymius* (Cotelerius, *Eccl. Graec. Monum.* ii. 200) ; (3) *S. Sabas.* (*ib.* iii. 220) ; (4) *Theodosius the Archimandrite* (only found in Latin, of doubtful authenticity) ; (5) *Cyriacus the Anchoret* ; (6) *S. Theognius the Ascetic, bp. of Cyprus* (Fabric. *Bibl. Graec. u.s.* ; Cave, *Hist. Lit.* p. i. 529). [E.V.]

D

Dalmatius (4), monk and abbat, near Constantinople at the time of the council of Ephesus (A.D. 431). His influence arose from his eminent piety, strength of character, and fiery zeal. Under Theodosius the Great he had served in the 2nd company of Guards, married, had children, and led a virtuous life. Feeling a call to a monastic life, he left his wife and children, except a son Faustus, and went to be instructed by abbat Isaac, who had dwelt in the desert since his infancy. Isaac at his death made him *Hegumenus*, superior of the monastery, under the patriarch Atticus. Consulted by councils, patriarchs, and emperors, he remained in his cell 48 years without quitting it. He is sometimes addressed as chief of the monasteries of Constantinople ; but it is uncertain whether this was a complimentary or official title. He is not to be confounded with Dalmatius, monk at Constantinople, bp. of Cyzicus ; because the latter was present at the council of Ephesus in that capacity.

During the supremacy of the Nestorian party at Ephesus, letters were conveyed by a beggar in the hollow of a cane from Cyril and the Athanasian or Catholic bishops to the emperor Theodosius II., the clergy and people at Constantinople complaining that they had been imprisoned three months, that the Nestorians had deposed Cyril and Memnon bp. of Ephesus, and that they were all in the greatest distress. A short memorial was added to the letter of the bishops, probably for Dalmatius. Dalmatius was greatly moved, and believed himself summoned to go forth at length from his retreat in the interests of truth. Accompanied by the monks of all the monasteries, led by their abbats, he went to the palace in a long procession, divided into two companies, and singing alternately; a vast crowd of sympathizers followed. The abbats were admitted to the emperor's presence; and the monks remained outside chanting. Returning to the people, the abbats asked them to go to the church of St. Mocius to hear the letter of the council and the emperor's reply. They went through the city, the monks chanting and carrying wax tapers. Great enthusiasm was excited against Nestorius. At the church the abbats read the letter of the bishops, which produced high excitement. Dalmatius, who was a presbyter, then mounted the pulpit, begged them to be patient, and in temperate and modest terms related his conversation with the emperor, and its satisfactory result. The emperor then wrote to Ephesus, ordering a deputation of each party to arrive at Constantinople. In a letter to Dalmatius the council acknowledged that to him only was owing the emperor's knowledge of the truth. Cyril, *Ep.* 23, etc., *Patr. Gk.* lxxvii.; *Concil. Gen.* i.; *Dalmatii Apol.* p. 477; St. Procl. CP. Episc. *Ep.* iii.; *Patr. Gk.* lxv. p. 876, lxxxv. col. 1797-1802; Ceillier, viii. 290, 395, 396, 407, 594; Fleury, bk. xxvi. [W.M.S.]

Damasus, pope, said to have been a Spaniard, the son of Antonius. On the death of Liberius (Sept. A.D. 366) the factions which had disgraced his election broke out with redoubled violence. The original root of bitterness had been Arianism; and Felix the Arian antipope [FELIX II.] had been expelled by Liberius. Seven days after the death of Liberius, Felix's partisans met and proclaimed Damasus pope in the Lucina [qy. the crypt of St. Lucina in the catacomb of Callistus ?]. Damasus had previously taken up a middle position between the contending parties, which may have specially recommended him to the electors, who could not hope to carry an extreme man. Yet, about the same time apparently the party of Liberius met in the Julian basilica and elected Ursicinus or Ursinus.

It is difficult to ascertain the truth with regard to the strife between the rival popes. Our most detailed account is by personal enemies of Damasus, and the incidents of the struggle are recorded under URSINUS.

Damasus used his success well, and the chair of St. Peter, even if, as his enemies alleged, acquired by violent means, was never more respected nor vigorous than during his bishopric. He appears as a principal opponent of Arian and other heretics. Bp. Peter of Alexandria was his firm friend all along; and was associated with him in the condemnation of Apollinaris (Soz. vi. 25), and in affixing the stigma of Arianism to Meletius of Antioch and Eusebius, who were upheld by Basil (Basil, *Ep.* cclxvi. iii. 597, ed. Bened.). On Meletius's death Damasus struggled hard to gain the chair of Antioch for Paulinus, and to exclude Flavianus; nor was he reconciled to the latter till some time later (Socr. v. 15).

His correspondence with Jerome, his attached friend and secretary, begins A.D. 376, and closes only with his death A.D. 384. Six of Jerome's letters to him are preserved, two being expositions of difficult passages of Scripture elicited by letters of Damasus asking the aid of his learning. Jerome's desire to dedicate to him a translation of Didymus's work on the Holy Ghost was only stopped by his death. In later letters Jerome speaks in high terms of Damasus; calls him "that illustrious man, that virgin doctor of the virgin church," "eager to catch the first sound of the preaching of continence"; who "wrote both verse and prose in favour of virginity" (*Epp.* Hieron. 22, 48). From this Milman (*Latin Christ.* i. 69) conjectures that Damasus was a patron of the growing monastic party—a not improbable conjecture, rendered more likely by the ardent attachment of Jerome, and the veneration in which the memory of pope Damasus was held by later times, when monasticism had taken firm root in the Roman church. But the best-known record of Damasus will always be his labour of love in the catacombs of Rome. Here he searched ardently and devotedly for the tombs of the martyrs, which had been blocked up and hidden by the Christians during the last persecution. He "removed the earth, widened the passages, so as to make them more serviceable for the crowd of pilgrims, constructed flights of stairs leading to the more illustrious shrines, and adorned the chambers with marbles, opening shafts to admit air and light where practicable, and supporting the friable *tufa* walls and galleries wherever it was necessary with arches of brick and stone work. Almost all the catacombs bear traces of his labours, and modern discovery is continually bringing to light fragments of the inscriptions which he composed in honour of the martyrs, and caused to be engraved on marble slabs, in a peculiarly beautiful character, by a very able artist, Furius Dionysius Filocalus. It is a singular fact that no original inscription of pope Damasus has ever yet been found executed by any other hand; nor have any inscriptions been found, excepting those of Damasus, in precisely the same form of letters. Hence the type is well known to students of Christian epigraphy as the 'Damasine character'" (*Roma Sotterranea*, by Northcote and Brownlow, p. 97). Damasus also laid down a marble pavement in the basilica of St. Sebastian, recording by an inscription the temporary burial in that church of SS. Peter and Paul (*ib.* p. 114). He built the baptistery at the Vatican in honour of St. Peter, where de Rossi thinks, from an inscription in the Damasine character, was an actual chair which went by the name of St. Peter's seat (*ib.* p. 393), and he drained the crypts of the Vatican, that the bodies buried there might not be disturbed by the overflow of water (*ib.* p. 334). He died in Dec. 384, after a pontificate of 18 years. Before his death he had prepared his own tomb above the catacomb of Callistus, giving his reason in an inscription in what is called the Papal crypt of that catacomb:

> "Hic fateor Damasus volui mea condere membra,
> Sed timui sanctos cineres vexare priorum"

(*ib.* p. 102). Cf. Hefele, *Conciliengeschichte*, vols. i. and ii. [G.H.M.]

Damianus (**2**), M. [COSMAS.]

Daniel (**9**) the Stylite, of the 5th cent., was a Mesopotamian by birth, and in his youth had visited Symeon the Stylite. After having lived a monastic life in convents for several years, at the age of 47 he received as a legacy the cowl of Symeon, and established his pillar 4 miles N. of Constantinople. The patriarch Gennadius ordained him presbyter against his will, standing at the foot of his column. Then the patriarch, by means of a ladder, administered the Eucharist, and received it in turn from the Stylite. He lived on his pillar for 33 years, and died at the age of 80. He was visited with reverence by kings and emperors as an oracle; but discouraged all who brought complaints against their bishops. Towards the end of his life, solicited eagerly by both sides, he took part in the dispute between the emperor Basiliscus, a Monophysite, and Acacius patriarch of Constantinople. Descending from his pillar, he appeared in the city, denounced Basiliscus, and inflamed the people with such zeal that Basiliscus published an orthodox edict. The following is his prayer before he began his life on the pillar: "I yield Thee glory, Jesus Christ my God, for all the blessings which Thou hast heaped upon me, and for the grace which Thou hast given me that I should embrace this manner of life. But Thou knowest that in ascending this pillar I lean on thee alone, and that to Thee alone I look for the happy issue of mine undertaking. Accept, then, my object; strengthen me that I finish this painful course; give me grace to end it in holiness." In his last will to his disciples, after commending them to the common Father of all, and to the Saviour Who died for them, Daniel bade them "hold fast humility, practise obedience, exercise hospitality, keep the fasts, observe the vigils, love poverty, and above all maintain charity, which is the first and great commandment; avoid the tares of the heretics; separate never from the church your mother: if you do these things your righteousness shall be perfect." Baronius places his death in A.D. 489. *Vita S. Daniel*, ap. Surium, ad diem ii. decemb. cap. xli. xlii. xliii.; Robertson, *Ch. Hist.* ii. 41-43, 274; Ceillier, x. 344, 403, 485. Baronius, ed. Theiner, vol. viii. *ad an.* 460, § 20; 464, § 2; 465, § 3, 12, 13; 476, § 48, 50, 51, 53; 489, § 4. [W.M.S.]

Dativus (3), celebrated senator, martyred under Diocletian Feb. 11, A.D. 304. In spite of orders to the contrary, a company of the faithful met in the town of Abitina, in the proconsulate of Africa, to celebrate Christian worship and communion, at the house of one Felix Octavius. Forty-nine men and women were surprised by the official and magistrates of the town. They marched cheerfully to their destination, chanting hymns and canticles, having at their head Dativus the senator and Saturninus the presbyter. They confessed Jesus Christ, were chained, and sent to Carthage. There the proconsul Anulinus examined them. Dativus, refusing to say who was the chief of their company, was tortured. As he lay under the iron, at a second examination, Dativus was accused by Fortunatianus, advocate, brother of the martyr Victoria, one of the arrested, of enticing her and other young girls to Abitina. Victoria, however, indignantly denied that she had gone there but of her own accord. The executioners continued tormenting Dativus, till the interior of his breast could be seen. He went on praying and begging Jesus Christ for patience. The proconsul, stopping the torture, asked him again if he had been present. "I was in the assembly," he answered, "and celebrated the Lord's Supper with the brethren." They again thrust the irons into his side; and Dativus, repeating his prayer, continued to say, "O Christ, I pray Thee let me not be confounded." And he added, "What have I done? Saturninus is our presbyter." Dativus was carried to gaol. Here he soon afterwards died. Many of his companions were also tortured, and most of them were starved to death in prison. Ruinart, *Acta Sinc. Mart.* p. 382; Ceillier, iii. 20, etc.; *AA. SS. Bolland.* Feb. ii. p. 513. [W.M.S.]

David (5), St. (*Degui*; Welsh, *Dewi*), the most eminent Welsh saint.

His Period.—The *Annales Cambriae*, our earliest authority for his existence, date his death A.D. 601; and one reading, which the *Monumenta* only gives in brackets, under A.D. 458, is: "St. Dewi nascitur anno tricesimo post discessum Patricii de Menevia" (M. H. B. 830, 831). Geoffrey of Monmouth dates his death A.D. 542, and William of Malmesbury A.D. 546. Ussher argues that he died A.D. 544, at the age of 82 (*Brit. Eccl. Ant.* Works, 1847; vi. 43, 44, Chron. Index, ad ann. 544); but Rice Rees, who has followed him in his computations, places his birth 20 years later, and fixes A.D. 566 as the last date possible for his death. The A.D. 601 of the *Ann. Camb.* is the date adopted by Haddan and Stubbs (*Councils*, i. 121, 143, 148), who remark that David would thus come into view just as the history of Wales emerges from the darkness that conceals it for a century after the departure of the Romans.

A *résumé* of authorities for his Life is given by Jones and Freeman (*Hist. of St. David's*, 240), and a full and careful list of all known materials, manuscript and printed, by Hardy (*Descr. Catal.* i. 766).

The Story of his Life.—The asserted facts of St. David's life, omitting such as are clearly legendary, meet with various degrees of credence from authors of repute. Rees, in his *Essay on Welsh Saints*, while rejecting several circumstances as manifestly fabulous or incredible, such as his going to Jerusalem to be consecrated, is disposed to accept enough to make a biographical narrative.

His father was (in medieval Latin) Xantus or Sanctus, prince of Keretica—*i.e.* modern Cardiganshire. David is said to have been educated first under St. Iltutus in his college (afterwards called from him Llanilltyd Fawr, or Lanwit Major), and subsequently in the college of Paulinus (a pupil of Germanus and one of the great teachers of the age), at Tygwyn ar Dâf (Rees, *Welsh Saints*, 178), or at Whitland in Carmarthenshire (Jones and Freeman); and here he spent ten years in the study of Holy Scripture. In course of time David became head of a society of his own, founding or restoring a monastery or college at a spot which Giraldus calls Vallis Rosina (derived, as is generally supposed, from a confusion between *Rhos*, a swamp, and *Rhosyn*, a rose), near Hen-Meneu, and this institution was subsequently named, out of respect to his memory, Ty Dewi, House of David, or St. David's. In those days, remarks Rees, abbats of monasteries were looked upon in their own neighbourhoods as bishops, and were styled such, while it is probable that they also exercised chorepiscopal rights in their societies (*Welsh Saints*, 182, 266; cf. Haddan and Stubbs, i. 142, 143). Such dignity David enjoyed before his elevation to the archbishopric of the Cambrian church. It was the Pelagian controversy that occasioned his advancement. To pronounce upon the great heresy then troubling the church, archbp. Dubricius convened a synod at Brefi, and David, whose eloquence put the troublers to confusion, made such an impression that the synod at once elected him archbp. of Caerleon and primate of the Cambrian church, Dubricius himself resigning in his favour. The locality of this synod, which holds a marked place in Welsh ecclesiastical traditions, was on the banks of the Brefi, a tributary of the Teifi; Llanddewi Brefi it was afterwards called, from the dedication of its church to St. David. It is 8 miles from Lampeter, and from recent archaeological discoveries has been identified with an important Roman station, the Loventium of the itineraries (Lewis, *Top. Dict. of Wales*; cf. Haddan and Stubbs, *Councils*, i. 117). The Pelagian heresy, however, still survived, and the new archbishop convened another synod, the issue of which was so decided as to gain it the name of the Synod of Victory. It is entered in the *Annales Cambriae*, "Synodus Victoriae apud Britones congregatur," under A.D. 569, but not with full confidence (M. H. B. 831). It is also mentioned, without a date, in the *Annales Menevenses* (Wharton, *Angl. Sac.* ii. 648). After residing for a while at Caerleon on Usk, where the seat of the primate was then established, David, by permission of king Arthur, removed to Menevia, the Menapia of the Itineraries, one of the ports for Ireland (Wright, *Celt, Roman, and Saxon*, 138). The Roman road Via Julia led to it; the voyage across was 45 miles; the Menapii, one of the tribes which held the E. coast of Ireland, were no doubt a colony from the opposite shore of Britain (*ib.* 43); David's baptism by the bp. of Munster indicates a religious connexion between Menevia and Ireland. The tradition of a mission of the British church to Ireland to restore the faith there, under the auspices of David, Gildas, and Cadoc (Haddan and Stubbs, *Councils*, i. 115) points the same way. May we not, therefore, assume that the see was removed because the tide of Saxon conquest drove the British church to cultivate closer relations with their Celtic brethren opposite?

As primate, David distinguished himself by saintly character and apostolic zeal, a glowing, not to say an overcharged, description of which is given in Giraldus. It is generally agreed that Wales was divided into dioceses in his time. Rees, in his learned essay on the Welsh saints, shews that of the dedications and localities of the churches of the principality, a large number terminate in David's native name, ddewi, or are otherwise connected with his memory (*Welsh Saints*, p. 52). These instances, moreover, abound in a well-defined district; and Rees has ingeniously used these circumstances as indicating the limits of the diocese of archbp. David's immediate jurisdiction (*ib.* pp. 197-199). David's successor was Cynog.

Jones and Freeman (*St. David's*, 246 seq.) conclude that we may safely accept as historical facts: that St. David established a see and monastery at Menevia early in the 7th cent., the site being chosen for the sake of retirement; that his diocese was co-extensive with the Demetae; that he had no archiepiscopal jurisdiction; that a synod was held at Brefi, in which he probably played a conspicuous part, but that its objects are unknown; and finally that of his immediate successors nothing is recorded (*ib.* 257). These writers convey a vivid impression of the "strange and desolate scenery" of the spot now named after St. David, and give some curious antiquarian details. Haddan and Stubbs (*Councils*, i. 115-120) give dates to the synod of Brefi and the synod of Victory, a little before 569 and in 569, later than Rees's latest possible date for David's death; and they regard the accounts given of the synods by Ricemarchus, and Giraldus after him, as purely fabulous, and directed to the establishment of the apocryphal supremacy of St. David and his see over the entire British church. They express much doubt as to the purpose of those assemblies being to crush Pelagianism. Valuable documentary information and references as to the whole subject of the early Welsh episcopate are given in Appendix C (*op. cit.*), and it is maintained that "there is no real evidence of the existence of any archiepiscopate at all in Wales during the Welsh period, if the term is held to imply jurisdiction admitted or even claimed (until the 12th cent.) by one see over another."

David was canonized by pope Calixtus *c.* A.D. 1120, and commemorated on Mar. 1 (Rees, *op. cit.* 201). [C.H.]

Decius. The reign of this emperor, though among the shortest in the Roman annals (A.D. 249-251), has gained a pre-eminence in ecclesiastical history altogether disproportioned to its place in general history. It was burnt in on the memories of men as a fiery trial, and occasioned many memorable controversies.

When Cn. Messius Decius Trajanus first appears in history it is with a grown-up son, himself between fifty and sixty, as a member of the Roman senate, in the last year of the reign of Philip the Arabian. The army elected him as emperor, and forced him to lead them into Italy. Near Verona they encountered Philip, who was defeated and slain (June 17, A.D. 249), and Decius began to reign. He associated his own son and Annius Maximus Gratus with him as Caesars.

The edict which made his name a byword of reproach may have been due to a desire to restore the rigorous morality of the old Roman life, and the old religion which gave that morality its sanctions. If we may judge by the confessions of the great Christian teachers, who owned that the church deserved its sufferings, the lives of its members did not then present a very lovely aspect. Christian men were effeminate and self-indulgent, trimming their beard and dyeing their hair; Christian women painted their faces, and brightened their eyes with cosmetics. The clergy were covetous and ambitious, looking on their profession as a path to wealth and influence. In addition to these evils they presented, even more than they had done in the days of the Antonines, the aspect of a secret society with a highly compact organization. That the late emperor had been supposed to favour it or even to have been secretly a member of it was enough to add another element to the policy which Decius now adopted.

That policy was opened early in A.D. 250 by an edict no longer extant,* of which we can form a fair estimate, partly from an account given by Gregory of Nyssa (*Vit. Greg. Thaum.*), and partly from the history of the persecution, as traced by Cyprian, in his epistles and the treatise *de Lapsis*, and by Dionysius of Alexandria (Eus. *H. E.* vi. 40-42). It did not order any sharp measures of extermination. Magistrates throughout the empire were ordered, under heavy penalties, to put pressure upon the worshippers of Christ to abjure Christianity. Fear did its work on many whose faith had never had any real groundwork in conviction. The seats of the magistrates were thronged with apostates, some rushing eagerly to be conspicuous among the first to offer sacrifice and sprinkle incense on the altar; some pale and trembling, as if about to be themselves sacrificial victims. In that crowd of renegades were, too, not a few base and feeble-hearted priests of the church. Others found an ingenious way of satisfying their conscience, and securing their position and life. The magistrates were not above accepting bribes, and for a reasonable money payment would give a certificate (*libellus*) that sacrifice had been duly offered, without making the actual performance of the rite compulsory. The *libellatici* were rightly branded by Christian feeling with a double note of infamy. They added dishonesty and falsehood to cowardice and denial. Bad as the *sacrificati*, the *thurificati*, might be, they were not so contemptible as these. Next, severe measures were brought to bear on the faithful. They were dragged before the prefects and other magistrates, questioned as to their faith, required to sacrifice, exposed to insults and outrages if they refused, thrust into prison, and, in many instances, ill-treated till they died. The wiser and more prudent bishops, such as Dionysius of Alexandria and Cyprian of Carthage, followed the counsel of their Lord (Matt. x. 23), and the example of Polycarp, fled from the storm themselves, and exhorted their followers to do the same. Some, who thus withdrew from the common life of men, never returned to it (*e.g.* Paul, the hermit of the Thebaid, and Maximus of Nice), and the Decian period has been commonly regarded, though with some exaggeration, as the starting-point of the anchoretic life. The wiser pastors continued, as far as they could, to watch over their flocks and keep them steadfast in the faith, even while exposed to taunts and suspicions of cowardice or deception. Others languished in prison, like the sufferers at Rome, of whom Cyprian tells, "*sine solatio mortis.*" Some courted death not in vain, or met it bravely.

*** A document purporting to give the text of the edict was published at Toulouse A.D. 1664, but is universally acknowledged to be spurious.**

The persecution of Decius (commonly reckoned as the seventh) may fairly be measured as to its extent, if not its actual severity, by the list of martyrs under it still found in the calendar of the Western church. It was more extensive and more systematic than any that had preceded it. Fabian, bp. of Rome, was among the foremost of the victims; Babylas of Antioch, Pionius of Smyrna (seized, it was said, while celebrating the anniversary of the martyrdom of Polycarp), Agatha of Sicily, Polyeuctes of Armenia, Carpus and his deacon of Thyatira, Maximus (a layman) of Asia, Alexander, bp. of Jerusalem, Acacius of the Phrygian Antioch, Epimachus and Nemesius of Alexandria, Peter and his companions of Lampsacus, Irenaeus of Neo-Caesarea, Martial of Limoges, Abdon and Sennen (Persians then at Rome), Cassian of Imola, Lucian a Thracian, Trypho and Respicius of Bithynia, the Ten Martyrs of Crete, have all found a place in the martyrologies of this period, and, after allowing uncertainty to some of the names, the list is enough to shew that there was hardly a province of the empire where the persecution was not felt. Among "confessors" (a title which seems to have been then, for the first time, used in this sense) were Origen, who was tortured on the rack, and the boy Dioscorus who, at the age of 15, offered himself for the crown of martyrdom, but was spared by the Alexandrian prefect in pity for his youth. To this reign belongs the well-known legend of the Seven Sleepers of Ephesus, told for the first time by Gregory of Tours (*de Glor. Martyr.* c. 95). Confessing the faith, like Dioscorus, in the prime of early manhood, they were, it was said, walled up in a cave, and left to die. They fell asleep, and the place acquired a local fame for its sanctity. In the reign of Theodosius (A.D. 447) the cave was opened, and the sleepers awoke, went forth, and were startled at the changes which they witnessed, temples destroyed and churches standing in their place. Their second life was, however, of short duration. They again lay down together and fell asleep, this time not to wake again.

Happily, the persecution was as short as it was severe. The attacks of the Goths (or the Carpi, probably a Gothic tribe) drew Decius and his son into Pannonia, where they fell in battle. In some respects the after-effects of the Decian persecution were more important than its direct results. It cleared off the crowd of half-hearted Christians, and left behind those who were prepared by its discipline for the severer struggles that were to come under Valerian and Diocletian. Questions arose as to the treatment of those who had apostatized (the *lapsi* of Cyprian's treatise). Were the *libellatici* to be dealt with on the same footing as the *thurificati*? Were either capable of readmission into the fold of Christ? Was that readmission to be conditional upon the church's normal discipline, or were the confessors to be allowed to give a certificate of absolution (the *libellus pacis*) to those whose weakness or repentance was sufficient reason for indulgence? Some of those who prided themselves, like many of the Roman confessors, on their constancy, looked down with scorn on the indulgence shewn by Cyprian and Cornelius to the *lapsi*, and even taunted the latter with having been a *libellaticus*. The tendency to ascetic rigorism of discipline would doubtless have shewn itself sooner or later in any case, but historically the Novatianist schisms had their beginning in the Decian persecution. Cf. Eus. *H. E.* vi. 39-45; Cyprian, *de Laps.*, and *Epp.* passim; the articles in this dict. on the persons named above; and an excellent paper on Decius by Hefele in Wetzer and Welte's *Kirchen Lexicon*. For the general history of the reign, see Gibbon (c. x.), whose narrative is based on Zosimus and Zonaras. [E.H.P.]

Demetrias, a Roman virgin to whom Jerome wrote his treatise (*Ep.* 130, ed. *Vall.*) on the keeping of virginity. Her family was illustrious at Rome, her grandmother Proba (who is much praised by Jerome) having had three sons, all consuls. Demetrias had in early life wished to take the vow of virginity, but feared her parents' opposition. They, however, fully approved, and it gladdened all the churches of Italy. Her father having died just before the sack of Rome by Alaric, the family sold their property and set sail for Africa, witnessing the burning of Rome as they left Italy; and, arriving in Africa, fell into the hands of the rapacious count Heraclian, who took away a large part of their property. Jerome exhorts Demetrias to a life of study and fasting; care in the selection of companions; consecration of her wealth to Christ's service; and to working with her own hands. He warns her not to perplex herself with difficult questions introduced by the Origenists; and recommends the study of Scripture. He exhorts her to prefer the coenobitic to the hermit life, and bears testimony, as he had done 30 years before to Eustochium, to the excellence of the virgin-state, notwithstanding the attacks made upon it. [W.H.F.]

Demetrius (2) succeeded Julianus A.D. 189, as 11th bp. of Alexandria (Eus. *H. E.* v. 22). He presided over the see for 43 years, and died A.D. 231-232 (*ib.* vi. 26). He appears to have been of an energetic and imperious nature. He took an active interest in the Catechetical School, and is said to have sent one of its early chiefs, PANTAENUS, on a [second ?] mission "to the Indians" on their own request (Hieron. *de Vir. Ill.* 36). After Clement had left Alexandria, he placed Origen at its head, *c.* 203 (Eus. *H. E.* vi. 5), and strenuously encouraged him to continue his work, when his indiscreet zeal had exposed him to misrepresentation (*ib.* vi. 8). Later (A.D. 217), he sent Origen to the Roman governor of Arabia, at the governor's earnest invitation (*ib.* vi. 19). Origen fulfilled his mission satisfactorily, but not long afterwards Demetrius's friendship for him was interrupted. [ORIGEN.] According to a late, and not very trustworthy, authority, Demetrius is reported to have written letters on the keeping of Easter, maintaining the view adopted at Nicaea (Eutychius, *Ann.* pp. 363 ff.; Migne, *Patrol.* vol. cxi.). Other legendary stories of his life are given in the *Chronicon Orientale* (pp. 72 f. ed. 1685), and more briefly by Tillemont (*Mémoires*, Origène, art .vii. tom. iii. p. 225, ed. Bruxelles).

The statement that Demetrius first changed the singular ecclesiastical arrangement of Egypt, by appointing three bishops in addition to the bp. of Alexandria, who had formerly governed the whole province, is probably correct, though the only direct authority for it is that of Eutychius, patriarch of Alexandria, in the 10th cent. (cf. Lightfoot, *Philippians*, p. 230). Possibly this change was due to special views on church government, which may have influenced Demetrius in his harsh judgment on the ordination of Origen beyond the limits of his jurisdiction. [B.F.W.]

Demophilus, bp. of Constantinople, A.D. 370; expelled 380; died 386; formerly bp. of Berea; born of good family in Thessalonica (Philostorg. *H. E.* ix. 14). On the death of Eudoxius in 370 he was elected by the Arians to the bishopric of Constantinople (Socr. *H. E.* iv. 14; Soz. *H. E.* vi. 13). The people, however, were much divided (Philostorg. *H. E.* ix. 10). The orthodox party chose Evagrius for their bishop, and he was ordained by Eustathius, the deposed bp. of Antioch. This was the signal for an outburst of fury on the part of the Arians. Eustathius and Evagrius were banished by Valens, and their followers bitterly persecuted (Socr. *H. E.* iv. 14, 16; Soz. *H. E.* vi. 13, 14). Demophilus, soon after his accession, went to Cyzicus in conjunction with Dorotheus, or Theodorus, of Heraclea, to procure the election of an Arian bishop, that see having been vacant since the banishment of Eunomius. But the people of Cyzicus refused to acknowledge them till they had anathematized Aetius, Eunomius, and their followers. They were then permitted to ordain a bishop chosen by the people. The bishop who was ordained straightway and clearly taught the consubstantial faith (Philostorg. *H. E.* ix. 13).

In 380 changed times came and made the reign of Theodosius I. and the patriarchate of Demophilus memorable. The emperor Theodosius offered to confirm him in his see, if he would subscribe the Nicene Creed. Demophilus refused, and was immediately ordered to give up his churches. He then called his followers together, and retired, with Lucius of Alexandria and others, to a place of worship without the walls (Socr. *H. E.* v. 7). The churches of Constantinople, which had for forty years been in Arian hands, were now restored to the orthodox; and similarly in other cities. It was, in fact, a general disestablishment of Arianism and re-establishment of Catholicism. Philostorgius (*H. E.* ix. 19) adds that Demophilus went to his own city, Berea. But this must have been some time afterwards, or he must have returned from exile, for he represented the Arian party at the synod held in Constantinople, A.D. 383 (Socr. *H. E.* v. 10; Soz. *H. E.* vii. 12). The same writer says that Demophilus was wont to throw everything into confusion, especially the doctrines of the church, and quotes from a sermon at Constantinople, in which he spoke of the human nature of the Saviour as lost in the divine, as a glass of milk when poured into the sea. Philostorg. *Patrol. Gk.* lxv.; Soz. and Socr. *Patrol. Gk.* lxvii. [P.O.]

Dianius or **Dianaeus,** for more than 20 years bp. of Caesarea in Cappadocia, a saintly man much venerated in the early church, notwithstanding his somewhat doubtful orthodoxy. He was almost certainly the bishop who baptized Basil the Great on his return from Athens, and ordained him lector (Basil, *de Sp. Sancto*, 29, p. 357). Basil speaks of him in terms of most affectionate respect, describing him as remarkable for his virtues, frank, generous, and attractive from his amiability, venerable both in aspect and in character (*Ep.* 51 [84]). We see him, however, in these troubled times weak and undecided, led by his peaceful disposition to deprecate controversy, and by his feebleness to side with the strongest; destitute of strong theological convictions, and wanting the clearness of thought to appreciate subtleties of doctrine. He was, therefore, too often found on the semi-Arian side of the church. If, as Tillemont holds, he is the Danius who heads the list of bishops to whom pope Julius directed his dignified reply to the insolent letter addressed to him from Antioch, he took a leading part in the synod held at that city in the early months of A.D. 340, by which the deposition of Athanasius was confirmed, and George of Cappadocia placed on the throne of Alexandria (*Epistola Julii*, apud Athanas. *Apolog.* ii. p. 239). He also took part in the famous synod of Antioch, *in Encaeniis*, A.D. 341, and was present at Sardica, A.D. 347, where, according to Hilary (p. 29), he joined in the anathema against Julius and Athanasius. His weakness of character was still more fatally shewn when, after the council of Constantinople, A.D. 359, the formula of Rimini was sought to be imposed on the church by the authority of the emperor. To the intense grief of Basil, Dianius yielded to pressure and signed the heretical document. Basil could not hold communion with one who had so far compromised his faith, and fled to Nazianzum. It was reported that he had anathematized his bishop, but this he indignantly denies (Basil, *Ep.* 51 [84]). Dianius keenly felt the absence of his eloquent and able young counsellor, especially when Julian endeavoured to re-establish paganism. After two years he recalled Basil, and declared that he had signed the creed of Rimini in the simplicity of his heart, hoping to restore peace to the distracted church, with no idea of impugning the faith of Nicaea. Basil, satisfied with Dianius's explanations, returned to his former post of adviser of the bishop till his death, which occurred soon after, probably A.D. 362. [BASILIUS OF CAESAREA.] [E.V.]

Didymus, head of the Catechetical School of Alexandria in the 4th cent., born A.D. 309 or 314 (Tillemont, *Mém.* x. 387). When only four years old he lost his sight from disease; and consequently was never taught, as he himself declared, even the usual rudiments of learning. But his extraordinary force of character and intense thirst for knowledge triumphed over all disadvantages. He prayed for inward light, "but added studies to prayers" (Rufin. ii. 7). He learned the alphabet by touch from engraved wooden tablets, and words and syllables by attentive listening. Thus he became master of various sciences (Socr. iv. 25; Soz. iii. 15; Theod. iv. 26), and attained a truly wonderful familiarity with the Scriptures. Athanasius made the blind scholar head of the Catechetical School, as a fitting successor to Pantaenus and Clement. He was the twelfth who occupied that chair. In his earlier manhood, Anthony, visiting Alexandria to support the Catholic cause against the Arians, entered Didymus's cell, and despite his modest reluctance obliged him to offer up prayers (Rosweyd. *Vit. Patr.* 944, 539, ed. 1617), and asked Didymus whether he was sad on account of his blindness. After the question had been twice repeated, Didymus owned that he did feel the affliction painfully. "Do not be distressed," rejoined the saintly hermit, "for the loss of a faculty enjoyed by gnats and flies, when you have that inward eyesight which is the privilege of none but saints." Jerome (*Ep.* 68; cf. Socr. iv. 29) stayed for a month at Alexandria in 386, mainly (see *Prolog. in Eph.*) to see Didymus and have Scripture difficulties explained by him (Soz. *l.c.*). "In many points," wrote Jerome in A.D. 400 (*Ep.* 84), "I give him thanks. I learned from him things which I had not known; what I did know, his teaching has helped me to retain." Rufinus was also, for a much longer time, a pupil of Didymus. Palladius (Rosweyd. *l.c.*), who visited him four times, states that he had a dream of the emperor Julian's death at the exact time it occurred in his Persian expedition. Sozomen says that in arguing for the Nicene faith, Didymus was successful by his extreme persuasiveness—he seemed to make every one a judge of the points in dispute (iii. 15); and Isidore of Pelusium (*Ep.* i. 331) and Libanius (*Ep.* 321) speak of his great ability.

Our fullest information about him is derived from Jerome, who frequently refers to him as his old teacher, and affectionately describes him as "my seer," in allusion to the contrast between his physical blindness and his keenness of spiritual and intellectual perception. Jerome translated into Latin Didymus's treatise *On the Holy Spirit*, and prefixed a preface, in which he spoke of the author as having "eyes like the spouse in the Song of Songs," as "unskilled in speech but not in knowledge, exhibiting in his very speech the character of an apostolic man, as well by luminous thought as by simplicity of words." Writing in 392 (*de Viris Illustr.* 109), Jerome gives a short biographical account of Didymus.

The extent to which Didymus may be called an Origenizer has been discussed. See Mingarelli's "Commentarius" prefixed to his edition of Didymus's *de Trinitate* (Bologna, 1769). In his extant writings there is no assertion of Origenian views as to the pre-existence of souls, and he affirms, more than once, the endless nature of future punishment; but seems to have believed that some of the fallen angels occupied a midway position between angels and demons, and would be ultimately forgiven. Neither Epiphanius nor Theophilus, nor indeed any one before the 6th cent. except Jerome, laid Origenism to his charge; and with regard to the alleged condemnation of his memory by the 5th general council, as he is never named in the Acts, the utmost that can be made of such a statement is, that the condemnation of Origen in that synod's 11th anathema (Mansi, ix. 383) was somewhat largely construed as carrying with it, by implication, the condemnation of other writers more or less identified with his school of thought. See Tillemont's "comparison of Didymus with St. Gregory of Nyssa" (x. 396). Didymus's work *On the Holy Spirit* was clearly a protest against Macedonianism (see Tillemont, x. 393).

His comments on the Catholic Epistles are extant, as translated by Epiphanius Scholasticus (see Galland. *Bib. Vet. Patr.* ii.). His notes on I. Peter shew a dislike of Chiliasm, as a carnal and frivolous theory; he asserts free will, opposes Manicheans, admits the possibility of faults on the part of angels being cleansed through Christ; and in words very characteristic of the indomitable student and teacher, rebukes Christians who neglect sacred studies and attend only to practical life (on I. Peter iii. 15). He comments briefly on II. Peter, but sets it aside as spurious and "not in the canon," although (see *infra*) in the *de Trinitate* he cites it as Petrine. The chief features of his remarks on St. John's three Epistles are, (1) the earnestness against Docetism, Valentinianism, all speculations injurious to the Maker of the world, (2) the assertion that a true knowledge of God is possible without a knowledge of His essence, (3) care to urge the necessity of combining orthodoxy with right action. In the notes on Jude, he says that Christ is called the only Sovereign because He is the only true God. He speaks of the doom of those who turn away absolutely to evil as hopeless.

His treatise *Against the Manicheans* (pub. by Combefis in his *Auctarium Novum*, 1672) begins with logical formulae, intended to disprove the existence of two unoriginated Principles. From the blame and punishment attached to evil, he infers that Satan and his followers are not evil by nature; he discusses the terms "by nature children of wrath" (which he understands to mean "really children of wrath"), "children of this world," "son of perdition," "generation of vipers," with the aim of shewing that they do not contravene the great moral facts of free will and responsibility. The devil, he urges, was created good, and became a devil by his own free will. If it be objected, why then did God make a being who was to become so pestilent? the objection really lies against the whole plan of God's moral government, which intends His rational creatures to become good by choosing goodness, and therefore leaves them capable of choosing evil, and drawing on themselves the result of such a choice. He also asserts the transmission of original sin: a Saviour born by ordinary generation would have incurred the sin entailed on Adam's whole posterity. His three books *On the Trinity* have not reached us in a perfect state. They are interesting as exhibiting the Athanasian character, so to speak, of his thought in presence of Anomoeans and of Macedonians. He admits II. Peter as genuine: perhaps the opinion he had formerly held as to its non-canonicity had been reconsidered. He is very earnest, almost in the style of the "Athanasian Creed," on the co-equality of the Divine Hypostases (he uses that term in the sense which the younger generation of Catholics had adopted since the earlier days of the Arian strife). He enforces the perpetuity of Christ's kingdom (as if in controversy with Marcellians), and speaks of the Virgin Mother as Theotokos (ii. 4). He bestows much time and pains on the Macedonian controversy. Occasionally he kindles and glows with strong devotional fervour, and concludes an eloquent passage on the glory of the Holy Trinity with a thrice-repeated Amen. Shortly before this passage he invokes the archangels, and expresses his belief in the intercession of the saints (ii. 7). [W.B.]

Dimoeritae, another name for the followers of Apollinarius, probably to be explained by a passage in a letter of Gregory of Nazianzum to Nectarius of Constantinople (*Ep.* 202, al. *Or.* 46). Gregory says that Apollinarius's book affirmed that He Who had come down from above had no νοῦς, but that τὴν θεότητα τοῦ Μονογενοῦς τὴν τοῦ νοῦ φύσιν ἀναπληρώσασαν. Hence, as the Apollinarians maintained that our Lord assumed only (διμοιρία) two of the three parts (σῶμα, ψυχή, νοῦς) of which perfect humanity consists, they were called Dimoeritae by Epiphanius, who says (*Haer.* lxxvii.) that "some denied especially the perfect Incarnation of Christ; some asserted His body consubstantial with His divinity; some emphatically denied that He had ever taken a soul; others not less emphatically refused to Him a mind."

Among the leaders of the Dimoeritae was one Vitalius. Both Gregory of Nazianzum and Epiphanius came in contact with him; the former while Vitalius was, it would seem, a presbyter, the latter when he had been made a bishop of the sect. Epiphanius at Antioch, in a long discussion with Vitalius, put the crucial question: "You admit the Incarnation, do you also admit that Christ took a mind (νοῦν)?" The answer was, "No." Epiphanius persisted: "In what sense then do you call Christ τέλειος?" The point was debated without results. Epiphanius urged that not only was nothing gained by excluding mind, as we understand it, from the nature of Christ; but also that by such exclusion much was lost which made His nature, character, and actions intelligible. Vitalius and his followers avoided Epiphanius's arguments by reverting to their favourite texts, *e.g.* "We have the mind of Christ" (I. Cor. ii. 16), etc.

The Dimoeritae probably existed, as a sect, for a few years only, either under that name or as Vitalians, Synusiasts, Polemians, Valentinians, after some favourite leader or opinion. Then they died out, or merged themselves into other bodies holding similar views, or were brought back to the church. The books, psalteries, and hymns composed and issued by Apollinarius and his principal followers were met, and their effects counteracted, by books and hymns such as have given to Gregory of Nazianzum a name among ecclesiastical song-writers. Epiphanius, *Panaria*, iii. 11; *Haer.* lxxvii. (ed. Dindorf, iii. 1, p. 454); Oehler, *Corpus Haereseolog.* ii. 330, etc.; and the usual Church histories, *e.g.* Neander, Niedner, Hase, Robertson, *s.v.* "Apollinarianism," should be consulted. [J.M.F.]

Dinooth, Dinothus, abbat of Bangor Iscoed,

a Welsh saint, placed by Rees between A.D. 500 and 542. Originally a North British chieftain, reverses drove him into Wales, where he found a protector in Cyngen, prince of Powys. Like many other British chieftains who lost their lands in the Saxon conquest (Rees, *Welsh Saints*, 207), Dinooth embraced a life of religion, and, under Cyngen, founded, in conjunction with his sons, Deiniol, Cynwyl, and Gwarthan, the monastery of Bangor on the Dee, of which he was the first abbat. Bede mentions his name in his narrative of the second conference at Augustine's Oak (*H. E.* ii. 2), but merely says, cautiously, "Tempore illo Dinoot abbas praefuisse *narratur*." Bede, who wrote a century and a quarter after Augustine's time, shews no special acquaintance with the internal affairs of the Britons, and we cannot help suspecting that the present uncertainty as to the chronology of Welsh hagiology existed when Bede wrote. A later statement makes the founder of Bangor alive in A.D. 602 or 603, and brings him to the conference, though he must have been in extremest old age, and would have had a mountain journey from the Dee to the lower Severn (see *D. C. A.* "Augustine's Oak"; also Haddan and Stubbs, iii. 40, 41, on Augustine's journey); it even reports the speech he is said to have made in the name of the British church in answer to Augustine. For this document see Haddan and Stubbs (*Councils*, i. 122), where the answer is quoted in the original Welsh with Spelman's Latin translation. Two copies of the original MS. exist in the Cottonian collection. It is accepted as genuine by Leland (Tanner, *Biblioth.* 1748, art. "Dinotus," p. 228), Stillingfleet (*Orig. Brit.* i. 536), Lappenberg (*Hist. of Eng.* i. 135). On the other hand, the document does not mention the name of Augustine, nor allude to one subject of the conference which is markedly noted by Bede, the evangelization of the Anglo-Saxons. In fact it contains no name whatever, but is a firm and temperate repudiation of papal authority, and an assertion of the supremacy of "the bp. of Caerleon upon Usk" over the British church. For any internal evidence to the contrary, the "Answer" might have been penned in reply to some demand made upon the British church by the see of Canterbury centuries after Dinooth. It bears upon that subject, and that alone.

We know less about Dinooth than about his famous monastery upon the right bank of the Dee, 10 or 12 miles from Chester. The name of Bangor ys y coed (Bangor under the wood) distinguishes it from other Bangors, especially that of Carnarvonshire, where Deiniol, the son of Dinooth, founded another monastery, which was soon afterwards made the seat of a bishopric. So numerous were the monks of Bangor Iscoed that, as Bede puts it, on their being divided into seven parts with a ruler over each, none of those parts consisted of less than 300 men, who all lived by the labour of their hands. It thus rivalled the Irish Bangor [COMGALL], and, from the learned men mentioned by Bede as residing there, must have been as much a college as a monastery. Augustine's prediction was levelled, not against this institution in particular, but the British church and people at large; "if they would not preach the way of life to the English nation, they should at their hands undergo the vengeance of death." The conjunction desired by Augustine ("una cum nobis," Bede) involved their ecclesiastical submission. "Dinooth's Answer," in recognizing this, may have appeared to some one in after-times a sufficient ground to assign the document to this occasion. The judgment came about 10 years afterwards, A.D. 613 (*Ann. Cambr.* and *Ann. Tighern.*, preferable to earlier dates, as 603 of Flor. Wig. and 606 or 607 of *A. S. C.*; cf. Haddan and Stubbs, i. 123), when Ethelfrid, the pagan king of Northumbria, invaded the Britons at Chester. Being about to give battle, he observed their "priests," who were there to pray for the soldiers, drawn up apart in a place of greater safety, and under the military protection of prince Brocmail. They had come chiefly from Bangor, after a three days' fast. The invader, regarding them as a contingent of his enemy, attacked them first and slew about 1,200, only 50 escaping. Bede either here uses the term "sacerdotes" and "monachi" as synonymous, or the priests were in charge of the monks, leading their devotions. It was a disastrous blow to Bangor, and was naturally handed down as a fulfilment of Augustine's words; but we do not hear that the monastery itself was attacked. Some 60 years later the annalists record "Combustio Bennchoriae Brittonum" (Hadd. and St. i. 125), probably referring to this Bangor of the Dee. Malmesbury (*G. R.* ed. Hardy, i. 66) describes the extensive ruins of the place in his day—"tot semiruti parietes ecclesiarum, tot anfractus porticuum, tanta turba ruderum, quantum vix alibi cernas"; the credibility of which description has been almost destroyed by sometimes translating the first clause, "the ruined walls of so many churches." The remains had nearly disappeared in the time of Camden. (Camd. ed. Gough, ii. 422, 429; Smith, ad. Bed. *E. H.* ii. 2; Tanner, *Notit.* ed. Nasmith, Flint. ii.) The site is on the road between Wrexham and Whitchurch, about 5 miles from each. Its modern state and surviving vestiges are described in Lewis (*Topog. Dict. of Wales*, art. "Bangor"). Leland's description is in his *Itinerary* (vol. v. p. 30, 2nd ed. Hearne). [C.H.]

Diocletian (*Docles, Diocles, Caius Valerius Diocletianus Jovius*), A.D. 284-305. The acts that make the reign of this emperor memorable in the history of the church belong to its closing years. Had he died before A.D. 303 he would have taken his place among the rulers whose general tolerance helped Christianity to obtain its victory. As it is, his name is identified with the most terrible of its persecutions. For three centuries men reckoned from the commencement of his reign as from the era of martyrs; and the date is still recognized in the Coptic Church as the basis of its chronology.

The earlier years of Diocletian concern us only in connexion with the struggle which came to a head when his work seemed nearly over. Elected by the soldiers in Bithynia at the age of 39, after the murder of Numerian, he was formally installed at Nicomedia. In A.D. 286 he chose Maximian as his colleague, gave him the title first of Cæsar and then of

Augustus, and sent him to command in the West, while he remained in the East, chiefly at Nicomedia, which he tried to make, by lavish outlay on its buildings, a new capital for the empire. It indicates his intention to uphold the religion of the state that he assumed the surname of Jovius, and gave to his colleague that of Herculius. Among the buildings with which he embellished the various provinces were temples of Zeus, Apollo, Nemesis, Hecate, at Antioch, of Isis and Serapis at Rome, of Isis at Phylae, of Mithras at Vindobona. He consulted haruspices and augurs as to the success of his enterprises, and in more difficult emergencies the oracle of the Milesian Apollo at Branchidae (Lactant. *de Mort. Pers.* cc. 10, 11).

The appointment of Constantius Chlorus and Galerius in A.D. 293 as Caesars under the two Augusti introduced new elements. Each was called on to prove his loyalty to the system into which he was adopted by a new marriage. Constantius divorced Helena and married Theodora, the step-daughter of Maximian. Galerius, also repudiating his former wife, received the hand of Valeria, the daughter of Diocletian and Prisca. To Constantius was entrusted the government of Gaul and Britain, to Galerius the provinces between the Adriatic and the Euxine. Diocletian kept the provinces of Asia under his own control. Maximian had those of Africa and Italy. The edict of Gallienus, A.D. 259, had placed Christianity in the number of *religiones licitae*, and there had been no formal persecution since. Diocletian and Maximian began by adopting the same policy; and the martyrdoms which are referred to the earlier years of their reign, like those of St. Maurice and the Theban Legion at Martigny (Octodurum), of St. Victor at Marseilles, of SS. Cosmas and Damian and others in Cilicia, if more than legendary, must be referred to special causes, and not to a general policy of persecution. The somewhat cloudy rhetoric of Eusebius in describing the condition of the church of this time indicates that the last struggle with the old religion could not long be averted. The most trusted and influential eunuchs of the household, Dorotheus and Gorgonius, were avowedly Christians and excused from attending at heathen sacrifices (Eus. viii. 1). Prisca the wife, and Valeria the daughter, of Diocletian were kept back from an open profession of faith; but their absence from all sacrifices made men look on them with suspicion (Lactant. *de Mort. Persec.* c. 15). The church of Nicomedia was the most conspicuous edifice in the city. The adherents of the old system had good reason for alarm. They saw in every part of the empire an organized society that threatened it with destruction. Symptoms of the coming conflict began before long to shew themselves. Malchus, the disciple of Plotinus (better known as Porphyry), wrote against the religion of the Christians while maintaining a tone of reverence towards Christ Himself, and so became in their eyes their most formidable opponent. Hierocles, first as *Vicarius* of Bithynia and afterwards, probably, as prefect of Egypt, fought against them with pen and sword, and published *Words of a Truth-lover to the Christians*, in which Christ was compared with Apollonius of Tyana. Within the imperial circle itself some were impatient of the tolerance of Diocletian. The mother of Galerius, who gave sacrificial banquets almost daily, was annoyed because Christian officers and soldiers refused to come to them. The cases of Maximilian of Theveste, in proconsular Africa, who (A.D. 295) had refused to serve as a soldier and take the military oath, as incompatible with his allegiance to Christ, and of Marcellus (A.D. 298), who at Tingis in Mauritania solemnly renounced his allegiance to the emperor rather than take part in idolatrous festivals, had probably alarmed Galerius himself (Ruinart, *Acta Sincera*, pp. 309, 312).

Occasions for decisive measures were soon found. Diocletian, who seems to have had a devout belief in divination, had offered sacrifice, and the haruspices were inspecting the entrails of the victim to see what omens were to be found there. The Christian officers and servants of the emperor were present as part of their duty, and satisfied their conscience by making the sign of the cross upon their foreheads. The diviners were, or pretended to be, struck with amazement at the absence, despite repeated sacrifices, of the expected signs. At last they declared their work hindered by the presence of profane persons. The emperor's rage was roused. His personal attendants and the officials in his palace were ordered to sacrifice under penalty of being scourged. Letters were sent to military officers bidding them to compel their soldiers to a like conformity under pain of dismissal. The mother of Galerius urged the emperor on, and found but a feeble resistance. He deprecated the slaughter and wished to confine the edict to servants of his household and soldiers. He would take counsel with his friends and consult the gods. One of the haruspices was accordingly sent to the oracle of the Milesian Apollo at Branchidae. The answer came, not from the priestess only, but, as it were, from the god himself speaking from the recesses of his cave, telling him that the presence of the self-styled "just ones" on the earth made it impossible for the oracles to speak the truth. This turned the scale and the emperor gave way. All he asked for was that bloodshed might, if possible, be avoided. Galerius had wished to condemn to the flames all who refused to sacrifice. After many divinations, the Feast of the Terminalia (Feb. 23) of A.D. 303 was chosen as the fit day for issuing the edict against the new society. At break of day the prefect, attended by officers and secretaries, went to the church of Nicomedia while Diocletian and Galerius watched the proceedings from the palace. The doors were broken open. Search was made for the image of the Christian's God, which they expected to find there. The books were burned, the church sacked. Fear of the fire spreading made Diocletian shrink from burning the church, but a body of pioneers with axes and crowbars razed it in a few hours. Next morning an edict ordained that (1) all churches were to be demolished; (2) all sacred books burnt; (3) all Christian officials stripped of their dignities, and deprived of civil rights, and therefore rendered liable to torture and other outrages; while Christian men who were not officials were to be reduced to slavery. A Christian who tore it down, with the sarcastic exclamation, "More triumphs of Goths and Sarmatians!" was seized, tortured, and burnt alive at a slow fire. Shortly after, a fire broke out in the palace and suspicion fell upon the Christians, notably upon the palace eunuchs. The use made of the occurrence to work upon Diocletian's fears justified the impression of Christian writers that it was a device contrived by Galerius and executed by his slaves. All who were suspected were examined by torture; within a fortnight there was another similar alarm, and now there was no limit to the old man's fury. His wife and daughter were compelled to free themselves from suspicion by joining in sacrifice. The eunuchs of his household, before so trusted, Dorotheus, Gorgonius, Petrus, were put to death. The persecution raged throughout the province. Some were burnt, some drowned, some thrust into dungeons. Altars were set up in every court of justice, and both parties to suits compelled to sacrifice. A second edict ordered that all the clergy, without option of sacrifice, should be imprisoned. Anthimus bp. of Nicomedia was beheaded (Eus. *H. E.* viii. 6). Hierocles as author and magistrate silenced by torture those whom he failed to convince. Letters were sent to Maximian and Constantius in the West, urging them to adopt like measures. The former was but too willing an instrument. The latter, more humane and disposed to a policy of toleration, was compelled to join in destroying the buildings of the Christians, and was glad if he could save their lives (Lactant. *de Mort. Persec.* cc. 12-16).

Individual martyrdoms may be found with more or less fulness in the *Acta Sincera* of Ruinart, in the *Annals* of Baronius, in most Church Histories, notably in Fleury, viii. and ix. Here we merely note the extent, continuance, and ferocity which distinguished this persecution from all others. In Syria, Palestine, Egypt, Western Africa, Italy, and Spain the passions of men were let loose, and raged without restraint. In Gaul and Britain only was there any safety. Constantius was said (Eus. *Vit. Const.* i. 16) to have shewn a marked preference for those who were true to their religion, and refused to sacrifice. Elsewhere every town in the empire witnessed acts of incredible cruelty. The wish to destroy all the sacred books of the Christians, and all the accessories of their worship, led men to seize on the deacons, readers, and others connected with the churches, and to torture them till they gave them up. In Dec. 303, Diocletian went to Rome to celebrate with Maximian the 20th anniversary of his accession. At the Vicennalia the licence of the people offended him, and he left after two weeks for Ravenna. There he was attacked by a severe illness, which detained him for some months. Slowly he made his way to Nicomedia, where he became worse. Prayers were offered for his recovery in all the temples. It was rumoured that his death was concealed till the arrival of Galerius. When he appeared to contradict the rumour, he was so altered that he could hardly be recognized. His mind, it was said, was seriously affected. Galerius came, but it was to press on the emperor the duty and expediency of resigning. Maximian had been already persuaded to do so. After a feeble resistance Diocletian yielded. The two Caesars were to become Augusti. He would fain have named Maxentius the son of Maximian and Constantine the son of Constantius to take their place; but Galerius coerced or persuaded him to appoint Maximin and Severus, in whom he hoped to find more submissive instruments. When the formal acts had been completed, the emperor laid aside his official names Diocletianus and Jovius, and returned to the simple Diocles of his youth. For the history of the following year see GALERIUS and CONSTANTINE. The retired emperor settled at Salona, on the coast of Dalmatia, and occupied himself with building and gardening, and refused to abandon his cabbages for the cares of the state. In 310 Maximian, after vainly struggling against the growing power of Constantine, who had succeeded Constantius, was compelled to end his life by his own hands. In 311 Galerius died in the agonies of a loathsome and horrible disease, and before his death confessed, by an edict of toleration, that the attempt which he had made to crush Christianity had failed. Diocletian survived to witness the alliance between Constantine and Licinius, to receive and decline an invitation to a conference with them at Milan, to hear that Constantine had charged him with conspiring first with Maxentius and then with Maximian, and had ordered his statue and that of Maximian to be thrown down in every part of the empire. In A.D. 313 the end came, some said through poison (Aurel. Vict. *Epist.* 39), to avoid a worse fate at the hands of Constantine and Licinius. It was characteristic of his fate as representing the close of pagan imperialism, that he was the last emperor who celebrated a triumph at Rome, and the last to receive the honour of apotheosis from the Roman senate (Preuss, p. 169). [E.H.P.]

Diodorus (3), presbyter of Antioch, and *c.* A.D. 379 bp. of Tarsus, of a noble family of Antioch, where he passed nearly the whole of his life until he became a bishop (Theod. *H. E.* iv. 24). He studied philosophy or secular learning at Athens, where he probably was an associate of Basil and Julian, the future emperor (Facund. lib. iv. c. 2, p. 59). On his return to his native city, Diodorus and his friend Flavian, also of noble birth (subsequently bp. of Antioch), embraced a religious life. Here, while still laymen, during the reign of Constantius, they exerted themselves energetically for the defence of the orthodox faith against the Arians, who were covertly supported by bp. Leontius, *c.* 350. They gathered the orthodox laity even by night around the tombs of the martyrs, to join in the antiphonal chanting of the Psalms, which, Theodoret tells us, was first instituted or revived by them, as a means of kindling religious zeal, after the model ascribed by tradition to the martyred bishop of their church, the holy Ignatius (Socr. *H. E.* vi. 8; Theod. *H. E.* ii. 24). These services strengthened the faithful to meet the persecutions. The weight of Diodorus and Flavian at Antioch was proved when in 350 their threat of withdrawal from communion induced Leontius to suspend AETIUS from the diaconate (Theod. *u.s.*). On the accession of Julian, his attempt to rekindle an expiring paganism provided a new field for the energies of Diodorus. With pen and tongue he denounced the folly of a return to an exploded superstition, and so called forth the scurrilous jests of Julian.

The persecution of the Catholic cause by the Arian Valens recalled Diodorus, now a presbyter, to his former championship of the Nicene faith. During the frequent banishments of Meletius, the spiritual instruction of his diocese was chiefly entrusted to him and Flavian, and Diodorus saved the barque of the church from being "submerged by the waves of misbelief" (Theod. *H. E.* v. 4). Valens having forbidden the Catholics to meet within the walls of cities, Diodorus gathered his congregation in the church in the old town S. of the Orontes. Immense numbers were there "fed by him with sound doctrine" (Chrys. *Laus Diodori*, § 4, t. iii. p. 749). When forcibly driven out of this church, he gathered his congregation in the soldiers' exercising ground, or "gymnasium," and exhorted them from house to house. The texts and arguments of his discourses were chiefly furnished by Flavian, and clothed by Diodorus in a rhetorical dress. His oratory is compared by Chrysostom to "a lyre" for melody, and to "a trumpet" for the power with which, like Joshua at Jericho, he broke down the strongholds of his heretical opponents. He also held private assemblies at his own house to expound the faith and refute heresy (Theod. *H. E.* iv. 25; Chrys. *l.c.*; Facund. iv. 22). Such dauntless championship of the faith failed not to provoke persecution. His life was more than once in danger, and he was forced to seek safety in flight (Chrys. *l.c.*). Once at least when driven from Antioch he joined his spiritual father Meletius in exile at Getasa in Armenia, where, in 372, he met Basil the Great (Basil, *Ep.* 187). The intimate terms of Diodorus and Basil are seen from the tone of Basil's correspondence.

Even more than for his undaunted defence of the catholic faith Diodorus deserves the gratitude of the church as head of the theological school at Antioch. He pursued a healthy common-sense principle of exposition of Holy Scripture, which, discarding alike allegorism and coarse literalism, sought by the help of criticism, philology, history, and other external resources, to develop the true meaning of the text, as intended by the authors (Socr. *H. E.* vi. 3; Soz. *H. E.* viii. 2; Hieron. *de Vir. Illust.* No. 119).

Meletius, on being restored to Antioch in 378, appointed Diodorus bp. of Tarsus and metropolitan of the then undivided province of Cilicia (Facundus, viii. 5). His career as bishop, according to Jerome (*l.c.*), was less distinguished than as presbyter. He took part in the great council of Antioch A.D. 379, which failed to put an end to the Antiochene schism, as well as in the 2nd oecumenical council at Constantinople A.D. 381. By the decree of the emperor Theodosius, July 30, 381, Diodorus was named as one of the orthodox Eastern prelates, communion with whom was the test of orthodoxy (*Cod. Theod.* lib. xvi. tit. i. 3; t. vi. p. 9). Meletius having died during the session of the council, Diodorus, violating the compact made to heal the schism, united with Acacius of Beroea in consecrating Flavian as bp. of Antioch, for which both the consecrating prelates were excommunicated by the bishops of the West (Soz. *H. E.* vii. 11). As Phalerius was bp. of Tarsus at a council at Constantinople in 394, the date of Diodorus's death is approximately fixed. Facundus and others tell us that he died full of days and glory, revered by the whole church and honoured by its chief doctors, by Basil, Meletius, Theodoret, Domnus of Antioch, and even by the chief impugner of the soundness of his faith, Cyril of Alexandria.

This high credit was disturbed by the Nestorian controversies of the next cent. His rationalizing spirit had led him to use language about the Incarnation containing the principles of that heresy afterwards more fully developed by his disciple Theodorus. Thus, not without justice, he has been deemed the virtual parent of Nestorianism and called "a Nestorian before Nestorius." It was his repugnance to the errors of Apollinarianism which led him to the opposite errors of Nestorianism. His sense of the importance of the truth of Christ's manhood caused him to insist on Its distinctness from His Godhead in a manner which gradually led to Its being represented as a separate personality. He drew a distinction between Him Who according to His essence was Son of God—the eternal Logos—and Him Who through divine decree and adoption became Son of God. The one was Son of God by nature, the other by grace. The son of man became Son of God because chosen to be the receptacle or temple of God the Word. It followed that Mary could not be properly termed the "mother of God," nor God the Word be strictly called the Son of David, that designation belonging, according to human descent, to the temple in which the Divine Son tabernacled. Diodorus therefore distinguished two Sons, the Son of God and the son of Mary, combined in the person of Christ. When, then, the great Nestorian controversy set in, Cyril clearly saw that, apart from the watchword Θεοτόκος, which had not arisen in the days of Diodorus, what men called Nestorianism was substantially the doctrine of Diodorus as developed by Theodorus of Mopsuestia, and that Nestorianism could only be fully crushed by a condemnation of the doctrines of Diodorus as the fountain head. This condemnation was most difficult to obtain. No name was held in so much reverence throughout the East. Cyril, however, was of far too determined a spirit to hesitate. If orthodox views of the Incarnation were to be established, the authority of Diodorus must, at any cost of enmity and unpopularity, be destroyed. Every means was therefore taken to enforce, by the aid of the emperor and the patriarch Proclus, his condemnation, together with that of his still more heretical pupil Theodorus. Cyril himself, in a letter to the emperor, described them in the harshest terms as the fathers of the blasphemies of Nestorius (Theodoret, t. v. p. 854), and in a letter to John of Antioch denounced them as "going full sail, as it were, against the glory of Christ." It is not surprising that Diodorus began to be looked upon with suspicion by those who had been accustomed to regard him as a bulwark of the faith, insomuch that Theodoret, when himself accused of Nestorian leanings, did not venture to quote the words of Diodorus in his defence, though he regarded him with reverence (σέβω), as "a holy and blessed father" (Theod. *Ep.* 16). In the hope of rehabilitating his credit, Theodoret wrote a treatise to prove the orthodoxy of Diodorus, which led Cyril to peruse them and to pronounce them categorically heretical (ib. *Epp.* 38, 52). All attempts, however, to depreciate the authority of Diodorus, both by Cyril and Rabbulas of Edessa, only exalted him in the estimation of the Nestorian party, and the opposition contributed to the formation of the independent and still existing Nestorian church, which looks upon Diodorus and Theodorus with deepest veneration as its founders. The presbyter Maris of Hardaschir, in Persia, translated the works of Diodorus into Persian, and they, together with those of Theodorus, were also translated into Armenian, Syriac, and other Oriental tongues (Neander, *Ch. Hist.* vol. iv. pp. 209, 284; Clark's trans. Liberat. *Breviar.* c. 10). Diodorus was naturally anathematized by Eutyches and his followers. Flavian III., also bp. of Antioch, was compelled by the Monophysites to pass an anathema on the writings of Diodorus and Theodorus in A.D. 499. The controversy respecting the orthodoxy of Diodorus was revived in the 6th cent. by the interminable disputes about "the Three Articles." There is a full defence of his orthodoxy by Facundus in his *Defensio Trium Capitulorum*" (lib. iv. c. 2). Photius asserts that Diodorus was formally condemned by the fifth oecumenical council held at Constantinople A.D. 553, but it does not appear in the acts of that council. Diodorus was a very copious author, the titles of between 20 and 30 distinct works being enumerated in various catalogues. The whole have perished, except some fragments, no less than 60 having been burnt, according to Ebed-Jesu, by the Arians. His writings were partly exegetical, mainly controversial. He wrote comments on all the books of O. and N. T., except the Ep. to the Hebrews, the Catholic Epistles (I. John however being commented on), and the Apocalypse. In these, according to Jerome (*de Vir. Illust.* No. 119), he imitated the line of thought of Eusebius of Emesa, but fell below him in eloquence and refinement. [E.V.]

Diognetus, Epistle to. The Greek writing known under this name was first printed in 1592 by Henricus Stephanus, along with a companion piece *To Greeks*, as hitherto unknown writings of Justin Martyr, taken by him from a single faded exemplar.

In his edition, as in the transcript in his own handwriting extant at Leyden, the writing *To Greeks* was not prefixed, but appended to the writing *To Diognetus*; but in the MS. from which he took the pieces (identified by Gebhardt with that collated by Cunitz at Strasburg, where it perished in 1870) three works, each ascribed by name to Justin, were followed by the two pieces *Of the Same to Greeks* and *Of the Same to Diognetus*. The correctness of the ascription of each of these two pieces to Justin was separately called in question by subsequent critics; but the connexion between the two pieces, the contrast in style presented by both alike to the spurious or dubious works of Justin to which in the MS. they were appended, and the fact that it was not directly to Justin Martyr, but to the author of the address *To Greeks* that the address *To Diognetus* was in the MS. ascribed, were forgotten.

In the MS., again, the text given under the heading *To Diognetus* was broken into *three* fragments by *two* clear breaks with marginal notes from the old 13th-cent. scribe, saying, "Thus I found a break in the copy before me also, it being very ancient." Of these two breaks the former, occurring near the end of c. vii., is ignored by Stephanus in his division of the writing into chapters. Whether more or less be missing, the writing comprised in cc. vii.-x. is plainly the continuation of the writing commenced in cc. i.-vii. In the concluding fragment (cc. xi. xii.), appended after the second break, the writer calls himself "disciple of apostles," and on this ground the writer *To Diognetus* has been included among the apostolic Fathers. But the contrast between cc. i.-x. and cc. xi. xii. is so great that critics have concluded the final appended fragment to be no part of the writing to Diognetus, but the peroration of another treatise by another writer.

No other ancient copy of the Greek of any of the writings published in 1592 has been found; but the writer *To Greeks*, with whom the writer *To Diognetus* was in the MS. immediately identified, has been plainly distinguished from Justin by the discovery and publication by Cureton in his *Spicilegium Syriacum* from a 6th or 7th cent. MS. of a Syriac version of an almost identical discourse ascribed to one "Ambrosius, a chief man of Greece, who became a Christian, and all his fellow-councillors raised a clamour against him." We may thus say that the true traditional writer *To Greeks* and *To Diognetus* is a certain otherwise unknown Ambrosius, convert like Justin from Hellenism to Christianity—the reply *To Greeks*, the assailants of the writer, being naturally followed by the response *To Diognetus*, the inquirer.

This conclusion is confirmed by internal evidence. The style of the two writings is identical. In each there is the same Attic diction joined with the same Roman dignity. Nay, in each there is the same occurrence of two contrasted styles, the same passage from the scornful vigour of the satirist to the joyous sweetness of the evangelist.

"Come, be taught," says the writer *To Greeks* (c. v.); and it seems that Diognetus came. Common as the name was, the only Diognetus known to us after Christ was a painting master who *c.* 133 had charge of the young Marcus Aurelius. Whether this was the Diognetus who came to the Christian teacher we do not know. The writing addressed to him is not in form an epistle, it seems rather to be a discourse delivered in a Christian Assembly into which the eminent inquirer had found his way. His coming implied a triple question: (i) "On what God relying, Christians despise death and neither reckon those gods who are so accounted by the Greeks, nor observe any superstition of Jews"; (ii) "What the kindly affection is that they have one for another"; and (iii) "What, in short, this new race or practice might be that has invaded society now and no earlier." To (i) the writer replies in cc. i.-vii., first bidding the Greek look at his manufactured gods (c. ii.), and convicting the Jews of vain oblations (c. iii.) and ungrateful service (c. iv.) to the Giver of all to all, then (c. v.) portraying the wondrous life of Christians, at home yet strangers everywhere, like the soul in the body of the world (c. vi.), and so (c. vii.) passing from the earthly things to the heavenly to tell how it was God Who implanted the Word by the mission of the Maker of all, sent as an imperial Son, in love, to be sent again as Judge. So the inquirer is answered that the reasons for non-compliance with Hellenism and Judaism are obvious, but the Christians' God is the one God of the Jews, and their religion consists of purity and charity, and was founded by the mission of the Son, Whom God will send again. At this point something has dropped out. The argument may be surmised to have continued after this fashion: "An end of all things is the doctrine of your Greek sages; but the Jews looked for a perpetual earthly kingdom, and when Christ proclaimed a kingdom not of this world, they slew Him, and yet He is not dead, and Christian worship is not to deny Him." For as resumed (c. vii.) after a break in the middle of a sentence, the discourse points to martyrdoms as "signs," not of the return but "of the presence" of the Lord, as though saying, "You see, He is still with us." Then proceeding (c. viii.) to contrast the follies of philosophy with the assurance wrought by the Father's revelation of Himself to faith, he explains (c. ix.) how God waited to shew forth what He had prepared till unrighteousness had been made manifest, and then, when the time came, Himself took our sins and gave His own Son for us and would have us trust Him. So (c. x.) he passes from expounding "on what God Christians rely" to expound "what the love is that they bear one to another," the outcome of their love to Him Who first loved them.

The first two questions of the inquirer are thus answered, and in answering them completely the third question, "What the new institution might be," would be answered along with them; but that answer seems not to be completed before the second break. It could not be complete till it had been carried further than merely saying that "it was God Who implanted the Word," and that He did so "when the time came." "The Word that appeared new" must have been "found old"; and this is the answer that we find in the final fragment (cc. xi. xii.) after the second break. The style has become different. We find ourselves listening to the peroration of a homily, before the withdrawal of the catechumens and the celebration of the mysteries. It does not follow that the final fragment does not belong to the preceding discourse. If Diognetus had shewn his desire for instruction by coming into a Christian assembly, the whole discourse may have been delivered before such an audience as is addressed in the peroration at the close. We are brought into a new region. The satirist of superstition and evangelist of atoning, justifying mercy is succeeded by a mystical believer in a Christ born anew in hearts of saints. The new thing is portrayed as "that which was from the beginning," yet ever new. "This is He that is ever reckoned a Son to-day." But what it is can be known only by taking up the cross and so coming to be with Christ in Paradise, "Whose tree if thou bearest fruit and if thou choosest thou shalt eat those things that with God are desired."

The loss of intervening matter makes the transition to the new region abrupt and the contrast patent. "The Lord's Passover cometh forth, and, teaching saints, the Word is gladdened." But the course is still straightforward and the guide is not diverse. The style is different only so far as is necessitated by the difference of subject. It exhibits the same anarthrous use of nouns, the same accumulation of clause on clause, not pursued too far; the same unexpected turns at the close of the sentences; the same union of dignity with sweetness, the same blending of Pauline with Johannine teaching; the same persistent subordination of doctrine to life. On these grounds we may venture to differ from the wide consent of critics in imagining a second nameless author.

It is worth noting that an Ambrose, of the consecration of Antioch, is said in a Syriac tradition to have been the third primate of Edessa and the East (Burkitt, *Early Eastern Christianity*, p. 29). The writer *To Greeks* and *To Diognetus* may have been this bringer of Greek Pauline Christianity to the regions beyond Euphrates conquered by Trajan and abandoned by Hadrian, and have been ancestor of the friend of Origen and of the great Milanese archbp. and of the legendary father of King Arthur.

Probably an old copy exhibited three works of Ambrosius—an avowal of Christianity, and answers *To Greeks* and *To Diognetus*, each a brave act as well as a solid work, the first now lost, the second a fine sample of a class of controversial works of which samples are numerous, the third, *To Diognetus*, preserved in fragments only, but unique, not apologetic merely, but catechetical, a portraiture of early Christianity not in its manifestation only, but in its springs, bringing us to the gates of the Paradise of God.

In free allied states like Antioch and Athens avowal of Christianity may have been tolerated when not suffered in Roman or subject regions. In the 2nd cent. the world was not yet all Roman.

The date of the writings may be determined with great probability, not with absolute certainty, except that, if genuine, they cannot be post-Nicene. The picture of the church presented to Diognetus pretty plainly belongs to a date earlier than the accession of Commodus. The chief school of Christian thought would seem still to be at Athens, though on the eve of its transference to Alexandria by Athenagoras. It is among the writings of Tatian, Melito, and Theophilus and the fragments of Apollinaris, Abercius, etc., that these pieces seem most at home. The writer seems to appear in his freshness beside Justin in his ripeness, and to be the meeting-point of the teachings of Justin and Marcion, as he is at the point of departure of Irenaeus, Tertullian, Hippolytus, and Origen on the one hand, and Praxeas, Noetus, and Sabellius on the other.

Lost in the crowd of predecessors whom Irenaeus and Clement hardly ever name and merged in Justin's shadow, convinced that God alone can reveal Himself, and content to be hidden in his Saviour's righteousness, the old writer has gradually emerged by virtue of an inborn lustre, at once the obscurest and most brilliant of his contemporaries, and has cast a glory on the early church while remaining himself unknown.

Authorities.—Gallandi, *ap.* Migne, *Patr. Gk.* ii. 1159 ff.; Bickersteth, *Christian Fathers,* (1838); Dorner, *Person of Christ*, i. 260 ff.; Hefele, *Patres Apostolici* (Tübingen, 1842); Neander, *Church History*, ii. 420, 425 (Bohn); Westcott, *Canon* (ed. 1875), pp. 85 ff.; Bunsen, *Hippolytus*, i. 187 ff., *Analecta Antenicaena*, i. 103 ff.; Donaldson, *Hist. Christ. Lit.* ii. 126 ff.; Davidson, *Intro. to N. T.* ii. 399; Harnack, *Patres Apostolici*, i. 205 ff. (Leipz. 1875, 2nd ed. 1878); Cureton, *Spicilegium Syriacum* (Lond. 1854); Ceillier, *Auteurs sacrés*, i. 412 (ed. 1865); Bigg, *Origins of Christianity*; Lightfoot and Harmer, *Apost. Fathers*, p. 487. An Eng. trans. of the *Ep. to Diognetus* is included in the *Ante-Nicene Lib.* and another by L. B. Radford is pub. cheaply by S.P.C.K. [E.E.B.]

Dionysia (1), virgin martyr at Lampsacus, A.D. 250. Seeing Nicomachus suddenly seized with madness and dying in horror, after having denied the faith under torture, and sacrificed to the heathen gods, Dionysia cried out, "Miserable and most wretched man! Why, for one hour's respite, didst thou take to thyself unceasing and indescribable punishment!" The proconsul Optimus hearing her, asked if she were a Christian. "Yes," she answered, "and that is why I weep for this unhappy man, who loses eternal rest by not being able to suffer a moment's pain." The proconsul dismissed her with a brutal order. Next day, having succeeded in maintaining her chastity, she escaped, and joined Andrew and Paul, two Christians who were being stoned to death. "I wish to die with you here," she said, "that I may live with you in heaven!" Optimus ordered her to be taken from Andrew and Paul, and beheaded, May 15, 250, the 2nd year of Decius. Ruinart, *Act. Sinc. Mart.* p. 159; Ceillier, ii. 118. [W.M.S.]

Dionysia (2), at Alexandria, A.D. 251, mother of many children, who, loving her Lord more than her children, died by the sword, along with the venerable lady Mercuria, without being tried by torture, as the prefect had succeeded so ill with Ammonarion that he was ashamed to go on torturing and being defeated by women (Dion. Alex. *ad* Fab. *ap.* Eus. *H. E.* vi. 41). [E.B.B.]

Dionysia (3), St., a Christian martyr in the 5th cent. According to the narrative of Victor Vitensis, her contemporary, she was a lady of rare beauty in Africa, who preferred tortures, shameful indignities, and death to renouncing her faith; a victim of the persecution of the orthodox or Catholic Christians by Hunneric, king of the Vandals. The date assigned for her martyrdom is 484.

See Victor Vitensis, *de Persecutione Africanâ*, V. c. 1; *ap.* Migne, *Patr. Lat.* lvii.; Tillem., *Mémoires*, t. xvi. (Paris, 1701, 4to); Baronius, *Annales Ecclesiastici*, t. viii. p. 463 (Lucae, 1741, fol.). [I.G.S.]

Dionysius (1), **Pseudo-Areopagita.** Under the name of Dionysius the Areopagite there has passed current a body of remarkable writings. Before shewing that the author of these writings was not the Dionysius converted by St. Paul (Acts xvii. 34), we must discriminate both of them from a third Dionysius, the St. Denys of France. The identity of all three was popularly believed for many cen turies, and even yet is maintained by some.

Was, then, the convert of St. Paul at Athens the first apostle of France? The answer would not seem doubtful from the statement of Sulpicius Severus, that the earliest martyrs in Gaul were under the reign of Aurelius (*Sacr. Hist.* ii. 46), *i.e.* after A.D. 160; and from the circumstance that neither the old martyrologies nor the old French chroniclers contain any hint of the identity of the two. Gregory of Tours (*Hist. Franc.* i. 30) fixes the coming of St. Denys into France as late as the reign of Decius, *i.e.* after A.D. 250; while Usuardus, who wrote his *Martyrologium* for Charlemagne, assigned Oct. 3 to the memory of the Areopagite, and Oct. 9 to that of the patron saint of France. The reasons for believing St. Denys of France to be the author of these writings are equally slight. Their style and subject-matter all betoken a philosophic leisure, not the active life of a missionary in a barbarous country; and a residence in the East is implied in the very titles of those to whom they are addressed. It is the opinion of Bardenhewer (*Patrol.* p. 538) that the writings of Stiglmayr and Koch (see under *Authorities, infra*) have proved "that the Areopagitica were nothing more than a composition written under an assumed name, and in reality dating from about the end of the fifth century."

We may deal with the writings under: (1) External History; (2) Nature and Contents.

(1) It is generally admitted that the first unequivocal mention of them is in the records of the conference at Constantinople in 532. The emperor Justinian invited Hypatius of Ephesus, and other bishops of the orthodox side, to meet in his palace the leaders of the Severians. During the debate, these alleged writings of the Areopagite were brought forward by the latter in support of their Monophysite views; and the objections of Hypatius have been preserved. If genuine, he asked, how could they have escaped the notice of Cyril and others? (Mansi, viii. col. 821); and this question has never been satisfactorily answered. Supposed traces of them have been pointed out in Origen; and other ingenious reasons, explaining their concealment for five centuries, have been confuted again and again. Still, whatever their parentage, they are henceforward never lost sight of. Writers of the school which had at first objected to them soon found how serviceable to their own cause they might be made. Thus a chain of testimony begins to be attached to them in unbroken continuity.

In the Western church we first find them mentioned by pope Gregory the Great (*c.* 590); but his manner of citing them makes it probable that he only knew them by report. In any case, they did not become generally known in the West till after A.D. 827, when Michael the Stammerer sent a copy to Louis le Débonnaire, son of Charlemagne. The abbey of St. Denys, near Paris, was thought the most fitting receptacle for such a treasure; and its abbat, the superstitious and unprincipled Hilduin, compiled a collection of *Areopagitica* in honour of the event. This work professes to be based on documents then extant, but is described in equally unfavourable terms by Sirmond and by Cave. In the next reign, that of Charles the Bald, a Latin trans. of all the Dionysian writings was made by the great scholar Joannes Erigena. It is first publicly mentioned by pope Nicholas I., in a letter to Charles in 861, and is warmly praised by Anastasius Bibliothecarius in 865.

(2) The Dionysian writings consist of four extant treatises: *On the Heavenly Hierarchy; On the Ecclesiastical Hierarchy; On the Names of God; On Mystic Theology*; after which come ten letters or fragments of letters.

This list, from one point of view, is complete as an exposition of the Dionysian system, and is also in its proper order. For we may take as its epitome the words of St. Paul with which the first sentence in the volume concludes: "For of Him and to Him are all things" (Rom. xi. 36). God, the centre towards which all tend, and at the same time the all-embracing circumference within which all are included; the constant streaming forth from Him, like rays from the visible sun, of divine influences whereby men are purified, illumined, and drawn upwards to Himself; man's powerlessness to know the real nature and being of God, while yet he may be drawn near to Him, in the mystic communion of a loving faith: such is, very briefly, the burden of the Dionysian strain. And if we take the *de Divinis Nominibus* as the central portion of the writings, and recognize the two *Hierarchies* as one consecutive whole, we have enough to fill up the outline sketched above. In the *Celestial* and *Ecclesiastical Hierarchies*, with their ninefold orders of heavenly and of earthly ministrations, we have the means, the machinery (so to speak), whereby God communicates Himself to man. In the *Divina Nomina* we have disclosed to us, so far as can be seen through veils and shadows, the Fountain-head of all light and being, the object of all thought and desire. In the *Mystic Theology* we have the converse of the path marked out in the *Hierarchies*, the ascent of the human soul to mystic union with God. The three great sections of the Dionysian writings thus answer very strikingly to the three elements of which he makes his hierarchy to consist: τάξις, ἐπιστήμη, and ἐνέργεια πρὸς τὸ θεοειδὲς ἀφοιουμένη (*Eccl. Hier.* iii. § 1).

Yet the author refers to a series of treatises, still more numerous than the preceding, as if he thought them necessary for the completion of his design. These are: *On Divine Hymns; Symbolic Theology; On the Objects of Intellect and Sense; Theological Outlines; On the Soul; On the Just Judgment of God.* To these are added by Sixtus Senensis and others: *On the Properties and Orders of Angels; The Legal Hierarchy.*

The question of these missing treatises is most perplexing. Did they ever exist? If so, what has become of them? Are they mere inventions of the author, designed to parry attacks on his own weak points, and to suggest the filling up of deficiencies which in reality he left unsupplied? This last seems very probable. But, if true, while our respect for the intellectual completeness of the author's mind is increased, our opinion of his moral straightforwardness must be diminished. However, he is certainly entitled to the credit of his conception of such a theological system, whether all the parts be duly filled in or not.

Limits of space do not here allow a minute analysis of the extant works. The *Heavenly Hierarchy* opens with what sounds almost like the keynote of the whole, the text πᾶσα δόσις ἀγαθή, κ.τ.λ. of Jas. i. 17. The language, in which the simple words of these Apostles are expanded and paraphrased, will convey no bad idea of the generally turgid style. To bring us to Himself, God graciously makes use of signs and symbols, and of intervening orders of ministers, by whose means we may be gradually raised to nearer communion with Him. Such an organization he calls a Hierarchy—"a sacred order, and science, and activity, assimilated as far as possible to the godlike, and elevated to the imitation of God proportionately to the Divine illuminations conceded to it" (*Cel. Hier.* iii. § 1, tr. by Westcott). The members of the Heavenly Hierarchy are the nine orders of Angels—the term Angel being sometimes used alike of all the orders, and sometimes, in a more proper and restricted sense, of the lowest of the nine. The names of the nine orders appear to be obtained by combining with the more obvious Seraphim, Cherubim, Archangels, and Angels, five deduced from two passages of St. Paul, Eph. i. 21 and Col. i. 16. In each of these passages four names are mentioned, of which three (ἄρχαι, ἐξουσίαι, κυριότητες) are common to both, while one is peculiar to each, δυνάμεις to the former, θρόνοι to the latter. The nine are subdivided into triads, ranged thus in descending order:

1. Seraphim, Cherubim, Thrones.
2. Dominations, Virtues, Powers.
3. Principalities, Archangels, Angels.

The long and important treatise *On the Names of God* (Περὶ θείων ὀνομάτων) has been shewn by Stiglmayr and Koch to contain an extract from Proclus's treatise *de Malorum Substitentia*; which has reached us in a Latin trans. It is an inquiry into the being and attributes of God as indicated by the Divine Names in Holy Scripture. These Names, like all outward channels of spiritual knowledge, can reveal His real nature but very imperfectly; and even so, not without prayer, which, like the golden chain of Homer, lifts us up to Heaven while we seem to be drawing it down to earth; or like the rope thrown out to mariners from a rock, which enables them to draw their ship nearer to the rock, while they pull as if they would draw the rock to them (*Div. Nom.* iii. § 1). The first thing thus revealed is God's goodness, the far-reaching effulgence of His being, which streams forth upon all, like the rays of the sun (*ib.* iv. § 1). Evil is nothing real and positive, but a defect, a negation only: Στέρησις ἄρα ἐστὶ τὸ κακόν, καὶ ἔλλειψις, καὶ ἀσθένεια, καὶ ἀσυμμετρία, κ.τ.λ. (*ib.* iv. § 32). As what we call cold is but a deficiency of heat; or darkness, of light; so what we call evil is a deficiency of goodness. When the sky grows dark, as evening sets in, that darkness is nothing positive, superadded to what existed before: we are conscious of gloom merely from the disappearance of the light, which was the true existence (*ib.* iv. § 24). This subject is pursued in a very noble train of thought to some length, and is followed by a discussion of still other names and titles, adapted to the infirmity of human understanding, under which God's attributes are made intelligible to us. That the author is conscious of his theory of evil not being logically complete appears from his briefly referring to another supposed treatise, Περὶ δικαίου καὶ θείου δικαιωτηρίου (*ib.* iv. § 35), for a settlement of the question how far evil, being such as is described, deserves punishment at the hands of God.

Of two legends, widely known in connexion with the name of Dionysius, from their insertion in the Breviary of the Latin church, one must be noticed here, as found in the present work. When Dionysius was present with Timothy, to whom he is writing, and James, ὁ ἀδελφόθεος, and Peter, ἡ κορυφαία καὶ πρεσβυτάτη τῶν θεολόγων ἀκρότης, and other disciples, "for the spectacle of the body which was the beginning of life and the recipient of God" (ἐπὶ τὴν θέαν τοῦ ζωαρχικοῦ καὶ θεοδόχου—al. φωτοδόχου—σώματος (*ib.* iii. § 2)), no one but the apostles surpassed Hierotheus, his preceptor, in the inspired hymns and praises which he uttered. This is generally considered to refer to a gathering of the apostles round the deathbed of the Holy Virgin. The language is vague, and the passage comes in with singular abruptness, as a sequel to one on the power of prayer. In the paraphrase of Pachymeres, the names of the apostles are omitted. The explanation of Barradas (quoted by Hipler, *ubi inf.* p. 48 n.) is that the gathering round the θεοτόκος really represents the assembly of believers for the reception of the Holy Eucharist, bending (as the words of one liturgy express it) "ante splendida et *theodocha* signa cum timore inclinati."

The short treatise on *Mystic Theology* indicates the means of approaching more nearly to God, previously set forth under the *Divine Names*, by reversing the procedure adopted in the Hierarchies. He who would aspire to a truer and more intimate knowledge of God must rise above signs and symbols, above earthly conceptions and definitions of God, and thus advance by negation, rather than by affirmation, κατ' ἀφαίρεσιν, not κατὰ θέσιν. Even in the Hierarchies (*Cel. Hier.* ii. § 3) Dionysius had spoken of ἀπόφασις as a surer way of penetrating the divine mystery than κατάφασις, and now enforces the same truth by an illustration which, if not taken directly from Plotinus, presents a striking parallel to one used by him—that of the sculptor, who, striving to fashion a beautiful statue, chips away the outer marble, and removes what was in fact an obstruction to his own ideal (*Myst. Theol.* c. ii.; cf. Plotinus, *de Pulchritudine*, ed. Creuzer, 1814, p. 62).

Of the *Letters*, the first two are little more than detached notes on points of the *Mystic Theology*—on our ἀγνωσία of God, and His transcendent nature. The third is a short fragment on the meaning of the word ἐξαίφνης in Mal. iii. 1, "The Lord . . . shall *suddenly* come to His temple," and its application to the Incarnation. The fourth, addressed, like the three previous ones, to the monk Caius, treats briefly of the Incarnation, and the nature of that human body with which Christ could walk upon the waters (cf. *Div. Nom.* ii. 9). The fifth, to Dorotheus, is on the meaning of the *divine darkness* (ὁ θεῖος γνόφος) spoken of in the *Mystic Theology*. The sixth, to Sosipater, teaches that labour is better spent in establishing truth than in confuting error. The seventh is a much longer letter, addressed to Polycarp, in which he bids him answer the taunts of the Sophist Apollophanes, by recalling the days when he and Dionysius were fellow-students at Hierapolis, and his own remark when they beheld the darkness of the Crucifixion: ταῦτα, ὦ καλὲ Διονύσιε, θείων ἀμοιβαὶ πραγμάτων. The exclamation attributed to Dionysius himself, as it appears in the Latin Breviary, *Aut Deus naturae patitur, aut mundi machina dissolvitur*, or, as it is given by Syngelus in his *Life*, Ὁ ἄγνωστος ἐν σαρκὶ πάσχει Θεός, κ.τ.λ., is not found in the Dionysian writings. The eighth letter, to a monk, Demophilus, is on gentleness and forbearance, and the topic is illustrated by a dream which St. Carpus had in Crete. The ninth, also a long letter, addressed to Titus, bp. of Crete, refers to matters treated in the *Symbolic Theology*. Many points are discussed in what to some would appear a strangely neologic spirit. The anthropomorphism of O.T., the bold metaphors of the Song of Songs (τὰς τῶν ᾀσμάτων προσύλους καὶ ἑταιρικὰς πολυπαθείας), and the like, can only be understood, he says, by true lovers of holiness, who come to the study of divine wisdom divested of every childish imagination (πᾶσαν τὴν παιδαριώδη φαντασίαν ἐπὶ τῶν ἱερῶν συμβόλων ἀποσκευαζομένοις). In this letter we seem to see before us a disciple of Philo. The tenth, and last, is a mere fragment, addressed to St. John the Divine, an exile in Patmos, foretelling his approaching release from confinement.

Authorities.—Isaac Casaubon, *de Rebus sacris Eccl. Exercitt. xxi.* (1615); Jean Launoy, *Varia de duobus Dionysiis* (1660); J. Dallaeus, *de Scriptis quae . . . circumferunter* (1666); P. F. Chifflet, *Opuscula quatuor* (1679); Ussher, *Dissertatio de Scriptis . . .* appended to his *Historia Dogmatica* (1690); M. Lequien, *Dissertatio Secunda*, prefixed to tom. i. of *Joannis Damasceni Op.* (1712); Cave, *Script. Eccl. Hist. Lit.* (1740); Brucker, *Hist. Crit.* tom. iii. (1766); J. L. Mosheim, *Commentatio de Turbata per Recentiores Platonicos Ecclesia* (1767); J. A. Fabricius, *Biblioth. Graeca*, tom. vii. (1801); J. G. Engelhardt, *de Dionysio Areop. Plotinizante* (1820); Milman, *Lat. Christ.* vol. vi. (1855); Dr. Franz Hipler, *Dionysius der Areopagite* (Regensburg, 1861); B. F. Westcott, Essay on Dionysius the Areopagite in the *Contemp. Rev.* May 1867; Dean Colet, *On the Hierarchies of Dionysius* (1869); J. Fowler, Essay on the works of St. Dionysius the Areopagite, in relation to Christian art, in the *Sacristy*, Feb. 1872; H. Koch, in *Theol. Quartalschrift*, 1895 and 1898; Stiglmayr in *Hist. Jahrbücher* (1895). [J.H.L.]

Dionysius (2), St., apostle of France, and first bp. of Paris. Concerning his identity and era there are three principal opinions.

(1) That he was Dionysius the Areopagite, formerly bp. of Athens, who came to Rome and was sent by Clement, bp. of Rome, to preach in Gaul. This is the tradition of the Greek church, and of those of Gaul, Germany, Spain, and Italy. The corresponding legend, shortly narrated in the Paris Martyrology, states that his companions were Rusticus, a presbyter, and Eleutherus, a deacon, and that all three were put to death by the sword under Sisinnius Fescenninus, prefect of Gaul. This is the opinion of Flavius Lucius Dexter, *d.* 444 (*Chronicon. Patr. Lat.* xxxi. 270).

(2) That, although not the Areopagite, he was sent by Clement or the successors of the apostles. This is held in a poem in honour of Dionysius, attributed with some probability to Venantius Fortunatus of Poitiers, who had written a poem on the same subject committing himself to no opinion (*Patr. Lat.* lxxxviii. 72, 98). It is also supported by Pagius in his notes on Baronius.

(3) That he was sent from Rome in the 3rd cent., and suffered martyrdom *c.* A.D. 250. This is held by Sulpicius Severus, *d.* A.D. 410, and Gregory of Tours, *d.* 595. Sulpicius says, "Under Aurelius, son of Antoninus, raged the fifth persecution. Then first were martyrdoms seen in Gaul, for the religion of God was late in coming over the Alps" (Severi, *Chronicon*, ii. 32, *Patr. Lat.* xx. 147). Gregory (*Hist. of the Franks*, bk. i. c. 28), speaking of the Decian persecution, quotes the *Hist. Passionis S. M. Saturnini*: "Under the consulship of Decius and Gratus, as is held in faithful recollection, the state of Toulouse began to have a bishop, St. Saturninus, her first and chief. These were the men sent: to Tours, Gatianus the bishop; to Arles, Trophimus the bishop; to Toulouse, Saturninus the bishop; to Paris, Dionysius the bishop, etc. Of these the blessed Dionysius, bishop of the Parisians, afflicted with many pains for the name of Christ, ended this present life under the sword." Probably, therefore, he died under the emperor Aurelian in A.D. 272 (cf. *Gall. Christ.* vii. 4). [W.M.S.]

Dionysius (3), bp. of Corinth, probably the successor of PRIMUS, placed by Eusebius in his *Chronicle* under A.D. 171 (see also Eus. *H. E.* ii. 25, iii. 4, iv. 21, 23, 35; Hieron. *Catal.* 27). He was the writer of certain pastoral letters, which gained so much authority in his own lifetime that heretics (probably the followers of Marcion) found it worth while, as he complains, to circulate copies falsified by interpolations and omissions. Eusebius mentions having met with 8 of these letters—viz. seven which he calls "Catholic Epistles," addressed to Lacedemon, Athens, Nicomedia, Gortyna and other churches in Crete, Amastris and other churches in Pontus, Cnossus, and Rome; and one to "his most faithful sister Chrysophora." Probably the letters were already collected into a volume and enumerated by Eusebius in the order they occurred there, or he would probably have mentioned the two Cretan letters consecutively. Nothing remains of them, except the short account of their contents given by Eusebius, and a few fragments of the letter to the Roman church which, though very scanty, throw considerable light on the state of the church at the time. Eusebius praises Dionysius for having given a share in his "inspired industry" to those in foreign lands. A bp. of Corinth might consider Lacedaemon and Athens as under his metropolitan superintendence, but that he should send letters of admonition to Crete, Bithynia, and Paphlagonia not only proves the reputation of the writer, but indicates the unity of the Christian community. A still more interesting proof of this is furnished by the letter to the Roman church, which would seem to be one of thanks for a gift of money, and in which he speaks of it as a custom of that church from the earliest times to send supplies to churches in every city to relieve poverty, and to support the brethren condemned to work in the mines, "a custom not only preserved, but increased by the blessed bp. Soter, who administered their bounty to the saints, and with blessed words exhorted the brethren that came up as an affectionate father his children." The epithet here applied to Soter is usually used of those deceased in Christ; but there are instances of its application to living persons, and Eusebius speaks of him as still bishop when the letter of Dionysius was written. This letter is remarkable also as containing the earliest testimony that St. Peter suffered martyrdom in Italy at the same time as St. Paul. The letters indicate the general prevalence of episcopal government when they were written. In most of them the bishop of the church addressed is mentioned with honour; Palmas in Pontus, Philip and Pinytus in Crete, Soter at Rome. That to the Athenians reminds them of a former bp. Publius, who had suffered martyrdom during persecutions which reduced that church very low, from which condition it was revived by the zeal of Quadratus, the successor of Publius. This form of government was then supposed to date from apostolic times, for in the same letter Dionysius the Areopagite is counted as the first bp. of Athens; but the importance of the bishop seems to be still subordinate to that of his church. The letters, including that to Rome, are each addressed to the church, not to the bishop; and Soter's own letter, like Clement's former one, was written not in his own name, but that of his church (ὑμῶν τὴν ἐπιστολὴν). The letters, indeed, of Dionysius himself were written in his own name, and he uses the 1st pers. sing. in speaking of them, but adds that they were written at the request of brethren. Eusebius mentions two, Bacchylides and Elpistus, at whose instance that to the churches of Pontus was written.

The letters also illustrate the value attached by Christians to their sacred literature. Dionysius informs the church of Rome that the day on which he wrote, being the Lord's day, had been kept holy, and that they had then read the letter of the Roman church, and would continue from time to time to read it for their instruction, as they were in the habit of reading the letter formerly written from the same church by the hand of Clement; and speaking of the falsification of his own letters, he adds, "No marvel, then, that some have attempted to tamper with the Scriptures of the Lord, since they have attempted it on writings not comparable to them (οὐ τοιαύταις)." Thus we learn that it was then customary to read sacred books in the Christian assemblies; that this practice was not limited to our canonical books; that attempts were made by men regarded as heretics to corrupt these writings, and that such attempts were jealously guarded against. The value attached by Christians to writings was regulated rather by the character of their contents than by the dignity of the writer; for while there is no trace that the letter of Soter thus honoured at Corinth passed beyond that church, the letter of Dionysius himself became the property of the whole Christian community. But we learn the pre-eminent authority enjoyed by certain books, called the Scriptures of the Lord, which we cannot be wrong in identifying with some of the writings of our N.T. Dionysius, in the very brief fragments remaining, shews signs of acquaintance with the St. Matt., the Acts, I. Thess., and the Apocalypse. There is, therefore, no reason for limiting to the O.T. the "expositions of the divine Scriptures," which Eusebius tells us were contained in the letter of Dionysius to the churches of Pontus. In speaking of attempts to corrupt the Scriptures, Dionysius probably refers to the heresy of Marcion, against which, we are told, he wrote in his letter to the church of Nicomedia, "defending the rule of truth." We cannot lay much stress on a rhetorical passage where Jerome (*Ep. ad Magnum*, 83) includes Dionysius among those who had applied secular learning to the refutation of heresy, tracing each heresy to its source in the writings of the philosophers. Dionysius had probably also Marcionism in view, when he exhorted the church of Gortyna "to beware of the perversion of heretics," for we are told that its bp. Philip had found it necessary to compose a treatise against Marcion. We may see traces of the same heresy in the subjects treated of in the letter to the churches of Pontus (the home of Marcion), to which Dionysius gave instructions concerning marriage and chastity (marriage having been proscribed by Marcion), and which he also exhorted to receive back those who returned after any fall, whether into irregularity of living or into heretical error. But the rigorist tendencies here combated were exhibited also, not only among the then rising sects of the Encratites and Montanists, but by men of undoubted orthodoxy. Writing to the Cnossians Dionysius exhorts Pinytus the bp., a man highly commended by Eusebius for piety, orthodoxy, and learning, not to impose on the brethren too heavy a burden of chastity, but to regard the weakness of the many. Eusebius reports Pinytus as replying with expressions of high respect for Dionysius, which were understood by Rufinus to imply an adoption of his views. But he apparently persevered in his own opinion, for he exhorts Dionysius to impart to his people some more advanced instruction, lest if he fed them always with milk instead of with more solid food, they should continue in the state of children.

We are not told anything of the time or manner of the death of Dionysius. It must have been before the Paschal disputes in A.D. 198, when we find Palmas of Pontus still alive, but a new bishop (Bacchylus) at Corinth. The Greek church counts Dionysius among martyrs, and the Menaea name the sword as the instrument of his death; but there is no authority for his martyrdom earlier than Cedrenus, *i.e.* the end of the 11th cent. The Roman church only counts him among confessors. The abbey of St. Denis in France claimed to be in possession of the body of Dionysius of Corinth, alleged to have been brought from Greece to Rome, and given them in 1215 by Innocent III. The pope's bull is given by the Bollandists under April 8. See Routh, *Rel. Sac.* (2nd ed.), i. 178-201. [G.S.]

Dionysius (6) of Alexandria. This "great bishop of Alexandria" (Eus. *H. E.* vi. *Praef.*) and "teacher of the catholic church" (Athan. *de Sent. Dion.* 6), was born, apparently, of a wealthy and honourable family (Eus. *H. E.* vii. 11, and Valesius *ad loc.*). He was an old man in A.D. 265 (Eus. *H. E.* vii. 27), and a presbyter in A.D. 233 (Hieron. *de Vir. Ill.* 69). His parents were Gentiles, and he was led to examine the claims of Christianity by private study (*Ep. Dion.* ap. Eus. *H. E.* vii. 7). His conversion cost him the sacrifice of "worldly glory" (Eus. *H. E.* vii. 11); but he found in Origen an able teacher (*ib.* vi. 29); and Dionysius remained faithful to his master to the last. In the persecutions of Decius he addressed a letter to him *On Persecution* (*ib.* vi. 46), doubtless as an expression of sympathy with his sufferings (*c.* A.D. 259), and on the death of Origen (A.D. 253) wrote to Theotecnus bp. of Caesarea in his praise (Steph. Gob. *ap.* Phot. Cod. 232). Dionysius, then a presbyter, succeeded Heraclas as head of the Catechetical School, at the time, as the words of Eusebius imply, when Heraclas was made bp. of Alexandria, A.D. 232-233 (Eus. *l.c.*). He held this office till he was raised to the bishopric, on the death of Heraclas, A.D. 247-248, and perhaps retained it till his death, A.D. 265. His episcopate was in troubled times. A popular outbreak at Alexandria (A.D. 248-249) anticipated by about a year (Eus. *H. E.* vi. 41) the persecution under Decius (A.D. 249-251). Dionysius fled from Alexandria, and, being afterwards taken by some soldiers, was rescued by a friend, escaping in an obscure retirement from further attacks. In the persecution of Valerian, A.D. 257, he was banished, but continued to direct and animate the Alexandrian church from the successive places of his exile. His conduct on these occasions exposed him to ungenerous criticism, and Eusebius has preserved several interesting passages of a letter (*c.* A.D. 258-259), in which he defends himself with great spirit against the accusations of a bp. Germanus (*ib.* vi. 40, vii. 11). On the accession of Gallienus, A.D. 260, Dionysius was allowed to return to Alexandria (*ib.* vii. 13, 21), where he had to face war, famine, and pestilence (*ib.* vii. 22). In A.D. 264-265 he was invited to the synod at Antioch which met to consider the opinions of Paul of Samosata. His age and infirmities did not allow him to go, and he died shortly afterwards (A.D. 265) (*ib.* vii. 27, 28; Hieron. *de Vir. Ill.* 69).

Dionysius was active in controversy, but always bore himself with prudence. In this spirit he was anxious to deal gently with the "lapsed" (Eus. *H. E.* vi. 42); he pressed upon Novatian the duty of self-restraint, for the sake of the peace of the church, A.D. 251 (*ib.* vii. 45; Hieron. *l.c.*); and with better results counselled moderation in dealing with the rebaptism of heretics, in a correspondence with popes Stephen and Sixtus (A.D. 256-257) (Eus. *H. E.* vii. 5, 7, 9). His last letter (or letters) regarding Paul of Samosata seem to have been written in a similar strain. He charged the assembled bishops to do their duty, but did not shrink from appealing to Paul also, as still fairly within the reach of honest argument (Theod. *Haer. Fab.* ii. 8). In one instance Dionysius met with immediate success. In a discussion with a party of Chiliasts he brought his opponents to abandon their error (Eus. *H. E.* vii. 24). His own orthodoxy, however, did not always remain unimpeached. When controverting the false teaching of Sabellius, the charge of tritheism was brought against him by some Sabellian adversaries, and entertained at first by his namesake Dionysius of Rome. Discussion shewed that one ground of the misunderstanding was the ambiguity of the words used to describe "essence" and "person," which the two bishops took in different senses. Dionysius of Rome regarded ὑπόστασις as expressing the essence of the divine nature; Dionysius of Alexandria as expressing the essence of each divine person. The former therefore affirmed that to divide the ὑπόστασις was to make separate gods; the latter affirmed with equal justice that there could be no Trinity unless each ὑπόστασις was distinct. The Alexandrine bishop had, however, used other phrases, which were claimed by Arians at a later time as favouring their views. Basil, on hearsay, as it has been supposed (Lumper, *Hist. Patrum,* xiii. 86 f.), admitted that Dionysius sowed the seeds of the Anomoean heresy (*Ep.* i. 9), but Athanasius with fuller knowledge vindicated his perfect orthodoxy. Dionysius has been represented as recognizing the supremacy of Rome in the defence which he made. But the fragments of his answer to his namesake (Athan. *de Sent. Dionysii,* ἐπέστειλε Διονυσίῳ δηλῶσαι . . . for the use of ἐπιστέλλω see Eus. *H. E.* vi. 46, etc.) shew the most complete and resolute independence; and there is nothing in the narrative of Athanasius which implies that the Alexandrine bishop recognized, or that the Roman bishop claimed, any dogmatic authority as belonging to the imperial see. To say that a synod was held upon the subject at Rome is an incorrect interpretation of the facts.

Dionysius was a prolific writer. Jerome (*l.c.*) has preserved a long but not exhaustive catalogue of his books. Some important fragments remain of his treatises *On Nature* (Eus. *Praep. Ev.* xiv. 23 ff.), and *On the Promises,* in refutation of the Chiliastic views of Nepos (Eus. *H. E.* iii. 28, vii. 24, 25); of his *Refutation and Defence,* addressed to Dionysius of Rome, in reply to the accusation of false teaching on the Holy Trinity (Athan. *de Sent. Dionysii*; *de Synodis,* c. 44; *de Decr. Syn. Nic.* c. 25); of his *Commentaries on Ecclesiastes* and on *St. Luke,* and of his books *Against Sabellius* (Eus. *Praep. Ev.* vii. 19).

The fragments of his letters are, however, the most interesting extant memorials of his work and character and of his time; and Eusebius, with a true historical instinct, has made them the basis of the sixth and seventh books of his history. The following will shew the wide ground covered:

A.D. 251.—To Domitius and Didymus. Personal experiences during persecution (Eus. *H. E.* vii. 11).

A.D. 251-252.—To Novatian, to the Roman Confessors, to Cornelius of Rome, Fabius of Antioch, Conon of Hermopolis; and to Christians in Alexandria, Egypt, Laodicaea, Armenia, on discipline and repentance, with pictures from contemporary history (*ib.* vi. 41, and vii. 45).

A.D. 253-257.—To Stephen of Rome, the Roman presbyters Dionysius and Philemon, Sixtus II. of Rome on Rebaptism (*ib.* vii. 4, 5, 7, 9).

A.D. 258-263.—To Germanus: incidents in persecution. Against Sabellians. A series of festal letters, with pictures of contemporary history (*ib.* vii. 11, 22 ff., 26).

A.D. 264.—To Paul of Samosata (vi. 40).

To these, of some of which only the titles remain, must be added an important canonical letter to Basilides, of uncertain date, discussing various questions of discipline, and especially points connected with the Lenten fast (cf. Dittrich, pp. 46 ff.). All the fragments repay careful study. They are uniformly inspired by sympathy and large-heartedness. His criticism on the style of the Apocalypse is perhaps unique among early writings for clearness and scholarly precision (Eus. *H. E.* vii. 25).

The most accessible and complete collection of his remains is in Migne's *Patr. Gk.* x. pp. 1233 ff., 1575 ff., to which must be added Pitra, *Spicil. Solesm.* i. 15 ff. A full monograph on Dionysius by Dittrich (Freiburg, 1867) supplements the arts. in Tillemont, Maréchal, Lumper, Moehler. An Eng. trans. of his works is in the *Ante-Nicene Lib.*, and his *Letters*, etc., have been ed. by Dr. Feltoe for the *Camb. Patristic Texts* (1904). [B.F.W.]

Dionysius (7), bp. of Rome; a Greek by birth, consecrated July 22, A.D. 259, on the death of Xystus, in the persecution of Valerian. His efforts against heresy are recorded. When Dionysius of Alexandria (*q.v.*) was accused of holding doctrines akin to those of Sabellius, the Roman Dionysius wrote to him, and extracted so satisfactory a defence that he declared him purged of suspicion (Athan. *Ep. de Sent. Dionys. Opp.* i. 252; see an Eng. trans. of the *Fragm. against Sabellius* in *Ante-Nicene Lib.*). In 264 the Alexandrian and Roman Dionysii acted together with the council of Antioch in condemning and degrading Paul of Samosata. Dionysius of Rome died Dec. 26, 269. [G.H.M.]

Dionysius (19), surnamed *Exiguus* because of his humbleness of heart, was a Scythian by birth, and a monk in the Western church under the emperors Justin and Justinian. To him we owe the custom of dating events from the birth of our Saviour, though he is now acknowledged to have placed the era four years too late. His collection of canons laid the foundation of canon law. He knew Latin and Greek fairly; though it is obvious that neither was his vernacular. His Latin translations form the bulk of his extant works. Cassiodorus speaks of his moral and intellectual qualities with well-deserved praise. His performances were not original discoveries, but improvements on those of others.

I. The period called after him was borrowed from Victorius of Aquitaine, who flourished 100 years earlier, and is said to have invented it. It is a revolution of 532 years, produced by multiplying the solar cycle of 28 by the lunar of 19 years. It is called sometimes "recapitulatio Dionysii." A note to § 13 of the preliminary dissertation to *l'Art de vérif. les dates* shews how he improved on his predecessor. His cycle was published in the last year of the emperor Justin, A.D. 527. It began with March 25, now kept as the festival of the Annunciation; and from this epoch all the dates of bulls and briefs of the court of Rome are supposed to run (Butler's *Lives of the Saints*, Oct. 15: note to the Life of St. Teresa). His first year had for its characters the solar cycle 10, the lunar 2, and the Roman indiction 4, thereby proclaiming its identity with the year 4714 of the Julian period, which again coincided with the 4th year of the 194th Olympiad, and the 753rd of the building of Rome. It was adopted in Italy soon after its publication; in France perhaps a century later. In England it was ordained A.D. 816, at the synod of Chelsea, that all bishops should date their acts from the Incarnation.

II. In his letter to bp. Stephen, to whom he dedicates his collection of Canons, he admits the existence of an earlier, but defective, Latin translation, of which copies have been printed and named, after his naming of it, *Prisca Versio* by Justellus and others. His own was a corrected edition of that earlier version, so far as regards the canons of Nicaea, Ancyra, Neo-Caesarea, Gangra, Antioch, Laodicea, and Constantinople—165 in all—together with 27 of Chalcedon: all originally published in Greek, and all, except the Laodicean, already translated in the *Prisca Versio*. The Laodicean, unlike the rest, are given in an abbreviated form, and the chronological order is interrupted to place the Nicene canons first. He specifies as having been translated by himself the 50 so-called canons of the Apostles, which stand at the head of his collection, which he admits were not then universally received; and, as having been appended by himself, the Sardican and African canons, which he says were published in Latin, and with which his collection ends. His collection speedily displaced that of the *Prisca*. Cassiodorus, his friend and patron, writes of it within a few years of his decease, "Quos hodie usu ecclesia Romana complectitur"; and adds, "Alia quoque multa ex Graeco transtulit in Latinam, quae utilitati possunt ecclesiasticae convenire" (*de Inst. Div. Litt.* c. 23). It seems certain, from what Cassiodorus says, that Dionysius either translated or revised an earlier translation of the official documents of the 3rd and 4th councils, as well as the canons of the 1st and 2nd.

III. He published all the decretal epistles of the popes he could discover from Siricius, who succeeded Damasus, A.D. 384, to Anastasius II., who succeeded Gelasius, A.D. 496. Gelasius, he says himself, he had never seen in life; in other words, he had never been at Rome up to Gelasius's death. By this publication a death-blow was given to the false decretals of the Pseudo-Isidore, centuries before their appearance. His attestation of the true text and consequent rendering of the 6th Nicene canon, his translating the 9th of Chalcedon into plain Latin, after suppressing the 28th, which, as it was not passed in full council he could omit with perfect honesty, and, most of all, the publicity which he first gave to the canons against transmarine appeals in the African code and to the stand made by the African bishops against the encroachments of pope Zosimus and his successors in the matter of Apiarius, are historical stumbling-blocks which are fatal to the papal claims. Misquotations of the Sardican canons, by which those claims were supported, are, moreover, exposed by his preservation of them in the language in which he avers they were published. Aloisius Vincenzi, writing on papal infallibility (*de Sacrâ Monarchiâ*, etc. 1875), is quite willing to abandon the Sardican canons in order to get rid also of the African code, which is a thorn in his side. [E.S.FF.]

Dioscorus (1), patriarch of Alexandria, succeeded Cyril about midsummer 444, receiving consecration, according to one report (Mansi, vii. 603), from two bishops only. He had served as Cyril's archdeacon. Liberatus says that he had never been married. It is difficult to harmonize the accounts of his character. Theodoret, whose testimony in his favour cannot be suspected, declared in a letter to Dioscorus, soon after his consecration, that the fame of his virtues, and particularly of his modesty and humility, was widely spread (*Ep.* 60); on the other hand, after he had involved himself in the Monophysite heresy, he was accused of having gravely misconducted himself in the first years of his episcopate (Mansi, vi. 1008). According to a deacon, Ischyrion, Dioscorus had laid waste property, inflicted fines and exile, bought up and sold at a high price the wheat sent by the government to Libya, appropriated and grossly misspent money left by a lady named Peristeria for religious and charitable purposes, received women of notorious character into his house, persecuted Ischyrion as a favourite of Cyril's, ruined the little estate which was his only support, sent a "phalanx of ecclesiastics, or rather of ruffians," to put him to death, and, after his escape, again sought to murder him in a hospital; in proof, Ischyrion appealed to six persons, one of whom was bath-keeper to Dioscorus (*ib.* 1012). According to a priest named Athanasius, Cyril's nephew, Dioscorus, from the outset of his episcopate ("which he obtained one knows not how," says the petitioner), harassed him and his brother by using influence with the court, so that the brother died of distress, and Athanasius, with his aunts, sister-in-law, and nephews, were bereft of their homes by the patriarch's malignity. He himself was deposed, without any trial, from the priesthood, and became, perforce, a wanderer for years. According to a layman named Sophronius, Dioscorus hindered the execution of an imperial order which Sophronius had obtained for the redress of a grievous wrong. "The country," he said, "belonged to him rather than to the sovereigns" (τῶν κρατούντων). Sophronius averred that legal evidence was forthcoming to prove that Dioscorus had usurped, in Egypt, the authority belonging to the emperor. He added that Dioscorus had taken away his clothes and property, and compelled him to flee for his life; and he charged him, further, with adultery and blasphemy (*ib.* 1029). Such accusations were then so readily made—as the life of St. Athanasius himself shews—that some deduction must be made from charges brought against Dioscorus in the hour of his adversity; and wrongs done by his agents may have been in some cases unfairly called his acts. Still, it is but too likely that there was sufficient truth in them to demonstrate the evil effects on his character of elevation to a post of almost absolute power; for such, in those days, was the great "evangelical throne." We find him, before the end of his first year, in correspondence with pope Leo the Great, who gave directions, as from the see of St. Peter, to the new successor of St. Mark; writing, on June 21, 445, that "it would be shocking (*nefas*) to believe that St. Mark formed his rules for Alexandria otherwise than on the Petrine model" (*Ep.* 11). In 447 Dioscorus appears among those who expressed suspicion of the theological character of Theodoret, who had been much mixed up with the party of Nestorius. It was rumoured that, preaching at Antioch, he had practically taught Nestorianism; and Dioscorus, hearing this, wrote to Domnus, bp. of Antioch, Theodoret's patriarch; whereupon Theodoret wrote a denial (*Ep.* 83) ending with an anathema against all who should deny the holy Virgin to be Theotokos, call Jesus a mere man, or divide the one Son into two. Dioscorus still assumed the truth of the charge (Theod. *Ep.* 86), allowed Theodoret to be anathematized in church, and even rose from his throne to echo the malediction, and sent some bishops to Constantinople to support him against Theodoret.

Then, in Nov. 448, the aged EUTYCHES, archimandrite of Constantinople and a vehement enemy of Nestorianizers, was accused by Eusebius, bp. of Dorylaeum, before a council of which Flavian was president, with an opposite error. He clung tenaciously to the phrase, "one incarnate nature of God the Word," which Cyril had used on the authority of St. Athanasius; but neglected the qualifications and explanations by which Cyril had guarded his meaning. Thus, by refusing to admit that Christ, as incarnate, had "two natures," Eutyches appeared to his judges to have revived, in effect, the Apollinarian heresy—to have denied the distinctness and verity of Christ's manhood; and he was deprived of his priestly office, and excommunicated. His patron, the chamberlain Chrysaphius, applied to Dioscorus for aid, promising to support him in all his designs if he would take up the cause of Eutyches against Flavian (Niceph. xiv. 47). Eutyches himself wrote to Dioscorus, asking him "to examine his cause" (Liberat. c. 12), and Dioscorus, zealous against all anti-Cyrilline tendencies in theology, wrote to the emperor, urging him to call a general council to review Flavian's judgment. Theodosius, influenced by his wife and his chamberlain, issued letters (Mar. 30, 449), ordering the chief prelates (patriarchs, as we may call them, and exarchs) to repair, with some of their bishops, to Ephesus by Aug. 1, 449 (Mansi, vi. 587).

This council of evil memory—on which Leo afterwards fastened the name of "Latrocinium," or gang of robbers—met on Aug. 8, 449, in St. Mary's church at Ephesus, the scene of the third general council's meeting in 431; 150 bishops being present. Dioscorus presided, and next to him Julian, or Julius, the representative of the "most holy bishop of the Roman church," then Juvenal of Jerusalem, Domnus of Antioch, and—his lowered position indicating what was to come—Flavian of Constantinople (*ib.* 607). The archbp. of Alexandria shewed himself a partisan throughout. He did indeed propose the acceptance of Leo's letter to the council, a letter written at the same time as, and expressly referring to, the famous "Tome"; but it was only handed in, not read, Juvenal moving that another imperial letter should be read and recorded. The president then intimated that the council's business was not to frame a new doctrinal formulary, but to inquire whether what had lately appeared—meaning, the statements of Flavian and bp. Eusebius on the one hand, those of Eutyches on the other—were accordant with the decisions of the councils of Nicaea and Ephesus—"two councils in name," said he, "but one in faith" (*ib.* 628). Eutyches was then introduced, and made his statement, beginning, "I commend myself to the Father, the Son, and the Holy Ghost, and the true verdict of your justice." After he had finished his address, Flavian desired that Eusebius, who had been his accuser, should be called in and heard. Elpidius, the imperial commissioner, vetoed this proposal on the ground that the judges of Eutyches were now to be judged, and that his accuser had already fulfilled his task, "and, as he thought, successfully": to let him speak now would be a cause of mere disturbance (*ib.* 645). This unjudicial view of the case was supported by Dioscorus. Flavian was baffled, and the council resolved to hear the acts of the synod of Constantinople which had condemned Eutyches. The episcopal deputy of Leo, with his companion the deacon Hilarus, urged that "the pope's letter" (probably including the "Tome" in this proposal) should be read first, but this was overruled; Dioscorus moved that the "acts" should be first read, and then the letter of the bp. of Rome. The reading began (*ib.* 649). When the passage was reached in which Basil of Seleucia and Seleucus of Amasia had said that the one Christ was in two natures after the incarnation, a storm of wrath broke out. "Let no one call the Lord 'two' after the union! Do not divide the undivided! Seleucus was not bp. of Amasia! This is Nestorianism." "Be quiet for a little," said Dioscorus; "let us hear some more blasphemies. Why are we to blame Nestorius only? There are many Nestoriuses" (*ib.* 685). The reading proceeded as far as Eusebius's question to Eutyches, "Do you own two natures after the incarnation?" Then arose another storm: "The holy synod exclaimed, 'Away with Eusebius, burn him, let him be burnt alive! Let him be cut in two—be divided, even as he divided!'" "Can you endure," asked Dioscorus, "to hear of two natures after the incarnation?" "Anathema to him that says it!" was the reply. "I have need of your voices and your hands too," rejoined Dioscorus; "if any one cannot shout, let him stretch out his hand." Another anathema rang out (*ib.* 737). Another passage, containing a statement of belief by Eutyches, was heard with applause. "We accept this statement," said Dioscorus. "This is the faith of the Fathers," exclaimed the bishops. "Of what faith do you say this?" asked Dioscorus. "Of Eutyches's: for Eusebius is impious" (ἀσεβής, *ib.* 740). Similar approbation was given to another passage containing the characteristic formula of Eutychianism: "I confess that our Lord was of two natures before the incarnation; but after the incarnation [*i.e.* in Him as incarnate] I confess *one* nature." "We all agree to this," said Dioscorus. "We agree," said the council (*ib.* 744). Presently came a sentence in which Basil of Seleucia had denounced the denial of two natures after the incarnation as equivalent to the assertion of a commixture and a fusion. This aroused once more the zealots of the Alexandrian party; one bishop sprang forward, shouting, "This upsets the whole church!" The Egyptians and the monks, led by Barsumas, cried out, "Cut him in two, who says two natures! He is a Nestorian!" Basil's nerves gave way; he lost, as he afterwards said, his perceptions, bodily and mental (*ib.* 636). He began to say that he did not remember whether he had uttered the obnoxious words, but that he had meant to say, "If you do not add the word 'incarnate' to 'nature,' as Cyril did, the phrase 'one nature' implies a fusion." Juvenal asked whether his words had been wrongly reported; he answered helplessly, "I do not recollect" (*ib.* 748). He seems to have been coerced into a formal retractation of the phrase "two natures"; but he added "hypostases" as explanatory of "natures," and professed to "adore the one nature of the Godhead of the Only-begotten, who was made man and incarnate" (*ib.* 828). Eutyches declared that the acts of the Constantinopolitan synod had been tampered with. "It is false," said Flavian. "If Flavian," said Dioscorus, "knows anything which supports his opinion, let him put it in writing . . . No one hinders you, and the council knows it." Flavian then said that the acts had been scrutinized, and no falsification had been found in them; that, for himself, he had always glorified God by holding what he then held. Dioscorus called on the bishops to give their verdict as to the theological statements of Eutyches. They acquitted him of all unsoundness, as faithful to Nicene and Ephesian teaching. Domnus expressed regret for having mistakenly condemned him (*ib.* 836). Basil of Seleucia spoke like the rest. Flavian, of course, was silent. Dioscorus spoke last, affirming the judgments of the council, and "adding his own opinion." Eutyches was "restored" to his presbyterial rank and his abbatial dignity (*ib.* 861). His monks were then released from the excommunication incurred at Constantinople. The doctrinal decisions of the Ephesian council of 431, in its first and sixth sessions, were then read. Dioscorus proposed that these decisions, with those of Nicaea, should be recognized as an unalterable standard of orthodoxy; that whoever should say or think otherwise, or should unsettle them, should be put under censure. "Let each one of you speak his mind on this." Several bishops assented. Hilarus, the Roman deacon, testified that the apostolic see reverenced those decisions, and that its letter, if read, would prove this. Dioscorus called in some secretaries, who brought forward a draft sentence of deposition against Flavian and Eusebius, on the ground that the Ephesian council had enacted severe penalties against any who should frame or propose any other creed than the Nicene. Flavian and Eusebius were declared to have constructively committed this offence by "unsettling almost everything, and causing scandal and confusion throughout the churches." Their deposition was decided upon (*ib.* 907). Onesiphorus, bp. of Iconium, with some others, went up to Dioscorus, clasped his feet and knees, and passionately entreated him not to go to such extremities. "He has done nothing worthy of deposition . . . . if he deserves condemnation, let him be condemned." "It must be," said Dioscorus in answer; "if my tongue were to be cut out for it, I would still say so." They persisted, and he, starting from his throne, stood up on the footstool and exclaimed, "Are you getting up a sedition? Where are the counts?" Military officers, soldiers with swords and sticks, even the proconsul with chains, entered at his call. He peremptorily commanded the bishops to sign the sentence, and with a fierce gesture of the hand exclaimed, "He that does not choose to sign must reckon with *me*." A scene of terrorism followed. Those prelates who were reluctant to take part in the deposition were threatened with exile, beaten by the soldiers, denounced as heretics by the partisans of Dioscorus, and by the crowd of fanatical monks (*ib.* vii. 68) who accompanied Barsumas, until they put their names to a blank paper on which the sentence was to be written (*ib.* vi. 601 seq. 625, 637, 988). They afterwards protested that they had signed under compulsion. Basil of Seleucia declared that he had given way because he was "given over to the judgment of 120 or 130 bishops; had he been dealing with magistrates, he would have suffered martyrdom." "The Egyptians," says Tillemont, "who signed willingly enough, did so after the others had been made to sign" (xv. 571; cf. Mansi, vi. 601).

Flavian's own fate was the special tragedy of the Latrocinium. He had lodged in the hands of the Roman delegates a formal appeal to the pope and the Western bishops (not to the pope alone; see Leo, *Ep.* 43, Tillemont, xv. 374). It was nearly his last act. He was brutally treated, kicked, and beaten by the agents of Dioscorus, and even, we are told, by Dioscorus himself (see Evagr. i. 1; Niceph. xiv. 47). He was then imprisoned, and soon exiled, but died in the hands of his guards, from the effect of his injuries, three days after his deposition (Liberatus, *Brev.* 19), Aug. 11,

449. He was regarded as a martyr for the doctrine of "the two natures in the one person" of Christ. Anatolius, who had been the agent (*apocrisiarius*) of Dioscorus at Constantinople, was appointed his successor.

Dioscorus and his council—as we may well call it—proceeded to depose Theodoret and several other bishops; "many," says Leo, "were expelled from their sees, and banished, because they would not accept heresy" (*Ep.* 93). Theodoret was put under a special ban. "They ordered me," he writes (*Ep.* 140), "to be excluded from shelter, from water, from everything."

Confusion now pervaded the Eastern churches. It was impossible to acquiesce in the proceedings of the "Latrocinium." Leo bestirred himself to get a new oecumenical council held in Italy: the imperial family in the West supported this, but Theodosius II. persisted in upholding the late council. In the spring of 450 Dioscorus took a new and exceptionally audacious step. At Nicaea, on his way to the court, he caused ten bishops whom he had brought from Egypt to sign a document excommunicating pope Leo (Mansi, vi. 1009, 1148; vii. 104), doubtless on the ground that Leo was endeavouring to quash the canonical decisions of a legitimate council. His cause, however, was ruined when the orthodox Pulcheria succeeded to the empire, and gave her hand to Marcian, this event leading to a new council at Chalcedon on Oct. 8, 451, which Dioscorus attended. The deputies of Leo come first, then Anatolius, Dioscorus, Maximus, Juvenal. At first Dioscorus sat among those bishops who were on the right of the chancel (*ib.* vi. 580). The Roman deputies on the opposite side desired, in the name of Leo, that Dioscorus should not sit in the council. The magistrates, who acted as imperial commissioners (and were the *effective* presidents), asked what was charged against him? Paschasinus, the chief Roman delegate, answered, "When he comes in" (*i.e.* after having first gone out) "it will be necessary to state objections against him." The magistrates desired again to hear the charge. Lucentius, another delegate, said, "He has presumed to hold a synod without leave of the apostolic see, which has never been done." (Rome did not recognize the "second general council" of 381; which, in fact, was not then owned as general.) "We cannot," said Paschasinus, "transgress the apostolic pope's orders." "We cannot," added Lucentius, "allow such a wrong as that this man should sit in the council, who is come to be judged." "If *you* claim to judge," replied the magistrates sharply, "do not be accuser too." They bade Dioscorus sit in the middle by himself, and the Roman deputies sat down and said no more. Eusebius of Dorylaeum asked to be heard against Dioscorus. "I have been injured by him; the faith has been injured; Flavian was killed, after he and I had been unjustly deposed by Dioscorus. Command my petition to the emperors to be read." It was read by Beronicianus, the secretary of the imperial consistory, and stated that "at the recent council at Ephesus, this good (χρηστός) Dioscorus, disregarding justice, and supporting Eutyches in heresy—having also gained power by bribes, and assembled a disorderly multitude—did all he could to ruin the Catholic faith, and to establish the heresy of Eutyches, and condemned us: I desire, therefore, that he be called to account, and that the records of his proceedings against us be examined." Dioscorus, preserving his self-possession, answered, "The synod was held by the emperor's order; I too desire that its acts against Flavian may be read"; but added, "I beg that the doctrinal question be first considered." "No," said the magistrates, "the charge against you must first be met; wait until the acts have been read, as you yourself desired." The letter of Theodosius, convoking the late council, was read. The magistrates then ordered that Theodoret should be brought in, because Leo had "restored to him his episcopate," and the emperor had ordered him to attend the council. He entered accordingly. The Egyptians and some other bishops shouted, "Turn out the teacher of Nestorius!" Others rejoined, "We signed a blank paper; we were beaten, and so made to sign. Turn out the enemies of Flavian and of the faith!" "Why," asked Dioscorus, "should Cyril be ejected?" (*i.e.* virtually, by the admission of Theodoret). His adversaries turned fiercely upon him: "Turn out Dioscorus the homicide!" Ultimately the magistrates ruled that Theodoret should sit down, but in the middle of the assembly, and that his admission should not prejudice any charge against him (*ib.* 592). The reading went on; at the letter giving Dioscorus the presidency, he remarked that Juvenal, and Thalassius of Caesarea, were associated with him, that the synod had gone with him, and that Theodosius had confirmed its decrees. Forthwith, a cry arose from the bishops whom he had intimidated at Ephesus. "Not one of us signed voluntarily. We were overawed by soldiers." Dioscorus coolly said that if the bishops had not understood the merits of the case, they ought not to have signed. The reading was resumed. Flavian being named, his friends asked why he had been degraded to the fifth place? The next interruption was in reference to the suppression, at the Latrocinium, of Leo's letter. Aetius, archdeacon of Constantinople, said it had not even been "received." "But," said Dioscorus, "the acts shew that I proposed that it should be read. Let others say why it was not read." "What others?" "Juvenal and Thalassius." Juvenal, on being questioned, said, "The chief notary told us that he had an imperial letter; I answered that it ought to come first; no one afterwards said that he had in his hands a letter from Leo." Thalassius (evidently a weak man, though holding the great see of St. Basil) said that he had not power, of himself, to order the reading of the letter (*ib.* 617). At another point the "Orientals," the opponents of Dioscorus, objected that the acts of Ephesus misrepresented their words. Dioscorus replied, "Each bishop had his own secretaries . . . taking down the speeches." Stephen of Ephesus then narrated the violence done to his secretaries: Acacias of Arianathia described the coercion scene. When the reader came to Dioscorus's words, "I examine the decrees of the Fathers" (councils), Eusebius said, "See, he said, 'I examine'; and *I* do the same." Dioscorus caught him up: "I said 'examine,' not 'innovate.' Our Saviour bade us examine the Scriptures; that is not innovating." "He said, Seek, and ye shall find," retorted Eusebius (*ib.* 629). One bishop objected to the record of "Guardian of the faith" as an acclamation in honour of Dioscorus, "No one said that." "They want to deny all that is confessed to be the fact," said Dioscorus; "let them next say they were not there." At the words of Eutyches, "I have observed the definitions of the council," *i.e.* the Ephesian decree against adding to the Nicene faith, Eusebius broke in, "He lied! There is no such definition, no canon prescribing this." "There are four copies," said Dioscorus calmly, "which contain it. What bishops have defined, is it not a definition? It is not a canon: a canon is a different thing." The bp. of Cyzicus referred to the additions made in the council of 381 to the original Nicene creed (*e.g.* "of the Holy Spirit and the Virgin Mary"). The Egyptians disclaimed all such additions. (Cyril, in fact, had never acknowledged that revised version of the Nicene formulary.) There was some further criticism of the profession of faith made by Eutyches; whereupon Dioscorus said, "If Eutyches has any heterodox opinion, he deserves not only to be punished, but to be burnt! My only object is to preserve the Catholic faith, not that of any man. I look to God, and not to any individual; I care for nothing but my own soul and the right faith" (*ib.* 633). Basil of Seleucia described what had taken place as regarded his own statements. "If you taught in such a Catholic tone," said the magistrates, "why did you sign the deposition of Flavian?" Basil pleaded the compulsory authority of a council of bishops. "On your own shewing," said Dioscorus, "you betrayed the faith for fear of men." Others who had given way with Basil cried, "We all sinned; we all ask pardon." "But," said the magistrates, "you said at first that you had been forced to sign a blank paper." The "peccavimus" was reiterated (*ib.* 639). When the reader came to the failure of Flavian's attempt to get Eusebius a hearing, Dioscorus threw the responsibility on Elpidius; so did Juvenal. Thalassius only said, "It was not my doing." "Such a defence," said the magistrates, "is no defence when the faith is concerned." "If," said Dioscorus, "you blame me for obeying Elpidius, were no rules broken when Theodoret was brought in?" "He came in as accuser." "Why then does he now sit in the rank of a bishop?" "He and Eusebius sit as accusers," was the answer; "and *you* sit as accused" (*ib.* 649). Afterwards the magistrates recurred to this topic: "Eusebius, at Constantinople, when accusing Eutyches, himself asked that Eutyches should be present. Why was not a like course taken at Ephesus?" No one answered (*ib.* 656). Cyril's letter to John of Antioch, "Laetentur coeli," was read as part of the acts of Ephesus. Theodoret, by way of clearing himself, anathematized the assertion of "two Sons." *All* the bishops—so the acts of Chalcedon say expressly—cried out, "We believe as did Cyril; we did so believe, and we *do*. Anathema to whoever does not so believe." The opponents of Dioscorus then claimed Flavian as in fact of one mind with Cyril, as clear of Nestorianism. The "Easterns" added, "Leo believes so, Anatolius believes so." There was universal protestation of agreement with Cyril, including even the magistrates, who answered, as it were, for Marcian and Pulcheria. Then came a fierce outcry against Dioscorus. "Out with the murderer of Flavian—the parricide!" The magistrates asked, "Why did you receive to communion Eutyches, who holds the opposite to this belief? Why condemn Flavian and Eusebius who agree with it?" "The records," answered Dioscorus, "will shew the truth." Presently, in regard to some words of Eustathius of Berytus, adopting Cyril's phrase, "one incarnate nature," as Athanasian, the Easterns cried, "Eutyches thinks thus, so does Dioscorus." Dioscorus shewed that he was careful to disclaim, even with anathema, all notions of a "confusion, or commixture," of Godhead and manhood in Christ. The magistrates asked whether the canonical letters of Cyril, recently read (*i.e.* his second letter to Nestorius, Mansi, vi. 660, and his letter to John, *ib.* 665, *not* including the third letter to Nestorius, to which the 12 anathemas were annexed) bore out the language as cited from Eustathius. Eustathius held up the book from which he had taken Cyril's language. "If I spoke amiss, here is the manuscript: let *it* be anathematized with me!" He repeated Cyril's letter to Acacius by heart, and then explained: "One nature" did not exclude the flesh of Christ, which was co-essential with us; and "two natures" was a heterodox phrase if (*i.e.* only if) it was used for a "division" of His person. "Why then did you depose Flavian?" "I erred" (*ib.* v. 677). Flavian's own statement, that Christ was of two natures after the incarnation, in one hypostasis and one person, etc., was then considered; several bishops, in turn, approved of it, including Paschasinus, Anatolius, Maximus, Thalassius, Eustathius. The Easterns called "archbp. Flavian" a martyr. "Let his next words be read," said Dioscorus; "you will find that he is inconsistent with himself." Juvenal, who had been sitting on the right, now went over to the left, and the Easterns welcomed him. Peter of Corinth, a young bishop, did the same, owning that Flavian held with Cyril; the Easterns exclaimed, "Peter thinks as does" (St.) "Peter." Other bishops spoke similarly. Dioscorus, still undaunted, said, "The reason why Flavian was condemned was plainly this, that he asserted two natures after the incarnation. I have passages from the Fathers, Athanasius, Gregory, Cyril, to the effect that after the incarnation there were not two natures, but one incarnate nature of the Word. If I am to be expelled, the Fathers will be expelled with me. I am defending their doctrine; I do not deviate from them at all; I have not got these extracts carelessly, I have verified them" (*ib.* vi. 684; see note in Oxf. ed. of Fleury, vol. iii. p. 348). After more reading, he said, "I accept the phrase 'of two natures,' but I do not accept 'two'" (*i.e.* he would not say,

"Christ has now two natures"). "I am obliged to speak boldly (ἀναισχυντεῖν); I am speaking for my own soul." "Was Flavian," asked Paschasinus, "allowed such freedom of speech as this man takes?" "No," said the magistrates significantly; "but then *this* council is being carried on with justice" (*ib.* 692). Some time later the Easterns denied that the whole council at Ephesus had assented to Eutyches's language; it was the language of "that Pharaoh, Dioscorus the homicide." Eustathius, wishing, he said, to promote a good understanding, asked whether "two natures" meant "two divided natures." "No," said Basil, "neither divided nor confused" (*ib.* 744). Basil afterwards, with Onesiphorus, described the coercion used as to the signatures (*ib.* 827). The reading went on until it was necessary to light the candles (*ib.* 901). At last they came to the signatures; then the magistrates proposed that as the deposition had been proved unjust, Dioscorus, Juvenal, Thalassius, Eusebius of Ancyra, Eustathius, and Basil, as leaders in the late synod, should be deposed; but this, it appears (*ib.* 976, 1041), was a provisional sentence, to be further considered by the council. It was received with applause, "A just sentence! Christ has deposed Dioscorus! God has vindicated the martyrs!" The magistrates desired that each bishop should give in a carefully framed statement of belief conformable to the Nicene "exposition," to that of the 150 Fathers (of Constantinople, in 381), to the canonical epistles and expositions of the Fathers, Gregory, Basil, Athanasius, Hilary, Ambrose, and Cyril's two canonical epistles published and confirmed in the first Ephesian council, adding that Leo had written a letter to Flavian against Eutyches. So ended the first session (*ib.* 935).

The second session was held Oct. 10 (*ib.* 937); Dioscorus was absent. After some discussion as to making an exposition of faith, which led to the reading of the creed in its two forms—both of which were accepted—and of Cyril's "two canonical epistles," and of Leo's letter to Flavian (the Tome), which was greeted with "Peter has spoken by Leo; Cyril taught thus; Leo and Cyril have taught alike," but to parts of which some objection was taken by one bishop, and time given for consideration, the usual exclamations were made, among which we find that of the Illyrians, "Restore Dioscorus to the synod, to the churches! We have all offended, let all be forgiven!" while the enemies of Dioscorus called for his banishment, and the clerics of Constantinople said that he who communicated with him was a Jew (*ib.* 976). In the third session, Sat. Oct. 13, the magistrates not being present, a memorial to the council from Eusebius of Dorylaeum, setting forth charges against Dioscorus, was read (*ib.* 985). It then appeared that Dioscorus had been summoned, like other bishops, to the session, and intimated his willingness to come; but his guards prevented him. Two priests, sent to search for him, could not find him in the precincts of the church. Three bishops, sent with a notary, found him, and said, "The holy council begs your Holiness to attend its meeting." "I am under guard," said he; "I am hindered by the officers" (*magistriani*, the subordinates of the "master of the offices," or "supreme magistrate of the palace," see Gibbon, ii. 326); and, after two other summonses, positively and finally refused to come. He had nothing more to say than he had said to former envoys. They begged him to reconsider it. "If your Holiness knows that you are falsely accused, the council is not far off; do take the trouble to come and refute the falsehood." "What I have said, I have said; it is enough." They desisted, and reported their failure. "Do you order that we proceed to ecclesiastical penalties against him?" asked Paschasinus, addressing the council. "Yes, we agree." One bishop said bittterly, "When he murdered holy Flavian, he did not adduce canons, nor proceed by church forms." The Roman delegates proposed a sentence, to this effect: "Dioscorus has received Eutyches, though duly condemned by Flavian, into communion. The apostolic see excuses those who were coerced by Dioscorus at Ephesus, but who are obedient to archbp. Leo" (as president) "and the council; but this man glories in his crime. He prevented Leo's letter to Flavian" (the acts of Ephesus say the letter to the council, *v. supra*) "from being read. He has presumed to excommunicate Leo. He has thrice refused to come and answer to charges. Therefore Leo, by us and the council, together with St. Peter, the rock of the church, deprives him of episcopal and sacerdotal dignity" (*ib.* 1045). A letter was written to Dioscorus, announcing that he was deposed for disregarding the canons and disobeying the council. Dioscorus at first made light of the sentence, and said that he should soon be restored; the council wrote to the two emperors, reciting his misdeeds, as before, and adding that he had restored the heterodox and justly-deposed Eutyches to his office, in contempt of Leo's letter, had done injury to Eusebius, and had received to communion persons lawfully condemned (*ib.* 1097). The deposition of Dioscorus was confirmed by the emperor; he was banished to Gangra in Paphlagonia, and died there in 454. Proterius, archpriest of Alexandria, who adhered to the council of Chalcedon, was placed in the see of St. Mark, but never gained the goodwill of his people as a body; they regarded Dioscorus, though *de facto* deposed, as their legitimate patriarch; and his deposition inaugurated the schism which to this day has divided the Christians of Egypt, the majority of whom, bearing the name of Jacobites, have always disowned the council of Chalcedon, and venerated Dioscorus as "their teacher" (Lit. Copt. St. Basil), and as a persecuted saint (see Neale, *Hist. Alex.* ii. 6). As to his theological position, there is, perhaps, little or nothing in his own words which might not be interpreted consistently with orthodoxy. Even as to his conduct, the charges brought by the Alexandrian petitioners at Chalcedon are too deeply coloured by passion to command our full belief; and a mere profligate oppressor would not have secured so largely the loyalty of Alexandrian churchmen. But his public acts in 449 exhibit the perversion of considerable abilities—of courage, resolution, clear-headedness—under the temptations of excessive power and the promptings of a tyrannous self-will. The brutal treatment of Flavian, which he practically sanctioned, in which perhaps he personally took part, has made his memory specially odious; and his name is conspicuous among the "violent men" of church history. [MONOPHYSITISM.] [W.B.]

Dioscorus (4), the eldest of four Nitrian monks, Dioscorus, AMMONIUS, Eusebius, and Euthymius, known from their stature as the "Tall Brethren," who became conspicuous in Chrysostom's early troubles. They were reluctantly induced by Theophilus, patriarch of Alexandria, to leave the desert and to submit to ordination. Eusebius and Euthymius became presbyters, and Dioscorus was consecrated bp. of Hermopolis. Weary of city life and uncongenial duties, and shocked by the avarice and other vices of Theophilus, Dioscorus and his brethren returned to their solitudes, though the indignant patriarch tried to deter them by violent menaces (Socr. *H. E.* viii. 12). As depositaries of dangerous secrets, they had become formidable to Theophilus, who resolved to wreak vengeance upon them. On the pretext of their adherence to the mystic views of Origen on the Person of the Deity, and their decided opposition to Anthropomorphism, which Theophilus had originally shared with them, Theophilus had them ejected from their monasteries and treated them with the utmost contumely and violence when they went to Alexandria to appeal (Pallad. p. 54). Having procured their condemnation at a packed synod at Alexandria, A.D. 401, Theophilus personally headed a night attack on their monastery, which was burnt and pillaged, and Dioscorus himself treated with violence and indignity (*ib.* p. 57). Driven from Egypt, the "Tall Brethren" took refuge in Palestine, but later resolved to appeal for protection to the emperor and to Chrysostom in person. Chrysostom manifested much sympathy, but contented himself with writing to Theophilus, urging his reconciliation with them. Theophilus's only reply was an angry remonstrance against his harbouring heretics and interfering with another see. He sent emissaries to Constantinople to denounce the brethren as magicians, heretics, and rebels. The monks then announced their intention of appealing to the secular power for a judicial investigation of the charges against them, and demanded that Theophilus should be summoned to answer for his conduct before a council. The superstitious reverence of the empress Eudoxia, all-powerful with the feeble Arcadius, secured them their desire, and Theophilus was ordered to appear at Constantinople. This appeal to the civil authority displeased Chrysostom, who declined to interfere further in the controversy. For the manner in which Theophilus turned the tables on Chrysostom, becoming the accuser instead of the accused, and securing his deposition, see CHRYSOSTOM; THEOPHILUS (8). His main object having been accomplished in the overthrow of his great rival, Theophilus now made no difficulty about reconciliation with the Nitrian monks, whom he publicly restored to communion on their simple petition. Dioscorus and Ammonius had, however, died not long before. Socr. *H. E.* vi. 16; Soz. *H. E.* viii. 17; Pallad. p. 157. [E.V.]

Docetism, the very early heresy that our blessed Lord had a body like ours, only in appearance, not in reality. St. Jerome scarcely exaggerates when he says (*adv. Lucif.* 23): "While the apostles were still surviving, while Christ's blood was still fresh in Judea, the Lord's body was asserted to be but a phantasm." Apart from N.T. passages, *e.g.* Eph. ii. 9, Heb. ii. 14, which confute this assertion, but do not bear clear marks of having been written with a controversial purpose, it appears from I. John iv. 2, II. John 7, that when these epistles were written there were teachers, stigmatised by the writer as prompted by the spirit of Antichrist, who denied that Jesus Christ had come *in the flesh*, a form of expression implying a Docetic theory. Those who held that evil resulted from the inherent fault of matter found it impossible to believe that the Saviour could be Himself under the dominion of that evil from which He came to deliver men, and they therefore rejected the Church's doctrine of a real union of the divine and human natures in the person of our Lord, but our Lord's pre-existence and superhuman nature was regarded as so essential a part of Christianity that with two exceptions, or perhaps even only one (*i.e.* JUSTINUS and perhaps CARPOCRATES), all the sects known as Gnostic ascribed to the Saviour a superhuman nature, some however separating the personality of that nature from His human personality, others reducing our Lord's earthly part to mere appearance. It is even doubtful whether we are not to understand in a technical sense the statement that he taught that "power" from the Father had descended on our Lord; that is to say, whether it was not his doctrine that one of the heavenly powers had united itself to the man Jesus. Teaching of this kind is unequivocally attributed to CERINTHUS, whose other doctrines, as reported by Irenaeus, have great resemblance to those of Carpocrates. It is in opposition to the theory which makes our Lord's claim to be Christ date, not from his birth, but from some later period, that Irenaeus (iii. 16) uses the argument, shewing his belief in the inspiration of the gospels, that Matthew might have said, "the birth of Jesus was in this wise," but that the Holy Spirit, foreseeing and guarding against the depravation of the truth, said by Matthew "the birth of Christ was on this wise." Baur (*Christliche Gnosis*, p. 258) makes Docetism common to all the Gnostics, holding that the theory which has just been described is in a certain sense Docetic; inasmuch as while holding Jesus to be a real man, visibly active in the work of redemption, it teaches that this is but deceptive appearance, the work being actually performed by a distinct personality, Christ. But it is more usual and more natural to use the word Docetism only with reference to those other theories which refuse to acknowledge the true manhood of the Redeemer. For example, we are told (Iren. i. 23) that, according to the system of Simon, the Redeemer (who, however, is not Jesus,* but Simon himself)

* Perhaps it is not correct to say "not Jesus," for Simon held a theory of the transmigration of souls, and may have claimed to be identical with Jesus. If this were so, however, he must have been later than the Simon of the Acts.

"had appeared among men as man, though he was not a man, and was thought to have suffered in Judea, though he did not suffer." According to the system of SATURNINUS (Iren. i. 24), the Saviour was without birth, without body, and without figure, and appeared a man in phantasm, not in truth. According to BASILIDES, as reported by Irenaeus (i. 24), Christ or Nous is not distinguished from Jesus, but is said to be an incorporeal power, who transfigured Himself as He willed; that He appeared on earth as man and worked miracles, but that He did not suffer; that it was Simon of Cyrene, who, being transfigured into the form of Jesus, was crucified, while Jesus Himself, in the form of Simon standing by, laughed at His persecutors, and then, incapable of being held by them, ascended up to Him Who had sent Him, invisible to them all. The Docetism here described is strenuously combated in the Ignatian Epistles in their Greek form, esp. in *ad Trall.* 9, 10, and *ad Smyrn.* 2. In these the writer emphasises the statements that our Lord was truly born, did eat and drink, was truly persecuted under Pontius Pilate, was truly crucified, and truly rose from the dead; and he expressly declares that these statements were made in contradiction of the doctrine of certain unbelievers, or rather atheists, who asserted His sufferings to be but seeming. This polemic is absent from the Syriac Ignatius, and an argument has hence been derived against the genuineness of the Greek form. But in order to make the argument valid, there ought to be proof that the rise of Docetism was probably later than the age of Ignatius, whereas the probability seems to be quite the other way. Saturninus holds such a place in all heretical lists, that he must be referred to the very beginning of the 2nd cent., and, as he taught in Antioch, may very possibly have been encountered by Ignatius. Polycarp also (*Ep.* 7) uses the words of I. John iv. 3 in such a way as to shew that Docetism was in his time troublesome.

In the forms of Docetism thus far described there is no evidence that there was involved any more subtle theory than that the senses of the spectators of our Lord's earthly life were deceived. The Docetism of VALENTINUS was exhibited in a more artificial theory, which is fully set forth in our art. *s.v.* It appears that Valentinus was only partly docetic. He conceded to Jesus the possession of a real body capable of really affecting the senses, but held that that body was made of a different substance from ours and was peculiar as regards its sustenance by earthly nutriment (Letter to Agathopus, *ap.* Clem. Alex. *Strom.* iii. 7, 451). Irenaeus, however (v. 1, 2, and more fully iii. 22), insists that the Valentinian doctrine did not practically differ from pure Docetism; for that if our Lord had not taken substance of flesh in the womb of the Virgin He could not have been the real man Who suffered hunger and thirst and weariness, Who wept at the grave of Lazarus, Who sweat drops of blood, from Whose wounded side came forth blood and water.

The Docetism of MARCION differed from that of preceding Gnostics. With them the great stumbling-block had been the sufferings of Christ, and accordingly it is the reality of Christ's passion and death that their antagonists sought to establish. Marcion, on the contrary, was quite willing to acknowledge the proof of our Lord's love exhibited in His sufferings and death, but it was repulsive to him to own His human birth, which according to his view would have made our Lord the debtor and the subject of the Creator of the world. Accordingly, while Basilides had admitted a real birth of the man Jesus, Valentinus at least a seeming birth in which the body elsewhere prepared was ushered into the world, Marcion would own no birth at all, and began his gospel with the sudden announcement that in the 15th year of Tiberius Christ * came down (by which we are to understand came down from heaven) to Capernaum, a city of Galilee (Tert. *adv. Marc.* iv. 7). Marcion's disciple Apelles so far modified his master's doctrine that he was willing to own that Jesus had a solid body, but denied that there had been a birth in which He had assumed it (Tert. *de C. C.* 6); and he held that of this body our Lord made only a temporary use, and that when He had shewn it to His disciples after His resurrection He gave it back to the elements from which He had received it (Hipp. *Ref.* vii. 38, 260). Something of this kind seems to have been also the view of the sect known as *Docetae*.

The fourth book of the dialogue against the Marcionites (Origen, i. 853) contains a polemic against Docetism which is represented as defended by Marinus the disciple of Bardesanes, who adopts the Valentinian notion that our Lord had come διὰ Μαρίας, not ἐκ Μαρίας, and who maintains that His earthly body was only such as the angels had temporarily assumed who ate and drank with Abraham. One argument on the orthodox side is used by several Fathers, and the form of words in which each has expressed himself has been much discussed in modern controversy. It occurs here in the form "If Christ were without flesh and blood, of what sort of flesh and blood are the bread and wine, the images (εἰκόνας) with which He commanded that the memorial of Him should be made?" (cf. Ign. *ad. Smyrn.* 7; Iren. iv. 18, v. 2; Tert. *adv. Marcion.* iv. 40). Of later heretics, the most considerable who maintained a Docetic theory are the Manicheans. In the controversy with them the orthodox had exactly the same points to establish as in the controversy with Marcion, viz. that Christ had come into the world, not merely as sent by the Father, but as really born of the Virgin; that He was truly incarnate, and did not assume the form of a body merely as did the angels whose appearances have been recorded; that He was circumcised, baptized, tempted; that His death was a real one, as was necessary in order that His resurrection also should be real (see in particular the disputation between Augustine and Faustus). With regard to the disputes in the 6th cent. concerning our Lord's body, see JULIANUS (**47**) of Halicarnassus, and *D. C. B.* (4-vol. ed.) under CORRUPTICOLAE and PHANTASIASTAE. It is well known that Mahommed

* There is a well-recommended various reading, "Deum" instead of "eum"; but Epiphanius (*Haer.* 42, p. 312) would scarcely have passed this over in silence had he found it in his Marcion.

also adopted the Docetic account of our Lord's crucifixion.

Besides formal heresies which have been tainted with Docetism, the same imputation has been cast on more than one of the Fathers. It is very strongly brought by Photius (*Bibl.* 109) against the hypotyposes of CLEMENT OF ALEXANDRIA. This book has not survived, but there is no doubt from his extant writings that Clement ascribed to our Lord a real body. In a fragment probably from the lost Hypotyposes preserved in a Latin trans. (p. 1009), he quotes from "the traditions" that when St. John handled the body of our Lord the flesh offered no resistance, but yielded place to the disciple's hand. Redepenning's conclusion (*Origenes,* ii. 391) is that Clement's doctrine deviated from that subsequently recognised as orthodox, not in respect of our Lord's body, the reality of which he acknowledged, but in holding that His body was directly united to the Divine Logos without the intervention of a human soul capable of feeling pain or suffering. Redepenning (*l.c.*) also discusses how far ORIGEN is chargeable with Docetism, on which also consult Huet's *Origeniana*, ii. Qu. iii. 10, 11.

The traditions referred to by Clement have been identified with the contents of a work of Leucius Charinus, purporting to relate travels of the apostles, of which an account is given by Photius (*Bibl.* 114), and from which extracts are also quoted in the Acts of the second council of Nicaea (*Actio* v.). In this work, which Grabe seems to have correctly regarded as Marcionite, it was taught that the Son was not man, but only seemed to be so; that He shewed Himself to His disciples sometimes young, sometimes old; sometimes a child, sometimes an old man; sometimes great, sometimes small; sometimes so great as to touch the heavens with His head; that His footsteps left no trace; and that He was not really crucified, but, according to Photius, another person in His place. The account given in the Nicene extracts of a vision seen by St. John on the mount of Olives, at the time of the crucifixion, teaches that the form crucified was not really our Lord, but does not suggest that it was any other person. [G.S.]

Domitianus (1), A.D. 81-96. This emperor, though placed by Lactantius (*de Mort. Persecut.* c. 3) and others among the persecutors of the church, can hardly be considered as having made any systematic effort to crush Christianity as such. Through the greater part of the empire the Christians seem to have been unmolested. The traces of persecution, such as they are, seem rather to belong to his general policy of suspicion and cruelty. Indirectly they are of interest in shewing how the new religion was attracting notice and spreading.

(1) Vespasian, before his death, had given orders (Eus. *H. E.* iii. 12) that inquiry should be made for all who claimed to be descendants of the house of David, seeking thus to cut off all who might incite the Jews to a fresh revolt. The fears of Domitian led him to continue the search, and Hegesippus (in Eus. *H. E.* iii. 19, 20) records one striking incident connected with it. The grandchildren of Judas, the brother of the Lord, were taken to Rome and brought into the emperor's presence. They acknowledged that they were of the kingly line, but stated that the only kingdom they looked for was one spiritual and angelic, to be manifested at the end of the world. The emperor, Hegesippus tells us, thought them beneath his notice, released them, and allowed them to go back to Judea, and put a stop to the *persecution against the church which he had begun.* This persecution was probably the inquiry itself. The Judean followers of the Christ, whom they habitually spoke of as the seed of David, would inevitably be suspected of being likely to appeal to the hopes of the conquered population.

(2) Towards the close of Domitian's reign a domestic tragedy occurred which there is good reason for connecting with the progress of Christianity. The emperor had a cousin named Flavius Clemens, whom at one time he held in high favour. He gave him his niece Flavia Domitilla in marriage, changed the names of his sons to Vespasian and Domitian and designated them as heirs to the empire, and nominated Clemens as his colleague in the consulship. Suddenly, almost within the year of his consulship, he put Clemens to death, banished his wife to Pandataria, and his daughter (or niece), who was also called Domitilla, to Pontia. Revenge for these acts had apparently no small share in the emperor's assassination. One of the most prominent conspirators concerned was Stephanus, an agent and freedman of the banished widow of Clemens. Thus the story is told by Suetonius (*Domit.* cc. 15, 17). It remains to see on what grounds church writers like Eusebius (*H. E.* iii. 18) claim the three members of the Flavian house as among the first illustrious martyrs of royal rank. (i) Flavius Clemens is described by Suetonius (*l.c.*) as "contemptissimae inertiae." A Christian would naturally be so described by men of his own rank and by the outer world, just as Tertullian complains that the Christians of his time were stigmatized, when other charges failed, as "infructuosi negotiis" (*Apol.* c. 42). (ii) The specific charge against Clemens and the two Domitillae is reported by Dio Cassius (lxvii. 14) and Xiphilinus (p. 766) to have been atheism. The same accusation, the latter adds, was brought against many others who shewed a bias towards Jewish customs. This again agrees with the general feeling of the Roman world towards the Christians at a later period, and may be regarded as the first instance of that feeling. (iii) Later tradition confirms these inferences. Jerome tells us (*Ep.* 27) how Paula visited Pontia on her way to Jerusalem, as already an object of reverence, and saw the three cells in which Domitilla and her two eunuchs Achilleus and Nereus had lived during their exile. They were said to have returned to Rome and suffered martyrdom under Trajan. A church on the Coelian Hill at Rome dedicated to S. Clement, in which a tablet was discovered in 1725 to the memory of Flavius Clemens, martyr, and described by Cardinal Albiani (*T. Flavii Clementis Viri Consularis et Martyris Tumulus Illustratus*, 1727), seems therefore to have commemorated the consul and not the writer of that name. The name of Clement of Alexandria, Titus Flavius Clemens, may be re-

garded as an indication of the honour in which the martyr's memory was held. On the whole, everything seems to indicate that the received tradition is true, and that the Christian church was almost on the point, even before the close of the 1st cent., of furnishing a successor to the imperial throne.

(3) With the reign of Domitian is also connected the legend of St. John's presence at Rome, and of his being thrown, before the Porta Latina, at the command of the emperor, into a cauldron of boiling oil, and then banished to Patmos. Tertullian (*de Praescript.* c. 36) is the first writer who mentions it. The apostle, as the chosen friend of the Son of David, may have been pointed out by the *delatores* of Ephesus as the descendants of Judas were in Judea. Tertullian, in speaking elsewhere (*Apol.* c. 5) of Domitian's conduct towards the church, describes him as only attempting a persecution, and then, thinking better of it, recalling those whom he had condemned to exile. In other accounts (Eus. *H. E.* iii. 20) the decree of recall was connected with the accession of Nerva. [E.H.P.]

Domitilla Flavia. [DOMITIANUS (1).]

Domnus I. (2), bp. of Antioch, appointed A.D. 269 on the deposition of Paul of Samosata, by the sole authority of the council, without any reference to the clergy and people, the bishops evidently fearing they might re-elect Paul (Eus. *H. E.* vii. 30). Paul, relying on the support of Zenobia, retained for two years the episcopal residence and its church. The orthodox section appealed to Aurelian after he had conquered Zenobia and taken Antioch, A.D. 272. The emperor decided that the right of occupation should belong to the party in communion with the bishops of Italy and the see of Rome. This decision was enforced by the civil power, and Paul was compelled to leave the palace in disgrace (Eus. *u.s.*). Domnus died A.D. 274, and was succeeded by Timaeus (Till. *Mém. eccl.* t. iv. p. 302; Neander, *Ch. Hist.* vol. i. p. 193, Clark's trans.; Neale, *Patr. of Antioch*, pp. 52-57). [E.V.]

Domnus II. (4), bp. of Antioch, a friend of Theodoret. He was nephew of John, bp. of Antioch, brought up under Euthymius the famous anchoret of Palestine. He was ordained deacon by Juvenal of Jerusalem on his visit to the Laura of Euthymus in A.D. 429. Two years afterwards, learning that his uncle the bp. of Antioch had become entangled in the Nestorian heresy, he besought Euthymius to allow him to go and extricate him. Euthymius counselled him to remain where he was, telling him that God could take care of his uncle without him; that solitude was safer for him than the world; that his design would not turn out to his ultimate advantage; that he might not improbably succeed to his uncle's dignity, but would become the victim of clever and unprincipled men, who would avail themselves of his simplicity, and then accomplish his ruin; but the old man's counsels were thrown away. Domnus left the Laura without even saying farewell to Euthymius (*Vita S. Euthymii*, cc. 42, 56, 57). He obtained such popularity at Antioch that on the death of his uncle, A.D. 441, he was appointed his successor, and at once ranked as the chief bishop of the Eastern world. In 445 he summoned a synod of Syrian bishops which confirmed the deposition of Athanasius of Perrha. In 447 he consecrated Irenaeus to the see of Tyre (Theod. *Ep.* 110; Labbe, *Concil.* t. iii. col. 1275); but Theodosius II., having commanded that the appointment should be annulled, Irenaeus being both a *digamus* and a favourer of the Nestorian heresy, Domnus, despite Theodoret's remonstrances, yielded to the imperial will (Theod. *u.s.*; *Ep.* 80). Ibas, bp. of Edessa, being charged with promulgating Nestorian doctrines (Labbe, *ib.* t. iv. col. 658), Domnus summoned a council at Antioch (A.D. 448), which decided in favour of Ibas and deposed his accusers (*ib.* 639 seq.). Domnus's sentence, though revoked by Flavian, bp. of Constantinople, was confirmed by three episcopal commissioners to whom he and the emperor Theodosius had committed the matter. Domnus was one of the earliest impeachers of the orthodoxy of Eutyches, in a synodical letter to Theodosius, *c.* 447 (Facundus, viii. 5; xii. 5). At the Latrocinium, held at Ephesus, Aug. 8, 449, on this matter, Domnus, in virtue of an imperial rescript, found himself deprived of his presidential seat, which was occupied by Dioscorus, while precedence over the patriarch of Antioch was given to Juvenal of Jerusalem (Labbe, *ib.* 115, p. 251). Cowed by the dictatorial spirit of Dioscorus, and unnerved by the violence of Barsumas and his monks, Domnus revoked his former condemnation of Eutyches, and voted for his restoration (*ib.* col. 258) and for the condemnation of Flavian (*ib.* col. 306). Domnus was, nevertheless, deposed and banished by Dioscorus. The charges against him were, approval of a Nestorian sermon preached before him at Antioch by Theodoret on the death of Cyril (Mercator, t. i. p. 276), and some expressions in letters written by him to Dioscorus condemning the perplexed and obscure character of Cyril's anathemas (Liberatus, c. 11, p. 74). He was the only bishop then deposed and banished who was not reinstated after the council of Chalcedon. At that council Maximus, his successor in the see of Antioch, obtained permission to assign Domnus a pension from the revenues of the church (Labbe, *ib.* col. 681; append. col. 770). Finally, on his recall from exile Domnus returned to the monastic home of his youth, and ended his days in the Laura of St. Euthymius, where in 452, according to Theophanes, he afforded a refuge to Juvenal of Jerusalem when driven from his see (Theoph. p. 92). [E.V.]

Donatus and **Donatism.** The Donatists were the first Christians who separated from the church on the ground of discipline, though the church had already been torn by heresies, such as Gnosticism and Manicheism, which had affected doctrines. It is important to remember that Donatism was not heresy, as the word is ordinarily understood. All heretics are, in one sense, schismatics, but all schismatics are not heretics; and the Donatists themselves protested, with justice, against being considered heretics.

Mensurius was bp. of Carthage during and after Diocletian's persecution (A.D. 303). Having been required by consul Anulinus to give up any copies of Holy Scripture in his possession, he had hid them, and passed off heretical works in their stead. The consul, learning the "pious fraud," declined to take further action. Mensurius felt it his duty to check the growing and inordinate reverence for martyrdom. He saw that there were too many would-be martyrs whose character would not bear close scrutiny, and, together with his archdeacon Caecilian, did his best to discountenance the reverence of good but mistaken Christians for these undeserving men. This naturally brought him into odium with those to whom martyrdom was the becoming conclusion of the Christian life.

During his lifetime the storm was brewing, and it fairly broke out when Caecilian succeeded him (A.D. 311). That appointment was felt to be a blow to all who magnified martyrdom. His opponents rested their principal objection on the fact that he had been ordained by a traditor, Felix of Aptunga; and proceeded to elect Majorinus as successor to Mensurius. The charge was a strange one to be made by Caecilian's chief opponent, SECUNDUS, bp. of Tigisis, for documents exist which prove Secundus himself a traditor, in spite of his boast to Mensurius. From that date Donatism, as it was afterwards called, had a separate and schismatical existence. Both sides appealed to Constantine, and the emperor at once subjected the alleged traditorship of Felix to a thorough examination by a council at Rome (A.D. 313), which decided in favour of Felix, cleared his character, and consequently declared the ordination of Caecilian valid. The subject was again exhaustively discussed before the consul Aelianus, who, at the bidding of Constantine, gave the Donatists another opportunity (A.D. 314), at Carthage, of proving their charge against Felix. The finding of the tribunal was unanimous: "Nemo in eum (Felicem) aliquid probare potuerit quod religiosissimas scripturas tradiderit vel exusserit."

Bp. Majorinus died A.D. 315, but had been a leader of little consequence. His followers had called themselves, for convenience' sake, the party of Majorinus; but after his death, if not before, they took the name—Donatists—by which they are best known. There were perhaps 2 bishops named Donatus; (1) of Casae Nigrae, who, before Caecilian's elevation, had shewn his schismatical tendencies; (2) the successor of Majorinus and surnamed "the Great." But this distinction has lately been questioned; see Sparrow Simpson, *St. Aug. and Afr. Ch. Divisions* (1910), p. 31; Monceaux, *Revue de l'Hist. de Religion* (1909).

In Donatus the Great personal hostility to Mensurius and Caecilian, and irritation against the decisions of Rome and Arles [CAECILIAN], of Aelianus and Constantine, led to a defiant attitude against both Church and State. The dissentients to Caecilian had, consistently enough, refused to his church the title of the Church of God, and appropriated that distinction to themselves. The Caecilianist clergy were condemned for their league with a traditor and their acts repudiated as invalid; hence those who followed Majorinus were rebaptized. But Constantine's edict (A.D. 316) took away from them their churches, and the heavy hand of Ursacius deprived them of their lives. The sectarians found in Donatus a man bold enough to denounce the imperial power and to infuse vigour into their strife against the Caecilianists. He was neither "the angel" his followers called him nor "the fiend" his opponents described him. He was a man of unquestionable ability, eloquence, and thoroughness—the Cyprian of his party, as St. Augustine called him; but also hard and unloving to foe, proud and overbearing to friend. Optatus and St. Augustine were justified in comparing with the proud "prince of Tyre" (Ezek. xxviii. 2) the man who in his lifetime permitted his followers to swear by his name and by his grey hairs, and could ask of the menial bishops, "What do you say to *my* party?" and who, after his death, was described by Donatists at the conference of Carthage as the miracle-worker, "the pride of the church of Carthage, the man with the reputation of a martyr."

When the soldiers of Ursacius appeared in N. Africa, Donatus was ready to resist them, and his courage infected the timid people and prelates. His name became the rallying-point for every man who had real or imaginary grievances against existing ecclesiastical, civil, and social powers, amongst others the Circumcellions. "They were a class of men," says St. Augustine, "who followed no kind of useful occupation, held their own lives in fanatical contempt, and thought no death too cruel for those who differed from them; they wandered about from place to place, chiefly in the country districts, and haunted the cells of the peasants for the purpose of obtaining food. Hence they were called 'Circumcelliones.'" The better class of Donatists turned away in horror from fanatics who imbrued their hands with the blood of the innocent as well as of the guilty; but the offer of partisanship having been once accepted, it was impossible to withdraw it altogether. Donatus, Parmenian, Petilian, and Cresconius in turn were forced to palliate as much as they could the actions of these allies, who preferred to be called Agonistici, Champions of Christ, and who rushed into the battle with "Deo laudes" as their war-cry, and with a weapon dubbed "Israelite" as their war-club.

Constantine soon found that Donatism was not to be put down by the sword. In A.D. 317 Ursacius was bidden hold his hand, and Caecilian was exhorted to treat his opponents kindly, and leave vengeance to God. The emperor's letter was a mixture of truth and sarcasm: "All schisms," he wrote, "are from the devil; and these Separatists proceed from him. What good can you expect from those who are the adversaries of God and the enemies of the holy church? Such men must split off from the church, and attach themselves to the devil. Surely we act most wisely, if we leave to them what they have wrenched from us. By patience and kindness we may hope to gain them. Let us leave vengeance to God. I rejoice to think that you meet their brutality with gentleness and good temper. As I understand that these men have destroyed a church in Constantinople, I have ordered my finance-minister to build you a new one. God grant that these mistaken Separatists may at last see their error and turn to the one true God!" It was not a letter calculated to soothe the

Donatists. They presently replied to the emperor that he must distinctly understand that they would have nothing to do with his "fool of a bishop" (*i.e.* Caecilian), and that he might do his worst. With this mutual contempt and recrimination matters ended for the time. Constantine during the remainder of his life ignored the Donatists; but they increased largely in numbers in their own districts—in A.D. 330 they held a synod attended by 270 bishops—and established a few insignificant stations elsewhere.

Constans, son of Constantine, succeeded to his father's N. African possessions; and, at first, endeavoured to conciliate the Donatists by kindness. He published (A.D. 340) an edict requiring the Donatists to return to the church, urging that "unity must now exist, because Christ was a lover of unity," and instructed his commissioners Ursacius (probably not the Ursacius already mentioned) and Leontius to distribute money, as alms, in Donatist as well as in Catholic churches. The Donatists spurned it as gold offered by the devil to seduce men from their faith. The sword of persecution was then unsheathed to deprive the Donatists of their churches; and the survivors regarded the victims as martyrs and their graves as platforms for preaching resistance. In A.D. 345 Gregorius travelled through the province, offering not only alms but valuable church plate to all who would accept the imperial invitation to submit. Donatus sent circular letters through all the provinces, forbidding the acceptance of any presents; and wrote to Gregorius in a scurrilous style. In A.D. 347 a third commission, composed of Paul, Macarius, and Taurinus, came to Donatus himself, with gold in their hands. The bishop listened impatiently, and at length broke out, "What has the emperor to do with the church?" They were words which meant much at the time, but have meant more since.

The language of Donatus was repeated from every Donatistic pulpit by preachers proclaiming the duty of separation from a church "which committed fornication with the princes of this world," and whose prelates were mere tools of an emperor. Such obloquy served to madden the fanatics, even though it brought upon them furious persecution. The Circumcellions rose, and frightful bloodshed followed. These "Christian champions" traversed the country, subverting everything. Slaves and debtors were deemed brothers; masters and creditors tyrants. The excesses of the Circumcellions were so great that Donatus and his brother-bishops were forced to appeal to Taurinus to check them. The Circumcellions kissed the hands which betrayed them, and turned their fury upon themselves. They longed for martyrdom. They invaded pagan temples that death might be found from the sword of some infuriated idolator; they entered courts of justice and frightened judges ordered their instant execution; travellers were stopped and threatened with instant death if they did not slay the suppliants. Days, hours, and places were named that an admiring crowd might witness them cast themselves headlong from some rock into the graves which their posterity would reverence as those of the martyrs. Macarius did not discriminate between moderate Donatist and extreme Circumcellionist. With an iron hand he crushed both. Donatus was banished, and died in exile. The church was triumphant. Optatus saluted Constans as the servant of God who had been privileged to restore unity; but many regretted that unity had been won at such a price. When Donatists afterwards called Christians "Macarians," in scornful allusion to the persecutor of their sect, St. Augustine replied: "Yes, we are Macarians, for that name means 'blessed,' and who is more blessed than Christ to Whom we belong?" but it was natural to him and worthy of him to add, "Don't let us call one another names. Don't cast at me the times of Macarius, and I won't remind you of the madness of the Circumcellions. Let us, as far as possible, work together, because we are all orphans."

It was probably soon after the cessation of the persecution that Gratus, Caecilian's successor, summoned a synod at Carthage, which established (1) the non-iteration of baptism, when duly administered in the name of the Trinity; (2) the necessary restrictions on reverence for martyrs, and on the assignment of that title.

In A.D. 361 Julian became emperor. His edict "recalled all the bishops and clergy banished in the reign of Constantius, and granted equal freedom to all parties of the Christian church." The Donatists were not included in this. Two of their bishops, Rogatian and Pontus, waited on the emperor; and left with full permission to return to their country. The return was marked by violence and murder. The Donatists treated the churches as places which had been profaned, washed the walls and altars, tore the vestments to pieces, threw the holy vessels outside and the sacred elements to the dogs. Then they reintroduced their rigorous discipline. Apostates were received only after most humiliating penance, laymen were rebaptized, and clerics reordained. For two years Donatism was in the ascendant and basked in the imperial sunshine. But the cry which went up from the dying Julian's lips (A.D. 363), "Galilean, Thou hast conquered," was also the cry which told the Donatist that his day of triumph had ended.

Donatus had been succeeded by Parmenian, perhaps the ablest and least prejudiced of the Donatist episcopacy. A foreigner by birth, and actually ignorant of many of the saddest and cruellest episodes of Donatist history, he entered upon his duties at Carthage free from the passionate views which marked so many of his followers, and disposed to rate lightly much that to them was of great importance. His literary merit was great and excited the admiration of Optatus, bp. of Milevi, and of St. Augustine, each of whom has left a statement of the current Donatist opinions. The theological disputations between Optatus and Parmenian are preserved in the great work of the former, and evidently Parmenian's opinions are honestly given. Optatus was a man of unquestioned piety, dialectical skill, and orthodoxy; perfectly indifferent to Circumcellion threats, bribery, or corruption; earnestly desirous for unity, if it could be obtained without sacrifice of principle; and he sought as much common ground as possible, before stating unhesitatingly where he and his opponent must part. If the usual tone of kindliness and courtesy is occasionally forgotten, if the title "brother" given to Parmenian is replaced by "Antichrist" when Donatus is mentioned, if cool, argumentative reasoning is sometimes dropped for defiant passionate utterance, the difference is intelligible in a character so full of both charity and zeal that St. Augustine called him "a second Ambrose of Milan."

There were two points about which, theoretically, both men were agreed: (1) That there was only one church; and (2) that in that one church there was only one baptism, and this not to be repeated. But disagreement soon began. "A church," said the Donatist, "in which traditors both existed and dispensed the sacraments was no church, and baptism administered by traditors was no baptism." Where, then, was the pure church? with the Catholic or Donatist? How far was the validity of the sacraments dependent upon the purity of the church and the personal character of those who dispensed them? These were old questions, but discussed between Optatus and Parmenian as they had never been before. [OPTATUS (6); PARMENIANUS.]

The existence of Donatism was next threatened by divisions within. "As Donatus," says St. Augustine, "sought to divide Christ, so was Donatus divided by the divisions which arose daily amongst his own followers." Rogatists and Maximianists, or individuals like Tichonius, arose to contest or moderate the views of the founders of the sect. [TICHONIUS.]

The fiercest blow to Donatism was, however, given by the Maximianist schism. [MAXIMIANUS (2).] Parmenian died A.D. 392, and was succeeded by Primian. Primian imposed a penance on one of his deacons, Maximian; the deacon protested, was excommunicated, and appealed to some neighbouring bishops, who took up his cause and respectfully solicited Primian to give them a hearing or to meet them. Primian declined. In A.D. 393 more than 100 malcontent bishops assembled in synod at Cabarsussis, summoned Primian before them, and, on his again refusing to notice them, recited his misdeeds in an elaborate document, excommunicated him, and elected Maximian, procuring his consecration at Carthage. The Donatists of Carthage, now divided into Primianists and Maximianists, had, in their turn, to experience the misery of altar set up against altar. "God," says St. Augustine, "was repaying to them the measure they had paid to Caecilian." Primian and his party were, however, much the stronger. The bps. of Numidia and Mauritania to the number of 310 sided with him; and at the council of Bagai (A.D. 394), presided over by Primian himself, Maximian was excommunicated, and his ordainers and coadjutors commanded to repent and return to the Primianist party before a certain date. The Maximianists shewed little disposition to acquiesce in this decision, and persecution began. Maximian's church was levelled to the ground and his house handed over to a heathen priest. The proconsul Seranus was asked to assist in carrying out the judgment of the council on the refractory. The Maximianists were hunted from place to place, and the treatment of the aged and beloved bp. of Membresa, Salvius, was scandalous and cruel beyond measure. But few Maximianists, however, returned to the main body; the majority struggled on as martyrs, rebaptizing and reordaining those who joined them. Donatism had received a mortal wound.

The action of the Catholic church and the state during this period further helped to check the extension of Donatism. Many Donatists, priests as well as laymen, disgusted with party squabbles and cruel excesses, turned their eyes to the church. They were met with kindness. In A.D. 393 a council met at Hippo under the presidency of Aurelius, bp. of Carthage. The measures passed were liberal in spirit and intention. They allowed returning Donatist clergy to retain their clerical position and functions, if they had not rebaptized, and if they brought their congregations with them; and decided that children of Donatists, even if they had received Donatist baptism, should not be excluded from the service of the altar.

The action of the state had varied according as political events had directed imperial attention to Donatists or removed it from them. Valentinian's edict (A.D. 373) deposing any clerical person who rebaptized, and Gratian's successive decrees—the first (A.D. 375) commanding the surrender of their churches; the second (A.D. 377) issued to the Donatist, Flavian, the imperial representative in Africa, enjoining further the confiscation of houses used by them; the third (A.D. 378) commanding the expulsion from Rome of one Claudian, who had gone there to propagate Donatist opinions—produced a good deal of misery; but the political disquiet connected with the murder of Gratian (A.D. 383), the wars between Maximus and Theodosius, the deposition of Maximus and restoration of Valentinian (A.D. 388), made it impossible to enforce these or similar injunctions, and for the time the Donatists enjoyed a comparative freedom from interference. In A.D. 392 Theodosius issued his laws against heretics generally, fining all such who performed priestly functions. This was not directed against the Donatists particularly, and was probably not enforced against them previous to the death of Theodosius (A.D. 395). That event was followed by Gildo's usurpation of power in Africa, and his alliance with one of the cruellest Donatist bishops, Optatus of Thamugas. The ravages committed were only stayed by Honorius's victory over Gildo (A.D. 398); and Theodosius's penalty was enforced by Seranus against Optatus and his followers. An edict of Honorius (A.D. 398) decreeing the punishment of death to all who dared to violate churches and maltreat the clergy was evidently directed against the Circumcellions.

Yet the position of the Donatist body was better than that of the Catholic church. The greater part of Africa was Donatist, the church lay crushed and oppressed. Towards the end of the 4th cent. it seemed almost as if the place of the ancient, Catholic, and Apostolic church would be taken by the new usurping sect. Then the good providence of God raised up St. AUGUSTINE, whose piety and ability shielded then and since the true church of Christ. In A.D. 391 he came to Hippo, and the popular vote at once pointed him out as the future successor of the aged Valerius. In A.D. 395 he was consecrated coadjutor-bishop. Hippo was a hot-bed of Donatism. In a letter (*Ep.* 33) to Proculeianus the Donatist bp. of Hippo, St. Augustine pathetically asks, "What has Christ done to us, that we rend His members asunder? Consider how sad a division reigns in Christian households and families. Husband and wife, who—in their married life—know no division, separate themselves at the altar of Christ! Children live with their parents in the same dwelling, but that dwelling is not also God's dwelling." Full of zeal, St. Augustine threw himself into the thick of the fight. His sermons attracted Donatists as well as Catholics, and the sectarians threatened his life; but his works had great effect. Men like Petilian were silenced; priests, laymen, and even whole communities came back to the church. Twice in 401 a council met at Carthage to deal with the supply of Catholic clergy; Donatist enticement or persecution having so reduced their number that many churches had no deacons and therefore no future means for supplying the higher offices. The council at Hippo had imposed restrictions upon Donatist clergy, who returned to the church, exercising their office. An appeal to pope Anastasius to remove these restrictions was allowed. St. Augustine set the example of receiving Donatist-ordained deacons, though apparently he declined to receive again—in an official capacity—those who had previously passed from the church to the sectarians. These measures, though accompanied by loving words of greeting, roused the Donatists. They were still a majority, powerful and persistent. They called to their aid the brutal fanaticism of the Circumcellions, especially against apostate Donatists and the Catholic clergy. Once again fire and sword levelled churches and destroyed altars. St. Augustine was threatened, tracked, and surrounded; Catholic priests were stopped in the road, and the choice offered them: "Promise to preach no more, or prepare for ill-treatment." Moderate-minded men among the Donatists looked on in horror, but were powerless to check the barbarities. The Catholics, before appealing to the state, desired (A.D. 403) a conference. The Donatist bishop, Primian, repelled their advances with insult, saying, "The sons of the martyrs and the brood of traditors can never meet." Equally unsuccessful were attempts of St. Augustine and Possidius to confer with leading Donatist bishops. At last a council at Carthage (A.D. 404) determined to appeal to Honorius to enforce the laws of Theodosius against the Donatists and restrict the excesses of the Circumcellions. But before the deputation reached the emperor, his anger was kindled by accounts from his own officers. The cruelty of the Donatists to two Catholic bishops, Servus and Maximinian of Bagai, made him little disposed to accept the gentler measures proposed by the council of Carthage; and in 405 he issued an edict, fining those who had inflicted ill-usage, and threatening the Donatist bishops and clergy with banishment. In the same year imperial laws forbade rebaptism, condemned the Donatists as heretics, confiscated their meeting-houses and the goods of those who rebaptized, excluded them from testamentary inheritance, and proclaimed to all "that the one and true Catholic faith of Almighty God was to be received." These and similar imperial edicts brought to the church many who had been wavering. The Catholics received them with love and forgiveness; and in some cities, as in Carthage, union between Catholics and Donatists was openly asserted and celebrated. But these edicts exasperated still further the more extreme Donatists. St. Augustine's own city, Hippo, and its neighbourhood suffered fearfully from the Circumcellions. In A.D. 409 St. Augustine complained bitterly (*Ep.* 111) of their plundering and ravages, their revengeful acts and cruelties to the Catholic bishops and laity. Letters to Donatist bishops or to imperial commissioners were of little use when the men to whom they referred would slay themselves if balked of their prey, or cast themselves into the fires they themselves had kindled. They heard of Stilicho's death (A.D. 408). Rightly or wrongly they had considered him the originator of the stern decrees lately issued, and hailed the news by joining with heathen in slaying, ill-using, or putting to flight the hated Catholic bishops. Fresh deputations went to Rome; St. Augustine wrote letters to the chief minister Olympius; and fresh edicts, enforcing previous laws, fines, and punishments, were sent to Africa.

About this time St. Augustine issued other works which throw much light on the Donatist controversy: (*a*) *On the One Baptism*, written between A.D. 406 and 411, an answer to a tract of Petilian's bearing the same title. (*b*) *Against Cresconius*, written A.D. 409. Cresconius objected to his party being called Donatists: "Not Donatus, but Christ was their founder. It was not heresy but schism which separated them and the Catholic church"; and Cresconius claimed that it was not they who were in schism, but the Catholics, who thereby had lost church and baptism.

The invasion of Rome by Alaric king of the Goths took place A.D. 408, and it was rumoured that the Donatists of Africa were ready to support the invader. The emperor Honorius rescinded his extreme decrees against heathen and schismatic; but in 410 a deputation of 4 bishops from Carthage again brought complaints against the Donatists to him. The deputation was charged to petition for a conference of Catholics and Donatists under imperial presidency. In Oct. 410 Honorius instructed the proconsul of Africa, Marcellinus, to make all necessary preparations and act as president at the debates. He issued an edict (Jan. 411) inviting Catholic and Donatist bishops to meet in June at Carthage and elect representatives, promising safe-conduct and suspending meanwhile all processes against Donatists. Both parties entered eagerly into the scheme: 286 Catholic and 279 Donatist bishops came to Carthage in May; and, after great difficulty in bringing the Donatists to the point, the president pronounced sentence. The official Acts and the testimony of Holy

Scripture were taken to have proved the unsoundness of the accusations against Caecilian, and of the view that one man, through the sinfulness of another, became therefore a partaker in that other's guilt. "I therefore," said Marcellinus, "warn all men . . . to hinder the assembling of Donatists in towns and villages, and to restore the churches to the Catholics. Every bishop of the community of Donatus must, on his return to his home, return to the one true church, or at least not impede the faithful execution of the law. If they have Circumcellions about them, and do not restrain and repress the excesses of these men, they shall be deprived of their places in the state."

The condemned Donatists, among whom were the principal bishops, smarting at their defeat, reviled Marcellinus and appealed to the emperor. The reply came (A.D. 412), terse and stern, and classed them as heretics. It bade them return to the church, fined them according to their rank and station, and in the event of contumacy confiscated their houses and goods. Many Donatists obeyed the edict, others scorned it. Whole communities, as at Cirta, bishops and laymen everywhere, returned to the church; some from conviction, others for reasons of expediency and comfort. The Circumcellions broke out afresh, fired churches, destroyed houses, cast into the flames those Scriptures which had been found to tell against them, and cruelly maltreated and even murdered ecclesiastics who expounded them. The less violent proclaimed with a sneer that the church chests and imperial coffers were enriched with the gold of the Separatists, and pointed to the death of Marcellinus (A.D. 413) as a divine judgment upon their unrighteous judge. In A.D. 414 a yet sterner decree announced that all Donatist church-buildings were to become the property of the Catholic church, and all Donatist clergy to be suspended and banished. Fines were doubled; confiscation and banishment stared the Separatists in the face; their testimony in courts of law was disallowed; their social condition was degraded to the lowest; that the penalties stopped short of death was owing chiefly to St. Augustine, who strove successfully to prevent others from imbruing their hands with the blood of mistaken fanatics. The church, to its credit be it recorded, by kindness and gentleness made the pain of defeat less bitter to its foes, while it did not neglect to avail itself of the advantages resulting from victory. As the Catholic bishops returned to their homes they spread everywhere the news of the victory, and in the following Lent publicly proclaimed it in their churches. Short summaries of the acts and judgment of the conference were circulated, one being by St. Augustine himself. These were intended principally for Catholics; others, as St. Augustine's "*ad Donatistas post collectionem*," were addressed to the sectarians who might be swayed by one-sided reports circulated by Donatist bishops, or by their slanderous abuse of Marcellinus and the Catholics. In 418 a council at Carthage passed resolutions regulating the proceedings, when Donatist bishops, clergy, and congregations came back to the church. Nothing could prove more clearly to what a large extent this had taken place. The church was no longer suppliant, but triumphant; and the change is observable also in some letters and acts of St. Augustine at this period, which may be said to be his last words on the great Donatist controversy. His work *de Correctione Donatistarum* is addressed to a soldier, Bonifacius, and is written in a style and language almost military in its stern enforcement of discipline. Bonifacius had asked the difference between the Arians and Donatists. St. Augustine, after answering the question, went on to speak of Donatists as "rebels against the unity of the church of Christ." The conference at Carthage and the emperor had laid down laws which they disobeyed, and thus deserved punishment (Dan. iii. 29). The Lord had commanded His disciples to compel the resisting to come to the marriage-feast, and that marriage-feast was the unity of the Body of Christ. The church was that Body; so long as a man lived, God in His goodness would bring him to repentance, and lead him to that church, which was the temple of the Holy Ghost; but outside that Body, the Church, the Holy Ghost gave no man life. The same strong statement recurs in his exhortation to Emeritus, the Donatist bp. of Caesarea. The majority of Emeritus's congregation had returned to the church. St. Augustine pleaded with the bishop: "Outside the church you may have everything except salvation. You may have offices, Sacraments, Liturgy, Gospel, belief, and preaching, in the name of the Trinity; but you can only find salvation in the Catholic Church."

The last letters of St. Augustine were addressed to a Donatist bishop Gaudentius. Marcellinus had been succeeded by Dulcitius, who endeavoured to carry out the strong laws against the Donatists with all possible mildness, and specially interested himself in restraining the fanaticism of the Circumcellions. Unfortunately, some words of his were taken to mean that he would punish them with death unless they returned to the church. Gaudentius and his congregation assembled in their church, determined to set fire to it and perish in the flames. Dulcitius contrived to stop this by a letter to Gaudentius, who in two letters defended his proposed action and the views of his party. Dulcitius appealed to St. Augustine, who answered Gaudentius's arguments. His work, *contra Gaudentium*, in two books, goes over the old ground, also exposing the folly and crime of suicide.

Donatism had now lived its life. No new champions appeared to defend it, and once again only did the schism lift up its head. Towards the end of the 6th cent. there was a momentary revival of energy and proselytism; but popes such as Leo and Gregory the Great and imperial laws were irresistible. The movement died out. The Donatists lingered on till the invasion of Africa by the Mahommedans swept them away or merged them into some other schismatical body.

See Optatus, ed. *Alba Spinaeus* (Par. 1631), or ed. Dupin (Antw. 1702); S. Augustini, *Opera*, vol. vii. (Par. ed. 1635); Vogel, "Donatisten" in Herzog's *Real-Encyclop.*; Hefele, do. in Wetzer's *Kirchenlexicon* and *Concil-Geschichte*;

Neander, *Church History*, iii. 258, etc. ed. Bohn; Niedner, *Lehrbuch d. Christlichen Kirchengeschichte*, 324; Robertson, *Hist. of the Christian Church*, i. 175, etc.; Hagenbach, *Kirchengeschichte*, i. 547; Ribbeck, *Donatus und Augustinus* (1858); M. Deutsch, *Drei Actenstücke zur Geschichte der Donatismus* (Berlin, 1875); Harnack, *Dog. Gesch.* (3rd. ed.) iii. 36 ff.; Thomasius, *Dog. Gesch.* (2nd ed.) i. 606 ff. [J.M.F.]

Dorothea, virgin, martyred with Theophilus the Advocate, and two other women, Christa and Callista, at Caesarea, in Cappadocia. Some doubt is entertained about these names, as they occur in no Greek menology or martyrology; but they are found in ancient Roman accounts; and details are given by the monk Usuard, bp. Ado, and Rabanus. They are celebrated on Feb. 6. Baronius, Bollandus, and Tillemont all place the death of Dorothea in the persecution of Diocletian.

She was a young girl of Caesarea in Cappadocia, famed so widely for Christian piety that when the governor Fabricius, Sapricius, or Apricius arrived he had her brought before him and tortured. Unable to persuade her to marry, he sent her to Christa and Callista that they might induce her to give up her faith. She converted them; whereupon the governor put them to death in a boiling cauldron.

Dorothea was again tortured, and shewed her joy for the martyrdom of Christa and Callista and for her own sufferings. The governor, insulted and enraged, ordered her head to be cut off. On her way to execution an advocate named Theophilus laughingly asked her to send him some apples and roses from the paradise of her heavenly bridegroom. The legend states that these were miraculously conveyed to him, although Cappadocia was then covered with snow. Theophilus was converted, tortured, and decapitated.

Dorothea's body is said to have been taken to Rome, and preserved in the church across the Tiber which bears her name. On her festival there is a ceremony of blessing roses and apples. Migne, *Dict. Hagiograph.* i. 779; Bollandus, *Acta Sanct.* Feb. i. p. 771; Tillem. *Hist. eccl.* p. 497 (Paris, 1702). [W.M.S.]

Dorotheus (3), a presbyter of Antioch, ordained by Cyril of Antioch (Hieron. *Chron.*) c. A.D. 290, who with his contemporary Lucian may be regarded as the progenitor of the sound and healthy school of scriptural hermeneutics which distinguished the interpreters of Antioch from those of Alexandria. Eusebius speaks of him with high commendation, as distinguished by a pure taste and sound learning, of a wide and liberal education, well acquainted not only with the Hebrew Scriptures, which Eusebius says he had heard him expounding in the church at Antioch, with moderation (μετρίως), but also with classical literature. He was a congenital eunuch, which commended him to the notice of the emperor Constantine, who placed him at the head of the purple-dye-house at Tyre Eus. *H. E.* vii. 32; Neander, *Eccl. Hist.* vol. ii. p. 528, Clark's trans.; Gieseler, *Eccl. Hist.* vol. i. p. 247, Clark's trans. [E.V.]

Dorotheus (7), bp. of Martianopolis in Moesia Secunda, and metropolitan; a zealous supporter of the doctrines of Nesturios, and a determined enemy of the title θεοτόκος. Preaching in Constantinople not long before the council of Ephesus, he declared that "if any one asserted that Mary was the mother of God he was anathema" (*Ep. Cyrill.* ap. Baluz. *Concil.* col. 402). He attended that council, A.D. 431, signing the appeal to the emperor against the dominant party (Baluz. 701), and joining in the documents warning the clergy and people of Hierapolis and Constantinople against the errors of Cyril, and announcing Cyril's excommunication (*ib.* 706, 725). He was deposed and excommunicated by Cyril and his friends. This deposition being confirmed by the imperial power, he was ordered by Maximinian's synod at Constantinople to be ejected from his city and throne. His influence, however, with his people was so great that they refused to receive his successor Secundianus, and drove him from the city (*Ep. Doroth. ad Cyrill.* Baluz. 750), whereupon Dorotheus was banished by the emperor to Caesarea in Cappadocia. Two letters of his to John of Antioch are preserved in the *Synodicon* (Nos. 78, 115; Baluz. 781, 816), expressing his anxiety at Paul's setting out to Egypt and his distress at hearing that terms had been come to with Cyril, and a third (No. 137; Baluz. 840) to Alexander of Hierapolis and Theodoret, proposing a joint appeal to the emperor. [E.V.]

Dorotheus (10), bp. of Thessalonica 515-520. He wrote on April 28, 515, to pope Hormisdas, urging him to labour for the peace of the church. He testifies respect for the see of Rome, and wishes to see the heresies of Nestorius and Eutyches everywhere condemned.

But in the spring of 517 we find him a Eutychian schismatic, seeking to exercise over the province of Thessalonica the rights which belonged to its metropolis when in communion with the Catholic church. He persecuted John bp. of Nicopolis, employing the secular arm and persuading the emperor Anastasius to support his faction. Complaints were brought to pope Hormisdas, who pointed out that he might regain his rights if he rejoined the Catholic church; but the papal legates Ennodius and Peregrinus were to bring the affair before the emperor, if bp. Dorotheus should persist. The emperor Anastasius refused the message of the legates, tried to corrupt them, and wrote to the pope saying that he could suffer insults, but not commands (July 11, 517). The death of the emperor almost exactly a year afterwards altered the balance against the Eutychians. Justin I., the Thracian, wrote, on his accession, to the pope, expressing his own wish and that of the principal Eastern bishops for the restoration of peace between East and West. Hormisdas, with the advice of king Theodoric, sent a third legation to Constantinople, Germanus bp. of Capua, John a bishop, Blandus a presbyter, and others. To these men at Constantinople Hormisdas wrote to inquire personally into the doings of the Eutychians at Thessalonica, and to cite bp. Dorotheus and his abettor Aristides the presbyter to Rome, that they might give account of their faith and receive resolution of their doubts. Two days before the arrival of the legates, Dorotheus baptized more than 2,000 people, and distributed the Eucharistic bread in large baskets, so that multitudes could keep it by them. On their arrival, the populace of Thessalonica, excited, as the legates thought, by Dorotheus, fell upon them, and killed John, a Catholic, who had received them in his house. News of these outrages arriving at Constantinople, the emperor Justin promised to summon Dorotheus before him. The pope wrote to his legates, saying that they must see Dorotheus deposed, and take care that Aristides should not be his successor. Dorotheus was cited before the emperor at Heraclea; he appealed to Rome, but the emperor thought it unadvisable to send him there, as his accusers would not be present. He was suddenly sent away from Heraclea, and the pope's legates, bp. John and the presbyter Epiphanius, who had remained at Thessalonica in his absence, wrote in alarm to the remaining legates at Constantinople lest Dorotheus and others should re-establish themselves in their sees by liberal use of money.

Dorotheus was now obliged by the emperor to send deputies to Rome to satisfy the pope. He accordingly wrote an agreeable letter, saying that he had exposed his life in defence of bp. John, when the populace had fallen upon him. Pope Hormisdas wrote back, saying that the crime was known to all the world, and required clearer defence; he remitted its examination to the patriarch of Constantinople. Hormisd. *Epp.*, *Patr. Lat.* lxiii. pp. 371, 372, 408, 445, 446, 452, 468, 473, 481, 499, etc.; Ceillier, x. 616, 618, 619, 625 626, 628, 632, 633. [W.M.S.]

Dositheus (1). The earliest ecclesiastical writers speak of a sect of Dositheans, which, though it never spread far outside Samaria, seems to have had some considerable duration in that quarter. It was rather a Jewish sect than a Christian heresy, for Dositheus was regarded rather as a rival than as a disciple of our Lord, but trustworthy information as to his history and his doctrines is very scanty. Only the name of himself and his sect occurs in Hegesippus's list of heresies, preserved by Eusebius (*H. E.* iv. 22). He is there placed next after Simon and Cleobius. The earliest detailed account of him is given in the Clementine writings, and it is not unlikely that their account was derived from the treatise on heresies of Justin Martyr. The *Recognitions* (ii. 8) and *Homilies* (ii. 24) agree in making Simon Magus a disciple of Dositheus, and the *Recognitions* would lead us to suppose that Dositheus was clearly the elder. They represent him as already recognised as the prophet like unto Moses, whom Jehovah was to raise up; when Simon with difficulty and entreaty obtained election among his 30 disciples. The *Homilies* make Simon and Dositheus fellow-disciples of John the Baptist, to whom in several places the author shews hostility. As our Lord, the Sun, had 12 apostles, so John, the Moon, had 30 disciples, or even more accurately answering to the days of a lunation, 29½, for one of them was a woman. On John's death Simon was absent studying magic in Egypt, and so Dositheus was put over his head into the chief place, an arrangement in which Simon on his return thought it prudent to acquiesce. Origen, who was acquainted with the *Recognitions*, probably had in his mind the story of the 30 disciples of Dositheus, when he says (*contra Celsum*, vi. 11) that he doubts whether there were then 30 Dositheans in the world (*ib.* i. 57) or 30 Simonians. *Recognitions* and *Homilies* agree that Simon after his enrolment among the disciples of Dositheus, by his disparagement among his fellow-disciples of their master's pretensions, provoked Dositheus to smite him with a staff, which through Simon's magical art passed through his body as if it had been smoke. Dositheus in amazement thereat, and conscious that he himself was not the Standing one as he pretended to be, inquired if Simon claimed that dignity for himself, and, being answered in the affirmative, resigned his chief place to him and became his worshipper. Soon after he died. Elsewhere (i. 54) the *Recognitions* represent Dositheus as the founder of the sect of the Sadducees, a sect which, according to their account, had its commencement only in the days of John the Baptist.

Next in order of the early witnesses to the activity of Dositheus is Hippolytus, who, as we learn from Photius (*Cod.* 121), commenced his shorter treatise on heresies with a section on the Dositheans. We gather the contents of this treatise from Epiphanius (*Haer.* 13), Philaster (4), and Pseudo-Tertullian, and the opening sentence of the latter, which relates to the Dositheans, is almost exactly reproduced by St. Jerome (*adv. Luciferianos*, iv. 304). The first section of the work of Hippolytus apparently contained a brief notice of pre-Christian sects, the foremost place being given to the Dositheans. Hippolytus seems to have adopted the account of the *Recognitions* as to the origin of the sect of the Sadducees, and to have also charged Dositheus with rejecting the inspiration of the prophets. A statement that Dositheus was a Jew by birth was understood by Epiphanius to mean that he had deserted from the Jews to the Samaritans, a change which Epiphanius attributes to disappointed ambition. Origen mentions Dositheus in several places (*cont. Celsum u.s.*, tract 27 in Matt. vol. iii. 851; in Luc. iii. 962; in Johann. iv. vol. iv. p. 237; *de Princ.* iv. 1-17); but only in the last two passages makes any statement which clearly shews that he had sources of information independent of the Clementine *Recognitions*; viz. in the commentary on John he speaks of books ascribed to Dositheus as being then current among his disciples, and of their belief that their master had not really died; and in *de Princ.* he asserts that Dositheus expounded Exod. xvi. 29 so as to teach that persons were bound to remain to the end of the sabbath as they found themselves at the beginning of it; if sitting, sitting to the end; if lying, lying, Epiphanius, who may have read Dosithean books, adds, from his personal investigations. to the details which he found in Hippolytus. He describes the sect as still existing, observing the Sabbath, circumcision, and other Jewish ordinances, abstaining from animal food, and many of them from sexual intercourse either altogether, or at least after having had children; but the reading here is uncertain. They are said to have admitted the resurrection of the body, the denial of which is represented as an addition made by the Sadducees to the original teaching of Dositheus. Epiphanius adds a story that Dositheus retired to a cave, and there, under a show of piety, practised such abstinence from food and drink as to bring his life to a voluntary end. This story appears, in a slightly different shape, in a Samaritan chronicle, of which an account is given by Abraham Ecchellensis ad *Hebed Jesu, Catal. lib. Chald.* p. 162, Rom. 1653, the story there being that it was the measures taken by the Samaritan high-priest against the new sect, especially because of their use of a book of the law falsified by Dositheus (there called Dousis), which compelled Dositheus to flee to a mountain, where he died from want of food in a cave. The notes of Ecchellensis are not given in Assemani's republication of Hebed Jesu (*Bibl. Or.* iii.). This account is taken from Mosheim (*v. infra*), and from De Sacy's *Chrestomathie Arabe*, i. 337.

It appears that the sect of Dositheans long maintained a local existence. In Hebed Jesu's catalogue of Chaldee books (Assemani, *Bibl. Or.* iii. 42) we read that Theophilus of Persia, who was later than the council of Ephesus, wrote against Dositheus. And Photius (*Cod.* 230) reports that he read among the works of Eulogius, patriarch of Alexandria (*d.* A.D. 608), one entitled *Definition against the Samaritans*, the argument of which is that the people of Samaria being divided in opinion as to whether the "prophet like unto Moses" was Joshua or Dositheus, Eulogius held a synod there (in the 7th year of Marcianus according to the MSS.; if we correct this to the 7th year of Maurice, it gives A.D. 588) and taught them the divinity of our Lord. The independent notices of the continued existence of the sect make it not incredible that Eulogius may have encountered it. He appears to have really used Dosithean books, and reports that Dositheus exhibited particular hostility to the patriarch Judah, and if he claimed to be himself the prophet who was to come, he would naturally be anxious to exclude the belief that that prophet must be of the tribe of Judah. The form (Dosthes) given by Eulogius for his name is a closer approach than Dositheus to the Hebrew Dosthai, which it probably really represents. Drusius (*de Sectis Hebraeorum*, iii. 4, 6) and Lightfoot (*Disquis. Chorograph. in* Johann. iv.) shew that this was, according to Jewish tradition, the name of one of the priests who was sent (II. Kings xvii. 27) to teach the manner of the God of the land, and that the same name was borne by other Samaritans.

There seems no ground for Reland's conjecture (*de Samaritanis*, v.) that Dositheus was the author of the Samaritan book of Joshua, since published by Juynboll (Leyden, 1848). Juynboll, p. 113, quotes the testimony of an Arabic writer, Aboulfatah (given more fully, De Sacy, p. 335), that the sect still existed in the 14th cent. This writer places Dositheus in the time of John Hyrcanus, *i.e.* more than a hundred years before Christ. Jost (*Gesch. des Judenthums*, i. 66) refers to Beer (*Buch der Jubiläen*) as giving evidence that the sect left traces in Abyssinia. Several critics who have wished to accept all the statements of the above-mentioned authorities, and who have felt the difficulty of making the founder of the sect of the Sadducees contemporary with John the Baptist, have adopted the solution that there must have been two Dosithei, both founders of Samaritan sects. But we may safely say that there was but one sect of Dositheans, and that there is no evidence that any ancient writer believed that it had at different times two heads bearing the same name. Considering that the sect claimed to have been more than a century old when our earliest informants tried to get information about its founder, we need not be surprised if the stories which they collected contain many things legendary, and which do not harmonise. Probably the Dositheans were a Jewish or Samaritan ascetic sect, something akin to the Essenes, existing from before our Lord's time, and the stories connecting their founder with Simon Magus and with John the Baptist may be dismissed as merely mythical. The fullest and ablest dissertation on the Dositheans is that by Mosheim (*Institutiones Historiae Christianae majores*, 1739, i. 376). Cf. Harnack, *Gesch. der Alt.-Chr. Lit. Theol.* pp. 152 f. [G.S.]

Dubhthach (*Duach*) (3), Mac Ui Lugair. When St. Patrick had come to Tara and was preaching before king Leogaire, we are told that the only one who rose on the saint's approach and respectfully saluted him was Dubhthach, the king's poet, who was the first to embrace the Christian faith in that place; and as Joceline says, "being baptized and confirmed in the faith, he turned his poetry, which in the flower and prime of his studies he employed in praise of false gods, to a much better use; changing his mind and style, he composed more elegant poems in praise of the Almighty Creator and His holy preachers." This was Dubhthach Mac Ui Lugair, descended from Cormach Caech, son of Cucorb, in Leinster. His name occupies a large space in ancient Irish hagiology as a famous poet and the ancestor of many well-known saints. He was the teacher of St. Fiacc (Oct. 12) of Sletty, and recommended him to St. Patrick for the episcopate. [FIACC.] In the compilation of the Seanchus Mor, said to have been carried on under the auspices of St. Patrick, St. Dubhthach was one of the nine appointed to revise the ancient laws. Colgan says he had in his possession some of the poems of St. Dubhthach (*Tr. Thaum.* 8 n5.): the *Poems of St. Dubhthach* are given in O'Donovan's *Book of Rights*, and with translations and notes in Shearman's *Loca Patriciana*. His dates are uncertain, but his birth is placed after 370, his conversion in 433, and his death perhaps after 479. See *Loca Patriciana*, by the Rev. J. F. Shearman, in *Journ. Roy. Hist. and Arch. Assoc. Ir.* 4 ser. vols. ii. iii., with Mr. R. R. Brash's papers in the same Journal, traversing several of Shearman's assertions; Ware, *Irish Writers*, 1; Ussher, *Eccl. Ant.* c. 17, wks. vi. 409-412, and *Ind. Chron.* A.D. 433; Todd, *St. Patrick*, 130, 424, 446. [J.G.]

Dubricius, Dubric (*Dibric, Dyfrig*), arch-bp. of Caerleon, one of the most distinguished names in the story of king Arthur as related by Geoffrey of Monmouth. Arthur makes him archbp. of the city of Legions (Galf. *Mon. Hist.* viii. 12); he crowns king Arthur (ix. 1);

makes an oration to the British army prior to the battle of Badon (ix. 4); and is the director of all the ecclesiastical pomp of the court. He was grandson of Brychan king of Brecknockshire, and two localities, vaguely described as the banks of the Gwain near Fishguard and the banks of the Wye in Herefordshire, are claimed for his birthplace. Rees decides in favour of the latter for the following reasons. In the district of Erchenfield, in the county of Hereford, are a church (Whitchurch) and two chapels (Ballingham and Hentland, subject to Lugwardine) dedicated to Dubricius, and all of them near the Wye. At Henllan (*i.e.* Old-church, now Hentland) he is said to have founded a college, and to have remained seven years before removing to Mochros much farther up the Wye, supposed to be the present Moccas. In corroboration of this tradition there were lately remaining, says Rees, on a farm called Lanfrother in Hentland, traces of former importance. This author further suggests that St. Devereux, seven miles to the west of Hereford, might be a Norman rendering of Dubricius. Rees grants, in support of Ussher, that he may have been appointed bp. of Llandaff about A.D. 470, and that he was raised by Ambrosius Aurelius, the brother of Uther and uncle of Arthur, to the archbishopric of Caerleon on the death of Tremounos or Tremorius, A.D. 490. It does not appear that Wales was then divided into dioceses, or that there were any established bishops' sees except Caerleon. The jurisdiction of its archbishop, according to the rule observable elsewhere in the empire, would be co-extensive with the Roman province of Britannia Secunda, and his suffragans were so many chorepiscopi, without any settled places of residence. The influence of Dubricius and the liberality of Meurig ab Tewdrig king of Glamorgan made the see of Llandaff permanent; whence Dubricius is said to have been its first bishop. It appears, however, that after promotion to the archbishopric of Caerleon he still retained the bishopric of Llandaff, where he mostly resided, and from which he is called archbishop of Llandaff; but that the title belonged rather to Caerleon is clear since upon his resignation David became archbp. of Caerleon and Teilo bp. of Llandaff. Dubricius is distinguished as the founder of colleges; and besides those on the banks of the Wye already mentioned he founded, or concurred in founding, the collegiate monasteries of Llancarvan, Caergorworn, and Caerleon. In his time the Pelagian heresy, which had been once suppressed by St. Germanus, had increased again to such a degree as to require extraordinary efforts for its eradication, and a synod of the whole clergy of Wales was convened at Brefi in Cardiganshire. The distinction earned by David on that occasion gave Dubricius an excuse for laying down his office, and, worn with years and longing for retirement, he withdrew to a monastery in the island of Enlli or Bardsey, where he died. Rees, who puts the chronology of Dubricius and David early, gives A.D. 522 for the date. He was buried in the island, where his remains lay undisturbed till A.D. 1120, when they were removed by Urban bp. of Llandaff and interred with great pomp in the new cathedral which had been rebuilt a short time before. His death was commemorated on Nov. 4, and his translation on May 29. The bones of the saint were with great difficulty discovered at Bardsey, the oldest writings having to be searched, as recorded in the *Liber Landavensis* (ed. Rees, 1840, p. 329). Such in the main is Rees's account of Dubricius (*Essay on the Welsh Saints*, 171-193). Of ancient materials an anonymous *Vita* in Wharton (*Angl. Sac.* ii. 667) is important as having been evidently compiled from earlier sources before the fables of Geoffrey of Monmouth appeared. Benedict of Gloucester wrote his *Vita* (*Angl. Sac.* ii. 656) after Geoffrey. Capgrave has also a Life (*N. L. A.* f. 87). For others see Hardy, *Des. Cat.* i. 40-44. Haddan and Stubbs, *Councils*, i. 146, 147, should be consulted on Dubricius's Llandaff bishopric, and on his connexion with Archenfield or Erchenfield; likewise Stubbs (*Registrum*, 154, 155) for the early and legendary successions to Llandaff and Caerleon. See also Ussher, *Brit. Eccl. Antiq.* Works, t. v. 510; Chron. Index, sub ann. 490, 512, 520-522. In regard to the period of Dubricius, authorities differ within limits similar to those assigned to St. David. The *Annales Cambriae* under A.D. 612 give the obit of Conthigirnus and bp. Dibric, whom the editors of the *Monumenta*, with an "ut videtur," name bps. Kentigern and Dubricius (M. H. B. 831). The *Liber Landavensis* also (80) gives this date, and it is adopted in Haddan and Stubbs (i. 146). Hardy (*Des. Cat.* i. 41) refers to Alford's *Annales*, A.D. 436, ss. 2, 3, 4, for some critical remarks on the probable chronology of the life of Dubricius. [C.H.]

E

Ebionism and **Ebionites.** The name Ebionite first occurs in Irenaeus (*c.* 180-190). It was repeated, probably from him, by Hippolytus (*c.* 225-235) and Origen († A.D. 254), who first introduced an explanation of the name. Others offered different explanations (*e.g.* Eus. † *c.* 340); while other writers fabricated a leader, "Ebion," after whom the sect was called (cf. Philastrius, Pseudo-Tertullian, Pseudo-Jerome, Isidore of Spain, etc.).

These explanations owe their origin to the tendency to carry back Ebionism, or the date of its founder, as far as possible. Thus the "Ebionite" was (according to his own statement) the "poor" man (אֶבְיוֹן), he who voluntarily strove to practise the Master's precept (Matt. x. 9) in Apostolic times (Acts iv. 34-37; cf. Epiphanius, *Haer.* xxx. c. 17); and the correctness of the etymology is not shaken by the Patristic scorn which derived the name from "poverty of intellect," or from "low and mean opinions of Christ" (see Eus. *H. E.* iii. 27; Origen, *de Princ.*, and *contr. Cel.* ii. c. 4; Ignat., *Ep. ad Philadelph.* c. 6, longer recension). "Ebion," first personified by Tertullian, was said to have been a pupil of Cerinthus, and the Gospel of St. John to have been directed against them both. St. Paul and St. Luke were asserted to have spoken and written against Ebionites. The "Apostolical Constitutions" (vi. c. 6) traced them back to Apostolic times; Theodoret (*Haer. Fab.* ii. c. 2) assigned them to the reign of Domitian (A.D. 81-96). The existence of an "Ebion" is, however, now surrendered. Ebionism, like Gnosticism, had no special founder; but that its birthplace was the Holy Land, and its existence contemporary with the beginning of the Christian Church, is, with certain reservations, probably correct. A tendency to Ebionism existed from the first; gradually it assumed shape, and as gradually developed into the two special forms presently to be noticed.

The records of the church of Jerusalem contained in *Acts* prove how strong was the zeal for the Law of Moses among the Jewish converts to Christianity. After the fall of Jerusalem (A.D. 70), the church was formed at Pella under Symeon, and the Jewish Christians were brought face to face with two leading facts: firstly, that the temple being destroyed, and the observance of the Law and its ordinances possible only in part, there was valid reason for doubting the necessity of retaining the rest; secondly, that if they adopted this view, they must expect to find in the Jews their most uncompromising enemies. As Christians they had expected a judgment predicted by Christ, and, following His advice, had fled from the city. Both prediction and act were resented by the Jews, as is shewn not only by the contemptuous term (Minim) they applied to the Jewish Christians (Grätz, *Gesch. d. Juden.* iv. p. 89, etc.), but by the share they took in the death of the aged bp. Symeon (A.D. 106). The breach was further widened by the refusal of the Jewish Christians to take part in the national struggles—notably that of Bar-Cocheba (A.D. 132)—against the Romans, by the tortures they suffered for their refusal, and lastly, by the erection of Aelia Capitolina (A.D. 138) on the ruins of Jerusalem. The Jews were forbidden to enter it, while the Jewish and Gentile Christians who crowded there read in Hadrian's imperial decree the abolition of the most distinctively Jewish rites, and practically signified their assent by electing as their bishop a Gentile and uncircumcised man—Mark (Eus. *H. E.* iv. 6). Changes hitherto working gradually now rapidly developed. Jewish Christians, with predilections for Gentile Christianity and its comparative freedom, found the way made clear to them; others, attempting to be both Jews and Christians, ended in being neither, and exposed themselves to the contempt of Rabbin as well as Christian (Grätz, p. 433); others receded farther from Christianity, and approximated more and more closely to pure Judaism. The Ebionites are to be ranked among the last. By the time of Trajan (96-117) political events had given them a definite organization, and their position as a sect opposed to Gentile Christianity became fixed by the acts which culminated in the erection of Aelia Capitolina.

The Ebionites were known by other names, such as "Homuncionites" (Gk. "Anthropians" or "Anthropolatrians") from their Christological views, "Peratici" from their settlement at Peraea, and "Symmachians" from the one able literary man among them whose name has reached us. [SYMMACHUS (2).] Acquaintance with Hebrew was then confined to a few, and his Greek version of O.T. was produced for the benefit of those who declined the LXX adopted by the orthodox Christians, or the Greek versions of Aquila and Theodotion accepted by the Jews. Many, if not most, of the improvements made by the Vulgate on the LXX are due to the Ebionite version (Field, *Origenis Hexaplarum quae supersunt*, Preface).

Ebionism presents itself under two principal types, an earlier and a later, the former usually designated Ebionism proper or Pharisaic Ebionism, the latter, Essene or Gnostic Ebionism. The earlier type is to be traced in the writings of Justin Martyr, Irenaeus, Hippolytus, Tertullian, etc.; the latter in those of Epiphanius especially.

(*a*) *Ebionism Proper.*—The term expresses conveniently the opinions and practices of the descendants of the Judaizers of the Apostolic age, and is very little removed from Judaism. Judaism was to them not so much a preparation for Christianity as an institution eternally good in itself, and but slightly modified in Christianity. Whatever merit Christianity had, it possessed as the continuation and supplement of Judaism. The divinity of the Old Covenant was the only valid guarantee for the truth of the New. Hence such Ebionites tended to exalt the Old at the expense of the New, to magnify Moses and the Prophets, and to allow Jesus Christ to be "nothing more than a Solomon or a Jonas" (Tertull. *de Carne Christi*, c. 18). Legal righteousness was to them the highest type of perfection; the earthly Jerusalem, in spite of its destruction, was an object of adoration "as if it were the house of God" (Iren. *adv. Haer.* i. c. 22 [*al.* c. 26]); its restoration would take place in the millennial kingdom of Messiah, and the Jews would return there as the manifestly chosen people of God. The Ebionites divided the life of Jesus Christ into two parts—one preceding, the other following, His Baptism. In common with Cerinthus and Carpocrates, they represented Him to have been "the Son of Joseph and Mary according to the ordinary course of human generation" (Iren. *l.c.*). They denied His birth of a Virgin, translating the original word in Isa. vii. 14 not παρθένος, but νεᾶνις. He was "a mere man, nothing more than a descendant of David, and not also the Son of God" (Tert. c. 14). But at His Baptism a great change took place. The event is described in the "Gospel according to the Hebrews" current among them, and the description is an altered expansion of the record of St. Matthew (iii. 13, 14). The Voice from heaven spake not only the words recorded by the Evangelist, but also the words, "This day have I begotten Thee" (Ps. ii. 7). A great light suddenly filled the place. John the Baptist asked, "Who art Thou, Lord?" and the Voice answered as before. John prostrated himself at the feet of Jesus, "I pray Thee, Lord, baptize me," but Jesus forbade him, saying, "Suffer it to be so," etc., etc. (Epiph. *Haer.* xxx. 13). The day of Baptism was thus the day of His "anointing by election and then becoming Christ" (cf. Justin Martyr. *Dial. c. Tryph.* c. xlix.), it was the turning-point in the life of Jesus: from that moment He was endued with power necessary to fill His mission as Messiah; but He was still man. The Ebionites knew nothing of either pre-existence or divinity in connexion with Him. They are said to have freed themselves from the common Jewish notion that the Messiah was to be an earthly king; they were not shocked, as were so many of the Jews, at the humbleness of the birth, the sufferings, and crucifixion of Jesus; but they agreed with them in looking upon the advent of Messiah as future, and in deferring the restitution of all things to the millennium. The Ebionites proper insisted that the Law should be strictly observed not only by themselves but by all. They quoted the words of Jesus (Matt. v. 17), and pointed to His practice (cf. Matt. xxvi. 55; John vii. 14, etc.). It was the natural tendency of this view to diminish the value of *faith* in Christ and a corresponding life. Of far greater moment to them, and as necessary to salvation, was the due observance of circumcision, the sabbath, the distinction between clean and unclean food, the sacrificial offerings—probably with the later Pharisaic additions (cf. Eus. *H.E.* vi. 17)—and the refusal of fellowship or hospitality to the Gentiles (cf. Justin, c. xlvii.). They even quoted the words of Jesus (Matt. x. 24, 25) as their warrant, and affirmed their motto to be: "We also would be imitators of Christ" (Origen, quoted by Schliemann). Jesus, they asserted, "was justified by fulfilling the Law. He was the Christ of God, since not one of the rest of mankind had observed the Law completely. Had any one else fulfilled the commandments of the Law, he would have been the Christ." Hence "when Ebionites thus fulfil the law, they are able to become Christs" (Hippolytus, *Refut. Omn. Haer.* vii. 34).

As might be expected, the Apostle Paul was especially hateful to them. They repudiated his official character, they reviled him personally. In language which recalls that of the Judaizers alluded to in *Corinthians* and *Galatians*, they represented him as a teacher directly opposed to SS. Peter, James, and John; they repudiated his Apostolical authority because (as they affirmed) he had not been "called of Jesus Christ Himself," nor trained in the Church of Jerusalem. They twisted into a defamatory application to himself his employment of the term "deceiver" (II. Cor. vi. 8); he was himself one of the "many which corrupted the word of God" (ii. 17); he proclaimed "deliverance from the Law" only "to please men" (Gal. i. 10) and "commend himself" (II. Cor. iii. 1). His personal character was held up to reproach as that of one who "walked according to the flesh" (x. 2), puffed up with pride, marked by levity of purpose (iii. 1) and even by dishonesty (vii. 2). They rejected his epistles, not on the ground of authenticity, but as the work of an "apostate from the Law" (Eus. iii. c. 27; Iren. *l.c.*). They even asserted that by birth he was not a Jew, but a Gentile (wresting his words in Acts xxi. 39) who had become a proselyte in the hope of marrying the High Priest's daughter, but that having failed in this he had severed himself from the Jews and occupied himself in writing against circumcision and the observance of the sabbath (Epiph. *adv. Haer.* I. xxx. 16, 25).

In common with the Nazarenes and the Gnostic-Ebionites, the Pharisaic Ebionites used a recension of the Gospel of St. Matthew, which they termed the "gospel according to the Hebrews." It was a Chaldee version written in Hebrew letters, afterwards translated into Greek and Latin by Jerome, who declared it identical with the "gospel of the Twelve Apostles" and the "gospel of the Nazarenes" (see Herzog, *Real-Encyklopädie*, "Apokryphen d. N. Test." p. 520, ed. 1877). In the Ebionite "gospel" the section corresponding to the first two chapters of St. Matt. was omitted, the supernatural character of the narrative being contradictory to their views about the person of Jesus Christ. It is difficult to say with certainty what other books of the N.T. were known to them; but there is reason to believe that they (as also the Gnostic-Ebionites) were familiar with the Gospels of St. Mark and St. Luke. The existence among them of the "Protevangelium Jacobi" and the Περιοδοὶ τοῦ Πέτρου indicates their respect for those Apostles.

(*b*) *Essene or Gnostic Ebionism.*—This, as the name indicates, was a type of Ebionism affected by external influences. The characteristic features of the ascetic Essenes were reproduced in its practices, and the traces of influences more directly mystical and oriental were evident in its doctrines. The different phases through which Ebionism passed at different times render it, however, difficult to distinguish clearly in every case between Gnostic and Pharisaic Ebionism. Epiphanius (*adv. Haer.* xxx.) is the chief authority on the Gnostic Ebionites. He met them in Cyprus, and personally obtained information about them (cf. R. A. Lipsius, *Zur Quellen-Kritik d. Epiphanios*, pp. 138, 143, 150 etc.).

Their principal tenets were as follows: Christianity they identified with primitive religion or genuine Mosaism, as distinguished from what they termed accretions to Mosaism, or the post-Mosaic developments described in the later books of O.T. To carry out this distinction they fabricated two classes of "prophets," προφῆται ἀληθείας, and προφῆται συνέσεως οὐκ ἀληθείας. In the former class they placed Adam, Noah, Abraham, Isaac, Jacob, Aaron, Moses, and Jesus; in the latter David, Solomon, Isaiah, Jeremiah, etc. In the same spirit they accepted the Pentateuch alone among the O.T. writings, and emasculated it; rejecting whatever reflected questionably upon their favourites. They held that there were two antagonistic powers appointed by God—Christ and devil; to the former was allotted the world to come, to the latter the present world. The conception of Christ was variously entertained. Some affirmed that He was created (not born) of the Father, a Spirit, and higher than the angels; that He had the power of coming to this earth when He would, and in various modes of manifestation; that He had been incarnate in Adam, and had appeared to the patriarchs in bodily shape; others identified Adam and Christ. In these last days He had come in the person of Jesus. Jesus was therefore to them a successor of Moses, and not of higher authority. They quoted from their gospel a saying attributed to Him, " I am He concerning Whom Moses prophesied, saying, A prophet shall the Lord God raise unto you like unto me," etc. (*Clem. Hom.* iii. c. 53), and this was enough to identify His teaching with that of genuine Mosaism. But by declining to fix the precise moment of the union of the Christ with the man Jesus—a union assigned by Pharisaic Ebionites to the hour of Baptism—they admitted His miraculous origin.

In pursuance of their conception that the devil was the " prince of this world " they were strict ascetics. They abjured flesh-meat, repudiating passages (*e.g.* Gen. xviii. 8) which contradicted their view ; they refused to taste wine, and communicated with unleavened bread and water. Water was to them " in the place of a god " ; ablutions and lustrations were imperative and frequent. But they held the married life in honour, and recommended early marriages. To the observance of the Jewish sabbath they added that of the Christian Lord's day. Circumcision was sacred to them from the practice of the patriarchs and of Jesus Christ ; and they declined all fellowship with the uncircumcised, but repudiated the sacrifices of the altar and the reverence of the Jew for the Temple. In common with the Ebionites proper, they detested St. Paul, rejected his epistles, and circulated stories discreditable to him. The other Apostles were known to them by their writings, which they regarded as inferior to their own gospel.

The conjecture appears not improbable that as the siege of Jerusalem under Titus gave an impetus to Ebionism proper, so the ruin under Hadrian developed Gnostic Ebionism. Not that Gnosticism began then to affect it for the first time, but that Gnostic ideas hitherto held in solution were precipitated and found a congenial home among men who through contact with oriental systems in Syria were already predisposed to accept them (cf. Mansel, *The Gnostic Heresies*, lect. viii.). This is further evident from the book of Elchasai and the Clementine literature. These works are the production of the Essene Ebionites ; and where they speak of Jesus Christ and His Apostles, His sayings and their lives, they do so, not in the words of the canonical Gospels and Epistles, but with additions or omissions, and a colouring which transforms (*e.g.*) St. Peter, St. Matthew, and St. James the Just into Essenes, and yet with that Gnostic tendency of thought which makes them lineal descendants of the Judaizers who imperilled the church at Colossae. (See Lightfoot, *Colossians*, p. 73, etc., and *Essenism and Christianity*, p. 397, etc.)

The Essene or Gnostic-Ebionites differed from the Pharisaic Ebionites in another respect. By missionary zeal, as well as by literary activity, they sought to obtain converts to their views. In the earlier part of the 3rd cent. the Ebionite Alcibiades of Apamea (Syria) repaired to Rome. He brought with him the book of Elchasai, and " preached unto men a new remission of sins (proclaimed) in the third year of Trajan's reign " (A.D. 101). Hippolytus, who gives an account of the matter (*Haer.* ix. c. viii. etc., ed. Clark), exposed the decided antinomianism which penetrated the teaching of the mythical teacher and of the pupil, but it is evident that many " became victims of the delusion." The immorality which the book—in imitation of the teaching of Callistus—indirectly encouraged probably attracted some, but would discredit the dogmatic views of the missionary.

Ebionite Christianity did not, however, last very long, neither did it exercise much influence west of Syria while it lasted. In Palestine the discomfiture accorded to " a certain one " (probably Alcibiades) who came to Caesarea *c.* A.D. 247 maintaining the " ungodly and wicked error of the Elkesaites " (Eus. vi. 38 ; cf. Redepenning, *Origines*, ii. p. 72) was in keeping with the reception accorded to less extreme Ebionite views from the time of the reconstitution of the mother-church at Aelia Capitolina. Judaism of every kind gradually passed out of favour. The attitude of the bishops of Palestine in the Paschal controversy of the 2nd cent. was that of men who wished to stand clear of any sympathy with Jewish customs ; the language of Justin Martyr and of Hegesippus was the language of the representatives of the Samaritan and the Hebrew Christianity of the day, not of the Ebionite. Outside of Palestine Ebionism had even less chance of survival. From the very first, the instructions and memories of St. Paul and St. John excluded it from Asia Minor ; in Antioch the names of Ignatius, Theophilus, and Serapion were vouchers for Catholic doctrine and practice ; and the daughter-churches of Gaul and Alexandria naturally preferred doctrine supplied to them by teachers trained in the school of these Apostles. Even in the church of Rome, whatever tendency existed in Apostolic times towards Ebionism, the separation—also in Apostolic times—of the Judaizers was the beginning of the end which no after-amalgamation under Clement could retard. The tone of the *Shepherd of Hermas*—a work which emanated from the Roman church during the first half of the 2nd cent. (see Lightfoot, *Galatians*, p. 99, n. 3)—however different from the tone of Clement and St. Paul, is not Ebionite, as a comparison with another so-called Roman and certainly later Ebionite work—the Clementine writings—shews. The end of Ebionism had actually come in the Roman church when in the 2nd cent. Jewish practices—notably as regards the observance of Easter—were unhesitatingly rejected. The creed of the Christian in Rome was the creed which he held from Irenaeus in Gaul and Polycarp in Asia Minor, and not from the Ebionite. When the above-named Alcibiades appeared in Rome (A.D. 219), Hippolytus denounced his teaching (that of Elchasai) as that of " a wolf risen up against many wandering sheep, whom Callistus had scattered abroad " : it came upon him as a novelty ; it had " risen up," he says, " in our own day " (*Haer.* ix. cc. 8, 12). This language is a proof of the oblivion which had certainly befallen any previous propagation of Ebionism in Rome.

For 200 years more Ebionism—especially of the Essene form—lingered on. A few Ebionites were left in the time of Theodoret, about the middle of 5th cent. ; the rest had returned to strict Judaism and the utter rejection of Christianity, or to a purer Christianity than that which Ebionism favoured.

The Patristic notices on the Ebionites will be found in the works referred to (cf. on their value, R. A. Lipsius, *Die Quellen d. ältesten Ketzergeschichte*, 1875). The literature on the subject is further collected by (*int. al.*) Schliemann, *Die Clementinen* (1844); Ritschl, *Die Entstehung d. alt-katholischen Kirche* (1857); Lightfoot, *Galatians*, Dissertation III. *St. Paul and the Three* (1876). [J.M.F.]

Edesius (3) shared the romantic fortunes of his brother Frumentius, the first bp. of Auxumis (Axum), in the 4th cent. The biographical details at our disposal consist of a lengthy narrative, introduced, on the authority of Edesius, by Rufinus into his *Ecclesiastical History* (lib. i. 9). This narrative has been copied, with slight deviations, by Socrates (*H. E.* i. 19), Sozomen (ii. 24), and Theodoret (i. 23, 24). Cf. also Baronius (*Ann.* 327, viii. ix. x.). Frumentius and Edesius, the young relatives of Meropius, a Syrian philosopher (merchant), accompanied him on a voyage of adventure to India. On their return to Phoenicia by way of the Red Sea, they landed "at a certain port," where there was "a safe haven," and there suffered from the barbarous assault of the "Indians," who murdered all the ship's company except the two youths, who were conveyed as prizes to the king. He appointed Frumentius and Edesius as his treasurer and cup-bearer respectively. By their means Christianity was introduced among "the Indians." Their names in Ethiopian documents given by Ludolf (*Hist. Eth.* iii. 2) are Fremonatos and Sydvacus (cf. Gesenius, *Aethiop. Kirche* in Ersch and Gruber, and Hoffmann in Herzog's *Encyc.*). The word "India" is used with the same indefiniteness as are Ethiopia and Libya elsewhere. From the times of Aristotle to those of Eratosthenes and of Hipparchus, India and Africa were believed to unite at some unknown point S. of the Indian Ocean (*Dict. Anc. Geogr.* vol. ii. p. 45, art. "India"; Pliny, vi. 22-24). These "Indians" were Abyssinians, as we see from the subsequent career of Frumentius. The king, according to Ludolf's Ethiopian Codex, was called Abreha, and on drawing near his end, offered their liberty to the two youths. The queen-mother earnestly besought them to remain, to undertake the education of the young prince Erazanes, and to assist her in the regency during his minority. They consented, and lost no opportunity of diffusing a knowledge of Christ. They sought out Christian merchants trading in the country, gathered Christian disciples, and built houses of prayer, "that worship might be offered, and the Roman ecclesiastical routine observed" (Soz. *l.c.*). They were not in orders, and Frumentius went to Alexandria and asked for a bishop to be sent to Abyssinia. Athanasius consecrated Frumentius himself. Edesius remained at Tyre and became a presbyter of the church there, where Rufinus met him. [H.R.R.]

Elagabalus. The short reign of this feeble and profligate emperor, though not coming into direct contact with the history of the Christian church, is not without interest as a phase of the religious condition of the empire. Varius Avitus Bassianus, as he was named at his birth, was of Phoenician descent, and born at Emesa, in Syria, *c.* A.D. 205. His mother, Julia Soëmia, and aunt, Julia Mammaea, were devoted to the worship of *El-gabal* (=God the Creator, or, according to less probable etymology, God of the Mountains), and he and his cousin Alexander Severus were in early childhood consecrated as priests of that deity, and the young Bassianus took the name of the god to whom he ministered.

Julia Mammaea had eclectic tendencies, and by her invitation the great Origen came to Antioch (probably, however, after the death of Elagabalus), and was received with many marks of honour. Eusebius, who relates the fact (*H. E.* vi. 21), speaks of her as a woman of exceptional piety (γυνὴ θεοσεβεστάτη εἰ καί τις ἄλλη γεγονυῖα), and we may trace her influence in the character of her son Alexander Severus. [SEVERUS (2).] After spending some time at Nicomedia, where he entered on his second consulship, Elagabalus proceeded in A.D. 219 (the year in which Callistus succeeded Zephyrinus as bp. of Rome) to the capital. His short reign there was a frenzy of idolatrous impurity. His jealousy and suspicion led him to imprison Alexander Severus, whose virtue attracted the admiration both of soldiers and people, and whom, at his mother's advice, he had adopted and proclaimed as Caesar soon after arriving in Rome. The troops rose and rescued their favourite. The two sisters, each with her son, appeared at the head of their supporters, and the followers of Severus were victorious. Soëmia and the boy-emperor were thrown into the Tiber (hence the epithet Tiberinus afterwards attached to him in derision), and the senate branded his name with eternal infamy. Dio. Cass. lxxvii. 30-41, lxxix.; Herodian, v. 4-23; Lamprid. *Elagab.*; Capitolin. *Macrinus*; Eutrop. viii. 13; Aurel. Victor, *de Caes.* xxiii., *Epit.* xxiii.) [E.H.P.]

Elesbaan, a king, hermit, and saint of Ethiopia during the 6th cent. (Rome, Oct. 27; Ethiopia, Ginbot, xx. May 15; cf. Ludolphus, p. 415), whose exact story is difficult to trace. (Cf. Ludolphus, *History of Ethiopia*, ed. 1684, p. 167; Lebeau, *Histoire du Bas Empire*, ed. 1827 viii. 47, note 4; Walch, in *Novi Commentarii Soc. Reg. Gottingen.* t. iv.; *Historia Rerum in Homeritide Saec.* vi. *Gestarum*, p. 4.) The importance of the crusades on which his fame rests is attested by Gibbon, who asserts that, had their purpose been attained, "Mahomet must have been crushed in his cradle, and Abyssinia would have prevented a revolution which has changed the civil and religious state of the world" (*Decline and Fall*, c. xlii. *sub fin.*). The details of the saint's wars and character are drawn from the *Acta S. Arethae*, extant in two forms: the earlier and more authentic, found by Lequien in the Colbert Library (*Oriens Christianus*, ii. 428), is referred by the Jesuit author of the *Acta Sanctorum* to the 7th cent. at latest; the later is, at best, but the recension of Simeon Metaphrastes, in the 10th cent.

It was probably during the later years of Anastasius's reign that Elesbaan succeeded his father Tazena on the throne of Ethiopia. His kingdom was greatly dependent for its welfare upon the goodwill and good order of the people of Yemen, the Homeritae, from whom it was separated by the narrow strait of Bab-el-Mandeb: for though the territory of the Homeritae the merchants of Syria and of Rome came to the great port of Adulis (cf. *Assemani Bibl. Orientalis*, i. p. 360), near whose ruins in Annesley Bay the Arabian traders still unlade their ships (cf. Henry Salt, *A Voyage to Abyssinia*, c. ix. p. 451). When Elesbaan succeeded, the Homeritae had greatly obscured the Christianity which they had received in the reign of Constantius, but the language of Cosmas Indicopleustes (Migne, *Patr. Gk.* vol. lxxxviii. p. 170) shews that it was not wholly extinct. The name of their king is variously written Dunaan and Dhu Nowas; by John of Asia as Dimion; by Theophanes as Damian. He had been made king *c.* 490, by the people whom he had freed from their gross tyrant Laknia Dhu Sjenatir; and having shortly after his accession forsworn idolatry and embraced Judaism, determined to enforce his new creed with the sword (cf. *Acta Sanctorum*, Oct. vol. x. p. 693). In retaliation for the sufferings of the Jews throughout the Christian empire, he exacted heavy tolls from all Christian merchants who came through his territory to the port of Aden and the Straits of Bab-el-Mandeb, and, according to John of Asia (cf. Assemani, *Bibl. Orientalis*, i. 360), put many Christians to death. Such action was injurious to the commerce of all the neighbouring peoples, but especially of Ethiopia; and Elesbaan soon after his accession sent a useless remonstrance, and then prepared for war. About A.D. 519 he crossed the straits, utterly defeated the Arabian forces, and driving the Jew to refuge in the hills, left a viceroy to bear Christian rule over the Homeritae and returned to Ethiopia (*ib.* p. 362). The time of this expedition is incidentally and approximately marked by Cosmas Indicopleustes, who tells us that he was at Adulis "*ἐν τῇ ἀρχῇ τῆς βασιλείας Ἰουστίνου τοῦ Ῥωμαίων βασίλεως*" (A.D. 518-527), when the king of the people of Axum, being about to war against the Homeritae, sent to ask the governor of Adulis for a copy of a certain inscription; which copy Cosmas and another monk were charged to make (Migne, *Patr. Gk.* vol. lxxxviii. p. 102).

The death of the viceroy, probably in A.D. 522 or 523, whom Elesbaan had left in Yemen, encouraged Dhu Nowas to come down from his hiding-place in the hills ("tanquam daemon carne indutus," *Acta Sanctorum*, Oct. xii. 316), and reassert himself as king of the Homeritae and champion of Judaism. Choosing a season when the Arabian Gulf would be an impassable barrier to the intervention of Elesbaan, he gathered a force which presently numbered 120,000 men and, having put to death all Christians whom he could find and turned their church into a synagogue, pressed on to Negran, the head-quarters of the Ethiopian vice-royalty, then held by Arethas the phylarch. He found the garrison forewarned and the gates closed; nor were they opened at his threats, when coming to the wall and holding up a wooden cross he swore that all who would not blaspheme the Crucified and insult the sign of His suffering should die. At last by treachery Dhu Nowas won an entrance, promising to hurt none of the citizens and only demanding an exorbitant tribute; but having entered, he began at once the reckless massacre which has left its mark even in the Koran (cf. Walch's paper in the *Göttingen Commentarii*, p. 25). Arethas and Ruma his wife died with a defiant confession on their lips; more than 4,000 Christian men, women, and children were killed (commemorated in the Roman calendar on Oct. 24); and from the fiery dyke into which the victims were thrown, Dhu Nowas received the name Saheb-el-Okhdud ("Lord of the Trench"). At this time, probably in Jan. 524, Simeon, bp. of Beth-Arsam, had been sent by the emperor Justin, together with Abraham, a priest of Constantinople, to gain the alliance of Mundhir III., king of the Arabians of Hira, a friend valuable alike for reasons of commerce and in regard to the war with Persia. As the ambassadors drew near the king (the story is told by Simeon in a letter to the abbat of Gabula), they were met by a crowd of Arabs crying that Christ was driven out of Rome and Persia and Homeritis; and they learnt that messengers were present from Dhu Nowas with letters to king Mundhir, in which they heard the long recital of the treachery by which Negran had been taken, of the insult to the bishop's tomb, of the slaughter of the Christians and the triumph of Judaism, the confession of the martyr Arethas, and the speech of Ruma urging the women of Negran to follow her to the abiding city of the divine Bridegroom, praying that the blood of the martyrs might be the wall of Negran while it continued in the faith, and that she might be forgiven for that Arethas had died first. They heard of her brutal murder, and the appeal of Dhu Nowas that Mundhir should at once enact a like massacre throughout his kingdom. Their own end must have seemed very near; but the courage of a soldier who stood forth as spokesman of the many Christians in Mundhir's army decided the hesitation of the king, and the ambassadors went away unhurt (but apparently unanswered) to Naaman, a port in the Arabian Gulf. There they heard more fully the story of the massacre, and especially of the constancy of a boy, who was afterwards known to the bp. of Asia at Justinian's court. Simeon of Beth-Arsam thus closes his letter, praying that the news may be spread throughout the church and the martyrs receive the honour of commemoration, and that the king of Ethiopia may be urged to help the Homeritae against the oppression of the Jew (cf. Assemani, *Bibl. Or.* i. 364-379). When this message reached Elesbaan, it was reinforced by a letter from Justin, elicited by the entreaties of Dous Ibn Dzi Thaleban, one of the few Christians who had escaped Dhu Nowas (cf. Wright, *Early Christianity in Arabia*, p. 56). This letter is given in the *Acta S. Arethae*; where also it is told how the patriarch of Alexandria, at the request of Justin, urged Elesbaan to invade Yemen, offering up a litany and appointing a vigil on his behalf, and sending to him the Eucharist in a silver vessel. Without delay Elesbaan collected a great army, which he divided into two parts; 15,000 men he sent southwards to cross at Bab-el-Mandeb and, marching through Yemen, divert the strength of Dhu Nowas's forces from the main body of the Ethiopians, which Elesbaan intended to send by sea to some place on the S. coast of Arabia. For the transport of these latter he appropriated 60 merchant vessels then anchored in his ports, adding ten more, built after the native fashion, the planks being held together by ropes. On the eve of the enterprise he went in procession to the great church of Axum, and there, laying aside his royalty, sued *in formâ pauperis* for the favour of Him Whose war he dared to wage; praying that his sins might be visited on himself, and not on his people. Then he sought the blessing, counsel, and prayers of St. Pantaleon; and received from within the doorless and windowless tower, where the hermit had lived for 45 years, the answer: "Ἔστω σὺν σοι ὁ συμβασιλεύων σοι." Thus the army was sent on its twofold route.

For the 15,000 Bab-el-Mandeb was indeed a gate of tears: they died of hunger, wandering in the desert. The main body was safely embarked, and sailed S. down the Gulf of Arabia towards the straits; which Dhu Nowas had barred by a huge chain, stretched across the space of two furlongs from side to side. Over this, however, first ten ships and then seven more, including that of the Ethiopian admiral, were lifted by the waves; the rest were driven back by stress of weather, but presently, the chain being, according to one account, broken, forced the passage, and passing the other seventeen, cast anchor farther along the coast. Meanwhile Dhu Nowas, having first encamped on the W. shore, where he thought his chain would force the Ethiopians to land, hurried from his position, and leaving but a few men to resist the smaller fleet, watched with his main army the movements of the rest. Those on the 17 ships under the Ethiopian admiral easily effected a landing near Aden, and defeating the troops opposed to them, pressed on to the chief city, Taphar, or Taphran, which surrendered immediately (cf. Wright, *op. cit.* 58-60). Discouraged by this disaster, the main body of the Arabians offered a feeble resistance; and Dhu Nowas saw that his downfall was very near. According to the Arabian historians, he threw himself from the cliff and died in the waves; according to the *Acta S. Arethae*, he bound his seven kinsmen in chains, and fastened them to his throne, lest they should fail to share his fate; and so awaited death at Elesbaan's own hand. The Arabic writers are unsupported in their story of the useless resistance of a successor Dhu Giadan; it was probably at the death of Dhu Nowas that the kingdom of the Homeritae ended, and Yemen became a province of Ethiopia. At Taphar Elesbaan is said to have built a church, digging the foundations for seven days with his own hands; and from Taphar he wrote of his victory to the patriarch of Alexandria. A bishop was sent from Alexandria and appointed to the see of Negran, but there are doubts as to both the orthodoxy and identity of this bishop. The king restored Negran, entrusting it to Arethas's son, rebuilding and endowing the great church, and granting perpetual right of asylum to the place where the bodies of the martyrs had lain, and then returned to Ethiopia (Boll. *Acta SS.* Oct. xii. 322), leaving a Christian Arab named Esimiphaeus or Ariathus, to be his viceroy over the conquered people. A part of Elesbaan's army, however, refused to leave the luxury of Arabia Felix, and not long after set up as rival to Esimiphaeus one Abrahah or Abraham, the Christian slave of a Roman merchant, who was strong enough to shut up the viceroy in a fort and seize the throne of Yemen. A force of 3,000 men was sent by Elesbaan, under a prince of his house, whom some call Aryates or Arethas, to depose the usurper; and it seems that Abrahah, like Dhu Nowas, sought safety among the mountains. But he soon (*c.* 540) came down and confronted the representative of Elesbaan; and at the critical moment the Ethiopian troops deserted and murdered their general. To maintain his supremacy and avenge his kinsman, Elesbaan sent a second army; but this, loyally fighting with Abrahah, was utterly defeated, and only a handful of men returned to Ethiopia. The Arabic historians record that Elesbaan swore to yet lay hold of the land of the Homeritae, both mountain and plain, pluck the forelock from the rebel's head, and take his blood as the price of Aryates's death; and they tell of the mixed cunning and cowardice by which Abrahah satisfied the Ethiopian's oath, and evaded his anger, winning at last a recognition of his dignity. Procopius adds that Abrahah paid tribute to Elesbaan's successor; and the Homeritae remained in free subjection to Ethiopia almost to the end of the century.

Records are extant, almost in the very words of the ambassadors, of two embassies from Justinian to Elesbaan. Joannes Malala, in writing of the first, had the autograph of the envoy whom Procopius (*de Bello Persico*, i. 20) calls Julian; Photius has preserved, in the third codex of his *Bibliotheca*, Nonnosus's story of his experience in the second mission. Julian must have been sent before 531, for Cabades was still living, and, according to Procopius, Esimiphaeus was viceroy of Homeritis. He was received by Elesbaan, according to his own account, with the silence of an intense joy; for the alliance of Rome had long been the great desire of the Ethiopians. The king was seated on a high chariot, drawn by four elephants caparisoned with gold; he wore a loose robe studded with pearls, and round his loins a covering of linen embroidered with gold. He received Justinian's letter with every sign of respect, and began to prepare his forces to take part in the Persian war even before Julian was dismissed from his court with the kiss of peace (Johannis Malalae, *Chronographia*, xviii. Bonn. ed. pp. 457, 458). Malala records no sequel of these preparations; Procopius complains that none occurred.

The second embassy was sent primarily to Kaisus or Imrulcays, the prince of the Chindini and Maaddeni, and only secondarily to the Homeritae and Ethiopians, probably in the last years of Elesbaan's reign. Nonnosus the envoy belonged to a family of diplomatists. But Photius does not state the purpose or result of this journey; only telling of the great herd of 5,000 elephants which Nonnosus saw between Adulis and Axum, and the pigmy negroes who met him on an island as he sailed away from Pharsan (Photii, *Bibliotheca*, Bekker's ed. pp. 2, 3).

The story of Elesbaan's abdication and seclusion is told in the *Acta S. Arethae*. Having accepted the fealty and recognized the royalty of Abrahah, and having confirmed the faith of Christ in Homeritis, he laid aside his crown and assumed the garb of a solitary. His cell is still shewn to the traveller; it was visited in 1805 by Henry Salt, and has been elaborately described by Mendez and Lefevre. There the king remained in solitude and great asceticism; and the year of his death is unknown. His crown he sent to Jerusalem, praying that it might be hung "in conspectu januae vivifici sepulchri." [F.P.]

Eleusius (2), bp. of Cyzicus, a prominent semi-Arian in the 2nd half of the 4th cent., intimately connected with Basil of Ancyra, Eustathius of Sebaste, Sophronius of Pompeiopolis, and other leaders of the Macedonian party. He is uniformly described as of high personal character, holy in life, rigid in self-discipline, untiring in his exertions for what he deemed truth, and, according to St. Hilary, more nearly orthodox than most of his associates (Hilar. *de Synod.* p. 133). The people of his diocese are described by Theodoret as zealous for the orthodox faith, and well instructed in the Holy Scriptures and in church doctrines, and he himself as a man worthy of all praise (Theod. *H. E.* ii. 25; *Haer. Fab.* iv. 3). Though usually found acting with the tyrannical and unscrupulous party, of which Macedonius was the original leader, and sharing in the discredit of their measures against the holders of the Homoousian faith, Eleusius was uncompromising in opposing the pronounced Arians, by whom he was persecuted and deposed. He held office in the Imperial household when suddenly elevated to the see of Cyzicus by Macedonius, bp. of Constantinople, *c.* 356 (Soz. *H. E.* iv. 20; Suidas, *s.v.* Ἐλεύσιος). He signalized his entrance on his office by a vehement outburst of zeal against the relics of paganism at Cyzicus. He shewed no less decision in dealing with the Novatianists, with whom a community of persecution had caused the Catholics to unite. He destroyed their church, and forbade their assemblies for worship (Socr. *H. E.* ii. 38; Soz. *H. E.* iv. 21; v. 15). He soon acquired great influence over his people by his religious zeal and the gravity of his manners. He established in his diocese a large number of monasteries, both for males and females (Suidas, *u.s.*). He took part in the semi-Arian council at Ancyra 358 A.D. (Hilar. *de Synod.* p. 127), and was one of the members deputed to lay before Constantius at Sirmium the decrees they had passed, condemnatory of the Anomoeans (Hilar. *u.s.*; Soz. *H. E.* iv. 13; Labbe, *Concil.* ii. 790). At the council of Seleucia, A.D. 359, he replied to the proposition of the Acacians to draw up a new confession of faith, by asserting that they had not met to receive a new faith, but to pledge themselves for death to that of the fathers (Socr. *H. E.* ii. 39, 40). Being commissioned with Eustathius of Sebaste, Basil of Ancyra, and others, to communicate the result of the synod to Constantius, Eleusius denounced the blasphemies attributed to Eudoxius so vigorously that the latter was compelled by the emperor's threats to retract (Theod. *H. E.* ii. 23). [EUDOXIUS; EUSTATHIUS OF SEBASTE.] The wily Acacians, however, speedily gained the ear of Constantius, and secured the deposition of their semi-Arian rivals, including Eleusius, A.D. 360. The nominal charge against him was that he had baptized and ordained one Heraclius of Tyre, who, being accused of magic, had fled to Cyzicus, and whom, when the facts came to his knowledge, he had refused to depose. He was also charged with having admitted to holy orders persons condemned by his neighbour, Maris of Chalcedon (Soz. *H. E.* iv. 24; Socr. *H. E.* ii. 42). His old patron, Macedonius of Constantinople, who had been got rid of at the same time, wrote to encourage him and the other deposed prelates in their adherence to the Antiochene formula and to the "Homoiousian" as the watchword of their party (Socr. *H. E.* ii. 45; Soz. *H. E.* iv. 27). The subtle Anomoean Eunomius was intruded into the see of Cyzicus by Eudoxius, who had succeeded Macedonius (Socr. *H. E.* iv. 7; Philost. *H. E.* v. 3). Eunomius failed to secure the goodwill of the people who refused to attend where he officiated, and built a church for themselves outside the town. On the accession of Julian, A.D. 361, Eleusius, with the other deposed prelates, returned to his see, but was soon expelled a second time by Julian, on the representation of the heathen inhabitants of Cyzicus, for his zeal against paganism (Soz. *H. E.* v. 15). At Julian's death Eleusius regained possession. He took the lead at the Macedonian council of Lampsacus, A.D. 365 (Socr. *H. E.* iv. 4). At Nicomedia, A.D. 366, he weakly succumbed to Valens's threats of banishment and confiscation, and accepted the Arian creed. Full of remorse, he assembled his people on his return to Cyzicus, confessed and deplored his crime, and desired, since he had denied his faith, to resign his charge to a worthier. The people, devotedly attached to him, refused to accept his resignation (*ib.* 6; Philost. *H. E.* ix. 13). In 381 Eleusius was the chief of 36 bishops of Macedonian tenets summoned by Theodosius to the oecumenical council of Constantinople in the hope of bringing them back to Catholic doctrine. This anticipation proved nugatory; Eleusius and his adherents obstinately refused all reconciliation, maintaining their heretical views on the Divinity of the Holy Ghost (Socr. *H. E.* v. 8; Soz. *H. E.* vii. 7). Similarly at the conference of bishops of all parties in 383, to which Eleusius was also invited as chief of the Macedonians, the differences proved irreconcilable, and the emperor manifested his disappointment by severe edicts directed against the Macedonians, Eunomians, Arians, and other heretics (Tillem. *Mém. Eccl.* vol. vi. passim). [E.V.]

Eleutherus (1), bp. of Rome in the reigns of Marcus Aurelius and Commodus, during 15 years, 6 months, and 5 days, according to the Liberian catalogue. Eusebius (*H. E.* v. *prooem.*) places his accession in the 17th year of Antoninus Verus (*i.e.* Marcus Aurelius), viz.

A.D. 177; which would make 192 the date of his death. But the consuls given in the Liberian catalogue as contemporary with his election and death are those of 171 and 185.

Hegesippus, quoted by Eusebius (*H. E.* iv. 22), states that when he himself arrived in Rome, Eleutherus was deacon of Anicetus, who was then bishop, and became bishop on the death of Soter, the successor of Anicetus (cf. Iren. *adv. Haeres.* iii. 3, and Jerome, *de Vir. Illustr.* c. 22).

Eleutherus was contemporary with the Aurelian persecution; and after the death of Aurelius the Christians had peace, in consequence, it is said, of the favour of Marcia, the concubine of Commodus; the only recorded exception in Rome being the martyrdom of Apollonius in the reign of Commodus (Eus. *H. E.* v. 21; Jerome, *Catal.* c. 42). The chief sufferers under Aurelius were the churches of Asia Minor and those of Lyons and Vienne in Southern Gaul, A.D. 177. In letters to Eleutherus by the hand of Irenaeus the latter churches made known, "for the sake of the peace of the churches" (*H. E.* v. 3), their own judgment, with that of their martyrs while in prison, respecting the claims of Montanus to inspiration.

The fact of the bp. of Rome having been especially addressed on this occasion has been adduced as an acknowledgment in that early age of his supreme authority. But the letters of the martyrs to Eleutherus do not appear, from Eusebius, to have had any different purport from those sent also to the churches of Asia and Phrygia, nor does their object seem to have been to seek a judgment, but rather to express one, in virtue, we may suppose, of the weight carried in those days by the utterances of martyrs. Their having addressed Eleutherus, as well as the churches where Montanus himself was teaching, is sufficiently accounted for by the prominence of the Roman bishop's position in the West, about which there is no dispute. Of the course taken by Eleutherus with respect to Montanus nothing can be alleged with certainty.

Besides the heresy of Montanus, those of Basilides, Valentinus, Cerdo, and Marcion were then at their height, and gained many adherents in Rome. Valentinus and Cerdo had come there between 138 and 142; Marcion a little later. There is, however, some difficulty in placing the sojourn in Rome of these heresiarchs in the episcopate of Eleutherus; Valentinus, according to other accounts, having died previously (see Tillem. *On Eleutherus*). Florinus and Blastus also, two degraded presbyters of Rome, broached during the episcopate of Eleutherus certain heresies, of which nothing is known except what may be gathered from the titles of certain lost treatises written against them by Irenaeus (Eus. *H. E.* v. 14, 15, 20, Pacian, *Ep.* i.). The visit of Irenaeus to Eleutherus gave the latter opportunity to become acquainted with the prevalent heresies, against which he became the most distinguished champion.

Especially interesting to Englishmen is the story connecting Eleutherus with the origin of British Christianity (Bede, *H. E.* c. iv.). [LUCIUS (16)]. This account, written some 500 years after the event, is the earliest mention of it in any historian. It seems pretty certain that it was from a Roman catalogue that Bede got his information, Gildas, his usual authority, being silent on the subject. In the hands of chroniclers after Bede the story receives several and growing additions. The story is first found in its simplest form in the Pontifical annals at Rome, in the 6th cent.; is introduced into Britain by Bede in the 8th; grows into the conversion of the whole of Britain in the 9th; and appears full-fledged, enriched with details, and connected with both Llandaff and Glastonbury, in the 12th. There is, however, nothing improbable in the original story itself, and it is more likely to have had some fact than pure invention for its origin, and the Welsh traditions about Lleirwg, though unnoticed by Gildas, may have been ancient and genuine ones, independent of Bede's account. Lingard takes this view, laying stress on the dedication of churches in the diocese of Llandaff to Lleirwg and the saints associated with him, and supposing him to have been an independent British prince outside the Roman pale. In confirmation of the story is alleged further the fact that, shortly after the time of Eleutherus writers first begin to speak of British Christianity. For Tertullian, Origen, and Arnobius are the first to allude to the triumphs of the Gospel, though partial, in this remote island. What they say, however, is quite consistent with the earlier, and other than Roman, origin of the British church; and it may be that it was the very fact of their having borne this testimony that suggested Eleutherus, a pope shortly anterior to their date, as one to whom the mission might be assigned. [J.B—Y.]

Elias (1) **I.**, bp. of Jerusalem, A.D. 494-513; an Arab by birth who was educated with Martyrius, in one of the Nitrian monasteries. Driven from Egypt by Timothy Aelurus, the two friends took refuge, A.D. 457, in the laura of St. Euthymius, who received them with great favour, and predicted that they would both be bishops of Jerusalem. After a time they quitted the laura, and Elias constructed a cell at Jericho. In 478 Martyrius succeeded Anastasius as bp. of Jerusalem, and was followed by Sallustius in 486, and in 494 by Elias. Moschus records that Elias practised total abstinence from wine both as monk and bishop (*Prat. Spiritual.* c. 25). His residence became the nucleus of a collection of cells of ascetics, which developed into a monastery adjacent to the church of the Anastasis (Cyril. Scythop. *Vit. S. Sabae*, c. 31). When Elias succeeded to the patriarchate, the Christian world exhibited a melancholy spectacle of discord. There were at least four great parties anathematizing one another. When the Monophysites (Acephali) in Syria, under the leadership of Xenaias of Hierapolis, broke into open insurrection, treating as heretics all who acknowledged the two natures, Elias was one of the chief objects of their attack. In 509 they demanded a confession of his faith, and Anastasius required him to convene a council to repudiate the decrees of Chalcedon. Elias declined, but drew up a letter to the emperor, containing a statement of his belief, accompanied by anathemas of

Nestorius, Eutyches, Diodorus, and Theodore of Mopsuestia. This was entrusted to members of the Acephali to convey to Constantinople. When opened, it was found to contain an anathema against the two natures. Elias reproached the bearers with having falsified the document and thus laid him open to the charge, which he found it very hard to refute, of having condemned the council of Chalcedon (Evagr. *H. E.* iii. 31; Theod. *Lect.* p. 561; Theophan. *Chronogr.* pp. 129, 130). Macedonius having been deposed A.D. 511, and Timotheus, an unscrupulous Monophysite monk, appointed to the see of Constantinople, Elias, whose principle appears to have been to accept the inevitable and to go the utmost possible length in obedience to the ruling powers, seized on the fact that he had abstained at first from anathematizing the council of Chalcedon, as a warrant for joining communion with him and receiving his synodical letter. Elias could not contend against his many unscrupulous enemies, and in 513 was driven from his see, dying in 518 in banishment at Aila on the Red Sea shore, aet. 88. Tillem. *Mém. Eccl.* xvi.; Cyril. Scythop. *Vita S. Euthymii*; and other authorities cited above. [E.V.]

Elkesai, Elkesaites (Ἡλχασαί, Hippolytus; Ἠλξαί, Ἐλκεσσαῖοι, Epiphanius; Ἑλκεσαιταί, Origen). A book bearing the name of *Elkesai* and purporting to contain angelic revelations, was, at the end of the 2nd cent., in high repute among certain Ebionite sectaries, who were most numerous in the district E. of the lower Jordan and the Dead Sea. This book first became known to orthodox writers in the 3rd cent., and we have accounts of it from three independent primary sources, Hippolytus, Origen, and Epiphanius. Hippolytus (*Ref.* ix. 12, p. 292) gives several extracts, and states that it was brought to Rome by a certain Alcibiades, a native of Apameia in Syria, and indicates that the time was during, or immediately after, the episcopate of Callistus—*i.e.* *c.* A.D. 222. The great controversy then agitating the church of Rome was whether, and with what limitations, forgiveness might be bestowed on grievous post-baptismal sin. Hippolytus took the side of rigour and Callistus of leniency. This book of Elkesai announced a new method of forgiveness of sin, asserted to have been revealed in the third year of Trajan, by which any person, no matter of what sins he might have been guilty (some of the very grossest are expressly mentioned), might obtain forgiveness by submitting to a new baptism with the use of a certain formula of which we shall speak presently. A similar baptism was prescribed as a remedy for the bite of a mad dog or a serpent or for disease. Hippolytus takes credit for resisting the teaching of Alcibiades, and blames Callistus for having, by the laxity of his doctrine and practice concerning church discipline, pre-disposed men's minds to the easy methods of forgiveness expounded in this book. Origen, in a fragment of a homily on the 82nd Psalm, preserved by Eusebius (*H. E.* vi. 38) and assigned by Redepenning to A.D. 247, speaks of the teaching of the Helcesaites, some specimens of which he gives, as having then but lately troubled the churches. Epiphanius, though a later witness, professes to speak from personal acquaintance with the book, and this is confirmed by his coincidence in a number of details with the other authorities. We may count the Pseudo-Clementine writings as a fourth source of information concerning the books of Elkesai. Hippolytus states that the book, according to its own account, had been obtained from Seres, in Parthia, by a righteous man named Elkesai; that its contents had been revealed by an angel 96 miles high, accompanied by a female of corresponding size; that the male was Son of God, and the female was called Holy Spirit. Epiphanius speaks of Elkesai as a false prophet. Probably this Elkesai was an imaginary personage, and we must reject the account of Epiphanius who assigns to him a certain part in the history of the Ebionite sects.

The book is evidently of Jewish origin. Jerusalem is made the centre of the world's devotion, and the right rule of prayer is to turn not necessarily to the East, but towards Jerusalem. The names of the book are formed from Hebrew roots. A further mark of Aramaic origin is the representation of the Holy Spirit as a female. The book ordered compliance with ordinances of the Jewish law, but condemned the rite of sacrifice, so involving the rejection of parts of O.T., and of the eating of flesh. The superiority of the forgiveness of sins by the washing of water over that by the fire of sacrifice is based on the superiority of water to fire (Hipp. ix. 14; Epiph. *Haer.* 19, p. 42; Clem. *Rec.* i. 48; *Hom.* xi. 26). It is taught that Christ is but a created being, but the greatest of creatures, being Lord over angels as well as over every other created thing. The name Great King is applied to Him (Epiph. *Haer.* 19, p. 41; Hipp. ix. 15; *Hom.* viii. 21). The formula of baptism runs, In the name of the Most High God and of His Son, the Great King; but this Great King is not exclusively identified with Jesus of Nazareth, for He appeared in the world in successive incarnations, Adam being the first. The book agreed with the Clementines in complete rejection of St. Paul. It taught the lawfulness of denying the faith under persecution (Eus. vi. 38; Epiph. 19), thus getting rid of the class of offences as to the forgiveness of which there was then most controversy.

The statement of the book that the revelation was made in the 3rd year of Trajan is of no historic value. The work, however, which was the common groundwork of the Clementine *Recognitions* and *Homilies* [CLEMENTINE LITERATURE] asserts that a new gospel was published (the Homilies add "secretly") after the destruction of the Holy Place; and it seems on other grounds probable that a number of Essenes, who had always held the Temple sacrifices in abomination, were brought to recognize Jesus as the true Prophet when the destruction of the Temple and the abolition of its sacrifices fulfilled His prediction. At this time, then, probably arose those Ebionite sects which combined a certain reverence for our Lord's utterances, and an acknowledgment of Him as a divine prophet, with the retention of a host of Essene usages and doctrines. Hence the book of Elkesai may have been, as it professed to be, a considerable time in secret circulation among the Ebionite sects before Alcibiades brought it to Rome, though it is also possible that it may have been then of quite recent manufacture.

It would seem to be long before the sect of Elkesaites disappeared. En-hedim, an Arabic author (*c.* A.D. 987) quoted by Chwolson (*Die Sabier*, i. 112, ii. 543), tells of a sect of Sabeans of the Desert who practised frequent religious washings, and who counted one El-Chasaiach as their founder. See Ritschl, *Zeitschrift für histor. Theol.* (1853), pp. 573 sqq., *Entstehung der altkatholischen Kirche*, pp. 234 sqq.; Hilgenfeld, *Nov. Test. extra Canonem Receptum*, iii. 153, where all the fragments of the book are collected; Uhlhorn, *Hom. u. Recog. des Clem. Rom.* p. 392; and Lightfoot's *Dissertation on the Essenes*, "Ep. to Colossians," pp. 118 sqq. [G.S.]

Elpidius (8), bp. of Laodicea in Syria at the close of the 4th cent. and opening of the 5th. He was originally a priest of Antioch under Meletius, whose confidence he enjoyed and with whom he resided (σύσκηνος) (Theod. *H. E.* v. 27). He shared in his master's sufferings under Valens, and accompanied by Flavian, attended him at the council of Constantinople A.D. 381 (Labbe, ii. 955). We next find him as bishop at a council at Constantinople A.D. 394 (Labbe, ii. 1151), and again at Constantinople at the close of A.D. 403, as a member of the council summoned by Chrysostom's enemies, and issuing in his deposition. Elpidius had been an intimate friend of Chrysostom at Antioch, and now lent the weight of his age and well-deserved reputation to the defence of his old associate. When the validity of the canons of the council of Antioch, of suspected orthodoxy, used by Chrysostom's enemies as an instrument to secure their object, came into question before the emperor, Elpidius adroitly turned the tables on Acacius and his party by proposing that the advocates of the canons should declare themselves of the same faith with those who had promulgated them (Pallad. *Dial.* c. 9, p. 80). After Chrysostom's deposition and exile, Elpidius exerted himself strenuously in his behalf, dispatching letters to bishops and faithful laity in all parts of the world, exhorting them to remain true to Chrysostom, and encouraging them to bear up against persecution. Chrysostom wrote to Elpidius shortly after his arrival at Cucusus in 404, thanking him most warmly, and giving him information concerning the place of his banishment, his companions, and his health (Chrys. *Ep.* 114). Four other letters from Chrysostom to Elpidius are extant, all written from Cucusus (*Epp.* 25, 138, A.D. 405; *Ep.* 131, A.D. 406; *Ep.* 142, A.D. 407).

Elpidius suffered for his fidelity to his friend in the persecution against the Joannite party under Atticus and Porphyry. In 406 he was deposed from his see, and was closely imprisoned in his house for three years (Pallad. *Dial.* p. 195). In 414 Alexander, succeeding Porphyry as bp. of Antioch, restored Elpidius to his see in a manner which testified deep reverence for his character, and pope Innocent heard of it with extreme satisfaction (Baron. 408, §§ 35, 37; Tillem. xi. 274). [E.V.]

Emilianus (8) (*Aemilianus, San Millan*), solitary; claimed by the Spanish Benedictines as joint patron of Spain with St. James (Sandoval, *Fundaciones de San Benito en España*, Madrid, 1601). The only original source of information about him is his Life by St. Braulio bp. of Saragossa, written about 50 years after his death, on the testimony of four of his disciples. St. Braulio gives no dates and no names of parents, but the common tradition is that St. Emilianus was born *c.* 473, and died *c.* 572. His birthplace and the site of his oratory have caused much controversy, Castile claiming him as born at Berceo, close to the existing monastery of San Millan, while Aragon urges Verdeyo, near Calatayud.

He began life as a shepherd, and while following his flock over the mountains had the dream which caused his conversion. He betook himself to St. Felix, a neighbouring hermit, for instruction in Catholic belief and practice. He soon left Verdejo for the mountains, wandering N.W. into the remotest parts between Burgos and Logrono. For 40 years he lived a hermit's life there, mostly on or near the peak of La Cogolla (according to the tradition of the monastery; there is no mention of the Cogolla of St. Braulio's life), whence the after-name of the monastery which commemorated him—San Millan de la Cogolla. Didymus, bp. of Tarrazona (Turiasso), much against the saint's will, ordained him presbyter, and gave him the cure of Vergegium. Here his entire unworldliness drew upon him the hatred of his brother clergy. He was accused before Didymus of wasting the goods of the church, and deprived of his cure. Thus released from an unwelcome office, Emilianus passed the rest of his life at an oratory near Vergegium. During this second retirement, although his personal asceticism increased rather than diminished, he allowed himself to be surrounded by a small circle of disciples, and became widely famed for charity and tenderness towards the poor. St. Braulio nowhere speaks of him as monachus, but only as presbyter. Tamayo de Salazar, *Martyr. Hisp.* vi. 109; *Esp. Sagrada*, l. 2; Mabillon, saec. i.; Yepes, *Chron. Benedictin.* i. ann. 572; Sanchez, *Poesias Cast. ant. al Siglo XV.* vol. ii. [M.A.W.]

Encratites (Ἐγκρατεῖς, Irenaeus; Ἐγκρατηταί, Clem. Alex.; Ἐγκρατῖται, Hippol.), heretics who abstained from flesh, wine, and the marriage bed, believing them essentially impure. Persons who so abstained called themselves continent (ἐγκρατεῖς, Iren. i. 28, p. 107); and the slightly modified form, Encratites, soon became a technical name to denote those whose asceticism was regarded as of a heretical character (Clem. Alex. *Paed.* ii. 2, p. 182; *Strom.* i. 15, p. 359, vii. 17, p. 900; Hippol. *Ref.* viii. 20, p. 276). We are not bound to suppose that all who were known by the name formed a single united sect. Irenaeus, *e.g.* (*l.c.*), says that some of the earliest of them were followers of Saturninus and Marcion; and it is reasonable to understand by this, not that they united in a single heretical body, but that, independently using the same mode of life and making the same boast of continence, they were known to the orthodox by the same name. The practice of such abstinence was older than Christianity. Not to speak of the Indian ascetics (to whom Clement of Alexandria refers as predecessors of the Encratites), the abstinence of the Essenes, both in respect of food and of marriage, is notorious. Josephus's account of the Essenes is referred to by Porphyry, who, like them, objected both to the use of animal food and to animal sacrifices. An interesting specimen of Pythagorean doctrine on this subject is his work περὶ ἀποχῆς τῶν ἐμψύχων, addressed to a friend who after trial of abstinence had wickedly relapsed into the use of flesh diet. He insists on the importance of keeping the soul, as far as possible, free from the bonds of matter, to which animal food tends to enslave it; on the wisdom of avoiding everything over which evil demons have power, viz. all material things, and especially animal food; and on the injustice of depriving of life for our pleasure animals akin to ourselves, having reason, emotions, sentiments, completely like ours.

The account given by Hegesippus of James the Just (Eus. *H. E.* ii. 23) shews that righteousness of the Essene type was clearly held in admiration in the Christian church; and I. Tim. iv. 3-6 shews that teachers had already arisen who inculcated such abstinence as a duty. But it does not appear that they held the Gnostic doctrine, that matter is essentially evil, and its creation the work of a being inferior or hostile to the Supreme; for the apostle's argument assumes as common ground that the things they rejected were creatures of the good God. We find from the Clementines that the Ebionite sects which arose out of Essenism permitted marriage, but disallowed flesh meat and wine; and that their doctrine respecting God's work of creation was quite orthodox. Hippolytus, too, who takes his account of the Encratites from his own acquaintance with them as a then existing sect, describes them as orthodox in doctrine concerning God and Christ, and differing from the church only in their manner of life. But the Gnostic teachers named by Irenaeus (*l.c.*) undoubtedly based their asceticism on the doctrine of the evil of matter, denying it to be the work of God, and consequently deemed it wrong, by generation, to bring new souls under the dominion of death, and expose them to the miseries of this life. A full discussion of their arguments occurs in the third book of Clement's *Stromateis* (though the name Encratites does not occur here), the principal writers whom he combats being MARCION, TATIAN, already mentioned by Irenaeus as a leader of that sect, and Julius CASSIANUS. The Gospel according to the Egyptians contained alleged sayings of our Lord, which they used in support of their doctrines. Epiphanius mentions that they used other apocryphal writings, such as the Acts of Andrew, John, and Thomas. This controversy seems to have been actively carried on in the last quarter of the 2nd cent. Eusebius (*H. E.* iv. 28) relates that Musanus, a writer early in that period, addressed a very effective dissuasive argument to certain brethren who had turned aside to that sect, then newly come into existence; and Theodoret (*Haer. Fab.* i. 21) mentions that another writer of the same date, Apollinaris, wrote against the Severian Encratites. Eusebius (iv. 29) derives this name Severians from a certain Severus, who became an Encratite leader shortly after Tatian. He adds that these Severians received the O.T. and the Gospels, only putting their peculiar interpretations on them, but reviled Paul, rejecting his epistles and also *Acts*. This shews Ebionite features, and these Severians may have been of Ebionite origin, for great diversity probably existed between the teaching of persons classed together as Encratites. The Severians are described by Epiphanius (*Haer.* 45) with all the features of an Ophite sect; but evidently from hearsay only, as he speaks of the sect as having almost died out; and Lipsius (*Q.-K. des Epiph.* 215) gives good reason for thinking that he found no article on them in previous heretical treatises. Epiphanius describes (*Haer.* 48) the Encratites as widely spread, enumerating seven different countries where they were then to be found. Evidently, therefore, there were in these countries heretics leading an ascetic life, though it would be unsafe to assert an absolute identity in their teaching. We may conclude Epiphanius mistaken in placing the Encratites after the Tatianites, as if they were a branch of the latter sect, the true relation being just the opposite. Some additional information about the Encratites is in the work of Macarius Magnes, pub. in Paris, 1876. He wrote *c.* 400, and enumerates (iii. 43, p. 151) some countries where the Encratites (whom he also called Apotactites and Eremites) were to be found. He was thus, probably, acquainted with the work of Epiphanius. But he adds that a defence of their doctrines in eight books had been published by a leader of theirs, Dositheus, a Cilician, in which he inveighed against marriage and the tasting of wine or partaking of flesh meat. In his account of the Samaritan DOSITHEUS, Epiphanius introduces some Encratite features not attested by other authorities, and may have allowed his knowledge of the doctrine of the one Dositheus to affect his account of the other. We cannot give much weight to the account of Philaster, who (72) assigns the name and doctrine of the Encratites to the followers of AERIUS; and we may wholly disregard the inventive "Praedestinatus" (who represents the Encratites as refuted by an Epiphanius, bp. of Ancyra), except to repeat his distinction between Encratite and Catholic abstainers—viz. the former asserted the food they rejected to be evil; the latter owned it to be good, too good for them. Canons of St. Basil on Encratite baptism (clxxxviii. can. 1; cxcix. can. 47) have given rise to some dispute, but it seems clear that St. Basil wished to reject the baptism of these Encratites, not because the orthodox formula of baptism was lacking, but because, regarding them as tainted with Marcionite error, he could not accept the verbal acknowledgment of the Father in the baptismal formula as atonement for the insult offered to the Creator, Whose work they looked on as evil. For a reference to these canons, as well as to the law of the Theodosian code (A.D. 381) against the Manicheans, who sheltered themselves under the name of Encratites, see APOSTOLICI. Not many years earlier the Encratites were an existing sect in

Galatia; for Sozomen (v. 11) records the sufferings of Busiris, at that time one of them, in the persecution under Julian. [G.S.]

Ennodius (1) Magnus Felix, bp. of Pavia, born at Arles (Ennod. *Ep.* lib. vii. 8) *c.* 473; connected with Romans of distinction (*ib.* iv. 25). The invasion of the Visigoths, and the consequent loss of his patrimony, caused him to migrate at an early age to Milan, where he was educated in the house of an aunt. In 489, the year in which Theodoric invaded Italy, his aunt died, and he was saved from beggary by marriage (*Eucharist. de Vit.*). A dangerous sickness (*Ep.* viii. 24) led him to serious thought and suggested the composition of his *Eucharisticon*, in which he reviews with penitence his past life. He was subsequently ordained deacon by Epiphanius bp. of Pavia, whose exhortations determined him to renounce his marriage, with the consent of his wife, who retired into a convent. In 494 he accompanied Epiphanius (Ennod. *Vit. Epiphan.* 234 A) on a mission to Gundebaud, king of the Burgundians, to procure the ransom of certain Ligurian prisoners. Upon the death of Epiphanius two years later he visited Rome, and gained reputation by composing an apology for pope Symmachus and the synod which acquitted him, as well as by a public panegyric in honour of Theodoric. The former of these was inserted in the *Acta Conciliorum*; the latter is generally included in collections of the *Panegyrici Veteres*. Under the next pope, Hormisdas, he succeeded Maximus II. in the see of Pavia, and was sent in 515, and again in 517, on an embassy to the emperor Anastasius to oppose the spread of the Eutychian heresy. Both embassies were unsuccessful. Anastasius, failing to corrupt or bend the bishop, had him placed on board an unseaworthy vessel. Ennodius, however, arrived safely in his diocese, which he continued to administer for four years. He died at the age of 48, and was buried in the church of St. Michael at Pavia, July 17, 521.

His writings exemplify throughout a profane tendency of thought and expression which Christian writers in Gaul were slow to abandon. Many of his letters suit the pen of a heathen rhetorician rather than of a Christian bishop. His illustrations are commonly drawn from Greek mythology. He speaks of divine grace as descending "de Superis," and sets the Fates side by side with Jesus Christ. His style is turgid, involved, and affected. He seems to shrink from making himself intelligible lest he should be thought commonplace, and the result is unattractive. His works are reprinted with notes in Migne's *Patr.* vol. lxiii. For his Life see Sirmond's ed.; Ceillier, *Auteurs sacr. et ecclés.* x. 569; for a just estimate of his literary merits, Ampère, *Hist. lit. de la France*, t. ii. c. vii. [E.M.Y.]

Ephraim (4) the Syrian, usually called Ephrem Syrus, from the Syriac form of his name Aphrem, was born in Mesopotamia, for he describes his home as lying between the Tigris and the Euphrates (*Opp. Syr.* i. 23), probably at Nisibis. As Edessa became the chief scene of his labours, he is generally styled the Edessene. It is comparatively certain that he died, as stated by St. Jerome, "in extreme old age," *c.* A.D. 373, and therefore was probably born *c.* A.D. 308.*

The story of his parents seeking to train him in idolatry is at variance with his own statements. In his Confession (*Opp. Gr.* i. 129) he says, "When I sinned, I was already a partaker of grace: I had been early taught about Christ by my parents; they who had begotten me after the flesh had trained me in the fear of the Lord. I had seen my neighbours living piously; I had heard of many suffering for Christ. My own parents were confessors before the Judge: yea, I am the kindred of martyrs." Or again, in his Syriac works (*Opp. Syr.* ii. 499): "I was born in the way of truth; and though my boyhood understood not the greatness of the benefit, I knew it when trial came."

In 337 Constantine the Great died, and Sapor, king of Persia, seized the opportunity of invading Mesopotamia. He commenced the siege of Nisibis in 338, and in 70 days had brought it to the verge of surrender. But Ephrem induced the aged bishop James to mount the walls and pray for the Divine succour. Shortly afterwards swarms of mosquitoes and horse-flies made the horses and elephants unmanageable, and Sapor withdrew his forces lest he should bring upon himself heavier chastisement. Before the end of 338 St. James died, when Ephrem probably left Nisibis, and after a short stay at Amid, to which city his mother is said to have belonged, travelled towards Edessa, the chief seat both of Christianity and of learning in Mesopotamia.

Knowing no handicraft and having no means of living, Ephrem there entered the service of a bath-keeper, but devoted his spare time to teaching and reasoning with the natives. While so engaged one day his words were overheard by an aged monk who had descended from his hermitage into the city, and being rebuked by him for still mingling with the world, Ephrem withdrew into a cavern among the mountains, adopted the monastic dress, and commenced a life of extreme asceticism, giving himself up to study and to writing. His works were widely diffused, and disciples gathered round him, of whom many rose to eminence as teachers, and several of whom he commemorates in his Testament. The growing fame of Basil, bp. of Caesarea in Cappadocia, inspired Ephrem with a strong desire to visit one who had been shewn him in a dream as a column of fire reaching from earth to heaven.

His journey to Caesarea is vouched for by Basil's brother Gregory, and by Ephrem himself in his Encomium on Basil.† Accompanied by an interpreter, he arrived on the eve of the Epiphany, and spent the night in the streets. The next morning they took their place in an obscure corner of the church, and Ephrem groaned in spirit as he saw Basil seated in a magnificent pulpit, arrayed in shining garments, with a mitre sparkling with jewels on his head, and surrounded by a multitude of clergy adorned with almost equal splendour. "Alas!" he said to his interpreter, "I fear

* St. Jerome's expression must not be forced too much.

† On the authenticity of this piece, which exists only in Greek, see Proleg. to Ephr. *Opp. Gr.* II. li.

our labour is in vain. For if we, who have given up the world, have advanced so little in holiness, what spiritual gifts can we expect to find in one surrounded by so great pomp and glory?" But when Basil began to preach, it seemed to Ephrem as though the Holy Ghost, in shape like a dove, sat upon his shoulder, and suggested to him the words. From time to time the people murmured their applause, and Ephrem twice repeated sentences which had fallen from the preacher's lips. Upon this Basil sent his archdeacon to invite him into his presence, which, offended at the saint's ragged attire, he did reluctantly, and only after he had been twice bidden to summon him. After embracing one another, with many florid compliments, Basil asked him how it was that, knowing no Greek, he had twice cheered the sermon, and repeated sentences of it to the multitude? And Ephrem answered, "It was not I who praised and repeated, but the Holy Ghost by my mouth." Under pressure from St. Basil, Ephrem consented to be ordained deacon. When Basil had laid his hands upon him, being suddenly endowed with the knowledge of Syriac, he said to Ephrem in that tongue, "O Lord, bid him arise," upon which Ephrem answered in Greek, "Save me, and raise me up, O God, by Thy grace." Doubtless Ephrem, travelling about with an educated companion, and having been an eminent teacher at Edessa, a place famous for its schools, had picked up some knowledge of Greek and Hebrew, some evidence of which we shall later gather from his own writings. Two instances are given in the *Acta* of the influence of Ephrem's teaching on St. Basil. It had been usual at Caesarea in the Doxology to say, Glory be to the Father, and to the Son, to the Holy Ghost; but after Ephrem's visit Basil inserted *and* before the third clause. Whereat the people in church murmured, and Basil defended himself by saying that his Syrian visitor had taught him that the insertion of the conjunction was necessary for the more clear manifestation of the doctrine of the Holy Trinity. The other instance is as follows: In Gen. i. 2 the LXX renders "The Spirit of God was borne upon the surface of the water." So St. Basil had understood it, but the Peshitta-Syriac version renders it, "The Spirit of God brooded upon the face of the waters," which Ephrem explained of the Spirit resting upon them with a warm and fostering influence as of a hen sitting upon her nest, and so endowing them with the power of bringing forth the moving creature that hath life. St. Basil gives two reasons for trusting his Syrian friend. First, that Ephrem led a very ascetic life; "for in proportion as a man abandons the love of the world, so does he excel in that perfection which rises above the world." Secondly, that "Ephrem is an acute thinker, and has a thorough knowledge of the divine philosophy," *i.e.* of the general sense of Holy Scripture. There is nothing to suggest that any appeal was made to the Hebrew, as Benedict suggests, though, in fact, the Syriac and Hebrew words are the same; and, curiously enough, in his own exposition (*Opp. Syr.* i. 8), Ephrem says that the words simply mean that a wind was in motion; for the waters were instinct, he argues, with no creative energy till the fourth day. From Caesarea, Ephrem was recalled to Edessa by the news that the city was assailed by numerous heresies. On his journey he rescued the people of Samosata from the influence of false teaching by a miracle, and on reaching home sought to counteract heresy by teaching orthodoxy in hymns. The fatalistic tenets of Bardesan, a Gnostic who flourished at the end of the 2nd cent., had been embodied in 150 psalms, a number fixed upon in irreverent imitation of the Psalter of David. His son Honorius had set these hymns to music, and so sweet were both the words and tunes that they were known by heart even by children and sung to the guitar. To combat their influence Ephrem composed numerous hymns himself, and trained young women, who were aspirants after the conventual life, to sing them in chorus. These hymns have no rhyme, nor do they scan, but are simply arranged in parallel lines, containing each, as a rule, seven syllables. Their poetry consists in their elevated sentiments and richness of metaphor, but their regular form was an aid to the memory, and rendered them capable of being set to music. The subjects of these hymns were the Life of our Lord, including His Nativity, Baptism, Fasting, and chief incidents of his ministry, His Passion, Resurrection, and Ascension. He wrote also on Repentance, on the Dead, and on Martyrs. Upon the Festivals of our Lord, we read, on the first days of the week, and on the days of martyrs, Ephrem gathered round him his choirs, and the whole city flocked to hear them, and the poems of Bardesan lost their influence. While thus occupied Basil endeavoured to persuade him to visit Caesarea again, intending to make him a bishop, but the saint even feigned madness rather than consent. Meanwhile he wrote upon the devastation committed by the Persians, the Maccabean martyrs, the Life of Constantine, and so on, until the accession of Julian rudely disturbed his studies. On his expedition against the Persians Julian had advanced as far as Haran, a town so famous for obstinate adherence to heathenism that Haranite in Syriac is equivalent to pagan, and there determined to hold a great sacrifice, to which he commanded the Edessenes to send chosen citizens to do him homage, and to grace by their presence his restoration of the old cult. But this met with such fierce opposition on the part of the people, and such an eager desire for martyrdom, that the embassy withdrew in haste, and Julian threatened Edessa with bitter vengeance upon his return. Ephrem, who had exerted himself to the utmost in this crisis, resumed his hermit life, quitting the mountains only for controversy with heretics or for charitable services. As a controversialist, Gregory of Nyssa relates of him with great approbation an act contrary to modern views of morality: The "insane and irrational Apollinaris" had written a treatise in two volumes containing much that was contrary to Scripture. These he had given in charge of a lady at Edessa, from whom Ephrem borrowed them, pretending that he was a disciple of Apollinaris and was preparing to defend his views. Before returning them he glued the leaves together, and then challenged the heretic to a public disputation. Apollinaris accepted the challenge so far as to consent to read from these books what he had written, declining more on account of his great age; but he found the leaves so firmly fastened together that he could not open them, and withdrew, deeply mortified by his opponent's unworthy victory.

Far more creditable is the last act recorded of Ephrem. While withdrawn in his rocky cavern he heard that Edessa had been visited by a severe famine. He came down to the city, and induced the richer citizens to bring out their secret stores of food, on condition, however, that Ephrem should himself take charge of them. He managed them with such skill, prudence, and honesty that they sufficed for the Edessenes and for numerous strangers also. The next year was one of great plenty, and Ephrem resumed his solitary life amidst the prayers and gratitude of all classes.

His death followed shortly afterwards, fully foreseen by himself, as his Testament proves. In this hymn, written in heptasyllabic metre, after playing upon his own name and professing his faith, he commands his disciples not to bury him beneath the altar, nor in a church, nor amongst the martyrs, but in the common burying-ground of strangers, in his gown and cowl, with no spices nor waxlights, but with their prayers. It ends with an account of Lamprotata, daughter of the prefect of Edessa, who earnestly sought permission to be buried in due time at Ephrem's feet.

The works of Ephrem were most voluminous. Sozomen (*Eccl. Hist.* iii. 16) says that he wrote three million lines, but a large proportion has perished. What remains is said by Bellarmine to be "pious rather than learned." The great edition of his works is that in six vols. fol., pub. at Rome in 1732-1743, under the editorship of the Maronite Peter Mobarek, better known by the Latin translation of his surname Benedict, and completed after his death by J. S. E. Asseman, titular bp. of Apamaea, who is answerable, however, for the translation of only vol. vi. pp. 425-687. The first three vols. consist of sermons and discourses in Greek with a Latin translation. Many of these are probably genuine, for Sozomen says that already in his lifetime works of Ephrem were translated into Greek, and as both Chrysostom and Jerome were acquainted with them, and Gregory of Nyssa quotes his Testament, it is certain that several of his writings were very soon thus made available for general use. But some pieces must be received with caution, and one (*Opp. Gr.* ii. 356 seq.) is almost certainly not genuine.

The other three vols. contain his Syriac works, the most important being his Exposition of O.T. Of the commentary upon the Gospels few traces remain, but Dionysius Barsalibi, bp. of Amid, says that Ephrem had followed the order of the Diatessaron of Tatian. As copies of Dionysius's own commentary exist in the British Museum, the Bodleian Library, and elsewhere, some portions of Ephrem's work, as well as some idea of Tatian's arrangement, might be obtained from it. A collection of Armenian translations of Ephrem's works, pub. in 4 vols. 8vo by the Mechitarists at Venice in 1836, includes one (in vol. iii.) of his commentary on St. Paul's epistles.

Following upon the commentary are 12 metrical expositions of portions of Scripture, such as the creation of man in God's image, the temptation of Eve, the translation of Enoch, etc., occupying pp. 316-319. Some of these, especially that upon the mission of Jonah and the repentance of the Ninevites, have been translated into English by the Rev. H. Burgess (Lond. 1856), the author also of *Select Metrical Hymns and Homilies of Ephraem Syrus* (two vols. Lond. 1853). These expositions are followed by 13 metrical homilies upon the Nativity, pp. 396-436. Next come 56 homilies against false doctrines (pp. 437-560); chiefly against Bardesan, Marcion, and Manes.

In vol. iii., after the *Acta S. Ephraemi* (i.-lxiii.), the first place is held by 87 homilies on the Faith, in answer to freethinkers. The last seven of these are called sermons upon the Pearl, which Ephrem takes as an emblem of the Christian faith, working out the idea with great beauty, though with that diffuseness which is the common fault of his writings. Three very long controversial homilies (pp. 164-208) follow, repeating many of the same thoughts.

A sermon against the Jews, preached on Palm Sunday (pp. 209-224), has been translated by the Rev. J. B. Morris into English.* Then follow 85 hymns (pp. 225-359) to be used at the burial of bishops, presbyters, deacons, monks, princes, rich men, strangers, matrons, women, youths, children, in time of plague, and for general use. These are trans. into Eng. in Burgess's *Select Metrical Hymns*.

Next come four short homilies on Free-will (pp. 359-366), partly following the order of the Syriac alphabet; then 76 homilies on Repentance (pp. 367-561). Next, 12 sermons on the Paradise of Eden (pp. 562-598); and finally, 18 sermons on miscellaneous subjects (pp. 599-687). Considerable activity has been displayed in editing other Syriac works of Ephrem—*e.g.* by Dr. J. J. Overbeck, in *S. Ephraemi Syri, Rabulae, Balaei, aliorumque Opera Selecta* (Oxf., Clarendon Press, 1865). Almost more important is "*S. Ephraemi Syri Carmina Nisibena*, ed. by Dr. G. Bickell, Lipsiae, 1866." Of these hymns, the first 21 treat of the long struggle between Sapor and the Romans for the possession of Nisibis, from its siege in 350 to just before its miserable surrender by Jovian in 363. The next 5 hymns have perished; in Nos. 26-30 the scene is Edessa, and the subject the schism there in the bishopric of Barses, A.D. 361-370. Bickell thinks these were written *c.* 370, towards the close of Ephrem's life. Hymns 31-34 treat of Haran and the many troubles its bishop, Vitus, endured from the pagans there. The other hymns (35-77) treat of the Overthrow of Death and Satan by our Lord, of the Resurrection of the Body in refutation of Bardesan and Manes,

* Morris (*Select Works of Ephr. Syrus*, Oxf. 1847) translated 13 rhythms on the Nativity, this against the Jews, the 80 rhythms on the Faith, 7 on the Pearl, and 3 long controversial homilies.

of Dialogues between Death, Satan, and Man, and of Hymns upon the Resurrection, not of a controversial but of a consolatory character. From the directions for singing given with each hymn, and the existence in most of them of a response or refrain noted in the MS. in red, the collection was evidently for liturgical use.

Bertheau edited a Syriac homily of St. Ephrem from a MS. at Rome (Göttingen, 1837), and another from the Museum Borghianum was pub. by Zingerle and Mösinger in *Monumenta Syriaca* (Innsbruck, 1869), vol. i. pp. 4-12; in vol. ii. (pub. 1878) numerous fragments from MSS. at Rome are found, pp. 33-51. In most Chrestomathies specimens of Ephrem's writings are given, and that by Hahn and Sieffert consists entirely of them.

As a commentator Ephrem holds a middle place between the literal interpretation of Theodore of Mopsuestia and the allegorical method of Origen. As Basil and Gregory were both strongly influenced by Origen, Ephrem's independence is the more remarkable. In commenting on Is. xxv. 7 (vol. ii. 61), he gives a statement of his method as follows: "Though the prophet is speaking of Sennacherib he has a covert reference to Satan. For the spiritual sense is usually the same as the ecclesiastical. The words therefore of the prophets concerning those things which have happened or were about to happen to the Jews are mystically to be referred to the future propagation of the church, and the providence of God and His judgments upon the just and upon evil-doers." Benedict, followed by Lengerke, instead of *ecclesiastical* translates *historical*; what Ephrem really says is that there is first the literal interpretation, and secondly a spiritual one, which generally refers to the church.

The question has often been asked whether he really possessed any competent acquaintance with Hebrew and Greek. He had not had a learned education, but nevertheless displays considerable knowledge, including some of physical science, and in his discourses on fate, freewill, etc., he manifests, without parade, a sufficient mastery of Greek philosophy to refute the Gnostic errors prevalent in the East. We need not be surprised, therefore, that Sozomen says (*H. E.* iii. 16) that Basil wondered at his learning.

The chief places which suggest some knowledge of Hebrew are as follow. Commenting on the creation of whales in Gen. i. 21 (*Opp. Syr.* i. 18), he says that they and leviathan inhabit the waters, behemoth the land; quoting not only Job xl. 15, but Ps. l. 10, which he translates, "And behemoth upon a thousand hills." Ephrem's rendering is perfectly possible, and must have been obtained from some Jewish source.

On I. Sam. iii. 11 he rightly says that both the Syr. and Heb. names for cymbal resemble the verb so translated. In I. Sam. xxi. 7 he correctly explains the word "detained" by noting that the Heb. word *neasar* signifies pressed or bidden away. In II. Kings iii. 4 he rightly says that the Syr. *nokdo* is really a Heb. word, and means "head shepherd."

These points might have been picked up from conversation with others, and there is a marked absence of acquaintance with the language in his commentary as a whole.

Of Greek he also shews but a very moderate knowledge, though a more real acquaintance with it than with Hebrew. His own words in *Opp. Syr.* ii. 317 are to the point: "Not from the rivulet of my own thought have I opened these things for thy drinking, for I am poor and destitute alike of meat and drink; but, like a bottle from the sea or drops from a caldron, I have begged these things from just men, who were lords of the fountain."

An example will shew him much more at home in Greek than in Hebrew. In I. Kings xiv. 3 (*Opp. Syr.* i. 480) the Syriac version has, instead of *cracknels*, a rare word signifying *sweetmeats*. Ephrem notices that the Greek has *grapes*, and gives this as an explanation of the Syriac; but makes no reference to the Hebrew word, which certainly signifies some kind of *cakes*, such as might rightly be called sweetmeats, but certainly is no kind of fruit.

From his intense devotion and piety, his hymns were largely adopted into the services of the church, and prayers also composed by him are found in most Oriental liturgies. His personal character deserves high praise. He was an extreme ascetic, passing his whole life in poverty, raggedness, humility, and gentleness. His gentleness has been denied on account of the fierce language sometimes used in controversial writings. We may, however, take his words in his Testament as literally true (*Opp. Gr.* ii. 396): "Throughout my whole life, neither by night nor day, have I reviled any one, nor striven with any one; but in their assemblies I have disputed with those who deny the faith. For if a wolf is entering the fold, and the dog goes not out and barks, the master beats the dog. But a wise man hates no one, or if he hates at all, he hates only a fool."

"His words reach the heart, for they treat powerfully of human joys and cares; they depict the struggles and storms of life, and sometimes its calm rest. He knows how to awaken terror and alarm, as he sets forth before the sinner his punishment, God's righteous judgment, his destined condemnation; he knows, too, how to build up and comfort, where he proclaims the hopes of the faithful and the bliss of eternal happiness. His words ring in mild, soft tones when he paints the happy rest of the pious, the peace of soul enjoyed by those who cleave to the Christian faith; they thunder and rage like a storm wind when he scourges heretics, or chastises pride and folly. Ephraim was an orator possessed of spirit and taste, and his poetical gifts were exactly those calculated to give weight and influence to his authority as a teacher among his countrymen" (Roediger). As such they venerated him, giving him especially the title of Malphono, the teacher; but one of his greatest services to the church was the marvellous variety and richness which he gave to its public worship. Ephraim's quotations from the Gospels have been collected by F. C. Burkitt (*Texts and Studies*, vol. vii. No. 2, Camb. Univ. Press). His Commentary on the Diatessaron was trans. into Latin by J. B. Aucher, and pub. in this form by G. Mösinger (Venice, 1876). See also J. H. Hill, *A Dissertation on the Gospel Commentary of S. Ephraim* (Edinburgh, 1896). The *Fragments* of S. Ephraim have been ed. by J. R. Harris for the (Camb. Univ. Press). [R.P.S.]

Ephraim (6) (*Ephrem*, *Ephraemius*, or, as Theophanes gives the name, *Euphraimius*), bp. of Antioch and patriarch, A.D. 527-545. The title, ὁ 'Αμίδιος, given him by Theophanes, indicates that he was a native of Amida in Armenia. He devoted the early part of his life to civil employments, and became Count of the East in the reign of Justin I. The city of Antioch having been nearly destroyed in A.D. 525 and 526 by earthquake and conflagration, Ephraim was sent by Justin as commissioner to relieve the sufferers and restore the city. The high qualities manifested in the fulfilment of these duties gained the affection and respect of the people of Antioch, who unanimously chose him bishop on the death of Euphrasius (Evagr. *H. E.* iv. 5, 6). His consecration is placed in A.D. 357. As bishop he exhibited an unwavering firmness against the heretical tendencies of his day. Theophanes says that he shewed "a divine zeal against schismatics" (*Chronogr.* p. 118). Moschus tells a story of his encounter near Hierapolis with one of the pillar ascetics, a follower of Severus and the Acephali (*Prat. Spiritual.* c. 36). Ephraim examined synodically the tenets of Syncleticus, metropolitan of Tarsus, who was suspected of Eutychian leanings but was acquitted (Phot. *Cod.* 228). In 537, at the bidding of Justinian, he repaired with Hypatius of Ephesus and Peter of Jerusalem to Gaza to hold a council in the matter of Paul the patriarch of Alexandria, who had been banished to that city and there deposed. In obedience to the emperor Justinian, Ephraim held a synod at Antioch, which repudiated the doctrines of Origen as heretical (Liberat. c. 23, *apud* Labbe, *Concil.* v. 777 seq.; Baronius, *Annal.* 537, 538). He was the author of a large number of theological treatises directed against Nestorius, Eutyches, Severus, and the Acephali, and in defence of the decrees of Chalcedon. In 546, yielding to severe pressure, he subscribed the edict Justinian had put forth condemning "the three chapters" (Facund. *Pro Defens. Trium Capit.* iv. 4). He did not survive the disgrace of this concession, and died in 547.

His copious theological works have almost entirely perished, and we have little knowledge of them save through Photius (*Biblioth. Cod.* 228, 229), who speaks of having read three of the volumes, but gives particulars of two only. Some few fragments of his defence of the council of Chalcedon, and of the third book against Severus, and other works, are given by Mai (*Bibl. Nov.* iv. 63, vii. 204) and are printed by Migne (*Patr. Gk.* lxxxvi. par. 2, pp. 2099 seq.). Theophanes, *Chronogr.* ad ann. 519, p. 118 D; Moschus, *Prat. Spiritual.* cc. 36, 37; Cave, *Hist. Lit.* i. 507; Fabric. *Bibl. Graec.* lib. v. c. 38; Le Quien, *Oriens Christ.* ii. 733). [E.V.]

Epiphanes, a Gnostic writer about the middle of the 2nd cent., or earlier. Clement of Alexandria (*Strom.* iii. p. 511) gives the following account of him. He was the son of CARPOCRATES, by a mother named Alexandria, a native of Cephallenia. He died at the age of 17, and at Same, a city of Cephallenia, a handsome temple and other buildings were raised in his memory; and at the new moon the Cephallenians were wont to celebrate his apotheosis as a god by sacrifices, libations, banquets, and the singing of hymns. He had been instructed by his father in the ordinary circle of arts and sciences, and in the Platonic philosophy. He was the founder of the "Monadic Gnosis," and from him flowed the heresy of those afterwards known as Carpocratians. He was the author of a work on Justice, which he made to consist in equality. He taught that, God having given His benefits to all alike and in common, human laws are censurable which instituted the distinction of *meum* and *tuum*, and which secure to one as his peculiar possession that to which all have an equal right. This communistic doctrine he extended to the sexual relations. Whatever may have been the origin of the phrase "Monadic Gnosis," the doctrine here described seems the direct opposite of Dualism. Instead of accounting for the existence of evil as the work of a hostile principle, this theory would represent moral evil as a mere fiction of human laws, perversely instituted in opposition to the will of the Creator.

There is a passage in Irenaeus (I. xi. 3, p. 54) which, it has been contended, gives us another specimen of the teaching of Epiphanes. In giving an account of the doctrines of some followers of Valentinus, after stating the theory of Secundus, he goes on to mention the description which another "illustrious teacher of theirs" (*clarus magister*) gives of the origin of the primary Tetrad. In this the first principle is stated to be one existing before all things, surpassing all thought and speech, which the author calls Oneliness (μονότης). With this Monotes co-existed a power which he calls Unity (ἑνότης). This Monotes and Henotes constituting absolute unity (τὸ ἓν οὖσαι) emitted (though not in any proper sense of that word) a principle the object of thought only, which reason calls Monad. And with this Monad co-existed a power consubstantial with it, which the author calls Unit (τὸ ἕν). From this Tetrad came all the rest of the Aeons. Pearson conjectured (see Dodwell, *Dissert. in Iren.* iv. §§ 25) that the "clarus magister" of the old Latin translation represented ἐπιφανὴς διδάσκαλος, and that this Epiphanes was a proper name, or at least that there was a play upon words referring to that name. The doctrine of the extract, then, which seems an attempt to reconcile the theory of a Tetrad with strong belief in the unity of the First Principle, might well be a part of the Monadic Gnosis, of which Epiphanes was said to be the author. Pearson's restoration of the Greek has since been pretty nearly verified by the recovery of the passage as reproduced by Hippolytus (*Ref.* vi. 38), where it runs ἄλλος δέ τις ἐπιφανὴς διδάσκαλος αὐτῶν. Here the word in question is plainly an adjective, and Tertullian so understood it, who translates (*adv. Valent.* 37) "insignioris apud eos magistri." On the other hand, Epiphanius understood the passage of Epiphanes. On examining what he tells of that heretic (*Haer.*

32), it is plain that Epiphanius has been following Irenaeus until, on coming to the words ἐπιφανὴς διδάσκαλος, he goes off to Clement of Alexandria, and puts in what he there found about Epiphanes. But Neander has made it almost certain that the person to whom Irenaeus really refers is MARCUS (17). He points out that these four names for the members of the primary Tetrad, Monotes, Henotes, Monas, and Hen, which the "illustrious teacher" (c. 11) speaks of as names of his own giving, occur again with a καθ' ἃ προείρηται in a passage cited from Marcus by name (Iren. i. 15, p. 74). [G.S.]

Epiphanius (1), bp. of Salamis in Cyprus, zealous champion of orthodox faith and monastic piety, was born at Besanduke, a village near Eleutheropolis in Palestine. As in 392, twelve years before his death, he was an aged man, we may conjecturally date his birth between 310 and 320. Much of his early lifetime was spent with the monks of Egypt, among whom he not only acquired a burning zeal for ecclesiastical orthodoxy and the forms of ascetic life then coming into favour, but also first came in contact with various kinds of heretics. When twenty years old he returned home and built a monastery near Besanduke, of which he undertook the direction. He was ordained presbyter by Eutychius, then bp. of Eleutheropolis. With St. Hilarion, the founder of Palestinian monasticism, Epiphanius early stood in intimate relation, and at a time when the great majority of Oriental bishops favoured Arian or semi-Arian views, he adhered with unshaken fidelity to the Nicene faith, and its persecuted champions, Eusebius of Vercelli and Paulinus of Antioch, whom Constantius had banished from their sees. In 367 he was elected bp. of Constantia, the ancient Salamis, in Cyprus, where for 36 years he discharged the episcopal office with the zeal he had shewn in his monastery. The whole island was soon covered with monastic institutions. With the monks of Palestine, and especially of his own monastery at Eleutheropolis, he continued as bishop to hold uninterrupted communication. People consulted him on every important question. Some years after his elevation to the episcopate, he addressed a letter to the faithful in Arabia, in defence of the perpetual virginity of Mary, afterwards incorporated in his great work, *Against all Heresies* (*Haer.* lxxviii.). Soon after, several presbyters of Suedra in Pamphylia invoked his assistance in their controversy with Arians and Macedonians. Similar applications came from other quarters; *e.g.* by an Egyptian Christian named Hypatius, and by a presbyter, Conops, apparently a Pisidian, who, with his co-presbyters, sought instruction in a long series of disputed doctrines. This was the origin of his Αγκυρωτός (*Ancoratus*) in 374, an exposition of the faith, which, anchor-like, might fix the mind when tossed by the waves of heresy. A similar occasion produced his great heresiological work, written in the years 374-377, the so-called Πανάριον, on which his fame chiefly rests. He wrote this at the request of Acacius and Paulus, two presbyters and heads of monasteries in Coele-Syria, and in it attacks the Gnostic sects of the 2nd and 3rd cents., and the Arians, semi-Arians, Macedonians, Apollinarians, Origenists, of his own time. About 376 he was taking an active part in the Apollinarian controversies. Vitalis, a presbyter of Antioch, had been consecrated bishop by Apollinaris himself; whereupon Epiphanius undertook a journey to Antioch to recall Vitalis from his error and reconcile him to the orthodox bp. Paulinus. His efforts, however, proved unsuccessful. Though not himself present at the oecumenical council of Constantinople, 381, which ensured the triumph of the Nicene doctrine in the Oriental churches, his shorter confession of faith, which is found at the end of his *Ancoratus* (c. 120) and seems to have been the baptismal creed of the church of Salamis, agrees almost word for word with the Constantinopolitan formula. He took no part in the synod held at Constantinople in 382; but towards the end of that year we find him associated with St. Jerome, Paulinus of Antioch, and the three legates of that synod, at a council held under bp. Damasus at Rome, which appears to have dealt with the Meletian and Apollinarian controversies. At Rome he was domiciled in the house of the elder Paula, who, under the spiritual guidance of St. Jerome, had dedicated her ample fortune to the poor and sick, and Epiphanius seems to have strengthened her in a resolution to forsake home and children for an ascetic life at a great distance from Rome. Early in 383, when the bishops were returning to their sees, Paula went on pilgrimage to the Holy Land. She stayed with Epiphanius in Salamis about 10 days. Somewhat later St. Jerome also visited Epiphanius, on his way to Bethlehem, bringing a train of monks to Cyprus, to salute "the father of almost the whole episcopate, the last relic of ancient piety." Thenceforward we find Epiphanius in almost unbroken intercourse with Jerome, in alliance with whom he began his Origenistic controversies. He had indeed already, in his *Ancoratus* (c. 54) and still more in his *Panarion*, attacked Origen as the ancestor of the Arian heresy.

On hearing that Origenism had appeared in Palestine, he hastened thither, in old age (A.D. 394), to crush it. His appearance sufficed to drive the *ci-devant* Origenist Jerome into the bitterest enmity with his former friends, who refused to repudiate their old attachment. Epiphanius, received with all honours by the bp. of Jerusalem, preached in the most violent manner in the church of the Resurrection. Bp. John, after expressing his disapproval by gestures only for a time, sent his archdeacon to beg him to abstain from speaking further on these topics. The sermon being over, Epiphanius, as he walked by the side of John to the church of the Holy Cross, was pressed upon by the people, as Jerome tells us, from all sides with tokens of veneration. Bp. John, irritated by the sermon, evidently preached against himself, took the next opportunity to preach against certain simple and uneducated persons who represented God to themselves in human form and corporeity. Whereupon Epiphanius rose, and expressing his full concurrence with this, declared that it was quite as necessary to repudiate the heresies of Origen as of the Anthropomorphists. He then hastened to join Jerome at Bethlehem, and required the monks there to renounce at once all church fellowship with the bp. of Jerusalem; but they entreated him to return to John. Epiphanius went back to Jerusalem the same evening, but immediately regretting the step, and without so much as speaking to the bishop, left Jerusalem again at midnight for his old monastery of Eleutheropolis. From there he continued to press the monks of Bethlehem to renounce church fellowship with the Origenist bp. John, and finally availed himself of the occasion provided by a deputation from Bethlehem, to ordain as presbyter Jerome's brother Paulinianus, and impose him on the community, as one who should administer the sacraments among them. This intrusion into the rights of another bishop Epiphanius endeavoured subsequently to excuse in a letter to John. His excuses were far from satisfying the bishop, who reported to other bishops this violation of the canons, and threatened the monks of Bethlehem with ecclesiastical penalties so long as they should recognize Paulinianus or persist in separation. Epiphanius and Jerome, continuing to insist on John publicly purging himself of Origenistic heresy, proceeded to invoke the mediation of Theophilus bp. of Alexandria. Theophilus's legate, a presbyter named Isidore, openly sided with John, and Theophilus himself, who at that time was reckoned an Origenist, designated Epiphanius, in a letter to the bp. of Rome, a heretic and schismatic.

According to another account, Theophilus accused him, as well as John, of Anthropomorphism. Epiphanius certainly received in this controversy little or no support from other bishops. He returned to his diocese, followed by Paulinianus. In this way the chief source of dispute between John and the monks of Jerusalem was removed, and Jerome provisionally renewed communion with the bp. of Jerusalem, as well as with his old friend Rufinus. A few years after the close of this first Origenist controversy, Epiphanius found himself involved in much more unpleasant transactions. Among the monks of Egypt the controversy between Anthropomorphists and Origenists continued to rage. Theophilus of Alexandria having in 398 directed a paschal epistle against the Anthropomorphists, a wild army of monks from the wilderness of Scete rushed into Alexandria, and so frightened the bishop that he thought his life depended on immediate concession. From that time Theophilus appears as a strong opponent of Origenism. In his paschal epistle of 399 he opposes the heresies of Origen in the most violent manner. [THEOPHILUS (9).]

Great joy was expressed by Epiphanius. "Know, my beloved son," he writes to Jerome, "that Amalek is destroyed to the very root; on the hill of Rephidim has been erected the banner of the cross. God has strengthened the hands of His servant Theophilus as once He did those of Moses." Epiphanius was soon drawn yet more deeply into these transactions. The bishops began on all sides to speak against the heresies of Origen.

Theophilus having involved himself in a separate conflict of his own with Chrysostom at Constantinople and finding his cause there opposed by the "Long Brothers" from Egypt [CHRYSOSTOM], made strenuous efforts to gain the assistance of Epiphanius against the action of those Origenistic monks, calling upon him to pass judgment upon Origen and his heresy by means of a Cypriote synod. Epiphanius assembled a synod, prohibited the works of Origen, and called on Chrysostom to do the same. He was then moved by Theophilus to appear personally, as an ancient combatant of heresy, at Constantinople. In the winter of 402 Epiphanius set sail, convinced that only his appearance was required to destroy the last remains of the Origenistic poison. Accompanied by several of his clergy, he landed near Constantinople. Chrysostom sent his clergy to give him honourable reception at the gates of the city, with a friendly invitation to take up his abode in the episcopal residence. This was rudely refused by the passionate old man, who declared himself unable to hold church communion with Chrysostom until he had expelled the "Long Brothers," and had subscribed a condemnation of the writings of Origen. This Chrysostom gently declined, with a reference to the synod about to be holden; whereupon Epiphanius at once assembled the many bishops already gathered at Constantinople, and required them all to subscribe the decrees of his own provincial council against the writings of Origen. Some consented willingly, others refused. Whereupon the opponents of Chrysostom urged Epiphanius to come forward at the service in the church of the Apostles, and openly preach against the Origenists and their protector Chrysostom. Chrysostom warned Epiphanius to abstain, and the latter may by this time have begun to suspect that he was but a tool in the hands of others. On his way to the church he turned back, and soon after, at a meeting with the "Long Brothers," confessed that he had passed judgment upon them on hearsay only, and, growing weary of the miserable business, determined to return home, but died on board ship in the spring of 403.

His story shews him as an honest, but credulous and narrow-minded, zealot for church orthodoxy. His frequent journeys and extensive reading enabled him to collect a large store of historical information, and this he used with much ingenuity in defending the church orthodoxy of his time. But he exercised really very small influence on dogmatic theology, and his theological polemics were more distinguished by pious zeal than by penetrating intelligence. His refutation of the doctrine of Origen is astoundingly superficial, a few meagre utterances detached from their context being all he gives us, and yet he boasted of having read 6,000 of Origen's works, a much larger number, as Rufinus remarks, than Origen had written.

Those of his time regarded Epiphanius as a saint; wherever he appeared, he was surrounded by admiring disciples, and crowds waited for hours to hear him preach. His biography, written in the name of Polybius, an alleged companion of the saint (printed in the edd. of Petavius and Dindorf), is little more than a collection of legends.

Among his writings the most important are the *Ancoratus* and *Panarion*. The *Ancoratus* comprises in 121 sections a prolix exposition, full of repetitions, of the doctrines of the Trinity, the true humanity of Christ and the resurrection of the body, with a constant polemic against Origen and the heresiarchs of his own time, especially Arians, Sabellians, Pneumatomachi, and Dimoirites (Apollinarians). The whole concludes with the Nicene creed in a twofold form with various additions. This work is chiefly of interest as a witness to the orthodoxy of its time. The *Panarion* is of much greater importance. It deals in three books with 80 heresies. The catalogue is essentially that already given in his *Ancoratus* (cc. 11 and 12). He begins with heresies existing at the time of our Lord's birth—Barbarism, Scythianism, Hellenism, Judaism, Samaritanism. The last three are subdivided; Hellenism and Samaritanism into four each, Judaism into seven. Then follow 60 heresies after the birth of Christ, from the Simonians to the Massalians, including some which, as Epiphanius acknowledges, were rather acts of schism than heresies. The extraordinary division of pre-Christian heresies is founded on a passage he often quotes (Col. iii. 11). Barbarism lasted from Adam to Noah, Scythianism from Noah to the migration of Peleg and Reu to Scythia. Hellenism, he thinks, sprang up under Serug, understanding thereby idolatry proper. Of the various Greek schools of philosophy, which he regards as particular heresies belonging to Hellenism and offers a complete list of them in the conclusion of his work, he shews himself but poorly informed. His communications concerning the various Jewish sects are for the most part worthless; and what he says of the Nasarenes and Ossenes (*Haer.* xviii. and xix.) is derived purely from respectable but misunderstood narratives concerning the Ebionites and Elkesaites. His accounts of the Jewish-Christian and Gnostic sects of the 2nd and 3rd cents. mingle valuable traditions with misunderstandings and fancies of his own. His pious zeal to excel all previous heresiologers by completing the list of heretics led him into strange misunderstandings, adventurous combinations, and arbitrary assertions. He often frames long narratives out of very meagre hints. The strangest phenomena are combined with a total absence of criticism, and cognate matters are arbitrarily separated. Yet he often copies his authorities with slavish dependence, and so enables critical commentators to collect a rich abundance of genuine traditions from his works. For the section from Dositheus to Noetus (*Haer.* xiii.-lvii.) he used a writing now lost, but of very great importance, which is also used by a contemporary writer, Philastrius of Brixia—viz. the work of Hippolytus, *Against all Heresies*. Besides this he used the well-known work of Irenaeus of Lyons. These narratives are often pieced together in very mechanical fashion, resulting in frequent repetitions and contradictory statements.

Besides these two, he had access to many original works of heretics themselves and numerous trustworthy oral traditions. Very valuable are his extracts (*Haer.* xxxi.) from an old Valentinian work, the Ep. of Ptolemaeus to Flora, which is quoted entire (xxxiii.), and the copious extracts from Marcion's gospel (xlii.). Against the Montanists (xlviii.) he uses an anonymous controversial work of great antiquity, from which Eusebius also (*H. E.* v. 17) gives large extracts; in his article on the Alogi (*Haer.* li.) he probably uses the work of Porphyry against the Christians. In the section against Origen (xliv.) copious extracts are introduced from Methodius, περὶ ἀναστάσεως. Several notices of heresies existing in Epiphanius's own time are derived from his own observation. The last main division of the *Panarion* (*Haer.* lxv.-lxxx.), where he carefully notes the different opinions of Arians, semi-Arians, Photinians, Marcellians, Pneumatomachi, Aerians, Aetians, Apollinarists, or Dimoirites, is one of the most important contemporary authorities for the Trinitarian and Christological controversies since the beginning of the 4th cent. Although a fanatical partisan, and therefore not always to be relied on, Epiphanius speaks almost everywhere from his own knowledge and enhances the value of his work by the literal transcription of important documents. Of far inferior value are his attempted refutations, which are further marred by fanatical abuse, misrepresentation of opinions, and attacks on character. He takes particular pleasure in describing real or alleged licentious excesses on the part of heretics; his refutations proper contain sometimes really successful argument, but are generally weak and unhappy. The work concludes with the section περὶ πίστεως, a glorifying description of the Holy Catholic Church, its faith, its manners, and its ordinances, of great and manifold significance for the history of the church at that time. Each section is preceded by a short summary. An Ἀνακεφαλαίωσις, probably the work of Epiphanius himself (preceded by a short extract from an epistle of Epiphanius to Acacius and Paulus, and followed by an extract from the section setting forth the Catholic faith), almost literally repeats the contents of these summaries. This Ἀνακεφαλαίωσις, a work used by St. Augustine and St. John Damascene, apparently circulated as an independent writing, as did bk. x. of the *Philosophumena* and the summary added to Hippolytus's σύνταγμα against all heresies and preserved in a Latin translation in the *Praescriptiones* of Tertullian. Of another more copious epitome-midway between the brevity of the Ἀνακεφαλαίωσις and the details of the *Panarion*, a large fragment was pub. by Dindorf from a Paris MS., No. 854, in his ed. of Epiphanius, vol. i. pp. 339-369, from a transcript made by Fr. Duebners (cf. also the various readings given by Dindorf from a Cod. Cryptoferrar. vol. iii. p. 2, praef. pp. iv.-xii.).

The best ed., that of W. Dindorf (Leipz. 1859-1862, 5 vols. sm. 8vo), contains all the genuine writings (the *Ancoratus*, *Anacephalaeosis*, *Panarion*, and *de Mensuris et Ponderibus* in the Gk. text, *de Gemmis* in all three text forms, and the two epistles in Jerome's trans.), and also the spurious homilies, the epitome, and the *Vita Epiphanii* of Polybius. Of works and treatises concerning Epiphanius may be mentioned the book attributed to the abbé Gervais, *L'Histoire et la vie de St.*

Épiphane (Paris, 1738); Tillemont, *Mémoires*, t. x. pp. 484 seq., 822 seq.; Fabricius, *Bibl. Graec.* ed. Harl. viii. pp. 261 seq.; Schröckh, *Christliche Kirchengeschichte*, t. x. pp. 3 ff.; Eberhard, *Die Betheiligung des Epiphanius an dem Streite über Origenes* (Trier, 1859); Lipsius, *Zur Quellenkritik des Epiphanios* (Wien, 1865). [R.A.L.]

Epiphanius (17), 16th bp., 5th patriarch of Constantinople, A.D. 520-535, succeeding John II.

The eastern empire was now rising to great splendour through the victories of its generals, Belisarius and Narses. Idolatry was universally suppressed, heathen books were burnt, pagan images destroyed, the professors of the old religion imprisoned and flogged. At Constantinople the zeal of Justinian for a church policy was shewn during the patriarchate of Epiphanius by laws (*e.g.* in 528 and 529) regulating episcopal elections and duties. These enactments, and the passivity of Epiphanius and his clergy, are remarkable proofs of the entire absence as yet of any claims such as the clergy later asserted for exclusively clerical legislation for the spirituality.

The first conspicuous office of Epiphanius was the charge of the catechumens at Constantinople. In 519, the year before his election, he was sent with bp. John and count Licinius to Macedonia to receive the documents "libellos," or subscriptions of those who wished reunion with the Catholic church, at the request of the apocrisiarius of Dorotheus bp. of Thessalonica. On Feb. 25, 520, he was elected bishop by the emperor Justin, with the consent of bishops, monks, and people. He is described in the letter of the synod of Constantinople to pope Hormisdas as "holding the right faith, and maintaining a fatherly care for orphans" (*Patr. Lat.* lxiii. 483). He accepted the conditions of peace between East and West concluded by his predecessor, the patriarch John, with pope Hormisdas; ratifying them at a council at Constantinople, where he accepted also the decrees of Chalcedon. Dioscorus, agent of Hormisdas at Constantinople, writes of his fair promises, but adds, "What he can fulfil we don't know. He has not yet asked us to communion" (*ib.* 482). Four letters remain of Epiphanius to Hormisdas, telling him of his election, sending him his creed, and declaring that he condemned all those whose name the pope had forbidden to be recited in the diptychs. Epiphanius adopts the symbol of Nicaea, the decrees of Ephesus, Constantinople, and Chalcedon, and the letters of pope Leo in defence of the faith. His second letter was accompanied by a chalice of gold surrounded with precious stones, a patina of gold, a chalice of silver, and two veils of silk, which he presented to the Roman church. In order to make the peace general, he advises the pope not to be too rigorous in exacting the extrusion of the names of former bishops from diptychs. His excuse for the bishops of Pontus, Asia, and the East is composed in very beautiful language. The answers of Hormisdas are given in the Acts of the Council of Constantinople held under Mennas. He trusts to the prudence and experience of Epiphanius, and recommends lenity towards the returning, severity to the obdurate. Epiphanius is to complete the reunion himself. (Labbe, *Concil.* iv. 1534, 1537, 1545, 1546, 1555, ed. 1671; *Patr. Lat.* lxiii. 497, 507, 523.) The severe measures by which Justin was establishing the supremacy of the Catholics in the East were arousing Theodoric, the Arian master of Italy, to retaliation in the West. Pope John I., the successor of Hormisdas, became thoroughly alarmed; and in 525, at the demand of Theodoric, proceeded to Constantinople to obtain the revocation of the edict against the Arians and get their churches restored to them (Marcellin. *Chron.* ann. 525; Labbe, *Concil.* iv. 1600). Great honour was paid to pope John in the eastern capital. The people went out twelve miles to receive him, bearing ceremonial tapers and crosses. The emperor Justin prostrated himself before him, and wished to be crowned by his hand. The patriarch Epiphanius invited him to perform Mass; but the pope, mindful of the traditional policy of encroachment, refused to do so until they had offered him the first seat. With high solemnity he said the office in Latin on Easter Day, communicating with all the bishops of the East except Timothy of Alexandria, the declared enemy of Chalcedon (Baron. 525, 8, 10; Pagi, ix. 349, 351; *AA. SS.* May 27; Schröckh, xvi. 102, xviii. 214-216; Gibbon, iii. 473; Milman, *Lat. Christ.* i. 302). In 531 the dispute between Rome and Constantinople was revived by the appeal of Stephen, metropolitan of Larissa, to pope Boniface, against the sentence of Epiphanius. Stephen was eventually deposed, notwithstanding his appeal. On June 5, 535, Epiphanius died, after an episcopate of 14 years and 3 months (Theoph. A.D. 529 in *Patr. Gk.* cviii. 477). All that is known of him is to his advantage.

Besides his letters to Hormisdas, we have the sentence of his council against Severus and Peter (*Patr. Gk.* lxxxvi. 783-786). Forty-five canons are attributed to him (Assemani, *Bibl. Orient.* 619). [W.M.S.]

Epiphanius (39) Scholasticus, an ecclesiastic *c.* A.D. 510, of whom we know scarcely anything except that he was the friend of CASSIODORUS, the celebrated head of the *Monasterium Vivariense*. He apparently bore the name Scholasticus, not so much because of any devotion to literature or theology, but in the sense that word frequently had in the middle ages, meaning a chaplain, amanuensis, or general assistant of any dignitary of the church (Du Cange, *Glossarium*, s.v.). In this relationship, in all probability, Epiphanius stood to his distinguished master, by whom he was summoned to take a part in urging his monks to classical and sacred studies, and especially to the transcription of manuscripts. To Epiphanius was assigned the translation into Latin of the histories of Socrates, Sozomen, and Theodoret. Cassiodorus revised the work, corrected faults of style, abridged it, and arranged it into one continuous history of the church. He then published it for the use of the clergy. The book attained a high reputation. It was known as the Tripartite History; and, along with the translation of Eusebius by Rufinus, it became the manual of church history for the clergy of the West for many centuries. The book is generally pub. as if Cassiodorus were its author, under the title of *Historiae Ecclesiasticae Tripartitae Epitome.*

Epiphanius translated several additional works, such as the commentaries of Didymus upon the Proverbs of Solomon and the seven Catholic Epistles, those of Epiphanius bp. of Cyprus upon the Canticles, and perhaps others, of which one survives, and may be found in Labbe (*Conc.* t. v.), namely, his *Codex Encyclicus*, a work to which he was also urged by Cassiodorus. It is a collection of letters addressed by different synods to the emperor Leo in defence of the decrees of the council of Chalcedon against TIMOTHEUS AELURUS. [W.M.]

Eraclius (1) (*Heraclius*, in the older editions *Eradius*), deacon of the church of Hippo A.D. 425, had inherited considerable property, part of which he spent in raising a "memoria" of the martyr [STEPHEN]; the rest he offered as a gift to the church. St. Augustine, fearing that the absolute acceptance of such a gift from so young a man might be the subject of future reproval or regret, caused Eraclius first to invest the money in land, which might be given back to him should any unforeseen reason for restitution arise. On becoming one of Augustine's clergy, Eraclius made his poverty complete by setting free a few slaves whom he had retained (Aug. *Serm.* 356, vol. v. 1387). In 426 Augustine was summoned to Milevis, to obviate some threatened dissensions. Severus, the late bishop, had designated his successor in his lifetime, but had made his choice known to his clergy only. This caused discontent, and the interference of Augustine was judged necessary to secure the unanimous acceptance of the bishop so chosen. Augustine, then in his 72nd year, was thus reminded of the expedience of securing his own church from similar trouble at his death, and he made choice of Eraclius, then apparently the junior presbyter of the church, to be his coadjutor and designate successor (*D. C. A.* i. 228). Only, though he had himself been ordained bishop in the lifetime of his predecessor, Valerius, he now held that this had been an unconscious violation of the Nicene canon against having two bishops in the same church, and therefore resolved that Eraclius, while discharging all the secular duties of the see, should remain a presbyter until his own death. To obviate future dispute, he assembled his people (Sept. 26, 426) to obtain their consent to the arrangement, having the notaries of the church in attendance to draw up regular "gesta" of the proceedings, which those present were asked to subscribe (*Ep.* 213, vol. ii. p. 788).

The capture of Hippo by the Vandals prevented the arrangements from taking effect, and Augustine does not appear to have had any successor in his see. Eraclius, in 427, held a private discussion with Maximinus, the Arian bishop, which led to a public disputation between Maximinus and Augustine (*Coll. cum Max.* viii. 650). Two sermons by Eraclius are preserved, the first of which, preached in Augustine's presence, is almost all taken up with compliments and apologies (v. 1523 and 72, Append. p. 131). [G.S.]

Ethelbert (1) **I.** (properly *Aethelberht* or *Aethelbriht*; Bede, *Aedilberct*), king of Kent, son of Irminric, and great-grandson of Oeric, surnamed Oisc, the son of Hengist, succeeded to the kingdom of the Kentishmen as the heir of the "Aescingas" in 560 (the date, 565, in the *Chronicle* is inconsistent with Bede's reckoning given below). Some years after his accession he provoked a conflict with Ceawlin, the West Saxon king, and Cutha, his brother, was defeated at Wimbledon with the loss of two ealdormen and driven back into Kent (*Sax. Chron.* A.658). Ethelbert had already married Bertha or Berhte, daughter of Charibert, king of Paris, on the understanding that she should be free to practise "the rites of her own Christian religion," under a bishop named Liudhard, chosen by her parents (Bede, i. 25). Ethelbert faithfully observed this compact, but shewed no curiosity about his wife's creed. She and her episcopal chaplain worshipped undisturbed in the old Roman-British church of St. Martin, on a hill E. of Ethelbert's city of Canterbury (Bede, i. 26). Ethelbert succeeded, on the death of Ceawlin in 593, to that pre-eminence among the Saxon and Anglican kings usually described as the Bretwaldadom (see Freeman, *Norm. Conq.* i. 542). Four years later, in the spring of 597, he was brought face to face with a band of Christian missionaries, headed by Augustine, whom pope Gregory the Great had sent to "bring him the best of all messages, which would ensure to all who received it eternal life and an endless kingdom with the true and living God" (Bede, i. 29). Ethelbert had sent word to the foreigners to remain in the Isle of Thanet, where they had landed, and "supplied them with all necessaries until he should see what to do with them." He soon came into the isle, and sitting down with his "gesiths" or attendant thanes in the open air (for he feared the effect of spells under a roof) listened attentively to the speech of Augustine. [AUGUSTINUS.] Then he spoke in some such words as Bede has rendered immortal. "Your words and your promises are fair; but seeing they are new and uncertain, I cannot give in to them, and leave the rites which I, with the whole race of the Angles, have so long observed. But since you are strangers who have come from afar, and, as I think I have observed, have desired to make us share in what you believe to be true and thoroughly good, we do not mean to hurt you, but rather shall take care to receive you with kindly hospitality, and to afford you what you need for your support; nor do we forbid you to win over to your faith, by preaching, as many as you can." He gave them a dwelling in Canterbury, N.W. of the present cathedral precinct. They began to make converts, as Bede tells us, through the charm of their preaching, and the still more powerful influence of consistent lives. Shortly afterwards Ethelbert expressed his belief in the truth of those promises which he had described as unheard-of, and was baptized; the time, according to Canterbury tradition, was June 1, the Whitsun-eve of 597, the place, undoubtedly, was St. Martin's. The king proved one of the truest and noblest of royal converts. He built a new palace at Regulbium or Reculver, abandoning his old abode to Augustine, now consecrated as archbishop, and adding the gift of various "needful possessions" (Bede, i. 26). He assisted Augustine in converting an old Roman-built church into "the cathedral church of the Holy Saviour," and also built, "after exhortation," a monastery outside the E. wall of the city, dedicated to SS. Peter and Paul, but afterwards known as "St Augustine's." He received by the hands of Mellitus, who, with others, joined the mission in 601, a letter of congratulation and exhortation from pope Gregory; and lent his aid as Bretwalda to arrangements for a conference, near the Bristol Channel, between his archbishop and some bishops of the ancient British church. Among the many "good services which he rendered to his people," Bede reckons those "dooms" or decrees which, "after the example of the Romans, he framed with the consent of his wise men," and among which he first of all set down what satisfaction (*bôt*) was to be made by any one who robbed the church, the bishop, or the clergy. For he was "minded to afford his protection to those whose doctrine he had received" (Bede, ii. 5). For these dooms, 90 in number, extant in the *Textus Roffensis*, see Thorpe's *Ancient Laws and Institutes of England*, p. 1. Ethelbert's nephew Sabert, the son of his sister Ricula, held the dependent kingship of the East Saxons, and embraced the faith under the persuasion of his uncle and overlord, who built a church of St. Paul in London for Mellitus as bishop of that kingdom. He also built at "Hrof's Castle," *i.e.* Rochester, a church of St. Andrew for a bishop named Justus; "gave many gifts to both prelates, and added lands and possessions for the use of those who were with them." It was doubtless in Ethelbert's reign and under his influence that Redwald, king of the East Angles, while visiting Kent, received baptism, although, as his after-conduct shewed, his convictions were not deep (Bede, ii. 19). After Bertha's death, Ethelbert married a young wife whose name is unknown. His last days must have been saddened by anxiety as to the future reign of his son Eadbald, who refused to receive the faith of Christ. Ethelbert died, after what Bede describes as a most glorious reign of 56 years, on Feb. 24, A.D. 616, and was buried beside his first wife in the "porticus" or transept of St. Martin, within the church of SS. Peter and Paul, leaving behind a memory held in grateful reverence as that of the first English Christian king (Hardy, *Cat. Mat.* i. 176, 214-216, 259). Cf. *The Mission of St. Augustine, according to the Original Documents*, by A. J. Mason, D.D. (Camb. 1897). [W.B.]

Etheria. [SYLVIA.]

Eucherius (1), St., bp. of Lyons, prob. born late in 4th cent.; except perhaps St. Irenaeus the most distinguished occupant of that see.

Authorities.—Sidonius Apollinaris, *Ep.* lib. iii. 8.; St. Isidorus, *de Ecclesiasticis Scriptoribus*, cap. xv.; Gennadius, *de Illustribus Ecclesiae Scriptoribus*, cap. lxiii.; Cassianus, some of whose *Collationes* (xi.-xvii.) are addressed to Eucherius and Honoratus. [CASSIANUS (11).]

Born in a high social position, he married Galla, a lady of his own station. Their two sons, Salonius and Veranius, received an ecclesiastical education in the monastery of Lerinum under St. Honoratus and Salvanius; and both appear, from the title of the commentary on *Kings*, falsely ascribed to Eucherius, to have become bishops during the lifetime of their father.

The civic duties of Eucherius (whatever they were) appear to have been discharged conscientiously and vigorously. Sidonius Apollinaris is loud in the praise of his friend as a layman, and compares him (*Ep.* viii.) to the Bruti and Torquati of old. But the world, then in a very turbulent and unsettled condition, palled upon Eucherius, and while still in the vigour of life he sought a retreat from its cares and temptations on the island of Lerinum, the smaller of the two isles now known as the Lérins, off Antibes; and subsequently on the larger one of Lero, now called *Sainte Marguerite.* Here he pursued an ascetic life of study and worship, devoting himself also to the education of his children. During this period he composed the two undoubtedly genuine works which we possess.

Intercourse, both personal and by correspondence, with eminent ecclesiastics tended to make widely known his deserved reputation for sanctity and for a varied and considerable learning, and *c.* 434 the church of Lyons unanimously, unsought, elected him bishop. He brought to the discharge of this office the influence and experience acquired in lay government, as well as the spiritual training and erudition won in his retirement. He was bishop some 16 years, the remainder of his life, and Claudianus Mamertus speaks of him as "magnorum sui saeculi pontificum longe maximus." He was succeeded by his son Veranius, while Geneva became the see of his other son Salonius.

Works.—1. *Epistola, seu Libellus, de laude Eremi.* This short treatise, addressed to St. Hilary of Arles, is assigned, with probability, to A.D. 428. The *Collationes* of Cassian, composed at the request of Eucherius, had given so vivid a picture of the hermits of the Thebaid as to call forth this epistle. The author calls attention to the blessings recorded in Holy Scripture as connected with lonely spots (*e.g.* the law was given in the wilderness and the chosen race fed with bread from heaven) and to the sanction given to retirement by the examples of Moses, Elijah, St. John Baptist, and our Lord Himself. In reference to this last he exclaims, "O laus magna deserti, ut diabolus, qui vicerat in Paradiso, in Eremo vinceretur"; and notices the withdrawal of Christ to solitude for prayer, and the fact of the Transfiguration taking place on a mountain.

2. *Epistola Paraenetica ad Valerianum cognatum.* "*De contemptu mundi et saecularis philosophiae.*" Its date is probably *c.* A.D. 432. Eucherius evidently desires his highly-placed and wealthy kinsman to follow him in retirement from the world. Valerian is reminded of the many saintly doctors of the church who had once occupied an exalted secular position; *e.g.* Clement of Rome, Gregory Thaumaturgus, Gregory Nazianzen, Basil, Paulinus of Nola, Ambrose, etc. The Latin of this epistle won the approbation of Erasmus, who published an edition, accompanied by scholia, at Basle, A.D. 1520.

3. *Liber formularum spiritalis intelligentiae*

[al. *de formâ spiritalis intellectûs*] *ad Veranium filium.* This is a defence of the lawfulness of the allegorical sense of Scripture, pleading the testimony of Scripture itself; *e.g.* Ps. lxxvii. [lxxviii. A.V.] 2, and the use of such phrases as "the hand of God," "the eyes of the Lord," etc., which cannot be taken *ad literam.* It displays a very extensive acquaintance with the Bible and anticipates many favourite usages of mediaeval mystics and hymn-writers; such as the term *anagoge* (ἀναγωγή) for the application of Scripture to the heavenly Jerusalem, identification of the *digitus Dei* with the Holy Spirit (St. Luke xi. 20, with St. Matt. xii. 28) and the like.

4. *Instructionum Libri Duo ad Salonium filium.* Of this treatise, the former book discusses difficulties in the O. and N.T., such as the scriptural evidence for the doctrine of the Holy Trinity; the permission of polygamy to the patriarchs; the existence of evil, which (with many other divines) he makes simply the privation of good, etc. The second book deals with Hebrew names, but does not display a very profound acquaintance with Hebrew. Eucherius quotes with much respect the version of the O.T. by Aquila.

There are also Homilies by him, and some other works are ascribed to him of doubtful authenticity.

Editions.—There is no complete edition of the writings of Eucherius. For this art. the *Bibliotheca Patrum Maxima* (Lugduni), A.D. 1677 (t. vi. p. 822), has been used. Cf. A. Gouillond, *St. Eucher. Lérins et l'Eglise de Lyon au Ve Siècle* (Lyons, 1881). [J.G.C.]

Euchites. *Doctrines and Practices.*—At the beginning of the last quarter of the 4th cent. or a little earlier, fanatics made their appearance in Syria, whose manner of life was said to have been introduced from Mesopotamia, and who were known by the Syriac name of Messalians or Massalians (מְצַלְיו), praying people. צְלָא *oravit* is found in the Chaldee (Dan. vi. 11; Ezra vi. 10). Epiphanius, whose account of them is the last article (80) of his work on heresies, translates the name (εὐχόμενοι), but in the next generation the Messalians had obtained a technical name in Greek also, and were known as Euchites (εὐχῆται or εὐχῖται). They professed to give themselves entirely to prayer, refusing to work and living by begging; thus differing from the Christian monks, who supported themselves by their labour. They were of both sexes, went about together, and in summer weather slept in the streets promiscuously, as persons who had renounced the world and had no possession or habitation of their own. Epiphanius dates the commencement of this sect from the reign of Constantius (*d.* A.D. 361). Theodoret (*H.E.* iv. 11; *Haer. Fab.* iv. 10; *Rel. Hist.* iii., *Vit. Marcian.* vol. iii. 1146) dates its beginning a few years later under Valentinian. There seems no foundation for the charge that the Euchites were derived from the Manichees. Epiphanius connects them with heathen devotees whom he calls Euphemites, and who it seems had also been known as Messalians. The Euchites appear never to have made any entrance into the West, but in the East, though probably at no time very numerous, they are heard of for centuries; and when the Bogomiles of the 12th cent. appeared, the name Messalian still survived, and the new heretics were accounted descendants of the ancient sect.

In the time of Epiphanius the Messalians scarcely were a sect, having no settled system nor recognized leader; and Epiphanius imputes to them no error of doctrine, but only criticizes their manner of life.

Two accounts of Euchite doctrine are apparently of greater antiquity than the authors who preserve them. One is given by Timotheus (*de Receptione Haer.* in Cotelier's *Mon. Ecc. Gr.* iii. 400). This writer was a presbyter of Constantinople in the 6th cent. His coincidences with Theodoret are too numerous to be well explained except on the supposition of common sources. These sources probably were the Acts of the councils of Antioch and Side, which contained summaries of Messalian doctrine. Theodoret may possibly also have used a Messalian book called *Asceticus*, the doctrines of which, Photius tells us, had been exposed and anathematized at the council of Ephesus in 431. Probably that book furnished the "heads of the impious doctrine of the Messalians taken from their own book" given by Joannes Damascenus (*de Haer.* ap. Cotelier, *Mon. Ecc. Gr.* i. 302, and *Opp.* Le Quien, i. 95), but which would seem also (see Wolf, *Hist. Bogomil.* p. 11) to have been separately preserved in two MSS. at Leipzig (*Acta Eruditorum*, 1696, p. 299; 1699, p. 157; and in the Bodleian, *Cod. Barocc.* 185).

They held that in consequence of Adam's sin every one had from his birth a demon, substantially united to his soul, which incited him to sin, and which baptism was ineffectual to expel. Dealing only with past sin, baptism did but shear off the surface growth, and did not touch the root of the evil. The true remedy was intense, concentrated prayer, continued till it produced a state from which all affections and volitions were banished (ἀπάθεια). In this the soul felt as sensible a consciousness of union with its heavenly bridegroom as an earthly bride in the embraces of her husband. Then the demon went out in the spittle or in the mucus of the nose, or was seen to depart in smoke or in the form of a serpent, and there was in like manner sensible evidence of the entrance of the Holy Spirit. St. Augustine (*Haer.* 57), who had some source of information independent of Epiphanius, ascribes to them a fancy that the Holy Spirit might be seen to enter in the appearance of innocuous fire, and the demon to pass out of the man's mouth in the form of a sow with her farrow. Possibly language intended by them metaphorically was misunderstood; for they described the soul of him who had not Christ in him as the abode of serpents and venomous beasts. They further thought that he who had arrived at the passionless state could see the Holy Trinity with his bodily eyes; that the three hypostases of the Trinity coalesced into one, which united itself with worthy souls. This doctrine no doubt furnishes the key to the account given by Epiphanius of the effacement of the sense of distinct personality in members of this sect. They held the possibility in the passionless state of a perfection in which sin was impossible; such a man needed neither instruction for his soul nor fasting to discipline his body, for delicate food and luxurious living could stir no evil desire in him. It is probably a misconception to suppose that they claimed that he could be guilty of licentious conduct without falling from perfection. The soul of him who was "spiritual," as they boasted themselves to be, was changed into the divine nature; he could see things invisible to ordinary men; and so some of them used to dance by way of trampling on the demons which they saw, a practice from which they were called Choreutae. The things they saw in their dreams they took for realities, and boasted that they then acquired a knowledge of future events, could see the condition of departed souls, and could read men's hearts. Both sexes might partake of this divine illumination, and they had female teachers, whom they honoured more than the clergy. The use of the Lord's Supper they regarded as a thing indifferent: it could neither benefit the worthy nor harm the unworthy receiver; but there was no reason for separating from the church by refusing it. They disparaged all the ordinary forms of Christian charity as compared with the merit of bestowing alms on one of their members. They had speculations about our Lord's humanity, of which the most intelligible is that the body which He assumed had been full of demons which it was necessary for Him to expel.

History.—The first whom we read of as a leader of the sect is Adelphius; hence "Adelphians" was one of their many names. He was a layman of Mesopotamia. Epiphanius speaks of them in his time as having no recognized leader. Theodoret tells that Flavian bp. of Antioch sent monks to bring the Messalian teachers at Edessa to Antioch. They denied their doctrines, and charged their accusers with calumny. Flavian then used an artifice afterwards repeated by Alexius Comnenus in the case of the Bogomiles. He affected to take their part, treated the aged Adelphius with great respect, and led him to believe that he would find in an aged bishop one able to understand and sympathize with views which younger men rejected only from want of experience. Adelphius, having been thus enticed into a full disclosure of his sentiments, was rebuked in the words addressed by Daniel to the wicked elder (Susanna, 52) and punished as convicted out of his own mouth. He and his party were beaten, excommunicated, and banished, and were not allowed, as they wished, the alternative of recantation, no confidence being felt in their sincerity, especially as they were found communicating in friendly terms with Messalians whom they had anathematized. Probably it was on this occasion that Flavian held a synod against them (Photius, 52), attended by three other bishops (Bizus of Seleucia, a Mesopotamian bishop, Maruthas, described by Photius as bp. of the Supharenians, and Samus) and by about 30 clergy. With Adelphius there were condemned two persons named Sabas, one of them a monk and a eunuch, Eustathius of Edessa, Dadoes, Hermas, Symeon, and others. Flavian informed the bishops of Edessa and neighbourhood what had been done, and received an approving reply. The Messalians banished from Syria went to Pamphylia, and there met new antagonists. They were also condemned by a council of 25 bishops held at Side and presided over by AMPHILOCHIUS of Iconium, which sent a synodical letter to Flavian, informing him of their proceedings. In their Acts Amphilochius gave a full statement of the Messalian tenets expressed in their own words. Photius represents the synod at Antioch just mentioned as having been called in consequence of the synodical letter from Side, but this is more than doubtful, though Theodoret also, in his *Eccl. Hist.*, mentions the proceedings in Pamphylia before mentioning those which resulted in the banishment of the Messalians to Pamphylia. We cannot fix the year of these proceedings, but *c.* 390 will probably not be far wrong. Measures were taken against the Messalians in Armenia also. Letoius bp. of Melitene obtained information from Flavian as to the proceedings in Antioch. Finding some monasteries in his diocese infected by this heresy, he set fire to them, and hunted the wolves from his sheepfold. A less zealous Armenian bishop was rebuked by Flavian for favour shewn to these heretics. In Pamphylia the contest lasted for several years. The orthodox leaders were another Amphilochius, bp. of Side, and Verinianus bp. of Perga, who were stimulated by energetic letters from Atticus bp. of Constantinople, and later, in A.D. 426, from the synod held for the consecration of Sisinnius, the successor of Atticus, in which Theodotus of Antioch and a bishop named Neon are mentioned by Photius as taking active parts. Messalianism had probably at that time given some trouble in Constantinople itself. Nilus (*de Vol. Paup. ad Magnam,* 21) couples with Adelphius of Mesopotamia, Alexander, who polluted Constantinople with like teaching, and against whom he contends that their idleness, instead of aiding devotion, gave scope to evil thoughts and passions and was inimical to the true spirit of prayer. Tillemont has conjectured that this was the Alexander who about this time founded the order of the Acoimetae (see *D. C. A. s.v.*), but the identification is far from certain. There is no evidence that the latter was a heretic save that his name has not been honoured with the prefix of saint; and his institution would scarcely have met with the success it did if it could have been represented as devised by a notorious Messalian to carry out the notions of his sect as to the duty of incessant prayer.

Between the accession of Sisinnius and the council of Ephesus in 431, John of Antioch wrote to Nestorius about the Messalians, and Theodosius legislated against them (xvi. Cod. Theod. *de Haer.* vol. vi. p. 187). At Ephesus Valerian of Iconium, and Amphilochius of Side, in the name of the bps. of Lycaonia and Pamphylia, obtained from the council a confirmation of the decrees made against the Euchites at Constantinople in 426 and the anathematization of the Messalian book, *Asceticus*, passages from which Valerian laid before the synod (Mansi, iv. 1477). Fabricius names Agapius, and Walch Adelphius, as the author of this book, but the writer is really unknown. These proceedings at Ephesus were unknown to Gregory the Great (*Ep.* vi. 14, *ad Narsem*, vol. vii. p. 361), but are mentioned by Photius, and the decree was read at the second council of Nicaea (Mansi, xii. 1025). The cause of Gregory's oversight may have been that his correspondent cited to him as Ephesine the Acts of the council of Antioch. We learn from the Ephesine decree that Messalianism had also been condemned at Alexandria, and Timotheus mentions Cyril as an antagonist of these heretics. In the *Ep. ad Calosyrium* (prefixed to the tract *adv. Anthropomorph.* vii. 363) Cyril rebukes certain monks who made piety a cloak for laziness, but there is no evidence that they were Euchites. The articles of the *Asceticus* were the subject of 24 anathemas by Archelaus (bp. of Caesarea in Cappadocia some time between the two Ephesine synods of 431 and 449), and of two letters by Heracleidas of Nyssa (*c.* 440). The next Euchite leader of whom we read is Lampetius, after whom his followers were called Lampetians, and who is said to have been the first of the sect to attain the dignity of priesthood. He had been ordained by Alypius, bp. of Caesarea (Cappadocia) in 458. He was accused to Alypius by the presbyter Gerontius, superior of the monks at Glitis, of undue familiarity with women, unseemly language, scoffing at those who took part in the musical services of the church as being still under the law when they ought to make melody only in their hearts, and of other Euchite doctrines and practices. The examination of the charges was delegated by Alypius to Hormisdas bp. of Comana, and Lampetius was degraded from the priesthood. He wrote a work called the *Testament*, answered by the Monophysite Severus, afterwards bp. of Antioch. A fragment of this answer is preserved in a catena belonging to New College, Oxford (Wolf, *Anecdota Graeca*, iii. 182). It insists on the duty of praising God both with heart and voice. The same catena contains an extract from another work of Severus against the Euchites, an epistle to a bp. Solon. Photius tells that in Rhinocorura two persons named Alpheus, one of them a bishop, defended the orthodoxy of Lampetius, and were in consequence deposed. He learned this from a letter written by Ptolemy, another bishop of the same district, to Timotheus of Alexandria. There have been at Alexandria several bishops of that name, but probably the Timotheus intended is the one contemporary with Lampetius (460-482).

The next Messalian leader of whom we read (in Timotheus) is Marcian, a money-changer, who lived in the middle of the 6th cent., and from whom these sectaries came to be called Marcianists. The correspondence of Gregory the Great, already referred to, arose out of the condemnation under this name, unknown in the West, in 595, of one John, a presbyter of Chalcedon. He appealed to the pope, who pronounced him orthodox, complaining that he had not even been able to make out from his accusers what the heresy of Marcianism was. In the 7th cent. Maximus, in his scholia on the Pseudo-Dionysius (II. 88), charges those whom he calls indifferently Lampetians, Messalians, Adelphians, or Marcianists, with giving but three years to ascetic life and the rest of their life to all manner of debauchery.

We hear no more of the Messalians till the Bogomile heresy arose in the 12th cent.

Of modern writers, the most useful are Tillemont, viii. 530; Walch, *Hist. der Ketz.* iii. 418; and Neander, *Ch. Hist.* iii. 323. [G.S.]

Eudoxius (2), 8th bp. of Constantinople (360-370), previously bp. of Germanicia and of Antioch, one of the most influential Arians. Between 324 and 331 St. Eustathius was bp. of Antioch. Eudoxius came to him seeking holy orders. Eustathius found his doctrine unsound and refused him. But when Eustathius was deposed, the Arians or Eusebians had everything their own way, and admitted Eudoxius to orders and made him bp. of Germanicia, on the confines of Syria, Cilicia, and Cappadocia. This bishopric he held at least 17 years, the dark period of the principal intrigues against Athanasius, and of the reigns of the sons of Constantine. In 341 was held, at Antioch, the council of the Dedication or Encaenia, under Placillus. Eudoxius of Germanicia attended. He was an Arian pure and simple, a disciple of Aetius, a friend of Eunomius. The council produced four creeds, in which the Eusebian party succeeded in making their doctrine as plausible as might be, and the second of these became known as the "Creed of the Dedication." Athanasius says that Eudoxius was sent with Martyrius and Macedonius to take the new creed of Antioch to Italy. This new creed may, however, have been the Macrostich, or Long Formula, drawn up at a later council of Antioch. In 343 or 347 the rival councils of Sardica and Philippopolis were held. At the latter was drawn up a creed more Arian than those of Antioch, and it was signed by Eudoxius. At the end of 347 Eudoxius was in attendance on the emperor in the West, when news came of the death of Leontius of Antioch. Excusing himself on the plea that the affairs of Germanicia required his presence, he hastened to Antioch, and, representing himself as nominated by the emperor, got himself made bishop, and sent Asphalus, a presbyter of Antioch, to make the best of the case at court. Constantius wrote to the church of Antioch: "Eudoxius went to seek you without my sending him. . . . To what restraint will men be amenable, who impudently pass from city to city, seeking with a most unlawful appetite every occasion to enrich themselves?" Meanwhile the new prelate was preaching open Arianism and persecuting the orthodox. In the first year of his episcopate at Antioch he held a council, which received the creed of Sirmium. An idea may be formed of his sermons from three different sources. Hilary of Poictiers, then in the East, heard Eudoxius in his cathedral, and wished his ears had been deaf, so horribly blasphemous was the language. Theodoret and Epiphanius report him as boasting that he had the same knowledge about God as God had about Himself.

A council was held at Seleucia in Sept. 359, the orthodox forming a very small minority. The majority signed the "Creed of the Dedication"; Eudoxius, who was present, was deposed by the less heretical party, and appears to have sought the shelter of the court at Constantinople. Here, by the aid of the Acacians, he secured his appointment as patriarch on the deposition of Macedonius, and on Jan. 27, 360, took possession of his throne in the presence of 72 bishops. On Feb. 15 the great church of Constantinople, St. Sophia, begun in 342 by the emperor Constantius, was dedicated. Eudoxius, mounting his episcopal throne before the expectant multitude of courtiers, ecclesiastics, and citizens, began with the words: "The Father is ἀσεβής, the Son is εὐσεβής." A great tumult of indignation arose on all sides in St. Sophia. The orator, unabashed, explained: "The Father is ἀσεβής because He honours nobody; the Son is εὐσεβής because He honours the Father." The new cathedral echoed with peals of uncontrollable laughter. Thus, says Socrates (ii. 43), these heresiarchs tore the church to pieces by their captious subtilties.

Eudoxius consecrated his friend Eunomius to the see of Cyzicus; but such complaints were brought to the emperor that he ordered Eudoxius to depose him. Eudoxius, terrified by menaces, persuaded him quietly to retire.

In 365 an attack was made on Eudoxius by the semi-Arians, now called Macedonians. Holding a meeting at Lampsacus, they signed the "Creed of the Dedication," cited Eudoxius and his party before them, and, as they did not come, sentenced them to deprivation; but Valens refused to confirm the proceedings. In 367 Valens, as he was setting out for the Gothic war, was induced by his wife to receive baptism from Eudoxius. In the same year he issued, doubtless under the advice of Eudoxius, an order that such bishops as had been banished by Constantius and had returned under Julian should again be exiled.

The years during which Eudoxius and Valens acted together were troubled by portents, which many attributed to the anger of Heaven at the cruelty of Valens in banishing bishops who would not admit Eudoxius to their communion. Eudoxius died in 370. He well deserves the character given him by Baronius, "the worst of all the Arians." Soz. *H. E.* iv. 26; Socr. *H. E.* ii. 19, 37, 40, 43; Theoph. *Chronogr.* § 38; Niceph. Callist. *H. E.* xi. 4; Theod. *H. E.* ii. 25; *Haer. Fab.* iv. 3; Epiph. *de Haeres.* lxxiii. 2; Athan. *ad Solit.* in *Patr. Gk.* xxvi. 572, 219, 589, 274, 580, 713, 601; Hilarius, *de Synod.*, *Patr. Lat.* x. 471, etc.; *Liber contr. Const. Imp.* §§ 665, 680, 573, etc. [W.M.S.]

Eulalius (1), an antipope, elected and ordained as bp. of Rome after the death of Zosimus at the close of 418, in opposition to Boniface I., who was finally established in the see, Eulalius being expelled from Rome by the emperor Honorius in April 419. The official letters which passed have been preserved in the Vatican, and are quoted at length by Baronius (*A. E.* ann. 418, lxxix. 419, ii.-xxxii.). They throw light on the conflicts attending the election of bishops, and on the powers exercised by the emperors in connexion therewith. First we have a letter (Dec. 29, 418) to Honorius at Ravenna from Symmachus the Praefectus Urbis, stating that, after he had warned the people to proceed to a new election without disturbance, Eulalius the archdeacon had been taken to the Lateran church by the clergy and people, duly elected, and ordained; while certain presbyters, accompanied by a crowd, had gone with Bonifacius, a presbyter, to the church of Theodora, and, though warned to do nothing rashly, had ordained him in the church of St. Marcellus, and thence took him to St. Peter's basilica. He requests the instructions of the emperor, with whom, he says, it rests to give judgment in such a case. Honorius replies (Jan. 3, 419) by ordering Boniface to be expelled from the city, and the authors of the sedition in his favour punished, Eulalius having been duly appointed according to the rule of Catholic discipline (competens numerus ordinantium, solemnitas temporis, locique qualitas) and the rival election being deficient in these respects. Symmachus replies (Jan. 8) that he has carried out the emperor's order, not without resistance on the part of Boniface, who had caused a messenger sent to forbid a procession to be beaten by the people; had held the procession; and had forcibly entered the city, but had been expelled by an opposing mob; while Eulalius had celebrated service in the basilica of St. Peter amid the acclamations of almost the whole city.

Meantime the presbyters who supported Boniface had sent a different account. They had been unable, they say, to assemble in the customary place, the Lateran church, because of its being occupied by Eulalius with a very small number of presbyters and an excited mob; they were the great majority of the clergy, supported by the better part of the laity; amid general acclamation they had elected Boniface, in whose ordination 70 priests and 9 bishops of divers provinces had concurred; whereas the bp. of Ostia, a sick old man almost at the point of death, had been brought against his will to assist in the ordination of Boniface's rival.

Having received this counter-statement, Honorius writes to Symmachus (Jan. 15), revoking his former edict; commanding the attendance at Ravenna (Feb. 8) of Boniface and Eulalius, with their respective supporters, before a synod.

The documents shew that the members of this synod were divided, and unable to come to a decision before Easter (Mar. 30), when custom required a bishop to celebrate in Rome. Honorius therefore decided to refer the case after Easter to a fuller synod, and commissioned Achilleus bp. of Spoleto to celebrate Easter in Rome, forbidding both claimants to be present there. He exacts obedience in a high tone of authority, and threatens with summary punishment all disturbers of the peace. The synod was to be held at Spoletum on June 13. Honorius sent private letters to several of the more important prelates, *e.g.* Paulinus of Nola, Augustine, and Aurelius of Carthage, and circular letters to the bishops of Africa and Gaul. The proposed assembly, however, never took place. Eulalius and his party, disregarding the imperial orders, entered Rome at mid-day, Mar. 18, and came into violent collision with Achilleus and his supporters, Symmachus and the Vicarius

Urbis narrowly escaping with their lives. Thereupon the emperor ordered (Mar. 25) Eulalius to be immediately expelled from the city. Eulalius refused to comply, and took violent possession of the Lateran church, but was eventually dislodged thence and expelled from Rome, an imperial edict (Apr. 3) excluding him from the see and confirming Boniface as bp. of Rome. The latter was welcomed as bishop by the whole population with joy and gratitude to the emperor.

Eulalius retired to Antium, near Rome, expecting the death of Boniface, who fell sick after his accession, but this hope failing, he made no further attempt to recover the see, though invited to do so by his partisans in Rome on the death of Boniface in 423. According to the *Liber Pontificalis*, he afterwards became bp. of Nepete.

From this account, extracted from contemporary documents, the following facts are evident. First, that with the ancient custom of election of a new bishop by the clergy, with the assent of the laity, and confirmation by provincial bishops, there was no desire on the part of the civil power to interfere. Secondly, that elections had come to be conducted in an irregular and tumultuous manner, giving rise [DAMASUS] to violent conflicts, with bloodshed even in the churches. Thirdly, that it was the necessity of restoring order, and adjudicating between rival claims, that led to the interposition of the emperor. Fourthly, that in this case the emperor did not insist on a right to decide on the validity of either election without first submitting the question to an episcopal synod. Fifthly, eventually, serious provocation being given, he settled the question on his own authority, without the sanction of a synod or regard to the canonicity of the original election. A statement in the *Liber Pontificalis* that Eulalius was deposed by a synod of 252 bishops is inconsistent with the contemporary evidence given above, and, as such, Baronius rejects it. [J.B—Y.]

Eulogius (4), bp. of Edessa. When a presbyter there he suffered in the persecution by Valens. Barses the bishop having been deposed and exiled, the orthodox refused to communicate with an Arian prelate, intruded into the see. Modestus the prefect commanded the leading ecclesiastics to obey the emperor and communicate with the new prelate. The whole body, led by Eulogius, offered so firm a resistance that Modestus sentenced them, 80 in number, to transportation to Thrace. The confessors received so much honour there that Valens relegated them, two and two, to distant localities, Eulogius with a presbyter Protogenes being sent to Antinous in the Thebaid. Though there was a Catholic bishop here the population was almost entirely pagan, and the two presbyters commenced missionary work among them. On the cessation of the persecution Eulogius and Protogenes returned to Edessa, where, Barses being dead, Eulogius was consecrated bishop by Eusebius of Samosata (Theod. *H. E.* iv. 18, v. 4). He attended the councils held at Rome in 369 (Labbe, ii. 894), Antioch in 379, and Constantinople in 381 (*ib.* 955). See Soz. vi. 34; and Migne's note 61, *Patr. Gk.* lxvii. 1394. [E.V.]

Eunomius (3) of Cappadocia, bp. of Cyzicus (360-364) after the expulsion of Eleusius. As the pupil and secretary of Aetius, he formulated his master's system with a preciseness which stamped the name of Eunomians instead of that of Aetians on the Anomoean heretics. He was distinguished by "a faculty of subtle disputation and hard mechanical reasoning" (Newman, *Arians*, c. iv. § 4), which subjected the Christian verities to strict logical processes, and rejected every doctrine that could not be shewn to be consistent with human reason. Neander further describes him as the decided enemy of asceticism, and of the growing disposition to worship saints and relics—in fact, the "Rationalist" of the 4th cent. (*Ch. Hist.* iv. p. 78, Clark's trans.).

The name of his birthplace is given as Dacora by Sozomen and Philostorgius, and as Oltiseris by Gregory Nyssen, who correctly places it on the confines of Cappadocia and Galatia (Soz. *H. E.* vii. 17; Philost. *H. E.* x. 6, xi. 5). Eunomius came of an honest, industrious stock. His father, an unpretending, hard-working man, supported his family by the produce of his land and by teaching a few neighbours' children in the winter evenings (Greg. Nys. *in Eunom.* i. p. 291). Eunomius inherited his father's independent spirit. He learnt shorthand, and became amanuensis to a kinsman and tutor to his children. The country becoming distasteful to him, he went to Constantinople, hoping to study rhetoric. Gregory Nyssen, who endeavours to blacken his character as much as possible, hints that his life there was not very reputable, but specifies no charges. It was reported that he worked as a tailor, making clothes and girdles. Before very long he returned to Cappadocia.

The fame of Aetius, then teaching at Alexandria, reaching Eunomius, he proceeded thither *c.* 356, and placed himself under his instruction, acting also as his amanuensis (Socr. *H. E.* ii. 35, iv. 7; Soz. *H. E.* vi. 27; Philost. *H. E.* iii. 20; Greg. Nys. *in Eunom.* i. p. 290). He accompanied Aetius to Antioch at the beginning of 358, to attend the Arian council summoned by Eudoxius, who had through court favour succeeded to the see of Antioch.

The bold front displayed by the Arians at this council, and the favour shewn to the flagrant blasphemies of Aetius and Eunomius, who did not scruple to assert the absolute unlikeness (*ἀνόμοιον*) of the Son to the Father, excited the strong opposition of the semi-Arian party, of which George of Laodicea, Basil of Ancyra, and Macedonius of Constantinople, were the highly respectable leaders. Under colour of the dedication of a church, a council was speedily held by them at Ancyra at which the Anomoean doctrines and their authors were condemned. A synodical letter was sent to the emperor denouncing the teaching of Eunomius and his master and charging the latter with being privy to the conspiracy of Gallus (Philost. *H. E.* iv. 8). These proceedings struck dismay into the Arian clique at Antioch, and Eunomius, now a deacon, was sent to Constantinople as their advocate. But, apprehended in Asia Minor by some imperial officers, he was banished by the emperor's orders to Midaeus or Migde in Phrygia; Aetius to Pepuza. Eudoxius found it prudent to retire to his native Armenia till the storm had blown over (Greg. Nys. *ib.* p. 291), but found means to reinstate himself in the emperor's favour, and at the close of 359 was chosen successor of Macedonius in the imperial see. Constantius had the utmost abhorrence of the Anomoeans and their teaching. Aetius was therefore sacrificed by the Arians as a scapegoat, while Eunomius was persuaded to separate himself reluctantly from his old teacher and conceal his heterodoxy, that he might secure a position of influence from which to secretly disseminate his views. Eudoxius procured for him from the emperor the bishopric of Cyzicus, vacant by the deposition of the semi-Arian ELEUSIUS; but after a while, weary of dissimulation, he began to propound his doctrines, at first privately, and then in public assemblies. Complaints of his heterodoxy were laid before Eudoxius, who, forced by Constantius, summoned Eunomius before a council of bishops at Constantinople, but sent him a secret message counselling flight. Eunomius, not appearing, was condemned in his absence, deposed, and banished (Theod. *Haer. Fab.* iv. 3; *H. E.* ii. 29; Philost. *H. E.* vi. 1). On this he broke altogether with his former associates, and headed a party of his own, called after him Eunomians, professing the extreme Anomoean doctrines of the general comprehensibleness of the Divine Essence, and the absolute unlikeness of the Son to the Father. The accession of Julian in 361 recalled Eunomius and Aetius among the other bishops banished by Constantius. They both settled in Constantinople during the reigns of Julian and his successor Jovian (Philost. *H. E.* vi. 7, vii. 6). The growing popularity of Eunomianism at Constantinople caused jealousy in Eudoxius, who took advantage of the commotions caused by the rebellion of Procopius on the accession of Valens in 364 to expel Eunomius and Aetius from the city. Eunomius retired to his country house near Chalcedon. Procopius having also taken refuge there in Eunomius's absence, Eunomius was accused of favouring his designs, and was in danger of being capitally condemned. Sentence of banishment to Mauritania was actually passed upon him, A.D. 367. But on his way thither, passing through Mursa, the Arian bishop Valens, by personal application to the emperor Valens, obtained the repeal of his sentence (*ib.* iv. 4-8). He was, the same year, again sentenced to banishment by Modestus, the prefect of the Praetorian guards, as a disturber of the public peace (*ib.* ix. 11). But he was again at Constantinople, or at least at Chalcedon, early in the reign of Theodosius, A.D. 379, to whom in 383 he, with other bishops, presented a confession of faith which is still extant. The next year Theodosius, finding some officers of the court infected with Eunomian views, expelled them from the palace, and having seized Eunomius at Chalcedon, banished him to Halmyris in Moesia, on the Danube. Halmyris being captured by the Goths, who had crossed the frozen river, Eunomius was transported to Caesarea in Cappadocia. The fact that he had attacked their late venerated bishop, Basil the Great, in his writings, made him so unpopular there that his life was hardly safe. He was therefore permitted to retire to his paternal estate at Dacora, where he died in extreme old age soon after A.D. 392, when, according to Jerome (*Vir. Illust.* c. 120), he was still living, and writing much against the church. His body was buried there, but transferred to Tyana, by order of Eutropius, *c.* 396, and there carefully guarded by the monks—to prevent its being carried by his adherents to Constantinople and buried beside his master Aetius, to whom he had himself given a splendid funeral (Soz. *H. E.* vii. 17; Philost. *H. E.* ix. 6, xi. 5).

Eunomianism, a cold, logical system, lacked elements of vitality, and notwithstanding its popularity at first, did not long survive its authors. In the following century, when Theodoret wrote, the body had dwindled to a scanty remnant, compelled to conceal themselves and hold their meetings in such obscure corners that they had gained the name of "Troglodytes" (Theod. *Haer. Fab.* iv. 3). St. Augustine remarked that in his time the few Anomoeans existing were all in the East and that there were none in Africa (Aug. *de Past. Cur.* c. 8, p. 278).

Eunomius endeavoured to develop Arianism as a formal doctrinal system; starting with the conception of God as the absolute simple Being, of Whom neither self-communication nor generation can be predicated. His essence is in this, that He is what He is of Himself alone, underived, unbegotten—and as being the only unbegotten One, the Father, in the strict sense of Deity, is alone God; and as He is unbegotten, inasmuch as begetting necessarily involves the division and impartation of being, so it is impossible for Him to beget. If that which was begotten shared in the θεότης of the Deity, God would not be the absolute unbegotten One, but would be divided into a begotten and an unbegotten God. A communication of the essence of God, such as that involved in the idea of generation, would transfer to the Absolute Deity the notions of time and sense. An eternal generation was to Eunomius a thing absolutely inconceivable. A begetting, a bringing forth, could not be imagined as without beginning and end. The generation of the Son of God must therefore have had its beginning, as it must have had its termination, at a definite point of time. It is, therefore, incompatible with the predicate of eternity. If that can be rightly asserted of the Son, He must equally, with the Father, be unbegotten. This denial of the eternal generation of the Son involved also the denial of the likeness of His essence to that of the Father, from which the designation of the party, "Anomoean," was derived. That which is begotten, he asserted, cannot possibly resemble the essence of that which is unbegotten; hence, equality of essence, "Homoousian," or even similarity of essence, "Homoiousian," is untenable. Were the begotten to resemble the unbegotten in its essence, it must cease to be unbegotten. Were the Father and the Son equal, the Son must also be unbegotten, a consequence utterly destructive of the fundamental doctrine of generation and subordination. Such generation, moreover, Eunomius held to be essentially impossible. If then, according to the teaching of the church, the

Son, Who is begotten, were of the same essence as the Father Who begets, there must be both an unbegotten and a begotten element in God. The essence of the Father and of the Son must therefore be absolutely dissimilar. And as Their essence, so also is Their knowledge of Themselves different. Each knows Himself as He is, and not as the other. The one knows Himself as unbegotten, the other as begotten. Since, therefore, the Son did not share in any way the essence of the Father, what is His relation to God, and to what does He owe His origin? Eunomius's answer lay in a distinction between the essence (οὐσία) and the energy (ἐνεργεία) of God. Neither movement nor self-communication being predicable of the Divine Essence, it is to the Divine Energy, conceived as separable from the Θεότης, that we must ascribe the calling into existence out of nothing of all that is. In virtue of this ἐνεργεία only can God be called Father, as it is by this that all that is, besides Himself, has come into being. Of these creations of the Divine Energy the Son or Logos holds the first place, as the instrumental creator of the world. In this relation likeness to the Father is predicable of the Son. The Son may in this sense be regarded as the express image and likeness of the ἐνεργεία of the Father, as He conferred on Him divine dignity in the power of creation. This made the immeasurable difference between the Son and all other created beings. He was produced by the Father, as an alone Being, the first or most perfect of all Beings, to be, by His will, His instrument in the creation of all other existences. God called Him into being immediately, but all other creatures mediately through Him. This teaching introduced a dualism into the essence of God Himself, when it drew a distinction between His essence and His will—the one being infinite and absolute, and the other relative and limited to finite objects. On the ground of this dualism Eunomius is charged by Gregory Nyssen with Manicheism. Eunomius regarded the Paraclete as sharing in the Divine nature in a still more secondary and derived sense, as no more than the highest and noblest production of the Only-begotten Son, given to be the source of all light and sanctification.

The entire want of spiritual depth and life in Eunomius is shewn by his maintaining that the Divine nature is perfectly comprehensible by the human intellect, and charging those who denied this with an utter ignorance of the first principles of Christianity. He accused them of preaching an unknown God, and even denied their right to be called Christians at all, since without knowledge of God there could be no Christianity; while he denied to those who did not hold his views as to the nature of God and the generation of the Son the possession of any true knowledge of the Divine Being. He held that Christ had been sent to lead other creatures up to God, the primal source of all existence, as a Being external to Himself, and that believers should not stop at the generation of the Son, but having followed Him as far as He was able to lead them, should soar above Him, as above all created beings, whether material or spiritual, to God Himself, the One Absolute Being, as their final aim, that in the knowledge of Him they might obtain eternal life. Eunomius's poor and low idea of the knowledge of God placed it merely in a formal illumination of the understanding and a theoretical knowledge of God and spiritual truth, instead of in that fellowship with God as made known to us in Christ and that knowledge which comes from love, which the church has ever held to be the true life of the soul. In harmony with this formal, intellectual idea of knowledge, as the source of Christian life, Eunomius assigned a lower place to the sacraments than to the teaching of the word, depreciating the liturgical, as compared with the doctrinal, element of Christianity. As quoted by Gregory Nyssen, he asserted that "the essence of Christianity did not depend for its ratification on sacred terms, on the special virtue of customs and mystic symbols, but on accuracy of doctrine" (Greg. Nys. *in Eunom.* p. 704). For fuller statements of the doctrinal system of Eunomius, see Dorner, *Doctrine of the Person of Christ*, div. i. vol. ii. pp. 264 ff., Clark's trans.; Neander, *Ch. Hist.* vol. iv. pp. 77 ff., Clark's trans.; Herzog, *Real-Encycl.* "Eunomius und Eunomianer" (from which works the foregoing account has been derived); Klose, *Geschichte und Lehre des Eunomius* (1833); Bauer, *Dreieinigkeit*, i. pp. 365-387; Meyer, *Trinitätslehre*, pp. 175 ff.; Lange, *Arianismus in seiner weiteren Entwickelung*.

Eunomius, as a writer, was more copious than elegant. Photius speaks very depreciatingly of his studied obscurity, the weakness of his arguments, and his logical power. Socrates estimates his style no less unfavourably (*H. E.* iv. 7). Notwithstanding these alleged defects, his writings, which Rufinus states were very numerous and directed against the Christian faith (*H. E.* i. 25), were much esteemed by his followers, who, according to Jerome, valued their authority more highly than that of the Gospels (Hieron. *adv. Vigil.* t. ii. p. 123). The bold blasphemies in these books caused their destruction. Successive imperial edicts, one of Arcadius, dated not more than four years after his death A.D. 398 (*Cod. Theod.* t. vi. p. 152; lib. xvi. 34), commanded that his books should be burnt, and made the possession of any of his writings a capital crime. Little of his writing remains, save some few fragments preserved in the works of his theological adversaries. His *Exposition of Faith* and his *Apologeticus* are the only pieces extant of any length.

(1) ἔκθεσις πίστεως, *Fidei libellus.* A confession of faith presented to Theodosius, A.D. 383 (Socr. *H. E.* vii. 12), first printed by Valesius in his notes to Socrates, afterwards by Baluze in *Conciliorum Nov. Collect.* i. 89, and in Fabricius, *Biblioth. Graeca*, v. 23.

(2) *Apologeticus*, in 28 sections. This is his most famous work, in which, with much subtlety, he seeks to refute the Nicene doctrine of the Trinity, especially the co-eternal and consubstantial divinity of Christ. Basil the Great thought the book worth an elaborate refutation, in five books, *adversus Eunomium* (Migne, *Patr. Gk.* xxx. 835). An English trans. was pub. by Whiston in his *Eunomianismus Redivivus* (Lond. 1711, 8vo).

Cave, *Hist. Lit.* i. p. 219; Fab. *Bibl. Graeca*,

viii. p. 261; Phot. *Cod.* 137, 138; Tillem. *Mém. Eccl.* vi. 501 ff. [E.V.]

Euphemitae, also known as *Messalians*, "praying people," and therefore reckoned by Epiphanius (*Haer.* 80) as predecessors of the Christian sect so called. Epiphanius, our sole informant, tells us that they were neither Christians, Jews, nor Samaritans, but heathen, believing in a plurality of gods, but offering worship only to one whom they called the Almighty. They built oratories, some of which exactly resembled Christian churches; in these they met at evening and early morn, with many lights, to join in hymns and prayer. We learn from Epiphanius with some surprise that some of the magistrates put several of these people to death for perversion of the truth and unwarranted imitation of church customs, and that in particular Lupicianus, having thus punished some of them, gave occasion to a new error, for they buried the bodies, held services at the spot, and called themselves *martyriani*. Epiphanius also charges a section of the Euphemites with calling themselves *Sataniani* and worshipping Satan, thinking that by such service they might disarm his hostility. It does not appear that Epiphanius means to assert that the Christian Euchites were historically derived from these heathen Euphemites, but merely that there was a general resemblance of practices between them. Tillemont conjectured (viii. 529) that the Euphemites of Epiphanius might be identical with the *Hypsistarii* of Greg. Naz., or less probably with the COELICOLAE of Africa. [EUCHITES.] [G.S.]

Euphemius (4), 3rd patriarch of Constantinople, succeeding Fravitta and followed by Macedonius II. He ruled six years and three months, A.D. 489-496, and died in 515. Theophanes calls him Euthymius. He was a presbyter of Constantinople, administrator of a hospital for the poor at Neapolis, untinged with any suspicion of Eutychian leanings, and is described as learned and very virtuous. Finding that Peter Mongus, the patriarch of Alexandria, anathematized the council of Chalcedon, he was so indignant that before he took his seat on the patriarchal throne he solemnly separated from all communion with him, and with his own hands effaced his name from the diptychs, placing in its stead that of Felix III. of Rome. For a year the strife between Mongus and Euphemius was bitter. Each summoned councils against the other; Euphemius even thought of persuading a council to depose Mongus; but at the end of Oct. 490 Mongus died.

To pope Felix the patriarch sent letters, as was usual, to announce his election, but received the reply that he might be admitted as a private member of the church Catholic, but could not be received in communion as a bishop, because he had not removed from the diptychs the names of his predecessors, Acacius and Fravitta.

At the death (probably in 489) of Daniel the Stylite on the pillar where he had lived for 33 years, Euphemius came with others to the foot of the pillar to attend his last moments. Anastasius, the future emperor, then an aged officer of the emperor Zeno, held Eutychian views, and, according to Suidas, formed a sect which met in some church of Constantinople. The patriarch appeared before the conventicle with menacing gestures and drove them from the spot. "If you must frequent the church," he exclaimed, "agree with her! or else no more enter into her gates to pervert men more simple than yourself." Henceforth, says the annalist, Anastasius kept quiet, for the sake of the glory that he coveted. As the emperor Zeno died in 491, this must have occurred within two years after the consecration of Euphemius, and it witnesses alike to his intrepidity and his influence. After the death of Zeno, the empress Ariadne procured the election of Anastasius, on the understanding that he was to marry her. The patriarch openly called him a heretic, unworthy of reigning over Christians, and refused to crown him, despite the entreaties of the empress and the senate, until Anastasius would give a written profession of his creed, promise under his hand to keep the Catholic faith intact, make no innovation in the church, and follow as his rule of belief the decrees of Chalcedon. Anastasius gave the writing under most solemn oaths, and Euphemius put it in charge of the saintly Macedonius, chancellor and treasurer of the church of Constantinople, to be stored in the archives of the cathedral (Evagr. iii. 32).

At the end of 491, or on Feb. 25, 492, pope Felix died. His successor Gelasius immediately announced his elevation to the emperor Anastasius, but took no notice of Euphemius, who had written at once to express his congratulations, and his desire for peace and for the reunion of the churches. Not obtaining an answer, he wrote a second time. Neither letter remains, but the reply of Gelasius shews that Euphemius, in congratulating the Roman church on its pontiff, added that he himself was not sufficiently his own master to do what he wished; that the people of Constantinople would never agree to disgrace the memory of their late patriarch Acacius; that if that were necessary, the pope had better write to the people about it himself, and send someone to try and persuade them; that Acacius had never said anything against the faith, and that if he was in communion with Mongus, it was when Mongus had given a satisfactory account of his creed. Euphemius subjoined his own confession, rejecting Eutyches and accepting Chalcedon. It seems also that Euphemius spoke of those who had been baptized and ordained by Acacius since the sentence pronounced against him at Rome, and pointed out how embarrassing it would be if the memory of Acacius must be condemned (Ceillier, x. 486). Replying to these temperate counsels, Gelasius allows that in other circumstances he would have written to announce his election, but sourly observes that the custom existed only among those bishops who were united in communion, and was not to be extended to those who, like Euphemius, preferred a strange alliance to that of St. Peter. He allows the necessity of gentleness and tenderness, but remarks that there is no need to throw yourself into the ditch when you are helping others out. As a mark of condescension he willingly grants the canonical remedy to all who had been baptized and ordained by Acacius. Can Euphemius possibly wish him to allow the names of condemned heretics and their successors to be recited in the sacred diptychs? Euphemius professed to reject Eutyches; let him reject also those who have communicated with the successors of Eutyches. Was it not even worse for Acacius to know the truth and yet communicate with its enemies? The condemnation of Acacius was *ipso facto* according to the decrees of ancient councils. If Peter Mongus did purge himself, why did not Euphemius send proofs of it? He is much vexed with Euphemius for saying that he is constrained to do things which he does not wish; no bishop should talk so about that truth for which he ought to lay down his life. He refuses to send a mission to Constantinople, for it is the pastor's duty to convince his own flock. At the tribunal of Jesus Christ it will be seen which of the two is bitter and hard. The high spirit of the orthodox patriarch was fired by this dictatorial interference. He even thought of summoning the pope himself to account; and as Gelasius was certainly even more suspicious of the emperor Anastasius, who was, despite the recantation which Euphemius had enforced, a real Eutychian at heart, it is very likely that, as Baronius asserts, the patriarch did not attempt to conceal the pope's antipathy to the emperor.

Nothing cooled the zeal of Euphemius for the council of Chalcedon. Anastasius harboured designs against its supporters; the patriarch gathered together the bishops who were at Constantinople, and invited them to confirm its decrees. According to Theophanes and Victor of Tunis, this occurred in 492 (Vict. Tun. *Chron.* p. 5); but in Mansi (vii. 1180) the event is placed at the beginning of the patriarchate of Euphemius, and the decrees are said to have been sent by the bishops to pope Felix III. Various jars shewed the continued rupture with Rome. Theodoric had become master of Italy, and in 493 sent Faustus and Irenaeus to the emperor Anastasius to ask to peace. During their sojourn at Constantinople the envoys received complaints from the Greeks against the Roman church, which they reported to the pope. Euphemius urged that the condemnation of Acacius by one prelate only was invalid; to excommunicate a metropolitan of Constantinople a general council was necessary (*ib.* viii. 16). Now occurred that imprudence which unhappily cost Euphemius his throne. Anastasius, tired of war against the Isaurians, was seeking an honourable way of stopping it. He asked Euphemius in confidence to beg the bishops at Constantinople (there were always bishops coming and going to and from the metropolis) to pray for peace and thus furnish him with an opportunity of entering on negotiations. Euphemius betrayed the secret to John the patrician, father-in-law of Athenodorus, one of the chiefs of the Isaurians. John hurried to the emperor to inform him of the patriarch's indiscretion. Anastasius was deeply offended, and thenceforth never ceased to persecute his old opponent. He accused him of helping the Isaurians against him, and of corresponding with them (Theoph. *Chronog.* A.D. 488). An assassin, either by Anastasius's own order or to gain his favour, drew his sword on Euphemius at the door of the sacristy, but was struck down by an attendant.

Anastasius sought other means to get rid of Euphemius. Theodorus speaks of the violence with which he demanded back the profession of faith on which his coronation had depended (Theod. Lect. ii. 8, 572 seq. in *Patr. Gk.* lxxxvi.). He assembled the bishops who were in the capital and preferred charges against their metropolitan, whom they obsequiously declared excommunicated and deposed. The people loyally refused to surrender him, but had soon to yield to the emperor.

Meanwhile Euphemius, fearing for his life, retired to the baptistery, and refused to go out until Macedonius had promised on the word of the emperor that no violence should be done him when they conducted him to exile. With a proper feeling of respect for the fallen greatness and unconquerable dignity of his predecessor, Macedonius, on coming to find him in the baptistery, made the attendant deacon take off the newly-given pallium and clothed himself in the dress of a simple presbyter, "not daring to wear" his insignia before their canonical owner. After some conversation, Macedonius (himself to follow Euphemius to the very same place of exile under the same emperor) handed to him the proceeds of a loan he had raised for his expenses. Euphemius was taken to Eucaïtes in 495, the fifth year of Anastasius. His death occurred 20 years later at Ancyra, whither, it is thought, the Hunnish invasion had made him retire. Elias, metropolitan of Jerusalem, himself afterwards expelled from his see by Anastasius, stood stoutly by Euphemius at the time of his exile, declaring against the legality of his sentence (Cyrillus, *Vita S. Sabae*, c. 69, apud Sur. t. vi.). In the East Euphemius was always honoured as the defender of the Catholic faith and of Chalcedon, and as a man of the highest holiness and orthodoxy. Great efforts were made at the fifth general council to get his name put solemnly back in the diptychs (Mansi, viii. 1061 E). The authorities for his Life are, Marcel. *Chron.* A.D. 491-495 in *Patr. Lat.* li. p. 933; Theod. Lect. *Eccl. Hist.* ii. 6-15 in *Patr. Gk.* lxxxvi. pt. i. 185-189; Theoph. *Chronog.* A.D. 481-489 in *Patr. Gk.* cviii. 324-337; St. Niceph. Constant. *Chronog. Brev.* 45 in *Patr. Gk.* c. p. 1046; Baronius, A.D. 489-495; Gelas. Pap. *Ep. et Decret.* i. in *Patr. Lat.* lix. 13. [W.M.S.]

Euprepius (4), bp. of Bizya in Thrace; one of 68 bishops who demanded that the opening of the council of Ephesus should be postponed until the arrival of John of Antioch. He signed on this occasion also for Fritilas bp. of Heraclea (*Synod. adv. Tragoed.* cap. 7, in Theod. *Opp.* t. v. in *Patr. Gk.* lxxxiv. 591). He nevertheless attended the council when it opened, signed the sentence against Nestorius and the "decretum de fide" (Mansi, iv. 1225 C, 1364 E). Euprepius is chiefly of interest from the memorial termed "Supplex libellus," which he and Cyril, bp. of Coele in the same province, jointly addressed to the fathers of the council (*ib.* 1478), stating that by an ancient custom in the European provinces a bishop sometimes had more bishoprics than one under his charge; that Euprepius was then administering the see of Arcadiopolis in addition to that of Bizya, while Cyril was acting similarly. The council was requested to rule that this custom might not be disturbed, and that Fritilas, bp. of Heraclea, might be forbidden to appoint bishops in those cities of Thrace which were then without bishops of their own. The prayer was granted, and it was decreed that the custom of the cities in question should be respected (Le Quien, *Or. Chr.* i. 1136, 1145). [E.V.]

Euric (1) (*Evarich, Evorich, Euthorik, Evarix*), king of the Visigothic kingdom of Toulouse from 466 to 484, and from 477 onwards master of almost the whole of Spain. Under him the Visigoth power reached its highest point. In the reign of his successor it was curtailed by the Franks, while in that of his father, Theodoric or Theodored I. (*d.* 451) and his brothers, Thorismund and Theodoric II., the country occupied by the Goths had still been reckoned as an integral part of the empire (" auxiliamini reipublicae," says Aetius to the Goths before the battle of Chalons, " cujus membrum tenetis," Jord. c. 36), while the Gothic state had found it necessary to submit again and again to the foedus with Rome. " Euric, therefore, king of the Visigoths," says Jord. c. 45, " seeing the frequent changes of the Roman princes " (and the weakness of the Roman kingdom, " Romani regni vacillationem," as he says in c. 46), " attempted to occupy the Gauls in his own right, *suo jure*." And again, " Totas Hispanias Galliasque sibi jam proprio jure tenens." Thus the pretence of the foedus was finally set aside, and in the interval between the fall of the western empire and the rise of the Ostrogoths and Franks, Euric appears as the most powerful sovereign of the West (Dahn, v. 100). In 466, the year of his accession, Euric sent legates to the Eastern emperor Leo, perhaps with a last thought of renewing the foedus. The negotiations came to nothing, and in 467 the Goths and Vandals made a defensive league against Leo, Anthemius, and Rikimir, who were about to attack Genseric. Beside his Vandalic auxiliaries in Gaul, Euric also had the support of a certain party among the provincials themselves, as is shewn by the evidence given at the trial of Arvandus, prefect of the Gauls, for treasonable correspondence with the Goths (Sidon. Apoll. i. 7), and in 468 he attacked the newly made Western emperor Anthemius simultaneously in Gaul and Spain, with the result that by 474 the Gothic dominion in Gaul would have extended from the Atlantic to the Rhone and Mediterranean, and from the Pyrenees to the Loire, but for one obstacle—the vigorous defence of Auvergne by Ecdicius, son of the emperor Avitus, and the famous bp. of Clermont, Sidonius Apollinaris (Sid. Apoll. vii. 1). The history of this dramatic struggle, preserved in the letters of Sidonius, throws valuable light on the politics of the 5th cent. It is the last desperate effort of the provincial nobility to avoid barbarian masters, and it is a fight, too, of Catholicism against Arianism. But it was unsuccessful. After besieging Clermont in 474, Euric withdrew into winter quarters, while Sidonius and Ecdicius, in the midst of a devastated country, organized fresh resistance. But with the spring diplomacy intervened. Glycerius, fearful for Italy, and hoping to purchase a renewal of the foedus, had in 473 formally ceded the country to Euric, a compact rejected by Ecdicius and Sidonius; and now Nepos, for the same reasons, sent legates to Euric, amongst them the famous Epiphanius of Pavia (Ennod. *Vita S. Epiph. AA. SS.* Jan. ii. p. 369), to treat for peace. Euric persisted in the demand for Auvergne, and accordingly, in return for a renewal of the foedus (" fidelibus animis foederabuntur," Sid. Apoll. ix. 5), Ecdicius and Sidonius were ordered to submit, and the district was given over to the revenge of the Goths. Ecdicius fled to the Burgundians, while Sidonius (see *Ep.* vii. 7, for his invectives against the peace —" Pudeat vos hujus foederis, nec utilis nec decori ! "), having vainly attempted to make favourable terms for the Catholics with Euric, was banished to Livia, near Narbonne (Sid. Apoll. viii. 3). By the influence of Euric's minister, Leo, he was released after a year's imprisonment, and appeared at the Gothic court at Bordeaux, where, during a stay of two months, he succeeded in obtaining only one audience of the king, so great was the crowd of ambassadors, and the pressure of important business awaiting the decision of Euric and his minister. In *Epp.* viii. 9, Sidonius has left us a brilliant picture of the Gothic king, surrounded by barbarian envoys, Roman legates, and even Persian ambassadors. The Gothic territory in Gaul was now bounded by the Loire, the Rhone, and the two seas, while in Spain a great many towns were already held by Gothic garrisons. Euric's troops easily overran the whole country at their next great advance. In 475 came the fall of Nepos and Augustulus, and the suspension of the empire of the West. The news aroused all the barbarian races in Gaul and Spain. Euric, with an Ostrogothic reinforcement under Widimer, crossed the Pyrenees in 477, took Pampelona and Saragossa, and annihilated the resistance of the Roman nobility in Tarraconensis. By 478 the whole peninsula had fallen to the Goths, except a mountainous strip in the N.W., relinquished probably by treaty to the Suevi. By this complete conquest of the peninsula, " a place of refuge was provided for the Goths . . . destined in the following generation to fall back before the young and all-subduing power of the Franks, called to a greater work than they " (Dahn, *Könige der Germanen*, v. 98). Fresh successes in Gaul followed close upon the Spanish campaign. Arles was taken, 480, Marseilles, 481, and ultimately the whole of Provence up to the Maritime Alps (Proc. b. G. i. 1, quoted by Dahn, *l.c.*), and the exiled Nepos, indeed, seems to have formally surrendered almost the whole of southern Roman Gaul to Euric. Euric was now sovereign from the Loire to the Straits of Gibraltar, and appears as the protector of the neighbouring barbarian races against the encroaching Franks (*Cass. Var.* iii. 3), taking the same position towards them as Theodoric the Great took later in the reign of Euric's son Alaric, Theodoric's son-in-law. Euric survived the accession of Chlodwig (Clovis) three years, dying before Sept. 485.

Euric's Personal Character, and his Persecu-

tions of the Catholics.—His commanding gifts and personality cannot be doubted. Even his bitterest enemy, Sidonius, speaks of his courage and capacity with unwilling admiration. "Pre-eminent in war, of fiery courage and vigorous youth," says Sidonius ("armis potens, acer animis, alacer annis," *Ep.* vii. 6), "he makes but one mistake—that of supposing that his successes are due to the correctness of his religion, when he owes them rather to a stroke of earthly good fortune." Euric was much interested in religious matters and a passionate Arian, not merely apparently from political motives, though his persecution of the Catholic bishops was dictated by sufficient political reasons. The letter of Sidonius quoted above throws great light upon Euric's relation to the Catholic church, and upon the state of the church under his government. "It must be confessed," he says, "that although this king of the Goths is terrible because of his power, I fear his attacks upon the Christian laws more than I dread his blows for the Roman walls. The mere name of Catholic, they say, curdles his countenance and heart like vinegar, so that you might almost doubt whether he was more the king of his people or of his sect. Lose no time," he adds, addressing his correspondent Basilius, bp. of Aix, "in ascertaining the hidden weakness of the Catholic state, that you may be able to apply prompt and public remedy. Bordeaux, Périgueux, Rodez, Limoges, Gabale, Eause, Bazas, Comminges, Auch, and many other towns, where death has cut off the bishops ["summis sacerdotibus ipsorum morte truncatis," a passage misunderstood later by Gregory of Tours, who speaks of the execution of bishops, *Hist. Franc.* ii. 25], and no new bishops have been appointed in their places . . . mark the wide boundary of spiritual ruin. The evil grows every day with the successive deaths of the bishops, and the heretics, both of the present and the past, might be moved by the suffering of congregations deprived of their bishops, and in despair for their lost faith." The churches were crumbling; thorns filled the open doorways; cattle browsed in the porches and on the grass round the altar. Even in town churches services were rare, and "when a priest dies, and no episcopal benediction gives him a successor in that church, not only the priest but the priest's office dies" ("sacerdotium moritur, non sacerdos"). Not only are vacancies caused by death: two bishops, Crocus and Simplicius, are mentioned as deposed and exiled by Euric. Finally, Sidonius implores the aid of Basilius, the position of whose bishopric made him diplomatically important ("per vos mala foederum currunt, per vos regni utriusque pacta conditionesque portantur") towards obtaining for the Catholics from the Gothic government the right of ordaining bishops, that "so we may keep our hold upon the people of the Gauls, if not *ex foedere*, at least *ex fide*."

Gregory of Tours in the next cent. echoed and exaggerated the account of Sidonius, and all succeeding Catholic writers have accused Euric of the same intolerant persecution of the church. The persecution must be looked upon, to a great extent, as political. The Catholic bishops and the provincial nobility were the natural leaders of the Romanized populations. The ecclesiastical organization made the bishops specially formidable (see Dahn's remarks on the Vandal king Huneric's persecutions, *op. cit.* i. 250). Their opposition threatened the work of Euric's life, and did, in fact, with the aid of the orthodox Franks, destroy it in the reign of his successor. But the persecution has a special interest as one of the earliest instances of that oppression in the name of religion, of which the later history of the Goths in conquered Spain is everywhere full (Dahn, v. 101). Euric, however, did not oppress the Romans as such. His minister Leo (Sid. Apoll. viii. 3), and count Victorius, to whom was entrusted the government of Auvergne after its surrender (*ib.* vii. 17; Greg. Tur. ii. 35), were of illustrious Roman families. It was probably by Leo's help that Euric drew up the code of laws of which Isidore and others speak (*Hist. Goth.* apud *Esp. Sagr.* vi. 486); Dahn, *Könige der Germanen, Vte Abth.* pp. 88-101, see list of sources and literature prefixed. For the ultra-Catholic view of the persecution, see Gams's *Kirchengesch. von Spanien*, ii. 1, 484. [M.A.W.]

Eusebius (1), succeeded Marcellus as bp. of Rome, A.D. 309 or 310. He was banished by Maxentius to Sicily, where he died after a pontificate of four months (Apr. 18 to Aug. 17). His body was brought back to Rome, and buried in the cemetery of Callistus on the Appian Way. Hardly anything was known with certainty about this bishop till the discoveries of de Rossi in the catacombs. That he was buried in the cemetery of Callistus rested on the authority of the Liberian *Deposit. Episc.* and the Felician catalogue. But ancient itineraries, written by persons who had visited these tombs, described his resting-place as not being the papal crypt in that cemetery, where all the popes (with two exceptions) since Pontianus had been laid, but in a separate one some distance from it. De Rossi found this crypt, and therein discovered, in 1852 and 1856, fragments of the inscription placed by pope Damasus over the grave, and known from copies taken before the closing of the catacombs. But it was previously uncertain whether it referred to Eusebius the pope or to some other Eusebius. All such doubt was now set at rest by the discovery, in the crypt referred to, of 46 fragments of a slab bearing a copy of the original inscription, and of the original slab, identified by the peculiar characters of Damasine inscriptions. The inscription is as follows:—

"Damasus Episcopus feci.
Heraclius vetuit lapsos peccata dolere
Eusebius miseros docuit sua crimina flere
Scinditur in partes populus gliscente furore
Seditio caedes bellum discordia lites
Extemplo pariter pulsi feritate tyranni
Integra cum rector servaret foedera pacis
Pertulit exilium domino sub judice laetus
Litore Trinacrio mundum vitamque reliquit.
Eusebio Episcopo et martyri."

We thus have revealed a state of things at Rome of which no other record has been preserved. It would seem that, on the cessation of Diocletian's persecution, the church there was rent into two parties on the subject of the terms of readmission of the lapsed to communion: that one Heraclius headed a party who were for readmission without the penitential discipline insisted on by Eusebius; that the consequent tumults and bloodshed caused "the tyrant" Maxentius to interpose and banish the leaders of both factions; and that Eusebius, dying during his exile in Sicily, thus obtained the name of martyr. It appears further, from the similar Damasine inscription on Marcellus, that the contest had begun before the accession of Eusebius, who, like Marcellus, had required penance from the *lapsi*. [MARCELLUS (3).] The way in which the name of Heraclius occurs in the inscription on Eusebius suggests that he may have been elected as an antipope (so Lipsius, *Chronologie der römischen Bischöfe*). At any rate, the subject of dispute was the same as had led to the first election of an antipope, viz. Novatian, after the Decian persecution, some 50 years before; though on the earlier occasion the question was whether the *lapsi* were to be readmitted to communion at all or not, the schismatics being on the side of severity; on the later occasion the question was only about the conditions of their readmission, the dissentients being on the side of laxity. In both instances the church of Rome, as represented by her lawful bishops, seems to have held a consistent and judicious course. [J.B—Y.]

Eusebius (5), of Alexandria, a writer of sermons, about whom Galland says "all is uncertain; nothing can be affirmed on good grounds as to his age or as to his bishopric" (*Bibl. Patr.* viii. p. xxiii.). It is uncertain whether he belongs to the 5th or the 6th cent. A complete list of sermons is given by Mai, as follows: 1. *On Fasting.* 2. *On Love.* 3. *On the Incarnation and its Causes.* 4. *On Thankfulness in Sickness.* 5. *On Imparting Grace to him that Lacks it.* 6. *On Sudden Death*, or, *Those that Die by Snares.* 7. *On New Moon, Sabbath, and on not Observing the Voices of Birds.* 8. *On Commemoration of Saints.* 9. *On Meals*, at such festivals. 10. *On the Nativity.* 11. *On the Baptism of Christ.* 12. *On "Art thou He that should come?"* 13. *On the Coming of John into Hades, and on the Devil.* 14. *On the Treason of Judas.* 15. *On the Devil and Hades.* 16. *On the Lord's Day.* 17. *On the Passion, for the Preparation Day.* 18. *On the Resurrection.* 19. *On the Ascension.* 20. *On the Second Advent.* 21. *On "Astronomers."* 22. *On Almsgiving, and on the Rich Man and Lazarus.* He adheres to the Catholic doctrines of the Trinity and the Incarnation. He uses the ordinary Eastern phrase, "Christ our God," speaks of Him as Maker of the world, as Master of the creation, as present from the beginning with the prophets, and as the Lord of Isaiah's vision. He calls the Holy Spirit consubstantial with the Father and the Son; in the sermon on *Almsgiving* he calls the Virgin Mother "Ever-Virgin," "Theotokos," and "our undefiled Lady." He insists on free will and responsibility. "God . . . saith, 'If you do not choose to hear Me, I do not compel you.' God could make thee good against thy will, but what is involuntary is unrewarded. . . . If He wrote it down that I was to commit sin, and I do commit it, why does He judge me?" If a man means to please God, "God holds out a hand to him straightway," etc. Before a man renounces the world (by a monastic vow), let him try himself, know his own soul. He who fasts must fast with "tongue, eyes, hands, feet"; his whole "body, soul, and spirit" must be restrained from all sinful indulgence. "Fast, as the Lord said, in cheerfulness, with sincere love to all men. But when you have done all this, do not think you are better than A. or B. Say you are unprofitable servants." People are not to blame wine, but those who drink it to excess; nor riches, but the man who administers them ill. Abraham had riches, but they harmed him not, etc. Some sentences shew a true spiritual insight: "What sort of righteousness exceeds the rest? Love, for without it no good comes of any other. What sin is worst? All sin is dreadful, but none is worse than covetousness and remembrance of injuries" (Serm. *On Love*). He has humour, too, which must have told: "On Sundays the herald calls people to church; everybody says he is sleepy, or unwell. Hark! a sound of harp or pipe, a noise of dancing: all hasten that way as if on wings" (*Hom. on the Lord's Day*, Galland. viii. 253). He depicts vividly the extravagance of Alexandrian wealth; the splendid houses glistening with marble, beds and carpets wrought with gold and pearls, horses with golden bridles and saddles, the crowds of servants of various classes—some to attend the great man when he rides out, some to manage his lands or his house, building, or his kitchen, some to fan him at his meals, to keep the house quiet during his slumber:—the varieties of white bread, the pheasants, geese, peacocks, hares, etc., served up at his table. The Christian should look forward to Sunday, not simply as a day of rest from labour, but as a day of prayer and Communion. Let him come in early morning to church for the Eucharistic service (the features of it are enumerated: the psalmody, the reading of Prophets, of St. Paul, of the Gospels, the Angelic and Seraphic hymns, the ceaseless Alleluia, the exhortations of bishops and presbyters, the presence of Christ "on the sacred table," the "coming" of the Spirit). "If thy conscience is clear, approach, and receive the Body and Blood of the Lord. If it condemns thee in regard to wicked deeds, decline the Communion until thou hast corrected it by repentance, but stay through the prayers [*i.e.* the communion service], and do not go out of the church unless thou art dismissed"; or again, "before the dismissal." He severely blames a layman who tastes food before the Liturgy is over, whether he communicates or not; but denounces those who communicate after eating (as many do on Easter Day itself) as if guilty of a heinous sin. (In this case, as in regard to premature departure from church, he does not scruple to refer to Judas.) He blames those who do not communicate when a priest, known to be of bad life, is the celebrant; for "God turneth not away, and the bread becomes the Body." He reproves those who are disorderly at the vigil services of a saint's festival, and at daybreak rise and cause great disturbances. "Inside the church, the priest is presenting the supplication . . . having set forth (προτεθεικώς) the Body and the Blood . . . for the salvation of the world: while, outside, amusements go on." He refers to the different functions of priest, deacon, reader, chanter, and subdeacon (ὑπηρέτης). He encourages invocation of saints.

Mai calls him a writer delightful from his "ingenuitas," his "Christian ac pastoralis simplicitas," and his "nativum dicendi genus" (*Patrum Nov. Biblioth.* ii. 499). [W.B.]

Eusebius (23) of Caesarea, also known as **Eusebius Pamphili.** Of extant sources of our knowledge of Eusebius the most important are the scattered notices in writers of the same or immediately succeeding ages, *e.g.* Athanasius, Jerome, Socrates, Sozomen, and Theodoret. At a later date some valuable information is contained in the proceedings of the second council of Nicaea (Labbe, *Conc.* viii. 1144 seq. ed. Colet.), and in the *Antirrhetica* of the patriarch Nicephorus (*Spicil. Solesm.* i. pp. 371 seq.) likewise connected with the Iconoclastic controversy. The primary sources of information, however, for the career of one who was above all a literary man must be sought in his own works. The only edition of them which aims at completeness is in Migne's *Patr. Gk.* vols. xix.-xxiv. See also the standard works of Cave (*Hist. Lit.* i. pp. 175 seq.), Tillemont (*Hist. Eccl.* vii. pp. 39 seq., 659 seq., together with scattered notices in his account of the Arians and of the Nicene council in vol. vi.), and Fabricius (*Bibl. Graec.* vii. pp. 335 seq. ed. Harles). The most complete monograph is Stein's *Eusebius Bischof von Cäsarea* (Würzburg, 1852). There is a useful English trans. of the *History* in the *Nicene and Post-Nicene Fathers*, by Mr. Giffert; cf. A. C. Headlam, *The Editions or MSS. of Eusebius*, in *Journal of Theol. Studies*, 1902, iii. 93-102.

The references in his own works will hardly allow us to place his birth much later than A.D. 260, so that he would be nearly 80 at his death. All notices of his early life are connected with Caesarea; and as it was then usual to prefer a native as bishop, everything favours this as the city of his birth.

Of his parentage and relationships absolutely nothing is known, but here, as a child, he was catechized in that declaration of belief which years afterwards was laid by him before the great council of Nicaea, and adopted by the assembled Fathers as a basis for the creed of the universal church. Here he listened to the Biblical expositions of the learned Dorotheus, thoroughly versed in the Hebrew Scriptures and not unacquainted with Greek literature and philosophy, once the superintendent of the emperor's purple factory at Tyre, but now a presbyter in the church of Caesarea (*H. E.* vii. 32). Here, in due time, he was himself ordained a presbyter, probably by that bp. Agapius whose wise forethought and untiring assiduity and openhanded benevolence he himself has recorded (*ib.*). Here, above all, he contracted with the saintly student PAMPHILUS that friendship which was the crown and glory of his life, and which martyrdom itself could not sever. Eusebius owed far more to Pamphilus than the impulse and direction given to his studies. Pamphilus, no mere student recluse, was a man of large heart and bountiful hand, above all things helpful to his friends (*Mart. Pal.* 11), giving freely to all in want; he multiplied copies of the Scriptures, which he distributed gratuitously (Eus. in Hieron. *c. Rufin.* i. 9, *Op.* ii. 465); and to the sympathy of the friend he united the courage of the hero. He had also the power of impressing his own strong convictions on others. Hence, when the great trial of faith came, his house was found to be not only the home of students but the nursery of martyrs. To one like Eusebius, who owed his strength and his weakness alike to a ready susceptibility of impression from those about him, such a friendship was an inestimable blessing. He expressed the strength of his devotion to this friend by adopting his name, being known as "Eusebius of Pamphilus."

Eusebius was in middle life when the last and fiercest persecution broke out. For nearly half a century—a longer period than at any other time since its foundation—the church had enjoyed uninterrupted peace as regards attacks from without. Suddenly and unexpectedly all was changed. The city of Caesarea became a chief centre of persecution. Eusebius tells how he saw the houses of prayer razed to the ground, the holy Scriptures committed to the flames in the market-places, the pastors hiding themselves, and shamefully jeered at when caught by their persecutors (*H. E.* viii. 2). For seven years the attacks continued. At Tyre also Eusebius saw several Christians torn by wild beasts in the amphitheatre (*ib.* 7, 8). Leaving Palestine, he visited Egypt. In no country did the persecution rage more fiercely. Here, in the Thebaid, they perished, ten, twenty, even sixty or a hundred at a time. Eusebius tells how he in these parts witnessed numerous martyrdoms in a single day, some by beheading, others by fire; the executioners relieving each other by relays and the victims eagerly pressing forward to be tortured, clamouring for the honour of martyrdom, and receiving their sentence with joy and laughter (*ib.* 9). This visit to Egypt was apparently after the imprisonment and martyrdom of Pamphilus, in the latest and fiercest days of the persecution. It was probably now that Eusebius was imprisoned for his faith. If so, we have the less difficulty in explaining his release, without any stain left on his integrity or his courage.

Not long after the restoration of peace (A.D. 313) Eusebius was unanimously elected to the vacant see of Caesarea. Among the earliest results of the peace was the erection of a magnificent basilica at Tyre under the direction of his friend Paulinus, the bishop. Eusebius was invited to deliver the inaugural address. This address he has preserved and inserted in his *History*, where, though not mentioned, the orator's name is but thinly concealed (*H.E.* ix. 4). This oration is a paean of thanksgiving over the restitution of the Church, of which the splendid building at Tyre was at once the firstfruit and the type. The incident must have taken place not later than A.D. 315. For more than 25 years he presided over the church of Caesarea, winning the respect and affection of all. He died bp. of Caesarea.

When the Arian controversy broke out, the sympathies of Eusebius were early enlisted on the side of Arius. If his namesake of Nicomedia may be trusted, he was especially zealous on behalf of the Arian doctrine at this time (Eus. Nicom. in Theod. *H. E.* i. 5, ἡ τοῦ δεσπότου μου Εὐσεβίου σπουδὴ ἡ ὑπὲρ ἀληθοῦς λόγου). But the testimony of this strong partisan may well be suspected; and the attitude of Eusebius of Caesarea throughout suggests that he was influenced rather by personal associations and the desire to secure liberal treatment for the heresiarch than by any real accordance with his views. Whatever his motives, he wrote to Alexander, bp. of Alexandria, remonstrating with him for deposing Arius and urging that he had misrepresented the opinions of the latter (Labbe, *Conc.* viii. 1148, ed. Colet). The cause of Arius was taken up also by two neighbouring bishops, Theodotus of Laodicea and Paulinus of Tyre. In a letter addressed to his namesake of Constantinople, Alexander complains of three Syrian bishops, "appointed he knows not how," as having fanned the flame of sedition (Theod. *H. E.* i. 3); while Arius himself claims "all the bishops in the East," mentioning by name Eusebius of Caesarea with others, as on his side (*ib.* i. 4). Accordingly, when he was deposed by a synod convened at Alexandria by Alexander, Arius appealed to Eusebius and others to interpose. A meeting of Syrian bishops decided for his restoration, though wording the decision cautiously. The synod thought that Arius should be allowed to gather his congregation about him as heretofore, but added that he must render obedience to Alexander and entreat to be admitted to communion with him (Soz. *H. E.* i. 15).

At the council of Nicaea (A.D. 325) Eusebius took a leading part. This prominence he cannot have owed to his bishopric, which, though important, did not rank with the great sees, "the apostolic thrones" (*ib.* 17) of Rome, Antioch, and Alexandria. But that he was beyond question the most learned man and most famous living writer in the church at this time would suffice to secure him a hearing. Probably, however, his importance was due even more to his close relations with the great emperor, whose entire confidence he enjoyed. He occupied the first seat to the emperor's right (*V. C.* iii. 11), and delivered the opening address to Constantine when he took his seat in the council-chamber (*ib.* i. prooem., iii. 11; Soz. *H. E.* i. 19). The speech is unfortunately not preserved.

Eusebius himself has left us an account of his doings with regard to the main object of the council in a letter of explanation to his church at Caesarea. He laid before the council the creed in use in the Caesarean church, which had been handed down from the bishops who preceded him, which he himself had been taught at his baptism, and in which, both as a presbyter and bishop, he had instructed others. The emperor was satisfied with the orthodoxy of this creed, inserting however the single word ὁμοούσιον, and giving explanations as to its meaning which set the scruples of Eusebius at rest. The assembled Fathers, taking this as their starting-point, made other important insertions and alterations. Moreover, an anathema was appended directly condemning Arian doctrines. Eusebius took time to consider before subscribing to this revised formula. The three expressions which caused difficulty were: (1) "of the substance of the Father" (ἐκ τῆς οὐσίας τοῦ πατρός); (2) "begotten, not made" (γεννηθέντα, οὐ ποιηθέντα); (3) "of the same substance" (ὁμοούσιον); and of these he demanded explanations. The explanations were so far satisfactory that for the sake of peace he subscribed to the creed. He had the less scruple in assenting to the final anathema, because the Arian expressions which it condemned were not scriptural, and he considered that "almost all the confusion and disturbance of the churches" had arisen from the use of unscriptural phrases. This letter, he concludes, is written to the Caesareans to explain that he would resist to the last any vital change in the traditional creed of his church, but had subscribed to these alterations, when assured of their innocence, to avoid appearing contentious (ἀφιλονείκως). See Hort's *Two Dissertations*, pp. 55 seq.

The settlement of the dispute respecting the time of observing Easter was another important work undertaken by the council. In this also a leading part has been assigned to Eusebius by some modern writers (*e.g.* Stanley, *Eastern Church*, p. 182, following Tillemont, *H. E.* vi. p. 668).

The hopes which Eusebius with others had built upon the decisions of the Nicene council were soon dashed. The final peace of the church seemed as far distant as ever. In three controversies with three distinguished antagonists, Eusebius took a more or less prominent part; and his reputation, whether justly or not, has suffered greatly in consequence.

(i) *Synod of Antioch.*—Eustathius, bp. of Antioch, was a staunch advocate of the Nicene doctrine and a determined foe of the Arians. He had assailed the tenets of Origen (Socr. *H. E.* vi. 13), of whom Eusebius was an ardent champion, and had charged Eusebius himself with faithlessness to the doctrines of Nicaea. He was accused in turn of Sabellianism by Eusebius (*ib.* i. 23; Soz. *H.E.* ii. 19). To the historian Socrates the doctrines of the two antagonists seemed practically identical. Nevertheless they were regarded as the two principals in the quarrel (Soz. *H. E.* ii. 18). A synod, mainly composed of bishops with Arian or semi-Arian sympathies, was assembled at Antioch, A.D. 330, to consider the charge of Sabellianism brought against Eustathius, who was deposed. The see of Antioch thus became vacant. The assembled bishops proposed Eusebius of Caesarea as his successor, and wrote to the emperor on his behalf, but Eusebius declined the honour, alleging the rule of the Church, regarded as an "apostolic tradition," which forbade translations from one see to another; and Euphronius was elected.

(ii) *Synods of Caesarea, Tyre, and Jerusalem.*—The next stage of the Arian controversy exhibits Eusebius in conflict with a greater than Eustathius. The disgraceful intrigues of the Arians and Meletians against Athanasius, which led to his first exile, are related in our art. ATHANASIUS. It is sufficient to say here that the emperor summoned Athanasius to appear before a gathering of bishops at Caesarea, to meet the charges brought against him. It is stated by Theodoret (*H. E.* i. 26) that Constantine was induced to name Caesarea by the Arian party, who selected it because the enemies of Athanasius were in a majority there (ἔνθα δὴ πλείους ἦσαν οἱ δυσμενεῖς), but the emperor may have given the preference to Caesarea because he reposed the greatest confidence in the moderation (ἐπιείκεια) of its bishop. Athanasius excused himself from attending, believing that there was a conspiracy against him, and that he would not have fair play there (*Festal Letters*, p. xvii, Oxf. trans.; Theod. *H. E.* i. 26; Soz. *H. E.* ii. 25). This was in 334. Athanasius does not mention this synod in his *Apology*.

The next year (A.D. 335) Athanasius received a peremptory and angry summons from Constantine to appear before a synod of bishops at Tyre. Theodoret (*l.c.*) conjectures (ὡς οἶμαι) that the place of meeting was changed by the emperor out of deference to the fears of Athanasius, who "looked with suspicion on Caesarea on account of its ruler." Athanasius, or his friends, may indeed have objected to Eusebius as a partisan; for the Egyptian bishops who espoused the cause of Athanasius, addressing the synod of Tyre, allege "the law of God" as forbidding "an enemy to be witness or judge," and shortly afterwards add mysteriously, "ye know why Eusebius of Caesarea has become an enemy since last year" (Athan. *Ap. c. Arian.* 77, *Op.* i. p. 153). The scenes at the synod of Tyre form the most picturesque and the most shameful chapter in the Arian controversy. After all allowance for the exaggerations of the Athanasian party, from whom our knowledge is chiefly derived, the proceedings will still remain an undying shame to Eusebius of Nicomedia and his fellow-intriguers. But there is no reason for supposing that Eusebius of Caesarea took any active part in these plots. Athanasius mentions him rarely, and then without any special bitterness. The "Eusebians" (οἱ περὶ Εὐσέβιον) are always the adherents of his Nicomedian namesake. But, though probably not participating in, and possibly ignorant of their plots, Eusebius of Caesarea was certainly used as a tool by the more unscrupulous and violent partisans of Arius, and must bear the reproach of a too easy compliance with their actions. The proceedings were cut short by the withdrawal of Athanasius, who suddenly sailed to Constantinople, and appealed in person to the emperor. The synod condemned him by default.

While the bishops at Tyre were in the midst of their session, an urgent summons from the emperor called them to take part in the approaching festival at Jerusalem (Eus. *V. C.* iv. 41 seq.; Socr. *H. E.* i. 33 seq.; Soz. *H. E.* ii. 26; Theod. *H. E.* i. 29). It was the ***tricennalia*** of Constantine. No previous sovereign after Augustus, the founder of the empire, had reigned for thirty years. Constantine had a fondness for magnificent ceremonial, and here was a noble opportunity (*V. C.* iv. 40, καιρὸς εὔκαιρος). The occasion was marked by the dedication of Constantine's new and splendid basilica, built on the site of Calvary. The festival was graced by a series of orations from the principal persons present. In these Eusebius bore a conspicuous part, finding in this dedication festival a far more congenial atmosphere than in the intrigues of the synod at Tyre. He speaks of the assemblage at Tyre as a mere episode of the festival at Jerusalem (ὁδοῦ δὴ πάρεργον). The emperor, he says, preparing for the celebration of this festival, was anxious to end the quarrels which rent the church. In doing so he was obeying the Lord's injunction, "Be reconciled to thy brother, and then go and offer thy gift" (cf. Soz. i. 26). This view of the emperor's motive is entirely borne out by Constantine's own letter to the synod at Tyre. Eusebius was greatly impressed by the celebration; but Tillemont, who shews strong prejudice against Eusebius throughout, altogether misstates the case in saying that he "compares or even prefers this assembly to the council of Nicaea, striving to exalt it as much as he can, for the sake of effacing the glory of that great council," etc. (vi. p. 284). But Eusebius says distinctly that "*after* that first council" this was the greatest synod assembled by Constantine (*V. C.* iv. 47); and so far from shewing any desire to depreciate the council of Nicaea, he cannot find language magnificent enough to sing its glories (iii. 6 seq.).

Arius and Euzoius had presented a confession of faith to the emperor, seeking readmission to the church. The emperor was satisfied that this document was in harmony with the faith of Nicaea, and sent Arius and Euzoius to Jerusalem, requesting the synod to consider their confession of faith and restore them to communion. Arius and his followers were accordingly readmitted at Jerusalem. Of the bishops responsible for this act, some were hostile to Athanasius, others would regard it as an act of pacification. The stress which Eusebius lays on Constantine's desire to secure peace on this, as on all other occasions, suggests that that was a predominant idea in the writer's own mind, though perhaps not unmixed with other influences.

(iii) *Synod of Constantinople.*—Athanasius had not fled to Constantinople in vain. Constantine desired pacification but was not insensible to justice; and the personal pleadings of Athanasius convinced him that justice had been outraged (*Ap. c. Arian.* 86). The bishops at the dedication festival had scarcely executed the request, or command, of the emperor's first letter, when they received another written in a very different temper (*ib.*; Socr. *H. E.* i. 34; Soz. *H. E.* ii. 27). It was addressed "to the bishops that had assembled at Tyre"; described their proceedings as "tumultuous and stormy"; and summoned them without delay to Constantinople. The leaders of the Eusebian party alone obeyed; the rest retired to their homes. Among those who obeyed was Eusebius of Caesarea. Of the principal events which occurred at Constantinople, the banishment of Athanasius and the death of Arius, we need not speak here. But the proceedings of the synod then held there (A.D. 336) have an important bearing on the literary history of Eusebius. The chief work of the synod was the condemnation of MARCELLUS, bp. of Ancyra, an uncompromising opponent of the Arians. He had written a book in reply to the Arian Asterius "the sophist," in which his zeal against Arian tenets goaded him into expressions that had a rank savour of Sabellianism. The proceedings against him had commenced at Jerusalem and were continued at Constantinople, where he was condemned of Sabellianism, and deposed from his bishopric (Socr. *H. E.* i. 36; Soz. *H. E.* ii. 33). Eusebius is especially mentioned as taking part in this synod (Athan. *Ap. c. Arian.* 87; cf. Eus. *c. Marc.* ii. 4, p. 115). Not satisfied with this, the dominant party urged Eusebius to undertake a refutation of the heretic. Two works against Marcellus were his response. Eusebius found also more congenial employment during his sojourn at Constantinople. The celebration of the emperor's *tricennalia* had not yet ended, and Eusebius delivered a panegyric which he afterwards appended to his *Life of Constantine.* The delivery of this oration may have been the chief motive which induced Eusebius to accompany the Arian bishops to Constantinople. It must have been during this same visit, though on an earlier day, that he delivered before the emperor his discourse on the church of the Holy Sepulchre, probably previously spoken also at the dedication itself. This oration has unfortunately not survived. It does not appear that Eusebius had any personal interview with Constantine before the council of Nicaea. Here, however, he stood high in the emperor's favour, as the prominent position assigned to him shews; and there seems thenceforward no interruption in their cordial relations. The emperor used to enter into familiar conversation with him, relating the most remarkable incidents in his career, such as the miraculous appearance of the cross in the skies (*V. C.* i. 28), and the protection afforded by that emblem in battle (ii. 9). He corresponded with him on various subjects, on one occasion asking him to see to the execution of fifty copies of the Scriptures for his new capital, and supplying him with the necessary means (iv. 36); and he listened with patience, and even with delight, to the lengthy and elaborate orations which Eusebius delivered from time to time in his presence. Constantine praises his eulogist's gentleness or moderation (iii. 60). Nor was Constantine the only member of the imperial family with whom Eusebius had friendly relations. The empress Constantia, the sister of Constantine and wife of Licinius, wrote to him on a matter of religious interest. In his reply we are especially struck with the frankness of expostulation, almost of rebuke, with which he addresses her (*Spicil. Solesm.* i. 383).

The great emperor breathed his last on May 22, A.D. 337; and Eusebius died not later than the close of 339 or the beginning of 340. In Wright's *Ancient Syrian Martyrology*, which cannot date later than half a century after the event, "the commemoration of Eusebius bp. of Palestine" is placed on May 30. If this represents the day of his death, as probably it does, he must have died in 339, for the notices will hardly allow so late a date in the following year. His literary activity was unabated to the end. Four years at most can have elapsed between his last visit to Constantinople and his death. He must have been nearly 80 years old when the end came. Yet at this advanced age, and within this short period, he composed the *Panegyric*, the *Life of Constantine*, the treatise *Against Marcellus*, and the companion treatise *On the Theology of the Church*; probably he had in hand at the same time other unfinished works, such as the *Theophania.* There are no signs of failing mental vigour in these works. The two doctrinal treatises are perhaps his most forcible and lucid writings. The *Panegyric* and the *Life of Constantine* are disfigured by a too luxuriant rhetoric, but in vigour equal any of his earlier works. Of his death itself no record is left. Acacius, his successor, had been his pupil. Though more decidedly Arian in bias, he was a devoted admirer of his master (Soz. *H. E.* iii. 2). He wrote a Life of Eusebius, and apparently edited some of his works.

Literary Works.—The literary remains of Eusebius are a rich and, excepting the *Chronicle* and the *Ecclesiastical History*, a comparatively unexplored mine of study. They may be classed as: A. *Historical*; B. *Apologetic*; C. *Critical and Exegetical*; D. *Doctrinal*; E *Orations*; F. *Letters.*

A. HISTORICAL.—(1) *Life of Pamphilus.*—Eusebius (*Mart. Pal.* 11), speaking of his friend's martyrdom, refers to this work as follows: "The rest of the triumphs of his virtue, requiring a longer narration, we have already before this given to the world in a separate work in three books, of which his life is the subject." He also refers to it 3 times in his *History* (*H. E.* vi. 32, vii. 32, viii. 13). The *Life of Pamphilus* was thus written before the *History*, and before the shorter ed. of—

(2) *The Martyrs of Palestine.*—This work is extant in two forms, a shorter and a longer. The shorter is attached to the *History*, commonly between the 8th and 9th books.

The longer form is not extant entire in the original Greek. In the Bollandist *Acta Sanctorum* (Jun. t. i. p. 64) Papebroch pub. for the first time in Greek, from a Paris MS. of the Metaphrast, an account of the martyrdom of Pamphilus and others, professedly "composed by Eusebius Pamphili." It had appeared in a Latin version before. The Greek was reprinted by Fabricius, *Hippolytus*, ii. p. 217. This is a fuller account of the incidents related in the *Mart. Pal.* 11 attached to the *History.* Their common matter is expressed in the same words, or nearly so. Hence one must have been an enlargement or an abridgment of the other.

Nor can it reasonably be doubted that the shorter form of the *Palestinian Martyrs* is Eusebius's own. It retains those notices of the longer form in which Eusebius speaks in his own person; and, moreover, in the passages peculiar to this shorter form, Eusebius is evidently the speaker. Thus (c. 11) he mentions having already written a special work in three books on the life of Pamphilus; and when recording the death of Silvanus, who had had his eyes put out (c. 13), mentions his own astonishment when he once heard him reading the Scriptures, as he supposed, from a book in church, but was told that he was blind and was repeating them by heart. Moreover, other incidental notices, inserted from time to time and having no place in the longer form, shew the knowledge of a contemporary and eyewitness.

The longer edition seems to be the original

form. It is an independent work, apparently written not very long after the events. It betrays no other motive than to inform and edify the readers, more especially the Christians of Caesarea and Palestine, to whom it is immediately addressed. "Our city of Caesarea" is an expression occurring several times (pp. 4 twice, 25, 30). "This our country," "this our city," are analogous phrases (pp. 8, 13).

In the shorter form the case is different. The writer does not localize himself in the same way. It is always "the city," never "this city," of Caesarea. The appeal to the Caesareans in recounting the miracle is left out (c. 4). The hortatory beginning and ending are omitted, and the didactic portions abridged or excised. The shorter form thus appears to be part of a larger work, in which the sufferings of the martyrs were set off against the deaths of the persecutors. The object would thus be the vindication of God's righteousness. This idea appears several times elsewhere in Eusebius, and he may have desired to embody it in a separate treatise.

(3) *Collection of Ancient Martyrdoms.*—Of this work Eusebius was not the author, but merely, as the title suggests and as the notices require, the compiler and editor. The narratives of martyrdoms were, in the eyes of Eusebius, not only valuable as history but instructive as lessons (*H. E.* v. praef.). Hence he took pains to preserve authentic records of them, himself undertaking to record those of his own country, Palestine, at this time; while he left to others in different parts of the world to relate those "quae ipsi miserrima viderunt," declaring that only thus could strict accuracy be attained (*H. E.* viii. 13, with the whole context). But he was anxious also to preserve the records of past persecutions. Hence this collection of *Martyrologies*. The epithet "ancient" (ἀρχαῖα) must be regarded as relative, applying to all prior to the "persecution of his own time" (ὁ καθ' ἡμᾶς διωγμός, according to his favourite expression). He himself refers to this collection for the martyrdom of Polycarp and others at Smyrna under Antoninus Pius A.D. 155 or 156 (iv. 15), for the documents relating to the sufferers in Gaul under M. Aurelius A.D. 177 (v. 1, seq.), and for the defence of Apollonius under Commodus A.D. 180-185 (v. 21). But it would probably comprise any martyrdoms which occurred before the long peace that preceded the outbreak of the last persecution under Diocletian.

[(4) *Chronicle.*—This work may be described in words suggested by the author's own account of it at the beginning of his *Eclogae Propheticae*, as "chronological tables, to which is prefixed an epitome of universal history drawn from various sources." The epitome occupies the first book, the tables the second. The tables exhibit in parallel columns the successions of the rulers of different nations, so that contemporary monarchs can be seen at a glance. Notes mark the years of the more remarkable historical events, these notes constituting an epitome of history. The interest which Christians felt in the study of comparative chronology arose from heathen opponents contrasting the antiquity of their rites with the novelty of the Christian religion. Christian apologists retorted by proving that the Grecian legislators and philosophers were very much later than the Hebrew legislator and later than the prophets who had testified of Christ and taught a religion of which Christianity was the legitimate continuation. In the *Praeparatio Evangelica* (x. 9) Eusebius urges this, quoting largely from preceding writers who had proved the antiquity of the Jews, *e.g.* Josephus, Tatian, Clement of Alexandria, and especially Africanus. This last writer had made the synchronisms between sacred and profane history his special study, and his chronological work, now lost, gave Eusebius the model and, to a great extent, the materials for his own *Chronicle.*

The Greek of Eusebius's own work has been lost, and until recent times it was only known through the use made of it by successors, particularly Jerome, who translated it into Latin, enlarging the notices of Roman history and continuing it to his own time. In 1606 Scaliger published an edition of the *Chronicle*, in which he attempted to restore the Greek of Eusebius, collecting from Syncellus, Cedrenus, and other Greek chronologers, notices which he believed himself able, mainly by the help of Jerome's translation, to identify as copied from Eusebius; but his restoration of the first book, where he had but little guidance from Jerome, did not inspire confidence, and has been proved untrustworthy. An Armenian trans. of the *Chronicle*, pub. in 1818, enables us now to state the contents of bk. i.

After pleading that early Greek and even Hebrew chronology present many difficulties, Eusebius, in the first section, gives a sketch of Chaldee and Assyrian history, subjoining a table of Assyrian, Median, Lydian, and Persian kings, ending with the Darius conquered by Alexander. The authors he uses are Alexander Polyhistor, and, as known through him, Berosus; Abydenus, Josephus, Castor, Diodorus, and Cephalion. He notes the coincidences of these writers with Hebrew history and suggests that the incredible lengths assigned to reigns in the early Chaldee history may be reduced if the "sari," said to be periods of 3,600 years, were in reality far shorter periods, and in like manner, following Africanus, that the Egyptian years may be in reality but months. An alternative suggestion in this first book is that some Egyptian dynasties may have been, not consecutive, but synchronous. The second section treats of Hebrew chronology, the secular authorities used being Josephus and Africanus. Eusebius notices the chronological difference between the Heb., LXX., and Samaritan texts, and conjectures that the Hebrews, to justify by patriarchal example their love of early marriages, systematically shortened the intervals between the birth of each patriarch and that of his first son. He gives other arguments which decide him in favour of the LXX, especially as it was the version used by our Lord and the apostles. In the period from the Deluge to the birth of Abraham, which Eusebius makes the initial point of his own tables, he follows the LXX, except that he omits the second Cainan, making 942 years; and thus placing the birth of Abraham in the year from the Creation 3184. He reckons 480 years between the Exodus and Solomon's temple, as in I. Kings. In the preface to his second book, he states that his predecessors had made Moses contemporary with Inachus, and 700 years earlier than the Trojan War. His own computation made Inachus contemporary with Jacob, and Moses with Cecrops, but he contends that this leaves Moses still nearly 400 years older than the capture of Troy, and older than Deucalion's Deluge, Phaethon's Conflagration, Bacchus, Aesculapius, Castor and Pollux, Hercules, Homer and the Seven Wise Men of Greece, and Pythagoras the first philosopher. Eusebius counts 442 years from the foundation of Solomon's temple to its destruction under Zedekiah. He reckons two prophetic periods of 70 years of captivity. One begins with the destruction of the temple, and ends with the 2nd year of Darius Hystaspis and the rebuilding of the temple under Zerubbabel. The other is from the first prophesying of Jeremiah in the 15th year of Josiah to the 1st year of Cyrus, when an altar was set up at Jerusalem and the foundations of the temple laid. In the tables Eusebius gives an alternative for this period, viz. from the 3rd year of Jehoiakim to the 19th of Cyrus. From the 2nd year of Darius, which he counts as the 1st year of the 65th olympiad, Eusebius counts 548 years to the preaching of our Lord and the 15th year of Tiberius, which he reckons as the 4th year of the 201st olympiad, and as the year 5228 from the creation of the world. There is every reason for thinking that more editions of the *Chronicle* than one were published by Eusebius in his lifetime. In its latest form it terminates with the Vicennalia of Constantine. Jerome says in his preface that as far as the taking of Troy his work was a mere translation of that of Eusebius; that from that date to the point at which the work of Eusebius closes, he added notices, from Suetonius and others, relating to Roman history; and that the conclusion from where Eusebius breaks off to his own time was entirely his own. G.S.]

(5) *Ecclesiastical History*.—From many considerations it seems clear that the *History* was finished some time in A.D. 324 or 325—before midsummer in the latter year, and probably some months earlier; and the earlier books even some years before this.

The work contains no indications that it was due to any suggestion from without, as some have supposed. If the author had been prompted to it by Constantine, he would hardly have been silent about the fact, for he is only too ready elsewhere to parade the flatteries of his imperial patron. Moreover, it was probably written in great measure, or at least the materials for it collected, before his relations with Constantine began. His own language rather suggests that it grew out of a previous work, the *Chronicle*.

He begins by enumerating the topics with which it is intended to deal: (1) the successions of the apostles with continuous chronological data from the Christian era to his own time; (2) the events of ecclesiastical history; (3) the most distinguished rulers, preachers, and writers in the church; (4) the teachers of heresy who, like "grievous wolves," have ravaged the flock of Christ; (5) the retribution which had befallen the Jewish race; (6) the persecutions of the church and the victories of the martyrs and confessors, concluding with the great and final deliverance wrought by the Saviour in the author's own day. He prays for guidance, since he is entering upon an untrodden way, where he will find no footprints, though the works of predecessors may serve as beacon-lights here and there through the waste. He considers it absolutely necessary (ἀναγκαιότατα) to undertake the task, because no one else before him had done so. The work, he concludes, must of necessity commence with the Incarnation and Divinity (οἰκονομίας τε καὶ θεολογίας) of Christ, because from Him we all derive our name. Accordingly he proceeds to shew that Christianity is no new thing, but has its roots in the eternal past. The Word was with God before the beginning of creation. He was recognized and known by righteous men in all ages, especially among the Hebrews; His advent, even His very names, were foretold and glorified; His society—the Christian church—was the subject of prophecy, while the Christian type of life was never without examples since the race began (i. 4, cf. ii. 1). "After this necessary preparation" (μετὰ τὴν δέουσαν προκατασκευήν, i. 5), he proceeds to speak of the Incarnation, its chronology and synchronisms in external history, the Herodian kingdom, the Roman empire, the Jewish priesthood, including a discussion of the Saviour's genealogy; thus shewing that it came in the fulness of time as a realization of prophecy (cc. 5-10). A chapter is devoted to the Baptist as the first herald (c. 11), another to the appointment of the Twelve and the Seventy (c. 12); a third to the mission sent by Christ Himself to Edessa, as recorded in the archives of that city (c. 13). We are thus brought to the time of the Ascension, and the first book ends. The second comprises the preaching of the apostles to the destruction of Jerusalem, the writer's aim being not to repeat the accounts in the N.T., but to supplement them from external sources. The third book extends to the reign of Trajan, and covers the sub-apostolic age, ending with notices of Ignatius, Clement, and Papias. The fourth and fifth carry us to the close of the 2nd cent., including the Montanist, Quartodeciman, and Monarchian disputes. The sixth contains the period from the persecution of Severus (A.D. 203) to that of Decius (A.D. 250), the central figure being Origen, of whom a full account is given. The seventh continues the narrative to the outbreak of the great persecution under Diocletian, and is largely composed of quotations from Dionysius of Alexandria, as the preface states. It is significant that the last forty years of this period, though contemporary with the historian, are dismissed in a single long chapter. It was a period of very rapid but silent progress, when the church for the first time was in the happy condition of having no history. The eighth book gives the history of the persecution of Diocletian till the "palinode," the edict of Galerius (A.D. 311). The ninth relates the sufferings of the Eastern Christians until the victory over Maxentius at the Milvian bridge in the West, and the death of Maximin in the East, left Constantine and

Licinius sole emperors. The tenth and last book, dedicated to Paulinus, gives an account of the rebuilding of the churches, the imperial decrees favourable to the Christians, the subsequent rebellion of Licinius, and the victory of Constantine by which he was left sole master of the Roman world. A panegyric of Constantine closes the whole.

Eusebius thus had a truly noble conception of the work which he had undertaken. It was nothing less than the history of a society which stood in an intimate relation to the Divine Logos Himself, a society whose roots struck down into the remotest past and whose destinies soared into the eternal future. He felt, moreover, that he himself lived at the great crisis in its history. Now at length it seemed to have conquered the powers of this world. This was the very time, therefore, to place on record the incidents of its past career. Moreover, he had great opportunities, such as were not likely to fall to another. In his own episcopal city, perhaps in his own official residence, Pamphilus had got together the largest Christian library yet collected. Not far off, at Jerusalem, was another valuable library, collected a century earlier by the bp. Alexander, and especially rich in the correspondence of men of letters and rulers in the church, "from which library," writes Eusebius, "we too have been able to collect together the materials for this undertaking which we have in hand" (*H. E.* vi. 20). Moreover, he had been trained in a highly efficient school of literary industry under Pamphilus, while his passion for learning has rarely been equalled, perhaps never surpassed.

The execution of his work, however, falls far short of the conception. The faults indeed are so patent as to have unjustly obscured the merits, for it is withal a noble monument of literary labour. We must remember his plea for indulgence, as one setting foot upon new ground, "nullius ante trita solo"; and as he had no predecessor, so he had no successor. Rufinus, Socrates, Sozomen, Theodoret, all commenced where he ended. The most bitter of his theological adversaries were forced to confess their obligations to him, and to speak of his work with respect. If we reflect what a blank would be left in our knowledge of this important chapter in history if the narrative of Eusebius were blotted out, we shall appreciate our enormous debt of gratitude to him.

Two points require consideration: (1) the range and adequacy of his materials, and (2) the use made of them.

(1) The range of materials is astonishing when we consider that Eusebius was a pioneer. Some hundred works, several of them very lengthy, are either directly cited or referred to as read. In many instances he would read an entire treatise for the sake of one or two historical notices, and must have searched many others without finding anything to serve his purpose, thus involving enormous labour. This then is his strongest point. Yet even here deficiencies may be noted. He very rarely quotes the works of heresiarchs themselves, being content to give their opinions through the medium of their opponents' refutations. A still greater defect is his considerable ignorance of Latin literature and of Latin Christendom generally. Thus he knows nothing of Tertullian's works, except the *Apologeticum*, which he quotes (ii. 2, 25, iii. 20, 33, v. 5) from a bad Greek translation (*e.g.* ii. 25, where the translator, being ignorant of the Latin idiom *cum maxime*, destroys the sense). Of Tertullian himself he gives no account, but calls him a "Roman." Pliny's letter he only knows through Tertullian (iii. 33) and he is unacquainted with the name of the province which Pliny governed. Of Hippolytus again he has very little information to communicate, and cannot even tell the name of his see (vi. 20, 22). His account of Cyprian, too, is extremely meagre (vi. 43, vii. 3), though Cyprian was for some years the most conspicuous figure in Western Christendom, and died (A.D. 258) not very long before his own birth. He betrays the same ignorance with regard to the bps. of Rome. His dates here, strangely enough, are widest of the mark when close upon his own time. Thus he assigns to Xystus II. († A.D. 258) eleven years (vii. 27) instead of months; to Eutychianus († A.D. 283) ten months (vii. 32) instead of nearly nine years; to Gaius, whom he calls his own contemporary, and who died long after he had arrived at manhood (A.D. 296), "about fifteen years" (vii. 32) instead of twelve. He seems to have had a corrupt list and did not possess the knowledge necessary to correct it. With the Latin language he appears to have had no thorough acquaintance, though he sometimes ventured to translate Latin documents (iv. 8, 9; cf. viii. 17). But he must not be held responsible for the blunders in the versions of others, *e.g.* of Tertullian's *Apologeticum*. The translations of state documents in the later books may be the semi-official Greek versions such as Constantine was in the habit of employing persons to make (*V. C.* iv. 32). See on this subject Heinichen's note on *H. E.* iv. 8.

(2) Under the second head the most vital question is the *sincerity* of Eusebius. Did he tamper with his materials or not? The sarcasm of Gibbon (*Decline and Fall*, c. xvi.) is well known: "The gravest of the ecclesiastical historians, Eusebius himself, indirectly confesses that he has related whatever might redound to the glory, and that he has suppressed all that could tend to the disgrace, of religion." The passages to which he refers (*H. E.* viii. 2; *Mart. Pal.* 12) do not bear out this imputation. There is no indirectness about them, but on the contrary they deplore, in the most emphatic terms, the evils which disgraced the church, and they represent the persecution under Diocletian as a just retribution for these wrongdoings. The ambitions, intriguing for office, factious quarrels, cowardly denials and shipwrecks of the faith —"evil piled upon evil" (κακὰ κακοῖς ἐπιτειχίζοντες)—are denounced in no measured language. Eusebius contents himself with condemning these sins and shortcomings in general terms, without entering into details; declaring his intention of confining himself to topics profitable (πρὸς ὠφελείας) to his own and future generations. This treatment may be regarded as too great a sacrifice to edification; but it leaves no imputation on his honesty. Nor again can the *special*

charges against his honour as a narrator be sustained. There is no ground whatever for the surmise that Eusebius forged or interpolated the passage from Josephus relating to our Lord, quoted in *H. E.* i. 11, though Heinichen (iii. pp. 623 seq., Melet. ii.) is disposed to entertain the charge. The passage is contained in all our extant MSS., and there is sufficient evidence that other interpolations (though not this) were introduced into the text of Josephus long before this time (see Orig. *c. Cels.* i. 47, Delarue's note). Another interpolation in Josephus which Eusebius quotes (ii. 23) was certainly known to Origen (*l.c.*). Doubtless also the omission of the owl in the account of Herod Agrippa's death (*H. E.* ii. 10) was already in some texts of Josephus (*Ant.* xix. 8, 2). The manner in which Eusebius deals with his very numerous quotations elsewhere, where we can test his honesty, sufficiently vindicates him from this unjust charge.

Moreover, Eusebius is generally careful to collect the best evidence accessible, and also to distinguish between different kinds of evidence. "Almost every page witnesses to the zeal with which he collected testimonies from writers who lived at the time of the events which he describes. For the sixth and seventh books he evidently rejoices to be able to use for the foundation of his narrative the contemporary letters of Dionysius; 'Dionysius, our great bp. of Alexandria,' he writes, 'will again help me by his own words in the composition of my seventh book of the history, since he relates in order the events of his own time in the letters which he has left' (vii. praef.). . . . In accordance with this instinctive desire for original testimony, Eusebius scrupulously distinguishes facts which rest on documentary from those which rest on oral evidence. Some things he relates on the authority of a 'general' (iii. 11, 36) or 'old report' (iii. 19, 20) or from tradition (i. 7, ii. 9, vi. 2, etc.). In the lists of successions he is careful to notice where written records failed him. 'I could not,' he says, 'by any means find the chronology of the bps. of Jerusalem preserved in writing; thus much only I received from written sources, that there were fifteen bishops in succession up to the date of the siege under Hadrian, etc.' (iv. 5)." [w.] "There is nothing like hearing the actual words" of the writer, he says again and again (i. 23, iii. 32, vii. 23; cf. iv. 23), when introducing a quotation. His general sincerity and good faith seem, therefore, clear. But his intellectual qualifications were in many respects defective. His credulity, indeed, has frequently been much exaggerated. "Undoubtedly he relates many incidents which may seem to us incredible, but, when he does so, he gives the evidence on which they are recommended to him. At one time it is the express testimony of some well-known writer, at another a general belief, at another an old tradition, at another his own observation (v. 7, vi. 9, vii. 17, 18)." [w.] In the most remarkable passage bearing on the question he recounts his own experience during the last persecution in Palestine (*Mart. Pal.* 9). "There can be no doubt about the occurrence which Eusebius here describes, and it does not appear that he can be reproached for adding the interpretation which his countrymen placed upon it. What he vouches for we can accept as truth; what he records as a popular comment leaves his historical veracity and judgment unimpaired." [w.] Even Gibbon (c. xvi.) describes the character of Eusebius as "less tinctured with credulity, and more practised in the arts of courts, than that of almost any of his contemporaries." A far more serious drawback is the loose and uncritical spirit in which he sometimes deals with his materials. This shews itself in diverse ways. (*a*) He is not always to be trusted in his discrimination of genuine and spurious documents. As regards the canon of Scripture indeed he takes special pains; lays down certain principles which shall guide him in the production of testimonies; and on the whole adheres to these principles with fidelity (see *Contemp. Rev.* Jan. 1875, pp. 169 seq.). Yet elsewhere he adduces as genuine the correspondence of Christ and Abgarus (i. 13), though never treating it as canonical Scripture. The unworthy suspicion that Eusebius forged this correspondence which he asserted to be a translation of a Syriac original found in the archives of Edessa has been refuted by the discovery and publication of the original Syriac (*The Doctrine of Addai the Apostle with an English Translation and Notes* by G. Phillips, Lond. 1876; see Zahn, *Götting. Gel. Anz.* Feb. 6, 1877, pp. 161 seq.; *Contemp. Rev.* May 1877, p. 1137; a portion of this work had been published some time before in Cureton's *Ancient Syriac Documents*, pp. 6 seq., Lond. 1864). Not his honesty, but his critical discernment was at fault. Yet we cannot be severe upon him for maintaining a position which, however untenable, has commended itself to Cave (*H. L.* i. p. 2), Grabe (*Spic. Patr.* i. pp. 1 seq.), and other writers of this stamp, as defensible. This, moreover, is the most flagrant instance of misappreciation. On the whole, considering the great mass of spurious documents current in his age, we may well admire his discrimination, as *e.g.* in the case of the numerous Clementine writings (iii. 16, 38), alleging the presence or absence of external testimony for his decisions. Pearson's eulogy (*Vind. Ign.* i. 8) on Eusebius, though exaggerated, is not undeserved. He is *generally* a safe guide in discriminating between the genuine and the spurious. (*b*) He is often careless in his manner of quoting. His quotations from Irenaeus, for instance, lose much of their significance, even for his own purpose, by abstraction from their context (v. 8). His quotations from Papias (iii. 39) and from Hegesippus (iii. 32, iv. 22) are tantalizing by their brevity, for the exact bearing of the words could only have been learnt from their context. But, except in the passages from Josephus (where the blame, as we have seen, belongs elsewhere), the quotations themselves are given with fair accuracy. (*c*) He draws hasty and unwarranted inferences from his authorities, and is loose in interpreting their bearing. This is his weakest point as a critical historian. Thus he quotes Josephus respecting the census of Quirinus and the insurrections of Theudas and of Judas the Galilean, as if he agreed in all respects with the accounts in St. Luke, and does not notice the chronological difficulties (i. 5, 9; ii. 11). He adduces the Jewish historian as a witness to the assignment of a tetrarchy to Lysanias (i. 9), though in fact Josephus says nothing about this Lysanias in the passage in question, but elsewhere mentions an earlier person bearing the name as ruler of Abilene (*Ant.* xx. 7. 1; *B. J.* ii. 11. 5). He represents this same writer as stating that Herod Antipas was banished to Vienne (i. 11), whereas Josephus sends Archelaus to Vienne (*B. J.* ii. 7. 3) and Herod Antipas to Lyons (*Ant.* xviii. 7. 2) or Spain (*B. J.* ii. 9. 6). He quotes Philo's description of the Jewish Therapeutae, as if it related to Christian ascetics (ii. 17). He gives, side by side, the contradictory accounts of the death of James the Just in Josephus and Hegesippus, as if they tallied (ii. 23). He hopelessly confuses the brothers M. Aurelius and L. Verus (v. prooem., 4, 5) from a misunderstanding of his documents, though in the *Chronicle* (ii. p. 170) he is substantially correct with regard to these emperors. Many other examples of such carelessness might be produced. (*d*) He is very *desultory* in his treatment, placing in different parts of his work notices bearing on the same subject. He relates a fact, or quotes an authority bearing upon it, in season or out of season, according as it is recalled to his memory by some accidental connexion. "Nothing can illustrate this characteristic better than the manner in which he deals with the canon of the N.T. After mentioning the martyrdom of St. Peter and St. Paul at Rome, he proceeds at once (iii. 3) without any further preface to enumerate the writings attributed to them respectively, distinguishing those which were generally received by ancient tradition from those which were disputed. At the same time he adds a notice of the Shepherd, because it had been attributed by some to the Hermas mentioned by St. Paul. After this he resumes his narrative, and then having related the last labours of St. John, he gives an account of the writings attributed to him (iii. 24), promising a further discussion of the Apocalypse, which, however, does not appear. This catalogue is followed by some fragmentary discussions on the Gospels, to which a general classification of all the books claiming to have apostolic authority is added. When this is ended, the history suddenly goes back to a point in the middle of the former book (ii. 15). Elsewhere he repeats the notice of an incident for the sake of adding some new detail, yet so as to mar the symmetry of his work." [W.] Examples of this fault occur in the accounts of the first preaching at Edessa (i. 13, ii. 1), of the writings of Clement of Rome (iii. 16, 38; iv. 22, 23, etc.), of the daughters of Philip (iii. 30, 39; cf. v. 17, 24), etc.

(6) *Life of Constantine*, in four books.—The date of this work is fixed within narrow limits. It was written after the death of the great emperor (May 337) and after his three sons had been declared Augusti (Sept. 337)—see iv. 68; and Eusebius himself died not later than A.D. 340. Though not professing to be such, it is to some extent a continuation of the *Ecclesiastical History*. As such it is mentioned by Socrates (*H. E.* i. 1), to whom, as to other historians, it furnishes important materials for the period. For the council of Nicaea especially, and for some portions of the Arian controversy, it is a primary source of information of the highest value. As regards the emperor himself, it is notoriously one-sided. The verdict of Socrates will not be disputed. The author, he says, "has devoted more thought to the praises of the emperor and to the grandiloquence of language befitting a panegyric, as if he were pronouncing an encomium, than to the accurate narrative of the events which took place." But there is no ground for suspecting him of misrepresenting the facts given, and with the qualification stated above, his biography has the highest value. It is a vivid picture of certain aspects of a great personality, painted by one familiarly acquainted with him, who had access to important documents. It may even be set down to the credit of Eusebius that his praises of Constantine are much louder after his death than during his lifetime. In this respect he contrasts favourably with Seneca. Nor shall we do justice to Eusebius unless we bear in mind the extravagant praises which even heathen panegyrists lavished on the great Christian emperor before his face, as an indication of the spirit of the age. But after all excuses made, this indiscriminate praise of Constantine is a reproach from which we should gladly have held Eusebius free.

B. Apologetic.—(7) *Against Hierocles.*—Hierocles was governor in Bithynia, and used his power ruthlessly to embitter the persecution which he is thought to have instigated (Lactant. *Div. Inst.* v. 2; *Mort. Pers.* 16; see Mason, *Persecution of Diocletian*, pp. 58, 108). Not satisfied with assailing the Christians from the tribunal, he attacked them also with his pen. The title of his work seems to have been ὁ Φιλαλήθης, *The Lover of Truth.* It was a ruthless assault on Christianity, written in a biting style. Its main object was to expose the contradictions of the Christian records. Eusebius, however, confines himself to one point—the comparison of Apollonius, as described in his Life by Philostratus, with our Saviour, to the disparagement of the latter. There is much difference of opinion whether Philostratus himself intended to set up Apollonius as a rival to the Christ of the Gospels [Apollonius of Tyana], but Hierocles at all events turned his romance to this use.

Eusebius refutes his opponent with great moderation, and generally with good effect. He allows that Apollonius was a wise and virtuous man, but refuses to concede the higher claims advanced on his behalf. He shews that the work of Philostratus was not based on satisfactory evidence; that the narrative is full of absurdities and contradictions; and that the moral character of Apollonius as therein portrayed is far from perfect. He maintains that the supernatural incidents, if they actually occurred, might have been the work of demons. In conclusion (§§ 46-48) he refutes and denounces the fatalism of Apollonius, as alone sufficient to discredit his wisdom.

(8) *Against Porphyry*, an elaborate work in 25 books: Hieron. *Ep.* 70 ad Magn. § 3 (i. p. 427, Vallarsi); *Vir. Ill.* 81.—No part of this elaborate refutation has survived. Yet

we may form some notion of its contents from the *Praeparatio* and *Demonstratio Evangelica*, in considerable portions of which Eusebius obviously has Porphyry in view, even where he does not name him. To Jerome and Socrates the refutation seemed satisfactory. Philostorgius (*H. E.* viii. 14) preferred the similar work of Apollinaris to it, as also to the earlier refutation of Methodius, but himself added another reply to Porphyry (*H.* E. x. 10). All the four refutations have alike perished, with the work which gave rise to them.

(9) *Praeparatio Evangelica.*—So Eusebius himself calls a treatise, which more strictly ought to have been called *Praeparatio Demonstrationis Evangelicae*, for it is an introductory treatise leading up to—

(10) The *Demonstratio Evangelica.*—These two treatises, in fact, are parts of one great work. They are both dedicated to Theodotus, an adherent of the Arian party, who was bp. of Laodicea for some thirty years.

In the absence of more direct testimony, we may infer that these works were begun during the persecution, but not concluded till some time after. The *Preparation* is extant entire, and comprises 15 books. The *Demonstration*, on the other hand, is incomplete. It consisted of 20 books, of which only the first ten are extant in the MSS. The *Preparation* sketches briefly what the Gospel is, and then adverts to the common taunt that the Christians accept their religion by faith without investigation. The whole work is an answer to this taunt. The object of the *Preparation* is to justify the Christians in transferring their allegiance from the religion and philosophy of the Greeks to the sacred books of the Hebrews. The object of the *Demonstration* is to shew from those sacred books themselves that Christians did right in not stopping short at the religious practices and beliefs of the Jews, but in adopting a different mode of life. Thus the *Preparation* is an apology for Christianity as against the Gentiles, while the *Demonstration* defends it as against the Jews, and " yet not," he adds, " *against* the Jews, nay, far from it, but rather *for* the Jews, if they would learn wisdom."

In the first three books of the *Preparation* he attacks the mythology of the heathen, exposing its absurdity, and refutes the physiological interpretations put upon the myths ; in the next three he discusses the oracles, and as connected therewith the sacrifices to demons and the doctrine of fate ; in the third three explains the bearing of " the Hebrew Oracles," and adduces the testimony of heathen writers in their favour ; in bks. x. xi. xii. and xiii. he remarks on the plagiarisms of the Greek philosophers from the Hebrews, dwelling on the priority of the Hebrew Scriptures, and shews how all that is best in Greek teaching and speculation agrees with them ; in bk. xiv. he points to the contradictions among Greek philosophers, shewing how the systems opposed to Christian belief have been condemned by the wisest Gentile philosophers themselves ; and lastly, in bk. xv., he exposes the falsehoods and errors of the Greek systems of philosophy, more especially of the Peripatetics, Stoics, and materialists of all schools. He claims to have thus given a complete answer to those who charge Christians with transferring their allegiance from Hellenism to Hebraism blindly and without knowledge. In the *Demonstration*, bks. i. and ii. are introductory (iii. 1. 1, τῶν προλεγομένων). In bk. i. a sketch is given of the Gospel teaching and reasons alleged why Christians, while adopting the Hebrew Oracles, should depart from the Jewish mode of life ; a distinction being drawn between Hebraism, the religion of all godly men from the beginning, and Judaism, the temporary and special system of the Jews, so that Christianity is a continuation of the former, but a departure from the latter. In bk. ii. testimonies from the prophets shew that the two great phenomena of the Christian Church had been long foretold—the general ingathering of the Gentiles and the general falling away of the Jews—so that the Christians " were only laying claim to their own " (iii. 1. 1). Bk. iii. begins the main subject of the treatise. He promises to speak of the *humanity* of Christ, as corresponding to the predictions of the prophets ; but the topics are introduced in a desultory way (*e.g.* that Christ was not a sorcerer, that the Apostles were not deceivers, etc.) without any very obvious connexion with the main theme. Bks. iv. and v. pass on to the *divinity* of Christ, both as the Son and as the Logos (see v. prooem. 1. 2), this likewise having been announced by the prophets. From bk. vi. onward to the end he treats of the *Incarnation* and *life* (ἐπιδημία) of our Lord as a fulfilment of prophecy, and of the manner of Christ's appearing, the place of His birth, His parentage and genealogy, the time of His advent and His works as in like manner foretold. In bk. x., the last which is extant, he reaches the Passion, treating of the traitor Judas and the incidents of the Crucifixion. What were the topics of the remaining ten books we have no data for determining, but may conjecture with Stein (p. 102) that they dealt with the burial, resurrection, and ascension, and perhaps also with the foundation of the Christian church and the Second Advent. The extant fragment of bk. xv. relates to the four kingdoms of Daniel ii. Jerome (*Comm. in Hos.* Praef. *Op.* vi. p. 18) speaks of Eusebius as " discussing some matters respecting the prophet Hosea " in bk. xviii. This great apologetic work exhibits the merits and defects which we find elsewhere in Eusebius ; the same greatness of conception marred by inadequacy of execution, the same profusion of learning combined with inability to control his materials, which we have seen in his *History*. The topics are not kept distinct ; yet this is probably the most important apologetic work of the early church. Its frequent, forcible, and true conceptions, more especially on the theme of " God in history," arrest our attention now, and must have impressed his contemporaries still more strongly ; while in learning and comprehensiveness it is without a rival. It exhibits the same wide acquaintance with Greek profane writers which the *History* exhibits with Christian literature. The number of writers quoted or referred to is astonishing (see Fabric. *Bibl. Graec.* vii. p. 346), the names of some being only known to us through Eusebius, while of several others he has preserved large portions not otherwise extant. He quotes not less than 21 works of Plato, and gives more than 50 quotations from the *Laws* alone. The impression produced by this mass of learning led Scaliger to call the work "divini commentarii," and Cave "opus profecto nobilissimum" (*H. L.* i. p. 178). An admirable ed. of the *Preparatio* was pub. in 1903 at the Oxford Press under the learned and accurate editorship of the late Dr. Gifford, with trans. and notes.

(11) The *Praeparatio Ecclesiastica* (Ἐκκλησιαστικὴ Προπαρασκευή) is not extant, nor is (12) the *Demonstratio Ecclesiastica* (Ἐκκλησιαστικὴ Ἀπόδειξις), but both are mentioned by Photius (*Bibl.* 11, 12.) The names suggest that these two works aimed at doing for the society what the *Praeparatio* and *Demonstratio Evangelica* do for the doctrines of which the society is the depositary.

(13) *Two Books of Objection and Defence*, only known from Photius (*Bibl.* 13).

(14) *The Divine Manifestation* (Θεοφάνεια), in five books, was long supposed to be lost, but fragments of the Greek original were published by Mai from Vatican MSS. in his *Script. Vet. Nov. Coll.* i. (1831), viii. (1833), and in 1842 the work was printed entire in a Syriac version by Dr. S. Lee, who in 1843 pub. an Eng. trans. with intro. and notes (*Eusebius, bp. of Caesarea, on the Theophania*, etc., Camb. 1843). By the aid of this version Mai (A.D. 1847) in his *Bibl. Nov. Patr.* iv. p. 310 (cf. p. 110) rearranged his Greek fragments.

The subject is, as the name *Theophania* suggests, the manifestation of God in the Incarnation of the Divine Word. The contents are: (i) An account of the *subject* and the *recipients* of the revelation. The doctrine of the Word of God is insisted upon, His person and working set forth. Polytheist and pantheist are alike at fault. The Word is essentially one. His relation to creation, and especially to man, and the pre-eminence, characteristics, destiny, and fall of man are dealt with. (ii) The *necessity* of the revelation. The human race was degraded by gross idolatry with its accompanying immoralities. The philosophers could not rescue it. Plato had the clearest sense of the truth, yet even he was greatly at fault. Meanwhile the demons of polytheism had maddened mankind, as shewn by human sacrifices and the prevalence of wars. The demons, too, had shewn their powerlessness; they could not defend their temples or foresee their overthrow. (iii) The *proof* of the revelation. Its excellency and power is seen in its *effects*. For this it was necessary that the Word should be incarnate, put to death, and rise again. The change which has come over mankind in consequence is set forth. (iv) The *proof* of the revelation, from the *fulfilment of Christ's words*—His prophecies respecting the extension of His kingdom, the trials of His church, the destinies of His servants, and the fate of the Jews. (v) The common heathen *objection* that Christ was a sorcerer and a deceiver, achieving His results by magic, is answered.

The place of writing of the *Theophania* is Caesarea (iv. 6), and it was plainly written after the triumph of Constantine and the restoration of peace to the church. The persecution is over, and the persecutors have met with their punishment (iii. 20, v. 52). Polytheism is fast waning, and Christianity is spreading everywhere (ii. 76, iii. 79).

(15) *On the Numerous Progeny of the Ancients.*—This lost treatise is mentioned in *Praep. Ev.* vii. 8. 29. It is doubtless the same work to which St. Basil refers (*de Spir. Sanct.* 29, *Op.* iii. p. 61) as *Difficulties respecting the Polygamy of the Ancients*. It would seem to have been an apologetic work, as it seems to have aimed at accounting for the polygamy of the patriarchs and the Jews generally, and reconciling it with the ascetic life, which in his own time was regarded as the true ideal of Christian teaching. This problem occurs again and again in his extant apologetic writings. In the reference in the *Praeparatio* Eusebius speaks of having discussed in this work the notices of the lives of the patriarchs and "their philosophic endurance and self-discipline," whether by way of direct narrative or of allegorical suggestion.

C. Critical and Exegetical—*i.e.* all works directed primarily to the criticism and elucidation of the Scriptures.

(16) *Biblical Texts.*—In his earlier years Eusebius was occupied in conjunction with Pamphilus in the production of correct Greek texts of the O.T. A notice of his later years shews him engaged in a similar work (*V. C.* iv. 36, 37). The emperor writes to Eusebius, asking him to provide 50 copies of the Scriptures for use in the churches of Constantinople, where the Christian population had largely multiplied. The manuscripts must be easily legible and handy for use, written on carefully prepared parchment, and transcribed by skilful caligraphers. He has already written, he adds, to the procurator-general (καθολικός) of the district (τῆς διοικήσεως), charging him to furnish Eusebius with the necessary appliances and has placed at his disposal two public waggons to convey the manuscripts, when complete, to the new metropolis. Eusebius executes the commission. The manuscripts were arranged, he tells us, in ternions and quaternions (τρισσὰ καὶ τετρασσά) and carefully prepared at great cost. The emperor wrote expressing his satisfaction with them.

(17) *Sections and Canons, with the Letter to Carpianus prefixed.*—Eusebius explains the origin and method of these sections and canons in the prefatory letter. Ammonius of Alexandria (*c.* 220) had constructed a Harmony or Diatessaron of the Gospels. He took St. Matthew as his standard, and placed side by side with it the parallel passages from the other three. The work of Ammonius suggested to Eusebius the plan which he adopted, but Eusebius desired to preserve the continuity of all the narratives. He therefore divided each gospel separately into *sections*, which he numbered continuously, and constructed a table of ten *canons*, containing lists of passages: canon i, common to all the four evangelists; canon ii, common to Matthew, Mark, Luke; canon iii, common to Matthew, Luke, John; canon iv, common to Matthew, Mark, John; canon v, common to Matthew and Luke; canon vi, common to Matthew and Mark; canon vii, common to

Matthew and John; canon viii, common to Luke and Mark; canon ix, common to Luke and John; canon x, passages peculiar to a single evangelist, so that this last canon contains four separate lists. The sections of the several gospels were numbered in black, and beneath each such number was a second number in vermilion, specifying the canon to which the section belonged. By turning to the canon so specified, the reader would see the numbers of the parallel sections in the other evangelists. For the history of the sections and canons in the MSS. see Scrivener's *Introd. to the Criticism of the N.T.*, pp. 54 seq. and *passim.* The sections and canons are marked in many editions of the Gk. Test., *e.g.* those of Tischendorf and Tregelles.

(18) Under the head of Biblical exegesis may be ranged several togographical works undertaken at the instance of Paulinus, bp. of Tyre.—(*a*) *Interpretation of the Ethnological Terms in the Hebrew Scriptures;* (*b*) *Chorography of Ancient Judaea, with the Inheritances of the Ten Tribes;* (*c*) *A Plan of Jerusalem and of the Temple.* This was accompanied with memoirs relating to the different localities. (*d*) *On the Names of Places in Holy Scripture*, entitled in the head of Jerome's version *de Situ et Nominibus Locorum Hebraicorum*, but elsewhere (*Vir. Ill.* 81) *Topica.* The first three, which perhaps should be regarded as parts of the same work, are mentioned in the preface to the fourth, which alone is extant. All were written at the instance of Paulinus, to whom (*d*) is dedicated. This last professes to give alphabetically "the designations of the cities and villages mentioned in Holy Scripture in their original language," with a description of the locality and the modern names. The names are transliterated with various success from the Hebrew. The value of this treatise arises from the close acquaintance which Eusebius had with the geography of Palestine in his own day. The work had already been translated into Latin by some unskilful hand before Jerome's time, but so unsatisfactorily that he undertook a new version. He omitted some important notices and made several changes, justified by his personal knowledge of Palestine.

(19) *On the Nomenclature of the Book of the Prophets.*—This work contains a brief account of the several prophets and the subjects of their prophecies, beginning with the minor prophets and following the order of the LXX.

(20) *In Psalmos*, a continuous commentary on the Psalms, which stands in antiquity and intrinsic merit in the first rank of patristic commentaries. The historical bearing of the several psalms is generally treated sensibly; the theological and mystical interpretations betray the extravagance common to patristic exegesis. The value of the work is largely increased by frequent extracts from the Hexaplaric versions and by notices respecting the text and history of the Psalter. The author possessed some acquaintance with Hebrew, though not always sufficient to prevent mistakes. This commentary had a great reputation, and was translated into Latin within a very few years of its publication by Eusebius of Vercellae.

(21) *Commentary on Isaiah.*—This work exhibits the same characteristics as the *Commentary on the Psalms.* Jerome is largely indebted to Eusebius, whom he sometimes translates almost word for word without acknowledgment. Eusebius occasionally inserts interesting traditions on the authority of a Hebrew teacher: *e.g.* that Shebna became high-priest and betrayed the people to Sennacherib; that Hezekiah was seized with sickness for not singing God's praises, like Moses and Deborah, after his victory. Sometimes he gives Christian traditions: *e.g.* that Judas Iscariot was of the tribe of Ephraim. This commentary is mentioned by Procopius in his preface, and is freely used by him and by later Greek commentators.

(22) *Commentary on St. Luke's Gospel.*—Not mentioned by Jerome or Photius. Some extracts remain.

(23) *Commentary on I. Corinthians.*—Such a work seems to be implied by Jerome's language, *Ep.* xlix., though he does not mention it in his *Catalogue.*

(24) *Commentaries on other Books of Scripture.*—Extracts are given from, or mention is made of, commentaries on *Proverbs*, *Song of Songs*, *Daniel*, *Hebrews*, and several other books (see Fabric. *op. cit.* p. 399). It is doubtful, however, whether such extracts (even when genuine) are from continuous commentaries or from exegetical or dogmatical works.

(25) *On the Discrepancies of the Gospels.*—This work consists of two parts, really separate works, and quoted as such: (i) *Questions and Solutions on the Genealogy of the Saviour, addressed to Stephanus;* (ii) *Questions and Solutions concerning the Passion and Resurrection of the Saviour, addressed to Marinus.* The difficulties do not always turn upon *discrepancies*—*e.g.* he discusses the question why Thamar is mentioned, and difficulties with respect to Bathsheba and Ruth. But the discrepancies occupy a sufficiently large space to give the name to the whole. The work exhibits the characteristic hesitation of Eusebius in a somewhat aggravated form. Alternative solutions are frequently offered, and he does not decide between them. But it is suggestive and full of interest. It is valuable also as preserving large fragments of Africanus, besides some important notices, such as the absence of Mark xvi. 9-16 from the most numerous and best MSS. From this storehouse of information later harmonists plundered freely, often without acknowledgment.

D. Doctrinal.—(26) *General Elementary Introduction.*—Five fragments of this work have been published by Mai. All deal with analogous topics, having reference to general principles of ethics, etc. It seems to have been a general introduction to theology, and its contents were very miscellaneous, as the extant remains shew.

(27) *Prophetical Extracts.*—This work contains prophetical passages from O.T. relating to our Lord's person and work, with explanatory comments, and comprises four books, of which the first is devoted to the historical books, the second to the Psalms, the third to the remaining poetical books and the other prophets, the fourth to Isaiah. The author explains that his main object is to shew that the prophets spoke of Jesus Christ as the pre-

existent Word, Who is "a second cause of the universe and God and Lord," and that they predicted His two advents. Thus the personality of the Logos is here the leading idea in his treatment of the prophecies.

(28) *Defence of Origen.*—This was the joint work of Pamphilus and Eusebius. The original has perished, but the first book survives in the translation of Rufinus (printed in Origen, *Op.* iv. App. pp. 17 seq. Delarue). Eusebius (*H. E.* vi. 3) says that the work was undertaken to refute "captious detractors"; probably referring especially to Methodius, who had written two works against Origen (Hieron. *Vir. Ill.* 93; Socr. *H. E.* vi. 13) and was attacked by name in the sixth book (Hieron. *c. Rufin.* i. 11). It was dedicated to the confessors of Palestine, especially Patermuthius (Phot. *Bibl.* 118), who was martyred the year after Pamphilus (Eus. *Mart. Pal.* 13). The first book contains an exposition of Origen's principles, especially of his doctrines respecting the Trinity and the Incarnation; then nine special charges against him are refuted, relating to the nature of Christ, the resurrection of the dead, metempsychosis, etc. In one of the later books the doctrine of fatalism was discussed (Rufin. *Apol.* i. 11, in Hieron. *Op.* ii. p. 582). Elsewhere also it was shewn that Origen in his mystical explanation of Adam and Eve, as referring to Christ and the church, only followed the traditional interpretation (Socr. *H. E.* iii. 7). In the same spirit precedents were quoted for his doctrines of the pre-existence of the soul and the restitution of all things (Anon. *Synod. Ep.* 198). The *Apology* also contained a full account of the life of Origen (Phot. *Bibl.* 118). Eusebius himself refers to bk. ii. for accounts of the controversy about Origen's ordination to the priesthood and his contributions to sacred letters (*H. E.* vi. 23), and to bk. vi. for the letters which Origen wrote to Fabianus and others in defence of his orthodoxy (*ib.* 36), and to the work generally for the part taken by Origen in theological controversy (*ib.* 33). Socrates (*H. E.* iv. 27) states that the panegyric of Gregory Thaumaturgus on Origen was given in this *Apology*.

(29) *Against Marcellus, bp. of Ancyra*, in two books.—The occasion of writing is explained by Eusebius himself (*c. Marc.* ii. 4, pp. 55 seq.). Marcellus had been condemned for Sabellianism, and deposed by a synod of Constantinople (A.D. 336), composed chiefly of the Arian friends of Eusebius. This work was undertaken at the wish of these friends to justify the decision. Certain persons considered that Marcellus had been unfairly treated, and Eusebius, being partly responsible for the decision, felt bound to uphold its justice. The work aims simply at *exposing* the views of Marcellus. [MARCELLUS (4).]

(30) *On the Theology of the Church, a Refutation of Marcellus*, in three books.—Eusebius had at first thought it sufficient merely to expose the opinions of Marcellus, leaving them to condemn themselves. But on reflection, fearing lest some might be drawn away "from the theology of the church" by their very length and pretentiousness, he undertook to refute them, and to shew that no single Scripture favours the view of Marcellus, but that, according to the approved interpretations, all Scripture is against him. Having done this, he will expound the true theology respecting our Saviour, as it has been handed down in the church from the beginning. Thus, as explained by its author, the aim of this second treatise is *refutation*, as that of the first was *exposure*. The first was mainly *personal*, the second is chiefly *dogmatical*.

The two treatises were first edited by bp. R. Montague (Montacutius) with trans. and notes (Paris, 1628) at the end of the *Demonstratio*, and this ed. was reprinted (Lips. 1688). The best ed. is that of Gaisford (Oxf. 1852), where they are in the same vol. with the work *Against Hierocles*. He revised the text and reprinted the trans. and notes of Montague. The fragments of Marcellus are collected by Rettberg (*Marcelliana*, Götting. 1794). The monographs on Marcellus, especially Zahn's *M. von Ancyra* (Gotha, 1867), are useful aids.

(31) *On the Paschal Festival.*—Eusebius (*Vit. Const.* iv. 35, 36) states that he addressed to Constantine "a mystical explanation of the significance of the festival," upon which the emperor wrote (*c.* 335), expressing himself greatly delighted, and saying that it was a difficult undertaking "to expound in a becoming way the reason and origin of the Paschal festival, as well as its profitable and painful consummation." A long fragment of this treatise was discovered and published by Mai. The recovered fragment contains: (1) A declaration of the figurative character of the Jewish Passover. (2) An account of its institution and of the ceremonial itself. (3) An explanation of the typical significance of the different parts of the ceremonial, with reference to their Christian counterparts. (4) A brief statement of the settlement of the question at Nicaea. (5) An argument that Christians are not bound to observe the time of the Jewish festival, mainly because it was not the Jewish Passover which our Lord Himself kept.

E. ORATIONS AND SERMONS.—(32) *At the Dedication of the Church in Tyre.*—This oration is inserted by Eusebius in his *History* (x. 4.) The new basilica at Tyre was a splendid building, and Eusebius addresses Paulinus, the bishop, as a Bezaleel, a Solomon, a Zerubbabel, a new Aaron or Melchizedek. He applies to the occasion the predictions of the Jewish prophets foretelling the rebuilding of the temple and the restoration of the polity. He gives thanks for the triumph of Christ, the Word of God, Who has proved mightier than the mightiest of kings. This magnificent temple, which has arisen from the ruins of its predecessor, is a token of His power. Then follows an elaborate description of the building, which, continues the orator, is a symbol of the spiritual church of Tyre, of the spiritual church throughout the world, in its history, its overthrow, its desolation, its re-erection on a more splendid scale, and in the arrangement of its several parts. But the spiritual church on earth is itself only a faint image of the heavenly Zion, where adoring hosts unceasingly sing the praises of their King.

(33) *At the Vicennalia of Constantine*, A.D. 325.—This oration, which is not extant, is mentioned *Vit. Const.* prooem. iii. 11. It seems to have been the opening address at the council of Nicaea, see *supra*.

(34) *On the Sepulchre of the Saviour*, A.D. 335.—This is mentioned *Vit. Const.* iv. 33, 46 seq. The circumstances of its delivery have been already described. It has been lost.

(35) *At the Tricennalia of Constantine*, A.D. 335 or 336.—This oration is commonly called *de Laudibus Constantini*. The orator, taking occasion from the festival, speaks of the Almighty Sovereign, and the Divine Word through Whom He administers the universe (§ 1). The emperor is a sort of reflection of the Supreme Word. The monarchy on earth is the counterpart of that in heaven (§§ 2, 3). The Word is the interpreter of the Invisible God in all things (§ 4). An emperor who, like Constantine, is sensible of his dependence on God, is alone fit to rule (§ 5). Periods and divisions of time are from God, as is all order throughout the universe. The number thirty (3 × 10) has a special symbolic significance, reminding us of the kingdom of glory (§ 6). The powers of wickedness and the sufferings of the saints were ended by Constantine, the champion and representative of God (§ 7). He waged war against idolatry, profligacy, and superstition (§ 8). What a change has been suddenly wrought! The false gods did not foresee their fate. The emperor, armed with piety, overthrew them. Churches rise from the ground everywhere (§ 8). The truth is proclaimed far and wide (§ 9). "Come now, most mighty victor Constantine," says the orator, "let me lay before thee the mysteries of sacred doctrines in this royal discourse concerning the Supreme King of the Universe." Accordingly he speaks of the person and working of the Divine Word, as mediator in the creation and government of the universe. Polytheism is condemned. As God is one, so His Word is one (§§ 11, 12). Humanity, led astray by demons and steeped in ignorance and sin, needed the advent of the Word (§ 13). It was necessary too that He should come clothed in a body (§ 14). His death and resurrection also were indispensable for the redemption of men (§ 15). The power of the Divine Word was evinced by the establishment of the church and the spread of the gospel (§ 16). It was manifested in our own time by the faith of the martyrs, by the triumph of the church over oppression, and by the punishment of the persecutors (§ 17). We have evidence of the divine origin of our faith in the prophetic announcements of Christ's coming, and in the fulfilment of His own predictions; more especially in the coincidence in time between the establishment of the Roman empire and the publication of the Gospel (§ 18).

(36) *In Praise of the Martyrs.*—This discourse is short and of little value; but the orator mentions, among those whom he invites his hearers to commemorate, almost every bishop of Antioch from the end of the 2nd cent. to his own time, so that it would seem to have been delivered at Antioch.

(37) *On the Failure of Rain*, mentioned by Ebedjesu, but apparently not elsewhere.

F. Letters.—(38) *To Alexander*, bp. of Alexandria, on behalf of Arius and his friends, complaining that they have been misrepresented.

(39) *To Euphration* (sometimes written incorrectly *Euphrasion*), bp. of Balanea in Syria, a strong opponent of the Arians (Athan. *de Fug.* 3, *Op.* i. p. 254; *Hist. Ar. ad Mon.* 5, *ib.* p. 274), who was present at the council of Nicaea. Athanasius refers to this letter as declaring plainly that Christ is not true God (*de Synod.* 17, *Op.* i. p. 584). An extract (containing the passage to which doubtless Athanasius refers) is quoted at the second council of Nicaea (*l.c.*). It insists strongly on the subordination of the Son.

(40) *To Constantia Augusta* (*Op.* ii. 1545), the sister of Constantine and wife of Licinius, who was closely allied with the Arians. Constantia had asked Eusebius to send her a certain likeness of Christ, of which she had heard. He rebukes her for the request, saying that such representations are inadequate in themselves and tend to idolatry. He states that a foolish woman had brought him two likenesses, which might be philosophers, but were alleged by her to represent St. Paul and the Saviour. He had detained them lest they should prove a stumbling-block to her or to others. He reminds Constantia that St. Paul declares his intention of "knowing Christ no longer after the flesh." This letter was quoted by the Iconoclasts, and this led their opponents to rake up all the questionable expressions in his writings, that they might blacken his character for orthodoxy.

(41) *To the Church of Caesarea*, written from Nicaea (A.D. 325) during or immediately after the council to vindicate his conduct. This letter is preserved by Athanasius as an appendix to the *de Decret. Syn. Nic.* (*Op.* i. p. 187; cf. § 3, *ib.* p. 166); in Socr. *H. E.* i. 8; in Theod. *H. E.* i. 11; in Gelasius Cyz. *Hist. Conc. Nic.* ii. 34 seq. (Labbe, *Conc.* ii. 264 seq. ed. Colet.); in the *Historia Tripartita*, ii. 11; and in Niceph. *H. E.* viii. 22. A passage towards the end (§§ 9, 10) which savours strongly of Arianism is wanting in Socrates and in the *Historia Tripartita*, but appears in the other authorities, and seems certainly to be referred to by Athanasius in two places (*de Decr. Syn. Nic.* 3, *l.c.*; *de Synod.* 13, *Op.* i. p. 581). It is condemned, however, by Bull (*Def. Fid. Nic.* iii. 9. 3) and Cave (*Diss. Tert. in Joh. Cleric.* p. 58, printed at the end of his *Hist. Lit.* vol. ii.) as a spurious addition, probably inserted by some Arian. The letter is translated and annotated by Newman in *Select Treatises of St. Athanasius*, pp. 59 seq. (Oxf. 1853).

In reviewing the literary history of Eusebius, we are struck first of all with the range and extent of his labours. His extant works, voluminous as they are, must have formed somewhat less than half his actual writings. No field of theological learning is untouched. He is historian, apologist, topographer, exegete, critic, preacher, dogmatic writer, in turn, and, if permanent utility may be taken as a test of literary excellence, Eusebius will hold a very high place indeed. The *Ecclesiastical History* is absolutely unique and indispensable. The *Chronicle* is a vast storehouse of information as to ancient monarchies. The *Preparation* and *Demonstration* are the most important contributions to theology in their own province. Even minor works, such as the *Martyrs of Palestine*, the *Life of Constan-*

tine, the *Questions addressed to Stephanus and to Marinus*, and others, would leave an irreparable blank if they were obliterated. His more technical treatises have the same permanent value. The *Canons and Sections* have not been superseded for their particular purpose. The *Topography of Palestine* is the most important contribution to our knowledge in its own department. In short, no ancient ecclesiastical writer has laid posterity under heavier obligations than has Eusebius by his great erudition. In the *History*, *Chronicle*, and *Preparation*, he has preserved a vast amount of early literature in three several spheres, which would otherwise have been irrecoverably lost. Moreover, he deserves the highest credit for his keen insight as to what would have permanent interest. He, and he only, has preserved the past in all its phases, in history, in doctrine, in criticism, even in topography, for the instruction of the future.

This is his real title to greatness. As an expositor of facts, an abstract thinker, or a master of style, it would be absurd to compare him with the great names of classical antiquity. His merits and his faults have been already indicated. His gigantic learning was his master rather than his slave. He had great conceptions, which he was unable adequately to carry out. He had valuable detached thoughts, but fails in continuity of argument. He was most laborious, yet most desultory. He accumulated materials with great diligence; but was loose, perfunctory, and uncritical in their use. His style is especially vicious. When his theme seems to him to demand a lofty flight of rhetoric, as in his *Life of Constantine*, his language becomes turgid and unnatural.

He is before all things an apologist. His great services in this respect are emphasized by Evagrius (*H. E.* i. 1, πείθειν οἷός τε εἶναι τοὺς ἐντυγχάνοντας θρησκεύειν τὰ ἡμέτερα); and doubtless his directly apologetic writings were much more effective than at this distance of time we can realize. Whatever subject he touches, his thoughts seem to pour instinctively into this same channel. If he treats of chronology, a main purpose is to shew the superior antiquity of the Hebrew oracles to the wisdom of the Greeks. If he writes a history of the church, it is because he sees in the course of events a vindication of the Divine Word. Even in an encomium of a sovereign, he soars aloft at once into the region of theology, for he sees in the subject of his panegyric the instrument of a higher power for the fulfilment of a divine economy. In so essentially technical a task as the division of the Gospels into sections, his underlying desire is to vindicate the essential unity of the evangelical narratives against gainsayers. This character as an apologist was due partly to the epoch in which he lived, and partly to his individual temper and circumstances. He stood, as it were, on the frontier line between two ages, with one foot in the Hellenism of the past and the other in the Christianity of the future, and by his very position was constrained to discuss their mutual relations. He was equally learned in the wisdom of the Greeks and in the Scriptures, while his breadth of sympathy and moderation of temper fitted him beyond most of his contemporaries for tracing their conflicts and coincidences. Like St. Paul on Mars' Hill, he sought the elements of truth in pre-existing philosophical systems or popular religions; and thus obtaining a foothold, worked onward in his assault upon paganism. The Greek apologists of the 2nd and 3rd cents. all, without exception, took up this position. Eusebius, through his illustrious spiritual ancestors, Origen and Pamphilus, had inherited this tradition from Alexandria. It was the only method which could achieve success in apologetics while Christianity stood face to face with still powerful forms of heathen worship. It is the only method which can hope for victory now, when once again the Gospel is confronted with the widespread religions of India and the farther East.

If we may judge from the silence of his contemporaries—and silence in this case is an important witness—Eusebius commanded general respect by his personal character. With the single exception of the taunt of Potammon, mentioned already, not a word of accusation is levelled against him in an age when theological controversy was peculiarly reckless and acrimonious. His relations to Pamphilus shew a strongly affectionate disposition; and it is more than probable that he was drawn into those public acts from which his reputation has suffered most by the loyalty of private friendship. His moderation is especially praised by the emperor Constantine; and his speculative opinions, as well as his personal acts, bear out this commendation. His was a life which was before all things laborious and self-denying. He was not only the most learned and prolific writer of his age; but he administered the affairs of an important diocese, and took an active part in all great questions which agitated the church.

His admiration for Constantine may be excessive, but is not difficult to understand. Constantine was unquestionably one of the very greatest emperors of Rome. His commanding personality must have been irresistible; and is enhanced by his deference towards the leading Christian bishops. He carried out a change in the relations between the church and the state incomparably greater than any before or after. Eusebius delighted to place Augustus and Constantine in juxtaposition. During the one reign the Word had appeared in the flesh; during the other He had triumphed over the world. The one reign was the counterpart and complement of the other.

A discussion of the theological opinions of Eusebius is impossible within our limits. Readers are referred to Baronius (*ad ann.* 340, c. 38 seq.), Petavius (*Dogm. Theol. de Trin.* lib. i. cap. xi. seq.), Montfaucon (*Praelim. in Comm. ad Psalm.* c. vi.), and Tillemont (*H. E.* vii. pp. 67 seq.) among those who have assailed, and Bull (*Def. Fid. Nic.* ii. 9. 20, iii. 9. 3, 11), Cave (*Hist. Lit.* ii. app. pp. 42 seq.), and Lee (*Theophania*, pp. xxiv. seq.) among those who have defended his opinions, from the orthodox point of view. A convenient summary of the controversy will be found in Stein, pp. 117 seq. His orthodoxy cannot be hastily denied. Dr. Newman, who cannot be accused of unduly favouring Eusebius, says that "in his own writings, numerous as they are, there is very little which fixes on Eusebius any charge, beyond that of attachment to the Platonic phraseology. Had he not connected himself with the Arian party, it would have been unjust to have suspected him of heresy" (*Arians*, p. 262). If we except the works written before the council of Nicaea, in which there is occasionally much looseness of expression, his language is for the most part strictly orthodox, or at least capable of explanation in an orthodox sense. Against the two main theses of Arius, (1) that the Word was a creature (κτίσμα) like other creatures, and (2) that there was a time when He was not, Eusebius is explicit on the orthodox side (e.g. *c. Marc.* i. 4, p. 22, *de Eccl. Theol.* i. 2, 3, pp. 61 seq., *ib.* i. 8, 9, 10, pp. 66 seq.). He states in direct language that the Word had no beginning (*Theoph.* ii. 3, cf. *de Laud. Const.* 2). If elsewhere he represents the Father as prior to the Son (e.g. *Dem. Ev.* iv. 3. 5, ὁ δὲ πατὴρ προϋπάρχει τοῦ υἱοῦ καὶ τῆς γενέσεως αὐτοῦ προϋφέστηκεν), this priority is not necessarily intended to be temporal, and his meaning must be interpreted by his language in other passages. Nor, again, do such expressions as "second existence," "second cause," necessarily bear an Arian sense; for they may be taken to imply that subordination which has ever been recognized by the orthodox. But though his language might pass muster, "his acts," it is said, "are his confession." This is the strongest point in the indictment. His alliance with the Arian party is indisputable; but the inference drawn from it may be questioned. He may have made too great concessions to friendship. His natural temper suggested toleration, and the cause of the Arians was, or seemed to be, the cause of comprehension, and he had a profound and rooted aversion to the Sabellianism of Marcellus and others, who were acting with Athanasius. Where we have no certain information as to motives, it seems only fair to accept his own statements with respect to his opinions.*

* "The remark has been made," writes Dr. Newman (*Arians*, p. 263), "that throughout his *Ecclesiastical History*, no instance occurs of his expressing abhorrence of the superstitions of Paganism," and that his custom is either to praise, or not to blame, such heretical writers as fall under his notice.

Nothing could be more erroneous as a statement of facts than Dr. Newman's language here. Even if it had been true, that there is no abhorrence of paganism expressed in the *History*, great parts of the *Praeparatio* and *Theophania*, the *Tricennial Oration* and the *Life of Constantine*, are an elaborate indictment of the superstitions and horrors of heathendom; so that the comparative silence in the *History* must be explained by the fact that this was not, except incidentally, his theme. On the attitude of Eusebius towards heresies, Newman's statement is still wider of the mark. It is difficult to see how language could surpass such expressions as, *e.g.*, i. 1; ii. 1, 13; iii. 26, 27, 28, 29, 32; iv. 7, 29, 30; v. 13, 14, 16-20, etc., "grievous wolves," "most abominable heresy," "like a pestilent and scabby disease," "incurable and dangerous poison," "most foul heresy, overshooting anything that could exist or be conceived, more abominable than all shame," "double-mouthed and two-headed serpent," "like venomous reptiles," "loathsome evil-deeds": these and similar expressions form the staple of his language when he comes athwart a heresy.

While the Arian controversy was still fresh, the part taken by Eusebius was remembered against him in the Greek church, and the orthodox Fathers are generally depreciatory. But as the direct interest of the dispute wore out, the tide turned and set in his favour. Hence from the 5th cent. onwards we find a disposition to clear him of any complicity in Arian doctrine. Thus Socrates (*H. E.* ii. 21) is at some pains to prove him orthodox; and Gelasius of Cyzicus (*H. S. N.* ii. 1) stoutly defends this "most noble tiller of ecclesiastical husbandry," this "strict lover of truth" ὁ φιλαληθέστατος), and says that if there be any suggestion, however faint, of Arian heresy (μικρόν τι τὰ 'Αρείου ὑπονοούμενα) in his sayings or writings, it was due to "the inadvertence of simplicity," and that Eusebius himself pleaded this excuse in self-defence. Accordingly he represents him as a champion of orthodoxy against Arian opponents. The tide turned again at the second council of Nicaea. As the Iconoclasts alleged his authority for their views, the opposite party sought to disparage him. "His own books," says Photius, "cry aloud that he is convicted of Arianism" (*Ep.* 73). A lasting injury was inflicted on his reputation by dragging him into the Iconoclastic dispute. In the Latin church he fared somewhat better. Jerome indeed stigmatizes the teacher to whom he was more largely indebted than perhaps to any other as "the chief of the Arians," "the standard-bearer of the Arian faction," "the most flagrant champion of the impiety of Arius." But the eminent services of Eusebius to Christian literature carried the day in the western church. Two popes successively vindicated his reputation. Gelasius declined to place his *History* and *Chronicle* on the list of proscribed works (*Decret. de Libr. Apocr.* 4). Pelagius II., when defending him, says: "Holy Church weigheth the hearts of her faithful ones with kindliness rather than their words with rigour" (*Ep.* 5. 921). Neither Gelasius nor Pelagius refers directly to the charge of Arianism. The offence which seemed to them to require apology was his defence of the heretic Origen.

A more remarkable fact still is the canonization of Eusebius, notwithstanding his real or supposed Arian opinions. In an ancient Syrian *Martyrology*, translated from the Greek, and already referred to, he takes his rank among the honoured martyrs and confessors of the church. Nor was it only in the East that this honour awaited him. In the *Martyrologium Hieronymianum* for xi. Kal. Jul. we find the entry "In Caesarea Cappadociae depositio sancti Eusebii" (Hieron. *Op.* xi. 578). The person intended was Eusebius, the predecessor of St. Basil [Eusebius (**24**)], as the addition "Cappadociae" shews, but the transcendent fame of the Eusebius of the other Caesarea eclipsed this comparatively obscure person and finally obliterated his name from the Latin calendars. The word "Cappadociae" disappeared. In Usuard the notice becomes "In Caesarea Palestinae sancti Eusebii historiographi" (with a *v. l.*); and in old Latin martyrologies, where he is not distinctly specified, the historian Eusebius is doubtless understood. Accordingly, in several

Gallican service-books the historian is commemorated as a saint (see Valois, *Testimonia pro Eusebio*); and in the *Martyrologium Romanum* itself he held his place for many centuries. In the revision of this *Martyrology* under Gregory XIII. his name was struck out, and Eusebius of Samosata substituted, under the mistaken idea that Caesarea had been substituted for Samosata by a mistake. The *Martyrologium Hieronymianum*, which contained the true key to the error, had not then been discovered. The *Eccl. Hist.*, according to the text of Burton, with intro. by Dr. Bright, is pub. by Oxf. Univ. Press, and a valuable Eng. trans. both of the *History* and of the *Life of Constantine* by Dr. McGiffert is in the *Post-Nicene Lib. of the Fathers*. A cheap trans. with life, notes, chronol. table, etc., is in Bohn's Library (Bell). The works of Eusebius have been ed. by T. Gaisford (Clar. Press, 9 vols.); and a revised text of the *Evang. Prep.* with notes and Eng. trans. by E. H. Gifford (Clar. Press, 4 vols.). The Bodleian MS. of Jerome's version of the *Chronicle* of Eusebius has been reproduced in collotype with intro. by J. K. Fotheringham (Clar. Press) [L.]

Eusebius (24), bp. of Caesarea in Cappadocia, by whom Basil the Great was ordained to the presbyterate. Eusebius was a layman, and unbaptized at the time of his elevation to the episcopate, A.D. 362. On the death of Dianius, the church of Caesarea was divided into two nearly equal factions, and the choice of a layman universally known and respected was the readiest way out of the dilemma. Military force had to be employed to overcome his reluctance and to compel the prelates to consecrate. No sooner were they free than the bishops endeavoured to declare their consecration of Eusebius void. But the counsels of the elder Gregory of Nazianzus prevailed (Greg. Naz. *Orat.* xix. 36, pp. 308, 309). Eusebius proved a very respectable prelate, but quite unequal to the circumstances of severe trial in which he soon found himself. One of the earliest acts of his episcopate was to ordain Basil priest. A coldness grew up between Eusebius and Basil, leading to Basil's three years' retirement to Pontus. [BASILIUS OF CAESAREA.] (Greg. Naz. *Orat.* xx. §§ 51-53; *Ep.* 19, 20, 169, 170.) In 366 Basil returned to Caesarea. Each had learnt wisdom from the past (Greg. Naz. *Orat.* xx. §§ 57-59), and harmonious relations existed unbroken to the death of Eusebius, A.D. 370.

Fleury states that Eusebius is reckoned by some as a martyr (Fleury, xv. 13, 14; xvi. 9, 14, 17), but Usuard probably confounds Eusebius of Cappadocia with Eusebius the historian. See Papebrochius in *AA. SS.* Boll. Jun. iv. 75; and on the other side, Tillem. *Mém.* vii. 39. [EUSEBIUS OF CAESAREA.] [E.V.]

Eusebius (34), bp. of Dorylaeum in Phrygia Salutaris, the constant supporter of orthodoxy against Nestorius and Eutyches alike. About Christmas A.D. 428, when Nestorius was asserting his heresy in a sermon at Constantinople, there stood up in church a layman of excellent character, distinguished for erudition and orthodox zeal, who asserted in opposition to Nestorius that the "eternal Word begotten before the ages had submitted also to be born a second time" (*i.e.* according to the flesh of the Virgin). This bold assertion of the faith caused great excitement in the church. (Cyril. Alex. *adv. Nestor.* i. 20 in Migne, vol. ix. p. 41 D; Marius Mercator, pars ii. lib. i.; *Patr. Lat.* xlviii. p. 769 B.) This was certainly, as Theophanes (*Chron.* p. 76) expressly says, our Eusebius, who thus was the first to oppose the Nestorian heresy (Evagr. *Hist.* i. 9 in *Patr. Gk.* lxxxvi. 2445). He was also the first to protest against the heretical utterances of Anastasius, the syncellus of Nestorius (Theophan. *Chron.* p. 76). He was a "rhetor" (Evagr. *l.c.*) distinguished in legal practice (Leont. Byzant. *cont. Nestor. et Eutych.* lib. iii. in *Patr. Gk.* lxxxvi. 1389) and an "agens in rebus" to the court (*Gesta de Nom. Acacii*, cap. i. in Galland. *Biblioth.* x. 667; cf. Tillem. xiv. n. xi. on Cyril of Alex.). Theophanes (*l.c.*) calls him a σχολαστικὸς of the empress.

After the sermon of St. Proclus against Nestorius, and before the orthodox had separated from the communion of Nestorius, in consequence of the council of Ephesus, there appeared, fixed in a public place, a document exposing the identity of Nestorius's doctrine with that of Paul of Samosata. This document common opinion attributed to Eusebius (Leont. Byzant. *u.s.*). It begins by conjuring its readers to make its contents known or give a copy of it to all bishops, clergy, and laity in Constantinople. It draws out the parallel between the doctrines of Nestorius and Paul of Samosata, who both deny that the child born of Mary was the Eternal Word; and ends with an anathema on him who denies the identity of the Only-begotten of the Father and the child of Mary. Eusebius must have been a priest at the time when St. Cyril wrote his five books against Nestorius (Cyril. Alex. *u.s.*—so much is implied in the τελῶν ἔτι ἐν λαικοῖς), i.e. *c.* 430. He was certainly bp. of Dorylaeum in 448. He himself states that he was poor (Labbe, *Conc.* iv. 221 D.). Common hostility to Nestorius had hitherto united Eusebius and Eutyches; but about this time Eusebius, perceiving the heretical tendencies of his friend, frequently visited him, and exhorted him to reconsider his ways (*ib.* 154 D). Finding him immovable, Eusebius presented a "libellus" against Eutyches at a council at Constantinople under Flavian, Nov. 8, 448 (*ib.* 151). He deplores the persistency of Eutyches in error, and demands that he should be summoned before the council to answer charges of heresy. His petition was granted, though with unwillingness. At the second session of the council (Nov. 12), Eusebius requested that the second letter of St. Cyril to Nestorius and his letter to John of Antioch should be read as representing the standard of orthodoxy. This led to a profession of the orthodox faith from Flavian, assented to by the other bishops. At the third session (Nov. 15) Eusebius found that Eutyches had refused to come, alleging a determination never to quit his monastery, and saying that Eusebius had been for some time (πάλαι) his enemy. [EUTYCHES (4).] Only on the third summons was he induced to appear. Meanwhile Eusebius pressed his point persistently and even harshly, behaving with such warmth that, as Flavian said, "fire itself seemed cold to him, in his zeal for orthodoxy." Finding that Eutyches had attempted to secure the adhesion of the other archimandrites to his views [FAUSTUS (28)], Eusebius urged that he should be immediately treated with the rigour he deserved (Labbe, iv. 211). Flavian still urged patience and moderation. At last, on Nov. 22, Eutyches appeared with a large monastic and imperial escort, and was examined. Eusebius said of Eutyches: "I am poor, he threatens me with exile; he has wealth, he is already depicting (ἀναζωγραφεῖ) the oasis for me." He feared also lest Eutyches should turn round and assent to the orthodox faith—thus causing him to be suspected of making calumnious charges (*ib.* 221, C, D, E). The crucial question he put to Eutyches was: "My lord archimandrite, do you confess two natures after the Incarnation, and do you say that Christ is consubstantial with us according to the flesh or not?" To the first part Eutyches would not assent; he was condemned by all the bishops, and sentence of deposition was passed. He at once wrote to pope Leo I. in his own defence (Leo Mag. *Ep.* xxi. 739), complaining of the "machinations" of Eusebius.

We next hear of Eusebius in Apr. 449 at the examination of the Acts of the council of Constantinople, which Eutyches had declared to have been falsified. With him were 14 of the 34 bishops who had condemned Eutyches (Labbe, iv. 235). Eutyches was represented by three delegates; Eusebius and others remonstrated against his absence, but the emperor's orders overruled them. Eusebius insisted that all examination into the case of Eutyches, and into any question other than the authenticity of the Acts, should be referred to a general council (*ib.* 268). The examination of the Acts does not seem to have brought to light any inaccuracy of importance. When Eusebius arrived in Ephesus early in Aug. 449, to attend the council, he apparently lodged with Stephen of Ephesus (*ib.* 111 D, E), but was not permitted to attend the meetings of the council, on the ground that the emperor had forbidden it (*ib.* 145 A, B). Flavian urged that he should be admitted and heard, but Elpidius, one of the imperial commissioners, opposed it (Hefele, *Concil.* ii. 355), and the same wish or command of the emperor was urged by Dioscorus at the council of Chalcedon also. When the passage in the acts of Constantinople was read where Eusebius pressed Eutyches to acknowledge the two natures after the Incarnation, the council burst forth, "Off with Eusebius! burn him!" (Labbe, iv. 224 A). Sentence of deposition was pronounced against Flavian and Eusebius, and they were imprisoned (Liberat. cap. xii.; Galland, xii. p. 140) and then sent into exile (*Gest. de Nom. Acac.* Galland, x. 668). Eusebius escaped to Rome, where Leo welcomed him and granted him communion. He was there till Apr. 481 (Leo Mag. *Ep.* lxxix. lxxx. 1037, 1041). Leo commends him to the care of Anatolius of Constantinople, the successor of Flavian, as one who had suffered much for the faith. Eusebius left Rome to attend the council of Chalcedon. He had addressed a formal petition to the emperor Marcian against Dioscorus, and appears in the council as his accuser. He complains more than once of the conduct of Dioscorus in excluding him from the council of Ephesus (Labbe, iv. 145, 156). His innocence, with that of St. Flavian, was fully recognized at the close of the 1st session of the council of Chalcedon (*ib.* 322, 323); but at the 3rd session, on Oct. 13, he presented a further petition against Dioscorus, on behalf of himself, of Flavian (τοῦ ἐν ἁγίοις), and of the orthodox faith. He urges the iniquities of Dioscorus at Ephesus, and begs for complete exculpation for himself and condemnation for Dioscorus (*ib.* 381). In the 4th session Eusebius took part in the case of certain Egyptian bishops who declined to condemn Eutyches, alleging that they were bound to follow their patriarch (*i.e.* Dioscorus), in accordance with the council of Nicaea. Eusebius has but one word to say, "ψεύδονται" (*ib.* 513 A). We find him later (5th session, Oct. 22) siding at first against the imperial officers, and the wishes of the Roman legates for making no addition to the council's definition of faith (*ib.* 558 D; cf. Bright, *Hist. of the Church*, p. 409). Afterwards, however, he assisted at the revision which made that definition a completer expression of the doctrine of Leo's tome. In the 11th session he (Labbe, iv. 699 A) voted for the deposition of both claimants to the see of Ephesus, Bassian and Stephen, as being both alike irregularly consecrated. In the 15th session (Oct. 23) he signed the much-contested 28th canon of the council on the position to be held by the see of Constantinople. [LEO I.] The last time his name appears is in the rescript of the emperor Marcian, June 452, which had for its special object to rehabilitate the memory of Flavian, but which secured also that the condemnation of the robber council should in no way injure the reputation of Eusebius and Theodoret (*ib.* 866). His name appears in the list of bishops signing the decrees of the council at Rome in 503, but this list certainly belongs to some earlier council (cf. Baron. ann. 503, ix.). Comparing him with Flavian, we cannot but feel his want of generosity in his treatment of Eutyches, whose superior in logical power and theological perception he undoubtedly was. But none can deny him the credit of having been a watchful guardian of the doctrine of the Incarnation all through his life, and a keen-sighted and persistent antagonist of error, whether on the one side or the other, who by his sufferings for the orthodox faith merits the title of confessor. [C.G.]

Eusebius (35) Emesenus, bp. of Emesa, now Hems, in Syria, *c.* 341-359. He was born at Edessa, of a noble family, of Christian parents, and from his earliest years was taught the Holy Scriptures. His education was continued in Palestine and subsequently at Alexandria. In Palestine he studied theology under Eusebius of Caesarea and Patrophilus of Scythopolis, from whom he contracted the Arian leanings which distinguished him to the end of his life. Jerome terms him "signifer Arianae factionis" (*Chron. sub. ann.* x. Constantii), and his Arian tenets are spoken of by Theodoret as too well known to admit question (Theod. *Eranist.* Dial. iii. p. 257, ed. Schulze). About A.D. 331 he visited Antioch. Eustathius had been recently banished, and the see was occupied by one of the short-lived Arian intruders, Euphronius, with whom Eusebius lived on terms of intimacy. Eusebius's high personal character and reputation for learning marked him out for the episcopate, and to avoid the office he repaired to Alexandria, where he devoted himself to philosophy. Returning to Antioch, Flaccillus (otherwise Placillus), the Arian bishop, received him into his episcopal residence and admitted him to his confidence. The Arian synod which met at Antioch A.D. 340, under the predominant influence of Eusebius of Nicomedia, to nominate a successor to the newly deposed Athanasius, offered the vacant throne to Eusebius, who, well knowing how Athanasius was beloved by the Alexandrians, resolutely declined, and Gregory was chosen in his stead. Eusebius, however, allowed himself to be created bp. of Emesa. This city, on the Orontes to the N.E. of the Libanus range, some distance N. of Laodicea, was famous for its magnificent temple of Elagabalus, the Syrophoenician sun-god. A report, based on Eusebius's astronomical studies, had reached the excitable inhabitants that their new bishop was a sorcerer, addicted to judicial astrology. His approach aroused a violent popular commotion, before which he fled to his friend and future panegyrist, George, bp. of Laodicea. By George's exertions, and the influence of Flaccillus of Antioch and Narcissus of Neronias, the Emesenes were convinced of the groundlessness of their suspicions, and Eusebius obtained quiet possession. He was a great favourite with Constantius, who took him on several expeditions, especially those against Sapor II., king of Persia. It is singular that the charge, which Sozomen attributes to mere malevolence, of Sabellianism was brought against one whose Arian leanings were so pronounced. Eusebius died before the end of A.D. 359. He was buried at Antioch (Hieron. *de Vir. Ill.* 101), and his funeral oration by George of Laodicea ascribed to him miraculous powers.

He was a very copious writer. Jerome, who speaks somewhat contemptuously of his productions, particularizes treatises against the Jews, the Gentiles, and the Novatianists, an exposition of *Galatians* in ten books, and a large number of very brief homilies on the Gospels. The greater part of his works is lost. Theodoret quotes with high commendation in his *Eranistes* (Dial. iii. p. 258, ed. Schulze) two passages on the impassibility of the Son of God, a truth for which he says Eusebius endured many and severe struggles. Theodoret also speaks of works of his against Apelles (*Haer. Fab.* i. 25) and Manes (*ib.* 26). All the extant remains of Eusebius are printed by Migne, *Patr.* t. lxxxvi. i. pp. 461 ff. Socr. *H. E.* ii. 9; Soz. *H. E.* iii. 6; Niceph. *H. E.* ix. 5; Tillem. *Mém. Eccl.* t. vi. p. 313; Cave, *Hist. Lit.* vol. i. p. 207; Oudin, t. i. p. 389.) [E.V.]

Eusebius (48), bp. of Laodicea, in Syria Prima; a native and deacon of Alexandria. In the persecution under Valerian, A.D. 257, when the venerable bp. Dionysius had been banished from Alexandria, Eusebius remained, ministering to those in prison and burying the martyrs, a faithful service gratefully commemorated in a letter of Dionysius (apud Eus. *H. E.* vii. 11). During the civil strife at the death of Valerian, when Alexandria was in revolt, A.D. 262, Aemilianus, who had assumed the purple, was driven into the strong quarter of the city called Bruchium, and besieged. Eusebius without, and his friend Anatolius within, the besieged quarter secured escape for all useless hands, including a large number of Christians, whom Eusebius received kindly, supplying them with food and medicine, and carefully tending the sick. To the synod of Antioch, A.D. 264, summoned to deal with Paul of Samosata, Dionysius bp. of Alexandria, being unable to be present through age, sent Eusebius as his representative. The see of Laodicea was then vacant, and the Laodiceans demanded Eusebius for their bishop, taking no refusal. As bp. of Laodicea he sat at the synod when Paul of Samosata was deposed, A.D. 270. He was succeeded by his old friend Anatolius. Eus. *H. E.* vii. 11, 32; Tillem. *Mém. Eccl.* iv. 304; Le Quien, *Or. Christ.* ii. 792; Neale, *Patriarchate of Alex.* i. 77. [E.V.]

Eusebius (60), bp. of Nicomedia. Our knowledge of his character is derived almost exclusively from the bitter language of his theological antagonists. He wielded an extraordinary influence over the fortunes of some of the great party leaders of the 4th cent. The fascination he exercised over the minds of Constantine and Constantius, his dexterity in utilizing both secular and ecclesiastical law to punish his theological enemies, his ingenuity in blinding the judgment of those not alive to the magnitude of the problem, and in persuading the unwary of the practical identity of his own views with those of the Catholic church, together with the political and personal ascendancy he achieved, reveal mental capacity and diplomatic skill worthy of a better cause. During 20 years his shadow haunts the pages of the ecclesiastical historians, though they seldom bring us face to face with the man or preserve his words. Even the chronology of his life is singularly uncertain.

It is difficult to understand the pertinacity and even ferocity with which Eusebius and his party pursued the Homoousian leaders, and to reconcile this with their well-accredited compromises, shiftings of front, and theological evasions. Dr. Newman (*Arians of Fourth Cent.* p. 272) admits their consistency in one thing, "their hatred of the sacred mystery." He thinks that this mystery, "like a spectre, was haunting the field and disturbing the complacency of their intellectual investigations." Their consciences did not scruple to "find evasions of a test." They undoubtedly compromised themselves by signature; yet they did not treat as unimportant that which they were wont to declare such but set all the machinery of church and empire in motion to enforce their latitudinarian view on the conscience of the church.

The Arian and the orthodox agreed as to the unique and exalted dignity of the Son of God; both alike described the relation between the first and second hypostasis in the Godhead as that which is imaged to us in the paternal and filial relation. They even agreed that the Son was "begotten of His Father before all worlds"—before the commencement of time, in an ineffable manner—that the Son was the originator of the categories of time and place, that "by His own will and counsel He has subsisted before time and before ages, as perfect God, only begotten and unchangeable" (*Letter of Arius to Eus. of Nic.* preserved by Theodoret, i. 5). They agreed that He was "God of God," "Light of Light," and worthy of all honour and worship. The orthodox went further, and in order to affirm that the Deity of the Son of God was absolute and not relative, infinite and not finite, asserted that He was of the same *οὐσία* with the Father. There Arius and Eusebius stopped, and, pressing the significance of the image of Father and Son by materialistic analogies into logical conclusions, argued that "generation" implied that "there was [a period, rather than a 'time'] when He was not," that "He was not before He was begotten." The one element, said they, which the Son did not possess by His generation was the eternal, absolute *οὐσία* of the Father. "We affirm," said Eusebius, in his one extant authentic letter, addressed to Paulinus of Tyre (Theod. i. 6), that "there is One Who is unbegotten, and that there also exists Another, Who did in truth proceed from Him, yet Who was not made out of His substance, and Who does not at all participate in the nature or substance of Him Who is unbegotten." *

If we follow out the logical conclusions involved in the denial of the orthodox statement on this transcendental theme, it is more easy to understand the abhorrence with which the dogmatic negations of the Arians were regarded by the Catholic church. The position of Arius and Eusebius involved a virtual Ditheism, and opened the door to a novel Polytheism. After Christianity had triumphed over the gods of heathendom, Arius seemed to be reintroducing them under other names. The numerical unity of God was at stake; and a schism, or at least a divarication of interests in the Godhead, shewn to be possible. Moreover, the "Divinity" of the Incarnate Word was on this hypothesis less than God; and so behind the Deity which He claimed there loomed another Godhead, between Whom and Himself antagonism might easily be predicated. The Gnosticism of Marcion had already drawn such antagonism into sharp outline, and the entire view of the person of the Lord, thus suggested, rapidly degenerated into a cold and unchristian humanitarianism.

The exigencies of historic criticism and of the exegesis of the N.T. compelled the Arian party to discriminate between the Word, the power, the wisdom of God, and the *Son*. They could not deny, since God could never have been without His "Logos," that the Logos was in some sense eternal. So they took advantage of the distinction drawn in the Greek schools between λόγος ἐνδιάθετος, identifiable with the wisdom, reason, and self-consciousness of God, and λόγος προφορικός, the setting forth and going out at a particular epoch of the divine energy. The latter they regarded as the λόγος which was made flesh and might be equated with the Son. "The external (prophoric) word was a created Being made in the beginning of all things as the visible emblem of the internal (endiathetic) word, and (used as) the instrument of God's purposes towards His creation" (Newman, *l.c.* 199; cf. Athan. *Hist. Conc. Arim. et Seleuc.* cap. ii. § 18).

* This phrase seems to class him with Heterousians or even Anomoeans, at that early period.

The orthodox party admitted the double use of the word λόγος, allowed that it answered to the eternal wisdom and also to the eternal manifestation of God, and discarding the trammels of the figurative expression by which the internal relations of the Godhead can alone be represented to us, declared that they could not carry the materialistic or temporal accompaniments of our idea of Father and Son into this "generation," and boldly accepted the sublime paradox with which Origen had refuted Sabellianism—viz. the "eternal generation of the Son." To suppose the relation between the Father and Son other than eternal was to be involved in the toils of a polytheistic emanation and Gnostic speculation. Compelled to formulate expressions about the infinite and eternal God, they concluded that any formula which divided the essence of God left infinity on the one side, and the finite on the other, *i.e.* that there would be, on this hypothesis, an infinite difference even in majesty and glory between the Father and the Son. This was blasphemy in the eyes of those who held the Divinity of the Son of God.

The controversy was embittered by the method in which Arius and Eusebius appealed to Holy Scripture. They urged that Godhead and participation in the divine nature were attributed to Christ in the same terms in which similar distinctions are yielded by God to other creatures, angelic, human, or physical (Theod. *H. E.* i. 6, 8). Thus Christ's rank in the universe might be indefinitely reduced, and all confidence in Him ultimately proved an illusion. The argument had a tone of gross irreverence, even if the leaders can be quite acquitted of blasphemous levity or intentional abuse.

One of the tactics of the Arian or Eusebian party was to accuse of Sabellianism those, like Athanasius, Eustathius, and Marcellus of Ancyra, who refused their interpretation of the relation between the Father and the Son. Doubtless many not versed in philosophical discussion were incapable of discriminating between the views of Sabellius and an orthodoxy which vehemently or unguardedly condemned the Arian position. Eusebius repudiated violently the Pantheistic tendency of the Sabellian doctrine. He is the most prominent and most distinguished man of the entire movement, and it has been plausibly argued that he was the teacher rather than the disciple of Arius. Athanasius himself made the suggestion. We learn on good authority, that of Arius himself, that they were fellow-disciples of Lucian of Antioch (*ib.* 5). Lucian afterwards modified his views and became a martyr for the faith, but his rationalizing spirit had had a great effect on the schools of Antioch. According to Ammianus Marcellinus, Eusebius was a distant relative of the emperor Julian, and therefore possibly of Constantine.

It may have been through the wife of Licinius and sister of Constantine that he received his first ecclesiastical appointment. This was the bishopric of Berytus (Beirout) in

Syria. We cannot say under what pretext he was translated to the see of Nicomedia, a city which was still the principal seat of the imperial court. In Nicomedia his ambitious spirit and personal relations with the imperial family gave him much influence. "He was," says Sozomen (*H. E.* i. 15), "a man of considerable learning, and held in high repute at the palace." Here were spun the webs by which the Arian conspiracy for a while prevailed over the faith and discipline of the church. One of the most authoritative documents of Arianism is a letter sent by Arius to Eusebius of Nicomedia, after his first suspension from presbyteral functions at Baukalis, Alexandria, in which he reminds Eusebius of their ancient friendship and briefly states his own views. [ARIUS.] Arius boasts that Eusebius of Caesarea, Theodotus of Laodicea, Paulinus of Tyre, Athanasius of Anazarbus, Gregory of Berytus, Aetius of Lydda, and *all the bishops of the East*, if he is condemned, must be condemned with him (Theod. *H. E.* i. 5). The alarm created by the conduct of Arius and his numerous friends in high quarters induced Alexander of Alexandria to indite his famous letter to Alexander of Constantinople, which is of an encyclical character and was sent in some form to Eusebius of Nicomedia and other prelates. Exasperated by its tone, Eusebius called a council in Bithynia (probably at Nicomedia itself) of the friends of Arius, who addressed numerous bishops, desiring them to grant communion to the Arians and requiring, Alexander to do the like (Soz. i. 15). These proceedings drew from Eusebius a written expression of his views, in a letter to Paulinus of Tyre, preserved by Theodoret (i. 6). Eusebius believed Alexander of Alexandria to be in doctrinal error, but not yet so far gone but that Paulinus might put him right. He tacitly assumed that the party of Alexandria asserted "*two* unbegotten beings," a position utterly denied by themselves. He repudiated strongly the idea that the Son was made in any sense out of the substance of God; declaring the Son "to be entirely distinct in nature and power," the method of His origination being known only to God, not even to the Son Himself. The verb "created," in Prov. viii. 22-26, could not, Eusebius said, have been used if the "wisdom" of which the prophet was speaking was ἐξ ἀποῤῥοίας τῆς οὐσίας: "For that which *proceeds* from Him Who is unbegotten cannot be said to have been created or founded either by Him or by another." The effect of the *word* "begotten" is reduced to a minimum by saying that the term is used of "things" and of persons entirely different in nature from God. "Men," "Israel," and "drops of dew" are in different scriptures said to be "begotten" of God. Therefore, Eusebius argued, the *term* cannot and does not carry similarity, still less identity of nature. At first the emperor Constantine treated the conflict as if capable of easy adjustment by a wise exercise of Christian temper. In 324 he wrote a joint letter, which he entrusted to Hosius of Cordova (Soz. *H. E.* i. 16), in which he called upon Alexander and Arius, for the sake of peace, to terminate their controversy. The dispute was a "trifling and foolish verbal dispute," and difference of judgment was, he urged, compatible with union and communion. Constantine had probably been led to this step by Eusebius of Nicomedia, and the strong pressure put upon Alexander to receive Arius into communion corresponds with the subsequent persistent demand of the Eusebians. The effort at mediation failed, although conducted with skilful diplomacy and tact by the venerable Hosius. As the dispute was no mere verbal quibble, but did in reality touch the very object of divine worship, the ground of religious hope, and the unity of the Godhead, the well-meant interference of the emperor merely augmented the acrimony of the disputants. Arius was again condemned by a council at Alexandria, and the entire East was disturbed. The angry letter of Constantine to Arius, which must have been written after his condemnation by the Alexandrian council and before the council of Nicaea, shews that the influence of Eusebius must now have been in abeyance.* Constantine was no theologian, but hated a recalcitrant subordinate in church or state, and hence the undoubted vacillation of his mind towards Alexander, Arius, Eusebius, and Athanasius. At the oecumenical council of Nicaea in 325, Eusebius defended the excommunicated presbyter and was the advocate and interpreter of his opinions before the council. We must give him credit for moral courage in risking his position as bishop and as court favourite for the sake of his theological views, and opposing himself almost single-handed to the nearly unanimous judgment of the first representative assembly of the Christian episcopate—a judgment fanned into enthusiasm by martyrs and monks from the African monasteries and accepted hurriedly but passionately by the emperor. The courage was of short duration, and made way for disingenuous wiles. Eusebius soon displayed an inconsistent and temporizing spirit. Whether or no they still held that the difference was merely verbal, when the Arian bishops in the council found that the Godhead of the Redeemer was declared by the vast majority to be of the very essence of Christian doctrine, they made every effort to accept the terms in which that Godhead was being expressed by the council, making signs to each other that term after term, such as "Power of God," "Wisdom of God," "Image of God," "Very God of very God," might be accepted because they could use them of such divinity as was "made" or constituted as such by the divine appointment. Thus they were becoming parties to a test, which they were intending to evade. The term *Homoousion*, as applied to the Son of God, rallied for a while their conscience, and Eusebius declared it to be untenable. According to Theodoret (i. 8), the "formulary propounded by Eusebius contained undisguised evidence of his blasphemy; the reading of it occasioned great grief to the audience on account of the depravity of the doctrines; the writer was covered with shame, and the impious writing was torn to pieces." The

* Tillemont, *Les Ariens*, note 5. The letter is preserved by Gelasius of Cyzicus (iii. 1) in Greek, and given by Baronius in Latin from a MS. in the Vatican. Bar. *Ann.* 319, vi.

inconsistency of the Arian party is exaggerated by Theodoret, for he adds, "the Arians unanimously signed the confession of faith adopted by the council." This is not precisely the case. There were 17 bishops (Soz. i. 20) * who at first refused their signatures, among them both the Eusebii, Theognis of Nicaea, Menophantus of Ephesus, Secundus of Ptolemais, Theonas, Patrophilus, Narcissus, Maris, and others. Eusebius of Caesarea, after long discussion, signed the symbol, which was in fact an enlargement of a formal creed that he had himself presented to the council, on the ground that the negative dogmata of the Arian party which were anathematized by the council could not be found in Scripture. Others of his party followed. According to Theodoret (i. 9), all, except Secundus and Theonas, joined in the condemnation of Arius; and Sozomen (i. 21) declares explicitly that Eusebius of Nicomedia, with others, "sanctioned" the decision of the synod as to the consubstantiality of the Son, and the excommunication of those who held the Arian formulae; but Sozomen goes on to say that "it ought to be known that Eusebius and Theognis, although they assented to the exposition of faith set forth by the council, neither agreed nor subscribed to the *deposition* of Arius." Sozomen, apparently, makes this refusal to sign, on the part of Eusebius and Theognis, to have been the reason or occasion of their own exile, and of the filling up by Constantine of their respective sees with Amphion and Chrestus. Philostorgius admits that the whole Arian party, except Secundus and Theonas, signed the symbol, but that they did it deceitfully (ἐν δόλῳ), with the mental reservation of ὁμοιούσιον (of similar substance) for ὁμοούσιον (of the same substance). He adds, according to his editor, that they did this under the direction of Constantina, the sister of Constantine; and further he relates that "Secundus, when sent into exile, reproached Eusebius for having signed, saying that he did so in order to avoid going into exile, and that Secundus expressed a confident hope that Eusebius would shortly be exiled, an event which took place three months after the council." Moreover, Athanasius (*de Decretis Syn. Nic.* cc. 3, 18) expressly says that Eusebius signed the formulary.

Notwithstanding their signature, for some reason Eusebius and Theognis were banished for nearly three years from their respective sees. Theodoret (*H. E.* i. 20) preserves a portion of a letter written by Constantine against Eusebius and Theognis, and addressed to the Nicomedians. The document displays bitter animosity, and, for so astute a prince, a curious simplicity. Constantine reveals a private grudge against Eusebius for his conduct when Licinius was contending with him, and professes to have seized the accomplices of Eusebius and to have possessed himself of damaging papers and trustworthy evidence against him. He reproaches Eusebius with having been the first defender of Arius and with having deceived him in hope of retaining his benefice. He refers angrily to the conduct of Eusebius in urging Alexandrians and others to communicate with the Arians. This pertinacity is suggested by Constantine as the actuating cause and occasion of his exile.

* Philostorgius mentions 22 names, but Hefele, following Socrates and Sozomen, limits them to 17.

Epiphanius (*Haer.* lxviii.) details the circumstances of the union of the Meletian schismatics with the Arians, and the disingenuous part taken by Eusebius in promising his good offices with the emperor, if they in their turn would promote the return of Arius to Alexandria, and would promise inter-communion with him and his party.

The terms of hatred and disgust with which Constantine speaks of Eusebius render his early return to Nicomedia very puzzling. Sozomen (ii. 16) and Socrates (i. 14) both record a letter (A.D. 328) from Eusebius and Theognis to "the *Bishops*," explaining their views, in which they say, "We hold the same faith that you do, and after a diligent examination of the word ὁμοούσιος, are wholly intent upon preserving peace, and are seduced by no heresy. Having proposed for the safety of the church such suggestions as occurred to us, and having certified what we deemed requisite, we signed the confession of faith. *We did not certainly sign the anathemas*—not because we impugned the confession of faith, but because we did not believe the accused to be what he was represented to us. . . . So far from opposing any of the decrees enacted in your holy synod, we assent to all of them—not because we are wearied of exile, but because we wish to avert all suspicion of heresy. . . . The accused having justified himself *and having been recalled from exile,* . . . we beseech you to make our supplications known to our most godly emperor, and that you immediately direct us to act according to your will." If this letter is genuine, it demonstrates the fact of their partial and incomplete signature of the symbol of Nicaea, and that the incompleteness turned on *personal* and not on doctrinal grounds. Other statements of Sozomen (ii. 27) are in harmony with it, but there are reasons for hesitating to receive these statements, and the letter itself is in obvious contradiction with the evidence of Philostorgius (i. 9) and Epiphanius (lxviii. 5) that Eusebius and Theognis signed the symbol, anathemas and all. Are we to believe these writers against the testimony of Sozomen and Socrates, who expressly give a consistent representation undoubtedly more favourable to Eusebius?

The most powerful argument of De Broglie and others against the genuineness of the letter, as being written from the exile of Eusebius, is the silence of Athanasius, who never uses it to shew the identity of the position and sentiments of Arius and Eusebius. Philostorgius recounts a rumour that after the council Eusebius desired to have his name expunged from the list of signatures, and a similar statement is repeated by Sozomen (ii. 21) as the possible cause of the banishment of Eusebius. The fact may, notwithstanding the adverse judgment of many historians, have been that Eusebius signed the formulary, expressing the view he took of its meaning, and discriminating between an anathema of certain positions and the persecution of an individual. A signature, thus qualified, may have saved him from immediate banishment. In the course of three months his sympathy with Arius and his underhand proceeding with the Meletians may have roused the emperor's indignation and led to his banishment. The probability that Arius was recalled first, as positively stated in what purports to be a contemporary document, is certainly greater than that merely *à priori* probability on which De Broglie insists. Moreover, if Arius had been restored to favour, the vacillating mind of Constantine may have been moved to recall the two bishops. At all events, *c.* 329, we find Eusebius once more in high favour with Constantine (Socr. *H. E.* i. 23), discharging his episcopal functions and persuading Constantine that he and Arius held substantially the creed of Nicaea. Thenceforward Eusebius used his great power at court and his ascendancy over the mind of Constantine to blast the character and quench the influence of the most distinguished advocates of anti-Arian views. He put all the machinery of church and state into operation to unseat Athanasius, Eustathius, Marcellus, and others; and, by means open to the severest reprehension, steadily and unscrupulously strove to enforce his latitudinarian compromise on the Catholic church. It is not difficult to trace his hand in the letter of Constantine threatening Athanasius, now archbp. of Alexandria, with deposition if he did not admit those anxious for communion. Moreover, Athanasius assures us that Eusebius wrote to him personally with the same object. The answers Athanasius gave to Eusebius and the emperor made it clear that the project could never succeed so long as Athanasius remained at Alexandria.

Meanwhile, considerable controversy had occurred between Eusebius of Caesarea and Eustathius of Antioch on the true meaning of the term Homoousios. Eustathius [EUSTATHIUS (3)], in his zeal for the Nicene faith, had strenuously refused to admit Arians into communion, and laid himself open, in the opinion of Eusebius of Caesarea, to the charge of Sabellianism (Soz. ii. 18). This provided the opportunity for Eusebius of Nicomedia to strike a blow at Eustathius, and nothing can exceed the treachery shewn by Eusebius on this occasion. His apparently friendly visit to Eustathius on his way to Jerusalem (Soz. ii. 19; Theod. i. 21), the gathering of his Arian supporters on his return to Antioch, shew the scheme to have been deeply laid. Here, A.D. 330 or beginning of 331, the council of his friends was held, at which the charge of Sabellianism was, according to Theodoret (i. 21) and Philostorgius (ii. 7), aggravated by the accusation brought by a woman, that Eustathius was the father of her child—a not uncommon device of the enemies of ecclesiastics. The upshot was that through this, and other vamped-up charges of disrespect to the emperor's mother, Eustathius was deposed and exiled by the Eusebians. The letter of Constantine upon the affair, and against heretics generally, brought the controversy to a lull, until the first attack upon Athanasius. The career of Eusebius of Nicomedia during the remaining ten years of his life is so closely intertwined with the romantic sufferings of Athanasius that it is difficult to indicate the part he took in the persecution of Athanasius without reproducing the story of this great hero of the Catholic faith. The first charge which Eusebius encouraged the Meletians to bring against Athanasius concerned his taxing the people of Egypt for linen vestments, and turned upon the supposed violence of Macarius, the representative of Athanasius, in overthrowing the altar and the chalice, when reproving (for uncanonical proceedings) Ischyras, a priest of the Colluthian sect. These charges were all absolutely disproved by Athanasius before Constantine at Nicomedia. On his return to Alexandria, Athanasius had to encounter fresh opposition. The preposterous story of the murder of Arsenius, with its grotesque accompaniments, was gravely laid at his door. [ATHANASIUS.] To this, at first, he disdained to reply. Eusebius declared even this to be a serious charge, and made much capital out of the refusal of Athanasius to attend the council at Caesarea, which was summoned, among other causes, to investigate it (Theod. i. 28). In 335, the partisan council of Tyre passed a sentence of deposition upon Athanasius, who had fled to Constantinople to appeal to the emperor, who summoned the whole synod of Tyre before him. Eusebius and a few of his party, Theognis, Patrophilus, Valens, and Ursacius, obeyed the summons, and confronted Athanasius; but abandoning the disproved charges upon which the sentence of deposition rested, they met him with new accusations likely to damage him in the view of the emperor. Constantine yielded to the malicious inventions of Eusebius, and banished Athanasius to Trèves, in Feb. 336. The cause of banishment is obscure, but twice over (*Ap.* § 87, *Hist. Ar.* § 50) Athanasius declares that Constantine sent him to Gaul to deliver him from the fury of his enemies. While Athanasius was in exile, Eusebius and his party impeached Marcellus of Ancyra for refusing to appear at the council of Dedication at Jerusalem, A.D. 335, and for Sabellianism, an implication of heresy to which he exposed himself while zealously vindicating his refusal to hold communion with Arians. [ASTERIUS (1); MARCELLUS.] Marcellus was deposed by the Eusebians, and not restored till the council of Sardica. At the council of Dedication at Jerusalem, Arius propounded a view of his faith which was satisfactory to the council, was received into communion there, and sent by Eusebius to Alexandria, whence, as his presence created great disturbance, he was summoned to Constantinople. There Arius died tragically on the eve of the public reception which Eusebius had planned. The death of Alexander of Constantinople followed very shortly, and the effort to elect Paul [PAULUS (18)] in his place (without the consent of the bp. of Nicomedia) roused the ire of Eusebius, who intrigued to secure his first deposition. Eusebius must still have retained the favour of Constantine, as he appears to have administered baptism to the dying emperor, May 337. Jerome says that by this act Constantine avowed himself an Arian. "But all history protests against the severity of this sentence" (de Broglie). Hefele supposes that Constantine regarded Eusebius as the great advocate of Christian unity. Moreover, in the eyes of Constantine, Eusebius was one who had signed the Nicene symbol, and had renounced the negations of Arius. The ecclesiastical historians give divergent statements as to when Eusebius was raised to the episcopate of Constantinople. Theodoret (i. 19) accuses Eusebius of unlawful translation from Nicomedia to Constantinople, "in direct violation of that canon which prohibits bishops and presbyters from going from one city to another," and asserts that this took place on the death of Alexander. There is, however, proof that Paul, who was twice banished through the influence of Eusebius, was the immediate successor of Alexander. Paul was nominated by Alexander, but the Eusebian party put forward Macedonius (Soz. iii. 4), and were defeated. The dispute roused the indignation of Constantius, and "through the machination of the enemies of Paul a synod was convened, and he was expelled from the church, and Eusebius, bp. of Nicomedia, was installed in the bishopric of Constantinople"; with this statement Socrates (ii. 7) agrees. For a while the education of Julian was entrusted to Eusebius, who had unbounded influence over Constantius.

In 340 the Eusebians held a synod at Antioch, at which Athanasius was once more condemned. In 341 (May) the council developed into the celebrated council *in Encaeniis*, held also at Antioch, at which, under the presidency of Eusebius or Placetus of Antioch, and with the assent and presence of Constantius, divers canons were passed, which are esteemed of authority by later oecumenical councils. These two councils are confounded and identified by Socrates (ii. 2) and Sozomen.

The cruel injustice to which Athanasius was subjected by long exile is freely attributed to Eusebius, as its mainspring and constant instigator. Nevertheless the last thing we are told about Eusebius by Socrates (ii. 13) is that he appealed from the council of Antioch to Julius, bp. of Rome, to give definite sentence as to Athanasius, but that before the sentence of Julius reached him, "immediately after the council broke up, breath went out of his body, and so he died," A.D. 342.

In addition to authors already cited, the following may be consulted: *The Orations of St. Athanasius against the Arians, according to the Benedictine Text, with an Account of his Life*, by William Bright, D.D.; Hefele, *History of the Christian Councils*, translated by Prebendary Clark and Mr. Oxenham, vols. i. and ii.; Möhler, *Athanasius der Grosse und die Kirche seiner Zeit* (1844); William Bright, D.D., *History of the Church from 313 to 451* (1869); Albert de Broglie, *L'Eglise et l'Empire* (1856), t. ii.; *The Arians of the Fourth Century*, by J. H. Newman (4th ed. 1876). [H.R.R.]

Eusebius (71), bp. of Pelusium, between Ammonius and Georgius. He was present at the council of Ephesus in 431 (Mansi, iv. 1127 A, 1219 B, 1366 D; v. 615 C). His contemporary Isidore, abbat of Pelusium, depicts him in the darkest colours, as a man of some taste and some ability, an "agreeable" preacher (*Ep.* i. 112; cf. v. 301), but hot-tempered (v. 196; cf. iii. 44) and easily swayed by men worse than himself (ii. 127; v. 451); his hands were not clear of simoniacal gain, which he employed in building a splendid church (i. 37; ii. 246); he "entrusted the flock to dogs, wolves, foxes" (v. 147), "the monasteries to herdsmen and runaway slaves" (i. 262); he was forgetful of the poor, and inaccessible to remonstrance (iii. 260). His confidants were Lucius the archdeacon, who was said to take money for ordinations (i. 29); Zosimus a priest, who disgraced his grey hairs by vices (i. 140; ii. 75, 205, etc.) and retained contributions meant for the poor (v. 210); and three deacons, Eustathius, Anatolius, and Maron (i. 223; ii. 28, 29, etc.), with whom Gotthius (ii. 10), Simon, and Chaeremon (v. 48, 373) are associated. The greediness of those who administered the church property was insatiable (v. 79). The offences of these men, or of some of them, were so gross that men cried out against them as effective advocates of Epicureanism (ii, 153, 230), and Isidore had to tell his correspondents that he had done his best (as, indeed, many of his letters shew, *e.g.* i. 140, 436; ii. 28, 39, etc.) to reclaim the offenders, but that the physician could not compel the patient to follow his advice, that "God the Word Himself" could not save Judas (iv. 205.) that a good man should not soil his lips by denouncing their conduct (iii. 229; v. 116), and that nothing remained but to pray for their conversion (v. 2, 105, etc.), and in the meantime to distinguish between the man and the office (ii. 52), and to remember that the unworthiness of the minister hindered not the effect of the sacraments (ii. 32). But the fullest account of the misgovernment of the church of Pelusium is given in the story of Martinianus (ii. 127), whom Eusebius had ordained, and made "oeconomus" or church steward. He played the knave and tyrant, treated the bishops as his tool, was more than once in peril of his life from the indignation of the citizens, went to Alexandria, was menaced by archbp. Cyril with excommunication, but returned and imputed to Cyril himself a participation in simony. Such things induced many to leave Pelusium in disgust; "the altar lacked ministers" (i. 38); a pious deacon, such as Eutonius, was oppressed by Zosimus (ii. 131) and attacked by the whole clergy, to some extent out of subserviency to the bishop (v. 564). Eusebius is not mentioned among the Fathers of the council of Chalcedon in 451. In 457 he and Peter, bp. of Majuma, assisted at the ordination of Timotheus Aelurus to the see of Alexandria (Evagr. *H. E.* ii. 8), and those who were parties to that proceeding are stated by Theodorus Lector (*H. E.* i. 9) to have been deposed bishops. The epistle of the Egyptian bishops to Anatolius (*Cod. Encyc.* in Mansi, vii. 533 A) represents the two bishops (here unnamed) who ordained Timotheus as having no communion with the Catholic church. Le Quien, *Or. Chr.* ii. 533; Tillem. *Mém.* xv. 747, 748, 782-788. [W.B. AND C.H.]

Eusebius (77), bp. of Samosata (360-373), the friend alike of Basil the Great, Meletius, and Gregory Nazianzen. All that is definitely known of Eusebius is gathered from the epistles of Basil and of Gregory, and from some incidents in the *Ecclesiastical History* of Theodoret. The fervent and laudatory phrases applied to him might suggest hyperbole if they were not so constant (*Epp.* xxviii. xxix. Greg. Naz. *Opp.* ed. Prunaeus, Colon. vol. i. 792; *Ep.* xxxiv.

Basilii opera, ed. Par. t. iii.). As bp. of Samosata in 361, he took part in the consecration of Meletius to the see of Antioch. Meletius was then in communion with the Arians, and a coalition of bishops of both parties placed the document affirming the consecration in the hands of Eusebius. Meletius soon proclaimed explicitly his Nicene Trinitarianism, and was banished by Constantius on the charge of Sabellianism. Meanwhile Eusebius had returned to Samosata with the written record of the appointment of Meletius to Antioch. The Arians, anxious to destroy this proof of their complicity, persuaded Constantius to demand, by a public functionary, the reddition of the document. Eusebius replied, "I cannot consent to restore the public deposit, except at the command of the whole assembly of bishops by whom it was committed to my care." This reply incensed the emperor, who wrote to Eusebius ordering him to deliver the decree on pain of amputation of his right hand. Theodoret says the threat was only meant to intimidate the bishop; if so, it failed, for Eusebius stretched out both hands, exclaiming, "I am willing to suffer the loss of both hands rather than resign a document which contains so manifest a demonstration of the impiety of the Arians."

Tillemont hesitates to claim for Eusebius, as many writers have done, the honour of being the Christian confessor in the persecutions under Julian. According to Greg. Naz. (*Orat. c. Julianum*, i. p. 133 B.C.), when suffering on the rack and finding one part of his body not as yet tortured, Eusebius complained to the executioners for not conferring equal honour on his entire frame. The death of Julian and the accession of Jovian gave liberty to the church.

During and after this temporary lull in the imperial patronage of the Arian party, the great exertions of Eusebius probably took place. He is represented as travelling in the guise of a soldier (Theod. iv. 13) through Phoenicia and Palestine, ordaining presbyters and deacons, and must thus have become known to Basil, who on the death of Eusebius of Caesarea wrote to Gregory (Bas. *Ep.* xlvii. Paris ed.), the father of Gregory of Nazianzus, advising the selection of Eusebius of Samosata for the vacant bishopric. The Paris editors of Basil plausibly suggest that the letter thus numbered was written by Gregory to Eusebius concerning Basil, rather than by Basil concerning Eusebius. The part which Eusebius did take in the election of Basil is well known. Basil's appointment gave Gregory extreme satisfaction (Greg. Naz. *Ep.* xxix.). He dilates on the delight which the visit of Eusebius to Caesarea had given the community. The bedridden had sprung from their couches, and all kinds of moral miracles had been wrought by his presence. Thereafter the correspondence between Basil and Eusebius reveals the progress of their joint lives, and throws some light upon the history of the church. The two ecclesiastics were passionately eager for one another's society, and appear to have formed numerous designs, all falling through, for an interchange of visits.

In 372 Eusebius signed, with Meletius, Basil, and 29 others, a letter to the Western bishops, in view of their common troubles from Arian opponents. The letter (Basil, *Ep.* xcii. Paris ed.), a melancholy Jeremiad, recounts disaster and disorder, uncanonical proceedings and Arian heresy. The Eastern bishops look to their brethren in Italy and Gaul for sympathy and advice, paying a tribute to the pristine purity which the Western churches had preserved intact while the Eastern churches had been lacerated, undermined, and divided by heretics and unconstitutional acts. Later in 372 Basil entreats Eusebius to meet him at Phargamon in Armenia, at an assembly of bishops (*Ep.* xcv.). If Eusebius will not or cannot attend the conference, neither will Basil; and (xcviii.) he passionately urges him to visit him at Caesarea. Letters from Eusebius appear to have been received by Basil, who once more (c.) begs a visit at the time of the festival of the martyr Eupsychius, since many things demanded mutual consideration. At the end of 372 Basil (cv.) managed the laborious journey to Samosata, and secured from his friend the promise of a return visit. This promise, said he, had ravished the church with joy. In 373 Basil urged Eusebius to fulfil his promise, and (cxxvii.) assured him that Jovinus had answered his expectations as bp. of Nicopolis. Jovinus was a worthy pupil of Eusebius, and gratified Basil by his canonical proprieties. Everywhere the θρέμματα of Eusebius exhibit the image of his sanctity. Other authorities (Tillem. *Art.* iii.) record that Jovinus relapsed afterwards into Arianism. The good offices of Eusebius were solicited by Eustathius of Sebaste, who had quarrelled with Basil. Basil's principle of "purity before reconciliation" convinced Eusebius of his wisdom and moderation. At the council of Gangra, probably in 372 or 373, Eustathius of Sebaste was condemned for Arian tendencies and hyperascetic practices. There is a difficulty in deciding who was the Eusebius mentioned *primo loco* without a see in the synodal letter. It may have been the bp. of Samosata, and as Basil entreated his advice as to Eustathius, he may have joined him, Hypatius, Gregory, and other friends whose names occur in this *pronunciamiento*. His age and moral eminence would give him this prominent position. The 20 canons of Gangra are detailed with interesting comment by Hefele, who thinks the chronology entirely uncertain. We venture the above suggestion, which would throw considerable light on the practical character of the bp. of Samosata. In 373 a letter of Basil (*Ep.* cxxxvi.) shews that Eusebius had successfully secured the election of a Catholic bishop at Tarsus. In consequence, he was eagerly entreated to visit Basil at Caesarea. He may have done so, and presided at the council of Gangra. An encyclical which Eusebius proposed to send to Italy was not prepared, but Dorotheus and Gregory of Nyssa were induced to visit Rome in 374. The Paris editors assign to 368 or 369 Basil's letters (xxvii. xxxi.) descriptive of his illness, and the famine that arrested his movements, but whensoever written, they reveal the extraordinary confidence put by Basil in his brother bishop. He had been healed by the intercessions of Eusebius, and now, all medical aid having failed Hypatius his brother, he sends him to Samosata to be under the care and prayers of

Eusebius and his brethren. It is remarkable that Eusebius was left undisturbed during the bitter persecutions of the orthodox by the emperor Valens. At length his hour came, and few pages in the history of the time are more vivid than those which portray the circumstances of his exile. Valens promised the Arian bp. Eudoxius, who had baptized him, that he would banish all who held contrary opinions. Thus Eusebius was expelled from Samosata (Theod. iv. 13). The imperial sentence ordered his instant departure to Thrace (*ib.* 14). Ceillier (v. 3) places this in 374. The officer who served the summons was bidden by Eusebius to conceal the cause of his journey. "For if the multitude (said Eusebius), who are all imbued with divine zeal, should learn your design, they would drown you, and I should have to answer for your death." After conducting worship, he took one domestic servant, a "pillow, and a book," and departed in the dead of night. The effect of his departure upon his flock is graphically described by Theodoret. The clamour, the weeping, the pursuit, the entreaties to return to Samosata and brave the wrath of the emperor, the humble submission of the bishop to the will of the prince on the ground of the authority of St. Paul, the refusal of costly gifts, the parting of the old man from his people, and the disappearance of the venerable confessor on his long and perilous journey to the Danube, are all told in a few striking sentences. Eusebius had excited a persistent and intense antagonism to the views of the Arians which assumed very practical forms. The Arian bp. Eunomius was avoided as if smitten with deadly and contagious pest. The very water he used in the public bath was wasted by the populace as contaminated. The repugnance being invincible, the poor man, inoffensive and gentle in spirit, retired from the unequal contest. His successor, Lucius, "a wolf and a deceiver of the flock," was received with scant courtesy. The children spontaneously burned a ball upon which the ass on which the Arian bishop rode had accidentally trodden. Lucius was not conquered by such manifestations, and took counsel with the Roman magistracy to banish all the Catholic clergy. Meanwhile Eusebius by slow stages reached the Danube when "the Goths were ravaging Thrace and besieging many cities." The most vigorous eulogium is passed upon his power to console others. At this dark time his faithfulness was a joy to the Eastern bishops. Basil congratulated Antiochus, a nephew of Eusebius, on the privilege of having seen and talked with such a man (*Ep.* clxviii.), and Gregory thought his prayers for their welfare must be as efficacious as those of a martyr. For Eusebius, concealed in exile, Basil contrived means of communication with his old flock. Numerous letters passed between the two, more in the tone of young lovers than of old bishops, and some interesting hints are given as to difficulty of communication. Eusebius was eagerly longing for letters, while Basil protested that he had written no fewer than four, which never reached their destination. To Eusebius (ccxxxix.) Basil complains bitterly of the lack of fair dealing on the part of the Western church, and mysterious hints are not unfrequently dropped as to the sentiment entertained at Rome with reference to himself, Eusebius, and Meletius. In 377 Dorotheus found that the two latter were, to the horror of Basil, reckoned at Rome as Arians. Eusebius suffered less from the barbarian ravages of the Goths than from this momentary assault on his honour. In 378 the persecuting policy of Valens was closed by his death. Gratian recalled the banished prelates, and gave peace to the Eastern church. Theodoret (*H. E.* v. 4, 5) expressly mentions the permission to Eusebius to return. Notwithstanding the apparently non-canonical character of the proceeding, Eusebius ordained numerous bishops on his way from Thrace to the Euphrates, including Acacius at Beroea, Theodotus at Hierapolis, Isidore at Cyrus, and Eulogius at Edessa. All these names were appended to the creed of Constantinople.

When taking part in the ordination of Maris at the little town of Dolica (Theod. *H. E.* v. 4), a woman charged with Arian passion hurled at Eusebius a brick, which fell upon his head, and wounded him fatally. Theodoret records that the aged bishop, in the spirit of the protomartyr and his Divine Lord, extorted promises from his attendants that they would make no search for his murderess. On June 22 the Eastern churches commemorate his so-called martyrdom. His nephew Antiochus probably succeeded to the bishopric of Samosata. Tillem. viii. 326; Ceillier, v. 5. [H.R.R.]

Eusebius (93), St., bp. of Vercellae (Vercelli), known for his zeal and sufferings in the cause of orthodoxy. He was born in Sardinia, ordained a "reader" at Rome, and in 340 consecrated bp. of Vercelli. St. Ambrose, in a letter to the church there (*Ep.* 63), especially commends him as the first Western bishop who joined monastic discipline with the discharge of episcopal duties. He took several of his clergy to live with him, and adopted a kind of monastic rule for their daily life. In 354 (Jaffé, *Reg. Pontif.* p. 15) he was asked by Liberius, bp. of Rome, to go with Lucifer of Cagliari and others to Constantius, to suggest the summoning of a council on the disputes between the Arians and the orthodox. The council was held in the next year at Milan. At first Eusebius absented himself, but ultimately yielded to the united solicitations of the Arian party, of Lucifer and Pancratius, the orthodox delegates of Liberius, and of the emperor. The proceedings were somewhat disorderly, and the action of the bp. of Milan was undecided. The practical question was whether the bishops present should sign a condemnation of Athanasius. Eusebius was so peremptory in refusing as to excite the anger of the Arianizing emperor, who banished him, together with some priests and deacons, to Scythopolis in Syria. Patrophilus, a leading Arian, was bp. there, and Eusebius calls him his "jailer." During his confinement here, two messengers arrived with money and assurances of goodwill from the churches of Vercelli and neighbourhood. In his reply Eusebius gave full particulars of his annoying treatment at Scythopolis. He was a troublesome prisoner, having twice all but starved himself to death because he would not accept provisions from Arian hands. After a while he was removed to Cappadocia, and thence to Egypt. From the Thebaid in Egypt he wrote to Gregory, bp. of Elvira in Spain, praising his anti-Arian constancy. Julian, succeeding Constantius in 361, permitted all banished bishops to return. Eusebius went to Alexandria to consult with Athanasius. The two bishops convoked a council in 362 at Alexandria. One of its objects was to end a schism at Antioch, and after it was over Eusebius went thither to bear a synodal letter or "tome" from the council to the Antiochenes. But Lucifer of Cagliari had preceded him and aggravated the schism by the hasty consecration of Paulinus as a rival bishop; and Eusebius immediately withdrew from Antioch. [MELETIUS; PAULINUS (6).] Lucifer renounced communion with Eusebius and with all who, in accordance with the decree of the Alexandrian council, were willing to receive back bishops who repented their connexion with Arian heresy. Leaving Antioch, Eusebius visited Eastern churches to confirm them in the orthodox faith. Thence he passed into Illyria, and so to Italy, which, in the words of Jerome, "put off its mourning on Eusebius's return." He now joined the zealous Hilary of Poictiers in endeavours to re-establish orthodoxy in the West. With this view they stirred up opposition to the Arianizing Auxentius, bp. of Milan, but were foiled by his profession of orthodoxy. This was in 364; nothing more is recorded of Eusebius until his death, placed by Jerome in 371.

His extant writings are three letters: one a brief reply to Constantius, that he would attend the council at Milan, but would do there whatever should seem to him right and according to the will of God; and the two to the church at Vercelli and to Gregory of Elvira. They are in Galland, *Bibl. Patrum*, and Migne, *Patr. Lat.* t. xii. Jerome says that Eusebius translated, omitting what was heterodox, the commentaries on the Psalms by his namesake of Caesarea; and also names him, with Hilary of Poictiers, as a translator of Origen and the same Eusebius; but nothing further is known of these translations. A famous *Codex Vercellensis* is thus described by Tregelles: "A MS. of the 4th cent., said to have been written by the hand of Eusebius bp. of Vercelli, where the codex is now preserved. The text is defective in several places, as might be supposed from its very great age. It was transcribed and pub. by Irici, at Milan, in 1748. . . . This MS. is probably the most valuable exemplar of the old Latin in its unaltered state." The chief authority for his Life is St. Jerome, who places him amongst his *Viri Illustres*, and alludes to him in his letters and elsewhere. There are several letters addressed to him by Liberius, and allusions to him in Athanasius. He is mentioned also by Rufinus, Theodoret, Sozomen, and Socrates. The *Sermones* relating to him among the works of Ambrose are admittedly spurious. In the *Journ. of Theol. Studies*, vol. i. p. 126, Mr. C. H. Turner raised the two questions whether Eusebius of Vercelli was the author of the Seven Books on the Trinity by the Pseudo-Vigilius of Thapsus, and whether he could have been the author of *Quicunque Vult*; and subsequently in the same vol. the Rev. A. E. Burn offered proof that Eusebius was the author of the work of Pseudo-Vigilius, but that there are strong reasons against supposing that he could have written *Quicunque*, although he says the latter theory throws new light on the history of the theological terms used in the creed. [J.LL.D.]

Eusebius (96), Aug. 14, presbyter, confessor at Rome A.D. 358, and by some styled martyr. From the earliest times his fame has been everywhere celebrated. A church dedicated to him is mentioned in the first council held at Rome under pope Symmachus, A.D. 498 (Mansi, viii. 236, 237). It was rebuilt by pope Zacharias, *c.* 742 (Anastas. *Lib. Pontif.* art. "Zacharias," No. 226). The facts of his history are very obscure. His Acts (Baluz. *Miscell.* t. ii. p. 141) relate that upon the recall of pope Liberius by Constantius, Eusebius preached against them both as Arians; and since the orthodox party, who now supported Felix, were excluded from all the churches, he continued to hold divine service in his own house. For this he was brought before Constantius and Liberius, when he boldly reproved the pope for falling away from Catholic truth. Constantius thereupon consigned him to a dungeon four feet wide, where he continued to languish for seven months and then died. He was buried by his friends and co-presbyters Orosius and Gregory, in the cemetery of Callistus, with the simple inscription "Eusebio Homini Dei." Constantius arrested Gregory for this, and consigned him to the same dungeon, where he also died, and was in turn buried by Orosius, by whom the Acts of Eusebius profess to have been written. The Bollandist and Tillemont point out grave historical difficulties in this narration, especially that Constantius, Liberius, and Eusebius never could have been in the city together. The whole matter is a source of trouble to Roman Catholic writers, because the saintly character of St. Eusebius, guaranteed by the Roman martyrology as revised by pope Gregory XIII., seems necessarily to involve the condemnation of Liberius. The Bollandists at great length vindicate the catholicity of Felix II., and are equally zealous champions of St. Eusebius. Tillemont and Hefele (*Hist. of Councils*, ii. § 81, "Pope Liberius and the Third Sirmian Formula") are equally decided opponents of Felix. [G.T.S.]

Eusebius (99), of Cremona, presbyter, a friend of St. Jerome, through whose writings he is known. He was with Jerome at Bethlehem in 393, and became the unconscious means of extending into Italy the strife concerning Origenism which had begun at Jerusalem. Epiphanius had written to John, bp. of Jerusalem, in vindication of his conduct on his recent visit to Palestine, A.D. 394. Eusebius, not knowing Greek, begged Jerome to translate it. This Jerome did in a cursory manner (*ad Pammachium, Ep.* 57, § 2, ed. Vall.), and the document was stolen from the cell of Eusebius by one whom Jerome believed to be in the service of Rufinus (*cont. Ruf.* iii. 4). Rufinus apparently sent the translated letter to Rome, accusing Jerome of having falsified the original. Eusebius remained at Bethlehem till Easter, 398, when he was obliged to return hastily to Italy.

On arriving in Rome, he became an agent of Jerome's party in the Origenistic controversy

He lived at first on good terms with Rufinus, who, however, afterwards accused him of having come to Rome "to bark against him." Rufinus was then engaged in translating the περὶ ἀρχῶν of Origen for the use of his friends, leaving out some of the most objectionable passages. Eusebius sent a copy of this to Bethlehem, where Jerome denounced it as a mistranslation. Rufinus replied that Eusebius had obtained an imperfect copy, either by bribing the copyist or by other wrong means, and had also tampered with the MS. St. Jerome, however, vehemently defends his friend from these accusations (*cont. Ruf.* iii. 5). Pope Anastasius being entirely ignorant of Origen and his teaching, Eusebius, together with Marcella and Pammachius, brought before him certain passages from Origen's writings (Anastasius ad Simplicianum in Jerome, *Ep.* 95, ed. Vall.), which so moved him that he at once condemned Origen and all his works. Eusebius being about to return to Cremona in 400, the pope charged him in the letter just quoted to Simplicianus, bp. of Milan, and he there set forth the same passages of Origen which he had laid before the pope. He was confronted, however, by Rufinus, who declared these passages to be false; and Eusebius continued his journey without having induced Simplicianus to condemn Origen. After this we hear nothing of Eusebius for some 20 years. He appears to have remained in Italy supporting Jerome's interests and corresponding with him. At the extreme end of Jerome's life we still find Eusebius writing to him and sending him books relating to the Pelagian heresy (ad Alyp. et Aug. *Ep.* 143), and receiving from Jerome the last of his Commentaries, that on Jeremiah (*Prol. to Comm. on Jer.* in vol. iv. 833). [W.H.F.]

Eusebius (126), eunuch, and grand chamberlain under Constantius II. Socrates (ii. 2, 16) relates that, after the death of Constantine in 337, Eusebius of Nicomedia and Theognis of Nicaea, bestirring themselves on behalf of the Arians, made use of a certain presbyter in high favour with Constantius, who had before been instrumental in recalling Arius from exile. He persuaded Eusebius the head chamberlain to adopt Arian opinions, and the rest of the chamberlains followed, and prevailed on the empress also. In 359 Eusebius was the mainspring of the plan of Eudoxius and others for dividing the council to be held on the subject of Arianism, making the Western bishops sit at Rimini, the Eastern at Seleucia; part of those in the secret were to sit at each council, and try to gain over their opponents to Arian views. Laymen of influence favoured the plan in order to please the chamberlain (Soz. *H. E.* iv. 16). On the death of Constantius in 361 Eusebius tried to curry favour with Julian by assuring him of the loyalty of the East (Amm. xxi. 15, § 4); but was unable to avert what Ammianus and Philostorgius represent as the just reward of his deeds. One of the first acts of Julian was to condemn him to death (*ib.* xxii. 3, § 12). Ammianus describes him as the prime mover of all the court intrigues of his day, and sarcastically calls the emperor one of his favourites (*ib.* xviii. 4, § 33). [W.M.S. AND M.F.A.]

Eustathius (3), bp. of Berrhoea in Syria, then of Antioch, *c.* A.D. 324-331, designated by Theodoret (*H. E.* i. 7) "the Great," one of the earliest and most vigorous opponents of Arianism, venerated for his learning, virtues, and eloquence (Soz. *H. E.* i. 2, ii. 19; Theod. *H. E.* i. 20), recognized by Athanasius as a worthy fellow-labourer for the orthodox faith (Athan. *Hist. Arian.* § 5). He was a native of Side in Pamphylia (Hieron. *de Vir. Illus.* c. 85). The title of "confessor" given him by Athanasius more than once (t. i. pp. 702, 812) indicates that he suffered in the persecution of Diocletian. As bp. of Berrhoea he was one of the orthodox prelates to whom Alexander of Alexandria sent a copy of his letter to Alexander of Constantinople, concerning Arius and his errors (Theod. *H. E.* i. 4). His translation from Berrhoea is placed by Sozomen after the council of Nicaea (Soz. *H. E.* i. 2). Theodoret states more correctly that he sat at that council as bp. of Antioch, and that his election to that see was the unanimous act of the bishops, presbyters, and faithful laity of the city and province (Theod. *H.E.* i. 7). According to Theodoret he was the immediate successor of Philogonius; but, according to the *Chronicle* of Jerome, Theophanes, and others, a certain Paulinus, not the Paulinus of Tyre, intervened for a short time (Tillem. vol. vii. p. 22, n. i. p. 646). At the council of Nicaea Eustathius occupied one of the first, if not the very first place among the assembled prelates (Facund. viii. 4). That he occupied the seat of honour at the emperor's right hand and pronounced the panegyrical address to Constantine is asserted by Theodoret (*H. E.* i. 7), but contradicted by Sozomen (*H. E.* i. 19), who assigns the dignity to Eusebius of Caesarea. Eusebius himself maintains a discreet silence, but he evidently wishes it to be inferred that the place of honour was his own (Eus. *de Vit. Const.* iii. 11). On his return to Antioch Eustathius banished those of his clergy suspected of Arian tenets and resolutely rejected all ambiguous submissions. Among those whom he refused to receive were Stephen, Leontius, ὁ ἀπόκοπος, and Eudoxius (who successively occupied his episcopal seat after his deposition), George of Laodicea, Theodosius of Tripolis, and Eustathius of Sebaste (Athan. *Hist. Arian.* § 5). In his writings and sermons he lost no opportunity of declaring the Nicene faith, and shewing its agreement with Holy Scripture. Theodoret (*H. E.* i. 8) specially mentions one of his sermons on Prov. viii. 22, and gives a long extract. The troubled relations of Eustathius with the two Eusebii may be dated from the council of Nicaea. At this synod Eusebius of Caesarea and Eustathius were rivals both in theological views and for favour with the emperor. To one of Eustathius's uncompromising orthodoxy, Eusebius appeared a foe to the truth, the more dangerous on account of his ability and the subtlety which veiled his heretical proclivities. Eustathius denounced him as departing from the Nicene faith. Eusebius retorted with the charge of Sabellianism. accusing Eustathius of holding one only personality in the Deity (Socr. *H. E.* i. 23; Soz. *H. E.* ii. 18; Theod. *H. E.* i. 21). Eusebius of Nicomedia and Theognis of Nicaea, in their progress of almost royal magnificence to

Jerusalem, passed through Antioch, and had a fraternal reception from Eustathius, and left with every appearance of friendship. Their inspection of the sacred buildings over, Eusebius returned to Antioch with a large cortège of partisan bishops—Aetius of Lydda, Patrophilus of Scythopolis, Theodotus of Laodicea, and Eusebius of Caesarea. The cabal entered Antioch with the air of masters. The plot had been maturing in their absence. Witnesses were prepared with charges against the bishop of incontinency and other gross crimes. Eustathius was summoned before this self-constituted tribunal, and, despite the opposition of the better-minded bishops and the absence of trustworthy evidence, was condemned for heresy, profligacy, and tyrannical conduct, and deposed from his bishopric. This aroused the indignation of the people of Antioch, who took up arms in defence of their beloved bishop. Some of the magistrates and other officials headed the movement. An artfully coloured account of these disturbances and Eustathius's complicity in them was transmitted to Constantine. A count was dispatched to quell the sedition and to put the sentence of the council into execution. Eustathius submitted to constituted authority. Accompanied by many of his clergy, he left Antioch without resistance or manifesting any resentment (Socr. *H. E.* i. 24; Soz. *H. E.* ii. 19; Theod. *H. E.* i. 21; Philost. *H. E.* ii. 7; Eus. *Vit. Const.* iii. 59). He appears to have spent the larger part of his exile at Philippi, where he died, *c.* 337. The date of his deposition was probably at the end of 330 or beginning of 331 (Tillem. *Mém. eccl.* vol. vii. note 3, *sur Saint Eustathe*; Wetter, *Restitutio verae Chronolog. rerum contra Arian. Gest.*; de Broglie, *L'Eglise et l'Empire*, c. vii.). The deposition of Eustathius led to a lamentable schism in the church of Antioch, which lasted nearly a century, not being completely healed till the episcopate of Alexander, A.D. 413-420.

Eustathius was a copious writer, and is much praised by early authorities (Soz. *H. E.* ii. 19; Hieron. *Ep.* 70 [84], ad Magnum). We possess only scattered fragments and one entire work, named by Jerome *de Engastrimytho adv. Origenem.* In this he attacks Origen with great vehemence, ridicules him as a πολυΐστωρ, and controverts his idea that the prophet Samuel was actually called up by the witch of Endor (Gall. *Vet. Patr. Bibl.* vol. iv., and Migne, *Patr.* vol. xviii. pp. 614 ff.). In *Texte und Untersuchungen* (1886), ii. 4, a new ed. of this treatise was edited by A. Zahn. Fabr. *Bibl. Graec.* vol. ix. pp. 131 ff. ed. Harles; Cave, *Hist. Lit.* i. 187; Migne, *Patr.* t. ix. pp. 131 ff.; Tillem. *u.s.* pp. 21 ff.; De Broglie, *op. cit.* t. ii. pp. 294 ff. [E.V.]

Eustathius (4), bp. of Sebaste (the modern *Siwas*) in Pontus, on the N. bank of the Halys, the capital of Armenia Minor (*c.* A.D. 357-380). Eustathius occupies a place more conspicuous than honourable in the unhappy dissensions between the adherents of the orthodox faith and the various shades of Arian, semi-Arian, and Anomoean heresy during the middle of the 4th cent. Originally a disciple of Arius, after repeated approaches to the Nicene faith, with occasional professions of accepting it, he probaby ended his days as a Eunomian heretic (Basil. *Ep.* 244 [82], § 9). Few in that epoch of conflicting creeds and formularies ever signed more various documents. Basil enumerates his signature of the formularies of Ancyra, Seleucia, Constantinople, Lampsacus, Nice in Thrace, and Cyzicus, which are sufficiently diverse to indicate the vagueness of his theology (Basil. *l.c.*). Eustathius thus naturally forfeited the confidence of all schools of theology. His personal character appears to have been high. There must have been something more than common in a man who could secure the affection and respect for many years of Basil the Great, as, in Basil's own strong language, "exhibiting something more than man" (*Ep.* 212 [370], § 2). As bishop he manifested his care for the sick and needy, and was unwearied in the fulfilment of duty. The system of coenobitic monasticism introduced by him into Asia Basil took as his model (Soz. *H. E.* iii. 14; Basil. *Ep.* 223 [79], § 3).

Eustathius was born in the Cappodocian Caesarea towards the beginning of the 4th cent. He studied at Alexandria under the heresiarch Arius (*c.* A.D. 320) (Basil. *Ep.* 223 [79], § 3; 244 [82], § 9; 263 [74], § 3). On leaving Alexandria he repaired to Antioch, where he was refused ordination on account of his Arian tenets by his orthodox namesake (Athan. *Solit.* p. 812). He was afterwards ordained by Eulalius (*c.* 331), but very speedily degraded by him for refusing to wear the clerical dress (Socr. *H. E.* ii. 43, Soz. *H. E.* iv. 24). From Antioch Eustathius returned to Caesarea, where he obtained ordination from the orthodox bp. Hermogenes, on declaring his unqualified adhesion to the Nicene faith (Basil. *Ep.* 244 [82], § 9; 263 [74], § 3). On the death of Hermogenes, Eustathius repaired to Constantinople and attached himself to Eusebius, the bishop there, "the Coryphaeus of the Arian party" (Basil. *ll.cc.*). By him he was a second time deposed (*c.* A.D. 342) on the ground of some unspecified act of unfaithfulness to duty (Soz. *H. E.* iv. 24). He retired again to Caesarea, where, carefully concealing his Arian proclivities, he sought to commend himself to the bishop, Dianius. His subsequent history till he became bp. of Sebaste is almost a blank. We must, however, assign to it the theological argument held by him and Basil of Ancyra with the audacious Anomoean, Aetius, who is regarded by Basil as in some sense Eustathius's pupil (Basil. *Ep.* 123, § 5). It was certainly during this period that Eustathius and his early friend the presbyter AERIUS founded coenobitic monachism in Armenia and the adjacent provinces (Epiphan. *Haer.* 75, § 2). The rule laid down by him for the government of his religious communities of both sexes contained extravagances alluded to by Socrates and Sozomen, which are not unlikely to have been the cause, otherwise unknown, of his excommunication by the council of Neo-Caesarea (Socr. *H. E.* ii. 43; Soz. *H. E.* iv. 24). While Eustathius was regulating his coenobitic foundations (*c.* 358) he was visited by Basil, who records the delight with which he saw the coarse garments, the girdle, the sandals of undressed hide, and witnessed the self-denying and laborious lives of Eustathius and his followers. His admiration for such a victory over the world and the flesh dispelled all suspicions of Arian sentiments, and the desire to spread them secretly, which had been rumoured (Basil. *Ep.* 223 [79], § 3). After Basil had retired to the banks of the Iris and commenced his own monastic life, he and his brother Gregory received frequent visits from Eustathius, who, with them, would visit Annesi, the residence of their mother Macrina, and spend there whole days and nights in friendly theological discussion (*ib.* § 5).

Eustathius's episcopate must have begun before 357, when Athanasius speaks of him as a bishop (Athan. *Orat. in Arian.* i. p. 290 ; *Solit.* p. 812). He was made bp. of Sebaste, according to the same authority, by the Arian party, who hoped to find him an able and facile instrument. His early companion Aerius was a candidate for the bishopric, and felt very mortified by his failure. Eustathius shewed him the utmost consideration, ordained him presbyter, and appointed him manager of a refuge for the poor, the foundation of which was one of the first acts of his episcopate. The final rupture between them is detailed under AERIUS. Somewhere about this time we may place Eustathius's conviction of perjury in the council of Antioch (see Socr. *H. E.* iv. 24), and his deposition by the obscure council of Melitene in Armenia *c.* A.D. 357 (Basil. *Ep.* 263 [74]). Neither of these events appears to have entailed any lasting consequences. Eustathius was one of the prelates at the semi-Arian synod summoned at Ancyra by George of Laodicea, before Easter A.D. 358, to check the alarming spread of Anomoean doctrines, and he, with Basil of Ancyra and Eleusius of Cyzicus, conveyed the synodal letter, equally repudiating the Anomoean and Homoousian doctrines, and declaring for the Homoiousion, to Constantius at Sirmium (Soz. *H. E.* iv. 13, 14 ; Basil. *Ep.* 263 [74], § 3). When the council met at Seleucia on Sept. 27, 359, Eustathius occupied a prominent place in its tumultuous and indecisive proceedings, and was the head of the ten episcopal deputies, Basil of Ancyra, Silvanus of Tarsus, and Eleusius of Cyzicus being other chief members, sent to Constantinople to lay their report before Constantius. Stormy discussions followed, in which Eustathius led the semi-Arians as against the pure Arians. He vehemently denounced the blasphemies of the bold Anomoean, Eudoxius, bp. of Antioch, and produced a formulary of faith declaring the dissimilarity of the Father and the Son, which he asserted to be by Eudoxius. All seemed to augur the triumph of orthodoxy when the arrival of Valens and Ursacius from Ariminum announcing the subjugation of the Western bishops and the general proscription of the Homoousion suddenly changed the scene. Constantius was overjoyed at the unexpected success, and after a protracted discussion, compelled Eustathius and the other Seleucian deputies to sign the fatal formulary. It was then, in Jerome's words, "ingemuit totus orbis et se esse Arianum miratus est" (Hieron. *in Lucif.* 19). This base concession profited the recreants little. The emperor summoned a synod, of which Acacius was the ruling spirit, at Constantinople in Jan. 360. Eustathius was deposed in a tyrannical manner, with Cyril of Jerusalem, Basil of Ancyra, Eleusius of Cyzicus, and other important prelates. Eustathius was not even allowed to defend himself. His former deposition by Eulalius was held sufficient (Socr. *H. E.* ii. 41-43 ; Soz. *H. E.* iv. 24). Constantius confirmed the sentence, exiled the bishops, and gave their sees to others. The death of Constantius in 361 and the accession of Julian witnessed the recall of Eustathius with the other banished bishops. He immediately repudiated his signature to the creed of Ariminum, and did all he could to shew his horror of pure Arianism. Sozomen tells us that, with Eleusius, Sophronius, and others of like mind, he held several synods, condemning the partisans of Acacius, denouncing the creed of Ariminum, and asserting the Homoiousion as the true mean between the Homoousion of the West and the Anomoeon of Aetius and his followers (*H. E.* v. 14). With the accession of Valens in 364, Arianism once more assumed ascendancy in the East. The semi-Arian party, or Macedonians as they now began to be called, met by imperial permission in council at Lampsacus A.D. 365, under the presidency of Eleusius, and repudiated the Acacian council of Constantinople (360) and the creed of Ariminum, renewed the confession of Antioch (*In Encaeniis*), and pronounced sentence of deposition on Eudoxius and Acacius (Socr. *H. E.* iv. 2-4 ; Soz. *H. E.* vi. 7). These proceedings irritated Valens, who required them to hold communion with Eudoxius, and, on their refusal, sentenced them to fine and banishment, giving their sees to others. To escape annihilation, the Macedonians sent deputies, Eustathius being one, to the Western emperor Valentinian and Liberius, bp. of Rome, who had repented his lapse in A.D. 357, offering to unite with them in faith. Before they arrived, Valentinian had left for Gaul, and Liberius, at first looking coldly on them as Arians, refused to receive them. On their giving a written adhesion to the Nicene Creed and the Homoousion, he received them into communion, and gave them letters in his name and that of the Western church to the prelates of the East, expressing his satisfaction at the proof he had received of the identity of doctrine between East and West (Socr. *H. E.* iv. 12 ; Soz. *H. E.* vi. 11). No mention was made of the new Macedonian heresy concerning the Holy Spirit, now infecting the Eastern church, of which Eustathius and the other deputies were among the chief promulgators. Eustathius and his companions at once repaired to Sicily, where a synod of bishops, on their profession of orthodoxy, gave them letters of communion. They then returned to their own country. A synod of orthodox bishops was assembled in 367 at Tyana, to receive the letters of communion from the West and other documents (Soz. *l.c.* ; Basil. *Ep.* 244 [82], § 5). Eustathius and his fellow-delegates, now recognized as true Catholics, were acknowledged as the rightful bishops of their sees. A council summoned at Tarsus to consolidate this happy reunion was prohibited by Valens, who, having committed himself to the Arian party, issued an edict expelling all bishops restored by Julian. Eustathius, to save himself, signed a formula at Cyzicus of Homoiousian character, which also denied the divinity of the Holy Spirit. Basil says tersely of Eustathius and his party, "they saw Cyzicus and returned with a different creed" (Basil. *u.s.* and § 9; 226 [73]).

On Basil's elevation to the episcopate in 370 Eustathius exhibited great joy, and professed an earnest desire to be of service to his friend. He recommended persons as fellow-helpers who, as Basil bitterly complains, turned out to be spies of his actions and words, interpreting all in a malevolent sense and reporting to their chief (*ib.* 223 [79], § 3). For their subsequent bitter relations, see BASILIUS OF CAESAREA. Eustathius heaped calumnies on the head of his former associate, openly charging him with Apollinarian and other heretical views, and encouraged the clergy of his diocese and province to form a rival communion. Demosthenes, the Vicar of the Prefect, an old enemy of Basil, strenuously forwarded this object. In 376 he visited Sebaste and other chief places in the province, oppressing Basil's adherents, whom he compelled to undertake onerous and costly public duties, and loading the followers of Eustathius with the highest honours (*ib.* 237 [264], § 2). Eustathius, seeing Arianism in the ascendant, openly sought communion with those whom he had repeatedly denounced. His deposition at Constantinople was not forgotten by the Arians, who had not hitherto recognized him as a canonical bishop. He now sought their goodwill by humiliating concessions. He had overthrown the altars of Basilides, bp. of Gangra, as an Arian, but now begged admission to his communion. He had treated the people of Amasea as heretics, excommunicating Elpidius for holding intercourse with them, and now earnestly sought their recognition. At Ancyra, the Arians refusing him public recognition, he submitted to communicate with them in private houses. When the Arian bishops met in synod at Nyssa he sent a deputation of his clergy to invite them to Sebaste, conducted them through the province with every mark of honour, allowed them to preach and celebrate the Eucharist in his churches, and withheld no mark of the most intimate communion (*ib.* 257 [72], § 3). These humiliations had but tardy and partial success in obtaining his public acknowledgment by the dominant ecclesiastics. His efforts to secure Arian favour and his effrontery in trading upon his former recognition by Liberius extorted from Basil a vehement letter of remonstrance, addressed to the bp. of Rome and the other Western bishops, depicting the evils inflicted on the Eastern church by the wolves in sheep's clothing, and requesting Liberius to declare publicly the terms on which Eustathius had been admitted to communion (*ib.* 263 [74], § 3). All Basil's efforts to obtain this mark of sympathy and brotherly recognition from the West were fruitless. He continued to be harassed by the unscrupulous attacks of Eustathius till his death in 379. If the see was vacated by his death, and not, as Hefele holds, with much probability, by his deposition at Gangra, Eustathius died soon after. In 380 Peter became bp. of Sebaste, and thus Basil's brother replaced Basil's most dangerous enemy.

The synod of Gangra, of uncertain date [*D. C. A.*, *s.v.*], is intimately connected with the name of Eustathius. The identity of the Eustathius there condemned with the bp. of Sebaste, though affirmed by every ancient authority, has been denied by Blondel (*De la primauté*, p. 138), Baronius (*Annal.* iii. ann. 361, n. 53), Du Pin (*Nouvelle bibliothèque*, ii. 339), and called in question by Tillemont (*Mém. eccl.* ix. note 28, *S. Basile*); but on careful investigation Hefele (*Hist. of the Church Councils*, ii. 325 ff. Engl. trans.) scouts the idea that another Eustathius is intended. C. F. Loofs, *Eust. of Seb.*, Halle, 1898. [E.V.]

Eustathius (22), bp. of Berytus (Beyrout), a time-serving prelate attached to the court, who kept steadily in view the aggrandizement and independence of his see of Berytus, then suffragan to Tyre. As a bishop of some consideration for theological knowledge, he was appointed commissioner, with Photius of Tyre and Uranius of Himera, by Theodosius II., A.D. 448, to examine the tenets of Ibas of Edessa, charged by the monastic party with favouring the Nestorian heresy. This commission, dated Oct. 26, 448, and addressed to Damasus, the secretary of state (Labbe, *Conc.* iv. 638), was opened at Berytus, Feb. 1, A.D. 449, in the residence of Eustathius, recently erected by him near his magnificent new church. Ibas indignantly disclaimed the blasphemies attributed to him, and produced a protest, signed by a large number of his clergy, that they had never heard him utter words contrary to the faith (*ib.* p. 637). The accusation broke down. But the investigation was revived a week or two afterwards at Tyre (*ib.* 635). Eustathius and his brother commissioners drew up a concordat, which was signed, Feb. 25, by Ibas and his accusers, and countersigned by Eustathius and Photius (*ib.* 632). At the second council of Ephesus, the disgraceful "Robbers' Synod," Aug. 8, 449, Eustathius, Eusebius of Ancyra, and Basil of Seleucia were the imperial commissioners (*ib.* 1079). Eustathius lent all his influence to Dioscorus and the dominant party against the venerable Flavian, voting for the rehabilitation of Eutyches and declaring that he had stated the true faith in perfect conformity to the doctrine of godliness (*ib.* 262). In 450, through the influence of pope Leo and his legates at Constantinople, Eustathius's name was erased from the diptychs of the church as an accomplice in Flavian's violent death. He and his associates, however, were allowed to retain their sees, in the hope that this leniency might lead them to repent (Leo Magn. *Ep.* 60). The feeble Theodosius II. being now replaced by the orthodox and vigorous Marcian, Eustathius found it politic to change his camp, and at the council of Chalcedon promptly abandoned Dioscorus, declaring his agreement in faith with Flavian, and with exaggerated expressions of penitence asking pardon for his share in the acts of the recent synod (Labbe, iv. 141, 176, 177). The abject humiliation of Eustathius and his party prevailed with the orthodox bishops, who acquitted them as mere tools of Dioscorus and received them as brothers (*ib.* 508-509). At a later session of the council, Oct. 20, the issue between Eustathius and Photius of Tyre was discussed (*ib.* 539). As a reward for his support of the court party at the "Latrocinium," Eustathius had obtained from Theodosius a decree giving metropolitical rank to Berytus (Lupus, *in Canon.* 950). Flavian's successor Anatolius, together with Maximus of Antioch and other court bishops, had consequently, at the close of 449, dismembered the diocese of Tyre and assigned five churches to the formerly suffragan see of Berytus (Labbe, iv. 542-546). Photius, disregarding this, and continuing to consecrate bishops for these churches, was excommunicated by Anatolius, and the prelates he had consecrated were deposed and degraded by Eustathius (*ib.* 530). Photius submitted to this interference on the threat of deposition, protesting that he did so by constraint. The council supported him, maintained the ancient prerogatives of the metropolitical see of Tyre, and pronounced the acts of Eustathius void.

When in 457 the emperor Leo, anxious to give peace to the church of Alexandria, dealt with the intrusion of Timothy Aelurus, Eustathius was consulted, and joined in the condemnation of that intruding patriarch (*ib.* 890). The church built by Eustathius at Berytus is described by Zacharias Scholasticus as *de mundi opificio*. Tillem. *Mém. eccl.* xv.; Le Quien, *Oriens Christ.* ii. 818; Cave, *Hist. Lit.* i. 440. [E.V.]

Eustochium, 3rd daughter of PAULA, the friend of Jerome, from whose writings all that is known of her is gathered. Born probably *c.* 370, she had shared from her earliest days the ascetic views of her mother, and was confirmed in them by frequenting the house of Marcella (Hieron. i. 952, ed. Vallarsi). Her uncle Hymettius, with his wife Praetextata (see Thierry's *St. Jérôme*, i. 161), endeavoured to wean her from these by inviting her to their house, changing her attire, and placing her among the mirrors and the flattery of a patrician reception-room (Hieron. i. 394, 683); but she resisted their seductions and took the vow of perpetual virginity, being the first Roman lady of noble birth to do so (i. 394). Jerome addressed to her his celebrated treatise *de Virginitate Servandâ* (i. 88), in which vivid pictures of Roman society enforce the superior sanctity of the state of virginity. This treatise excited great animosity against Jerome, and was one cause of his leaving Rome and returning to Palestine. Paula and Eustochium resolving to go there also, embarked in 385 at Portus. At Bethlehem they built and managed the hospice and convent, and from her mother's death in 404 Eustochium was its head till her own death in 418, two years before that of Jerome. Many passages in Jerome's writings give a picture of her character and manner of life. Small in stature (i. 290), she had great courage and decision of character (i. 394), and followed the ascetic teaching of Jerome and her mother with unwavering confidence and enthusiasm (i. 402, 403). She spoke Greek and Latin with equal facility, and learnt Hebrew to sing the Psalms in the original (i. 720). Jerome praises her skill in the training of virgins, whom she led in all acts of devotion (i. 290) and to whom she set an example by undertaking all menial offices (i. 403). She was eager to increase her knowledge of the Scriptures, and to her importunity Jerome ascribes the writing of many of his commentaries, which were dedicated to her and her mother, and afterwards to her and her niece the younger Paula, who, with the younger Melania, was her coadjutor in her convent work and her study of Scripture. She is reckoned a saint in the Roman church, her festival being Sept. 28. [W.H.F.]

Eustochius (6), patriarch of Jerusalem, in succession to Peter, and, according to Papebroch, from A.D. 544 to 556. On the death of Peter, Eustochius, oeconomus of the church of Alexandria but residing at Constantinople, was favoured by the emperor Justinian in preference to Macarius, an Origenist, who had been first elected. At the synod of Constantinople, 553, Eustochius was represented by three legates, Stephanus bp. of Raphia, Georgius bp. of Tiberias, Damasus bp. of Sozusa or Sozytana (Mansi, ix. 173 C.); and when the acts in condemnation of Origenism were sent by the emperor to Jerusalem, all the bishops of Palestine except Alexander of Abila confirmed them. But in the monasteries of that province, and especially in that named the New Laura, the partisans of the proscribed opinions grew daily more powerful, notwithstanding the resolute efforts of the patriarch against them. In 555, after eight months of persistent admonition, Eustochius went in person, with the dux Anastasius, to the New Laura, and forcibly expelled the whole body, replacing them by 60 monks from the principal laura and 60 from other orthodox monasteries of the desert, under the prior Joannes. Origenism was thus rooted out of Palestine. According to Victor Tununensis, Eustochius was removed from the patriarchate, and Macarius restored. Cyrillus Scythopol. in Coteler. *Monum. Eccles. Graec.* iii. 373; Evagr. *H. E.* iv. 37, 38; Victor Tunun. in *Patr. Lat.* lxviii. 962 A; Theoph. *Chronog.* A.M. 6060; Papebroch, *Patriarch. Hierosol.* in Boll. *Acta SS.* Intro. to vol. iii. of May, p. xxvii.; Le Quien, *Or. Chr.* iii. 210. Pagi (ann. 561 iii.) discusses the chronology. See also Clinton, *F. R.* 537, 557. [C.H.]

Euthalius (5), a deacon of Alexandria, afterwards bp. of Sulca; fl. A.D. 459. This date is confirmed by the fact that his works are dedicated to Athanasius the Younger, who was bp. of Alexandria about that time. Euthalius appears to have been then a deacon, devoted to the study of the N.T. text. He is now best known as the author of the Euthalian Sections.

The books of N.T. were written without any division into chapters, verses, or words. The first steps towards such a convenient division seem to have proceeded from the wish for easy reference to parallel passages. This was done by what are known as the Ammonian Sections, together with the Eusebian Canons. [EUSEBIUS OF CAESAREA.] Ammonius of Alexandria, in the 3rd cent., is generally credited with dividing the gospels into sections, but the principle had not been applied to other books of N.T. Euthalius introduced a system of division into all those not yet divided, except the Apocalypse, which spread rapidly over the whole Greek church and has become, by its presence or absence, a valuable test of the antiquity of a MS. In the Epp. of St. Paul, Euthalius tells us, he adopted the scheme of a certain "father," whose name is nowhere given. But by his other labours, and the further critical apparatus which he supplied, Euthalius procured for it the acceptance it soon obtained. In *Romans* there were 19 capitula; in *Galatians*, 12; in *Ephesians*, 10; in *I. Thessalonians*, 7;

in *II. Thessalonians*, 6; in *Hebrews*, 22; in *Philemon*, 2; and so on.

Three points in connexion with the text especially occupied Euthalius.

(1) The Larger Sections or Lessons. Fixed lessons for public worship no doubt passed from the synagogue into the Christian church, at least as soon as the canon was settled. But there seems to have been little or no uniformity in them. Individual churches had divisions of their own. The scheme proposed by Euthalius, however, speedily became general in all Greek-speaking churches. The whole N.T., except the Gospels and Apocalypse, was divided into 57 portions of very varying length (in *Acts* there were 16; in the Pauline Epp. 31; 5 in *Rom.*; 5 in *I. Cor.*; 4 in *II. Cor.*; in the Catholic Epp. 10; 2 in *James*; 2 in *I. Pe.*; 1 in *II. Pe.*, etc.) Of these, 53 were for Sundays, which seem alone to have been provided for in the Alexandrian *Synaxes*, and Mill supposes that the other 4 were for Christmas, Good Friday, Easter, and Epiphany (Proleg. in N.T. p. 90).

(2) The smaller divisions were the well-known στιχοι—*i.e.* "lines" (Lat. *versus*), each containing either a few words complete in themselves, or as much as it was possible to read without effort at one breath. Like that of the capitula formerly spoken of, the plan of these "verses" was not introduced by Euthalius. It had already been adopted in some of the poetical books, and in poetical parts of the prose books of the O.T. The LXX had occasionally employed it. It had been sanctioned by Origen. The Vulgate had used it, and it is found in the psalms of the Vatican and Sinaitic MSS. It had been partially applied to N.T., for Origen speaks of the 100 στίχοι of *II.* and *III. John*, of a few in St. Paul's Epistles, and very few in *I. John*; while Eustathius of Antioch, in the 4th cent., is said to reckon 135 from John viii. 59 to x. 31 (Scrivener, *Intro. to Codex D*, p. 17). But these figures shew that many of these divisions cannot have been στίχοι in the strict sense, but of very unequal length, and generally much larger. What was before partially and imperfectly done Euthalius extended upon better principles and with greater care. In *Rom.* he made 920 such στίχοι; in *Gal.* 293; in *Eph.* 312; in *I. Thess.* 193; in *II. Thess.* 106; in *Heb.* 703; in *Philemon*, 37; and so on.

(3) The third part of his labour was an enumeration of all the quotations from O.T., and even from profane writers, found in those books of N.T. of which he treated. These he numbered in one catalogue; assigned to the various books whence they were taken in a second; and quoted at length in a third. If we may look upon the *Argumenta* as really the work of Euthalius, and not, as Zacagnius argues (*Praef.* p. 60), as the production of a later hand, he went also into the substance and meaning of the books edited by him, as the *Argumenta* contain short and excellent summaries of them. Euthalius also wrote a short Life of St. Paul, prefixed to his work on the 14 epistles of that apostle, but it is bald and meagre. It has been said that he also wrote comments on *Acts* and *Luke*; and that in an ancient catena on *Romans* there were fragments of his writings; but these statements seem to be ncorrect (*ib.* p. 71).

In later life he became a bishop, and was known as Episcopus Sulcensis. Scrivener suggests Sulci in Sardinia as the only see of that name (*Intr.* p. 53, n. 1), but so distant a place is unlikely. Zacagnius thinks that Sulca may represent Psilca, a city of the Thebaid near Syene; but Galland throws doubt on this, and the point must be left unsolved.

His works remained long unknown, but in 1698 they were ed. and pub. at Rome by Laurentius Alexander Zacagnius, praefect of the Vatican Library, in vol. i. of his *Collectanea Monumentorum Veterum Ecclesiae Graecae ac Latinae*, in the long preface of which different questions relating to Euthalius are discussed with much care. This ed. has been printed in Galland (*Biblioth. Pat.* x. 197) and in Migne (*Patr. Gk.* lxxxv. 621). Notices of Euthalius may be found in the *Prolegomena of N.T.* of Wetstein and Mill, and in Scrivener's *Intro. to the Criticism of N.T.* But much light has recently been thrown on Euthalius by Dean Armitage Robinson in his "Euthaliana" (*Texts and Stud.* iii. 3), and in an article "Recent Work on Euthalius" in the *Journ. of Theol. Stud.* vol. vi. p. 87, Oct. 1904. In the latter art. the recent work on the subject by Von Soden and Zahn is noticed. [W.M.]

Eutherius (2), bp. of Tyana, a leader of the Nestorians at the council of Ephesus, A.D. 431, and for some time afterwards. Before the council he was in active correspondence with John of Antioch, about the alleged Apollinarianism of Cyril of Alexandria and his adherents (Theod. *Ep.* 112; Migne, *Patr. Gk.* lxxxiii. 1310). His name occurs in the various documents addressed to, and issued by, the members of his party collectively at this council. On July 18 John and his adherents were deposed and excommunicated, and Eutherius among them (*Act. Co. Eph.* acta v. 654); his sentence being confirmed at Constantinople before the end of the year. After his return home we find him in friendly correspondence with Firmus of Caesarea, notwithstanding the part Firmus had taken in his excommunication (Firm. *Ep.* 23; *Patr. Gk.* lxxvii. 1498). Firmus was sent to Tyana to ordain a successor to Eutherius, and met with great opposition from the citizens, who were much attached to their bishop. Longras also, the imperial officer in command of the Isaurian troops there, interfered; and both Firmus and the person whom he had ordained were compelled to flee. The newly ordained bishop renounced his orders, and seems to have returned to lay life (Theod. *Ep. Hypomnesticon Alex. Hierapolis Synodicon*, c. 45). After the reconciliation of Cyril and John of Antioch, Eutherius wrote to John to remonstrate with him on his inconsistency and want of loyalty to what he once contended for (*ib.* c. 73, *u.s.* 681); to Alexander of Hierapolis, who was opposed to the reconciliation, a long letter ably defending the position which they and others were still determined to maintain (*ib.* c. 201, *u.s.* 815); and to Helladius bp. of Tarsus, who had also written to Alexander, to encourage him in his opposition, expressing great joy at what he had done (*ib.* c. 74, *u.s.* 684). Eutherius was ultimately banished to Scythopolis, and from thence to Tyre, where he died (*ib.* c. 190, *u.s.*).

He is the author of a treatise in 17 chapters, with a prefatory letter addressed to Eustathius bp. of Parnassus, which Photius ascribed to Theodoret (Phot. *Biblioth.* c. xlvi. Migne, *Patr. Gk.* ciii. 79), and which has since been attributed by some to Maximus the Martyr, and by others to Athanasius (Garner's notes on Marius Mercator in *Patr. Lat.* xlviii. 759, 1086, 1087; Fabricius, *Biblioth. Graec.* ed. Harles, viii. 304), in which he subjects the "Scholia" of Cyril of Alexandria, "de Incarnatione Unigeniti" (Mar. Merc. *u.s.* 1066) to elaborate and searching criticism. [T.W.D.]

Euthymius (4), abbat in Palestine, born in 377, at Melitene in Armenia, and placed at an early age under the direction of its bishop, Otreius. After his ordination as priest he was placed in charge of all the monasteries in and near the place. Finding this too great an interruption to his meditations, in his 29th year he escaped to Jerusalem to visit the holy places, and found a home with a community of separate monks at Pharan, 6 miles from Jerusalem. With another hermit, Theoctistus, he used to take long walks into the desert of Cutila at sacred seasons. On one of these occasions, in the 5th year of his stay at Pharan, they came to a tremendous torrent with a cavern on one of its banks. Here they determined to live, lost to the world. They were, however, discovered by some shepherds, who sent them gifts. The fathers of Pharan also found them out, and came at times to see them. About 411 Euthymius began to receive disciples. They turned the cavern into a church, and built a monastery on the side of the ravine. Theoctistus had charge of it. In 420 Euthymius erected a laura, like that of Pharan, on the road from Jerusalem to Jericho, where he would see inquirers on Saturdays and Sundays, and his advice was always given with captivating sweetness and humility. In 428 the church of his laura was consecrated by Juvenal, the first patriarch of Jerusalem, accompanied by the presbyter Hesychius and the celebrated Passarion, governor of a monastery in Jerusalem.

A new turn was given to the life of Euthymius by a cure which he effected for Terebon, son of Aspebetus, prince of the Saracens, who, hearing of his fame, brought the afflicted boy to his gloomy retreat with a large train of followers. The prayers of Euthymius are said to have restored health to the patient, and the whole company believed on the Lord Jesus. Euthymius ordered a little recess for water to be hollowed out in the side of the cave, and baptized them on the spot, the father taking the name of Peter. His brother-in-law Maris joined the community of anchorets, bestowing all his wealth for the enlargement of the buildings. The story spread over Palestine and the neighbouring countries, and Euthymius was besieged with applications for medical assistance and prayer.

Peter, bp. of the Saracens, on his way to the council at Ephesus, A.D. 431, visited Euthymius, who exhorted him to unite with Cyril of Alexandria and Acacius of Melitene, and to do in regard to the creed whatever seemed right to those prelates. When the council of Chalcedon issued its decrees (451), two of his disciples, Stephen and John, who had been present, brought them to their master. The report of his approval spread through the desert, and all the recluses would have shared it but for the influence of the monk Theodosius, whose life and doctrine appear to have been equally unsatisfactory, who even tried hard to persuade Euthymius to reject Chalcedon, but without success.

The empress Eudoxia, an energetic Eutychian, after the death of her husband in 450, went to Jerusalem, and being urged by her brother Valerius to become reconciled to the Catholic church, determined to consult Euthymius. She built a tower about 4 miles S. of his laura, and sent to him Cosmas, guardian of the so-called True Cross at Constantinople, and Anastasius, a bishop. Euthymius came; and after giving his blessing to the empress, advised her that the violent death of her son-in-law, Valentinian, the irruption of the Vandals, the captivity of her daughter Eudoxia and of her grandchildren, might all be attributed to her Eutychian opinions. She should abjure her schism, and embrace the communion of Juvenal, patriarch of Jerusalem. The empress obeyed, and her example was followed by a multitude of monks and laymen. A celebrated anchoret also, Gerasimus, owed his separation from Eutychianism to Euthymius. Euthymius died in 473; his obsequies were celebrated by the patriarch Anastatius and a large number of clergy, among whom are mentioned Chrysippus, guardian of the Cross, and a deacon named Fidus. See Cotelier's ed. of the *Vita Euthymii* by Cyrillus Scythopolitanus (Cot. *Eccl. Graec. Monum.* iv. 1, Paris, 1692). [W.M.S.]

Eutyches (4) and **Eutychianism.** Eutyches was archimandrite of a monastery near Constantinople. For 70 years (as he told pope Leo) he had lived a monastic life, and during 30 out of them had presided over his 300 monks. He was a staunch upholder of the views and conduct of Cyril of Alexandria, who had even sent him, as a special mark of favour, a copy of the Acts of the council of Ephesus, A.D. 431. By whom he was first accused, whether by Theodoret in his *Eranistes*, or by his former friend, Eusebius of Dorylaeum, or by Domnus of Antioch, it seems difficult to decide (cf. Hefele, ii. 319; Martin, 75-78); but it is clear that to Eusebius are due the definite charges first brought against him at Constantinople in 448.

Flavian, who succeeded Proclus in 447 as archbishop, convened a synod in Constantinople on Nov. 8, 448, to consider some questions between the metropolitan of Sardis and two of his suffragan bishops. Eusebius of Dorylaeum was present, and at its conclusion complained that Eutyches defamed "the holy Fathers and himself, a man who had never been suspected of heresy," alleging himself prepared to convict Eutyches of being untrue to the orthodox faith. Flavian listened in astonishment, and suggested that Eusebius should first privately discuss with Eutyches the points in dispute. Eusebius retorted that he had already done this unsuccessfully; he, therefore, implored the synod to summon Eutyches before them, not only to induce him to give up his views, but to prevent infection spreading further. Two deputies, a priest and a deacon, were instructed to read to Eutyches the complaint, and to invite him to attend the synod, which met again on Nov. 12. Eusebius asked first for the recital of (*a*) Cyril's first letter to Nestorius, (*b*) the approbation of that letter by the council of Ephesus, and (*c*) Cyril's letter to John of Antioch; secondly, that all present should express acceptance of these documents as true expositions of the Nicene Creed. Flavian and the bishops present accepted these propositions, and a resolution to the same effect was sent to the absentees for their approval and signature. The synod professed its belief in "Jesus Christ the only-begotten Son of God, perfect God and perfect man, of a reasonable soul and body subsisting, begotten before all ages, without beginning; of the Father according to the Godhead, but in these last days for our sake and for our salvation born of the Virgin Mary, according to the manhood; consubstantial with the Father, as touching His Godhead, and consubstantial with the mother, as touching His manhood." "We confess that Jesus Christ, after the Incarnation, was of two natures in one Hypostasis and in one Person; one Christ, one Son, one Lord. Whosoever asserts otherwise, him we exclude from the clergy and the church" (Mansi, vi. 679). At the third session, Nov. 15, the deputies announced that Eutyches refused to appear before the synod, alleging that Eusebius had long been his enemy, and had grossly slandered him, for he (Eutyches) was ready to assent to and subscribe the statements of the holy Fathers at Nicaea and Ephesus. Certain expressions used by them were, in his opinion, mistakes; in such cases he turned to Holy Scripture, as a safer guide than the Fathers. He worshipped one nature, and that the nature of God incarnate. Reading from a little book which he fetched, Eutyches then, according to the deputies, first protested against a statement falsely ascribed to him—viz. that the Logos had brought His body from heaven—and next asserted his inability to find in the writings of the Fathers their belief that our Lord Jesus Christ subsisted of two Persons united in one Hypostasis; adding, that even if he did find such a statement, he must decline to accept it, as not being in Holy Scripture. In his belief, He Who was born of the Virgin Mary was very God and very man, but His body was not of like substance with ours. Eusebius struck in, "This is quite enough to enable us to take action against Eutyches; but let him be summoned a second time." Two priests were now sent to tell Eutyches that his replies had given great offence; he must come and explain them, as well as meet the charges originally brought against him. They took with them a note saying that if he still refused to appear, it might be necessary to deal with him according to canonical law, and that his determination not to leave his cell was simply an evasion. During their absence, Eusebius brought forward a further charge. Eutyches, he asserted, had written and circulated among the monks a little book on the faith, to which he had requested their signatures. The statement was evidently an exaggeration, but was of sufficient importance for priests and deacons to be at once sent to the neighbouring monasteries to make inquiries. Meanwhile Mamas and Theophilus returned. They reported that they had encountered many obstacles. The monks round the door of the monastery had affirmed the archimandrite to be ill; one Eleusinius had presented himself as representing Eutyches; and it was only on the assurance that the letter, of which they were the bearers, contained neither hard nor secret messages that they at last procured an audience. To the letter Eutyches replied that nothing but death should make him leave his monastery, and that the archbishop and the synod might do what they pleased. In his turn, he wished them to take a letter; and on their refusal announced his intention of sending it to the synod. Eusebius at once broke out, "Guilty men have always some excuse ready; we must bring Eutyches here against his will." But at the desire of Flavian, two priests (Memnon and Epiphanius) and a deacon (Germanus) were sent to make another effort. They took a letter exhorting Eutyches not to compel the synod to put in force canonical censure, and summoning him before them two days later (Nov. 17). The synod met on Nov. 16. During the session, information was brought to Flavian that certain monks and deacons, friends of Eutyches, and Abraham, archimandrite of a neighbouring monastery, requested an audience. They were at once admitted. Abraham informed the archbishop that Eutyches was ill, and had deputed him to speak for him. Flavian's reply was paternal and conciliatory. He regretted the illness of Eutyches, and, on behalf of those present, expressed their willingness to wait till he was restored. "Let him remember," he continued, "that he is not coming among strangers, but among men who would receive him with fatherly and brotherly affection, and many of whom have hitherto been his friends. He has pained many, and must defend himself. Surely if he could leave his retirement when the error of Nestorius imperilled the faith, he should do as much when his own orthodoxy is in question. He has but to acknowledge and anathematize his error, and the past shall be forgiven. As regards the future, he must give assurance to us that he will only teach conformably to the doctrines of the Fathers." The archbishop closed with significant words: "You (monks) know the zeal of the accuser of Eutyches. Fire itself seems to him cold in comparison with his burning zeal for religion. God knows I have besought him to desist; but, as he persisted, what could I do? Do you suppose that I have any wish to destroy you, and not rather gather you together? It is the act of an enemy to scatter, but the act of a father to gather."

The fifth session opened on Wed. Nov. 17, and as the result of its deliberations, Eutyches was informed that he would be expected on Nov. 22, and, if he failed to appear, would be deprived of his clerical functions and monastic dignity. A sixth session met on Sat. Nov. 20, and agreed that Eutyches might be accompanied on the Monday following by four friends. Eusebius said that when Mamas and Theophilus had visited Eutyches, the archimandrite used expressions not reported to the synod, but which threw great light on his opinions. At the request of the bishops, Theophilus narrated what had occurred. Eutyches, he said, had wished to argue with them, and in the presence of several of his monks had put these questions: "Where, in Holy Scripture, is there any mention of two natures? Which of the Fathers has declared that God the Word has two natures?" Mamas had replied that the argument from silence was insufficient. "The word ὁμοούσιος does not occur in Holy Scripture; we owe it to the definitions of the Fathers. And similarly we owe to them the affirmation of the two natures." Theophilus had then asked if Eutyches believed that God the Word was "perfect (τέλειος) in Christ," and "Do you believe that the man made flesh was also perfect (in Him)?" He answered "Yes" to both questions, whereupon Theophilus urged, "If in Christ be perfect God and perfect man, then do these perfect (natures) form the one Son. Why will you not allow that the one Son consists of two natures?" Eutyches replied: "God forbid that I should say that Christ consists of two natures, or dispute about the nature of God. Let the synod depose me, or do what they please. I will hold fast by the faith which I have received." Mamas substantiated the truth of this report, adding that what led to the discussion was a remark of Eutyches: "God the Word became flesh to restore fallen human nature," and the question which he (Mamas) had put: "By what nature, then, is this human nature taken up and restored?" Flavian naturally asked why this conversation had not been reported before: it was a lame but thoroughly Oriental answer to reply: "Because we had been sent, not to question Eutyches about his faith, but to summon him to the synod. We gave you his answer to the latter point. No one asked us about the former, and therefore we held our peace."

The seventh, last, and weightiest session met on Mon. Nov. 22. Eutyches at last presented himself, accompanied by a multitude of soldiers, monks, and others, who refused to allow him to enter till assured that he should depart as free as he entered. A letter from the emperor (Theodosius II.) was presented. "I wish," it said, "for the peace of the church, and steadfast adherence to the orthodox doctrines of the Fathers at Nicaea and Ephesus. And because I know that Florentius the patrician is a man approved in the faith, I desire that he should be present at the sessions of a synod which has to deal with matters of faith." The synod received the letter with shouts, "Long live the emperor! His faith is great! Long live our pious, orthodox, high-priest and emperor (τῷ ἀρχιερεῖ βασιλεῖ)." Florentius was conducted to his seat, the accuser (Eusebius) and the accused (Eutyches) took their places, and the session began by the recital of all the papers bearing on the point at issue. Cyril's letter to John of Antioch was again read, in which occurred the following: "We confess our Lord Jesus Christ . . . consubstantial with the Father, according to the Godhead, and consubstantial with us according to the manhood; for a union of the two natures was made; wherefore we confess one Christ, one Son, one Lord. And in accordance with the perception of the unconfused union (τὴν τῆς ἀσυγχύτου ἑνώσεως ἔννοιαν), we confess the Holy Virgin θεοτόκος, because God the Word was made flesh, and became man and united to Himself by conception the temple taken from her." Eusebius exclaimed, "Certainly Eutyches does not acknowledge this; he has never believed it, but taught the very opposite to every one who came to him." Florentius desired that Eutyches should be asked if he assented to these documents or not. Eutyches was interrogated; and when the archbishop put the plain question: "Do you confess that Christ is of two natures?" Eutyches answered, "I have never yet presumed to dispute about the nature of my God; that He is consubstantial with us have I never said. I readily admit that the Holy Virgin is consubstantial with us, and that our God was born of her flesh." Flavian, Florentius, Basil of Seleucia, and others, pressed upon him: "If you admit that Mary is consubstantial with us, and that Christ took His manhood from her, it naturally follows that He, according to His manhood, is consubstantial with us." Eutyches answered: "I do not say that the body of man has become the body of God; but in speaking of a human body of God I say that the Lord became flesh of the Virgin. If you wish me to add that His body is consubstantial with ours, I will do so; but I cannot use the word consubstantial in such a manner as to deny that He is the Son of God." Flavian's retort was just: "You will then admit this from compulsion, and not because it is your belief." Finally, the synod desired Eutyches to make a full explanation, and to pronounce an anathema on opinions opposed to the documents which had been recited. Eutyches replied that he would, if the synod desired it, make use of language (viz. consubstantial with us, and of two natures) which, in his opinion, was very much open to question; "but," he added, "inasmuch as I do not find such language either in Holy Scripture or in the writings of the Fathers, I must decline to pronounce an anathema on those who do not accept it, lest—in so doing—I should be anathematizing the Fathers." Florentius asked: "Do you acknowledge two natures in Christ, and His consubstantiality with us?" "Cyril and Athanasius," answered Eutyches, "speak of two natures before the union, but of one nature after the union." "If you do not acknowledge two natures after the union," said Florentius, "you will be condemned. Whosoever refuses the formula 'of two natures' and the expression 'two natures' is unorthodox;" to which the synod responded with the cry, "And to receive this under compulsion (as would Eutyches) is not to believe in it. Long live the emperor!" The sentence was pronounced: "Eutyches, formerly priest and archimandrite, hath proved himself affected by the heresy of Valentinus and Apollinaris, and hath refused—in spite of our admonition—to accept the true faith. Therefore we, lamenting his perverseness, have decreed, through our Lord Jesus Christ, blasphemed by him, that he be excluded from all priestly functions, from our communion, and from his primacy in his monastery." Excommunication was pronounced upon all who should consort with and abet him, and the sentence was signed by 32 (? 28) bishops, and 23 archimandrites. Eutyches left the council-chamber muttering an appeal to Rome.

The monks rallied round Eutyches, and the influence of the minister Chrysaphius, his godson, was exerted in his behalf. Eutyches himself wrote to the emperor and to many of the bishops, and placarded notices about Constantinople, protesting against his sentence and justifying his teaching. Of his letters the most important is to pope Leo. In it he accuses Eusebius of acting at Satan's bidding, not in the interests of orthodoxy, but with the intention of destroying him. He repeats that he could not accede to the demands of the synod, acknowledge two natures in Christ, and anathematize all who opposed this doctrine, because Athanasius, Gregory, Julius, and Felix had rejected the expression "two natures," he himself having no wish to add to the creed of Nicaea and Ephesus, nor to define too particularly the nature of God the Word. He adds that he had desired the synod to lay the matter before the pope, promising to abide by his decision; but this not having been granted, he, being in great danger, now implored the pope to give an unprejudiced judgment, and to protect him.

Flavian, on his part, circulated the decree of excommunication. He charged the monks to obey it, and communicated it to the emperor, the pope, and provincial bishops. His interviews with the emperor were marked by great suspicion on the part of the latter; and his letter to Leo was forestalled by that of Eutyches and a second was required before the pope was satisfied. Leo eventually gave Eutyches his answer in the celebrated *Epistola Dogmatica ad Flavianum.*

Court favour inclined to Eutyches; and early in 449 the emperor appointed a commission to examine a charge of falsification of the acts of the late synod of Constantinople, proffered by Eutyches against Flavian. No such falsification was proved, and the commission had no choice but to confirm the sentence pronounced by the synod; but an agitation was thereby advanced, which was productive of the greatest misery.

A council had already been summoned by the emperor to meet at Ephesus. Eutyches and Dioscorus, patriarch of Alexandria, had demanded it, and their position had been supported by Chrysaphius. The imperial summons was in the names of Theodosius II. and Valentinian III., and was dated May 30, 449. It stated the cause of the summons to be the doubts and disputes which had arisen concerning the faith; it invited Dioscorus to present himself with ten metropolitans and ten bishops at Ephesus on Aug. 1; and it extended the invitation to other bishops, Theodoret of Cyrus (Kars) being exempted unless specially summoned by the council.

The synod—the "Latrocinium," or "Robber Synod," as posterity was taught to call it by Leo—first met on Aug. 8, 449. "Flavian was presented as an oppressor and Eutyches as a victim, and terrible was the day on which it opened. The true faith received in the East a shock from which it has never completely recovered since. The church witnessed the separation from herself of nations which have never returned to her, and perhaps never will" (Martin). Leo was not present except by his legates, who brought the famous tome, or doctrinal letter, to Flavian, and letters to the emperor, the archimandrites, the council, and others. In his letter to Theodosius (June 13, 449) Leo expresses his regret that "the foolish old man" (Eutyches) had not given up opinions condemned by the synod of Constantinople, and intimates his wish that the archimandrite should be received again if he would keep his promise to the pope, and amend what was erroneous in his views. In the letter to Pulcheria (same date), the pope considers Eutyches to have fallen into his error "through want of knowledge rather than through wickedness"; to the archimandrites of Constantinople he states his conviction that they do not share the views of Eutyches, and exhorts them to deal tenderly with him should he renounce his error; and to the synod he quotes the confession of St. Peter, "Thou art the Christ, the Son of the living God" (Matt. xvi. 16) as embodying belief in the two natures, and argues that if Eutyches had rightly understood these words, he would not have swerved from the path of truth. In most of these Leo refers to the tome as containing the true teaching of the church.

A synod stigmatized as "a gang of robbers" was not likely to permit the recital of a document condemnatory of Eutyches, the man they were pledged to acquit. It was presented, but shelved.

For the history of the synod, in its relation to Eutyches, see Dioscorus. The Christian world was rent in pieces by its proceedings. Egypt, Thrace, and Palestine ranged themselves with Dioscorus and the emperor; Syria, Pontus, Asia, Rome, protested against the treatment of Flavian and the acquittal of Eutyches. Dioscorus excommunicated Leo, Leo Dioscorus. Theodosius applauded and confirmed the decisions of the synod in a decree which denounced Flavian, Eusebius, and others as Nestorians, forbad the elevation of their followers to episcopal rank, deposed them if already bishops, and expelled them from the country. Leo wrote to the emperor Theodosius, to the church at Constantinople, and to the anti-Eutychian archimandrites. He asked for a general council.

The wrangle was suddenly silenced by the death of Theodosius (July 450). Under Marcian orthodoxy triumphed again: "Eutychianism, as well as Nestorianism, was conquered" (Leo). Marcian assented at once and cordially to the pope's request for a council. Anatolius convened a synod of such bishops, archimandrites, priests, and deacons as were at Constantinople, and in the presence of the Roman legates subscribed the tome, and, together with the whole assembly, anathematized Eutyches, Nestorius, and their followers. Leo's wish for a council was not now so urgent. The danger had passed away. Eutychianism and Nestorianism had been anathematized; his own tome had been everywhere accepted; of more immediate importance, in his opinion, was the practical question, how best and most speedily to reconcile the penitent and to punish the obstinate. The war in the West, the invasion of Gaul by Attila, would prevent the bishops of the West from attending a council in Italy, where he wished it to be. Nestorianism was still powerful among the bishops of Syria, and would unquestionably bias the views of many, should a council be called in the East, as the emperor desired. He feared that the men who would unite for the condemnation of Eutychianism would find means for a triumph of Nestorianism over orthodoxy. But, in deference to the emperor's convictions, he consented to send representatives to the future council, while he urged that no fresh discussion should be allowed whether Eutyches was heretical or not, or whether Dioscorus had judged rightly or not, but that debate should turn upon the best means of reconciling and dealing mercifully with those who had gone wrong. For a similar reason he urged the emperor's wife, Pulcheria, to cause the removal of Eutyches from the neighbourhood of Constantinople, and to place an orthodox abbat at the head of his monastery.

The fourth great council of the church met at Chalcedon on Oct. 8, 451. For its general history see DIOSCORUS. During the first session the secretaries read the documents descriptive of the introduction of Eutyches at the synod of Ephesus (the Latrocinium) and the reading of his paper. At words attributing to Eutyches the statement, "The third general council (that of Ephesus, 431) hath directly forbidden any addition to the Nicene Creed," Eusebius of Dorylaeum exclaimed, "That is untrue." "You will find it in four copies," retorted Dioscorus. Diogenes of Cyzicus urged that Eutyches had not repeated the Nicene Creed as it then stood; for the second general council (Constantinople, 381) had certainly appended (against Apollinaris and Macedonius) to the words "He was incarnate," the words "by the Holy Ghost of the Virgin Mary," though he considered this an explanation rather than an addition; but the Egyptian bishops present disclaimed (as Cyril had previously done) any such revised version of the Nicene confession and greeted the words of Diogenes with loud disapproval. Angry words were again interchanged when the reader continued: "I (Eutyches) anathematize all who say that the flesh of our Lord Jesus Christ came down from heaven." "True," interrupted Eusebius, "but Eutyches has never told us whence Christ did take His manhood;" and Diogenes and Basil of Seleucia affirmed that Eutyches, though pressed upon this point at Constantinople, had refused to speak out. Dioscorus now, and to his honour, protested: "Let Eutyches be not only punished, but burnt, if he holds heterodox opinions. I only care to preserve the Catholic faith, not that of any individual man"; and then he turned upon Basil for having said one thing at Constantinople and another at Ephesus. "I did so," pleaded Basil, "out of fear of the majority. Before a tribunal of magistrates I would have remained firm even to martyrdom; but I did not dare oppose (a tribunal of) the Fathers (or bishops)." This plea for pardon was adopted by the others. "Yes, we all sinned (at Ephesus); we all implore forgiveness."

At the 4th session (Oct. 17) 18 anti-Eutychian priests and archimandrites, headed by Faustus, were admitted. They were questioned about a petition addressed to Marcian previous to the opening of the council, by Carosus and other Eutychians, who styled themselves archimandrites. Faustus replied that only two of the petitioners (Carosus and Dorotheus) were archimandrites, the rest were men who lived in martyries or were unknown to them. The imperial commissioners commanded that Carosus and the others should be summoned. Twenty came, and then the petition was read. It was an impassioned appeal to the emperor to prevent an outbreak of schism, to summon a council, and meanwhile forbid the expulsion of any man from his church, monastery, or martyry. In a second document the Eutychians excused themselves for not having previously attended, on the ground that the emperor had forbidden it. "The emperor," it proceeded, "had assured them that at the council the creed of Nicaea only should be established, and that nothing should be undertaken previous to this." It urged that the condemnation of Dioscorus was inconsistent with the imperial promise; he and his bishops should therefore be again called to the council, and the present schism would be removed. If not, they declared that they would hold no communion with men who opposed the creed of the 318 Fathers at Nicaea. To prove their own orthodoxy they appended their signatures to that creed and to the Ephesian canon which confirmed it. Aetius, archdeacon of Constantinople, reminded these petitioners that church discipline required monks to accept from the bishops instructions in matters of faith. In the name of the council he demanded, "Do you assent to their decision or not?" "I abide by the creed of Nicaea," answered Carosus; "condemn me and send me into exile. . . . If Eutyches doth not believe what the Catholic church believes, let him be anathema." The appeal of Faustus and other anti-Eutychian archimandrites to the emperor was now ordered to be read. The Eutychian archimandrite Dorotheus immediately asserted the orthodoxy of Eutyches. The commissioners retorted, "Eutyches teaches that the body of the Redeemer is not of like substance to ours. What say you to that?" Dorotheus avoided a direct answer by quoting the language of the Constantinopolitan creed in this form, "Incarnate of the Virgin and made man," and interpreting it in an anti-Nestorian sense; but he declined to attest the language used on this point by Leo in his tome. The commissioners were now on the point of passing judgment, when the Eutychians asserted that the emperor had promised them an opportunity of fair debate with their opponents in his presence. It was necessary to ascertain the truth of this, and the sitting of Oct. 17 ended. On Oct. 20 the council met again. Alexander, the priest and periodeutes ("visitor," see Suicer, *Thesaur.* i. n.), who had been deputed to see the emperor, informed the council that he and the decurion John had been sent by the emperor to the monks, with a message to the effect that had he (the emperor) considered himself able to decide the point in dispute, he would not have convened a council. "I now charge you," continued the emperor, "to attend the council and learn from them what you do not yet know. For what the holy general council determines, that I follow, that I rest in, and that I believe." The imperial language was greeted with loud acclamations. The Eutychians were granted 30 days' consideration, after which, should they remain contumacious, they would be deprived of ecclesiastical rank and office. From Leo's correspondence (*Epp.* 136, 141, 142) it would seem that Carosus and Dorotheus persisted in their views and were ejected by Marcian from their monastery. On Oct. 22, in the 5th session, the memorable "Definition of faith agreed upon at the council of Chalcedon" was recited and received with the unanimous cry, "This is the faith of the Fathers; this is the faith of the Apostles. We all assent to it. We all think thus." It was signed by the metropolitan and by the imperial commissioners. After declaring "the sufficiency of the wise and saving creed" of Nicaea and Constantinople, inasmuch as that creed taught "completely the perfect doctrine concerning the Father, the Son, and the Holy Spirit, and fully explained the Incarnation of the Lord to those who received it faithfully," it goes on to admit that some "dare to corrupt the mystery of the Lord's Incarnation, others (*i.e.* the Eutychians) bring in a confusion and mixture (σύγχυσιν καὶ κρᾶσιν), and absurdly imagine the nature of the flesh and of the Godhead to be one, and teach the monstrous doctrine that the Divine nature of the Only-begotten was a commixture capable of suffering . . . Therefore the present holy, great, and oecumenical council . . . has added for the confirmation of the orthodox doctrines, the letter of Leo written to Flavian for the removal of the evil opinions (κακονοία) of Eutyches. For it is directed against those who attempt to rend the mystery of the Incarnation into a duad of Sons; it repels from the sacred congregation those who dare to say that the Divinity of the Only-begotten is capable of suffering; it is opposed to those who imagine a mixture or confusion of the two natures of Christ; it drives away those who fancy that the form of a servant which was taken by Him of us is of an heavenly or any other substance; and it condemns those who speak of two natures of the Lord before the union, and feign one after the union. . . . We then," was the conclusion, "following the holy Fathers, all with one consent teach men to confess one and the same Son, one Lord Jesus Christ; the same perfect in Godhead and also perfect in manhood: truly God and truly man, of a reasonable soul and body; consubstantial with the Father according to the Godhead, and consubstantial with us according to the manhood; in all things like unto us without sin; begotten before all ages of the Father according to the Godhead, and in these latter days, for us and for our salvation, born of Mary, the Virgin Mother of God, according to the Manhood; one and the same Christ, Son, Lord, Only-begotten, to be acknowledged in two natures, inconfusedly, unchangeably, indivisibly, inseparably (ἐν δύο φύσεσιν ἀσυγχύτως, ἀτρέπτως, ἀδιαιρέτως, ἀχωρίστως γνωριζόμενον), the distinction of natures being by no means taken away by the union, but rather the property of each nature being preserved, and concurring in one person and one hypostasis, not parted or divided into two persons, but one and the same Son and Only-begotten, God the Word, the Lord Jesus Christ, as the prophets from the beginning have declared concerning Him, and the Lord Jesus Christ Himself has taught us, and the creed of the holy Fathers has delivered to us." "Writing, composing, devising, or teaching any other creed" was declared unlawful, with penalties: "bishops and clergy were to be deposed, monks and laymen anathematized."

On Oct. 25 Marcian, accompanied by Pulcheria and the court, opened and closed the sixth session. In his address he explained that he appeared in person, as Constantine had done before him, not to overawe and coerce any, but to strengthen and confirm the faith: his efforts and prayers were alike directed to one end, that all might be one in true doctrine, hold the same religion, and honour the true Catholic faith. The archdeacon Aetius recited in his presence the confession of faith approved at the previous session, and when the emperor asked if it expressed the opinion of all, shouts arose from all sides, "This is the belief of us all! We are unanimous, and have signed it unanimously! We are all orthodox! This is the belief of the Fathers; this is the belief of the Apostles; this is the belief of the orthodox; this belief hath saved the world! Long live Marcian, the new Constantine, the new Paul, the new David! Long live Pulcheria, the new Helena!"

Imperial edicts speedily followed the close of the council (Nov. 1). One, dated Mar. 13, 452, was especially directed against the Eutychians. They had persisted in disseminating their "foolishness" in spite of the council and the emperor. Marcian warned them that their contumacy would be sharply punished; and on July 28, Eutychians and Apollinarians were deprived of their priests and forbidden to hold meetings or live together in monasteries; they were to be considered incapable of inheriting property under a will or devising property to their co-sympathizers; and were to be reckoned unfit for military service. Eutychian priests who had seceded from their post in the church and the monks from Eutyches's own monastery were banished from Roman territory. Their writings were to be burnt, and the composer and circulator of such works was to be punished with confiscation of goods and with exile. Dioscorus and Eutyches were exiled, but the latter died probably before the sentence was carried into effect.

"With none of those who have been the authors of heresies among Christians was blasphemy the first intention; nor did they fall from the truth in a desire to dishonour the Deity, but rather from an idea which each entertained, that he should improve upon his predecessors by upholding such and such doctrines." These words of the church historian Evagrius (i. 11) follow his account of the second (*i.e.* the Robber) synod of Ephesus, which restored Eutyches. They express the belief of a judicially-trained mind within little more than 100 years after the events in question, and are in substance reproduced by "judicious" Hooker (*Eccl. Pol.* v. c. 52). Cyril "had given instance in the body and soul of man no farther than only to enforce by example against Nestorius, that a visible and invisible, a mortal and an immortal substance, may united make one person." Eutyches and his followers took those words of Cyril "as though it had been his drift to teach, that even as in us the body and the soul, so in Christ God and man make but *one nature*. . . . He became unsound (in belief) by denying the difference which still continueth between the one and the other nature." It was "real, though erring reverence" which led him, in the first instance, to broach his opinions. His "narrow mind, stiffened by seclusion, and bewildered by harassing excitement" (Bright) was in no state in the day of his trial before the synod of Constantinople to perceive to what his teaching logically conducted, nor to accept the qualifications or paraphrases kindly offered. He passed away, but Eutychianism exists still (Pusey, *Councils of the Church*, p. 25). It never has and never will yield to edicts like those of Marcian. The right faith has been defined by the great council which opposed both it and Nestorianism. "We must keep warily a middle course, shunning both that distraction of Persons, wherein Nestorius went away, and also this latter confusion of natures, which deceived Eutyches" (Hooker). [MONOPHYSITISM.]

Consult Mansi, *Sacr. Conc. Collectio*, vi. vii.; Tillem. *Mémoires*, etc. xv.; Bright, *History of the Church* (313-451); and other works mentioned above. [J.M.F.]

Eutychianus (3), bp. of Rome from Jan. 275 to Dec. 283, during a period of 8 years, 11 months and 3 days, and buried in the cemetery of Callistus. The truth of the record in the Liberian Catalogue has been confirmed by the discovery by De Rossi (*Rom. Sot.* ii. 70), in the papal crypt of the cemetery, of fragments of a slab inscribed ΕΥΤΥΧΙΑΝΟϹ ΕΠΙϹ (Eutychianus episcopus). Ten decreta appear as his in the collections of Gratian, Ivo, and others. [J.B—Y.]

Eutychius (18), St., patriarch of Constantinople. His biography, composed by his chaplain Eustathius, has been preserved entire. Eutychius was born at Theium in Phrygia *c.* 512. His father Alexander was a general under Belisarius. Eutychius took the monastic habit at Amasea at the age of 30, *c.* 542.

As an archimandrite at Constantinople he stood high in favour with the patriarch Mennas, at whose death in 552 he was nominated by Justinian to the vacant chair.

At the beginning of 553 Eutychius wrote to pope Vigilius, making his profession of the Catholic faith, declaring his acceptance of the four councils and the letters of St. Leo, and requesting Vigilius to preside over the council that was to be held on the question of the Three Chapters. Vigilius refused, and Eutychius shared the first place in the assembly with the patriarchs Apollinarius of Alexandria and Domninus of Antioch. At the second session the pope excused himself again, on the ground of ill-health. The subscription of Eutychius to the Acts of this synod, which sat from May 5 to June 2, 553, is a summary of the decrees against the Three Chapters.

Eutychius came into violent collision with Justinian in 564, when the emperor adopted the tenets of the Aphthartodocetae. Eutychius, in a long address, demonstrated the incompatibility of that theory with Scripture; but Justinian insisted on his subscribing to it, and finding him uncompromising, ordered his arrest. On Jan. 22, 565, Eutychius was at the holy table celebrating the feast-day of St. Timotheus in the church adjoining the Hormisdas palace (cf. du Cange, *Cpolis. Chr.* lib. ii. p. 96, lib. iv. p. 93, ed. 1729), when soldiers broke into the patriarchal residence, entered the church, and carried the patriarch away, first to a monastery called Choracudis, and the next day to that of St. Osias near Chalcedon. The 8th day after this outrage Justinian called an assembly of princes and prelates, to which he summoned Eutychius. The charges against him were trifling and absurd: that he used ointments, ate delicate meats, and prayed long. Cited thrice, Eutychius replied that he would only come if he were to be judged canonically, in his own dignity, and in command of his clergy. Condemned by default, he was sent to an island in the Propontis named Principus, and afterwards to his old monastery at Amasea, where he spent 12 years and 5 months. On the death of Joannes Scholasticus, whom Justinian had put in the patriarchal chair, the people of Constantinople loudly demanded the return of Eutychius. Justin II. had succeeded Justinian, and had associated with himself the young Tiberius. The emperors immediately sent an honourable deputation to Amasea to bring back Eutychius, who returned with great joy to Constantinople in Oct. 577. An immense concourse met him, shouting aloud, "Blessed is he that cometh in the name of the Lord," and "Glory to God in the highest, on earth peace." In questionable imitation of our Lord he entered on an ass's colt, over garments spread on the ground, the crowd carrying palms, dancing, and singing. The whole city was illuminated, public banquets were held, new buildings inaugurated. Next day he was met by the two emperors with conspicuous honour at the church of the Virgin in Blachernae. He then proceeded to the great church, which was filled from end to end, mounted the pulpit, and blessed the multitude. He was six hours distributing the communion, as all wished to receive from his own hands.

Towards the end of his life Eutychius maintained that after the resurrection the body will be more subtle than air, and no longer palpable. Gregory the Great, then residing at Constantinople as delegate of the Roman church, felt himself bound to oppose this opinion. The emperor Tiberius talked to the disputants separately, and tried to reconcile them; but the breach was persistent. Eutychius breathed his last quietly on Sunday after Easter Day, Apr. 5, 582, aged 70 years. Some of his friends told Gregory that, a few minutes before his end, he touched the skin of his hand, saying, "I confess that in this flesh we shall rise again" (Paul. Diac. *Vit. Greg. Mag.* lib. i. capp. 9, 27-30; *Vit. Greg.*

ex ejus Script. lib. i. cap. 5, §§ 6-8; Greg. Mag. *Moral.* xiv. §§ 72-74).

The chronology of his life here followed is that fixed by Henschen in his introductory argument to the Life by Eustathius (Boll. *Acta SS.* 6 Ap. i. 550). His literary remains are his letter to pope Vigilius already mentioned, printed in Greek and Latin by Mansi (ix. 186), and by Migne (*Patr. Lat.* lxix. 63; *Patr. Gk.* lxxxvi. 2401), and some fragments of a *Discourse on Easter and the Holy Eucharist* (Migne, *Patr. Gk.* lxxxvi. 2391). In this treatise Eutychius argues against the Quartodecimans, against the Hydroparastatae who used water instead of wine at communion (he says that the only apostolic tradition is the mixture of both), against certain schismatic Armenians who used only wine, and against some Greeks and Armenians who adored the elements as soon as they were offered and before consecration. The lost work of Eutychius was a discourse on the manner of existence of reasonable natures in space, a sort of physical theory of the future life. *Patr. Gk.* lxxxix. §§ 2270-2389; Bolland. *AA. SS.* Ap. i. 548; *ib.* App. p. lix. in Greek; Surius, *de Prob. Hist. SS.* Apr. p. 82; Evagr. iv. 37; Theoph. *Chronogr.* 193, 201, 202, 203, 210, 211, 212, 213; Cave, i. 527. [W.M.S.]

Euzoïus (1), Arian bp. of Antioch, the companion and intimate friend of Arius from an early age. He was one of 11 presbyters and deacons of that church, deposed together with Arius by Alexander bp. of Alexandria, *c.* 320 (Socr. *H. E.* i. 6; Soz. *H. E.* i. 15; Theod. *H. E.* i. 4, ii. 311; Athan. *de Syn.* p. 907). He was again condemned and banished, with Arius, by the council of Nicaea, A.D. 325. When Arius was recalled from banishment, and summoned to the emperor's side in 330, he was accompanied by Euzoïus, by this time a priest. Both regained the emperor's confidence by an evasive declaration of their faith and a professed acceptance of the creed of Nicaea (Socr. *H. E.* i. 25, 26; Soz. *H. E.* ii. 27). He accompanied Arius to Jerusalem at the great gathering of Eusebian bishops for the dedication of the church of the Anastasis, Sept. 13, 335, and with him was received into communion by the council then held (Soz. *l.c.*; Athan. *de Synod.* p. 891). In 361 Constantius, having banished Meletius, bp. of Antioch, summoned Euzoïus from Alexandria, and commanded the bishops of the province to consecrate him. A few months later Constantius, being seized with a fatal fever, summoned the newly appointed bishop, Euzoïus, to his bedside on Nov. 3, 361, and received from him the sacrament of baptism. Whether this was at Antioch or Mopsucrene in Cilicia is uncertain (Athan. *ib.* 907; Philost. *H. E.* vi. 5). On the accession of Valens, Euzoïus was urged by Eudoxius to convene a synod of bishops at Antioch to take off Aetius's sentence, and this he ultimately did, *c.* 364 (*ib.* vii. 5). On the death of Athanasius in 373, Euzoïus was, at his own petition, dispatched by Valens, with Magnus the imperial treasurer and troops, to instal the imperial nominee, the Arian Lucius of Samosata, instead of Peter the duly elected and enthroned bishop. This commission was carried out with shameless brutality and persecution of the orthodox (Socr. *H. E.* iv. 21; Theod. iv. 21, 22). Euzoïus's death is placed by Socrates in 376 at Constantinople (*H. E.* iv. 35). Le Quien, *Or. Chr.* ii. 713; Baron. *Ann.* ad ann. 325, lxxix.; 335, xlix. [E.V.]

Evagrius (5), known as Evagrius of Antioch, was consecrated bishop over one of the parties in Antioch in 388 or 389, and must have lived until at least 392. Socr. *H. E.* v. 15; Soz. *H. E.* vii. 15; Theod. *H. E.* v. 23; Hieron. *de Vir. Ill.* cap. 25; Ambrose, *Ep.* lvi.

Evagrius belonged to the Eustathian division of the orthodox church at Antioch, of which he became a presbyter. After the schism at Antioch caused by Lucifer's consecration of Paulinus, Evagrius left Antioch, and accompanied Eusebius of Vercelli to Italy in 363 or 364. Here he zealously co-operated with Eusebius in restoring peace to the churches distracted by the results of the council of Ariminum, and re-establishing orthodoxy on the terms laid down by the synod of Alexandria in 362. He also afforded pope Damasus important aid against Ursicius and his faction, A.D. 367. At Milan he resolutely withstood the Arian bp. Auxentius. After nine or ten years he returned to the East, with Jerome, with the view of healing the schism that still divided the church of Antioch. He called at Caesarea to visit Basil in the autumn of 373, and found him suffering from ague. He was commissioned by the Western bishops to return to Basil the letters he had sent them, probably relating to the Meletian schism, as unsatisfactory, and to convey terms dictated by them, which he was to embody in a fresh letter to be sent into the West by some duly authorized commissioners. Only thus would the Western prelates feel warranted in interfering in the Eastern church, and making a personal visit (Basil, *Ep.* 138 [8]). On his return to Antioch, Evagrius wrote in harsh terms to Basil, accusing him of a love of controversy and of being unduly swayed by personal partialities. If he really desired peace, let him come himself to Antioch and endeavour to re-unite the Catholics, or at least write to them and use his influence with Meletius to put an end to the dissensions. Basil's reply is a model of courteous sarcasm. If Evagrius was so great a lover of peace, why had he not fulfilled his promise of communicating with Dorotheus, the head of the Meletian party? It would be far better for Evagrius to depute some one from Antioch, who would know the parties to be approached and the form the letters should take (*ib.* 156 [342]). On the death of Paulinus, A.D. 388, Evagrius manifested the hollowness of his professed desire for peace by becoming himself the instrument of prolonging the schism. He was ordained by the dying bp. Paulinus, in his sick-chamber, without the presence or consent of any assisting bishops, in direct violation of the canons. Flavian had been consecrated by the other party on the death of Meletius, A.D. 381. Thus the hope of healing the schism was again frustrated (Socr. *H. E.* v. 15; Theod. *H. E.* v. 23). A council was summoned at Capua, A.D. 390, to determine whether Flavian or Evagrius was lawful bp. of Antioch, but found the question too knotty, and relegated the decision to Theophilus of Alexandria and the Egyptian bishops.

The death of Evagrius deprived Flavian of his rival. This was not before 392, in which year Jerome speaks of him as still alive (*de Vir. Ill.* c. 125). Jerome praises treatises on various subjects which he heard Evagrius read while still a presbyter, but which he had not yet published. He translated into Latin the Life of St. Anthony by St. Athanasius (Migne, *Patr. Gk.* xxvi. 835-976). Its genuineness has been much disputed, but the balance of critical judgment seems in its favour. [J.C.G. AND E.V.]

Evagrius (12) **Ponticus,** anchoret and writer, born at Ibora in Pontus Galaticus, according to Tillemont, in 345. He was ordained reader by Basil, and deacon by Gregory Nyssen, who took him to the council of Constantinople, A.D. 381, *teste* his pupil Palladius (*Hist. Lausiac.* c. 86, p. 1010). Gregory Nyssen thought so highly of Evagrius as a theologian and dialectician that he left him behind in Constantinople to aid the newly appointed bishop, Nectarius (who, before his consecration, was a layman destitute of theological training) in dealing with heretics. The imperial city proved a dangerous home for the young deacon. The wife of an ex-prefect conceived a guilty passion for him, which he returned. The husband's jealousy was awakened, and Evagrius only escaped assassination by a timely flight, being warned of his peril by a dream (Soz. *H. E.* vi. 30). Jerusalem was the place of his retreat. Here he was hospitably received by Melania the elder, by whom he was nursed during a severe attack of fever, and who, perceiving the weakness of his disposition, led him to embrace an ascetic life as the only safeguard against the temptations of the flesh. Evagrius went to Egypt, where, after two years spent in great austerities in the Nitrian desert, he plunged still deeper into the solitude, and practised severer mortifications in the cells of Scetis. Here the two Macarii were his instructors and models in the ascetic life. After enduring many terrible temptations, recorded by Palladius, and having obtained mastery over his bodily passions, he became qualified to instruct others in asceticism. Palladius became his companion and disciple in 391. Among his other disciples were Rufinus, and Heraclides of Cyprus, afterwards bp. of Ephesus (*ib.* viii. 6). Palladius gives several anecdotes illustrative of the height of ascetic virtue attained by Evagrius and his fellow-hermits. On one occasion he threw into the fire a packet of letters from his parents and other near friends lest their perusal should re-entangle him in worldly thoughts (Cassian, v. 32; Tillem. x. 376). Theophilus, the metropolitan of Alexandria, desired to make him a bishop, and Evagrius fled to resist his importunities (Socr. *H. E.* iv. 23). Evagrius remained in the cells of Scetis until he died, worn out with austerities, in the 17th year of his recluse life, A.D. 398, at the age of 54, "signis et prodigiis pollens" (Gennad. *Illust. Vir.* c. xi.). He was a zealous champion of the doctrines of Origen, for which he fell under the lash of Jerome, whose enmity had also been aroused by his having been the instructor of Rufinus during his sojourn in Egypt and having enjoyed the patronage of Melania. Jerome speaks in contemptuous terms of his writings (*ad Ctesiph.*), especially of his book περὶ ἀπαθείας, when combating the tenet ascribed to the Origenists that a man could raise himself to a superiority to temptation (*i.e.* as Jerome says, "becoming either a stone or god") and live without sin. He also charges him with being a precursor of Pelagius (*in Pelag.* p. 260), and including in his book *de Monachis* many who never were monks at all, and also Origenists who had been condemned by their bishops. The existing remains of his writings are printed by Galland, *Bibl. Patr.* vii. 551-581, and Migne, *Patr.* vol. 86. Socrates, Gennadius, Palladius, and Suidas, *sub voc.* "Macarius," mention as by him: (1) *Monachus*, on "active virtue," in 100 chapters. (2) *Gnosticus*. (3) *Antirrheticus*, a collection of passages of Scripture against the eight divisions of evil thoughts. (4) A *Century of Prayers*. (5) 600 *Gnostic Problems*. (6) A *Letter to Melania*. (7) A book, περὶ ἀπαθείας. (8) 100 *Sentences for the Use of Anchorets living simply*. (9) *Short Sentences*. (10) Στιχηρά, in two books, one addressed to monks, and the other to a virgin dedicated to God. (11) *Liber de rerum monachalium rationibus*. (12) *Scholion de tetragrammato Dei nomine*. Oudin, i. 883; Tillem. *Mém. eccl.* x. pp. 368 ff.; Fabr. *Bibl. Graec.* ix. 284, ed. Harles; Dupin, *Hist. Eccl.* iii. 1; Cave, *Hist. Lit.* i. 275; cf. O. Zickler, *Evagrius Ponticus* (Munich, 1893); J. Dräseke, "Zu Evag.-Pont." in *Zeitschrift für wissensch Theol.* 1894, xxxvii. 125 ff. [E.V.]

Evagrius (17), an ecclesiastical historian, who wrote six books, embracing a period of 163 years, from the council of Ephesus A.D. 431 to the 12th year of the emperor Mauricius Tiberius, A.D. 594. He was born at Epiphania in Coelesyria A.D. 536 or 537, but accompanied his parents to Apamea for his education, and from Apamea seems to have gone to Antioch, the capital of Syria, and entered the profession of the law. He received the surname of Scholasticus, a term then applied to lawyers (Du Cange, *Glossarium*, s.v.), gained great favour with Gregory bp. of Antioch, and was chosen by him to assist in his judgments. He seems to have won general esteem and goodwill, for on his second marriage the city was filled with rejoicing, and great honours were paid him by the citizens. He accompanied Gregory to Constantinople, and successfully advocated his cause when he was summoned to answer there for heinous crimes. He also wrote for him a book containing "reports, epistles, decrees, orations, disputations, with sundry other matters," which led to his appointment as quaestor by Tiberius Constantinus and by Mauricius Tiberius as master of the rolls, "where the lieutenants and magistrates with their monuments are registered" (Evagr. vi. 23). This is his own account of his promotion.

His death must have occurred after 594, in which year he wrote his history at the age of 58 (iv. 28). His other works have perished. The history was intended as a continuation of those of Eusebius, Socrates, Sozomen, and Theodoret. He sought all sources of information at his command—the writings of Eustathius the Syrian, Zosimus, Priscus, Joannes Rhetor, Procopius of Caesarea, Agathus, and other good authors—and resolved to bring their scattered information together "that the famous deeds which slumbered in the dust of forgetfulness might be revived; that they might be stirred with his pen, and presented for immortal memory" (Pref. to his *Hist.*).

Despite his unnecessarily inflated style, he largely attained his end. He is a warm, often an enthusiastic writer, orthodox in his sentiments, and eager in his denunciations of prevailing heresies. Jortin indeed has condemned him as "in points of theological controversy an injudicious prejudiced zealot" (*Remarks on Eccl. Hist.* ii. p. 120); but Evagrius was a lawyer, not a theologian, and we must look to him for the popular rather than the learned estimate of the theological controversies of his time. His credulous enthusiasm led him to accept too easily the legends of the saints, but in other respects he shews many of the best qualities of an historian. Not a few original documents, decrees of councils, supplications to emperors, letters of emperors and bishops, etc., are preserved in his pages, forming most important authorities for the events to which they relate. Goss (in Herzog) especially praises his defence of Constantine against the slanders of Zosimus. In his general arrangement he follows the reigns of the emperors of the East from Theodosius the Younger to Maurice; but the arrangement of details is faulty. There is often great spirit in the narrative, an excellent specimen of which is his account of the council of Chalcedon (ii. 18). The work is chiefly valuable in relation to the Nestorian and Eutychian heresies, and the councils of Ephesus and Chalcedon. The first ed. of the *History* is that of Valesius, with notes (Paris, 1673) reprinted at Camb. in *Hist. Eccl. Scriptores cum notis Valesii et Reading*, and repub. by the Clar. Press. The latest and best ed. is by Bidez and Parmentier (Lond. 1849) in *Byzantine Texts* edited by J. B. Bury. See also Krumbacher's *Gesch. der Byz. Lit.* 2nd ed. p. 246. There is a fair Eng. trans. by Meredith Hanmer (Lond. 1619) along with a trans. of Eusebius and Socrates, and more recent ones pub. by Bagster in 1847 and in Bohn's Lib. (Bell). [W.M.]

Evaristus (called *Aristus* in the Liberian Catalogue), bp. of Rome at the beginning of the 2nd cent. With respect to the exact date and duration of his episcopate, as well as the names and order of succession of his predecessors [LINUS; CLETUS; CLEMENT], ancient accounts are greatly at variance. Eusebius (*H. E.* iii. 34, iv. 1) gives Clemens as his immediate predecessor, the third year of Trajan (101) as the date of his accession, and 9 years as the duration of his episcopate; but in his *Chronicle* he makes the latter 7 years (*Chron.* iv. 1). Irenaeus, an older authority, who probably got his information when at Rome in the time of Eleutherus towards the end of the cent., also makes Clemens his predecessor, but gives no dates (*adv. Haeres.* iii. 3, 3). The Liberian (A.D 354) and subsequent Roman Catalogues, as well as Augustin and Optatus, represent him as succeeding Anacletus, and the former authorities give A.D. 96 as the commencement of his episcopate, and between 13 and 14 years as its duration. The best and probably final authority on the order and dates of the early era of Rome is Bp. Lightfoot's *Apostolical Fathers*, part i. [J.B—Y.]

Evodius (1), according to early tradition, first bp. of Antioch (Eus. *Chron.* ann. Abr. 2058; *H. E.* iii. 22). His episcopate has indirectly the older testimony of Origen, who speaks of Ignatius as the second bishop after Peter (*in Luc. Hom.* 6, vol. iii. p. 938; see also Eus. *Quaest. ad Steph. ap* Mai, *Scr. Vet.* i. p. 2). This tradition has all the appearance of being historical. Ignatius early acquired such celebrity that it is not likely the name of an undistinguished person would have been placed before his, if the facts did not require this arrangement. The language used about episcopacy in the Ignatian epistles agrees with the conclusion that Ignatius was not the first at Antioch to hold the office. As time went on, the fitness of things seemed to demand that Ignatius should not be separated from the Apostles. Athanasius (*Ep. de Synodis*, i. 607) speaks of Ignatius as coming after the Apostles without mention of any one intervening; Chrysostom makes him contemporary with the Apostles (*Hom. in Ignat.* vol. ii. p. 593); the *Apostolic Constitutions* (vii. 46) have recourse to the expedient adopted in the parallel case of Clement of Rome, the hypothesis of a double ordination, Evodius being said to have been ordained by Peter, Ignatius by Paul. Theodoret (*Dial.* I. *Immutab.* iv. 82, Migne) and others represent Ignatius as ordained by Peter. The authorities are given at length by Zahn (*Patres Apostol.* ii. 327).

There is reason to believe that the earliest tradition did not include an ordination even of Evodius by Peter; for the chronicle of Eusebius places the departure of Peter from Antioch three years, or, according to St. Jerome's version, two years before the ordination of Evodius. The chronology of the early bishops of Antioch has been investigated by Harnack (*Die Zeit des Ignatius*). He infers that the earliest list must have contained only names of bishops of Antioch without any note of lengths of episcopates, but still that Eusebius must have had the work of some preceding chronologer to guide him. We may well believe, as Harnack suggests, that Eusebius got his chronology of early bishops of Antioch from Africanus, to whom he acknowledges his obligation, and whose chronicle has generally been believed to be the basis of that of Eusebius. If the belief had been entertained at the beginning of the 3rd cent. that Evodius had been ordained by Peter, it is incredible that Africanus would have assigned a date which absolutely excludes an ordination by Peter. The date assigned by the chronicle of Eusebius to the accession of Evodius appears to have no historic value, and thus, while we accept the episcopate of Evodius as an historic fact, we have no data for fixing his accession, but may safely place it considerably later than A.D. 42. [G.S.]

Eznik (*Eznig*, *Esnig*), an Armenian doctor of the church in the 5th cent. His native place was Koghb or Kolp (whence he was called the Kolpensian), and he was a disciple of the patriarch Sahak (Isaac) and Mjesrop, the *praeceptor Armeniae*. Besides his mother tongue he understood Persian, Greek, and

Syriac. During long journeys through Syria, Mesopotamia, and Greece he added to his theological learning, becoming thoroughly acquainted with ecclesiastical literature. Later he was made a bishop, and as such took part in the synod of Artashast, A.D. 450, which repelled the demands of the Persian viceroy, Mihr-Nersh, that the Armenians should adopt Zoroastrianism, in an epistle marked with dignity, courage, and faith.

He died an aged man, as bp. of Bagrewand (Pakrewand) in the province of Airerat (cf. Neumann, *Geschichte der Armenischen Literatur*, pp. 42 seq.). His main work is *The Destruction of False Doctrines*, still preserved in the Armenian original (pub. by the Mechitarists of St. Lazarus in the collection of Armenian classics, Venice, 1826). There is a good German trans. by J. M. Schmid (Leipz. 1900), *Biblioth. der alten armen. Lit.* i. The whole is divided into 4 books—the 1st combats the Gentile doctrine of the eternity of matter, the 2nd the Zoroastrian religion, the 3rd Greek philosophy, the 4th the Gnostic sect of the Marcionites. The immediate occasion of the work was the conflict between Armenian Christianity and Parsism. The 4th book is of value for the history of heresy. The representation given of the Marcionite doctrine of Principias, and the various myths concerning the origin of the human race, its corruption by matter, the mission of Christ, His crucifixion, descent into hell, and victory over the Demiurge, contain much peculiar and characteristic, but much also belonging to the later developments, not the original forms, of Marcionitism. [R.A.L.]

F

Fabianus (1) (called by the Greeks and in the Liberian Catalogue *Fabius*, by Eutychius and in the Alexandrian Chronicle *Flavianus*), bp. of Rome from early in Feb. 236 to Jan. 20, 250, and a martyr. Eusebius relates that, the brethren being assembled in the church to choose a successor to Anteros, Fabianus, a layman lately come from the country, being indicated as the chosen of Heaven by a dove settling on his head, the people acclaimed him as worthy and placed him on the episcopal throne (*H. E.* vi. 29). That the choice proved a good one is witnessed by Cyprian, who rejoices that "his honourable consummation had corresponded to the integrity of his administration" (*Ep.* 39, cf. 30).

In the Liberian Catalogue (A.D. 354) he is said to have divided the regions of the city among the deacons, and to have been martyred Jan. 20, 250. In the Felician Catalogue (A.D. 530) and in later editions of the *Liber Pontificalis* it is added that he made also seven subdeacons to superintend the seven notaries appointed to record faithfully the acts of the martyrs; also that he caused to be brought to Rome by sea the body of Pontianus (the predecessor of his predecessor Anteros), martyred in Sardinia, and buried it in the cemetery of Callixtus on the Appian Way; in which cemetery he too was buried. It is remarkable that, though the Roman calendar designates all the first 30 bishops of Rome except two as saints and martyrs, Fabianus is the first, except Telesphorus and Pontianus, whose martyrdom rests on any good authority (cf. also Eus. *H. E.* vi. 39; Hieron. *de Ill. Vir.* c. 54; Cypr. *Epp.* 39, 30). Fabianus was among the earliest victims of the Decian persecution. Fragments of a slab bearing the inscription ΦΑΒΙΑΝΟϹ + ΕΠΙ + ΜΡ (Fabianus episcopus martyr), together with others inscribed with the names of Anteros, Lucius, and Eutychianus, Roman bishops of the same period, have been found in what is called the papal crypt of the cemetery of Callixtus, thus attesting the accounts given of the place of his burial (*Roma Sotterranea*, by Northcote and Brownlow).

Fabianus is specially named by Eusebius (*H. E.* vi. 36) as one among many bishops to whom Origen wrote in defence of his own orthodoxy. Cyprian mentions him (*Ep.* 59) as having, with Donatus bp. of Carthage, written a letter severely censuring one Privatus, an heretical bp. of Lambaesa in Numidia, who had been condemned by a synod of 90 bishops at Lambaesa for "many and grievous faults." Nothing more is known about Fabianus with certainty. Great doubt rests on the story (accepted by Andreas du Chesne, in *Vit. Pontif.*, and in the main by the Bollandists) of his having been the founder of the seven Gallic churches of Toulouse, Arles, Tours, Paris, Narbonne, Clermont, Limoges; to which he is said to have sent respectively Saturninus, Trophimus, Gratianus, Dionysius, Paulus, Astremonius, and Martialis as missionary bishops. The story is absent from early records, and is disputable also on other grounds. Still more improbable is the story, accepted by the Bollandists and Baronius, and resting mainly on the authority of the Acts of St. Pontius, that the emperor Philip and his son became Christians, and were baptized by Fabianus. [PHILIPPUS (5).] Three spurious decretals are attributed to Fabianus. There are also ten decreta assigned to him by Gratian and others, on matters of discipline. [J.B—Y.]

Fabiola (1), a noble Roman lady, a friend of St. Jerome, who wrote for her two dissertations (*Ep.* lxiv. and lxxviii. ed. Vall.) on the dress of the high priest, and on the stations of the Israelites in the desert; and also a memoir of her in his touching letter to Oceanus (*Ep.* lxxvii. ed. Vall.) in the year of her death, 399. Thierry (*St. Jerome*, ii. 11) has worked up the intimations about her into an interesting and dramatic story. She was descended from Julius Maximus and extremely wealthy; a woman of a lively and passionate nature, married to a man whose vices compelled her to divorce him. She then accepted a second husband, the first being still alive. It is probable that this step separated her from Paula and the other friends of Jerome, and from church communion, and may account for the fact that we hear nothing of her during Jerome's stay at Rome. After the death of her second husband she voluntarily went through a public penance. Having publicly renewed her communion with the church, she sold all her possessions, and determined to administer the vast sums thus acquired for the good of the poor. She supported monasteries in various parts of Italy and the adjacent islands, and joined Pammachius in the institution of a hospital (νοσοκομεῖον), where she gathered in the sick and outcasts, and tended them with her own hands. In 395 she suddenly appeared at Bethlehem, making the journey with her kinsman Oceanus. Several causes prevented Bethlehem from becoming her home. The Origenistic strife divided Jerome and his friends from Rufinus and Melania, and the new-comers did not escape the discord. Oceanus warmly espoused the side of Jerome; Fabiola seems to have stood aloof. But efforts were made, if we may believe Jerome (*cont. Ruf.* iii. 14), to draw them into the camp of the adversary. Letters in which Rufinus was praised, fraudulently taken from the cell of Jerome's friend Eusebius, were found in the rooms of Fabiola and Oceanus. But this proceeding failed to cause a breach between Fabiola and Jerome. Jerome bears witness to the earnestness with which she attached herself to his teaching. The two treatises above mentioned are the results of her importunity (*Ep.* xiv. ed. Vall.).

Jerome was seeking a suitable dwelling-place for her, and engaged in writing his treatise on the mystical meaning of the high priest's garments, when the inroad of the Huns caused a panic in Palestine. Jerome and his friends hurried to the sea-coast at Joppa, and had hired vessels for flight, when the Huns abandoned their purpose and turned back. Jerome, with Paula and Eustochium, returned to Bethlehem; but Fabiola went on to Rome.

The last three years of her life were occupied with incessant activity in good works. In conjunction with Pammachius she instituted at Portus a hospice (xenodochium), perhaps taking her model from that established by Jerome at Bethlehem; and it was so successful that, as Jerome says, in one year it become known from Parthia to Britain. But to the last her disposition was restless. She found Rome and Italy too small for her charities, and was purposing some long journey or change of habitation when death overtook her A.D. 399. Her funeral was celebrated as a Christian triumph. The streets were crowded, the hallelujahs reached the golden roof of the temples. Jerome's book on the 42 stations (mansiones) of the Israelites in the desert was dedicated to her memory. [W.H.F.]

Faustus (11), sometimes called "the Breton," from having been born in Brittany, or (as Tillemont thinks) in Britain, but more generally known as Faustus of Riez from the name of his see. Born towards the close of the 4th cent., he may have lost his father while he was young, for we only hear of his mother, whose fervid piety made a great impression on all who saw her. Faustus studied Greek philosophy, but in a Christian spirit; mastered the principles of rhetoric, and may have pleaded for a time at the bar.

While still youthful (probably *c.* 426 or a little later) he entered the famous monastery of Lerins, then presided over by St. Maximus. Here he became a thorough ascetic and a great student of Holy Scripture, without, however, giving up his philosophic pursuits. Here he probably acquired the reputation, assigned to him by Gennadius, of an illustrious extempore preacher. He became a presbyter, and *c.* 432 or 433 succeeded Maximus as abbat of Lerins. His tenure was marked by a dispute with his diocesan Theodore, bp. of Fréjus, concerning their respective rights. The third council of Arles was convened by Ravennius, bp. of Arles, for the sole purpose of settling this controversy. The decision left considerable ecclesiastical power in the hands of the abbat. The epistle of Faustus to a deacon named Gratus (*al.* Gratius or Gregorius), who was heretical on the union of the two natures in the Person of Christ, belongs also to this period.

Faustus next succeeded St. Maximus in the episcopate of Riez in Provence. Baronius places this as late as 472, but Tillemont (*Mém.* vi. p. 775) as early as 462 or even 456. Faustus continued as bishop the stern self-discipline which he had practised as monk and abbat. He often retired to Lerins, becoming known throughout and beyond his diocese as one who gave succour to those sick whether in body or mind. He seems to have taken a stern view of late repentances, like those so prevalent at an earlier period in the church of N. Africa. In the councils of Arles and of Lyons a presbyter named Lucidus, accused of having taught fatalism through misunderstanding Augustine, was induced to retract; and Leontius, bp. of Arles, invited Faustus to compose a treatise on grace and free choice.

Faustus appears from Sidonius to have had some share in the treaty of 475 between the emperor Nepos and Euric king of the Visigoths, which Tillemont and Gibbon agree in regarding as discreditable to the Roman empire. It wrested Auvergne and subsequently Provence from an orthodox sovereign, and gave them to an Arian. This was unfortunate for Faustus, who *c.* 481 was banished, probably because of his writings against Arianism. His banishment is naturally attributed to king Euric, on whose death in 483 he returned to Riez. His life was prolonged until at least A.D. 492, possibly for some years later.

His writings have not come down to us in a complete and satisfactory condition. The following are still accessible:—

(1) *Professio Fidei.*—He opens with a severe attack on the teaching of Pelagius as heretical, but expresses a fear of the opposite extreme, of such a denial of man's power as a free agent as would virtually amount to fatalism.

(2) *Epistola ad Lucidum Presbyterum.*—Here, too, he anathematizes the error of Pelagius; but also any who shall have declared that Christ did not die for all men, or willeth not that all should be saved.

(3) *De Gratiâ Dei et Humanae Mentis libero Arbitrio.*—After again censuring Pelagius, the writer argues strongly on behalf of the need of human endeavour and co-operation with the Divine aid. In his interpretation of passages of Holy Scripture (*e.g.* Exod. iv. 21, vii. 13; Rom. ix. 11-26) which favour most Augustinianism, he is most extreme and least successful. Many passages might almost have come from the pen of some Arminian controversialist at the synod of Dort. In cap. x. of bk. ii., which is entitled *Gentes Deum Naturaliter Sapuisse,* Faustus calls attention to the lan-

guage of Daniel towards Nebuchadnezzar and his censure of Belshazzar, as a heathen recognition of God (Dan. iv. and v.). He also appeals for the same purpose to the first chapter of Jonah, the repentance of the Ninevites (Jon. iii.) and the language of Jeremiah (xviii. 7-10). Perhaps the famous expression in the apology of Tertullian, *O testimonium animae naturaliter Christianae*, might be considered to favour the view of heathendom here taken by Faustus.

(4) *Ad Monachos Sermo.*—The tone of this short letter resembles that of his other writings. He refers to excommunication as a terrible weapon only to be used in the last resort. It is sad to see monks go back to the world, especially if, after doing so, they retain their monastic dress. As usual, he is energetic in his appeals to the human element in religion. "Use your will. Resist the devil. Cherish all graces, especially obedience and humility."

(5) *De Ratione Fidei Catholicae.*—The former part is a brief statement of the case against Arianism. It explains the distinction between *Persona* and *Natura* in reference to our Lord's Incarnation, and appears to be addressed to an orthodox but perplexed friend, whom the author treats as a superior. The second portion is metaphysical, and discusses the nature of the soul, which Faustus seems to pronounce material. Claudius Mamertus, in his *de Statu Animae*, wrote against Faustus on this point. Faustus may, however, not have meant to do more than draw a marked distinction between the Creator and the creature; arguing, as he does, *nihil credendum incorporeum praeter Deum.*

(6) *Homilia de S. Maximi Laudibus.*—A eulogy of his predecessor.

(7) *Epistolae.*—Two have already been described. The other 17 epistles touch upon problems of metaphysics and theology.

Faustus was of unimpeachably good character; of an earnest, active, ascetic life; orthodox on the central doctrine of the Christian faith and suffering exile for it as a confessor; but stigmatized as a semi-Pelagian, and consequently by many authorities, both ancient and modern, denied the title of saint. But his own flock at Riez, deeply moved by his life and preaching, and warmly attached to his memory, insisted on giving him a local canonization as *Sanctus Faustus Reiensis*; they erected a basilica, dedicated in his name, and kept Jan. 18 as his festival. The first complete ed. of his works was pub. by A. Engelbrecht in *Corpus Script. Eccl. Lat.* vol. xxi.; cf. other publications of Engelbrecht on the same subject. [J.G.C.]

Felicissimus (1), deacon of Carthage, whom Novatus associated with himself in the management of a district called Mons (Cyp. *Ep.* 41). He was the chief agent (*signifer seditionis, Ep.* 59) of the anti-Cyprianic party, which combined the five presbyters originally opposed to Cyprian's election with the later-formed party for the easy readmission of the lapsed (*Epp.* 43, 45). Cyprian (*Ep.* 52) definitely states that Felicissimus had been, when the persecution arose, on the point of being tried before the presbytery on charges of homicidal cruelty to his father and wife. Like other African and Spanish deacons (Neander, vol. i. p. 324, ed. Bohn), he acquired influence through his administration of church property and was able to threaten with excommunication any who accepted relief or office from Cyprian's commissioners. The latter excommunicated him (*Ep.* 42) with Cyprian's consent. The mild resolution of the council of 252, making easy the readmission of the lapsed on earnest repentance [CYPRIANUS], destroyed his *locus standi.* The party then coalesced with that of PRIVATUS (2), who consecrated Fortunatus anti-bishop; and Felicissimus sailed for Rome to conciliate or intimidate Cornelius into recognizing him (*Ep.* 59). Failing here, the party melted quietly away. [E.W.B.]

Felicitas (1), commemorated on Nov. 23; martyr at Rome with her seven sons, under Antoninus Pius, and, according to their Acts, at his personal command, Publius being prefect of the city, *c.* A.D. 150. It is almost certain that there was no authorized persecution under ANTONINUS PIUS, but public calamities stirred up the mob to seek for the favour of the gods by shedding Christian blood (Julii Capitolini, *Vita Antonini Pii*, c. 9). Doubtless, in some such way, Felicitas and her children suffered. In her Acts Publius the Prefect is represented as commanded by Antoninus to compel her to sacrifice, but in vain, though he appeals to her maternal affection as well as her fears. He then calls upon each of her sons, Januarius, Felix, Philippus, Sylvanus, Alexander, Vitalis, Martialis, with a similar want of success, the mother exhorting them, "Behold, my sons, heaven, and look upwards, whence you expect Christ with His saints." The prefect, having tortured some of them, reported to the emperor, at whose command they were beheaded. Their martyrdom is commemorated by Gregory the Great, in *Hom.* 3 *super Evang.* where, preaching in a church dedicated to her, he lauds Felicitas as "Plus quam martyr quae septem pignoribus ad regnum praemissis, toties ante se mortua est. Ad poenas prima venit sed pervenit octava" (*Mart. Vet. Rom.* Hieron., Bedae, Adonis, Usuardi). [G.T.S.]

Felicitas (2), Mar. 7; martyr at Carthage with Perpetua, Revocatus, Saturninus, and Secundinus, all catechumens, and baptized after their arrest. Felicitas and her companions having been interrogated by Hilarianus, the proconsul, and remaining steadfast, were condemned to be thrown to the beasts on the anniversary of the young Geta's accession. Felicitas, being in the eighth month of her pregnancy, and the law not permitting women in her condition to be executed, was greatly distressed at the delay of her martyrdom. Prayer was therefore made that God might grant her an earlier delivery, and this accordingly took place a few days after. While the pangs of labour were upon her, the jailer, hearing some exclamations of pain, said, "If thy present sufferings are so great, what wilt thou do when thou art thrown to the wild beasts? This thou didst not consider when thou refusedst to sacrifice." Whereupon she answered, "What I now suffer I suffer myself, but then there will be another Who will suffer for me because I also shall suffer for Him." They were all put to death together in A.D. 202 or 203, during the reign of Severus, whose latter years were marked by a very rigorous persecution (Ael. Spart. *Sever. Imp.* § 27 in *Hist. August. Scriptt.*). Few martyrdoms are better attested than this. The ancient Roman calendar, pub. by Bucherius, and dating from *c.* 360, mentions only three African martyrs, viz. Felicitas, Perpetua, and Cyprian. Their names are in the canon of the Roman Mass, which mentions none but really primitive martyrs. Their martyrdom is mentioned by Tertullian in *de Anima*, lv., and treated at length in three sermons (280, 281, 282) by St. Augustine, while their burial at Carthage, in the Basilica Major, is asserted by Victor Vitensis, lib. i. *de Pers. Vandal.* There are three texts of these *Acts*—the original Lat. text, an ancient Gk. version, and a shorter Lat. text, probably an excerpt from the Gk. version. For all three texts see the ed. of Dean J. A. Robinson in *Texts and Studies*, i. 2; cf. also von Gebhardt's *Acta.* [G.T.S.]

Felix (1) **I.**, bp. of Rome, probably from Jan. 5, 269, to Dec. 30, 274, in the reigns of Claudius and Aurelian. The Liberian Catalogue (354) names the consuls of the years above mentioned as those contemporary with his accession and death, and gives 5 years, 11 months, and 25 days as the duration of his episcopate; while the Liberian *Depositio Episcoporum* gives Dec. 30 as the date of his death. Later and less trustworthy authorities, including the *Liber Pontificalis*, differ as to the date and duration of his episcopate. He appears in the Roman Calendar as a saint and martyr, his day being May 30. His martyrdom is asserted, not only in the later editions of the *Liber Pontificalis*, but also in the early recension of 530, known as the Felician Catalogue. Notwithstanding this testimony, his martyrdom seems inconsistent with the silence of the Liberian Catalogue, and with his name appearing in the *Depositio Episcoporum*, not the *Depositio Martyrum* of the same date.

Nothing is known with certainty of his acts, except the part he took in the deposition of Paul of Samosata from the see of Antioch. A synod at Antioch (A.D. 290) having deposed this heretical bishop and appointed Domnus in his place, announced these facts in letters addressed to Maximus and Dionysius, bps. of Alexandria and Rome, and to other Catholic bishops. Felix, who had in the meantime succeeded Dionysius, addressed a letter on the subject to Maximus and to the clergy of Antioch, fragments of which are preserved in the *Apologeticus* of Cyril of Alexandria, and in the Acts of the council of Ephesus, and which is also alluded to by Marius Mercator, and by Vincent of Lerins in his *Commonitorium*; cf. Harnack, *Gesch. der alt. Ch. Lit.* i. 659. Three decretals, undoubtedly spurious, are assigned to him (Harduin, *Concil.*). [J.B.]

Felix (2) **II.**, bp. of Rome after the exile of pope Liberius (A.D. 355). He has a place in the Roman calendar as a saint and martyr, and in the Pontifical and in the Acts of St. Felix and St. Eusebius as a legitimately elected and orthodox pope, persecuted by the emperor and the Arian faction. Contemporary and other ancient writers (Faustus and Marcellinus, Hilary, Athanasius, Jerome, Rufinus, Sozomen, and Theodoret) unanimously represent him, on the contrary, as an interloper placed in the see violently and irregularly by the emperor and the Arians, and do not allude to his martyrdom. The following is the account given by Marcellinus and Faustus, two contemporary Luciferian presbyters of Rome, who must have had good opportunity of knowing the truth. It occurs in the preface to their *Libellus Precum* addressed to the emperors Valentinian, Theodosius, and Arcadius during the pontificate of Damasus, who succeeded Liberius, and by whom the writers complain of being persecuted. Immediately on the banishment of Liberius all the clergy, including the archdeacon Felix, swore to accept no other bishop during the life of the exiled pope. Notwithstanding, the clergy afterwards ordained this Felix, though the people were displeased and abstained from taking part. Damasus, pope after Liberius, was among his perjured supporters. In 357 the emperor visited Rome, and, being solicited by the people for the return of Liberius, consented on condition of his complying with the imperial requirements, but with the intention of his ruling the church jointly with Felix. In the third year Liberius returned, and the people met him with joy. Felix was driven from the city, but soon after, at the instigation of the clergy who had perjured themselves in his election, burst into it again, taking his position in the basilica of Julius beyond the Tiber. The faithful and the nobles again expelled him with great ignominy. After 8 years, during the consulship of Valentinianus and Valens (*i.e.* A.D. 365), on the 10th of the Calends of Dec. (Nov. 22), Felix died, leaving Liberius without a rival as bp. of Rome till his own death on the 8th of the Calends of Oct. (Sept. 24), 366. The other writers mentioned tell us that the election and consecration of Felix took place in the imperial palace, since the people debarred the Arians from their churches; that three of the emperor's eunuchs represented the people, the consecrators being three heretical bishops, Epictetus of Centumellae, Acacius of Caesarea, and Basil of Ancyra; and it was only the Arian section of the clergy, though apparently a large one, that supported Felix.

A very different account is given in the Pontifical and in the *Acts* of St. Felix and of St. Eusebius; the former account is undoubtedly to be preferred. But though Felix, as well as Liberius, has obtained a place in the list of lawful popes, and has even been canonized, it is thus evident that his claim is more than doubtful. Accordingly, Augustine, Optatus, and Eutychius (as did Athanasius, Jerome, and Rufinus) exclude him from their lists of popes. In the Roman church, however, his claim to the position appears to have remained unquestioned till the 14th cent., when, an emendation of the Roman Martyrology having been undertaken in 1582, under pope Gregory XIII., the question was raised and discussed. Baronius at first opposed the claims of Felix; a cardinal, Sanctorius, defended them. The question was decided by the accidental discovery, in the church of SS. Cosmas and Damian in the forum, of a coffin bearing the inscription, "Corpus S. Felicis papae et martyris, qui damnavit Constantium." In the face of this, Baronius was convinced, and retracted all he had written (Baron. *ad Liberium*, c. lxii.). Accordingly Felix retained his place in the Martyrology, though the title of pope was afterwards expunged from the oratio for his day in the breviary. What became of the inscribed slab is not known, and in the absence of any knowledge of its date, its testimony is valueless. [J.B—Y.]

Felix (3) III. (otherwise II.), bp. of Rome from Mar. 483 to Feb. 492. The clergy having met in St. Peter's church to elect a successor to Simplicius, Basilius (Praefectus Praetorio and Patrician) interposed in the name of his master Odoacer the Herulian, who since 476 had ruled the West as king of Italy, alleging, as a fact known to his hearers, that Simplicius before his death had conjured the king to allow no election of a successor without his consent; and this to avoid the turmoil and detriment to the church that was likely to ensue. Basilius expressing surprise that the clergy, knowing this, had taken independent action, proceeded in the king's name to propound a law prohibiting the pope then to be elected and all future popes from alienating any farms or other church possessions; declaring invalid the titles of any who might thus receive ecclesiastical property; requiring the restitution of alienated farms with their proceeds, or the sale for religious uses of gold, silver, jewels, and clothes unfitted for church purposes; and subjecting all donors and recipients of church property to anathema. The assembled clergy seem to have assented to this, and to have been then allowed to proceed with their election, their choice falling on Caelius Felix, the son of a presbyter also called Felix. The Roman synod under pope Symmachus (498-514) protested against this interference of laymen with the election of a pope, and Symmachus consented to declare it void, but required the re-enaction of the law against the alienation of farms, etc.

The pontificate of this Felix was chiefly remarkable for the commencement of the schism of 35 years between Rome and the Eastern patriarchates. In 451 the council of Chalcedon had condemned the Monophysite or Eutychian heresy, adopting the definition of faith contained in the famous letter of pope Leo I. to Flavian, patriarch of Constantinople. The council had also enacted canons of discipline, the 9th and the 17th giving to the patriarchal throne of Constantinople the final determination of causes against metropolitans in the East; and the 28th assigning to the most holy throne of Constantinople, or new Rome, equal privileges with the elder Rome in ecclesiastical matters, as being the second after her, with the right of ordaining metropolitans in the Pontic and Asian and Thracian dioceses, and bishops among the barbarians therein. This last canon the legates of pope Leo had protested against at the council, and Leo himself had afterwards repudiated it, as contrary (so he expressed himself) to the Nicene canons, and an undue usurpation on the part of Constantinople. In connexion with the heresy condemned by the council of Chalcedon and with the privileges assigned by its canons to Constantinople, the schism between the East and West ensued during the pontificate of Felix.

The condemnation of Monophysitism at Chalcedon by no means silenced its abettors, who in the church of Alexandria were especially strong and resolute. They supported Peter Mongus as patriarch; the orthodox supporting first Timotheus Solofacialus, and on his death John Talaia. [ACACIUS (7); JOANNES (11).] Felix, in a synod at Rome, renewed his predecessor's excommunication of Peter Mongus, addressed letters to the emperor Zeno and Acacius, patriarch of Constantinople. Acacius is urged to renounce Peter Mongus, and induce the emperor to do the same. Felix sent also a formal summons for Acacius to appear at Rome and answer the charge of having disregarded the injunctions of Simplicius. The letter to Zeno implored the emperor to refrain from rending the seamless garment of Christ, and to renew his support of the one faith which had raised him to the imperial dignity, the faith of the Roman church, against which the Lord had said that the gates of hell should not prevail; but both the emperor and Acacius continued to support Peter. The papal legates having returned to Rome, Felix convened a synod of 67 Italian bishops, in which he renewed the excommunication of Peter Mongus, and published an irrevocable sentence of deposition and excommunication against Acacius himself. The sentence of excommunication was served on Acacius by one of those zealous champions of Felix, the Sleepless Monks ("Acoemetae"), who fastened it to the robe of the patriarch when about to officiate in church. The patriarch discovered it, but proceeded with the service, and then, in a calm, clear voice, ordered the name of Felix, bp. of Rome, to be erased from the diptychs of the church. This was on Aug. 1, 484. Thus the two chief bishops of Christendom stood mutually excommunicated, and the first great schism between the East and West began. The emperor and the great majority of the prelates of the East supported Acacius; and thus the patriarchates of Alexandria, Antioch, and Jerusalem, as well as Constantinople, remained out of communion with Rome.

Another noted Monophysite, called Peter Fullo (*i.e.* the Fuller), had excited the orthodox zeal of Felix, patriarch of Antioch. He had added to the Tersanctus the clause, "Who wast crucified for us," and was charged with thus attributing passibility to the Godhead. To him, therefore, from a Roman synod, Felix addressed a synodical letter in which, in the name of Peter, the chief of the apostles and the head of all sees, he pronounced his deposition and excommunication.

In 489 Acacius died, and was succeeded by Flavitas, or Fravitas. Felix, on hearing of the vacancy of the see, wrote to Thalasius, an archimandrite of Constantinople, warning him and his monks (who appear throughout to have espoused the cause of Rome) to communicate with no successor till Rome had been fully apprised of all proceedings and had declared the church of Constantinople restored to its communion. Flavitas having died within four months after his accession, the popes' letter to him was received by his successor Euphemius. Felix, though satisfied as to the faith of Euphemius, insisted on the erasure of the name of Acacius, which condition being demurred to, the breach continued.

After his rupture with the East, Felix helped to reconstitute the African church, which had cruelly suffered at the hands of the Arian Vandals. This persecution, which had raged under king Hunneric, who died in 484, ceased under his successor Gundamund, when a number of apostates sought readmission to catholic communion. A synod of 38 bishops held at Rome under Felix in 488 issued a synodical letter dated Mar. 15, laying down terms of readmission. Felix died Feb. 24, 492.

His extant works are 15 letters (Migne, *Patr. Lat.* lviii. 893 ff.). Gratian gives also a decretum as his, to the effect that the royal will should yield to priests in ecclesiastical causes. The ancient authorities for his Life are his letters and those of his successor Gelasius, the Breviarium of Liberatus Diaconus, and the Histories of Evagrius and Nicephorus Callistus. [J.B—Y.]

Felix (4) IV. (otherwise III.; see FELIX II.), bp. of Rome (July 526—Oct. 530) during 4 years, 2 months, and 14 or 18 days (Anastas. *Biblioth.*). The same authority states that he built the basilica of SS. Cosmas and Damian, restored that of the martyr St. Saturninus, and was buried, on Oct. 12, in the basilica of St. Peter. There is little to be told of him, except the circumstances of his appointment. His predecessor, John I., had died in prison at Ravenna, into which he had been thrown by Theodoric the Ostrogoth, who then ruled the West as king of Italy. Theodoric took the unprecedented step of appointing his successor on his own authority, without waiting for the customary election by clergy and people. This high-handed proceeding seems to have been at length acquiesced in. No subsequent king or emperor laid claim to a like power of interference in the appointment of popes, though the confirmation of elections by the civil power was insisted on, and continued till the election of Zachary in 752, when the confirmation of the exarch of Ravenna, as representing the Eastern emperor, was first dispensed with under the Carlovingian empire. The same freedom of election by clergy and people continued to be the theory till the appointment was given to the College of Cardinals during the pontificate of Nicholas II., A.D. 1059. For previous interventions of the civil power see BONIFACIUS II., EULALIUS (1), FELIX III., SYMMACHUS, LAURENTIUS (10). The only further event known as marking the pontificate of Felix is the issue of an edict by Athalaric, the successor of Theodoric, requiring all civil suits against ecclesiastics to be preferred before the bishop and not the secular judge. The edict was called forth by Felix, with the Roman clergy, having complained to the king that the Goths had invaded the rights of churches and dragged the clergy before lay tribunals. It extended only to the Roman clergy, "in honour of the Apostolic see" (Cassiodor. lib. 8, c. 24). Justinian I. afterwards extended it, though with an appeal to the civil tribunal, to all ecclesiastics (Justin. *Novel.* 83, 123).

For this pope's letter, esp. letter to Caesarius of Arles, requiring probation from candidates for the priesthood before their ordination, see Migne, *Patr. Lat.* lxv., An important *decretum* of this pope was made known by Amelli in 1882, and edited by Mommsen in *Neuer Archiv fur älter deutsch. Gesch. Kunde*, 1886. See Duchesne, *La Succession du pape Félix IV.* (Rome, 1883). [J.B—Y.]

Felix (26) I., bp. of Aptunga, in proconsular Africa. Felix was one of those who laid hands on Caecilian as bp. of Carthage, if not the sole officiating bishop, A.D. 311 (Aug. *Brevie. Coll.* iii. 14, 26; 16, 29). The Donatist party, having failed in the Court of Inquiry at Rome, under Melchiades, Oct. 2, 313, to establish their case against Caecilian, turned their attack on Felix, whom they sought to convict of the infamous crime of "tradition" in the persecution of Maximus, A.D. 303. The emperor gave orders to Aelianus, the proconsul of Africa, to hold an inquiry on the spot, which took place on Feb. 15, 314 (Aug. *Post. Coll.* 38, 56; *Ep.* 43, 3-14; 88; *c. Cresc.* iii. 61) at Carthage, in the presence of many who had held municipal offices at the time of the persecution. In vain the prosecution relied on a chain of fraudulent evidence elaborately concocted. The proconsul pronounced the complete acquittal of Felix, which was confirmed by the emperor, and repeated in a letter to Verinus, or Valerius, the vicar of Africa, A.D. 321. The whole case was brought up again at Carth. Conf., A.D. 411, when Augustine argued that there was no doubt of the completeness of the imperial decision. Aug. *c. Cresc.* iii. 81, iv. 79; *de Unic. Bapt.* 28; *Brev. Coll.* 41, 42; *Post. Coll.* 56; *Mon. Vet. Don.* iii. pp. 160-167 and 341-343, ed. Oberthür; Bruns. *Concil.* i. 108; Routh, *Rel. Sacr.* iv. 92. [H.W.P.]

Felix (174), bp. of Tubzoca (perhaps Thibaris in Numidia). His story illustrates the first edict of persecution issued by Diocletian in Feb. 303, and the special severity with which it was worked in the West under the emperor Maximian. This edict did not authorize death as a punishment, but simply prohibited the assembly of Christians for religious worship; ordered the destruction of churches and sacred documents, and authorized torture. Official notice of its publication arrived at Tubzoca on June 5, and the overseer of the city, Magnellianus, summoned first the clergy and then the bishop, and demanded the sacred writings. Felix replied, "It is better that I should be burned rather than the Holy Scriptures, since it is better to obey God rather than man." Three days were given him for reconsideration, during which time he was committed to the private custody of Vincentius Celsinus, a leading citizen. Upon his continued refusal he was sent to the proconsul Anulinus at Carthage, June 24. By him the bishop was twice examined. With the edict there seems to have been sent by Maximian the praetorian prefect or commander of the emperor's guard, to secure its due execution. To him, upon his final refusal, Felix and his companions were delivered for transporation into Italy, arriving after four days' sail in Sicily. At Agrigentum, Catana, Messana, and Taurominium they were received with great honour by the Christians. Thence they were carried by the prefect to

Venusia, in Apulia, where, having again called upon Felix to surrender the sacred writings, he condemned him to death for disobedience. Felix suffered by beheading, Aug. 30, on which day he is commemorated by Bede. There is considerable confusion as to details in different versions of the Acts, which d'Achery and Baluze have in vain endeavoured to remedy. *Martyr. Vet. Roman.* Bedae, Adonis, Usuardi; Baronius, *Annal.* A.D. 302, cxvii.-cxxiii.; Ruinart, *Acta Sincera*; Surius; d'Acherii *Spicileg.* t. xii. 634; Baluz. *Miscell.* t. ii. p. 77; Tillem. v. 202. [G.T.S.]

Felix (186) of Nola. [PAULINUS (8).]

Felix (212). [SCILLITAN MARTYRS.]

Firmilianus (1), St., bp. of Caesarea in Cappadocia, one of the greatest prelates of his time. In 232 he already occupied his see (Eus. vi. 26, 27), though Cave (*Hist.* i. p. 123) speaks of 233 as the year of his elevation. When Origen soon after left Egypt, Firmilian induced him to visit Cappadocia; subsequently he paid Origen long visits in Judaea to advance his own knowledge of theology (Eus. *l.c.*). He urged Dionysius of Alexandria to attend the council of Antioch, held to repudiate Novatianism (*ib.* vi. 46; cf. Routh, *R. S.* iii. 51).

In 256 he is addressed by Cyprian in a letter now lost as to the Asiatic practice of rebaptizing those baptized by heretics. In his long reply (Cyp. *Ep.* 75) Firmilian describes it as impossible to add much to the strength of Cyprian's arguments. He is clear as to the antiquity of the practice in Asia, which he regards as ratified by the action of the council of Iconium in the case of the Montanists. He speaks of several meetings of the Cappadocian bishops, one immediately before his writing. Baronius, Labbe, and other Roman writers have been anxious to prove that the baptismal dispute originated with Firmilian and the East, but the attempt is against the whole tenor of Cyprianic correspondence as well as the express statement of Eusebius (vii. 3). To Firmilian the see of Jerusalem appears to be the central see, so far as such an idea arises. He presided at Antioch, A.D. 266, in the first synod held to try Paul of Samosata, and visited Antioch twice on this business (*Concil. Antioch. contr. Paul. Samos.* in Routh, *R. S.* iii. 304; Eus. vii. 30). Imposed upon by Paul's promises, he procured the postponement of a decision against him. But when it was necessary to convene another synod in 272, Firmilian, who was to have again presided, died on his journey, at Tarsus. To his contemporaries his 40 years of influential episcopate, his friendship with Origen and Dionysius, the appeal to him of Cyprian, and his censure of Stephanus might well make him seem the most conspicuous figure of his time.

Routh (vol. iii. p. 149) points to him as one of the oldest authorities who states with precision the anti-Pelagian doctrine. Basil (*de Spiritu Sancto*, xxix.) speaks of his discourses as early testimonies to the exactness of his own doctrine, and quotes his agreement with Cyprian on baptism in the epistle to Amphilochius (*Ep.* 188). [E.W.B.]

Flavianus (4) I., bp. of Antioch, 381-404. Born at Antioch, of a distinguished family, he was still very young when his father's death left him heir of his considerable property. As bishop he continued to occupy the family mansion at Antioch, which he devoted to the reception of the sick and distressed of his flock. Chrysostom, in his highly coloured eulogium pronounced on receiving priest's orders at his hands, records that he was remarkable from his earliest years for temperance and contempt of luxury, although early deprived of parental control and exposed to temptations incident to youth, wealth, and good birth. Theodoret (*H. E.* ii. 24) relates that, when a half-concealed Arianism was triumphing, Flavian, with his friend Diodorus (afterwards bp. of Tarsus), left his home and adopted the life of a solitary. The necessities of the times soon recalled them to Antioch, where as laymen they kept alive an orthodox remnant. Leontius was then the intruding bp. of Antioch, and, while a Eusebian at heart, sought by temporizing to preserve a hollow peace in his church. The counsel of the orthodox bp. Eustathius, before he was expelled from Antioch (*c.* 328), was that his adherents should maintain the unity of the church and continue in communion with his successors in the see; but there was no small risk of their being thus gradually absorbed by the Eusebians and losing hold of the Catholic faith. This danger was strenuously met by Flavian and Diodorus. They rallied the faithful about them, accustomed them to assemble round the tombs of the martyrs, and exhorted them to adhere steadfastly to the faith. They are said by Theodoret to have revived the antiphonal chanting of the Psalms, which tradition ascribed to Ignatius (*ib.* ii. 24; Socr. *H. E.* vi. 8). Leontius endeavoured to check the growing influence of these gatherings by causing them to be transferred from the martyries without the walls to the churches of the city, but this only increased their popularity and strengthened the cause of orthodoxy. Flavian and Diodorus became all-powerful at Antioch; Leontius, being unable to resist them, was compelled to retrace his steps (Theod. ii. 24).

Leontius was succeeded by Eudoxius, then by the excellent Meletius, who was deposed, and in 361 by Euzoïus, the old comrade of Arius. Euzoïus was repudiated with horror by all the orthodox. Those who had till now remained in communion with the bishops recognized by the state, separated themselves and recognized Meletius as their bishop. The old Catholic body, however, who bore the name of Eustathians, would not submit to a bishop, however orthodox, consecrated by Arians, and continued to worship apart from their Meletian brethren, as well as from Euzoïus, having as leader Paulinus, a presbyter highly esteemed by all parties. This schism between two orthodox bodies caused much pain to Athanasius and others. A council at Alexandria, early in 362, wisely advised that Paulinus and his flock should unite with Meletius, who had now returned from exile; but the precipitancy of Lucifer of Cagliari perpetuated the schism by ordaining Paulinus bishop. The Arian emperor Valens came to reside at Antioch in June 370; and this was the signal for a violent persecution of the orthodox. Meletius was banished a third time, and the duty of ministering to the faithful under their prolonged trials devolved on Flavian and Diodorus. The Catholics, having been deprived of their churches, took refuge among ravines and caverns in the abrupt mountain ranges overhanging the city. Here they worshipped, exposed to the assaults of a rude soldiery, by whom they were repeatedly dislodged. The persecution ceased with the death of Valens in 378. The exiles were recalled, and Meletius resumed charge of his flock. His official recognition as the Catholic bp. of Antioch was more tardy. Gratian had commanded that the churches should be given up to prelates in communion with Damasus, bp. of Rome, and that Arian intruders should be expelled. But here were two bishops with equal claims to orthodoxy, Paulinus and Meletius, and a third, Vitalian, who held Apollinarian views. Sapor, a high military officer, to whom Gratian had committed the execution of the edict, was much perplexed. Flavian convinced him that the right lay with Meletius. The separation, however, still continued. Paulinus declined the proposal of Meletius that they should be recognized as of equal authority and that the survivor should be sole bishop. The Oriental churches recognized Meletius, the West and Egypt Paulinus (*ib.* v. 1-3). In 381 Flavian accompanied Meletius to the council of Constantinople, during the session of which Meletius died. Gregory of Nazianzus entreated his brother-bishops to heal the schism by recognizing Paulinus as orthodox bp. of Antioch (Greg. Naz. *de Vita Sac.* v. 1572 seq. p. 757). But this, however right in itself, would have been a triumph for the Westerns. The council was composed of Oriental bishops, and, in spite of the remonstrances of Gregory, Flavian was elected to succeed Meletius. Flavian cannot be altogether excused for this continuance of the schism; and the less so if, as Socrates (v. 5) and Sozomen (vii. 3, 11) state, he was one of the six leading clergy of Antioch who had sworn not to seek the bishopric themselves at the death of Meletius or Paulinus, but to acknowledge the survivor. This charge, however, is rendered very doubtful by the absence of reference to it in the letters of Ambrose or any contemporary documents published by adherents of Paulinus during the controversy. Flavian was consecrated by Diodorus of Tarsus and Acacius of Beroea with the ratification of the council. Paulinus remonstrated in vain (Theod. v. 23), but his cause was maintained by Damasus and the Western bishops and those of Egypt; while even at Antioch, though most of the Meletians welcomed Flavian with joy (Chrys. *Hom. cum Presbyt. fuit ordinatus*, § 4), some, indignant at his breaking an engagement, real or implied, separated from his communion and joined Paulinus (Soz. vii. 11). The West refused all intercourse with Flavian, and the council at Aquileia in Sept. 381 wrote to Theodosius in favour of Paulinus, and requested him to summon a council at Alexandria to decide that and other questions. Theodosius acquiesced, but selected Rome. The Eastern prelates declined to attend, and held a synod of their own at Constantinople in 382. Even here the bishops of Egypt, Cyprus, and Arabia recognized Paulinus, and demanded the banishment of Flavian, who was supported by the bishops of Palestine, Phoenicia, and Syria (Socr. v. 10). A synodal letter was, however, dispatched to Damasus and the Western bishops, recognizing Flavian's consecration as legitimate (Theod. v. 9). Paulinus himself attended the council at Rome, accompanied by Epiphanius and his ardent supporter Jerome. At this council the West refused to acknowledge Flavian as canonically elected. It is said that they even excommunicated him and his two consecrators (Soz. vii. 11). The two rivals continued to exercise episcopal functions for their respective flocks. Consequently church discipline became impossible. Early in his episcopate Flavian exercised his authority against the Syrian sect of perfectionists known as Euchites or Messalians, and to make himself acquainted with their doctrines, which it was their habit to conceal, he condescended to an unworthy act of deception.

In 386 Flavian ordained Chrysostom presbyter, and Chrysostom preached a eulogistic inaugural discourse (Chrys. *u.s.* §§ 3, 4). The sedition at Antioch and the destruction of the Imperial Statues, 387, shewed Flavian at his best. When the brief fit of popular madness was over and the Antiochenes awoke to their danger, Flavian at their entreaty became their advocate with the emperor, starting immediately on his errand of mercy (Chrys. *de Statuis*, iii. 1, xxi. 3). The success of his mission was complete. Though Paulinus died in 388, the schism continued; for on his deathbed he had consecrated Evagrius, a presbyter of his church, as his successor (Socr. v. 15; Soz. vii. 15; Theod. v. 23). Theodosius summoned Flavian to meet him at a synod at Capua. Flavian excused himself as winter was setting in, but promised to obey the emperor's bidding in the spring (Theod. v. 23). Ambrose and the other leading Western prelates urged Theodosius to compel Flavian to come to Rome and submit to the judgment of the church. Flavian replied to the emperor that if his episcopal seat only was the object of attack, he would prefer to resign it altogether. The knot was before long cut by the death of Evagrius. Flavian's influence prevented the election of a successor. The Eustathians, however, still refused to acknowledge Flavian, and continued to hold their assemblies apart (Soz. vii. 15, viii. 3; Socr. v. 15). This separation lasted till the episcopate of Alexander, 414 or 415. The division between Flavian and Egypt and the West was finally healed by Chrysostom, who took the opportunity of the presence of Theophilus, patriarch of Alexandria, at Constantinople for his consecration in 398, to induce him to become reconciled with Flavian, and to join in dispatching an embassy to Rome to supplicate Siricius to recognize Flavian as canonical bishop of Antioch. Their mission was entirely successful (Socr. v. 15; Soz. viii. 3; Theod. v. 23). To shew that all angry feeling had ceased, and to conciliate his opponents, Flavian put the names of Paulinus and Evagrius on the diptychs (Cyril. Alex. *Ep.* 56, p. 203). Flavian lived long enough to see the deposition and exile of Chrysostom, against which he protested with his last breath. His death probably occurred in 404 (Pallad. *Dial.* p. 144; Soz. viii. 24; Theophan. p. 68). He governed the church of Antioch for 23 years; and Tillemont thinks it probable that he lived to the age of 95. The Greek church commemorates him on Sept. 26.

He left behind certain homilies, of which a few fragments are preserved. Theodoret, in his *Eranistes*, quotes one on John i. 14 (*Dial.* i. p. 46), another on St. John the Baptist (*ib.* p. 66), on Easter, and the treachery of Judas (*Dial.* iii. p. 250) or the *Theophania*, and a passage from his commentary on St. Luke (*Dial.* ii. p. 160). [E.V.]

Flavianus (8), 18th bp. of Constantinople, between Proclus and Anatolius, for about two or three years. He is described by Nicephorus as being at his election guardian of the sacred vessels of the great church of Constantinople, with a reputation for a heavenly life. At the time of his consecration Theodosius II. was staying at Chalcedon. Chrysaphius his minister immediately plotted against the new patriarch. Foiled in an attempt to extort a present of gold to the emperor for acknowledging his elevation, Chrysaphius, with the empress Eudocia for an ally, planned two methods of attack against Flavian—the direct subversion of the authority of the emperor's sister Pulcheria; and the support of Eutyches, to whom the archbishop was opposed. Pulcheria had devoted herself to a religious life; let the emperor order the prelate to ordain her a deaconess. Flavian, receiving the emperor's command to this effect, and beyond measure grieved, sent a private message to Pulcheria, who divined the scheme, and to avoid a struggle retired to Hebdomum, where for a time she led a private life (Theoph. *u. infr.*).

Flavian having assembled a council of 40 bishops at Constantinople Nov. 8, 448, to compose a difference between the metropolitan bp. of Sardis and two bishops of his province, Eusebius, bp. of Dorylaeum, appeared and presented his indictment against Eutyches. The speech of Flavian remains, concluding with this appeal to the bp. of Dorylaeum: "Let your reverence condescend to visit him and argue with him about the true faith, and if he shall be found in very truth to err, then he shall be called to our holy assembly, and shall answer for himself." For the particulars of this great controversy see DIOSCORUS and EUTYCHES. When, on Aug. 8, 449, the Latrocinium assembled at Ephesus, Eutyches violently attacked the archbishop.

On Aug. 11, 449, Flavian expired at Hypepe in Lydia from the effects of the barbarous ill-usage which resulted from this attack. When Pulcheria returned to power, after her brother's death, she had Flavian's remains, which had been buried obscurely, brought with great pomp to Constantinople. It was more like a triumph, says the chronicler, than a funeral procession.

Among the documents which touch on the career of Flavian are the reply of Petrus Chrysologus, archbp. of Ravenna, to a circular appeal of Eutyches, and various letters of Theodoret. Leo wrote Flavian a beautiful letter before hearing that he was dead.

Leo. Mag. *Epp.* 23, 26, 27, 28, 44; Facund, *Pro Trib. Capit.* viii. 5; xii. 5; Evagr. ii. 2. etc.; Liberatus Diac. *Breviar.* xi. xii.; Soz. *H. E.* ix. 1; Theophan. *Chronogr.* pp. 84-88, etc.; Niceph. Constant. xiv. 47. [W.M.S.]

Flavianus (16) **II.**, bp. of Antioch, 498-512, previously a monk in the monastery of Tilmognon, in Coelesyria (Evagr. *H. E.* iii. 32), and at the time of his consecration "apocrisiarius" or nuncio of the church of Antioch at the court of Constantinople (Vict. Tunun. *Chron.*; Theophan. *Chronogr.* p. 122). Before his consecration Flavian passed for an opponent of the decrees of Chalcedon, and on his appointment he sent to announce the fact to John Haemula, bp. of Alexandria, with letters of communion, and a request for the same in return (Evagr. iii. 23). He speedily, however, withdrew from intercourse with the patriarchs of Alexandria, and joined the opposite party, uniting with Elias of Jerusalem and Macedonius of Constantinople (Liberat. c. 18, p. 128). Flavian soon found a bitter enemy in the turbulent Monophysite Xenaias or Philoxenus, bp. of Hierapolis. On Flavian's declaring for the council of Chalcedon, Xenaias denounced his patriarch as a concealed Nestorian. Flavian made no difficulty in anathematizing Nestorius and his doctrines. Xenaias demanded that he should anathematize Diodorus, Theodore, Theodoret, and others, as necessary to completely prove that he was not a Nestorian. On his refusing, Xenaias stirred up against him the party of Dioscorus in Egypt, and charged Flavian before Anastasius with being a Nestorian (Evagr. iii. 31; Theophan. p. 128). Anastasius used pressure, to which Flavian yielded partially, trusting by concessions to satisfy his enemies. He convened a synod of the prelates of his patriarchate which drew up a letter to Anastasius confirming the first three councils, passing over that of Chalcedon in silence, and anathematizing Diodorus, Theodore, and the others. Xenaias, seeking Flavian's overthrow, required of him further a formal anathema of the council of Chalcedon and of all who admitted the two natures. On his refusal, Xenaias again denounced him to the emperor. Flavian declared his acceptance of the decrees of Chalcedon in condemning Nestorius and Eutyches, but not as a rule of faith. Xenaias having gathered the bishops of Isauria and others, induced them to draw up a formula anathematizing Chalcedon and the two natures, and Flavian and Macedonius, refusing to sign this, were declared excommunicate, A.D. 509 (Evagr. *u.s.*; Theophan. p. 131). The next year the vacillating Flavian received letters from Severus, the uncompromising antagonist of Macedonius, on the subject of anathematizing Chalcedon, and the reunion of the Acephali with the church (Liberat. c. 19, p. 135). This so irritated Macedonius that he anathematized his former friend, and drove with indignation from his presence the apocrisiarii of Antioch (Theophan. p. 131). On the expulsion of Macedonius, A.D. 511, Flavian obeyed the emperor in recognizing his successor Timotheus, on being convinced of his orthodoxy, but without disguising his displeasure at the violent and uncanonical measures by which Macedonius had been deposed. This exasperated Anastasius, who readily acceded to the request of Xenaias and Soterichus that a council should be convened, ostensibly for the more precise declaration of the faith on the points at issue, but really to depose Flavian and Elias of Jerusalem; but it was broken up by the emperor's mandate, to the extreme vexation of Soterichus and Xenaias, without pronouncing any sentence (Labbe, *Concil.* iv. 1414, vii. 88; Theophan. *u.s.*; Coteler. *Monum. Eccl. Graec.* iii. 298). Flavian's perplexities were increased by the inroad of a tumultuous body of monks from Syria Prima, clamouring for the anathematization of Nestorius and all supposed favourers of his doctrines. The citizens rose against them, slew many, and threw their bodies into the Orontes. A rival body of monks poured down from the mountain ranges of Coelesyria, eager to do battle in defence of their metropolitan and former associate. Flavian was completely unnerved, and, yielding to the stronger party, pronounced a public anathema in his cathedral on the decrees of Chalcedon and the four so-called heretical doctors. His enemies, determined to obtain his patriarchate for one of their own party, accused him to the emperor of condemning with his lips what he still held in his heart. The recent disturbances at Antioch were attributed to him, and afforded the civil authorities a pretext for desiring him to leave Antioch for a time. His quitting Antioch was seized on by the emperor as an acknowledgment of guilt. Anastasus declared the see vacant, sent Severus to occupy it, and banished Flavian to Petra in Arabia, where he died in 518. Eutych. Alex. *Annal. Eccl.* p. 140; Marcell. *Chron.*; Theophan. p. 134; Evagr. *H. E.* iii. 32. [E.V.]

Florentius (50), a chief minister of state at Constantinople under Theodosius II. and Marcian, a man of the highest reputation for soundness of faith, purity of life, and statesmanlike wisdom (Labbe, *Concil.* iv. 220). He was consul in A.D. 429, patrician in 448, prefect of the praetorian guards, and the high dignity of prefect of the East was bestowed on him a seventh time by Marcian in 450.

In 448, when Flavian had resolved to put Eutyches on his trial for heretical doctrine, Theodosius demanded that Florentius should have a seat at the synod as his representative. Hitherto the ostensible reason for the presence of imperial officers at ecclesiastical synods was the preservation of order. The ground expressly assigned by the emperor for requiring the admission of Florentius, viz. that the matters under discussion concerned the faith, was a startling innovation which Flavian withstood as long as he dared (Acac. *Hist. Brevicul.* p. 112; Liberat. *Breviar.* c. xi.; Labbe, *Concil.* iv. 247). On the opening of the trial Florentius took his seat among the metropolitans, next to Seleucus, bp. of Amasea (Labbe, 238; Liberat. p. 60), and disclaimed all desire to dogmatize, or to forget his position as a layman; but he took a very leading and authoritative part in the discussion, and manifested a strong leaning towards the acquittal of Eutyches. But his efforts to induce Eutyches to acknowledge the two natures in Christ or to adopt language which might satisfy the council were fruitless, and the interests of orthodoxy compelled him to assent to his condemnation (Labbe, 507, 517). As Eutyches left the hall he lodged with Florentius an appeal against his condemnation to the churches of Rome, Alexandria, and Jerusalem. The bishop availed himself of the plea that the trial was closed to exclude the registration of the appeal (*ib.* 244). When the council of Chalcedon met, Florentius was present with other high civil dignitaries; but there is no record of the part he took. We have letters to Florentius from Theodoret (*Ep.* 89), Isidore of Pelusium (*Ep.* lib. i. 486), and Firmus of Caesarea (*Ep.* 29). [E.V.]

Florinus (1), for some time in the latter half of the 2nd cent. a presbyter at Rome, deprived for falling into heresy. He is known from two notices (v. 15, 20) in Eusebius, taken from writings of Irenaeus against Florinus. One is an interesting fragment of a letter to Florinus, in which Irenaeus records his youthful recollections of Polycarp, representing how that bishop, whose good opinion Florinus had once been anxious to gain, would have been shocked at his present opinions. The fragment contains unmistakable internal evidence of genuineness. The title of the letter to Florinus was *On Monarchy, or that God is not the Author of Evil*, and Eusebius remarks that Florinus seems to have maintained the opposite opinion. Later writers have naturally followed the report of Eusebius. Philaster (79) refers to an unnamed heretic, who taught that things which God made were in their own nature evil. Augustine (66) calls the anonymous heretic Florinus and, with little probability, makes him the founder of a sect of Floriniani. He probably arrived at this result by combining the notice in Eusebius with Philaster's mention in another place of Floriani. The work of Irenaeus which we possess does not mention Florinus, and has no trace of the letter, nor does Tertullian, in dealing with the same subject, employ the letter to Florinus. If Florinus ever in a heretical sense made God the author of evil, his errors afterwards took the opposite direction, and he became a Valentinian. In reply to him Irenaeus composed his work *On the Ogdoad*. If the controversy of Irenaeus with Florinus was earlier than the publication of the treatise on heresies, we should expect some trace of it therein; and the fact that, after the publication of a treatise dealing so fully with Valentinianism, a separate treatise on the Ogdoad was necessary, may point to the controversy having arisen later. In favour of the later date is also the fact that there is extant a Syriac fragment (Harvey, ii. 457), purporting to be an extract from a letter of Irenaeus to Victor of Rome concerning Florinus, a presbyter, who was a partisan of the error of Valentinus, and had published an abominable book. Florinus is not named by Epiphanius, Philaster, or Pseudo-Tertullian who has so many notices of Roman heretics; and it is likely, therefore, that he was not named in the earlier work of Hippolytus, nor in the lectures of Irenaeus, on which that work was founded; he is not named in the later work of Hippolytus, nor by Tertullian. This silence is not easily explained if either Florinus or any school of Floriniani were any source of danger after his exposure by IRENAEUS (cf. Zahn, *Forschungen*, iv. 283-308). [G.S.]

Fortunatus (17), **Venantius Honorius Cle-**

mentianus, bp. of Poictiers, and the last representative of Latin poetry in Gaul, was born *c.* 530 at Ceneta, the modern Ceneda, near Tarvisium (Treviso) (*Vit. Sanct. Martin.* lib. iv. 668). He seems to have resided at an early age at Aquileia, where he came under the influence of one Paulus, who was instrumental in his conversion. Paulus Diaconus (*Hist. Langobard.* lib. ii. 23) relates that he studied grammar, rhetoric, and poetry at Ravenna. In gratitude for his recovery from blindness, he set out on a pilgrimage to the tomb of St. Martin of Tours *c.* 565. Crossing the Alps and passing into Austrasia, he visited king Siegbert, for whom he composed an epithalamium on his marriage with Brunehault, couched in terms of extravagant flattery. Euphronius bp. of Tours and Fortunatus became close friends (*Miscell.* iii. 1-3). After completing his pilgrimage, he continued to travel in Gaul, because of the disturbed state of Italy, due to the incursions of the Lombards, but finding an additional inducement in the society of Rhadegund of Poictiers, for whom he conceived a Platonic attachment. She was the daughter of Bertharius, king of the Thuringians, and had been espoused against her will to Lothair I., king of Neustria, but had separated from him, and retired in 550 to Poictiers, where she founded the convent of St. Croix, more for literary than for religious seclusion, appointing her own domestic Agnes the first abbess. At what date Fortunatus visited Poictiers is uncertain, but he was induced to become chaplain and almoner to the convent. Rhadegund employed her poet-chaplain in correspondence with the prelates of Gaul, and despatched him from time to time on delicate missions. He thus became intimate with Gregory of Tours, Syagrius of Autun, Felix of Nantes, Germanus of Paris, Avitus of Clermont, and many others, to whom his poems are addressed. He also composed Lives of the saints, theological treatises, and hymns, including the famous *Vexilla Regis*, composed for a religious ceremony at Poictiers. The *Pange Lingua*, though generally ascribed to his pen, was more probably composed, as Sirmond has shewn (*in Notis ad Epist. Sidon. Apollin.* lib. iii. *Ep.* 4), by Claudianus Mamertus. Fortunatus was ordained priest, and, subsequently to the death of Rhadegund in 597, succeeded Plato in the bishopric of Poictiers; but died early in the 7th cent.

His works comprise: (1) Eleven Books of Miscellanies, chiefly in elegiac verse, interesting for the light they throw upon the manners of the time and the history of art (*Miscell.* i. 12; iii. 13), but as literature all but worthless.

(2) The Life of St. Martin of Tours in four books, consisting of 2,245 hexameter lines, hastily composed, and little more than a metrical version of Severus Sulpicius's incomparably better prose.

(3) An elegiac poem in three cantos, written in the character, and evidently under the inspiration, of Rhadegund. The first, *de Excidio Thuringiae*, is dedicated to her cousin Amalfred (or Hermanfred); the second is a panegyric of Justin II. and his empress Sophia, who had presented Rhadegund with a piece of the true cross.

(4) A collection of 150 elegiac verses addressed to Rhadegund and Agnes, and a short epigram *ad Theuchildem*.

(5) The Lives of eleven saints—Hilary of Poitiers, Germain of Paris, Aubin of Angers, Paternus of Avranches, Rhadegund of Poictiers, Amant of Rodez, Médard of Noyon, Remy of Rheims, Lubin of Chartres, Mauril of Angers, and Marcel of Paris—but the first book of the Life of Hilary and the Lives of the three last-named saints ought probably to be attributed to another Fortunatus. To these must be added an account of the martyrdom at Paris of St. Denys, St. Rusticus, and St. Eleutherius.

His style is pedantic, his taste bad, his grammar and prosody seldom correct for many lines together, but two of his longer poems display a simplicity and pathos foreign to his usual style—viz. that on the marriage of Galesuintha, sister of Brunehaut, with Chilperic, and his Elegy upon the Fall of Thuringia.

The latest and best ed. of his works is by Leo and Krusch (Berlin, 1881-1885). A good earlier ed. by Luchi is reprinted in Migne's *Patr. Lat.* lxxxviii. Augustin Thierry, *Récits mérovingiens*, t. ii. Recit. vi.; and Ampère, *Hist. lit. de la France*, t. ii. c. 13. [E.M.Y.]

Fortunatus (18), a bp. who has been confounded with Venantius Fortunatus, bp. of Poictiers. Born at Vercellae, he migrated into Gaul, and became intimate with St. Germanus, who induced him to write the Life of St. Marcellus. He was probably the author of bk. i. of the Life of St. Hilary of Poictiers, and of three other Lives of saints ascribed to his more distinguished namesake. He died at Celles, in the diocese of Sens, *c.* 569. Rivet, *Hist. lit. de la France*, t. iii. p. 298. [E.M.Y.]

Forty Martyrs, The. Three groups occur as such:—

(1) Forty soldiers, who suffered under Licinius, 320, at Sebaste in Armenia. A list of their names is given in the martyrology of Ado under March 11. [See SEBASTE, FORTY MARTYRS OF, in *D. C. A.*] They were young, brave, and noted for their services. The emperor having ordained that the military police of the cities should offer sacrifices, the governor called upon these forty to comply. They refused, and withstood both bribes and threats. Thereupon a new punishment was devised. They were immersed for a whole night in a frozen pond, a hot bath being placed within sight for any who might choose to avail themselves of it, their doing so, however, being the sign of apostasy. The trial was too great for one. He left the pond and flung himself into the bath, but as soon as he touched the hot water he died. The number of forty was not, however, broken. The sentinel who watched the bath saw in a vision angels descend and distribute rewards to all in the pond. The guard at once stripped off his clothing and took the vacant place in the pond. Next morning they were all flung into fires. There was one Melito, younger and more vigorous than the rest, whose resolution they thought they might shake. His mother, however, who was present, herself placed him in the executioner's cart, saying: "Go, my son, finish this happy voyage with thy comrades, that thou mayst not be the last presented to God." Their relics were carefully preserved and carried to various cities, where many churches

were built in their honour. The mother Emmelia, and the sister Macrina, of St. Basil obtained some for their monastery near the village of Annesi in Pontus, where already a church had been built in their honour (Greg. Nys. *Vit. S. Macrin.*). Sozomen (*H. E.* ix. 2) tells a strange story about another set of their relics. In addition to the authorities quoted, consult Pitra, *Analect. Sacr.* t. i. p. 599, in *Spicil. Solesmense.* Their popularity throughout the entire East has ever been very great (cf. Dr. Zirecek, *Geschichte der Bulgaren*). In Burton's *Unexplored Syria*, App. ii., a church in their honour is noted at Huns, near Damascus; cf. also Melchior de Vogüé, *Les Églises de la terre sainte*, p. 367.

(2) Another set of Forty Martyrs in Persia, 375, is commemorated on May 20 (Assemani, *Mart. Orient.* i. 141). Among them were the bishops Abdas and Ebed-Jesu. Ceillier, iii. 82, 336; Bas. *Menol.*

(3) Under Dec. 24 Forty Virgin Martyrs under Decius at Antioch in Syria are noted in *Mart.* Hieron., Adon., Usuard. [G.T.S.]

Fravitta, 23rd bp. of Constantinople A.D. 489. Our chief authority is Nicephorus Callistus, who relates that on the death of Acacius, the emperor Zeno placed on the altar of the great church of Constantinople two sheets of paper. On one was written a prayer that God would send an angel to inscribe on the blank sheet the name of him whom He wished to be the patriarch. A fast of 40 days with prayer was ordered. The church was given into the custody of a confidential eunuch, the imperial chamberlain, and the imperial seal set on the casket containing the papers. A presbyter named Fravitta was in charge of the suburban church of St. Thecla. Fired with ambition, he paid the eunuch large sums, and promised him more, to write his name on the blank sheet. At the end of the 40 days the casket was opened; the name of Fravitta was found, and he was enthroned amid universal acclamations. Within 4 months he died, and the powerful eunuch was pressing his executors for the promised gold. They revealed the odious tale to the emperor. The forger was turned out of all his employments and driven from the city. Zeno, ashamed of his failure, entrusted the election of the new patriarch to the clergy.

Such is the account of Nicephorus Callistus. In the correspondence between Zeno, Fravitta, and pope Felix on the appointment there is no trace of this story.

Fravitta at one and the same time wrote letters to Peter Mongus asking for his communion, and a synodal to pope Felix begging his sanction and co-operation. This document was carried to Rome by Catholic monks of Constantinople who had always kept separate from Acacius and his friend Mongus. An accompanying letter of Zeno showed great affection for Fravitta; Zeno had only laboured for his appointment because he thought him worthy and to restore peace and unity to the churches. Pope Felix, delighted with the letters, had Zeno's read aloud to the deputation and all the clergy of Rome, who expressed loud approval. When the pope, however, wished the monks from Constantinople to undertake that the names of Acacius and Mongus should be rejected from the diptychs, they replied that they had no instructions on that point. The joy of the pope was finally destroyed by the arrival at Rome of a copy of the letter which Fravitta had sent to Mongus. Directly contrary to that which Felix had received, it actually denied all communion with Rome. The pope would not hear a word more from the monks. Whether the story of Nicephorus Callistus be true or not, Fravitta stands disgraced by this duplicity. Niceph. Callist. xvi. 19, *Patr. Gk.* cxlvii. § 684, p. 152; Joann. Zonar. *Annal.* xiv. iii. *Patr. Gk.* cxxxiv. § 53, p. 1214; Liberat. Diac. *Brev.* xviii. *Patr. Lat.* lxviii.; Felicis Pap. *Ep.* xii. and xiii. *Patr. Lat.* lviii. p. 971; Evagr. iii. 23, *Patr. Gk.* lxxxvi. part ii.; Theoph. *Chronogr.* 114, *Patr. Gk.* cviii. p. 324. [W.M.S.]

Fructuosus (1), M., bp. of Tarragona in the 3rd cent. The *Acta* of his martyrdom and of his two deacons and fellow-sufferers, Eulogius and Augurius, are the most ancient Spanish *Acta*, and marked by a realistic simplicity which contrasts very favourably with many of the *Acta* of Diocletian's persecution. Prudentius made use of them in his hymn to the martyrs (*Felix Tarraco Fructuose vestris*, etc., Peristeph. vi.), and they are largely quoted by St. Augustine (Serm. 273, Migne, *Patr. Lat.* xxxviii.). Under Valerian and Gallienus in the consulate of Aemilianus and Bassus (A.D. 259), Aemilianus Praeses of Tarragona issued an edict against the Christians, compelling all to sacrifice to the gods. Hearing this, bp. Fructuosus and the whole church of Tarragona gave themselves to unceasing prayer. One night, after Fructuosus had retired, four *apparitores* appeared at his gate and summoned him and his deacons before the Praeses. This was Sunday, and they remained in prison till Friday, enjoying, however, some intercourse with the brethren outside. Fructuosus even baptized a catechumen within the prison. Appearing before the Praeses, all three simply and steadfastly avowed their faith. Finally the Praeses asked Fructuosus, "Art thou the bishop of the Christians?" He answered, "I am." The Praeses retorted, "*Thou wast,*" and gave orders for them to be scourged and burnt alive. On their way to the amphitheatre Christians and heathens alike crowded around in sympathy. Some offered Fructuosus a cup of aromatic strengthening drink. He refused, saying, "It is not yet time to break the fast" (it being Friday, and ten o'clock; the Friday fast lasting till three). At the gate of the amphitheatre Fructuosus addressed the people. "Be of good cheer; a pastor shall not be wanting to you, nor shall the love and promise of God fail you, either here or hereafter. For this which you behold is but the infirmity of an hour." After the flames were kindled, the ligatures binding their hands were quickly burnt; then Fructuosus, *consuetudinis memor*, fell on his knees and so passed away.

This is the account of the *Acta* printed by Tamayo in the *Martyr. Hisp.* (vol. i. Jan. 21) from a 14th-cent. calendar in the library of the cathedral of Astorga. It omits important points contained in the Bollandist *Acta* (*A.A. S.S.* Jan. ii.), which are the same as those printed by Florez (*Esp. Sag.* xxv.). [M.A.W.]

Frumentius. [EDESIUS, 3.]

Fulgentius (3), Fabius Claudius Gordianus, bp. of Ruspe, b. 468, d. 533. His life was mostly spent in the provinces of N.W. Africa ruled by the Vandal kings, Genseric, Hunneric, and Thrasimund, and he suffered from their persecutions. The writings of Fulgentius himself, a biographical memoir prefixed to his works and addressed to bp. Felicianus, his successor, supposed to be by Ferrandus, a deacon of Carthage, and a treatise *de Persecutione Vandalica*, by Victor Vitensis in 487 (Migne, *Patr. Lat.* t. lviii.), are the principal sources of information for the Vandal persecution in Africa. Every refinement of cruelty seems to have been visited upon the presbyters, bishops, and virgins of the N. African church during the reigns of Genseric and Hunneric. At the first incursion of the Vandals the whole country was desolated, houses of prayer and basilicas razed, neither age nor sex spared, the tombs of the martyrs rifled for treasure, bishops banished from their sees, virgins basely used, and every effort made to alienate the people from the Catholic faith. At the commencement of Hunneric's reign (Victor, lib. ii.) a gleam of sunshine cheered the church, during which the vacant see of Carthage was filled by Eugenius, whose extraordinary virtues are duly recorded by his biographers. His popularity excited the rage and animosity of the conquerors, who forbade their own people to enter his church. Those who disobeyed were submitted to torture; some were blinded, and many died of the inhuman treatment. Women were scalped, stripped, and paraded through the streets. Victor says, "We knew many of these." Nor did the orthodox alone suffer. Jocundus, the Arian patriarch, was burned alive, and Manicheans were hunted down like wild beasts. At the end of his 2nd year Hunneric refused all position in the court or executive to any but Arians, and banished to Sardinia all who refused to conform; heavy pecuniary fines were imposed whenever a bishop was ordained; many Christian women died under inhuman cruelties, and many were crippled for life. In 486 the bishops and priests were exiled into the desert, and in his 8th year Hunneric issued an edict, still preserved (*ib.* iii.), summoning the Homoousians to renounce their faith, fixing a date for their submission and for their churches to be destroyed, books burned, and pastors banished. The consequences of this edict are detailed with horrible circumstantiality by Victor, and even Gibbon considers them inhumanly severe. The cruelties of the Diocletian persecution were equalled, if not surpassed, by these efforts to extirpate the Homoousian faith. Gordian, the grandfather of Fulgentius, a senator of Carthage, was exiled by Genseric. His two sons returned home during an interval of grace to find their property in the hands of Arian priests. Not being allowed to remain at Carthage, they settled at Telepte in the province of Byzacene. One of them, Claudius, married Maria Anna, a Christian lady, who gave birth in 468 to Fulgentius. His mother was careful that he should study the Greek language, and would not allow him to read Roman literature until he had committed to memory the greater part of the poems of Homer and of the plays of Menander. He displayed great talent for business and much versatility. His fine character recommended him to the court, and he was appointed fiscal procurator of the province. But after perusing Augustine's comment on Ps. xxxvi. (xxxvii. Heb.), he was attracted by the "pleasures of a mind at peace with God, which fears nothing but sin." Hunneric having banished the bishops to the neighbouring deserts, young Fulgentius began to retire from society and devote himself to prayer and various austerities. One of these exiled bishops, FAUSTUS, had formed a little monastery not far from Telepte, to which Fulgentius betook himself. Owing to the persecution, and at the advice of Faustus, Fulgentius removed to another small monastery, under abbat Felix, between whom and Fulgentius sprang up an enduring friendship. They divided the superintendence of the monastery between them, Fulgentius undertaking the duties of teacher. Troubles from an incursion of the Numidians compelled them to settle at Sicca Veneria or Siccensis (*Vita*, c. ix.). An Arian presbyter in the neighbourhood, alarmed at the influence exercised by the saintly Felix and Fulgentius, laid a plot to rob and torture them. The little company again migrated to Ididi in Mauritania, and here Fulgentius, reading the *Institutiones Cassiani*, resolved to go to Egypt and the Thebaid to follow a more severe rule of mortification. At Syracuse he was kindly received by bp. Eulalius, who discouraged his going to the Thebaid, as it was separated by a "perfidious heresy and schism from the communion of St. Peter," *i.e.* the Monophysite doctrine and the schism to which that led in the Egyptian church after the council of Chalcedon, A.D. 451. The advice was followed, and for some months he resided near Syracuse. In 500 he visited Rome, was present at the gorgeous reception given to Theodoric, and that year returned to Africa. He received from Sylvester, primarius of Byzacene, a site for a spacious monastery which was at once crowded; thence he retired to a lonely island, which lacked wood, drinkable water, and access to the mainland. Here he occupied himself with manual toil and spiritual exercises. Felix, having discovered his retreat, persuaded Faustus to ordain Fulgentius a presbyter, and, under pain of excommunication, to compel a return to his monastery. This was shortly after the death of Hunneric and accession of Thrasimund, who, though an Arian, was more liberal than his predecessors (Gibbon, Smith's ed. vol. iv. c. 37). The little seaport of Ruspe, on a projecting spur of the coast near the Syrtis Parva, had remained without a bishop, and desired Fulgentius, who was taken by force from his cell to Victor the primate of Byzacene and consecrated as its bishop in 508, when 40 years old. He made no change in his costume or daily regimen. His first demand from his people was a site for a monastery, and his old friend Felix was summoned to preside over it. But Thrasimund dismissed Fulgentius and other newly elected bishops to Sardinia. Here, in the name of the 60 exiles, he wrote important letters on questions of theological and ecclesiastical importance.

His literary faculty, knowledge of Scripture, and repute as a theologian, probably induced Thrasimund to summon him to Carthage, and ten objections to the Catholic faith were presented to him. His reply was his earliest treatise, viz. *One Book against the Arians, Ten Answers to Ten Objections.* The third objection resembles a common argument of the earlier Arians, viz. that Prov. viii. 22, John xvi. 29, Ps. ii. 7, and other passages imply that the Son is "created," "generated in time," and therefore not of the same substance with the Father, to which Fulgentius replied that they all refer to the Incarnation, and not to the essence of the Son of God. He used the argument of Athanasius, which makes the customary worship of the Son of God verge either on Polytheism or Sabellianism if we do not at the same time recognize the consubstantiality of the Son. To deny, said Fulgentius, the Catholic position, produces the dilemma that the Son of God was either from something or from nothing. To suppose that He was made "out of nothing" reduces Him to the rank of a creature; while to suppose that He was made "from something," in essence different from God, involves a coeternal Being, and some form of Manichean dualism. Fulgentius laid the greatest emphasis on the unity of God's essence, and assumed, as a point not in dispute, that Christ was the object of Divine worship. This throws some light upon the later Arianism. The reply was not considered satisfactory by Thrasimund, who sent another group of objections, which were to be read to Fulgentius. No copy was to be left with him, but he was expected to return categorical answers: a statement vouched for by the opening chapters of the *ad Trasimundum Regem Vandalorum Libri tres* (cf. Schroeckh, *Christliche Kirchengeschichte*, xviii. 108). Bk. i. treats "of the Mystery of the Mediator, Christ, having two natures in one person"; bk. ii. "of the Immensity of the Divinity of the Son of God"; bk. iii. "of the Sacrament of the Lord's Passion." In bk. i. Fulgentius displays great familiarity with Scripture, and endeavours to establish the eternal generation of the Logos, and the birth in time of the Christ, when the Logos took flesh, and endeavours to shew that by "flesh" is meant the whole of humanity, body and reasonable soul, just as occasionally by "soul" is denoted not only reasonable soul but body as well. In bk. i. he shews that the whole of humanity needed redemption, and was taken into union with the Eternal Word; in bk. ii. that nothing less than Deity in His supreme wisdom and power could effect the redemption. In many ways he argues the immensity of the Son and of the Spirit of God. In bk. iii. he opposes strongly not only *Patripassianism*, but all *theopathia*, Θεοπασχιτισμός and the supposition that the Deity of Christ felt *substantialiter* the sorrows of the Cross. The dyophysite position is urged with remarkable earnestness, and held to be completely compatible with the unity of the person of Christ. The personality of the Christ the Son of God is distinguished from the personality of the Father, with an almost semi-Arian force, while he holds that the nature and substance of the Father and the Son are one and the same. "Sicut inseparabilis est unitate naturae sic inconfusibilis permanet proprietate personae" (lib. iii. c. 3). (Cf. "unus omnino; non confusione substantiae; sed unitate personae," of the Athanasian Creed.) Yet though Christ emptied Himself of His glory, He was full of grace and truth. The two natures were united, not confused, in Christ. But as there was taken up into His one personality the reasonable soul and flesh of man, not a human personality, but human nature, He could weep at the grave of Lazarus and die upon the Cross. Chap. 20 shews conclusively that Fulgentius must have read as the text of Heb. ii. 9, χωρὶς Θεοῦ rather than χάριτι Θεοῦ, as he lays repeated emphasis on the *sine Deo.* The author of the *Vita* assures us that Thrasimund secured the assistance of an Arian bishop, Pinta, to reply to these three books, and that Fulgentius rejoined. The existing work entitled *Pro Fide Catholica adv. Pintam Episcopum Arianum, liber unus* (*Opp.* Migne's ed. pp. 708-720) cannot be the work of Fulgentius. The indignation of the Arian party at Carthage led to what is called his second exile. In the dead of night Fulgentius was hurried on board a vessel bound for Sardinia. On reaching Calaris (Cagliari) in Sardinia, he was received by the exiles with great enthusiasm and reverence. Here he remained until the king died in 523, and displayed extraordinary energy in literary, polemical, and monastic work. With the assistance of Brumasius, the "antistes" of the city, he built another monastery, where more than 40 monks lived under a strict rule of community of property. The equity, benevolence, and self-abnegation of these coenobites are extolled in high terms, and Fulgentius is especially commended for his sweetness and gentleness to the youngest and weakest, which was never disturbed except when bound by his office and vows to act with severity towards insubordination or sin. Symmachus, bp. of Rome, wrote a letter of congratulation to these valiant champions of Christ (*Anast. in Symmacho*, Baron. ann. 504). During this period the majority of his extant letters were penned, for the most part in answer to difficult theological questions, and then also Fulgentius revealed his strong agreement with Augustine on predestination, grace, and remission of sin, at a time when these doctrines were being called in question by the semi-Pelagians of S. Gaul and N. Africa. Cf. Neander, *General Church History*, Clark's trans. vol. iv. 417 ff.; Shedd, *Hist. of Christian Doctrine*, vol. ii. 104 ff.; Wiggers, *Augustinismus und Pelagianismus*, II. Theil, 369-393; Schroeckh, xviii.

The most extended of these dissertations is *ad Monimum, libri tres. I. De duplice praedestinatione Dei. II. Complectens tres quaestiones. III. De vera expositione illius dicti: et verbum erat apud Deum.* Monimus was an intimate friend of Fulgentius, and, on perusing Augustine's *de Perfectione Justitiae Hominis*, had thought that that Father taught predestination to sin as well as to virtue. Fulgentius assured Monimus that God does not predestinate men to sin, but only to the punishment merited by sin, quoting Ezk. xviii. 30. "Sin," said he, "is not in Him, so sin is not from Him. That which is not His work cannot be His predestination." No constraint of the will is meant by predestination, but the disposition of Divine grace by which God pardons one, though He may punish another, gives grace to one who is unworthy of it, even if He find another worthy of His anger. Bk. ii. is occupied with Arian questions as to the Trinity, and the Divinity of the Holy Spirit. The rigidity of his ecclesiastical theory is here conspicuous. The charity, the sacrifices, the services of heretics are of no avail, since they are separated from the Catholic Church. Bk. iii. replies to the Arian interpretation of "apud Deum" in John i. 1; to their theory that if it had been said "verbum est in Deo," we might have thence deduced the identity of the two natures, that "apud" implies separation and dissimilarity. His *argumentum ad hominem* is very ingenious; the exegetical argument which follows is feeble.

During this period Fulgentius wrote the *Liber ad Donatum de Fide Orthodoxa et Diversis Erroribus Haereticorum* (*Ep.* viii. Migne), elsewhere described as a letter to the Carthaginians. His object was succinctly to characterize Sabellian, Arian, Macedonian, and Manichean heresy; he condemns Photinus, and the errors of Eutyches and Nestorius by name, declaring that the true doctrine of the church was to assert the two natures, as against Eutyches, and to repudiate the two persons, against Nestorius. During his residence in Sardinia an important letter was written to Euthymius, *de Remissione Peccatorum* (§ xiv. Ceillier, p. 527, Migne). The question was asked by Euthymius, a devout laic, whether remission of sins was possible after death. After a broad description of what remission of sin is, Fulgentius declares the human conditions to be "faith," "good works," and "time," but it can only be secured in the Catholic church, which has power to remit all sin except the sin against the Holy Ghost, which he declares to be "final impenitence." The utmost stress is laid upon the irreversible condition of the soul at death. All merits are attributed to Divine grace (Wiggers, *op. cit.* p. 382).

The 3 books, *de Veritate Praedestinationis et Gratia Dei* (Migne, p. 604), are addressed to *John and Venerius*, to whom other letters were also sent during the 2nd exile (*Ep.* xv. Ceillier, § x.) on the doctrines of Faustus of Rhegium (de Riez, Riji, sometimes Galliarum).

Fulgentius lays down, in opposition to Faustus, that grace can neither be known nor appreciated until given; that so long as man is without it, he resists it by word or deed. Faustus had spoken of an imperishable grain of good in every man which is nourished by grace. Free will is this spark of heavenly fire, not obliterated by the fall. Fulgentius urged that there may be free will, but not free will to that which is good.

In 523 Thrasimund died, and his successor, Hilderic, allowed the return of the Catholic bishops, and the election of new ones in the churches still vacant. The bishops were received at Carthage with transports of joy, and none with greater enthusiasm than Fulgentius, who was welcomed with triumphal arches, lamps, torches, and banners. On arriving at Ruspe, he yielded in the monastery entire deference to Felix, took the position of the humblest neophyte, and only suggested more vigorous work for the clerics, more frequent fasting for the monks. In 524 a council was held at Juncensis, apparently to enforce a more rigid attention to the canons. Fulgentius was called to preside. His precedence was disputed by a bishop called Quodvultdeus, but confirmed by his brethren. After the council, Fulgentius besought out of charity that his brethren would transfer this nominal precedence to his rival, thus heaping on his head coals of fire. The primate of Carthage, Boniface, sought the presence of Fulgentius at the dedication of a new church, and wept tears of joy under his powerful discourse. During this period Fulgentius wrote his great work against Fabianus, fragments only of which remain. They discuss a variety of interesting problems bearing on the Divinity of the Holy Spirit and other elements of Trinitarian doctrine. The *Sermones* which remain, by their flowing eloquence, antithetic style and tender sensibility, attest the power of Fulgentius. He powerfully discriminates between the Son and the Trinity, and clearly implies the double procession of the Holy Spirit. He claims that the Father had created everything by the Son. Men are only wounded by the poison and malice of creatures by reason of their sins. The mightiest beings are submitted to man. There is no evil in nature. He draws weighty distinctions between the sins of the just and the wicked.

Ferrandus the deacon asked whether he might count upon the salvation of an Ethiopian, who had come as a catechumen eagerly desiring baptism, but had died at the moment of baptism. Fulgentius starts with the thesis that faith is the indispensable condition of salvation, baptism or no baptism. Heretics and enemies of the church will not be saved by baptism. The Ethiopian had given evidence of faith, and was baptized, though then unconscious, both conditions being indispensable to salvation. He is therefore saved. But he reprobates baptism of the really dead, for baptism removes the stain and curse of original sin, the seat of which is the soul. If the soul is severed from the body, baptism is worthless. He decides that the benefits of the Eucharist are contained in baptism, and hence, he says, for many centuries past, infants are not fed with the Eucharist after their baptism.

In another correspondence Fulgentius argues that the passion was Christ's *quâ* His whole *person*, but quâ *nature* it was the experience of His flesh only. His soul and body were separated at death. His soul went to Hades, His body to the grave, but His Divine nature at that very moment filled all space and time, together with the Father and the Holy Spirit.

Many of the same arguments are repeated in the *Letter Addressed to the Monks of Scythia*, who accepted all the decisions of Chalcedon, anathematized Pelagius, Julian, and even Faustus, and asked for further light. The reply of Fulgentius and 15 other bishops consists of 67 chapters. The points of chief interest are that Fulgentius denied that the Virgin was conceived immaculate, and that when speaking of the eternal generation of the Son, he used the bold expression, "ex utero Patris." He laid the strongest emphasis on the Monergistic hypothesis of regeneration, and weakened the universalism of God's love by declaring that "all" does not mean "all men," but "all kinds of men."

While pursuing his literary work with such industry, Fulgentius retired from his monastery at Ruspe to another on the island of Circina, and redoubled his self-mortifications. Here his health gave way. When told that a bath was absolutely necessary to prolong his life, he obstinately refused to break his rule. He died in Jan. 533, in his 65th year and the 25th of his episcopate, and Felicianus was elected his successor the same day.

The most complete ed. of his works was issued in Paris (1684) by L. Mangeant. The whole, with many letters to which he replied, is in Migne, *Patr. Lat.* t. lxv.; Schroeckh, *Kirchengeschichte*, xvii. xviii. 108 ff. [H.R.R.]

Fulgentius (4) Ferrandus, a disciple and companion of Fulgentius of Ruspe (3); sharing his exile to Sardinia during the persecution by the Arian kings of the Vandals. Ferrandus received the hospitality of St. Saturninus at Cagliari, and on the death of Thrasimund, A.D. 523, returned to Carthage, where he became a deacon. In all probability he was the author of the *Vita* prefixed to the works of Fulgentius of Ruspe, and dedicated to Felicianus. Hoffmann, *Lex.* s.n.; Herzog, *Encycl.* art. by Wagenmann; Petrus Pithaeus, in preface *Lectori*, prefixed to *Breviatio Canonum Ferrandi*, Cod. Canonum, p. 303.

Two letters of Ferrandus to Fulgentius are extant (Migne, *Patr.* lxv. pp. 378-435), with the lengthy and careful replies of the latter. For the former see FULGENTIUS (3). The second asked concerning:—1. The Separability of the Persons of the Trinity. 2. Whether the Divinity of the Christ suffered on the cross, or the Divine Person suffered only in the flesh. The fifth question concerned the double gift of the cup to the apostles, as mentioned in St. Luke's gospel. Ferrandus was often appealed to for his own theological judgment. His collected writings (*Biblioth. Patr.* Chiffletius, 1649) preserve one entitled *de Duabus in Christo naturis*, and an *Epistola Anatolio de quaestione an aliquis ex Trinitate passus est*. He is also the author of a *Breviatio canonum ecclesiasticorum* (*Codex Canonum*, F. Pithaeus, and *Miscellanea Ecclesiastica*, Petrus Pithaeus, pp. 303 ff.), a collection and digest of 232 canons of the earliest councils, Nicaea, Laodicea, Sardica, Constantinople, Carthage, etc., chiefly appertaining to the election, ordination, and character of bishops, presbyters, and deacons; the feasts of the church; the duties of virgins, catechumens, etc. It is thought to have been compiled during the reign of Anastasius (d. 518). Ferrandus appears to have had his knowledge of the Greek councils through a translation and digest of such canons as had been previously in use in Spain. The mention of later synods and writings has led others to believe that the *Breviatio* was compiled *c.* 547. [CANON LAW, *D. C. A.*] Ferrandus took a not unimportant part in the violent discussions produced by the edict of Justinian I. (the *Capitula Tria*), which condemned certain passages from Theodoret, Theodore of Mopsuestia, and Ibas of Edessa. Ferrandus was backed by the vehemently orthodox and dyophysite spirit of the N. African church, and in a letter (546) to Anatolius and Pelagius, two deacons of the Roman church, whom Vigilius instructed to communicate with him, declared against the reception of the edict of Justinian. The most complete ed. of his works is by Chiffletius (Dijon, 1649). The two letters to Fulgentius of Ruspe are in Sirmond's and Migne's edd. of *Fulgentii Opp.* [H.R.R.]

Fundanus (1) Minucius, proconsul of Asia in the reign of Hadrian. He received the imperial instructions applied for by his predecessor Granianus as to how Christians were to be dealt with (Justin. Mart. *Apol.* i. § 69; Eus. *H. E.* iv. 9). [HADRIANUS (1).] This rescript seems to shew that a Christian was not to be tried merely for being a Christian, but only for some definite breach of the law. As this might be due to principles, Christianity would remain still punishable, but only in overt act. [C.H.]

G

Galenus, Claudius, physician, born A.D. 130 at Pergamus, flourished chiefly at Rome under the Antonines, and died in 200 or 201. For a full account see *D. of G. and R. Biogr.* He belongs to church history only because of a few incidental words referring to Christianity that occur in his voluminous writings. Thus in his *de Pulsuum Differentiis* (lib. iii. cap. 3, *sub. fin.* in *Opp.* t. viii. p. 657, ed. Kühn) he writes: "It is easier to convince the disciples of Moses and Christ than physicians and philosophers who are addicted to particular sects"; and (lib. ii. cap. 4, p. 579) he condemns the method of Archigenes, who requires his dicta to be received absolutely and without demonstration, "as though we were come to the school of Moses and of Christ." In the *de Renum Affectuum Dignotione* (Kühn, t. xix.) there are other references, but that treatise is spurious. An Arabic writer has preserved a fragment of Galen's lost work, *de Republicâ Platonis*, which reads: "We know that the people called Christians have founded a religion in parables and miracles. In moral training we see them in nowise inferior to philosophers; they practise celibacy, as do many of their women; in diet they are abstemious, in fastings and prayers assiduous; they injure no one. In the practice of virtue they surpass philosophers; in probity, in continence, in the genuine performance of miracles (verâ miraculorum patratione—does he mean the Scripture miracles, on which their religion was based?) they infinitely excel them" (Casiri, *Biblioth. Arabico-Hispana,* vol. i. p. 253). For apologetic remarks on Galen's testimony see Lardner's *Credibility* (*Works*, vol. vii. p. 300, ed. 1838). [C.H.]

Galerius, emperor. (*Gaius Galerius Valerius Maximianus* on his coinage; called *Maximus* in some Acts of martyrs, that having apparently been his name until Diocletian changed it; see Lact. *Mort.* 18; nicknamed *Armentarius* from his original occupation.) He was a native of New Dacia, on the S. of the

Danube. His mother Romula had fled thither for refuge from the predatory Carpi, who pillaged her own country on the N. side (Lact. *Mort.* 9; Aur. Vict. *Epit.* xl. 17). As a youth he was a neatherd, but soon joined the army under Aurelian and Probus. Without education or virtues, he raised himself by undoubted military gifts, until he was selected (together with Constantius) by Diocletian to fill the office of Caesar of the East in Diocletian's famous scheme for the reorganization of the empire, A.D. 292. He married Valeria, the Christian daughter of Diocletian. There were no children of the marriage, which was anything but happy, but the gentle Valeria adopted her husband's bastard son Candidian. Galerius had none of the gifts of a ruler, nor any appreciation of his father-in-law's policy, but his authority with the army made him a useful coadjutor. Five years after his call to the Caesarship (A.D. 297) he was sent to conduct the chief war of the reign of Diocletian, the last which ever gave the Capitol a triumph, against Narses, king of Persia. After an unsuccessful first campaign, he utterly routed Narses, and forced him to purchase peace at the cost of five provinces near the source of the Tigris.

The year 303 brought Galerius prominently into contact with the church. He had conceived a hatred for the Christians, originating (so far as we can see) almost wholly in his fanatical superstition and aversion to Christian morality. His mother was a noted votaress of the Phrygian orgies, and plied her son continually with entreaties to demolish Christianity. She was supported by the magician and so-called Platonist THEOTECNUS (Cedr. vol. i. p. 47, ed. Bonn), who had also acquired an ascendancy over Galerius. The winter of 302-303 was spent by Galerius at Nicomedia, where he used every effort to compel the reluctant Diocletian to annul the legislation of GALLIENUS, to break the forty years' amity between the empire and the church, and to crush Christianity. Step by step he gained his points, until Diocletian consented to proscribe the open profession of Christianity and to take all measures to suppress it, *short of bloodshed* (Lact. *Mort.* 11, "rem sine sanguine transigi"). The first edict of Diocletian, however, was not strong enough to content Galerius. The demolition of buildings which proclaimed the power of the church, the prohibition of synaxis, the burning of the books used in the Christian ritual, the civic, social, and military degradation of Christians, were too slow ways of abolishing it. His one desire was to remove Diocletian's expressive clause, that "no blood was to be shed in the transaction." A fire broke out in the part of the palace where Diocletian lived. Lactantius, then resident at Nicomedia, asserts that it was set alight by Galerius, whose object was to persuade the Augustus that his trusty Christian chamberlains were conspiring against him; but on application of torture to the whole household, they were acquitted. A fortnight later another occurred, and Galerius (who, ostensibly to escape assassination, perhaps really to avoid discovery, immediately departed) convinced Diocletian of the existence of a Christian plot, and the emperor signed his second edict, ordering the incarceration of the *entire clergy*, though even now there was to be no bloodshed.

In putting these edicts into execution Galerius shews occasional signs of a reluctant intention to adhere to the principles of Diocletian's legislation. His return to his own province in 304 was marked by a sudden crowd of martyrdoms where the edicts had before not even been published, but his conduct in the case of St. ROMANUS shews that, when directly appealed to, he felt bound to forbid the capital punishment of even obstreperous Christians (Eus. *Mart. Pal.* ii.). The time was coming, however, when Galerius was to have more liberty of action. In 304, probably during a total collapse of Diocletian's health, the so-called Fourth Edict was issued by Maximian, no doubt in conjunction with Galerius, making death the penalty of Christianity. Diocletian began to recover in March 305, and abandoned his long-held intention of abdicating on May 1 in that year, not improbably because of the commotion which had been caused by the Fourth Edict. Galerius, who had long coveted the promised diadem, would brook no more delay, and with much violence compelled the enfeebled Augustus to retire, leaving himself nominally second to Constantius, whose death in July 306 left Galerius supreme.

Political troubles which followed did not divert Galerius from persecution. On Mar. 31, 308, he issued, in conjunction with his nephew Maximin, a bloody edict against the Manicheans (*Cod. Greg.* ed. Hänel, lib. xiv. p. 44*). For the date see the present writer's essay on *The Persecution of Diocletian*, p. 279. The same year saw an order to substitute mutilation for death in cases of Christianity; as Eusebius says (*Mart. Pal.* ix), "The conflagration subsided, as if quenched with the streams of sacred blood." But the relaxation was only for a few months. The autumn of 308 saw a new edict issued, which began a perfect reign of terror for two full years, the most prolific in bloodshed of any in the history of Roman persecutions; and the vast majority of persons who in the East (for the persecution in the West had ceased with the accession of Constantine and usurpation of Maxentius) are celebrated as "martyrs under Diocletian" really suffered between 308 and 311. This part of the persecution bears marks, however, of the influence of Maximin Daza rather than of Galerius. Towards the close of 310 Galerius was seized with an incurable malady, partially caused by his vicious life. This gradually developed into the frightful disease vulgarly known as being "eaten of worms." The fact rests not only on the authority of the church historians (Eus. *H. E.* viii., xvi. 3 ff.; Lact. *Mort.* 33), but also upon that of the pagan Aurelius Victor (*Epit.* xl. 4) and the fragment known as Anonymous Valesii. Galerius, face to face with so awful a death, thought (apparently) that a compromise might be effected with the God of the Christians, whom he undoubtedly recognized as an active and hostile power. From his dying-bed was issued his famous Edict of Toleration, bearing the signatures also of Constantine and of Licinius, which virtually put an end to the "Persecution of Diocletian." This most extraordinary document may be read in full in Eus. *H. E.* viii. 17, and Lact. *Mort.* 34. The origin of the persecution is ascribed to the fact that the Christians had wilfully departed from the "institutions of the ancients which had peradventure been first set on foot by their own forefathers," and had formed schismatical assemblies on their own private judgment. Primitive Christianity is here meant by the phrase *instituta veterum*, and the edicts were asserted to have had no object but to bring the Christians back to it. But Galerius was now determined, under certain unspecified conditions, to allow Christianity once more and to permit the building of churches. In return, the Christians are told to pray to their God for the recovery of Galerius.

Thus did the dying persecutor try to pose as a kind reformer, and to lead the God of the Christians to remit his temporal punishment. "The Unknown God to Whom he had at last betaken himself gave no answer to his insolent and tardy invocation" (De Broglie, i. 207). The edict was posted at Nicomedia on April 30; he died on May 5 or 13, 311. [A.J.M.]

Galla (5) Placidia, daughter of Theodosius I., by his second wife Galla. When in 410 Rome was captured by Alaric, Placidia was taken prisoner, but was treated with great respect (Olympiod. *ap.* Phot. *Biblioth.* lxxx.; Zos. *Hist.* vi. 12), and in Jan. 414, at Narbona in Gaul, married Ataulphus, who had succeeded his uncle Alaric. After the death of Ataulphus, Placidia returned to Italy, A.D. 416, and dwelt with her paternal uncle Honorius, at Ravenna. In Jan. 417 she married Constantius. By him she had two children, Valentinian and Honoria (Olympiod. *u.s.*) Her influence over Constantius was soon shewn in his active persecution of the Pelagians (Prosp. *Chron. s.a.* 418), when, in Feb. 421, Honorius admitted Constantius to a share of the empire. On Sept. 11, 421, Constantius died. Placidia again took up her abode with Honorius at Ravenna, but their mutual affection being replaced by bitter hate, which occasioned serious disturbances in the city, she and her children were sent to Theodosius II. at Constantinople (Olympiod. *u.s.*). On the death of Honorius in Aug. 423, Theodosius declared for Valentinian. Valentinian being but a child, the authority of Placidia was now supreme, and among her first acts was the issue of three edicts in rapid succession for the banishment of all "Manicheans, heretics, and schismatics, and every sect opposed to the Catholic faith" (*Cod. Theod.* XVI. v. 62, July 17; *ib.* 63, Aug. 4; *ib.* 64, Aug. 6, 425, all dated from Aquileia), meaning especially the adherents of the antipope Eulalius, who were still numerous in Rome. These edicts were soon followed by another of great severity, directed against apostates (*Cod. Theod.* XVI. vii. 8, Apr. 7, 426).

In 427 the machinations of Aetius put Placidia in conflict with her tried friend Boniface, count of Africa, who, in despair, appealed for help to the Vandals, and Africa was overrun by their forces. Placidia explained matters to Boniface, and urged him to do his best to repair the injury which the empire had sustained. But it was too late; the Vandals were masters of the country, and Africa was lost (Procop. *Bell. Vandal.* i. 4; Augustine, *Ep.* 220; Gibbon, c. xxxiii.).

In 449 Placidia was at Rome with Valentinian. The legates of Leo had just returned from the Robber Council of Ephesus. Leo bitterly bewailed the doings of that assembly to Placidia, who immediately wrote to Theodosius and his sister Pulcheria, intreating them to interfere in defence of the faith of their ancestors and to procure the restoration of Flavian, the deposed bp. of Constantinople (Conc. Chalced. pt. i. *Ep.* 26, 28, 30; Labbe, iv. 53, 55, 58). She died soon afterwards at Rome, and was buried at Ravenna (Idatius, *Chr. s.a.*; Gibbon, *u.s.*). [T.W.D.]

Gallienus, P. Licinius, emperor, son of Valerian, appointed by the senate coadjutor to his father very shortly after Valerian's succession in Aug. 253. In 260 his father's captivity in Persia left him politically irresponsible.

One great act brings him into church history. On his father's fall, he was legally bound to put every clergyman to death wherever found, and to deal in almost as summary a fashion with all other Christians. [VALERIAN.] Gallienus had had three years' experience of the difficulty and wearisomeness of this task. The "Thirty Tyrants," moreover, were foes formidable enough to attract what little attention could be spared from pleasure. Accordingly, in 261 he issued a public edict, by which Christianity was for the first time put on a clearly legal footing as a *religio licita*. This edict is the most marked epoch in the history of the church's relation to the state since the rescript of Trajan to Pliny, which had made Christianity distinctly a *religio illicita*. The words in which Eusebius describes the edict (the text of which is lost) imply no more than that actual *persecution* was stopped (*H. E.* vii. 13), which might have been done without a legal recognition of Christianity; but Eusebius has preserved a copy of the encyclical rescript which the emperor addressed to the Christian bishops of the Egyptian province, which shews that the position of "the bishops" is perfectly recognized by the pagan government. The rescript informs the bishops that orders have been issued to the pagan officials to evacuate the consecrated places; the bishops' copies of the rescript will serve as a warrant against all interference in reoccupying. Thus formally, universally, and deliberately was done what Alexander Severus had done in an isolated case in a freak of generosity—*i.e.* the right of the Corpus Christianorum to hold property was fully recognized. If Christianity had not been explicitly made a *religio licita*, this would have been impossible. The great proof, however, of the footing gained by the church through Gallienus's edict lies in the action of his successor Aurelian in the matter of Paul of Samosata. Though Aurelian's bigoted sun-worship and hatred of the church were well known, and his death alone prevented a great rupture, the Catholics were so secure of their legal position as actually to appeal to the emperor in person to decide their dispute; and Aurelian, as the law then stood, not only recognized the right of the church to hold property, but also to decide internal disputes (though they concerned property) according to her own methods. [A.J.M.]

Gallus (1) Caesar, son of Julius Constantius (youngest brother of Constantine the Great) and his first wife Galla; born A.D. 325 at Massa Veternensis near Siena in Tuscany (Amm. xiv. 11, 27). In the general massacre of the younger branches of the imperial family on the death of Constantine in 337, two young brothers were alone preserved—Gallus who was ill of a sickness which seemed likely to be mortal, and Julian a child of seven.

Both were brought up as Christians, and entered with apparent zeal into the externals of the Christian life. In 350 Gallus received the dignity of Caesar, which the childless Constantius bestowed upon him on succeeding to the sole government of the empire by the death of his brother Constans. In the West Constantius was distracted by the usurpation of Magnentius in Gaul, while in the East the Persians were a perpetual source of alarm. Gallus had to make a solemn oath upon the Gospels not to undertake anything against the rights of his cousin, who similarly pledged himself to Gallus. He received at the same time the strong-minded and unfeminine Constantina as his wife, and Lucilianus, the count of the East, as his general (Zos. 2, 45. Philost. iv. 1 refers to the oath between Constantius and Gallus; cf. *Chron. Pasch.* p. 540; Zonaras, xiii. 8).

The records of his short reign at Antioch come to us chiefly from Ammianus (lib. xiv.). They are almost entirely unfavourable to him. His defence of the frontier against the Persians was indeed successful (Zos. 3, 1; Philost. iii. 28, speaks strongly on this point), but his internal policy was disastrous.

Besides the report of his harsh and open misgovernment, accounts of secret treason meditated by him were conveyed to Constantius. The emperor, with his usual craft, sent an affectionate letter and desired his presence, as he wished to consult him on urgent public business (Amm. xiv. 11, 1). When he arrived at Petovio in Noricum, he was seized by the count Barbatio, deprived of his imperial insignia, and conveyed, with many protestations that his life was safe, to Flanon in Dalmatia, where he was closely guarded. The all-powerful eunuch Eusebius was then sent to interrogate him upon his various crimes. Gallus did not deny them, but blamed his wife. Constantius ordered his execution, which took place towards the close of 354.

His instruction had been Arian under the direction of Constantius, and he seems to have been influenced not a little by the Anomoean Aetius. This notorious man had been sent to him to be put to death as a heretic. Gallus spared him on the intercession of Leontius, bp. of Antioch, and became very friendly with him. According to Philostorgius, he made him his religious instructor, and attempted by his means to recall Julian to the faith, when he heard that he was wavering (Philost. *H. E.* iii. 27). There is no reason to doubt that the young Caesar was a zealous Christian after a sort, and that he was distressed by his brother's danger of apostasy. [J.W.]

Gallus (11), abbat, the apostle of Switzerland. One primary authority is the *Vita S. Galli*, compiled by Walafrid Strabo, abbat of Reichenau (A.D. 842-849), and pub. by Surius (*Vitae Sanct.* Oct. 16, t. iv. 252 seq., Colon. 1617), by Mabillon (Acta SS. O.S.B. ii. 215 seq.), and Migne (*Patr. Lat.* cxiii. 975 seq.). Another *Vita S. Galli*, ex MS. St. Gall. 553, is published by Portz (*Mon. Germ. Hist.* ii. 189). The original documents are to be found in Wartmann's *Nerkundenbuch der Abtei St. Gallen*, vols. i.-iii. 1865-1882.

He undoubtedly was of Irish birth, and his original name was Cellach, Calech, or Caillech. Trained at Bangor, in the famous school of St. Comgall, he accompanied Columbanus into Gaul, A.D. 585, and in his exile from Luxeuil along the Rhine into Switzerland, and, apparently from his aptness at learning the languages, proved a most useful assistant in preaching to the Suevi, Helvetii, and neighbouring tribes. [COLUMBANUS.] When Columbanus in 612 left Switzerland to escape the persecution of the Burgundian court, Gallus was detained at Bregenz by a fever, but as soon as he could, returned to his friend the priest Willimar, at Arbona on the S. shore of the Lake of Constance, and devoted his remaining years to the conversion of the wild tribes inhabiting this eastern frontier of Austrasia. On the banks of the Steinaha or Steinach he built his cell and oratory, in the midst of a thick forest. Twelve others accompanied him. His collection of rude huts determined the site of the town and monastery of St. Gall. When the see of Constance became vacant in 616, the episcopate was urgently pressed upon him, and again in 625, but he declined, and was allowed to nominate his deacon John, a native of the place. The sermon he preached at John's consecration is extant in Latin—a wonderful specimen of Irish erudition, simple yet full of vigour, learned and devout, giving an abstract of the history of God's dealings from the creation, of the fall and redemption, of the mission of the apostles and calling of the Gentiles, and ending with a powerful appeal to Christian faith and life, which gives some idea of the state of the corrupt and barbarous society he was seeking to leaven. Beyond these few incidents we know little. He died Oct. 16, 645 or 646, at Arbona, aged 95, but some propose an earlier date.

The oratory of St. Gall gave rise to one of the most celebrated monasteries of the middle ages, and its library to this day stands unrivalled in the wealth and variety of its ancient manuscripts. (For an account of the school of St. Gall and its cultivation of the fine arts, see *Hist. lit. de la France,* iv. 243-246.) [J.G.]

Gaudentius, bp. of Brescia (Brixia), successor of PHILASTER (Philastrius) *c.* A.D. 387. Of the early life of Gaudentius nothing is known for certain. He was probably a native of Brescia; at any rate, he was well known there in his youth. From the language which he uses in reference to his predecessor he appears to have been intimately acquainted with him (though Tillemont is wrong in his interpretation of the words "ego . . . minima ejus pars"). He had a brother Paul, in deacon's orders ("frater carnis et spiritus germanitate carissime"—though his metaphorical use of similar language in speaking of St.

Peter and St. Paul as "vere consanguinei fratres, . . . sanguinis communione germanos" makes the point somewhat doubtful). While still a young man he went on pilgrimage to the Holy Land, as many of his contemporaries did (cf. Hieron. *Epp.* 44, 48). His way lay through Cappadocia. At Caesarea he made the acquaintance of two nieces of St. Basil, "mothers" of a convent there, who gave him some ashes of the famous Forty of Sebastia, which had been given to them by their uncle. These ashes, or rather the Forty themselves, he says, were his "faithful companions" on the rest of the journey; and at a later time he deposited them, with other relics which he had collected, in a basilica which he built at Brescia and called the *Concilium Sanctorum.* At Antioch, probably, he became acquainted with St. John Chrysostom, who never forgot the warmth of affection which he then shewed. Gaudentius was in the East when Philaster of Brescia died. The people of Brescia elected him to be their bishop. They were rash enough to bind themselves with an oath, so Gaudentius says, that they would have him and no other. A deputation of them was sent out to him, reinforced by urgent letters from St. Ambrose and other bishops of the province. Gaudentius resisted, but the Eastern bishops among whom he was sojourning went so far as to threaten to excommunicate him if he would not comply. At last his resistance broke down. He returned, and was consecrated to the vacant see, presumably by St. Ambrose himself. The address which was delivered on that day, according to custom, by the newly consecrated bishop has been preserved (*Serm.* xvi.). St. Ambrose was present at the delivery of it, and was expected to follow it up with an address of his own.

The episcopate of Gaudentius was not, so far as we know, eventful. But there was one remarkable adventure in the course of it. In the year 404 or 405 he was chosen, along with two other bishops and two Roman priests, to bear to the Eastern emperor Arcadius an epistle from his Western colleague Honorius, and from Innocent I. of Rome and the Italian bishops, urging that an oecumenical council should be convened, to examine the case of St. John Chrysostom, who had been deposed and banished from Constantinople. Palladius (*Dial.* c. 4), who accompanied the envoys and who gives us this information, does not, indeed, mention the see of the envoy Gaudentius; but no other bearer of the name is so likely to have been chosen as the bp. of Brescia. The mission was ineffectual, and such sufferings were inflicted upon the envoys as might well earn for Gaudentius his title of "Confessor." He received a warm letter of thanks from St. Chrysostom (*Ep.* 184) for his exertions on his behalf. The letter probably refers to exertions preparatory to the mission, or the reference to the fate of the mission would have been more explicit.

How long Gaudentius held his see is not certain. In his sermon on Philaster he mentions that it is the fourteenth time that he has pronounced his yearly panegyric; but as the date of his consecration to the episcopate is conjectural, this indication is not decisive. That he was still bishop in 410 appears from the fact that the learned Rufinus dedicated to him, in or about that year, his trans. of the *Clementine Recognitions*, in which he describes him as "nostrorum decus insigne doctorum," and says that every word that fell from him deserved to be taken down for the benefit of posterity. Rufinus refers particularly to his knowledge of Greek; and though he does not directly name the see which he held, the identification is aided by his statement that the Gaudentius to whom his work was dedicated was heir to the virgin Silvia—probably the Silvia, sister-in-law of Rufinus the well-known *praefectus orientis*, to whom Gamurrini attributes, though probably without good reason, the *Peregrinatio* he discovered in 1884. This Silvia is known to have been buried at Brescia (Gamurrini, *Peregrinatio*, p. xxxvi; Butler, *Lausiac Hist.* i. p. 296, ii. pp. 148, 229). Gaudentius was buried in a church at Brescia, which is thought to be the same as his own *Concilium Sanctorum.*

Gaudentius was not a writer. The most modest of men, he thought it enough if he might instruct the flock committed to him by word of mouth (*Praefatio ad Benivolum*). But there was a leading magistrate of Brescia named Benivolus, who had formerly (in 386) thrown up his situation in the imperial service rather than abet the attacks of Justina upon St. Ambrose. This man, one year, was hindered by sickness from attending the Easter services. He begged Gaudentius to write down for him the addresses which he had failed to hear. Gaudentius complied. In addition to the eight discourses on the directions in Exodus concerning the Passover and two on the Marriage at Cana, which had been delivered during that Eastertide, he sent also four on various Gospel texts, and a fifth on the Maccabean martyrs. Besides these fifteen sermons sent to Benivolus, four occasional sermons of his are in existence, taken down in shorthand and published (apparently) without his consent. They were delivered respectively on the day of his own consecration, at the dedication of his new basilica, at Milan by desire of St. Ambrose on the feast of St. Peter and St. Paul, and on the anniversary of his predecessor's death. To these sermons are added two expository letters, one to a man named Serminius on the Unjust Steward, the other to his brother Paul on the text "My Father is greater than I."

Gaudentius felt himself bound, like others of his time, to give "spiritual," *i.e.* allegorical, interpretations of his texts. These are often in the highest degree fantastic, and have drawn upon their author the severe criticism of Du Pin (*Bibl. eccl.* siècle v. pt. i.). But Gaudentius generally prepares for them by a literal interpretation, and when he does so, the exegesis is usually marked by good sense. Gaudentius is interested in textual criticism, and more than once remarks on the correspondence or conflict between the Latin text, as he knows it, and the Greek. He is an independent interpreter himself (*Serm.* xix., "Ego tamen pro libertate fidei opportunitatem dictorum secretus traxi ad," etc.), and vindicates the like freedom for others (*Serm.* xviii. "Nulli praejudicaturus, qualiter interpretari voluerit"). When dealing with moral subjects there is a fine elevation in his utterance. As a theologian he has a firm grasp on the Nicene doctrine as taught by St. Ambrose. Arianism is a defeated foe (*Serm.* xxi. "Furentem eo tempore Arianam perfidiam"), but one that still needs vigorous refutation. In regard to other doctrinal points, it may be observed that, however strongly Gaudentius expresses himself about the Holy Eucharist in the terms of his age (*Serm.* ii. 244), he insists characteristically that the Flesh and Blood of Christ are to be spiritually understood (*ib.* 241, "Agni carnes, id est, doctrinae ejus viscera"). He puts much faith in the intercessions of the saints, though he does not directly speak of invoking them (*Serm.* xvii. xx. xxi. *ad fin.*). He dwells with emphasis on the supernatural character of our Lord's birth, not only of His conception (*e.g. Serm.* viii. 270, ix. 281). His style is easy; his sentences often admirably terse and pointed (*e.g. Praef.* 227, "Si autem justus es, nomen quidem justi praesumere non audebis; *Serm.* vii. 265, "Quod Deus majorem causam tunc ulciscendi habeat, si in exiguis rebus, ubi nulla difficultas est observandi, pervicaci tantum spiritu contemnatur"). His sermons preserve a good many interesting notes of the life of the time (*e.g. Serm.* xiii., the beggars at the church door, the dread of the barbarian invasions, the landowner who leaves his labourers to be supported by the church, the horses and mules adorned with gold and silver, the heathen altar allowed to remain on a Christian man's estate). His vocabulary is rather interesting; he uses popular words (*e.g. brodium*) on the one hand, and recherché words (*e.g. peccamen, victorialis*) on the other. It has been made the subject of a special study by Paucker (*Zeitschr. f. d. österreich. Gymnasien,* xxxii. pp. 481 ff.).

The chief ed. of his works is that of Paolo Gagliardi (Galeardus), canon of Brescia, pub. at Padua in 1720, or rather the second and improved ed. of 1738, printed at Brescia. This is reprinted in Migne's *Patr. Lat.* vol. xx. Accounts of Gaudentius and his works will be found in Tillemont, t. x. pt. 2; in Nirschl, *Lehrbuch d. Patrologie* (Mainz, 1883), ii. pp. 488 ff.; in Hauck-Herzog *Realencycl.* vi. (by Leimbach); and in Wetzer and Welte, *Kirchenlex.* v. (by Hefele). [A.J.M.]

Gaudentius (7), Donatist bp. of Thamugada (Temugadi), a town of Numidia, about 14 Roman miles N.E. of Lambesa (Ant. *Itin.* 34, 2), one of the seven managers on the Donatist side in Carth. Conf., A.D. 411 (*Mon. Vet. Don.* pp. 288, 408, ed. Oberthür). His name is chiefly known by his controversy with St. Augustine, *c.* 420. Dulcitius had informed him what was the course intended by the imperial government towards the Donatists. Gaudentius replied in two letters, which Dulcitius sent to Augustine, whose reply to them in two books entitled *contra Gaudentium* (Aug. *Opp.* vol. ix. 707-751, ed. Migne) may be regarded as representing the close of the Donatist controversy (vol. i. p. 895). The Donatist cause, already languishing, from this time fell into a decay, to which these treatises of St. Augustine materially contributed. Sparrow Simpson, *S. Aug. and African Ch. Divisions* (1910), pp. 133-137. [H.W.P.]

Gelasius (1) **I.**, bp. of Rome after Felix III. (or II.) from Mar. 492 to Nov. 496, during about 4½ years. At the time of his accession the schism between the Western and Eastern churches, which had begun under his predecessor, had lasted more than 7 years. Its occasion had been the excommunication, by pope Felix, of Acacius, patriarch of Constantinople, for supporting and communicating with Peter Mongus, the once Monophysite patriarch of Alexandria, who had, however, satisfied Acacius by subscribing the Henoticon, and afterwards the Nicene creed. There had been other grounds of complaint against Acacius, notably his disregard of the authority of the Roman see; but the above had been the original cause of quarrel. [Felix III.; Acacius (7).]

Acacius being now dead, the dispute concerned only the retention of his name in the diptychs of the Eastern church. Felix had demanded its erasure as a condition of intercommunion with his successors, but they had refused to comply. The patriarch of Constantinople was now Euphemius; the emperor Anastasius. On his accession Gelasius wrote a respectful letter to the emperor, who did not reply. To Euphemius the new pope did not write, as was usual, to inform him of his accession. Euphemius, however, wrote twice to Gelasius, expressing a strong desire for reconciliation between the churches, and a hope that Gelasius would, through condescension and a spirit of charity, be able to restore concord. He insisted that Acacius himself had been no heretic, and that before he communicated with Peter Mongus the latter had been purged of heresy. He asked by what synodical authority Acacius had been condemned; and alleged that the people of Constantinople would never allow his name to be erased; but suggested that the pope might send an embassy to Constantinople to treat on the subject. Gelasius, in his reply, couched in a tone of imperious humility, utterly refuses any compromise. He speaks of the custom of the bishops of the apostolic see notifying their elevation to inferior bishops as a condescension rather than an obligation, and one certainly not due to such as chose to cast in their lot with heretics. He treats with contempt the plea of the determined attitude of the people of Constantinople. The shepherd ought, he says, to lead the flock, not the flock control the shepherd. The letter thus asserts in no measured terms the supremacy of the see of Rome, and the necessity of submitting to it. "We shall come," he concludes, "brother Euphemius, without doubt to that tremendous tribunal of Christ, with those standing round by whom the faith has been defended. There it will be proved whether the glorious confession of St. Peter has left anything short for the salvation of those given to him to rule, or whether there has been rebellious and pernicious obstinacy in those who were unwilling to obey him."

In 493 Gelasius wrote a long letter to the Eastern bishops. Its main drift was to justify the excommunication of Acacius by asserting that he had exceeded his powers in absolving Peter Mongus without the authority of the Roman see, and plainly asserts the supremacy of the apostolic see over the whole church as due to the original commission of Christ to St. Peter, and as having always existed prior to, and independent of, all synods and canons. He speaks of "the apostolical judgment, which the voice of Christ, the tradition of the elders, and the authority of canons had supported, that it should itself always determine questions throughout the church." As to the possibility of Acacius being absolved now, having died excommunicate, he says that Christ Himself, Who raised the dead, is never said to have absolved those who died in error, and that even to St. Peter it was on earth only that the power of binding and loosing had been given. Such a tone was not calculated to conciliate. The name of Gelasius himself was therefore removed from the diptychs of the Constantinopolitan church. Gelasius wrote a long letter to the emperor in a similar vein, and exhorted him to use his temporal power to control his people in spiritual as well as mundane matters. This letter is noteworthy as containing a distinct expression of the view taken by Gelasius of the relations between the ecclesiastical and civil jurisdictions. Each he regards as separate and supreme in its own sphere. As in secular things priests are bound to obey princes, so in spiritual things all the faithful, including princes, ought to submit their hearts to priests; and, if to priests generally, much more to the prelate of that see which even supreme Divinity has willed should be over all priests, and to which the subsequent piety of the general church has perpetually accorded such pre-eminence. Gelasius also wrote on the same subjects to the bishops of various provinces, including those of East Illyricum and Dardania. In his address to the last he enlarges on its being the function of the Roman see, not only to carry out the decisions of synods, but even to give to such decisions their whole authority. Nay, the purpose of synods is spoken of as being simply to express the assent of the church at large to what the pope had already decreed and what was therefore already binding. This, he says, had been the case in the instance of the council of Chalcedon. Further, instances are alleged of popes having on their own mere authority reversed the decisions of synods, absolved those whom synods had condemned, and condemned those whom synods had absolved. The cases of Athanasius and Chrysostom are cited as examples. Lastly, any claim of Constantinople (contemptuously spoken of as in the diocese of Heraclea) to be exempt from the judgment of "the first see" is put aside as absurd, since "the power of a secular kingdom is one thing, the distribution of ecclesiastical dignities another."

In 495 Gelasius convened a synod of 46 bishops at Rome to absolve and restore to his see Misenus of Cumae, one of the bishops sent by pope Felix to Constantinople in the affair of Acacius, who had been then won over, and in consequence excommunicated. Before receiving absolution this prelate was required to declare that he "condemned, anathematized, abhorred, and for ever execrated Dioscorus, Aelurus, Peter Mongus, Peter Fullo, Acacius, and all their successors, accomplices, abettors, and all who communicated with them." Gelasius died in Nov. 496.

A curious treatise of his called *Tomus de Anathematis Vinculo* refers to those canons of the council of Chalcedon, giving independent authority to the see of Constantinople, of which pope Leo had disapproved, setting forth that the fact of this council having done something wrongly did not impair the validity of what it had rightly done, and that the approval of the see of Rome was the sole test of what was right. The tract contains further arguments as to Rome alone having been competent to reconcile Peter Mongus or to absolve Acacius, and in reference to the idea of the emperor having had power in the latter case without the leave of Rome, the same distinction between the spheres of the ecclesiastical and civil jurisdictions is drawn as in the letter to the emperor. Melchizedek is referred to as having in old times been both priest and king; the devil, it is said, in imitation of him, had induced the emperors to assume the supreme pontificate; but since Christianity had revealed the truth to the world, the union of the two powers had ceased to be lawful: Christ, in consideration of human frailty, had now for ever separated them, leaving the emperors dependent on the pontiffs for their everlasting salvation, the pontiffs on the emperors for the administration of all temporal affairs. Milman (*Lat. Christ.*) remarks on the contrast between the interpretation of the type of Melchizedek and that given in the 13th cent. by pope Innocent IV., who takes Melchizedek as prefiguring the union in the pope of the sacerdotal and royal powers.

Two other works are attributed to Gelasius in which views are expressed not easily reconciled with those of his successors. One is a tract, the authenticity of which has not been questioned, against the Manicheans at Rome, in which the practice, adopted by that sect, of communion in one kind is strongly condemned. His words are, "We find that some, taking only the portion of the sacred body, abstain from the cup of the sacred blood. Let these (since I know not by what superstition they are actuated) either receive the entire sacraments or be debarred from them altogether; because a division of one and the same mystery cannot take place without great sacrilege." Baronius evades the obviously general application of these words by saying that they refer only to the Manicheans.

The treatise *de Duabus Naturis*, arguing against the Eutychian position that the union of the human and divine natures in Christ implies the absorption of the human into the divine, adduces the Eucharist as the image, similitude, and representation of the same mystery, the point being that as, after consecration, the natural substance of the bread and wine remains unchanged, so the human nature of Christ remained unchanged notwithstanding its union with divinity. His words are: "The sacraments of the body and blood of Christ which we take are a divine thing, inasmuch as through them we are made partakers of the divine nature; and yet the substance or nature of bread and wine ceases not to be." This language being inconsistent with the doctrine of transubstantiation, Baronius first disputes the authorship of the treatise, and secondly, seeks to explain the words away. But if the authoritatively enunciated views of Gelasius on the relations between civil and ecclesiastical authority, on communion in one kind and on transubstantiation, are inconsistent with those subsequently endorsed by Rome, yet, on the other hand, few, if any, of his successors have gone beyond him in their claims of supreme and universal authority belonging by divine institution to the Roman see.

Among his works is a treatise *Decretum de Libris Recipiendis*, fixing the canonical books of Scripture, and distinguishing between ancient ecclesiastical writers to be received or rejected. It bears signs of a later date, having been first assigned to Gelasius by Hincmar of Rheims in the 7th cent. The most memorable of the works attributed to him is the *Gelasian Sacramentary*, which was that in use till Gregory the Great revised and abbreviated it. A new ed. was edited by H. A. Wilson (Oxf. 1894). See also C. H. Turner, in the *Jl. of Theol. Studies* (1900-1901), i. 556 ff. [SACRAMENTARY in *D. C. A.*] A Sacramentary in several books found in the queen of Sweden's library, and published by Thomasius in 1680, is supposed to be the Gelasian one. The main authorities for his Life, besides the *Liber Pontificalis*, are the letters of himself and his contemporaries, and his other extant writings. [J. B—Y.]

Gelasius (13) of Cyzicus, in 2nd half of the 5th cent., author of a work on the history of the council of Nicaea, entitled by Photius *The Acts of the First Council in Three Books*. Our only knowledge of the author is derived from himself. Photius acknowledges his inability to determine who he was. We learn from Gelasius's own words that he was the son of a presbyter of Cyzicus, and, while still residing in his father's house, fell in with an old parchment volume which had belonged to Dalmatius, bp. of Cyzicus, containing a long account of the proceedings of the council of Nicaea. This document not supplying all the information he desired, Gelasius examined the works of other writers, from which he filled up the gaps. He mentions the work of an ancient writer named John, a presbyter otherwise unknown, the works of Eusebius of Caesarea and Rufinus (whom he calls a Roman presbyter), who were both eye-witnesses, and many others. From these and other sources Gelasius compiled his history of the Nicene council. It is sometimes taken for granted that it contains a complete collection of the synodal acts of the council. There is, however, no evidence of the existence of such a collection, or of any one having seen or used it. Athanasius had none such to refer to (cf. Athan. *de Decret. Syn. Nic.* l. 2), and certainly we do not possess it in Gelasius (cf. Hefele, *Hist. of Councils*, Eng. trans. 263, 264). From the work itself we learn that it was composed in Bithynia. As an historical authority it is almost worthless. Its prolix disputations and lengthy orations are, as Cave has justly remarked, evidently the writer's own composition. Dupin's verdict is still more severe. "There is neither order in his narrative, nor exactness in his observations, nor elegance in his language, nor judgment in his selection of facts, nor good sense in his judgments." Instances of his untrustworthiness are seen in his statements that the council was summoned by pope Sylvester, and that Hosius of Cordova presided as his delegate; and he devotes many chapters (ii. 11-24) to disputations on the divinity of the Holy Spirit, which had not then come into controversy at all. The work is in vol. ii. of Labbe's collection (col. 103-286) and in those of Harduin and Mansi. Phot. *Biblioth.* Codd. 15, 88, 89; Fabric. *Biblioth. Graec.* v. 24, vi. 4; Cave, *Hist. Lit.* i. 454; Dupin, iv. 187; Le Quien, *Or. Christ.* iii. 568. [E.V.]

Gennadius (10), 21st bp. of Constantinople, 458-471, between Anatolius and Acacius. His first public appearance was in an attack on Cyril, in two works, *c.* 431 or 432, *Against the Anathemas of Cyril*, and *Two Books to Parthenius*. In the latter he exclaims, "How many times have I heard blasphemies from Cyril of Egypt? Woe to the scourge of Alexandria!" In 433 Gennadius was probably one of those who became reconciled with Cyril.

In 458 he was a presbyter at Constantinople and designated by Leo to fill the see as a man of spotless reputation, on whom no suspicion had ever breathed, and of holy life and conspicuous learning. From the beginning of his episcopate Gennadius proved his zeal for the Catholic faith and the maintenance of discipline. His discretion was before long tested. Timothy Aelurus, chased from the see of Alexandria by order of the emperor, had obtained leave to come to Constantinople, intending, by a pretence of Catholicism, to re-establish himself on his throne. Gennadius, urged by Leo, bp. of Rome, June 17, 460, did his utmost to prevent the voyage of Timothy, and to secure the immediate consecration of an orthodox prelate for Alexandria. All happened as Leo desired; Timothy Aelurus was banished to the Chersonese, and Timothy Solofaciolus was chosen bp. of Alexandria in his stead. An appointment which Gennadius made about this time, that of Marcian, who had been a Novatianist, but had come over to the orthodox church, to the important post of chancellor of the goods of the church of Constantinople, shewed his liberality, penetration, and desire for order. Two Egyptian solitaries told John Moschus a story which is also told by Theodorus Lector. The church of St. Eleutherius at Constantinople was served by a reader named Carisius, who led a disorderly life. Gennadius severely reprimanded him in vain. According to the rules of the church, the patriarch had him flogged, which was also ineffectual. The patriarch sent one of his officers to the church of St. Eleutherus to beg that holy martyr either to correct the unworthy reader or to take him from the world. Next day Carisius was found dead, to the terror of the whole town. Theodorus also relates how a painter, presuming to depict the Saviour under the form of Jupiter, had his hand withered, but was healed by the prayers of Gennadius.

Gennadius ordained Daniel the Stylite presbyter, as related in that saint's life, at the request of the emperor Leo, standing at the foot of the Pharos and performing the ceremonies there. The buying and selling of holy orders was a crying scandal of the age. Measures had been taken against simony by the council of Chalcedon. In 459 or 460 Gennadius, finding the evil practice unabated, held a council at Constantinople to consider it. An encyclical was issued, adding anathema to the former sentence.

Gennadius died in 471, and stands out as an able and successful administrator, for whom no historian has anything but praise, if we except the criticism naturally aroused by his attack in his younger days against Cyril of Alexandria, an attack which the unmeasured language of Cyril perhaps excuses.

Gennadius wrote a commentary on Daniel and many other parts of O.T. and on all the epistles of St. Paul, and a great number of homilies. Of these only a few fragments remain. The principal are on Gen., Ex., Ps., Rom., I. and II. Cor., Gal., and Heb., and are interesting specimens of 5th-cent. exegesis. That on *Romans*, a series of explanatory remarks on isolated texts, is the most important. He fails to grasp the great central doctrine of the epistle, but shews thought and spiritual life. Gennadius, CP. Patr., *Patr. Gk.* lxxxv. p. 1611, etc.; Bolland. *AA. SS.* Aug. 25, p. 148; Ceillier, x. 343. [W.M.S.]

Gennadius (11) Massiliensis, presbyter of Marseilles, who died in 496.

If we accept his *de Viris Illustribus* as it is commonly published, we are warranted in classing Gennadius of Marseilles with the semi-Pelagians, as he censures Augustine and Prosper and praises Faustus. Moreover, the very laudatory account of St. Jerome at the commencement of the book seems inconsistent with the hostile reference to that father under the art. Rufinus in the same catalogue.

The *de Viris Illustribus* in its most commonly accepted form was probably published *c.* 495, and contains, in some ten folio pages, short biographies of ecclesiastics between 392 and 495. Although lacking the lively touches of his great predecessor, Jerome, the catalogue of Gennadius exhibits a real sense of proportion. The greater men stand out in its pages, and it conveys much real and valuable information. With due allowance for the bias referred to, it may be regarded as a trustworthy compilation.

His other treatise, entitled *Epistola de Fide meâ*, or *de Ecclesiasticis Dogmatibus Liber*, begins with a profession of faith in the three creeds, interwoven with the names of those who are considered by the writer (with occasionally questionable accuracy) to have impugned this or that article of belief. Gennadius considers (like later writers, *e.g.* Aquinas) that all men, even those alive at the second Advent, will have to die (7). But this conviction, though derived from a widespread patristic tradition, is, he admits, rejected by equally catholic and learned Fathers. Of the theories concerning the soul of man subsequently known as the creationist and the traducianist views, he espouses the creationist. He will not allow the existence of the spirit as a third element in man besides the body and the soul, but regards it as only another name for the soul (19). Heretical baptism is not to be repeated, unless it has been administered by heretics who would have declined to employ the invocation of the Holy Trinity (52). He recommends weekly reception of the Eucharist by all not under the burden of mortal sin. Such as are should have recourse to public penitence. He will not deny that private penance may suffice; but even here outward manifestation, such as change of dress, is desirable. Daily reception of holy communion he will neither praise nor blame (53). Evil was invented by Satan (57). Though celibacy is rated above matrimony, to condemn marriage is Manichean (67). A twice-married Christian should not be ordained (72). Churches should be called after martyrs, and the relics of martyrs honoured (73). None but the baptized attain eternal life; not even catechumens, unless they suffer martyrdom (74). Penitence thoroughly avails to Christians even at their latest breath (80). The Creator alone knows our secret thoughts. Satan can learn them only by our motions and manifestations (81). Marvels may be wrought in the Lord's name even by bad men (84). Men can become holy without such marks (85). The freedom of man's will is strongly asserted in this short treatise, but the commencement of all goodness is assigned to divine grace. The language of Gennadius is here not quite Augustinian; but neither is it Pelagian, and the work was long included among those of St. Augustine.

The *de Viris Illustribus* is given in most good edd. of the works of St. Jerome, and is ed. by Dr. Richardson in the *Lib. of Nicene and Post-Nicene Fathers*; the *Liber de Ecclesiasticis Dogmatibus* is in the Appendix to t. viii. of the Benedictine ed. of St. Augustine (p. 75). Cf. C. H. Turner in *J. of Theol. Studies* (1905), vii. 78-99, who prints a new text of the *Liber de Eccl. Dogm.* [J.G.C.]

Genovefa (*Geneviève*), patron saint of Paris and of France. The most ancient records tell the story of her life as follows: About A.D. 430 St. Germanus of Auxerre and St. Lupus of Troyes, proceeding to England to combat the Pelagian heresy, stayed one evening at Nanterre, then a village, about 7 miles from Paris. The villagers assembled to see the two renowned prelates, and a little girl attracted the notice of St. Germanus. He learnt that her name was Genovefa, her parents' names Severus and Gerontia. The parents were summoned, and bidden rejoice in the sanctity of their daughter, who would be the means of saving many. Addressing himself to the child, he dwelt on the high state of virginity, and engaged her to consecrate herself. Before departing St. Germanus reminded her of her promise, and gave her a brazen coin marked with the cross, to wear as her only ornament. Henceforth miracles marked her out as the spouse of Christ. When St. Germanus arrived in Paris on a second journey to Britain, he asked tidings of St. Genovefa, and was met with the murmurs of her detractors. Disregarding their tales, he sought her dwelling, humbly saluted her, shewed the people the floor of her chamber wet with her secret tears, and commended her to their love. When the rumour of Attila's merciless and irresistible progress reached Paris, the terrified citizens were for fleeing with their families and goods. But Genovefa assembled the matrons and bade them seek deliverance by prayer and fasting rather than by flight. The Huns were diverted through the efficacy of her prayers, as after-ages believed (*c.* 448). Her abstinence and self-inflicted privations were notable. From her 15th to her 50th year she ate but twice a week, and then only bread of barley or beans. Thereafter, by command of her bishops, she added a little fish and milk. Every Saturday she kept a vigil in her church of St. Denys, and from Epiphany till Easter remained immured in her cell. Before her death Clovis, of whose conversion a later legend has made her the joint author with Clotilda, began to build for her the church which later bore her name. Unfinished at his death, it was completed by Clotilda, and dedicated to SS. Peter and Paul. Upon Genovefa's death (Jan. 3, 512) she was buried in it.

The chief authority for her history is an anonymous author, who asserts that he wrote 18 years after her death, therefore *c.* A.D. 530. This life was first published by Jean Ravisi, of Nevers, in his *Des Femmes illustres* (Paris, 1521), and then by Surius, with corrections in the style (Jan. 3); again, by the Bollandists, in 1643, from better MSS., together with another Life differing only in unimportant particulars (*Acta SS.* Jan. 1, 138 seq.). The Life of St. Germanus of Auxerre by Constantius (c. 5, Boll. *Acta SS.* Jul. vii. 211), and that part of St. Genovefa's which relates to him, almost certainly have a common source, or else one is taken from the other, with slight alterations. That episode being subtracted, there is nothing in the remainder which might not be the work of a later age. The history, therefore, must be accepted with great doubt. Innumerable Lives of St. Genovefa have appeared in France in modern times, mostly of a devotional character, and useless for critical or historical purposes. Saintyves, *Vie de Ste. Geneviève*; Baillet, *Vies des saints*, Jan. 3, t. ii. 417; Bédouet, *Hist. et culte de Ste. G.* (Paris, 1866); Lefeuve, *Hist. de Ste. G.* c. xiii. (Paris, 1842); Fleury, *Hist. ecclés.* lxix. 22, lxxiv. 39; Dulaure, *Hist. de Paris*, i. 240-241. [S.A.B.]

Genseric, king of the Vandals, the illegitimate son of king Godigiselus, reigned in Spain jointly with his legitimate brother GUNDERIC, and on the death of the latter, A.D. 428, became sole sovereign. He is said to have been originally a Catholic, but early in life embraced the Arian heresy.

Before the death of Gunderic, Boniface, count of Africa, forced to seek safety in revolt, invited the Vandals to invade Africa. Genseric readily accepted, and in May 429, according to Idatius (in 427 according to Prosper), crossed into Africa with 50,000 warriors, who poured over the fertile and defenceless provinces. Carthage, Cirta, and Hippo Regius alone withstood the tide of invasion. The Vandals especially ravaged the churches, basilicas, cemeteries, and monasteries. Bishops and priests were tortured to compel them to disclose the church treasures. Victor mentions two who were burnt alive—the venerable Papinian, one of his predecessors in the see of Vita, and Mansuetus, bp. of Urci. Hippo was besieged, but through the efforts of count Boniface, who had returned to his allegiance, supported by an army of allied Goths, the Vandals were obliged by famine, after a siege of 14 months, to abandon the attempt. St. Augustine died in Aug. A.D. 430, in the 3rd month of the siege (Possidius, Life of St. Aug. in Migne, *Patr. Lat.* xxxii. 59). Soon afterwards Boniface, defeated with great loss, returned to Italy. Genseric concluded at Hippo, on Feb. 10, 435, a peace with Valentinian, undertaking to pay a tribute for the territories he had conquered, and to leave unmolested those still held by Valentinian, sending his son Hunneric as a hostage. In 437 Genseric began to persecute the Catholic bishops in the ceded territories, of whom Possidius Novatus and Severianus were the most illustrious, and not only took their churches from them, but banished them from their sees. Four Spaniards, Arcadius, Probus, Paschasius, and Eutychius, who were faithful servants of Genseric, but who refused at his command to embrace Arianism, were tortured and put to death. Paulillus, a younger brother of Paschasius and Eutychius, was cruelly scourged and reduced to slavery.

Genseric, after procuring the restoration of his son, took Carthage by surprise, Oct. 19, 439. The bishops and noble laity were stripped of their possessions and offered the alternative of slavery or exile. Quodvultdeus, bp. of Carthage, and a number of his clergy were compelled to embark in unseaworthy ships, but reached Naples in safety. All the churches within the walls of Carthage were handed over from the Catholics to the Arians, and also many of those outside, especially two dedicated to St. Cyprian. The Arians in this were, however, only meting out to the Catholics treatment such as they received where the latter party was the stronger. Genseric ordered funeral processions of the Catholics to be conducted in silence and sent the remainder of the clergy into exile. Some of the most distinguished clergy and laity of these provinces petitioned the king to be allowed to live in peace under the Vandals. He replied, "I have resolved to let none of your race and name escape. How then do you dare to make such a demand?" and was with difficulty restrained by the entreaties of his attendants from drowning the petitioners in the adjoining sea. The Catholics, deprived of their churches, were obliged to celebrate the divine mysteries where and as best they could. In 440 Genseric equipped a fleet, with which he ravaged Sicily and besieged Palermo. At the instigation of Maximus, the leader of the Arians in Sicily, he persecuted the Catholics, some of whom suffered martyrdom. According to Prosper, he was recalled by news of the arrival in Africa of count Sebastian, son-in-law of count Boniface, but Idatius places his arrival ten years later. Sebastian had come as a friend to take refuge at his court, but Genseric, who feared his renown as a statesman and general, tried to convert him to Arianism, that his refusal might supply a pretext for putting him to death. Sebastian evaded his demands by a dexterous reply, which Genseric was unable to answer, but some other excuse for his execution was shortly found. In A.D. 441 a new peace was concluded, by which Valentinian retained the three Mauritanias and part of Numidia, and ceded the remainder of his African dominions to Genseric, who divided the Zeugitane or proconsular province, in which was Carthage, among the Vandals and kept the rest in his own possession. Universal oppression of the natives followed. Then Genseric discovered a plot among his nobles against himself, and tortured and executed many of them. Probably from alarm at this conspiracy, he began a new and severer persecution. The Catholics were allowed no place for prayer or the ministration of the sacraments. Every allusion in a sermon to Pharaoh, Nebuchadnezzar, or Holofernes was regarded as aimed at the king, and the preacher punished with exile. Among the bishops now banished, Victor mentions Urbanus of Girba, Crescius, a metropolitan who presided over 120 bishops, Habetdeus of Teudela, and Eustratius of Suffectum. Felix of Adrumetum was banished for receiving a foreign monk. Genseric prohibited the consecration of new bishops in place of those banished. In 454, however, he yielded to Valentinian's requests so far as to allow Deogratias to be consecrated for Carthage. The see had remained vacant since the banishment of Quodvultdeus 15 years before. In 455 Genseric, at the invitation of Eudoxia, Valentinian's widow, sailed to Italy, and took Rome without a blow. At the intercession of Leo the Great, he abstained from torturing or massacring the inhabitants and burning the city, but gave it up to systematic plunder. For 14 days and nights the work of pillage continued, the city was ransacked of its remaining treasures, and Genseric then returned unmolested to Africa, carrying much booty and many thousand captives, including the empress Eudoxia and her two daughters. The elder became the wife of his son Hunneric; the younger, with her mother, was eventually surrendered to the emperor Leo.

The whole of Africa now fell into the hands of Genseric, and also Sicily, Sardinia, Corsica, and the Balearic Islands. His fleets yearly sailed from Carthage in the early spring, and ravaged all the Mediterranean coasts. When leaving Carthage on one of these expeditions, the helmsman asked Genseric whither he should steer. "Against those," he replied, "who have incurred the wrath of God." His object was not only to plunder, but to persecute. Spain, Italy, Dalmatia, Campania, Calabria, Apulia, Bruttium, Venetia, Lucania, Epirus, and the Peloponnese all suffered from his ravages. After the death of Deogratias, A.D. 457, Genseric did not allow any more bishops to be consecrated in the proconsular province, the peculiar domain of the Vandals, so that of the original number of 164 only three were left in Victor's time. One Proculus was sent to compel the bishops to give up all their books and the sacramental vessels. When they refused, they were seized by force and the altar-cloths made into shirts for the soldiers. St. Valerian, bp. of Abbenza, was expelled from that town. No one was allowed to receive him into their house or permit him to remain on their land, and he was long obliged to lie by the roadside. At Regia the Catholics had ventured at Easter to take possession of their church. The Arians, headed by a priest named Adduit, attacked the church, part forcing an entrance with drawn swords and part shooting arrows through the windows. The reader was killed in the pulpit by an arrow, and many worshippers slain on the altar-steps. Most of the survivors were executed by Genseric's orders. Genseric, by the advice of the Arian bishops, commanded all officials of his court to embrace Arianism. According to Victor's account, Armogast, one of the number, refused, and was tightly bound with cords, but they broke like a spider's web; and when he was hung head downwards by one foot, he seemed to sleep as peacefully as if in his bed. His persecutors, unable to overcome his resolution, were about to kill him, but were dissuaded by an Arian priest, lest he should be reverenced as a martyr. He was accordingly compelled to labour in the fields and afterwards to tend cattle near Carthage.

The emperor Majorian in 460 assembled a fleet of 300 vessels at Carthagena to recover Africa. His plans were betrayed to the Vandals, who surprised and carried off the greater part of his ships. Genseric, however, in alarm, concluded peace with Majorian. In 468 Leo collected a mighty armament of 1,113 ships, each containing 100 men (Cedrenus, 350, ed. Dindorf.), under the command of his brother-in-law Basiliscus. The main armament landed at the Hermaean promontory (Cape Bon), about 40 miles from Carthage. Genseric, by means, it was generally believed, of a large bride, induced Basiliscus to grant a truce for five days. He used this time to man all the ships he could, and, the wind becoming favourable, attacked the Romans and sent fire-ships among their crowded vessels. Panic and confusion spread through the vast multitude, most of whom tried to fly, but a few fell fighting gallantly to the last. After this victory Genseric regained Sardinia and Tripoli, where the Roman arms had met with success, and ravaged the Mediterranean coasts more cruelly than before, till a peace was concluded between him and the emperor Zeno. Genseric, at the request of the emperor's ambassador Severus, released those prisoners who had fallen to his own or his sons' lot, and allowed him to ransom as many others as he could (Malchus, *de Legationibus*, 3, ed. Dindorf), and, at Leo's entreaty, allowed the churches of Carthage to be reopened and the exiled bishops and clergy to return. Soon afterwards he died, on Jan. 24, 477.

According to the description of Jornandes (*de Gothorum Origine*, c. 33, in Cassiodorus, i. 412, in Migne, *Patr. Lat.* lxix. 1274), Genseric was of moderate stature and lame from a fall from his horse. He was a man of few words, and thus better able to conceal the deep designs he had conceived. He scorned luxury, was greedy of empire, passionate, skilful in intrigue, and cruel; but it must be remembered that all our informants are writers who hated and dreaded himself and his nation both as heretics and enemies. With every allowance for Salvian's rhetoric (*de Gubernatione Dei*, vii. in Migne, *Patr. Lat.* liii.), it must be admitted that his description of the morals of the Vandals and those of the dissolute Carthaginians show the former in a more favourable light than the latter.

Genseric's name is variously spelt Gizericus, Gaisericus, Geisericus, and Zinzirichus. The sources for the above account are the *Chronicles* of Prosper and Idatius (in Migne, *Patr. Lat.* li.) ; Procopius, *de Bello Vandalico*, i. 3-7 ; Isidorus, *de Regibus Gothorum* (Isid. *Opp.* vii. 130-133, in Migne, *Patr. Lat.* lxxxiii. 1076) ; and Victor Vitensis, *de Persecutione Vandalica*, i. (in Migne, *Patr. Lat.* lviii.). Gibbon, cc. xxxiii. xxxvi. and xxxvii., may also be consulted ; and Ruinart's dissertation in his appendix to Victor Vitensis, and Ceillier, *Histoire des auteurs sacrés*, x. c. 28. [F.D.]

Georgius (3), bp. of Laodicea ad mare in Syria Prima (335-347), who took part in the Trinitarian controversies of the 4th cent. At first an ardent admirer of the teaching of Arius and associated with Eusebius of Nicomedia, he subsequently became a semi-Arian, but seems ultimately to have united with the Anomoeans, whose uncompromising opponent he had once been, and to have died professing their tenets (Newman, *Arians*, pt. ii. p. 275). He was a native of Alexandria. In early life he devoted himself with considerable distinction to the study of philosophy (Philost. *H. E.* viii. 17). He was ordained presbyter by Alexander, bp. of Alexandria (*ib.*; Eus. *Vit. Const.* iii. 62). Having gone to Antioch, he endeavoured to mediate between Arius and the Catholic body. To the Arians he shewed how, by a sophistical evasion based on I. Cor. xi. 12 (τὰ δὲ πάντα ἐκ τοῦ Θεοῦ), they might accept the orthodox test Θεὸν ἐκ Θεοῦ (Socr. *H. E.* ii. 45 ; Athan. *de Synod.* p. 887). The attempt at reconciliation completely failed, and resulted in his deposition and excommunication by Alexander, on the ground of false doctrine and of the open and habitual irregularities of his life (Athan. *ib.* p. 886 ; *Apol.* ii. p. 728 ; *de Fug.* p. 718 ; Theod. *H. E.* ii. 9). Athanasius styles him "the most wicked of all the Arians," reprobated even by his own party (*de Fug.* 718). After his excommunication at Alexandria, he sought admission among the clergy of Antioch, but was steadily rejected by Eustathius (Athan. *Hist. Arian.* p. 812). On this he retired to Arethusa, where he acted as presbyter, and, on the expulsion of Eustathius, was welcomed back to Antioch by the dominant Arian faction. He was appointed bp. of Laodicea on the death of the Arian Theodotus (Athan. *de Synod.* p. 886 ; *Or.* i. p. 290 ; Soz. *H. E.* vi. 25). As bishop he took a leading part in the successive synods summoned by the Arian faction against Athanasius. He was at the councils of Tyre and Jerusalem in 335 (Athan. *Apol.* ii. p. 728 ; Eus. *Vit. Const.* iv. 43), and that of the Dedication at Antioch in 341 (Soz. *H. E.* iii. 5). Fear kept him from the council of Sardica in 347, where the bishops unanimously deposed him and many others as having been previously condemned by Alexander, and as holding Arian opinions (Theod. *H. E.* iii. 9 ; Labbe, *Concil.* ii. 678 ; Athan. *Apol.* ii. p. 765 ; *de Fug.* p. 718). Of this deposition George took no heed, and in 358, when Eudoxius, the newly appointed bp. of Antioch, openly sided with Aetius and the Anomoeans, George earnestly appealed to Macedonius of Constantinople and other bishops, who were visiting Basil at Ancyra to consecrate a newly erected church, to lose no time in summoning a council to condemn the Anomoean heresy and eject Aetius. His letter is preserved by Sozomen (*H. E.* iv. 13 ; Labbe, *Concil.* ii. 790). At Seleucia, in 359, when the semi-Arian party was split into two, George headed the more numerous faction opposed to that of Acacius and Eudoxius, whom, with their adherents, they deposed (Socr. *H. E.* ii. 40). On the expulsion of Anianus from the see of Antioch, George was mainly responsible for the election of Meletius, believing him to hold the same opinions as himself. He was speedily undeceived, for on his first entry into Antioch Meletius startled his hearers by an unequivocal declaration of the truth as laid down at Nicaea. Indignant at being thus entrapped, George and his fellows lost no time in securing the deposition and expulsion of a bishop of such uncompromising orthodoxy (Theod. *H. E.* ii. 31 ; Philost. *H. E.* v. 1 ; Socr. *H. E.* ii. 44 ; Soz. *H. E.* iv. 28). Gregory Nyssen mentions a letter by George relating to Arius (*in Eunom.* i. 28), and Socrates quotes a panegyric composed by him on the Arian Eusebius of Emesa, who was his intimate friend and resided with him at Laodicea after his expulsion from Emesa and by whose intervention at Antioch he was restored to his see (Socr. *H. E.* i. 24, ii. 9). He was also the author of some treatises against heresy, especially that of the Manicheans (Theod. *Haer. Fab.* i. 28 ; Phot. *Bibl.* c. 85 ; Niceph. *H. E.* vi. 32). [E.V.]

Georgius (4), commonly called of Cappadocia (Athan. *Ep. ad Episc.* 7) ; Arian intruding bp. of Alexandria (356-361). He was born, according to Ammianus Marcellinus, at Epiphania in Cilicia (xxii. 11, 3), and, if so, must have been Cappadocian only by descent. Gregory Nazianzen describes him as not purely free-born (*Orat.* xxi. 16), and as "unlearned," but he undoubtedly collected a library which Julian, no bad judge, describes as "very large and ample," richly stored with philosophical, rhetorical, and historical authors, and with various works of "Galilean" or Christian theology (*Epp.* 9, 36). In Feb. 356, after Athanasius had retired from Alexandria in consequence of the attack on his church, which all but ended in his seizure, he heard that George was to be intruded into his throne, as Gregory had been 16 years previously. George arrived in Alexandria, escorted by soldiers, during Lent 356 (*de Fug.* 6). His installation was a signal for new inflictions on Alexandrian church-people. "After Easter week," says Athanasius (*ib.*), "virgins were imprisoned, bishops led away in chains" (some 26 are named in *Hist. Arian.* 72) ; "attacks made on houses" ; and on the first Sunday evening after Pentecost a number of people who had met for prayer in a secluded place were cruelly maltreated by the commander, Sebastian, a "pitiless Manichean," for refusing to communicate with George.

The intruding bishop was a man of resolution and action (Soz. iii. 7). Gregory of Nazianzus, who disparages his abilities, admits that he was like a "hand" to the Arians, while he employed an eloquent prelate—probably Acacius—as a "tongue." He belonged to the Acacian section of the party, and was consequently obnoxious to the semi-Arians, who "deposed him" in the council of Seleucia. He allowed the notorious adventurer Aetius, founder of the Anomoeans or ultra-Arians, to officiate as deacon at Alexandria, after having been ordained, as Athanasius tells us (*de Synod.* 38), by Leontius of Antioch, although he afterwards "compelled" the Arian bishops of Egypt to sign the decree of the Acacian synod of Constantinople of 360 against Aetius (Philost. iii. 2). He induced Theodore, bp. of Oxyrynchus, to submit to degradation from the ministry and to be reordained by him as an Arian bishop (*Lib. Marcell. et Faustini*, Sirmond. i. 135). He managed to keep the confidence of Constantius, who congratulated the Alexandrians on having abandoned such "grovelling teachers" as Athanasius and entrusted their "heavenward aspirations" to the guidance of "the most venerable George" (Athan. *Apol. to Const.* 30, 31). But George was far from recommending his form of Christianity either to the orthodox or to the pagans of Alexandria. "He was severe," says Sozomen, "to the adherents of Athanasius," not only forbidding the exercise of their worship, but "inflicting imprisonment and scourges on men and women after the fashion of a tyrant"; while, towards all alike, "he wielded his authority with more violence than belonged to the episcopal rank and character." He was "hated by the magistrates for his supercilious demeanour, by the people for his tyranny" (Soz. iv. 10, 30). He stood well with Constantius, who was guided theologically by the Acacians; and it was easy for the "pope" of Alexandria to embitter his sovereign (as Julian says he did, *Ep.* 10) against the Alexandrian community, to name several of its members as disobedient subjects, and to suggest that its grand public buildings ought by rights to pay tax to the treasury (Ammian. etc.). He shewed himself a keen man of business, "buying up the nitre-works, the marshes of papyrus and reed, and the salt lakes" (Epiph. *Haer.* lxxvi.). He manifested his anti-pagan zeal by arbitrary acts and insulting speeches, procured the banishment of Zeno, a prominent pagan physician (Julian, *Ep.* 45), prevented the pagans from offering sacrifices and celebrating their national feasts (Soz. iv. 30), brought Artemius, "duke" of Egypt, much given to the destruction of idols (Theod. iii. 18), with an armed force into the superb temple of Serapis at Alexandria, which was forthwith stripped of images, votive offerings, and ornaments (Julian, *l.c.*; Soz. *l.c.*). On Aug. 29, 358, the people broke into the church of St. Dionysius, where George was then residing, and the soldiers rescued him from their hands with difficulty and after hard fighting. On Oct. 2 he was obliged to leave the city; and the "Athanasians" occupied the churches from Oct. 11 to Dec. 24, when they were again ejected by Sebastian. Probably George returned soon after he had quitted the Seleucian council, *i.e.* in Nov. 359. The news of Julian's accession arrived at Alexandria Nov. 30, 361. George was in the height of his pride and power: he had persecuted and mocked the pagans (Socr. iii. 2; Maff. Frag.; Ammian.), who now, being officially informed that there was an emperor who worshipped the gods, felt that the gods could at last be avenged. The shout arose, "Away with George!" and "in a moment," says the Fragmentist, they threw him into prison, with Diodorus and Dracontius, the master of the mint, who had overthrown a pagan altar which he found standing there (Ammian.). The captives were kept in irons until the morning of Dec. 24. Then the pagan mob again assembled, dragged them forth with "horrible shouts" of triumph, and kicked them to death. They flung the mangled body of George on a camel, which they led through every part of the city, dragging the two other corpses along with ropes, and eventually burned the remains on the shore, casting the ashes into the sea.

The Arians, of course, regarded George as a martyr; and Gibbon took an evident pleasure in representing "the renowned St. George of England" as the Alexandrian usurper "transformed" into a heroic soldier-saint; but bp. Milner (*Hist. Inquiry into the Existence and Character of St. George*, 1792) and others have shewn that this assumption of identity is manifestly false, the St. George who is patron saint of England being of an earlier date, though of that saint's life, country, or date we have no certain information, such traditions as we possess being given in the next art. [W.B.]

Georgius (43), M., Apr. 23 (Μεγαλομάρτυς, Bas. *Men.*); traditionally the patron saint of England, a military tribune and martyr under Diocletian at Nicomedia, A.D. 303. He was a native of Cappadocia and of good birth. Some time before the outbreak of the great persecution he accompanied his mother to Lydda, in Palestine, where she possessed property. As soon, however, as he heard of the publication of the first edict (Feb. 23, 303), he returned to Nicomedia, where, as some think, he was the celebrated person who tore down the imperial proclamation, and then suffered death by roasting over a slow fire (Eus. *H. E.* viii. 5). [DIOCLETIAN.] The earliest historical testimony to the existence and martyrdom of St. George is an inscription in a church at Ezr'a or Edhr'a, in S. Syria, copied by Burckhardt and Porter, and discussed by Mr. Hogg in two papers before the Royal Society of Literature (*Transactions*, vi. 292, vii. 106). This inscription states that the building had been a heathen temple, but was dedicated as a church in honour of the great martyr St. George, in a year which Hogg, by an acute argument, fixes as 346. (For another view, however, which assigns the inscription to 499, see Böckh's *Corp. Inscript. Graec.* ed. Kirchhoff, t. iv. No. 8627.) His name occurs again in another inscription in the church of Shaka, 20 miles E. of Ezr'a, which Hogg dates A.D. 367. (Böckh, *l.c.* No. 8609, cf. 8630; for other instances of transformations of heathen temples into churches and hospitals in the 4th and 5th cent., see Böckh, *l.c.* 8645, 8647.) The council assembled at Rome by pope Gelasius, A.D. 494 or 496 (Hefele, *Concil.* i. 610, iii. 219, ed. Paris, 1869), condemned the Acts of St. George, together with those of Cyricus and Julitta, as corrupted by heretics, but expressly asserted that the saints themselves were real martyrs and worthy of all reverence (cf. Pitra, *Spicil. Solesmen.* iv. 391, for a repetition, three centuries later in the East, of this condemnation by the patriarch Nicephorus, in his *Constit. Eccl.*). Thenceforward the testimonies to his existence rapidly thicken, but decrease in value. Gregory of Tours in the 6th cent. mentions him as highly celebrated in France, while in the East his cultus became universally established (cf. Fleury, *H. E.* xxxiv. 46) and churches were erected in all directions in his honour, one of the most celebrated being that built, probably by Justinian, over his tomb at Lydda, whither his relics had been transferred after his martyrdom. This church still exists. (For an engraving of it, see Thomson's *Land and Book*, ii. 292; cf. Robinson's *Biblical Researches*, iii. 51-55, with Le Quien, *Oriens Christian.* iii. 1271, for full particulars of St. George's connexion with Lydda.) Another is at Thessalonica; described in Texier and Pullan, *Byzantine Architecture*, pp. 132-142, where strong reasons are given for assigning its erection to Constantine (cf. Procopius, *de Aedif.* iii. 4, ed. Bonn).

The Medieval Legends.—The Arians of the 5th cent. seem to have corrupted his acts for their own purposes. Their story is that he was arrested by Datianus, emperor of Rome, or, according to others, of Persia, by whom he was in vain ordered to sacrifice to Apollo. The magician Athanasius undertook to confound the saint. After various attempts the magician was converted and baptized, as well as the queen Alexandra. After many miracles and various tortures, St. George was beheaded. It is strange that, notwithstanding the decrees of Rome and Constantinople, this Arian corruption became the basis of all subsequent legends, and even found its way into the hymns of St. John Damascene in honour of St. George (Mai. *Spicil. Rom.* t. ix. p. 729; Ceillier, xii. 89). The addition of a horse and a dragon to the story arose out of the imaginations of medieval writers. The dragon represents the devil, suggested by St. George's triumph over him at his martyrdom (cf. Eus. *Vita Constant.* iii. 3). When the race of the Bagratides ascended the throne of Georgia at the end of the 6th cent., they adopted St. George slaying the Dragon as part of their arms (Malan, *Hist. of Georgian Ch.* pp. 15, 29). The horse was added during the Frankish occupation of Constantinople as suitable, according to medieval ideas, to his rank and character as a military martyr. St. George was depicted on a horse as early as 1227, according to Nicephorus Gregoras (*Hist. Byzant.* viii. 5), where will be found a curious story concerning a picture in the imperial palace at Constantinople, of St. George mounted upon a horse, which neighed in the most violent style whenever an enemy was about to make a successful assault upon the city. The earliest trace we can now find of the full-grown legend of St. George and the dragon, and the king's daughter Sabra, whom he delivered, is in the *Historia Lombardica*, popularly called the *Golden Legend*, of Jacobus de Voragine, archbp. of Genoa, A.D. 1280, and in the breviary service for St. George's Day, till revised by pope Clement VIII. Thence it became the foundation of the story as told in Johnson's *Historie of the Seven Champions of Christendom*, and the old ballad of *St. George and the Dragon*, reprinted in the third volume of Percy's *Reliques*, many features of which Spenser reproduces in his *Faëry Queen.* Busbecq in the 16th cent. found in the heart of Asia Minor a legend of the Turkish hero Chederles, to whom were ascribed exploits similar to those of St. George (*Ep.* 1, pp. 93, 95, ed. 1633), and he found Georgian Christians venerating above every image that of St. George on horseback, regarding him as having conquered the evil one (*Ep.* 3, p. 209).

Connexion with England.—St. George's story was well known in England from the 7th cent., most probably through the Roman missionaries sent by Gregory. Arculf, the early traveller, when returning to his bishopric in France, was carried northward to Iona, *c.* 699, where he told the monks the story of St. George, whence, through Adamnan and Bede, it became widely known in Britain. St. George has a place in the Anglo-Saxon ritual of Durham assigned to the early part of the 9th cent., pub. by the Surtees Society A.D. 1840, and among the publications of the Percy Society we have an Anglo-Saxon *Passion of St. George*, the work of Aelfric, archbp. of York A.D. 1020-1051, ed. by Hardwick A.D. 1850, in whose preface is much interesting information on this point. His special fame, however, in this country arose immediately out of the early Crusades. William of Malmesbury (*Gesta Reg. Angl.* ed. Sir T. D. Hardy, ii. 559) tells us that, when the Crusaders were hard pressed by the Saracens at the battle of Antioch, June 28, 1089, the soldiers were encouraged by seeing "the martyrs George and Demetrius hastily approaching from the mountainous districts, hurling darts against the enemy, but assisting the Franks" (cf. Gibbon, cap. lviii.; Michaud's *Hist. of Crusades*, i. 173, ed. Lond.; on the military fame of St. Demetrius see Böckh, *Corp. Inscrip.* iv. 8642; Du Cange, *Gloss.* i. 974; Texier, *op. cit.* pp. 123-132). This timely apparition at the very crisis of the campaign led the Crusaders, among whom were a large contingent of Normans under Robert, son of William the Conqueror, to adopt St. George as their patron. During the campaigns of Richard I. in Palestine, St. George appeared to him and so became a special favourite with the Normans and English (Itin. of Richard I. in *Chron. of Crusades*, ed. Bohn, p. 239). In 1222 a national council at Oxford ordered his feast to be kept as a lesser holiday throughout England. He was not, however, formally adopted as patron saint of England till the time of Edward III., who founded St. George's chapel at Windsor in 1348. In 1349 Edward joined battle with the French near Calais, when, "moved by a sudden impulse," says Thomas of Walsingham, "he drew his sword with the exclamation, Ha! St. Edward, Ha! St. George, and routed the French" (cf. Smith's *Student's Hume*, cap. x. § 8). From that time St. George replaced St. Edward the Confessor as patron of England. In 1350, according to some authorities, the order of the Garter was instituted under his patronage, and in 1415, according to the *Constitutions* of archbp. Chichely, St. George's Day was made a major double feast, and ordered to be observed like Christmas Day. In the first Prayer Book of Edward VI. St. George's feast was a red-letter day, and had a special epistle and gospel. This was changed in the next revision (Ashmole, *Order of the Garter*; Anstis, *Register*; Pott, *Antiquities of Windsor and History of Order of Garter*, A.D. 1749). The influence of the Crusades also led to St. George becoming the patron of the republic of Genoa, the kingdoms of Aragon and Valencia, and to the institutions of orders of knighthood under his name all over Europe (cf. *AA. SS.* Boll. Apr. iii. 160). In N. Syria his day is still observed as a great festival (Lyde, *Secret Sects of N. Syria*, Lond. 1853, p. 19).

Controversy.—The consentient testimony of all Christendom till the Reformation attested the existence of St. George. Calvin first questioned it. In his *Institutes*, lib. iii. cap. 20, § 27, when arguing against invocation of saints, he ridiculed those who esteem Christ's intercession as of no value unless "accedant Georgius aut Hippolytus aut similes larvae," where, unfortunately for himself, he places Hippolytus in the class of ghosts or phantoms together with St. George. Dr. Reynolds, early in the 17th cent., was the first to confuse the orthodox martyr of Lydda with the Arian bp. of Alexandria. [GEORGIUS (4).] Against him Dr. Heylin argued in an exhaustive treatise (*Hist. of St. George of Cappadocia*), giving (pp. 164-166) a very full list of all earlier authors who had referred to St. George, including a quotation from a reputed treatise by St. Ambrose, *Liber Praefationum*, which is not now extant. The controversy was continued during the 18th cent. Dr. Milner wrote in defence of the historical reality of St. George, provoked doubtless by Gibbon's well-known sneer in c. xxiii. of his history. See further *Mart. Vet. Rom.*, *Mart.* Adon., *Mart.* Usuard., which all fix his martyrdom at Diospolis in Persia (cf. Herod. ed. Rawlinson, i. 72, v. 49, vii. 72); Hogg, however, well suggests the Bithynian town of that name, which was in the Persian empire under Cyrus (*Pasch. Chron.* ed. Bonn, p. 510; Sym. Metaphrast.; *Magdeburg. Centur.* cent. iv. cap. xii.; Ceillier, xi. 404, xii. 58, 89, 297; Alban-Butler, *Lives of Saints*; Malan, *Hist. of the Georgian Church*, pp. 28, 51, 54, 72; E. A. Wallis Budge, *The Martyrdom and Miracles of St. George of Cappadocia*: the Coptic texts ed. with an Eng. trans., Lond. 1888). [G.T.S.]

Germanus (8), St., bp. of Auxerre, born probably *c.* 378, at Auxerre, near the S. border of what was afterwards Champagne. The parents of German caused him to be baptized and well educated. He went to Rome, studied for the bar, practised as an advocate before the tribunal of the prefect, on his return married a lady named Eustachia, and rose to be one of the six dukes of Gaul, each of whom governed a number of provinces (Gibbon, ii. 320), Auxerre being included in German's district. German, having been ordained and nominated as his successor by Amator, bp. of Auxerre, was, on the latter's death, unanimously elected, and consecrated on Sun. July 7, 418. His wife became to him as a sister; he distributed his property to the poor; he became a severe ascetic, and, as his biographer Constantius says, a "persecutor of his body," abstaining from salt, oil, and even from vegetables, from wine, excepting a small quantity much diluted on Christmas Day or Easter Day, and from wheat bread, instead of which he ate barley bread with a preliminary taste of ashes (*cinerem praelibavit*). He wore the same hood and tunic in all seasons, and slept on ashes in a framework of boards. "Let any one speak his mind," says Constantius, to whom some details of German's life must have come down not free from exaggeration, "but I positively assert that the blessed German endured a long martyrdom." Withal he was hospitable, and gave his guests a good meal, though he would not share it. He founded a monastery outside Auxerre, on the opposite bank of the Yonne, often crossing in a boat to visit the abbat and brethren.

Pelagianism had been rife in its founder's native island of Britain; and the British clergy, unable to refute the heretics, requested help from the church, we may say from their mother church, of Gaul. Accordingly a numerous synod unanimously sent to Britain German and Lupus, bp. of Troyes, both going the more readily because of the labour involved. So says Constantius, who is followed closely by Bede (i. 17). But Prosper of Aquitaine, a contemporary, in his *Chronicle* for A.D. 429, says that pope Celestine, "at the suggestion of the deacon Palladius, sent German as his representative" (*vice sua*) into Britain; and in his *contra Collatorem*, written *c.* 432, speaks of Celestine as "taking pains to keep the Roman island" (Britain) "Catholic" (c. 21 or 24). The truth probably lies in a combination of the pope's action with the councils, at any rate as regards German. Lupus is not included by Prosper—of him evidently Celestine took no thought, but, we may reasonably believe, gave some special commission to German either before (so Tillemont, *Mémoires*, xiv. 154) or at the time of the Gallic synod: it is not probable that, as Lingard supposes, the synod's commission was only to Lupus and German "sent" by the pope alone (*Angl. Sax. Ch.* i. 8).

When the two prelates reached Nanterre near Paris, German saw in the crowd which met them the girl GENOVEFA, whom he bade live as one espoused to Christ, and who became "St. Geneviève of Paris." Arrived in Britain, the bishops preached the doctrines of grace in churches and on the country roads with great effect; till the Pelagian leaders challenged them to a discussion, apparently near Verulam. A great multitude assembled: the two bishops, appealing to Scripture in support of the Catholic position, silenced their opponents, and the shouts of the audience hailed their victory. German and Lupus then visited the reputed tomb of the British protomartyr Alban; and Constantius adds the famous tale of the Alleluia Victory. The Britons were menaced by Picts and Saxons; German and Lupus encouraged them to resist, catechized and baptized the still heathen majority in their army, and then, shortly after Easter 430, stationing them in a narrow glen, bade them at the invaders' approach repeat thrice the Paschal Alleluia. The Britons sent the shout ringing through the defile; the enemy was seized with panic, and "faith without the sword won a bloodless victory."

In 447 German was again entreated by British churchmen to aid them against Pelagianism. He took with him Severus, bp. of Trèves, a disciple of Lupus, and having on his way vindicated Genovefa against calumniators, landed in Britain, triumphed again over the Pelagians, and procured their banishment from the island. Welsh traditions record his many activities on behalf of the British church. They lay the scene of the Alleluia victory at Maes-garmon near Mold; they speak of colleges founded by German, of national customs traced to his authority; and although much of this is legendary and the stories in Nennius about his relations with king Vortigern apocryphal, he probably did more for British Christianity than Constantius records. He had no sooner returned home than another occasion for his humane intervention arose. The Armoricans, whose country had not yet acquired (through British immigration) the name of Brittany, were in chronic revolt against the empire, hoping to obtain favourable terms for Armorica. German set forth at once for Italy, and on June 19, 448, reached Milan; proceeding to Ravenna, he obtained pardon for the Armoricans, but unfortunately news came that they had again revolted, and his mission proved in vain. German was soon afterwards taken ill. His lodging overflowed with visitors; a choir kept up ceaseless psalmody by his bedside. He died July 31, 448, having been bishop 30 years and 25 days. His body was embalmed, and a magnificent funeral journey to Gaul attested the reverence of the court. He was buried in a chapel near Auxerre on Oct. 1. Constantius's Life is in Surius, *de Probatis Sanctorum Historiis*, vol. iv. A metrical Life and a prose account of his "miracles," both by a monk named Hereric, are in *Acta Sanctorum*, July 31. [W.B.]

Germanus (18) (*Germain*), St., 20th bp. of Paris, born at Autun of parents of rank named Eleutherius and Eusebia (*c.* 496), and educated at Avalon and Luzy (Lausia). In due time he was ordained deacon, and three years later priest. He was next made abbat of the monastery of St. Symphorian at Autun, by bp. Nectarius. In 555, being present at Paris on some mission to Childebert, when that see was vacant by the death of Eusebius, he was raised to the archbishopric. His great object seems to have been to check the unbridled licence of the Frank kings, and to ameliorate the misery produced by constant civil war. In 557 he was present at the third council of Paris, and appears to have exercised considerable influence over Childebert, whose edict against pagan revelry on holy days may have been due to St. Germanus (Migne, *Patr. Lat.* lxxii. 1121), and likewise the building by Childebert of the church of St. Vincent to receive the stole of that martyr which he had brought from Spain. (See the charter given by Aimoin, *de Gest. Franc.* ii. 20, ed. Jac. du Brevi, Paris, 1602, and cf. *Hist. Litt. de la France*, iii. 270). This church was said to have been consecrated by St. Germanus on the day Childebert died (Dec. 23, 558). Childebert's successor Clotaire was, according to Venantius Fortunatus, at first not equally amenable, but a sickness changed his disposition. Germanus's death is variously dated 575, 576, and 577. He was buried in an oratorium near the vestibule of the church of St. Vincent; and in 754 his body was removed with great ceremony into the church itself, in the presence of Pippin and his son Charles the Great, then a child. The church henceforth was called St. Germain des Prés.

There is extant by St. Germanus a treatise on the Mass, or exposition of the old Gallic Liturgy (*Patr. Lat.* lxxii. 89; cf. Ceillier, xi. 308 seq., for the reasons for ascribing it to him). Among his writings is also generally counted the privilege which he granted to his monastery exempting it from all episcopal jurisdiction (*c.* 565). Its authenticity has been vehemently attacked and defended (see Migne, *Patr. Lat.* lxxii. 81 *n.* and the authorities there referred to). St. Germanus's Life was written by Venantius Fortunatus, his contemporary and friend, but the work is little else than a string of miracles. It may be found in Mabillon's *Acta SS. Ord. S. Bened.* i. 234-245 (Paris, 1668-1701). See also Boll. *Acta SS.* Mai. vi. 774 sqq.; *Gall. Christ.* vii. 18-21; Mansi, ix. 747, 805, 867, 869; and, for the monastery, the *Dissertatio* of Ruinartius, in Bouquet, ii. 722. [S.A.B.]

Gervasius (1), June 19 (Us.); Oct. 14 (Bas. *Menol.*). Martyr with Protasius at Milan, under Nero. These two brothers were sons of Vitalis, whose martyrdom at Ravenna and mythical acts are recorded in *Mart.* Adon. Apr. 28. After 300 years, and when their memory had entirely faded, God is said to have revealed their place of burial to St. Ambrose in a dream. [AMBROSIUS.] The empress Justina was striving to obtain one of the churches of Milan for Arian worship, and help was needed to sustain the orthodox in their opposition to the imperial authority. Just at this time a new and splendid basilica was awaiting consecration. The people, as a kind of orthodox demonstration, wished it consecrated with the same pomp and ceremonial as had been used for another new church near the Roman Gate. Ambrose consented, if he should have some new relics to place therein. He therefore ordered excavations to be made in the church of St. Nabor and St. Felix, near the rails which enclosed their tomb. The search was rewarded by the discovery of the bodies of "two men of wondrous size, such as ancient times produced" (Amb. *Ep.* xxii. § 2), with all their bones entire and very much blood. They were removed to the church of St. Fausta, and the next day to the new Ambrosian church, where they were duly enshrined. At each different stage St. Ambrose delivered impassioned and fanciful harangues. In that on their enshrinement he claims that they had already expelled demons, and restored to sight a blind butcher, one Severus, who was cured by touching the pall that covered the relics. The Arians ridiculed the matter, asserting that Ambrose had hired persons to feign themselves demoniacs. The whole story has afforded copious matter for criticism. Mosheim (cent. iv. pt. ii. c. 3, § 8), Gibbon (c. xxvii.), Isaac Taylor (*Ancient Christianity*, vol. ii. 242-272), consider the thing a trick got up by the contrivance and at the expense of St. Ambrose himself. Two distinct points demand attention: 1st, the finding of the bodies; 2nd, the reputed miracles. The discovery of the bodies may have been neither a miracle nor a trick. Churches were frequently built in cemeteries, and excavation might easily chance upon bodies. Some, moreover, have fixed Diocletian's persecution as the time of their martyrdom, and St. Ambrose, as the official custodian of the church records, might therefore have some knowledge of their resting-place, and in times of intense theological excitement men have often imputed to dreams or supernatural assistance that for which, under calmer circumstances, they would account in a more commonplace way. It is hardly possible to read through the epistle of St. Ambrose to his sister Marcellina (*Ep.* xxii.), in which he gives an account of the discovery, and still imagine that such genuine enthusiasm could go hand in hand with conscious knavery and deceit. There remains the question of the miracles to which St. Ambrose and St. Augustine testify (*de Civit. Dei*, xxii. 8; *Confess.* ix. 7; *Ser.* 286 and 318). These were of two kinds: the restoration of demoniacs and the healing of a blind man. As to the demoniacs, we cannot decide. At times of religious excitement such cases have occurred, and can be accounted for on purely natural grounds. They belong to an obscure region of psychological phenomena. The case of the blind man, whose cure is reported by St. Augustine, then resident at Milan, as well as by St. Ambrose, stands on a different footing, and is the one really important point of the narrative with which Taylor fails effectively to grapple. We must observe, also, in favour of the miracle that St. Ambrose called immediate attention to it, and that no one seems to have challenged the fact of the blindness or the reality of restoration to sight; and further Severus devoted himself in consequence as a servant of the church wherein the relics were placed, and continued such for more than 20 years. On the other hand, we have no means of judging as to the nature of the disease in the man's eyes. He was not born blind, but had contracted the disease, being a butcher by trade. He might therefore have only been affected in some such way as powerful nervous excitement might cure, but for which he and St. Ambrose would naturally account by the miraculous power of the martyrs. In the *Criterion of Miracles*, by bp. Douglas (pp. 130-160, ed. 1803), there are many acute observations on similar reputed miracles in the 18th cent. *Mart. Rom. Vet.*, Adon., Bedae, Usuard.; *Kal. Carthag.*; *Kal. Front.*; Tillem. *Mém.* ii. 78, 498; Fleury, *H. E.* viii. 49, xviii. 47; Ceill. v. 386, 490, ix. 340. [G.T.S.]

Gildas (*Gildasius, Gildus, Gillas*), commemorated Jan. 29. In medieval Lives Gildas appears in a well-defined individuality, but a more critical view detects so many anachronisms and historical defects that it has been questioned, first, whether he ever lived, and secondly, whether there were more Gildases than one. Though he is mentioned by name, and his writings quoted from by Bede, Alcuin, William of Newburgh, Geoffrey of Monmouth, and Giraldus Cambrensis, there is no memoir of him written within several centuries of his supposed date, and the two oldest, on which the others are based, are ordinary specimens of the unhistorical tone of mind of the 11th and 12th cents. To surmount the chronological and historical difficulties, Ussher, Ware, Bale, Pitseus, Golgan, and O'Conor have imagined at least two of the name, perhaps even four or six, about the 5th and 6th cents. These have received distinguishing designations, and thus have obtained a recognized position in history. But the more probable and more generally received opinion is that there is but one Gildas, who could not have lived earlier than about the end of the 5th cent. or later than that of the 6th. The oldest authority is *Vita Gildae, auctore monacho Ruyensi anonymo*, ed. by the Bollandists (*Acta SS.* Jan. 29, iii. 573 seq.), and attributed to the 11th cent. or earlier. The other was written by Caradoc of Llancarvan in the 12th cent. (Engl. Hist. Soc. 1838). (For pub. and MS. Lives see Hardy's *Descript. Cat.* i. pt. i. 151-156, pt. ii. 799.) With what seems more or less a common groundwork of fact, these Lives have much that is irreconcilable. "Nor need this seem so very strange," says O'Hanlon (*Irish Saints*, i. 473-474), "when both accounts had been drawn up several centuries after the lifetime of Gildas, and when they had been written in different centuries and in separate countries. The diversities of chronological events, and of persons hardly contemporaneous, will only enable us to infer that the sources of information were occasionally doubtful, while the various coincidences of narrative seem to warrant a conclusion that both tracts were intended to chronicle the life of one and the same person. It deserves remark, however, that" (quoting from *Mon. Hist. Brit.* i. pt. i. 59, n.) "both are said to have been born in Scotland. One was the son of Nau, the other of Cau: the eldest son [? brother] of one was Huel, of the other Cuil. Both lives have stories of a bell, both Gildases go to Ireland, both go to Rome, and both build churches. The monk of Ruys quotes several passages from Gildas's *de Excidio*, and assigns it to him: and Caradoc calls him 'Historiographus Britonum,' and say that he wrote *Historiae de Regibus Britonum*." Bp. Nicolson (*Eng. Hist. Libr.* 32, 3rd ed.) concludes that Gildas "was monk of Bangor about the middle of the 6th cent.; a sorrowful spectator of the miseries and almost utter ruin of his countrymen by a people under whose banner they had hoped for peace." Those who believe there was only one Gildas do not entirely agree as to his dates, one for his birth being sought between A.D. 484 and 520, and one for his death between A.D. 565 and 602. In his *de Excidio Britanniae* he says he was born in the year of "obsessionis Badonici montis" (c. 26). The *Annales Cambriae* place the "bellum Badonis" in 516, and the *Annales Tigernachi* Gildas's death in 570: these dates are probably nearest the truth. By those who suppose there were two or more bearing the same name, "Albanius" is placed in the 5th cent. (425-512, Ussher), and "Badonicus" in the 6th (520-570, Ussher).

The writing ascribed to Gildas was long regarded as one treatise, *de Excidio Britanniae*; but is now usually divided into the *Historia Gildae* and *Epistola Gildae*. The former is a bare recital of the events of British history under the Romans, and between their withdrawal and his own time; the latter a querulous, confused, and lengthy series of bitter invectives in the form of a declamatory epistle addressed to the Britons, and relating specially to five kings, "reges sed tyrannos," named Constantinus, Aurelius, Conan, Vortiporus, Cuneglasus and Maglocunus.* Many, though probably without quite sufficient reason, regard the latter as the work of a later writer, and as intended in the ecclesiastical differences of the 7th and 8th cents. for purely polemical purposes, while others would place it even later still. See useful notes on both sides in *Notes and Queries*, 4th ser. i. 171, 271, 511, and on the side of genuineness and authenticity, *Hist. lit. de la France*, t. iii. 280 seq. Bolland. *Acta SS.* Jan. 29, iii. 566-582; Colgan, *Acta SS.* 176-203, 226-228; Lanigan, *Eccl. Hist. Ir.* i. c. 9; Ussher, *Brit. Eccl. Ant.* cc. 13-17, and Ind. *Chron.*; Wright, *Biog. Brit. Lit.* Ang.-Sax. per. 115-135. See Haddon and Stubbs, *Councils*, etc. vol. i. pp. 44-107; Th. Mommsen (*Mon. Ger.*); *Dict. of Nat. Biog.* vol. xxi. An Eng. trans. of Gildas's work is in Bohn's Lib. (*O. E. Chronicles*). [J.G.]

Glycerius (5), a deacon in Cappadocia, who caused Basil much annoyance by his extravagant and disorderly proceedings *c.* 374. Being a vigorous young man, well fitted for the humbler offices of the church, and having adopted the ascetic life, he was ordained deacon by Basil, though to what church is doubtful. It is variously given as Venesa, Veësa, Venata, and Synnasa. His elevation turned the young man's head. He at once began to neglect the duties of his office, and gathered about him a number of young women, partly by persuasion, partly by force, of whom he took the direction, styling himself their patriarch, and adopting a dress in keeping with his pretensions. He was supported by the offerings of his female followers, and Basil charges him with adopting this spiritual directorship in order to get his living without work. The wild and disorderly proceedings of Glycerius and his deluded adherents created great scandal and caused him to be gravely admonished by his own presbyter, his chorepiscopus, and finally by Basil himself. Glycerius turned a deaf ear, and having swelled his fanatical band by a number of young men, he one night hastily left the city with his whole troop against the will of many of the girls. The scandal of such a band wandering about under pretence of religion, singing hymns, and leaping and dancing in a disorderly fashion, was increased by the fact that a fair was going on, and the young women were exposed to the rude jests of the rabble. Fathers who came to rescue their daughters from such disgrace were driven away by Glycerius with contumely, and he carried off his whole band to a neighbouring town, of which an unidentified Gregory was bishop. Several of Basil's letters turned on this matter, the further issue of which is not known. [E.V.]

Glycerius (8), emperor of the West, afterwards bp. of Salona. In Mar. 473, being then *comes domesticorum*, he assumed the imperial title at Ravenna in succession to Olybrius; but the emperor of the East, Leo I. the Thracian, set up Julius Nepos, who was proclaimed at Ravenna late in 473 or early in 474, and marched against Glycerius and took him prisoner at Portus. (See art. GLYCERIUS in *D. of G. and R. Biogr.*) Glycerius has been reckoned bp. of Portus, of Milan, and of Salona. The *Chronicon* of Marcellinus Comes under A.D. 474 states that Glycerius "imperio expulsus, in portu urbis Romae ex Caesare episcopus ordinatus est, et obiit" (*Patr. Lat.* li. 931); on the strength of which he has been named bp. of Portus, as by Paulus Diaconus, who writes: "Portuensis episcopus ordinatur" (*Hist. Misc.* lib. xv. in *Patr. Lat.* xcv. 973 B). Cappelletti and Ughelli (who calls him Gulcerius) assign him to that see between Petrus and Herennius (Ug. *Ital. Sac.* i. 111; Capp. *Le Chiese d' Ital.* i. 497). Evagrius, on the other hand, relates (*H. E.* ii. 16) that Nepos appointed Glycerius bp. of the Romans ἐς Σάλωνας, scarcely, however, intending to say, as Canisius understands him, that Glycerius was made bp. of Rome. He must mean (writing as a Greek) that Glycerius was ordained bp. for Salona by the Roman ecclesiastical authorities, and that his see belonged to the Roman or western part of the empire and to that patriarchate rather than the Byzantine. Jornandes likewise states that Nepos "Glycerium ab imperio expellens, in Salona Dalmatiae episcopum fecit" (Jorn. *de Reg. Succ.* in Muratori, *Rer. Ital. Script.* t. i. p. 239 B). It is therefore best to understand with Canisius (note on the passage in Evagrius, *vid. Patr. Gk.* lxxxvi. pt. 2, p. 2546) that the deposition of Glycerius took place at Portus, where at the same time he was appointed to Salona. Thus also Farlati (*Illyr. Sac.* ii. 117-120). The principality of Dalmatia belonged to Nepos independently of the imperial title. Thither he retired before his successful competitor Orestes, and was brought into contact once more with Glycerius. Photius (*Biblioth. Cod.* 78) mentions the now lost *Byzantine History* of Malchus the Sophist as stating that Nepos, having divested Glycerius of his Caesarian authority and invaded "the empire of the Romans," ordained him, made him a bishop, and finally perished by his machinations (*insidiis petitus*), not "was assassinated," as stated by Gibbon. Farlati assigns six years to his episcopate, placing his death in 480.

The supposition that he was bp. of Milan rests on very slender ground. Ennodius, bp. of Pavia, who dedicates short poems to several successive bishops of Milan, inscribes one to Glycerius, whom he places between Martinianus and Lazarus (carm. 82, in *Patr. Lat.* lxiii. 349); but there is nothing in the verses to identify him with the ex-emperor. Enno-

* Skene (*Four Anc. Books of Wales*, i. 63, 64) regards them as contemporary rulers, living, one in Devon and Cornwall, two in Wales, and two probably in the N. of Ireland.

dius, in his Life of Epiphanius, bp. of Pavia, mentions the emperor Glycerius as shewing so much veneration for that saint as to accept his intercession for some people in the diocese of Pavia, who had incurred the imperial displeasure (Ennod. *Vit. Epiphan.* in *Patr. Lat.* lxiii. 219 A). These are the sole grounds on which Gibbon hazards, doubtfully, the statement (*Decl. and Fall*, vol. iv. p. 295, ed. Smith) that Glycerius was promoted by Orestes from Salona to the archbishopric of Milan in reward for his assassination of Nepos. [C.H.]

Gnosticism. The zeal with which a learner commences the study of ecclesiastical history is not unfrequently damped at an early stage, when he finds that, in order to know the history of religious thought in the 2nd cent., he must make himself acquainted with speculations so wild and so baseless that it is irksome to read them and difficult to believe that time was when acquaintance with them was counted as what alone deserved the name of "knowledge." But it would be a mistake to think too disdainfully of those early heretics who go by the common name of Gnostics. In the first place, it may be said in their excuse that the problems which they undertook to solve were among the most difficult with which the human intellect has ever grappled—namely, to explain the origin of evil, and to make it conceivable how the multiplicity of finite existence can all have been derived from a single absolute unconditioned principle. And besides, these speculators only did what learned theologians have constantly since endeavoured to do—namely, combine the doctrines which they learned from revelation with the results of what they regarded as the best philosophy of their own day, so as to obtain what seemed to them the most satisfactory account and explanation of the facts of the universe. Every union of philosophy and religion is the marriage of a mortal with an immortal: the religion lives; the philosophy grows old and dies. When the philosophic element of a theological system becomes antiquated, its explanations which contented one age become unsatisfactory to the next, and there ensues what is spoken of as a conflict between religion and science; whereas, in reality, it is a conflict between the science of one generation and that of a succeeding one. If the religious speculations of the 2nd cent. appear to us peculiarly unreasonable, it is because the philosophy incorporated with them is completely alien to modern thought. That philosophy gave unlimited licence to the framing of hypotheses, and provided that the results were in tolerable accordance with the facts, no other proof was required that the causes which these hypotheses assumed were really in operation. The *Timaeus* of Plato is a favourable specimen of the philosophic writings which moulded the Gnostic speculations; and the interval between that and a modern treatise on physics is fully as wide as between Gnosticism and modern scientific theology. So it has happened that modern thought has less sympathy with heretical theories deeply coloured by the philosophy of their own time than with the plain common sense of a church writer such as Irenaeus, which led him to proceed by the positive historical method, and reject what was merely fanciful and speculative. And it may be said that deeply important as were some of the particular questions discussed in the conflict between the church and Gnosticism, an even more important issue of that conflict was the decision of the method by which religious knowledge was to be arrived at. The Gnostics generally held that the Saviour effected redemption by making a revelation of knowledge, yet they but feebly attempted to connect historically their teaching with his; what was derived from Him was buried under elements taken freely from heathen mythologies and philosophies, or springing from the mere fancy of the speculator, so that, if Gnosticism had triumphed, all that is distinctively Christian would have disappeared. In opposition to them, church writers were led to emphasize the principle that that alone is to be accounted true knowledge of things divine which can be shewn by historical tradition, written or oral, to have been derived from the teaching of Christ and His apostles, a principle the philosophic justice of which must be admitted if Christ be owned as having filled the part in the enlightenment of the world which orthodox and Gnostics alike attributed to Him. Thus, by the conflict with Gnosticism reverence in the church was deepened for the authority of revelation as restraining the licence of human speculation, and so the channel was marked out within the bounds of which religious thought continued for centuries to flow.

We deal here with some general aspects of the subject, referring to the articles on the chief Gnostic teachers for details as to the special tenets of the different Gnostic sects.

Use of the Word Gnosticism.—In logical order we ought to begin by defining Gnosticism, and so fixing what extension is to be given to the application of the term, a point on which writers are not agreed. Baur, for instance, reckons among Gnostics the sectaries from whom the Clementine writings emanated, although on some of the most fundamental points their doctrines are diametrically opposed to those commonly reckoned as Gnostic. We conform to more ordinary usage in giving to the word a narrower sense, but this is a matter on which controversy would be only verbal, Gnosticism not being a word which has in its own nature a definite meaning. There is no difficulty in naming common characteristics of the sects commonly called Gnostic, though perhaps none of them is distinctive enough to be made the basis of a logical definition. They professed to be able to trace their doctrine to the apostles. Basilides was said to have learned from a companion of St. Peter; gospels were in circulation among them which purported to have been written by Philip, Thomas, and other apostles; and they professed to be able to find their doctrines in the canonical scriptures by methods of allegorical interpretation which, however forced, could easily be paralleled in the procedure of orthodox writers. If we made our definition turn on the claim to the possession of such a Gnosis and to the title of Gnostic, we should have to count Clement of Alexandria among Gnostics and *I. Timothy* among Gnostic writings; for the church writers refused to surrender these titles to the heretics and, claiming to be the true Gnostics, branded the heretical Gnosis as "falsely so called." If we fix our attention on the predominance of the speculative over the practical in Gnosticism, which, as Baur truly remarks, led men to regard Christianity less as a means of salvation than as furnishing the principles of a philosophy of the universe, we must allow that since their time very many orthodox writings have been open to the same criticism. We come very close to a definition if we make the criterion of Gnosticism to be the establishment of a dualism between spirit and matter; and, springing out of this, the doctrine that the world was created by some power different from the supreme God, yet we might not be able to establish that this characteristic belongs to every sect which we count as Gnostic; and if we are asked why we do not count such sects as the Manicheans among the Gnostics, the best answer is that usage confines the word to those sects which arose in the ferment of thought when Christianity first came into contact with heathen philosophy, excluding those which clearly began later. A title of honour claimed by these sectaries for themselves, and at first refused them by their opponents, was afterwards adopted as the most convenient way of designating them.

We have no reason to think that the earliest Gnostics intended to found sects separated from the church and called after their own names. Their disciples were to be Christians, only elevated above the rest as acquainted with deeper mysteries, and called γνωστικοί, because possessed of a Gnosis superior to the simple faith of the multitude. Probably the earliest instance of the use of the word is by Celsus, quoted by Origen, v. 61, where, speaking of the multiplicity of Christian sects, he says that there were some who professed to be Gnostics. Irenaeus (i. xxv. 5, p. 104), speaking of the Carpocratians and in particular of that school of them which Marcellina established at Rome, says that they called themselves Gnostics. It is doubtless on the strength of this passage that Eusebius (*H. E.* iv. 7), quoting Irenaeus in the same context, calls Carpocrates the father of the sect called that of the Gnostics. In the habitual use of the word by Irenaeus himself it does not occur as limited to Carpocratians. Irenaeus, in his first book, when he has gone through the sects called after the names of heretical teachers, gives in a kind of appendix an account of a number of sects in their general characteristics Ophite, but he does not himself use that name. He calls them "multitudo Gnosticorum," tracing their origin to Simon Magus, and counting them as progenitors of the Valentinians. And constantly we have the expression Basilidians, Valentinians, etc., "et reliqui Gnostici," where, by the latter appellation, the Ophite sects are specially intended. The form of expression does not exclude from the title of Gnostic the sects named after their founders; and the doctrine of the Valentinians is all through the work of Irenaeus a branch of "Gnosis falsely so called"; yet it is usually spoken of less as Gnosticism than as a development of Gnosticism, and the Valentinians are described as more Gnostic than the Gnostics, meaning by the latter word the Ophite sects already mentioned. In the work of Hippolytus against heresies, the name is almost exclusively found in connexion with the sect of the Naassenes or Ophites, and three or four times it is repeated (v. 2, p. 93; 4, p. 94; 11, p. 123) that these people call themselves Gnostics, claiming that they alone "knew the depths." The common source of Epiphanius and Philaster had an article on the Nicolaitanes, tracing the origin of the Gnostics to Nicolas the Deacon (see also Hippolytus, vii. 36, p. 258, and the statement of Irenaeus [II. ii. p. 188] that Nicolaitanism was a branch of Gnosis). Epiphanius divides this article into two, making the Gnostics a separate heresy (*Haer.* 26). Hence ancient usage leaves a good deal of latitude to modern writers in deciding which of the 2nd-cent. sects they will count as Gnostic.

Classification of Gnostic Sects.—Some general principles of philosophic classification may be easily agreed on, but when they come to be applied, it is found that there are some sects to which it is not obvious where to assign a place, and that some sects are separated whose affinities are closer than those of others which are classed together. A very important, though not a complete, division is that made by Clement of Alexandria (*Strom.* iii. 5) into the ascetic and licentious sects: both parties agreeing in holding the essential evil of matter; the one endeavouring by rigorous abstinence to free as much as possible man's soul from the bondage to which it is subjected by union with his material part, and refusing to marry and so enthral new souls in the prisons of bodies; the other abandoning as desperate any attempt to purify the hopelessly corrupt body, and teaching that the instructed soul ought to hold itself unaffected by the deeds of the body. All actions were to it indifferent. The division of Neander is intended to embrace a wider range than that just described. Taking the common doctrine of the Gnostic sects that the world was made by a Being different from the supreme God, he distinguishes whether that Being was held to have acted in subordination to the Supreme, and on the whole to have carried out his intentions, or to have been absolutely hostile to the supreme God. Taking into account the generally acknowledged principle that the Creator of the world was the same as the God worshipped by the Jews, we see that Gnostics of the second class would be absolutely hostile to Judaism, which those of the former class might accept as one of the stages ordained by the Supreme in the enlightenment of the world. Thus Neander's division classifies sects as not unfriendly to Judaism or as hostile to it; the former class taking its origin in those Alexandrian schools where the authority of such teachers as Philo had weight, the latter among Christian converts from Oriental philosophy whose early education had given them no prejudices in favour of Judaism. Gieseler divides into Alexandrian Gnostics, whose teaching was mainly influenced by the Platonic philosophy, and Syrian strongly affected by Parsism. In the former the emanation doctrine was predominant, in the latter dualism. Undoubtedly the most satisfactory classification would be if it were possible, as Matter suggested, to have one founded on the history of the generation of the sects, distinguishing the school where Gnosticism had its beginning, and naming the schools which successively in different places altered in different directions the original scheme. But a good classification of this kind is rendered impossible by the scantiness of our materials for the history of Gnosticism. Irenaeus is the first to give any full details, and he may be counted two generations later than Valentinus; for Marcus, the disciple of Valentinus, was resisted by one whom Irenaeus looked up to with respect as belonging to the generation above his own. The interval between Valentinus and the beginning of Gnosticism was, moreover, probably quite as great as that between Valentinus and Irenaeus. The phrase used by Hippolytus in telling us that the Naassenes boasted that they alone "knew the depths" was also a watchword of the false teachers reprobated in the Apocalypse (Rev. ii. 24). We can hardly avoid the inference that these Naassenes inherited a phrase continuously in use among heretical teachers since before the publication of the *Revelation*. Of the writers who would deny the pastoral epistles to be St. Paul's, a large proportion date the *Revelation* only 2 or 3 years after St. Paul's death; therefore, whether or not it was St. Paul who wrote of the "falsely called knowledge," it remains probable that heretical pretenders to Gnosis had arisen in his lifetime. If the beginnings of Gnosticism were thus in apostolic times, we need not be surprised that the notices of its origin given by Irenaeus more than a century afterwards are so scanty; and that the teachers to whom its origin has been ascribed, Simon, Menander, Nicolas, Cerinthus, remain shadowy or legendary characters. It follows that conclusions as to the order of succession of the early Gnostic sects and their obligations one to another are very insecure. Still, some general facts in the history of the evolution of Gnosticism may be considered fairly certain; and we are disposed to accept the classification of Lipsius and count three stages in the progress of Gnosticism, even though there may be doubt to what place a particular sect is to be assigned. The birthplace of Gnosticism may be said to be Syria, if we include in that Palestine and Samaria, where church tradition places the activity of those whom it regards as its founders, Simon and Menander. It may also be inferred from the use made of O.T. and of Hebrew words that Gnosticism sprang out of Judaism. The false teaching combated in *Colossians*, which has several Gnostic features, is also distinctly Jewish, insisting on the observance of sabbaths and new moons. The Epp. to *Timothy* and *Titus*, dealing with a somewhat later development of Gnosticism, describe the false teachers as "of the circumcision," "professing to be teachers of the law" and propounders of "Jewish fables." It is not unlikely that what these epistles characterize as "profane and old wives' fables" may be some of the Jewish Haggadah of which the early stages of Gnosticism are full. The story of Ialdabaoth, *e.g.*, told by Irenaeus (i. 30), we hold to date from the very beginning of Gnosticism, if not in its present shape, at least in some rudimentary form, as fragments of it appear in different Gnostic systems, especially the representation of the work of Creation as performed by an inferior being, who still fully believed himself to be the Supreme, saying, "I am God, and there is none beside me," until, after this boast, his ignorance was enlightened. The Jewish Cabbala has been asserted to be the parent of Gnosticism; but the records of Cabbalistic doctrine are quite modern, and any attempt to pick out the really ancient parts must be attended with uncertainty. Lipsius (p. 270, and Grätz, referred to by him) shews that the Cabbala is certainly not older than Gnosticism, its relation to it being not that of a parent, but of a younger brother. If there be direct obligation, the Cabbala is the borrower, but many common features are to be explained by regarding both as branches from the same root, and as alike springing from the contact of Judaism with the religious beliefs of the farther East. Jewish Essenism especially furnished a soil favourable to the growth of Gnosticism, with which it seems to have had in common the doctrine of the essential evil of matter, as appears from the denial by the Essenes of the resurrection of the body and from their inculcation of a disciplining of man's material part by very severe asceticism. (See Lightfoot, *Colossians*, 119 seq.) Further, the Ebionite sects which sprang out of Essenism, while they professed the strongest attachment to the Mosaic law, not only rejected the authority of the prophetical writings, but dealt in a very arbitrary manner with those parts of the Pentateuch which conflicted with their peculiar doctrines. We have parallels to this in theories of some of the early Gnostic sects which referred the Jewish prophetical books to the inspiration of beings inferior to Him by Whom the law was given, as well as in the arbitrary modes of criticism applied by some of the later sects to the books of Scripture. A form of Gnosticism thus developed from Judaism when the latter was brought into contact with the mystic speculations of the East, whether we suppose Essenism to have been a stage in the process of growth or both to have been independent growths under similar circumstances of development. Lipsius notes as the characteristics of those sects which he counts as belonging to the first stage of Gnosticism that they still move almost or altogether within the circle of the Jewish religious history, and that the chief problem they set themselves is the defining the relation between Christianity and Judaism. The solutions at which they arrive are very various. Those Jewish sects whose Essenism passed into the Ebionitism of the Clementines regarded Christianity as essentially identical with Judaism, either religion being sufficient for salvation. These sects are quite orthodox as to the Creation, their utmost deviation (if it can be called so) from the received belief being the ascription of Creation to the immanent wisdom of God. Other Jewish speculators came to think of the formation of matter as accomplished by a subordinate being, carrying out, it may be, the will of the Supreme, but owing to his finiteness and ignorance doing the work with many imperfections. Then came the theory that this subordinate being was the God of the Jews, to which nation he had issued many commandments that were not good, though overruled by the Supreme so as to carry out His ends. Lastly came the theory of the Cainites and other extreme Ophite sects, which represented the God of the Jews as the determined enemy of the Supreme, and as one whose commands it was the duty of every enlightened Gnostic to disobey. With all their variety of results, these sects agreed in the importance attached to the problem of the true relations of Judaism to Christianity. They do make use of certain heathen principles of cosmogony, but these such as already had become familiar to Syriac Judaism, and introduced not so much to effect a reconciliation between Christianity and heathenism as to give an explanation of the service rendered to the world by the publication of Christianity, the absolute religion. This is made mainly to consist in the aid given to the soul in its struggles to escape the bonds of finiteness and darkness, by making known to it the supersensual world and awaking it to the consciousness of its spiritual origin. Regarding this knowledge as the common privilege of Christians, the first speculators would count their own possession of it as differing rather in degree than in kind ; and so it is not easy to draw a sharp line of distinction between their doctrine on the subject of Gnosis and that admitted as orthodox. Our Lord had described it as the privilege of His disciples to know the mysteries of the kingdom of heaven ; later when His followers learned of a suffering Messiah, and of the fulfilment in Jesus of the types of the Mosaic law, they felt that the veil had been removed for them, and that they enjoyed a knowledge of the meaning of the O.T. Scriptures to which their unconverted brethren were strangers. This feeling pervades the Ep. to the *Hebrews,* and still more that of Barnabas. Another doctrine which St. Paul describes as a mystery formerly kept secret, but now revealed through his gospel, is the admission of the Gentiles on equal terms with the Jews to the inheritance of the kingdom of Christ. It was no part of orthodox Christian doctrine that all Christians possessed the true Gnosis in equal degree. Some required to be fed with milk, not with strong meat, and had not their senses exercised by reason of use to discern between good and evil. Clement of Alexandria distinguished between faith and knowledge. The difference, therefore, between the Gnostic doctrine and that of the church mainly depends on the character of what was accounted knowledge, much of the Gnostic so-called knowledge consisting in acquaintance with the names of a host of invisible beings and with the formulae which could gain their favour.

Gnosticism, in its first stage, did not proceed far outside the limits of Syria. What Lipsius counts as the second stage dates from the migration of Gnostic systems to Alexandria, where the myths of Syriac Gnosis came to be united to principles of Grecian philosophy. Different Gnostic systems resulted according as the principles of this or that Grecian school were adopted. Thus, in the system of Valentinus, the Pythagorean Platonic philosophy predominates, the Stoic in that of the Basilidians as presented by Hippolytus. In these systems, tinged with Hellenism, the Jewish religion is not so much controverted or disparaged as ignored. The mythological personages among whom in the older Gnosis the work of creation was distributed are in these Hellenic systems replaced by a kind of abstract beings (of whom the Valentinian aeons are an example) which personify the different stages of the process by which the One Infinite Spirit communicates and reveals itself to derived existences. The distinction between faith and knowledge becomes sharpened, the persons to whom faith and knowledge respectively are to serve as guides being represented as essentially different in nature. The most obvious division of men is into a kingdom of light and a kingdom of darkness. The need of a third class may have first made itself felt from the necessity of finding a place for members of the Jewish religion, who stood so far above heathenism, so far below Christianity. The Platonic trichotomy of body, soul, and spirit afforded a principle of threefold classification, and men are divided into earthly (ὑλικοί or χοϊκοί), animal (ψυχικοί), and spiritual (πνευματικοί). In these Hellenic Gnostic systems the second class represents not Jews but ordinary Christians, and the distinction between them and the Gnostics themselves (who are the spiritual) rests on an assumed difference of nature which leaves little room for human free will. Salvation by faith and corresponding works is disparaged as suitable only for the psychical, the better sort of whom may, by this means, be brought to as high a position in the order of the universe as their nature is capable of ; but the really spiritual need not these lower methods of salvation. It suffices for them to have the knowledge of their true nature revealed for them to become certain of shaking off all imprisoning bonds and soaring to the highest region of all. Thus ordinary historical Christianity runs the risk of meeting the same fate in the later Gnostic systems that befell Judaism in the earlier. The doctrines and facts of the religion are only valued so far as they can be made subservient to the peculiar notions of Gnosticism ; and the method of allegorical interpretation was so freely applied to both Testaments that all the solid parts of the religion were in danger of being volatilized away.

The natural consequence of this weakening of the historic side of Christianity was the removal of all sufficient barrier against the intrusion of heathen elements into the systems ; while their moral teaching was injuriously affected by the doctrine that the spiritual were secure of salvation by necessity of their nature and irrespectively of their conduct. Gnosticism, in its third stage, struggles in various ways to avoid these faults, and so again draws nearer to the teaching of the Catholic church. Thus the DOCETAE of Hippolytus allow of immense variety of classes, corresponding to the diversity of ideas derived from the world of aeons, which each has received ; while again they deny to none a share in our Lord's redemption, but own that members of different sects are entitled, each in his degree, to claim kinship with Jesus and to obtain forgiveness of sins through Him. So again in one of the latest of the Gnostic systems, that of PISTIS SOPHIA, there is no assertion of an essential diversity of nature among men, but the immense development of ranks and degrees in the spiritual world, which that work professes to reveal, is used so as to provide for every man a place according to his works. In the system of Marcion, too, the theory of essentially different classes is abandoned; the great boast of Christianity is its universality; and the redemption of the Gospel is represented, not as the mere rousing of the pneumatic soul to consciousness of privileges all along possessed, but as the introduction of a real principle of moral life through the revelation of a God of love forgiving sins through Christ.

We add brief notes on a few main points of the Gnostic systems.

Creation and Cosmogony.—Philo (*de Op. Mund.*) had inferred from the expression, "Let *us* make man," of *Genesis* that God had used other beings as assistants in the creation of man, and he explains in this way why man is capable of vice as well as virtue, ascribing the origin of the latter to God, of the former to His helpers in the work of creation. The earliest Gnostic sects ascribe the work of creation to angels, some of them using the same passage in *Genesis* (Justin. *Dial. cum Tryph.* c. 67).

Doctrine with respect to Judaism.—The doctrine that the Creator of the world is not the supreme God leads at once to the question, What then is to be thought of the God of the Jews, who certainly claimed to have created the world? This question is most distinctly answered in the doctrine of the Ophite system (*Iren.* i. 30). According to it he who claimed to be a jealous God, acknowledging none other, was led by sheer ignorance to make a false pretension. He was in truth none other than the chief of the creative angels, holding but a subordinate place in the constitution of the universe. It was he who forbad to Adam and Eve that knowledge by which they might be informed that he had superiors, and who on their disobedience cast them out of Paradise.

Doctrine concerning the Nature of Man.—With the myth, told by Saturninus, of the animation of a previously lifeless man by a spark of light from above, he connected the doctrine, in which he was followed by almost all Gnostic sects, that there would be no resurrection of the body, the spark of light being taken back on death to the place whence it had come, and man's material part being resolved into its elements. Saturninus is said to have taught the doctrine, antagonistic to that of man's free will, that there were classes of men by nature essentially different, and of these he counted two—the good and the wicked. The doctrine became common to many Gnostic systems that the human frame contained a heavenly element struggling to return to its native place.

Redemption and Christology.—The Gnostic systems generally represent man's spirit as imprisoned in matter, and needing release. The majority recognize the coming of Christ as a turning-point in human affairs, but almost all reduce the Redeemer's work to the impartation of knowledge and the disclosure of mysteries. With regard to the nature of Christ, the lowest view is held by Justinus, who describes Jesus but as a shepherd boy commissioned by an angel to be the bearer of a divine revelation, and who attributes to Him at no time any higher character. Carpocrates makes Jesus a man like others, only of more than ordinary steadfastness and purity of soul, possessing no prerogatives which other men may not attain in the same or even higher degree if they follow, or surpass, His example. Besides furnishing an example, He was also supposed to have made a revelation of truth, to secret traditions of which the followers of Carpocrates appealed. At the opposite pole from those who see in the Saviour a mere man are those who deny His humanity altogether. We know from St. John's epistle that the doctrine that our Lord had not really come in the flesh was one which at an early time troubled the church.

Authorities.—The great work of Irenaeus against heresies is the chief storehouse whence writers, both ancient and modern, have drawn their accounts of the Gnostic sects. It was primarily directed against the then most popular form of the heresy of Valentinus, and hence this form of Gnosticism has thrown all others into the shade, and many modern writers when professing to describe Gnosticism really describe Valentinianism. Irenäeus was largely copied by Tertullian, who, however, was an independent authority on Marcionism; by Hippolytus, who in his work against heresies adds, however, large extracts from his independent reading of Gnostic works; and by Epiphanius, who also gives a few valuable additions from other sources. The *Stromateis* of Clement of Alexandria, though provokingly desultory and unsystematic, furnish much valuable information about Gnosticism, which was still a living foe of the church. The writings of Origen also yield much important information. The matter, not borrowed from Irenaeus, to be gleaned from later heresiologists is scanty and of doubtful value.

Modern works which have made valuable contributions to the knowledge of Gnosticism include Neander, *Genetische Entwickelung* (1818), and *Church Hist.* vol. ii. (1825 and 2nd ed. 1843, trans. in Clarke's series); Burton, *Bampton Lectures* (1829); Baur, *Christliche Gnosis* (1835); *Die christliche Kirche der drei ersten Jahrhunderte* (1853, 2nd ed. 1860); and Mansel, *The Gnostic Heresies* (1875). [G.S.]

Gordianus (7), father of pope Gregory the Great, was a noble Roman of senatorial rank, and descended from a pope Felix (Joann. Diac. *in Vit. S. Gregorii*; Greg. *Dialog.* l. 4, c. 16). John the Deacon says that Felix IV. (*acc.* 523) was his ancestor; but this pope being described as a Samnite, whereas Gregory is always spoken of as of Roman descent, Felix III. (*acc.* 467) is more probable. A large property accrued to Gregory on his father's death. Gordianus is described as a religious man, and thus contributing to the eminently religious training of his son, though not canonized after death, as were his wife Silvia, and his two sisters, Tarsilla and

Aemiliana. John the deacon (*op. cit.* l. 4, c. 83) describes two pictures of him and his wife Silvia remaining to the writer's time (9th cent.) in the *Atrium* of St. Andrew's monastery, where they had been placed by St. Gregory himself, the founder of the monastery. Gordianus is represented as standing before a seated figure of St. Peter (who holds his right hand) and as clothed in a chestnut-coloured *planeta* over a *dalmatic*, and with *caligae* on his feet. Gordianus is designated "Regionarius," from which, as well as from his dress, Baronius supposes that he was one of the seven cardinal deacons of Rome, it having been not uncommon, he says, for married men, with the consent of their wives, to embrace clerical or monastic life. As to the dress, he adduces two of St. Gregory's epistles (*Ep.* 113, l. i. ind. 2, and *Ep.* 28, l. 7, ind. 1) to shew that the dalmatic and caligae were then part of the costume of Roman deacons. But the meaning of the title "regionarius" is uncertain. It occurs in St. Gregory's *Ep.* 5, l. 7, ind. 1, in *Ep.* 2 of pope Honorius I. (regionarius nostrae sedis); in Aimoinus, *de Gestis Francorum*, pt. 2, p. 247 (regionarius primae sedis); in *Vit. Ludovici Pii*, ann. 835 (regionarius Romanae urbis); and in Anastasius, *On Constantine* (Theophanes regionarius). In two of these instances, those from Honorius and Aimoinus, the persons so designated are expressly said to be subdeacons. It seems to have denoted an office connected with the city of Rome and the apostolic see, but certainly not one confined to deacons. As to the dress, it is merely originally ordinary lay costume, the planeta, rather than the casula, having been worn by persons of rank. St. Gregory himself, in his portrait in the same monastery described by John the deacon, wears precisely the same dress, even to the colour of the planeta, only having the pallium over it, to mark his ecclesiastical rank. [J.B—Y.]

Gratianus (5) (*Flavius Gratianus Augustus*), emperor 375-383, son of Valentinian, was born at Sirmium in 359, while his father was still an officer in the army. When Valentinian was chosen emperor by the soldiers in 364, Gratian was not five years old. On Aug. 24, 367, Valentinian, at Amiens, declared him "Augustus."

When Valentinian died in 375, the infant child of his second wife Justina (Valentinian II.) was proclaimed Augustus by his principal officers (Amm. xxx. 10), in reliance upon the youth and good nature of Gratian, who was at Treves, and who recognized his young brother almost immediately. Justina fixed her court at Sirmium; and the Western empire was perhaps nominally divided between the two brothers, Gratian having Gaul, Spain, and Britain, and Valentinian, Italy, Illyricum, and Africa (Zos. iv. 19). But this division must have been simply nominal, as Gratian constantly acted in the latter provinces (see Tillem. *Emp.* v. p. 140, and cf. the laws quoted *infra*). For the first years of his reign, till the death of his uncle Valens, Gratian resided chiefly at Trèves, whence most of his laws are dated. His first acts were to punish with death some of the prominent instruments of the cruelties committed in the name of justice and discipline, which had disgraced his father's later years, especially the hated Maximinus. Another act, doubtless at the beginning of his reign, shewed his determination to break with paganism more effectually than his predecessors had done. This was his refusal of the robe of pontifex maximus, when it was brought to him according to custom by the pontifices; thinking (as the heathen historian tells us) that it was unlawful for a Christian (Zos. iv. 36). The title appears indeed to some extent on coins and inscriptions, but it is not easy to fix their date.

The Eastern empire was, meanwhile, in the hands of the incompetent Valens, in great danger from Goths. In 378 the Alamanni Lentienses passed the Rhine in great force and threatened the Western empire, but were heavily defeated by Gratian at Argentaria, near Colmar (Amm. xxxi. 10). This set him free to move towards the East; and at Sirmium he heard of the defeat of his uncle at Adrianople, Aug. 7, and of his ignoble death (*ib.* 11, 6; 12, 10). The situation was extremely critical for an emperor not 20 years of age. The barbarians were in motion on all the frontiers. The internal condition of the West was insecure, from the tacit antagonism between the two courts, and the East was now suddenly thrown upon his hands, as Valens had left no children. Gratian shewed his judgment by sending for the younger Theodosius, son of the late count Theodosius and about 13 years older than himself, who after his father's execution was living in retirement upon his estates in Spain (Victor, *Ep.* 72, 74, etc.; cf. Themist. *Orat.* 14, p. 183 A). Theodosius, loyal and fearless like his father, was at once entrusted with command of the troops as magister militum. His successes over the barbarians (probably Sarmatians) encouraged Gratian to appoint him emperor of the East with general applause (Theod. v. 5, 6).

Gratian returned from Sirmium by way of Aquileia and Milan, at which places he passed some parts of July and Aug. 379. He had previously been brought into contact with St. Ambrose, and had received from him the two first books of his treatise *de Fide*, intended specially to preserve him against Arianism. This teaching had its due effect; and he now addressed a letter to the bp. of Milan (see *infra*). St. Ambrose sent him two more books of his treatise, and probably had personal intercourse with him. Gratian then went on to his usual residence at Treves, but during the following years resided much more frequently at and near Milan, especially in winter; his intercourse with St. Ambrose resulting in his confirmation in the Catholic faith. There was, however, another side to this practical neglect of the Gallic provinces. The Western provincials—never very contented—felt the absence of the imperial court. If Gratian had continued to reside at Treves, the rebellion of Magnus Maximus might never have taken place, and certainly would not have grown so formidable.

The influence of St. Ambrose is shewn by the ecclesiastical laws (see *infra*), and in the removal of the altar of Victory from the senate-house at Rome in A.D. 381 (St. Ambr. *Ep.* 17, 5; Symm. *Ep.* 61, ad init. et ad finem). The heathen senators, though in the minority, were accustomed to offer incense on this altar, and to touch it in taking solemn oaths (Ambr. *Ep.* 17, 9). It had been removed or covered up during the visit of Constantius, but was again restored under Julian, and Valentinian's policy had been against interference with such matters (Symm. *l.c.*). Its removal now caused great distress to the heathen party, who met in the senate-house and petitioned Gratian for its restoration. But the Christians, who had absented themselves from the curia, met privately, and sent a counter-petition through pope Damasus to Ambrose, who presented it to the emperor (Ambr. *l.c.*). The weight of this document enabled the advisers of Gratian to prevent his giving the heathen party a hearing. This blow was soon followed by another even more telling—the confiscation of the revenues of the temple of Victory, and the abolition of the privileges of the pontiffs and vestals, a measure extended to other heathen institutions (*ib.* 3-5; 18, 11 f.; *Cod. Theod.* xv. 10, 20).

These laws were followed by a famine in Italy, especially in Rome, which the pagans naturally ascribed to sacrilege (Symm. *l.c.*).

A much more serious danger was the revolt of Magnus Maximus, a former comrade of Theodosius in Britain, who was probably jealous of his honours, and was now put forward as emperor by the soldiers. [MAXIMUS (**2**).] This rising took place A.D. 383 in Britain, whence the usurper passed over to the mouth of the Rhine, gathering large bodies of men as he went. Gratian set out to meet him, with his two generals Balio and Merobaudes, the latter a Frank by birth. The two armies met near Paris, and Gratian was deserted by nearly all his troops (Zos. iv. 35; Ambr. *in Ps.* 61, 17). Only 300 horse remained faithful. With these he fled at full speed to Lyons. The governor received him with protestations of loyalty, and took a solemn oath on the Gospels not to hurt him. Gratian, deceived by his assurances, took his place in his imperial robes at a feast, during or soon after which he was basely assassinated (Aug. 25) at the age of 24, leaving no children. The traitor even denied his body burial (Ambr. *l.c.*, and 23 f.; Marcell. *sub anno*).

Gratian was amiable and modest—in fact, too modest to be a good governor in these rough times. He was generous and kind-hearted, of an attractive disposition and beautiful person. His tutor Ausonius had taken pains to inspire him with tastes for rhetoric and versification. He was chaste and temperate, careful in religious conduct, and zealous for the faith. His great fault was a neglect of public business through devotion to sport, especially to shooting wild beasts with bow and arrows in his parks and preserves (Amm. *l.c.*; Victor, *Ep.* 73). He once killed a lion with a single arrow (Aus. *Epig.* 6); and St. Ambrose alludes to his prowess in the chase, adopting the language of David's elegy over Jonathan—"Gratiani sagitta non est reversa retro" (*de Obitu Valent.* 73; cf. the old Latin of II. Sam. i. 22).

The ecclesiastical policy of Gratian was more important than his civil or military government. His reign, coinciding with that of Theodosius, saw orthodox Christianity for the first time dominant throughout the empire. His measures in behalf of the church were often tainted with injustice towards the sects. But it is probable that the laws were very imperfectly carried out (see Richter, p. 327). His first general law against heretical sects is dated from Trèves, May 1, 376, and speaks of a previous law of the same kind (*Cod. Theod.* xvi. 5, 4), which may, however, be one of Valens (and Valentinian).

In 377, shortly before the death of Valens, he condemned rebaptism, and ordered the Donatist churches to be restored to the Catholics and their private meeting-houses confiscated (*Cod. Theod.* xvi. 6, 2). The death of Valens was naturally the signal for the disciple of St. Ambrose to restore the Catholics of the East to their possessions. He recalled all those whom his uncle had banished, and further issued an edict of toleration for all Christian sects, except the Eunomians (extreme Arians, see Soz. vi. 26), Photinians, and Manicheans (Socr. v. 2; Soz. vii. 1). Theodoret (v. 2) appears to confuse this with the later edict of Gratian and Theodosius. On the strong representations of Idacius of Merida, the Priscillianists, an enthusiastic sect of Gnostics numerous in Spain (Sulpicius Severus, *Chron.* ii. 47, 6), were also excepted.

On his return from Sirmium, Gratian wrote the following affectionate and interesting autograph (Ambr. *Ep.* 1, 3) letter to St. Ambrose: "I desire much to enjoy the bodily presence of him whose recollection I carry with me, and with whom I am present in spirit. Therefore, hasten to me, religious priest of God, to teach me the doctrine of the true faith. Not that I am anxious for argument, or wish to know God in words rather than in spirit; but that my heart may be opened more fully to receive the abiding revelation of the divinity. For He will teach me, Whom I do not deny, Whom I confess to be my God and my Lord, not raising as an objection against His divinity that He took upon Himself a created nature like my own [non ei obiciens, quam in me video, creaturam]. I confess that I can add nothing to the glory of Christ; but I should wish to commend myself to the Father in glorifying the Son. I will not fear a grudging spirit on the part of God. I shall not suppose myself such an encomiast as to increase His divinity by my praises. In my weakness and frailty I utter what I can, not what is adequate to His divinity. I desire you to send me a copy of the same treatise, which you sent before [*de Fide*, i. ii.], enlarging it by a faithful dissertation on the Holy Spirit: prove that He is God by arguments of Scripture and reason. May the Deity keep you for many years, my father, and worshipper of the eternal God, Jesus Christ, Whom we worship." St. Ambrose replies, excusing his non-attendance upon the emperor, praising the expressions of his faith, and sending two fresh books of his treatise. For the new book, *de Spiritu Sancto*, he asks time, knowing (as he says) what a critic will read them. The subject was at this moment being largely discussed in the Eastern church.

It is assumed by De Broglie that the bishop and the emperor did not meet at this time, but St. Ambrose writes in the letter just quoted,

§ 7, "veniam plane et festinabo ut jubes," and two laws of Gratian's are dated from Milan in July and Aug. 379 (*Cod. Just.* vi. 32, 4, July 29, and *Cod. Theod.* xvi. 5, 5, Aug. 3, to Hesperius Pf. Praet. de haereticis), the second of which may shew the influence of St. Ambrose. It forbids the heresies against which former imperial edicts had been directed, and especially that of rebaptism (the Donatists), and revokes the recent tolerant edict of Sirmium.

About this time must be dated the occurrences mentioned by St. Ambrose in *de Spiritu Sancto*, i. §§ 19-21. The empress Justina, an Arian, had obtained from Gratian a basilica for the worship of her sect, to the great distress of the Catholics. He restored it, however, apparently of his own motion, to their equal surprise and delight, perhaps A.D. 380 (cf. Richter, n. 30, p. 692 ; *de Spiritu Sancto*, § 20, neque enim aliud possumus dicere, nisi sancti Spiritus hanc priore gratiam, quod ignorantibus omnibus subito Basilicam reddidisti). St. Ambrose also obtained another victory over the Arians in 380 in his journey to Sirmium, where Justina apparently also went. In spite of her vehement opposition, he succeeded in consecrating an orthodox bishop to the metropolitan see of Illyria, and thus laid the foundation for the suppression of heresy in that quarter of the empire (Paulinus, *Vita Ambrosii*, 11).

Gratian evidently agreed in the important edict issued by his colleague Theodosius on Feb. 27, 380, from Thessalonica to the people of Constantinople. This remarkable document declared the desire of the emperors that all their subjects should profess the religion given by St. Peter to the Romans and now held by the pontiff Damasus, and Peter, bp. of Alexandria—that is to say, should confess the one deity and equal majesty of the three persons of the Blessed Trinity, Father, Son, and Holy Spirit ; and further, that they alone who hold this faith are to be called *Catholics*, and their places of meeting *churches* ; while the rest are branded as heretics, and are threatened with an indefinite punishment (*Cod. Theod.* xvi. 1, 2 ; cf. the law of the next year, which mentions various Catholic bishops of the East, whose communion was to be the test of orthodoxy, including Nectarius of Constantinople—perhaps the reference to Damasus had given offence). De Broglie says of these laws, " It was impossible to abjure more decidedly the pretension of dogmatizing from the elevation of the throne, which had been since Constantine the mania of all the emperors and the scourge of the empire " (vol. v. p. 365). But correct dogmatism is still dogmatism, and the definition of truth by good emperors kept up the delusion that the right of perpetual interference with religion was inherent in their office.

In May 383, at Padua, Gratian issued a penal law against apostates, and those who try to make others apostatize from Christianity.

In 381 he summoned the council of Aquileia (which met on Sept. 5) to decide the cases of the Illyrian bishops Palladius and Secundianus, who were accused of Arianism. Their condemnation put an end to the official life of Arianism in that important district (Ambr. *Ep.* 9). The records of this council are preserved by St. Ambrose, (following his 8th epistle in the Benedictine ed.), who took the chief part in it, though he did not technically preside. The same council took up the case of pope Damasus and besought the emperor to interfere against the partisans of the antipope Ursinus (*ib.* 11). The relations of Gratian with the see of Rome are somewhat obscure, but some extension of its privileges and pretensions dates from this reign. According to the documents first published by Sirmond, a synod held in Rome soon after Gratian's accession made large demands for ecclesiastical jurisdiction and particularly asked that the bp. of Rome should only be judged by a council of bishops or by the emperor in person. Gratian in his rescript to Aquilinus the vicar (of Rome ?) grants and confirms several privileges, but says nothing of the latter request. Some doubt hangs over the whole of these documents. (See Godefroy, *Cod. Theod.* vol. vi. appendix, pp. 17, 18 ; Baron. *Annals*, sub anno 381, §§ 1, 2 ; Tillem. *Damase*, arts. 10 and 11. Greenwood, *Cathedra Petri*, vol. i. pp. 239-242 ; Hefele, *Councils*, § 91, does not even hint at their existence.)

In consequence of the success of the council of Aquileia St. Ambrose was anxious to call together an oecumenical assembly at Rome to settle the dispute between Nectarius and Maximus, who both claimed the see of Constantinople, and pressed the emperor Theodosius on the point (*Epp.* 13 and 14), who, however, naturally viewed this interference with coldness (Theod. v. 8, 9). A council, nevertheless, met at Rome, but without doing much beyond condemning the Apollinarians.

Returning to Milan, St. Ambrose took leave of the young emperor for the last time. Their intercourse had always been tender and affectionate, and was the last thought of the emperor before his death.

We may here mention an instance of their relations, which may have been at this or at any other period of their friendship (de Broglie, to make a point, puts it here, vol. vi. p. 45, but neither Paulinus, § 37, nor Sozomen, vii. 25, gives any hint of date). A heathen of quality was condemned to death for abusing Gratian and calling him an unworthy son of Valentinian. As he was being led to execution, Ambrose hurried to the palace to intercede for him. One Macedonius, master of the offices, it would seem, ordered the servants to refuse him admittance, as Gratian was engaged in his favourite sport. Ambrose went round to the park gates, entered unperceived by the huntsmen, and never left Gratian till he had overcome his arguments and those of his courtiers and obtained remission of the sentence. "The time will come," he said to Macedonius, " when you will fly for asylum to the church, but the church doors will be shut against you." The anecdote of the criminal is told by Sozomen, *l.c.* ; the words to Macedonius are given by Paulinus, *u.s.* [J.W.]

Gregorius (3), surnamed *Thaumaturgus*, bp. of Neocaesarea in Pontus, *c.* 233-270 ; born *c.* 210 at Neocaesarea on the Lycus, the modern Niksar ; the son of wealthy and noble heathen parents. Christianity had as yet made little progress in that neighbourhood, there being only 17 Christians in the whole region (Greg. Nys. *Vita Thaum.*; Migne, *Patr. Gk.* xlvi. 954). The extraordinary success of the episcopal labours of the young missionary and the romantic details with which later hands embellished them secured for him the well-known title of *Thaumaturgus*. This repute cannot be set down as exclusively due to the credulousness of the age, for as Lardner (*Cred.* ii. 42, § 5) remarked, besides Gregory of Nyssa, such writers as Basil, Jerome, and Theodoret distinguished him, as above others, "a man of apostolic signs and wonders" (cf. Dr. J. H. Newman, *Essays on Miracles*, p. 263). No light is thrown upon his thaumaturgic renown by his extant writings, which are conspicuous for their philosophic tone, humility, self-distrust, and practical sense. He must have been a man of singular force of character and weighty judgment. Heretics claimed the sanction of his name for their speculations, thus indirectly revealing the confidence in which he was held by all parties.

Gregory (originally Theodorus) stated that his father died and he himself passed through a remarkable spiritual crisis in his 14th year. He attributed the change of sentiment to "the Divine Logos, the Angel of the counsel of God, and the common Saviour of all." He left it, however, doubtful in what precisely the change consisted. His mother having suggested the pursuit of rhetoric, he was advised to study specially Roman law and become an alumnus of the celebrated school of jurisprudence at Berytus in Syria. His sister needed an escort to Palestine to join her husband in his high position under the Roman governor at Caesarea. The young Gregory and his brother Athenodorus took this opportunity to travel. "My guardian angel" (says he) "on our arrival at Caesarea handed us over to the care and tuition of Origen," and the brothers, abandoning their journey, remained there under the personal spell of the teacher for five years. The mental processes by which Gregory was led to Christ throw considerable light on the mind of Origen and the methods of Christian education in the 3rd cent. These details are preserved in a panegyric on Origen, which before leaving Caesarea the young student pronounced to a great assembly in the presence of his master. They differ in several particulars from the account of Gregory of Nyssa (Greg. Nys. *Vita Thaum.*; Migne, *Patr. Gk.* vol. xlvi. pp. 893-958). According to Gregory's own statements (*Orat. de Orig.* c. vi.), Origen enticed his pupils first to the study of philosophy, which he recommended as a duty to the Lord of all, "since man alone of all creatures is deemed by his Creator as worthy to pursue it." "A thoughtful man, if pious, must philosophize," says he, so "at length, like some spark lighting on our soul, love was kindled and burst into flame within us, a love to the Holy Logos, the most lovely object of all, Who attracts all to Himself by His unutterable beauty." "Only one object seemed worthy of pursuit, philosophy and the master of philosophy, this divine (θεῖος) man." His love to Origen was like that of Jonathan for David. Gregory praises Origen for his Socratic discipline, and for the way in which his teacher probed his inmost soul with questions, pruned his native wildness and repressed his exuberance. He was taught to interrogate his consciousness, and critically to investigate reasonings and the meanings of words. Origen accustomed his pupils first to the dialectic method of inquiry, and then, in Aristotelian fashion, fed them to contemplate the "magnitude, the wondrousness, the magnificent, and absolutely wise construction of the world." He seems to have followed (strangely enough) the order of the sciences in Comte's classification of the branches of human knowledge. Thus, he began with "the immutable foundation of all, geometry, and then" (says Gregory) "by astronomy he lifted us up to the things highest above us." He reduced things to their "pristine elements," "going over the nature of the whole and of each several section," "he filled our minds with a rational, instead of an irrational, wonder at the sacred oeconomy of the universe and the irreprovable constitution of all things." These words and much more that might be quoted from the Panegyric are a strange comment on the thaumaturgic actions freely attributed to Gregory. Morals followed physics, and emphasis is laid by Gregory on the practical experience by which Origen desired his pupils to verify all theories, "stimulating us by the deeds he did more than by the doctrines he taught." He urged the study of Grecian philosophy for the direct culture of their moral nature. The end of the entire discipline was "nothing but this: By the pure mind make thyself like to God, that thou mayest draw near to Him and abide in Him." Origen advised Gregory to study all the writings of the philosophers and poets of old, except the Atheists, and gave reasons for a catholic and liberal eclecticism, and, with a modern spirit, disclaimed the force of prejudice and the misery of half-truths and of fixed ideas, and the advantage of "selecting all that was useful and true in all the various philosophers, and putting aside all that was false." Gregory says of his master: "That leader of all (ἀρχηγὸς πάντων) who speaks in undertones (ὑπηχῶν) to God's dear prophets and suggests to them all their prophecy and their mystic and divine word, has so honoured this man Origen as a friend as to appoint him to be their interpreter." Evidently to Gregory the gift of interpretation was as much a divine *charisma* as prophecy itself. So great were the joys thus placed within his reach that he adds with rapture, "He was truly a paradise to us, after the similitude of the Paradise of God." He regrets his departure from Caesarea, as Adam might bewail his expulsion from Eden, having to eat of the soil, to contend with thorns and thistles, and dwell in darkness, weeping and mourning. He says, "I go away of my own will, and not by constraint, and by my own act I am dispossessed, when it is in my option to remain."

The influence of Origen's teaching upon Gregory and Athenodorus is confirmed by Eusebius (*H. E.* vi. 30), who adds that "they made such improvement that both, though very young, were honoured with the episcopate in the churches of Pontus."

Gregory of Nyssa describes Gregory of Neocaesarea as spending much time in Alexandria, and says that before his baptism, while resident there, he displayed a high tone of moral propriety. A residence in Alexandria may have occurred in the five years that Gregory and his brother were under the direction of Origen. These years were probably interrupted by the persecution under Maximinus Thrax (reigned July 235 to May 238), which was aimed especially at the leaders of the church. Origen may then have gone into retirement and left his pupils at liberty to travel into Egypt. If Gregory's baptism was deferred until Origen could return to Caesarea, it must have taken place at the close of their intercourse after the death of Maximin and the accession of Gordian in 238. Reckoning backwards the five years, Gregory did not reach Caesarea before 233, and probably later; and did not leave the "Paradise" until 238 at the earliest, when he pronounced his Panegyric. This document is of interest from the testimony it bears to the doctrine of the Trinity and the light it throws upon the faith of Gregory. Bp. Bull has laid great emphasis upon the passage (*Orat. de Origine*, cap. iv.) in which Gregory offers his praise to the Father, and then to "the Champion and Saviour of our souls, His first-born Word, the Creator and Governor of all things, . . . being the truth, the wisdom, the power of the Father Himself of all things, and besides being both in Him and absolutely united to Him (ἀτεχνῶς ἡνώμενος), the most perfect and living and animate word of the primal mind." Bp. Bull rightly calls attention to the prae-Nicene character of these phrases, whioh yet substantially agree with the deliverance of the Nicene Fathers (*Def. Nic. Creed*, vol. i. p. 331). They are of importance in estimating the authenticity and significance of other documents.

Immediately on his return to Neocaesarea Gregory received a letter from Origen (*Philocalia*, c. 13), revealing the teacher's extraordinary regard for his pupil, whom he describes as "my most excellent lord and venerable son." Gregory is exhorted to study all philosophies, as a preparation for Christianity and to aid the interpretation of Holy Scripture. He is thus to spoil the Egyptians of their fine gold, in order to make vessels for the sanctuary, and not idols of his own. He is then urged with some passion to study the Scriptures, and to seek from God by prayer the light he needs (see *Ante-Nic. Library*, Origen's works, vol. i. 388-390, for a translation of this letter). Shortly after his return Gregory became bishop of his native city, and one of the most celebrated (διαβόητος) bishops of the age (Eus. *H. E.* vi. 30, and vii. 14). The curious details of his ordination are referred to in Basil's *Menol. Graec.* (Nov. 17), where it is stated that he was ordained by Phaedimus, bp. of Amasea, when the two were at a distance from each other. Our only guide for the subsequent details of his life is Gregory of Nyssa. Some of that writer's most extraordinary statements are in a measure vouched for by his brother Basil the Great, and by Rufinus in his expansion of the history of Eusebius. As the later father tells the story, the young and saintly student, on reaching home, was entreated by the entire population to remain as their magistrate and legislator. Like Moses, he took counsel of God, and retired into the wilderness, but, unlike Moses, he married no wife, and had virtue only for his spouse. Then we are told that Phaedimus, bp. of Amasea, sought to consecrate him by guile, but failed, and adopted the expedient of electing and ordaining him by prayer when he was distant a journey of three days. We are assured that this induced Gregory to yield to the summons, and to submit afterwards to the customary rites. Gregory only demanded time for meditation on the truths of the Christian faith before accepting the commission. This meditation issued in the supposed divine revelation to him in the dead of the night of one of the most explicit formularies of the creed of the church of the 3rd cent., "after he had been deeply considering the reason of the faith, and sifting disputations of all sorts." Gregory saw a vision of St. John and the mother of the Lord, and the latter commanded the former to lay before Gregory the true faith. Apart from this romance, the formulary attributed to Gregory is undoubtedly of high antiquity, and Lardner (*Credibility*, vol. ii. p. 29) does not argue with his wonted candour in his endeavour to fasten upon it signs of later origin.* It is singularly free from the peculiar phrases which acquired technical significance in the 4th cent., and yet maintains a most uncompromising antagonism to Sabellian and Unitarian heresy. Moreover, Gregory of Nyssa asserts that when he uttered his encomium, the autograph MS. of this creed was in possession of the church at Neocaesarea. He adds that the church had been continually initiated (μυσταγωγεῖται) by means of this confession of Gregory's faith. This statement Basil confirmed (*Ep.* 204, Bas. *Opp.* Paris ed. t. iii. p. 303), saying that in his tender age, when residing in Neocaesarea, he had been taught the words of Gregory by his sainted grandmother Macrina, and (*de Spir. Sancto*, c. 29, *ib.* p. 62) he declared the tenacity with which the ways and words of Gregory had been preserved by that church, even to the mode of reciting the doxology. Moreover, Basil attributed to his influence the orthodoxy of a whole succession of bishops from Gregory to the Musonius of his own day (*Ep.* 204). In addressing the Neocaesareans (*Ep.* 207, *ib.* p. 311), he warns them against twisting the words of Gregory. The formulary must be

* The Creed is as follows in Bull's trans. :—"There is one God, Father of Him Who is the living Word, subsisting Wisdom and Power and Eternal Impress (χαρακτηρος ἀϊδίου), Perfect Begetter of the Perfect, Father of the only-begotten Son. There is one Lord, Alone of the alone, God of God, Impress and Image of the Godhead, the operative Word; Wisdom comprehensive of the system of the universe, and Power productive of the whole creation; true Son of true Father, Invisible of Invisible, and Incorruptible of Incorruptible, and Immortal of Immortal, and Eternal of Eternal. And there is one Holy Ghost, Who hath His being of God, Who hath appeared (that is to mankind, δηλαδὴ τοῖς ἀνθρώποις, a clause which Greg. of Nyssa gives, but which is not found in some of the codices) through the Son, Image of the Son, Perfect of the Perfect; Life, the Cause of all them that live; Holy Fountain, Holiness, the Bestower of sanctification, in Whom is manifested God the Father Who is over all and in all, and God the Son, Who is through all. A perfect Trinity, not divided nor alien in glory and eternity and dominion."

distinguished from the ἔκθεσις τῆς κατὰ μέρος πίστεως, which is now found among the dubious writings of Gregory, and which even Labbe confounded with it. A very important sentence which has been variously attributed to the saint and his biographer follows the formula as given in the Life. Dr. Burton referred it to Gregory of Nyssa. Modern editors call attention to the fact that Gregory of Nazianzus (*Orat.* 10) refers to the closing sentences as the substance of the formula itself. It runs as follows: "There is therefore nothing created or servile in the Trinity; nor anything superinduced, as though previously non-existing and introduced afterwards. Never therefore was the Son wanting to the Father, nor the Spirit to the Son; but there is ever the same Trinity, unchangeable and unalterable" (cf. Migne, *Patr. Gk.* vol. x. p. 988). Great difference of opinion has prevailed as to the genuineness of this document; thus Bingham, Bull, Cave, Tillemont (iv. 327), Ceillier, Hahn (cf. Dorner's *Person of Christ,* A. ii. 482), Mohler (*Athan.* i. 105), have defended it, and Lardner, Whiston, Münscher, Gieseler, Herzog (*Abriss der Kirchengesch.* i. 122), contest it. Neander divided it into two parts, the one genuine revealing its Origenistic source, and the other of later growth. Dr. Caspari has, in an appendix to his great work, *Alte und neue Quellen zur Geschichte des Taufsymbols und der Glaubensregel* (1879), defended it with great erudition, and concludes that there is nothing in the formula incompatible with its being the production of a pupil of Origen. He shews, moreover, that it must have been produced between A.D. 260 and 265.

There can be little doubt that the missionary labour of Gregory was great and successful, and that his personal influence was extraordinary. A few of the marvellous occurrences detailed by Gregory of Nyssa are referred to by Basil and Rufinus. Basil tells us (*de Spir. Sancto, l.c.*) "that Gregory was a great and conspicuous lamp, illuminating the church of God, and that he possessed, from the co-operation of the Spirit, a formidable power against the demons; that he turned the course of rivers by giving them orders in the name of Christ; that he dried up a lake, which was the cause of strife to two brothers; and that his predictions of the future made him the equal of the other prophets; . . . that by friends and enemies of the truth he was regarded, in virtue of his signs and prodigies, as another Moses." But Gregory of Nyssa expands into voluminous legend the record of these deeds. With the exception of a reference to the river Lycus, the Panegyric of Gregory of Nyssa contains no verifying element, giving neither names, dates, nor places for these astounding portents. They were, as Dr. Newman observes, wrought at such times and seasons as to lead to numerous conversions. They were described as well-known facts in a hortatory address and in ecclesiastical style. But they contrast very forcibly with the philosophical bias of Gregory's mind, and they are not referred to until a century after their occurrence.

One of the most interesting facts introduced by his panegyrist refers to Gregory's selection of an obscure person, Alexander the charcoal burner, as bishop over the neighbouring city of Comana. He was preferred to men of eloquence and station by reason of his humble self-consecration to God, and justified the choice by reason of his excellent discourse, holy living, and martyr death.

The great missionary success of Gregory and the rapid growth of the Church must have preceded the persecution under Decius, which began in 250 and 251. The edict was ferocious, and, in the hands of sympathetic governors, cruelly carried out. [DECIUS.] Gregory advised those who could do so to save themselves and their faith by flight and concealment. His enemies pursued him into his retreat, but Gregory of Nyssa says that they found in place of the bishop and his deacon two trees. This "prodigy" differs so profoundly (as do others in the same writer) from the N.T. miracles, both in character and motive, that they form an instructive hint as to the ethnic and imaginative source of the whole cycle.

In 257 Gregory returned to Neocaesarea, and when, in 258, peace was restored to the church, he ordered annual feasts in commemoration of the martyrs. He is credited by his biographer with the doubtful wisdom of hoping to secure the allegiance of those who had been in the habit of worshipping idols, by arranging ceremonials in honour of the martyrs resembling that to which they had been accustomed. This time-serving is an unfavourable indication of character, and does something to explain the melancholy defection from moral uprightness and honour of many of his supposed converts. The conversion of the heathen is said to have been greatly quickened by a fearful plague which was partly, at least, due to Gregory's miraculous powers.

At his death the number of heathen who now remained in his diocese is said to have dwindled to 17, the exact number of Christians found there when Phaedimus consecrated him (*Vit. Thaum. l.c.* p. 954). But the Christianity of the Neocaesareans must have been in many cases of a very imperfect kind, if we may judge from one of the most authentic documents referred to his pen, and entitled *Epistola Canonica S. Gregorii . . . de iis qui in barbarorum incursione idolothyta comederant, et alia quaedam peccata commiserant.* Numerous authorities, Dodwell (*Dissertationes in Cyprianum*), Ceillier (vol. ii. p. 444), question the genuineness of the last, the eleventh, of canons, but the conviction widely prevails that the previous ten are genuine. They refer to the circumstances which followed the ravages of the Goths and Boradi in Pontus, and Asia Minor generally, during the reign of Gallienus. The prevailing disorder tempted numerous Christians in Pontus to flagrant acts of impiety and disloyalty. Some took possession of the goods of those who had been dragged into bondage. Others identified themselves with the barbarians, actually helping the heathen in their uttermost cruelty towards their brethren. These facts are gathered from the "canons" in which Gregory denounced strenuously the commission of such crimes, and assigned to them their ecclesiastical penalty. The bishop does not linger over the mere ceremonial uncleanness that might follow from enforced consumption of meat offered to idols, and exonerates from blame or any ecclesiastical anathema women who had, against their will, lost their chastity; but he lays great emphasis on the vices and greed of those who had violated Christian morality for gain and personal advantage. Different degrees of penalty and exclusion from church privilege were assigned, and those were argued on ground of Scripture alone. The epistle containing these canons was addressed to an anonymous bp. of Pontus, who had asked his advice, *c.* 258, towards the end of his episcopate. It reveals the imperfect character of the wholesale conversions that had followed his remarkable ministry.

Other works have been wrongly attributed to Gregory; *e.g.* ἔκθεσις τῆς κατὰ μέρος πίστεως, which Vossius published in Latin in 1662, among the works of Gregory, and which Cardinal Mai (*Scrip. Vet.* vii. p. 170) has presented in Greek from the *Codex Vaticanus.* It is given by Migne (*l.c.* pp. 1103-1123). The best interpretation of the title is, "A creed not of all the dogmas of the church, but only of some, in opposition to the heretics who deny them" (*Ante-Nicene Library*, vol. xx. p. 81). It differs from the former confession in its obvious and technical repudiation of Arianism, and its distinct references to the later Nestorian, and Eutychian heresies. Other treatises and fragments given in edd. of his works, and also trans. in *A.-N. L.*, are: *Capitula duodecim de Fide*, with interpretation, attributed by Gretser to Gregory (ed. Ratisbon, 1741). *Ad Tatianum Disputatio de Animâ*, which must have been written by a medieval philosopher when the philosophy of Aristotle was beginning to exert a new influence (Ceillier). Four *Homiliae*, preserved by Vossius, on "the Annunciation to the Holy Virgin Mary," and on "Christ's Baptism," are totally unlike the genuine writing of Gregory; they are surcharged with the peculiar reverence paid to the Mother of our Lord after the controversy between Nestorius and Cyril, and they adopt the test-words of orthodoxy current in the Arian disputes. Two brief fragments remain to be added, one a comment on Matt. vi. 22-23, from a Catena, *Cod. MS.* and pub. by Galland, *Vet. Patr. Bibl.* xiv. 119, and a discourse, *in Omnes Sanctos*, preserved with a long *Epistola praevia* by Mingarelli.

Gregory was present at the first council at Antioch (264) to try Paul of Samosata. His brother Athenodorus accompanied him, and they are named among the most eminent members of the council (Eus. *H. E.* vii. 28).

Gregory was buried in the church he had built in Neocaesarea, and commemorated on Nov. 17 (*Cal. Ethiop.*) and Nov. 23 (*Cal. Arm.*).

Editions of his Works.—The most noted have been those of Gerard Vossius, 1640, in 4to, and in 1622, in folio. They had been published in *Bibl. Patr. Cologne* in 1618. The Panegyric on Origen by Sirmond, 1605, 4to. De la Rue included it in his ed. of *Origensis Opera*, vol. iv. The various fragments attributed to Gregory are all pub. by Migne (*Patr. Gk.* vol. x.). See esp. Ryssel, *Gregorius Thaumaturgus* (Leipz. 1880). His *Address to Origen* and Origen's *Letter to Gregory* have been trans. with intro. and notes by W. Metcalfe (S.P.C.K.). There are also translations of his works in the *Ante-Nic. Lib.* vol. vi. [H.R.R.]

Gregorius (7), St., "the Illuminator" (*Gregor Lusavoritch*), "the sun of Armenia," the apostle, first patriarch and patron saint of Armenia, *c.* 302-331. Of his life and times the best if not the only authorities are Agathangelos, who was secretary to Tiridates king of Armenia, the persecutor and afterwards the convert of Gregory, and Simeon Metaphrastes. A French trans. of the former was printed in vol. i. of the *Historiens del' Arménie* (1867), by Victor Langlois. The Life of St. Gregory by Metaphrastes (Migne, *Patr. Gk.* cxv. 941-996) is evidently drawn from Agathangelos. The silence of all Greek writers about Gregory is remarkable. The Rev. S. C. Malan trans. the Life and Times of St. Gregory the Illuminator from the Armenian work of the Vartabed Matthew, which is the main source of the following sketch.

Gregory was born *c.* 257 in Valarshabad, the capital of the province of Ararat in Armenia. His father Anak, or Anag, a Parthian Arsacid, of the province of Balkh, murdered, *c.* 258, Chosroes I. of Armenia. The dying king commanded the whole family of Anak to be slain, but an infant was saved, carried to the Cappadocian Caesarea, there brought up in the Christian faith, and baptized Gregorius.

Tiridates III., son of Chosroes, recovered the kingdom *c.* 284 by the help of Diocletian, whose favour he had gained and whose hatred of Christianity he had imbibed. Gregory became his servant, and was raised to the rank of a noble. In the first year of his reign Tiridates went to the town of Erez (Erzenga) in Higher Armenia, to make offerings to Anahid, the patron-goddess of Armenia; but Gregory, refusing to take any part in this idolatry, endeavoured to turn the king from his idols, and spoke to him of Christ as the judge of quick and dead. Then followed what are known as "the twelve tortures of St. Gregory," borne with unsurpassed fortitude (but see Dowling's *Armenian Church*, S.P.C.K. 1910). After two years Tiridates ordered the saint to be thrown into a muddy pit infested with creeping creatures, into which malefactors were wont to be hurled, in the city of Ardashat, and there he lived for 14 years, being fed by a Christian woman named Anna. This is one of several traces in the story of an already-existing Christianity in Armenia.

The king's barbarous treatment of a community of religious women, who *c.* 300 took refuge within his domains and built a convent outside the city of Valarshabad, brought a plague upon him and his people, which was only relieved when Gregory was fetched from the pit. Gregory instructed the people, and at his order they built three churches where the King's crimes had been perpetrated, and he called the place Etchmiadzin (the descent of the Only-begotten), its Turkish name being Ütch-Kilise (Three Churches). Gregory was consecrated bp. for Armenia *c.* 302, by Leontius, bp. of Caesarea in Cappadocia. His cathedral was in Valarshabad. He destroyed the idol temples, "conquering the devils who inhabited them"—*i.e.* the priests and supporters of the old religion—and baptized the king and his court in the Euphrates. This national conversion occurred before Constantine had established the church in the Roman empire, and Armenia was thus the first kingdom to adopt Christianity as the religion of the state. Gregory encouraged the reading of the Holy Scriptures, both of the O. and N. T. He wrote letters to St. James of Nisibis, requesting him to compose homilies on faith, love, and other virtues. In 325 Gregory is said to have been summoned to the council of Nicaea, but, being himself unable to go, sent his son, who brought back the decrees for the Armenian church. The venerable patriarch greatly rejoiced on reading them, and exclaimed, "Now let us praise Him Who was before the worlds, worshipping the most Holy Trinity and the Godhead of the Father, Son, and Holy Ghost, now and ever, world without end, Amen," which words are said after the Nicene Creed in the Armenian church (Malan. p. 327, n.). After filling the country with churches and ministers, schools and convents, he retired in 331 to lead a solitary life among the caves of Manyea in the province of Taran, having previously consecrated his son Arisdages bishop in his stead. Gregory died in the wilderness A.D. 332, and the shepherds, finding his dead body without knowing whose it was, erected over it a cairn of stones.

The Bollandists have printed Agathangelos and other Lives of Gregory. *ActaSS.* viii. Sept. pp. 295-413; Basil. *Men.* Sept. 30, in Migne, *Patr. Gk.* cxvii.; Le Quien, *Or. Chr.* i. 1355, 1371. In honour of her founder the Armenian church has been called the Armeno-Gregorian. Saint-Martin (*Mém. sur l'Arménie*, i. 436) and Langlois (*Historiens*, ii. 387) date his consecration A.D. 276. [L.D.]

Gregorius (8), *the Cappadocian*, appointed by Arianizing bishops at Antioch in the beginning of 340—not, apparently, of 339, as the *Festal Index* says, and clearly not at the Dedication Festival in 341 as Socrates says (ii. 20)—to supersede Athanasius in the see of Alexandria. As a student in the schools of Alexandria he had received kindness from Athanasius (Greg. Naz. *Orat.* xxi. 15). He arrived on Mar. 23 (cf. *Fest. Ind.*), Athanasius having retired into concealment. That Gregory was an Arian may be inferred from his appointment. Athanasius says, in an encyclical letter of the time, that his sympathy with the heresy was proved by the fact that only its supporters had demanded him, and that he employed as secretary one Ammon, who had been long before excommunicated by bp. Alexander for his impiety (*Encycl.* c. 7). Athanasius tells us that on Good Friday, Gregory having entered a church, the people shewed their abhorrence, whereupon he caused the prefect Philagrius publicly to scourge 34 virgins and married women and men of rank, and to imprison them. After Athanasius fled to Rome, Gregory became still more bitter (Athan. *Hist. Ar.* 13). We hear of him as "oppressing the city" in 341 (*Fest. Ind.*). Auxentius, afterwards Arian bp. of Milan, was ordained priest by him (Hilar. *in Aux.* 8). The council of Sardica, at the end of A.D. 343, pronounced him never to have been, in the church's eyes, a bishop (*Hist. Ar.* 17). He died, not by murder, as Theodoret says (ii. 4) through a confusion with George, but after a long illness (*Fest. Ind.*), about ten months after the exposure of the Arian plot against bp. Euphrates—*i.e. c.* Feb. A.D. 345. This date, gathered from Athanasius (*Hist. Ar.* 21) is preferable to that of the *Index*, Epiphi 2=June 26, 346. [W.B.]

Gregorius (12) **Baeticus**, St., bp. of Eliberi, Elvira, or Granada, *c.* 357-384; first mentioned as resisting the famous Hosius of Cordova, when under the persecution of Constantius Hosius gave way so far as to admit Arian bishops to communion with him. This must have been in or before A.D. 357, the year of Hosius's death. At the council of Ariminum Gregorius was one of the few bishops who adhered to the creed of Nicaea, and refused to hold communion with the Arian Valens, Ursacius, and their followers. Our authority for this is a letter to Gregorius by Eusebius of Vercellae from his exile in the Thebaid (printed among the works of St. Hilary of Poitiers, ii. 700, in Migne, *Patr. Lat.* x. 713). Eusebius there acknowledges letters he had received from Gregorius, giving an account of his conduct, and commends him highly for having acted as became a bishop. Gams, however (*Kirchengesch.* ii. 256-259, 279-282), maintains that Gregorius was one of the bishops who fell into heresy at Ariminum, and further identifies him with the Gregorius in the deputation sent by the council to Constantius and headed by Restitutus of Carthage, who assented to and subscribed an Arian formula of belief at Nice, in Thrace, Oct. 10, 359, and held communion with the Arian leaders, Valens, Ursacius, and others (St. Hilary of Poitiers, *ex Opere Historico Fragmentum* 8, in Migne, *Patr. Lat.* x. 702).

Gregorius is generally supposed to have been one of the leaders of the schism originated by Lucifer of Cagliari. This theory is supported by the terms of praise applied to him by the Luciferians Faustinus and Marcellus in their *Libellus Precum ad Imperatores* (c. 9, 10, 20, 25, 27, in Migne, *Patr. Lat.* xiii. 89, 90, 97, 100, 102); and also by the way St. Jerome, in his *Chronicle* under the date 374=A.D. 370 (in Migne, *Patr. Lat.* xxvii. 695), couples him with Lucifer of Cagliari, saying that the latter with Gregorius a Spanish, and Philo a Libyan, bishop, "nunquam se Arianae miscuit pravitati." Florez, however (*Esp. Sagr.* xii. 121), maintains that no certain proof of this theory exists. Gams, on the other hand (*op. cit.* ii. 310-314), maintains that even before the death of Lucifer, Gregorius was the recognized head of the sect. On the authority of the *Libellus Precum*, c. 25, he considers that Gregorius, after Lucifer's return from exile in 362, visited him in Sardinia; and he identifies with Gregorius the bishop mentioned in c. 63 as at Rome under the assumed name of Taorgius, and as having consecrated one Ephesius as bp. of the Luciferians there, an event which he dates between 366 and 371. From the *Libellus Precum* and the Rescript of Theodosius in reply addressed to Cynegius, Gregorius was apparently alive in 384. In none of the above passages is his see mentioned, as he is called only episcopus Hispaniarum or Hispaniensis, but it is supplied by St. Jerome, *de Vir. Illust.* c. 105 (Hieron. *Op.* ii. 937, in Migne, *Patr. Lat.* xxiii. 703). Opinions have been much divided as to the book *de Fide*, attributed to him by Jerome. The Bollandists (*Acta SS.* Ap. iii. 270) say "etiamnum latet." It was formerly supposed to be the *de Trinitate* now ascribed to Faustinus. Gams (p. 314) thinks that this, though really written by Faustinus, is the work to which St. Jerome alludes.

The materials for a Life of Gregorius are thus scanty, the *Libellus Precum* being of very doubtful authority, and widely different estimates have been formed of him. But the two charges of Arianism and Luciferianism seem mutually destructive. [F.D.]

Gregorius (13) **I.,** bp. of Nazianzus in Cappadocia, father of Gregorius Nazianzenus. [GREGORIUS (14).] Originally a member of the Hypsistarii, a sect numerous in Cappadocia, he was converted to the Catholic faith, married a lady named Nonna, and was soon afterwards consecrated bp. of Nazianzus, *c.* 329. He was a pillar of the orthodox party, though weak enough to sign the creed of Ariminum in deference to Constantius, A.D. 360. He took part in the ordination of Basil to the see of Caesarea [BASILIUS]; he opposed the attempts of the emperor Valens, A.D. 371, to overthrow the Catholic faith; yet he, as well as Basil, was spared the banishment inflicted on many bishops (Socr. iv. 11). After an episcopate of 45 years, he died A.D. 374. His son frequently mentions his good father, both in his sermons and his verses, and pronounced a funeral oration over him. Greg. Naz. *Oratio* xviii. in Migne, *Patr. Gk.* xxxv. 330; Le Quien, *Oriens Christ.* i. 411. [L.D.]

Gregorius (14) **Nazianzenus,** bp. (370-390) of Sasima and of Constantinople, has been fortunate in his biographers. He left them abundant materials in his works, especially in a large collection of letters and a long autobiographical poem.

St. Gregory takes his distinctive title from Nazianzus, a small town in S.W. Cappadocia, near which, in a district known as the Tiberine (*Ep.* ii. *Op.* ii. 2; Basil, *Ep.* iv.), at a village called Arianzus, where his father had an estate, he was born. Both his parents are known to us. His father bore the same name [GREGORIUS (13)] and belonged in early life to the sect of the HYPSISTARII (*Orat.* xviii. 5; *Op.* i. 333). His mother's name was Nonna, a child of Christian parents (Philtatius and Gorgonia), and is praised by her son as a model of Christian virtues. To her life and prayers he attributes his father's conversion.

The date of his birth we may reasonably fix from his own words in 325-329.

Nonna, in fulfilment of a vow, dedicated him to the Lord, but not by baptism. She taught him to read the Scriptures, and led him to regard himself as an Isaac offered in sacrifice to God, Who had given him to another Abraham and Sarah. He, as another Isaac, dedicated himself. He rejoices to tell of the examples set him at home and of the bent given to his studies by companionship with good men. The tutor to whose care the brothers were committed was Carterius, perhaps the same who was afterwards head of the monasteries of Antioch and instructor of Chrysostom (Tillem. *Mémoires*, ix. 370).

At Caesarea in Cappadocia probably was commenced Gregory's friendship with Basil, which, tried by many a shock, survived them all, and was the chief influence which moulded not only the life of both friends, but also the theology of the Christian church. Gregory and his brother went to Caesarea in Palestine to pursue the study of oratory (*Orat.* vii. 6, *Op.* ii. 201); Caesarius departing thence to Alexandria, and Gregory remaining to study in the school made famous by Origen, Pamphilus, and Eusebius. Thespesius was then the master of greatest renown, and Euzoïus was a fellow-pupil with Gregory (Hieron. *de Eccles. Script.* c. 113). From Palestine Gregory went to Alexandria (*Orat. l.c.*). Here Didymus filled the chair of Pantaenus, Clement, and Origen, and Athanasius the episcopal throne, though probably an exile at the time. Gregory pressed on to Athens. A ship of Aegina offered him passage (*Orat.* xviii. 31, *Op.* i. 351). Off Cyprus a fierce storm struck her. The thunder, lightning, darkness, creaking of the yards, shaking of the masts, cries of the crew, appeals for help to Christ, even by those who before had not known Him, all added to the terror of the scene. The storm continued 22 days, during which they saw no chance of deliverance. Gregory's chief fear was lest he should die without baptism. In prayer he dedicated himself again to God, and sought for help. The prayer was answered, and the rescued crew were so affected that they all accepted Gregory's God.

Among the Athenian sophists of the day, none were more famous than Himerius and Proaeresius, with whom Gregory continued the study of oratory. At Athens Gregory and Basil were together again (*Orat.* xliii. 15; *Op.* i. 781); Gregory rendering the freshman Basil various friendly offices, such as exempting him from the rough practical joking which all who joined the Athenian classes had to pass through. [BASILIUS.] The Armenians, jealous of the newcomer, whose fame had preceded him, and with some of the old feeling of antagonism against Cappadocia, tried to entrap him in sophistical debates. When they were being defeated, Gregory, feeling the honour of Athens at stake, came to the rescue, but soon saw their real object, and left them to join his friend (*Orat.* xliii. 16, 17; *ib.* 782, 783). These things are trifles, but had important effects. The two friends, rendered obnoxious to their companions, were bound the more closely to each other. Their fellow-students, for various reasons, bore various names and surnames. The two friends were, and desired to be called, Christians; they had all things in common, and "became as one mind possessing two bodies" (*Orat.* xliii. 20, 21; *ib.* 785, 786; *Carm.* xi. 221-235; *Op.* ii. 687). Among other students then at the university was Julian the Apostate. Gregory claims that he had even then discerned his character in his very looks; and that he used to warn their fellow-students that Rome was cherishing a serpent (*Orat.* v. 24, *Op.* i. 162).

Gregory must have spent at Athens probably not less than ten years. He went there a beardless youth; he left about his 30th year. To the effect of those years the matter and form alike of his work bear witness.

Leaving probably about the beginning of 356, Gregory went first to Constantinople, wishing to see the new Rome before his return to Asia. Here he unexpectedly met his brother Caesarius, journeying to Nazianzus from Alexandria. The mother had longed to see both her sons return together, and

Gregory has left a touching account of their meeting; and at this point some of the biographers fix his baptism. Gregory himself tells us that he now laid down the plan of his life. Every power he possessed was to be devoted to God; but the way seemed divided into two, and he knew not which to take. Elias, the sons of Jonadab, the Baptist, were types of the life that attracted him; but on the other hand was the study of the Scriptures, for which the desert offered no opportunities; and the advanced age of his parents presented claims which seemed to be imperative duties. He resolved to live the strict life of an ascetic and yet perform the duties of society (*Carm.* i. *de Rebus suis*, l. 65 seq.; *Op.* ii. 635), but denying himself even the pleasure of music (*ib.* l. 69).

But in the midst of various trifling irritations of domestic duty, which went far to mar the life he had marked out for himself, Gregory heard from Basil, who had resolved to found a coenobitic system in Pontus, and asked his friend to join him. Gregory answered by proposing to Basil to join them at the Tiberine, where the ascetic life in common could be followed and the duties of home performed (*Ep.* i. *Op.* ii. 1). Basil did visit Arianzus, but remained only a short time. From Caesarea he again wrote to Gregory, after which Gregory set out for Pontus. One substantial result of their joint labours is preserved in the *Philocalia*, a series of extracts from the exegetical works of Origen. Gregory himself speaks of this work, which he sent as a present to his friend Theodosius of Tyana (*Ep.* cxv. *Op.* ii. 103). We know from Gregory's own words also that he took part in composing the famous "Rules" of Basil. It is not clear how long he remained in Pontus. Clemencet thinks two or three years, and the supposition agrees with Gregory's regret that he had but tasted enough of the life there to excite his longing for more (*Orat.* ii. 6, *Op.* i. 14). The silence of Gregory with regard to his return may be due to another cause. Constantius had required the bishops throughout the empire to accept the creed of Rimini (A.D. 359-360), and the bp. of Nazianzus, though hitherto faithful to the Nicene doctrine, did so. The monks of his diocese were devoted to Athanasius, and there followed a division in the church, which Gregory alone could heal. He induced the bishop to make a public confession of orthodoxy, and delivered a sermon on the occasion (*Orat.* vi. *Op.* i. 179 seq.). If this division at Nazianzus occurred in 360, we have the reason of Gregory's return (Tillem. *Mém.* ix. 345; Schröckh, *Kirchengesch.* xiii. 287; Ullmann, *Gregorius von Nazianz.* s. 41). If with Clemencet and others (*Op.* i. pp. xciv. seq.) it is assigned to 363-364, we must suppose that the return was due to the general claim of filial duty. In any case he came to Nazianzus, and received letters from Basil asking him to return to Pontus (*Ep.* vi. *ad fin.*, *Op.* ii. p. 6). The aged bishop felt the need of support and help, and resolved to overrule the scruples which made Gregory shrink from the responsibilities of the priesthood. The ordination occurred on one of the high festivals, probably at Christmas, A.D. 361 (Nicetas, ii. 1021; Tillem. *Mém.* ix. 352). Nicetas assumes that the congregation compelled Gregory to accept ordination (cf. *Carm.* xi. *de Vitâ suâ*, 345-348, *Op.* ii.) Such forced ordinations were not unknown (Bingham, *Orig. Eccles.* iv. 2-5 and ix. 7, 1). Basil was in the same way made priest.

Gregory preached in the church at Nazianzus on the Easter Day following his ordination, and had expected that a crowded church would have welcomed his return and have applauded his first sermon; but the church was almost deserted. Gregory could not be ignorant of the cause of this estrangement. His flight from the work of the priesthood demanded an explanation, and Gregory determined to give an answer worthy of the question and of himself. It is contained in the second oration (*Op.* i. ii. 65). In no part of his writings do we find proof of greater study. It is practically a treatise on the pastoral office, and forms the foundation of Chrysostom's *de Sacerdotio* and of the *Cura Pastoralis* of Gregory the Great, while writers in all ages have directly or indirectly drawn largely from it. The earlier part treats of the reasons for his flight: (1) he was wholly unprepared for the ordination; (2) he had always been attracted by the monastic life; (3) he was ashamed of the life and character of the mass of the clergy; (4) he did not at that time, he did not now—and this reason weighed with him most of all—think himself fit to rule the flock of Christ and govern the minds of men" (*Orat.* ii. 9). He then discusses for 40 sections the duties and difficulties of the true pastor (*ib.* 10-49). "His first duty is to preach the word, and this is so difficult that to fulfil it ideally would require universal knowledge. Theological knowledge is absolutely necessary, especially of the doctrine of the Trinity, lest he fall into the Atheism of Sabellius, or the Judaism of Arius, or the Polytheism too common among the orthodox. It is necessary to hold to the truth that there is one God, and to confess that there are three persons, and attributes proper to each; but for this there is need of the Spirit's help. Much more is it difficult to expound it to a popular audience, both from the preacher's imperfection and the people's want of preparation. Zeal not according to knowledge leads men away from the truth. Then, there is the desire of vainglory, with inexperience, and her constant attendant, rashness, inconstancy, based on ignorance of the Scripture; and a subjective eclecticism which ends in an uncertain creed, and leads men to doubt of truth, as if a blind or deaf man were to place the evil not in himself but in the light of the sun or the voice of his friend. It is more easy to instruct minds wholly ignorant than those which have received false teaching; but the work of weeding, as well as that of sowing, must be done. The work of a spiritual ruler is like that of a man trying to manage a herd of beasts, old and young, wild and tame. He must, therefore, be single in will to rule the whole body, manifold to govern each member of it. Some must be fed with milk; some with more solid food. For all this who is sufficient? There are spiritual hucksters who adulterate the word of truth; but it is better to be led than to lead others, and to learn than attempt to teach what one does not know. Men are foolish if they do not know their own ignorance; rash, if they know it, and yet lightly undertake this work. The Jews did not allow young men to read all parts of the Scriptures; but in the church there is no such bound placed between teaching and learning. A mere boy, who does not know the very names of the sacred writings, if he can babble a few pious words, and these caught by hearing, not by reading, becomes a teacher. Men spend more time and pains in learning to dance or play the flute than teachers of things divine and human spend in studying them. The love of vainglory is at the root of this evil. The true ideal is to be found in the lives of disciples like Peter or Paul, who became all things to all men that they might gain some. The false teachers incur great danger, and the pastor's sin causes the public woe. The prophets dwelt on the fearful position of the shepherds who feed themselves; the apostles and Christ Himself taught what the true shepherds should be; and His condemnation of Scribes and Pharisees includes all false teachers." Day and night did these thoughts possess Gregory. He was aware of the objections of priests that the candle should be placed on the candlestick, and the talent not hidden; but no time of preparation for the priesthood can be too long, and haste is full of danger. He dreaded both its duties and its dignity. "He who has not learned to speak the hidden wisdom of God, and to bear the cross of Christ, should not enter upon the priesthood. For himself, he would prefer a private life. A great man ought to undertake great things; a small man small things. Only that man can build the tower who has wherewith to build it." Such are the reasons Gregory gives for his flight. He adds those which led to his return. "(1) The longing he had for them and which he saw they had for him; (2) the white hairs and feeble limbs of his holy parents—the father who was to him as an angel, and the mother to whom he owed also his spiritual birth. There is a time for yielding as for everything else; (3) the example of the prophet Jonah—and this weighed most with him, for every letter of Scripture is inspired for our use—who deserved pardon, but he himself would not if he still refused. The denunciations of disobedience in Holy Scripture are no less severe than those against the unworthy pastor. On either side is danger. The middle is the only safe course—not to seek the priesthood, nor yet to refuse it. There is a merit in obedience; but for disobedience there is hardly any remedy. Some holy men are more, others less, forward to undertake rule. Neither are to be blamed."

Such is the general character of the famous Τοῦ Αὐτοῦ Ἀπολογητικός. Did it alone remain to us, Gregory must still have been thought of as one of the four pillars of the Greek church, and we should still read the chief traits of his personal character. It was written in 362. Julian the Apostate had entered Constantinople on Dec. 11, 361, and persuaded Gregory's brother Caesarius to remain at court. Gregory was then with Basil, who had indignantly rejected like advances, and he blushes that the son of a bishop should accept them. It made their father weary of life, and had to be hidden from their mother (*Ep.* vii. *Op.* ii. 7). The effect of this letter upon Caesarius we may judge from his declaration before Julian: "In a word, I am a Christian, and I mean to be one," and from the exclamation of the emperor: "O happy father of such unhappy children!" (*Orat.* vii. 13, *Op.* i. 206; cf. De Broglie, *Constance,* ii. 207). Gregory esteemed the victory of Caesarius as a more precious gift than the half of the empire (*Orat.* vii. 14, *ad init.*). But Julian had bitter revenge in store. He ordered that no Christian should teach profane literature. This caused Gregory to compose many of the poems now extant, probably as reading-books for Christian schools. Towards the end of 363 or the beginning of 364 he wrote two Invectives against Julian (*Orat.* iv. *Op.* i. 78-147; *Orat.* v. *ib.* 147-175). The emperor had fallen, pierced by an arrow, in the previous June. The orator in these philippics held him up as the sum of all that was vile. In the first sentence he is called "the dragon, the apostate, the Assyrian, the common enemy, the great mind" (Is. x. 12, LXX); and this sentence is typical. These orations, looked at dispassionately, remind us rather of Demosthenes or Cicero than of a Christian bishop. The admirers of the saint find it still more difficult to explain the panegyric on the Arian Constantius, which these discourses contain. He is "the most divine and Christ-loving of emperors, and his great soul is summoned from heaven. The sin of his life was the inhuman humanity which spared Julian" (*Orat.* iv. 34 seq., *Op.* i. 93 seq.). Gregory, indeed, speaks elsewhere of three things of which Constantius repented when dying: (1) the murder of his relations; (2) that he had named Julian Caesar; (3) that he had given himself to the dogma of the newer creed (*Orat.* xxi. 26, *Op.* i. 403 A). Yet he knew that the emperor gave his support to impiety, and framed laws against the orthodox doctrine (*Orat.* xxv. 9, *Op.* i. 461 A); nor could he have been ignorant that it was by Euzoïus that baptism was administered to the penitent. The character of Constantius is clearly used as an oratorical contrast to that of Julian.

While Gregory was thus employed at Nazianzus, Basil returned from Pontus to Caesarea, where Eusebius had been made bishop, and was ordained against his will. He informed his friend of this, and Gregory replied in a letter which is important as shewing his thoughts about the position in which both he and Basil had been placed. "Now the thing is done it is necessary to fulfil one's duty—such at least is the way in which I look at it—especially in the present distress, when many tongues of heretics are raised against us, and not to disappoint the hopes of those who have put their faith in us and in our past life" (*Ep.* viii. *Op.* ii. 8). A difference arose ere long between Eusebius and Basil. Its origin is not known, and Gregory thought it better that it should not be (*Orat.* xliii. 28, *Op.* i. 792). It shews Gregory in the character of peacemaker. The warm friend of Basil, he was no less an admirer of the bishop, and an advocate for the rights of authority. Invited by the bishop to fill the place vacated by Basil's retirement to Pontus, he does not hesitate to assert that the treatment of Basil was unjust and to demand reconciliation with his friend as the price of his own influence (*Epp.* xvi.-xx. *Op.* ii. 16). An indignant reply from Eusebius only called forth stronger letters from the same standpoint (*Epp.* xvii. and xviii. *Op.* ii. 17, 18), and an equally plain letter to Basil, telling him that Eusebius was disposed to be reconciled to him, and urging him to be first in the victory of submission (*Ep.* xix. *ib.*). Hereupon Basil returned to Caesarea, and gave his powerful aid to the bishop in the dangers threatening the church, or rather became bishop in reality, while Eusebius was still so in name—" the keeper of the lion, the leader of the leader" (*Orat.* xliii. 33, *Op.* i. 796). When peace was thus established, Gregory returned again to Nazianzus. Here new troubles awaited him. Caesarius had been chosen by Valens to be treasurer of Bithynia, and once more his brother was distressed at seeing him among the servants of an adversary of the true faith. On Oct. 11, 368, Nicaea was almost destroyed by an earthquake. Gregory made this the ground of an earnest appeal to Caesarius to abandon his office (*Ep.* xx. *Op.* ii. p. 19). He was on the point of yielding when he suddenly died. The funeral oration delivered by Gregory is placed by Jerome first in the list of the orator's celebrated works (*Catal. Scrip. Eccles.* 117). It narrates, in the language of fraternal love, the deeds of a noble life, and seeks in that of Christian submission to console his parents and his friends (*Orat.* vii. *Op.* 198, et seq.). Sixteen epitaphs remain to shew how often Gregory mourned his loss (*Ep.* vi.-xxi. *Op.* ii. 1111-1115). The death of Caesarius brought trouble to Gregory from the administration of his estate which had been left to the poor. Against extortioners who tried to seize it he appealed to his friend Sophronius, prefect of Constantinople (*Ep.* xxix. *Op.* ii. 24) ; and his troubles called forth the kind offices of Basil. He himself tells us plaintively how he would gladly have fled these business worries, but felt it his duty to share the burden with his father (*Carm.* xi. 375-380, *Op.* ii. 695). About the same time another loss befell the house of Nazianzus in the death of Gorgonia, and once again Gregory delivered a funeral discourse of most touching gracefulness (*Orat.* viii. *Op.* i. 218 et seq.). These sorrows weighed heavily on Gregory's spirit ; and while in public discourses he sought to console others, his private poems shew how hard he found it to console himself. " Already his whitening hairs shew his grief, and his stiffening limbs are inclining to the evening of a sad day" (*Carm. de Rebus suis*, i. 177-306, *Op.* ii. 641 sqq.). In 370 Eusebius died in the arms of Basil, who at once invited Gregory to Caesarea on the plea that he was himself *in extremis*. The latter regarded this as a pretext, and in a tone of mingled affection and reproach declined to go until after the election of the archbishop (*Ep.* xl. *Op.* ii. 34). The invitation to the bp. of Nazianzus to be present at the election was answered, as all the editors with almost certainty judge, by the hands of the son. He dwells upon the importance of the position and the special qualifications for it possessed by Basil, and promises his assistance if they propose to elect him (*Ep.* xli. *Op.* ii. 35). He wrote also to Eusebius of Samosata by the hands of the deacon Eustathius, urging him to go to Caesarea and promote Basil's election (*Ep.* xlii. *Op.* ii. 37). Eusebius yielded to this request, but the vote of the aged bp. of Nazianzus was also needed. An illness he had disappeared as soon as he started. The son thought it prudent to remain at home, but sent by his father's hands a letter to Eusebius, expressing his esteem and excusing his absence, and referring to the miracle of his father's restored health (*Ep.* xliv. *Op.* ii. 39). He did not go even after the election, but contented himself at first with writing letters which witness to his wisdom and affection (*Epp.* xlv. and xlvi. *Op.* ii. 40, 41). When the storm had subsided he went in person, but declined the position of first among the presbyters, or probably that of coadjutor bishop (τήνδε τῆς καθέδρας τιμήν, *Orat.* xliii. 39, *Op.* i. 801), which Basil offered him. But in the opposition caused by the bishops defeated in the election, and in the persecution organized by the prefect Modestius at the command of Valens, Gregory was foremost as a personal friend and as a defender of the faith (Socr. iv. 11).

In 370 Valens made a civil division of Cappadocia into two provinces, and in 372 Anthimus, bp. of Tyana, claimed equal rights with the bp. of Caesarea—*i.e.* the rights of metropolitan of Cappadocia Secunda, of which Tyana was the capital. Basil resisted this claim, and Gregory, who had returned to Nazianzus, offered, in a letter full of affectionate admiration (*Ep.* xlviii. *Op.* ii. 40), to visit and support his friend and went to Caesarea. Thence they proceeded together to the foot of Mount Taurus in Cappadocia Secunda, where was a chapel dedicated to St. Orestes, and where the people were accustomed to pay their tithes in kind. On their return they found the mountain-passes at Sasima guarded by followers of Anthimus. A struggle took place, and Gregory implies that he was personally injured (*Carm.* xi. 453, *Op.* ii. 699). He seems soon afterwards to have returned to Nazianzus, whither he was followed by Basil, who had resolved (by way of securing his own rights) to make Sasima a bishopric, and Gregory the first bishop. In this he was aided by the elder Gregory, and the son yielded against his own will (*Orat.* ix. *Op.* i. 234-238). At the last moment he fled, but was pursued by Basil, and at length consecrated (*Orat.* x. *Op.* i. 239-241). But he still put off the duties of his see, until Basil sent Gregory of Nyssa to remonstrate. But Anthimus was again prepared to resist by armed force, and Gregory finally abandoned duties which he had never willingly accepted. Basil wrote reproaching him, and he replied in the same tone. " He would not fight with the warlike Anthimus, for he was himself little experienced in war, and liable to be wounded, and one, moreover, who preferred repose. Why should he fight for sucking-pigs and chickens, which after all were not his own, as if it were a question of souls and of canons ? And why should he rob the metropolis of the illustrious Sasima?" (*Ep.* xlviii. *Op.* ii. 44). The "illustrious Sasima" must be described in the words of the poem, *de Vitâ suâ*: "On a much frequented road of Cappadocia, at a point where it is divided into three, is a halting-place, where is neither water nor grass, nor any mark of civilization. It is a frightful and detestable little village. Everywhere you meet nothing but dust, noises, waggons, howls, groans, petty officials, instruments of torture, chains. The whole population consists of foreigners and travellers. Such was my church of Sasima" (*Carm.* xi. 439-446, *Op.* ii. 696). Other letters were exchanged, but nothing could change his determination. He was at length prevailed upon by his father to leave the mountains, whither he had fled for refuge, and to become coadjutor at Nazianzus. This did not deliver him from the quarrel between Basil and Anthimus, for Nazianzus was in the new province of Cappadocia Secunda, and the bp. of Tyana soon visited the Gregories and sought to gain them to his cause. They held firm to Basil, but Anthimus then asked the son to interfere between Basil and himself, and to seek a conference. The option of having one at all, its time and place if resolved upon, all was left to Basil's will, and yet he felt injured and expressed his dissatisfaction at Gregory's conduct. The latter felt and said, in plain terms, "that his friend was puffed up by his new dignity, and unmindful of what was due to others. He had himself offended Anthimus by his firm Basilism (βασιλισμόν). Was it just that Basil should be offended for the same reason?" (*Ep.* l. *Op.* ii. 44). He soon gave further proof of affection by taking an active part in the election of Eulalius as bp. of Doaris, and by a remonstrance on the subject of Basil's teaching, which he felt was due from his friendship. He had heard men cavil at Basil's orthodoxy, and assert that he did not hold the Divinity of the Third Person in the Trinity; and humbly asked him, for the sake of silencing his detractors—he himself had no doubt—to express in definite words what he held as the true doctrine (*Ep.* lviii. *Op.* ii. 50). Basil did not accept the friendly letter in the same spirit. Gregory saw from his reply that it had given pain, in spite of his care. Yet he submits, and will place himself entirely in Basil's hands (*Ep.* lix. *Op.* ii. 53).

The year 373 was an "annus mirabilis" for Nazianzus, and called forth two remarkable discourses from Gregory. An epidemic among their cattle, a season of drought, and a destructive tempest in harvest reduced the people to absolute poverty. They turned in their need to the church, and compelled Gregory to address them. The discourse seems to have been impromptu. Gregory "regrets that he is the constrained speaker rather than his father—that the stream is made to flow while the fountain is dry—and then urges that divine punishments are all in mercy, and that human sins are the ordinary causes of public woes"; then plainly puts before his hearers the special sins of their city and invites them to penitence and change of life (*Orat.* xvi. *Op.* i. 299). The inability of the inhabitants to pay the imperial taxes led to an insurrection. At the approach of the prefect with a body of troops they took refuge in the church, and he consented to hear Gregory's plea. While the Invective against Julian reminds us of the Philippics or the *de Coronâ*, we have here an oration which has borne without injury comparison with the *pro Ligario* or *pro Marcello*, or Chrysostom's plea for Eutropius or Flavian (Benoît, p. 355). The first part points the afflicted people to the true source of comfort; the second is addressed to princes and magistrates. "The prefect was subject to the authority of the teacher, which was higher than his own. Did he wield the sword? it was for Christ. Was he God's image? so were the poor suffering people. The most divine thing was to do good; let him not lose the opportunity. Did he see the white hair of the aged bishop, and think of his long, unblemished priesthood, whom, it may be, the very angels found worthy of homage (λατρείας), and did not that move him?" "I adjure you by the name of Christ, by Christ's emptying Himself for us, by the sufferings of Him Who cannot suffer, by His cross, by the nails which have delivered me from sin, by His death and burial, resurrection and ascension; and lastly, by this common table where we sit together, and by these symbols of my salvation, which I consecrate with the same mouth that addresses to you this prayer—in the name, I say, of this sacred mystery which lifts us up to heaven!" He concluded by praying "that the prefect may find for himself such a judge as he should be for them, and that all meet with merciful judgment here and hereafter" (*Orat.* xvii. *Op.* i. 317 et seq.) Early in 374 the elder Gregory died, and the son delivered a discourse, at which his mother Nonna and his friend Basil were present, and which was an eulogy of both his parents and of his friend (*Orat.* xviii. *Op.* i. 327). Nonna survived her husband only a few months, and died as she knelt at the Holy Table (*Epit.* lxv.-c. *Op.* ii. 1133-1149). The brother and sister were already dead. Gregory was left alone. His first care was to devote his large fortune wholly to the poor, reserving only a small plot of land at Arianzus; and then to invite the bishops to elect a successor to the see. Fear lest the church should be rent by heresy induced him to exercise the office temporarily. Two reasons determined him not to preach at Nazianzus again—(1) that he may cause them to elect a bishop to succeed his father; (2) that his silence may check the mania for theological discussion which was spreading through the Eastern church and leading everybody to teach the things of the Spirit without the Spirit.

For two years after the bishop's death Gregory in vain pressed for the election of a successor. His love of retirement was now, as all through life, a powerful influence, and towards the end of 375 he disappeared suddenly, and found refuge for 3 years at Seleucia in Isauria, at a monastery devoted to the virgin Thecla (*Carm.* xi. 549, *Op.* ii. 701).

In the beginning of 379 Basil died, and Gregory wrote to comfort his brother Gregory of Nyssa. He could neither visit Basil in illness nor be present at his funeral, for he was himself then dangerously ill (*Ep.* lxxvi. *Op.* ii. 65), but he expressed his love in 12 epitaphs. A letter from Gregory to Eudocius the rhetorician, written soon after, speaks of the loss which made him regard death as "the only deliverance from the ills which weighed upon him" (*Ep.* lxxx. *Op.* ii. 72).

But the chief work of his life yet lay before him. At the Nicaean council, Alexander, then bp. of Constantinople, signed the decrees which condemned Arius. He was succeeded by Paul, who was devoted to the true faith, and suffered martyrdom in A.D. 351. For 30 years after the death of Paul, Constantinople was the battle-ground of a constant war with heresy. The followers of Manes and Novatus, Photinus and Marcellus, Sabellius and Apollinaris, were numerous there; and the adherents of the Nicene faith, few in number, humiliated, crushed, having neither church nor pastor, were obliged to conceal themselves in remote quarters of the city (Benoît, *Grég. de Naz.* p. 397). They applied to Gregory to help them, and many bishops urged their plea. For a long time he was unwilling to leave his retirement, but then came the conviction that he dared not refuse this summons. The date of his arrival at Constantinople is not certain, but was probably before Easter, 379 (Tillem. *Mém.* ix. 799). A prayer, in the form of a poem, indicates the spirit with which he entered upon his new work (*Carm.* iii. *Op.* ii. 667), and another poem shews what that work involved. New Rome "had passed through the death of infidelity; there was left but one last breath of life. He had come to this city to defend the faith. What they needed was solid teaching to deliver them from the spider-webs of subtleties in which they had been taken" (*Carm.* xi. 562-611, *Op.* ii. 705, 6). In a private house, where he himself was lodged by relations, his work was begun. It was to him "an Anastasia, the scene of the resurrection of the faith" (*Orat.* xlii. 26, *Carm.* xi. 1079, *Op.* ii. 731); the house was too small for the multitudes that flocked to it, and a church was built in its place. His fame, as a theologian, rests chiefly on the discourses delivered at the Anastasia. His first work was to gather the scattered members of the flock and instruct them in the practical duties of Christianity and the danger of empty theological discussions (*Carm.* xi. 1210-1231, *Op.* ii. 737-739). Again and again in the early discourses does he dwell on the truth that only through personal holiness can a man grasp any idea of the Holy One (*Orat.* xx. and *Orat.* xxii. *Op.* i. 376-384 and 597-603). Gregory was exposed to the attacks of all parties. His origin, person, clothing, were made objects of ridicule. They would have welcomed a polished orator with external graces; but his manner of life had made him prematurely old, and his gifts to the poor had made him in appearance and reality a poor man. One night, a mob, led by monks, broke into the place of meeting and profaned the altar and sacred elements. Gregory escaped, but was taken before the judges as a homicide; "but He Who knew how to save from the lions was present to deliver him" (*Carm.* xi. 665-678, *Op.* ii. 709). "He cared not that they attacked him—the stones were his delight; he cared only for the flock who were thus injured" (*ib.* 725 et seq.). His chief sorrow was to come from a division in the flock itself. This started from the schism of Antioch, which had spread through the whole church; but the immediate question was one of competition for the bishopric. Gregory had kept aloof from this quarrel, but some of his followers took an active part in it, and endeavoured to draw from him a decision for one or other of the rivals. Some seem to have favoured Paulinus, some Meletius. Gregory preached a sermon on Peace (*Orat.* xxii. *Op.* i. 414-425), dwelling "on its blessings, and the inconsistency of their faith, servants of the God of peace as they claimed to be, and their practice. Their duty was to remain united when the faith was not in question; to weaken the present struggle by keeping out of it, and thus to do the rivals a greater service than by fighting for them" (*ib.* 14, p. 423). Soon afterwards the news of the establishment of peace reached Constantinople, and was followed by peace in the little church of the Anastasia. Gregory, though ill, preached almost certainly on this occasion another sermon on Peace (*Orat.* xxiii. *Op.* i. 425-434), thankfully celebrating its return, and urging those present who were divided from them by heresy "to be at peace with them by acceptance of the true faith. It was the work of the sacred Trinity to give the faithful peace among themselves. The sacred Trinity would heal also this wider breach." At the close of this sermon he promises to deal more fully with the questions at issue between the followers of the Nicene faith and their opponents. This he did in the five theological discourses which soon followed (*Orat.* xxvii.-xxxi. *Op.* i. 487-577; *vide infra*). Other important discourses belong to the same period, of which the most remarkable are a second on the Divinity of the Holy Spirit, preached at Whitsuntide 381 (?) (*Orat.* xli. *Op.* ii. 731-744), and one on Moderation in Discussions—a frequent subject with Gregory—in which heresy is traced to its absence (*Orat.* xxxii. *Op.* ii. 579-601). He delivered also three (?) panegyrics, the subjects of which were Cyprian, whose name was held in deserved honour in Constantinople (*Orat.* xxiv. *Op.* i. 437-450); Athanasius, whose memory was specially dear to Gregory as the champion of Nicene orthodoxy, and who had died but a few years before (A.D. 373) (*Orat.* xxi. *Op.* i. 386-411); and the Maccabees (?), whose heroism might well have been specially intended for an example in the present struggle (*Orat.* xv. *Op.* i. 287-298). The last two, especially that on Athanasius, are counted by all judges, from Jerome downwards, among Gregory's noblest works (*Script. Eccles.* 117).

Jerome became about this time a disciple of Gregory and loved to tell how much he had learned from his teacher.

Another stranger who came to Constantinople professed himself a disciple of the now famous theologian. He bore the name of Maximus, and represented himself as descended from a line of martyrs, and as having suffered much through his adherence to the Nicene faith. Professing himself an ardent admirer of Gregory's sermons, this man was planning the overthrow of his teacher, and hoped even to establish himself in the episcopal chair. He had an important ally in

Peter, bp. of Alexandria, who had recognized Gregory as practically bp. of the orthodox in Constantinople (*Carm.* xi. 858-931), but now joined in the plot against him. Gregory was ill in bed, when one night Maximus with his followers went to the church to be consecrated by 5 suffragans sent from Alexandria for the purpose. While they were preparing for the ceremony, day began to dawn, and a mob, excited by the sudden news, rushed in, drove them from the church, and compelled Maximus to flee from Constantinople. Retiring to Alexandria, he demanded that Peter should find him another bishopric or relinquish his own. He was silenced by the prefect and banished.

In connexion with the story of Maximus, Gregory tells us that he one day uttered the words, "My beloved children, keep intact this Trinity which I, your most happy father, have delivered to you, and preserve some memorial of my labours." One of the hearers saw the hint, and people of all ages, conditions, and ranks vied with each other in cries of affection for him and hatred for his foes (*Carm.* xi. 1057-1113, *Op.* ii. 729-731), and one cried, "If you go, you will banish the doctrine of the Trinity as well as yourself" (*ib.* 1100). At this Gregory promised to remain until the arrival of some bishops who were expected at the council, but retired for a while to the country to recruit his shattered health.

On Nov. 24, 380, Theodosius made his formal entry into Constantinople. One of his first cares was to restore to the orthodox the churches of which they had been deprived by the Arians. Gregory was summoned, and early on the morning of Nov. 26, in the presence of an immense crowd, Theodosius and Gregory entered the church of the Holy Apostles. A thick fog enveloped the building, but at the first accents of the chants the rays of the sun fell upon the vestments of the priests and the swords of the soldiers, and brought to Gregory's mind the glory of the Tabernacle of old. At the same time there arose a cry like thunder demanding that he should be bishop. "Silence!—silence!" he cried. "This is the time to give thanks to God. It will be time enough, hereafter, to settle other things." The service was continued without further interruption. Only one sword was drawn, and that was put back unstained into its sheath (*Carm.* xi. 1325-1390). In no part of Gregory's life is his true excellence of character more clearly seen than here; to his spirit of moderation and forgiveness is it to be attributed that this great religious revolution was effected without shedding one drop of blood. He tells one incident which reveals his spirit towards his foes. While he was ill in bed an assassin who had attempted his life entered his room, and, stung by conscience, fell weeping and speechless at his feet. Gregory said to him, "May God preserve you! It is nothing wonderful that I whom He hath saved should be merciful to you. Your bold deed has made you mine. Take care to walk, henceforth, worthy of God and of me." Gregory adds that this deed softened the feeling of the citizens towards him.

Not long after the entry into the metropolitical church—perhaps the very next day—the enthusiasm of the multitude led them to attempt to place Gregory by force in the episcopal chair. Yet there were traces of jealousy, and false motives were freely attributed to him. Always sensitive, he delivered in the presence of Theodosius a sermon "concerning himself, and to those who said that he wished to be bp. of Constantinople, and concerning the favours which the people had shewn towards him" (*Orat.* xxxvi. *Op.* i. 633-643). It is a forcible *Apologia pro Vitâ suâ.* "He would have been ashamed to seek that bishopric, bowed down as he was by old age and physical weakness. They said that he had sought another's bride (Constantinople): he had really refused his own (Sasima)" (*ib.* vi. 638, 639). The emperor and the court were present; questions greater than personal ones arose to Gregory's mind, and the discourse became an eloquent appeal to princes, sages, philosophers, professors, philologists, orators, to weigh their responsibilities and fulfil their duties.

Another discourse preached before Theodosius is the only one of Gregory's extant discourses which is a homily in the narrower sense of a definite exposition and application of a passage of Scripture (*Orat.* xxxvii. *Op.* i. 644-660). The text was Matt. xix. 1-12. Gregory first shews that "the reason why Christ moved from place to place was that He might heal the more persons. For the salvation of the world He had moved from heaven to earth. This was the cause of His voluntary humiliation, which men who understood it not had dwelt upon as contradicting His divinity, though divine names and attributes are applied to Him. Christ answered some questions (Matt. xix. 3, 4); others He did not answer (Luke xx. 2, 4). The preacher would follow Christ's example" (*ib.* v. 648, 649). "Christ answered fully their question about divorce. The preacher applying the teaching of Christ protests against the injustice of the Roman law, which distinguished between the adultery of the woman and that of the man. Men made it, and therefore it was directed against women (*ib.* vi. 649). Marriage for the first time is lawful, the second time an indulgence; more than the second, sinful; but virginity is a higher state (*ib.* v. iii.-x. 650-652). Husbands, wives, virgins, eunuchs, priests, laymen, all have their duties." He exhorts them to fulfil these, and, as in almost every discourse, passes on to the duty of believing in the doctrine of the Trinity.

Three other important discourses of Gregory, which belong also to the ministry at Constantinople, can only be mentioned. (1) On the Nativity [Dec. 25, 380 ?] (*Orat.* xxxviii. *Op.* i. 661-675; (2) On the Epiphany [Jan. 6, 381 ?] (*Orat.* xxxiv. *ib.* 676-691); (3) On Holy Baptism (*Orat.* xl. *ib.* 691-729).

Theodosius had long intended to summon a general council, and in May, A.D. 381, the synod of the 150 bishops who formed the second oecumenical council was held in the capital of the East. Socrates tells us that the object of the council was to confirm the Nicene faith and to appoint a bishop for Constantinople (*Hist. Eccl.* v. 8; cf. Soz. vii. 7; Theod. v. 7; Mansi, *Collect. Concil.* iii. 523). No Western bishop is mentioned as present, and the attempt to shew that Damasus of Rome was either consulted or represented is futile; but 36 bishops who were followers of Macedonius were present, and every effort was made to induce them to accept the Nicene faith. Meletius, the venerable bp. of Antioch, was at first president. The consecration of Maximus was at once pronounced void. The wish of Theodosius that Gregory should be chosen for the vacant see was well known; and the only bishop who opposed it was Gregory himself. He was by force placed in the episcopal chair. But he had this hope—alas! a vain one—that, "as position gives influence, he should be able, like a choragus who leads two choirs, to produce harmony between opposing parties" (*Carm.* xi. 1525-1545, *Op.* ii. 755). Meletius dying, the new archbishop naturally succeeded him as president of the council, but who should succeed him as bp. of Antioch? It is said that the two bishops, Meletius and Paulinus, had agreed that the survivor should be the sole bishop, and that to this agreement the chief clergy and laity of both parties were sworn. Meletius himself expressed an earnest wish for it from his death-bed, but a strong party, both within and without the council, was soon organized against it. Gregory has given us, in the poem *de Vitâ suâ*, a résumé of his own speech on the question (*Carm.* xi. 1591-1679, *Op.* ii. 759-763). "Now God had given the means of peace, let them confirm Paulinus in the episcopal office, and when the two should pass away, let them elect a new bishop. . . . For himself, he sought their permission to resign the office which they had conferred upon him, and he would gladly retire to some desert far away from evil men." He could scarcely have expected that this address would be received with favour, for the Meletian party was overpoweringly strong in the synod, and Paulinus had not been invited; but he was not prepared for the storm which followed. "There arose a cry like that of a number of jackdaws, and the younger members attacked him like a swarm of wasps" (*ib.* 1680-1690). He left the synod never to return to it. For a while illness was opportunely (καλῶς) the reason of his absence (*ib.* 1745), but the council proceeded to name Flavian as successor of Meletius; and Gregory, finding that his opinion had little weight, withdrew altogether and left the official residence, which was close to the church of the Holy Apostles (*Carm.* xi. 1778, *Op.* ii. 769). This led to earnest entreaties from the people that he would not desert his flock (*ib.* 1785-1795). Moved for a while by these prayers, he yet persisted in his determination, which was strengthened by the arrival of bishops from Egypt and Macedonia. The East and the West were now opposed to each other, and "prepared for the battle like wild boars, sharpening their terrible tusks" (*ib.* 1804). The new members of the synod did not object to Gregory personally; but his election was probably in itself obnoxious as an act of Meletius. It was clearly opposed, they urged, to the 15th canon of the Nicene council, which forbad any bishop, presbyter, or deacon to pass from one city to another. By that canon he ought to be sent back to Sasima. Gregory's party urged that he was released from that obligation by an equal authority, as another general council had elected him bp. of Constantinople; but it could not be expected that this plea would be accepted by bishops who were not a party to that act, nor was Gregory himself justified in speaking of the Nicene canons as obsolete. Gregory exhorted the council to think of higher things and mutual harmony. "He would be another Jonah to pacify the angry waves. Gladly would he find retirement and rest. He had but one anxiety, and that was for his beloved doctrine of the Trinity (*ib.* 1828-1855). He left the synod, glad at the thought of rest from his labours; sorrowful as one who is robbed of his children." The synod received his resignation with satisfaction, as removing a chief ground of dissension, and probably of jealousy also (*ib.* 1869; *Carm.* xii. 145-148, *Op.* ii. 787). Gregory went from the assembly to the emperor, who unwillingly consented. Gregory's only remaining care was to reconcile those who had been opposed to him and to bid farewell to his friends. He delivered a public statement of his position and a public farewell to the council and his church towards the end of June, 381 (*Orat.* xlii. *Op.* i. 748-768), before the synod and in the presence of a congregation which filled every corner of the church, and among whom no eye was dry. "Was there needed proof of his right to the bishopric? He would render his accounts. Let his work answer. He found them a rude flock, without a pastor, scattered, persecuted, robbed. Let them look round and see the wreath which had been woven—priests, deacons, readers, holy men and women. That wreath he had helped to weave. Was it a great thing to have established sound doctrine in a city which was the centre of the world? In that, too, he had done his part. Had he ever sought to promote his own interests? He could appeal like another Samuel. No; he had lived for God and the church, and kept the vows of his priesthood. All this he had done through the Holy Trinity and by the help of the Spirit. He would present to the synod his church as the most precious offering. The reward he asked was that they would appoint some one with pure hands and prudent tongue to watch over it; and that to the white hairs and worn-out frame of an old man, who could hardly then preach to them, they would allow the longed-for rest. Let them learn to prove these his last words—bishops to see the evil of the contentions which were among them; people to disregard externals and love priests rather than orators, men who cared for their souls rather than rich men." He then pronounced his lengthened farewell "to the beloved Anastasia, to the large temple, to the churches throughout the city, to the apostles who inhabited the temple, to the episcopal throne, to the clergy of all degrees, to all who helped at the holy table, to the choruses of Nazareans, to the virgins, wives, widows, orphans, poor; to the hospitable houses, to the crowds of hearers; to prince and palace and their inhabitants; to the Christ-loving city, to Eastern and Western lands; above all, to angels, protectors of the church and of himself; to the Holy Trinity, his only thought and treasure." With this pathetic climax, unsurpassed elsewhere even by Gregory himself, he concluded his last discourse in Constantinople. He left the city and retired to Nazianzus. Here he received a letter from Philagrius, an old friend of Caesarius and himself, animadverting upon his retirement. His answer breathes the same spirit as the poem *de Vitâ suâ* and the farewell sermon. "He was tired of fighting against envy and against venerable bishops, who destroyed the peace and put their personal squabbles before questions of faith" (*Ep.* lxxxvii. *Op.* ii. 76). Among the letters belonging to this period, two addressed to Nectarius, who was chosen to succeed Gregory at Constantinople, deserve special note, as shewing that he cherished for him and the church nothing but the most entire goodwill (*Epp.* lxxxviii. and xci. *Op.* ii. 77, 78). Gregory's difficulties were not yet at an end. On his return to Nazianzus he found that church in confusion, chiefly through the teaching of the Apollinarians (*Carm.* xxxi. *Op.* ii. 870-877). He tried to find a bishop who would stem the evil, but was thwarted by the presbyters and by the desertion of seven bishops who had promised to support him. His candidate had been hitherto engaged in secular affairs, but he thought him the most promising. He seems to have succeeded in naming another as bishop, and then to have retired to Arianzus. But very shortly he was again urged to take the governance of the church at Nazianzus and check the rapidly spreading Apollinarianism, and, in spite of his own strong disinclination, he agreed to do so. During this second administration the prefect Olympius threatened to destroy the city in consequence of a seditious attack, and it was saved only by a pacific letter from the bishop (*Ep.* cxli. *Op.* ii. 118-120). Other letters of the same kind shew Gregory as the father of the city, watching over all its interests with loving care.

But he felt that his constant illness unfitted him for his duties, and we find him writing to the archbp. of Tyana earnestly beseeching him to take steps to appoint another bishop. "If this letter did not affect its purpose, he would publicly proclaim the bishopric vacant rather than that the church should longer suffer from his own infirmity" (*Ep.* clii. *Op.* ii. 128). Eulalius, Gregory's colleague and relation, and the man of his choice, was elected in his stead. Gregory's satisfaction is expressed in a letter to Gregory of Nyssa (*Ep.* clxxxii. *Op.* ii. 149). Gregory withdrew to Arianzus, and spent in retirement the six remaining years of life. To this period belong certainly a large number of poems and letters; and probably two discourses, one on the Festival of St. Mamas, which was kept with special honour around Nazianzus on the first Sun. after Easter (καινὴ κυριακή), and one on the Holy Passover (*Orat.* xliv. and xlv. *Op.* i. 834-868).

Gregory at first retired to the little plot at Arianzus which he had retained when all his other property was given to the poor. Here a shady walk with a fountain was his favourite resort (*Carm.* xliv. 1-24, *Op.* ii. 915-917). But even this peaceful spot was denied him, and he was "driven forth without city, throne, or children, but always full of cares for them, as a wanderer upon the earth" (*Carm.* xliii. 1-12, *Op.* 913-915). He found a temporary resting-place at a tomb consecrated to martyrs at Carbala, a place of which nothing is known, and which the Bollandists suppose (Mai. ii. 424 F) to be another name for the plot at Arianzus. He was driven thence by a relative named Valentinian, who settled near with the female members of his family, as from another Paradise by another Eve. Οἰκαρχίαις δὴ γυναικῶν οὕτως ὑποχωρήσομεν, ὥσπερ ἐχιδναίοις ἐπιδρομαῖς (*Ep.* cciii. *Op.* ii. 169). The poems and letters of this period speak of constant illness and suffering, with but short intervals of relief. A frame never strong had given way under the severe asceticism of the earlier and the burden of the later life. "I suffer," he says in one of the letters, "and am content, not because I suffer, but because I am for others an example of patience. If I have no means to overcome any pain, I gain from it at least the power to bear it, and to be thankful as well in sorrowful circumstances as in joyous; for I am convinced that, although it seems to us the contrary, there is in the eyes of the Sovereign Reason nothing opposed to reason, in all which happens to us" (*Ep.* xxxvi. *Op.* ii. 32). Besides physical sufferings he had to bear intense spiritual agony, which at times took from him all hope either in this world or the next. In the thick of the spiritual combat he, like other great souls, learnt the lessons he was to teach to the world. His death must be assigned to about the 11th year of Theodosius, *i.e.* A.D. 389 or 390.

Gregory's extant works are contained in two fol. vols. of the Benedictine edition. Vol. i. consists of 45 sermons, of which some have been noticed in this article. Vol. ii. includes 243 letters—theological, pastoral, political, domestic; the will of Gregory, taken from the archives of the church of Nazianzus, and the poems arranged in two books. The dogmatic poems are 38 in number. No. 10 (74 iambics) is on the Incarnation, against Apollinaris. No. 11 (16 hexameters and pentameters) is also on the Incarnation. Nos. 12-29 are mnemonic verses on the facts of Holy Scripture, apparently meant for school use. Nos. 29-38 are prayers or hymns addressed to God. The moral poems are 40 in number. No. 1 (732 hexameters) is a eulogy of virginity. Nos. 2-7 in various metres, deal with kindred subjects, exhortations and counsels to virgins and monks, and the superiority of the single life. Nos. 8-11 are on the secular and religious life, and exhortations to virtue; Nos. 12 and 13 on the frailty of the human nature. No. 14 is a meditation on human nature in 132 hexameters and pentameters. It ranks with No. 1 among the most beautiful of Gregory's poems. The remainder of the poems in this section are on such subjects as the baseness of the outer man; the blessedness of the Christian life; the sin of frequent oaths and of anger; the loss of dear friends; the misery of false friends. Four are satires against a bad-mannered nobleman (26 and 27); misers (28); feminine luxury (29). There are 99 poems relating to his own life. One of them (No. 11, *de Vitâ suâ*) is an autobiography extending to 1,949 lines, to which another (No. 12, *de Seipso et de Episcopis*) adds 836 lines more. Among the historical poems is an epistle to

Nemesius, an eminent public man, shewing him the errors of paganism, and urging him to accept Christianity. These poetic epistles are of considerable length, and shew the varied interests and practical wisdom of the writer. There are 129 epitaphs and 94 epigrams, most of which are short poems, with little in them of the modern epigram, though some shew (*e.g.* 10-14, Εἰς Ἀγαπητούς) that the pen of Gregory could, when occasion required, be pointed with adamant. No less than 64 (31-94), belonging probably to the writer's youth, are upon the spoilers of tombs. If the statement of Jerome and Suidas, that Gregory wrote 30,000 verses, is to be understood literally, more than a third of them are now unknown.

In forming an estimate of Gregory's literary position, we have to consider (1) his poems, (2) his letters, and (3) his orations. Of each kind of writing there are abundant materials to form a judgment. (1) Two criticisms of the poems from very different standpoints may help us to arrive at the true mean. To Dr. Ullmann (*Gregorius*, ss. 200-202) they are "inferior to the letters, the product of old age, whereas the true vein of poetry must have shewn itself in earlier life; cramped by their subject-matters, which did not admit of originality; prosaic thoughts wrapped in poetic forms; involved and diffusive"; though he admits that some of the short pieces are poetry of a high order, and that the didactic aim of Gregory is to be taken into account. "Still they could never be more than a poor substitute for the older poetry of Greece." Villemain considers the poems the finest of all Gregory's works. He instances one especially (*de Humanâ naturâ*), "the severe charm of which seems to have anticipated the finest inspirations of our melancholy age, while it preserves the impress of a faith still fresh and honest, even in its trouble. . . . His funeral eulogies are hymns; his invectives against Julian have something of the malediction of the prophets. He has been called the 'Theologian of the East.' He ought to have been called rather 'the Poet of Eastern Christendom'" (*Tableau de l'éloquence chrétienne au 4me siècle*, p. 133). (2) Gregory's extant letters, though upon very various subjects, and often written under the pressure of immediate necessity, are almost invariably finished compositions. (3) A higher place has been claimed in this article for Gregory's orations than for his poems. He is now held to be greater than Basil, or even Chrysostom, and to have combined "the invincible logic of Bourdaloue; the unction, colour, and harmony of Massillon; the flexibility, poetic grace, and vivacity of Fénelon; the force, grandeur, and sublimity of Bossuet. . . . The Eagle of Meaux has been especially inspired by him in his funeral orations; the Swan of Cambrai has followed him in his treatise on *The Existence of God*" (Benoît, p. 721). He was an orator by training and profession. For this he studied at Caesarea, Alexandria, and Athens, and was the acknowledged chief in the schools of the rhetoricians. The oratory of the Christian pulpit was the creation of Gregory and Basil. It was based on the ancient models, and was akin, therefore, to the speeches of Demosthenes and Cicero, rather than to the modern sermon. It has been charged against the sermons of Gregory that they are not expositions of Scripture. As compared with the homilies of Chrysostom, for example, they certainly are not (except one: *Orat.* xxxvii. *Op.* i. 644-660); the nature of the case made it impossible that they should be. But the margin of every page abounds with references to Scripture, and no reader can fail to see with Bossuet that "Gregory's whole discourse is nothing but a judicious weaving of Scripture, and that he manifests everywhere a profound acquaintance with it" (*Défense de la tradition*, etc., iv. 2; Benoît, p. 723).

Great as was the position of Gregory as a writer, he left his chief mark upon history as a theologian. He alone beyond the apostolic circle has been thought worthy to bear the name "Theologus" which had been appropriated to St. John. Ullmann (*Gregorius*, etc. ss. 209-352), following Clemencet (*Op.* i. xlix.-lxxviii.), has arranged under their separate headings his views on the articles of faith. Within our present limits we can only refer to them as contained in the five famous theological discourses at Constantinople (*Orat.* xxvii.-xxxi. *Op.* i. 487-579).

(1) The first, Κατὰ Εὐνομιάνων, urges that "to discourse about God is a task of the greatest difficulty, not fitted for all times or all persons, nor to be undertaken in the presence of all persons. . . . The teacher of theology ought first to practise virtue. There is abundant scope for work to refute the older teaching of the pagan philosophers, or to discuss simpler questions of science and theology; but as to the nature of God our words should be few, for we can know but little in this life."

(2) Περὶ θεολογίας. Gregory reasserts here his favourite position, that "it is the pure mind only that can know God. . . . . The theologian beholds part of God, but the divine nature he can neither express in words nor comprehend in thought. The higher intelligence of angels even cannot know Him as He is. That there is a creating and preserving cause, we can know, as the sound of an instrument bears witness to its maker and player; that God is, we know, but what He is, and of what nature He is, and where He is, and where He was before the foundation of the world, we cannot know. The Infinite cannot be defined. We can only predicate negative attributes, for the nature of the divine essence is beyond all human conception."

(3) Περὶ Υἱοῦ. The two previous discourses were introductory. He now passes to the next subject. "The three earliest opinions concerning God were anarchia, polyarchia, and monarchia. The two former could not stand, as leading to confusion rather than the order of the universe. We hold that there is a monarchia, but that God is not limited to one person. If unity is divided, it becomes plurality. But if there is equal dignity of nature, and agreement of will, and identity of movement, and convergence to unity of those things which are of unity (and this cannot be the case in created things), there may be distinction in number without by any means involving distinction in essence and nature.

Unity, therefore (μονάς), from the beginning going forth to duality (εἰς δυάδα), constituted a Trinity (μέχρι τριάδος). Human words fail to express the generation and procession, and it is better to keep to scriptural terms; but the writer has in his thoughts an overflowing of goodness, and the Platonic simile of an overflowing cup applied to first and second causes. The generation and procession are eternal, and all questions as to time are inapplicable." Gregory then proceeds to state and answer the common objections of his adversaries.

(4) Περὶ Υἱοῦ. Another discourse on the same subject. Gregory has already answered the objection, that some passages of Scripture speak of the Son as human. He here exhaustively examines, under ten objections, the scriptural language applied to our Lord, and then passes to an exposition of the names (*a*) common to the Deity, (*b*) peculiar to the Son, (*c*) peculiar to the Son as man.

(5) Περὶ τοῦ Ἁγίου πνεύματος. Gregory commences this oration by referring to the difficulties arising because many who admitted the divinity of the Son regarded that of the Holy Ghost as a new doctrine not found in Holy Scripture. He expresses, in the strongest terms, his own belief in the divinity of the Third Person. "The Holy Spirit is holiness. Had the Spirit been wanting to the divine Trinity, the Father and the Son would have been imperfect." The most eminent pagan philosophers had had a glimpse of the truth, for they spoke of the "Mind of the Universe," the "Mind without," etc.

No conception of the subtlety of thought or beauty of expression in these discourses of Gregory can be given in an outline. Critics have rivalled each other in their praise, and many theologians have found in them their own best thoughts. A critic who cannot be accused of partiality towards Gregory has given perhaps the truest estimate of them. "A substance of thought, the concentration of all that is spread through the writings of Hilary, Basil, and Athanasius; a flow of softened eloquence which does not halt or lose itself for a moment; an argument nervous without dryness on the one hand, and without useless ornament on the other, gives these five discourses a place to themselves among the monuments of this fine genius, who was not always in the same degree free from grandiloquence and affectation. In a few pages and in a few hours Gregory has summed up and closed the controversy of a whole century." De Broglie, *L'Eglise et l'empire*, v. 385; Benoît, *Grégoire*, etc. 435, 436.

Little is needed for the study of Gregory's life and works beyond the admirable Benedictine ed. referred to above (Migne, *Patr. Gk.* xxxv.-xxxviii.), and the Lives by Ullmann (*Greg. von Naz. der Theologe*, 2. Aufl., Gotha, 1867; pt. i. of earlier ed. trans. by Cox, Oxf. 1855) and Benoît (*St. Grég. de Naz.*, Paris, 1876). For a well-known comparison of Gregory and Basil see Newman's *Church of the Fathers*, pp. 116-145, 551. Gregory's *Five Theol. Orations* have been ed. by A. J. Mason (Camb. Univ. Press, 1899). See also Duchesne, *Histoire de l'Egl.* vol. ii. ch. xii. Some of his works are trans. into Eng. in the *Post-Nic. Fathers*. [H.W.W.]

Gregorius (15) **Nyssenus,** bp. of Nyssa in Cappadocia (372-395), younger brother of Basil the Great, and a leading theologian of the Eastern church. He and his brother and their common friend Gregory Nazianzen were the chief champions of the orthodox Nicene faith in the struggle against Arianism and Apollinarianism, and by their discreet zeal, independency of spirit, and moderation of temper, contributed chiefly to its victory in the East. He was one of ten children of Basil, an advocate and rhetorician of eminence, and his wife Emmelia (Greg. Nys. *de Vit. S. Macr.*, *Opp.* ed. Morel. t. ii. pp. 182-186). We may place Gregory's birth *c.* 335 or 336, probably at Caesarea. He did not share his eldest brother's advantage of a university training, but was probably brought up in the schools of his native city. That no very special pains had been devoted to his education we may gather from the words of his sister Macidora on her deathbed, in which she ascribed the high reputation he had gained to the prayers of his parents, since "he had little or no assistance towards it from home" (*ib.* iii. 192). A feeble constitution and natural shyness disposed him to a literary retirement. His considerable intellectual powers had been improved by diligent private study; but he shrank from a public career, and appears after his father's death to have lived upon his inheritance, without any profession. That his religious instincts did not develop early appears from his account of his reluctant attendance at the ceremonial held by his mother Emmelia in honour of the "Forty Martyrs." A terrifying dream, which seemed to reproach him with neglect, led him to become a "lector" and as such read the Bible lections in the congregation (Greg. Naz. *Ep.* 43, t. i. p. 804). He would seem, however, to have soon deserted this vocation for that of a professor of rhetoric. This backsliding caused great pain to his friends and gave occasion to the enemies of religion to suspect his motives and bring unfounded accusations against him. Gregory Nazianzen, whose affection for him was warm and sincere, strongly remonstrated with him, expressing the grief felt by himself and others at his falling away from his first love. The date of this temporary desertion must be placed either before 361 or after 363, about the same time as his marriage. His wife was named Theosebeia, and her character answered to her name. She died some time after Gregory had become a bishop, and, according to Tillemont, subsequently to the council of Constantinople, A.D. 381. Expressions in Gregory Nazianzen's letter would lead us to believe that both himself and his friend were then somewhat advanced in life; and from Theosebeia being styled Gregory Nyssen's "sister" we may gather that they had ceased to cohabit, probably on his becoming a bishop (Greg. Naz. *Ep.* 95, t. i. p. 846; Niceph. *H. E.* xi. 19).

Gregory soon abandoned his profession of a teacher of rhetoric. The urgent remonstrances of his friend Gregory Nazianzen would have an earnest supporter in his elder sister, the holy recluse Macrina, who doubtless used the same powerful arguments which had induced Basil to give up all prospect of worldly fame for the service of Christ. Probably also the profession he had undertaken proved increasingly distasteful to one of Gregory's sensitive and retiring disposition, and he may have been further discouraged by the small results of his exertions to inspire a literary taste among youths who, as he complains in letters to his brother Basil's tutor Libanius, written while practising as a rhetorician (Greg. Nys. *Ep.* 13, 14), were much more ready to enter the army than to follow rhetorical studies. He retired to a monastery in Pontus, almost certainly that on the river Iris presided over by his brother Basil, and in close vicinity to Annesi, where was the female convent of which his sister Macrina was the superior. In this congenial retreat he passed several years, devoting himself to the study of the Scriptures and the works of Christian commentators. Among these it is certain that Origen had a high place, the influence of that writer being evident in Gregory's own theological works. At Pontus, *c.* 371, he composed his work *de Virginitate,* in which, while extolling virginity as the highest perfection of Christian life, he laments that he had separated himself from that state (*de Virg.* lib. iii. t. iii. pp. 116 seq.). Towards the close of his residence in Pontus, A.D. 371, circumstances occurred displaying Gregory's want of judgment in a striking manner. An estrangement had arisen between Basil and his aged uncle, the bp. Gregory, whom the family deservedly regarded as their second father. The younger Gregory took on himself the office of mediator. Straightforward methods having failed, he adopted crooked ones, and forged letters to his brother in their uncle's name desiring reconciliation. The letters were indignantly repudiated by the justly offended bishop, and reconciliation became increasingly hopeless. Basil addressed a letter to his brother, which is a model of dignified rebuke. He first ridicules him with his simplicity, unworthy of a Christian, reproaches him for endeavouring to serve the cause of truth by deception, and charges him with unbrotherly conduct in adding affliction to one already pressed out of measure (Basil. *Ep.* 58 [44]).

In 372 (the year Gregory Nazianzen was consecrated to the see of Sasima) Gregory was forced by his brother Basil to accept reluctantly the see of Nyssa, an obscure town of Cappadocia Prima, about ten miles from the capital, Caesarea. Their common friend, Eusebius of Samosata, wrote to Basil to remonstrate on his burying so distinguished a man in so unworthy a see. Basil replied that his brother's merits made him worthy to govern the whole church gathered into one, but he desired that the see should be made famous by its bishop, not the bishop by his see (*ib.* 98 [259]). These words have proved prophetic.

Gregory's episcopate fell in troublous times. Valens, a zealous Arian, being on the throne, lost no opportunity of forwarding his own tenets and vexing the orthodox. The miserable Demosthenes [BASILIUS] had been recently appointed vicar of Pontus to do all in his power to crush the adherents of the Nicene faith. After petty acts of persecution, in which the semi-Arian prelates joined with high satisfaction, as a means of retaliating on Basil, a synod was summoned at Ancyra at the close of 375, to examine some alleged canonical irregularities in Gregory's consecration, and to investigate a frivolous charge brought against him by a certain Philocharis of having made away with church funds left by his predecessor. A band of soldiers was sent to arrest Gregory and conduct him to the place of hearing. A chill on his journey brought on a pleuritic seizure and aggravated a painful malady to which he was subject. His entreaties to be allowed to halt for medical treatment were disregarded, but he managed to elude the vigilance of the soldiers and to escape to some place of concealment where his maladies could be cared for. Basil collected a synod of orthodox Cappadocian bishops, in whose name he addressed a dignified but courteous letter to Demosthenes, apologizing for his brother's non-appearance at Ancyra, and stating that the charge of embezzlement could be shewn to be false by the books of the treasurers of the church; while, if any canonical defect in his ordination could be proved, the ordainers were those who should be called to account, an account which they were ready to render (*ib.* 225 [385]). Basil wrote also to a man of distinction named Aburgius, begging him to use his influence to save Gregory from the misery of being dragged into court and implicated in judicial business from which his peaceful disposition shrank (*ib.* 33 [358]). Another synod was summoned at Nyssa by Demosthenes A.D. 376, through the instrumentality of Eustathius of Sebaste. Still Gregory refused to appear. He was pronounced contumacious and deposed by the assembled bishops, of whom Anysius and Ecdicius of Parnasse were the leaders, and they consecrated a successor, whom Basil spoke of with scorn as a miserable slave who could be bought for a few oboli (*ib.* 237 [264], 239 [10]). Gregory's deposition was followed by his banishment by Valens (Greg. Nys. *de Vit. Macr.* t. ii. p. 192). These accumulated troubles utterly crushed his gentle spirit. In his letters he bewails the cruel necessity which had compelled him to desert his spiritual children, and driven him from his home and friends to dwell among malicious enemies who scrutinized every look and gesture, nay his very dress, and made them grounds of accusation. He dwells with tender recollection on the home he had lost—his fireside, his table, his pantry, his bed, his bench, his sackcloth—and contrasts it with the stifling hole in which he was forced to dwell, of which the only furniture was straitness, darkness, and cold. His only consolation is in the assurance that his brethren would remember him in their prayers (Greg. Nys. *Epp.* 18, 22). His letters to Gregory Nazianzen have unfortunately perished, but his deep despondency is shewn by the replies. After his expulsion from his see his namesake wrote that, though denied his wish to accompany him in his banishment, he went with him in spirit, and trusted in God that the storm would soon blow over, and he get the better of all his enemies, as a recompense for his strict orthodoxy (Greg. Naz. *Ep.* 142, t. i. p. 866). Driven from place to place to avoid his enemies, he had compared himself to a stick carried aimlessly hither and thither on the surface of a stream; his friend replies that his movements were rather like those of the sun, which brings life to all things, or of the planets, whose apparent irregularities are subject to a fixed law (*ib.* 34 [32], p. 798). Out of heart at the apparent triumph of Arianism, Gregory bids him be of good cheer, for the enemies of the truth were like serpents, creeping from their holes in the sunshine of imperial favour, who, however alarming their hissing, would be driven back into the earth by time and truth. All would come right if they left all to God (*ib.* 35 [33], p. 799). This trust in God proved well founded. On the death of Valens in 378 the youthful Gratian recalled the banished bishops, and, to the joy of the faithful, Gregory was restored to Nyssa. In one of his letters he describes with graphic power his return. The latter half of his journey was a triumphal progress, the inhabitants pouring out to meet him, and escorting him with acclamations and tears of joy (Greg. Nys. *Ep.* 3, Zacagni; No. 6, Migne). On Jan. 1, 379, Basil, whom he loved as a brother and revered as a spiritual father, died. Gregory certainly attended his funeral, delivering his funeral oration, to which we are indebted for many particulars of Basil's life. In common with Gregory's compositions generally, it offends by the extravagance of its language and turgid oratory (Greg. Nys. *in Laud. Patr. Bas.* t. iii. pp. 479 seq.). Gregory Nazianzen, who was prevented from being present by illness, wrote a consolatory letter, praising his namesake very highly, and saying that his chief comfort now was to see all Basil's virtues reflected in him, as in a mirror (Greg. Naz. *Ep.* 37 [35], p. 799). One sorrow followed close upon another in Gregory's life. The confusion in the churches after the long Arian supremacy entailed severe labours and anxieties upon him for the defence of the truth and the reformation of the erring (*de Vit. Macr.* t. ii. p. 192). In Sept. 379 he took part in the council held at Antioch for the double purpose of healing the Antiochene schism (which it failed to effect) and of taking measures for securing the church's victory over the lately dominant Arianism (Labbe, *Concil.* ii. 910; Baluz. *Nov. Concil. Coll.* p. 78). On his way back to his diocese, Gregory visited the monastery at Annesi, over which his sister Macrina presided. He found her dying, and she expired the next evening. A full account of her last hours, with a detailed biography, is given by him in a letter to the monk Olympius (*de Vit. S. Macrinae Virg.* t. ii. pp. 177 seq.). In his treatise *de Anima et Resurrectione* (entitled, in honour of his sister, τὰ Μακρίνια) we have another account of her deathbed, in which he puts long speeches into her mouth, as part of a dialogue held with him on the proofs of the immortality of the soul and the resurrection of the body, the object of which was to mitigate his grief for Basil's death (t. iii. pp. 181 seq.). [Macrina the Younger.] After celebrating his sister's funeral, Gregory continued his journey to his diocese, where an unbroken series of calamities awaited him. The Galatians had been sowing their heresies. The people at Ibora on the borders of Pontus, having lost their bishop by death, elected Gregory to the vacant see. This, in some unexplained way, caused troubles calling for the intervention of the military. These difficulties being settled, he set out on a long and toilsome journey, in fulfilment of a commission from the council of Antioch "to visit and reform the church of Arabia" (t. iii. p. 653)—*i.e.* of Babylon. He found the state of the church there even worse than had been represented. The people had grown hardened in heresy, and were as brutish and barbarous in their lives as in their tongue. From his despairing tone we judge that the mission met with but little success. At its termination, being near the Holy Land, he visited the spots consecrated by the life and death of Christ. The emperor put a public chariot at his disposal, which served him and his retinue "both for a monastery and a church," fasting, psalmody, and the hours of prayer being regularly observed all through the journey (t. iii. p. 658). He visited Bethlehem, Golgotha, the Mount of Olives, and the Anastasis. But the result of this pilgrimage was disappointment. His faith received no confirmation, and his religious sense was scandalized by the gross immorality prevailing in the Holy City, which he describes as a sink of all iniquity. The church there was in an almost equally unsatisfactory state. Cyril, after his repeated depositions by Arian influence, had finally returned, but had failed to heal the dissensions of the Christians or bring them back to unity of faith. Gregory's efforts were equally ineffectual, and he returned to Cappadocia depressed and saddened. In two letters, one to three ladies resident at Jerusalem, Eustathia, Ambrosia, and Basilissa (t. iii. pp. 659 seq.), the other the celebrated one *de Euntibus Hierosolyma*, he declares his conviction not of the uselessness only but of the evil of pilgrimages. "He urges . . . the dangers of robbery and violence in the Holy Land itself, of the moral state of which he draws a fearful picture. He asserts the religious superiority of Cappadocia, which had more churches than any part of the world, and inquires in plain terms whether a man will believe the virgin birth of Christ the more by seeing Bethlehem, or His resurrection by visiting His tomb, or His ascension by standing on the Mount of Olives" (Milman, *Hist. of Christianity*, bk. iii. c. 11, vol. iii. p. 192, note). There is no sufficient reason for questioning the genuineness of this letter. We next hear of Gregory at the second general council, that of Constantinople, A.D. 381 (Labbe, *Concil.* ii. 955), accompanied by his deacon Evagrius. There he held a principal place as a recognized theological leader, τῆς ἐκκλησίας τὸ κοινὸν ἔρεισμα, as his friend Gregory Nazianzen had at an earlier period termed him. That he was the author of the clauses then added to the Nicene symbol is an unverified assertion of Nicephorus Callistus (*H. E.* xii. 13). It was probably on this occasion that he read to Gregory Nazianzen and to Jerome his work against Eunomius, or the more important parts of it (Hieron. *de Vir. Ill.* c. 128). Gregory Nazianzen having been reluctantly compelled to ascend the episcopal throne of Constantinople, Gregory Nyssen delivered an inaugural oration now lost, and, soon after, a funeral oration on the venerable Meletius of Antioch, which has been preserved (Socr. *H. E.* iv. 26; *Oratio in funere Magni Meletii*, t. iii. pp. 587 seq.). Before the close of the council the emperor Theodosius issued a decree from Heraclea, July 30, 381, containing the names of the bishops who were to be regarded as centres of orthodox communion in their respective districts. Among these Gregory Nyssen appears, together with his metropolitan Helladius of Caesarea and Otreius of Melitene, for the diocese of Pontus (*Cod. Theod.* l. iii. *de Fide Catholica*, t. vi. p. 9; Socr. *H. E.* v. 8). Gregory, however, was not made for the delicate and difficult business of restoring the unity of the faith. He was more a student than a man of action. His simplicity was easily imposed upon. Open to flattery, he became the dupe of designing men. His colleague Helladius was in every way his inferior, and if Gregory took as little pains to conceal his sense of this in his personal intercourse as in his correspondence with Flavian, we cannot be surprised at the metropolitan's dignity being severely wounded. Helladius revenged himself by gross rudeness to Gregory. Having turned out of his way to pay his respects to his metropolitan, Gregory was kept standing at the door under the midday sun, and when at last admitted to Helladius's presence, his complimentary speeches were received with chilling silence. When he mildly remonstrated, Helladius broke into cutting reproaches, and rudely drove him from his presence (*Ep. ad Flavian.* t. iii. pp. 645 seq.). Gregory was present at the synod at Constantinople in 383, when he delivered his discourse on the Godhead of the Second and Third Persons of the Trinity (*de Abraham*, t. iii. pp. 464 seq.; cf. Tillem. *Mém. ecclés.* ix. p. 586, *S. Grég. de Nysse*, art. x.), and again at Constantinople in A.D. 385, when he pronounced the funeral oration over the little princess Pulcheria, and shortly afterwards over her mother the empress Flaccilla. Both orations are extant (t. iii. pp. 514 seq., 527 seq.). During these visits to Constantinople, Gregory obtained the friendship of Olympias, the celebrated deaconess and correspondent of Chrysostom, at whose instance he undertook an exposition of the Canticles, a portion of which, containing 15 homilies, he completed and sent her (*in Cant. Cantic.* t. i. pp. 468 seq.). Gregory was present at the synod at Constantinople A.D. 394, under the presidency of Nectarius, to decide between the claims of Bagadius and Agapius to the see of Bostra in Arabia (Labbe, *Concil.* ii. 1151). At the request of Nectarius Gregory delivered the homily bearing the erroneous title, *de Ordinatione*, which is evidently a production of his old age (t. ii. pp. 40 seq.). His architectural taste appears in this homily. It is probable that he did not long survive this synod. The date of his death was perhaps A.D. 395.

Gregory Nyssen was a very copious writer, and the greater part of his recorded works have been preserved. They may be divided into five classes: (1) *Exegetical*; (2) *Dogmatical*; (3) *Ascetic*; (4) *Funeral Orations and Panegyrical Discourses*; (5) *Letters*.

(1) *Exegetical.*—What exegesis of Holy Scripture he has left is of no high value, his system of interpretation being almost entirely allegorical. To this class belong his works on the *Creation*, written chiefly to supplement and defend the great work of his brother Basil on the *Hexaemeron*. These include (i) περὶ τῆς ἑξαημέρου, dedicated to his youngest brother Peter, bp. of Sebaste. It is also called *Apologeticus*, as it contains a defence of the actions of Moses and of some points in Basil's work. (ii) A treatise on the creation of man, written as a supplement to Basil's treatise (vol. i. p. 45; Socr. *H. E.* iv. 26), the fundamental idea of which is the unity of the human race—that humanity before God is to be considered as one man. It is called by Suidas τεῦχος θαυμάσιον. (iii) Also two homilies on the same subject (Gen. i. 26), frequently appended to Basil's *Hexaemeron*, and erroneously assigned to him by Combefis and others. There is also a discourse (t. ii. pp. 22-34) on the meaning of the image and likeness of God in which man was created. (iv) A treatise on the *Life of Moses* as exhibiting a pattern of a perfect Christian life; dedicated to Caesarius. (v) Two books on the *Superscriptions of the Psalms*, in which he endeavours to shew that the five books of the Psalter are intended to lead men upward, as by five steps, to moral perfection. (vi) Eight homilies expository of *Ecclesiastes*, ending with c. vii. 13, "less forced, more useful, and more natural" (Dupin). (vii) Fifteen homilies on the *Canticles*, ending with c. vi. 9; dedicated to Olympias. (viii) Five homilies on the *Lord's Prayer*, "lectu dignissimae" (Fabric.). (ix) Eight homilies on the *Beatitudes*. (x) A discourse on 1 Cor. xv. 28, in which he combats the Arian perversion of the passage as to the subjection of the Son. (xi) A short treatise on the witch of Endor, Ἐγγαστρίμυθος, to prove that the apparition was a demon in the shape of Samuel; addressed to a bishop named Theodosius.

(2) *Dogmatical.*—These are deservedly regarded as among the most important patristic contributions towards a true view of the mystery of the Trinity, hardly, if at all, inferior to the writings of Basil. (i) Chief, both in size and importance, is his great work *Against Eunomius*, written after Basil's death, to refute the reply of Eunomius to Basil's attack upon his teaching, and to vindicate his brother from the calumnious charges of his adversary. (ii) Almost equally important are the replies to Apollinaris, especially the *Antirrheticus adversus Apollinarem*. These are not only valuable as giving the most weighty answer on the orthodox side to this heresy, but their numerous extracts from Apollinarian writings are really the chief sources of our acquaintance with those doctrines. The same subjects are treated with great accuracy of thought and spiritual insight in (iii) *Sermo Catecheticus Magnus*, a work in 40 chapters, containing a systematized course of theological teaching for catechists, proving, for the benefit of those who did not accept the authority of Holy Scripture, the harmony of the chief doctrines of the faith with the instincts of the human heart. This work contains passages asserting the annihilation of evil, the restitution of all things, and the final restoration of evil men and evil

spirits to the blessedness of union with God, so that He may be "all in all," embracing all things endued with sense and reason—doctrines derived by Gregory from Origen. It has been asserted from the time of Germanus of Constantinople that these passages were foisted in by heretical writers (Phot. *Cod.* 233, pp. 904 sqq.); but there is no foundation for this hypothesis. The concluding section of the work, which speaks of the errors of Severus, a century posterior to Gregory, is evidently an addition of some blundering copyist. It must be acknowledged that in his desire to exalt the divine nature Gregory came dangerously near the doctrines afterwards developed by Eutyches and the Monothelites, if he did not actually enunciate them. While he rightly held that the infinite Logos was not imprisoned in Christ's human soul and body, he does not assign the proper independence to this human soul and will. Hooker quotes some words of his as to the entire extinction of all distinction between the two natures of Christ, as a drop of vinegar is lost in the ocean (*Eccl. Pol.* t. ii. 697), which he deems so plain and direct for Eutyches that he "stands in doubt they are not his whose name they carry" (*ib.* bk. v. c. iii. § 2; cf. Neander, *Ch. Hist.* vol. iv. p. 115, Clark's trans.).

(3) The class of his *Ascetical Writings* is small. To it belong his early work *de Virginitate*; his *Canonical Epistles* to Letoius, bp. of Melitene, classifying sins, and the penances due to each; etc.

(4) The chief *Funeral Orations* are those on his brother Basil, on Meletius, on the empress Flaccilla, and on the young princess Pulcheria. We have also several panegyrical discourses and some homilies.

(5) The extant *Epistles* are not numerous. The chief are that to *Flavian*, complaining of contumelious treatment by Helladius, and the two on *Pilgrimages to Jerusalem.*

All previous edd. of his collected works trans. into Latin were greatly surpassed in elegance and accuracy by that of Paris, 1603, under the superintendence of Front du Duc. The first ed. of the Greek text with a Latin trans. appeared from Morel's press at Paris in 1615 in two vols. fol., also ed. by Du Duc. Other complete reprints, including his epistles and other *additamenta*, are by Galland (*Bibl. Vet. Patr.* t. vi.) and Migne (*Patr. Gk.* xliv.-xlvi.). A good critical ed. of his works is, however, much wanted. Such an ed. was commenced by Forbes and Oehler in 1855, but very little has appeared. In the *Journ. of Theol. Stud.*, 1902, is an art. by J. H. Srawley on the text of the *Orat. Cat.*, and in 1903 the same writer ed. it for the *Camb. Univ. Texts.* Another useful ed. of it was pub. in 1909 in Gk. and French by Meridier in *Textes et Documents* of Hemmer and Lejay. An Eng. trans. is in the *Post-Nic. Fathers.* The familiar letters published by Zacagni and Caraccioli are very helpful towards forming an estimate of Gregory's character. They shew us a man of great refinement, with a love for natural beauty and a lively appreciation of the picturesque in scenery and of elegance in architecture. Of the latter art the detailed description given in his letter to Amphilochius (*Ep.* 25) of an octagonal "martyrium" surmounted by a conical spire, rising from a clerestory supported on eight columns, proves him to have possessed considerable technical knowledge. It is perhaps the clearest and most detailed description of an ecclesiastical building of the 4th cent. remaining to us. His letter to Adelphius (*Ep.* 20) furnishes a charming description of a country villa, and its groves and ornamental buildings. Cave, *Hist. Lit.* vol. i. pp. 244 sqq.; Ceillier, *Auteurs ecclés.* t. vii. pp. 320 sqq.; Oudin, I. diss. iv.; Schröckh, *Kirchengesch.* Bd. xiv. 1-147; Tillem. *Mém. ecclés.* t. ix.; Dupin, cent. iv.; Fabric. *Bibl. Graec.* t. ix. pp. 98 sqq. [E.V.]

Gregorius (16), bp. of Merida from *c.* 402; known to us only from the decretal of Innocent I. addressed *ad universos episcopos in Tolosa* (should be *qui in Toleto congregati sunt*). Innocent's letter (which Jaffé dates 404) is concerned partly with the schism of those bishops of Baetica and Carthaginensis who refused to acknowledge the authority of the council held at Toledo A.D. 400, which re-admitted to communion the once Priscillianist bishops, Symphosius and Dictinius, and partly with certain irregularities in the manner of ordination then prevalent in Spain. The pope lays down that although, strictly speaking, the illegal ordinations already made ought to be cancelled, yet, for the sake of peace and to avoid tumults, what is past is to be condoned. The number of canonically invalid ordinations recently made is, he says, so great that otherwise the existing confusion would be made worse instead of better. "How many have been admitted to the priesthood who, like Rufinus and Gregory, have after baptism practised in the law courts? How many soldiers who, in obedience to authority, have been obliged to execute harsh orders (severa praecepta)? How many curiales who, in obedience also, have done whatever was commanded them? How many who have given amusements and spectacles to the people (voluptates et editiones populo celebrarunt) have become bishops?" (See Gams's comments on Can. 2 of council of Eliberi. ii. 1, 53.) "Quorum omnium neminem ne ad societatem quidem ordinis clericorum, oportuerat pervenire" (see *Decret.* cap. iv. Tejada y Ramiro; *Col. de Can.* ii.). In cap. v. we have the second mention of Gregory. "Let the complaint, if any, of Gregory, bp. of Merida, ordained in place of Patruinus [who presided at C. Tol. I.] be heard, and if he has suffered injury *contra meritum suum*, let those who are envious of another's office be punished, lest in future the spirit of faction should again inconvenience good men."

From these notices it appears that Gregory succeeded Patruinus in the metropolitan see of Merida shortly after the council of Toledo in 400, that in his youth and after baptism he had practised as an advocate; that his election to the bishopric was therefore, strictly speaking, illegal, and that his appointment had met with great opposition. Innocent's letter would naturally confirm him in his see and discredit the party of opposition. It was probably during Gregory's pontificate that the irruption of Vandals, Alani, and Suevi into Spain took place (in the autumn of 409, Idat. ap. *Esp. Sagr.* iv. 353), and those scenes of horror and cruelty took place of which Idatius has left us a vivid, though possibly exaggerated, picture. After a first period of indiscriminate devastation and plunder, the invaders, settling down, divided the provinces among themselves by lot (Idat. *l.c.* ann. 411). In this division Lusitania and Carthaginensis fell to the Alani, themselves to be shortly destroyed by the Goths under Walga (418), and Merida with its splendid buildings and Roman prestige, with all the other great cities of S. Spain, "submitted to the rule of the barbarians who lorded it over the Roman provinces." Innocent's letter concerning Gregory is extremely valuable for Spanish church history at the time. *Esp. Sagr.* xiii. 163; Gams, *Kirchengesch.* ii. 1, 420. [M.A.W.]

Gregorius (31) Theopolitanus, bp. of Antioch A.D. 569-594. In his earliest youth he devoted himself to a monastic life, and became so celebrated for his austerities that when scarcely past boyhood he was chosen superior of the Syrian laura of Pharon or Pharan (Moschus), called by Evagrius the monastery of the Byzantines. Sergius the Armenian in the monastery of the Eunuchs near the Jordan was earnestly importuned by Gregory to conduct him to his venerable master, another Sergius, dwelling by the Dead Sea. When the latter saw Gregory approach, he cordially saluted him, brought water, washed his feet, and conversed with him upon spiritual subjects the whole day. Sergius the disciple afterwards reminded his master that he had never treated other visitors, although some had been bishops and presbyters, as he had treated father Gregory. "Who father Gregory may be," the old man replied, "I know not; but this I know, I have entertained a patriarch in my cave, and I have seen him carry the sacred pallium and the Gospels" (Joann. Mosch. *Prat. Spirit.* c. 139, 140, in *Patr. Lat.* lxxiv. 189). From Pharan Gregory was summoned by Justin II. to preside over the monastery of Mount Sinai (Evagr. *H. E.* v. 6). On the expulsion of Anastasius, bp. of Antioch, by Justin in 569, Gregory was appointed his successor. Theophanes (*Chron.* A.D. 562, p. 206) makes his promotion take place from the Syrian monastery. His administration is highly praised by Evagrius, who ascribes to him almost every possible excellence. When Chosroes I. invaded the Roman territory, A.D. 572, Gregory, who was kept informed of the real state of affairs by his friend the bp. of Nisibis, then besieged by the Roman forces, vainly endeavoured to rouse the feeble emperor by representations of the successes of the Persian forces and the incompetence of the imperial commanders. An earthquake compelled Gregory to flee with the treasures of the church, and he had the mortification of seeing Antioch occupied by the troops of Adaormanes, the general of Chosroes (Evagr. *H. E.* v. 9). The latter years of his episcopate were clouded by extreme unpopularity and embittered by grave accusations (*ib.* c. 18). In the reign of Maurice, A.D. 588, a quarrel with Asterius, the popular Count of the East, again aroused the passions of the excitable Antiochenes against their bishop. He was openly reviled by the mob, and turned into ridicule on the stage. On the removal of Asterius, his successor, John, was commissioned by the emperor to inquire into the charges against Gregory, who proceeded to Constantinople, accompanied by Evagrius as his legal adviser, *c.* 589, and received a triumphal acquittal (*ib.* vi. 7). He returned to Antioch to witness its almost total destruction by earthquake, A.D. 589, barely escaping with his life (*ib.* c. 8). In the widespread discontent of the imperial forces, the troops in Syria on the Persian frontier broke out into open mutiny. Gregory, who by his largesses had made himself very popular with the troops, was dispatched to bring them back to their allegiance. He was suffering severely from gout, and had to be conveyed in a litter, from which he addressed the army so eloquently that they at once consented to accept the emperor's nominee, Philippicus, as their commander. His harangue is preserved by his grateful friend Evagrius (*ib.* c. 11-13). Soon after, his diplomatic skill caused him to be selected by Maurice as an ambassador to the younger Chosroes, when compelled by his disasters to take refuge in the imperial territory, A.D. 590 or 591, and Gregory's advice was instrumental in the recovery of his throne, for which the grateful monarch sent him some gold and jewelled crosses and other valuable presents (*ib.* c. 18-21). In spite of his age and infirmities, Gregory conducted a visitation of the remoter portions of his patriarchate, which were much infected with the doctrines of Severus, and succeeded in bringing back whole tribes, as well as many separate villages and monasteries, into union with the catholic church (*ib.* c. 22). After this he paid a visit to Simeon Stylites the younger, who was suffering from a mortal disease (*ib.* c. 23). Soon after he appears to have resigned his see into the hands of the deposed patriarch Anastasius, who resumed his patriarchal authority in 594, in which year Gregory died (*ib.* c. 24). His extant works consist of a homily *in Mulieres unguentiferas* found in Galland and Migne (*Patr. Gk.* lxxxviii. p. 1847), and two sermons on the *Baptism of Christ*, which have been erroneously ascribed to Chrysostom. Evagrius (vi. 24) also attributes to Gregory a volume of historical collections, now lost. Fabric. *Bibl. Graec.* xi. 102; Cave, *Hist. Lat.* i. 534. Cf. Huidacher in *Zeitschr. für Kathol. Theol.* 1901, xxv. 367. [E.V.]

Gregorius (32) Turonensis, bp. of Tours (*c.* 573-594). His life we know chiefly from his own writings. The *Vita per Odonem Abbatem*, generally pub. with his works, is almost entirely based upon what he says of himself.

Gregory himself gives a list of his works. At the end of his History he says, "Decem libros historiarum, septem miraculorum, unum de vitis Patrum scripsi: in Psalterii tractatum librum unum commentatus sum: de cursibus etiam ecclesiasticis unum librum condidi" (bk. x. 31, *sub fin.*). Of these all are extant except the commentary on the Psalms, of which only fragments exist, collected in vol. iii. of Bordier's ed. pp. 401 sqq. His History is in vol. ii. of Bouquet, and in the collections of La Bigne, Duchesne, and Migne. There are valuable edd. by the Société de l'Histoire de France, with French trans. and notes, viz. the *Hist. eccl. des Francs*, edited by MM.

Guadet et Taranne (4 vols. 1836-1838), and *Les Livres des miracles et autres opuscules*, including the *Vita*, extracts from Fortunatus, etc., by M. H. L. Bordier (4 vols. 1857-1864). But the best and most recent ed. is that of W. Arndt and Br. Krusch in *Mon. Germ. Hist. Script Rez. Merov.* i. This contains an *Index, Orthographica, Lexica et Grammatica.* Of the commentaries and works bearing on his life and writings, the most important and thorough are Löbell's *Gregor von Tours und seine Zeit* (2nd ed. 1869), and Gabriel Monod's *Etudes critiques sur l'époque mérovingienne*, pt. i. 1872, being fasc. No. 9 of the *Bibliothèque de l'école des hautes études.*

Georgius Florentius (subsequently called Gregorius, after his great-grandfather) was born Nov. 30, 538. Previous authorities have generally given the year 543, from the passage in the *Vita* which states that he was 30 years old at the time of his consecration, *i.e.* in 573.

Members of both parents' families had held high office in church and state. His paternal grandfather Georgius and his maternal great-grandfather Florentius (*V. P.* 8, 1) had been senators at Clermont. Gallus, son of Georgius and uncle of Gregory, was bp. of Auvergne; another uncle, Nicetius or Nizier, bp. of Lyons (*H.* v. 5; *V. P.* 8); another, Gundulf, had risen to ducal rank (*H.* vi. 11). Gregory, bp. of Langres, and originally count of Autun, was his great-grandfather, and all the previous bishops of Tours, except five, had been of his family (v. 50). It is with justifiable pride, therefore, that he asserts (*V. P.* 6) that none in Gaul could boast of purer and nobler blood than himself. His father appears to have died early, and Gregory received most of his education from his uncle Gallus, bp. of Auvergne. Being sick of a fever in his youth, he found relief by visiting the shrine of St. Illidius, the patron saint of Clermont. The fever returned, and Gregory's life was despaired of. Being again carried to St. Illidius's shrine, he vowed to dedicate himself to the ministry if he recovered, nor would he quit the shrine till his prayer was granted (*V. P.* 2, 2).

Armentaria, Gregory's mother, returned to Burgundy, her native country, and Gregory apparently lived with Avitus, at first archdeacon, afterwards bp. of Auvergne, who carried on his education, directing his pupil rather to the study of ecclesiastical than of secular works. Gregory looked upon Avitus as in the fullest sense his spiritual father. "It was his teaching and preaching that, next to the Psalms of David, led me to recognize that Jesus Christ the Son of God had come into the world to save sinners, and caused me to reverence and honour those as the friends and disciples of Christ who take up His cross and follow in His steps" (*V. P.* 2, Intro.). By Avitus he was ordained deacon, probably *c.* 563 (Monod. 29).

Of Gregory's life before he became bp. of Tours few details are known. He appears to have been well known at Tours (*Mir. Mart.* i. 32, *Vita*, c. ii.), for it was in consequence of the expressed wish of the whole people of Tours, clergy and laity, that Sigebert appointed him, in 573, to the see. He was consecrated by Egidius of Rheims. He was known to and favoured by Radegund the widow of Clotaire I., foundress of St. Cross at Poictiers, who, according to Fortunatus, helped to procure his election (*Carm.* v. 3).

The elevation of Gregory was contemporary with the renewed outbreak of civil war between Sigebert and Chilperic, the former of whom had inherited the Austrasian, the latter the Neustrian, possessions of their father Clotaire I. (d. 561). The possession of Touraine and Poitou was in some sort the occasion of the war, and these countries suffered from the ravages of both parties. Gregory's sympathies were naturally with Sigebert (*Vita S. Greg.* § 11), and the people of Tours were generally (*H.* iv. 50), though not unanimously (iv. 46), on the same side. Chilperic, according to Gregory, was even more cruel and regardless of human life than the other Merovingian princes; he was the "Nero and Herod of his age" (vi. 46); he not only plundered and burned throughout the country, but specially destroyed churches and monasteries, slew priests and monks, and paid no regard to the possessions of St. Martin (iv. 48). Tours remained under Chilperic till his death in 584, and some of the best traits in Gregory's character appear in his resistance to the murderous violence of the king and the truculent treachery of Fredegund. Thus he braved their wrath, and refused to surrender their rebellious son Meroveus (v. 14), and their enemy Guntram Boso who had defeated and killed Theodebert (v. 4), both of whom had taken sanctuary at the shrine of St. Martin; and Gregory alone of the bishops dared to rebuke Chilperic for his unjust conduct towards Praetextatus, and to protect Praetextatus from the vengeance of Fredegund (v. 19); and when Chilperic wanted to force on his people his views of the doctrine of the Trinity, Gregory withstood him. Chilperic recited to Gregory what he had written on the subject, saying, "I will that such shall be your belief and that of all the other doctors of the church." "Do not deceive yourself, my lord king," Gregory replied; "you must follow in this matter the teaching of the apostles and doctors of the church, the teaching of Hilary and Eusebius, the confession that you made at baptism." "It appears then," angrily exclaimed the king, "that Hilary and Eusebius are my declared enemies in this matter." "No," said Gregory; "neither God nor His saints are your enemies," and he proceeded to expound the orthodox doctrine of the Trinity. Chilperic was very angry. "I shall set forth my ideas to those who are wiser than you, and they will approve of them." "Never," was the answer, "it would be no wise man, but a lunatic, that would adopt such views as yours" (v. 45).

Gregory had a persistent enemy in Leudastes, count of Tours (v. 49). When removed from office because of his misdeeds, he endeavoured to take revenge on Gregory by maligning him to the king, that he was going to deliver over the city to Childebert, Sigebert's son, and finally that Gregory had spread a report of Fredegund's adultery. Chilperic summoned a council of the bishops of the kingdom at Braine, near Soissons, to investigate the charge, and it was found that the accusation rested solely on the evidence of Leudastes and Riculfus. All agreed that the witness of an inferior was not to be believed against a priest and his superior, and Gregory was acquitted on condition of solemnly disclaiming on oath all cognizance of the charge. Leudastes fled; Riculfus was condemned to death: at Gregory's intercession he was spared death, but not horrible torture (v. 48-50; *Grégoire de Tours au concile de Braine*, par S. Prioux, Paris, 1847, is a mere réchauffé of Gregory's own account of these proceedings, and of no independent critical value). The subsequent fate of Leudastes illustrates the best side of Gregory's character. After being a fugitive in different parts of Gaul, Leudastes presented himself at Tours to have his excommunication removed with a view to marrying and settling there. He brought letters from several bishops, but none from queen Fredegund, his principal enemy, and when Gregory wrote to her, she asked Gregory to postpone receiving back Leudastes into communion till further inquiry had been made. Gregory, suspicious of Fredegund's design, warned Leudastes's father-in-law, and besought him to induce Leudastes to keep quiet till Fredegund's anger was appeased. "This advice," says Gregory, "I gave sincerely, and for the love of God, but Leudastes suspected treachery, and refused to take it: so the proverb was fulfilled which I once heard an old man tell, 'Always give good counsel to friend and foe; the friend will take it, the foe will despise it.'" Leudastes went to the king to get his pardon; Chilperic was willing, but warned him to be careful till the queen's wrath was appeased. Leudastes rashly tried to force forgiveness from the queen. Fredegund was implacable and furious, and Leudastes was put to death with great cruelty. "He deserved his death," says Gregory, "for he had ever led a wicked life" (*H.* vi. 32).

During the wars that followed the death of Chilperic in 584, Touraine and Poitou desired to be subject to Childebert, Sigebert's son, *i.e.* to resume their allegiance to the Austrasian king, but were compelled to submit to Guntram, king of Orleans and Burgundy (vii. 12, 13), and under his power they remained till restored to Childebert by the treaty of Andelot in 587, in concluding which Gregory was one of Childebert's commissioners (iv. 20). Guntram died in 593. Childebert succeeded him as the treaty had provided, and the latest notice in Gregory's writings is the visit of Childebert to Orleans after Guntram's death (*Mir. S. Martin*, iv. 37). Gregory himself died Nov. 17, 594.

His activity was not confined to the general affairs of the kingdom. He was even more zealous for the welfare of his own and neighbouring dioceses. His later years were much occupied with the disturbances caused by Chrodieldis in the nunnery at Poictiers which had been founded by Gregory's friend St. Radegund. His first interference was ineffectual (ix. 39 sqq.), but the disturbance having increased, Guntram and Childebert appointed a joint commission of bishops to inquire into the matter. Gregory was one of Childebert's commissioners, but refused to enter upon the work until the civil disturbance had been actually repressed (x. 15, 16). He had a great deal of trouble also with another rebellious nun, Berthegunda (ix. 33, x. 12).

Gregory magnifies the sanctity and power of Tours's great patron St. Martin. He maintained the rights of sanctuary of the shrine in favour of the most powerful offenders, and in spite of the wrath of Chilperic and Fredegund (*e.g.* Meroveus, Guntram Boso, Ebrulfus, vii. 22, 29). He was a builder of churches in the city and see, and especially a rebuilder of the great church of St. Martin (x. 31). He did his best to arbitrate in and appease the bloody feuds of private or political partisanship (vii. 47) and was a rigorous and effectual defender of the exemption of the city from increased taxation (ix. 20). Evidently a man of unselfish earnestness and energy, he was popular with all in the city.

Gregory began to write first as bishop, his subject being the *Miracles of St. Martin.* Venantius Fortunatus in 576 alludes to the work, probably to the first two books, which, however, were not completed till 583, the third book not before 587, and the fourth was still incomplete at Gregory's death. The *Gloria Martyrum* was composed *c.* 585. Gregory wrote also the *Gloria Confessorum* (completed 588) and the *Vitae Patrum*, the latter being continued till the time of his death.

The History appears to have been written contemporaneously with the *Miracles of the Saints*, most probably in several divisions and at different times. Giesebrecht, who has carefully investigated the internal evidence, comes to the following conclusions. The History was originally written at three separate periods, and falls into three separate divisions. Bks. i.-iv. and the first half of bk. v. were probably composed *c.* 577; from the middle of bk. v. to the end of the 37th chapter of bk. viii. in 584 and 585; the remainder in 590 and 591. The last chapter of the last book is an epilogue, separately composed; for the history as a history is unfinished. Gregory would probably have carried it on at least to the death of Guntram in Mar. 593. As in the case of the books of the Miracles, Gregory appears to have revised his History, and we find in the earlier books insertions and references to Gregory's other works and to events of later date. This revision does not appear to have reached further than the end of bk. vi.; hence several MSS., and these the most ancient, contain only the first six books, and the authors of the *Hist. Epit.* and of the *Gesta Reg. Franc.* appear to have known only these. Monod substantially agrees with Giesebrecht as to the dates.

Gregory begins his History with the Creation, and his first book consists largely of extracts from Eusebius, Jerome, and Orosius (*Hist.* i. *Prol.* sub fin. cc. 34, 37). In bk. ii., which treats of the Frankish conquests, he still owes much to Orosius and to the Lives of the Saints, and quotes from Renatus Frigiderius and Sulpicius Alexander (ii. 9), two 5th-cent. writers, whose works are not extant. Thereafter he writes directly from oral tradition and authorities. Bks. iii. and iv., dealing with events down to 575, are, compared with those which follow, meagre and unchronologically arranged, giving prominence to events in Auvergne and Burgundy (Monod, p. 102). From 575 the narrative becomes fuller and more systematic, the intervals of time being regularly marked. (Giesebrecht, pp. 32-34. Monod, in his 4th chap., investigates the comparative value in different parts of the work of the documentary and oral sources of the History.)

Gregory apologizes more than once for the rudeness of his style. But rough though this might be, he was far from lacking learning or culture such as his age could afford. Though ignorant of Greek, he had a fair acquaintance with Latin authors, quoting or referring to Livy, Pliny, Cicero, Aulus Gellius, etc. (Monod, 112). He does not attempt to make his History a consistent and well-balanced whole, nor to subordinate local to general interests. The fullness of his recital of particular events depends not upon intrinsic importance but upon the amount of information he has at command. So too he follows the dramatic method, putting speeches into the mouths of individuals which are the composition of the author. Even where he depends upon written authorities he is, in detail, untrustworthy. Where he can be compared with writers now extant, as in the first two books of the History, his inaccuracy is seen to be considerable. He transcribes carelessly, and often cites from memory, giving the substance of that which he has read, and that not correctly (see instances ap. Monod, pp. 80 sqq.). Little confidence can be placed in his narrative of events outside of Gaul, and the less the farther the scene of action is removed from Gaul. His sincerity and impartiality have been attacked on various grounds: that he unduly favours the church, or that he traduces the church in his accounts of the wickedness of the bishops of the time, or that he traduces the character of the Franks (Kries, *de Gregorii Turonensis episcopi vita et scriptis*, Breslau, 1859), whether from motives of race-jealousy or any other. Gregory looks upon history as a struggle of the church against unbelief in heathen and heretics and worldly-mindedness in professing Christians. Hence he begins his History with a confession of the orthodox faith. The epithet *ecclesiastica* applied to the History from Ruinart's time is a misnomer in the modern sense, for Gregory specially defends his method of mixing things secular and religious. With a man so passionate and impressionable as Gregory, the fact of his being a priest and the bishop of the see of St. Martin, the ecclesiastical and religious centre of Gaul, does influence his feelings and actions towards individuals. But ecclesiastical prejudices did not prevent him recording events as related to him. He shews no rancour in treating of the Frankish conquerors, such as would be natural in the victim of an oppressed nationality. After the first days of the conquest there was no political subjection of Roman to Teuton as such; Romans were not excluded from offices and dignities because of their birth (pp. 101-118).

Gregory's work remains, despite all, as the great and in many respects the only authority for the history of the 6th cent., and his fresh and simple, though not unbiassed, narrative is of the greatest value. He tells us exactly what the Franks were like, and what life in Gaul was like; and he gives us the evidence upon which his judgment is founded. [T.R.B.]

Gregorius (51) I. (*The Great*), bp. of Rome from Sept. 3, 590, to Mar. 12, 604; born at Rome probably *c.* 540, of a wealthy senatorial family. The family was a religious one; his mother Silvia, and Tarsilla and Aemiliana, the two sisters of his father Gordianus, have been canonized. Under such influences his education is spoken of by his biographer, John the deacon, as having been that of a saint among saints. Gregory of Tours, his contemporary, says that in grammar, rhetoric, and logic he was accounted second to none in Rome (*Hist.* x. 1). He studied law, distinguished himself in the senate, and at an early age (certainly before 573) was recommended by the emperor Justin II. for the post of praetor urbis. After a public career of credit, his deep religious ideas suggested a higher vocation; and on his father's death he kept but a small share of the great wealth that came to him, employing the rest in charitable uses, and especially in founding monasteries, of which he endowed six in Sicily, and one, dedicated to St. Andrew, on the site of his own house near the church of SS. John and Paul at Rome. Here he himself became a monk. The date of his first retirement from the world, and its duration, are uncertain, as are also the exact dates of subsequent events previous to his accession to his see; but the most probable order of events is here followed. During his seclusion his asceticism is said to have been such as to endanger his life had he not been prevailed on by friends to abate its rigour; and it may have partly laid the foundation of his bad health in later life. Gregory Turonensis speaks of his stomach at this time being so enfeebled by fast and vigil that he could hardly stand. Benedict I., having ordained him one of the seven deacons (*regionarii*) of Rome, sent him as his apocrisiarius to Constantinople, and he was similarly employed in 579 by Benedict's successor Pelagius II. After this Gregory resided three years in Constantinople, where two noteworthy events occurred: his controversy with Eutychius, the patriarch, about the nature of the resurrection body; and the commencement of his famous work *Magna Moralia*. Recalled by Pelagius to Rome, he was allowed to return to his monastery, but was still employed as the pope's secretary. During his renewed monastic life and in his capacity of abbat he was distinguished for the strictness of his own life and the rigour of his discipline. One story which he tells leaves an impression of zeal carried to almost inhuman harshness. A monk, Julius, who had been a physician and had attended Gregory himself, night and day, during a long illness, being himself dangerously ill, confided to a brother that, in violation of monastic rule, he had three pieces of gold concealed in his cell. This confession was overheard, the cell searched, and the pieces found. Gregory forbade all to approach the offender, even in the agonies of death, and after death caused his body to be thrown on a dunghill with the pieces of gold, the monks crying aloud, "Thy money perish with thee" (Greg. *Dial.* iv. 55).

On Feb. 8, 590, Pelagius II. died, Rome being then in great straits. The Lombards were ravaging the country and threatening the city, aid being craved in vain from the distant emperor; within famine and plague were raging. Gregory was at once unanimously chosen by senate, clergy, and people to succeed Pelagius; but to him his election was distressing, and he wrote to the emperor Mauricius imploring him not to confirm it. His letter was intercepted by the prefect of Rome, and another sent, in the name of senate, clergy, and people, earnestly requesting confirmation. Before the reply of the emperor reached Rome, Gregory aroused the people to repentance by his sermons, and instituted the famous processional litany, called Litania septiformis. The emperor confirmed the election of Gregory, who fled in disguise, was brought back in triumph, conducted to the church of St. Peter, and immediately ordained on Sept. 3, 590 (Anastas. Bibliothec. and *Mortyrol. Roman.*).

After his accession he continued in heart a monk, surrounding himself with ecclesiastics instead of laymen, and living with them according to monastic rule. In accordance with this plan a synodal decree was made under him in 595, substituting clergy or monks for the boys and secular persons who had formerly waited on the pope in his chamber (*Ep.* iv. 44). Yet he rose at once to his new position. The church shared in the distress and disorganization of the time. The fires of controversy of the last two centuries still raged in the East. In Istria and Gaul the schism on the question of the Three Chapters continued; in Africa the Donatists once more became aggressive against the Catholics. Spain had but just, and as yet imperfectly, recovered from Arianism. In Gaul the church was oppressed under its barbarian rulers; in Italy, under the Arian Lombards, the clergy were infected with the demoralization of the day. The monastic system was suffering declension and was now notoriously corrupt. Literature and learning had almost died with Boëthius; and all these causes combined with temporal calamities led to a prevalent belief, which Gregory shared, that the end of all things was at hand. Nor was the position of the papacy encouraging to one who, like Gregory, took a high view of the prerogatives of St. Peter's chair. Since the recovery of Italy by Justinian (after the capture of Rome by Belisarius in 536) the popes had been far less independent than even under the Gothic kings. Justinian regarded the bishops of Rome as his creatures, to be appointed, summoned to court, and deposed at his pleasure, and subject to the commands of his exarch at Ravenna. No reigns of popes had been so inglorious as those of Gregory's immediate predecessors, Vigilius, Pelagius I., Benedict, and Pelagius II. He himself describes the Roman church as "like an old and violently shattered ship, admitting the waters on all sides, its timbers rotten, shaken by daily storms, and sounding of wreck" (*Ep.* i.).

Gregory may be regarded, first, as a spiritual ruler; secondly, as a temporal administrator and potentate; lastly, as to his personal character and as a doctor of the church.

Immediately after his accession he sent, according to custom, a confession of his faith to the patriarchs of Constantinople, Alexandria, Antioch, and Jerusalem, in which he declared his reception of the first four general councils, as of the four gospels, and his condemnation of the Three Chapters—*i.e.* the writings of three deceased prelates, Theodorus, Theodoret, and Ibas, supposed to savour of heresy, and already condemned by Justinian and by the fifth council called oecumenical. The strong language in which he exalts the authority of the four councils as "the square stone on which rests the structure of the faith, the rule of every man's actions and life, which foundation whoever does not hold is out of the building," is significant of his views on the authority of the church at large, while his recognition of the four patriarchs as coordinate potentates, to whom he sends an account of his own faith, expresses one aspect of the relation to the Eastern churches which then satisfied the Roman pontiffs. He lost no time in taking measures for the restoration of discipline, the reform of abuses, the repression of heresy, and the establishment of the authority of the Roman see, both in his own metropolitan province and wherever his influence extended. That jurisdiction was threefold—episcopal, metropolitan, and patriarchal. As bishop he had the oversight of the city; as metropolitan of the seven suffragan, afterwards called cardinal, bishops of the Roman territory, *i.e.* of Ostia, Portus, Silva Candida, Sabina, Praeneste, Tusculum, and Albanum; while his patriarchate seems to have originally extended (according to Rufinus, *H. E.* i. [x.] 6) over the suburban provinces under the civil jurisdiction of the vicarius urbis, including Upper Italy, Sicily, Sardinia, and Corsica. But being the only patriarch in the West, he had in fact claimed and exercised jurisdiction beyond these original limits, including the three other vicariates into which the prefecture of Italy was politically divided: N. Italy, with its centre at Milan, W. Illyricum, with its capital at Sirmium, and W. Africa, with its capital at Carthage. Before his accession a still wider authority had been claimed and in part acknowledged. As bishops of the old imperial city, with an acknowledged primacy of honour among the patriarchs, still more as occupants of St. Peter's chair and conservators of his doctrine, and as such consulted and appealed to by various Western churches, the popes had come to exercise a more or less defined jurisdiction over them all. The power of sending judges to hear the appeals of condemned bishops, which had been accorded to pope Julius by the Western council of Sardica in 343, had been claimed by his successors as perpetually belonging to the Roman see and extended so as to involve the summoning of cases to be heard at Rome; and a law had been obtained by Leo I. from Valentinian (445) by which the pope was made supreme head of the whole Western church, with the power of summoning prelates from all provinces to abide his judgment. On the assumption of such authority Gregory acted, being determined to abate none of the rights claimed by his predecessors.

In the year of his accession (590) he endeavoured, though without result, to bring over the Istrian bishops, who still refused to condemn the Three Chapters. With this view he appointed a council to meet at Rome, and obtained an order from the emperor for the attendance of these bishops. They petitioned for exemption, saying that their faith was that formerly taught them by pope Vigilius, and protesting against submission to the bp. of Rome as their judge. The emperor countermanded the order, and Gregory acquiesced.

In 591 his orthodox zeal was directed with more success against the African Donatists. It was the custom in Numidia for the senior bishop, whether Donatist or Catholic, to exercise metropolitan authority over the other bishops. Such senior now happened to be a Donatist, and he assumed the customary authority. Gregory wrote to the Catholic bishops of Numidia, and to Gennadius, exarch of Africa, urging them to resist such a claim (*Ep.* i. 74, 75), and the Donatist bishop was deposed, but the sect continued in Africa as long as Christianity did. This is not the only instance of Gregory, like others of his age, not being averse to persecution as a means of conversion. In Sicily he enjoined rigorous measures (*summopere persequi*) for the recovery of the Manicheans to the church (*Ep.* iv. 6); there, and in Corsica, Sardinia, and Campania, the heathen peasants and slaves on the papal estates were by his order compelled to conform, not only by exactions on such as refused, but also by the imprisonment of freemen, and the corporal castigation (*verberibus et cruciatibus*) of slaves (*Ep.* iii. 26; vii. ind. ii. 67), and in France he exhorted queen Brunichild to similar measures of coercion (*Ep.* vii. 5). On the other hand, there are three letters of his, written in the same year as those about the African Donatists, which evince a spirit of unusual toleration towards Jews. They are addressed to three bishops, Peter of Tarracina, Virgilius of Arles, and Theodorus of Marseilles. The first had driven the Jews from their synagogues, and the last two had converted a number by offering them the choice of baptism or exile. Gregory strongly condemns such proceedings, "because conversions wrought by force are never sincere, and those thus converted seldom fail to return to their vomit when the force is removed." (*Ep.* i. 34, i. 45; cf. *Ep.* vii. ind. i. 26, vii. ind. ii. 5, vii. 2, 59.) Yet he had no objection to luring them into the fold by the prospect of advantage, for in a letter to a deacon Cyprian, who was steward of the papal patrimony in Sicily, he directs him to offer the Jews a remission of one-third of the taxes due to the Roman church if they became Christians, saying, in justification, that though such conversions might be insincere, their children would be brought up in the bosom of the church (*Ep.* iv. 6, cf. *Ep.* xii. 30). In such apparent inconsistencies we may see his good sense and Christian benevolence in conflict with the impulses of zeal and the notions of his age.

Gregory was no less active in reforming the church itself. Great laxity was prevalent among the monks, of which the life of Benedict, the founder of the Benedictine order, affords ample evidence. Several of Gregory's letters are addressed to monks who had left their monasteries for the world and marriage. He issued the following regulations for the restoration of monastic discipline: no monk should be received under 18 years of age, nor any husband without his wife's consent (in one case he orders a husband who had entered a monastery to be restored to his wife [*Ep.* ix. 44]); two years of probation should always be required, and three in the case of soldiers; a professed monk leaving his order should be immured for life; no monk, though an abbat, should leave the precincts of his monastery, except on urgent occasions; under no pretext should any monk leave his monastery alone, on the ground that "Qui sine teste ambulat non rectè vivit." He provided for the more complete separation of the monastic and clerical orders, forbidding any monk to remain in his monastery after ordination, and any priest to enter a monastery except to exercise clerical functions, or to become a monk without giving up his clerical office; and further exempting some monasteries from the jurisdiction of bishops. This last important provision was extended to all monasteries by the Lateran synod, held under him in 601.

He was no less zealous in his correction of the clergy. Several bishops under his immediate metropolitan jurisdiction and elsewhere he rebuked or deposed for incontinency and other crimes. His own nuncio at Constantinople, Laurentius the archdeacon, he recalled and deposed. From the clergy generally he required strict chastity, forbidding them to retain in their houses any women but their mothers, sisters, or wives married before ordination, and with these last prohibiting conjugal intercourse (*Ep.* i. 50, ix. 64). Bishops he recommends to imitate St. Augustine in banishing from their houses even such female relatives as the canons allow (*Ep.* vii. ind. ii. 39; xi. 42, 43). In Sicily the obligation to celibacy had, in 588, been extended to subdeacons. This rule he upheld by directing the bishops to require a vow of celibacy from all who should in future be ordained subdeacons, but acknowledging its hardship on such as had made no such vow on their ordination, he contented himself with forbidding the advancement to the diaconate of existing subdeacons who had continued conjugal intercourse after the introduction of the rule (*Ep.* i. ind. ix. 42).

He also set himself resolutely against the prevalent simony, forbidding all bishops and clergy to exact or accept fee or reward for the functions of their office; and he set the example himself by refusing the annual presents which it had been customary for the bishops of Rome to receive from their suffragans, or payment for the pallium sent to metropolitans, which payment was forbidden to all future popes by a Roman synod in 595.

In 592 began a struggle in reference to discipline with certain bishops of Thessaly and Dalmatia, in the province of Illyricum. Hadrianus of Thebes had been deposed by a provincial synod under his metropolitan the bp. of Larissa, and the sentence had been confirmed by John of Justiniana Prima, the primate of Illyricum. The deposed prelate appealed to Gregory, who, after examining the whole case, ordered the primate to reinstate Hadrianus (*Ep.* ii. ind. xi. 6, 7). He also ordered Natalis, bp. of Salona in Dalmatia and metropolitan, under pain of excommunication, to reinstate his archdeacon Honoratus whom he had deposed (*Ep.* ii. ind. x. 14, 15, 16). In both instances he appears to have been obeyed. Not so, however, in the case of Maximus, who succeeded Natalis as bp. of Salona and metropolitan in the same year. Maximus having been elected in opposition to Honoratus, whom Gregory had recommended, the latter disallowed the election, and wrote to the clergy of Salona forbidding them to choose a bishop without the consent of the apostolic see. Meanwhile the emperor had confirmed the election. After protracted negotiations, lasting 7 years, during which 17 letters were written by Gregory, the emperor committed the settlement of the dispute to Maximianus, bp. of Ravenna, with the result that Maximus, having publicly begged pardon of the pope and cleared himself from the charge of simony by an oath of purgation at the tomb of St. Apollinaris, was at last acknowledged as lawful bp. of Salona (*Ep.* iii. ind. xii. 15, 20; iv. ind. xiii. 34; v. ind. xiv. 3; vi. ind. xv. 17; vii. ind. i. 1; vii. ind. ii. 81, 82, 83). In the West beyond the limits of the empire Gregory also lost no opportunity of extending the influence of his see and of advancing and consolidating the church. Reccared, the Visigothic king of Spain, renounced Arianism for Catholicism at the council of Toledo in 589, and Gregory heard of this from Leander, bp. of Seville, whom he exhorted to watch over the royal convert. He sent Leander a pallium to be used at mass only. He wrote to Reccared in warm congratulation, exhorting him to humility, chastity, and mercy; thanking him for presents received, and sending in return a key from the body of St. Peter, in which was some iron from the chain that had bound him, and a cross containing a piece of the true cross, and some hairs of John the Baptist (*Canones Eccles. Hispan.*). There is no distinct assumption, in these letters, of jurisdiction over the Spanish church, and this is the only known instance of a pallium having been sent to Spain previously to the Saracen invasion. The ancient Spanish church does not seem to have been noted for its dependence on the Roman see (see Geddes, *Tracts*, vol. ii. pp. 25, 49; Gieseler, *Eccles. Hist.* vol. ii. p. 188). With the Frank rulers of Gaul Gregory carefully cultivated friendly relations. In 595, at the request of king Childeric, he conferred the pallium on Virgilius of Arles, the ancient metropolitan see, whose bishop pope Zosimus had confirmed in his metropolitan right, and made vicar as early as 417. Not long after Gregory began a correspondence with queen Brunichild, in which he exhorts her to use her power for the correction of the vices of the clergy and the conversion of the heathen. Another royal female correspondent, cultivated and flattered with a similar purpose, and one more worthy of the praise conferred, was Theodelinda the Lombard queen. To 599 is assigned the extensive conversion of the Lombards to Catholicism, brought about after the death of king Antharis through the marriage of this Theodelinda, his widow, with Agilulph duke of Turin, who consequently succeeded to the throne. With this pious lady, a zealous Catholic, Gregory kept up a highly complimentary correspondence, sending her also a copy of his four books of dialogues.

Over the church in Ireland, then bound by no close tie of allegiance to the see of Rome, he endeavoured to extend his influence, writing in 592 a long letter to the bishops.

Not content with thus influencing, consolidating, and reforming the existing churches throughout the West, he was also a zealous missionary, and as such the founder of our English, as distinct from the more ancient British, Christianity. [AUGUSTINE.]

Of his relations with Constantinople and the Eastern church, the year 593 affords the first example. Having heard of two presbyters, John of Chalcedon and Anastasius of Isauria, being beaten with cudgels, after conviction on a charge of heresy, under John the Faster, then patriarch of Constantinople, Gregory wrote twice to the patriarch, remonstrating with him for introducing a new and uncanonical punishment, exhorting him to restore the two presbyters or to judge them canonically, and expressing his own readiness to receive them at Rome. Notwithstanding the patriarch's protest, the presbyters thereupon withdrew to Rome and were received and absolved by Gregory after examination (*Ep.* ii. 52, v. 64). In other letters we find him saying, "With respect to the Constantinopolitan church, who doubts that it is subject to the apostolical see?" and "I know not what bishop is not subject to it, if fault is found in him" (*Ep.* vii. ind. ii. 64, 65). But the most memorable incidents in this connexion are his remonstrances against the assumption by John the Faster of the title of oecumenical or universal bishop. They began in 595, being provoked by the repeated occurrence of the title in a judgment against an heretical presbyter which had been sent to Rome. The title was not new. Patriarchs had been so styled by the emperors Leo and Justinian, and it had been confirmed to John the Faster and his successors by a general Eastern synod at Constantinople in 588, pope Pelagius protesting against it. Gregory now wrote to Sabinianus, his apocrisiarius at Constantinople, desiring him to use his utmost endeavours with the patriarch, the emperor, and the empress, to procure the renunciation of the title; and when this failed, he himself wrote to all these in peculiarly strong language. The title he called foolish, proud, pestiferous, profane, wicked, a diabolical usurpation; the ambition of any who assumed it was like that of Lucifer, and its assumption a sign of the approach of the king of pride, *i.e.* Antichrist. His arguments are such as to preclude himself as well as others from assuming the title, though he implies that if any could claim it it would be St. Peter's successors. Peter, he says, was the first of the apostles, yet neither he nor any of the others would assume the title universal, being all members of the church under one head, Christ. He also states (probably in error) that the title had been offered to the bp. of Rome at the council of Chalcedon, and refused. Failing entirely to make an impression at Constantinople, he addressed himself to the Eastern patriarchs. He wrote to Eulogius of Alexandria and Anastasius of Antioch, representing the purpose of their brother of Constantinople as being that of degrading them, and usurping to himself all ecclesiastical power. They, however, were not thus moved to action; they seem to have regarded the title as one of honour only, suitable to the patriarch of the imperial city; and one of them, Anastasius, wrote in reply that the matter seemed to him of little moment. The controversy continued after the death of John the Faster. Gregory instructed his apocrisiarius at Constantinople to demand from the new patriarch, Cyriacus, as a condition of intercommunion, the renunciation of the proud and impious title which his predecessor had wickedly assumed. In vain did Cyriacus send a nuncio to Rome in the hope of arranging matters: Gregory was resolute, and wrote, "I confidently say that whosoever calls himself universal priest, or desires to be so called in his elation, is the forerunner of Antichrist." At this time he seems to have gained a supporter, if not to his protest, at any rate to the paramount dignity of his own see, in Eulogius of Alexandria, whom he had before addressed without result. For in answering a letter from that patriarch, he acknowledges with approval the dignity assigned by him to the see of St. Peter, and expresses adroitly a curious view of his correspondent, as well as the patriarch of Antioch, being a sharer in it. "Who does not know," he says, "that the church was built and established on the firmness of the prince of the apostles, by whose very name is implied a rock? Hence, though there were several apostles, there is but one apostolic see, that of the prince of the apostles, which has acquired great authority; and that see is in three places, in Rome where he died, in Alexandria where it was founded by his disciple St. Mark, and in Antioch where he himself lived seven years. These three, therefore, are but one see, and on that one see sit three bishops, who are but one in Him Who said, I am in My Father, and you in Me, and I in you." But when Eulogius in a second letter styled the bp. of Rome universal pope, Gregory warmly rejected such a title, saying, "If you give more to me than is due to me, you rob yourself of what is due to you. Nothing can redound to my honour that redounds to the dishonour of my brethren. If you call me universal pope, you thereby own yourself to be no pope. Let no such titles be mentioned or ever heard among us." Gregory was obliged at last to acquiesce in the assumption of the obnoxious title by the Constantinopolitan patriarch; and it may have been by way of contrast that he usually styled himself in his own letters by the title since borne by the bps. of Rome, "Servus servorum Dei." Evidently Gregory and his opponents took different views of the import of the title contended for. They represented it as one simply of honour and dignity, while he regarded it as involving the assumption of supreme authority over the church at large, and especially over the see of St. Peter, whence probably in a great measure the vehemence of his remonstrance. In the different views taken appears the difference of principle on which pre-eminence was in that age thought assignable to sees in the East and West respectively. In the East the dignity of a see was regarded as an appanage of a city's civil importance, on which ground alone could any pre-eminence be claimed for Constantinople. In the West it was the apostolical origin of the see, and the purely ecclesiastical pre-eminence belonging to it from ancient times, to which especial regard was paid. Thus viewed, the struggle of Gregory for the dignity of his own see against that of Constantinople assumes importance as a protest against the Erastianism of the East. It certainly would not have been well for the church had the spiritual authority of the bps. of Rome accrued to the subservient patriarchs of the Eastern capital.

As a temporal administrator and potentate Gregory evinced equally great vigour, ability, and zeal, guided by address and judgment. The see of Rome had large possessions, constituting what was called the patrimony of St. Peter, in Italy, Sardinia, and Corsica, and also in more remote parts, *e.g.* Dalmatia, Illyricum, Gaul, and even Africa and the East. Over these estates Gregory exercised a vigilant superintendence by means of officers called "rectores patrimonii" and "defensores," to whom his letters remain, prescribing minute regulations for the management of the lands, and guarding especially against any oppression of the peasants. The revenues accruing to the see, thus carefully secured, though with every possible regard to humanity and justice, were expended according to the fourfold division then prevalent in the West—viz. in equal parts for the bishop, the clergy, the fabric and services of the church, and the poor. This distribution, publicly made four times a year, Gregory personally superintended. His own charities were immense, a large portion of the population of Rome being dependent on them: every day, before his own meal, a portion was sent to the poor at his door; the sick and infirm in every street were sought out; and a large volume was kept containing the names, ages, and dwellings of the objects of his bounty.

A field for the exercise of his political abilities was afforded by his position as virtual ruler of Rome at that critical time. His letters and homilies gave a lamentable account of the miseries of the country, and he endeavoured to conclude a peace between Agilulph, the Lombard king, who was himself disposed to come to terms, and the exarch Romanus. These endeavours were frustrated by the opposition of Romanus, who represented Gregory to the emperor as having been overreached by the crafty enemy. The emperor believed his exarch, and wrote to Gregory in condemnation of his conduct. In vain did Gregory remonstrate in letters both to the emperor and to the empress Constantina, complaining to the latter not so much of the ravages of the Lombards as of the cruelty and exactions of the imperial officers; but though small success crowned his efforts, whatever mitigation of distress was accomplished was due to him.

In 601 an event occurred which shews Gregory in a less favourable light, with respect to his relations to the powers of the world than anything else during his career. Phocas, a centurion, was made emperor by the army.

He secured his throne by the murder of Mauricius, whose six sons had been first cruelly executed before their father's eyes. He afterwards put to death the empress Constantina and her three daughters, who had been lured out of the asylum of a church under a promise of safety. Numerous persons of all ranks and in various parts of the empire are also said to have been put to death with unusual cruelty. To Phocas and his consort Leontia, who is spoken of as little better than her husband, Gregory wrote congratulatory letters in a style of flattery beyond even what was usual with him in addressing great potentates (*Ep.* xi. ind. vi. 38, 45, 46). His motive was doubtless largely the hope of obtaining from the new powers the support which Mauricius had not accorded him in his dispute with the Eastern patriarch. This motive appears plainly in one of his letters to Leontia, to whom, rather than to the emperor, with characteristic tact, he intimates his hopes of support to the church of St. Peter, endeavouring to work upon her religious fears.

Gregory lived only 16 months after the accession of Phocas, dying after protracted suffering from gout on Mar. 12, 604. He was buried in the basilica of St. Peter.

Immediately after his death a famine occurred, which the starving multitude attributed to his prodigal expenditure, and his library was only saved from destruction by the interposition of the archdeacon Peter.

The pontificate of Gregory the Great is rightly regarded as second to none in its influence on the future form of Western Christianity. He lived in the period of transition from Christendom under imperial rule to the medieval papacy, and he laid or consolidated the foundation of the latter. He advanced, indeed, no claims to authority beyond what had been asserted by his predecessors; yet the consistency, firmness, conscientious zeal, as well as address and judgment, with which he maintained it, and the waning of the power of the Eastern empire, left him virtual ruler of Rome and the sole power to whom the Western church turned for support, and whom the Christianized barbarians, founders of the new kingdom of Europe, regarded with reverence. Thus he paved the way for the system of papal absolutism that culminated under Gregory VII. and Innocent III.

As a writer he was intellectually eminent; and deserves his place among the doctors of the church, though his learning and mental attitude were those of his age. As a critic, an expositor, an original thinker, he may not stand high; he knew neither Greek nor Hebrew, and had no deep acquaintance with the Christian Fathers; literature for its own sake he set little store by; classical literature, as being heathen, he repudiated. Yet as a clear and powerful exponent of the received orthodox doctrine, especially in its practical aspect, as well as of the system of hagiology, demonology, and monastic asceticism, which then formed part of the religion of Christendom, he spoke with a loud and influential voice to many ages after his own, and contributed more than any one person to fix the form and tone of medieval religious thought.

He was also influential as a preacher, and no less famous for his influence on the music and liturgy of the church; whence he is called "magister caeremoniarum." To cultivate church singing he instituted a song-school in Rome, called *Orphanotrophium*, the name of which implies also a charitable purpose. Of it, John the deacon, after speaking of the cento of antiphons which Gregory had carefully compiled, says: "He founded a school of singers, endowed it with some farms, and built for it two habitations, one under the steps of the basilica of St. Peter the Apostle, the other under the houses of the Lateran Palace. There to the present day his couch on which he used to recline when singing, and his whip with which he menaced the boys, together with his original antiphonary, are preserved with fitting reverence" (*Vit. Greg.* ii. 6). It is generally alleged that, whereas St. Ambrose had in the latter part of the 4th cent. introduced at Milan the four authentic modes or scales, called, after those of the ancient Greek music, Dorian, Phrygian, Lydian, Mixo-Lydian, St. Gregory added to them the four plagal, or subsidiary, modes called Hypo-Dorian, Hypo-Phrygian, Hypo-Lydian, and Hypo-Mixo-Lydian, thus enlarging the allowed range of ecclesiastical melody.

His Septiform litany was so called from being appointed by him to be sung by the inhabitants of Rome divided into seven companies, viz. of clergy, laymen, monks, virgins, matrons, widows, and of poor people and children. These, starting from 7 different churches, were to chant through the streets of Rome, and meet for common supplication in the church of the Blessed Virgin. He also appointed "the stations"—churches at which were to be held solemn services in Lent and at the four great festivals; visiting the churches in person, and being received with stately ceremonial.

His extant works of undoubted genuineness are: (1) *Expositio in beatum Job, seu Moralium* lib. xxxv. In this celebrated work (begun at Constantinople before he was pope and finished afterwards) "the book of Job is expounded in a threefold manner, according to its historic, its moral, and its allegorical meaning. The moral interpretation may still be read with profit, though rather for the loftiness and purity of its tone than for the justness of the exposition." As to the allegorical interpretation, "names of persons, numbers, words, even syllables, are made pregnant with all kinds of mysterious meanings" (Milman, *Hist. of Latin Christianity*). (2) *Libri duo in Ezechielem*: viz. 22 homilies on Ezekiel, delivered at Rome during its siege by Agilulph. (3) *Libri duo in Evangelia*: viz. 40 homilies on the gospels for the day, preached at various times. (4) *Liber Regulae Pastoralis*, in 4 parts; a treatise on the pastoral office, addressed to a bp. John to explain and justify the writer's former reluctance to undertake the burden of the popedom. This work was long held in the highest esteem. Leander of Seville circulated it in Spain; the emperor Mauricius had it translated into Greek; Alfred the Great translated it into English; a succession of synods in Gaul enjoined a knowledge of it on all bishops; and Hincmar, archbp. of Rheims in the 9th cent., says that a copy of it was delivered, together with the book of canons, to bishops at their ordination, with a charge to them to frame their lives according to its precepts (*in Praefatione Opusculi* 55 *Capitulorum*). (5) *Dialogorum libri IV. de vita et miraculis patrum Italicorum, et de aeternitate animae*. The authenticity of this work has been doubted; apparently without adequate grounds. It is written in the form of dialogues with the archdeacon Peter, and contains accounts of saintly persons, prominent among whom is Benedict of Nursia, the contemporary founder of the Benedictine order. It abounds in marvels, and relates visions of the state of departed souls, which have been a main support, if not a principal foundation, of the medieval doctrine about purgatory. The *Dialogues* were translated into Anglo-Saxon by order of Alfred (Asser. *Gest. Alf.* in *Mon. Hist. Brit.* 486 E). (6) *Registrum Epistolarum*, in 14 books, of which the 13th is wanting; a very varied collection of 838 letters to persons of all ranks, which gives a vivid idea of his unwearied activity, the multifariousness of his engagements and interests, his address, judgment, and versatility. (7) *Liber Sacramentorum*. This, the famous Gregorian Sacramentary, was an abbreviated arrangement in one vol., with some alterations and additions, of the sacramentary of pope Gelasius, which again had been founded on an older one attributed to pope Leo I. John the deacon says of Gregory's work, "Sed et Gelasianum codicem, de Missarum solemniis multa subtrahens, pauca convertens, nonnulla superadjiciens, in unius libelli volumine coarctavit" (Joann. Diac. *in Vit. Greg.* ii. 17; cf. Bede, *H. E.* ii. 1). The changes made by Gregory were principally in the Missae, or variable offices for particular days; in the *Ordo Missae* itself only two alterations are spoken of as made by him, viz. to the part of the canon beginning, "Hanc igitur oblationem," he added the words, "Diesque nostros in tua pace disponas, atque ab aeterna damnatione eripi et in electorum tuorum jubeas grege numerari"; and the transference of the Lord's Prayer from after the breaking of bread to its present place in the canon (*Ep. ad Joann. Syrac.* lib. ix. *Ep.* 12). Whatever uncertainty there may be as to the original text of Gregory's sacramentary as a whole, it is considered certain that the present Roman canon and, except for certain subsequent additions, the ordinarium are the same as what he left. [SACRAMENTARY in *D. C. A.*] (8) *Liber Antiphonarius*, a collection of antiphons for mass. To what extent this was original, or how far it may have been altered since Gregory's time, is uncertain.

Of the following works attributed to Gregory, the genuineness is doubtful: (1) *Liber Benedictionum*; (2) *Liber Responsalis seu Antiphonarius*; (3) *Expositiones in librum I. Regum*; (4) *Expositiones super Canticum Canticorum*; (5) *Expositio in* vii. *Pss. Paenitentiales*; (6) *Concordia quorundam testimoniorum sacrae Scripturae*. There are also 9 hymns attributed to him with probability.

Of his personal appearance an idea may be formed from a description given by John the deacon of a portrait preserved to his own day (9th cent.) in St. Andrew's monastery, "in absidicula post fratrum cellarium"; which he concludes to have been painted during the pope's life and by his order. That this was the case is inferred from the head being surmounted, not by a *corona*, but by a *tabula* ("tabulae similitudinem"), which John says is the mark of a living person, and by the appended inscription:

> "Christe potens Domine, nostri largitor honoris
> Indultum officium solita pietate guberna."

The figure is of ordinary size, and well formed; the face "most becomingly prolonged with a certain rotundity"; the beard of moderate size and somewhat tawny; in the middle of his otherwise bald forehead are two neat little curls twisting towards the right; the crown of the head is round and large; dark hair, decently curled, hangs under the middle of the ear; he has a fine forehead; his eyebrows are long and elevated, but slender; the pupils of the eyes are of a yellow tinge, not large, but open, and the under-eyelids are full; the nose is slender as it curves down from the eyebrows, broader about the middle, then slightly curved, and expanding at the nostrils; the mouth is ruddy; the lips thick and subdivided; the cheeks regular ("compositae"); the chin rather prominent from the confines of the jaws; the complexion was "aquilinus et lividus" (*al.* "vividus"), not "cardiacus," as it became afterwards, *i.e.* he had in the picture a dark but fresh complexion, though in later life it acquired an unhealthy hue. (See Du Cange for the probable meaning of the words.) His countenance is mild; his hands good, with taper fingers, well adapted for writing. The dress he wears is of interest—a chestnut-coloured *planeta* over a *dalmatica*, which is precisely the same dress as that in which his father is depicted, and therefore not then a peculiarly sacerdotal costume. [GORDIANUS.] He is distinguished from his father by the *pallium*, the then form and mode of wearing which are intimated by the description. It is brought from the left shoulder so as to hang carelessly under the breast, and, passing over the right shoulder, is deposited behind the back, the other end being carried straight behind the neck also to the right shoulder, from which it hangs down the side. In the left hand is a book of the Gospels; the right is in the attitude of making the sign of the cross (Joann. Diac. *in Vit. Greg.* l. 4, c. 83). John describes also his *pallium*, woven of white linen and with no marks of the needle in it; his phylactery (or case for relics), of thin silver, and hung from the neck by crimson cloth, and his belt ("baltheus"), only a thumb's breadth wide—which, he says, were preserved and venerated on the saint's anniversary, and which he refers to as shewing the monastic simplicity of Gregory's attire (*ib.* c. 8).

Our chief authorities for the Life of Gregory are his own writings, especially his letters, of which a trans. (*Selecta Epp.*) is in *Lib. of Post.-Nic. Fathers*. Among ancient writers Gregory of Tours (his contemporary), Bede, Paul Warnefried (730), Ado Trevirensis (1070), Simeon Metaphrastes (1300), Isidorus Hispalensis, have detailed notices of him.

Paul the deacon in the 8th cent., and John the deacon, a monk of Cassino, in the 9th cent., wrote Lives of him (Greg. *Op.* ed. Benedict). The Benedictine ed. of his works has a fuller Life, using additional sources. An important work on *Gregory the Great, his Place in Thought and History*, was pub. by the Rev. F. H. Dudden, in two vols. 4to, 1905 (Lond., Longmans). A cheap popular Life by the author of this art. is pub. by S.P.C.K. in their *Fathers for Eng. Readers*; see also a monograph on *Pope Gregory the Great and his Relation with Gaul*, by F. W. Kellett (Camb. Univ. Press). [J.B—Y.]

Gundobald, 4th king of the Burgundians (Greg. Tur. *Hist. Franc.* ii. 28). The kingdom of the Burgundians, which extended from the Vosges to the Durance and from the Alps to the Loire, was divided between Gundobald and his surviving brother Godegiselus, the former having Lyons for his capital, the latter Geneva (Greg. Tur. *Hist. Franc.* ii. 32; Ennodius, *Vita S. Epiphanii*, 50-54; Boll. Jan. ii. 374-375; cf. Mascou, *Hist. of the Ancient Germans*, xi. 10, 31, and Annotation iv.). In 500 Clovis, who had married Gundobald's niece, defeated Gundobald at Dijon, with the aid of Godegiselus who fought against his brother, and imposed a tribute. But on Clovis's departure he renounced his allegiance, and besieged and killed his brother, who had triumphantly entered Vienne. Henceforth till his death he ruled the whole Burgundian territory (Marius Avent. *Chron.*, Migne, *Patr. Lat.* lxxii. 795, 796; Greg. Tur. ii. 32, 33; *Epitomata*, xxii.-xxiv.; Richter, *Annalen*, 37, 38). About this time was held under his presidency at Lyons a conference between the Catholics, led by Avitus, and the Arians, led by Boniface. According to the Catholic account of it which survives, the heretics were utterly confounded. The narrative is in the *Spicilegium*, iii. 304 (Paris, 1723), Mansi, viii. 242, and excerpta from it in *Patr. Lat.* lxxi. 1154. Gundobald died in 516, leaving his son, the Catholic Sigismund, as his successor.

In spite of the unfavourable testimony of Catholic writers, there are many indications that Gundobald was for his time an enlightened and humane king. The wisdom and equity of his government are evidenced by the *Loi Gombette*, the Burgundian code, called after him, which, though probably not taking its present shape entirely till his son's reign, was enacted by him. Its provisions in favour of the Roman, or old Gallic inhabitants, whom in most respects it put on an equality with the conquerors, entitles it to be called the best barbarian code which had yet appeared (Greg. Tur. ii. 33; *Hist. lit. de la France*, iii. 83 sqq.; *L'Art de vérifier les dates*, x. 365, Paris, 1818). For the code see Bouquet, iv. 257 seq., and Pertz, *Leges*, iii. 497 seq.

Though he professed Arianism, Gundobald did not persecute, but secured the Catholics in the possession of their endowments, as Avitus testifies (*Ep.* xxxix. *Patr. Lat.* lix. 256). The circumstances relied on by Revillout (*De l'Arianisme des peuples germaniques*, 180, 181), who takes the opposite view, are trivial, compared with the testimony of Avitus and the silence of Gregory. Gundobald's whole correspondence with Avitus and the conference of Lyons demonstrate the interest he took in religious subjects and his tolerance of orthodoxy. Several of the bishop's letters survive, answering inquiries on various points of doctrine, *e.g.* the Eutychian heresy (*Epp.* 3 and 4), repentance *in articulo mortis*, and justification by faith or works (*Ep.* 5). One only of Gundobald's remains (*Ep.* 19), asking an explanation of Is. ii. 3-5, and Mic. iv. 4. These letters are in Migne, *Patr. Lat.* lix. 199, 202, 210, 219, 223, 236, 244, 255, and commented on in Ceillier's *Hist. générale des auteurs sacrés*, x. 554 sqq. He probably died an Arian. According to Gregory, he was convinced and begged Avitus to baptize him in secret, fearing his subjects; but Avitus refused, and he perished in his heresy (*Hist. Franc.* ii. 34, cf. iii. prologue). But there are two passages in Avitus's letters (*Ep.* v. sub fin. *Patr. Lat.* lix. 224, "Unde cum laetitiam—orbitatem," and *Ep.* ii. sub init. *Patr. Lat.* lix. 202, "Unicum simul—principaliter de tuenda catholicae partis veritate curetis") which seem almost to imply that he was then a Catholic. See too Gregory's story of the piety of his queen (*de Mirac. S. Juliani*, ii. 8). [S.A.B.]

Guntramnus (2) (*Guntchramnus, Gunthrannus, Gontran*), St., king of Burgundy, son of Clotaire I. and Ingundis (Greg. Tur. *Hist. Franc.* iv. 3). Upon his father's death in 561, the kingdom was divided by lot between the three sons. Guntram had the kingdom of Burgundy, which then extended from the Vosges to the Durance, and from the Alps to the Loire. Orleans was his nominal capital, but his ordinary residence was at Châlon-sur-Saône (iv. 21, 22). His pacific and unenterprising disposition made his reign uneventful. He died in 593, in the 33rd year of his reign, on Mar. 28, on which day the martyrologies commemorate him as a saint, and was buried in the monastery church of St. Marcellus, his own foundation at Châlons.

Though the church has canonized Guntram, it is perhaps doubtful whether his virtues would stand out brightly on any other background than the utter darkness of Merovingian times. His chief merit seems to have been the avoidance of the terrible excesses which characterized some of his family, and this was perhaps as much due to the feebleness of his nature as to any positive inclination towards well-doing. Even his clerical eulogists admit that as regards women his morals were by no means scrupulous (Aimoin, iii. 3, *Patr. Lat.* cxxxix. 693). When provocation or panic was absent he was mild, and even merciful, but on occasion he readily committed the barbarities of his age. The merest suspicion or accusation connected with his personal safety sufficed to throw him into a panic, when torture was freely applied to obtain confessions. Assassination was the haunting fear of his life, and he always wore arms and continually strengthened the escort which attended him everywhere, except in church (vii. 8, 18, viii. 11, 44). His apprehension at times was almost comic. Gregory tells us that one Sunday at church in Paris, when the deacon had enjoined silence for the mass, Guntram turned to the people and said, "I beseech you, men and women who are present, do not break your faith to me, but forbear to kill me as you killed my brothers. At least let me live three years, that I may rear up the nephews whom I have adopted, lest mayhap, which God forbid, you perish together with those little ones when I am dead, and there is no strong man of our race to defend you" (vii. 8, cf. Michelet, *Hist. de France*, i. 231, "Ce bon homme semble chargé de la partie comique dans le drame terrible de l'histoire mérovingienne").

On the other hand, mere abstinence from wanton wrong-doing and aggression must be counted for a virtue in his family and age. For the crowning evil of the time, the incessant civil wars which devastated France, he was in no way responsible. Though frequently in combat, it was always to repel the aggression of others, except in his Gothic wars, which he probably regarded as crusades against heretics. The profuse almsgiving which he practised (*e.g.* vii. 40) shewed a real, if mistaken, desire for the good of his subjects.

But it was his warm friendship to the church and clergy which procured him the rank of a saint. St. Benignus of Dijon, St. Symphorian of Autun, and St. Marcellus of Châlon-sur-Saône were founded or enriched by him, and in the last he established and provided for perpetual psalmody after the model of St. Sigismund's foundation at St. Maurice (Fredegar. *Chron.* xv.; Aimoin, *Hist. Franc.* iii. 81, *Patr. Lat.* cxxxix. 751). Bishops were his constant advisers, and his favourite solution of all complications was an episcopal council (Greg. Tur. v. 28; vii. 16; viii. 13, 20, 27). He commended himself to them also by his respect for church ceremonies and his frequent and regular attendance at religious services, and especially by his freedom and condescension in eating, drinking, and conversing with them (vii. 29; viii. 1-7, 9, 10; ix. 3, 20, 21; x. 28). Gregory says, "You would have thought him a priest as well as a king" (ix. 21). "With priests he was like a priest," says Fredegarius (*Chron.* i.), and "he shewed himself humble to the priests of Christ," says Aimoin (*u.s.*). Chilperic once intercepted the letter of a bishop, in which it was written that the transition from Guntram's sway to his was like passing from paradise to hell (Greg. Tur. vi. 22). In estimating Guntram's character, therefore, we must always remember that our information comes from this favoured class. Especially does this apply to Gregory of Tours, who was on very friendly terms with him (viii. 2-7, 13; ix. 20, 21), and who ascribes miracles to his sanctity during his lifetime (ix. 21; cf. too Paulus Diaconus, *de Gest. Langob.* iii. 33, Migne, *Patr. Lat.* xcv. 535, and Aimoin. iii. 3, *Patr. Lat.* cxxxix. 693). There is extant an edict of Guntram addressed to the bishops and judges commanding the observance of the Sabbath and holy days, in conformity with the canon of the 2nd council of Mâcon. It is dated Nov. 10, 585, and is in Mansi, ix. 962, and Boll. *Acta SS.* Mar. iii. 720; cf. *Hist. lit. de la France*, iii. 369 seq.). [S.A.B.]

H

Habibus (2) (*Abibus*), deacon, martyr at Edessa in the reign of Licinius; mentioned in the Basilian *Menologium*, Nov. 15, with the martyrs Gurias and Samonas, in whose tomb he was laid; at Dec. 2 he has a separate notice. Simeon Metaphrastes in his lengthened account of those two martyrs (the Lat. in Surius, *de Prob. Hist. SS.* Nov. 15, p. 342, the Lat. and Gk. in *Patr. Gk.* cxvi. 141) similarly embodies the history of Habib. Assemani notices him in his *Bibl. Orient.* (i. 330, 331) from Metaphrastes, but not in his *Acta Martyrum.* The original Syriac account of Habib which Metaphrastes abridged has been discovered, and was ed. in 1864 by Dr. Wright with a trans. by Dr. Cureton (*Ancient Syriac Documents*, p. 72, notes p. 187). The Syrian author, whose name was Theophilus, professes to have been an eyewitness of the martyrdom (which he places on Sept. 2) and a convert. The ancient *Syrian Martyrology*, another discovery trans. by Dr. Wright (*Journ. Sac. Lit.* 1866, p. 429), likewise commemorates Habib on Sept. 2. Theophilus says that in the month Ab (*i.e.* Aug.) in the year 620 of the kingdom of Alexander of Macedon, in the consulate of Licinius and Constantine, in the days of Conon, bp. of Edessa, the emperor commanded the altars of the gods to be everywhere repaired, sacrifices and libations offered and incense burnt to Jupiter. Habib, a deacon of the village of Telzeha, went privately among the churches and villages encouraging the Christians not to comply. The Christians were more numerous than their persecutors, and word reached Edessa that even Constantine "in Gaul and Spain" had become Christian and did not sacrifice. Habib's proceedings were reported to Licinius, who sentenced him to die by fire. When this news reached Edessa, Habib was some 50 miles off at Zeugma, secretly encouraging the Christians there, and his family and friends at Telzeha were arrested. Hereupon, Habib went to Edessa and presented himself privately to Theotecnus, the head of the governor's household. This official desired to save Habib and pressed him to depart secretly, assuring him that his friends would soon be released. Habib, believing that cowardice would endanger his eternal salvation, persisted in surrender, and was led before the governor. On refusing to sacrifice, he was imprisoned, tortured, and then burned, after he had at great length uncompromisingly exposed the sin and folly of idolatry. The day of his imprisonment was the emperor's festival, and on the 2nd of Ilul (Sept.) he suffered. His dying prayer was, "O king Christ, for Thine is this world and Thine is the world to come, behold and see that while I might have been able to flee from these afflictions I did not flee, in order that I might not fall into the hands of Thy justice. Let therefore this fire in which I am to be burned be for a recompense before Thee, so that I may be delivered from that fire which is not quenched; and receive Thou my spirit into Thy presence through the Spirit of Thy Godhead, O glorious Son of the adorable Father."

The year is given by Baronius, who had only Metaphrastes to guide him, as A.D. 316 (*A. E.* ann. 316, xlviii.). Assemani (*Bibl. Or.* i. 331) with the same materials decides for 323. The details of Theophilus might seem to settle the point; but if his era is that of the Seleucidae, Ilul 2, 620 was Sept. 2, 309, and Licinius only became master of the East in 313. The date therefore is still a difficulty. [C.H.]

Hadrianus (1), **Publius Aelius,** emperor 117-137. Born in 76, and placed, at the age of ten, on his father's death, under the guardianship of his cousin, Ulpius Trajanus, afterwards emperor, Hadrian was in his youth a diligent student of Greek literature, and entered on his career as military tribune in Lower Moesia in 95. On the death of Nerva in 97, Trajan became emperor, and Hadrian, on whom he bestowed such favours that men looked for a formal adoption, served in the wars with the Dacians, Pannonians, Sarmatians, and Parthians. During the campaign against the last-named, Trajan, leaving Hadrian in command of the army and of the province of Syria, started for Rome, but died at Selinus in Cilicia in 117. Hadrian had himself proclaimed emperor by the army, communicated the election to the senate, and received their formal sanction. His external policy was marked by the abandonment of any idea of extending the eastern frontier of the empire beyond the Euphrates. Having gained popular favour by gladiatorial games, large donations, and the remission of arrears of taxes, Hadrian devoted himself for several years from 120 to a personal inspection of the provinces. In 120-121 he visited Gaul, Germany, and Britain, erecting fortresses and strengthening the frontier defences, of which an example is his Roman wall from the Solway to the mouth of the Tyne. We may find traces, perhaps, of the eclectic tendency of his mind in the altars dedicated to Mithras and to an otherwise unknown goddess named Coventina or Conventina, found near the wall not far from Hexham.* In 122 he came to Athens, which became his favourite residence, and the same eclectic tendency led him to seek initiation in the Eleusinian mysteries (A.D. 125). On the death, probably self-sought, of his favourite Antinous, a Bithynian page of great beauty and genius, Hadrian paid his memory the divine honours given to emperors. Constellations were named after him, cities dedicated to him, incense burnt in his honour, and the art market flooded with statues and busts representing his exceeding beauty. The apotheosis of Antinous was the *reductio* at once *ad absurdum* and *ad horribile* of the decayed polytheism of the empire (Eus. *H. E.* iv. 8; Justin, *Apol.* i. 39). In 131 the emperor began to execute the plan, conceived earlier in his reign, of making Jerusalem a Roman colonia, and rebuilding it as *Aelia Capitolina*, thus commemorating both the *gens* to which the emperor belonged and its consecration to the Capitolian Jupiter. At first the proposal was received tranquilly. The work of rebuilding was placed in the hands of a Jew, Aquila of Pontus, and the Jews petitioned for permission to rebuild their temple. They were met with studied indignity, and a plough was drawn over the site of the sacred place in token of its desecration. The city was filled with Roman emigrants, the Jews were forbidden to enter the city, but allowed, as if in bitter irony, on the anniversary of its capture by Titus to bewail their fate within its gates. On one of the gates a marble statue of the unclean beast was a direct insult to Jewish feeling, while Christian feeling was outraged by a statue of Jupiter on the site of the resurrection and of Venus on that of the crucifixion. Trees and statues were placed on the platform of the temple, and a grove to Adonis near the cave of the nativity at Bethlehem. Such persistent defiance of national feeling roused widespread indignation, which burst out under a leader whom we know by his assumed name of Bar-Cocheba ("the son of a star")—a name probably suggested by the imagery of Balaam (Num. xxiv. 17), possibly also by the recollection of the "star in the east" of Matt. ii. 2. He is described by Eusebius (*H. E.* iv. 3) as a murderer and a robber (φονικὸς καὶ λῃστρικὸς) of the Barabbas type, but was recognized by Akiba, the leading rabbi of the time, as the Messiah, seized 50 fortresses and 985 villages, and established himself in the stronghold of Bethera, between Caesarea and Lydda (rebuilt by Hadrian and renamed Diospolis). The Christians of Palestine, true to the apostolic precept of submission to the powers that be, took no part in the insurrection, and were accordingly persecuted by the rebel leader and offered the alternative of denying the Messiahship of Jesus or the penalty of torture and death (*ib.* iv. 8). Severus was recalled from Britain, the rebellion suppressed with a strong hand, and edicts of extreme stringency issued against the Jews, forbidding them to circumcise their children, keep the Sabbath, or educate their youth in the Law. Akiba died under torture, and a secret school for instruction in the Law, continuing the rabbinic traditions, was formed at Lydda (Jost, *Judenthum*, ii. 7). To the Christian church in Judaea the suppression of the revolt and the tolerant spirit of the emperor brought relief. They left Pella, where they had taken refuge during the siege of Jerusalem by Titus, and returned to the holy city. Its 15 successive bishops had all been Hebrews, but now the mother-church of the world first came under the care of a gentile bishop (Eus. *H. E.* iv. 5).

In his general treatment of Christians, Hadrian followed in the footsteps of Trajan. The more cultivated members of the church felt that in addressing the tolerant, eclectic emperor, "curiositatum omnium explorator," as Tertullian calls him (*Apol.* c. 5), they had a chance of a favourable hearing, and the age of apologists began. QUADRATUS presented his *Apologia*, laying stress on the publicity of the works of Christ, and appealing to still surviving eye-witnesses. ARISTIDES addressed to the emperor (A.D. 133) a treatise, extant and admired in the time of Jerome, in defence of the Christians, and was said even to have been admitted to a personal hearing. Early in his reign, but probably a little later, an Asiatic official of high character, Serenius Granianus, applied to Hadrian for instructions

* See a paper by Mr. Clayton in the *Transactions of the Newcastle Archaeological Society* for 1875. Some archaeologists consider Conventina a Latinized form of the name of some British goddess. The fact that Hadrian when in Spain summoned a *conventus* of all Romans resident there suggests that the goddess was perhaps the personified guardian of such a *conventus* held in Britain.

as to the treatment of Christians, complaining that their enemies expected him to condemn them without a trial. The emperor thereupon addressed an official letter to Minucius Fundanus, proconsul of Asia, regulating the mode of procedure against the persecuted sect. No encouragement was to be given to common informers (συκοφάνται) or to popular clamour. If the officials of the district (ἐπαρχιῶται) were confident that they could sustain a prosecution, the matter was to be investigated in due course. Offenders against the laws were to be punished; but, above all things, the trade of the informer was to be checked (Eus. *H. E.* iv. 8, 9). The character of Hadrian may be inferred from his policy. He had not the zeal of a persecutor nor the fear that leads to cruelty. His philosophy and his religion did not keep him from the infamy of an impure passion of the basest type. He adapted himself without difficulty to the worship of the place in which he was. At Rome he maintained the traditional sacred rites which had originated under the republic, and posed as the patron of Epictetus and the Stoicism identified with his name. At Athens he was initiated in the Eleusinian mysteries, and rose to the dignity of an Epoptes in the order, as one in the circle of its most esoteric teaching. He became an expert in the secrets of magic and astrology. To him, as he says in his letter to Servianus, the worshippers of Serapis and of Christ stood on the same footing. Rulers of synagogues, Christian bishops, Samaritan teachers, were all alike trading on the credulity of the multitude (Flavius Vopiscus, *Saturn.* cc. 7, 8). According to a later writer, Lampridius (*in Alex. Sev.* c. 43), his wide eclecticism led him at one time to erect temples without statues, which he intended to dedicate to Christ. He was restrained, it was reported, by oracles, which declared that, if this were done, all other temples would be deserted and the religion of the empire subverted. But the absence of contemporary evidence of such an intention, on which Christian apologists would naturally have lain stress, leads us to reject Lampridius's explanation of these temples as an unauthenticated conjecture. More probably, as Casaubon suggests (*Annot. in Lamprid.* c. 43), they were intended ultimately to be consecrated to Hadrian himself. So the imperial Sophist—the term is used of Hadrian by Julian (*Caesares*, p. 28, ed. 1583) —passed through life, "holding no form of creed and contemplating all," and the well-known lines—

"Animula, vagula, blandula,
Hospes, comesque corporis,
Quae nunc abibis in loca,
Pallidula, rigida, nudula?
Nec, ut soles, dabis jocos"
(Spartian. *Vit. Hadr.*)

shew a like dilettanteism in him to the last.

A reign like that of Hadrian naturally, on the whole, favoured the growth of the church. The popular cry, "Christianos ad loenes," was hushed. Apologetic literature was an appeal to the intellect and judgment of mankind. The frivolous eclecticism of the emperor and yet more his deification of Antinous were enough to shake the allegiance of serious minds to the older system. Tolerance was, however, equally favourable to the growth of heresy; and to this reign we trace the rise and growth of the chief Gnostic sects of the 2nd cent., the followers of SATURNINUS in Syria, of BASILIDES, CARPOCRATES, and VALENTINUS in Egypt, of MARCION in Pontus (Eus. *H. E.* iv. 7, 8). Cf., besides the authorities cited, Gibbon, *Decline and Fall*, c. iii.; Milman, *Hist. of Christ.* bk. ii. c. vi.; Lardner, *Jewish and Heathen Testimonies*, c. xi. [E.H.P.]

Hecebolius or **Hecebolus**, a rhetor at Constantinople in the reign of Constantius, who professed himself a "fervent" Christian, and was therefore selected by that emperor as one of the teachers of Julian (Socr. iii. 1, 13). After the death of Constantius, however, Hecebolius followed the example of his former pupil and became a "fierce pagan" (γοργὸς Ἕλλην; Socr. *u.s.* 13). He was in great favour with Julian, and appears to have been one of his familiar correspondents (Julian, *Ep.* 19, ed. Heyler, p. 23; Ἑκηβόλῳ), and seems to have had some civil office at Edessa. The Arians of that city, "in the insolence of wealth," had violently attacked the Valentinians. Julian wrote to Hecebolius to say that, "since they had done what could not be allowed in any well-governed city," "in order to help the men the more easily to enter the kingdom of heaven as it was prescribed" by their "most wonderful law, he had commanded all moneys to be taken away from the church of the Edessenes, that they might be distributed among the soldiers, and that its property should be confiscated to his private treasury; that being poor they might become wise and not lose the kingdom of heaven which they hoped for" (Julian, *Ep.* 43, ed. Heyler, p. 82; Baron. *s.a.* 362, xiii.; Soz. vi. 1). Such appropriation of church property was one of the crimes of which Julian was accused after his death (Greg. Naz. *adv. Jul. Orat.* iii.). The emperor adds that he had charged the inhabitants of Edessa to abstain from "riot and strife," lest "they themselves" should suffer "the sword, exile, and fire." The last sentence in the letter appears to intimate that he would hold Hecebolius personally responsible for the future good conduct of the city. After the death of Julian and the reversal of the imperial policy, Hecebolius ostentatiously professed extreme penitence for his apostasy and prostrated himself at the church door, crying to all that entered, "Trample upon me—the salt that has lost its savour" (Socr. iii. 13; Baron. *u.s.*=Matt. v. 13). Baronius assumes the identity of the magistrate of Edessa with the "rhetor" of Constantinople (*s.a.* 362, xiii. xiv.), but Tillemont regards them as different persons (*Mém.* vii. 331, 332). Libanius mentions a Hecebolius, but gives us no clue to his history (*Ep.* 309). [T.W.D.]

Hedibia (EDIBIA), a lady in Gaul, who corresponded with St. Jerome (then at Bethlehem) *c.* 405. She was descended from the Druids, and held the hereditary office of priests of Belen (= Apollo) at Bayeux. Her grandfather and father (if *majores* is to be taken strictly) Patera and Delphidius (the names being in each case derived from their office) were remarkable men. Of Patera, Jerome says in his *Chronicle*, under A.D. 339, "Patera rhetor Romae gloriosissime docet."

Delphidius was a writer in prose and verse and a celebrated advocate. Ammianus Marcellinus (xviii. 1) tells of his pleading before the emperor Julian. Both became professors at Bordeaux (Ausonius, *Carmen*, Prof. Burd. iv. and v.). The wife and daughter of Delphidius became entangled in the Zoroastrian teaching of Priscillian, and suffered death in the persecution of his followers (Sulp. Sev. *Hist. Sac.* ii. 63, 64; Prosper Aquit. *Chron.*; Auson. *Carmen*, v.). Hedibia was a diligent student of Scripture, and, finding no one to assist her, sent, by her friend Apodemius, a list of questions to Jerome. He answered them in a long letter (*Ep.* 120, ed. Vall.). We hear of her again as a friend of Artemia, wife of Rusticus, on whose account she again wrote to Jerome (*Ep.* 122, ed. Vall.). [W.H.F.]

Hegesippus (1), commonly known as the father of church history, although his works, except a few fragments which will be found in Routh (*Rel. Sacr.* i. pp. 207-219) and in Grabe (*Spicil.* ii. 203-214), have perished. Nothing positive is known of his birth or early circumstances. From his use of the Gospel according to the Hebrews, written in the Syro-Chaldaic language of Palestine, his insertion in his history of words in the Hebrew dialect, and his mention of unwritten traditions of the Jews, Eusebius infers that he was a Hebrew (*H. E.* iv. 22), but possibly, as conjectured by Weizsäcker (Herzog, *Encyc.* v. 647), Eusebius knew this as a fact from other sources also. We owe our only information as to his date to a statement of his own, preserved by Eusebius (iv. 22), which is understood to mean that at Rome he compiled a succession of the bishops of the Roman see to the time of Anicetus, whose deacon was Eleutherus. After this statement Hegesippus is represented as adding, "and to Anicetus succeeds Soter, after whom Eleutherus." Much as the interpretation of these words has been disputed, it does not seem difficult to gather that Hegesippus means that the list of bishops compiled by him at Rome was drawn from the authentic records of the church there. That list closed with Anicetus. He was afterwards able to add the names of Soter and Eleutherus. It thus appears that he was at Rome in the days of Anicetus and made his inquiries then, but did not publish them till considerably later. But Anicetus, according to Lipsius (*Chronologie der römischen Bischöfe*), was bp. of Rome 156-167, and Eleutherus 175-189. Hegesippus had thus written much of his history previous to A.D. 167, and published it in the time of Eleutherus, perhaps early in his episcopate. Any difficulty in accepting these dates has been occasioned by the rendering given to another passage of Eusebius (iv. 8), where he quotes Hegesippus as speaking of certain games (ἀγών) instituted in honour of Antinous, a slave of Hadrian, of which he says ἐφ' ἡμῶν γενόμενος (a better established reading than γινόμενος). But these words seem simply to mean that the games had been instituted in his own time, thus illustrating the μέχρι νῦν of the preceding sentence. Hadrian reigned 117-138, so that if Hegesippus published *c.* 180, being then well advanced in life, he might well remember the times of that emperor. This derives confirmation from a statement of Jerome, generally regarded as somewhat extravagant, that the life of Hegesippus had bordered on the apostolic age ("vicinus apostolicorum temporum," *de Vir. Ill.* c. 22). But there is no extravagance in the remark. If Hegesippus was born *c.* 120 or earlier, he may well be described as having lived near the times of St. John. We may, therefore, fix the bloom of Hegesippus's life about the middle of the 2nd cent.

His history embraced, so far as we may judge from its fragments, numerous miscellaneous observations, recollections, and traditions, jotted down without regard to order, as they occurred to the author or came under his notice during his travels. Jerome tells us that the work contained the events of the church from Palestine to Rome, and from the death of Christ to the writer's own day. It is not a regular history of the church, Weizsäcker well remarking that, in that case, the story of James the Just ought to have been found in the first book, not in the last.

Its general style was thought plain and unpretending, says Jerome, and with this description what remains sufficiently agrees. The question of its trustworthiness is of greater moment. The account given in it of James the head of the church in Jerusalem has led to many charges against Hegesippus of not having been careful enough to prove what he relates. He has been thought to be contradicted by Josephus, who tells us that "Ananus, the high-priest, assembled the Sanhedrin of judges, and brought before them the brother of Jesus Who was called Christ, whose name was James, and some others. And, when he had formed an accusation against them, he delivered them to be stoned" (*Ant.* xx. 9, 1). We may be permitted to doubt, however, whether the sentence thus referred to was carried out, for not only was it unlawful for the Sanhedrin to punish by death without consent of the Roman authorities, but Josephus informs us immediately after that the charge of the citizens against Ananus was, that it was not lawful for him to assemble a Sanhedrin without the procurator's assent, nothing being said of the stoning to death. Further, Eusebius, who has preserved the narrative of Hegesippus, and the early Fathers who allude to it, appear to have placed in it implicit confidence; and there is nothing improbable in most, if not even in all, of the particulars mentioned. Eusebius speaks of him in the most commendatory terms, and quotes him on numerous occasions (see *H. E.* ii. 23; iii. 11, 16, 20, 32; iv. 8, 11, 22), illustrating his own words in iv. 8, πλείσταις κεχρήμεθα φωναῖς. Such confidence appears to have been deserved. Hegesippus had an inquiring mind, and had travelled much; he endeavoured to learn all he could of the past and present state of the churches that he visited: at Corinth the first epistle of Clement excited his curiosity; at Rome the history of its early bishops. All this, and his unpretending and unexaggerated style, shows him as very far from being either a hasty observer or a credulous chronicler.

An important question remains: Was Hegesippus of the Judaizing Christian party? Baur looks upon him as representing the narrowest section of the Jewish Christians, even as a most declared enemy of St. Paul, travelling like a commissioned agent in the interests of the Judaizers (*K. G.* i. p. 84; so also Schwegler, *Nachap. Zeit*, i. p. 342, etc.). This view is founded mainly upon an extract from his works, preserved in Photius (see in Routh, *R. S.* i. p. 219), where Hegesippus comments on the words, "Eye hath not seen, nor ear heard, neither have entered into the heart of man the things which God hath prepared for the just," "Such words are spoken in vain, and those who use them lie against the Holy Scriptures and the Lord Who says, 'Blessed are your eyes for they see, and your ears for they hear.'" It is argued that Hegesippus is here directly attacking St. Paul's words in I. Cor. ii. 9; and the inference is that Hegesippus was keenly Judaic. We know that the Gnostics were in the habit of so using the words in question, and that they described by means of them the very essence of that spiritual insight which the neophyte who had just sworn the oath of allegiance to them received, "And when he [*i.e.* he who is about to be initiated] has sworn this oath, he goes on to the Good One, and beholds 'whatever things eye hath not seen, and ear hath not heard, and which have not entered into the heart of man" (Hippolytus, *Ref. of all Heresies*, i. p. 193, T. & T. Clark). It is much the more probable inference, therefore, that Hegesippus refers to this Gnostic misinterpretation of the words and not to St. Paul (cf. Routh, *R. S.* i. p. 281; Ritschl, *Die Entstehung der Altk. Kirche*, p. 267; Hilgenfeld, *Die Apost. Väter*, p. 102). Further, Hegesippus must have known that Clement, whose epistle he approved, quotes in c. xxxiv., for a purpose precisely similar to that of the apostle, the very passage in question, though with a slight variation in the words. How, then, can he have held the contrary opinion as to the use made of it by St. Paul? It is obviously a *particular application* of the passage, different from that of the apostle, that he has in view.

In the light of these considerations, Hegesippus appears to have been not a Judaizing but a Catholic Christian; and, if so, he becomes a witness not only for the catholicity in the main of the Christian church of the 2nd cent., but for the extent to which Catholic truth prevailed in it, for his evidence, whatever its purport, has reference to the condition of the church upon a large scale. Either, therefore, over this wide extent the church was as a whole marked by a narrow Judaic spirit, or over the same wide extent it was catholic in spirit, with heretical sects struggling to corrupt its faith. If our verdict be in favour of the latter view, it becomes impossible to look at Hegesippus in the light in which he has been presented by the Tübingen school. We must regard him as a Catholic, not as a Judaizing Christian, and his statements as to the condition of the church in his day become a powerful argument against, rather than in favour of, the conclusions of that school. Cf Zahn, *Forschungen*. 1900, vi. 228-273. [W.M.]

Hegesippus (2) (*Egesippus*), the alleged author of a work of which a translation from Greek into Latin, or what purported to be such, appeared *c.* 400, and is commonly referred to as *de Bello Judaico* or as *de Excidio Urbis Hierosolymitanae*. It is mainly taken from the *Wars* of Josephus. The translator freely adds to his author, sometimes from the later books of the *Antiquities* of Josephus, sometimes from Roman historians and other sources, and also freely composes speeches for the actors.

The work is that of an earnest defender of the Christian faith. An approximation to his date is supplied by several passages; as when he speaks of Constantinople having long become the second city of the Roman empire (iii. 5, p. 179), and of Antioch, once the metropolis of the Persians, being in his time the defence of the Byzantines against that people. He also speaks of the triumphs of the Romans in "Scotia" and in "Saxonia," using language strikingly similar to that of Claudian (*c.* 398) (v. 18, p. 299; Claud. *de iv. Cons. Honor.* 31-34). The work early acquired a considerable reputation. Some have ascribed the translation to Ambrose. The Benedictines, however, strongly reject the Ambrosian authorship, asserting that it contains nothing whatever in Ambrose's style; while Galland earnestly contends for it, and reprints an elaborate dissertation of Mazochius which he regards as conclusive (Galland. *Biblioth. Patr.* vii. prolegom. p. xxix.). The editors of the *Patrologia* incline to reject the Ambrosian authorship, though they print it among his writings (xv. 1962). The most correct edition (Marburg, 1858, 1864, 4to) was commenced by Prof. C. F. Weber of Marburg, and completed after his death by Prof. Julius Caesar, who elaborately discussed the authorship and date (pp. 389-399). Cf. G. Landgraf, "Die Hegesippus Frage" in *Archiv. f. Latin Lexicogr.* (1902), xii. 465-472, who decides in favour of the Ambrosian authorship. [T.W.D.]

Helena (1), said to have been the companion of SIMON Magus. According to Justin Martyr (*Apol.* i. 26) and Irenaeus (i. 23, p. 99), who possibly makes use of a lost work of Justin's, she was a prostitute whom Simon had purchased from a brothel at Tyre and led about, holding her up to the veneration of his disciples. Giving himself out to be the Supreme Power and the Father above all, he taught, says Irenaeus, that "she was the first conception of his mind, the mother of all things, by whom in the beginning he conceived the thought of making the angels and archangels; for that this Conception proceeded forth from him and, knowing her father's wishes, descended to the lower world, and produced the angels and powers, by whom also he said that this world was made. But after she had produced them, she was detained by them through envy . . . and . . . confined in a human body, and for ages passed into other female bodies, as if from one vessel into another. He said, also, that she was that Helen on account of whom the Trojan war was fought; . . . that after passing from one body to another, and constantly meeting with insult, at last she became a public prostitute, and that she was 'the lost sheep.' On this account he had come that he might first of all reclaim her and free her from her chains, and then give salvation to men through the knowledge of himself." The same story is told by Hippolytus (*Ref.* vi. 19, p. 174), Tertullian (*de Anima*, 34), Epiphanius (*Haer.* 21), Philaster (*Haer.* 29), Theodoret (*Haer. Fab.* i. 1). Tertullian evidently knows no more than he read in Irenaeus; but Hippolytus, who had read the Μεγάλη Ἀποφάσις, gives some additional particulars, *e.g.* that Simon allegorized the story of the wooden horse and of Helen and her torch. The wooden horse must also have been mentioned in the earlier treatise against heresies, used by Epiphanius and Philaster, both of whom state that Simon expounded it as representing the ignorance of the nations. Epiphanius, then, it may be believed, did not invent some other particulars, in which he differs from or goes beyond Irenaeus. He states that Simon called this conception (Ennoea) Prunicus and Holy Spirit; and he gives a different account, in some respects, of the reasons for her descent into the lower world. According to this account, she was *sent* in order to rob the Archons, the framers of this world, of their power, by enticing them to desire her beauty, and setting them in hostility to one another.

The honour paid to Helena by the followers of Simon was known to Celsus, who says (v. 62) that certain Simonians were also called Heleniani, from Helena, or else from a teacher Helenus. We are told also by Irenaeus and Hippolytus that the Simonians had images of Simon as Jupiter and of Helen as Minerva, which they honoured, calling the former lord, the latter lady. This adaptation of the myth of Athene springing from the head of Zeus to the alleged relation of Ennoea to the first Father is of a piece with the appropriation of other Grecian myths by these heretics.

The doctrine thus attributed to Simon has close affinity with that of other Gnostic systems, more especially that of the Ophites, described at the end of bk. i. of Irenaeus, except that in the Simonian system one female personage fills parts which in other systems are distributed among more than one. But in several systems we have the association with the First Cause of a female principle, his thought or conception; and we have the myth of the descent of a Sophia into the lower material regions, her sufferings from the hostility of the powers who rule there, her struggles with them, and her ultimate redemption. Peculiar to Simon is his doctrine of the transmigration of souls and his identification, by means of it, of himself and his female companion with the two principal personages of the Gnostic mythology. Simon, moreover, persuaded his followers not only to condone his connexion with a degraded person, but to accept the fact of her degradation fully admitted as only a greater proof of his redemptive power. We find it easier to believe, therefore, that the story had a foundation in fact than that it was imagined without any. On the other hand, it does not seem likely that Simon could have been the first Gnostic, it being more credible that he turned to his account a mythology already current than that he could have obtained acceptance for his tale of Ennoea, if invented for the first time for his own justification.

Baur has suggested (*Christliche Gnosis*, p. 308) that Justin in his account of the honours paid at Samaria to Simon and Helena may have been misled by the honours there paid to Phoenician sun and moon divinities of similar names. On this and other cognate questions see SIMON. Suffice it here to say that one strong fact in support of his theory, viz. that in the Clementine Recognitions (ii. 14, preserved in the Latin of Rufinus) the companion of Simon is called Luna, may have originated in an early error of transcription. She is Helena in the corresponding passage of the Clementine Homilies, ii. 23; and we find elsewhere the false reading Selene for Helene, *e.g.* in Augustine (*de Haer.* 1). [G.S.]

Helena (2), St., or **Flavia Julia Helena Augusta,** first wife of Constantius Chlorus, and mother of Constantine the Great, born *c.* 248, died *c.* 327.

Little is known for certain of her life, except that she was mother of Constantine the Great and when about 80 years old undertook a remarkable pilgrimage to Palestine, which resulted in the adornment and increased veneration of the holy places.

She was doubtless of humble parentage, being, according to one story, the daughter of an innkeeper (Anon. Valesii 2, 2, "matre vilissima," Ambrose, *de Obitu Theodosii*, § 42, p. 295). Constantius when he made her acquaintance was a young officer in the army, of good family and position, nearly related, by the female line, to the emperor Claudius, and appears to have at first united her to himself by the looser tie then customary between persons of such different conditions (Hieron. *Chron.* anno. 2322; Orosius, vii. 25; *Chron. Pasch.* A.D. 304, vol. i. p. 516, ed. Bonn; Zos. ii. 8). The relation of "concubinatus" might be a lifelong one and did not necessarily imply immorality. In outward appearance it differed nothing from the ordinary civil marriage by mutual consent, and was sometimes called "conjugium inaequale." Her son Constantine, apparently her only child, was born probably in 274, at Naissus in Dardania, the country where his father's family had for some time been settled. After his birth Constantius probably advanced Helena to the position of a lawful wife. That she had this position is expressly stated by some of our authorities, but the very emphasis of their assertion implies that there was something peculiar about the case (Eus. *H. E.* viii. 13, 12, παῖδα γνήσιον . . . καταλιπών and the inscription from Salerno given below). Respect for Constantine would naturally prevent writers in his reign from stating the circumstances in detail. It may be, however, that his law to legitimatize the children of a concubine "per subsequens matrimonium" was suggested by his mother's experience.

After living with Constantius some 20 years Helena was divorced on the occasion of his elevation to the dignity of Caesar in 292; the Augustus Maximian, in choosing him for his colleague, requiring this, as a matter of policy, in order that Constantius might marry his own step-daughter, Theodora (Eutrop. *Brev.* ix. 22; Victor, *de Caesaribus*, 39; *Epitome*, 54)—a proceeding which has parallels in Roman history. The looseness of the marriage tie among the Romans is a quite sufficient explanation of these acts, without supposing any offence or misconduct on the part of the wife, or any special heartlessness on that of the husband. We know nothing of her life during the remainder of her husband's reign. When Constantine succeeded in 306, he probably recalled his mother to the court, but direct proof of this is wanting. We have a coin stamped HELENA. N.F. *i.e. nobilissima femina*, with a head on one side and a star in a laurel crown upon the other, perhaps struck in her honour whilst Constantine was still Caesar. The statement of Eusebius that Constantine paid his mother great honours, and caused her to be proclaimed Augusta to all the troops, and struck her image on gold coins, is no doubt correct, but is unfortunately unaccompanied by dates (*Vita Const.* iii. 47). Silver and copper coins are found with the name *Flavia Helena Augusta*, struck in her lifetime. Others with the remarkable epigraph *Fl. Jul. Helenae Aug.* were struck at Constantinople and Trèves as memorials after her death, and Theodora was also similarly commemorated, to mark the reconciliation of the two branches of the family. Helena is styled Augusta in inscriptions, but in none necessarily earlier than 320 (Mommsen, *Inscr. Neap.* 106, given below; *Inscr. Urbis Romae, C. I. L.* v. 1134-1136).

Eusebius also tells us that through Constantine she became a Christian (*V. C.* iii. 57), and is supported (whatever the support may be worth) by the probably spurious letters preserved in the Acts of St. Silvester. [CONSTANTINE.] We must therefore reject the story which ascribes his conversion to his mother's influence (Theod. i. 18, and the late and fabulous Eutychius Alexandrinus, pp. 408, 456, ed. Oxon.).

The following inscription from Salerno marks the power of Helena in her son's court: "To our sovereign lady Flavia Augusta Helena, the most chaste wife of the divine Constantius, the mother of our Lord Constantine, the greatest, most pious and victorious Augustus, the grandmother of our Lords *Crispus and* Constantine and Constantius, the most blessed and fortunate Caesars, this is erected by Alpinius Magnus, vir clarissimus, corrector of Lucania and Bruttii, devoted to her excellence and piety" (Mommsen, *u.s.* Orell. 1074, Wilmanns 1079).

In 326 Crispus was put to death on an obscure charge by his father's orders. Tradition attributes this dark act to Fausta; and Helena's bitter complaints about her grandson's death are said to have irritated Constantine to execute his wife by way of retribution (Vict. *Epit.* 41, Fausta conjuge ut putant suggerente Crispum filium necari jussit. Dehinc uxorem suam Faustam in balneas ardentes conjectam interemit, cum eum mater Helena dolore nimie nepotis increparet).

Eusebius speaks strongly of her youthful spirit when she, in fulfilment of a vow, made her pilgrimage to the Holy Land, notwithstanding her great age, nearly 80 years (*V. C.* iii. 42, cf. 46). She received almost unlimited supplies of money from her son and spent it in royal charities to the poor and bounties to the soldiery; as well as using her power to free prisoners and criminals condemned to the mines and to recall persons from exile (*ib.* 44). She was a frequent attendant at the church services, and adorned the buildings with costly offerings (*ib.* 45). Her death cannot have been earlier than 327, because she did not make her pilgrimage until after the death of Crispus. Tillemont puts it in 328, and it may have been later. (See further, Clinton, *F. R.* ii. 80, 81.) Her body was carried with great pomp to "the imperial city," *i.e.* probably, Constantinople (Eus. *V. C.* iii. 47; Socr. i. 17, thus glosses the phrase—εἰς τὴν βασιλεύουσαν νέαν Ῥώμην). It was believed, however, in the West that she was buried at Rome, and there is a tradition that in 480 her body was stolen thence by a monk Theogisus and brought to Hautvilliers in the diocese of Rheims. Others say that it is still in the porphyry vase in the church of Ara Coeli (Tillem. *Mém.* t. vii. n. 7). The place too of her death is strangely uncertain. Eusebius's silence would imply that she died in Palestine; but if the traditions of her bounty to the people and church of Cyprus on her way home are of any value, it must have been somewhere nearer Rome or Constantinople. These traditions may be seen in M. de Mas Letrie's *Hist. de l'Ile de Chypre sous les Lusignan* (Paris, 1852-1861); *Church Qtly. Rev.* vol. vii. pp. 186 f. [J.W.]

Invention of the Cross.—It is in connexion with this famous story that the name of Helena is especially interesting to the student of church history. Its truth has been much discussed, and we will briefly summarize the evidence of the ancient authorities.

(1) In the very interesting itinerary of the anonymous Pilgrim from Bordeaux to Jerusalem, generally referred to A.D. 333, seven years after the date assigned to the finding of the cross (Migne, *Patr. Lat.* xiii. 771), we have a description of the city, and many traditional sites of events both in O. and N. T. are mentioned. Among these are the house of Caiaphas with the pillar at which our Lord was scourged, the praetorium of Pontius Pilate, the little hill (*monticulus*) of Golgotha, and, a stone's throw from it, the cave of the resurrection. On the latter spot a beautiful basilica erected by Constantine is noticed, as also on Mount Olivet and at Bethlehem. Yet there is no allusion to the cross, nor is the name of Helena mentioned.

(2) The Life of Constantine by Eusebius was written probably in 338, five years after the visit of the Bordeaux Pilgrim. He records the visit of Helena to Jerusalem, but does not connect her name with the place of Crucifixion nor with the Holy Sepulchre. He tells us that Constantine built a house of prayer on the site of the Resurrection and beautified the caves connected with our Lord's Birth and Ascension, and that he did so in memory of his mother, who had built two churches, one at Bethlehem, the other on the Mount of Ascension. Thus of the three famous caves, Eusebius connects Helena not with that of the Resurrection, but only with the other two. He indeed says that these were not the only churches she built, but it is hardly conceivable that he should have left the one on the site of the Resurrection unspecified. The original motive of her journey, he says, was to return thanks to God for His peculiar

mercies to her family and to inquire as to the welfare of the people of the country. His account of the discovery of the Holy Sepulchre by Constantine is not free from difficulty. It is not easy to say whether he represents its discovery as being before or after the death of Helena. His language is general, but the presumption is that, if it had been before, her name would have been connected with the event. He does not imply that any difficulty was experienced in finding the site of the tomb, but there is nothing as to the cross. All his words bear upon the Resurrection, not the Passion, of our Lord. But in Constantine's letter to Macarius, bp. of Jerusalem, which he inserts, there are one or two expressions of which the same cannot be said. Allowing for the excesses of hyperbolical language, it is still hard to understand the words, "When the cave was opened, the sight which met the eyes excelled all possible eulogy, as much as heavenly things excel earthly," unless some kind of memorial other than the tomb itself was discovered; and immediately afterwards we have two expressions referring definitely to our Lord's Passion. The first is, *τὸ γὰρ γνώρισμα τοῦ ἁγιωτάτου ἐκείνου πάθους ὑπὸ τῇ γῇ πάλαι κρυπτόμενον*; and the second, *ἀφ' οὗ* (since) *τοῦ σωτηρίου πάθους πίστιν εἰς φῶς προήγαγεν* (sc. the tomb). At the same time it is difficult to believe that, had the cross or any part of it been discovered, it should not have been more exactly described, and the most probable explanation is that *πάθος* is used to describe the whole scene of Redemption, of which the Resurrection was a part (Eus. *Vit. Const.* iii. 26-42, *Patr. Gk.* xx. 1086). That the place was very early venerated is proved by Eusebius's statement (*Comm. on Ps.* lxxxvii. 18) that marvels (*θαύματα*) were even then wrought at the tomb of Christ.

(3) Cyril of Jerusalem, whose catechetical lectures were delivered, he says, upon the very spot where our Lord was crucified, and, as we know from other sources, not more than 20 years after the alleged discovery (viz. in 346), has three allusions to the wood of the cross (iv. 10, x. 19, xiii. 4). The most definite is in x. 19, where he describes it as "until to-day visible amongst us" (*μεχρὶ σήμερον παρ' ἡμῖν φαινόμενον*), "and now filling nearly the whole world by means of those who in faith take from it." In his letter to Constantius, which, however, is of doubtful authenticity [Cyril], it is distinctly stated that the cross was discovered in the reign of Constantine (c. 3). The first quotations prove that it was believed in his day that the real wood of our Lord's cross had been discovered, but do not give the grounds of the belief. Nor, though he speaks of the cross, does he connect it with St. Helena. Thus none of our three earliest authorities speak of her as the discoverer.

(4) St. Chrysostom, writing probably before 387, speaks of the wood of the true cross (*Patr. Gk.* xlviii. 826).

(5) Sulpicius Severus (*c.* 395) tells us that Helena built three basilicas (not two, as in Eusebius), one on each of the sites of the Passion, Resurrection, and Ascension. The site of the Passion, he says, was discovered by Helena, but he does not add that it was by supernatural help. Three crosses were discovered, and the right one ascertained by the miraculous restoration to life of a dead body (*Hist. Sacr.* i. 33, *Patr. Gk.* xx. 148).

(6) St. Ambrose, writing in 395, says that Helena was inspired by the Spirit with the desire to search for the cross, that she distinguished the true cross by its title (thus differing from Sulpicius and all later writers), that two of the nails were used by the emperor, one being fixed in his crown and the other employed as a bit for his bridle (*de Obitu Theodosii*, c. 41 ff., *Patr. Gk.* xvi. 1399).

(7) Rufinus (writing in 400, according to the Life in Migne's ed.) tells us further that not only was the journey inspired by God, but that the place of the Passion was miraculously revealed; that the three crosses were found "confuso ordine," and the title separately; that the true cross was discovered by the miraculous healing of a sick lady (not the revival of a corpse, as above); that part of the wood was sent to Constantine, and part left at Jerusalem in a silver casket (cf. *μεχρὶ σήμερον φαινόμενον* in Cyril's description above). (*H. E.* i. 7, 8, *Patr. Gk.* xxi. 475.)

(8) Paulinus of Nola, writing (*c.* 403) to Sulpicius Severus, and sending him a piece, as he says, of the true cross brought from Jerusalem by Benedicta Melanius, adds an account of its original discovery, because, as he says, it is so difficult to credit. He says that Helena went to rescue the holy places, adorned the site of our Lord's Birth in addition to the other three sites, and discovered the place of the Passion by the concurrent testimony of many Jews and Christians in the city. He adds that, though pieces were frequently taken from the cross, its original bulk was miraculously preserved (*Ep.* xxxi. 4, *Patr. Gk.* lxi. 325).

(9) St. Jerome, in his *Comm. on Zech.* xiv. 20 (*Patr. Lat.* xxv. 1540), probably written A.D. 406, mentions the nail from the cross which was used for the emperor's bridle, as related in many other writers, and in *Ep.* lviii. (*ib.* xxii. 581) speaks of the images of Jove and Venus which stood until the time of Constantine on the sites of the Resurrection and of the Passion respectively.

(10) St. Cyril of Alexandria (*c.* 420) mentions as a report (*φασί*) that the wood of the cross had been found at different times (*κατὰ καιρούς*) with the nails still fixed in it (*Comm. on Zech.* xiv. 20, *Patr. Gk.* lxxii. 271).

(11) Socrates (*c.* 430) informs us that Helena was told in a night vision to go to Jerusalem; that she found the site of the Passion with difficulty, though he alludes to no supernatural aid; that Macarius suggested the means of distinguishing the true cross, viz. by applying it to a woman on the point of death; that the empress erected "new Jerusalem" on the site (a phrase evidently taken from Eusebius); and that the emperor put one of the nails on his statue at Constantinople, as many inhabitants testified (*H. E.* i. 17, *Patr. Gk.* lxvii. 118).

(12) Sozomen (*c.* 430) claims good authority for his account, and states that Constantine, in gratitude for the council of Nicaea, wished to build a church on Golgotha; that Helena about the same time went to Palestine to pray and to look for the sacred sites. He does not, however, mention any divine impulse. The

difficulty of discovery was caused, he says, by the Greeks having defiled them to stop the growing θρησκεία; the site of the Sepulchre was made known, as some say, by a Hebrew living in the East, from documentary evidence, but more probably by signs and dreams from God. He says that the crosses were found near the same spot (ἑτέρωθι περὶ τὸν αὐτὸν τόπον) as they had been left by the soldiers in confused order, the inscription still remaining on the tablet. He mentions two miracles: the healing of a woman with an incurable disease and the raising of a corpse, combining the other accounts; and adds that the greater part of the cross was still preserved at Jerusalem (*H. E.* ii. 1, 2, *Patr. Gk.* lxvii. 929).

(13) Theodoret (*c.* 448) inserts the letter of Constantine to Macarius, and follows the order of Eusebius, representing, however, Helena's journey, more definitely than Eusebius does, as consequent upon the finding of the Sepulchre by Constantine. But his account seems inconsistent. The crosses, he says, were found *near* the Lord's tomb—παρὰ τὸ μνῆμα τὸ Δεσποτικόν (*H. E.* i. 16, 17, *Patr. Gk.* lxxxii. 955).

(14) St. Leo (454), in writing to Juvenal, bp. of Jerusalem, speaks of the constant witness borne at Jerusalem to the reality of Christ's Passion by the existence of the cross (*Ep.* cxxxix. 2, *Patr.* liv. 1106).

(15) St. Gregory of Tours (d. 595) adds that discovery was made on May 3, 326; that, during a great storm which occurred soon after, Helena put one of the nails into the sea, which was at once calmed; that two more were used for the emperor's bridle, and the fourth placed on the head of his statue; that the lance, crown of thorns, and pillar of scourging were preserved and worked miracles (*Lib. Mirac.* i. 5, *Patr. Lat.* lxxi. 709), and the cross found by the aid of a Jew, afterwards baptized as Quiriacus (*Hist. Franc.* i. 34, *Patr. Lat.* lxxi. 179).

Thus no detailed story is found until nearly 70 years after the event, and then in the West only. The vagueness of St. Cyril of Alexandria is particularly observable. Small differences of detail occur; the last author cited adds several particulars not included in the other accounts, and there are features in the story which look like invention or exaggeration. On the whole, considering that our earliest authorities do not represent Helena as the discoverer and that the story gradually develops, it seems probable that she had no part in the discovery of the cross, even if it took place, which itself seems exceedingly doubtful. That the site of the Holy Sepulchre was discovered, or supposed to be discovered, in the reign of Constantine, there seems every reason to believe; and it is easy to understand how marvels would grow up around it. [M.F.A.]

Heliodorus (7), bp. of Altinum near Aquileia, *c.* 400, had served originally as a soldier, but had been ordained before we first hear of him. He belonged to a band of friends drawn together at Aquileia, *c.* 372, for the study of Scripture and the practice of asceticism, which included St. Jerome, Evagrius afterwards bp. of Antioch, Rufinus, Bonosus, and Chromatius afterwards bp. of Aquileia. The passion for asceticism and the troubles which arose about Jerome made the companions resolve, under the guidance of Evagrius, to go to Syria and Antioch. Heliodorus went on to Jerusalem, where he enjoyed the hospitality of Florentius, who, having devoted himself to the ascetic life, employed his wealth in the entertainment of pilgrims (Hieron. *Ep.* iv. ed. Vall.). Returning to Antioch, he found Jerome resolved to go into the solitude of the desert of Chalcis. Heliodorus felt that he himself had a call to the pastoral life, having a sister and a nephew dependent on him (Hieron. *Ep.* lx. 9, ed. Vall.). He therefore returned to his native Aquileia, holding out to his friend some hopes that he might rejoin him one day in the desert (*ib.*). Jerome wrote to him on his return to Italy a letter, reproaching him for turning back from the more perfect service, which afterwards had a great effect in furthering asceticism and became so celebrated that a Roman lady, Fabiola, knew it by heart (Hieron. *Ep.* lxxvii. 9, ed. Vall.; *Ep.* xiv. 11). But their friendship was never broken. Heliodorus continued in the pastoral office, and not long afterwards became bp. of Altinum. He was present in 381 as a bishop at the council of Aquileia. In after-years he was closely allied with Chromatius, bp. of Aquileia, and they both kept up communications with Jerome, then residing at Bethlehem. They took a warm interest in Jerome's translation of the Scriptures, and frequently wrote to him, exhorting him to complete the long-delayed work. They supported amanuenses to assist him; and by the grateful mention of their aid in the prefaces to the books last translated, their names are for ever associated with the great work of the Vulgate ("Preface to the Books of Solomon and to Tobit," Jerome's *Works*, vol. ix. 1305, x. 26; Migne's ed. of Vallarsi's *Jerome*). Cappelletti (*Le Chiese d'Italia*, v. 516, 610) reckons his successor in the see of Altinum to have been Ambrosius, A.D. 407. [W.H.F.]

Helladius (4), bp. of Tarsus *c.* 430, a disciple of St. Theodosius of Antioch, after whose death (*c.* 412) he presided over the monastery he had founded near Rhosus in Cilicia. Having spent 60 years in monastic life, he succeeded Marianus, bp. of the metropolitan see of Tarsus (Theod. *Vit. Patr.* c. 10). His episcopate illustrates the stormy period of the council of Ephesus. He was one of those who protested against commencing the council before the arrival of John of Antioch and the Oriental bishops (Baluz. *Nov. Concil. Coll.* p. 697), and he joined the opposition council (*conciliabulum*) presided over by John upon his arrival. He supported the counter-remonstrances addressed to the emperors by Nestorius (*ib.* 703), and his name is appended to the synodal letter to the clergy and laity of Hierapolis (*ib.* 705) and to that to John of Antioch and Theodoret and the other members of the Oriental deputation to Theodosius (*ib.* 725). Helladius steadily ignored the deposition of Nestorius and withheld all recognition of Maximian as his successor. John of Antioch wrote, commending his action (*ib.* 752, c. 48). When the rival leaders sought peace, Helladius kept aloof, and on the receipt of the six articles drawn up by John at a council at Antioch, which ultimately opened the way for reconcilation, he and Alexander of Hierapolis rejected the terms and all communion with Cyril. He wrote to Alexander that, wearied by the struggle and sick at heart at the defection of his fellow-combatants, he longed to retire to a monastery, and was only restrained by his care for his flock (*ib.* 770, c. 68). The year 433 saw the concordat between Cyril and John confirmed, to the indignation of the irreconcilable party. A synod held by Helladius at Tarsus indignantly repudiated the "execrable agreement," and declared that the condemnation could not be removed from "the Egyptian" until he had "anathematized his own anathematisms." The firmness of Helladius rejoiced Alexander, who wrote that he intended to hold a synod himself, begging Helladius, whom he regarded as his leader, to attend it and sign its decrees (*ib.* 713, c. 110; 814, c. 111; 815, c. 114). Helladius with Eutherius of Tyana next drew up a long letter to pope Sixtus, giving their account of the council of Ephesus and begging him as a new Moses to save the true Israel from the persecution of the Egyptians. This was sent round to obtain the signatures of other bishops (*ib.* 817 sqq. c. 117). At this period we have a letter from Theodoret, complaining that Helladius refused to answer him and seemed to regard him as a deserter. Theodoret had accepted Cyril's letter because he found it orthodox, but he would never desert Nestorius (*ib.* 813, c. 110). The resolution of Helladius now began to break down. The concordat was accepted by an increasing number of Oriental prelates and he was left more and more alone. John wrote to complain of his obstinacy (*ib.* 842, c. 140). Theodosius threatened to put the civil power in motion against him and the other recusants. He, Alexander, Theodoret, and Maximian were ordered to accept the concordat or resign their sees. All eventually yielded except Alexander. The quaestor Domitian and Theodoret both urged Helladius to submit (*ib.* 829, c. 125; 859, c. 160), and this was made easier by the death of Maximian, Apr. 12, 434, and the succession of the saintly Proclus (Socr. *H. E.* vii. 41). The orthodoxy of the new bishop was readily acknowledged by Helladius (Baluz. 850, c. 148), who, having determined on yielding, wrote to Alexander to explain his conduct (*ib.* 862, c. 164). Alexander bitterly reproached him with his weakness (*ib.* 863, c. 164), but the latter convoked the bishops of his province, whose synodical letters to Theodosius declared their complete acceptance of all required of them: admission of the decrees of the council of Ephesus, communion with Cyril, the ratification of Nestorius's sentence of deposition, and the anathematization of him and his adherents (*ib.* 887, c. 192). Helladius thus saved himself from deposition and exile at the expense of consistency. He had now to justify his conduct to Nestorius, whom he had repeatedly promised never to forsake. The task was no easy one; nor can we say that he fulfilled it with any honour to himself. He wrote Nestorius that though through men's evil deeds everything had turned out directly contrary to his prayers, his feeling towards him remained unchanged, and that, as he knew he was still struggling for true piety, he believed that he would joyfully endure all laid upon him, and that he hoped he might be reckoned with him at the last judgment, when his soul, tried by so many and great temptations, would shine forth. He excuses himself for joining Theodoret and those who had accepted the concordat, as the letters produced from Cyril were in perfect harmony with apostolical traditions (*ib.* 888, c. 193). Then Helladius passes from the history. The letters are printed by Chr. Lupus (*Ep. Ephesinae*, Nos. 68, 111, 114, 144, 154, 193) and by Baluze, *Concil. Nov. Collect.* in the *Tragoedia Irenaei*, cc. 68, 111, 114, 117, 130, 164, 192, 193. Tillem. *Mém.* t. xiv.; Le Quien, *Or. Christ.* t. ii. p. 874; Cave, *Hist. Lit.* t. i. p. 418. [E.V.]

Helvidius, a Western writer who, like Novatian and Pelagius, Jovinian and Vigilantius, put forward opinions on anthropological subjects opposed to the generally received teaching of the church in their day. The only extant contemporary notice of him is the short tract against him by St. Jerome (*Opp.* ii. p. 203-230, ed. Vall.), written when they were both at Rome, while pope Damasus was alive. It appeared, according to Vallarsius, A.D. 383. St. Jerome says he had put off answering him for some time: "Ne respondendo dignus fieret, qui vinceretur"; and he describes him throughout as "hominem rusticanum, et vix primis quoque imbutum literis" (§ 1); besides being wholly unknown to him: "Ego ipse, qui contra te scribo, quum in eadem urbe consistam, albus, ut aiunt, aterve sis, nescio." St. Jerome speaks of his own work in writing to Pammachius as "librum contra Helvidium *de beatae Mariae virginitate perpetuâ*" (*Ep.* xlviii. § 17), this being what his opponent had denied in the first instance, though the outcome of his opinions had been to rank virginity below matrimony. Helvidius sought countenance for his first point in the writings of Tertullian and Victorinus. St. Jerome shews (§ 17) he had misrepresented the latter; of Tertullian, whose writings may still speak for themselves, he merely says, "Ecclesiae hominem non fuisse." But, in any case, he retorts with much force: What avail straggling opinions against primitive truth? "Numquid non possum tibi totam veterum scriptorum seriem commovere: Ignatium, Polycarpum, Irenaeum, Justinum Martyrem, multosque alios apostolicos et eloquentes viros, qui adversus Ebionem, et Theodotum Byzantium, Valentinum, haec eadem sentientes, plena sapientiae volumina conscripserunt. Quae si legisses aliquando, plus saperes." This argument is just as suitable to our own as it was to patristic times, never losing anything by repetition. What had Helvidius to oppose to it in this case? Nothing, unless his adversary misrepresents him, but novel interpretations of Scripture by himself. St. Jerome therefore refutes him only so far as to point out that there is no necessity for understanding any of the passages adduced by him otherwise than the church had understood them hitherto; but that, in any case, the interpretations of them offered by Helvidius were delusive. For the application of the views of Helvidius to the question of the perpetual virginity of the Lord's mother see Lightfoot, *Galatians*, pp. 247-282, and Murray's

Illus. B. D. (1908), art. JAMES. As Jerome nowhere charges Helvidius with having been "a disciple of Auxentius," the Arian bp. of Milan, or "an imitator of Symmachus," the champion of idolatry, we may well ask with Vallarsius where Gennadius, who wrote more than a century later, got authority for both statements (*de Script. Eccl.* c. 33) which Cave repeats in part (*Hist. Lit.* i. 278). Neither St. Ambrose nor St. Augustine mentions him when, in writing on *Virginity*, they join St. Jerome in condemning his views. His followers constitute the 84th of the heresies enumerated by the latter. [E.S.FF.]

Henoticon, The, or *Instrument of Union*, a document owing its existence to Acacius, the patriarch of Constantinople, and probably the production of his pen, put forth by the emperor Zeno, A.D. 482, on his restoration to the throne, after the discomfiture of the usurper Basiliscus, with the view of putting an end to the dissensions caused by what Gibbon calls "the obstinate and sanguinary zeal of the Monophysites." Like every endeavour, however well meant, to cover radical differences by a vague comprehensiveness, it not only failed to secure union but aggravated the divisions it was intended to cure, and created a schism which divided the East and West for nearly 40 years, lasting down to the reign of Justinian and the popedom of Hormisdas.

The immediate cause of its issue was the dissension between the rival occupants of the patriarchal see of Alexandria. On the death of Timotheus Salofaciolus in 482, John Talaia, the oeconomus of the Alexandrian church, was elected by the orthodox party. He at once, according to custom, dispatched synodical letters to the chief bishops of Christendom, to notify his election. Those addressed to Simplicius of Rome and Calandion of Antioch were duly received; but the letters for Acacius and Zeno were delayed, and Acacius heard of John's appointment from another quarter. Thinking the seeming neglect a studied insult, Acacius and Gennadius, bp. of Hermopolis Minor, a relation of Timotheus Salofaciolus, and "apocrisiarius" or legate of the see of Alexandria, who conceived that he too had been slighted by the new patriarch, determined to compass his overthrow. They represented to Zeno that Talaia was unworthy of the patriarchate, both as having replaced the name of Dioscorus on the diptychs, and as having perjured himself by accepting the see of Alexandria, after having, as was asserted, taken an oath that he would not seek for it. Zeno readily gave credence to these charges, and when it was further represented that, if he recognized Peter Mongus, the deposed patriarch, peace would be restored, he wrote to Simplicius, stating his grounds for hesitating to sanction the appointment of John, and urging the restoration of Peter Mongus to put an end to the distractions of the church. Simplicius replied, June 482, that he would delay recognizing John as patriarch until the grave charges brought by Zeno could be investigated; but he utterly refused to allow the elevation of a convicted heretic such as Peter Mongus to the patriarchal see. His return to the true faith might restore him to communion, but could not render him worthy to be a chief ruler of the church (Liberat. Diac. *Breviar.* cc. 16, 17; Evagr. *H. E.* iii. 12). This opposition roused the indignation of Zeno, who issued imperative commands to Pergamius, the new prefect of Egypt, then about to sail for Alexandria, and to Apollonius the governor, to expel John Talaia and seat Peter Mongus in his place. Acacius persuaded Zeno to present himself to the world in the novel character of an expounder of the faith of the Catholic church. The "Henoticon" was drawn up, and as it did not directly mention the council of Chalcedon and a hypothetical allusion in it was capable of being construed in a depreciatory sense, it could be accepted by those who, like Mongus, had hitherto rejected that council's decrees. The friends of Mongus undertook that he would adopt it, and on this he was recognized by Zeno and Acacius as the canonical patriarch and his name inserted in the diptychs.

The "Henoticon" was directed to the bishops and people in Alexandria, Egypt, Libya, and Pentapolis; but, as Tillemont has remarked (*Mém. eccl.* xvi. 327), it was really addressed only to those who had separated themselves from the church, *i.e.* to the Monophysites or semi-Eutychians. The original document is given by Evagrius (*H. E.* iii. 14) and in a not very clear Latin translation by Liberatus (*Breviar.* c. 18; Labbe, *Concil.* v. 767). It commences by stating that "certain abbats, hermits, and other reverend persons had presented to the emperor a petition, supplicating him to restore the unity of the churches, and enlarging on the lamentable results of the late divisions." On this account, and knowing also that the strength and shield of the empire rested in the one true faith declared by the holy Fathers gathered at Nicaea, confirmed by those who met at Constantinople and followed by those who had condemned Nestorius at the council of Ephesus, the emperor declares that "the creed so made and confirmed is the one only symbol of faith, and that he has held, holds, and will hold no other, and will regard all who hold another as aliens, and that in this alone those who desire saving baptism must be baptized." All who hold other views he anathematizes, and recognizes the twelve chapters of Cyril as a symbolical book. The document then proceeds to declare the orthodox faith, viz. "that our Lord Jesus Christ is the only-begotten Son of God, and Himself God, incarnate, consubstantial with the Father according to His Godhead, and consubstantial with us according to His manhood, that He came down from heaven, and was incarnate by the Holy Ghost of the Virgin Mary, Mother of God, and that He is One Son, not two." That "it was this one and the same Son of God Who wrought miracles, and endured the sufferings which He underwent voluntarily in His flesh." Those "who divide or confound the natures, or admit only a phantastical incarnation," are to be rejected, "since the incarnation without sin of the Mother of God did not cause the addition of a Son, for the Trinity remained even when one Person of the Trinity, God the Word, became incarnate." It asserts that this is no new form of faith, and anathematizes all who have ever thought, or do think, "anything to the contrary, either now or at any other time, either at Chalcedon or in any other synod," especially Nestorius and Eutyches and their followers. It closes with an earnest appeal to all to return to the church which, "as a loving mother, opens her longing arms to receive them."

Such was the document which was to "combine all the churches in one harmonious confederacy." It was "a work of some skill, of some adroitness, in attempting to reconcile, in eluding, evading difficulties; it is subtle to escape subtleties" (Milman, *Hist. of Lat. Christ.* bk. iii. c. i. vol. i. p. 248). The crucial test of the unity or duality of the natures of the Incarnate Word is left an open question, on which a difference of opinion might be lawfully permitted. Gibbon's verdict is by no means an unfair one, that "it accurately represents the Catholic faith of the incarnation without adopting or disclaiming the peculiar terms of the hostile sects" (vol. vi. p. 44, c. xlvii.). But its fatal error was its feebleness, and that it endeavoured to substitute for real unity of doctrine a fictitious cohesion of discordant elements. The Monophysites who subscribed were to be admitted into communion without being required to give up their distinctive doctrines; while their opponents were left free to maintain the authority of the decrees of Chalcedon and the tome of Leo. The resulting peace was naturally more apparent than real and satisfied no one. The Catholic party, zealous in their advocacy of the council of Chalcedon, had no liking for a document which disparaged its authority and suggested the possible erroneousness of its decisions. The Monophysites, on the other hand, clamoured for a more definite condemnation of a council which they regarded as heretical. The high Chalcedonian party, chiefly consisting of the monastic orders, condemned the "Henoticon" as tainted with Eutychianism, and, on the other hand, the Eutychians or Monophysites, indignant with Mongus for turning traitor to their cause, separated themselves, and, forming a distinct body without any chief leader and not holding communion with the patriarch, were designated "the headless sect," "Acephali." A third body of dissidents was formed by the high ecclesiastical party, who were offended at the presumption of the emperor in assuming a right to issue decrees on spiritual matters, "a right," writes Milman, (*u.s.* p. 235), "complacently admitted when ratifying or compulsorily enforcing ecclesiastical decrees, and usually adopted without scruple on other occasions by the party with which the court happened to side." A fourth party was that of the centre or moderates, who were weary of strife, or too loyal or too cowardly to resist the imperial power. This party of the centre was in communion with Peter Mongus, who had at once signed the "Henoticon," and had had it read in church at a public festival and openly commended it to the adoption of the faithful. Violence and falsehood characterized the conduct of Mongus. As soon as he felt himself safe in his seat, his overbearing temper knew no bounds. He removed from the diptychs the names of Proterius and Timotheus Salofaciolus, disinterring the remains of the latter and casting them out of the church; inserted the names of Dioscorus and Timotheus Aelurus; and anathematized the council of Chalcedon and the tome of Leo. When called to account by Acacius, he coolly denied the anathemas, and professed his acceptance of the faith as declared at Chalcedon. He wrote to the same effect to Simplicius, expressing a desire to be received into communion by him (Evagr. *H. E.* iii. 17; Liberat. *Breviar.* c. 18). Such double-dealing estranged many of his own party, and the discussions of which the unhappy "instrument of union" was the parent were still further aggravated by the cruel persecution of the orthodox throughout the whole of Egypt by the new patriarch. In bold defiance of the prohibitions of the emperor, all, whether clerics, monks, or laymen, who refused to accept the "Henoticon" were subjected to expulsion and serious maltreatment (Evagr. *H. E.* iii. 22). At this crisis Simplicius died, A.D. 483. The first act of his successor, Felix II., was an indignant rejection of the "Henoticon," as an insult to the council of Chalcedon, as an audacious act of the emperor Zeno, who dared to dictate articles of faith, and as a seed-plot of impiety (Theod. *Lect.* ap. Milman, *u.s.* p. 236). He also anathematized all bishops who had subscribed this edict. This anathema included nearly all the bishops of the East. A strong admonitory letter was addressed by Felix to Acacius, and another in milder terms to Zeno, the authors of the "Henoticon." All remonstrance proving vain, Felix fulminated an anathema against Acacius, deposing and excommunicating him, July 28, A.D. 484 (Liberat. c. 18; Labbe, *Concil.* iv. 1072). This anathema severed the whole of the Eastern church from the West for nearly 40 years. [ACACIUS.] Neither emperor nor patriarch took much heed of the condemnation of the Roman see, and continued to press the "Henoticon" everywhere, ejecting bishops who withheld their signatures and refused to communicate with Peter Mongus (Theoph. p. 114; Liberat. c. 18; Vict. Tunun. *Chron.*; Tillem. *Mém. eccl.* xvi. p. 168; Aece, *Art.* xcv.). Calandion, patriarch of Antioch, was deposed, and Peter the Fuller reinstated. Thus the three chief sees of the East were in constrained communion and nearly all the suffragan bishops had been silenced or deposed. Zeno and Acacius had "made a solitude and called it peace." It would be tedious to narrate in detail the subsequent issues of this unhappy attempt to force discordant elements into external union which continued under Acacius's successors and under the emperor Anastasius. Anastasius required toleration of the bishops who were forbidden to force the decrees of Chalcedon on a reluctant diocese or to compel one which had accepted that council to abandon it. Those who violated this law of toleration were deposed with impartial severity (Evagr. *H. E.* iii. 30). Euphemius was deposed from Constantinople A.D. 495. Macedonius, his successor, began by subscribing the "Henoticon," but overawed by the obstinate orthodoxy of the "Acoemetae" and other monastic bodies of Constantinople, whom he had undertaken to reconcile to that instrument, he became an ardent partisan of the council of Chalcedon, and, after having headed the religious tumults in the city which at one time threatened Anastasius's throne, was in his turn deposed and succeeded by Timotheus, A.D. 511. The new patriarch not only signed the "Henoticon," but pronounced an anathema on the council of Chalcedon. Flavianus, accused of being a concealed Nestorian, was ejected from Antioch in A.D. 512, where the Monophysite Severus, who had raised religious riots in the streets of Alexandria and Constantinople, reigned supreme. Elias of Jerusalem, though making large concessions to the Catholic party, refused to go all lengths with them, and was deposed in 513. "Throughout Asiatic Christendom it was the same wild struggle. Bishops deposed quietly, or, where resistance was made, the two factions fighting in the streets, in the churches. Cities, even the holiest places, ran with blood" (Milman, *u.s.* p. 245).

The "Henoticon," so fruitful a source of dissension in the East, became also the watchword of rival parties in the West. Gelasius, succeeding Anastasius II., sought to re-unite the churches by the proposal, couched in the very spirit of the "Henoticon," that Acacius's name should be quietly left on the diptychs. On his death in 498 a contested election ensued, exasperated by differences of opinion on the "Henoticon" and the schisms in the East. Two rival pontiffs were consecrated on Dec. 22, A.D. 499—Laurentius an advocate of union, and Symmachus its uncompromising opponent. Theodoric decided in favour of Symmachus, who had received the largest number of votes. This choice was fatal to the restoration of peace in the East on the terms of the "Henoticon." Pope and emperor hurled at one another charges of heresy and messages of defiance. The turbulent orthodox party at Constantinople was supported in its obstinate resistance to the emperor by the Roman see. The rebellion of Vitalian, characterized by Gibbon as "the first of the religious wars," whose battle-cry was the council of Chalcedon, was countenanced by Symmachus's still more haughty successor, Hormisdas, who reaped the fruits of the humiliation of the aged Anastasius and became "the dictator of the religion of the world." The demand of Hormisdas for the public anathematization of the authors and maintainers of the "Henoticon" was indignantly rejected by Anastasius. The conflict only ended with the life of Anastasius, who died worn out by strife at the age of nearly 90 years, A.D. 518. His successor, Justin, was an unlettered soldier of unbending orthodoxy. The new patriarch, John of Cappadocia, "a man of servile mind though unmeasured ambition," was prepared to adopt any course which would secure his power. He had seconded all the measures of Anastasius, but at the demand of the mob he now hastily assembled a synod of 40 bishops, which anathematized all upholders of the "Henoticon," recalled the banished bishops, and deposed the so-called usurpers. All heretics, *i.e.* those who refused the council of Chalcedon, were made incapable of civil or military office. Hormisdas profited by the favourable opportunity to press his demands, which were admitted without question. The names of the patriarchs Acacius, Fravitta, Euphemius, and Macedonius, together with those of the emperor Zeno and Anastasius, were erased from the diptychs, and Acacius was branded with a special anathema. Fresh disturbances were created when it was found that Hormisdas demanded the condemnation of all who had communicated with Acacius, and turned a deaf ear to the repeated applications of both emperor and patriarch for some relaxation of these terms (Evagr. *H. E.* iv. 4; Labbe, *Concil.* iv. 1542; Natal. Alexand. *Hist. Eccl.* t. ii. p. 448). Hormisdas at last consented that Epiphanius, John's successor, should act for him in receiving churches into communion. Some honoured names were allowed to remain on the diptychs, and eventually Euphemius, Macedonius, Flavian of Antioch, Elias of Jerusalem and some others who had died during the separation, were admitted to the Roman Calendars (Tillem. *Mém. eccl.* t. xvi. p. 697; Bolland. Apr. 25, p. 373).

Thus ended the unhappy schism. The "Henoticon," without being formally repealed, was allowed to sink into oblivion. The four oecumenical councils, including Chalcedon, were everywhere received, save in Egypt, and one common creed expressed the religious faith of the Christian world. Gibbon, *Decline and Fall*, c. xlvii.; Tillem. *Mém. eccl.* vol. xvi. "Acace"; Schröckh, *Kirchengesch.* vol. xviii.; Migne, *Patr.* t. lviii.; Evagr. *H. E.* libb. iii. iv.; Liberat. *Breviar.*; Walch, *Ketzerhist.* vol. vi.; Fleury, *Hist. eccl.* t. vi. vii.; Neander, *Ch. Hist.* vol. iv. pp. 253 ff. (Clarke's trans.); Dorner, *Person*, div. ii. vol. i. pp. 123 ff.; Milman, *Hist. of Lat. Christ.* vol. i. bk. iii. cc. i. iii. [E.V.]

Heracles, patriarch of Alexandria, A.D. 233–249; brother of the martyr Plutarch, one of Origen's converts (Eus. *H. E.* vi. 3). From being a pupil he became an assistant in teaching to Origen, who left the school to him when he retired from Alexandria to Caesarea (*ib.* 15, 26). Heraclas retained the school but a short time, for on the death of Demetrius he was elected to the archiepiscopal throne. Heraclas did not adopt any of his teacher's peculiar views, but voted for his deprivation both from his office as teacher and from his orders and for his excommunication at the two synods held by Demetrius, nor when elected bishop did he attempt to rescind these sentences. Eusebius (*ib.* 31) narrates a visit paid to Heraclas by Africanus the annalist on hearing of his great learning, and (*ib.* vii. 7), on the authority of his successor Dionysius, gives his rule respecting the treatment of heretics. Le Quien, *Oriens Christ.* ii. 392; Phot. *Cod.* 118; *Acta SS.* Boll. Jul. 3. 645–647. [L.D.]

Heracleon (1), a Gnostic described by Clement of Alexandria (*Strom.* iv. 9, p. 595) as the most esteemed (δοκιμώτατος) of the school of Valentinus; and, according to Origen (*Comm. in S. Joann.* t. ii. § 8, *Opp.* t. iv. p. 66), said to have been in personal contact (γνώριμος) with Valentinus himself. He is barely mentioned by Irenaeus (ii. 41) and by Tertullian (*adv. Valent.* 4). The common source of Philaster and Pseudo-Tertullian (*i.e.* probably the earlier treatise of Hippolytus) contained an article on Heracleon between those on Ptolemaeus and Secundus, and on Marcus and Colarbasus.

The chief interest that now attaches to Heracleon is that he is the earliest commentator on the N.T. of whom we have knowledge. Origen, in the still extant portion of his commentary on St. John, quotes Heracleon nearly 50 times, usually controverting, occasionally accepting his expositions. We thus recover large sections of Heracleon's commentary on cc. i. ii. iv. and viii. of St John. There is reason to think that he wrote commentaries on St. Luke also. Clement of Alexandria (*Strom.* iv. 9) expressly quotes from Heracleon's exposition of Luke xii. 8; and another reference (25 *Eclog. ex Script. Proph.* p. 995) is in connexion with Luke iii. 16, 17, and so probably from an exposition of these verses. The fragments of Heracleon were collected by Grabe (*Spicileg.* ii. 85, etc.), and reprinted as an appendix to Massuet's, Stieren's, and Migne's editions of Irenaeus.

The first passage quoted by Clement bears on an accusation brought against some of the Gnostic sects, that they taught that it was no sin to avoid martyrdom by denying the faith. No exception can be taken to what Heracleon says on this subject. "Men mistake in thinking that the only confession is that made with the voice before the magistrates; there is another confession made in the life and conversation, by faith and works corresponding to the faith. The first confession may be made by a hypocrite: and it is one not required of all; there are many who have never been called on to make it, as for instance Matthew, Philip, Thomas, Levi [Lebbaeus]; the other confession must be made by all. He who has first confessed in his disposition of heart will confess with the voice also when need shall arise and reason require. Well did Christ use concerning confession the phrase 'in Me' (*ἐὰν ὁμολογήσῃ ἐν ἐμοί*), concerning denial the phrase 'Me.' A man may confess 'Him' with the voice who really denies Him, if he does not confess Him also in action; but those only confess 'in Him' who live in the confession and in corresponding actions. Nay, it is He Whom they embrace and Who dwells in them Who makes confession 'in them'; for 'He cannot deny Himself.' But concerning denial, He did not say whosoever shall deny 'in Me,' but whosoever shall deny 'Me'; for no one that is 'in Him' can deny Him. And the words 'before men' do not mean before unbelievers only, but before Christians and unbelievers alike; before the one by their life and conversation, before the others in words." In this exposition every word in the sacred text assumes significance; and this characteristic runs equally through the fragments of Heracleon's commentary on St. John, whether the words commented on be our Lord's own or only those of the Evangelist. Thus he calls attention to the facts that in the statement "all things were made by Him," the preposition used is *διά*; that Jesus is said to have gone *down* to Capernaum and gone *up* to Jerusalem; that He found the buyers and sellers *ἐν τῷ ἱερῷ*, not *ἐν τῷ ναῷ*; that He said salvation is *of* the Jews not *in* them, and again (iv. 40) that our Lord tarried *with* the Samaritans, not *in* them; notice is taken of the point in our Lord's discourse with the woman of Samaria, where He first emphasizes His assertion with "Woman, believe Me"; and though Origen occasionally accuses Heracleon of deficient accuracy, for instance in taking *the* prophet (i. 21) as meaning no more than *a* prophet; "in three days" (ii. 19) as meaning no more than "on the third day"; yet on the whole Heracleon's examination of the words is exceedingly minute. He attempts to reconcile differences between the Evangelists, *e.g.* our Lord's ascription to the Baptist of the titles "Elias" and "prophet" with John's own disclaimer of these titles. He finds mysteries in the numbers in the narrative—in the 46 years which the temple was in building, the 6 husbands of the woman of Samaria (for such was his reading), the 2 days our Lord abode with the people of the city, the 7th hour at which the nobleman's son was healed. He thinks it necessary to reconcile his own doctrine with that of the sacred writer, even at the cost of some violence of interpretation. Thus he declares that the Evangelist's assertion that all things were made by the Logos must be understood only of the things of the visible creation, his own doctrine being that the higher aeon world was not so made, but that the lower creation was made by the Logos through the instrumentality of the Demiurge. Instances of this kind where the interpreter is forced to reject the most obvious meaning of the text are sufficiently numerous to shew that the gospel was not written in the interests of Valentinianism; but it is a book which Heracleon evidently recognized as of such authority that he must perforce have it on his side.

He strives to find Valentinianism in the Gospel by a method of spiritual interpretation. Thus the nobleman (*βασιλικός*, iv. 47) is the Demiurge, a petty prince, his kingdom being limited and temporary, the servants are his angels, the son is the man who belongs to the Demiurge. As he finds the *ψυχικοί* represented in the nobleman's son, so again he finds the *πνευματικοί* in the woman of Samaria. The water of Jacob's well which she rejected is Judaism; the husband whom she is to call is no earthly husband, but her spiritual bridegroom from the Pleroma; the other husbands with whom she previously had committed fornication represent the matter with which the spiritual have been entangled; that she is no longer to worship either in "this mountain" or in "Jerusalem" means that she is not, like the heathen, to worship the visible creation, the Hyle, or kingdom of the devil, nor like the Jews to worship the creator or Demiurge; her watering-pot is her good disposition for receiving life from the Saviour. Though the results of Heracleon's method are heretical, the method itself is one commonly used by orthodox Fathers, especially by Origen. Many orthodox parallels to Heracleon's exposition could be adduced, *e.g.* that the cords with which our Lord drove the traffickers from the temple represent the power of the Holy Spirit; the wood to which He assumes they were attached, the wood of the cross. Origen even occasionally blames Heracleon for being too easily content with more obvious interpretations. Heracleon at first is satisfied to take "whose shoe latchet I am not worthy to loose" as meaning no more than "for whom I am not worthy to perform menial offices," and he has Origen's approbation when he tries, however unsuccessfully, to investigate what the shoe represented. It does not appear that Heracleon used his method of interpretation controversially to establish Valentinian doctrine, but, being a Valentinian, readily found those doctrines indicated in the passages on which he commented.

One other of his interpretations deserves mention. The meaning which the Greek of John viii. 44 most naturally conveys is that of the pre-Hieronymian translation "mendax est sicut et pater ejus," and so it is generally understood by Greek Fathers, though in various ways they escape attributing a father to the devil. Hilgenfeld and Volkmar consider that the Evangelist shews that he embraced the opinion of the Valentinians and some earlier Gnostic sects that the father of the devil was the Demiurge or God of the Jews. But this idea was unknown to Heracleon, who here interprets the father of the devil as his essentially evil nature; to which Origen objects that if the devil be evil by the necessity of his nature, he ought rather to be pitied than blamed.

To judge from the fragments we have, Heracleon's bent was rather practical than speculative. He says nothing of the Gnostic theories as to stages in the origin of the universe; the prologue of St. John does not tempt him into mention of the Valentinian Aeonology. In fact he does not use the word aeon in the sense employed by other Valentinian writers, but rather where according to their use we should expect the word Pleroma; and this last word he uses in a special sense, describing the spiritual husband of the Samaritan woman as her Pleroma—that is, the complement which supplies what was lacking to perfection. We find in his system only two beings unknown to orthodox theology, the Demiurge, and apparently a second Son of Man; for on John iv. 37 he distinguishes a higher Son of Man who sows from the Saviour Who reaps. Heracleon gives as great prominence as any orthodox writer to Christ and His redeeming work. But all mankind are not alike in a condition to profit by His redemption. There is a threefold order of creatures: First, the Hylic or material, formed of the ὕλη, which is the substance of the devil, incapable of immortality. Secondly, the psychic or animal belonging to the kingdom of the Demiurge; their ψυχή is naturally mortal, but capable of being clothed with immortality, and it depends on their disposition (θέσις) whether they become sons of God or children of the devil; and, thirdly, the pneumatic or spiritual, who are by nature of the divine essence, though entangled with matter and needing redemption to be delivered from it. These are the special creation of the Logos; they live in Him, and become one with Him. In the second class Heracleon seems to have had the Jews specially in mind and to have regarded them with a good deal of tenderness. They are the children of Abraham who, if they do not love God, at least do not hate Him. Their king, the Demiurge, is represented as not hostile to the Supreme, and though shortsighted and ignorant, yet as well disposed to faith and ready to implore the Saviour's help for his subjects whom he had not himself been able to deliver. When his ignorance is removed, he and his redeemed subjects will enjoy immortality in a place raised above the material world.

Besides the passages on which he comments Heracleon refers to Gen. vi.; Isa. i. 2; Matt. viii. 2, ix. 37; xviii. 11; Rom. i. 25, xii. 1; I. Cor. xv. 54; II. Tim. ii. 13. Neander and Cave have suggested Alexandria as the place where Heracleon taught; but Clement's language suggests some distance either of time or of place; for he would scarcely have thought it necessary to explain that Heracleon was the most in repute of the Valentinians if he were at the time the head of a rival school in the same city. Hippolytus makes Heracleon one of the Italian school of Valentinians; but the silence of all the authorities makes it unlikely that he taught at Rome. It seems, therefore, most likely that he taught in one of the cities of S. Italy; or "Praedestinatus" may be right in making Sicily the scene of his inventions about Heracleon.

The date of Heracleon is of interest on account of his use of St. John's Gospel, which clearly had attained high authority when he wrote. The mere fact, however, that a book was held in equal honour by the Valentinians and the orthodox seems to prove that it must have attained its position before the separation of the Valentinians from the church; and, if so, it is of less importance to determine the exact date of Heracleon. The decade 170-180 may probably be fixed for the centre of his activity. This would not be inconsistent with his having been personally instructed by Valentinus, who continued to teach as late as 160, and would allow time for Heracleon to have gained celebrity before Clement wrote, one of whose references to Heracleon is in what was probably one of his earliest works. He had evidently long passed from the scene when Origen wrote. (Neander, *Gen. Entwick.* 143, and *Ch. Hist.* ii. 135; Heinrici, *Val. Gnosis*, 127; Westcott, *N. T. Canon.* 299.) The Gk. text of *The Fragments of Heracleon* has been ed. with intro. and notes by A. E. Brooke (Camb. Univ. Press). [G.S.]

Heraclides (5) Cyprius, bp. of Ephesus; a native of Cyprus, who had received a liberal education, was versed in the Scriptures, and had passed some years in ascetic training in the desert of Scetis under Evagrius. He then became deacon to Chrysostom, and was in immediate attendance on him. On the deprivation of Antoninus, bp. of Ephesus, A.D. 401, there being a deadlock in the election through the number of rival candidates and the violence of the opposing factions, Chrysostom brought Heraclides forward, and he was elected by the votes of seventy bishops to the vacant see. The election at first only increased the disturbance, and loud complaints were made of the unfitness of Heraclides for the office, which detained Chrysostom in Asia

(Socr. *H. E.* vi. 11; Soz. *H. E.* viii. 6; Pallad. p. 139). At the assembling of the synod of the Oak, A.D. 403, Heraclides was summoned to answer certain specified charges brought against him by Macarius, bp. of Magnesia, a bishop named Isaac, and a monk named John. Among these charges was one of holding Origenizing views. The urgency with which the condemnation of Chrysostom was pressed forward retarded the suit against Heraclides, which had come to no issue when his great master was deposed and banished. After Chrysostom's second and final exile in 404, Heraclides was his fellow-sufferer. He was deposed by the party in power, and put in prison at Nicomedia, where, when Palladius wrote, he had been already languishing for years. A eunuch who, according to Palladius, was stained with the grossest vices, was consecrated bp. of Ephesus in his room (Pallad. *Dial.* ed. Bigot. p. 139). On the ascription to this Heraclides of the *Lausiac History* of Palladius, under the name of *Paradisus Heraclidis*, see PALLADIUS (7); also Fabricius, *Bibl. Graec.* x. 117; Ceillier, vii. 487. [E.V.]

Hermas (2). In the latter half of the 2nd cent. there was in circulation a book of visions and allegories, purporting to be written by one Hermas and commonly known as *The Shepherd.* This book was treated with respect bordering on that paid to the canonical Scriptures of N.T., and was publicly read in some churches. A passage from it is quoted by Irenaeus (iv. 20, p. 253) with the words, "Well said the Scripture," a fact which Eusebius notes (*H. E.* v. 8). Probably in the time of Irenaeus the work was publicly read in the Gallican churches. The mutilated commencement of the *Stromateis* of Clement of Alexandria opens in the middle of a quotation from *The Shepherd*, and about ten times elsewhere he cites the book, always with a complete acceptance of the reality and divine character of the revelations made to Hermas, but without suggesting who Hermas was or when he lived. Origen, who frequently cites the book (*in Rom.* xvi. 14, vol. iv. p. 683), considered it divinely inspired. He suggests, as do others after him, but apparently on no earlier authority, that it was written by the Hermas mentioned in Rom. xvi. 14. His other quotations shew that less favourable views of the book were current in his time. They are carefully separated from quotations from the canonical books, and he generally adds a saving clause, giving the reader permission to reject them; he speaks of it (*in Matt.* xix. 7, vol. iii. p. 644) as a book current in the church but not acknowledged by all, and (*de Princ.* iv. 11) as despised by some. Eusebius (iii. 25) places the book among the orthodox νόθα with the Acts of Paul, Revelation of Peter, Epistle of Barnabas, etc. Elsewhere (iii. 3), while unable to place it among the ὁμολογουμένα because rejected by some, he records its public use in churches and by some most eminent writers, and that it was judged by some most necessary for elementary instruction in the faith. Athanasius (*Ep. Fest.* 39, vol. i. pt. ii. p. 963) classes it with some of the deutero-canonical books of O.T. and with *The Teaching of the Apostles* as not canonical, but useful for catechetical instruction. It is found in the Sinaitic MS. following the Ep. of Barnabas, as an appendix to the N.T. After the 4th cent. it rapidly passed out of ecclesiastical use in the East.

The Western tradition deserves more attention, as internal evidence shews the book to have been composed at Rome. The MURATORIAN FRAGMENT on the Canon tells us that it had been written during the episcopate of Pius by his brother Hermas, a period which the writer speaks of as within then living memory. He concludes that the book ought to be read but not publicly in the church among the prophetic writings, the number of which was complete, nor among the apostolic. The statement that the book not only might but ought to be read is a high recognition of the value attributed to it by the writer, and we gather that at least in some places its use in church was then such as to lead some to regard it as on a level with the canonical Scriptures. Tertullian, in one of his earliest treatises, *de Oratione*, has a reference to its influence on the practice of churches which shews it to have enjoyed high authority at the time, an authority which Tertullian's argument does not dispute. It had probably been used in church reading and translated into Latin, since Tertullian describes it by the Latin title *Pastor*, and not by a Greek title, as he usually does in the case of Greek writings. Some ten years later, after Tertullian had become a Montanist, and the authority of *The Shepherd* is urged in behalf of readmitting adulterers to communion, he rejects the book as not counted worthy of inclusion in the canon, but placed by every council, even those of the Catholic party, among false and apocryphal writings (*de Pudic.* c. 10). Quoting *Hebrews*, he says that this is at least more received than that apocryphal *Shepherd* of the adulterers (c. 20). The phrase "*more* received" warns us to take *cum grano* Tertullian's assertion as to the *universal* rejection of *The Shepherd*; but doubtless the distinction between apostolic and later writings was then drawn more sharply, and in the interval between Tertullian's two writings *The Shepherd* may have been excluded from public reading in many churches which before had admitted it. The Liberian papal catalogue (probably here, as elsewhere, following the catalogue of Hippolytus) states that under the episcopate of Pius his brother Ermas wrote a book in which the commands and precepts were contained which the angel gave him when he came to him in the habit of a shepherd. Yet, while refusing to assign the book to apostolic times, it makes no doubt of the reality of the angelic appearance to Hermas. Later biographical notices of popes state that the message given to Hermas was that Easter should always be celebrated on a Sunday. These clearly shew that by then all knowledge of the book had been lost; and further notices shew a confusion between the name of Hermas and that of his book, which imply that the book was no longer in use. Jerome, when quoting Eusebius about the book (*de Vir. Ill.* 10, vol. ii. 845), adds that among the Latins it was almost unknown. He speaks contemptuously of it (*in Habac.* i. 14, vol. vi. 604), for it seems certain that the book of Hermas is here referred to. It is marked in the Gelasian decree as apocryphal. Notwithstanding, there are indications that some use of the book continued in the West, *e.g.* the fact being that there still exist some 20 MSS. of the Latin version. In the African church of the 4th cent. we find from the list in the *Codex Claromontanus* (Westcott, *Canon N. T.* p. 557) that it was placed with the Acts of Paul and the Revelation of St. Peter as an appendix to the N.T. books; and it occupies a similar place in the Sinaitic MS., the only Greek Bible known to have contained it. But in some existing Latin MSS. it is placed with the apocryphal books of O.T.

The book is in three parts. The first part consists of visions. Hermas tells that he who had brought him up had sold him to Rome to a lady named Rhoda; that after a considerable time he renewed his acquaintance with her and began to love her as a sister; that he saw her one day bathing in the Tiber and assisted her out of the water; that admiring her beauty he thought how happy he should be if he had a wife like her in person and disposition. Further than this his thought did not go. But a little time after he had a vision. He fell asleep, and in his dream was walking and struggling on ground so rugged and broken that it was impossible to pass. At length he succeeded in crossing the water by which his path had been washed away, and coming into smooth ground knelt to confess his sins to God. Then the heavens were opened and he saw Rhoda saluting him from the sky. On his asking her what she did there, she told him that she had been taken up to accuse him, because God was angry with him for having sinned in thought against her. Then Hermas was overwhelmed with horror and fear, not knowing how he could abide the severity of God's judgment, if such a thought as his was marked as sin. Rhoda now passes out of his dream and he sees a venerable aged lady clad in shining garments sitting on a great white chair and holding a book in her hand. She asks why he, usually so cheerful, is now so sad. On telling her, she owns what a sin any impure thought would be in one so chaste, so single-minded and so innocent as he; but tells him that this is not why God is displeased with him, but because of the sins of his children, whom he, through false indulgence, had allowed to corrupt themselves, but to whom repentance was open if he would warn them. Then she reads to him out of her book, but of all she reads he can remember nothing save the last comforting sentence, and that all which preceded was terrible and threatening. She parted from him with the words, "Play the man, Hermas." Hermas was an elderly man with a grown-up family, and Rhoda must have been at least as old as himself. If the tale is an invented one, this is certainly an incongruity; but if it be a true story, it is quite conceivable that the thought may have occurred to Hermas, who seems to have been not happy in his family relations, how much happier it would have been for him if Rhoda had been his wife; and that afterwards, in a dream, this thought may have recurred to his memory as a sin to be repented of. The vision presents all the characteristics of a real dream; the want of logical connexion between the parts, the changes of scene, the fading out of Rhoda as principal figure and the appearance of the aged lady in her room; the substitution of quite a different offence for the sinful thought which weighed on his conscience at the beginning; the physical distress in his sleep at first presenting the idea of walking on and on without being able to find an outlet, afterwards of mental grief at words spoken to him; the long reading of which only the words spoken immediately before awaking are remembered,—all these indicate that we are reading not a literary invention like the dream of the *Pilgrim's Progress*, but the recital, a little dressed up it may be, of a dream which the narrator really had. In another vision, a year after, he saw again the lady and her book, and received the book to copy, but still it conveyed no idea to his mind. He then set himself by fasting and prayer to learn its meaning, and after about a fortnight was gratified. He learns, too, that the lady is not, as he had imagined, the sibyl, but the church, and that she appeared as old because she was created first of all, and for her sake the world was made. *Ephesians*, which probably suggested this doctrine of the pre-existence of the church, is one of the N.T. books of whose use by Hermas there are clear traces. In subsequent visions we have a different account of the matter; he sees in each a woman more and more youthful in appearance, whom he is taught to identify with the church of his former vision; and it is explained that he saw her old at first because the spirit of Christians had been broken by infirmity and doubt, and afterwards more youthful as by the revelations made him their spirit had been renewed. After his first two visions Hermas watched eagerly for new revelations, and set himself to obtain them by fasting and prayer. In those later visions, while the pictures presented to his mind are such as we can well believe to have been dream representations, the explanations given of them have a coherence only to be found in the thoughts of a waking man. This is still more true of the second and third parts of the work. At the end of the first part he has the vision in which he sees a man dressed like a shepherd, who tells him that he is the angel of repentance and the guardian to whose care he had been entrusted. From this shepherd he receives, for his instruction and that of the church, the "Commandments," which form the second, and the "Similitudes," which form the third, part of the work. The Similitudes were probably suggested by N.T. parables, though the frigid compositions of Hermas fall infinitely below these.

The literary merits of the work of Hermas are of little importance compared with the fundamental question as to the date of the book and whether it claims to be an inspired document, the writer of which aspires to no literary merit, save that of faithfully recording the revelations made him. Are we to suppose that Hermas in relating his visions intended no more than to present edifying lessons in an allegorical form, and that it was merely as an instructive fiction that the book was regarded when it was introduced into public reading in the church? Donaldson says: "If the book be not inspired, then either the writer fancied he had seen these visions, or tried to make other people fancy this, or he clothed the work in a fictitious form designedly and undisguisedly. If he did the first, he must have been silly. If he did the second, he must have been an impostor." But as he believes the author to have been "an honest, upright, and thoughtful man," he concludes that he did the third, "as multitudes of others have done after him, with John Bunyan at their head." If we took this view we could lay no stress on anything the author tells us about himself and his family. These details might be fictitious, as the angels, the towers, and the beasts of the visions. We could not even assume that his name was Hermas, for the narrator of the visions, who bears this name, might be an imaginary personage. But we ourselves feel bound to reject this as altogether mistaken criticism, and as an application to the 2nd cent. of the standards of to-day. To us it seems plain that, whatever the author intended, the first readers of Hermas did not receive the book as mere allegorical fiction. Bunsen (*Hippolytus and his Age*, i. 315) tells us that Niebuhr used to pity the Athenian (*sic*, Qu. *Roman?*) Christians for being obliged to listen to this "good but dull novel." If the authorities of the church regarded it merely as a novel, would they have appointed it for public reading? At the end of the century Clement and others shew no doubt of the reality of the visions. Were the men of a couple of generations earlier likely to have been more severe in their judgments, and would an angelic appearance seem to them so incredible that one who related it would be regarded as the narrator of a fiction that he did not intend to be believed? The book itself contains directions to the rulers of the Roman church to send the volume to foreign churches. If we suppose it really was sent to them stamped as a prophetic writing by the authority of the Roman church, we have an explanation of the consideration, only second to that of the canonical Scriptures, which it enjoyed in so many distant churches. A man at the present day might publish a story of visions, and be persuaded that his readers would not take him seriously, but no one in the 2nd cent. would be entitled to hold such a persuasion, and if the book of Hermas was accepted as inspired, the writer cannot be acquitted of the responsibility of having foreseen and intended this result. Mosheim, *de Rebus Christ. ante Const.* 163, 166, holds that the writer must either have been "mente captus et fanaticus," or else "scientem volentemque fefellisse," the latter being the opinion to which he inclines, believing that the lawfulness of pious frauds was a fixed opinion with many Christians at the date of the composition we are discussing. We maintain, however, that it is possible to disbelieve in the inspiration of Hermas without imputing folly either to him who made the claim or to those who admitted it. We must not regard the men of the 2nd cent. as fools because their views as to God's manner of teaching His church were different from those which the experience of so many following centuries has taught us. A Christian cannot regard them as fools for believing that in the time of our Lord and His apostles a great manifestation of the supernatural was made to the world. How long and to what extent similar manifestations would present themselves in the ordinary life of the church only experience could shew, and they are not to be scorned if their expectations have not been borne out by later experience. In particular, if we are to set down as fools all who have believed that supernatural intimations may be given in dreams, our list would be a long one, and would include many eminent names; and though modern science may regard visions as phenomena admitting a natural explanation, it is not reasonable to expect such a view from the science of the 2nd cent. What Hermas tells of his personal history and of the times and circumstances of his visions conveys to us the impression of artless truth. His information about himself is contained in incidental allusions, not very easy to piece together; and the author of a fictitious narrative would not have conveyed so obscurely what he tells about his hero. He would probably also have made him a man of some eminence, holding high church office, whereas Hermas always speaks of the presbyters as if he were not one of them, and could have no motive for making his hero one engaged in trade unsuccessfully and not very honestly, and an elderly man with a termagant wife and ill brought-up children. On the other hand, if the book be true history, it is very much to the point that Hermas should get a revelation, directing his wife to keep her tongue in better order, and his children to pay more respect to their parents; nor need we suppose Hermas guilty of dishonesty in thus turning his gift of prophecy to the advantage of his family comfort; for nothing can be more natural than that the thoughts which troubled his waking moments should present themselves in his visions. There is nothing incredible in the supposition that the pictures of the first vision did present themselves to the mind of Hermas as he relates them. They must have been very vivid, and have impressed him strongly. Still, it is a year before he has another vision. After this he begins to fast and pray and look out eagerly for more revelations. Finally he comes to believe himself to be under the constant guardianship of the shepherd angel of repentance, and he ascribes all the lessons he desires to teach to the inspiration of this heavenly monitor. But perhaps his language expresses no more than his belief in the divine inspiration under which he wrote, for elsewhere he states that he does not regard the personages of his visions as having objective reality, and those things which in the earlier part are represented as spoken to him by the church are afterwards said to have been spoken by God's Spirit under the form of the church. That he sincerely believed himself to be the bearer of a divine message appears to be the case. A summary of his convictions would serve also for those of a man in many respects very unlike, Savonarola, (*a*) that the church of his time had corrupted itself, and had become deeply tainted with worldliness; (*b*) that a time of great tribulation was at hand, in which the dross should be purged away; (*c*) that there was still an intervening time, during which repentance was possible and would be accepted; (*d*) that he was himself divinely commissioned to preach that repentance.

Date and Authorship.—Antiquity furnishes authority for three suppositions: (*a*) the author was the Hermas to whom a salutation is sent in Rom. xvi. 14; or (*b*) brother to Pius, bp. of Rome at the middle of the 2nd cent.; or (*c*) contemporary with Clement who was bishop at the very beginning of that century or the end of the preceding. The first may be set aside as a highly improbable guess of Origen. The author shews no wish to be taken for the apostolic Hermas, but distinctly speaks of the apostles as all dead. A forger could have found many more suitable names than Hermas, one of the least prominent in N.T., and of which, except in connexion with this book, there is no trace in ecclesiastical tradition. If our view of the book be correct, the author had no motive for antedating it. His prophecy announced tribulation close at hand and only a short intervening period for repentance. To represent such a prophecy as being already 50 or 100 years old would be to represent it as having failed, and in fact *The Shepherd* did lose credit when it had been so long in existence. Hermas seems to have thought that, if the worldliness of the church could be repented of and reformed, it would be possible to keep it pure during the brief remainder of its existence. He announced therefore forgiveness on repentance for sins of old Christians prior to the date of his revelation, but none for those of new converts, or for sins subsequent to his revelation. To date his revelation 50 years back would have defeated his own purpose and made his message inapplicable to those whom he addressed. Again the acceptance of the book by the church of Rome is inexplicable if it were introduced by no known person, containing, as it does, revelations purporting to have been given among themselves and to a leading member of their church. If the first readers of the work of Elchesai or of the Clementine homilies asked, Why did we never hear of these things before? these books had provided an answer in the fiction that the alleged authors had only communicated them under a pledge of strict secrecy; in this book, on the contrary, Hermas is directed (*Vis.* iii. 8) to go after three days and speak in the hearing of all the saints the words he had heard in his vision. Elsewhere he enables us to understand how this direction could be carried out. We learn (*Mand.* 11) that certain persons were then recognized in the church as having prophetic gifts, and that at the Christian meetings for worship, if after prayer ended one of them were filled with the Holy Spirit, he might speak unto the people as the Lord willed. The simplest explanation how the Roman Church came to believe in its inspiration seems, then, to be that it had previously admitted the inspiration of its author, that he held the position of a recognized prophet as in the East did Quadratus and Ammia of Philadelphia (Eus. *H. E.* v. 16), and that he really did publicly deliver his message in the church assembly. As the 2nd cent. went on, the public exercise of prophetic powers in the church seems to have ceased, and when revived by Montanus and his followers had to encounter much opposition. The ensuing controversy led the church to insist more strongly on the distinction between the inspiration of the canonical writers and that of holy men of later times, and the Muratorian fragment exhibits the feeling entertained towards the end of the cent. that the list of prophetic writings had been closed and that no production of the later years of the church could be admitted.

But if, as we think, the Hermas of *The Shepherd* is not a fictitious character, but a real person known in the church of Rome in the 2nd cent., we incline to follow Zahn in relying more on his connexion with Clement than with Pius. Zahn places *The Shepherd* *c.* 97; but if we assign that date to the epistle of Clement we ought to allow a few years for that letter to have obtained the celebrity and success which the notice in Hermas implies. That notice need not necessarily have been published in the lifetime of Clement, for Hermas is not instructed to deliver his message immediately, but only after the completion of his revelations, and this may have been after Clement's death.

Are, then, any indications of date in the book inconsistent with such an early date?

There is much affinity between the leading ideas of Montanism and of the book of Hermas, especially as to the fall of many in the church from the ideal of holiness. The question was asked, Was it possible to renew such again to repentance? In both our Lord's second coming was eagerly looked forward to, and a knowledge of God's coming dealings with His church sought for from visions and revelations. But the teaching of Hermas is less rigorous than the Montanistic, and all that is special to Montanism is unknown to him.

Hermas directs his efforts almost exclusively to combating the relaxation of morality in the church; he scarcely notices doctrinal errors, and no reference to Gnostic doctrines can be found in his book, unless it be a statement (*Sim.* v. 7) that there were some who took licence to misuse the flesh on account of a denial of the resurrection of the body. But these false teachers seem to have been all in the church, not separate from it. In the passage which seems most distinctly to refer to Gnostics (*ib.* ix. 22), they are described as "wishing to know everything and knowing nothing," as "praising themselves that they have understanding, and wishing to be teachers, though they were really fools." Yet, he adds, "to these repentance is open, for they were not wicked, but rather silly and without understanding." The seeds of Gnosticism had begun to spring up even in apostolic times; but we cannot think that Hermas would have written thus after Gnosticism had become dangerous to the Roman church.

Hermas rebukes the strifes for precedence among Christians (*Vis.* iii. 9; *Mand.* ix.; *Sim.* viii. 7), and it is difficult to find in his book evidence of the existence of the episcopal form of government or of resistance to its introduction. He appears to use ἐπίσκοπος as synonymous with πρεσβύτερος and always speaks of the government of the church as in the hands of the elders, without hinting that one elder enjoyed authority over others. Clement, indeed, is recognized as the organ by which the church of Rome communicated with foreign churches; but we are not told that implied a pre-eminence in domestic rule. Similarly, though we infer that the presbyters had seats of honour in the church assemblies, we are not told that one had a seat higher than the rest. Either it was not the case or it was too much a matter of course to be mentioned. But a message regarding dissensions is sent τοῖς προηγουμένοις τῆς ἐκκλησίας καὶ τοῖς πρωτοκαθεδρίταις. It is a very forced explanation of the last plural noun to suppose it means some one of the προηγούμενοι who desired to make himself the first, nor have we reason to think that the word implies any sarcasm. It is more natural to understand that besides the presbyters there were others, such as the teachers and prophets (*Mand.* xi.), who in church assemblies were given seats of honour.

The church had at the time of this writing enjoyed a good deal of quiet, but this had evidently been broken by many harassing persecutions, in which some had apostatized. Usually their danger is described as no more than of loss of goods and of injury to worldly business; but there had been (though perhaps not recently) martyrs who had given their lives and endured crosses and wild beasts for the Name of the Son of God. They could have saved themselves by denial or by committing idolatry. Thus they suffered *as Christians*, and it has been inferred that the date must be later than the well-known letter of Trajan to Pliny which first made the profession of Christianity unlawful. Yet it seems possible to assign an earlier date to *The Shepherd*, and to *I. Peter* which is affected by the same argument, when we remember that Trajan only gave imperial sanction to the rule on which Pliny had been acting already, and on which others had probably been acting previously; for Pliny implies that trials of Christians were then well known. And it may be argued that after the edict of Trajan obstinate profession of Christianity was liable to be punished with death, whereas in the time of Hermas it seems to have been punished only by fine or imprisonment. Hermas lost his business in the persecution, having been betrayed, it seems, by his children. At the time of the visions he was apparently farming. Zahn, who places the persecution under Domitian, ingeniously conjectures (p. 133) that Hermas was one of those to whom, as Dion Cassius tells (68, 2), Nerva made restitution by giving land instead of the goods of which they had been despoiled by Domitian.

It is disappointing to have to add that an ordinary Christian of to-day would find in the book neither much interest nor edification, and that the historical student finds in it much less help than he might expect. Hermas is absorbed in trying to bring about a practical reform; he shews much less interest in doctrine, in which possibly as a layman he was perhaps not accurately instructed; he never quotes either O. or N. T., nor is his language much influenced by Scripture phraseology, and some would describe him as having preached not the Gospel, but merely a dry morality. The inference was natural, if Pauline Christianity is so much in the background in Hermas, that he must have been an anti-Pauline Jewish Christian; and this may seem confirmed by the fact that the N.T. book which has most stamped itself on his mind is the Ep. of St. James. Yet a closer examination finds no real trace of Judaism in him. It is scarcely credible that one brought up a Jew should seem so unfamiliar with O.T.* The Jewish nation and its privileges are not even mentioned, nor the distinction between Jew and Gentile. Michael is not the guardian angel of the nation, but of the Christian church.

The only express quotation is from the lost apocryphal book of Eldad and Modad. His use of either O. or N. T. not being indicated by formal quotation, but only by coincidences of language or thought, there is room for difference of opinion as to his use of particular books. The proofs of the use of the Epp. of James and of Ephesians seem decisive, and only a little less strong in the case of I. Peter and I. Cor. Of his use of the Gospel and Revelation of St. John we are persuaded, though we admit that the evidence is not conclusive. We believe also that the knowledge of sayings of our Lord which Hermas unmistakably exhibits was obtained from our Synoptic Gospels, the coincidences with St. Mark (see Zahn, p. 457) being most striking.

Where Hermas had lived before he was sold to Rome we can only conjecture. According to a reading which there seems no good ground to question, he supposes himself in one of his visions to have been transported to Arcadia, and Mahaffy says (*Rambles in Greece*, p. 330, 2nd ed.) that the scenery he describes suits that in Arcadia, and does not suit the neighbourhood of Rome. Zahn conjectures that Hermas was born in Egypt because the architecture of the tower of Hermas's visions resembles the description in Josephus of the Jewish temple in the Egyptian Heliopolis.

The Shepherd has been edited by Hilgenfeld (*Nov. Test. ext. Can. Rec.* 1866) and Gebhardt and Harnack (*Patres Apostolici*, 1877). The latter ed. is indispensable, and contains a full list of editions, and of works treating of Hermas. Some interesting discussion is to be found in the reviews of Gebhardt's ed. by Overbeck (Schurer, *Theol. Literaturzeitung*, 1878), Donaldson in *Theological Review* (1878), and Zahn, *Göttingen gelehrte Anzeigen* (1878). Zahn, *Der Hirt des Hermas* (1868), is the work from which we have learned most. Another ed. is by Funk (*Pat. Apost.* Tübingen, 1878). *A Collation of the Athos Codex of the Shepherd* with intro. by Dr. Lambros, trans. and ed. with preface and appendices by Dr. J. A. Robinson, has been pub. by Camb. Univ. Press; a cheap Eng. trans. of *The Shepherd* by Dr. C. Taylor (2 vols.) by S.P.C.K.; and in

*** The contrast is striking if we compare the fullness of O.T. quotation in Clement's ep. with the scantiness in Hermas. Harnack noted seven passages which seem to shew acquaintance with O.T. Four of these relate to passages quoted in N.T. books which seem to have been read by Hermas; the other three are doubtful.**

Ante-Nic. Fathers, vol. ii. See also F. Spitta, *Zur Gesch. und Lit. der Urchristenthums*, vol. ii. (Göttingen, 1898), and Funk, in *Theol. Quartalschr.* lxxxi. and lxxxv. [G.S.]

Hermenigild (*Ermenigild*), St., Visigoth Catholic prince in Spain, son of the Arian king Leovigild. Hermenigild and Reccared were sons of Leovigild's first wife (Joh. Bicl. apud *Esp. Sagr.* vi. 378), who was dead in 569. The dates of their births are unknown (? 560-562), but Hermenigild was the elder. In 573 both sons were made "consortes regni" (*ib.*). Most probably between 573 and 575 (cf. Greg. Tur. iv. 38) Hermenigild was betrothed to the Catholic Frankish princess Ingunthis, the daughter of Sigibert of Rheims. In 579 (Joh. Bicl. *l.c.* 381) Ingunthis, then 12 years old, reached Spain, and, owing to dissensions between her and her Arian grandmother, Leovigild sent the newly married pair to a distance, assigning to Hermenigild the government of Baetica, or part of it, with Seville for a capital (*ib.*). Here later in 579 (cf. Görres, *Kritische Untersuch. über den Aufstand und das Martyrium des Westgoth. Königsohnes Hermenigild*, in *Zeitschrift für Hist. Theol.* 1873, i. n. 83; Dahn, *Kön. der Germ.* v. 137, gives 580 as the year) Hermenigild renounced Arianism, was confirmed in the Catholic faith by Leander the Catholic metropolitan of Seville, and took the name of Joannes (Greg. Tur. v. 39; Greg. Magn. *Dial.* iii. 31; Paul. Diac. iii. 21). This was immediately followed by the rebellion of Hermenigild (Joh. Bicl. *l.c.*), who shortly afterwards formed a close alliance with the Byzantines in the south, and with the recently catholicized Suevi in the north, *i.e.* with the two most formidable enemies of his father's state and power (cf. Dahn, v. 138). Thus the struggle shaped itself as a conflict of confessions and nationalities, of Arianism and Catholicism, of Goth and Roman, although Leovigild had adherents among the provincials, and Hermenigild counted some Gothic partisans (*ib.* 140).

It was not till the end of 582 that Leovigild felt himself strong enough to attack his son. Seville fell in 584 (Joh. Bicl. *l.c.* 383), and shortly afterwards Hermenigild was captured in or near Cordova (*ib.*; Greg. Tur. v. 39, vi. 43), deprived of the government of Baetica, and exiled to Valencia. In 585 Hermenigild was put to death (Joh. Bicl. 384). Isidore does not mention her death at all. Gregory of Tours mentions it in passing (*Hist. Fr.* viii. 28). Upon the account given by Gregory the Great *alone* (*Dial.* iii. 31) rests the claim of Hermenigild to be considered not as a rebel suffering the penalty of a political crime, but as a martyr for the Catholic faith. According to the pope, Hermenigild, after a painful imprisonment, was beheaded on the night of Easter Sunday, by his father's *apparitores*, because he had refused to receive the sacrament from the hands of an Arian bishop. After the execution, miracles were not wanting to substantiate his claim to veneration. In his grave, according to Gregory, were laid the foundations of Visigothic Catholicism; for, after Leovigild's death, his son Reccared was converted by Leander and led the whole people of the Visigoths to the true faith. [M.A.W.]

Hermes (1) Trismegistus. Under this title we have a variety of writings of uncertain date and unknown authorship originating in Egypt. The name "Hermes Trismegistus" never belonged to any single writer. Jamblichus, at the beginning of his treatise *de Mysteriis*, tells us that "Hermes, who presides over speech, is, according to ancient tradition, common to all priests; he it is who exists in all of them. That is why our ancestors attributed all discoveries to him, and issued their works under the name of Hermes." There was, in fact, a long-continued series of books called "hermetic," extending over several centuries. Tertullian, however (*cont. Valent.* c. 15), speaks of Hermes Trismegistus as a master in philosophy; and the extant hermetic books have, whatever their date, philosophical and spiritual relations of a very interesting kind. They belong, as is now generally agreed, to the neo-Platonic school; and gather up in a synthesis, the artificiality of which is not at first sight apparent, large elements of all the different factors of religious belief in the Roman world or the 2nd and 3rd cents. The two principal are the Ποιμάνδρης (the "Shepherd of Men"), and the Λόγος τέλειος (or "Discourse of Initiation"), otherwise called "Asclepius." These two works, together with a variety of fragments, have been translated into French by M. Louis Ménard (Paris, 1867), and accompanied with a preliminary essay of much interest on the hermetic writings and their affinities generally. His most important fragments are from a work entitled Κόρη κόσμου (the "Virgin of the World"), a dialogue between Isis and her son Hôrus on the origin of nature and of animated beings, including man. Other less noticeable works attributed to Hermes Trismegistus are named in *D. of G. and R. Biogr.* (*s.v.*).

It is not to be assumed that these, the Ποιμάνδρης, and Λόγος τέλειος, are by the same author; but from their great similarity of tone and thought, this is possible. Both works are quoted by Lactantius (who ascribed to them the fabulous antiquity and high authority which the early Fathers were wont to attribute to the Sibylline books); and must have been written before *c.* 330, when Lactantius died. The historical allusions in the Asclepius distinctly point to a time when heathenism was about to perish before the increasing power of Christianity. Hence both these works were probably written towards the close of the 3rd cent.

Three motives are discernible in them. First, the endeavour to take an intellectual survey of the whole spiritual universe, without marking any points where the understanding of man fails and has to retire unsatisfied; this is a disposition which, under different forms and at different times, has been called Pantheism or Gnosticism (though the Gnostic idea of an evil element in creation nowhere appears in these treatises). The ideas of the author are presented with a gorgeous material imagery; and, speaking generally, he regards the material world as interpenetrated by the spiritual, and almost identified with it. The power and divine character which he attributes to the sun and other heavenly bodies are peculiarly Egyptian, though this also brings him into affinity with Stoic, and even with Platonic, views. Secondly, this Pantheism or Gnosticism is modified by moral and religious elements which certainly might to some degree be paralleled in Plato, but to which it is difficult to avoid ascribing a Jewish and even a Christian origin. Great stress is laid on the unity, the creative power, the fatherhood and goodness of God. The argument from design also appears (*Poemander*, c. 5). Even the well-known terms of baptism and regeneration occur, though in different connexions, and the former in a metaphorical sense. One of the chapters of the *Poemander* is entitled "The Secret Sermon on the Mountain." The future punishments for wrongdoing are described with emphasis, but there is no moral teaching in detail. Thirdly, these intellectual and religious elements are associated with a passionate and vigorous defence of the heathen religion, including idol worship, and a prophecy of the evils which will come on the earth from the loss of piety. They are thus the only extant lamentation of expiring heathenism, and one that is not without pathos. But for the most part the style is hierophantic, pretentious, and diffuse. See further Fabric. *Bibl. Graec.* vol. i. pp. 46-94; Baumgarten Crusius, *de Lib. Hermeticorum Origine atque Indole* (Jena, 1827); and Chambers, *The Theol. and Philos. Works of Her. Tris.* (Edin. 1882). [J.R.M.]

Hermias (5), a Christian philosopher, author of the *Irrisio Gentilium Philosophorum*, annexed in all *Bibliothecae Patrum* to the works of Athenagoras (Migne, *Patr. Gk.* vi. 1167). It was published in Greek and Latin at Basle in 1553. It consists of satirical reflections on the opinions of the philosophers, shewing how Anaxagoras, Empedocles, Pythagoras, Epicurus, etc. agree only in repelling and refuting one another. Who the author was seems to have baffled all inquiries. Some identify him with Hermias Sozomen the ecclesiastical historian. Even the martyr of May 31 has been suggested (Ceillier, vi. 332). Cave (i. 81) attributes the work to the 2nd cent. As it was plainly written when heathenism was triumphant, Ceillier (*u.s.*) places it under Julian. Neander (*H. E.* ii. 429, ed. Bohn) regards Hermias as "one of those bitter enemies of the Greek philosophy whom Clement of Alexandria thought it necessary to censure, and who, following the idle Jewish legend, pretended that the Greek philosophy had been derived from fallen angels. In the title of his book he is called the philosopher; perhaps he wore the philosopher's mantle before his conversion, and after it passed at once from an enthusiastic admiration of the Greek pilosophy to extreme abhorrence of it" (Du Pin, *H. E.* t. i. p. 69, ed. 1723). The latest ed. is by H. Diels, in *Doxographi Graeci* (Berlin, 1879). [G.T.S.]

Hermogenes (1), a teacher of heretical doctrine towards the close of 2nd cent., the chief error ascribed to him being the doctrine that God had formed the world, not out of nothing, but out of previously existing uncreated matter. Tertullian wrote two tracts in answer, one of which is extant, and is our chief source of information about Hermogenes. The minuteness with which his arguments are answered indicates that Tertullian is replying to a published work of Hermogenes, apparently written in Latin. Another doctrine of Hermogenes preserved by Clement of Alexandria (*Eclog. ex Script. Proph.* 56, p. 1002), being unlike anything told of him by Tertullian, was conjectured by Mosheim (*de Rebus Christ. ante Const.* p. 435), to belong to some different Hermogenes. But the since recovered treatise on heresies by Hippolytus combines in its account of Hermogenes (viii. 17, p. 273) the doctrines attributed to him by Clement and by Tertullian. Probably Clement and Hippolytus drew from a common source, namely, the work "against the heresy of Hermogenes," which, Eusebius tells us (*H. E.* iv. 24), was written by Theophilus of Antioch, and which is mentioned also by Theodoret (*Haer. Fab.* i. 19), who probably drew from it his account of Hermogenes, in which he clearly employs some authority different from the tenth book, or summary, of Hippolytus, of which he makes large use of elsewhere. Theodoret adds that Hermogenes was also answered by Origen, from which it has been supposed that he refers under this name to the summary now ascribed to Hippolytus; but there is no evidence that Theodoret regarded this work as Origen's (see Volkmar, *Hippolytus und die römischen Zeitgenossen*, p. 54), so that some lost work of Origen's must be presumed. The passages cited are all our primary authorities about Hermogenes, except some statements of Philaster (see below).

A considerable distance of time and place separates the notices by Theophilus and Tertullian. THEOPHILUS survived the accession of Commodus in 180, but probably not more than two years. Hence 180 would be our latest date for the teaching of Hermogenes, which may have been earlier. He probably had disciples at Antioch, and therefore must have taught at or near there, and any writing of his answered by Theophilus must have been written in Greek. Tertullian's tract against Hermogenes is assigned by Uhlhorn (*Fundamenta Chron. Tert.* p. 60) to A.D. 206 or 207. In it Hermogenes is spoken of as still living ("ad hodiernum homo in saeculo") and coupled with one Nigidius in the work on Prescription, c. 30, as among the heretics "who still walk perverting the ways of God." There are indications that the work to which Tertullian replies was in Latin, and every reason to think that Hermogenes (though probably, as his name indicates, of Greek descent) was then living in Carthage, for Tertullian assails his private character, entering into details in a way which would not be intelligible unless both were inhabitants of the same city. The same inference may be drawn from the frequency of Tertullian's references to Hermogenes in works of which his errors are not the subject (*de Monog.* 16; *de Praescrip.* 30, 33; *adv. Valent.* 16; *de Animâ*, 1, 11, 21, 22, 24); for apparently proximity gave this heretic an importance in his eyes greater than was otherwise warranted. Tertullian describes him as a turbulent man, who took loquacity for eloquence and impudence for firmness. Two things in particular are shocking to his then Montanist principles, that Hermogenes was a painter, and that he had married frequently. Neander and others have supposed that the offence of Hermogenes was that he painted mythological subjects. But there is no trace of this limitation in Tertullian's treatise, which shews all through a dislike of the pictorial art, and Tertullian seems to have considered the representation of the human form absolutely forbidden by the 2nd commandment. As for the charge of frequent marriages, if Hermogenes, who in 207 would be advanced in life, was then married to a third wife, a writer so fond of rhetorical exaggeration as Tertullian might describe him as one who had formed a practice of marrying (*nubit assidue*), or who had "married more women than he had painted." Tertullian's language may imply that Hermogenes had also endeavoured to prove from Scripture that a second marriage was not unlawful.

With regard to the doctrines of Hermogenes, the language of Hippolytus suggests that he denied the physical possibility of creation from nothing; but in the representation of Tertullian no stress is laid on the philosophic maxim, "Nihil ex nihilo," and the eternal existence of matter seems only assumed to account for the origin of evil. The argument of Hermogenes was, either God made the world out of His own substance, or out of nothing, or out of previously existing matter. The first or emanation hypothesis is rejected, since He Who is indivisible and immutable could not separate Himself into parts, or make Himself other than He had ever been. The second is disproved by the existence of evil, for if God made all things out of nothing unrestrained by any condition, His work would have been all good and perfect like Himself. It remained, therefore, that God must have formed the world out of previously existent matter, through the fault of which evil was possible. Further, God must have been always God and Lord, therefore there must always have existed something of which He was God and Lord. Tertullian replies that God was always God but not always Lord, and appeals to Genesis, where the title God is given to the Creator from the first, but the title Lord not till after the creation of man. Concerning Tertullian's assertion that God was not always Father, see Bull, *Def. Fid. Nic.* iii. 10. From the assertion of Hermogenes that God was always Lord of matter, Neander inferred that he must have denied any creation in time, and held that God had been from eternity operating in a formative manner on matter. Tertullian does not appear to have drawn this consequence, and (c. 44) assumes as undisputed some definite epoch of creation. But the account of Hippolytus shews Neander to have been right. With regard to the general argument, Tertullian shews that the hypothesis of the eternity of matter relieves none of the difficulties of reconciling the existence of evil with the attributes of God. If God exercised lordship over matter, why did He not clear it of evil before He employed it in the work of creation? Or why did He employ in His work that which He knew to be evil? It would really, he says, be more honourable to God to make Him the free and voluntary author of evil than to make him the slave of matter, compelled to use it in His work, though knowing it to be evil. He contends that the hypothesis of Hermogenes amounts to Ditheism, since, though he does not give to matter the name of God, he ascribes to it God's essential attribute of eternity. He asks what just claim of lordship God could have over matter as eternal as Himself; nay, which might claim to be the superior; for matter could do without God, but God, it would seem, could not carry out His work without coming to matter for assistance. In the discussion every word in the Mosaic account of creation receives minute examination and there is a good deal of strained verbal interpretation on both sides. But the authority, and apparently the canon, of Scripture were subjects on which both were agreed. Tertullian holds Scripture so exclusive an authority that its mere silence is decisive, and, since it does not mention pre-existent matter, that those who assert its existence incur the woe denounced against those who add to that which is written.

Though the word "materialist" is first heard of in this controversy, the views of Hermogenes were very unlike those now known by that name, and it is doubtful whether our word matter exactly corresponds to the *hyle* of Hermogenes. This apparently included the ideas of shapelessness and disorderly motion, so that all the sensible world could not, as in our modern language, be described as material. That which became κόσμος ceased to be *hyle*, and, in fact, Tertullian does not admit the existence of matter in the sense of Hermogenes. Hermogenes held matter to be infinite and refused to apply to it any predicate. It is without form, and is described as in a perpetual state of turbulent restless motion, like water boiling in a pot. It is not to be called good, since it needed the Deity to fashion it; nor bad, since it was capable of being reduced to order. It is not to be called corporeal, because motion, one of its essential attributes, is incorporeal, nor incorporeal because out of it bodies are made. Hermogenes repudiated the Stoic notion that God pervades matter, or is in it like honey in a honeycomb; his idea was that the Deity, without intermixing with matter, operated on it by His mere approach and by shewing Himself, just as beauty affects the mind by the mere sight of it (a very appropriate illustration for a painter) or as a magnet causes motion without contact merely on being brought near. By this approach part of matter was reduced to order and became the κόσμος, but part remains unsubdued; and this, it is to be supposed, was in the theory of Hermogenes the source of evil. Tertullian acutely remarks that this language about God's drawing near to matter as well as the use of the words above and below with reference to the relative position of God and matter cannot be reconciled with the doctrine of Hermogenes as to the infinity of matter.

The lost tract of Tertullian against Hermogenes discussed the origin of the soul, which Hermogenes ascribed to matter, Tertullian to the breath of life inspired by God at the formation of man (Gen. ii. 7). Tertullian accuses his opponent of mistranslation in substituting "Spirit" for "breath," apparently in order to exclude the possibility of interpreting this part of the verse of the communication of the soul, since the Divine

Spirit could not be supposed capable of falling into sin. This supplies one indication that the tract to which Tertullian replies was in Latin; and Hermogenes, as a Greek by birth, would probably not use the current Latin translation of the Bible, but render for himself.

The opinion of Hermogenes (not mentioned by Tertullian, but recorded by Clement, Hippolytus, and Theodoret) is that our Lord on His ascension left His body in the sun and Himself ascended to the Father, a doctrine which he derived or confirmed from Ps. xix., "He hath placed his tabernacle in the sun." (Theodoret adds that Hermogenes taught that the devil and the demons would be resolved into *hyle*. This agrees very well with the doctrine that the soul derived its origin from matter.) It is a common point of Gnostic doctrine that our Lord's nature was after the passion resolved into its elements and that only the purely spiritual part ascended to the Father. But on no other point does Hermogenes approach Gnostic teaching; in his theory of creation, he recognizes neither emanation from God nor anything intervening between God and matter; his general doctrine was confessedly orthodox and he would seem to have no wish to separate from the church nor to consider himself as transgressing the limits of Christian philosophic speculations.

It remains to notice Philaster's confused account of Hermogenes. It would not cause much difficulty that he counts (*Haer.* 53) the Hermogenians as a school of Sabellians, called after Hermogenes as the Praxeani were after Praxeas. Though the silence of Tertullian leads us to believe that Hermogenes himself was orthodox on this point, his followers may very possibly have allied themselves with those of Praxeas against their common opponent. But in the next section Philaster tells of Galatian heretics, Seleucus and Hermias, and attributes to them the very doctrines of Hermogenes that matter was co-eternal with God, that man's soul was from matter, and that our Lord deposited His body in the sun in accordance with the Psalm already quoted. It is beyond all probability that such a combination of doctrines could have been taught independently by two heretics and it is not likely that Hermogenes had disciples in Galatia; we may therefore reasonably believe that Philaster's Hermias is Hermogenes. Philaster, however, attributes to his heretics other doctrines which we have no reason to think were held by Hermogenes: that evil proceeded sometimes from God, sometimes from matter; that there was no visible Paradise; that water-baptism was not to be used, seeing that souls had been formed from wind and fire, and that the Baptist had said that Christ should baptize with the Holy Ghost and with fire; that angels, not Christ, had created men's souls; that this world was the only "infernum," and that the only resurrection is that of the human race occurring daily in the procreation of children. Philaster may have read tracts not now extant, in which Tertullian made mention of Hermogenes, and possibly if we had the lost tract *de Paradiso* it might throw light on Philaster's statements. But we may safely reject his account as untrustworthy, even though we cannot now trace the origin of his confusion.

The tract against Hermogenes has been analysed by writers on Tertullian; *e.g.* Neander, *Antignosticus*, p. 448, Bohn's trans.; Kaye, *Tertullian*, p. 532; Hauck, *Tertullian*, p. 240. Consult also arts. *s.v.* in Tillemont, iii. and Walch, *Hist. der Ketz.* i. 576; and E. Heintzel, *Hermogenes* (Berlin, 1902). [G.S.]

Hesychius (3) (*Hesechius*), bp. of an Egyptian see, mentioned as the author, with Phileas, Theodorus, and Pachumius, of a letter to Meletius, schismatic bp. of Lycopolis in Egypt. The letter, given in a Latin version in Gallandius, *Bibl. Patrum*, iv. 67, is a remonstrance to Meletius on his irregular ordinations in other dioceses, and was written (*c.* 296) when the authors were in prison and Peter of Alexandria alive. The martyrdom of Hesychius under Galerius, with Phileas, Pachumius, and Theodorus, is recorded in Eus. *Hist. Eccl.* viii. 13. This Hesychius has been usually identified with the reviser of the text of the LXX, and of N.T., or at least of the Gospels, which obtained extensive currency in Egypt. There are no grounds for questioning the truth of this conjecture. This Hesychian recension is mentioned more than once by Jerome, who states that it was generally accepted in Egypt, as that of his fellow-martyr, Lucian of Antioch, was in Asia Minor and the East (Hieron. *Praef. in Paralipom. ad Chromat. Ep.* 107, repeated in *Apologia II. adv. Rufin.* vol. i. p. 763, Paris, 1609). Jerome also refers to it as "exemplaria Alexandrina" (*in Esai.* lviii. 11). We know little or nothing more of this edition of the LXX. It was doubtless an attempt, like that of Lucian, to purify the text in use in Egypt, by collating various manuscripts and by recourse to other means of assistance at hand. Jerome speaks with some contempt of his labours in the field of O.T. recension, and still more of his and Lucian's recension of the Gospels. If we interpret his words strictly, Hesychius, as well as Lucian, added so much to the text as to lay them open to the charge of falsifying the Gospels and rendering their work "apocryphal" (Hieron. *Praef. in Evang. ad Damasum*). The words of the famous Decretal of Gelasius (*c.* 500) "On ecclesiastical books," which are, however, regarded by Credner (*Zur Gesch. d. K.* p. 216) as additions to the original decree "made at the time it was republished in Spain under the name of Hormisdas, *c.* 700-800" (Westcott, *Hist. of Can.* p. 448, n. 1), are equally condemnatory: "Evangelia quae falsavit Isicius [Hesychius]—Apocrypha" (Labbe, *Conc.* iv. 126). Westcott pronounces Hug's speculations as to the influence of this recension, "of which nothing is certainly known," "quite unsatisfactory" (*ib.*). [E.V.]

Hesychius (25), presbyter of Jerusalem in the first half of 5th cent., a copious and learned writer whose comments on Holy Scripture and other works gained a great reputation. Considerable confusion exists as to the authorship of several of the treatises ascribed to him—a confusion which it is hopeless entirely to remove. It is possible that some were written by the bp. of Salona. [HESYCHIUS (6).] It is altogether a mistake to speak of Hesychius as bp. of Jerusalem. According to the Greek Menology, Mar. 28, he was born and educated at Jerusalem, where "by meditating on the Scriptures he obtained a deep acquaintance with divine things." On reaching manhood he left home and devoted himself to a solitary life in the desert, where he "with bee-like industry gathered the flowers of virtue from the holy Fathers there." He was ordained presbyter against his will by the patriarch of Jerusalem, and spent the rest of his life there or at other sacred places. Hesychius the presbyter is mentioned by Theophanes, who, in 412, speaks of him as "the presbyter of Jerusalem," and in 413 records his celebrity for theological learning. He is mentioned in the Life of St. Euthymius by Cyril of Scythopolis (Coteler. *Eccl. Graec. Monum.* t. ii. p. 233, § 42), as accompanying Juvenal, patriarch of Jerusalem, to the consecration of the church of the "laura" of St. Euthymius, A.D. 428 or 429, and as received with much honour by the abbat. He is said by Allatius (*Diatriba de Simeonibus*, p. 100) to have been Chartophylax or Keeper of the Records of the church of the Anastasis at Jerusalem. His death can only be placed approximately *c.* 438. He is twice mentioned by Photius, who shares to some extent in the confusion as to the Hesychii, and assigns him no date. In *Cod.* 275 Photius quotes a rhetorical passage from a sermon on James the Lord's brother and David (θεοπάτωρ), evidently delivered at Jerusalem. Hesychius compares Bethlehem and Sion, to the great advantage of the latter, and, in a manner very natural in a presbyter of Jerusalem, elevates St. James's authority above that of St. Peter in the council of Jerusalem.

Of several of the numerous works attributed to this author, all we can say is that they bear the name of Hesychius in one of its forms, but whether actually the composition of the presbyter of Jerusalem or of some other Hesychius it is difficult, if not impossible, to determine. Tillemont feels no insuperable difficulty in assigning them all to the same author, but confesses that fuller light might lead to a different conclusion.

(1) *In Leviticum Libri VII. Explanationum Allegoricarum sive Commentarius*, dedicated to the deacon Eutychianus, is the most extensive work extant under the name of Hesychius. It has frequently been printed. The earliest editions are those of Basle (1527, fol.) and Paris (1581, 8vo). It is in the various *Bibliothecae Patrum*, as that of Lyons, t. xii. p. 52, and the *Vet. Patr. Bibl.* of Galland, t. xi.

(2) *Commentaries on the Psalms.*—Harles and Fabricius, *Bibl. Graec.* vol. vii. p. 549, speak of many portions of this work existing in MS., especially one in the University Library of Cambridge containing Pss. lxxvii.-cvii. The only portions printed are the *Fragmenta in Psalmos*, extracted from the Greek *Catena in Psalmos*, with a Latin trans. by Balthazar Corderius. These are very sensible and useful, and lead us to wish for the publication of the whole. See Faulhaber, *Hesych. Hierosol. Interpr. Is. Proph.* 1900 sqq.; att. to Faulhaber in *Theol. Quartalschr.* 1901. The Commentary on the Psalms att. to Athanasius (Migne, *Patr. Gk.* xxvii.) is by Hesychius.

(3) Στιχηρὸν sive *κεφάλαια in XII. Prophetas et Esaiam*, an epitome of the 12 Minor Prophets and Isaiah, section by section.

(4) *Fragments of Commentaries* on Ezk., Dan., Acts, James, I. Peter, and Jude.

(5) *Difficultatum et Solutionum Collectio.*—A harmonizing of 61 discrepant passages in the Gospel history, generally characterized by sound common sense and a reluctance to force an unreal agreement.

(6) Eight *Sermons*, or *Fragments of Sermons.*

(7) Ἀντιρρητικὰ καὶ Εὐκτικά. *Two Centuries of Moral Maxims on Temperance and Virtue and Instructions on Prayer*, addressed to one Theodotus.

(8) *The Martyrdom of Longinus the Centurion.*—The author, according to Fabricius, belonged to a much later period than the one who wrote the works previously enumerated.

(9) *An Ecclesiastical History*, of which a fragment is given in the Acts of the council of Constantinople, A.D. 353, *Collat. Quinta*, condemnatory of Theodore of Mopsuestia.

Cave, *Hist. Lit.* t. i. p. 570; Fabricius, *Bibl. Graec.* ed. Harles, t. vii. pp. 548-551; Galland, *Vet. Patr. Bibl.* t. xi.; Migne, *Patr. Gk.* vol. xciii. pp. 781-1560. [E.V.]

Hesychius (27) Illustris, a copious historical and biographical writer, the son of an advocate and born at Miletus. His distinctive name (Ἰλλούστριος) was the official title conferred by Constantine the Great on the highest rank of state officers. Nothing is known of him except that he lived in the reigns of Anastasius, Justin, and Justinian, and that his literary labours were cut short by grief at the premature death of a son named John. Suidas doubts whether he was a Christian on the somewhat precarious ground of his omission of all ecclesiastical writers in his work on men of learning. But very substantial reasons have been produced on the other side by Cave (*Hist. Lit.* t. i. p. 518) and accepted by Fabricius. His chief work was a *Universal History* in six books and in a synoptical form through a period of 1920 years, reaching from Belus, the reputed founder of the Assyrian empire, to the death of Anastasius I., A.D. 518. The whole has perished except the initial portion of bk. vi., which has been several times printed under the title of *Constantinopolis Origines*, or *Antiquitates*. It was published by George Dousa, and ascribed to Georgius Codinus (Heidelberg, 1596), and subsequently by Meursius, under the name of its real author, appended to his *de Viris Claris* (Lugd. Bat. 1613). It was followed by a supplement, recording the reign of Justin, and the early years of Justinian. This, as the work of a contemporary whose official position enabled him to obtain accurate information, must have been of great historical value, and its loss is very much to be regretted. Hesychius also wrote a series of biographical notices of learned men, which, going over very much the same ground as the work of Diogenes Laertius, has been supposed to be an epitome of the *Vitae Philosophorum*. A comparison of the two will shew that the differences are too great to admit this idea. This work has been printed by Meursius (Lugd. Bat. 1613). Without sufficient grounds Hesychius Illustris has been identified with the lexicographer of

Alexandria. Cave, *l.c.*; Suidas, *s.v.*; Photius, *Cod.* 69; Fabr. *Bibl. Graec.* t. vii. p. 544; Thorschmidius, *de Hesychio Illustri*, ap. Orellium *Hesychii Opera*. [E.V.]

Hieracas (*Hierax*), an Egyptian teacher, from whom the sect of Hieracitae took their name. Our knowledge of him is almost entirely derived from Epiphanius (*Haer.* 67, p. 709), who states that he was contemporary with the Egyptian bp. Meletius and Peter of Alexandria, and lived under Diocletian's persecution. This agrees very well with the notice of him by Arius (*vide infra*), so that he may be placed at the very beginning of the 4th cent. Epiphanius treats him with more respect than other founders of heretical sects, and is willing to believe that he practised asceticism *bonâ fide*, which, in the case of his followers, he counts but as hypocrisy. According to Epiphanius, Hieracas lived at Leontopolis, in Egypt, abstaining from wine and animal food; and by his severity of life and the weight of his personal character did much to gain reception for his doctrines, especially among other Egyptian ascetics. He had great ability and learning, being well trained in Greek and Egyptian literature and science, and wrote several works in both languages. Epiphanius ascribes to him a good knowledge of medicine, and, with more hesitation, of astronomy and magic. He practised the art of calligraphy, and is said to have lived to 90 years of age, and to have retained such perfect eyesight as to be able to continue the practice of his art to the time of his death. Besides composing hymns, he wrote several expository works on Scripture, of which one on the Hexaemeron is particularly mentioned. It was, doubtless, in this work that he put forward a doctrine censured by Epiphanius, viz. the denial of a material Paradise. Mosheim connects this with his reprobation of marriage, imagining that it arose from the necessity of replying to the objection that marriage was a state ordained by God in Paradise. Neander, with more probability, conceives that the notion of the essential evil of matter was at the bottom of this as well as of other doctrines of Hieracas. This would lead him to allegorize the Paradise of Genesis, interpreting it of that higher spiritual world from which the heavenly spirit fell by an inclination to earthly matter. This notion would also account for a second doctrine, which, according to Epiphanius, he held in common with Origen, viz. that the future resurrection would be of the soul only, not of the material body; for all who counted it a gain to the soul to be liberated by death from the bonds of matter found it hard to believe that it could be again imprisoned in a body at the resurrection. The same notion would explain the prominence which the mortification of the body held in his practical teaching; so that, according to this view, Hieracas would be referred to the class of Gnostic ENCRATITES. The most salient point in his practical teaching was, that he absolutely condemned marriage, holding that, though permitted under the old dispensation, since the coming of Christ no married person could inherit the kingdom of heaven. If it was objected that the apostle had said, "marriage is honourable in all," he appealed to what the same apostle had said "a little further on" (I. Cor. vii.), when he wished all to be as himself and only tolerated marriage "because of fornication," *i.e.* as the lesser of two evils. Thus it appears that Hieracas believed in the Pauline origin of *Hebrews*, and his language seems to indicate that in his sacred volume that epistle preceded I. Corinthians. He received also the pastoral epistles of St. Paul, for he appeals to I. Tim. ii. 11 in support of another of his doctrines, viz. that children dying before the use of reason cannot inherit the kingdom of heaven; and asks if he who strives cannot be crowned unless he strive lawfully, how can he be crowned who has never striven at all? Arius, in his letter to Alexander in defence of his views concerning our Lord's Person (Epiph. *Haer.* 69, 7, p. 732; Athan. *de Syn.* i. 583; Hilar. *de Trin.* vi. 5, 12), contrasts his own doctrine with that of Valentinus, of Manichaeus, of Sabellius, of Hieracas; and presumably all these teachers, by rejection of whom he hopes to establish his own orthodoxy, were reputed as heretics. Hieracas, according to Arius, illustrated the relation between the first two Persons of the Godhead by the comparison of a light kindled from another, or of a torch divided into two, or, as Hilary understands it, of a lamp with two wicks burning in the same oil.

His doctrine concerning the Holy Spirit is more questionable. He was influenced by the book of the Ascension of Isaiah, which he received as authoritative. In it Isaiah is represented as seeing in the seventh Heaven, on the right and left hand of God respectively, two Beings like each other, one being the Son, the other the angel of the Holy Spirit Who spake by the prophets. Hieracas inferred that the latter Being, Who makes priestly intercession with groanings that cannot be uttered, must be the same as Melchisedek, who also was "made like unto the Son of God," and "who remaineth a priest for ever." These tenets are ascribed to Hieracas by Epiphanius, whose account is abridged by Augustine (*Haer.* 47), by Joannes Damascenus (66), and by "Praedestinatus" (47). The continued existence of the sect is assumed in a story told by Rufinus (*Hist. Mon.* 28, p. 196) of Macarius, who, when he had failed to confute the cunning arguments of a Hieracite heretic to the satisfaction of his hearers, vanquished him by successfully challenging him to a contest as to which could raise a dead body. Rufinus does not make the story turn on the fact that Hieracas denied the resurrection of the flesh. [G.S.]

Hierocles (1), a native of a small town in Caria, born at latest *c.* 275. He was a Neoplatonic philosopher, to be distinguished from the 5th-cent. philosopher HIEROCLES (2). Lactantius supposed him to have been in early life a Christian, as he displayed in his writings such intimate knowledge of Scripture and Christian teaching. He must have been an active and able administrator, as he seems to have risen rapidly by his own exertions. In an inscription at Palmyra (*Corp. Inscript. Lat.* t. iii. no. 133) his name occurs as ruler of that city under Diocletian and Maximian, Galerius and Constantius being Caesars. Here he probably came in contact with Galerius and impressed the Caesar with a respect for his abilities on his famous Persian expedition, when the first seeds of the persecution were sown, 297-302. The expression reiterated by Lactantius, that he was the "author and adviser of the persecution," lends support to this view. He was translated as prefect in 304 or 305 to Bithynia after the persecution broke out, and in 305 or 306 was promoted to the government of Alexandria, as is proved by the fact that Eusebius records the martyrdom of Aedesius at Alexandria as occurring by his orders a short time after that of Apphianus, which he dates Apr. 2, 306 (cf. Eus. *Mart. Pal.* cc. iv. v.; Epiphanius, *Haer.* lxviii.; Assem. *Mart. Orient.* ii. 195). Hierocles seems to have there displayed the same bloodthirsty cruelty as marked another philosophic persecutor, Theotecnus. He wrote a book against Christianity, entitled Λόγος φιλαλήθης πρὸς τοὺς Χριστιανούς, in which he brought forward various scriptural difficulties and alleged contradictions and instituted comparisons between the life and miracles of Jesus Christ and of Apollonius of Tyana. To this Eusebius replied in a treatise yet extant, *Liber contra Hieroclem*, wherein he shews that Apollonius was "so far from being comparable to Jesus Christ that he did not deserve to be ranked among the philosophers" (Du Pin, *H. E.* i. 155, art. "Eusebius"). Duchesne, in an acute treatise on the then lately discovered works of Macarius Magnes (Paris, Klinksieck, 1877), suggests that the work of Hierocles embodied the objections drawn by Porphyry from Holy Scripture, and that the work of Macarius was a reply to them, and suggests that Hierocles wrote his book while ruling at Palmyra before the persecution. Coming from a man in his position, it would carry great weight in the region of the Euphrates. Macarius, therefore, as a dweller in that region (Duchesne, p. 11), and Eusebius, replied. Fleury, *H. E.* t. ii. l. viii. § 30; Tillem. *Mém.* xiii. 333; *Hist. des Emp.* iv. 307; Neander, *H. E.* t. i. pp. 201, 240, ed. Bohn; Macar. Mag. ed. Blondel; Mason, *Dioclet. Persec.* pp. 58, 108; Herzog, *Real-Encyc.* art. "Hierocles." Dr. Gaisford, of Oxford, pub. in 1852 the treatises of Eusebius against Hierocles and against Marcellus. [G.T.S.]

Hierocles (2), a philosopher, generally classed among the neo-Platonists, who lived at Alexandria in the first half of 5th cent., and delivered lectures of considerable merit. His character is spoken of by Damascius (quoted by Suidas) in high terms. When sojourning at Constantinople he came into collision with the government (or, as Kuster interprets it, with the Christian authorities) and was severely beaten in the court of justice, possibly (as Zeller conjectures) for his adherence to the old religion. He was then banished, and retired to Alexandria. His teacher in philosophy was Plutarch the neo-Platonist; Theosebius is mentioned as his disciple.

His principal extant work is a commentary on the *Golden Verses* attributed to Pythagoras. His entire remains have been ed. by bp. Pearson, P. Needham (Camb. 1709), Gaisford (1850), and Mullach (1853). See the last vol. of Zeller's *Greek Philosophy*, pp. 681-687.

Hierocles appears to have been a reconciler between the old and the new. Doubtless a sincere adherent of the heathen religion, its distinctive features melt away in his hands and his soft and tender tone recalls the accents of Christian piety, *e.g.* in the following passages from his commentary on the *Golden Verses*: "No proper cause is assignable for God to have created the world but His essential goodness. He is good by nature; and the good envies none in anything" (p. 20, ed. Needham). "What offering can you make to God, out of material things, that shall be likened unto or suitable to Him? . . . For, as the Pythagoreans say, God has no place in the world more fitted for Him than a pure soul" (p. 24). "'Strength dwells near necessity.' Our author adds this to shew that we must not measure our ability to tolerate our friend by mere choice, but by our real strength, which is discovered only by actual necessity. We have all in time of need more strength than we commonly think" (p. 52). "We must love the unworthy for the sake of their partnership in the same nature with us" (p. 56). "We must be gentle to those who speak falsely, knowing from what evils we ourselves have been cleansed. . . . And gentleness is much aided by the confidence which comes from real knowledge" (p. 110). "Let us unite prayer with work. We must pray for the end for which we work, and work for the end for which we pray; to teach us this our author says, 'Go to your work, having prayed the gods to accomplish it'" (p. 172).

The reasons adduced by Hierocles for belief in a future state are strictly moral, and quite remote from subtlety: "Except some part of us subsists after death, capable of receiving the ornaments of truth and goodness (and the rational soul has beyond doubt this capability), there cannot exist in us the pure desire for honourable actions. The suspicion that we may suffer annihilation destroys our concern for such matters" (p. 76).

Not less noteworthy are his views respecting Providence. God, he says, is the sole eternal author of all things; those Platonists who say that God could only make the universe by the aid of eternal matter are in error (p. 246, from the treatise περὶ προνοίας). Man has free will; but since the thoughts of man vacillate and sometimes forget God, man is liable to sin: what we call fate is the just and necessary retribution made by God, or by those powers who do God's will, for man's actions, whether for merit or demerit (p. 256; cf. p. 92). Hence the inequality in the lots of men. Pain is the result of antecedent sin; those who know this know the remedy, for they will henceforward avoid wrongdoing and will not accuse God as if He were the essential cause of their suffering (pp. 92, 94).

The approximation of heathen philosophy to Christianity is the most interesting point to be noticed in connexion with Hierocles. He never, in his extant works, directly mentions Christianity; what degree of tacit opposition is implied in his philosophy is a difficult question. His philosophy has points more specially characteristic of Platonism and neo-Platonism, *e.g.* his belief in the pre-existence of man and in the transmigration of souls. With Porphyry and Jamblichus, however, he denied that the souls of men could migrate into the bodies of animals.

We conclude by quoting a passage on Marriage; shewing the singularly modern and Christian type of his mind. "Marriage is expedient, first, because it produces a truly divine fruit, namely children, our helpers alike when we are young and strong, and when we are old and worn. . . . But even apart from this, wedded life is a happy lot. A wife by her tender offices refreshes those who are wearied with external toil; she makes her husband forget those troubles which are never so active and aggressive as in the midst of a solitary and unfriended life; sometimes questioning him on his business pursuits, or referring some domestic matter to his judgment, and taking counsel with him upon it: giving a savour and pleasure to life by her unstrained cheerfulness and alacrity. Then again in the united exercise of religious sacrifice, in her conduct as mistress of the house in the absence of her husband, when the family has to be held in order not without a certain ruling spirit, in her care for her servants, in her careful tending of the sick, in these and other things too many to be recounted, her influence is notable. . . . Splendid dwellings, marbles and precious stones and myrtle groves are but poor ornaments to a family. But the heaven-blessed union of a husband and wife, who have all, even their bodies and souls, in common, who rule their house and bring up their children well, is a more noble and excellent ornament; as indeed Homer said. . . . Nothing is so burdensome but that a husband and wife can easily bear it when they are in harmony together, and willing to give their common strength to the task." [J.R.M.]

Hieronymus (4) (*Jerome*), St. The full name is Eusebius Hieronymus.

Among the best accounts of St. Jerome are: *Saint Jérôme, la Société chrétienne à Rome et l'émigration romaine en Terre Sainte*, par M. Amédée Thierry (Paris, 1867), and *Hieronymus sein Leben und Werken* von Dr. Otto Zöckler (Gotha, 1865); the former gives a vivid, artistic, and, on the whole, accurate picture of his life, with large extracts in the original from his writings, the latter a critical and comprehensive view of both. These contain all that is best in previous biographers, such as the Benedictine Martianay (Paris, 1706), Sebastian Dolci (Ancona, 1750), Engelstoft (Copenhagen, 1797); to which may be added notices of Jerome in the *Acta Sanctorum*, *Biblia Sacra*, Du Pin's and Ceillier's *Histories of Ecclesiastical Writers*, the excellent article in the *D. of G. and R. Biogr.*, the Life of Jerome prefixed to Vallarsi's ed. of his works, which has a singular value from its succinct narrative and careful investigation of dates.

He was born *c.* 346 at Stridon, a town near Aquileia, of Catholic Christian parents (Pref. to *Job*), who, according to the custom then common, did not have him baptized in infancy. They were not very wealthy, but possessed houses (*Ep.* lxvi. 4) and slaves (*cont. Ruf.* i. c. 30), and lived in close intimacy with the richer family of Bonosus, Jerome's foster-brother (*Ep.* iii. 5). They were living in 373, when Jerome first went to the East (xxii. 30), but, since he never mentions them later, they probably died in the Gothic invasion (377) when Stridon was destroyed. He had a brother Paulinian, some 20 years younger (lxxxii. 8), who from 385 lived constantly with him. He was brought up in comfort, if not in luxury (xxii. 30) and received a good education. He was in a grammar school, probably at Rome, and about 17 years old, when the death of the emperor Julian (363) was announced (*Comm. on Habakkuk*, i. 10). Certainly it was not much later than this that he was sent with his friend Bonosus to complete his education at Rome, and they probably lived together there. The chief study of those days was rhetoric, to which Jerome applied himself diligently, attending the law courts and hearing the best pleaders (*Comm. on Gal.* ii. 13). Early in his stay at Rome he lived irregularly and fell into sin (*Ep.* vi. 4, xiv. 6, xlviii. 20). But he was drawn back, and finally cast in his lot with the Christian church. He describes how on Sundays he used to visit, with other young men of like age and mind, the tombs of the martyrs in the Catacombs (*Comm. in Ezek.* c. 40, p. 468); and this indicates a serious bent, which culminated in his baptism at Rome while Liberius was pope, *i.e.* before 366. While there he acquired a considerable library (*Ep.* xxii. 30) which he afterwards carried wherever he went. On the termination of his studies in Rome he determined to go with Bonosus into Gaul, for what purpose is unknown. They probably first returned home and lived together for a time in Aquileia, or some other town in N. Italy. Certainly they at this time made the acquaintance of Rufinus (iii. 3) and that friendship began between him and Jerome which afterwards turned out so disastrously to both (see Augustine to Jerome, *Ep.* cx.). Hearing that they were going into Gaul, the country of Hilary, Rufinus begged Jerome to copy for him Hilary's commentary on the Psalms and his book upon the Councils (*Ep.* v. 2); and this may have fostered Jerome's tendency towards ecclesiastical literature, which was henceforward the main pursuit of his life. This vocation declared itself during his stay in Gaul. He went with his friend to several parts of Gaul, staying longest at Trèves, then the seat of government. But his mind was occupied with scriptural studies, and he made his first attempt at a commentary. It was on the prophet Obadiah, which he interpreted mystically (pref. to *Comm. on Obadiah*).

The friends returned to Italy. Eusebius, bp. of Vercellae, had a few years before returned from banishment in the East, bringing with him Evagrius, a presbyter (afterwards bp.) of Antioch, who during his stay in Italy had played a considerable part in church affairs (*Ep.* i. 15). He seems to have had a great influence over Jerome at this time; and either with him or about the same time he settled at Aquileia, and from 370 to 373 the chief scene of interest lies there, where a company of young men devoted themselves to sacred studies and the ascetic life. It included the presbyter Chromatius (afterwards bp. of Aquileia), his brother Eusebius, with Jovinus the archdeacon; Rufinus, Bonosus, Heliodorus (afterwards bp. of Altinum), the monk Chrysogonus, the subdeacon Niceas, and Hylas the freedman of the wealthy Roman lady Melania; all of whom are met with later in Jerome's history. They were knit together by close friendship and common pursuits; and the presence of Evagrius, who knew the holy places and hermitages of the East, gave a special direction to their ascetic tendencies. For a time all went well. The baptism of Rufinus took place now (Ruf. *Apol.* i. 4). It was Jerome's fortune to become, wherever he lived, the object of great affection, and also of great animosity. Whatever was the cause (*Ep.* iii. 3), the society at Aquileia suddenly dispersed.

The friends went (probably early in 373) in different directions. Bonosus retired to an island in the Adriatic and lived as a hermit (vii. 3). Rufinus went to the East in the train of Melania. Jerome, with Heliodorus, Innocentius, and Hylas, accompanied Evagrius to Palestine. Leaving his parents, sister, relations and home comforts (xxii. 30), but taking his library, he travelled through Thrace, Pontus, Bithynia, Galatia, Cappadocia and Cilicia, to Antioch. The journey was exhausting, and Jerome had a long period of ill-health, culminating in a fever. Innocentius and Hylas died from the same fever. Heliodorus went to Jerusalem. During his illness (*ib.*) Jerome had his bent towards scriptural studies and asceticism confirmed. While his friends stood by his bed expecting his death, he felt himself, in a trance, carried before the throne of God, and condemned as being no Christian but a Ciceronian, who preferred worldly literature to Christ. From this time, though he continued to quote the classics profusely, his literary interest was wholly with the Bible and church writings. It seems likely that, as soon as his health was restored, he determined to embrace the solitary life. He wrote to Theodosius (ii.), who was apparently a kind of chief of the hermits in the desert of Chalcis, asking to be received among them, and thither he proceeded about the autumn of 374.

He was now about 28 years old. The desert of Chalcis, where he lived for 4 or 5 years (374-379), was in the country of the Saracens, in the E. of Syria (v.). It was peopled by hermits, who lived mainly in solitude, but had frequent intercourse among themselves and a little with the world. They lived under some kind of discipline, with a ruling presbyter named Marcus (xvii.). Jerome lived in a cell, and gained his own living (xvii. 3); probably, according to the recommendation he gives later to Rusticus (cxxv.), cultivating a garden, and making baskets of rushes, or, more congenially, copying books. He describes his life in writing to Eustochium (xxii. 7), 9 or 10 years later, as one of spiritual struggles. "I sat alone; I was filled with bitterness: my limbs were uncomely and rough with sackcloth, and my squalid skin became as black as an Ethiopian's. Every day I was in tears and groans; and if ever the sleep which hung upon my eyelids overcame my resistance, I knocked against the ground my bare bones, which scarce clung together. I say nothing of my meat and drink, since the monks even when sick use cold water, and it is thought a luxury if they ever partake of cooked food. Through fear of hell, I had condemned myself to prison; I had scorpions and wild beasts for my only companions." His literary talent was by no means idle during this period. He wrote letters to his friends in Italy, to Florentius at Jerusalem (v.-xvii.), and to Heliodorus (xiv.) on the Praises of the Desert, chiding him for not having embraced the perfect life of solitude. A Jew who had become a Christian was his instructor in Hebrew (xviii. 10), and Jerome obtained from one of the sect of the Nazarenes at Beroea the Gospel according to the Hebrews, which he copied, and afterwards translated into Greek and Latin (*de Vir. Ill.* 2, 3). He was frequently visited by Evagrius (*Ep.* vii. 1), who also acted as the intermediary of his communication with his friends in Aquileia, and later with Damasus at Rome (xv. 5). But again, owing chiefly to his vehement feelings and expressions, he made enemies. He was driven away by the ill-will of his brother-monks. At first, as we see from his letter to Heliodorus, he was satisfied with his condition; but his last years in the desert were embittered by theological strife, relating to the conflicts in the church at Antioch, from which he was glad to escape. The see of Antioch was claimed by three bishops, Vitalis the Arian, Meletius, acknowledged by Basil and the orthodox bishops of the East (Basil, *Ep.* 156, to Evagrius), and Paulinus, supported by pope Damasus and the stronger anti-Arian party of Rome. Between Meletius and Paulinus the dispute was mainly verbal, but none the less bitter. Jerome complains that the Meletians, not content with his holding the truth, treated him as a heretic if he did not do so in their words (*Ep.* xv. 3). He appealed to Damasus, strongly protesting his submission to Rome (xv. xvi.). Finding his position more and more difficult, he wrote to Marcus, the chief presbyter of the monks of Chalcis (xvii.), in the winter of 378, professing his soundness in the faith, declaring that he was ready, but for illness, to depart, and begging the hospitality of the desert till the winter was past. Proceeding in the spring of 379 to Antioch, he stayed there till 380, uniting himself to the party of Paulinus, and by him was ordained presbyter against his will. He never celebrated the Eucharist or officiated as presbyter, as appears from many passages in his works. There are extant no letters and only one work of this period, the dialogue of an orthodox man with a Luciferian. Lucifer of Cagliari having taken part in the appointment of Paulinus, a corrective was needed for the more extreme among the Western party at Antioch; and this was given in Jerome's dialogue, which is clear, moderate, and free from the violence of his later controversial works. It exhibits a considerable knowledge of church history, and contains the account of the council of Ariminum, with the famous words (c. 19): "Ingemuit totus orbis et Arianum se esse miratus est." In 380 Jerome went to Constantinople until the end of 381. He sought the instruction of Gregory Nazianzen, who had taken charge of the orthodox church there in 379, and frequent allusions in his works witness to his profiting greatly from his master's mode of interpreting Scripture. He calls him "praeceptor meus" (*de Vir. Ill.* 117) and appeals to his authority in his commentaries and letters (*Comm. on Ephes.* v. 3; *Epp.* l. 1, lii. 8, etc.). He was also acquainted with Gregory of Nyssa (*de Vir. Ill.* 128). He was attacked, while at Constantinople, with a complaint in the eyes, arising from overwork, which caused him to dictate the works he now wrote. This practice afterwards became habitual to him (pref. to *Comm. on Gal.* iii.), though he did not wholly give up writing with his own hand; and he contrasts the imperfections of the works which he dictated with the greater elaboration he could give those he himself wrote. He wrote no letters here; but his literary activity was great. He translated the Chronicle of Eusebius, a large work, which embraces the chronology from the creation to A.D. 330, Jerome adding the events of the next 50 years. He translated the Homilies of Origen on Jer. and Ezk., possibly also on Isa., and wrote a short treatise for Damasus on the interpretations of the Seraphim in Isa. vi., which is improperly placed among the letters (*Ep.* xviii.). These works mark the epoch when he began to feel the importance of Origen as a church-writer, though daring even then to differ from him in doctrine, and also to realize the imperfections of the existing versions of the Scriptures. In the treatise on the Seraphim, and again in the preface to the Chronicle, we find him contrast the various Gk. versions of O.T., studies which eventually forced on him the necessity of a translation direct from the Hebrew. What were his relations to the council of Constantinople in 381 we do not know. It is certain, however, that pope Damasus desired his presence in Rome at the council of 382, which reviewed the Acts of that council, and that he went in the train of bps. Paulinus of Antioch and Epiphanius of Constantia (Salamis) in Cyprus (cxxiii. 10; cxxvii. 7).

Bible Work.—His stay in Rome, from the spring of 382 to Aug. 385, was a very eventful and decisive period in his life. He made many friends and many enemies; his knowledge and reputation as a scholar greatly increased, and his experience of Rome determined him to give himself irrevocably and exclusively to his two great interests, scriptural study and the promotion of asceticism. He undertook, at the request of Damasus, a revision of the version of the Psalms (vol. x. col. 121). He translated from the LXX; and his new version was used in the Roman church till the pontificate of Pius V. He, also at the request of Damasus, revised the N.T., of which the old Versio Itala was very defective. The preface addressed to Damasus (*ib.* col. 557) is a good critical document, pointing out that the old version had been varied by transcribers, and asking, "If any one has the right version, which is it?" It was intended as a preface to the Gospels only; but from the record of his works in the list of ecclesiastical writers (*de Vir. Ill.* 135), which states that he had restored the N.T. according to the original Greek, as well as from other passages (*e.g. Ep.* xxvii. 3), we infer that the whole version was completed (see Vallarsi's pref. to vol. x.; also Murray's *Illus. B. D.* (1908), art. VULGATE). He also, at the request of Damasus and others, wrote many short exegetical treatises, included among his letters (on *Hosanna*, xix. xx.; *Prodigal Son*, xxi.; *O.T. Names of God*, xxv.; *Halleluia and Amen*, xxvi.; *Sela and Diapsalma*, xxviii.; *Ephod and Seraphim*, xxix.; *Alphabetical Psalms*, xxx.; "*The Bread of Carefulness*," xxxiv.). He began also his studies on the original of O.T. by collating the Gk. versions of Aquila and the LXX with the Heb. (xxxii., xxxvi. 12), and was thus further confirmed in the convictions which led to the Vulgate version. He translated for Damasus the Commentary of Origen on the *Song of Songs* (vol. x. p. 500), and began his translation of the work of Didymus, the blind Origenistic teacher of Alexandria, on the Holy Spirit, which he did not complete till after his settlement at Bethlehem, probably because of the increasing suspicions and enmity of clergy and people, whom he speaks of as the senate of the Pharisees, against all that had any connexion with Origen (pref. to *Didymus on the Holy Spirit*, vol. ii. 105), which cause also prevented him continuing the translation of Origen's Commentaries, begun at Constantinople. Jerome was Origen's vehement champion and the contemptuous opponent of his impugners. "The city of Rome," he says, "consents to his condemnation . . . not because of the novelty of his doctrines, not because of heresy, as the dogs who are mad against him now pretend; but because they could not bear the glory of his eloquence and his knowledge, and because, when he spoke, they were all thought to be dumb" (*Ep.* xxxiii. 4).

Asceticism.—The other chief object of his life increased this enmity, although it also made great advances during his stay at Rome. Nearly fifty years before, Athanasius and the monk Peter (334) had sown the seeds of asceticism at Rome by their accounts of the monasteries of Nitria and the Thebaid. The declining state of the empire had meanwhile predisposed men either to selfish luxury or monasticism. Epiphanius, with whom Jerome now came to Rome, had been trained by the hermits HILARION and HESYCHAS; he was, with Paulinus, the guest of the wealthy and noble Paula (cviii. 5), the heiress of the Aemilian race; and thus Jerome was introduced to one who became his life-long friend and his chief support in his labours She had three daughters: Blessila, whose death, after a short and austere widowhood, was so eventful to Jerome himself; Julia Eustochium, who first among the Roman nobility took the virgin's vow; and Paulina, who married Jerome's friend Pammachius. These formed part of a circle of ladies who gradually gathered round the ascetic teacher of scriptural lore. Among them were MARCELLA, whose house on the Aventine was their meeting-place; her young friend Principia (cxxvii.); her sister the recluse Asella, the confidant of Jerome's complaints on leaving Rome (xlv.); Lea, already the head of a kind of convent, whose sudden death was announced whilst the friends were reading the Psalms (xxiii.); Furia, the descendant of Camillus, sister-in-law to Blesilla, and her mother Titiana; Marcellina and Felicitas, to whom Jerome's last adieus were sent on leaving Rome (xlv.); perhaps also, though she is not named till later, the enthusiastic Fabiola, less steady, but more eager than the rest (lxxvii.). These ladies, all of the highest patrician families, were already disposed to the ascetic life. Contact with the Eastern bishops added a special interest in Palestine; and the presence of Jerome confirmed both these tendencies. He became the centre of a band of friends who, withdrawn from a political and social life which they regarded as hopelessly corrupt, gave themselves to the study of Scripture and to works of charity. They knew Greek; learned Hebrew that they might sing the Psalms in the original; learned by heart the writings of their teacher (lxxvii. 9); held daily meetings whereat he expounded the Scriptures (xxiii. 1), and for them he wrote many of his exegetical treatises. The principles he instilled into their minds may be seen in many of his letters of this period, which were at once copied and eagerly seized both by friends and enemies. The treatise which especially illustrates his teaching at this time is addressed to Eustochium on the Preservation of Virginity (xxii.). Jerome's own experience in the desert, his anti-Ciceronian dream at Antioch, his knowledge of the desert monks, of whom he gives a valuable description, were here used in favour of the virgin and ascetic life; the extreme fear of impurity contrasts strangely with the gross suggestions in every page; it contains such a depreciation of the married state, the vexations of which ("uteri tumentes, infantium vagitus") are only relieved by vulgar and selfish luxury, that almost the only advantage allowed it is that by it virgins are brought into the world; and the vivid descriptions of Roman life—the pretended virgins, the avaricious and self-indulgent matrons, the dainty, luxurious, and rapacious clergy—forcible as they are, lose some of their value by their appearance of caricature. Another treatise written during this period, against the layman Helvidius, the pupil of Auxentius of Milan, on the perpetual virginity of Mary, though its main points are well argued, exhibits the same fanatical aversion to marriage, combined with a supercilious disregard of his opponent which was habitual to Jerome. [HELVIDIUS.]

A crisis in Jerome's fortunes came with the end of 384. Damasus, who had been pope for nearly 20 years, was dying, and amongst his possible successors Jerome could not escape mention. He had, as he tells us, on first coming to Rome, been pointed out as the future pope (xlv. 3). But he was entirely unfitted by character and habit of mind for an office which has always required the talents of the statesman and man of the world, rather than those of the student, and he had offended every part of the community. The general lay feeling was strongly opposed to asceticism (xxvii. 2). At the funeral of Blesilla (xxxix. 4) the rumour was spread that she had been killed by the excessive austerities enjoined upon her; the violent grief of her mother was taken as a reproach to the ascetic system, and the cry was heard, "The monks to the Tiber!" Jerome, though cautioned by his friends to moderate his language (xxvii. 2), continued to use the most insulting expressions towards all who opposed him. It is not surprising that the Roman church should have deemed him unfitted to be its head, and that Jerome himself should, in his calmer reflections, have felt that Rome was ill-suited to him, and that in attempting, with his temper and habits, to carry out his conception of Christianity in Rome he had been vainly trying "to sing the Lord's song in a strange land" (xlv. 6). Siricius, the successor of Damasus, had no sympathy with Jerome either then or in the subsequent Origenistic controversy. The party of friends on the Aventine was broken up. Jerome counsels Marcella (xliv.) to leave Rome and seek religious seclusion in the country. Paula and Eustochium preferred to go with him to Palestine. In Aug. 385 Jerome embarked, with all that was dearest to him, at Portus, and in his touching and instructive letter to Asella (xlv.) bade a final farewell to Rome. Accompanied by his brother Paulinian and his friend Vincentius (*cont. Ruf.* iii. 22), he sailed direct to Antioch. Paula and Eustochium (*Ep.* cviii., where all these incidents are narrated), leaving Paulina, then of marriageable age, and her young brother Toxotius, embarked at the same time, but visited Epiphanius in Cyprus on their way. The friends were reunited at Antioch, as winter was setting in. Paula would brook no delay, and, despite the inclemency of the season, they started at once for Palestine. They visited Sarepta, Acre, Caesarea, Joppa, Lydda, and Emmaus, arriving at Jerusalem early in 386. The city was moved at their coming, and the proconsul prepared a splendid reception for them in the Praetorium; but they only stayed to see the holy places, and, after visiting spots of special interest in the S. of Palestine, journeyed on into Egypt. There the time was divided between the two great objects of Jerome's life, the study of Scripture and the promotion of asceticism. At Alexandria he sat, though already grey-haired (lxxxiv. 3), at the feet of Didymus, the great Origenistic teacher, whom, in contrast to his blindness, Jerome delights to speak of as "the seer." (See in his praises the preface to the commentary on Ephesians.) Jerome had already, as we have seen, translated in part his book on the Holy Spirit; and now, at the request of his distinguished pupil, Didymus composed his Commentary on Hosea and Zechariah (Hieron. pref. to *Hosea*, and *de Vir. Ill.* 109). Pausing at Alexandria only 30 days, they turned to the monasteries of Nitria, where they were received with great honour. At one time they were almost persuaded to remain in the Egyptian desert, but the attractions of the holy places of Palestine prevailed; and sailing from Alexandria to Majoma, they settled at Bethlehem, in the autumn of 386. There Jerome lived the remaining 34 years of his life, pursuing unremittingly and with the utmost success the two great objects of his life.

Bethlehem, First Period, 386-392. *Monasteries.*—Their first work was to establish themselves at Bethlehem. A monastery and a convent were built, over which Jerome and Paula respectively presided (*Ep.* cviii. 14, 19). There was a church in which they met on

Sundays, and perhaps oftener (cxlvii.); and a hospice for pilgrims, of whom a vast number came from all parts to visit the holy places (*Epp.* xlvi. lxvi.; *cont. Vigilantium,* 13, 14). These institutions were mainly supported by Paula, though, towards the end of her life, when she by her profusion had become poor, their support fell upon Jerome, who, for this purpose, sold his estate in Pannonia (*Ep.* lxvi.). He lived in a cell (cv. and *cont. Joan. Jerus.*), in or close to the monastery, surrounded by his library, to which he continually added, as is shewn by his constant reference to a great variety of authors, sacred and profane, and by his account of obtaining a copy of the Hexapla from the library at Caesarea (*Comm. on Titus,* c. 3, p. 734). He describes himself as living very moderately on bread and vegetables (*Ep.* lxxix. 4); he was not neglectful of his person, but recommended a moderate neatness of dress (lii. 9, lx. 10). We do not read of any special austerities beyond the fact of his seclusion from the world, which he speaks of as a living in the fields and in solidude, that he might mourn for his sins and gain Christ's mercy (*cont. Joan. Jerus.* 41). He did not officiate in the services, but his time was greatly absorbed by the cares (*Ep.* cxiv. 1) and discipline (cxlvii.) of the monastery and by the crowds of monks and pilgrims who flocked to the hospice (lxvi. 14; *adv. Ruf.* i. 31). He expounded the Scriptures daily to the brethren in the monastery. Sacred studies were his main pursuit, and his diligence is almost incredible. "He is wholly absorbed in reading," says Sulpicius; "he takes no rest by day or by night; he is ever reading or writing something." He wrote, or rather dictated, with great rapidity. He was believed at times to have composed 1,000 lines of his commentaries in a day (pref. to bk. ii. of *Comm. on Ephes.* in vol. vii. col. 507). He wrote almost daily to Paula and Eustochium (*de Vir. Ill.* 135); and, though many of his letters were mere messages, yet almost all were at once published (*Ep.* xlix. 2), either by friends or enemies. There were many interruptions. Besides the excessive number of ordinary pilgrims, persons came from all parts, and needed special entertainment. The agitated state of the empire also was felt in the hermitage of Bethlehem. The successive invasions of the Huns (*Ep.* lxxvii. 8) and the Isaurians (cxiv.) created a panic in Palestine, so that, in 395, ships had been provided at Joppa to carry away the virgins of Bethlehem, who hurried to the coast to embark, when the danger passed away. These invasions caused great lack of means at Bethlehem (cxiv. 1), so that Jerome and his friends had to sell all to continue the work. Amidst such difficulties his great literary works were accomplished. Immediately on settling at Bethlehem, he set to work to perfect his knowledge of Hebrew with the aid of a Jew named Bar Anina (called Barabbas by Jerome's adversaries, who conceived that through this teacher his version was tainted with Judaism; see Ruf. *Apol.* ii. 12). Their interviews took place at night (*Ep.* lxxxiv.), each being afraid of the suspicions their intercourse might cause. He also learned Chaldee, but less thoroughly (pref. to *Daniel,* vol. ix. col. 1358). When any unusual difficulty occurred in translation or exposition, he obtained further aid. For the book of Job he paid a teacher to come to him from Lydda (pref. to *Job,* vol. ix. col. 1140); for the Chaldee of Tobit he had a rabbi from Tiberias (pref. to *Tobit,* vol. x.). The Chronicles he went over word by word with a doctor of law from Tiberias (pref. to *Chron.*). The great expense entailed was no doubt in part defrayed by Paula. At a later time, when his resources failed, Chromatius of Aquileia, and Heliodorus of Altinum, supported the scribes who assisted him (pref. to *Esther,* addressed to Chrom. and Hel.).

Bible Work.—The results of his first six years' labours may be thus summed up. The commentary on Eccles. and the translation of Didymus on the Holy Spirit were completed; commentaries were written on Gal. Eph. Tit. and Philemon; the version of N.T. begun in Rome was revised; a treatise on Pss. x.-xvi. was written; and translations made of Origen's Commentaries on St. Luke and the Psalms. Jerome, who had long before felt the great importance for scriptural studies of a knowledge of the localities (pref. to *Chron.*), turned to account his travels in Palestine in his work on the names of Hebrew places, mainly translated from Eusebius, and gave to the world what may be called "Chips from his Workshop," in the book on Hebrew proper names and the Hebrew questions on Gen., a work which he seems to have intended to carry on in the other books as a pendant to his translations. Further, as a preparatory work to the Vulg., he had revised the Latin version of O.T. then current (which was imperfectly made from the LXX), by a comparison of Origen's Hexapla (pref. to *Joshua,* vol. ix. 356; pref. to *Chron.* vol. ix. col. 1394; pref. to *Job,* vol. ix. col. 1142; *Ep.* lxxi. *ad Lucinium*). This work, though not mentioned in the Catalogue (*de Vir. Ill.* 135), certainly existed. Jerome used it in his familiar expositions each day (*cont. Ruf.* ii. 24). Augustine had heard of it and asked to see it (*Ep.* cxxxiv., end), but it had, through fraud or neglect, been lost; and all that remains of it is Job, the Psalms, and the preface to the books of Solomon (vol. x.). The Vulgate itself was in preparation, as we find from the Catalogue; but as it was not produced for some years, what had been done thus far was evidently only preliminary and imperfect work.

Besides his work on the Scriptures, Jerome had designed a vast scheme of church history, from the beginning to his own time, giving the lives of all the most eminent men; and as a preliminary to this, and in furtherance of asceticism, he wrote Lives of MALCHUS and HILARION. The minuteness of detail in these works would have made a church history on such a scale impossible; and the credulity they shew throws doubt on Jerome's capacity for such work.

A far more important work for the purposes of the church historian is the book which is variously called the "Catalogue of Church Writers," the "Book on Illustrious Men," or the "Epitaphion" (though it includes men then living). Some portions are taken from Eusebius, but the design and most of the details are original. It includes the writers of

N.T., and church teachers of East and West up to Jerome's own time, and even men accounted heretics and non-Christians like Seneca, whose works were of importance to the progress of human thought.

The letter which Jerome wrote in the name of Paula and Eustochium to Marcella at Rome (*Ep.* xlvi.), the only letter preserved from these first six years, expresses an enthusiastic view of their privileges in reading the Scriptures in the tongue and country in which they were written. The crowds who came from all parts seem to them to be so many choirs, engaged in services of praise, each in their own tongue. The very ploughmen chant Hallelujahs. Far from the Babylon of Rome, they associate with the saints of Scripture and find in the holy places the gate of heaven. This view of Palestine is always present to Jerome, however much he has to confess the actual secularization of Jerusalem (lviii. 4); and it makes his Biblical work not merely one of learning but of piety.

Second Period, 393-404.—Private letters of Jerome abound during this period, and illustrate his personal history.

To this period belong the many external difficulties at Bethlehem already mentioned. During almost the whole of 398 Jerome was ill, and again in 404-405 (lxxiv. 6, cxiv. 1). He was disturbed also by the controversy or schism between the monks of Bethlehem and the bp. of Jerusalem; and an injury to his hand prevented his writing. Poverty was also overtaking him. Paula had spent her fortune in lavish charity, and Jerome sent his brother Paulinianus to their former home to sell the remains of their property to support the monasteries (lxvi. 14). The sad quarrel between Jerome and Rufinus began in 394; see under the controversies (*infra*) which occupied so much of this period.

Commentaries.—Jerome had begun his commentaries on the Minor Prophets in 391 (*de Vir. Ill.* 135); they form four books, and were published at long intervals up to 406. In 397 he wrote his commentary on Matthew, the last on the N.T. It was finished, with great haste and eagerness (*Ep.* lxxiii. 10), in Lent 398, as he was recovering from an illness. After a long interval the commentary on Isaiah followed, and thereafter he wrote upon the Great Prophets only.

The Vulgate.—That which we now call the Vulgate, and which is in the main the work of Jerome, was during his life the Bible of the learned and only by degrees won general acceptance. The *editio vulgata* in previous use was a loose translation from the LXX, almost every copy varying. Jerome had begun very early to read the O.T. in Gk. Here the same difficulty met him. The LXX version was confronted, in Origen's Hexapla, with those of Theodotion, Aquila, and Symmachus, and with two others called Quinta and Sexta. Where they differed, who was to decide? This question is asked by Jerome as early as the preface to the Chronicle of Eusebius (381) and was constantly repeated in defence of his translation. He seems to have distinctly contemplated this work from the moment of his settlement at Bethlehem, and a great deal of the labour of his first years there may be regarded as preliminary to it. It was begun within the first few years. But, in so elaborate a work, it was impossible that the first copies should be perfect. It is probable that the whole, or larger part, was gone through at an early date and given to his friends or the public after a more mature revision, according as his health or courage allowed. He distinctly purposed to publish it from the first. Yet the actual publication was made in a fragmentary and hesitating manner. At times he speaks of portions as extorted from him by the earnest requests of his friends (pref. to *Gen.* vol. ix. etc.). Some parts he represents as done in extreme haste; the books of Solomon as the work of three days (pref. in vol. ix. col. 1307); Tobit and Judith were each that of a single day. He shews in his prefaces extreme sensitiveness to attacks upon his work, and speaks of it often as an ungrateful task. Of the Apocrypha he translated only parts, and these very cursorily (pref. to Tobit, vol. x.), doubtless because of his comparative indifference to the Apocrypha, his opinion of which is quoted in Art. vi. of the 39 Articles, from the preface to the Books of Solomon (vol. ix. ed. 1308). Samuel and Kings were published first, then Job and the Prophets, then Ezra, Nehemiah and Genesis. All these were finished in or before 393; but here occurred a break, due partly, no doubt, to unsettlement and panic caused by the invasion of the Huns in 395. In 396 the work was resumed at the entreaty of Chromatius and Heliodorus, who sent him money to support the necessary helpers (pref. to Books of Solomon). The Books of Solomon were then completed (398) and the preface indicates an intention to continue the work more systematically. But the ill-feeling excited by his translation made him unwilling to continue, and his long illness in 398 intervened. He tells Lucinius that he had then given his servants the whole except the Octateuch to copy (*Ep.* xlix. 4). But, from whatever cause, the work was not resumed till 403-404, in which years the remainder was completed, namely, the last four books of Moses, Joshua and Judges, Ruth and Esther. His friends collected the translations into one volume, and the title of Vulgate, which had hitherto applied to the version before in use (pref. to *Ezk.* vol. ix. col. 995, pref. to *Esther*, vol. ix. 1503), in time came to belong to an edition which is in the main the work of Jerome.

Controversies.—Controversial works at this period occupied a share of Jerome's energies out of all proportion to their importance.

Against Jovinian.—Jovinian was a Roman monk, originally distinguished by extreme asceticism, who had adopted freer opinions. He put off the monastic dress and lived like other men. The book of Jovinian was sent to Jerome about the end of 393, and he at once answered it in two books. He warmly attacks Jovinian as a renegade and as a dog who has returned to his vomit.

Origenism.—The second great controversy in which Jerome was now engaged arose about Origenism, which embraces in its wide sweep Epiphanius, bp. of Cyprus, John, bp. of Jerusalem, Theophilus, bp. of Alexandria, St. John Chrysostom, the pope Anastasius, and above all Jerome's former friend Rufinus—a controversy by which the churches of the East and the West were long and deeply agitated. It divides itself, as far as Jerome is concerned, into two distinct parts: the first represented by his writing against John of Jerusalem, and extending from 494-499, when peace was made between them; the second represented by three books directed against Rufinus, the first two written in 401, the third in 402.

Jerome's own relation to Origen is not difficult to understand, though it laid him open to the charge of inconsistency. He had become acquainted with his works during his first enthusiasm for Greek ecclesiastical learning and had recognized his as the greatest name in Christian literature, worthy of comparison with the greatest of classical times (see esp. *Ep.* xxxiii.). The literary interest was to Jerome, then as at all times, more than the dogmatic; deeply impressed by the genius and learning of the great Alexandrine, his praise, like his subsequent blame, was without reason or moderation. He spoke with entire commendation of his commentaries, and even of the Τόμοι, or Chapters, which included the book περὶ Ἀρχῶν (which may be translated either *On First Principles* or *On the Powers* on which the chief controversy afterwards turned). "In his work," he says (pref. to trans. of Origen on *Jer.* vol. v. col. 611), "he gave all the sails of his genius to the free breath of the winds, and receding from the shore, went forth into the open sea." It was not the peculiarities of Origen's dogmatic system, but the boldness of his genius, that appealed to the mind of Jerome. From the first he shewed a certain independence, nor did he ever give his adherence to Origen's peculiar system. He quoted without blame even such theories as the possible restoration of Satan, but never gave his personal assent to them. Even when, afterwards, he became a violent opponent of Origenism, he shewed discrimination. He continued to use Origen's commentaries, and even in some points of doctrine commended his exposition. His vehement language, however, makes him appear first a violent partisan of Origen, and later an equally violent opponent. The change, moreover, has the appearance of being the result, not so much of a great conviction, as of a fear of the suspicion of heresy.

John, bp. of Jerusalem, and Rufinus.—During the first year of Jerome's stay at Bethlehem he was on good terms with both John the bp. and Rufinus, who had been established with Melania on Mount Olives since 377. John, who succeeded Cyril a few months before Jerome and Paula arrived in 386, was on familiar terms with Rufinus whom he ordained, and there is no sign that he was ill-disposed towards Jerome. The troubles originated in the visit to Jerusalem of a certain Aterbius, otherwise unknown (*cont. Ruf.* iii. 33), who scattered accusations of Origenistic heresy among the foremost persons at Jerusalem, and joining Jerome with Rufinus on account of their friendship, charged them both with heresy. Jerome made a confession of his faith which satisfied this self-appointed inquisitor; but Rufinus refused to see him, and with threats bade him begone. This was apparently in 393. In 394 Epiphanius, bp. of Salamis in Cyprus, who in his book on heresies had formally included the doctrines of Origen, visited Jerusalem, and strife broke out in the church of the Resurrection, where Epiphanius's pointed sermon against Origenism was taken as reflecting so directly upon John that the bishop sent his archdeacon to remonstrate and stop him. John, after he had delivered a long sermon against Anthropomorphism, was requested by Epiphanius, amidst the ironical applause of the people, to condemn Origenism with the same earnestness; and then Epiphanius came to the monastery at Bethlehem declaring John a heretic, and, after attempting to elicit some anti-Origenistic confession from the bishop, finally at night left his house, where he had been a guest, for the monastery. Epiphanius, convinced that John was on the verge of heresy, advised Jerome and his friends to separate themselves from their bishop; and provided for the ministrations of their church by ordaining Jerome's brother Paulinian.

John now appealed to Alexandria and to Rome against Jerome and his friends as schismatics. Theophilus of Alexandria at once took John's side, but, becoming an anti-Origenist later, opened communication with Jerome, of which the latter gladly availed himself. Jerome was thenceforward the minister of Theophilus in his communication with the West in the war against Origen; and thus completely united himself with the anti-Origenistic party. Rufinus, when he arrived in Rome with Melania in 397, found the contest about Origenism at its height, but ignorance on the subject was so great that pope Anastasius, even though induced to condemn Origen, plainly admitted in his letter to John of Jerusalem (Hieron. ii. 677, Vallarsi's Rufinus [Migne's *Patr.* xxi.] 408) that he neither knew who Origen was nor what he had written. Rufinus being asked by a pious man named Macarius to give an exposition of Origen's tenets, made the translation of the περὶ Ἀρχῶν which is now published in Origen's works and is the only extant version. This translation was at once the subject of dispute. Jerome's friends complained that Rufinus had given a falsely favourable version. Rufinus declared that he had only used the just freedom of a critic and translator in omitting passages interpolated by heretics, who wished to make Origen speak their views, and in translating Eastern thoughts into Western idioms. But the real complaint against Rufinus rested on personal grounds. In his preface he had seemed to associate Jerome, as the translator of Origen, with Origen's work, and to shield himself under Jerome's authority. Jerome and his friends, extremely sensitive of the least reproach of heresy and having already taken a strong part against Origen, trembled for his reputation. Rufinus's preface was sent to him by Pammachius and Oceanus, with the request (*Ep.* lxxxii.) that he would point out the truth, and would translate the περὶ Ἀρχῶν as Origen had written it. Jerome did so, and with his new translation sent a long letter (lxxxiv.) to his two friends, which, though making too little of his former admiration for Origen, in the main states the case fairly and without asperity towards Rufinus. The same may be said of his letter (lxxxi.) to Rufinus himself, possibly in answer to one from Rufinus ("diu te Romae moratum sermo proprius indicavit"), which speaks of their reconciliation and remonstrates, as a friend with a friend, against the mention Rufinus had made of him. "There are not many," he says, "who can be pleased with feigned praise" ("fictis laudibus"). This letter, unfortunately, did not reach Rufinus. He had gone to Aquileia with the ordinary commendation ("literae formatae") from the pope. Siricius had died; his successor, Anastasius, was in the hands of Pammachius and Marcella (cxxvii.), who were moving him to condemn Origen. Anastasius, though ignorant on the whole subject, was struck by passages shewn him by Eusebius in Jerome's translation of the περὶ Ἀρχῶν, which had been given him by Marcella (Rufin. *Apol.* ii.), and proceeded to condemn Origen. He also was persuaded to summon Rufinus (Rufinus [Migne's *Patr. Lat.* xxi.] 403) to Rome to make a confession of his faith; and wrote to John of Jerusalem, expressing his fear as to Rufinus's intentions and his faith (see the letter in Jerome's *Works*, ii. 677, Rufinus, 408). Jerome's friends kept his letter to Rufinus, so that Rufinus was prevented from learning Jerome's actual dispositions towards him. He only knew that the latter's friends were in some way involving him in the condemnation they had procured against Origen and which the emperors themselves had now ratified (Anastasius to John, *u.s.*). To Anastasius, therefore, he replied in a short letter, excusing himself from coming to Rome, but giving an explicit declaration of his faith. But from Jerome he was wholly alienated. His friend Apronianus at Rome having sent him the letter of Jerome to Pammachius and Oceanus, he replied in the document which is called his *Apology*, with bitter feelings against his former friend. He did not scruple to use against him the facts known to him through their former intimacy, such as the vows made in consequence of his anti-Ciceronian dream, which he declared Jerome to have broken, and he allowed himself to join in the carping spirit in which Jerome's enemies spoke against his translation of the Scriptures. This document was privately circulated among Rufinus's friends at Rome. It became partly known to Pammachius and Marcella, who, not being able to obtain a copy, sent him a description of its contents, with such quotations as they could procure. Jerome at once composed the two first books of his *Apology* in the form of a letter to his Roman friends. Its tone is that of one not quite willing to break through an old friendship, but its language is strong and at times contemptuous. It was brought to Rufinus at Aquileia, who answered in a letter meant for Jerome's eyes alone, which has not come down to us. From Jerome's reply we know that it was sharp and bitter, and declared his ability to produce facts which if known to the world would blast Jerome's character for ever. Jerome was estranged by extracts from Rufinus's *Apology*. Then Rufinus himself sent him a true copy, and the result was a final rupture. Augustine, to whom Jerome sent his book, writes (Hieron. *Ep.* cx. 6) with the utmost sorrow at the scandal; he declares that he was cast down by the thought that "persons so dear and so familiar, united by a chain of friendship which had been known to all the church," should now be publicly tearing each other to pieces. He writes like one who has an equal esteem for both the combatants, and only desires their reconciliation. But Jerome never ceased to speak of his former friend with passionate condemnation and contempt. When Rufinus died in Sicily in 410 he wrote: "The scorpion lies underground between Enceladus and Porphyrion, and the hydra of many heads has at last ceased to hiss against me" (pref. to *Comm. on Ezk.*). In later years he sees the spirit of Rufinus revived in Pelagius (pref. to *Comm. on Jer.* bk. i.), and even in letters of edification he cannot refrain from bitter remarks on his memory (*Ep.* cxxv. 18, cxxxiii. 3).

Vigilantius.—A fourth controversy was with Vigilantius (*cont. Vig.* liber unus), a Spanish monk, into whom, as Jerome says, the soul of his former opponent Jovinian had passed, a controversy further embittered by mutual accusations of Origenism, and in which Jerome's violence and contemptuousness passes all bounds. Vigilantius had stayed at the monastery at Bethlehem in 396, on the introduction of Paulinus. In a letter to Vigilantius in 396, Jerome accuses him of blasphemous interpretations of Scripture derived from Origen. He treats him as a vulgar fool, without the least claim to knowledge or letters. He applies to him the proverb Ὄνῳ λύρα, turns his name to Dormitantius, and ends by saying he hopes he may find pardon when, as Origen holds, the devil will find it. Vigilantius is said by Gennadius (*de Scr. Eccl.* 35) to have been an ignorant man, though polished in words. But he was as far in advance of Jerome in his views of the Christian life as he was behind him in literary power. His book, written in 404, was sent by Riparius to Jerome, who replied (*Ep.* cix.), dismissing the matter with contempt. Afterwards, probably finding the opinions of Vigilantius gaining ground, he, at the request of certain presbyters, wrote his treatise against him. It is a short book, dictated, he states, *unius noctis lucubratione*; his friend Sisinnius, who was to take it, being greatly hurried. Vigilantius maintained that the honour paid to the martyrs' tombs was excessive, that watching in their basilicas was to be deprecated, that the alleged miracles done there were false; that the money collected for the "poor saints at Jerusalem" had better be kept at home; that the hermit life was cowardice; and, lastly, that it would be well that presbyters should be married before ordination. Jerome speaks of these accusations as being so openly blasphemous as to require neither argument nor the production of testimonies against them, but merely the expression of the writer's indignation. He does not admit even a grain of truth in them. "If you do not honour the tombs of the martyrs," he says, "you assert that they were not wrong in burning the martyrs." He himself believes the miracles, and values the intercession of the saints. This is the treatise in which Jerome felt most sure he was in the right, and the only one in which he was wholly in the wrong.

Augustine.—The exchange of letters between Jerome and Augustine, though begun with something of asperity, ended in edification. Jerome heard of Augustine soon after his conversion (386); and Augustine, eight years his junior, had a great respect (which did not prevent criticism) for Jerome and his work. Augustine's friend Alypius stayed with Jerome in 393, and Jerome heard with satisfaction of the great African's zeal for the study of Scripture and of his rising fame. In 394 Augustine, then coadjutor bp. of Hippo (succeeding in 395), having had his attention no doubt called to Jerome's works by Alypius, wrote the letter (among Jerome's, lvi.) which originated the controversy. It related to the interpretation of the dispute of St. Paul and St. Peter at Antioch, recorded in Gal. ii. The letter is written in a grave tone, but perhaps with something of assumption, considering the great position of Jerome. Augustine commends him for translating Greek commentaries into Latin, and wishes that in his translations of O.T. he would note very carefully the places in which he diverges from the LXX. He then notes that Jerome, in his *Commentary on the Galatians*, had maintained that the dispute was merely feigned, that Peter had pretended to act so as to incur Paul's rebuke, in order to set before the church the incongruity of a Christian continuing under Mosaic law. This appeared to Augustine to impute to the apostles an acted lie. This letter was committed, together with other works of Augustine on which Jerome's opinion was desired, to Profuturus, a presbyter, who being, before he sailed, elected to a bishopric in N. Africa, turned back, and soon after died. He had neither transmitted the letter to Jerome nor returned it to Augustine; but it was seen by others and copied, so that the attack on Jerome was widely known in the West while entirely unknown to Jerome at Bethlehem. Augustine, discovering that his letter had not reached Jerome, wrote a second (among Jerome's, lxvii.), again entering into the question, asking Jerome to confess his error and to sing a palinode for the injury done to Christian truth. Paulus, to whom this letter was committed, proved untrustworthy, and let it be circulated without being transmitted to Jerome. It was seen by a deacon, Sisinnius, who, coming to Bethlehem some five years afterwards, either brought a copy or described its contents to Jerome. Meanwhile Augustine heard, through pilgrims returning from Palestine, the state of the facts and the feelings aroused by them. He wrote a short letter to excuse himself (among Jerome's, ci.), pointing out that what he had written was not, as seemed to be supposed, a book for publication, but a personal letter expressing to a friend a difference of opinion. He begged Jerome to point out similarly any points of his writings he might think wrong, and concluded with an earnest wish for some personal converse with the great teacher of Bethlehem. Jerome replied in a letter (cii.) in which friendship struggled with suspicion and resentment. He sent some of his works, including those last written, against Rufinus. As to Augustine's works, he says he knows little of them, but intimates that he might have much to say in criticism. He insinuates that Augustine might be seeking honour by attacking him, but warns him that he too can strike hard. Augustine replied in a letter (among Jerome's, civ.) written with demonstrations of profound respect, but in which, after explaining how his first letter had miscarried, he again enters into questions of Biblical literature. He commends Jerome's new translations of N.T., but begs him not to translate O.T. from the Heb., enforcing his wish by the story of a parish in Africa being scandalized and almost broken up by its bishop reading Jonah in Jerome's new version. In this version as then read, *ivy* was substituted for *gourd* in c. iv. When the bishop read "ivy" the people rose and cried out "gourd," till he was obliged to resort to the received version, lest he should be left without any followers. Augustine recommends Jerome to translate from the LXX, with notes where his version deviates from the received text. Jerome answers that he has never received Augustine's original letter, but has only seen what purports to be a copy. "Send me," he says, "your letter signed by yourself, or else cease from attacking me. As to your writings, which you put forward so much, I have only read the Soliloquies and the Commentary on the Psalms, and will only say that in this last there are things disagreeing with the best Greek commentaries. Let me beg you in future, if you write to me, to take care that I am the first whom your letter reaches." Augustine now (in 404) sent by a presbyter Praesidius authentic copies of his two original letters (written nine or ten years before), accompanied by one in which he begged that the matter might be treated as between friends, and not grow into a feud like that of Jerome and Rufinus, which he deeply lamented. On receipt of this Jerome at once wrote (*Ep.* civ.) a full answer to Augustine's principal letters (in Hieron. lvi. lxvii. civ. cx.), and on the question of St. Peter at Antioch appealed to the great Eastern expositors of Scripture. Augustine replied in a long letter (in Jerome's, cxvi.) on the chief question, adding many expressions tending to satisfy Jerome as to their personal relations. Jerome appears to have been more than satisfied; perhaps even to have been convinced. The only allusions in his later writings to this controversy seem to favour Augustine's view. Augustine wrote two letters to him a few years later on the origin of souls (cxxxi.), and on the meaning of the words, "He that offends in one point is guilty of all" (cxxxii.). Jerome's reply (cxxxiv.) is wholly friendly. He refers to a request in one of Augustine's former letters (civ.) for translations from the LXX, saying that these had been stolen from him, and adds, "Each of us has his gift; there is nothing in your letters but what I admire; and I wish to be understood as assenting to all you say, for we must be united in order to withstand Pelagianism." Augustine, on his part, shewed a remarkable deference to Jerome's opinion on the origin of souls, as to which after five year she still hesitated (Hieron. *Ep.* cxliv.) to give a definite answer to his friend Optatus because he had not received one from Jerome; and he sent Orosius, probably referring to this very question, to sit, as Orosius himself says, at the feet of Jerome (*de Lib. Arb.* 3). The remaining letters shew a constant increase of friendship. The two great teachers, though from somewhat different points of view, laboured together in combating Pelagianism; and, having been to each other for a while almost as heretics, stand justly side by side as canonized doctors of Latin Christianity.

Last Period, 405-420. *Old Age and Troubles.*—This last period of Jerome's life was full of external dangers and towards its close agitated by controversy. In 405 the Isaurians devastated the N. of Palestine, the monasteries of Bethlehem were beset with fugitives, and Jerome and his friends were brought into great straits for the means of living. The winter was extremely cold, and Jerome was laid low by a severe illness in Lent 406 (*Ep.* cxiv.) which left him weak for a long time. The barbarian invasions culminated in the sack of Rome by Alaric in 410. In this last calamity, which seemed to be ushering in the end of the world (cxxiii.), Pammachius and Marcella died. Emigration from Italy to Africa and Syria set in, and the more religious among the fugitives flocked to Jerusalem and Bethlehem (pref. to bks. iii. and vii. of *Comm. on Ezk.*). Jerome was not unaffected by the evil political influences of the time. He represents himself as watched by enemies, who made it dangerous for him even to express his sense of the miseries of the empire. In his *Commentary on the Monarchies in Daniel* he reflects on the low state to which the Roman empire had fallen and its need of support from barbarians; and these words were taken as reflecting on Stilicho, the great half-Vandal general, the father-in-law and minister of Honorius, and the real ruler of the empire. Stilicho, whom Jerome afterwards speaks of (*Ep.* cxxiii. 17) as "the half-barbarian traitor who armed the enemy against us with our own resources," appears to have heard of Jerome's expressions in his commentary and to have taken great offence, and Jerome believed that he was meditating some revenge against him when he was put to death ("Dei judicio," pref. to bk. xi. of *Comm. on Is.*) by order of his imperial relative. In the year following the sack of Rome Palestine suffered from an incursion of barbarians from which Jerome barely escaped (*Ep.* cxxvi. 2). He was very poor (pref. to *Comm. on Ezk.* bk. viii.), but made no complaint of this. His best friends had passed away—Paula in 403, Pammachius and Marcella in 410 (pref. to *Comm. on Ezk.* bk. i.). Of his Roman friends, Oceanus, Principia, and the younger Fabiola alone remained (*Epp.* cxx. cxxvii.); Eustochium had very possibly (as Thierry supposes) less authority than her mother in the management of the convent, and this left room for irregularities like those related in Jerome's letter (cxlvii.) to Sabinianus. Eustochium died in 418 (pref. to *Comm. on Jer.* bk. i.). Jerome's days were taken up by the monastery and the hospice (pref. to *Comm. on Ezk.* bk. viii.) and he could only dictate his commentaries at night; he was even glad when winter came and gave him longer nights for this purpose (*ib.*). He was growing weak with age and frequent illnesses, and his eyesight, which had originally failed nearly 40 years before (Constantinople, 380), was so weak that he could hardly decipher Heb. letters at night (*ib.*). Controversy arose again with Pelagius (pref. to *Comm. on Jer.* bks. i.-iv.), and Jerome's relations with the bp. of Jerusalem can hardly have been smooth (*Ep.* cxxxvii.). On the other hand, his brother Paulinian was still with him; the younger Paula, daughter of Toxotius and Laeta (cvii. cxxxiv.), survived him and replaced her aunt Eustochium in managing the monasteries. Albina, and the younger Melania with her husband Pinianus (cxliv.), came to live with him; he had kindly relations with persons in many countries; and the only leading man of the Western church was his friend. Amidst all discouragements, he continued his Biblical studies and writings with no sign of weakness to the end.

Pelagianism.—The Pelagian controversy was forced upon his notice. He had not antecedently formed any strong opinion on it, and had been connected in early life with some of the leading supporters of Pelagius (pref. to *Comm. on Jer.* bk. iv.). But no great question could now arise in the church without an appeal to Jerome, and his correspondence necessarily embraced this subject (*Epp.* cxxxiii. cxxxviii.). Orosius, the friend of Augustine, came to reside at Bethlehem in 414, full of the council of Carthage and of the thoughts and doings of his teacher; and when in 415 Pelagius and Coelestius came to Palestine, Jerome was in the very centre of the controversy. A synod was held under John of Jerusalem [Joannes (**216**)] in July 415 with no result; and at a synod at Diospolis in 416 Pelagius was acquitted, partly, it was believed, because the Eastern bishops could not see their way in matters of Western theology and in judging of Latin expressions. But the mind of the church generally was against him, and Jerome was called upon to give expression to it. Ctesiphon from Rome wrote to him directly on the subject and drew a long reply (cxxxiii.). Augustine addressed to him two letters on points bearing upon the subject (cxxxi. cxxxii.), and in his letter on the origin of souls insinuated that Jerome's creationism might identify him with Pelagius's denial of the transmission of Adam's sin (cxxx. 6). Pelagius sometimes quoted Jerome as agreeing with him (pref. to *Comm. on Jer.* bk. i.), sometimes attacked passages in his commentaries (*id.* bk. iv.) and depreciated his translation of the Scriptures (pref. to *Dial. against Pelag.*). Orosius, who withstood Pelagius in the synod of Jerusalem with little success, appealed (*de Libero Arbitrio contra Pelagium*) to Jerome as a champion of the faith. Jerome wrote, therefore, in 3 books, the dialogue against the Pelagians, an amplification of his letter to Ctesiphon, in which Atticus (the Augustinian) and Critobulus (the Pelagian) maintain the argument. It turns upon the question whether a man can be without sin if he so wills. Its tone is much milder than that of Jerome's other controversial writings, with the single exception of the dialogue against the Luciferians. But still he is dealing with a heretic, and heresy is under the ban of the church and of heaven. This terrible doom contrasts somewhat sharply with the balanced argument, in which Jerome appears not as a thorough-going predestinarian, but a "synergist," maintaining the coexistence of the free will, and reducing predestination to God's foreknowledge of human determination (see the *Dialogue*, esp. i. 5, ii. 6, iii. 18). Nevertheless, the partisans of Pelagius were irritated to bitterness and violence. A crowd of Pelagian monks attacked, partly threw down, and partly burned the monasteries of Bethlehem, some of the inmates were slaughtered, and Jerome only escaped by taking refuge in a tower stronger than the rest. This violence, however, was their last effort. A strong letter from pope Innocentius (cxxxvii.) to John of Jerusalem (who died soon after, 418) warned him that he would be held accountable for any future violence, and Jerome received a letter (cxxxvi.) assuring him of the pope's protection. Jerome's letters to Riparius (cxxxviii.), Apronius (cxxxix.), and Augustine (cxli. cxliii.), speak of the cause of Augustine as triumphant, and of Pelagius, who is compared to Catiline, leaving Palestine, though Jerusalem is still held by some powerful adversary, who is compared to Nebuchadnezzar (cxliv.). There was, however, in the East no strong feeling against Pelagius. His cause was upheld by Theodore of Mopsuestia, who in a work, of which parts are extant (in Hieron. vol. ii. pp. 807-814), argues against Augustine and Jerome (whom he calls "Aram"), as "those who say that men sin by nature and not by will." In the West a work was written by Anianus, a deacon of Celeda, of which a copy was sent to Jerome (cxliii. 2) by Eusebius of Cremona, but to which he was never able to reply.

Letters.—The letters of this period of Jerome's life are mostly ones of counsel to those who asked his advice. Among these may be mentioned that to Ageruchia (cxxiii.), exhorting her to persevere in her estate as a widow, and giving as deterrents from a second marriage some touches of Roman manners and a remarkable account of the sack of Rome; to the virgin Demetrias (cxxx.), who had escaped from the burning of Rome and fallen into the hands of count Heraclian in Africa; and to Sabinianus (cxlvii.) the lapsed deacon, who had brought disorder into the monasteries, and from which letter a whole romance of monastic life might be constructed. Jerome wrote also the Memoir of Marcella (cxxvii.), who died from ill-treatment in the sack of Rome, addressing his letter to her friend Principia; but he was too dejected and infirm to write the Epitaphium of Eustochium, who died two years before him (cdxviii.). Other letters relate to scriptural studies; cxix., to Minucius and Alexander, learned presbyters of the diocese of Toulouse, on the interpretation of the words, "We shall not all sleep, but we shall all be changed"; cxx., to Hebidia, a lady of a remarkable family whose father and grandfather were orators, poets, professors, and priests of Apollo Belen at Bayeux; cxl., to the presbyter Cyprian, an exposition of Ps. xc.; cxxiv., to Avitus, on the περὶ Ἀρχῶν; cxxix., on how Palestine could be called the Promised Land; and cxlvi., to Evangelus an African presbyter, containing the well-known theory of Jerome on the relative positions of bishops, priests, and deacons.

Commentaries on Greater Prophets.—Of Bible work in his later years we have only the Commentaries on the Greater Prophets: on Daniel in 407; on Isaiah in 16 books, written in the intervals of business and illness, and issued at various times from 408-410; on Ezekiel, from 410-414; and on Jeremiah, cut short at c. xxxii. by Jerome's last illness. The prefaces to these are remarkable documents and very serviceable for the chronology of Jerome's life. Those on Ezekiel record the sack of Rome, the death of Rufinus (bk. i.), the immigration from Rome (bks. iii. and vii.), the rise of Pelagianism (bk. vi.); and bk. ix. of the commentary speaks of the invasion of Rome by count Heraclian. Jerome was prevented from taking up the commentary on Jeremiah till after the death of Eustochium (418), and thus his last work was written in the year (419) which intervened between Eustochium's death and his own. Yet not only is the work full of vigour, but the prefaces shew a renewal of controversial ardour against Pelagius, whom he speaks of as "Scotorum pultibus praegravatus" (bks. i. and iii.). That controversy and the business of the pilgrims (bk. iv.) shortened his time for the commentary (bk. iii.), which, though intended to be short (bk. i.), required his excuses in the last preface (bk. vi.) for its growing length.

Death.—It is generally believed that a long sickness preceded the death of Jerome, that after 419 he was unable to work at all, that he was attended in this illness by the younger Paula and Melania; that he died, according to the *Chronicle* of Prosper of Aquitania, on Sept. 20, 420, and that he was buried beside Paula and Eustochium near the grotto of the Nativity. His body was believed to have been subsequently carried to Rome and placed in the church of Sta. Maria Maggiore on the Esquiline. Legends, such as that, immortalized by the etching of Albert Dürer, of the lion which constantly attended him, and of the miracles at his grave, are innumerable.

Writings now Extant.—Vallarsi's ed. contains a complete table of contents which may be usefully consulted. In our list the date of time and place at which each was composed, and the volume in Vallarsi's ed., are added.

I. Bible Translations :—

(1) *From the Hebrew.*—The Vulgate of O.T., written at Bethlehem, begun 391, finished 404, vol. ix.

(2) *From the LXX.*—The Psalms as used at Rome, written in Rome 383; and as used in Gaul, written at Bethlehem *c.* 388. The book of Job, being part of the translation of LXX made between 386 and 392 at Bethlehem, the rest being lost (*Ep.* cxxxiv.), vol. x.

(3) *From the Chaldee.*—Tobit and Judith, Bethlehem, A.D. 398.

(4) *From the Greek.*—The Vulgate version of N.T., made at Rome between 382 and 385.

II. Commentaries :—

(1) *Original.*—Ecclesiastes, vol. iii. A.D. 388; Isaiah, vol. iv. 410; Jeremiah, i.-xxxii. 41, vol. iv. 419; Ezekiel, vol. v. 410-414; Daniel, vol. v. 407; Minor Prophets, vol. vi. at various times between 391 and 406; Matthew, vol. vii. 387; Galatians, Ephesians, Titus, Philemon, vol. vii. 388: all at Bethlehem.

(2) *Translated from Origen.*—Homilies on Jer. and Ezk., vol. v. Bethlehem, date doubtful; on Luke, vol. vii. Bethlehem, 389; Canticles, vol. iii. Rome and Bethlehem, 385-387.

There is also a commentary on Job, and a specimen of one on the Psalms, vol. vii.; and the translation of Origen's Homilies on Isaiah, all attributed to Jerome, vol. iv.

III. Books illustrating Scripture:—

(1) Book of Hebrew Names, or Glossary of Proper Names in O.T.; Bethlehem, 388; vol. iii. 1.

(2) Book of Questions on Genesis, Bethlehem, 388; vol. iii. 301.

(3) A translation of Eusebius's book on the Sites and Names of Hebrew Places, Bethlehem, 388; vol. iii. 121.

(4) Translation of Didymus on the Holy Spirit, Rome and Bethlehem, 385-387; vol. ii. 105.

IV. Books on Church History and Controversy (all in vol. ii.):—

(1) Book of Illustrious Men, or Catalogue of Ecclesiastical Writers, Bethlehem, A.D. 392.

(2) Dialogue with a Luciferian, Antioch, 379.

(3) Lives of the Hermits: Paulus, Desert, 374; Malchus and Hilarion, Bethlehem, 390.

(4) Translation of the Rule of Pachomius; Bethlehem, 404.

(5) Books of ascetic controversy: against Helvidius, Rome, 383; against Jovinian, Bethlehem, 393; against Vigilantius, Bethlehem, 406.

(6) Books of personal controversy: against John, bp. of Jerusalem, Bethlehem, 398 or 399; against Rufinus, i. and ii. 402, iii. 404.

(7) Dialogue with a Pelagian, Bethlehem, 416.

V. General History:—Translation of the *Chronicle* of Eusebius, with Jerome's additions, vol. viii., Constantinople, 382.

VI. Letters:—The series of letters, vol. i. *Ep.* i. Aquileia, 371; ii.-iv. Antioch, 374; v.-xvii. Desert, 374-379; xviii. Constantinople, 381; xix.-xlv. Rome, 382-385; xlvi.-cxlviii. Bethlehem, 386-418.

The works attributed to Jerome but not genuine, which are given in Vallarsi's ed., are: A Breviary, Commentary, and Preface on the Psalms, vol. vii.; some Greek fragments, and a Lexicon of Hebrew Names, the Names of Places in the Acts, the Ten Names of God, the Benedictions of the Patriarchs, the Ten Temptations in the Desert, a Commentary on the Song of Deborah, Hebrew Questions in Kings and Chronicles, an Exposition of Job, vol. iii., three letters in vol. i., and 51 in vol. xi., and several miscellaneous writings in vol. xi., most of which are by Pelagius.

Criticism.—(1) As a Bible translator, Jerome deserves the highest place for his clear conviction of the importance of his task and his perseverance against great obstacles. This is shewn especially in his prefaces, which are of great value as shewing his system. He took very great pains, but not with all alike. The Chronicles he went over word by word with his Hebrew teacher; Tobit he translated in a single day. His method was, first, never to swerve needlessly from the original; second, to avoid solecisms; third, at all risks, even that of introducing solecisms, to give the true sense. These principles are not always consistently carried out. There is sometimes undue laxity, which is defended in the *de Optimo Genere Interpretandi*; sometimes an unnecessary literalism, arising from a notion that some hidden sense lies behind the words, but really depriving the words of sense. His versions were during his lifetime both highly prized and greatly condemned. His friend Sophronius translated a great part of them into Greek and they were read in many Eastern churches in Jerome's lifetime. After his death they gradually won universal acceptance in the West, and were finally, with some alterations (mostly for the worse), stamped with the authority of the Roman church at the council of Trent. See Vallarsi's preface to vol. ix., and Zöckler, pt. II. ii. *Hieronymus als Bibel Uebersetzer.*

(2) As an expositor, Jerome lacks originality. His Commentaries are mostly compilations from others, whose views he gives at times without any opinion of his own. This, however, makes them of special value as the record of the thoughts of distinguished men, such as Origen. His derivations are puerile. His interpretation of prophecy is the merest literal application of it to events in the church. He is often inconsistent, and at times seems to veil his own opinion under that of another. His allusions to the events of his own time as illustrations of Scripture are often of great interest. His great haste in writing (pref. to bk. ii. of *Comm. on Eph.* and pref. to bk. iii. of *Comm. on Gal.*), his frequent weak health and weak eyes, and his great self-confidence caused him to trust his memory too much.

(3) The books on Hebrew Names, Questions on Genesis, and the Site and Names of Hebrew Places shew a wide range of interest and are useful contributions to Biblical knowledge, especially the last-named, which is often appealed to in the present day. But even here he was too ready to accept Jewish tales rather than to exercise independent judgment.

In theology, properly so called, he is weak. His first letter to Damasus on the Trinitarian controversies at Antioch shews a clear perception of what the church taught, but also a shrinking from dogmatic questions and a servile submission to episcopal authority. He accepted without question the damnation of all the heathen. His dealings with Origen shew his weakness; he surrendered his impartial judgment as soon as Origen's works were condemned. In the Pelagian controversy his slight realization of the importance of the questions contrasts markedly with the deep conviction of the writings of Augustine. In some matters, which had not been dealt with by church authority, he held his own; *e.g.* as to the origin of souls he is decided as a creationist. He puts aside purgatory and scoffs at millenarianism. His views on the Apocrypha and on the orders of the Christian ministry have become classical.

(4) For church history he had some considerable faculty, as is shewn by the dialogue with a Luciferian. His knowledge was great and his sympathies large, when there was no question of church condemnations. His book *de Viris Illustribus* is especially valuable and

his defence of it against Augustine's criticism shews him to have the wider culture and greater knowledge. But the lives of the hermits incorporate legend with history. In controversy his ordinary method is to take as absolute truth the decisions of bishops and even the popular feeling in the church and to use all his powers in enforcing these. His own life and documents which give its details are his best contributions to church history.

(5) His knowledge of and sympathy with human history generally was very like that of monks of later times. He had much curiosity and considerable knowledge. His translation of the *Chronicle* of Eusebius shews his interest in history, but is very uncritical. The mistakes of Eusebius are not corrected but aggravated by the translator; his own additions shew that his critical faculty was not such as to guard against the admission of considerable errors; and his credulity constantly reveals itself. He nowhere shews even the rudiments of a philosophy of history. He knew both the events of his time and facts lying beyond the usual range. He was acquainted with the routes to India, and mentions the Brahmans (*Epp.* xxii. lxx. etc.) and Buddha (*adv. Jov.* i. 42). Events like the fall of Rome deeply impressed him; but he deals with these very much as the monks of the middle ages dealt with the events of their time. He is a recluse, with no political sagacity and no sense of human progress.

(6) His letters are the most interesting part of his writings. They are very various; vivid in feeling and graphic in their pictures of life. The letters to Heliodorus (xiv.) on the praise of hermit life; to Eustochium (xxii.) on the preservation of virginity in the mixed life of the Roman church and world; to Asella (xlv.) on his departure from Rome; to Nepotian (lii.) on the duties of the presbyters and monks of his day; to Marcella from Paula and Eustochium (xlvi.), giving the enthusiastic description of monastic life among the holy places of Palestine; to Laeta (cvii.) on the education of a child whose grandfather was a heathen priest, whose parents were Christians, and who was herself to be a nun; to Rusticus (cxxv.), giving rules which shew the character of the monastic life in those days,—all these are literary gems; and the Epitaphia of Blesilla (xxxix.), Fabiola (lxxvii.), Nepotianus (lx.), Paula (cviii.), and Marcella (cxxvii.) form a hagiography of the best and most attractive kind.

Style.—His style is excellent, and he was rightly praised as the Christian Cicero by Erasmus, who contrasts his writings with monkish and scholastic literature. It is vivid, full of illustrations, with happy turns, such as "lucus a non lucendo," Ὀνῳ̂ λύρα, "fac de necessitate virtutem," "Ingemuit totus orbis et Arianum se esse miratus est." The scriptural quotations and allusions are often overdone and forced, but with no unreality or cant; and he never loses his dignity except in some controversial personalities.

Character.—He was vain, and unable to bear rivals; extremely sensitive as to the estimation of his contemporaries, especially the bishops; passionate and resentful, but at times suddenly placable; scornful and violent in controversy; kind to the weak and poor; respectful in dealing with women; entirely without avarice; extraordinarily diligent, and nobly tenacious of the main objects of his life.

Influence.—His influence grew through his life and increased after his death. "He lived and reigned for a thousand years." His writings contain the whole spirit of the church of the middle ages; its monasticism, its contrast of sacred things with profane, its credulity and superstition, its deference to hierarchical authority, its dread of heresy, its passion for pilgrimages. To the society which was thus in a great measure formed by him, his Bible was the greatest boon which could have been given. But he founded no school and had no inspiring power; there was not sufficient courage or width of view in his spiritual legacy. As Thierry says, "There is no continuation of his work; a few more letters of Augustine and Paulinus, and night falls over the West." A cheap popular Life of St. Jerome by E. L. Cutts is pub. by S.P.C.K. in their *Fathers for Eng. Readers.* A trans. of his principal works is in the *Lib. of Nic. and Post.-Nic. Fathers.* The Bp. of Albany has in preparation (1911) a trans. of the *Epistolae Selectae* (ed. Hurter). [W.H.F.]

Hierotheus, a writer whose works are quoted by the Pseudo-Dionysius, who styles him his teacher. Two long extracts are preserved in the *de Divinis Nominibus* of the Pseudo-Dionysius (c. 2, §§ 9, 10; c. 4, §§ 15-17), and there are incidental references to him elsewhere. In the first extract (c. 2, § 9 fin.) his *Theological Institutes* (θεολογικαὶ στοιχειώσεις) are cited; in the second his *Amatory Hymns* (ἐρωτικοὶ ὕμνοι). His writings most probably belong to the school of Edessa, and should be dated about the middle or end of 5th cent. In confirmation of this view Dr. Westcott has noted a statement in Assemani (*Biblioth. Orient.* ii. 290, 291) that Stephen Bar-Sudaili, abbat of a monastery at Edessa, published a book under the name of Hierotheus to support his own mystic doctrines. Assemani says that this abbat held the doctrine of final restoration as taught by Origen, and was abused for it by Xenaias and James of Sarug, bp. of Batnae (*Bibl. Or.* i. 303, ii. 30-33; Ceillier, x. 641; Westcott on Dionys. Areop. in *Contemporary Rev.* May, 1867). The mystical views in the works of Hierotheus and Dionysius easily lend themselves to the support of that theory. According to Assemani (ii. 291), Bar-Sudaili wrote under the name of Hierotheus to prove "finem poenarum aliquando futurum, nec impios in saeculum saeculorum puniendos fore, sed per ignem purgandos; atque ita et malos daemones misericordiam consequuturos esse, et cuncta in divinam naturam transmutanda, juxta illud Pauli, ut sit Deus omnia in omnibus." In Mai's *Spicilegium Romanum* (iii. 704-707) will be found other fragments of this writer, translated from some Arabic MSS. Their theology savours, however, more of the 4th and 5th cents. than of the 1st. But see A. L. Frothingham, *Stephen Bar-Sudaili and the Book of Hierotheos* (Leyden, 1886). [G.T.S.]

Hilarianus (1), Quintus Julius (*Hilarion*), a Latin Chiliast writer, *c.* 397, author of two extant treatises. The first, *Expositum de Die Paschae et Mensis*, after having disappeared for several centuries, was printed in 1712, with a dissertation by Pfaffius to prove that it was written A.D. 397. Hilarian supports the Latins against the Greeks, in agreement with pope Victor and the council of Nicaea.

The second treatise, *Chronologia sive Libellus de Mundi Duratione*, is founded on a dispute about the date of the end of the world. The author counts 5,530 years from the Creation to the Passion; gives the world 6,000; and would therefore end it *c.* 498.

The following is a sketch of his chronology:

From the Creation to the Deluge	2237	years.
,, ,, Deluge to the Call of Abraham	1012	,,
,, thence to the Exodus	430	,,
,, ,, ,, Samuel	450	,,
,, ,, ,, Zedekiah	514	,,
The Captivity lasted	70	,,
Thence to the Passion	887	,,

He believes that after the close of the apocalyptic thousand years will come the loosing of Satan, the seducing of the nations Gog and Magog, the descent of fire from heaven upon their armies; then the second resurrection, the judgment, the passing away of the old things and the bringing in of the new heavens and new earth; "impii in ambustione aeterna; justi autem cum Deo in vita aeterna" (c. 19). His style is barbarous. La Bigne, *Biblioth. Vet. Patr.* 1609, t. vii.; 1618, t. v. pt. i.; 1654, t. vii.; 1677, t. vii. Migne, *Patr. Lat.* xiii. col. 1094-1114; Cave, i. 252; Ceillier, vi. 288. A new ed. of *de Mundi Duratione* was pub. by C. Frisk in *Chronica Minora* (Leipz. 1892). [W.M.S. AND J.G.]

Hilarion (1), a hermit of Palestine (d. 371). Jerome wrote his Life in 390, quoting Epiphanius, Hilarion's disciple. Jerome certainly considered his *Lives of the Hermits* as historical (*Vit. Malchi*, i.); but the marvels of the Life of Hilarion have induced some to believe it to be a mere romance (Israel in Hilgenfeld's *Zeitschrift* for 1880, p. 128, but see Zöckler's *Jerome*, 179). No attempt is made in this art. to separate fact from fiction. The Life of Hilarion in any case shews the ideal on which monasticism was nourished in the 4th cent.

Hilarion was born at Thabatha, 5 miles S. of Gaza, *c.* 300, of heathen parents, who sent him for education to Alexandria. There he shewed great talents and proficiency in rhetoric, which then comprehended nearly the whole of a liberal education. He was of a disposition which made him beloved by all. He became a Christian, and, turning from the frivolous pleasures of the circus and theatre, spent all his leisure in the assemblies of the church. Hearing of the monastic retreat of Anthony, he became his disciple for a time, but found that the multitude who resorted to Anthony made life with him a city life rather than one of retirement. Though but fifteen years old, he determined to become a hermit. He returned to Palestine and found his parents dead, gave away his goods to his brothers and the poor, and went to live in a desert place 7 miles from the Christian city of Majoma near Gaza. The boy hermit was clad in a sackcloth shirt, which he never changed till it was worn out, a cloak of skins which Anthony had given him, and a blanket such as peasants wore. His daily sustenance was 15 carices (a sort of figs). He cultivated a little plot of ground and made baskets of rushes, so as not to be idle. His disordered fancy summoned up a thousand temptations of Satan, but he overcame them all by calling on the name of Christ. He dwelt 12 years in a little cabin made by himself of woven reeds and rushes; after that in a hut only 5 feet high, still shewn when Jerome was in Palestine, and more like a sepulchre than a house.

The fame of his sanctity spread rapidly, and he was reputed to be a worker of miracles and an exorcist. Men of all ranks (whose names and abodes are circumstantially recorded) suffering from hysteric affections, then attributed to demons, were healed. An officer of Majoma, whose duty it was to rear horses for the Circensian games and who had been always beaten through a spell laid upon his chariot by the votaries of Marnas, the idol of Gaza, won the race when the saint had poured water upon his chariot wheels. Hilarion had many disciples, whom he formed into societies and went on circuits to visit them; and many stories were told of his shrewdness and penetration in rebuking their weaknesses.

But the crowds who flocked about him made him feel no longer a hermit; and in his 63rd year, the year of the death of Anthony (which was miraculously made known to him), he resolved to set out on his wanderings. Men crowded round him to the number of 10,000, beseeching him not to depart. Business ceased throughout Palestine, the minds of men being wholly occupied with hopes and fears about his departure; but he left them, and with a few monks, who seem soon to have left him, he went his way, never to return. He first turned towards Babylon, then to Egypt. He fled to the Oasis, and afterwards sailed for Sicily. There he lay hid for a time; but his disciple Hesychius at last discovered him. He again set forth in search of solitude; but wherever he went his miracles betrayed him. He at length arrived in Cyprus, the home of his friend Epiphanius. There he found a solitary and inaccessible place, still called by his name, where he lived the last three years of his life, often in the company of Hesychius and Epiphanius. His body was buried in the grounds of a lady named Constantia, but Hesychius disinterred it, and carried it to Majoma in Palestine. Constantia died of grief, but the translation caused joy throughout Palestine, where its anniversary was observed as a festival. *Vita S. Hilarionis*, in Jerome's *Works*, vol. ii. 13-40, ed. Vall.; Soz. iii. 14, vi. 32; *Vit. Patrum*, lib. v. c. 4, § 15, p. 568, in Migne's *Patr. Gk.* vol. lxxiii. His name occurs in the *Byzantine Calendar*, Oct. 21, as "Our Father Hilarion the Great." [W.H.F.]

Hilarius (7) Pictaviensis, St. (*Hilary of Poictiers*), d. A.D. 368.

Authorities.—(1) His own writings. These furnish so much information that the biography in the Benedictine ed. of Hilary's works is mainly drawn from them. (2) Hieron. *de Viris Illustribus* (*seu Scriptorum Eccles. Catalogus*), c. 100. Also *in Esaiam*, c. lx., *in Psalm.* lviii. (A.V. lix.), in the prooemium in lib. ii. *Comm. ad Gal.* (3) St. Augustine, *de Trinitate*, lib. x. c. 6, lib. xv. c. 2. (4) Cassian, *de Incar-*

natione, lib. vii. (5) St. Gregory of Tours, *de Gloriâ Confessorum*, c. 2. (6) Fortunatus, whose identification is uncertain. [FORTUNATUS (**17**) and (**18**).] (7) Cassiodorus, *Institut. Divin.* lib. i. c. 16.

Life.—Hilary is believed to have been born of illustrious stock in Poictiers. St. Jerome (*in Gal.*) distinctly asserts this, but some authorities name more vaguely the *province* of Aquitaine, rather than the *capital.* He enjoyed a good education in the Latin classics, and evidently was specially fond of the writings of Quintilian.

About A.D. 350, Hilary, then a married man but, it would seem, still young, appears to have become a Christian. He depicts himself as gradually rising first above the attractions of ease and plenty; then aiming at knowledge of truth and the practice of virtue. The books of Moses and the Psalms gave him abundant help in his desire to know God; in his consciousness of weakness the writings of apostles and evangelists aided him, more especially the Gospel of St. John, with its clear and emphatic teaching on the incarnation of the co-eternal Son. His conversion was essentially due to the study of Holy Scripture.

After his baptism he became an edifying example of a good Christian layman. He must have remained a layman for some few years. His wife's name is unknown, but a daughter, his only child, was called Abra (*al.* Apra *seu* Afra). About 353 the see of Poictiers became vacant by death. The popular voice fixed upon Hilary as the new bishop, and he was raised *per saltum* to the episcopate. He amply justified the choice.

Two years after his consecration a visit from St. Martin, which was regarded as a compliment to the orthodoxy and zeal of Hilary, proved a prelude to an active struggle against the Arian party in Gaul, then headed by Ursacius, Valens, and Saturninus, of whom Saturninus occupies, in the writings of the orthodox, an evil pre-eminence, being represented as immoral, violent, and apt to seek the aid of the civil power against the defenders of the creed of Nicaea. Hilary unites with Sulpicius Severus in censuring Saturninus more than his comrades. The course pursued by Ursacius and Valens, though less violent, was extremely fitful and uncertain, and a majority of the bishops of Gaul, led by Hilary, formally separated themselves from the communion of all three. Many even of those who had leant towards Arianism now threw in their lot with Hilary, who received them on condition that they should be approved by the confessors then suffering exile. At a council at Béziers, in Languedoc, Saturninus probably presiding, Hilary (with some other orthodox bishops) was present, but declares that he was refused a hearing. The emperor Constantius received from Saturninus an account of this gathering, and at once resolved to banish to Phrygia Hilary and one of his allies, St. Rhodanus, bp. of Toulouse. Hilary believed that the accusation laid against him before the emperor involved a charge of gross impropriety of conduct. As this event occurred soon after the council of Béziers and before that of Seleucia, its date is assigned to the middle of 356. During this exile of somewhat more than three years Hilary had a good deal of liberty and much enforced leisure. He employed it in examining the condition of religion in Asia Minor, forming an exceedingly unfavourable impression, especially as regarded his episcopate, and in composition and an attempt to remove misunderstandings, especially between the bishops of the East and those of Gaul; for the Gallicans imagined all in Asia to be sheer Arians, while the Orientals supposed their brethren in Gaul to be lapsing into Sabellianism. Hilary's treatise *de Synodis* belongs to this period (358 or 359), and also his great work *de Trinitate.*

The fourth year (359) of Hilary's exile witnessed the council of Rimini in the West and that of Seleucia in the East. The emperor apparently intended the decisions of these two assemblies, if accordant, to be conjointly regarded as the decree of one oecumenical council. Hilary was compelled by the secular authorities to attend that of Seleucia, Constantius himself having convoked it. He found there three sections: the orthodox, semi-Arian, and ultra-Arian or Anomoean. Although his presence was of great service in explaining the true state of things in Gaul, the language of the Acacians so shocked him that he retired from the assembly. These Anomoeans were nevertheless condemned there.

From Seleucia Hilary went to Constantinople and was granted an interview with the emperor. Here the Arians, having joined the Anomoeans, were in great force, and, having gathered another council in the Eastern capital, tried to reverse their failure at Seleucia. A challenge from Hilary to discuss the questions at issue publicly, in presence of the emperor, on the evidence of Holy Scripture, was, as he informs us, declined; and Constantius sent his prisoner back to Gaul, without formally annulling the sentence of banishment or allowing him perfect liberty. The energies of Hilary in Gaul were chiefly concerned with the Arians, but his acts (though by no means all his writings) in Phrygia with the semi-Arians. His attitude towards these two forms of error was by no means identical. Arianism he regarded as a deadly heresy, with which anything like compromise was impossible. But with semi-Arianism, or at any rate with certain leading semi-Arians, he thought it quite possible to come to an understanding; and it will be seen in the account of his works how earnestly he strove to act as a peacemaker between them and the supporters of the creed of Nicaea. The three succeeding years (A.D. 360-362) were partly occupied by his rather dilatory journey homeward, and after his return by efforts which, though of a conciliatory character, all aimed at the restoration of the faith as set forth at Nicaea. His joy at reaching Poictiers (where he was warmly welcomed) and at finding in health his wife, his daughter, and his disciple St. Martin, was dashed by the scenes witnessed during his progress. Constantius had banished all bishops who had refused to accept the formula promulgated at Rimini (Socr. *H. E.* ii. 37; confirmed by Soz. iv. 19, and by St. Jerome in his treatise *adv. Luciferianos*). Hilary and his more ardent friends were not prepared at once to refuse communion to all who had been betrayed into accepting the Riminian decrees. He gathered in different parts of Gaul assemblies of bishops for mutual explanation, apparently with great success. Hilary's former opponent, Saturninus, bp. of Arles, vainly attempted to thwart this work, and Saturninus soon found himself deserted and practically, perhaps even formally, excommunicated by the Gallican episcopate.

Hilary now ventured, despite the unrepealed sentence of banishment, to journey into N. Italy and Illyria, to bring these provinces into spiritual conformity with Gaul. He arrived in Italy A.D. 362 and was greatly encouraged and assisted by St. Eusebius of Vercelli. These two friends, especially in remote districts, into which a fair statement of the points at issue had not penetrated, created a considerable impression, though not equal to that produced in Gaul. Possibly Lucifer of Cagliari proved an obstacle. That this ardent and ultra-Athanasian supporter of orthodoxy disapproved of one of the conciliatory manifestos of Hilary will be seen below; and as on another ground he had broken with Eusebius and was opposed to all communion with any who had accepted the decrees of Rimini, he could not have viewed their career with satisfaction.

Hilary, nevertheless, remained in Italy until the late autumn of 364. Valentinian, who became emperor in Feb. 364, found him at Milan in November. A serious altercation between Hilary and Auxentius, bp. of Milan, attracted his attention. The generally charitable tone adopted by Hilary towards his ecclesiastical opponents warrants our accepting his unfavourable report of Auxentius. According to Hilary, the profession of the creed of Nicaea made by Auxentius was thoroughly insincere, though he persuaded Valentinian that he was acting in good faith; and, as a natural result, Hilary was commanded to return to Gaul and at once obeyed, but to the bishops and the church at large made known his own convictions respecting the real character of the bp. of Milan.

Hilary spent more than three years at Poictiers after his return from Italy. These years, especially the last two, were comparatively untroubled. He died calmly on Jan. 13, 368, though in the Roman service-books his day is Jan. 14, so as not to interfere with the octave of the Epiphany.

Writings.—I. EXEGETICAL.—(1) *Exposition of the Psalms* (*Commentarii in Psalmos*).—The comments embrace Ps. i., ii.; ix.-xiii. (and perhaps xiv.); li.-lxix.; xci.-cl. (The numbers are the Vulgate reckoning, *e.g.* li. is lii., and lxix. is lxx. in A.V.) The treatment is not critical, but reveals a deeply sincere and high-toned spirit. Jerome's translation was yet to come when Hilary wrote. As was natural, he leant mainly and somewhat too confidently upon the LXX, but took full advantage of the comments of Origen. He seeks a *via media* between the literal sense, and that reference of everything to Christ which marks some later commentators, both patristic and medieval.

(2) *Commentarii in Matthaeum.*—This is the earliest gospel commentary in the Western church; all previous ones being either, like that of Origen, in Greek, or, if in Latin, only partial, as some tractates of St. Cyprian. In the next century the work of Hilary was somewhat overshadowed by the commentaries produced by the genius of St. Augustine and the learning of St. Jerome in the West, and by the eloquence of St. Chrysostom in the East. Although he may have made some use of the writings of Origen, there is much that is curious and sometimes acute as well as devout that seems to be really his own. Jerome and Augustine frequently quote it. It was probably composed before his banishment to Phrygia in 356.

On the expressions concerning divorce (Matt. v. 31, 32), Hilary regards Christian marriage as absolutely indissoluble. His endeavours to solve difficulties, such as that of the genealogies of our Lord, indicate a real willingness to face them and are not devoid of acuteness. On "the brethren of the Lord" Hilary uses the powerful argument that Christ would not have committed the Virgin Mother to the care of St. John if she had had children of her own, and he adopts the view, usually connected with the name of Epiphanius, that they were children of Joseph by a former wife.

Hilary's respect for the LXX led him to embrace the Alexandrian rather than the Palestinian canon of O.T. He occasionally cites some portions of the Apocrypha (as Judith, Wisdom, and Maccabees) as Scripture. He is earnest in urging the study of Scripture, and lays much stress on the need of humility and reverence for reading them with profit. Both the Word and the Sacraments become spiritual food for the soul.

II. DOGMATICAL.—*Libri XII. de Trinitate.*—For *de Trinitate* some copies read *contra Arianos*, others *de Fide*, and others some slight varieties of a like kind. But *de Trinitate* appears on the whole the most suitable; and as Hilary's is the most ancient extant exposition of St. Matthew by a Latin father, so the *de Trinitate* is the first great contribution, in Latin, to the discussion of this great dogma. Bk. i. treats of natural religion, and how it leads up to revelation. Bk. ii. especially discusses the baptismal formula (Matt. xxviii. 19); bk. iii. the union of the two natures in Christ; bk. iv. that this coexistence of two natures does not derogate from the unity of His Divine Person. Bk. v. urges, as against heretics, the testimony of the prophets (*ex auctoritatibus propheticis*) in favour of the propositions of bk. iv. Bk. vi. is mainly occupied with refutations of Sabellian and Manichean doctrines. Bk. vii. shews how the errors of Ebionites, Arians, and Sabellians overthrow each other, thus illustrating a principle asserted in bk. i. § 26: "Lis eorum est fides nostra." Bk. viii. contains a demonstration of the unity of God, and shews that it is nowise affected by the Sonship of Christ. Bk. ix. replies to the Arian appeal to certain texts, *e.g.* Mark xiv. 32, Luke xviii. 19, John v. 19, xiv. 28, xvii. 3. Bks. x. and xi. similarly discuss, *e.g.*, Matt. xxvi. 38, 39, 46, Luke xxiii. 46, John xx. 17, and 1 Cor. xv. 27, 28. Bk. xii. is also expressly written against Arianism. It includes a passage of much beauty, which bears a slight resemblance to the devout and eloquent pleading of Wisd. ix.

The work is a longer, more methodical, and more consecutive anti-Arian argument than Athanasius himself found time to indite. Viewed intellectually, it must perhaps be ranked above Hilary's commentary on Scripture. Its recognition of the rights of reason as well as of faith, combined with its sense of human ignorance and of our need of humility, its explanation of many difficulties and of the meaning of the terms employed; the endeavour (though not always successful) to adapt to his subject the imperfect medium of Latin, its many felicitous descriptions, both of the temper in which we ought, and the spirit in which we ought not, to approach the study of these mysteries; the mode of his appeals to Holy Scripture,—all form very striking features. The book evidently produced a great impression. A high compliment is paid it by the historian Socrates: "Both [*i.e.* Hilary and Eusebius of Vercelli] nobly contended side by side for the faith. Hilary, who was an eloquent man, set forth in his book the dogmas of the Homoousion in the Latin tongue . . . and powerfully confuted the Arian dogmas" (*H. E.* iii. 10). It marks an epoch in the history of dogmatic theology in the Western church. Its influence declined in the next century and throughout the earlier and later middle ages. About 416, some 56 years after its publication, the 15 books *de Trinitate* of the great bp. of Hippo appeared. St. Augustine became *the* doctor *par excellence* of the West, and the labours of Hilary, most effective at their appearance, became somewhat neglected and obscured. The errors of Pelagianism, perhaps some anticipations of Nestorianism, had certainly by the time of Augustine tended to bring into clearer relief some particular phases and elements of Christian doctrine. Development in this sense is fully recognized by the Lutheran Dorner and by the Anglican Prof. Hussey. Nor can it be called a novel theory. "By the very events," writes the historian Evagrius, "by which the members of the church have been rent asunder have the true and faultless dogmas (τὰ ὀρθὰ καὶ ἀμώμητα δόγματα) been the more fully polished and set forth, and the Catholic and apostolic church of God hath gone on to increase and to a heavenward ascent" (*H. E.* i. 11). "Many things," says Augustine himself, "pertaining to the Catholic faith, while in course of agitation by the hot restlessness of heretics, are, with a view to defence against them, weighed more carefully, understood more clearly, and preached more earnestly; and the question mooted by the adversary hath become an occasion of our learning." * The intentions of Hilary were so thoroughly good that both his studies of Holy Scripture and the influence of the three later oecumenical councils would doubtless have saved him from some serious mistakes, if he had lived to hear of their decisions. It is true, as the Benedictine editor points out, that Hilary's note upon Ps. liii. 8 condemns not only Apollinaris, but (by anticipation) Nestorius and Eutyches as well. Nevertheless, such mistakes as Hilary did make are all connected with the subject, which has been summed up in so masterly a manner by Hooker (*E. P.* bk. v. cc. lii.-liv., esp. § 10 of liv.), viz. the union of the two natures in the one divine personality of Christ. The chief of these mistakes are as follows: In *de Trinitate*, bk. x., Hilary seems to approach to a denial of the truth that the Incarnate Lord took man's nature from His Virgin Mother, of her substance. This is probably only an incautious over-statement of the article, "He was conceived of the Holy Ghost." For the language in other passages of this book and on Pss. cxxxviii. and lxv. implies a complete acceptance of the *Homo ex substantiâ Matris*. Some laxity of usage appears in regard to the terms *Verbum* and *Spiritus*. Certainly the former word seems necessary instead of the latter in the phrase (bk. x.) "Spiritus sanctus desuper veniens naturae se humanae carne immiscuit." Dom Coutant points out similar confusion of language in Tertullian and Lactantius, and even in St. Irenaeus and St. Cyprian. St. Gregory and St. Athanasius seem inclined to palliate it.

A more serious error is Hilary's apparent want of grasp of the truth of our Lord's humanity in all things, sin alone excepted. At times he seems to speak of our Lord's natural body as if endued with impassibility (*indolentia*), and of His soul as if not obnoxious to the human affections of fear, grief, and the like. This and the other mistakes of Hilary are more or less palliated by Lanfranc, by the two great schoolmen Peter Lombard and Aquinas, and by Bonaventure. Hilary also meets with indulgence from Natalis Alexander; and, above all, is defended by his Benedictine editor, Dom Coutant, who, as Cave justly remarks, "naevos explicare, emollire et vindicare satagit." A sort of tradition was handed down to Bonaventure by a schoolman, William of Paris, that Hilary had made a formal retractation of his error concerning the *indolentia*, which he had ascribed to our Lord. This seems very doubtful; nevertheless, the language of his later books, *e.g.* on the Pss., appears to recognize the reality of both the mental and bodily sufferings of Christ.

III. Polemical.—(1) *Ad Constantium Augustum Liber Primus.*—This address, probably Hilary's earliest extant composition, is a petition to the emperor—evidently written before Hilary's exile, at the close of 355 or early in 356—for toleration for the orthodox in Gaul against the persecution of Arian bishops and laymen. These assaults Hilary represents as both coarse and cruel. He names some supporters of Arianism, both in the East and in Gaul. Among the latter, Ursacius and Valens occupy a painful prominence. He urges that it is even on political grounds a mistake for the emperor to allow such proceedings; among his Catholic subjects will be found the best defenders of the realm against internal sedition and barbarian invasion. The excellent tone of this address is admitted on all sides.

(2) *Ad Constantium Augustum Liber Secundus.*—This second address is subsequent to Hilary's exile, having been presented to the

* Dean Hook, in his University Sermons preached before 1838, called attention to this as a favourite opinion of St. Augustine's. Bp. Moberly, in his *Discourses on the Great Forty Days* (preface and discourse iv.) shewed the difference between this view and the modern Roman theory of development.

emperor in 360. Hilary protests his innocence of all charges brought against him. He is still *in effect* a bishop in Gaul, ministering to his flock through the clergy. He would gladly meet the man whom he regards as the author of his exile, Saturninus, bp. of Arles. He is anxious to plead for the faith in the council about to be summoned. He will argue from Holy Scripture, but warns the emperor that every heretic maintains his creed to be agreeable to Scripture. He is deeply conscious of the injury wrought to Christianity in the sight of the outer world by the distractions of so many rival councils and professions of faith.

(3) *Contra Constantium Augustum Liber.*—This book is addressed to the bps. of Gaul. Jerome is almost certainly mistaken in asserting its composition to be later than the death of Constantius. Internal evidence sufficiently confutes the idea, though its existence probably did not become widely known until after that event (361). Hilary's tone is now utterly changed. He has given up all hope of influencing Constantius. The emperor, too, on his side, has altered the traditional line of policy against opponents. He is here charged, not with persecution, but with the enticements of bribes, of good dinners, of flatteries and invitations to court. Hilary appears to have laid aside his usual self-restraint, perhaps to have lost his temper, and to have forgotten his usual respectfulness and charity of language. Constantius has become, in his eyes, an Antichrist, who would fain make a present of the world to Satan. The entire letter shews that Hilary had lost all hope of any aid to the faith being granted by Constantius, and it is at least just to give its due weight to the remark of Möhler that, "if we drive men to despair, we ought to be prepared to hear them speak the language of despair."

(4) *De Synodis Fidei Catholicae contra Arianos et praevaricatores Arianis acquiescentes*; also occasionally referred to as *de Fide Orientalium*; and sometimes, though less frequently, as *de Synodis Graeciae*, or even simply as *Epistola*. Internal evidence furnishes a satisfactory approximation to the date of its composition, viz. in 358 or very early in 359. It is a letter from Hilary, an exile in Phrygia, to his brother-bishops in Gaul, who had asked for an explanation of the numerous professions of faith which the Orientals seemed to be putting forth. Hilary, although (as we have seen from his subsequent second letter to Constantius) deeply conscious of the harm wrought by these proceedings, wrote back a thorough *Irenicon*, for such must the *de Synodis* among all his writings be especially considered. Praising his Gallic brethren for firmness in opposing Saturninus and for their just condemnation of the second formula proposed at Sirmium, he desires that they and their brethren in Britain (*provinciarum Britanniarum episcopi*) should come to Ancyra or to Rimini in a conciliatory frame of mind. Just as the orthodox *Homoousion* may be twisted into Sabellianism, even so may the unorthodox *Homoiousion* be found patient of a good interpretation. It may be shewn to those well disposed that, rightly understood, complete similarity in reality involves identity. The faith professed at Sardica was, he maintains, substantially sound. It asserted the external origin of the Son from the substance of the Father, and condemned the heresy of Photinus, "quae initium Dei filii ex partu Virginis mentiebatur." Hilary appeals to the more peace-loving among the semi-Arian bishops to accept both terms in their true sense. "Date veniam, Fratres, quam frequenter poposci. *Ariani non estis; cur negando homoousion censemini Ariani?*" (§ 88). Here comes in that remarkable statement, that he had never, before his exile, heard the Nicene Creed, but had made it out for himself from the Gospels and other books of N.T.

A peacemaker is often suspected on one side, sometimes upon both. His first letter to Constantius, his commentary on St. Matthew, his confessorship as shewn in his exile, did not save Hilary from suspicion. By some he was held to have conceded too much to the semi-Arians. This opinion was voiced by Lucifer of Cagliari, the earnest but somewhat harsh-minded representative of that extreme wing which might be called more Athanasian than Athanasius. Some apologetic notes, shewing much courtesy and gentleness, appended by Hilary to a copy sent to Lucifer, were first published in the Benedictine ed. (Paris, 1693).

(5) *Liber contra Auxentium.*—Written A.D. 365, under Valentinian, who had become emperor in 366. Hilary was convinced that the profession of orthodoxy made by Auxentius was thoroughly insincere. The emperor accepted the position avowed by Auxentius, entered into communion with him, and ordered Hilary to leave Milan. Hilary obeyed at once, but, as the sole resource left him, published this address to the church at large. Hence its other titles, viz. *contra Arianos vel Auxentium Mediolanensem*, and *Epistola ad Catholicos et Auxentium*. It forms a curious commentary upon church history by bringing into vivid relief the utterly changed character of the temptations to which Christians were now exposed as compared with those of the ante-Nicene period. Hilary's view must be considered a rather one-sided one. He sees clearly the evils of his own day, but hardly realizes what must have been the trials of the times of Nero, Decius, and Galerius. The concluding part makes out a strong case against Auxentius. It is difficult to believe that he was not an Arian at heart. Hilary, like some of his contemporaries, declares that the ears of the people have become purer than the hearts of the bishops. He begs those who shrink from breaking off communion with Auxentius, whom he calls an angel of Satan, not to let their love of mere walls and buildings seduce them into a false peace. Antichrist may seat himself within a church; the forests and mountains, lakes and prisons, are safer. It must be remembered, in palliation of Hilary's strong language respecting the bp. of Milan, that he regarded him not as an open foe, but as a betrayer of truth by false pretences. Rufinus, who speaks of Hilary as a "confessor fidei Catholicae," entitles this work "librum instructionis plenissimae." *

(6) *Fragmenta Hilarii.*—These fragments were first published in 1598 by Nicolaus Faber, who got them from the library of Father

* **Rufinus**, ***de Adulteratione Librorum Origenis.***

Pithou. They possess considerable value in the elucidation of the history of the period embraced by Hilary's episcopate. It is claimed that they are the remnants of a book by Hilary mentioned by Rufinus, and described by Jerome as *Liber contra Valentem et Ursacium*, which contained a history of the councils of Rimini and Seleucia. On this book Hilary expended much labour, having begun it in 360 and completed it in 366. The 15 fragments occupy some 80 folio pages. They are, with one exception, recognized as genuine by Tillemont and by Ceillier. Whether, however, all the other documents cited in these fragments can be depended upon has been disputed. Respecting the genuineness of the commentaries given by Dom Pitra, opinions may fairly differ; and happily there is in that case no disturbing influence at work as there is in the case of these fragments. If we accept them as authentic, the case against LIBERIUS is certainly darkened. But this is precisely the conclusion which certain modern critics (such as, *e.g.*, the anonymous editor of Dom Ceillier) are for very obvious reasons most anxious to avoid.

(7) *Epistola ad Abram Filiam suam* (*c.* 358).—Hilary, during his exile, learnt that there was some prospect of his daughter Abra, though only in her 13th year, being sought in marriage. He draws a mystic portrait of the heavenly bridegroom, which is evidently intended to suggest the superiority of a religious celibacy, but leaves her an entirely free choice, only desiring that the decision should be really her own. He encloses a morning and an evening hymn. On any difficulties in the letter or the hymns, Abra is to consult her mother. The *Hymnus matutinus*, a very brief one, is still extant. The *Hymnus vespertinus* is more disputed, but Cardinal Mai makes a fair case for it, though it does not satisfy Dom Coutant and Dom Ceillier. Two other hymns by Hilary, commencing respectively "Hymnum dicat turba fratrum" (a hymn on the life of our Lord) and "Jesus refulsit omnium" (on the Epiphany) are given by Thomassy in his *Hymnarium*. Dom Pitra gives some verses of considerable beauty on our Lord's childhood, which seem to be Hilary's. The letter to Abra is considered doubtful by some critics, and rejected by Cave, but upon insufficient evidence.

The best ed. of Hilary is the Benedictine by Coutant (Paris, 1693), or its reprint with a few additions by Maffei (Verona, 1730). The *de Trinitate* is in Hurter's *Ss. Pat. Opusc.* (Innsbrück, 1888).

In conclusion, it must be observed that, though Hilary in his *de Trinitate* (lib. vi. 36-38) speaks of Peter's *confession* as the foundation of the church, he, in other writings, more especially in his commentary on the Psalms, is inclined to make Peter himself, whom he terms *caelestis regni janitorem*, the foundation. In the *fragmenta* we find a letter from the fathers of Sardica to pope Julius, which certainly does refer to the Roman see as the head see. If Hilary approved of this document, he may very probably have allowed to Rome a primacy, at any rate, in the West. But this is a somewhat slender foundation to build a superstructure upon; and it is singular to find Ceillier's editor, in his anxiety to damage the authority of the *fragmenta*, somewhat injuring the credit of the only one brief sentence in the extensive works of Hilary which can be cited as a recognition, however indirect, of the Roman primacy (Ceillier, iv. p. 63, note). In practice Hilary did not often take his stand upon authority. The metropolitan see of Arles was in his time occupied by the Arian Saturninus, Hilary's chief opponent in his earlier day. He had not been long bishop when, by force of character, will, intellect, and confessorship, he came into the first rank of champions. The idea of controversy being settled by the *fiat* of any one bishop, whether of Rome or elsewhere, had never dawned upon his mind. No leave was asked when he descended into Italy to confront Auxentius. A cheap popular Life of Hilary of Poictiers, by J. G. Cazenove, is pub. by S.P.C.K. in their *Fathers for Eng. Readers*, and a selection of his works is in the *Lib. of Nic. and Post-Nic. Fathers*. Cf. also an art. in *Journ. of Theol. Stud.* Apr. 1904, by A. J. Mason on "The First Latin Christian Poet." [J.G.C.]

Hilarius (17) **Arelatensis** (*Hilary of Arles*), St., bp. of Arles and metropolitan.

Authorities.—(1) References to himself in his biography of his predecessor, Honoratus of Arles. (2) *Vita Hilarii*, usually assigned to St. Honoratus, bp. of Marseilles, a disciple of Hilary (Boll. *Acta SS.* 5; Mai. ii. 25). (3) Gennadius, *Illust. Vir. Catal.* § 67. (4) St. Leo (*Ep.* 89, *al.* 10). (5) Councils of Riez, 439, Orange and Vaison, 442, Rome, 445 (Labbe, *Concil.* t. i. pp. 1747, 1783), Vienne, 445 (Natalis Alexander, *Hist. Ecclesiastica*, t. v. p. 168, art. viii. *de Concilio Romano in causâ Hilarii Arelatensis*). (6) Notices of St. Hilary are also to be found in the writings of St. EUCHERIUS (who dedicated to him his book *de Laude Eremi*), of St. Isidore, of Sidonius Apollinaris, and others; and very specially in certain writings of St. Prosper and St. Augustine, to which references will be found below.

The place of his birth, probably in 401, was apparently that part of Gallia Belgica called later Austrasia. He was of noble family. His education was, according to the standard of the age, a thoroughly liberal one, including philosophy and rhetoric. That in rhetoric he became no mean proficient is proved by the graceful style of the one assured composition of his which is extant.

The early ambition of Hilary's mind lay in the direction of secular greatness. Both station and culture gave him every prospect of success, and he appears to have ably discharged the duties of some dignified offices in the state, though we are not informed of their precise nature. He must have been very young when the example and the entreaties of his friend and kinsman Honoratus of Arles induced him to renounce all secular society for the solitude of the isle of Lérins. He sold his estates to his brother, and gave the proceeds partly to the poor, partly to some monasteries which needed aid. At Lérins he became a model monk in the very best and highest sense; but after a period probably not exceeding two years his friend Honoratus, being chosen (A.D. 426) bp. of Arles, obtained the comfort of Hilary's companionship in his new duties.

Honoratus died Jan. 16, 429, and Hilary at once prepared to return to Lérins, but the citizens of Arles compelled him to occupy the vacant see. As bishop, he lived in many respects like a monk, though by no means as a recluse. Simply clad, he traversed on foot the whole of his diocese and province. At home he dwelt in a seminary with some of his clergy. For the redemption of captives he earned money by tilling the earth and planting vines, and did not scruple to sell on emergencies sacred church vessels, substituting others of meaner material. He continued his studies, was constant in meditation and prayer, and as a preacher produced a great impression, by his excellent matter and delivery.

The canons passed by the councils of Riez and of Orange, over which Hilary presided in 439 and 442 respectively, were in the main of a disciplinary character; at Riez a special canon, the seventh, insisted strongly on the rights of the metropolitan. It seems undeniable that Hilary was inclined to press the claims of this office to a degree which amounted to usurpation; partly, perhaps, in regard to the geographical extent of the jurisdiction claimed by him for the see of Arles, and certainly with respect to the rights of the clergy, the laity, and the comprovincial bishops.

But before dealing with his important contest with pope Leo, we must interpose a few words on the semi-Pelagianism of which he has been accused. In 429, the year in which he became bishop, two letters (225 and 226 in the Benedictine ed. of St. Augustine) were addressed to the great bp. of Hippo, one by Prosper, and one by another Hilary, a layman. In the former, Prosper, after recounting various shades of dissent manifested in S. Gaul from the Augustinian teaching on predestination, expressly names Hilary, bp. of Arles, among the recalcitrants. Prosper refers in terms of high encomium to Hilary, and intimates that in all other respects the bp. of Arles was an admirer and supporter of Augustine's teaching. He believed, indeed, that Hilary had some intention of writing to Augustine for explanation on the points at issue. The epistle of Hilary the layman, though its statement is more brief and general, entirely confirms that of Prosper.

If on this evidence, and also from the respect shewn by him to Faustus of Riez, we are compelled to class Hilary of Arles with the semi-Pelagians, it must be recognized that he is a supporter of their views in their very mildest form. That Hilary had some grounds for fearing that Augustine's teaching might imperil the acknowledgment of man's free agency is admitted by many of our historians, *e.g.* Canons Bright (*Hist. of Church*, p. 307) and Robertson (*Hist. of Chr. Church*, bk. iii. cc. ii. and vii.). St. Germain of Auxerre, who went twice over to Britain to contend against Pelagianism, was a companion of the bp. of Arles on at least one of his tours through Gaul. Out of this tour, undertaken by Hilary as metropolitan, there arose the important contest between the bps. of Arles and Rome which ended in procuring for the Roman see a great increase of authority, both in respect of territory and of power. The struggle is in many respects a remarkable one. Each side was well championed. Leo and Hilary were men of saintly piety, earnest and energetic in the discharge of their duties. Each conscientiously believed himself in the right; both were apt to be hasty and high-handed in carrying out their views of ecclesiastical government. Hilary found at Besançon (Vesontio), or according to some at Vesoul, a bp. named Chelidonius, the validity of whose position was assailed on the two grounds that he had married a widow while yet a layman, and that he had previously, as a lay magistrate, pronounced sentences of capital punishment. Hilary held a council at Vienne in 444, and we learn from his biographer and from the testimony of Leo that by its sentence Chelidonius was deposed from the episcopate and appealed to Rome in person. Although it was now midwinter, Hilary went on foot across the Alps. Presenting himself to Leo, he respectfully requested him to act in conformity with the canons and usages of the universal church. Persons juridically deposed were known to be serving the altar in Rome. If Leo found this to be the case, let him, as quietly and secretly as he pleased, put a stop to such violation of the canons. If Leo would not do this, Hilary would simply return home, as he had not come to Rome to bring any accusation. It seems probable, however, that he would have listened if Leo had been content with suggesting a rehearing of the cause in Gaul. Leo declined to take this view. Although Gaul was not a portion of the Roman patriarchate, the Roman pontiff resolved to assert over that region a claim similar to that which he had just failed to establish in Africa. [Leo.] He summoned a council or conference in which Hilary, for the sake of peace, consented to take part. Several bishops were present, including Chelidonius. Hilary, with much plainness of speech, defended his conduct. Leo had him put under guard; but Hilary contrived to escape and (apparently in Feb. 445) returned to Arles. Leo found the charge of marriage with a widow *not proven* against Chelidonius; and formally (as he had already done informally) pronounced him restored to his rank of bishop and to his see. Not content with the reversal of Hilary's sentence, Leo proceeded to deprive the bp. of Arles of his rights as a metropolitan, and to confer them on the bp. of Vienne. He further charged Hilary with having traversed Gaul attended by a band of armed men, and with hastily, without waiting for election by the clergy and laity, consecrating a new bishop in place of Projectus, a bishop (according to Hilary within his province) who was at that time ill. Leo availed himself of his great influence with Valentinian III. to obtain an imperial rescript against Hilary, as one who was injuring the peace of the church and rebelling against the majesty of the empire. This celebrated document, which virtually promised the support of the secular arm to the claim of the Roman pontiff to be a universal bishop, was issued in 445, and was addressed to the Roman general in Gaul, Aetius.

In this controversy Protestant historians, as a rule, take the side of Hilary. But Roman Catholics are much divided. Writers of the ultramontane school, as Rohrbacher or the

Italian Gorini (cited in the recent edition of Dom Ceillier), are severe upon Hilary and profess to regard the emperor's rescript as only stating explicitly a principle always recognized. But the Gallicans, as Quesnel and Tillemont, strongly defend Hilary.

It must be said for him that his conviction, that the see of Arles gave him metropolitical power over the whole of Gaul, was based upon no small amount of cogent testimony. The case in favour of this has been ably summed up by Natalis Alexander (*H. E.* § v. c. v. art. 8), and by the Rev. W. Kay in a note to the Oxf. trans. of Fleury (Lond. 1844). But if it hold good for the case of Chelidonius, it is not equally clear for that of Projectus. That Hilary should escape from Rome, when he found the secular authority employed to detain him, was only natural and justifiable. That he should take soldiers with him in making his visitations may be reasonably ascribed (as Fleury suggests) to the disturbed state of the country. As regards Projectus, he may have strayed beyond the ill-defined limits of his province and most certainly violated canonical rule. But there is no reason to doubt that Hilary, in so acting, really believed that Projectus would not recover, and wished to provide against an emergency. As for Hilary's exceeding freedom of language in the presence of Leo, which greatly shocked Leo and probably others among the audience, it must be remembered that the bp. of Arles was always wont to speak very plainly. Moreover, as a friend of Hilary, the prefect Auxiliaris subsequently observed, "Roman ears were very delicate."

Those who are willing to accept pleas on behalf of Hilary do not thereby commit themselves to unreserved censure on pope Leo. The encouragement to interference in the affairs of S. Gaul was undeniably very great. Strong as was the case for the jurisdiction of Arles over most of the Gallican sees, the authority over Narbonensian Gaul had long been claimed for the bp. of Vienne. A contest between Patroclus of Arles and Proculus of Marseilles had already been carried to a former bp. of Rome, Zosimus, in 422 (some 22 years before the case of Hilary), though the result had not been encouraging to the partisans of Rome, since Zosimus misjudged it and his successor Boniface referred it back to the prelates of Gaul. But Leo, though at times dwelling more upon St. Peter's confession of faith than on his personal position, in all his letters bearing on the contest with Hilary repeats continually the text (Matt. xvi. 18) on which other bishops of Rome had dwelt so much, and appeals to it as if no other interpretation had ever been heard of, and as in itself his sole and sufficient justification.

Leo's recourse to the emperor's aid has been severely censured; and Tillemont declared concerning the famous law of June 6, 445, that "in the eyes of those who have any love for the church's liberty or any knowledge of her discipline, it will bring as little honour to him whom it praises as of injury to him whom it condemns" (Tillem. *Mém. eccl.* t. xv. art. xx. p. 83). Baronius (as Tillemont naturally adds) is fully justified in appealing to this act of Valentinian as a proof of the powerful aid lent by the emperors towards establishing the greatness and authority of the pope.

Of the remaining four years of Hilary's life, after his return to Gaul, we know little more than that they were incessantly occupied with the discharge of his duties. Practically the acts of Leo do not appear to have affected his position (see Hallam, *Middle Ages*, vol. ii. c. vii. pt. i. and Fleury), and Hilary never acknowledged their validity; though an appeal to Leo was made after Hilary's death for the restoration of its ancient metropolitical rights to Arles. The attempts of Hilary through friends to conciliate Leo availed little. But when, after the death of Hilary (May 5, 449), the prelates of the provinces announced to Leo that Ravennius had been elected and duly consecrated, Leo wrote an acknowledgment which sounds like a virtual retractation of his imputations on the motives and character of Hilary and most justly entitled him a man "of holy memory."

Writings.—Waterland (*Critical History of the Athanasian Creed*) argues that Hilary of Arles was the author of the (so-called) *Creed of St. Athanasius*, but this remains only an ingenious conjecture. Among other doubtful works assigned to Hilary must be classed certain poems on sacred subjects: (1) *Poema de septem fratribus Maccabaeis ab Antiocho Epiphane interfectis.* (2) A poem, more frequently attributed to Prosper Aquitanus and generally included in his works, entitled *Carmen de Dei Providentiâ.* (3) *Carmen in Genesim.* This poem (which, like the two preceding, is in hexameters) has been more often ascribed to the earlier Hilary, bp. of Poictiers. The Benedictine editors reject it with some indignation from the genuine works of Hilary of Poictiers; remarking, however, that this does not involve its attribution to Hilary of Arles. But despite faults—theological, grammatical, and metrical—the poem is curious as a real attempt at that blending of the Christian and classic elements of literature displayed in after-ages so brilliantly, though after all with questionable success, by such able scholars as the Jesuit Casimir and the Presbyterian Buchanan.

We have the authority of Hilary's biographer for asserting that he did compose some poetry (*versus*), wrote many letters, an explanation of the Creed (*Symboli Expositio*—this is a main element in Waterland's argument) and sermons for all the church's festivals (*Homiliae in totius Anni Festivitates*). These were apparently extant when Honoratus wrote. Two only survive: (1) *Epistola ad Eucherium Episcopum Lugdunensem.* (2) *Vita Sancti Honorati Arelatensis Episcopi.* This may be read in the Bollandist *Acta Sanctorum*, for Jan. 16. [J.G.C.]

Hilarius (18) (*Hilarus*), bp. of Rome from Nov. 19 (or 17, Bolland.), 461, to Sept. 10, 467, succeeding Leo I. after a vacancy of nine days. He was a native of Sardinia and, when elected pope, archdeacon of Rome. He had been sent, when a deacon, as one of the legates of pope Leo to the council at Ephesus called Latrocinium (449), and is especially mentioned in the Acts of the council as having protested against the deposition of Flavian. After the council, Flavian having died from the violent treatment he had undergone, Hilarius, fearing with reason the like usage, escaped from Ephesus and travelled by by-roads to Italy. A letter from Hilarius, addressed after his return to the empress Pulcheria, gives an account of these transactions (Baron. ad ann. 449, and *Act. Concil. Chalced.*). His short pontificate is chiefly memorable for his assertion of the authority of the see of Rome in Gaul and Spain. His predecessor Leo, during his struggle with St. Hilary of Arles for supremacy in Gaul, had obtained from Valentinian III. a famous rescript (445) confirming such supremacy to the fullest extent both in Gaul and elsewhere [LEO]; and to such extent it was accordingly claimed by Hilarius. Soon after his accession he wrote (Jan. 25, 462) to Leontius, bp. of Arles and exarch of the provinces of Narbonensian Gaul, announcing the event and referring to the deference due to the Roman see. In the same year he wrote a second letter to Leontius, who had deferentially congratulated the pope on his accession, and had begged him to continue the favour shewn to the see of Arles against opponents of its jurisdiction. The pope, in his reply, commends his correspondent's deference to St. Peter and desires that the discipline of the Roman church should prevail in all churches. Rusticus, metropolitan of Narbonne, had nominated his archdeacon Hermes as his successor, but had failed to obtain Leo's approval. On the death of Rusticus, Hermes had been accepted by the clergy and people of Narbonne as their metropolitan bishop. On this, Frederic, king of the West Goths, an Arian, wrote to acquaint the pope with the "wicked usurpation" and "execrable presumption" of Hermes. Accordingly Hilarius wrote a third letter to Leontius, in which he adopts the language of Frederic, and requires Leontius to send to Rome a statement of the affair, signed by himself and other bishops (Hil. *Ep.* vii. Labbe). The matter was now brought before a synod at Rome (462), and Hermes was declared degraded from the rank of metropolitan, but allowed to retain his see. Hilarius notified this decision in a letter dated Dec. 3, 462, to the bishops of the provinces of Vienne, Lyons, Narbonensis prima and secunda, and the Pennine Alps, which letter also contained regulations for the discipline of the church in Gaul (Hil. *Ep.* viii. Labbe). In 463 Hilarius again interposed in the affairs of the church in Gaul; and on this occasion not only Leontius of Arles but also Mamertus, metropolitan of Vienne, fell under his displeasure. The city Diae Vocontiorum (Die in Dauphine) had been assigned by pope Leo to the jurisdiction of Arles; but Mamertus had, notwithstanding, ordained a bp. of that see. Hilarius, again deriving his information from an Arian prince, Gundriac the Burgundian king, wrote a severe letter to Leontius, censuring him for not having apprized the holy see, and charging him to investigate the matter in a synod and then send to Rome a synodal letter giving a true account of it. Mamertus seems to have continued to assert his claim to jurisdiction in spite of the pope; for in Feb. 464 we find two more letters from Hilarius, a general one to the Gallican bishops, and another to various bishops addressed by name, in the former of which he accuses Mamertus of presumption and prevarication, threatens to deprive him of his metropolitan rank and disallows the bishops whom he had ordained till confirmed by Leontius. The second letter is noteworthy in that the pope rests his claim to supremacy over Gaul on imperial as well as ecclesiastical law; alluding probably to the rescript of Valentinian III. "He [*i.e.* Mamertus] could not abrogate any portion of the right appointed to our brother Leontius by my predecessor of holy memory; since it has been decreed by the law of Christian princes that whatsoever the prelate of the apostolic see may, on his own judgment, have pronounced to churches and their rulers . . . is to be tenaciously observed; nor can those things ever be upset which shall be supported by both ecclesiastical and royal injunction" (Hil. *Epp.* ix. x. xi. Labbe). Baronius finds it needful to account for St. Leo and St. Hilarius having so bitterly inveighed against St. Hilary and St. Mamertus by saying that popes may be deceived on matters of fact, and, under the prepossession of false accusations, persecute the innocent (Baron. ad ann. 464).

In 465 Hilary exercised over the Spanish church the authority already brought to bear on that of Gaul, but this time on appeal. Two questions came before him. First, Silvanus, bp. of Calchorra, had been guilty of offences against the canons; and his metropolitan, Ascanius of Tarragona, had in 464 sent a synodal letter on the subject to the pope, requesting directions (*Inter Hilar. Epp.*, *Ep.* ii. Labbe). Secondly, Nundinarius, bp. of Barcelona, had nominated his successor, and after his death the nomination was confirmed by the metropolitan Ascanius and his suffragans. But they wrote to the pope desiring his concurrence and acknowledging the primacy of St. Peter's see. Both these letters were considered in a synod at Rome. On the second case it was decided that Irenaeus, the nominated bishop, should quit the see of Barcelona and return to his former one, while the Spanish bishops were ordered to condone the uncanonical acts of Silvanus (Hil. *Epp.* i. ii. iii. and *Concil. Rom.* xlviii. Labbe).

In 467 the new emperor Anthemius was induced by one Philotheus, a Macedonian heretic whom he had brought with him, to issue a general edict of toleration for heretics. This was, however, revoked before coming into effect, and pope Gelasius (*Ep. ad Episc. Dardan.*) says that this was due to Hilarius having in the church of St. Peter remonstrated with the emperor and induced him to promise on oath that he would allow no schismatical assemblies in Rome. In the same year Hilarius died. He appears in the Roman Calendar as a saint and confessor. In remembrance of his deliverance at Ephesus from the trials that procured him the title of confessor, he built, after he became pope, in the baptistery of Constantine near the Lateran, two chapels dedicated to St. John Baptist and St. John the Evangelist, to the latter of whom he attributed his deliverance. The chapel to the Evangelist bore the inscription, "Liberatori suo Johanni Evangelistae, Hilarus famulus Christi" (Bolland. *citing* Caesar Rasponus).

The extant writings of Hilarius are his letters referred to above. Anastasius Bibliothecarius mentions his decreta sent to various parts, confirming the synods of Nice, Ephesus, and Chalcedon, condemning Eutyches, Nestorius, and all heretics, and confirming the domination and primacy of the holy Catholic and apostolic see (*Concil. Rom. u.s.*; Thiel. *Epp. Pontiff. Rom.* i.). [J.B—Y.]

Hippolytus (2) Romanus. Though so celebrated in his lifetime, Hippolytus has been but obscurely known to the church of subsequent times. He was at the beginning of the 3rd cent. unquestionably the most learned member of the Roman church, and a man of very considerable literary activity; his works were very numerous, and their circulation spread from Italy to the East, some having been translated into Syriac, Arabic, Armenian, Ethiopic, and perhaps other languages. His name assumes various disguises, as Poltus in the popular memory of Italy, in Egypt as Abulides. There is evidence also that he took a very active part in the affairs of his own church; but there are no contemporary witnesses to inform us concerning his personal history. A century after his death Eusebius evidently knew nothing of him beyond what he could infer from such works of his as had reached him. These works were soon superseded by those of other more able and learned writers. Scarcely one has come down to us without mutilation, and the authenticity of almost every work assigned to him has been disputed. Yet his celebrity survived, and various legends, not always carefully distinguished from the authentic history of the saint, arose. It has been disputed whether Hippolytus was a presbyter or a bishop; and if a bishop, of what see; whether he laboured in Italy or Arabia; whether he was orthodox or a schismatic; whether he was a martyr, and if so, by what death he died. At length the recovery of the work on heresies, now by general consent attributed to him, cleared away some obscurities in his personal history, though many questions can still receive only doubtful answers.

The earliest notice of Hippolytus is by Eusebius in two passages (*H. E.* vi. 20, 22). In the first, speaking of ecclesiastical writers of whom letters were then preserved in the library at Jerusalem, Eusebius mentions "likewise Hippolytus, who was bishop of another church somewhere." In the second he gives a list of the works of Hippolytus which he had met with (not including any letters), this being probably the list of those in the library at Caesarea, but adds that many other works by him might be found elsewhere.

If the earliest witnesses give no certain information as to where Hippolytus laboured, they enable us to determine when he lived. Eusebius says that he wrote a work on the Paschal feast, in which he gives a sixteen-years' Easter table, and accompanies it with a chronology, the boundary of his calculations being the first year of the emperor Alexander, *i.e.* A.D. 222. In 1551, in some excavations made on the Via Tirburtina, near Rome, a marble statue was found, representing a venerable person sitting in a chair, clad in the Greek pallium. The back and sides of the chair contain Greek inscriptions. The back has a list of works presumably written by the person represented. One side has a sixteen-years' cycle, exactly corresponding to the description of Eusebius and beginning with the first year of Alexander. Other evidence makes it certain that this cycle is that of Hippolytus. The works sufficiently agree with those ascribed to Hippolytus by Eusebius and Jerome; and no doubt is entertained that Hippolytus is the person commemorated. The list of Paschal full moons in the cycle gives accurately the astronomical full moons for the years 217-223 inclusive. For the next eight years the true full moons are a day or two later than those given, and after that deviate still further; so that after two or three revolutions of the cycle the table would be useless. This table must, then, have been framed about the time specified, A.D. 222, and the chair must be a nearly contemporary monument, for it is not conceivable that the table would be put on record, to do its author honour, after it had been tried long enough to make its worthlessness apparent. Further, the inscription is in Greek, and the early Roman church contained a large section, if not a majority, of foreigners, whose habitual language was Greek. This inscription must have been placed before that section had disappeared and Latin had become the exclusive language of the church. A further proof of antiquity is furnished by the list of writings, which is independent of those of Eusebius and Jerome, and which no one in the West could have drawn up long after the death of Hippolytus. The date thus fixed agrees with what we otherwise know, that Hippolytus was a contemporary of Origen, Jerome telling us that it appeared from a homily of Hippolytus then extant that it had been delivered in Origen's hearing. We know from Eusebius (*H. E.* vi. 14) that Origen visited Rome in the reign of Caracalla and episcopate of Zephyrinus, *i.e.* some time in the years 211-217. In one of these years he might thus have heard Hippolytus preach. We must place the commencement of the activity of Hippolytus as early as the 2nd cent. Photius tells us that the treatise of Hippolytus *Against all the Heresies* professed to be a synopsis of lectures delivered by Irenaeus. The simplest supposition seems to be that Hippolytus heard Irenaeus lecture in Rome. Eusebius tells of one visit of Irenaeus to Rome *c.* 178. A note in a Moscow MS. of the martyrdom of Polycarp (Zahn's *Ignatius*, p. 167) represents him as teaching at Rome several years before. It is not unlikely that Irenaeus came again to Rome and there delivered lectures against heresies. The time could not have been long after the beginning of the last decade of the 2nd cent. It has been shewn that the author of the cycle engraved on the chair must also have been the author of a chronicle, a Latin translation of which is extant, the last event in which is the death of the emperor Alexander (235). In that year an entry in the Liberian Catalogue of bishops of Rome records that Pontianus the bishop, and Hippolytus the presbyter, were transported as exiles to the pestilent island of Sardinia. It is difficult to believe that the

Hippolytus here described as presbyter is not our Hippolytus, and probably both he and Pontianus gained the title of martyrs by dying in the mines. From the "depositio martyrum" of the Liberian Catalogue it appears that the bodies of Pontianus and Hippolytus were both deposited on the same day (Aug. 13), the former in the cemetery of Callistus, the latter in that on the Via Tiburtina, and it is natural to think that both bodies were brought from Sardinia to Rome. The translation of Pontianus, we are told, was effected by pope Fabianus, probably in 236 or 237. A very different account of the martyrdom of Hippolytus is given by Prudentius (*Peristeph.* 11), who wrote at the beginning of the 5th cent. His story is that Hippolytus had been a presbyter, who was torn in pieces at Ostia by wild horses, like the Hippolytus of mythology. Prudentius describes the subterranean tomb of the saint and states that he saw on the spot a picture representing this execution, and that this martyrdom was commemorated on Aug. 13. He gives an account of the crowds who flocked to the commemoration and a description of a stately church, with a double row of pillars, which Döllinger considers was the church of St. Laurence († 258), a saint whose cultus attained much greater celebrity, and who was also buried on the Via Tiburtina, his church being adjacent to the tomb of Hippolytus.

The picture which Prudentius saw may well have been originally intended to depict the sufferings of the mythological Hippolytus, and, being inscribed with that name, have been ignorantly copied or transferred by Christians to adorn the resting-place of the martyr of that name. The tale told by Prudentius is plainly the offspring of the picture, and the authentic evidence of the deposition, on Aug. 13, on the Via Tiburtina of the remains of a Hippolytus who is coupled with Pontianus indicates the real owner of the tomb, of whom, in the century and a half which passed before Prudentius visited it, all but his name and the day of his feast had been forgotten.

What light has been cast upon his history by the recovery of the treatise against heresies? The portion previously extant had been known under the name of Origen's *Philosophumena*. We make no scruple in treating this as the work of Hippolytus, for this is the nearly unanimous opinion of critics, Lipsius alone hesitating and cautiously citing the author as Pseudo-Origenes. From this work it appears that he took an active part in the affairs of the Roman church in the episcopates of Zephyrinus and Callistus. Döllinger has shewn that, without imputing wilful misstatement to Hippolytus, it is possible to put on all that he relates about CALLISTUS a very much more favourable interpretation than he has done; and with regard to the charge that Callistus in trying to steer a middle course between Sabellianism and orthodoxy had invented a new heresy, the retort may be made that it was Hippolytus himself who in his dread of Sabellianism had laid himself open to the charge of Ditheism. But the point to which Döllinger called attention, with which we are most concerned here, is that Hippolytus in this work never recognizes Callistus as bp. of Rome. He says that Callistus had aspired to the episcopal throne and that on the death of Zephyrinus "he supposed himself to have obtained what he had been hunting for." But Hippolytus treats him only as the founder of a school (διδασκαλεῖον) in opposition to the Catholic church, using the same word with regard to Noetus (*cont. Haer. Noeti*, Lagarde, p. 44), of whom he says that when expelled from the church he had the presumption to set up "a school." Hippolytus says that Callistus and his party claimed to be the Catholic church and gloried in their numbers, though this multitude of adherents had been gained by unworthy means, namely, by improper laxity in receiving offenders. Callistus had received into his communion persons whom Hippolytus had excommunicated. He adds that this school of Callistus still continued when he wrote, which was plainly after the death of Callistus, and he refuses to give its members any name but Callistians. Evidently the breach between Hippolytus and Callistus had proceeded to open schism. But if Hippolytus did not regard Callistus as bp. of Rome, whom did he so regard? To this question it is difficult to give any answer but Döllinger's: Hippolytus claimed to be bp. of Rome himself. In the introduction to his work, Hippolytus claims to hold the episcopal office; he declares that the pains which he took in the confutation of heresy were his duty as successor of the apostles, partaker of the grace of the Holy Spirit that had been given to them and which they transmitted to those of right faith, and as clad with the dignity of the high priesthood and office of teaching and guardian of the church. Afterwards we find him exercising the power of excommunication upon persons, who thereupon joined the school of Callistus. Thus we seem to have a key to the difficulty that Hippolytus is described in the Liberian Catalogue only as presbyter, and yet was known in the East universally as bishop, and very widely as bp. of Rome. His claim to be bishop was not admitted by the church of Rome, but was made in works of his, written in Greek and circulating extensively in the East, either by himself in the works or more probably in titles prefixed to them by his ardent followers. We have also a key to the origin of the tradition that Hippolytus had been a Novatianist. He had been in separation from the church, and the exact cause of difference had been forgotten. Against another hypothesis, that Hippolytus was at the same time bp. of Portus and a leading presbyter of Rome, Döllinger urges, besides the weakness of the proof that Hippolytus was bp. of Portus, that there is no evidence that Portus had then a bishop, and that, according to the then constitution of the church, the offices of presbyter and bishop could not be thus combined. Döllinger contends that the schism could not have occurred immediately on the election of Callistus; but there is exactly the same reason for saying that Hippolytus refused to recognize Zephyrinus as bishop, as that he rejected Callistus; for he speaks of the former also as "imagining" that he governed the church. In consistency, then, Döllinger ought to have made the schism begin in the time of Zephyrinus, and so de Rossi does, adding a conjecture of his own, that the leader of the schism had been Victor's archdeacon, and had in that capacity obtained his knowledge of the early life of Callistus, and that he was actuated by disappointment at not having been made bishop on Victor's death. On the other hand, to make a schism of which no one in the East seems to have ever heard begin so early ascribes to it such long duration as to be quite incredible. For it continued after the death of Callistus, some time after which the account in the treatise on heresies was plainly written, and Döllinger thinks it even possible that it may have continued up to the time of the deportation of Pontianus and Hippolytus to Sardinia. He regards with some favour the hypothesis that this banishment might have been designed to deliver the city from dissensions and disputes for the possession of churches between the adherents of the rival leaders. It seems to us most likely that Pontianus and Hippolytus were banished early in the reign of Maximin as the two leading members of the Christian community. We find it hard to refuse the explanation of von Döllinger, which makes Hippolytus the first anti-pope; but the difficulties arising from the fact that the existence of so serious a schism has been absolutely unknown to the church from the 4th cent. to the 19th are so great, that if we knew of any other way of satisfactorily explaining the language of Hippolytus we should adopt it in preference. We are not told who consecrated Hippolytus as bishop, but a schism in inaugurating which bishops thus took the lead must have been a serious one: it lasted at least 5 or 6 years, and, if we make it begin in the time of Zephyrinus as we seem bound to do, perhaps 20 years, and it had as its head the most learned man of the Roman church and one whose name was most likely to be known to foreign churches. Yet the existence of this schism was absolutely unknown abroad. All Greek lists of the popes, as well as the Latin, include Callistus, and make no mention of Hippolytus; and the confessed ignorance of Eusebius about the see of Hippolytus is proof enough that he was not in possession of the key to the difficulty. In the Novatianist disputes which commenced about 15 years after the death of Hippolytus, when many would still be alive who could have remembered the controversy between him and Callistus, we find no allusion on either side to any such comparatively recent schism of which a man holding rigorist views resembling those of Novatian was the head. Bearing in mind the excitement caused in the case of Novatian, we ask, Was the question who was bp. of Rome regarded as a matter of such purely local concern that controversy could go on at Rome for years and the outside world know nothing of it, and *that* although the unsuccessful claimant was a person on other grounds very widely known? Is it conceivable, if Hippolytus really set up a rival chair to Callistus, that he, whose books and letters widely circulated in the East, made no attempt to enlist on his side the bishops of the great Eastern sees? Or is it likely, if Hippolytus had started a long-continued and dangerous schism at Rome, that the predominant party should have completely condoned his offence, that he should have been honoured for centuries as a saint and a martyr, and that his name should have been handed down with no hint of that schism until words of his own came to light to suggest it? These improbabilities in the theory hitherto most generally received, amount almost to impossibilities, though we confess it difficult to find a satisfactory substitute. We can only suggest that if there were at the time, as there are grounds for supposing, a Greek congregation at Rome, the head of it is very likely to have been Hippolytus, and the head of such a congregation might naturally be entrusted with the episcopal power of admitting or excluding members, since doubtful cases could scarcely be investigated by a Latin-speaking pope. The supposition that he may have received episcopal consecration, besides explaining the enigmatical dignity ἐθνῶν ἐπίσκοπος ascribed by Photius to Caius, would give a less violently improbable account of the claim of Hippolytus to episcopal dignity than the theory that he had been consecrated as anti-pope. As he was probably the last holder of his anomalous office, it is not surprising if no remembrance was retained of its exact constitution; but it is in the nature of things probable that the period when the church of Rome was Greek and when it was Latin should be separated by a bilingual period; and it is not unnatural that the arrangements made during that interval should be forgotten when the need for them had passed. The severity of the persecutions at Rome under Decius and Valerian seems to have obliterated much of the recollections of the history of the early part of the century. Whether Hippolytus was bishop or presbyter, he wrote his attacks on Callistus in Greek and addressed them to Greek-speaking people, and there is no evidence that he made any assault on the unity of the Latin-speaking church. This may account for the faintness of the impression which his schismatic language produced and for the facility with which it was pardoned. That the arrogance and intemperance of language which he displayed did not deprive him of permanent honour in the Roman church is to be accounted for by the leniency with which men treat the faults of one who has real claims to respect. Hippolytus was a man of whose learning the whole Roman church must have been proud; he was of undoubted piety, and of courage which he proved in his good confession afterwards. The way of return would not be made difficult for such a man when he really wished all dissension to end.

The preceding discussions have told all that is known of the life of Hippolytus. We now proceed to enumerate his works; acknowledging the great help of the list of Caspari, *Taufsymbol und Glaubensregel*, iii. 377.

(1) Most completely associated with his name is the 16 years' cycle (mentioned by Eusebius and Jerome, *u.s.*), and the little treatise in which he explained it. This is among the list of works on the statue, Ἀπόδειξις χρόνων τοῦ πάσχα καὶ τὰ ἐν τῷ πίνακι. That the cycle engraved on the statue is undoubtedly that of Hippolytus is not only proved by facts already pointed out and by its interpre-

tation of the 70 weeks of Daniel in the manner peculiar to Hippolytus, but is placed beyond doubt by its literal agreement with a Syriac version of the cycle of Hippolytus preserved in a chronological work by Elias of Nisibis (Lagarde, *Analecta Syriaca*, p. 89). The cycle of 8 years used by Greek astronomers for harmonizing lunar and solar years is much older than Hippolytus. What was novel in the scheme of Hippolytus was his putting two eight-years' cycles together in order to exhibit readily the days of the week on which the full moons fell. The cycle of Hippolytus is not astronomically correct, and, as the Syriac writer correctly states, the error accumulates at the rate of three days for every sixteen-years' cycle. Of this Hippolytus has no suspicion, and he supposed that he could by means of his cycle determine all Paschal full moons future or past.

(2) Eusebius, in the passage where he has spoken of the work on the Paschal feast just considered (*τὸ περὶ τοῦ πάσχα σύγγραμμα*). proceeds with a list of the *other* works of Hippolytus he had met with, among which is one *περὶ τοῦ πάσχα*. The use of the definite article in the first case might suggest that Eusebius only knew one such work, and mentions it the second time in its order in his collection of works of Hippolytus. But it may be considered certain that Hippolytus treated doubly of the Paschal celebration: in (1) giving rules for finding Easter; in another writing, which probably was an Easter-day sermon, treating of its doctrinal import.

(3) Among the works enumerated on the statue is a chronicle. The list runs *χρονικῶν πρὸς Ἕλληνας*, and it has been questioned whether this describes two separate works, or a chronicle written with a controversial object; but the remains of the chronicle itself shew it to have been written for the instruction of Christians and not as a polemic against heathenism. The chronicle records the death of the emperor Alexander, and therefore the deportation of Hippolytus and Pontianus to Sardinia could not have taken place under Alexander as the later Papal Catalogue has it, but under Maximin. It follows, also, that this chronicle is likely to be the latest work of Hippolytus, and therefore that a passage common to it and to the later treatise on heresy was taken from an earlier work, a supposition which presents no difficulty.

(4) We pass now from the chronological to the anti-heretical writings; first, the treatise against all heresies, which may have been the earliest work of Hippolytus. It is mentioned in the lists of both Eusebius and Jerome, and a passage is quoted from it in the Paschal Chronicle, though it is not in the list on the chair as we have it, which shews that we cannot build any conclusion on the absence of a name therefrom. The fullest account of this treatise is given by Photius (*Cod.* 121). He describes it as a small book, *βιβλιδάριον*, against 32 heresies, beginning with the Dositheans and ending with Noetus and the Noetians; that it purported to be an abstract of discourses of Irenaeus; was written in a clear, dignified style, though not observant of Attic propriety. It denied St. Paul's authorship of *Hebrews*. It was probably published in the early years of the episcopate (199-217) of Zephyrinus, to lead up to an assault on Noetianism, then the most formidable heresy at Rome.

(5) A work, or rather a fragment, bearing in the MS. the title of *Homily of Hippolytus against the Heresy of one Noetus*, appears on examination to be not a homily, but the conclusion of a treatise against more heresies than one. It begins: "Certain others are privily introducing another doctrine, having become disciples of one Noetus." It proceeds to refute the Noetian objection that the assertion of the distinct personality of our Lord contradicts those texts of Scripture which declare the absolute unity of God. At the end of this discussion he says, "Now that Noetus also has been refuted, let us come to the setting forth of the truth, that we may establish the truth, against which all so great heresies have arisen, without being able to say anything." The orthodoxy of the tract seems unsuspected by Tillemont, Ceillier, Lumper, and others. It was formally defended by bp. Bull, and was published by Routh (*Ecc. Script. Opusc.*) as a lucid exposition of orthodox doctrine. When, however, it came to light that the teaching of Hippolytus had been censured by pope Callistus, Döllinger had no difficulty in pointing out features in it open to censure. Though Hippolytus acknowledges the Logos to have been from eternity dwelling in God as His intelligence, he yet appears to teach that there was a definite epoch determined by the will of God, prior no doubt to all creation, when that Logos, which had previously dwelt impersonally in God, assumed a separate hypostatic existence, in order that by Him the world should be framed and the Deity manifested to it. Thus, beside God there appeared another; yet not two Gods, but only as light from light, a ray from the sun. Hippolytus also teaches that it was only at the Incarnation that He Who before was the Logos properly became Son, though previously He might be called Son in reference to what He was to be. Döllinger imagines that this emanation doctrine of Hippolytus may, in the controversies of the time, have been stigmatized as Valentinian, and that thus we may account for a late authority connecting this heresy with his name.

(6) *Refutation of all Heresies.*—In 1842 Minoides Mynas brought to Paris from Mount Athos, besides other literary treasures, a 14th-cent. MS. containing what purported to be a refutation of all heresies, divided into 10 books. Owing to mutilation, the MS. begins in the middle of bk. iv.; but from the numbering of the leaves it is inferred that the MS. had never contained any of the first three books. Miller, who published it in 1851 for the Univ. of Oxford, perceived that it belonged to the work published under the name of Origen's *Philosophumena* by Gronovius, and afterwards in the Benedictine ed. of Origen, though it had been perceived that the ascription to Origen must be erroneous, as the author claims the dignity of high priesthood, and refers to a former work on heresies, while no such work is said to have been composed by Origen. Miller in his edition reprinted the *Philosophumena* as bk. i. of the *Elenchus*, but ascribed the whole to Origen, an ascription which was generally

rejected. Jacobi, in a German periodical, put forward the claims of Hippolytus, a theory which was embraced by Bunsen (*Hippolytus and his Age*, 1852; 2nd ed., *Christianity and Mankind*, 1854) and Wordsworth (*St. Hippol. and the Ch. of Rome*, 1853, 2nd ed. 1880), and completely established by Döllinger (*Hippolytus und Kallistus*, 1853). From the book itself we infer that the author lived at Rome during the episcopates of Zephyrinus and Callistus, and for some time afterwards; that he held high ecclesiastical office, and enjoyed much consideration, being not afraid to oppose his opinion on a theological question to that of the bishop, and able to persuade himself that fear of him restrained the bishop from a course on which he otherwise would have entered. Hippolytus satisfies these conditions better than any one else for whom the authorship has been claimed. Further, the hypothesis that Hippolytus was the author gives the explanation of the prevalent Eastern belief that he was bp. of Rome, of the tradition preserved by Prudentius that he had been once in schism from the church, and of the singular honour of a statue done him; for as the head of a party his adherents would glorify his learning and prolific industry. That the work on heresies connects itself with six distinct works of Hippolytus makes the ascription certain. A trans. of the *Refutation* and of other fragments is in the vol. *Apost. Fathers* in *Ante-Nic. Lib.* (T. & T. Clark).

(*a*) *The Treatise against the Thirty-two Heresies.*—The author begins by saying that he had a long time before (πάλαι) published another work against heresy, with less minute exposure of the secret doctrines of the heretics than that which he now proposes to make. Of those for whom the authorship has been claimed, Hippolytus is the only one whom we know to have published a previous work on heresies. The time between the two works would be 20 years at least.

(*b*) *The Treatise on the Universe.*—At the end of the *Refutation* (x. 32, p. 334, Plummer's trans.) the author refers to a previous work of his, περὶ τῆς τοῦ παντὸς οὐσίας, and among the works ascribed to Hippolytus on the statue we read, πρὸς Ἕλληνας καὶ πρὸς Πλάτωνα ἢ καὶ περὶ τοῦ παντός. Photius remarks that the author of the work on the universe also wrote the *Labyrinth*, according to a statement at the end of that work. Now, bk. x. begins with the words, "The labyrinth of heresies." We may, then, reasonably conclude that what Photius knew as the *Labyrinth* was our bk. x., which was known by its first word.

(*c*) *The Chronicle and the Treatise on the Psalms.*—The enumeration of the 72 nations among whom the earth was divided (x. 30), and which the author states that he had previously given in other books, precisely agrees with that in the *Chronicle* of Hippolytus; and though this chronicle was probably later than the *Refutation*, Hippolytus wrote commentaries on Genesis, where this enumeration would naturally be given in treating of c. x., and he appears to have been, like many prolific writers, apt to repeat himself. This same enumeration is given in his commentary on the Psalms (No. 29 *infra*).

(*d*) *The Tract against Noetus.*—On comparing this tract with the exposition of the truth given at the end of the *Refutation*, the identity of doctrine, and sometimes of form of expression, decisively proves common authorship. The same doctrine is found, that the Logos, Which had from eternity dwelt in the Deity as His unspoken thought, afterwards assumed a separate hypostatic existence, differing from created things not only in priority but also because they were out of nothing, He of the substance of the Godhead; and being the framer of the universe according to the divine ideas (in the Platonic sense of the word) which had dwelt in Him from the first. That the Son's personal divinity was not by the original necessity of His nature, but given by an act of the divine will, is stated more offensively than in the earlier tract. He says to his reader, "God has been pleased to make you a man, not a god. If He had willed to make you a god He could have done so; you have the example of the Logos."

(*e*) *The Treatise on Antichrist.*—In c. ii. of this treatise (Lagarde, p. 2), when telling how the prophets treated not only of the past but of the present and the future, he uses language in some respects verbally coinciding with what is said in the *Elenchus* (x. 33, p. 337).

The evidence which has been produced amounts to a demonstration of the Hippolytine authorship. The title of the work would be φιλοσοφούμενα ἢ κατὰ πασῶν αἱρέσεων ἔλεγχος; the name *Philosophumena* properly applying to the first 4 books, the *Elenchus* to the last 6. Its chief value to us consists, in addition to the light cast on the disputes in the church of Rome at the beginning of the 3rd cent., in its extracts from otherwise unknown Gnostic writings, inserted by the author to shame these sects by an exposure of their secret tenets. Its attack on the character of pope Callistus was fatal to its circulation. No doubt when a reconciliation was effected at Rome all parties desired to suppress the book. Bk. i. was preserved as containing a harmless and useful account of the doctrines of heathen philosophers; and bk. x., which presented no cause for offence (there being nothing to indicate that the heretic Callistus mentioned in it was intended for the bp. of Rome), also had some circulation and was seen by Theodoret and Photius. But these two writers are the only ones in whom we can trace any knowledge of bk. x., which was certainly not used by Epiphanius. The rest of the work is mentioned by no extant writer, and but for the chance preservation of a single copy in the East would have altogether perished.

(7) *The Little Labyrinth.*—Eusebius (*H. E.* v. 27) gives some long extracts from an anonymous work against the heresy of Artemon. Internal evidence shews that the writer was a member of the Roman church and speaks of things that occurred in the episcopate of Zephyrinus as having happened in his own time. On the other hand, Zephyrinus is described as Victor's successor, language not likely to be used if Zephyrinus were at the time bishop, or even the last preceding bishop. The writer's recollection too does not appear to go back to the episcopate of Victor. The date would therefore be soon after the episcopate of Callistus. Theodoret (*Haer. Fab.*

ii. 5) refers to the same work as known in his time under the name of the *Little Labyrinth* and attributed by some to Origen; though Theodoret considers this assumption disproved by the difference of style. Photius (*Cod.* 48) ascribes to Caius a book called the *Labyrinth*, which we have identified with the summary of the *Elenchus*. He does not mention the *Little Labyrinth*, but adds that it was said that Caius had composed a special treatise against the heresy of Artemon. We have no reason to think that the *Labyrinth* of Photius and the *Little Labyrinth* of Theodoret were the same; on the contrary, the latter was probably identical with the treatise against Artemon, which Photius expressly distinguishes from his *Labyrinth*. Internal evidence, and the fact that we have some external evidence for the authorship of Caius and none for that of Hippolytus, cause us to give our verdict for Caius.

(8) *The Work against Bero and Helix.*—A certain Anastasius of the 7th cent. is the earliest authority for designating Hippolytus as bp. of Portus. He so calls him in sending to Rome extracts made by him at Constantinople from what purported to be a treatise of Hippolytus, περὶ θεολογίας καὶ σαρκώσεως, against the above-named heretics, his adversaries having hindered Anastasius from getting possession of the entire work. Döllinger (p. 295) has given conclusive reasons for regarding this as no work of Hippolytus, but as a forgery not earlier than the 6th cent. The technical language of these fragments is also that of the controversies of the 5th cent., and quite unlike that of the age of Hippolytus. It was doubtless Anastasius who supplied another passage from the discourse περὶ θεολογίας produced at the Lateran Council in 649.

(9) A Syriac list of the writings of Hippolytus given by Ebed Jesu, a writer of the very beginning of the 14th cent. (Assemani, *Bibl. Or.* iii. 1, p. 15), contains a work whose Syriac title is translated by Ecchelensis *de Regimine*, by Assemani *de Dispensatione*. Adopting the latter rendering and taking "dispensatio" to be equivalent to οἰκονομία, we should conclude its subject to be our Lord's Incarnation. It may therefore be identical with (8). If the other rendering be adopted, the work would relate to church government, and might be identical with some part of (21).

(10) *The Treatise against Marcion.*—Mentioned in the catalogues of Eusebius and Jerome, but nothing of it remains.

(11) On the statue is enumerated a work περὶ τἀγαθοῦ καὶ πόθεν τὸ κακόν. This may well have been an anti-Marcionite composition, and possibly that mentioned by Eusebius (10).

(12) *Defence of the Gospel and Apocalypse of St. John.*—We may probably class among anti-heretical writings the work described on the chair as ὑπὲρ τοῦ κατὰ Ἰωάννην εὐαγγελίου καὶ ἀποκαλύψεως, and in the list of Ebed Jesu as "a defence of the Apocalypse and Gospel of the apostle and evangelist John." The work on the Apocalypse mentioned by Jerome we take to be different, and we notice it among the exegetical works. Hippolytus in his extant remains constantly employs the Apocalypse, and his regard for it is appealed to by Andrew of Caesarea (*Max. Bibl. Patr.* v. 590). It has been supposed that Caius was the writer, replied to by Hippolytus, who ascribes the Apocalypse and the Gospel to Cerinthus; but the arguments for supposing that Caius rejected the Apocalypse are inconclusive, and it is highly improbable that he, an orthodox member of the Roman church, rejected the Gospel of St. John.

(13) One argument in support of the view just referred to is that Ebed Jesu (*u.s.*) enumerates among the works of Hippolytus *Chapters* (or heads) *against Caius*, which, it has been conjectured, were identical with (12). But Ebed Jesu reckons the two works as distinct. What other heresy of Caius Hippolytus could have confuted is unknown.

(14) It is hard to draw the line between controversial and dogmatic books. Thus, with regard to the treatise cited by Anastasius Sinaita (Lagarde, No. 9, p. 90), περὶ ἀναστάσεως καὶ ἀφθαρσίας, which may be the same as that described on the statue as περὶ Θεοῦ καὶ σαρκὸς ἀναστάσεως and by Jerome as *de Resurrectione*, we cannot tell whether it was a simple explanation of Christian doctrine or directed against the errors of heretics or heathens.

(15) A controversial character more clearly belongs to another work on the same subject, a fragment of which is preserved in Syriac (Lagarde, *Anal. Syr.* p. 87), and contains what Stephen Gobar (Photius, *Cod.* 232) noted as a peculiarity of Hippolytus, found also in both his treatises against heresy, viz. that he makes Nicolas the deacon himself, and not any misunderstood saying of his, the origin of the errors of the Nicolaitanes. Here he is charged with maintaining that the resurrection has passed already and that Christians are to expect none other than that which took place when they believed and were baptized.

(16) One work at least Hippolytus specially directed to the heathen, and though this is not included in the list of Jerome he probably alludes to it (*Ep. ad Magnum*, i. 423) where he classes Hippolytus with others who wrote "contra gentes." On the chair we read χρονικῶν πρὸς Ἕλληνας καὶ πρὸς Πλάτωνα ἢ καὶ περὶ τοῦ παντός. We might take πρὸς Ἕλληνας as a distinct work, or with what precedes or with what follows. That the last is the true construction appears both from the title given in one of the MSS., in which a fragment is preserved, ὁ λόγος πρὸς Ἕλληνας ὁ ἐπιγεγραμμένος κατὰ Πλάτωνα περὶ τῆς τοῦ παντὸς αἰτίας, and from the fact that the same fragment contains addresses to the Greeks. This, then, is evidently the treatise περὶ τῆς τοῦ παντὸς οὐσίας, mentioned at the end of the *Elenchus*, and of which Photius speaks in a passage already referred to (*Cod.* 48). He says that the treatise was in two short books, that it shewed that Plato was inconsistent; that the Platonic philosopher Alcinous had spoken falsely and absurdly about the soul, matter, and the resurrection; and that the Jewish nation was much older than the Greek. The theory of the universe embodied in this work made all things consist of the four elements, earth, air, fire, or water. Things formed of more elements than one are subject to death by the dissolution of their component parts, but things formed of one element (*e.g.* angels,

formed of fire alone) are indissoluble and immortal. Angels also have no female, for from water the generative principle is derived. Man is made of all four elements, his soul being formed of air and called ψυχή, because this element is colder than the other three. The principal extant fragment contains a description of Hades as a place underground where souls are detained until the judgment. The gate is guarded by an archangel. When the angels appointed to that service conduct thither righteous souls, they proceed to the right to a place of light called Abraham's bosom, where they enjoy continued present pleasures with the expectation of still greater happiness in the future. The wicked, on the other hand, are hurried down to the left into a place of darkness where is the lake of fire, into which no one has yet been cast, but which is prepared for the future judgment. There they not only suffer present temporary punishments, but are tormented by the sight and smoke of that burning lake and the horrible expectation of the punishment to come. The sight of the righteous also punishes them, between whom and them a great gulf is fixed; and while the bodies of the righteous will rise renewed and glorified, theirs will be raised with all their diseases and decay. Bunsen conjectures that Hippolytus may have taken some points for which he has not Scripture authority from the Apoalypse of Peter.

(17) *The Demonstration against the Jews.*—The Greek text of a fragment of a work bearing this title was first published by Fabricius (vol. ii. 1) from a copy supplied by Montfaucon from a Vatican MS. There is no external evidence to confirm the ascription in the MS. of this work to Hippolytus. The mutilated list on the chair begins *-ους*; but it is bare conjecture which completes this into πρὸς Ἰουδαίους. There is nothing in the fragment which forbids us to suppose Hippolytus the writer. It shews that the Jews have no reason to glory in the sufferings they inflicted on Jesus of Nazareth, for it had been foretold that the Messiah should so suffer, and these sufferings had been the cause of the misery afterwards endured by the Jewish nation.

(18) We pass now to dogmatic writings. Jerome, in his list of the writings of Hippolytus, gives "Προσομιλία de laude Domini salvatoris." This is the homily delivered in the presence of Origen.

(19) *The Work on Antichrist.*—Of all the writings of Hippolytus this is the only one extant in a perfect state, or nearly so. It appears in Jerome's list with the title *de Antichrista*; Photius calls it περὶ Χριστοῦ καὶ ἀντιχρίστου; and the title it bears in the MS. from which the first printed edition was made is περὶ τοῦ σωτῆρος ἡμῶν Ἰησοῦ Χριστοῦ καὶ περὶ τοῦ ἀντιχρίστου. The work is addressed to one Theophilus, and the author cautions him against communicating to unbelievers what he was about to teach him, quoting Paul's directions to Timothy, "the things thou hast heard of me commit thou to *faithful men*." The doctrine of the treatise as to the coming overthrow of the Roman power would give good reason for this caution. Jerome's title best describes the treatise, of which, after some introductory remarks on prophetic inspiration, Antichrist is almost exclusively the subject. The later title has some justification in the parallel between Christ and Antichrist, with which he begins, shewing how the deceiver had sought in all things to liken himself to the Son of God. He was to be, like Christ, a lion (Deut. xxxiii. 22), a king, a lamb (Rev. xiii. 11), he was to come in the form of a man, and to be of the circumcision; he was to send out false apostles and gather in a people, and as the Lord had given a seal to those who believe in Him, so should he, etc. The writer then quotes fully all the prophecies of Antichrist, and concludes that he shall be of the tribe of Dan; that Daniel's four kingdoms are the Babylonian, Median, Grecian, and Roman; that the ten toes of the image are ten kings among whom the Roman empire should be divided, that from among these Antichrist should arise and overthrow three of the kings, viz. those of Egypt, Libya, and Ethiopia, and make an expedition against Tyre and Berytus, and then should gain the submission of the Jews, hoping to obtain vengeance by their means; that he should shew himself forth as God, and persecute to the death those who refuse to worship him; that he should reign three years and a half and then that he and his kingdom should be destroyed by Christ's second coming. For the problem of the number of the beast, while other solutions mentioned by Irenaeus are noticed, that of Λατεῖνος is preferred. This is one of many coincidences shewing that Hippolytus used the treatise of Irenaeus against heresies and enumerated (§ iv.) by Overbeck in an able monograph on this tract *Quaestionum Hippol. specimen.* Overbeck discusses also the points of contact between this tract and Origen, deciding that these may be accounted for without supposing either writer indebted to the other.

(20) The text of a homily *on the Holy Theophany* was communicated to Fabricius by Gale from a MS. still preserved at Cambridge. There is also extant a Syriac translation of great part of this homily, viz. to the end of c. 7 (Wright, *Catal. of Syr. MSS. of Brit. Mus.* ii. 842). The ascription of the MSS. is not confirmed by any external evidence, nor is this homily mentioned in any list of the Hippolytine works, nor quoted by any ancient author. We do not, however, see anything in it which Hippolytus might not have written, and Wordsworth has pointed out a remarkable coincidence with the Refutation, viz. that in both man is spoken of as becoming a god by the gift of new birth and immortality.

(21) On the chair is enumerated περὶ χαρισμάτων ἀποστολικὴ παράδοσις. It is doubtful whether this is the title of one work or two. For various speculations see Fabricius, p. 83. The most probable theory is that it treated of Montanist claims to inspiration.

(22) On the chair we have words which have been read ᾠδαὶ εἰς πάσας τὰς γραφάς. If the line describes only a single work it may denote hymns, one in praise of each of the books of Scripture and perhaps giving a poetical account of its contents.

(23) *On the Hexaemeron.*—We now pass to the exegetical writings. This work is given in the lists of Eusebius and Jerome. The

latter states (*Ep.* liv., *ad Pammach. et Ocean.* vol. i. p. 525) that Ambrose had made use of it in his work on the same subject.

(24) εἰς τὰ μετὰ τὴν ἑξαήμερον (Eus.). *In Genesim* (Hieron.). From this we suppose the account of the 72 nations to have been taken.

(25) *On Exodus.*—This we only know from Jerome's list. No quotations have been preserved, though Magistris makes a doubtful suggestion that Theodoret's citations from the λόγος εἰς τὴν ᾠδὴν τὴν μεγάλην are from a commentary on the Song of Moses (Ex. xv.).

(26) There is extant a fragment (Lagarde, 51) of a commentary on "the blessings of Balaam"; and Trithemius also ascribes to Hippolytus a commentary on *Numbers.* An Arabic catena on the Pentateuch, of which a portion was pub. by Fabricius, ii. 33-44, and the whole of *Gen.* by Lagarde, *Materialien zur Kritik und Geschichte des Pentateuchs*, contains numerous extracts from an Hippolytus whom it describes as the expounder of the Targum. It is generally admitted that the scholia do not belong to our Hippolytus.

(27, 28) Theodoret cites several passages from the *Discourse on Elkanah and Hannah.* Another part of *Samuel* was the subject of a special treatise called by Jerome *de Saul et Pythonissa*, and in Gk. εἰς τὴν ἐγγαστρίμυθον, for so an imperfect line on the chair is generally, and, as we believe, correctly, completed.

(29) *The Commentary on the Psalms.*—The eixstence of this work is testified by Jerome and by the inscription on the chair. Yet elsewhere when writing to Augustine Jerome gives a list of commentators on the Psalms (*Ep.* cxii., vol. i. p. 754), leaving out Hippolytus and counting Eusebius as the next Greek commentator after Origen, either through mere forgetfulness or because Jerome had only read, of Hippolytus, homilies on particular Psalms and some general observations on the whole book. Theodoret quotes from the commentary on Pss. ii. xxiii. and xxiv., and on the ᾠδὴ μεγάλη, which may mean Ps. cxix. These quotations may be from separate homilies, and not from the present work. A fragment published by Bandini comments on Ps. lxxviii. Several other fragments of doubtful genuineness are given by Magistris (Migne, x. 722). Hippolytus classifies the Psalms according to their authors and inscriptions, and explains that they are all called David's because he originated the institution of temple psalmody, as the book of Esther is called after her, and not after Mordecai, of whom it has much more to tell, because Esther, by her act of self-sacrifice, was the originator of the whole deliverance. Hippolytus points out that the Psalms are not in chronological order, and supposes that Ezra did not find them all at once and placed them in books as he found them. The Greek, on the contrary, supposes that the chronological order was deranged to establish a mystical connexion between the number of a Psalm and its subject. Eusebius here follows Hippolytus.

(30) *On Proverbs.* Mentioned in Jerome's list. Some fragments have been preserved in catenae (Lagarde, pp. 196-199). Others pub. by Mai (*Bib. Nov. Pat.* vii.) will be found in Migne (p. 6).

(31, 32) Jerome enumerates a commentary on *Ecclesiastes*; both Eusebius and Jerome one on the *Song of Songs.* Lagarde gives one fragment from the former (No. 136, p. 200) and four from the latter (No. 35, p. 200; and *Anal. Syr.* p. 87). One of these states that Hezekiah suppressed the works of Solomon on natural history, because the people sought in them for the recovery of their diseases, instead of seeking help from God.

(33, 34, 35) Jerome enumerates a commentary on *Isaiah*; Eusebius one on parts of *Ezekiel.* Assemani states (*Bibl. Or.* i. 607) that there is Syriac testimony to the existence of one on *Jeremiah.*

(36) *On Daniel.*—In Jerome's list. It is the subject of an article by Photius; is quoted by several other writers, and large fragments of it remain. In a most valuable contribution to Hippolytine literature, Bardenhewer (Freiburg, 1877) collects all the notices of this work, discusses the different extant fragments, and restores the original as far as possible. Catenae quote passages from the commentary of Hippolytus on Susanna, but the early lists do not mention this as a separate treatise, and Bardenhewer is probably right in thinking that it was the commencement of the commentary on Daniel, to which book that of Susanna was then commonly prefixed. The list of Ebed-Jesu attributes to Hippolytus an exposition of Susanna and of Daniel the Little. This writer's list of O.T. books includes Daniel, Susanna, and Daniel the Little. There is no evidence what is meant by the last. Hippolytus supposes Susanna to have been the daughter of the high-priest Hilkiah (II. Kings xxii. 4) and sister to the prophet Jeremiah, and he probably, like Africanus, identified her husband with the Jehoiachin who was kindly treated by Evil-Merodach. Hippolytus thought, like so many of the Fathers, that the persons, institutions, and events of O.T. included, beside their literal meaning, a typical representation of things corresponding in the new dispensation. The remains of the commentary on *Daniel* contain a theory attested by Photius, that our Lord had come in the year of the world 5500, and that its end should be in the year 6000, that is, not until 500 years after the Incarnation. In Scripture proof of this calculation, Hippolytus appeals to the 5½ cubits which he finds in Ex. xxv. 10; to the sixth hour, John xix. 14, which denotes half a day or 500 years; and to Rev. xvii. 10. This 5500 years must be understood as round numbers, for the *Chronicle* of Hippolytus counts the exact number of years as 5502.

(37) *On Zechariah.*—Known only from Jerome's list and the prologue to his commentary on Zechariah.

(38) *On Matthew.*—We know of this from the prologue to Jerome's commentary on Matthew; and Theodoret quotes from a discourse on the parable of the talents, which, however, may have been a separate homily.

(39) *On Luke.*—Two fragments are given by Mai (Lagarde, p. 202), and Theodoret has preserved part of a homily on the two thieves.

(40) *On the Apocalypse.*—In the list of Jerome, and mentioned by Jacob of Edessa (Eph. Syr. *Opp. Syr.* i. 192) and Syncellus, 358. Some fragments are preserved in an Arabic

Catena on the Apocalypse (Lagarde, *Anal. Syr.* app. pp. 24-27). It appears that Hippolytus (who is described as pope of Rome) interpreted the woman (Rev. xii. 1) to be the church; the sun with which she is clothed, our Lord; the moon, John the Baptist; the twelve stars, the twelve apostles; the two wings on which she was to fly, hope and love. He understood xii. 10 to speak, not of an actual swallowing up by the earth of the hostile armies, but only that they wandered about in despair. He understood by the wound of the beast (xiii. 3) the contempt and refusal of obedience with which Antichrist would be received by many at first; and by the healing of it the subsequent submission of the nations. The two horns (xiii. 11) are the law and the prophets, for this beast will be a lamb outwardly, though inwardly a ravening wolf. Of the number of the beast, beside the Irenaean solutions, Lateinos, Euanthas, and Teitan, he gives one of his own, Dantialos, a name possibly suggested by the theory that Antichrist was to be of the tribe of Dan. The kings of the East (xvi. 12) come to the support of Antichrist. Armageddon is the valley of Jehoshaphat. The five kings (xvii. 13) are Nebuchadnezzar, Cyrus, Darius, Alexander and his four successors. The next is the Roman empire, whose time was not yet completed; the seventh, who had not yet come, was Antichrist.

This enumeration includes all the works for which there is evidence of Hippolytine authorship, unless we add the letters with which it would seem Eusebius was acquainted. The list of genuine writings is quite enough to establish the immense literary activity of Hippolytus, especially as an interpreter of Scripture; and his labours must have given a great impulse to the study of God's word. As a writer he must be pronounced active rather than able or painstaking. Yet he must be admitted to deserve the reverence his literary labours gained from his contemporaries and the honour paid him at his death. For centuries afterwards his name was obscured; but his glory blazed out again when in the time of Charlemagne his relics were transferred to France. For some interesting particulars of this translation see Benson, *Journ. of Classical and Sacred Philology*, i. 190. We quote his account of the visit of pope Alexander III. to his shrine in the church of St. Denys in 1159. "On the threshold of one of the chapels he paused to ask, 'Whose relics it contained?' 'Those of St. Hippolytus,' was the answer. 'I don't believe it—I don't believe it' ('Non credo—non credo'), replied the infallible authority. 'The bones of St. Hippolytus were never removed from the holy city.' But St. Hippolytus, whose dry bones apparently had as little reverence for the spiritual progeny of Zephyrinus and Callistus as the ancient bishop's tongue and pen had manifested towards these saints themselves, was so very angry that he rumbled his bones inside the reliquary with a noise like thunder ('ut rugitus tonitrui putaretur'). To what lengths he might have gone if rattling had not sufficed we dare not conjecture. But the pope, falling on his knees, exclaimed in terror, 'I believe, O my Lord Hippolytus—I believe; pray be quiet.' And he built an altar of marble there to appease the disquieted saint."

Literature.—Arts. on Hippolytus are to be found in Tillem. vol. iv.; Ceillier, vol. i.; Fabr. *Bibl. Gr.* vii. 183, ed. Harles, where is the best account of the older bibliography. The discovery of the *Refutation* made a good deal of the older literature antiquated. We have already referred to some of the more important writings which that discovery elicited. The more important special dissertations on the other works have been referred to under their respective sections. The most important discussion on the life and works of Hippolytus is that in vol. xi. of part i. of Bp. Lightfoot's *Apost. Fathers*, pp. 137-477. [G.S.]

Hippolytus (5): Aug. 10 (Bas. *Men.*), Aug. 13 (*Mart. Vet. Rom.* Usuard.). An apocryphal martyr, first mentioned in the 5th or 6th cent. His story, as given in the martyrology of Ado, is taken from the spurious acts of St. Laurentius the Roman archdeacon, where we are told that that saint, when arrested, was delivered by the prefect Valerian into the custody of Hippolytus, a high military officer, who was converted and at once baptized by him, and thereupon sentenced to be torn asunder by wild horses. Döllinger, in *Hippolytus and Callistus* (Plummer's trans.), pp. 28-39 and 51-60, discusses the rise and development of this legend, which has largely helped to confuse the story of the genuine Hippolytus, the Roman presbyter and writer of the 3rd cent. (*q.v.*) (cf. Bunsen's *Christianity and Mankind*, i. 426). Döllinger fixes the composition of this story between the time of pope Liberius and that of Leo the Great, a period of about 70 years. The whole subject is in a state of great confusion in the martyrologies, which Döllinger has striven, with his usual critical power and vast knowledge, to arrange in some consistent order. Yet the impartial reader must feel sorely perplexed between the opposing theories of Döllinger and Bunsen. (Cf. for the more modern traditions regarding this martyr, Aug. Hare's *Walks in Rome*, ii. 139.) [G.T.S.]

Honorius (1), Flavius Augustus, emperor, b. 384, d. 423. A full account of him is given in the *Dict. of Classical Biogr.* He was declared emperor of the West in 394 at Milan, where he remained almost uninterruptedly till 399. He and his brother Arcadius seem to have been only ill-informed spectators of the tremendous events passing around them.

There is an important enactment against paganism in the first year of Honorius's reign (*Cod. Theod.* XVI. x. 13) which forbids all sacrifices and apparently all public assemblage for pagan worship. The legislation against heresy is varied and stringent. In XVI. v. 25 of the *Theodosian Code* all Theodosius's coercive edicts were re-enacted in their sharpest form and all concessions revoked. The Eunomians in particular were excluded from rights of military service, legal testimony and inheritance, though this special severity was relaxed soon after (v. 27), in accordance with Theodosius's edicts (XVI. v. 22-24). All heretical congregations were forbidden, and their celebration of the holy mysteries, with ordination either of bishops or presbyters, altogether interdicted. Two more of the five severe edicts of this year provided that slight error or deviation ("vel levi argumento a tramite Catholica") shall be unsparingly crushed. Penalties for neglect of statutes on heresy are made capital (XVI. v. 28), and c. 29 is inquisitorial and applies to all employés and officials, civil or military. All found to be "culpae hujus affines" are to be expelled from the service and the city. This is dated Nov. 23, Constantinople, so that Arcadius, or rather Eutropius, may be its author.

It is difficult to say how strictly the Honorian edicts against heresy were carried out, but no such persecution as that of St. Chrysostom is laid to the account of the emperor of the West. There is doubt, however, that the ecclesiastical legislation of 396 and following years was very severe. On March 2, 396 (*T. C.* XVI. v. 30), all heretical places of assemblage were confiscated and all meetings interdicted. By edicts 31 and 32 the Eunomian clergy were banished and inquiries were directed to be made after their leaders. XVI. vii. 6 deprived all apostates of testamentary power, their property was to go to their natural heirs; and by XVI. x. 14 all privileges of pagan priesthood or ministry were done away. The Jews were protected by three edicts (XVI. viii. 11-13).

The following edicts on church matters extend over 397 and 398. The Apollinarians were banished from Constantinople (*T. C.* XVI. v. 33) on Apr. 1, which was the only coercive measure of the year, and does not belong to Honorius. By XVI. ii. 30, Jan. 31, all ancient privileges were confined to bishops and clergy, with the proviso "Nihil extraordinarii muneris ecclesiae, vel sordidae functionis agnoscatur," repeated in XI. xvi. 22 (June 4). The Jews were protected from popular tumults (XVI. viii. 12, 13), and equal privileges and respect shewn to high-priests and patriarchs as to the higher Christian clergy. In 398 there were severe statutes on heresy. By *T. C.* XVI. v. 34 (Constantinople, but in Honorius's fourth consulship) Eunomian and Montanist clergy were banished from all cities and deprived of civic rights. If detected performing their rites in the country they were to be banished and the building confiscated, their books seized and burned, and keeping them was a capital offence. The Manicheans were specially attacked A.D. 399 (c. 35), and those who harboured them were threatened. C. 36 allowed testamentary rights to the Eunomians, but forbad them to assemble or to celebrate the mysteries. Their clergy ("ministri sceleris, quos falso nomine antistites vocant) were to be banished. Clerical rights of sanctuary for criminals were formally refused (*de Poenis*, ix. xl. 16), but intercession was permitted. This claim seems to have been pressed by the clerical and monastic body by violent means, which the authorities had difficulty in restraining. Cases in which "tanta clericorum ac monachorum audacia est, ut bellum velint potius quam judicium" were to be referred to the emperor for severer adjudication. Bishops were to punish the offences of monks. Debtors, public and private, including some unhappy curiales, had claimed sanctuary in churches (IX. xlv. 3). They were to be removed "manu mox injecta." No cleric or monk was to assert sanctuary by forcible defence for condemned criminals (XI. xxx. 7). Bishops were recommended to ordain clergy from the monastic orders (VI. ii. 32).

Ambrose had successfully resisted the reintroduction of the altar or statue of Victory into the senate-house in 384; and by 399 it may have appeared to Honorius's advisers that the time was come when paganism might be hastened out of existence. The paganism of the Roman senate and people was connected with the proudest associations of their public and domestic history, and it lingered long in the old patrician houses of the metropolis and among the rustic population. This was a source of weakness in keeping Christian emperors away from Rome. It may have been intended to end this division by direct attempts at suppressing paganism. The death-struggle of a paganism long fostered, and quite without real devotion, contributed to the final overthrow of Rome. Its immediate result in the life of Honorius seems to have been the undermining of Stilicho. The eunuch influence in both Eastern and Western courts had always been against him. There seems no doubt that Stilicho was opposed to anything which thinned his muster-rolls and weakened the hearts of his followers. Athanasius had advised Jovian (Broglie, *L'Eglise et l'Empire romain*, vol. v. p. 362) to bear with error; to bear witness to truth as emperor, but trust for its victory to the God of truth. Stilicho hardly reached this, as is proved by the many laws against heretics and idolaters in the code; but the accusations of Orosius (vi. 37) and the hostility of Zosimus on the pagan side seem to justify Gibbon's honourable estimate of him. In any case he had a few years of glory to come, and his great enemy was preparing for the defeats of Pollentia and Verona. In 398-399 Alaric was declared master-general of Eastern Illyricum by Arcadius, and raised on barbarian bucklers as king of Visigoths, with one man only between him and Rome (*de Bello Getico*, 503). Between 400 and 403 he had crossed Pannonia to the Julian Alps, taken Aquileia, subdued Istria and Venetia, and was threatening Milan. Honorius, now in his 15th year, thought only of flight into Gaul; but Alaric, overthrown by Stilicho at Pollentia and Verona, was allowed or compelled to retreat, and Honorius went with Stilicho to Rome to celebrate the last triumph of the empire (A.D. 404). The customary games took place with great magnificence, and on this occasion St. Telemachus sacrificed himself by attempting to separate the gladiators. Honorius seems not to have prevented their exhibition, though there are traces of an attempt to substitute hunting scenes, races, and grand cavalry displays, among which seems to have been the ancient game of Troy. After a stay of some months at Rome, during which he appears to have honestly done all in his power to conciliate the senate, clergy, and people, Honorius determined (A.D. 404) to fix his residence in the fortress of Ravenna, which was almost impregnable on the land side and afforded easy escape by sea. The Milanese entertained an affection for Honorius, and desired his return; but he had soon good reason to feel that his choice of residence had been a wise one, both strategically and for his own comfort.

The anti-pagan legislation of 399-400 prepared for the consummating decree of confiscation in 408. *T. C.* XVI. x. 15 prohibited sacrifice, but restrained the destruction of temples, as monumental public works. In July there was an edict (c. 16) for the destruction of rural temples ("sine turba ac tumultu"). Some concession was found necessary, for, in Sept., Tit. x. 17 allowed the usual civic festivals and days of enjoyment ("festos et communem laetitiam"), but strictly without sacrifice. This is commented on by Gibbon in his 23rd chap., on the "Decay of Paganism," vol. iii. p. 16, where he points out how offerings of produce without sacrifice might be used, and the various evasions by which absolutely pagan celebration might elude Christian rule. Such usages might remain for ages, and be carried bodily into Christian country life by popular custom. This is matter of historical experience in all countries; and the May or Beltane, and other strange rites of the Teutonic races, bear witness to it in our own day. There was a final injunction this year (c. 18) against destroying temples, if sacrifices in them had been thoroughly discontinued. XVI. v. 35 was a severe edict against the Manicheans and their harbourers in Africa (June). In July (c. 36) the Eunomians were released from intestacy and allowed freedom of movement. Their meetings were still forbidden and their profane mysteries made a capital offence. As the crudest form of Arianism, this heresy seems to have specially vexed Honorius and his advisers. An edict (*de Religione*, XVI. xi. 1) gave bishops a claim to special authority in causes involving religious questions. "Quoties de religione agitur episcopos convenit agitare." Ecclesiastics were to find substitutes in the curiae, appeals being allowed (XI. xxx. 58, 59).

In A.D. 400 the games were forbidden during Lent and the week before Easter, also on Christmas Day and Epiphany. Civic banishment and exclusion from society was decreed on bishops and clergy deprived or degraded by their fellow-clergy for seditious conduct (XVI. ii. 35). Sons of priests were not to be forced into the ministry (XII. i. 166).

The single edict of A.D. 401 on ecclesiastical matters, addressed to Pompeianus, proconsul of Africa, excepted bishops and clergy actively employed in sacred duties from the "auraria pensio," apparently (see Brissonus, *Dict.*) a tax on commercial men.

In 404 there were 14 decrees, chiefly on religious matters. Of XVI. viii. 15, 16, 17, *de Judaeis*, 15 renews the general privileges of their patriarchs; 16 deprives or exempts Samaritans from military responsibilities; 17 withdraws the prohibition of A.D. 400 as to collections in the synagogues. XVI. ii. (37 Aug.) releases from prison various clerical persons concerned in popular tumults in Constantinople, but expels them, with all other foreign bishops and clergy, from the city. XVI. iv. 4, 5 (*De his qui super Religione contendunt*) coerces "the orthodox, who now forsake the holy churches, and assemble elsewhere ('alio convenire conantur'), and venture to dissent from the religion of Acacius, Theophilus, and Porphyrius," now dominant in Constantinople—Nov. Tillemont considers that all these edicts refer to the tumults which took place in 404 on the persecution of St. Chrysostom, except that which refers to officials, issued in Jan. The saint was not exiled till June.

There were 5 religious decrees out of 18 in 405. Two related to the Manichean and Donatist heresies, former statutes being put in force or threatened: "Una sit catholica veneratio, una Salus sit, Trinitatis par sibique congruens Sanctitas expetatur." XVI. vi. 3, 14 were against the repetition of baptism, which some persons seem to have thought might be repeated not only after heresy, but for forgiveness of repeated sins. Persons guilty of rebaptizing others were deprived of all their property, which was, however, secured to their heirs if orthodox. The contumacious were threatened with loss of all civil rights, and there was a heavy fine for connivance.

The irruption of the pagan and ferocious Radagaisus is dated by Gibbon 406, by Tillemont 405. He had to capitulate and was beheaded, and so many of his Germans were sold as slaves that their price fell to a single gold piece. After this invasion and in his desperate circumstances as the last general of Italy's last army, Stilicho apparently turned towards his worthiest enemy and felt the necessity of making terms with Alaric. Stilicho was slain at Ravenna Aug. 23, 408.

Alaric now (Oct. 408) crossed the Alps on pretence of a large claim of money. Honorius fled to Ravenna, and Alaric besieged Rome for the first time, but accepted a large ransom in 409 and withdrew into Tuscany. He renewed the siege in the same year, and Rome submitted. Attalus was proclaimed emperor by him. In 410 the capture and sack of Rome followed. Alaric died before the end of the year, and in 412 the Goths under Adolf withdrew into Gaul, where Adolf remained until driven into Spain about 3 years after.

A.D. 407, 408. *T.C.* XVI. v. 40, 41 included the Manichean, Phrygian, and Priscillianist sects in the liabilities of the Donatists, *i.e.* loss of rights of property and succession, gift, sale, contract, will, and right to restrain orthodox slaves from worship. Heresy was expressly made a public offence, because *crimen in religione divina in omnium fertur injuriam*, but by c. 41 simple "confessio" or acknowledgment of error and return to orthodox service sufficed for restoration to all rights, and Honorius shewed genuine anxiety to recall his people to the right path on easy terms. XVI. ii. 38 enacted clerical immunities for Africa.

In 408, XVI. viii. 18 stated that at the feast of Purim ("Aman ad recordationem") the Jews were accustomed to burn or insult the cross. This was to cease, their other ceremonies were "infra contemptum Christianae legis," and might continue. There were 6 statutes on heretics and pagans—XVI. v. 42-45, with XVI. x. 19, and V. xiv. 7—and XVI. ii. 36, *de Episcopis*. Enemies to the Catholic faith were forbidden to serve in the emperor's palace guard. All statutes against Donatists, Manicheans, and Priscillianists were to be fully enforced, and a new sect called Caelicolae were, with them, to be deprived of all buildings for public assemblage. Donatists who had not yet confessed their heresy, but only withdrawn from Catholic service (" saevae religionis obtentu ") were included. Certain Jews and Donatists had insulted the Sacraments, and were to be punished; illegal assemblage for heretical worship was again prohibited. XVI. ii. 39 provided that a degraded cleric who had renounced clerical office should be at once made a curialis and forbidden to resume his orders.

A.D. 409. *De Haereticis*, XVI. v. 46, Jan., 47, June. Two edicts to enforce laws on Jews, Gentiles, or pagans, and heretics. Tillemont says that the death of Stilicho caused a general outbreak of heretics, the Donatists of Africa in particular asserting that his laws against them were now abrogated. Two edicts in March and July forbad amusements (" voluptates ") on Sunday and exempted Jews from public calls on their Sabbath (II. viii. 25, 26).

In 410 there were 4 decrees (out of 19) on heresy. The Montanists, Priscillianists, and others were forbidden military service, and other means of exemption from curial burdens (XVI. v. 48). To the intestacy of the Eunomians was added the reversion of bequests to the fisc, if no orthodox heir survive; c. 51 altogether abrogated a former imperial oraculum or rescript, by which certain heretics had been allowed to meet in secret. XVI. xi. 3 confirmed all existing religious statutes.

A.D. 411, 412. XVI. v. 52, Jan. Heavy fines, or total confiscation of property, on obstinate Donatists. Pressure was to be exercised by masters on their slaves, and by the local authorities on coloni. Heretical clergy banished from Africa (c. 53). Jovinian and others, his followers, to be corporally punished and banished to island of Boas, on coast of Dalmatia. XVI. ii. 40, 41, *de Episcopis*. Church properties exempted from fugatio (a kind of land-tax by acreage, Brisson), also from repairs of public roads and bridges. By c. 41 clergy were to be tried only before their bishops and unnecessary scandal avoided by only bringing accusations which could be definitely proved. For perfect tolerance towards the Jews, XVI. viii. 20, 21.

In 418 Wallia and his Visigoths were settled in the S.W. of France with Toulouse for their capital. Britain was entirely lost, and the Armoricans were maintaining themselves in independence. A fresh revolt under another Maximus seems not to have been suppressed till 422. Wallia, however, acted in Spain as a feudal ally of the empire, won a succession of victories over the Alani, Vandals, and Suevi, and restored great part of the peninsula to Honorius, who is said by Prosper's *Chronicle* to have entered Rome in triumph a second time. The Burgundians occupied the two provinces which still bear their name, and the Franks were settled on the Rhine. All continued to acknowledge the title of Honorius, and to hold titles from the empire; and all accepted the civil law and magistracy of Rome. Honorius himself had confirmed the independence of Britain and Armorica *c.* 410, and died of dropsy in his 40th year (423), Aug. 27.

His later legislation has little historical interest, but the enactments on paganism and heresy from 413 to 423 were as follows: Two against repetition of baptism, A.D. 413; two against Donatists, v. 54, 55. These comprise (XVI. vi. 6, 7) the settlement effected by Marcellinus on Honorius's part at Carthage, between the orthodox and the Donatists, which, Tillemont says, brought the heresy to an end. Against any public assemblage for heretical purposes, v. 56. By v. 57 Montanist congregations were forbidden; their clergy to be banished if they attempted to ordain others. Harbourers to be deprived of the house or property where the heretic remained. Their places of meeting, if any were left standing, to be the property of the church. By c. 58 houses of Eunomian clergy were confiscated to the fisc; or any in which second baptism has been administered. Their clergy were exiled, and they were again deprived of testamentary and military rights. All these, except the last, were addressed to Africa. By III. xii. 4 marriage with a deceased wife's sister or husband's brother was forbidden. XVI. x. 20. All pagan priests were required to return to their native place. Confiscation to the church or the emperor of lands and grounds used for pagan purposes. To become a pagan was now a capital offence. In 416 Gentiles, or persons guilty of participation in pagan rites, were excluded from the army and from official or judicial positions. In 423 Honorius renewed all his edicts against heresy, with special mention of Manicheans, Phrygians, Priscillianists, Arians, Macedonians, Eunomians, Novatianists, and Sabbatiani. XVI. v. 59, 60. He was able to say that he believed there were very few pagans remaining, and so far his persecution may seem to have been successful, as with the Donatists and others. Other and more powerful causes were at work, and error and idolatry were taking other forms. The remarkable statute (XVI. x. 22 and 23) ran thus: " Paganos, si qui supersunt, quanquam jam nullos esse credamus, promulgatorum legum jam dudum praescripta compescant." The next (c. 23) stated that pagans caught in acts of idolatrous ceremonial ought to be capitally punished, but are only subject to loss of property and exile. He denounced the same sentence in c. 24 on Manicheans and Pepuzitae, who were worse than all other heretics, saying, " quod in venerabili die Paschatis ab omnibus dissentiant." He ended with a strong caution against any violence on Christian pretences to pagans or Jews leading quiet and legal lives, with penalty of triple or fourfold restitution. Two more decrees this year restored all fabrics taken from the Jews, even for church purposes; or, in case the holy mysteries had been celebrated in such buildings, equal accommodation should be provided for the former holders.

Honorius possessed no character except a timid docility, but with some natural goodness of heart or gentleness, otherwise he could not have continued to reign so disastrously for 28 years. It must be remembered, in excuse of his coercive action, that persecution was no invention of his or Theodosius's, but an inheritance of the empire. Such questions as the expediency or the possibility of perfect toleration, the limits of pressure or coercion, and what body in the state is to exercise it, have been debated in theory and hewn out in practice, from the beginnings of society, and are still unsettled. Nor can they be solved, unless the relation of the individual conscience to the public, and of the individual soul to the church, were accurately known and defined. That there is a point at which the church militant must cease to strive with invincible ignorance or determined error, leaving them to the civil power, as civil dangers or nuisances only, seems a rule which the sad experience of 1800 years has but imperfectly taught the Christian world. Only the great spirit of Athanasius seems to have anticipated it in his day, though he did not always act on it. The world knew no tolerance, and never had known it in Honorius's time; and his position as emperor compelled him to do as other emperors had done before him. The temptation to a Christian emperor to hold heresy or paganism an offence against the State, which he personified (at least on earth, and in heathen theory in heaven), was too much for man. Without asserting that all the faults of the Christian church may be traced to the fatal gift of Constantine, we cannot doubt that her alliance with the temporal power proved as dangerous as her investiture with temporal rule was fabulous. Pagan emperors had claimed to rule as personal and present divinity, and this claim had always specially embittered their persecution of the Christian faith. It was never, in fact, withdrawn; the ruler of Rome was invested with an awe beyond man, and that, in fact, descended to the mediaeval popedom. Constantine himself had allowed his statues to be worshipped with incense and lights, and so most unhappily encouraged the earlier iconodulism of half-Christianized Greeks. But the connexion he instituted between the temporal and spiritual power tempted a Christian despot like Theodosius, under guidance of a great representative of the church, to think that God was surely with them in whatever persecuting edict they set forth; and thus Justinian's words, "Sacrilegii instar est dubitare" (*Cod.* IX. xxix. 3), were literally meant, and logically, if not conscientiously, believed. The empire could not forget its traditions. Excuses which are admitted by Christians for Aurelius or Diocletian ought to be considered in behalf of Theodosius and his sons. The fierceness and necessities of their age must be allowed as palliations.

Theodosius's 15 edicts in 15 years, from 380-384, extend over the ministers, assemblies and persons of heretics, and make not only the Manichean heresy punishable by death, but the Quartodeciman error as to keeping Easter. Ambrose, like other Churchmen, could not abstain from the use of the mighty arm of flesh at his command, and the institution of inquisitors must certainly have been an ecclesiastical measure. It should be remembered that the Christian faith had by its own influences so elevated and organized the influence of the human conscience as to have become a temporal power by the nature of things. The Christian spiritual power ruled men's persons and fortunes; the bishop was in fact obeyed by his large share of the population, and became a temporal magistrate because men made him arbitrate for them. (See Guizot, *Civ. in Europe*, lect. ii. p. 34, ed. Bohn.) He was consequently involved with the civil power in coercive measures of all kinds and in all directions.

Lastly, the empire was divided between Rome and Constantinople, but Italy between Rome and Milan or Ravenna. Ambrose must have felt that the remaining paganism of Rome was his chief difficulty, and his influence must have been accordingly exerted on Honorius in his first days. Hence, perhaps, his supineness and indifference to the fate of Rome, and perhaps, in a great degree, the paralysis of Italian defence as soon as the barbaric genius of Stilicho was withdrawn.

A coin of Honorius is figured in Smith's *Dict. of G. and R. Biogr.* s.v. The countenance has an inexpressiveness which may have belonged to him in a special degree, but extends to most portraiture after the 3rd cent. Another represents the emperor in the paludamentum, bearing a globe and the labarum. On another, with Vota Publica, are two emperors with nimbi, which is important evidence of the derivation of that symbol from imperial effigies (see Tyrwhitt, *Art Teaching of Prim. Ch.*, *Index* "Nimbus"). [R.ST.J.T.]

Hormisdas (3), bp. of Rome after Symmachus from July 26, 514, to Aug. 6, 523, Anastasius and Justin being successively emperors of the East and Theodoric ruling the West as king of Italy. Hormisdas was a native of Frusino in Campania. Pope Silverius (*acc.* 536) is said to have been his son (Liberat. *Breviar.* 22). The memorable event of his pontificate was the restoration of communion between Rome and Constantinople, which had been interrupted since 484, in connexion with the Eutychian heresy. [FELIX III.; ACACIUS.] The first overtures were made in 515 by the emperor Anastasius, being moved thereto by Vitalian, a Scythian, the commander of the imperial cavalry, who, having taken up the cause of orthodoxy, made himself master of Thrace, Scythia, and Mysia, and marched with an army of Huns and Bulgarians to the gates of Constantinople. Anastasius had to procure peace by assenting to 3 conditions, one being that he should summon a council at Heraclea, the pope being invited and free discussion allowed (Theophan. *Chron. ad an. Imp. Anast.* 23). In 515 the emperor wrote to Hormisdas, desiring his concurrence in restoring unity to the church by means of such a council; and Hormisdas, after a guarded reply, sent legates to Constantinople with letters to the emperor and Vitalian, and a statement of the necessary conditions for union. These were: (1) The emperor should issue to all bishops of his dominion a written declaration accepting the council of Chalcedon and the letters of pope Leo. (2) A like declaration should be publicly signed by the Eastern bishops, who should also anathematize Nestorius, Eutyches, Dioscorus, Aelurus, Peter Mongus, Peter the Fuller, and Acacius, with all their followers. (3) Persons exiled for religion should be recalled and their cases reserved for the judgment of the apostolic see. (4) Such exiles as had been in communion with Rome and professed the catholic faith should first be recalled. (5) Bishops accused of having persecuted the orthodox should be sent to Rome to be judged. Thus the emperor proposed a free discussion in council; the pope required the unqualified acceptance of orthodoxy, and submission to himself as head of Christendom, before he would treat at all. He did not reject the idea of a council, but, from his point of view, none was wanted. The Easterns had but to renounce their errors and accept the terms of reconciliation dictated by the apostolic see, and peace would be at once restored.

This attempt failed, as Anastasius, though now professing orthodoxy, demurred to erasing the name of Acacius from the diptychs. But he continued his overtures. In 516 he sent two distinguished laymen to Rome with a letter to Hormisdas. But Hormisdas continued resolute, and the emperor dismissed the bishops already assembled at Heraclea for the intended council. In a letter to Avitus of Vienne (517) the pope, referring to this embassy, complains of the fruitless and perfidious promises of the Greeks, but rejoices at the faithfulness of the churches of Gaul, Thrace, Dardania, and Illyricum, which had stood firm against persecution in the communion of Rome. It appears that 40 bishops of Illyricum and Greece had renounced obedience to their metropolitan of Thessalonica and sent to Hormisdas to seek communion with Rome (Theophan. *Chron.*).

Hormisdas, building on the emperor's political necessities, sent in 517 a second embassy to the East with increased demands. They were charged with a rule of faith (*regula fidei*) for the signature of all who desired reconciliation with Rome which was more exacting than any previous document. The signers were to declare that, mindful of the text "Thou art Peter," etc., the truth of which has been proved by the immaculate religion ever maintained by the apostolic see, they profess in all things to follow that see, and to desire communion with it. Accordingly they were to accept the decrees of Chalcedon and the "tome" of pope Leo, and also all letters on religion he had ever written; and not only to anathematize Nestorius, Eutyches, Dioscorus, Timothy Aelurus, Peter Fullo, and Acacius, with all their followers, but also exclude from their diptychs all who had been "sequestrated from catholic communion," which is explained to mean communion with the apostolic see. Such demands ended the negotiations, and Anastasius peremptorily dismissed the legates, and sent a reply to Hormisdas (July 11, 517) which ended: "We can bear to be injured and set at naught; we will not be commanded" (Hormisd. *Epp. post. Ep.* xxii. Labbe).

Persecutions were now renewed in the East. The monasteries of the orthodox in Syria Secunda were burnt and 350 monks massacred. The survivors sent a deputation to the pope, acknowledging in ample terms the supremacy of "the most holy and blessed patriarch of the whole world," "the successor of the Prince of the Apostles," and "the Head of all." They implore him to exercise his power of binding and loosing in defence of the true faith, and to anathematize all heretics, including Acacius (*ib.*). To this appeal Hormisdas replied in a letter to all the orthodox in the East, exhorting them to steadfastness in the faith of Chalcedon, and to patience under present straits (in Act. V. *Concil. Constantin.* Labbe, vol. v. p. 1111).

The death of Anastasius (July 9, 518) and the accession of the orthodox Justin changed the aspect of affairs. During divine service at Constantinople, while John the Cappadocian (who had lately succeeded Timotheus as patriarch) was officiating, the populace, who had been all along on the orthodox side, seem to have made a riot in the church in the impatience of their orthodox zeal, crying, "Long live the emperor!" "Long live the patriarch!" They would not brook delay. By continued cries, by closing the doors of the church and saying they would not leave it till he had done what they wanted, they compelled him to proclaim the acceptance of the four general councils, including Chalcedon. A synod, attended by some 40 bishops, ratified what the patriarch had done. Letters were sent to various Eastern metropolitans, including those of Jerusalem, Tyre, and Syria Secunda, who forthwith reported to the synod the full acceptance of orthodoxy by their several churches (*ib.* p. 1131, etc.). Coercive measures were used by Justin. In two edicts he ordered the restoration of the orthodox exiled by Anastasius, the acknowledgment of the council of Chalcedon in the diptychs of all churches, and declared heretics incapable of public offices, civil or military.

The pope insisted upon the erasure of the name of Acacius and the subscription of the rule of faith rejected by Anastasius as the first steps to restoration of communion. In 519 Hormisdas sent a legation to Constantinople, charged with letters to the emperor and patriarch, and also to the empress Euphemia and other persons of distinction, including three influential ladies, Anastasia, Palmatia, and Anicia. They carried with them the *libellus* described above, to be signed by all who desired reconciliation.

At Constantinople they were met by Vitalian, Justinian, and other senators, and received by the emperor in the presence of the senate and a deputation of four bishops to represent the patriarch. The *libellus* was read; the bishops had nothing to say against it, and the emperor and senators recommended them to accept it. The patriarch proved unwilling to sign it as it stood; but at length, after much contention, it was agreed that he might embody the *libellus* unaltered in a letter, with his own preamble. This was done, the names of Acacius and his successors in the see, Fravitas, Euphemius, Macedonius, and Timotheus, and of the emperors Zeno and Anastasius, were erased from the diptychs; the bishops of other cities, and the archimandrites who had been previously reluctant, now came to terms; and the legates wrote to the pope expressing thankfulness that so complete a triumph had been won without sedition, tumult, or shedding of blood. The patriarch's preamble was a protest against the claim of Rome to dictate terms of communion to Constantinople and an assertion of the co-ordinate authority of his own see. He says, "Know therefore, most holy one, that, according to what I have written, agreeing in the truth with thee, I too, loving peace, renounce all the heretics repudiated by thee: for I hold the most holy churches of the elder and of the new Rome to be one; I define that see of the apostle Peter and this of the imperial city to be one see." The same view of the unity of the two sees is expressed in his letter to Hormisdas. Even Justin, in his letter to the pope, guards against implying that the authority of Constantinople was inferior to that of Rome, saying that "John, the prelate of our new Rome, with his clergy, agrees with you," and that "all concur in complying with what is your wish, as well as that of the Constantinopolitan see." Peace being thus concluded at Constantinople, a deputation was sent to Thessalonica, headed by bp. John, the papal legate, to receive the submission of that church. Dorotheus, bp. of Thessalonica, tore the *libellus* in two before the people, and declared that never would he sign it or assent to such as did. Hormisdas, on hearing of this, wrote to the emperor, requiring that Dorotheus should be deposed. But Dorotheus was summoned to Constantinople to be tried, sent thence to Heraclea while his cause was being heard, and eventually allowed to return to his see. He and his church were now restored to Catholic communion, and he wrote a respectful letter to the pope (A.D. 520) expressing great regard for him personally and for the apostolic see. Hormisdas replied that he was anxious to believe in his innocence, and in his being the author of the peace now concluded, but expressed dissatisfaction that he "delayed even to follow those whom he ought to have led," and hoped he would "repel from himself the odium of so great a crime, and in reconciliation to the faith would at length follow the example of those who had returned." It thus seems clear that Dorotheus, though professing orthodoxy and restored by the emperor to his see, had not so far fully complied, if he ever did, with the pope's terms (*Inter Epp.* Hormisd. lxii. lxiii. lxxii. lxxiii.).

Notwithstanding the general triumph of orthodoxy throughout the East, except at Alexandria, the unbending pertinacity of Hormisdas still caused difficulties. In 520 the emperor Justinian and Epiphanius (who had succeeded John as patriarch) wrote urgent letters to him on the subject. They alleged that, though the condition was complied with in the imperial city, yet no small part of the Orientals, especially in the provinces of Pontus, Asia, and Oriens, would not be compelled by sword, fire, or torments to comply, and they implored the pope not to be more exacting than his predecessors. The pope persisted in his demand, and urged Justin, as a duty, not to shrink from coercion. He authorized Epiphanius to deal at his discretion with various cases (*ib.* lxxii. *Concil. Constant.* act. V. Labbe, vol. v. p. 1119).

A nice question, arising out of the now defined orthodox doctrine of One Person and Two Natures in Christ, came before Hormisdas for settlement. There being but one Personality in the Incarnate Word, and that Divine, it seemed correct to say that this Divine Person suffered; and yet to say this seemed to attribute passibility to the Godhead. It was undoubted Nestorian heresy to deny that He Whom the Blessed Virgin brought forth was God. But He Who was brought forth was the same with Him Who suffered on the Cross. On the other hand "God was crucified" had been a favourite Monophysite formula, used to emphasize their doctrine of the absorption of the human nature into the divine; and great offence had formerly been given to the orthodox by the addition of "Who wast crucified for us" to the Trisagion by Peter Fullo. The adoption of this addition at Constantinople under Anastasius had caused a popular tumult, and it was probably its abrogation during the reaction under Justin that caused certain Scythian monks to defend the formula, and to maintain that "ONE of the holy and undivided Trinity" suffered. The question was laid before the legates of Hormisdas, when in Constantinople, A.D. 519. They decided against the Scythian monks, arguing that the faith had been fully and sufficiently defined at Chalcedon and in the letter of pope Leo, and that the formula of the monks was an unauthorized novelty, likely to lead to serious heresy. The monks contended that its adoption was necessary for rendering the definitions of Chalcedon distinct against Nestorianism. Vitalian seems to have supported them. Justin and Justinian begged the pope to settle the question. He wrote to desire that the monks should be kept at Constantinople; but they managed to get to Rome to lay their case before him (*Ep.* lxxix. Labbe). At length they left Rome, having publicly proclaimed their views there. Hormisdas does not seem to have actually condemned the expression of the monks, though annoyed by their propounding it, but spoke strongly against it as an unnecessary novelty. In the end, however, their view triumphed. For in 533 the emperor Justinian issued an edict asserting that "the sufferings and miracles are of one and the same—for we do not acknowledge God the Word to be one and Christ another, but one and the same: for the Trinity remained even after the Incarnation of the One Word of God, Who was of the Trinity; for the Holy Trinity does not admit of the addition of a fourth person. We anathematize Nestorius the man-worshipper, and those who think with him, who deny that our Lord Jesus Christ, the Son of God and our God, Incarnate, made man, and crucified, was One of the holy consubstantial Trinity" (*Lex Justinian.* A.D. 533, *Cod.* I. i. 6; Joann. Pap. ii. *Epp.* in *Patr. Lat.* lxvi. 18 B), and it has since been accounted orthodox to affirm that God suffered in the flesh, though in His assumed human, not in His original divine, nature. (See Pearson *On the Creed*, art. iv.).

Hormisdas died early in Aug. 523, having held the see 9 years and 11 days. He, as well as all the popes during the schism with the East, except the too conciliatory Anastasius, has had his firmness acknowledged by canonization, his day in the Roman Calendar being Aug. 6. His extant writings consist of letters, 80 being attributed to him, one of which, to St. Remigius (in which he gives him vicariate jurisdiction over the kingdom of Clovis which he had converted), is probably spurious, as it implies that Clovis was still reigning, though he had died in 511, more than two years before the election of Hormisdas. Most of the remaining 70 letters refer to the affairs of the East, several to the metropolitan see of Nicopolis in Epirus (Hormisd. vi.-ix., xvii.-xxii.).

Three letters of Hormisdas (xxiv.-xxvi.), to John, bp. of Tarragona, Sallustius, bp. of Seville, and the bishops of Spain in general, give the two prelates vicariate jurisdiction over E. and W. Spain, exhort against simony and other irregularities, and direct the regular convention of synods. Cf. Thiel, *Epp. Pontiff. Rom.* i.

Hormisdas had great administrative and diplomatic abilities, was singularly uncompromising and firm of purpose, and one of the most strenuous and successful assertors of the supremacy of the Roman see. [J.B—Y.]

Hosius (1), (*Osius*), a confessor under Maximian, and bp. of Corduba, the capital of the province of Baetica in Spain. He took a leading part on the catholic side in the controversies of the first half of the 4th cent. For nearly 50 years he was the foremost bishop of his time, held in universal esteem and enjoying unbounded influence. Eusebius says, "He was approved for the sobriety and genuineness of his faith, had distinguished himself by the boldness of his religious profession, and his fame was widely spread" (*Vit. Cons.* bk. ii. cc. 63, 73). Socrates calls him "the celebrated Hosius" (*H. E.* ii. 29). Sozomen says: "He was honoured for his faith, virtuous life, and steadfast confession of truth" (*H. E.* i. 16). Athanasius is never weary of repeating his praises. "Of the great Hosius," he says, "who answers to his name, that confessor of a happy old age, it is superfluous for me to speak, for he is not an obscure person, but of all men the most illustrious" (*Apol. de Fugâ*, § 7). Considering his great renown and his prominent part in affairs, it is remarkable how very little is known of his personal history. There seems no reason to doubt Eusebius, Athanasius, and others, who make him a native of Spain. Athanasius says (*Hist. Arian.* § 45) that when Hosius was more than 100 years old, and had been more than 60 years a bishop, he was summoned by Constantius from Spain to Sirmium, and there subscribed an Arian formula about the middle of A.D. 357. Soon afterwards he returned to his native country and died. We may probably, therefore, place his birth *c.* 256, as Tillemont does (*Mém.* t. vii. p. 302, 4to ed.).

The common view that he suffered for the Christian faith in Diocletian's persecution between 303 and 305 is more than doubtful. We have his own testimony in his letter to Constantius (the son of Constantine) preserved by Athanasius (*Hist. Arian.* § 44). "I was a confessor at the first, when a persecution arose in the time of your grandfather Maximian." These words can hardly refer to the general persecution enjoined by Diocletian. The allusion seems to be to the persecution of which the chief promoter was Maximian, the Augustus and colleague, not the son-in-law, of Diocletian. Maximianus Herculius was made Caesar in 285, and Augustus in 286, as is shewn by coins and inscriptions (cf. Clinton, *Fasti Romani*, vol. i. p. 328), and for six years the Roman empire was divided between these two rulers, Diocletian having the East and Maximian the West. In 292 a further partition of the empire took place by the appointment of two Caesars, Constantius Chlorus (the father of Constantine) and Galerius Maximianus. When Constantius was made Caesar in 292, Maximian's half of the empire was subdivided. "Cuncta quae trans Alpes Galliae sunt Constantio commissa; Africa Italiaque Herculio" (Aur. Vict. *de Caesar*, xxxix. 30). On the abdication of Diocletian and Maximian in 305, Gaul, with Italy and Africa, was given to Constantius, and the rest of the empire to Galerius. But Constantius, content with the dignity of Augustus, refused to administer Italy and Africa (Eutropius, x. 1). Orosius similarly says that Constantius, "Italiam, Africam, Hispaniam et Gallias obtinuit. Sed, vir tranquillissimus, Gallia tantum Hispaniaque contentus, Galerio caeteris patribus cessit" (*Hist.* vii. 25). Constantius, says Sozomen (*H. E.* i. 6), was not willing that Christianity should be accounted unlawful in the countries beyond the confines of Italy, *i.e.* in Gaul, Britain, or the region of the Pyrenaean mountains as far as the western ocean. These facts shew that in the division of the empire Spain was always an appendage of Gaul, and under the same administration. If so, it was under the jurisdiction of Constantius, and, as both Lactantius and Eusebius affirm, that Constantius took no part in the persecution of the Christians, it could not have been in his period that Hosius became a confessor. When, then, did he suffer? We have his own testimony that he had been a confessor in the time of Maximian. Probably it was in some special and local persecution carried out under the orders of Maximianus Herculius while he was sole ruler of the West, before Constantius was appointed Caesar in 292, and much before the general persecution authorized by the edicts of Diocletian in 303. It is very probable that between 286 and 292, while Maximian was sole ruler of the West, there were many martyrdoms in Spain as well as in Gaul and Italy. Hosius would have been then between 30 and 36 years old, and it is far more likely that he suffered persecution and witnessed a good confession then than later under the mild rule of Constantius. Beyond Hosius's own statement, we have no contemporary evidence upon the subject.

As the bishops and officers of the church generally suffered first in the outbreaks of persecution, it is more than probable that Hosius was already bp. of Corduba when he became a confessor. His earliest public act with which we are acquainted was his presence as bp. of Corduba at the synod of Elvira, but the date of this synod, like that of other events in his history, is involved in much obscurity. Mendoza, who has written more fully upon it than any other author, is of opinion that it should be placed in 300 or 301. Nineteen bishops from different parts of Spain were present, hence it may be regarded as representing the whole church of Spain. The president was Felix of Acci (Guadix) in Baetica, probably the oldest bishop present. The name of Hosius comes next. As a rule the order of signatures to the Acts of councils indicates the order of precedence among the bishops, either according to the date of their consecration or the importance of their episcopal sees (Hefele,

Hist. of Councils, vol. i. 64, Eng. trans.). As Hosius was probably not over 45 years old, his high position could not have been due to his age, but must have been in right of his see. We infer, therefore, that Corduba then held the first place among the cities of Spain.

It is now very difficult to form a true conception of Corduba in its ancient grandeur. In the 1st and the beginning of the 2nd cents. Spain reached a very high development in the social system of Rome. Roman influence had so spread in Baetica that the natives had forgotten their own language. Roman schools were opened in the coloniae and municipia, the most brilliant being at Corduba and Osca. For nearly two centuries Spain produced men remarkable in all kinds of culture. Lucan and the two Senecas were born at Corduba, its schools thus furnishing rivals even to Vergil and Cicero. In the time of Hosius this intellectual activity had considerably declined, and pre-eminence in literary culture had passed to the province of Africa. But Corduba must still have retained a high place in the social development of the time. A man called to such an important see would most probably be one of some personal distinction. Baronius (ad ann. 57) attaches little importance to this synod, which he suspects of Novatianist tendencies. The very first canon, indeed, decrees that adults who have sacrificed to idols have committed a capital crime and can never again be received into communion. Such a denial of pardon to those who lapsed under persecution was the chief error of Novatian (Socr. *H. E.* iv. 28). The Novatianist discipline was very rigid in other respects also, especially with reference to carnal sins, and many of the canons of Elvira relate to such offences, and their stern and austere spirit shews how deeply the Fathers at Elvira were influenced by Novatianist principles. Though we cannot trace the hand of Hosius in the composition of these canons, yet as he was a leading member of the synod, its decrees would doubtless be in harmony with his convictions.

For 12 or 13 years after this synod nothing is known of his life. He then seems to have been brought into close personal relations with the emperor Constantine, and thenceforward his acts form part of the history of his time. It would be interesting to know how Hosius acquired the great influence over Constantine which it is believed he exercised up to the time of the Nicene council. But there is not a single passage in any ancient writer which relates the origin of their connexion.

The absence of Hosius from the synod of Arles, Aug. 1, 314, the most numerously attended council that had hitherto been held in Christendom, is remarkable. Bishops from Italy, Gaul, Spain, and Britain were assembled as representatives of the whole Western church. Constantine was absent, being engaged in his first war with Licinius in Pannonia. Possibly Hosius may have been in attendance upon the emperor, as we learn from Eusebius (*Vit. Const.* ii. 4) that in this campaign Constantine took with him "the priests of God," for the benefit of their prayers and "to have them constantly about his person, as most trusty guardians of the soul." Traces exist of the presence of Hosius at the imperial court in 316, when the Donatists, having been condemned at the council in Nov. at Milan by the emperor himself, spread abroad a report, as we learn from Augustine (*cont. Ep. Parmen.* lib. i. c. 8, vol. ix. p. 43, ed. Migne), that by the advice of Hosius, a friend of Caecilian, the catholic bp. of Carthage, they had been condemned.

In the relations between Christianity and paganism there is ground for thinking that the position of Hosius at this time must have been somewhat of a representative one on the Christian side; otherwise it is difficult to understand why the emperor should have addressed to him a law declaring free such slaves as were emancipated in the presence of the bishops or clergy (A.D. 321; *Cod. Theod.* lib. iv. tit. 7, col. 379, Hänel's ed.). By the end of 323 Constantine had become sole master of the Roman empire in the East and West, and took measures for the re-establishment of religious concord throughout his dominions. To this end, says Socrates (*H. E.* i. 7), "he sent a letter to Alexander, bp. of Alexandria, and to Arius, by a trustworthy person named Hosius, who was bp. of Corduba in Spain, whom the emperor greatly loved and held in the highest estimation," urging them not to contend about matters of small importance (Eus. *Vit. Const.* ii. 63). That Hosius, a bishop of the Western church, and speaking only Latin, should be sent to a city in the East in which Greek civilization had reached its highest development is a striking proof of the high opinion that the emperor had of him. Moreover, his mission gave him precedence as an imperial commissioner over the bp. of Alexandria, whose see ranked next to that of Rome. It is not very clear what Hosius did at Alexandria, the accounts being very imperfect and confused. He apparently devoted himself with great earnestness to refuting the dogmas of Sabellius (Socr. *H. E.* iii. 7), but as to his steps with reference to Arius, history is silent. We know, however, that he failed to extinguish the flame which the Arians had lighted. Finding it impossible to terminate these controversies, he had to return to Constantine and acknowledge that his mission had failed. The emperor thereupon, probably by his advice (Sulpit. Sever. *Hist.* ii. 55, "Nicaena synodus auctore illo [Hosio] confecta habebatur"), resolved to convoke an oecumenical council and to invite bishops from all quarters. The council was held at Nicaea in 325. The part of Hosius in it has been much discussed. (1) Was he the president of the council, and if so (2) did he preside as legate of the pope? There is no doubt of his very prominent position. Unfortunately no complete account of the acts of the synod is extant, if such ever existed.

(1) Roman Catholic writers, such as Baronius, Nat. Alexander (vol. vii. p. 390), Fleury, Alzog, and Hefele (*Conc.* i. 39), maintain that he was president, but as the legate of the pope. They refer to Gelasius (lib. i. c. 5), who says, "Osius ex Hispanis, . . . Silvestri Episcopi maximae Romae locum obtinebat"—ἐπέχων καὶ τὸν τόπον, Mansi, ii. 806 D. There is a little ambiguity in these words. A man may occupy a place which rightly belongs to another, but it does not follow that he is his representative because he sits in his seat. At this

epoch, although the bp. of Rome held the first place among all his brethren, partly because Rome was the principal city in the world, yet his ecclesiastical jurisdiction does not appear to have extended beyond the churches of the ten provinces of Italy, called in the versio prisca of the 6th Nicene canon "suburbicaria loca." The churches of the East were mainly under the jurisdiction of the metropolitans of Alexandria or Antioch, and these great bishops would not brook the interference of their Western brethren. Moreover, the great strength of Christianity lay then in the East. The West was still imperfectly Christianized. It is difficult, therefore, to believe that Hosius presided at the council of Nicaea—an Eastern synod—as legate of the pope.

(2) But when we inquire why the usual order of precedence was departed from, we are a little at a loss for a satisfactory answer. Du Pin (*Nouv. Bib.* t. ii. pt. 2, p. 315) thought that Hosius presided because already acquainted with the question at issue and highly esteemed by the emperor. Similarly Schröckh (*Kirchengeschichte*, Thl. v. § 336). This seems the most probable explanation. It would be difficult to understand how the bishop of a see in Spain took precedence over the great patriarchs of the East if he had not been appointed by the emperor. Hosius was at the height of his reputation and enjoying the fullest confidence of his imperial master. He was, says Dean Stanley (*Eastern Church*, lect. iii.), "as the world-renowned Spaniard, an object of deeper interest to Christendom than any bp. of Rome could at that time have been." The power of the popes of Rome was not yet sufficiently consolidated for their claim to preside to have been admitted. Eleven years before, at the great council of the West at Arles in 314, the emperor appointed Marinus, bp. of Arles, to preside, while pope Silvester was represented there, as at Nicaea, by two presbyters and two deacons (cf. Hefele, *Conc.* i. 181). The council of Nicaea was convoked by Constantine, and there is good reason to believe that Hosius held the foremost place by his appointment. He is believed to have been the emperor's adviser in ecclesiastical matters. The part that Constantine, then only a catechumen, took in the proceedings at Nicaea shews that he must have received some instruction as to the debated questions from an orthodox teacher. It is very unlikely that he could have of himself given such a philosophical explanation of the Homoousion as he did (see the letter addressed by Eusebius to the Christians at Caesarea and preserved by Socrates, *H. E.* i. 8). Again, the emperor's letter to the churches respecting the council (Eus. *Vit. Const.* iii. 17-20) bears unmistakable traces of the hand of a theologian. Dean Milman (*Hist. of Christianity*, vol. ii. p. 364, crown 8vo ed.) calls the letter of Constantine to Arius and Alexander "in its spirit a model of temper and conciliation. It is probable that the hand of Hosius is to be traced in its composition. His influence was uniformly exercised in this manner. Wherever the edicts of the government were mild, conciliating, and humane, we find the bp. of Corduba."

At the conclusion of the council Hosius seems to have returned to Corduba. For nearly 20 years he lived in retirement in his own diocese. No trace of a return to the court of Constantine remains, and it does not appear that they ever met again. We must look to the history of the time for some explanation of the cause for these altered relations. Constantine left Asia Minor for Rome, which he reached *c.* July 326. His brief stay there was marked by deeds of cruelty. In the midst of the Vicennalia the people of Rome heard with regret that his son Crispus had been put to death. Not long afterwards the young Licinianus, his nephew, a boy of 12, was killed, at the suggestion, it is said, of the empress Fausta, whom retribution soon overtook. There followed a great number of public executions. The true causes of these events are involved in mystery, but Constantine is said to have become a prey to remorse. A great change certainly took place in his character after he became sole master of the Roman empire. He was spoiled by prosperity (Eutropius, lib. x. cc. 4, 6). He became arrogant and impatient of counsel, distrustful and suspicious. This moral deterioration was accompanied with great vacillation in his religious opinions. A few years after the council of Nicaea he fell under Arian influences. Arius was recalled; and at the instigation of Eusebius of Nicomedia and his adherents, Athanasius was condemned upon a false charge and banished to Gaul (A.D. 335). Not long before his death, in 337, Constantine received baptism from Eusebius of Nicomedia, an Arian bishop. This change in the character and opinions of Constantine was the true cause of his altered relations with Hosius. As the influence of the Arians over his mind increased, that of his old counsellor would of necessity decline.

Hosius does not appear to have been present at any of the synods between those of Nicaea and Sardica, nor to have taken any public part in the controversies between Athanasius and the Arians during 20 years. In 345 the emperor Constans summoned Athanasius to Milan from Rome, and informed him that he had been urged by certain bishops (believed to have been pope Julius, Hosius, and Maximinus of Trèves; cf. Hilar. *Frag.* 2, p. 16) to use his influence with his brother Constantius, that a council might be called to settle the questions concerning him, the place of meeting to be Sardica. Athanasius while in Milan was directed by Constans to go to Gaul to meet Hosius and travel with him to Sardica (Athan. *Apol. ad Const.* c. 4). Hosius was now nearly 90 years old. So long a journey implies considerable vigour of body, and that age had not changed his convictions nor impaired his zeal. Nor had his long retirement lessened his influence or the unbounded respect felt for him by his contemporaries. In the encyclical letter of the council of Sardica to be found in Athanasius (*Apol. contr. Arian.* c. 44), Hosius is spoken of as "one who on account of his age, his confession, and the many labours he had undergone, is worthy of all reverence." His presidency in this case is affirmed in express terms by Athanasius (*Hist. Arian.* c. 16): "The great Hosius was president of the council." The Acts shew him as the life and soul of the synod, proposing most of the canons and taking the foremost part in the proceedings. The synod afforded a great opportunity for his wisdom and conciliatory spirit. He specially sought to conciliate the Eusebian party, of which he writes to Constantine (*ib.* c. 44): "On my own account I challenged the enemies of Athanasius, when they came to the church where I generally was, to declare what they had against him. This I did once and again, requesting them if they were unwilling to appear before the whole council, yet to appear before me alone." The Eusebians, however, rejecting all overtures, held a synod of their own at Philippopolis, whence they sent an encyclical letter to the churches, condemning Hosius, Julius, bp. of Rome, and others, chiefly for holding communion with Athanasius. Hosius, they said, had also always been a persecutor of a certain Marcus of blessed memory, a strenuous defender of evil men, and a companion of wicked and abandoned persons in the East (Hilar. *Frag.* iii. t. ii. col. 674, ed. Migne).

Until 354 we hear nothing further of him. An extant letter written to him by pope Liberius, early in 354, shews the great respect in which he was held. Liberius writes, full of grief, because Vincentius of Capua, one of his legates in whom he had placed great confidence, at a synod consisting chiefly of the Eusebian party, held at Arles in 353, had consented under constraint to give up communion with Athanasius (*ib.* vi. t. ii. col. 688).

During his long life Hosius had preserved an unblemished name and been a consistent and uncompromising supporter of the Nicene faith. At length, when 100 years old, he gave way for a brief moment to the violence of his persecutors, and consented under torture to hold communion with Valens and Ursacius (Athan. *Hist. Arian.* 45), a concession which has been much magnified and misrepresented.

In 355 a synod was convoked by Constantius at Milan, which deserved, says Tillemont (*Mém.* t. vi. p. 362), the name of a robber synod even more than did the false council of Ephesus. At this synod the Eusebians first openly declared in favour of the dogmas of Arius, and endeavoured to secure their acceptance by the church. The emperor called upon the orthodox bishops, under penalty of banishment, to join in the condemnation of Athanasius. Most of them gave way, and consented to condemn Athanasius and to hold communion with the Arians (Rufinus, lib. i. c. 20). The few who stood firm were banished, bound with chains, to distant provinces: Dionysius, exarch of Milan, to Cappadocia, or Armenia; Lucifer to Syria; Eusebius of Vercelli into Palestine (cf. Athan. *Apol. Const.* 27). In 366 Liberius, bp. of Rome, was summoned to Milan, where Constantius was residing, and allowed three days to choose between signing the condemnation of Athanasius or going into exile. He chose the latter, and was banished to Beroea in Thrace. From the first the object of the Arians had been to gain the great Hosius. "As long as he escaped their wicked machinations they thought they had accomplished nothing. We have done everything, they said to Constantius. We have banished the bishop of the Romans, and before him a very great number of other bishops, and have filled every place with alarm. But these strong measures are as nothing, nor is our success at all more secure so long as Hosius remains. Begin then to persecute him also, and spare him not, ancient as he is. Our heresy knows not to honour the hoary hairs of the aged" (Athan. *Hist. Arian.* § 42). At their solicitation the emperor had previously summoned Hosius to Milan, *c.* A.D. 355. On his arrival he urged him to subscribe against Athanasius and hold communion with the Arians. The old man, full of grief that such a proposal should have been even made to him, would not for one moment listen to it. Severely rebuking the emperor and endeavouring to convince him of his error, he withdrew from the court and returned to his own country. Constantius wrote frequently, sometimes flattering, sometimes threatening him. "Be persuaded," he said, "and subscribe against Athanasius, for whoever subscribes against him thereby embraces with us the Arian cause." Hosius remained fearless and unmoved, and wrote a spirited answer to Constantius, preserved by Athanasius, the only extant composition by Hosius (*ib.* § 44). The emperor continued to threaten him severely, intending either to bring him over by force or to banish him, for, says Socrates (*H. E.* ii. 31) the Arians considered that this would give great authority to their opinions. Finding that Hosius would not subscribe, Constantius sent for him to Sirmium and detained him there a whole year. "Unmindful," says Athanasius (*l.c.*), "of his father's love for Hosius, without reverence for his great age, for he was then 100 years old, this patron of impiety and emperor of heresy used such violence towards the old man that at last, broken down by suffering, he was brought, though with reluctance, to hold communion with Valens and Ursacius, but he would not subscribe against Athanasius" (A.D. 357). He says elsewhere (*Apol. pro Fug.* § 7) that Hosius "yielded for a time to the Arians, as being old and infirm in body, and after repeated blows had been inflicted upon him above measure, and conspiracies formed against his kinsfolk." Socrates gives similar testimony (*l.c.*; cf. Newman, *Arians*, c. iv. § 3).

It is difficult to determine which of the confessions of faith drawn up at Sirmium was actually signed by Hosius. Whether there was only one synod of Sirmium, or two or three at intervals of a few years, is also a question upon which opinions have differed widely. The predominant opinion is expressed by Valesius in a note to Socrates (*H. E.* ii. 30), viz. that there were three synods there, each issuing a different creed. The first, in 351, at which Photinus was deposed, published a confession in Greek. At the second, in 357, Hosius was compelled to be present and his subscription was obtained by force to a creed written in Latin, called by Hilarius "blasphemia apud Sirmium per Osium et Potamium conscripta" (*Opp.* ed. Migne, t. ii. col. 487). The third Sirmian creed, called the "Dated Creed" from its naming the consuls, was agreed upon at a convention of bishops in May 359. This was the creed afterwards produced by Ursacius and Valens at the synod of Ariminum (cf. Athan. *de Synod.* 48). Socrates, indeed (*H. E.* ii. 30), says that three creeds were drawn up at the same synod of Sirmium as that which deposed Photinus (A.D. 351)—one in Greek and two in Latin—neither of which agreed together. But this is clearly an error. Sozomen says (*H. E.* iv. 12) that "Hosius had certainly, with the view of arresting the contention excited by Valens, Ursacius, and Germinius, consented, though by compulsion, with some other bishops at Sirmium to refrain from the use of the terms Homoousion and Homoiousion, because such terms do not occur in the Holy Scriptures and are beyond the understanding of men." These very expressions occur in the creed set forth at Sirmium in Latin, and afterwards translated into Greek, which Socrates gives (*l.c.*), and there is no room to doubt that this was the confession which Hosius signed.

It may be doubted, says Dean Stanley (*East. Ch.* lect. vii. c. 3), " whether in his own age the authority of Hosius in the theological world was not even higher than that of Athanasius." The Arians, therefore, would naturally make the most of the concession wrung from him. Those who constantly slandered Athanasius would not have many scruples about calumniating Hosius. Epiphanius (*Haer.* 73), about 20 years later, says that the Arians thought they could condemn the teaching of the church as to the Homoousion by producing letters fraudulently procured from the venerable Hosius, stating that the substance was dissimilar. Sozomen says (*H. E.* iv. 12) that Eudoxius, bp. of Antioch, *c.* 358, upheld the heresy of Aetius, that the Son is dissimilar to the Father, and rejected the terms Homoousion and Homoiousion. When he received the letter of Hosius he spread a report that Liberius had also made the same admission (iv. 15). These letters were most probably spurious. There is reason also to believe that the creed actually signed by Hosius was interpolated and sent into the East in his name. This may perhaps explain the expression of Hilarius (*contr. Constantium*, c. 23, col. 580, ed. Migne, vol. ii.) when he speaks of " deliramenta Osii et *incrementa* Ursacii et Valentis " (cf. Newman's notes to Athanasius, Eng. trans. vol. i. p. 162).

Exaggerated reports of the fall of Hosius were spread by the Arians far and wide. His perversion was their strongest argument against the Catholic party in Gaul. To this a contemporary writer, Phoebadius, bp. of Agennum, replies (*Lib. contra Arian.* c. 23, *Patr. Lat.* ed. Migne, vol. xx. col. 30) : " Novit enim mundus quae in hanc tenuerit aetatem qua constantia apud Sardicam et in Nicaeno tractatu assensus sit et damnaverit Arianos. . . . Si nonaginta fere annis male credidit, post nonaginta illum recte sentire non credam." The Donatists also, whose views Hosius had opposed equally strongly, did not fail to calumniate him. Augustine vindicates his memory (*Lib. contra Parmen.* lib. i. c. 4, § 7, ed. Migne, vol. ix. col. 38). Marcellus and Faustinus, two presbyters who were followers of Lucifer of Cagliari, relate (*Libellum ad Theodos. c.* 383 or 384) that on the return of Hosius to Spain, Gregory, bp. of Elvira, refused to hold communion with him, and as Hosius was in the act of pronouncing his deposition he was struck dumb and fell from his seat. It is very possible that the first part of the story may have had some foundation, as a letter is extant (Hilar. *Frag.* xii. t. ii. col. 713, ed. Migne) from Eusebius of Vercelli to Gregory of Spain (*c.* 360), congratulating him on having withstood the transgressor Hosius. Among ancient writers, no one has referred to the lapse of Hosius so bitterly as Hilary of Poictiers. This is the more remarkable as he had never heard of the Nicene Creed until he went into exile (Hilar. *de Syn.* c. 91, ad fin. vol. ii. col. 545, ed. Migne). He charges Hosius and Potamius, bp. of Lisbon, with having drawn up the second creed of Sirmium, which he designates in one place (*Opp.* ed. Migne, t. ii. col. 487) as the " blasphemia," in another (col. 599) as " deliramenta Osii"; and says (col. 539) that his fall was due to his having been too anxious to get away from Sirmium and die in his own country. These hard sayings occur in Hilary's treatise *de Synodis*, written probably in 358, a year after the second synod of Sirmium, at which Hosius was forced to be present. Hilary himself tells us (*de Syn.* c. 63, t. ii. col. 533) that the majority of those with whom he was then living in exile had no true acquaintance with God—in other words, held Arian opinions—" Ex majori parte Asianae decem provinciae intra quas consisto, vere Deum nesciunt." Whatever tidings came to him would therefore reach him through Arian channels. His means of information are not to be compared with those of Athanasius. He is, moreover, the only ancient writer who says that Hosius had any hand in the composition of the creed of the second council of Sirmium, and any combination between Hosius and Potamius, the reputed author with him of this confession, is for other reasons most improbable. The one had been all his life a consistent supporter of the Nicene Creed, the other a renegade. Moreover, Hosius at this time was about 100 years old. At such an age men do not willingly invent new creeds ; they are far more likely to cling tenaciously to old ones.

Sulpicius Severus (*c.* 404 or 405) speaks of the lapse of Hosius as resting on a popular rumour which seemed quite incredible unless extreme old age had enfeebled his powers and made him childish (*Hist. Sac.* lib. 2).

To clear his memory from the charges of Hilary it is sufficient to point out that the synod of Sardica spoke of Hosius as a man of a " happy old age, who, on account of his age, his confession, and the many labours he has undergone, is worthy of all reverence." So public a testimony to his high character is enough to silence all detraction, and the affectionate and reverential language in which the great Athanasius describes the passing frailty of his venerable friend, the father of the bishops, is very different from the furious and intemperate tone in which it is referred to by Hilary. " This true Hosius, and his blameless life," says Athanasius, " were known to all." As he relates the violence used towards him, he expresses only the tenderest commiseration for his friend ; but against Constantius, his persecutor, his indignation knows no bounds (*Hist. Arian.* 46).

There is some doubt whether Hosius succumbed to the violence used against him at Sirmium and died there in 357, or whether, after subscribing the Arian formula, he was permitted to end his days in Spain. This involves the further question—whether before his death he recanted, and was readmitted into the Catholic church, or retained his Arian opinions to the last. The story told by the Luciferians and the charges brought against his memory by his old enemies the Donatists serve at least to shew that, according to ecclesiastical tradition, he died in Spain. The question is fully examined by Baronius (sub ann. 357, cc. xxx.-xxxvii.), who does not believe the story told by the Luciferians. The story of the apostate Marcellinus is not confirmed by any contemporary writer. Had it been true, it must have been known to Athanasius, who says distinctly that Hosius yielded to the outrages of the Arians "for a time, as being old and infirm in body" (*Apol. pro Fug.* § 5), and that "at the approach of death, as it were by his last testament, he bore witness to the force which had been used towards him, and abjured the Arian heresy and gave strict charge that no one should receive it" (*Hist. Arian.* 45). These words prove that his lapse was but a temporary one, that he died in communion with the church, and in the midst of his friends. Hilary's words as to his anxiety to leave Sirmium and be buried in his own country imply that he obtained his wish to return to Spain. The date of his death is a little uncertain, but from Marcellinus we learn that it was soon after his return to Spain and before the concession he had made to the Arians had become widely known. As the treatise of Athanasius (*Hist. Arian.*) was written between 358 and 360, it must have been before that period. Some writers favour the end of 357; others think he lived till 359.

His profound acquaintance with Christian doctrine was combined with a singularly blameless and holy life. He seems to have had great tact and judgment and a conciliatory disposition. The shadow cast upon his name by the concession extorted from him by the Arians must not be allowed to obscure the rightful honour due to him for his labours and sufferings on behalf of the Catholic faith. "Even Christianity," says Dean Milman (*Hist. of Christianity*, vol. ii. p. 427, ed. 1875), "has no power over that mental imbecility which accompanies the decay of physical strength, and this act of feebleness ought not for an instant to be set against the unblemished virtue of a whole life."

A very full account of his life, and a discussion of various points in his history, will be found in Gams (*Die Kirchengesch. von Spanien*, Band ii. pp. 1-309, Regensburg, 1864). See also Hefele, *Conciliengesch.* vols. i. and ii., of which there is an Eng. trans.; Tillemont, *Mém.* t. vii. p. 300, 4to ed.; Dom Ceillier, *s.v.* t. iii. 392, new ed.; Zahn, *Const. der Gr. u. die Kirche*, 1876; Florez, *España Sagrada*, La Provincia de Bética, vol. ix. and x. (Madrid, 1754). [T.D.C.M.]

Hunneric (*Ugnericus, Hunerix, Honorichus*), eldest son and successor (Jan. 24, 477) of Genseric, king of the Vandals. Sent to Rome in his youth as a hostage for the observance of the treaty his father had made with Valentinian III., he married (462), after the sack of Rome, the captive Eudocia, eldest of the daughters of that emperor. Soon after he ascended the throne he ordered diligent search to be made for Manicheans, of whom he burnt many and exiled more across the sea, being commended for this by Victor. His subjects were oppressed with taxes and exactions, but he relaxed the strictness of his father's laws against the orthodox, and, at the intercession of his sister-in-law Placidia, the widow of the emperor Olybrius, and the emperor Zeno, allowed (A.D. 481) a bp. of Carthage (Eugenius) to be elected, the see having been vacant since the death of Deogratias in 457. He made this concession upon condition that a similar liberty should be allowed the Arian bishops and laity in Zeno's dominions, or else the newly elected bishops and all other orthodox bishops with their clergy would be banished to the Moors.

To secure the succession to his son, Hunneric sent his brother Theodoric into exile and put to death his wife and children. The Arian patriarch of Carthage, who was supposed to favour Theodoric, was burnt alive, and many of his clergy shared his fate or were thrown to wild beasts; nor did Hunneric spare the friends his father had commended to him on his death-bed if suspected of being inclined to support his brother. Hunneric now took measures against the orthodox. The influence of Eugenius on the Vandals was especially dreaded by the Arian clergy, at whose suggestion the king forbade him to preach in public or to allow persons in Vandal dress to enter Catholic churches. The bishop replied that the house of God was open to all. A great number of Catholics, being the king's servants, wore the Vandal dress. Men were therefore posted at the church doors with long rakes, with which any person entering in Vandal dress was seized by the hair as so to tear off hair and scalp together. Many died in consequence. Hunneric next deprived Catholics who held posts at the court or belonged to the army of their offices and pay; many of the former were forced to work in the fields near Utica and the latter were deprived of their property and exiled to Sicily or Sardinia. A law confiscating the property of deceased bishops and imposing a fine of 500 solidi on each new bishop was contemplated, but abandoned for fear of retaliatory measures against the Arians in the Eastern empire. Virgins were hung up naked with heavy weights attached to their feet, and their breasts and backs burnt with red-hot irons, to extort, if possible, a confession of immorality, which might be used against the bishops and clergy. Many expired under the torture and the survivors were maimed for life. A body of Catholic bishops, priests, deacons, and laity, numbering 4,976, was sent into banishment among the savage Moors of the desert. Victor gives a touching description of their sufferings during their marches by day and in crowded dens at night.

These cruelties were only the prelude of a more extensive and systematic persecution. Hunneric, on Ascension Day, 483, published an edict to Eugenius, and the other Catholic or, as he termed them, Homoousian bishops, ordering them to assemble at Carthage on Feb. 1, to meet the Arian bishops in conference and decide the points in controversy between them, promising them a safe-conduct. Even before the conference, however, the persecution began. Victor tells of various bishops cruelly beaten and sent into exile, while on Sept. 20, Laetus, bp. of Nepta, was burnt to terrify the rest of the Catholic party. When the meeting assembled, the Catholics were indignant to find Cyrila, the Arian patriarch, in the presidential chair. After mutual recriminations the orthodox presented a statement of their belief and their arguments for it. The Arians received it with indignation, as in it the orthodox claimed the name of Catholics, and falsely suggested to the king that the disturbance was the fault of their opponents. Hunneric seized this pretext for publishing, on Feb. 25, an edict he had already prepared and distributed to the magistrates throughout his dominions, ordering all churches of the orthodox party to be handed over with their endowments to the Arians, and further, after reciting the penalties imposed on the Donatists in 412 and 414 by edicts of Honorius (*Codex Theodosianus*, XVI. v. 52, 54), enacting that the Catholics should be subject to the same penalties and disabilities. Pardon was promised to those who should renounce Catholicism before June 1. Persecution, however, began before the three months' grace had expired. The first to suffer were the bishops assembled at Carthage. They were expelled from the town with nothing but the clothes they had on, and were obliged to beg their bread. The inhabitants were forbidden to give them shelter or food under pain of being burnt alive with their whole families. While outside the walls in this miserable state, they were summoned to meet at the Temple of Memory persons sent by the king, and were required to take an oath to support the succession of Hilderic, the king's son, and to hold no correspondence with countries beyond the sea. On these conditions the king promised to restore them their churches. Some took the oath, but others refused, excusing themselves by the precept "Swear not at all." They were then told to separate, the names and sees of the bishops of each party were taken down, and they were all sent to prison. A few days afterwards those who had taken the oath were told that, as they had infringed the precept of the Gospel, the king banished them to the country, assigning them land to cultivate, on condition that they should not chant, pray, baptize, ordain, or receive any into the church. To those who had refused was said, "You refused to swear because you did not wish our master's son to succeed him. Therefore you are exiled to Corsica, where you shall cut timber for our master's navy." Of the 466 attending the council, 88 fell away to Arianism; of the others one was a martyr, one a confessor, 46 were banished to Corsica, and the rest to the country parts of Africa.

Meanwhile throughout Africa a most cruel persecution raged, neither age nor sex being a protection; some were cruelly beaten, others hung, and some burnt alive. Noble ladies were stripped naked and tortured in the public streets. Victorian, a former proconsul of Carthage, was the most illustrious victim of the persecution. Victor's fifth book is full of accounts of the constancy and suffering of the Catholics. Eugenius was entrusted to the custody of the cruel Antonius, the Arian bp. of a city in Tripoli, where his hardships brought on a stroke of paralysis. Bp. Habetdeus was bound and gagged by Antonius and forced to undergo the rite of a second baptism, which was imposed also by force or fraud upon many of the orthodox. The Vandals, who had renounced Arianism, were treated with peculiar cruelty. Some had their eyes put out, others their hands, feet, noses, or ears cut off. Hunneric, to insult Uranius, and Zeno who had sent him to intercede for the Catholics, ordered some of the cruellest scenes of torture to be enacted in the streets through which he had to pass on his way to the palace.

The most celebrated event of the persecution occurred at Typasa, a seaport town of Mauritania. A former notary of Cyrila's having been consecrated as the Arian bishop of that town, the greater part of the citizens took ship to Spain. A few, not finding room on board, remained, whom the Arian bishop on his arrival endeavoured, first by persuasion and then by threats, to induce to become Arians. They refused, and having assembled in a house, began publicly to celebrate the divine mysteries. The bishop thereupon dispatched secretly to Carthage an accusation against them to the king, who sent an officer with orders to have their tongues cut out and their right hands cut off before the assembled province in the forum. This was done, but they continued to speak as plainly as before. This is attested by Victor, who was probably an eye-witness; by the eye-witnesses Aeneas of Gaza, the Platonic philosopher (*Theophrastus*, in Migne, *Patr. Gk.* lxxxv. 1000), Justinian (*Cod.* i. 27), and Marcellinus (*Chron.* in Migne, *Patr. Lat.* li. 933), all of whom had seen some of these persons at Constantinople; by Procopius (*de Bello Vandalico*, i. 8); Victor Tununensis (*Chron.* in Migne, *Patr. Lat.* lxviii. 946); and pope Gregory the Great (*Dial.* iii. 32 in Migne, *Patr. Lat.* lxxvii. 293), and has generally been considered not only a miracle, but the most remarkable one on record after apostolic times. The variety of the witnesses and the consistency of their testimony on all material points give it claims to belief, such as few apparently preternatural events possess. Dr. Middleton was the first to suggest (*Free Inquiry*, 313-316) that, assuming the account true, it by no means follows that the event was miraculous, a position he maintains by instances of a person born without a tongue, and of another who had lost it by disease, who were able to speak. Mr. Twistleton (*The Tongue not Essential to Speech*) has shewn this explanation probable. He gives numerous cases of similarly mutilated persons in Eastern countries, and of persons in England whose tongues had been removed by surgical operations, who could still pronounce distinctly all letters except *d* and *t*; one of the latter he had actually seen and conversed with. He sums up by saying: "The final result seems to be that questions connected with the phenomenon of speech in the African confessors are purely within the domain of natural science, and that there is no reason for asserting or suspecting any miraculous intervention in the matter." The persecution continued to rage till Hunneric died, on the following Dec. 11. Like the persecutor Galerius his body mortified, and bred worms.

Sources.—Victor Vitensis, *de Persecutione Vandalica*, ii. iv. and v. in Migne, *Patr. Lat.* lviii., with Ruinart's Appendix; *Procopius de Bello Vandalico*, i. 8; Appendix to Prosper's *Chron.* in Migne, *Patr. Lat.* li. 605; *Chron.* of Victor Tununensis in *ib.* lxviii. Gibbon (c. xxxvii.) gives a good narrative of the persecution, and Ceillier (*Auteurs sacrés*, x. 452-462) may also be consulted. [F.D.]

Hyginus (1), bp. of Rome after Telesphorus, probably from 137 to 141. Our early authorities for the dates and duration of his episcopate are confused, as in the case of other bishops of that early period. Anastasius (*Lib. Pontif*) says that he was a Greek, son of an Athenian philosopher, of unknown genealogy. Several spurious decretals are assigned to him. See *Mart. Rom.* under Jan. 11; also Lightfoot, on the Early Roman successions, *Apost. Fath.* part i. vol. i. [J.B—Y.]

Hypatia (1). Socrates (*H. E.* vii. 15) says: "There was a lady in Alexandria, by name Hypatia, daughter of the philosopher Theon. She advanced to such a point of mental culture as to surpass all the philosophers of her age and to receive the office of lecturer in the Platonic school, of which Plotinus had been the founder, and there expound all philosophic learning to any desirous of it. Students of philosophy came from all quarters to hear her. The dignified freedom of speech, which her training had implanted in her, enabled her to appear even before the public magistrates with entire modesty; none could feel ashamed to see her take her station in the midst of men. She was reverenced and admired even the more for it, by reason of the noble temperance of her disposition. This then was the woman upon whom malicious envy now made its attack. She was wont to have frequent communications with Orestes [the prefect]; this aroused enmity against her in the church community. The charge was that it was through her that Orestes was prevented from entering upon friendly relations with the bishop [Cyril]. Accordingly some passionate fanatics, led by Peter the Reader, conspired together and watched her as she was returning home from some journey, tore her from her chariot, and dragged her to the church called Caesarium; there they stripped her and killed her with oyster shells, and, having torn her in pieces, gathered together the limbs to a place called Cinaron, and consumed them with fire. This deed occasioned no small blame to Cyril and the Alexandrian church; for murders, fightings, and the like are wholly alien to those who are minded to follow the things of Christ. This event happened in the fourth year of the episcopate of Cyril, in the consulships of Honorius (for the tenth time) and Theodosius (for the sixth time) in the month of March, at the season of the fast" (*i.e.* Mar. 415). Little can be added to this. Synesius of Cyrene (afterwards bp. of Ptolemais) was a devoted disciple of hers. According to Suidas, she married Isidorus. No trustworthy account connects Cyril directly with her murder. [J.R.M.]

Hypatia (2). In the synodical book of the council of Ephesus is given a letter, from its style evidently the work of a female writer (unnamed), which is falsely attributed to Hypatia (1) the philosopher of Alexandria. It complains of the condemnation and banishment of Nestorius, which took place 17 years after the death of Hypatia. The writer is struck by the teaching of the Christians that God died for men; she founds her plea for Nestorius on an appeal to reason and Scripture. Baluze, *Concil. App.* p. 837 (Paris, 1683, fol.); Ceillier, viii. 387. [W.M.S.]

Hypatius (19), presbyter and hegumenus in the first half of the 5th cent. of the monastery in Bithynia, once presided over and afterwards abandoned by Rufinus. His Life, by Callinicus his disciple (Boll. *Acta SS.* 17 Jun. iii. 303), tells how his zeal brought him into collision with his lukewarm bishop Eulalius of Chalcedon. Understanding that Nestorius, before his formal accusation, was broaching novel opinions, Hypatius had the patriarch's name removed from the office books of the church adjoining his monastery (§§ 14, 38, 51, 53). Eulalius, alarmed at this daring act, which amounted to an excommunication of the all-powerful patriarch, remonstrated and threatened, but Hypatius undauntedly persisted. Again, when Leontius, the prefect of Constantinople, was about to re-establish at Chalcedon the Olympic games abolished by Constantine, Hypatius, finding that Eulalius would do nothing, openly declared that he would by main force defeat this restoration of idolatry at the head of his monks, though it should cost him his life. Leontius, having had warning of this opposition, relinquished the project and returned to Constantinople (§ 45). A certain ascetic archimandrite, Alexander, from Asia Minor, having taken up his abode in the capital with 100 monks, gained much reputation for sanctity, but in consequence of his bold rebukes of the imperial household was ordered to leave. The exiles betook themselves to the church of Hypatius, but Eulalius, obeying orders from the palace, had them beaten and expelled. Hypatius immediately welcomed them into his monastery and dressed their wounds. The bishop threatened fresh violence, but the rustic neighbours volunteered a defence, and a riot was imminent when a messenger from the empress ordered that they should not be molested. Alexander and his party retired in peace and founded a monastery near, the inmates bearing the name of Acoemetae, the Sleepless (§ 57; Acoemetae in *D. C. A.*, and the Bollandist account of their founder in *Acta SS.* Jan. i. 1018). [C.H.]

I

Ibas, bp. of Edessa *c* A.D. 435-457, a Syrian by birth. His name in Syriac is *Ihiba* or *Hiba* = Donatus. He appears first as a presbyter of the church of Edessa during the episcopate of Rabbulas, and warmly espousing the theological views which his bishop uncompromisingly opposed. He was an ardent admirer of the writings of Theodore of Mopsuestia, which he translated into Syriac and diligently disseminated through the East. The famous theological school of Edessa, of which, according to some accounts, Ibas was head, and to which the Christian youth from Persia and adjacent lands resorted for education, offered great facilities for this propagation of Theodore's tenets. The growing popularity of doctrines which appeared to him decidedly heretical caused Rabbulas much alarm, and he endeavoured to get Theodore's works anathematized and burnt. The church of Edessa was generally favourable to Theodore's teaching, and Ibas was supported by the majority against their bishop. He attended the council of Ephesus in 431 as a presbyter, was cognizant of Cyril's autocratic conduct (*Ep. ad Mar.*; Labbe, *Conc.* iv. 662), and wrote in 433 the letter to Maris, then or subsequently bp. of Hardaschir in Persia, to which subsequent events gave celebrity. Maris had been at Edessa previous to the Nestorian controversy, and Ibas wrote this letter to tell him what had occurred since his visit. Though evidently written under great exasperation, it shews Ibas as a man of independent judgment, free from party spirit. Nestorius is severely censured in it for refusing the title θεοτόκος to the Virgin, and Ibas accuses Cyril of Apollinarianism, and denounces the heresy of his 12 chapters, charging him with maintaining the perfect identity of the manhood and Godhead in Christ, and denying the Catholic doctrine of the union of two Natures in One Person (Labbe, iv. 661, v. 510). Rabbulas dying in 435 or 436, a reactionary wave made Ibas his successor. This was very distasteful to those who held the strong anti-Nestorian views of their late bishop, and they speedily planned to secure his deposition, by spreading charges against him of openly preaching heretical doctrines. The accusations soon reached the ears of Theodosius II. and Proclus, patriarch of Constantinople. To Proclus the matter appeared so serious that towards the close of 437 he wrote to John of Antioch, as the leading prelate of the East, though really having no canonical jurisdiction over Osrhoene, begging him to persuade Ibas, if innocent, to remove the scandal by condemning publicly certain propositions chiefly drawn from Theodore's writings against the errors of Nestorius. The same demand was made by Proclus of all the Eastern bishops; but Ibas and the bishops generally refused to condemn Theodore's propositions (*ib.* v. 511-514). Though foiled so far, the malcontents at Edessa maintained their hostile attitude to their bishop. Their leaders were four presbyters, Samuel, Cyrus, Eulogius, and Maras, acting at the instigation of one of Ibas's own suffragans, Uranius, bp. of Himeria, a pronounced Eutychian. Domnus, who had in 442 succeeded his uncle John as bp. of Antioch, visiting Hierapolis for the enthronization of the new bp. Stephen, the conspirators chose that moment for action. Cyrus and Eulogius formally laid before Domnus the accusation against Ibas, signed by about 17 clergy of Edessa, and supported by 30 (*ib.* iv. 658). Ibas, when starting for Hierapolis to pay his respects to Domnus, heard of the accusation, and at once summoned his clergy, pronounced excommunication on Cyrus and Eulogius as calumniators, threatened the same treatment to all who participated in their proceedings. No immediate step seems to have followed the presentation of the libel. In 445 Ibas was summoned by Domnus to the synod held at Antioch in the matter of Athanasius of Perrha, but he excused himself by letter (*ib.* iv. 739). The sympathies of Domnus inclined to Ibas, and he shewed no readiness to entertain the charges brought against him. At last, in Lent 448, the four chief delators presented their indictment before Domnus and the council of the East in a manner too formal to be neglected. Domnus consequently summoned Ibas to appear before him after Easter to answer the charges. The council was held at Antioch, and was attended by only a few bishops. The existing Acts bear only nine signatures (*ib.* iv. 643). Ibas in person answered the 18 charges, mostly of a frivolous character and destitute of proof: *e.g.* that he had appropriated a jewelled chalice to his own use; that the wine at the Eucharist was inferior in quality and quantity; the malversation of sums given for the ransom of captives; simoniacal ordinations and the admission of unfit persons to the ministry and episcopate, especially his nephew Daniel, stated to be a scandalous person, whom he had made bp. of Charrae. The most weighty charges were that he had anathematized Cyril and charged him with heresy; that he was a Nestorian; and especially that at Easter 445, in the presence of his clergy, he had spoken the blasphemous words, "I do not envy Christ His becoming God, for I can become God nc less than He." "This is the day that Jesus Christ became God" (*ib.* iv. 647-654; Liberat. c. 12). The first charge he acknowledged, the others he indignantly repudiated as base slanders. Only two of the accusers appeared. Samuel and Cyrus had gone to Constantinople, in defiance of the terms on which the excommunication had been taken off, to lay their complaint before the emperor and patriarch, the favourable feeling of Domnus towards the accused being too evident for them to hope for an impartial trial. Domnus and the council declined to proceed in the absence of the chief witnesses, and the case seemed to be postponed indefinitely (Labbe, iv. 642 seq.; Theod. *Ep.* 111). Eulogius and Maras, thereupon, hastened to join their fellow-conspirators at Constantinople, where they found a powerful party strongly hostile to the Eastern bishops, Theodoret in particular. Their faction was soon strengthened by the arrival of Uranius, the prime mover of the whole cabal, and half a dozen more Edessene clergy. The emperor and Flavian, who had succeeded Proclus as patriarch, listened to their complaints, but declined to hear them officially. The case was remitted to the East, and by an imperial commission, dated Oct. 26, 448, Uranius of Himeria, Photius of Tyre, just elected Sept. 9, 448, on the deposition of Irenaeus, and Eustathius of Berytus were deputed to hear it, and Damascius, the tribune and secretary of state, was dispatched as imperial commissioner. The whole proceeding was manifestly illegal. It was contrary to the canons that bishops should be subjected to the judgment of other bishops, two belonging to another province, on the strength of an imperial decree. No one, however, protested. The imperial power was regarded as absolute. The tribunal also was grossly unfair. One of the three judges, Uranius, was ringleader of the movement against Ibas; the other two had obtained their sees by the instrumentality of Uranius (Martin, *Le Brigandage d'Ephèse*, pp. 118-120). Tyre was named as the place of trial. The exasperation stirred up there by the blasphemies charged against Ibas was so great that it was thought politic to remove the trial to Berytus to avoid disturbances (Labbe, iv. 636). The court sat in the hall of Eustathius's episcopal residence. The indictment was produced by Ibas's accusers. Ibas laid before his judges a memorial signed by many of his clergy, denying that he had ever uttered the alleged blasphemies (*ib.* iv. 667-671). Only three witnesses supported the accusation, and brought forward a copy of the celebrated letter to Maris (*ib.* iv. 659-662). The commissioners, avoiding any judicial decision, brought about a friendly arrangement. His enemies agreed to withdraw their accusations on Ibas promising that he would forget the past, regard his accusers as his children, and remit any fresh difficulty for settlement to Domnus; and that, to avoid suspicion of malversation, the church revenues of Edessa should be administered, like those of Antioch, by oeconomi. Ibas gave equal satisfaction on theological points. He engaged to publicly anathematize Nestorius and all who thought with him on his return, and declared the identity of his doctrine with that agreed upon by John and Cyril, and that he accepted the decrees of Ephesus equally with those of Nicaea as due to the inspiration of the Holy Spirit. The concordat was signed, Uranius alone dissenting, Feb. 25, 449 (*ib.* iv. 630-648). The truce had no elements of permanence, and a very few weeks saw it broken. The Eutychian party, resolved on the ruin of Ibas and irritated at their failure at Berytus, left no stone unturned to overthrow it. All-powerful at Constantinople through the intrigues of Chrysaphius, Dioscorus and his partisans easily obtained from the feeble emperor, indignant at the condemnation of Eutyches, an edict summoning a general council at Ephesus for Aug. 1, 449. Reports diligently spread in Edessa during his absence of Ibas's heterodoxy made his reception so unfavourable that he was obliged to leave the town and call upon the "magister militiae" for a guard to protect him. He soon discovered that all appeal to the civil power was idle; he was regarded as a public enemy to be crushed at all hazards. The count Chaereas as civil governor of Osrhoene, but with secret instructions from Constantinople emanating from Chrysaphius and Eutyches, was deputed to arrest and imprison him and reopen the suit. When Chaereas entered Edessa, Apr. 12, 449, to commence the trial, he was met by a turbulent body of abbats and monks and their partisans, clamouring furiously for the immediate expulsion and condemnation of Ibas and his Nestorian crew. Ibas was "a second Judas," "an adversary of Christ," an "offshoot of Pharaoh." "To the fire with him and all his race." Two days later the inquiry began in the absence of Ibas amid violent interruptions. All Edessa knew that Chaereas had come merely to ratify under the colour of judicial proceedings a sentence of condemnation already passed. Chaereas, however, was moving too slowly for their hatred, and on Sun. Apr. 17 the excitement in church was so violent that the count was compelled to promise that the verdict of the synod of Berytus should be reviewed and a new investigation commenced. This began on Apr. 18; all the old charges were reproduced by the same accusers, amid wild yells of "Ibas to the gallows, to the mines, to the circus, to exile" drowning every attempt at explanation or defence. Chaereas, as had been predetermined, addressed a report to the imperial government, declaring the charges proved; and on June 27 the emperor, acknowledging the receipt of the document, ordered that a bishop who would command the confidence of the faithful should be substituted for Ibas (Perry, *The Second Synod of Ephesus*; Martin, *u.s.* t. ii. c. ix.). Only a legally constituted synod could depose him, but meanwhile his enemies' malice could be gratified by his maltreatment. He was forbidden to enter Edessa, apprehended and treated as the vilest of criminals, dragged about from province to province, changing his quarters 40 times and being in 20 different prisons (Labbe, iv. 634; Liberat. c. 12; Facund. lib. vi. c. 1). The council of Ephesus, so notorious for its scandalous violence, which gained for it, from Leo the Great (*Ep.* 95), the title of the "Gang of Robbers," opened on Aug. 3. One of its objects was to get rid finally of Ibas. This was the work of the second session, held on Aug. 22. Ibas was not cited to appear, being then in prison at Antioch (Labbe, iv. 626, 634). Before the witnesses were allowed to enter, the three bishops who had conducted the investigation at Tyre and Berytus were asked for an account of their proceedings. Instead of declaring the fact that, after examination made, they had acquitted Ibas, they made pitiful excuses as to their inability to arrive at the truth from the distance of the place of trial to Edessa, and endeavoured to shift the burden by saying that an investigation had subsequently been held at Edessa itself, which had received the approbation of the emperor, and that the wisest course for the council would be to inquire what was the decision there. This advice was followed. The monks of Edessa and the other parties to the indictment were admitted, and the whole of the depositions and correspondence read to the assembly. As the reading of the document ended, wild maledictions burst forth, invoking every kind of vengeance, temporal and eternal, on the head of this "second Iscariot," this "veritable Satan." "Nestorius and Ibas should be burnt alive together. The destruction of the two would be the deliverance of the world." Eulogius, the presbyter of Edessa, who had been one of the first accusers of Ibas before Domnus, followed with a summary of the proceedings from their commencement, specifying all the real or supposed crimes laid to his charge. The question of deposition was put to the council, and carried *nem. con.* Among those who voted for it were Eustathius of Berytus and Photius of Tyre, who had previously acquitted him ont he same evidence. The sentence was that he should be deposed from the episcopate and priesthood, deprived even of lay communion, and compelled to restore the money of which it was pretended he had robbed the poor. Ibas, twice acquitted, was condemned without being heard or even summoned; and no protest was raised in his favour, even by those who, a few months before, had given him their suffrage (Martin, *u.s.* t. iii. c. ii. p. 181; Labbe, iv. 674; *Chron. Edess.* anno 756; Assemani, *Bibl. Or.* i. 202). We have no certain knowledge of what befel Ibas on his deposition. At the beginning of 451 the deposed and banished bishops were allowed to return from exile, but the question of their restoration was reserved for the fourth general council which met at Chalcedon A.D. 451. In the 9th session, Oct. 26, the case of Ibas came before the assembled bishops. On his demand to be restored in accordance with the verdict of Photius and Eustathius at Berytus and Tyre, the Acts of that synod were read, and the next day the pope's legates gave their opinion that Ibas, being unlawfully deposed, should be at once restored. After much discussion this was carried unanimously. The legates led the way, declaring his letter to Maris orthodox, and commanding his restitution. All the prelates agreed in this verdict, the condition being that he should anathematize Nestorius and Eutyches and accept the tome of Leo. Ibas consented without any difficulty. "He had anathematized Nestorius already in his writings, and would do so again ten thousand times, together with Eutyches and all who teach the One Nature, and would accept all that the council holds as truth." On this he was unanimously absolved, restored to his episcopal dignity, and voted as bp. of Edessa at the subsequent sessions (Labbe, iv. 793, 799; Facund. lib. v. c. 3). Nonnus, who had been chosen bishop on his deposition, being legitimately ordained, was allowed to retain his episcopal rank, and on Ibas's death, Oct. 28, 457, quietly succeeded him as metropolitan (Labbe, iv. 891, 917). The fiction that Ibas had disowned the letter to Maris at Chalcedon (Greg. Magn. lib. viii. *Ep.* 14), as he was asserted by Justinian to have done before at Berytus, as having been forged in his name, is thoroughly disproved by Facundus (lib. v. c. 2, lib. vii. c. 5). A controversy concerning his letter to Maris arose in the next century, in the notorious dispute about the "Three Articles," when the letter was branded as heterodox (together with the works of Theodore of Mopsuestia and Theodoret's writings in favour of Nestorius) in the edict of Justinian, and was formally condemned in 553 by the fifth general council, which pronounced an anathema, in bold defiance of historical fact, against all who should pretend that it and the other documents impugned had been recognized as orthodox by the council of Chalcedon (Evagr. *H. E.* iv. 38; Labbe, v. 562-567). Ibas is anathematized by the Jacobites as a Nestorian (Assemani, t. i. p. 202). According to the *Chronicle* of Edessa, Ibas, during his episcopate, erected the new church of the Apostles at Edessa, to which a senator gave a silver table of 720 lb. weight, and Anatolius, praefectus militum, a silver coffer to receive the relics of St. Thomas the Apostle, who was said, after preaching in Parthia, to have been buried there (Socr. *H. E.* iv. 18).

Ibas was a translator and disseminator of the writings of others rather than an original author. His translations of the theological works of Theodore of Mopsuestia, Diodorus of Tarsus, Theodoret, and Nestorius, were actively spread through Syria, Persia, and the East, and were very influential in fostering the Nestorian tenets which have, even to the present day, characterized the Christians of those regions. His influence was permanent in the celebrated theological school of Edessa, in spite of the efforts of Nonnus to eradicate it, until its final overthrow and the banishment of its teachers to Persia. Tillem. *Mém. eccl.* t. xv.; Assemani, *Bibl. Orient.* t. i. pp. 199 seq., t. iii. pp. 70-74; Cave, *Hist. Lit.* t. i. p. 426; Facund. *Defens. Trium. Capitul.*; Schröckh, xv. 438, xviii. 307-311; Perry, *Acts of the Second Council of Ephesus*; Abbé Martin, *Actes du Brigandage d'Ephèse*; *Le Pseudo-synode d'Ephèse.* [E.V.]

Idatius (3) (*Idacius*; surnamed *Lemicensis*), bp. of Aquae Flaviae (Chaves or Chiaves) in Gallicia, from *c.* 427 to 470, and author of a well-known *Chronicle* which was one of the various continuations of Jerome. Our only sources for his life are notices in his own work, for the meagre Life by Isidore in *de Vir. Ill.* c. ix. is merely a summary of Idatius's own prologue. The existing material was elaborately sifted and put together by Florez (*Esp. Sagr.* iv., Madrid, 1749), and less completely by Garzon, whose ed. of Idatius was pub. at Brussels in 1845 by P. F. X. de Ram.

Birthplace and Bishopric.—Idatius tells us in the prologue to his *Chronicle* that he was born "in Lemica civitate," "Lemica" being a copyist's error for Limica in Portugal. He was born *c.* 388, shortly after the execution of Priscillian and his companions at Trèves, and about the time when, as he tells us in his *Chronicle* (ad. ann. 386), the Priscillianists, falling back on Spain after the death of their chief, took a special hold on the province of Gallicia. About A.D. 400 he was in Egypt and Palestine, where, as he says (Prolog. and *Chron.* ad ann. 435), he, "et infantulus et pupillus," saw St. Jerome at Bethlehem, John bp. of Jerusalem, Eulogius of Caesarea, and Theophilus of Alexandria. His return to Gallicia may be dated *c.* 402 (Florez, *Esp. Sagr.* iv. 301). In 416, seven years after the irruption of the Suevi, Alani, and Vandals into the peninsula, Idatius entered the ministry, for so we must understand the entry in the *Chron. Parvum* (see below) under that year, "Idatii conversio ad Dominum peccatoris" (cf. Florez, *l.c.* p. 302), and in 427 he was made bishop (see Prol. *Esp. Sagr.* iv. 348). In 431 the rule of the Suevi had become so intolerable that Idatius was sent by the Gallician provincials to Aetius in Gaul to ask for help. He returned in 432, accompanied by the legate Censorius, after whose departure from Gallicia the bishops persuaded Hermeric, the Suevian king, to make peace with the provincials. For about 24 years Gallicia enjoyed tranquillity compared with the rest of Spain, and the Gallician bishops found themselves to some extent free to deal with the prevalent Priscillianist and Manichean doctrines, which had even infected some of the episcopate (*Ep. Leo Magn. ad Turribium*; Tejada y Ramiro, *Colecc. de Can.* etc. ii. p. 889). Between 441 and 447 must be placed the letter of Turribius to Idatius and Ceponius (? bp. of Tuy) on the Priscillianist apocryphal books (*Esp. Sagr.* xvi. 95; Tejada y Ramiro, ii. 887). In 444-445, the confessions of certain Roman Manicheans having disclosed the names of their co-believers in the provinces, letters were sent to the provinces by pope Leo warning the bishops (Prosper ad ann. 444; see Garzon's note 6, ed. De Ram, p. 83). Accordingly we find Idatius and Turribius in 445 holding a trial of certain Manicheans discovered at Astorga, no doubt by aid of the papal letters, and forwarding a report of the trial to the neighbouring metropolitan of Merida, evidently to put him on his guard. In 447, in answer to various documents from St. Turribius on the Gallician heresies, Leo sent a long decretal letter to Spain to be circulated by him, urging the assembly of a national council, or at least of a Gallician synod, in which, by the efforts of Turribius and of Idatius and Ceponius, "fratres vestri," a remedy might be devised for the prevailing disorder. Probably the synod never actually met, for Idatius's *Chronicle*, which rarely omits any ecclesiastical news he could give, does not mention it.

In the troubled times after the flight and execution of Rekiar, Idatius fell a victim to the disorders of the country. His capture at Aquae Flaviae by Frumari (July 26, 460) was owing mostly, no doubt, to his importance as a leader and representative of the Roman population, but partly, perhaps, as Florez suggests, to the hatred of certain Gallician Priscillianist informers (their names are Latin; cf. *Chron.* ad ann.) who had felt the weight of his authority. He was released in 3 months, and after his return to Chiaves lived at least 8 years under the Suevian kingdom which he had too hastily declared to be "destructum et finitum" in 456 (? "*pene* destructum," as Isidore, his copyist in *Hist. Suevorum*, eod. loc.), but which took a new lease, on Frumari's death (464), under Remismund. His *Chronicle* ends with 469, and he must have died before 474, the year of the emperor Leo's death, under whom Isidore places that of Idatius (*Esp. Sagr.* iv. 303, ed. De Ram, pp. 15, 39).

Chronicle.—The prologue to the *Chronicle*, composed apparently after its completion, at any rate in the extreme old age of its author, gives a full account of its intention, sources, and arrangement. It was intended to continue the *Chronicle* of Eusebius and Jerome, Idatius including his own works in one vol. with theirs (ed. De Ram, p. 48, note 3, and p. 59, note 4), and he divides it into two parts, the first starting from 379, where Jerome breaks off, and ending 427, when Idatius was made bishop; the second extending from 427 to the end. In the first division Sulpicius and Orosius seem to have been his main authorities, together with the works of SS. Augustine and Jerome (*Esp. Sagr.* iv. 335, 356), and the lives and writings of certain contemporary bishops (John of Jerusalem, *l.c.* 357, Paulinus of Beziers, *ib.*, Paulinus of Nola, 358, etc.). "Thenceforward" (*i.e.* from 427), he says, describing his second division, "I, undeservedly chosen to the office of the episcopate, and not ignorant of all the troubles of this miserable time, have added both the falling landmarks ('metas ruituras') of the oppressed Roman empire, and also what is more mournful still, the degenerate condition of the church order within Gallicia, which is the end of the world, the destruction of honest liberty by indiscriminate appointments (to bishoprics), and the almost universal decay of the divine discipline of religion, evils springing from the rule of furious men and the tumults of hostile nations." This is the note of the whole *Chronicle*, which gives a vivid and invaluable picture of one most important scene in the great drama of the fall of the Western empire, and without which we should be almost in the dark as to events of the first half of the 5th cent. in Spain. Idatius describes the entry of the Vandals, Alani, and Suevi into the Peninsula in Oct. 409, and the two following years of indiscriminate pillage and ruin before the division of the country by lot amongst the invaders.

The *Chronicle* altogether embraces 91 years. On the chronology of the last five years and on possible interpolations of certain chronological notes by the copyist, see ed. De Ram, p. 39, also Florez, iv. 310.

The Fasti Idatiani were first attributed to Idatius by Sirmond, partly because in the ancient MS. from which he printed the *Chronicle* the *Fasti* followed immediately, and partly because he believed that there was strong internal evidence for the Idatian authorship (*Op.* 1728, ii. 287). This opinion has been generally adopted, notably by Dr. Mommsen (*Corpus Inscr. Lat.* i. 484). Florez is an exception, but his grounds are extremely slight (see *Esp. Sagr.* iv. 457, and Garzon's answer, ed. De Ram, p. 41). The history of the *Fasti* has now been cleared up with great learning and acuteness by Holder-Egger in the *Neues Archiv der Gesellschaft für ältere Deutsche Geschichtskunde*, ii. pp. 59-71. His general conclusions are (1) that the *Fasti Idatiani* are one of two derivatives of certain consular Fasti put together at Constantinople in 4th cent., the *Chronicon Paschale* (Migne, *Patr. Gk.* xcii.) being the other. (2) That the common source of the *Fasti* and of the *Chron. Pasch.* was itself compiled at Constantinople from older Roman Fasti, such as are still preserved in the Chronographus of 354 (Mommsen, *op. cit.* i. 483; Wattenbach, *Deutschlands Geschichtsquellen*, p. 48), the notices peculiar to Constantinople beginning from 330, when Byzantium became the second capital of the empire. (3) That after 390-395, when the *Chron. Pasch.* branches off from the *Fasti Idatiani*, a copy of the Constantinople Fasti came westward, received certain additions in Italy and then reached Spain, where a Spanish reviser and continuator gave them the shape under which we now know them as the *Fasti Idatiani*. That Idatius the author of the *Chronicle* revised the *Fasti* Holder-Egger does not believe, but is inclined to hold that their agreement is best explained by the theory that Idatius *used* but did not compose the *Fasti*. His arguments on this point seem scarcely conclusive, and he is indeed prepared to admit that *certain* trifling additions to and alterations in the *Fasti* were probably made by Idatius. For the latter use of the *Fasti Idatiani*, the East Roman Fasti as the Ravenna annals are the West Roman Fasti (Wattenbach, i. 49), see Holder-Egger's art. *Die Chronik des Marcellinus Comes und der Oströmischen Fasten, Neues Archiv*, etc. ii. 44.

The *Chronicon Parvum Idatii* is the work of an unskilful abbreviator of the larger *Chronicle*, who adds a continuation to the time of Justinian. It must not be confused with the *excerpta* from Idatius made under Charles the Great.

Besides the references already given see Adolf Ebert, *Allgemeine Gesch. der Litt. des Mittelalters im Abendlande*, i. 1874; Teuffel, *Gesch. der Römischen Litt.* 1875. [M.A.W.]

Ignatius (1), St. (called *Theophorus*), Oct. 17, the 2nd bp. of Antioch (*c.* 70-*c.* 107), between Evodius and Hero. He is sometimes reckoned the 3rd bishop, St. Peter being reckoned the first (Bosch, *Pat. Ant.* in Boll. *Acta SS.* Jul. iv. introd. p. 8; Le Quien, *Or. Chr.* ii. 700).

The question of the life and writings of Ignatius, including the connected subject of the Ep. of Polycarp to the Philippians, has been described by M. Renan as the most difficult in early Christian history next to that of the fourth gospel.

I. About 165 Lucian in his satire *de Morte Peregrini* relates (cc. 14-41) that Peregrinus was made a prisoner in Syria. The Christians of Asia Minor sent messengers and money to him according to their usual custom when persons were imprisoned for their faith. Peregrinus wrote letters to all the more important cities, forwarding these by messengers whom he appointed (ἐχειροτόνησε) and entitled νεκραγγέλους and νερτεροδρόμους. The coincidence of this *story* with that of Ignatius, as told afterwards by Eusebius, would be alone a strong evidence of connexion. The similarity of the *expressions* with the πρέπει χειροτονῆσαί τινα ὃς δυνήσεται θεοδρόμος καλεῖσθαι of *ad Pol.* vii. would, if the words stood alone, make it almost certain that Lucian was mimicking the words of the epistle. These two probabilities lead us to believe that the composition was by one acquainted with the story and even some of the letters of Ignatius. (Renan, i. 38; Zahn, i. 517; Pearson, i. 2; Denzinger, 85; Lightfoot, ii. See *Authorities* at the foot of this art.)

Theophilus, bp. of Antioch (fl. before 167), has a coincidence with Ignat. *ad Eph.* xix. 1, where the virginity of Mary is said to have been concealed from the devil. Irenaeus, *c.* 180 (*adv. Haer.* iii. 3, 4), bears witness that Polycarp wrote to the Philippians, and (v. 28) mentions how a Christian martyr said, "I am the bread-corn of Christ, to be ground by the teeth of beasts that I may be found pure bread"—words found in Ignat. *ad Rom.* iv. 1. The passage of Irenaeus is quoted by Eusebius (*H. E.* iii. 36) as a testimony to Ignatius. Origen, early in 3rd cent., *Prol. in Cant.* (*Op.* ed. Delarue, iii. 30), writes, "I remember also that one of the saints, by name Ignatius, said of Christ, 'My love was crucified'"—words found in Ignat. *ad Rom.* vii. 2. Origen also (*Hom. in Luc.* vol. iii. 938) says, "I find it well written in one of the epistles of a certain martyr, I mean Ignatius, 2nd bp. of Antioch after Peter, who in the persecution fought with beasts at Rome, that the virginity of Mary escaped the prince of this world" (Ignat. *ad Eph.* xix. 1).

Eusebius, early in 4th cent., gives a full account which explains these fragmentary allusions and quotations. In his *Chronicle* he twice names Ignatius as 2nd bp. of Antioch after the apostles; in one case adding that he was martyred. In his *Ecclesiastical History*, besides less important notices of our saint and of Polycarp, he relates (iii. 22, 37, 38, iv. 14, 15) how Ignatius, whom he calls very celebrated among the Christians, was sent from Syria to Rome to be cast to the beasts for Christ's sake. When journeying under guard through Asia he addressed to the cities near places of his sojourn exhortations and epistles. Thus in Smyrna, the city of Polycarp, he wrote to Ephesus, Magnesia, and Tralles. He wrote to the Romans, begging them not to impede his martyrdom. Of this epistle Eusebius appends § v. at length. Then he tells how Ignatius, having left Smyrna and come to Troas, wrote thence to the Philadelphians and Smyrnaeans and to Polycarp. One sentence from *Smyr.* iii. Eusebius copies as containing a saying of Christ not otherwise handed down. The *Apostolical Constitutions*, in their uninterpolated form as known to us through the Syriac trans. of the *Didascalia*, in several places coincide very strikingly with the shorter Greek or 7 Vossian epistles. An epistle which passes under the name of Athanasius, and which if not by him is by a contemporary writer, quotes a passage from *ad Eph.* vii. 2, as written by Ignatius, who after the apostles was bp. of Antioch and a martyr of Christ. (See, as to the genuineness of this epistle, Cureton, lxviii.; Zahn, i. 578.) St. Basil (ed. Ben. ii. 598) quotes, without naming Ignatius, the familiar sentence from *ad Eph.* xix. 1, concerning Satan's ignorance of the virginity of Mary. St. Jerome's testimony is dependent on that of Eusebius. St. Chrysostom (*Op.* vol. ii. 592) has a homily on St. Ignatius which relates that he was appointed by the apostles bp. of Antioch; was sent for to Rome in a time of persecution to be there judged; instructed and admonished with wonderful power all the cities on the way, and Rome itself when he arrived; was condemned and martyred in the Roman theatre crying, Ἐγὼ τῶν θηρίων ἐκείνων ὀναίμην; and his remains were transferred after death with great solemnity to Antioch. (Zahn [i. 33-49] does not believe that the genuine writings of Chrysostom shew that he was acquainted with the writings of Ignatius. But see the other side powerfully argued by Pearson, i. 9; Denzinger, 90; Lipsius, ii. 21.) Theodoret frequently cites the 7 Vossian epistles, and mentions Ignatius as ordained by St. Peter and made the food of beasts for the testimony of Christ. Severus, patriarch of Antioch (513-551), has a long catalogue of sayings from Ignatius, in which every one of the 7 epistles is laid under contribution. These are to be found in Syr. in Cureton, in Gk. in Zahn (ii. 352). Cureton furnishes also a large collection of Syriac fragments, in which passages taken from the 7 Vossian epistles are declared to have the force of canons in the church.

II. We possess also a multitude of Acts of the martyrdom of St. Ignatius, which, if we could accept them, would supply very particular accounts of his life and death. Of these Ussher published 3 in whole or part: one in Lat. from two related MSS.; another in Lat. from the Cottonian library; a third in Gk. from a MS. at Oxford. The Bollandists published a Latin martyrdom in the *Acta SS.* for Feb. 1; Cotelerius a Gk. one by Symeon Metaphrastes. Ruinart, and afterwards Jacobson (*Pat. Ap.* ii.), printed a Gk. MS. from the Colbertine collection (MS. Colb.); J. S. Assemani found a Syriac one which may be the same as that partly printed by Cureton (i.). Aucher, and afterwards Petermann (p. 496), published an Armenian one. Dressel printed a Gk. version of the 10th cent. (MS. Vat.). The 9 are reducible to 5, possessing each a certain independence. But of these MS. Colb. and MS. Vat. are by far the most valuable, being completely independent, while the remaining versions are mixtures of these two.

MS. Colb. (see Zahn, ii. p. 301) relates the condemnation of Ignatius by Trajan in Antioch, and incorporates the Ep. to the Romans. This MS. bears marks of interpolation, and its chief value lies in its incorporation of the Ep. to the Romans. The other epistles the author of the MS. has not read carefully. We conclude that this martyrdom, written in the 4th cent., assumed its present form after the first half of the 5th.

MS. Vat. (Zahn, ii. 307) omits all judicial proceedings in Antioch. Ignatius is sent for by Trajan to Rome, as a teacher dangerous to the state; an argument takes place before the senate between the emperor and the saint; the lions kill him, but leave the body untouched, and it remains as a sacred deposit at Rome. Thus MS. Vat. seems to have arisen on the basis of an account of the journey and death of the saint, extant at the end of the 4th cent. On the whole, the martyrdoms are late and untrustworthy compositions, wholly useless as materials for determining the question of the epistles; we are thrown back on Eusebius.

III. Eusebius in the *Chronicle* (ed. Schöne, ii. 152, 158, 162) omits (contrary to his custom) the durations of the episcopates of Antioch. We can, therefore, place Ignatius's death any time between Ab. 2123, Traj. 10, and 2132, Traj. 19. In *H. E.* iii. 22, Eusebius, in a general way, makes the episcopates of Symeon and Ignatius contemporary with the first years of Trajan and the last of St. John and (iii. 36) with Polycarp and Papias. We may date his epistles, journey, and death in any year from 105 to 117. Funk fixes it at 107.

In 1878 Harnack published a tract (*Die Zeit des Ign.* Leipz.) impugning the tradition that Ignatius was martyred under Trajan. The argument rests upon the acts of the martyrdom being proved by Zahn, with the general assent of all his critics, to be untrustworthy; the date of the saint's death thus resting wholly on the testimony of Eusebius, who shews that he had no data except the untrustworthy information of Julius Africanus (Harnack, pp. 66 sqq.). But it is very improbable that Eusebius had no tradition save through Africanus, or the latter no tradition save four names.

The theory of Volkmar, which the author of *Supernatural Religion* (i. 268) regarded as "demonstrated," was that the martyrdom of Ignatius happened not in Rome but in Antioch, upon Dec. 20, 115 (on which day his feast was kept), in consequence of the excitement produced by an earthquake a week previously; but it is now known from the ancient Syriac *Menologion*, published by Wright (*Journ. Sac. Lit.* Jan. 1866, p. 45), that the feast was originally kept not upon Dec. 20, but upon Oct. 17. (Zahn, i. 33, and Lightfoot, ii. 352, note §, are to be corrected in accordance with this discovery.)

The other details in the martyrdoms and elsewhere are but expansions from hints supposed to be found in the letters, of which we find an instance in the long dialogue between Ignatius and Trajan upon the name Θεοφόρος. There is no reason to suspect the genuineness of this addition to the saint's name. It is given untranslated in the 4th-cent. Syriac version. The interpolator found it in his copy, for it stands in all his epistles except that to Polycarp and in all the MSS. of the shorter translation, both Greek and Latin. The 4th-cent. writers, regarding it as a title of honour, do not quote it; in the 6th it came to be regarded as a name.

The tradition that Ignatius was martyred at Rome can be traced higher than the records of Eusebius and Origen. The designation of world-famed, which Eusebius gives him, shews the general tradition; and the words of Origen are to the same effect. The testimony of Irenaeus, which Eusebius adduces as perfectly agreeing with the tradition known to him, dates but 70 years after the fact. True, these expressions come from writers who knew the epistles; but the mere existence of the epistles at such a date, even if they were spurious, would be sufficient proof of the existence of the tradition; and it is impossible that such a story should have arisen so soon after Trajan, if it had contradicted known facts or prevalent customs of his reign.

Eusebius clearly wrote with the collection of letters before him, and knew of no other collection besides the 7 he mentions. These he arranges according to place and time of writing, gives his quotation from Romans as out of "the Epistles," and cites Irenaeus's quotation from Ignatius, as proof of that writer's knowledge of them, although Irenaeus did not mention the author's name.

IV. The gradual presentation of the various Ignatian documents to the modern world is related in the introduction to Cureton's *Corpus Ignatianum* and is briefly as follows. Late in the 15th and in the beginning of the 16th cents. 12 epistles, purporting to be by Ignatius, were given to the world, first in Latin translations, then in the original Greek, together with three others manifestly spurious, which existed in Latin alone. The epistles which bear non-Eusebian titles were soon suspected of spuriousness, and it was proved that the text of the Eusebian, as then known, was interpolated. Ussher first restored the genuine text by means of a Latin translation which he discovered, and his arguments (except as to his doubt whether Ignatius wrote separately to Polycarp) were confirmed by Vossius's publication of the Medicean MS. Thenceforward we have had the longer and the shorter (or Vossian) recensions, the former containing the 7 Eusebian epistles in a longer text and also epistles of Mary of Castabala to Ignatius, with his reply, of Ignatius to the Tarsians, Philippians, Antiochenes, and Hero, his successor; the Vossian comprising only the Eusebian letters and those in a shorter text. The longer recension has had few defenders, while the shorter had many and early assailants, moved especially by its support of episcopacy. Of these Daillé was perhaps the ablest, but he was sufficiently answered by bp. Pearson. The genuineness of the longer recension as a whole is now generally denied, the time and method of its interpolations and additions being the only points for consideration.

Cureton in 1839 transcribed from Syriac MSS. in the Brit. Mus. a fragment of the martyrdom of Ignatius and of the Ep. to the Romans therein contained. In 1847 he discovered, among Syriac MSS. acquired in the meantime, three epistles of Ignatius, viz. to Polycarp, to the Ephesians, and to the Romans, transcribed in the 6th or 7th cent. These epistles are in a form considerably shorter even than the shorter recension of the earlier time. Cureton believed this the sole genuine text, and argued the point very ably, but with a confidence which in its contrast with the present state of belief should be a warning to all who are tempted to be too positive on this difficult controversy. Many scholars at the time accepted the Curetonian theory, and Bunsen wrote a voluminous work in its defence. The Armenian version, first printed, though very incorrectly, in 1783, is mentioned by Cureton, who failed to perceive the effect its testimony was to have upon his own argument. The correct publication and due estimate of the Armenian version are due to Petermann. According to him, it was rendered out of Syriac in the 5th cent., and agrees with Ussher's Latin MS. in that, while it contains several post-Eusebian epistles united with the Eusebian, the latter are free from any systematic interpolations such as are in the longer recension.

V. *Date of the Longer Recension.*—The latest ancient writer who cites only the Eusebian epistles in the uninterpolated text is the monk Antonius in the early part of the 7th cent. (Cureton, p. 176; Zahn, ii. 350). Severus of Antioch, 6th cent. (Cureton, 212; Zahn, 352) cites all the Eusebian epistles in a text free from interpolations.

We cannot doubt that in Ussher's MS. and in the Armenian translation we have (minute textual criticism apart) the 7 epistles as the Fathers from Eusebius to Severus of Antioch and as the interpolator had them. The arguments of Ussher upon this point remain unanswered. But the Armenian, with the Syriac translation from which it sprang, brings back the composition of the six additional epistles to A.D. 400 at latest; and these are undoubtedly the work of the same hand which interpolated the others. On the other hand, the interpolation cannot have been before 325, or Eusebius would have cited or alluded to it; moreover, it shews undoubted marks of dependence on his history. The period of the interpolator is thus fixed at the latter part of the 4th cent. His doctrine, as Ussher shewed (p. 221), is stark Arianism.

Several names in Pseudo-Ignatius are borrowed from the period A.D. 360 to 380 (Philost. iii. 15; Theod. i. 5, v. 7; Socr. iii. 25, iv. 12). The titles of the new letters are also easily accounted for in the same period. Pseudo-Ignatius interests himself against the Quartodecimans; proving that they must have been still strong when he wrote, which was not the case at the conclusion of the 4th cent. These oppositions point to the period 360-380. Thus all historical indications point to the 2nd half of the 4th cent. as the date of the interpolations.

Zahn conjectures the interpolator to have been Acacius, the scholar, biographer, and successor of Eusebius at Caesarea, who, as Sozomen (iv. 23) informs us, was regarded as heir to the learning as well as the position of that divine. The roughness of the known character of Acacius (*c.* 360) agrees with the abusiveness of Pseudo-Ignatius.

Different Syriac translations of Greek works give similar citations from Ignatius in somewhat varying language; probably because the authors cited from memory an existing Syriac version. Zahn contends that the Armenian version came from the one Syriac translation in the 5th cent., and from it the extracts were taken, perhaps somewhat later, which Cureton mistook for the original epistles. The connexion in which Cureton's epistles were found is that of a series of extracts from Fathers whose remaining works are not to be supposed rendered doubtful by their absence from this Syriac MS., and Petermann (xxi.) has corrected Bunsen's supposition that the concluding words of the MS. imply that the epistles of Ignatius, as known to the writer, were all comprised in what he copied. Zahn (pp. 199, 200) compares the Syriac extracts numbered i. and ii. in *Corp. Ignat.*, taken as they were, beyond doubt, from the existing Syriac translation, with S. Cur. (*i.e.* Cureton's *Syriac Epp.*); and apparently succeeds in making out that the same translator, whose work is presented in a fragmentary form in S. Cur., meets us in these extracts. *E.g.* the expression *θηριομαχεῖν*, and many other peculiar words, are similarly rendered; though no. i. seems sometimes to preserve better the text from which it was copied. We might cull from S. Cur. itself certain proofs that it was not the original. Moreover, there are certain passages in it which are plainly not complete in themselves. It is surely a quite sufficient motive to suppose that the epitomator intended to make one of those selections of the best parts of a good work, which in all ages have been practised upon the most eminent writers without disrespect. Hefele (see Denzinger, pp. 8, 196) thinks he can discern the practical ascetic purpose of the selection, and we observe that very naturally the abbreviator begins each epistle with a design of taking all that is most edifying; but his resolution or his space fails him before the end, when he abridges far more than at the beginning. His form of Ephesians has alone an uniform character of epitome from the first; but a number of personal names plainly fit to be omitted come very early. Denzinger powerfully urges (pp. 77 seq.) the certainty that the Monophysites would have complained when the seven epistles were quoted against them had these been spurious, and he and Uhlhorn have fully shewn how entirely the epitomator is committed to any doctrines in the shorter recension which can be found difficult. What a useless and objectless task then would any one have in interpolating and extending Cureton's three into the seven! Upon the whole case we can pronounce with much confidence that the Curetonian theory is never likely to revive.

VI. The Ep. to the Romans differs from the other six Eusebian letters in being used by some authors who use no others and omitted by some who cite the others. Zahn suggests that it did not at first belong to the collection, but was propounded by itself, with or without a martyrdom. This seems supported by the fact that it escaped the interpolations which the other epistles suffered at the hand, probably, of Acacius.

VII. The circumstances of the journey and martyrdom of Ignatius, gathered from the seven epistles and from that of Polycarp, are as follows: He suffers under a merely local persecution. It is in progress at Antioch while he is in Smyrna, whence he writes to the Romans, Ephesians, Magnesians, and Trallians. But Rome, Magnesia (xii.), and Ephesus (xii.) are at peace, and in Troas he learns that peace is restored to the church in Antioch. Of the local causes of this Antiochene persecution we are ignorant, but it is not in the least difficult to credit. The imagined meeting of the emperor and the saint is not found in the epistles; it is "the world" under whose enmity the church is there said to suffer. All now recognize that, according to the testimony of the letters, Ignatius has been condemned in Antioch to death, and journeys with death by exposure to the beasts as the settled fate before him. He deprecates interposition of the church at Rome (quite powerful enough at the end of the 1st cent. to be conceivably successful in such a movement) for the remission of a sentence already delivered. The supposition of Hilgenfeld (i. 200) that prayer to God for his martyrdom, or abstinence from prayer against it, is what he asks of the Romans seems quite inadmissible, and we could not conceive him so assured of the approach of death if the sentence had not been already pronounced. The right of appeal to the emperor was recognized, and could be made without the consent of the criminal, but not if the sentence had proceeded from the emperor himself. Thus the Colbertine Martyrdom, which makes Trajan the judge at Antioch, contradicts the epistles no less than the Vatican which puts off the process to Rome. MS. Colb. brings Ignatius by sea to Smyrna; but Eusebius, who had read the epistles, supposes the journey to be by land, and he is clearly right. The journey "by land and sea" (*ad Rom.* v.) may easily refer to a voyage from Seleucia to some Cilician port, and thence by road. The ordinary way from Antioch to Ephesus was by land, and Ignatius calls the messenger to be sent by the Smyrnaeans to Antioch θεοδρόμος (*Pol.* vii.). Ignatius did not, as was usual, pass through Magnesia and Ephesus, but left the great road at Sardis and came by Laodicea, Hierapolis, Philadelphia, and perhaps Colossae, as he had certainly visited Philadelphia and met there the false teachers from Ephesus (Zahn, 258 seq. also 266 seq.). The churches written to were not chosen at random, but were those which had shewn their love by sending messengers to him. The replies were thus, primarily, letters of thanks, quite naturally extending into admonitions.

We find him in the enjoyment of much freedom on his journey, though chained to a soldier. In Philadelphia he preaches, not in a church, but in a large assembly of Christians; in Smyrna he has intercourse with the Christians there and with messengers of other churches. He has much speech with the bishops concerning the state of the churches. That of Ephesus he treats with special respect, and anticipates writing a second letter (*ad Eph.* xx.); that of Tralles he addresses in a markedly different manner (*ad. Tr.* 2, 12). He must, therefore, have had time in Smyrna to acquaint himself with the condition of the neighbouring churches. If the writing of epistles under the circumstances of his captivity should cause surprise, it must be remembered that they are only short letters, not books. The expression βιβλίδιον, which in Eph. xx. he applies to his intended second missive, is often applied to letters. He dictated to a Christian, and thus might, as Pearson remarks, have finished one of the shorter letters in an hour, the longest in three. Perpetua and Saturus wrote in prison narratives as long as the epistles of Ignatius (*Acta SS. Perp. et Fel.* Ruinart). A ten days' sojourn would amply meet the necessities of the case; and there is nothing in the treatment to which the letters witness inconsistent with that used to other Christian prisoners, *e.g.* St. Paul. The numberless *libelli pacis*, written by martyrs in prison, and the celebrations of the holy mysteries there with their friends, shew that the liberty given Ignatius was not extraordinary; especially as the word εὐεργετούμενοι which he applies to his guard points, doubtless, to money given them by the Christians. Ignatius is always eager to know more Christians and to interest them in each other. The news of the cessation of persecution in Antioch stirs him to urge Polycarp to take an interest in that church. The great idea of the Catholic church is at work in him. He does not deny that his request that messengers should be sent to Antioch is an unusual one, but dwells upon the great benefit which will result (*Pol.* 7; *Sm.* 11; *Phil.* 10). But when Polycarp, a few weeks or months afterwards, writes to the Philippians, the messenger had not yet been sent. Ignatius had but lately passed through Philippi, by the Via Egnatia to Neapolis. The Philippians immediately after wrote to Polycarp, and forwarded a message to the

Antiochenes, expecting to be in time to catch the messenger for Antioch before his departure. Ignatius had plainly been suggesting the same thoughts to them as to Polycarp; and this would be plainer still if the reading in Eus. *H. E.* iii. 36, 14 (ἐγράψατέ μοι καὶ ὑμεῖς καὶ Ἰγνάτιος) were more sure, and thus a second letter had been received by Polycarp from Ignatius. But this second epistle, if written, has been lost. Polycarp wrote immediately after receiving the epistle of the Philippians. He speaks of the death of Ignatius, knowing that the sentence in Antioch made it certain; probably knowing also the date of the games at which he was to die. But he is not acquainted with any particulars, since he asks for news concerning the martyr and those with him (*Ep. Pol.* xiii.), and at the request of the Philippians forwards all the epistles of Ignatius to which he had access, viz. those to the Asiatic churches; but not all that he knew to have been written.

VIII. The chief difficulty in accepting the epistles as genuine has always arisen from the form of church government which they record as existing and support with great emphasis. They display the threefold ministry established in Asia Minor and Syria, and the terms Ἐπίσκοπος and πρεσβύτερος are applied to perfectly distinct orders—a state of things and use of language which are argued to be wholly incompatible with a date early in the 2nd cent. Hence Daillé derived his "palmary argument" (c. xxvi., answered by Pears. ii. 13).

It is noteworthy that the testimony of the epistles on this point extends no further than the localities named. To the Romans Ignatius only once names the office of a bishop, and that in reference to himself; and in Polycarp's Ep. to the Philippians there is no mention of any bishop, while the deacons and presbyters are addressed at considerable length. The standpoint of the epistles is perfectly consistent with the supposition that episcopacy existing from the times of the apostles in Asia Minor and Syria and believed by the Christians there to be a divinely ordained institution, made its way gradually into other parts of the church, and that those who most valued it might yet know that it did not exist in churches to which they wrote, or not be assured that it did, and might feel it no part of their duty to enter upon a controversy concerning it.

Zahn fairly observes that there is no attempt, even in those epistles where obedience to the bishop is most urged, to recommend it in opposition to other forms of church government. Not only is the supposition that Ignatius was introducing episcopacy utterly out of the question, but none of the epistles bear the slightest trace of any recent introduction of it in the places in which it exists. The presbyterate is everywhere identified with the episcopate in its claims to obedience, and those who resist the one resist the other. It is extremely hard to reconcile these characteristics with the supposition that the letters were forged to introduce the rule of bishops or to uplift it to an unprecedented position in order to resist the assaults of heresy.

A good deal of uncertainty remains as to the relations which the smaller congregations outside the limits of the cities held in the Ignatian church order to the bishops of the cities. No provision appears for episcopal rule over country congregations whose pastors are not in the "presbytery"—an uncommon expression in antiquity, but used 13 times by Ignatius.

The duties the epistles ascribe to bishops are very similar to those which St. Paul (Acts. xx.) lays upon presbyters. Only in one place (*Pol.* 5) do they speak of the preaching of the bishop; and it is not peculiar to him, but common with the presbyters. The deacons have duties wholly distinct, concerned with the meat and drink given to the poor and with the distribution of the mysteries of the Eucharist. But the presbyters are very closely united with the bishop. They are not his vicars, but his συνέδριον (*Phil.* 8; *Pol.* 7), and yet the bishop is by no means a mere president of the college of presbyters. Zahn shews that even though the development of episcopacy were thought to have taken place through the elevation of one of a college to a presidency in those parts where it did not exist in the end of the 1st cent., it would still be impossible to hold this of Asia. The youth of many of the earliest Asiatic bishops puts this theory entirely out of the question there. Whatever development is implied in the passage from the state of things represented in I. Pet. and I. Tim. to organized episcopacy, took place, according to the testimony of all records both of Scripture and tradition, in the 30 years between the death of St. Paul and the time of Domitian, had Asia Minor for its centre, and was conducted under the influence of St. John and apostolic men from Palestine, in which country Jerusalem offers the records of a succession of bishops more trustworthy perhaps than that of any other see. Now the Syrian churches were from the first in closest union with Palestine. Thus all the most undoubted records of episcopacy in the subapostolic age centre in the very quarters in which our epistles exhibit it, a weighty coincidence in determining their authenticity.

It is certainly somewhat startling to those accustomed to regard bishops as the successors of the apostles that Ignatius everywhere speaks of the position of the apostles as corresponding to that of the existing presbyters, while the prototype of the bishop is not the apostles, but the Lord Himself. It would be hasty, however, to infer that Ignatius denied that the office and authority of the apostles was represented and historically succeeded by that of the bishops. The state of things visibly displayed when the Lord and His apostles were on earth is for Ignatius the type of church order for all time. (See Bp. Harold Browne, *The Strife and the Victory*, 1872, p. 62.) If, however, the epistles had been forged to support episcopacy, they would not have omitted an argument of such weight as the apostolical authority and succession.

The duty of submission is with Ignatius the first call upon each member of the church, and exhortations to personal holiness go hand in hand with admonitions to unity and obedience. The word ὑποτάσσεσθαι denotes the duty of all, not (be it marked) towards the bishop alone, but towards authority in all its steps

(*Mgn.* 13 and 7). But the bishop represents the principle of unity in the church.

Sprintzl ingeniously argues (p. 67) that the supremacy of the bp. of Rome is taught by Ignatius, on the ground that, first, he teaches the supremacy of the Roman church over others (*Rom. prooem.*), and secondly, the supremacy of the bishop in every church. But the explanation of the passage in Romans is very doubtful, and the marked omission of any mention of the bp. of Rome seems inconsistent with any supremacy apart from the natural position of his church.

The emphatic terms in which these letters propose the bishop as the representative of Christ have always presented a stumbling-block to many minds, even apart from the question of date. But before we pronounce these expressions exaggerated, we must remember that obedience to the bishop is valued by the writer for the sake of unity, while unity is for him the only fence against the heresy to which small and disunited bodies are subject (*Phil.* 4, 8; *Mgn.* 1, etc). Identification of the position of the church ruler with that of the Lord would be more easy to a writer of an age very close to Christ than to one of later date. When the divine nature of the Lord and His elevation in heaven came through lapse of time to overshadow the remembrance of His life on earth, it seemed a superhuman claim on the part of any office to say that it represented Him. But it would naturally be otherwise when the recollection of His human intercourse with men was fresh; for why should not men represent one so truly man? Thus the strong expressions may really be a mark of early date.

IX. In *Sm.* 8 is first found the phrase Catholic church—an expression pronounced by Lipsius (iii.) to prove of itself the later date of the epistles. Such a decision is very precarious, even if, with Lipsius, we reject the testimony of the Martyrdom of Polycarp to the use of the expression. Sprintzl remarks that the phrase "Where Jesus Christ is, there is the Catholic church" naturally follows upon the preceding statement of the relation of the bishop to the particular church: what the bishop is to it, that Christ is to the Catholic church at large. Thus to Ignatius the church of each place is a miniature of the church at large (*Sm.* 8) and its unity is guarded by all the sanctions of the Christian faith. The one faith is, in the epistles, the bond of the church. "The gospel" is that which the apostles proclaimed (*Phil.* 5); not the four written gospels, but the substance of the message of salvation.

We find in the epistles the germ of the great ideas of worship afterwards developed in the church. The altar-idea and the temple-idea as applied to the church are there (*Eph.* 5; *Mgn.* 7; *Phil.* 4). The Eucharist holds its commanding place (*Rom.* 7; *Phil.* 4, and probably *Eph.* 5), though what its rites were at this early period is hard to answer from the letters. Ἀγάπη (*Sm.* 8) is applied to the Eucharist, and ἀγαπᾶν (*Sm.* 7) means to celebrate it. In Ignatian phraseology Εὐχαριστία is used where the blessing of Holy Communion is denoted, Ἀγάπη means the whole service of which the consecration is only a moment. In *Sm.* 7 those who speak against the gifts of God are plainly those who deny τὴν εὐχαριστίαν σάρκα εἶναι τοῦ σωτῆρος ἡμῶν Ἰησοῦ Χριστοῦ. Christians observed the Lord's Day, not the Jewish Sabbath (*Mgn.* 8, 9).

X. As to the theology of the epistles, there have been great differences of opinion. The more significant theological statements are uncontroversial, though called out by heresies to which the writer opposes his conception of the nature of Christ. The originality and reality of the revelation in Christ is the great point with him. Hence follows the unreasonableness of Judaizing, which he sometimes presses in terms apparently inconsistent with the recognition of Jewish Christians as really believers. But probably, like St. Paul, he is treating the question from the Gentile standpoint alone. Prophets and the law are worthy of all honour in Christ; πάντα ὁμοῦ καλά ἐστιν ἐὰν ἐν ἀγάπῃ πιστεύητε. The prophets were Christians in spirit, and Christ raised them from the dead (*Mgn.* 9). They were believers in Christ; yea, even the angels must believe in His blood (*Sm.* 6). But for this practical and real salvation finding its expression in history the heretics would substitute a shadowy representation of religious notions in a merely apparent and unreal life of Christ. Therefore we find Ignatius constantly adding the word ἀληθῶς to his records of the acts of Christ (*Sm.* 3, 4; *Tr.* 10). Ἐν σαρκί is an equivalent phrase. The Blood is named with or instead of the Flesh to shew that the Lord had in death the same bodily constitution as in life, of which the faithful partake in the Eucharist. Being real flesh, Christ was the New Man, and the revelation of God in the earth (*Eph.* 18). He is an eternal Person, but He is God's Son, as born of Mary and of God. When the writer speaks of an outcoming of Christ from God, he means the Incarnation, and not anything previous. Though he uses the epithet ἀΐδιος with Λόγος, yet he does not seem to mean that it is *as* Λόγος that the Lord is eternal. It is as incarnate and as man that He is the Logos of God. His twofold nature furnishes the explanation of the opposite attributes ascribed to Him (*Eph.* 7; *Pol.* 3). Baur and Lipsius have discovered Patripassianism in the last-quoted passage. But this accusation is inconsistent with all the rest of the epistles, and seems, indeed, to have been since abandoned by Lipsius. In opposition to Baur's assertion that except in one suspected place there is no mention of Christ as Son of God, Zahn finds himself able to enumerate 29 such cases. The epistles lay vast stress upon the Godhead of the Lord; it is because of this that His birth is the entrance of the New Man, and His death the resurrection of the faithful. To them He stands in a personal and practical relation, which makes Him their God. His present invisible relation to them involves an increase of the activity of His Godhead, and of its revelation to men (*ad Rom.* 3; *ad Eph.* 15); but He was always God. Therefore Ignatius can speak of the blood and of the suffering of God (*Eph.* 1; *Rom.* 6). The τρία μυστήρια κραυγῆς, the three mysteries loudest in proclamation of truth to those who can hear, are the Incarnation, Birth, and Death of Christ, hid in their real significance from the devil and from the unbelieving. The terms Son and Λόγος are not applied to express the relations of the Divine Persons. Ignatius is content to maintain on the one hand the unity of God, on the other the eternal personality of Christ.

XI. The question what special heresies are denounced in the epistles possesses, in relation to their date, an importance scarcely below that of episcopacy. All, except Romans, contain warnings against heresy, and the exhortations to unity and submission to authority derive their urgency from this danger. It was long a question whether two forms of heresy, Judaic and Docetic, or only one, Judaeo-docetic, were aimed at. But already in 1856, despite the arguments of Hilgenfeld (i. 230), it appeared to Lipsius (i. 31) that the question was decided in the latter sense. The heretics were wandering teachers, ever seeking proselytes (*Eph.* 7), and all the denunciations of heresy are directed against that mixture of Judaism with Gnosticism, represented by some whom Ignatius met in his journey (*Mgn.* 8, 10, 11; *Tr.* 9; *Sm.* 1). The idea of Ritschl (*Entst. der altk. Kirche*, p. 580) that they were Montanist teachers met with little favour.

Cureton and others have thought to find direct allusions to the teaching of Valentinus in the epistles (but see Pearson II. vi.). But the allusion Λόγος ἀπὸ Σιγῆς προελθών (*Mgn.* 8) is not applicable to Valentinus.

Basilides is probably early enough, and disciples of his might have been wandering in Asia Minor; Cerinthus too was of this age. I. and II. John contain warnings against Docetism, which Polycarp (*Ep.* 7) applies to the heretics of his own time, which was also that of Ignatius. Of all the heretics whom Bunsen and others have supposed the epistles to denounce, Saturninus alone can be proved to have held the doctrines they condemn.

XII. From the epistles, as Hilgenfeld (i. 225-226) truly remarks, different critics, according to their bias, have derived in some cases the very highest, and in some the very poorest, notion of the writer's character. The letters are indeed more characteristic than any we have between St. Paul and the great Fathers of the 4th cent.; but they give no record of the writer's surroundings or of his ways in his diocese when the times were quiet. His name is Latin; his style very Semitic. He had not seen the Lord or the apostles, and was not, as MS. Colb. makes him, a fellow-pupil with Polycarp of St. John. It is perhaps somewhat precarious to infer with Zahn, from his strong terms of self-reproach (*Eph.* 21; *Mgn.* 14), that he had led an un-Christian or anti-Christian life in early years. His longing for death is extreme, but is really for life under another and better form. We do not know that he courted martyrdom before his judges, since we only meet him after he has been condemned and is well used to the idea. All his exhortations have the one burden and object, closer union with Christ. He bids others seek, and seeks himself, that union in permanence and perfection which the Holy Eucharist gives here in part. He does not imagine death in itself to have any value (*Rom.* 4; *Tr.* 3, 4; *Eph.* 12; *Sm.* 4). The prayers he asks are not for his death, but for his due preparation (*Eph.* 21; *Mgn.* 14; *Tr.* 12, 13). For an interesting summary of the moral aspect of the Ignatian epistles in respect to the personality of the writer and to the ideal which his teaching presents, see Sprintzl, pp. 244 sqq.

XIII. The great majority of critics, whether adverse to the genuineness of the epistles or not, have recognized that the seven epistles professing to be of Ignatius, as shewn by the individuality of the author there displayed, and the one of Polycarp, form an indivisible whole. Romans, indeed, is the brightest and most interesting of the letters. This is because its chief subject is his personal eagerness for martyrdom; he is writing to the place where he expects to suffer, and to people who can help or hinder his object.

The Ep. of Polycarp contains a witness for the whole body of epistles, which (if it be genuine) renders almost all others superfluous; since it mentions letters written to Smyrna by Ignatius, and by Polycarp collected and sent to Philippi; and intimates the existence of others. Thus those who believe the Ignatian letters to be a production late in the 2nd cent. are forced to consider the Ep. of Polycarp a fraud also, in whole or in part. For its satisfactory defence see Lightfoot, *Cont. Rev.* 1875. With it we may consider the genuineness of the Ignatian epistles proved. For a forger late in the 2nd cent., it would have been impossible to avoid mentioning Polycarp's connexion with the apostles, or alluding to the epistles to the seven Asiatic churches in Revelation; they are never mentioned. In all historical fictions of antiquity, reiterated pains are taken to make the facts to be maintained understood. In Ignatius they are hard to reach; the writer is not thinking of readers who have all to learn from him. Lastly, no ancient fiction has succeeded in individualizing character to the degree here displayed; *e.g.* in the picture of the false teachers. The improbabilities on which the author of *Supernatural Religion*, and even, though less decidedly, Hilgenfeld (17), rely to prove the whole story an undoubted fabrication, are recognized by M. Renan as established facts, even though he does not believe that the epistles we possess are those to which the story refers. Finally, by the great work of Bp. Lightfoot the genuineness of the seven Vossian epistles may be regarded as completely established. The *Epp.* of Ignatius in the longer and shorter recensions and the Syr. version were in *Patr. Apost.* ed. G. Jacobson (Clar. Press); and a trans. of the *Epp.* together with the *Martyrdom* and spurious *Epp.* are in the *Ante-Nic. Lib.*

Authorities.—Ussher, *Dissertatio de Ig. et Pol.* (1644), in *Works* by Elrington, vii. 87-295; Joannis Dallaei, *de Scriptis quae sub Dion. Areop. et Ig. Ant. nominibus circumferuntur*, lib. ii. (Genev. 1666); Pearson, *Vindiciae Ignatianae* (ed. nov. Oxf. 1852); Zahn, i. *Ignatius von Antiochien*, p. 629 (Gotha, 1873), ii. *Patrum Apostolicorum Opera*, fasc. ii. (Lips. 1876); Hilgenfeld, i. *Die apostolischen Väter* (Halle, 1853), ii. in his *Zeitsch.* 1874, pp. 96 seq.; Lightfoot, i. in Phil. pp. 208-210, ii. in *Cont. Rev.* (Feb. 1875); Petermann, *S. Ign. Ep.* (Lips. 1849); Harnack, *Die Zeit des Ignatius* (Leipz. 1878); Cureton, *Corpus Ignatianum* (Lond.

1849); Denzinger, *Ueber die Aechtheit der Ign. Briefe* (Würzburg, 1849); Renan, i. *Les Evangiles* (Paris, 1877), ii. in *Journal des Savants* (1874); Uhlhorn, i. in *Zeitschrift für hist. Theol.* (1851, 283), ii. in *Herzogs Encyc.*; Funk, *Op. Pat. Ap.* (ed. 5, Tübing. 1878).

Cureton (*Corp. Ign.*) or (better still, except for Syriac scholars) Zahn (ii.) will furnish the student with all the documents and ancient testimonies. The special treatise of Zahn on Ignatius is, as Bp. Lightfoot remarks, little known in England, and is of an exhaustive character. The reader will understand that, while we have not hesitated to dissent from it where necessary, we have freely availed ourselves of its pages. The Epistles of Ignatius have been pub. in a cheap trans. by J. R. Srawley (S.P.C.K. 2 vols.) [R.T.S.]

Innocentius (12) **I.**, bp. of Rome, after Anastasius, from May 402, to Mar. 12, 417.

The circumstances of his time and the character and talents of Innocent render his pontificate important. Christianity had now for nearly a century been the religion of the emperors; paganism was fast becoming a system of the past; the capture of Rome by Alaric during his pontificate, regarded as the divine judgment on the heathen city and causing the dispersion and ruin of the remains of the heathen nobility, completed the downfull of the ancient order. With the ascendancy of the church had grown that of the hierarchy, and especially of the head of that hierarchy in the West, the Roman bishop. The need of centres of unity and seats of authority to keep the church together amid doctrinal conflicts; the power and importance hence accruing to the patriarchal sees, and especially to Rome as the one great patriarchate of the West, the see of the old seat of empire and the only Western one that claimed apostolic origin; the view now generally received of the bp. of Rome as the successor of the prince of the apostles; the removal of the seat of empire to Constantinople, leaving the pope, when there was but one emperor, the sole Western potentate, and when there were two, as in Innocent's time, the fixing of the imperial residence at Ravenna instead of Rome,—such were among the causes of the aggrandizement of the Roman see. The Western church had been comparatively free from the controversies which had divided the East, nor had the popes taken much personal part in them; but they had almost invariably supported the orthodox cause, received and protected the orthodox under persecution, and, after watching with quiet dignity the Eastern struggle, had accepted and confirmed the decisions of orthodox councils. Hence Rome appeared as the bulwark of the cause of truth, and its claim to be the unerring guardian of the apostolic faith and discipline gained extensive credence. Innocent himself was eminently the man to enter into, and make the most of, the position he was called to occupy. Unstained in life, able and resolute, with a full appreciation of the dignity and prerogatives of his see, he lost no opportunity of asserting its claims, and under him the idea of universal papal supremacy, though as yet somewhat shadowy, was already taking form. At his accession the empire had for seven years been divided between the two sons of Theodosius, Arcadius and Honorius; the latter, now 18 years of age, under the control of the great general Stilicho, ruling in the West. Two years after Innocent's accession (A.D. 404) he fixed his residence at Ravenna.

I. West. (i) *Illyria.*—Immediately after his election Innocent wrote to Anysius, bp. of Thessalonica, informing him of the event and giving him the oversight of the churches of eastern Illyria. The prefecture of Illyria had been dismembered since 388, the Eastern part, including Dacia and Macedonia, being assigned to the Eastern empire, but popes Damasus and Siricius had continued to claim ecclesiastical jurisdiction over the separated portion, delegating their authority to the bishops of Thessalonica. Innocent thus made no new claim, nor did he hereby assert any authority over the East generally (Innoc. *Ep.* 1; Galland. *Bibl. Patr.*). When Rufus, some years after, succeeded Anysius as bp. of Thessalonica, a letter was at once sent to him, reversing the vicariate commission, defining its extent, and reminding him that his jurisdiction was derived from the favour of the apostolic see only. In 414 we find Innocent exercising authority of a summary kind, without the intervention of the bp. of Thessalonica, in East Illyria. The bishops of Macedonia had sent him a synodal letter, desiring directions as to: (1) Whether persons ordained by one Bonosus, a deceased heretical bishop, might be admitted to the priesthood. (2) Whether persons who had married widows might be ordained and made bishops, for which allowance they pleaded the custom of their church. (3) They had asked leave to raise to the episcopate one Photinus, who had been condemned by Innocent's predecessors, and to depose a deacon called Eustatius. Some at least of these questions had already been decided by Innocent, for he expresses surprise and displeasure at their being again mooted. He then authoritatively decides them. Those who had married widows he debars from ordination, citing the prohibition of such marriages to the high-priest under the Mosaic law. Those ordained by Bonosus are debarred the priesthood by the law of the Roman church (*lex nostrae ecclesiae*), which admitted to lay communion persons baptized by heretics, but did not recognize their orders. The Nicene canon about the Novatianists, he says, applied to them only, and the condonation by Anysius had only been a temporary expedient. The question whether those who had married one wife before and another after baptism were to be accounted deuterogamists, and so incapable of ordination, he discussed at length also in other epistles.* He decides that they are to be so accounted, for baptism is not the commencement of a new life in such sort as to relax the obligations of a previous marriage. Though with hesitation and much anxiety, he allows the promotion of Photinus, notwith-

* Cf. *Epp.* ii. iii. *Bibl. Patr.* Galland. St. Jerome, in one of his letters, strongly maintains the opposite view to Innocent, and Jerome's view was probably the prevalent one at the time, for he speaks of the number of persons ordained, and even advanced to the episcopate, after marrying a second wife after baptism, being large enough to compose a council.

standing the condemnation of him by previous popes, on the ground that they had been imposed on by false reports; and he disallows the deposition of Eustatius (*Ep.* xvii. Galland.). Another epistle, addressed to the bishops of Macedonia, confirms the deposition of Babalius and Taurianus, who had appealed to Rome from the sentence of the bishops of their province. This appeal the bishops seem to have taken amiss, for Innocent presses upon them the advantage of having their judgment revised (*Ep.* xviii. Galland.).

(ii) *Gaul.*—Victricius, bp. of Rouen, having been in Rome towards the end of 403 (*Ep. ad Victric.* § 14, and Paul. Nolan. *Ep. ad Victric.* xxxvii. 1), applied to the pope soon after for information as to the practice and discipline of the Roman church. Innocent sent him a letter containing 14 rules, of which he says that they are no new ones, but derived by tradition from the apostles and fathers, though too generally unknown or disregarded. He directs Victricius to communicate them to the bishops and others, with a view to their future observance. Among them were: (1) No bishop may ordain without the knowledge of his metropolitan and the assistance of other bishops. (3) Ordinary causes against bishops are to be determined by the other bishops of the province, saving always the authority of Rome. (4) Greater causes, after the judgment of the bishops, are to be referred to the apostolic see, "as the synod [referring, probably, to the canons of Sardica] has decreed." (6, 7) No layman who has married a widow, or been twice married, may be ordained. (8) No bishop may ordain any one from another diocese without leave of its bishop. (9) Converts from Novatianism and Montanism are to be received by imposition of hands only, without iteration of baptism; but such as, having left the church, had been rebaptized by heretics, are only to be received after long penance. (10) Priests and Levites who have wives are not to cohabit with them. This rule is supported by argument, resting mainly on the prohibition of intercourse with their wives to priests under the old law before officiating. Christian priests and Levites, it is argued, ought always to be prepared to officiate. (11) Monks, taking minor orders, may not marry. (12) Courtiers and public functionaries are not to be admitted to any clerical order; for they might have to exhibit or preside over entertainments undoubtedly invented by the devil, and were liable to be recalled to his service by the emperor, so as to cause much "sadness and anxiety." Victricius is reminded of painful cases he had witnessed in Rome, when the pope had with difficulty obtained from the emperor the exemption even of priests from being recalled to his service. (13) Veiled virgins who marry are not to be admitted even to penance till the husband's death; but (14) such as have promised virginity, but have not been "veiled by the priest," may be reconciled after penance.

In 405 Innocent was similarly consulted by another bp. of Gaul, Exsuperius of Toulouse, whom he commends for referring doubtful questions to the apostolic see, and gives him the following directions: (1) Priests or deacons who cohabit with their wives are to be deprived, as pope Siricius had directed. The prohibition of conjugal intercourse to the priests in O.T. before officiating is adduced as before; also St. Paul's injunction to the Corinthian laity to abstain for a time, that they might give themselves unto prayer; whence it follows that the clergy, to whom prayer and sacrifice is a continual duty, ought always to abstain. When St. Paul said that a bishop was to be the husband of one wife, he did not mean that he was to live with her, else he would not have said, "They that are in the flesh cannot please God"; and he said "having children," not "begetting" them. The incontinence of clergy whom the injunction of pope Siricius had not reached may, however, be condoned; but they are not to be promoted to any higher order. (2) To the question whether such as had led continually loose lives after baptism might be admitted to penance and communion at the approach of death, Innocent replies that, though in former times penance only and not communion was accorded in such cases, the strict rule may now be relaxed, and both given. (3) Baptized Christians are not precluded from inflicting torture or condemning to death as judges, nor from suing as advocates for judgment in a capital case. Innocent, however, elsewhere precludes Christians who had been so engaged from ordination (*Ep.* xxvii. *ad Felicem*). (4) To the question how it was that adultery in a wife was more severely visited than in a husband, it is replied that the cause was the unwillingness of wives to accuse their husbands, and the difficulty of convicting the latter of transgression, not that adultery was more criminal in one case than in the other. (5) Divorced persons who marry again during the life of their first consort and those who marry them are adulterers, and to be excommunicated, but not their parents or relations, unless accessory. Lastly, a list is given of the canonical books of Scripture, the same as are now received by the church of Rome; while certain books, bearing the names of Matthias, James the Less, Peter, John, and Thomas, are repudiated and condemned.

(iii) *Spain.*—In 400 had been held the first council of Toledo, mainly to deal with Priscillianists returning to the church. Two such bishops, Symphorius and Dichtynius, with others, had been received by the council; but certain bishops of Baetica still refused to communicate with them. A Spanish bishop, Hilary, who had subscribed the decree of the council of Toledo, went with a priest, Elpidius, to Rome, to represent this to the pope; complaining also of two bishops, Rufinus and Minicius, who had ordained other bishops out of their own province without the knowledge of the metropolitan; and of other prevalent irregularities with respect to ordinations. The complainants do not appear to have been commissioned by any synod, or other authority of the Spanish church, to lay these matters before the pope, but Innocent took the opportunity to address a letter, after a synod held at Rome, to the bishops of the Toledo council, advising or directing them; though without asserting, as he does to other churches, the authority of the Roman see. He condemns those who refused to communicate with reconciled Priscillianists, and directs the bishops to inquire into the cases of Rufinus and Minicius and to enforce the canons. As to other prevalent irregularities—such as the ordination of persons who had, after baptism, pleaded as advocates, served in the army, or as courtiers (*curiales*) been concerned in objectionable ceremonies or entertainments—he directs that such past irregularities should be condoned for fear of scandal and disturbance, but avoided in the future. He insists, as so often in his letters, on the incapacity for ordination of such as had married widows or had married twice, and again protests that baptism cannot annul the obligation of a previous marriage. He supports these prohibitions by arguments from O.T. and from St. Paul, "Husband of one wife" (*Ep.* iii. *Bibl. Patr.* Galland.). We do not know how this admonitory letter was received in Spain.

(iv) *Africa.*—In 412 or 413 Innocent wrote to Aurelius, bp. of Carthage, requesting him to announce in synod the day for keeping Easter in 414, with the view of its being announced, as was then customary, to the church by the bp. of Rome (*Ep.* xiv. Galland.). Towards the end of 416 he received synodal letters from councils at Carthage and Milevis in Numidia, and from St. Augustine (who had taken part in the latter council), with four other bishops, on the Pelagian controversy; to all of which he replied in Jan. 417. This correspondence illustrates the relations then subsisting between the West African church and Rome. (For such relations at an early period see STEPHANUS; CYPRIANUS; SIXTUS II.) The synodal letters inform Innocent of the renewal of the condemnation of Pelagius and Coelestius pronounced five years previously at Carthage, and very respectfully request him to add the authority of the apostolical see to the decrees of their mediocrity ("ut statutis nostrae mediocritatis etiam apostolicae sedis auctoritas adhibeatur"); setting forth the heresies condemned, and arguments against them. They recognize the weight that the pope's approval would carry, but do not at all imply that the validity of their own condemnation depended on it. The five bishops imply some doubt as to his probable action, having heard that there were some in Rome who favoured the heretic; and they await the result with suspense, fear, and trembling. Innocent, in replying, assumes much greater dependence on the see of Rome on the part of the Africans than their language had implied, and asserts very large claims to general authority. He commends the bishops of the Carthaginian synod for referring the matter to his judgment, as knowing what was due to the see of the apostle from whom all episcopal authority was derived; and for having observed the decrees of the Fathers, resting on divine authority, according to which nothing done, even in remote and separated provinces, was to be considered settled till it had come to the knowledge of the Roman see and been confirmed by its authority, that all waters proceeding from the fountain of their birth, the pure streams of the uncorrupted head, might flow through the different regions of the whole world. The abundant stream of Rome, flowing, the bishops hoped, from the same fountain-head as the smaller stream of Africa, becomes in Innocent the fountain-head from which all streams must flow. He addresses the bishops of the Milevetan synod in the same strain. He then proceeds to condemn the Pelagian heresy in strong terms and to anathematize all its abettors and supporters. To adduce proofs, he says, is unnecessary, since his correspondents had said all that was wanted. He declines to accede to their suggestion that he should make overtures to Pelagius, or send for him to Rome. It is for the heretical, he says, to come to me of his own accord, if ready to retract his errors; if not ready, he would not obey my summons; if he should come, repudiate his heresy, and ask pardon, he will be received (*Epp.* Augustine, xc.-xcv.; *Epp.* Innoc. clxxxi.-clxxxiii. Galland.).

In a letter to Decentius, bp. of Eugubium in Umbria (dated A.D. 416), the claims of the Roman see are no less strongly asserted than in the letters to the African bishops. Innocent tells him that no one can be ignorant of the obligation of all to observe the traditions, and those alone, which the Roman church had received from St. Peter, the prince of the apostles, and which that church ever preserved—especially as no churches had been founded in Italy, Gaul, Spain, Africa, Sicily, or the interjacent islands, except by St. Peter or his successors. The letter proceeds to require observance of various Roman usages. (1) The pax in the Eucharist must be given after communion, not before. (2) The names of such as offer oblations at the Eucharist are not to be recited by the priest before the sacrifice, or the canon. (3) Infants after baptism may not be confirmed by unction except by the bishop; but priests may anoint other parts of the body than the forehead, using oil blessed by the bishop. (4) Saturday as well as Friday in each week is to be observed as a fast, in commemoration of the whole time Christ was in the grave. (5) Demoniacs may receive imposition of hands from priests or other clergy commissioned by the bishop. (6) St. James's direction that the sick are to call for the *elders* of the church does not preclude the bishop from administering the unction; but not only priests, but any Christian may anoint, using chrism prepared by the bishop. Penitents, however, to whom the other sacraments are denied, may not receive unction, "quia genus sacramenti est." It appears plain from the way the unction of the sick is spoken of that it was then used with a view to recovery, not as a last rite. (7) One Roman custom, that of sending, on the Lord's day, the Eucharist consecrated by the bishop to the presbyters throughout the city, that all on that day at least may partake of one communion, is not to be observed where it involved carrying the sacrament to great distances. Even in Rome it is not taken to the priests in the various cemeteries (*Epp.* xxv. Galland.).

II. EAST.—In 404 Innocent began to intervene in the affairs of the East in the matter of St. Chrysostom, who had been deposed and driven from Constantinople after the synod of the Oak in 403, and finally expelled on June 20, 404. A letter reached Innocent from Chrysostom himself, another from the 40 bishops who remained in his communion, a third from his clergy. That from Chrysostom (given by Palladius in his *Dialogus de Vita S. Johan. Chrysost.*) was addressed to the bps. of Rome, Aquileia, and Milan, as the three great bishops of the West. It requests them to protest against what had been done, and to continue in communion with the writer. To all these letters Innocent replied that, while still in communion with both parties, he reprobated the past proceedings as irregular, and proposed a council of Easterns and Westerns, from which avowed friends and enemies of the accused should be excluded. A second letter arrived from Theophilus, patriarch of Alexandria, with the Acts of the synod of the Oak, shewing that Chrysostom had been condemned by 36 bishops, of whom 29 were Egyptians. Innocent's brief reply is that he cannot renounce communion with Chrysostom on the strength of the past futile proceedings and demands that Theophilus should proffer his charges before a proper council, according to the Nicene canons. Communications from Constantinople continued to reach Innocent, one from about 25 bishops of Chrysostom's party, informing him of Chrysostom's banishment to Cucusus and the burning of his cathedral church. To them and to the banished prelate the pope sent letters of communion, being unable to render help. Cruel persecution of the friends of Chrysostom, set afoot by the Eastern emperor Arcadius, brought a number of letters to Rome from oppressed bishops and clergy, and the resort thither of many in person, including Anysius of Thessalonica, Palladius of Helenopolis (the author of the *Dialogus de Vit. S. Johan. Chrysost.*), and Cassianus, famous afterwards as a monk and a writer. Innocent represented the matter to the emperor Honorius, who wrote thrice to his brother Arcadius on the subject. His third letter, sent under the advice of a synod assembled by the pope at his request, urged the assembling of a combined council of Easterns and Westerns at Thessalonica. He desired Innocent to appoint five bishops, two priests, and one deacon as a deputation from the Western church; and these he charged with this third letter, in which he requested his brother to summon the Oriental bishops. He also sent letters addressed to himself by the bishops of Rome and Aquileia, as specimens of many so addressed, and as representing the opinion of the Western bishops on the question at issue (Innoc. *Ep.* ix. Galland.; Pallad. *Dialog.* c. iii.). The deputation was accompanied by four Eastern bishops who had fled to Rome. It failed entirely. Persecution was continued in the East; Honorius contemplated a war against his brother, but was deterred by a threatened invasion of the Goths; and Innocent, failing in his attempt to bring about an impartial council, separated himself from the communion of Atticus, Theophilus, and Porphyrius.

This appeal of St. Chrysostom and his friends involved no acknowledgment of any authority of the Roman bishop over the Eastern church. They apply to him not as a superior or a judge, but as a powerful friend whose support they solicit. Chrysostom's letter, which in Roman editions appears as addressed to the pope alone, was really written to the three principal bishops of the West. Its contents leave no doubt of this. Honorius, in his letters to his brother, speaks of the Western bishops generally having been applied to, and quotes their views as of equal moment with that of the bishops of Rome. Innocent in his replies makes no claim to adjudicate, nor does he make any assertion of the universal supremacy of his see, such as appears in his letters to the Africans and to Decentius, but recommends a council of Easterns and Westerns as the proper authoritative tribunal. For a view of papal claims over the East less than a century later see FELIX III. and ACACIUS (7).

After the death of Chrysostom the pope and all the West remained for some time out of communion with Constantinople, Alexandria, and Antioch. The church of Antioch was the first to be reconciled, when bp. Alexander in 413 replaced the name of Chrysostom in the diptychs of his church, and sent a legation to Rome to sue for restoration of communion. This was cordially granted in a synodal letter signed by 20 Italian bishops. Innocent wrote to Alexander congratulating him warmly and desiring a frequent interchange of letters. At the same time Acacius of Beroea, one of Chrysostom's bitterest opponents, was received into communion by Innocent through Alexander, to whom the letter of communion was sent for transmission. Atticus of Constantinople was reconciled a few years later. Moved partly by the threatening attitude of the populace, and partly by the advice of the emperor, he consented, with a bad grace, to place Chrysostom's name on the diptychs, and was received into communion. The church of Alexandria was the last to come to terms. Theophilus's nephew Cyril, succeeding him Oct. 18, 412, was urged by Atticus to yield, and did so at last, though not till 417, ten years after the death of Chrysostom. Throughout Innocent appears to have acted with dignity, fairness, firmness, and moderation. Alexander having, later, consulted the pope as to the jurisdiction of his patriarchal see of Antioch, Innocent replied that in accordance with the canons of Nice (*Can.* vi.) the authority of the bp. of Antioch extended over the whole diocese, not only over one province. *Diocese* is here used, in its original sense, to denote a civil division of the empire comprising many provinces. The Oriental diocese here referred to included 15 provinces, over the metropolitans of which the patriarchal jurisdiction of Antioch is alleged to extend.

Two more letters, written in the last year of his life, further illustrate Innocent's attitude towards the churches of the East. St. Jerome had been attacked in his cell at Bethlehem by a band of ruffians and had narrowly escaped; the two noble virgins, Eustochium and her niece Paula, living in retirement under his spiritual direction, had been driven from their house, which had been burnt, and some of their attendants killed. The party of Pelagius was suspected. Innocent wrote to Jerome, offering to exert "the whole authority of the apostolic see" against the offenders, if they could be discovered, and to appoint judges to try them; and to John, bp. of Jerusalem, who was no friend to Jerome, in an authoritative tone, reproving him severely for allowing such atrocities within his jurisdiction (*Epp.* xxxiv. xxxv. Galland.).

III. Alaric.—There were three Gothic invasions of Italy—the first under Alaric, the second under Radagaisus, the third led by Alaric himself, who laid siege to Rome A.D. 408. Innocent was within the city, the emperor at Ravenna. Famine and plague having ensued during the siege, Zosimus, the heathen historian, alleges that Pompeianus, the prefect of the city, having been persuaded by certain Etruscan diviners that their spells and sacrifices, performed on the Capitol, could draw down lightnings against the enemy, Innocent was consulted and consented, but the majority of the senators refused (v. 40). Sozomen mentions the circumstance but does not implicate Innocent (ix. 6). It seems highly improbable that Innocent would sanction such rites of heathenism. In 409 the offer of a ransom led Alaric to raise the siege, and two deputations were sent to the emperor at Ravenna to induce him to sanction the terms agreed on. The first having failed, Innocent accompanied the second, and thus was not in the city when it was finally taken on Aug. 24, 410. Alaric's invasion was regarded as a judgment on heathen rather than Christian Rome, and as a vindication of the church, the pope's providential absence being compared by Orosius to the saving of Lot from Sodom. Undoubtedly the event was a marked one in the supersession of heathenism by Christianity. The destruction of the old temples, never afterwards restored, the dispersion and ruin of families which clung most to the old order, the view that judgment had fallen on old heathen Rome, which its deities had been powerless to protect, all helped to complete the triumph of the church and to add importance to the reign of Innocent. Soon after this great event Augustine (A.D. 413) began his famous work, *de Civitate Dei*, though he took 13 years to complete it, in which he sees a vision of the kingdom of God rising on the ruins of the kingdom of the world—a vision which gradually took more distinct shape in the idea, already more or less grasped by Innocent, of a Catholic Christendom united under the Roman see.

Innocent's *Epistolae et Decreta* are printed in Galland's *Bibl. Pat.* t. viii. and in Migne, *Patr. Lat.* t. xx. Cf. *Innocent the Great* by C. H. C. Pirie-Gordon (Longmans ; 4 maps and 8 genealogical tables). [J.B—Y.]

Irenaeus (1), bp. of Lyons. Very little is known of his personal history except that he was a native of Asia Minor ; in early youth had seen and heard bp. Polycarp at Smyrna ; afterwards came into Gaul, and during the persecution of 177 carried, as presbyter of Lyons, a letter from the Gallican confessors to the Roman bp. Eleutherus (174 or 175-189) ; after the death of bp. Pothinus of Lyons (177) became his successor (Eus. *H. E.* v. 5), and was still bishop in the time of bp. Victor, who succeeded Eleutherus at Rome (189-198 or 199) ; and that he took a leading part in all ecclesiastical transactions and controversies of the time. St. Jerome speaks of him (*de Vir. Ill.* 35) as having flourished in the reign of Commodus (180-192). His birth is assigned to widely distant epochs. The earliest and the latest dates proposed are 50 years apart (97-147). Various considerations lead us to fix on *c.* 126, or possibly *c.* 136, as the latest admissible date.

Of his youthful literary training and culture we can only judge from his writings, which shew some acquaintance with the Greek poets and philosophers ; he cites Homer, Hesiod, Pindar, and Plato. Of his Christian training he tells us that, besides instructions from Polycarp, he had other teachers, "Presbyters" (of Asia Minor), whom he designates as mediate or immediate disciples of the apostles (*Haer.* ii. 22, 5 ; iv. 27, 1 ; 32, 1 ; v. 5, 1 ; 30, 1 ; 33, 3 ; 36, 1). Whether he was personally acquainted with Papias, whom he mentions so frequently, is uncertain. If he was in Rome A.D. 156 he doubtless continued his studies there. The time of his removal into Gaul is unknown, but there were close ties between the missionary church of Gaul and the mother-churches of Asia Minor. At the time of the persecution, to which the aged bp. Pothinus fell a victim in the 17th year of Marcus Aurelius, A.D. 177 (cf. my *Chronologie der römischen Bischöfe*, p. 185), Irenaeus was a presbyter at Lugdunum. That Irenaeus wrote the epistle of the Gallican confessors to the churches of Asia Minor and Phrygia, which so vividly describes the persecution (ap. Eus. *H. E.* v. 1), is an uncertain conjecture. There is indeed a fragment preserved by Oecumenius and assigned to Irenaeus (*Fragm. Graec.* xiii. ap. Harvey, ii. 482 seq.), which really stands in very close connexion with that epistle, mentioning in a similar way the calumny about "Thyestean banquets," which rested on depositions wrung from tortured slaves, the endeavours of the persecutors to force the martyrs Sanctus and Blandina to make a like confession, and Blandina's answer, which, though not identical with that in the epistle, is nearly related to it. Irenaeus's mission to Rome was undertaken to intercede with bp. Eleutherus for the Montanists of Asia Minor in the name and on behalf of the Gallican confessors (Eus. *H. E.* v. 3, 4). That another object of the journey was that Irenaeus himself might obtain episcopal consecration at Rome is an unproved assertion of some Roman Catholic authors. The common assumption that there was then no episcopal see but Lyons in all Gaul is hardly warranted by the fact that in the narrative of the persecution at Vienne a deacon only and no bishop is mentioned. A better argument is that Eusebius (*H. E.* v. 23) appears to speak of Irenaeus as bishop of all the churches of Gaul. But neither can be regarded as a sure proof.

As bp. of Lyons Irenaeus was distinguished for his zeal for the conversion of the heathen (cf. the Acts of St. Ferreolus and his companions, Boll. *Acta SS.* 16 Jun. iii.), and yet more by his conflicts with heretics and his strenuous endeavours to maintain the peace of the church, in true accord with his name Εἰρηναῖος (Peace-man). His great work *Against all Heresies* was probably written during his episcopate. The preface informs us that he then first wrote as an ecclesiastical writer. We subsequently find him exerting himself to protect the churches of his native country (Asia Minor) from Roman pretensions and aggression. The Roman bp. Victor was endeavouring to compel these churches, which had hitherto kept Easter, with the Jews, on Nisan 14, to conform to the practice of Rome. On their refusal to abandon the custom of their forefathers, their reasons being given in a letter addressed to Victor by Polycrates, bp. of Ephesus, he had cut them off from his communion. This harsh treatment was highly disapproved by many even of those who, like the Roman bishop, kept Easter on the Sunday following the equinoctial full-moon. Among these was Irenaeus himself. In the name of all the Gallican churches he remonstrated with Victor, in a writing of which a considerable fragment is extant, reminding him of the example set by his predecessors, who had found no occasion in these differences of paschal observance for excommunicating their brethren of Asia Minor. Irenaeus (as Eusebius further informs us, *H. E.* v. 23) also appealed to other foreign bishops, but without any effect on the harsh determination of the Roman. Another writing of Irenaeus mentioned by Eusebius (*H. E.* v. 20), which seems to have referred to the same subject, was entitled περὶ σχίσματος and addressed to Blastus, head of the Roman Quartodecimans.

How long Irenaeus was bishop is uncertain. His death is commonly assigned to 202 or 203. This rests on the assumption that he was martyred under Septimius Severus. But such a martyrdom is by no means established. Tertullian, Hippolytus, Eusebius, Epiphanius, Ephrem, Augustine, Theodoret, are silent. In the Syriac fragments Irenaeus is frequently spoken of as "a disciple of Polycarp, bishop and martyr," but not himself honoured with the martyr's title either there or in any quotations from his writings. The first witness for his martyrdom is found in Jerome's commentary on Isaiah, written *c.* 410, where (c. 64) Irenaeus is spoken of as *vir apostolicus episcopus et martyr*; but when elsewhere treating *ex professo* of his life and writings (*de Vir. Ill.* c. 35), Jerome is silent as to his martyrdom. As Dodwell conjectures, the words *et martyr* may be an interpolation. If not, Jerome must have learnt the alleged fact subsequently to 392, when the *de Viris Illustribus* was written. There is no witness for it earlier than the 5th cent.

Writings.—The chief was the great work in five books against Gnosticism entitled Ἔλεγχος καὶ ἀνατροπὴ τῆς ψευδωνύμου γνώσεως, *Detectio et eversio falso cognominatae agnitionis.* (The full Greek title is found in Eus. *H. E.* v. 7; Phot. *Bibl. Cod.* 120 and elsewhere; cf. also frequent references to it by Irenaeus in the *praefationes* to bks. ii. iv. v. and the conclusion of bk. iv.) It is commonly cited under the briefer title πρὸς αἱρέσεις (*contra Haereses*). We possess it entire in the Latin version only, which, however, must have been made from the Greek original very soon after its composition, since the Latin was used by Tertullian some ten years after, in his tractate *adv. Valentinianos.* Its translator was a Celt (witness the barbarous Latinity); probably one of the clergy of Lyons. Most of the original work being now lost, the slavish literality of the translator imparts to his version a very high value. Many obscurities of expression, arising in part from a misunderstanding of the Greek idiom, admit an easy solution when translated back into Greek. Beside this Latin version, which appears to have soon superseded the Greek original in the Western church, there was a Syriac translation, of which numerous fragments are extant and were first put together by Harvey in his ed. of Irenaeus (ii. 431 seq.). They are derived from the Brit. Mus. collection of Nitrian MSS., some of which are as old as the 6th, 7th, and 8th cents. (cf. Harvey, ii. 431, note). To these are added (Nos. xxi. xxxi. and xxxii.) fragments of an Armenian interpolated version first published by Pitra in his *Spicilegium Solesmense,* t. i. (Paris, 1852). Of these No. xxi. only is taken from the work *Against Heresies.* The almost entire agreement between these Syriac fragments and the Old Latin version further witnesses its genuineness and fidelity. The Greek original, said to have been still extant in the 16th cent., was made great use of by Hippolytus (or whoever wrote the *Philosophumena*), Epiphanius, and Theodoret. To the numerous extracts in these writers, esp. the first two, we owe the greater part of the original Greek of bk. i.—the preface and cc. 1-21 entire, and numerous fragments besides. Of the other books, the Greek has come down to us in isolated passages, mostly through citations by Eusebius. The ed. of Wigan Harvey (2 vols. Camb. 1857) is based on a careful collation of the Codices Claromont. and Arundel. His *Prolegomena* contain minute investigations into the origin, characteristics and main phenomena of Gnosticism, as well as concerning the life and writings of Irenaeus.

Against Heresies was written in Gaul. (Irenaeus says so expressly, lib. i. praef. 3, cf. i. 13, 7. We follow Massuet's division of chapters.) The date of composition is determined iii. 3, 3, in which he speaks of Eleutherus as then twelfth in succession to the apostles on the episcopal chair of Rome (νῦν δωδεκάτῳ τόπῳ τὸν τῆς ἐπισκοπῆς ἀπὸ τῶν ἀποστόλων κατέχει κλῆρον Ἐλεύθερος). According to this, the third book was written at the earliest A.D. 174 or 175, at the latest A.D. 189 (cf. *Chronologie der röm. Bischöfe,* pp. 184 sqq.). The commencement and completion of the work were possibly some years apart, but we cannot put the date of bks. iv. and v. so late as the episcopate of Victor (189-198 or 199). We may tentatively assume 182, the mid-period of Eleutherus's episcopate, or (since the first two books alone appear to have been written immediately after each other—cf. the prefaces to bks. ii. and iii.-v.) we may propose from A.D. 180 to 185 as the date of the whole work. To assign a more exact date is hopeless. That Irenaeus wrote as bishop, and not earlier than 178 as presbyter, is by far most probable, though it cannot be drawn with absolute certainty from the words of the preface to bk. v. to which Massuet appeals.

As *the first external motive* for its composition, Irenaeus himself mentions (lib. i. praef.; ii. 17, 1; iii. praef.) the request of a friend for some instruction as to the heretical opinions of the Valentinians and how to refute them. The recent spread of the Valentinian sect through the Rhone district had already led Irenaeus to acquaint himself particularly with their writings and tenets. The dangerous character of their teaching had been fully recognized by others, whom he modestly designates as *multo nobis meliores*; but these had been (iv. praef.) unable through ignorance of the Valentinian "rule" or system of doctrine to adequately refute it. That it was his first object to refute Valentinianism, and only in a secondary and occasional way to attack other heresies, is evident from the whole construction and arrangement of bk. i., which is almost exclusively occupied with the Valentinians, and in a great measure bk. ii. also. Irenaeus repeatedly observes that he who refutes the Valentinians at the same time refutes all other heresies (cf. ii. 31, 1) "destructis itaque his qui a Valentino sunt, omnis haereticorum eversa est multitudo," an assertion of which he proceeds (31, 1-35, 5) to give detailed proof, in reference to various heretical parties. Thus in the preface to bk. iv. he speaks of the "doctrina eorum qui sunt a Valentino" as a "recapitulatio omnium haereticorum," and in bk. ii. of having taken them as an example of the way in which all heretics are to be refuted ("tanquam speculum habuimus eos totius eversionis"). In bks. iii. iv. and v. the circle of vision is enlarged. Taking the Scriptures for his guide, he goes through in order the fundamental doctrines of Gnosticism, and besides Valentinian dogmas reviews the cognate ones of other heretical schools, specially of the Marcionites, but nowhere gives such a connected view and refutation of other Gnostic systems as of the Valentinian in bk. ii.

His sources were primarily the writings of the heretics themselves. In the preface of bk. i. he speaks of the ὑπομνήματα of disciples of Valentinus, and observes that he has been in personal communication with some of them. More particularly it is the school of Ptolemaeus, an ἀπάνθισμα τῆς Οὐαλεντίνου σχολῆς, whose dogmatic system he sets himself to describe. The detailed account (*c. Haer.* i. 1-7) describes its development in the Western or Italian form, and this from several writings, one of which Clemens Alexandrinus also made use of in the *excerpta ex scriptis Theodoti*, cc. 44-65. From another source were derived additional details, cc. 11 and 12, of various opinions within the Valentinian system and of Valentinus himself, Secundus, Ptolemaeus, and others; c. 13, 1-5, cc. 14 and 15 are concerned with Marcus, his magic arts and theories about the symbolism of letters and numbers, concluding with a citation of some Iambic Senarii, written against him by a "Divinae aspirationis Senior et Praeco veritatis" (ὁ θεόπνευστος πρεσβύτης καὶ κῆρυξ τῆς ἀληθείας). The same authority is further designated, after the quotation, as "amator Dei senior," which Epiphanius expresses by ὁ θεοφιλὴς πρεσβύτης.

Two other sources, from which Irenaeus may have derived acquaintance with Gnostic opinions, have been conjectured by Harnack (*Zur Quellenkritik der Geschichte des Gnosticismus*, p. 56) for the information in bks. iii.-v. concerning the details of Marcion's system, which with the Valentinian is the heresy most frequently referred to in that portion. These were Marcion's own writings and a refutation of Marcion by a presbyter of Asia Minor.

It would be of great interest to obtain more exact impressions of those other presbyters to whose words and writings Irenaeus makes frequent reference. Besides the "God-loving elder," from whom he borrows the Iambic Senarii against Marcus, Irenaeus cites on various occasions from "presbyters and disciples of the apostles"; under which title, besides Polycarp, bp. Papias of Hierapolis must certainly be included. From bk. iv. of Papias's Λογίων κυριακῶν ἐξηγήσεις Irenaeus cites the saying traditionally attributed to our Lord on the alleged testimony of St. John concerning the glories of His millennial kingdom (v. 33, 3 sqq.).

Of the writings of Polycarp there is no certain trace in Irenaeus, but he held in faithful remembrance his oral utterances. He knows indeed several writings of the bp. of Smyrna (*Ep. ad Florin.* ap. Eus. v. 20) and specially mentions Polycarp's Ep. to the Philippians (*Haer.* iii. 3, 4). Of the works of Justin Martyr Irenaeus knew and used—besides the Syntagma against all Heresies, and the possibly identical Syntagma against Marcion—the first Apologies, without, however, citing it (*Quellen der ältesten Ketzergeschichte*, p. 63). From which of Justin's works the citation, v. 26, 2, is derived cannot be decided. With far greater confidence we may assume Irenaeus to have used the *Memoirs* of Hegesippus (iii. 3, 3; 4, 3, cf. *Quellen der ält. Ketzergesch.* p. 73), and he makes one citation from the Ep. of Ignatius to the Romans (v. 28, 4), but without mentioning his name.

Irenaeus's great work is divided into five books. Bk. i. contains a detailed account of the Valentinian system, together with a general view of the opinions of the other sects. Bk. ii. undertakes to exhibit the unreasonableness and self-contradiction of the doctrines of Valentinianism. His chief object here is to combat the doctrine of the Demiurge or Creator as a subordinate existence outside the Pleroma, of limited power and insight, and separated from the "Father" by an infinite chasm. He also controverts the Valentinian doctrine concerning the Pleroma and its antithesis the Kenoma, the theory of Emanations, of the Fall of Achamoth, and the formation of the lower world through the sufferings of the *Sophia*; and finally, at great length, the Gnostic teaching concerning souls, and the distinction between Psychici and Pneumatici. Bks. iii. iv. and v. contain the refutation of Gnostic doctrines from Holy Scripture, preceded by a short dissertation on the sources of Christian truth. The one foundation of the faith is the gospel transmitted first by oral tradition and subsequently committed to writing. The Gnostics allow neither the refutation of their doctrines out of Scripture nor disproof from tradition. Against the one they appeal to a secret doctrine handed down among themselves, against the other to their own higher knowledge (gnosis). Irenaeus meets them by stating the characteristics of genuine apostolic tradition as ensuring the right interpretation of Holy Scripture. The chief *media* and transmitters of this tradition are the apostolic churches and their episcopal succession from the apostles themselves (*Haer.* iii. 1-4). He proceeds to give the proof from

Scripture—first, against the doctrine of the Demiurge, then against the Gnostic Christology. There is but one God, Creator of the world and Father of our Lord Jesus Christ, Who is the Son, the Eternal God-Logos, and has truly been made Flesh in order to redeem mankind from its fall in Adam. Under this head he combats the errors of both Docetae and Ebionites, and, returning to his main purpose, attacks the chief Gnostic doctrine in a refutation of Marcion's attempt to distinguish between the *Good* God and the *Just* or Judicial God. This occupies him at the close of bk. iii. Bk. iv. is directed against the same doctrine. Irenaeus now attacks the distinction made between the lawgiver and the Father, shewing the identity of the divine revelation in O. and N. T., the close connexion between law and gospel, and the typical pre-announcement of the N.T. in the Old. He shews that eternal happiness or endless misery will befall men from the same God, as reward or as punishment for their own free choice of good or evil. Bk. v. gives a detailed proof of the resurrection of the body and of the millennial kingdom.

Of other writings of Irenaeus, fragments only, or bare names, have been preserved. Whether he ever carried out the intention, announced i. 27, 4 and iii. 12, 12, of writing a special treatise against Marcion, cannot be determined. Eusebius (*H. E.* v. 8) mentions this intention, and elsewhere (*H. E.* iv. 25) reckons Irenaeus, with Philip of Gortyna and Modestus, among authors who had written against Marcion. Of his *Epistle to Florinus*, Eusebius has preserved a considerable fragment. FLORINUS was an older contemporary of Irenaeus and a disciple of Polycarp. He was afterwards a presbyter at Rome, and was deposed, apparently for heresy (Eus. *H. E.* v. 15). The epistle of Irenaeus, addressed to him, bore also, according to Eusebius (*H. E.* v. 20), the title περὶ μοναρχίας ἢ περὶ τοῦ μὴ εἶναι τὸν Θεὸν ποιητὴν κακῶν, which implies that he had adopted Gnostic opinions. The "God" whom he apparently regarded as the author of evil was the Gnostic Demiurge. He afterwards, according to Eusebius, inclined to Valentinianism; whereupon Irenaeus addressed him in another treatise, περὶ ὀγδοάδος, from which Eusebius quotes the concluding words, conjuring the copyists to make an accurate and faithful transcript of his words. The epistle περὶ μοναρχίας is regarded by Leimbach (*Zeitschrift für lutherische Theologie,* 1873, pp. 626 seq.) and Lightfoot (*Contemp. Rev.* 1875, May, p. 834) as one of Irenaeus's earliest writings. Leimbach would date it between 168 and 177, but his arguments are trivial. Of far greater importance is Lightfoot's argument that the treatise περὶ ὀγδοάδος was probably written before the great work *Against Heresies*, since its detailed treatment of the Valentinian system would have made a special tractate on the Ogdoad superfluous. But Lightfoot seems to have overlooked the fragmentary portion of an epistle to Victor of Rome, preserved among the Syriac fragments of Irenaeus (*Fragm.* xxviii. ap. Harvey, ii. p. 457), which is introduced with the words, "And Irenaeus, bp. of Lyons, to Victor, bp. of Rome, concerning Florinus, a presbyter who was a partisan of the error of Valentinus, and published an abominable book, thus wrote:" whereupon follows the fragment itself. From these words it appears that the epistle from which the fragment was taken could not have been written till after the first three books *Against Heresies*, probably not till after the completion of the whole, and, at the earliest, *c.* 190.

If Eusebius is right in making the deposition of the Roman presbyter Blastus contemporaneous with that of Florinus ,the epistle addressed to the former by Irenaeus and entitled περὶ σχίσματος (Eus. *H. E.* v. 20) must belong to the same period. Blastus was, according to Eusebius, the head of the Roman Montanists (*H. E.* v. 15)—cf. also Pacianus, *Ep. ad Sympronian.* c. 1—and, according to Pseudo-Tertullian (*Libell. adv. Omn. Haereses,* 22), a Quartodeciman. Both are probably correct. We know that the Montanists of Asia Minor (like the Christians there) kept Easter on Nisan 14 (cf. Schwegler, *Montanismus,* p. 251); it is therefore quite credible that Blastus, as a Montanist, may have conformed to Quartodeciman practice, and, as a member of the Roman presbytery, may have sought to introduce it into Rome. But if Blastus be the one referred to in another Syriac fragment (*Fragm.* xxvii. ap. Harvey, ii. 456), he was not an Asiatic but an Alexandrian; and on this supposition his Quartodecimanism must have come from his close connexion with the Montanists of Asia Minor, since the Paschal calendar of Alexandria was the same as that of Rome. One can, moreover, quite understand bp. Victor's responding to any attempt on Blastus's part to create a schism in the Roman church by introducing the Asiatic custom, with deposition from the presbyteral office. Such a breach of discipline in his own diocese (the actual spectacle of some Roman Christians keeping Easter with the Asiatics on Nisan 14, and in opposition to the ancestral custom of the bps. of Rome) would naturally excite him to uncompromising harshness towards the brethren of Asia Minor generally; so that on these refusing to conform to the Roman custom, he at once cut off the churches of the Asiatic province and the neighbouring dioceses from his church-communion (cf. my art. in *Zeitschrift für wissenschaftliche Theologie,* 1866, pp. 192 seq., and *Chronologie der röm. Bischöfe,* p. 174). These ecclesiastical troubles moved the man of peace, Irenaeus, to send letters of remonstrance to both Blastus and bp. Victor. To the former, which according to Eusebius bore the title περὶ σχίσματος, may possibly be assigned the Syriac fragment (xxvii. ap. Harvey, ii. 456) introduced with the following words: "Irenaeus, bp. of Lyons, who was a contemporary of Polycarp, disciple of the apostle, bp. of Smyrna and martyr, and for this reason is held in just estimation, wrote to an Alexandrian that it is right, with respect to the Feast of the Resurrection, that we should celebrate it upon the first day of the week." But inasmuch as we know from Eusebius (*H. E.* v. 24) that Irenaeus wrote on the same subject to several persons, it is possible that this Alexandrian may have been another than Blastus. Of the letter to Victor Eusebius (*ib.*) has preserved a considerable extract showing that the current controversies regarded also the mode and duration of the antecedent Paschal fast. Some kept one day, others two days, others several days; some again reckoned their fast-day at 40 hours of day and night (οἱ δὲ τεσσαράκοντα ὥρας ἡμερινάς τε καὶ νυκτερινὰς συμμετροῦσι τὴν ἡμέραν αὐτῶν). But these differences of practice resting on ancient custom—so Irenaeus proceeds to say—have never yet disturbed the church's peace and unity of faith. For although former bishops of Rome, from Xystus to Soter, had never kept Nisan 14, they had always maintained full communion with any who came from dioceses where it was observed; *e.g.* Polycarp, whom Anicetus permitted to celebrate in his own church, both separating afterwards in peace. No title is given by Eusebius to this epistle, but according to the *Quaestiones et Responsa ad Orthodoxos* of Pseudo-Justin (c. 115) it was entitled περὶ τοῦ Πάσχα (cf. *Fragm. Graec.* vii. ap. Harvey, ii. 478). In the same work Pseudo-Justin tells us further that the old Christian custom of refraining from kneeling on Easter Day, as a sign of Christ's resurrection, is carried back by Irenaeus to apostolic times, and the observance of this custom continued through the season of Pentecost, as the whole period (of 50 days after Easter) was regarded as equal to Easter Day itself.

Of other writings of Irenaeus Eusebius mentions (*H. E.* v. 26) a short tractate, πρὸς Ἕλληνας, which bore also the title περὶ ἐπιστήμης, an ἐπίδειξις τοῦ ἀποστολικοῦ κηρύγματος, addressed to a certain Marcian; and a βιβλίον διαλέξεων διαφόρων, in which he is said to have cited *Hebrews* and the *Wisdom of Solomon.* Jerome, apparently copying Eusebius, makes, however, a distinction (*de Vir. Ill.* 35) between the λόγος πρὸς Ἕλληνας and the περὶ ἐπιστήμης ("scripsit . . . contra Gentes volumen breve et de Disciplina aliud"). The tractate on Apostolical Preaching addressed to Marcian appears to have been a catechetical work on the Rule of Faith. The βιβλίον διαλέξεων διαφόρων appears, in accordance with the early usage of the word διαλέξεις (cf. Harvey, i. p. clxvii. sqq.), to have been a collection of homilies on various Scripture texts. Rufinus incorrectly renders διαλέξεις by *Dialogus*; Jerome by *Tractatus.* From these homilies were probably taken the numerous Gk. fragments found in various catenae, containing expositions of various passages of the Pentateuch and the historical books of O.T. and of St. Matthew and St. Luke (*Fr. Graec.* xv.-xxiii., xxv.-xxix., xxxi., xxxiii., xxxiv., xxxix., xl., xlii.-xlvii.), as well as the Syriac fragment of an exposition of the Song of Solomon (*Fr. Syr.* xxvi. ap. Harvey, ii. 455) and the Armenian homily on the Sons of Zebedee (*Fr. Syr.* xxxii. ap. Harvey, ii. 464 sqq.). To the same collection would also belong a tractate on the History of Elkanah and Samuel, mentioned in a Syriac manuscript (Harvey, ii. 507 note).

His Theology and Influence on Ecclesiastical Development.—Irenaeus, with Tertullian, Hippolytus, Cyprian, on the one side, and Clemens Alexandrinus and Origen on the other, was a main founder of the ancient Catholic church, as it rose amid conflicts with Gnosticism and Montanism, out of the church of the post-apostolic era. Baur and the Tübingen school were wrong in explaining the development of primitive Catholic Christianity as the fruit of a compromise effected by the Pauline and Petrine parties soon after the middle of the 2nd cent. to overcome the new opposition. The earliest post-apostolic form of Christianity was no mere product of conflicting antitheses of the apostolic time, or of their reconciliation. The Jewish-Christian communities of Palestine and Syria formed, even towards the end of the 1st cent., a small and vanishing minority as compared to the swelling dimensions of the Gentile church. That to some extent Jewish-Christian influences did operate upon Gentile Christianity during the former half of the 2nd cent. need not wholly be denied; yet the one feature in which we are most tempted to trace them—the conception of the gospel as a new law—is quite as much the outcome of an internal development within the Gentile church itself. The ultimate triumph of Christian universalism, and the recognized equality between Jewish and Gentile members of the church of the Messiah, was a fruit of the life-long labours of St. Paul. The new Christian community, largely Gentile, regarded itself as the true people of God, as the spiritual Israel, and as the genuine heir of the church of the O.T., while the great mass of Jewish unbelievers were, as a penalty for their rejection of the true Messiah, excluded from the blessings of the kingdom of God. To this new spiritual Israel were speedily, in part at least, transferred the forms of the O.T. theocracy, and all the Jewish Scriptures were received as divinely inspired documents by the new church. But, whereas St. Paul had emphasized the antithesis between law and gospel, the Gentile churches after his time attached themselves more closely to the doctrinal norm of the older apostles, and laid stress on the continued validity of the law for Christians; though, as it was impossible to bind Gentiles to observe the ceremonial law, its precepts were given, after the example of the Jewish religious philosophy of Alexandria, a spiritual interpretation. Already, in *Hebrews,* we find the relations between O. and N. T. viewed under the aspect of Type and Anti-type, Prophecy and Fulfilment. The later Gentile Christianity learned to see everywhere in O.T. types of the gospel revelation, and thus combined freedom from the Mosaic ceremonial law with the maintenance of the entire continuity of the O. and N. T. revelation. The Moral Law, as the centre and substance of the Mosaic revelation, remained the obligatory norm of conduct for Gentile Christians; Christ had not abrogated the law of Moses, but fulfilled and completed it. The theological learning of the time confines itself too exclusively to a typological interpretation of O.T. So much the greater, on the other hand, is the influence exercised upon these writers by heathen philosophic culture. In the Apologists of the middle portion of the 2nd cent.—Justin, Tatian, Theophilus, Athenagoras—this influence appears specially strong. Justin makes constant endeavours to comprehend Christianity under the then generally accepted forms of philosophical speculation, and to commend it as a manifestation of the highest reason to the cultured minds of his time. In this way he became the first founder of a Catholic system of theology. The doctrine of the Divine Logos as the "Second God," the Mediator through Whom all divine revelation is transmitted, was already for Justin an apologetic weapon, remained thence forward a standing basis for the philosophical defence of Christianity, and proved in after-times the strongest weapon in the church's armoury in the conflict with Gnostic opinions.

The widespread appearance of the manifold forms of Gnosticism in the 2nd cent. is a most significant proof of the far-reaching influence exercised by pagan thought and speculation on the Gentile church of that age. The danger from the influx on all sides of foreign thought was all the greater because the Gentile churches had as yet but a feeble comprehension of the ideas specially belonging to Christianity. The conflict with Gnosticism gradually gave fresh vigour to that revival of fundamental Christian and Pauline thought which distinguishes the theology of Irenaeus and of other early "Catholic" doctors at the end of the 2nd and beginning of the 3rd cent. from the simpler and poorer view of Christian truth presented in the works of the early Apologists. The perils with which the Gnostic speculation menaced the Christian system were, on the one hand, concerned with that which formed a common groundwork for Christianity and Judaism—*i.e.* first and specially the Monotheistic principle itself, and then the doctrines of Divine Justice, Freedom of the Will, and Future Retribution; on the other hand, they had regard to the traditions peculiar to Christianity concerning the historical person and work of Jesus Christ, the genuine human realism of His life and sufferings, the universal application of His redeeming work to all believers, and the external and historical character of that final restitution to which Christians looked forward. The Monotheistic idea, the divine μοναρχία, was assailed by the Gnostic doctrine of the Demiurge, the Pleroma, and the series of Aeons; and the universally accepted doctrine of our Lord's Incarnation and Messiahship by the various forms of Gnostic docetism. Further, the whole ethical basis of Christian religion was destroyed by the distinctions which Gnostic teachers made between two or three separate classes of mankind, and by their view of redemption as a purely theoretical process, or as the impartation of true knowledge (gnosis) to *those only* who by their own originally pneumatic nature had from the beginning been predestined to reception into the heavenly realm of light. Instead of the Christian doctrine of Freewill and consequent responsibility, they taught an iron heathenish metaphysical Necessity, which arbitrarily determined the fortunes of men; instead of a future divine recompense according to the measure of faith and works, a one-sided over-estimation of mere knowledge as the one condition of ultimate salvation; instead of the original Christian notion of the final consummation as a series of great outward visible occurrences, the resurrection of the flesh, a day of final judgment, and the setting up on earth of a millennial kingdom, they taught the spiritualistic conception of a saving deliverance of pneumatic souls and their translation into the upper world; whereas for the *Psychici* was reserved only a limited share in such knowledge and salvation, and for the material ("hylic" or "choic") man and for the earthly bodies of men, nothing but an ultimate and complete annihilation. It cannot be denied that both the Gentile Christianity of that era and the Catholic theology of following times appropriated various elements nearly related to these Gnostic speculations. A Catholic gnosis also appeared, which differed essentially from that heretical gnosis in intending to maintain unimpaired the received foundations of Christian faith. Yet, in truth, the idealistic speculations of the Alexandrine school were separated from those of the heretical gnosis by very uncertain lines of demarcation, and were afterwards, in some essential points, rejected by the church. Irenaeus, in contradistinction to the Alexandrine doctors, appears to have been less concerned with setting up a Catholic in opposition to the heretical gnosis, than with securing the foundations of the common Christian faith by *strengthening the bands of existing church unity.* He recognizes certain subjects which, as lying outside the rule of faith delivered to all, might be safely entrusted to the deeper and more searching meditations and inquiries of the more enlightened, but these related only to a clearer understanding of the details of the history of divine revelation, the right interpretation of parables, insight into the divine plan of human salvation (why God should bear with such long-suffering the apostasy of angels and the disobedience of man at the Fall), the differences and unity of the two Testaments, the necessity for the Incarnation of the Logos, the second coming of Christ at the end of time, the conversion of the heathen, the resurrection of the body, etc. (*Haer.* i. 10, 3). These questions would arise in the course of the Gnostic controversy, but the form in which Irenaeus presents them assumes everywhere a clear antithesis to Gnostic speculation and a firm retention of the Catholic rule of faith. Only in quite an isolated form is once named the question why one and the same God should have created the temporal and the eternal, the earthly and the heavenly; while Irenaeus insists strongly on the narrow bounds of human knowledge and insight, and on the impossibility for mortal man to know the reasons for everything (ii. 25, 3; 28, 1), and is never weary of chastising the arrogant presumption of the *Pneumatici* who exalt themselves above the *Creator*, while their impotence in the presence of His works is manifest to all (ii. 30, 1 sqq.).

His theoretical refutation of Gnostc opinions, *e.g.* in bk. ii., is full of acute remarks. His main purpose is to repel the Gnostic assault on the divine monarchia. He shews that by the separation of the Creator from the highest God, the absolute being of God Himself is denied. Neither above nor beside the Creator Himself can there be any other principle, for so God Himself would cease to be the all-embracing Pleroma, and being limited from without would cease to be infinite. And so again, if the Pleroma be separated from all beneath it by an immeasurable discrepancy, a third principle is introduced, which limits the other two, and is greater than both, and the questions concerning the limiting and the limited become boundlessly insoluble. He urges similar arguments against the doctrine of creative angels. If their creative energies are independent of the Godhead, God ceases to be God; if dependent upon Him, He is represented as needing inferior assistants. Against the assumption of a vacuum (κένωμα, σκιὰ κενώματος) outside the Divine Pleroma, he remarks that, if the world be thought of as produced out of this void and formless substratum without the knowledge of the προπατώρ, then the attribute of omniscience is denied Him. Nor can it be explained why for such endless times He should have left that space thus empty. Again, if God did actually beforehand form this lower world for Himself in thought, then was He its real creator. In that case its mutability and transient duration must have been fore-willed by the Father Himself, and not be due to any defect or ignorance on the part of an inferior maker. The origin of the κένωμα also is incomprehensible. If it be an emanation from the Divine Pleroma, that Pleroma itself must be burdened with emptiness and imperfection. If it be self-originated, it is really as absolute as the Father of all Himself. Such a defect, again, in the Pleroma, like a spot on a garment, would have been at once removed, in the very beginning, had the Divine Father been able to remove it; if otherwise, the blame of letting it remain so long must fall upon Him, and He will have to be accounted, like the heathen Jupiter, repentant over His own ways. Nay, if He was unable to remove this defect in the beginning, He cannot remove it now. The imperfection of this lower world leads back then to the conclusion that there must have been something void or formless, dark or disorderly, an element of error or infirmity in the Father Himself or in His Pleroma. The like thought recurs in the further argument that the temporal and transient could not have been made after the image of the unchangeable and eternal without introducing into it an alien element of mutability. The image must be like its prototype, and not opposed to it, and therefore the earthly material composite cannot be the image of that which is spiritual without drawing down the spiritual into its own sphere of materialism. The same objection is made to the notion that the corporeal may be an image or shadow of the spiritual world. It is only something corporeal that can cast a shadow. Again, if it be maintained that the Creator could not make the world out of Himself, but only after a foreign archetype, the same must be true of the Divine Father. He also must have derived, from some other source, the archetype of that higher world of which He was the maker, and so on. The question about type and archetype would thus be drawn out into infinity (ii. 1-8). But inasmuch as we must stop at some original at last, it is far more reasonable to believe that the Creator and the One only God are one and the same (ii. 16, 1 sqq.).

In the interest of the same absolute divine Perfection and Unity, Irenaeus controverts the Valentinian doctrine of the Aeons. Besides noting the arbitrary way in which the Pleroma is made to consist of 30 Aeons, neither more nor less (ii. 12, 1; 15, 1; 16, 1), he finds fault with the anthropomorphic conceptions behind the whole theory of emanations. The fact that the Propator Himself is reckoned as an Aeon, the unemanate, unborn, illimitable, formless One placed in the same class with emanations and births and limitations and forms, destroys the absolute perfection of the divine Nature (ii. 12, 1). Again, the separation from the Godhead of its own indivisible elements, the conception of the divine Ἔννοια, the divine Νοῦς, the divine Λόγος, etc., as so many hypostases, which in various stages have issued from its bosom, is an unwarrantable transfer of human passions and affections to the divine, which, on the contrary, is all Ἔννοια, all Νοῦς, all Λόγος, and knows of no such division from itself (ii. 13). He subjects to acute criticism the manner in which each Aeon is supposed to have been produced: was it without substantial separation, as the ray proceeding from the sun, or was it hypostatical, as one human being is personally distinct from all others, or was it by organic growth, as the branch from the tree? He asks whether these emanations are all of the same substance with those from which they proceed and contemporaneous with them, or have come forth in different stages? Whether they are all simple and alike, as spirits and lights, or composite and corporeal and of various forms? (ii. 17, 1 sqq.). He insists on carrying to their literal consequences the mythological conceptions which regarded the Valentinian Aeons as so many distinct personalities, produced according to human analogy among themselves; and he offers the alternative, that they must either be like their original Parent the Father and therefore impassible as He is (in which case there could be no suffering Aeon like the Valentinian Sophia), or different from Him in substance and capable of suffering, upon which the question arises, how such differences of substance could come to exist in the unchangeable Pleroma.

So acute a polemic must have equally served the interests of philosophy by its maintenance of the absolute character of the divine idea and of religion by its assertion of the divine monarchia. Irenaeus, like other opponents of Gnosticism, was clearly convinced that the whole system betrayed influences of heathen thought. The theory that everything must return to the originals of its component parts, and that God Himself is bound by this Necessity, so that even He cannot impart to the mortal immortality, to the corruptible incorruption, was derived by the Gnostics from the Stoics; the Valentinian doctrine of the Soter as made up from all the Aeons, each contributing thereto the flower of his own essence, is nothing more than the Hesiodic fable about Pandora.

Yet the Gnostics wished and meant to be Christians, and indeed set up a claim to possess a deeper knowledge of Christian truth than the Psychici of the church. Like their opponents, they appealed to Scripture in proof of their doctrines, and also boasted to be in possession of genuine apostolical traditions, deriving their doctrines, some from St. Paul, others from St. Peter, others from Judas, Thomas, Philip, and Matthew. In addition to the secret doctrine which they professed to have received by oral tradition, they appealed to alleged writings of the apostles or their disciples. In conducting his controversy on these lines with the Valentinians, Irenaeus remarks first on their arbitrary method of dealing with Scripture; and describes their mode of drawing arguments from it as a "twisting ropes of sand" (i. 8, 1; ii. 10, 1). They indulge in every kind of perverse interpretation, and violently wresting texts out of their natural connexion put them arbitrarily together again after the manner of the centos made from Homer (i. 9, 4). He compares this proceeding to that of a bungler who has broken up a beautiful mosaic portrait of a king made by skilful artists out of costly gems, and puts the stones together again to form an ill-executed image of a dog or fox, maintaining that it is the same beautiful king's portrait as before (i. 8, 1). Since the Gnostics specially exercised their arts of interpretation on our Lord's parables, Irenaeus repeatedly lays down principles on which such interpretation should be made (ii. 10, 2; 20, 1 sqq.; 27, 1 sqq.). Dark and ambiguous passages are not to be cleared up by still darker interpretations nor enigmas solved by greater enigmas; but that which is dark and ambiguous must be illustrated by that which is consistent and clear (ii, 10, 1). Irenaeus himself in interpreting Scripture, especially when he indulges in allegory, is not free from forced and arbitrary methods of exposition (cf. *e.g.* the interpretations of Judg. vi. 37, in *Haer.* iii. 17, 3; Jon. ii. 1 sqq. *Haer.* iii. 20, 1; Dan. ii. 34, *Haer.* iii. 21, 7); but in opposition to the fantastic interpretations which characterize the Valentinian school, he represents for the most part the historical sense of the written Word. His main purpose in the last three books is to refute the Gnostics out of Scripture itself. Irenaeus quotes as frequently from N.T. as from O.T. Whereas formerly men had been content with the authority of O.T. as the documentary memorial of divine revelation, or with the Lord's own words in addition to the utterances of law and prophets, they now felt more and more impelled, and that by the very example of the Gnostics themselves, to seek a fixed collection of N.T. Scriptures and to extend to them the idea of divine inspiration. The Gnostics in their opposition to O.T., which they supposed to have proceeded from the Demiurge or some subordinate angelic agency, had appealed to writings real or supposed of the apostles as being a more perfect form of divine revelation, and the first point to be established against them was the essential unity of *both* revelations—Old and New. Bk. iv. is almost wholly devoted by Irenaeus to the proof of this point against Marcion. It is one and the same Divine Spirit that spake both in prophets and apostles (iii. 21, 4), one and the same Divine Authority from which both the law and its fulfilment in Christ proceeds. The O.T. contains presages and fore-types of Christian Revelation (iv. 15; 15, i.; 19, i. etc.); the literal fulfilment of its prophecies proves that it came from the same God as the N.T., and is therefore of the same nature (iv. 9, 1). The prophets and the gospels together make up the totality of Scripture ("universae Scripturae," ii. 27, 2). That the Bible is one divinely inspired whole is thus clearly enunciated. Even Justin Martyr seems to regard the gospels rather as memoirs (ἀπομνημονεύματα) by apostles of the Lord's words and actions than as canonical Scriptures; but Irenaeus cites passages from the gospels as inspired words of the Holy Spirit, using the same formulae of citation as for O.T. (iii. 10, 4; 16, 2; cf. ii. 35, 4 and 5), and similarly from the epistles and Apocalypse (iii. 16, 9; v. 30, 4). The two main divisions of the N.T. canon are for him the gospels and the apostolic writings (τὰ εὐαγγελικὰ καὶ τὰ ἀποστολικά, i. 3, 6). These two already constitute a complete whole, like the Scriptures of the O.T., and he therefore blames the Ebionites for using only the gospel of St. Matthew, the Docetae only that of St. Mark, Marcion St. Luke's gospel only and the Pauline epistles, and even these not unmutilated (iii. 11, 7 and 12, 12). He remarks that those "unhappy ones" who reject the gospel of St. John cast away also the divine prophetic spirit of which it contains the promise (iii. 11, 9). But he equally condemns the use of apocryphal writings. The teachers of Alexandria, with laxer notions about inspiration, made use of such without scrupulosity. Irenaeus draws a clear line of demarcation between canonical Scriptures and apocryphal writings. He blames the Valentinians for boasting to possess "more gospels than actually exist" (iii. 11, 9) and the Gnostic Marcus for having used besides our Gospels "an infinite number of apocryphal and spurious works" (i. 20, 1). He considers himself able to prove that there *must* be just four gospels, neither more nor less. The proof is a somewhat singular one. From the four regions of the earth, the four principal winds, the fourfold form of the cherubim, the four covenants made by God with man, he deduces the necessity of one fourfold gospel (iii. 11, 8). This gospel first orally delivered, and then fixed in writing, Irenaeus designates the *fundamentum et columna fidei nostrae* (iii. 1, 1). The N.T. canon of Irenaeus embraces nearly all now received; viz. the four gospels, twelve epistles of St. Paul (the omission of *Philemon* appears to be accidental), I. Peter, I. and II. John, the Acts, and the Revelation. The omission of III. John is most probably accidental also. From St. James there is probably a quotation at iv. 16, 2 (cf. Jas. ii. 23), and the frequently recurring expression "lex libertatis" appears to have been borrowed from Jas. i. 25. The possible references to Hebrews are uncertain. Resemblances, perhaps echoes, are found in several places (cf. Harvey's Index), and Eusebius testifies (*H. E.* v. 26) that both *Hebrews* and the *Wisdom of Solomon* are mentioned by Irenaeus in his διαλέξεις διάφοροι. The epistle is cited as a Pauline work in one fragment only, the second Pfaffian (*Fr. Graec.* xxxvi. ap. Harvey.)

Irenaeus in his controversy with the Gnostics

assumes the possibility that we might have had to be without N.T. Scriptures altogether. In this case we should have to inquire of the tradition left by the apostles of the churches (iii. 4, 1: "quid autem si neque apostoli quidem Scripturas reliquissent nobis, nonne oportebat ordinem sequi traditionis quam tradiderunt iis quibus committebant, ecclesias?"). But the Gnostics also appealed to an apostolical tradition. Irenaeus complains that when one would refute them from the Bible they accused it of error, or declared the interpretation to be doubtful. The truth can only be ascertained, they said, by those who know the true tradition (iii. 2, 1). But this teaching is identical with that of Irenaeus himself, and he insists on finding this true tradition in the rule of faith (κανὼν τῆς ἀληθείας, *Regula Fidei*), as contained in the Baptismal Confession of the whole church (i. 9, 4; cf. 22, 1). Irenaeus thus obtains a sure note or token by which to distinguish the genuine apostolical tradition (ἡ ὑπὸ τῆς ἐκκλησίας κηρυσσομένη ἀλήθεια, i. 9, 5; *praeconium ecclesiae*, v. 20, 2; *apostolica ecclesiae traditio*, iii. 3, 3; or simply παράδοσις, *traditio*, i. 10, 2; iii. 2, 2 and frequently) from the so-called apostolical secret doctrine to which the Gnostics made their appeal. The Baptismal Confession (or *Credo*) acquired its complete form only through the conflicts of the Gnostic controversy. In the writings of Irenaeus, as in those of his contemporaries, it is cited in various, now longer now shorter, forms. This is no proof that one or other of these was the actual form then used in baptism. The probability is far greater that the shorter form of the old Roman *credo* still preserved to us was that already used in the time of Irenaeus. (Caspari, *Ungedruckte*, etc. *Quellen zur Geschichte des Taufsymbols und der Glaubensregel*, tom. iii. 1875, pp. 3 sqq.) The variations as we find them in the creeds of the Eastern churches appear to have been introduced in order to express, with greater distinctness, the antithesis of Christian belief to Gnostic heresy. So here a special emphasis is laid on the belief in "*One* God the Father Almighty, Who made heaven and earth," and in "one Jesus Christ, the Son of God, Who became flesh for our salvation." This rule of faith Irenaeus testifies that the church, scattered over the whole οἰκουμένη, delivers as with one mind and mouth, even as she has herself received it from the apostles and their disciples (i. 10, 1 and 2). A clear, determinate note is thus given by which to distinguish the genuine Christian tradition from that of heresy. To the pretended secret doctrine of the latter is opposed the public preaching of the faith of the apostolic churches; to the mutability and endless varieties of Gnostic doctrines the unity of the church's teaching; to their novelty her antiquity, and to their endless subdivisions into schools and parties the uniformity and universality of her traditional witness. That only which, from the times of the apostles, has been handed down in unbroken tradition by the elders of the church and publicly and uniformly taught in the churches, that doctrine which at all times and in every place may be learned by inquiry from the successors of the apostle in their teaching office, that alone is the Christian apostolic truth (i. 10, 2; iii. 2, 2; 3, 1, 3, 4; 4, 1 seq.; 24, 1; iv. 33, 7 seq.; v. 20, 1).

The learned church antiquarian Hegesippus had, *c.* 170, undertaken long journeys to assure himself of the general agreement of Christian communities in their doctrinal traditions; in each apostolic church he had set himself to inquire for the unbroken succession of its pastors and their teaching, and records with satisfaction the result of his investigations: "In every succession in every city it is still maintained as the law announces and as the prophets and the Lord." And again, "So long as the sacred choir of the apostles still lived, the church was like a virgin undefiled and pure, and not till afterwards in the times of Trajan did error, which so long had crept in darkness, venture forth into the light of day" (ap. Eus. *H. E.* iv. 22; iii. 32). Irenaeus is specially emphatic in everywhere contrasting the vacillation and variety of heretical opinions with the uniform proclamation of one and the same apostolic witness in all the churches of the world (i. 8, 1; 10, 1). Truth, he remarks, can be but one; while each heretical teacher proclaims a different doctrine of his own invention. How impossible is it that truth can have remained so long hidden from the church and been handed down as secret doctrine in possession of the few! She is free and accessible to all, both learned and ignorant, and all who earnestly seek her find. With almost a shout of triumph he opposes to the unstable, ever-changing, many-headed doctrinal systems and sects of Gnosticism, with their vain appeals to obscure names of pretended disciples of the apostles or to supposititious writings, the one universal norm of truth which all the churches recognise. "The church, though dispersed through the whole world, is carefully guarding the same faith as dwelling in one and the same house; these things she believes, in like manner, as having one soul and the self-same heart; these, too, she accordantly proclaims, and teaches, and delivers, as though possessing but one mouth. The speeches of the world are many and divergent, but the force of our tradition is one and the same." And again: "The churches in Germany have no other faith, no other tradition, than that which is found in Spain, or among the Celts, in the regions of the East, in Egypt and in Libya, or in these mid parts of the earth." He compares the church's proclamation of the truth to the light of the sun, one and the same throughout the universe and visible to all who have eyes. "The mightiest in word among the presidents of the churches teaches only the same things as others (for no one here is above the Master), and the weak in word takes nothing away from what has been delivered him. The faith being always one and the same, he that can say much about it doth not exceed, he that can say but little doth not diminish" (i. 10, 2). "The tradition of the apostles made manifest, as it is, through all the world can be recognized in every church by all who wish to know the truth" (iii. 3, 1). But this light from God shines not for heretics because they have dishonoured and despised Him (iii. 24, 2). Cf. also the first of Pfaffian fragments (*Fr. Graec.* xxxv.).

The argument from antiquity is also employed by Irenaeus on behalf of church tradition. If controversies arise about matters of faith, let recourse be had to the most ancient churches in which the apostles themselves once resided and a decisive answer will then be found. This oral apostolic tradition exists even in the churches among barbarous nations, in whose hearts the Spirit, without ink or parchment, has written the old and saving truth (iii. 4, 1 and 2). But while thus the genuine tradition may, in the apostolic churches, be traced back through the successions of the elders to the apostles themselves, the sects and their doctrines are all of later origin. There were no Valentinians before Valentinus, no Marcionites before Marcion. Valentinus himself and Kerdon (Marcion's teacher) did not appear in Rome till the time of Hyginus the ninth bishop after the apostles, Valentinus flourished under Pius, Marcion under Anicetus (iii. 4, 3). All these founders of sects were much later than the apostles (iii. 21, 3) and the first bishops to whom they committed the care of the churches (v. 20, 1). In contradistinction to their ψευδώνυμος γνῶσις the true gnosis consists in the doctrine of the apostles and the maintenance of the pure and ancient constitution of the church (τὸ ἀρχαῖον τῆς ἐκκλησίας σύστημα) throughout the world (iv. 33, 7). The main point then, on which all turns, is the clear proof of a pure transmission of apostolic teaching through immediate disciples of the apostles themselves and *their* disciples after them. What is the tradition of the elders (πρεσβῦται, πρεσβύτεροι), *i.e.* the heads of apostolic churches who stood in direct communication with the apostles themselves or with their disciples ?—is the question, therefore, which Irenaeus is everywhere asking. These elders are the guardians and transmitters of the apostles' teaching. As in the preceding generation Papias had collected the traditions of "disciples of the Lord," so now Irenaeus is collecting reminiscences of *their* disciples, mediate or immediate, a Polycarp, a Papias, etc., and as Hegesippus had been careful to inform himself as to the succession of pastors from apostolic times, so Irenaeus, in opposition to the doctrines of the Gnostics, appeals not only to the ancestral teaching maintained in churches of apostolic foundation, such as Rome, Smyrna, Ephesus, but also to the lists of those men who, since the apostles, had presided over them (iii. 3).

The main representatives therefore of genuine apostolical tradition are for Irenaeus the bishops of the churches as successors of the apostles and guardians of their doctrines. In the episcopate, as a continuation of the apostolic office, he finds the one sure pledge of the church's unity and the maintenance of her doctrine. Although the expression ἐκκλησία καθολική, which came into vogue towards the end of the 2nd cent., does not occur in his writings, the thing itself is constantly before him, *i.e.* the conception of one true church spread over the earth, and bound together by the one true Faith, in contrast to the manifold and variegated and apostate forms of "heresy." Its external bond of unity is the episcopal office. The development of monarchical episcopacy was a primary consequence of the conflict with Gnosticism, and its origination out of simpler constitutional forms betrays itself in a mode of expression derived indeed from earlier times, but still common to Irenaeus, with Tertullian, Clemens Alexandrinus, Hippolytus, and others, the use, namely, of the official titles, πρεσβύτεροι and ἐπίσκοποι, to designate alternately the same persons. Πρεσβύτεροι in this context are, in the first place, "elders," *i.e.* "ancients" or fathers, who represent the immediate connexion of the early church with the apostolic time. This name or title is then transferred to the heads of churches, inasmuch as they in succession to the apostles have been faithful transmitters of what was handed down to them. The true unbroken apostolical succession and *praeconium ecclesiae* is therefore attributed to the same persons, now as πρεσβύτεροι now as ἐπίσκοποι (iii. 3, 2, cf. iii. 2, 2 ; iv. 26, 2, 4, 5 ; Ep. ad Victorem ap. Eus. *H. E.* v. 24) ; nay, in so many words, the "successio episcopalis" was assigned to the πρεσβύτεροι (iv. 26, 2). By these "presbyters," however, we are certainly to understand heads of churches (especially those of apostolic foundation), who alone were capable of acting as the guardians and maintainers of church unity. The episcopate is for Irenaeus no mere congregational office, but one belonging to the whole church ; the great importance attached by his contemporaries to the proofs of a genuine apostolical succession rests on the assumption that the episcopate was the guardian of the church's unity of teaching, a continuation, in fact, of the apostolic teaching-office, ordained for that purpose by the apostles themselves. The bishop, in reference to any particular congregation, is a representative of the whole Catholic church, the very idea of catholicity being indebted for its completion to this more sharply defined conception of the episcopal office. In the episcopate thus completely formed the Catholic church first manifested herself in organic unity as "the body of Christ." As formerly the apostles, so now the bishops, their successors, are the "ecclesia repraesentativa." Only through the episcopate as the faithful guardian and transmitter of the apostolical tradition do such congregations retain their hold on visible church unity and their possession of the truth (cf. iv. 33, 7). The significance of the episcopal office rests therefore on the fact of an apostolical succession, and on this historical connexion of the bishops with the apostolic era depends the certainty of their being possessed of the true tradition. That this assurance is not illusory is proved by the actual uniformity of church teaching throughout the world, the agreement of all the apostolic churches in the confession of the same truth (iii. 3, 3). Beyond this historical proof of the church's possession of the true teaching through her episcopate, the argument is not carried further by Irenaeus. The later dogma of a *continua successio Spiritus Sancti, i.e.* of an abiding special gift of the Holy Spirit attached to the episcopate of apostolical succession, has nevertheless some precursive traces in his writings. Though the Holy

Spirit is a *scala ascensionis ad Deum*, of which all the faithful are partakers, yet the guidance of the church by the Spirit is mediated by apostles, prophets, and teachers, and they who would have the guidance of the Spirit must come to the church. "For, where the church is, there is the Spirit of God, and where the Spirit of God is, there is the church and all grace—the Spirit, moreover, is the truth" (iii. 24, 1). Expressly therefore is the "*charisma veritatis*" attached to the episcopal succession (iv. 26, 2), not as a gift of inspiration enabling the bishops to discover fresh truths, but rather as such guidance as enables them to preserve the original truth. Therefore it is more particularly the churches of apostolical foundation, and in the West specially the church of Rome, which can give the surest warrant for the true and incorrupt tradition. In this sense the much-disputed passage is to be understood in which some would find a witness for the primacy of the Roman church: "For with this church must, on account of her more excellent origin ('propter potiorem principalitatem,' *i.e. διὰ τὴν διαφορωτέραν ἀρχήν*), every church, that is, all the faithful coming from all quarters, put themselves in agreement, as being the church in which at all times by those who come from all quarters the tradition derived from the apostles has been preserved" (iii. 3, 2). The *potentior principalitas* denotes here not only the superior antiquity of the Roman church as the greatest, oldest, and most widely known (*i.e.* in the West, where Irenaeus was writing), but also her nobler origin as founded by those "two most glorious apostles Peter and Paul." The mention of the "faithful coming from all quarters" points again to the position of the great world's metropolis as a centre of intercourse, and therefore the place in which Christians could most easily convince themselves of the oneness of apostolical tradition in the whole church. Obscurations and corruptions of that tradition, quite possible in remoter churches, would at Rome be soonest discovered and most easily removed. It is not of any Roman lordship over other churches or a primatial teaching-office committed to the Roman bishop that Irenaeus is here speaking, but only of the surer warrant offered by the position of that church for the uncorrupt maintenance of the apostolical traditions. So, after reckoning the succession of Roman bishops down to Eleutherus, his own contemporary, Irenaeus proceeds: *τῇ αὐτῇ τάξει καὶ τῇ αὐτῇ διαδοχῇ, ἥ τε ἀπὸ τῶν ἀποστόλων ἐν τῇ ἐκκλησίᾳ παράδοσις καὶ τὸ τῆς ἀληθείας κήρυγμα κατήντηκεν εἰς ἡμᾶς* (iii. 3, 3). But just the same he says of the church of Ephesus founded by St. Paul, and till the times of Trajan under the guidance of St. John: *ἀλλὰ καὶ ἡ ἐν Ἐφέσῳ ἐκκλησία ὑπὸ Παύλου μὲν τεθεμελιωμένη, Ἰωάννου δὲ παραμείναντος αὐτοῖς μέχρι τῶν Τραϊανοῦ χρόνων, μάρτυς ἀληθής ἐστι τῆς ἀποστολικῆς παραδόσεως* (iii. 3, 4).

The unity of the Catholic church, thus secured by the continuance of the apostolic office, is regarded by Irenaeus as mainly a *doctrinal unity*. Of her *guardianship of sacramental grace* he gives hints only. Yet he is certainly on the way to that conception when he singles out the continuance of spiritual gifts as a special note of the true church, meaning thereby not merely the *charisma veritatis*. but also the gifts of prophecy and miracle (ii. 32, 4; cf. iii. 11, 9). He is not less decided in opposing schismatics, who destroy the church's unity (iv. 26, 2; 33, 7), than heretics who corrupt her doctrine. In internal divisions among the faithful he never wearies in urging the interests of peace. Neither in the Montanistic movement nor in the Paschal controversy does he see grounds for the severance of church communion. At the same time he determinedly opposes that separatist temper, which, denying the presence of the Spirit in the church, would claim His gifts exclusively for its own sect or party. Even if we are not warranted in identifying with the Montanists those "false prophets" of whom he speaks (iv. 33, 6) as with lying lips pretending to prophesy, any more than those who (iii. 11, 9) deny the gospel of St. John—all the more applicable to them is the following description: "Men who bring about schisms, devoid of true love to God, seeking their own advantage rather than the unity of the church; wounding and dividing for petty reasons the great and glorious body of Christ, and so far as in them lies destroying it; speaking peace, but acting war, and in sober truth straining out the gnat and swallowing the camel. For no reformation which they could bring about would outweigh the evils produced by their schism" (iv. 33, 7). The great importance attached by Irenaeus to the maintenance of church unity rests for him on the assumption that the church being sole depositary of divine truth is the only trustworthy guarantee of human salvation. While himself sharing, with the Montanists, not only the hope of the millennial kingdom but also the expectation of its outward visible glory (v. 32-36) and delighting in reminiscences of what the "elders" (Papias) have handed down concerning it as from the lips of the apostle St. John (v. 33, 3), Irenaeus does, on the other hand, with his conception of the church as an outward visible institution of prime necessity for human salvation, pave the way for that catholic ideal, which, in contrast to the dreams and aspirations of Montanism, would substitute for a glorious vision of the future the existing church on earth as God's visible kingdom. When the visible church as an outward institution comes to be regarded as the essential medium of saving grace, all its forms and ordinances at once acquire a quasi-legal or sacramental character. The church is for Irenaeus an earthly paradise, of the trees of which every one may eat, while heresy has only the forbidden tree of knowledge, whose fruits are death-bringing (v. 20, 2). As the church's faith is the only faith which is true and saving (iii. praef.), so is he alone a Christian man who conforms to the church's institutions and laws (cf. iii. 15, 2; v. 20, 1). The church's sacrifices, the church's prayers, the church's works alone are holy (iv. 18, 1 sqq.; ii. 32, 5).

This essentially *legal* conception of Christianity was also that of the generation which followed the apostles. The great Catholic doctors gave to this legal conception of the church a further development. For Tertullian, Clement, and Origen the work of Christ was primarily the promulgation of a new divine law. Irenaeus calls indeed Christianity the N.T. of freedom (iii. 12, 14; iv. 16, 5; 34, 3; cf. iii. 10, 5), but simply in reference to the exemption of Gentile Christians from obedience to the Mosaic ceremonial law. In antithesis to Marcion, who derived the Mosaic law from the Demiurge, the gospel from the good God, Irenaeus maintained the substantial identity of both covenants ("unius et ejusdem substantiae sunt," iv. 9, 1; cf. 9, 2; 13, 3, etc.). When he appropriates the Pauline antithesis of bondage and liberty (cf. also iv. 9, 1 seq.; 13, 2; 16, 5; 18, 2; 34, 1 seq., etc., etc.), the religious premises which led up in St. Paul's mind to that antithesis are perhaps wanting to Irenaeus. The N.T. consists for him in a body of divine prescripts. The bondsman and undisciplined has indeed one law, the free, the justified by faith, another (iv. 9, 1); but inasmuch as the nucleus of both Testaments is one and the same—namely, those natural precepts (*naturalia praecepta*) (iv. 13, 4; cf. 15, 1) which have from the beginning impressed themselves on the mind of man—it follows that the evangelical law of liberty (iv. 34, 4) differs only quantitatively, not qualitatively, from that of Moses. This difference consists on the one hand in the abolition of the precepts of the ceremonial law, which for the Israelites themselves had but a temporary purpose and validity, to restrain from idol worship, to uphold external discipline, or to serve as precursors and symbols of spiritual precepts (iv. 13, 2; 14, 1 sqq.; 15, 1; 16, 3 sqq.; 19, 1; 23, 1 seq.; 24, 1 seq.), and on the other in the reinforcement of those natural precepts which have come down to us from the beginning (iv. 9, 2; 13, 1; 16, 5). The laws of liberty (*decreta libertatis*) do not annul the duty of obedience; the difference between sons and servants from this point of view consists in the sons having a larger faith (iv. 32, 2) and exhibiting a more ready obedience (iv. 11, 4). Accordingly, the antithesis between the two Testaments is not an antithesis of fear and love. Love is the greatest commandment under the O.T. (iv. 12, 3). Fear continues as a precept under the New. Christ has even enlarged the precept of fear—the children must fear as well as love more than the servants (iv. 16, 5). On the one side the children indeed are free, on the other they are still servants (iv. 14, 1). The two lawgivings differ only in the number and greatness (*multitudine et magnitudine*) of their commandments. The law of liberty, being the greater, is given not for Jews only, but for all nations (iv. 9, 2); but the precepts of a perfect life (*consummatae vitae praecepta*) are for both Testaments the same (iv. 12, 3).

The new precepts which characterize Christianity are, in the first place, the ordinances and institutions of the church. Among other distinguishing notes of the new law Irenaeus further emphasizes that Christians believe not in the Father only but also in the Son, that they do as well as say, and that they abstain from evil desires as well as from evil works (iv. 13, 1). Even while largely using Pauline language in speaking of Justification by Faith (iv. 5, 5; 9, 1; 16, 2; 21, 1), his legal conception is still there. Faith is opposed by Irenaeus to the ψευδώνυμος γνῶσις of the heretics, and essentially consists in the reception of the *Regula Fidei*, the Rule of Faith; it is therefore simply defined as obedience to the will of God (iv. 16, 5), *i.e.* a moral duty, and not, as for St. Paul, the subjective form in which a new religious life and relation is first constituted.

This *legal* conception leads Irenaeus further to insist on the freedom of the will, and on salvation as conditioned by a man's own ethical self-determination. All Catholic practical theology tends to limit the free forgiveness of sins to the moment of baptism, and after that to make salvation dependent on a godly life and the performance of good works. In the same spirit Irenaeus quite innocently puts in juxtaposition justification by obedience to the natural precepts and justification by faith: "naturalia legis per quae homo justificatur quae etiam ante legislationem custodiebant qui fide justificabantur et placebant Deo" (iv. 13, 1). He is led thus strongly to insist on the moral law by his opposition to the Gnostic teaching that the spiritual man is exempted from it and obtains salvation through his higher gnosis. His energetic assertion of the freedom of the will has also a polemical object —to refute the Valentinian dualistic doctrine, which made the salvation of the spiritual man the result of his original *pneumatic* nature (cf. esp. iv. 37). But this perfectly justifiable opposition leads Irenaeus to put too much in the background the doctrine of divine grace as the only source of human salvation. He even puts it as a divine requirement that in order to the Spirit's resting upon them, Christians must, beside their baptismal vocation, be also adorned with works of righteousness (iv. 36, 6). This seems inconsistent with the Pauline teaching that it is only by the gift of the Spirit that Christians are enabled to do good works at all. But, on the other hand, he says that the Spirit dwells in men as God's creation, working in them the will of the Father and renovating into the newness of Christ (iii. 17, 1). As dry ground, without dew from heaven, can bear no fruit, so neither can the soul perform good works without the irrigation of the water of life (iii. 17, 2).

If in his legal conception Irenaeus may be said to anticipate the mode of thought which characterizes the Catholicism of a later time, the same cannot be said of his teaching on the sacraments. Indeed the sacramental side of Catholic theology did not take shape till through and after the Montanistic and Novatianist controversies. Whereas both these parties insisted on finding the church's sanctity in the spiritual endowments and personal holiness of individual members, "Catholics" sought for the note of holiness mainly in the church's sacramental ordinances, or in marvellous operations of the Holy Spirit in certain functions of her public life. The chief organ of these operations would be the episcopate, which thus came to be viewed as not merely the guardian of doctrinal purity, but also the bearer of supernatural grace and powers, and following the type of the O.T. priesthood as a kind of mediator between God and men. This side of the Catholic ideal of the church is not yet developed in the writings of Irenaeus. On the contrary, he insists on the original Christian conception of the universal priesthood and outpouring of the Spirit on all believers (iv. 20, 6 sqq.; v. 6, 1; cf. iv. 13, 2 sqq.; 33, 1 sqq.), first, as against the Gnostics, and their claims to an exclusive possession of the divine πνεῦμα, and, secondly, against the false prophets, and their denial of the presence of the Spirit in the church (iii. 11, 9; iv. 33, 6). The sacramental idea of grace imparted through the church is for Irenaeus restricted to baptism as a divine institution for the salvation of man, the type of which is the ark of Noah (iv. 36, 4). Of priestly absolution and its sacramental significance he nowhere speaks; on the contrary, he adopts the saying of an elder which has a somewhat Montanistic ring about it—that after baptism there is no further forgiveness of sins (iv. 27, 2). This, as is clear from the epistle of the Gallican confessors, is not meant to exclude the possibility of indulgence being extended to the fallen under any circumstances. The familiar thought of the Ignatian epistles, that separation from the episcopal altar is a separation from the church herself, also finds no distinct utterance in the writings of Irenaeus. But in his time the ministration of the Eucharist by bishops and presbyters was undoubtedly a long-established custom. In regard to the dogma of the Holy Communion Irenaeus, like Justin Martyr, expresses the thought that through the invocation of Christ's name over the earthly elements the Divine Logos does actually enter into such mysterious connexion with the bread and wine as to constitute a union of an earthly and a heavenly πρᾶγμα similar to that which took place at the Incarnation itself. In virtue of this union of the Logos with the bread and wine those earthly substances are made the flesh and blood of Christ; and it appears to have been with Irenaeus a favourite thought, that through the partaking of Christ's flesh and blood in the Holy Communion our earthly bodies are made partakers of immortality (iv. 18, 4 seq.; 33, 2; v. 2, 2 seq.; cf. also iv. 17, 5 seq.; 18, 1 sqq., and the second Pfaffian fragment, *Fr. Graec.* xxxvi. ap. Harvey).

The chief significance of Irenaeus as a theologian consists in his doctrine concerning the *Person and Work of Christ.* The doctrine of Christ's Godhead was for the Gentile Christianity of the post-apostolic age the theological expression of the absolute significance of that divine revelation which was enshrined in His person and work. While the Gnostics regarded Christ as only one among numerous eradiations of the divine essence, thereby imperilling on the one hand the truth of the divine monarchia, and on the other the absolute and final character of the gospel revelation, the opposing doctrine of the Godhead of the Logos, and of His Incarnation in Jesus Christ, provided the exact theological truth and formula of which the Christian conscience felt the need, in order to gather into one the scattered elements which the multitude of Gnostic Aeons were dividing. Following the guidance of St. John's gospel, the more philosophically cultured teachers of the church—Justin, Theophilus, Tatian, Athenagoras, the Alexandrine Clemens, Origen, Tertullian, and Hippolytus—found in the doctrine of the Divine Logos the classical expression which they needed for the unique and absolute character of the gospel revelations. It was in antithesis both to the Gnostic doctrine of Aeons and the psilanthropism of the Ebionites that the Divine Logos or Eternal Thought of God Himself was conceived of as the personal organ of all divine revelation Which had issued from the inner life of the Divine Paternity. His manifestation in the flesh is therefore the climax of all the revelations of God in the world. This Logos-doctrine Irenaeus adopted. The invisible Father is visible in the Logos (iv. 20, 7). The divine "Pleroma" (Irenaeus borrows the Gnostic term to express the fulness of divine perfection, ii. 1, 3 seq.) is revealed therein. God Himself is all Intelligence, all Thought, all Logos; what He thinks He utters, what He utters He thinks; the all-embracing divine intelligence is the Father Himself, Who has made Himself visible in the Son (ii. 28, 5). The infinite, immeasurable Father is, in the words of some old teacher of the church, become measurable and comprehensible in the Son ("immensus Pater in Filio mensuratus"), for the Son is the "measure of the Father," the manifestation of the Infinite in finite form (iv. 4, 2). In contrast with Tertullian, Irenaeus's first great purpose and object is to emphasize the absoluteness and spirituality of God, and therefore to reject anything like a physical emanation (*prolatio*) of the Logos, lest God should be made into something composite, and something other than His own infinite thought (*principalis mens*), or His own Logos (ii. 28, 5). The older teachers of the Logos-doctrine conceived the generation of the Logos after the analogy of the temporal process from thinking to speaking, and assumed that His issuing from the Father as a distinct person, *i.e.* the outspeaking of the inward divine thought, first took place at the creation. Tertullian represented the same conception in a more sensuous form. The Father is for him the whole Godhead, the Son "portio totius"; and on this point he expressly recognizes the resemblance between his view and that of the Gnostics (*c. Drax.* 8). Irenaeus, on the other hand, is driven by his own opposition to the Gnostic doctrine of Aeons to reject anything like a προβολή or *prolatio* from the Godhead as a limitation of His infinity or an anthropomorphism. He is therefore the first doctor of the church who maintained with the utmost distinctness the eternal coexistence of the Son with the Father ("semper coexistens Filius Patri," ii. 30, 9; iii. 18, 1). His frequent designation of the Son and Holy Spirit as the "Hands of God" is a figurative expression to denote Their being not so much emanations of the Godhead as organs of its creative energy. To presumptuous endeavours to comprehend the way in which the Son comes from the Father he opposes our human ignorance, and mocks at the vain attempts of those who would transfer human relations to the Infinite and Unchangeable One ("quasi ipsi obstetricaverint prolationem enunciant," ii. 28, 6). These polemics, if directed primarily against the

Gnostics, are not less applicable to the emanistic theories of other teachers. On the other hand, the clearly marked division between the Logos-doctrine of an Hippolytus and Tertullian and the Patripassian conception of it can hardly be said to exist for Irenaeus, who often speaks as if the eternal Logos were but the self-revealing side of the otherwise invisible and hidden Godhead, without one's being always able to see how the personal distinction between the two can be thus maintained. His doctrine of the Logos was developed (unlike that of Tertullian and Hippolytus) without any direct reference to Patripassianism (of which no mention is made in his writings), while the true human personality of the Son is maintained against the Gnostics with as much decision as His true Godhead against the Ebionites.

His conception of the Logos as the one great and absolute organ of all divine revelations leads Irenaeus, as it did Justin Martyr and the other Apologists, to refer back to His agency all the *pre-Christian manifestations of God* (iv. 20, 7 seq.). But Irenaeus is the first Christian doctor who expressly applies this thought, in his conflict with the Gnostics, to the origination of the Mosaic law (iv. 9). "Both Testaments proceeded from one and the same head of the family (*paterfamilias*), our Lord Jesus Christ, the Word of God, Who spake (of old) to Abraham and to Moses" (cf. iv. 12, 4). But Irenaeus nowhere maintains the precepts of the old ceremonial law as obligatory upon Christians.

The fulfilment of all previous revelations is attained in the personal manifestation of the Logos in the flesh. By the Incarnation of the Son the divine purpose in creation, the union (*adunatio, communio, commixtio*) of God and man, has been accomplished, and the end is brought back to the beginning (iv. 20, 2, 4; 33, 4; v. 2, 1, *et passim*).

Together with the Logos *the Spirit of God* is often spoken of as an organ of divine revelation. It is not, however, easy to determine their right relation one to the other. The designation of the Holy Spirit as Wisdom (*Sapientia*) reminds us of the Alexandrine phraseology, in which λόγος and σοφία are also distinguished without the distinction being fully worked out or consistently adhered to. Irenaeus uses the term "Sapientia" of the Divine Spirit always. But the comprehension of his meaning is made somewhat difficult by his sometimes speaking of our communion with the Son as mediated by the Spirit (v. 36, 2), and sometimes of the historical manifestation of the Logos as the mean whereby men become partakers of the Spirit of the Father (iv. 38, 2). The solution probably is that Irenaeus uses the term "Spirit of God" in now a narrower, now a wider sense. In the narrower sense the Spirit is the organ of Divine Revelation in the heart and consciousness of man, and so distinguished from the Logos as the universal organ of Divine Revelation to all creatures and all worlds (v. 1, 1; cf. iii. 21, 4; iv. 33, 1, 7, etc.). In the wider sense the Spirit is the inner Being of God Himself in contradistinction to the material universe and the σάρξ (*caro*) or human corporeity. The former sense is always to be assumed where the Spirit is distinguished from the Logos as another divine hypostasis, "progenies et figuratio Dei" (iv. 7, 4; 20, 1 seq.); the latter, where the Spirit is spoken of as "the bread of immortality" (iv. 38, 1) and the life-giving principle from which endless life wells forth (v. 12, 2). It is with this latter meaning that Irenaeus, speaking of the humanity of Jesus Christ, expresses a thought, often recurred to by later theologians, that the Spirit is the anointing (*unctio*, χρίσμα) and bond of unity between the Father and the Son. The Holy Spirit is in fact, for him, also the uniting principle between God and man. God through the Spirit imparts Himself to man; man through the Incarnation enters into God (v. 1, 1). This last thought leads us on to the grand conception which Irenaeus entertains of the development of the whole human race from Adam up to Christ. Man was not from the first, according to Irenaeus, made perfect and immortal, but designed, in God's purpose concerning him, to become so. But this can only be through the Spirit of God, and in order that man may be made partaker of the Spirit and thereby united to God, it was necessary that the Logos should become incarnate (iv. 38, 1 sqq.). The image of God (εἰκὼν τοῦ Θεοῦ), for which man was created, could not become visible before the Incarnation, and so man lost this image, the likeness of God, the possession of the Spirit (v. 16, 2), falling into sin by his own fault, and thereby coming not only under the power of natural death, but rendered incapable of exhibiting the image of God (v. 12, 2; 23, 1 seq.). Thus though Irenaeus regards sin, not like the Gnostics as a necessity of nature, but as man's own free act, he yet works out the thought that God has permitted the existence of evil because only by the contrast could goodness be appreciated, like health after sickness, light after darkness, life after death (iv. 37, 7; 39, 1). Without sin there would have been no consciousness of need, no desire for union with God, no thankfulness for His mercy (iii. 20, 1 sqq.). The chief aim of Irenaeus in these disquisitions is again his conflict with Gnostic error, especially that of Marcion, who explained the origin of evil in the universe by the theory of two Gods—the highest and an inferior one. Irenaeus appropriates the language of the prophet (Isa. xlv. 6, 7), *I am the Lord: I make peace, and create evil*, and works out the thought that for the very sake of destroying evil a final *recapitulatio totius iniquitatis* may be necessary (v. 29, 2). Two equally significant thoughts must be distinguished in the full doctrine of Irenaeus concerning the Incarnation of the Logos and the divine purpose in the Incarnation: the idea of humanity being raised to perfection in Christ through union with the divine nature, and that of the victory gained by humanity in the God-man its Head over sin and the devil.

The Incarnation is for Irenaeus not merely an historical fact, but has for its basis the eternal divine predestination of man. It was only by God becoming man that man could attain the predestined end of his original creation. The perfecting of humanity in Christ is also a realisation of the true idea of humanity—the Logos first assimilating Himself to man, and then man to Himself ("semet ipsum homini et hominem sibimet ipsi assimilans"). "In past times it was said indeed that man had been made after God's image, but it was not shewn. For the Logos was still invisible after Whose image man had been made. And on this very account did man also easily forfeit the likeness. But when the Logos of God became flesh He established both points: He truly exhibited the [divine] image, by Himself becoming that which was the image of Himself, and firmly restored the likeness by making man to be like the unseen Father" (v. 16, 2). Man's destination is to be like God, and by the attainment of this likeness God's great purpose is accomplished of indwelling in man, and so of uniting man to Himself (iii. 20, 2). Hence follows the necessity that He by Whom the perfecting of man was accomplished should be Himself both God and man. Irenaeus is therefore as strongly opposed to the Ebionitic as to the Docetic error. To the Ebionites he objects that they do not receive the doctrine of the commixture of the heavenly wine with the earthly water, the union of God and man, but, retaining the leaven of the old birth (after the flesh), abide in mortal flesh and in that death which disobedience has incurred (v. 1, 3; iii. 19, 1). It was necessary that the Logos should become man in order that man, receiving the Logos and obtaining the sonship, might become son of God. We could not obtain incorruption and immortality except by being united to that which is incorruptible and immortal. Only through the absorption of the one by the other can we become partakers of the divine Sonship (iii. 19, 1; cf. iii. 18, 7). On the other hand, in opposition to Gnostic Docetism, Irenaeus insists no less strongly on the reality of the Incarnation of the Logos. If this were but putative, salvation would be putative also (iv. 33, 5). The mediator between God and man must belong to both in order to unite both (iv. 18, 7). If we are truly to know God and enter into fellowship with the Divine Logos, our teacher must Himself have become man. We need a teacher Whom we can see and hear, in order to be followers of His deeds and doers of His words (v. 1, 1). This fundamental thought—that the divine nature of which we are to be partakers can be brought nigh to us only in the form of a genuine human existence—is expressed elsewhere still more emphatically, when Irenaeus insists that Christ, in order to conduct the human race to its divine destination, must Himself belong to it, and take upon Him human flesh and all the characteristics of humanity; that if man is to be raised to God, God must come down to man (iv. 33, 4, πῶς ἄνθρωπος χωρήσει εἰς Θεόν, εἰ μὴ ὁ Θεὸς ἐχωρήθη εἰς ἄνθρωπον). The second Adam, the head of our spiritual humanity, must Himself come of the race of Adam in order to unite the end with the beginning (iii. 22, 3 seq.; 23, 1; iv. 34, 4; v. 1, 3; 16, 1 seq.). The profound conception of a *recapitulatio* (ἀνακεφαλαίωσις) of humanity in Christ is one to which Irenaeus perpetually recurs. (See iii. 18, 1; 22, 1, 3; 23, 1; iv. 38, 1; v. 1, 2 seq.; 14, 1; 23, 2; 36, 3; cf. iv. 40, 3; v. 16, 2). It was needful that Christ should recapitulate and pass through all the stages of an ordinary human life in order to consecrate each of them in us, by a likeness to Himself in each (ii. 22, 4; iii. 18, 7), and that He should come at the end of time in order to conduct all who from the beginning had hoped in Him to eternal life in fellowship with God (iv. 22, 1 seq.; cf. 27, 1). As Christ was typically pre-formed in Adam (iii. 22, 3), so was Adam's destiny accomplished in Christ (v. 1, 3; 16, 2 seq.). The Spirit of God descended on the Son of God made man that in Him He might accustom Himself to an indwelling in the human race (iii. 17, 1). Man was to grow used to receive God, and God to indwell in man (ii. 20, 2).

With this thought of the *recapitulatio* of the human race in Christ is combined another of equal depth and significance—that of *the victory over sin* and *deliverance of sin's captives* from the power of Satan by the *obedience* of Christ. This deliverance or redemption was necessary before the divine purpose of the union of God and man could be accomplished. For if man, created by God for life, but corrupted by the serpent, had not returned to life, but been wholly subjected to death's power, God would then have been defeated, and the devil's iniquity proved itself stronger than His holy will. But God, triumphant and magnanimous, has by the second Adam (Christ) bound the strong man and spoiled his goods, and deprived death of its prey, and brought back man once slain to life. He who by false promises of life and the likeness of God had bound man in the chains of sin has now been justly made captive in his turn, and his prisoner, man, set free (iii. 23, 1 seq.; cf. 18, 7; iv. 21, 3). The power of the devil over man consisted in man's sin, and the apostasy into which the devil had seduced him (v. 21, 3), but now the disobedience of one man has been repaired by one man's obedience (iii. 18, 7; 21, 10). The first Adam was *initium morientium*, the second Adam *initium viventium*, Who needed to be both God and man, no less in order to become the saviour than to be the perfecter of mankind (iii. 22, 4; v. 1, 3). Only One Who was Himself man could overcome man's enemy, and bind in his turn him by whom man had been bound; in this way alone could the victory over the enemy be altogether just. So, on the other hand, only One Who was also God could accomplish a redemption which should be stable and sure (iii. 18, 7; v. 21, 3). Christ must be truly man to be as man truly tempted, must be born of a woman to deliver those who by a woman had been brought under the devil's power, and must truly live and suffer as a man in order as man to fight and triumph. Again, He must also be the Logos in order to be glorified, in order as the strong one to overcome the enemy in whose power the whole human race found itself (iii. 18, 6, 7; 19, 3; iv. 33, 4; v. 17, 3; 21, 1; 22, 1); and finally, that man might learn that it is not through himself but only through God's mercy that he obtains incorruption (v. 21, 3). The recapitulation of mankind in Christ consists therefore not only in man's original destiny being accomplished by the beginner of a new humanity, but also in His taking up and conducting to a triumphant issue, at the end of time, the conflict wherein, at the beginning, man had been overcome. The victory of God made man is man's victory, since all humanity is summed up (recapitulated) in Christ. Man must himself leave the evil one bound with the same chains wherewith he himself had been bound—the chains of transgression (v. 21, 3); but the first man could not thus have triumphed, having been by him seduced and bound, but only the second man, the Son of God, after Whose image Adam was created, and Who has become man in order to take back His old creation ("antiquam plasmationem") into Himself (iv. 33, 4). The devil had obtained *his* dominion over the first man by deceit and violence; whereas the redemption of the new race had taken place not with violence but, as became God, by free persuasion ("secundum suadelam, quemadmodum decebat Deum suadentem, non vim inferentem, accipere quae vellet," v. 1, 1). The dominion of the devil is an unjust dominion, for he, like a robber, has seized and taken to himself what did not belong to him, estranged us from our original godlike nature, and made us into his own disciples. Divine justice demands that what the devil has obtained by conflict should in a lawful conflict be won back from him. The Son of God deals, according to His own sense of right, with the apostasy itself, redeeming from it, at a price, that which was His own ("non deficiens in sua justitia juste etiam adversus ipsam conversus est apostasiam, ea quae sunt sua redimens ab ea," v. 1; 1; cf. 24, 4). Christ came not snatching with deceit that which was another's, but justly and graciously resuming that which was His own; justly in regard to the apostasy (the evil one) from whose power He redeemed us with His own blood, and graciously in reference to us whom He so redeemed (v. 2, 1). The persuasion (*suadela*) of which the Son of God made use consisted, so far as the devil was concerned, in his free consent to accept the redemption price of the Lord's death for his prisoners; and so the Lord redeemed us, giving His soul for our souls and His flesh for our flesh (v. 1, 1). Two thoughts are here to be distinguished. The first is that of Christ's *victorious* conflict with the evil one, maintaining, spite of all his temptations, full and entire obedience to the Father, unmasking Satan as rebel and deceiver, and thereby proving Himself the strong one (v. 21, 2 seq.). The second is that of redemption through Christ's blood, which is expressly represented as a price paid to the devil and by him voluntarily received. The first thought is developed mainly with reference to the temptation in the wilderness. In the third temptation the evil one is completely exposed and called by his true name, the Son of God appears as victor, and, by His obedience to the divine command, absolves the sin of Adam (v. 21, 2). With this chain of thought, complete in itself, the other theory of a redemption-price paid in the blood of Christ, is placed in no connexion. It is *not* said that the devil, acting up to his rights, caused the Saviour's death, which indeed is represented from another point of view as a price legitimately offered and paid down to him (v. 1, 1). The thought, moreover, subsequently worked out by Origen, that the devil deceived himself with the hope of bringing under his power One Whom he was too weak to hold, is not found in Irenaeus. But along with this conception of the redemption-price offered to the devil appears another thought, that man has been reconciled to God by the sacrifice of the body of Christ and the shedding of His blood (v. 14, 3).

It must be allowed that Irenaeus gives no complete dogmatic theory with regard to the nature of Christ's work of redemption, for his theological speculations nowhere appear as an independent system, but are simply developed in polemical contrast to those of the heretical gnosis. By this conflict with Gnosticism the currents of Christian religious thought were once more put in rapid movement and problems which had exercised St. Paul were again before the church.

A new letter of St. Irenaeus of considerable importance was discovered in 1904 by an Armenian scholar in the Church of the Virgin at Erivan in Russian Armenia, and trans. into German with notes by Dr. Harnack (1907). It was written to his friend Marcian and possibly intended as a manual for catechising (Drews, *Der lit. Charakter der neuernt deckten Schrift des Iren.* 1907). For an account of it see Essay VI. in Dr. Knowling's *Messianic Interpretation* (S.P.C.K. 1911).

Literature.—The *Vita Irenaei* of Feuardent and that of Peter Halloix; the *Dissertationes in Irenaeum* of Dodwell and those of Massuet; the Prolegomena of Harvey (*Preliminary Matter*, I. *Sources and Phenomena of Gnosticism*; II. *Life and Writings of St. Irenaeus*); Tillemont, *Mémoires*, iii. 77 sqq. and 619 sqq.; Lipsius, *Die Zeit des Irenaeus von Lyon und die Entstehung der altkatholischen Kirche* in Sybel's *Histor. Zeitschrift*, xxviii. pp. 241 sqq.; Lightfoot, *The Churches of Gaul*, in *Contemp. Review*, Aug. 1876, pp. 405 sqq.; the posthumous work of Dean Mansel, *The Gnostic Heresies of the First and Second Centuries* (London, 1875). Some translations of Irenaeus are in the *Ante-Nic. Fathers*, and bk. iii. of *adv. Haer.* has been trans. by H. Deane with notes and glossary (Clar. Press). A critical ed. of *adv. Haer.* is pub. by the Camb. Univ. Press in 2 vols. [R.A.L.]

Irenaeus (7), count of the empire and subsequently bp. of Tyre, while a layman took a zealous interest in theological controversies and was ardently attached to the cause of his personal friend Nestorius. In 431 Irenaeus unofficially accompanied Nestorius to the council of Ephesus (Labbe, *Concil.* iii. 443), employing his influence in behalf of his friend to the great irritation of Cyril and his party (*ib.* 749, 762; Baluze, 496, 524). When, five days after Cyril had hastily secured the condemnation of Nestorius, the approach of John of Antioch and the Eastern bishops was announced, Irenaeus, accompanied by a guard of soldiers, hurried out to apprise them of the high-handed proceedings of the council. He was followed by deputies from the council, who, as Memnon relates, were at the count's instigation maltreated by the soldiers, and prevented from having an audience with John (Labbe, *ib.* 764; Mercator, ii. praef. xxvii.). To counteract the influence of Dalmatius and the monastic party at Constantinople, the

Eastern bishops deputed Irenaeus to proceed thither with letters to the emperor and the leading officers of state, narrating their side (Labbe, *ib.* 717-720). Irenaeus obtained an audience of Theodosius, and his statement of the proceedings was so convincing that Theodosius was on the point of pronouncing the condemnation of Nestorius illegal, when the arrival of John, the Syncellus of Cyril, entirely frustrated his efforts.

The decree of Theodosius which banished Nestorius, Aug. 435, pronounced the same sentence against Irenaeus and a presbyter named Photius, as propagators of his impiety. Stripped of his honours, his property confiscated, he was deported to Petra (Baluz. p. 884, c. clxxxviii, clxxxix.), and passed 12 years in his Arabian banishment without once participating in Christian ordinances. His time was spent in the preparation of a history of the troubled scenes in which he had taken part, known as the *Tragoedia Irenaei*. The invectives in this work against Theodoret, Ibas, and all who had questioned Nestorius's perfect orthodoxy, render it probable that it was written early in his banishment, and that the lapse of time brought calmer thoughts. His doctrinal views seem also to have received some modification during this period, for at its close the banished heretic suddenly reappeared as the unanimous choice of the bishops of the province of Phoenicia for the vacant metropolitical see of Tyre, their choice being ratified by the leading members of the episcopate of Pontus and Palestine and accepted with warm commendation by Proclus of Constantinople. The date of his ordination as bp. of Tyre must have been before the end of 446. Since the reconciliation of John of Antioch and Cyril, a kind of truce had existed between the two parties—the Egyptians and Orientals—which this elevation of a leading Nestorian sympathiser to the episcopate rendered no longer possible. Irenaeus had been consecrated by Domnus, the patriarch of Antioch, who, therefore, was the first object of attack. He was plied with missives from the dominant clerical party at Constantinople, asserting that the election of a convicted heretic and a *digamus* was *ipso facto* null and void and charging him under severe threats to proceed to a fresh election. The emperor's name was adroitly kept in the background; but it was implied that the malcontents were acting with his sanction. Domnus turned for counsel to Theodoret, who replied that "it was better to fall under the ill-will of man than to offend God and wound one's own conscience." But the ruin of Irenaeus had been resolved on, and Theodosius was compelled to seal with his imperial authority the act of deposition. An edict was issued (Feb. 17, 448), renewing those formerly published against the Nestorians, and commanding that Irenaeus should be deposed from his see, deprived of the dress and title of priest, compelled to live as a layman in his own country and never set foot again in Tyre. Domnus, unwilling to consecrate a successor, sought to temporise, until fear of ulterior consequences prevailed over his scruples, and Photius was made bp. of Tyre, Sept. 9, 448 (*Actes du Brigand.* pp. 134, 143), and Irenaeus disappears entirely from the scene. The Latrocinium in 449 confirmed his deposition, after that of Ibas and Daniel of Charrae, and passed an anathema on him (Martin, *Actes du Brigandage*, pp. 82-86; Evagr. *H. E.* i. 10). As Irenaeus is not mentioned at the council of Chalcedon, he was probably no longer alive.

During the latter part of his career Irenaeus enjoyed the friendship and confidence of Theodoret, who speaks highly of his orthodoxy, magnanimity, liberality towards those in adversity, especially those who had known better times, and of his other virtues (*Ep.* 35, 110), and wrote him frequent letters.

Irenaeus's great historical work, the *Tragoedia*, has unfortunately perished and is only known to us from an ill-executed Latin translation of large portions of it, made subsequently to the time of Justinian by a partisan of "the Three Chapters." The anonymous translator, who has given very little more than the letters and other documents, invaluable for the light thrown on the transactions of the period, together with the summaries of Irenaeus and some interpolations and explanations of his own, sometimes barely intelligible, entitled his work *Synodicon.*

Tillem. *Mém. eccl.* xiv. 606-608, 613, 614 *et passim*; xv. 264-266, 578, 579 *et passim*; Cave, *Hist. Lit.* i. 437; Le Quien, *Or. Christ.* ii. 807; Labbe, *Concil.* tom. iii. *passim*; Baluze, *Nov. Coll. Concil.* passim; Abbé Martin, *Le Brigandage d'Ephèse*, pp. 82-95, 183. [E.V.]

Isaacus (7) **I.**, St. (*Sahag the Great, Parthev the Parthian*), catholicos of the church of Greater Armenia for 40 or 51 years, 390-441. Moses of Khorene states that he belonged to the house of the founder of the Armenian church, Gregory the Illuminator. His long patriarchate is remarkable for the invention of the Armenian characters by Mesrob, the translation of the Scriptures into the Armenian language, and the commencement of the golden age of Armenian literature; for the revision of the Armenian liturgy, first translated from the Greek by Gregory, which has continued unaltered ever since in the Armeno-Gregorian church; and for the destruction of the independence of Armenia. At the commencement of his patriarchate Isaac visited the Persian king at Ctesiphon, where, on behalf of his sovereign, he acknowledged Armenia to be tributary to Persia. Owng to the troubled state of the country he was virtually ruler for several years. In 428, from which date Armenian chronology becomes more certain (St. Martin, *Mém. sur l'Arménie*, i. 320, n.), the Persian king deposed Ardaces IV., the last of the Armenian Arsacidae, and Isaac retired into Western Armenia, either by order of the Persian monarch or through the enmity of the satraps of his own country, whom it is said he had offended by refusing to join in their plans. Whilst in Western Armenia (428-439) he sent Mesrob to Constantinople with letters to Theodosius II., and the general Anatolius, who was commissioned by the emperor to build the city of Theodosiopolis (called Garin by the Armenians, Erzeroum by the Turks), near the sources of the Euphrates, as a place of refuge for Isaac. Meanwhile the Persian kings set up others as patriarchs in his stead, but at length the Armenian satraps repented and invited Isaac to resume his throne. This he refused to do, but appointed one administrator in his stead, according to some Mastentzes, according to Moses of Khorene Samuel, nominated by the Persian king. After the death of his vicar he seems to have partially resumed his episcopal functions over the whole Armenian community. On account of the patriarch's expulsion, the archbp. of Cappadocian Caesarea disallowed the ordination of bishops, which had been conceded to Isaac; but by the influence of the Persians all connexion between Armenia and Caesarea was from this time forth broken off—a fact which tended towards the isolation of the Armenian church. Isaac did not attend the general council of Ephesus. He died at the age of 110 years, being the last Armenian patriarch of the family of Gregory the Illuminator; he was followed to the grave in six months by his friend Mesrob. Moses of Khorene, bk. iii. cc. xlix.-lxviii., in Langlois, *Hist. de l'Arménie*, ii. 159-173; St. Martin, *Mém. sur l'Arménie*, i. 437; Galanus, *Hist. Arm.* c. vii.; Le Quien, *Oriens Christ.* i. 1375; Malan, *Life of St. Gregory*, p. 28. [L.D.]

Isaacus (14) Ninivita, anchorite and bishop towards the end of the 6th cent. An anonymous Life prefixed to his works states that he was by birth a Syrian, and, with his brother who became abbat, entered the great monastery of St. Matthew at Nineveh. Afterwards he retired to a lonely cell, where he long remained. Isaac's fame as an anchorite became so great that he was raised to the bishopric of Nineveh, which, however, he resigned on the very day of his consecration, owing to an incident which convinced him that his office was superfluous in a place where the gospel was little esteemed. Feeling also that episcopal functions interfered with the ascetic life, he finally retired to the desert of Scete or Scetis, where he died. Lambecius (*Comment.* lib. v. pp. 74 sqq.), Cave (*Hist. Lit.* i. 519) and others confuse him with another Isaacus Syrus.

Works.—Ebedjesu (*Cat.* p. 63) writes that "he composed seven tomes on spiritual guidance, and on divine mysteries, judgments, and government." A considerable number, though not all, of these discourses are extant in Syriac, Arabic, and Greek MSS. in the Vatican and other libraries. Fifty-three of his homilies were rendered from Greek into Latin, *c.* 1407, by a monk who freely abridged and altered the order of his original. In this form they appear in the various *Bibliothecae Patrum*, as a continuous treatise entitled *de Contemptu Mundi*, uniformly but wrongly attributed to Isaacus Antiochenus.

He is much quoted by the old Syrian writers. His style teems with metaphor; his matter is often interesting, both theologically and historically. He treats mainly of the ascetic life, its rules and spiritual experiences. Watching, fasting, silence, and solitude are means to self-mastery. There are three grades of anchorites—novices, proficients, and the perfect. The worth of actions is gauged by the degree of the love of God which inspires them. By the thoughts which stir within, a man may learn to what grade of holiness he has risen. There are three methods by which every rational soul can approach unto God—viz. love, fear, divine training. He who has gotten love feeds on Christ at all times, and becomes immortal (John vi. 52). Sermons 8, 47, 48 (B. M. cod. 694) treat of the alternations of light and darkness, the deep dejection and sudden ecstasy to which anchorites were subject. For the former Isaacus prescribes holy reading and prayer—"infer tibi violentiam ad orandum, et praestolare auxilium, et veniet tibi te ignorante." Serm. 23 is directed against those who asked, If God be good, why did He create sin, Gehenna, Death, and Satan? Elsewhere Isaacus says that there is a natural faculty whereby we discern good from evil, to lose which is to sink lower than one's natural state; and this faculty precedes faith, and leads us thereto. There is also a faculty of spiritual knowledge which is the offspring of faith. He explains the "many mansions" of heaven as meaning the different capacities of the souls abiding there—a difference not of place but of grace.

Zingerle (*Mon. Syr.* i. 97 sqq.) has published Serm. 31, *On the natural offspring of the virtues*, and Serm. 43, *On the various grades of knowledge and faith.* Other titles are, *On the differences of revelations and operations in holy men*; *In how many ways the perception of things incorporeal is received by the nature of man* (B. M. cod. 694, 14 and 24); *That it is wrong without necessity to desire or expect any sign manifested through us or to us* (do. 695, 46).

A short tract, *de Cogitationibus* (περὶ λογισμῶν), attributed to this Isaacus, is given in Migne, vol. lxxxvi., along with the *de Contemptu Mundi.* A book, *de Causa Causarum* or *Liber Generalis ad Omnes Gentes*, treating of God and the creation and government of the universe, has been assigned to this Isaacus; it really belongs to Jacobus Edessenus (fl. 710), see Pohlmann, *Zeitschr. d. Morgenland. Gesellsch.* (1861), p. 648.

Cf. Wright's Cat. Syr. MSS. in Brit. Mus. vol. ii. pp. 569-581; *de Contemptu Mundi* in Migne, *Patr. Curs. Gk.* lxxxvi. pp. 811-885; Assem. *Bibl. Orient.* i. 444-463, iii. 104, etc.; Cave, *Hist. Lit.* i. 519; Fabric. *Biblioth. Graec.* xi. 114-122 Harl.; Casimir Oudin, *Comment. de Scriptor. Eccl.* i. coll. 1400-1405; Ceillier, xii. 100. [C.J.B.]

Isaacus (21), a Donatist who, together with Maximianus, met his death at Carthage in consequence of the cruel punishment inflicted by order of the proconsul of Africa, A.D. 348. The history is related by a fellow-Donatist named Macrobius; and though he does not mention the name of the proconsul, doubtless the tragedy took place in connexion with the mission into Africa of Paulus and Macarius. The narrative is told in barbarous Latin and a rhetorical style so turgid as to suggest the suspicion of exaggeration in the details. But these, horrible as they are, agree too well with what we know to have taken place in other cases. Maximianus suffered first, but Isaac provoked the anger of the judges by his taunting exclamations and was forthwith compelled to undergo a treatment no less brutal. Having been first scourged with "plumbata," a whip armed with leaden bullets, and then beaten with sticks, they were both cast into prison, but Isaac disappointed the further violence of his tormentors by death. This took place on a Saturday. Crowds immediately flocked to the prison, singing hymns as if it were the eve of Easter, and they watched beside the corpse to ensure it Christian burial. To disappoint this intention, the proconsul on the day following gave orders that both the living man and the dead body should be cast together into the sea. To execute this command, the soldiers were obliged to clear the way from the prison by force, and many persons were wounded in the struggle. The two victims were thrown into the sea at some distance from each other in baskets weighted with sand to ensure their sinking. But the action of the waves, caused, according to the writer's belief, by divine interposition, tore away the sand, and after six days brought the two bodies together to shore, where they were received with welcome by their fellow-Christians on their way to the churches and received Christian burial, the malice of those who had sought to deprive them of it being thus gloriously defeated.

Notwithstanding the inflated style of the narrative (very different, as Mabillon remarks truly, from that of the existing accounts of the deaths of true Catholic martyrs), and notwithstanding the very slight notice St. Augustine takes of the event, into which he acknowledges that he had made very little inquiry, and also despite his evident success in convicting some accounts of Donatist martyrdoms of inaccuracy, if not of direct falsehood, there seems no reason for doubting the substantial truth of this narrative, especially as Marculus, in Dec. of the same year, suffered death for a similar cause and with similar circumstances of cruelty. Neither can we doubt that the cause for which these men suffered was essentially one of religion. True, St. Augustine compares such cases to that of Hagar, and elsewhere argues in favour of the duty of the state as the guardian of truth to repress heresy and insinuates that those guilty of this offence are punished not so much on account of religion as of treason or disloyalty; but we must bear in mind that (1) the proceedings here related took place six years before St. Augustine's birth, and had not been repeated in his time, and that thus he was no witness either to the truth or falsehood of the narratives; (2) the behaviour and language of Isaac remind us more of an angry partisan than a Christian martyr; (3) the glaring faults of the narrative in style and temper do not extenuate the treatment which, after every allowance for exaggeration, the sufferers must have endured. Aug. *Tr. in Joann.* xi. 15; *c. Cresc.* iii. 49, 54; Mabillon, *Vet. Anal.* p. 185; *Mon. Vet. Don.* No. 29, pp. 237, 248, ed. Oberthür; Ceillier, v. 106; Morcelli, *Africa Christiana*, ii. 249. [H.W.P.]

Isaacus (28). Several eminent solitaries of the Egyptian deserts in the 4th cent. bore this name. The references are scattered up and down in the *Vitae Patrum*, and it is not always clear which Isaac is intended. The following seem to be distinct persons.

(i) Abbat **Isaacus,** presbyter of the anchorites in the Scetic desert (ἡ Σκῆτις, Copt. Schiêt), S.W. of Lake Mareotis. At 7 years of age he withdrew from the world, A.D. 358, and attached himself to Macarius of Alexandria, the disciple of St. Anthony. Palladius relates of abbat Isaac that he knew the Scriptures by heart, lived in utter purity, and could handle deadly serpents (κεράσται) without harm. He lived in solitude for 50 years, his followers numbering 150. Certain anecdotes in the *Apophthegmata Fatrum* appear to belong to him. "Abbat Isaac was wont to say to the brethren, Our fathers and abbat Pambo wore old bepatched raiment and palm husks (σεβένια); nowadays ye wear costly clothing. Hence! It was ye who desolated the district." (Scetis was overrun, *c.* 395, by the Mazices, a horde of merciless savages.)

Cassianus, who was in Scetis A.D. 398, conversed with Isaacus, to whom he assigns the 9th and 10th of his Conferences (*Collationes*), which treat of prayer. In the former Isaacus distinguishes four kinds of prayer, according to I. Tim. ii. 1 (*Collat.* 9, cc. 9-14). Then he expounds at length the Lord's Prayer (cc. 18-23). The highest type, however, is prayer "unuttered, unexpressed," like that of Christ on the mountain or in the garden (c. 25, *de qualitate sublimioris orationis*). In c. 36 he advises short and frequent petitions ("frequenter quidem sed breviter"), lest, while we linger, the foe suggest some evil thought.

The 10th *Conference* begins by relating how the patriarch Theophilus of Alexandria scandalized the Scetic anchorites by his Paschal Letter denouncing Anthropomorphism, and how the aged abbat Serapion, though convinced of his error, could not render thanks with the rest, but fell a-weeping and crying, "They have taken my God from me!" Cassianus and the other witnesses asked Isaacus to account for the old man's heresy. Isaacus made it a survival of heathen ideas of Deity in a simple and unlettered mind (cc. 1-5). Isaacus proceeds to shew how to attain to perfect and unceasing prayer. That will be realized when all our love and desire, every aim, effort, thought, all that we contemplate, speak of, hope for, is God; when we are united with Him by an enduring and indissoluble affection. C. 10 gives as a prayer suited to all emergencies the verse Ps. lxx. 1. Ill prays he who only prays when upon his knees. He prays never, who even upon his knees is distracted by wandering thoughts. Such as we would be found when praying, such should we be before we pray.

When 50 years old Isaacus was expelled from his desert by Theophilus of Alexandria, albeit that prelate had made bishops of seven or eight of his anchorites. Isaacus turned for succour to St. Chrysostom and Olympias. He was still living in A.D. 408.

Sources.—Pallad. *Dialog. de Vita Chrysost.* in *Patr. Gk.* xlvii. 59, 60; *Cassiani Massil. Collat.* 9, 10, in Migne, xlix. 770 sqq.; *Apophthegmata Patr. ib.* lxv. 223; a number of anecdotes headed περὶ τοῦ Ἀββᾶ Ἰσαὰκ τοῦ πρεσβυτέρου τῶν Κελλίων, but referring to several persons, cf. *de Vit. Patr.* lib. iii. col. 752, in Migne, lxxiii.; Tillem. *Mém.* viii. 650, 617, 648, and 813, n. vi.; Ceillier, viii. 174-177.

(ii) **Isaacus,** presbyter and abbat of the Nitrian desert, sometimes called Presbyter of the Cells (Κελλία N. of Nitria). The chief account of this Isaacus is also in Palladius (*Dialog.* Migne, xlvii. coll. 59, 60). He was head of 210 recluses. His charity and humility were famous. He built a hospital for the sick and for the numerous visitors to his community. Like Isaacus of Scetis, he was an adept in the Scriptures. Like him, too, after 30 years in the desert, he was driven forth *c.* 400 by the patriarch Theophilus, who had chosen a number of his disciples to be bishops. The *Apophthegmata Patrum* gives some stories about Isaac of the Cells. "The abbat Isaac said, In my youth I lived with abbat Cronius. Old and trembling as he was, he would never bid me do anything; he would rise by himself, and hand the water-cruse (τὸ βαυκάλιον) to me and the rest. And abbat Theodore of Phermè, with whom also I lived, would set out the table by himself and say, 'Brother, if thou wilt, come and eat.' I said, 'Father, I came to thee to profit: why dost not bid me do somewhat?' He answered never a word; but when the old men asked him the same thing, he broke out with, 'Am I Coenobiarch, that I should command him? If he like, what he sees me doing, he will himself do.' Thenceforward I forestalled the old man's purposes. And I had learned the lesson of doing in silence."

It appears that, after the persecution of Theophilus, Isaacus had returned to his desert. In the *Apoph. Patr.*, Migne, t. lxv. 223, 239, there are other anecdotes concerning him (cf. Tillem. *Mém.* viii. 623-625).

(iii) **Isaacus,** called Thebaeus, an anchorite of the Thebaid, probably not identical with (ii), although Cronius, the master of the Cellia, at one time lived in the Thebaid (*Vit. Patr.* lib. vii. col. 1044, Migne, t. lxxiii.). Alardus Gazaeus, the Benedictine annotator of Cassianus, writes (*Collat.* 9 *ad init.*) that there were two chief anchorites named Isaac; one who lived in the Scetic desert, and another called Thebaeus, often mentioned in the *Vitae Patrum* and in *Pratum Spirituale*, c. 161.

Once Isaac ("de Thebaida," *Vit. Patr.* v.) had banished an offending brother from the congregation. When he would have entered his cell, an angel stood in the way. "God sends me to learn where you wish Him to bestow the solitary whom you have condemned." The abbat owned his fault and was forgiven, but was warned not to rob God of His prerogative by anticipating His judgments. Isaac Thebaeus used to say to the brethren, "Bring no children hither. Four churches in Scetis have been desolated, owing to children."

Sources.—Apoph. Patr. col. 240, in Migne, lxv.; *de Vit. Patr.* lib. v. in Migne, lxxiii. (version of an unknown Greek author by Pelagius, *c.* 550), coll. 909, 918; *de Vit. Patr.* iii. col. 786 (prob. by Rufinus).

(iv) **Isaacus,** disciple of St. Apollos, probably lived at Cellia. He was accomplished in every good work. On his way to the church he would hold no converse with any, and after communion he would hurry back to his cell, without waiting for the cup of wine and the food (παξαμάτης) usually handed round among the brethren after service. "A lamp goes out, if one hold it long in the open air; and if I, kindled by the holy oblation, linger outside my cell, my mind grows dark" (*Apoph. Patr.* col. 241). [C.J.B.]

Isaacus (29) Senior, mentioned in an anonymous Life of Ephraim the Syrian among the more distinguished disciples of Ephraim who were also Syriac writers. He is cited by Joannes Maro (*Tract. ad Nest. et Eutych.*), by Bar-hebraeus (*Hist. Dynast.* 91), and by many other Syriac and Arabic authors, most of whom, however, confuse him with Isaac presbyter of Antioch (Assemani, *B. O.* i. 165). Gennadius in his *de Scriptor. Eccl.* c. 26, says: "Isaac wrote, concerning the Three Persons of the Holy Trinity and the Incarnation of the Lord, a book of very dark disputation and involved discourse; proving that there are three Persons in the one Godhead, each possessing a *proprium* peculiar to himself. The *proprium* of the Father is that He is the origin of the others, yet Himself without origin; that of the Son is that, though begotten, He is not later than His begetter; that of the Holy Ghost is that It is neither made nor begotten, and yet is from another. Of the Incarnation he writes that two Natures abide in the one Person of the Son of God." This chapter precedes those about Marcarius and Evagrius Pontinus, who lived *ante* 400. It is hence inferred that Isaac flourished about the end of the 4th cent. (Cave, i. 415, places him *c.* 430 (?), but some put him a century earlier.)

The work of Isaac, not unfairly described by Gennadius, is entitled *Libellus Fidei SS. Trinitatis et Incarnationis Domini.* It is a brief treatise, and is printed in Migne, *Patr. Gk.* xxxiii. In a codex Pithoeanus, *teste* Sirmond, the title is *Fides Isaacis* (or *Isacis*) *ex Judaeo.* Hence Isaac Senior has been identified by Tillemont (viii. 409) with Isaac the converted Jew who calumniated pope Damasus. Assemani thinks that the silence of Gennadius and his epitomizer Honorius renders it doubtful that Isaac Senior, the author of the *Libellus Fidei,* was a Jew. Cf. also Galland. vii. *Prol.* p. xxv.; Ceillier, vi. 290; Mansi, iii. 504 B; Pagi, *Crit.* ad ann. 378, xx. [C.J.B.]

Isaacus (31) Antiochenus, born at Amid (Diarbekir) in Mesopotamia, called "the Great" and "the Elder," a priest of Antioch in Syria, said to have visited Rome. His teacher was Zenobius the disciple of St. Ephraim, not (as Cave) Ephraim himself. The *Chronicle of Edessa* speaks of him as an archimandrite, without specifying his monastery, which was at Gabala in Phoenicia. He died *c.* 460. He is sometimes confused with Isaacus of Nineveh. Bar-hebraeus (*Hist. Dynast.* p. 91) unjustly brands him as a heretic and a renegade. He was author of numerous works in Syriac, of which the chief were polemics against the Nestorians and Eutychians, and of a long elegy on the overthrow of Antioch by the earthquake of 459. He also wrote a poem on the Ludi Seculares, held by Honorius in his sixth consulship (A.D. 404), and another on the sack of Rome by Alaric (A.D. 410). Jacobus of Edessa reckons him among the best writers of Syriac. His poems are extant in MSS. in the Vatican and other European libraries. Many of them are wrongly ascribed to St. Ephraim, and included amongst his works in the Roman edition. In discourse No. 7 Isaacus speaks of relic-worship and holy days. Besides Sunday, many Christians observed Friday, the day of the Passion. No. 9 attacks prevalent errors on the Incarnation. Here Isaacus seems to fall into the opposite heresies, failing to distinguish Nature from Person; but elsewhere he uses language unmistakably orthodox. Assemani thinks his words have been tampered with by Jacobite copyists. No. 24, Christ suffered as man, not as God. No. 50 touches on future retribution: "The fault is temporal, the punishment eternal." This aims at those Syrian monks who had adopted the opinion of Origen on this subject. No. 59 is a hymn asserting, against the Cathari or Novatianists, that fallen man recovers innocence not only by baptism, but also by penitence. No. 62 is a hymn of supplication, lamenting the disasters of the age, *e.g.* the inroads of Huns and Arabs, famine, plague, and earthquake. Johannes Maro quotes two discourses not found in the Vatican MSS. The first, on Ezekiel's chariot, clearly asserts two natures and one person in Christ: "duo aspectus, una persona; duae naturae, unus salvator." Similarly, the second, on the Incarnation. Bickell printed both, so far as he found them extant (*S. Isaac. Op.* i. 50, 52).

The library of the British Museum possesses about 80 of the discourses, hymns, prayers, etc., of St. Isaacus in MSS., ranging from the 6th to the 12th cent. Dr. Bickell, in the preface to his edition of the works of Isaac, gives a list of 178 entire poems, and of 13 others imperfect at the beginning or end (179-191); three prose writings dealing with the ascetic life (192-194); five sermons in Arabic, on the Incarnation, etc. (195-199); and a sermon in Greek, on the Transfiguration, usually assigned to St. Ephraim (200).

See *S. Isaaci Antiocheni opera omnia ex omnibus quotquot exstant codd. MSS. cum varia lectione Syr. Arab.* primus ed. G. Bickell, vol. i. 1873, ii. 1877; Gennadius, *Vir. Illustr.* 66; Assem. *Bibl. Orient.* i. 207-234; Cave, *Hist. Lit.* i. 434; Ceillier, x. 578; Wright's *Cat. Syr. MSS. Brit. Mus. General Index*, p. 1289.

The poems of Isaac are important for the right understanding of the doctrines of the Nestorians, Eutychians, Novatianists, Pelagians, and other sects; besides being authorities for the events, manners, and customs of the writer's age. [C.J.B.]

Ischyras (2) (*Ischyrion*, Soz.), Egyptian pseudo-presbyter and finally bishop; a slanderer of Athanasius. His story, which begins under the predecessor of Athanasius, is made out from scattered passages in the *Apol. c. Arian.*, and a slight outline is given by Socrates (i. 27). He belonged to a hamlet in the Mareotis too small for a church of its own (§ 85, ed. Migne) and there had a conventicle attended by seven persons at most (77, 83). He did not bear a good moral character (63) and was once charged with insulting the emperor's statues (vol. i. 185 B, *n.*). The Alexandrian synod of 324 disallowed his orders and pronounced him a layman (74, 75), disproving his pretensions to have been ordained by bp. Meletius, in whose *breviarium* his name did not appear (11, 28, 46, 71). He had given out that he was a presbyter of the pseudo-bishop Colluthus (2), but no one out of his own family believed him, as he never had a church, and no one in the neighbourhood looked on him as a clergyman (74, 75). He never attended ecclesiastical assemblies as a presbyter (28). In spite of the synod, he continued to act as a presbyter, and was doing this in the cottage of Ision when Athanasius, being on a visitation in the Mareotis, sent his presbyter Macarius to bid him desist. When Macarius reached the house, Ischyras was reported ill in his cell or in a corner behind the door (28, 63, 83), certainly not officiating at the Eucharist (41). This occurrence may be assigned to *c.* 329, between the latest date (June 8, 328) possible for the consecration of Athanasius and Nov. 330, when the troubles broke out. Ischyras on his recovery went over to the Meletians, in conjunction with whom he framed his accusation against Macarius (63), and through Macarius against Athanasius. In the spring of 331 (see vol. i. p. 184, and Hefele, ii. 13) the three Meletians accused Macarius at Nicomedia of having broken a chalice, overturned a holy table, and burnt service books on the occasion of his visit. As his friends became ashamed of him (63), Ischyras confessed the fabrication to the archbishop and implored forgiveness (16, 28, 63, 74). This would be in mid-Lent 332. In the summer of 335 Ischyras, having meanwhile been gained over by the Eusebians, revived the accusation before the council of Tyre (13), and accompanied the synodal commission to the Mareotis to investigate its truth (27). For his reward his Eusebian patrons procured (85) an imperial order for the erection of a church for him at a place called Pax Secontaruri, and the document recognized him as a "presbyter." They afterwards obtained for him the episcopal title (16, 41), and he figures as bp. of Mareotis among the bishops assembled at Sardica in 343 (Socr. ii. 20; Soz. iii. 12, here "Ischyrion"). He afterwards withdrew to Philippopolis (Hilar. *Frag.* iii. in *Patr. Lat.* x. 677 A; Mansi, iii. 139), at which synod his name is corruptly written Quirius. No other instance of a bp. of Mareotis occurs. Le Quien, *Or. Chr.* ii. 530. [T.W.D.]

Isdigerdes (1) **I.** (*Jezdedscherd, Yazdejirdus, Yezdegerdes*; Ἰσδιγέρδης and Ἰσδεγέρδης by the Greeks; in Armenian *Yazgerd*; on his coins, יזדכרתי, *i.e. Izdikerti*), king of Persia, surnamed Al Aitham (the Wicked), known in history as Isdigerd I., though an obscure and uncertain predecessor of the same name makes Mordtmann reckon him as Isdigerd II. Rawlinson thinks the best evidence favours 399 for the commencement of his reign, and 419 or 420 for his death. He was son of Sapor III., succeeding his brother Vararanes IV., and succeeded by his son Vararanes V. He reigned at Ctesiphon. With the Romans he appears to have lived in peace; Agathias (*Hist.* iv. 26, p. 264, ed. Bonn, 1828) and Theophanes (*Chron.* i. 125, 128, p. 69, ed. Bonn, 1839) relate how the emperor Arcadius on his death-bed directed his son Theodosius to be put under Isdigerdes's tutelage. (Petavius, *Rat. Temp.* pt. i. l. vi. c. 15, p. 249, Lugd. 1710; Greg. Abul-Pharajius, *Hist. Comp. Dyn.* i. p. 91, Oxf. 1663.) For a time he was almost a Christian, and as

Socrates (*H. E.* vii. 8) says, gave every facility for the propagation of the gospel, yet probably closed his days in persecuting the church. Under the example and influence of Maruthas, bp. of Martyropolis in Mesopotamia, who had been sent on an embassy from the Romans early in his reign, he was very favourably disposed towards Christianity and the church in Persia had peace with full liberty of worship and church-building. He overcame and exposed the impostures of the magi, with the assistance of Maruthas and other Christians, and miracles are said to have been wrought before him for the confirmation of the gospel. A second visit of Maruthas seems to have deepened the impression (Socr. *ib.*), but the indiscreet and impetuous zeal of one of Maruthas's companions, Abdas bp. of Susa, lost this royal convert to the faith. Abdas burned one of the temples of fire (Theod. *H. E.* v. 39). This offence Isdigerd was prepared to overlook, if Abdas would rebuild the burned pyreion; failing this, the king threatened to burn down and destroy all Christian churches in Persia. Abdas, esteeming it morally wrong to rebuild the temple, refused to comply, and the churches were burned. Abdas was among the first of the martyrs, and a persecution commenced in or towards the end of Isdigerd's reign, which his son and successor Vararanes or Bararanes carried on with most revolting cruelty and which was only ended by the presence of the Roman legions. From the odium of this persecution the memory of Isdigerd is specially shielded by Socrates (*H. E.* vii. 18-21), who throws it on his son; but Theodoret (v. 39) probably gives the truer account, though Isdigerd had probably neither the time nor inclination to carry out his edicts with severity. His character is described as noble and generous, tarnished only by this one dark spot in the last year of his reign or in a brief period in the middle of it. For the best modern literature of this reign, see ISDIGERDES (2). [G.T.S.]

Isdigerdes (2) **II.,** king of Persia, the son and successor of Vararanes V. All modern writers place his death A.D. 457, but differ somewhat as to the length of his reign. For its commencement Rawlinson thinks the best evidence is for 440. Soon after he declared war against the Roman empire. Theodosius II. shortly made peace with him, and Isdigerd then undertook a war, which continued many years (443-451), against the Tatars of Transoxiana. He attempted to force the Zoroastrian religion on Christian Armenia. In this he was ably seconded by his vizier Mihr-nerses, whose proclamation, still extant, embodies the Zoroastrian objection to Christian doctrine [MESROBES]. It was answered in a council of eighteen Armenian bishops, headed by the patriarch Joseph, at Ardashad in 450. This document, also extant, is a lengthened apology for Christianity and contains a detailed confession of faith, with a resolution of adhering to it couched in these terms: "Do thou therefore inquire of us no further concerning these things, for our belief originates not with man. We are not taught like children; but we are indissolubly bound to God, from Whom nothing can detach us, neither now, nor hereafter, nor for ever, nor for ever and ever" (*Hist. of Vartan*, tr. by Neumann, 1830). Isdigerd's attempt to convert Armenia to Zoroastrianism was manifestly dictated by a desire to detach the country from the Christian Roman empire. In 451 he attacked the Armenians. They endeavoured to secure the help of the emperor Marcian, who was, however, paralysed through fear of Attila and the Huns. In 455 or 456 the Persians triumphed in a great battle, wherein the patriarch Joseph and many nobles were taken prisoners and martyred. Agathias, iv. 27; Tabari, *Chronique*, iii. 127; Clinton, *Fasti Romani*, i. p. 546; Tillem. *Emp.* vi. 39; Saint-Martin, *Mém. sur l'Armén.* vol. i. p. 322; Pathkanian, *Histoire des Sassan.* in *Journal Asiatique* (1866), pp. 108-238; Mordtmann, *Zeitschrift der deutschen Morgenlandischen Gesellschaft*, t. viii. 70; Rawlinson's *Seventh Or. Monarchy* (1876), c. xv. p. 301, where other authorities will be found. Pathkanian's article gives a list of writers who have treated of this period. Isdigerd II. was succeeded by Perozes. [G.T.S.]

Isidorus (13), archbp. of Seville, 600-636. Notwithstanding his prominent place in Spanish ecclesiastical history, the known facts of his life are few, and considerable uncertainty attaches to many points. It appears certain that his father was of the province of Cartagena, and that for some reason his parents left there for Seville either before or very shortly after his birth. It is not certain, therefore, whether Isidore was born at Seville or Cartagena, but probably at the latter. Arevalo (i. 122) decides for Seville; so Dupin: Florez (*Esp. Sag.* ix. 193, x. 120) is in favour of Cartagena. All things tend to shew that his parents died when he was very young. He was the youngest of the family. Leander, the eldest, was archbp. of Seville *c.* 579-599, and Fulgentius was bp. of Astigi or Ecija in the province of Seville. Isidore was archbp. of Seville for nearly 40 years, and died in 636. Leander received the pall from Gregory the Great in 599. Gams fixes 600 as the year of Leander's death, and consequently of Isidore's succession (ii. 41). To date the birth of Isidore *c.* 560 will not be far wrong. His early manhood was probably passed in a monastery, where he could pursue the studies which afterwards made him famous. Most probably he never belonged to a coenobite order.

We meet his name in connexion with the so-called decree of Gunthimar, the Gothic king, and a supposed synod of Toledo in 610 assigning metropolitan rank to the see of Toledo. In the list of subscriptions appended to the *Decretum* in the conciliar collections (*e.g.* Mansi, x. 511) Isidore stands second, following the king. He next appears as presiding over the second council of Seville in Nov. 618 or 619, in the reign of king Sisebut (Mansi, x. 555). The church of Seville is spoken of as the "holy Jerusalem." The governor of the city, Sisisclus, and the treasurer Suanilanus were present. The decrees set forth fully the doctrine of the Person of Christ against the Acephali, supporting it with appeals to Scripture, the Apostles' Creed, and the Fathers. This document was signed by 8 bishops, of whom Isidore subscribed first as metropolitan of Baetica. Some uncertainty hangs over Isidore's presence at a council held at Toledo *c.* 625.

The fourth council of Toledo was held in 633, in the extreme old age of Isidore and shortly before his death, soon after Sisenand came to the throne. It met in the basilica of St. Leocadia, and was composed of prelates from Gaul and Narbonne, and from all the provinces of Spain. The king, with his court magnates, was present, and threw himself on the earth before the bishops, and with tears and sighs entreated their intercession with God, and exhorted them to observe the ancient decrees of the church and to reform abuses. The council issued 75 decrees, for a summary of which see *D. C. A.* ii. 1968. They were signed by the six metropolitan archbishops of Spain. This council was the only one in which they were all present, and was the most numerously attended of all Spanish synods. Isidore signed first as the oldest metropolitan and oldest bishop present (Mansi, x. 641). The council probably expressed with tolerable accuracy the mind and influence of Isidore. It presents a vivid picture of the church of Spain at that period. The position and deference granted to the king is remarkable, and nothing is said of allegiance to Rome. The church is free and independent, yet bound in solemn allegiance to the acknowledged king. The relations of the church to the Jews are striking, and the canons shew that there were many Jews in the Spanish community and that the Christian church had not yet emancipated itself from the intolerance of Judaism. This council was the last great public event of Isidore's life. He died three years afterwards. As he felt his end approaching he distributed his goods lavishly among the poor, and is said to have spent the whole day for six months in almsgiving. In his last illness he performed public penance in the church of St. Vincentius the martyr, gathered around him the bishops, the religious orders, the clergy, and the poor, then, as one bishop invested him with the penitential girdle, and another strewed ashes on his head, he made a pious and eloquent prayer, translated in full by Gams, received the Body and Blood of Christ in the sacrament, took affectionate leave of all present, retired to his cell, and in four days died.

Isidore was undoubtedly the greatest man of his time in the church of Spain. He was versed in all the learning of the age, and well acquainted with Greek, Latin, and Hebrew. His works shew him as a man of varied accomplishments and great versatility of mind; and the prominent place he long filled in his own country sufficiently indicates his general ability and character. His eloquence struck all who heard him with astonishment, and he represented in himself all the science of his time. His language is studiously scriptural. He is quoted as holding predestinarian views, but his language seems hardly to go so far. At the 8th council of Toledo, in 653, the epithet *Egregius* was applied to him, and confirmed at the 15th council of Toledo, 688. Popes and councils vied in doing him honour, till Benedict XIV. permitted the office of St. Isidore to be recited with the antiphon "O doctor optime," and the gospel, "Vos estis sal terrae."

His works are many and multifarious. (1) His *Etymologies* or *Origins* was, according to Braulio and Ildefonsus, his last work. It is in 20 books, and treats of the whole circle of the sciences in a very concise, methodical, and convenient manner. It is for the period a really wonderful work, and the authors quoted in it shew his wide classical reading. The subjects of the books are: i. Grammar in 44 chapters, containing an immense amount of information in a convenient form. ii. Rhetoric and dialectics, in 31 chapters. iii. The four mathematical sciences: *i.e.* arithmetic, 9 chapters; geometry, 5 chapters; music, 9 chapters; and astronomy, 48 chapters; algebra not being yet invented. iv. Medicine, in 13 chapters. v. Laws, 27 chapters; Times, 12 chapters. vi. Ecclesiastical books and offices, 19 chapters. vii. Of God, angels, and the orders of the faithful, 14 chapters. viii. The church and divers sects, 11 chapters. ix. Languages, nations, kingdoms, warfare, citizens, and relationships, 7 chapters. x. An alphabetical index and explanation of certain words. A vast amount of erroneous ingenuity is displayed in deriving all the words of the Latin language from itself: *e.g.* "*Nox*, a nocendo dicta, eo quod oculis noceat. *Niger*, quasi *nubiger*, quia non serenus, sed fusco opertus est. Unde et nubilum diem tetrum dicimus. *Prudens*, quasi *porro videns:* perspicax enim est, et incertorum praevidet casus. *Cauterium* dictum quasi *cauturium* quod *urat*," etc. xi. Of men and portents, in 4 chapters. xii. Animals, in 8. xiii. The universe (*mundus*), in 22. xiv. The earth and its parts, in 9. xv. Buildings, land-surveying, roads, etc., in 16. xvi. Mineralogy, stones, weights, measures, and metals, in 27. xvii. Agriculture, in 11. xviii. War and various games, in 69. xix. Ships, architecture, clothes of various kinds, in 34. xx. Food, domestic and agricultural implements, carriages, harness, etc., in 16. The treatise, which in the Roman edition occupies two quarto vols., is a singular medley of information and ignorance, and presents a remarkable picture of the condition of life and knowledge at the time. In bk. v., under the head of "De discretione temporum," is a chronological summary of sacred and secular history from Adam to Heraclius, concluding in these striking words: "Eraclius xvii nunc agit imperii annum: Judaei in Hispania Christiani efficiuntur. Residuum sextae aetatis soli Deo est cognitum." The whole period (after an idea common in Augustine) is divided into six ages, ending with Noah, Abraham, Samuel, Zedekiah, Julius Caesar, Heraclius. In bk. vi. is an introductory account of the several books of the Bible. It is probably not possible to overrate the value and the usefulness of this treatise to the age in which Isidore lived, and indeed for many ages it was the best available handbook.

(2) *Libri Differentiarum sive de Proprietate Sermonum.*—Bk. i. treats of the differences of words, often with acuteness and accuracy. Bk. ii. treats in 40 sections and 170 paragraphs of the differences of things, *e.g.* between Deus and Dominus, Substance and Essence, etc.

This is, in fact, a brief theological treatise on the doctrine of the Trinity, the power and nature of Christ, Paradise, angels, and men. He elaborately defines words denoting the members of the body, sin, grace, freewill, the law and the gospel, the active and contemplative life, virtues, vices, and the like.

(3) *Allegoriae quaedam Sacrae Scripturae.*—A spiritual interpretation of the names of Scripture characters: 129 from O. T. and 121 from N. T.; the latter being often from our Lord's parables, miracles, etc., as the ten virgins, the woman with the lost piece of money, the man who planted a vineyard, and the like. The angered king who sent his armies and destroyed those murderers and burnt up their city is interpreted of God the Father, who sent Vespasian Caesar to destroy Jerusalem. He shews an intimate acquaintance with Scripture and with the wonderful way it had then permeated the teaching and life of the church. The treatise is of intrinsic interest.

(4) Somewhat similar to the last is *de Ortu et Obitu Patrum qui in Scriptura Laudibus Efferuntur*; 64 chapters on O.T. characters and 21 on New, from Adam to Maccabaeus and from Zacharias to Titus. The genuineness of this treatise has been much doubted.

(5) *Proomeia in Libros Vet. et Nov. Test.*—Very brief introductions to the several books of O. and N.T., including Tobias, Judith, Esdras, and Maccabees, "ex quibus quidem Tobiae, Judith, et Maccabaeorum, Hebraei non recipiunt. Ecclesia tamen eosdem intra canonicas scripturas enumerat."

(6) *Liber Numerorum qui in sanctis Scripturis occurrunt.*—A mystical treatment of numbers from one to sixty, omitting some after twenty.

(7) *Quaestiones tam de Novo quam de Veteri Testamento.*—A series of 41 questions on the substance and teaching of Scripture with appropriate answers. Some are very interesting.

(8) *Secretorum Expositiones Sacramentorum, seu Quaestiones in Vetus Testamentum.*—A mystical interpretation of the principal events recorded in the books of Moses, Joshua, Judges, Samuel, Kings, Ezra, Maccabees. The preface states that he has gathered the opinions of ancient ecclesiastical writers, viz. Origen, Victorinus, Ambrose, Jerome, Augustine, Fulgentius, Cassianus, and pope Gregory the Great. Gen. is treated of in 31 chapters Ex. in 59, Lev. in 17, Num. in 42, Deut. in 22, Josh. in 18, Judg. in 9 (including 1 on Ruth), I. Kings (*i.e.* Sam.) in 21, II. Kings in 6, III. Kings in 8, IV. Kings in 8, Ezra in 3, Mac. in 1. The mystical method of interpretation is pursued to an excessive degree.

(9) *De Fide Catholica ex Veteri et Novo Testamento contra Judaeos.*—Addressed to his sister Florentina and apparently written at her request. It treats of the person of Christ from His existence in the bosom of the Father before the world was till His ascension and return to judgment; and the consequences of the Incarnation, viz. the unbelief of the Jews, the ingathering of the Gentiles, the conversion of the Jews at the end of the world, and the cessation of the Sabbath.

(10) *Sententiarum Libri* iii.—A kind of manual of Christian faith and practice, treating of God and His attributes. It discourses also upon the world, the origin of evil, angels man, the soul, and senses of the flesh, Christ and the Holy Spirit, the church and heresies, the heathen nations, the law, seven rules or principles for the understanding of Scripture, the difference between the two Testaments, symbol and prayer, baptism and communion, martyrdom, the miracles wrought by the saints, Antichrist and his works, the resurrection and judgment, hell, the punishment of the wicked, and the glory of the just. Great use is made throughout of the works of Augustine and Gregory.

(11) *De Ecclesiasticis Officiis* treats of the services of the church, and of clerics, their rules and orders, the tonsure, the episcopal office, vicars episcopal, presbyters, deacons, sacristans and subdeacons, readers, psalmists, exorcists, acolytes, porters, monks, penitents, virgins, widows, the married, catechumens, exorcism, salt, candidates for baptism, the creed, the rule of faith, baptism, chrism, imposition of hands, and confirmation.

(12) *Synonyma de lamentatione animae peccatricis.*—One of the most curious of Isidore's works; a kind of soliloquy between Homo and Ratio. Homo begins by lamenting his lost and desperate condition in consequence of sin, and Ratio undertakes to direct him aright to a higher and holier condition issuing in the bliss of eternal felicity.

(13) *Regula Monachorum.*—This treatise led some to suppose Isidore a Benedictine monk, the only order then established in the West; but Gams thinks the proof not sufficient.

(14) Thirteen short letters follow: to bp. Leudefred of Cordova; to Braulio, to whom he speaks of giving a ring and a pall; to Helladius of Toledo on the fall of a certain bp. of Cordova; to duke Claudius, whom he congratulates on his victories; to Massona, bp. of Merida; and to archdeacon Redemptus.

(15) *De Ordine Creaturarum.*—This book has been doubted by some, and, though Arevalo maintains it to be genuine, he prints it in smaller type. Gams reckons it as Isidore's. It treats of faith in the Trinity, spiritual creation, the waters above the firmament, the firmament of heaven, the sun and moon, the devil and the nature of demons, the nature of waters and course of the ocean, Paradise, the nature of man after sin, the diversity of sinners and their place of punishment, purgatorial fire and the future life.

(16) *De Natura Rerum Liber.*—One of the most celebrated of Isidore's treatises, dedicated to king Sisebut (acc. A.D. 612), one of the best kings of Spain, whose death was universally lamented by the Goths. Isidore discourses of the days, the night, the seasons, the solstice and equinox, the world and its five zones, heaven and its name, the planets, the waters, the heavens, the nature, size, and course of the sun, the light and course of the moon, the eclipse of sun and moon, the course of the stars, the position of the seven planets, the light of the stars, falling stars, the names of the stars and whether they have any soul, thunder, lightning, the rainbow, clouds, showers, snow, hail, the nature and names of the winds, the signs of storms, pestilence, the heat, size, and saltness of the ocean, the river Nile, the names of sea and rivers, the position

and motion of the earth, mount Etna, and the parts of the earth. He gives diagrams to illustrate his meaning. For a full analysis of the sources of this book see Gustavus Bekker's ed. (Berlin, 1857).

(17) *Chronicon.*—A very brief summary of the principal events from the creation of the world to the reign of the emperor Heraclius and of king Sisebut. Hertzberg gives an elaborate analysis of the sources of Isidore's two chronicles in the *Forschungen zur deutschen Gesch.* xv. 289.

(18) *Historia de regibus Gothorum, Wandalorum et Suevorum.*—The Goths, according to Isidore, were descended from Gog and Magog, and of the same race as the Getae. They first appeared in Thessaly in the time of Pompey, and in that of Valerian devastated Macedonia, Greece, Pontus, Asia, and Illyricum. The history is brought down to 621, the reign of king Swintila. Isidore praises the Goths highly; and Spaniards of his time esteemed it an honour to be reckoned Goths. This brief sketch is invaluable as our chief authority for the history of the West Goths. Of the Vandals we learn less from him, and his sketch of the Suevi is very brief, the former compressing 123 years into a single page, and the latter 177 in the same space. The Vandals entered Spain under Gunderic and were destroyed on the fall of Gelimer; the Suevi entered under Hermeric in 409 and became incorporated with the Gothic nation in 585.

(19) *De Viris Illustribus liber.*—Many Greeks and Latins had treated of the Christian writers before Isidore, but he determined to give a brief outline of those whom he had read himself. The list embraces 46 names, and Braulio has added that of Isidore himself in the celebrated "Praenotatio librorum S. Isidori a Braulione edita." Among the 46 are Xystus the pope, Macrobius the deacon, Theodore of Mopsuestia, Hosius of Cordova, Eusebius of Dorylaeum, Chrysostom, Hilary of Arles, Gregory the pope, Leander his own brother, and Maximus of Saragossa. This is a valuable summary of important facts in ecclesiastical history, but too often disfigured by the fierce and illiberal polemical spirit of the day—*vide, e.g.*, his remarks on the death of Hosius.

Other minor works assigned, some doubtfully, to Isidore need not be enumerated.

His Latin is not pure. He uses many Spanish words, and Arevalo has collected no fewer than 1,640 words which would not be understood by the ordinary reader or would strike him as strange. The style is feeble and inflated, having all the marks of an age of decadence. He was a voluminous writer of great learning, well versed in Holy Scripture, of which he manifests a remarkable knowledge, had a trained and cultivated mind, but was rather a receptive and reproductive writer than one of strong masculine and original mind. He was a very conspicuous ornament of the Spanish church and shed great glory on the age he adorned. He did much to hand on the light of Christianity and make it effectual to the amelioration of a semi-barbarous nation, and his character contrasts favourably with those of a later period.

A full list of the Lives of Isidore up to his time may be seen in Chevalier's *Sources historiques du Moyen-âge*, p. 1127, including those of Henschen in Boll. *Acta SS.* 4 Apr. i. 327; Arevalo in his ed. of Isidore's Works; Florez, *Esp. Sag.* ix. 173 (ed. 1752); Dupin, *Eccl. Writ.* t. ii. p. 1 (ed. 1724); Ceillier, xi. 710; Cave, i. 547; Gams, *Kirchengeschichte von Spanien* (3 vols. 8vo, Regensburg, 1862-1874; the great want of this excellent work is an adequate index; the first vol. alone has a "Register"). Arevalo's ed. of Isidore's works has been reprinted by the Abbé Migne in his *Patr. Lat.* lxxxi.-lxxxiv., with the addition of an eighth vol., containing the *Collectio Canonum* ascribed to Isidore; vols. lxxxv.-lxxxvi. of Migne contain *Liturgia Mozarabica secundum Regulam Beati Isidori.* There is an excellent ed. of the *de Natura Rerum Liber* by G. Becker (Berlin 1857). Prof. J. E. B. Mayor has given a list of editions and authorities in his *Bibliographical Clue to Latin Literature*, p. 212. [S.L.]

De Reg. Gothorum, Vandalorum, et Suevorum.—The histories, of all Isidore's works, have the most practical value for the present day. The *Historia Gothorum* is still to us, as it was to Mariana, one of the main sources of Gothic history. Upon the histories in general was based all the later medieval history-writing of Spain. A most valuable contribution was made to our knowledge of the exact place of the histories in historical work by Dr. Hugo Hertzberg (Göttingen, 1874) in his *Die Historien und die Chroniken des Isidorus von Sevilla: Eine Quellenuntersuchung, Erster Th., die Historien.* Dr. Hertzberg's great merit lies in the clearness with which he shews exactly how Isidore worked, what were the kind and amount of his material, and the method employed in working it up.

Dr. Hertzberg's general conclusions are, that Isidore neither possessed large material nor used what he had well. In no case did he take *all* that earlier chronicles offered him, but only extracts; his choice and arrangement of statements are often bad, and the proper chronological order frequently disregarded. Notwithstanding these drawbacks, the permanent historical value of certain portions of the *Hist. Goth.* is very great. From the reign of Euric, where Idatius breaks off, Isidore becomes for a time our only informant. He alone preserves the memory of Euric's legislation, while our knowledge of Visigothic history under Gesalic, Theudis, Theudigisel, Agila, and Athanagild rests essentially on his testimony. In the prominent reigns of Leovigild and Recared, Joh. Biclarensis becomes our great source, but Isidore's additions are important. From Recared to Suinthila he is again our best and sometimes our only source. The *Hist. Vand.* is, however, historically valueless, as we possess the sources from which it is a mere extract, and the same may almost be said of the *Hist. Suev.* Just where Isidore might have drawn most from oral testimony and thus supplied a real gap in our historical knowledge, viz. in the 100 years of Suevian history between Remismund and Theodemir, he fails us most notably. The whole missing cent. is dismissed in one vague sentence which tells us nothing.

For a complete catalogue of the nine MSS. of the longer form of the text, and the two MSS. of the shorter, as well as of the editions of both texts, see Dr. Hertzberg's *Diss.* 8-18. He gives a complete analysis of both texts according to the sources. For general references see Potthast, *Bibl. Hist. Med. Devi.* The longer text of the histories is printed in *Esp. Sagr.* vi. with an introduction and long notes by Florez. [M.A.W.]

Isidorus (24). [BASILIDES.]

Isidorus (31) Pelusiota, an eminent ascetic, theologian, and spiritual director in 5th cent., born at Alexandria (Photius, *Bibl.* 228). His family was probably of high rank. The wide range of his reading, as shewn by his familiarity with Greek poets, historians, orators, and philosophers, witnesses to the best Alexandrian education. He also felt the full influence of that great development of Egyptian monasticism which was encouraged by the seclusion of Athanasius during his third exile and by the persecution of the "holy solitaries" after his death, and which made so deep an impression on the as yet unconverted Augustine (*Confess.* viii. 6; cf. Isid. *Ep.* i. 173, alluding to "the blessed Ammon"). Isidore resolved to adopt the monastic life in its coenobitic form, as it had been organized by Pachomius at Tabenna and was being exhibited by various communities in the Upper Thebaid which followed his rule, by others in the Lower Thebaid, and the 5,000 inmates of the cells of Nitria (cf. Fleury, bk. xx. c. 9). The place he selected was near Pelusium, an ancient border-town at one of the Nile mouths. Jerome says it had "a very safe harbour" and was a centre of all "business connected with the sea" (*Comm. in Ezech.* ix. 30), but its inhabitants were proverbial for dulness (Hieron. *Ep.* lxxxiv. 9). It was the capital of the province of Augustamnica Prima, and as such the seat of a "corrector" or governor. When Isidore first knew it, it was "rich and populous" (*Ep.* iii. 260). It suffered much from the maladministration of a Cappadocian named Gigantius. Believing that monastic life was the "imitation and receptacle of all the Lord's precepts" (*Ep.* i. 278), Isidore became a thorough monk in his ascetic self-devotion. Whether he became abbat Tillemont considers uncertain (xv. 101). We know from Facundus (*Def. Tri. Capit.* ii. 4), and, indeed, virtually from himself (*Ep.* i. 258), that he was ordained a presbyter, very likely by bp. Ammonius (*Ep.* ii. 127), clearly not by his successor Eusebius, whom Isidore depicts as the centre of an ecclesiastical scandal which was to him a standing grief and offence.

Perhaps this ecclesiastical degeneracy near his own home led Isidore to generalize somewhat too despondingly as to its prevalence all around. Alluding to Eusebius's love of church-building he says: "It was not for the sake of walls, but of souls, that the King of Heaven came to visit us." "Could I have chosen, I would have rather lived in apostolic times, when church buildings were not thus adorned but the church was decked with grace, than in these days, when the buildings are ornamented with all kinds of marble, and the church is bare and void of spiritual gifts" (*Ep.* ii. 246; cf. ii. 88). "Once pastors would die for their flocks; now they destroy the sheep by causing the soul to stumble. . . . Once they distributed their goods to the needy; now they appropriate what belongs to the poor. Once they practised virtue; now they ostracize [a favourite phrase with Isidore] those who do. . . . I will not accuse *all*" (iii. 223). "Once men avoided the episcopate because of the greatness of its authority; now they rush into it because of the greatness of its luxury. . . . The dignity has lapsed from a priesthood into a tyranny, from a stewardship into a mastership [δεσποτείαν]. For they claim not to administer as stewards, but to appropriate as masters" (v. 21, to a bishop). "It is not long since the church had splendid teachers and approved disciples;" and it might be so again if bishops would "lay aside their tyranny and shew a fatherly interest in their people . . . but until that foundation is well laid, I think it idle to talk about the top-stone" (v. 126). He would say to worldly and arrogant prelates, "Abate your pride, relax your superciliousness, remember that you are but ashes. . . . Do not use the arms of the priesthood against the priesthood itself" (v. 131). "When those who were crowned with the priesthood led an evangelical and apostolical life, the priesthood was naturally dreaded by the sovereignty; but now it is the sovereignty which is dreaded by the priesthood, or rather by those who seem to discharge it but by their conduct insult it" (v. 268, to Cyril). "Some . . . openly reproach priests; others pay them outward respect but in secret revile them. . . . This does not surprise *me*. As they do not act like those of old, they are treated differently. Those of old corrected kings when they sinned; these do not correct even rich subjects; and if they try to correct some poor man, they are reproached as having been convicted of the same offences" (v. 278). So, speaking to an ambitious deacon about I. Tim. iii. 1, he corrects a misapprehension. "Paul did not say, '*Let* every one desire the episcopate.' . . . It is a work, not a relaxation; a solicitude, not a luxury; a responsible ministration, not an irresponsible dominion; a fatherly supervision, not a tyrannical autocracy" (iii. 216). Elsewhere he complains that bishops would receive persons excommunicated by other bishops, to the ruin of the discipline of souls (iii. 259), and that in their bitter contests these official peacemakers would fain devour each other (iv. 133). The secularization of the episcopal character he traces in one letter to the excessive honour paid by emperors to bishops, and adds: "There *are* bishops who take pains to live up to the apostolic standard; if you say, 'Very few,' I do not deny it; but . . . many are called, few are chosen." Isidore exhibits an intense habitual moral earnestness, vigilant against all that implied or might tend to sin (v. 17, 208). His downright censures, delivered under a serious conviction that he was specially appointed for the purpose (i. 389; cf. Tillem. xv. 102), naturally made him enemies among the higher clergy, who tried to put him under some sort of ban, and thereby "unintentionally set a crown upon his head" (*Ep.* v. 131). But he was not less stern to faults in other orders, such as the inhospitality (i. 50), gluttony (i. 392), or "pugnacity" (i. 298) of monks; their neglect of manual labour (i. 49), the disorderliness of those who haunted cities and frequented public shows, as if all that "the angelic life" required were "a cloak, a staff, and a beard" (i. 92; cf. i. 220, and Chalcedon, can. 4). He rebukes a physician who is morally diseased (*Ep.* i. 391), denounces a homicide who went "swaggering" through Pelusium (i. 297), warns a wicked magistrate to flee from eternal punishment (i. 31), remonstrates with a soldier for invading the cells of monks and teaching them false doctrine (i. 327), and with a general for attempting to take away the privilege of sanctuary (i. 174), etc. In a letter probably addressed to Pulcheria he reprobates the conduct of some imperial envoys, who had compromised their Christianity in the negotiation of a peace (iv. 143).

The two great church questions in which Isidore took a decided part brought him into collision with his own patriarch, Cyril of Alexandria. The first related to the recognition of St. Chrysostom's memory as worthy of the reverence of faithful Christians. Theophilus of Alexandria had practically procured his deposition and exile; the West had supported Chrysostom while he lived and afterwards had suspended communion with churches which would not insert his name in their diptychs. Antioch had yielded; even Atticus of Constantinople had done so for peace' sake. Cyril, the nephew and successor of Theophilus, held fast to his uncle's position. Isidore had loved and honoured "holy John," if he had not, as Nicephorus says (xiv. 30), been instructed by him. In a letter to a grammarian he quotes Libanius's panegyric on his oratory (*Ep.* ii. 42); to another Isidore he specially recommends "the most wise John's" commentary on the Romans (v. 32); in another letter, recommending his treatise "on the Priesthood," he calls him "the eye of the Byzantine church, and of every church" (i. 156); and he describes the "tragedy of John" in the bitter words: "Theophilus, who was building-mad, and worshipped gold, and had a spite against my namesake" (see Socr. vi. 9), was "put forward by Egypt to persecute that pious man and true theologian" (*Ep.* i. 152). Similarly he wrote to Cyril: "Put a stop to these contentions: do not involve the living Church in a private vengeance prosecuted out of duty to the dead, nor entail on her a perpetual division [αἰώνιον διχόνοιαν] under pretence of piety" (i. 570, transl. by Facund.). Cyril took this advice, and the "Joannite" quarrel came to an end, probably in 417-418 (Tillem. xiv. 281; see Photius, *Bibl.* 232).

The other matter was far more momentous. When Cyril was at the council of Ephesus endeavouring to crush Nestorianism, Isidore wrote to him: "Prejudice does not see clearly; antipathy does not see at all. If you wish to be clear of both these affections of the eyesight, do not pass violent sentences, but commit causes to just judgment. God... was pleased to 'come down and see' the cry of Sodom, thereby teaching us to inquire accurately. For many of those at Ephesus accuse you of pursuing a personal feud, instead of seeking the things of Jesus Christ in an orthodox way. 'He is,' they say, 'the nephew of Theophilus,'" etc. (*Ep.* i. 310; cf. a Latin version, not quite accurate, by Facundus, *l.c.*). He had, however, no sympathy with Nestorius: in the close of the letter he seems to contrast him with Chrysostom; in the next letter he urges Theodosius II. to restrain his ministers from "dogmatizing" to the council, the court being then favourable to Nestorius. Isidore was, indeed, very zealous against all tendencies to Apollinarianism: he disliked the phrase, "God's Passion," he insisted that the word "Incarnate" should be added—it was the Passion of Christ (*Ep.* i. 129); he urged on Cyril the authority of Athanasius for the phrase, "*from* two natures" (i. 323), and he even uses the yet clearer phrase, ultimately adopted by the council of Chalcedon, "*in* both natures" (i. 405); but he repeatedly insists on the unity of the Person of Christ, the God-Man, which was the point at issue in the controversy (i. 23, 303, 405). He says that "the Lamb of God," as the true Paschal victim, "combined the fire of the divine essence with the flesh that is now eaten by us" (i. 219); in a letter to a Nestorianizing "scholasticus" he calls the Virgin (not simply Theotokos, but) "Mother of God Incarnate" (Θεοῦ σαρκωθέντος μητέρα," i. 54). When Cyril, two years later, came to an understanding with John of Antioch, Isidore exhorted him to be consistent and said that his most recent writings shewed him to be "either open to flattery or an agent of levity, swayed by vainglory instead of imitating the great athletes" of the faith, etc. (i. 324). Perhaps these letters were "the treatise to" (or against) Cyril, which Evagrius ascribes to Isidore. Isidore was better employed when he uttered warnings against the rising heresy of Eutychianism: "To assert only one nature of Christ after the Incarnation is to take away both, either by a change of the divine or an abatement of the human" (i. 102); among various errors he mentions "a fusion and comixture and abolition of the natures," urging his correspondent, a presbyter, to cling to the "inspired" Nicene faith (iv. 99).

His theology was generally characterized by accuracy and moderation. In a truly Athanasian spirit (cf. Athan. *de Decr. Nic.* 22) he writes, "We are bound to know and believe *that* God is, not to busy ourselves as to *what* He is" (*i.e.* attempt to comprehend His essence; *Ep.* ii. 299). He is emphatic against the two extremes of Arianism and Sabellianism. "If God was always like to Himself, He must have been always Father; therefore the Son is co-eternal" (i. 241, cf. i. 389); and Eunomians exceed Arians in making the Son a servant (i. 246). Sabellians misinterpret John x. 30, where ἕν shews the one essence, and the plural ἐσμεν the two hypostases (i. 138). In the Trinity, the Godhead is one, but the hypostases are three (i. 247). In Heb. i. 3 the ἀπαύγασμα indicates the co-eternity, the χαρακτήρ the personality; it is in things made that "before" and "after" have place, not in "the dread and sovereign Trinity" (iii. 18; cf. the *Quicunque*, ver. 25). The belief in three Persons in one essence excludes alike Judaism and polytheism (*Ep.* iii. 112). Of John xiv. 28 he observes that "greater" or "less than" implies identity of nature (i. 422). On Phil. ii. 6 seq. he argues that, unless Christ was equal to the Father, the illustration is irrelevant; if He was equal, then it is pertinent. (iv. 22. The passage is interesting as shewing that he, like St. Chrysostom, while interpreting οὐχ ἁρπαγμὸν—θεῷ of the condescension, understood St. Paul to mean, "Christ could afford to waive the display of His co-equality, just because He did *not* regard it as a thing to which He had no right.") He explains Rom. iii. 25: when no other cure for a man's ills was possible, "God brought in the Only-begotten Son as a ransom; one Victim, surpassing all in worth, was offered up for all" (iv. 100). He contends that the divinity of the Holy Spirit—denied by Macedonians—is involved in the divinity of the Son (i. 20). Against the denial of the latter doctrine he cites a number of texts and explains the "humble language" used by Jesus as the result of the "economy" of the Incarnation, whereas the "lofty language" also used by Him would be inexplicable if He were a mere man (iv. 166). "Baptism," he writes to a count, "does not only wash away the uncleanness derived through Adam's transgression, for that much were nothing, but conveys a divine regeneration surpassing all words—redemption, sanctification, adoption, etc.; and the baptized person, through the reception of the sacred mysteries [of the Eucharist: cf. i. 228], becomes of one body with the Only-begotten, and is united to Him as the body to its head" (iii. 195). He censures such abstinence as proceeds from "Manichean or Marcionite principles" (i. 52); notices the omissions in the Marcionite gospel (i. 371); accuses Novatianists of self-righteous assurance (i. 100), but is credulous as to the scandalous imputations against the Montanists, much resembling the libels which had been circulated against the early Christians (i. 242). His letters illustrate the activity of Jewish opposition to the Gospel. They tell us of a few who cavilled at the substitution of bread for bloody sacrifices in the Christian oblation (i. 401); of one who criticized the "hyperbole" in John xxi. 25 (ii. 99); of another who argued from Haggai ii. 9 that the temple would yet be restored (iv. 17). Although Paganism, as a system and organized power, was defunct (i. 270), yet its adherents were still voluble; they called Christianity "a new-fangled scheme of life" (ii. 46), contemned its principle of faith (v. 101), disparaged Scripture on account of its "barbaric diction" and its defects of style (iv. 28), sneered at the "dead Jesus," the Cross, the Sepulchre, and the "ignorance of the apostles" (iv. 27), and Isidore heard one of them, a clever rhetorician, bursting into "a broad laugh" at the Passion, and presently put him to silence (iv. 31). He wrote a "little treatise" (λογίδιον) to prove that there was "no such thing as fate" (iii. 253), and a book "against the Gentiles" to prove that divination was "nonsensical" (ii. 137, 228), thus using in behalf of religion the "weapons and syllogisms of its opponents, to their confusion" (iii. 87). Both are now lost. His familiarity with heathen writers—among whom he criticizes Galen (iv. 125)—gave him great advantages in discussion with unbelievers; and he takes occasion from a question as to Origen's theory about the lapse of souls to cite a variety of opinions still current, apparently among those who still rejected the Gospel. "Some think that the soul is extinguished with the body . . . some have imagined that all is governed by chance; some have entrusted their lives to fate, necessity, and fortune . . . some have said that heaven is ruled by providence, but the earth is not" (iv. 163). He speaks of the harm done to the Christians' argument by Christians' misconduct: "If we overcome heretics, pagans, and Jews by our correct doctrine, we are bound also to overcome them by our conduct, lest, when worsted on the former ground, they should think to overcome on the latter, and, after rejecting our faith, should adduce against it our own lives" (iv. 226).

Very many of his letters are answers to questions as to texts of Scripture. Like Athanasius, he sometimes gives a choice of explanations (*e.g.* i. 114); although a follower of Chrysostom, he shews an Alexandrian tendency to far-fetched and fantastic interpretation, as when he explains the live coal and the tongs in Isa. vi. 7 to represent the divine essence and the flesh of Christ (i. 42), or the carcase and the eagles to mean humanity ruined by tasting the forbidden fruit and lifted up by ascetic mortification (i. 282), or when "he that is on the house-top" is made to denote a man who despises the present life (i. 210). He reproves a presbyter for criticizing mystical interpreters (ii. 81), but says also that those who attempt to make the whole of O.T. refer to Christ give an opening to pagans and heretics, "for while they strain the passages which do *not* refer to Him, they awaken suspicion as to those which without any straining *do* refer to Him" (ii. 195). With similar good sense he remarks that St. Paul's concessions to Jewish observance were not a turning back to the law, but an "economy" for the sake of others who had not outgrown it (i. 407). Again, he observes that church history should relieve despondency as to existing evils, and that even the present state of the church should remove mistrust as to the future (ii. 5). Difficulties about the resurrection of the body are met by considering that the future body will not be like the present, but "ethereal and spiritual" (ii. 43). He admits that ambition is a natural motive and can be turned to good (iii. 34). Ascetic as he was, he dissuades from immoderate fasting, lest an "immoderate reaction" ensue (ii. 45). Obedience to the government, when it does not interfere with religion, is inculcated, because our Lord "was registered and paid tribute to Caesar" (i. 48). But he exhorts Theodosius II. (probably soon after his accession) to "combine mildness with authority" (i. 35), intimating that his ears were too open to malicious representations (i. 275); and he speaks to a "corrector" in the manly tones so seldom heard in those days, except from the lips of typical Christians: "He who has been invested with rule ought himself to be ruled by the laws; if he himself sets them aside, how can he be a lawful ruler?" (v. 383). He considers that the genealogy traced through Joseph proves that Mary also sprang from

David (i. 7); that the fourth beast in Daniel meant the Roman empire (i. 218); that the 70 weeks extended from the 20th year of Artaxerxes to the 8th of Claudius (iii. 89); that *Hebrews* was by St. Paul (i. 7). He interprets Mark xiii. 32 evasively (i. 117). He corrects the confusion between the two Philips (i. 447). His shrewdness and humour, occasionally tinged with causticity, appear in various letters. "I hear that you have bought a great many books, and yet . . . know nothing of their contents;" take care lest you be called "a book's-grave," or "moth-feeder"; then comes a serious allusion to the buried talent (i. 127). He tells a bishop that he trains the younger ministers well, but spoils them by over-praising them (i. 202). He hears that Zosimus can say by heart some passages of St. Basil and suggests that he should read a certain homily against drunkards (i. 61). He asks an ascetic why he "abstains from meat and feeds greedily on revilings" (i. 446). His friend Harpocras, a good "sophist" (whom he recommends for a vacant mastership, v. 458, and urges to keep his boys from the theatre and hippodrome, v. 185), had written a sarcastic "monody," or elegy, on Zosimus and his fellows, as already "dead in sin"; Isidore, whom he had requested to forward it to them, defers doing so, lest he should infuriate them against the author; however, he says in effect, if you really mean it to go, send it yourself, and then, if a feud arises, you will have no one else to blame (v. 52). He remarks that "some people are allowed to be tempted to cure them of the notion that they are great and invincible persons" (v. 39). He points out to a palace chamberlain the inconsistence of being glib at Scripture quotations and "mad after other people's property" (i. 27). But for all this keenness and didactic severity, and in spite of his expressed approval of the use of torture (i. 116), he impresses us as a man of kindly disposition, warm in his friendships (see *Epp.* i. 161, ii. 31, v. 125). He observes that "God values nothing more than love, for the sake of which He became man and obedient unto death; for on this account also the first-called of His disciples were two brothers . . . our Saviour thus intimating that He wills all His disciples to be united fraternally" (i. 10). In this spirit he says of slaves, "Prejudice or fortune . . . has made them our property, but we are all one by nature, by the faith, by the judgment to come" (i. 471); and he tells how a young man came to his cell, asked to see him, was introduced by the porter, fell at his feet in tears in silence, then, on being reassured, said that he was the servant of Iron the barrister, and had offended his master in ignorance, but too deeply for pardon. "I cannot think," writes Isidore, "that the true Christian Iron, who knows the grace that has set all men free, can hold a slave" (οἰκέτην ἔχειν, i. 142). This tenderness is in harmony with the candour ("si sainte et si belle," says Tillemont, xv. 104) with which he owns that when he has tried to pray for them who have deliberately injured him, he has found himself doing so "with his lips only." "Not that I doubt that some have attained that height of excellence: rather, I rejoice at and rejoice with them, and would desire to reach the same point" (v. 398).

Isidore's letters naturally contain allusions to the religious customs or opinions of his age: such as pilgrimage to the shrines of the saints, as of St. Peter (ii. 5; cf. i. 160 on that of Thecla, and i. 226 on the martyrs who "guard the city" of Pelusium); the benediction given by the bishop "from his high chair," and the response "And with thy spirit" (i. 122); the deacon's linen garment, and the bishop's woollen "omophorion" which he took off when the gospel was read (i. 136); the right of sanctuary (i. 174); the wrongfulness of exacting an oath (i. 155).

His death cannot be placed later than 449 or 450 (see Tillem. xv. 116).

Two thousand letters of his, we are told, were collected by the zealously anti-Monophysite community of Acoemetae, or "sleepless" monks, at Constantinople, and arranged in 4 vols. of 500 letters each. This collection appears to be identical with the extant 2,012 letters, distributed, without regard to chronology, into 5 books (see Tillem. xv. 117, 847), of which the first three were edited by Billius, the fourth by Rittershusius, and the fifth by Andrew Schott, a Jesuit; the whole being included in the ed. pub. at Paris in 1638. Many of the letters are, in effect, repetitions. See Bouuy, *De S. Isid. Pel.* lib. iii. (Nîmes, 1885); also C. H. Turner and E. K. Lake in *Journ. of Theol. Stud.* vol. vi. pp. 70, 270. [W.B.]

Ivo, St. (*Yvo*), June 10, a supposed Persian bp. in Britain, after whom the town of St. Ives in Hunts was named. His Life was written by the monk Goscelin when resident at Ramsey, towards the end of 11th cent., based on a more diffused account by a previous abbat Andrew, who collected his information while in the East on a pilgrimage to Jerusalem in 1020. Goscelin's Life is printed in Boll. *Acta SS.* 10 June ii. 288. It describes Ivo as a missionary bishop, a star of the East, a messenger of the true Sun, divinely marked out for work in Britain. Quitting Persia, he passed through Asia and Illyricum to Rome, enlightening every place he visited. From Rome he proceeded to Gaul, where the admiring king and nobles would have detained him, but he pushed forward to Britain with his three companions. There he rescued the people from idolatry. The first-fruit of his labours was "a youth of patrician dignity named Patricius, the son of a Senator." Passing into Mercia, Ivo settled at the vill of Slepe, 3 English leucae (Gosc. c. 2, § 8) from Huntedun. There he laboured many years, died, and was buried. About 100 lustra (c. 1, § 4) had passed since the bishop's death, when a peasant of Slepe struck with his plough a stone sarcophagus, within which were found, besides human remains, a silver chalice and insignia of the episcopal rank. Slepe being one of the estates of the abbey of Ramsey, 8 leucae (c. 2, § 8) distant, abbat Eadnoth was informed of this. The same night a man of Slepe saw in a vision one robed as a bishop, with ornaments like those in the sarcophagus, who said he was St. Ivo and wished to be removed to the abbey, with two of his companions, whose burial-places he described. The translation was accordingly effected, and on the spot where the saint was found a church was dedicated to him, connected with which was a priory as a cell of the parent abbey. The spot was thenceforth known as St. Ives. A later hand adds that *temp.* Henry I. the relics of the two companions were re-translated to St. Ives. As Ramsey abbey was founded about 991 or a little earlier (*Mon. Hist. Brit.* 580 D; *Monast. Angl.* ii. 547), Eadnoth the first abbat (*Liber Eliens.* ed. Stewart, p. 188) would be living *c.* 1000 (the common date of the translation is 1001). Reckoning back 100 lustra or 400 years (computing by the four-year lustrum), we arrive at A.D. 600 as about the period of Ivo's death, and this is the year given by Florence of Worcester (*Chron.* in *M. H. B.* 526). His mission at Slepe must thus be placed *c.* 580-600, which nearly corresponds with the reign of the emperor Maurice, with whom Diceto (in Gale, iii. 559) makes him contemporary. Thus Ivo's Mercian mission preceded the arrival of Augustine by about half a generation and anticipated by some 70 years the conversion of Mercia as narrated in Bede. The obvious improbability of this leaves the monks of Ramsey responsible for the legend.

Possibly there may be here a lingering tradition of old British Christianity and a reminiscence of its Oriental origin, leaving the period out of the question. It would not be surprising if a British remnant should have survived in that locality as late as the Conquest. There are indications that Britons did actually maintain themselves in E. Mercia and the fastnesses of the fens long after the conversion of the English race. Moreover, the name of Patrick gives the story a Celtic look, and the locality might have been a sort of eastern Glastonbury. The Celtic element in the first conversion of the Mercian Angles was likely to prolong the vitality of Celtic traditions. If there was Celtic blood surviving in the fens when Ramsey was founded, the Oriental colouring of the legend is accounted for. The stone sarcophagus may have been a genuine Roman relic, furnishing a material basis for the story and suggesting the occasion. If the above inferences are not unreasonable, the legend of St. Ivo contains a reminiscence that the Christian missionaries who reached Britain from the East came by way of Gaul and of the tradition of their having been sent from Rome.

Slepe is found in Domesday and is still the name of one of the manors of St. Ives.

The priory of St. Ives, the ruins of which survive, is described in *Monast. Angl.* ii. 631. In the time of Brompton (Twysd. p. 883) no saint in England was so eminent as St. Ivo at Ramsey for the cure of diseases.

The story was written again by John of Tynemouth in 14th cent., in whose *Sanctilogium*, before the MS. was burnt, it stood No. 70 (Smith, *Cat. Cotton MSS.* p. 29). It was one of those adopted by Capgrave in 15th cent. for his *Nova Legenda* (ff. 199) and so is preserved. This version states that the pope commissioned him to Britain. The MS. Lives of Ivo are mentioned by Hardy (*Desc. Cat.* i. 184-186), and the Life by Goscelin exists as a Bodleian manuscript in a fuller form than the recension given by the Bollandists, the Life in Capgrave being another abridgment. One of the MSS. mentioned by Hardy purports to be the very Life by abbat Andrew referred to by Goscelin. [C.H.]

J

Jacobus (4) or **James,** bp. of Nisibis in Mesopotamia, called "the Moses of Mesopotamia," born at Nisibis or Antiochia Mygdoniae towards the end of 3rd cent. He is said to have been nearly related to Gregory the Illuminator, the apostle of Armenia. At an early age he devoted himself to the life of a solitary, and the celebrity he acquired by his self-imposed austerities caused Theodoret to assign him the first place in his *Religiosa Historia* or *Vitae Patrum*—where he is entitled ὁ μέγας. During this period he went to Persia for intercourse with the Christians of that country and to confirm their faith under the persecutions of Sapor II. Gennadius (*de Script. Eccl.* c. 1) reports that James was a confessor in the Maximinian persecution. On the vacancy of the see of his native city he was compelled by the popular demand to become bishop. His episcopate, according to Theodoret, was signalized by fresh miracles.

In 325 he was summoned to the council of Nicaea (Labbe, *Concil.* ii. 52, 76). A leading part is ascribed to him by Theodoret in its debates (Theod. *u.s.* p. 1114). He is commended by Athanasius, together with Hosius, Alexander, Eustathius, and others (*adv. Arian.* t. i. p. 252). According to some Eastern accounts, James was one whom the emperor Constantine marked out for peculiar honour (Stanley, *Eastern Church*, p. 203). His name occurs among those who signed the decrees of the council of Antioch, *in Encaeniis*, A.D. 341, of more than doubtful orthodoxy (Labbe, *Concil.* ii. 559), but no mention of his being present at this council occurs elsewhere (Tillem. *Mém. eccl.* t. vi. note 27, *les Arensi;* Hefele, *Councils*, ii. 58, Eng. tr.). That the awfully sudden death of Arius at Constantinople, on the eve of his anticipated triumph, A.D. 336, was due to the prayers of James of Nisibis, and that on this emergency he had exhorted the faithful to devote a whole week to uninterrupted fasting and public supplication in the churches, rests only on the authority of one passage, in the *Religiosa Historia* of Theodoret, the spuriousness of which is acknowledged by all sound critics. The gross blunders of making the death of the heresiarch contemporaneous with the council of Nicaea, and of confounding Alexander of Alexandria with Alexander of Constantinople, prove it an ignorant forgery. In the account of the death of Arius obtained by Theodoret from Athanasius (Theod. *H. E.* i. 14; Soz. *H. E.* ii. 20) no mention is made of James, nor in that given by Athanasius in his letter to the bishops. As bp. of Nisibis James was the spiritual father of Ephrem Syrus, who was baptized by him and remained by his side as long as he lived. Milles, bp. of Susa, visiting Nisibis to attend a synod for settling the differences between the bps. of Seleucia and Ctesiphon, *c.* 341, found James busily erecting his cathedral, towards which, on his return, Milles sent a large quantity of silk from Adiabene (Assemani, *Bibl. Or.* tom. i. p. 186). On the attempt, three times renewed, of Sapor II. to make himself master of Nisibis, A.D. 338, 346, 350, James maintained the faith of the inhabitants in the divine protection, kindled their enthusiasm by his words and example, and with great military genius and administrative skill thwarted the measures of the besiegers. For the tale of the final siege of 350, which lasted three months, and of the bishop's successful efforts to save his city, see Gibbon, c. xviii. vol. ii. pp. 385 ff. or De Broglie, *L'Eglise et l'Empire*, t. iii. pp. 180-195. See also Theod. *u.s.* p. 1118; *H. E.* ii. 26; Theophan. p. 32. Nisibis was quickly relieved by Sapor being called away to defend his kingdom against an inroad of the Massagetae. James cannot have long survived this deliverance. He was honourably interred within the city, that his hallowed remains might continue to defend it. When in 363 Nisibis yielded to Persia, the Christians carried the sacred talisman with them. (Theod. *u.s.* p. 1119; Soz. *H. E.* v. 3; Gennad. *u.s.* c. 1.)

Gennadius speaks of James as a copious writer, and gives the titles of 26 of his treatises. Eighteen were found by Assemani in the Armenian convent of St. Anthony at Venice, together with a request for some of his works from a Gregory and James's reply. Their titles—*de Fide, de Dilectione, de Jejunio, de Oratione, de Bello, de Devotis, de Poenitentia, de Resurrectione*, etc.—correspond generally with those given by Gennadius, but the order is different. In the same collection Assemani found the long letter of James to the bishops of Seleucia and Ctesiphon, on the Assyrian schism. It is in 31 sections, lamenting the divisions of the church and the pride and arrogance which caused them, and exhorting them to seek peace and concord. These were all published with a Latin translation, and a learned preface establishing their authenticity, and notes by Nicolas Maria Antonelli in 1756; also in the collection of the Armenian Fathers, pub. at Venice in 1765, and again at Constantinople in 1824. The Latin translation is found in the *Patres Apostolici* of Caillau, t. 25, pp. 254-543. The liturgy bearing the name of James of Nisibis, said to have been formerly in use among the Syrians (Abr. Ecchell. *Not. in Catal. Ebed-Jesu*, p. 134; Bona, *Liturg.* i. 9) is certainly not his, but should be ascribed to James of Sarug (Renaudot, *Lit. Or.* t. ii. p. 4). James of Nisibis is commemorated in Wright's *Syrian Martyrology*, and in the Roman martyrology, July 15. Assemani, *Bibl. Or.* t. i. pp. 17 sqq., 186, 557, 652; Tillem. *Mém. eccl.* t. vii.; Ceillier, *Ant. eccl.* t. iv. pp. 478 sqq.; Fabricius, *Bibl. Graec.* t. ix. p. 289; Cave, *Hist. Lit.* t. i. p. 189. [E.V.]

Jacobus (13) Sarugensis, bp. of Batnae, a little town in the district of Sarug in Osrhoëne. He enjoyed an extraordinary reputation for learning and holiness and was sainted alike by orthodox and heretics. The Syrian liturgies commemorate him with St. Ephraim as "os eloquentissimum et columnam ecclesiae."

Two Lives are extant in the Vatican and one in the Brit. Mus. (Cod. dcccclx. 46, dated A.D. 1197). The oldest and best is the spirited eulogium by his disciple Georgius, perhaps a bishop of the Arabs. The other two, which are anonymous and later than 10th cent., are in close agreement with it. According to them, Jacobus was born at Kurtom on the Euphrates, A.D. 452, and was taught in one of the schools of Edessa (according to Mares the Nestorian).

The anonymous Life (Vat.) states that Jacobus was made bp. of Batnae ("urbis Sarug") when 67½ years old, A.D. 519, and that he died 2½ years afterwards, *i.e.* A.D. 521. Before A.D. 503, Joshua Stylites tells us, Jacobus was a *periodeutes* or visitor of the district of Batnae, a middle rank between the episcopate and the priesthood. Cf. Ep. 16 in the Brit. Mus. Cod. dclxxii. The Stylite adds that Jacobus composed many homilies on Scripture, psalms, and hymns; which proves his fame already established in 503.

Renaudot (t. ii. *Liturgg. Orientt.*) has charged Jacobus with Monophysitism, a charge which Assemani and Abbeloos shew to be unwarranted. Timotheus of Constantinople (fl. 6th cent. *ad init.*) calls him "orthodox," Isaacus Ninivita and Joannes Maro quote him as such, and Joshua the Stylite, his contemporary, calls him venerable. The Maronites, always hostile to Nestorians and Jacobites, honour him as a saint. Further, he began his episcopate under Justin, by whose orders Severus was driven from Antioch, Philoxenos from Hierapolis, and other heretics from Mesopotamia and Syria. Had Jacobus been a Monophysite, he would have shared their fate. Not a single Catholic writer of the 5th, 6th, or 7th cent., says Assemani, has so accused him. Bar-hebraeus and the Life in the Brit. Mus., indeed, allege that he communicated with Severus, and Dionysius in his *Chronicon* asserts that St. Jacobus of Sarug would not communicate with Paul of Antioch, because the latter confessed the two natures. But Dionysius is contradictory in his dates. Some passages of the extant hymns speak of the single nature of Christ, but may be interpolated. There is direct evidence that after the council of Chalcedon the Monophysites began to tamper with texts (cf. Evagr. iii. 31). They even attributed whole works, written in their own interests, to such men as Athanasius and Gregory Thaumaturgus. Jacobus Edessenus testifies that a certain poem was falsely ascribed by the Jacobite sect to the bp. of Batnae shortly after his decease (Bar-hebr. *Horr. Myst. ad* Gen. vi.). A silly poem against the council of Chalcedon (*Cod. Nitr.* 5 fol. 139) is proved by internal evidence to be spurious. His writings in general supply ample proof of orthodoxy on the doctrines in question.

Works.—He was a very voluminous writer. Bar-hebraeus says that he employed 70 amanuenses in writing his homiletic poems, of which 760 exist, besides expositions, epistles, hymns, and psalms. Georgius, in his panegyric, gives a list of his poetic writings which treat of the great men of O.T., of angels, and of the mysteries of the Son of God. The anonymous Life (Vat.) states that his homilies (*mim'rê*) numbered 763. Of these many may be lost; most of those which survive are unedited.

Prose Works.—(1) An anaphora or liturgy (Renaud. *Lit. Or.* ii. 556-566) beginning *Deus*

Pater, qui es tranquillitas! also found in Ethiopic (Brit. Mus. Cod. cclxi. 11, "Anaphora of holy Mar Jacob the Doctor, of Batnan of Serug." Also Codd. cclxiii. and cclxxiii.).

(2) An order of Baptism; one of four used by the Maronites (Assemani, *Cod. Lit.* ii. 309).

(3) An order of Confirmation (*ib.* iii. 184).

(4) A number of epistles—the Brit. Mus. Cod. dclxxii. (dated A.D. 603) contains 34 in a more or less perfect state, including (*a*) Ep. to Samuel, abbat of St. Isaacus at Gabûla; on the Trinity and Incarnation. "The Father unbegotten, the Son begotten, the Spirit proceeding from the Father, and receiving from the Son." (*b*) Ep. to the Himyarite Christians. (*c*) Ep. to Stephen bar-Sudaïl of Edessa, proving from reason and Scripture the eternity of heaven and hell. (*d*) Ep. to Jacobus, an abbat of Edessa, explaining Heb. x. 26, I. John v. 16, etc. (*e*) Ep. to bp. Eutychianus against the Nestorians.

(5) Six Homilies: on Nativity, Epiphany, Lent, Palm Sunday, The Passion, The Resurrection (Zingerlé, *Sechs Homilien des heilig. Jacob von Sarug*, Bonn, 1867).

Poetic Works.—Assemani gives a catalogue of 231, with headings and first words. Very few have been printed. The subjects are chiefly the personages and events of O. and N. T., esp. the words and deeds of Christ. Jacobus is very fond of an allegorical treatment of O.T. themes.

Wright's *Cat. Syr. MSS.*, pp. 502-525, gives an account of upwards of 40 MSS. and fragments of MSS., containing metrical discourses, and letters and a few homilies in prose, by St. Jacobus. Jacobus Edessenus classed the bp. of Batnae with St. Ephraim, Isaacus Magnus, and Xenaias Mabugensis, as a model writer of Syriac. Assem. *Bibl. Or.* i. 283-340; Cave, ii. 110; Abbeloos, *de Vitâ et Scriptt. S. Jacobi Batn. Sarugi in Mesop. Episc.* (Lovan. 1867); Matagne, *Act. Sanct.* xii. Oct. p. 824; Bickell, *Consp. Syr.* 25, 26. [C.J.B.]

Jacobus (15) or **James Baradaeus** (*Al Baradai, Burdoho, Burdeono, Burdeana*, or *Burdeaya*, also *Phaselita*, or *Zanzalus*), ordained by the Monophysites bp. of Edessa (*c.* A.D. 541), with oecumenical authority over the members of their body throughout the East. By his indomitable zeal and untiring activity this remarkable man rescued the Monophysite community from the extinction with which persecution by the imperial power threatened it, and breathed a new life into what seemed little more than an expiring faction, consecrating bishops, ordaining clergy, and uniting its scattered elements in an organization so well planned and so stable that it has subsisted unharmed through all the many political and dynastic storms in that portion of the world, and preserves to the present day the name of its founder as the Jacobite church of the East. Materials for his Life are furnished by two Syriac biographies by his contemporary, John of Asia, the Monophysite bp. of Ephesus ordained by him, printed by Land (*Anecdota Syriaca*, vol. ii. pp. 249-253, pp. 364-383), and by the third part of the *Eccles. History* of the same author (Payne Smith's trans. pp. 273-278, 291).

The surname Baradaeus is derived from the ragged mendicant's garb patched up out of old saddle-cloths, in which, the better to disguise his spiritual functions from the unfriendly eyes of those in power, this indefatigable propagator of his creed performed his swift and secret journeys over Syria and Mesopotamia.

James Baradaeus is stated by John of Ephesus to have been born at Tela Mauzalat, otherwise called Constantina, a city of Osrhoëne, 55 miles due E. of Edessa, towards the close of 5th cent. His father, Theophilus Bar-Manu, was one of the clergy of the place. In pursuance of a vow of his parents, James, when two years old, was placed in that monastery under the care of abbat Eustathius, and trained in Greek and Syriac literature and in the strictest asceticism (Land, *Anecdot. Syr.* t. ii. p. 364). He became remarkable for the severity of his self-discipline. Having on the death of his parents inherited their property, including a couple of slaves, he manumitted them, and made over the house and estate to them, reserving nothing for himself (*ib.* 366). He eventually became a presbyter. His fame spread over the East and reached the empress Theodora, who was eagerly desirous of seeing him, as one of the chief saints of the Monophysite party of which she was a zealous partisan. James was with much difficulty induced to leave his monastery for the imperial city. Arriving at Constantinople, he was received with much honour by Theodora. But the splendour of the court had no attractions for him. He retired to one of the monasteries of the city, where he lived as a complete recluse. The period spent by him at Constantinople—15 years, according to John of Ephesus—was a disastrous one for the Monophysite body. Justinian had resolved to enforce the Chalcedonian decrees universally, and the bishops and clergy who refused them were punished with imprisonment, deprivation, and exile. Whole districts of Syria and the adjacent countries were thus deprived of their pastors, and the Monophysites were threatened with gradual extinction. For ten years many churches had been destitute of the sacraments, which they refused to receive from what were to them heretical hands. The extreme peril of the Monophysites was represented to Theodora by the sheikh Harith, and by her instrumentality the recluse James was drawn from his cell and persuaded to accept the hazardous and laborious post of the apostle of Monophysitism in the East. A considerable number of Monophysite bishops from all parts of the East, including Theodosius of Alexandria, Anthimus the deposed patriarch of Constantinople, Constantius of Laodicea, John of Egypt, Peter, and others, who had come to Constantinople in the hope of mitigating the displeasure of the emperor and exciting the sympathies of Theodora, were held by Justinian in one of the imperial castles in a kind of honourable imprisonment. By them James was consecrated to the episcopate, nominally as bp. of Edessa but virtually as a metropolitan with oecumenical authority. The date is uncertain, but that given by Assemani (A.D. 541) is probably correct. The result proved the wisdom of the choice. Of the simplest mode of life, inured to hardship from his earliest years, tolerant of the extremities of hunger and fatigue, "a second Asahel for fleetness of foot" (Abulpharagius), fired with an unquenchable zeal for what he regarded as the true faith, with a dauntless courage that despised all dangers, James, in his tattered beggar's disguise, traversed on foot the whole of Asia Minor, Syria, Mesopotamia, and the adjacent provinces, even to the borders of Persia, everywhere ordaining bishops and clergy, by his exhortations or his encyclical letters encouraging his depressed co-religionists to courageously maintain their faith against the advocates of the two natures, and organizing them into a compact spiritual body. By his indefatigable labours "the expiring faction was revived, and united and perpetuated. . . . The speed of the zealous missionary was promoted by the fleetest dromedaries of a devout chief of the Arabs; the doctrine and discipline of the Jacobites were secretly established in the dominions of Justinian, and each Jacobite was compelled to violate the laws and to hate the Roman legislator" (Gibbon, vol. vi. p. 75, ed. 1838). He is stated to have ordained the incredible number of 80,000 clergy. John of Ephesus says 100,000 (Land, *Anecdot. Syr.* ii. 251), including 89 bishops and two patriarchs. His wonderful success in reviving the moribund Monophysite church aroused the emperor and the Catholic bishops. Orders were issued and rewards offered for his apprehension. But, in his beggar's garb, aided by the friendly Arab tribes and the people of Syria and Asia, he eluded all attempts to seize him, and lived into the reign of Tiberius. The longer of the two Lives of James, by John of Ephesus (Land, *u.s.* pp. 364-383), must be consulted for the extent and variety of his missionary labours and for the miracles which illustrated them.

James failed miserably when he attempted to govern the vast and heterogeneous body he had created and organized. The simplicity and innocence of his character, as described by his contemporary John of Ephesus (*H. E.* iv. 15), disqualified him for rule, and put him in the power of "crafty and designing men about him, who turned him every way they chose, and used him as a means of establishing their own powers." His unhappy dissensions with the bishops he had ordained clouded the closing portion of James's long life. The internecine strife between the different sections of the Monophysite party is fully detailed by John of Ephesus, who records with bitter lamentation the blows, fighting, murders, and other deeds "so insensate and unrestrained that Satan and his herds of demons alone could rejoice in them, wrought on both sides by the two factions with which the believers—so unworthy of the name—were rent," provoking "the contempt and ridicule of heathens, Jews, and heretics" (*H. E.* iv. 30). For a full account see John of Ephesus, *op. cit.* (Payne Smith's trans. pp. 48 sqq., 81 sqq., 274 sqq.).

One of these party squabbles was between James and the bps. Conon and Eugenius, whom he had ordained at Alexandria—the former for the Isaurian Seleucia, the latter for Tarsus—who became the founders of the obscure and short-lived sect of the "Cononites," or, from the monastery at Constantinople to which a section of them belonged, "Condobandites" (John of Ephesus, *H. E.* i. 31, v. 1-12; trans. *u.s.* pp. 49-65). Each anathematized the other, James denouncing Conon and his companion as "Tritheists," and they retaliated by the stigma of "Sabellian."

A still longer and more widespreading difference arose between James and Paul, whom he had ordained patriarch of Antioch (*H. E.* i. 41, p. 81). Paul and the other three leading bishops of the Monophysites had been summoned to Constantinople under colour of taking measures for restoring unity to the church, and, proving obstinate in the adherence to their own creed, were thrown into prison for a considerable time and subjected to the harshest treatment. This prolonged persecution broke their spirit, and one by one they all yielded, accepting the communion of John the patriarch of Constantinople and the "Synodites," as the adherents of the Chalcedonian decrees were contemptuously termed by their opponents, "lapsing miserably into the communion of the two natures" (*ib.* i. 41, ii. 1-9, iv. 15). Paul, stung with remorse for his cowardice, escaped into Arabia, taking refuge with Mondir, son and successor of Harith. On hearing of his defection James at once cut Paul off from communion; but at the end of three years, on receiving the assurance of his contrition, his act of penitence was laid before the synod of the Monophysite church of the East, and he was duly and canonically restored to communion by James, who notified the fact by encyclic letters (*ib.* iv. 15). Paul's rehabilitation caused great indignation among the Monophysites at Alexandria. They clamoured for his deposition, which was carried into effect by Peter, the intruded patriarch, in violation of all canonical order; the patriarch of Antioch (Paul's position in the Monophysite communion) owning no allegiance to the patriarch of Alexandria (*ib.* iv. 16). James allowed himself to be persuaded that if he were to visit Alexandria the veneration felt for his age and services would bring to an end the unhappy dissension between the churches of Syria and Egypt, and though he had denounced Peter, both orally and in writing, he was induced not only to hold communion with him but to draw up instruments of concord and to give his formal assent to the deposition of Paul, only stipulating that it should not be accompanied by any excommunication (*ib.* 17). The intelligence was received with indignation and dismay in Syria on James's return. The schism which resulted between the adherents of James and Paul, A.D. 576, "spread like an ulcer" through the whole of the East, especially in Constantinople. In vain did Paul entreat James to discuss the matters at issue between them calmly, promising to abide by the issue. In vain did Mondir put himself forward as a peacemaker. James shrank from investigation, and caused an obstinate refusal to be returned to all overtures of accommodation (*ib.* 20, 21). Wearied out at last, and feeling the necessity for putting an end to the violence and bloodshed which was raging unchecked, James suddenly set out for Alexandria, but never reached it. On the arrival of his party, including several bishops, at the monastery of

Cassianus or Mar-Romanus on the Egyptian frontier, a deadly sickness attacked them, and James himself fell a victim to it, July 30, 578. His episcopate is said to have lasted 37 years, and his life, according to Renaudot (*Lit. Or.* ii. 342), 73 years.

A liturgy bearing the name of "Jacobus Bordayaeus" is given by Renaudot (*Lit. Or.* t. ii. pp. 332-341), who confuses him, as Baronius does (*ad ann.* 535), with Jacobus Baradaeus. That this liturgy is correctly assigned to the Jacobite church is proved by the special memorial of their founder, "memento Domine omnium pastorum et doctorum ecclesiae orthodoxae . . . praecipue vero Jacobi Bordaei," as well as by the special condemnation of those who "impiously blasphemed the Incarnation of the Word, and divided the union in nature (*unionem in natura*) with the flesh taken from the holy mother of God" (*ib.* 337, 338). The *Catechesis*, the chief dogmatical formulary of the Jacobites, "totius fidei Jacobiticae norma et fundamentum" (Cave, *Hist. Lit.* i. 524), though adjudged to be his by Cave, Abraham Ecchellensis, and others, together with the *Encomium in Jacobitas*, and an Arabic Homily on the Annunciation, are discredited by Assemani on philological and chronological grounds. [E.V.]

Joannes (11) I., surnamed *Talaia*, patriarch of Alexandria and afterwards bp. of Nola. From having been a presbyter in the monastery of the Tabennesians at Canopus near Alexandria, he was known as Tabennesiotes (Pagi, *Critic.* s.a. 482, xix.; Mansi, vii. 1178 B). Previous to the expulsion of Salofaciolus from his see of Alexandria, and after his restoration, John held the office of oeconomus under him (*Brevic. Hist. Eutych.* Mansi, vii. 1063; Liberat. *Breviar.* c. 16 in Migne, *Patr. Lat.* lxviii. 1020). Shortly afterwards John was sent by the Catholics of Alexandria to the emperor Zeno, to thank him for the restoration of Salofaciolus, and to pray that when a vacancy occurred in the see they might choose his successor. He obtained an edict from the emperor complying with this request (Evagr. *H. E.* iii. 12), and after his return became greatly distinguished as a preacher in Alexandria (*Brevic. Hist. Eutych.* u.s.). Salofaciolus died A.D. 482, and the Catholics then elected John (*ib.*). The Monophysites elected Peter Mongus, then in exile (Liberat. c. 17; Theophan. *s.a.* 476). John sent the usual synodic announcement of his election to Simplicius, bp. of Rome, but neglected to direct one to ACACIUS, bp. of Constantinople, only sending one to his friend Illus, who was then in that city, with instructions to make what use of it he thought fit, and accompanying it with a letter addressed to the emperor. When the magistrianus whom John employed as his messenger to Constantinople arrived there, he found that Illus had gone to Antioch, whither he followed him with the synodic. On receiving it at Antioch Illus delivered the synodic to Calandio, then recently elected to the patriarchate of that see (Liberat. cc. 17, 18). Acacius, taking offence at not receiving a synodic from John, joined the Monophysites in their appeal to the emperor against him, and prevailed upon Zeno to write to Simplicius, praying him not to acknowledge John (Simplic. *Ep.* 17, July 15, A.D. 482, in Mansi, vii. 992). Without waiting for the reply of Simplicius, Zeno instructed the civil authorities to expel John. Thus driven from Alexandria, Talaia went to Illus at Antioch, and thence to Rome (Liberat. c. 18). There he was favourably received by Simplicius, who at once wrote to Acacius on his behalf (*Ep.* 18, Nov. 6, 482, in Mansi, vii. 995). Acacius replied that he did not recognize John, but had received Mongus into communion by command of Zeno; and Simplicius rejoined, blaming Acacius in no measured terms (Liberat. c. 18). Simplicius died March 2, 483, but John was warmly supported by his successor Felix III., who cited Acacius to answer certain charges brought against him by Talaia, and wrote to the emperor praying him to withdraw his countenance from Mongus and restore John (*Libell. Citationis ad Acac.* Mansi, vii. 1108; Felic. *Ep.* 2, A.D. 483, in *ib.* 1032). On the return of his legates from Constantinople, Felix held a synod at Rome which excommunicated Acacius for his persistent support of Mongus (*Ep.* 6, July 28, 484, in *ib.* 1053). Felix wrote to inform Zeno of this, and to let him know that "the apostolic see would never consent to communion with Peter of Alexandria, who had been justly condemned long since" (*Ep.* 9, Aug. 1, 484, in *ib.* 1065). Felix did not obtain his end, and John seems to have remained at Rome until the death of Zeno and the succession of Anastasius, A.D. 491, to whom John had shewn kindness at Alexandria after his shipwreck. Presuming that Anastasius would not be unmindful of this, John went to Constantinople to appeal to him. On hearing of his arrival Anastasius at once ordered him to be exiled, and John made his escape and returned to Rome (Theophan. *s.a.* 484, p. 118; Victor Tunun. *s.a.* 494, in Migne, *Patr. Lat.* lxviii. 948). Felix died Feb. 25, 492, but his successor, Gelasius I., equally interested himself in John (Gelas. *Epp.* 13, 15, in Mansi, viii. 49 seq., *c.* 493-495).

All these efforts to procure his reinstatement were of no avail; John never returned to Alexandria, but received, as some compensation, the see of Nola in Campania, where, after many years, he died in peace (Liberat. c. 18). During his episcopate there he apparently wrote an ἀπολογία to Gelasius, in which he anathematized the Pelagian heresy, Pelagius himself, and Celestius, as well as Julianus of Eclana. Phot. *Biblioth.* Cod. liv.; Le Quien, *Or. Christ.* ii. 417, 419; Remondini, *Del Nolana Eccl. Storia*, iii. 56-59; Ughelli, *Ital. Sacr.* vi. 251; Tillem. *Mém.* xvi. 313 seq.; Hefele, *Concil.* ii. 604 seq. [T.W.D.]

Joannes (31), bp. of Antioch (429-448). Our knowledge of him commences with his election as successor to Theodotus in the see of Antioch. In 429 the bishops of the East, according to the aged Acacius of Beroea, congratulated themselves on having such a leader (Labbe, iii. 386); but the troubles which rendered his episcopate so unhappily famous began immediately to shew themselves. His old companion and fellow-townsman Nestorius had just been appointed to the see of Constantinople, and had inaugurated his episcopate with a sermon in the metropolitan church repudiating the term "Mother of God," θεοτόκος. Celestine, the Roman pontiff, summoned a synod of Western bishops in Aug. 430, which unanimously condemned the tenets of Nestorius, and the name of John of Antioch appears in the controversy. The support of the Eastern prelates, of whom the patriarch of Antioch was chief, being of great importance, Celestine wrote to John, Juvenal of Jerusalem, Rufus of Thessalonica, and Flavian of Philippi, informing them of the decree passed against Nestorius (Baluz. p. 438, c. xv.; Labbe, iii. 376). At the same time Cyril, patriarch of Alexandria, wrote to John calling upon him, on pain of being separated from the communion of the West, to accept Celestine's decision and unite with him in defending the faith against Nestorius (Baluz. p. 442, c. xviii.; Labbe, iii. 379). Such a declaration of open hostility against an old friend, of whose virtual orthodoxy he was convinced, was very distasteful to John. He dispatched a letter full of Christian persuasiveness, by the count Irenaeus, to Nestorius, in his own name, and that of his brother-bishops Archelaus, Apringius, Theodoret, Heliades, Melchius, and the newly appointed bp. of Laodicea, Macarius, entreating him not to plunge the church into discord on account of a word to which the Christian ear had become accustomed, and which was capable of being interpreted in his own sense. He enlarged on the danger of schism, warning Nestorius that the East, Egypt, and Macedonia were about to separate from him, and exhorted him to follow the example of Theodorus of Mopsuestia in retracting words which had given pain to the orthodox, since he really held the orthodox faith on these points (Baluz. p. 445, c. xxi.; Labbe, iii. 390 seq.). John wrote also to count Irenaeus, Musaeus bp. of Antarada, and Helladius bp. of Tarsus, who were then at Constantinople, hoping to avail himself of their influence with Nestorius (Baluz. p. 688). Nestorius's reply indicated no intention of following John's counsels. He declared himself orthodox in the truest sense. He had no rooted objection to the term θεοτόκος, but thought it unsafe, because accepted by some in an Arian or Apollinarian sense. He preferred Χριστοτόκος, as a middle term between it and ἀνθρωποτόκος. He proposed to defer the discussion to the general council which he hoped for (*ib.* p. 688).

The divergence of the Antiochene and Alexandrian schools of thought in their way of regarding the mystery of the Incarnation lay at the root of this controversy about the term, and it was brought into open manifestation by the publication of Cyril's twelve "anathematisms" on the teaching of Nestorius. Nestorius, on receiving these fulminations at the end of 430, at once sent copies of them to John, together with his two sermons of Dec. 13 and 14, in which he professed to have acknowledged Mary as the "Mother of God" (*ib.* p. 691, c. iv.). John declared himself horror-stricken at the Apollinarian heresy which characterized Cyril's articles. He made them known far and wide, in Cappadocia, Galatia, and through the East generally, accompanying them with earnest appeals to the bishops and the orthodox everywhere to openly repudiate the grave errors they contained (*ib.* p. 838, No. xxxvi. *Ep. Alexandri Episc.*). His letter to Firmus is preserved (Baluz. p. 691, c. iv.), in which he expresses abhorrence of the "capitula," which he considers so unlike Cyril both in style and doctrine that he cannot believe they are his, and calls upon Firmus, if they reach Pontus, to get them abjured by the bishops of the province, without naming the supposed author. He rejoices over Nestorius's public acceptance of the test-word, in the two sermons he has sent him, which has quieted the storm and restored tranquillity to the church of Constantinople. John was also careful to have Cyril's heretical formularies refuted by able theologians. [ANDREAS SAMOSATENSIS; THEODORET.]

The breach between the two patriarchs was complete. Each denounced the other as heretical. A larger arena was supplied by the general council summoned by Theodosius to meet at Ephesus at Pentecost, 431. John's arrival having been delayed more than a fortnight beyond the time fixed for the opening of the council, he wrote that Antioch was 42 days' journey from Ephesus, at the fastest. He had been travelling without interruption for 30 days; he was now within five or six stages of Ephesus. If Cyril would condescend to wait a little longer, he hoped in a very few days to arrive (*ib.* p. 451, c. xxiii.). Cyril would not delay. On Mon. June 22, 431, 198 bishops met in the church of St. Mary the Virgin, and in one day Nestorius was tried, condemned, sentenced, deposed, and excommunicated. Five days later, Sat. June 27, John arrived with 14 bishops. His reasons for delay were quite sufficient. His patriarchate was a very extensive one. His attendant bishops could not leave their churches before the octave of Easter, Apr. 26. The distances some of them had to travel did not allow them to reach Antioch before May 10. John's departure had been delayed by a famine at Antioch and consequent outbreaks of the populace; their progress was impeded by floods (Labbe, iii. 602); the transport broke down; many of the bishops were aged men, unfit for rapid travelling. There was nothing to support Cyril's accusation that John's delay was intentional.

Cyril sent a deputation of bishops and ecclesiastics to welcome John, apprise him in the name of the council of the deposition of Nestorius and that he must no longer regard him as a bishop (*ib.* iii. 761). John, who had already heard from count Irenaeus of the hasty decision of the council, refused to admit the deputation, and they complained that they were rudely treated by the guard whom Irenaeus had sent to do honour to and protect the Eastern bishops. The deputation were compelled to wait for some hours at the door of the house where John took up his quarters, exposed to the insults of the soldiers and the attendants of the Orientals (*ib.* 593, 764), while a rival council was being held within. The bishops who sided with John had hastened to his lodgings, where, "before they had shaken the dust off their feet, or taken off their cloaks" (Cyril. *Ep. ad Colest.* Labbe, iii. 663), the small synod—the "conciliabulum" their enemies tauntingly called it—of 43 bishops, passed a sentence of deposition on

Cyril and Memnon, bp. of Ephesus, and of excommunication on all the other prelates of the council, until they should have condemned Cyril's "capitula," which they declared tainted not only with Apollinarian, but with Arian and Eunomian heresy (*ib.* 596, 637, 657, 664 *passim*). The sentences of excommunication and deposition were posted up in the city. There John vouchsafed an audience to the deputies of the other council. They communicated its decrees as to Nestorius, but received, they asserted, no reply but insults and blows (*ib.* 764). Returning to Cyril they formally complained of John's treatment, of which they shewed marks on their persons. The council immediately declared John separated from their communion until he explained this conduct.

John's attempts to reduce Cyril and his adherents to submission by his own authority proved fruitless, and he had recourse to the emperor and the ecclesiastical power at Constantinople. Several letters were written to Theodosius, to the empresses Pulcheria and Eudocia, the clergy, the senate, and the people of that city (Labbe, iii. 601-609; Liberat. c. vi.) to explain the tardiness of John's arrival and to justify the sentence pronounced on Cyril, Memnon, and the other bishops. Theodosius wrote to the council, declaring their decisions null (Labbe, iii. 704). The letter reached Ephesus June 29. John and his friends welcomed it with benedictions, assuring the emperor that they had acted from pure zeal for the faith which was imperilled by the Apollinarianism of Cyril's "anathematisms." Relying on imperial favour, John strove in vain to persuade the Ephesians to demand a new bishop in the place of Memnon. Meantime, the legates of Celestine had arrived from Rome, and the council, strengthened by their presence and the approbation of the bp. of Rome, proceeded, July 16, to summon John before them. Their deputation was informed that John could hold no intercourse with excommunicated persons (*ib.* 640). On this the council declared null all the acts of John's "conciliabulum," and, on his persisting, separated him and the bishops who had joined him from the communion of the church, pronounced them disqualified for all episcopal functions, and published their decree openly (*ib.* 302).

Two counter-deputations from the opposite parties presented themselves to Theodosius in the first week of September at Chalcedon. John himself did not shrink from an open defence of the orthodoxy of Nestorius, declaring his deposition illegal and exposing the heresy of Cyril's anathematisms (Baluz. pp. 837, 839). To support their evidently failing cause, John and his fellow-deputies wrote to some leading prelates of the West, the bps. of Milan, Aquileia, and Ravenna, and Rufus of Thessalonica, laying before them in earnest terms the heretical character of Cyril's doctrines (Theod. *Ep.* 112; Labbe, iii. 736), but apparently without favourable result. The victory was substantially with the Cyrillian party. After six audiences the emperor, weary of the fruitless strife, declared his final resolve. Nestorius, generally abandoned by his supporters, was permitted to retire to his former monastery of St. Euprepius at Antioch. Maximian, a presbyter of Constantinople, in defiance of the protest of John and his party, was consecrated (Oct. 25) bp. of the imperial see in his room. Memnon and Cyril were reinstated: the former to remain at Ephesus as bishop; Cyril and the other bishops to return home. John and the Orientals were only not formally condemned because the dogmatic question had not been discussed. Before he retired vanquished, John delivered a final remonstrance. The churches of Chalcedon were closed against the Oriental bishops, but they had obtained a spacious hall for public worship and preaching. Large crowds assembled to listen to the powerful sermons of Theodoret and the milder exhortations of John. The mortification with which John left Chalcedon was deepened by the events of his homeward journey. At Ancyra he found that letters from its bp. Theodotus, who was one of the eight deputies of the council, as well as from Firmus of Caesarea, and Maximian the newly appointed bp. of Constantinople, had commanded that he and his companions should be regarded as excommunicate.

From Ancyra John proceeded to Tarsus. Here, in his own patriarchate, he immediately held a council, together with Alexander of Hierapolis and the other deputies, at which he confirmed the deposition of Cyril and his brother-commissioners (Baluz. 840, 843, 847). Theodoret and the others engaged never to consent to the deposition of Nestorius. On reaching Antioch, about the middle of Dec., John summoned a very numerously attended council of bishops, which pronounced a fresh sentence against Cyril and wrote to Theodosius, calling upon him to take measures for the general condemnation of the doctrines of Cyril, as contrary to the Nicene faith which they were resolved to maintain to the death (Socr. *H. E.* vii. 34; Liberat. c. vi.; Baluz. p. 741, c. xxxix.). Soon after his return to Antioch John, accompanied by six bishops, visited the venerable Acacius of Beroea, whose sympathy in the controversy had greatly strengthened and consoled him. The old man was deeply grieved to hear the untoward result of their proceedings.

The battle was now over and the victory remained with Cyril. His return to Alexandria was a triumphal progress (Labbe, iii. 105). But the victory had been purchased by a schism in the church. Alexandria and Antioch were two hostile camps. For three years a bitter strife was maintained. The issue, however, was never doubtful. John, alarmed for his own safety, soon began to shew symptoms of yielding. The emperor, at the urgent demand of Celestine, had pronounced the banishment of Nestorius. John might not unreasonably fear a demand for his own deposition. It was time he should make it clear that he had no real sympathy with the errors of the heresiarch. The pertinacity with which Nestorius continued to promulgate the tenets which had proved so ruinous to the peace of the church irritated John. The newly elected bp. of Rome, Sixtus, who had warmly embraced Cyril's cause, in a letter addressed to the prelates of the East in the interests of reunion, A.D. 432, declared that John might be received again into the Catholic church, provided he repudiated all whom the council of Ephesus had deposed and proved by his acts that he really deserved the name of a Catholic bishop (Coteler. *Mon. Eccl. Graec.* i. 47). Cyril was disposed to limit his requirements to the condemnation of Nestorius and the recognition of Maximian. John summoned Alexander of Hierapolis, Andrew of Samosata, Theodoret, and probably others, to Antioch and held a conference to draw up terms of peace. It was agreed that if Cyril would reject his anathematisms they would restore him to communion. Propositions for union were dispatched by John to Cyril. John and his fellow-bishops next sought the intervention of Acacius of Beroea, who was universally venerated, in the hope that his influence might render Cyril more willing to accept the terms (Baluz. 756, c. liii.; Labbe, iii. 1114). Cyril, though naturally declining to retract his condemnation of Nestorius's tenets, opened the way for a reconciliation with John. John, eager to come to terms with his formidable foe, declared himself fully satisfied of Cyril's orthodoxy; his explanation had removed all the doubt his former language had raised (Labbe, iii. 757, 782). Paul, bp. of Emesa, was dispatched by John to Alexandria to confer with Cyril and bring about the much-desired restoration of communion (*ib.* 783). These events took place in Dec. 432 and Jan. 433. Cyril after some hesitation signed a confession of faith sent him by John, declaring in express terms "the union of the two natures without confusion in the One Christ, One Son, One Lord," and confessing "the Holy Virgin to be the Mother of God, because God the Word was incarnate and made man, and from His very conception united to Himself the temple taken from her" (Labbe, iii. 1094; Baluz. pp. 800, 804; Liberat. 8, p. 30), and gave Paul of Emesa an explanation of his anathematisms which Paul approved (Labbe, iii. 1090). Cyril then required acceptance of the deposition of Nestorius, recognition of Maximian, and acquiescence in the sentence passed by him on the four metropolitans deposed as Nestorians; terms acceded to by Paul. Each party was desirous of peace and disposed to concessions. Paul, placing in Cyril's hand a written consent to all his requirements, was admitted to communion and allowed to preach at the Feast of the Nativity (Cyril. *Ep.* 32, 40; Labbe, iii. 1095; Liberat. c. 8, p. 32). John, however, sent letters stating that neither he nor the other Oriental bishops could consent so hastily to the condemnation of Nestorius, from whose writings he gave extracts to prove their orthodoxy (Baluz. p. 908). Cyril and the court began to weary of so much indecision, and, to bring matters to a point, a document drawn up by Cyril and Paul was sent for John to sign (Cyril, *Epp.* 40, 42), together with letters of communion to be given him if he consented. Fresh delays ensued, but at last, in Apr. 433, the act giving peace to the Christian world was signed and dispatched to Alexandria, where it was announced by Cyril in the cathedral on Apr. 23. John, in a letter to Cyril, stated that in signing this document he had no intention to derogate from the authority of the Nicene Creed, and expressly recognized Maximian as the lawful bp. of Constantinople in place of Nestorius, sometime bishop, but deposed for teaching which merited anathema. He also wrote a circular letter of communion addressed to pope Sixtus, Cyril and Maximian (Labbe, iii. 1087, 1090, 1094, 1154; Cyril, *Ep.* 41). The East and West were once more at one. Cyril testified his joy in the celebrated letter to John, commencing "Let the heavens rejoice, and let the earth be glad" (Labbe, iii. 1106-1111). John wrote to Theodosius thanking him for the peace which his efforts had procured, and begged him to render it universal by restoring the deposed bishops.

This accommodation was far from being satisfactory to the extreme members of either party. Isidore of Pelusium and other adherents of Cyril expressed a fear that he had made too large concessions; while John had given great offence to many of his warmest supporters, who accused him of truckling to powerful advocates of a hollow peace to secure his position as bishop. Theodoret refused to abandon Nestorius. Alexander of Hierapolis broke off communion with his patriarch John (Baluz. pp. 799, 832). During the next two years John sought to force the bishops of his patriarchate to accept the terms of peace. Theodoret's unwillingness to abandon Nestorius and rooted dislike to Cyril's articles raised a coldness between him and John which was much strengthened by an unwarrantable usurpation on John's part, who at the close of 433 or beginning of 434 had ordained bishops for Euphratesia. This aggression caused serious irritation among the bishops of the province, who, led by Theodoret, withdrew from communion with John. John unhappily continuing his acts of usurpation, the disaffection spread. Nine provinces subject to the patriarch of Antioch renounced communion with John, who had at length to request the imperial power to force them into union by ejecting the bishops who refused the agreement he had arranged with Cyril. Theodoret, yielding to the entreaties of James of Cyrus and other solitaries of his diocese, consented to a conference with John and was received by his old friend with great cordiality. All reproaches were silenced, and as John did not insist on his accepting the sentence against Nestorius, he embraced the concordat, and returned to communion with John and Cyril (*ib.* pp. 834-836). The way towards peace had been smoothed by the death of Nestorius's successor, Maximian, Apr. 12, 434, and the appointment as archbp. of Constantinople of the saintly Proclus, who, in the early part of the Nestorian controversy, had preached the great sermon on the Theotokos (Socr. *H. E.* vii. 40; Baluz. p. 851). Proclus's influence was exerted in favour of peace, and so successfully that all the remonstrant bishops, except Alexander of Hierapolis and five others, ultimately accepted the concordat and retained their sees. Alexander was ejected in Apr. 435. John made a strong representation to Proclus in 436 that Nestorius in his retirement was persisting in his blasphemies and perverting many in Antioch and throughout the East (Baluz. p. 894), and formally requested Theodosius to expel him from the East and deprive him of the power of doing mischief (Evagr. *H. E.* i. 7; Theophan. p. 78). An edict was accordingly issued that all the heresiarch's books should be burnt, his followers called "Simonians" and their meetings suppressed (Labbe, iii. 1209; Cod. Theod. XVI. v. 66). The property of Nestorius was confiscated and he was banished to the remote and terrible Egyptian oasis.

Nestorian doctrines were too deeply rooted in the Eastern mind to be eradicated by persecution. Cyril, suspecting that the union was more apparent than real and that some of the bishops who had verbally condemned Nestorius still in their hearts cherished his teaching, procured orders from the Imperial government that the bishops should severally and explicitly repudiate Nestorianism. A formula of Cyril's having been put into John's hands for signature, John wrote in 436 or 437 to Proclus to remonstrate against this multiplicity of tests which distracted the attention of bishops from the care of their dioceses (Labbe, iii. 894).

Fresh troubles speedily broke out in the East in connexion with the writings of the greatly revered Theodore of Mopsuestia and Diodorus of Tarsus, whose disciple Nestorius had been. The bishops and clergy of Armenia appealed to Proclus for his judgment on the teaching of Theodore (*ib.* v. 463). Proclus replied by the celebrated doctrinal epistle known as the "Tome of St. Proclus." To this were attached some passages selected from Theodore's writings, which he deemed deserving of condemnation (*ib.* 511-513). This letter he sent first to John requesting that he and his council would sign it (Liberat. p. 46; Facundus, lib. 8, c. 1, 2). John assembled his provincial bishops at Antioch. They expressed annoyance at being called on for fresh signatures, as if their orthodoxy was still questionable, but made no difficulty about signing the "Tome," which they found worthy of all admiration, both for beauty of style and the dogmatic precision of its definitions. But the demand for the condemnation of the appended extracts called forth indignant protests. They refused to condemn passages divorced from their context, and capable, even as they stood, of an orthodox interpretation. A fresh schism threatened, but the letters of remonstrance written by John and his council to Proclus and Theodosius put a stop to the whole matter. Even Cyril, who had striven hard to procure the condemnation of Theodore, was compelled to desist by the resolute front shewn by the Orientals, some of whom, John told him, were ready to be burnt rather than condemn the teaching of one they so deeply revered (Cyril. *Epp.* 54, 199). Theodosius wrote to the Oriental bishops that the church must not be disturbed by fresh controversy and that no one should presume to decide anything unfavourable to those who had died in the peace of the church (Baluz. p. 928, c. ccxix.). The date of this transaction was probably 438. It is the last recorded event in John's career. His death occurred in 441 or 442. Tillem. *Mém. eccl.* t. xiv. xv.; Ceillier, *Auteurs eccl.*; Cave, *Hist. Lit.* i. 412; Neander, *Church. Hist.* vol. iv., Clarke's ed.; Milman, *Latin Christ.* vol. i. pp. 141-177; Bright, *Hist. of Church*, pp. 310-365. [E.V.]

Joannes (113), surnamed *Silentiarius*, bp. of Colonia and afterwards one of the most celebrated of the monks. His Life was written by Cyril of Scythopolis. He was born in 454, at Nicopolis in Armenia. His father and mother, noble and wealthy Christians, gave him a Christian education. John consecrated himself to God when 18 years old, built a church at Nicopolis in honour of the Virgin Mary, and taking ten brethren set up a monastery. In his 28th year (*c.* 481) the bp. of Sebastia, metropolitan of the district, at the request of the people of Colonia, consecrated him bishop of that see against his will. He continued his monastic life, specially avoiding the baths. "He thought it the greatest of all virtues never to be washed"; "determined never to be seen, even by his own eyes, without his clothes." His character had the happiest effect on his own family.

When he had been bp. ten years he went to Constantinople with an appeal to the emperor. Here he embarked on a ship unknown to his friends, made his way to Jerusalem, and dwelt there in a hospital for old men, wherein was an oratory of George the Martyr, but was supernaturally guided to the community of St. Sabas, who presided over 150 anchorets and received John, and appointed him to some petty office. A guest-house was being built; the former bp. of Colonia, the noble of the Byzantine court, fetched water from a torrent, cooked for the builders, brought stones and other materials for the work. Next year the steward appointed John to the humble duty of presiding over the kitchen. At the end of three years he was appointed steward. Sabas, ignorant of his ecclesiastical rank, considering it high time for John to be ordained, took him to Jerusalem, and introduced him to archbp. Elias. John was obliged to confess that he was a bishop. Archbp. Elias wondered at his story, summoned Sabas, and excused John from ordination, promising that from that day he should be silent and nobody should molest him. He never left his cell for four years afterwards, and was seen by none but the brothers who served him, except at the dedication of a church in the community, when he was obliged to pay his respects to archbp. Elias. The patriarch was captivated with his conversation and held him in lifelong honour. In 503 John went into the desert of Ruba. Here he remained silent about seven years, only leaving his cave every third or fourth day to collect wild apples, the usual food of the solitaries.

Sabas eventually persuaded John to return to his old community when 56 years old, A.D. 510. Here he continued to live a life that seemed to the people of those days absolutely angelical and many stories are told of his miraculous endowments. He must have died *c.* 558. Cyril. Mon. ap. *AA. SS.* Bolland. 13 Mai. iii. 232; Baron. *Annal.* ad ann. 457, lviii. etc.; Ceillier, xi. 277. [W.M.S.]

Joannes (124) **II.**, surnamed *Cappadox*, 27th bp. of Constantinople, 517-520, appointed by Anastasius after an enforced condemnation of Chalcedon. His short patriarchate is memorable for the celebrated Acclamations of Constantinople, and the reunion of East and West after a schism of 34 years. At the death of Timothy, John of Cappadocia, whom he had designated his successor, was presbyter and chancellor of the church of Constantinople.

On July 9, 518, the long reign of Anastasius came to a close, the orthodox Justin succeeding. On Sunday, July 15, the new emperor entered the cathedral, and the archbishop, accompanied by twelve prelates, was making his way through the throngs that crowded every corner. As he came near the raised dais where the pulpit stood shouts arose, "Long live the patriarch! Long live the emperor! Why do we remain excommunicated? Why have we not communicated these many years? You are Catholic, what do you fear, worthy servant of the Trinity? Cast out Severus the Manichee! O Justin, our emperor, you win! This instant proclaim the synod of Chalcedon, because Justin reigns." These and other cries continued. The procession passed into the inclosure, but the excited congregation went on shouting outside the gates of the choir in similar strains: "You shall not come out unless you anathematize Severus," referring to the heretical patriarch of Antioch. The patriarch John, having meanwhile gained time for thought and consultation, came out and mounted the pulpit, saying, "There is no need of disturbance or tumult; nothing has been done against the faith; we recognize for orthodox all the councils which have confirmed the decrees of Nicaea, and principally these three—Constantinople, Ephesus, and the great council of Chalcedon."

The people were determined to have a more formal decision, and continued shouting for several hours, mingling with their former cries such as these: "Fix a day for a festival in honour of Chalcedon!" "Commemorate the holy synod this very morrow!" The people being thus firm, the deacon Samuel was instructed to announce the desired festival. Still the people continued to shout with all their might, "Severus is now to be anathematized; anathematize him this instant, or there's nothing done!" The patriarch, seeing that something must be settled, took counsel with the twelve attendant prelates, who agreed to the curse on Severus. This extemporaneous and intimidated council then carried a decree by acclamation: "It is plain to all that Severus in separating himself from this church condemned himself. Following, therefore, the canons and the Fathers, we hold him alien and condemned by reason of his blasphemies, and we anathematize him." The domes of St. Sophia rang with shouts of triumph and the crowd dispersed. It was a day long remembered in Constantinople.

The next day the promised commemoration of Chalcedon took place. Again as the patriarch made his processional entrance and approached the pulpit clamours arose: "Restore the relics of Macedonius to the church! Restore those exiled for the faith! Let the bones of the Nestorians be dug up! Let the bones of the Eutychians be dug up! Cast out the Manichees! Place the four councils in the diptychs! Place Leo, bp. of Rome, in the diptychs! Bring the diptychs to the pulpit!" This kind of cry continuing, the patriarch replied, "Yesterday we did what was enough to satisfy my dear people, and we shall do the same to-day. We must take the faith as our inviolable foundation; it will aid us to reunite the churches. Let us then glorify with one mouth the holy and consubstantial Trinity." But the people went on crying madly, "This instant, let none go out! I abjure you, shut the doors! You no longer fear Amantius the Manichee! Justin reigns, why fear Amantius?" So they continued. The patriarch tried in vain to bring them to reason. It was the outburst of enthusiasm and excitement long pent up under heterodox repression. It bore all before it. The patriarch was at last obliged to have inserted in the diptychs the four councils of Nicaea, Constantinople, Ephesus, and Chalcedon, and the names of Euphemius and Macedonius, patriarchs of Constantinople, and Leo, bp. of Rome. Then the multitude chanted for more than an hour, "Blessed be the Lord God of Israel, for He hath visited and redeemed His people!" The choir assembled on the raised platform, and, turning eastwards, sang the Trisagion, the whole people listening in silence. When the moment arrived for the recitation of the names of the defunct bishops from the diptychs, the multitude closed in silence about the holy table; and when the deacon had read the new insertions, a mighty shout arose, "Glory be to Thee, O Lord!"

To authenticate what had been done, John assembled on July 20 a council of 40 bishops, who happened to be at the capital. The four general councils and the name of Leo, bp. of Rome, were inscribed in the diptychs. Severus of Antioch was anathematized after an examination of his works in which a distinct condemnation of Chalcedon was discovered. John wrote to John of Jerusalem and to Epiphanius of Tyre, telling them the good news of the acclamations and the synod. His letters were accompanied by orders from Justin to restore all who had been banished by Anastasius, and to inscribe the council of Chalcedon in the diptychs. At Jerusalem and at Tyre there was great joy. Many other churches declared for Chalcedon, and during the reign of Justin 2,500 bishops gave their adhesion and approval. Now came the reconciliation with Rome. The emperor Justin wrote to the pope a fortnight after the scene of the acclamations, begging him to further the desires of the patriarch John for the reunion of the churches. John wrote saying that he received the four general councils, and that the names of Leo and of Hormisdas himself had been put in the diptychs. A deputation was sent to Constantinople with instructions that Acacius was to be anathematized by name, but that Euphemius and Macedonius might be passed over in silence.

The deputies arrived at Constantinople on Mar. 25, 519. Justin received the pope's letters with great respect, and told the ambassadors to come to an explanation with the patriarch, who at first wished to express his adherence in the form of a letter, but agreed to write a little preface and place after it the words of Hormisdas, which he copied out in his own handwriting. Two copies were sent by the legates to Rome, one in Greek, the other in Latin. Emperor, senate, and all present were overjoyed at this ratification of peace.

The sting of the transaction still remained; they had now to efface from the diptychs the names of five patriarchs and two emperors—Acacius, Fravitta, Euphemius, Macedonius, and Timotheus; Zeno and Anastasius. All the bishops at Constantinople gave their consent in writing; so did all the abbats, after some had raised a difficulty. On Easter Day the pacification was promulgated. The court and people, equally enthusiastic, surged into St. Sophia. The vaults resounded with acclamations in praise of God, the emperor, St. Peter, and the bp. of Rome. Opponents, who had prophesied sedition and tumult, were signally disappointed. Never within memory had so vast a number communicated. The emperor sent an account of the proceedings throughout the provinces and the ambassadors forwarded their report to Rome, saying that there only remained the negotiations with Antioch. John wrote to Hormisdas to congratulate him on the great work, and to offer him the credit of its success. Soon after, Jan. 19, 520, John died.

Baronius, *ad ann.* 518, x.–lxxvii. 520, vii.; Fleury, ii. 573; *Acta SS.* Bolland. 18 Aug. iii. 655; Theoph. *Chronogr.* § 140, *Patr. Gk.* cviii.; Niceph. Callist. iii. 456, *Patr. Gk.* cxlvii.; Photius, iii. § 287 a, *Patr. Gk.* ciii.; Avitus, *Ep.* vii. *Patr. Lat.* lix. 227; Hormisdas, *Epp.*, *Patr. Lat.* lxiii. p. 426, etc. [W.M.S.]

Joannes (125) III., surnamed *Scholasticus*, "*The Lawyer*," 32nd bp. of Constantinople (Apr. 12, 565–Aug. 31, 577), born at Sirimis, in the region of Cynegia, near Antioch. There was a flourishing college of lawyers at Antioch, where he entered and did himself credit. This was suppressed in 533 by Justinian. John was ordained and became agent and secretary of his church. This would bring him into touch with the court at Constantinople. When Justinian, towards the close of his life, tried to raise the sect of the Aphthartodocetae to the rank of orthodoxy, and determined to expel the blameless Eutychius for his opposition, the able lawyer-ecclesiastic of Antioch, who had already distinguished himself by his great edition of the canons, was chosen to carry out the imperial will.

Little is known of his episcopal career. Seven months after his appointment Justinian died. The new emperor, Justin II., was crowned by the patriarch, Nov. 14, 565. John himself died shortly before Justin.

One of the most useful works of that period was the Digest of Canon Law formed by John at Antioch. Following some older work which he mentions in his preface, he abandoned the historical plan of giving the decrees of each council in order and arranged them on a philosophical principle, according to their matter. The older writers had sixty heads. He reduced them to fifty. To the canons of the councils of Nicaea, Ancyra, Neocaesarea, Gangra, Antioch, Ephesus, and Constantinople, already collected and received in the Greek church, John added 89 "Apostolical Canons," the 21 of Sardica, and the 68 of the canonical letter of Basil. Writing to Photius, pope Nicholas I. cites a harmony of the canons which includes those of Sardica, which could only be that of John the Lawyer. When John came to Constantinople, he edited the *Nomocanon*, an abridgment of his former work, with the addition of a comparison of the imperial rescripts and civil laws (especially the Novels of Justinian) under each head. Balsamon cites this without naming the author, in his notes on the first canon of the Trullan council of Constantinople. In a MS. of the Paris library the *Nomocanon* is attributed to Theodoret, but in all others to John. Theodoret would not have inserted the "apostolical canons" and those of Sardica, and the style has no resemblance to his. In 1661 these two works were printed at the beginning of vol. ii. of the *Bibliotheca Canonica* of Justellus, at Paris. Photius (*Cod.* lxxv.) mentions his catechism, in which he established the Catholic teaching of the consubstantial Trinity, saying that he wrote it in 568, under Justin II., and that it was afterwards attacked by the impious Philoponus. Fabricius considers that the Digest or Harmony and the *Nomocanon* are probably rightly assigned to John the Lawyer. Fabricius, xi. 101, xii. 146, 193, 201, 209; Evagr. *H. E.* iv. 38, v. 13, *Patr. Gk.* lxxxvi. pt. 2; Theoph. *Chronogr.* 204, etc., *Patr. Gk.* cviii.; Niceph. Callist. iii. 455, *Patr. Gk.* cxlvii.; Victor Tunun. *Patr. Lat.* lxviii. 937; Baronius, *ad. ann.* 564, xiv. xxix.; 565, xvii.; 578, 5; *Patr. Constant.* in *Acta SS.* Bolland. Aug. i. p.* 67. [W.M.S.]

Joannes (126) IV. (surnamed *The Faster*, *Jejunator*, sometimes also *Cappadox*, and thus liable to be confused with the patriarch John II.), 33rd bp. of Constantinople, from Apr. 11, 582 to Sept. 2, 595. He was born at Constantinople of artisan parents, and was a sculptor. In 587 or 588 he summoned the bishops of the East in the name of "the Oecumenical Patriarch" to decide the cause of Gregory, archbp. of Antioch, who was acquitted and returned to his see. Pelagius II., bp. of Rome, solemnly annulled the acts of this council. In 593 we find John severely blamed by pope Gregory for having allowed an Isaurian presbyter named Anastasius, accused of heresy, to be beaten with ropes in the church of Constantinople.

In 595 the controversy was again rife about the title of universal bishop. Gregory the Great wrote to his legate Sabinianus forbidding him to communicate with John. In the case of a presbyter named Athanasius, accused of being to some extent a Manichee, and condemned as such, Gregory shews that the accuser was himself a Pelagian, and that by the carelessness, ignorance, or fault of John the Faster the Nestorian council of Ephesus had actually been mistaken for the Catholic, so that heretics would be taken for orthodox, and orthodox condemned as heretics!

His Writings.—Isidore of Seville (*de Script. Eccl.* 26) attributes to him only a letter, not now extant, on baptism addressed to St. Leander. John, he says, "propounds nothing of his own, but only repeats the opinions of the ancient Fathers on trine immersion."

But there are extant four works attributed to John the Faster. (1) His Penitential, *Libellus Poenitentialis*, or, as it is described in bk. iii. of the work of Leo Allatius, *de Consensu Utriusque Ecclesiae* (Rome, 1655, 4to), *Praxis Graecis Praescripta in Confessione Peragenda.* The Greeks of the middle ages always attributed this and (2) to John the Faster.

(2) *Instructio, qua non modo confitens de confessione pie et integre edenda instituitur, sed etiam sacerdos, qua ratione confessiones excipiat, poenitentiam imponat et reconciliationem praestet informatur.*

(3) *Homily on Penitence, Continence, and Virginity.* Often printed among Chrysostom's homilies, but now agreed not to be Chrysostom's. Montfaucon, Vossius, and Pearson held it to be by John the Faster; Morel and Savile printed it among Chrysostom's works.

(4) *Homily on False Prophets and False Doctrine.* Attributed occasionally to Chrysostom, by Peter Wastel to John of Jerusalem, but by Vossius, Petavius, and Cave to John the Faster.

(5) A set of *Precepts to a Monk*, in a MS. at the Paris library.

Migne reproduces the Penitential, the Instructions for Confession, and the Homily on Penitence in *Patr. Gk.* lxxxviii. 1089. See also Baronius, *ad. ann.* 588-593; *AA. SS.* Bolland. Aug. 1, p. 69; Fleury, ii. bk. xxxiv. c. 44, etc.; Ceillier, xi. 427, etc.; Fabricius, *Bibl. Graec.* xi. 108, xii. 239. [W.M.S.]

Joannes (160) (called *of Asia* and *of Ephesus*), Monophysite bp. of Ephesus, born *c.* 516, and living in 585, a Syriac writer whose chief work was his *History of the Church*, in the extant portion of which he describes himself once as "John, who is called superintendent of the heathen and Breaker of Idols" (ii. 4), and twice as "John who is over the heathen, who was bp. of Ephesus" (ii. 41; iii. 15). Elsewhere he styles himself, "John bp. of Ephesus" (iv. 45), or simply, "John of Ephesus" (v. 1); and, lastly, "John of Asia, that is, John of Ephesus" (v. 7). Hence John of Ephesus is clearly the historian so often mentioned by Syriac writers as John bp. of Asia, "Asia" meaning the district of which Ephesus was the capital.

Dr. Land (*Johann von Ephesus der erste syrische Kirchenhistoriker*) discusses his identification with one or other of his numerous namesakes who wrote during the same period; and has pronounced in the negative.

What we know of the personal history of John of Ephesus is gathered from the meagre extracts from pt. ii. of his great work, preserved in the *Chronicon* of Dionysius; and from the extant pt. iii., which is to some extent an autobiography. Dionysius (*ap.* Assemani, *Bibl. Or.* 83-90) tells us that John's birthplace was Amid in N. Mesopotamia. He stood high in the confidence of the emperor Justinian, by whom he was commissioned in 542 as "Teacher of the heathen" in the four provinces of Asia, Caria, Phrygia, and Lydia. His success was such that in four years 70,000 persons adopted Christianity. In the third part of his history (ii. 44) John mentions that Deuterius was 35 years his fellow-labourer, and his successor in Caria. Together they had built 99 churches and 12 monasteries. John tells (iii. 36-37) how the work began among the mountains round Tralles. His chief monastery, Darira, rose upon the site of a famous temple which he had demolished.

In 546 he was entrusted with an inquiry into the secret practice of pagan rites by professing Christians. Members of all ranks were inculpated: Phocas, prefect of the capital, being informed against, poisoned himself. John was appointed to instruct the accused in Christian doctrine; and an imperial edict prescribed conversion within three months! Theophanes tells us that heathens and heretics were to be excluded from public office.

From pt. iii. of John's history we learn that in the 2nd year of Tiberius (A.D. 579), upon the rumour of a heathen plot to destroy the Christians of Baalbec, the emperor ordered an officer named Theophilus to suppress paganism in the East. Torture, crucifixion, the sword, wild beasts, were among the means employed. Numbers were accused; the prisons teemed with victims of every rank; and a permanent inquisition was established for their trial.

As bp. of Ephesus or "Asia," John appears to have supervised all the Monophysite congregations of Asia Minor. His 30 years of influence at the court of Justinian and his high personal qualities gave him very considerable authority among his own party. He tells us (v. 1) that in the reign of Justin II. he "was dwelling in the royal city and controlling all the revenues of all the congregations of the Faithful there and in every place." In a chapter written A.D. 581 he mentions his old intimacy with Tiberius at the court of Justin: "He and I were often together, and stood with the other courtiers before the serene Justin" (iii. 22).

John suffered grievously in the persecution instigated first by John Scholasticus, whom he calls John of Sirmin, and afterwards by Eutychius. Together with Paul of Aphrodisias (subsequently patriarch of Antioch), Stephen, bp. of Cyprus, and the bp. Elisha, John of Ephesus was imprisoned in the patriarch's palace. In the heated debates which followed, the four Monophysite bishops stoutly charged John of Sirmin with breach of the canons in annulling the orders of their clergy, and, when the patriarch demanded of them "a union such as that between Cyril of Alexandria and John of Antioch," declared their willingness provided they might drive out the council of Chalcedon from the church, as Cyril had driven out Nestorius. The vacillating emperor, of whom John testifies that for six years he had been friendly to the "orthodox," attempted to secure peace by drawing up a dogmatic formula, in the shape of an imperial edict, which he sent to the four captive bishops for revision. Their changes were admitted, but the "Nestorians and semi-Nestorians" of the court—so John puts it—scared the timid emperor into further alterations, of which the chief was an inserted clause, "that the customs of the church were to be maintained," which meant that the obnoxious council was still to be proclaimed from the diptychs. Weary of the dispute, and probably not understanding its grounds, Justin now signed the document, and required the subscription of John of Ephesus and his companions. They declined, and 33 days passed in constant wrangling between them and the patriarch. Meanwhile they were kept under close guard; the patriarch's creatures stripped them of everything; friends were denied admittance to their prison; and their personal followers were also confined in the dungeons of the palace. The misery of the four bishops was aggravated by the reproaches of the leading Monophysite laymen, who supposed that their obstinacy alone hindered a compromise which would stop the persecution. The cunning patriarch was careful to encourage this belief. At last his victims gave way, the patriarch promising upon oath that the council of Chalcedon should be sacrificed. The four bishops twice communicated with him; but when they reminded him of his promise, he referred them to the pope; he could not, for their sakes, risk a schism from Rome. Our historian touchingly describes the sorrow of himself and his companions over this fraud; even their opponents pitied them, until they once more faced them with galling taunts, which led to a second imprisonment (i. 17-25). The emperor made further fruitless attempts at conciliation. The upshot of a discussion before the senate was that the four bishops boldly uttered their anathema "upon the whole heresy of the two natures," and renounced communion with their deceivers for ever. Thereupon they were sentenced to "banishment." The sentence was at once carried out. They never saw each other again. John of Ephesus was confined in the hospital of Eubulus at Constantinople. Though helpless from gout and exposed to swarms of vermin, he was denied all assistance. As he lay in his filthy prison, it seemed to him that his feverish thirst was slaked and his misery comforted by a heavenly visitant, whose coming he describes with much pathos and simplicity. After a year he was removed to an island, where he remained 18 months, when the Caesar Tiberius ordered his release. For three years, however, he was under surveillance, until the patriarch died (A.D. 578). Before the outbreak of this persecution, John of Ephesus and Paul of Aphrodisias had argued publicly with Conon and Eugenius, the founders of the Cononites, nicknamed Tritheites, in the presence of the patriarch and his synod, by command of Justin (v. 3). Conon had vainly tried to win the support of John, who proved to him that he was a heretic and afterwards wrote him a letter of warning (v. 1-12). Eutychius, who, upon the death of John of Sirmin, was restored to the patriarchal throne, was hardly more tolerant of Monophysites than its late occupant. Persecution was renewed, and John of Ephesus again met with disgraceful injustice. By another imprisonment Eutychius wrung from him the resignation of a property which Callinicus, a chief officer of the court, had bestowed, and which John had largely improved and converted into a monastery. After being further deprived of his right of receiving five loaves at the public distributions, for which he had paid 300 darics, John was released.

Tiberius, Justin's successor, though unwilling to persecute, was overcome by popular clamour. The mob of the capital groundlessly suspected their new emperor of Arian leanings (iii. 13, 26). An edict was therefore published ordering the arrest of Arians, Manicheans, etc. Under cover of this, the "orthodox" were once more harried and plundered. The first victim was John of Ephesus (iii. 15), who had now lived many years and suffered much in Constantinople. He and his friends were incarcerated at Christmas in a miserable prison called the Cancellum (A.D. 578 ?); and after much fruitless argument were finally ordered to leave the city.

It is greatly to our historian's credit that, during the bitter strife which raged long among the Monophysites themselves, in the matter of the double election of Theodore and Peter to succeed Theodosius as their patriarch of Alexandria, he maintained an honourable neutrality, standing equally aloof from Paulites and Jacobites, although his sympathies were with Theodore, the injured patriarch (iv. 9-48). John wrote his account of this pernicious quarrel in 583, the 2nd year of Maurice; for he says that it had already lasted 8 years (iv. 11), and that he is writing an outline of events from the year of Alexander 886 (A.D. 575) onwards (iv. 13). In his anxiety to heal the schism, John sent 10 epistles to "the blessed Jacob" [JACOBUS BARADAEUS], protesting his own neutrality, and urging reconciliation between the two factions (iv. 46); and after Jacob's death (A.D. 581) his party made overtures to John of Ephesus, then living at the capital, to induce him to recognize Peter of Callinicus as patriarch of Antioch in place of Paul (iv. 45). In reply the historian rebuked them for violating the canons. John accuses both sides of an utter want of mutual charity, and an entire aversion to calm examination of the grounds of their quarrel. He adds that he has briefly recorded the main facts from the outset to the current year, 896 (A.D. 585)—the latest date observable in his work.

The Ecclesiastical History.—John states (pt. iii. bk. i. c. 3) that he has already written a history of the church, "beginning from the times of Julius Caesar, as far as to the sixth year of the reign of Justin II., son of the sister of Justinian." If, as Dr. Payne Smith assumes, pt. i. was a mere abridgment of Eusebius, its loss is not a great one. The disappearance of pt. ii. is more unfortunate, as it would probably have furnished much important matter for the reign of Justinian. It brought the history down to 571. Pt. iii. continues it to *c.* 585, thus covering the period between the 6th year of Justin II. and the 4th of Maurice. It was called forth by the persecution above mentioned, which broke out in the 6th or 7th year of Justin, and the writer often apologizes for want of chronological order, occasional repetitions, and even inconsistencies of statement (see esp. i. 3; ii. 50), as defects due to the stress of untoward circumstances: "This should be known to critics: many of these stories were penned in time of persecution . . . people conveyed away the papers inscribed with these chapters, and the other papers and writings, into divers places, and in some instances they remained hidden so long as two or three years in one place or another" (ii. 50). John had no memoranda of what he had already written, and never found opportunity for revision. With these drawbacks, the work possesses special interest as an original account. John was contemporary with most of the characters described; he writes of what he himself saw and heard and of doings in which he was personally concerned. For 30 years he was a trusted servant of Justinian; and Gibbon would probably have recognized in the second part of his history a valuable gauge of the servility and the malice of Procopius. Had Gibbon possessed the third part of John's work, he would hardly have surmised that "the sentiments of Justin II. were pure and benevolent," or believed that the four last years of that emperor "were passed in *tranquil* obscurity" (cf. iii. 1-6); had he read what John has to say of the worthless stepson of Belisarius he might have rated "the gallant Photius" less highly; and he would have learned that it was the thoughtless improvidence of Tiberius which forced the unhappy Maurice to appear a grasping niggard (cf. iii. 11; v. 20). As regards chronology, Assemani, who did not love a Monophysite, accuses John of inaccuracy, asserting that he used a peculiar Greek era, making almost all Justinian's acts and his death ten years later than the dates assigned by Evagrius, Theophanes, and Cedrenus. But in pt. iii. (v. 13) John gives the usual date for Justinian's death—Nov. 14, 876 [565]. Of Theophanes Gibbon has said that he is "full of strange blunders" and "his chronology is loose and inaccurate"; his verdict in regard to John of Ephesus would have been very different.

His attitude to the great controversy of his day is that of one thoroughly convinced that his own party holds exclusive possession of the truth. The Monophysites are "the orthodox," "the faithful"; their opponents "Synodites," "Nestorians," or at least "half-Nestorians"; the synod of Chalcedon is "the stumbling-block and source of confusion of the whole church"; "it sunders Christ our God into two natures after the Union, and teaches a Quaternity instead of the holy Trinity" (i. 10, 18); the four bishops taunt the patriarch with "the heresy of the two natures, and the blasphemies of the synod, and of the tome of Leo" (i. 18). Yet John does not labour to blacken the memory of his adversaries; the strong terms in which he speaks of the pride of power and savage tyranny of John Scholasticus are warranted or at least excused by facts (i. 5, 12, 37); and Baronius denounces John of Sirmin in language equally decided (*H. E.* ad ann. 564). In regard to Eutychius, John protests his adherence to truth: "Although we declare ourselves opposed to the excellent patriarch Eutychius, yet from the truth we have not swerved in one thing out of a hundred; nor was it from eagerness to revile and ridicule that we committed these things to writing" (iii. 22). His impartiality is manifest in his description of the great schism which rent asunder his own communion; unsparing in his censure of both factions, he refers their wicked and worse than heathenish rancour to the instigation of devils (iv. 19, 22, 39). Credulous John was, but credulity was a common attribute of his age. More serious objection might be taken to his approval of the cruelties connected with the suppression of heathenism (iii. 34) and his intolerance of "heresy" other than his own. In 550 he dug up and burnt the bones of Montanus, Maximilla, and Priscilla, the false prophets of Montanism (Extr. *ap.* Dionys.). Herein also he shared the temper of his contemporaries. The spirit of persecution is not the peculiar mark of any age, church, or sect. Apart from these blemishes we may recognize in him an historian who sincerely loved truth; a bishop who was upright and devoted; and a man whose piety rested upon a thorough knowledge of Scripture.

His style, like that of most Syriac writers, is verbose and somewhat unwieldy, but has the eloquence of simple truth and homely pathos.

The Third Part of the Ecclesiastical History of John of Ephesus was first edited from the unique MS. in the Brit. Mus. by Dr. Cureton (Oxf. 1853)—a splendid reproduction of the original—and translated into English by Dr. Payne Smith (Oxf. 1860) and into German by Schönfelder (München, 1862). These versions are of great assistance, many chapters being defective in the original. [C.J.B.]

Joannes (216) II., bp. of Jerusalem, 386-417, in succession to Cyril; a prelate known to us chiefly through the invectives of Jerome, and hence particularly difficult to estimate. Imbued with that tendency of Eastern church teachers which formed their chief difference from those of the Western church, he with difficulty brought himself to acquiesce in the condemnation of Origenism or to take any steps against Pelagius, with whom he was brought in contact at the close of his episcopacy, and the presence of Jerome and other immigrants from Italy, and the anti-Origenistic vehemence of Epiphanius of Salamis and Theophilus of Alexandria, made it impossible for him to escape the reproach of laxity and even at times of heresy.

Born between 350 and 356 (Hieron. *Ep.* lxxxii. 8, ed. Vall.), he passed as a young man some time among the monks of Nitria in Egypt. There he, no doubt, imbibed his affection for Origen's teaching, and probably became acquainted with two persons who had much to do with his own subsequent history and with that of the Origenistic controversy—the monk Isidore (one of the Long Monks) and Rufinus. During the troublous times before the accession of Theodosius, when Arianism was in the ascendant, he declined, *teste* Jerome (*cont. Joan. Jerus.* 4), to communicate with the orthodox bishops exiled by Valens. But no imputation of Arianism rests upon him. He was evidently esteemed very highly, and of great eloquence (*ib.* 41) and subtlety of mind. His flatterers compared him with Chrysippus, Plato, and Demosthenes (*ib.* 4). He was little more than 30 years old (Hieron. *Ep.* lxxxii. 8, ed. Vall.) when chosen to succeed Cyril as bp. of Jerusalem. It was a see of great importance, subject in certain respects to the metropolitan at Caesarea, but acting at times independently; of great wealth (*cont. Joan. Jerus.* 14), and of great interest for its holy places, which were visited by pilgrims from all parts. It had also a special interest from the settlements of distinguished persons from the West, which made it during his episcopate a focus of Christian and literary activity, and with two of which, that of Rufinus and Melania on the Mount of Olives, and of Jerome and Paula at Bethlehem, he was destined to have close but similar relations. Jerome accuses him of making a gain of his bishopric and living in luxury (*Comm. in Joann.* c. 14, and *Ep.* lvii. 12); but this may be only the common animus of monk against bishop, embittered by momentary resentment. The clergy of Jerusalem were certainly attached to him. Rufinus thought it a sufficient defence of his own faith to say that it was that preached at Jerusalem by the holy bp. John (Ruf. *Apol.* i. 13). But the most important testimony is given by the pope Anastasius, in a letter to him in 401, a time when the adversaries of John, Pammachius, and Marcella had access to the pope, and only two or three years after Jerome's Philippic was composed. Anastasius speaks of the splendour of his holiness and his divine virtues; his eminence and his praise are so conspicuous that he cannot find words equal to his merits. He accounts it an honour to have received praise from one of so serene and heavenly a disposition, the splendour of whose episcopate shines throughout the world (see Vallarsi's *Rufinus*, pp. 408, 409; Migne's *Patr. Lat.* xxi.).

When John became bishop, Rufinus had already been settled on the Mount of Olives some nine years, and Jerome and his friends were just entering on their work at Bethlehem. At first he lived in impartial friendship with them both, seeking out Jerome especially ("nos suo arbitrio diligebat," Hieron. *Ep.* lxxxii. 11, ed. Vall.), and making use of Rufinus, whom he ordained, as a learned man, in business which required his special talents. After some six years their peace was disturbed. A certain Aterbius (Hieron. *cont. Ruf.* iii. 33), who by his officious insinuations and imputations of Origenistic heresy caused the first breach between Jerome and Rufinus, had, no doubt, some dealings with the bishop also; and, probably through him, the suspicions of Epiphanius, the venerable bp. of Salamis, were aroused. When Epiphanius came to Jerusalem in 394, the strife broke out. For the controversy see EPIPHANIUS (1) and HIERONYMUS (2). During the dispute between Jerome and Rufinus, John in no way intervened. Zöckler (*Hieron.* p. 249) thinks him to have inclined rather to the side of Jerome. We certainly find Jerome, in a letter to Theophilus, in commendation of his encyclical (*Ep.* lxxxvi., ed. Vall.), pleading for his bishop. John had accepted a person under the ban of Theophilus who had come from Jerusalem to Alexandria, and thus had incurred the wrath of that fierce prelate; but Jerome represented that Theophilus had sent no letters condemnatory of this person, and that it would be rash to condemn John for a supposed fault committed in ignorance. As regards Rufinus, John wrote a letter to pope Anastasius, the tenor of which can be only dimly inferred from the pope's extant reply. John was apparently less anxious to defend Rufinus than to secure his own freedom from implication in the charges made against Rufinus by Jerome's friends at Rome. The pope, with fulsome expressions of esteem for John, bids him put such fears away and judge Rufinus for himself. He professes to know nothing about Origen, not even who he was, while yet he has condemned his opinions; and as to Rufinus, he only says that, if his translation of the works of Origen implies an acceptance of his opinions (a matter which he leaves to his own conscience), he must see where he can procure absolution. That John was not then in familiar communication with Rufinus, but was with Jerome, may be inferred from the fact that Jerome used this letter in his controversy with Rufinus (*cont. Ruf.* ii. 14), while Rufinus did not know of its existence, and, when he heard of it, treated it as an invention of Jerome (*ib.* iii. 20). The reconciliation of John with the monks of Bethlehem is further attested by Sulpicius Severus (*Dial.* i. 8), who had stayed six months at Bethlehem, and says that John had entrusted to Jerome and his brother the charge of the parish of Bethlehem. A letter from Chrysostom to John in 404 (Migne's *Patr. Gk.* vol. lii.) shews that he had taken Chrysostom's part; then we hear nothing more of John for 12 or 13 years, when the Pelagian controversy brings him forward once more. Pelagius and Coelestius, having come in 415 to Jerusalem, were encountered by Orosius, the friend of Augustine, who had come to visit Jerome, and afterwards by the Gaulish bishops Heros and Lazarus. Orosius, who recounts these transactions in the first nine chaps. of his *Liber de Arbitrii Libertate*, addressed himself to John, as did also Pelagius; but John was not willing to accept without inquiry the decrees of the council of Carthage and resented their being pressed upon him by Orosius. The two parties were in secret conflict for some time, till John determined on holding a synod to end the strife, on July 28, 415. John was the only bishop present; the rest were presbyters and laymen. He shewed some consideration towards Pelagius, allowing him, though a layman, to sit among the presbyters; and when there was a clamour against Pelagius for shewing disrespect for the name and authority of Augustine, John, by saying, "I am Augustine," undertook both to ensure respect to that great teacher and not to allow his authority to be pressed too far against his antagonist. "If," cried Orosius, "you represent Augustine, follow Augustine's judgment." John thereupon asked him if he was ready to become the accuser of Pelagius; but Orosius declined this duty, saying that Pelagius had been condemned by the African bishops, whose decisions John ought to accept. The proceedings were somewhat confused from the necessity of employing an interpreter. Finally, it was determined to send a letter to pope Innocentius and to abide by his judgment. Meanwhile, John imposed silence upon both parties. This satisfied neither. The opinions of Pelagius continued to be spread by private intercourse, and Augustine wrote to remonstrate with John against the toleration of heresy. On the arrival of the Gaulish bishops Heros and Lazarus, another synod was held at Diospolis (416) under the presidency of Euzoïus, the metropolitan bp. of Caesarea, in which John again took part. Augustine, in his work against Julianus, records the decision of this council, which was favourable to Pelagius, but considers his acquittal due to uncertainties occasioned by difference of language, which enabled Pelagius to express himself in seemingly orthodox words; and both in this work and in his letter to John he treats John as a brother-bishop whom he holds in high esteem. Meanwhile, the more intemperate partisans of Pelagius resorted to open violence. The dialogue of Jerome against the Pelagians, though mild compared with his other controversial works, incensed them, and they proceeded to burn the monasteries of Bethlehem. The attitude of John at this time cannot be gathered with any certainty. That he was in any way an accomplice in such proceedings is incredible. Nothing of the sort appears from the letters of Jerome, though he speaks in a resigned manner of his losses. Complaints, however, of the ill-treatment of Jerome and the Roman ladies at Bethlehem reached pope Innocent, who wrote to John a letter (Hieron. *Ep.* cxxxvii., ed. Vall.) of sharp rebuke. He does not imply that John had been accessory to the violence; but, considering that a bishop ought to be able to prevent such acts or at least relieve their consequences, he bids him take care that no further violence is done, on pain of the laws of the church being put in force against him. The view here taken of these transactions, which is that of Zöckler (*Hieron.* pp. 310-316), is opposed by Thierry (*St. Jerome*, bk. xii. c. iii.), who looks upon John as a partisan of Pelagius and as the enemy of Jerome to the end. John was now at the close of his career. Possibly the letter of Innocentius never reached him, for it can hardly have been written, as Vallarsi shews (pref. to Hieron. *sub. litt.* cxxxv.-cxxxviii.), before 417, and John died (see Ceillier, vii. 497, etc.) on Jan. 10 in that year. After a troubled episcopate of 30 years and a life of from 60 to 65 years, failing health may have prevented his exercising full control in this last and most painful episode of his career.

Several works are attributed to him (see Ceillier, vii. 97, etc.). Gennadius (30) mentions one which he wrote in his own defence; but no work of his is extant. He must, therefore, always be viewed through the medium of other, mostly hostile, writers, and through the mists of controversy. [W.H.F.]

Joannes (217) III., bp. of Jerusalem, 513-524. On the banishment of Elias, bp. of Jerusalem, by the emperor Anastasius, John, deacon of the Anastasis, was forcibly thrust into his episcopal seat by Olympius, prefect of Palestine, on his engaging to receive Severus of Antioch into communion and to anathematize the decrees of Chalcedon (Cyrill. Scythop. *Vit. S. Sab.* cc. 37, 56). Such an engagement awoke the orthodox zeal of St. Sabas and the other fathers of the desert, who successfully used their influence with the new-made bishop to prevent the fulfilment of the compact, which Olympius lacked sufficient firmness to enforce. Anastasius, recalling Olympius, dispatched in his room a name-sake of his own, who had offered to forfeit 300 pounds of gold if he failed to induce John to fulfil his agreement, A.D. 517. The prefect Anastasius surprised the unsuspicious bishop and threw him into prison until he should fulfil his promise. This step delighted the populace, who regarded John as having obtained Elias's seat by fraud. Zacharias, one of the leading men of Caesarea, gaining a secret interview with the imprisoned bishop, persuaded him to feign assent to Anastasius's requirements and promise, if he would release him from prison, to publicly signify, on the following Sunday, his agreement to the original conditions. Anastasius, believing John's professions, liberated him. On the Sunday a vast concourse assembled, including 10,000 monks. Anastasius was present with his officials to receive the expected submission. John, having ascended the ambo, supported by Theodosius and Sabas, the leaders of the monastic party, was received with vociferous shouts, "Anathematize the heretics!" "Confirm the synod!" When silence was secured, John and his two companions pronounced a joint anathema on Nestorius, Eutyches, Soterichus of the Cappadocian Caesarea, and all who rejected the decrees of Chalcedon. Anastasius, utterly unprepared for this open violation of the compact, was too much terrified by the turbulent multitude, evidently prepared for violence, and hastily escaped to Caesarea. The emperor, though furious, had too much on his hands to attend to ecclesiastical disputes at Jerusalem, and John was allowed to go unpunished. The death of Anastasius in 518, and the succession of Justin, changed the whole situation. Orthodoxy was now in the ascendant. The whole East followed the example of the capital, and John could, without fear of consequences, summon his synod to make the same profession of faith with his brother-patriarch in the imperial city, and was received into communion by pope Hormisdas, at the request of Justin (*ib.* c. 60). John died A.D. 524, after an episcopate of 11 years. Theophan. *Chronogr.* p. 136; Tillem. *Mém. eccl.* xvi. 721; Fleury, *H. E.* livre xxi. cc. 27, 28; Le Quien, *Or. Christ.* iii. 185. [E.V.]

Joannes (346) I., bp. of Rome after Hormisdas, Aug. 13, 523, to May 18, 526. The emperor Justin, having during the pontificate of Hormisdas restored the churches in the East to orthodoxy and communion with Rome, continued to shew his orthodox zeal by the persecution of heretics. Having already suppressed the Eutychians and Nestorians, he issued in 523 a severe edict against Manicheans, condemning them, wherever found, to banishment or death (*Cod. Justin.* leg. 12). Justin's edict had debarred other heretics from public offices, but had excepted the Arian Goths because of his league with Theodoric, the Gothic king of Italy. Soon afterwards, however, he proceeded against the Arians also, ordering all their churches to be consecrated anew for the use of the Catholics. Theodoric, who, though an Arian, had hitherto granted toleration to Catholics in his own dominions, remonstrated with the emperor by letter, but without effect. He therefore applied to the bp. of Rome, whom he sent for to Ravenna, desiring him to go to Constantinople to use his influence with the emperor, and threatening that, unless toleration were conceded to Arians in the East, he would himself withhold it from Catholics in the West. John went (A.D. 525), accompanied by five bishops and four senators. The unprecedented event of a visit by a bishop of Rome to Constantinople caused a great sensation there. He was received with the utmost respect by acclaiming crowds and by the emperor. Invited by the patriarch Epiphanius to celebrate Easter with him in the great church, he consented only if seated on a throne above that of the patriarch. He officiated in Latin and according to the Latin rite. None were excluded from his communion except Timotheus, patriarch of Alexandria (Theophan.; Marcellin. Com.). Anastasius (*Lib. Pontif.*) states that the emperor, though now in the 8th year of his reign, bowing to the ground before the vicar of St. Peter, solicited and obtained the honour of being crowned by him. There is concurrence of testimony that John obtained a cessation of Justin's measures against the Arians. Baronius and Binius, anxious to clear a pope from tolerating heresy, insist that John dissuaded the emperor from the concessions demanded. Against this supposition Pagi (*Critic.*) cites the following: "Justin, having heard the legation, promised that he would do all, except that those who had been reconciled to the Catholic faith could by no means be restored to the Arians" (*Anonym. Vales.*); "The venerable pope and senators returned with glory, having obtained all they asked from Justin" (Anastasius); "Justinus Augustus granted the whole petition, and restored to the heretics their churches, according to the wish of Theodoric the heretical king, lest Christians, and especially priests, should be put to the sword" (*Auctor. Chron. Veterum Pontificum*); "Having come to Augustus, they requested him with many tears to accept favourably the tenour of their embassy, however unjust; and he, moved by their tears, granted what they asked, and left the Arians unmolested" (*Miscell.* lib. 15, *ad ann.* vi. Justin). Whatever the cause, it is certain that John and the legates were, on returning, received with displeasure by Theodoric and imprisoned at Ravenna, where the pope died on May 18, 526. His body was buried in St. Peter's at Rome on May 27, on which day he appears in the Roman Martyrology as a saint and martyr. See also *Fragm. Vales.* Greg. Dial. i. iii. c. 2. [J.B—Y.]

Joannes (347) II. (called *Mercurius*), bp. of Rome after Boniface II., Dec. 31, 532, to May 27, 535, a Roman by birth who had been a Roman presbyter (Anastas. *Lib. Pont.*) The canvassings and contests then usual delayed the election 11 weeks. Church funds were used and sacred vessels publicly sold for bribery (*Ep. Athalaric. ad Joann. pap.*; Cassiodor. *Variar.* l. ix.; *Ep.* 15).

The most noteworthy incident of his brief reign is a doctrinal decision, in which he appears at first sight to differ from one of his predecessors. Pope Hormisdas had in 522 written in strong condemnation of certain Scythian monks who had upheld the statement that "One of the Trinity" (*Unus ex Trinitate*) "suffered in the flesh." His rejection of the phrase had at the time been construed so as to imply heresy (*Ep.* Maxent. *ad* Hormisd.), and now the *Acoemetae*, or "Sleepless Monks," of Constantinople argued from it in favour of the Nestorian position that Mary was not truly and properly the mother of God; saying with reason that, if He Who suffered in the flesh was not of the Trinity, neither was He Who was born in the flesh. The emperor Justinian, supported by the patriarch Epiphanius, having condemned the position of the "Sleepless Monks," they sent a deputation to Rome, urging the pope to support their deduction from the supposed doctrine of his predecessor. The emperor, having embodied his view of the true doctrine in an imperial edict, sent it with an embassy to Rome and a letter requesting the pope to signify in writing to himself and the patriarch his acceptance of the doctrine of the edict, which he lays down as indubitably true, and assumes to be, as a matter of course, the doctrine of the Roman see (*Inter. Epp.* Joann. II. Labbe). But the edict was a distinct assertion of the correctness of the phrase contended for by the Scythian monks and so much objected to by Hormisdas. Its words are, "The sufferings, as well as miracles, which Christ of His own accord endured in the flesh are of one and the same. For we do not know God the Word as one and Christ as another, but one and the same" (Lex. Justin. *Cod.* 1, i. 6). In his letter Justinian expresses himself similarly.

John, having received both deputations, assembled the Roman clergy, who at first could come to no agreement. But afterwards a synod convened by the pope accepted and confirmed Justinian's confession of faith. To this effect he wrote to the emperor on Mar. 25, 534 (Joann. II. *Ep.* ii.; Labbe) and to the Roman senators, laying down the true doctrine as the emperor had defined it, and warning them not to communicate with the "Sleepless Monks."

It is true that we do not find in the letters of Hormisdas any distinct condemnation of the phrase itself, however strongly he inveighed against its upholders, as troublesome and dangerous innovators. But the fact remains that a doctrinal statement which one pope strongly discountenanced, as at any rate unnecessary and fraught with danger, was, twelve years afterwards, at the instance of an emperor, authoritatively propounded by another. Justinian's view, which John accepted, has ever since been received as orthodox.

In 534 John, being consulted by Caesarius of Arles as to Contumeliosus, bp. of Riez in Gaul, wrote to Caesarius, to the bishops of Gaul, and to the clergy of Riez, directing the guilty bishop to be confined in a monastery.

A letter assigned to this pope by the Pseudo-Isidore, addressed to a bp. Valerius, on the relation of the Son to the Father, is spurious. [J.B—Y.]

Joannes (348) III., bp. of Rome, after Pelagius, July 18, 560, to July 12, 573, ordained after a vacancy of 4 months and 17 days, was the son of a person of distinction at Rome (Anastas. *Lib. Pont.*). There are two incidents in which his name appears. Two bishops in Gaul had been deposed by a synod held by order of king Guntram at Lyons under the metropolitan Nicetius. The deposed prelates obtained the king's leave to appeal to Rome, and John III. ordered their restoration (Greg. Turon. *Hist.* l. v. cc. 20, 27). The second incident is mentioned by Anastasius (*Lib. Pont. in Vit. Joann. III.*), and by Paulus

Diaconus (i. 5). The exarch Narses, having retired to Naples, there invited the Lombards to invade Italy. The pope went to him, and persuaded him to return to Rome. This incident, discredited by Baronius (*Ann.* 567, Nos. 8-12) is credited by Pagi and Muratori (cf. Gibbon, c. xlv.). [J.B—Y.]

Joannes (444) Presbyter, a shadowy personage of the sub-apostolic age, the reasons for belief in his existence being solely derived from an inference drawn by Eusebius from language used in a passage of Papias. In the middle of the 3rd cent. Dionysius of Alexandria (Eus. *H. E.* vii. 25) had maintained on critical grounds that the author of the fourth gospel and of the Catholic epistle could not also have been the author of the Apocalypse. Dionysius takes for granted that the author of the gospel was John the apostle, and has no difficulty in conceding that the name of the author of the Apocalypse was also John, since the writer himself says so; but urges that he never claims to be the apostle. He calls himself simply John, without adding that he was the disciple whom Jesus loved, or who leaned on our Lord's breast, or the brother of James, or in any way forcing us to identify him with the son of Zebedee. Now, there were many Johns, and it is said that there were two tombs in Ephesus, each called John's. Except in the statement last made, Dionysius does not pretend to have found any actual trace of any John of the apostolic age besides John the apostle and John Mark. His argument is merely that if we have good critical reasons for believing the authors of the gospel and of the Apocalypse to be distinct, the fact that both bore the name John does not force us to identify them. Some 75 years later Eusebius found historic evidence for regarding as a fact what Dionysius had suggested as a possibility. He produces from the preface to the work of Papias an extract, for a fuller discussion of which see PAPIAS. What concerns us here is that Papias, speaking of his care in collecting oral traditions of the apostolic times, says, "On any occasion when a person came in my way, who had been a follower of the elders, I would inquire about the discourses of the elders—what was said by Andrew, or by Peter, or by Philip, or by Thomas or James, or by John or Matthew or any other of the Lord's disciples, and what Aristion and the Elder John, the disciples of the Lord say" (Lightfoot's trans.). Eusebius points out that as the name John occurs here twice: the first time in a list of apostles, no doubt representing John the apostle; the second time in a different list, after the name of Aristion and with the title elder prefixed, it must represent a different person. Thus the John whose traditions Papias several times records is the elder, not the apostle. We find thus, remarks Eusebius, that "the account of those is true who have stated that two persons in Asia had the same name, and that there were two tombs in Ephesus, each of which, even to the present time, bears the name of John." "It is likely that the second (unless we allow that it was, as some would have it, the first) beheld the revelation ascribed to John" (*H. E.* iii. 39). Although Eusebius does not here name Dionysius of Alexandria, he plainly had in mind that passage of his writings which he gives at length elsewhere. The ambiguous way in which he speaks of the Apocalypse shews that his personal inclination was to pronounce it non-apostolical, but that he was kept in check by the weight of authority in its favour. The silence of Eusebius indicates that the other passages in Papias where John was mentioned contained no decisive indications what John was intended.

Modern writers have not been unanimous in their judgment on this criticism of Eusebius. Several reject it, judging Papias to be mentioning one John twice. So Milligan (*Journal Sac. Lit.* Oct. 1867), Riggenbach (*Jahrb. für deutsche Theol.* xiii. 319), Zahn (*Stud. und Krit.* 1866, p. 650, *Acta Johannis*, 1880, p. cliv.). But a far more powerful array of critics endorses the conclusion of Eusebius—*e.g.* Steitz (*Stud. und Krit.* 1868, p. 63), Lightfoot (*Contemp. Rev.* Aug. 1875, p. 379), Westcott (*N. T. Canon.* p. 69); while less orthodox critics with one consent base their theories with confidence on John the Elder being as historical as SS. Peter or Paul.

The argument of Eusebius, on the other hand, seems to have made little impression at the time and his successors seem to know only of one John and go on speaking of Papias as the hearer of John the apostle. In this they follow Irenaeus; and it is an important fact that Irenaeus, who was very familiar with the work of Papias of which he made large use and whose Eastern origin ought to have acquainted him with the traditions of the Asiatic church, shews no symptom of having heard of any John but the apostle, and describes Papias (v. 33, p. 333) as a hearer of John and a companion of Polycarp. That Polycarp was a hearer of John the apostle is stated explicitly by Irenaeus in his letter to Victor (Eus. *H. E.* v. 24; see also his letter to Florinus, v. 20). That Polycarp was made bp. of Smyrna by John the apostle is stated by Tertullian (*Praes.* v. 30) and was never doubted by subsequent writers. Polycrates, appealing to the great lights of the church of Asia (Eus. v. 24), names John, who leaned on our Lord's breast, who sleeps at Ephesus, but says nothing about any second John buried there or elsewhere. The silence of Dionysius of Alexandria is positive proof that no tradition of a second John had reached him. If he knew and remembered the passage in Papias it did not occur to him to draw from it the same inference as Eusebius. Neither, though he mentions the two monuments at Ephesus, both bearing the name of John, does he say what would have been very much to his purpose, that he had heard that they were supposed to commemorate different persons; and in fact Jerome, who in his "catalogue" repeats the story, tells us that some held that the same John was commemorated by both.* The Acts of Leucius are notoriously the source whence the Fathers, from the 4th cent., derived Johannine traditions. While disagreeing with

* Zahn (*Acta Johannis*, p. cliv. sqq.) tries to prove that one memorial church was erected outside the walls where John was buried; the other inside on the site of the house where he resided and had celebrated his last communion.

Zahn's opinion that Leucius was earlier than Papias, it is highly probable that he was a full century earlier than Eusebius, and we can assert, with as much confidence as such a thing can be asserted of a book of which only fragments remain, that Leucius mentioned no John but the apostle. If when Leucius put his stories together any tradition had remained of a second John, this would surely have been among the Leucian names of the apostle's disciples, so many of which we are able to enumerate. Eusebius had not thought of his theory at the time of his earlier work, the *Chronicle*, in which he describes Papias as a disciple of the evangelist. Jerome also is not self-consistent, speaking in one way when immediately under the influence of Eusebius, at other times following the older tradition. In the East the only trace of the theory of Eusebius is that the *Apostolic Constitutions* (vii. 46) make John ordain another John, as bp. of Ephesus in succession to Timothy. The writers who used the work of Papias do not seem to suspect that any John but the apostle was the source of his information. One fragment (Gebhardt and Harnack, 2nd ed. No. iii. p. 93) was preserved by Apollinarius, who describes Papias as a disciple of John; some authorities add "the apostle," but wherever John is mentioned without addition no other is meant. Anastasius of Sinai (Gebhardt, No. vi.) describes Papias as ὁ ἐν τῷ ἐπιστηθίῳ φοιτήσας and No. vii. as ὁ Ἰωάννου τοῦ εὐαγγελιστοῦ φοιτητής; Maximus confessor (No. ix.) describes him as συνακμάσαντα τῷ θείῳ εὐαγγελιστῇ Ἰωάννῃ. An anonymous but ancient note even makes Papias the scribe who wrote the gospel from the apostle's dictation. Thus Eusebius stands completely alone among ancient authorities, differing alike from his predecessors and successors. It by no means necessarily follows that he was wrong. If he has correctly interpreted the language of Papias, the authority of so ancient a witness outweighs that of any number of later writers. We can conceive either that there were two Johns in Asia, and that the latter's fame was so absorbed by the glory of his greater namesake that all remembrance of him was lost; or else we may imagine that the second John, the source of apostolic traditions to the Asiatic churches, was held in such high consideration that, though not really so, he passed in common fame as the apostle.

The supposition that John the apostle was never in Asia Minor has been embraced by Keim (*Jesu von Nazara*), Scholten (*Der Apostel Johannes in Kleinasien*) and others. But except that the recognition of the residence of a different John in Asia opens the possibility of a confusion, their reasons for disbelief in the apostle's residence in Asia are worthless. There is an immense mass of patristic testimony that John the apostle lived to a great age and died in Asia in the reign of Trajan.

If, then, both John the apostle and the elder taught in Asia, can we transfer to the second anything traditionally told of the first? Dionysius and Eusebius transfer to him the authorship of the Apocalypse, but those who now divide the Johannine books between these two Johns unanimously give the Apocalypse to the first. St. Jerome assigns to "the Elder" the two minor epistles, and this is a very natural inference from their inscription. That is a modest one, if the writer could have claimed the dignity of apostle; but if not, it seems arrogant to designate himself as *the* elder when there must have been elders in every city. There is also a great assumption of authority in the tone of the 3rd epistle. The writer sends his legates to the churches of the district, is angry if these legates are not respectfully received, and addresses the churches in a tone of command. It may be suggested as an explanation of this, that the writer knew himself to be the sole survivor in the district of the first Christian generation; and it agrees with this that Papias describes him as a disciple of our Lord, yet speaks of him in the present tense while he speaks of the apostles in the past. But this hypothesis is scarcely tenable if we believe what is told of the great age attained by the apostle John, who is said to have lived to the reign of Trajan. This hardly leaves room for any one who could claim to have heard our Lord to acquire celebrity after the apostle's decease. Further, no one who used the fourth gospel only could know that there had been an apostle named John. Even our Lord's forerunner, called in other gospels John the Baptist, in this is simply John, as if there were no need to distinguish him from any other. The apostle alone would not feel such need, therefore if he were the author of the gospel, all is intelligible; but if the author were his disciple, is it conceivable that he should thus suppress the name of his great master and predecessor in labour in Asia; and if beside the apostle there were in our Lord's circle another John, is it conceivable that the writer should not have distinguished between them?

Thus the Eusebian interpretation of Papias must stand on its own merits. It obtains no confirmation from independent testimony, nor does it solve any perplexing problems. It is certainly possible that we with our more powerful instruments of criticism may be able to resolve a double star which had appeared to the early observers single. Yet considering how much closer and more favourably circumstanced they were, we have need to look well that the mistake is not our own. One Eusebian argument must then be rejected, namely, that by calling his second John the elder, Papias meant to distinguish him from the apostle. This would be so if he had called the first John an apostle, but actually he calls him an elder. If we suppose, as do Lightfoot and others, that he uses the word elder in two different senses, at least the word cannot be used the second time *to distinguish him* from those to whom it is applied the first time. If it is to distinguish him from any one it is from Aristion, to whom, though also called a disciple of the Lord, this name is not applied. Hence Eusebius's second argument, that Papias by placing John after Aristion meant to assign to him a less honourable place, fails since John is given a title of dignity which is refused to Aristion. Some light is thrown on the sense in which the word elder is applied to John by Papias in his preface by the fact that one of his traditions is told with the formula, "These things the elder used to say." This must surely mean more than that the authority cited was one of the many presbyters of the church and we cannot help connecting with it the fact revealed by the minor Johannine epistles, that there was some one in the Asiatic church who spoke of himself, and no doubt was habitually spoken of by others, as "the Elder."

The only Eusebian argument then that remains is that Papias mentions the name John twice over and therefore may be presumed to speak of two Johns. But might he not first enumerate John in his list of seven apostles, concerning whom he had been able to glean traditions, and a second time in his shorter list of men of the first Christian generation who had survived to his own day? Papias wrote for the men of his time, to whom the facts were well known, and the idea of being misunderstood would no more occur to him than it would to us, if we spoke of one of our leading statesmen at one moment by his surname only, the next with the addition of his title or Christian name. The second time the title "elder" is used it does not mean "one of the first generation of Christians," for Aristion to whom the title is refused was that; it does not mean merely one holding the office of presbyter, for then the phrase "*the* elder" would have no meaning. What remains but that the second John had the same right to the title as Andrew, Peter, and the rest to whom it is given in the beginning of the sentence?

Hence while we own the Eusebian interpretation of Papias to be a possible one, we are unable to see that it is the only possible one; and therefore while willing to receive the hypothesis of two Johns, if it will help to explain any difficulty, we do not think the evidence strong enough to establish it as an historical fact; and we frankly own that if it were not for deference to better judges, we should unite with Keim in relegating, though in a different way, this "Doppelgänger" of the apostle to the region of ghostland. [G.S.]

Joannes (504), surnamed *Climacus*, *Scholasticus*, or *Sinaita*. At the age of 16 he entered the monastery of Mount Sinai, subsequently became an anchoret, and at 75 abbat of Mount Sinai. At the entreaty of John abbat of Raïthu he now composed his works, the *Scala Paradisi* and the *Liber ad Pastorem*; from the title (κλῖμαξ) of the first of these he gained his name of Climacus (Climakos). It contains his experiences in the spiritual life, with instructions for the attainment of a higher degree of holiness, and is dedicated to the abbat of Raïthu who afterwards wrote a commentary upon it (*Patr. Gk.* lxxxviii. 1211-1248). Returning into solitude, John died at an advanced age early in the 7th cent. Boll. *Acta SS.* Mart. iii. 834; Migne, *u.s.* 631-1210; a new ed. of the Gk. text of his works was pub. in 1883 at Constantinople by Sophronius Eremites; Surius, *de Probatis Sanct. Historiis*, Mar. 30. [I.G.S.]

Joannes (507) Saba, a native of Nineveh, fl. in 6th cent.; an orthodox monk of Dilaita or Daliatha, a small town on the W. bank of the Euphrates. His works are 30 discourses and 48 epistles, of which Syriac and Arabic MSS. exist in the Roman libraries. Though abounding in digressions, the style is marked by persuasive eloquence. They are headed: "On the divine gifts and spiritual solaces vouchsafed to monks for their comfort and delight." Assem. *Bib. Or.* i. 433-444, iii. i. 103, 4; Bickell, *Consp. Syr.* p. 26. [C.J.B.]

Joannes (509), called *of Bêth-Rabbân* or *Bêthnarsi*, disciple and successor in the 6th cent. of Jacobus the founder of the monastery of Bêth-Haba. Jesujab, bp. of Nineveh, stated that Joannes had been a monk 70 years before his departure from Bêth-Haba; 30 years he had lived as a solitary, 40 with Jacobus as a coenobite. Joannes was for some time in the monastery of Bêth-Rabbân, which was subject to the same abbat as Bêth-Haba. Ebedjesu (*ap.* Assem. *Bibl. Or.* III. i. 72) states that he wrote a commentary on Ex., Lev., Num., Job, Jer., Ezk., and Prov., also certain tracts against Magi, Jews, and heretics. He also wrote prayers for Rogation days, a prayer on the death of Chosroes I. (d. 579), and on a plague which befel Nisibis, besides paracletic addresses for each order in the church (*i.e.* metrical discourses read in the office of the dead), a book of questions relating to O. and N. T., psalms, hymns, and chants. One of his hymns is in the *Mosul Breviary*, p. 61, and in a MS. in the Brit. Mus. (Wright, *Cat.* p. 135). Rosen and Forshall (*Cat. MSS.* xii. 3 n.) mention another hymn of his. Cf. also Lelong, *Bibl. Sacr.* ii. 794. [C.J.B.]

Joannes (520), surnamed *Moschus* and *Eucratas* (also *Everatas* and *Eviratus*, corruptions of Eucratas as Fabricius remarks), a monk, author of *Pratum Spirituale*, *c.* 620. The materials of his Life are to be collected from his book (which exhibits no historical arrangement), a brief notice by Photius (*Cod.* 199) and a Greek Vatican MS. of which Migne has printed a Latin version entitled *Elogium Auctoris*. This document extends the chronological material, and purports to have been composed while the laura of St. Sabas in Palestine was standing.

Photius states that Moschus commenced the recluse life in the monastery of St. Theodosius, perhaps *c.* 575. In the *Pratum* Moschus is found at two monasteries named after two Theodosii, near Antioch and Jerusalem respectively. The one intended by Photius is a laura founded *c.* 451 by the younger St. Theodosius a little E. of Jerusalem (Boll. *Acta SS.* Jan. i. 683). The *Pratum* (c. 92) shews Moschus at this spot, described as "in the desert of the holy city," Gregory being archimandrite. In the reign of Tiberius (*Prat.* 112) John Moschus was sent by his superior on monastic business with a companion, Sophronius Sophista (said to have been afterwards patriarch of Jerusalem), to Egypt and Oasis. This circumstance, unnoticed by Photius, is assigned by the *Elogium* to the beginning of the reign of Tiberius (*i.e.* 578). The absence was perhaps temporary, and Moschus's more protracted wanderings in Egypt may be assigned to a much later day. His Palestine life lasted more than 25 years, and Sophronius Sophista is frequently mentioned as his companion, once with a remark that it was "before he renounced the world." Photius states that he began monastic life at St. Theodosius, he afterwards resided with the monks of the Jordan desert and in the new laura of St. Sabas. The *Pratum* fills up this outline. The laura of Pharon (Φαρών, Φαρῶν, Φαρᾶ, Pharan in the Latin version) was his residence for ten years (40). It was within burying distance of Jerusalem (42), and near the laura of Calamon and that of the Towers of Jordan (40). The laura of Calamon where Moschus visited was near Jordan (157, 163). Another ten years (67) he resided at the laura of Aeliotae. This also was near Jordan (134) and still under the rule of its founder Antonius (66). Moschus was at Jerusalem at the consecration of the patriarch Amos (149), probably therefore A.D. 594 (Le Quien, *Or. Chr.* iii. 246); he records having ascended from "holy Gethsemane" to the "holy mount of Olives" (187). He resided at the laura of St. Sabas, called New Laura (3,128) near the Dead Sea (53), and a few miles E. of St. Theodosius (Boll. *u.s.*). He visited the μονή of the eunuchs near "holy Jordan" (135-137), the xenodochium of the fathers at Ascalon (189), and Scythopolis (50). That he held the office of a κανόναρχος is a mistake of Fabricius, citing *Prat.* 50, where it is a narrator, not Moschus, who thus describes himself. From the wilderness of Jordan and the New Laura, says Photius, John went to Antioch and its neighbourhood, the *Elogium* adding that this occurred when the Persians attacked the Romans because of the murder (Nov. 27, 602) of the emperor Maurice and his children. In 603 Chosroes declared war against Phocas. The *Pratum* shews Moschus at Antioch or Theopolis (88, 89) and at Seleucia while Theodorus was bp. (79); but as this bp. is not otherwise known we get no date (Le Quien, *Or. Chr.* ii. 780). He visited the μοναστήριον (also μονή) of the elder St. Theodosius, on the Rhosicus Scopulus, a mountain promontory between Rhosus in the gulf of Issus and Seleucia (80-86, 95, 99). At a village six miles from Rhosus, in the seventh indiction (*i.e.* between Sept. 1, 604, and Aug. 31, 605), he heard the story of Joannes Humilis. From those parts, says Photius, he went to Alexandria and Oasis and the neighbouring deserts. This was his principal visit to Egypt, the only one noticed by Photius and the most prominent one in the *Elogium*, which states his reason for leaving Syria to have been the invasion of the empire by the Persians, *i.e.* when Chosroes overran N. Syria in and after 605 (as detailed by Rawlinson, *Seventh Monarchy*, 501, 502). At Alexandria Moschus remained eight years (as the Latin version renders χρόνους ὀκτώ, *Prat.* 13 *fin.*) in the μοναστήριον of Palladius (69-73). The names of monastic localities in and about Alexandria occur in *Prat.* 60, 105, 110, 111, 145, 146, 162, 177, 184, 195. There are recorded also visits to the Thebaid cities of Antinous and Lycus (44, 143, 161), to the laura of Raythu (115, 116, 119) on the Red Sea shore (120, 121), and to Mount Sinai (122, 123). Photius states that from Egypt Moschus went to Rome, touching at some islands en route, and at Rome composed his book. What drove him from Egypt appears in the *Elogium*. The holy places had fallen into the hands of the enemy and the subjects of the empire were terror-stricken. This again assists the chronology; for as the Persians obtained possession of Jerusalem in 615 and in 616 advanced from Palestine and took Alexandria (Rawl. 503, 504), the rumour of their approach would cause the retirement of Moschus in one of those years. The *Pratum* (185) records a visit to Samos. The *Elogium* relates how on his deathbed at Rome he delivered his book to Sophronius, requesting to be buried if possible at Mount Sinai or at the laura of St. Theodosius. Sophronius and 12 fellow-disciples sailed with the body to Palestine, but, hearing at Ascalon that Sinai was beset by Arabs, took it up to Jerusalem (in the beginning of the eighth indiction, *i.e.* c. Sept. 1, 620) and buried it in the cemetery of St. Theodosius.

The work of Moschus consists of anecdotes and sayings collected in the various monasteries he visited, usually of eminent anchorets of his own time, as he states in his dedicatory address to Sophronius; but some whose stories were related belonged to an earlier period, *e.g.* John of Sapsas. The work is now distributed in 219 chapters, but was originally comprised, says Photius, in 304 narrations (διηγήματα). The discrepancy may be partly due to arrangement, as some chaps. (*e.g.* 5, 55, 92, 95, 105) contain 2 or even 3 distinct narrations, introduced by the very word διήγημα. Moschus (*To Sophron.*) compares the character of his worthies to various flowers in a spring meadow, and names his work accordingly Λειμών (*Pratum*). In the time of Photius some called it Νέον Παραδείσιον (*Hortulus Novus*), and it has since been named *Viridarium*, Νέος Παράδεισος (*Novus Paradisus*) and Λειμωνάριον. The title *Pratum Spirituale* apparently originated with the first Latin translator, said by Possevinus to have been Ambrosius Camaldulensis (*ob.* 1439), who translated numerous works of the Greek Fathers (Oudin. iii. 2437). The *Pratum* in this version forms lib. x. of Rosweyd's *Vitae Patrum* (1615), which Migne reprinted in 1850 (*Pat. Lat.* lxxiv.), prefixing to the *Pratum* the *Elogium Auctoris* already described. In 1624 an incomplete Greek text made its appearance, accompanying the Latin, furnished by Fronto Ducaeus in vol. ii. of the *Auctarium* to the 4th ed. of La Bigne's *Magna Bibliotheca Patrum.* In La Bigne's ed. of 1654 it stands in vol. xiii. p. 1057. In 1681 Cotelier (*Eccles. Gr. Mon.* ii. 341) supplied more of the Greek and gave an independent Latin translation of some parts. In 1860 Migne (*Pat. Gk.* lxxxvii. 2814) reprinted the thus augmented Greek, leaving a gap of only three chaps. (121, 122, 132), retaining the Latin of Ambrosius throughout. Other bibliographical particulars, including an account of the Italian and French versions, will be found in Fabricius (*Bibl. Gr.* x. 124, ed. Harles). The authorship of the *Pratum* used sometimes to be attributed to Sophronius, in whose name it is cited by John of Damascus (*de Imagin.* orat. i. 328, ii. 344, iii. 352 in *Patr. Gk.* xciv. 1279, 1315, 1335) and likewise in actio iv. of the seventh synod in 787 (Mansi, xiii. 59). John Moschus and his book are treated by Cave (i. 581) and more fully by Ceillier (xi. 700). Dupin gives an analysis of the *Pratum* for illustrations of church discipline (Eng. trans. 1722, t. ii. p. 11).

Cf. S. Vailhé, *St. Jean Mosch.* in *Echos d'orient*, 1901. [C.H.]

Joannes (564) Philoponus, a "grammaticus" of Alexandria; a distinguished philosopher, a voluminous writer (Suidas, *s.v.* Ἰωάννης Τρ.), and one of the leaders of the Tritheites of the 6th cent. (Sophron. *Ep. Synodic. Co. Const.* A.D. 680; act. xi. in Mansi, xi. 501; Leont. Byzant. *de Sect.* act. v. in Migne, *Patr. Gk.* lxxxvi. i. 1232). From his great industry he acquired the surname of Philoponus. He was a native of Alexandria. His earliest known appearance as an author was in his περὶ αἰδιότητος, a reply to Proclus Diadochus. It shows great dialectic ability and learning, the quotations in it covering the whole range of the literature of his own and previous times (Fabricius, *Bibl. Gr.* ed. Harles, x. 652-654), and is said by Suidas to have been a complete refutation of the great neo-Platonist and to have convicted him of gross ignorance (*s. v.* Πρόκλος).

Apparently about the same time Philoponus was engaged in a controversy with Severus, the deposed bp. of Antioch (Suidas, *s.v.* Ἰωαν; Galland. *Bibl. Vet. Patr.* xii. 376; Cureton, *Fragments*, 212, 245 seq.). To the same period may be assigned a treatise *de Universali et Particulari*, described by Assemani in his catalogue of Syriac MSS. (*Bibl. Or.* i. 613).

At the request of Sergius (ordained patriarch of Antioch by the Monophysites *c.* 540) Philoponus wrote his Διαιτητής, *Arbiter*, the Umpire. It is an attempt to shew that the doctrine which he and his followers held upon the subject of the union of the two natures in the person of our Lord was dialectically necessary. The argument is admirably condensed by Prof. Dorner in his *History of the Development of the Doctrine of the Person of Christ* (Clark's trans. ii. l. 416).

At what period Philoponus distinctly avowed what is known as Tritheism (Eulog. *Patr. Alex. Orat.* Phot. ccxxx. ed. Schott. p. 879) does not clearly appear, but it must have been before the middle of the 6th cent. as Mar Abas, "Primas Orientis" (d. 552) was one of his converts to that doctrine (Assem. *Bibl. Or.* ii. 411). Notwithstanding this, if not because of it, the emperor Justinian sent one of his officers named Stephanus to Alexandria to summon Philoponus to Constantinople "in causâ fidei," but he wrote excusing himself because of age and infirmity. In his letter he urged Justinian to issue an edict prohibiting the discussion of the "two natures."

On the death of Joannes Ascusnaghes, the founder of the Tritheites, his *Demonstrationes* were sent to Philoponus at Alexandria. The latter then wrote a treatise on the subject and sent it to his friend at Constantinople. The Monophysites, finding that this publication brought them into great disrepute, appealed to the emperor Justin II., who had married Sophia, a granddaughter of the empress Theodora, and was known to be favourable to their party. He complied with their request, and the matter was committed to Joannes Scholasticus, who had succeeded Eutychius on his refusal to subscribe the Julianist edict of Justinian, A.D. 565 (Greg. Bar-hebr.; Asseman. *Bibl. Or.* ii. 328).

We hear no more of Philoponus until 568, when, John, patriarch of Constantinople, having delivered a catechetical discourse on the "Holy and consubstantial Trinity," he published a treatise in reply to it. Photius is unsparing in his criticism of this work, charging the author with having perverted the authorities whom he quotes (*Bibl.* lxxv.). Philoponus must now have been very old, but apparently lived some years longer.

During his lifetime the Tritheites appear to have been united under his leadership (Tim. Presb. *Recept. Haer.* in *Patr. Gk.* lxxxvi. i. 62), but after his decease they became divided because of the opinions he had maintained on the resurrection-body, both in his writings against the heathen and in a special work on this subject. This last was in several books, of which Photius speaks in no respectful terms (*Bibl.* xxi. xxiii.), though it found great favour with that section of the Monophysites which persevered in their adherence to Philoponus and with Eutychius the Catholic patriarch of Constantinople. [EUTYCHIUS (18).] Those Tritheites who still followed him were distinguished as Philoponiaci, or Athanasiani because of Athanasius's prominence amongst them (Schonfelder, *Die Tritheiten*, app. to his German trans. of John of Ephesus, 269, 274, 297), while their opponents were called Cononitae, after Conon of Tarsus who wrote a reply to the Περὶ ἀναστάσεως.

Philoponus wrote numerous other works, many of them non-theological. His work *de Aeternitate Mundi* has been ed. by Rabe (Leipz. 1899); his *de Opificis Mundi* by Reichardt (Leipz. 1897), and a *Libellus de Paschale* by Walter (Jena, 1899). [T.W.D.]

Joannes (565) Scythopolita, a scholasticus of Scythopolis in Palestine. Photius had read a work of his in 12 books, *Against Separatists from the Church* or *Against Eutyches and Dioscorus*, written at the request of a patriarch Julianus, probably Julian patriarch of Antioch, A.D. 471-476 (Phot. *Cod.* 95, in *Patr. Gk.* ciii. 339 n). John of Scythopolis was also the author of παραθέσεις or commentaries on the Pseudo-Dionysius, which had a wide circulation for some centuries. Among the Syriac MSS. in the Brit. Mus. there is a Syriac trans. of Dionysius, with an introduction and notes by Phocas bar-Sergius of Edessa, a writer of the 8th cent. The notes are largely a translation of the παραθέσεις (Wright, *Cat. Syr. MSS.* pt. ii. p. 493). Cf. Loofs, *Leontius von Byzanz.* (1887). [T.W.D.]

Jordanis (*Jornandes*, the Gothic name, on his becoming an ecclesiastic was changed to Jordanis, Wattenbach, p. 62), historian of the Goths (and probably bp. of Crotona, in Brutium) in the middle of 6th cent.

I. *Authorities.*—Grimm, *Kleinere Schriften*, iii. 171, etc.; Ebert, *Geschichte der Christlich Lat. Lit.* (Dahn, 1875); *Die Könige der Germanen*, ii. 243-260, for Jordanis's use of words of constitutional importance; *Anekdoton Holderi* (Hermann Usener, Bonn, 1877); and for other authorities, Wattenbach, p. 55.

II. *Writings.*—His only works of which we have certain knowledge are the *de Breviatione Chronicorum* (more commonly but wrongly called *de Regnorum Successione*) and the *de Getarum Origine et Rebus Gestis.*

(1) The *de Breviatione Chronicorum* (Mura-

tori, *Scriptores Rerum Ital.* i. 222-242) is a compendium of the history of the world, of little value, and only important as indicating the strong feeling of the Goth Jordanis that the power of the Roman empire was to last to the end of time.

(2) The *de Getarum Origine et Rebus Gestis* is one of the most important works written during the period of the Teutonic settlements in Western Europe. In amount of matter it may equal about 20 pages of this Dict. Its contents are most conveniently arranged under four heads (cf. Ebert. p. 532).

1 (c. i. 13). The work opens with a geographical account of the world and in particular of N. Europe and the island "Scandza." Jordanis then identifies the Goths with the Scythians, whose country he describes, and praises their learning and bravery. He then recounts their wars with the Egyptians and Amazons, and, identifying the Goths with the Getae, describes the deeds of Telephus and Tomyris. Cyrus, Xerxes, Alexander the Great, Caesar and Tiberius are mentioned. With chap. 18 he suddenly passes to the devastation of the banks of the Danube by the Goths and their victory over the Romans. He then pauses to give fuller details about the royal Gothic race of the Amali.

2 (c. 14-23). He carries the genealogy of the Amali down to Mathasuentha, the granddaughter of Theodoric and widow of Vitigis, who had just married, as he tells us, Germanus brother of Justinian. He then returns to the Goths and their movement into Moesia and Thracia. Claiming for the emperor Maximus a Gothic father, he thus raises the Goths to high honour. The deeds of Ostrogotha are then related, the victory over the Gepidae, the expeditions to Asia Minor, and Geberich's conquest of the Vandals. After Geberich came Hermanaric conqueror of the Heneti and many other tribes.

3 (c. 24-47). This division begins with an account of the Huns, their victory over the Goths, and the death of Hermanaric. He traces the separation of the Visigoths from the Ostrogoths, and follows their history. He shortly recounts Alaric's invasion of Italy, and introduces the story of Attila's invasion of Gaul and defeat. The battle of Châlons is described at considerable length. At the close of the section he describes the subjugation of Italy by Odoacer and the deposition of Augustulus.

4 (c. 48-60). Jordanis now returns to the Ostrogoths, once more mentions the defeat of Hermanaric, and this leads him to speak of the death of Attila. He describes the movement of the Ostrogoths into Pannonia, the reign of Theodemir and the birth of Theodoric. The dealings of Theodoric with Zeno, his entrance into Italy and his victory over Odoacer are recounted. The outline of the fortunes of the Goths in Italy is related very briefly, and the work closes with the captivity of Vitigis, and another mention of the marriage of Mathasuentha with Germanus.

His own words in the dedication of the *de Getarum Origine* or History of the Goths, convey an impression that he had written an abstract from memory of a three days' reading of the History of the Goths by Cassiodorius, adding extracts of his own from Latin and Greek writers, and that the beginning, middle, and end of the work were his own composition. It might certainly have been supposed that the preface at least was the composition of Jordanis himself. But the most convincing evidence of the writer's want of originality has been shewn by the discovery made by Von Sybel with reference to this preface (Schmidt, *Zeitschrift für Geschichte*, vii. 288). It is largely a literal copy of the introduction by Rufinus to his trans. of Origen's Comm. on Romans.

If the general view of the *History of the Goths* by Jordanis, first propounded by Schirren, and afterwards worked out by Köpke, Bessel, and others, be true, the place of Jordanis as a historian is but low. He does not acknowledge several authorities whom he largely uses and displays an array of authorities whom he only knows at second-hand. But it must be remembered that Jordanis does not claim originality, except under the clause in the preface ("initium finemque et plura in medio mea dictione permiscens"). The substratum of the whole work must still be ascribed to Cassiodorius. Is it, then, possible to disentangle the work of Cassiodorius from the setting in which Jordanis has placed it? A complete separation can, from the circumstances of the case, hardly be possible. Yet we may be tolerably sure that, though many of the extracts bear the traces of the treatment and colouring of Jordanis, enough remains of the lost work to bring us in to close contact with the mind and words of Cassiodorius, and, to a certain extent, to enable us to understand his purpose in his great work.

The history of the Goths was certainly completed before the death of Athalaric in 534 (*Variae*, ix. 25); Köpke and others suppose *c.* 533. Since the discovery of the *Anekdoton Holderi*, however, it has become practically certain that the Gothic History of Cassiodorius was composed some years before 533; probably not later than 521.

In two passages of his *Variae* Cassiodorius refers to his Gothic History. By far the more important passage, of which nearly every word helps to shew his purpose, is in ix. 25, where Cassiodorius describes his History in a letter addressed nominally by king Athalaric to the senate in 534.

Cassiodorius clearly shews that his primary object was not literary, but political. He saw the growing antagonism between Goths and Romans and Theodoric's efforts to lessen it. He saw the king trying to combine the old and the new elements and to form a kingdom in which both could live with mutual respect. He determined to assist by his writing his master's plans. He would try to draw the Goths and Romans together by shewing that both nations were alike honourable for the antiquity of their race and the glory of their history. He would tell the Goths of the greatness of the Roman empire, with whom they fought in ancient days, and would shew the Romans that the kingly family of the Amali was as noble as any Roman house. No one was better fitted than he to write a history of the Goths. His real knowledge of ancient writers, his constant opportunities of converse with the king and Gothic nobles, his father's share and his own in all the later or contemporary events, provided him with ample material. In the earlier part of the work we can clearly see from Jordanis how the political theory of Cassiodorius was worked out. He adopted the belief that the Getae and the Goths were the same nation. Further, he accepted the identity of the Goths with the Scythians, a theory stated by several Greek writers. Thus the Goths were brought into contact or conflict with the great nations of antiquity and even the Amazons appear as Gothic women. Yet even with all the notices he could collect from Greek or Roman authorities and the stories and sagas he heard at the court of Ravenna, his stock of accurate information about the early history of the Goths cannot have been large. The very theory with which he wrote shews that much must be accepted with reserve.

Thirty years later the Gothic bishop, in his adaptation of the work, shewed that he rested his hopes of the future quite as much on the Roman empire as on the Gothic race itself. However little individuality as a historian Jordanis may have had, it lay with him to choose and adapt his extracts from Cassiodorius in accordance with his own feelings, and there is enough of himself in the work to enable us to catch something of his spirit. For him the end of the great struggle between Goths and Romans had come; the war between Totila and Belisarius, or Narses, which was yet going on, had no supreme interest. The race of the Amali, with which he was connected and on which all his hopes were centred, had ceased to rule the Goths. His desires for the future rested rather on the union of the brother of the emperor with the granddaughter of Theodoric than on the issue of a struggle which he probably and rightly thought hopeless. His Catholic sympathies, rejecting the idea of an Arian ruler, and his family pride, alike contributed to this result. Three times he alludes to the marriage of Mathasuentha, widow of Vitigis (with whom she had been brought captive to Constantinople), to Germanus, brother of the emperor Justinian (cc. 14, 48, 60). In c. 60 he tells how Germanus died, leaving an infant son: "Item Germanus: in quo conjuncta Aniciorum gens cum Amala stirpe spem adhuc utriusque generis Domino praestante promittit."

Jordanis was the first since Tacitus to treat the history of the Teutonic nations from their side. The eternity of the Roman empire had impressed itself on the mind of Jordanis. The idea, therefore, that the Goths were equally learned and ancient must have been a support to him (and others like him) when Theodoric was ruling almost as a miniature emperor in Italy. But the thought of a union between the imperial family and the Amali could alone satisfactorily reconcile his hopes for the great family to which he belonged and his belief in the church and empire of Rome. This traditional belief in the empire and church was destined never to be altogether broken in Italy. After two centuries of struggles between rival principles in church and state the next Italian ecclesiastic who attained importance as a historian, Paulus Diaconus, himself, like Jordanis, of Teutonic race, was able to witness the return of imperial power of old Rome and to have friendly intercourse with the new Teutonic emperor. To Jordanis the first Teutonic historian of a Teutonic race such a possibility was unknown, and he could only fix fruitless hopes on a union of the Greek and the Goth to solve his difficulties. For the spirit of the age and times which we thus seem to gather from Jordanis's work we owe him a debt of gratitude, and also for his preservation, if only in a broken form, of fragments from the greatest work of Theodoric's great secretary.

The most important editions of the History of the Goths are: Muratori, *Scriptores Rev. Ital.* i. 187-241 (Medial. 1723). Migne, *Patr. Cursus*, lxix. Appendix to works of Cassiodorius. Jordanis, *de Getarum Origine et Rebus Gestis*, ed. C. A. Closs (Stuttg. 1861). In the *Monumenta Germaniae* the two works of Jordanis are undertaken by Mommsen himself. *Neues Archiv. D. G. F. ältere Deutschen Geschichtskunde*, ii. 5.

III. *Life.*—Jordanis tells us that his grandfather was notary to Candac, chief of the Alani in Moesia, that he himself was a notary before becoming an ecclesiastic, that he was of the Gothic race and apparently connected with the royal family of the Amali. We know from his own writings no more, and nothing further can be absolutely certain. But a discovery, first made by Cassel, has led to an extremely important and very highly probable conjecture about his identity. The name of one Jordanes Crotonensis, bp. of Crotona (now Cotrone) in Bruttium is found, with those of several other bishops, appended to a document sometimes called the Damnatio Theodori, issued by pope Vigilius in Aug. 551 at Constantinople. If this should be our Jordanis, it becomes exceedingly probable that the Vigilius to whom the *Chronicle* of Jordanis is dedicated and sent, along with the History of the Goths, is pope Vigilius. Vigilius was pope from 537 to 555. He had been made pope by the influence of Belisarius at Rome, at the request of the empress Theodora. After the issue of the Three Chapters by Justinian, which Vigilius apparently dared not sign when in Italy, the pope was summoned to Constantinople, which he reached on Christmas Day, 547. He was retained at Constantinople, or in the neighbourhood, for seven years, till he at last obtained permission from Justinian to return to Italy. At Constantinople he was much persecuted by the emperor and his party, who tried to force him to sign a confession of faith in accordance with their views. He was bold enough to excommunicate the bp. of Caesarea, and then, fearing the emperor's wrath, took sanctuary in the basilica of St. Peter in Constantinople. While in this church with his companions, and, among others, several Italian bishops, he issued (Aug. 551) the document in which the name of Jordanes, bp. of Cotrona, is found.

Several considerations make it exceedingly probable that Jordanis wrote his work at Constantinople. His almost complete ignorance of the later and contemporary events in Italy is thus explained, and his detailed acquaintance, shewn in several passages, with the affairs of the empire accounted for.

The bp. of Cotrona lived not far from the monastery in Bruttium (monasterium Vivariense) to which Cassiodorius had retired after his active life as a statesman. Here Jordanis first saw the 12 books of the Gothic history, and was allowed by the steward of Cassiodorius a second perusal of the work. When he was, as we presume, with the pope in Constantinople he was suddenly called upon to write his Gothic history, and, as he tells us, had to make the best of what materials he had at hand or could remember. The *de Getarum Origine et Rebus Gestis* was the result. [A.H.D.A.]

Josephus (2), catholicos of Armenia (Le Quien, *Or. Christ.* i. 1079). St. Martin (*Mém. sur l'Arm.* i. 437) places him between Mesrob and Melidé, giving his dates as 441-452, but these figures do not represent his place in the series accurately. The Persian king contemporary with him was Isdigerd II., and the governor of Armenia was an Armenian Christian Vasag, prince of the Siounians (442-452). Joseph was one of the band of Armenian scholars trained under Mesrob and Isaac the Great and afterwards in the schools of Athens and Constantinople. [MESROBES.] He returned to Armenia probably *c.* 434. His patriarchate occurred at a most critical period, when Isdigerd II. was endeavouring to supplant the Christianity of Armenia by Zoroastrianism. For a full contemporary account of this see Elisha Vartabed's *Hist. of Vartan,* trans. from the Armenian by Neumann and Langlois. Isdigerd issued a proclamation to the Armenians—one of the utmost valuable ancient Zoroastrian documents we possess. A reply was issued in 450 by a synod of 17 bishops held at Ardashad. The name of Joseph, bp. of Ararat, heads the subscriptions (Neum. 13, 14, 87), the province of Ararat being one of 15 into which Armenia was divided. This seems Joseph's first appearance in these events. The reply is given in full by Elisha; for the spirit of it see ISDIGERD II. Exasperated by that bold manifesto, the king ordered the leading Armenian princes to appear before him, and they, depositing a confession of their faith with Joseph, obeyed (*ib.* 21). In the royal capital on the feast of Easter, 450, they were summoned into the king's presence, and peremptorily ordered to adore the sun on its rising the next day. Finding Isdigerd inexorable, they feigned compliance, and Isdigerd, accepting the act as a formal submission of their country, sent them home accompanied by a band of magi, who, supported by a large military force, were to instruct the Armenians in the Zoroastrian religion and laws. On the appearance of this armed mission the bishops went among their flocks exhorting them to resist. The people were resolved, and a Holy League was formed. On behalf of his distressed country Joseph appealed to the emperor Theodosius II., but shortly afterwards (July 28, 450) Theodosius died, and Marcian his successor would not help (*ib.* 36, 37). The Armenian Christians nevertheless assembled in arms, 60,000 in number, among them Joseph, Leontius the priest, many other priests and a multitude of deacons. On June 2, 451, at the Dekhmud, a tributary of the Araxes (St. Martin, i. 41), led by their prince Vartan they were disastrously defeated (Neum. 51). A fortress where the priests had taken refuge fell. Joseph and Leontius, when about to be put to death, asked to be sent to the king, hoping to make terms for their people. They were sent, but would not waver in their steadfastness (*ib.* 63, 66). Thus much Elisha relates of Joseph in his 7th chap., his last as Neumann believes. In an 8th chap. added by Langlois in 1867, and in another Armenian writer, Lazarus of Barb (c. 48 in Langlois, ii. 315), it is stated that in the 6th year of Isdigerd (*i.e.* 455) and on the 25th of the month Hroditz, the patriarch Joseph, Sahag, bp. of Reschdouni, the priests Arsenius, Leontius, Mousché, and the deacon Kadchadch were executed in the province of Abar, near Révan, a village of the Moks. Lazarus (*l.c.*) records his dying words. On the position of Abar see Langlois (t. ii. p. 186, note 1), and Neumann (p. 77, note 18). [LEONTIUS (**74**).] [G.T.S.]

Joshua (1) **Stylites,** a Syrian monk, a native of Edessa, entered the monastery of Zuenin near Amida in Mesopotamia. After some years he determined to imitate St. Simeon and live the rest of his days on a column, from which he derives his distinguishing name. Before this he had written in 507 the history of his times from 495, entitled, *History of the Calamities which befel Edessa, Amida, and all Mesopotamia.* A full description, with quotations from the original Syriac, is given by Assemani (*Bibl. Or.* i. 260). It was published at Leipzig in 1878, in the *Abhandlungen für die Kunde des Morgenlandes*, in the original Syriac, with a French trans. by Abbé Paulin Martin. The translator describes it as the most ancient history extant in Syriac, and specially valuable because of Joshua's personal share in the events. His text corrects many omissions and mistakes in Assemani's abstract. He fixes its composition between 510-515, and classes Joshua as a Monophysite, while Assemani regarded him as orthodox. [I.G.S. AND G.T.S.]

Jovianus (1), **Flavius,** Christian emperor from June 27, 363, to Feb. 16, 364. The authorities for the Life of Jovian are generally the same as those for that of Julian. The fifth oration of Themistius, and certain tracts printed among the works of St. Athanasius, are important for the special points of his edict of toleration and dealings with the Arians. There is a useful Life of Jovian by the Abbé J. P. R. de la Bléterie (Paris, 1748, 2 vols., and 1776, 1 vol.), containing also a translation of some of Julian's works.

Life.—Jovian was born *c.* A.D. 331. His father, the count Varronianus, was an inhabitant of the territory of Singidunum (Belgrade) in Moesia, the country which gave birth to so many emperors (Victor, *Epit.* 68). At the time of his unexpected elevation he was the first of the imperial bodyguard, a position of no very great distinction (Amm. xxv. 5, 4).

Julian died of a wound at midnight, between June 26 and 27, 363, in the midst of his retreat from Persia, leaving his army surrounded by active enemies. Early in the morning the generals and chief officers met to choose an emperor. Saturninus Secundus Sallustius, the prefect of the East, a moderate heathen, who was respected also by Christians, was elected; but he refused the dangerous honour, and Jovian was chosen.

The new emperor was a Christian and a firm adherent of the Nicene faith. He had, indeed, some claim to the honours of a confessor under his predecessor, but Julian, it is said, did not wish to part with so good an officer (Socr. iii. 22). He was in other respects a man of no very marked ability (Amm. xxv. 5, 4; Eutropius, x. 17). He was a generous, bluff, and hearty soldier, popular with his companions, fond of jest and merriment, and addicted to the pleasures common in the camp (Vict. *Epit.* 6; Amm. xxv. 10, 15). He had a bright and open face, always cheerful, and lighted with a pair of clear grey eyes. His figure was extremely tall and his gait rather heavy, and it was long before an imperial wreath could be found to fit him. He was only a moderate scholar, and in this and many other points was a strong contrast to Julian (Amm. *l.c.*).

Though he was a sincere believer, we cannot credit the statement of Rufinus that he would not accept the empire till he had obliged all his soldiers to become Christians (*H. E.* ii. 1). But the greater part of the army did, no doubt, return without difficulty to the profession of faith to which they had been accustomed under Constantius. The labarum again became their standard; and Jovian's coins present, besides the ☧, the new and striking type (now so familiar) of the ball surmounted by the cross, the symbol of the church dominating the world (see Eckhel, *Num. Vet.* viii. p. 147). Ammianus notes that sacrifices were offered, and entrails of victims inspected on the morning of Jovian's inauguration to decide on the movements of the army (xxv. 6, 1). But directly the reins of power were in his hands such things apparently ceased at once.

We need not describe at length the perplexities of the Roman generals in their endeavours to escape from Persia, and the protracted negotiations with Sapor, to whose terms Jovian felt it imperative to submit (Eutrop. *Brev.* x. 17; Amm. xxv. 7, 8). The terms were ignoble and humiliating: the cession of the five Mesopotamian provinces which Galerius had added to the Roman dominions, and of the fortresses of Nisibis and Singara, the former of which had been the bulwark of the empire since the reign of Mithridates. No less disgraceful was the sacrifice of Arsaces, king of Armenia, the firm ally of the Romans and a Christian prince, allied to the house of Constantine by his marriage with Olympias (Amm. *ib.* 9-12; cf. Greg. Naz. *Or.* v. 15). But probably no better terms could have been obtained without the loss of nearly all the army.

After crossing the Tigris with difficulty, the Roman forces marched for six days through very desert country to the fortress of Ur, where they were met by a convoy of provisions (Amm. xxv. 8, 16). The scenes at Nisibis were heartrending when the inhabitants were bidden leave their homes. Jovian, however, was firm (xxv. 9, 2). The Persian standard was hoisted on the citadel, in token of the change of ownership and the weeping and broken-hearted people were settled in the suburb of Amida. The emperor proceeded to Antioch. The remains of Julian were sent to be buried at Tarsus, where he had intended to reside on his return from the Persian war.

The consternation of the pagans at the news of the death of Julian and the accession of Jovian was as sudden and as marvellous as the triumph of the Christians. All Antioch made holiday, churches, chapels, and even theatres being filled with cries of joy, and taunts at the discomfiture of the heathen party. "Where are the prophecies and foolish Maximus? God has conquered and His Christ" (Theod. iii. 28). St. Gregory was writing his bitter and brilliant invectives at Nazianzus, where but a few months before the Christian population had trembled at the approach of Julian (*Orat.* iv. and v., the στηλιτευτικοί: they were probably *not* delivered from the pulpit; see p. 75 of the Benedictine ed. Paris, 1778). Some acts of violence were committed, especially in the destruction of temples and altars, and more were apprehended. At Constantinople a prefect of Julian's appointment was in danger of his life (Sievers, *Libanius*, p. 128; cf. Lib. *Epp.* 1179, 1186, 1489). Heathen priests, philosophers, rhetoricians, and magicians hid themselves in fear, or were maltreated by the populace. Libanius himself was in peril at Babylon, and was accused before Jovian of never ceasing his ill-omened lamentations for his dead friend, instead of wishing good fortune to the new reign (Liban. *de Vitâ suâ*, vol. i. pp. 93, 94, ed. Reiske; cf. Sievers, *Libanius*, pp. 128 ff.; Chastel, *Destruction du Paganisme*, pp. 154, 155, who, however, is not accurate in all details). Libanius was saved by the intervention of a Cappadocian friend, who told the emperor that he would gain nothing by putting him to death, as his orations would survive him and become current. This looks as if his *Monody* was already written and known at least by report, though probably only delivered to a select circle of friends. The *Epitaphius* was probably not completed and published till five or six years later (Sievers, p. 132).

To appease this disturbed state of feeling Jovian issued an edict that all his subjects should enjoy full liberty of conscience, though he forbade the practice of magic (Themistis *Oratio*, v. pp. 68-70; cf. Chastel, p. 156). This was probably one of the earliest of his laws. It is impossible to reconcile the positive statements of Themistius with that of Sozomen, that Jovian ordered that Christianity should be the only religion of his subjects (Soz. vi. 3); and Socrates, who quotes the oration of Themistius, says that all the temples were shut, and that the blood of sacrifices ceased to flow (iii. 24). Jovian may very probably have *strongly recommended* the Christian faith in his edicts without pretending to enforce it, and the cessation of sacrifice seems to have been a popular rather than a directly imperial movement (the passage in Libanius's *Monodia*, vol. i. p. 509, appears to refer to *Constantius* rather than Jovian; and that in the *Epitaphius*, pp. 619, 620, was probably written later). Jovian allowed the philosophers Maximus and Prisan, the intimate friends of Julian, to enjoy the honours they had received during Julian's reign (Eus. *Vita Maximi*, p. 58, ed. Boissonade, 1822).

The reaction under Jovian, so far as it was directed by his orders, consisted rather in favours granted to Christians than in acts of oppression towards paganism. The edict of toleration was perhaps issued at Antioch, which he reached some time in Oct., having been at Edessa on Sept. 27 (*Cod. Theod.* vii. 4, 9=*Cod. Just.* xii. 37, 2; it is omitted by accident in Hänel's *Series Chronologia*, p. 1654, but is given by Godefroy and Kruger). He restored the immunities of the clergy, and the stipends paid to the virgins and widows of the church, and such part of the allowance of corn which Julian had withdrawn as the state of public finances allowed (Soz. vi. 3; Theod. i. 11, iv. 4). A count named Magnus, who had burned the church of Berytus in the late reign, was ordered to rebuild it, and nearly lost his head (Theod. iv. 22, p. 180 B). At the same time probably Jovian issued a law condemning to death those who solicited or forced into marriage the virgins of the church (*Cod. Theod.* ix. 25, 2, this law is addressed to Secundus, prefect of the East, and is dated at Antioch, Feb. 19, a day or two after Jovian's death according to most accounts. Either we must read *Ancyrae* or suppose the month wrongly given, see the commentators *ad loc.*).

Jovian is remembered in church history on account of his connexion with St. Athanasius more than any other of his actions. The death of Julian was, it is said, revealed to his companion Theodore of Tabenne, and the bishop took courage to return to Alexandria. Here he received a letter from the new emperor praising him for his constancy under all persecutions, reinstating him in his functions, and desiring his prayers (Athan. *Op.* i. 622= vol. ii. col. 812, ed. Migne). Jovian in another letter (no longer extant) desired him to draw up a statement of the Catholic faith. He accordingly summoned a council, and wrote a synodal letter, stating and confirming the Nicene Creed (*l.c.* and Theod. iv. 3). Armed with this, he set sail for Antioch (Sept. 5, 363), where he met with a most gracious reception. The leaders of other ecclesiastical parties had been able to gain little beyond expressions of the emperor's desire for unity and toleration. The Arians, and especially bp. Lucius, who had been set up as a rival of Athanasius, followed Jovian about in his daily rides in hopes of prejudicing him against the champion of Catholicity (*l.c.* pp. 624, 625=vol. ii. col. 819 ff.). The bluff emperor reining up his steed to receive their petitions, and his rough and sensible answers mixed with Latin words to their old and worn-out charges and irrelevant pleas, stand out with singular vividness. We can almost hear him saying, "Feri, feri," to his guard, in order to be rid of his troublesome suitors.

Little seems to have been effected by Athanasius with the Arians at Antioch, and Jovian was disappointed in his endeavour to terminate the schism between the Catholic bps. Meletius and Paulinus (Basil, *Ep.* 89, vol. iii. p. 258, ed. Gaume). A coldness ensued between Meletius and Athanasius, and the latter was led to recognize the bishop of the Eustathians as the true head of the Antiochene church on his making a declaration of orthodoxy. Soon after this he returned in triumph to Alexandria.

Jovian quitted Antioch in Dec., and came by forced marches to Tarsus, where he adorned the tomb of Julian. At Tyana, in Cappadocia, he received the news that Malarich had declined the charge of Gaul, and that Jovinus still continued in his own position, but faithful to the new regime. Jovian also learned that his father-in-law Lucillianus had been murdered at Rheims in an accidental mutiny of the Batavian cohorts (Amm. xxv. 10; Zos. iii. 35). The deputies of the Western armies saluted their new sovereign as he descended from Mount Taurus. With them was Valentinian, so soon to be his successor, whom he appointed captain of the second division of scutarii (Amm. xxv. 10, 9).

Another and a heavier blow followed—the news of the loss of his father Varronianus, whom he had for some time hoped to associate with himself in the consulship of the ensuing year. The loss was softened by the arrival of his wife Charito and infant son Varronianus, who, it was determined, should fill the place destined for his grandfather. The inauguration of the new consuls took place on Jan. 1 at Ancyra (Amm. xxv. 10, 11; cf. Themist. *Or.* v. p. 71). Zonaras (*Annal.* xiii. 14) says that Charito never saw her husband after his elevation, but this seems a mistake (see De Broglie, iv. p. 485 n.). The oration of Themistius was, it seems, delivered at this time.

Jovian still pushed on, notwithstanding the inclemency of the weather, and arrived at an obscure place called Dadastané, about halfway between Ancyra and Nicaea. About Feb. 16, after a heavy supper, he went to bed in an apartment recently built. The plaster being still damp, a brazier of charcoal was brought in to warm the air, and in the morning he was found dead in his bed, after a short reign of only 8 months. (Amm. xxv. 10, 12, 13, describes his death; the date is variously given as Mar. 16, 17, and 18; see Clinton.) He was buried at Constantinople, and after 10 days' interval Valentinian succeeded.

Owing to the shortness of Jovian's reign, inscriptions relating to him (other than those on milestones) are very rare, but there is one over the portal of the church of Panaghia at Palaeopolis in Corfu. It may be found in the *Corpus Inscr. Graec.* vol. iv. 8608, from various authorities, and was also copied on the spot by bp. Wordsworth of Lincoln in 1832, who alone gives the first line: "*αὔτη πύλη τοῦ κυρίου δίκεοι εἰσελεύσοντε* [i.e. *δίκαιοι εἰσελεύσονται*] *ἐν αὐτῇ.* [J.W.]

Jovinianus (2), condemned as a heretic by synods at Rome and Milan *c.* 390. Our fullest information about him is derived from St. Jerome, who wrote two books, *adversus Jovinianum*. From these we learn that he had been a monk, living austerely, but adopted certain views which led him to substitute luxury in dress and personal habits and food for the asceticism of the convent, the opinions ascribed to him by Jerome being: (1) A virgin is no better as such than a wife in the sight of God. (2) Abstinence is no better than a thankful partaking of food. (3) A person baptized with the Spirit as well as with water cannot sin. (4) All sins are equal. (5) There is but one grade of punishment and one of reward in the future world. We learn further from St. Augustine (lib. i. *contra Julian.* c. ii.), and from the letter of the Milanese synod to Siricius (Ambros. *Op. Ep.* 42), that Jovinian maintained tenets as to the Virgin Mary's virginity in giving birth to Jesus Christ in opposition to the orthodox view. He was living at Rome (Hieron. *Prolog. adv. Pelag.*), and wrote in Latin (*ib.* lib. ii. *adv. Jovin.* § 37). Certain Christians at Rome, amongst them Jerome's correspondent Pammachius, brought the book to the notice of Siricius, bp. of Rome, who called a meeting of his clergy and condemned the new heresy. Hoping for protection from Theodosius, who was now at Milan, Jovinian and his friends proceeded thither; but Siricius sent three of his presbyters with a letter of warning to the church at Milan. Ambrose responded warmly to Siricius, and with eight other bishops endorsed the sentence passed by the Roman church. In a letter by Ambrose in the name of the synod of Milan to Siricius conveying this judgment, it is stated that the emperor "execrated" the impiety of the Jovinianists, and that all at Milan who had seen them shunned them like a contagion. In 409 Jerome, writing against Vigilantius, refers to Jovinian as having recently died.

The heresies of Jovinian would be especially obnoxious to the great ecclesiastics of his time, who were wont to insist strongly upon the merit of virginity and of abstinence. Jerome writes against Jovinian, he says, in answer to an appeal made by holy brethren at Rome who desired that he should crush the Epicurus of the Christians with evangelical and apostolic vigour. The vigour of the reply was a little too much even for them (*quod nimius fuerim*). His praise of virginity seemed to do some wrong to marriage. Accordingly Pammachius (*prudenter et amanter*, as Jerome acknowledges) thought it best to suppress the copies of Jerome's answer. But the books had already circulated too much to be recalled. Whatever Jerome wrote was seized upon by friends or enemies, and quickly made public (*Ep.* 48, 49). Jovinian is not accused of any worse immorality than an indulgence in good living, which was probably exaggerated rhetorically by Jerome. Augustine reproaches him with having led consecrated virgins of advanced age to accept husbands. He himself abstained from marriage, merely because of the troubles involved in it. See Hieron. lib. i. *adv. Jov.* § 3; August. *de Haer.* § 82, lib. ii. *de Nupt. et Concep.* § 23; *Retract.* lib. ii. § 23; also Haller, *Jovinianus sein Leben und seine Lehre* in *Texte und Untersuch.* xvii. new ser. (Leipz. 1897). [J.LL.D.]

Juliana (8), mother of the virgin DEMETRIAS, to whom we have letters from Jerome, Augustine, pope Innocent, and Pelagius. She was of noble birth, being connected through her mother Proba and her husband Olybrius with some of the greatest families of Rome, and was possessed of great wealth. When her daughter proposed to take vows of virginity, she refrained from influencing her; but when Demetrias appeared in the church clad in the dress of a virgin she shewed her great delight at this step. She supported the cause of Chrysostom at Rome and entertained his messengers. His thanks were conveyed in a letter from his place of exile (A.D. 406), exhorting her to hold fast and aid in allaying the waves of controversy (Chrys. *Ep.* 169). She fled with her daughter to Africa from Rome when it was sacked by Alaric, but fell into the rapacious hands of count Heraclion, who robbed her of half her property. She was commended to the African churches by pope Innocent in a laudatory letter (*Ep.* 15), which takes the rank of a decree in the collection of papal rescripts by Dion. Exig. (Coll. Dec. 39; Hieron. *Ep.* 130, ed. Vall.). She became acquainted with Augustine while in Africa, and she and her daughter had relations with Pelagius, who wrote a long letter to Demetrias (given among the *Supposititi*a of Jerome; ed. Vall. vol. xi.) vindicating free will by her example. Augustine, with Alypius, wrote to Juliana (Aug. *Ep.* 188, A.D. 418), arguing that all the virtues of Demetrias were from the grace of God. [W.H.F.]

Julianus (15) (*Eclanensis*), bp. of Eclana or Aeculanum (Noris, *ad Hist. Pelag.* in *Opp.* iv. 747, ed. 1729-1732), near Beneventum (*ib.* i. 18, in *Opp.* i. 178; Pagi, *Critic*, s.a. 419, ix.), a distinguished leader of the Pelagians of 5th cent. A native of Apulia (August. *Opus Imperf.* vi. 18 in *Patr. Lat.* xlv. 1542), his birth is assigned to *c.* 386 (Garner, *Diss.* i. *ad part.* i. *Opp.* Mar. Merc. c. 6, in *Patr. Lat.* xlviii. 291). His father was an Italian bishop named Memor or Memorius (Mar. Merc. *Subnot.* iv. 4, Garner's *n.* g. *u.s.* p. 130; Pagi, *u.s.*; Cappelletti, *Chies. Ital.* xx. 19) and his mother a noble lady named Juliana (Mar. Merc. *u.s.*). Augustine of Hippo was intimate with the family, and wrote of them in terms of great affection and respect, *c.* 410 (*Ep.* 101; Noris, *Opp.* i. 422, iv. 747). Julian, *c.* 404, became a "lector" in the church over which his father presided, and while holding that office married a lady named Ia. Paulinus, afterwards bp. of Nola, composed an elaborate *Epithalamium*, which represents him as on terms of great intimacy with the family (*Poem.* xxv. in *Pali.* lxi. 633). By *c.* 410 Julian had become a deacon, but whether Ia was then living does not appear.

He was consecrated to the episcopate by Innocent I. *c.* 417 (Mar. Merc. *Commonit.* iii. 2), but the name of his see is variously given. Marius Mercator, who was his contemporary, distinctly speaks of him as "Episcopus Eclanensis" (*Nestor. Tract.* praef. § 1, Migne, 184; *Theod. Mops.* praef. § 2, Migne, 1043). Innocent I. died Mar. 12, 417. Up to that date Julian had maintained a high reputation for ability, learning, and orthodoxy, and Mercator concludes that he must have sympathized with Innocent's condemnation of the Pelagians (*Commonit.* iii. 2). Yet there is reason to believe that even Innocent had ground for at least suspecting his proclivities (August. *cont. Julian.* i. 13). When the cases of Pelagius and Coelestius were reopened by Zosimus, shortly after the death of Innocent, Julian seems to have expressed himself strongly in their favour in the hearing of Mercator (*Subnot.* vii. 2; Noris, *Opp.* i. 183); and when ZOSIMUS issued his *Epistola Tractoria* against the Pelagians (A.D. 417; Jaffé, *Reg. Pont. Rom.* 417) and sent it to the bishops of the East and West for subscription, Julian was among those who refused. He was accordingly deposed, and afterwards exiled under the edicts issued by the emperor Honorius in Mar. 418 (Mar. Merc. *Commonit.* iii. 1). Julian now addressed two letters to Zosimus (August. *Op. Imp.* i. 18), one of which was very generally circulated throughout Italy before it reached the pontiff. Of this Mercator has preserved some fragments (*Subnot.* vi. 10-13, ix. 3). Of the other we have no remains (Pagi, *Critic.* A.D. 418, lvii.).

About the same time Julian addressed a letter to Rufus, bp. of Thessalonica (410-431), on his own behalf and that of 18 fellow-recusants. Rufus was vicarius of the Roman see in Illyricum (Innocent's ep. to Rufus, June 17, 412, in Mansi, viii. 751) and just then in serious collision with Atticus the patriarch of Constantinople. As Atticus was a strenuous opponent of the Pelagians (Noris, *Opp.* iv. 884), Julian and his brethren perhaps thought Rufus might be persuaded to favour them (*ib.* i. 201, 202). Zosimus died Dec. 26, 418, and was succeeded by Boniface I., Apr. 10, 419. The letter of Julian to Rufus, with another to the clergy of Rome which he denied to be his (August. *Op. Imp.* i. 18), were answered by Augustine in his *contra Duas Epistolas Pelagianorum.* Julian avows an earnest desire to gain the aid of the Oriental bishops against the "profanity of Manicheans," for so he styles the Catholics (*cont. Duas. Ep.* ii. 1); accuses Zosimus of tergiversation and the Roman clergy of having been unduly influenced in their condemnation of the Pelagians (ii. 3); charges both with various heresies (ii. 2-5); and protests that by their means the subscriptions of nearly all the Western bishops had been uncanonically extorted to a dogma which he characterizes as "non minus stultum quam impium" (iv. 8, § 20 *init.*). Garnier assigns the letter to Rufus and the two to Zosimus to A.D. 418 (*ad Primam Partem,* diss. i. Migne, 292).

When Julian addressed his two letters to Zosimus he was preparing a reply to the first of Augustine's two books *de Nuptiis et Concupiscentiâ* (Mar. Merc. *Subnot.* praef. § 7), which he addressed to a fellow-recusant named Turbantius, whose prayers he earnestly asks that the church may be delivered from the defilement of Manicheism (*ib.* iii.). He sent some extracts from the work, which was in four books, and apparently entitled *Contra eos qui nuptias damnant et fructus earum diabolo assignant* (August. *de Nuptiis et Concupisc.* ii. 4, § 11), to Valerius, who forwarded them to his friend Augustine, who at once rejoined in a second book *de Nuptiis et Concupiscentiâ* (August. *Retract.* ii. 53). When Julian's work subsequently came into his hands, Augustine published a fuller rejoinder in his *contra Julianum Pelagianum.* Augustine freely quotes his antagonist, and we see that Julian again insisted upon the Manicheism of his opponents (lib. ii. *passim*); again charged Zosimus with prevarication (iii. 1, vi. 2), and elaborated the whole anthropology for which he contended.

When driven from the West, Julian and some of his fellow-exiles went into Cilicia and remained for a time with Theodorus, bp. of Mopsuestia (Mar. Merc. *Theod. Mops.* praef. § 2), who is charged by Mercator with having been one of the originators of Pelagianism (*Subnot.* praef. § 1, *Symb. Theod. Mops.* praef. § 2) and who wrote against Augustine (Phot. *Bibl. Cod.* 177; Mar. Merc. Garnier, *ad Prim. Partem,* diss. vi.). Meanwhile the rejoinder of Augustine had reached Julian, who answered it in 8 books, addressed to Florus, a fellow-recusant (*Co. Eph.* A.D. 431, actio v. in Mansi, iv. 1337; Mar. Merc. *Subnot.* praef.). Mercator has given various extracts (*Subnot.* passim), but it is best known from Augustine's elaborate *Opus Imperfectum,* which was evoked by it (August. *Opp.* t. x. in *Patr. Lat.* xlv. 1050), but left incomplete. On the death of Boniface I. and the succession of Celestine I. in Sept. 422, Julian apparently left Cilicia and returned to Italy, probably hoping that the new pontiff might reconsider the case of the Pelagians, especially as a variance had then arisen between the Roman see and the African bishops. Celestine repulsed him, and caused him to be exiled a second time (Prosper. *contr. Collator.* xxi. 2, in *Patr. Lat.* li. 271). Julian was also condemned, in his absence, by a council in Cilicia, Theodorus concurring in the censure (Mar. Merc. *Symb. Theod. Mops.* praef. § 3; Garnier, *ad Prim. Part.* diss. ii. Migne, 359). On this Julian went to Constantinople, where the same fate awaited him both from Atticus and his successor Sisinnius (A.D. 426, 427) (Garnier, *u.s.* 361; *Coelest. ad Nestor.* in Mansi, iv. 1025). On the accession of Nestorius to the patriarchate (A.D. 428) the expectations of Julian were again raised, and he appealed both to Nestorius and to the emperor Theodosius II. Both at first gave him some encouragement (Mar. Merc. *Nestor. Tract.* praef. § 1), which may be why there is no mention of the Pelagians in the celebrated edict which the emperor issued against heresies at the instance of Nestorius (*Cod. Theod.* XVI. v. 65, May 30, 428; Socr. *H. E.* vii. 29). The patriarch wrote to Celestine more than once in his behoof and that of his friends (Nestor. *Ep.* to Celest. in Mansi, iv. 1022, 1023), but the favour he shewed them necessitated his defending himself in a public discourse delivered in their presence, and translated by Mercator (*u.s.* Migne, 189 seq.). In 429 Mercator presented his *Commonitorium de Coelestio* to the emperor, wherein he carefully relates the proceedings against the Pelagians and comments severely upon their teaching. Julian and his friends were then driven from Constantinople by an imperial edict (Mar. Merc. *Commonit.* praef. § 1). Towards the close of 430 Celestine convened a council at Rome, which condemned Julian and others once more (Garnier, *u.s.* diss. ii.). Whither he went from Constantinople does not appear, but he with other Pelagians seem to have accompanied Nestorius to the convent of Ephesus, A.D. 431, and took part in the "Conciliabulum" held by Joannes of Antioch (*Relat. ad Coel.* in Mansi, iv. 1334). Baronius (*s.a.* 431 lxxix.) infers from one of the letters of Gregory the Great (lib. ix. ind. ii. ep. 49 in *Patr. Lat.* xv. lxxvii. 981) that the "Conciliabulum" absolved Julian and his friends, but Cardinal

Noris (*Opp.* i. 362) has shewn that the council repeat their condemnation of the Pelagians, expressly mentioning Julian by name (*Relat. u.s.*; Mar. Merc. *Nestor. Tract.* praef. § 2).

Sixtus III., the successor of Celestine (July 31, 432), when a presbyter, had favoured the Pelagians, much to the grief of Augustine (*Ep.* 174). Julian attempted to recover his lost position through him, but Sixtus evidently treated him with severity, mainly at the instigation of Leo, then a presbyter, who became his successor, A.D. 440 (Prosper. *Chron.* s.a. 439). When pontiff himself, Leo shewed the same spirit toward the Pelagians, especially toward Julian (*de Promiss. Dei*, pt. iv. c. 6 in *Patr. Lat.* li. 843). We hear no more of Julian until his death in Sicily, *c.* 454 (Gennad. *Script. Eccl.* xlv. in *Patr. Lat.* lviii. 1084; Garnier, *u.s.* diss. i. Migne, 297).

Some years after his death Julian was again condemned by Joannes Talaia, formerly patriarch of Alexandria, but *c.* 484 bp. of Nola in Italy (Phot. *Bibl. Cod.* liv.; *s.f.* August. *Opp.* in *Patr. Lat.* xlv. 1684).

Julian was an able and a learned man. Gennadius speaks of him as "vir acer ingenio, in divinis Scripturis doctus, Graeca et Latina lingua scholasticus" (*u.s.*). He was of high character, and especially distinguished for generous benevolence (Gennad. *u.s.*), and seems actuated throughout the controversy by a firm conviction that he was acting in the interests of what he held to be the Christian faith and of morality itself.

Besides his works already mentioned, Bede speaks of his *Opuscula* on the Canticles, and among them of a "libellus" *de Amore*, and a "libellus" *de Bono Constantiae*, both of which he charges with Pelagianism, giving from each some extracts (*in Cantica*, praef. Migne, 1065-1077). Garnier claims Julian as the translator of the *Libellus Fidei a Rufino Palaestinae Provinciae Presbytero*, which he has published in his ed. of Marius Mercator (*ad Primam Partem*, dissert. v. Migne, 449, dissert. vi. Migne, 623), and as the author of the *Liber Definitionum seu Ratiocinationum*, to which Augustine replied in his *de Perfectione Justitiae* (note 6 in Mar. Merc. *Subnot.* Migne, 145, 146). Cf. A. Bruckner, *Julian von Eclanum* (Leipz. 1897) in *Texte und Untersuch.* xv. 3. [T.W.D.]

Julianus (27), bp. of Cos, the friend and frequent correspondent of Leo the Great. He was by birth an Italian. Being educated at Rome (Leo. Mag. *Ep.* lxxxi. 1042; Migne, *Ep.* cxiii. 1190) he was acquainted with Latin as well as Greek (*Ep.* cxiii. 1194) and was thus useful to Leo, who was ignorant of Greek. Leo found in him a man after his own heart. He describes him as a "part of himself" (*Ep.* cxxv. 1244). Long experience led him to put the fullest confidence in his orthodoxy, erudition, watchfulness, and zeal (*Ep.* xxxv. 875, xci. 1066). Nothing could exceed the value of such a man to Leo to watch over the interests of the faith and the Roman see in the East. Julian was present at the council of Constantinople in 448 and professed his belief in the "two natures in one Person"—an expression which Dioscorus could not tolerate when he heard it read at Chalcedon—and subscribed the condemnation of Eutyches (Labbe, *Concilia*, iv. 188 B, 231 B). In Apr. 449 he was present at the synod in Constantinople, granted by the emperor at the demand of Eutyches to verify the records of the former council. Here we find him disputing occasionally the exact accuracy of the "Acta" (Labbe, iv. 231 (2), c. 234 (2) B; Tillem. xv. 511). He wrote to Leo a letter which produced two replies dated the same day, June 13, 449, the first of a long series of letters from Leo to Julian (*Epp.* xxxiv. xxxv.). The latter of the two contains an elaborate dogmatic statement against Eutyches. After this Julian became one of the pope's chief mediums for impressing his wishes and policy on the East. [LEO.] Through the Eutychian troubles Julian remained true to the faith and suffered so much that, as he tells Leo, he thought of retiring to Rome (*Ep.* lxxxi. 1042). It was JULIUS of Puteoli, however, not this Julian, who was papal legate at the council of Ephesus. Leo commended Julian to the favour of Pulcheria and Anatolius of Constantinople as one who had always been faithful to St. Flavian (*Epp.* lxxix. lxxx. 1037, 1041, dated Apr. 451). In June 451 he begs him to associate himself with his legates, Lucentius and Basil, to the council of Chalcedon (*Ep.* lxxxvi. 1063). He is commended to Marcian the emperor as a "particeps" with them (*Ep.* xc. 1065). His exact position at that council appears somewhat ambiguous. He is not mentioned among the legates in the letter of Leo to the council (*Ep.* xciii. 1070), but in the Acts of the council is always spoken of as holding that position (Labbe, iv. 80 C, 852 C, 559 E). In the list of signatures he does not appear among the legates of Rome, yet higher than his own rank, as bp. of Cos, would entitle him to appear, and among the metropolitans (cf. Tillem. xv. 645, and note, 43). His condemnation of Dioscorus, with reasons assigned, appears in the acta of the third session of the council (Labbe, iv. 427 C). In the matter of the claims of BASSIAN and Stephen to the see of Ephesus, he gives his voice first for setting both aside, then for allowing a local council to choose (701 D, 703 D). He displeased Leo by not resisting the 28th canon of the council in favour of the claims of Constantinople (*Ep.* xcviii. 1098), and by writing to Leo begging him to give his assent to it (*Ep.* cvii. 1172). After this, however, he is in as good favour as ever. From Mar. 453 he was apocrisiarius or deputy of the see of Rome at the court of Constantinople. Leo requests him to remain constantly at court, watching zealously over the interests of the faith (*Epp.* cxi. 1187, cxiii. 1190, "speculari non desinas"; cf. Tillem. xv. 761). In Mar. 453 Leo requested him to make a complete translation of the Acts of the council of Chalcedon (*Ep.* cxiii. 1194). Julian seems to have returned to his diocese in 457 (cf. Tillem. xvii. 762, 791) and wrote a reply, in his own name only, to the circular letter of the emperor Leo on the excesses of Timothy Aelurus and the authority of the Chalcedonian council. [LEO, emperor.] Julian urges that Timotheus should be punished by the civil power and maintains strongly the authority of the council. "For where were assembled so many bishops, where were present the holy Gospels, where was so much united prayer, there, we believe, was also present with invisible power the author of all creation" (Labbe, iv. 942 ; *Or. Chr.* i. 935). After this no more is known of him. [C.G.]

Julianus (47), bp. of Halicarnassus in the province of Caria; a leader of the Monophysites. In 511 he was active in conjunction with Severus and others in instigating the emperor Anastasius to depose Macedonius, patriarch of Constantinople (Theod. Lect. ii. 26). Theophanes erroneously speaks of him as bp. of Caria before he was bp. of Halicarnassus (*Chron.* A.C. 503, in *Patr. Gk.* cviii. 362). On the accession of Justin I. in 518, severe measures were taken against the Monophysites and Julian was driven from his see. He went to Alexandria, followed quickly by Severus on his expulsion from Antioch (Liberatus, *Brev.* c. 19; Evagr. *H. E.* iv. 4; Vict. Tunun. *Chron.* s.a. 539). Timotheus the successor of Dioscorus the younger received both kindly, and they settled near the city. Shortly afterwards a monk appealed to Severus as to whether the body of our Lord should be called corruptible. He answered that the "fathers" had declared that it should. Some Alexandrians hearing this asked Julian, who said that the "fathers" had declared the contrary. In the fierce controversy thus evoked the Julianists charged the Severians with being Phthartolatrae or Corrupticolae, while the Severians charged the Julianists with being Phantasiastae and Manicheans (Liberatus, *u.s.*; Tim. Presb. *de Recept. Haer.* in *Patr. Gk.* lxxxvi. 58; Niceph. Call. *E. H.* xviii. 45). The designation by which the Julianists were more generally known was Aphthartodocetae or Incorrupticolae (Jo. Damasc. *de Haer.* § 84). Much was written on either side. The only writings of Julian that remain are his *Ten Anathemas*, a Syriac version by Paulus, the deposed bp. of Callinicus, being published by Assemani (*MSS. Cod. Biblioth. Apost. Vatic. Catalog.* iii. 230, 231). A Latin trans. of this valuable document is given by Gieseler in his *Commentatio qua Monophysitarum veterum variae de Christi persona opiniones imprimis ex ipsorum effatis recens editis illustrantur* (P. ii. p. 5). Three letters from Julian to Severus, also translated by Paulus, and several fragments are among the Syrian MSS. in the Brit. Mus. (Wright, *Cat. Syr. MSS.* pt. ii. 554, 929, 960, 961, pt. iii. 1059). Assemani also gives three letters of his to Severus from the Syriac MSS. in the Vatican (*u.s.* iii. 223).

Leontius of Byzantium tells us that Julian earnestly contended for the "Incorruptibility," because he considered the view of Severus made a distinction (διαφοράν) between the body of our Lord and the Word of God, to allow of which was to acknowledge two natures in Him (*de Sect.* act v. 3, in *Patr. Gk.* lxxxvi. 1230). This explanation is also given by Theodorus Rhaituensis (*de Incarnat.* in *Patr. Gk.* xci. 1498) and is fully sustained, especially by the eighth *Anathema* as pub. by Gieseler. He was certainly no Phantasiast and far from being a Manichean; but, as Dorner justly observes, in asserting "the supernatural character of our Lord's body," Julian and his followers did not intend to deny its "reality," but only aimed at "giving greater prominence to His love by tracing not merely His sufferings themselves, but even the possibility of suffering" to His self-sacrifice (*Person of Christ*, ed. Clark, ii. i. 129). Jo. Damasc. *Orth. Fid.* iii. 28; Eus. Thess. *contr. Andr.*; Phot. *Bibl. Cod.* 162; Thom. Aquin. *Sum.* p. iii. q. i. art. 5 concl.

Julian by some means recovered his see of Halicarnassus, but in the council of Constantinople A.D. 536, under Agapetus bp. of Rome, he was again deposed (Theoph. *s.a.* 529; Mansi, viii. 869; *Libell. Syn.* in Labbe, v. 276). After this he disappears, but his opinions continued to spread long afterwards, especially in the East; where his followers ultimately divided, one part holding "that the body of our Lord was absolutely (κατὰ πάντα τρόπον) incorruptible from the very 'Unio' itself" (ἐξ αὐτῆς τῆς ἑνώσεως); another, that it was not absolutely incorruptible but potentially (δυνάμει) the reverse, yet could not become corruptible because the Word prevented it; and a third that it was not only incorruptible from the very "Unio," but also increate (οὐ μόνον ἄφθαρτον ἐξ αὐτῆς ἑνώσεως, ἀλλὰ καὶ ἄκτιστον). These last were distinguished as Actistitae. Tim. Presb. *u.s.* 43; Leont. Byzant. *contr. Nestor. et Eutych.* ii. in *Patr. Gk.* lxxxvi. 1315, 1358; Id. *de Sect.* act x. *ib.* 1259; Anastas. Sinait. *Viae Dux*, c. 23, in *Patr. Gk.* lxxxix. 296; Isaac. Arm. Cath. *Orat. contr. Armen.* c. 1, in *Patr. Gk.* cxxxii. 1155; Id. *de Reb. Arm. ib.* 1243.

Four scholastici from Alexandria visited Ephesus *c.* 549, and prevailed upon bp. Procopius to avow himself a Julianist. In 560, immediately after his decease, seven of his presbyters, who were also Julianists, are said to have placed the hands of his corpse on the head of a monk named Eutropius, and then to have recited the consecration prayer over him.* Eutropius afterwards ordained ten Julianist bishops, and sent them as missionaries east and west, among other places to Constantinople, Antioch, and Alexandria, and into Syria, Persia, Mesopotamia, and the country of the Homerites (Asseman. *Bibl. Or.* i. 316, ii. 86, 88, iii. pt. ii. ccccl v.; Wright, *Cat. Syr. MSS.* ii. 755).

By A.D. 565 the emperor Justinian had become an Incorruptibilist. He issued an edict avowing his change of opinion and gave orders that "all bishops everywhere" should be compelled to accept Julianism (Evagr. *H. E.* iv. 39; Theoph. *s.a.* 557; Cedrenus, *Comp. Hist.* ed. Bonn. i. 680; Pagi, *Critic.* s.a. 565, ii.). This naturally encountered great opposition, especially, among others, from Anastasius patriarch of Antioch (A.D. 559-569) and Nicetius bp. of Trèves (527-566) (Nicetius, *Ep.* 2 in *Patr. Lat.* lxviii. 380). But the Gaianites of Alexandria took courage from the edict to erect churches in that city, and elected Helpidius, an archdeacon, as their bishop (Theoph. *u.s.*). He almost immediately incurred the displeasure of the emperor and died on his way to Constantinople, whither he had been summoned. They then united with the Theodosians under Dorotheus, who, Theophanes says, was one of that party, but who

* The corpse of Julian is said to have been treated in the same manner by his personal followers (Isaac. Arm. Cath. *de Reb. Arm.* u.s. 1248).

both Sophronius of Jerusalem and John of Ephesus, the latter of whom especially was likely to be much better informed than the Chronographer, say was a Julianist (Sophron. *Ep. Syn.* in *Patr. Gk.* lxxxvii. 3191; *Jo. v. Eph. Kirchengesch. uebers,* v. Schönfelder, i. 40, p. 47). Justinian died Nov. 565.

The Julianists were still numerous at Alexandria during the patriarchate of Eulogius (Phot. *Bibl. Cod.* 227) and continued so still later. Sophronius of Jerusalem speaks of "Menas Alexandrinus, Gaianitarum propugnator" as his contemporary (*u.s.* 3194), and Anastasius Sinaita relates a public disputation with the Gaianites of that city in which he took part (*Viae Dux,* u.s. 150 seq.). They were known in the West as late as the commencement of 7th cent. (Greg. I. *Ep.* lib. ix. ind. ii. ep. 68, *ad Eus. Thessal.* in *Patr. Lat.* lxxvii. A.D. 601; Jaffé, *Reg. Pont.* 145; Eus. Thessal. *u.s.*). In Armenia they were very numerous in the time of Gregory Bar-hebraeus (Assemani, *u.s.* ii. 296; Dorner, *u.s.* 13 n.).

Julian achieved a very high reputation as a commentator on the Scriptures. Nicetas bp. of Heraclea, *c.* 1077, selected many of the most striking passages in his *Catena Graecorum Patrum in Beatum Job* from Julian's exegetical and other writings. This catena was first published by Patricius Junius, with a Latin trans. (London, 1637, fol.), and afterwards in Greek only at Venice (1792, fol.). The quotations from Julian are in the "Proemium" and pp. 37, 45, 66, 93, 170, 178, 228, 230, 273, 437, 465, 480, 505, 539, 547-613, of the former of these editions. Fabric. *Bibl. Gr.* ed. Harles, viii. 647, 650; Cave, i. 495; Ceillier, xi. 344. Cf. Usener in Lietzmann's *Katenen, Freib. in Breisq* (1897), p. 28, and the Rhein *Mur. f. Phil.* 1900, iv. p. 321; also Loofs in *Leont. von Byzanz.* (Leipz. 1887), i. p. 30. [T.W.D.]

Julianus (73), missionary priest to the Nubians in the reign of Justinian. John of Ephesus (R. Payne Smith's trans. pp. 251 seq.) and Bar-hebraeus (in Asseman. *Bibl. Or.* ii. 330) give an account of him. He was an old man of great worth, and one of the clergy in attendance on Theodosius, the Monophysite patriarch of Alexandria, then residing at Constantinople. Julian had long desired to Christianize the Nobadae or Nubians, a wandering people E. of the Thebais and beyond the limits of the empire, which they greatly harassed. The empress Theodora warmly encouraged the undertaking and consulted Justinian about it, who became interested but objected to Julian as a Monophysite, and named another instead, whilst Theodora persisted in favouring Julian. John of Ephesus describes fully the rival missions and the triumph of the empress's schemes. Julian reached the Nubian court first, won over the king and secured the rejection of the emperor's envoy when he arrived. Thus the Nubians were gained to the Monophysite creed and to the jurisdiction of Theodosius. After labouring there two years Julian placed Theodore, a Thebaid bishop, in charge and returned to Constantinople, where he soon afterwards died. For the subsequent history of the mission see LONGINUS. [T.W.D.]

Julianus (103), Flavius Claudius, emperor, often called Julian the Apostate; born A.D. 331; appointed Caesar, Nov. 6, 355; proclaimed Augustus, Apr. 360; succeeded Constantius as sole emperor, Nov. 3, 361; died in Persia, June 27, 363. For the authorities for Julian's life, see *D. C. B.* (4-vol. ed.), *s.v.*

The first and still in some respects the best English account of Julian is to be found in Gibbon's *Decline and Fall of the Roman Empire,* cc. 19, 22-24—a forcible and on the whole very just picture. Like some other cold and sceptical people (*e.g.* Strauss), Gibbon despised Julian's superstitious enthusiasm, and, though he cannot restrain some sneers at the church and the orthodox faith, this part of his history has generally met with comparative favour at the hands of Christian critics. Mr. J. W. Barlow on *Gibbon and Julian* in the Dublin *Hermathena* for 1877 endeavours to shew that Gibbon, in order to gain a reputation for impartiality, is unfair to the emperor, whom he thinks morally and intellectually the best man "of the whole series." In the first three quarters of the last century little or nothing was published in England specially on this subject. An interesting and valuable essay, written for a Cambridge historical prize by the Hon. Arthur Lyttelton, has been kindly placed at the disposal of the writer of this article, who owes to it several important references. It is embodied in the *Church Qtly. Rev.* for Oct. 1880, vol. xi. pp. 24-58, *The Pagan Reaction under Julian,* which gives a fresh and vigorous view of the subject. Mr. Gerald H. Rendall's Hulsean Essay for 1876, *The Emperor Julian; Paganism and Christianity* is decidedly the best account of Julian's religious position in English, perhaps in any modern language. In French we have the invaluable Tillemont and other writers of church history. Besides the articles in vol. iv. of the *Empereurs* there is a special treatise on the *Persécution de l'Eglise par J. l'Apostat,* in vol. vii. of the *Mémoires.* We miss, however, a critical treatment of the authorities and wide generalizations in Tillemont. He also seems to exaggerate the scope of the law against Christian professors. The fullest history of Julian is that of Albert de Broglie in vols. iii. and iv. of his *L'Eglise et l'empire romain au quatrième siècle* (Paris, 1866, etc.). This is indispensable to the student of the period. Its general attitude is that taken in this article, but he is too anxious to make points to be careful of minute accuracy, and therefore of entire fairness, and his references often want correction. These volumes were reviewed by C. Martha in the *Revue des deux mondes* for Mar. 1867, vol. lxviii. pp. 137-169, who paints the emperor more favourably. In German J. F. A. Mücke, *Flavius Claudius Julianus: nach den Quellen* (Gotha, 1867 and 1869, 2 parts) is the most complete modern account. Fr. Rode, *Geschichte der Reaction Kaiser Julians gegen die christliche Kirche* (Jena, 1877); a useful study, and generally very accurate, paying proper attention to chronology. The writer takes up something of the same position as Keim does in his essay on Constantine's conversion—striving after fairness towards the church, without accepting its doctrines. He admires Julian's books against the Christians as anticipating the line of modern critical theology in many points, pp. 102, 103; cf. p. 32, n. 10.

§ 1. *Early years of Julian as a Christian* (A.D. 331-351). § 2. *Conversion to heathenism* 351-355. § 3. *Julian as Caesar* from Nov. 6, 355 to Nov. 3, 361. § 4. *Residence at Constantinople as Augustus*, Nov. 3, 361 to May, 362. § 5. *Journey through Asia Minor*, May to July, 362. § 6. *Residence at Antioch*, July, 362 to March 5, 363. § 7. *Persian campaign and death*, March 5 to June 27, 363.

§ 1. *Early Years of Julian as a Christian* (A.D. 331-351).—Flavius Claudius Julianus was the youngest son of Julius Constantius, the half-brother of Constantine the Great. His mother, Basilina, was of the noble family of the Anicii, and daughter of Julianus the praetorian prefect, whose name was given to her son. Julian was born at Constantinople in the latter part of A.D. 331, the year after the dedication of the new capital.

Upon the death of Constantine in May 337, and the accession of his three sons, there was a general massacre of the male branches of the younger line of the Flavian family descended from Constantius Chlorus and his second wife Theodora. In this tragedy there perished the father and eldest brother of Julian, his paternal uncle, his cousins the Caesars Delmatius and Hanniballian, and four other members of the family. Julian and his elder half-brother Gallus, who was sick of an illness which was expected to be mortal, were alone preserved, by the compassion or the policy of Constantius (cf. Socr. *H. E.* iii. 1; Greg. Naz. *Or.* iii. p. 58 B. Julian, *ad S. P. Q. Athen.* p. 270 C, gives the list of those who perished, and ascribes their deaths to Constantius, who he says wished at first to slay both himself and Gallus). Julian is said to have owed his life to the interference of Mark, bp. of Arethusa, who gave him sanctuary in a church (Greg. Naz. *Or.* iii. p. 80 C). The boy was taken charge of by his mother's family, and his education conducted under the direction of the Arian Eusebius, bp. of Nicomedia, who was distantly related to him (Amm. xxii. 9. 4; cf. Soz. v. 2). When Eusebius was translated in 388 to the see of Constantinople Julian probably went with him, and attended the schools of that city (cf. Libanius, ἐπιτάφιος, ed. Reiske, i. p. 525; Julian, *Ep.* 58; and Rode, *Die Reaction Julians*, p. 22, n. 10). His constant attendant and guardian was his mother's slave Mardonius, whose influence evidently had great power in moulding the character and tastes of his pupil, and who insisted strongly on a staid and perhaps rather pedantic demeanour (Liban. *l.c.*; Jul. *Misopogon*, pp. 351 seq.; Mücke, in his *Julianus nach den Quellen*, zweite Abtheilung, pp. 6 and 9, makes a curious blunder in supposing that Julian disliked Mardonius). Though educating him only for a private position, he set before him a high standard, and particularly held up to his imitation the names and characters of "Plato, Socrates, Aristotle, and Theophrastus" (*Misop.* p. 353 B). He kept him from the theatre and the circus, and taught him rather to love the Homeric descriptions of Phaeacia and Demodocus and Calypso's isle, and the cave of Circe (*ib.* 351 D). Such teaching doubtless fed the naturally dreamy temperament of his pupil. Julian tells us that from a child he had a strange desire of gazing at the sun, and that he loved to spend a clear night in looking fixedly at the moon and stars, so that he almost gained the character of an astrologer (Jul. *Or.* iv. *ad regem Solem* ad init.; cf. the fable, *Or.* vii. p. 229, in which he speaks of himself as entrusted by Zeus to the sun's guardianship).

These pleasant days of freedom were brought to an abrupt conclusion by the command of Constantius. The death of his relative Eusebius (in 342) deprived Julian of a powerful protector, when he was about 11 years old; and soon after (probably in 343 or 344) the emperor recalled Gallus from exile, and sent the two brothers to the distant palace of Macellum in Cappadocia. Here for six years they were kept under surveillance, with no lack of material comforts, but apart from young men of their own age and with only the society of their slaves (Greg. Naz. *Or.* iii. p. 58 B; Julian, *ad Ath*, p. 271 C). Their seclusion was only once broken by a visit from Constantius (Jul. *ad Ath.* p. 274, probably in 347, see laws of the *Cod. Theod.* in this year). Masters and teachers were not wanting, especially of that form of Arianism to which Constantius was devoted; and Julian now, if not before, made a considerable verbal acquaintance with the Bible, an acquaintance which frequently appears in his writings. He and Gallus were admitted to the office of *Reader* in the church—a proof that he had been baptized, though no mention of his baptism is recorded. They interested themselves zealously in the building of chapels over the relics of certain martyrs (Greg. Naz. *Or.* iii. p. 58; Soz. v. 2). The success of Gallus in this building and the ill-success of Julian was remarked at the time, and was (afterwards, at any rate) considered as an omen of his apostasy (Greg. Naz. *l.c.* p. 59).

In the spring of 351 Constantius felt himself forced by the burden of empire to take a colleague, and Gallus was appointed Caesar. Julian with difficulty was permitted to leave Macellum, and seems to have returned for a short time to Constantinople; there he studied grammar with Nicocles, and rhetoric with Hecebolius then a zealous Christian (Socr. *H. E.* iii. 1). Constantius, fearing lest his presence in the capital might lead to his becoming too popular, ordered him to remove to Nicomedia (Liban. *Epitaph.* p. 526, προσφωνητικός, p. 408). Hecebolius exacted a promise from his pupil that he would not attend the lectures of the famous heathen sophist Libanius; Julian kept his promise, perhaps fearing to excite suspicion by outward intercourse with a chief partisan of the old religion, but contented himself with a study of the written lectures of the master (Liban. *l.c.* 526 seq. Libanius does not *name* Hecebolius, but the description seems to point to him: Sievers, *Libanius*, p. 54, n. 5, supposes Nicocles to be meant). Others, however, in Nicomedia besides Libanius attracted the attention of the young prince. He here learnt to know some of the more mystical of the heathen party, to whom paganism was still a reality and the gods living beings, visions of whom were to be seen by night and whose power still worked signs and wonders. "He is sent to the city of Nicomedes," says Libanius, "as a place of less importance than Constantinople. But this was the beginning of the greatest blessings both to himself and the world. For there was there a spark of the mantic art still smouldering, which had with difficulty escaped the hands of the impious. By the light of this" (turning to Julian) "you first tracked out what was obscure, and learnt to curb your vehement hatred of the gods, being rendered gentle by the revelations of divination" (Liban. *Prosphoneticus*, ed. Reiske, 1, p. 408).

While Julian was thus having his first experience of the inner circle of heathen life, Gallus met his brother for the last time as he passed through Bithynia to undertake the government of the East with which Constantius had invested him (Liban. *Epitaph*. p. 527, διὰ τῆς Βιθυνίας). The two brothers, according to Julian's account, corresponded but rarely after this, and on few subjects (Jul. *ad Ath*. p. 273; Liban. *Epitaph*. p. 530). Gallus, it is said, having reason at a later date to suspect his brother's change of belief, sent the Arian Aetius to confer with him (Philostorgius, 3, 27). Julian, if we may believe Libanus, sent Gallus good advice on his political conduct, which had he followed he might have preserved both the empire and his life (Liban. *ad Jul. cos*. p. 376, ed. Reiske).

§ 2. *Conversion to Heathenism* (A.D. 351-355).—The secret apostasy of Julian was the result of his residence at Nicomedia, though it was not completed there. The chief agent in effecting it was the neo-Platonist Maximus of Ephesus, a philosopher, magician, and political schemer. The fame of the wisdom of Aedesius first attracted Julian to Pergamus, but he, being old and infirm, recommended him to his pupils, Chrysanthius and Eusebius. The latter was, or pretended to be, an adversary of the theurgic methods of Maximus, and a follower of the higher and more intellectual Platonism, and used to finish every lecture by a general warning against trickery and charlatans. Julian, much struck with this, took the advice of Chrysanthius upon the point, and asked Eusebius to explain what he meant. The latter replied by an account of Maximus, which gave a new edge of the already keen curiosity of Julian. "Some days ago" (he went on) "he ran in and called our company together to the temple of Hecate, thus making a large body of witnesses against himself. . . . When we came before the goddess and saluted her, he cried, 'Sit down, dearest friends, and see what will happen, and whether I am superior to ordinary men.' We all sat down, then he burnt a grain of frankincense, and as he repeated some sort of chant to himself he so far succeeded in the exhibition of his power that first the image smiled and then even appeared to laugh. We were confounded at the sight, but he said, 'Let none of you be disturbed at this, for in a moment the torches which the goddess has in her hands will be lighted up'—and before he had done speaking light actually burned in the torches. We then retired, being amazed and in doubt at the wonder which had taken place. But do not you wonder at anything of this kind, just as I also through the purifying effects of reason conceive it is nothing of great importance." Julian (says Eunapius) hearing this, exclaimed, "Farewell, and keep to your books, if you will; you have revealed to me the man I was in search of" (Eunapius, *Vita Maximi*, pp. 48-51, ed. Boissonade). It is difficult to believe that Eusebius was not in league with Chrysanthius to bring Julian under the influence of Maximus. The young prince hurried off to Ephesus, and there threw himself with eagerness into the teaching of his new master, which seems exactly to have suited his fantastic temperament. Julian had no practical Christianity to fall back upon. The sense of being watched and suspected had sunk deeply into his mind at Macellum, and he had learnt to look upon Constantius not only as his jailor, but as the murderer of his nearest relations. This naturally did not incline him to the religion inculcated by Arian or semi-Arian court bishops, who probably laid stress upon their peculiar points of divergence from the orthodox faith, and neglected the rest of Christian theology. Julian therefore conceived of Christianity, not as a great body of truth satisfying the whole man, but as a set of formulas to be plausibly debated and distinguished. On the other hand, he had a real, though pedantic, love of Hellenic authors and literature, and a natural dislike to those who destroyed the ancient monuments of the old faith. His characteristic dreaminess and love of mystery found satisfaction in the secret cults to which men like Maximus were addicted—all the more zealously as public sacrifice was difficult or dangerous. He was by nature ardent and superstitious, and never fell into good hands. The pagan coterie soon discovered the importance of their convert, and imbued him with the notion that he was the chosen servant of the gods to bring back again Hellenic life and religion. By the arts of divination a speedy call to the throne was promised him, and he vowed to restore to the temples if he became emperor. (Libanius, *Epitaph*. pp. 529 and 565, who agrees substantially with Socrates, iii. 1, p. 168, and Sozomen, v. 2, p. 181; cf. Theod. iii. 1). For the present, however, the fulfilment of such hopes seemed distant, and Julian for ten years pretended zeal for Christianity (Liban. *Epitaph*. p. 528; Amm. xxii. 5, 1; Socr. iii. 1; Soz. v. 2). He had, indeed, good reason to fear the suspicions of his cousin. In 354 Gallus was craftily removed from his government and executed [GALLUS], and Julian was apprehended, on obscure charges (Amm. xv. 2, 7—the charge of leaving Macellum without permission seems strange, since the brothers had been released from their retirement some four years before). For seven months he was confined in N. Italy near the court, being removed from place to place (Jul. *ad Ath*. p. 272 D; Liban. *Epitaph*. p. 530; cf. Jul. *ad Themist*. p. 260 A)—an imprisonment brought to an end by the intervention of the gentle empress Eusebia, who procured for him an interview with Constantius, and leave to return to his studies (Jul.

ad Ath. pp. 272, 274; *Or.* 3, p. 118 B). At first he determined to retire to his mother's property in Bithynia, Constantius having confiscated all the estates of his father (Jul. *ad Ath.* p. 273; *Ep.* 40, p. 417 A, to Iamblichus—an interesting letter written 3 years later, and not concealing his religious opinions). He had hardly arrived in Asia Minor when the suspicions of Constantius were aroused by two reports brought by informers, one of treasonable proceedings at a banquet given by Africanus, the governor of Pannonia Secunda at Sirmium, the other of the rising of Silvanus in Gaul (Jul. *ad Ath.* p. 273 C, D; cf. Amm. xv. 3, 7 seq.). The first was no doubt connected in his mind with Julian, who had just passed through that country, and whom he in consequence recalled, but on his way back received permission, or rather command, to turn aside into Greece, a privilege which Eusebia had procured for him (*ad Ath.* 273 D; *Or.* 3, p. 118 C). He thus could gratify a long-cherished wish of visiting Athens. The young prince was naturally well received by professors and sophists, such as Prohaeresius and Himerius, then teaching at Athens. He had a turn for philosophy, and could discourse eagerly, in the modern neo-Platonic fashion, about the descent and the ascent of souls. He was surrounded by a swarm of young and old men, philosophers and rhetoricians, and (if we may believe Libanius) gained favour as much by his modesty and gentleness as by the qualities of his intelligence (Liban. *Epitaph.* p. 532). Two of the most distinguished of his familiars among his fellow-students at this time were the future bishops Basil and Gregory Nazianzen, then as always close and intimate friends. Gregory, however, seems to have detected something of his real character; he noticed an air of wildness and unsteadiness, a wandering eye, an uneven gait, a nervous agitation of the features, an unreasoning and disdainful laugh, an abrupt, irregular way of talking, which betrayed a mind ill at ease with itself, and exclaimed, "What a plague the Roman empire is breeding! God grant I may be a false prophet!" (*Or.* pp. 161, 162). Gregory, who had many friends among the professors, may well have been aware of the real state of the young prince's mind, and of his nightly visits to Eleusis, where he could indulge his religious feelings without reserve. Maximus had introduced him to the hierophant there, a great miracle-worker who was in league with the heathen party in Asia Minor (Eunapius, *Vita Maximi*, pp. 52, 53).

§ 3. *Julian as Caesar* (from Nov. 6, 355, to Nov. 3, 361 — death of Constantius).—About May 355 Julian was permitted to go to Athens, but a few months later was summoned again to the court (Jul. *ad Ath.* p. 273 D). He left the city in low spirits and with many tears, and, stretching out his hands to the Acropolis, besought Athena to save her suppliant—an act which, he tells us, many saw him perform (*ib.* p. 475 A). Those who did so could hardly have doubted his change of religion, and there were doubtless many sympathizers who looked to him as the future restorer of the old faith. He first crossed the Aegean to Ilium Novum, where he visited the antiquities under the guidance of the then Christian bp. Pegasius, who delighted him by omitting the sign of the cross in the temples, and otherwise shewing heathen sympathies (Jul. *Ep.* 78 — the letter, first edited by C. Henning, in *Hermes*, vol. ix.). On his arrival at Milan, Constantius was absent, but Julian was well received by the eunuchs of the empress (*ad Ath.* pp. 274, 275 B). His first impulse was to write to his protectress and implore her to obtain leave for him to return home; but on demanding a revelation from the gods, he received an intimation of their displeasure and a threat of disgraceful death if he did so, and, in consequence, schooled himself to yield his will to theirs, and to become their instrument for whatever purposes they chose (*ib.* pp. 275, 276; cf. Liban. *ad Jul. consulem*, t. 1, p. 378). Constantius soon returned, and determined, under the persevering pressure of his wife and notwithstanding strong opposition, to give the dignity of Caesar to his sole remaining relative (Amm. xv. 8, 3; Zos. 3, 1). On Nov. 6, 355, Julian received the insignia in the presence of the army at Milan, and was given control of the prefecture of Gaul (*i.e.* Spain, Gaul, Britain, and Germany), and especially of the defence of the frontiers (*ad Ath.* p. 277 A; Amm. *l.c.*). As he drew the unwonted garb around him in place of his beloved pallium, he was heard to mutter the line of Homer, to which his wit gave a new shade of meaning:

"Him purple death and destiny embraced"

(Amm. xv. 8, 17). At the same time he received, through the management of Eusebia, the emperor's sister Helena as his bride, and the gift of a library from the empress herself (*Or.* iii. p. 123 D). Thus the reconciliation of the cousins was apparently complete. Julian produced a spirited panegyric upon the reign and just actions of Constantius, which it seems right to assign to this date (*Or.* 1; cf. Spanheim's notes, p. 5). He set out, on Dec. 1, for his new duties with a small retinue, from which almost all his personal followers were carefully excluded (Amm. xv. 8, 17, 18; Jul. *ad Ath.* p. 277 B, C). Of his four slaves, one was his only confidant in religious matters, an African named Euhemerus (*ad Ath.* p. 277 B; Eunap. *Vita Maximi*, p. 54). His physician, Oribasius, who had charge of his library, was only allowed to accompany him through ignorance of their intimacy (*ad Ath. l.c.*; Eunap. *Vita Oribasii*, p. 104). He entered Vienne with great popular rejoicing (for the province was hard-pressed by the barbarians) and possibly with secret expectations amongst the heathen party, which had been strong in the time of Magnentius. A blind old woman, learning his name and office as he passed, cried out, "There goes he who will restore the temples of the gods!" (Amm. xv. 8, 22).

During the next five years the young Caesar appears as a strenuous and successful general and a popular ruler. The details of his wars with the Franks and Alamanns, the Salii and Chamavi, will be found in Ammianus and Zosimus. Perhaps we ought to recollect that he was his own historian, writing "commentaries" (now no longer extant) which were no doubt intended to rival those of the author of the *Gallic War*. After an expedition against the Franks in the autumn of 357 he wintered for the first time at Paris, which became a favourite abode of his. He gives a well-known description of his φίλη Λουκετία in the *Misopogon* (pp. 340 seq.). His military successes endeared him to both troops and people. His internal government, particularly as lightening public burdens, was equally popular. He had specially to contend with the avarice of Florentius, the praetorian prefect, who desired to increase the *capitatio*, and who, on Julian's refusal to sign the indiction, complained of him to Constantius (Amm. xvii. 3, 2, and 5, in 357). Constantius, while reproving him for discrediting his officer, left him a practically free hand, and the tax, which on his entering Gaul was 25 aurei a head, had been reduced to 7 when he left (Amm. xvi. 5, 14; cf. xvii. 3, 6).

His ambition was to imitate Marcus Aurelius as a philosopher upon the throne, and Alexander the Great as a model in warfare (*ad Themist.* p. 253). His table was very plainly furnished, and he refused all the luxuries which Constantius had written down for him as proper for a Caesar's board (Amm. xvi. 5, 3). His bed was a mat and a rug of skins, from which he rose at midnight, and, after secret prayer to Mercury, addressed himself first to public business and then to literature. He studied philosophy first, then poetry, rhetoric, and history, making himself also fairly proficient in Latin. His chamber was ordinarily never warmed; and one very cold night, at Paris, he was nearly suffocated by some charcoal in a brazier, but erroneously attributed it to the dampness of the room (*Misopogon*, p. 341). All this attracted the people, but was not agreeable to many of the courtiers. Julian knew that he was surrounded by disaffected officials and other spies upon his conduct, and continued to conceal his religious sentiments, and to act cautiously towards his cousin. During his administration of Gaul he produced another panegyric upon Constantius, and one upon Eusebia, though the exact occasion of neither can be determined (*Or.* 2 and 3). In these orations Julian, though indulging to the full in classical parallels and illustrations, takes care to hide his change of religion. He speaks even of his prayers to God for Constantius, naturally indeed and not in a canting way (*Or.* 3, p. 118 D). Nor did he hesitate to join with him in issuing a law denouncing a capital penalty against those who sacrifice to or worship idols (*Cod. Theod.* xvi. 10, 6, Apr. 356), in repressing magic and all kinds of divination with very severe edicts (*ib.* ix. 16, 4-6, in 357 and 358), in punishing renegade Christians who had become Jews (*ib.* xvi. 8, 7), and in granting new privileges to the church and clergy, and regulating those already given (*ib.* xvi. 2, 13-16; the last as late as Mar. 361). To have hinted at dislike to any of these measures would, indeed, have aroused at once the strongest suspicions. One of the edicts against magic, which threatens torture for every kind of divination, seems almost personally directed against Julian (*Cod. Theod.* ix. 16, 6, dated July 5, 358, from Ariminum). The effect upon his conscience of condemning as a public officer what he was secretly practising must have been hardening and demoralizing. For Julian was not without thought on such subjects. At another time he declared he would rather die than sign the oppressive edict brought him by Florentius (Amm. xvii. 3, 2); and in his later famous decree against Christian professors he writes vehemently of the wickedness of thinking one thing and teaching another (*Ep.* 42).

In Apr. 360 Constantius ordered the flower of the Gallic auxiliaries to be sent to aid him in his expedition against the Persians (Amm. xx. 4). This request produced great irritation among men who had enlisted on the understanding that they were not to be required to cross the Alps—an irritation fomented no doubt by the friends of Julian, particularly, it is said, by Oribasius (Eunap. *Vita Oribasii*, p. 104). The troops surrounded the palace at Paris and demanded that their favourite should take the title of Augustus (*ad Ath.* p. 284; Amm. xx. 4, 14). Julian, according to his own account, was quite unprepared for such a step, and would not accede till Jupiter had given him a sign from heaven. This sign was no doubt the vision of the Genius of the Empire, who declared that he had long been waiting on his threshold and was now unwilling to be turned away from it. Yet he warned him (so Julian told his intimates) that his residence with him would in no case be for long (Amm. xx. 5, 10; cf. Lib. *ad Jul. cos.* p. 386). We have no reason, however, to think that Julian had any real hesitation, except as to the opportuneness of the moment. When he came down to address the troops, he still appeared reluctant, but the enthusiasm of the soldiers would take no denial, and he was raised in Gallic fashion upon a shield, and hastily crowned with a gold chain which a dragoon (*draconarius*) tore from his own accoutrements. He promised the accustomed donative (Amm. xx. 4, 18), which the friends of Constantius, it would seem, secretly tried to outdo by bribes (*ad Ath.* p. 285 A). The discovery of their intrigue only raised the popular enthusiasm to a higher pitch, and Julian felt strong enough to treat with his cousin. He dispatched an embassy with a letter declining to send the Gallic troops, who (he declared) positively refused to go, and could not be spared with safety; but he offered some small corps of barbarian auxiliaries. He related the action of the army in proclaiming him Augustus, but said nothing of his own wish to bear the title. As a compromise he proposed that Constantius should still appoint the praetorian prefect, the chief governor of that quarter of the empire, but that all lesser offices should be under his own administration (*ib.* D, and for particulars, Amm. xx. 8, 5-17), who gives the substance of the letter at length). But to these public and open requests he added a threatening and bitter private missive, which had the effect, whether intentionally or not, of rendering his negotiations abortive (Amm. *l.c.*).

Such a state of things could only end in war, but neither party was in a hurry to precipitate it. In Vienne Julian celebrated the fifth anniversary of his appointment, and appeared for the first time in the jewelled diadem which had become the symbol of imperial dignity (Amm. xxi. 1, 4). Meanwhile both Eusebia and Helena had been removed by death, and with them almost the last links which united the cousins. Julian still kept up the pretence of being a Christian. At Epiphany, 361, he kept the festival solemnly and even ostentatiously, joining in the public prayers and devotions (*ib.* 2). He witnessed calmly the triumphant return of St. Hilary after his exile, and permitted the Gallic bishops to hold a council at Paris (S. Hilarii, *Frag. Hist.* pp. 1353, 1354). His name also appears, after that of Constantius, attached to a law issued on Mar. 1 at Antioch, giving privileges to Christian ascetics. But all this was mere dissimulation for the sake of popularity. In secret he was anxiously trying, by all possible heathen means, to divine the future (Amm. xxi. 1, 6 seq.). He sent in particular for the hierophant of Eleusis, with whose aid he performed rites known to themselves alone (Eunap. *Vita Maximi*, p. 53; cf. Amm. xxi. 5, 1, "placata ritu secretiori Bellona").

The irritation against Constantius was further increased by an arrogant letter, addressed of course to the *Caesar* Julian, requiring his immediate submission and merely promising him his life. Julian, on receiving this, uttered an exclamation which betrayed his religion: "He would rather commit himself and his life to the gods than to Constantius" (Zos. iii. 9, 7). The moment seemed now come for action. In a speech to the soldiers in which he referred in ambiguous language to the will of the God of heaven—"arbitrium dei caelestis"—he called upon them to take the oath of allegiance and follow him across the Alps. He spoke in general terms of occupying Illyricum and Dacia, and then deciding what was to be done (Amm. xxi. 5). Having thus secured the Western provinces, he made a rapid and successful passage through N. Italy, receiving its submission. He reached Sirmium without opposition, having ordered the different divisions of his army to concentrate there. Then he took and garrisoned the important pass of Succi (Ssulu Derbend) on the Balkans, between Sardica and Philippopolis, thus securing the power to descend into Thrace. For the time he established his quarters at Naissus (Nish), and awaited further news. From there he wrote to the senate of Rome against Constantius, and in self-defence to the Athenians, Lacedemonians, and Corinthians (Zos. iii. 10).

The Athenian letter was possibly entrusted to the Eleusinian hierophant, who returned home about this time. It was perhaps also under his guidance that Julian underwent the secret ceremonies of initiation described by Gregory Nazianzen (*Or.* 4, 52-56, pp. 101-103). According to common report, he submitted to the disgusting bath of blood, the taurobolium or criobolium, through which the worshippers of Mithra and Cybele sought to procure eternal life. Julian's object, it is said, was not only to gain the favour of the gods, but also to wash away all defilement from previous contact with the Christian mysteries. This miserable story is yet a very credible one. Existing monuments prove that many pagans of position continued the taurobolium till the end of the 4th cent. (see the inscriptions in Wilmanns, *Exempla Inscr. Lat.* 107-126).

Such secret incidents preceded Julian's public declaration of his change of religion. At Naissus or Sirmium he threw off the mask, and professed himself openly a heathen. Of his first public sacrifice he wrote with exultation to his friend Maximus: "We worship the gods openly, and the greatest part of the troops who accompanied me profess the true religion. We have acknowledged our gratitude to the gods in many hecatombs. The gods command me to consecrate myself to their service with all my might, and most readily do I obey them. They promise us great returns for our toils if we are not remiss" (*Ep.* 38, p. 415 c).

Now came the news of his cousin's sudden death at Mopsucrene, at the foot of Mount Taurus, on Nov. 3, and Julian learnt that he was accepted without opposition as the successor designated by his dying breath, a report of which we cannot guarantee the truth (Amm. xxii. 2, 6).

§ 4. *Julian as Augustus at Constantinople* (from Nov. 3, 361, to May 362).—Julian hastened to Constantinople, through the pass of Succi and by Philippopolis and Heraclea, entering the Eastern capital amid general rejoicings on Dec. 11. He conducted the funeral of Constantius with the usual honours; laying aside all the imperial insignia, except the purple, and marching in the procession, touching the bier with his hands (Liban. *Epitaph.* p. 512, cf. Greg. Naz. *Or.* 5, 16, 17, pp. 157, 158). Constantius was buried near his father in the Church of the Apostles, but whether Julian entered it is not stated.

Almost his next act was to appoint a special commission under the presidency of Saturninus Sallustius Secundus (to be distinguished from the prefect of the Gauls) to bring to justice the principal supporters of the late government. Julian himself avoided taking part in it, and allowed no appeal from its decisions. The commission met at Chalcedon, and acted with excessive rigour.

Julian next turned his attention to the palace, with its swarm of needless and overpaid officials, eunuchs, cooks, and barbers, who battened on bribes and exactions. All these he swept away, to the general satisfaction (Amm. xxii. 4; Liban. *Epit.* p. 565).

Towards Christians he adopted a policy of toleration, though desiring nothing more keenly than the humiliation of the Church. His object was to set sect against sect by extending equal licence to all (cf. Amm. xxii. 5). He issued an edict allowing all bishops exiled under Constantius to return, and restoring their confiscated property (Socr. iii. 1, p. 171). On the other hand, the extreme Arian, Aetius, as a friend of Gallus, received a special invitation to court (*Ep.* 31). A letter "to Basil," seemingly of the same date, and of similar purport, may possibly have been addressed to St. Basil of Caesarea (*Ep.* 12; De Broglie assumes this, t. iv. pp. 133, 235, n.). To Caesarius, a court physician of high repute and the brother of Gregory, Julian shewed great attention, and strove for his conversion.

He even entered into a public discussion on religion with him, and was much mortified by the ill success of his rhetoric (Greg. Naz. *Ep.* 6; *Orat.* vii. 11-14). The Donatists, Novatianists, and perhaps some extreme Arians were not loth to appear before the new emperor, who sought to destroy unanimity by extending free licence to all Christian sects, but there is no trace of any important Catholic leader falling into the snare. In the same spirit he ordered Eleusius, Arian bp. of Cyzicus, to restore the ruined church of the Novatianists within two months (Socr. ii. 38, p. 147; iii. 11; cf. *Ep.* 52, p. 436 A). Toleration was also extended to the Jews, from a real though imperfect sympathy. Their ritual seemed to Julian a point of contact with Hellenism, and with their rejection of an Incarnate Saviour he was quite in harmony. He approved of their worship of the Creator, but could not tolerate their identification of Him with the God Whose especial people they claimed to be —and Whom he, in his polytheism, imagined to be an inferior divinity (S. Cyril. *in Jul.* iv. pp. 115, 141, 201, 343, 354, ed. Spanheim).

The great task which lay nearest his heart was the restoration of heathenism to its former influence and power, and its rehabilitation both in theory and practice. He composed an oration for the festival of the sun, no doubt that celebrated on Dec. 25, as the "Natalis Solis invicti," in connexion with the winter solstice. Though Constantinople had never been a heathen city, or polluted with public heathen ceremonies, he called this "the festival which the imperial city celebrates with annual sacrifices" (*Orat.* 4, p. 131 D). The main body of the oration is occupied with the obscure theory of the triple hierarchy of worlds: the *κόσμος νοητός* or "intelligible world," the *κόσμος νοερός* or "intelligent," and the *κόσμος αἰσθητός* the "visible" or "phenomenal." In each of these three worlds there is a central principle, who is the chief object of worship and the fountain of power; the Sun king being the centre of the intermediate or "intelligent" world. This ideal god was evidently a kind of counterpoise in Julian's theology to the Word of God, the mediator of the Christian Trinity (*μέση τις, οὐκ ἀπὸ τῶν ἄκρων κραθεῖσα, τελεία δὲ καὶ ἀμιγὴς ἀφ' ὅλων τῶν θεῶν ἐμφανῶν τε καὶ ἀφανῶν καὶ αἰσθητῶν καὶ νοητῶν, ἡ τοῦ βασιλέως* Ἡλίου *νοερὰ καὶ πάγκαλος οὐσία*, p. 139 B, and *τῶν νοερῶν θεῶν μέσος ἐν μέσοις τεταγμένος κατὰ παντοίαν μεσότητα*. Cf. Naville, *Jul. l'A. et sa philosophie du polythéisme*, pp. 102 seq.). This oration should be read in connexion with the *fifth* oration "on the Mother of the Gods," which he delivered at her festival, apparently at the vernal equinox, and while still at Constantinople. It is chiefly an allegorical platonizing interpretation of the myth of Attis and Cybele, very different from the modern reference of it to the circle of the seasons.

In the practice of all superstitious ceremonies, whether public or mystic, Julian was enthusiastic to the point of ridiculous ostentation. He turned his palace into a temple. Every day he knew better than the priests themselves what festival was in the pagan calendar, and what sacrifice was required. He himself acted as attendant, slaughterer, and priest, and had a passion for all the details of heathen ritual (Liban. *Epitaph.* p. 564, *ad Jul. cos.* pp. 394 seq.; Greg. *Orat.* 5, 22, p. 161; de Broglie, iv. pp. 126, 127). No previous emperor had so highly prized his office of pontifex maximus, which Julian valued as equal to all the other imperial prerogatives (*χαίρει καλούμενος ἱερεὺς οὐχ ἧττον ἢ βασιλεύς*, Liban. *ad Jul. cos.* p. 394). In this capacity he apparently attempted to introduce something of the episcopal regimen into the loose system of the heathen priesthood, himself occupying the papal or patriarchal chair (cf. Greg. *Or.* 4, ii. p. 138). Thus he appointed Theodorus chief priest of Asia and Arsacius of Galatia, with control over inferior priests; the hierophant of Eleusis was set over Greece and Lydia, and Callixene made high priestess of Pessinus. (*Ep.* 63 *Theodoro* is early in his reign, and the long *Fragmentum Epistolae* may be a sequel to it; *Ep.* 49 *Arsacio* is later, as is that to Callixene, *Ep.* 21. The appointments of the hierophant and of Chrysanthius are described by Eunapius, *Vita Maximi*, pp. 54, 57.) As chief pontiff he issued some remarkable instructions to his subordinates, some of which have been preserved. His "pastoral letters," as they may properly be called, to the chief priests of Asia and Galatia, shew a striking insight into the defects of heathenism considered as a religious ideal, and a clear attempt to graft upon it the more popular and attractive features of Christianity. He regrets several times that Christians and Jews are more zealous than Gentiles, especially in charity to the poor (*Ep.* 49, pp. 430, 431; in *Frag.* p. 305 he refers to the influence of the Agapé and similar institutions. In *Ep.* 63, p. 453 D, he describes the persistency of the Jews in abstaining from swine's flesh, etc.). He promises large endowments of corn for distribution to the indigent and the support of the priesthood; and orders the establishment of guest-houses and hospitals (*ξενοδοχεῖα, καταγώγια ξένων καὶ πτωχῶν*, Soz. v. 16, Jul. *Ep.* 49, p. 430 C). In the very spirit of the Gospel he insists on the duty of giving clothing and food even to enemies and prisoners (*Frag.* pp. 290-291). "Who was ever impoverished," he writes, "by what he gave to his neighbours? I, for my part, as often as I have been liberal to those in want, have received back from them many times as much, though I am but a bad man of business; and I never repented of my liberality" (*Frag.* p. 290 C). Elsewhere he enters into minute details on the conduct and habits of the priesthood. He fixes the number of sacrifices to be offered by day and night, the deportment to be observed within and without the temples, the priest's dress, his visits to his friends, his secret meditations and his private reading. The priest must peruse nothing scurrilous or indecent, such as Archilochus, Hipponax, or the old comedy; nothing sceptical like Pyrrho and Epicurus; no novels and love-tales; but history and sound philosophy like Pythagoras, Plato, Aristotle, and the Stoics; and must learn by heart the hymns to the gods, especially those sung in his own temple (*Frag.* pp. 300-301; cf. *Ep.* 56, to Ecdicius, ordering him to train boys for the temple choirs). He must avoid theatres and taverns, and all public resorts where he is likely to hear or see anything vulgar or indecent (*Frag.* p. 304 B, C; *Ep.* 49, p. 430 B). Not only priests, but the sons of priests, are forbidden to attend the "venationes" or spectacles of wild beasts (*Frag.* p. 304 D). The true priest is to be considered superior, at least in the temple, to any public official, and to be honoured as the intercessor between gods and men (*Frag.* p. 296 B, C; cf. the edict to the Byzantine against applauding himself in the Tychaeum, *Ep.* 64). He, however, who does not obey the rules laid down for his conduct, is to be removed from his office (*Frag.* p. 297; *Ep.* 49, p. 430 B); and we possess an edict of Julian's suspending a priest for three months for injury done to a brother priest (*Ep.* 62).

Further, "he intended," says Gregory (*Or.* iv. 111, p. 138), "to establish schools in all cities, and professorial chairs of different grades, and lectures on heathen doctrines, both in their bearings on moral practice and in explanation of their abstruser mysteries." Of such lectures, no doubt, he wished his own orations on the Sun and the Mother of the Gods to be examples. Besides this imitation of Christian sermons and lectures, he desired to set up religious communities of men and women, vowed to chastity and meditation (*ἁγνευτήριά τε καὶ παρθενεύματα καὶ φροντιστήρια*, cf. Soz. v. 16). These were institutions familiar to Oriental heathenism, but out of harmony with the old Greek spirit of which Julian professed himself so ardent an admirer. He was, indeed, unconsciously less a disciple of Socrates than of the Hindu philosophy, a champion of Asian mysticism against European freedom of thought.

Julian used not only his literary and personal influence and pontifical authority in favour of the worship of the gods, but also his imperial power. The temples where standing were reopened, or rebuilt at the expense of those who had destroyed them, and received back their estates, which had been to some extent confiscated under Constantius (Amm. xxii. 4, 3, "pasti ex his quidam templorum spoliis"; Liban. *Epitaph.* p. 564, describes the general plan of restitution; cf. his *Ep.* 624, *πᾶσι κηρύξας κομίζεσθαι τὰ αὐτῶν.*) A friend of the gods was as a friend of the emperor's, their enemy became his (Liban. *l.c.* and more strongly p. 617). Yet direct persecution was forbidden and milder means of conversion practised (*Ep.* 7 to Artabius; Liban. 564). Julian even bore with some patience the public attacks of the blind and aged Maris, Arian bp. of Chalcedon, who called him an "impious atheist," while he was sacrificing in the Tychaeum of Constantinople. Julian replied only with a scoff at his infirmity: "Not even your Galilean God will heal you." Maris retorted, "I thank my God for my blindness which prevents me from seeing your apostasy," a rebuke which the emperor ignored (Soz. v. 4, where we must of course read *τυχαίῳ* for *τειχίῳ*, cf. Jul. *Ep.* 64, *Byzantinis*). Not a few persons of position apostatized, among them Julian's maternal uncle Julianus, his former tutor Hecebolius, the officials Felix, Modestus, and Elpidius, and the former bp. of Ilium Novum, Pegasius, all of whom were rewarded by promotion. (Philost. vii. 10; Socr. iii. 13; Liban. *pro Aristophane*, pp. 435, 436, and *Ep.* 17; Greg. Naz. *Or.* iv. 62, p. 105; Jul. *Ep.* 78; cf. Sievers, *Libanius*, p. 105. On the readiness of many of these converts to return to the church cf. Asterius of Amasea, *Hom. in Avaritiam*, p. 227, and *Hom.* xix. in *Psalm.* v. p. 433, Migne.) But the number of these new converts was less than might perhaps have been expected from the divided state of the church and the low standard of court Christianity under Constantius. It was far less, no doubt, than Julian's sanguine expectations. Caesarius, as we have seen, stood firm, and so did three prominent officers in the army, destined to be his successors in the empire—Jovian, Valentinian, and Valens (Valentinian was banished, Soz. vi. 6; Philost. vii. 7; cf. Greg. *Or.* iv. 65, p. 106). The steadfastness of the court and the army was indeed sorely tried. The monogram of Christ was removed from the Labarum, and replaced by the old S.P.Q.R.; and heathen symbols again began to appear upon the coinage, and upon statues and pictures of the emperor, so that it was difficult to pay him respect without appearing to bow to an idol. (Greg. *Or.* iv. 80, 81, pp. 116, 117; Socr. vi. 17. Socrates probably somewhat exaggerates. The obscure letter of Julian to a painter, *Ep.* 65, appears to reprimand him for painting him without his customary images in his hands or by his side.) Julian even condescended to a trick to entrap a number of his soldiers, probably of the praetorian guard, by persuading them to offer incense when receiving a donative from his hands (Soz. v. 17; Greg. *Or* iv. 83, 84, pp. 118, 119; cf. Rode, p. 62). Some of the soldiers, on discovering the snare from the jeers of their companions, protested loudly and threw down their money; and Julian, in consequence, dismissed all Christians from his bodyguard (Greg. *l.c.*; Socr. iii. 13). Many common soldiers were doubtless less firm, and conformed, at least outwardly, but the subsequent election of Jovian by the army of Persia looks as if their conviction was not deep). (Liban. *ad Jul. cos.* Jan. 1, 363, p. 399; Greg. *Or.* iv. 64, 65, p. 106; St. Chrys. *de Babyla contra Julianum*, § 23, vol. ii. pp. 686, 687, ed. Gaume; cf. Sievers, *Libanius*, pp. 107-109). It was pretty well understood that no Christian official would be promoted to high civil functions, while converts like Felix and Elpidius were. Julian is reported to have stated in an edict that the Christian law forbade its subjects to wield the sword of justice, and therefore he could not commit the government of provinces to them. Such a sentiment would be characteristic, and this edict is probably an historical fact (Rufin. i. 32), but perhaps did not extend to persons already in office or in the army, unless they offered resistance to the course of events. Other measures were aimed at the clergy as a body, and intended to reduce the church generally to the position which it held before Constantine. The church suffered as much perhaps as private owners of property by the order to restore the temples and refund temple lands. The clergy and widows who had received grants from the municipal revenues were deprived of them and obliged to repay their previous receipts—an act of great injustice (Soz. v. 5). The church lost its power of inheritance, and its ministers the privileges of making wills and of jurisdiction in certain cases (Jul. *Ep.* 52, p. 437 A, *Bostrenis*). But perhaps what was felt most of all was the loss of immunity from personal taxation and from the service of the curiae or municipal councils, who were held responsible for the taxes of their district. A short decree issued on Mar. 13, 362, made all persons, formerly privileged as Christians, liable to the office of decurion (*Cod. Theod.* xii. 1, 50). We may readily admit that the church would have been safer and holier without some of its privileges, which bound it too closely to the state. But to abolish them all at once, without warning, was a very harsh proceeding, which caused much suffering, and Ammianus only spoke the general opinion when he censured the conduct of his hero (Amm. xxv. 4, 21, cf. xxii. 9, 12). A Greek decree of apparently the same date, addressed *to the Byzantines*—*i.e.* the citizens of Constantinople—extended this measure to all privileged persons whatsoever, except those who had "done public service in the metropolis"—*i.e.* probably, those who had as consuls or praetors exhibited costly games for the public amusement (*Ep.* 11); a later decree also confirming the "chief physicians" in their immunities (*Cod. Theod.* xiii. 3-4, nearly equivalent to *Ep.* 25*).

In the spring of this year, while he was still at Constantinople, the affairs of the church of Alexandria attracted Julian's attention, and led to the first decided step which violated his policy of personal toleration. The intruded Arian bishop, George of Cappadocia, had made himself equally detested by pagans and Catholics. On Dec. 24 he was foully murdered by the former (without any intervention of Christians) in a riot. Dracontius, master of the mint, who had overturned an altar recently set up in his office, and Diodorus, who was building a church and gave offence to pagan prejudices by cutting short the hair of some boys employed under him, were both torn to pieces in the same sedition (Amm. xxii. 11, 9). Julian wrote an indignant reprimand to the people, but inflicted no punishment (*Ep.* 10, Amm. *l.c.*; cf. Julian's letter to Zeno, *Ep.* 45). On Feb. 22 St. Athanasius was again seated upon his throne amid the rejoicing of the people. Julian saw in him an enemy he could not afford to tolerate. He wrote to the Alexandrians (apparently at once), saying that one so often banished by royal decree ought to have awaited special permission to return; that in allowing the exiled bishops to come back he did not mean to restore them to their churches; Athanasius, he feared, had resumed his "episcopal throne," to the great disgust of "god-fearing Alexandrians." He therefore ordered him to leave the city at once, on pain of greater punishment (*Ep.* 26). Athanasius braved the emperor's wrath and did not leave Alexandria, except, perhaps, for a time. Public feeling was with him, and an appeal was apparently forwarded to the emperor to reconsider his sentence. (*Ep.* 51, written probably in Oct. 362, speaks of Athanasius as ἐπιζητούμενος by the Alexandrians.) The sequel of this appeal will appear later.

Another change of policy about this time shewed a further advance in intolerance and inconsistency. Julian determined to take the control of education into the hands of the state. On June 17, while *en route* between Constantinople and Antioch, he issued an edict, promulgated at Spoleto, to the Western empire, on June 28. This document said nothing about Christian teachers, but required for all professors and schoolmasters a diploma of approval from the municipal council in every city before they might teach. This was to be forwarded to himself for counter-signature (*Cod. Theod.* xiii. 3, 5). This power of veto was no doubt aimed at Christian teachers; and another edict, supposed to have been issued soon after, struck an open and violent blow at the church. This may have been issued even earlier; it can hardly have been much later (*Ep.* 42, with no title or date). It declares that "only a cheat and a charlatan will teach one thing while he thinks another. All teachers, especially those who instruct the young, ought . . . not to oppose the common belief and try to insinuate their own. . . . Now Homer, Hesiod, Demosthenes, Herodotus, Thucydides, Isocrates, and Lysias all founded their learning upon the gods, and considered themselves dedicated to Hermes or the Muses. It is monstrous, then, that those who teach these writers should dishonour their gods. I do not wish them to change their religion that they may retain their offices, but I give them the choice, either not to teach, or, if they prefer to do so, to teach at the same time that none of these authors is guilty of folly or impiety in his doctrine about the gods. . . . If teachers think these authors which they expound wise, and draw philosophy from them, let them emulate their religion. If they think them in error, let them go to the churches of the Galileans and expound Matthew and Luke, who forbid our sacrifices. I wish, however, the ears and tongues of you Christians may be 'regenerated,' as you would say, by these writings which I value so much."

Christians considered the decree practically to exclude them from the schools. For Julian expressly orders all teachers to *insist* on the religious side of their authors. Grammar-schools were to become seminaries of paganism. No indifferent or merely philological teaching was to be allowed. No sincere Christian parents therefore could send their sons to such schools. A quotation given by Gregory, as if from this decree, is not found in the text of the edict as we have it (*Or.* 4, 102, p. 132). Perhaps he may be quoting some other of Julian's writings, *e.g.* the books against the Christians. The words are characteristic: "Literature and the Greek language are naturally ours, who are worshippers of the gods; illiterate ignorance and rusticity are yours, whose wisdom goes no further than to say 'believe.'" The last taunt is borrowed from Celsus (Origen, *c. Celsum*, i. 9).

Two celebrated men gave up their posts rather than submit to this edict—Prohaeresius of Athens, whom many thought superior to Libanius, and C. Marius Victorinus of Rome. Julian had already made overtures to the former (*Ep.* 2), and even offered to except him from the action of the edict; but he refused to be put in a better condition than his fellows (Hieron. *Chron.* sub anno 2378; cf. Eunap.

Prohaeresius, p. 92; *Himerius*, p. 95; and *Frag.* 76, p. 544, ed. Boissonade). Victorinus was equally famous at Rome, and his constancy was a subject of just glory to the church (see the interesting account of his conversion, etc. in August. *Conf.* viii. 2-5).

Attempts were made to supply the place of classical literature by putting historical and doctrinal portions of Scripture into Greek prose and verse. Thus the elder APOLLINARIS wrote 24 books in hexameters, which were to form a substitute for Homer, on the Biblical history up to the reign of Saul, and produced tragedies, lyrics, and even comedies on Biblical subjects (Soz. v. 18). The younger Apollinaris reduced the writings of the N.T. into the form of Platonic dialogues (Socr. iii. 16); and some of the works of Victorinus in Latin, such as the poem on the seven Maccabean brothers, and various hymns, may have been written with the same aim (cf. Teuffel, *Gesch. der Röm. Lit.* § 384, 7), as also the Greek tragedy, still extant, of *Christus patiens*. Whatever their merit, these books could not properly supply the place of the classical training; and if Julian had lived and this edict had been put in force for any time, it would have been a very dangerous injury to the faith. (Socrates has some very good remarks on this subject, iii. 16.)

§ 5. *Julian's Journey through Asia Minor*—(May to July 362).—After a sojourn of about five months in Constantinople Julian began to think of foreign affairs. Fears of internal resistance were removed by the surrender of Aquileia, which had been seized by some troops of Constantius. He determined upon an expedition against Persia, the only power he thought worthy of his steel. Shortly after May 12 he set out upon a progress through Asia Minor to Antioch. He passed through Nicaea into Galatia, apparently as far as Ancyra, from which place, perhaps, he dispatched the edict about education just described (Amm. xxii. 9, 5. If the law, *Cod. Just.* i. 40, 5, is rightly attributed to Julian, he was at Ancyra on May 28, to which visit belongs a somewhat hyperbolical inscription celebrating his triumphant march from the Western Ocean to the Tigris, beginning, DOMINO TOTIVS ORBIS | IVLIANO AVGVSTO | EX OCEANO BRI | TANNICO (*C. I. L.* iii. 247, Orell. 1109, Wilmanns 1089). From Ancyra he visited Pessinus in Phrygia to pay homage to the famous sanctuary of the Mother of the Gods, at which he offered large and costly presents (Amm. *l.c.*; Liban. *ad Jul. cos.* p. 398). The oration in honour of this deity, who, with the Sun-god, was Julian's chief object of veneration, was probably delivered earlier; but he took occasion about this time to vindicate the doctrine of Diogenes from the aspersions of false and luxurious cynics (*Or.* vi. εἰς τοὺς ἀπαιδεύτους κύνας, delivered about the summer solstice, p. 181 A). He was not satisfied with the progress of heathenism amongst the people of the place (*Ep.* 49, *Arsacio pontifici Galatiae*, ad fin.). At Ancyra, according to the Acts of the Martyrs, a presbyter named Basil was accused of exciting the people against the gods and speaking injuriously of the emperor and his apostate courtiers. Basil was cruelly treated in his presence, and, after a second trial, was put to death by red-hot irons (Boll. Mar. 22; also in Ruinart, *Acta Mart. Sincera*, p. 599; Soz. p. 11). [BASILIUS OF ANCYRA.] Julian left Ancyra, according to the same Acts, on June 29, and soon after was met by a crowd of litigants, some clamouring for a restoration of their property, others complaining that they were unjustly forced into the curia, others accusing their neighbours of treason. Julian shewed no leniency to the second class, even when they had a strong case, being determined to allow as few immunities as possible. To the rest he was just and fair, and an amusing instance is recorded of the summary way he disposed of a feeble charge of treason (Amm. xxii. 9, 12; cf. xxv. 4, 21).

In Cappadocia his ill-humour was roused by finding almost all the people Christian. "Come, I beseech you," he writes to the philosopher Aristoxenus, "and meet me at Tyana, and shew us a genuine Greek amongst these Cappadocians. As far as I have seen, either the people will not sacrifice, or the very few that are ready to do so are ignorant of our ritual" (*Ep.* 4). He had already shewn his anger against the people of Caesarea, the capital of the province, who had dared, after his accession, to destroy the Temple of Fortune, the last that remained standing in their city. According to Sozomen (v. 4), he erased the city from the "list of the empire and called it by its old name Mazaca." He fined the Christians 300 pounds of gold, confiscated church property, and enrolled the ecclesiastics in the militia of the province, besides imposing a heavy poll-tax on the Christian laity. But either these severe measures must have been justified by great violence on the part of the Christians or Sozomen's account is exaggerated; for Gregory Nazianzen says that it is perhaps not fair to reproach him with his violent conduct to the Caesareans, and speaks of him as "justly indignant" (*Or.* 4, 92, p. 126). Such mild language in this instance may well make us attach more weight to Gregory's statements as to Julian's misdoings on other occasions. The emperor was further incensed by the tumultuous election of Eusebius to the bishopric of Caesarea, in which the soldiers of the garrison took part. This Eusebius was still a catechumen, but a man of official rank and influence, known to be an enemy of the emperor (Greg. *Or. in Patrem*, xviii. 33, p. 354). The elder Gregory firmly resisted the remonstrances of the governor of the province, who was sent to him by Julian, and the storm passed away (*ib.* 34, p. 355). "You knew us," cried Gregory, "you knew Basil and myself from the time of your sojourn in Greece, and you paid us the compliment which the Cyclops paid Ulysses, and kept us to be swallowed last" (*Or.* 5, 39, p. 174). The silence of Gregory may be taken as clenching the arguments from style against the genuineness of the supposed correspondence between Julian and St. Basil, which would otherwise be assigned to this date (see pp. 490 f.). The letters referred to are *Epp.* 40, 41, in the editions of St. Basil, the first of these=Jul. *Ep.* 75 (77 Heyler); cf. Rode, p. 86, note 11.

A more pleasant reception awaited Julian in the neighbouring province, Cilicia. Entering it by the famous pass of the Pylae Ciliciae, he was met by the governor, his friend Celsus, once his fellow-student, and probably his confidant at Athens, who greeted him with a panegyric—a greeting more agreeable to Julian than the customary presents made to emperors in their progresses (Amm. xxii. 9, 13; Liban. *Epit.* p. 575, and *Ep.* 648). Julian shewed his high esteem for his encomiast by taking him up into his chariot and entering with him into Tarsus, a city which evidently pleased him by its welcome. Celsus accompanied him to the southern boundary of his province, a few leagues N. of Antioch. Here they were met by a large crowd, among whom was Libanius (Liban. *de Vita Sua*, p. 81; *Ep.* 648; see Sievers, *Libanius*, p. 91). He reached Antioch before July 28, the date of a law found in both the Codes, permitting provincial governors to appoint inferior judges or *judices pedanei* (*Cod. Theod.* i. 68 = *Cod. Just.* iii. 3, 5; cf. *C. I. L.* iii. 459).

§ 6. *Julian's Residence at Antioch* (July 362 to March 5, 363).—The eight months spent at Antioch left Julian yet more bitter against the church, and less careful to avoid injustice to its members, in fact countenancing persecution even to death, though in word still forbidding it and proclaiming toleration. (Libanius says that Julian spent *nine* months at Antioch, *Epit.* p. 578, 15, but it is hard to make more than *eight*.) The narrative of this period may be divided into an account of (*a*) his relations with the citizens of Antioch; (*b*) his relations to the church at large; (*c*) attempt to rebuild the temple at Jerusalem.

(*a*) *Internal State of Antioch.*—On his entrance into the city Libanius greeted him in a speech in which he congratulated him on bringing back at once the ancient rites of sacrifice and the honour to the profession of rhetoric (*Prosphoneticus Juliano*, ed. Reiske, i. p. 405). But other sounds saddened Julian with a presage of his coming doom. It was the festival of the lamentation for Adonis, and the air resounded with shrieks for the lover of Venus, cut down in his prime as the green corn fails before the heat of the summer sun. This ill-omened beginning was followed by other equally unpropitious circumstances, and the residence of Julian at Antioch was a disappointment to himself and disagreeable to almost all the inhabitants. He was impatient, or soon became so, to engage upon his Persian campaign; but the difficulty of making the necessary preparations in time determined him to pass the winter at the Syrian capital (Liban. *Epit.* p. 576; Amm. xxii. 10, 1). He had anticipated much more devotion on the part of the pagans and much less resistance on that of the Christians. He was disgusted to find that both parties regretted the previous reign—"Neither the Chi nor the Kappa" (*i.e.* neither Christ nor Constantius) "did our city any harm" became a common saying (*Misopogon*, p. 357 A). To the heathens themselves the enthusiastic form of religion to which Julian was devoted was little more than an unpleasant and somewhat vulgar anachronism. His cynic asceticism and dislike of the theatre and the circus was unpopular in a city particularly addicted to public spectacles. His superstition was equally unpalatable. The short, untidy, long-bearded man, marching pompously in procession on the tips of his toes, and swaying his shoulders from side to side, surrounded by a crowd of abandoned characters, such as formed the regular attendants upon many heathen festivals, appeared seriously to compromise the dignity of the empire. The blood of countless victims flowed everywhere, but seemed to serve merely to gorge his foreign soldiery, especially the semi-barbarous Gauls; and the streets of Antioch were disturbed by their revels (Amm. xxii. 12, 6). Secret rumours spread of horrid nocturnal sacrifices and of the pursuit of arts of necromancy from which the natural heathen conscience shrank only less than the Christian. The wonder is, not that Julian quarrelled with the Antiochenes, but that he left the city without a greater explosion than actually took place.

Not a little of the irritation between the emperor and the citizens was centred upon the suburb of the city, called Daphne, a delicious cool retreat in which, as it was fabled, the nymph beloved by Apollo had been transformed into a laurel. Here was a celebrated temple of the god, and a spring that bore the name of Castalian, in former days the favourite haunt of the gay, the luxurious, and the vicious. Gallus had counteracted the genius loci by transposing to it the relics of the martyr bp. Babylas, whose chapel was erected opposite the temple of Apollo. The worship of the latter had almost ceased, and Julian, going to Daphne in Aug. (Loüs), to keep the annual festival of the Sun-god, was surprised to find no gathering of worshippers. He himself had returned for the purpose from a visit to the temple of Zeus Casius, several leagues distant. To his disgust the city had provided no sacrifice, and only one poor priest appeared, offering a single goose at his own expense. Julian rated the town council soundly (*Misop.* pp. 361 D, seq.). He took care that in future sacrifices should not be wanting, and eagerly consulted the oracle and unstopped the Castalian spring. After a long silence he learnt that Apollo was disturbed by the presence of the "dead man," *i.e.* Babylas. "I am surrounded by corpses," said the voice, "and I cannot speak till they are removed" (Soz. v. 19; Chrys. *de S. Bab.* § 15, p. 669; Liban. *Monodia in Daphnen*, vol. iii. p. 333). All the corpses were cleared away, but especially that of the martyr (Amm. xxii. 12, 8; *Misop.* p. 361 B). A remnant of religious awe perhaps prevented Julian from destroying the relics of which his actions practically acknowledged the power, and they were eagerly seized by the Christians and borne in triumph to Antioch. The procession along the five miles from Daphne to the city chanted aloud Ps. xcvii.: "Confounded be all they that worship carved images and that delight in vain gods." Julian, incensed by this personality, forced the prefect Sallustius, much against his will, to inquire into it with severity and punish those concerned. One young man, Theodorus, was hung upon the rack (*equuleus*) and cruelly scourged with iron nails for a whole day, till he was supposed to be dying. Rufinus, the church historian, who met him in after-life, asked him how he bore the pain. Theodorus replied that he had felt but little, for a young man stood by him wiping off the sweat of his agony and comforting him all the time (Rufin. i. 35, 36, referred to by Soc. iii. 19, and given in Ruinart, *Acta Martyrum*, p. 604, ed. Rabisbon. 1859). The anger of Julian was also braved by a widow named Publia, the head of a small community of Christian virgins, who sang in his hearing the Psalms against idols and against the enemies of God. She was brought before a court and buffeted on the face with severity, but dismissed (Theod. iii. 19).

Shortly after the translation of the relics of St. Babylas to Antioch, on the night of Oct. 22, the temple of Daphne itself was burnt to the ground. The heathens accused the Christians of maliciously setting it on fire; they attributed it to fire from heaven and the prayers of St. Babylas. A story also got about that Asclepiades the cynic had left a number of lighted candles burning in the shrine (Amm. xxii. 13; Soz. v. 20; Chrys. *de S. Bab.* § 17, p. 674). Julian's wrath was intense. He accused the Christians of the deed, and suspected the priests of knowing about it (*Misop.* pp. 346 B, 361 B, C). As a punishment he ordered the cathedral church of Antioch to be closed, and confiscated its goods (Amm. xxii. 13, 2; Soz. v. 8). The order was executed by his uncle Julianus, now count of the East, with all the zeal of a new convert and with circumstances of disgusting profanity. Theodoret, a presbyter, who still collected a congregation of the faithful, was tortured and beheaded (Ruinart, *Acta Mart.* p. 605). The Christian account tells us that Julian reproved his uncle as having brought him into disgrace, but in the *Misopogon* he gives him nothing but praise (*ib.* p. 607, *Misop.* p. 365 C). The count's miserable death, which followed soon after, was naturally treated as a judgment from heaven (Soz. v. 8; Theod. iii. 12, etc.). That of Felix, another renegade, had, a little earlier, been equally remarkable for its suddenness. The two were regarded as a presage of the emperor's own doom, for now that Julianus and Felix were gone, Augustus would soon follow, a play upon the imperial title *Julianus Felix Augustus* (Amm. xxiii. 1, 5). This was a trivial saying, but calculated to disquiet and irritate a mind like Julian's.

Antioch meanwhile was afflicted by a dearth, which almost became a famine, and the emperor's efforts to alleviate it failed. He imported a large quantity of grain from Egypt, and fixed the market price at a low figure. Speculators bought up his importations, and would not sell their own stores, and soon there was nothing in the markets. Julian declared that the fault was in the magistrates, and tried in vain to infuse some of his own public spirit into the farmers and merchants (Liban. *Epit.* p. 587). The town council were sent to prison (Amm. xxii. 14, 2; Liban. *Epit.* p. 588). Their confinement, however, did not last a day, and they were released by the intercession of Libanius, who tells us that he was not deterred from his petition by the sarcastic hint that the Orontes was not far off (*de Vita Sua*, vol. i. p. 85). The whole winter, indeed, was clouded with misfortunes. On Dec. 2 the rest of Nicomedia was destroyed by earthquake, and a large part of Nicaea suffered with it (Amm. xxii. 13, 5). News was brought that Constantinople was in danger from the same cause, and some suggested that the wrath of the earth-shaker Poseidon must be appeased. This gave Julian, who had a real affection for the city, an opportunity of showing his enthusiasm. He stood all day long in the open air, under rain and storm, in a fixed and rigid attitude, like an Indian yogi, while his courtiers looked on in amazement from under cover. It was calculated afterwards that the earthquake stopped on the very day of the imperial intercession, and Julian, it is said, took no harm from his exposure (Liban. *Epit.* p. 581). But this partial success did not make him feel secure of the favour of the gods. He was convinced that Apollo had deserted Daphne and the other deities were not propitious. Even the day of his entering the consulship, Jan. 1, 363, graced with an oration of Libanius (*ad Jul. imp. consulem*), was disfigured by a bad omen: a priest fell dead on the steps of the temple of the Genius. This was the more annoying, as he had no doubt intended to make his fourth consulship mark a new era by taking as his colleague his old friend Sallustius prefect of the Gauls, an honour paid to no one outside the imperial family since the days of Diocletian (Amm. xxiii. 1, 1). At the same time too he received news of the failure of the attempt (see (*c*), *infra*) to rebuild the temple at Jerusalem (Amm. xxiii. 1, 3).

Meanwhile his designs for involving the city in heathen rites caused considerable excitement and odium. He profaned the fountains of the city of Daphne according to Christian ideas, and consecrated them according to his own, by throwing into them a portion of his sacrifices, so that all who used them might be partakers with the gods, and for a similar reason ordered all things sold in the market, such as bread, meat, and vegetables, to be sprinkled with lustral water. The Christians complained but followed the precept of the apostle in eating freely all things sold in public, without inquiry (Theod. iii. 15). Two young officers, Juventinus and Maximinus, were one day lamenting this state of things, and quoted the words from the Greek Daniel, c. iii. 32, "Thou hast delivered us to a lawless king, to an apostate beyond all the heathen that are in the earth." Their words were repeated by an informer, and they were ordered to appear before the emperor. They declared the cause of their complaint, the only one (as they said) which they had to bring against his government. They were thrown into prison, and friends were sent to promise them large rewards if they would change their religion; but they stood firm, and were beheaded in the middle of the night, on the charge of having spoken evil of the emperor (Chrys. *in Juvent. et Max.* 3; cf. Theod. iii. 15). The date of this "martyrdom" may have been Jan. 25, as it appears in Latin calendars (Boll. Jan. p. 618).

Julian discharged his spleen upon the Antiochenes by writing one of the most remarkable satires ever published—the *Misopogon.* "He had been insulted," says Gibbon, "by satires and libels; in his turn he composed, under the title of *The Enemy of the Beard*, an ironical confession of his own faults aud a severe satire on the licentious and effeminate manners of Antioch. The imperial reply was publicly exposed before the gates of the palace, and the *Misopogon* still remains a singular monument of the resentment, the wit, the humanity, and the indiscretion of Julian" (*Decline and Fall*, c. 24, vol. 3, p. 8, ed. Bohn). Julian's own philosophic beard gives the title to the pamphlet, which throws much light upon the character of the emperor. In form it is a dialogue between himself and the people, in which he describes his own virtues under the colour of vices, and their vices as if they were virtues. Occasionally he lays aside his irony and directly expresses his indignation against them, and reveals his own character with a humorous simplicity that in turn attracts and repels us. This pamphlet was written in the seventh month of his sojourn at Antioch, probably, that is, in the latter half of Jan.; and he left the city in the first week of March. "I turn my back upon a city full of all vices, insolence, drunkenness, incontinence, impiety, avarice, and impudence," were his last words to Antioch (Liban. *Legatio ad Jul.* pp. 469 seq.).

(*b*) *Julian's Relation to the Church at Large during his Residence at Antioch.*—The general object of the emperor's policy was to degrade Christianity and to promote heathenism by every means short of an edict of persecution or the imposition of a general penalty on the profession of the faith.

We do not possess the text of many of Julian's edicts, a number of which were naturally removed from the statute book. We know that he ordered the temples to be reopened and their estates to be restored, but we do not know the terms in which this order was couched. Probably he used bitter language against the "atheists" and "Galileans," ordering all chapels of martyrs built within the sacred precincts to be destroyed, and all relics of "dead men" to be summarily removed. Something of this kind must have been the σύνθημα or "signal," of which he speaks in the *Misopogon* as having been followed by the neighbouring "holy cities" of Syria with a zeal and enthusiasm which exceeded even his wishes (*Misop.* p. 361 A; Soz. p. 20, *ad fin.*, mentions an order to destroy two Christian chapels near the temple of Apollo Didymaeus at Miletus). This confession from his own mouth goes far to justify the statements of his opponents. Riots occurred in consequence of this "signal" in many cities, particularly of Syria and the East, where the Christians were numerous and popular passion was strong. The details of Julian's relation to some of these cases form perhaps the gravest stains upon his character.

The earliest case after his entry into Antioch which can be dated exactly was that of Titus, bp. of Bostra, in Arabia Auranitis. Julian had informed Titus that he should be held responsible for any breach of the peace (Soz. v. 15, p. 102 B). The bishop answered by a memorial, declaring that the Christian population was equal in numbers to the heathen but that under his influence and that of their clergy they were careful to abstain from sedition (*ib.*). Julian on Aug. 1, 362, replied by a public letter to the people of Bostra, representing this language as an impertinence, and calumniating Titus as the accuser of the Christian body. After quoting the memorial of Titus, he proceeds: "These are the words of the bishop concerning you. Observe, he does not ascribe your regularity to your own inclination; unwillingly, he says, you refrain 'by his exhortations.' Do you then use your wills, and expel him as your accuser from your city. . . . Such is their fate who turn from the worship of the immortal gods to dead men and relics" (*Ep.* 52).

A month or two later, probably in Oct., he continued his attack upon Athanasius, the first acts of which have already been described. The great champion had never left Alexandria, or had soon returned. Julian was thoroughly enraged to find his first order had not been executed. He wrote angrily to the prefect Ecdicius: "I swear by great Serapis if he does not leave Alexandria and every part of Egypt, by the 1st of Dec., I will fine your cohort a hundred pounds of gold. You know that I am slow to condemn, but when I have condemned much slower in pardoning," adding in his own hand, "I am thoroughly pained at being treated in this way with contempt. By all the gods, no sight, or rather no news, of your doings could give me greater pleasure than that of Athanasius being driven from Egypt, the scoundrel who in my reign has dared to baptize Greek ladies of rank. Let him be expelled" (*Ep.* 6). At the same time he wrote to the people of Alexandria, mingling personal abuse of their bishop with arguments to enforce the worship of Serapis and the visible gods, the sun and moon, and to depreciate the worship of "Jesus, Whom neither you nor your fathers have seen," and "Whose doctrine has done nothing for your city." "We have long ago ordered him," he concludes, "to leave the city, now we banish him from the whole of Egypt" (*Ep.* 51). The news of these decrees was brought to Athanasius on Oct. 23, and he felt it time to depart. "Be of good heart," he said to those who clustered round him, "it is but a cloud; it will soon pass" (Ruf. i. 32; *Festal Epistles, Chronicle*, p. 14, for the date). During the rest of Julian's reign he lived in retirement in the monasteries of the Egyptian desert.

To Hecebolius (who was perhaps his old master advanced to some place of authority) he wrote concerning a sedition at Edessa, in much the same terms as he had written to the people of Bostra, but apparently with more justice. "I have always used the Galileans well, and abstained from violent measures of conversion; but the Arians, luxuriating in their wealth, have treated the Valentinians in a manner which cannot be tolerated in a well-ordered city. In order, therefore, that they may enter more easily into the kingdom of Heaven in the way which their wonderful law bids them, I have ordered all the money of the church of Edessa to be seized for division amongst the soldiers, and its estates to be confiscated" (*Ep.* 43, cf. Rufin. i. 32; Socr. iii. 13). This twisting of the gospel precept against the church is a close parallel to the alleged edict forbidding Christians to exercise the sword of the magistrate, and supports its authenticity (so Rode, p. 85, n. 9, see *supra*). Another disturbance was reported as occurring between the cities of Gaza and Maiuma in Palestine. The latter, originally a suburb of Gaza, had been raised by Constantius to the rank of an independent corporation. The people of Gaza had successfully petitioned the new emperor for a withdrawal of these privileges, and now in their exultation attacked their neighbours, and set fire to their chapels, with other acts of violence. Three brothers of a respectable family named Eusebius, Nestabus, and Zeno, were murdered with circumstances of great atrocity. The people were considerably alarmed by fear of what the emperor might do, and the governor arrested some of the ringleaders, who were brought to Antioch. In this case Julian's sense of justice seems entirely to have deserted him. Not only was no reprimand addressed to the people of Gaza, but the governor was himself put on his trial and deprived of his office. "What great matter is it if one Greek hand has slain ten Galileans?" were words well calculated to bear bitter fruit wherever they were repeated, and equivalent, as Gregory argues, to an edict of persecution (Greg. *Or.* 4, 93, p. 127; Sozomen—a Gazene himself—v. 9). Rode accepts most of this story, but rejects without sufficient reason the words attributed to Julian, p. 92, n. 12, who did and said many things in a fit of passion, of which his cooler judgment disapproved. Disturbances against the Christians broke out in many parts of Palestine. Holy places and holy things were profaned, and Christian people maltreated, tortured, and destroyed, sometimes in the most abominable manner (*Chron. Pasch.* p. 546, ed. Bonn.; Soz. v. 21; Philost. vii. 4).

Meanwhile Mark, bp. of Arethusa, a small town in Syria, who was said to have saved the life of the infant Julian, had refused to pay for the restoration of a temple which he had destroyed in the preceding reign. He was scourged in public, his beard was torn, his naked body was smeared with honey and hung up in a net exposed to the stings of insects and the fierce rays of the Syrian sun. Nothing could be wrung from him, and he was at last set free, a conqueror (Greg. *Or.* 4, 88-91, pp. 122-125; Soz. v. 10). Wherever he went, he was surrounded by admirers, and this case became a warning to the more temperate and cautious pagans not to proceed to extremities. Libanius intercedes for an offender, lest he should turn out another Mark (*Ep.* 730); and Sallust, the prefect of the East, admonished Julian for the disgrace this fruitless contest with an old man brought upon the pagan cause (Greg. *l.c.*; Sallust's *name* is not mentioned, but his office and character are described with sufficient clearness).

(*c*) *Attempt to rebuild the Temple at Jerusalem.*—Julian had apparently for some time past wished to conciliate the Jewish people, and was quite ready to grant Jehovah a place amongst the other local deities (cf. *Frag.* p. 295 C; St. Cyril. in Spanheim's *Julian*, pp. 99, 100, and p. 305, on Sacrifice). It seems probable, therefore, that his chief motive in wishing to restore the temple at Jerusalem was the desire to increase the number of divinities who were propitious to him, and to gain the favour of the Jewish God in the prosecution of his Persian campaign. This is substantially the account given by Socrates, who tells us that he summoned the Jews to him and asked why they did not offer sacrifice. They replied that it was not lawful for them to do so, except at Jerusalem, and he therefore determined to rebuild the temple of Solomon (Socr. iii. 20). This account agrees best with the statements of the emperor himself in his epistles and in his books against the Christians, and other motives attributed to him may be considered as subordinate (cf. Greg. *Or.* 5, 3, p. 149; Rufin. i. 37; Soz. v. 21). There is, however, an air of great probability in the statement of Philostorgius that he wished to falsify the prediction of our Blessed Lord as to the utter destruction of the temple (vii. 9). Nor could the enmity of the Jews against the Christians be otherwise than very pleasing to him (Greg. *l.c.* ἐπαφῆκε καὶ τὸ Ἰουδαίων φῦλον ἡμῖν). Julian provided very large sums for the work, and entrusted its execution to the oversight of Alypius of Antioch, an officer who had been employed by him in Britain and who was his intimate personal friend (Amm. xxiii. i. 2; *Epp.* 29 and 30 are addressed to him). The Jews were exultant and eager to contribute their wealth and their labour. The rubbish was cleared away and the old foundations were laid bare. But a stronger power intervened. To quote the words of Ammianus: "Whilst Alypius was strenuously forcing on the work, and the governor of the province was lending his assistance, fearful balls of flames, bursting out with frequent assaults near the foundations, and several times burning the workmen, rendered access to the spot impossible; and in this way the attempt came to a standstill through the determined obstinacy of the element" (xxiii. 1, 3). No doubt the Christians saw in this defeat of their oppressor not only a miracle of divine power, but a peculiarly striking fulfilment of the old prophecies in which fire is so often spoken of as the emblem and instrument of judgment (*e.g.* Deut. xxxii. 22, Jer. xxi. 14, and particularly, perhaps, the historical description of Lam. iv. 11, "The Lord hath accomplished His fury; He hath poured out His fierce anger, and hath kindled a fire in Zion, and it hath devoured the foundations thereof"). They thought also, of course, of our Lord's own words, now more completely verified than ever. Julian retained his wide knowledge of the text of Scripture, as we see by his writings, and these prophecies doubtless irritated him by their literal exactness. The "globi flammarum prope *fundamenta* erumpentes" of the heathen historian are an undesigned coincidence with the words of Hebrew prophecy.

From heathen testimonies, and from the fathers and historians of the church, Dr. Newman has put together the following detailed account of the occurrence, in which he chiefly follows Warburton. The order of the incidents is, of course, not certain, but only a matter of probable inference; nor can we guarantee the details as they appear in the later writers. "They declare as follows: The work was interrupted by a violent whirlwind, says Theodoret, which scattered about vast quantities of lime, sand and other loose materials collected for the building. A storm of thunder and lightning followed; fire fell, says Socrates, and the workmen's tools, the spades, the axes, and the saws were melted down. Then came an earthquake, which threw up the stones of the old foundation, says Socrates; filled up the excavation, says Theodoret, which had been made for the new foundations; and, as Rufinus adds, threw down the buildings in the neighbourhood, and especially the public porticoes in which were numbers of the Jews who had been aiding in the undertaking, and who were buried in the ruins. The workmen returned to their work; but from the recesses, laid open by the earthquake, balls of fire burst out, says Ammianus; and that again and again as often as they renewed the attempt. The fiery mass, says Rufinus, raged up and down the street for hours; and St. Gregory, that when some fled to a neighbouring church for safety the fire met them at the door and forced them back, with the loss either of life or of their extremities. At length the commotion ceased; a calm succeeded; and, as St. Gregory adds, in the sky appeared a luminous cross surrounded by a circle. Nay, upon the garments and the bodies of the persons present crosses were impressed, says St. Gregory; which were luminous by night, says Rufinus; and at other times of a dark colour, says Theodoret; and would not wash out, adds Socrates. In consequence the attempt was abandoned" (Newman, Essay on Miracles in *Early Eccl. Hist.* p. clxxvii.). All these incidents present a picture consistent with the extraordinary operations of the forces of nature. Even for the luminous crosses there are curious parallels in the history of storms of lightning and volcanic eruptions (see those collected by Warburton and quoted by Newman, p. clxxxii. notes). The cross in the sky has its likeness in the effects of mock suns and parhelia. But even so, a Christian may still fairly assert his right to call the event a miraculous interposition of God's providence. It fulfilled all the purposes we can assign to the Scripture miracles. It gave "an impression of the present agency and of the will of God." It seemed to shew His severe disapproval of the attempt and fulfilled the prophecy of Christ. It came, like the vision of Constantine, at a critical epoch in the world's history. It was, as the heathen poet has it, a "dignus vindice nodus." All who were present or heard of the event at the time thought it, we may be sure, a sign from God. As a miracle it ranges beside those Biblical miracles in which, at some critical moment, the forces of nature are seen to work strikingly for God's people or against their enemies.

§ 7. *Julian's Persian Campaign and Death* (Mar. 5 to June 27, 363).—Julian's route into Persia is marked with considerable exactness; the first part of it by a letter which he wrote to Libanius from Hierapolis (*Ep.* 27). At Beroea, the modern Aleppo, he "conversed with the senate on matters of religion—all praised my discourse, but few only were convinced by it" (*Ep.* 27, p. 399 D).

At Batnae (the scenery of which he compared to that of Daphne) he found ostentatious preparations for sacrifice upon the public roads, but thought them too obviously studied and too redolent of personal flattery. Leaving Edessa on his left hand, probably as a city too distinctly Christian to be visited with comfort, he had reached Carrhae, a place of vigorous pagan traditions, on Mar. 19. At some distance from the town there was a famous temple of the Moon, in which it was worshipped both as a male and a female deity, and near which the emperor Caracalla had been murdered (Herodian. iv. 13, 3; Spartian. *Caracallus*, 6, 6; 7, 3). Julian made a point of visiting it and offered sacrifices "according to the local rites." Of his secret doings in this temple there are different accounts. Ammianus had heard that he invested his relative Procopius, who was his only companion, with his paludamentum, and bid him seize the empire in case he died in the campaign on which they were engaged (Aram. xxiii. 3, 2). Among Christians a report was current that he offered a human sacrifice. The story ran that he sealed up the temple and ordered it not to be opened till his return: and that after the news of his death people entered it and found a woman hanging by the hair of her head, and her body cut open as if to search for omens (Theod. iii. 26).

On Mar. 27 he was at Callinicum and celebrated the festival of the Mother of the Gods (Amm. xxiii. 3, 7). At the beginning of Apr. he came to Circesium (Carchemish) at the junction of the Chaboras and the Euphrates. Here he received distressing letters from his friend Sallustius in Gaul, urging him to give up his campaign as he felt sure that the gods were unfavourable (Amm. xxiii. 5, 6). At Zaitham (where Ammianus first begins to speak in the first person) they saw the high mound which marked the burial-place of the emperor Gordian. The historian records numerous portents on their march; among them, a lion which appeared at Dura gave rise to a curious dispute between the Etruscan augurs and the philosophers who followed in his train. The former shewed from their books that it was an ill omen; the latter (amongst whom were Maximus and Priscus) had historical precedents to prove that it need not be so regarded. A similar dispute occurred next day as to the meaning of a thunderstorm (xxiii. 5, 10 seq.). Such superstitious discussions were not likely to embolden the soldiery; but Julian decided in favour of the philosophers, animated the army with his own courage, and tried to dispel the prejudice that the Romans had never invaded Persia with success. One of his most important officers, Hormisdas (elder brother of Sapor, the reigning king of Persia), had angered the nobles of his country by threats, had been imprisoned by them, and escaped to the court of Constantine. He became apparently a sincere Christian, yet remained a useful and trusted officer of Julian. By his intervention several Assyrian towns opened their gates to the invaders (xxiv. 1, 6, etc.). The country was inundated by the natives, and it required all Julian's inventive quickness and personal example to carry the army through the marshes. After various successes he arrived at the bank of the Tigris, at the ruins of the old Greek city of Seleucia opposite Ctesiphon. He forced the passage of the river by a very vigorous and dangerous movement in the face of the enemy, and found himself under the walls of the capital (xxiv. 6, 4-14). But no threats or sarcasms could draw the inhabitants from their impregnable defences, and Sapor himself made no appearance. Part of the Roman army had been left in Mesopotamia, where the two ambitious generals, Procopius and Sebastianus, fell out, and the support expected from Arsaces was not forthcoming. But though Sapor did not appear to give battle, he sent a secret ambassador with offers of an honourable peace, the exact terms of which are unknown to us (Liban. *Epit.* p. 608; Socr. iii. 21; Ammianus is here defective). These Julian declined, against the advice of Hormisdas. He was fired with all sorts of vague and enthusiastic projects; he longed to visit the plain of Arbela and to overrun the whole Persian empire (Liban. *Epit.* p. 609). These ideas were kindled into action by the arts of a certain Persian noble, who pretended to be a deserter, indignant against his sovereign, but who in reality played the part of a second Zopyrus (Greg. Naz. *Or.* 5, 11, p. 154; cf. Aurel. Victor. *Epit.* 67; Soz. vi. 1, p. 218). Julian's fleet presented a difficulty, and he determined upon the hazardous measure of burning it, except a very few vessels, which were to be placed on wheels. This was done at Abuzatha, where he halted five days (Zos. iii. 26). A short time of reflection and a discovery that his Persian informants were deceiving him made him regret his decision. He attempted too late to save some of the ships. Only twelve out of some 1,100 were still uninjured. What had been intended to be a triumphant progress almost insensibly became a retreat. The Persian cavalry were perpetually harassing the outskirts of the army, and though beaten at close quarters were continually appearing in fresh swarms. The few ships that remained were insufficient to build a bridge by which to open communications with Mesopotamia. Nothing was left but to proceed along the E. bank of the Tigris to the nearest friendly province, Corduene in S. Armenia, as quickly as possible. This was determined on June 16, only ten days before the death of Julian (Amm. xxiv. 8, 5). How far he had previously penetrated into the interior is not easy to determine. In the next few days the Romans fought several battles with success, but not such as to ensure them a quiet march forwards. They suffered from want of food, and Julian shared their privations on an equality with the commonest soldier (Amm. xxv. 2, 2). On the night of June 25, as he was studying some book of philosophy in his tent, he had a vision (as he told his intimates) of the Genius of the Republic leaving his tent in a mournful attitude, with a veil over his head and over the cornucopia in his hand—reminding him by contrast of his vision of the night before he was proclaimed Augustus. He shook off his natural terror, and went out into the night air to offer propitiatory sacrifices, when he received another shock from the appearance of a brilliant meteor, which he interpreted as a sign of the wrath of Mars, whom he had already offended (xxv. 2, 4; cf. xxiv. 6, 17). When day dawned the Etruscan diviners implored him to make no movement that day, or at least to put off his march for some hours. But his courage had returned with daylight, and he gave the order to advance. Sudden attacks of the enemy from different quarters threw the army into confusion, and Julian, excited by the danger, rushed forward without his breastplate, catching up a shield as he went. As he raised his hands above his head to urge his men to pursue, a cavalry spear from an unknown hand grazed his arm and lodged in his right side. He tried to draw out the spear-head, but the sharp edges cut his fingers. He threw up his hand with a convulsive motion, and fell fainting from his horse (xxv. 3, 7, compared with other accounts), uttering a cry which is differently reported. Some said he threw his own blood towards heaven with the bitter words, "O Galilean, Thou hast conquered!" (Theod. iii. 25). Others thought they heard him reproach the gods, and especially the Sun, his patron, for their desertion (Philost. vii. 15; Soz. vi. 2). He was borne to his tent and his wound dressed, no doubt by his friend Oribasius. For a moment he revived, and called for a horse and arms, but a gush of blood shewed how weak he really was. On learning that the place was called Phrygia he gave up all hope, having been told by some diviner that he should die in Phrygia. He addressed those who stood around him in a highly philosophic speech in the style of Socrates, of which Ammianus has preserved a report. He considered that death was sent him as a gift from the gods. He knew of no great faults he had committed either in a private station or as Caesar. He had always desired the good of his subjects, and had endeavoured to be a faithful servant of the republic. He had long known the decree of fate, that his death was impending, and thanked the supreme God that it came, not in a disgraceful or painful way, but in a glorious form. He would not discuss the appointment of his successor, lest he should pass over one who was worthy, or endanger the life of some one whom he thought fit, but hoped that the republic would find a good ruler after him. He then distributed his personal effects to his intimate friends, and asked among others for Anatolius, the master of the offices. Sallustius (the prefect of the East) replied that he was *happy*. Julian understood that he had fallen, but lamented the death of his friend with a natural feeling which he had restrained in thinking of his own. Those who stood round could no longer restrain their grief, but he still kept his habit of command, and rebuked them for their want of high feeling. "My life gives me confidence of being taken to the islands of the blest, to have converse with heaven and the stars; it is mean to weep as if I had deserved to be condemned to Tartarus" (Liban. *Epit.* p. 614, *ἐπετίμα τοῖς τε ἄλλοις, καὶ οὐχ ἥκιστα (τοῖς φιλοσόφοις) εἰ τῶν βεβιωμένων αὐτὸν εἰς μακάρων νήσους ἀγόντων, οἱ δὲ ὡς ἀξίως ταρτάρου βεβιωκότα δακρύουσιν*: Amm. xxv. 3, 22, "humile esse caelo sideribusque conciliatum lugeri principem dicens").

His last moments were spent in a difficult discussion with Maximus and Priscus on "the sublimity of souls." In the midst of this debate his wound burst afresh, and he called for a cup of cold water, drank it, and passed away quietly at midnight on the evening of June 26, having not yet reached the age of 32 (Amm. xxv. 3, 23; 5, 1; Socr. iii. 21, etc.).

It was never found out who threw the fatal spear, though the Persians offered a reward. The suggestion of Libanius that it was a Christian was such as he would naturally make in his bitterness (*Epit.* pp. 612, 614). Gregory, Socrates, and Rufinus consider it uncertain whether it was a Persian or one of his own soldiers (Greg. *Or.* v. 13, p. 155; Ruf. i. 36; Socr. iii. 21). Sozomen notices the suspicion of Libanius, and defends it in a spirit which cannot but be condemned (Soz. vi. 1).

The news of Julian's death and that the army had elected a Christian, Jovian, to succeed him caused enormous rejoicings, especially in Antioch. Jovian was obliged to make peace by ceding the five Mesopotamian provinces, including Nisibis, which had been the bulwark of the empire in the East. Procopius was ordered to carry back the body to Tarsus, where it was interred with pagan ceremonies opposite that of Maximinus Daïa.

Character.—Julian's story leaves the impression of a living man far more than that of most historical personages. The most opposite and unexpected estimates of him have been formed. He has been admired and pitied by religious-minded men, detested and satirized by sceptics and atheists. His own friend Ammianus despised his superstition, and paints it in terms not much weaker than the invectives of Gregory and Chrysostom; Gibbon sneers at him alternately with his Christian opponents. A. Comte wished to appoint an annual day for execrating his memory in company with that of Bonaparte, as one of the "two principal opponents of progress," and as the "more insensate" of the two (*System of Positive Polity*, Eng. trans. vol. i. p. 82; an ordinance afterwards withdrawn, *ib.* vol. iv. p. 351). Strauss treats him as a vain, reactionary dreamer, comparable to medievalists who tried to stay the march of modern thought. On the other hand, pietistic historians like Arnold, Neander, and even Ullmann, unlike the ancient writers of the church, are tolerant and favourable.

The simple reason of this divergence is, of course, that the strongest force working in him was a self-confident religious enthusiasm, disguised under the form of self-surrender to a divine mission. Such a character constantly appears in different lights, and some of those who have judged him have looked chiefly at the sentimental side of his life, without considering his actions; while others have estimated him by his actions apart from his principles—the more so because he was inconsistent himself in his conduct, and sometimes acted with, sometimes against, his principles; and hence any one who chooses to take a partial view may easily find a justi fication in the positive statements of this or that historian, or of Julian himself.

A Christian who attempts to judge Julian without prejudice will probably go through several phases of opinion before he comes to a final estimate. All but the cold-hearted will sympathize, to some extent at least, with his religious enthusiasm, and with the sacrifices which he was ready to make in its behalf. It is impossible to doubt that he had a vein of noble sentiment, and a lofty and, in many ways, unselfish ambition. He had a real love of ideal beauty, and of the literary and artistic traditions of the past. There was something even pathetic in his hero-worship and his attachment to those whom he supposed to be his friends. If he was often pedantic and imitative, if he had a somewhat shallow and conceited manner, yet we must confess that much of this was the vice of the age, and this pettiness was thrown off in critical moments. Under strong excitement he often became simple, great, and natural.

Or again, many persons will sympathize with his conservative instincts, and his wish to retain what was great in the culture and art of past ages; while others will be attracted by his mystic speculations and ascetic practices, which were akin to much that has been valued and admired in many great names in the history of the church. But on reflection we see that all this was combined with a ruling spirit and view of things which was essentially heathen, and therefore fundamentally defective, as well as antagonistic, to all that we hold dearest and most vital. Julian was at bottom thoroughly one-sided. He was enthusiastic and even passionate in his religion; but it was the passion of the intellect and senses rather than of the heart.

Much of his natural warmth of feeling had been chilled and soured by the sense of injustice and secret enmity under which he so long laboured. He could not forget the murder of his nearest relations, nor the suspicions, intrigues, and actual personal indignities of which he was the subject. What we know of his early surroundings inclines us to suppose that their influence for good was but slight. His relation, Eusebius of Nicomedia, does not bear a high character. His pedagogue Mardonius was evidently more heathen than Christian in his sympathies, and a time-serving creature like Hecebolius was not likely to make much impression upon his pupil.

We have endeavoured to give a fair general estimate of this remarkable character, with the full consciousness how hazardous such an estimate is. If any one wishes for a catalogue of qualities, which can, as it were, be ticketed and labelled, he cannot do better than read Ammianus's elaborate award (xxv. 4). The historian takes the four cardinal virtues—temperance, prudence, justice, and courage—and gives a due amount of praise tempered with some fault-finding under each head. His chastity and abstinence were remarkable. He aimed at justice, and to a great extent earned a high reputation for it. He was liberal to his friends, and careless of his own comforts and conveniences in a very remarkable degree; while he did much to lighten and equalize the burden of taxation upon his subjects. His successes in Gaul gained him the affection of the people, and his popularity with the soldiers may be gathered from the manner in which the dwellers in northern and western lands followed him into the midst of Persia. He may be said to have quelled a military tumult by the threat of retiring into private life. The lighter qualities of his character present him in rather a disagreeable aspect. He was loquacious and inconsistent in small things and in great. He was extremely superstitious, and even fanatical in his observance of religious rites, to a degree that made him appear trifling and undignified even to his friends. His manner was obviously irritating, and such as could not inspire respect in his subjects; and, on the other hand, he was too eager to gain popular applause. No one can doubt his cleverness and ability as a writer, but the greater number of his writings do not shew method, and they are often singularly deficient in judgment. An exception, perhaps, may be made in respect to the first oration to Constantius, the letter to the Athenians, and the Caesars. The latter, however, was a strange performance for one who was himself an emperor.

In person he was rather short, and awkwardly though very strongly built. His features were fine and well-marked, and his eyes very brilliant; his mouth was rather over-large and his lower lip inclined to droop. As a young man he grew a beard, but was required to cut it off when he became Caesar, and seems only to have grown it again after taking possession of Constantinople. At Antioch it was allowed to grow to a great size. His neck was thick, and his head hung forward, and was set on broad and thick shoulders. His walk was ungraceful; and he had an unsteady motion of the limbs. There is a fine life-size statue of Julian, of good and artistic workmanship, in the ruined hall of his palace in the garden of the Hôtel Clugny at Paris. It is figured as the frontispiece to E. Talbot's translation of his works.

Theory of Religion.—Julian's theory was too superficial and occasional to leave much mark upon the history of thought. His book against Christianity became indeed a favourite weapon with infidels, but he never founded a school of positive belief. He was, in fact, an enthusiastic amateur, who employed some of the nights of a laborious career of public business in writing brilliant essays in the neo-Platonic manner. He tells us that the oration in praise of the Sun took him three nights (p. 157 C); that on the Mother of the Gods was composed, "without taking breath, in the short space of one night" (p. 178 D). Such work may astonish us even now, but it is not surprising that it should be incomplete, rambling, and obscure.

There are, however, certain constantly recurring thoughts which may be regarded as established principles with Julian. Julian forms one of that long line of remarkable men in the first four centuries after Christ who endeavoured to give a rational form to the religion and morality of the heathen world in opposition to the growing power of Christianity—men whose ill-success is one of the strongest proofs of the deadness of their own cause, and the vitality of that against which they strove. Seneca, Plutarch, Epictetus, Marcus Aurelius, Celsus, Plotinus, Porphyry, Iamblichus, and Hierocles were in this sense precursors of Julian. We may define the objects of their efforts on behalf of paganism as:

(1) To unite popular beliefs in many gods with some conception of the unity of the divine being, and to give some consistent, if not rational, account of the origin of the world and of the course of human history.

(2) To defend the myths and legends of heathenism, and generally to establish heathen morals on a higher basis than mere custom.

(3) To satisfy the yearnings of the soul for the knowledge of God, while rejecting the exclusive claims of the Jewish and Christian revelation.

(1) *Doctrine as to the Nature of God.*—The birth of Christ took place in the fulness of time, *i.e.* when mankind had been prepared for it, by many influences bearing them towards the acceptance of a revelation. One of the most important of these preparations was the movement towards monotheism. The old simple belief in many gods living together in a sort of upper world was gone, and thinking men would accept no system which did not assume the supremacy of one divine principle, and in some degree "justify" the action of Providence in dealing with mankind as a whole. But the worship of many gods had too deep a hold upon the fancy and affections, as well as the mind, of the people to be surrendered without a long struggle, and various methods were advanced to shelter and protect the current belief. The systems thus formed were naturally all more or less pantheistic, finding unity in an informal abstraction from the phenomena of nature. But, as we should expect to be the case on European soil, they were neither logically pantheistic in the abstract way of the Hindu philosophical sects nor sharply dualistic like the speculations of the Gnostics and Manicheans. The more practical minds of the Graeco-Roman world were satisfied to give an account of things as they appeared without overpowering and paralyzing themselves by the insoluble question as to the existence and potencies of matter; and thus they were at once more inconsistent and less absurd than some of their contemporaries. While looking upon matter as something degrading, and upon contact with it as a thing to be avoided, they nevertheless did not define matter to be non-existent, or merely phenomenal, nor did they regard it as absolutely evil. In the same way, while they lost all true hold upon the personality of God, and believed in the eternity of the world (*e.g.* Jul. *Or.* iv. p. 132 C), they used the terms creation and providence, and spoke of communion with and likeness to God. Into an eclectic system of this kind it was not difficult to incorporate the gods of the heathen world, and to make them subserve a sort of philosophy of history. With Julian they take a double position: (*a*) as intermediate beings employed in creation who protect the Supreme Being from too intimate contact with the world; (*b*) as accounting for the difference between nations, and so enabling men to uphold traditional usages without ceasing to hold to one ideal law and one truth (Jul. *Or.* vi. p. 184 C, *ὥσπερ γὰρ ἀλήθεια μία, οὕτω δὲ καὶ φιλοσοφία μία*).

The chief source of information on this part

of Julian's theory is his *Fourth Oration, in praise of the Sovereign Sun.* The most striking feature of the theology proper of this system is its triple hierarchy of deities and worlds. Such a triple division was a common feature of neo-Platonism and had its roots in thoughts current before the Christian era; but it was no doubt emphasized by later theorists as a counterpoise to the Christian doctrine of the Trinity. That of Julian was probably borrowed from Iamblichus of Chalcis (uncle, it has been supposed, of his correspondent), to whom he frequently appeals in terms of the highest veneration (*e.g. Or.* iv. p. 146 A, 150 D, 157 D; see Ueberweg, *Hist. of Philosophy*, § 69, vol. i. pp. 252-254, Eng. trans.).

According to this belief there are three worlds informed and held together by three classes of divine beings. The highest and most spiritual is the *κόσμος νοητός*, or "intelligible world," the world of absolute immaterial essences, the centre of which is the One or the Good, who is the source of beings and of all beauty and perfection to the gods who surround him (p. 133 C). Between this highly elevated region and the grosser material world comes the *κόσμος νοερός*, or "intelligent world," the centre of which is the sovereign sun, the great object of Julian's devotion. He receives his power from the Good, and communicates it not only to the gods around him, but also to the sensible world, the *κόσμος αἰσθητός*, in which we live. In this sphere the "visible disk" of the sun is the source of light and life, as the invisible sun is in the intelligible world. Any one who will read this oration with care will be convinced that Julian wished to find in his sovereign sun a substitute for the Christian doctrine of the second person of the blessed Trinity, and this appears in particular on pp. 141, 142 (cf. Naville, p. 104; Lamé, pp. 234 ff.). The position specially given to the sun is a proof of the advance of Oriental thought in the Roman empire, and it was certainly no new idea of Julian's. Amongst others, Aurelian and Elagabalus had made him their chief divinity, and Constantine himself had been specially devoted to the "Sol invictus." Julian, we have seen, had from his childhood been fascinated with the physical beauty of the light. Towards the close of the century we find Macrobius arguing somewhat in the spirit of some modern inquirers that all heathen religion is the product of solar myths. Yet it is curious to observe the shifts to which Julian is put to prove this doctrine out of Homer and Hesiod, and from the customs of the ancient Greeks and Romans (pp. 135-137 and 148 ff.). He seems, indeed, conscious of the weakness of his arguments from the poets, and dismisses them with the remark that they have much that is human in their inspiration, and appeals to the directer revelations of the gods themselves—we must suppose in the visions which he claimed to receive (p. 137 C).

The connexion of this theory with the national gods is nowhere distinctly worked out. It is, in fact, part of the pantheistic character of this belief that the idea of the personality of the gods recedes or becomes prominent, like the figures in a magic lantern, according to the subject under discussion, without any shock to the dreamy neo-Platonist. At one time they are mere essences or principles, at another they are Zeus, Apollo, Ares, etc., ruling and directing the fortunes of nations, and imposing upon them a peculiar type of character and special laws and institutions. At one moment they are little more than the ideas of Plato, at another they are actual *δαίμονες*, acting as lieutenants of the Creator. This last view is in essentials the same as that put forward by Celsus (probably in the reign of Marcus Aurelius) in his book, known to us from its refutation by Origen (bk. v. cc. 25-33). It is the view asserted at length by Julian in his books against the Christians, especially as a defence of the customs and institutions of antiquity against the innovations of the religion which strove to break down all prejudices of class and nation. (St. Cyril. *adv. Jul.* iv. pp. 115, 116, 130, 141, 143, 148, etc.; cf. *Fragmentum Epistolae*, p. 292 C, D, *ἄνθρωποι τοῖς γενεάρχαις θεοῖς ἀποκληρωθέντες, οἱ καὶ προήγαγον αὐτούς, ἀπὸ τοῦ δημιουργοῦ τὰς ψυχὰς παραλαμβάνοντες ἐξ αἰῶνος*; for the subject generally, see Naville, c. iii. "Les Dieux Nationaux.") It is easy to see how fatal such a doctrine must be to moral progress. If everything is as it is by the will of the gods, no custom, however revolting, lacks defence. It is strange that, after the refutation of this absurdity by Origen, any one should have been bold enough to put it forward as a serious theory (cf. Orig. *contra Celsum*, v. cc. 25-28 and 34-39).

With regard to the relation of images and sacrifices to the gods, who are worshipped by these means, there is an interesting passage in the *Fragment of the Letter to a Priest* (pp. 293 ff.). He warns his correspondent not to consider images as actually receiving worship, nor to suppose that the gods really need our sacrifices. But he defends their use as suitable to our own bodily condition (*ἐπειδὴ γὰρ ἡμᾶς ὄντας ἐν σώματι σωματικὰς ἔδει ποιεῖσθαι τοῖς θεοῖς καὶ τὰς λατρείας, ἀσώματοι δέ εἰσιν αὐτοί*, p. 293 D). "Just as earthly kings desire to have honour paid them and their statues without actually *needing* it, so do the gods. The images of the gods are not the gods, and yet more than mere wood and stone. They ought to lead us up to the unseen. And yet being made by human art, they are liable to injury at the hands of wicked men, just as good men are unjustly put to death like Socrates, and Dion, and Empedotimus. But their murderers afterwards were punished by divine vengeance, and so have sacrilegious persons manifestly received a due reward in my reign" (pp. 294 C to 295 B).

(2) *Defence of Pagan Morality.*—We have already described at some length Julian's attempts to raise the morality of his heathen subordinates, especially in the priesthood. He was conscious of a defect, and strenuously set himself to remedy it, though he could do little more in the way of quotation of texts than allege a few general maxims drawn from ancient writings as to kindness to the poor, etc. His strongest argument is one that might well have made him hesitate—the shame of being so much outdone by the "Galileans." Another branch of this subject was the relation of

morality to Greek mythology, and with this he busied himself on two occasions, about the same time. The two orations, *The Praise of the Mother of the Gods* and *Against the Cynic Heraclius*, were probably both delivered about the time of the vernal equinox, while he was still at Constantinople, A.D. 362. In the first of these he gives an elaborate explanation of the story of Attis; in the second he rebukes Heraclius for his immoral teaching in the form of myths, and gives an example of one which he thinks really edifying, which describes his own youth under the protection of the gods.

The explanation of the myth of Attis is important as a specimen of Julian's theology. According to modern interpreters, this myth, as well as that of Adonis in its hundred forms, describes merely the succession of the seasons; Julian adapts it to his speculations on the triple hierarchy of worlds. With him the mother of the gods is the female principle of the highest and most spiritual world. He calls her the lady of all life, the mother and bride of great Zeus, the motherless virgin, she who bears children without passion, and creates things that are together with the father (p. 166 A, B). Here we are landed into the full obscurity of Gnostic principles and emanations, and the whole story is evidently only a kind of converse arrangement of that which meets us in the Valentinian myth of Achamoth (see Mansel, *Gnostic Heresies*, lects. 11, 12). Attis is a principle of the second or intelligent world, "the productive and creative intelligence, the essence which descends into the farthest ends of matter to give birth to all things" (p. 161 C). It is difficult to see how he is distinguished in his functions with regard to creation from the sovereign sun, but this is only one of the many weak points of this fanciful exposition. His material type in the lowest world is the Milky Way, in which philosophers say that the impassible circumambient ether mingles with the passible elements of the world (p. 165 C). The mother of the gods engages Attis to remain ever faithful to herself, that is, to look always upward. Instead of this, he descends into the cave, and has commerce with the nymph, that is, produces the visible universe out of matter. The sun, who is the principle of harmony and restraint, something like the Valentinian Horus (ὅρος), sends the lion or fiery principle to put a stop to this production of visible forms. Then follows the ἐπτομή of Attis, which is defined as the ἐποχὴ τῆς ἀπειρίας, the limit placed upon the process into infinity. The part played by the sun is indicated by the season at which the festival took place, the vernal equinox, when he produces equality of day and night (p. 168 C, D). All this is explained as a mere passionless eternal procedure on the part of the supposed gods. A real creation proceeding from God's love and good pleasure was a thought far above the scope of this philosophy, to which the world was as personal as the so-called gods.

Enough has been said to shew how thoroughly pantheistic was Julian's interpretation of the myths; how destructive of any true conception of the divine nature, how thoroughly unmoral, how utterly incapable of touching the heart, was his theology. Yet he felt the need of some personal commerce with God, however inconsistent such a wish was with his intellectual view of divine things.

(3) *Intercourse with God.*—When Julian was in Asia Minor under the influence of the philosophers Eusebius and Chrysanthius, and heard the details of the wonderful works of Maximus, he said (according to Eunapius), "Farewell, and keep to your books if you will; you have revealed to me the man I was in search of" (Eunap. *Vita Maximi*, p. 51). This story has been discredited by some, who think it strange that so great a lover of books as Julian should speak slightingly of them. But it is confirmed by his own language in his *Oration on the Sun* (p. 137 C): "Let us say farewell to poetic descriptions; for they have much that is human mixed up with the divine. But let us go on to declare what the god himself seems to teach us both about himself and the other gods" (ix. 11, 5). Julian here appeals from a book revelation, as it were, to a direct instruction given him in the numerous visions in which he was visited by the gods.

We have already noticed Julian's enthusiasm for the mysteries and his love of all rites and practices which promised a closer intercourse with the gods. He could never bring himself to acquiesce in the colder methods of some of the masters of the neo-Platonic school. He was not satisfied with the intellectual ecstasy described by Plotinus, nor with the self-purification of Porphyry, who generally rejected sacrifice and divination (Ueberweg, *Hist. of Philosophy*, § 68, notes, vol. i. p. 251, Eng. trans.). The party of Iamblichus, to which Julian belonged, required something approaching a control of a god (*theurgy*), a quasi-mechanical method of communication with him, which could be put in force at will, and the result of which could only be called a "Bacchic frenzy" (*Or.* vii. pp. 217 D and 221 D, etc.). Julian was duped by men who were half deceivers and half deceived. He is one among many who are forced by an inward conviction to believe in supernatural revelation, but who will only have it on their own terms. Libanius tells us that Julian knew the forms and lineaments of the gods as familiarly as those of his friends, and we have mentioned the visions which appeared to him at great crises of his life. He himself says, "Aesculapius often healed me, telling me of remedies" (St. Cyril. *adv. Jul.* viii. p. 234), and elsewhere he speaks of this deity as a sort of incarnate Saviour (*Or.* iv. p. 144 B, C). This temper of mind, while it speaks in high-flown, positive language of the knowledge of God and pours contempt on the uninitiated, yet means something by "knowledge" very different from the sober and bracing certainty attained by Christian faith, hope, and love. Here, as elsewhere, the pantheistic temper speaks grandly, but feels meanly. Death indeed is looked forward to with some composure as the emancipation of the divine element in man from darkness. Julian several times prays for a happy death, and expected after it to be raised to communion with the gods. His orations to the Sun and the Mother of the Gods both conclude with such prayers, and we have seen how he actually met his end (Liban. *Ep.* p. 614; Amm.

xxv. 3, 22). But the doctrine of the ascent (*sublimitas*) of souls, on which he was conversing with Maximus and Priscus when that end came, was a very different thing from the Christian's hope. It was, in fact, the same in substance as the barren and deadening Oriental doctrine of transmigration; and it is remarkable that Julian, who felt himself so favoured by the heavenly powers, in one of his most ardent prayers to the sun, looks forward to a felicity which has no certainty of being eternal (*Or.* iv. p. 158 c; see some good remarks on the contrast between this and the Christian doctrine in Naville, pp. 59 ff.).

Julian's Polemic against Christianity.—How near measures against Christianity were to his heart may be seen in his prayer to the Mother of the Gods, where he speaks of "cleansing the empire from the stain of atheism" as the great wish of his life (*Or.* v. p. 180 B). He preferred, however, the method of persuasion to that of constraint, and his books against the Christians are an evidence of this temper. He begins by saying that he wishes to give the reasons which have convinced him that the Galilean doctrine is a human invention (Cyr. ii. p. 39). He then goes on to attack the narratives of the Bible as fabulous. He allows that the Greeks have monstrous fables likewise (p. 44), but then they have philosophy, while Christians have nothing but the Bible, and are in fact barbarians. If Christians attack the idolatry of heathens, Julian retorts, "you worship the wood of the cross, and refuse to worship the ancile which came down from heaven" (Cyr. vi. p. 194). On the whole, he does not spend much time in such questions, but accepts the Bible as a generally true narrative, and rather attacks Christianity on grounds of supposed reason, and in connexion with and in contrast to Judaism.

We may follow Naville in considering the main body of his works under three heads: (1) his polemic against the monotheism of the O.T.; (2) his attack upon the novel and aggressive character of Christian doctrine; (3) especially against the adoration of Christ as God, and the worship of "dead men," such as the martyrs (cf. Naville, pp. 175 ff.).

(1) *Against the Monotheism of the O.T.*—Julian regarded the gods of polytheism as links or intermediaries between the supreme God and the material world, and so as rendering the conception of creation easier and more philosophical. He contrasts Plato's doctrine of creation in the *Timaeus* with the abrupt statements of Moses, "God said," etc. (pp. 49-57). One might almost suppose (he urges) that Moses imagined God to have created nothing incorporeal, no intermediate spiritual or angelic beings, but to have Himself directly organized matter (p. 49). He proceeds to argue against the supposition that the supreme God made choice of the Hebrew nation as a peculiar people to the exclusion of others. "If He is the God of all of us, and our common creator, why has He abandoned us?" (p. 106). Both in acts and morals the Hebrews are inferior. They have been always in slavery, and have invented nothing. As for morality, the imitation of God amongst the Jews is the imitation of a "jealous God," as in the case of Phinehas (Cyr. v. pp. 160-171). The worst of our generals never treated subject nations so cruelly as Moses treated the Canaanites (vi. p. 184). The only precepts in the Decalogue not held in common by all nations are the commandments against idolatry and for the observance of the sabbath. The true view, to his mind, was that the God of the Jews was a local, national god, like those of other peoples, far inferior to the supreme God (iv. pp. 115, 116, 141, 148, etc.). Sometimes he seems inclined to accept Jehovah as the creator of the visible world, while at other times he throws doubt upon this assumption; but in any case he considered Him a true object of worship (*Ep.* 25, *Judaeis.* But in Cyril. iv. p. 148 he blames Moses for confounding a partial and national god with the Creator). Further, the Jewish usages of temples, altars, sacrifices, purifications, circumcision, etc., were all observed to have a close resemblance to those of heathenism, and were a foundation for many reproaches against the Galileans, who had abandoned so much that was laudable and respectable (vi. p. 202; vii. p. 238; ix. pp. 298, 299, 305, etc.).

(2) *Julian's Attack upon Christianity as a Novel and Revolutionary Religion.*—In the same spirit he puts Christianity much below Judaism. "If you who have deserted us had attached yourself to the doctrines of the Hebrews, you would not have been in so thoroughly bad a condition, though worse than you were before when you were amongst us. For you would have worshipped one God instead of many gods, and not, as is now the case, a man, or rather a number of miserable men. You would have had a hard and stern law, with much that is barbarous in it, instead of our mild and gentle customs, and would have been so far the losers; but you would have been purer and more holy in religious rites. As it is, you are like the leeches, and suck all the worst blood out of Hebraism and leave the purer behind" (Cyr. vi. pp. 201, 202). It was thus natural that St. Paul should be the special object of his dislike. "He surpasses all the impostors and charlatans who have ever existed" (Cyr. iii. p. 100). Julian accuses the Jewish Christians of having deserted a law which Moses declared to be eternal (ix. p. 319). Even Jesus Himself said that He came to fulfil the law. Peter declared that he had a vision, in which God shewed him that no animal was impure (p. 314), and Paul boldly says, "Christ is the end of the law"; but Moses says, "Ye shall not add unto the word which I command you, neither shall ye diminish ought from it"; and "Cursed is every one that continueth not in all things" (Cyr. ix. p. 320=Deut. iv. 2, xxvii. 27; cf. x. pp. 343, 351, 354, 356, 358, where he attacks Christians for giving up sacrifice, circumcision, and the sabbath, and asserts that Abraham used divination and practised astrology). He sneers at baptism, which cannot cure any bodily infirmity, but is said to remove all the transgressions of the soul—adulteries, thefts, etc.—so great is its penetrating power! (vii. p. 245). The argument against the Christian interpretation of prophecy is also remarkable. He comments textually on the blessing of Judah, Gen. xlix.

10; on the prophecy of Balaam, Num. xxiv. 17; on that of Moses, Deut. xviii. 15-18; and on that of Emmanuel, Is. vii. 14; and tries to shew that they have no reference outside Judaism itself, though the last is evidently a difficulty to him (pp. 253, 261, 262).

(3) *The Worship of Jesus as God and the Adoration of the Martyrs* are the great objects of Julian's attacks. His argument is partly concerned with the prophecies just quoted, partly with the N.T. itself. He asserts that Moses never speaks of "the first-born Son of God," while he does speak of "the sons of God," *i.e.* the angels, who have charge of different nations (Gen. vi. 2). But Moses says expressly, "Thou shalt worship the Lord thy God, and Him only shalt thou serve" (Cyr. ix. p. 290). Even if the prophecy of Emmanuel in Is. refers to Jesus, it gives you no right to call His mother *θεοτόκος*. How could she bear God, being a human creature like ourselves? And how is her son the Saviour when God says, "I am, and there is no Saviour beside Me"? (viii. p. 276).

"John began this evil. You have gone on and added the worship of other dead men to that of the first dead man. You have filled all things with tombs and sepulchres; though Jesus speaks of 'whited sepulchres full of dead men's bones and all uncleanness'" (p. 335). "Why, then, do you bow before tombs? The Jews did it, according to Isaiah, to obtain visions in dreams, and four apostles also probably did so after their master's death" (p. 339). (The reference is to Is. lxv. 4, "which remain among the graves and lodge among the monuments": the words *δι' ἐνύπνια* are added in the Greek version.) In his letter to the Alexandrians he puts with equal force the folly of adoring a man, and not adoring the sun and the moon, especially the former, the great sun, the living, animated, intelligent, and beneficent image of the intelligible or spiritual Father (*Ep.* 51, p. 434). It is strange to find this slighting disregard for men as objects of worship in one who assumed that he was a champion of pure Hellenism, especially in an emperor who succeeded a long line of deified emperors. A great deal of his dislike to what he considered the Christian doctrine arose, doubtless, from aristocratic pride. He looked down upon Christ as a Galilean peasant, a subject of Augustus Caesar (Cyr. vi. p. 213). "It is hardly three hundred years since He began to be talked about. During all His life He did nothing worth recording, unless any one reckons it among very great acts to have cured halt and blind people, and to exorcize demoniacs in the villages of Bethsaida and Bethany" (vi. p. 191). He looked upon Christians as parvenus who had assumed a position of power for which they were not fitted, and exercised it wantonly in destroying temples and prosecuting their own heretics, etc. "Jesus and Paul never taught you this. They never expected that Christians would fill so important a place, and were satisfied with converting a few maidservants and slaves, and by their means to get hold of their mistresses, and men like Cornelius and Sergius. If under the reigns of Tiberius and Claudius they have succeeded in convincing a single distinguished person, you may hold me for a liar in every thing" (vi. p. 206).

It is remarkable that Julian shews practically no appreciation of the need of redemption or of the contrast between Christian and heathen life. This we must ascribe in great measure to the misfortune of his early training, to the Arianism of his teachers, and the unloveliness and unlovingness of his early surroundings. Some allowance must also be made for the corruption and extravagance of some forms of popular religion, and for the rash and violent acts of fanaticism committed by many Christians. The superstitious cultus of martyrs, for instance, was no doubt disavowed by the highest minds of the 4th cent., such as St. Athanasius and St. Augustine. But in the masses newly converted from paganism it formed a natural centre for much of the old superstition and fanaticism (Athan. *Or. cont. Arian.* ii. 32; August. *de Vera Relig.* 55; and esp. *cont. Faustum*, xx. 21).

But besides all this there was in the family of Constantine generally a hardness and self-assertion, though accompanied with strong religious pressure, which made them inaccessible to Christian feeling on the subject of sin. The members of it believed strongly in their providential vocation to take a great part in religious questions, but were very rarely troubled by scruples as to their personal unworthiness. Julian's own character, as we have seen, was specially inconsistent, but its ruling element was self-confidence, which he disguised to himself as a reliance upon divine direction. In conclusion, we may draw attention to some of Julian's admissions. He accepts the account of the Gospel miracles. He rejects the Gnostic interpretation of St. John, which separated the Word of God from the Christ. He witnesses to the common use of the term *θεοτόκος* long before the Nestorian troubles. His remarks about martyr-worship and the adoration of the cross have some importance as facts in the history of Christian worship.

On *the Coins* of Julian see *D. C. B.* (4-vol. ed.) *s.v.* We conclude that from policy Julian did not make any general issue of coins with heathen inscriptions or strongly marked heathen symbols which would have shocked his Christian subjects. The statements of Socrates and Sozomen are in perfect harmony with this conclusion. [J.W.]

Julianus (105) Sabas, Oct. 18, an anchorite, whose history Theodoret tells. Sabas or Sabbas, says Theodoret, was a title of veneration, meaning an elder, corresponding with "abbas" or father, commonly applied to anchorites in the East. His cave was in Osrhoëne; he practised extraordinary asceticism and endured extremes of heat and fatigue. In 372, on the expulsion of Meletius, bp. of Antioch, the triumphant Arian party gave out that Julian had embraced their views; whereupon Acacius (subsequently bp. of Berrhoea), accompanied by Asterius, went to Julian and induced him to visit Antioch, where his presence exposed the slander and encouraged the Catholics. He returned to his cave and there died. Theod. *H. E.* iii. 19, iv. 24; *Hist. Religios.* No. ii.; *Menol. Graec.* Sirlet.; Ceillier, viii. 238; Wright, *Cat. Syr. MSS.* ii. 700, iii. 1084, 1090. [C.H.]

Julius (5), bp. of Rome after Marcus, Feb. 6, 337, to Apr. 12, 352, elected after a vacancy of four months. His pontificate is specially notable for his defence of Athanasius, and for the canons of Sardica enacted during it. When Julius became pope, Athanasius was in exile at Trèves after his first deposition by the council of Tyre, having been banished by Constantine the Great in 336. Constantine, dying on Whitsunday 337, was succeeded by his three sons, by whose permission Athanasius returned to his see. But the Eusebians continuing their machinations, the restoration of Athanasius was declared invalid; and one Pistus was set up as bp. of Alexandria in his stead. A deputation was now sent to Rome to induce Julius to declare against Athanasius and acknowledge Pistus; but having failed to convince the pope, desired him to convene a general council at which he should adjudicate upon the charges against Athanasius. Socrates (*H. E.* ii. 11) and Sozomen (*H. E.* iii. 7) state that Eusebius wrote to Julius requesting him to judge the case. But this is not asserted by Julius, and is improbable. Julius undertook to hold a council wherever Athanasius chose, and seems to have sent a synodical letter to the Eusebians apprising them of his intention. The dates of the events that followed are not without difficulty.

Early in 340 Pistus had been given up as the rival bishop, and one Gregory, a Cappadocian, violently intruded by Philagrius the prefect of Egypt into the see; and the Lenten services had been the occasion of atrocious treatment of the Catholics of Alexandria. Athanasius, having concealed himself for a time in the neighbourhood and prepared an encyclic in which he detailed the proceedings, seems to have departed for Rome about Easter 340, and to have been welcomed there by Julius, who, after his arrival, sent two presbyters, Elpidius and Philoxenes, with a letter to Eusebius and his party fixing Dec. 340, at Rome, for the proposed synod. The Eusebians refused to come, and detained the envoys of Julius beyond the time fixed. Elpidius and Philoxenes did not return to Rome till Jan. 341, bringing then a letter, the purport of which is gathered from the reply of Julius to be mentioned presently. Julius suppressed this letter for some time, hoping that the arrival of some Eusebians in Rome might spare him the pain of making it public, and in this hope he also deferred the assembling of the council. But no one came. The Eusebians now shewed themselves by no means prepared to submit to his adjudication, but took advantage of the dedication of a new cathedral at Antioch to hold a council of their own there, known as the "Dedication council" (probably in Aug. 341) and attended by 97 bishops. They prepared canons and three creeds, designed to convince the Western church of their orthodoxy, confirmed the sentence of the council of Tyre against Athanasius, and endeavoured to prevent his restoration by a canon with retrospective force, debarring even from a hearing any bishop or priest who should have officiated after a canonical deposition. Julius meanwhile had made public their letter, and, not yet knowing of the proceedings at Antioch, assembled his council in the church of the presbyter Vito at Rome, apparently in Nov. 341, Athanasius being stated to have been then a year and a half in Rome. It was attended by more than 50 bishops. Old and new accusations were considered; the Acts of the council of Tyre, and those of the inquiry in the Mareotis about the broken chalice, which had been left at Rome by the Eusebian envoys two years before, were produced; witnesses were heard in disproof of the charges and in proof of Eusebian atrocities; and the result was the complete acquittal of Athanasius and confirmation of the communion with him, which had never been discontinued by the Roman church. Marcellus of Ancyra, who had been deposed and banished on a charge of heresy by a Eusebian council at Constantinople in 336 and had been 15 months in Rome, was declared orthodox on the strength of his confession of faith which satisfied the council. Other bishops and priests, from Thrace, Coelesyria, Phoenicia, Palestine, and Egypt, are said by Julius in his subsequent synodal letter to have been present to complain of injuries suffered from the Eusebian party. Socrates (*H. E.* ii. 15) and Sozomen (*H. E.* iii. 8) say that all the deposed bishops were reinstated by Julius in virtue of the prerogative of the Roman see, and that he wrote vigorous letters in their defence, reprehending the Eastern bishops and summoning some of the accusers to Rome. But there seems much exaggeration here. Paul certainly, the deposed patriarch of Constantinople (whom Eusebius had succeeded and who is mentioned by Socrates and Sozomen among the successful appellants), was not restored till the death of his rival in 342, and then only for a time and not through the action of Julius; nor did Athanasius regain his see till 346. Indeed, Sozomen himself acknowledges (iii. 10) that Julius effected nothing at the time by his letters in favour of Athanasius and Paul, and consequently referred their cause to the emperor Constans. Julius's real attitude and action are best seen in the long letter he addressed to the Easterns at the desire of the Roman council, which has been preserved entire by Athanasius (*Apol. contra Arian.* 21-36). He begins by animadverting strongly on the tone of the letter brought to him by his envoys, which was such, he says, that when he had at last reluctantly shewn it to others they could hardly believe it genuine. His own action had been complained of in the letter. He therefore both defends himself and recriminates: "You object to having your own synodal judgment [that of Tyre] questioned in a second council. But this is no unprecedented proceeding. The council of Nice permitted the re-examination of synodical Acts. If your own judgment were right, you should have rejoiced in the opportunity of having it confirmed; and how can you, of all men, complain, when it was at the instance of your own emissaries, when worsted by the advocates of Athanasius, that the Roman council was convened? You certainly cannot plead the irreversibility of a synodical decision, having yourselves reversed even the judgment of Nice in admitting Arians to communion. If on this ground you complain of my receiving Athanasius, much more may I complain of your asking me to acknowledge Pistus, a man alleged by the envoys of Athanasius to have been condemned as an Arian at Nice and admitted by your own representatives to have been ordained by one Secundus, who had been so condemned. It must have been from chagrin at being so utterly refuted in his advocacy of Pistus that your emissary Macarius fled by night, though in weak health, from Rome." He next refers sarcastically to an allegation of his correspondents as to the equality of all bishops, made either in justification of their having judged a bp. of Alexandria or in deprecation of the case being referred to Rome. "If, as you write, you hold the honour of all bishops to be equal, and unaffected by the greatness of their sees, this view comes ill from those who have shewn themselves so anxious to get translated from their own small sees to greater ones." He here alludes to Eusebius himself, who had passed from Berytus to Nicomedia, and thence to Constantinople. Having treated as frivolous their plea of the short time allowed them to get to the Roman council, he meets their further complaint that his letter of summons had been addressed only to Eusebius and his party, instead of the whole Eastern episcopate. "I naturally wrote to those who had written to me." He adds emphatically, "Though I alone wrote, I did so in the name of, and as expressing the sentiments of, all the Italian bishops." He then justifies at length his action and that of the Roman council. The letters of accusation against Athanasius had been from strangers living at a distance, and contradicted one another: the testimonies in his favour from his own people, who knew him well, had been clear and consistent. He exposes the false charges about the murder of Arsenius and the broken chalice, and the unfairness of the Mareotic inquiry. He contrasts the conduct of Athanasius, who had come of his own accord to Rome to court investigation, with the unwillingness of his accusers to appear against him. He dwells on the uncanonical intrusion of Gregory the Cappadocian by military force into the Alexandrian see, and on the atrocities committed to enforce acceptance of him. "It is you," he adds, "who have set at nought the canons, and disturbed the church's peace; not we, as you allege, who have entertained a just appeal, and acquitted the innocent." After briefly justifying the acquittal of Marcellus from the charge of heresy, he calls upon those to whom he writes to repudiate the base conspiracy of a few and so remedy the wrong done. He points out what would have been the proper course of procedure in case of any just cause of suspicion against the bishops. This part of his letter is important, as shewing his own view of his position in relation to the church at large. "If," he says, "they were guilty, as you say they were, they ought to have been judged canonically, not after your method. All of us [*i.e.* the whole episcopate] ought to have been written to, that so justice might be done by all. For they were bishops who suffered these things, and bishops of no ordinary sees, but of such as were founded by apostles personally. Why, then, were you unwilling to write to us [*i.e.* to the Roman church] especially about the Alexandrian see? Can you be ignorant that this is the custom; that we should be written to in the first place, so that hence [*i.e.* from this church] what is just may be defined? Wherefore, if a suspicion against the bishop had arisen there [*i.e.* in Alexandria], it ought to have been referred hither to our church. But now, having never informed us of the case, they wish us to accept their condemnation, in which we had no part. Not so do the ordinances of St. Paul direct; not so do the Fathers teach: this is pride, and a new ambition. I beseech you, hear me gladly. I write this for the public good: for what we have received from the blessed Peter I signify to you." This language will hardly bear the inferences of Socrates (ii. 8, 17) and of Sozomen (iii. 10), that, according to church law, enactments made without the consent of the bp. of Rome were held invalid. It certainly implies no claim to exclusive jurisdiction over all churches. All that Julius insists on is that charges against the bishops of great sees ought, according to apostolic tradition and canonical rule, to be referred to the whole episcopate; and that, in the case of a bp. of Alexandria at least, custom gave the initiative of proceedings to the bp. of Rome. In this reference to custom he probably has in view the case of Dionysius of Alexandria, the charges against whom had been laid before Dionysius of Rome. The allegation in the earlier part of his letter of the fathers of Nice having sanctioned the reconsideration of the decisions of synods is more difficult to account for. He may be alluding to the action of the Nicene council * in entertaining the case of Arius after he had been synodically condemned at Alexandria. The action of pope Julius appears open to no exception, for if the synod consisted of Westerns only, that was because the Easterns refused to attend it, though Julius had convened it at the suggestion of their own emissaries; and, after all, the Roman synod only confirmed the continuance of communion with Eastern prelates whom it deemed unjustly condemned. It had no power to do more. Still, the action of Julius may have served as a step towards subsequent papal claims of a more advanced kind; and it probably suggested the canons of Sardica, pregnant with results, which will be noticed presently.

Athanasius remained still in Rome, till, in his fourth year of residence there—probably in the summer of 343—he received a summons from Constans, now sole emperor of the West, to meet him at Milan (Athan. *Apol. ad Imp. Constantium*, 4), about the holding of a new council, at which both East and West should be fully represented. With the concurrence of the Eastern emperor Constantius, this council was summoned at the Moesian town of Sardica on the confines of their empires, probably towards the end of 343. The scheme of united action failed, the Eastern bishops holding a separate synod at Philippopolis. The rest met at Sardica under the

* This indeed was one of the purposes which the emperor had at heart in convening it. Just as the synod of Arles had also met by his orders to reconsider the acquittal of St. Caecilian, decreed in the previous synod of Rome under Melchiades.—E.S.FF.

venerable Hosius of Cordova. In some editions of the Acts of the council he is designated one of the legates of the Roman see. But this designation seems due only to the desire, which appears in other cases, of assigning the presidency of all councils to the pope. According to Athanasius (*Apol. contra Arian.* 50), Julius was represented by two presbyters, Archidamus and Philoxenes, whose names appear in the signatures to the synodal letter of the council after that of Hosius. Hosius undoubtedly presided, and there is no sign of his having done so as the pope's deputy either in the Acts of the council or in the letter sent to Julius at its close. Nor can the initiative of the council be assigned to Julius, for this is inconsistent with the statement of Athanasius, who calls God to witness that when summoned to Milan he was entirely ignorant of the purpose of the summons, but found that it was because " certain bishops " there had been moving Constans to induce Constantius to allow a general council to be assembled (*Apol. ad Imp. Constantium*, 4). If Julius had been the mover, it is unlikely that Athanasius, who was with him at Rome, would have been ignorant of the purpose of his summons or would have spoken only of " certain bishops." The council was convened by the emperors on their own authority, to review the whole past proceedings, whether at Tyre, Antioch, or Rome, without asking the pope's leave or inviting him to take the lead. It confirmed and promulgated anew all the decisions of the Roman council, decreed the restoration of the banished orthodox prelates, and excommunicated the Eusebian intruders. It also passed 21 canons of discipline, 3 being of special historic importance. The extant Acts of the council give them thus. Canon III. (*al.* III., IV.) " Bp. Osius said: This also is necessary to be added, that bishops pass not from their own province to another in which there are bishops, unless perhaps on the invitation of their brethren there, that we may not seem to close the gate of charity. And, if in any province a bishop have a controversy against a brother bishop, let neither of the two call upon a bishop from another province to take cognizance of it. But, should any one of the bishops have been condemned in any case, and think that he has good cause for a reconsideration of it, let us (if it please you) honour the memory of the blessed Apostle St. Peter, so that Julius, the Roman bishop, be written to by those who have examined the case; and, if he should judge that the trial ought to be renewed, let it be renewed, and let him appoint judges. But, if he should decide that the case is such that what has been done ought not to be reconsidered, what he thus decides shall be confirmed. *Si hoc omnibus placet?* The synod replied, *Placet.*" Canon IV. (*al. V.*) " Bp. Gaudentius said: Let it, if it please you, be added to this decree that when any bishop has been deposed by the judgment of bishops who dwell in neighbouring places, and he has proclaimed his intention of taking his case to Rome, no other bishop shall by any means be ordained to his see till the cause has been determined in the judgment of the Roman bishop." Canon V. (*al.* VII.) " Bp. Osius said: It has seemed good to us (*placuit*) that if any bishop has been accused, and the assembled bishops of his own region have deposed him, and if he has appealed to the bishop of the Roman church, and if the latter is willing to hear him, and considers it just that the inquiry should be renewed, let him deign to write to the bishops of a neighbouring province, that they may diligently inquire into everything, and give their sentence according to the truth. But if the appellant in his supplication should have moved the Roman bishop to send a presbyter [*al.* presbyters] 'de suo latere,' it shall be in his [*i.e.* the Roman bishop's] power to do whatever he thinks right. And if he should decide to send persons having his own authority to sit in judgment with the bishops, it shall be at his option to do so. But if he should think the bishops sufficient for terminating the business, he shall do what approves itself to his most wise judgment." * In these canons we notice, *firstly*, they were designed to provide what recent events had shewn the need of, and what the existing church system did not adequately furnish — a recognized court of appeal in ecclesiastical causes. The canons of Nice had provided none beyond the provincial synod, for beyond that the only strictly canonical appeal was to a general council, which could be but a rare event and was dependent on the will of princes. The need was felt of a readier remedy. *Secondly*, this remedy was provided by giving the Roman bishop the power to cause the judgment of provincial synods to be reconsidered; but only on the appeal of the aggrieved party, and only in certain prescribed ways. He might refuse to interfere, thus confirming the decision of the provincial synod; or he might constitute the bishops of a neighbouring province as a court of appeal; he might further, if requested and if he thought it necessary, send one or more presbyters as his legates to watch the proceedings, or appoint representatives of himself to sit as assessors in the court. But he was not empowered to interfere unless appealed to, or to summon the case to Rome to be heard before himself in synod; still less, of course, to adjudicate alone. *Thirdly*, it is evident that this course was sanctioned for the first time at Sardica. The canons, on the face of them, were not a confirmation of a traditional prerogative of Rome. The words of Hosius were, " Let us, if it please you, honour the memory of the blessed Apostle St. Peter," *i.e.* by conceding this power to the Roman bishop. *Fourthly*, the power in question was definitely given only to the then reigning pope, Julius, who is mentioned by name; and it has hence been supposed that it was not meant to be given his successors (cf. Richer. *Hist. Concil. General.* t. i. c. 3, § 4). But the arrangement was probably at any rate intended to be permanent, since the need for it and the grounds assigned for it were permanent. *Fifthly*, since it was the causes of

* The editions of these canons, extant in Greek and Latin translations, vary in their wording and arrangement of them, but all agree in the drift as given above. Doubts have been entertained of their authenticity, but they are generally accepted. See Gieseler, Eccl. Hist. 2nd period, div. 1, c. iii. note 7.

Eastern bishops that led to the enactment, the canons were probably meant to apply to the whole church, and not to the Western only. The Greek canonists, Balsamon and Zonaras, maintain their narrower scope; and it is true that, the council having consisted of Westerns only, they were never accepted by the churches of the East. But though the council of Sardica was not in fact oecumenical, the emperors had intended it to be so, and the Roman canonists call it so in virtue of the general summons. They, however, regard it as an appendage to that of Nice; and probably its canons were from the first added at Rome to those of Nice as supplementary to them, since in the well-known case of Apiarius, the African presbyter (A.D. 417), pope Zosimus quoted them as Nicene; and pope Innocent (A.D. 402) seems previously to have done the same in defending his appellate jurisdiction over Gaul. In the African case the error was eventually exposed by reference to the copies of the Nicene canons preserved at Constantinople and Alexandria, and the Africans thereupon distinctly repudiated the claims of Rome which rested upon this false foundation. But Boniface and Celestine, the successors of Zosimus, refer to these canons as Nicene, as did Leo I. in 449; and this continued to be the Roman position. The persistence of the popes in quoting them as Nicene after the mistake had been discovered is an early instance of Roman unfairness in support of papal claims. It is further a significant fact that in some Roman copies the name of Sylvester was substituted for that of Julius, as if with an intention of throwing their date back to the Nicene period. The scope also of the canons came in time to be unduly extended, being made to involve the power of the pope to summon at his will all cases to be heard before himself at Rome. Our proper conclusion seems to be that, though probably intended by their framers to bind the whole church, their authority was not really adequate to the purpose; and that the popes afterwards appealed to them unfairly in support of their claims by misrepresenting both their authority and their scope.

At the close of its sittings the council of Sardica addressed letters to the two emperors, to Julius, to the church of Alexandria, to the bishops of Egypt and Libya, and an encyclic "to all bishops." In that to Julius the reason he alleged for not attending—viz. the necessity of remaining in Rome to guard against the schemes of heretics—is allowed as sufficient; and he is presumed to have been present in spirit. The documents sent him and the oral report of his emissaries would inform him of what had been done, but it was thought fit to send him also a brief summary: The most religious emperors had permitted the council to discuss anew all past proceedings, and hence the following questions had been considered: (1) The definition of the true faith; (2) The condemnation or acquittal of those whom the Eusebians had deposed; (3) The charges against the Eusebians themselves of having unjustly condemned and persecuted the orthodox. For full information as to the council's decisions he is referred to the letters written to the emperors; and he is directed, rather than requested ("tua autem excellens prudentia disponere debet, ut per tua scripta," etc.), to inform the bishops of Italy, Sardinia, and Sicily of what had been done, that they might know with whom to hold communion. A list is appended of those excommunicated by the synod. The whole drift of the letter is inconsistent with the council having been convened by the pope himself, or held in his name, or considered dependent on him for ratification of its decrees. He is not even charged with the promulgation of them, except to bishops immediately under his jurisdiction. The only expression pointing to his pre-eminent position is that it would appear to be best and exceedingly fitting ("optimum et valde congruentissimum") that "the head, that is the see of St. Peter," should be informed respecting every single province. Nor is there in the letter to the Alexandrians, or in the encyclic to all bishops, any reference to him as having initiated or taken part in the council; only in the latter a passing allusion to the previous council which he ("comminister noster dilectissimus") had convened at Rome. The letter to Julius is signed, first by Hosius, and then by 58 other bishops, being probably those present at the close of the council. But as many as 284 are given by Athanasius (*Apol. contra Arian.* 49, 50) as having assented to its decrees and signed its encyclic letter. They include, from various parts of the West with a few from the East 78, from Gaul and Britain 34, from Africa 36, from Egypt 94, from Italy 15, from Cyprus 12, from Palestine 15.

Not till Oct. 346, some three years after the council, was Athanasius allowed to return to his see. Before that he again visited Rome, and was again cordially received by Julius, who wrote a letter of congratulation to the clergy and laity of Alexandria, remarkable for its warmth of feeling and beauty of expression. He regards the return at last of their beloved bishop after such prolonged affliction as a reward granted to their unwavering affection for him, shewn by their continual prayers and their letters of sympathy that had consoled his exile, as well as to his own faithfulness. He dwells on the holy character of Athanasius, his resoluteness in defence of the faith, his endurance of persecution, his contempt of death and danger. He congratulates them on receiving him back all the more glorious for his long trials and fully proved innocence. He pictures vividly his welcome home by rejoicing crowds at Alexandria. The letter is the more admirable for the absence of all bitterness towards the persecutors.

The only further notice of Julius is of his having received the recantation of Valens and Ursacius, two notable opponents of Athanasius who had been condemned at Sardica. They had already recanted before a synod at Milan, and written a pacific letter to Athanasius; but went also of their own accord, A.D. 347, to Rome, and presented a humble apologetic letter to Julius, and were admitted to communion (Athan. *Hist. Arian. ad Monachos*, 26; Hilar. *Fragm.* i.). Their profession however (in which they owned the falsity of their charges against Athanasius and renounced Arian heresy), proved insincere.

For when, after the defeat of Constans in 350 and the defeat of Maxentius in 351, the tide of imperial favour began to turn, they recanted their recantation, which they said had been made only under fear of Constans. But Julius, who died Apr. 12, 352, was spared the troublous times which ensued. The fresh charges now got up, and sent to him and the emperor, arrived at Rome too late for him to entertain them. [LIBERIUS.]

His only extant writings are the two letters, to the Eusebians and the Alexandrians, referred to above. Ten *decreta* are ascribed to him in the collections of Gratian and Ivo. One is interesting for its allusion to certain usages in the celebration of the Eucharist—viz. using milk, or the expressed juice of grapes, instead of wine; administering the bread dipped in the wine, after the manner of the Greeks at the present day; and using a linen cloth soaked in must, reserved through the year and moistened with water, for each celebration. All these are condemned, except the use of the unfermented juice of the grape, in which (it is said) is the efficacy of wine, in case of need, if mixed with water, which is declared always necessary to represent the people, as the wine represents the blood of Christ.

Julius was buried, according to the Liberian and Felician Catalogues, "in coemeterio Calepodii ad Callistum" on the Aurelian Way, where he had built a basilica. [J.B—Y.]

Julius (9) (*Julianus*), bp. of Puteoli (*Gesta de Nom. Acacii*, in Labbe, iv. 1079 D), probably the bp. Julius to whom, A.D. 448, Leo the Great entrusted the execution of certain disciplinary measures in the church of Beneventum (Leo Mag. *Ep.* xix. 736). Certainly he, with Renatus the presbyter and HILARUS the deacon, carried to Flavian of Constantinople the famous "tome" of St. Leo in June 449, and acted as his legate in the "Robber" council of Ephesus (Leo Mag. *Ep.* xxxiii. 866, Migne). The legates are described by Leo as sent *de latere meo* (*Ep.* xxxii. 859, xxxiv. 870. He was not the first pope to use this phrase; see the Ballerini *in loc.* Migne). Because Julius appears in the "acta" of the council most frequently as Julianus he has been confused with Julian of Cos. That it was our Julius who was the papal legate at Ephesus is proved by Leo's letter to the latter (xxxiv. 870) and by the fact that the legate did not know Greek, which Julian of Cos certainly did (see JULIANUS (27); Labbe, iv. 121 B; Tillem. xv. note 21, pp. 901-902). Evagrius (*H. E.* i. x.), Prosper (*Chron*), and *Gesta de Nom. Acac.* (in Labbe, iv. 1079 D), call the papal legate Julius, not Julianus (see also Marianus Scotus, *Chron.* ann. 450 in *Patr. Lat.* cxlvii. 726). On Quesnel's hypothesis, that Julius and not Renatus died on the road to Ephesus, and that Julian took his place, cf. Tillemont, *l.c.*, and Hefele, *Concil.* ii. 368, 369. On their arrival at Ephesus the legates lodged with Flavian; on the ground that they had lived with him and been tampered with by him (συνεκροτήθησαν, Lat. *munerati*), Eutyches took exception to their impartiality as judges (Labbe, iv. 149 B).

The assertion of Liberatus (*Breviarium*, c. xii.) that the Roman legates could not take part in the council ("assidere non *passi sunt*" are his words) because the precedence was not given to them as representing Rome, and because Leo's letter was not read, is not in harmony with the acta of the council (see Tillem. xv. notes 26 and 27, p. 904). They undoubtedly did take part in the proceedings of the council, and Julius ranked after Dioscorus. His interpreter, as he could not speak Greek, was Florentius, bp. of Sardis (Labbe, iv. 122 B). We read that he made several efforts to resist DIOSCORUS, especially urging that Leo's letter should be read, but he does not seem to have been so prominent in opposition as Hilarus the deacon (*ib.* 128 B, 149 B, 302 D). Leo, however, expresses high commendation of the conduct of his legates generally. They protested in the council, he says, and declared that no violence should sever them from the truth (*Ep.* 45, 922). He speaks to Theodosius, the emperor, of intelligence having been brought him of the acts of the synod by the bishop whom he had sent, as well as by the deacon (*Ep.* xliii. 902); but this in other letters (xliv. 911, xlv. 919) is corrected by the statement that only Hilarus escaped to Rome. What happened to Julius we do not know, nor do we hear of him subsequently (Ughelli, *Italia Sacra*, vi. 272). Ughelli and Cappelletti (xix. 647, 669) name him Julianus and make him 6th bp. of Puteoli between Theodore and Stephen. [C.G.]

Junilius (Ἰούνιλος, *Junillus*), an African by birth, hence commonly known as Junilius Africanus. He filled for seven years in the court of Justinian the important office of quaestor of the sacred palace, succeeding the celebrated Tribonian (Procop. *Anecd.* c. 20). Procopius tells us that Constantine, whom the Acts of the 5th general council shew to have held the office in 553, succeeded on the death of Junilius, which may therefore be placed a year or two earlier. Junilius, though a layman, took great interest in theological studies. A deputation of African bishops visiting Constantinople, one of them, PRIMASIUS of Adrumetum, inquired of his distinguished countryman, Junilius, who among the Greeks was distinguished as a theologian, to which Junilius replied that he knew one Paul [PAUL OF NISIBIS], a Persian by race, who had been educated in the school of the Syrians at Nisibis, where theology was taught by public masters in the same systematic manner as the secular studies of grammar and rhetoric elsewhere. Junilius had an introduction to the Scriptures by this Paul, which, on the solicitation of Primasius, he translated into Latin, breaking it up into question and answer. Kihn identifies this work of Paul with that which Ebedjesu (Asseman. *Bibl. Or.* III. i. 87; Badger, *Nestorians*, ii. 369) calls *Maschelmonutho desurtho*. The work of Junilius was called "Instituta regularia divinae legis," but is commonly known as "De partibus divinae legis," a title which really belongs only to chap. i. It has been often printed in libraries of the Fathers (*e.g.* Galland, vol. xii.; Migne, vol. lxviii.). The best ed., for which 13 MSS. were collated, is by Prof. Kihn of Würzburg (*Theodor von Mopsuestia*, Freiburg, 1880), a work admirable for its thorough investigations, and throwing much light on Junilius.

The introduction does not, as has been

often assumed, represent an African school of theology, but the Syrian; and Kihn conclusively shews that (although possibly Junilius was not aware of it himself) it is all founded on the teaching of THEODORE of Mopsuestia.

Junilius divides the books of Scripture into two classes. The first, which alone he calls Canonical Scripture, are of perfect authority; the second added by many are of secondary (*mediae*) authority; all other books are of no authority. The first class consists of (1) *Historical Books:* Pentateuch, Josh., Judg., Ruth, Sam., and Kings., and in N.T. the four Gospels and Acts; (2) *Prophetical* (in which what is evidently intended for a chronological arrangement is substituted for that more usual): Ps., Hos., Is., Jl., Am., Ob., Jon., Mic., Nah., Hab., Zeph., Jer., Ezk., Dan., Hag., Zech., and Mal. (he says that John's Apocalypse is much doubted of amongst the Easterns); (3) *Proverbial or parabolic:* the Prov. of Solomon and the Book of Jesus the Son of Sirach; (4) *Doctrinal:* Eccles., the 14 epp. of St. Paul in the order now usual, including Heb., I. Pet., and I. Jn. In his second class he counts (1) *Historical:* Chron., Job, Esdras (no doubt including Neh.), Judith, Est., and Macc.; (3) *Proverbial:* Wisdom and Cant.; (4) *Doctrinal:* the Epp. of Jas., II. Pet., Jude, II. III. Jn. Lam. and Bar. were included in Jer. Tobit is not mentioned, but is quoted in a later part of the treatise. Kihn is no doubt right in regarding its omission as due to the accidental error of an early transcriber; for no writer of the time would have designedly refused to include Tobit even in his list of deuterocanonical books. Junilius gives as a reason for not reckoning the books of the second class as canonical that the Hebrews make this difference, as Jerome and others testify. This is clearly incorrect with regard to several of them, and one is tempted to think (*pace* Kihn) that Junilius himself added this reference to Jerome and did not find it in his Greek original. The low place assigned to Job and Cant. accords with the estimate formed by Theodore of Mopsuestia. Junilius quotes as Peter's a passage from his second epistle, which he had not admitted into his list of canonical books. He describes Ps., Eccles., and Job as written in metre (see Bickell, *Metrices Biblicae Regulae*). The work of Junilius presents a great number of other points of interest, *e.g.* his answer, ii. 29, to the question how we prove the books of Scripture to have been written by divine inspiration.

The publication of the work Kihn assigns to 551, in which year the *Chronicle* of Victor Tununensis records the presence at Constantinople of the African bishops Reparatus, Firmus, Primasius, and Verecundus. He thinks that Junilius probably met Paul of Nisibis there as early as 543. We do not venture to oppose the judgment of one entitled to speak with so high authority; but we should have thought that the introduction into the West of this product of the Nestorian school of theology took place at an earlier period of the controversy about the Three Chapters than 551. It is not unlikely that Primasius paid earlier visits to Constantinople than that of which we have evidence. A commentary on Gen. i. wrongly ascribed to Junilius is now generally attributed to Bede. [G.S.]

Justina (5), empress, second wife of Valentinian I., a Sicilian by birth, and, *teste* Zosimus (iv. 19 and 43), the widow of Magnentius, killed in 353. Valentinian may have divorced his first wife (*Chron. Pasch.* 302), and then espoused Justina, probably in 368.

She was an Arian, but during her husband's lifetime concealed her opinions (Ruf. *H. E.* ii. 15, in Migne, *Patr. Lat.* xxi. 523). She, however, endeavoured to prevent him from allowing St. Martin of Tours to enter his presence (Sulp. Sev. *Dial.* ii. in *ib.* xx. 205). After her husband's death she at once used her influence as mother of the infant emperor Valentinian II. to advance the interests of her sect, and soon came into collision with St. Ambrose. Their first contest was probably *c.* 380, when St. Ambrose was summoned to Sirmium to take part in the consecration of Anemius as bishop of that see, the empress being desirous that the new bishop should be consecrated by the Arians (Paulinus, *Vita S. Ambrosii*, in *ib.* xiv. 30).

After the murder of Gratian and the seizure by Maximus of Spain, Gaul, and Britain in 383, Justina (who, with her infant son, was residing in the imperial palace at Milan) had recourse to her former opponent St. Ambrose. She placed her son in his hands, and induced him to undertake the delicate task of going as ambassador to Maximus, to persuade him to be contented with Gratian's provinces and to leave Valentinian in undisturbed possession of Italy, Africa, and Western Illyricum (St. Ambrose, *Epp.* 20, 21, 24; Id. *de Obitu Valentiniani*, 1182 in *Patr. Lat.* xvi. 1001, 1007, 1035, 1368). His mission was successful, at any rate for a time; but the ungrateful Justina assailed him at Easter 385 with the object of obtaining a church at Milan for the use of her fellow-Arians. For an account of this memorable struggle see AMBROSIUS. By a constitution (*Cod. Theod.* xvi. 1, 4), dated Jan. 21, 386, and drawn up at her direction (Soz. *H. E.* vii. 13), those who held the opinions sanctioned by the council of Ariminum were granted the right of meeting for public worship, Catholics being forbidden under pain of death to offer opposition or to endeavour to get the law repealed.

When danger again threatened, Justina again had recourse to Ambrose's services. After Easter 387 he was sent to Trier to ask that the body of Gratian should be restored to his brother and to avert Maximus's threatened invasion of Italy (*Ep.* 24). His mission was unsuccessful; Maximus crossed the Alps in the autumn and made himself master of Italy without striking a blow. Valentinian and his mother and sisters fled by sea to Thessalonica, whence she sent to Theodosius imploring his help. Zosimus (iv. 44) narrates how she overcame his reluctance by the charms of her daughter, the beautiful Galla, whose hand paid for his assistance. (See Duc de Broglie, *L'Eglise et l'emp.* iii. 228.) In 388, the year of her son's restoration, Justina died (Soz. *H. E.* vii. 14; Ruf. *H. E.* ii. 17). [F.D.]

Justinianus (6) **I.**, Roman emperor (275-565).

I. *Life and Character.*—Justinian was born

most probably in 483 at Tauresium, on the borders of Illyricum and Macedonia, a spot probably a little S. of Uskiub, the ancient Scupi (see Procop. *Aedif.* iv. 1, and Tozer, *Highlands of European Turkey*, ii. p. 370). After his accession he built at his birthplace a city which he named Justiniana Prima and made the capital of the province and seat of an archbishop. [The tale regarding his Slavonic origin started by Alemanni in his notes to the *Anecdota* of Procopius seems to be baseless; see art. in *Eng. Hist. Rev.* Oct. 1887, by the present writer.] Early in life he came to Constantinople, and attached himself to his uncle Justin, who, serving in the imperial guards under the emperors Zeno and Anastasius, had risen to high place. At Constantinople Justinian diligently studied law, theology, and general literature, and the influence of his uncle doubtless procured him employment in the civil service of the state. When Justinian was 35, the emperor Anastasius was succeeded by Justin, an illiterate soldier, weakened by age, to whom the help of his more active nephew was almost indispensable. Ecclesiastical affairs and the general administration of the state fell under the control of Justinian. He became co-emperor in 527, and on Justin's death, a month later, assumed without question the sole sovereignty of the Roman world, retaining it till his death in 565, at the age of 82, when he was peaceably succeeded by his nephew Justin II.

In 526 he married Theodora, a woman of singular beauty, and still more remarkable charms of manner and intellect, said to have been a native of Cyprus and a comedian. The gossip of the time, starting from this undoubted fact, has accumulated in the *Anecdota*, or unpublished memoirs, ascribed to, and no doubt written by (although there has been a controversy on the point), Procopius, a variety of scandalous tales regarding her earlier career. [THEODORA.] She soon acquired an almost unbounded dominion over Justinian's mind, and was commonly regarded as the source of many of his schemes and enterprises. She died in 548, and he did not marry again.

Most of what we know directly about Justinian comes from PROCOPIUS, which does not diminish the difficulty of forming a comprehensive and consistent view of his abilities and character. For Procopius wrote of him with servility in his lifetime, and reviled him in the *Anecdota*, a singular book which did not come to light till long afterwards. Setting aside exaggerations in both directions, it may be concluded that Justinian was a man of considerable, if not first-rate, abilities. He was well educated, according to the ideas and customs of the time, and more or less conversant with many branches of knowledge. Procopius accuses him of being a barbarian both in mind and speech, which probably means only that he spoke Greek like an Illyrian provincial (*Anecd.* c. 14). His artistic taste is shewn by the many beautiful buildings which he erected, two among which—those of St. Sophia at Constantinople and St. Vitalis at Ravenna (though it does not appear that he had any share in designing this latter)—have had the unique distinction of becoming architectural models for subsequent ages, the one for the East and the other for the West. Several hymns still used in the orthodox Eastern church are ascribed to his pen, and he is the author of a treatise against the Monophysites, which Cardinal Mai has published. The records of his government and administration shew that he possessed great ingenuity and enterprise; but the enterprise was often prompted more by vanity and lust of power than by regard to the welfare of his people, and his ingenuity was not guided by prudence or by a solid knowledge of the economical conditions of prosperity. There was much more cleverness than wisdom about him; we see in his policy few indications of deep and statesmanlike foresight. The chief feature of his character is his extraordinary industry. He seemed to live for work, and toiled harder than any of his own clerks. He was naturally abstemious and regular in life, observing the church fasts very strictly, able to go long without food, taking little sleep, and spending most of his time, when not actually giving audiences, in pacing up and down the rooms of the palace listening to readers or dictating to an amanuensis. He cared little for vulgar pleasures (though he shewed an excessive partiality for the blue faction, he does not appear to have been personally addicted to the games of the circus), and yielded to no influences except those of his wife Theodora. We are told that he was easy of access—a rare merit in the despotic centre of a highly formal court—pleasant and reassuring in manner, but also deceitful and capable of treachery and ingratitude. How far this ingratitude was in the most notable case, that of Belisarius, excused by apprehensions of danger, is a problem not wholly solved or soluble. Wantonly cruel he does not seem to have been, and on several occasions shewed an unexpected clemency, but he shrank from no severities that his intellect judged useful.

In person he was well formed, rather above the middle height, with a ruddy and smiling countenance. Besides his effigy on coins, we have two probably contemporary portraits among the mosaics of Ravenna—one in the apse of the church of San Vitale, built in his reign, in which he appears among a number of other figures; the other now preserved in the noble church of Sant' Apollinare in Urbe.

II. The political events of his reign may be read in Procopius, Agathias, Theophanes (all three in the Bonn ed. of the Byzantine historians), in the ecclesiastical history of Evagrius, in Gibbon (see cc. xl.-xliii. for a full and brilliant picture of Justinian's times), and in Le Beau (*Histoire du bas empire*, vols. viii. and ix., with St. Martin's notes). Finlay (*Greece under the Romans*, vol. i. of new ed.) has some valuable remarks, as also Hertzberg, *Griechenland unter der Römer*, vol. iii.; see also Dahn, *Prokopios von Caesarea*. At Justinian's accession the empire was generally at peace. An expedition was dispatched in 533, under Belisarius, which landed in Africa without opposition and reduced the whole Vandal kingdom to submission in little more than three months. The Vandals who survived seem to have been rapidly absorbed into the African population; anyhow, we hear no more of them. The fleet of Belisarius received in rapid succession the submission of Sardinia, Corsica, and the Balearic Isles. Orthodoxy was re-established there and in Africa. Justinian directed the laws against heretics to be put in force against the Arians and Donatists in Africa, and their meetings to be altogether forbidden (Baron. *ad ann.* 535). The orthodox bishops met in a council, at which 207 prelates were present (Baron. *ad ann.* 535). The orthodox churches of Africa were restored to the full enjoyment of their rights, property, and privileges. But the African church and province never regained its former prosperity. The misgovernment of the imperial lieutenants completed the ruin which the Vandals had begun, and the wild Moorish tribes encroached in all directions on the Roman population. Great part of the country, once the most productive part of the Roman dominions, relapsed into solitude and neglect; the Christians there were still divided by the mutual jealousies of Donatists, Arians, and orthodox.

The success of his enterprise against the Vandals encouraged Justinian to attempt the recovery of Italy from the Ostrogoths, who had held it and Sicily since the invasion under Theodoric in 493-494. The emperors at Constantinople considered themselves, ever since the extinction of the Western branch of the empire in 476, *de jure* sovereigns of Italy and the whole West, regarding the Gothic kings partly as their lieutenants, partly as mere usurpers. Justinian dispatched Belisarius from Constantinople with a fleet and over 7,000 men in the autumn of 535. He reduced Sicily easily in a few weeks. Then he attacked Italy, occupying Rome in Dec. 536. The Ostrogoths had shortly before risen against their king Theodahad, and chosen Witigis, whom Belisarius took at Ravenna and carried to Constantinople, leaving the imperial power supreme in Italy. Totila, whom the Goths chose in the room of Witigis, recovered fortress after fortress from the incompetent generals who succeeded Belisarius, till he was master of most part of Italy; and at length restored the Gothic kingdom to a better position than it had held since the death of Theodoric. But in 552 his army was defeated, and himself slain by Narses, and with him died the last hopes of the Gothic kingdom of Italy. After Narses had destroyed Butelin and his host in a great battle near Casilinum in Campania, 544, the small remains of the Gothic nation either passed into Spain and Gaul to mingle with other barbarians or were lost among the Roman population of Italy, which now was finally in Justinian's hands. It was, however, a desolated and depopulated Italy. Nor was it long left to his successors.

The third great struggle of Justinian's reign was against the Persian empire, then under Kobad and Chosroes Anushirvan in the zenith of its power. After several campaigns Chosroes concluded in 533, on obtaining from the emperor 11,000 pounds of gold, a peace which gave rest to the eastern provinces. In 539 war broke out again, and also a revolt against Justinian in Armenia, a part of whose people appealed to the Persians for help. Chosroes commanded a vast force, which the Roman generals were quite unable to resist in the open field. In 540 Antioch, far the greatest town of the eastern part of the empire, was sacked, and many thousand inhabitants carried to a new city, built for them near Ctesiphon, his own capital. Towards the end of Justinian's reign the fighting slackened; a peace for 50 years was concluded in 562 on terms humiliating to Justinian, who undertook to pay yearly 30,000 gold pieces. This peace lasted only 10 years; but the war which began in 572 lies outside Justinian's reign.

Less famous, but perhaps even more ruinous, were the contests which Justinian had to maintain against the barbarians of Scythia and the Danube. From the Alps to the Black Sea, the N. border of the empire was the scene of seldom intermitted warfare. The various tribes whom the Roman historian calls Huns, and who included the race subsequently distinguished as Bulgarians, poured from the S. of what is now Russia down upon Thrace, ravaged it and Macedonia, penetrated on one occasion to the isthmus of Corinth, and six years before Justinian's death, in 559, appeared in great force under the walls of Constantinople, from which they were repulsed by the skill and vigour of Belisarius. In the N.W. provinces villages were destroyed, cultivated land laid waste, and immense numbers of the inhabitants carried into slavery. The only serious efforts the emperor made against these enemies (besides the building of fortresses) were by diplomacy. His policy was to foment hostilities between neighbouring tribes, taking sometimes one, sometimes another, into alliance with the empire, and offering large presents, often so regular as to amount to a kind of blackmail, to buy them off for the moment or induce them to turn their arms against some other barbarian power. His activity as a negotiator was unwearied. Embassies from all parts of the barbarian world arrived at Constantinople, excited the wonder of the people by their strange garb and manners, and returned home laden with gifts and promises. Even the tribes of the Baltic and the Turks of Central Asia seem to have thus come into relations with him. His policy was much blamed in his own time (see esp. Procop. *Anecd.*), and may appear shortsighted as supplying fresh inducements to the barbarians to renew their attacks and letting them know the wealth of the capital; but perhaps no other policy was possible, and the incidental advantages of Roman influence and culture upon the border tribes may have been considerable.

III. We possess no systematic account of the internal state of the empire in Justinian's time, and depend only upon occasional notices by historians like Procopius and Agathias, and a study of Justinian's legislative measures. The civil service was, and had long been, in a high state of efficiency. Such alterations as Justinian made tended to perfect this organization and to render all its members more completely subservient to the crown. He spent enormous sums not only on his wars but in the erection of churches, fortresses, and public buildings of every kind (a list will be found in the *de Aedificiis* of Procopius), and was therefore always in want of money. Oppressive as taxation had been before, he seems to have made it even more stringent; and when the land-tax and other ordinary sources of revenue failed, he was driven to such expedients as the sale of public offices, and even to the prostitution of justice and the confiscation of the property of private persons. Though the instances of this rest chiefly on the untrustworthy authority of the *Anecdota* of Procopius (who ascribes the worst to the immediate action of the empress), stories in other historians give some support to the accusation. On one occasion he attempted to debase the coin, but was checked by a threatened insurrection in the capital. The same charges of venality and extortion are brought against Tribonian, John of Cappadocia, and others of Justinian's ministers. The administration of justice must have been greatly improved by the promulgation of the whole binding law in the *Codex*, *Pandects*, and *Institutes*; and great importance was evidently attached to the maintenance of the law schools of Berytus and Constantinople; corruption may, however, have largely prevailed among the judges. Brilliant as Justinian's reign may appear to us, the sufferings endured by the people from war, taxation, the persecution of heretics, the blows struck at the privileges of various classes and professions, as well as from the great plague and from destructive earthquakes, made his rule unpopular, as shewn by the rebellions in Africa and the disaffection of the reconquered Italians. In Constantinople, not to speak of minor seditions, there occurred a tremendous insurrection in Jan. 532, arising out of a tumult in the hippodrome, and apparently due, partly to resentment at the maladministration of John of Cappadocia, partly to the presence in the city of a large number of starving immigrants. The revolters held the city for some days, set fire to some of the finest buildings, drove Justinian into his palace fortress, and proclaimed Hypatius, nephew of the deceased emperor Anastasius, emperor. Having no concerted plan of action, part of them were induced to abandon the rest, who were then surprised and slaughtered by the imperial guards under the command of Belisarius. It is said that 30,000 people perished in this rising, which is known as the Nika sedition, from the watchword used by the rebels. (See an interesting account by W. A. Schmidt, *Der Aufstand in Constantinopel unter Kaiser Justinian.*)

He made efforts to open up new channels for the traffic in silk, and ultimately succeeded, through the boldness of two Persian monks, who conveyed the eggs of the worm in a hollow cane from China to the empire. The manufacture of silk was thus no longer at the mercy of the Persians, who had stopped the supply in time of war, and the culture of the silk-worm became an important branch of industry in the Roman East.

As a whole, the faults of Justinian's domestic government appear greatly to outweigh its merits. His subjects had grown tired of him long before his death; but later ages looked back to his reign as a period of conquest abroad and magnificence at home, and accepted the surname of the Great.

IV. *Ecclesiastical policy* occupied no small share of Justinian's thoughts and care.

During the lifetime of Justin I., he sought to re-establish the communion of the churches of Constantinople and Rome, which had been interrupted owing to the Monophysite controversies. On his accession in 527 he professed himself a zealous supporter of the Two Natures and the decrees of Chalcedon, and the firmness of his throne was no doubt partly due to this coincidence of his theological views with those of the bulk of his subjects in Constantinople, Thrace, and Asia Minor. He had great confidence in his own powers as a theologian, and took an active part in all the current controversies. A diligent student and having some literary pretensions, he read and wrote much on theological topics. His ecclesiastical policy apparently had two main objects, not, however, consistently pursued—the maintenance of the orthodox doctrine of the Four Councils, and especially of Chalcedon, and the reconciliation of the Monophysites, or at least the inducing by apparent concessions the more moderate Monophysites to accept the decrees of Chalcedon. There was in his court an active, though probably concealed, Monophysite party, headed by, and sheltering itself under, the empress Theodora. One of the emperor's first acts was to summon a conference of leading theologians on both sides, so as to bring about a reconciliation. After several sittings, however, in one of which Justinian delivered a long allocution, vital points were reached on which neither side could yield, and the conference was dissolved. Among the Monophysite leaders were Severus, deposed from the patriarchate of Antioch in the time of Justin, and Anthimus, bp. of Trebizond. They seem to have acquired much influence in Theodora's coterie, and, probably owing to her, Anthimus was raised in 535 to the patriarchate of Constantinople, in spite of the doctrinal suspicions attaching to him. Pope Agapetus, having heard of these suspicions, and disapproving, as Rome was wont to do, of translations from one bishopric to another, refused to communicate with the patriarch till he should have purged himself from the charge of heresy, and insisted that, when purged, Anthimus should return to Trebizond. Justinian (perhaps owing to the support which Theodora seems to have given Anthimus) was at first displeased and resisted, but Agapetus prevailed. Anthimus was deposed, and Mennas, head of the hospitium of Samson in Constantinople, appointed in his place and consecrated by Agapetus, who soon afterwards died. By the directions of Justinian, Mennas called a local synod, which met during May and June 536 (Mansi, viii.; cf. Hefele, *Conciliengeschichte*, ii. pp. 742-753), and deposed Anthimus from his see of Trebizond. The synod anathematized Severus, Peter of Apamea, and Zoaras as suspected of Monophysitism. In Aug. 536 Justinian issued an edict addressed to Mennas confirming all that the synod had done.

After this there appears to have been a comparative calm in the ecclesiastical world of Constantinople, till the emperor's attention was called to the growth of Origenistic opinions in the East, and especially in Syria.

About the beginning of the 6th cent. there had been in the monasteries of Palestine, and particularly in that great one called the New Laura, a considerable diffusion of Origen's opinions, which excited the alarm of St. Sabas and of the patriarch Peter of Jerusalem. The latter in 543 induced Pelagius, apocrisiarius of the Roman bishop, to make representations to the emperor on the subject, and sent with him four monks to accuse the followers of Origen. The four monks were supported by Mennas the patriarch. Two Origenist bishops, Theodore Ascidas, archbp. of Caesarea in Cappadocia, and Domitian, bp. of Ancyra, resided usually at Constantinople and had much influence with the emperor. Nevertheless they seem to have] feared the charge of heresy too much to resist the monks from Palestine, and perhaps did not own their attachment to Origen's writings. Anyhow, the emperor promptly condemned the accused opinions, issuing a long edict addressed to the patriarch Mennas, in which he classes Origen among the heretics, and singles out for anathema ten particular doctrines contained in his writings. A local council, convoked by Mennas, dutifully echoed the emperor's edict, publishing its anathemas against 14 propositions drawn from Origen, and condemning his person.

Theodore and Domitian had submitted, but their mortification drove them to take action in another way, and thus to awaken a long, needless, and most mischievous controversy. Justinian was at work upon a treatise on the Incarnation, whereby he trusted to convince and conciliate the stubborn Acephali (or extremer Monophysites) of Egypt. Theodore, according to our authorities, suggested to him that a simpler way of winning back those who disliked the council of Chalcedon would be to get certain writings condemned which that council had approved, but which the Monophysites disliked as being of a distinctly Nestorian tendency. (See Liberatus *ap.* Galland. *Bibl. Patr.* xii. 160, as to Theodore, and Facundus, bk. i. c. 2, as to Domitian of Ancyra; cf. Evagr. *H. E.* iv. 38; *Vita S. Sabae.*) They singled out 3 treatises for condemnation, which soon became famous as the τρία κεφάλαια (*tria capitula*), which we usually translate Three Chapters, but would be better called the Three Articles, viz. the writings of Theodore of Mopsuestia, the treatise of Theodoret against Cyril and his twelve articles, and the letter of (or attributed to) Ibas, bp. of Edessa, to the Persian bp. Maris. Later, the term τρία κεφάλαια came to mean both the persons and writings impugned. This latter is the usual sense in the authors of the time (*e.g.* Facundus of Hermiane, whose treatise is entitled *Defensio pro Tribus Capitulis*) and in the protocols of the fifth general council. The Nestorians still appealed to Theodore as their highest authority, and triumphantly pointed to the fact that he had never been condemned. Against Theodoret and Ibas the case was weaker. Both had joined in anathematizing Nestorius at Chalcedon, and been restored to their sees. But both had attacked Cyril, who, though claimed by the Monophysites, was also a bulwark of orthodoxy, and the ep. to Maris was a violent assault on the council of Ephesus. It might therefore be with some show of plausibility alleged that the authority of that council was not established while these assailants seemed to be protected by the aegis of Chalcedon.

Seconded by Theodora (says Liberatus, *u.s.*), Theodore Ascidas and Domitian persuaded Justinian to compose and issue a treatise or edict against the Three Articles. Desisting from his book against the Acephali, he forthwith composed the suggested edict, which was issued between 543 and 545, probably in 545. It has perished, only three or four short extracts being preserved by Facundus. It was circulated through the church for the signatures of the bishops. The four Eastern patriarchs were naturally afraid of reopening any question as to the authority of Chalcedon. Mennas, after some hesitation, signed, but subject to a promise given him on oath, that he might withdraw his signature if the bp. of Rome refused to agree. The other three, Ephraim of Antioch, Peter of Jerusalem, Zoilus of Alexandria, under real or imagined threats of deposition, obeyed and signed, and after more or less intimidation and the offer of various rewards, the great majority of bishops through Syria, Asia Minor, Greece, and Macedonia signed also. In the West, the bishops having less to lose and being accustomed to face Arian potentates, Justinian found a less ready compliance. The bishops of Africa led the opposition, and were largely supported by those of Italy, Gaul, Illyricum, and Dalmatia. In Rome much alarm was produced by the arrival of the edict, and by the emperor's command to Vigilius, lately chosen pope, to repair to Constantinople. Theodora enforced by terrible threats his appearance. Vigilius, not venturing openly to oppose the emperor, and fearing the anger of Theodora, had also to reckon with the all but universal loyalty to the council of Chalcedon of the Roman church and of the Western churches generally, and so temporized. He arrived in Constantinople in 547, having delayed nearly a year in Sicily. In 548 he issued a document called the *Judicatum*, condemning the Three Articles, saving, however, the authority of Chalcedon. In 548 Theodora died, but Justinian was now thoroughly committed against the Three Articles. He continued to coerce the recalcitrant bishops of Africa, depriving some of their sees, and, after various negotiations with Vigilius, issued in 551 a second edict against the Three Articles addressed to the whole Christian world, which has been preserved under the name of the Confession of Faith, ὁμολογία πίστεως Ἰουστινιανοῦ αὐτοκράτορος (Mansi, ix. 537). This edict is really a theological treatise, taking the writings of the three impugned doctors and discovering heresies in them by minute scrutiny and inference. Vigilius was required to subscribe it, but refused, and took refuge in the basilica of St. Peter at Constantinople, and afterwards in the church of St. Euphemia at Chalcedon. Here he remained, until the emperor, anxious for his concurrence in summoning a general council as the only solution for the dissensions, induced him to withdraw his censure of the edict. He then returned to Constantinople to await the opening of the council. The first sitting was on May 5, 553.

Eutychius, who, upon the death of Mennas in Aug. 552, had become patriarch of Constantinople, presided. By him sat Apollinaris of Alexandria and Domninus of Antioch. Eustochius of Jerusalem was represented by 3 bishops. Altogether 151 bishops were present at the opening, while 164 signed at the end, the very large majority belonging to the East. Six from Africa attended, but more than 20 were kept away by Vigilius, who himself refused to attend, but sent his views in writing in a document called the *Constitutum* (Mansi, ix. 61), presented, not to the council, but to Justinian himself, who refused to receive it. Justinian addressed a letter to the fathers, reproaching Vigilius, and requiring his name to be struck out of the diptychs, as having by his defence of Theodoret and Ibas excluded himself from the right to church-fellowship. He also produced evidence that the pope had solemnly promised, both to himself and Theodora, to procure the condemnation of the Three Articles. Thereupon the council, troubling no further about the pope, proceeded to examine the writings impugned. (Hefele, *u.s.* 267-274. For the *Acta* see Mansi, vol. ix. and under CONSTANTINOPLE, *D. C. A.*) Theodore of Mopsuestia was anathematized absolutely, and anathema was pronounced against Theodoret's treatise in opposition to Cyril's Twelve Articles and against the letter to Maris, which passed under the name of Ibas. A series of 14 articles, or anathemas, was prepared, most of them corresponding closely with the articles of Justinian's ὁμολογία πίστεως, in which the orthodox faith as to the Trinity and Incarnation was restated. The first four general councils and their decrees were formally accepted, and art. 11 anathematizes Arius, Eunomius, Macedonius, Apollinarius, Origen, Nestorius, Eutyches, and their adherents. It has been often supposed that the opinions of Origen and his followers were formally condemned at this council. (See Evagr. iv. 38; Theoph. *Chronogr.* p. 354 of Bonn ed. vol. i.) But this has arisen from confounding the former local council under Mennas in 543 with this general council. Origen is only referred to in its general anathema, and thus no particular doctrines of his have ever been condemned by the whole church. The 14 articles were subscribed at the last sitting, on June 2, 553, by all the 164 bishops, headed by Eutychius of Constantinople. Eight African bishops signed. Justinian sent the decrees all over the empire for signature by the bishops. Little opposition was experienced in the East. The monks of the New Laura, who attacked the decrees, were chased out by the imperial general Anastasius. The council had threatened with deposition any bishops or other clerics who should teach or speak against it. We hear, however, of only one bishop, Alexander of Abydus, who was deposed. Vigilius and the Western ecclesiastics who had signed the *Constitutum* appear to have held out for some time, but in Dec. 553 Vigilius issued a letter (Mansi, ix. 414), addressed to the patriarch Eutychius, in which he owns that he was in the wrong and is now glad to confess it. He then anathematizes Theodore, Theodoret, and the letter of Ibas, without prejudice to the authority of the council of Chalcedon, which of course never meant to approve these heresies. Being then released by Justinian, Vigilantius set off for Rome, but died in Syracuse upon his way. A serious schism followed in the West. The bishops of Dalmatia and Illyricum were hottest in their opposition to the anathemas of the fifth council, and their archbp. Frontinus was taken to Constantinople and thence banished to Upper Egypt. A manifesto by Justinian, addressed to some Western bishops (*ib.* 589), has been supposed to be an answer to remonstrances from these Illyrians. The resistance in Africa was broken by similar violent means, a good many bishops being deposed and imprisoned in convents, under the auspices of the metropolitan Primasius of Carthage, and by the secular arm of the governor. In Gaul and Spain there was great discontent, though not a complete breach with Rome; while in N. Italy the bishops of Tuscany, the province of Milan, and Istria and Venetia, broke off communion with the pope. The patriarchate of Aquileia, afterwards removed to Grado, and finally divided into the two small patriarchates of Grado and Aquileia, arose out of this schism, which did not end till the beginning of the 8th cent. Ultimately the whole Western church was brought by the efforts of the popes to recognize the fifth general council. The effect, however, which Justinian had been encouraged to expect was not attained. Not a single Monophysite seems to have returned to the orthodox church. The Egyptian Acephali in particular were as stubborn as ever.

Justinian in his last days himself lapsed into heresy. The doctrine that the body of Christ was insensible to fleshly passions and weaknesses, was in fact incorruptible, and so not ordinary flesh at all, had been broached early in the century by bp. JULIAN of Halicarnassus, a leading Monophysite, in opposition to the view of Severus, patriarch of Antioch, that Christ's body was corruptible up to the resurrection, and only afterwards ceased to be so. Justinian published an edict declaring the doctrine of Julian orthodox and requiring the assent of all patriarchs and bishops to this new article. Eutychius of Constantinople was deposed for rejecting the edict. Before more could be done, Justinian died (A.D. 565) and the controversy at once collapsed, for his successor took comparatively slight interest in theological questions.

The general character of Justinian's ecclesiastical policy has been sufficiently indicated. In spite of his protestations of respect for the clergy, the important place they held at his court, and the privileges which his legislation gave them, he never hesitated to resort to despotism and banishment to bend them to his will. No previous Roman emperor had been so much interested in theological disputes, nor arrogated to himself so great a right of interference even with the popes. His control of the fifth council was much more direct and considerable than his predecessors exercised at Ephesus and Chalcedon.

Justinian was through his life a resolute, though not always consistent, persecutor. Nestorians and Eutychians were punished with deposition from ecclesiastical office, excommunication, and occasionally with banishment. Manicheans, Gnostics, and Montanists were more severely dealt with, deprived of all civil rights and forbidden to meet for worship. These penalties were often enforced with much cruelty and sometimes produced sanguinary contests. The Montanists of Phrygia, being required to undergo baptism, shut themselves up in their churches, killed their wives and children, and set fire to the buildings. Similar rigours were inflicted on Jews and Samaritans, though the Jews, as a serviceable element in the population, seem to have in practice fared somewhat better than the others. It is not very easy to determine precisely how far the laws directed against heathenism were carried out. They punish apostasy with death, require all persons to undergo baptism, deprive pagans of all civil rights and privileges, and forbid any public pagan worship. In spite of this, a great number of pagans continued to exist even among the cultivated and wealthy classes of the capital. An inquisition at Constantinople in the 3rd year of Justinian's reign (Theoph. *Chron.* p. 153) shewed a large number of pagans in the higher official classes. An ordinance was then issued, forbidding all civil employment to persons not orthodox Christians and three months were allowed for conversion. Not long before, Justinian had taken away all the churches of the heretics, except one of the Arians, and given them to the orthodox (*ib.* 150). Energetic inquiries through W. Asia Minor are said to have led to the enforced baptism of 70,000 persons. Among the mountain tribes of Taygetus paganism survived till the days of Basil I. (867-886). Only at Athens, however, did persons of intellectual and social eminence continue to openly avow themselves heathens. The professors of its university, or at least the most distinguished among them, were not Christians. Although speculative moralists and mystics, making philosophy their rule of life, rather than worshippers of the old deities of Olympus, their influence was decidedly anti-Christian. In 528, on the discovery of crypto-paganism in his capital, Justinian issued several stringent constitutions, one of which, forbidding " persons persisting in the madness of Hellenism to teach any branch of knowledge," struck directly at the Athenian professors. In 529 he sent a copy of the *Codex Constitutionum*, containing this ordinance, to Athens, with a prohibition to teach law there, and shortly after the teaching of philosophy was similarly forbidden, and the remaining property of the Platonic Academy was seized for public purposes. This finally extinguished the university. Its head, Damascius, a neo-Platonist of Syrian birth, and by conviction a resolute heathen, and six of his colleagues proceeded (in 532) to the court of Chosroes, king of Persia, at Ctesiphon, but soon returned to the Roman empire, in which Chosroes secured for them, by a treaty he negotiated with Justinian, the freedom to live unbaptized and unmolested. They did not, however, settle again in Athens, which rapidly became a Christian city even in externals, its temples being turned into churches. So one may ascribe to Justinian the extinction in the Roman world of open and cultivated paganism as well as of the Platonic philosophy.

V. *Justinian's legislation* falls under two principal heads—his work as a codifier and consolidator of pre-existing law ; and his own new laws, some of which were incorporated in the *Codex Constitutionum*, while others, published subsequently, remain as detached statutes, and go by the name of the Novels (*Novellae Constitutiones*). The vast changes involved in the establishment of Christianity had rendered much of the old law, though still formally unrepealed, practically obsolete. There was therefore overwhelming necessity for sweeping reforms both in the substance and in the outward form and expression of the law. Such reforms had been attempted in the time of THEODOSIUS II., when the Theodosian Codex, containing a collection of the later constitutions, had been prepared and published A.D. 438. This, however, dealt only with the imperial constitutions, not with the writings of the jurists ; and now, nearly a century later, the old evils were found as serious as ever, while the further changes in society had made the necessity for abolishing antiquated enactments even greater.

Justinian set to work so promptly after his accession that he had probably meditated already upon the measures which were called for and fixed his eyes on the men to be used as instruments. He began with the easier part of the task, the codification of *jus novum*, the imperial constitutions of more recent date. A commission was appointed in Feb. 528 to go through the whole mass of constitutions and select for preservation those still in force and of practical importance. In Apr. 529 the *Codex Constitutionum* was formally promulgated, and copies sent into every province of the empire, with directions that it should supersede all other constitutions previously in force. (See Const. *Summa Reipublicae* prefixed to the *Codex*.)

The next step was to deal with the *jus vetus*, the law contained in the writings of the authorized jurists, which practically included so much of the old *leges*, *senatus consulta*, and *edicta* as retained any practical importance. But there were many differences of opinion among the jurists whose writings had legal authority. Justinian accordingly issued a series of 50 constitutions, known as the *Quinquaginta Decisiones*, settling the disputed points (see Const. *Cordi Nobis* prefixed to the *Codex*). At the same time a large number of other ordinances were promulgated, amending the laws and abolishing obsolete provisions. The ground being thus cleared, he appointed a commission of 16 lawyers, under the presidency of Tribonian. Their instructions were chiefly : to collect into one body all best worth preserving in the writings of the authorized jurists, making extracts so as to avoid both repetition and contradiction, and give one statement of the law upon each of the many points where discrepant views had formerly prevailed. Redundancies were to be cut off, errors in manuscripts or in expression set right, alterations introduced where necessary, no *antinomia* (contradiction) allowed to remain, nothing repealed which had been already enacted in the *Codex*. Obsolete rules of law were to be passed over. The work was to be distributed into 50 books. The constitution containing these directions is dated Dec. 530. The commissioners promptly set to work, reading no less than 2,000 treatises for the purpose of making extracts. The work, to which the names of *Digesta* or *Pandectae* (Πανδέκται—all receivers) are indifferently given by Justinian, was completed in the autumn of 533 and published with two prefatory constitutions on Dec. 16. Each book is divided into titles, each title into extracts. The total number of titles is 432, and of extracts from 39 jurists 9,123. The whole book is published as an imperial constitution, deriving its force from the imperial sanction, which abrogated all pre-existing law, except that contained in the *Codex* and subsequently published constitutions. No judge nor advocate might travel out of the four corners of these two new statutes, the *Codex* and the *Digesta*.

While the Digest was in progress, Justinian directed three of the chief commissioners—Tribonian, Theophilus professor of law in the university of Constantinople, and Dorotheus professor of law at Berytus (Beyrut in Syria, the other great law-school of the empire)—to prepare an elementary manual for educational purposes, based on the existing treatises, and especially on the deservedly popular *Institutes* of Gaius, but brought up to the state of the law as changed by recent emperors and by Justinian himself. This treatise, dealing in four books with the law of Persons, of Things, and of Actions, was published shortly before the Digest, not only as a text-book for teaching, but also as a law, a constitution with full imperial authority. It is the treatise now known as Justinian's *Institutiones*.

On Nov. 16, 534, a revised *Codex*, including constitutions published since 529, and omitting laws that had been in the interval repealed or become unnecessary, was issued with an introductory constitution (now prefixed to it) called *Cordi nobis*, abrogating the former edition altogether. The *Codex* we now have is this new one. It is divided into 12 books and 765 titles, containing 4,652 constitutions, the earliest dating from Hadrian, while far the larger part of the constitutions in the *Codex* were more recent, and perhaps half of them the work of the Christian emperors.

Between 534 and the end of Justinian's reign a large number of new laws appeared, the majority during the lifetime of Tribonian (d. 545). These are called *Novellae Constitutiones post Codicem* (νεαραὶ διατάξεις), or shortly *Novellae* (νεαραί), Novels. They mostly have the form of edicts or general laws rather than of the earlier *rescripta*. They do not appear to have ever been gathered into one officially sanctioned volume (although this had originally been promised, see Const. *Cordi nobis*), but several private collections were made, from which our present text is derived. (See as to the Novels Biener, *Gesch. der Novellen Justinians*, and generally as to the history and edd. of the *Corpus Juris*, Rudorff, *Römische Rechtsgeschichte*, Leipz. 1857.)

The Corpus Juris Civilis, consisting of the four parts already mentioned—the *Codex*, the *Digesta*, the *Institutiones*, and the *Novellae*—became under Justinian the sole law of the Roman empire, was accepted in the early Middle Ages as the law of Germany, S. France, and Italy, and has exerted a great influence on the jurisprudence even of countries which, like England, repudiate (except in special departments) its authority. As we now understand by codification the reduction of the whole law into one scientific system of rules, new in form and expression though mostly old in substance, the work of Justinian would be better described as a Consolidation than a Codification. On the whole, it may be said that he exercised a wise discretion in attempting no more, and many as are the faults in the arrangement of his *Codex* and *Digest* and in the occasional disproportion of treatment, the work was done decidedly better than other literary and scientific productions of Justinian's age would have led us to expect.

The Corpus Juris held its ground as the supreme law book of the empire for little more than three centuries. Much of the earlier law had then become obsolete, and something shorter, less elaborate, more adapted to the needs and lower capacities of the time was required. Accordingly the emperors, Basil the Macedonian, Constantine, and Leo the philosopher, directed the preparation of a new law book, which, revised and finally issued under Leo *c.* 890, received the name of the Basilica, or Imperial Code. It contains, in 60 books, a complete system of law for the Eastern empire, retaining a great deal of the substance of the Corpus Juris, but in a wholly altered form; the extracts from the *Codex* of constitutions, and those from the Pandects and Novels being all thrown into one new *Codex*, and intermingled with later matter. It is in Greek; is much less bulky than the Corpus Juris, and has come down to us imperfect. The best ed. is Haimbach's (Leipz. 1833-1851), with supplement by Zacharia (Leipz. 1846). The *Codex* is cited in Herzog. vol. ix. (1901), according to the ed. of P. Krüger (Berlin, 1877); the *Novellae* according to the ed. of C. E. Zacharias a Lingenthal (2 vols. Leipz. 1881).

The new legislation of Justinian is contained partly in the *Codex* and partly in the Novels. The legal changes made by the constitutions of the first seven years of his reign, which have been incorporated in the *Codex*, are often merely solutions of problems, or settlements of disputes which had perplexed or divided the earlier jurists. These were promulgated in the *Quinquaginta Decisiones* already mentioned. A considerable number more relate to administrative subjects; while the rest are miscellaneous, running over the whole field of law. For his ecclesiastical constitutions see articles in *D. C. A.*, to which this subject more properly belongs. A few remarks may, however, be profitably made here on the emperor's ecclesiastical laws as contained firstly in the *Codex Constitutionum*, where they are abbreviated; and, secondly, in the Novels, where they appear at full and often wearisome length. The earlier ones are in the *Codex*, the Novels extend from 534 to 565.

In Justinian's *Codex* the first 13 titles of bk. i. are occupied by laws relating to Christian theology and doctrine. Title I., styled "De

Summa Trinitate et Fide Catholica et ut nemo de ea publice contendere audeat," contains (besides extracts from laws of earlier emperors) four laws by Justinian, beginning with the fifth, some of which have been taken into the *Codex* from the *Collectio Constitutionum Ecclesiasticarum*, laying down the true orthodox faith as defined by the first four general councils, and anathematizing "Nestorius the man-worshipper, Eutyches the insane, Apollinaris the soul destroyer," and all who agree with these heretics. One of these constitutions is an edict addressed by Justinian to pope John (as well as to Epiphanius, patriarch of Constantinople), with the reply of the pope confirming the edict as a declaration of the faith. Title II., "De Sacrosanctis Ecclesiis et de rebus et privilegiis earum," contains eight laws by Justinian dealing chiefly with legacies to churches or other charitable uses, and with the management of church property. Title III. is, "De Episcopis et clericis et orphanotrophiis et xenodochiis et brephotrophiis et ptochotrophiis et asceteriis et monachis et privilegiis eorum et castrensi peculio et de redimendis captivis et de nuptiis clericorum vetitis seu permissis." Sixteen laws in it (less than one-third in number, but more than half in bulk) are by Justinian, and treat of a great many topics, including the election and qualifications of bishops and priests, the choice of heads (ἡγούμενοι, αι) of monasteries and nunneries, the observance of a pure and strict life in monasteries, the management of church property by the bishop and steward, with various provisions relating to charitable foundations, to the residence of the clergy at their churches, the regular maintenance of divine service there, and to wills of property for church purposes. Title IV., "De Episcopali Audientia et de diversis capitulis quae ad jus curamque et reverentiam pontificalem pertinent," is almost equally miscellaneous in its contents. Fourteen constitutions in it are by Justinian. The fifth, "De Haereticis et Manichaeis et Samaritis," contains a selection of persecuting or disabling laws from the time of Constantine down to and including Justinian's own. The penalties threatened, and the general severity of tone, steadily increase as time goes on, and the number of different kinds of heretics included in the denunciations is enlarged. In one case (c. 21) a distinction is drawn by the emperor between various degrees of heresy and infidelity. "Manichaeis Borboritis et paganis, necnon Samaritis et Montanistis et Ascodrogitis et Ophitis omne testimonium sicut et alias legitimas conversationes sancimus esse interdictum. Aliis vero haereticis tantum modo judicialia testimonia contra orthodoxos, secundum quod constitutum est, volumus esse inhibita." Title VI., "Ne sanctum baptisma iteretur"; VII., "De Apostatis"; VIII., "Nemini licere signum Salvatoris, Christi humi vel in silice vel in marmore aut insculpere aut pingere"; IX., "De Judaeis et coelicolis"; and X., "Ne Christianum mancipium haereticus vel paganus vel Judaeus habeat vel possideat vel circumcidat," are comparatively short and contain only laws of earlier emperors. In XI., "De Paganis Sacrificiis et Templis," is an interesting collection of various enactments against paganism from the famous edict of Constantius (A.D. 353) onwards, concluding with a general command to all heathens to be baptized forthwith, on pain of losing all their property and all civic rights; while death is the penalty for any one who, having been baptized, relapses into heathenism. All sacrifices, or other acts of pagan worship, are strictly forbidden and severely punishable; all gifts of property to any heathen temple or purpose are confiscated, the temples being all destroyed or appropriated to other uses, and the teaching of paganism, and indeed any teaching by any pagan, is absolutely prohibited. Titles XII. and XIII., "De his qui ad ecclesias confugiunt vel ibi exclamant," and "De his qui in ecclesiis manumittuntur," are less important. They illustrate the growth of the right of sanctuary in churches, and the practice of manumission there. With title XIV., "De Legibus et Constitutionibus Principum et edictis," ordinary civil legislation begins. A good many references to ecclesiastical matters, and especially to the jurisdiction of the bishops, are scattered through other parts of the *Codex*. It is clear from this summary that neither Justinian nor his predecessors intended to frame a complete body of laws or rules for the government of the church, its hierarchical constitution and administration, much less for its internal discipline or its ritual. These things had been left to be settled by custom, by the authority of patriarchs, metropolitans, and bishops, by the canons of councils as occasion arose. Not that the civil monarch supposed such to lie beyond his scope, for in Constantinople the emperors, and Justinian most of all, regarded themselves as clothed with a supreme executive authority over the religious no less than the secular society. The distinction afterwards asserted in the West between the temporal and spiritual powers had not then been imagined. No Eastern ecclesiastic denied the emperor's right to summon general councils, direct them, and confirm their decrees. But the emperors had been content to leave to churchmen the settling of what were regarded as more or less technical and professional matters, which they were fittest to settle. The narrow and bigoted spirit, which runs through the persecuting laws included in the *Codex*, is fully as conspicuous in Justinian's own as in those of any of his predecessors. Moreover, by re-enacting them he made himself responsible for all that they contained. In that age of the world it was believed possible to stamp out heresy by a sufficiently vigorous exercise of the arm of flesh. Paganism was in fact thus stamped out, though in one or two mountainous districts of Greece and perhaps of Asia Minor it lingered secretly for 2 or 3 centuries more.

The topics of the Novels, or constitutions issued by Justinian from 535 till his death in 565, are very various. Of the 153 to which the 168 appearing in the largest collection may be reduced, 33, forming the largest group, relate to ecclesiastical and religious matters. Next in number come those dealing with civil and military administration. Marriage and the legal relations arising therefrom are dealt with in various Novels. Justinian was fond of tinkering at this subject, and not always successfully. The most remarkable provisions are in Novels 117 (§§ 10 and 12) and 134 (§ 11), in which he greatly limits the freedom of divorce previously allowed, almost indeed abolishing it. But this severity was found unmaintainable: such complaints arose that in 566, ten years after the 134th Novel appeared, Justin II., nephew and successor of Justinian, repealed (Nov. cxl.) the penalties provided by it and by the 117th, leaving the law as it had stood under earlier sovereigns. The Novels have a great many provisions regarding dowries, simplifying a rather complicated branch of the law and securing the interests of the wife. Several constitutions, prompted by a desire for moral reformation, deal with criminal law, several relate to guardianship, the position of freedmen, and other parts of the law of persons, and nine deal with the law of obligations; none of them of any great importance. Among the ecclesiastical Novels, several groups may be distinguished. One group contains those which deal with the temporal rights and relations of the church and her ministers as holders of property. Eight constitutions may be referred to it, most of which are occupied with the length of time needed for a good title to lands originally belonging to the church to be acquired by adverse enjoyment; and with the conditions under which ecclesiastical lands might be alienated for a term or in perpetuity. Both topics gave Justinian much trouble and he was sometimes obliged to modify his enactments. A second group comprises constitutions merely local in application, referring to a particular province (*e.g.* Nov. 37 to Africa), church (*e.g.* Nov. 3 to the Great Church of Constantinople, Nov. 40 to the Church of the Resurrection at Jerusalem), or see (*e.g.* Nov. 11 to the privileges of the archiepiscopal chair of Justiniana Prima in Illyricum). To a third and more important group may be referred the 13 constitutions dealing with ecclesiastical organization and discipline, the mode of choosing bishops and other clerics, their qualifications, the jurisdiction of bishops, the restrictions on the jurisdiction of civil courts in causes where clerics are concerned (a matter of great interest in view of the questions which were to occupy medieval Europe), the rights, immunities, and position generally of the clergy (*e.g.* the exemption of a bishop from *patria potestas*, Nov. 81, the devolution of the property of a cleric dying intestate without legal heirs, Nov. 131, § 13), the regulations under which a church or oratory might be built, endowed, and consecrated, the internal discipline of monasteries and regulation of monastic life. A fourth and last group includes four ordinances levelled at heretics (a good many provisions affecting whom incidentally occur in other Novels, especially in those of the third group). One of these four, called Edictum de Fide, is a short appeal to heretics to return to the safe teaching and anathematizings of the Catholic church (Nov. 132); another is directed against Jews and Samaritans, refusing them immunities from public burdens such as their exclusion from public offices and honours might otherwise have appeared to imply (Nov. 45); a third deprives heretic women of the privileges granted by Justinian's laws to women in respect of their dowry; and the fourth is a sentence of deposition and anathema against Anthimus patriarch of Constantinople, Severus patriarch of Antioch, Peter of Apamea, Zoaras, and others charged with Monophysitism, issued in confirmation of the sentence passed by the synod at Constantinople under the patriarch Mennas in 536. The most generally remarkable characteristics of these ecclesiastical statutes, apart from their spirit of bitter intolerance, are the strong disposition to favour the church, the clerical order, and the monastic life; and the assumption throughout of a complete right of control by the imperial legislator over all sorts of ecclesiastical affairs and questions. Although there are some matters, such as ritual, penance, etc., touched not at all or very slightly, still the impression conveyed here, as in the *Codex*, is that the civil power claimed a universal and paramount right of legislating for the church; nor is there any distinction laid down or recognized between matters reserved for the legislative action of the church in her synods and those which the emperor may deal with. He always speaks with the utmost respect of the sacred canons, sometimes quotes them, professes to confirm them, and (Nov. 131, § 1) expressly declares that all the canons of the four great general councils are to have the force and rank of laws (τάξιν νόμων ἐπέχειν). But there is no admission of the exclusive right of the church or of any ecclesiastical dignitary or body to legislate on any particular topics; this is indeed implicitly excluded by the laws, especially those in bk. i. of the *Codex*, which deal with the most specially spiritual of spiritual questions, the cardinal doctrines of the Christian faith. It is therefore not surprising that the African bishops who wrote against him in the matter of the Three Articles complain of his conduct as arrogating to the magistrate what belonged of right to the duly constituted officers of the church. Subsequent history shows that the Eastern emperor always maintained his authority over the church; while different political conditions enabled the Western patriarch and the Western church generally to throw off the control of the civil power and even extend its own jurisdiction over civil causes.

These ecclesiastical Novels throw much light on the state of the 6th-cent. Eastern church, and the evils which it was thought necessary to remedy. We hear once or twice of the ignorance of the clergy, persons being sometimes ordained who could not read the prayers used in the sacramental services of the Supper and Baptism (Novs. 6, 137). Irregularities in monastic life were frequent, as appears from the penalties threatened (Novs. 5, 133). Bishops too often resided away from their sees, so that a prohibition to the administrator to send money to them while absent was needed (Nov. 6, § 3; Nov. 123, § 9). That a bishop must be unmarried, and a priest either unmarried or married only once and to a virgin, was insisted on. The habit of building churches without funds sufficient for their due maintenance and service is checked

(Novs. 57, 67), as also that of having private chapels, or celebrating the sacred mysteries in houses (Novs. 58, 131). The often neglected canonical direction to hold provincial synods twice, or at least once, a year is renewed (Nov. 138). The substance of the enactments contained in these Novels and in the *Codex*, upon such matters as the election of bishops, celibacy of clergy, permanency of monastic vows, etc., will be found under the appropriate heads in *D. C. A*. The regulations regarding a monastic life have a special interest as very shortly anterior to the creation of the rule of St. BENEDICT of Nursia, who was a contemporary of Justinian. [J.B.]

Justinus (2) Martyr, St., son of Priscus, grandson of Bacchius; born at Flavia Neapolis, hard by the ruins of ancient Sychem (now Nablous), in Palestine (*Apol.* i. 1). He calls himself a Samaritan (*Dial.* c. 120, § 349 C), so that his family had probably settled there definitely; but he is obviously not a Samaritan by blood or religion; nothing in his writing would point to such an origin. He has not heard, even, of Moses or of the prophets until well on in life; he classes himself among those Gentiles to whom the Gospel was opened so largely when the main mass (*Apol.* i. 53, § 88 B) of the house of Jacob, in which he includes by name the Samaritans as well as the Jews, rejected it. He speaks of being brought up in heathen customs, being uncircumcised (*Dial.* c. 29, § 246 C), and receiving a thoroughly Greek education (*Dial.* c. 2, § 219). The name of his grandfather is Greek; of his father and himself Latin. What we know of him is gathered almost entirely from his own writings, and chiefly from his famous description of the studies through which he passed to his conversion, given in his *Dialogue* with the New Tryphon. The opening of the *Dialogue* discovers Justin walking in the colonnades of a city, which Eusebius identifies with Ephesus (*H. E.* iv. 18), shortly after the wars of the Romans against Bar-Cocheba in 132-136 (*Dial.* c. 1, § 217). To the Jew, who greets him as a philosopher, he recounts his philosophic experiences, though we gain but little clue as to where or at what time these experiences occurred. He speaks of his first longing to share in that wisdom "which is verily the highest possession, the most valued by God, to Whom it alone leads and unites us"; when with this hope he went successively to a Stoic teacher, a Peripatetic, and a famous Pythagorean, but in each case to no purpose. Much grieved at this, he thought of trying the Platonics, whose fame stood high. He went chiefly to one lately settled in his town, who was thought highly of by his school; advanced some way with him, giving him the greater part of every day; was delighted with the perception of the Incorporeal; the contemplation of the Ideas "gave wings to my mind, quickly I thought to become wise, and expected that, if it were not for my dull sight, I should be in a moment looking upon God; for this sight is the fulfilment of the Platonic philosophy." "While in this frame of mind I one day had a wish for quiet meditation, away from the beaten track of men, and so went to a bit of ground not far from the sea; and there, just as I was nearing the place where I looked to be alone with my thoughts, an old man, of a pleasant countenance, and with a gentle and dignified mien, came following me a little behind." The old man asked Justin, "'For what are you come here?' 'I delight,' I answered, 'in these strolls, in which I can hold converse with myself, without interruption; a place like this is most favourable for such talking as I love.' 'Ah! you are a lover of talk, and not of action or of reality,' he said. 'You are one, I suppose, who cares more for reasons than for facts, for words than for deeds.' 'And how, indeed,' I answered, 'can a man act more efficiently than in exhibiting the reason that governs all, or than in laying hold of it, and there, borne aloft on it, looking down on others who stray helplessly below, and do nothing sane, or dear to God? Without philosophy and right reason there is no possible wisdom. Every man, therefore, ought to esteem philosophy as his noblest work, and to let all else come second or third to it; for by philosophy things are made right and acceptable, without it they become common and vulgar.' 'Philosophy, then, is the true cause of happiness, is it?' he asked in reply. 'Yes, indeed, it is,' I said, 'it and it alone.'"

A discussion follows on the possibility of philosophy giving the true knowledge of God, which is Happiness; at its close Justin confesses that his philosophy supplies no clear account of the soul, of its capacity to perceive the Divine, nor of the character of its life; the old man speaks with a decision that he professes to owe neither to Plato nor to Pythagoras, who are the bulwarks of philosophy. What teacher is there who can give certainty where such as these fail? asks Justin. The old man replies that there have been men, far older than all these philosophers, men blessed and upright and beloved of God, who spoke by the spirit of God, and are called Prophets. These alone have seen the truth, and spoken it to men; not as reasoners, for they go higher than all argument, but as witnesses of the truth, who are worthy to be believed, since the events foretold have come to pass and so compel us to rely on their words, as do also the wonders they have worked to the honour and glory of God the Father and of His Christ. "Pray thou, then, that the gates of the Light may be opened too for thee; for these things can only be seen and known by those to whom God and His Christ have given understanding." Justin saw the old man no more; but in his soul the flame was fired and a passion of love aroused for these prophets, the friends of Christ; and as he reflected upon it he found that here indeed lay the one and only sure and worthy philosophy.

This is all we know of his conversion. The scene is, perhaps, idealized; it has a savour of Plato; but the imagination of Justin was hardly equal to producing, unaided, such vivid detail of scenery and character. The description would imply that he was somewhat advanced in study, but not past the enthusiasms of earlier life. The event, apparently, occurred in Flavia Neapolis, *i.e.* "*our* town," in which the Platonist teacher had settled;

but "our town" may mean that in which he and Tryphon were conversing, *i.e.*, according to Eusebius, Ephesus. It must have been before the Bar-Cocheba wars, if it is from them that Tryphon was flying when Justin met him. The conversion takes the form of a passage from the imperfect to the perfect philosophy; throughout his life it retains that impress. He was not rescued from intellectual despair, but was in the highest condition of confidence when the old man met him. The aim with which he started on his studies was achieved when he became a Christian. Hence he is not thrown into an attitude of antagonism to that which he leaves; his new faith does not break with the old so much as fulfil it. He still, therefore, calls himself the philosopher, still invites men to enter his school, still wears the philosopher's cloak (*Dial.* i. § 217; Eus. *H. E.* iv. 11; cf. the Acts of Justin). From the first, philosophy had been pursued with the religious aim of attaining the highest spiritual happiness by communing with God; the certified knowledge of God, therefore, professed by the prophets, and made manifest in Christ, comes to him as the crown of his existing aspiration.

One other motive he records to have affected his conversion, *i.e.* his wondering admiration at the steadfastness of Christians under persecution. "When I was still attached to the doctrine of Plato, and used to hear the accusations hurled against Christians, and yet saw them perfectly fearless in the face of death and of all that is terrible, I understood that it was impossible they should be living all the time a life of wickedness and lust" (*Apol.* ii. 12, § 50 A). This appeal, which the moral steadfastness of the Christians had made to him, he continually brings to bear upon others (i. 8, § 57; i. 11, § 58 E, etc.). Perhaps, too, the lack of moral reality and energy in the doctrines of philosophy was not unfelt by Justin, for his words seem sometimes to recall the old man's taunt, "You are a man of words, and not of deeds" (cf. i. 14, § 61 E, "For Christ was no Sophist, but His word was the power of God").

We have no details of his life after baptism. He seems to have come to Rome, and, perhaps, to have stayed there some time, according to Eusebius (*H. E.* iv. 11). His peculiar office was to bring the Christian apologetic into the publicity of active controversy in the schools. The collision with Tryphon in the Colonnades is probably but a specimen of the intellectual intercourse which Justin challenged by wearing the philosopher's cloak. The introduction to the *Dialogue* appears to record a familiar habit. The *Second Apology* mentions a dispute with Crescens the Cynic (3, § 43, B, C). The memory of Justin's characteristic attitude is recorded by Eusebius: "It was then that St. Justin flourished, who, under the dress of a philosopher, preached the word of God, and defended the truth of our faith by his writings as well as by his words"; and the Acts of his martyrdom speak of Justin as sitting in the house of Martinus, a recognized place of meeting for Christians, and there conversing with any who visited him, imparting to them the true doctrine. The persons condemned with him are companions whom he has gathered about him and converted. "I took delight," says one of them, Evelpistus, "in listening to Justin's discourse."

When persecution fell sharply upon the church, he was in the van of those who considered it their first duty to make public to their judges the doctrine and life so foully accused (*Apol.* i. 3, § 54). So, in the *Dialogue* with Tryphon, he speaks of the guilt he would incur before the judgment seat of Christ if he did not freely and ungrudgingly open to them his knowledge of the meaning of Scripture (*Dial.* c. 58, § 280 B).

This freedom of apologetic crowned itself towards the close of Justin's life in the three works which alone can be accepted as undoubtedly authentic: the two *Apologies* and the *Dialogue with Tryphon the Jew*. This same freedom brought him to his death.

The secret cause of his seizure is supposed by Eusebius to have been the enmity of an opponent whom he had convicted of ignorance, Crescens the Cynic. "Crescens," Tatian writes, "who made himself a nest in Rome, while professing to despise death, proved his fear of it by scheming to bring Justin and myself to death as to an evil thing" (*Or.* c. 32; cf. Eus. *H. E.* iv. 16). For the reality of his violent death for Christ we have the indubitable testimony of his historic title, Justin Martyr. For the actual account of it we are dependent on the Acts of his martyrdom, which embody, probably without serious change, the simple and forcible tradition which the 3rd cent. retained of the death-scene. They have the appearance of containing genuine matter. According to these, he and his companions are brought before Rusticus, the prefect of the city, and are simply commanded to sacrifice to the gods, without any mention of Crescens, or of Justin's *Apologies* to the emperors. Justin, on examination, professes to have found the final truth in Christianity, after exploring all other systems; this truth, he declares, consists in adoring the one God, Who has made all things, visible and invisible, and Jesus Christ, the Son of God, Who was foretold by the prophets to be coming into the world to preach salvation and teach good doctrine. He declares that Christians meet wherever they choose or can, seeing that their God is not limited to this or that place, but fills heaven and earth; but that he himself, on this, his second visit to Rome, held meetings for his followers in the house of one Martinus only, near the baths of Timotinus. After a brave refusal to sacrifice, and an assurance of salvation in Christ, he and those with him were condemned to be beaten with rods and beheaded. They died praising God and confessing their Saviour. The faithful secretly carried their bodies to a fit burial.

Such are the fragments left to us of his life; between what dates do they fall? The title of the *First Apology* is decisive; it is addressed to the "Emperor Titus Aelius Antoninus Pius, Augustus, Caesar; to Verissimus his son, philosopher, and to Lucius, the natural son of a philosophic Caesar, the adopted son of a pious Caesar." Here we have Antoninus Pius as sole emperor, with his two imperial companions, adopted by him as sons at the request of Hadrian, *i.e.* Marcus Aurelius and Lucius Verus (cf. Neander, *Ch. Hist.* [trans.] vol. ii. 446, 1851). With this the Eusebian tradition agrees; according to it, the first *Apology* was addressed to Antoninus; in the *Chronicon* it is assigned to *c.* 141, the fourth of that reign. Antoninus reigned from 137 to 161; will 141 suit Justin's language?

According to some, this is not early enough, for the title omits to salute Aurelius as Caesar, which he became publicly in 140. Against this lie several weighty objections: (1) Lucius Verus is called, possibly philosopher, certainly "ἐραστὴς παιδείας," lover of culture; but by 140 he is only ten years old. (2) Marcion is in the *Apology* the greatest type of heresy, "with a following spread over every race of men." Justin's language seems to belong to a time when Marcion's pre-eminence had overshadowed the earlier heretics (cf. Lipsius, *Die Quellen der Ketzergeschichte*, 1875, pp. 21, 22), and this could hardly be till well after 140. It was under Antoninus (according to general authority, cf. Tertullian, Clement, etc.) that Marcion succeeded in putting himself in the front, and arrived at Rome. Yet, already before the *Apology*, Justin has written a book against him, with other heretics (*Apol.* i. 26, § 70 C). It is difficult to attribute to Marcion this immense position in the very first years of Antoninus (cf. *contra*, Semisch, *Justin*, p. 73, 1840). (3) Justin professes to be writing 150 years after our Lord's birth, a round number, it is true, but in a context where the object is to diminish the interval. Without very positive evidence against it, the year 148—*i.e.* Justin's A.D. 150—should be taken as the approximate date. These reasons would place the first *Apology* near the end of the first half of the reign of Antoninus. This would not conflict with two other references to times—to the deification of Antoninus, *i.e.* 131 (*Apol.* i. 29, § 72), and to the wars of Bar-Cocheba, 132, 136 (31, § 72). Both have the same formula: τῷ νῦν γεγενημένῳ πολέμῳ and 'Αντινόου τοῦ νῦν γεγενημένου. The expression is vague, but requires the two events to be well within the memories of Justin's readers.

The address of the second *Apology* has at last, after many confusions, been determined to refer to Antoninus again, and Marcus Aurelius. It is indirect, and found in 2, § 42 C, where a single emperor is definitely meant, and in the last chapter, where the rulers are spoken of in the plural; in 2, § 43 B there are two people in office, Pius the αὐτοκράτωρ, and a philosopher, who is saluted as son of Caesar; and continued reference is made to the mingled piety and philosophy of these personages. These two, with the well-known titles, can hardly be other than Antoninus and Marcus Aurelius. This is made almost a certainty when we consider that the second *Apology* seems to have followed close upon the first and bears all the mark of a sequel or appendix (cf. Volkmar, in *Theolog. Jahrb.* 1855, N. 14; cf. Hort, in *Journ. of Classic and Sacred Philol.* vol. iii. p. 155 (1857), of which much use is made in the art.). This is clear, among other things, from the references in the second to the first *Apology* (*Apol.* ii. 4, § 43; 6, § 45; 8, § 46) as to a writing close at hand and freshly remembered. The date of the *Apologies* may be thrown back as far in the reign of Antoninus as is consistent with the prominence attributed to Marcion.

Of the date of Justin's birth we have nothing certain. Epiphanius states that he died when 30 years old. The evidence is not forthcoming. For the date of his conversion we have scarcely any evidence except that it was before the wars of Bar-Cocheba, 132-136 (*Dial.* i. 1, § 217). Eusebius supposes he was unconverted at the date of Antinous, A.D. 131 (*H. E.* iv. 8), but it is doubtful if Eusebius had any ground for this except *Apol.* i. 29, § 72, which certainly does not require it.

The genuineness of the three writings already mentioned is universally accepted. The first *Apology* definitely pronounces itself to be Justin's; the second obviously belongs to the first; the *Dialogue* claims to be written by a Samaritan, who had addressed the emperor—its personal history of the writer exactly tallies with Justin's attitude towards philosophy in the *Apologies*. The peculiar phrase ἀπομνημονεύματα τῶν 'Αποστόλων occurs in these three works, and in them alone. The whole tone of the works agrees with the period assigned. The external evidence gathered by Eusebius is strong and unbroken (cf. Eus. *H. E.* iv. 18).

But it is otherwise with an *Oratio ad Graecos*; a λόγος παραινετικὸς πρὸς "Ελληνας, or *Cohortatio ad Graecos*; a fragment, περὶ 'Αναστάσεως; and a book, περὶ Μοναρχίας, which must be classed as very doubtful; others are decidedly not genuine.

Several works of Justin have been entirely lost: (1) The book *Against all Heresies*, to which he refers in *Apol.* i. 26, § 70. (2) *Against Marcion*, referred to by Irenaeus (iv. *contra Haer.* c. 14; cf. v. 26), supposed by some to be part of (1). (3) A book called Ψάλτης, and (4) περὶ ψυχῆς, in which he contrasts his own doctrine with that of the Greek philosophers (Eus. *H. E.* iv. 18).

"Many other works of his," says Eusebius, "are in the hands of the brethren." Evidently he must have written a great deal, and the three undoubted works still extant perhaps account for this voluminous character of his writings. For these three pieces are written loosely and unsystematically, and read like the outpouring of a mind that had ranged widely in heathen literature and philosophy, and had massed a large store of general knowledge, which could be easily and effectively brought to bear upon current topics, without any scrupulous regard to the artistic or symmetrical appearance of the result.

Justin's writing, especially in the first *Apology*, is full of direct and striking force; it moves easily and pleasingly; his thinking is fresh, healthy, vigorous, and to the point; his wide knowledge is used with practical skill; his whole tone and character are immensely attractive by their genuineness, simplicity, generous high-mindedness, and frank and confident energy.

In the first *Apology*, composed with much more care and completeness than the second, he defines and justifies his position of apologist before the rulers, with supreme dignity and confidence. He calls upon them to let it be seen whether they are the loyal guardians of right and lovers of culture, which they are reported to be. He demands for himself and his fellows the justice of an exact and critical examination, without regard to prejudice, superstition, irrational panic, or any long-established evil fame. It is, as it were, for the sake of the governors and their justice that he seems to be asking a trial, for, "as for us Christians," he proudly declares, "we do not consider that we can suffer any ill from any one, unless we are convicted of wickedness or evil-doing; you can kill us indeed, but damage us you cannot" (*Apol.* i. 2, 54 A); "Princes who prefer prejudice to truth can do no more harm than robbers in a desert" (*Apol.* i. 12, § 59 E). So he opens his *Apology*, which can be roughly divided into three divisions, cc. 3-23, in which he refutes, generally, the false charges made against Christianity; cc. 23-61 exhibiting the truth of the Christian system and how it has got misunderstood; cc. 61-68 revealing the character of Christian worship and customs.

The charges against the Christians, encountered in pt. i., are: (1) The very fact of Christianity is itself treated as a punishable crime (c. iv.). (2) Atheism (c. vi.). How can they with any justice be called atheists, who reverence and worship the Father of all Righteousness, the Son Who came from the Father and taught us this, the whole Host of Angels and the Prophetical Spirit? "These are they whom we honour in reason and truth, offering our knowledge of them to all who will learn of us." (3) That some Christians have been proved malefactors. Yes, very likely, for we all are called Christians however much we vary. Therefore let every one be tried on his merits. If convicted of evil, let him pay the penalty, only as an evil-doer, not as a Christian. If innocent of crime, let him be acquitted though a Christian. (4) Christians are charged with aiming at a kingdom. But this can hardly be a kingdom on earth; for, then, we should be ruining all our hopes of it by our willingness to die for Christ. Yet we never attempt to conceal our faith; and here Justin makes a direct appeal. "Surely," he cries, "we are the best friends that a ruler could desire, we who believe in a God Whose eye no crime can escape, no falsehood deceive; we who look for an eternal judgment, not only on our deeds, but even on our thoughts! So our Master, Jesus Christ, the Son of God, has taught us." For the reality and true character of this faith in God through Christ, he offers the proof of the Christian's moral conversion. "We who once delighted in adultery, now are become chaste; once given to magic, now are consecrated to the one good God; once loving wealth above all things, now hold all our goods in common, and share them with the poor; once full of hatred and slaughter, now live together in peace, and pray for our enemies, and strive to convert our persecutors." All this is emphasised by our belief in the resurrection of the body, in which we shall hereafter suffer pain for all our sins done here (c. 18). Is this incredible? Yet it is believed not only by us, but by all who turn to magic rites, to spiritualists, to witches, to frenzied seers, to oracles at Dodona or Delphi; by Empedocles and Pythagoras, Plato and Socrates, by Homer and Virgil.

Here begins a defence of Christian doctrine, on the ground of its likeness to doctrines already held in heathenism (c. 21). We alone are hated, even though we hold the same as the Greeks; we alone are killed for our faith, even though we do nothing bad.

(C. 30.) He turns to a new objection. "How do you know the genuineness of your Christ, or that He was not some clever magic-worker?" Justin's answer is, by the proof of prophecy. The books of the Jews, translated in the LXX, in spite of the bitter hatred of the Jews against us, speak, years before the event, of us and of our Christ.

(C. 46.) A new objection: were all men irresponsible before 150 years ago, when Christ was born under Quirinus? No; there were Christians before Christ, men who lived in the power of the Word of God, Socrates and Heraclitus, Abraham and Elias.

(C. 56.) The demons have deceived men before Christ by the tales of Polytheism; and, after Christ, by the impieties of Simon, Menander, and Marcion: but have never been able to make men disbelieve in the end of the world and the judgment to come, nor to conceal the advent of Christ.

(Cc. 61-67.) He has spoken of Faith in Christ and Regeneration of Life; he will now tell what this exactly means; and so proceeds to describe the baptism by which the regeneration is effected; the reasons for this rite; its accomplishment in the Name of the Nameless God called the Father, in the Name of the Son Jesus Christ crucified under Pontius Pilate, and in the Name of the Holy Spirit Who spake by the Prophets. He describes (c. 65) the Eucharistic Feast to which the baptized are admitted, and gives a brief account of the character to be attributed to the bread and wine then consecrated and of the authority on which this rests.

He speaks once more of the feast, as it recurs on the Sundays, when they all assemble together, and (c. 68) closes rather abruptly, with the personal directness which throughout gives dignity to the *Apology*. "If my words seem to you agreeable to reason and truth, then give them their due value; if they strike you as trifling, then treat them lightly as trifles; but, at least, do not decree death against those who do nothing wrong, as if they were enemies of the state. For, if you continue in iniquity, we foretell that you will not be able to escape the future judgment of God; we shall be content to cry, God's will be done!"

He adds an epistle of Hadrian to Minucius Fundanus, by which he could claim a fair trial; but he would rather ask that as a matter of plain justice than by right of law or precedent. This letter of Hadrian's, we are told by Eusebius, was preserved by Justin in its Latin form (*H. E.* iv. 8), and thrown by him into Greek. Its style suits the age of Hadrian (Otto, ed. of Justin, vol. i. note on p. 190); it is considered genuine by Aubé, Ueberweg, doubted by Keim (*Theol. Jahrb.* t. xv. Tüb. 1856, p. 387). It gives so little to the Christians, that it seems hardly likely to be fictitious.

The second *Apology*, possibly an appendix to the first (Otto, ed. p. lxxxi.; Volkmar, *Baur und Zell. Theolog. Jahrb.* t. xiv. Tüb. 1855; Keim, *Protest. K.-Z.* Ber. 1873, n. 28, col. 619), anyhow written at no long interval after the first, begins abruptly with an appeal directly to the Romans, but in reality addressed to the imperial rulers (cf. cc. 3, 14, 15), together with the whole people. These rulers, under whom the affairs which led to the *Apology* occurred, are, it has been argued, the emperor Pius and the philosopher Marcus Aurelius, and, according to a suggested reading, Lucius Verus son of Caesar. The opening betrays by its suddenness, and emphasizes by dwelling on the speed with which the *Apology* had been produced, the excitement under which it was composed. "Things had happened within the last two days in Rome," such as the irrational actions of the magistrates, which had driven Justin to write an *Apology* for his own people, who are, though the Romans know it not and will not have it, their brothers, of like feelings with themselves.

(C. 2.) He relates the case which had so fired him with indignation; it is very typical of what Christians were subject to. The dissolute wife of a dissolute man is converted and is anxious to separate from her husband. He holds out some hopes of amendment, so she forces herself to remain, but he plunges into worse debauchery. She sends a writ of divorce and leaves him. Then this "good and noble husband" bethought himself of accusing her of being a Christian. While her case was pending, a certain Ptolemaus, the wife's master in the faith, whom Urbicus had imprisoned, is challenged with being a Christian. Ptolemaus, brought up before Urbicus, is asked, "Are you a Christian?" and on confessing it is at once condemned to death. Lucius a Christian publicly challenges Urbicus to justify a decision which punished a man simply for the name of Christian. "You, too, are a Christian, I suppose?" is the only answer he gets from Urbicus; and on confessing it he is condemned to death, declaring as he goes that he is glad to be free of rulers so unjust and to depart to the Father and King of Heaven. A third in the same way passes to a like punishment; "And I myself," breaks in Justin, "look for the same fate, for I, too, have enemies who have a grudge against me, and are likely enough to take this way of avenging themselves; Crescens especially, the sham philosopher, whom I have convicted of entire ignorance about the Christianity which he slanders."

(C. 4.) It may be said in scorn, "Be off, then, to your God in Heaven by killing yourselves, and trouble us no longer!" But Christians believe the world to be made by God to fulfil His purpose; they are not at liberty to destroy, as far as in them lies, the human race, for whom the world was created. Nor yet can we deny our faith; for this would be to allow its guilt and to lie, and would leave you in your evil prejudices.

(C. 5.) "Why does God not help His own?" He spares to punish and destroy the evil world, for the sake of this holy seed, the Christians, who are the real reason why God still preserves the order of nature, which the fallen angels have so corrupted.

The effect of these *Apologies* upon the rulers of Rome is unknown; but Justin's expectation of death was not disappointed, and Marcus Aurelius still mistrusted the motives which made Christians martyrs and saw no reason to stay the outcry of the Roman crowd when it demanded Christian victims. It remained a legal crime to be a Christian. Indeed, according to Roman ideas of government, it could hardly cease to be criminal as long as Christianity continued its private and peculiar organization and found it impossible to conform to the tests of good citizenship, such as the oath to the emperor. The *Apologies* never hint at concession on such points, but persist that their present position is entirely innocent. Their vigour must have revealed the irreconcilability of Christian life with the mass of pagan custom and temper in which the solidity of Rome had its foundation.

The *Dialogue* with Trypho follows the first *Apology*, and probably the second also, between 142 and 148 according to Hort; in 155 (Volkmar); or in 160-164 (Keim). It was written to report to a dear friend, Marcus Pompeius (cf. c. 8, § 225 D; c. 141, § 371 B), a discussion which Justin had held with the Jews during the Bar-Cocheba wars. The discussion represents the Christian polemic against the Jews; but Trypho makes his advance as a philosopher rather than as a Jew, and it is Justin who turns the talk to the Jewish Scriptures by expressing his surprise at a Jew being still engaged in searching for truth in the pagan philosophers when he possessed already in those Scriptures the authorized exponent of revealed wisdom, for the sake of whose secured certainty Justin himself had left all other human systems. Trypho is, indeed, a curious type of Judaism; a light and superficial inquirer in the courts of the schools, surrounded by a band of loud and lively friends, he begins with a reference to a Socratic at Argos, who had taught him to address courteously all who wore the philosopher's cloak, in the hope of finding, through the pleasant interchange of thoughts, something useful to both. He smiles gracefully as he inquires what opinion Justin holds about the gods, and, apparently, justifies his philosophic studies in the face of Scripture, by claiming that the philosophers are equally with Moses searchers after the Being of God. The noisy friends having been avoided by retirement to a quiet seat, Trypho opens the question with the air of a free and tolerant seeker after truth; he has read the Gospel, and found in it a morality too high for real practice, and is ready to acknowledge the piety of the better Christians. What he wonders at is that with so much goodness, they should nevertheless live as Gentiles without keeping the pure laws of God, *e.g.* the Sabbath and circumcision, by which He separates the holy from sinners; he wonders, too, how those who place their hope in a man can yet hope for a reward from God. He would gladly have all this explained (cf. c. 57, § 280 A; c. 68, § 293 A). Trypho, then, is no fierce Jewish opponent, prepared to attack, but adopts the tone almost of an inquirer. It is the Jew under a new aspect that we find here, the Jew of culture, of open and tolerant mind, with the easy courtesy of the literary world. Before such apparent openness and easy-going lightness it is perhaps not without artistic skill that Justin hints at the fierce and implacable hatred of Jew against Christian which had tortured and slain Christians without pity under Bar-Cocheba and made Jews everywhere the most violent and remorseless of the church's slanderers and persecutors (c. 108, § 335).

The *Dialogue* takes two days. Some fresh friends of Trypho join him on the second day (c. 118, § 346 C); he speaks sometimes of them as if only two, at other times as if many. One is named Mnaseas (c. 85, § 312). They shout disapproval once, as if in a theatre (c. 122, § 351 A). The whole is spoken as they sit on some stone seats in the gymnasium, Justin being about to sail on a voyage.

The actual argument begins at c. 10. The points especially raised by Trypho were two, *i.e.* how the Christians could profess to serve God and yet (1) break God's given law, and (2) believe in a human Saviour (cf. c. 10, § 227 D). The purity of Christian living is acknowledged; the problem is its consistency with its creed.

Justin's argument may be roughly divided into three parts (Otto, Prolegomena). In cc. 11-47 he refutes Trypho's conception of the binding character of the Jewish law, which refutation involves him also in a partial answer to the second part of the problem, *i.e.* the nature of the Christ in Whom they trust; for the passing away of the Law turns on the character of the Christ of Whom it prophesies. In cc. 48-108 he expounds the absolute divinity of Christ, His pre-existence, incarnation, passion, resurrection, and ascension, by virtue of which the belief in Him is proved consistent with belief in God alone. In c. 109 he passes to the necessary outcome of these two principles—the conversion of the Gentiles, the new Israel, and the abandonment of the old Israel, unless they accept the new covenant. The whole is rested on the Scriptures, on the interpretation of prophecy. Justin starts with a claim to believe absolutely in the God of Israel; here is his common ground with Trypho (c. 11)—both accept the old revelation (c. 68, § 298 A; cf. 57, § 279 B; 56, § 277 D). "I should not endure your argument," Trypho says (c. 56, § 277 D), "unless you referred all to the Scriptures; but I see you try to find all your reasons in them, and announce no other God but the Supreme Creator of the world."

The *Dialogue,* therefore, is a perfect storehouse of early Christian interpretation of Scripture. This forms its wonderful value; it carries us back to that first effort at interpretation which dates from St. Peter's speech at the election of Matthias, and knits itself so closely with the walk to Emmaus, when the Scriptures were first opened and it was seen from them that Christ must suffer. The O.T. is still the sacred guide and continual companion of the Christian life, the type of the *written* revelation; everything is there. Yet by the side of it we already feel in Justin that a new power has appeared, a fresh canon is forming, another book is beginning to assert itself. The work is full of crucial interest, just because Justin appears at the moment when this is gradually becoming clear.

In the two *Apologies* and the *Dialogue* Justin covers a large part of the theological field. His treatment is peculiarly typical of the earliest form of Christian speculation outside and beyond the immediate lines laid down by the apostolic writings. The apostolic Fathers were rather practical than speculative. The doctrinal works of people like Melito of Sardis are lost. In the Apologists Christianity, according to its preserved records, first prominently applies itself to the elucidation of its dogmatic position, and of them Justin is among the earliest and the most famous. But in considering his theology we must remember that we only possess his exoteric utterances. He is not spontaneously developing the Christian's creed, but is striving, under the stress of a critical emergency, to exhibit it most effectively and least suspiciously to an alien and unsympathetic audience, prepared not merely to discuss but to judge and kill. The whole position tended to quicken the natural tendency of Justin's mind towards an optimistic insistence on likenesses and agreements, rather than on differences between himself and his opponents. This is not said to discredit his utterances, but simply in order to consider them, as all intelligent criticism must consider them, under their actual historical conditions. Justin is on what is yet new ground to a great extent; he is pioneering, he is venturing along unmarked and unexamined roads. Christian doctrine is still forming itself under his hands, even on some essential and cardinal points.

Justin's *Theology,* then, begins in the presence of (1) Jewish Monotheism, and (2) of the Primal and Absolute and Universal Cause of all Existence, posited by the philosophic consciousness of paganism. He has to state how his conception of the Deity stands to these.

He answers, that he believes (1) in a God identical with the God of the Jews: "There is no other God, nor ever has been, but He Who made and ordered the Universe; that very God Who brought your fathers, Trypho, out of Egypt, the God of Abraham, Isaac, and Jacob" (*Dial.* 11, § 228 A). This God of creation is the one cause of all existence, therefore known as the Father: ὁ πατὴρ τῶν ὅλων (*ib.* 114, § 342 A), or τῶν πάντων (*Apol.* i. 8, § 57 A). In *Apol.* ii. 6, § 44 D, he sums up all the names by which the absolute God may be known, πατήρ, Θεός, κτίστης, κύριος, δεσπότης. This is his cardinal and prevailing expression for God the Father—that He is the Maker and Ordainer and Lord of all creation. (2) But, besides the Father, Justin undertakes to exhibit the Divinity of a Second Person, the Son, ὁ μόνος λεγόμενος κυρίως υἱός (*Apol.* ii. 6, § 44), υἱὸν αὐτοῦ τοῦ ὄντως Θεοῦ (*ib.* i. 13, § 60 C), to whom is allotted the second place, in honour and worship, after the ἄτρεπτον καὶ ἀεὶ ὄντα Θεὸν γεννήτορα τῶν ἁπάντων. He is, primarily, ὁ Λόγος, the Word of God, with God before creation began, συνὴν τῷ πατρὶ πρὸ πάντων τῶν ποιημάτων (*Dial.* 62, § 285 D). With Him the Father communicated (προσομιλεῖ), having begotten Him before all things (γέννημα ὑπὸ τοῦ Θεοῦ ἐγεγέννητο). The manner of this begetting is spoken of as a projection (τῷ ὄντι ἀπὸ τοῦ πατρὸς προβληθὲν γέννημα). Such is the Λόγος, called by Solomon the Wisdom, who co-existed with the Father at that moment when, at the beginning, by Him the Father made and perfected all things (*Apol.* ii. 6, § 44 E; *Dial.* 62, § 285 D). He it is Who is ὁ Θεός, ἀπὸ τοῦ πατρὸς τῶν ὅλων γεννηθείς, and Who is known as the Word, and the Wisdom, and the Power, and the Glory of Him Who begat Him (*Dial.* 61, § 284 A, B). The Son is the instrument of "Creation" (δι' αὐτοῦ πάντα ἔκτισε); hence (in addition to His primal names, Λόγος, Υἱός) called Χριστός, κατὰ τὸ κεχρίσθαι τὰ πάντα δι' αὐτόν; but this name is in itself of unknown significance, just as the title "God" is no real name, but rather expresses a natural opinion, inborn in man, about an unutterable fact. Christ's Being, therefore, as well as the Father's, is beyond all human expression, and is known only economically; for, if this is true of the title Χριστός, it can hardly but be true of the higher names, Λόγος and Υἱός. This Λόγος is identical with the Man Jesus, conceived through the will of the Father on behalf of man, named Jesus as being a Man and a Saviour. Justin holds, then, the entire Divinity of Him Who was born a Man and crucified under Pontius Pilate. Nothing can be more pronounced or decided than his position; it is brought to the front by the necessities of his arguments both with the Jew and the Gentile. He starts with this position, that he worships as God, a man Christ Jesus; it is this that he has to justify to the Gentile (cf. *Apol.* i. 21, 22, § 67). "In that we say," he says, "that the Word, Which is the first-begotten of God, has been born without human mixture, as Jesus Christ, our Master, Who was crucified and died, and rose again;" or, again, "Jesus Christ, Who alone was begotten to be the only Son of God, being the Word of God, and the first-born and the Power of God (πρωτότοκος καὶ δύναμις), became Man by the will of the Father, and taught us these things." He justifies the possibility of these statements to the emperors by appeals to Greek mythology, *i.e.* he is so fast bound to this belief that he has to run the risk of all the discredit that will attach to it in the minds of the philosophic statesmen to whom he is appealing from its likeness to the debasing fables which their intellectualism either rationalized or discarded. That Justin is conscious of this risk of discredit is clear from cc. 53 and 54 of the first *Apology*, with which we may compare the taunt of Trypho (*Dial.* 67, § 219 B). So again, in the *Dialogue*, it is the Christian worship of a man that puzzles Trypho; and the first necessity for Justin is to exhibit the consistency of this with the supreme monarchy of God. "First shew me," asks Trypho (*ib.* c. 50), "how you can prove there is any other God besides the Creator of the universe?" and this not in any economical sense, but verily and indeed (cf. *ib.* 55, § 274 C); and Justin accepts the task, undertaking to exhibit Jesus, the Christ, born of a virgin, as Θεὸς καὶ Κύριος τῶν δυνάμεων (*ib.* 36, § 254 E), to shew Him to be, at the same time, both Θεὸς καὶ Κύριος, and also ἀνὴρ καὶ ἄνθρωπος (*ib.* 59, § 382 C). The rigour with which this is posited may be tested by the crucial case of the appearance to Abraham at Mamre. Here, it is allowed, after a little discussion, that no angelic manifestation satisfies the language used by Scripture. It is certainly God Himself Who is spoken of. Justin undertakes to prove that this cannot be God the Father, but must be other than He Who created all things—"*other*," he means, "in number, in person, not in will or spirit" (*ib.* 56, § 276 D, ἕτερος, ἀριθμῷ λέγω ἀλλ' οὐ γνώμῃ). So, again, he applies to this Divine Being the tremendous words delivered to Moses from the midst of the burning bush, and he will not suffer this to be qualified or weakened by any such subtle distinctions as Trypho attempts to draw between the angel seen of Moses and the voice of God that spoke. He insists, against any such subtleties, that whatever Presence of God was actually there manifested was the Presence, not of the Supreme Creator, Who cannot be imagined to have left His Highest Heaven, but of that Being Who, being God, announces Himself to Moses as the God Who had shewn Himself to Abraham, Isaac, and Jacob. To Him, therefore, apply the words "I am that I am." By these two cases, specimens of a hundred others drawn from Law and Psalm and Prophets, it will be seen how clearly the problem was present to Justin, and how definitely he had envisaged its solution so far as the O.T. was concerned; in direct collision with the Monotheism of the Jew, he defends himself, not by withdrawing or modifying his assertions, but by discovering the evidence for His dual Godhead in the very heart of the ancient Revelation itself; not in any by-ways or minor incidents, but in the very core and centre of those most essential manifestations of God to Abraham, Jacob, Moses, and Joshua, on the truth of which the whole fabric of Jewish faith and worship was reared.

Justin has next to consider in what relation these two Divine Beings stand to each other. Given the existence of a Second Person Who can so effectually identify Himself with the First as to be called ὁ Θεός, how can we conceive the harmony and unity of such a duality? Justin is clear that the distinction between the two Beings is real; it is a numerical distinction. The Word is no mere emanation of the Father, inseparable from Him as the light is inseparable from the sun. He is a real subsistence, born of the Father's Will (*Dial.* 128, § 358 B). The words used, therefore, to express their relation are words of companionship, of intercourse, of συνῆν, προσομιλεῖ (cf. *ib.* 62, § 285 C, D, where he brings out the fact of this personal intercourse as involved in the consultations at the creation of man). They are two distinct Beings, but yet must be One in order not to dissolve the absoluteness of the only Godhead. Such a unity may be pictured by the connexion between a thought and the Reason that thinks it, or by the unity of a flame with the fire from which it was taken. Each of these examples of the unbroken unity has the shortcoming that they compel us to think of a stage prior to the dual condition in which that which is now dual was single. What, then, of the existence of the Word before It became the προβληθὲν γέννημα? Justin is content with the statements: (1) That "before all things," already "at the beginning," this projection had been effected, the two Persons were already distinct (cf. *ib.* 62, § 285 D; 56, § 276 C, τὸν καὶ πρὸ ποιήσεως κόσμου ὄντα Θεόν). (2) That besides this actual projection of the Λόγος there is a state which may be described as a condition of inner companionship with God the Creator (συνῆν). This precedence is never distinctly asserted to be temporal by Justin. In the *Dialogue* the συνών is stated to be eternal in exactly that sense in which the γέννημα is eternal, *i.e.* as being "before all things."

Justin does not appear to definitely pronounce on the question how the process of Begetting consists with the absolute eternity of the Personal Word begotten. There is no precise realization of a Λόγος ἐνδιάθετος and προφορικός. He hardly seems conscious of this difficulty in his two analogies of the thought and the flame; he is satisfied with expressing, by them, the unity, and yet distinctness, of the Father and the Son. He is content to state that this unity in difference existed from the very first, before all created things. His analysis seems hardly to have pressed back to the final question, which Arian logic discovered to lie behind all minor issues, *i.e.* was there a moment when the Father was not yet a Father? Such a suspension of analysis is not unnatural, since Justin, in the writings before us, hardly enters on the contemplation of the Nature of God in and to Himself. It is always as the source of all things—the Father, the Maker, the Lord of the Universe—that he presents God to us. It is God in His relation to His works that we contemplate. What He was in Himself before all His works does not seem considered, and it is therefore all the more sufficient to state that God came to the making of the world already dual in character. The moment at which creation was to begin found the Son already existent, as ὁ Θεός, in personal intercourse with the Father. With this he leaves us, only affirming that that character of paternity which constitutes the relation of God to the world had a prior and peculiar significance and reality in the relation that united the absolute God and His Word (cf. *Apol.* ii. 6, § 44, ὁ μόνος λεγόμενος κυρίως υἱός).

Justin's metaphysic, then, culminates in the assertion of this essential Sonship pre-existent to the creation. This being so, his language remains as indecisive on the ulterior question of the origin of the Sonship as is the language of Proverbs on the eternity of the Wisdom. In both cases the utmost expression for eternity that their logic had attained to is used. It is useless to press them for an answer to the puzzles of a later logic, which carried the problem back into that very eternity which closed their horizon. It was inevitable that the natural and unsystematized language used before the Arian controversy should be capable of an Arian interpretation. Since the Father is indeed slone ἀγέννητος, the sole unoriginate fount of the Divine life, the expressions used about Him, and about the Son, must necessarily impute to Him an underivative, to the Son a derivative Being; and must, therefore, tend to class the Son rather with the rest of τὰ γενητά than with the sole ἀγενητόν. It could only be at the end of a most subtle and delicate reflection that Christian logic could possibly realize that it was bound, if it would be finally consistent with itself, to class the derived Being of the Son, by virtue of the absolute eternity of its derivation, on the side of τὸ ἀγενητόν rather than on that of τὰ γενητά. Justin, in the full flush of readiness to sweep in to the service of faith the dear and familiar language of his former Platonism, may have left himself unguarded and careless on this uttermost point of the philosophy of the Incarnation; but it will not easily be doubted—by any one who has observed how he develops the full divinity of the Son over all the ground which his logic covered with a boldness and a vigour that, in face of the inevitable obstacles, prejudices, misunderstandings excited by such a creed, are perfectly astonishing—what answer he would have given if the final issue of the position had once presented itself definitely to him.

Justin had also affirmed the *moral* unity of the Son with the Father. This is not stated to be the ground of the Unity. The analogies of the thought and of the flame, on the contrary, imply a unity of substance to be the ground of the κυρίως υἱότης, but it is introduced in order to explain the consistency of his belief with the reality of a single supreme Will in the Godhead (*Dial.* 56, § 274), and the explanation naturally led him to affirm the complete subordination of the Son to the will of the Father. The Son is the expression of the Father's mind, the δύναμιν λογικήν, which He begat from Himself. He is the interpreter of His Purpose, the instrument by which He designs. In everything, therefore, the Son is conditioned by the supreme Will; His office, His very nature, is to be ὁ ἄγγελος, ὁ ὑπηρέτης. All His highest titles, υἱός and λόγος, as well as others, belong to Him by virtue of His serving the Father's purpose and being born by the Father's Will (ἐκ τοῦ ἀπὸ τοῦ πατρὸς θελήσει γεγενῆσθαι, *ib.* 61, § 284 B). "I say that He never did anything but what the Maker of the world, above Whom there is no God at all, willed that He should do" (*ib.* 56, § 276). The Father is above all. Trypho would not endure to listen to Justin if he did not hold this (*ib.* 56, § 278 B). The Son is then subordinate, and perfectly subordinate, but this subordination is such that it can allow the Son to identify Himself utterly with the Father, as with Moses at the bush, and so to be called ὁ Κύριος and ὁ Θεός.

In the expression "born of the Father's Will" we are once more close to Arian controversy. Was there, then, a moment when the Father had not yet willed to have a Son? If so, how can the Son be eternal? Yet, if not, how was the Father's will free? Justin has no such questions put to him. He states this dependence of the Son for His very Being on the Will of the Father without anxiety as to His right to be named ὁ Θεός, and to receive worship in the absolute sense in which a Jew would understand that title and that worship. And here, again, surely it was inevitable that the Christian consciousness should have so stated frankly the subordinate and dependent character of the eternal Sonship, before it appreciated the subtle puzzle that would ensue when logic began its critical work upon the novel and double-sided conception. Subordination of the Son to the Father must represent the immediate, primary, natural, and intelligible method of presenting to the reflecting mind the reconciliation of the duality of Persons with the unity of Will. The very name of Son, or of the Word, implied it. So far, too, the logic inherited from the philosophies would supply the needful formula. It would take time to discover that Christianity held implicitly, in its faith in the entire Divinity of the Son, a position which, if ever it was to be made consistent with the explicit formula of the subordination, must necessitate an entirely new and original logical effort, such as would justify the synthesis already achieved by the Christian's intuitive belief in the absolute Divinity of a dependent and subordinate Son. This new logical effort was made when Athanasius recognized the dilemma into which the old logic of the Schools had thrown the Christian position, and, instead of abandoning either of the alternatives, evolved a higher logic, which could accept both. For it must be remembered, if we are to be impartial to Justin, that the Nicene controversy was not closed by the church throwing over the subordination, while the Arian threw over the entire Divinity of the Son. Nicaea confessed the subordination, and made it theoretically consistent with the absolute Divinity. This being so, the only possible test by which to try Justin (who certainly held both the divinity and the subordination) would be to ask whether, if he had seen the dilemma, he would have held the subordination of the Son to be the primary and imperative truth to the logical needs of which the fulness of the divine Sonship must be thrown over, or whether he would have felt the latter truth to be so intimately essential that a novel logic must be called into existence which should interpret it into accordance with the subordination. It cannot but be felt that Justin's *faith* is a great deal more pronounced and definite than his Platonic logic; that the one is clear and strong where the other is vague and arbitrary; and, if so, that in a conflict between the two his faith would have remained supreme. Justin's temper of mind is the complete reverse of that of Arius.

On the ministerial activities of the Son for the Father Justin is much more explicit.

The Word has one chief mission from the Father, that of interpreting Him to man; hence He received the name of ἄγγελος (cf. *Dial.* 56, § 275). He accomplishes this (1) to the Jews by means of the Theophanies and through the lips of the prophets. The Word is the direct inspirer Whose spirit moves the prophets, and Whose words they speak (cf. *Apol.* i. 36, § 76 D). The whole manifold Scripture, with all its many parts and voices, is, as it were, a great play written by a single author, the Word of God, Who alone speaks through all the characters displayed. Of this Justin gives instances in cc. 37, 38, 39. Again, He is not only the *inward* force, but the *outward* object also, to Which all prophecy is directed. The Jewish Scripture has in Him a permanent aim, a fixed canon; it all arranges itself round Him (cf. *Apol.* i. 31, § 73 A). To foretell Him and His work is the one purpose of prophecy. By it His whole life in its main outlines is described, His advent, His birth from the virgin, His coming to man's estate, His curing of the sick, His raising the dead, His being hated, and unknown, and crucified, His death, resurrection, and ascension, His divine sonship, His mission of the apostles, His success among the Gentiles (*ib.* i. 31, § 73). (2) Justin attributes a revelation of the Word to the Gentiles, as well as to the Jews; to them He is the ἄγγελος, the interpreter of the Father, not by *prophetic* anticipations, but by *partial* manifestation, of Himself. Every man in every race possesses a germ of the Word, by the power of which men knew what truth they did know, and did what good they did do; above all, the philosophers and lawgivers who, in their rational inquiries and speculations, were obeying the measure of the Word within them (κατὰ λόγου μέρος . . . δι' εὑρέσεως καὶ θεωρίας, *ib.* ii. 10, § 48 C). It is Justin who promulgates the famous formula: Ὅσα παρὰ πᾶσι καλῶς εἴρηται ἡμῶν τῶν Χριστιανῶν ἐστι (*ib.* ii. 13, § 51). "We do not believe less, but more, than Empedocles and Pythagoras, Socrates and Plato," he says: "we approve what they rightly said; but our doctrine is higher than theirs;" and so too with the Stoics, poets, and historians (cf. *ib.* i. 18, § 65 C; ii. 10, 13). This is the principle the Alexandrians are to develop. These ancient friends of Christ, for their obedience to the Word, were hated as Christians are hated, as impious and curious busy-bodies; chief of them was Socrates, who was martyred for Christ. With him are mentioned Heraclitus, Musonius the Stoic, etc. In the exercising of human reason to search out God such as these obeyed the power of the Word, the Reason of God (λόγῳ πειραθέντες τὰ πράγματα θεωρῆσαι καὶ ἐλέγξαι . . . διὰ λόγου ζητήσεως θεοῦ τοῦ ἀγνώστου ἐπίγνωσιν; *ib.* ii. 10, § 48; cf. i. 5, § 55 E: λόγῳ ἀληθεῖ καὶ ἐξεταστικῶς). This general differs from the Christian revelation in the *partial* character of the λόγος σπερματικός; each philosopher, etc., saw only a part of the Word. Hence the contradictions of the philosophic system, the inconsistencies of human law; some had one right part, some another. Christians possess the *whole* Word of God, in the person of Christ Jesus; they, therefore, hold the canon of truth which distinguishes all that was good and true of old, from the false and the confused with which it was mixed (*ib.* ii. 9, 10, § 47). This distinction is radical; "since the germ and image of something, given to man according to the measure of his capacity, is quite distinct from that very thing itself which permits itself, by its own favour, to be so given and communicated" (*ib.* ii. 13, § 51 C). This clear distinction exhibits the full reality of the personality attributed by Justin to the Word revealed in Christ; it is personality which distinguishes itself so decisively from the influence and energy which it exercises; it is it again which makes the distinction between a partial and a complete revelation to be so radical. The completeness of the Christian revelation lies in its being the revelation of Christ's Person (cf. *ib.* ii. 10, § 48, ὅς ἐστι Χριστός; ii. 13, § 51). Hence, the Revelation of the Word concentrates itself in the Incarnation; for so only, and then only, is the Word Himself in His *personal* reality, as distinct from all his activities, and superior to all His influences, made manifest and actual to man. "Our truth is more sublime than all human doctrine," says Justin, "on account of the entirety with which the Divine Reason has appeared, for our sakes, as Christ, being manifested as body, and reason, and spirit" (*ib.* ii. 10, § 48 B). It is because the Word of the absolute and ineffable God has "become a man for our sakes, sharing our passions, and curing our ills," that we surpass all the philosophers whose wisdom we claim to be ours (*ib.* ii. 13, § 50). Christians now can worship and love the Word. They possess in Him a doctor who will authoritatively determine the truth, separating it from the confusions introduced by the demons (*ib.* ii. 13, § 51; ii. 9, § 48 B). He has thus made the certain and secure revelation of the Father, which Socrates pronounced to be so difficult and perilous by the way of human reasoning; and He has made this revelation effective and universal, by being Himself no mere reasoner, but the very Power of the Ineffable God (δύναμίς ἐστι τοῦ Πατρός, *ib.* ii. 10, § 49 A; cf. i. 23, § 68 B). This Power of God avails to ensure security of truth to those even who cannot use reasoning effectively, to artisans and utterly unlearned people. The identification of the man Christ Jesus with the antecedent Word of God is entire and unhesitating. Nothing can exceed Justin's preciseness. "Christ Who was known in part by Socrates, for He was and is the Word which is in every man, and foretold things both by the prophets and in His own Person, when He took upon Him our nature and taught these things" (*ib.* ii. 10, § 49 A). Here it is identically the same Person Who is known to Socrates, and inspires the prophets, and taught mankind in the flesh (cf. *ib.* i. 23: "Jesus Christ, Who is the Word of God, His First-born, His Power, His only Son, was also made man"; cf. i. 63, § 96 A). In consequence of the pre-existence, the Incarnation could only be effected by a supernatural birth. Because the Christ existed personally in Himself before the ages and then endured to be born as a man, He could not be begotten by man, but must be born solely by the will of the Father Who originally begat Him. Such a birth would be unnecessary for a human Christ; those, therefore, who held that God's Christ was not pre-existent or divine, would not hold that He was born supernaturally of a virgin. So Justin claims that Trypho might accept the proofs that Jesus was Christ, even though he should fail to convince him of the eternal pre-existence and virgin-birth of Jesus (*Dial.* 48, § 267 B); and here Justin confesses that some who are called Christians and acknowledge Jesus to be Christ, yet hold Him to be a man born of men. He himself could never agree with them even if the main mass of Christians were to turn against him; but he speaks of these Ebionites with a mildness that is rather startling in view of the immense strength and definiteness of his own belief, with which his own church, as he tells us, fully agreed. Apparently he is justifying the possibility of the *pis aller*, which he proposes to Trypho. It is a novelty to Trypho, it seems, to hear of there being such Christians: he expects them to hold what Justin holds. Evidently, the common church faith in the pre-existence and divinity of Christ is so entire that it already has a theology which is anxious to use the agony in the garden and the bitter cry on the cross as proofs that Christ was actually a man Who could suffer pain (*ib.* 103, § 331 D, etc.), as if it were the humanity that was more likely to be doubted than the divinity. This supernatural birth is justified by Isaiah's prophecy (which he accuses the Jews of having corrupted, by changing παρθένος into νεᾶνις, and which the demons have caricatured in the myth of Perseus) (*ib.* 68, § 294); by Psalm cx.: "From the womb I begat Thee" (*ib.* 63, 286 D); and from many other texts in which Justin sees it foreshadowed that the blood of Christ would come not by human mixture, but solely by the will of God (*Apol.* i. 32, § 74; *Dial.* 76, § 301). His language on this goes so far that it seems sometimes hardly consistent with the perfect manhood of Christ. He is "*like* a son of man," *i.e.* not born of human seed. His blood is called the "blood of the grape," because it came not to Him from man, but direct from the will of the Father. He is the "stone cut without hands," etc.

The purpose of the Incarnation is to save men from evil deeds and evil powers, and to teach assured truth (*Apol.* i. 23, § 68 C; ἐπ' ἀλλαγῇ καὶ ἐπαναγωγῇ τοῦ ἀνθρωπείου γένους; ii. 9 § 48, B). He brings to bear the full divine energy (ἡ δύναμις τοῦ Πατρός) on a race diseased and deceived through the action of devils. So He is the medicine to cure (*ib.* ii. 13, § 51 D), which He becomes by sharing our humanity (τῶν παθῶν τῶν ἡμετέρων συμμέτοχος). He is therefore called the Saviour (*ib.* i. 61, § 94 A), in Whom we receive remission of sins and regeneration. His mode of action is by (1) teaching, as the Word, which is no mere persuasive argument but is a Power penetrating deeper than the sun into the recesses of the soul (*Dial.* 121, § 350 A), enabling us not only to hear and understand, but to be saved (*Apol.* ii. 12, § 49). His truth is an absolute canon by which to sift the true from the false in human speculations, since He, the Entire Word, distinguishes with certainty, amid the confusion of the philosophies, that in them which is His own working. So completely and uniquely authoritative is He, that it is by His teaching alone that men rightly know and worship the one Father and God (*ib.* i. 13). (2) He saves, secondly, by suffering on the cross: so sharing in all the reality of our flesh (cf. *Dial.* 98, § 324 D, γέγονεν ἄνθρωπος ἀντιληπτικὸς παθῶν). He destroys death by death. He gains possession of men by the cross (*cf ib.* 134, § 364 C, δι' αἵματος καὶ μυστηρίου τοῦ σταυροῦ κτησάμενος αὐτούς). By His blood

He loosens the power of the devil (*ib.* 94, § 322 A); He removes death (*ib.* 105, § 332); by His blood He purifies those who believe (*Apol.* i. 32, § 74 A): hence, He, as crucified, is the Priest, the Eternal High Priest (*cf. Dial.* 116, 343 E). Man's power to keep blameless, and to drive out devils, follows the economy of His Passion (*ib.* 31, § 247 D). Hence He is called βοηθός and λυτρωτής (*ib.* 30, § 247 C), the hope of Christians is hung on the crucifixion of Christ (*ib.* 96, § 323 C). By His stripes we are healed (*ib.* 17, § 234 E, 336 D). So He is the Paschal Lamb, Who saves from death by the sprinkling of blood (*ib.* 111, § 338 C). He saved, by submitting to that which all men deserved for sin, *i.e.* the curse pronounced on all who kept not the law; therefore He was crucified, because the curse lay on crucifixion; but He was no more under God's curse when He endured our curse than was the brazen serpent, which was ordered by God, though He had condemned all images. God saved of old by an image without violating the Second Commandment; He saves now, by a Crucified, those who are worthy of the curse, without, for that, laying His curse on the Crucified. It is the Jews, and not God, who now fulfil the text by "cursing Him that hung on the tree" (*ib.* 96, 323). This cross and suffering the Father willed for man's sake, that on His Christ might fall the curse of all men: He willed it, knowing that He would raise Him again from this death, as Christ testified on the cross by His appeal to the Father. This coming of Christ to be despised, to suffer, to die, is justified by many appeals to prophecy, especially to Ps. xxii. (*ib.* 98, § 325), to Jacob's blessing, Gen. xlix. 8, 12, etc. It is the "hidden power of God which is exhibited in the crucified Christ" (*ib.* 49, § 269 C). This power (ἰσχὺς τοῦ μυστηρίου τοῦ σταυροῦ, *ib.* 91, § 318 B) began to manifest its hidden efficacy from the day of the resurrection; those who have faith in the cross, and exercise penitence, are, through the power of Christ, the great and eternal priest, stripped of the filthy garments of sin, and clothed with new robes, and made priests, through whom everywhere sacrifices are offered (*ib.* 116, § 344). Christ Himself is raised from the grave, to be led up into heaven, by the Father, there to dwell until He shall strike down all the devils His enemies and the number of the elect righteous shall be fulfilled, when He will be shewn in glory on the throne of His manifested kingdom. Then will be the great judgment of devils and sinners which is delayed solely for the sake of gathering in all who may yet be willing to believe and repent (*Apol.* i. 45, § 82 D; ii. 7, § 45 B); till it comes, Christ sends down power on His Apostles, by which they, and all who will, consecrate themselves to the one God (*ib.* i. 50, § 86 B; 49, § 85 B). This present efficacy of Christ is evident in the power of Christians over devils, who are bound and expelled by their adjuration (cf. *Dial.* 76, § 302 A). This power, offered to all, manifests itself especially among the Gentiles, and is rejected by Jew and Samaritan, as many a prophecy had foretold (*ib.* 91, § 319 A; cf. 120, § 348, etc. to end of *Dial.*). It calls men by the road of faith into friendship and blessing, penitence, and compunction, and assures them of a kingdom to come, eternal and incorruptible (cf. *ib.* 139, § 369 A). All on whom the power of the cross comes are gathered with one mind into one synagogue, one church, a church born of and called by His name, addressed by the Word in Scripture as His daughter, "Hearken, O daughter" (*ib.* 63, § 287 B). This church is described, with St. Paul, as one body, ἓν καλεῖται καὶ ἔστι σῶμα (*ib.* 42, § 261 A).

The eternal kingdom comes with Christ's second advent, in glory, as judge. He will judge every man, up to Adam himself (*ib.* 132, § 362 A); then shall sinners and devils weep, for to them He will allot a place in that eternal fire which will destroy this world; believers He will admit to the kingdom, recalling the dead to life and establishing them in an eternal and indissoluble kingdom, themselves incorruptible, immortal, painless (*ib.* 117, § 345, B). This is the Melchisedec, King of Salem, eternal Priest of the Most High, Who will remake a new heaven and a new earth, into which holy land His circumcised shall enter (*ib.* 113, § 341 A). This kingdom is generally spoken of as in heaven, as not earthly (cf. *Apol.* i. 11, § 59 A, etc.); it is a home with God, for the sake of which Christians easily despise all earthly delights and lusts and the fear of death. In one famous passage in the *Dialogue* (80, § 306 B; cf. 113, § 341 A) he accepts the Jewish belief of a millennium in a restored and beautified Jerusalem; he claims to have dealt already with this point, though no such explanation is in the *Dialogue*; many share this belief with him, he says, yet many pious and orthodox Christians reject it; only those who are, according to Justin, ὀρθογνώμονες κατὰ πάντα Χριστιανοί, hold this faith with him, based on Is. lxv. 17 and on the Revelation of "one of themselves, by name John, an apostle of Christ," who speaks of a first resurrection and then a second eternal resurrection and judgment of all men. Evidently there are no words of our Lord's to support this belief; it is a pious opinion, resting on the literal reading of the Apocalypse, held by the most strict believers, but not necessary to a pure and true faith (καθαρὰ καὶ εὐσεβὴς γνώμη). Far different are those who deny the future resurrection of the body altogether and believe in an immediate entrance of the souls of Christians into heaven: "let Trypho beware of deeming such to be Christians at all." The resurrection of the body is a cardinal point of Justin's creed (cf. *Apol.* i. 18 ff.); essential to the reality of future punishment, and to the fullness of a Christian's security against all loss in death, and justified by an appeal to the wonder of our first creation and to Christ's miracles (*Dial.* 69, § 296 A).

When this Advent will be, we know not, though it may be soon. It will be preceded by the appearance of the Man of Iniquity.

On the action of the Third Person, Justin is not so definite; he is continually speaking of Him, but His person and office are not always distinguished with precision from those of the Second Person. He is there, in Justin's creed, a recognized element in it, constantly occurring; but apparently Justin's metaphysic had not yet had time or occasion to dwell on this point with anxiety or exactness. The most definite mention of Him is in the typical formula for the object of Christian worship and sacramental service; here He is distinctly allied to the First and Second Persons as the alone Third, Who shares with Them the adoration of Christians and the ministration of grace (cf. *Apol.* i. 13, § 60 E, Πνεῦμα προφητικὸν ἐν τρίτῃ τάξει τιμῶμεν, where he is explaining what it is that Christians worship); again (*ib.* i. 60, § 93 B), he claims for the Spirit the truth of that τὸ τρίτον which Plato was supposed to have suggested. Here, as in the former case, the τρίτον is parallel to ἡ δευτέρα χώρα, the place of the Son, and must, therefore, be understood in something of the same significance as that; and that "second place" signified, we know, a difference in number, in fact, in personality, not a mere logical distinction; yet it included such a unity of substance and will that the terminology of the Godhead could be directly applied to it, with the exception of those symbols of absolute supremacy, *i.e.* the titles, "Father," "Creator," etc. As the Holy Spirit is directly included within the lines of the object worshipped, so is He directly implicated in the divine action upon men: thus the baptismal and sacrificial formula unite His name with that of the Father and the Son (*ib.* i. 61, § 94 A; 65, § 97 D; 67, § 98 C). He, with the Son, is the medium by which praise and thanksgiving are offered to the Father; His is the third name in the might of which the Christian receives regeneration. One curious passage gives Him a strange place: Justin refutes (*ib.* i. 6, § 56 C) the charge of atheism by claiming that Christians honour and adore (σεβόμεθα καὶ προσκυνοῦμεν) "both God the Father, and the Son Who came from Him, and the host of good angels that follow Him, and are made like to Him, and the Prophetic Spirit also." Here the angels are brought in front of the Spirit, through the need, probably, of expressing their unity with Christ by virtue of which they become the objects of Christian reverence (ἐξομοιουμένων). Several attempts have been made to avoid this sudden introduction of the angels, by various interpreters (cf. Otto's note *in loc.* ed. vol. i. 1, 21); but it is hardly possible to read the passage otherwise than as it stands. It must be explained by its position; Justin is quite precise and clear in other passages, where the position attributed to the Holy Spirit is definitely marked, and this sentence, therefore, must be interpreted in accordance with them, not they be confused by it. The angels are best introduced in close company with that Divine Person to Whom they are peculiarly attached, and from Whom especially they derive their title to sanctity (cf. *Dial.* 31, § 247 E; *Apol.* i. 52, §§ 87-88; *Dial.* 61, § 284 B), our Lord being Himself ὁ ἄγγελος, and being therefore named ἀρχιστράτηγος, the captain of the angelic host. Only through Him can they be reverenced; while the Holy Spirit receives worship by right of Himself. Justin, by throwing in at the end σεβόμεθα with προσκυνοῦμεν, covers all the varieties of adoration that his inclusion of angels may have made requisite; and he adds λόγῳ καὶ ἀληθείᾳ τιμῶντες, as if to suggest that there were carefully guarded lines of distinction in the Christian's worship. Elsewhere he shews himself perfectly conscious of the impossibility of paying absolute worship to any but God alone (*Apol.* i. 16, § 63); in order to justify the adoration of Christ, he knows clearly that he must shew Him to be higher than all angels (*Dial.* 56, § 276). The whole argument with the Jew exhibits the precision of Justin's distinction between God and His angelic ministers; but, on the other hand, his language in this unique passage evidences the reverential service that could be offered, according to Christian use, to those who had been fashioned into the likeness of Christ.

The Holy Spirit is concerned with creation (*ib.* i. 60, § 93 B), in His distinct personal fullness, as ὁ τρίτος, with a third station peculiar to Himself (τρίτη χώρα) in the Godhead. His main office is with inspiration; He is τὸ Πνεῦμα τὸ προφητικόν; this is His cardinal name. He speaks as Himself to man, using men as His organ (διὰ Μωϋσέως προεμήνυσε, *ib.* i. 60, § 93 B); here, since the words follow the statement of the place of the Holy Spirit in the Triad, they must definitely intend Him, in His distinction from the Word, to be the spring of inspiration; so, too, in the formula of baptism, it is the name of προφητικός, which marks His distinction from the Word; and we must, therefore, apply to Him, in His separate right and existence, the constantly recurring use of this name (cf. *ib.* i. 38, § 77 C; 47, § 84 A, etc., etc.), on all which occasions He is spoken of as the direct author and speaker of prophecy, and prophecy is spoken of as peculiarly the note of God (*ib.* i. 30, § 72 B, etc.). This Spirit is one throughout; It spoke once in Elias, and afterwards in the Baptist (*Dial.* 49, § 268). Yet Justin sometimes attributes to the Word this action of inspiration which gives to the Spirit His name (cf. *Apol.* i. 36, § 76 D); the prophets speak through the Word which moves them (so again *ib.* i. 33, § 75 D, θεοφοροῦνται λόγῳ θείῳ; cf. *Dial.* 61, § 284 C; 62, § 285; 63, § 236 D). In both cases it is the *effective agency* by which the prophets are stirred to speak which is attributed to the Word; and Justin attributes this on grounds which he expects the heathen emperors to acknowledge, it is language they must understand (*Apol.* i. 33). The action of God on man is so intimately bound up with the Word, in Justin, that it is wonderful how much inspiration he attributes to the Spirit, rather than how little.

Justin holds very decisively the belief (1) in good angels, attached intimately to our Lord (cf. former quotations), messengers of God in O. and N. T., fed in heaven on some manna (*Dial.* 57, § 279 C), accompanying Christ in His glory on the last day; and (2) more particularly in bad angels, to whom the earth and man had been committed by God (*Apol.* ii. 5, § 44 A), but who overstepped their limits in wicked intercourse with women, who, from them, bore sons, the devils; they reduced the human race to servitude, by deceitful magic, and by terror, and by instituting sacrifices, etc., to themselves, for which they lusted now that they had known the passion of fleshly desires: they sowed the seeds of war, adultery, crime. Chief among them is the Serpent, the tempter of Adam and Eve, the Devil, Satanas, a name ascribed to him by our Lord Himself at His temptation, signifying Apostate and Serpent (*ib.* i. 28, § 71 B; *Dial.* 103, § 331 B).

The problem of the *human soul* occupies the chief place in the account of Justin's conversion; the philosophers were felt to be uncertain and insecure in their conception of it, especially as regards its immortality, its consequent transmigration, and its relation to the divine substance. Justin holds that the soul is no particle of the absolute mind; has no life in itself; is created; is not life, but partaker of life, so that it could perish; but receives immortality by the will of God, as is proved by a mass of practical testimony, by the word of Revelation, and by its consonance with the needs of justice; this immortality includes as its essential requisite the resurrection of the body, without which Justice could not fulfil itself; it will be given both to the just and to the unjust (cf. *Dial.* 4, 5, 6; *Apol.* i. 21, § 67 D; 18, 19, § 65), though it is only rightly "immortality" for the just; for the others, eternal fire.

Man, according to Justin, has been imprisoned in sin since the fall of Adam, the first man, deceived of the devil, who fell greatly by deceiving Eve; hence "ye shall die" (*Dial.* 124, § 353 D, *ὁμοίως τῷ Ἀδὰμ καὶ τῇ Εὔᾳ ἐξομοιούμενοι, θάνατον ἑαυτοῖς ἐργάζονται*), though originally made *θεῷ ὁμοίως ἀπαθεῖς καὶ ἀθανάτους* (cf. *ib.* 88, § 316 A). Man, as the angels, was made incorruptible, if he kept God's laws. This Biblical view falls in with his account of the whole human race, as sinning through the deceit of evil angels who made them think their own bad passions possible in gods. This evil state, thus brought on, is spoken of as a tyranny from which man had to be delivered by another (cf. *ib.* 116, § 344 A; *Apol.* ii. 6, § 45 A); Christ comes *ἐπὶ καταλύσει τῶν δαιμόνων*. The whole race is under the curse; for, if the Jews were, by the laws of Moses, much more were the Gentiles with their horrible idolatry (*Dial.* 95, § 322 D). Only by Christ is the curse removed; He, our Israel, wrestles for us with the devil (*ib.* 125, § 354 D). Only by His grace are the devils made subject. But Justin combines with this a great anxiety to keep man's free-will intact; he is continually explaining himself on this point. Man is never deserted of God; he possesses, after the fall, the germinal *Λόγος*, by which he discerns between good and evil, between true and false (cf. *ib.* 93, § 320 D; *Apol.* ii. 10).

The gift of Christ to man is primarily remission of sins (cf. *Dial.* 116, § 344, etc.), effected through penitence on man's part, excited by his call into true faith in the Creator; by Christ's power, sin is stripped off and remitted; we are made regenerate (*Apol.* i. 61, § 94 D). This regeneration accomplished and the truth being now known and confessed, we become bound, and fit, to accomplish a good life, to keep the commandments, to attain eternal life (*ib.* i. 65, § 97 C). We are clothed with garments prepared of Christ (*Dial.* 116, § 344); we are to imitate God's own virtues, to exhibit ourselves worthy of His counsel by works (*Apol.* i. 10, § 58 B). The entire change of character is beautifully given in *Apol.* i. 14, § 61, 15, etc.

The most effective guard of this pure living is belief in the resurrection of the body; for this hope consecrates the entire man to the holiness of the eternal kingdom and renders real the sense of future punishment; we shall *feel* torture, hereafter, in our bodies; without this, future pain would be unreal and meaningless (*ib.* i. 18, § 65). God will raise and endue with incorruptibility the dead bodies, now dissolved and scattered like seeds over the earth (*ib.* i. 19).

This human race will endure until the number of those willing to become Christians is complete. It is because God acts by the free choice of man that He does not destroy evil by force, but offers men the chance of escape, and gives them time to use the chance (*Dial.* 102, § 329 A). The punishment that awaits sinners, when the end comes, will be by fire and for ever. On this Justin is very pronounced (cf. *Apol.* i. 8, § 57 B): "an eternal punishment" (*αἰώνιον κόλασιν*), he says, "and not a mere period of a thousand years," *ἀπαύστως κολάζεσθαι* (*Dial.* 45, § 264 B); the kingdom is *αἰώνιος καὶ ἄλυτος*, the *κόλασις πυρὸς* is *αἰώνιος* too (*Dial.* 117, § 345). He uses the language freely and frankly, unhampered, apparently, by his theory of the soul, which makes its immortality dependent on the Will of God, Who wills it in the shape of Holiness (cf. Iren. bk. iii. 36; cf. *Apol.* i. 21, § 67). He justifies the existence of reward and punishment by the forcible argument, that, without them, you are compelled to believe God indifferent to good and evil, or else good and evil to have no real actuality; both which beliefs are impious. The judgment is the witness of God's regard to the reality of the distinction (cf. *Apol.* ii. 9, § 47 E; i. 28, § 71 C).

The church is that society of Christians in which the power of the regeneration is faithfully manifested and the pure knowledge revealed in Christ loyally held; so Justin is anxious to explain that not all so-called Christians are real Christians, any more than all so-called philosophies mean the same thing (*ib.* i. 7, § 56 D). Many, professing to confess Christ, hold impious and immoral doctrine, with whom the "disciples of the true and pure doctrine" do not communicate; they are marked as heretical by assuming the names of their founders, *e.g.* Marcion, Valentinus, Basilides (*Dial* 35, § 253 D).

The true Christians hold "the pure teaching of Jesus Christ"; possess "a pure and pious doctrine" based on Scripture, and the words of Christ, not on human doctrine (*ib.* 48, § 269 D); prove them true by holiness (cf. *Apol.* i. 26, § 70 B); heretics may be capable of any wickedness for all Justin knows. He himself has written a work against all the heresies (*ib.* i. 26, § 70 C). The heresies confirm true believers in the faith, since Christ foretold them (cf. *Dial.* 82, § 308 B; 35, § 253 C), though they lead many away.

True believers are admitted to the body by the rite of baptism, on their acceptance of Christian verity and their promise to live accordingly (*Apol.* i. 61, § 93 E). This baptism is the true circumcision of the Spirit (*Dial.* 43, § 261 D); works with the cross to expiate our sins (*ib.* 86, § 314 A); is appointed by Christ Himself for the remission of sins; and is our regeneration, by which we are born again out of a state of sin into Light and Holiness; so called "Illumination," φωτισμός (*Apol.* i. 61, 74). It presupposes penitence and a confession of faith (*ib.* i. 61, 65). Baptism admits to the brotherhood, the assembly, where common prayers are made (*ib.* i. 65, § 97 C), the kiss of peace given, and the Eucharist offered by the leader of the brethren, ὁ προεστώς; who takes the bread and water and wine brought him, and sends up praise and glory to the Father, in the Name of the Son and the Holy Spirit; at the end of his thanksgiving the people give their consent by saying, "Amen"; after this thanksgiving, εὐχαριστία, the deacons administer the elements, with which thanks have been offered (τοῦ εὐχαριστηθέντος ἄρτου), to each one present and carry some to the absent. This food is itself called the Eucharist; no one may eat of it who does not believe the truth taught and has not been washed by baptism; for it is not ordinary bread or wine, κοινὸν ἄρτον, but "in the very manner that Jesus Christ becoming incarnate by the word of God, had, for our salvation, both flesh and blood, so have we been taught that the food, which has been made a thanksgiving by the word of prayer which He gave us, by which food our own flesh and blood are, through a process of transformation, nourished, is both the flesh and the blood of that same incarnate Jesus." He proceeds to quote, from the books of the apostles, the account of the institution of the Last Supper, and compares it with the initiatory offerings in the mysteries of Mithra (*ib.* i. 65-66, § 97). In this passage the Incarnation is spoken of, as elsewhere, as the work of the Word Himself; though He is Himself the Incarnate One (cf. *ib.* i. 32, 74 B, ὁ λόγος ὃς σαρκοποιηθεὶς ἄνθρωπος γέγονεν). The principle of the Eucharist is found in the principle of the Incarnation (though the analogy is hardly to be pressed into details); it is the flesh and blood of Christ, taken for our salvation, that are identified with the food; which food is itself so intimately allied with our flesh and blood that it still nourishes our actual bodies κατὰ μεταβολήν, though it is the flesh and blood of Jesus, after the word of prayer, δι' εὐχῆς λόγου (by some rendered, "prayer of His word," cf. Otto's notes, p. 181 of 3rd ed.), which He Himself instituted, *i.e.* the words ordained by Christ, given by Justin as "Do this in remembrance of Me: this is My body: this is My blood." In the *Dialogue,* 117, § 345 A, Justin speaks again of the "dry and liquid food" in which memorial is made by Christians, according to a received institution, of the suffering of the Son of God, τὸ πάθος ὃ πέπονθε. This memorial is there identified with those prayers and thanksgivings, offered by holy people, which alone are the sacrifices perfect and well-pleasing to God, in contrast with the Jewish sacrifices, and in fulfilment of Mal. i. 10. These sacrifices (θυσίαι) occur at the Eucharist of the bread and of the cup; the spiritual sacrifice of praise is then and there alone accomplished, by God's injunction. Isa. xxxiii. 13 is fulfilled in the bread which our Christ ordered us (παρέδωκεν) to offer (ποιεῖν) for a memorial of His having taken to Himself a body, and so become passible (παθητός) (*Dial.* 70, § 296 E).

Justin mentions, beside the Eucharist which followed the baptism, that the Christians met every Sunday (ἡ τοῦ ἡλίου ἡμέρα), the day on which God began creation and raised Christ (*Apol.* i. 67, § 97). All came in who could, from country and town, to one place; the memorials of the apostles or the books of the prophets were read publicly; then, the leader preached and admonished; after which all rose together and prayed; then the Eucharist is administered as before described. At such times, offertories were made of voluntary gifts, laid in the hands of the leader, who distributed them to the sick, widows, etc. "Ever," says Justin, "do we remind ourselves of this rite" which followed our baptism; and "ever we live together; we who are rich give to the poor; and for everything that we have we bless the Creator of all through Jesus Christ and the Holy Spirit" (*ib.* i. 67); sending up to Him solemn prayers (πομπάς) and hymns, not deeming Him to be in need of blood and libations and sweet smells (*ib.* i. 13, § 60 C). Sunday, then, was observed as a peculiar day (cf. *Dial.* 24, 241 B); this is in contrast with σαββατίζειν, and "regarding the stars," which mean, distinctly, keeping the Jewish feasts; this the main body of Christians repudiated, so that it was by most treated as a criminal heresy to keep the sabbath, and they refused to hold communion with those Christians who still held to these Jewish customs. This severity Justin condemns; but his whole argument with Trypho accepts thoroughly the abolition of the Fourth Commandment. The sabbath symbolizes Moses, and Christians hope not in Moses but in Christ; the Christian does not think himself pious for keeping one day idle, but for keeping a continual sabbath. The sabbath was given for the hardness of the Jews' hearts (cf. *ib.* 10, § 227 B, etc.; 19, § 237 C; 21, § 238),

Justin's conception of the Law is very strong and decided. Definite as he is against Marcion, in his belief in the revelation of the true God made in O.T., he yet takes an extreme view of the partial, local and temporal character of the law. He bases himself, mainly, on his principle of the complete universality of God: God is everlasting, throughout all time, over all people; He is Judge of all the earth; His justice must be alike everywhere. Hence He cannot shut up His relations to man within the limits of a law addressed to a single people, and for a limited period of time (*Dial.* 23, § 240 E; 93, 320 C). Facts prove this: for God was well-pleased with Abel, Enoch, Noah, Melchisedec, though they were uncircumcised and kept no sabbaths (cf. *ib.* 19, § 236 C). Again, if virtue lay in the mere act of circumcision, women would be in a worse case than men (*ib.* 23, § 241 C). It would be against God's nature to value such rites, and limitations, and new sacrifices, for their own sake, as if the good lay in them. Did the Law, then, not come from Him? Yes; but God in it accommodated Himself to the Jews; it was for you Jews alone that it was necessary; because you forgot Him, He had to decree your sabbaths; because you fell away to idols, He had to demand of you sacrifices (*ib.* 19, § 236 E). He ordered you a temple, lest you should worship images. All was done to distinguish the Jewish race from the heathen; and this, not on account of the race's virtue, so much as for its proneness to evil. To justify this, Justin appeals to the "everlasting voice of prophecy"; he quotes the many words of the prophets in which sabbaths and sacrifices are declared unpleasing and unavailing. "I am not inventing all this," he says, but "this is what David sang, Isaiah preached, Zechariah proclaimed, Moses wrote" (*ib.* 29). Where the prophets insist on the laws, it was because of the people's sin (*ib.* 27, § 244 B). But Justin has, still, to account for the Law being, in a relative sense, worthy of God; and this He does by distinguishing two elements in it, one eternal, the other temporal; the two stand to each other chiefly as sign and reality; so Justin discovers in the temporal provisions of the Law allegories of eternal truths. This is what was meant when Moses gave minute rules about meats and herbs and drinks; it was to symbolize the moral laws (cf. *ib.* 20, § 237 C), but the Jewish people took it literally. They supposed, *e.g.*, some herbs to be evil, some good; while, in truth, God meant all to be good, if it was profitable to men. The circumcision under Joshua was allegorical (cf. *ib.* iii. § 332). So, again, meat was a symbol of Christ; so, too, the Passover Lamb, and the scape-goats (*ib.* 40, 41, § 259 A). But if the Law was allegorical, symbolic, it necessarily ceased when the reality came. So it ended with Christ Who has enabled us to sever the eternal from the temporal elements: He is the test and canon of what was real in the Law (*ib.* 67, § 292 C).

If Christ took away sin, He took away the reason for the Law; He gave us the circumcision of the heart, which made the carnal circumcision needless (cf. *βαπτίσθητε τὴν ψυχὴν ἀπὸ ὀργῆς καὶ ἰδού, τὸ σῶμα καθαρόν ἐστι*: *ib.* 14, 231 D). Justin does not consider that such a principle as this negatives the necessity of an outward baptism, or of an outward Sunday; for both these he holds. Prophecy speaks of a new covenant to be made in a Christ; and this for Jew as well as for Gentile, for both are to be saved in the same Christ (*ib.* 64, § 287 B). Why, then, did Christ keep the Law? Out of the economy of God; He accepted the Law as He accepted the Cross, and the becoming-man: it was in order to carry out the Father's will; but He was not justified by keeping the Law; otherwise He could not be the Saviour of all men (*ib.* 67, § 292 A) nor have introduced a new covenant. The admission of the eternal significance of Christ necessarily carries us back behind the Law, to the conditions under which all men had always lived (*ib.* 23, § 241 B).

The failure of the Jews to believe in the Christ is no argument for their being right; for it is foretold all along that the Gentiles are the children of prophecy, the true Israel, the perfect proselytes; it is of them that all the good promises are spoken. The whole of the end of the *Dialogue* is devoted to shewing this.

We realize in Justin the complete Gentilism of the Christianity of 140 A.D. He regards the Law rather as an evidence of peculiar evil, than of peculiar good, in the Jews; so he even says in scorn that circumcision only serves to mark them out for condemnation, as the accursed who are forbidden to enter Jerusalem; it enables the Romans to exclude them from the Holy Land.

But if Justin is hard upon the Law, he is very different towards Prophecy. On Prophecy, on Scripture, he relies absolutely; he asks to be believed, only so far as he can prove his truth by Scripture. It is the word of God, given by God through the Word, or chiefly through the Spirit. This is reiterated continually. The whole O.T. is as a great drama, with various actors, but of which there is a single author, the Spirit of God (*Apol.* i. 36, § 76 D). It is a unity; so that Justin does not believe that any one part can contradict any other; rather he would feel bound to confess his own ignorance, where such seemed the case (*Dial.* 65, § 289 C). His definition is: "Certain men existed among the Jews, God's prophets, through whom the prophetic spirit foretold things before they occurred" (*Apol.* i. 31, § 72 B). Moses he calls the first; after Moses he speaks of an "eternal prophecy going forth" (*ib.* i. 31; *Dial.* 30, § 247 A). They foretold Christ, His coming, His birth from a virgin, His man's estate, His curing disease and raising the dead, His being hated and despised and fixed to a cross, His death, resurrection, and ascension, His being, and being called, the Son of Uod, His sending out apostles, His success among the Gentiles (*Apol.* i. 31, § 73 A).

Justin offers a very storehouse of Christian interpretations of Scripture, such as cannot be classified briefly; the strongest lines lie:—

(1) In the exhibition of the divine plurality, through which Justin can, while retaining the absolute purity and separateness of God the Father such as the Jewish monotheism made imperative, yet justify and correlate all the manifold manifestations of Himself by God under local and temporal qualifications, all receiving their true and complete elucidation in the Incarnation. He Whose nature it is to be the expression and exhibition of the Father's will, was at the tent door with Abraham, in the dream with Jacob, in the burning bush with Moses, at the camp side with Joshua, above the cherubim with Isaiah, and now is made man of Mary (cf. *Dial.* 75, § 301 A).

(2) Justin ably gathers into one the many-sided characteristics of the Messianic prophecy—the many human, mingled with the many divine, names attributed to the Christ: He is man—yet to be adored; He is suffering, yet triumphant; He saves His people, He is rejected by His people. Justin, in the paradox of the Cross, has a key to the endless paradox of prophecy. All the shifting double-sided revelations of Godhead and manhood, of triumph and suffering, meet in a crucified king. He can give a unity of solution to a Christ Who is called "Angel of great Counsel" and "Man" by Ezekiel, "As a Son of man" by Daniel, "Servant" or "Child" by Isaiah, "Christ" and "God" and "Adorable" by David, "Christ" and "the Stone" by many, "Wisdom" by Solomon, "Joseph, Judah, and the Star" by Moses, "the Morning Star" by

Zechariah, "Suffering," and "Jacob," and "Israel" by Isaiah, and "Rod," and "Flower," and "Corner-stone" "cut without hands," and "Son of God," Who is "despised and rejected," yet also is proclaimed "King of Kings, King of Hosts, King of Glory," and is "Set on the right hand of God," "Born of a virgin," yet "Existent before all the world," "the power of God, the glory of God," "the Word," "the Lord," "the Captain of the Hosts," "King," "Priest," yet also "Man," "the Stone," "the Child," "the Sufferer" (*ib.* 126, § 355 B; 61, § 284 A; 34, § 251 D). In giving force to this last characteristic of the Christ, *i.e.* ὁ παθητός, at the same time that he gave reality to the highest title, ὁ θεὸς προσκυνητός, Justin shews his power over the Jew, who can only hover aimlessly between the two, unable to deal with or accept either the lowest or the highest. Justin declares that no one ever understood the prophecy of the sufferings, until Christ opened it to His apostles.

(3) He is powerful in his deduction from prophecy of the failure, unbelief, and ruin of the Jewish race—as the favoured people; and in the change of the manifestation of God from them to the Gentiles. Here he had much to use which was only a stumbling-block to strict Jewish reliance on blood and privilege.

(4) He is successful in exhibiting the *newness* of Christ's covenant, the *New* Law, the *New* Heart; under this conception the continual discontent of God with the old sacrifices and sabbaths gains intensity of meaning; the calls to wash and be clean, and put away sins, are vivified; the prophetic types of a new and wider dispensation are brought into daylight. Cf. the whole latter part of the *Dialogue.*

Where Justin is weakest is, naturally, in knowledge. He is ignorant of the original tongue and very arbitrary in his interpretation of details; he uses Christ as the accepted key to the whole complicated history, in a way that to a believer is often full of devotional suggestiveness, but to an unbeliever has no argumentative force. Instances may be found in such chaps. as 77, 78 of the *Dialogue,* or c. 81, etc. He often takes the wrong sense of a passage. He interprets the passages condemnatory of the Jewish sacrifices, etc., in a way that wins them a new meaning from Christ, but is certainly not their intended meaning. He can only meet Trypho's sharp criticism on this point by appealing to his own presumption that God's approval of the Law can only have been an accommodation to the people's sins (*Dial.* 27, § 244 B).

Prophecy is to Justin the main form of Christian evidences; and this for Gentile as much as for Jew. It is to prophecy he turns to prove that the Christian story of the Incarnation is not a poetic tale, without foundation; Greek mythology offers no testimony to its own reality (*Apol.* i. 54, § 89 A). Christ's miracles were no magic or conjuring because they were foretold (*ib.* i. 30, 31, § 72 A). Justin is shy of arguing from miracles: there had been too much false wonder-working for him to appeal to them. The miracles of the old Prophets he speaks of as worthy to win them credit, since they were coincident with a lofty desire to reveal God and with prophecy of Christ (*Dial.* 7, § 225 A). Christ's miracles are to be believed on the ground of prophecy (*Apol.* i. 30). Miracles are, to him, proofs, when they have been testified to, but cannot stand alone as evidence.

The other evidence to which Justin appeals is the (1) purity of Christian precepts (*Apol.* i. 14, § 61); (2) their constancy under torture (*ib.* ii. 12, § 50 A; *Dial.* 110, § 337 B); (3) the consecrated lives of uncorrupt virginity, the conversion of penitents to holiness (*Apol.* i. 15, 62 B, C; cf. *ib.* i. 29, § 71 E); (4) the exorcising of demons (*ib.* ii. 6, § 45 B); (5) the existence of prophetical gifts in the church (cf. *Dial.* 82, § 308 B), as well as of gifts of spiritual power (*ib.* 35, § 254 B), miracle, and healing (*ib.* 39, § 258 A).

We may briefly ask what knowledge Justin shows of (1) Jewish, and (2) Gentile learning.

(1) He refers frequently to Jewish modes of interpreting texts and seems used to dealing with them (cf. *ib.* 50, § 269 D); but perhaps he knows them rather in their polemic against Christians than in their own inner teaching. He charges them with escaping from texts against them by throwing doubts on the LXX, while all the Messianic texts that can be accommodated to human affairs they attach to whom they choose, but not to Christ (*ib.* 63, § 294 B). Thus they attribute the fulfilment of the triumphs spoken of in the Psalms to Solomon, in Isaiah to Hezekiah (*ib.* 64, § 287 A; 77, § 302 B). Justin does not seem to know of any Jewish theorizing on the problem of the Λόγος. The Jews expect a purely human Christ (*ib.* 49, § 268 A), to be heralded by Elias in person, and anointed by him; till which time the Christ is to be in obscurity; He will not even know Himself (*ib.* 110, § 336 C). The texts that speak of Christ as passible, yet as God and adorable, they are compelled, Justin says, to attribute to Christ, but they refuse to allow this Jesus to be the Christ, though they have to confess that the Christ will suffer and be worshipped. The divinity of Christ is, according to this, forced upon the Jews' belief by Christian logic, but they do not know what to make of it, and are in straits.

(2) As to Gentile philosophy, Justin's general knowledge was evidently large; but it is a question how far he held to any system accurately or scientifically; he sits pretty loosely to them all. He places Plato highest, and delights in his doctrine of Eternal Ideas, but no definite Platonic formulae are used; the Ideas do not appear; the doctrine of the Word has general relations to Platonism, but that is all; it is itself utterly unlike any teaching in Plato; it belongs to the process of thought which has its roots in O.T., and works through Philo up into Christianity. He gives us nothing of Plato's except the account of the "X" as the law of creation, in the Timaeus, which Justin supposes him to have taken from the account of the brazen serpent; and the statement of the triad character of things, which is taken from an epistle attributed till lately to Plato. He declares Plato's account of creation from formless matter to have been taken from Genesis; but he only means this in the most general way, for he seems to fancy that Plato's formula is consistent with Moses'

statement that this formless matter had itself been made by God (cf. *Apol.* i. 59, § 92 D). It is obvious that Justin's relation to Platonism is quite external; he holds the Christian formulae, and whenever he detects a likeness to them in Plato, he delights in bringing it out, without regard to context or system; these likenesses are entirely arbitrary and superficial, and can never be pressed. Justin's canon of truth is absolutely in Scripture; from that standpoint his kindly love for Plato pleases itself in exhibiting in him fragmentary resemblance to the truth; but if these fragments of truth are rooted in error, so much the worse for Plato; Justin has no idea of following them down. There is something to be said for his connexion with Stoicism; he approved their morals, and found them right, to some extent, as to the ultimate end of Nature; but objects strongly to their physical doctrines, their belief in fate, their physico-Pantheistic conception of God, by which they must either identify God with evil and change, or else deny the reality of evil (*ib.* ii. 7, 8); he considers their physics inconsistent with their ethics. Musonius and Heraclitus he honourably distinguishes; of the Epicureans he speaks scornfully (*ib.* ii. 15, § 52 B).

One problem remains to be considered, *i.e.* the relation of Justin to our four Gospels. The amount and frequency of his references to our Lord's life and words, in the generation immediately preceding the day in which the present Gospels emerge, secure and alone, into the full daylight of history, make him of salient importance in determining their character; and the state of the present controversy, which has detected the subtle transition, through which the gospel story passed, from the conditions of a living, oral tradition to those of formal written exemplars, increases the importance of Justin, as he begins the definite references to *written* records, of a fixed character, capable of being used for devotional purposes. Are these records identical in substance and in form with our Gospels?

(1) The substantial characteristics of our Lord's life, down even to minute details, are, obviously, the same for Justin as for us. We can compose, from his quotations, a full summary of the whole gospel life, from the angel's message to the Virgin until the ascension, entering into many particulars, illustrating prophecies, supplying the very words of our Lord, in many instances relating all the circumstances; and, as a whole, it is perfectly clear that the lines which limit and determine in detail our Gospel did so, too, to his. The same body of facts is selected; the same character, the same limits preserved, the same characteristics brought forward; the same motives, the same interests are concerned; the same prophetic aspects dwelt upon. This is noticeable, when we remember how very special and remarkable a choice must have been originally exercised upon our Lord's life, to select and retain the peculiar fragments, no more and no less, which are collected and sorted by our Synoptists.

(2) Justin makes some additions or changes in detail to this main story; so few that they can be mentioned and their character seen. He had a genealogy which, whether ours or not, he attributed to Mary, not to Joseph; Cyrenius he calls the first procurator of Judaea; our Lord's birthplace is a cave; the Magi come from Arabia; *all* the children in Bethlehem are killed; our Lord is not "comely of aspect"; He made ploughs and yokes, emblems of righteousness; the Baptist *sat* by Jordan; a fire shone in Jordan at our Lord's baptism, and the words from heaven complete the text of the second Psalm; the Jews ascribed our Lord's miracles to magic; John ceased his mission at our Lord's public appearance. The Lord said, "There shall be schisms and heresies"; and "In whatsoever I find you, in that will I judge you."

Of these several are, probably, confusions or amplifications of Justin's own; some represent additions found in various texts of our present Gospels, and were, probably, floating, popular, traditional interpretations of various passages. The only remaining points definitely distinct are, the home of the Magi, the cave of the Nativity, the posture of the Baptist, the two sayings of our Lord. Does Justin, then, take these from tradition or from any uncanonical gospel? We must hypothesize the gospel that he used, if it is not ours; for we have no relic of it in our hands, and here the remark seems convincing (Sanday, *Gospels in the Second Century*, p. 101) that this gospel, if it existed, belongs not to an earlier but to a *later* stage of the story than our canonical works.

That they were *books* that he used he tells us frequently; it is all "written"; the books are called by a name peculiar to Justin, ἀπομνημονεύματα τῶν Ἀποστόλων; they are records of our Lord's sayings and doings, written either by apostles or their followers (*Apol.* i. 66, § 98 B; *Dial.* 103, § 333 D). These books constitute τὸ εὐαγγέλιον (*ib.* 10, § 227 E); a quotation is referred to this εὐαγγέλιον (*ib.* 100, § 326 C); the ἀπομνημονεύματα are themselves called εὐαγγέλια, he tells us, if the text is right (*Apol.* i. 66). All this points obviously to the existence of various records, "written either by apostles or by their followers," constituting altogether a single story, τὸ εὐαγγέλιον. So far our Gospels exactly correspond. More than this, it is almost incredible that he should not have known *Matthew*, at least; besides the general mass of reference, which exhibits remarkable resemblance to this Gospel, he has marked notices that distinguish *Matthew* from the other forms of the evangelical tradition: the visit of the Magi, the descent into Egypt, Joseph's suspicions of Mary, texts, elsewhere unparalleled, from the Sermon on the Mount, the application of Is. xlii. 1-4 to the colt with the ass; above all, the comment of the disciples upon the identification of the Baptist with Elias (*Dial.* 49, § 269 A; Matt. xviii. 11-13), the expressions ἔνοχος εἰς (Matt. v. 22), ἀγγαρεύσει (v. 41), etc., etc. The resemblance to *Luke* in places where we can distinguish St. Luke's peculiar work from the general tradition are in a few cases almost impossible to resist, such as the quotation of xviii. 27 (*Apol.* i. 20, § 66); the use of the unique expression ἰσάγγελοι, xx. 35-36; and the most remarkable expressions at the annunciation, ἐπισκιάζειν δύναμις ὑψίστου, etc., which are directly Lucan. Cf., also, the last word on the cross. The only statement entirely peculiar to *Mark* is the naming of the sons of Zebedee. Thus not only is the whole body of quotation accounted for with a few rare exceptions, from our Gospels, but in some cases where SS. Matthew and Luke affect by their individuality the common original tradition Justin reproduces them.

The inexactness of quotation is the one opposing element. Justin is inexact, it is true, in his O.T. quotations, but he is more than three times as inaccurate in his N.T. ones. It is intensely difficult to know how much to discount for free combination which Justin uses extensively, how much for lack of memory, how much for mere paraphrase; or to determine, after such discounting, how much evidence remains to shew Justin's use of any other gospel besides our own. But if Justin used some form of the gospel not now in the canon, it was either a text used by the side of *Matthew* and *Luke*, and not differing from them in any degree more than they differ from each other; and if so, it would multiply the evidence for the authenticity of the narrative embodied in our canon; or else it was a text compounding and combining with some freedom the other two; and if so, it supposes these canonical gospels to be already the formal authorities. The supposition that Justin used a perfectly distinct form of the gospel story from any we now possess is met by the invincible difficulty that, though *ex hypothesi* of sufficient importance and acceptance to be used in the public offices of the metropolitan church as late as the boyhood of St. Irenaeus, it has, nevertheless, totally disappeared.

As to *John*, the main argument against its use is that from silence. Justin is full of doctrine on the subject of the Word, on the pre-existence and divine authority of Christ, yet no words from the Johannine discourses appear in his work. This argument has necessarily great weight, yet any single distinct reference to *John* must outweigh such a negative. Is there any such reference?

In *Dial.* 88 Justin attributes to the Baptist himself the words of the prophet, φωνὴ βοῶντος. This attribution is one of those remarkable distinctions peculiar to St. John's Gospel. We know of no other ground for it. Twice (in *Apol.* i. 22, § 68 B, and *Dial.* 69, § 296 A) he speaks of our Lord healing people infirm ἐκ γενετῆς: the only recorded instance of this is the blind man in Jn. ix. 20, ἐκ γενετῆς. In *Apol.* i. 61, Justin, it can hardly be doubted, is paraphrasing Jn. iii. 3-5. He is referring to a definite statement of our Lord; and the statement—a most marked and peculiar one—occurs here only. Justin refers to it in a way that makes it hardly possible to suppose him unacquainted with the continuation in *John.* In its context in the *Apology* the reference to the physical impossibility of a literal new birth is singularly awkward (cf. Otto, note *in loc.*). Justin, moreover, claims that he is believing Christ's own teaching when he believes in His Divine pre-existence; which would be more intelligible of *John* than of the other Gospels (*Dial.* 48, § 267 D). There is, again, a notice of our Lord (*ib.* 106, § 333) which receives its proper interpretation only in Jn. xiii. and xvii.; Christ, says Justin, knew that the Father gave everything to Him, and Himself demanded this. Such are the possible direct references, rare, indeed, but in one case, at least, remarkably noticeable. Indirectly, Justin holds a doctrine of the Word, clear, pronounced, decisive, such as finds no home or base for itself but in the Fourth Gospel. This doctrine Justin does not originate; it is the accepted, familiar, Christian faith put forth for the whole body, as their common belief, without hesitation, apology, anxiety, scruple, or uncertainty. It presents the exact features of the Johannine teaching; the universalism of the Philonic Λόγος is identified with, and made concrete by, the living, vivid individualism of the Incarnate Messiah. The synthesis is done, is complete, without confusion or doubt. Justin is as definite, as full of sanctioned certainty on the reality of this doctrine of the Incarnate Word, as he is on the facts and discourses represented by our Synoptists. The Life of our Lord is already for him the Life as it is in fusion with the dogma of the Word—the Life as it is under the manipulation that is displayed in the Fourth Gospel. Have we any cause of sufficient force to have achieved so decided a result but the Gospel of St. John? (Cf. Thoma, in *Zeitsch. für Wissenschaft. Theolog.* pt. 4 (1875, Leipz.): an elaborate discussion which concludes, "Justin *cites* only the Synopt., but he thinks and argues with the Fourth Gospel, evidencing its existence, but not its apostolicity"; but cf. on last point, Westcott, *Canon of N.T.* p. 100.)

In connexion with this there must be mentioned a passage in *Dial.* 123, § 353 B, in which, if not the gospel, then the first ep. of St. John can hardly be supposed absent from the writer's mind. The peculiar conjunction of καλούμεθα καὶ ἐσμέν is essentially Johannine (I. John iii. 1, 2); as is the connexion of "sonship" with keeping τὰς ἐντολάς. Justin, again, knows the writings of the Valentinians, and this (according to the evidence of Hippolytus and Irenaeus) must have involved a knowledge of the Fourth Gospel. Altogether, the problem presented by his not quoting *John* is far easier to solve than the problem of his not knowing it.

As to the rest of the canon, Justin mentions the Apocalypse by name, attributing it to St. John (*Dial.* 81, § 308 A). He can hardly but be thinking of *Romans* in *ib.* 23, § 241 B. He has references to *I. Corinthians* (*ib.* 14, § 231 D; 111, § 333 C; *Apol.* 1, 60, § 93), and to *II. Thessalonians* (*Dial.* 32, § 110). He constantly repeats the πρωτότοκος πάσης κτίσεως, which suggests *Colossians*; he has references which seem to recall *Hebrews* (*ib.* 13, § 229 D; *Apol.* i. 12, § 60, ἀπόστολος . . . Ἰησοῦς Χριστός); his words appear in several places to point to *Acts* (cf. *Apol.* 50, § 86 B; 40, § 79 A). Everywhere he exhibits traces of St. Paul; and his controversy with Marcion must have involved a complete acquaintance with the theology and language of the great apostle.

Throughout Justin claims to shew forth, with a certainty attested by sacrifice and death, a solid body of certified doctrine, which *apostolic* authority sealed and secured; Christ, as He had been foretold by prophets and announced to the world by apostles, is the assured ground of his faith (cf. *Dial.* 119, § 343 A; *Apol.* i. 39, 42). The apostles are the twelve bells on the border of the high-priest's garment, with the sound of whose ringing the whole world has been filled (*Dial.* 42, § 263 C); the apostles are the evangelical preachers in whose person Isaiah cried, "Lord, who hath believed our report?" the apostles are "the brethren in the midst of whom" Christ gives praise unto God (*ib.* 106, § 333 C). The *Apologies* have been pub. in Eng. in the *Ante-Nic. Fathers* (T. & T. Clark) and in a cheap form in the *A. and M. Theol. Lib.* (Griffith). [H.S.H.]

Justinus (3), a Gnostic writer, author of several books, only known to us by the abstract which Hippolytus (*Ref. Haer.* v. 23, p. 148) has given of one of them, called the book of Baruch. The account which that book gives of the origin and history of the universe makes it to have sprung from three underived principles, two male, one female. The first of these is the Good Being, and has no other name; He is perfect in knowledge, and is remote from all contact with the created world, of which, however, He is afterwards described as the Ultimate Cause. It is the knowledge of this Good Being which alone deserves the name, and it is from the possession of it that these heretics claimed the title of Gnostics. The second principle is called Elohim, the Father of the creation, deficient in knowledge, but not represented as subject to evil passion. The third, or female principle, identified with the earth, is called Eden and Israel, destitute of knowledge and subject to anger, of a double form, a woman above the middle, a snake below. Of her, Elohim becomes enamoured, and from their intercourse spring 24 angels—12 paternal, who co-operate with their father and do his will, and 12 maternal, who do the mother's will. The principal part is played by the third paternal angel, Baruch, the chief minister of good, and the third maternal, Naas, or the serpent, the chief author of evil.

Lipsius regards this work of Justinus as probably written later than the middle of 2nd cent., representing in its fundamental ideas one of the oldest, perhaps the very oldest, form of Gnosticism, and as exhibiting the passage of Jewish Christianity into Gnosis. We cannot share this view. On comparing the system of Justinus with that of the Ophite sect described by Irenaeus (i. 30), the points of contact are found to be too numerous to be all accidental. In the system of these Ophites the commencement is made with two male principles, and one female. On the whole, we feel bound to refer the system of Justinus to the latest stage of Gnosticism, when a philosophy, in which any unproved assumption was regarded as sufficiently justified by any remote analogy, had reached its exhaustion, and when its teachers were forced to seek for novelty by wilder and more audacious combinations; and we are not disposed to quarrel with the verdict of Hippolytus that he had met with many heretics, but never a worse one than Justinus. [G.S.]

Justinus (12) **I.,** proclaimed emperor (July 9, 518) on the death of the emperor Anastasius by the troops under his command and by the people (*Chron. Pasch.* 331, in *Patr. Gk.* xcii. 858), the choice being approved by the senate (Marcell. *Chron.*). He was a man of no education, and the affairs of the state were managed chiefly by his prudent minister Proclus the quaestor and afterwards by his nephew and eventual successor Justinian. For the most memorable event of his reign, the end of the schism between the Eastern and Western churches, see HORMISDAS. For his relations with Persia see CHOSROES I. in *D. C. B.* (4-vol. ed.).

In 523 Justin issued a constitution against the Manicheans and other heretics (*Codex*, i. tit. v. 12). The former were punished with exile or death; other heretics, pagans, Jews, and Samaritans, were declared incapable of holding a magistracy or entering military service. The allied Goths were exempted from these provisions. Because of the persecution of his Arian co-religionists, Theodoric sent pope John I. in 525 to Constantinople to remonstrate with the emperor. [EPIPHANIUS (17)]

In Apr. 527 Justin caused Justinian, who had long taken the chief part in government, to be proclaimed emperor and crowned, and on Aug. 1 died, in his 75th year. [F.D.]

Justinus (13) **II.,** emperor, nephew of Justinian, son of his sister Vigilantia. He was appointed Curopalates or Master of the Palace by his uncle (Corip. i. 138). The night Justinian died, a deputation of the senate, headed by the patrician Callinicus, hurried to his house and persuaded him to accept the crown. In the early morning he was saluted emperor by the populace in the hippodrome. The same day (Nov. 14, 565) he was crowned by the patriarch John (Theophan. *Cron.* in *Patr. Gk.* cviii. 525), and received the homage of the senate and people in the hippodrome.

Justin, on his accession, declared himself an adherent of the decrees of Chalcedon, and restored to their sees the bishops who had been banished by his predecessor (Venantius Fortunatus, *ad Justinum*, 25-26, 39-44, in *Patr. Lat.* lxxxviii. 432). The edict is given in probably a corrupt form by Evagrius (*H. E.* v. 1, in *Patr. Gk.* lxxxvi. 2789), and also by Nicephorus Callistus (*H. E.* xvii. 33). Soon afterwards another edict was published, given at length by Evagrius (*H. E.* v. 4), in which, after setting forth the orthodox belief as to the doctrines of the Trinity and the Incarnation, he exhorted all to return to the Catholic Church, which should remain firm and unchanged for ever; and that no one should for the future dispute about persons or syllables, probably referring to the person of Theodore and the writings of Theodoret and Ibas, and also to the question as to the Incorruptibility of the body of Christ. This edict gained general approval, as all interpreted it in favour of their own views, but none of the various sects returned to communion, in consequence of the emperor's declaration that no change was to be made in the church. Justin also early in his reign sent Photinus, the stepson of Belisarius, with full powers to reconcile the churches of Egypt and Alexandria, but his mission seems to have been fruitless.

For the secular events of his reign see JUSTINUS II., *D. of G. and R. Biogr.*

In May 568 a rescript was issued to Spes-in-Deum, the archbp. of the Byzacene province in Africa, confirming the privileges of his church and synod by which he was the sole judge of charges brought against any bishops or clergy within his jurisdiction, and in Nov. (Clinton, *Fasti*, 825) a law (*Nov.* cxlix.) was promulgated addressed to the bishops and leading men of each province directing them to choose the governors (*praesides*) themselves and to submit the names to the emperor, who would invest them with their offices. At the end of 570 or the beginning of 571, Anastasius, bp. of Antioch, was deposed and Gregorius substituted in his place. [ANASTASIUS SINAITA (1); GREGORIUS (31).] On May 18, 572, a stringent law was passed against the Samaritans (*Nov.* cxliv.). They were declared incapable of inheriting under a will or an intestacy and of exercising testamentary powers except in favour of Christians. Otherwise the goods of the deceased were forfeited to the treasury. For the sake of agriculture farmers were exempted from these provisions. Samaritans were also declared incapable of holding any civil or military employments. Baptized Samaritans who observed the sabbath or other rites of their creed were punished with perpetual exile. A Samaritan was declared incapable of having a Christian slave; if he bought one, the slave *ipso facto* became entitled to his freedom; while a Samaritan slave became free on embracing Christianity. Justin at length was seized with madness, and died, Oct. 5, 578, after reigning nearly 13 years. [F.D.]

Juvenalis (2) succeeded Praylius as bp. of Jerusalem *c.* 420. The ruling object of his episcopate was the elevation of the see of Jerusalem from the subordinate position it held in accordance with the seventh of the canons of Nicaea, as suffragan to the metropolitan see of Caesarea, to a primary place in the episcopate. Juvenal coveted not merely metropolitan, but patriarchal rank, and in defiance of all canonical authority claimed jurisdiction over the great see of Antioch, from which he sought to remove Arabia and the two Phoenicias to his own province. Scarcely had he been consecrated bp. of Jerusalem when he proceeded to assert his claims to the metropolitan rank by his acts. A letter of remonstrance against the proceedings of the council of Ephesus, sent to Theodosius by the Oriental party, complains that Juvenal had ordained in provinces over which he had no jurisdiction (Labbe, *Concil.* iii. 728). Cyril of Alexandria wrote to Leo, then archdeacon of Rome, informing him of this and begging that his unlawful attempts might have no sanction from the apostolic see. Juvenal, however, was far too useful an ally against Nestorius for Cyril lightly to discard. When the council met at Ephesus, Juvenal was allowed to take precedence of his metropolitan of Caesarea and to occupy the position of vice-president of the council, coming next after Cyril himself (*ib.* iii. 445), and was regarded in all respects as the second prelate in the assembly. The arrogant assertion of his supremacy over the bp. of Antioch, and his claim to take rank next after Rome as an apostolical see, provoked no open remonstrance. At the "Latrocinium" Juvenal occupied the third place, after Dioscorus and the papal legate, by the special order of Theodosius (*ib.* iv. 109). When the council of Chalcedon met, one of the matters before it was the dispute as to priority between Juvenal and Maximus, bp. of Antioch. The contention ended in a compromise agreed on in the Seventh Action. Juvenal surrendered his claim to the two Phoenicias and to Arabia, on condition of being allowed metropolitical jurisdiction over the three Palestines (*ib.* iv. 613). The claim to patriarchal authority over the bp. of Antioch put forward at Ephesus was discreetly dropped. The terms arranged between Maximus and Juvenal received the consent of the assembled bishops (*ib.* 618). Maximus, however, soon repented his too ready acquiescence in Juvenal's demands, and wrote a letter of complaint to pope Leo, who, replying June 11, 453, upheld the authority of the Nicene canons, and promised to do all he could to maintain the ancient dignity of the see of Antioch (Leo Magn. *Ep. ad Maximum*, 119 [92]). No further action, however, seems to have been taken either by Leo or by Maximus. Juvenal was left master of the situation, and the church of Jerusalem from that epoch has peaceably enjoyed the patriarchal dignity.

On the opening of the council at Ephesus, June 22, 431, Juvenal took a prominent part in the condemnation of Nestorius. As one of the eight legates deputed by the council, he aided in the consecration of Maximian in Nestorius's room, Oct. 25, 431 (Labbe, iii. 780; Baluz 571 seq.). In retaliation, John of Antioch and the Orientals on their way back from Ephesus held a synod at Tarsus, which excommunicated Cyril and the deputies of the council, Juvenal at their head (Baluz. 939).

When, in 449, the "Latrocinium" met at Ephesus, Juvenal was the first to sign the instrument of Flavian's deposition (Labbe, iv. 306). The natural consequence of this open patronage of heresy was that the name of Juvenal, together with those of Dioscorus and the other bishops of the "Latrocinium," was removed from the diptychs of Rome and other orthodox churches (Leo Magn. *Ep. ad Anatolium*, 80 [60]). This alarmed Juvenal, and he faced completely round at Chalcedon in 451, denouncing the doctrines he had supported two years before at Ephesus. The place he occupied in the council indicated that he had been compelled to abate somewhat of his overweening pretensions. Anatolius of Constantinople and Maximus of Antioch both took precedence of him, as did the Roman legates and Dioscorus (Labbe, iv. 79 *et passim*). The proceedings had not advanced far when Juvenal, seeing the course events were taking, rose up with the bishops of Palestine in his train, and crossed over from the right, where he had been sitting with the Alexandrine prelates, to the Orientals on the left amid shouts of "Welcome, orthodox one! It is God Who has brought thee over here" (*ib.* 178). This desertion of his old friends barely saved him. Evidence being read as to the violence with which Flavian's condemnation had been enforced, and the brutality with which he had been treated, the imperial commissioners proposed Juvenal's deposition, together with that of Dioscorus, Eusebius, and the others who had taken a leading part in these disgraceful transactions (*ib.* 323). Juvenal evidently felt that consistency must now be sacrificed to the maintenance of his position, and having given his vote and signature to the deposition of Dioscorus (*ib.* 458) and signed the tome of Leo (*ib.* 798), the objections of the commissioners were overruled. Juvenal and his four companions were allowed to resume their seats, amid a shout of welcome, "This is the Lord's doing." "Many years to the orthodox! This is the peace of the churches" (*ib.* 509). He subsequently took part in drawing up the declaration of faith (*ib.* 559-562) and signed the letter sent to Leo (Baluz. 1370). We have a Latin translation of a synodical letter written in his own name and that of the bishops of Palestine, A.D. 453, to the archimandrites, presbyters, and monks of the province confirming the decrees of Chalcedon (Labbe, iv. 889).

His enjoyment of his newly acquired dignity was speedily disturbed. The decrees of Chalcedon were not at all acceptable to a large number of the archimandrites and monks of Palestine, who generally held Eutychian views, and they, in 452, addressed letters to Marcian and to Pulcheria against the conduct of their bishop. The emperor and empress administered severe rebukes to the remonstrants (*ib.* 874, 879). The imperial displeasure, however, failed to repress the turbulence of the malcontents, and under the leadership of Theodosius, a fanatical Monophysite monk, patronized by the empress-dowager Eudocia, who had made Jerusalem her home, they threw the whole province into confusion. Juvenal's life was threatened. The walls and gates were guarded to prevent his escape. But he concealed himself, and together with Domnus made his way to the desert, whence he fled to Constantinople and laid his complaints against Theodosius and his partisans before the emperor (*ib.* 858; Cyrill. Scythop. *Euthym. Vit.* 82; Evagr. *H. E.* ii. 5; Theophan. p. 92). Marcian took decided measures to restore order. After holding possession for two years, Theodosius was expelled from Jerusalem, 453, and Juvenal was restored. Eudocia returned to Jerusalem, and renewed communion with Juvenal, her example proving influential to bring back the large majority both of monks and laity to the cathedral church (*Euthym. Vit.* 86). One of Juvenal's first acts on his restoration was to hold a council which issued a synodical letter to the two Palestines, declaring the perfect orthodoxy of the decrees of Chalcedon and denying that anything had there been altered in, or added to, the Nicene faith (Labbe, iv. 889). Mutual ill-will and suspicion still embittered the relations of Juvenal to his province, and Evagrius complains of the evils which had followed his return (Evagr. *H. E.* ii. 5). Leo (Sept. 4, 454) offered congratulations on his restoration, but told him plainly that he had brought his troubles on himself by his condemnation of Flavian and admission of the errors of Eutyches, and that having favoured heretics he cannot now blame them. Leo expressed his satisfaction that he had come to a better mind, and advised him to study his tome to confirm him in the faith (Leo Magn. *Ep.* 139 [171]). In 457 Leo addressed Juvenal among the metropolitans of the East, with reference to the troubles at Alexandria, urging him to defend the faith as declared at Chalcedon (*Ep.* 150 [119]).

The statement of Basil of Seleucia that Juvenal first "began to celebrate the glorious and adorable salvation-bringing nativity of the Lord" (*Patr. Gk.* lxxxv. 469) must be interpreted to mean that he separated the celebration of the Nativity and the Epiphany, which, till then, had been kept on the same day, Jan. 6. We may gather from a letter professing to be addressed by the bp. of Jerusalem to the bp. of Rome that this change was in accordance with the Western practice. Basil of Seleucia, being a contemporary of Juvenal and associated with him in his public acts, may be regarded as trustworthy evidence for the fact. According to Basil, Juvenal built a basilica in honour of St. Stephen on the site of his martyrdom, for which the empress Eudocia furnished the funds. The death of Juvenal probably occurred in 458 (cf. Tillem. *Note sur Juvenal*, xv. 867). He was succeeded by Anastasius. Tillem. *Mém. eccl.* xv.; Ceillier, xiii. 247; Cave, *Script. Eccl.* i. 419; Oudin, i. 1270.) [E.V.]

Juvencus, C. Vettius Aquilinus, a Christian poet, by birth a Spaniard, descended from a noble family. He was a presbyter, and composed his poem on the gospels during the reign of peace established by Constantine (*Hist. Ev.* iv. 808 sqq.; Hieron. *de Vir. Ill.* c. 84; Ep. lxx. *Chronica* ad 332 A.D.). His works shew an acquaintance with the chief Latin poets.

(i) *Historia Evangelica.* This is the only extant work attributed to him on the authority of St. Jerome. It is an hexameter poem on our Lord's life, based upon the gospels. It is of interest as the first Christian epic, the first effort to tell the gospel story in a metrical form. Its chief merit lies in its literal adherence to the text. Commencing with the events of Luke i. ii. (i. 1-258), it passes to the account of St. Matthew (i. 18), and follows that to the end, omitting only a few short passages (xiii. 44-53, xx. 29-34, xxi. 10-13, xxiii. 15-26, 29-36, xxiv. 28), rarely supplemented from the other Synoptists (v. i. 355, ii. 43), but having large extracts from St. John, viz. i. 43–iv. (lib. ii. 99-348), v. 19-47 (ii. 639 sqq.), xi. (iv. 306-404). It is saved from baldness by a clear fluent style, which shews a knowledge of Vergil, Ovid, and Lucan. It seems to have been widely known from the first and quoted with approval by St. Jerome (*ad* Matt. ii. 11), pope Gelasius, Venantius Fortunatus (*de Vita S. Martini*, 1), Isidore, Jonas Scotus, Bede, and Alcuin (Migne, *Prolegg.* col. 42 sqq.). It has been edited no less than 30 times. The best separate edd. are by Reusch (Frankfort, 1710); Arevalo (Rome, 1792) (reprinted in Migne); and esp. Huemer (Vienna, 1891) in *Corpus Script. Eccl. Lat.* xxiv. Cf. Gebser, *de C. Vett. Aq. Vita et Scriptis* (lib. i. with intro. and notes), Jena, 1827; C. Marold, *Ueber d. Evang.-buch des Juvencus in seinen Verhältniss z. Bibeltext in Zeitschr. für wissenschaft. Theol.* xxxiii. p. 329 (1890); *Kritische Beiträge zur Hist. Evang. des Juvencus* von Dr. J. Huemer in *Wiener Studien* (Vienna, 1880), pp. 81-112.

(ii) St. Jerome (*u.s*) attributes to him "nonnulla eodem metro ad sacramentorum ordinem pertinentia," but these are not extant.

(iii) *Historia Vet. Testamenti.* Only extant in parts, and its authorship doubtful.

(iv) Some later writers attribute hymns to him, but there is no trace of any except the canticles in *Hist. Ev.* and *Hist. Vet. Test.* [W.L.]

K

Kentigern (*Conthigernus, Cyndeyrn, Kentegernus, Quentigern, Mongah, Munghu, Mungo*, bp. of Glasgow and confessor). St. Kentigern shares, with St. Ninian and St. Columba, the highest honour among the early evangelizers of Scotland. The time, extent, and sphere of St. Kentigern's missionary enterprise are sufficiently recognized. Strictly speaking, there is only one Life of St. Kentigern known, that by Joceline of Furness, written probably *c.* 1180, for bp. Joceline of Glasgow (A.D. 1174-1199), from two earlier memoirs, but there is an older fragment which was probably one of the two used by him. From these all others are derived.

St. Kentigern, perhaps better and more popularly known as St. Mungo, was a Strathclyde Briton. His parentage is doubtful. He was born at Culross in Perthshire. From his master there he secretly departed, and travelling westward, crossing the Forth probably near Alloa, arrived at Carnock near Stirling, and thence was led by the oxen which carried the corpse of Fregus to Cathures, now Glasgow, where St. Ninian had already consecrated a cemetery. There he took up the unfinished work of St. Ninian. The picture presented of the time and field of his labour is a deplorable one. He was consecrated by a single bishop, called for the purpose from Ireland (c. 11). He was raised to the episcopate in his 25th year (c. 12), but all we know of the date is that it was before his departure to Wales. Ussher places it in 540, which is accepted by Stubbs (*Reg. Sacr. Angl.* 157). At Glasgow he formed a monastic school, and a beautiful account is given (cc. 12-18) of the man, his austere life and humble piety. He had a wide province, which he traversed mostly on foot, and his message was to the lapsed from the faith and to the morally degraded, as well as to the ignorant pagans. The disorders in the kingdom, and probably the increasing power of the pagan faction, induced the bishop to leave his see and find refuge in Wales a few years after his consecration (A.D. 543, Ussher). On his way he spent some time in Cumberland, where his work is marked by churches still dedicated to him (c. 23); thence he advanced as far as Menevia, where he visited St. David, and then appears to have returned northwards, settling for a time on the banks of the Clwyd and building his church at its confluence with the Elwy, at Llanelwy, now St. Asaph's, in Flintshire (cc. 23-25), *c.* 545 (Stubbs). The monastery which he erected at Llanelwy was soon filled. Old and young, rich and poor, prince and peasant, flocked to it, and we have a very graphic picture of how monasteries were raised in ancient days before stone was used for such erections, and how the *laus perennis* was carried out in large communities, such as this must have been with its 965 brethren in their "threefold division of religious observance" (cc. 24-25).

Meanwhile the sovereign had changed, and, as a direct consequence, the religious feeling of the kingdom of Strathclyde. Rhydderch Hael, son of Tudwal Tudglud, had come to the throne, and at the battle of Ardderyd (now Arthuret, on the Esk near Carlisle), had defeated (573) the heathen party under Gwendolen, at Ceidio, whereby his kingdom was made to extend from the Clyde to the Mersey, and thus to the confines of St. Kentigern's Welsh see. The first-fruit of this battle was the recall of St. Kentigern to his Cumbrian diocese by Rhydderch, who, himself of Irish extraction, had received the Christian faith during his exile in Ireland. This date is of importance, giving one fixed point in St. Kentigern's chronology. Rhydderch's call he at once obeyed; and consecrating his disciple St. Asaph to fill his place in N. Wales, returned to Strathclyde, but went no farther than Holdelm (now Hoddam, Dumfriesshire), where for some years (probably eight) he had his episcopal seat. His leaving Llanelwy was a cause of much lamentation, and a great number of the monks accompanied him. At Hoddam a joyous welcome was given to the saint by king Rhydderch, who is represented (cc. 31-33) as going out with his people to meet him and as conceding to him all power over himself and his posterity. At Glasgow the still more famous meeting took place between St. Columba and St. Kentigern. The districts they evangelized were contiguous. Their meeting was typical of the two currents of Christian faith and practice running alongside and overflowing the land—viz. the Irish and the Welsh—which were to come in contact again at the great rampart of the Grampian range and give their character to the Scotic and the Pictish churches. The dedications to the N. of Glasgow, and on Deeside in Aberdeenshire, make it probable that St. Kentigern had extended his labours into the regions of the South Picts, and up, at least, to the dividing line between them and the Northern. His death is variously dated from 601 to 614; the Welsh authorities generally giving 612, as in *Annales Cambriae*; but the true date is probably 603 (Skene, *Celt. Scot.* ii. 197 n.; Bp. Forbes, *Lives*, etc., 369-370). He died on Sun., Jan. 13, and was buried where the cathedral of Glasgow now stands. The favourite name in dedications is St. Mungo. There are none to him in Wales, but there are in Cumberland at Aspatria, Bromfield, Caldbeck, Crosfeld (in Kirkland), Crosthwaite, Grinsdale, Lethington, Mungrisedale (in Greystock), and Sowerby. His chief dedication and episcopal seat, which, as in like cases, was near, but not quite at the ancient civil capital, Alclwyd or Dumbarton, is the cathedral church of Glasgow; and there appears to have been a Little St Mungo's kirk outside the city walls. [J.G.]

L

Lactantius (1), Lucius Caelius (or **Caecilius) Firmianus**, a well-known Christian apologist of the beginning of the 4th cent.: "Rhetor erat ille, non theologus: neque inter ecclesiae doctores locum unquam obtinuit," as bp. Bull says of him (*Def. Fid. Nic.* ii. 14, 4, and iii. 10, 20). Lactantius, enumerating previous Christian apologists, seems only conscious of three—Minucius Felix, Tertullian, and St. Cyprian—but this is explained by supposing that he limits himself to his countrymen, viz. African apologists. St. Jerome mentions an *Itinerary* written by him, in hexameter verse, of his route from Africa to Nicomedia, as though he were then leaving home for the first time. The African church produced, as did no other country, a succession of learned advocates or rhetoricians, men of the world, who embraced Christianity from conviction, and wrote vigorously in its defence, culminating in St. Augustine, each employing Latin with the freedom of a vernacular, and in the case of Lactantius with so much purity as to have procured for him the title of the Christian Cicero; while Italy produced no Christian apologists and, till St. Ambrose, no great theologian. Divines and men of letters, as well as emperors, had to be sought in the provinces. In all his empire Constantine could find no better preceptor for his eldest son Crispus, then destined to succeed him at Rome, than this African Latin. This brought him to Gaul *c.* 313, the first date we can fix in his career on any tangible grounds. Lactantius had previously been invited to set up a school of rhetoric at Nicomedia. There, doubtless, he was converted on witnessing the superhuman constancy displayed by the Christians, and by his "best beloved" Donatus in particular, on whose sufferings in the tenth and savagest persecution, under Diocletian, he dwells with so much tenderness (*de Morte Persecut.* cc. 16, 35, and 52). Donatus, he tells us himself, had lain in prison six years when the edict of Galerius, published A.D. 311, procured his release. In Gaul, Lactantius died, perhaps in the year of the Nicene council, A.D. 325. To judge from his extant writings, he must have been somewhat austere, soured it may be by failures, as he had no mean estimate of his own powers (*de Opif. Dei*, c. 1; *Inst.* v. 1-4): a man of few and warm rather than of many friends; thoughtful, learned, conscientious, and pure. Eusebius (*Chron.* A.D. 319) speaks of him as having always been so poor as frequently to have lacked the necessaries of life. St. Jerome says it was his ill-success in getting pupils at Nicomedia, from its being a Greek city, that induced him to write. St. Jerome gives a list of his writings, but whether in the order in which they were published or not he omits to say. The first he names is the *Symposium*, which he calls a youthful performance; the second is the *Itinerary*; the third, the *Grammarian*. Then comes the well-known treatise *de Irâ Dei*, still extant, which St. Jerome calls *pulcherrimum;* next, his *Institutions*, in seven books, extant also, on which his fame principally rests; next, his own epitome of the same work, *In Libro uno acephalo* ("a compendium of the last three books only," as Cave explains it; but the first half was claimed by Pfaff to have been recovered A.D. 1712 from a Turin MS., and its genuineness, though disputed, is still maintained). The seventh work named by St. Jerome was in two books, addressed to Asclepiades; both are now lost. The eighth, which had disappeared also, was claimed by Baluze as recovered by him; it was published in 1679 at the commencement of his second book of *Miscellanies*, but with the title *Liber ad Donatum Confessorem de Mortibus Persecutorum*, instead of *de Persecutione Liber unus*, which is that of St. Jerome. Judged by its contents, the first is the more accurate title. His four books of letters to Probus, two to Severus, and two to his pupil Demetrian, which St. Jerome regards as eight consecutive books (in Gal. ii. 4), are lost. The twelfth and last work assigned to him by St. Jerome is *de Opificio Dei, vel Formatione Hominis*. The tract *de Morte Persecutorum* ends with the joint edict of Licinius and Constantine, published at Nicomedia by the former, A.D. 313, at which the author lays down his pen in celebrating the triumph of God, with thankful joy and prayers day and night for its continuance. He could not have written thus after the differences between Licinius and Constantine had commenced, and the former joined the ranks of the persecutors; he therefore probably published it when leaving Nicomedia for Gaul. The first chapter of his tract *de Opificio Dei* shews it to have been written after, probably only just after, his conversion, and "Quam minime sim quietus, et in summis necessitatibus" are just the words that might have been wrung from a recent convert in a heathen capital, where Christians were having to choose daily between death and their faith, and his old pupils were leaving him on learning what he had become. Supposing Lactantius to have been converted about midway in the persecution under Diocletian at Nicomedia, and then betaken himself to writing, *penuriâ discipulorum*, as St. Jerome says, there was abundance of time for the composition of all his extant works during the rest of his abode there, with the exception of his *Epitome.* His *Epitome* and the confessedly later insertions in his *Institutions*—*e.g.* his appeals to Constantine (i. 1, ii. 1, vii. 26), his mention of the Arians, and of the Catholic church, his promise of a separate work on heresies (iv. 30) which it would seem he never fulfilled—would all naturally fall within the period of his removal to Gaul and tutorship to the heir-apparent, to whom he could have scarce failed to dedicate any fresh work, had such been afterwards written. Was he the pupil or hearer of Arnobius in his younger days that St. Jerome makes him in one place (*de Vir. Illust.* c. 80), or contemporary with Arnobius, as we might infer from another (*Chron.* A.D. 326)? There is nothing in their works to connect them, and at the commencement of his fifth book, in specifying, *ex iis qui mihi noti sunt* (c. 1), those who had written against the assailants of Christianity previously to himself, he could scarcely have passed over the work of Arnobius, if already published, and still less if Arnobius, besides being an African, had been his old preceptor. We therefore prefer following St. Jerome in his continuation of Eusebius, and making Lactantius and Arnobius independent: Lactantius possibly the older of the two. Eusebius finds a place for Lactantius in his *Chronicon*, but none for his supposed master. The work of

Arnobius is limited to a refutation of the polytheism of the day and the popular objections to Christianity; that of Lactantius, like the *City of God* by St. Augustine, which cites Lactantius with approval (xviii. 23), first exposes the false religions, but also expounds the true. It has been analysed by Cave briefly (*Hist. Lit.* i. 162), by Le Nourry thoroughly (*ap.* Migne, *Patr. Lat.* vi. 825), by Dupin, with his accustomed vivacity (*E. H.* vol. i. 185-187, Eng. trans. by W. W.), and by Mountain (*Summary of the Writings of Lactantius*, i. 129). It is trans. in full, with notes, in the *Ante-Nicene Lib.* (T. & T. Clark).

The tract *de Opificio Dei* may challenge comparison with Cicero's *de Naturâ Deorum* in point of style and is far superior to it in depth and originality. The tract *de Irâ Dei*, against the Epicureans and Stoics, is intended to prove God as capable of anger as of compassion and mercy. The tract *de Morte Persecutorum* is a collection of historical facts tending to show that all the emperors who persecuted the Christians died miserably, and may be compared with Spelman's *de non Temerandis Ecclesiis* of modern times.

As for his theology, the indulgence should be shewn him that all breakers of new ground may claim. Tertullian was the model that he looked up to most: and no writer had as yet eclipsed Origen. His account of the origin of all things (*Inst.* ii. 9) reminds us of the speeches of Raphael and Abdiel in *Paradise Lost* (v. 577 and 808). We cannot read his latest exposition of the Incarnation (*Epit.* c. 43) without discovering in it some well-known phrases of the Athanasian Creed—*e.g.* "The same person is the Son of God and of man, for He was twice born: first of God in the Spirit before the origin of the world; and afterwards in the flesh of man, in the reign of Augustus." Dupin, after having expatiated on his many merits, sums up very justly: "He is accused of doubting whether the Holy Ghost was the third Person, and to have sometimes confounded him with the Son, and sometimes with the Father; but it may be alleged in his defence that he meant nothing else but that the name of the Spirit in Scripture is common to the Father and the Son. But whatever the matter is, we find no footsteps of this error in any of his works, what are now remaining; though in some places he takes occasion to speak of the Holy Ghost. He seems to be of opinion that the Word was generated in time; but it is an easy matter to give a Catholic sense to that expression, as we have seen it done to others: and we may be with justice allowed to do so, since he plainly establishes the Divinity of the Word in that very place."

For further particulars see besides authorities already cited, Le Nourry (*Apparat. ad Bibl. Max. Vet. Pat.* t. ii. diss. 3), Fabricius (*Bibl. Lat.* lib. xi.), Oudin (*de Script. Eccl.* t. i. p. 307), Lardner (*Cred.* pt. ii. bk. i. c. 65), Schramm (*Anal. Op. SS. Pat.* vol. vii. p. 250), Fessler (*Inst. Patrol.* vol. i. p. 328), *Nouv. Biog. Gen.* vol. xxviii. p. 611. See esp. Brandt in *Sitzungsberichte der phil.-histor. Klasse der Kgl. Akud der Wissensh.* (Vienna, 1889-1891), cxviii.-cxxv. [E.S.FF.]

Laeghaire (2) (*Lagerie*, phonet cally *Leary*), pagan monarch of Ireland, reigning at Tara in the county of Meath. In the fifth year of his reign St. Patrick, having spent the winter in the counties of Down and Antrim, in the spring determined to hold his Easter festival near Laeghaire's palace. The monarch, surrounded by his nobles and his Druid priests, saw with wonder and rage the distant light of the Christian paschal fire which was to quench the lights of heathendom, and rode over in force to Ferta-fer-Feic to expel the intruder. But mollified by the stranger's address, or frightened by his words of power, he allowed the Christian mission to be established. We can hardly believe that he continued a persecutor while such progress was made in the spread of the Gospel around him and in his own family. His queen may perhaps have become a Christian; his two daughters, Fedhelm the ruddy and Eithne the fair, were certainly converted and numbered among the saints. Several of his descendants (Reeves, *St. Adamnan*, 173) are beatified.

He probably died a pagan. The *Four Masters* give the date as 458, but 463 is more likely (*Ann. Tig.*, *eo an.*, ap. O'Conor, *Rer. Hib. Script.* iv. 111). He reigned probably 35 years. His body was carried to and buried at Tara, in the S.E. side of the external rampart, with his weapons upon him, and his face turned towards the Lagenians, as if still fighting against them. *Vitae S. Patricii*, ap. Colgan, *Tr. Thaum.* pass.; Lanigan, *Ch. Hist. Ir.* i. c. 5; Moore, *Hist. Ir.* i. c. 10; O'Hanlon, *Ir. Saints*, i. 163 seq.; Nennius, *Hist.* c. 59, ap. *Mon. Hist. Brit.* pt. ii. 72; Keating, *Gen. Hist. Ir.* B. ii. pp. 325 seq.; *Four Mast.* by O'Donovan, i. 144-145 *n.* g; Wills, *Ill. Ir.* i. 60; Skene, *Celt. Scot.* ii. 100 seq. 428 seq.; Todd, *St. Patrick*, 436 seq.; Joyce, *Irish Names of Places*, 2nd ser. 230-231. [J.G.]

Lampetius. [EUCHITES.]

Laurentius (10), antipope, elected on the same day as Symmachus, four days after the decease of Anastasius II., which, according to Pagi (*Critic. in Baron.*), occurred on Nov. 22, 498, Laurentius being brought forward in the interests of concession, Symmachus in the interests of unbending orthodoxy. Fierce conflicts ensued. The members of the senate as well as the clergy were arrayed in two parties. At length it was agreed to refer the settlement to Theodoric the Ostrogoth, now reigning at Ravenna as king of Italy, and he pronounced Symmachus the lawful pope (Anastas.). Laurentius at first acquiesced, and accepted the see of Nucerina, but his partisans at Rome recalled him, and for three years after his election Rome was divided into two parties, headed by Festus and Probinus on the side of Laurentius, and by Faustus on the side of Symmachus. Anastasius states that "those who communicated with Symmachus were slain with the sword; holy women and virgins were dragged from their houses or convents, denuded and scourged; there were daily fights against the church in the midst of the city; many priests were killed; there was no security for walking in the city by day or night. The ex-consul Faustus alone fought for the church." His account implies that more influential laymen were on the side of Laurentius, but that the clergy generally adhered to Symmachus. The matter was finally settled in the "synodus palmaris," the proceedings of which are supposed to be given under *Synod. Romana III. sub Symmacho,* the date of which is x. Kal. Novembris. Laurentius is said, in a fragment of a catalogue of the popes printed from a remarkably ancient MS. by Joseph Blanchinus in his ed. of Anastasius, to have retired to a farm of the patrician Festus, and to have died there, "sub ingenti abstinentia." This account evidently emanated from the party of Laurentius, if not from Festus himself (cf. Pagi's note on Baronius, ann. 502 i.).

Authorities.—Anastasius (*in Vit. Symmachi*); *Frag. Cat. Pontif.* in Anastas. Bibl. ed. 1718-1835, Rome, t. iv. *Prolegom.* p. lxix.; Theodorus Lector (lib. ii.), Theophanes (*Chron.* p. 123, ed. Paris), and Nicephorus (lib. 16, c. 35); Acts of Councils under Symmachus; *Libellus Apologeticus* of Ennodius written in justification of Symmachus after his final triumph. [J.B—Y.]

Laurentius (15), surnamed *Mellifluus,* thought to have been bp. of Novara *c.* 507. A Laurentius, surnamed Mellifluus, from the sweetness with which he delivered homilies, is mentioned by Sigebert (*Scr. Eccl.* c. 120 in *Patr. Lat.* clx. 572) as the author of a treatise *de Duobus Temporibus,* viz. one period from Adam to Christ, the other from Christ to the end of the world. That this Laurentius was the presbyter who instructed Gaudentius the first bp. of Novara was maintained by Cotta, an outline of whose arguments may be seen in the *Acta Eruditorum* (suppl. t. ii. pp. 525, 526, ed. Lips. 1696). La Bigne (*Max. Bibl. Pat.* t. ix. p. 465, Lugd. 1677) suspects that Laurentius Mellifluus was bp. of Novara, and subsequently the 25th bp. of Milan who is praised by Ennodius in his first *Dictio.* La Bigne grounds his opinion on certain allusions of Ennodius in his second *Dictio,* which was sent to Honoratus, bp. of Novara (*e.g. Patr. Lat.* lxiii. 269 B). Other corroborative passages have been adduced by Mabillon (*ut inf.*), as where Ennodius describes Laurentius bp. of Milan pacifying his haughty brethren by honeyed words of conciliation ("blandimentorum melle," *ib.* 267 A). The historians of literature usually therefore designate Laurentius Mellifluus bp. of Novara, but he is not admitted by the historians of the see, as Ughelli (*Ital. Sac.* iv. 692) and Cappelletti (*Le Chiese d'Ital.* xiv. 526). Three extant treatises are ascribed to Laurentius Mellifluus, viz. two homilies, *de Poenitentia* and *de Eleemosyna,* printed by La Bigne in his *Bibliotheca,* and a treatise *de Muliere Cananaea,* printed by Mabillon with a note on the author, supporting the view of La Bigne, in his *Analecta* (p. 55, ed. 1723). The homilies are in La Bigne (*Max. Bib. Pat.* t. ix. p. 465, Lug. 1677) and the three treatises in Migne (*Patr. Lat.* lxvi. 87) with both La Bigne's and Mabillon's notices of the author. Cave mistakenly says (i. 493) that the *de Duobus Temporibus* is lost, for it is evidently the homily *de Poenitentia,* which opens with an exposition of the "duo tempora," which terms he employs somewhat in the sense of the two dispensations for the divine pardon of sin. The sin inherited from Adam is in baptism entirely put away through the merits of Christ. Christ the second Adam simply cancelled the sin derived from the first Adam. Original sin therefore corresponds, in a manner, with the pre-Christian period. For actual transgression each person is himself alone responsible and is to be released from it by penitence, with which the treatise is mainly occupied, and so has received its present title. For other notices see Ceillier (xi. 95), Dupin (*Eccl. Writ.* t. i. p. 540, ed. 1722), Tillem. (*Mém.* x. 259, 260). [C.H.]

Laurentius (36), Aug. 10, archdeacon of Rome, and martyr under Valerian, A.D. 258. Cyprian (*Ep.* 82 *al.* 80 *ad Successum*) mentions the rescript of Valerian directing that bishops, presbyters, and deacons should forthwith be punished, and records the martyrdom of Xystus bp. of Rome, in accordance with it on Aug. 6. Laurentius, the first of the traditional seven deacons of Rome, suffered four days afterwards. The genuine Acts of this martyrdom were lost even in St. Augustine's time, as he tells us (*Ser.* 302, *de Sancto Laurent.*) that his narration was gained from tradition instead of reciting the Acts as his custom was (S. Ambr. *de Off.* i. 41). Laurentius suffered by burning over a slow fire, the prefect thinking thus to extort the vast treasures which he believed the Christians to have concealed. He was buried in the Via Tiburtina in the cemetery of Cyriaca by Hippolytus and Justinus, a presbyter, where Constantine the Great is said to have built a church in honour of the martyr, which pope Damasus rebuilt or repaired. Few martyrdoms of the first three centuries are better attested than this one. St Laurentius is commemorated in the canon of the Roman Mass. His name occurs in the most ancient Calendars, as Catalog. Liberianus or Bucherianus (4th cent.), in the Calendar of Ptolemeus Silvius (5th cent.), and in others described under CALENDAR in *D. C. A.* (cf. Smedt, *Introd. ad Hist. Ecclesiast.* pp. 199-219, 514). He is commemorated by Prudentius in his *Peristeph.* (*Mart. Rom. Vet.*; *Mart.* Adon., Usuard.; Tillem. *Mém.* iv. 38; Ceillier, ii. 423; Fleury, *H. E.* vii. 38, xi. 36, xviii. 33). Cf. Fronton, *Ep. et Dissert. Eccl.* p. 219 (1720), where, in a note on Aug. 10, in *Rom. Kal.*, an accurate account is given of the churches built at Rome in his honour. [G.T.S.]

Leander (2), metropolitan bp. of Seville from (?) 575 to 600. His life covers the most important period of Visigothic Christianity, and with LEOVIGILD, HERMENIGILD, and RECCARED he plays an indispensable part in that drama, half-political, half-religious, which issued in the conversion council of 589. All that is historically known of the origin of the famous family, which included his two brothers ISIDORE and FULGENTIUS, and their only sister FLORENTINA, is derived from the opening sentence in Isidore's Life of Leander (*de Vir. Ill.* c. 41; *Esp. Sagr.* v. 463) and from the concluding chapter of Leander's *Regula,* or *Libellus ad Florentinam* (*Esp. Sagr.* ix. 355). Their father was Severianus "Carthaginensis Provinciae." At some unknown date, while Florentina was a child, the family left their native place (*Libell. ad Florent.* c. 21), and settled probably at Seville. It is probable that Leander was born between 535 and 540. He would thus be a youth at the time of the family exile. Before 579, the date of the outbreak of the Hermenigild rebellion, he had been a monk, and then raised to the metropolitan see of Seville, perhaps at that time the most important ecclesiastical post in Spain. The Catholics under the Arian king Leovigild had especial need of able and faithful leaders. Probably Leander saw the opportunity of the Catholics in Hermenigild's youth and the Catholicism of his wife Ingunthis, and this conjecture is warranted by the evidence that the persuasive and eloquent bishop, who afterwards led the conversion council, laid the first stone of his great work in the conversion and rising of Hermenigild against his Arian king and father Leovigild. Leovigild's Arian council of 581 was succeeded by civil war between father and son in 582. Hermenigild had already endeavoured to strengthen himself by alliances with the Catholic Suevi in the N. and the Catholic Byzantines in the S. and E. In connexion with this last alliance we next hear of Leander at Constantinople, "cum—te illuc injuncta pro causis fidei Visigothorum legatio perduxisset," says Gregory the Great, describing in after-years (Pref. in *Moralia, Patr. Lat.* lxxv. 510) his first friendship with Leander.

The exact date of this mission is unknown (see Görres, *Zeitschrift für historische Theologie,* i. 1873, p. 103); but we incline to place it in 583, about the beginning of the siege of Seville, when effectual support from the empire might have given victory to Hermenigild. In 584 Seville fell and Hermenigild was captured at Cordova. Thenceforward Arianism was triumphant, and that persecution of the Catholics by Leovigild, which is described by Isidore (*Hist. Goth. Esp. Sagr.* vi. 491) and Gregory of Tours (*Hist. Franc.* v. 39), was carried actively forward. In Apr. or May 586 occurred the death of Leovigild and the accession of his second son Reccared; and Leander, on receiving information as to the state of affairs, appears to have hurried home from Constantinople. (Cf. what Lucinian says of his "haste" on the journey homewards from Constantinople, *Ep. Licin. ad Greg. Pat. Esp. Sagr.* v.) In Feb. 587 the preliminary synod took place at Toledo, in which Reccared and his nobles abjured Arianism, and notice of the step was sent to the provinces.

The Conversion Council.—In 589 a great gathering at Toledo of the king and queen, the court, and 62 bishops, Arian and Catholic, changed the whole outer face of Visigothic history and entirely shifted its centre of gravity. The causes which led to it had been long at work (cf. Dahn, *Könige der Germanen,* v. on the *political* causes); but this third council of Toledo remains one of the most astonishing and interesting events in history. For a detailed sketch of the proceedings see RECCARED. Here we are only concerned with Leander's share in it. "Summa tamen synodalis negotii," says the contemporary bp. of Gerona, Joannes Biclarensis, "penes Sanctum Leandrum Hispal. ecclesiae episcopum et beatissimum Eutropium monasterii Servitani abbatem fuit." This justifies us in attributing to Leander the main outline of the proceedings and the wording of a large proportion of the Acts. Reccared's speeches are probably to be traced to him. They are quite in accordance with Leander's known style, especially with that of the homily which concludes the council and was avowedly written and delivered by him. The homily (*Homilia Sancti Leandri in laudem ecclesiae ob conversionem gentis*) is an eloquent and imaginative piece of writing, with an undercurrent of reference to the great semi-religious, semi-political struggle which marked the reign of the last Arian king. "The peace of Christ, then," says Leander, "has destroyed the wall of discord which the devil had built up, and the house which division was bringing to ruin is united in and established upon Christ the corner-stone." Tejada y Ramiro, *Colecc. de Can. de la Igl. Española,* ii. 247-260; Gams, *Kirchengeschichte von Spanien,* ii. (2), 6, 41; Dahn, v. 159, vi. 434; Helfferich, *Entstehung und Geschichte der Westgothen Recht,* 33-46; Hefele, iii. 44-49.

First Synod of Seville.—Eighteen months after the conversion council, Leander, as metropolitan of Baetica, and in obedience to the 18th canon of the council of 589, summoned the bishops of Baetica to a provincial synod in the cathedral of Seville, "in ecclesia Hispalensi Sancta Jerusalem" (cf. Florez, ix. on the use of "Sancta Jerusalem"). The Acts, on matters disciplinary, are drawn up in the form of a letter to the absent bp. Pegasius of Astigi (Ecija).

Correspondence with Gregory the Great.—Gregory and Leander, first made friends at Constantinople between 575 and 585, when Gregory was apocrisiarius of Pelagius II. at the East-Roman court. In May 591 Gregory, now pope, wrote a long letter to Leander (*Ep.* lib. i. 43, *apud* Migne, *Patr. Lat.* lxxvii. 497) in answer to his old friend, who had congratulated him on his elevation, reported the Visigothic conversion and the third council of Toledo, and inquired as to the form of baptism to be thenceforward observed in Spain, whether by single or threefold immersion. The pope expressed his joy in the conversion of the Visigoths, declaring that Leander's accounts of Reccared have made him love a man of whom he has no personal knowledge. Let Leander look to it diligently that the work so well begun may be perfected. In a country where unity of faith had never been questioned, single or threefold immersion might be observed indifferently, as representing either the Unity or the Trinity of the Godhead; but as in Spain the Arian mode of baptism had been by threefold immersion, it would be well henceforward to allow one immersion only, lest the heretics be supposed to have triumphed and confusion ensue. Finally, the pope sent Leander certain codices; part of the *Homilies on Job,* which he had asked for, were to follow, as the *librarii* had not been able to finish the copy in time.

Gregory's second letter, dated July 595, is a note accompanying the gift of the *Regula Pastoralis* with pts. i. and ii. of the *Moralia.*

The Pallium.—In Aug. 599 Gregory wrote to Reccared, Claudius Dux of Lusitania, and Leander. The letter to Leander announces the gift of the pallium, to be worn at the celebration of Mass, "solemnia Missarum." To Reccared the pope writes: "To our honoured brother and fellow-bishop Leander we have sent the pallium as a gift from the see of the blessed apostle Peter, which we owe to ancient custom (*antiquae consuetudini*), to your deserts, and to his dignity and goodness." The exact force of the gift of the pallium to Leander has been much disputed. Florez (ix. 167) maintains it was nothing more than a mark of honour and distinction, and did not carry with it the apostolic vicariate, which had, however, been bestowed on his predecessors in the see, ZENO and SALLUSTIUS, by popes Simplicius and Hormisdas (Tejada y Ramiro, ii. 962, 1015). In support of his supposition that pallium and vicariate were not necessarily combined, he quotes the case of bp. Auxanius of Arles, successor of St. Caesarius, to whom pope Vigilius gave the pallium when the vicariate had been previously bestowed (Vigil. *Ep.* vii. *apud* Migne, *Patr. Lat.* lxix. 27). Gams, however, holds that in Gregory's mind at any rate the pallium carried with it the vicariate, and that the phrase *antiquae consuetudini* is to be taken as referring to the vicariates of Zeno and Sallustius, and as implying the recognition by Gregory of an ancient claim on behalf of the see of Seville to represent the apostolic see in Spain. The various other bestowals of the pallium on Western bishops by Gregory, especially the cases of Augustine of Canterbury (*Ep.* xi. 64, 65) and Syagrius of Autun (ix. 108), should be studied in connexion with the case of Leander (cf. Walter, *Lehrbuch des Kirchenrechts*, pp. 308, 277, and Thomassin, *Discipline de l'Eglise*, ii. i. cc. 25, 26). Very soon after the arrival of the pallium, at latest in 600, Leander died, shortly before the king, whose constant friend and adviser he had been.

Works.—The *Libellus ad Florentinam* consists of an introductory letter and 21 chapters, which constitute the *Regula.* The style is easy and flowing, rising at time to real pathos and sweetness, as in the beautiful concluding chapter with its well-known reference to Isidore. Its laudation of the celibate life and depreciation of marriage are quite in the taste of the time, and, to judge from can. 5 of C. Tol. iii., seem to have been then in Spain a distinguishing mark of the Catholic as opposed to the Arian clergy.

The *Homily* noticed above is the only other work of Leander now extant. Isidore, however, in his Life of his brother (*de Vir. Ill.* c. 41) speaks of three controversial treatises against the Arians, composed by him during his exile from Spain under Leovigild. Isidore's description shews that they were especially intended to meet the arguments and expose the pretensions of the Arian council of 581. The last-named was probably in categorical answer to the *libellus* issued after the synod by the Arian bishops and expressly anathematized by the conversion council (Joh. Bicl. *ad an.* 581; Tejada y Ramiro, ii. p. 224).

Authorities.—Besides those already quoted, Baron. *Ann. Eccl.* A.D. 583, 584, 585, 589, 591, 595, 599; Nicolas Antonio, *Bibl. Vet.* ed. Bayer, 1788, i. 290; *de Castri Bibl. Española,* ii. 280; Aguirre, *Coll. Max. Conc. Hisp.* iii. 281-302; Fabric. *Bibl. Lat.* iv. 252, ed. 1754; Mabillon, *Ann. Ord. S. Bened.* i. 287; *AA. SS.* Boll. March ii. 275; Amador de los Rios, *Hist. Coll. de la Lit. Españ.* i. 312, 323; Montalembert, *Moines de l'Occident,* ii. [M.A.W.]

Leo (1) I., emperor (surnamed the Great, the Thracian, and the Butcher), born *c.* 400 in the country of the Bessi in Thrace, proclaimed emperor Feb. 7, 457, and crowned by Anatolius, patriarch of Constantinople, being the first Christian sovereign to receive his crown from the hands of a priest. Immediately upon the news of Marcian's death, religious troubles broke out in Alexandria, where the Monophysite party murdered the patriarch Proterius (Proteius), substituting for him Timothy Aelurus. The orthodox bishops of Egypt fled to the emperor to make complaint. Anatolius, bp. of Constantinople, reported their sad case to pope Leo, who energetically seconded their efforts for redress. The emperor, distracted by the demands of pope and patriarch on the one hand, of Aspar and the heretical party on the other, addressed a circular letter to Anatolius and all other metropolitans, commanding them to assemble their provincial councils, and advise him—(1) whether the decrees of the council of Chalcedon should be held binding; (2) as to the ordination of Timothy Aelurus. He also consulted the three most celebrated ascetics of the time, Symeon Stylites, James the Syrian, and Baradatus. We possess in the *Codex Encyclius* the answers of all the bishops and hermits consulted, a most valuable monument of ecclesiastical antiquity. It was apparently composed by imperial order by some unknown Greek, translated into Latin at the order of the senator Cassiodorus by Epiphanius Scholasticus, and first published in modern times by Laurentius Surius. It is in all collections of the councils, but in full only in Labbe and Coss. *Concil.* i. 4, pp. 890-980 (cf. Cave, *Scriptt. Lit. Hist.* i. 495; Tillem. *Mém.* xv. art. 167). The bishops, in Aug. 458, replied, unanimously upholding the decrees of Chalcedon and rejecting the ordination of Timothy, who, however, maintained his position at Alexandria till 460.

In 468 Leo sent an expedition under the command of Basiliscus, his brother-in-law, against the Arian Vandals of N. Africa, who were bitterly hostile to him on account of his orthodoxy. Aspar and Ardaburius secretly arranged with Basiliscus for its failure, as they feared any diminution of the great Arian power. The emperor, having discovered the conspiracy, put Aspar and Ardaburius to death, and banished Basiliscus A.D. 469. The Gothic guards, in revenge, raised a civil war in Constantinople, under one Ostrys, a friend of Aspar, and attacked the palace, but were defeated. Leo thereupon issued a severe edict against the Arians and forbade them holding meetings or possessing churches.

In another quarter controversy burst forth. Gennadius, patriarch of Constantinople, dying in 471, was succeeded by Acacius, whom Leo admitted a member of the senate, where no ecclesiastic had hitherto sat. Acacius obtained from Leo an edict confirming the 28th canon of Chalcedon, which raised Constantinople to the same ecclesiastical level as Rome. Pope Simplicius resisted the claim, and a bitter controversy ensued, lasting many years and most fruitful in divisions (Milman, *Lat. Christ.* lib. iii. c. i.).

Leo was very active in church legislation. He made laws in 466 confirming the right of asylum to churches; in 468 forbidding any persons save Christians to act as advocates. In 469 he issued an edict against simoniacal contracts and one of almost puritan strictness upon the observance of Sunday. He forbade judicial proceedings on that day, and even the playing of lyre, harp, or other musical instrument (*Chron. Pasch.* A.D. 467, where the words of the edict are given). The same year he passed stern laws against paganism and issued a fresh edict in favour of hospitals. In 471 a law was published, apparently elicited by the troubles at Antioch, commanding monks not to leave their monasteries. When Isocasius, a philosopher and magistrate of Antioch, was forced by torture to accept baptism at Constantinople, the emperor seems to have personally superintended the deed (Joan. Malalas, *Chronogr.* lib. xiv.). Leo died Feb. 3, 474, aged 73, and was succeeded by his grandson Leo II. Evagr. *H. E.* lib. ii.; Procopii, *de Bell. Bandal.*; Theoph. *Chronogr.* [G.T.S.]

Leo (5) I., the Great, saint, bp. of Rome, A.D. 440-461. We know but little of him before his papacy. He himself and Prosper of Aquitaine call Rome his "patria" (Prosp. *Chron.*, *Patr. Lat.* li. 599; Leo Mag. *Ep.* xxxi. 4, p. 85, Migne). His birth must have been about the last decade of the 4th cent. He is said (Vig. Taps. *contra Eutych.* lib. iv.) to have been baptized by Celestine; but if so, this must have been while Celestine was still a simple priest. There is no trace in his writings that his education comprised any study of pagan authors, and he was throughout life ignorant of Greek (*Epp.* cxxx. 3, p. 1258; cxiii. 4, p. 1194); but his elaborate style indicates considerable training in composition. In 418 we hear, in the letters of St. Augustine (*Epp.* cxci. cxciv. 1), of a certain acolyte Leo, the bearer of a letter from Sixtus, afterwards pope, to Aurelius of Carthage and apparently also of pope Zosimus's letter in condemnation of Pelagianism, addressed to Aurelius, St. Augustine, and the other African bishops. The mention of Sixtus, with whom Leo was afterwards connected, and the date of the occurrence, would lead us to identify this acolyte with Leo the Great. If so, it is interesting that he should have come in contact early in life with the greatest of Latin theologians. Under the pontificate of Celestine (422-432) he was a deacon, or (according to Gennadius, *de Vir. Illus.* 61) archdeacon of Rome. His important place in the church is shewn by two incidents. In 430 the treatise of Cassian, *de Incarnatione*, against the Nestorians, was written at Leo's exhortation, and dedicated to him with every expression of respect (Cassian, *de Incarn. Praef.* Migne, *Patr. Lat.* i. p. 11). In 431, during the council of Ephesus, St. Cyril of Alexandria wrote to Leo against the ambitious design of Juvenal of Jerusalem to obtain for his see the dignity of a patriarchate (*Ep.* cxix. 4, p. 1216). In 439 Leo, on the alert against the Pelagians, urged the pope to offer a vigilant resistance to the movements of Julian of Eclanum, who was seeking to obtain readmission to the church without any real recantation of his errors (Prosper, *Chron.*, *Patr. Lat.* li. 598). Very soon after, Leo was sent on an important civil embassy to Gaul. The Western empire was in a condition of extreme weakness. Nominally governed by Placidia and her youthful son Valentinian III., the real power lay almost wholly in the hands of the general Aetius, at this moment engaged in a quarrel in Gaul with general Albinus. It is a sign of the important civil position held by Leo the deacon that he was chosen to endeavour to bring about a reconciliation (Prosper, *Chron.*, *Patr. Lat.* li. p. 599). During his prolonged absence pope Sixtus died, and Leo was promptly elected, and an embassy sent to recall him to Rome. "More than forty days," says Prosper, "the Roman church was without a bishop, awaiting with wonderful peace and patience the arrival of the deacon Leo." He was consecrated Sept. 29, 440. The first of his extant works is a brief sermon on this occasion, *de Natali Ipsius*, in which he praises God and returns thanks to the people, asking their prayers for the success of his ministry. (For date of consecration see Ballerini's note, *Patr. Lat.* lv. 193; Tillem. xv. note 2 on St. Leo.)

It was a difficult and trying time. The Eastern empire was in its normal state of "premature decay," the Western empire was tottering to its fall. Africa was already a prey to Genseric and the Vandals. The devastation of the African church was well-nigh complete. The church at large was in evil case. Without, she was encompassed by the Arian powers; within the Manicheans, the Priscillianists, the Pelagians and the semi-Pelagians, were disturbing her peace; in the East Nestorianism was still rife. There was an extraordinary paucity of men capable of leading, whether in church or state. A man was needed capable of disciplining and consolidating Western Christendom, that it might present a firm front to the heretical barbarians and remain in unshaken consistency through that stormy period which links the ancient with the modern world. The church, preserving her identity, must give the framework for the society which was to be. That she might fulfil her function, large sacrifices must be made to the surpassing necessity for unity, solidity, and strength. Leo was the man for the post: lofty and severe in life and aims, rigid and stern in insisting on the rules of ecclesiastical discipline; gifted with an indomitable energy, courage, and perseverance, and a capacity for keeping his eye on many widely distant spheres of activity at once; inspired with an unhesitating acceptance and an admirable grasp of the dogmatic faith of the church, which he was prepared to press everywhere at all costs; finally, possessed with, and unceasingly acting upon, an overmastering sense of the indefeasible authority of the church of Rome as the divinely ordained centre of all church work and life, he stands out as the Christian representative of the imperial dignity and severity of old Rome, and is the true founder of the medieval papacy in all its magnificence of conception and uncompromising strength. His is a simple character, if regarded with sympathy, not hard to understand and appreciate; representing strongly that side of the developing life of the church specially identified with Rome—authority and unity; and a special interest attaches to his history from the fact that he stands so much alone, as almost the one considerable man in Christendom. "The dignity of the imperial name may be said to have died with Theodosius the Great." Among churchmen Augustine was just dead, Cyril very soon to die. The best-known names are those of Theodoret, Prosper, Cassian, and Hilary of Arles. There was not even an imposing representative of heresy; "on the throne of Rome, alone of all the great sees, did religion maintain its majesty, its sanctity, its piety" (Milman, *Lat. Christianity*, vol. i. p. 228). In such an age and in such a position, a strong man like Leo could exercise an abiding influence.

In strengthening the framework of the church, Leo was playing an important part in the reconstruction of civil society. In 452 Attila, having spread desolation over the plains of Lombardy, was encamped upon the Mincius, ready to advance towards Rome. In this extremity Leo, accompanied by the consular Avienus and the prefect Trigetius, met the barbarian, and Attila, yielding to their persuasions, consented to withdraw beyond the Danube.

The terms were discreditable enough to the Roman empire; but that the confidence and courage of St. Leo in meeting the fearful Hun made a great impression on the Eastern as well as the Western world may be seen from the somewhat curious allusion to it by the Eastern bishops in the appeal to pope Symmachus *c.* 510 (*Patr. Lat.* lxii. p. 63). "If your predecessor, the archbp. Leo, now among the saints, thought it not unworthy of him to go himself to meet the barbarian Attila, that he might free from captivity of the body not Christians only, but Jews and pagans, surely your holiness will be touched by the captivity of soul under which we are suffering." No doubt later ages have exaggerated the importance of Leo's action, as may be seen in Baronius's account and that of later Roman Catholic writers (*Ann.* 452, § 56 seq.). Later tradition has also introduced the well-known legend which represents Attila as confessing himself overawed by a miraculous presence, the apparition of St. Peter, and, according to another account, of St. Paul also, threatening him with instant death if he refused to yield. (Baronius boldly maintains the legend, which can plead no respectable evidence. See Tillem. xv. 751, etc.) Again, in 455, when Genseric and the Vandals were at the gates of Rome, the defenceless city, "without a ruler and without a standing force," found its sole hope in the dauntless courage of Leo. Unarmed, at the head of his clergy, he went outside the walls to meet the invader and succeeded in restraining the cruelty and licence of devastation. What exactly the barbarian promised, and how much of his promise he kept, is not quite certain, but at least "the mediation of Leo was glorious to himself, and, in some degree, beneficial to his country" (Gibbon). To neither of these two encounters between Leo and the barbarians do we find allusion in his extant writings. Clearly, if Leo was the "saviour of his country," he was not inclined to boast of it. He had little to complain of in the submissiveness of the Western emperor in his relations with himself. Nothing can exceed the ecclesiastical authority which is recognized as belonging to the pope in the constitution of Valentinian, which accompanied Leo's letter into Gaul in 448 when Leo was in conflict with Hilary of Arles (Leo Mag. *Ep.* xi.). This constitution, which has the names of both emperors, Eastern and Western, at its head, speaks of the "merits" of St. Peter, the dignity of Rome and the authority of a council as conspiring to confirm the primacy of the Roman bishops. It declares that it is necessary for the peace of all that all the churches ("universitas") should recognize him as their ruler, and that his decree on the subject of the Gallic church would be authoritative even without imperial sanction; yet by way of giving this sanction, it asserts that "no bishops, whether of Gaul or of other provinces, are to be allowed, contrary to ancient customs, to attempt anything ("ne quid tentare") without the authority of the venerable man, the pope of the eternal city; but that the one law for them and for all is "quicquid sanxit vel sanxerit apostolicae sedis auctoritas"; and if any bishop summoned to Rome neglect to come, the provincial magistrate (moderator) is to compel him. Nothing could be stronger than this language; the document, however, must be considered entirely Western, the result of pressure put by Leo on the feeble mind of Valentinian. (See Tillem. xv. 441, who calls it "une loy . . . trop favorable à la puissance du siége [de S. Léon] mais peu honorable à sa piété.") That Valentinian and his family were much under Leo's influence is proved also by the letters which in the early part of 450 he induced him, his mother Placidia, and his wife Eudoxia, to write to Theodosius II., the Eastern emperor, in the interest of Leo's petition for a council in Italy, all which letters reiterate the views of Leo and assert the loftiest position for the see of Rome (Leo Mag. *Epp.* liv.-lviii.). Theodosius, however, was not so amenable to Leo's wishes. In the matter of the councils, the pope had to submit to the emperor. It was the emperor who summoned the council of Ephesus in 449 (*Epp.* xxix. 840, xxx. 851); Leo speaking always respectfully of him * (xxxi. 856, 840), but being inclined to complain at least of the short notice (857). The emperor decided the occasion, place, and time; and the pope apologizes for not attending in person (*ib.*). Again, after the disastrous termination of the Ephesine synod, Leo cannot obtain from the emperor his request for a gathering in Italy. The summoning of councils still depended on the "commandment and will of princes"; and Leo gives a constant practical recognition to the interference of the Eastern empire in ecclesiastical appointments and affairs generally (*Ep.* lxxxiv. c. 3, etc.; cf. also cliii. 1, remembering that Aspar was an Arian, Tillem. *Empereurs*, vi. 366). In general Leo conceives of the right relation of the empire

* Considering the tone official language then took Leo cannot be accused of exaggerated flattery.

and the church as a very intimate one. "Human affairs cannot," he says, "be safe unless the royal and sacerdotal authority combine to defend the faith" (*Ep.* lx. 983). He tells the emperor Leo on his accession that his empire is given him "not only to rule the world, but to defend the church" (*Ep.* clvi. 1323). When he praises an emperor he ascribes to him a "sacerdotal" mind (*e.g. Ep.* clv. 1319). The civil power is constantly called upon, at any rate in the East, where Leo could not always depend on the ecclesiastical authorities, to do the work of the church (*Epp.* cxii. 1189, cxv. 1203, cxxxvi.), and he justifies the execution of Priscillian in the previous century on the ground "that though the lenity of the church, contented with a sacerdotal sentence, is averse from taking a bloody revenge, yet at times it finds assistance in the severe commands of Christian princes, because the fear of punishment for the body sometimes drives men to seek healing for the soul" (*Ep.* xv. 696).

As an ecclesiastical ruler we will consider Leo first in his relation to the various heresies in the West. Septimus, bp. of Altina, in the province of Aquileia, writes (*Ep.* i. Migne) to inform Leo that Pelagian ecclesiastics are being admitted to communion in that province without recantation, are being reinstated into their ecclesiastical degrees, and allowed, contrary to the canons, to wander from church to church. Leo writes to the metropolitan to complain, desiring him to summon a provincial synod and extract from suspected persons a condemnation of Pelagian errors (i. 591). Of his struggle with the Manicheans we know more. Recent troubles, especially the capture of Carthage by Genseric in 439, had driven many of these heretics to Rome. They were to be seen there moving about with pale faces, in mean apparel, fasting, and making distinctions of meats. They seem to have professed Catholicism and done their best to escape attention (Leo Mag. *Serm.* xvi. 4, xxxv.; *Ep.* xv. 16, p. 708). The vigilance of Leo, however, was too much for them. Of this sect he had a particular horror. Their heresy is a mixture, he says, of all others, while it alone has no element of good in it (*Serm.* xvi. 4, xxiv. 5). Accordingly, in the beginning of 444, Leo made a diligent search for them. A large number, both of teachers and disciples, and among them their bishop, were tried in the presence of numerous authorities, ecclesiastical and civil, a "senatus amplissimus," as Valentinian calls it, at which confession was made of the most hideous immoralities in their secret assemblies (*Epp.* vii. p. 624, xv. 16, p. 708; *Serm.* xvi. 4, and Constitutio Valent., *Ep.* viii.). Those who remained impenitent were banished *in perpetuum* by the civil power, and a constitution of Valentinian reviving the previous laws against the sect, dated June 19, 445, put them under all kinds of civil penalties. Leo, by sermons (ix. xvii. xxiv. xxxv. xlii.) and a circular letter to the bishops of Italy (*Ep.* vii.), did all he could to publish their infamy, and his exertions appear to have stirred up other bishops, both in the East and West, to similar activity (Prosper and Idatius, *Chron.*, *Patr. Lat.* li. 600, 882). Theodoret, writing in 449, counts this exhibition of zeal against the Manicheans one of St. Leo's greatest titles to fame (Leo Mag. *Ep.* lii. c. 2). In 447 we find Leo sending an account of these proceedings to Turribius, bp. of Astorga (*Ep.* xv. 16, 708). At this period the Priscillianists were exercising a very disastrous influence in Spain. St. Turribius, their active opponent, wrote to Leo for advice, and Leo replies in July 447 (*Ep.* xv.). He views the heresy as a mixture of Manicheism with other forms of evil, heretical and pagan, and exhorts Turribius to gather a synod of all the Spanish provinces to examine into the orthodoxy of the bishops; with this view he sends letters to the bishops of the various provinces, but urges that at least a provincial synod of Gallicia should be held (c. 17). We find subsequent allusions to a Gallician council, to which Leo is said to have written (Labbe, *Conc.* v. 837 A; Idat. *Chron.* xxiii.), and to a council of various provinces at Toledo in 447, which is said to have acted "cum praecepto papae Leonis" (Labbe, ii. 1227 B; cf. Tillem. xv. 555 seq.; Ceillier, x. 668). Though we hear still of Novatianism and Donatism in Africa (*Ep.* xii. 6), Leo did not take any special measures against these nor other heresies in the West.

Leo's introduction to Eastern disputes is a somewhat curious one. Eutyches early in 448 wrote to Leo apparently deploring the revival of Nestorianism. Leo replied on June 1, applauding his solicitude, and apparently heard no more of Eutyches till early in 449 he received two letters announcing his condemnation in the council of Constantinople—one from the emperor Theodosius, the other from himself. Eutyches (*Ep.* xxi.) appeals to the judgment of the Roman pontiff. Leo, however, maintains a cautious attitude; writes to Flavian (*Ep.* xxiii.) complaining that he has sent him no information about the condemnation of Eutyches, that the appeal of the condemned to Rome was, according to his own account, not received and he himself hastily condemned, though he professed himself ready to amend anything in his faith which should be found at fault. At the same time Leo writes to the emperor, lamenting his ignorance of the true state of the case (*Ep.* xxiv.). Meanwhile, it appears that Flavian had really written soon after the close of the council to inform Leo, and to Domnus of Antioch and other prelates. His letter, however (*Ep.* xxii.) had not reached Leo by the end of Feb. 449. Had it arrived, it would have been calculated to give Leo a clearer view of the dogmatic question at issue. Flavian's second letter to Leo, in reply to his (*Ep.* xxvi.), contains no allusions to Leo's complaints of his silence and want of consideration; he characterizes Eutyches's representations as crafty and false, explains clearly the drift of his teaching, and urges the pope to send his subscription to the condemnation, and to keep the emperor on the right side (*ib.* p. 788); the matter, he adds, only needs his assistance to keep it all straight. Leo, now confirmed in his adhesion to Flavian, writes briefly in May 449, assuring him of his sympathy (*Ep.* xxvii.), followed in June by "the tome" (*Ep.* xxviii.), one of the most justly celebrated of pontifical decrees—nominally a letter to an individual bishop, but really addressed to all the world, Western as well as Eastern. At the same time, Leo sent letters directed against Eutyches's doctrine, and calling attention to his tome, to Pulcheria, Faustus, Martin, and the other archimandrites of Constantinople, to the Ephesine council itself, and two to his close friend JULIAN of Cos (*Epp.* xxxi.-xxxv.). Meanwhile Theodosius, at the instance of Eutyches, had directed the assembling of a council, which, professing to be aimed at Nestorianism only, excited much alarm in the minds of Eastern prelates and in that of Leo, who, though praising the emperor's zeal for religion, ventures to hint that there is no occasion for assembling a synod in a matter where there is no possibility of doubt—an opinion which he expresses more strongly to Flavian. Theodosius had sent a request that Leo would be present at the council. This, as he writes to Pulcheria, the circumstances of the city would not permit; and there would, as he tells Theodosius, be no precedent for such a course (*Epp.* xxxi. 857; xxxvii. 887). He sent ("de latere suo") three legates to represent on his behalf the spirit at once of severity and mercy (*Epp.* xxix. p. 841; xxxiv. c. 2; xxxiii. p. 866). They seem to have left Rome before June 23. Apparently at the beginning of Oct. news reached Rome that the council had been packed and managed by Dioscorus; that Leo's tome had not been read; that Eutyches had been reinstated, St. Flavian and Eusebius condemned and deposed; finally, that of Leo's legates one only had barely escaped to tell the tale; and though Leo was ignorant of the crowning enormity of the murder of St. Flavian, his indignation boils over (*Epp.* xliii. p. 904; xliv. p. 912; xlv. p. 921; cxx. 3, p. 1224; xlv. 2). The proceedings of the council are characterized as a "sceleratissimum facinus"; "it was no synod at all, but a "latrocinium," a den of robbers; its acts are null and void; it cuts to the root of the Christian faith (*Epp.* xliv. i. p. 913; lxxxv. i. p. 1051; xcv. 2; xlv. 2, p. 923; xliv. 1, 913). Still, Leo is more indignant than dismayed (*Ep.* xlviii.). The fearful and half-anticipated result of the synod only stirs his energies. There was then sitting at Rome a council apparently representing the whole West, and assembled to consider the present emergency (*Epp.* lxi. 1; xlv. 2; xlvi. 2; lxix. p. 1008). In his own name and that of the council Leo addresses letters to various quarters. The church of Constantinople and the archimandrites (*Epp.* l. li.) are exhorted to be loyal to the faith and to Flavian, whose death was not yet known in Rome, and they are assured that no one who usurps his place can be in the communion of Rome or a true bishop (p. 934). Besides those letters (*Epp.* xliii. xliv. xlv.), there are two to the emperor, urgently requesting that a more oecumenical council may be held in Italy. Till this has been done, Leo begs the emperor by all that is most sacred to allow everything to remain as it was before the first decision at Constantinople (*Ep.* xliv. 2, p. 915). This request, made in the name of all the bishops and churches of the West ("nostrae partes," xliv. 3), is accompanied by the strongest condemnation of the Ephesine council and backed up by an appeal to the empress Pulcheria (*Ep.* xlv.). The ground of the request is especially the appeal of Flavian to Rome—an appeal for the justification of which Leo offers the authority of a Nicene canon (*Ep.* xliv. 916; *vid. inf.*).

On Dec. 25 Leo, still surrounded by his council, presses his request to the emperor again (*Ep.* liv.); and in Mar. 450 writes again to stir up Pulcheria, the archimandrites (*Ep.* xi.), and the clergy and people of Constantinople, to press his petition for a "plenaria synodus," and "next to the divine assistance to aim at obtaining the favour of the Catholic princes" (*Epp.* lix. 5, 981, lx. lxi.). Meanwhile, taking the opportunity of Valentinian's presence in Rome with his wife Licinia Eudoxia (Theodosius's daughter) and his mother, Galla Placidia, Leo gets them all to write letters urging the Eastern emperor to do what he wished (*Epp.* lv. lvi. lvii.). Galla Placidia wrote at the same time to Pulcheria, expre ing detestation of the Ephesine synod, and describing how Leo, when solemnly asking their intercession with Theodosius, could hardly speak for grief (*Ep.* lviii.).

In his replies to Valentinian, Placidia, and Eudoxia (*Epp.* lxii. lxiii. lxiv.) Theodosius asserts his continued orthodoxy, but professes his complete satisfaction with the Ephesine synod. His reply to Leo is not preserved, but contained an absolute refusal to do what he wished. Leo had another cause of anxiety. Anatolius had written to him in the end of 449, telling him of his election to succeed Flavian (*Ep.* liii.). Anatolius had been Dioscorus's representative at Constantinople, and what security had Leo for his orthodoxy? Moreover, he had simply announced his consecration, without asking for Leo's consent to it. Leo wrote in July 450 to Theodosius, whom he still addresses with the utmost respect, requiring that Anatolius should read the Catholic Fathers and the Ep. of Cyril, without overlooking his own Ep. to Flavian, and then make a public profession of adherence to their doctrine, to be transmitted to the apostolic see and all bishops and churches. This he demands somewhat peremptorily, sending legates to explain his views, and renewing his request for an Italian council (*Ep.* lxix.). This letter he backs up with others to Pulcheria, Faustus, and the archimandrites (*Epp.* lxx. lxxi. lxxii.). Leo appears even now to have been full of hope (*Ep.* lxxiii. to Martin), though Dioscorus had the audacity to excommunicate him and the emperor was all against him. But before his legates could reach Constantinople, his chief cause of anxiety was removed. Theodosius died, July 450, and was succeeded by Pulcheria, always Leo's friend, who united to herself as emperor, Marcian, equally zealous for his cause. Dioscorus's hopes were gone. The letter of the new emperor (*Ep.* lxxiii.), announcing his election, promised the council to be held specially under Leo's influence ("te auctore"), and the letter which followed the arrival of Leo's messengers at Constantinople asked him either to come to the East to assist at it or, if that was impossible, to let the emperor summon the Eastern, Illyrian, and Thracian bishops to some place "ubi nobis placuerit" (*Ep.* lxxvi.). We hear nothing of Leo's requirement that it should be in Italy, though he did not cease to wish that it should be there (*Ep.* xcv. 1). Meanwhile Anatolius had willingly signed the tome, as had "all the church of Constantinople, with a number of bishops"—it appears that it was sent for signature to all the metropolitans (*Ep.* lxxxviii. 3; Labbe, iv. 546 c)—the bishops banished for adherence to Flavian were recalled, and all honour shewn to Flavian's body (*Ep.* Pulcheria, lxxvii.). At the same time a large number of the bishops who had been induced by fear to assent to the decrees of the Ephesine synod (by July 451 almost all) had testified their sorrow, and, though by the decision of the papal legates not yet admitted to the communion of Rome, were allowed the privileges of their own churches; Eutyches was banished, though not far enough to satisfy Leo, and everywhere "the light of the Catholic faith was shining forth" (*Epp.* lxxx. 2; lxxxiv. 3; cxxxii. p. 1053). The legates, who returned at once, carried back a number of letters to their master, and in Apr. 451 we have a number of letters from him, expressing genuine satisfaction. He commends all that has been done, praises the "sacerdotal" zeal of Marcian, the diligent watchfulness of Pulcheria, and rejoices in Anatolius's adhesion to the truth (*Epp.* lxxviii. lxxix. lxxx.; cf. lxxxv. 3). He praises the conduct of his legates and confirms their wish that the names of those bishops, Dioscorus, Juvenal, and Eustathius, who had taken a chief part in the crimes of the council of Ephesus should not be recited at the altar (lxxx. 3; lxxxv. 2). As for the council, he wishes it postponed, but has to yield to the emperor, and writes to him in June 451 (*Ep.* lxxxix.), nominating the legates to represent him. He makes it a point that his legates should preside, and that the question of the true faith should not be treated as an open one (*Ep.* xc.; cf. xciii.). If Leo, presiding in the person of his legates, secures the position of his see, and if the prohibition of maintaining heretical positions ("nec id liceat defendi, quod non liceat credi") gives security to the faith, there will be no cause of anxiety about the council, but a caution is still needed that the condemnation of Eutyches must not be an excuse for any rehabilitation of Nestorianism (*Ep.* xciii. end). When the synodal letter of the council of Chalcedon (*Ep.* xcviii.) reached Leo, it was couched in terms highly complimentary to himself, and brought the best news as regards the question of faith. Eutyches had been finally condemned and Dioscorus deposed. Leo expresses his satisfaction (*Ep.* to Marcian, civ.). The faith of the church was unmistakably asserted. In Mar. 453 he tells Maximus of Antioch (*Ep.* cxix.) that "the glory of the day is everywhere arisen." "The divine mystery of the Incarnation," he tells Theodoret, "has been restored to the age"; "it is the world's second festivity since the advent of the Lord" (*Ep.* cxx.).

While on this score Leo had every cause for joy, there was one decree of the council against which his legates had protested and which stirred his utmost indignation—viz. the 28th decree on the dignity of the see of Constantinople, which seemed to imperil the unique position of the see of Rome.

Before treating of this, we will take a general review of the position and influence of Leo as bp. of Rome up to this point of his pontificate. The age into which Leo was born was one which demanded, above all else, a firm consistency and therefore centralization in the church. It was an age of little intellectual energy, and was to be succeeded by ages of still less. The world wanted above all things unity and strength, and this was found in taking Rome for a centre and a guide both in faith and in discipline. Accordingly the papal supremacy made a great stride during Leo's life. He has been well called "the first pope," "the Cyprian of the papacy," for we associate with Leo's name the first clear assertion that metropolitans and patriarchs are subject in some way, still undefined, to Rome. What is Leo's own view of his position? In his sermons preached on his "birthday," *i.e.* the day of his consecration—an occasion on which a provincial council used annually to be assembled at Rome—he expresses his sense of his own insignificance but of the magnitude of his position and of the presence of St. Peter in his see, "ordinatissima totius ecclesiae charitas in Petri sede Petrum suscipit" (*Serm.* ii. 2; cf. iii. 3; v. 4). St. Peter is the rock; St. Peter alone has to "strengthen his brethren" (iii. 3; iv. 3). Not only has he the primacy (iii. 4) but is the channel through which is given whatever graces the other apostles have, and so, though there are many bishops and pastors, yet Peter governs them all by his peculiar office ("proprie"), whom Christ governs by His supreme authority ("principaliter"); thus "great and wonderful is the share in its own power which the divine condescension assigned to this man" (lv. 2). Just as the faith of Peter in Christ abides, so also does the commission of Christ to Peter, and "Peter's care rules still all parts of the church" (iii. 2; v. 4). Thus the see of Rome is the centre of sacerdotal grace and of church authority; it represents Peter, "from whom, as from a head, the Lord wills that His gifts should flow out into the whole body, so that he should know he has no share in the divine mystery who has dared to retire from the solid foundation of Peter" (*Ep.* x. 1, *in re* Hilary of Arles). The see of Rome again, occupies in the ecclesiastical world more than the position which the empire of Rome occupies in the secular—"gens sancta, civitas sacerdotalis et regia, caput orbis effecta latius praesidet religione divina quam dominatione terrena"—because the Roman empire uniting the world was just the divine preparation for the spread of the universal Gospel (*Serm.* lxxxii. 1 and 2). This, then, is his theory: let us see how he put it in practice. We see him standing as in a watch-tower, with his eye on every part of the Christian world, zealous everywhere for the interests of the faith and of discipline, and, wherever he sees occasion, taking the opportunity of insinuating the authority of his see, not only in the West, but in the East. The "authority of the apostolic see" to regulate discipline and depose bishops is asserted very absolutely to the bishops of Aquileia and of the home provinces in the beginning of his pontificate; as for the heretics, "obediendo nobis, probent se esse nostros" (*Epp.* i. v. iv.).

With something more of apology (though with the precedent of his predecessors), he asserts his authority—"*in order to prevent usurpations*" in Illyria (*Ep.* v. 1). As his predecessors had done, he appointed a vicegerent, Anastasius of Thessalonica, to whom he wishes the Illyrian bishops to submit as to himself. He is to be to the metropolitans as they are to the ordinary bishops, and a regular system of provincial administration is ordained, by which the assent of the papal vicarius is required for all episcopal elections and by which metropolitans are to be ordained actually by him (*Ep.* vi. 4; but cf. xiv. 6, where the latter point is modified). Biennial provincial councils, summoned by the metropolitans, referring graver matters to a representative synod, summoned by the vicar, whence again difficult questions are to be referred to Rome, are to maintain provincial discipline (*Epp.* xiv. 7; xiii. 2). Moreover, any individual bishop can appeal from the metropolitan directly to Rome, as Atticus, the metropolitan of Epirus Vetus, actually did some years later, securing the pope's interference against the cruel treatment of Anastasius (*Ep.* xiv. 1, p. 685). This supremacy of the papal vicar, which is of great historical importance, seems to have been accepted without remonstrance by the Illyrian churches (*Ep.* xiii. 1). Meanwhile, in 445, a letter from Dioscorus of Alexandria, probably announcing his succession to St. Cyril, gave Leo an opportunity of dictating to the church of Alexandria (*Ep.* ix.). That church owned St. Mark for her founder; should not the church of St. Mark be in complete accord with the church of St. Mark's master? On the strength of this relation between the churches, Leo gives Dioscorus detailed directions about days of ordination and the celebration of mass. About the same time the restless energy of Leo was engaged in his famous controversy with St. Hilary of Arles. This controversy (for which see HILARY), which is of special importance as being the first case in which "the supremacy of the Roman see over Gaul was brought to the issue of direct assertion on the pope's part, of inflexible resistance on the part of his opponent," arose out of an appeal of a bishop, Celidonius, to Rome against the judgment of Hilary. Though some blame attaches to Hilary, Leo's conduct was imperious, precipitate, unjust, and not over-scrupulous. The temptation to press a disputed claim of the Roman see and extend the Roman prerogative was too strong; Leo's violent language about the saintly Hilary (*Ep.* x.), his high-handed treatment of Gallic rights, and his attempt to give a sort of primacy in Gaul to Leontius on the mere score of age cannot be defended. He seems conscious that he is treading on doubtful ground in the beginning of his letter to the Gallic bishops, for he is careful to assert that there is nothing *new* in his proceedings, and that he is *only defending the Gallic bishops from the aggressions of Hilary.* He professes to consult them (c. 4); he fortifies himself with an imperial edict, for which he must be held mainly responsible (*vid. sup.*); though he apparently excluded Hilary from his communion, he did not venture to depose him from his episcopal functions, and on his death speaks of him as "sanctae memoriae" (*Ep.* xl.; cf. Tillem. xv. 80, 89). The peremptory orders of Leo seem to have obtained but inadequate execution in Gaul (Tillem. xv. 86) as shown in the election of Ravennius, Hilary's successor. Leo had desired (*Ep.* lxvi. 2) that the privileges he took from Hilary should be given to the bp. of Vienne; but the latter seems to have taken no part in the consecration of Ravennius, yet Leo speaks of his consecration as constitutionally conducted and divinely inspired (*Epp.* xl. xli.) and appears in the directions he gives Ravennius to recognize him as a metropolitan (*Ep.* xlii.; Tillem. xv. 93). Of the way Ravennius was consecrated, the bp. of Vienne seems to have made no complaint. He did, however, complain of the ordination by Ravennius of a bp. of Vaison (*Ep.* lxvi. 1). This complaint was followed on the other side by a petition from 19 bishops of the three provinces formerly subject to Arles, asking for the restoration to that see of its former dignity. Leo had now an opportunity to mediate. However imperfectly subservient to Leo's wishes the Gallic church had hitherto been, the tone of this letter is sufficiently abject. The pope's authoritative attitude and the imperial edict had done their work. They simply put themselves in Leo's hands. They ground the claim of Arles on ancient custom, civil dignity, and specially on the fact that in Trophimus that town had had the first Gallic bishop, and Trophimus had been sent by St. Peter; they even claim for Arles a certain authority over all Gaul as the vicegerent of the Roman see. Having received this appeal, so satisfactory in its tone, and the counter-complaint from Vienne, Leo proceeded to divide the authority. He examined carefully, he says, the rival claims of Vienne and Arles, and ultimately assigned a limited authority over four churches to the bp. of Vienne, and the rest of the province of Vienne to Arles; of the claims of Arles to larger metropolitan rights, he says nothing (*Ep.* lxvi.). This decision seems to have been acquiesced in by Ravennius, but did not finally stop the disputes of the rival sees (Tillem. xv. 95, 96). Leo sent also his tome to Ravennius for distribution in Gaul and secret communications, "quae committenda litteris non fuerunt," by the mouth of the messengers.

Probably *c.* 446 we find Leo correcting some scandals and asserting his authority in the church of Africa, too weak and disorganized now, from the devastations of Genseric and the recently concluded war, to resist interference as in the days of Celestine. He had sent a representative to make inquiries into alleged violations of discipline there in the election of bishops; on receiving his report, Leo wrote (*Ep.* xii. to the bishops of Mauretania Caesariensis) assuming complete authority over the administration of their church. He even received an appeal from an African bishop, LUPICINUS, and reversed the decision of the African church in receiving him to communion.

In 447 we have seen Leo entering into the affairs of the church of Spain, distracted like the African with barbarian invasions, and dictating the course to be pursued against the Priscillianist heretics; and the same year he sharply reprimanded the Sicilian bishops for the alienation of church property, of which complaints had been laid before him in a Roman synod by the clergy of the despoiled churches (*Ep.* xvii.). The Eutychian controversy went far to aggrandize the position of Rome as the seat of dogmatic truth and the refuge of oppressed orthodoxy. Rome's pretensions to a superior jurisdiction are older than her claims to be the source of dogmatic truth. The claim of infallibility was yet unheard, but it went far to lay the ground of this claim that in the last great controversy about the Incarnation Rome's utterance became the standard of orthodoxy. The glory of being the safest dogmatic guide coalesced with increasing authority as the centre of discipline and government. True, the letter of Leo to Flavian went out for signature east and west on the authority of a council; there is no approach to a claim to dogmatic authority as bp. of Rome on Leo's part; still, the letter was Leo's letter and the stream of things was running in the direction of his exaltation. Moreover, the position of Rome at this period made Leo the recipient of appeal after appeal. Eutyches, Flavian, Eusebius, Theodoret, the presbyters Basil and John (*Ep.* lxxxvii.), made, or were supposed to have made, appeals, and gave Leo opportunities of asserting an old claim. The council of Sardica had framed a canon, allowing appeals from discontented bishops to pope JULIUS. This canon, with the others of this council, was in the Roman church included with the canons of Nicaea, and as such had been quoted by the popes; but that it was not Nicene, the African church had shewn quite clearly in the time of Zosimus. Though Leo could not be ignorant of this fact, he still alleges the authority of Nicaea for the right of appeal (*Ep.* liv. p. 917, in the case of Flavian). No "custom of the Roman church" can justify this. (For the Roman canons, see collection in Migne's *Patr. Lat.* lv. *init.*; Gieseler, *Eccl. Hist.* § 92.)

Leo appears to make no exact or definite claim over the Eastern bishops through the Eutychian controversy. He professes his "universalis cura" for the welfare of the whole church (*Ep.* lxxv.) and claims to be kept fully alive to what goes on in the East (cf. *Ep.* to Flavian, xxiii.), while the power of excluding from his own communion gave him some hold on episcopal elections, which he requires to be notified to him with satisfactory proofs of the orthodoxy of new bishops (cf. his language at his confirmation of Anatolius's election); "nostra communio" all through his writings is an expression of much meaning and weight. Moreover, we have seen that he claimed a right of receiving appeals from all parts of the Christian world, and we shall see him trying to annul the authority of a canon of Chalcedon which displeased him. But when he writes his celebrated letter to Flavian, on the subject of the true faith of the Incarnation, he writes in a tone no wise different from that adopted by St. Cyril in his letters against Nestorius. The bp. of Ravenna (Peter Chrysologus), at the beginning of the Eutychian controversy, wrote to Eutyches recommending him to listen to Rome, because "the blessed Peter who lives and presides in his own see gives the truth of the faith to those who seek it" (*Ep.* xxv. *ad fin.*), but there is nothing of this tone in Leo's own words. He classes his letter with that of Cyril (*Epp.* lxvii.; lxix. 1006): "non aspernetur Anatolius," he says, "etiam meam epistolam recensere, quam pietati patrum per omnia concordare reperiet" (lxx. 1010). After the council of Chalcedon, he commends his own letter as confirmed by the council and witnessed to by patristic testimony (*e.g. Ep.* cxx. to Theodoret, c. 4; cf. esp. *Ep.* cx. 3, 117, where he fortifies himself by the authority of St. Athanasius, and *Ep.* cxxiii. 2, where he speaks of his tome simply as "synodalia decreta"; *Ep.* cxxxix. 4; Leo attached the "testimonia patrum" to his tome after the Robber council, *Ep.* lxxxviii. 3).

Of the Eastern bishops, THEODORET, in making his appeal (*Ep.* lii.), addresses Leo in language very reverential to his see: "If Paul betook himself to Peter that he might carry back from him an explanation to those who were raising questions at Antioch about their conversation in the law, much more do I," etc.; but while he admits it expedient that the pope should have the first place ("primas") in all things, he grounds this position on (1) the greatness of Rome; (2) the continuous piety of the church; (3) the possession of the tombs of St. Peter and St. Paul: not the sort of prerogatives on which Leo would ground his primacy. Flavian addresses Leo in a way entirely consistent with the dignity of his own see. He informs him of the condemnation of Eutyches (*Ep.* xxii.), but only that Leo may *put the bishops subordinate to him on their guard*; and when Flavian asks for Leo's subscription (*Ep.* xxvi.), he asks it for an already canonically made deposition. At the council of Chalcedon, Leo was treated with all possible respect. He had required (*Ep.* lxxxix. to Marcian) that his legates should preside, "on account of the inconstancy of so many of his brethren." Certainly the doubtful orthodoxy of so many of the chief Eastern bishops, and the connexion of Anatolius with Dioscorus, would have made it difficult to find any one so fit as the Roman legates to preside. Moreover, all the influence of Marcian and Pulcheria was on the side of Leo, "giving him entire authority" (Theodor. Lector. lib. i.), except as regards the *place* of the council; hence there were reasons enough for giving him the presidency, even if Leo had not been Leo and Rome Rome. As it was, there was no direct opposition and the influence of his legates was strong enough to enforce in great measure his wishes as to Dioscorus. When the synod proceeded to read Leo's tome, some Illyrian and other bishops raised doubts on certain expressions in it. Explanations were given and conferences held, where those points were shewn by the legates and others to be in agreement with the doctrines of councils and the Ep. of Cyril (Labbe, iv. 367 C, D; 491 D). Finally, his letter was unanimously received, because it was in agreement with the decrees of Nicaea, Constantinople, and Ephesus, and the Epp. of St. Cyril (pp. 471 seq.). "Peter," the bishops cried, "spoke thus by Leo! Leo teaches truly! Cyril taught so! Eternal the memory of Cyril! Leo and Cyril teach alike! This is the faith of the Fathers!" (367, 368).

Thus Leo's letter was treated by the council like the letter of any other highly respected churchman; and in the eighth session of the council Leo's decision on the orthodoxy of Theodoret was not accepted till that bishop had satisfied the synod that he really was orthodox (621 C, D). On one or two points especial reverence for Leo was shewn in the council. According to the Acts of the council, the form in which the papal legates expressed the condemnation of Dioscorus was, "The archbishop of the great and elder Rome, *through us and through the holy synod now present*, together with the . . . apostle Peter, who is the rock . . . has stripped Dioscorus of all sacerdotal dignity" (426 C). This "sentence" indeed exists in a widely different form, as sent by Leo himself to the Gallic bishops (*Ep.* ciii.), in which Leo is described as "head of the universal church," and condemns "by us his vicars with the consent of the synod." The *Acta* are probably the best authority, as we do not know exactly whence Leo's version came. In any case, the papal legates were regarded as *passing sentence on Dioscorus with the consent of the council* (cf. *Patr. Lat.* li. p. 989, note b; Evagr. *H. E.* ii. 4). The title "oecumenical archbishop" is used of Leo in the plea of Sophronius against Dioscorus (Labbe, iv. 411 D), and "bishop of all the churches," or "of the oecumenical church," by the papal legates.* It is, perhaps, in mistaken allusion to these expressions of individuals that pope Gregory I. states that the bishops of Rome were called "universales episcopi" by the council of Chalcedon (Greg. Mag. *Epp.* lib. v. ep. xviii. 743, Migne) and that the title thus offered had been consistently rejected (pp. 749, 771, 919). The synodical letter (*Ep.* xcviii.) which the assembled bishops wrote to Leo was highly complimentary. They speak of him as the "interpreter to all of the blessed Peter." He has presided by his legates as "the head over the members" (c. 1). It is he who took away his dignity from Eutyches (c. 2). They express indignation at the monstrous attempt which Dioscorus made to excommunicate Leo, "he to whom the Saviour intrusted the care of the vine" (c. 3); but all this language, so acceptable to Leo, serves to usher in a very unpleasant matter. The first council of Constantinople had decreed that the bishop of that place should have the primacy of honour after the bp. of Rome, because "it is itself new Rome" (Labbe, ii. 947 C). Leo's statement, that this canon had never taken effect, is entirely untrue. On the contrary, the precedence of honour had become an extensive jurisdiction (Tillem. xv. pp. 701 seq.); and this jurisdiction had now been sanctioned by the 28th canon of the council of Chalcedon, which professed to confirm the canon of Constantinople. "The Fathers," they say, "gave with reason the primacy to the chair of old Rome, because that was the royal city, and, with the same object in view, the 180 pious bishops gave equal primacy (τὰ ἴσα πρεσβεῖα) to the chair of new Rome" (which phase, however, is afterwards explained by the words "*being next after* old Rome"); this addition to the rank of new Rome is grounded on her imperial position; it is then further allowed that the see of Constantinople should have the right of ordaining the metropolitans of Pontus, Asia, and Thrace, and certain other bishops (Labbe, iv. 795 D seq.). From the discussion on this subject the papal legates had retired, saying they had no directions from Rome in the matter; but when the Eastern bishops had confirmed the canon, they demanded and obtained another session, when they protested in vain against it (Labbe, iv. sess. 12). Doubtless the bishops had been partly inspired by jealousy of Rome. Leo's oft-repeated sneer, that they had been compelled to sign, they stoutly denied in session (*ib.* 809, 813 B seq.). This canon the council announce to Leo: their object, they say, was to secure order and good discipline, and it was made at the wish of the emperor, the senate, and the citizens (*Ep.* xcviii. 1097): they therefore express a good hope that Leo will not resist it as his legates did. At the same time, Leo received letters from Marcian, Anatolius (*Epp.* c. ci.), and Julian, expressing joy at the successful suppression of heresy and endeavouring to conciliate him in regard to the 28th canon. Anatolius writes in as conciliatory a tone as possible, urging that the jurisdiction actually reserved for Constantinople is less than custom had sanctioned, repeating that it was at the wish of emperor, senate, and consuls that the canon was passed, and complaining gently of the conduct of the legates after so much deference had been shewn them. It would seem from the words of the "Commonitorium" which he intrusted to his legates (Labbe, iv. 829 E) that Leo had had some inkling of what the council might do in this respect. Indeed Eusebius of Dorylaeum stated in session that he had actually read this canon to Leo, when at Rome, in presence of some clerics from Constantinople, and that he had accepted it (815 B). Leo is, however, now extremely indignant. A very angry tone runs through the letters to Marcian, Pulcheria, Anatolius, and Julian (*Epp.* civ.-cvii.). He urges that when Anatolius's antecedents were so doubtful, an attitude of humility would have best beseemed him (*Epp.* civ. c. 2; cv. 3; cvi. 5), that secular importance cannot confer ecclesiastical privilege, "alia enim est ratio rerum saecularium, alia divinarum" (civ. 3), and that the canon is in flat contradiction to the unalterable decrees of Nicaea, alluding probably to the sixth canon, on the rights of certain metropolitans. He treats very scornfully the assent of the Chalcedonian bishops; it is an "extorta subscriptio"; what can it avail against the protest of the legates? (*Ep.* cv. 1055). He thinks just as little of the decree of Constantinople (*Ep.* civ. 2). He charges Anatolius with having diverted the council from its own proper object to subserve his ambitious purposes (*Ep.* cvi. 2), and finally takes up the cudgels for Antioch and Alexandria, though the bishops of those sees, Theodoret and Maximus, had signed the decree—which indeed does

* Lest we attach too much importance to these flattering titles in the Eastern world, we should notice that the same title is applied to *Dioscorus* at Ephesus (Labbe, iv. 270, 472 A, 479 E; Tillem. xv. 564).

not appear to interfere with the prerogatives which the canon of Nicaea assigned them (cf. Tillem. xv. p. 709), while not only had custom long allowed to Constantinople a position of superior dignity, but that position had been secured to her by a council, of the authority of which Leo had no right to speak so scornfully. The exhortations to avoid ecclesiastical ambition which Leo frequently uses and his contention for the canons of Nicaea did not come with a good grace from a bp. of Rome. If anything can justify Leo's claims, surely it is not the council of Nicaea. In Feb. 453 the emperor wrote to Leo, begging him to send as soon as possible his confirmation of the Acts of Chalcedon, that none might be able to shelter themselves under the excuse that he had not confirmed them (*Ep.* cx.). Leo replied, Mar. 11, to the council and to the emperor (*Epp.* cxiv. cxv.), saying that, if Anatolius had shewn his letters, which he had motives for concealing, no doubt could have existed as to his approval of the decrees of the council, "that is, *as regards faith* ("in sola videlicet causa fidei, quod saepe dicendum est"), for the determination of which alone the council was assembled by the command of the Christian prince and the assent of the apostolic see" (cxiv. 1). To the emperor he sent his assent to the decrees concerning faith and the condemnation of the heretics as a matter of obedience to him, and begged him to make his assent universally known (cxv. 1204, cf. also *Epp.* cxxvi. cxxvii.).

Despite the reverential speeches of council, emperor, and bishops to Leo, neither this canon nor the attitude of the council towards Leo's tome, nor indeed Leo's own way of talking about it, give modern Romanists any great cause for satisfaction with the council of Chalcedon.

Meanwhile, in maintaining the cause of the faith, Leo was asserting his prerogative in many quarters. In 451 Leo's tome was approved in a council under Eusebius of Milan, which sent him a highly complimentary letter (*Ep.* xcvii.), in which, however, the tome is commended as agreeing with St. Ambrose, just as it was by the council of Chalcedon as agreeing with St. Cyril.

About 452 the East was troubled by the tumultuous proceedings of the Eutychian monks in Palestine, headed by one Theodosius, who elected a bishop in place of Juvenal, seized Jerusalem, and committed all sorts of violences (Tillem. xv. § 138, etc.). These disturbances caused Leo great anxiety (*Ep.* cix.), and drew from him (*Ep.* cxxiv.) a clear and admirable exposition of the faith, as lying between Nestorian and Eutychian error. On the death of Marcian in 457 Eutychian risings were attempted in Constantinople and Alexandria (*Epp.* cxl. cxliv.). Leo (*Ep.* cxlv.), writing to congratulate the emperor Leo on his accession, urged him to active measures against the heretics, and by constant letters did all he could to keep Anatolius and Julian also zealous for the Chalcedonian decrees and the suppression of heresy. He urged that the question of the faith should not again be allowed to come into discussion. He complained to Basil, the new bp. of Antioch, that he had not, "according to ecclesiastical custom," notified his consecration to him, and addressed other letters against Timotheus Aelurus to the bishops of Thessalonica, Jerusalem, Corinth, and Dyrrhachium, which he sends for distribution to Julian (*Epp.* cxlix. cl. clii.). He sent the expressions of agreement to his tome from the bishops of Gaul and Spain in a letter to Aetius, and wrote (Oct. 11, 457) condoling with the refugee Egyptian Catholics now in Constantinople (*Epp.* cliv. clv. clx.). "They are not," he says, "exiles from God." Meanwhile, a circular letter from the emperor, asking all the metropolitans to summon provincial councils and collect the opinions of their bishops on the conduct of Timotheus Aelurus and the authority of the Chalcedonian decrees, gave Leo an opportunity of again impressing his views on the emperor, and urging him to make up by his zeal for any laxity in Anatolius (*Ep.* clvi. c. 6). He had both to resist all inclination on the emperor's part to listen to the suggestions which accused his doctrine of Nestorianism, and to oppose strongly the idea of assembling another council, which the emperor had entertained. When the emperor dropped the idea of a council, he proposed, wherever the suggestion may have come from, a conference between some of the Eutychian heretics and an envoy of the pope (*Ep.* clxii.). This again Leo could not consent to, for it involved the discussion of the faith which had been once for all determined, as if it were an open question ("patefacta quaerere, perfecta retractare, definita convellere"). He sent legates, not, however, to dispute, but to teach "what is the rule of the apostolic faith"; and some time in the same year addressed to Leo a long dogmatic epistle (*Ep.* clxv.) sometimes, called the "second tome," closely parallel to the epistle he had before sent for the instruction of the Eutychian monks of Palestine. To it is attached a collection of testimonies, more ample than he had previously sent to Theodosius. In 460 Leo saw his wishes realized in the expulsion of Timotheus Aelurus, who, however, was allowed to come to Constantinople. Leo writes in June to congratulate the emperor on his energy against Aelurus, and to impress on him the need of a pious and orthodox bishop for Alexandria ("in summo pontifice," *Ep.* ccxix. c. 2). At the same time he writes to Gennadius, the new bp. of Constantinople, who had succeeded Anatolius in 468, urging him to be on his watch against Aelurus, whose arrival at Constantinople he deplored and who appeared likely to have a considerable following there. The bishop elected for Alexandria, Timotheus Solofaciolus, met with Leo's warm approval.

The letters which Leo wrote at this time (Aug. 461) to Timotheus, his church, and some monks of Egypt (*Epp.* clxxi. clxxiii.) are the last public documents of his life. Before his death Leo saw the peace of the church of Alexandria established and orthodoxy supreme, for a period at least of 16 years, in the elevation to its throne of Timothy Solofaciolus.

Though Leo was heedless of the rights of national churches, harsh and violent in his treatment of Hilary, and not always very scrupulous in his assertions about the canons of Nicaea, personal ambition was with him wholly merged in the sense of the surpassing dignity of his see, and his zeal was alway high-minded and inspired by an overmastering passion for unity in faith and discipline, and it might have fared ill with that faith and discipline in those days of weakness and trouble if a man of his persistence, integrity, piety, and strength had not been raised up to defend and secure both the one and the other. The notes of the discipline which he enforced were authority, uniformity, and antiquity, the authorities to which he appealed Scripture, tradition, and the decrees of councils or the holy see. His zeal for uniformity shewed itself in the beginning of his reign by his care that the whole of Christendom should celebrate Easter on the same day. In 444, according to the Roman calculation, it fell on Mar. 26, according to the Alexandrian on Apr. 23. In this difficulty Leo wrote to St. Cyril, who replied, of course, in favour of the Alexandrian computation, and Leo had to surrender his point: "non quia ratio manifesta docuerit, sed quia unitatis cura persuaserit," and the Roman cycle gave way to the Alexandrian (*Epp.* lxxxviii. xcvi. cxxi. cxxii. cxxiii. [from Proterius of Alexandria], cxxxvii. cxxxviii.). Where it did not clash with his own he could support the authority of other bishops. He maintained the rights of metropolitans and reproved a bishop for appealing to himself in a difficulty instead of consulting his metropolitan (*Ep.* cviii. 2). The bishop was to rule with a strong hand. He must know the law and must not shrink from enforcing it, for it is "negligent rulers who nourish the plague, while they shrink from applying to it an austere remedy," and the "care of those committed to us requires that we should follow up with the zeal of faith those who, themselves destroyed, would destroy others" (*Epp.* i. 5; iv. 2; vii.). Among his disciplinary directions were regulations forbidding the ordination of slaves (*Ep.* iv.), which, though justified on the ground that they are not free for the Lord's service, are couched in language breathing more of the Roman patrician than of the Christian bishop (cf. "quibus nulla *natalium* dignitas suffragatur," "tanquam servilis vilitas hunc honorem capiat," "sacrum ministerium talis consortii vilitate polluitur"). Moreover a second marriage, or the marriage of a widow or divorced woman, was a bar to orders (*Epp.* iv. 2, 3; xii. 5), and those in orders, even subdeacons, must abstain from "carnale connubium, ut et qui habent, sint tanquam non habentes, et qui non habent, permaneant singulares" (*Epp.* xiv. 4 and clxvii. 3). The day of ordination and consecration was to be Sunday only (*Ep.* vi.) or Saturday night (*Ep.* ix.). The proper antecedents of the consecration of a bishop he declared to be "vota civium, testimonia populorum, honoratorum arbitrium, electio clericorum" (*Ep.* x. 4, 6; ccxvii. 1). In case of a division of votes the metropolitan must decide and be guided by the preponderance of supporters and of qualifications (*Ep.* xiv. 5). When ordained no cleric was to be allowed to wander; he must remain in his own church (*Ep.* i.; cf. xiii. 4; xiv. 7). All must rise in due order from the lower to the higher grades (*Ep.* xii. 4; cf. *Ep.* xix.). Unambiguous condemnation of heresy is to be required before ordination from those who are suspected; and those who are reconverted must give up hope of promotion (*Epp.* xviii.; cxxxv. 2). The multiplication of bishops in small places where they are not needed is forbidden (c. 10). As he insists on the relative dignity of different parts of the body of Christ (*Ep.* cxix. 6), so he reasons that each part should fulfil only its own functions. Laymen and monks—*i.e.* those *extra ordinem sacerdotalem*—are not to be allowed to preach (*Epp.* cxix.; cxx. 6). He would enforce local discipline by insisting on provincial councils. Baptism was only to be given at Easter or Pentecost, except in cases of necessity (*Epp.* xvi. and clxviii.). For the Mass, the rule of the Roman church, which he would enforce on Alexandria also, is that where the church will not hold all the faithful, it should be celebrated on the same day as often as is necessary for them all to "offer" (*Ep.* ix. 2). As to ecclesiastical penance, believing that "indulgence of God cannot be obtained except by sacerdotal supplication," he gives rules for receiving penitents, etc. (*Epp.* cviii. 2; clxvii. 2, 7-14), and directs that in ordinary cases ("de penitentia quae a fidelibus postulatur") private confession, first to God and then to the priest, should be substituted for public confession, the scandals in which might deter from penitence altogether (*Ep.* clxviii.). The laity under penitential discipline are exhorted to abstain from commerce and the civil law courts (*Ep.* clxvii. 10, 11), and even those who have at any time been penitents are advised to abstain from marriage and ordered to abstain from military service (cc. 12-13). Neo of Ravenna asked whether returned captives who had no memory of baptism should be baptized. On this, as a "novum et inauditum" point, Leo consulted the synod, "that the consideration of many persons might lead more surely to the truth" (*Ep.* clxvi. p. 1406). He greatly dreads appearing to sanction a repetition of baptism, but decides that where no remembrance is possible and no evidence can be obtained, baptism may be given. Leo had a strong opinion on usury. "Fenus pecuniae," he says, "est funus animae." "Caret omni humanitate" (*Serm.* xvii.), and it is forbidden to the laity as to the clergy (*Ep.* iv. 2, 4). "Penitence," he says, "is to be measured not by length of time, but by sorrow of heart" (*Ep.* clix. 4); "not instituting what is new, but restoring what is old," is his canon of reformation (*Ep.* x. 2). Among his rules for episcopal government we may notice the following as characteristic: "Integritas praesidentium salus est subditorum, et ubi est incolumitas obedientiae ibi sana est forma doctrinae" (xii. 1); or this: "sic est adhibenda correptio, ut semper sit salva dilectio"; or this: "constantiam mansuetudo commendet, justitiam lenitas temperet, patientia contineat libertatem."

Leo's theology is to be gathered chiefly from some six or seven dogmatic epistles and from his sermons (*Epp.* xxviii. the tome to Flavian, xxv. to Julian, lix. to the church of Constantinople, cxxiv. to the monks of Palestine, cxxxix. to Juvenal, clxv. the "second tome," to the emperor Leo, all written between 449 and 458). These epistles are wholly occupied with the controversial statement of the doctrine of the Incarnation. His others are devoted almost entirely to discipline and organization. Of his genuine sermons 96 remain, five, "de natali suo" (*vid. sup.*), on the see of St. Peter; six, "de collectis," on the duty of almsgiving; nine, "de dec. mens. jejunio," on the duty of almsgiving, prayer, and fasting; ten, "de Nativitate," theological and practical discourses on the Incarnation; eight, "in Epiphaniae solemnitate," containing more narrative than do the Christmas sermons, and specially applicable to an age no longer tried by persecution; twelve, for Lent, on fasting and works of mercy; one on the Transfiguration; nineteen on the passion, preached on Sundays and Wednesdays in Holy Week, being devotional and practical commentaries on the Gospel narrative; two for Easter, preached on the eve; two for Ascensiontide; three for Pentecost, containing theological statements; four for the Pentecostal fast; four on the feasts on St. Peter, St. Paul, and St. Lawrence; nine on the fast of the seventh month; one on the Beatitudes; and one against Eutyches when some Egyptian merchants arrived who tried to justify the doings of the Egyptian Eutychians.

Leo's style is generally forcible, and always to the point—businesslike and severe, epigrammatic and terse in expression. No doubt the love of epigram and antithesis, characteristic of his age, always tends to simple mannerism and obscurity, but in Leo the tendency is under control; he is almost always weighty and clear, and sometimes eloquent. To impress his meaning, he has no objection whatever to repeating himself (*Serm.* xxv. *init.*). Some epistles (*e.g. Epp.* cxxiv. and clxv.) are extremely similar even in language. His sermons are in very much the same style as his epistles. Sozomen (vii. 19) says "that in his day in Rome neither bishop nor any one else teaches the people in the church." This statement is denied and its meaning disputed (cf. notes *in loc.* and Migne, *Patr.* lv. p. 197), but at least we should judge from Leo's sermons that there is no tradition of pulpit eloquence behind him. His tone is that of the Christian bishop, reproving, exhorting, and instructing with the severity of a Roman censor (Milman, *Lat. Christianity*, i. 233). Sometimes indeed he rises to eloquence, but generally speaks with a terse brevity, more adapted, but for its epigrams which would catch the ear, to be read than merely listened to. The sermons are mostly very short, and the practical aspect of the truth as opposed to the speculative is specially prominent. If Christ has renewed our nature, we must live up to the possibilities of the nature He has renewed. The mystery of the Incarnation is incomprehensible by the understanding; but for that let us rejoice, "sentiamus nobis bonum esse quod vincimur" (*Serm.* xxix.). Christ *must* be God and man—man to unite us to Himself, God to save us, "Expergiscere igitur, o homo, et dignitatem tuae cognosce naturae; recordare te factum ad imaginem Dei, quae etsi in Adam corrupta in Christo tamen est reformata" (xxvii. 6).

Leo's theological statements are always characterized by great clearness, fulness, strength, an intense reverence for dogma, and a deep conviction of its supreme importance. His theology is throughout of the *Western* type, for he is wholly on the practical, not on the speculative, side of theology. Philosophical theory, speculation on the relation of the Persons in the Trinity, there is none, only a clear and powerful grasp upon the dogma as an inexpugnable truth of quite incomparable practical importance. Moreover, his statement of the doctrine of the Trinity is Western, tallying with the Athanasian Creed, with none of the Eastern doctrine of "subordination" remaining, "In Trinitate enim divina, nihil dissimile, nihil impar est, ut omnibus existentiae gradibus exclusis, nulla ibi Persona sit anterior, nulla posterior" (*Serm.* lxxv.; lxxvi. 2, cf. *Serm.* xxii. 2, where he interprets "My Father is greater than I" of the *Incarnate* Son only). Being ignorant of Greek, he could not be versed in Eastern theology; but in the "testimonia patrum" (*Ep.* ccxv.), more Greek than Latin fathers are quoted (of course from translations).

His Doctrine of the Incarnation.—This was produced in antagonism to Eutychianism and is coloured by this antagonism. The Eutychianism which he opposes is not so much the particular doctrine of the particular man as that which he represents—namely, the denial of the real and permanent humanity of Jesus Christ. He presents a dilemma to Eutyches: either, he says, denying as you do the two natures in Christ, you must hold the impiety of Apollinaris, and assert that the Deity was converted into flesh and became passible and mortal, or if you shrink from that you fall into the Manichean madness of denying the reality of the body and the bodily acts (*Ep.* cxxiv. 2). If he can escape from this dilemma, he is sure to be only veering to the opposite pole of Arianism. For Christ is spoken of as being "raised," "exalted," etc. What is exalted if the humanity is not real? You must assert the divinity of Christ to be an inferior one, capable of exaltation (*Ep.* lix. 3). Thus Eutyches is to Leo the representative of the "Manichean impiety," as he is fond of calling it, which denies the reality of our Lord's manhood. This gives him his starting-point to assert our Lord's true and perpetual humanity, while avoiding the contrary Nestorian error of abstracting from His perfect divinity, which was always being charged upon the anti-Eutychians, "in integra ergo veri hominis perfectaque natura verus natus est Deus, totus in suis, totus in nostris . . . humana augens, divina non minuens" (*Ep.* xxviii. 3). The human nature was really created and really assumed; created in being assumed (*Ep.* xxxvi. 3). There is the whole of human nature, body and soul, and the whole of the divine (*Ep.* xxxv. 2); each nature remains distinct in its operations, "glorificata permanet in glorificante, Verbo scilicet operante quod Verbi est et carne exsequente quod carnis est. Unum horum coruscat miraculis, aliud succumbit injuriis"; "proprietas divinae humanaeque naturae individua permanet." All through the life he traces the duality of the operations in the unity of the Person (*Epp.* xxviii.; cxxiv. 5). And so perfect is this unity that what is proper to one nature can be ascribed to the other (" communicatio idiomatum," c. 5). The unity is not a mere inhabitation of the Creator in the created nature, but a real mingling of the one nature with the other, though they remain distinct (*Serm.* xxiii. § 1), and the result is " ut idem esset dives in paupertate, omnipotens in abjectione, impassibilis in supplicio, immortalis in morte " (*Ep.* xxxv. 2). Just as the visible light is contaminated by none of the filth on which it sheds itself, so the essence of the eternal and incorporeal light could be polluted by nothing which it assumed (*Serm.* xxxiv. 4).

In proof of this doctrine of the Incarnation Leo appeals to several classes of evidence, sometimes to the analogies of reason—why, he urges, cannot the divinity and humanity be one person, when soul and body in man form one person? (*Ep.* xxvi. 2); constantly to Scripture—the very source of heresy is that man will not labour " in the broad fields of Holy Scripture " (" in latitudine SS.," *Ep.* xxviii. 1 and 2); constantly to the creeds and the past of the church (for he hates novelty)—it is the creed which introduces us to Scripture (*Ep.* cxxviii. 1); we need not blush to believe what apostles and those whom they taught, what martyrs and confessors believed (*Epp.* clxv. 9; clii.); but Leo very often and very characteristically appeals also to consequences, and looks at a doctrine in the light of the necessities of the church's life. What becomes of the salvation of our human nature if Christ have it not? How can He be the Head of the new race? How can He clothe our human nature with His divine? (" Caro enim Christi velamen est verbi, quo omnis qui ipsum integre confitetur induitur," *Ep.* lix. 4). What is the meaning of the Holy Communion of His Body and Blood, the very purpose of which is that, receiving the virtue of the heavenly food, we may pass into (" transeamus in ") His flesh Who became our flesh? (*Ep.* lix. 2; *cf.* also *Serm.* xci. 3). What becomes of the resurrection and ascension; nay, what becomes of His mediation? How does He reconcile man to God if He have not the whole of humanity, except sin? (*Ep.* cxxiv. 6, 7, and *Serm.* xxv. 5, etc.).

The Atonement.—Leo holds the view once prevalent, but now utterly abandoned, which may be stated out of his writings as follows. Man in his fallen state was in slavery to the devil, and, as by his own free will he had fallen, justly so. The devil had certain rights over him which he would retain unless that humanity which he had conquered could conquer him again. In redeeming man, God chose to overcome the devil rather by the rule of justice than of power. To this end He became Man. The Incarnation deceived the devil. He knew not with Whom he was matched. He saw a Child suffering the sorrows and pains of childhood; he saw Him grow by natural stages to manhood, and having had so many proofs that He was mortal He concluded that He was infected with the poison of original sin. So he set in force against Him, as though exercising a right upon sin-stained humanity, all methods and instruments of persecution, thinking that, if He, Whose virtues exceeded so far those of all saints, must yield to death and His merits availed not to deliver Him, he would be secure of every one else for ever. But in persecuting and slaying Christ, Whom was he slaying? One Who was *man*, but sinless, Who owed him nothing, and thus, by exacting the penalty of iniquity from Him in Whom he had found no fault, he went beyond his right. The covenant which bound man to the devil was thus broken. His injustice in demanding too much cancelled the whole debt of man due to him. Man was free. (*Serm.* xxii. 3, 4; lxix. 3; *cf.* xvi. 1, lxi. 4. The nails which pierced our Lord's hands and feet transfixed the devil with perpetual wounds, lxiv. 2, 3.) Thus, to effect our redemption, Christ must have been both man and God; and it was necessary that He should suffer and die by the operations of the devil; and His death has a value different in kind from that of all the saints (*Serm.* lxiv. 2, 3; lix. 1). On the cross of Christ the oblation of human nature was made by a saving victim (lv. 3). His death, the Just for the unjust, was a price of infinite value (lvi. 3; lvii. 4). According to this theory, the price was paid to the devil and man was free; " redemptio aufert captivitatem et regeneratio mutat originem et fides justificat peccatorem " (xxii. 4). Nothing is said about—there is hardly clear room left for—an oblation to God. Elsewhere, however, Leo speaks of Christ as offering a " new and true sacrifice of reconciliation to His Father " (*Serm.* lix. 5; cf. *Ep.* cxxiv. 2, where the sacrifice is clearly conceived as offered to the Father. Cf. also *Serm.* lxiv. 2, 3).

The Doctrine of Grace.—Living, though Leo did, in a time when this doctrine was still in dispute, and mixed up, as he had been, in part of the dispute, we have little in his genuine works on the subject. He speaks of it indeed (*Ep.* i. 3) in orthodox terms. " The whole gift of God's works depends upon the previous operation of God [' omnis bonorum operum donatio, divina praeparatio est '], for no man is justified by virtue before he is [justified] by grace, which is to every man the beginning of righteousness, the fount of good, and the source of merit." Nothing in us, he implies, can antedate the operation of grace; all in us needs the salvation of Christ; but this grace of God which alone justifies was given, not for the first time, but in larger measure (" aucta non coepta ") by Christ's birth, and this " sacrament of great holiness " (the Incarnation) was so powerful, even in its previous indications (" tam potens etiam in significationibus suis "), that they who hoped in the promise received it no less than they who accepted the gift " (*Serm.* xxii. 4). On this subject he often dwells; the Incarnation is the consummation of a previous presence and operation of the Son (*Serm.* xxv. 4). All through the O.T. men were justified by the same faith, and made part of the body of Christ by the same sacrament (*Serm.* xxx. 7; liv. 1). This same truth comes out in his sermons on Pentecost. There is perfect equality, he there says, in the Trinity. " It is eternal to the Father to be the Father of the co-eternal Son. It is eternal to the Son to be begotten of the Father out of all time. It is eternal to the Holy Spirit to be the Spirit of the Father and the Son; so that the Father has never been without the Son, nor the Son without the Father, nor the Father and the Son without the Spirit. Thus the unchangeable Deity of the blessed Trinity is one in substance, undivided and inseparable in operation, concordant in will, alike in power, equal in glory." "What the Father is, that is the Son, and that is the Holy Spirit"; and what the Father does, that does the Son, and that does the Holy Spirit. There was no beginning to the operation of the Holy Spirit upon man since his creation. The descent at Pentecost was not the "beginning of a gift, but the addition of fulness" ("adjectio largitatis") (*Serm.* lxxvi. 3). The difference has lain not in the virtue and reality of the gifts, but in their *measure* (cf. on the unity of divine purpose and love, from first to last of the divine economy, the end of c. 3 of "the tome").

Leo holds that the "merits" of saints can work wonders and aid the church on earth (*Serm.* v. 4). He often speaks of St. Peter assisting his people with his prayers (xii. xiii. xvi. *ad. fin.*, etc.) and with his merits (lxxxi. 4). So also of St. Laurence (lxxxv.). He attributes the deliverance of the city from the barbarians to the "care of the saints" (lxxxiv. 1). The Leonine *Sacramentary*, which certainly contains much of Leo's age, is full of such prayers as "adjuva nos, Domine, tuorum prece sanctorum, ut quorum festa gerimus sentiamus auxilium" (cf. *Ep.* lviii. *init.*; ci. 3, for similar sentiments). But he never speaks of the blessed Virgin as aiding, nor of any saints but St. Peter, St. Paul (*Serm.* lxxxii. *fin.*), and St. Laurence; nor does he invoke them, or direct them to be invoked, though he believes that they are aiding the church by their patronage, prayers, or merits. Elsewhere, distinguishing the value of the deaths of the saints from that of Christ, he very zealously guards the prerogative of Christ as the real source of merit.

To relics he makes no allusion, except where he rejoices that those of St. Flavian had been brought back to Constantinople (*Ep.* lxxix. 2), and perhaps when, writing to Eudocia and Juvenal in Palestine, he seeks to stir their faith through the local memorials of Christ's passion (*Epp.* cxxxix. 2; cxxiii.). Comparing his works with Gregory's, we are struck by the total absence of superstition in Leo. His sermons "are singularly Christian—Christian as dwelling almost exclusively on Christ: His birth, His passion, His resurrection" (Milman, *Lat. Christ.* i. p. 233). We find constant reference to the special dangers and wants of his time—*e.g.* warnings against the prevalent Manicheism. When he converted a number of Manicheans, he at once applied his sermon, regardless of repeating himself, to instruct them (*Serm.* xxv. 1). He reproves the people for forsaking the commemoration of the deliverance of the city, probably from Genseric, which he had instituted on the feast of SS. Peter and Paul, for games and spectacles, and he exhorts them to gratitude to God (lxxxiv.). He reproves idolatrous practices in the church. Magic, charms, cabalistic doctrines, even a worship of the rising sun, were in vogue. Christians, on their way into St. Peter's basilica, would turn and bow to the sun (lxxxiv. 2; xxvii. 4). This worship, which, as he says, was half pagan, akin to that of the Priscillianists and Manicheans, and half due to ignorance in people who really meant to worship the Creator, but which in any case was akin to idolatry, he deeply deplores and earnestly prohibits.

Leo especially urges purity, strictness, and severity of life, in an age no longer disciplined by persecutions. "Kings now," he says, "do not so much pride themselves on being born to empire as rejoice that they are reborn in baptism." The devil tries by avarice and ease those whom troubles could not alienate (xxxvi. 3). Hence the interest of his sermons in Lent and at the other fasts of the "Quattuor Tempora" and those (on almsgiving) "de Collectis." * Prayers, fasting, and almsgiving are, in his view, the three chief parts of Christian duty. "By prayer the mercy of God is sought; by fasting, the lusts of the flesh are extinguished; by almsgiving, our sins are atoned for ['redimuntur']." "The most effectual petition for pardon lies in alms and fasting, and the prayer which is assisted by such suffrages rises more speedily to the ears of God" (xii. 4, xvi. 2). He uses almsgiving in a large sense almost equivalent to love (xliv. 2). "Alms destroy sins" (*Serm.* vii., quoted from Ecclus. iii. 30), "abolish death, extinguish the penalty of eternal fire" (x.). It is a grace without which we can have no other (x.). "He who has cleansed himself by almsgiving need not doubt that even after many sins the splendour of the new birth will be restored to him" (xx. *ad fin.*). But we must look how we give, so as not, *e.g.*, to overlook the retiring; we must "understand about" the poor (ix. 3; "Beatus qui *intelligit super*," Ps. xl. 1). Our gifts should go to those who do not yet believe as well as to Christians (xli. 3), and special thoughtfulness is enjoined for slaves. What God looks to is, he often insists, not the amount, but the spirit of the gift: "ibi censetur qualitus actionis, ubi invenitur initium voluntatis" (xciv. 1); "nulli parvus est census, cui magnus est animus" (*Serm.* xl. 4); and gifts given not in the spirit of faith, though ever so large, avail nothing (xliv. 2). Love, he insists, is the fulfilling of the law. Truth and mercy, faith and love, go together. "There is no love without faith, no faith without love" (cf. esp. *Serm.* xlv.). Fasting, too, is constantly enjoined. Virtue is a very narrow mean (xliii. 2), and strict self-discipline is ever absolutely necessary. But fasting is a means, not an end. It must not proceed from any belief in matter being evil in itself. "No substance is evil, and evil in itself has no nature" (xlii. 4). The object of fasting is to make the body apt for pure, holy, and spiritual activity—to subject the flesh to the reason and spirit. "A man has true peace and liberty when the flesh is ruled by the judgment of the mind, and the mind is directed by the government of God" (xxxix. 2; xlii. 2). He insists strongly on this dominion of the mind. Otherwise "parum est si carnis substantia tenuatur et animae fortitudo non alitur"; "continendum est a cibis

* *I.e.* at that stated period of the year when offerings were made in the Roman church, by an old custom instituted in place of a still older pagan solemnity; cf. *Admonit.* in *Serm.* vi. Migne.

sed multo magis ab erroribus jejunandum" (xci. 2). The "abstinentia jejunantis" must be the "refectio pauperis" (xiii.); "sentiant humanitatem nostram aegritudines decumbentium, imbecillitates debilium, labores exulum, destitutio pupillorum et desolatarum maestitudo viduarum" (xl. 4). Fasting without such works of mercy is not a purification of the soul, but a mere affliction of the flesh (xv.). In Lent, prisoners are to be set free and debts forgiven (xli. 3). If a man cannot fast from bodily weakness, let him do works of love (lxxxvii. 3). Through all Leo's sermons in penitential seasons there runs a great sense of the unity of the church's work and the co-operation of all her members in the penitential discipline and prayers. "The fullest abolition of sins is obtained when the whole church joins in one prayer and one confession" (lxxxviii. 3). The merit of holy obedience is the strength of the church against her enemies (lxxxviii. 2, 3). Public acts are better than individual ones (lxxxix. 2). Leo's remedies for sins—as well those of habitual laxity as the more venial and accidental—are self-examination, penitential works, fasts, prayers, works of mercy and moral self-discipline as the means of purification (cf. l. 1, 2; lxxxviii. 3; xli. 1; xliii. 3). Forgiveness of injuries (xliii. 4) and the exercise of love (xlv.) are insisted on from this point of view: "qui potuit malitia pollui, studeat benignitate purgari" (xlv. 4). The Christian is purified by moral effort and discipline and his sanctification is his purification (but cf. xcii. 1; l. 1, 2; lxxxviii. 5).

Another aspect of Leo's work as an ecclesiastical writer remains to be considered. "The collect as we have it is Western in every feature: in that 'unity of sentiment and severity of style' which Lord Macaulay has admired; in its Roman brevity and majestic conciseness, its freedom from all luxuriant ornament and all inflation of phraseology" (Bright, *Ancient Collects*, append. 206); and there is no early Western writer to whose style it bears a closer resemblance and with whose character it is more consonant than that of Leo, its reputed inventor. How much of Leo's work the fragment of the *Sacramentary* attributed to him by its first editor in 1735, P. Joseph Blanchinius, actually contains, it is impossible to say. "Muratori holds it to be a series of Missae, clumsily put together by a private person at the end of the 5th cent., containing much that [Leo] wrote." Certainly it is Roman, certainly the oldest Roman *sacramentary*, and certainly it contains much which is in the style and expresses the doctrine of St. Leo. As certainly Leo's work, Quesnel with propriety specifies two noble "prefaces," for the consecration of a bishop and a presbyter ("Deus honorum omnium," and "Domine sancte," § xxvii. 111 and 113, Migne), and an "Allocutio archidiaconi ad episcopum pro reconciliatione poenitentium" (at the end of the *Sacramentary* in Migne's ed.). In the *Liber Pontificalis* the addition of the words "sanctum sacrificium, immaculatam hostiam" to the Canon of the Mass is ascribed to Leo (Migne, *Patr.* liv. p. 1233). Collects in the English Prayer-book derived from the Leonine *Sacramentary* are those for the 3rd Sun. after Easter (referring originally to those who had been baptized on Easter Eve), the 5th Sun. after Trinity (suggested originally by the disasters of the dying Western empire), and the 9th, 13th, and 14th Sundays after Trinity. (See Bright, pp. 208, 209).

Before concluding this notice of Leo as a theologian, we must mention a statement of Gennadius (*de Script. Eccles.* lxxxiv.; *Patr. Lat.* lviii. 1107), that the letters of pope Leo on the true Incarnation of Christ are said to have been addressed to their various destinations, and dictated ("ad diversos datae et dictatae") by Prosper of Aquitaine. It is also stated that one or two of Leo's sermons are found in one MS. assigned to St. Prosper. But Gennadius himself attributes "the tome," the chief of Leo's letters on the Incarnation, absolutely to his own hand (c. lxx.). It is very probable that Leo should have brought Prosper, "doctissimus illorum temporum," with him from Gaul to Rome, to assist him in his conflicts with heresy: he may have been secretary to him, as Jerome was to pope Damasus *; he may specially have exerted himself for St. Leo against the Pelagians. But the unity and individuality of style which run all through St. Leo's writings, and which appear not least strongly marked in his dogmatic epistles, forbid us to attribute to Prosper in any sense their *authorship*, though he may have assisted in their composition. (Cf. Tillem. xv. p. 540, xvi. 25, and note 7 on St. Prosper; Arendt, *Leo der Grosse*, p. 417, etc.)

Leo is said to have restored the silver ornaments of the churches of Rome after the ravages of the Vandals, and repaired the basilicas of St. Peter and St. Paul, placing a mosaic in the latter which represented the adoration of the four-and-twenty elders; and to have built a basilica in honour of St. Cornelius, established some monks by the church of St. Peter, instituted guardians, called at first "cubicularii," and afterwards "capellani," for the tombs of the apostles (Tillem. xv. art. 73; *Vita Anastasii*, Migne, *Patr. Lat.* liv. 55, 1234); and received St. Valentine, bp. of Passau, at Rome and sent him to missionary work in Rhaltia (Tillem. xv. 175).

Leo died in 461 (Marcell. *Chron.*, etc.), possibly on Nov. 10 (Tillem. xv. n. 73). He was buried in the church of St. Peter, where, it is said, no previous pope not a martyr was buried (Anast. *Vita Pontif.*, *Patr. Lat.* liv. p. 60, Migne). He has been honoured as a *saint* and *confessor*. Benedict XIV. in 1754 decreed him the title of a *doctor ecclesiae* (*Patr. Lat.* lv. 835). He is commemorated in the Roman church on Apr. 11; in the Eastern on Feb. 18 (*AA. SS.* Apr. ii. p. 15).

The genuine works of Leo which we possess are 96 sermons and 173 letters. On works ascribed to him (the *de Vocatione*, etc.) consult discussions in Migne's *Patr. Lat.* For history of edd. see Schoenemann's *Notitia Hist.-Lit. in S. Leonem*, prefixed to Migne's ed. The most famous editions of his whole works

* It appears probable that *Ep.* cxx. (to Theodoret) was written by a secretary, and that Leo's personal salutation is added at the end. See concluding words, "et alia manu, Deus te incolumem custodiat, frater charissime." Cf. conclusion of *Ep.* cxxxiii. (Proterius to Leo), and Marcian's letter, *Ep.* c.

are Quesnel's (Paris, 1675), a work of consummate learning, but condemned by the popes because of its strong Gallican opinions, and the ed. of the Ballerini (Venice, 1753-1757), which re-edited Quesnel in the Roman interest. This is now the standard ed. and is reproduced in the *Patr. Lat.* of Migne, vols. liv. lv. lvi. Select sermons and letters of St. Leo have been edited by H. Hurter, S.J., in *Sanc. Patrum Opuscula Selecta*, vols. xiv. and xxv. There is an Eng. trans. of selected sermons, with theological notes and "the tome" in the original by Dr. Bright (Lond. 1862).

Materials and Authorities.—i. Leo's own works. ii. The contemporary chronicles of Prosper, Idatius, etc.; *Acta* of council of Chalcedon, etc. iii. Various Lives of Leo, church histories, etc., especially (1) a very brief life in *Hist. de Vitis Romanorum Pontificum* of Anastasius Bibliothecarius (9th cent.) in Migne's *Patr. Lat.* cxxviii. pp. 299 sqq.; (2) *De Vita et Gestis S. Leonis* in *ib.* lv. 153 sqq.; (3) The exhaustive, accurate, and impartial *Mémoire* of Tillemont (*Mém. eccl.* xv. 414–832), (4) Ceillier's *Auteurs sacrés*, vol. x. (for Leo's works); (5) The Bollandist Life by Canisino, *AA. SS.* Apr. ii. 15, of very little value; and, omitting various partisan lives on both sides; (6) an admirable judgment of Leo's life and works, viewing him chiefly as the architect of the papacy, in Böhringer's *Die Kirche Christi und ihre Zengen*, i. 4, pp. 170-309; (7) Milman's, *Lat. Christ.* vol. i. c. 4, an excellent account of Leo and his time; (8) Bright's *Hist. of the Church*, cc. xiv. xv.; (9) Alzog's *Grundriss der Patr.* § 78; and (10) "Leo I." in Herzog's *Real-Encycl.* A short popular Life by the present writer is pub. by S.P.C.K. in their series of *Fathers for Eng. Readers*. A trans. of Leo's letters and sermons is ed. by Dr. Feltoe in the *Lib. of Nic. and Post-Nic. Fathers*. [C.G.]

Leontius (2), bp. of Antioch, A.D. 348-357; a Phrygian by birth (Theod. *H. E.* ii. 10), and, like many leading Arians, a disciple of the celebrated teacher Lucian (Philostorg. iii. 15). When the see of Antioch became vacant by the removal of Stephen, the emperor Constantius effected the appointment of Leontius, who strove to avoid giving offence to either Arians or orthodox. One of the current party tests was whether the doxology was used in our present form or in that which the Arians (*ib.* 13) maintained to be the more ancient, "Glory be to the Father, *through* the Son, *in* the Holy Ghost." Those who watched Leontius could never make out more of his doxology than "world without end. Amen" (Theod. ii. 19). Among the orthodox of his flock were two ascetics, Flavian and Diodorus, who, though not yet advanced to the priesthood, had very great influence because of their holy lives. To them Theodoret ascribes the invention of the practice of dividing the choir into two and chanting the Psalms of David antiphonically, a use of the church of Antioch which legend soon attributed to its martyr-bishop Ignatius (Socr. vi. 8). They assembled the devout at the tombs of the martyrs and spent the whole night in singing of hymns. Leontius could not forbid this popular devotion, but requested its leaders to hold their meetings in church, a request with which they complied. Leontius foresaw that on his death the conduct of affairs was likely to fall into less cautious hands, and, touching his white hairs predicted, "When this snow melts there will be much mud." The orthodox, however, complained that he shewed manifest bias in advancing unworthy Arians. In particular he incurred censure by his ordination to the diaconate of his former pupil Aetius, afterwards notorious as an extreme Arian leader. On the strong protest of Flavian and Diodorus Leontius suspended Aetius from ecclesiastical functions. Philostorgius (iii. 27) relates that Leontius subsequently saved the life of Aetius by clearing him from false charges made to the emperor Gallus. When Athanasius came to Antioch, he communicated not with Leontius and the dominant party, but with the ultra-orthodox minority called Eustathians, who had refused to recognize any other bishop while the deposed Eustathius was alive and who worshipped in private conventicles. Leontius accused Athanasius of cowardice in running away from his own church. The taunt stung Athanasius deeply. He wrote his *Apologia de Fuga* in reply to it, and always speaks bitterly of Leontius, seldom omitting the opprobrious epithet ὁ ἀπόκυπος. He even (*de Fug.* 26) accuses the aged bishop of criminality in his early relations with Eustolium. If there had been any proof of this, Leontius would have been deposed not for mutilation but for corrupting a church virgin; and if it had been believed at Antioch the respect paid him by orthodox members of his flock would be inconceivable. The censure of so great a man irretrievably damaged Leontius in the estimation of succeeding ages, and his mildness and moderation have caused him to be compared to one of those hidden reefs which are more dangerous to mariners than naked rocks. Yet we may charitably think that the gentleness and love of peace which all attest were not mere hypocrisy, and may impute his toleration of heretics to no worse cause than insufficient appreciation of the serious issues involved. The *Paschal Chronicle*, p. 503, quotes the authority of Leontius for its account of the martyrdom of Babylas. Leontius died at the end of 357 or beginning of 358. Athanasius, writing in 358, *Hist. Ar.*, speaks of him as still living, but perhaps the news had not reached Athanasius. [G.S.]

Leontius (62), a scholasticus of Byzantium, and afterwards a monk in Palestine, who wrote *c.* 610 a Gk. treatise *de Sectis* (*Patr. Gk.* lxxxvi. 1193; Cave, i. 543; Ceillier, xi. 666). Cf. Fessler Jungmann, *Inst. Patr.* ii. 2, p. 95; but esp. F. Loofs, *Leontius von Byzanz und die Gleichnamigen Schrifts teller der Griechischen Kirche* (Leipz. 1887); also Herzog's *Encycl.* 3rd ed. *s.v.* "Leonz. von Byzanz." [T.W.D.]

Leontius (74), priest and martyr of Armenia in the reign of Isdigerd II. of Persia. He acted a conspicuous part in the stand of the Armenian church against the court of Persia, as related chiefly in the *History of Vartan* by Elisha Vartabed and in the historical work of Lazarus of Barb. In Nov. 450 700 magian priests, sent under escort to instruct the Armenians in the court religion, arrived at Ankes in the centre of Armenia. There having lain encamped for 25 days, they ordered the church to be broken open. Thus commenced the persecuting violence of Persia. Leontius, putting himself at the head of his people, drove the magian party to flight, after which divine service went on in the church unmolested through the day. A general rising followed, and in 451 66,000 Armenian Christians mustered under prince Vartan in the plain of Artass to encounter the Persian army. Joseph and a large body of his clergy, including Leontius, were present to encourage the Christian forces (Lazarus, § 34 in Langl. ii. 296, 297; Elisha, *u. inf.*). Leontius, who is everywhere mentioned with Joseph, and is usually the orator, as he is the chief inspirer, of the whole movement, delivered a fervent address before the battle (given fully by Langlois), dwelling on the examples of Phineas, Elijah, Gideon, and other famous believers in O.T. (Langl. ii. 218). The battle (June 2, 451, *ib.* 298 note) was lost and a remnant found refuge in the stronghold of Pag. This too was taken and many clergy were put to death. Joseph, Leontius, and their companions, were taken to the court of Persia, and put on their defence. Finally they and four others were executed on the 25th of the month Hroditz in the 16th year of Isdigerd (A.D. 455), in the province of Abar, near a village of the Mogs named Révan. The account of the martyrdom has every appearance of being a genuine coeval record, simple, natural, unlegendary. Lazarus himself wrote in the following generation, and his position gave him access to the best authorities, which he describes, especiallv assuring his readers that he faithfully reports the last words of the martyrs. The most severely dealt with was Leontius, he being regarded as the chief instigator of the Armenian resistance. The general history of these events may be read in Saint-Martin's *Le Beau*, t. vi. pp. 258-318. [C.H.]

Leovigild (LEUVICHILD), Arian king of the Visigoths in Spain from 569 to Apr. or May 586. His reign and that of his successor, the convert RECCARED, represent the crisis of Visigothic history, religious and political.

Upon the death of Athanagild in the winter of 567, the Gothic throne remained unfilled until in 568 Leova, *dux* of the Septimanian province, was made king by the magnates of Gallia Gothica. In 569 he assigned to his younger brother Leovigild the government of the Spanish portion. In the first year of his reign Leovigild married Goisvintha, the widow of his predecessor Athanagild and a strong Arian (Greg. Tur. *H. F.* v. 39). By a previous marriage he had two sons, Hermenigild and Reccared. Leovigild faced the situation with success. His first campaign (A.D. 569) was against the Byzantine settlers and garrisons of the Baza and Malaga districts. For 20 years Cordova had refused to acknowledge the lordship of the Goths, and the great town of the Baetis had been the headquarters of the Imperialist and Catholic power in the Peninsula. Its fall (early in 572 ?) was a heavy blow to the imperial cause in Spain (Joannes Bicl. *Esp. Sagr.* vi. 377). In 572 (573 according to J. Bicl.) Leova died, and Leovigild remained master of both divisions of the kingdom.

Hermenigild's Rebellion.—In 572 (or 573) the king had made both the sons of his first marriage "consortes regni" (J. Bicl. p. 378), and before 580 both were betrothed to Frankish princesses, Hermenigild to his step-niece Ingunthis, granddaughter of Goisvintha, Leovigild's second wife, Reccared to Ingunthis's first cousin, Rigunthis, daughter of Chilperic and Fredegonde. In 580 Hermenigild's bride, a girl of 12 or 13, passed the Pyrenees, "cum magno apparatu" (Greg. Tur. v. 39), having been exhorted on her way by bp. Fronimius of Agde to hold fast her orthodox profession in the midst of the Arian family into which she had married, and who no doubt expected her to become an Arian. She stood firm, and dissension speedily arose with her Arian grandmother. In order to secure family peace Leovigild assigned to Hermenigild and Ingunthis the town of Seville, where the influence of his wife, says Gregory of Tours—of the famous metropolitan of Baetica, Leander, according to Gregory the Great, *Dial.* iii. 41—converted Hermenigild to Catholicism (*Hist. Fr.* v. 39; Paul. Diac. W. iii. 21). He was confirmed in the orthodox faith by Leander. The son thus placed himself in opposition to his father and to all the Gothic traditions, and was brought into natural alliance with the forces threatening the Gothic state, with the Byzantines in the S., the Suevi in the N., and the disaffection smouldering among Leovigild's provincial subjects. The young couple may well have appeared to the Catholics convenient instruments for dealing a deadly blow at the heretical Gothic monarchy; while in the case of the Byzantines a strictly political motive would also be present.

The peril was a grave one. Leovigild, with a combination of energy and prudence, assembled a council of Arian bishops (581, mentioned in C. Tol. iii. as occurring in the 12th year of Leovigild), which drew up a formula designed to facilitate the conversion of Catholics to Arianism. Rebaptism was no longer demanded as heretofore. Converts should give glory to the Father "per Filium in Spiritu Sancto." (The Gloria Patri plays an important part in the history of Spanish Arianism. Cf. Greg. of Tours's conversation with Leovigild's envoy, the Arian Oppila—*Hist. Franc.* vi. 40, and C. Tol. iii.) A *libellus* containing the decisions of the council was widely circulated (C. Tol. iii. 16; Tejada y Ramiro, ii.) and other temptations were offered to the Catholic bishops and clergy. Isidore and Joannes mournfully confess that many yielded. The king also began to pay scrupulous respect to Catholic feeling and belief and to Catholic saints, and to pray in Catholic churches (Greg. Tur. vi. 18). "I believe," he is reported to have said, "with firmness that Jesus Christ is the Son of God, equal to the Father, but I do not at all believe that the Holy Ghost is God, since in no book of Scripture do we read that He is God." By such means Leovigild endeavoured to secure the Catholic party within the territory outside Hermenigild's influence.

During 581 and 582 Hermenigild had assumed a more and more formidable position, but Leovigild marched S. to the siege of Seville, which lasted through 583 into 584, and after the fall of Seville up the Guadalquivir valley to Cordova. Here the rebellion collapsed.

The imperial prefect was bribed to give up Hermenigild, who took refuge in a church, whence he was tempted by the promises of his father and brother. Leovigild embraced and pardoned him within the church, but as soon as he was drawn thence is reported to have ordered him to be despoiled of his royal dress and of his servants (*Hist. Franc.* vi. 43). He was conveyed to Toledo, and thence exiled to Valencia (A.D. 584) (Joh. Bicl. p. 383), and in 586 met his death at Tarraco at the hands of Sisebert. Upon this brilliant success followed the final incorporation of the Suevi with the Gothic state in 585.

Persecution of the Catholics.—Leovigild had crushed the Catholic and Byzantine conspiracy of which Hermenigild had been the instrument, and there followed an outbreak of that savage and fanatical temper so characteristic of the Visigothic race. The persecuting temper of the Arian kings, however, had always some political justification. The Catholic church was the natural foe of her Arian rulers, and when her attempts to shake them off failed, it was inevitable that the penalty should fall heavily on her and on her bishops. Leander of Seville was banished, Fronimius of Agde was obliged to fly into Merovingian territory (*Hist. Franc.* ix. 24), an Arian bishop was sent to Merida, and Masona, after ineffectual attempts by the king to win him over to Arianism, was imprisoned (Paulus Emerit. *Esp. Sagr.* xiii. p. 369). From the signatures at the conversion council it is evident that in many sees, especially within the newly annexed Suevian territory, a large but indefinite number of Catholic bishops were replaced by Arians. (On the general subject of the persecution, cf. Greg. Tur. v. 39, and for various doubtful details of it, see Greg. Tur. *Glor. Conf.* xii.; *Glor. Mart.* lxxxii.; and *de Vit. et Mir. Patr. Emerit.* c. xi.)

Leovigild died in Apr. or May, 586, at Toledo, according to some reports constant to the beliefs in which he had lived, according to others—less trustworthy—a repentant convert to Catholicism, mourning over the unrighteous death of his first-born son.

"Leovigild's reign," says Dahn, "represents the last attempt to maintain the Gothic state in its traditional aspects and character by the strenuous use of all possible weapons against its traditional dangers—war with Catholicism, chastisement of the nobility, reinvigoration of the monarchy, and defence of it against its hostile neighbours" (v. 150). An Arian monarchy, strong in all directions—towards its own pillars and supporters, the Gothic nobles, towards foreign outsiders, and towards its natural enemy Catholicism—this appears to have been Leovigild's ideal. To its influence may be traced most of the actions of his government, the association of his sons, his treatment of the rebellious and murderous nobles, his attitude towards the Catholic bishops, and, above all, certain alterations in the outer aspects of Gothic kingship which mark his reign and shew him prepared to accept just so much of Roman custom as would further his ends.

The conversations which Gregory of Tours reports between himself and Leovigild's Arian envoys on their way through Tours to Soissons or Paris (*H. F.* v. 44; vi. 40) throw much light upon the every-day social relations between Arianism and Catholicism at the time.

Sources.—Joannes Biclarensis, abbat of Biclaro and bp. of Gerona, a contemporary of Leovigild, his *Chronicon*, apud Florez. *Esp. Sagr.* vi.; Isidore of Seville, writing *c.* 630, *Hist. Goth.* ib.; Paulus Diaconus Emeritensis, fl. 650, *de Vit. et Mir. Patr. Emeritensium Esp. Sagr.* xiii. Dahn's *Könige der Germanen* remains the best account of the reign in point of insight and treatment; an exhaustive discussion of all the moot points is that by Prof. F. Görres, "*Kritische Untersuchungen über den Aufstand und das Martyrium des westgothischen Königssohnes Hermenigild,*" in *Zeitschrift für hist. Theol.* (1873). [M.A.W.]

Leucius (1), the reputed author of large apocryphal additions to the N.T. history, which originated in heretical circles, and which, though now lost, were much current in early times. The fullest account is that given by Photius (*Cod.* 114), who describes a book, called *The Circuits of the Apostles*, which contained the Acts of Peter, John, Andrew, Thomas, and Paul, and purported to have been written by Leucius Charinus. This second name Charinus is peculiar to Photius, earlier writers calling the author simply Leucius, a name variously altered by transcribers. Photius characterizes the book as in style utterly unlike the genuine N.T. writings, and full of folly, self-contradiction, falsehood, and impiety. It taught the existence of two gods—an evil one, the God of the Jews, having Simon Magus as his minister, and a good one, from Whom Christ came. It confounded the Father and the Son; denied the reality of Christ's Incarnation, and gave a Docetic account of His life on earth and especially of His crucifixion. It condemned marriage and regarded all generation as the work of the evil principle; denied that demons were created by God; related childish stories of miraculous restoration to life, of both men and cattle; and in the Acts of John used language which the Iconoclasts regarded as favouring them. From this description we can identify as the same work a collection of Apostolic Acts, from which extracts were read at the 2nd council of Nicaea (*Actio* v., Mansi, xiii. 167), the story of Lycomedes (see *D. C. B.* 4-vol. ed.) being that made use of by the Iconoclasts, and the Docetic tales being from this work. In the council was next read a citation from Amphilochius of Iconium, denouncing certain heretical Acts of the Apostles, and in particular arguing against the truth of a story, evidently that to which we have just referred, because it represented St. John as on the Mount of Olives during the crucifixion, and so contradicted the gospel, which relates that he was close to the Cross. With this evidence that the work read by Photius was in existence before the end of the 4th cent., we may probably refer to the same source a statement of Epiphanius (*Haer.* 51, p. 427) that Leucius was a disciple of John and joined his master in opposing the Ebionites. Church writers frequently reject the doctrine of heretical apocrypha and yet accept stories told in such documents as true, provided there were no doctrinal reason for rejecting them. The Docetic Leucius, who denied the true manhood of our Lord, was at the opposite pole from the Ebionites, who asserted Him to be mere man, and therefore the Acts of John might well have contained a confutation of Ebionism. The Acts of Leucius were in use among the Manichees in the time of St. Augustine. Faustus the Manichean (bk. 30, c. 4, vol. viii. p. 447) appeals to Acts of the four apostles mentioned by Photius (Peter, Andrew, Thomas, and John), charging the Catholic party with wrongly excluding them from their canon. In several places Augustine refers to the same Acts (*Cont. Adimant.* 17, viii. 137, 139; *Cont. Faust.* xxii. 79, p. 409; *Cont. adv. Leg. et Proph.* i. 20, p. 570), and he names as the author Leutius, the name being written in some MSS. Levitius or Leuticius (*Act. cum Felice*, ii. 6, p. 489; see also *de Fid.* cc. 5, 38, App. pp. 25, 33). In the passage last cited, the writer, supposed to be Evodius of Uzala, a contemporary of Augustine, quotes from the Acts of Andrew a story of Maximilla, the wife of the proconsul Egeas under whom St. Andrew suffered, who, to avoid having intercourse with her husband, without his knowledge substituted her maid in her own place; and on another occasion, when she and her companion were engaged hearing the apostle, an angel, by imitating their voices, deceived the husband into the belief that they were still in her bedchamber. This story, which agrees with what Photius tells of the author's condemnation of sexual intercourse, is much softened in the still extant Acts of Pseudo-Abdias, which are an orthodox recasting of a heretical original. We find still the names of Maximilla and Egeas; but Maximilla does not refuse intercourse with her husband, and only excites his displeasure because, on account of her eagerness to hear the apostle, she can be with him less frequently; and, without any angelic deception, providential means are devised to prevent Egeas from surprising his wife at the Christian meeting. These Augustinian notices enable us to infer that it was the same work Philaster had in view when he stated (*Haer.* 88) that the Manichees had Acts purporting to be written by disciples of St. Andrew, and describing apostle's doings when he passed from Pontus into Greece. He adds that these heretics had also Acts of Peter, John, and Paul, containing stories of miracles in which beasts were made to speak; for that these heretics counted the souls of men and of beasts alike (see Epiph. *Haer.* 66, p. 625). In the Gelasian decree on apocryphal books we read: "Libri omnes, quos fecit Leucius discipulus diaboli, apocryphi," where we have various readings, Lucianus and Seleucius (Thiel, *Epp. Rom. Pont.* 463). In the spurious correspondence between Jerome and Chromatius and Heliodorus, Jerome is represented as giving an orthodox version of certain authentic additions to St. Matthew's narrative, of which a heretical version had been given by Leucius (or, as it is printed, Seleucus), the author of the Acts already mentioned. In the letter of Innocent to Exsuperius (Mansi, iii. 1041) he condemns documents bearing the name of Matthew, of James the Less, of Peter and Paul written by Leucius, of Andrew written by Xenocharis and Leonidas the philosophers, and of Thomas. It has been conjectured that in Xenocharis an adjective has been joined with a proper name, and that we have here a corruption of Charinus. In the Latin version of the apocryphal *Descensus Christi ad inferos* (Tischendorf, *Evan. Apoc.* p. 369), two sons of the aged Simeon, named Leucius and Charinus, are represented as having died before our Lord, and as miraculously returning to bear witness to His triumphs in the under world. The writer clearly borrowed these names from the apocryphal Acts; did he there find warrant for regarding them as the names of distinct persons, or was Photius right in reporting both names to have been given to the same person? It would seem that only the Acts of John and perhaps of Peter named Leucius as their author: the necessities of the fiction would require the Acts of Andrew to be attested by a different witness, possibly Charinus, and it is conceivable that Photius may have combined the names merely from his judging, no doubt rightly, that all the Acts had a common author. Concerning the Acts of Paul in use among the Manicheans see LINUS and THECLA. Besides the authorities already cited, the Acts of Leucius are mentioned by Turribius, a Spanish bp. of the first half of the 5th cent., from whom we learn that they were used by the Priscillianists, and that the Acts of Thomas related a baptism, not in water but in oil, according to the Manichean fashion; and by Pseudo-Mellitus (Fabric. *Cod. Apoc. N.T.* ii. 604), who acknowledges the truth of apostolic miracles related by Leucius, but argues against his doctrine of two principles. Pacian (*Ep.* i. 2; Migne, *Patr. Lat.* xiii. 1053) says, "Phryges nobiliores qui se animatos a Leucio mentiuntur, se institutos a Proculo gloriantur." On this passage Zahn (see *infra*) mainly relies for dating the Acts of Leucius earlier than 160. But no other writer mentions a Montanist use of these Acts, and on this subject the authority of Pacian does not count for much. The context does not indicate that he had much personal knowledge of the sect, and his heretical notices appear to be derived from the Syntagma of Hippolytus, where we have no reason to think that he would have found any mention of Leucius. It is highly probably that Pacian, as well as others of his contemporaries, believed that Leucius was a real companion of St. John, and therefore no doubt earlier than Montanus; but that he had any means of real knowledge as to this we have no reason to believe. Besides those authorities which mention Leucius by name, others speak of apocryphal Acts, and probably refer to the same literature. Thus the *Synopsis Scripturae* ascribed to Athanasius (ii. 154) speaks of books called the Travels (περίοδοι) of Peter, of John, and of Thomas; and by the second the Leucian story is probably intended. Eusebius (iii. 25) tells of Acts of Andrew and of John; Epiphanius (*Haer.* 47) states that the Encratites used Acts of Andrew, John, and Thomas; that the Apostolici relied on Acts of Andrew and Thomas (*ib.* 61); and that those whom he calls Origeniani used Acts of Andrew (*ib.* 63). It is worth remarking that it is of the three apostles, Thomas, Andrew, and John, whose travels were written by Leucius, that Origen (*ap.* Eus. *H. E.* iii. 1) can tell where the lot of their preaching had fallen, viz. India, Scythia, and Asia respectively.

The testimonies we have cited are not earlier than the 4th cent., and several of them speak of Leucius as a Manichean; but Grabe, Cave, Mill, Beausobre, Lardner, and others consider that he lived in the 2nd cent.; and, as he therefore could not have been a Manichean, was probably a Marcionite. Some have identified him with the Marcionite LUCANUS. But no Marcionite would have chosen for the heroes of his narrative the Jewish apostles, John, Thomas, and Andrew. Beausobre (*Manichéisme*, i. 350) gives six arguments for the early date of Leucius, not one of which is conclusive, all being vitiated by the tacit assumption that Leucius was a real person, and not, as we hold, merely the fictitious name of an imaginary disciple of St. John, whom the forger chose to make the narrator of the story.

Zahn (*Acta Johannis*, 1880) published some new fragments of Leucius, which increase our power of recognizing as Leucian things which different fathers have told without naming their authority. The Leucian character of these fragments is verified by various coincidences with the old. Names recur, *e.g.* Lycomedes. There is a story of a miracle performed on one Drusiana, who had submitted to die rather than have intercourse with her husband. This agrees with that of Maximilla and Egeas in revealing the violently Encratite principles of the author; cf. that told in the *Acts of Thomas* (Tischendorf, *Acta Apoc.* p. 200). Zahn has argued the case for the early date of Leucius in a much more scientific way than previous supporters of the same thesis. He tries to shew that there are statements in earlier writers really derived from Leucius, though his name is not given. All Zahn's arguments do not seem to us conclusive, yet enough remains valid to lead us to regard the Leucian Acts as of the same age as the travels of Peter (which are the basis of the Clementines) and the Acts of Paul and Thecla. When a writer, who in one place quotes Leucius, elsewhere makes statements we know to be Leucian, they doubtless come from Leucius though he does not there name his authority; *e.g.* Epiphanius names Leucius only once, but we may safely count as derived from Leucius his reference to the manner of John's death (*Haer.* 79, 5) and to John's virginity (*ib.* 28, 7; 78, 10). Further, in the immediate context of the passage where Epiphanius names Leucius, he names other heretics of the apostolic age, and the presumption that he found these names in Leucius becomes almost a certainty when in one of the new Leucian fragments one of them, Cleobius, is found as that of a person in John's company. Other names in the same context are Claudius, Merinthus, and the Pauline Demas and Hermogenes; concerning whom see the Acts of Thecla and the so-called Dorotheus (*Paschal Chron.* ed. Dindorf, ii. 124). The Augustinian and Hieronymian notices may be treated similarly. We can identify as Leucian several statements* which are described as found "in ecclesiastica historia" or "in patrum traditionibus," and hence probably others reported with the same formulae are from the same source.

We next enumerate some of the statements which may be characterized as Leucian, naming some of the early writers who have repeated them. (1) A Leucian fragment (Zahn, p. 247) tells how John's virginity had been preserved by a threefold interposition of our Lord, breaking off the Apostle's designs each time that he attempted to marry. There is a clear reference to this story in a sermon ascribed to Augustine (Mai, *Nov. Pat. Bib.* I. i. 378), and from this source probably so many of the Fathers have derived their opinion of John's virginity, concerning which the canonical Scriptures say nothing (Ambros. *de Inst. Virg.* viii. 50, vol. iii. 324; Ambrosiaster on II. Cor. xi. 2, vol. iv. 2, 232; Hieron. *in Isaiam*, c. 56, vol. iv. p. 658; *adv. Jovin.* I. 26, vol. ii. 278; August. *cont. Faust.* xxx. vol. x. 535, *in Johan.* c. 21, vol. iv. 1082; Epiph. *Haer.* 58, 4). The Leucian Acts, in conformity with their strong Encratism, seem to have dwelt much on the apostle's virginity, describing this as the cause of our Lord's love to him, and as the reason for his many privileges, particularly the care of the virgin mother. In *Pistis Sophia* the name of the apostle John has usually the title ὁ παρθένος appended, and we may therefore set down *Pistis Sophia* as post-Leucian, but uncertainty as to its date prevents us from drawing any further inference. The earliest mention of John's virginity is found in the epithet "spado" given to St. John by Tertullian (*de Monog.* 17), whence Zahn infers that Tertullian must have used the Acts of Leucius. We think Zahn does not sufficiently allow for the probability in the case of one who is said to have lived so long, that a true tradition that he never married might have been preserved in the churches of Asia. Zahn contends that because Jerome uses the word "eunuchus," not "spado," he is not copying Tertullian, but that both writers use a common source, viz. Leucius. But when the passage in Tertullian is read with the rest of the treatise, it appears more likely that the epithet is Tertullian's own. (2) Other evidence of Tertullian's acquaintance with Leucius is found in his story of St. John's having been cast into burning oil. Speaking of Rome he says, "Ubi apostolus Johannes, posteaquam in oleum igneum demersus nihil passus est, in insulam relegatur." What was Tertullian's authority? Now, though none of the extant fragments of Leucius relate to this, yet that these Acts contained the story is probable from the following evidence. Jerome (vol. vii. p. 655) commenting on Matt. xx. 23 states on the authority of "ecclesiasticae historiae" that the apostle had been "missus in ferventis olei dolium, et inde ad suscipiendam coronam Christi athleta processerit, statimque relegatus in Pathmos insulam." Now Abdias, whose work is notoriously based on Leucius (*Hist. Ap.* v. 2, Fabric. *Cod. Ps. N.T.* ii. 534), has "proconsul jussit eum velut rebellem in

* In particular an account of a hymn supposed to have been sung on the night before the crucifixion by the apostles holding hands and forming a circle about our Lord (see Aug. *Ep.* 237 *ad Ceretium*, vol. ii. p. 849).

dolio ferventis olei mergi, qui statim ut conjectus in aeneo est, veluti athleta, unctus non adustus de vase exiit." The second passage will be seen to be the original, Jerome's use of *athleta* receiving its explanation from Abdias. This conclusion is strengthened by another passage in Jerome (*adv. Jovin.* i. 26, vol. ii. 278), where, though he names Tertullian as his authority, he gives particulars not found in him, viz. the "dolium ferventis olei," and that the apostle came out fresher and more vigorous than he had entered. We feel forced to believe that Jerome, who certainly used Leucius, found in it the statement about the boiling oil; and then there is a strong case for suspecting that this was also the authority of Tertullian. But though Tertullian names Rome as the scene of the miracle, it may be doubted whether this was so in the Greek Leucius. The mention by Abdias of a "proconsul" suggests Asia. Hippolytus, however, agrees with Tertullian in placing John at Rome (*de Christo et Antic.* 36). Some of the earliest Fathers who try to reconcile Matt. xx. 23 with the fact that John did not suffer martyrdom, do not mention this story of the baptism in oil (Origen, *in loc.* De la Rue, iii. 719). A later story makes John miraculously "drink a cup" of poison with impunity.

(3) An acquaintance with Leucius by Clement of Alexandria has been inferred from the agreement of both in giving on John's authority a Docetic account of our Lord. The "*traditions of Matthias*" may have been Clement's authority; but that John is appealed to no doubt gives probability to the conjecture that Clement's source is the Acts which treat of St. John, a probability increased on an examination of the story told by Clement (*Hypotyp. ap.* Eus. *H. E.* vi. 14) as to John's composition of the Fourth Gospel at the request of his friends. In the Muratorian Fragment the request is urged by the apostle's fellow-bishops in Asia; he asks them to fast three days, begging for a revelation of God's will, and then it is revealed to Andrew that John is to write. The stories of Clement and the Muratorian writer are too like to be independent; yet it is not conceivable that one copied from the other; therefore they doubtless used a common authority, who was not Papias, else Eusebius, when he quotes the passage from Clement, would scarcely have failed to mention it. Now, several later writers (Jerome in pref. to *Comm. on Matt.*, a writing pub. as St. Augustine's—Mai, *Nov. Pat. Bibl.* I. i. 379—Victorinus in his *Scholia* on the Apoc., Galland. iv. 59; and others, see Zahn, p. 198) tell the same story, agreeing, however, in additional particulars, which shew that they did not derive their knowledge from either the Muratorian writer or Clement. Thus they tell that the cause of the request that John should write was the spread of Ebionite heresy, which required that something should be added concerning the divinity of our Lord to what St. John's predecessors had told about His humanity; and that, in answer to their prayers, the apostle, filled with the Holy Ghost, burst into the prologue, "In the beginning was the Word." Other verbal coincidences make it probable that this story was found in the Acts of Leucius, which Epiphanius tells us contained an account of John's resistance to the Ebionite heresy; and if so, Leucius is likely to have been Clement's authority also.

Combining the probabilities under the three heads enumerated, there seems reasonable ground for thinking that the Leucian Acts were 2nd cent., and known to Clement and Tertullian. Irenaeus, however, shews no sign of acquaintance with them, and Clement must have had some other source of Johannine traditions, his story of John and the robber being, as Zahn owns, not derived from Leucius; for no later writer who tells the story shews any sign of having had any source of information but Clement.

We cannot follow Zahn in combining the two statements of Theodoret (*Haer. Fab.* iii. 4) that the Quartodecimans appealed to St. John's authority, and that they used apocryphal Acts, and thence inferring that Leucius represented St. John as sanctioning the Quartodeciman practice. If so, we think other traces of this Leucian statement would have remained. Theodoret would have found in Eusebius that the churches of Asia appealed to St. John as sanctioning their practice, and that may have been a true tradition.

A brief notice will suffice of other probable contents of the work of Leucius. He appears to have mentioned the exile to Patmos, and as resulting from a decree of the Roman emperor; but that the emperor was not named is likely from the variations of subsequent writers. Zahn refers to Leucius the story of St. John and the partridge, told by Cassianus, who elsewhere shews acquaintance with Leucius. A different story of a partridge is told in a non-Leucian fragment (Zahn, 190). The Leucian Acts very possibly contained an account of the Virgin's death. [Mellitus.] But the most important of the remaining Leucian stories is that concerning St. John's painless death. Leucius appears to have given what purported to be the apostle's sermon and Eucharistic prayer on the last Sunday of his life. Then after breaking of bread—there is no mention of wine—the apostle commands Byrrhus (the name occurs in the Ignatian epistles as that of an Ephesine deacon) to follow him with two companions, bringing spades with them. In a friend's burying-place they dig a grave, in which the apostle laid himself down, and with joyful prayer blessed his disciples and resigned his soul to God. Later versions give other miraculous details; in particular that which Augustine mentions (*in Johann.* xxi. vol. 3, p. 819), that St. John lay in the grave not dead but sleeping, the dust heaped over him showing his breathing by its motions. For other Johannine stories, see Prochorus.

Besides the Acts Leucius has been credited with a quantity of other apocryphal literature. If, as we believe, he is only a fictitious personage, it is likely enough that the author of the romance wrote other like fictions, though our information is too scanty for us to identify his work. But there is no trustworthy evidence that he affixed the name of Leucius to any composition besides the Acts of Peter and John. From the nature of the case an apostle's martyrdom must be related by one of the apostles' disciples, but such a one would not be regarded as a competent witness to the deeds of our Lord

Himself, and accordingly apocryphal gospels are commonly ascribed to an apostle, and not to one of the second generation of Christians. The only apparent evidence for a connexion of the name of Leucius with apocryphal gospels is the mention of the name in the spurious letter of Jerome to Chromatius and Heliodorus, a witness unworthy of credit even if his testimony were more distinct. Probably the orthodox, finding in the Acts which bore the name of Leucius plain evidence that the writer was heretical in his doctrine of two principles, still accepted him as a real personage of the sub-apostolic age, and when they met with other apocryphal stories, the doctrine of which they had to reject as heretical while willing to accept the facts related as mainly true, Leucius seemed a probable person to whom to ascribe the authorship. [LINUS.] [G.S.]

Liberatus (7) Diaconus, archdeacon of Carthage, a Latin writer on the Nestorian and Eutychian heresies, an account of which he wrote entitled, *Breviarium Causae Nestorianorum et Eutychianorum*, in which he records some circumstances of his life. He visited Rome in the pontificate of John II. on the affair of the Acoemetae order of monks (c. 20). In 535 he was deputed to Rome, with the bps. Caius and Peter, by the council of Carthage, to consult John II. as to how conforming Arian bishops should be received. They arrived about the time of the pope's death (he was buried May 27, 535), and his successor Agapetus (consecrated June 3, 535) replied to the synod by the three envoys (Mansi, viii. 849). Liberatus was an ardent defender of the *Three Chapters*, and undertook many journeys in that cause. On his return home he composed his *Breviarum*, so named as being an abridgment in 24 chapters of a history which, beginning with the ordination of Nestorius in 428, reached to the meeting of the fifth synod in 553. The work was probably written *c.* 560. Liberatus intimates in his preface that he collected his materials from the *Ecclesiastical History* which had been recently translated from the Greek into Latin (as Garnier thinks, the *Historia Tripartitia* of Cassiodorus), from the Acts of the councils, and from episcopal letters. The *Breviarum* was ed. with copious notes and dissertations by Garnier in 1675 (8vo, Paris), and this ed. is reprinted by Migne (*Patr. Lat.* lxviii. 969). Accounts of Liberatus will be found in Dupin (*Eccl. Wr.* t. i. p. 558, ed. 1722), Ceillier (xi. 303), Cave (i. 527), Fabric. (*Bibl. Lat.* t. iv. p. 272, ed. Mansi, 1754). [C.H.]

Liberius (4), ordained bp. of Rome May 22, 352 (*Catalog. Liber.*), as successor to Julius I. The assassination of Constans (A.D. 350) and the subsequent defeat of Magnentius in 351 had left Constantius sole emperor. New charges against Athanasius were sent to the emperor and Julius the pope, and the latter dying before they reached him, the hearing of fell to his successor Liberius. These charges were that Athanasius had influenced Constans against Constantius, corresponded with Magnentius, used an unconsecrated church in Alexandria, and disregarded an imperial summons calling him to Rome (Athan. *Apol. ad Constantium*). They were considered, together with an encyclic of 75 Egyptian bishops in behalf of Athanasius, by a council under Liberius at Rome in 352, and on this occasion the first charge of compliance with heresy is alleged against Liberius. Among the fragments of Hilary (*Fragm. IV.*) there is a letter purporting to be addressed by Liberius to his "beloved brethren and fellow-bishops throughout the East," declaring that he agrees and communicates with them, and that Athanasius, having been summoned to Rome and refused to come, is out of communion with himself and the Roman church. Bower (*Hist. of the Popes*), Tillemont (*Vie de S. Athan.* t. viii. art. 64, note 68), and Milman (*Lat. Christ.* bk. i. c. 2), accept this letter as genuine. Baronius, the Benedictine editors of the works of Hilary, Hefele (*Conciliengesch.* bk. v. § 73)—the last very positively—reject it as an Arian forgery; their principal, if not only, ground being the improbability of his writing it.

The death of Magnentius in the autumn of 353 left Constantius entirely free to follow his own heretical bent, when Liberius certainly stood forth as a fearless champion of the cause under imperial disfavour. He sent Vincentius of Capua, with Marcellus, another bp. of Campania, to the emperor, requesting him to call a council at Aquileia to settle the points at issue. Constantius being himself at Arles, summoned one there, which was attended in behalf of Liberius by legates. The main object of the leaders of the council, in which Valens and Ursacius took a prominent part, was to extort from the legates a renunciation of communion with Athanasius. After a fruitless attempt to obtain from the dominant party a simultaneous condemnation of Arius, the legates at length complied. Paulinus of Trèves refused, and was consequently banished (Sulp. Sev. l. 2; Hilar. *Libell. ad Const.*; id. *in Fragm.*; *Epp.* Liber. *ad Const. et Eus.*). Liberius, on hearing the result, wrote to Hosius of Cordova much distressed by the weakness of his messenger Vincentius, and to Caecilianus, bp. of Spoletum (Hilar. *Fragm. VI.*).

Subsequently (A.D. 354), most of the Western bishops having, under fear or pressure, expressed agreement with the East, Lucifer, bp. of Cagliari, being then in Rome, was, at his own suggestion, sent by Liberius to the emperor, to demand another council. The result was a council at Milan in the beginning of 355, attended by 300 Western bishops and but few Easterns. In spite of the bold remonstrances of Eusebius of Vercelli, Lucifer, Dionysius of Milan, and others, the condemnation of Athanasius was decreed, and required to be signed by all under pain of banishment. The pope's three legates were among the few who refused and were condemned to exile (see Sulp. Sev. l. 2; Athan. *Hist. Arian. ad Monachos*). Liberius at Rome still stood firm. He wrote to Eusebius (*ap. Act.* Eus.) congratulating him on his steadfastness, and sent an encyclic (*ib. et* Hilar. *Fragm. VI.*) to all the exiled confessors, encouraging them, and expressing his expectation of soon suffering like them. The emperor failed to turn him by threats or bribes. Finally Leontius, the prefect of Rome, was ordered to apprehend him and he was taken to Milan (see Athan. *op. cit.* c. 35 seq.). Theodoret (l. ii. c. 13) recounts in detail his interview with the emperor there.

"I have sent for you," said Constantius, "the bishop of my city, that you may repudiate the madness of Athanasius, whom the whole world has condemned." Liberius continued to insist that the condemnation had not been that of a fair and free council, or in the presence of the accused, and that those who condemned him had been actuated by fear or regard to the emperor's gifts and favour. Liberius having warned the emperor against making use of bishops, whose time ought to be devoted to spiritual matters, for the avenging of his own enmities, the latter finally cut short the discussion by saying, "There is only one thing to be done. I will that you embrace the communion of the churches, and so return to Rome. Consult peace, then, and subscribe, that you may be restored to your see." "I have already," Liberius replied, "bidden farewell to the brethren at Rome; for I account observance of the ecclesiastical law of more importance than residence at Rome." "I give you three days," the emperor said, "to make up your mind: unless within that time you comply, you must be prepared to go where I may send you." Liberius answered, "Three days or three months will make no difference with me: wherefore send me where you please." Two days having been allowed him for consideration, he was banished to Beroea in Thrace (A.D. 355). The emperor sent him, on his departure, 500 pieces of gold, which he refused, saying, "Go and tell him who sent me this gold to give it to his flatterers and players, who are always in want because of their insatiable cupidity, ever desiring riches and never satisfied. As for us, Christ, Who is in all things like unto the Father, supports us, and gives us all things needful." To the empress, who sent him the like sum, he sent word that she might give it to the emperor, who would want it for his military expeditions; and that, if he needed it not, he might give it to Maxentius (the Arian bp. of Milan) and Epictetus, who would be glad of it. Eusebius the eunuch also offered him money, to whom he said, "Thou hast pillaged the churches of the whole world, and dost thou now bring alms to me as a condemned pauper? Depart first, and become thyself a Christian." His banishment was followed by a general triumph of the Arian party. In Alexandria Athanasius was superseded by George of Cappadocia, the orthodox there cruelly persecuted, and Athanasius compelled eventually to take refuge among the hermits and coenobites of Egypt. In Gaul, in spite of the fearless protest of Hilary of Poictiers, the orthodox were persecuted and banished, and there also heresy triumphed. With regard to Rome, we find traces of two conflicting stories, one gathered from the practically unanimous testimony of contemporary or ancient writers of repute, some of whom have been our authorities so far—viz. Athanasius (*Hist. Arian. ad Monach.* 75), Jerome (*Chron. in ann. Abram.* mccclx.), Rufinus (*H. E.* x. 22), Socrates (*H. E.* ii. 37), Sozomen (*H. E.* iv. 8, 11), Theodoret (*H. E.* ii. 14), together with Marcellinus and Faustus, two contemporary Luciferian presbyters of Rome, in the preface to their *Libellus Precum*, addressed to the emperors Valentinian, Theodosius, and Arcadius, during the pontificate of Damasus, the successor of Liberius. The other, in conflict therewith, is in the Pontifical and the Acts of Martyrs. From the former authorities we learn that immediately after the exile of Liberius all the clergy, including the deacon FELIX (archdeacon according to Marcellinus and Faustus), swore before the people to accept no other bishop while Liberius lived. The populace, who appear throughout strongly on his side, debarred the Arians from the churches, so that the election of a successor, on which the emperor was determined, had to be made in the imperial palace. The deacon Felix was there chosen and consecrated, three of the emperor's eunuchs representing the people on the occasion, and three heretical bishops, Epictetus of Centumellae, Acacius of Caesarea, and Basilius of Ancyra being the consecrators. It seems probable that a considerable party among the clergy at least concurred in this consecration. Marcellinus and Faustus say that the clergy ordained him, while the people refused to take part; and Jerome states that after the intrusion of Felix by the Arians very many of the clerical order perjured themselves by supporting him. Felix appears to have been himself orthodox, no distinct charge of heresy being alleged by his accusers; only that of connivance with his own unlawful election by Arians in defiance of his oath, and of communicating with them. Two years after the exile of Liberius (A.D. 357), Constantius went to Rome, and Theodoret tells us that the wives of the magistrates and nobles waited on the emperor, beseeching him to have pity on the city bereaved of its shepherd and exposed to the snares of wolves. Constantius was so far moved as to consent to the return of Liberius on condition of his presiding over the church jointly with Felix. When the emperor's order was read publicly in the circus, there burst forth the unanimous cry, "One God, one Christ, one bishop!" There appears to have been some delay before the actual return of Liberius, who was required to satisfy the emperor by renouncing orthodoxy and Athanasius. This he was now, in strange contrast to his former firmness, but too ready to do. It appears that bp. Fortunatian of Aquileia had been employed by the Eusebians to persuade him (Hieron. *Catal. Script.* 97), and that Demophilus of Beroea had personally urged him to comply (*Ep.* Liber. *ad Orient. Episc. ap.* Hilar. *Fragm. VI.*). Hilary (*Fragm. VI.*) gives letters written by Liberius from Beroea at this time. One is to the Eastern bishops and presbyters; from which we give extracts, with Hilary's parenthetical comments: "I do not defend Athanasius: but because my predecessor Julius had received him, I was afraid of being accounted a prevaricator. Having learnt, however, that you had justly condemned him, I soon gave assent to your judgment, and sent a letter to that effect by bp. Fortunatian of Aquileia, to the emperor. Wherefore Athanasius being removed from the communion of us all (I will not even receive his letters), I say that I have peace and communion with you and with all the Eastern bishops. That you may be assured of my good faith in thus writing, know that my lord and brother Demophilus has deigned in his benevolence to expound to me the true Catholic faith which was treated, expounded, and received at Sirmium by many brethren and fellow-bishops of ours. (*This is the Arian perfidy :—This I have noted, not the apostate ;—the following are the words of Liberius.*) This I have received with a willing mind (*I say anathema to thee, Liberius, and thy companions*), and in no respect contradict ; I have given my assent, I follow and hold it. (*Once more, and a third time, anathema to thee, prevaricator Liberius !*) Seeing that you now perceive me to be in agreement with you in all things, I have thought it right to beseech your holinesses to deign by your common counsel and efforts to labour for my release from exile and my restoration to the see divinely entrusted to me." Another is to Ursacius, Valens, and Germinius, begging their good offices, and excusing his apparent delay in writing, as above, to the Oriental bishops. Before sending that letter he had already, he says, condemned Athanasius, as the whole presbytery of Rome could testify, to whom he seems to have previously sent letters intended for the emperor's eye. He concludes, "You should know, most dear brethren, by this letter, written with a plain and simple mind, that I have peace with all of you, bishops of the Catholic church. And I desire you to make known to our brethren and fellow-bishops Epictetus and Auxentius that with them I have peace and ecclesiastical communion. Whoever may dissent from this our peace and concord, let him know that he is separated from our communion." In giving this letter, Hilary again expresses his indignation in a note : "Anathema, I say to thee, prevaricator, together with the Arians." A third is to Vincentius of Capua, the bishop whose defection at Milan he had once so much deplored. In this he announces that he had given up his contention for Athanasius, and had written to say so to the Oriental bishops, and requests Vincentius to assemble the bishops of Campania and get them to join in an address to the emperor, "that I may be delivered from my great sadness." He concludes, "God keep thee safe, brother. We have peace with all the Eastern bishops, and I with you. I have absolved myself to God ; see you to it : if you have the will to fail me in my banishment, God will be judge between me and you."

No sufficient grounds exist for doubting the genuineness of the fragment of Hilary which contains these letters, or of the letters themselves. It is resolutely denied by Hefele (*Conciliengeschichte,* Bd. v. § 81) and by the Jesuit Stilting in the work of the Bollandists (*Acta SS.* Sept. t. vi. on Liberius), but their arguments are weak, resting chiefly on alleged historical difficulties and on the style of the letters. All the great Protestant critics accept them ; and among the Roman Catholics Natalis Alexander, Tillemont, Fleury, Dupin, Ceillier, Montfaucon, Constant, and Möhler. Dr. Döllinger does the same. Dr. Newman also (*Arians of the Fourth Century*) quotes them without any note of suspicion. Baronius accepts the letters to the Eastern bishops and to Vincentius, but rejects that to Valens and Ursacius, though only on the ground of its implied statement that Athanasius had been excommunicated by the Roman church. A refutation of Hefele's arguments is contained in P. le Page Renouf's *Condemnation of Pope Honorius* (Longmans, 1868), from which an extract, bearing on the subject, is given in Appendix to the Eng. trans. of Hefele's work (Clark, Edin. 1876). Even if the fragment of Hilary could be shewn to be spurious, the general fact of the fall of Liberius would remain indisputable, being attested by Athanasius (*Hist. Arian.* 41 ; *Apol. contr. Arian.* 89), Hilary (*contra Const. Imp.* 11), Sozomen (iv. 15), and Jerome (*Chron. et de Vir. Illustr.* 97). It was never questioned till comparatively recent times, when a few papal partisans—especially Stilting (*loc. cit.*), Franz Anton Zaccaria (*Dissert. de Commentitio Liberii lapsu*), Professor Palma (*Praelect. Histor. Eccles.* t. i. pt. ii. Romae, 1838)—have taken up his defence, relying primarily on the silence of Theodoret, Socrates, and Sulpicius Severus on his fall. Others, as Hefele, endeavour to extenuate its extent and culpability.

In the letter to the Eastern bishops Liberius speaks of having already accepted the exposition of the faith agreed upon "by many brethren and fellow-bishops" at Sirmium. It is a little uncertain what confession is here meant. There had been two noted synods of Sirmium and both had issued expositions of doctrine. The first in 351, assembled by the Eusebians, adopted a confession which asserted against Photinus and Marcellus of Ancyra the pre-existent divinity of the Son before His human birth and, but for its omission of the term *consubstantial,* was not heretical. Hilary of Poictiers (*de Syn.* 38 sqq.) allows it to be orthodox. Baronius and the Benedictine editors of Hilary (with whom agrees Dr. Döllinger in his *Papst-fabeln des Mittelalters*) maintain that this was the creed accepted by Liberius at Beroea. The formula of the second Sirmian synod, assembled in 357 by Constantius at the instance of the Anomaeans, prohibited both the definitions, *homoousios* and *homoiousios*, as being beyond the language of Scripture, and declared the Father to be in honour, dignity, and majesty greater than the Son, and, by implication, that the Father alone may be defined as without beginning, invisible, immortal, impassible. The doctrine expressed was essentially that of the Homoeans, though the phrase "like-unto the Father," from which they got their name, was not yet adopted. This may have been the creed accepted by Liberius at Beroea. His credit is not much saved by supposing it to have been the former one, since his letters are sufficient evidence of his pliability. Whichever it was, his acceptance was not enough to satisfy the emperor, who, having gone from Rome to Sirmium, summoned him thither, where he was required to sign a new formula, apparently prepared for the occasion. This was, according to Sozomen, concocted from three sources : first, the creed of the old Antiochene council of 269, in which the term *consubstantial,* alleged to be used heretically so as to compromise the Son's Personality by Paul of Samosta, was condemned ; secondly, one of the creeds issued by the Eusebian council at Antioch in 341, which omitted that term; and thirdly, the first Sirmian creed, above described. Sozomen adds that he signed also a condemnation of those who denied the Son to be *like* the Father according to substance and in all respects. When Liberius is said by some writers to have been summoned from Beroea to the *third* synod of Sirmium, and to have signed the *third* Sirmian confession, we must not understand those sometimes so called, viz. of May 359 (when a distinctly Homoean formula, prepared by bp. Mark of Arethusa, was subscribed), but the compilation above described.

Liberius was now allowed to return to Rome. Felix was compelled by the populace to retire from the city after tumults and bloodshed. Attempting afterwards to obtain a church beyond the Tiber, he was again expelled.

Two ways have been resorted to of excusing, in some degree, the compliance of Liberius. One, taken by Baronius and Hefele, is that the formulae he subscribed were capable of being understood in an orthodox sense, and so subscribed by him, though otherwise intended by the emperor: that "Liberius renounced the formula ὁμοούσιος, not because he had fallen from orthodoxy, but because he had been made to believe that formula to be the cloak of Sabellianism and Photinism" (Hefele). Baronius, however, condemns him so far as to say that his envy of Felix and his longing for the adulation to which he had been used at Rome led to his weakness. The other way is that of Bellarmine, who acknowledges his external but denies his internal assent to heresy: a view which saves his infallibility at the expense of his morality. The facts remain that in his letters from Beroea he proclaimed his renunciation of Athanasius and his entire agreement and communion with the Easterns, and that at Sirmium he signed a confession drawn up by semi-Arians, which was intended to express rejection of the orthodoxy for which he had once contended. Athanasius, Sozomen, Hilary, and Jerome all allude to his temporary compliance with heresy in some form as a known and undoubted fact. Athanasius, however, unlike Hilary, speaks of it with noble tolerance. He says, "But they [*i.e.* certain great bishops] not only supported me with arguments, but also endured exile; among them being Liberius of Rome. For, if he did not endure the affliction of his exile to the end, nevertheless he remained in banishment for two years, knowing the conspiracy against me" (*Apol. contra Arian.* 89). Again, "Moreover Liberius, having been banished, after two years gave way, and under fear of threatened death subscribed. But even this proves only their [*i.e.* the Arians'] violence, and his hatred of heresy; for he supported me as long as he had free choice" (*Hist. Arian. ad Monach.* 41). Once in possession of his see and surrounded by his orthodox supporters, Liberius appears to have resumed his old position of resolute orthodoxy. In 359 were held the two councils at Ariminum in the West and Seleucia in the East, resulting in the almost universal acceptance for a time of the Homoean formula, which Constantius was now persuaded to force upon the church in the hope of reconciling disputants. This called forth the famous expression of Jerome (*Dial. adv. Lucifer.* 19), "The whole world groaned, and wondered to find itself Arian." Liberius was not present at Ariminum, nor is there any reason to suppose that he assented to the now dominant confession. Jerome's language is rhetorical, and, on the other hand, Theodoret (*H. E.* ii. 22) gives a letter from a synod of Italian and Gallican bishops held at Rome under pope Damasus, stating that the Ariminian formula had the assent neither of the bp. of Rome, whose judgment was beyond all others to be expected, nor of Vincentius, nor of others besides.

The death of Constantius (A.D. 361) and the accession of Julian the Apostate having left the orthodox free from direct persecution, Athanasius returned once more in triumph to Alexandria (A.D. 362). In the council, famous for its reassertion of orthodoxy, then held at Alexandria, Liberius seems to have taken no prominent part. The glory of restoring orthodoxy and peace to the church is mainly due, not to the bp. of Rome, but to Athanasius, Eusebius of Vercelli, and Hilary of Poictiers.

Liberius comes next under notice in the last year of his episcopate, and during the reign of Valentinian and Valens, who became, at the beginning of 364, emperors of the West and East respectively, Valentinian being a Catholic, Valens an extreme and persecuting Arian. His persecutions extending to the semi-Arians as well as to the orthodox, caused the former to incline to union with the latter and to the position that the difference between them was one rather of words than of doctrine. They came about this time to be called Macedonians, and now turned to the Western emperor and the Roman bishop for support in their distress, sending three bishops as a deputation to Valentinian and Liberius, with instructions to communicate with the church of Rome and to accept the term "consubstantial." Valentinian was absent in Gaul, but Liberius received them (A.D. 366). At first he rejected their overtures because of their implication in heresy. They replied that they had now repented, and had already acknowledged the Son to be in all things like unto the Father, and that this expression meant the same as "consubstantial." He required a written confession of their faith. They gave him one, in which they referred to the letters brought by them from the Eastern bishops to him and the other Western bishops; anathematized Arius, the Sabellians, Patripassians, Marcionists, Photinians, Marcellianists, and the followers of Paul of Samosata; condemned the creed of Ariminum as entirely repugnant to the Nicene faith; and declared their entire assent to the Nicene creed. They concluded by saying that if any one had any charge against them, they were willing it should be heard before such orthodox bishops as Liberius might approve. Liberius now admitted them to communion, and dismissed them with letters, in the name of himself and the other Western bishops, to the bishops of the East who had sent the embassy.

Liberius died in the autumn of 366 (Marcell. and Faust.), having thus had a notable opportunity of atoning by his latest official act for his previous vacillation.

His extant writings are the letters referred

to above. There is also a discourse of his given by St. Ambrose (*de Virginibus*, lib. iii. c. 1) as having been delivered when Marcellina (the sister of Ambrose, to whom he addresses his treatise) made her profession of virginity. The discourse is interesting as containing the earliest known allusion to the keeping of the Christmas festival, while the way in which Ambrose introduces it shews the estimation in which Liberius was held, notwithstanding his temporary fall. [J.B—Y.]

Licentius (1). [ROMANIANUS.]

Linus (1), accounted the first bp. of Rome after the apostles, and identified by Irenaeus (iii. 2) with the Linus from whom St. Paul sent greetings to Timothy (II. Tim. iv. 21). For the question of the order of succession of the alleged earliest bishops of Rome, and of the positions held by the persons named, see CLEMENS ROMANUS. As Linus there is no difference of opinion, since in all the lists he comes first. Eusebius (*H. E.* iii. 13) assigns 12 years to his episcopate; the Liberian Catalogue 12 years, 4 months, and 12 days, from A.D. 55 to 67; the Felician Catalogue 11 years, 3 months, and 12 days. These cannot be accepted as historical, nor can the statements of the last-named catalogue, that he died a martyr, and was buried on the Vatican beside the body of St. Peter on Sept. 24. [J.B—Y.]

Under the name of Linus are extant two tracts purporting to contain the account of the martyrdom of SS. Peter and of Paul. These were first printed in 1517 by Faber Stapulensis as an appendix to his *Comm. on Saint Paul's Epistles*. These Acts of Linus have so many features common with the Leucian Acts [LEUCIUS] that the question arises whether we have not in Linus either a translation of a portion of the collection described by Photius or at least a work for which that collection supplied materials. Linus does not profess to give a complete account of the acts of the two apostles. He begins by briefly referring to (as if already known to his readers) the contest of St. Peter and Simon Magus, his imprisonments and other sufferings and labours, and then proceeds at once to the closing scenes. The stories of the martyrdom of the two apostles are quite distinct, there being no mention of Paul in the first nor of Peter in the second. The apostles' deaths are immediately brought about, not by Nero himself, but by his prefect Agrippa, a name, we may well believe, transferred by a chronological blunder from the reign of Augustus. This name, as well as some others mentioned by pseudo-Linus, occur also in the orthodox Acts of Peter and Paul published by Tischendorf and by Thilo. The alleged cause of Agrippa's animosity exhibits strongly the Encratite character common to Linus and the Leucian Acts. St. Peter, we are told, by his preaching of chastity had caused a number of matrons to leave the marriage bed of their husbands, who were thus infuriated against the apostle.

The intention to destroy Peter is revealed by MARCELLUS and other disciples, who pressingly entreat him to save himself by withdrawing from Rome. Among those who thus urge him are his jailors, Martinianus and Processus, who had already received baptism from him, and who represent that the plan to destroy Peter is entirely the prefect's own and has no sanction from the emperor, who seems to have forgotten all about the apostle. Then follows the well-known story of *Domine quo vadis*. St. Peter yields to his friends' entreaties, and consents to leave Rome, but at the gate he meets our Lord coming in, Who, on being asked whither He is going, replies, "To Rome, in order to be crucified again." The apostle understands that in his person his Master is to be crucified, and returns to suffer. Linus tells of the arrest of Peter, and lays the scene of the crucifixion at the Naumachia near Nero's obelisk on the mountain. St. Peter requests to be crucified head downwards, desiring out of humility not to suffer in the same way as his Master. A further reason is given, that in this way his disciples will be better able to hear his words spoken on the cross, and a mystical explanation is given of the inverted position which bears a very Gnostic character. An alleged saying of our Lord is quoted which strongly resembles a passage from the Gospel according to the Egyptians, cited by Julius Cassianus (Clem. Al. *Strom.* iii. 13, p. 553, see also Clem. Rom. ii. 12), "Unless ye make the right as the left, the left as the right, the top as the bottom, and the front as the backward, ye shall not know the kingdom of God." Linus relates how during Peter's crucifixion God, at the request of the apostle, opened the eyes of his sorrowing disciples, and so turned their grief into joy. For they saw the apostle standing upright at the top of his cross, crowned by angels with roses and lilies, and receiving from our Lord a book, out of which he reads to his disciples. This story has a good deal of affinity with that told by Leucius of a vision of our Lord during His crucifixion, seen by St. John on the Mount of Olives. The story of Peter's crucifixion head downwards was in the Acts known to Origen, who refers to it in his Comm. on Gen. (Eus. *H. E.* iii. 1). Linus relates that Marcellus took Peter's body from the cross, bathed it in milk and wine, and embalmed it with precious spices; but the same night, as he was watching the grave, the apostle appeared to him, and bid him let the dead bury their dead and himself preach the kingdom of God.

The second book, which treats of St. Paul, relates the success of his preaching at Rome. The emperor's teacher, his hearer and close friend, when he cannot converse with him, corresponds with him by letter. The emperor's attention is called to the matter by a miracle worked by Paul on his favourite cupbearer, Patroclus, of whom a story is told exactly reproducing that told of Eutychus in *Acts*. Nero orders St. Paul's execution, Paul turns his face to the east, offers a prayer in Hebrew, blesses the brethren, binds his eyes with a veil lent by a Christian matron, Plautilla, and presents his neck to the executioner. From his trunk there flows a stream of milk—a circumstance referred to by Ambrose and by Macarius in a work not later than *c.* 400. A dazzling light makes the soldiers unable to find the veil; returning to the gate they find that Plautilla has already received it back from Paul, who has visited her accompanied by a band of white-robed angels. The same evening, the doors being shut, Paul appears to the emperor, foretells his impending doom, and terrifies him into ordering the release of the prisoners he had apprehended. The story ends with an account of the baptism of the three soldiers who had had charge of St. Paul, and been converted by him. After his death he directs them to go to his grave, where they find SS. Luke and Titus praying and receive baptism at their hands.

Lipsius infers, from the coincidences of the tolerably numerous N.T. citations in Linus with the Vulg., that our present Latin Linus must be later than Jerome; but he does not seem to have appreciated the conservative character of Jerome's revision or to have consulted the older versions. We have found no coincidence with the Vulg. which is not equally a coincidence with an older version; and in one case, "relinque mortuos sepelire mortuos suos," the text agrees with the quotations of Ambrose, Jerome's translation being "dimitte." We conjecture the compiler to have been a Manichean, but he is quite orthodox in his views as to the work of creation, the point on which Gnostic speculation was most apt to go astray. [G.S.]

Lucanus (1), or **Lucianus,** Marcionite (*Lucanus*, Pseudo-Tert. 18; Philast. 46, and so probably their source, the Syntagma of Hippolytus; Tertull. *de Resur. Carn.* 2; Λουκᾶνος, Orig. *cont. Cels.* ii. 27; on the other hand, Λουκιανός Hippol. *Ref.* vii. 37; Epiph. *Haer.* 43). The former is the better attested form, and more likely to have been altered into the other. The Lucianites are reckoned as a sect distinct from the Marcionites, as well by Origen as by Hippolytus and his followers; but lack of authentic report of any important difference in doctrine leads us to believe that Lucanus did not separate from Marcion, but that after the latter's death Lucanus was a Marcionite teacher (probably at Rome), whose celebrity caused his followers to be known by his name rather than by that of the original founder of the sect. They may have been so called in contradistinction to the Marcionites of the school of Apelles, who approached more nearly to the orthodox. Origen's language (οἶμαι) implies that he had no very intimate knowledge of the teaching of Lucanus; he will not speak positively as to whether Lucanus tampered with the Gospels. Epiphanius owns that, the sect being extinct in his time, he had difficulty in obtaining accurate information about it. Tertullian alone (*u.s.*) seems to have direct knowledge of the teaching of Lucanus. He accuses him of going beyond other heretics who merely denied the resurrection of the body, and of maintaining that not even the soul would rise, but some other thing, neither soul nor body. Neander (*Ch. Hist.* ii. 189) interprets this to mean that Lucanus held that the ψυχή would perish and the πνεῦμα alone be immortal; and possibly this may be so, though Tertullian's language would lead us to attribute to Lucanus a theory more peculiar to himself than this would be. Some commentators, taking a jest of Tertullian's too literally, have, without good reason, ascribed to Lucanus a doctrine of transmigration of souls of men into bodies of brutes. They have, however, the authority of Epiphanius (*Haer.* 42, p. 330) for regarding this doctrine as one likely to be held by a Marcionite. Lucanus has been conjectured to be the author of the apocryphal Acts which bore the name of LEUCIUS, and Lardner treats the identification as certain. Even, however, if it were certain that the Acts of Leucius were Marcionite, not Manichean, and as early as the 2nd cent., there is no ground for this identification but the similarity of name. [G.S.]

Lucianus (8), a famous satirist, the wittiest, except Aristophanes, of all the extant writers of antiquity. Born (probably *c.* 120) at Samosata on the Euphrates, the son of poor parents, he gradually betook himself to the composing and reciting of rhetorical exercises, which he did with continually increasing success as he journeyed westwards, visiting Greece, Italy, and Gaul, where his success reached the highest pitch. As in course of time his rhetorical vein exhausted itself, he betook himself, when about 40 years old, to that style of writing—dialogue—on which his permanent fame has rested. About the same time he returned eastwards through Athens, and was at Olympia in A.D. 165, when he saw the extraordinary self-immolation by fire of the sophist Peregrinus. A little later he visited Paphlagonia, where he vehemently attacked, and made a bitter enemy of, the impostor Alexander of Abonoteichos. Of the extraordinary success of this man in deluding the weak and credulous minds of the rude people of those parts, and even the cultivated senators of Rome, Lucian has left us an animated account in the *False Prophet* (ψευδόμαντις). Lucian once had an interview with him, and stooping down, instead of kissing his hand, as was the custom, bit it severely. Luckily he had a guard of two soldiers with him, sent by his friend the governor of Cappadocia (a proof of Lucian's importance at this time), or he would have fared badly at the hands of the attendants of Alexander. The latter pretended reconciliation, and subsequently lent Lucian a ship to return home in, but gave secret instructions to the crew to throw him overboard on the voyage. The master of the ship, however, repented, and Lucian was landed at Aegialos, and thence conveyed to Amastris in a ship belonging to the ambassadors of king Eupator. He endeavoured to get Alexander punished for this piece of treachery, but the latter's influence was too strong. Of his later years we know but little; he was, however, appointed by the emperor (probably Commodus) to a post of honour and emolument in Egypt.

We do not know the cause, manner, or time of his death. His writings, with all their brilliancy, do not convey the impression of a warm-hearted man; the *Peregrinus* is especially noticeable for the hard unconcern with which he describes both the self-sacrificing love of the Christians and the tragic self-sought death of the sophist. For cool common sense and determination to see everything in its naked reality, apart from the disturbing influences of hope, fear, enthusiasm, or superstition, he has never in any age been surpassed. His most essential characteristic could not be better described than in his own words, in the dialogue entitled Ἁλιεύς, or the *Fisherman*: "I am a hater of imposture, jugglery, lies, and ostentation, and in short of all that rascally sort of men; and there are very many of them" (§ 20). Shortly after he says very candidly that there was some danger of his losing his power of esteem and love, for want of opportunities of exercising it; whereas opportunities in the contrary direction were ample and frequent.

For a complete analysis of his works see *D. of G. and R. Biogr., s.v.* Here it must suffice to indicate his relations to the religious influence of his time, and, above all, to Christianity.

The progress of experience, the leisure of research, had in his time shattered all real belief in the gods of ancient Greece and Rome in the minds of cultured men. But the vast crowd of deities, which the conflux of so many nations under the protecting shadow of Rome had gathered together, received, collectively and separately, a certain respect from the most incredulous. To the statesman, the gods of Rome were the highest symbol of the power of the imperial city; as such, he required for them external homage, to refuse which might be construed as rebellion against the state. Philosophers feared lest, if the particular acts of special deities were too rudely criticized, the reverence due to the gods in their remote and abstract sanctity might decay. Hence both classes favoured the sway of religious beliefs to which they had themselves ceased to adhere. The multitude was tossed about from religion to religion, from ceremony to ceremony, from rite to rite, in the vain hope that among so many supernatural powers some might lead men rightly to safety and happiness. The urgent need felt for guidance and the actual deficiency of sound guidance formed a combination favourable to the designs of greedy impostors. The Stoic philosophers, it is true, had formed a moral system capable of impressing on intellectual minds a remarkable self-restraint and large elements of virtue. But in hopefulness, the living sap which gives virtue its vitality, the Stoic was grievously deficient; and hence his philosophy was powerless with the multitude, and apt to degenerate into a hypocritical semblance even with its learned professors. There probably was never a time when so great a variety of hypocrisies and false beliefs prevailed among men. Such a world Lucian, with a cold, penetrating intellect, described with an audacity seldom paralleled. The ordinary method of his satire on the mythology of Greece and Rome consists in simply exhibiting the current legends as he finds them, stripped of the halo of awe and splendour with which they had habitually been surrounded, to the amused and critical reader. Sometimes his attack is more direct—as in the *Ζεὺς Τραγῳδός*, Jupiter the Tragedian, where the plain insinuation is that the general profession of belief in the gods was simply occasioned by the odium and alarm which a contrary assertion would excite. Not so sweeping in extent, but still more unreserved in exposing the doings of the heathen deities, is the treatise *περὶ θυσιῶν*, on Sacrifices. The *Ζεὺς Τραγῳδός* shews Lucian's disbelief in any divine governance of the world; the treatise *περὶ πένθους*, on Mourning, his disbelief in immortality.

But what was Lucian's attitude towards Christianity, which in his age was beginning to be known as no inconsiderable power in all parts of the Roman world? Two dialogues have to be considered in answering this question—*Ἀλέξανδρος ἢ Ψευδόμαντις*, Alexander, or the False Prophet; and *περὶ τῆς Περεγρίνου τελευτῆς*, Concerning the death of Peregrinus; for the Philopatris may be dismissed at once as pretty certainly no genuine work of its reputed author.

The most sympathetic allusion to the Christians by the genuine Lucian is in the "Alexander," where the Christians are joined with the Epicureans (whom Lucian much admired) as persistent and indomitable opponents of that fine specimen of rascality. A much fuller and more interesting account of the Christians is contained in the other work named. This (together with the Philopatris) was placed on the Index Expurgatorius, and hence does not appear in the first and second Aldine editions of Lucian (Venice, 1503 and 1522). Yet all that it says about the early Christians is very highly to their credit, except in attributing to them a too great *εὐήθεια*, a simplicity and guilelessness which rendered them liable to be deceived by worthless pretenders to sanctity. The passage contains one or two statements—that about the new Socrates, and the eating forbidden food—which it is difficult to think strictly accurate. Peregrinus Proteus was a cynic philosopher who flourished in the reign of the Antonines, and who, after a life of singularly perverted ambition, burnt himself publicly at the Olympian games, A.D. 165. We quote the passage from Francklin's translation:

"About this time it was that he learned the wonderful wisdom of the Christians, being intimately acquainted with many of their priests and scribes. In a very short time he convinced them that they were all boys to him; became their prophet, their leader, grand president, and, in short, all in all to them. He explained and interpreted several of their books, and wrote some himself, insomuch that they looked upon him as their legislator and high priest, nay, almost worshipped him as a god. Their leader, whom they yet adore, was crucified in Palestine for introducing this new sect. Proteus was on this account cast into prison, and this very circumstance was the foundation of all the consequence and reputation which he afterwards gained, and of that glory for which he had always been so ambitious; for when he was in bonds the Christians, considering it as a calamity affecting the common cause, did everything in their power to release him, which when they found impracticable, they paid him all possible deference and respect; old women, widows, and orphans were continually crowding to him; some of the most principal of them even slept with him in the prison, having bribed the keepers for that purpose; there were costly suppers brought in to them; they read their sacred books together, and the noble Peregrinus (for so he was then called) was dignified by them with the title of the New Socrates. Several of the Christian deputies from the cities of Asia came to assist, to plead for, and comfort him. It is incredible with what alacrity these people support and defend the public cause—they spare nothing, in short, to promote it. Peregrinus being made a prisoner on their account, they collected money for him, and he made a very pretty revenue of it. These poor men, it seems, had persuaded themselves that they should be immortal, and live for ever. They despised death, therefore, and offered up their lives a voluntary sacrifice, being taught by their lawgiver that they were all brethren, and that, quitting our Grecian gods, they must worship their own sophist, who was crucified, and live in obedience to his laws. In compliance with them they looked with contempt on all worldly treasures, and held everything in common—a maxim which they had adopted without any reason or foundation. If any cunning impostor, therefore, who knew how to manage matters came amongst them, he soon grew rich by imposing on the credulity of these weak and foolish men. Peregrinus, however, was set at liberty by the governor of Syria, a man of learning and a lover of philosophy, who withal well knew the folly of the man, and that he would willingly have suffered death for the sake of that glory and reputation which he would have acquired by it. Thinking him, however, not worthy of so honourable an exit, he let him go. . . . Once more, however, he was obliged to fly his country. The Christians were again his resource, and, having entered into their service, he wanted for nothing. Thus he subsisted for some time; but at length, having done something contrary to their laws (I believe it was eating food forbidden amongst them), he was reduced to want, and forced to retract his donation to the city, and to ask for his estate again, and issued a process in the name of the emperor to recover it; but the city sent messages to him commanding him to remain where he was, and be satisfied."

It would seem from the above that community of goods, in some degree or other, was practised among the early Christians to a later date than is generally supposed. Lucian confirms the general opinion as to the continual liability to persecution of the Christians of those ages. Moreover, though considering them weak and deluded people, he charges them with no imposture or falsehood, though he was very prone to bring such charges. In fact, did we know nothing of the early Christians but what he here records, his account would raise our interest in them in a very high degree; even their too great simplicity is not an unlovable trait.

There is an excellent trans. of Lucian by Wieland into German (Leipz. 1788-1789, 6 vols. 8vo), and one of great merit into Eng. by Dr. Francklin in 2 vols. 4to (Lond. 1780) and 4 vols. 8vo (Lond. 1781). For other edd. and trans. see *D. of G. and R. Biogr.* [J.R.M.]

Lucianus (12), priest of Antioch, martyr; born at Samosata *c.* 240, educated at Edessa under a certain Macarius, a learned expounder of Holy Scripture (Suidas, *s.v.*). Lucianus went to Antioch, which held a high rank among the schools of the East and was then, owing to the controversies raised by Paulus of Samosata, the great centre of theological interest. There he was probably instructed by Malchion, who seems to have been the true founder of the celebrated Antiochene school of divines, of whom Lucian, Chrysostom, Diodorus, Theodoret, and Theodore of Mopsuestia were afterwards some of the most distinguished. During the controversies after the deposition of Paulus, Lucian seems to have fallen under suspicion. Some have thought that he cherished sentiments akin to those of Paulus himself, which were of a Sabellian character, while others think that in opposing Paulus he used expressions akin to Arianism (cf. Newman's *Arians*, p. 7, and c. i. § 5). This latter view is supported by the creed presented at the council of Antioch, A.D. 341, and purporting to be drawn up by St. Lucian, which is extremely anti-Sabellian. He was separated from the communion of the three immediate successors of Paulus—Domnus, Timaeus, and Cyrillus. During the episcopate of Cyrillus he was restored, and became with Dorotheus the head of the theological school, giving to it the tone of literal, as opposed to allegorical, exposition of Scripture which it retained till the time of Chrysostom and Theodore of Mopsuestia. Lucian produced, possibly with the help of Dorotheus, a revised version of the LXX, which was used, as Jerome tells us, in the churches of Constantinople, Asia Minor, and Antioch, and met with such universal acceptance that it received the name of the Vulgate (Vulgata, Κοινή), while copies of the LXX in general passed under the title of Lucianea (Westcott, *Hist. of Canon*, p. 360). He also wrote some doctrinal treatises, and a commentary on Job. See Routh, *Reliq. Sacr.* v. 3-17.

In the school of Lucian the leaders and supporters of the Arian heresy were trained. Arius himself, Eusebius of Nicomedia, Maris of Chalcedon, Leontius of Antioch, Eudoxius, Theognis of Nicaea, and Asterius appealed to him as their authority (but see ARIUS) and adopted from him the party designation of Collucianists (De Broglie, *L'Eglise et l'Empire*, i. 375). Lucian became afterwards more conservative, and during Diocletian's persecution he encouraged the martyrs to suffer courageously, but escaped himself till Theotecnus was appointed governor of Antioch, when he was betrayed by the Sabellian party, seized and forwarded to Nicomedia to the emperor Maximinus, where, after delivering a speech in defence of the faith, he was starved for many days, tempted with meats offered to idols, and finally put to death in prison, Jan. 7, 311 or 312. His body was buried at Drepana in Bithynia, where his relics were visited by Constantine, who freed the city from taxes and changed its name to Helenopolis. A fragment of the apology delivered by the martyr has been preserved by Rufinus and will be found in Routh, *l.c.* Dr. Westcott, *l.c.*, accepts it as genuine.

As to whether Lucian the martyr and Biblical critic was the same person as Lucian the excommunicated heretic, Ceillier, Fleury, and De Broglie take one side, Dr. Newman the other. The former contend that neither Eusebius, Jerome, nor Chrysostom mentions his lapse in early life. But their notices are very brief, none of them are professed biographers, and we cannot depend much upon mere negative evidence. On the other hand we have the positive statements of Alexander, bp. of Alexandria (in Theod. *H. E.* i. 3, and Philostorg. *H. E.* ii. 14 and 15; see also

Epiphan. *Ancorat.* c. 33), which, together with the fact that the Arian party at Antioch sheltered themselves behind a creed said to have been "written in the hand of Lucian himself, who suffered martyrdom at Nicomedia" (Soz. *H. E.* iii. 5), outweigh the improbability involved in the silence of the others. He may easily have been 30 years in church communion when he died, and with the 4th-cent. Christians a martyrdom like his would more than atone for his early fall.

The creed of Lucian is in Hefele, *Hist. of Councils*, ii. 77, Clark's ed.; cf. Soz. *H. E.* iii. 5, vi. 12. Bp. Bull maintains its authenticity and orthodoxy (*Def. of Nic. Creed*, lib. iv. c. xiii. vi. § 5). Wright's *Syriac. Mart.* Eus. viii. 13, ix. 6; Chrysost. *Hom.* in Lucian, in Migne, *Patr. Gk.* t. l. p. 520; Gieseler, *H. E.* i. 248; Neander, *H. E.* ii. 498. Neander gives the numerous references to Lucian in St. Jerome's writings. [G.T.S.]

Luciferus I., bp. of Calaris (Cagliari) in Sardinia, mentioned first in a letter of pope Liberius to Eusebius of Vercelli. Moved by great anxiety about the efforts then being made (A.D. 354) to procure a condemnation of Athanasius by the Western bishops, Lucifer had come from Sardinia to Rome, and Liberius accepted his offer to go as an envoy to Constantius to ask him to summon a council. The council met at Milan in 354. The Arian party, supported by the emperor, was strong in it, and a proposal to condemn Athanasius was immediately brought forward, but resisted by Lucifer with such vehemence that the first day's meeting broke up in confusion and his opponents prevailed on the emperor to confine him in the palace. On the fourth day he was released. The subsequent discussions of the council were held in the palace and Constantius himself apparently took part in them. The proceedings were irregular and disorderly, and after some personal altercations the emperor sent Lucifer into exile. His banishment lasted from 355 to 361, and was mostly spent at Eleutheropolis in Palestine, subject to the persecutions of the Arian bp. Eutychius. During his banishment, and probably at Eleutheropolis, his books or pamphlets on the controversy were written. Lucifer addresses Constantius in them with a remarkable vigour of denunciation. He evidently courted persecution, and even martyrdom. He compares the emperor to the worst kings that ever reigned, and regards him as more impious than Judas Iscariot. He sent his vehement invective by a special messenger to Constantius himself. Astonished at this audacity, the emperor ordered Florentius, an officer of his court, to send the book back to Lucifer to ask if it were really his. The intrepid bishop replied that it was and sent it back again. Constantius must be allowed to have shewn magnanimity in leaving these violent effusions unpunished. There may, however, have been some additional hardship in the removal of Lucifer from Palestine to the Thebaid, where he remained till the death of Constantius in 361. Hearing of his arrival in Egypt, Athanasius sent a letter from Alexandria, full of praise and congratulations, asking him to let him see a copy of his work. After receiving it, Athanasius thanked him in a still more laudatory letter, and calls him the Elias of the age.

Very soon after his accession, A.D. 361, Julian permitted the exiled bishops to return to their sees. Lucifer and Eusebius of Vercelli were both in the Thebaid, and Eusebius pressed his friend to come with him to Alexandria, where a council was to be held under the presidency of Athanasius, to attempt to heal a schism at Antioch. Lucifer preferred to go straight to Antioch, sending two deacons to act for him at the council. Taking a hasty part in the affairs of the much-divided church at Antioch, where the Catholic party was divided into two sections, the followers of Meletius and the followers of Eustathius, Lucifer ordained Paulinus, the leader of the latter section, as bp. of the church. When Eusebius arrived at Antioch, bringing the synodal letter of the council and prepared to settle matters so as to give a triumph to neither party, he was distressed to find himself thus anticipated by the action of Lucifer. Unwilling to come into open collision with his friend, he retired immediately; Lucifer stayed, and declared that he would not hold communion with Eusebius or any who adopted the moderate policy of the Alexandrian council, which had determined that those bishops who had merely consented to Arianism under pressure should remain undisturbed.

After remaining some time at Antioch, Lucifer returned to Sardinia, and continued, it would seem, to occupy his see. Jerome (*Chron.*) states that he died in 371. To what extent he was an actual schismatic remains obscure. St. Ambrose remarks that "he had separated himself from our communion" (*de Excessu Satyri*, 1127, 47); and St. Augustine, "that he fell into the darkness of schism, having lost the light of charity" (*Ep.* 185, note 47). But there is no mention of any separation except Lucifer's own repulsion of so many ecclesiastics; and Jerome, in his dialogue against the Luciferians (§ 20), calls him *beatus* and *bonus pastor*. (See a quotation from the *Mém. de Trevoux* in Ceillier, vol. iv. p. 247.)

The substance of Lucifer's controversial pamphlets consists of appeals to Holy Scripture, and they contain a very large number of quotations from both Testaments. His writings are in Migne's *Patr. Lat.* t. xiii. His followers, if they ever formed a distinct organization, disappeared in a few years. Jerome's dialogue *adv. Luciferianos* purports to be the report of a discussion between an orthodox Christian and a Luciferian. The dialogue was written *c.* 378, seven years after the death of Lucifer. Five or six years later an appeal was made to the emperor by the Luciferian presbyters. [J.LL.D.]

Lucius (1) **I.,** bp. of Rome, after Cornelius, probably from June 25, 253, to Mar. 5, 254, or thereabouts. These dates are arrived at by Lipsius (*Chronol. der röm. Bischöfe*) after elaborate examination of conflicting data.

The Decian persecution having been renewed by Gallus, and Cornelius having died in banishment at Centumcellae, Lucius, elected in his place at Rome, was himself almost immediately banished. His banishment was of very short duration; for Cyprian, in his one extant letter addressed to him, while alluding to his election as recent, congratulates him also on his return (*Ep.* 61). A large number of Roman exiles for the faith appear from this letter to have returned to Rome with Lucius. In a letter to his successor Stephen (*Ep.* 68), Cyprian calls both Lucius and Cornelius "blessed martyrs," but probably uses the word to include confessors. For, though the Felician and later editions of the *Liber Pontificalis* say that Lucius was beheaded for the faith, the earlier Liberian Catalogue mentions his death only; and it is in the Liberian *Depositio Episcoporum*, not *Martyrum*, that his name is found. With regard to the then burning question of the reception of the *lapsi*, on which the schism of Novatian had begun under his predecessor Cornelius, he continued the lenient view which Cornelius, in accord with St. Cyprian of Carthage, had maintained (Cypr. *Ep.* 68). The Roman Martyrology, the Felician, and other editions of the *Liber Pontificalis*, rightly assign the cemetery of Callistus as his place of burial, and De Rossi has discovered, in the Papal crypt, fragments of a slab bearing the inscription ΛΟΥΚΙC. Six decreta, addressed to the churches of Gaul and Spain, are assigned to Lucius by the Pseudo-Isidore, and three others by Gratian—all undoubtedly spurious. [J.B—Y.]

Lucius (**11**), the third Arian intruded into the see of Alexandria, an Alexandrian by birth, ordained presbyter by George. After the murder of that prelate Lucius seems to have been regarded as head of the Arians of Alexandria; but Socrates's statement (iii. 4), that he was at that time ordained bishop, is corrected by Sozomen (vi. 5) and earlier authorities. At the accession of Jovian, according to the *Chronicon Acephalum*, a Maffeian fragment, four leading Arian bishops put him forward to address the new emperor at Antioch, hoping to divert Jovian's favour from Athanasius. Records of these interviews are annexed to Athanasius's epistle to Jovian, and appear to have been read by Sozomen, who summarizes the complaints urged against the great hero of orthodoxy. The records are vivid and graphic. Lucius, Bernicianus, and other Arians presented themselves to Jovian at one of the city gates when he was riding into the country. He asked their business. They said they were "Christians from Alexandria," and wanted a bishop. He answered, "I have ordered your former bishop, Athanasius, to be put in possession." They rejoined that Athanasius had for years been under accusation and sentence of banishment. A soldier interrupted them by telling the emperor that they were the "refuse" of "that unhallowed George." Jovian spurred his horse and rode away. Lucius does not reappear until 367, when, having been consecrated, says Tillemont (vi. 582), "either at Antioch, or at some other place out of Egypt," he attempted to possess himself of the bishopric, and entered Alexandria by night on Sept. 23, and "remained in a small house," next the precinct of the cathedral. In the morning he went to the house where his mother still lived; his presence excited general indignation, and the people beset the house. The prefect Latianus and the dux Trajanus sent officers to expel him, who reported that to do so publicly would imperil his life, whereupon Tatianus and Trajanus, with a large force, went to the house, and brought him out at 1 p.m. on Sept. 24. On Sept. 25 he was conducted out of Egypt (*Chron. Praevium* and *Acephalum*). Athanasius died on May 2, 373, being succeeded by Peter; but the prefect Palladius attacked the church, and Peter was either imprisoned or went into hiding. Euzoïus, the old Arian bp. of Antioch, easily obtained from Valens an order to install Lucius. Accordingly Lucius appeared in Alexandria, escorted, as Peter said in his encyclical letter (Theod. iv. 25), not by monks and clergy and laity, but by Euzoïus, and the imperial treasurer Magnus, at the head of a large body of soldiers; while the pagan populace intimated their friendly feeling towards the Arian bishop by hailing him as one who did not worship the Son of God and who must have been sent to Alexandria by the favour of Serapis. Lucius surrounded himself with pagan guards, and caused some of the orthodox to be beaten, others to be imprisoned, exiled, or pillaged, for refusing his communion, these severities being actually carried out by Magnus and Palladius as representing the secular power. Gregory of Nazianzus calls him a second Arius, and lays to his charge the sacrileges and barbarities of the new Arian persecution (*Orat.* xxv. 12, 13). He took an active part in the attack on the monks of Egypt; finding them immovably attached to the Nicene faith, he advised that their chief "abbats," the two Macarii, should be banished to a little pagan island; but when the holy men converted its inhabitants, the Alexandrian people made a vehement demonstration against Lucius, and he sent the exiles back to their cells (Neale, *Hist. Alex.* i. 203). When the Arian supremacy came to an end at the death of Valens, in 378, Lucius was finally ejected, and repaired to Constantinople, but the Arians of Alexandria still regarded him as their bishop (Socr. v. 3). He lived for a time at Constantinople, and contributed to the Arian force which gave such trouble to Gregory of Nazianzus, during his residence in the capital as bishop of the few Catholics, from the beginning of 379. In Nov. 380 the Arian bp. Demophilus was expelled, and Lucius went with him. Theodoret (iv. 21) confounds Lucius with another Arian prelate of that name, also a persecutor, who usurped the see of Samosata (Tillem. vi. 593). [W.B.]

Lucius (**16**) (*Lleirwg, Lles, Lleufer-Mawr, Lleurwg*), a mythical character represented as the first Christian king in Britain. By William of Malmesbury (*Ant. Glast.* ii.), and more especially by Geoffrey of Monmouth (*Brit. Hist.* iv. v.), besides later writers, Lucius is assigned a most important place in the Christianizing of Britain.

I. As represented by Geoffrey of Monmouth, whose narrative has made the deepest impression on popular history, Lucius was descended from Brutus, the founder and first king of Britain, and succeeded his father Coillus, son of Meirig or Marius. Like his father, he sought and secured the friendship of the Romans. The fame of the Christian miracles inspired him with such love for the true faith that he petitioned pope Eleutherus for teachers, and on the arrival of the two most holy doctors, Faganus and Duvanus, received baptism along with multitudes from all countries. When the missionaries had almost extinguished paganism in the island, they dedicated the heathen temples to the service of God, and filled them with congregations of Christians; they fully organized the church, making the flamens into bishops, and the arch-flamens into archbishops, and constituting 3 metropolitans with 28 suffragan bishops. Lucius largely endowed the church, and, rejoicing in the progress of the gospel, died at Gloucester (Malmesbury says at Glastonbury) A.D. 156, without leaving any issue (Baron. *Ann.* A.D. 183; Cressy, *Church Hist. Brit.* iii.iv. at great length and diffuseness; *Lib. Landav.* by Rees, 26, 65, 306, 309, but much shorter).

II. Parallel to the preceding, but without such minute details, is the legend in the Welsh Triads and genealogies, which are of very uncertain date and authority. Lleirwg, Lleurwg, or Lles, also named or surnamed Lleufer-Mawr ("the great luminary," as all the names express the idea of brightness, corresponding to the Latin Lucius), son of Coel ap Cyllin ap Caradog or Caractacus ap Bran, was a Welsh chieftain of Gwent and Morganwg in the S. of Wales. Two of the Triads (*Myv. Arch.* ii. 63, 68) state that he founded the church of Llandaff, which was the first in Britain, and endowed it with lands and privileges, giving the same also to all those persons who first embraced the gospel. The Welsh Triads would place him about the middle of the 2nd cent. (Rees, *Welsh Saints*, c. 4; Williams, *Emin. Welsh.* 276; *Lib. Landav.* by Rees, 309 n.; Lady Ch. Guest, *Mabinogion*, ii. 130; Stephens, *Lit. Cymr.* 69.)

III. In tracing the rise and growth of the legend there is comparatively little difficulty. Gildas makes no allusion to it. The earliest English author to notice it is Bede (*Chron.* A.D. 180): "Lucius Britanniae rex, missâ ad Eleutherium Romae episcopum epistolâ, ut Christianus efficiatur, impetrat"; and again *H. E.* i. c. 4.

The source from which Bede received the name of Lucius, and his connexion with Eleutherus, is shewn by Haddan and Stubbs (*Counc.* etc. i. 25) to have been a later interpolated form of the *Catalogus Pontificum Romanorum* (*ap.* Boll. *Acta SS.* 1 Apr. i. p. xxiii. *Catalogi Veteres Antiquorum Pontificum*). The original *Catalogue*, written shortly after 353, gives only the name and length of pontificate by the Roman consulships, but the interpolated copy (made *c.* 530) adds to the *Vita S. Eleutheri* "Hic accepit epistolam a Lucio Britanniae Rege ut Christianus efficeretur per ejus mandatum." Haddan and Stubbs conclude: "It would seem, therefore, that the bare story of the conversion of a British prince (*temp. Eleutheri*) originated in Rome during the 5th or 6th cents., almost 300 or more years after the date assigned to the story itself; that Bede in the 8th cent. introduced it into England, and that by the 9th cent. it had grown into the conversion of the whole of Britain; while the full-fledged fiction, connecting it specially with Wales and with Glastonbury, and entering into details, grew up between cents. 9 and 12."

Of the dates assigned to king Lucius there is an extreme variety, Ussher enumerating 23 from 137 to 190, and placing it in his own *Ind. Chron.* in 176, Nennius in 164, and Bede (*Chron.*) in 180, and again (*H. E.*) in 156. But the chronology is in hopeless confusion (see Haddan and Stubbs, i. 1-26). Ussher (*Brit. Eccl. Ant.* cc. iii.-vi.) enters minutely into the legend of Lucius, accepting his existence as a fact, as most other authors have done. His festival is usually Dec. 3. [J.G.]

IV. A final explanation of the Lucius legend was given by Dr. Harnack in 1904 in the *Sitzungsberichte der Königl. Preuss. Akademie der Wissensch.* xxvi.-xxvii.. A recovered fragment of the *Hypotyposes* of Clement of Alexandria suggested to him that the entry in the *Liber Pontificalis* was due to a confusion between Britannio and Britio. Dr. Harnack shews that the latter word almost undoubtedly refers to the birtha or castle of Edessa. Bede probably misread Britio in the *Liber Pontificalis* as Britannio, and referred the entry in consequence to Britain, whereas it relates to the conversion of Edessa in the time of Lucius Abgar IX. Harnack further shews that the original quotation was probably transferred from Julius Africanus to the *Lib. Pont.* See the review of the question in *Eng. Hist. Rev.* xxii. (1907) 769. Thus the mythic king Lucius of Britain finally disappears from history. [H.G.]

Lupus (2). [GERMANUS (8).]

M

Macarius (1) 1., bp. of Jerusalem, the 39th from the Apostles, Hermon being his predecessor. His accession is placed by Tillemont in 311 or 312. In a list of defenders of the faith, Athanasius (*Orat. I. adv. Arian*, p. 291) refers to Macarius as exhibiting "the honest and simple style of apostolical men." A letter was addressed to him and other orthodox bishops by Alexander of Alexandria (Epiph. *Haer.* lxix. 4, p. 730). He attended the council of Nicaea in 325 (Soz. i. 17; Theod. *H. E.* i. 15). During his episcopate, A.D. 326 or 327, HELENA paid her celebrated visit to Jerusalem. Macarius was commissioned by the emperor Constantine, A.D. 326, to see to the erection of a basilica on the site of the Holy Sepulchre. The emperor's letter is given by Eusebius (*de Vita Const.* iii. 29-32), Socrates (*H. E.* i. 9) and Theodoret (*H. E.* i. 17). Constantine subsequently (*c.* 330) wrote to Macarius with the other bishops of Palestine about the profanation of the sacred terebinth of Mamre by idolatrous rites (Euseb. *u.s.* 52, 53). The emperor also presented Macarius with a vestment of gold tissue for the administration of the sacrament of baptism, as a token of honour to the church of Jerusalem (Theod. *H. E.* ii. 27). The death of Macarius is placed by Sozomen (*H. E.* ii. 20) between the deposition of Eustathius, A.D. 331, and the council of Tyre, A.D. 335. He was succeeded by Maximus. [E.V.]

Macarius (9) Magnes, a writer of the end of the 4th cent. Four centuries after, his name had sunk into almost complete oblivion, when in the course of the image controversy a quotation from him was produced on the iconoclastic side. Nicephorus, then or afterwards patriarch of Constantinople, had never heard of him, and only after long search could he procure a copy of the work containing the extract (*Spicilegium Solesmense*, i. 305). Nicephorus evidently had no knowledge of the author except from the book itself. The words Macarius Magnes may be both proper names, or else may be translated either as the blessed Magnes or as Macarius the Magnesian. Nicephorus understood Macarius as a proper name, and so he found it understood in the title of the extract which he discusses, but will not undertake to say whether Magnes is a proper name or a geographical term. He concludes that Macarius was a bishop, because the title described the author as ἱεράρχης and the very ancient MS. from which his information was derived contained a portrait of the author in a sacerdotal dress. He dates Macarius as 300 years later than the "Divine and Apostolic preaching," as could be gathered from two passages in the work. The work, called *Apocritica*, was addressed to a friend named Theosthenes, and contained objections by a heathen of the school of Aristotle, together with replies by Macarius. Nicephorus finds that the extract produced by the Iconoclasts had been unfairly used, the context shewing that Macarius referred only to heathen idolatry and not to the use of images among Christians. But Nicephorus had no favourable opinion of him on the whole, thinking he discerned Manichean, Arian, or Nestorian tendencies, and especially agreement with "the impious and senseless Origen" as to the non-eternity of future punishments. Macarius again sank into obscurity, only some very few extracts from his writings being found in MSS. of succeeding centuries. Near the end of the 16th cent. he became again the subject of controversy through the Jesuit Turrianus, who had found a copy of the *Apocritica* in St. Mark's Library at Venice, which when afterwards sought for had disappeared. In 1867 there was found at Athens what there is good reason to believe was this copy, which, by theft or otherwise, had found its way to Greece. This was pub. by Paul Foucart (Paris, 1876). Shortly after Duchesne pub. a dissertation on Macarius (Paris, 1877), with the text of all the attainable fragments of Macarius's homilies on Genesis. The *Apocritica* consisted of five books: of these we have only the third complete; but enough remains to shew that the work purports to contain a report of a *viva voce* discussion between the author and a Grecian philosopher. In form it is perhaps unique. It is not a mere dialogue; nor does it proceed in the Platonic method of short questions and answers. Each speech of the heathen objector is made up of some half-dozen short speeches, each dealing with different objections. To these Macarius severally replies, and then follow a few lines of narrative introducing a new set of objections. We doubtless have here a unique specimen of genuine heathen objections of the 4th cent. The blows against Christianity are dealt with such hearty goodwill and with so little restraint of language that a Christian would certainly have regarded it as blasphemous to invent such an attack. That Macarius did not invent the objections is further shewn by his sometimes missing their point, and by his answers being often very unsatisfactory. There is also a clear difference in style between the language of the objector and of the respondent. It has therefore been inferred that Macarius reproduces the language as well as the substance of the arguments of a heathen, and then arises the question, "Does the dialogue record a real *viva voce* discussion with a heathen objector, or are the heathen objections from a published work against Christianity, and if so, whose?"

The earliest Christian apologists defended their religion against men who had a very vague knowledge of it. But towards the close of the 3rd cent. a systematic attack was made on our religion by its most formidable adversary, Porphyry, founded on a careful study of our sacred books. Three or four of the Macarian objections have been at least ultimately derived from Porphyry. They do not appear to be verbally copied from him; and the Macarian objector places himself 300 years after St. Paul's death, which, with every allowance for round numbers, is too late for Porphyry. Again, there is scarcely any resemblance between the objections in Macarius and what we know of those of the emperor Julian. Great part of these last is directed against the O.T., those of Macarius almost exclusively against the New; and the Macarian objections are not attacks of a general nature on the Christian scheme, but rather attempts to find error or self-contradiction in particular texts, *e.g.* how could Jesus say, "Me ye have not always," and yet "I am with you always, even to the end of the world"? Intermediate in time between Porphyry and Julian was Hierocles, and Duchesne ably advocates the view that the discussion in Macarius is fictitious, and that his book contains a literal transcript of parts of the lost work of Hierocles. We are ourselves inclined to believe that while no doubt Macarius or the heathen philosophers whom he encountered drew the substance of their arguments, and even in some cases their language, from previous heathen writings, yet on the whole the wording is Macarius's own. We give a few specimens of the objections with Macarius's solutions, with a warning that the selection is scarcely fair to Macarius, since it is not worth while printing such of his answers as an apologist of to-day would give.

Ob. Jesus told His disciples "Fear not them who can kill the body," yet when danger was threatening Himself, He prayed in an agony that the suffering might pass away. His words then were not worthy of a Son of God, nor even of a wise man who despises death.

Sol. We must see what it was our Lord really feared, when He prayed. The devil had seen so many proofs of His divinity that he dared not assault Him again, and so there was danger that that Passion which was to be the salvation of the world should never take place. Our Lord dissembles, therefore, and pretends to fear death, and thus deceiving the devil, hastens the hour of his assault; for when He prayed that His cup might pass, what He really desired was that it should come more speedily. He thus caught the devil by baiting the hook of His divinity with the worm of His humanity, as it is written in Ps. xxii., "I am a worm, and no man," and in Job xli., "Thou shalt draw out the dragon with a hook."—The doctrine that the devil was thus deceived is taught by many Fathers, *e.g.* Gregory Nyssen. Gregory the Great, commenting on Job xli. 1, uses language strikingly like that of Macarius; but the common source of Macarius and the rest was Origen's Comm. on Ps. xxii.

Ob. How can Jesus say "Moses wrote of Me," when nothing at all of the writings of Moses has been preserved? All were burnt with the temple, and what we have under the name of Moses was written 1,180 years after his death by Ezra and his company.

Sol. When Ezra rewrote the books of Moses, he restored them with perfect accuracy as they had been before: for it was the same Spirit Who taught them both.

Ob. "If they drink any deadly thing it shall not hurt them." If so, candidates for bishoprics ought to be tested by offering them a cup of poison. If they dare not drink, they ought to own that they do not really believe the words of Jesus; and if they have not faith for the cures promised in the same context and the power to remove mountains, no ordinary Christian is now a believer, nor even any bishops or presbyters.

Sol.—Christ's words are not to be understood literally. Working cures is no test of faith: for such are often performed by unbelievers or atheists. It is not to be supposed Christ intended His disciples to do what He never did Himself, and He never moved a literal mountain. What He meant by mountains was demons, and we have in Jer. li. 25 this metaphorical use of the word mountain. —Here we have another coincidence with Ambrose (in Ps. xxxvi. 35 (Vulg.); Migne, i. 1000), both no doubt being indebted to Origen.

It is important to note that St. Mark, as read by the objector and by Macarius, contained the disputed verses at the end, as is seen also from his mentioning that out of Mary Magdalen had been cast seven devils (see Orig. *Adv. Cels.* ii. 55). He speaks of the author of *Hebrews* as the Apostle, no doubt intending St. Paul. He appears to have used II. Peter (see p. 180). The phrase "the canon of the N.T." occurs p. 168.

With respect to idolatry the heathen apologist argues: None of us supposes wood or stone to be God, or thinks that if a piece be broken off an image, the power of the Deity represented is diminished. It was by way of reminder that the ancients set up temples and images, that those who come to them might think of God and make prayers according to their needs. You do not imagine a picture of your friend to be your friend; you keep it merely to remind you of him, and to do him honour. Our sacrifices are not intended to confer benefit on the Deity, but to shew the love and gratitude of the worshipper. We make our images of Deity in human form as being the most beautiful we know.

We have not space to give other answers of Macarius, though some are clever enough. Sufficient has been quoted to show the allegorical style of interpretation which Macarius used. Other examples could be easily added: *e.g.* the clouds by which Paul expected to be caught up mean angels (p. 174); the three measures of meal (Matt. xiii.) mean time, past, present, and future; the thong (shoe-latchet) which could not be loosed is the tie between our Lord's humanity and divinity (p. 93); the four watches of the night (Matt. xiv. 25) mean the ages of the patriarchs, of the law, of the prophets, and of Christ; in Elijah's vision the strong wind was the patriarchal dispensation which swept away the worship of idols; the earthquake was the law of Moses, at the giving of which the mountains leaped like rams; the fire was the word of prophecy (Jer. xx. 9); the still small voice was the message of Gabriel to Mary. Macarius thus belonged to the Alexandrian school of allegorical interpretation, as might be expected from the great use he makes of Origen, not to the Syrian literal school. [DIODORUS.] Alexandria might also be suggested by the fact that Macarius has some scientific knowledge. He admires extremely (p. 179) the skill of geometers in being able to find a square equal in area to a triangle; he knows the astronomical labours of Aratus, and is aware that in the discussion of celestial problems the earth is treated as a point. On the other hand, many indications point to the East as his abode. He measures distances by parasangs (p. 138); when speaking (p. 7) of the diversities which exist among the population of a great city, he chooses Antioch as his example. Speaking of the ascetic life, he draws his instances not from the celebrated solitaries of Egypt, but those of the East. In a short list of heretics the Syrian Bardesanes is included. The woman healed of an issue of blood is said to have been Berenice, queen of Edessa, a notion likely to have been derived from a local tradition. In a question of language which became the subject of much dispute in the East he sides with those who speak of τριῶν ὑποστάσεων ἐν οὐσίᾳ μιᾷ.

Crusius pointed out, and the suggestion has been adopted by Möller (Schürer, *Theol. Lit. Zeit.* 1877, p. 521), that at the Synod of the Oak in 403, one of the accusers of Heracleidas of Ephesus was a Macarius, bp. of Magnesia. His identification with our Macarius seems highly probable. It is not a weighty objection that one of the charges brought against Heracleidas was Origenism, while Macarius, as we have seen, was largely indebted to Origen. Macarius had other grounds of hostility to Heracleidas, and we have no knowledge that his own admiration of Origen was such as to induce him to incur the charge of heresy for his sake, or to refrain from bringing the charge of Origenism against an opponent. The Magnesian Macarius sufficiently satisfies the conditions of time and place.

Duchesne conjectures that Macarius may probably have visited Rome. Of the heroes of the Eastern church he names only Polycarp, telling of him a story found elsewhere. Of Westerns he names Irenaeus of Lyons, Fabian of Rome, and Cyprian of Carthage. He has the story told in the Latin Abdias (Fabric. *Cod. Ap. N. T.* p. 455) of flowing milk instead of blood from St. Paul's headless body (p.

182). The duration of St. Peter's episcopate is made only a few months (p. 102). [G.S.]

Macarius (12), presbyter of Athanasius. Early in his episcopate, perhaps in 329 or 330 (if his consecration was on June 8, 328, as Hefele reckons, *Councils*, ii. 4), ATHANASIUS, on a visitation in Mareotis, was informed that a layman named Ischyras was exercising priestly functions. Macarius was sent to summon the offender before the archbishop, but Ischyras being ill, his father was requested to restrain him from the offence. Ischyras, recovering, fled to the Meletians, who invented the accusation that Macarius, by order of Athanasius, had forced the chapel of Ischyras, overthrown his altar, broken the chalice, and burnt the sacred books (Athan. *Apol. c. Ar.* c. 63; Socr. i. 27; Hilar. Pict. *Fragm.* ii. § 18). Macarius is next found at the imperial court at Nicomedia on a mission with another priest, Alypius, when three Meletian clergy, Ision, Eudaemon, Callinicus, brought their accusation against Athanasius in reference to the linen vestments. Macarius and Alypius were opportunely able to refute the calumny (Socr. i. 27; Soz. ii. 22). This may have been late in 330 or early in 331; Pagi's date 328 seems too early. Macarius and the three Meletians were still there when Athanasius arrived (331) on a summons from Constantine; the Meletians brought against the archbishop the fresh charge of supplying money to Philumenus and Macarius was charged with the breaking of the chalice (Hefele, ii. 13). The charge was easily disproved. Macarius again assisted Athanasius when charged with the murder of Arsenius. When Arsenius had been found alive and John Arcaph had confessed the fraud, Macarius was sent to Constantinople to inform Constantine of the collapse of the whole calumny (Athan. *Apol. c. Ar.* cc. 65, 66). Macarius was dragged in chains before the council at Tyre in 335, and when the commission was sent by that council to Mareotis to investigate the affair of the chalice, which was still charged against Athanasius, Macarius was not allowed to accompany it, but was left in custody at Tyre. Athan. *Apol. c. Ar.* cc. 71, 72, 73; Mansi, ii. 1126, 1128, B, C; Hefele, ii. 14-23; Tillem. viii. 19-23. [C.H.]

Macarius (17). Two hermits or monks of this name both lived in Egypt in the 4th cent.; their characters and deeds are almost indistinguishable. The elder is called the Egyptian, the younger the Alexandrine. One of them was a disciple of Anthony and the master of EVAGRIUS, and one of them dwelt in the Thebaid. Jerome speaks of Rufinus (*Ep.* iii. 2, ed. Vall. A.D. 374) as "being at Nitria, and having reached the abode of Macarius." Yet Rufinus, who lived 6 years in Alexandria and the adjoining monasteries, describes the residence of Macarius (*Hist. Mon.* 29)—which he names Scithium and says was a day and a half's journey from the monasteries of Nitria—from the accounts of others rather than as an eye-witness. Rufinus, however, seems to have seen both hermits (*Apol. Ruf.* ii. 12). The stories about them are of a legendary character. Rufinus, *Hist. Mon.* 28, 29, and *Hist. Eccl.* ii. 4, 8; Palladius, 19, 20; Soz. iii. 13; Socr. iv. 18; Gennad. *d. V. Ill.* 11; *Martyrolog. Rom.* Jan. 5 and 15. [W.H.F.]

Macarius (24), a Christian of Rome who (end of 4th cent.) wrote on the divine providence in opposition to heathen notions of fate and astrology. Finding some difficulties, he dreamed of a ship bringing relief to his doubts. Rufinus just at this time arriving from Palestine, Macarius saw in this the interpretation of his dream and sought from him light from the Greek fathers. Rufinus trans. for him Origen's eulogy on the martyr Pamphilus (said by Jerome to be really by Eusebius) and also Origen's περὶ Ἀρχῶν, the publication of which led to violent controversy. [HIERONYMUS; ORIGEN.] Jerome calls him Ὄλβιος, saying, "Tunc discipulus Ὄλβιος, vere nominis sui si in talem magistrum non impegisset" (*Ep.* cxxvii. *ad Princ.* ed. Vall.) [W.H.F.]

Macedonius (2), bp. of Constantinople. At bp. Alexander's death in 336 party feeling ran high. His orthodox followers supported Paul, the Arians rallied round Macedonius. The former was ordained bishop, but did not hold his bishopric long. The emperor Constantius came to Constantinople, convened a synod of Arian bishops, banished Paul, and, to the disappointment of Macedonius, translated Eusebius of Nicomedia to the vacant see (A.D. 338). Eusebius's death in 341 restarted hostilities between the partisans of Paul and Macedonius. Paul returned, and was introduced into the *Irene* church of Constantinople; Arian bishops immediately ordained Macedonius in St. Paul's church. So violent did the tumult become that Constantius sent his general Hermogenes to eject Paul for a second time. His soldiers met with open resistance; the general was killed and his body dragged through the city. Constantius at once left Antioch, and punished Constantinople by depriving the people of half their daily allowance of corn. Paul was expelled; Macedonius was severely blamed for his part in these disturbances, and for allowing himself to be ordained without imperial sanction; but practically the Arians triumphed. Macedonius was permitted to officiate in the church in which he had been consecrated. Paul went to Rome, and he and Athanasius and other orthodox bishops expelled from their sees were sent back by Julius with letters rebuking those who had deposed them. Philip the prefect executed the fresh orders of the emperor in hurrying Paul into exile to Thessalonica, and in reinstating Macedonius, but not without bloodshed (Socr. ii. 16).

Macedonius held the see for about six years, while letters and delegates, the pope and the emperors, synods and counter-synods, were debating and disputing the treatment of Paul and Athanasius. In 349 the alternative of war offered by Constans, emperor of the West, induced Constantius to reinstate Paul; and Macedonius had to retire to a private church. The murder of Constans (A.D. 350) placed the East under the sole control of Constantius, and Paul was at once exiled. Imperial edicts followed, which permitted the Arians to claim to be the dominant faction in the church.

Macedonius is said to have signalled his return to power by acts which, if truly reported, brand him as a cruel bigot. The Novatianists suffered perhaps even more fearfully than the orthodox and some of them were stung into a desperate resistance: those of Constantinople removing the materials of their church to a distant suburb of the city; those at Mantinium in Paphlagonia daring to face the imperial soldiers sent to expel them from their home. "The exploits of Macedonius," says Socrates (ii. 38), "on behalf of Christianity, consisted of murders, battles, incarcerations, and civil wars."

An act of presumption finally lost him the imperial favour (A.D. 358). The sepulchre containing the relics of Constantine the Great was in danger of falling to pieces, and Macedonius determined to remove them. The question was made a party one. The orthodox assailed as sacrilege "the disinterment of the supporter of the Nicene faith," the Macedonians pleaded the necessities of structural repair. When the remains were conveyed to the church of Acacius the Martyr, the excited populace met in the church and churchyard; so frightful a carnage ensued that the place was filled with blood and slaughtered bodies. Constantius's anger was great against Macedonius because of the slaughter, but even more because he had removed the body without consulting him.

When Macedonius presented himself at the council of Seleucia (A.D. 359), it was ruled that being under accusation it was not proper for him to remain (Socr. ii. 40). His opponents, Acacius, Eudoxius, and others, followed him to Constantinople, and, availing themselves of the emperor's indignation, deposed him (A.D. 360) on the ground of cruelty and canonical irregularities. Macedonius retired to a suburb of the city, and died there.

He is said to have elaborated the views with which his name is connected in his retirement. His doctrine was embraced by Eleusius and others; and Marathonius brought so much zeal to the cause that its upholders were sometimes better known as Marathonians. Their grave, ascetic manners and pleasing and persuasive eloquence secured many followers in Constantinople, and also in Thrace, Bithynia, and the Hellespontine provinces. Under the emperor Julian they were strong enough to declare in synod at Zele in Pontus their separation from both Arians and orthodox. In 374 pope Damasus and in 381 the council of Constantinople condemned their views, and they gradually ceased to exist as a distinctive sect. For authorities, consult the scattered notices in Socrates, Sozomen; Hefele, *Conciliengeschichte*, i.; the usual Church histories and HOLY GHOST in *D. C. B.* (4-vol. ed. 1882). [J.M.F.]

Macedonius (3) **II.,** patriarch of Constantinople A.D. 495. For an account of his election see EUPHEMIUS (4). Within a year or two (the date is uncertain) he assembled a council, in which he confirmed in writing that of Chalcedon, and openly professed, as he always did, his adhesion to the orthodox faith. In 507 Elias, patriarch of Jerusalem, who had been unwilling to sanction the deposition of Euphemius, united himself in communion with Macedonius. The heterodox emperor Anastasius employed all means to oblige Macedonius to declare against the council of Chalcedon, but flattery and threats were alike unavailing. An assassin named Eucolus was even hired to take away his life. The patriarch avoided the blow, and ordered a fixed amount of provisions to be given monthly to the criminal. The people of Constantinople were equally zealous for the council of Chalcedon, even, more than once, to the point of sedition. To prevent unfavourable consequences, Anastasius ordered the prefect of the city to follow in the processions and attend at the assemblies of the church. In 510 the emperor made a new effort. Macedonius would do nothing without an oecumenical council at which the bp. of great Rome should preside. Anastasius, annoyed at this answer, and irritated because Macedonius would never release him from the engagement he had made at his coronation to maintain the faith of the church and the authority of the council of Chalcedon, sought means to drive him from his chair. He sent Eutychian monks and clergy, and sometimes the magistrates of the city, to load him with public outrage and insult. This caused such a tumult amongst the citizens that the emperor was obliged to shut himself up in his palace and to have vessels moored near in case flight should be necessary. He sent to beg Macedonius to come and speak with him. Macedonius went and reproached him with the sufferings his persecutions caused the church. Anastasius pretended to be willing to alter this, but at the same time made a third attempt to tamper with the orthodoxy of the patriarch. One of his instruments was Xenaïas, an Eutychian bishop. He demanded of Macedonius a declaration of his faith in writing; Macedonius addressed a memorandum to the emperor insisting that he knew no other faith than that of the Fathers of Nicaea and Constantinople, and that he anathematized Nestorius and Eutyches and those who admitted two Sons or two Christs, or who divided the two natures. Xenaias, seeing the failure of his first attempt, procured two infamous wretches, who accused Macedonius of an abominable crime, avowing themselves his accomplices. They then charged him with Nestorianism, and with having falsified a passage in an epistle of St. Paul, in support of that sect. At last the emperor commanded him to send by the hands of the master of the offices the authentic copy of the Acts of the council of Chalcedon signed with the autographs of the bishops. Macedonius refused, sealed it up, and hid it under the altar of the great church. Thereupon Anastasius had him carried off by night and taken to Chalcedon, to be conducted thence to Eucaïta in Pontus, the place of the exile of his predecessor. In 515 pope Hormisdas worked for the restitution of Macedonius, whom he considered unjustly deposed; it had been a stipulation in the treaty of peace between Vitalian and Anastasius that the patriarch and all the deposed bishops should be restored to their sees. But Anastasius never kept his promises, and Macedonius died in exile. His death occurred *c.* 517, at Gangra, where he had retired for fear of the Huns, who ravaged all Cappadocia, Galatia, and Pontus. Theod. Lect. ii. 573-578, in *Patr. Gk.* lxxxvi.; Evagr. III. xxxi. xxxii. in *ib.* 2661; Mansi, viii. 186, 198; Vict. Tun. *Chron.* in *Patr*

Lat. lxviii. 948; Liberat. vii. in *ib.* 982; Theoph. *Chron.* 120-123, 128, 130, 132. [W.M.S.]

Macrina (1), *the Elder,* the paternal grandmother of Basil and Gregory Nyssen, resident at and probably a native of Neocaesarea in Pontus. Both Macrina and her husband, of whose name we are ignorant, were deeply pious Christians. Macrina had been trained on the precepts of the celebrated bp. of Neocaesarea, Gregory Thaumaturgus, by some of his hearers. In the persecution of Galerius and Maximin, Macrina and her husband, to save their lives, left home with a slender equipment and escaped to a hill forest of Pontus, where they are said to have lived in safe retirement for seven years. On the cessation of the persecution, A.D. 311, they returned to Neocaesarea. On the renewal of the persecution they appear to have again suffered. Their goods were confiscated and Macrina and her husband obtained the right to be reckoned among confessors of the faith (Greg. Nys. *de Vit. S. Macr.* t. ii. pp. 178, 191). In due time their son Basil married Emmelia, and became the father of ten children, the eldest bearing her grandmother's name Macrina, and the second that of his father Basil. This boy, afterwards the celebrated bp. of Caesarea, Basil the Great, was brought up from infancy by his grandmother Macrina, at her country house at Annesi, to which she seems to have retired after her husband's death (Basil. *Ep.* 204 [75], § 6; 223 [79], § 3). Her death cannot be placed before 340. [E.V.]

Macrina (2), *the Younger,* the eldest child of her parents Basil and Emmelia, by her position in the family and still more by her force of character, high intellectual gifts, and earnest piety, proved the well-spring of good to the whole household, and so contributed largely to form the characters of her brothers. To her brother Basil in particular she was ever a wise and loving counsellor. Basil was born *c.* 329, and Macrina probably *c.* 327. She received her name from her paternal grandmother. She was very carefully educated by her mother, who was more anxious that she should be familiar with the sacred writers than with heathen poets. Macrina committed to memory the moral and ethical portion of the books of Solomon and the whole of the Psalter. Before her twelfth year she was ready at each hour of the day with the Psalm liturgically belonging to it (Greg. Nys. *de Vita S. Macr.* ii. 179). Her personal beauty, which, according to her brother Gregory, surpassed that of all of her age and country, and her large fortune, attracted many suitors. Of these her father selected a young advocate, of good birth and position, and when he was cut off by a premature death, Macrina resolutely refused any further proposals of marriage (*ib.* 180). After her father's death (*c.* 349) she devoted herself to the care of her widowed mother, the bringing up of her infant brother Peter, and the supervision of the interests of her family. Emmelia was left burdened with a large and extensive property, and the maintenance of and provision for nine children. Of the greater part of this load Macrina relieved her. They resided then, or soon afterwards, on the paternal estate near the village of Annesi, on the banks of the Iris, near Neocaesarea, which Macrina never left. Basil returned from Athens *c.* 355 elated with his university successes. Macrina taught him the enthusiastic love for an ascetic life which she herself felt (*ib.* 181). Brother and sister settled on their p ternal estate on opposite banks of the Iris. The premature death of her most dearly loved brother Naucratius, on a hunting expedition, 357, strengthened her resolution to separate from the world, and she persuaded her mother also, who was nearly broken-hearted at their loss, to embrace the ascetic life. The nucleus of the sisterhood was formed by their female servants and slaves. Devout women, some of high rank, soon gathered round them, while the birth and high connexions of Macrina and her mother attracted the daughters of the most aristocratic families in Pontus and Cappadocia to the community (*ib.* 184, 186). Among its members were a widow of high rank and wealth, named Vestiana, and a virgin named Lampadia, who is described as the chief of the band (*ib.* 197). Macrina took to her retreat her youngest brother Peter (*ib.* 186). The elevation of her brother Basil to the see of Caesarea, 370, became a stimulus to a higher pitch of asceticism. Peter was ordained presbyter by his brother (*ib.* 187), probably in 371. In 373 Emmelia died, holding the hands of Macrina and Peter and offering them to God with her dying breath, as the first-fruits and tenths of her womb, and was buried by them in her husband's grave at the chapel of the "Forty Martyrs." Macrina sustained her third great sorrow in the death (Jan. 1, 379) of Basil, whom she had long regarded with reverential affection. Nine months after, her brother Gregory Nyssen paid her a visit. Owing to his banishment under Valens and other persecutions it was eight or nine years since they had met. He found the aged invalid, parched with fever, stretched on planks on the ground, the wood barely covered with a bit of sackcloth. The pallet was carefully arranged to face the east. On her brother's approach she made a vain effort to rise to do him honour as a bishop; Gregory prevented her, and had her placed on her bed (*ib.* 189). With great self-command Macrina, *ἡ μεγάλη*, as he delights to call her, restrained her groans, checked her asthmatic pantings, and putting on a cheerful countenance endeavoured to divert him from the present sorrow. She ventured to speak of Basil's death; Gregory completely broke down; and when her consolations proved unavailing, she rebuked him for sorrowing like those who had no hope for one fallen asleep in Christ. Gregory defending himself, she bid him argue out the point with her. After a somewhat prolix controversy, Macrina, as though under divine inspiration—*καθάπερ θεοφορουμένη τῷ ἁγίῳ Πνεύματι*—her words pouring out without stay, like water from a fountain (*ib.* 189), delivered the long discourse on the resurrection and immortality of the soul which Gregory has recorded—more probably in his own than his dying sister's words—in the *de Anima ac Resurrectione Dialogus*, entitled *τὰ Μακρίνια* (*Opp.* t. iii. pp. 181-260). On the conclusion of this remarkable discourse (in which the purificatory nature of the fire of hell is unmistakably set forth, the anguish being in exact proportion to the rootedness of the sinful habits—*μέτρον τῆς ἀλγηδόνης ἡ τῆς κακίας ἐν ἑκάστῳ ποσότης ἐστίν*, p. 227), she noticed that her brother was weary and sent him to rest awhile in an arbour in the garden. Towards the close of the same day he revisited her bedside. She began a thankful review of her past life, recounting God's mercies to her (*ib.* 191, 192). At last her voice failed, and only by the motion of her lips and her outspread hands—*διαστολὴ τῶν χειρῶν*—was she known to be praying. She signed her eyes, mouth, and breast with the cross. Dusk came on; lights were brought in; she immediately attempted to chant the *ἐπιλύχνιος εὐχαριστία*—but "silently with her hands and with her heart." She once more signed herself on the face with the cross, gave a deep sigh, and finished her life and her prayers together (*ib.* 195). Round her neck was found an iron cross, and a ring containing a particle of the true cross (*ib.* 198). She was buried by her brother in the grave of her parents in the chapel of the "Forty Martyrs," about a mile from her monastery. Gregory was assisted in carrying the bier by Araxius the bishop of the diocese (probably Ibora), and two of the leading clergy. After her death many miracles said to have been performed by her were reported to Gregory (*ib.* 199, 202-204). Tillem. *Mém eccles.* ix. 564-573. [E.V.]

Magnentius, Flavius Popilius, emperor, 350-353. He rose under Constantius to the rank of count; and Constans gave him command of the Jovian and Herculian legions embodied by Diocletian and Maximian I. On Jan. 18, 350, he was proclaimed emperor instead of Constans, then absent on a hunting expedition. Constans fled, but was murdered at Helena or Elve at the foot of the W. Pyrenees. Gaul and all the Western Empire, including Italy, Sicily, Spain, and Africa, submitted to the new emperor. Socrates (*H. E.* ii. 26) says that the general confusion of affairs now encouraged the enemies of Athanasius to accuse him to Constantius; and Athanasius indignantly disclaims any correspondence or connexion with Magnentius, in the apology to Constantius; some false charge of the kind may have been made (Athan. vol. i. pp. 603 seq. Migne).

On Sept. 28, 351, the battle of Mursa on the Drave was fought, which deprived Magnentius of nearly all his provinces excepting Gaul. His last centre of operations was Lyons, and he fell upon his sword in Aug. 353. His coins, as Tillemont says (*Hist. des Emp.* iv. p. 354), prove his profession of Christianity; and he employed bishops in his negotiations with Constantius (Athan. *op. cit.* p. 606). But his usurpation began an unbroken career of crimes, and Athanasius's somewhat pithy summary of him (*ib.* 603) as *τὸν διάβολον Μαγνέντιον* is confirmed after their fashion by Zosimus and Julian. [R.ST.J.T.]

Majorianus, Julius Valerius, declared emperor of the West Apr. 1, 457, at Columellae, six miles from Ravenna. Tillemont argues (*Emp.* vi. 634) that he did not become emperor till some months later. Majorian apparently remained at Ravenna till Nov. 458, the year of his consulship, which was marked by a series of remarkable laws, which may be found among the "Novels" at the end of the Theodosian Code. An outline of these laws is given by Gibbon; the seventh enacted that a *curialis* who had taken orders to avoid the duties of his position, if below the rank of a deacon, should be at once reduced to his original status, while, if he had been ordained deacon, priest, or bishop, he was declared incapable of alienating his property. The sixth law, intended to encourage marriage, forbade nuns to take the veil before the age of forty. A girl compelled by her parents to devote herself to perpetual virginity was to be at liberty to marry if at her parents' death she was under 40. The whole of this law, except the restrictions on the testamentary power of widows, was repealed by Majorian's successor, Severus. It is remarkable that the Catalogue of the Popes given by the Bollandists (*AA. SS.* Apr. i. 33) states that Leo the Great forbad a woman taking the veil before 60 years of age, or according to a various reading 40, and that the 19th canon of the council of Agde (Mansi, viii. 328), following the law of Majorian, fixes the age at 40.

On his arrival at Lyons, before the close of 458, Majorian was greeted by Sidonius with a long panegyric (*Carm.* v.). At Arles, Mar. 28, 460, he issued a law declaring ordinations against the will of the person ordained to be null; subjected an archdeacon who had taken part in such an ordination to a penalty of ten pounds of gold to be received by the informer, and referred a bishop guilty of the same offence to the judgment of the apostolic see. By the same law parents who compelled a son to take orders against his will were to forfeit to him a third part of their property.

On Majorian's return to Italy in 461 Ricimer excited a mutiny in the army against him at Tortona, forced him to abdicate on Aug. 2, and five days afterwards caused him to be assassinated on the banks of the Ira. [F.D.]

Majorinus, a reader in the church at Carthage, holding some domestic office in the household of Lucilla, who was, through her influence, chosen bp. in opposition to CAECILIAN. This Augustine and Optatus denounced as an act of rebellion, and it was undoubtedly one of the first steps towards definite schism, A.D. 311. His party afterwards became known by the greater name of DONATUS. One of his consecrators was Silvanus, Donatist bp. of Cirta, who was afterwards proved before Zenophilus to have been a "traditor." Majorinus died *c.* 315. Aug. *Epp.* 43; 3, 16; 89; *c. Parm.* iii. 11, 18; *c. Cresc.* ii. 3; iii. 30, 32; iv. 9; *de Haer.* 69; Opt. i. 14, 15, 19; *Mon. Vet. Don.* iv. ed. Oberthür; Tillemont, *Mem.* vi. 15, 19, 24, 699, 700; Sparrow Simpson's *Aug. and Afr. Ch. Divisions* (1910), p. 18. [H.W.P.]

Malchion, a presbyter of Antioch in the reigns of Claudius and Aurelian, conspicuous for his prominent part in the deposition of the bp. of Antioch, Paul of Samosata, in 272. He was famed as a rhetorician and was a learned man well acquainted with heathen writers, from whom he was accustomed to make quotations (Hieron. *Ep.* lxx. 4), and held, while a presbyter of the church, the office of president of the faculty of rhetoric (Eus. vii. 29). The bishop having announced or implied doctrines concerning the nature of Christ which appeared to Malchion and most of his co-presbyters to be identical with the heresy of Artemon, he engaged him in a public discussion, which was taken down by shorthand writers and published. He compelled Paul unwillingly to unveil his opinions, and exhibited him to the assembly as a heretic. A great council of bishops and presbyters having then been called together, and having condemned Paul, Malchion was chosen to write the letter denouncing him as a heretic and a criminal to the bishops of Rome and Alexandria, and through them to the world. The letter and the report of the discussion were known in the 4th and 5th cents. by Eusebius and Jerome; the latter enrolled Malchion in his list of illustrious church-writers, while the former cites at length the principal portions of the condemning letter (Eus. *H. E.* vii. 29, 30; Hieron. *de Vir. Ill.* c. 71). A trans. of the existing fragments of Malchion are in the *Ante-Nic. Lib.* (T. & T. Clark). [W.H.F.]

Malchus (1), one of the earliest hermits in Syria, was seen in extreme old age by Jerome in 374 and told him the story of his life, which was written down by Jerome 16 years afterwards. He was born at Nisibis near Edessa, and was the only son of a proprietor of that district. He fled from his parents when they importuned him to marry, and joined one of the monastic establishments in the desert of Chalcis. As life advanced he desired to revisit his home. The caravan was surprised by Arabs; he was made a slave, and set to feed flocks. He worked faithfully, and everything prospered in his hands. His master required him to marry a woman who was his companion in slavery. Malchus pretended to comply, but secretly told the woman that he would rather die by his own hand than break his vow of continency. He found her of the same mind, and indeed she had a husband living. The pair agreed, though living separately, to pass as man and wife. After a time they escaped to the Roman settlements in Mesopotamia. Finding the abbat of his monastery dead, Malchus took up his abode in the hamlet of Maronia, near Antioch, his reputed wife living with the virgins near. Maronia came by inheritance to Evagrius, afterwards bp. of Antioch, in whose company Jerome came from Italy in 374; and the story of the aged hermit confirmed Jerome in his desire for the life in the desert, on which he entered in 375 (Hieron. *Vita Malchi, Opp.* vol. ii. 41, ed. Vall.). [W.H.F.]

Mamertus (1), St., 18th bp. of Vienne, the elder brother of Claudian the poet, whom he ordained priest, and who is said to have assisted him in his episcopal labours. Our first authentic information about him is in 463. The see of Die had been included by pope Leo in the province of Arles, but Mamertus had consecrated a bishop of it. Gundeuchus, or Gundioc, king of the Burgundians, complained to pope Hilary, who took up the matter warmly, addressing a letter, Feb. 24, 464, to various prelates, solemnly warning Mamertus. Mamertus was still alive at the death of his brother in 473 or 474 (Sid. Apoll. *Ep.* iv. 11, in *Patr. Lat.* lviii. 515), but how long after is unknown.

Though not the inventor of Rogations or Litanies, Mamertus was undoubtedly the founder of the Rogation Days. Litanies of the kind were, on the evidence of Basil, in use in the East and, on that of Sidonius, in the West, but Mamertus first systematized them on the three days preceding Ascension Day. The story of their institution has been given by his contemporary Sidonius, by Avitus, Gregory of Tours, and others. Vienne, in some year before 474, had been terrified by portents and calamities. To atone for the sins of which these calamities were thought to be the penalties, Mamertus, with the joyful assent of the citizens, ordained a three days' fast, with processions and an ordered service of prayer and song, which, for greater labour, was to take place outside the city. Its successful issue ensured its permanence, and from Vienne it spread over France and the West. Already in 470 or 474 Sidonius had established these services at Clermont, and looked to them as his chief hope in the threatened invasion of the Goths. In 511 the first council of Orleans recognized them and directed their continuance (Mansi, viii. 355). For accounts of this institution see Ceillier, x. 346; Bingham, *Antiquities*, iv. 281 sqq. (1855); Smith, *D. C. A.* art. "Rogation Days"; *Gall. Christ.* xvi. 15. [S.A.B.]

Mamertus (2), **Claudianus Ecdicius**, a learned writer of the last half of the 5th cent., one of the literary school of which Sidonius Apollinaris is the best-known member. He was a native of Gaul, and brother of the more famous Mamertus, archbp. of Vienne. Trained from his earliest years for the monastic life, he was educated in all the stores of Greek, Roman, and Christian literature. During his brother's archbishopric he worked as a presbyter in Vienne, and served so effectually as his right hand that some writers have represented him as a "bishop" under his brother. This, however, seems the result of a misinterpretation (cf. Sirmondi, i. p. 539). As presbyter he was specially useful in training the clergy, organizing the services of the church, and arranging the order of Psalms and Lessons for the year, and perhaps we may attribute to his influence the regular use of litanies upon Rogation Days established by his brother. He was no less eminent for intellectual power. When, *c.* 470, Faustus, bp. of Riez, published anonymously a treatise asserting the corporeality of the soul, Sidonius and other friends applied to Mamertus as best qualified to answer it, and the *de Statu Animae* was the result. Sidonius also mentions with warm praise a hymn he had written, and represents him as a great centre of intellectual discussion, "hominum aevi, loci, populi sui ingeniosissimus," full of learning, eager for argument, patient with those who could not understand, and, in his work as a priest, thoughtful for all, open-handed, humble, not letting his benevolence be known, the adviser and helper of his brother in all diocesan matters. He died *c.* 474, and his epitaph, composed by Sidonius, is the chief source of information about his life. (Sid. Apoll. *Ep.* iv. 2, 3, 11, v. 2; Gennadius, *de Scrip. Ill.* cc. 67 (?) and 83; and the Preface to his own work, *de Statu Animae*.)

Besides two letters of his, we have (1) the

book mentioned above, *de Statu Animae*, and (2) some poems of doubtful authorship. Sidonius (*u.s.*) mentions with special praise a hymn by Claudian, but does not give its name. One scholiast says that it was the well-known "Pange lingua gloriosi," and one MS. of Gennadius (*u.s.*) states that that hymn was written by Claudian. It is, however, ordinarily found ascribed to Fortunatus (v. Daniel, *Thes. Hymnol.* iii. p. 285, iv. p. 68).

Fabricius has also attributed to him an hexameter poem of 165 lines, "contra vanos poetas ad collegam," found in a Paris MS. without any author's name.

Possibly there should be assigned to him also a few smaller poems found among the works of the heathen poet Claudian, viz. two short hexameter poems entitled "Laus Christi" and "Carmen Paschale," some short epigrammatic praises of the paradox of the Incarnation, an elegiac account of Christ's miracles, an elegiac appeal to a friend not to criticize his verses too severely, and two short Greek hexameter addresses to Christ, Εἰς τὸν σωτῆρα and Εἰς τὸν δεσπότην Χριστόν.

The works are in Migne, vol. liii.; *Bibl. Vet. Patr.* Lugd. 1677, vi. p. 1050; ed. Galland. x. p. 417, and in the *Corpus Script. Eccl. Lat.* vol. xi. (1885); the poems in Fabricius, *Poet. Christ.* p. 777. The *de Statu Animae* has been separately edited, notably by Peter Mosellanus (Basil, 1504), Barth (Cycneae, 1655), Schulze (Dresden, 1883). [W.L.]

Mammaea or **Mamaea, Julia,** the daughter of Julia Moesa, and niece of Julia Domna, the wife of the emperor Septimius Severus. She played for a short time a conspicuous part in Roman history, not without some interesting points of contact with the Christian church. By her marriage with the Syrian Gessius Marcianus she became the mother of Alexander Severus, and soon afterwards was a widow. With her mother and her sister Soaemias, the mother of ELAGABALUS, she went, at the command of Macrinus after the death of Caracalla, to reside at Emesa. On the election of her nephew Elagabalus as emperor, she went with him and her son Alexander, then 13 years old, to Rome, and it speaks well for her prudence and goodness that she continued to secure the life of her son from the jealous suspicions of the tyrant and to preserve him from the fathomless impurity which ran riot in the imperial court. There are sufficient reasons for assigning this watchfulness to at least the indirect influence of Christian life and teaching. Possibly, as in the time of Nero, there may have been disciples of the new faith among the slaves of Caesar's household, whom she learnt to respect and imitate. On the death of Elagabalus, A.D. 222, and the election of her son by the Praetorian Guard, she attained great influence. Her leanings to the Christian society were shewn more distinctly when she was with the emperor at Antioch, and hearing that Origen, already famous as a preacher, was at Caesarea, invited him to visit them with the honour of a military escort, welcomed him with all honour, and listened attentively as he unfolded the excellence of the faith of Christ (Eus. *H. E.* vi. 21). It does not appear that she ever made a definite profession of belief, and her religion, though it won from Eusebius (*l.c.*) the epithets of θεοσεβεστάτη and εὐλαβής, and from Jerome (*de Script. Eccles.* c. 54) that of *religiosa*, was probably of the syncretistic type then prevalent, which shewed itself, in its better form, in Alexander's adoption of Christian rules of action, and in his placing busts of Christ, Abraham, Orpheus, and Apollonius of Tyana in his private oratory (Lamprid. *Vit. Sev.* c. 29, 43), and in its worst when Elagabalus wished to build a temple on the Capitol in which Jews, Samaritans, Christians, and Romans were to unite in worshipping the Deity whose name he had adopted. Both mother and son, in consequence of these tendencies, came under the lash of Julian, who sneers at the childish unwisdom of the latter in submitting his own will to Mammaea's and gratifying her greed of gain (*de Caesarr.* p. 315), and represents him as weakly bemoaning his disaster. Mammaea shared her son's fate when the troops rose and murdered him in Gaul, and her last moments were embittered by her son's reproaches for the pride and avarice which had wrought their common ruin (Gibbon, cc. vi. and vii. and authorities cited above). [E.H.P.]

Manes (called also *Mani* among Oriental writers, Μανιχαῖος and *Manichaeus* among Greeks and Latins). The lives of all ancient heretics have suffered much from the misrepresentations of their opponents. In the case of Manes there is the additional difficulty that we have two contradictory accounts in the Western and Eastern traditions. The Western story is derived from the Acts of Archelaus, bp. of Caschar; the Eastern from Persian and Arabian historians. Our earliest authentic notice of him is in Eusebius (*H. E.* vii. 31), where he is described "as a barbarian in life, both in speech and conduct, who attempted to form himself into a Christ, and then also proclaimed himself to be the very Paraclete and the Holy Spirit. Then, as if he were Christ, he selected twelve disciples, the partners of his new religion, and after patching together false and ungodly doctrines, collected from a thousand heresies long since extinct, he swept them off like a deadly poison, from Persia, upon this part of the world." The *Acta Archelai* were forged by some romancing Greek between A.D. 330 and 340, as we first find them quoted by Cyrill. Hieros. (*Catech.* vi., written A.D. 348-350), and Eusebius in his history, pub. 326-330, knows nothing of them. If genuine, it is scarcely possible that Eusebius, living but a few miles from Jerusalem and with all the imperial resources at his back, could have been ignorant of a dispute which must have made such a noise all over Syria and Mesopotamia. [ARCHELAUS.]

Upon the story told by the Syrian, Persian, and Arab historians and chroniclers known to Beausobre he places much more reliance than upon the Western tradition (pt. i. liv. ii. cc. i.-iv.). It runs thus: Manes was born *c.* 240, and descended from a Magian family. He was well educated in Greek, music, mathematics, geography, astronomy, painting, medicine, and the Scriptures. Being very zealous for the faith, he was ordained priest while yet young, but becoming a heretic he went to the court of Sapor, whom he proselytized to his views, *c.* 267, but as soon as he opened his views more fully the king resolved to put him to death. In fact, a real revival of Zoroastrian doctrine had taken place under his reign, and as soon as Manes disclosed his full plan it was seen to involve the overthrow of the national religion. He then fled into Turkestan, where he gained many disciples, used his talents to adorn a temple with paintings, and hiding himself in a cave for 12 months produced his gospel in a book embellished with beautiful figures. He returned to Persia, and presented this to king Hormisdas, who protected him and embraced his views. This king, dying within two years, was succeeded by Varanes I. A.D. 273, who was at first favourable to Manes. The national priesthood, however, becoming alarmed at the power of his sect, challenged him to a disputation before the king, after which he was condemned to die as a heretic. According to some he was crucified, according to others cut in two or flayed alive (Hyde, *Rel. Vet. Pers.* p. 283; Renaudot, *Hist. Pat. Alex.* pp. 40-49; Eutych. *Annal. Alex.* t. i. p. 387; Hotting. *Hist. Orient.* i. 3). Varanes instituted a general persecution of the Manicheans after his death. Eutychius (*l.c.*) reports a savage jest of his on this subject. He put to death 200 Manicheans, and caused them to be buried with their heads down and their feet projecting above ground. He then boasted he had a garden planted with men instead of trees. The persecution was so severe that adherents of the sect fled into all the neighbouring lands—India, China, Turkestan, etc. The pretext of the persecution was that the spread of the sect was hostile to the human race through their opposition to marriage (Assem. *Bibl. Or.* iii. 220).

Since Beausobre's time the sources of Oriental knowledge have been much enlarged, and modern research inclines more and more to trust the concordant testimony of Persian, Arabic, and Armenian historians, as opposed to the Byzantines, about the affairs of W. Asia. According to these Eastern authorities, the father of Manes came originally from Persia to Babylon, where Manes was born. One day his father heard in a temple a voice saying, "Eat no flesh, drink no wine, and abstain from women," whereupon he founded the sect of the Mugtasila or the Washers, identical with the Sabians of the Marshes between the Tigris and Euphrates, still found near Bassora. In this sect Manes was brought up, being instructed in all the knowledge of his time. At 12 years old an angel announced to him that when older he should abandon that sect. At 24 the same angel summoned him to found Manicheism in these words: "Hail, Manes, from me and from the Lord which has sent me to thee and chosen thee for his work. Now he commands thee to proclaim the glad tidings of the truth which comes from him, and bestow thereon thy whole zeal." Manes, according to one tradition, entered on his office the day that Sapor, son of Artaxerxes, succeeded to the throne, Sun. Apr. 1, 238, as Flügel determines by a lengthened calculation (pp. 146-149). According to another (p. 85) Manes appeared in the 2nd year of the emperor Gallus, A.D. 252 (pp. 150-162). He claimed to be the Paraclete promised by Christ, and derived his dogmas from Persian and Christian sources. Before Manes met Sapor he travelled for 40 years through various countries. Upon his return he invited Fîruz, the brother of Sapor and son of Artaxerxes, to accept his doctrines. Through him he was introduced to Sapor, who shewed him great respect, though he had previously intended to slay him. He promised reformation of his own life and freedom to Manes's adherents to preach their views. Already the sect had spread into India, China, and Turkestan. Manes was put to death by Varanes I. (272-276), and his body, cut in two, was suspended over the two gates of the city Dschundîsâbûr, pp. 99, 329-334. A version of his history which later research has brought to light is in Albîrûnî's *Chronology of Ancient Nations*, trans. by E. Sachau and pub. by the Oriental Trans. Fund in 1879. It is a most important document, and well deserves the praise the learned editor lavishes upon it in his introduction. In many particulars it strikingly confirms the narrative of an-Nadîm given by Flügel, both being probably derived from Manichean sources. Albîrûnî was a native of Khiva, A.D. 973-1048, and lived and wrote near there. This work proves him to have possessed vast literary resources no longer available, but some of which may yet be found in Central Asia. (Cf. art. by Thomas on *Recent Pehlvi Decipherments* in *Jour. Asiat. Soc.* 1871, p. 417.) The writings of Manes were very numerous. From Albîrûnî's work we learn that some were still in existence in the 11th cent. They were written in Persian and Syriac, and, according to Muhammad ben Ishak, in a character peculiar to the Manicheans. Of this alphabet Flügel in his commentary, p. 167, gives a copy. It contained more letters than the Syriac, and was chiefly used by the Manicheans of Samarkhand and Transoxania, where the Marcionites who still existed there in the 10th cent. used a similar character. The names of his books, according to Beausobre, are his Gospel; his Treasure of Life; Book of Chapters; Treatise about the Faith, which Beausobre (t. i. p. 427) believes identical with his Mysteries (μυστήρια, Epiph. *Haer.* lxvi. 14), of which too he gives an analysis, with which cf. the very different one by Muhammad ben Ishak in Flügel, p. 102; Book about the Giants, known in Syriac at the court of Baghdad so late as the 9th cent. (*Jour. Asiat.* Mar. 1835, p. 260). According to Epiphanius he also wrote treatises on astronomy, astrology, and magic. To his Fundamental Epistle Augustine replies in his treatise *cont. Ep. Fundamenti.* This last seems to have been specially popular in Africa. In Fabric. (*Bibl. Graec.* lib. v. c. i.) will be found a collection of fragments from his epistles and a list of his works. [G.T.S.]

Manicheans (Μανιχαῖοι, Epiph. *Haer.* lxvi., where they are also called Ἀκουανῖται, from Ἀκούας, one of their leaders, who carried the heresy from Mesopotamia to Eleutheropolis). For the personal history of Manes see last art. We now treat of the origin, principles, cultus, literature, and history of the sect called after him; which was, indeed, not so much a definite sect as a vast indefinite spiritual and intellectual movement, which from its very vastness eludes, or at least renders very difficult, definite historical treatment.

(1) *Origin and Principles of Manicheism.*—For the fountain of the Manichean heresy we must turn to India (see Baur, *Das Manichäische Religionssystem*, Tübingen, 1831, pp. 433-451, where there is satisfactory evidence that elements derived both from Buddhism and from Zoroastrism are found in the Manichean system). Darmester recognized the influence of the *Zend-Avesta* and Zoroastrism upon Manicheism: cf. *Zend-Avesta* in *Sacred Books of the East*, t. iv. intro. p. xxxvii. For a thorough exposition of this system see the two large works of Beausobre, Baur's vol. of 500 pp., and Neander's *Church Hist.* (Bohn's ed.), t. ii. pp. 157-195. We must content ourselves with sketching the leading principles of the sect. Manes probably at first merely desired to blend Christianity and Zoroastrism together. From Zoroastrism he took his Dualism, which consisted of two independent principles absolutely opposed to each other, with their opposite creations: on the one side God (Ahura-Mazda), the original good from whom nothing but good can proceed; on the other side original evil (Angro-Mainyus), whose essence is wild, self-conflicting tumult, matter, darkness, a world full of smoke and vapour. The powers of darkness, contending in wild rage, approached so near in their blind struggle to the realm of light that a gleam from that hitherto unknown kingdom reached them, whereupon they strove to force their way into it. The good God, in order to guard His boundaries, produced the Aeon Mother of Life, by whom the first or spiritual man was produced, together with the five elements, wind, light, water, fire, and matter, to carry on the struggle; which, however, are not identical with the actual elements, but are the elements of the higher world, of which the mundane and actual elements are a copy framed by the Prince of Darkness, a view we find worked out by the Cathari of the 12th cent. (Gieseler, *H. E.* iii. 452). Primitive man is worsted by the spirits of darkness, who take from him some of his armour, which is his soul (ψυχή). He prays to the Light-King, who sends the Spirit of Life, who rescues him and raises him once more to the Light-Kingdom. Meanwhile the Powers of Darkness had succeeded in swallowing part of the luminous essence of the primeval heavenly man, which they proceeded to shut up in material bodies, as in a prison. But this very violence is the means of their destruction. The Divine Spirit is only enclosed in the material prisons for a time and with a view to final deliverance. To illustrate this Manes used a parable. A shepherd sees a wild beast about to rush into the midst of his flock. He digs a pit and casts into it a kid; the beast springs into the pit to devour his prey, but cannot extricate himself. The shepherd, however, delivers the kid and leaves the lion to perish (*Disp. c. Archel.* c. 25; Epiph. *Haer.* lxvi. c. 44). The Spirit of Life at once began his preparations for purifying the souls which had been mixed up with the kingdom of darkness. That part of the soul which had not been affected by matter he placed in the sun and moon, whence it might send forth its influence to release and draw back towards itself, through the refining processes of vegetable and animal life, kindred souls diffused through all nature; for the sun and moon play as important a part in the Manichean as they do in the Persian, Indian, and Mithraic systems (C. B. Stark, *Zwei Mithraeen*, Heidelberg, 1864, p. 43). To prevent this gradual despiritualization the powers of darkness resolve to produce a being in whom the soul of nature, which was ever striving after liberty, might be securely imprisoned. This is man as he is now, shaped after the image of the primitive man with whom they originally waged war. He was formed by the prince of darkness, and embraces in himself the elements of both worlds, the soul springing from the Light-Kingdom, the body from that of darkness. The powers of darkness now perceive that the light-nature, by concentrating itself in man, has become powerful. They therefore seek to attach him by every possible enticement to the lower world. Here comes in the Manichean story of the Fall, which resembles that of the Ophites. The Powers of Darkness invited man to partake of all the trees of Paradise, forbidding only the tree of Knowledge. But an angel of light, or Christ Himself, the Spirit of the Sun, counteracted their artifices in the shape of the serpent, the parts of the Biblical narrative being thus reversed, God's share being ascribed to the devil and vice versa. The Manichean standpoint with respect to the Fall determined their attitude towards the whole O.T., which they rejected as the work of the evil principle. Likewise their theory about the creation of the material part of man determined their view of the Incarnation, which they regarded as wholly Docetic; if a material body was a prison and a burden to the spirit of man, Christ could scarcely voluntarily imprison His divine Spirit in the same. "Moreover, the Son, when He came for man's salvation, assumed a human appearance, so that He appeared to men as if He were a man, and men thought He had been born" (Epiph. *Haer.* lxvi. 49). This Docetic view of the Incarnation destroyed the reality of His life, His death, resurrection, and ascension, and struck at the root of all historical Christianity, so that we find at last some later Manicheans maintaining a distinction between the mundane or historical Christ, who was a bad man, and the spiritual Christ, Who was a divine deliverer (Gieseler, *H. E.* iii. 407, note 28). They attached a mystical signification to orthodox language about our Lord, whereby they could use it to deceive the unwary. Thus they could speak of a suffering son of man hanging on every tree—of a Christ crucified in every soul and suffering in matter. They gave their own interpretation to the symbols of the suffering Son of Man in the Lord's Supper (cf. Petrus Sic. *Hist. Man.* in Bigne's *Bib. PP.* xvi. 760). For a thorough exposition of the relations between Manicheism and Buddhism see Baur, *l.c.* pp. 433-451, where he points out Buddhist influence on Manichean doctrines as to the opposition between matter and spirit, upon the creation and end of the world, and upon moral questions. The most striking points of contact are metempsychosis (Baur, *l.c.* p. 440), and the stress laid upon

gnosis. The former is the outer way, whereby souls can return thither whence they have descended. The latter is the inner and highest way (cf. Colebrooke's *Essays*, ii. 382, 389, for the universal influence of this view in India). In both systems asceticism was the practical result of the opposition between matter and spirit; the more matter could be crushed, the nearer the spirit came to its original source (cf. Lassen, *Ind. Alterthum.* iii. 408-415).

(2) *Organization.*—Perhaps, however, it is on the practical organization of the system that Buddhist influence is most clearly seen. Manicheism differed from Gnosticism, for the latter did not wish to alter anything in the constitution of the existing church, but only desired to add to the Confession of Faith for the ψυχικοί a secret doctrine for the πνευματικοί; while Manes, as the Paraclete, set up a new church instead of the old, which, even in the persons of the apostles, had been corrupted by Jewish traditions. In the Manichean church the gradations were similar to those among the Buddhists (cf. H. H. Wilson's *Opp.* t. ii. p. 360, *Essay on Buddha and Buddhism*). There was first the great body consisting of the auditores, from whom a less strict course of life was demanded, and one of whose leading duties was to supply the other and higher class, the Elect or Perfect, with food and other necessaries. From these last an ascetic life was demanded. They should possess no property, were bound to a celibate and contemplative life, abstaining from all strong drinks and animal food. They should hurt no living thing, from a religious reverence for the divine life diffused through all nature. Not only should they take no life, but not even pull up a herb or pluck fruits or flowers (Aug. *cont. Faust.* v. 6, vi. 4). Thus Epiphanius (*Haer.* lxvi. c. 28) tells us that when their followers presented one of the Elect with food, he first addressed it thus: "I have neither reaped nor ground, nor pressed nor cast thee into the oven. All these things another has done, and brought thee to me. I am free from all fault." Upon which he said to his disciple, "I have prayed for thee," and let him go (cf. Von Wegnern, *de Manich. Indulgent.* pp. 69 seq.). Here is an essential Pantheism, a tendency which Manicheism manifestly draws from Buddhism (Hodgson, *Jour. Roy. As. Soc.* 1835, p. 295; Matter, *Hist. du Gnostic.* t. ii. 357) and which develops further in the course of its history. St. Augustine noted this point in his reply to Faustus, ii. 5, xii. 13; cf. Aug. *Epp.* 165, 166, c. iii. § 7; *Ep.* 74 *ad* Deuterium Episcop.; Toll. *Insig.* p. 137; Muratorii, *Anecd. Ambros. Biblioth.* ii. 112. Manes derived from Christianity another element of his system. As the Paraclete promised by Christ, he, after Christ's example, chose twelve apostles, in whom the government of the sect was placed. At their head there was a thirteenth, representing Manes and presiding over all (Flügel's *Mani*, pp. 97, 298, 316; Baur, *l.c.* p. 305); subordinate to them there were 72 bishops, under whom were presbyters, deacons, and travelling missionaries, a constitution which lasted to the 13th cent. and possibly may not be yet quite extinct.

(3) *Cultus.*—The Manicheans had their own peculiar rites, though their mystical interpretation of language enabled them to hold the highest position in the Christian ministry, as in an-Nadim's time, A.D. 987, it enabled them to conform externally to the Mohammedan system (Flügel's *Mani*, pp. 107, 404-408). Thus Eutychius, Pat. Alex. *Annal.* t. i. p. 515 (cf. Renaudot, *Hist. Patr. Alexand.* p. 101), tells how Timotheus, Pat. Alex., discovered Manicheans among the Egyptian bishops at the council of Constantinople by permitting the bishops and monks to eat flesh on Sundays, which the Manicheans would not do. Their worship consisted in prayers and hymns. They had neither temples, altars, incense, nor images. They fasted on Sunday. They regarded Easter lightly, as a festival which in their system had no meaning. They observed Pentecost, but not Christmas or Epiphany. Their great festival was that of Bema, held in March in memory of their founder's death. An empty chair or pulpit, richly upholstered, was then placed in their assembly, as a symbol of his presence, while one of his works, probably his *Fundamental Epistle*, was read, together with the records of his martyrdom (cf. Aug. *Reply to Fund. Epist.* c. viii.; *cont. Faust.* xviii. 5). As to their sacraments, the authorities vary much. Beausobre (t. ii. *liv.* ix. c. vi.) maintained strongly that they baptized even infants, and that in the name of the Trinity. On the other hand Augustine, *de Haer.* c. xlvi.; *cont. Ep. Pelag.* lib. ii. and other places cited by Beausobre, *l.c.* p. 714 n.; Cedren. *Hist. Comp.*, *Opp.* t. i. col. 831, Migne's *Patr. Gk.* t. cxxi., expressly assert that they rejected baptism with water; and Timotheus C. P. in his *Form. Recep. Haer.* classes them among those heretics who must receive baptism on joining the church, a rule which seems to have prevailed from the 4th cent. (Beveridge, *Cod. Canon. Eccles. Primit.* lib. ii. c. 12; Basil. *Ep.* clxxxviii.). Certainly their practice in the 12th cent. would support this latter view, as they then substituted their Consolamentum or laying on of hands—which they called the baptism of the Holy Ghost—for water baptism, which they scorned (cf. Gieseler, *H. E.* iii. 397, 410 n.). For the Manicheans to admit baptism with water would seem inconsistent with their fundamental principle of the essentially evil nature of matter (cf. Tertull. *cont. Marcion.* i. 23). But we cannot expect perfect consistency, as in another respect they seem to have retained from the Zoroastrian system an exaggerated reverence for water. As to their Eucharist there is the same diversity of testimony and a similar accusation of filthy practices. They celebrated the communion, substituting water for wine, the use of which they abhorred. About the disgusting ceremonial of Ischas, which Cyril. Hier. (*Cat.* vi.), Augustine (*Haer.* xlvi.), and Pope Leo I. (*ser. v. De Jejun. x. Mens.*) accuse them of adding to their communion in a foul manner, see Beausobre, liv. ix. cc. 7-9 in t. ii. pp. 720-762.

Manicheism has been the prolific parent of false gospels. [Leucius (1); Manes.] But the work of forgery was due not so much to Manes as to his followers, and it is almost certain that Manicheism merely adopted many apocryphal writings.

(4) *History after Death of Manes.*—(i) *In the East*, where they originated, the Manicheans made rapid progress, spreading, as an-Nadîm (Flügel's *Mani*, p. 105, cf. p. 394) tells us, into various lands. During their persecution upon the death of Manes, they fled into Transoxania, whence they maintained a constant communication with Babylon, their original seat, as the head of the sect always remained there till the Mohammedan invasion. They spread into S. Armenia and Cappadocia, where they found material ready to their hand in the HYPSISTARII of that region (Matter, *Gnosticism*, ii. 392), whence they came into immediate contact with Europe. A proof of their activity in Armenia is found in the work of Eznig, one of the leading writers of Armenia in the 5th cent., pub. by the Mekhitarite monks at Venice in 1826 under the title *Refutatio Errorum Persarum et Manichaeorum.* Their progress seems to have been intensified by the Mazdakite movement in the 5th cent., which was only a revival of Manicheism. It displayed the same missionary activity which manifested itself in an aggression upon the orthodox of Armenia, A.D. 590, noted by the Armenian historian Samuel of Ani. He gives us a list of Manichean works which they introduced into Armenia, including the Penitence or Apocalypse of Adam (pub. by Renan in the *Jour. Asiat.* 1853, t. ii. p. 431), the Explanation of the Gospel of Manes, the Gospel of the Infancy, the Vision of St. Paul, and the Testament of Adam.

(ii) *In the West* the first notice of an advance is found in an edict (given in Gieseler, *H. E.* i. 228) of Diocletian, directed to Julian, proconsul of Africa, dated prid. kal. Apr. 287, wherein Manichean leaders are condemned to the stake, and their adherents punished with decapitation and confiscation of all their goods, as following "a new and unheard-of monster, which has come to us from the Persians, a hostile people, and has perpetrated many misdeeds." The genuineness of this edict has been challenged, but is defended by Neander, *H. E.* ii. 195, n. The chief ground for disputing it is the silence of the Fathers, specially of Eusebius. But the argument *e silentio* is never a safe one, and Ambrosiaster mentions it when commenting upon II. Tim. iii. 7. It is addressed to the proconsul of Africa, where the Manicheans were making great progress. This coincides with the fact, known independently, that Manes sent a special envoy to Africa, where, during the 4th cent., Manicheism flourished, both among the monks and clergy of Egypt and in proconsular Africa, ensnaring souls like St. Augustine; and where they must have been very numerous and powerful, since, notwithstanding the severe and bloody laws enacted against them by Valentinian, A.D. 372, and Theodosius, A.D. 381, they assembled, taught, and debated in public in Augustine's time. Yet in some places these laws were not empty threats, for the heathen rhetorician Libanius appealed in behalf of the Manicheans of Palestine (*Ep.* 1344). Probably, as in the case of the pagan persecutions, the vigour with which they were enforced varied with the dispositions of local magistrates. From Africa the sect spread into Spain, Gaul, and Aquitaine (Philast. *Haer.* c. 61, 84), where it may have originated Priscillianism (Muratori, *Anecd. ex Ambros. Biblioth. Codic.* ii. 113, ed. 1698). Later we find the Arian king Hunneric persecuting it in Africa, together with the orthodox, A.D. 477 (Vict. Vit. *Hist. Persec. Wand.* ii. *init.*). We of course find the sect at Constantinople and at Rome. Constantine the Great commissioned a certain Strategius—who, under the name of Musonianus, rose to be praetorian prefect of the East—to report upon it (Ammian. Marcell. xv. 13); while again, 200 years later, in the end of the 5th and beginning of the 6th cent., Manicheism in the Mazdakite movement made an imperial convert in Anastasius I. At Rome they were found from ancient times. Lipsius in *Jahrb. Prot. Theol.* 1879, art. on *Neue Stud. zur Papst-Chronologie*, p. 438, discusses a constitution of pope Anastasius I. A.D. 398, enacted on account of their recent immigration from beyond the seas. After the barbarian invasion of Africa they fled to Rome in great numbers, and pope Leo I. was active in their repression. Leo says that the Manicheans, whom, with the aid of the civil magistrates, he arrested, acknowledged their dissolute practices; whereupon Valentinian III. published a very severe law against them. Notwithstanding all the papal efforts, renewed from age to age, we still find the sect at Rome in 7th cent., under Gregory the Great (cf. Greg. Mag. lib. ii. *Ep.* 37; Gieseler, *H. E.* t. ii. p. 491, Clark's ed.).

(5) *Remains of the Sect and of its Literature.*—In the Yezedees, or Devil-worshippers of Mosul, and the Ansairees of Syria, we have their direct representatives; while mingled with the doctrines of the Sabians or Hemerobaptistae, who still linger in the neighbourhood of Harran, we have a large Manichean element. See Badger's *Nestorians*, t. i. cc. ix. x.; Lyde's *Asian Mystery*, and Layard's *Nineveh*, c. ix., as confirming this view by several interesting facts, cf. also *Notes sur les sectes de Kurdistan*, par T. Gilbert, in *Jour. Asiat.* 1873, t. ii. p. 393. Cahier maintained, in *Mel. archéol.* i. 148, that the Bogomili and the Massalians, branches of the same sect, still existed (1888) in Russia. We still possess some specimens of their literature, and a critical examination of Mohammedan MSS. and a complete investigation of the interior state of Western and Central Asia would probably reveal them in still larger abundance (Beausob. *Hist. Man.* t. i. p. 366, and n. 4). Renan published in 1853, in the *Jour. Asiat.* a Syriac document called the Apocalypse of Adam, which he shewed to be one of those brought by the Manicheans into Armenia in 590 A.D. and condemned in the celebrated Gelasian decree. See Harnack, *Dogmengesch.* vol. ii. (4th ed. 1909), pp. 513-527. [GELASIUS.] [G.T.S.]

Mar Aba or **Mar-Abas.** [NESTORIAN CHURCH; THOMAS (8).]

Marana and **Cyra,** two ladies of birth and education of Beroea in Syria, who in their youth devoted themselves to a solitary life of the extremest austerity, which they had persevered in for 42 years when Theodoret wrote his *Religiosa Historia.* According to Theodoret they left home with some female servants whom they had inspired with the same ascetic fervour and built a small stone enclosure, open to the sky, the door of which they closed up with mud and stones, their only means of communication with the outer world being a small window through which they took in food. Only females were allowed to converse with Marana, and that only at Easter; Cyra no one had ever heard speak. For their maidens a small hovel was constructed within earshot, so that they could encourage them by their example and by their words to a life of prayer and holy love. Theodoret often visited these recluses and in honour of his priestly office they unwalled their door and admitted him into the enclosure, which he found devoid of any protection against the heat or cold, rain or snow. Their heads and the whole upper part of their bodies were enveloped in long hoods, entirely concealing their faces, breasts, and hands. They wore chains of iron round their necks, waists, and wrists, of such weight as to prevent Cyra, who was of weak frame, from raising herself upright. These they laid aside at Theodoret's request, but resumed after he left. Their fastings equalled in length those of Moses and David. Fired with a desire to visit holy sites, they made a pilgrimage to Jerusalem, not eating once on the journey nor as they returned, and only breaking their fast at Jerusalem. They practised the same rigid abstinence on a second pilgrimage to the tomb of St. Thecla at the Isaurian Seleucia. Theod. *Hist. Relig.* c. 29; Basil. *Menol.* Feb. 28; Tillem. ii. 64; Ceill. x. 63. [E.V.]

Marcella, the friend of Jerome, from whose writings and memoir of her (*Ep.* cxxvii. ed. Vall.) she is chiefly known. She was descended from the illustrious Roman family of the Marcelli, and had great wealth. Her mother Albina was a widow when Athanasius came as an exile to Rome in 340. From Athanasius and his companions she heard of Anthony and the monasteries of the Thebaid, and received her first impulse towards the ascetic life. She married, but her husband died after seven months, and she refused a second marriage offered her by the wealthy Cerealis, a man of consular rank but advanced in years. Her ascetic tendency was confirmed by the coming to Rome of the Egyptian monk Peter in 374. She was the first in the city to make the monastic profession. She continued to live with her mother in their palatial residence on the Aventine, but with the utmost simplicity. She was not immoderate in her asceticism, and followed the counsels of her mother, from whose society she never departed.

When Jerome came to Rome in 382, she sought him out because of his repute for Biblical learning, and made him, at first against his will, her constant companion. A circle of ladies gathered round her, and her house became a kind of convent dedicated to the study of the Scriptures, and to psalmody and prayer. Marcella was eager for information, and would not accept any doubtful explanation, so that Jerome found himself in the presence of a judge rather than a disciple. At times she took her teacher to task for his severity and quarrelsomeness (*Ep.* xxvii. 2, ed. Vall.). He wrote for her some 15 different treatises on difficult passages of Scripture and church history; and on his departure in 385 hoped that she might have accompanied her intimate friends Paula and Eustochium to Palestine. A letter written by those two ladies on their settlement at Bethlehem (in Jerome, *Ep.* xliv. ed. Vall.) invites her in glowing terms to come and enjoy with them the Holy Land; but she remained at Rome. After her mother's death in 387 she retired to a little house outside the city with her young friend Principia and devoted her whole time to good works. She still had a keen interest in Jerome's theological pursuits, and when Rufinus came to Rome and disputes arose as to his translation of Origen's περὶ Ἀρχῶν, she threw herself eagerly into the controversy. Having, in conjunction with Pammachius and Oceanus, ascertained Jerome's view of the matter, she urged the pope Anastasius (400-403) to condemn Origen and his defenders; and, when he hesitated, went to him and pointed out the passages which, she contended, though veiled in Rufinus's translation, demanded the pope's condemnation. Anastasius completely yielded, and like Theophilus of Alexandria condemned Origen and his upholders. "Of this glorious victory," says Jerome, "Marcella was the origin."

She lived till the sack of Rome by Alaric. The Goths, supposing her to be affecting poverty to conceal her wealth, used personal violence, but at her entreaty spared Principia, and at last allowed them to take sanctuary in St. Paul's church. Her faith made her seem hardly sensible of her sufferings, but she only survived a few days and died in the arms of Principia, leaving all she had to the poor. Jerome, ed. Vall. *Epp.* 23-29, 32, 34, 37-44, 46, 97, 127. [W.H.F.]

Marcellina (2), a sister of St. Ambrose, older than himself. His three books *de Virginibus,* addressed to her, were written by her request. From iii. 1 we learn that she was admitted as a consecrated virgin at Rome on Christmas Day, by pope Liberius, in the presence of a large concourse of virgins and others. The address then given by Liberius is recorded by Ambrose from what Marcellina had often repeated to him. Ambrose praises her devotion and advises her to relax the severity of her fasting. She is mentioned by him (*Ep.* v.) as a witness to the virginal purity of Indicia. A constant correspondence was kept up with her brother. She is his "domina soror vitae atque oculis praeferenda." He wrote three of his most important letters to her: *Ep.* xx. describes his conflict with Justina and her son the younger Valentinian; xxii. announces the discovery of the bodies of the martyrs Gervasius and Protasius; xli. reports a sermon in which he had reproved Theodosius. In his discourse on the death of his brother Satyrus, Ambrose speaks of the warm family affection which bound the three together, and of the sister's grief (*de Excessu Satyri,* §§ 33, 76). [J.LL.D.]

Marcellinus (1), bp. of Rome after Caius from June 30, 296, to Oct. 25 (?), 304, elected after a vacancy of about two months; called Marcellianus by Jerome, Nicephorus, and in the *Chronogr. Syntomon* (853). The above dates are those of the Liberian Catalogue (354) and appear correct. In other records his chronology is very uncertain, partly, it would seem, owing to a confusion between him and his successor Marcellus. He is omitted altogether in the Liberian *Depositio Episcoporum* and *Depositio Martyrum* (see Lipsius, *Chronol. der röm. Bisch.* p. 242). The main question about him is his conduct with regard to the persecution under Diocletian. The Liberian Catalogue says only that it occurred in his time—"quo tempore fuit persecutio." Eusebius (*H. E.* vii. 32) intimates that he was in some way implicated in it—ὃν καὶ αὐτὸν κατείληφεν ὁ διωγμός. The Felician Catalogue (530) says: "In which time was a great persecution: within 30 days 16,000 persons of both sexes were crowned with martyrdom through divers provinces; in the course of it Marcellinus himself was led to sacrifice, that he might offer incense, which thing he also did; and having after a few days been brought to penitence, he was by the same Diocletian, for the faith of Christ, together with Claudius Quirinus and Antoninus, beheaded and crowned with martyrdom. The holy bodies lay for 26 days in the street by order of Diocletian; when the presbyter Marcellus collected by night the bodies of the saints, and buried them on the Salarian Way in the cemetery of Priscilla in a cell (*cubiculum*) which is to be seen to the present day, because the penitent [pope] himself had so ordered while he was being dragged to execution, in a crypt near the body of St. Crescentio, vii. Kal. Maii." Most probably the statements of his having offered incense and of the place of his burial are true, but his martyrdom is at least doubtful. The charge of having yielded to the edict of Diocletian, which required all Christians to offer incense to the gods, appears from Augustine to have been alleged afterwards as a known fact by the African Donatists. True, Augustine treats it as probably a calumny, and says it "is by no means proved by any documentary evidence" (*de Unico Baptism. c. Petilian.* c. 16, § 27). Further, Theodoret (*H. E.* i. 2) speaks apparently with praise of the conduct of Marcellinus in the persecution: τὸν ἐν τῷ διωγμῷ διαπρέψαντα. On these grounds Bower, in his history of the popes, warmly maintains his innocence. But it is difficult to account for the introduction of the story into the pontifical annals themselves and its perpetuation as a tradition of the Roman church, unless there had been foundation for it. Even Augustine, however anxious to rebut the charge, can only plead the absence of evidence; he does not deny the tradition, or even the possibility of its truth. The expression of Theodoret is too vague to count as evidence. In the story of the martyrdom there is nothing in itself improbable, and it is quite possible that Marcellinus recovered courage and atoned for his temporary weakness. But there is such a significant absence of early evidence of the martyrdom as to leave it not only unproved but improbable. His name does not appear in the Liberian *Depositio Martyrum*, nor in Jerome's list, and, apart from the legendary complexion of the Felician narrative (including the statement of 16,000 having suffered in 30 days), the addition of the glory of martyrdom to popes in the later pontifical annals is too frequent to weigh against the silence of earlier accounts. Further, the omission of his name also from the *Depositio Episcoporum* may be due to his unfaithfulness, if that had not really been atoned for by martyrdom. His burial in the cemetery of Priscilla instead of that of Callistus, where his predecessors since Zephyrinus (236) had been interred, may be accepted without hesitation, the Felician Catalogue being apparently trustworthy as to the burial-places of popes, and the place where he lay being spoken of as well known in the writer's day. A reason for the change of place, independent of the alleged wish of the penitent pope himself, is given by De Rossi (*Rom. Sotteran.* ii. p. 105), viz. that the Christian cemeteries had been seized during the persecution, so that it had become necessary to construct a new one. It appears (*ib.* i. p. 203; ii. p. 105) that the Christians did not recover their sacred places till Maxentius restored them to pope Miltiades; and this accounts for the fact, that of the two popes between Marcellinus and Miltiades, the first, Marcellus, was also buried in the cemetery of Priscilla, but the second, Eusebius, as well as Miltiades himself, again in that of Callistus (*Catal. Felic.*); though not in the old papal crypt, a new one having presumably been constructed by Miltiades. In recensions of the pontifical annals later than the Felician the cemetery of Priscilla is said to have been acquired from a matron of that name by Marcellus, the successor of Marcellinus; but in the Felician account Marcellinus himself appears as having already secured a place of burial there. The cemetery itself was, according to De Rossi, one of the oldest in Rome, with extensive workings in it at a deep level, which he supposes to have been made during the persecution, when the old burial-place of the faithful on the Appian Way was no longer available. The Salarian Way, where the cemetery of Priscilla was, lies far from the Appian, being on the opposite side of the city, towards the N. [J.B—Y.]

Marcellinus (7), Flavius, a tribune and afterwards a notary (Böcking, *Not. Dig. Occ.* p. 408), brother to Apringius, afterwards proconsul of Africa, where Marcellinus appears to have usually resided. He was a Christian of high character, taking much interest in theological matters. In 410 he was appointed by Honorius to preside over a commission of inquiry into the disputes between the Catholics and Donatists, an office for which he was singularly well qualified, and which on the whole he discharged (in 411) with great moderation, good temper, and impartiality, though not without giving offence to the Donatists, who accused him of bribery (Aug. *Ep.* 141; *Cod. Theod.* xvi. 11, 5). With Augustine an intimate friendship subsisted which the behaviour of Marcellinus at the conference no doubt tended to strengthen; several letters were exchanged between them, and Augustine addressed to him his three books *de Peccatorum Meritis et Remissione*, his book *de Spiritu et Littera*, and the first two books of his great work *de Civitate Dei*, which he says that he undertook at his suggestion (Aug. *Retract.* ii. 37; *de Civ. Dei.* i. praef. ii. 1). Excepting letters about the conference (*Epp.* 128, 129), the correspondence appears to have been carried on chiefly during 412. It arose mainly out of the anxiety of Marcellinus for his friend Volusianus, who, notwithstanding the efforts of his mother to induce him to become a Christian, was swayed in a contrary direction by the worldly society in which he lived. In 413 occurred the revolt of Heraclian, suppressed by Marinus, count of Africa, who, bribed by the Donatists, as Orosius insinuates, arrested and imprisoned Marcellinus and Apringius. Several African bishops joined in a letter of intercession on behalf of the prisoners, whose prayer Caecilianus affected to support, and he even paid an express visit to Augustine, giving him the strongest hope that they would be released, with solemn asseverations of absence of hostility on his own part. But on the following day, Sept. 15 or 16, they were both put to death. Augustine mentions their edifying behaviour in prison. See Dr. Sparrow Simpson's *S. Aug. and Afr. Ch. Divisions* (1910), pp. 102-126. [H.W.P.]

Marcellus (3), bp. of Rome probably from May 24, 307, to Jan. 15, 309, the see having been vacant after the death of Marcellinus, 2 years, 6 months, and 27 days (Lipsius, *Chronologie der röm. Bischöf.*).

This pope appears as a martyr in the Roman Martyrology, and in the later recensions of the *Liber Pontificalis*, a story being told that he was beaten, and afterwards condemned to tend the imperial horses as a slave. No trace of this legend, or indeed of his being a martyr at all, appears in the earlier recensions of the Pontifical, including the Felician. But a light is thrown on the circumstances which probably led to his title of "Confessor" by the monumental inscriptions to him and his successor Eusebius, placed on their tombs by pope Damasus. That to Marcellus (Pagi, *Critic.* in Baron. *ad ann.* 309; *in Actis S. Januar.*; De Rossi, *Rom. Sotter.* vi. p. 204) reads:

"Veridicus rector lapsis quia crimina flere
Praedixit, miseris fuit omnibus hostis amarus.
Hinc furor, hinc odium sequitur, discordia lites,
Seditio, caedes; solvuntur foedera pacis.
Crimen ob alterius, Christum qui in pace negavit,
Finibus expulsus patriae est feritate tyranni.
Haec breviter Damasus voluit comperta referre
Marcelli ut populus meritum cognoscere posset."

It would appear from these lines, together with those on Eusebius [Eusebius (1)], that when persecution ceased at Rome conflicts arose in the Christian community as to the terms of readmission of the *lapsi* to communion; that Marcellus after his election had required a period of penance before absolution; that this stern discipline evoked violent opposition, the subjects of it being doubtless numerous and influential; that the church had been split into parties in consequence, and riots, anarchy, and even bloodshed, had ensued; that "the tyrant" Maxentius had interposed in the interests of peace and banished the pope as the author of the discord. He was not really so, the inscription implies, but "another," for whose "crime" he suffered, *i.e.* the leader and instigator of the opposition, who had "denied Christ in time of peace" by condoning apostasy and subverting discipline after persecution had ceased. But Marcellus was made the victim, and thus was a "confessor" (or, in the wider sense of the word, a "martyr"), if not strictly for the faith, at any rate for canonical discipline and the honour of Christ. The "other" referred to was probably the Heraclius spoken of in the inscription on Eusebius as having "forbidden the lapsi to mourn for their sins," and who was banished in the next episcopate by "the tyrant" as well as the pope—"Extemplo pariter pulsi feritate tyranni." As Marcellus, unlike Eusebius, is not said in the Damasine inscription to have died in exile, and as he was certainly buried at Rome, like his predecessor in the cemetery of Priscilla on the Salarian Way (*Catal. Felic.*), he may have been allowed to return to his see. [J.B—Y.]

Marcellus (4), bp. of Ancyra, believed to have been present at the synod held there in 315; but nothing can be proved from subscriptions doubtful in themselves. St. Athanasius, writing in 358 (*Hist. ad Mon.* 76), calls him an old man *then*; so that his age could have been no bar to his being *bishop* A.D. 315. He was certainly present, 325, at the Nicene council, where he obtained a good report, as pope Julius tells the Eusebians (Mansi, ii. 1215), for having contended earnestly for the Catholic faith against the Arians. Later, in refuting the heterodox writings of Asterius, he was accused of falling into doctrines combining the errors of Sabellius and Paul of Samosata, but his attachment to St. Athanasius and the orthodox cause may have subjected his book to unfair criticism. Anyhow the Eusebians, piqued at his absence from the synod of Tyre and afterwards the festivities at Jerusalem, A.D. 335, in honour of the dedication of the church of the Holy Sepulchre, called upon him to render account of the opinions advanced in it, and to recant them, and, according to Socrates, extorted a promise that he would burn the offending book. For not having at once done this, he was deposed in the synod held, by command of the emperor, at Constantinople by the chiefs of that party, in Feb. 336, when Eusebius of Nicomedia presided, and Eusebius of Caesarea was charged by the assembled bishops with the task of refuting the work of Marcellus. Basil the semi-Arian was appointed to the see vacated by him (Socr. i. 36). Condemned at Constantinople, Marcellus betook himself to Rome, apparently without loss of time. It must have been almost the first act of Julius, after his election (Feb. 6, 337), to receive Marcellus into communion. Marcellus could have scarcely left Rome when the Eusebian deputies, Macarius and two deacons, arrived (A.D. 339), hoping to persuade Julius to join them in unseating St. Athanasius who had returned from exile without being synodically restored. This led to Athanasius coming to Rome about Easter 340, and to a synod of more than 50 bishops assembled at Rome by pope Julius in Nov. 341.

Marcellus was at Rome then, having been admitted by Julius to communion on a previous visit; and Julius followed the precedent suggested by Marcellus at his previous visit, and adopted in his case, viz. that of sending presbyters to the Eusebians with the object of bringing them to Rome to confront an opponent already there. Neither Julius nor his bishops ventured to restore Marcellus or St. Athanasius to their respective sees. They merely gave their collective voice for admitting them to communion, and declared their innocence. It was now that Marcellus testified to Julius and the assembled bishops that his attempt to return to Ancyra, A.D. 338-339, had only provoked such flagrant scenes as had happened more recently at Alexandria when St. Athanasius was expelled (*Apol. c. Arian.* § 33, cf. Hil. *Frag.* iii. 9).

"Marcellus," Athanasius says, in his history to the monks (§ 6), "went to Rome, made his apology, and then at their request gave them his faith in writing, of which also the Sardican council approved." The Sardicans grounded their verdict in his favour on the book which Eusebius had maligned, but which they pronounced consistent with orthodoxy. "For he had not, as they affirmed, attributed to the Word of God a beginning from Mary, nor any end to His kingdom; but had stated His kingdom to be without beginning or end" (*Apol. c. Arian.* § 47). Hence they declared him faultless and free from taint. St. Hilary, who also says nothing of his profession, bears them out in their decision on the book; adding that Marcellus was never again tried or condemned in any subsequent synod (*Frag.* ii. 21-23). Against such testimony—living, competent, and explicit—as this, it is plainly not for moderns to contend, the book being no longer extant to speak for itself; and therefore we must—in spite of all Cave may urge to the contrary (*Hist. Lit.* i. 202), and after him Cardinal Newman (*Library of the Fathers*, xix. 503) and the learned writer of art. EUSEBIUS in this work—conclude with Montfaucon (*Diatr.* c. iii.), that, strongly as the extracts from it may read in Eusebius, whose party bias betrays itself in every line, yet "read by the light of what precedes and follows," as say the Sardican fathers, they may all be interpreted in a sense not conflicting with orthodoxy. St. Hilary, moreover, speaks with unwonted weight, as he proclaims the fact loudly that Marcellus subsequently by some rash utterances and his evident sympathy with his former disciple, Photinus, the ejected from Sirmium, came at last to be suspected of heretical leanings by all; and notably that he was, though privately, put out of communion by St. Athanasius, on which Marcellus abstained from church himself (*Frag.* ii. 23). Possibly such a rash utterance was in the mind of St. Hilary when he said to Constantius: "Hinc Marcellus Verbum Dei cum legit, nescit," and then adds: "Hinc Photinus hominem Jesum Christum cum loquitur, ignorat," classing them both in the same category. In the work of St. Epiphanius against heresies the Photinians rank first (71), and the Marcellians follow (72); yet even there the inference is, that the latter had been led astray by the former. St. Epiphanius does not mention the work of Eusebius against Marcellus, but gives extracts from one against him by Acacius, the successor of Eusebius at Caesarea, but not, as he says, because he thinks it any more conclusive than the Sardican fathers thought the work of Eusebius. But he criticizes the profession made by Marcellus in writing to pope Julius on the principle "Qui s'excuse s'accuse." This profession, what both Marcellus himself and St. Athanasius call his "ἔγγραφον πίστιν," which, he says expressly, he gave to pope Julius before leaving Rome, and which St. Epiphanius gives at full length. St. Athanasius says it was exhibited to the Roman and Sardican councils as well; but we have no other proof of this. It is but one of three different professions exhibited at different times on behalf of Marcellus—all characterized by the same suspicious surroundings, as will be shewn in due course. The two first are given by St. Epiphanius (*Haer.* lxxii.); the third was exhumed by Montfaucon. Dr. Heurtley (*de Fide et Symbolo*, p. 24) took this creed of Epiphanius as the earliest specimen of a Western creed. It was as certainly the baptismal creed of the West as it was *not* that of the local church of Rome (*ib.* pp. 89-133). For *had it been* the creed of the church of Rome, would not St. Athanasius have characterized it as such; would not Julius have recognized and applauded the adoption of his own formula? No doubt Marcellus picked it up in the Danubian provinces, or at Aquileia, in his way to Rome. It is identical with the creed commented upon by St. Augustine, which follows it in Heurtley (*op. cit.*), saving in the expression τὸν γεννηθέντα ἐκ Πνεύματος ἁγίου, etc., which is suspiciously peculiar, and may well have excited the misgivings of St. Epiphanius. Now this creed Marcellus never ventures to call the creed of his own church, yet must have meant that Julius should think it so, as he designates it "what he had been taught by his spiritual fathers, had learnt from holy Scripture, and preached in church," and he begs Julius to enclose copies of it to those bishops with whom he was corresponding, that any to whom he was unknown might be disabused of wrong notions formed of him from hostile statements. By way of preface, he recites, to condemn them, the principal errors held by his enemies; and affirms several points on which his own faith had been questioned. Whether by his own contrivance or otherwise, this profession was never made public, nor appealed to by him again. It satisfied Julius, and Julius may have communicated it to his correspondents among the Western bishops and to St. Athanasius on his arrival in Rome: but it cannot be proved to have been formally brought before the 50 bishops afterwards assembled there, and there is no proof that it was so much as named at Sardica. In dealing with Easterns, anyhow, the creed in which he professes his faith was that of Nicaea. This profession is extant as well as the other, and was being employed by his disciples in their own justification when it was placed in the hands of St. Epiphanius. It is headed "Inscription of the faith of Marcellus." Yet it can hardly be thought accidental that his own assent is not explicitly given by subscription either to this or the third formula, produced on his behalf. Montfaucon, preoccupied with his own discovery, seeks to connect it with this second profession, with which it has nothing whatever to do. Evidently Marcellus aimed at being an Eastern to the Easterns, and a Western to the Westerns.

Finally, neither of these professions would seem to have sufficed for him in extreme old age, but he must construct a third, intended this time for St. Athanasius himself. The date fixed for it by Montfaucon is 372, not earlier, to give time for some letters that passed on the subject of Marcellus in 371, between St. Athanasius and St. Basil, elected to the see of Caesarea the year before; not later, because St. Athanasius died in 373, and Marcellus himself in 374. But if Montfaucon had dated it 373, he would have got rid of the very difficulty which perplexed him most, viz. the absence of the name of St. Athanasius amongst its countersigners (*Diatr.* c. vi. 4). Far from having been received by St. Athanasius and his colleagues, the signatures affixed to this "aureum opusculum," as Montfaucon in his enthusiasm calls it, are such as go far towards impeaching its genuineness, or else depriving it of the least weight. Surely the signatures to it should have been *not* of those to whom it was delivered, but *from whom* it emanated! The document purports to be the work of a gathering of the church of Ancyra under their father Marcellus; and it may well have been dictated by a man of his advanced years, recapitulating and repudiating all the various errors amid which his chequered life had been passed. As no other name is given but his own and that of his deacon Eugenius who was charged with its delivery, we may well doubt whether any third person had a hand in it. The reference in it to the commendatory letters given to its bearer by the bishops of Greece and Macedonia seems consistent with its having been addressed, and expedited through their good offices, to St. Athanasius (*Diatr. ib.* § 2). Basil (*Epp.* 59, 125, 239, 265, ed. Ben.) is just as disgusted at Marcellus having been received into communion in the West under Julius, as at Eustathius having been similarly received under Liberius (*Epp.* 226, 244, 263). He looked upon both as trimmers, as indeed their acts prove them; and heterodox at heart, in spite of their repeated disclaimers, and undeserving of any trust. There was one point of which Marcellus never lost sight and traded upon through life, with whatsoever errors he was charged. "Se communione Julii et Athanasii, Romanae et Alexandrinae urbis pontificum, esse munitum"—as St. Jerome puts it (*de Vir. Illust.* c. 86). Some may, possibly, consider that he duped them both; and the second more, by a good deal, than the first. All that remains to be said of Marcellus is, that although restored at Sardica, and included in the general letter of recall issued subsequently by the emperor Constantius and preserved by St. Athanasius (*Apol. c. Arian.* § 54), he never seems to have regained his see. Basilius certainly was in possession of it at the second council of Sirmium A.D. 351, when he refuted Photinus; and either he, or Athanasius his successor, with whom St. Basil corresponded in 369 (*Ep.* 25), was in possession A.D. 363, and joined in the petition recorded by Socrates (iii. 25) to the emperor Jovian. St. Athanasius, according to Cardinal Newman, upheld him "to *c.* 360," but attacked his tenets pointedly, though without naming him, in his fourth oration against the Arians. The short essay demonstrating this is of the highest interest—Introd. to Disc. iv. pp. 503 seq. vol. xix., also vols. viii. and xiii. (p. 52, note l.), of *Lib. of the Fathers.* Cf. Montfaucon, *Diatr. de causâ Marcelli,* vol. ii. collect. Nov. Pat. Praef. 41 seq.; Newman's *Arians*; Rettberg's Pref. in Migne, *Patr. Gk.* xviii. 1299; Wetzer's *Restit. Ver. Chronol.*; and Larroque's *Diss. de Phot. Haeret.* [ATHANASIUS; EUSEBIUS OF CAESAREA.] [E.S.FF.]

Marcia. In 183 a conspiracy against the emperor Commodus was detected and put down, in which the emperor's sister Lucilla and his cousin Quadratus had been prime movers. On the execution of Quadratus and the confiscation of his property, his concubine Marcia became the concubine of Commodus and obtained the highest favour with him. She was granted all the honours due to an acknowledged empress, save that of having the sacred fire borne before her. The emperor's coins displayed her figure in the garb of an Amazon, and he himself took the title Amazonius, and gave it to a month of the year. She was all-powerful with him, and used her influence on behalf of the Christians, obtaining for them many benefits. This fact, stated by Dion Cassius (or possibly by his epitomizer Xiphilinus), has led to the suspicion that she was a Christian herself, a suspicion not disproved by her position as concubine; for the Christian code then dealt tenderly with the case of a female slave unable to refuse her person to her master, and, provided she shewed the fidelity of a wife, did not condemn her (*Const. Apost.* viii. 32). We now know from Hippolytus that the eunuch who brought Marcia up, and who retained a high place in her confidence, was a Christian presbyter. This sufficiently accounts for her Christian sympathies; and the epithet φιλόθεος, which Hippolytus applies to her, would have been different if, besides being friendly to the Christians, she had been a Christian herself.

Marcia, whose intimacy with her fellow-servant Eclectus had given occasion for remark, ultimately became his wife. She appears to have had resolution and spirit corresponding to her favourite Amazonian dress. She was put to death in 193 by Didius Julianus, to avenge the death of Commodus, which she had planned and carried out to save her own life. For the original authorities, see ECLECTUS. [G.S.]

Marciani. [EUCHITES.]

Marcianus (3), Nov. 2 (*Menol. Graec.* Sirlet. and *Mart. Rom.*), a celebrated solitary in the desert of Chalcis in Syria (Theod. *Rel. Hist.* c. 3); a native of Cyrrhus and of good family. In the desert he built himself within a narrow enclosure a cell in which he could neither stand upright nor lie at full length. In course of time he admitted to his society, but in separate dwellings, two disciples—Eusebius, his successor in the cell, and Agapetus. At some distance he established an abode, under the care of Eusebius, for those who desired to pursue a monastic life under regulations framed by him. Agapetus retired and became bp. of Apamea. Towards the end of his life Marcian allowed himself to be visited by all who pleased, women excepted, but only after the festival of Easter. About 382 he was visited by Flavian, the new bp. of Antioch, in company with four of the most eminent bishops of Syria—Acacius of Berrhoea, Eusebius of Chalcis, Isidore of Cyrrhus, and Theodotus of Hierapolis—besides some religious laymen of high rank. They came to listen to his wisdom, but he persisted in humble silence, and only observed that such as he could not expect to profit men while the word and works of God were so continually appealing to men in vain. Living in the Arian reign of Valens, Marcian's great influence was steadily exerted on the side of orthodoxy and he was an uncompromising opponent of all the prevailing heresies. He zealously upheld the Nicaean rule of Easter and broke off communion with the venerable solitary Abraham in the same desert until he gave up the old Syrian custom and conformed to the new one. Tillemont (viii. 483, xiv. 222) places his death *c.* 385 or 387. The Roman Martyrology commemorates him on Nov. 2. His disciple Agapetus founded two monasteries, one called after himself at Nicerta in the diocese of Apamea, and another called after Marcian's disciple Simeon. From them sprang many, all observing the rules of Marcian. His disciple Basil erected one at Seleucobelus. Tillem. viii. 478, x. 533, xi. 304, xii. 20, xiv. 222, xv. 340, 349 ; Dupin, i. 455, ed. 1722 ; Ceill. x. 52 ; Baron. *A. E.* ann. 382, lxviii. [C.H.]

Marcianus (4), Jan. 10, presbyter and oeconomus of the great church of Constantinople. The authorities for his Life are Theodorus Lector (*H. E.* i. 13, 23, in *Patr. Gk.* lxxxvi.), the *Basilian Menology*, Jan. 10, a *Vita* from Simeon Metaphrastes (Boll. *Acta SS.* 10 Jan. i. 609) ; and notices in the Bollandist Lives of St. Auxentius (14 Feb. ii. 770), St. Isidore the martyr of Chios (15 Mai. iii. 445), and St. Gregory Nazianzen (9 Mai. ii. 401 C, note *n*). Tillemont (xvi. 161) devotes an article to him. He was originally a layman of the Cathari or Novatianists (Theod. L. i. 13), and was then intimate with Auxentius, who was a Catholic (*Vit. Auxent. u.s.*). He was appointed oeconomus by the patriarch Gennadius, therefore after 458 ; and made it a rule that the clergy of Constantinople should retain for their own churches the offerings made in them and no longer pay them over to the great church (Theod. L. i. 13). His erection of the remarkable (θαυμαστὸν) church of the Anastasia or Holy Resurrection and of the church of St. Irene is mentioned in the *Basilian Menology* and by Codinus (*Aedif. Cp.* p. 88, ed. Bekker), the latter adding that he also built a hospital for the sick. The church of Irene (transformed from an idol temple) was on the shore (*Vit.* § 14) at "the passage" (Codin.). The Anastasia was (Codin.) a refoundation of the humble oratory in which St. Gregory ministered, and Marcian bought the site (then occupied by dealers in materials for mosaic work) because there had been found St. Gregory's commentaries (ὑπομνήματα), wherein he had, 50 years before, predicted the restoration of the building in greater size and beauty. The adornment of Marcian's church was subsequently completed by Basil the Macedonian, who added the golden ceiling. How Marcian saved his new church in the conflagration of Sept. 2 by his prayers and tears, while mounted on the roof with the Holy Gospels in his hands, is related by Theodore Lector (i. 23), the *Vita*, the *Basilian Menology*, Theophanes (A. C. 454), and Cedrenus (p. 348, ed. Bekker, p. 610). The year as fixed by Clinton (*F. R.* i. 666) was 465. Codinus's mention of 50 years makes the rebuilding of the Anastasia *c.* 425, as the Bollandist Lives of St. Gregory (*u.s.*) and St. Isidore (*u.s.*) say, long therefore before Marcian became oeconomus. He is stated to have placed the relics of St. Isidore in the church of St. Irene (*ib.*). An account of the two churches, very full as to the Anastasia, is given in Du Cange (*Cpolis. Chr.* lib. iv. pp. 98, 102, ed. 1729). Tillemont dates Marcian's death 471, and has minor notices of him at ii. 231, iii. 354, v. 98, ix. 416, xvi. 59, 70. [C.H.]

Marcianus (8), Flavius, emperor of the East 450-457. For his civil history see *D. of G. and R. Biogr.*

On his accession he found the world distracted by the Eutychian controversy. Theodosius had taken the part of Eutyches and upheld the decision of the "Latrocinium" of Ephesus. His death caused a complete revolution in the church in the East. Pulcheria had always been on the side of pope Leo and orthodoxy and naturally chose for her husband one who shared her views. Marcian, in his first letter to Leo (S. Leonis, *Ep.* lxxiii. in Migne, *Patr. Lat.* liv. 900), speaks of the assembling of a council under Leo's influence. For the correspondence between Marcian, Pulcheria, and Leo relating to the proposed council see LEO I. The disturbed state of the ecclesiastical atmosphere was probably the motive of Marcian's law of July 12, 451, against brawling in churches and holding meetings in private houses or in the streets (Codex, lib. i. tit. xii. 5). The same year Eutyches was banished, though not so far from Constantinople as Leo (*Ep.* lxxxiv.) wished, and orders were issued by the emperor convening a council. Originally intended to meet at Nicaea on Sept. 1, pressure of public business prevented the emperor, then in Thrace, from going so far from Constantinople, so the bishops assembled at Nicaea were directed to repair to Chalcedon (Mansi, vi. 552, 558). For a detailed account of the proceedings of the council see DIOSCORUS and EUTYCHES. Marcian and Pulcheria were present only at the sixth session on Oct. 25, when the emperor made short speeches in Greek and Latin to the assembled bishops, who received him and the empress enthusiastically as a new Constantine and a new Helena. [EUTYCHES.]

After the council separated Marcian proceeded to enforce its decrees by a series of edicts. The first two, dated Feb. 7 and Mar. 13, 452, confirmed the decisions of the council and prohibited public arguments on theological questions that had been settled by them once for all, as thereby the divine mysteries were exposed to the profane gaze of Jews and pagans (Mansi, vii. 475-480). A third, of July 6, repealed the constitution promulgated by Theodosius at the instigation of the Eutychians against Flavian and his adherents Eusebius and Theodoret (*ib.* 497-500). A fourth, dated July 28 (*ib.* 501-506), imposed heavy penalties and disabilities on the Eutychians. Another law, dated Aug. 1, 455, reenacted the same provisions with trifling variations and subjected the Eutychians to all penalties imposed upon the Apollinarists by former emperors (*ib.* 517-520). The emperor wrote to the monks of Alexandria by Joannes the Decurio (*ib.* 481), exhorting them to abandon their errors and to submit to the decrees of Chalcedon. The troubles at Alexandria, however, were too great to be appeased by words. The arrival of Proterius, the bishop appointed in place of Dioscorus, led to violent riots (Evagr. 229, 293).

Palestine was likewise in a disturbed state. Some of the monks of the defeated side, who had attended the council, on their return, headed by Theodosius, a violent monk who had been their leader in the council, stirred up an insurrection of the whole body of desert monks (*ib.* 293). Juvenalis, bp. of Jerusalem, had, after his return, to fly for his life. Severianus, bp. of Scythopolis, was killed by an assassin sent in pursuit of Juvenalis; Jerusalem was seized by the infuriated monks; houses were burnt, murders were perpetrated, the prisons broken open and criminals released, and finally Theodosius was elected bishop. Marcian, hearing of the outrages, wrote to the archimandrites, monks, and inhabitants of Jerusalem, rebuked them sharply, ordered the punishment of the guilty, and placed a garrison in Jerusalem (Mansi, vii. 487-495).

Marcian also took measures to suppress the last remnants of paganism. By a law of Nov. 12, 451 (*Codex*, lib. i. tit. xi. 7), he forbade, under pain of death, the reopening of the closed temples, and the offering sacrifices, libations, or incense in them, or even adorning them with flowers, and at the end of his law of Aug. 1, 455, directed the strict enforcement of the laws against paganism.

In Apr. 454 he passed a law granting to nuns, deaconesses, and widows the power of making testamentary dispositions in favour of the church or clergy and repealing all previous contrary enactments. In Apr. 456 he passed another (*ib.* tit. iii. 25, and tit. iv. 13), by which proceedings against the oeconomus or other clerics of the churches in Constantinople were to be taken at the plaintiff's desire either before the archbishop or the prefect of the city, and no oaths tendered to clerics, who were forbidden to swear by the laws of the church and an ancient canon.

Dying Jan. 457 (Theod. Lect. 565), aged 65, after a reign of 6½ years, he was buried in the church of the Apostles at Constantinople (Cedrenus, 607, in *Patr. Gk.* cxxi. 659). [F.D.]

Marcion, a noted and permanently influential heretic of the 2nd cent.

Life.—Justin Martyr (*Apol.* cc. 26, 58) mentions Simon and Menander as having been instigated by demons to introduce heresy into the church, and goes on to speak of Marcion as still living, evidently regarding him as the most formidable heretic of the day.* He states that he was a native of Pontus who had made many disciples out of every nation, and refers for a more detailed refutation to a separate treatise of his own, one sentence of which has been preserved by Irenaeus (iv. 6). This work seems to have been extant in the time of Photius (*Cod.* 154). Irenaeus also states that Marcion came from Pontus. He adds that thence he came to Rome, where he became an adherent, and afterwards the successor, of Cerdo, a Syrian teacher who, though he made public confession and was reconciled, privately continued teaching heretical doctrine, was betrayed by some of his hearers, and again separated. Irenaeus places the coming of Cerdo to Rome in the episcopate of Hyginus, which lasted four years, ending, according to Lipsius, 139, 140, or 141. Irenaeus places the activity of Marcion at Rome under Anicetus ("invaluit sub Aniceto"), whose episcopate of 12 years began in 154. He says (iii. 3) that Marcion meeting Polycarp at Rome (probably 154 or 155) claimed recognition, on which Polycarp answered, "I recognize thee as the firstborn of Satan." Irenaeus contemplated (iii. 12) a separate treatise against Marcion. There is no direct evidence of his having carried out this design, but as its proposed method is stated to have been the confutation of Marcion by means of his own gospel, and as this is precisely the method followed by Tertullian, who is elsewhere largely indebted to Irenaeus, the work of Irenaeus may have been then written and known to Tertullian. It has been stated under HIPPOLYTUS how the contents of the lost *Syntagma* of Hippolytus are inferred. It appears to have named Sinope as Marcion's native city (Epiph. 42, Philast. 45), of which his father was bishop; and to have stated that he was obliged to leave home because he seduced a virgin and was excommunicated by his father (Epiph., Pseudo-Tert. 17). Epiphanius tells, apparently on the same authority, that Marcion, his frequent entreaties for absolution having failed, went to Rome, where he arrived after the death of Hyginus, that he begged restoration from the presbyters there, but they declared themselves unable to act contrary to the decision of his venerated father. The mention of presbyters as then the ruling power in the church of Rome, and their professed inability to reverse the decision of a provincial bishop, indicate a date earlier than that of Epiphanius; but Epiphanius further states that Marcion's quarrel with the presbyters was not only because they did not restore him to church communion, but also because they did not make him bishop. This has been generally understood to mean bp. of Rome, and possibly Epiphanius intended this, but he does not say so. His words are *ὡς οὐκ ἀπείληφε τὴν προεδρίαν τε, καὶ τὴν εἴσδυσιν τῆς ἐκκλησίας.* It is absurd that an excommunicated foreigner should dream of being made bishop of a church from which he was asking in vain for absolution. Epiphanius must have misunderstood some expression he found in his authority, or Marcion must have been already a bishop (possibly one of his father's suffragans), been deposed, and was seeking at Rome both restoration to communion and recognition of his episcopal dignity. Optatus alone directly countenances the latter view, speaking of Marcion (iv. 5, p. 74) as "ex episcopo factus apostata." But there is some indirect confirmation in the fact which we learn from Adamantius (i. 15; xvi. 264, Lommatz.) that Marcion was afterwards recognized as bishop by his own followers and was

* Though the form Μαρκιανοί (*Trypho* 35) suggests followers of Marcus, we think Marcion is intended.

the head of a succession of Marcionite bishops continuing down to the writer's own day. The Marcionites appear to have had no difference with the orthodox as to the forms of church organization. Tertullian's words are well-known, "faciunt et favos vespae, faciunt et ecclesias Marcionitae" (*adv. Marcion.* iv. 5). We may conclude that episcopacy was the settled constitution of the church before the time of the Marcionite schism, else Marcion would not have adopted it in his new sect, and it seems more likely that Marcion had been consecrated to the office before the schism than that he obtained consecration afterwards, or by his own authority took the office to himself and appointed others to it, a thing unexampled in the church, of which we should surely have heard if Marcion had done it. Many critics have believed that the statement as to the cause of Marcion's excommunication arose from the misunderstanding of a common figurative expression, and that it meant that Marcion by heresy had corrupted the pure virgin church. We are inclined to adopt this view, not on account of the confessed austerity of Marcion's subsequent life and doctrines, which are not inconsistent with his having fallen into sins of the flesh in his youth, but because the story goes on to tell of Scripture difficulties propounded by Marcion to the Roman presbyters and of his rejection of their solutions. If the question had been whether pardon were to be given for an offence against morality, neither party would have been likely to enter into theological controversy, whereas such discussion would naturally arise if the cause of excommunication had been heresy.

The story proceeds to say that he asked the Roman presbyters to explain the texts, "A good tree cannot bring forth evil fruit," and "No man putteth a piece of new cloth unto an old garment," texts from which he himself deduced that works in which evil is to be found could not proceed from the good God, and that the Christian dispensation could have nothing in common with the Jewish. Rejecting the explanation offered him by the presbyters, he broke off the interview with a threat to make a schism in their church. The beginning of Marcionism was so early that the church writers of the end of the 2nd cent., who are our best authorities, do not themselves seem able to tell with certainty the story of its commencement. But we know that the heresy of Marcion spread itself widely over many countries. Epiphanius names as infected by it in his time, Rome and Italy, Egypt, Palestine, Arabia, Syria, Cyprus, and even Persia. Its diffusion in the latter half of the 2nd cent. is proved by its antagonists in numerous countries: Dionysius in Corinth writing to Nicomedia, Philip in Crete, Theophilus in Antioch, besides Modestus (Eus. iv. 25), Justin, Irenaeus, Hippolytus, Clement of Alexandria, Rhodo, and Tertullian. Bardesanes wrote in Syriac against the heresy (*ib.* iv. 30), as did Ephrem Syrus later.

Now, Marcion would seem to have travelled much and probably used his journeys to propagate his doctrines. Ephrem Syrus speaks of him as wandering like Cain, but possibly only refers to his leaving his country for Rome (Hymn 56, Assemani, *Bibl. Or.* i. 119). Tertullian constantly describes him as "nauclerus"; Rhodo (*ap.* Eus. v. 13) calls him ναύτης, according to a reading which we believe to be right, though the word is wanting in some MSS. His travels seem more likely to have preceded than to have followed his settling in Rome under Anicetus. Unless, therefore, the story of the interview with the Roman presbyters is to be rejected altogether, we think it must be taken date and all. The interview must be placed immediately after the death of Hyginus and we must suppose Marcion then to have left Rome on his travels and only to have settled there permanently some years later, first as a member of Cerdo's school and afterwards as his successor.

The authorities as to the chronology of his life are very conflicting. The statement on which we can most rely is that he taught in Rome during the episcopate of Anicetus. We have no good warrant to extend his activity later, for we can give no credit to Tertullian when he names Eleutherus (*de Praesc.* 30) in connexion with the excommunication of Marcion. If Marcion did not survive Anicetus he may have been born *c.* 100. The *Chronicle* of Edessa names 138 for the beginning of Marcionism, and with this agrees the first year of Antoninus given by the Fihrist (Flügel's *Mani*, p. 85). This date is not improbable, if we suppose an Oriental preaching of the heresy to have preceded its establishment at Rome; A.D. 150 is a not unlikely date for Justin Martyr's *Apology*, and 12 years' growth is not too much for Marcionism to attain the formidable dimensions that work indicates. If Justin Martyr's work is dated earlier, the date of Marcionism will be similarly affected.

The time of Marcion's death is unknown, but he probably did not survive Anicetus. The only works he is known to have left are his recensions of the Gospel and Pauline Epistles; his *Antitheses*, in which by comparing different passages he tried to shew that the O.T. contradicted the New, and also itself; and Tertullian refers to a letter of his, then extant, as proving that he had originally belonged to the Catholic church (*adv. Marc.* i. 1; iv. 4; *de Carn. Christ.* ii.). We learn from Rhodo (Eus. v. 13) that after his death his followers broke up into sects, among the leaders of which he names Apelles, who only acknowledged one first principle; Potitus and Basilicus, who counted two; and Syneros, who counted three (*Ref.* vii. 31). Other Marcionite teachers mentioned are Prepo, an Assyrian, by Hippolytus, Lucanus by Tertullian; Pitho and Blastus (the latter probably erroneously) by Theodoret (*Haer. Fab.* i. 25). Epiphanius says (*de Mens. et Pond.* 17) that Theodotion, the translator of O.T., had been a Marcionite before his apostasy to Judaism, and Jerome (*de Vir. Illust.* 56) states that Ambrosius was one before his conversion by Origen. These sectaries were formidable to the church, both from their numbers and the strictness of their life. They were very severe ascetics, refusing flesh meat, wine, and the married life. Unlike some Gnostics who taught that it was no sin to escape persecution by disguising their faith, the Marcionites vied with the orthodox in producing martyrs. Eusebius tells (iv. 15) that the same letter of the church of Smyrna from which he drew his account of the martyrdom of Polycarp, told also of the martyrdom of a Marcionite presbyter, Metrodorus, who, like Polycarp, suffered at Smyrna by fire, and in the same persecution. When, later, the Montanists appealed in proof of their orthodoxy to the number of their martyrs, they were reminded that this could be equally pleaded for the Marcionites (Eus. v. 16). Other Marcionite martyrs mentioned by Eusebius are a woman who suffered under Valerian at Caesarea in Palestine (iii. 12), and a Marcionite bp. Asclepius, who in the Diocletian persecution was burned alive at Caesarea on the same pyre as the orthodox Apselamus (*Mart. Pal.* c. 10). The strictness of the Marcionite discipline is proved by the unfriendly testimony of Tertullian, who tries by their practice to convict of falsity the Marcionite theory, that a good God could not be the object of fear: "If so, why do you not take your fill of the enjoyments of this life? Why do you not frequent the circus, the arena, and the theatre? Why do you not boil over with every kind of lust? When the censer is handed you, and you are asked to offer a few grains of incense, why not deny your faith? 'God forbid!' you cry—'God forbid!'"

At the end of the Diocletian persecution the Marcionites had a short interval of freedom of worship. An inscription has been found over the doorway of a house in a Syrian village (Le Bas and Waddington, *Inscriptions*, No. 2558, vol. iii. p. 583) bearing a Syrian date corresponding to the year commencing Oct. 1, 318. This is more ancient than any dated inscription belonging to a Catholic church. With the complete triumph of Christianity, Marcionite freedom of worship was lost. Constantine (Eus. *de Vit. Const.* iii. 64) absolutely forbade their meeting for worship in public or private buildings. Their churches were to be given to the Catholics; any private houses used for schismatical worship to be confiscated. But the dying out of Marcionism was probably less the result of imperial legislation than of the absorption of the older heresy by the new wave of Oriental dualism which in Manicheism passed over the church. The Theodosian Code (xvi. tit. v. 65) contains a solitary mention of Marcionites. They were not extinct in the fifth cent., for Theodoret, writing to pope Leo (*Ep.* 113, p. 1190), boasts that he had himself converted more than a thousand Marcionites. In *Ep.* 145 the number of converts rises to ten thousand; in *Ep.* 81 they are said to be the inhabitants of eight villages. In his Church History (v.) Theodoret tells of an unsuccessful effort made by Chrysostom for their conversion. Probably this survival of Marcionism was but a local peculiarity. But as late as 692 the council in Trullo thought it worth while to make provision for the reconciliation of Marcionites, and there is other evidence of lingering remains so late as the 10th cent. (Flügel's *Mani*, pp. 160, 167).

Doctrine.—There is a striking difference of character between the teaching of Marcion and of others commonly classed with him as Gnostics. The systems of the latter often contain so many elements derived from heathenism, or drawn from the fancy of the speculators, that we feel as if we had scarcely any common ground with them; but with Marcion Christianity is plainly the starting-point, and the character of his system harmonizes with his being the son of a Christian bishop and brought up as a Christian. But he has been perplexed by the question of the origin of evil, and is disposed to accept the solution, much prevalent in the East then, that evil is inextricably mixed up with matter, which therefore could not be the creation of the Supreme. He tries to fit in this solution with his Christian creed and with the Scriptures; but naturally only by a mutilation of both can he force an agreement. Indeed, he sometimes has even to alter the text, *e.g.* "I am not come to destroy the law, but to fulfil," into "I am not come to fulfil the law, but to destroy." Still, the arbitrary criticism of Marcion has more points of contact with modern thought than the baseless assumptions of other Gnostics. A modern divine would turn away from the dreams of Valentinianism in silent contempt; but he could not refuse to discuss the question raised by Marcion, whether there is such opposition between different parts of what he regards as the word of God, that all cannot come from the same author.

The fundamental point of difference between Marcion and the church was concerning the unity of the first principle. Marcion plainly asserted the existence of two Gods, a good one and a just one. What he meant to convey by these words Beausobre well illustrates by a passage of Bardesanes, preserved by Eusebius (*Praep. Evan.* vi. 10). He says that animals are of three kinds: some, like serpents and scorpions, will hurt those who have given them no provocation; some, like sheep, will not attempt to return evil for evil; others will hurt those only that hurt them. These three may be called evil, good, and just respectively. Marcion then thought the infliction of punishment inconsistent with perfect goodness, and would only concede the title of just to the God of O.T., who had distinctly threatened to punish the wicked. The God, he said, whose law was "An eye for an eye, and a tooth for a tooth," was a just God, but not the same as that good God whose command was, "If any smite thee on the one cheek, turn to him the other also." The command, "Thou shalt love him that loveth thee and hate thine enemy" was that of a just God; "Love thine enemy" was the law of the good God. Further, the God of O.T. had said of Himself, "I create evil"; but since from a good tree evil fruit cannot spring, it follows that He who created evil cannot Himself be good. He could not be the Supreme, for He was of limited intelligence, not being able to find Adam when he hid himself, and obliged to ask, "Where are thou?", and also obliged to come down to see before He could know whether Sodom had done according to its cry. Marcion's theory was that the visible creation was the work of the just God; the good God, whose abode he places in the third or highest heaven and whom apparently he acknowledged as the creator of a high immaterial universe, neither concerned Himself with mankind nor was known by them, until, taking compassion on the misery to which they had been brought by disobedience to their Creator who was casting them into his hell, He interfered for their redemption. The Marcionite denial of the unity of the first principle was variously modified. Some counted three first principles instead of two: a good Being who rules over the Christians, a just one over the Jews, a wicked one over the heathen. Others, since the world was supposed to be made out of previously existent matter, held that matter was a fourth self-originated principle. Marcion himself only counted two ἀρχαί, but used the word in the sense of ruling powers, for it does not appear that he regarded matter as the creation either of his good or his just God, and therefore it should rightly have been reckoned as an independent principle. Tertullian, indeed, argues that Marcion, to be consistent, should count as many as nine gods. In all these systems the good Being was acknowledged to be superior to the others, so it was not a violent change to assume that from this principle the others were derived; and Apelles and his school drew near the orthodox and taught that there was but one self-originated principle. The ascription of creation and redemption to different beings enabled the church writers to convict the Marcionite deity of unwarrantable interference with what did not belong to him. This interference was the more startling from its suddenness, for Marcion's rejection of O.T. obliged him to deny that there had been any intimation of the coming redemption, or any sign that it had been contemplated beforehand. His God then suddenly wakes up to trouble himself about this earth; stoops down from his third heaven into a world about which, for thousands of years, he had given himself no concern; there kidnaps the sons and servants of another, and teaches them to hate and despise their father and their king, on whose gifts they must still depend for sustenance, and who furnishes the very ground on which this new God's worshippers are to kneel, the heaven to which they are to stretch out their hands, the water in which they are baptized, the very eucharistic food for which a God must be thanked to whom it had never belonged.

Marcion's rejection of O.T. prophecy did not involve a denial that the prophets had foretold the coming of a Christ; but the Christ of the prophets could not be our Christ. The former was to come for the deliverance of the Jewish people; the latter for that of the whole human race. The former was to be a warrior—Christ was a man of peace; Christ suffered on the cross—the law pronounced accursed him that hangeth on a tree; the Christ of the prophets is to rule the nations with a rod of iron, kings are to set themselves against Him, He is to have the heathen for His inheritance and to set up a kingdom that shall not be destroyed. Jesus did none of these things, therefore the Christ of the prophets is still to come. Tertullian successfully shews that if Jesus was not the Christ of the prophets, He must have wished to personate Him, coming as He did at the time and in the place which the prophets had foretold, and fulfilling so many of the indications they had given. What Marcion supposed his own Christ to be has been disputed. Some have supposed that he did not distinguish him from his good God, for Marcion's Gospel was said to have commenced: "In the 15th year of Tiberius God came down to Capernaum, a city of Galilee, and taught on the sabbath days" (Tert. *adv. Marc.* iv. 7); but we believe the true reading here is "eum," not "deum," and that Marcion held his Christ to be a saving Spirit (i. 19), but did not confound him with the Supreme. Marcion's Gospel told nothing of the birth of Christ, and Marcion's "came down" has a very different meaning from what it has in the original passage (Luke vi. 31), in Marcion's use meaning "came down from heaven." In fact, the story of Christ's birth would represent Him as a born subject of the Demiurge, deriving from his bounty the very body in which He came; so it was preferred to tell the improbable tale of a divine teacher unheard-of before making a sudden appearance in the synagogue. That Christ had a real earthly body Marcion of course could not admit. See Docetism for an account of Marcion's doctrine on this subject, and that of his disciple Apelles, who on this point as on others approached more nearly to the orthodox. It was an obvious argument against the Docetic theory that if our Lord's body were not real we could have no faith that His miracles were real, nor in the reality of His sufferings and death, which Marcion was willing to regard as an exhibition of redeeming love; nor in the reality of His resurrection. Marcion, like the orthodox, taught that the death of our Lord was followed by a "descent into hell"; but Irenaeus tells us that he taught that there Cain, the people of Sodom, and others condemned in O.T. as wicked, received Christ's preaching and were taken up by Him into His kingdom; but that Abel, Enoch, Noah, Abraham, the prophets, and other righteous men imagined that the Demiurge was tempting them as on other occasions, and so, being afraid to join themselves to Christ and accept deliverance from Him, were left in the underworld. Christ's salvation, according to Marcion, affected the soul only, and did not affect the body, of which he held there would be no resurrection. Indeed, none of those who regarded matter as essentially evil could believe that evil would be made eternal by a material resurrection. Tertullian points out that sin originates with the soul, not the body, and pronounces it unfair that the sinful soul should be redeemed and the less guilty body punished. On unredeemed souls no punishment would be inflicted by Marcion's good God—he would merely abandon them to the vengeance of the Demiurge; but Tertullian shewed that if direct punishment were inconsistent with perfect goodness, such abandonment must be equally so.

The Marcionite system as described by Esnig has more of a mythic than of a rationalistic character, and if we accept this as the original form of Marcionism, Marcion owed more to the older Gnostics than we should otherwise have supposed. Marcion is said by Esnig to have taught that there were three heavens: in the highest dwelt the good God, in the second the God of the Law, in the lowest His angels; beneath lay Hyle, or matter, having an independent existence of its own. By the help of Hyle, which played the part of a female principle, the God of the Law made this world, after which he retired to his heaven; and each ruled in his own domain, he in heaven and Hyle on earth. Afterwards the God of the Law, beholding how goodly this earth was, desired to make man to inhabit it, and for this purpose requested the co-operation of Hyle. She supplied the dust from which man's body was made, and he breathed in his spirit, and made him live. He named him Adam, gave him a wife, and placed him in Paradise. There they lived, honouring and obeying their Maker, in joy and childlike innocence, for as yet they had no children. Then the Lord of Creation, seeing that Adam was worthy to serve Him, devised how he might withdraw him from Hyle and unite him to himself. He took him aside, and said, "Adam, I am God, and beside me there is no other; if thou worshippest any other God thou shalt die the death." When Adam heard of death he was afraid, and gradually withdrew himself from Hyle. When Hyle came after her wont to serve him, Adam did not listen to her, but withdrew himself. Then Hyle, recognizing that the Lord of Creation had supplanted her, said, "Seeing that he hates me and keeps not his compact with me, I will make a number of gods and fill the world with them, so that they who seek the true God shall not be able to find him." Thus she filled the world with idolatry; men ceased to adore the Lord of Creation, for Hyle had drawn them all to herself. Then was the Creator full of wrath; and as men died he cast them into hell, both Adam, on account of the tree, and the rest. There they remained 29 centuries. At length the good God looked down from the highest heaven and beheld what misery men suffered from Hyle and the Creator. He took compassion on those plagued and tortured in the fire of hell, and he sent his son to deliver them. "Go down," he said, "take on thee the form of a servant, and make thyself like the sons of the law. Heal their wounds, give sight to their blind, bring their dead to life, perform without reward the greatest miracles of healing; then will the God of the Law be jealous, and will instigate his servants to crucify thee. Then go down to hell, which will open her mouth to receive thee, supposing thee to be one of the dead. Then liberate the captives whom thou shalt find there, and bring them up to me." This was done. Hell was deceived and admitted Jesus, who emptied it of all the spirits therein and carried them up to his Father. When the God of the Law saw this he was enraged, rent his clothes, tore the curtain of his palace, darkened his sun, and veiled his world in darkness. After that, Jesus came down a second time, but now in the glory of his divinity, to plead with the God of the Law. When the Creator saw Jesus thus appear, he was obliged to own that he had been wrong in thinking that there was no other god but himself. Then Jesus said, "I have a controversy with thee, but I will take no other judge between us than thine own law. Is it not written in thy law that whoso killeth another shall himself be killed; that whoso sheddeth innocent blood shall have his own blood shed? Let me, then, kill thee and shed thy blood, for I was innocent and thou hast shed my blood." Then he recounted what benefits he had bestowed on the Creator's children, and in return had been crucified; and the Creator could make no defence, seeing himself condemned by his own law, and he said: "I was ignorant; I thought thee but a man, and did not know thee to be a God; take the revenge which is thy due." Then Jesus left him and betook himself to Paul, and revealed to him the way in which we should go. All who believe in Christ will give themselves to this good and righteous man. Men must withdraw themselves from the dominion of Hyle; but all do not know how this is to be done.

Though this mythical story differs much in complexion from other ancient accounts of Marcionite doctrine, we cannot absolutely reject it; for there is nothing in it inconsistent with Marcion's known doctrines or such as a Gnostic of his age might have taught. It is, indeed, such a system as he might have learned from the Syriac Gnostic Cerdo. But Marcion must have given the mythic element little prominence, or it would not have so disappeared from the other accounts.

Discipline and Worship.—In rites Marcion followed the church model. Thus (Tert. *adv. Marc.* i. 14) he had baptism with water, anointing with oil, a mixture of milk and honey was given to the newly baptized, and sacramental bread represented the Saviour's Body. Wine was absent from his Eucharist, for his principles entirely forbade wine or flesh meat. [ENCRATITES.] Fish, however, he permitted. He commanded his disciples to fast on Saturday, to mark his hostility to the God of the Jews, who had made that His day of rest. Marriage he condemned. A married man was received as a catechumen, but not admitted to baptism until he had agreed to separate from his wife (*ib.* i. 29 and iv. 10). This probably explains the statement of Epiphanius that the Marcionites celebrated the mysteries in the presence of unbaptized persons. The sect could not have flourished if it discouraged married persons from joining it; and if it admitted them only as catechumens, that class would naturally be granted larger privileges than in the Catholic church.* Nor need we disbelieve the statement of Epiphanius that a second or a third baptism was permitted. If a member married, or one who had put away his wife took her back, it is not incredible that on repentance a second baptism was necessary before restoration to full privileges of membership. Again, since the baptism of a married person was only permitted *in articulo mortis*, it would sometimes happen that catechumens were surprised by death before baptism, and it is not incredible that in such cases the device of a vicarious baptism may have been resorted to, as Chrysostom tells in speaking on the passage in Corinthians about being baptized for the dead. Epiphanius states that Marcion per-

* They justified their practice by an appeal to Gal. vi. 6 (see Hieron. *in loc.*).

mitted females to baptize. The Marcionite baptism was not recognized by the church. Theodoret tells that he baptized those whom he converted. (See also Basil. *Can.* 47, *Ep.* 199.) He tells also that he had met an aged Marcionite who, in his hostility to the Creator, refused to use his works, a principle which could not possibly be carried out consistently.

Canon of Scripture.—Marcion's rejection of the O.T. involved the rejection of great part of the New, which bears witness to the Old. He only retained the Gospel of St. Luke (and that in a mutilated form), and ten Epp. of St. Paul, omitting the pastoral epistles. In defence of his rejection of other apostolic writings, he appealed to the statements of St. Paul in Galatians, that some of the older apostles had not walked uprightly after the truth of the gospel, and that certain false apostles had perverted the gospel of Christ. Marcion's Gospel, though substantially identical, as far as it went, with our St. Luke's, did not bear that Evangelist's name. That it was, however, an abridgment of St. Luke was asserted by all the Fathers from Irenaeus and not doubted until modern times. Then it was noticed that in some cases where Marcion is accused by Epiphanius or Tertullian of having corrupted the text, his readings are witnessed by other ancient authorities. We have the means of restoring Marcion's Gospel with sufficient exactness. Tertullian goes through it in minute detail; Epiphanius also has made a series of minute notes on Marcion's corruptions of the text; some notices are also found in the Dialogue of Adamantius. Combining these independent sources, we obtain results on which we can place great confidence. It clearly appears that Marcion's Gospel and our St. Luke's in the main followed the same order and were even in verbal agreement, except that the latter contains much not found in the former. So that the affinity of the two forms is certain, and the only choice is whether we shall regard the one as a mutilation or the other as an interpolated form. The theory that the shorter form was the original was for some time defended by Ritschl and Baur, who, however, were obliged to yield to the arguments of Hilgenfeld and Volkmar. In Volkmar's *Das Evangelium Marcions* the differences between the two forms of the Gospel are examined in minute detail, especially with reference to their doctrinal bearings; and it is found that the only theory which will explain the facts is that Marcion's is a mutilated form. His form exhibits a hostility to Judaism, the Mosaic law, and the work of the Creator, of which there is not a trace in genuine Pauline Christianity. Dr. Sanday (*Gospel in the Second Cent.*, p. 204) has made a careful linguistic comparison of the portion of our St. Luke which Marcion acknowledges with that which he omits, the result being a decisive proof of common authorship; the part omitted by Marcion abounding in all the peculiarities which distinguish the style of the third evangelist. The theory, therefore, that Marcion's form is the original may be said to be now completely exploded. Dr. Sanday notes further that the text of St. Luke used by Marcion has some readings recognized by some other ancient authorities, but which no critic now accepts. The inference is that when Marcion used St. Luke's Gospel it had been so long in existence, and had been copied so often, that different types of text had had time to establish themselves. It has been argued that Marcion could not have known our Fourth Gospel, else he would have preferred this, as being more strongly anti-Jewish. But the Fourth Gospel is not anti-Jewish in Marcion's sense, and he would have had even more trouble in mutilating it to make it serve his purpose. At the very outset Christ's relation to the Jewish people is described in the words, "He came unto His own"; the Jewish temple is called His Father's house; salvation is said to be of the Jews; contrary to Marcion's teaching, Christ is perpetually identified with the Christ predicted in O.T.; the Scriptures are "they which testify of Me," "Moses wrote of Me," "Had ye believed Moses ye would have believed Me." Great importance is attached to the testimony of John the Baptist, who, according to Marcion, like the older prophets, did not know the true Christ; and the miracle of turning water into wine would alone have condemned the Gospel in Marcion's eyes. In short, the Fourth Gospel is strongly anti-Marcionite. See esp. Zahn's *Gesch. des N.T. Kanons*, i. 587-718 and ii. 409-529.

Marcion's *Apostolicon* consisted of ten epistles, in the order: Gal., I. and II. Cor., Rom. (wanting the last two chapters), I. and II. Thess., Eph. (called by Marcion the Ep. to the Laodiceans), Col., Philippians, Philemon. Concerning the order of the last two, Tertullian and Epiphanius differ. The Acts and the pastoral epistles are rejected. The *Apostolicon* was known to Jerome, who notes two or three of its readings. The most careful attempt to restore it is by Hilgenfeld (*Zeitschrift f. histor. Theol.* 1855). It becomes apparent that Marcion struck out from the Epistles which he acknowledged some passages which conflicted with his theory and also made some few additions. The arbitrary character of such criticism would destroy all claim to originality for Marcion's text of the Gospel, even if that claim had not otherwise been sufficiently refuted. [G.S.]

Marcus (6), bp. of Rome, probably from Jan. 18 to Oct. 7, 336, having been ordained 18 days after the death of his predecessor Sylvester. The above dates, from the Liberian Catalogue and *Depositio Episcoporum*, are confirmed by St. Jerome (*Chron.*), who gives him a reign of 8 months, and are consistent with historical events. He is said (*Catal. Felic.* and Anastasius) to have ordained that the bishops of Ostia should consecrate the bishops of Rome and bear the pallium, and to have been buried in the cemetery of Balbina on the Via Ardeatina, "in basilica quam coemiterium constituit." Baronius notices this as the earliest mention of the pallium. The cemetery of Balbina, called also that of St. Mark from this pope's interment there and variously spoken of in old itineraries as on the Ardeatine and Appian Ways, has been identified as lying between the two by De Rossi, who supposes the "basilica" to have been a chapel, or *cella memoriae*, built by Marcus at the entrance of an existing cemetery and intended as a place of burial. Interment near the surface of the ground seems about this time to have begun to supersede the use of subterranean catacombs. [J.B—Y.]

Marcus (14), surnamed *Eremita*, mentioned by Nicephorus Callistus as ὁ πολυθρύλλητος ἀσκητής, said to have lived in the reign of Theodosius II. and to have been a disciple of St. Chrysostom (Niceph. *H. E.* xiv. 30). Nicephorus speaks later of the works of a Μάρκος ἀσκητής, apparently the same man. Of these he had seen a collection of 8 and another of 32, dealing with the ascetic life (*H. E.* xiv. 54). Photius (*Bibl. Cod.* 200) gives an account of 8 works of Marcus the monk, all of which are extant with one doubtful exception. His works, pub. in *Patr. Gk.* lxv. 905, preceded by two disquisitions on the author by Gallandius and Fessler, are:

(1) περὶ νόμου πνευματικοῦ, a collection of short aphorisms, inculcating especially the duties of humility and constant prayer.

(2) περὶ τῶν οἰομένων ἐξ ἔργων δικαιοῦσθαι shews that as slaves of God we have no wages to expect. All is of grace, which is given τελεία in baptism, and afterwards in measure proportioned to our obedience.

(3) περὶ μετανοίας shews repentance to be necessary for all.

(4) ἀπόκρισις πρὸς τοὺς ἀποροῦντας περὶ τοῦ θείου βαπτίσματος, an important treatise on the doctrine of baptism, states distinctly that by the grace of baptism original sin is put away and the baptized are in exactly the condition Adam was before the fall.

(5) and (9) πρὸς Νικόλαον and περὶ νηστείας are ascetic treatises.

(7) ἀντιβολὴ πρὸς σχολαστικόν defends monastic life against a man of the world.

(8) συμβουλία νοὸς πρὸς τὴν ἑαυτοῦ ψυχήν shews that the root of evil is in ourselves.

(10) εἰς τὸν Μελχισεδέκ, against heretics who argued from the language of *Hebrews* that Melchizedek was the Son of God.

(6) κεφάλαια νηπτικά, generally included among the works of Marcus, but not mentioned by Photius, From external and internal evidence it would seem to be wrongly ascribed to Marcus. [M.F.A.]

Marcus (17), a Gnostic of the school of Valentinus, who taught in the middle of the 2nd cent. His doctrines are almost exclusively known to us through a long section (i. 13-21, pp. 55-98) in which Irenaeus gives an account of his teaching and his school. Both Hippolytus (*Ref.* vi. 39-55, pp. 200-220) and Epiphanius (*Haer.* 34) have copied their account from Irenaeus; and there seems no good reason to think that either had any direct knowledge of the writings of Marcus. But Clement of Alexandria clearly knew and used them. Although Jerome describes Marcus as a Basilidian (*Ep.* 75 *ad Theod.* i. 449), what Irenaeus reports clearly shews him as a follower of Valentinus. Thus his system tells of 30 Aeons, divided into an Ogdoad, a Decad, and a Dodecad; of the fall and recovery of Sophia; of the future union of the spirits of the chosen seed with angels as their heavenly bridegrooms. What Marcus added to the teaching of his predecessors is perhaps the most worthless of all that passed under the name of "knowledge" in the 2nd cent. It merely contains magical formulae, which the disciples were to get by heart and put trust in, and puerile speculations, such as were in vogue among the later Pythagoreans, about mysteries in numbers and names. Marcus found in Scripture and in Nature repeated examples of the occurrence of his mystical numbers, four, six, eight, ten, twelve, thirty. If so great mysteries were contained in names, it naturally followed that to know the right name of each celestial power was a matter of vital importance; and such knowledge the heretical teachers promised to bestow. They had formulae and sacraments of redemption. They taught that the baptism of the visible Jesus was but for the forgiveness of sins, but that the redemption of Him Who in that baptism descended was for perfection; the one was merely psychical, the other spiritual. Of the latter are interpreted the words in which our Lord spoke of another baptism (Luke xii. 50; Matt. xx. 22). Some conferred this redemption by baptism with special invocations; others added or substituted various anointings; others held that these applications could not procure spiritual redemption—only by knowledge could such redemption be effected. This knowledge included the possession of formulae, by the use of which the initiated would after death become incomprehensible and invisible to principalities and powers, and leaving their bodies in this lower creation and their souls with the Demiurge, ascend in their spirits to the Pleroma. Probably the Egyptian religion contributed this element to Gnosticism. Some of these Marcosian formulae were in Hebrew, of which Irenaeus has preserved specimens much corrupted by copyists. Marcus, as Irenaeus tells us, used other juggling tricks by which he gained the reputation of magical skill. A knowledge of astrology was among his accomplishments, and apparently some chemical knowledge, with which he astonished and impressed his disciples. The eucharistic cup of mingled wine and water was seen under his invocation to change to a purple red; and his disciples were told that this was because the great CHARIS had dropped some of her blood into the cup. Sometimes he would hand the cup to women, and bid them in his presence pronounce the eucharistic words; and then he would pour from their consecrated cup into a much larger one held by himself, and the liquor, miraculously increased at his prayer, would be seen to rise up and fill the larger vessel. He taught his female disciples to prophesy. Casting lots at their meetings, he would command her on whom the lot fell boldly to utter the words which were suggested to her mind, and such words were accepted by the hearers as prophetic utterances. He abused the influence he thus acquired over silly women to draw much money from them, and, it is said, even to gain from them more shameful compliances. He is accused of having used philtres and love charms, and at least one, if not more, of his female disciples on returning to the church confessed that body as well as mind had been defiled by him. Some of his followers certainly claimed to have been elevated, by their knowledge and the redemption they had experienced, above ordinary rules of morality. If we are sometimes tempted to be indulgent to Gnostic theories as the harmless dreams of well-meaning thinkers perplexed by problems too hard for them, the history of Marcus shews how these speculations became a degrading superstition. Everything elevating and ennobling in Christ's teaching disappeared; the teachers boasted of a sham science, having no tendency to make those who believed it wiser or better; the disciples trusted in magical rites and charms not more respectable than those of the heathen; and their morality became of quite heathen laxity.

Marcus appears to have been an elder contemporary of Irenaeus, who speaks of him as though still living and teaching. Irenaeus more than once tells of the resistance to Marcus of a venerated elder, from whom he quotes some iambic verses, written in reprobation of that heretic. Though we learn from Irenaeus that the Rhone district was much infested by followers of Marcus, it does not appear that Marcus was there himself, and the impression left is that Irenaeus knew the followers of Marcus by personal intercourse, Marcus only by his writings. We are told also of Marcus having seduced the wife of one of the deacons in Asia (*διάκονόν τινα τῶν ἐν τῇ Ἀσίᾳ*), and the most natural conclusion is that Asia Minor was the scene where Marcus made himself notorious as a teacher, probably before Irenaeus had left that district; that it was a leading bishop there who resisted Marcus; and that the heretic's doctrines passed into Gaul by means of the extensive intercourse well known to have then prevailed between the two countries. The use of Hebrew or Syriac names in the Marcosian school may lead us to ascribe to Marcus an Oriental origin. [G.S.]

Mari. [NESTORIAN CHURCH.]

Marinus (4), a military martyr in the reign of Gallienus, at Caesarea in Palestine, under a judge named Achaeus, A.D. 262. He was distinguished by his birth, riches, and services. When Marinus was about to be made a centurion, another aspirant declared him to be a Christian and unable therefore to sacrifice to the emperors. The judge granted him three hours to choose between death and compliance. As Marinus came out of the praetorium, Theotecnus the bishop led him into the church. Placing him by the altar, he raised his cloak, and pointing to the sword by his side, and presenting him with the book of the gospels, told him to choose which he wished. Without hesitation he extended his hand and took the book. "Hold fast then—hold fast to God," said Theotecnus, "and strengthened by Him mayest thou obtain what thou hast chosen: go in peace." He was immediately executed, and buried by a Christian senator named Astyrius. The narrative of Eusebius was probably that of an eye-witness, perhaps the bishop. It is a moot question whether this martyrdom resulted from persecution or from military law. Dr. F. Görres, in an art. in *Jahrb. Prot. Theologie*, 1877, p. 620, on "Die Toleranzedicte des Kaisers Gallienus," suggests that Marinus could not legally have suffered under Gallienus, who had already issued his edict of toleration, but that it must have taken place by command of Macrianus, who had revolted from Gallienus and taken possession of Egypt, Palestine, and the East, and was, as we learn from Eus. vii. 10, 13, 23 (cf. Trebell. Pollio, ed. H. Peter. *Scriptt. Hist. Aug.* t. ii. Gallieni duo. cc. i.–iii. xxx. Tyranni, cc. xiii. xiv.) the moral author of the Valerian persecution. When possessed of imperial authority, Macrianus vented his hate on the Christians whom Gallienus favoured. Eus. vii. 15, 16; Neander, *H. E.* ed. Bohn, i. 194; Ceill. ii. 394; Tillem. iv. 21; Pagi, *Crit.* i. 276, nr. x. xi.). [G.T.S.]

Maris (2) (*Mares, Magnus, Marius*), bp. of Chalcedon, a prominent Arian (Le Quien, *Or. Chr.* i. 599), said to have been a disciple of the martyr Lucian of Antioch (Philost. *H. E.* ii. 14; Tillem. v. 770, vi. 253, 646). He wrote in support of Arian opinions before the council of Nicaea (Athan. *de Syn.* § 17; Tillem. vi. 646). At the council he joined with Eusebius of Nicomedia, Theognis, Ursacius, and Valens against Athanasius (Socr. i. 8, 27), and was one of five who were unwilling to subscribe on account of the term *ὁμοούσιον* (i. 8). Maris at length yielded (Soz. i. 21; Nicet. Chon. *Thesaur.* v. 8; cf. Vales. note 71, *ad* Soz. i. 21). He was one of 17 who held out against the council and supported Arius, according to Gelasius (Mansi, ii. 818; cf. 878 B). His name occurs among the subscribers (*ib.* ii. 696). Philostorgius states (in Nicet. Chon. *Thes.* v. 8) that Maris, Eusebius, Theognis, expressed to the emperor their repentance for having signed, stating that they had complied only through fear of him, and that the emperor indignantly banished them to Gaul. Maris assisted at the council of Tyre in 335, and was one of the commission to Mareotis (Athan. *Ap. c. Ar.* §§ 13, 72; Theod. *H. E.* i. 28; Mansi, ii. 1125 D, 1130 B, 1143 D; Tillem. viii. 35, 42, 49). In 335 he was one of the deputies sent to Constantinople against Athanasius (Socr. i. 35; Tillem. vi. 290). He frequently wrote to pope Julius against Athanasius (Hilar. *Frag.* ii. § 2, in *Patr. Lat.* x. 632, here written Marius; Theod. *H. E.* ii. 6 *al.* 8; Tillem. vii. 270). In 341 he attended the council of Antioch and is named in the Ep. of Julius (*Ap. c. Ar.* § 20; Tillem. vi. 312). In 342 he was of the party who secured the appointment of Macedonius to the see of Constantinople (Socr. ii. 12; Tillem. vi. 323, 493). The same year he was one of four bishops deputed by Constantius to Constans (Socr. ii. 18; Athan. *de Syn.* § 25; Tillem. vi. 326; Hefele, *Conc.* ii. 80, 83). Sozomen (iii. 10) omits Maris here. That he was present at the council of Sardica (343-344) appears certain, although his name is not among the signatures (Tillem. viii. 95, 686, 688; Hefele, ii. 92, n. 3). At the council of Philippopolis his name is again absent, and among the subscriptions occur Thelaphius as bp. of Chalcedon (Mansi, ii. 138), probably by a clerical error. In 359 he defended the doctrine of the Anomoeans against Basil (Philostorg. iv. 12; Tillem. vi. 483) and was at the council of Ariminum (Socr. ii. 41; Soz. iv. 24), and in 360 at the council of Constantinople (*ib.*; Hefele, ii. 271; Tillem. vi. 487). In 362 Maris, then advanced in age and blind, at an interview with Julian, severely rebuked his apostasy, whereupon the emperor tauntingly observed, "Thy Galilean God will not heal thy sight." "I thank God," retorted Maris, "for depriving me of the power of beholding thy face" (Socr. iii. 12; Soz. v. 4; Tillem. vii. 332). He was living in the reign of Jovian (Philostorg. viii. 4; Tillem. viii. 764) and must be the Magnus of Chalcedon at the council of Antioch in 363 (Socr. iii. 25; Mansi, iii. 371, 372, 511). In an anonymous Life of Isaacius abbat of Constantinople (iii. 12 in Boll. *Acta SS.* Mai. vii. 254 B), Maris is said to have been present at the council of Constantinople in 381, a statement which may safely be rejected. [C.H.]

Marius (1) Mercator, a writer, of whom, until the last quarter of the 17th cent., nothing was known except indirectly through the writings of St. Augustine, who in his work *de Octo Quaestionibus Dulcitii*, mentions him as his son, *i.e.* his friend or pupil, and who addressed to him a letter, containing a long passage identical with one in that work (*Ep.* 193, *de Oct. Quaest. Dulc.* qu. 3).

Probably a native of Africa, in Rome in 417 or 418, and thought by Baluze to have outlived the council of Chalcedon, A.D. 451. When Julian of Eclana was lecturing at Rome in 418 in favour of Pelagianism, Mercator replied to him, and sent his reply to St. Augustine, to whom not long afterwards Mercator forwarded a second treatise. Whether these two works exist or not is doubtful, but a treatise called *Hypognosticon*, or *Hypermesticon*, in six books, included in vol. x. of St. Augustine's works (ed. Migne, p. 1611), has been thought to be the one in question. Five of the books treat of Pelagianism, and the sixth of Predestination. The letter of Augustine, forwarded by Albinus, A.D. 418, expresses admiration of the learning of Marius and discusses points submitted for consideration.

The works of Marius Mercator, being chiefly translations, some of them from his own writings in Greek, appear in Migne in the following order, together with much matter more or less relevant to the principal subject. Part I. 1. *Commonitorium super nomine Coelestii.*—A memorial against the doctrines of Coelestius and Julian, disciples of Pelagius, written in Greek, and presented by Mercator to the emperor Theodosius II. and to the church of Constantinople, A.D. 429, translated by himself into Latin. It contains a history of Pelagianism and an account of its doctrines, and an appeal to Julian to abandon them. 2. A treatise, to which the *Commonitorium* is a preface, against Julian, entitled *Subnotationes in verba Juliani*, written after the death of Augustine, A.D. 430. 3. Translations of various works relating to Pelagianism, including the creed of Theodore of Mopsuestia, with a preface and a refutation of the creed by Mercator. Part II. Concerning the Nestorian heresy, including extracts from Theodore of Mopsuestia, with preface and refutations by Mercator. Extracts from Theodoret bp. of Cyrus, against Cyril, and from his letters, with remarks by Mercator.

Marius Mercator appears to have been a layman, but an able theologian. His learning, zeal, and ability entitle him to a respectable place among ecclesiastical writers. Migne, *Patr. Lat.* xlviii.; Ceillier, viii. 36. [H.W.P.]

Marius (2), St., 3rd bp. of Lausanne, whither he is said to have transferred the see from Avenches, between Chilmegisilus and Magnerius (Gams, p. 283), or Arricus (*Gall. Christ.* xv. 329). He is better known as Marius Aventicensis, the chronicler. He was born at Autun, of parents of high rank. At about the age of 43 he was made bishop (A.D. 575). He constructed a church at Paterniacum (Payerne) on his own property, and made various donations to it. In 585 he was present at the 2nd council of Mâcon (Mansi, ix. 958), and after an episcopate lasting 20 years and 8 months died on the last day of 596, in his 64th year. At the council of Mâcon, in 585, he signed himself "episcopus ecclesiae Aventicae." The authors of the *Gallia Christiana* publish a metrical epitaph of unknown date, which represents him as fabricating with his own hands the sacred vessels for his church and ploughing his own glebe. His *Chronicon* is a work of some historical importance. Though extremely brief it furnishes information with reference to Burgundy and Switzerland during the period embraced by it which is found nowhere else, and serves to correct the bias of Gregory of Tours against the Arians of Burgundy. It takes up the chronicle of Prosper of Aquitaine in 455 and carries it to 581, continuing his method of marking the years by consulates, and commencing the indictions with 523. An anonymous author has carried it to 623. For an account and criticism of it see *Hist. Litt.* iii. 401; Cave, i. 538; Ceillier, xi. 399, 400; Wattenbach, *Deutschlands Geschichtsquellen*, i. 47; Richter, *Annalen*, p. 37 and refs. there given. It is in Bouquet, *Recueil*, ii. 12-19, and Migne, *Patr. Lat.* lxxii. 791-802. [S.A.B.]

Martinianus (1), legendary martyr with PROCESSUS at Rome. According to the Acts of LINUS, these were the two soldiers into whose charge Peter had been given. They were converted by him in prison, and for their baptism, Peter, by making the sign of the cross, caused a fountain, still shewn in the Mamertine prison, miraculously to spring from the rock. After their baptism the two soldiers give Peter as much liberty as he desires, and when news comes that the prefect Agrippa is about to put him to death, earnestly urge him to withdraw. Peter at first complies, but returns to custody in consequence of the well-known vision *Domine quo vadis.* According to a notice in Praedestinatus (*Haer.* 86), which has the air of being more historical than most of the stories of that author, their cult was already in vogue in the reign of the pretender Maximus, *i.e.* before the end of the 4th cent. According to this story, Montanists got temporary possession of their relics and claimed them as belonging to their sect. Lipsius conjectures that their cult began in the episcopate of Damasus, when great exertions were made to revive the memory of the saints of the Roman church. To this period may be referred the Acts of Processus and Martinianus (Bolland. *AA. SS.* July i. 303). They are clearly later than Constantine, containing mention of offices which did not exist till his time. They are evidently based on the

Acts of Linus, but the story receives considerable ornament. Their commemoration is fixed for July 2 in the Sacramentary of Gregory the Great (vol. ii. 114), who also mentions a church dedicated to them, and tells of a miraculous appearance of them (*Hom. in Evang.* ii. 32, vol. i. 1586). On the whole subject, see Lipsius (*Petrus-Sage*, pp. 137 seq.). [G.S.]

Martinus (1), St., bp. of Tours in the latter portion of 4th cent. Of all the prelates of that age he made the deepest impression upon the imagination of France and of a considerable part of Western Christendom.

Authorities.—The authorities practically resolve themselves into one, Sulpicius Severus, who mentions Martin in his *Sacra Historia* (lib. ii. cc. xlv. seq.), in connexion with the important case of Priscillian. [PRISCILLIANUS.] Of three dialogues composed by Sulpicius, two treat *de Virtutibus B. Martini*. An epistle, addressed to a presbyter named Eusebius (some say addressed to Desiderius), is composed *contra Aemulos Virtutum B. Martini*; and two more, written respectively to a deacon named Aurelius and to the author's mother-in-law Bassula, narrate the circumstances of Martin's death. Finally, we have a biography, *de Beati Martini Vitâ Liber*. In Horn's ed. of Sulpicius (Amsterdam, 1665), an 8vo of some 570 pages, including notes, at least a sixth part is occupied with St. Martin. St. Gregory of Tours devotes 3 books out of his 7 on miracles to those wrought by the relics of St. Martin, and references to Martin in his *Church History* again shew the large space in the mind of France occupied by our saint. We possess two versified biographies of St. Martin. Neither the later, in 4 books, by Venantius Fortunatus, merely adapted from the writings of Sulpicius, nor the earlier, more elegant poem, in 6 books, by Paulinus, has any claim to be considered an independent authority. Sozomen (*H. E.* iii. 16) has a brief account of Martin.

Life.—He was born at Sabaria in that part of Pannonia which is now Lower Hungary. He apparently lived at least 80 years (316-396).*

A.D. 316-336.—His father, a soldier in the Roman army, rose to be a military tribune. Martin's infancy was passed at Pavia in Italy, where his father was for some time stationed, and there he received his education, apparently a pagan one. But even in boyhood his real bent was made manifest, and at the age of ten he fled to a church and got himself enrolled as a catechumen against the wish of his parents. His father succeeded in checking for a season the boy's desire for a monastic career. An imperial edict ordered the enrolment of the sons of veterans, and Martin, who had become a wanderer among churches and monasteries, was, through his father's action, compelled to serve. Though living with much austerity, he won the affection of his fellows during his three years' service. During this period, between Martin's 15th and 18th year, we must place a well-known incident, which is thoroughly characteristic. At Amiens, in a winter of unusual severity, he met at the city gate a poor man naked and shivering. His comrades did not heed the sufferer's petitions, and Martin's purse was empty. But Martin with his sword divided his cloak and gave one half to the beggar. That night Martin, in a dream, saw Christ Himself clad in that half cloak. He regarded his dream as a call to baptism, which he straightway received. At the request of his military tribune, he stayed in the army two years after baptism.*

* Although some of the dates are well established, considerable uncertainty prevails respecting others. Thus though his length of life seems unquestioned, its limiting dates are not quite settled. It is difficult to reconcile some of the statements of Severus with the chronology set forth by Gregory of Tours.

A.D. 336-360.—The next important event in his career was his first visit to St. Hilary of Poictiers. Martin was his guest for a considerable time, and Hilary was anxious to ordain him deacon. Martin refused on the plea of unworthiness, but accepted the more lowly office of exorcist. Soon after he conceived it his duty to visit his parents and convert them from paganism. In crossing the Alps Martin fell in with a band of robbers, and was brought with hands bound before the chief, who asked who he was. He answered, "A Christian." To the further query whether he feared, he promptly replied that he never felt more secure, but that he grieved for the condition of his captors. The robber is said to have been converted. Martin's mother, with many more in Illyricum, became a convert to Christianity; his father remained a heathen. Arianism was particularly prevalent there, and Martin stood forth as an almost solitary confessor for the faith. He was publicly scourged and compelled to depart. Gaul being in a state of confusion in consequence of the exile of Hilary, Martin went to Italy, and for a short time found a safe retreat at Milan. But the bp. Auxentius, a leader among the Arians, severely persecuted him, and at length drove him away. He retired to the island of Gallinaria (now Galinara) off the coast of the Riviera.

A.D. 360-371.—Hilary being permitted to return home, Martin kept his promise and returned to Gaul, an attempt to meet Hilary at Rome having failed. Having settled near Poictiers, Martin founded, some five miles off at Locociagum (Lugugé), what is considered the earliest monastic institution in Gaul. Hilary gave him the site. If, as seems to be implied by Sulpicius, Martin returned to Gaul immediately after Hilary, his monastic life commenced A.D. 360. After 11 years in his monastery, his reputation led to his election to the see of Tours. It required what is called a pious fraud to entice him from his monastery; a leading citizen of Tours, having pretended that his wife was ill, begged Martin to come and visit her. A crowd of the people of Tours and from neighbouring cities had been gathered together, and the all but unanimous desire was for the election of Martin. The few opponents objected that his personal appearance was mean, his garments sordid, his hair unkempt. One of the objectorswas a bishop named Defensor. At service that day the reader, whose turn it was to officiate, failed, through pressure of the crowd, to arrive in time. A bystander took up a psalter and read the verse which in A.V. stands thus: "Out of the mouths of babes and sucklings hast Thou ordained strength

* The chronology is here painfully confused.

because of Thine enemies, that Thou mightest still the enemy and the avenger." But in the version then employed in Gaul, the concluding words were: " ut destruas inimicum et *defensorum.*" It is characteristic of the age that at this point a loud shout was raised by Martin's friends and his enemies were confounded, the reader's choice of the verse being regarded as a divine inspiration. Opposition thenceforth ceased, and Martin was duly consecrated.

A.D. 371-396.—To a great extent the new bp. of Tours continued to be the monk. He built a monastery two miles from the city, where 80 scholars, some of them noble, pursued a severe discipline. The art of transcribing was cultivated by the younger brethren. In time several cities obtained bishops from this institution. Unlike Hilary, whose controversies with Arians and semi-Arians formed his chief polemical work, bp. Martin was especially called upon to fight paganism. The country people in Gaul were still largely heathen. Martin, as portrayed by Sulpicius, simply lives in an atmosphere of marvels. During the first years of his episcopate the record is especially abundant, though his biographer declares he is restricting himself to a few specimens.

Martin must be regarded as the great evangelizer of the rural districts of Gaul, especially in the considerable and not very defined diocese of Tours. His work and influence are facts which no historian of France can omit. Twice he came across the path of emperors—namely, Valentinian I. and Maximus. Valentinian, the ruler of the West (364-375), for a time (in 368) fixed his seat of empire at Trèves. Martin repaired thither, for some unspecified reason. Moved by his Arian wife Justina, the great opponent of St. Ambrose, the emperor refused an audience. Martin within a week made his way into the palace. The emperor, indignant at the intrusion, declined to rise, until his chair caught fire and compelled him to move forward. Convinced of the divine aid, Valentinian granted all Martin's requests and took him into favour. Martin accepted the royal hospitality but declined all personal presents.

Somewhat different were the relations of Martin with the emperor Maximus, who, after the flight of Valentinian II., fixed his capital also at Trèves. Martin declined from Maximus such invitations as he had accepted from Valentinian, declaring it impossible to banquet with one "who had dethroned one emperor and slain another." The excuses of Maximus, however, induced Martin to appear at the imperial board. The seat assigned to him was among the very highest. In the middle of the feast the proper functionary offered, according to custom, a goblet to the sovereign. Maximus ordered that it should first be given to Martin, expecting to himself receive it from the bishop. But Martin handed the goblet to his chaplain, holding it wrong to allow the emperor higher honour than a presbyter. The bishop's conduct was admired, though no other prelate had acted thus even at the repast of secular dignitaries of inferior rank.

The intercourse of Martin with Maximus involved the bishop in the difficulties which troubled the church in connexion with the Priscillianist error. The leading opponent of Priscillian was the Spanish bp. Ithacius.

Priscillian, though condemned by a local council, was supported by some bishops, who consecrated him to the vacant see of Avila. The members of the council thereupon had recourse to the civil power; while the friends of Priscillian sought the aid of Damasus, bp. of Rome. Failing to obtain it, they betook themselves to Milan, where the great Ambrose was bishop. But St. Ambrose shewed them no more favour than Damasus. In 384 Ithacius went to Trèves to seek an interview with Maximus, and obtained the summoning of a council at Bordeaux. This all recognized as within the fair limits of imperial authority. But Priscillian, on his arrival at Bordeaux, instead of defending his cause by argument, appealed to the emperor. The Ithacians had already committed themselves to the permission of a considerable amount of state interference. Priscillian now came to Trèves and Ithacius followed. Martin objected to a case of heresy being left to a secular tribunal, begged Ithacius not to press the charges against Priscillian before such a court, and besought Maximus not to allow any other punishment of the accused beyond excommunication. Finding that he must leave Trèves and return home, Martin obtained a promise from the emperor that there should be no bloodshed. The trial of Priscillian, which had been delayed until Martin's departure, was now eagerly pressed on, at the instance of two bishops, Magnus and Rufus. The emperor seems to have been sincerely convinced that the heretical teaching of the Priscillianists involved gross immoralities; and, accordingly, in 385 Priscillian was executed with several of his adherents, while others were exiled.

This was the first instance of the capital punishment of a heretic. St. Martin and St. Ambrose protested, and refused communion with the bishops responsible for this sentence.

Martin paid a visit to Trèves later to plead that some of Gratian's officers might be spared. He found there a number of bishops gathered for the consecration of a new bishop, Felix, to the vacant see of Trèves. These prelates had, with one exception, communicated with the adherents of Ithacius, and had endeavoured unsuccessfully to prevent Martin's entrance into the city. The information that those for whose lives he came to plead were doomed, and that a sort of raid against Priscillianism was contemplated, induced Martin to change his mind, especially as he feared that the charge of sympathy with heresy might plausibly be imputed to himself and to others of ascetic life who had taken the same line. Martin evidently considered himself in a situation which involved a cruel and perplexing question of casuistry. Felix was himself a good man and well fitted for the vacant see. Still, Martin would not have communicated, but for the impending danger to the lives of innocent men and to the cause of religion. On his journey homeward, which he commenced on the day after his communion, he sat down in the vast solitude of a forest, near the village of Andethanna, and again debated with himself whether he had acted aright or not. It seemed to him that an angel appeared and told him that his compunction was right, but that he had had no choice. Henceforth he must be more careful. Martin believed that his power of working miracles and of relieving the oppressed was diminished ever after this unfortunate event. To escape such risks in the future, he never, for the remaining 16 years of his life, attended any synod or gathering of bishops. Sulpicius believes that in due time he regained his supernatural powers. The remainder of his career was spent in the conversion of his diocese, amidst constant prayer and toil. His death was calm, pious, and edifying. It probably occurred in 397, on Nov. 11, a date well known throughout the N. of England as the term-day of Martinmas. His funeral is said to have been attended by 2,000 monks. He is specially named among confessors in the Mass of pope Gregory, with Linus, Cletus, Hilary, Augustine, and 13 more. One of the oldest churches in England is that of St. Martin at Canterbury; and the earliest apostle of Scotland, St. Ninian, having heard of Martin's death while labouring in Galloway, dedicated to him the first stone church of the country, *Candida Casa*.

A cheap popular Life of St. Martin of Tours by J. C. Cazenove is pub. by S.P.C.K. in their *Fathers for Eng. Readers.* [J.G.C.]

Martinus (2), bp. of Dumium in Gallicia, and afterwards metropolitan bp. of Braga, died *c.* 580; a person of importance, about whom our information is scanty.

Our chief sources are: (1) Isidore, (*a*) his Life in *de Vir. Ill.* c. 35, (*b*) a reference in *Hist. Suevorum, Esp. Sagr.* vi. 505; (2) Gregory of Tours—(*a*) *de Mirac. Scti. Martini Tur.* i. 11; (*b*) *Hist. Franc.* v. 38; (3) some Acts of councils of Braga; (4) a letter and poem addressed to him by Venantius Fortunatus (Migne, *Patr. Lat.* lxxxviii.).

Life.—According to Gregory of Tours and Venantius Fortunatus, Martin was a native of Pannonia ("Pannonia Quiritis," Venantius). He had travelled to the Holy Land, and had in the East acquired such a knowledge of letters that he was held second to no scholar of his day. Thence (*ex Orientis partibus*) he came to Galicia, arriving "ad portum Galliciae" (? Portucale) on the same day as the relics of St. Martin of Tours, for which Arianus or Theodoric I., king of the Suevi, had shortly before petitioned the guardians of the saint's shrine. In 561, about eleven years after his arrival in the country, he attended the first council of Braga, presided over by Lucretius, metropolitan bp. of Braga. The Acts of the council, which are in an unusual and highly artificial shape, were probably compiled by Martin, the person of the greatest literary pretensions then in Gallicia.

This council evidently marks an era of revival and reformation in Galicia, probably under the auspices of the orthodox and energetic Martin. The only mention of Arianism in it throughout occurs in a letter of pope Vigilius which was read. Probably this indirect handling, and the penalties decreed generally against intercourse with heretics, were all that the bishops felt themselves strong enough to venture against a creed which had been shortly before the religious confession of the Suevian nation, and had no doubt still many friends in high places. Eleven years later another council was held at Braga, and Martin now occupied the metropolitan see as successor to Lucretius, the bishops addressing him in unusually submissive terms. Eleven bishops were present from the two synods of Lugo and Braga, which here appear as two distinct metropolitan dioceses for the first and only time in authentic history.

We may probably place the correspondence of Martin with Venantius Fortunatus between 572 and 580. In 580 Martin died, greatly mourned by the people of Gallicia. His memory is celebrated on Mar. 30.

Works.—(1) *Formula Vitae Honestae,* as he himself calls it in the preface, otherwise *de Differentiis Quatuor Virtutum* (so Isid. *l.c.*), or *de Quatuor Virtutibus Cardinalibus*—a little tract extremely popular in the middle ages, and frequently printed during the 15th and 16th cents. The best ed. is by Hasse in *Sen. Op.* iii. 468, where he describes the *Formula* as more frequently read and quoted in the middle ages than any of the genuine works of Seneca, to whom it was ascribed in early editions. There is an ed. by A. Weidner (Magdeburg, 1871). Cf. Fabricius, *Bibl. Med. Ae. Inf. Lat.* iii., *Bibl. Latina,* ed. 1773, ii. 119.

(2) *De Moribus,* a tract consisting of maxims from various sources. (Haase, xx.)

(3) *De Correctione Rusticorum.*—In this interesting tract Martin discusses the origin of idolatry and denounces the heathen customs still remaining in Galicia. His theory is that the fallen angels or demons assumed the names and shapes of notoriously wicked men and women who had already existed, such as Jove, Venus, Mars; that the nymphs, Lamias, and Neptune are demons with power to harm all who are not fortified with the sign of the cross, and who shew their faithlessness by calling the days of the week after the heathen gods. The observance of calends, the propitiation of mice and moths by presents of bread and cloth, auguries, the observance of the New Year on Jan. 1 instead of on the March equinox, when in the beginning God "divided the light from the darkness" by an equal division, the burning of wax tapers at stones, trees, streams, and crossways, the adornment of tables, the pouring of corn over the log on the hearth, the placing of wine and bread in the wells, the invocation of Minerva by the women at their spinning, the worship of Venus, the incantation of medicinal herbs, divination by birds and by sneezing, are all denounced as pagan superstitions, offensive to God and dangerous to him who practises them. The sign of the cross is to be the remedy against auguries and all other diabolical signs. The holy incantation, viz. the Creed, is the Christian's defence against diabolical incantations and songs.

(4) *De Trina Mersione,* a letter to a bp. Boniface on threefold immersion in baptism.

(5-9) *Pro Repellenda jactantia, de Superbia, Exhortatio Humilitatis, de Ira, de Pascha,* 5 small tracts, first pub. by Tamayo de Salazar in vol. ii. of his *Martyrol. Hisp.* and rightly considered genuine (Gams, ii. (1) 473).

(10) *De Paupertate,* a short tract, consisting of excerpts from Seneca, sometimes attributed to Martin, but not mentioned by

Florez or by Nicolas Antonio (*Bibl. Vat.* Bayer's ed. Haase, *l.c.* xx. 458).

Martin's Translations.—Besides his adaptations of Latin Stoical literature, Martin produced or superintended many translations from the Greek. The chief are (*a*) the *Capitula Martini*, a collection of 84 canons, which had great vogue and influence in the middle ages. These "capitula sive canones orientalium antiquorum patrum synodis a venerabili Martino episcopo, vel ab omni Bracarensi synodo excerpti," were incorporated in the earliest form of the Spanish *Codex Canonum*. With it they passed into the pseudo-Isidorian collection, and so obtained widespread influence. The sources of the collection cannot be all ascertained, they are not exclusively from *Greek* sources. They are, with some corrections, in Brun's *Canones Apostolorum*, (Berlin, 1839), ii. 43. (*b*) *Interrogationes et Reponsiones Plurimae*, sct. *Aegyptiorum Patr.*, trans. from an unknown Greek source by a deacon Paschasius in the monastery of Dumium, with a preface by Martin, at whose command the work had been undertaken (Rosweyd, *Vitae Patrum*, lib. vii. p. 505, and Prolegomenon, xiv.; Florez, *Esp. Sagr.* xv. 433).

Was Martin a Benedictine?—The great Benedictine writers unhesitatingly answer in the affirmative. (So Mabillon, *Annales O. S. B.* and *Bibliothèque générale de l'Ordre de Saint Benoît*, ii. 203.) But it is on the whole most probable that Martin adopted one of the various older rules still current in the contemporary monasteries of S. Gaul, with some of which we know him to have had relations. About 100 years later his illustrious successor in the sees of Dumium and Braga, St. Fructuosus, drew up a monastic rule for his monastery of Compludo, which was mainly an abbreviation of the Benedictine rule, but contained also provisions not found in that rule. This is the only piece of historical evidence connecting the Benedictine rule with Visigothic Catholicism. (Migne, *Pat. Lat.* lxxxvii. 1096; Yepés, *Chron. del Ord. de S. Benito*, i. for the ultra-Benedictine view. On the general subject of monasticism in Gothic Spain cf. Dahn, *Könige der Germanen*, vi.)

Martin's Personality.—That Martin played an important and commanding part in his generation all that remains of him suggests. His life appears to have been greatly influenced by the parallel so often drawn by his contemporaries between him and the greater Martin of Tours. We may also regard him to some extent as a piece in a political game. If Martin the missionary, *ex Orientis partibus*, effected the Suevian conversion, his career is one element in a scheme of European politics which can be traced through the greater part of 6th cent., and in which the destruction of the Suevian kingdom by Leovigild 5 years after Martin's death, and the West Gothic conversion to Catholicism under Reccared, are important incidents. (Gams, *Kirchengesch. von Spanien*, ii. (1) 471.) [M.A.W.]

Martyrius (3), bp. of Jerusalem, 478-486, a Cappadocian by birth, who had embraced a solitary life in the Nitrian desert. The violent proceedings of Timothy Aelurus drove him and other orthodox monks from Egypt, and he took refuge, A.D. 457, together with his fellow-solitary Elias, also subsequently bp. of Jerusalem, in the house of St. Euthymius, who received them with great favour (Cyrill. Scythop. *Vit. S. Euthym.* cc. 94, 95). After a time Martyrius retired to a cave 2 miles W. of the laura, which became the site of a considerable monastery (*ib.*). Martyrius and Elias were present at the death and burial of St. Euthymius, A.D. 473, after which Anastasius bp. of Jerusalem ordained them presbyters, attaching them to the church of the Resurrection (*ib.* cc. 105, 110, 112). Anastasius dying A.D. 478, Martyrius succeeded him as bp. of Jerusalem (*ib.* 113). His church was then rent asunder by the Eutychian Aposchistae, of whom Gerontius was the head. He succeeded in bringing back these schismatic monks to the unity of the church (*ib.* 123, 124). Cyrillus Scythopolitanus tells us that he died in the 8th year of his patriarchate, A.D. 486 (*Vit. S. Sab.* c. 19; Eutych. t. ii. p. 103). Le Quien, *Or. Christ.* iii. 171; Tillem. *Mém. eccl.* xvi. 332 seq. [E.V.]

Masona (*Massona, Mausona*, Mansi, ix. 1000; x. 478), bp. of Merida from *c.* 571 to *c.* 606. Except for the *de Vita et Miraculis Patrum Emeritensium*, a series of Lives attributed to Paulus Diaconus, a supposed writer of the 7th cent. (printed by Florez, *Esp. Sagr.* xiii., by Aguirre, *Coll. Max. Conc. Hisp.* ii. 639, and elsewhere), our information concerning Masona is extremely scanty.

Joannes Biclarensis says under A.D. 573, the 5th year of Leovigild, "Masona Emeritensis Ecclesiae Episcopus in nostro dogmate clarus habetur"; and at the third council of Toledo, the famous conversion council of 589, Masona presided, his signature "*Ecclesiae Catholicae* Emeritensis Metropolitanus Episcopus Provinciae Lusitaniae" being at the head of all the episcopal signatures, and immediately following that of Reccared. Between these two dates 16 years of great importance to the Gothic state had elapsed, comprising the rebellion of Hermenigild and the submission of Reccared to Catholicism. From the notice by Joannes Biclarensis 9 years earlier, it is evident that at the outbreak of the rebellion Masona was one of the most prominent Catholic bishops in S. Spain, and therefore would have considerable influence upon the position assumed by Merida in the contest. In 589 the great aim of the Catholic party was achieved, and the Visigothic state became, at least officially, Catholic. Eight years later a gathering of bishops at Toledo, under the presidency of Masona, passed two canons, one insisting upon the celibacy of bishops, priests, and deacons, the other reserving the endowments of a church for the benefit of its priests and other clerks, as against possible exactions from the bishop. This assembly was perhaps a chance gathering of a number of bishops in the capital, who took the opportunity to formulate rules on two important disciplinary points. If it was a duly summoned national council, the Acts were purposely or accidentally omitted from the original redaction of the Spanish *Codex Canonum* made within the first 40 years of 7th cent. Our last notice of Masona occurs in a letter, dated Feb. 28, 606, to him from Isidore in answer to an inquiry on a matter of discipline. In 610 his successor, Innocentius, signed the *Decretum Gundemari*.

The above *Vita* remains to be considered. If it be a genuine piece of 7th-cent. biography, it gives full and valuable information on his life and also on the general condition of the Spanish church in the 6th and 7th cents. But the Latin of the first three chaps. seems to make it impossible to refer them to 7th cent. The legendary and marvellous character of the remainder, and the desire apparent throughout to exalt the ecclesiastical importance of Merida, is, on the other hand, no argument against genuineness, as contemporary parallels might easily be quoted. The facts it gives regarding Masona are briefly: his Gothic extraction, his education in the church of St. Eulalia, his persecution at the hands of Leovigild, who sent two Arian bishops, Sunna and Nepopis, at different times, to undermine Masona's influence and oust him from his church, his intercourse with Leovigild at Toledo, where his resistance to the king's demand led to his exile, and his final restoration to his see after Leovigild's various supernatural warnings. After Reccared had succeeded and publicly embraced Catholicism, a struggle took place in Merida between Masona and Sunna. Sunna joined with two Gothic *Comes*, Segga and Witteric, in a plot for murdering Masona which was miraculously frustrated, and Witteric, afterwards the Gothic king of that name, confessed all to Masona, who was not only protected by miracles, but by the strong arm of the Catholic Claudius Dux of Lusitania (known to us from other sources, as are Sunna and Segga, cf. Isid. *Hist. Goth.* ap. *Esp. Sagr.* v. 492; Joann. Bicl. *op. cit.* 385, 386; and ep. Greg. Magn.; Aguirre Catalani, *Coll. Max. Conc. Hist.* ii.). Reccared decided that Sunna should either recant his Arianism or go into exile. He chose the latter, retired into Mauritania and there came to a miserable end. Masona lived to an honoured old age, procuring in his last hours the miraculous punishment of his archdeacon Eleutherius, who had abused the powers entrusted to him by the failing bishop.

It is not improbable that the *Vita* represents the 7th-cent. tradition. Isidore expressly mentions the exile of bishops among Leovigild's measures of persecution (*Hist. Goth. l.c.* p. 491), and it is most likely that Masona was exiled *c.* 583, after the fall of Merida, and restored, not during the lifetime of Leovigild, as his enthusiastic biographer declares, but upon the accession of Reccared, who sought to reverse his father's policy. Dahn, *Könige der Germanen*, v. 141; R. de Castro, *Biblioteca Españoles*, ii. p. 348; Nicolas Antonio, *Bibl. Vet.* Bayer's ed. i. p. 373; note by Morales to the *Memoriale Sanctorum* of St. Eulogius apud *Hist. Illust.* iv. 282. [M.A.W.]

Maternus (3), Julius Firmicus, an acute critic of pagan rites and doctrines and a vigorous apologist for the Christian faith, known from his treatise *de Errore Profanarum Religionum*, composed between 343 and 350, very valuable for its details of the secret rites of paganism. It describes every leading form of idolatry then current and gives us information not found elsewhere. It discusses the idolatry of the Persians, Egyptians, Assyrians, the Greek mysteries, the ceremonies and formulae used in the Mithraic worship. Some of the details on this last are very curious, some liturgical fragments being inserted. In opposition to the heathen orgies he presents the pure mysteries of Christianity in his preface, now almost completely lost, and from c. xxiv. to the end. He concludes with earnestly exhorting the emperors to suppress paganism by force; thus giving one of the earliest specimens of Christian intolerance. The work illustrates the small amount of philological and etymological science possessed by the ancients. Maternus, arguing against the Egyptians that Sarapis was originally the patriarch Joseph, derives the name Sarapis from Σαρᾶς ἀπό, because Joseph was the descendant of Sarah. The work is valuable for Biblical criticism, as in it are found quotations from the versions used in N. Africa in St. Cyprian's time. There are probably embodied in it some fragments of the ancient Greek writer Evemerus, whose work upon paganism, now lost, was largely used by all the Christian apologists. In Migne's *Patr. Lat.* t. xii. is reprinted an ed. of Maternus, pub. by Munter at Copenhagen in 1826, with an introductory dissertation discussing the whole subject. A contemporary pagan Julius Firmicus Maternus, usually styled Junior, wrote a work (between 330 and 360) on judicial astrology, mentioned by Sidon. Apoll. in *Ep. ad Pont. Leont.* Upon this see the above dissertation. There is some reason to suppose that he was converted to Christianity and was identical with the subject of our art. See C. H. Moore, *Jul. Firm. Mat. der Heide und der Christ.* (Munich, 1897). [G.T.S.]

Maurus (2), St., founder and abbat of the Benedictine monastery of Glanfeuil or St. Maur-sur-Loire. He is better known, as Herzog says, to tradition than to history, but the primary authority is Gregorius Mag. (*Dial.* ii. cc. 3 seq.). His Life, written by Faustus Cassinensis, and re-written with alterations by Odo or Eudes, at one time abbat of Glanfeuil, is given by Mabillon (*Acta SS. O. S. B.* saec. i. 274 seq.) and the Bolland. (*Acta SS.* Jan. i. 1039 seq.). [FAUSTUS (31)]. St. Maurus, better known in France as St. Maur, was when 12 years old entrusted by his father Equitius, an Italian nobleman, to the charge of St. Benedict at Subiaco (or at Monte Cassino) and trained in monastic rule. By St. Benedict he was sent into Gaul *c.* 543, and established his monastery on the Loire by favour of King Theodebert. He introduced the Benedictine rule, and was the chief means of its acceptance in France, but the details of his work are not given. He died A.D. 584. His monastery, secularized in 16th cent., was in the middle ages one of great influence, and the "Congregation of St. Maur" has done much from the 17th cent. to elevate the tone of the monastic orders. The genuineness of his life in all its stages has been disputed. Ceillier, *Sacr. Aut.* xi. 157, 170, 610; Herzog, *Real-Encycl.* ix. 201; Cave, *Lit. Hist.* i. 574; Mosheim, *Hist. Ch. Ch.* cent. xvii. § 2, pt. i. c. 1. [J.G.]

Maxentius (4), Joannes, presbyter and archimandrite. His monastery (*Sugg. Diosc.* in Labbe, iv. 1520) appears to have been situated within the jurisdiction of Paternus, bp. of Tomi (Köstendje), the capital of Scythia

Minor (Dobrudscha), who subscribed the synodical letter of the council held at Constantinople, A.D. 520, as "Provinciae Scythiae Metropolitanus" (Labbe, iv. 1525). About 517 a controversy arose at Constantinople, in which the credit of the council of Chalcedon (A.D. 451) was considered to be seriously involved (Hormisd. epp. 15, 16 in Mansi, viii. 418 and Labbe, iv. 1454, 1455). An active part was taken by certain Scythian monks, with Maxentius as their leader, who earnestly contended for the position "unus de Trinitate in carne crucifixus est" as essential to the exclusion of the heresy of Nestorius on the one hand and of Eutyches on the other (*Suggestio Dioscuri*, Labbe, iv. 1513, May 13, 519; Desprez, *Proleg. Fulgent. Rusp.* in Migne, lxv. 109). The dispute was at its height in 519, when Germanus bp. of Capua, bp. Joannes, Blandus a presbyter, Felix and Dioscorus deacons, arrived at Constantinople from Hormisdas bp. of Rome, to negotiate a reconciliation of the two churches (Baronius, *s.a.* lxxxvii.). At the same time the writings of Faustus the semi-Pelagian bp. of Riez were also the subject of fierce debate at Constantinople, the Scythian monks contending that they were heretical. Among the chief antagonists of the monks were a deacon named Victor, Paternus bp. of Tomi, and other Scythian bishops (*Sugg. Germ. Joann. Fel. Diosc. et Bland.* in Labbe, iv. 1514). Both parties had influential supporters in the imperial court, the monks being vigorously upheld by Vitalian, then apparently in great favour with the emperor Justin, who held the office of magister militum (Evagr. *H. E.* iv. 3; *Suggest. Diosc. u.s.*), and their opponents no less so at first by Justinian, who already held high office under his uncle (Vict. Tunun. *s.a.* 518; Justinian, *ad Hormisd.* Labbe, iv. 1516). Soon after the arrival of the Roman legates at Constantinople the Scythian monks appealed for their help, and Maxentius, in their name, drew up "de Christo Professio," explanatory of their faith, which they sent with the appeal (Migne, *Patr. Gk.* lxxxvi. 75, 79). They protest that it is from no disrespect to the council of Chalcedon, but in its defence, that they contend for their position on the subject of the Trinity, and declare that they anathematize all who either oppose that council or hold its decisions to be imperfect. They also denounce the teaching of Pelagius and Coelestius, and the followers of Theodore of Mopsuestia, as "contradictory to that of the apostle." They further pray the papal legates to hear their accusations against Victor and Paternus (May 30, 519, Labbe, iv. 1509; *Suggest. Legat. u.s.* 1514, June 29, 519; Hormisd. *Suggest. Diosc. et al.* May 30, 519; Labbe, iv. 1519; *Suggest. German. et al.* June 29, 519; *ib.* 1514; Hormisd. *Ep.* 67, *ad Justinian.*; *ib.* 1518). The legates, at the urgent request of the emperor Justin and Vitalian, consented to hear the case, but without pronouncing a decision. Failing to obtain satisfaction at Constantinople, the monks determined to send four of their number, Achilles, John, Leontius, Mauritius, to lay the whole case before Hormisdas at Rome (Justinian, *Ep. ad Hormisd.* Labbe, iv. 1516). The four departed for the West early in May 519, and Justinian and the Roman legates duly notify their departure to Hormisdas, and pray him to reject their appeal.

Hormisdas delaying to hear the four envoys, others were sent to join them, Maxentius apparently being one. Meanwhile Justinian changed his opinion of the monks and became their advocate (Justinian. *ad Hormisd.*; Hormisd. *Ep.* 66, *ad* Justinian. Sept. 2, 519, *u.s.* 1518). The controversy seems to have involved a considerable number of the clergy of the East, especially those of Jerusalem, Antioch, and Syria Secunda (Justin. *ad Hormisd. u.s.* 1520, Jan. 19, 520; *Deprec. et Supplic. ab Hieros. et al. u.s.* 1542). An active correspondence followed between Constantinople and Rome, during which Possessor, an African bp. exiled by the Arians, wrote to Hormisdas, requesting his opinion as to the orthodoxy of the writings of Faustus and urging that Vitalian and Justinian were equally anxious to hear from Hormisdas on the subject (Possess. *Ep. Afr. Relat.* Labbe, iv. 1530, received at Rome July 18, 520). Shortly after the dispatch of this letter Vitalian was put to death (Procop. *Hist. Arc.* 6, *Op.* ed. Bonn, iii. 46; Vict. Tunun. *s.a.* 523).

The deputation at Rome, finding the Roman legates at Constantinople too strong for them, and therefore having little hope of success with Hormisdas, resolved to appeal to the African bishops then in exile in Sardinia, some of whom, as Fulgentius of Ruspe, enjoyed a high reputation for ability as well as orthodoxy. In drawing up the appeal they again appear to have employed Maxentius. It was divided into eight chapters. In the fourth they elaborately defend the position they had maintained at Constantinople. At the close of the fifth they solemnly protest their acceptance of the councils of Nicaea, Constantinople, Ephesus, and Chalcedon, the letters of Leo anathematizing the writings of Theodore of Mopsuestia and Nestorius his disciple, and all writings opposed to the Twelve Chapters of the blessed Cyril against Nestorius; anathematizing in addition, Eutyches and Dioscorus (Petr. Diac. *de Incarnat. et Gratia*, Migne, *Patrol.* lxv. 442-451). This appeal was responded to by Fulgentius, bp. of Ruspe, in his well-known *de Incarnatione et Gratia Domini nostri Jesu Christi*, in which the exiled bishops express their hearty approval of the confession of faith which the appeal contained (Fulgent. *Ep.* 17, *Op. u.s.* 451-493). The monks, after being detained at Rome 14 months, had now returned to the East. Before they left they drew up a further protestation of their faith, which they caused to be affixed to the statues of the emperors (Hormisd. *Ep.* 70, *ad Possess.*; Labbe, iv. 1531). This, probably, was the "contra Nestorianos capitula" of the collected works of Maxentius. The title, however, hardly corresponds to the contents, which consist of 12 anathemas, the 9th being directed against the Eutychians, and the remaining three against Pelagius and Coelestius and their followers (Migne, *Patr. Gk.* lxxxvi. 86).

Maxentius and his friends, having returned to Constantinople, sent a copy of the writings of Faustus of Riez to Fulgentius and the other exiles in Sardinia, requesting him and his brethren to send their opinion of these (*ib.* lxv. 145). Meanwhile Fulgentius wrote his *de Veritate Praedestinationis*, addressed to Joannes presbyter and Venerius deacon, two of the Scythian monks (*ib.* 603-671), speaking of the monks in the highest terms. On Aug. 13, 520, Hormisdas replied to the letter received from Possessor on July 18, speaking of the monks with unmeasured reproach. They are scatterers of "poison under the pretence of religion," and he writes now so that, should they return to Constantinople, they might not deceive those who did not know of their conduct at Rome. He does not, however, commit himself to any opinion as to the position "unum de Trinitate," but refers to it in very general terms, saying, "The reverend wisdom of the Fathers has defined what is Catholic doctrine . . . what need, therefore, to raise any further controversy, when the Christian faith is limited by canonical books, synodical decrees, and the constitutions of the Fathers within fixed and immovable limits?" Nor is he much more explicit as to the writings of Faustus. He says that he does not receive him nor any one not approved by the authority of the Fathers, but adds, that if he agrees with "right faith and sound teaching" he is to be admitted; if not, he is to be rejected, and concludes with telling Possessor that "although what the Roman, that is the Catholic, church follows and maintains on the subject of free-will and the grace of God may be gathered from various books of the blessed Augustine, and especially from those addressed to Hilary and to Prosper; nevertheless, there are certain special documents preserved in the ecclesiastical archives, which, if Possessor has not, and wishes to see, he will send him" (Hormisd. *Ep. 70, ad Possess.*; Labbe, iv. 1530-1532). This letter was widely circulated as an encyclic, and when it came into the hands of Maxentius he at once replied to it in his *ad Ep. Hormisdae Responsio*, Migne, lxxvii. 94-112. The reply is in every way a remarkable document. The archimandrite refuses to believe the letter can have been written by Hormisdas, but argues that whether it was so or not, its author was "unquestionably a heretic," as he considers that to "maintain that Christ, the Son of God, is one of the Trinity is to contend about words." He also takes the writer to task for having virtually decided that, although the writings of Faustus were not authoritative, they were still to be read.

We hear nothing more of Maxentius and the Scythian monks until after Hormisdas died in Aug. 523. The encyclic of Hormisdas had now reached the exiled bishops in Sardinia, though there is no reason to believe that they had also seen the *Responsio* of Maxentius, and they had had ample leisure for consideration of the second appeal addressed to them from Constantinople. They accordingly met in council and sent the monks a reply in the form of a synodical letter. They acknowledge the receipt of the letter of Maxentius and his brethren, and say they rejoice that they "hold a right opinion on the grace of God, by whose light the free will of the human mind is illuminated, and by whose aid it is controlled," and express sorrow that any should question the Catholic faith on the point (c. 2).

The position for which John Maxentius and his brethren contended was afterwards formally approved by a council at Rome in 532 (Labbe, iv. 1761) and elaborately defended in 534 by John II. bp. of Rome, who argued that it had always been held by Catholics in the very form used by the Scythian monks, quoting Proclus patriarch of Constantinople and others (*Ep.* 3 in Labbe, iv. 1751; Jaffé, *Reg. Pont.* 73; Pagi, *Crit. s.a.* 533). The council of Constantinople of 553 anathematized all who questioned it (collat. viii. anath. 10, Labbe, v. 575). Yet Baronius (*s.a.* 519 cii.) is unsparing in his condemnation of the monks as impugners of the Catholic faith. They have found an able defender in Cardinal Noris (*Hist. Pelagiana*, ii. 18, in *Op.* i. 474-596; esp. c. 20, pp. 498-504; *Hist. Controv. de Univ. ex Trinit. passe*, cc. 4-8; *Op.* iii. 800-854), and Pagi (*Crit. s.a.* 519, vi.) accepts his vindication as conclusive. [T.W.D.]

Maximianus (1) I., M. Aurelius Valerius (Herculius), emperor of Rome A.D. 286-305 with Diocletian, 306-308 with Maxentius or Constantine; compelled to strangle himself Feb. 310, being probably 60 years old (Tillem. "Diocletian," vol. iv. p. 7, *Hist. des Emp.*). A Pannonian soldier of humble birth but great military ability and unresting activity, he was created Caesar in 285 by Diocletian, and Augustus in 286. (For the chief events in his history see DIOCLETIAN, CONSTANTINE, and MAXENTIUS in *D. of G. and R. Biogr.*) The Diocletian persecution began in A.D. 303, and Maximian joined in it. He is said in the *de Mortibus Persecutorum* to have been the worthy brother of Diocletian, and Eusebius speaks of his death in the same retributive tone as of the other emperors except Constantius and Constantine (*H. E.* viii. 13).

The military talents and activity of Maximianus were of the greatest value to the Western empire and in Africa, and while under Diocletian's influence or direction he seconded him honestly and well. He was a barbarian soldier without honour, principle, or education; crime was familiar to him, though he seems not to have practised cruelty for its own sake. He is accused of the usual sensual excesses, though not to the same extent as Maxentius. [R.ST.J.T.]

Maximianus (2), the man from whom a special sect among the Donatists derived its name; that schism within a schism, which rent it asunder and helped to bring about its ultimate overthrow. He is said to have been related to Donatus the Great, and was a deacon at Carthage when, at the death of Parmenian, Primian was appointed bp. of the Donatists there A.D. 391. Primian found fault with four of his deacons, especially Maximian, whom he appears to have disliked most. He tried to persuade the "Seniors" of Carthage to condemn them all, but they refused, and Primian then proceeded to excommunicate Maximian, who was ill and unable to appear. The Seniors summoned Primian to meet them to explain this arbitrariness, but he refused. They then wrote to the bishops of the district, entreating them to meet and inquire into the case. Forty-three met at Carthage; and their proceedings, notwithstanding the violence of the supporters of

Primian, who was himself absent, resulted in his condemnation. In June or July 393, at a second meeting of Donatist bishops at Cabarsussum, a town of Byzacene, Primian was more formally condemned, his deposition pronounced, and a resolution apparently passed that Maximian should be appointed in his place. He was accordingly ordained at Carthage by 12 bishops. But Primian was not crushed by this, for at a council of 310 bishops at Bagai, Apr. 24, 394, at which he himself presided, the supporters of Maximian, of whom none were present, were condemned in most opprobrious language. Notwithstanding the defection of the Maximianists, who appear to have rebaptized those who joined them, the validity of their baptism was not denied by the other Donatists, a point which Augustine frequently uses against them. Unremitting persecution induced many Maximianists to return at length to the Donatist community, but of Maximian himself we hear little or nothing subsequently; other names are most prominent in the party's history. Aug. *c. Cresc.* iii. 16, 59, iv. 3, 4, 6-9, 55, 57; *En. Ps.* (Vulg.) xxxvi. 19, 20, 23, 29; *Ps.* cxxiv. 5; *Epp.* 43, 26, 76; 44, 71; 53, 3; 141, 6; 185, 17; *de Gest. Emer.* 9; *c. Parm.* i. 9; Tillem. *Mém.* vi. 65-72; Morcelli, *Afr. Chr.* vol. ii. pp. 310-326; Ribbeck, *Aug. und Don.* pp. 206-236. [H.W.P.]

Maximianus (5), archbp. of Constantinople, A.D. 431. The action of the council of Ephesus had thrown the churches of Constantinople into direst confusion. A large proportion of the citizens held strongly to Nestorius; the clergy, with one voice, agreed in the anathema; and when the deposition became a fact no longer to be disputed, the excitement was continued about the election of a successor. After four months, agreement was arrived at in the election of Maximian. He had led a monastic life and had entered presbyteral orders; his action in building, at his own expense, tombs for the remains of holy men had obtained for him a reputation of sanctity. In principles he followed the former archbishops, Chrysostom, Atticus, and Sisinnius. Pope Celestine wrote to him in highly complimentary terms on his elevation. The appointment was made by the unanimous vote of clergy, emperor, and people. The letter of Maximian announcing to the pope his succession is lost, but that to S. Cyril remains, with its high eulogium on Cyril's constancy in defending the cause of Jesus Christ. It was the custom for occupants of the principal sees on election to send a synodical letter to the most considerable bishops of the Christian world, asking for the assurance of their communion. Maximian sent his synodical to the Easterns as to the others. Communion was refused by Helladius of Tarsus; and, we may conclude, by Eutherius of Tyana, Himerius of Nicomedia, and Dorotheus of Martianopolis, as Maximian deposed them. John of Antioch approved the refusal of the bp. of Tarsus, and praised him for having declined to insert the name of Maximian in the diptychs of his church. Maximian's earnest appeal for reunion continued. Pope Sixtus wrote to him several times, urging him to extend his charity to all whom he could possibly regain. Maximian spared no effort, and although he was in closest harmony with St. Cyril, he pressed him strongly to give up his anathemas, which seemed an insurmountable obstacle to reunion. He even wrote to the emperor's secretary Aristolaus the tribune, who was greatly interested in the question of peace, almost complaining that he did not press Cyril enough on the point, and to his archdeacon Epiphanius. Harmony being restored, John of Antioch and the other Eastern bishops wrote Maximian a letter of communion indicating their consent to his election and to the deposition of Nestorius. Cyril wrote to him, attributing the blessed result to the force of his prayers. A letter to Maximian from Aristolaus, which Maximian caused to be read in his church to his people, was pronounced spurious by Dorotheus of Martianopolis, evidently because it took the side of Maximian so decidedly. Maximian held the see of Constantinople from Oct. 25, 431, to Apr. 12, 434. Of all his letters, only that to St. Cyril is extant. Mansi, v. 257, 259, 266, 269, 271, 273, 286, 351; Baluz. *Nov. Coll. Conc.* 581 seq. ed. 1681; Socr. vii. 35, 40; Liberat. Diac. *Brev.* 19; Ceill. viii. 394. [W.M.S.]

Maximinus (2) **I.,** Roman emperor, A.D. 235-238. C. Julius Verus Maximinus is conspicuous as the first barbarian who wore the imperial purple, and as one of the emperors whose names are connected with the ten persecutions recorded by ecclesiastical historians. Born in Thrace of a Gothic father and an Alan mother, eight feet high and of gigantic strength, he attracted the notice of Septimius Severus, and rose into favour with Alexander Severus. When that emperor fell into disfavour with his troops, Maximinus seized his opportunity and organized a conspiracy which ended in the murder of Alexander and his mother at Mayence in 235. The praetorian guards elected him emperor, and their choice was confirmed by the senate.

The hostility of Maximinus to his Christian subjects was probably because of the favour they had enjoyed from the eclectic or syncretic sympathies of Alexander Severus. They would appear to him, as to other emperors, a secret, and therefore a dangerous, society, the natural focus of conspiracies and plots. The persecution was limited in its range, and probably was effectual chiefly in removing the restraints which the leanings of Alexander had imposed on the antagonism of the populations and governors of the provinces.

Pontianus, bp. of Rome, was banished with the presbyter Hippolytus to Sardinia, and died there in 235, and, according to Baronius (*Ann.* 137, 138), his successor Anteros met a like fate in 238. Origen thought it expedient to seek safety with his friend Firmilianus, bp. of the Cappadocian Caesarea. That province was under the government of Serenianus, whom Firmilianus describes (*ap.* Cyprian, *Ep.* 75) as "acerbus et dirus persecutor." Frequent earthquakes had roused the panic-stricken population to rage against the Christians as the cause of all disasters (Orig. *in Matt.* xxiv. 9). This was all the more keenly felt after the comparatively long tranquillity which they had enjoyed under Alexander Severus and his predecessors. From his retirement Origen addressed two treatises *On Martyrdom* and *On Prayer* to his disciple Ambrosius, a deacon of the church of Alexandria (Eus. *H. E.* vi. 28), and Protoctetus, a presbyter of Caesarea, both of whom were taken as prisoners to Germany (Orig. *Exhort. ad Mart.* 41).

The tyranny of Maximin brought about the revolt in Mauritania, which for three months raised the two GORDIANS to the throne of the Caesars. At Aquileia his troops, suffering from famine and disease, became disaffected. A party of praetorian guards rose, and he, with his son and the chief ministers of his tyranny, were slain in his tent. Their heads were cut off and exhibited on the battlements to the gaze of the citizens. [E.H.P.]

Maximinus (3) **II.** (*Jovius*), emperor, A.D. 305-3 Galerius Valerius Maximinus, originally called Daza, played a somewhat prominent part in the complications following on the abdication of DIOCLETIAN and MAXIMIANUS I. Those emperors were succeeded as *Augusti* by GALERIUS and CONSTANTIUS, who appointed as Caesars Daza, under the name of Maximinus, and Severus. On the death of Constantius (A.D. 306) Galerius assigned the provinces beyond the Alps to Constantine, but conferred the vacant title of *Augustus* on Severus, leaving that of Caesar to Constantine and Maximin. Severus was put to death A.D. 307, and Galerius made Constantine and Licinius *Augusti*, assigning Illyricum to the latter. Maximin, who was in charge of Syria and Egypt, jealous of this promotion of others to a higher position than his own, assumed, under the convenient plea that his troops compelled him, the title of Augustus, and added to it the epithet Jovius, which had been borne before by Diocletian (Eus. *H. E.* viii. 13; ix. 9). On the death of Galerius in 311, Maximin received the provinces of Asia Minor in addition to Syria and Egypt, and Licinius those of Eastern Europe. The decisive victory of Constantine at Milvian Bridge in 312, and the betrothal of Constantine's sister to Licinius, alarmed Maximin, who determined on immediate hostilities. At Heraclea he was encountered by the army of Licinius, and utterly routed. In 24 hours he reached Nicomedia, 160 miles from the scene of his defeat, and made his way to Tarsus, where after a few days' despair he poisoned himself. As a final insult to his memory all inscriptions to his honour were destroyed, his statues disfigured and thrown from their pedestals (ix. 11). His character is pre-eminent for brutal licentiousness and ferocious cruelty. The provinces of Asia, Syria, and Egypt groaned for six years under him, and of all the persecutors in that last great struggle between the old and new religions none were so infamous for their cruelties. Though he joined for a time, on the advice of the dying Galerius, with Constantine and Licinius in a decree of toleration in 311, he renewed the persecution with greater vigour within a few months (viii. 17). The sufferings of the Christians in Alexandria drew the hermit Anthony from his desert seclusion to exhort them to steadfastness. Of the martyrs of Palestine, to whom Eusebius dedicates a whole book of his history, most suffered by his orders and many in his presence. Heralds were sent through Caesarea ordering all men to sacrifice to the gods, and on his refusal, Appian, a youth of twenty, was tortured and slain. Ulpian and his brother Aedesius were slain at Tyre, Agapius was thrown into the amphitheatre at Caesarea to fight with a bear and so lacerated that he died the next day. Theodosia, a virgin of Tyre, was drowned, Silvanus tortured, and the confessors of Phaeno in Palestine sent to the mines (Eus. *de Mart. Palest.* c. 4). Silvanus, the aged bp. of Emesa, was thrown into a den of wild beasts. Peter, bp. of Alexandria, with many other bishops, was beheaded (*ib. H. E.* ix. 6). The church of Antioch supplied yet more illustrious martyrs. On the application of an embassy from that city, headed by Theotecnos, which he himself had prompted, he forbade the Christians to hold their wonted meetings in its catacombs (ix. 2). Hesychius and Lucian, the latter a presbyter, famous for learning and saintliness, were summoned to the emperor's presence at Nicomedia, half starved to death, and then tempted with a luxurious banquet as the price of their apostasy, and on their refusal to deny their faith were thrown into prison and put to death (ix. 6). Decrees, which Eusebius (ix. 7) copied from a pillar in Tyre, were issued, ascribing the famines, earthquakes, and pestilences to the wrath of the gods at the spread of the creed which was denounced as atheistic, and decreeing, at the alleged request of the Syrians themselves, perpetual banishment against all who adhered to their denial of the state religion. Even the Armenians, though outside the emperor's dominions, and old allies of Rome, were threatened with war, because they were Christians (ix. 8), and this at a time when thousands were dying of starvation from a prolonged famine followed by pestilence. From Nicomedia and the neighbouring cities the Christians were banished by an imperial edict, issued here as elsewhere, as at the request of the citizens themselves (ix. 9). Not till after his defeat by Licinius did the tyrant, in the rage of his despair, turn against the priests, prophets, and soothsayers who had urged him on, and, as a last resource, within less than a year after his edicts of extermination, issue a decree of toleration and order the restitution of property taken from the Christians and brought into the imperial treasury (ix. 10). [E.H.P.]

Maximinus (4), St., 5th archbp. of Trèves (*c.* 332-349), known to us from the part he played in the history of Athanasius. In Feb. 336 the latter was banished by the emperor Constantine to Trèves, then the seat of government of his eldest son Constantine II. Maximin received him with honour, became his zealous partisan and friend, and was thenceforth numbered among the champions of orthodoxy in the West (Hieron. *Chron.* an. 346, Migne, *Patr. Lat.* xxvii. 682; Athan. *Ep. ad Episc. Aegypt.* § 8; *Apologia ad Imp. Const.* § 3, ed. Benedict. i. 278, 297; Hilarius, *Hist. Frag.* ii. ed. Maff. ii. 634, in *Patr. Lat.* x. 644). For the probable influence of Athanasius's sojourn on the struggle between Arianism and orthodoxy and the growth of monasticism in the West, see Rettberg, *Kirchengeschichte,* i. 187, 188. Athanasius left Trèves in June 338, and in 340 Maximin was called upon to entertain and assist Paul, the banished bp. of Constantinople. His efforts resulted in Paul's restoration in 341. In 342 a deputation of four Arian bishops arrived at Trèves, hoping to win Constans to their views. They brought a creed of compromise, but Maximin was inflexibly hostile, refused them communion, and was mainly instrumental in securing the rejection of their proposals (Hilar. *Hist. Frag.* iii. ed. Maff. ii. 662, 663, in *Patr. Lat.* x. 674, 675). In 343 Maximin was present at the council of Milan (*Hist. litt. de la France*, i. B. 111). Whether he was also at the great council of Sardica, 343 or 344, is not quite certain, but he assented to its decisions (Athan. *Apol. contr. Arianos*, § 50, ed. Benedict. i. 168; Hilar. *ib.* ii. 647, in *Patr. Lat.* 659). His prominent part in the conflict with Arianism is shewn by the special excommunication pronounced against him at the heretical council of Philippopolis (*Hist. Frag.* iii. 27).

Maximin's cult was established from very early times. The legends that collected round his name are embodied in two biographies, one by an anonymous monk of St. Maximin in 8th cent. (Boll. *Acta SS.* Mai. vii. 21-25), the other by a Lupus, who, in the opinion of Ceillier (xii. 511) and others, was Lupus, bp. of Châlons. It is in Migne, *Patr. Lat.* cxix. 665-680. According to their story, Maximin was a native of Poitou, brother of Maxentius, bp. of Poictiers. Drawn to Trèves by the favour of St. Agricius, he was ordained by him and succeeded him in the see. Against the Arian heresy, then in the ascendant, he boldly contended and suffered much persecution. He summoned a council at Cologne, which condemned Euphratas, the bp. of that city, who denied the divinity of Christ. (This council is now admitted to be fictitious; see Baron. *Ann.* 346, vii. sqq.; Rettberg, *Kirchengeschichte Deutschlands*, i. 131). He died in Aquitaine after an episcopate of 17 years, and was buried there. For the early history of his famous monastery see Gall. *Christ.* xiii. 523 sqq.; Rettberg, *u.s.* i. 474. [S.A.B.]

Maximinus (6), Arian bp. of Hippo Regius, who came with the Gothic soldiers into Africa A.D. 427, 428, and held a discussion with St. Augustine on the Trinity. Augustine, later, replied in 2 books, which, with that which contains the discussion, exhibit the arguments for and against the Arian doctrine. The line of argument taken by Augustine resembles so strongly that expressed in our Athanasian creed that if this were lost it might almost be supplied from this treatise. August. *Coll. cum Max.* and *Contra Max.* i. ii. *Opp.* vol. viii. pp. 719-810, ed. Migne; *Vit. Poss.* 17; Ceillier, vol. ix. 359-361. [H.W.P.]

Maximus (2) Magnus, Christian emperor in the West, A.D. 383-388.

Authorities.—Besides the regular historians, of whom Zosimus (iv. 35-46) gives most original matter, St. Ambrose has special notices, *Epp.* 24 (narrative of his embassies), 20, § 23, and 40, § 23; Symmachus, *Ep.* ii. 31; Sulpicius Severus, almost contemporary, *Chron.* ii. 49-51, *Vita S. Martini*, 20, *Dialogus*, ii. 6, iii. 11. The best modern books are De Broglie, *L'Eglise et l'Empire au IVme siècle* (Paris, 1866), vol. vi. and H. Richter, *Weströmische Reich* (Berlin, 1865), pp. 568 ff., cf. T. Hodgkin, *Italy and her Invaders* (Oxf. 1880), vol. i. pp. 147-155.

History.—Magnus Maximus was a Spaniard by birth (Zos. iv. 35) and a dependant of the family of Theodosius, with whom he served in Britain. In 383 he was proclaimed emperor by the soldiers in Britain, where he held some command, apparently not a very high one. He landed in Gaul at the mouth of the Rhine, and was met by the army of Gratian somewhere near Paris. The troops came over to him, and Maximus suddenly found himself in possession of the western provinces. Gratian was killed at Lyons, Aug. 25, and, as was generally reported, by the orders of Maximus himself. The Western empire was thus in great danger, since Valentinian II. was a mere weak boy, and Theodosius was occupied in the East. It shews the position of St. Ambrose that he was chosen by the empress-mother, Justina, to treat for peace at this crisis (S. Ambr. *Ep.* 24, §§ 3, 5, 7). Peace was made, Maximus being acknowledged as Augustus and sovereign of the Gauls, side by side with Valentinian and Theodosius.

This state of things lasted for some years, during which Maximus, who had been baptized just before his usurpation, busied himself much with church affairs, being desirous to obtain a reputation for the strictest orthodoxy. Western writers, Sulpicius Severus and Orosius, though treating Maximus as a usurper, give him, on the whole, a good character, Sulpicius making exception on the score of his persecution of the Priscillianists and his love of money (Sulp. *Dial.* ii. 6; Oros. vii. 34). Thus Maximus was in general an able and popular ruler, at least in his own dominions, giving his subjects what they most wanted, some feeling of security and peace. But we must join in the censure passed upon his treatment of the Priscillianists by pope Siricius (synod of Turin, A.D. 401, can. 6, Hefele, *Councils*, § 113), St. Ambrose, and St. Martin of Tours. Ambrose, indeed, was a political opponent, but Maximus courted Siricius, and was very obsequious to Martin. The Priscillianist heretics, who held a mixture of Gnostic, Manichean, and Sabellian opinions, had been condemned by a synod at Saragossa in 380. Their opponents, Ithacius bp. of Ossonuba, and Idacius bp. of Emerita, found in Maximus a ready instrument of persecution. The Priscillianists were ordered to appear before a synod at Bordeaux in 384, where one of their chiefs, bp. Instantius, was condemned as unworthy of the episcopal office. Priscillian denied the competency of the synod, and appealed to the emperor. St. Martin besought him to abstain from bloodshed, and to remit the case to ecclesiastical judges. Ithacius, their most vehement accuser, did not hesitate to charge Martin himself with Priscillianism, but, for a time, better influences prevailed, and Maximus promised that no lives should be taken. After Martin's departure, however, other bishops persuaded Maximus to remit the case to a secular judge, Evodius, and finally the emperor condemned Priscillian and his companions, including a rich widow Euchrocia, to be beheaded. Instantius and some others were exiled. A second synod, held at Trèves in 385, approved by a majority the conduct of Ithacius, and urged Maximus to further measures of confiscation. St. Martin returned to intercede for some of his friends, and with this purpose communicated with the faction of Ithacius, who were then consecrating a bishop. There can be no doubt that Maximus wished to be regarded as a champion of catholicity, and to use this merit as a political instrument. As early as 385 he seems to have written to pope Siricius, professing his ardent love of the Catholic faith, offering to refer the case of a priest Agricius, whom the pope complained of as wrongly ordained, to ecclesiastical judges anywhere within his dominions. (This letter is only given at length by Baronius, *s.a.* 387, §§ 65, 66; cf. Tillemont, *Les Priscillianistes*, art. 10. The part about Agricius is given by Hänel, *s.a.* 385, from other MSS., thus confirming the genuineness of the letter.) At the beginning of 387 the struggle about the basilicas gave him a pretext for interfering on the Catholic side with the court of Milan, a proceeding which he may have thought would gain him the sympathy of his old opponent St. Ambrose. He wrote a threatening letter to Valentinian II., which we still possess, bidding him desist from the persecution of the church (Soz. vii. 13; Theod. v. 14. This letter is given only by Baronius, *s.a.* 387, §§ 33-36, cf. Tillem. *Saint Ambroise*, art. 48. Its genuineness seems not absolutely certain). Justina, in this emergency, again used the political skill and intrepidity of St. Ambrose, whose loyalty was unshaken and whose disinterestedness was universally recognized. Ambrose went on a second embassy to Maximus, of which he has left us a lively record in his 24th epistle. He set out after that memorable Easter which witnessed the baptism of St. Augustine, and found the emperor at Trèves. His high spirit and sincerity seem to have disappointed Maximus, who found fault with him for acting against his interest, accused count Bauto of turning barbarians upon his territory, and refused to restore the still unburied remains of Gratian; thus clearly shewing that he meant war. Ambrose's refusal to communicate with the Ithacians was the final offence, and the emperor suddenly commanded him to depart (cf. *Ep.* 24, § 3, for his judgment on this party). On his return to Milan Ambrose warned Valentinian to prepare for war, but his wise counsels were disregarded. A second ambassador Domninus was sent, and was entirely deceived by the soft words of Maximus, who persuaded him that Valentinian had no better friend than himself, and cajoled him into taking back into Italy a part of his army, under pretence of serving against the barbarians who were invading Pannonia. Having thus cleverly got his soldiers across the Alps, he followed rapidly in person, and entered Italy as an invader (Zos. iv. 42). Justina and her son and daughters fled to Theodosius at Thessalonica. Maximus was thus left in possession of Italy. The details of the campaign that followed belong to secular history. Theodosius defeated the troops of Maximus at Siscia and Petovio, and seized the emperor himself at Aquileia, where he was put to death, after some form of trial (Zos. iv. 46; Pacatus, 43, 44), on July 25 or August 28, 388, after a reign of rather more than five years. His son Victor, whom he had named Augustus, was put to death shortly after. Andragathius, his able general, who was accused of the murder of Gratian, threw himself into the Adriatic. It is not said what became of Marcellinus, who had been defeated at Petovio.

Legend.—The connexion of Maximus with Britain is obscure, but it has given rise to a considerable aftergrowth of legend. He is called "Rutupinus latro" by Ausonius, perhaps merely because he started from Richborough to invade Gaul. Welsh tradition has incorporated him into its genealogies of saints and royal heroes, under the name of Macsen Wledig, or Guledig, a title considered to be equivalent to imperator. (See H. Rowland's *Mona Antiqua Restaurata*, pp. 166 ff., ed. 2, Lond. 1766, and cf. Skene's *Four Ancient Books of Wales*, vol. i. pp. 45, 48, vol. ii. 405. He is usually called *Macsen*, which rather suggests a confusion with Maxentius, but Skene quotes his Welsh name also as *Maxim*, i. p. 48.) The "dream of Maxen Wledig" in the *Mabinogion* (ed. Guest, vol. iii. pp. 263-294, Lond. 1849) represents him as already emperor of Rome, and brought to Britain by a dream of a royal maiden Helen Luyddawc or Luyddog, daughter of Eudav (= Octavius?) of Caer Segont, or Carnarvon, and then returning after seven years with his brother-in-law Kynan to reconquer his old dominions. Another mythical account describes Kynan as raising an army of sixty thousand men, who afterwards settled in Armorica. The desolation of Britain thus left the country exposed to the attacks of the Picts and Saxons (cf. *Mabinogion, l.c.* pp. 29 ff.; R. Rees, *Essay on Welsh Saints*, pp. 104, 105, Lond. 1836; Nennius, *Hist. Brit.* § 23). A further development of the legend represents St. Ursula and her company of virgins as sent out as wives for these emigrated hosts. The term *Sarn Helen* applied to Roman roads in N. Wales is explained as referring to the wife of Maximus.

It is difficult to say what historical facts may be at the bottom of this. That the withdrawal of Roman troops by Maximus exposed Britain to invasion is an obvious fact, and is already asserted by Gildas (*Historia*, cc. 10, 11). The colonization of Armorica by some of his auxiliaries is also possible enough. On the other hand, the name of Helen *may* merely be borrowed from the mother of Constantine, and *Sarn Helen* may be explained as *Sarn-y-lleng*, "the legion's causeway," just as the story of the cutting out the tongues of the women of Armorica by Kynan's soldiers appears to be only an etymological myth to explain the name Llydaw applied to that country. For further refs., see R. Williams, *Biogr. Dict. of Eminent Welshmen* (Llandovery, 1852), art. "Maxen Wledig." [J.W.]

Maximus (3), Petronius, emperor of the West, A.D. 455; a descendant of the Maximus who usurped the empire in the time of Gratian (Procopius, *Bell. Vand.* i. 4). He was of one of the noblest and wealthiest families of Rome, was three times prefect of Rome and twice consul. To avenge the insult his wife had received from Valentinian III. (see Procopius, *u.s.*), he caused him to be assassinated on

Mar. 16 or 17, 455. Maximus then seized the vacant throne, and compelled Eudoxia, the widow of Valentinian, to marry him a few days after her husband's death, his own wife having died shortly before. He also gave her daughter Eudocia to his son Palladius, whom he created Caesar (Idatius, *Chronicon* in *Patr. Lat.* li. 884). The outraged Eudoxia summoned Genseric king of the Vandals to avenge and deliver her. Genseric sailed with a mighty armament for Rome. Maximus endeavoured to fly, but the people and soldiery, headed by Valentinian's officers, rose against him, stoned him, tore him limb from limb and flung his mangled body into the river, probably on June 12, 455 (*Chronicon Cuspinianum*); thus he reigned rather under 3 months. The chronology is discussed at length by Tillemont in a note (*Emp.* vi. 628). [F.D.]

Maximus (9), bp. of Alexandria, 14th "successor of St. Mark," had been a presbyter under bp. Dionysius. During the Decian persecution, after Dionysius had been carried away by some Christians of Mareotis into Libya, Maximus with three other presbyters "kept themselves concealed in Alexandria, secretly carrying on the oversight of the brethren" (Dionys. to Domitius and Didymus, *ap.* Euseb. vii. 11). It is surprising that their ministrations were undetected by the inquisitorial severity of the local government, which found victims among the virgins of the church (see Eus. vi. 41). Seven years later, when Valerian's persecution began, we find Maximus attending his bishop (who calls him his "fellow-presbyter") to the tribunal of the prefect Aemilianus, as involved with him, and three deacons and a Roman lay Christian, in the charge of contumacious rejection of the gods who had "preserved the emperor's sovereignty," and whose worship was in accordance with "natural" law. He was banished with Dionysius to Cephro in the Libyan frontier, sharing in the rough reception the heathen inhabitants gave to the bishop and assisting him in the preaching which ere long won over "not a few" of them to "the word then sown among them for the first time." After a while the party were removed to Colluthion, much nearer to Alexandria (*ib.* vii. 11). When Dionysius, "worn out with years," died early in 265 (in Mar. according to Le Quien, *Oriens Christ.* ii. 395; Neale says Feb., *Hist. Alex.* i. 39, 83), Maximus was appropriately elected to succeed him. Maximus died on Sun. Apr. 9, 282 (Le Quien, ii. 396) and was succeeded by Theonas. [W.B.]

Maximus (10), bp. of Jerusalem, the 40th in succession from the apostles, succeeded Macarius on his death, A.D. 336. He had been a confessor in one of the persecutions (Theod. *H. E.* ii. 26)—according to Philostorgius (*H. E.* iii. 12) that of Maximian—in which he had lost one eye and had the sinews of one arm and one thigh severed while still serving as a presbyter at Jerusalem. He appears to have had no strength of character, being honest but timid, his simplicity making him the tool of the stronger and more designing. His career is consequently inconsistent. He attended the council of Tyre, A.D. 335, being admitted to a seat, together with Marcellus of Ancyra, Asclepas of Gaza, and others, as among those least committed to the cause of Athanasius, whose presence would give an air of impartiality to its deliberations, whom, also for their close vicinity, it would not have been decent to exclude (De Broglie, *L'Eglise et l'Empire*, ii. 326). The part he took is variously represented. According to Socrates (*H. E.* ii. 8) and Sozomen (*H. E.* iii. 6), he assented to the deposition of Athanasius. Rufinus, however (*H. E.* i. 17), records the dramatic incident that the aged confessor Paphnutius of the Thebaid, whose mutilated form had attracted so much attention at Nicaea, when he saw Maximus vacillating, took him by the hand and led him over to the small band of Athanasius's supporters, saying that it did not become those who bore the tokens of their sufferings for the faith to consort with its adversaries. Sozomen, who here, as elsewhere, is not consistent, records the same incident (*H. E.* ii. 25). We know little of the part taken by Maximus in the Arian troubles between the council of Tyre, A.D. 335, and that of Sardica. But if he had refused complicity when the solemn recognition of Arius was made by the 200 bishops assembled for the dedication of Constantine's church at the council of Jerusalem, it could hardly fail to have been recorded. The silence of all historians throws doubt on Rufinus's statement that Maximus remained always faithful to the cause of Athanasius. He, however, refused to attend the council of the Dedication assembled by the Eusebians at Antioch, A.D. 341, at which the sentence of the council of Tyre against Athanasius, to which he had been an assenting party, was confirmed. On this occasion he had been put on his guard in time; and, conscious of his weakness, discreetly kept away, fearing lest he might, as at Tyre, be carried away (συναρπαγεὶς) against his will and led to acquiesce in measures of which he would afterwards repent (Socr. *H. E.* ii. 8; Soz. *H. E.* iii. 6). At Sardica he was once more on the orthodox side and his name stands first of the Palestinian bishops who signed the synodical letters (Athan. *Apolog. I. ad Const.* p. 768). A little later he warmly welcomed Athanasius when passing through Jerusalem to resume his seat at Alexandria, summoning an assemblage of bishops to do honour to him, by the whole of whom, with two or three exceptions, Athanasius was solemnly received into communion. Congratulatory letters on the recovery of their chief pastor were written to the Egyptian bishops, and Maximus was the first to affix his signature (Socr. *H. E.* ii. 24; Soz. *H. E.* 21, 22; Athan. *Apol. I. ad Const.* p. 775; *Hist. Arian. ad Solit.* § 25; Labbe, *Concil.* ii. 92, 625, 679). Jerome states that Maximus died in possession of his bishopric, A.D. 350 or 351, and that Cyril was appointed to the vacant see. [E.V.]

Maximus (11), the Cynic; the intrusive bp. of Constantinople, A.D. 380. A native of Alexandria of low parentage, he boasted that his family had produced martyrs. He was instructed in the rudiments of the Christian faith and received baptism, but sought to combine the Christian profession with Cynic philosophy. Gregory Nazianzen describes him as having had no regular occupation, but loitering about in the streets, like a shameless dog, foul and greedy (κύων, κυνίσκος, ἀμφόδων ὑπηρέτης). More than once he earned a flogging for his misdeeds and was finally banished to the Oasis. We hear of him next at Corinth, with a high reputation for religion, leading about a band of females—" the swan of the flock "—under colour of devotion (*Carm.* cxlviii. p. 450). Soon after Gregory Nazianzen had begun to reside there, Maximus shifted to Constantinople. Gregory devotes a considerable number of the biting iambics of his poem, *de Vita Sua*, to this man, who, however, before long completely gained his ear and heart. Maximus professed the most unbounded admiration for Gregory's discourses, praising them in private and in public. His zeal against heretics was most fierce and his denunciations of them uncompromising. The simple-hearted Gregory was completely duped by Maximus, even delivering a panegyrical oration, in the man's own presence in full church, before the celebration of the Eucharist, inviting him to stand by his side and receive the crown of victory. Meanwhile, Maximus was secretly maturing a plot for ousting his unsuspicious patron from his throne. He imposed upon Peter of Alexandria, who lent himself to Maximus's projects. Maximus found a ready tool in a presbyter of Constantinople envious of Gregory's talents and popularity (*de Vit.* p. 13). Others were gained by bribes. Seven unscrupulous sailors were dispatched from Alexandria to mix with the people and watch for a favourable opportunity for carrying out the plot. When all was ripe they were followed by a bevy of bishops, with secret instructions from the patriarch to consecrate Maximus. The conspirators chose a night when Gregory was confined by illness, burst into the cathedral, and commenced the consecration. They had set the Cynic on the archiepiscopal throne and had just begun shearing away his long curls when the day dawned. The news quickly spread and everybody rushed to the church. The magistrates appeared with their officers; Maximus and his consecrators were driven from the cathedral, and in the tenement of a flute-player the tonsure was completed. Maximus repaired to Thessalonica to lay his cause before Theodosius. He met with a cold reception from the emperor, who committed the matter to Ascholius, the much respected bp. of that city, charging him to refer it to pope Damasus. We have two letters from Damasus asking for special care that a Catholic bishop may be ordained (Migne, *Patr. Lat.* xiii. pp. 366-369; *Epp.* 5, 5, 6). Maximus returned to Alexandria, and demanded that Peter should assist him in re-establishing himself at Constantinople. Peter appealed to the prefect, by whom Maximus was driven out of Egypt. As the death of Peter and the accession of Timotheus are placed Feb. 14, 380, these events must have occurred in 379. When the second oecumenical council met at Constantinople in 381, Maximus's claim to the see of Constantinople was unanimously rejected, the last of its original four canons decreeing " that he neither was nor is a bishop, nor are they who have been ordained by him in any rank of the clergy " (Labbe, *Concil.* ii. 947, 954, 959).

Maximus appealed from the Eastern to the Western church. In the autumn of 381 a synod held either at Aquileia or at Milan under Ambrose's presidency considered Maximus's claims. Having only his own representations to guide them, and there being no question that Gregory's translation was uncanonical, while the election of Nectarius was open to grave censure as that of an unbaptized layman, Maximus also exhibiting letters from Peter the late venerable patriarch, to confirm his asserted communion with the church of Alexandria, it is not surprising that the Italian bishops pronounced decidedly in favour of Maximus and refused to recognize either Gregory or Nectarius. A letter of Ambrose and his brother-prelates to Theodosius (*Ep.* xiii. c. i. § 3) remonstrates against the acts of Nectarius as no rightful bishop, since the chair of Constantinople belonged to Maximus, whose restoration they demanded, as well as that a general council of Easterns and Westerns, to settle the disputed episcopate and that of Antioch, should be held at Rome. In 382 a provincial synod held at Rome, having received more accurate information, finally rejected Maximus's claims (Hefele, *Hist. of Councils*, i. pp. 359, 378, 381, Eng. trans.). Jerome tells us that Maximus sought to strengthen his cause by writing against the Arians, and presented the work to Gratian at Milan. He appears also to have written against Gregory, the latter replying in a set of caustic iambics (*Carm.* clxviii. p. 250) expressing astonishment at one so ignorant venturing on a literary composition. Theod. *H. E.* v. 8; cf. Soz. *H. E.* vii. 9; Greg. Naz. *Orat.* xxii. xxviii.; *Carm.* 1 *de Vita sua*; *Carm.* cxlviii.; Tillem. *Mém. eccl.* ix. 444-456, 501-503. [E.V.]

Maximus (15), patriarch of Antioch. After the deposition of Domnus II., patriarch of Antioch, by the " Latrocinium " of Ephesus, A.D. 449, Dioscorus persuaded the weak Theodosius to fill the vacancy with one of the clergy of Constantinople. Maximus was selected and ordained, in violation of all canonical orders, by Anatolius bp. of Constantinople, without the official sanction of the clergy or people of Antioch. Maximus, though owing his elevation to an heretical synod, gained a reputation for orthodoxy in the conduct of his diocese and province. He dispatched " epistolae tractoriae " through the churches subject to him as metropolitan, requiring the signatures of the bishops to Leo's famous " tome " and to another document condemning both Nestorius and Eutyches (Leo Magn. *Ep. ad Paschas.* 88 [68], June 451). Having thus discreetly assured his position, he was summoned to the council of Chalcedon in Oct. 451, and took his seat without question, and when the illegal acts of the " Latrocinium" were quashed, including the deposition of the other prelates, a special exception was made of the substitution of Maximus for Domnus on the express ground that Leo had opened communion with him and recognized his episcopate (Labbe, iv. 682). His most important controversy at Chalcedon was with Juvenal of Jerusalem regarding the limits of their respective patriarchates. It was long and bitter; at last a compromise was accepted by the council, that Antioch should retain the two Phoenicias and Arabia and that the three Palestines should form the patriarchate of Jerusalem (*ib.* 614-618). Maximus was among those by whom the Confession of Faith was drawn up (*ib.* 539-562), and stands second, between Anatolius of Constantinople and Juvenal of Jerusalem, in the signatories to the decree according metropolitical rank to Constantinople (*ib.* 798).

The next notice of Maximus is in a correspondence with Leo the Great, to whom he had appealed in defence of the prerogatives of his see. Leo promised to help him against either Jerusalem or Constantinople, exhorting him to assert his privileges as bp. of the third see in Christendom (*i.e.* only inferior to Alexandria and Rome). Maximus's zeal for the orthodox faith receives warm commendation from Leo, who exhorts him as "consors apostolicae sedis" to maintain the doctrine founded by St. Peter "speciali magisterio" in the cities of Antioch and Rome, against the erroneous teaching both of Nestorius and Eutyches, and to watch over the churches of the East generally and send him frequent tidings. The letter, dated June 11, 453, closes with a desire that Maximus will restrain unordained persons, whether monks or simple laics, from public preaching and teaching (Leo Magn. *Ep.* 109 [92]). Two years later, A.D. 455, the episcopate of Maximus came to a disastrous close by his deposition. The nature of his offence is nowhere specified. We do not know how much longer he lived or what became of him. Tillem. *Mém. eccl.* t. xv. *passim*; Le Quien, *Oriens Christianus*, t. ii. p. 725. [E.V.]

Maximus (16), bp. of Turin, writer, reckoned as Maximus II., the third bishop, by Cappelletti (*Le Chiese d'Ital.* xiv. 12, 14, 76), who puts a Maximus I. in 390 as the first bishop Ughelli (*Ital. Sac.* iv. 1022) counts them as one (cf. Boll. *Acta SS.* 25 Jun. v. 48). He was present at the council of Milan in 451 and signed the letter to pope Leo (Leo, *Ep.* 97; Labbe, iv. 583). He was also at the council of Rome in 465, where his name appears next after pope Hilary's, apparently on account of his seniority (Labbe, v. 86). Gennadius of Massilia (d. 496) gives a sketch of his works, most of which are still extant, but strangely says that he died in the reign of Arcadius and Honorius, *i.e.* before 423. This has led some to think that there were two bishops of this name, but the early date given by Gennadius seems irreconcilable with the many allusions to Nestorian doctrines in the homilies on the Nativity, and the general opinion is that he is wrong (Gennad. *de Scrip. Eccl.* c. xl. in *Patr. Lat.* lviii. 1081). The works of Maximus are in vol. lvii. of Migne's *Patrologia Latina*. They consist of 117 homilies, 116 sermons, 3 tractates on baptism, 2 (of very doubtful authority) entitled respectively *contra Paganos* and *contra Judaeos*, and a collection of expositions *de Capitulis Evangeliorum* (also doubtful). Many of the sermons and homilies were formerly ascribed to St. Ambrose, St. Augustine, St. Leo, etc. Several are on the great church festivals.

Points of interest in the homilies and sermons are: the notice of fixed lections (*e.g.* Hom. 36 and 37); abstinence from flesh meat in Lent (Hom. 44); no fasting or kneeling at prayer between Easter and Pentecost (Hom. 61). In Hom. 62, on the other hand, he mentions that the vigil of Pentecost was observed as a fast. This custom therefore probably originated in his time. St. Leo, mentioning the fast of Pentecost, makes it clear that he means the fast immediately following the festival. In Hom. 83 Maximus comments on the creed, which is exactly the same as the Roman creed given by Rufinus. Among contemporary events alluded to may be noticed the synod of Milan in 389, at which Jovinian was condemned (Hom. 9). Seven homilies (86-92) refer to the terror of the city at an impending barbaric invasion, apparently Attila's inroad, 452. Another homily (94) refers to the destruction of the church of Milan on the same occasion. He several times refers to superstitions in his diocese, their observance of the Calends of Jan. (16), their tumults during an eclipse (100), the idolatry still lurking among the lower orders (Serm. 101, 102). There are homilies on the feast of the Nativity of St. John the Baptist, on St. Lawrence, St. Cyprian, St. Agnes, and St. Eusebius of Vercelli, and several on the festival of SS. Peter and Paul which are worth particular attention. In some of these he uses very decided language on the supremacy of St. Peter, *e.g.*, speaking of him as the keystone of the church (Hom. 54), the "magister navis" (Serm. 114); and as entrusted with "totius Ecclesiae gubernacula" (Hom. 70). But in other places he speaks of St. Peter as supreme in discipline, St. Paul in doctrine, and remarks "inter ipsos quis cui praeponatur incertum est" (72). Nowhere does he allude to the church of Rome as inheriting exclusively the supremacy of St. Peter. Gennadius mentions a work of Maximus *de Spiritali Baptismi Gratia*, and three treatises on this subject, formerly ascribed to St. Augustine, are published by Migne with the works of Maximus, on the strength of three ancient MSS., one of which the church of Turin possesses. Nothing in their style is against Migne's conclusion. The first treatise dwells on the significance of the anointing of the ears before baptism; the second gives an interrogatory creed identical with the one mentioned above in the homilies, and alludes to the custom of baptizing on the third day after the profession of faith; the third speaks of the anointing of the head after baptism, by which is conferred the full regal and sacerdotal dignity spoken of by St. Peter, and of the custom of washing the feet at the same time, after the example of Christ. See F. Savio's *Gli Antichi Veseovi d'Italia* (Turin, 1899), p. 283. [M.F.A.]

Maximus (24), an ecclesiastical writer, placed by Eusebius (*H. E.* v. 27) in the reign of Severus and episcopate of Victor, *i.e.* in the last decade of 2nd cent. Eusebius says the subject of his work was the origin of evil and whether matter had been created, and elsewhere (*Praep. Ev.* vii. 22) entitles it, "Concerning Matter" (περὶ τῆς ὕλης), and preserves a long extract, from which it appears to have been in dialogue form. Routh, whose *Reliquiae Sacrae* (ii. 87) is by far the best ed. of the remains of Maximus, pointed out that the same fragment is in the dialogue on free will ascribed to Methodius, and that other things are common to the work on free will and the dialogue of Origen against the Marcionites, so that both authors probably drew from Maximus. That the work is rightly ascribed to Maximus the testimony of Eusebius is decisive; and St. Jerome says in his *Catalogue*, that Methodius wrote on free will, while Photius has preserved large extracts from what he knew as the work of Methodius on free will, which clearly prove that it incorporated much of Maximus. The style, moreover, of the opening of the dialogue on free will resembles Methodius, and differs from that of the part concerning matter. We leave, then, to Methodius the rhetorical introduction to his dialogue, but the context appears clearly to shew that the part which belongs to Maximus begins earlier than the portion quoted by Eusebius and printed by Routh. It must include the statement of the views of the speaker, who maintains matter to have existed from eternity, destitute of qualities, and also the announcement of the presence of the third speaker, who afterwards takes up the controversy, on the hypothesis that matter had been from the first possessed of qualities. In Methodius, the defender of the eternity of matter is apparently represented as a Valentinian, for his speeches are marked Val.; and so also in Adamantius. In Maximus he seems to be no heretic, but a sincere inquirer after truth. He propounds the difficulty concerning the origin of evil; if evil was at any time created, then something came out of nothing, since evil did not exist before; and God Who created it must take pleasure in evil, which we cannot admit. He then offers the solution that, co-eternally with God, there existed matter, destitute of form or qualities, and borne about in a disorderly manner; that God took pity on it, separated the best parts from the worst, reduced the former to order, and left the latter behind as being of no use to Him for His work, and that from these lees of matter evil sprang. The most successful part of the orthodox speaker's reply is where he shews that this hypothesis does not relieve God of the charge of being the author of evil.

Galland conjectures that the author of the dialogue is the Maximus who was 26th bp. of Jerusalem, and whom Eusebius, in his Chronicle, places about the reign of Commodus. It does not absolutely disprove this, that Eusebius, though he twice speaks of the writings of Maximus, does not mention that he was a bishop; probably Eusebius found in the book he used no mention of the author's dignity, and knew no more than we do whether he was the bp. of Jerusalem. But there seems increasing reason to think that Eusebius erroneously attributed to Maximus the work of Methodius: see Zahn in *Zeitschr. für Kirchengesch.* ix. 224-229, and J. A. Robinson, *The Philocalia of Origen* (Camb. 1893), pp. xl.-xlix. [G.S.]

Maximus (25) of Ephesus. A "master of theurgic science," commonly reckoned among the neo-Platonic philosophers, the interest of whose life consists merely in the fact that he supplied an essential link in the transit of the emperor Julian from Christianity to paganism. The account given by Eunapius, in his Life of Maximus, shews exactly how this was. Julian, while still under tutelage and in early youth, with the natural self-will of a vigorous mind, had rebelled in secret against his Christian instructors and betaken himself to Greek philosophy as a liberal and congenial study. This bent was not disallowed by the emperor Constantius, who thought it safe when compared with political ambitions. But philosophy at that era indicated much more than quiet intellectual research. It was a name of power, to which all whose sentiments flowed with a strong current towards the traditionary heathenism had recourse for self-justification; and it was natural that Julian, once he had attached himself to this study, should instinctively seek for more practical advantages from it than the mere increase of theoretical wisdom. Maximus, though flashy and meagre as a philosopher, was better supplied with an ostentatious show of practical power than any of his philosophic rivals. The amiable rhetorician Libanius, the aged sage Aedesius, could please Julian, but evidently were lacking in the force which could move the world. But when Aedesius, compelled by increasing infirmity, resigned Julian to the tuition of his two followers, Chrysanthius and Eusebius, Julian began to be struck with the terms in which these two spoke of their old fellow-pupil Maximus. Chrysanthius, indeed, alone seemed to admire him; Eusebius affected to depreciate him; but this feigned depreciation was calculated to excite the interest of Julian. For what Eusebius spoke of in this slighting manner was a certain miraculous power possessed by Maximus, of which he gave one or two casual instances. Julian had never seen miracles like those with which Maximus was credited; so he bade Eusebius stick to his learning and hurried off to Maximus. That skilful adept, after a solemn preparation of his imperial pupil, in which he was aided by Chrysanthius, described to Julian the revered religious authority of the hierophant of Eleusis, whose sacred rites were among the most famous in Greece, and urged him to go thither. He went, and was imbued with a teaching which combined a mysterious exaltation of the power of the Greek deities with hints of his own personal aggrandizement. By such acts as these, and by his initiation into the Eleusinian mysteries, he passed over to paganism, though his having done so was still unknown to the world. When, Constantius being dead, he became sole master of the Roman empire, he did not forget his instructors. He sent for Chrysanthius and Maximus; they consulted the sacrificial omens; the signs were unfavourable, and dissuaded them from accepting the invitation. Chrysanthius trembled, and refused to go; the more ambitious Maximus declared it unworthy of a wise man to yield to the first adverse sign, and went. He was received by Julian with extraordinary honours, but by his haughtiness and effeminate demeanour earned the censure even of the heathen, among whom was the partial panegyrist Eunapius. After the death of Julian he was severely and even cruelly treated by Valentinian and Valens, and though released for a time, was beheaded by order of

Valens in 371, on a charge of having conspired against him. His personal appearance is described by Eunapius as impressive. The four extant letters of Julian to him (Nos. 15, 16, 38, 39) consist of such indiscriminate panegyric that they tell little of his real character or views. For other authorities see *D. of G. and R. Biogr.* [J.R.M.]

Melania (1), a Roman lady of Spanish extraction, daughter of Marcellinus, who had been consul; born *c.* 350. Her husband died when she was only 22 years old, leaving her with three children, of whom two died immediately after their father. Full of ascetic enthusiasm, she rejoiced to be now more free to serve Christ, left her son to the charge of the urban praetor, and, though winter was beginning, sailed for the East (Hieron. *Ep.* xxxix. 4; *Chron. Ann.* 377, vol. viii. ed. Vall.), *c.* 372. She seems to have been acquainted with Jerome and his friends, who at that time formed an ascetic society at Aquileia. Her slave Hylas accompanied Jerome to Syria (Hieron. *Ep.* iii. 3), and Rufinus, from whom Jerome had then recently separated (*ib.*), was with her in 374 in Egypt, and possibly in Palestine (*ib.* iv. 2). During their stay in Egypt the persecution of the orthodox by Valens arose. Rufinus was imprisoned. Melania, who had only been in Egypt six months, went with a large body of exiled bishops, clergy, and anchorets to a place near Diocaesarea in Palestine, where she supported them at her own expense. Apparently she was joined by Rufinus after a time, and they went together to Jerusalem. There she established herself at the Mount of Olives, where, says Jerome (*Chron.* A.D. 377, properly 375), she was such a wonderful example of virtues, and especially of humility, that she received the name of Thecla. She formed a community of 50 virgins and was the means of reconciling to the church a large body of heretics called Πνευματομάχοι. Her house was open to all. Amongst those who visited her was EVAGRIUS, whom she persuaded to embrace the monastic life (A.D. 388). She knew John bp. of Jerusalem intimately, and no doubt shared with Rufinus in the friendship of Jerome and Paula when they settled at Bethlehem in 386, and afterwards in his contention with them. In 397 she returned with Rufinus to Italy, to confirm her granddaughter Melania the younger (*q.v.*) in the practice of asceticism. She was received by Paulinus at Nola with great honour, and brought him a piece of the true cross set in gold, sent by John bp. of Jerusalem. She took up her abode at Rome, where she no doubt assisted Rufinus through the controversy as to his translation of Origen's works. She lived probably with her son Publicola and his wife Albina and their two children, the younger Publicola, and the younger Melania, with her husband Pinianus. Palladius, when he came to Rome to plead the cause of Chrysostom, stayed with them. She desired to induce her granddaughter Melania and Pinianus to take vows of separation, and was much displeased that, though willing to vow continency, they would not separate from each other's society. In her vehement enthusiasm she spoke of her conflicts with those who resisted her asceticism as "fighting against wild beasts." In 408, Italy being threatened with the invasion of Alaric, and her son Publicola having died, she determined to leave Rome. Rufinus, having quitted Aquileia on the death of his father, went with her and her daughter-in-law Albina, the younger Publicola, Melania and Pinianus. She had been to Africa in 400 with a letter from Paulinus to Augustine (Aug. *Ep.* xiv.), and it was now determined that she should go to Sicily and thence to Africa, in both which countries she had estates. In Sicily Rufinus died. She passed on to Africa with the others; and, after vainly attempting to induce Melania and Pinianus to embrace the monastic state, went on to her former habitation on the Mount of Olives, and 40 days after died, aged 60. Palladius, *Hist. Laus.* c. 118; Paulinus, *Epp.* 29, 31, 45, 94. [W.H.F.]

Melania (2), daughter of Publicola son of MELANIA (1); born at Rome *c.* 383. She married Pinianus when exceedingly young, yielding to the wish of her father, though she was already imbued with the ascetic teachings of her grandmother, then living at Jerusalem. The young husband and wife were induced by Melania the elder in 397 to take a vow of continence, but refused to separate. They accompanied the grandmother from Rome (A.D. 408) to Sicily and Africa; but, when she returned to Jerusalem, they remained at Sagaste, attaching themselves to the bp. Alypius and enjoying the friendship of Augustine. On the death of the elder Melania the still considerable remains of her estates became the property of her granddaughter. She gave away those in Gaul and Italy, but kept those in Sicily, Spain, and Africa; and this led to the attempt of the people of Hippo to induce PINIANUS to become a priest of their church. In the scene in which a promise was exacted from them to remain at Hippo, Melania shewed great courage. When through the rapacity of the rebel count Heraclian she was denuded of her property and thus set free from the promise to remain at Hippo, she accompanied her husband to Egypt, and, after staying among the monastic establishments of the Thebaid and visiting Cyril at Alexandria, eventually went to Palestine, and, together with her mother Albina, settled at Bethlehem in 414. There they attached themselves to Jerome, and to the younger Paula, who then presided over the convent. Their ascetic convictions had so developed that they now accepted that separation which the elder Melania had vainly urged in her lifetime. Pinianus became the head of a monastery and Melania entered a convent. By the settlement of Melania at Bethlehem the feud was extinguished which had separated the followers of Rufinus from those of Jerome; and although in his letter to Ctesiphon (cxxiii. 3, ed. Vall., date 415) Jerome still has a bitter expression about the elder Melania, in his last letter to Augustine (cxliii. 2, ed. Vall.) in 419, Albina, Pinianus, and Melania are joined with Paula in their reverential greetings. Their intercourse with Augustine continued, and in answer to their questions on the Pelagian controversy he wrote his treatise *On Grace and Original Sin*, A.D. 418. Melania apparently lived on for many years. Photius says that she came to Constantinople in 437 and obtained his conversion and baptism at the hands of Proclus. Palladius, *Hist. Laus.* 119, 121; Augustine, *Epp.* 125, 126, and *de Grat. Christi*, ii. and xxxii., Surius, p. 380, Dec. 31; Photius, *Cod.* 53, p. 44. [W.H.F.]

Meletius (2) (*Melitius*), bp. of Lycopolis, consecrated not long before the beginning of the Arian controversy. The see of Lycopolis stood next in rank to that of Alexandria, of which Peter, afterwards martyr, was then bishop (A.D. 300-311). Meletius took advantage of Peter's flight from persecution (Soz. *H. E.* i. 24) to intrude into his and other dioceses, ordain priests, and assume the character of primate of Egypt. A protest against his conduct by four incarcerated Egyptian bishops, Hesychius, Pachomius, Theodore, and Phileas, urged that his act was uncalled-for and carried out without consulting them or Peter, involving a breach of the rule which forbade one bishop to intrude into the diocese of another. Meletius ignored the protest. The bishops were martyred, and Meletius went to Alexandria. He was received by the two elders, Isidore and the afterwards famous Arius; probably at their instigation he excommunicated two visitors appointed by Peter, and replaced them by others. The archbp. of Alexandria then wrote forbidding his flock to have fellowship with Meletius until these acts had been investigated. A synod of Egyptian bishops under Peter deposed Meletius (A.D. 306) for his irregular acts and insubordination. Athanasius and Socrates affirm indeed that the degradation of Meletius was specially due to his having "denied the faith during persecution and sacrificed"; but in this they probably express only the popular belief which could not otherwise explain why orthodox bishops were imprisoned and martyred, while Meletius passed through the length and breadth of the land unhindered. The council of Nicaea in its comments upon, and condemnation of, Meletius, takes no note of impiety; and the statement of Epiphanius—Meletius "was orthodox in his belief, and never dissented from the creed of the church in a single point. He was the author of a schism, but not of alterations of belief"—is probably true of the bishop, if not of his followers. Meletius retorted upon his deposers by separating himself and his followers. Peter preached against the Meletians, and rejected their baptism (Soz. i. xv.); Meletius retaliated by abusing Peter and his immediate successors Achillas and Alexander. At length the whole question was considered by the council of Nicaea. The 2nd, 4th, and 6th canons refer directly or indirectly to the Egyptian schism; and in a synodical epistle addressed by the bishops assembled there "to the holy and great church of the Alexandrians and to the beloved brethren throughout Egypt, Libya, and Pentapolis," the "contumacy of Meletius and of those who had been ordained by him" is dealt with (Socr. i. 9; Theod. i. 9). The line adopted was one of "clemency"; although Meletius is described as "strictly speaking wholly undeserving of favour." He was permitted to remain in his own city and retain a nominal dignity, but was not to ordain or nominate for ordination. The council decreed that those who had received appointments from him should be confirmed by a more legitimate ordination and then admitted to communion and retain their rank and ministry, but were to be counted inferior to those previously ordained and established by Alexander; nor were they to do anything without the concurrence of the bishops of the Catholic and apostolical church under Alexander. Meletius himself was to be an exception; "To him," said the bishops, "we by no means grant the same licence, on account of his former disorderly conduct. If the least authority were accorded to him, he would abuse it by again exciting confusion."

It is doubtful whether Meletius was at the council; but he did not resist its decrees. At Alexander's request he handed in a list of his clerical adherents, including 29 bishops, and in Alexandria itself 4 priests and 3 deacons. Meletius retired to Lycopolis, and during Alexander's lifetime remained quiet; but the appointment of Athanasius to the see of Alexandria was the signal for union of every faction opposed to him, and in the events which followed Meletius took a personal part. The uncompromising sternness of Athanasius was contrasted with the "clemency" of the council and of Alexander; Arian and Meletian, schismatic and heretic banded together against the one man they dreaded, and so pitiless and powerful was their hate that it wrung from him the comment on the pardon accorded to Meletius by the council of Nicaea "Would to God he had never been received!"

Before his death, the date of which is not known, Meletius nominated, contrary to the decree of the Nicene council, his friend John as his successor (Soz. ii. 21), a rank accorded to him and recognized by that council of Tyre (A.D. 335) in which the Eusebians and others deposed Athanasius (*ib.* ii. 25). "In process of time," says Sozomen (ii. 21), "the Meletians were generally called Arians in Egypt." Originally differences in doctrine parted them; but their alliance for attack or defence gradually led the Meletians to adopt Arian doctrines [ARIUS] and side with Arian church politics. The Meletians died out after the 5th cent.; the monks described by Theodoret (i. 9) being among the latest and most eccentric of the sect. "They neglected sound doctrine, and observed certain vain points of discipline, upholding the same infatuated views as the Jews and Samaritans." Consult Walch, *Ketzerhistorie*; Neander, Bright, and the usual church historians. [J.M.F.]

Meletius (3), bp. of Antioch, previously of Sebaste in Armenia (Soz. *H. E.* iv. 28; Theod. *H. E.* ii. 31), or according to Socrates (*H. E.* ii. 44), of Beroea in Syria.

He came to Antioch (A.D. 361) when the see had been vacated through the disorderly translation of Eudoxius to Constantinople (A.D. 360) and the city was still a focus for theological rancour and dispute. The Eustathians, now under the venerated priest Paulinus, represented the orthodox party with whom Athanasius was in communion; the Eudoxians were Arian or semi-Arian. Meletius owed his appointment to the joint application to Constantius of both parties, and each counted on his support. His arrival was greeted by an immense concourse. It was reported that he maintained the doctrines of the council of Nicaea. He was entreated to give a brief synopsis of his doctrine; and his declaration "the Son is of the same substance as the Father," at once and unequivocally proclaimed him an upholder of the essential doctrine of Nicaea. The applause of the Catholics was met by the cries of the infuriated Arians. The Arian archdeacon sprang forward and stopped the bishop's mouth with his hand. Meletius instantly extended three fingers towards the people, closed them, and then allowing only one to remain extended, expressed by signs what he was prevented from uttering. When the archdeacon freed his mouth to seize his hand, Meletius exclaimed, "Three Persons are conceived in the mind, but we speak as if addressing One" (Theod. and Soz.). Eudoxius, Acacius, and their partisans were furious; they reviled the bishop and charged him with Sabellianism; met in council and deposed him; and induced the emperor, "more changeable than Aeolus," to banish him to his native country and to appoint Euzoïus, the friend of Arius, in his place. The Catholics repudiated Euzoïus, but did not all support Meletius. The Eustathian section could not conscientiously unite with one who, however orthodox in faith, had received consecration from Arian bishops; neither would they communicate with his followers who had received Arian baptism. Schism followed. The Meletians withdrew to the Church of the Apostles in the old part of the city; the followers of Paulinus met in a small church within the city, this being allowed by Euzoïus out of respect for Paulinus.

The death of Constantius (Nov. 361) and the decrees of toleration promulgated by Julian permitted the banished bishops to return. An effort was at once made, especially by Athanasius and Eusebius bp. of Vercelli, to establish unity in order to resist the pagan emperor; and this was one of the principal objects of a council held at Alexandria in 362 (Hefele, *Conciliengeschichte*, i. 727), where it was ordered that Paulinus and his followers should unite with Meletius, and that the church, thus united, should in the spirit of fullest toleration receive all who accepted the Nicene creed and rejected the errors of Arianism, Sabellianism, Macedonianism, etc. Eusebius of Vercelli and Asterius of Petra were commissioned to proceed to Antioch, taking with them the synodal letter (*Tomus ad Antiochenos*), which was probably the work of Athanasius. The prospects of peace had, however, been fatally imperilled before the commissioners reached the city. Lucifer, bp. of Calaris, had gone direct to Antioch instead of to the council of Alexandria. He appears to have repeatedly exhorted both Meletians and Eustathians to unity; but his sympathies were strongly with the latter; and, when the former opposed him, he took the injudicious step of consecrating Paulinus as bishop. "This was not right," Theodoret justly protests (iii. 5). When Eusebius reached Antioch, he found that "the evil had, by such unwise measures, been made incurable." The long connexion of Athanasius with the Eustathians made him unwilling to disown Paulinus, who accepted the synodal letter; and attempts at union were suspended.

During the short reign of Julian Meletius remained at his post. Jovian's death (A.D. 364) and the edict of Valens re-expelling the bishops recalled by Julian once more drove Meletius into exile. Two devoted Antiochians, Flavian and Diodorus, rallied the persecuted who refused to communicate with the Arian Euzoïus and assembled them in caverns by the river side and in the open country. Paulinus, "on account of his eminent piety" (Socr. iv. 2), was left unmolested. During the 14 years which followed, bitterness and alienation were rife amongst the followers of Meletius and Paulinus. Basil (*Ep.* 89) recommended Meletius to write to Athanasius, who, however, would not sever the old ties between himself and the Eustathians. The death of Athanasius (A.D. 373) did not improve matters. His successor Peter, with Damasus of Rome, spoke in 377 of Eusebius and Meletius as Arians (Basil, *Ep.* 266). The Western bishops and Paulinus suspected Meletius and the Easterns of Arianism; the Easterns imputed Sabellianism to the Westerns.

Gratian, becoming sovereign of the whole empire in 378, at once proclaimed toleration to all sects, with a few exceptions (Socr. v. 2), amongst which must have been the Arians of Antioch (Theod. v. 2). Sapor, a military chief, went there to dispossess the partisans of Euzoïus and to give the Arian churches to the orthodox party. He pacified the Meletians by handing the churches over to them, and the animosity of the two parties was for the time allayed by the six principal presbyters binding themselves by oath to use no effort to secure consecration for themselves when either Paulinus or Meletius should die, but to permit the survivor to retain the see undisturbed.

In 379 a council at Antioch under Meletius accepted the synodal letter of Damasus (A.D. 378), which, known as "the Tome of the Westerns," was sent in the first instance to Paulinus; and two years later (381) Meletius—though disowned by Rome and Alexandria—was appointed to preside at the council of Constantinople. He was greeted by the emperor Theodosius with the warmest affection (*ib.* v. 6, 7). During the session of the council, Meletius died. His remains finally rested by those of Babylas the Martyr at Antioch.

The schism ought now to have ended. Paulinus was still alive, and should have been recognized as sole bishop. The Meletian party, however, irritated by his treatment of their leader, secured the appointment of FLAVIAN; and a fresh division arose, "grounded simply on a preference of bishops" (Socr. v. 269). The history of the Meletians now merges into that of the Flavianists. The schism was practically ended in Flavian's lifetime, 85 years after the ordination of Paulinus by Lucifer. [J.M.F.]

Melito, bp. of Sardis, held in the middle of the 2nd cent. a foremost place among the bishops of Asia as regards personal influence and literary activity. Shortly before the end of that cent. his name is mentioned by Polycrates of Ephesus in his letter to Victor of Rome (Eus. *H. E.* v. 24) as one of the luminaries of the Asiatic church by whose authority its Quartodeciman practice had been commended. The next extant mention of him some 20 years later is in the *Little Labyrinth* (Eus. v. 28). He is there appealed to as one of the writers, older than Victor of Rome, who had spoken of our Lord as being God as well as man. A reference to him in a lost work of Tertullian, known to us through a citation by Jerome in the art. *s.v.* in his Catalogue (c. 24), shews his high reputation in Tertullian's time. Our fullest information is from the notices in Eusebius (*H. E.* iv. 13, 26), who gives a list of Melito's works with which he was acquainted, together with 3 extracts.

His *Apology* presented to the emperor Marcus Aurelius may have been his latest work. It is placed under A.D. 170 in Jerome's translation of the Chronicle of Eusebius, but the date may be more safely inferred from a passage preserved by Eusebius. Melito, addressing Marcus Aurelius, and speaking of Augustus, says, "Of whom you have become the much-wished-for successor, and shall be so with your son if you keep that philosophy which took its beginning with Augustus," etc. That he here says "with your son," not "with your brother," is evidence that the date is later than the death of Lucius Verus, in 169. Commodus was associated in the empire with his father in 176. The passage quoted does not shew whether this association had already taken place or was only anticipated. In 177 persecutions of Christians were raging violently all over the empire. Melito's memorial seems to have been written at the very first beginning of that persecution. The Christians seem to be suffering more in their property than in their persons, and Melito is able to express a doubt whether the emperor had sanctioned the cruelties, and a belief that, when he had examined the case, he would interfere in their favour. Melito declares that Nero and Domitian were the only emperors who had sanctioned persecutions of Christians, and probably from this passage Tertullian derived his argument that only bad emperors had persecuted the Christians. On the other side, as forbidding interference, Melito quotes the letter of Hadrian to Fundanus, and letters of Antoninus, at a time when Aurelius himself was associated in the government, to the people of Larissa, of Thessalonica, and of Athens. One extract from the Apology preserved in the *Paschal Chronicle* (p. 483, Dindorf) gave rise to some discussion in the early Socinian controversy. "We are not worshippers of senseless stones, but adore one only God, Who is before all and over all, and [over] His Christ truly God the Word before all ages." The second "over" given in Rader's ed. of the Chronicle does not appear in the latest ed. (Dindorf's).

An Apology is extant in a Syriac trans. in one of the Nitrian MSS. in the Brit. Mus., which bears the heading, "The oration of Melito the Philosopher held before Antoninus Caesar, and he spoke to Caesar that he might know God, and he shewed him the way of truth, and began to speak as follows." Probably the Syriac translator, finding in his Greek original that the Apology was "addressed" to the emperor, made a blunder in supposing it delivered *viva voce*. It was printed in Syriac, with English trans. by Cureton (*Spicileg. Syr.*) and by Pitra, with a Latin trans. by Renan (*Spicil. Solesm.* vol. ii.) which has been revised in Otto's *Apologists*, vol. ix. Although this Syriac Apology appears complete, it contains none of the passages cited by Eusebius, and its character seems entirely different from that of the work known to Eusebius. The latter was mainly intended to induce the emperor to stop the persecution by shewing that the Christians did not deserve the treatment inflicted. The Syriac Apology is a calm argument against the absurdities of polytheism and idolatry, such as might have been written with the hope of making a convert of the emperor, but does not exhibit any of the mental tension of one suffering under unjust persecution. The Syriac Apology is, therefore, probably not the same as that from which Eusebius made extracts. Did, then, Melito write two apologies? The *Paschal Chronicle* records an Apology of Melito under both A.D. 164 and 169, but this is clearly only a double mention of one Apology, probably caused by the double mention in Eus. iv. 13, 26. The ascription of the Syriac Apology to Melito is probably an error, though the document is perhaps not much later. There are slight, but we think decisive, traces of the use of Justin Martyr's Apology: it must therefore be later than that. It is addressed to an emperor Antoninus, who might have been Pius, Aurelius, Caracalla, or Elagabalus. Probably one of the latter two is intended. The writer's point of view seems to be Syrian. In enumerating heathen idolatries he omits (as we should not expect from Melito writing in Asia Minor) Cybele and the Ephesian Diana; while he speaks in much detail of Syrian objects of worship, and seems to be personally acquainted with the city of Mabug, the Syrian Hierapolis. The admonition, "If they wish to dress you in a female garment, remember that you are a man," suggests Elagabalus rather than any of the other emperors mentioned. One other passage supports a presumption of Syrian authorship. The writer speaks of the world as destined to suffer from three deluges—one of wind, one of water, one of fire; the first two already past, the third still to come. The deluge of wind is that by which the tower of Babel was supposed to have been destroyed (see the Sibylline verses quoted by Theophilus, *ad Autol.* ii. 31, and also Abydenus, quoted by Eus. *Praep. Evan.* ix. 14). "Flood of wind" occurs in the work called *The Cave of Treasures* (Cureton, *Spicil. Syr.* p. 94), and in the Ethiopic book of Adam (Ewald's *Jahrbücher der Bibl. Wiss.* 1853). It has been contended that the reference to the deluge of fire shews acquaintance with II. Peter; but it seems to us that this can by no means be positively asserted. On N.T. allusions in this Apology see Westcott (*N. T. Canon*, p. 219). Against placing it so late as Elagabalus it may be urged that its conclusion, if interpreted naturally, speaks of the emperor as having children; and though the apologist might be merely expressing a wish on behalf of the emperor's unborn successors, it is simpler to refer the work to the time of Caracalla, who spent some time in Syria. There seem also traces that Tertullian, who was acquainted with the Eusebian Apology of Melito, also used this one. Such perhaps may be the identification of Serapis with Joseph and the remark that the old heathen gods were practically less honoured than the emperors, since their temples had to pay taxes.

Of other works of Melito the περὶ τοῦ πάσχα is first in the list of Eusebius. The date is limited by the opening sentence which Eusebius quotes: "In the proconsulate over Asia of Servilius Paulus, at the time that Sagaris suffered martyrdom, there took place much dispute at Laodicea about the Paschal celebration ἐμπεσόντος κατὰ καιρὸν in those days, and these things were written." Rufinus here reads "Sergius Paulus," and this appears from other authorities to have been the real name of the proconsul in question, probably within the limits 164-166.

The appeal of Polycrates to the authority of Melito makes it clear that the latter, in his work on Easter celebration, took the Quartodeciman side. Eusebius says that the work of Melito drew forth another, no doubt on the opposite side, from Clement of Alexandria. It has been conjectured that Melito was the Ionian whom Clement (Eus. *H. E.* v. 11) enumerates as among his teachers. It should be noticed that the extant fragments of Melito refute the notion that Quartodecimanism was inconsistent with the reception of the Fourth Gospel. Melito speaks of our Lord's three years' ministry after His baptism, which he could not have learned from the Synoptists. He accounts for the fact that a ram, not a lamb, was substituted as a sacrifice for Isaac, by the remark that our Lord, when He suffered, was not young like Isaac, but of mature years. Possibly here may be an indication that Melito held the same theory concerning our Lord's age as Irenaeus and other Asiatics, derived no doubt from John viii. 57. The whole passage shews that Melito believed strongly in the atoning efficacy of Christ's death, and looked on Him as the sacrificial lamb. The word he uses is ἀμνός, as in the Gospel, not ἀρνίον, as in the Apocalypse.

The next work of Melito from which Eusebius has given an extract is called *Selections*, addressed to a friend named Onesimus, who had asked Melito to make selections from the law and the prophets of passages concerning our Saviour, and concerning all our faith, and also to give him accurate information as to the number and order of the O.T. books. Melito relates that he had gone up to the East to the place where the things were preached and done, and had accurately learned the books of the O.T. He enumerates the five books of Moses, Joshua, Judges, Ruth, four of Kings, two of Chronicles, Psalms of David, Proverbs of Solomon, also called Wisdom, Ecclesiastes, Song of Songs, Job; of the Prophets, Isaiah, Jeremiah, the twelve Minor Prophets in one book, Daniel, Ezekiel, Esdras. The last, no doubt, includes Nehemiah and possibly Esther, which is otherwise omitted. This list gives the Hebrew canon adopted by the Church of England; but gives a different order of the books from that of Josephus, and does not attempt to make the number of books 22. The expressions "the Old Books," "the Books of the O.T.," shew clearly that the church of Melito's time had a *New* Testament canon.

Eusebius enumerates other works of Melito as being known to him. The titles enable us imperfectly to guess at their contents, and sometimes the titles themselves are uncertain. (4) τὰ περὶ πολιτείας καὶ προφητῶν, very likely two separate works "on Christian Conversation" and "on the Prophets" coupled together by Eusebius, because contained in the same volume in the Caesarean Library. (5) περὶ ἐκκλησίας. It has been conjectured that the breaking out of Montanism may have made it necessary to insist on the authority of the church. (6) περὶ κυριακῆς. Possibly the Quartodeciman controversy led to discussion about the Lord's Day. This word κυριακή, used in Rev. i. 10, is found also in Ignatius's Ep. to the Magnesians, c. 9, and in the letter of Dionysius of Corinth to Soter (Eus. iv. 33). (7) περὶ φύσεως ἀνθρώπου. (8) περὶ πλάσεως. This book on the formation of man, and (7) on the nature of man, if that be the reading, are conjectured to have been directed against Gnostic theories. (9) περὶ ὑπακοῆς πίστεως αἰσθητηρίων. What was the subject of a treatise on the obedience of faith of the senses has perplexed ancient as well as modern readers of this list. Jerome thinks that a περὶ may have dropped out of the text, and that there were two treatises, one on the Obedience of Faith, one on the Senses. (10) περὶ ψυχῆς καὶ σώματος καὶ νοός, probably on Human Nature. (11) περὶ λουτροῦ. (12) περὶ ἀληθείας, perhaps an apologetic work in commendation of Christianity. (13) περὶ κτίσεως καὶ γενέσεως Χριστοῦ. Ancient writers with one consent apply to our Lord the Κύριος ἔκτισέ με ἀρχὴν ὁδῶν αὐτοῦ of Prov. viii. 22. For a full discussion of this verse see Athan. *Or. Cont. Ar.* ii. 44. (14) περὶ προφητείας. A work with the same title written, or intended to be written, by Clement of Alexandria, was directed against the Montanists (*Strom.* iv. 13, p. 605), and this may also have been the design of this work of Melito, if the Montanist controversy had broken out before his death. (15) περὶ φιλοξενίας. (16) ἡ κλείς. What was the nature of this work we have no information. A Latin work entitled *Melitonis Clavis Sanctae Scripturae* mentioned by Labbe in 1653 as preserved in the library of the Clermont College is a medieval Latin composition. (17) (18) τὰ περὶ τοῦ διαβόλου καὶ τῆς ἀποκαλύψεως Ἰωάννου. The form of expression would indicate that both subjects were discussed in a single treatise. (19) περὶ ἐνσωμάτου θεοῦ. It would be natural to translate this, On God Incarnate, and we have other evidence that Melito wrote on the Incarnation. When he speaks of the two natures which our Lord combined, there is no trace of anthropomorphism in the attributes which he ascribes to the Divine nature. On the other hand Origen, commenting on Gen. i. 26 (vol. viii. 49, Lomm.) and arguing against the Anthropomorphites, says "of whom is Melito, who has left a certain treatise, περὶ τοῦ ἐνσώματον εἶναι τὸν θεόν." Probably Origen made a mistake, and that the subject of Melito's treatise was the Incarnation. But it is not impossible that a writer as orthodox as Melito may have held the opinions which Origen imputes to him.

The list given shews Melito's great activity as a writer, and the wide range of his writings.

Of spurious writings ascribed to Melito, we need only mention a commentary on the Apocalypse, the ascription to Melito apparently having been made by the fraud or ignorance of some transcriber, and not intended in the work itself, which is a compilation from various writers, some as late as the 13th cent. Through two works, *de Passione S. Joannis* and *de Transitu b. Mariae*, with which Melito's name was connected, it became widely known in the West, though with various disguises of form, such as Mileto, Miletus, and Mellitus, the last being the most common.

The remains of Melito are given by Routh (*Rel. Sac.* i. 113-153), and more fully by Otto (*Corp. Apol. Chr.* ix. 375-478). See also Piper (*Stud. und Krit.* 1838, p. 54), Westcott (*N. T. Canon*, p. 218), Lightfoot (*Contemp. Rev.* Feb. 1876). Cf. esp. Harnack, *Die Überlieferung der Apologeten* (*Text. und Untersuch.* I. 240), and *Gesch. der Alt. Chr.* lib. i. 246 ff. [G.S.]

Mellitus, the first bp. of London and third archbp. of Canterbury. He was not one of the original missionaries who accompanied Augustine to Britain, but was sent by St. Gregory in 601 to strengthen the hands of the newly consecrated archbishop and to convey to him the pall. Mellitus, accompanied by Laurentius, whom Augustine had sent to Rome, and by Justus, Paulinus, and Rufinianus, left Rome *c.* July 22, 601. They carried letters of commendation to the bps. of Vienne, Arles, Lyons, Gap, Toulon, Marseilles, Châlons on the Saône, Metz, Paris, Rouen, and Angers; to Theodoric, Theodebert, and Clothair, kings of the Franks, and also to queen Brunichild. These names probably indicate the route of the missionaries, and there is no evidence to support Ussher's conjecture that they visited Columbanus at Luxeuil on the way. To Augustine Mellitus brought also the answers which Gregory sent to the questions laid before him by Laurentius, and a supply of church furniture, "all things which were needed for worship and the ministry of the church, sacred vessels, altar-cloths, church ornaments, priestly and clerical robes, relics of saints and martyrs, and several books" (Bede, *H. E.* i. 29). Some account of the remains of St. Gregory's benefaction, preserved at Canterbury in the 15th cent., is given by Elmham (ed. Hardwick, pp. 96 seq.). Augustine, having received from the pope authority to consecrate bishops for the newly converted nation, chose Mellitus for the see of London. That city, properly the capital of the East Saxons, was then under Ethelbert, king of Kent, who had prevailed on the dependent kings of the East Saxons to receive Christianity, and who now founded the church of St. Paul as the cathedral of the new bishopric. No distinct date is given by Bede for the consecration of Mellitus, but it must have occurred some time between the winter of 601 and the early summer of 604, the most probable date for the death of Augustine.

Mellitus continued undisturbed in his see during the reign of Ethelbert. He joined in the letter addressed by Laurentius to the Irish bishops (Bede, *H. E.* ii. 4), and in 609 went to Rome to treat with pope Boniface IV. on matters necessary for the welfare of the English church. The precise object of this journey is not mentioned by the historian, who, however, tells us that Mellitus was present at a council on Feb. 27, 610, subscribed to the decrees, and subsequently carried them to the English church. The purpose of this council was to secure the peace of the monastic order and two versions of a decree are extant (Labbe, *Conc.* v. 619; Mansi, *Conc.* x. 504; Haddan and Stubbs, iii. 64, 65). Bede adds that Mellitus also brought letters from the pope to Ethelbert, Laurentius, and the whole clergy and people of the English (W. Malmesb. *G. P.* lib. i.; Haddan and Stubbs, iii. 65). The monks of St. Augustine's also shewed a bull of Boniface IV., dated Feb. 27, 611, addressed to Ethelbert, mentioning the request presented by Mellitus, and confirming the privileges of St. Augustine's (Elmham, *u.s.* pp. 129-131; Thorn, *ap.* Twysden, c. 1766; Haddan and Stubbs, iii. 67-69).

On the death of Ethelbert the newly-founded church was in danger of dissolution. Mellitus and Justus fled to Gaul, and Laurentius was only saved by a miracle from the disgrace of following them. Bede tells very circumstantially the story of Mellitus's flight. The sons of the Christian king Sebert had continued to be pagans. Seeing the bishop celebrate the holy communion and give the Eucharist to the people, they presumptuously asked, "Why do you not give us the white bread which you used to give to Saba our father and still give to the people?" The bishop replied that if they would be baptized they should have the bread. They refused the sacrament of initiation, but still demanded the bread. On Mellitus's persistence in refusing it, they banished him. He fled to Kent and afterwards to Gaul, whence he was recalled by Laurentius after the conversion of Eadbald. He probably remained at Canterbury until the death of Laurentius in 619, when he succeeded to the vacant see, which he held till 624. That his activity was impaired by gout is nearly all that is preserved about him. Bede mentions that he consecrated a church to the Blessed Virgin within the precincts of St. Augustine's monastery, and that, a great fire at Canterbury occurring in a place termed the "martyrdom of the four crowned martyrs," he was carried there and at his prayer a wind drove the flames southwards and saved the city (*H. E.* ii. 16, 17). [S.]

Menander, a Samaritan false teacher in the early part of the 2nd cent. Our knowledge of him is probably all derived, either directly or indirectly, from Justin Martyr. What he tells directly (*Apol.* i. 26, 56) is, that Menander was a native of the Samaritan town Capparatea, and a disciple of Simon, and, like him, had been instigated by the demons to deceive many by his magic arts; that he had had success of this kind at Antioch, where he had taught, and had persuaded his followers that they should not die; and that, when Justin wrote, some of them survived, holding this persuasion. Justin wrote a special treatise against heresies, and from this, in all probability, was derived the somewhat fuller account given by Irenaeus (i. 23, p. 100). According to this, Menander did not, like Simon, declare himself to be the chief power, but taught that that power was unknown to all. He gave the same account as Simon of the creation of the world—viz. that "it had been made by angels" who had taken their origin from the Ennoea of the supreme power. He put himself forward as having been sent by the invisible powers to mankind as a Saviour, enabling men, by the magical power which he taught them, to get the better of these creative angels. He taught that through baptism in his own name his disciples received a resurrection, and should thenceforward abide in immortal youth. Irenaeus evidently understood this language literally, and the history of heretical sects shews that it is not incredible that such promises may have been made; but the continuance of a belief which the experience of the past must have disproved indicates that a spiritual interpretation must have been found. Cyril of Jerusalem (C. I. 18) treats the denial of a literal resurrection of the body as a specially Samaritan heresy.

Irenaeus (iii. 4, p. 179), having spoken of Valentinus and Marcion, says that the other Gnostics, as had been shewn, took their beginnings from Menander, the disciple of Simon; and there is every probability that it was from the "Samaritan" Justin that Irenaeus learned his pedigree of Gnosticism, viz. that it originated with the Samaritan Simon, and was continued by his disciple Menander, who taught at Antioch, and that there Saturninus (and, apparently, Basilides) learned from him.

The name Menandrianists occurs in the list of Hegesippus (Eus. *H. E.* iv. 22). Tertullian evidently knows only what he has learned from Irenaeus (*de Anim.* 23, 50; *de Res. Carn.* 5). The same may be said of all later writers, and it is scarcely worth while to mention the imaginary condemnation of these heretics by Lucius of Rome, invented by "Praedestinatus." [G.S.]

Mennas, patriarch of Constantinople, 536-552. On the deposition of ANTHIMUS, Mennas, superior of the great convent of St. Samson at Constantinople, was elected to the see. Pope Agapetus was then at Constantinople, having presided at the council there which dealt with the case of Anthimus, and himself consecrated Mennas. Mennas accepted the council of Chalcedon; he was a Catholic, well known for his knowledge and integrity. On May 2, 536, he presided at a council assembled by Justinian at Constantinople at the request of 11 bishops of the East and of Palestine, and of 33 other ecclesiastics, to finish the case of Anthimus, and to decide those of Severus of Antioch, Peter of Apamea, and the Eutychian monk Zoara. The request had been made to pope Agapetus, who had died on Apr. 22, before the council could be held. The result of the council was that, Anthimus having been sought for in vain, he was forbidden to resume his episcopate of Trapezus and deposed from his rank; the others were anathematized. Mennas obtained from Justinian the passing of a law, dated Aug. 6, 536, confirming the Acts of this council. He also sent them to Peter of Jerusalem, who held a council to receive them. On Sept. 13, 540, pope Vigilius wrote to Mennas and to the emperor Justinian, by the hands of Dominicus the patrician. He endeavoured to carry on the influence which Agapetus had over the affairs of the church of Constantinople. He confirmed the anathemas pronounced by Mennas against Severus of Antioch, Peter of Apamea, Anthimus, and other schismatics, offering communion again to all who should come to a better mind. Mennas died on Aug. 5, 552, just before the second great council of Constantinople, called the fifth general. It was in the midst of the angry discussions about the "Three Chapters." Mennas had signed the declaration of faith addressed to pope Vigilius by Theodore of Corsaria and others to satisfy his protests and to preserve the peace of the church.

In the controversies which gave rise to the Lateran council in 649, a Monothelite writing was brought forward by Sergius patriarch of Constantinople as a genuine work of Mennas, supposed to be addressed to pope Vigilius. But in the third council of Constantinople, Nov. 10, 680, this document was proved to be the composition of the monk George, who confessed himself its author.

Mansi, viii. 869, 870, 960, ix. 157, etc., x. 863, 971, 1003, xi. 226, etc.; Liberatus, *Brev.* xxi. in *Patr. Lat.* lxviii. 1039 (see also the dissertations at the end of that volume); Vigil. Pap. *Ep.* in *Patr. Lat.* lxix. 21, 25; Agapet. Pap. *Ep.* in *Patr. Lat.* xlviii.; Evagr. iv. 36 in *Patr. Gk.* lxxxvi. pt. 2, 416, etc.; Ceillier, xi. 121, 194, 968, xii. 922, 947, 953. [W.M.S.]

Merlinus. The prophecies of Merlin, which had great influence in the middle ages, represented the enduring hate of the Welsh for the English conquerors, and were probably the composition of Merddin, son of Morvryn, whose patron, Gwenddolew, a prince in Strathclyde, and an upholder of the ancient faith, perished A.D. 577 at the battle of Arderydd, fighting against Rhydderch Hael, who had been converted by St. Columba to Christianity. When the northern Kymry were driven into Wales, Cornwall, and Brittany, they re-localized the story of Merlin in their new abodes. Merddin is now represented as a Christian, and said to be buried in Bardsey, the island of the Welsh saints; but much of his career is passed in Cornwall, which was long under the same dynasty as South Wales, even after the English got possession of the coast at Bristol, and broke the connexion by land between the two districts. As the mass of tradition grew into the shape in which we find it in Nennius, and later on in Geoffrey, Merlin becomes a wholly mythical character, the prophet of his race. It is not till Geoffrey of Monmouth that we find the boy called Merlin and made the confidant of Utherpendragon and of Arthur, and able to bring the stones of Stonehenge from Ireland. Nennius does not mention Merlin among the early bards, and the poems attributed to him were really composed in the 12th cent., when there was a great outburst of Welsh poetry (Stephens, *Literature of the Kymry*, § 4). Among these poems there is a dialogue between Merddin and his sister Gwenddydd ("The Dawn"), which contains prophecies as to a series of Welsh rulers. The story of Merlin made an impression abroad as well as in England. Layamon alludes to several of his prophecies and they soon gained popular fame. A *Vita Merlini* in Latin hexameters, also attributed, though wrongly, to Geoffrey of Monmouth, was printed by the Roxburghe Club, 1830; the later English forms of the story by the Early English Text Society. The one fact embodied in the legend is the long-continued enmity of the Kymry to the English invaders; but even this almost disappeared when the story became part of the great romance of Arthur. [C.W.B.]

Mesrobes, one of the most celebrated patriarchs and historians of Armenia, born in 354 at the town of Hasecasus, now Mush (Tozer's *Turkish Armenia*, p. 286) and educated under Nerses Magnus, the fourth patriarch of Armenia from St. Gregory the Illuminator, to whom also Mesrobes acted as secretary, an office which he likewise filled in the court of king Varaztad till dethroned by the Romans A.D. 386 (Langlois, *Fragm. Hist. Graec.* t. v. pt. ii. pp. 297-300). He then took holy orders and sought a solitary life. He became coadjutor to the patriarch Sahag in 390, when he devoted himself to the extirpation of the remains of idolatry still existing in Armenia. Under him a great revival of Armenian literature took place. From the introduction of Christianity Syriac had become the dominant language, a knowledge of it being deemed a necessary qualification for holy orders (cf. Agathang. *Hist. Tiribat.*; Zenob. *Hist. Daron.* in Langlois, *l.c.* pp. 179, 335, *Disc. Prelim.* p. xiv.; Goriun, *Hist. de S. Mesrop*; Vartan, *Hist. d'Arménie*, p. 51, Venice, 1862). Mesrobes devoted himself to revive the ancient Armenian culture, some fragments of which can yet be traced in Moses Chorenensis. He was an accomplished Greek, Persian, and Syriac scholar, but wished to revive a national literature. His first step was to restore, if not to invent, an alphabet for the Armenian tongue instead of depending on the Syriac character. He induced the patriarch Sahag, alias Isaac, to convoke a national council at the city of Vagharschabad to consider the question, at which the king Vram-Schapouh assisted. Learning that a Syrian bishop, one Daniel, possessed an ancient Armenian alphabet, Mesrobes sent a priest named Abel to him, who brought it back. It is supposed to have consisted of 22 or 27 letters. With this as a basis and with the help of various persons who possessed some traditionary knowledge of ancient Armenian, as Plato chief librarian at Edessa and two learned rhetoricians, Epiphanius and Rufinus, he composed the alphabet which the Armenians adopted in 406, the seven vowels having been made known, it was said, by direct revelation from heaven (cf. Langl. *l.c. Disc. prélim.* p. xv.; Moses Choren. *Hist. Armén.* lib. iii. cc. 52, 53, and for minute details of the whole question, Karékin, *Hist. de la litt. Armén.* pp. 8 seq. Venice, 1865; *Jour. Asiat.* 1867, t. I, p. 200). Mesrobes attracted great numbers to his schools and sent the ablest pupils to study at Edessa, Athens, Constantinople, Alexandria, Antioch, and even Rome, whence they brought back the most authentic copies of the Scriptures, the Fathers, Acts of the councils, and the profane writers. These young scholars endeavoured to adapt the Armenian tongue to the rules of Greek grammar, translating into Armenian the grammar of Dionysius the Thracian, an ed. of which with a French trans. was pub. at Paris in 1830. This Hellenizing movement among them in cent. 5 was analogous to similar ones in cents. 6, 7, 8, among the Persians and Monophysites, and in cent. 9 among the Arabs, movements to which we owe the preservation of some of the most precious monuments of antiquity, as Tatian's long-lost *Diatessaron*, pub. at Venice out of the Armenian in 1875, cf. *Qtly. Rev.* Apr. 1881, art. on the "Speaker's Commentary on N.T." (cf. Renan, *Hist. des lang. sémit.* p. 297). Among the disciples of Mesrobes were all the leading writers of Armenia, including Leontius presb. and mart., Moses Taronensis, Kioud of Arabeza, afterwards patriarch, Mamprus lector, Jonathan, Khatchig, Joseph of Baghin, Eznig, Knith bp. of Terchan, Jeremiah, Johannes of Egegheats, Moses Chorenensis, Lazarus of Barb, Gorium biographer of Mesrobes, Elisaeus (Langl. *l.c.*; Neumann's pref. to *Hist. of Vartan* in Public. of Orient. Trans. Fund, London, 1830). The Armenian church through their labours possessed a vernacular edition of the Bible in 410. Mesrobes also invented an alphabet for Georgia similar to the Armenian but containing 28 letters. Both alphabets had the letters arranged after the Greek order. The Armenians attribute to him the settlement of their liturgy. Sahag died Sept. 9, 440, and was succeeded as bishop by Mesrobes, until he died on Feb. 19, 441. The Life of Mesrobes by Goriun, pub. by the Mekhitarite Fathers at Venice in 1833, was trans. into German and pub. by Dr. B. Welte (Tübingen, 1841). See Moses Choren. *Hist. Armén.* lib. iii. cc. xlvii. lii.-liv. lvii. lviii. lx. lxi. lxvi. lxvii. for copious details of his life, and an art. by Petermann *s.v.* in Herzog's *Real Encyklop.* [G.T.S.]

Methodius (called also *Eubulius*), commemorated June 20 (Basil, *Menol.*) and Sept. 18 (*Mart. Rom.*), a Lycian bp. highly distinguished as a writer, bp. first of Olympus, afterwards of Patara, early in 4th cent. Jerome (*Cat.* 83), Socrates (vi. 13), and Maximus (*in Schol.* Dionys. Areop. 7) state that he was bp. of Olympus. Leontius of Byzantium calls him bp. of Patara, and he is thus known to all later Greek authorities. Jerome's unsupported statement that he was translated to Tyre was probably due to a transcriber's error for Patara in the authority which Jerome followed.

Jerome states that "he was crowned with martyrdom at the end of the last [*i.e.* Diocletian's] persecution; or as some affirm under Decius and Valerian, at Chalcis in Greece." The earlier date is inconsistent with the facts that Methodius wrote against Porphyry and that Eusebius speaks of him as a contemporary (*ap.* Hieron. *Apol. adv. Rufin.* I. vol. ii.). The martyrdom of a Lycian or Phoenician bp. at a place so remote as Euboea must also be pronounced incredible. The places were not then even under the same ruler, Greece being under Licinius and the Eastern provinces under Maximin. Accordingly Sophronius, the Greek translator of St.

Jerome, substitutes for Chalcis "in Greece," "in the East," whence some modern critics have concluded that Methodius suffered at Chalcis in Syria. But no weight can fairly be attached to this correction of Sophronius; and it is more probable that a Methodius whose name tradition had preserved as a martyr at Chalcis under Decius was wrongly identified with the better-known Lycian bishop. The evidence that the latter was a martyr at all is weak, and the silence of Eusebius is a difficulty; but Theodoret calls him bishop and martyr, as do the late Greek writers, while the Menaea make the mode of death decapitation.

Methodius wrote much, and his works were widely read and highly valued. Jerome several times refers to him: Epiphanius calls him ἀνὴρ λόγιος καὶ σφόδρα περὶ τῆς ἀληθείας ἀγωνισάμενος; Gregory Nyssen or Anastasius Sinaita (for the authorship is disputed), ὁ πολὺς ἐν σοφίᾳ; Andrew of Caesarea, ὁ μέγας; Eustathius of Antioch, ὁ τῆς ἁγίας ἄξιος μνήμης, and he is quoted by Theodoret, besides many later writers. Photius has preserved copious extracts (*Codd.* 234-237); other shorter extracts are to be found in Catenae, and others are given in the Nitrian MSS. (see Wright, *Cat. MSS. Syr. in Brit. Mus.*). The works of which we have knowledge are:

(1) The only one extant entire is the *Symposium*, or Banquet of the Ten Virgins. It reveals Methodius as an ardent admirer of Plato, from whom he probably derived his preference for dialogue form. In the present case he has not only imitated him in several passages, but has taken from him the whole idea of his work. As in Plato's Symposium the praises of Love are celebrated, so here are proclaimed the glories of Virginity. The imitation of the form of Plato's work is even kept up in not presenting the dialogue directly, but as reported by one present at it. Eubulius, or Eubulium, receives from a virgin Gregorion an account of a banquet in the gardens of Areté, not under Plato's plane-tree, but under an agnus-castus, in which ten virgin guests, at their hostess's command, pronounce ten successive discourses in praise of chastity. At the end of the banquet the victor Thecla leads off a hymn, to which the rest standing round as a chorus respond. But Methodius has caught very little of Plato's style or spirit. He has little dramatic power, and there is often little to distinguish one speaker from another. Of his general soundness on our Lord's Divinity there can be no doubt; and we have not found anything in the writings ascribed to him which an orthodox man might not have written, especially before the Arian disputes had made caution of language necessary. Elsewhere (*Cod.* 162) Photius mentions Methodius with Athanasius and other great names as one from whose writings Andrew had produced extracts garbled and falsified so as to teach heresy.

(2) In the Catalogue of Jerome he gives the first place to the writings of Methodius against Porphyry. He elsewhere refers to them (in *Comm. in Dan. Pref.* c. 13, vol. v. pp. 618, 730; Apol. ad Pammach. vol. i.; *Ep.* 70 ad Magnum, i. 425), stating in *Ep.* 70 that they ran to 10,000 lines. Philostorgius (viii. 14) rates the reply of Apollinarius to Porphyry as far superior to either that by Eusebius or by Methodius. All three replies have perished.

(3) *On the Resurrection.*—This work has been lost, but large extracts have been preserved by Epiphanius, *Haer.* 64, and by Photius, *Cod.* 234, see also Johan. Damasc. *de Imag. Orat.* 2. The text as given by Combefis and reprinted by Migne suppresses the heretical portions of the Epiphanian extracts. This work also is in the form of a Platonic dialogue, and is in refutation of Origen. The Origenist speakers deny the materiality of the resurrection body, and urge that it is enough if we believe that the same form shall rise again, beautified and glorified. In heaven our bodies will be spiritual; and so St. Paul teaches: "It is sown a natural body; it is raised a spiritual body"; "Flesh and blood shall not inherit the kingdom of God." Man had been originally in Paradise, that is, in the third heaven (II. Cor. xii.), having there none but a spiritual body; having sinned he was cast down to earth, where God made him "coats of skins," that is to say, for a punishment clad him in our present gross material bodies, which clog and fetter the soul and out of which spring our temptations to sin; for without the body the soul cannot sin. When we rise therefore to dwell where sin cannot be, we shall be like the angels, liberated from the flesh which has burdened us here. In reply, Methodius acutely points out the inconsistence of teaching that the soul cannot sin without the body, and at the same time that the body had been imposed on the soul as a punishment for sins previously committed; and in truth the body is an instrument for good as well as for evil. Paradise and the third heaven are not identified (II. Cor. xii.); two distinct revelations are spoken of. It is said that we shall hereafter be *as* the angels, that is, like them, not subject to change or decay; but not that we shall be angels or without earthly bodies. God does not make mistakes; if He had meant us to be angels He would have made us so at first. His creatures are diverse: besides angels, there are thrones, principalities, and powers. By death He does not design to turn us into something different in kind from what He at first meant us to be; but only as an artificer, when a work of his is polluted with stains which cannot otherwise be removed, melts it down, and makes it anew; so by death we shall be remade free from the pollution of sin. Similarly the world will not be destroyed, but made into a new and purer earth, fit for the risen saints.

(4) *De Pythonissa.*—Jerome tells us that this work, now lost, was directed against Origen. We may presume, therefore, that its scope was the same as that bearing the same title by Eustathius of Antioch, viz. to refute the opinion held by Origen after Justin Martyr that the soul of Samuel was under the power of Satan, and was evoked by the magical art of the witch of Endor. Methodius's view, however, could not have been the same as that of Eustathius, for a passage at the close of Photius's extracts from the treatise on the Resurrection implies a belief that the appearance of Samuel was real.

(5) *Xeno.*—Socrates (vi. 13), expressing his indignation against the reviling of Origen by worthless writers who sought to get into notice by defaming their betters, names Methodius as the earliest of Origen's assailants; adding that he had afterwards by way of retractation expressed admiration of him in a dialogue entitled Xeno. We believe the dialogue referred to by Socrates to be identical with (6). There is nothing in Methodius's confutations of Origen inconsistent with his having felt warm admiration for the man; and he has certainly followed him in his allegorical method of interpretation.

(6) Περὶ τῶν γενητῶν.—This work "on things created" is only known by extracts preserved by Photius (*Cod.* 235). It is a refutation of Origenist doctrine as to the eternity of the world, the principal arguments with which Methodius deals being that we cannot piously believe that there ever was a time when there was no Creator, no Almighty Ruler, and that there cannot be a Creator without things created by Him, a Ruler without things ruled over, a παντοκράτωρ without κρατούμενα. Further, that it is inconsistent with the unchangeableness of God to suppose that, after having passed ages without making anything, He suddenly took to creating. The orthodox speaker deals with his opponent by the Socratic method of question and answer. Photius's extracts begin with a discussion of the text, "Cast not your pearls before swine"; and we have near the commencement the phrase, μαργαρίτας τοῦ ξενῶνος. It is hard to get good sense by translating "pearls of the guest-chamber"; and with the knowledge we have that one of Methodius's dialogues was called Xeno, we are disposed to think that Xeno was one of the speakers in this dialogue, and that we are to translate "Xeno's pearls," *i.e.* pearls which Xeno presumably had mentioned, or else that the words τοῦ Ξενῶνος have got transposed and ought to be prefixed to the extract, the whole being taken from a speech by this interlocutor. Photius says that Methodius calls Origen a centaur, and interpreters have puzzled as to what he could have meant. In the extracts preserved the orthodox speaker addresses his Origenist interlocutor as ὦ Κένταυρε without the slightest air of uttering a sarcasm, so that we should be disposed to think that the name of the Origenist speaker in this dialogue was Centaurus.

(7) *On Free Will.*—[Maximus (24)].

For the works of Methodius see Migne, vol. xviii.; Eng. trans. in Schaff's *Ante-Nicene Fathers;* Jahn; S. Methodii opera, and S. Method. Platonizans, Halis. Sax. 1865. [G.S.]

Miltiades (1), an active Christian writer of the 2nd cent. Eusebius tells us (*H. E.* v. 17) that, besides leaving other records of his diligent study of the divine oracles, he composed a treatise "against the Greeks," another "against the Jews," and an "Apology" addressed to the rulers of this world on behalf of the school of philosophy to which he belonged. It is a natural inference from the plural "rulers" that there were, when Miltiades wrote, two emperors, probably Aurelius and Verus. The Apology may be supposed to have been a learned plea for toleration of Christianity, the purity of whose doctrines may have been favourably contrasted with the teaching of heathen philosophy. It is not extant, but seems to have had at the time a high repute. The writer of the "Little Labyrinth" (Eus. v. 28) names Miltiades in company with Justin, Tatian, and Clement among the writers in defence of the truth or against contemporary heretics who, before Victor's episcopate, had distinctly asserted the divinity of Christ. Tertullian (*adv. Valentin.* 5) names him with Justin Martyr and Irenaeus as a writer against heresy, giving him the appellation, evidently intended in an honourable sense, "Sophista Ecclesiarum." St. Jerome twice mentions him (*Catal.* 39; *Ep. ad Magnum*, vol. i. p. 427), but gives no clear indication that he knew more of him than he had learned from Eusebius.

Great obscurity hangs over his relation to Montanism, owing to a strange confusion, either on the part of Eusebius or of his copyists, between the names Miltiades and Alcibiades. In *H. E.* v. 2 Eusebius tells a story about one of the Lyons confessors named Alcibiades, and, going on to speak about Montanism, mentions an Alcibiades as among its leaders. After the death of Montanus, his sect seems to have been known in Phrygia by the name of its leader for the time being; and in an anti-Montanist document preserved by Eusebius, v. 16, the sect is called the party of Miltiades. This is the reading of all the MSS.; yet having regard to the earlier passage, editors are disposed here to substitute Alcibiades for Miltiades. If we are not permitted to think that there might have been Montanists of both names, it would seem more natural to make the opposite correction. In c. 16 there was nothing to lead copyists astray; in c. 2 Eusebius, having named an Alcibiades just before, might easily by a slip of the pen have repeated the same name. This view is strengthened by the fact that at the close of the Muratorian fragment, a name transcribed as "Mitiades" occurs as that of one the ecclesiastical use of whose writings was totally rejected by the church. This would be explained by the supposition that a Miltiades had written records of Montanist prophesyings or some other document, which that sect had regarded as inspired and admitted to church use. But the case is complicated further in c. 17 of Eusebius. He begins by saying that the anti-Montanist document mentioned Miltiades as having written against Montanus; and then, having given extracts from the document, goes on to give the account we have already used of the other works of Miltiades. But the extract, according to the reading of all the MSS., names not Miltiades but Alcibiades as the author of an anti-Montanist treatise, "that a prophet ought not to speak in ecstasy." Here editors are compelled to correct the Alcibiades of the extract into Miltiades to make Eusebius consistent; yet this leaves it unexplained why transcribers should go so strangely wrong. Cf. Otto, *Corpus Apol.* ix. 364. [G.S.]

Miltiades (2) (*Melchiades*), bp. of Rome after Eusebius, from July 2, 310, to Jan. 10 or 11, 314, the see having been vacant for 10 months and 14 days. The long vacancy is accounted for by the circumstances of his predecessor's death in exile and the divided state of the Roman church at the time.

The pontificate of Miltiades was marked by the accession, and so-called conversion, of Constantine the Great, and the definite termination of Diocletian's persecution. To Miltiades the possessions of the Christians at Rome, including the cemeteries, were at length restored by Maxentius: "Melchiades was recorded to have sent deacons with letters from the emperor Maxentius and from the prefect of the Praetorium to the prefect of the city, that they might recover possession of what had been taken away in the time of persecution, and which the aforesaid emperor had ordered to be restored" (Augustine, *Brevic. Collat. cum Donat.; die* iii. c. 34). Constantine, after the defeat and death of Maxentius (Oct. 28, 312), promulgated at Milan in 313 with Licinius the full edict of toleration known as "the Edict of Milan," which Licinius proclaimed in June 313 at Nicomedia in the East. All these important events were during the episcopate of Miltiades, who would be a personal witness of Constantine's entry into Rome after the battle of the Milvian bridge, with the labarum borne aloft, and the monogram of Christ marked upon the shields of his soldiers. But the pope's name does not become prominent until the complications which soon arose in connexion with the African Donatists. Constantine, according to Optatus, was greatly annoyed at being called upon to settle disputes among the clergy, but he complied with the request, nominating three Gallic bishops whom he commanded to go speedily to Rome to adjudge the matter in conjunction with Miltiades. He wrote a letter preserved by Eusebius, addressed to Miltiades and an unknown Marcus. There is no evidence, in this or other acts of Constantine, that he regarded the bp. of Rome as the sole or necessary judge of ecclesiastical causes on appeal. He was, indeed, careful to refer spiritual cases to the spirituality, and he naturally and properly referred the chief cognizance of a case arising in W. Africa to the Roman see, though not to the pope singly, but to him assisted by assessors whom he named himself. The three bishops of Gaul are named in the letter as colleagues of Miltiades and Marcus, and it appears from Optatus that 15 Italian bishops were added to the conclave, summoned, we may suppose, by Miltiades himself, so that he might hear the case canonically in synod with the assistance of the Gallic assessors. The decisions of the conclave were duly transmitted to Constantine, whom they fully satisfied (*Ep. Constant. ad vicar. Africae; ejusd. ad Episc. Syrac.*—Labbe, i. p. 1445; Eus. *H. E.* x. 5). Moved, however, by the continued complaints of Donatus and his party, he summoned the general synod of Arles (A.D. 314) with a view to a final settlement. In these further proceedings the bp. of Rome does not appear to have been consulted by the emperor, or regarded as possessing any position of supremacy. Constantine, professing great reverence for the episcopate in general, and recognizing the right of the clergy to settle cases purely ecclesiastical, himself set in motion and regulated ecclesiastical proceedings, delegated their administration to such ecclesiastics as he chose, and certainly shewed no peculiar deference to the Roman see. Nor do we find any protest on the part of the church of his day against his mode of procedure.

The fact that the conclave under Miltiades met in the Lateran palace (in the house of the empress Fausta) is adduced by Baronius (A.D. 312) as proving the tradition true that Constantine had made over that palace to the pope as a residence. But it is not known with any certainty when the popes came into permanent possession of the Lateran.

Miltiades was, in the time of St. Augustine, accused by African Donatists of having, as one of the presbyters of pope MARCELLINUS, with him given up the sacred books and offered incense under the persecution of Diocletian. Augustine treats the whole charge as unsupported by documentary evidence, and probably a calumny; and we find no mention of any such charge against Miltiades during his life, when the party of Donatus was likely to have made a strong point of it had it been known of them. Further, in the conference with the Donatists held A.D. 411 by order of the emperor Honorius the charge was alleged, but all proof of it broke down (Augustine, *u.s.*).

Miltiades was buried, as his predecessors since Pontianus till the commencement of persecution had been, in the cemetery of St. Callistus on the Appian Way. There also he had deposited the remains of his immediate predecessor Eusebius (*Depos. Episc. Liber.*). Yet neither of these two popes (according to early recensions of the Pontifical) lay in the old papal crypt of that cemetery, but each in a separate *cubiculum* apart from it. De Rossi supposes the approaches to the old crypt to have been blocked up by the Christians to save it from profanation; and the state in which the passages leading to it have been found confirms this supposition. He has identified positively the *cubiculum* of Eusebius, but that of Miltiades only conjecturally (see Northcote and Brownlow, *Rom. Sotter.* p. 146). Miltiades was the last pope buried in this cemetery. [J.B—Y.]

Minucius Felix, Marcus, one of the earliest and most pleasing of the Latin Christian apologists. His personal history can only be gathered from his own book. The earliest writer to mention him by name is Lactantius (*Institut.* v. 1), who describes him as a lawyer, "non ignobilis inter causidicos loci," but Lactantius may be merely drawing a natural inference from the introduction to the book itself, where Minucius tells how he had taken advantage of the court holidays to leave Rome for Ostia, "ad vindimeam feriae judiciariam curam relaxaverant." St. Jerome three times mentions Minucius (*Ep.* 48 *ad Pammach.* vol. i. p. 221; *Ep* 70 *ad Magnum*, vol. i. p. 427; *de Vir. Illust.* c. 58, vol. ii. p. 883), and describes him as "insignis causidicus Romani fori"; but it seems clear that Jerome drew this description from Lactantius, whom he quotes. It has been attempted to deduce the date of Minucius from the place which Jerome assigns him in his list of illustrious men; but there is no evidence that Jerome really knew more than we know ourselves.

Still more may the same be said of Eucherius, who speaks of Minucius (*Ep. ad Valer.* in *Patr. Lat.* l. 719). The *gens Minucia* was widely spread at Rome, and an inscription (Gruter, p. 918) shows among its families one with the cognomen Felix.

The only extant work of Minucius is a dialogue entitled "Octavius," modelled on the philosophical works of Cicero, whose writings, particularly *de Natura Deorum* and *de Divinatione*, Minucius has carefully studied. Minucius recalls a conversation of his lately deceased friend Octavius which resulted in the conversion to Christianity of their common friend Caecilius. He tells how Octavius had come to Rome, and gives a charming description of the morning walk on the beach taken by the three friends after they had gone from Rome to Ostia, until at last they sat down for rest and serious discussion on large stones placed for protection of the baths. At the beginning of the walk the heathen Caecilius, as they were passing an image of Serapis, had saluted it, as was customary, by kissing hands, whereupon Octavius charged Minucius with culpable negligence in having allowed his friend to continue in such degrading superstition. Caecilius challenges Octavius to a formal dispute. The little treatise then divides itself into two parts, containing first a lively attack by Caecilius on the Christian doctrines and practices, then a reply, about twice as long, by Octavius, refuting and retorting the heathen arguments. Each point of the attack is dealt with in order. Caecilius confesses himself vanquished, gladly ranging himself on the conquering side.

The following is an abstract of the arguments used by Caecilius on the heathen side. He censures the presumption of the Christians, who, though unlettered men, venture to pronounce positively on questions about which the greatest philosophers have doubted; he denies that there is any good ground for believing in the existence of a God, since the chance concourse of atoms will sufficiently account for the origin of the world, while the prosperity of the wicked and the misfortunes of the good shew that the world is governed by no Providence. Then shifting his ground, he urges the duty of worshipping the gods whom their ancestors had worshipped, and the folly of rejecting what universal experience and the consent of all nations had found to be salutary. Each nation had its peculiar god: the Romans, the most religious of all, worshipped gods of all nations, and so had attained the highest prosperity. The power of their deities had been exhibited in many oracles and prodigies; only one or two philosophers had ventured to deny their agency, and one of these, Protagoras, had in consequence been banished by the Athenians. Was it not then deplorable that the gods should be assailed by men of the dregs of the people, who, collecting credulous women and silly men, banded them in a fearful conspiracy, cemented by secret and detestable rites? Tales are repeated, for some of which the authority of Fronto is cited, of the initiation of Christian neophytes by partaking of the blood of a slaughtered infant, and other customary charges. If these things were not true, at least the obscurity in which they shrouded their rites shewed that they were such as they had cause to be ashamed of. These members of an illegal society dreaded to bring their doctrines into the light of day; they had no altars, no temples, no images, and were not even in their manner of worship like the Jews, the only people besides themselves who worshipped that wretched lonely God Who had not been able to save His own people from captivity; yet wished to meddle with everything and pry into every thought and every action. Nor was this the only absurdity of Christian doctrine. They threatened destruction to the world, which always had lasted and was bound together by fixed laws, and said that one day it would be burnt up. Yet for themselves, who were not eternal like the world, but were seen to be born and die, they dared to hope for immortality, and expect that their dust and ashes would live again. In the prospect of this imaginary life they gave up all enjoyment of their real present life, trusting in a God Whose impotence was exhibited in their daily sufferings from which He was unable to save His worshippers. In fine, if the Christians had any modesty, let them give up philosophy, of which their want of education had made them incapable; or if they must philosophize, let them follow that greatest of philosophers, Socrates, whose maxim was, "What is above us we have nothing to do with," otherwise the result will be either the destruction of all religion or the adoption of anile superstition.

Octavius replies that a hearing shall not be refused to the arguments of Christians because of their low worldly condition. Reason is the common property of all men. It is the rich who, intent on their wealth, are too often unable to lift their eyes to things divine. Some of those afterwards recognized as the greatest philosophers were at first despised as poor and plebeian. He then establishes, by the ordinary arguments from the order of the universe, the existence and providence and unity of God, confirming his conclusions by the authority of various philosophers, whose opinions respecting the Deity he extracts from Cicero's treatise. In proof how natural is the belief in God's unity, he appeals to the common use of the singular Deus, both in common speech and in the writings of the poets. He shews that the gods whom the heathen worshipped were but deified men, and exposes the absurdity of the fables commonly told of them, the folly of image-worship, and the cruelty and licentiousness of the rites by which the gods were honoured. He shews that it is false that the Romans owed their prosperity to their religion, since it was by a multitude of irreligious acts that their empire grew, and because their original native gods, to whom, if to any, must be ascribed the origin of their greatness, had been deposed from their position by the adoption of gods of the conquered peoples. He traces the source of all idolatry to the operation of the demons who, having lost their first estate, desired to draw others into the same ruin as themselves, who inspired oracles, wrought fictitious cures and other pretended miracles to deceive men, and were also the inventors and instigators of the calumnies against Christianity. All this was attested by their own confession when exorcised by Christians. Turning to the charges made against the Christians, Octavius not only denies and refutes them, but retorts them on the heathen, who had been the more ready to believe that others had been guilty of them because they had done the like themselves. If the Christians had not temples, or images, or altars, it was because they would not degrade the majesty of the infinite God by limiting Him to a narrow place. Man himself was God's best image, a holy life the best sacrifice that could be offered Him. God is invisible, but so is the wind whose effects we witness; so is our own soul; the sun itself, the source of all light, we cannot look at. As for the Christian doctrines which Caecilius had represented as absurd and incredible, different heathen philosophers had taught a future destruction of the world by fire or otherwise; some of them had taught a transmigration of souls, a doctrine quite as difficult as that of the resurrection of the body and less natural. The doctrine of a future life is recommended by countless analogies of nature; and though men whose lives are bad dislike to believe in future retribution, and prefer to think that death ends all, yet the current popular belief in Pyriphlegethon and Styx, a belief derived from information given by demons and from the Jewish prophets, shews how deep-seated is the conviction that the time will come when it shall not be well with the wicked. Nor is it to be thought that God deals ill with His worshippers because He does not give them a larger share of prosperity in this life: the Christians do not covet earthly riches; they look on trials as their discipline, persecutions as their warfare, in which they are not deserted by their God, but combat under His eye. The Romans honour with their praises such sufferers as Mucius Scaevola and Regulus, yet the heroism of these men has been repeatedly surpassed by that of Christian women and children. Lastly, we need not be disturbed by the failure of sceptical philosophers to arrive at any certain knowledge of truth. These men's lives gave the lie to their professions of wisdom; we, whose excellence is in life and not merely in word, may boast that we have succeeded in finding what they sought in vain, and have only cause for gratitude that a revelation was reserved for our hands which was denied to them.

It will be seen how meagre Minucius is in his exposition of Christian doctrine, thus differing from all the other apologists. The doctrines of the unity of God, the resurrection of the body, and future retribution make up nearly the whole of the system of Christian doctrine which he sets forth. The doctrine of the Logos, so prominent in the apologies of Justin, Athenagoras, and Tertullian, is absent; our Lord's name is not mentioned, and though from the manner in which Octavius repels the charge that the Christians worshipped a man who had been punished for his crimes, it may reasonably be inferred that he believed our Lord to be more than man, yet this is not plainly stated. Minucius clearly shews that the topics he omits are excluded, not from disbelief in, or ignorance of, them, but from a designed limitation of the objects of his work, because at the end, when Caecilius has declared himself satisfied on the main questions of the existence of God and of Providence and of the general truth of the Christian religion, he asks for another conversation, not because of remaining doubts, but because he desires to be taught other things still necessary to perfect instruction. It cannot be accident that Minucius does not imitate the entire unreserve with which Justin speaks of Christian doctrines and Christian rites. The work of Minucius was doubtless intended mainly to influence intelligent heathen; and we must infer that in the West at least the feeling prevailed when Minucius wrote which made Christians fear to cast their pearls before swine. One striking difference between Minucius and Justin is the former's complete omission of the argument from prophecy, yet the inspiration of the Jewish prophets is incidentally recognized (c. 35). Minucius never mentions the writings of either O. or N. T., and has scarcely any coincidence of language with them. There is (c. 29) an echo of Jer. xvii. 5, and perhaps (c. 34) of I. Cor. xv. 36, 42.

His date is generally agreed to have been before 250, somewhere about which time Cyprian published his *de Idolorum Vanitate*, in which large use is made of Minucius. A nearer limit depends on settling the relation of Minucius to Tertullian. His dialogue and the apology of Tertullian have in common so many arguments, sometimes in nearly the same words, that one of the two undoubtedly used the work of the other, but as to which was the follower critics have held opposite opinions. The difficulty is mainly caused by the excellent use both writers have made of their materials, whencesoever obtained, and the thoroughness with which they have incorporated them. We have already shewn the perfect workmanship of the dialogue of Minucius. Tertullian's *Apology* is equally excellent, though its plan is entirely different. It is an advocate's speech, written for presentation to heathen magistrates to convince them that Christians did not deserve persecution. It is more loosely constructed, and evidently more hastily written, than that of Minucius, but bears a strong stamp of originality. Many points briefly touched on in Minucius are expanded in Tertullian, so that either Minucius has abridged Tertullian or Tertullian has used and developed the suggestions of Minucius. This has furnished the best argument for the priority of Tertullian. Tertullian, it has been said, is one of the most original of writers, Minucius quite the reverse. We have already mentioned his obligations to Cicero; his work is also largely indebted to Seneca, besides containing traces of Juvenal and other writers. Is it not, then, most natural to believe that as he has drawn his arguments for Theism from Cicero, he has taken his defence of Christianity from Tertullian? In the common matter there are considerable differences as to arrangement and form of expression. If Tertullian were the original, Minucius would have a change of arrangement forced on him by the plan of his work, while the changes in form of expression either improve the Latinity or make the sentence more pointed; whereas if Minucius were the original, Tertullian's changes can hardly have any other object than to disguise his obligation. Notwithstanding, a very careful comparison of the common matter led Ebert (*K. Sächs. Ges. der Wissenschaften; philol.-histor. Classe*, Bd. v.) to consider Minucius the original, and Ebert's ability in arguing the case obtained for a time general acceptance of his opinion. But recently new evidence has been obtained. The dialogue would seem to describe Minucius as a native of Cirta and fellow-townsman of Fronto, of whom he speaks as "Cirtensis noster," while Octavius refers to him as "Fronto tuus." Now at Cirta (Constantine in Algeria) the French have found six inscriptions containing the name of Caecilius Natalis (Mommsen, *Lat. Insc.* viii. 6996 and 7094-7098). This Caecilius was chief magistrate of Cirta in 210, and on the completion of five years of office raised at his own expense a triumphal arch in honour of Caracalla, brazen statues in honour of "Indulgentia domini nostri," exhibited "ludos scenicos" for seven days, and in other ways exhibited munificence. See an art. by Dessau (*Hermes*, 1880, p. 471). We see no good reason for refusing to identify this Caecilius Natalis with the Caecilius of the dialogue. He is not likely to have been a Christian when discharging the functions just described; the conversation related by Minucius would therefore have occurred somewhat later than 215; and the composition itself might be a score of years later. We thus fall back on the opinion held by the best critics before the publication of Ebert's memoir, that the work of Minucius was written in the peaceful days of Alexander Severus, say A.D. 234.

A useful ed. is in Gersdorf's *Bibl. Pat. Ecc.* (Leipz. 1847), one with variorum notes in vol. iii. of Migne's *Patr. Lat.*, an excellent one by Holden (Camb. 1853), and one by Halm (Vienna, 1867) founded on a new collation of the MS., which may therefore be regarded as the best authority for the text, but contains only critical notes. See also Waltzing, *Bibliographie raisonnée de Min. Fel.* in *Muséon Belge* (1902), vi. pp. 216 ff.; also G. Bossier in *La fin du Paganisme*, 3rd ed. (Paris, 1898), i. 261. There is an English trans. in the *Lib of Ante-Nic. Fathers.* [G.S.]

Miro (*Mirio, Mirus*), king of the Suevi in Spain, 570-583.

Authorities.—Greg. Tur. *Hist. Franc.* v. 42, vi. 43; *Joannes Bicl.* ap. *Esp. Sagr.* v. 377, 380, 383; Isid. *Hist. Suev. ib.* 506; Acts of the second council of Braga; Tejada y Ramiro, *Colecc. de Lan. de la Igl. Esp.* ii. 620; *Formula Honestae Vitae*, by Martin of Braga; Pref. *Esp. Sagr.* xv. 383.

Miro represents a period in the history of the Suevian kingdom of Gallicia, when, having renounced the Arianism imposed upon them in the 5th cent. by their then existing relations to the Visigoths, the Suevi entered into alliance with the Franks on the one hand and probably the Eastern empire on the other, with the view of checking the power of the Arian West-Gothic king LEOVIGILD, which at the beginning of Miro's reign threatened the absorption of the Suevian state in the kingdom of Toledo, a result actually achieved two years after Miro's death. The known facts of his reign, which although few in number are often contradictorily given by the authorities, are as follows. In 572 the second council of Braga, a kind of supplementary council to the more important gathering of 561 [MARTINUS (2)] was held, and the king is specially mentioned as contributing to its assembly. In the same year Miro conducted an expedition against the Ruccones in Cantabria, one of the restless Basque tribes, with whom Suevi and Goths alike were perpetually at war. Four years later Miro's great West-Gothic contemporary Leovigild appeared on the borders of Gallicia. Miro sued for peace, and obtained it for a short time. In 580 the Catholic rebellion of HERMENIGILD against his father Leovigild broke out, and the rebellious son became the centre of Frankish, Suevian, and Byzantine policy in the peninsula. In 580 we hear of envoys sent by Miro to Guntchramn of Burgundy, Leovigild's worst enemy, and intercepted and detained on the way by Leovigild's ally, Chilperic of Soissons. In 583 Miro set out from Gallicia at the head of an army destined to raise the siege of Seville, then closely invested by Leovigild. He was met on the way by Leovigild, and, according to Gregory of Tours, who is evidently best informed on the matter, withdrew homewards, and died shortly after from the effects of the bad air and water of S. Spain. The two Spanish sources, Joannes Biclarensis and Isidore, say that he died before Seville, and describe him as assisting Leovigild in the siege of the town. On the reconciliation of these conflicting accounts, cf. Dahn, *Könige der Germanen*, vi. 571; and Görres, *Kritische Untersuch. über den Aufstand und das Martyrium der Westgoth. Königssohnes Hermenigild*, in *Zeitschrift für Hist. Theol.* 1873, I. Miro's relations to Martin of Braga, the Catholic leader and organizer of Gallicia during his reign and that of his father, seem to have been intimate and friendly. Martin's principal work, *Formula Vitae Honestae*, is dedicated to him, and the *Exhortatio Humilitatis*, printed among Martin's works, is also probably addressed to him (*Esp. Sagr.* xv. Appendix). [M.A.W.]

Modestus (3), prefect of the Praetorium, persecutor of the Catholics under the emperor Valens (Socr. iv. 16; Soz. vi. 18; Theod. *H. E.* iv. 18; Tillem. vi. 510, 555, 562, 574), who commissioned him to offer Basil the choice between deposition and communion with the Arians. A severe sickness having supervened, which he regarded as a judgment for his insolent behaviour, he entreated Basil to visit his sick-bed, humbly asked pardon, and commended himself to his prayers. Attributing his recovery to St. Basil's intercessions, he regarded him with the greatest reverence (Greg. Naz. pp. 352, 353). From this time Basil's influence with Modestus was so great that persons came from a great distance to request letters from him to the prefect. Six of these remain (Basil. *Epp.* 104 [279], 110 [277], 111 [276], 279 [274], 280 [275], 281 [278]), in which Basil claims immunity from taxes for all ministers of the church, begs for a lessening of the taxes for the impoverished inhabitants of the Taurus range, commends to him a friend summoned to the capital by legal charges, etc. Basil addresses Modestus with the respect due to his high official position, and expresses much gratitude for his readiness to listen to his requests. [E.V.]

Monnica, St. The name of this most celebrated of Christian mothers is spelt thus (not *Monica*) in the oldest MSS. of the writings of St. Augustine.

Her birthplace, nowhere explicitly named, may be assumed to be Tagaste, the home of her husband, Patricius. Her family was, probably, like his in point of social grade, *curialis* (*Possidii Vita Aug.* c. 2)—*i.e.* contributed a member or members to the senate of the colonia. Her parents' names are not known. They were consistent Christians; their home was (*Conf.* ix. 8) "domus fidelis, bonum membrum Ecclesiae." Monnica was born 331 or 332. Her early domestic training was pure and severe, under the strong hand of an aged and trusted Christian nurse, who had once carried the child's father in her arms. By her Monnica and her sisters (no brothers are mentioned) were taught to abstain entirely from drinking even water between meal-times, with the aim of guarding them beforehand against habits of intemperance when, after marriage, they should become "dominae apothecarum et cellariorum" (*ib.*). Yet Monnica, when scarcely past her early childhood, was on the verge of a confirmed love of wine, as she confessed long after to her son (*ib.*). She was married, at what age we know not, to Patricius of Tagaste, "vir curialis"; a man passionate ("ferox"), immoral, and not formally a member of the church; perhaps what would now be called an "adherent." * With him Monnica lived patiently and faithfully, till at the age of 40 she was left a widow, tenderly attached to his memory, and longing to be laid at death in his grave (*ib.* ix. 11). He was rough and eager, but not ungenerous; and she was permitted to win him to the Saviour before his end. A curious picture of the manners of that time and region appears (*ib.* ix. 9) when Monnica, surrounded by her married female friends, and seeing on some of them, "quarum viri mansuetiores erant [Patricio]," the marks of blows, inflicted even on their faces, counselled them to adopt, for protection, her own method of calm and unwavering submission. The mother of Patricius was an inmate of the home, and her also Monnica completely won to respect and affection, in spite of the slanders of the female slaves, by a union of filial obedience with vigour as a mistress.

She bore children more than once, for Augustine not only mentions a brother expressly (*ib.* ix. 11, etc.) but was the uncle of many nephews and nieces (*Vita Benedictina Aug.* c. i.). Augustine was born when Monnica was 23 years old, and when, as we gather from his language about her whole influence, she was already a Christian in the noblest sense, strong in the power of spiritual holiness, and ardently prayerful for the salvation of her child, and therefore for his personal acceptance of the faith. It is a sign of the popular Christian opinion and usage at the time that she did not bring him as an infant to baptism but merely to the initiation of a catechumen (*Conf.* i. 11; vi. 16), the sign of the cross and the salting with salt. She evidently thought that baptism required evidence of a previous true change of will.* In early boyhood, in extreme illness, he implored to be baptized, and she hastened to procure it; but on his sudden recovery again resolved to delay (*ib.* i. 11).

* *Conf.* vi. 16 states that both Augustine's *parentes* procured his initiation as an infant catechumen.

Monnica joined cordially with Patricius in securing the highest education for Augustine and in stimulating his studies; and even during her widowhood made every effort to maintain him in them. But his impurity and unbelief caused her agonizing distress, aggravated by his cynical conduct. For a time she declined his presence beneath her roof and at her table, "aversans et detestans blasphemias [filii]" (*ib.* iii. 11); but a memorable dream altered her decision. She saw a radiant being ("juvenum splendidum, hilarem, atque arridentem sibi") approach her as she stood on a wooden beam ("regula") bewailing her son's spiritual ruin; and he bade her be consoled, for where she was, there too her son should be. Augustine suggested that this might portend his mother's unbelief; but she instantly rejoined that the words were not "Where he is, there thou shalt be." This was snine years before his conversion. About the same time she received the well-known consolation from a bishop, wearied ("substomachans taedio") with her entreaties that he would reason with her son: "Go, prythee; the son of those tears cannot perish" (*ib.* 12).

She sorely bewailed Augustine's resolve to migrate to Italy, and would not leave his side; and when he escaped her, affecting to bid a friend good-bye on board ship and persuading her to spend the night in a chapel dedicated to Cyprian, she would not give him up. Beside herself with grief (*ib.* v. 8), she took ship and followed him, and on a stormy voyage consoled the terrified sailors, assuring them that she had seen a vision which promised safety (*ib.* vi. 1). Augustine arrived before her at Milan, and was already under the influence of Ambrose, but not yet won to the orthodox faith ("non manichaeus, sed neque catholicus christianus"); but she calmly assured him of her certainty that she should see him a believer before she died (*ib.*).

The ministrations of Ambrose she attended with great and reverent delight ("diligebat illum virum sicut angelum Dei"), and gave a striking proof of her feeling in submitting at once to his judgment on a point that must have touched her nearly. She had been used to bring oblations of vegetables, bread, and wine to the shrines of the African martyrs, and began the like practice at Milan. But Ambrose had forbidden the usage, partly because it was much abused to intemperance, partly (a significant fact) because it so closely resembled the pagan parentalia. Augustine owns that probably his mother would have obeyed none but Ambrose in such a case; to him, however, she yielded without a murmur. Ambrose fully understood Monnica's strength of Christian character and delighted to praise her to her son (*ib.* vi. 2). At Milan she was a

* We do not ignore the discussions upon this incident; see *e.g.* Wall on Infant Baptism, pt. ii. c. iii. § 11. But we think the *Confession* does *not* imply that *Patricius* interfered to defer Augustine's baptism.

most devout and diligent worshipper; liberal in alms; daily attending the Eucharist ("nullum diem praetermittebat oblationem ad altare [Domini]"), and was twice daily in the church, not to gossip there ("non ad vanas fabulas et aniles loquacitates") but to hear the word and pray (*ib.* v. 9). During the struggle of Ambrose with the Arian empress-mother Justina (385) Monnica was the most devout among the host of worshippers who gathered for vigils and prayers in the church (*ib.* ix. 7). The hymns of Ambrose she greatly loved, and treasured in her memory; the dialogue *de Beatâ Vitâ* closes with some noble words from Monnica, introduced by a quotation from the hymn "Fove precantes, Trinitas."

The final crisis of her son's conversion was instantly reported to her by Augustine and Alypius, to her extreme delight (*ib.* viii. 12), though it involved not only his baptism but his acceptance of a life of celibacy. Between his conversion and baptism she retired with him to Cassiciacum, the campagna of his friend Verecundus. The dialogues *de Ordine* and *de Beatâ Vitâ* give a charming picture of this retirement, spent in holy intercourse and in lofty thought lighted up with eternal truth. Monnica appears as an interlocutor in both dialogues, conspicuous for strength of native sense, and occasionally speaking with a vigour and spirit evidently reported from the life; a woman who might have shone at any period for intellectual gifts. "We fairly forgot her sex, and thought that some great man was in our circle" (*de B. V.* § 10). At the close of the dialogue she speaks of the bliss of the Eternal Vision: "This beyond dispute is the blessed life, the perfect; at which we must look to be enabled to arrive, hastening on in solid faith, joyful hope, and burning love" (*ib. ad fin.*). In the dialogue *de Ordine* Augustine speaks of his mother's "ingenium, atque in res divinas inflammatus animus" (ii. § 1).

She was now near the end. Her son, an orthodox believer, was about to return with her to Africa. They were lodging at Ostia, and making the last preparations for the voyage (*Conf.* ix. 10). Augustine records a conversation with his mother as they sat at a window looking on the viridarium of the house—a delightful colloquy ("colloquebamur soli valde dulciter"), rising from theme to theme of subtle but holy thought to the height of the beatific vision. The "colloquy" was surely no mere monologue on Augustine's part, if he has drawn his mother truly in his two dialogues. It closed with a solemn utterance from her: "she had done with the wish to live; her son was a believer, and fully consecrated; what did she there?" (*ib.*). Five days later she was taken ill ("decubuit febribus"), and at once recognized the end. Her long-cherished wish to lie in the grave of Patricius was gone. "Nothing," she said, "is far from God. There is no fear lest He, at the last day, should not know whence to raise me up." "So on the ninth day of her illness, in the 56th year of her age, and in the 33rd of my own, that devout and saintly soul was released from the body." She died in the presence of Augustine, of another son, of her grandson Adeodatus, so soon to follow her, and of many others ("omnes nos") (*ib.* 11, 12).

Augustine's grief was great. The burial was tearless ("cum ecce corpus elatum est, imus redimus sine lacrymis"), but another time of anguish followed, and a vain effort for relief at the bath. Then sleep came and a calmer waking, and now Augustine, like his blessed mother, found help in an Ambrosian hymn, "Deus creator omnium," and at last could weep calmly. He records his prayers for the departed soul, and begs those of the reader.

Monnica's character was equally strong, lively, and tender by nature and refined by grace to extraordinary elevation. Augustine lavishes his unique eloquence upon her heavenly tone of life and influence and the intensity of her longings for the salvation of the souls she loved. He calls her his mother both in the flesh and in the Lord. His whole being was due, under God, to Monnica. Christians who knew her "dearly loved her Lord in her, for they felt His presence in her heart" (*ib.* 10). She was an eager student of the Scriptures (*de Ord.* i. § 32). In Brieger's *Zeitschrift für Kirchengeschichte,* vol. i. p. 228, is printed (from Riese's *Anthologia Latina,* fasc. ii. p. 127) an epitaph on Monnica, bearing the name of *Bassus, ex-consul*; probably Anicius Bassus, consul A.D. 408, and therefore a contemporary of Augustine's. The lines are:

In tumulo Monicae. (*sic.*)

Hic posuit cineres genetrix castissima prolis
  Augustine tui altera lux meriti,
Qui servans pacis caelestia jura sacerdos
  Commissos populos moribus instituis.
Gloria vos major gestorum laude coronat
  Virtutum mater felicior subolis.

In the last couplet Monnica and her son are, apparently, addressed together. The pentameter apostrophizes Monnica as "Mother of Virtues," and Augustine as her yet "happier offspring"; happier, it may be, as a *celibate* saint. This epitaph is an interesting proof of the religious reverence accorded from the first to Monnica. Brieger's *Zeitschrift* also mentions the *translation of the bones of Monnica* from Ostia to Rome, in 1430, in the reign of Martin V., and at the expense of Mapheus Veghius. The relics were deposited in a chapel dedicated on the occasion to Augustine, and on the sarcophagus were inscribed the following lines, a curious and instructive advance upon the older epitaph in their ascription of mediatorial powers to Monnica:

Hic Augustini sanctam venerare parentem,
  Votaque fer tumulo, quo jacet illa, sacro.
Quae quondam gnato, toti nunc Monica mundo
  Succurrit precibus, praestat opemque suis.*

This translation is dated, in the Roman Martyrology, April 9. Monnica appears as a saint in the Roman calendar, Sancta Monica vidua, Apr. 4, and not infrequently as a figure in medieval art. Scheffer's picture, painted 1845, "St. Augustin et sa mère," gives a noble modern realization of Monnica.

Together 'neath the Italian heaven
They sit, the mother and her son,
He late from her by errors riven,
Now both in Jesus one:
The dear consenting hands are knit,
And either face, as there they sit,
Is lifted as to something seen
Beyond the blue serene.

* v. l. *sibi*, as the epitaph appears in Papebroch, *Acta Sanctorum Maii*, t. i. p. 491.

Such, we believe, is the ordinary interpretation of the picture; as if it represented the colloquy at Ostia. But an interesting passage in Mrs. Jameson's *Sacred and Legendary Art*, p. 314, seems to shew that Scheffer had in view some moment before Augustine's conversion; perhaps that recorded *Conf.* vi. 1, when Monnica assures Augustine that she should yet see him a believer. [H.C.G.M.]

Monoimus (a form, possibly representing the Jewish name Menaham), an Arabian Gnostic of 2nd cent. His name had been only preserved by a brief notice in Theodoret (*Haer. Fab.* i. 18) until the recovery of the lost work of Hippolytus against heresies shewed that from this work Theodoret derived his knowledge. Hippolytus gives a short abstract of the doctrine of Monoimus and an extract from a letter of his to one Theophrastus. The system described might at first seem one of mere pantheism; but a closer examination shews Christian elements in it, so that it is rightly classed as a heresy, and not as a form of heathenism. There is an express quotation from Colossians and a probable reference to the prologue of St. John's Gospel. The starting-point of the speculation is the ascription in N.T. of the work of creation to the Son of Man, whence it was inferred that the first principle was properly called Man. It follows that it is a mistake to look for God in creation; we must seek Him in ourselves, and can best find him by the study of the involuntary operations of our own soul. The relation between the "Man" and "Son of Man" exists from beyond time. The latter is derived from the former, but, it would seem, by an immediate and eternal necessity of His nature, just as from fire is necessarily derived the light which renders it visible. Thus, concerning the first principle, the Scriptures speak both of a "being" and a "becoming" (ἦν καὶ ἐγένετο), the first word properly applying to the "Man," the second to the "Son of Man." The speculations of Monoimus, as reported to us, relate only to the creation; we are told of none as to redemption.

His use of the phrases "Man" and "Son of Man" reminds us of the system of the Naassenes (Hippol. *Ref.* § 7; see also our art. GNOSTICISM), and a closer examination shews that Monoimus is really to be referred to that sect, although Hippolytus has classed them separately; for Monoimus describes his first principle as bisexual, and applies to it the titles "Father, Mother, the two immortal names," words taken out of a Naassene hymn. But there is a common source of this language in the Ἀπόφασις μεγάλη of Simon, this passage also being clearly the original of the description given by Monoimus of the contradictory attributes of his first principle. Further traces of the obligations of Monoimus to Simon are found in the reference to the six powers instrumental in creation, which answer to Simon's six "roots," while a similar indebtedness to Simon on the part of the Naassene writer in Hippolytus is found on comparing the anatomical speculations connected with the name Eden (v. 9; vi. 14). It is more doubtful whether there is any relation of obligation between Monoimus and the Clementine Homilies; both contrast "the Son of Man" with those "born of women" (*Hom.* ii. 17). Monoimus has mysteries in connexion with the number 14, shewing that he attached importance to Paschal celebration. [G.S.]

Monophysitism. The passionate protest raised in Egypt against the heresy of NESTORIUS, supported as it was by court influence, was carried so far that it led to a strong reaction. The Nestorian heresy was condemned because it tended to separate Christ into two beings, one God and the other man, and to regard the inhabitation of the latter by the former as differing in degree only from the inhabitation by the Deity of the patriarchs and prophets of the Old Dispensation. The cruel persecution of Nestorius himself (who, though he undoubtedly went too far in some of his statements, was willing to qualify many of them), the harsh treatment of the learned and holy Theodoret, and the forcible suppression of the teaching of the Syrian school, produced great indignation, and when the emperor Theodosius II. died, and was succeeded in 450 by Marcian, the reaction against Monophysitism broke out all the more fiercely in consequence of the violence and long duration of these measures of repression. Cyril had died in 444, and had been succeeded by Dioscorus, a man of equally violent passions and uncharitable spirit, but of far less self-control and diplomatic skill. Cyril had himself been guilty of confounding the divine and human natures of Christ as completely as Nestorius had been guilty of dividing them, and as long as he and Theodosius II. survived, what was afterwards condemned as Monophysite heresy was in the ascendant. Extremes very frequently meet, and it was not unfairly contended that Cyril, when he insisted on the personal supremacy of the Logos over the Manhood, had practically divided the Person of Christ as much as Nestorius had, when he taught that the human nature was no more than a mere adjunct to the Godhead (Dorner, *On the Person of Christ*, I. div. ii. pp. 67-71, where, however, there seems some "confusion of substance" in the way in which the author treats the question whether the Godhead could itself suffer pain, augmentation, or diminution through association with the manhood).

History of the Controversy.—When Theodosius and Cyril, with the aid of Rabbulas, endeavoured altogether to suppress the Syrian school in the East, considerable resistance was offered. As early as 435 Cyril had begun to resume his attacks on the reputation of Diodorus and Theodore. Even the patriarch Proclus [NESTORIUS] endeavoured to moderate the violence of Cyril's methods. John of Antioch informed the latter that the Syrian bishops would rather be burned than condemn their great teacher Theodore. The emperor was prevailed upon to forbid further proceedings, and Cyril himself found it necessary to yield. But he kept up the irritation by writing a treatise on the oneness of Christ's Person, to which Theodoret felt bound to reply, so that though repressive measures were abandoned, the controversy continued. Dioscorus, Cyril's successor, was not inclined to let it drop. He intrigued at Constantinople, and encouraged two monks named EUTYCHES and Barsumas to insist on something which approached very near to the absorption of the Manhood by the Godhead of Christ. Theodoret came forward once more (447) with his *Eranistes* (contributor to a *club* repast), a work in which he contended that the Logos was ἄτρεπτος (unchangeable), ἀσυγχύτος (*i.e.* His two natures were incapable of being confounded), and ἀπαθής (*i.e.* the Godhead was incapable of suffering). Dioscorus next wrote to the patriarch of Antioch accusing Theodoret of Nestorianism; and when Theodoret defended himself with temper and moderation, pointing out that he had condemned those who had denounced the term θεοτόκος and divided the Person of Christ, and appealing to the authority of Alexander, Athanasius, Basil, and Gregory, Dioscorus encouraged his monks to anathematize Theodoret openly in the church (448). By imperial decree Theodoret was ordered to keep in his own diocese, and not to cause synods to be summoned at Antioch or elsewhere. Just then a synod was held at Constantinople (448), under the patriarch Flavian (who had lately succeeded Proclus, and who is sometimes confounded with Flavian of Antioch, who died *c.* 408), for the dispatch of general business, and Eusebius, bp. of Dorylaeum in Phrygia, brought a complaint against the abbot Eutyches as a disturber of the public peace. Flavian bade him visit Eutyches; for Eutyches, like Dalmatius, had gained great credit for piety by never leaving his cell. Eusebius declined to do this, and Eutyches, when summoned, refused to come forth. When he found that he was about to be condemned for contumacy, he came forth, but brought a large assembly of monks, notables, and even soldiers in his train. By this means he secured a safe return to his monastery, but his adversaries continued to attack him, and to charge him with calling Christ's Body God's Body, and with asserting that It was not ὁμοούσιον with other bodies. When questioned, he denied that our Lord possessed two natures after His Incarnation. He was therefore deposed and excommunicated. The party of Eutyches had recourse to court intrigue, and the empress Eudocia contrived to deprive her sister-in-law Pulcheria, who favoured Flavian, of all her influence with the emperor. Eutyches next demanded a new trial, but though the emperor granted his request, Flavian refused to revise the sentence. Eutyches then, relying on the support of Dioscorus and the emperor, and also of Leo of Rome, whose predecessor had condemned Nestorius, appealed to an oecumenical council. But he tried to secure his safety by declaring his willingness to confess the two natures in the one Christ, if Dioscorus and Leo of Rome should require it. Flavian wished the matter to remain as it had been settled at Constantinople, but he was overruled, and a synod called together at Ephesus in 449.

Of this synod Dioscorus, not Flavian, was appointed president, and Flavian was present rather as an accused person than as a judge. The violence displayed at it by Dioscorus and his party caused it to be universally rejected by the Catholic church. It obtained the name of the Synod of Brigands, or Robber Synod (Latrocinium), which it has ever since retained. By trickery and tumult the bishops were forced to declare that there was but one nature in Christ, and the patriarch Flavian was so roughly handled at the council that he died shortly after of the injuries he had received. Flavian and Eusebius of Dorylaeum were deposed. Domnus of Antioch yielded to the clamour, in spite of the warnings of Theodoret, but he also was afterwards deposed. Theodoret was exiled to the monastery in which he had been brought up. For fuller details of this synod see DIOSCORUS; EUTYCHES. Within a few months, however, the situation underwent a great change. Theodosius died (450), and was succeeded by Marcian. The new emperor had previously espoused Pulcheria, who had contrived to regain her influence over the deceased emperor before his death, and who had already honoured the remains of the martyred patriarch Flavian with a public funeral. The bishops who had disgraced themselves by their craven submission to the decrees of the "Robber Synod"—"chameleons," as Theodoret calls them—now further disgraced themselves by as sudden a recantation. Leo, who had sent four representatives to Ephesus, had by this time learned from them the true history of the proceedings there. One of them, Hilary the deacon, had made a formal protest against these proceedings. Hilary had also taken with him from Ephesus the appeal of Flavian for a rehearing of the case in Italy. Leo now determined, if possible, to decide the question himself. As in the Arian, so in the Nestorian and Monophysite controversies, the West displayed a marked capacity for seizing on the salient points of the question at issue, which the Easterns often failed to grasp in consequence of their taste for metaphysical subtleties. Leo himself was a man "of strong character, undaunted courage, and clear, practical understanding," though "more skilled in liturgical than in theological questions" (Dorner). He was also by no means averse from making these controversies a means for increasing the prestige of his see. Socrates (*H. E.* vii. 7, 12) has remarked on the use which the patriarchs of Rome and Alexandria alike were making at this period of all opportunities of adding to their secular importance. Accordingly Leo held several synods at Rome in which the decrees of the "Robber Synod" were rejected. And even before the assembling of that synod he had written his celebrated letter to Flavian which, though suppressed at Ephesus, was afterwards read at Chalcedon, and accepted as an accurate statement of the doctrine handed down from the first in the church. He now made use of Flavian's appeal to him to procure the assembling of a council at Rome. But the emperor was too politic to permit this, and sent out letters for a council to be held at Nicaea. Such serious riots, however, broke out there that the emperor ultimately resolved to assemble it at Chalcedon, on the opposite side of the Bosphorus to Constantinople, where he could more easily prevent disturbances. There 630 bishops assembled. Leo now pretended that it was not only contrary to ecclesiastical custom, but derogatory to his dignity, for him to be present at the council. He further claimed to exercise the presidency through his five delegates, but his claim was not admitted, and Anatolius, the new patriarch of Constantinople, was associated with the absent Leo in the office of president. The delegates of Leo protested against Dioscorus being allowed to sit with his brother-patriarchs, considering the very serious imputations under which he lay, and they stated that unless their demands were acceded to, they would withdraw from the council. It should be remarked in passing that the presence and action of Leo's delegates dispose of the objections some theologians and historians have made against the oecumenical character of the synod. Eusebius of Dorylaeum now demanded that his petition against Dioscorus should be read. It was couched in the following striking terms (so Evagr. *H. E.* ii. 4): "I have been wronged by Dioscorus; the faith has been wronged; the bishop Flavian has been murdered, and, together with myself, unjustly deposed by him. Give directions that my petition is to be read." It was read accordingly. Eusebius is further declared by Evagrius (ii. 2) to have accused Dioscorus to the emperor of having personally inflicted the injuries of which Flavian died. Dioscorus was convicted of having suppressed Leo's letter to Flavian at the "Robber Synod"; he was deposed; the bishops deposed by him—Theodoret and Ibas among them—were reinstated; and Leo's letter to Flavian accepted by the council amid loud shouts of "Peter has spoken by Leo; Cyril and Leo teach alike." Dioscorus was deposed, but permission was given to the Egyptian bishops to defer their subscription to the Acts of the synod until their new patriarch had been consecrated. Eutyches also was condemned. The proceedings of the council were decidedly tumultuous. One day Theodoret was howled down by the Egyptian bishops; the day after Dioscorus met with a similar reception from the Syrian bishops. Some of the laity who were present as representatives of the emperor openly remarked on the unseemliness of such conduct on the part of bishops. The treatment of the venerable Theodoret was especially unseemly. The reason for which he was howled down was his refusal to anathematize Nestorius until he had an opportunity of explaining his position, though this was the position eventually accepted by the Catholic church at large—namely, the rejection at once of the doctrine of two hypostases, and of the doctrine of only one nature, in Christ. It was only in consequence of the emperor's intervention that the reception of Theodoret by the council was secured.

The resolution first proposed to the synod was not adopted, it being considered too favourable to the party of Dioscorus. The Roman delegates threatened to leave the council unless Leo's letter were accepted as an authoritative statement of doctrine. If this were not done, they intimated that the question should be settled at Rome. As many points of importance connected with the relations between the churches of the East and of the West remained unsettled, especially the question of the *status* of the patriarch of Constantinople, some of the Eastern prelates feared the prolongation of these disputes which would result from the retirement of Leo's representatives. Therefore, though not without many energetic protests, Leo's letter was recognized, at the request of the emperor, and a definition of doctrine in accordance with that letter was drawn up. The synod first recognized the creed put forth at Nicaea (325), and next the enlarged form of it adopted at Constantinople (381). Whether such a creed was actually promulgated at Constantinople has been disputed of late. But much of the evidence existing in 451 has disappeared, and it seems hardly safe to conclude from the silence of contemporary writers that the 630 bishops at Chalcedon had been misinformed on so vital a point. The synod went on to condemn the vain babblings (κενοφωνίας) of those who denied to the Virgin the title of θεοτόκος, as well as those who, on the other hand, affirmed a confusion and mixture (σύγχυσιν καὶ κρᾶσιν) in Christ, under the foolish impression that there could be one nature (consisting) of the Flesh and the Deity in Him, and who, in consequence of (this) confusion, resorted to the amazing suggestion that the divine nature of the Only-begotten was capable of suffering. After having formally accepted Leo's treatise as in conformity with this statement, the decree went on to declare that Jesus Christ was "Perfect in Godhead and Perfect in Manhood, truly God and truly Man; that He was possessed of a reasonable or rather *rational* (λογικῆς) soul and body, of the same substance (ὁμοούσιον) with the Father according to His Godhead, and of the same substance with us as regards His Manhood"; and that He is "to be recognized as existing in two natures, without confusion, without change, indivisibly, and inseparably (ἀσυγχύτως, ἀτρέπτως, ἀδιαιρέτως, ἀχωρίστως), the distinction of the natures being in no way removed by their union, but rather the speciality (ἰδιότης) of each nature being preserved, coalescing (συντρεχούσης) in one Person (πρόσωπον) and one hypostasis, not divided nor separated into two Persons, but being one and the same Son, and Only-begotten, God the Word, the Lord Jesus Christ." There can be no doubt that the decision thus promulgated was a sound one, and that, as Leo did not fail to remark pertinently more than once, the doctrines condemned at the two councils of Ephesus and Chalcedon pointed out two rocks on which the doctrine of Christ might be shipwrecked. "The Catholic church," he goes on to say, "could not teach the Humanity of Christ apart from His true Divinity, nor His Divinity without His true Humanity" (*Letter to Flavian*, c. 5). Yet he did not feel compelled, as Dorner observes, to explain "the internal relations of the two natures." That was, and has remained, a mystery which the human intellect has been unable to unravel. All he had to do was to lay down the particular propositions which, when enunciated by too daring theologians, were in plain conflict with the express teaching of God's

Word, and must therefore tend to mislead mankind on points essential to their salvation. The general reception of the *via media* laid down by the council, emphasised as it was at two subsequent councils held at Constantinople [see below and NESTORIUS], leaves no doubt that it represents the mind of Christendom upon the point. This conclusion is further accentuated by the fact that, though some Nestorian and Monophysite communities continue to exist, even they are no longer unwilling to hold communion with those who receive the doctrines promulgated by the council on the questions at issue.

The resistance against the decrees of the council of Chalcedon has nevertheless been even more formidable than against those of Ephesus, and the communities still in existence which are separated from the church at large on the question of the decrees of Chalcedon are more numerous, less scattered, and more thoroughly organized than those called into existence by the decrees of Ephesus. Yet this can hardly be attributed to the more harmless character of Monophysitism, because as a fact the opinions advocated by Dioscorus and Eutyches were pushed to far greater extremes and far less carefully qualified than those expressed by theologians so competent as Theodore of Mopsuestia and Theodoret of Cyrus. The survival, in forms so fully organized, of Monophysitism seems rather due to the break-up of the Roman empire, and the progressive decline of its political power, as well as to the spread of Mohammedanism in N. Africa and Armenia. In both cases the attempt at translation of Greek ideas into the Syrian and Egyptian vernacular had been an additional reason for the long continuance of the controversy.

A violent controversy at once sprung up, and a schism was organized, followed by violent disturbances. But it is notable that Dioscorus disappears from history after his deposition. His adversaries did not subject him to the same severities as those under which Nestorius perished. He had reason to be thankful that the fair-minded and gentle-hearted Theodoret was the leader of his opponents, and not the hard, intolerant, and relentless Cyril. Marcian contrived to restore order. But on his death fresh tumults arose. A rival patriarch, Timotheus Aelurus, was nominated, and Proterius, who had succeeded Dioscorus, was slain. The new emperor, Leo, deposed Timotheus. But the schism continued. The emperor Zeno next (482) issued his famous HENOTICON, in which, while Nestorius and Eutyches were anathematized, twelve chapters (or selections) from the works of Cyril were accepted. But Zeno's manner of life evoked no enthusiasm, and Philoxenus—favourably known to us as the patron of the Philoxenian-Syriac version of the Scriptures—"Peter the clothier," and Severus, organized a formidable Monophysite party in Syria, Egypt, and Constantinople respectively. Justinian, emperor from 527-565, did his utmost to support the decrees of Chalcedon, while his consort, the famous, or, as some historians prefer to put it, the infamous, Theodora, did her best to thwart her husband, at the instance of some ecclesiastical intriguers who had contrived to worm themselves into her confidence. For the controversy of the "Three Chapters" see NESTORIUS. Its result was to encourage Monophysitism, and that form of Christian belief rooted itself in Armenia, Mesopotamia, Egypt, and ultimately in Abyssinia. The Coptic (the word Coptic is etymologically the same as Egyptian) church has remained as a separate body in Egypt to the present day. The Maronites in Armenia form another community which owes its existence to the Monophysite controversy. The Monophysites called their orthodox opponents *Melchites*, on the ground that they had accepted their opinions from the civil government and its head, the emperor; while the orthodox bestowed on their opponents the name of *Jacobites*, from Jacob of Edessa, an enthusiastic disseminator of Monophysite views.

It is unnecessary to follow out in full detail the history of the Monophysite schism. It only remains to mention that a reaction dating from the condemnation of the "Three Chapters" issued in Monotheletism, or the assertion of only *one will* in Christ. This controversy led to the summoning of a *sixth* oecumenical council at Constantinople in 680, in which Monotheletism was condemned, after having been anathematized at Rome, under Martin I., in 649. Communion between the East and the West had been broken off for some time on this point, and pope Honorius, like his predecessors Liberius and Vigilius, fell into suspicion of heresy in the course of the controversy. But the decision of the above-mentioned council restored the interrupted communion, and more friendly relations between the East and the West continued to subsist for above 300 years. The Coptic church, persecuted first by its orthodox sister, and afterwards by the Mohammedans, has obstinately maintained a precarious and downtrodden existence from the 6th cent. to the present moment. It has practically ceased to be heterodox, and in 1843 proposals for union with the Orthodox church would have been carried into effect, but that when the Moslem Government heard of them, the Coptic patriarch was invited to take coffee with a prominent Government official, and went home to die of poison. Since the British occupation in 1882 the Coptic church has begun to emerge from its long period of depression. The lay Copts have become educated and even wealthy. Though but a seventh of the population, they own one-fifth of the property of their country. One of their number became prime minister—the first Coptic prime minister for a very long period—but was unfortunately murdered in an outburst of political and religious fanaticism early in 1910. Though the Coptic clergy are still ignorant and fanatical, and the aged patriarch refuses to take any steps towards their better education, the laity have extorted a permission from him for the appointment of a certain number of laity authorized to give instruction to their co-religionists on the truths of the Christian religion. The educated laity are decidedly friendly towards the Anglican church. Two missions to the Copts have been sent of late years from England, one in 1843 and the other in the last decade of the 19th cent. Neither of them were successful, and the

Copts will probably be allowed for the future to carry out the much-needed reforms in their system in their own way. The Maronites of the Lebanon have remained apart from the Orthodox church of the East up to the present time, but the French political influence in the Lebanon since 1860 has caused a considerable number of them to join the church of Rome. The church of Abyssinia, though its Liturgy shows some beautiful traces of the purer ages of Christianity, has fallen into many superstitions and corruptions. Yet that church has had sufficient vitality to claim representation among the numerous churches and denominations which now gather at the cradle of Christianity, and not the least imposing religious edifice to be seen at Jerusalem is the Abyssinian church.

General Effect of the Controversies about the Person of Christ.—It may not be out of place, in conclusion, to endeavour to arrive at some estimate of the influence of these prolonged and bitter controversies upon the history of the Christian church. On the surface that influence appears unfavourable. Not only was the church of Christ broken up into antagonistic sections which mutually hated each other, but a divided Christendom fell an easy victim to the Mohammedan invader. Western theology, when deprived of the balance afforded by the more purely intellectual characteristics predominant in the East, crystallized into a Roman mould. Not even the revival of letters cured this evil, and we find that even post-Reformation theology has not altogether escaped from the long domination of purely Western forms of thought. But to stop short here would be one-sided and superficial. The effect of these prolonged controversies has undoubtedly been to clear up the confusion which long existed in the Christian mind about the relations of the three Persons (or *distinctions*) in the Trinity, and of the two natures in the one Christ. The two conflicting tendencies at work in the Nestorian and Monophysite heresies were (1) the disposition to divide the Redeemer into two separate beings, united to one another for God's purpose of salvation, and (2) the disposition either (*a*) to make the Redeemer a Being compounded out of two other beings, God and Man, being Himself neither one nor the other, or (*b*) to regard the Humanity of Christ as swallowed up by His Divinity. Of these two forms of Monophysite doctrine the former is ultimately unthinkable. An Infinite Being and a finite one cannot possibly coalesce into a third being, which is neither the one nor the other. The second view, though in itself by no means inconceivable, has been felt to contradict the definite statements of Scripture on the nature of the union between God the Word and the Man Christ Jesus, and is therefore inadmissible. The controversy, pursued with great virulence for about a century and a half, ended by the definite establishment of a mean between the two extremes, namely, that Christ consisted of two separate natures, the Godhead and the Manhood, conjoined into one Personality or Individuality, *i.e.* one ultimate source of thought and action. Not that there was only one mind, or one will, in the Personality underlying these two natures, but that the action of the lower will was confined within certain limits, and ultimately determined by the fiat of the Divine and Higher Will. If it was permitted to the theologian to speak of a *communicatio idiomatum* (transfer of attributes), this involved no confusion nor amalgamation of the two natures, no absorption of the one by (or into) the other. Each remains separate and complete. But some attributes of the one nature may be spoken of as transferred to the other, by reason of the inseparable conjunction of both in the One Person (ὑπόστασις or πρόσωπον). Thus if, as is sometimes the case, God is spoken of as suffering or dying, it is not to be supposed that the Godhead, as such, is capable of suffering or of death. The expression is only permissible in consequence of the inseparable conjunction of Christ's Godhead and Manhood in one Personality. The same caution must be borne in mind when the Blessed Virgin is spoken of as θεοτόκος. God cannot be brought forth into this world as man is brought forth. Yet the Divine Word and the Man Christ Jesus are inseparably one. Another point must not be lost sight of. In the Nestorian and Monophysite controversies the word Hypostasis is applied to the Personal Mind and Will which separates the Being thus indicated from any other existence. But when, as in the Arian controversy, the word Hypostasis is applied to the so-called Persons in the Godhead, it is not used to indicate separate sources of thought and action, but is employed to denote certain eternal distinctions declared in Holy Scripture to exist within the Godhead Itself, where there can be only one Mind and Will. We confess that the Father's sole prerogative is to originate, the Son's to reveal, the Spirit's to guide, direct, inspire. But all these prerogatives co-exist harmoniously in Him, Who is above all, and through all, and in us all. The decisions of the four great oecumenical councils are thus a standing witness to the fact that the church, from the beginning till now, has taught consistently that Jesus Christ was (1) ἀληθῶς (truly), (2) τελέως (completely), (3) ἀδιαιρέτως (indivisibly), and (4) ἀσυγχύτως (without confusion [of nature]) the Word, or Son of the Eternal God, Who in the last times, "for us men and for our salvation," took upon Him our flesh, and manifested Himself to the world "in the form of a bond-slave," and that His two natures remained separate and uncombined. And so, being at once Perfect God and Perfect Man, He is able, not only to reconcile God and Man, and to destroy the empire of sin in the latter, but can in the end present us, reconciled and saved, as perfect and unblamable before the God and Father of us all.

Bibliography.—Our authorities are nearly the same as those given under NESTORIUS. We have no longer the help of Socrates, but Evagrius is vivid, and generally accurate, though often very credulous. He accepts implicitly the decisions of Ephesus and Chalcedon, and of the latter he gives a detailed and careful summary. The letters of Theodoret, and the collection of the letters of other men of mark in his day, found in many editions of his works [NESTORIUS] are full of information on the Monophysite controversy. In later times Monophysitism does not seem to have attracted the attention of writers to the same extent as Nestorianism has done. There is no work on the former corresponding to those of Assemani and Badger on the latter. Neander, Dorner, Canon Bright, and, more recently, Mr. Bethune Baker are as useful here as on Nestorianism. Canon Bright has also translated and edited Leo's Sermons on the Incarnation. Gieseler is strangely brief on the controversy in the 5th cent., but has more information on its later developments. Mr. Wigram's *Intro. to the Hist. of the Assyrian Church* (S.P.C.K. 1910) has some chapters on the later developments of Monophysitism in the East. [J.J.L.]

Monothelitism. [MONOPHYSITISM.]

Montanus (1), a native of Ardabau, a village in Phrygia, who, in the latter half of the 2nd cent., originated a widespread schism, of which traces remained for centuries.

I. *Rise of Montanism.*—The name Montanus was not uncommon in the district. It is found in a Phrygian inscription (Le Bas, 755) and in three others from neighbouring provinces (Boeckh—3662 Cyzicus, 4071 Ancyra, 4187 Amasia). Montanus had been originally a heathen, and according to Didymus (*de Trin.* iii. 41) an idol priest. The epithets "abscissus" and "semivir" applied to him by Jerome (*Ep. ad Marcellam*, vol. i. 186) suggest that Jerome may have thought him a priest of Cybele. That after his conversion he became a priest or bishop there is no evidence. He taught that God's supernatural revelations did not end with the apostles, but that even more wonderful manifestations of the divine energy might be expected under the dispensation of the Paraclete. It is asserted that Montanus claimed himself to be the Paraclete; but we believe this to have merely arisen out of the fact that he claimed to be an inspired organ by whom the Paraclete spoke, and that consequently words of his were uttered and accepted as those of that Divine Being. We are told that Montanus claimed to be a prophet and spoke in a kind of possession or ecstasy. He held that the relation between a prophet and the Divine Being Who inspired him was the same as between a musical instrument and he who played upon it; consequently the inspired words of a prophet were not to be regarded as those of the human speaker. In a fragment of his prophecy preserved by Epiphanius he says, "I have come, not an angel or ambassador, but God the Father." See also Didymus (*u.s.*). It is clear that Montanus here did not speak in his own name, but uttered words which he supposed God to have put into his mouth; and if he spoke similarly in the name of the Paraclete it does not follow that he claimed to be the Paraclete.

His prophesyings were soon outdone by two female disciples, Prisca or Priscilla and Maximilla, who fell into strange ecstasies, delivering in them what Montanus and his followers regarded as divine prophecies. They had been married, left their husbands, were given by Montanus the rank of virgins in the church, and were widely reverenced as prophetesses. But very different was the sober judgment formed of them by some of the neighbouring bishops. Phrygia was a country in which heathen devotion exhibited itself in the most fanatical form, and it seemed to calm observers that the frenzied utterances of the Montanistic prophetesses were far less like any previous manifestation of the prophetic gift among Christians than they were to those heathen orgiasms which the church had been wont to ascribe to the operation of demons. The church party looked on the Montanists as wilfully despising our Lord's warning to beware of false prophets, and as being in consequence deluded by Satan, in whose power they placed themselves by accepting as divine teachers women possessed by evil spirits. The Montanists looked on the church leaders as men who did despite to the Spirit of God by offering the indignity of exorcism to those whom He had chosen as His organs for communicating with the church. It does not appear that any offence was taken at the substance of the Montanistic prophesyings. On the contrary, it was owned that they had a certain plausibility; when with their congratulations and promises to those who accepted them they mixed a due proportion of rebukes and warnings, this was ascribed to the deeper art of Satan. What condemned the prophesyings in the minds of the church authorities was the frenzied ecstasy in which they were delivered.

The question as to the different characteristics of real and pretended prophecy was the main subject of discussion in the first stage of the Montanist controversy. It may have been treated of by Melito in his work on prophecy; it was certainly the subject of that of Miltiades περὶ τοῦ μὴ δεῖν προφήτην ἐν ἐκστάσει λαλεῖν; it was touched on in an early anonymous writing against Montanism [ABERCIUS], of which large fragments are preserved by Eusebius (v. 16, 17). Some more of this polemic is almost certainly preserved by Epiphanius, who often incorporates the labours of previous writers and whose section on Montanism contains a discussion which is clearly not Epiphanius's own, but a survival from the first stage of the controversy. We learn that the Montanists brought as Scripture examples of ecstasy the text "the Lord sent a deep sleep (ἔκστασιν) upon Adam," that David said in his haste (ἐν ἐκστάσει) "all men are liars," and that the same word is used of the vision which warned Peter to accept the invitation of Cornelius. The orthodox opponent points out that Peter's "not so" shews that in his ecstasy he did not lose his individual judgment and will. Other similar instances are quoted from O.T.

The same argument was probably pursued by Clement of Alexandria, who promised to write on prophecy against the Montanists (*Strom.* iv. 13, p. 605). He notes it as a characteristic of false prophets ἐν ἐκστάσει προεφήτευον ὡς ἂν Ἀποστάτου διάκονοι (i. 17, p. 369). Tertullian no doubt defended the Montanist position in his lost work in six books on ecstasy.

Notwithstanding the condemnation of Montanism and the excommunication of Montanists by neighbouring bishops, it continued to spread and make converts. Visitors came from far to witness the wonderful phenomena;

and the condemned prophets hoped to reverse the first unfavourable verdict by the sentence of a larger tribunal. But all the leading bishops of Asia Minor declared against it. At length an attempt was made to influence or overrule the judgment of Asiatic Christians by the opinion of their brethren beyond the sea. We cannot be sure how long Montanus had been teaching, or how long the excesses of his prophetesses had continued; but in 177 Western attention was first called to these disputes, the interference being solicited of the martyrs of Lyons, then suffering imprisonment and expecting death for the testimony of Christ. They were informed of the disputes by their brethren in Asia Minor, the native country no doubt of many of the Gallic Christians. Eusebius in his Chronicle assigns 172 for the beginning of the prophesying of Montanus. A few years more seems necessary for the growth of the new sect in Asia before it forced itself on the attention of foreign Christians, and the Epiphanian date 157 appears more probable, and agrees the vague date of Didymus, "more than 100 years after the Ascension." Possibly 157 may be the date of the conversion of Montanus, 172 that of his formal condemnation by the Asiatic church authorities.

Were the Gallic churches consulted by the orthodox, by the Montanists, or by both? and what answer did the Gallic Christians give? Eusebius only tells us that their judgment was pious and most orthodox, and that they subjoined letters which those who afterwards suffered martyrdom wrote while yet in prison to the brethren in Asia and Phrygia and also to Eleutherus, bp. of Rome, pleading (or negotiating, πρεσβεύοντες) for the peace of the churches. If, as has been suggested, the last expression meant entreating the removal of the excommunication from the Montanists, Eusebius, who begins his account of Montanism by describing it as a device of Satan, would not have praised such advice as pious and orthodox.

We think that *the Montanists had appealed to Rome*; that the church party solicited the good offices of their countrymen settled in Gaul, who wrote to Eleutherus representing the disturbance to the peace of the churches (a phrase probably preserved by Eusebius from the letter itself) which would ensue if the Roman church approved what the church on the spot condemned. We have no reason to think of Rome as then enjoying such supremacy that its reversal of an Asiatic excommunication would be quietly acquiesced in. Yet the Asiatic bishops might well be anxious how their decision would commend itself to the judgment of a stranger at a distance. To such a one there would be nothing incredible in special manifestations of God's Spirit displaying themselves in Phrygia, while the suggestion that the new prophesying was inspired by Satan might be repelled by its admitted orthodoxy, since all it professed to reveal tended to the glory of Christ and to the increase of Christian devotion. To avert, then, the possible calamity of a breach between the Eastern and Western churches, the Gallic churches, it would appear, not only wrote, but sent Irenaeus to Rome at the end of 177 or the beginning of 178. This hypothesis relieves us from the necessity of supposing this πρεσβεία to have been unsuccessful, while it fully accounts for the necessity of sending it.

The Asiatic churches laid before the Christian world justification for their course. Their case was stated by one of their most eminent bishops, Claudius Apolinarius of Hierapolis. Apolinarius gives the signatures of different bishops who had investigated and condemned the Montanist prophesyings. One of these, Sotas of Anchialus, on the western shore of the Black Sea, was dead when Apolinarius wrote; but Aelius Publius Julius, bp. of the neighbouring colony of Debeltus, gives his sworn testimony that Sotas had tried to cast the demon out of Priscilla but had been hindered by the hypocrites. We learn from a later writer that Zoticus of Comana and Julianus of Apamea similarly attempted to exorcise Maximilla, and were not permitted to do so. Another of Apolinarius's authorities adds weight to his signature by appending the title martyr, then commonly given to those who braved imprisonment or tortures for Christ. The result was that the Roman church approved the sentence of the Asiatic bishops, as we know independently from Tertullian.

II. *Montanism in the East, second stage.*—For the history of Montanism in the East after its definite separation from the church, our chief authorities are fragments preserved by Eusebius of two writers, the anonymous writer already mentioned and Apollonius of Ephesus. The date of both these writings is considerably later than the rise of Montanism. Apollonius places himself 40 years after its first beginning. In the time of the Anonymous the first leaders of the schism had vanished from the scene. Montanus was dead, as was Theodotus, an early leader in the movement, who had probably managed its finances, for he is said to have been towards it a kind of ἐπίτροπος. The Anonymous states that at the time he wrote 13 full years had elapsed and a 14th had begun since the death of Maximilla. Priscilla must have died previously, for Maximilla believed herself to be the last prophetess in the church and that after her the end would come.

Themiso seems to have been, after Montanus, the head of the Montanists. He was at any rate their leading man at Pepuza; and this was the headquarters of the sect. There probably Montanus had taught; there the prophetesses Priscilla and Maximilla resided; there Priscilla had seen in a vision Christ come in the form of a woman in a bright garment, who inspired her with wisdom and informed her that Pepuza was the holy place and that there the New Jerusalem was to descend from heaven. Thenceforth Pepuza and the neighbouring village Tymium became the Montanist holy place, habitually spoken of as Jerusalem. There Zoticus and Julianus visited Maximilla, and Themiso was then at the head of those who prevented the intended exorcism.

Montanus himself probably did not live long to preside over his sect, and this is perhaps why it is seldom called by the name of its founder. The sectaries called themselves πνευματικοί, spiritual, and the adherents of the church ψυχικοί, carnal, thus following the usage of some Gnostic sects. In Phrygia itself the Catholics seem to have called the new prophesying after its leader for the time being. Elsewhere it was called after its place of origin, the Phrygian heresy. In the West the name became by a solecism the Cataphrygian heresy.

Apparently after Themiso MILTIADES presided over the sect; the Anonymous calls it the heresy *τῶν κατὰ Μιλτιάδην*. One other Montanist of this period was Alexander, who was honoured by his party as a martyr, but had, according to Apollonius, been only punished by the proconsul, Aemilius Frontinus, for his crimes, as the public records would testify. We cannot, unfortunately, fix the date of that proconsulship.

Taking the Eusebian date, 172, for the rise of Montanism, Apollonius, who wrote 40 years later, must have written *c.* 210. The Epiphanian date, 157, would make him 15 years earlier. The Anonymous gives us a clue to his date in the statement that whereas Maximilla had foretold wars and tumults, there had been more than 13 years since her death with no general nor partial war, and the Christians had enjoyed continual peace. This, then, must have been written either before the wars of the reign of Severus had begun or after they had finished. The latest admissible date on the former hypothesis gives us 192, and for the death of Maximilla 179. It is hardly likely that in so short a time all the original leaders of the movement would have died.

Before the end of the 2nd cent. Montanist teachers had made their way as far as Antioch; for Serapion, the bishop there, wrote against them, copying the letter of Apolinarius. It is through Serapion that Eusebius seems to have known this letter.

Early in the 3rd cent. the church had made converts enough from Montanists born in the sect for the question to arise, On what terms were converts to be received who had had no other than Montanist baptism? Matter and form were perfectly regular; for in all essential points of doctrine these sectaries agreed with the church. But it was decided, at a council held at Iconium, to recognize no baptism given outside the church. This we learn from the letter to Cyprian by Firmilian of Caesarea in Cappadocia, when the later controversy arose about heretical baptism. This council, and one which made a similar decision at another Phrygian town, Synnada, are mentioned also by Dionysius of Alexandria (Eus. vii. 7). Firmilian speaks as if he had been present at the Iconium council, which may be dated *c.* 230.

So entirely had the Catholics ceased to regard the Montanists as Christian brethren that, as stated by the Anonymous, when persecution by the common enemy threw confessors from both bodies together, the orthodox persevered till their final martyrdom in refusing to hold intercourse with their Montanist fellow-sufferers; dreading to hold any friendship with the lying spirit who animated them. Epiphanius states that in his time the sect had many adherents in Phrygia, Galatia, Cappadocia, and Cilicia, and a considerable number in Constantinople.

III. *Montanism in the West.*—If we set aside the worthless Praedestinatus, there is no evidence whatever that any Roman bp. before Eleutherus had heard of Montanism, and the history of the interference of the Gallic confessors in 177 shews that it was then a new thing in the West. The case submitted to Eleutherus no doubt informed him by letter of the events in Phrygia; but apparently no Montanist teachers visited the West at this time, and after the judgment of Eleutherus the whole transaction seems to have been forgotten at Rome. It was in a subsequent episcopate that the first Montanist teacher, probably Proclus, appeared at Rome. There was no reason to regard him with suspicion. He could easily satisfy the bishop of his perfect orthodoxy in doctrine; and there was no ground for disbelieving what he might tell of supernatural manifestations in his own country. He was therefore either received into communion, or was about to be so and to obtain authority to report to his churches in Asia that their commendatory letters were recognized at Rome, when the arrival of another Asiatic, Praxeas, changed the scene. Praxeas could shew the Roman bp. that the Montanist pretensions to prophecy had been condemned by his predecessors, and probably the letter of Eleutherus was still accessible in the Roman archives. The justice of this previous condemnation Praxeas could confirm from his own knowledge of the Montanist churches and their prophesyings; and his testimony had the more weight because, having suffered imprisonment for the faith, he enjoyed the dignity of a martyr. The Montanist teacher was accordingly put out of communion at Rome. This story, which has all the marks of probability, is told by Tertullian (*adv. Prax.*), who probably had personal knowledge of the facts. The bishop could only be Zephyrinus, for we cannot go later; and as predecessors in the plural number are spoken of, these must have been Eleutherus and Victor. The conclusion which we have reached, that Montanism made no appearance in the West before the episcopate of Zephyrinus, is of great importance in the chronology of this controversy.

The formal rejection of Montanism by the Roman church was followed by a public disputation between the Montanist teacher Proclus, and Caius, a leading Roman presbyter. Eusebius, who read the record of it, says it took place under Zephyrinus. The Montanist preachers, whatever their failures, had one distinguished success in the acquisition of Tertullian. Apparently the condemnation of the Roman bishop was not in his mind decisive against the Montanist claims, and he engaged in an advocacy of them which resulted in his separation from the church. His writings are the great storehouse of information as to the peculiarities of Montanist teaching. The Italian Montanists were soon divided by schism arising out of the violent Patripassian controversy at Rome at the beginning of the 3rd cent. Among the Montanists, Aeschines was the head of the Patripassian party, and in this it would appear from an extract in Didymus that he followed Montanus himself; Proclus and his followers adhered to the orthodox doctrine on this subject.

IV. *Montanism and the Canon.*—The most

fundamental innovation of Montanist teaching was the theory of an authorized development of Christian doctrine, as opposed to the older theory that Christian doctrine was preached in its completeness by the apostles and that the church had merely to preserve faithfully the tradition of their teaching. The Montanists did not reject the apostolic revelations nor abandon any doctrines the church had learned from its older teachers. The revelations of the new prophecy were to supplement, not to displace, Scripture. They believed that while the fundamental truths of faith remained unshaken, points both of discipline and doctrine might receive correction. "A process of development was exhibited in God's revelations. It had its rudimentary principle in the religion of nature, its infancy in the law and the prophets, its youth in the gospel, its full maturity only in the dispensation of the Paraclete. Through His enlightenment the dark places of Scripture are made clear, parables made plain, those passages of which heretics had taken advantage cleared of all ambiguity" (Tert. *de Virg. Vel.* i.; *de Res. Carn.* 63). Accordingly Tertullian appeals to the new revelations on questions of discipline, *e.g.* second marriages, and also on questions of doctrine, as in his work against Praxeas and his treatise on the Resurrection of the Flesh. Some have thought it a thing to be regretted that the church by her condemnation of Montanism should have suppressed the freedom of individual prophesying. But each new prophetic revelation, if acknowledged as divine, would put as great a restraint on future individual speculation as words of Scripture or decree of pope or council. If Montanism had triumphed, Christian doctrine would have been developed, not under the superintendence of the church teachers most esteemed for wisdom, but usually of wild and excitable women. Thus Tertullian himself derives his doctrine as to the materiality and the form of the soul from a revelation made to an ecstatica of his congregation (*de Anima*, 9). To the Montanists it seemed that if God's Spirit made known anything as true, that truth could not be too extensively published. It is evident from quotations in Epiphanius and Tertullian that the prophecies of Maximilla and Montanus were committed to writing. To those who believed in their divine inspiration, these would practically form additional Scriptures. Hippolytus tells that the Montanists "have an infinity of books of these prophets whose words they neither examine by reason, nor give heed to those who can, but are carried away by their undiscriminating faith in them, thinking that they learn through their means something more than from the law, the prophets, and the gospels." Didymus is shocked at a prophetical book emanating from a female, whom the apostle did not permit to teach. It would be a mistake to suppose that the Montanistic disputes led to the formation of a N.T. canon. On the contrary, it is plain that when these disputes arose Christians had so far closed their N.T. canon that they were shocked that any modern writing should be made equal to the inspired books of the apostolic age. The Montanist disputes led to the publication of lists recognized by particular churches, and we consider that it was in opposition to the multitude of Montanist prophetic books that Caius in his disputation gave a list recognized by his church. The controversy also made Christians more scrupulous about paying to other books honours like those given to the books of Scripture, and we believe that it was for this reason that the *Shepherd* of Hermas ceased to have a place in church reading. But still we think it plain from the history that the conception of a closed N.T. canon was found by Montanism and not then created.

V. *Montanist Doctrines and Practices.*—The church objected, as against Montanism, to *any* addition being made to the teaching of Scripture. What, then, was the nature of the additions actually made by the Montanists?

(1) *New Fasts.*—The prophetesses had ordained that in addition to the ordinary Paschal fast of the church two weeks of what was called Xerophagy should be observed. In these the Montanists abstained, not only from flesh, wine, and the use of the bath, but from all succulent food, *e.g.* juicy fruit, except on Saturday and Sunday. The weekly stations also, or half fasts, which in the church ended at three p.m., were by Montanists usually continued till evening. The church party resisted the claim that these two new weeks of abstinence were divinely obligatory. The real question was, Had the prophetess God's command for instituting them? This particular revelation only came into prominence because at recurring intervals it put a marked difference between Montanists and Catholics, similar to that which the Paschal fast put between Christians and heathen.

(2) *Second Marriages.*—On this subject again the difference between the Montanists and the church really reduces itself to the question whether the Paraclete spoke by Montanus. Second marriages had before Montanus been regarded with disfavour in the church. Tertullian deprecates them with almost as much energy in his pre-Montanist work *ad Uxorem* as afterwards in his Montanist *de Monogamia.* But however unfavourably such marriages were regarded, their validity and lawfulness were not denied. St. Paul had seemed to declare that such marriages were not forbidden (Rom. vii. 3; I. Cor. vii. 39), and the direction in the pastoral epistles that a bishop should be husband of one wife seemed to leave others free.

(3) *Church Discipline.*—The treatise of Tertullian (*de Pudicitia*) shews a controversy of Montanists with the church concerning the power of church officers to give absolution. The occasion was the publication, by one whom Tertullian sarcastically calls "Pontifex Maximus" and "Episcopus Episcoporum," of an edict of pardon to persons guilty of adultery and fornication on due performance of penance. Doubtless a bp. of Rome is intended, and as Hippolytus tells (ix. 12) of Callistus being the first to introduce such laxity in granting absolution, it seems plain that Callistus was referred to. Tertullian holds that for such sin absolution ought never to be given. Not that the sinner was to despair of obtaining God's pardon by repent-

ance; but it was for God alone to pardon; man might not.

We refer to our art. TERTULLIAN for other doctrines which, though advocated by Tertullian in his Montanist days, we do not feel ourselves entitled to set down as Montanistic, in the absence of evidence that Tertullian had learned them from Montanus, or that they were held by Eastern Montanists. The bulk of what Tertullian taught as a Montanist he probably would equally have taught if Montanus had never lived; but owing to the place which Montanism ascribed to visions and revelations as means of obtaining a knowledge of the truth, his belief in his opinions was converted into assurance when they were echoed by prophetesses who in their visions gave utterance to opinions imbibed from their master in their waking hours.

VI. *Later History of Montanism.*—We gather from Tertullian's language (*adv. Prax.*) that it was some time before his persistent advocacy of Montanism drew excommunication on himself. To this interval we refer the Acts of Perpetua and Felicitas, in the editor of which we may perhaps recognize Tertullian himself. Both martyrs and martyrologist had clearly been under Montanist influences: great importance is attached to visions and revelations, and the editor justifies the composition of new Acts, intended for church reading, on the grounds that the "last days" in which he lived had witnessed, as had been prophesied, new visions, new prophecies, new exhibitions of the mighty working of God's Spirit, as great as or greater than in any preceding age. Yet the martyrs are evidently in full communion with the church. The schism which soon afterwards took place appears to have been of little importance either in numbers or duration. We hear nothing of Montanists in the writings of Cyprian, whose veneration for Tertullian would scarcely have been so great if his church were still suffering from a schism which Tertullian originated. In the next cent. Optatus (i. 9) speaks of Montanism as an extinct heresy, which it were slaying the slain to refute. Yet there were some who called themselves after Tertullian in the 4th cent. Augustine (*Haer.* 86) at Carthage heard that a well-known church which formerly belonged to the Tertullianists had been surrendered to the Catholics when the last of them returned to the church. He had evidently heard no tradition as to their tenets, and set himself to search in Tertullian's writings for heresies which they presumably may have held. Elsewhere in the West Montanism entirely disappears.

In the East, we have already mentioned the councils of Iconium and of Synnada. There is a mention of Montanism in the Acts of Achatius (Ruinart, p. 152). Though these Acts lack external attestation, internal evidence strongly favours their authenticity. Their scene is uncertain; the time is the Decian persecution A.D. 250. The magistrate, urging Achatius to sacrifice, presses him with the example of the Cataphrygians, "homines antiquae religionis," who had already conformed. Sozomen (ii. 32) ascribes the extinction of the Montanists, as well as of other heretical sects, to the edict of Constantine depriving them of their places of worship and forbidding their religious meetings. Till then, being confounded by heathen rulers with other Christians, they could meet for worship, and, even when few in number, keep together; but Constantine's edict killed all the weaker sects, and among them the Montanists, everywhere except in Phrygia and neighbouring districts, where they were still numerous in Sozomen's time. He says (vii. 18) that, unlike Scythia, where one bishop ruled over the whole province, among these Phrygian heretics every village had its bishop. At last the orthodox zeal of Justinian took measures to crush out the remains of the sect in Phrygia, and the Montanists in despair gathered with wives and children into their places of worship, set them on fire, and there perished (Procop. *Hist. Arc.* 11). In connexion with this may be taken what is told of John of Ephesus in the same reign of Justinian (Assemani, *Bibl. Or.* ii. 88), that A.D. 550 he had the bones dug up and burned of Montanus and of his prophetesses Carata, Prisca, and Maximilla. What is disguised under the name Carata we cannot tell. It is hardly likely that Montanism survived the persecution of Justinian. Besides Cataphrygians they were often called from their headquarters, Pepuzans, which Epiphanius counts as a distinct heresy. The best monograph on Montanism is by Bonwetsch (Erlangen, 1881). See also Zahn, *Forschanger zur Gesch. des N.T. Kanons*, etc. (1893), v. 3 ff., on the chronology of Montanism. [G.S.]

Montanus (3), bp. of Toledo, *c.* 523–*c.* 531.

Authorities.—(1) His Life by Ildefonsus (*de Vir. Ill.* c. 3). (2) Two letters printed by Loaysa (*Conc. Hisp.* p. 88), Aguirre (*Coll. Max. Conc. Hisp.* ii. 159), and Florez (*Esp. Sagr.* v. 409, 415). (3) The Acts of the second council of Toledo (Tejada y Ramiro, *Coll. de Can. de la Igl. Esp.* ii. 701).

His Life.—The facts related by Ildefonsus are meagre. We are told that Montanus was the successor of Celsus in the "prima sedes" of the province of Carthaginensis; that he defended and maintained his office; that he wrote two letters on points of church discipline, one to the inhabitants of Palencia, the other to a certain Turibius, a "religious"; and that he rebutted a scandalous accusation by the help of a miracle wrought in his favour. These Acts of the second council of Toledo are curious and important, and have been suspected of at least containing interpolations, if not of being altogether supposititious, but there seems no sufficient reason for doubting their genuineness. The council opened on May 17 in the 5th year of Amalaric (A.D. 527) according to the reckoning generally adopted since Florez's day, 531 according to the older reckoning. The bishops began by expressing their intention of adding to the *Codex Canonum* certain provisions not already contained in the ancient canons on the one hand, and of reviving such prescriptions as had fallen into disuse on the other. The material of these canons is common to most of the various Spanish councils of the first half of 6th cent. It is the concluding passage of the Acts which makes the council of special interest in Spanish ecclesiastical history. "According to the decrees of ancient canons, we declare that,

God willing, the council shall be held in future 'apud' our brother, the bishop Montanus, so that it will be the duty of our brother and co-bishop Montanus, *who is in the metropolis*, to forward to our co-principals, bishops of the Lord, letters convening the synod when the proper time shall arrive." An expression of thanks "to the glorious king Amalaric," with regard to whom the bishops pray that "throughout the unnumbered years of his reign he may continue to afford us the licence of carrying through all that pertains to the cultus fidei," concludes the Acts. In the words in italics is contained the first mention of Toledo as the ecclesiastical metropolis of Carthaginensis, the first indication of that commanding position to which the see was to attain under its 7th-cent. bishops. The passage also indicates the relations of Montanus with king Amalaric. Relying upon his support, upon the physical advantages of Toledo, and upon an ecclesiastical tradition capable of various interpretations, Montanus sought permanently to exalt the power and position of his see. But the time was not yet come, and the question still remained an open one in 589 when Leovigild fixed the seat of the consolidated Gothic power at Toledo, and practically settled the long-vexed question. Cartagena was in the hands of Byzantium, whereas the bp. of Toledo was the bishop of the urbs regia. It took some time to accomplish, but the *Decretum Gundemari* as a first step, and the Primacy Canon of the 12th council of Toledo as a second, were the inevitable ecclesiastical complements of physical and political facts. Hefele, *Conc. Gesch.* ii. 700; *Esp. Sagr.* v. 131, c. iii. [M.A.W.]

Moses (3) (*Moyses*), Roman presbyter (? of Jewish origin), a leading member of an influential group of confessors in the time of Cyprian, about the commencement of the Novatianist schism. The others were Maximus, Nicostratus, Rufinus, Urbanus, Sidonius, Macarius, and Celerinus. They wrote early in the persecution, urging the claims of discipline on the Carthaginian confessors (*Ep.* 27) (cf. Tillem. t. iii. Notes s. Moyse, t. iv., S. Cyp. a. xv., Lipsius, *Chr. d. röm. Bisch.* p. 200), and Moyses signed the second letter of the Roman clerus (viz. *Ep.* 30), drawn up by Novatian according to Cyprian (*Ep.* 55, iv.), and he wrote with the other confessors *Ep.* 31 to Cyprian (*Ep.* 32). When they had been a year in prison (*Ep.* 37), or more accurately 11 months and days (Liberian Catalogue, Mommsen, *Chronogr.* v. Jahre 354, p. 635), *i.e. c.* Jan. 1, 251, Moyses died and was accounted a confessor and martyr (*Ep.* 55). Shortly before his death he refused to communicate with *Novatian and the five presbyters* who sided with him (ἀποσχίσασιν) because he saw the tendency of his stern dogma (Cornelius to Fabius of Antioch, Eus. vi. 43, κατιδών).

Moyses' severance was not because Novatian had already left the Catholics, which he did not do till June 4, after the election of Cornelius; and Novatus, who induced it, did not leave Carthage for Rome until April or May (Rettberg, p. 109). Moyses' great authority remained a strong point in Cornelius's favour, when the rest of the confessors (*Ep.* 51) after their release threw their influence on the side of Novatian as representing the stricter discipline against Cornelius. The headship of the party belonged after Moyses' death to MAXIMUS (3). [E.W.B.]

Moses (5), of Khoren (*Moses Khorenensis*)—called by his countrymen the Father of History—the poet, grammarian, and most celebrated writer of Armenia, was the nephew and disciple of St. Mesrob, the founder of Armenian literature. [MESROBES.] Born at Khoren or Khorni, a town of the province of Darou, he was one of a band of scholars sent by Mesrob to study at Edessa, Constantinople, Alexandria, Athens, and Rome. There he accumulated very wide historical knowledge (cf. *Hist. Armen.* iii. 61, 62). Returning to Armenia, he assisted St. Mesrob in translating the Bible into his native language, a work which was accomplished between 407 and 433. This fixes his birth in the early part of cent. v.; though some place it in the latter part of cent. iv. Beyond his literary activity we do not know much about his life. He succeeded Eznig as bp. of Pakrevant, where he displayed great spiritual activity. According to the medieval Armenian chronicler, Samuel of Ani, he died in 488, aged 120. The following works attributed to him are extant: (1) *Hist. of Armenia*, (2) *Treatise on Rhetoric*, (3) *Treatise on Geography*, (4) *Letter on Assumption of B. V. M.*, (5) *Homily on Christ's Transfiguration*, (6) *Oration on Hripsinia, an Armenian Virgin Martyr*, (7) *Hymns used in Armenian Church Worship*. He wrote also 2 works now lost, viz. *Commentaries on the Armenian Grammarians*, of which fragments are found in John Erzengatzi, an Armenian writer of cent. xiii., and *Explanations of Armenian Church Offices*, of which we have only some fragments in Thomas Ardzrouni (cent. vii.). The *Hist. of Armenia* is perhaps the work of a later writer, but it is in some respects one of the most important historical works of antiquity. It embodies almost our only remains of pre-Christian Armenian literature and preserves many songs and traditions retained at that time in popular memory. For special studies of it see Dulaurier in *Journ. Asiat.* Jan. 1852. It is also very valuable because it preserves extensive remains of Assyrian, Chaldean, Syrian, and Greek writers. Moses had studied long at Edessa, where the library was very rich in ancient Assyrian chroniclers. This work also throws much light on the history of the Roman empire in cents. iv. and v., and its struggles against the renewed Persian empire and the efforts of Zoroastrianism. It has been translated into Italian by the Mechitarite Fathers (Venice, 1841); into French by V. Langlois in *Historiens anciens de l'Arménie* (Paris, 1867). See also Æ. Carrière, *Moise de Khoren, etc.* (Paris, 1891); Id., *Nouvelles sources de Moise de Kh.* (Vienna, 1894); Id., *La légende d'Abgar, dans l'hist. de Moise de Kh.*; also F. C. Conybeare in *Byzant. Zeitschr.* (1901), x. 489 seq. [G.T.S.]

Muratorian Fragment, a very ancient list of the books of N.T. first pub. in 1740 by Muratori (*Ant. Ital. Med. Aev.* iii. 851) and found in a 7th or 8th cent. MS. in the Ambrosian Library at Milan. The MS. had come from the Irish monastery of Bobbio, and the fragment seems to have been a copy of a loose leaf or two of a lost volume. It is defective in the beginning, and breaks off in the middle of a sentence, and the mutilation must have taken place in the archetype of our present copy. This copy was made by an illiterate and careless scribe, and is full of blunders; but is of the greatest value as the earliest-known list of N.T. books recognized by the church. A reference to the episcopate of Pius at Rome ("nuperrime temporibus nostris") is usually taken to prove that the document cannot be later than *c.* 180, some 20 years after Pius's death (see *infra*). This precludes Muratori's own conjecture as to authorship, viz. that it was by Caius the presbyter, *c.* 196; and Bunsen's conjecture that Hegesippus wrote it has nothing to recommend it. It is generally agreed that it was written in Rome. Though in Latin, it bears marks of translation from the Greek, though Hesse (*Das. Mur. Frag.*, Giessen, 1873) and others maintain the originality of the Latin.

The first line of the fragment evidently concludes its notice of St. Mark's Gospel; for it proceeds to speak of St. Luke's as in the 3rd place, St. John's in the 4th. A notice of St. Matthew's and St. Mark's must have come before, but we have no means of knowing whether the O.T. books preceded that notice. The document appears to have dealt with the choice of topics in the Gospels and the point where each began (cf. Iren. iii. 11). It is stated that St. Luke (and apparently St. Mark also) had not seen our Lord in the flesh. For its story as to the composition of St. John's Gospel see LEUCIUS. The document goes on to say that by one and the same sovereign Spirit the same fundamental doctrines are fully taught in all concerning our Lord's birth, life, passion, resurrection, and future coming. At the date of this document, therefore, belief was fully established in the pre-eminence of the four Gospels, and in their divine inspiration. Next comes the Acts, St. Luke being credited with purposing to record only what fell under his own notice, thus omitting the martyrdom of St. Peter and St. Paul's journey to Spain. Thirteen epistles of St. Paul are then mentioned. (*a*) epistles to churches, in the order: I. and II. Cor., Eph., Phil., Col., Gal., I. and II. Thess., Rom. It is observed that St. Paul addressed (like St. John) only seven churches by name,* shewing that he addressed the universal church. (*b*) Epistles to individuals: Philemon, Titus, and two to Timothy, written from personal affection, but hallowed by the Catholic church for the ordering of ecclesiastical discipline. Next follow words which we quote from Westcott's trans.: "Moreover there is in circulation an epistle to the Laodiceans, and another to the Alexandrians, forged under the name of Paul, bearing on [*al.* 'favouring'] the heresy of Marcion, and several others, which cannot be received into the Catholic church, for gall ought not to be mingled with honey. The epistle of Jude, however, and two epistles bearing the name of John, are received in the Catholic [church] (or, are reckoned among the Catholic [epistles]). And the book of Wisdom, written by the friends of Solomon in his honour [is acknowledged]. We receive, moreover, the Apocalypses of St. John and St. Peter only, which latter some of our body will not have read in the church." Marcion entitled his version of Eph. "to the Laodiceans," and there is a well-known pseudo-Pauline epistle with the same title. It has been generally conjectured that by the epistle "to the Alexandrians," *Hebrews* is meant; but it is nowhere else so described, has no Marcionite tendency, and is not "under the name of Paul." The fragment may refer to some current writing which has not survived, or the Ep. of Barnabas might possibly be intended. Though only two Epp. of John are mentioned, the opening sentence of I. John had been quoted in the paragraph treating of the Gospel, and our writer may have read that epistle as a kind of appendix to the Gospel, and be here speaking of the other two. The mention of Wisdom in a list of N.T. books is perplexing. Perhaps we should read "ut" for "et"; and the Proverbs of Solomon and not the apocryphal book of Wisdom may be intended. There may be an inaccurate reference to Prov. xxv. 1 (LXX). The fragment next says that the *Shepherd* was written "very lately, in our own time" in the city of Rome, his brother-bishop Pius then occupying the chair of the Roman church; that, therefore, it ought to be read, but not in the public reading of the church. The text of the last sentence of the document is very corrupt, but evidently names writings which are rejected altogether, including those of Arsinous, Valentinus, and Militiades, mention being also made of the Cataphrygians of Asia.

Westcott has shewn that no argument can be built upon the omissions (Ep. of James, both Epp. of Peter, and Hebrews) of our fragment, since it shews so many blunders of transcription, and some breaks in the sense. Certainly I. Peter held, at the earliest date claimed for the fragment, such a position in the Roman church that entire silence in respect to it seems incredible. Of disquisitions on our fragment we may name Credner, *N. T. Kanon*, Volkmar's ed. 141 seq. 341 seq.; Routh, *Rell. Sac.* i. 394; Tregelles, *Canon Muratorianus*; Hesse, *op. cit.*; Westcott, *N. T. Canon*, 208 seq. 514 seq.; and esp. Zahn, *Gesch. der N.T. Kanons*, ii. 1 (1890), pp. 1-143; also Lietzman's *Das Mur Frag.* (Bonn, 1908), besides countless arts. in journals, *e.g.* Harnack, in *Text und Unters.* (1900); Overbeck, *Zur Geschichte des Kanons* (1880); Hilgenfeld, *Zeitschrift* (1881), p. 129. Hilgenfeld (*Kanon*, p. 44), and Bötticher (De Lagarde) in Bunsen's *Hippolytus* i. 2nd ed. *Christianity and Mankind*, attempted its re-translation into Greek; an ed., with notes and facsimile by S. P. Tregelles, is pub. by the Clar. Press. The present writer expressed in 1874 (*Hermathena* i.) an opinion which he now holds with more confidence that

* *I.e.* "nomination," which might suggest the acknowledgment as St. Paul's of *Hebrews* as not addressed to a church by name. But no mention of that epistle follows, as we should in that case expect. Cyril's mention of Paul's Epp. to Seven Churches (*de Exhort. Mort.* 11, cf. Tert. *adv. Jud.* and Optatus, *de Schism. Don.* ii. 3) and the language of Augustine (*de Civ. Dei.* xvii. iv. 4), Victorinus of Padua (*in Apoc.* 1) and Pseudo-Chrys. (*Op. imperf.* in Matt. i. 6, pp. vi. xvii. Bened. ed.) suggest the acquaintance of those writers with our document.

the fragment was written in the episcopate of Zephyrinus. The words "temporibus nostris" must not be too severely pressed. We have no evidence that the writer was as careful and accurate as Eusebius, who yet speaks (iii. 28, cf. v. 27) of a period 50 or 60 years before he was writing as his own time. There are also indications from the history of the varying position held by the *Shepherd* that the publication of our fragment may have been between Tertullian's two tracts *de Oratione* and *de Pudicitia* (see *D. C. B.* 4-vol. ed. *s.v.*); and if it be true that MONTANISM only became active in the Roman church in the episcopate of Zephyrinus, the date of the Muratorian document is settled, for it is clearly anti-Montanist. If we regard it as written in the episcopate of Zephyrinus, Muratori's conjecture that Caius wrote it becomes possible; and we know from Eusebius that the disputation of Caius with Proclus, written at that period, contained, in opposition to Montanist revelations, a list of the books reverenced by the Catholic church. [G.S.]

Musonius (1), bp. of Neocaesarea, on whose death in A.D. 368 Basil wrote a long letter of consolation to his widowed church (*Ep.* 28 [62]), lauding him greatly and designating him no unworthy successor of Gregory Thaumaturgus. He describes him as a rigid supporter of old customs and the ancient faith, endeavouring to conform his church in all things to the primitive model. His watchful care had preserved his church from the storms of heresy ravaging all neighbouring churches. In so great reverence was he held that, though by no means the oldest of the bishops, the presidency in council was always his. He must have attained the episcopate comparatively young, for, though he ruled the church of Neocaesarea many years, he was not very aged when he died. Though Musonius had been prejudiced against Basil, and regarded his election to the episcopate with no friendly eyes, so that, though they were united in faith and in opposition to heresy, they were unable to co-operate for the peace of the church, Basil mentions him in a second letter to the Neocaesareans as the "blessed Musonius," the follower of the traditions of Gregory Thaumaturgus, "whose teaching was still sounding in their ears" (*Ep.* 210 [64]). [E.V.]

N

Narcissus (1), bp. of Jerusalem. Clinton (*Fasti Romani*) accepts the date A.D. 190 for the commencement of his episcopate. He was the 15th of the Gentile bishops of Jerusalem, reckoning from Marcus, A.D. 136, and the 30th in succession from the apostles (Eus. *H. E.* v. 12). According to the *Synodicon*, Narcissus presided over a council of 14 bishops of Palestine held at Jerusalem A.D. 198, on the Paschal controversy, and took part in that at Caesarea on the same subject under the presidency of Theophilus, bp. of the city (Labbe, *Concil.* i. 600). Eusebius speaks of the synodical letter of these bishops as still extant in his time (Eus. *H. E.* v. 23). Narcissus was conspicuous in the church of his day (Neale, *Patriarch. of Antioch*, p. 34; Eus. *H. E.* v. 12). Eusebius records a miracle traditionally ascribed to him, whereby water was converted into oil one Easter Eve, when the oil required for the great illumination had failed (Eus. *H. E.* vi. 9). The sanctity of his life raised against him a band of slanderers. Narcissus, stung by their calumny, abdicated his bishopric, and retired to the remotest part of the desert, where for several years he lived the ascetic life he had long coveted, no one knowing the place of his concealment.

Having been sought for in vain, the neighbouring bishops declared the see vacant, and ordained Dius as his successor, who was succeeded by Germanicus, and he by Gordius. During the episcopate of Gordius, Narcissus reappeared. Shortly after his disappearance the falsity of the charges against him, Eusebius tells us, had been proved by the curses imprecated by the false accusers having been fearfully made good. This, having eventually reached Narcissus's ears, probably led to his return. He at once resumed the oversight of his see at the earnest request of all (*ib.* 9, 10). In the 2nd year of Caracalla, A.D. 212 (Eus. *Chronicon*), Alexander, a Cappadocian bishop, a confessor in the persecution of Severus, visiting the holy city in fulfilment of a vow, was selected by the aged Narcissus as his coadjutor and eventual successor. Eusebius preserves a fragment of a letter written by Alexander to the people of Antinous, in which he speaks of Narcissus as being then in his 116th year, and as having virtually retired from his episcopal office (Eus. *H. E.* vi. 11). Epiphanius states that he lived ten years after Alexander became his coadjutor, to the reign of Alexander Severus, A.D. 222 (Epiph. *Haer.* lxvi. 20). This, however, is very improbable. Tillem. *Mém. eccl.* iii. 177 ff. [E.V.]

Nebridius (4), an intimate friend of St. Augustine, and probably of about the same age, described by him as very good and of a very cautious disposition. While Augustine was at Carthage under the influence of Manichean doctrine, it was partly through Nebridius and Vindicianus that he was induced to give up his belief in astrology, or, as it was then called, mathematics. Nebridius had already abandoned Manicheism and delivered lectures against it, A.D. 379 (Aug. *Conf.* iv. 3; vii. 2, 6). When Augustine removed from Rome to Milan as a lecturer in rhetoric, A.D. 384, Nebridius, out of love for him, determined to leave his home and mother, and take up his abode with Augustine and Alypius there, "for no other reason," says Augustine, "than that he might live with me in most ardent pursuit of truth and wisdom" (*ib.* vi. 7, 10). By and by Nebridius undertook to assist Verecundus in his grammar lectures at his earnest request and that of Augustine. This duty he performed with great care and discretion (*ib.* viii. 6). Soon after Nebridius appears to have taken up the notion of the Docetae, that our Lord took human nature not in reality but only in outward appearance, an error which, after a period of unknown length, he recanted. Soon after the conversion of Augustine he died, a true Catholic, having induced his household to join him in the change. "He is now," says Augustine with confidence, "in the bosom of Abraham" (*ib.* ix. 3, 4).

Though a much-loved friend, Nebridius was a troublesome correspondent, most persevering in his inquiries, which were sometimes very difficult to answer, and not satisfied with brief replies or always ready to make allowance for his friend's occupations (Aug. *Ep.* 98, 8). Of the 12 letters which remain of their correspondence, two only are addressed by Nebridius to Augustine. Those of Augustine are very long, chiefly on metaphysical subjects of extreme subtlety. [H.W.P.]

Nectarius (4), archbp. of Constantinople A.D. 381-397 or 398, successor to St. Gregory of Nazianzus. When Gregory resigned, Nectarius was praetor of Constantinople. He was of noble family, born at Tarsus in Cilicia, an elderly man, widely known for his admirable character, still only a catechumen. Preparing for a journey to Tarsus, he called on the bp. of Tarsus, Diodorus, who was attending the council, to ask if he could take letters for him. The appearance and manners of his visitor struck Diodorus so forcibly that he at once determined that he should be advanced as a candidate; and, alleging some other business, took the praetor to call on the bp. of Antioch, who, though laughing at the idea of such a competitor, asked Nectarius to put off his journey a short time. When the emperor Theodosius desired the bishops at the council to suggest candidates, reserving to himself the right of choosing one of them, the bp. of Antioch put at the bottom of his list, in compliment to the bp. of Tarsus, the name of the praetor. The emperor, reading the lists, declared his choice to be Nectarius. The Fathers were amazed. Who and what was this Nectarius? He was not even baptized. Astonishment at the emperor's unexpected choice was great. Even the bp. of Tarsus seems not to have known this disqualification. The startling information did not move Theodosius. The people of Constantinople were delighted at the news. The whole council agreed. Nectarius was baptized. The dress of a neophyte was changed for the robes of the bishop of the imperial city. The praetor, a few days previously a catechumen, became at once president of the second general council. He ruled the church upwards of 16 years, and made an admirable prelate. His name heads the 150 signatures to the canons of the second general council. The 3rd canon declares that "the bp. of Constantinople shall hold the first rank after the bp. of Rome, because Constantinople is new Rome."

The bishops of the West were not disposed to accept the election, and asked for a common synod of East and West to settle the succession. Accordingly the emperor Theodosius, soon after the close of the second general council, summoned the bishops of his empire to a fresh synod—not, however, as the Latins wished, at Alexandria, but at Constantinople. There were assembled here, early in the summer of 382, very nearly the same bishops who had been at the second general council. On arriving they received a letter from the synod of Milan, inviting them to a great general council at Rome. They replied that they must remain where they were, because they had not made preparations for so long a journey, and were only authorized by their colleagues to act at Constantinople. They sent three of their number—Syriacus, Eusebius, and Priscian—with a synodal letter to pope Damasus, archbp. Ambrose, and the other bishops assembled in council at Rome.

The Roman synod to which this letter was addressed was the 5th under Damasus. No certain account remains of its proceedings, nor of how its members treated the question of Nectarius. Theodosius, however, sent commissaries to Rome in support of the statements of his synod, as we learn from the letters of pope Boniface. In his 15th letter (to the bishops of Illyria) he shews that the church in Rome had finally agreed to recognize both Nectarius and Flavian. St. Ambrose, in his 63rd letter, adduces the election of Nectarius as an approval of his own by the East.

Six graceful letters from Nectarius remain in the correspondence of his illustrious predecessor Gregory. In the first he expresses his hearty good wishes for his episcopate. The last is of great importance, urging him not to be too liberal in tolerating the Apollinarians.

In 383 a third synod at Constantinople was held. In spite of the decrees of bishops and emperor, the Arians and Pneumatomachians continued to spread their doctrines. Theodosius summoned all parties to the imperial city for a great discussion in June, hoping to reconcile all differences. Before the proceedings, he sent for the archbishop and told him of his intention that all questions should be fully debated. Nectarius returned home, full of profound anxiety, and consulted the Novatianist bp. Agelius, who agreed with him in doctrine and was held in high personal esteem. Agelius felt himself unsuited for so grave a controversy; but he had a reader, Sisinnius, a brilliant philosopher and theologian, to whom he proposed to entrust the argument with the Arians. Sisinnius suggested that they should produce the testimonies of the old Fathers of the church on the doctrine of the Son, and first ask the heads of the several parties whether they accepted these authorities or desired to anathematize them. The archbishop and the emperor gladly agreed to this scheme. When the bishops met, the emperor asked: Did they respect the teachers who lived before the Arian division? They said, Yes. He then asked: Did they acknowledge them sound and trustworthy witnesses of the true Christian doctrine? The divisions this question produced shewed that the sectaries were bent on disputation. The emperor ordered each party to draw up a written confession of its doctrine. When this was done, the bishops were summoned to the imperial palace, Nectarius and Agelius for the orthodox, Demophilus (formerly bp. of Constantinople) for the Arians, Eleusius of Cyzicus for the Pneumatomachians, and Eunomius for the Anomoeans. The emperor received them with kindness and retired into a room alone with their written confessions. After praying God for enlightenment, he rejected and destroyed all except that of the orthodox, because the others introduced a division into the Holy Trinity. The sectaries thereupon sorrowfully returned home. The emperor now forbade all sectaries, except the Novatianists, to hold divine service anywhere, to publish their doctrines or to ordain clergy, under threat of severe civil penalties.

In 385 died Pulcheria, the emperor's daughter, and his wife Placilla. The archbishop asked Gregory of Nyssa to preach the funeral sermons on both occasions.

Towards the close of his episcopate Nectarius abolished the office of presbyter penitentiary, whose duty appears to have been to receive confessions before communion. His example was followed by nearly all other bishops. The presbyter penitentiary was added to the ecclesiastical roll about the time of the Novatianist schism, when that party declined to communicate with those who had lapsed in the Decian persecution. Gradually there were fewer lapsed to reconcile, and his duties became more closely connected with preparation for communion. A disgraceful occurrence induced Nectarius to leave the participation in holy communion entirely to individual consciences and abolish the office.

Nectarius died in 397 or 398, and was succeeded by St. John Chrysostom. (Theod. *H. E.* v. viii. etc.; Socr. *H. E.* v. viii. etc.; Soz. *H. E.* vii. viii. etc.; Theoph. *Chronogr.* 59, etc.; Nectarii Arch. CP. *Enarratio* in *Patr. Gk.* xxxix. p. 1821; Mansi, *Concil.* t. iii. p. 521, 599, 633, 643, 694, etc.; Hefele, *Hist. Christ. Councils*, tr. Oxenham (Edinb. 1876), vol. ii. pp. 344, 347, 378, 380, 382, etc. [W.M.S.]

Nemesius (4), bp. of Emesa in the latter half of 4th cent., of whom nothing is certainly known but that he wrote a rather remarkable treatise, *περὶ φύσεως ἀνθρώπου*, *de Natura Hominis*, of which cc. ii. and iii. wrongly appear as a separate work, entitled *περὶ ψυχῆς*, *de Anima*, among the writings of Gregory Nyssen. Le Quien (*Or. Christ.* ii. 839) places Nemesius fifth among the bishops of Emesa, between Paul I., who attended the council of Seleucia, A.D. 359, and Cyriacus, the friend of Chrysostom. The date of his writing is tolerably certain from his mentioning the doctrines of Apollinaris and Eunomius and the Origenists, but not those of Nestorius, Eutyches, or Pelagius. He could hardly have avoided mentioning Pelagius if his teaching had been known to him, in the part of his treatise relating to free will. That he was bp. of Emesa is stated in the title of his treatise in the various MS. copies, and by Maximus (ii. 153, ed. Combefis) and Anastasius Sinaita (*Quaest.* xviii. and xxiv.) in quoting his work. He is also quoted, though without his name, by Joannes Damascenus, Elias Cretensis, Meletius, Joannes Grammaticus, and others. The treatise is an interesting work which will well reward perusal, and has received much praise from able judges of style and matter. Nemesius establishes the immortality of the soul against the philosophers, vindicates free will, opposes fatalism, defends God's providence, and proves by copious examples the wisdom and goodness of the Deity. He gives indications that he was not ignorant of the circulation of the blood and the functions of the bile (cc. xxiv. xxviii. pp. 242, 260, ed. Matthaei). The best ed. is by C. F. Matthaei (Halae, 1802), reprinted by Migne in *Patr. Gk.* The treatise has been translated into most modern European languages, into Italian by Pizzimenti (no date), English, G. Wilkes (1636 and 1657), German by Osterhammer (Salzburg, 1819), and French by J. R. Thibault (Paris, 1844). Cf. M. Evangelides, *Nemesius und seine Quellen* (Berlin, 1882). [E.V.]

Nero (1), Claudius Caesar, emperor (Oct. 13, 54, to June 9, 68). For our purpose the interest of Nero's life centres in his persecution of the Christians. For his general history see Merivale, cc. lii.-lv. During his early reign Christianity was unmolested and seems to have spread rapidly at Rome. No doubt it received a great impetus from the preaching of St. Paul during the two years after his arrival, probably early in 61. But before long a terrible storm was to burst on the infant church. On the night of July 16, 64, a fire broke out in the valley between the Palatine and the Aventine. That part of the city was crowded with humble dwellings and shops full of inflammable contents. The lower parts of the city became a sea of flame. For six days the fire raged till it reached the foot of the Esquiline, where it was stopped by pulling down a number of houses. Soon after a second fire broke out in the gardens of Tigellinus near the Pincian, and raged for three days in the N. parts of the city. Though the loss of life was less in the second fire, the destruction of temples and public buildings was more serious. By the two fires three of the 14 regions were utterly destroyed, four escaped entirely, in the remaining seven but few houses were left standing. Nero was at Antium when the fire broke out, and did not return to Rome till it had almost reached the vast edifice he had constructed to connect his palace on the Palatine with the gardens of Maecenas on the Esquiline.

The horrible suspicion that Nero himself was the author of the fire gained strength. This is asserted as a positive fact by Suetonius (c. 38), Dion (lxii. 16), and Pliny the Elder (xvii. 1), the last being a contemporary, but Tacitus alludes to it only as a prevalent rumour. Whether well founded or not, and whether, supposing it true, the emperor's motive was to clear away the crooked, narrow streets of the old town in order to rebuild it on a new and regular plan, or whether it was a freak of madness, need not be discussed here. At any rate Nero found it necessary to divert from himself the rage of the people and put the blame upon the Christians.

The only author living near the time of the persecution who gives an account of it is Tacitus. After describing the origin of Christianity he proceeds: "First were arrested those who confessed, then on their information a vast multitude was convicted, not so much on the charge of arson as for their hatred of the human race. Their deaths were made more cruel by the mockery that accompanied them. Some were covered with the skins of wild beasts and torn to pieces by dogs; others perished on the cross or in the flames; and others again were burnt after sunset as torches to light up the darkness. Nero himself granted his gardens (on the Vatican) for the show, and gave an exhibition in the circus, and, dressed as a charioteer, mixed with the people or drove his chariot himself. Thus, guilty and deserving the severest punishment as they were, yet they were pitied, as they seemed to be put to death, not for the benefit of the state but to gratify the cruelty of an individual" (*Ann.* xv. 44). This narrative has been the subject of very various interpretations. Lightfoot (*Phil.* 24-27) considers that the Christians were at this time sufficiently numerous and conspicuous to attract the fury of the populace. The ambiguity of Tacitus leaves it doubtful whether those first arrested "confessed Christianity" or "confessed they were guilty of the burning." Schiller (*Geschichte des röm. Kaiserreichs unter Nero,* 435) argues that "fateri" in Tacitus is always used of the confession of a crime. According to his view, as many of the shops near the circus where the fire originated were occupied by Jews, suspicion would fall upon them, which would be strengthened by the fact that the Transtiberine, the Ghetto of that time, was one of the few quarters that had escaped the fire. At that time Jews and Christians lived in the same part of the town and in the same manner. Weiszäcker (*Jahrbücher für Deutsche Theologie*, xxi. 269, etc.) considers, with much probability, that Nero and his advisers having selected the Christians as the victims of the popular indignation, those first seized were conspicuous members and were charged as incendiaries, and from them the names of others were ascertained and these treated in the same way. Thus a vast number were arrested, so many that all could not have been guilty of arson. Why Nero selected the Christians must remain uncertain. The Jews, who at first sight would seem more likely scapegoats, as being more conspicuous and probably more unpopular, were strong enough to make Nero hesitate to attack them. A Jewish persecution in Rome might excite a dangerous revolt in Judea. The Christians, however, were conspicuous and numerous enough to furnish a plentiful supply of victims, but too few and weak to be formidable. From the allusions of St. Clement (Ep. to Cor. c. 6), a little more information can be obtained. Like Tacitus, he speaks of the vast multitude, and mentions that women underwent terrible and unholy tortures.

The persecution was probably confined to Rome. There is little evidence of it extending to the rest of the empire. The Acts of the saints mentioned by Tillemont (*Mém. eccl.* ii. 73-89) are all more or less fabulous, and even if authentic there seems little or no ground for placing them in the reign of Nero. The accounts in *Acts* of the journeys of St. Paul shew how easily an outbreak of popular fury might be excited by Jews or heathens, who, either on religious or private grounds, were hostile to the new doctrine, and how easily in such an outbreak a conspicuous Christian might be murdered without any state edict against Christianity, or without the public authorities interfering at all, and it is not unreasonable to suppose that, when Nero set the example of persecution, many provincial magistrates would take a harsher view than previously of the case of any Christian brought before them.

The question of the connexion between Nero and Antichrist was brought into prominence by M. Renan. The significance of the Neronian persecution lies in the fact that it was the first. Hitherto the attitude of state officials to Christianity had on the whole been favourable; at worst they treated it with contemptuous indifference. All this was now suddenly changed. The head of the state had made a ferocious attack on the infant church. Henceforth the two powers were in more or less violent antagonism till the struggle of 250 years was closed by the conversion of Constantine. Whatever the date of the Apocalypse, it can hardly be doubted that the Neronian persecution with all its horrors was vividly present to the mind of the author. To have perished obscurely by his own hand seemed both to pagans and Christians too commonplace an end for a monster who for 14 years had filled such a place in the eyes and the minds of men. Few had witnessed his death, so that the notion easily arose that he was still alive, had taken refuge with the Parthians, and would reappear. Tacitus mentions (*Hist.* i. 2; ii. 8, 9) the appearance of two false Neros, and Suetonius (c. 56) alludes to another. In the days of his prosperity diviners had predicted his fall and that he would gain a new dominion in the East and Jerusalem and at last regain the empire (*ib.* c. 40).

According to the theory of M. Reuss (*Hist. de la théol. chrétienne*, i. 429-452), adopted by Renan, the Apocalypse was written during the reign of Galba, *i.e.* at the end of 68 or beginning of 69, when men's minds were agitated, especially in Asia Minor, by the appearance of a false Nero in the island of Cythnus (Tac. *Hist.* ii. 8). M. Reuss interprets the first six heads of the first beast as the emperors Augustus, Tiberius, Caius, Claudius, Nero, and Galba, of whom the first five were dead, while the sixth, Galba, was then reigning. As he was 73 years old his reign must soon terminate; a seventh was to follow and reign for a short time, after which one of the emperors supposed to be dead was to reappear as Antichrist. The first four emperors had not been hostile to the Christians, and none of them, except Caius, had died a violent death. Nero therefore alone answers the description. Finally M. Reuss interprets the number of the beast as the numerical value of the letters of the words Νέρων Καῖσαρ when written in Hebrew, and explains the existence of the ancient variant reading 616 by supposing it due to a Latin reader who had found the solution, but pronounced the name Nero and not Neron. Whether this theory be well founded or not, the opinion that Nero would return as Antichrist certainly continued for centuries. Commodianus, who probably wrote *c.* 250, alludes to it (xli. in Migne, *Patr. Lat.* v. 231), and even in the 5th cent. St. Augustine (*de Civ. Dei*, xx. 19, in *ib.* xli. 686) mentions that some then believed he would rise again and reappear as Antichrist, and that others thought he had never died, but would appear at the appointed time and recover his kingdom. Another view was that Nero would be the precursor of Antichrist (Lact. *Mortes* 2, Sulp. Sev. *Dial.* ii. 14 in *Patr. Lat.* vii. 197; xx. 211.) [F.D.]

Nerva, Roman emperor, A.D. 96-98. M. Cocceius Nerva was the third in succession of a family conspicuous for legal and administrative power in the first century of the empire.

On the assassination of Domitian by Stephanus, the freedman and agent of Domitilla, he was elected as emperor by the soldiers, the people, and the senate, and reversed the policy of his predecessor. The connexion of Stephanus with Domitilla, if she and Flavius Clemens were indeed Christians, may indicate that the movement that placed Nerva on the throne was in part, at least, designed to further a more tolerant system of government than that of Domitian. Such, at any rate, was its effect. St. John was recalled from his exile in Patmos (Eus. *H. E.* iii. 20). The crowd of *delatores*, who had preferred accusations of treason, atheism, and Judaism, which fell most heavily on the Christians, were banished, and those who had been sent to prison or exile on these charges were recalled and set at liberty. Other measures of the emperor, though not distinctly Christian, tended in the same direction. [E.H.P.]

Nestorian Church. This is the name given in modern times to those whom 5th-cent. writers called simply "Easterns"; by which they meant the church that existed to the east of them, outside the boundary of the Roman empire, in the kingdom that was at first Parthian, and later Sassanid Persian. The body is also called "east Syrian" (the term Syrian implying use of the Syriac language rather than residence in "Syria"), and sometimes also "Chaldean" or "Assyrian."

Foundation of the Church.—During the course of the 1st cent. Christianity spread from Antioch, not only to the west but also eastwards, and in particular it extended to Edessa, then the capital of the little "buffer state" of Osrhoene, situated between the Roman and Parthian empires. The political independence of the state ended in 216, but it had lasted long enough to give a definite character to the local church, which was marked off by its Syriac vernacular and Oriental ways of thought from the Greek Christianity to the west of it. Missionaries went out from Edessa to the east again, and founded two daughter-churches, one in Armenia and one in what was then Parthia, the latter of which is the subject of this article.

The first two "apostles" and founders of this church were Adai (=Thaddeus) and Mari. Tradition identified the former with either the disciple of Christ—a statement hard to reconcile with the recorded fact that he was still able to travel in the year 100—or with one of "the Seventy." He is known to have preached in Assyria and Adiabene before the close of the 1st cent., and to have consecrated his disciple Paqida as first bishop of the latter province, in A.D. 104 (*Hist. of Mshikha-zca*); while the statement of the "doctrine of Adai" that the apostle died in peace at Edessa has the ring of truth in it. The later history of the church in that place is outside our subject.

Of Mari, his companion, little is known certainly (his life is a mere piece of hagiography), but he appears to have penetrated into the southern provinces of the Parthian kingdom, to have preached without much success at the capital, Seleucia-Ctesiphon, and to have died in peace at Dor-Koni. There seems no reason to doubt the historic character of both these teachers; and later tradition added that St. Thomas the Apostle, passing through this country on his way to India, was co-founder of the church with them.

The Church under the Arsacids and Sassanids.—Under Parthian rule, which was tolerant, and where the state religion was an outworn and eclectic paganism, the new faith spread rapidly and easily. There was no persecution by the government, though converts from one special religion, Zoroastrianism, had sometimes to face it, from the powerful hierarchy of that faith, the Magians. Thus the church had more than 20 bishops, and these were distributed over the whole country when, in 225, the 2nd Persian replaced the Parthian kingdom, and the Arsacid dynasty gave way to the Sassanid. This revolution was to its authors a revival of the old kingdom destroyed by Alexander, and the Persian nation rose again with a national religion, that of Zoroaster. It made no effort to destroy the Christianity that it found existing, but, like Islam later, tolerated it as the religion of a subject race, and so put it into the position that it still occupies in those lands, though the dominant religion has changed. Christians became a *melet* (a subject race organized in a church), recognized by the government, but despised by it. For them to proselytize from the state faith was a crime, punishable with death, though they were allowed to convert pagans. Apostasy from Christianity to the established faith meant worldly prosperity, but there was no persecution, though there was often oppression, by the government, until the adoption of Christianity by the Roman emperor (the standing enemy of the shah-in-shah) made every Christian politically suspect. Thus Persia continued to be a refuge for many Christians from Roman territory during the "general" persecutions of the 3rd cent., and the church grew, both by conversions and by the advent of "captivities," largely Christian in faith, brought by conquerors like Sapor I. from Roman territory.

Episcopate of Papa.—Though it extended rapidly elsewhere, the church made little progress in the capital, and there was no bishop there, and only a few Christians, till late in the 3rd cent. In 270 Akha d'Abuh', bp. of Arbela, joined with others in consecrating Papa to that see, and this man became its first bishop since the days of Mari. In later days legend supplied the names of earlier holders of what had then become a patriarchal throne, and indeed made Akha d'Abuh' himself one of the series, and told how in A.D. 170 he was recognized by the four "western patriarchs" as the fifth of the band.

Papa, as bp. of the capital, soon claimed to be the chief bishop of the church, its catholicos; the claim was favoured by the circumstances of the time, as in his days all the "greater thrones" were obtaining jurisdiction over the lesser sees within their sphere of attraction, and the patriarchates so formed were soon to be recognized at Nicaea. The conditions of *melet* life also tend to produce some one head, through whom the government can deal with the people. Papa, however, so claimed the honour as to produce irritation, and a council met in 315 to judge his claim. It was very adverse to Papa, who refused in anger to bow to its decision. "But is it not written, 'He that is chief among you . . .'?" said one bishop, Miles of Susa. "You fool, I know that," cried the catholicos. "Then be judged by the Gospel," retorted Miles, placing his own copy in the midst. Papa, in fury, struck the book with his fist, exclaiming, "Then speak, Gospel!—speak!" and, smitten with apoplexy or paralysis, fell helpless as he did so. After such a sacrilege and such a portent his condemnation naturally followed, and his archdeacon Shimun bar Saba'i was consecrated in his room.

Papa, on recovery, appealed for support to "the Westerns," *i.e.* not to Antioch or Rome (the "Nestorian" church never deemed herself subject to either of them), but to the nearest important sees to the west of him, Nisibis and Edessa. These supported him on the whole, but their advice did not, apparently, go beyond recommending a general reconciliation and submission to the see of Seleucia-Ctesiphon, on the ground that it would be for the good of the whole church that it should have a catholicos. This recommendation was carried out, all parties being a little ashamed of themselves. Papa was recognized as catholicos, with Shimun as colleague, *cum jure successionis*, and the right of the throne concerned to the primacy has never since been disputed. Papa survived these events for 12 years, and so was ruling during the council of Nicaea, though neither he nor any bishop of his jurisdiction (which did not then include Nisibis) was present at that gathering. Arianism passed by this church absolutely, and the fact is both a testimony to its isolation and a merciful dispensation. Church history might have been very different had that heresy found a national *point d'appui*.

Persecution of Sapor II.—Shimun succeeded Papa, and in his days the church had to face the terrible "forty years' persecution" of Sapor II. The acceptance of Christianity by the Roman empire meant terrible suffering for the church outside it, in that any outbreak of the secular rivalry of the two empires meant thereafter persecution for the church in one of them. This was inevitable, and the same dilemma exists to-day. Given a state professing a certain variety of militant religion (Zoroastrianism or Islam), how can loyalty to it be compatible with profession of the religion of its rivals? Constantine, like some Czars, liked playing the general protector of Christians; and Christians looked to him as naturally as, in the same land, they have since looked to Russia.

Thus, when Sapor made war on Constantius in 338, persecution commenced almost as a matter of course. Shimun the catholicos was one of the first victims, 100 priests and clerics suffering with him; and the struggle thus inaugurated continued until the death of Sapor in 378, in which time 16,000 martyrs, whose names are recorded, died for their faith.

This greatest of persecutions was not, of course, uniformly severe at all times in all provinces, and both it and others after it were rather the releasing of the "race-hatred" of Zoroastrianism against Christianity than the ordered process of law against a *religio illicita*. Thus, it resembled both in outline and detail the "Armenian massacres" of a later age. Clergy, of course, and celibates of both sexes, who were numerous, were specially marked, and so were the Christian inhabitants of the five provinces about Nisibis, when their surrender by the emperor Jovian in 363 handed them over to a notorious persecutor.

Practically, though not absolutely, the trial ended with the death of Sapor; but the exhausted church could do little to reorganize herself until a formal firman of toleration had been obtained. The influence of Theodosius II. secured this in 410 from the then shah-in-shah, Yezdegerd I.

Council of Isaac.—The church was then formally put into the position that it had, previously to the persecution, occupied practically: it was made a *melet* in the Persian state, under its catholicos, Isaac; it was allowed to hold a council, under his presidency and that of the Roman ambassador, Marutha; and it now for the first time accepted the Nicene Creed. Canons were also passed for the proper organization of the body, and some of these are based on Nicene rules. The church shewed its independence, however, by dealing very freely with the canons even of that council.

Seemingly, the council of Constantinople was accepted also at this time, but it was not thought to deserve special mention.

A period of rapid growth followed the enfranchisement and organization of the church that had proved its power to endure, and 26 new sees were added in 15 years to the 40 existing in 410, these including Merv, Herat, Seistan, and other centres in central Asia. Internal troubles arose, however, caused by the quarrels of Christians, and by their habit of "using pagan patronage"—*i.e.* applying to non-Christians of influence—in order to escape censure, to gain promotion, etc. The habit was, of course, destructive of all discipline. A council held in 420 to deal with this, under the catholicos Yahb-Alaha, and another Roman ambassador, Acacius of Amida, could only suggest the acceptance of the rules of several Western councils—Gangra, Antioch, Caesarea—without considering whether rules adapted for the West would for that reason suit the East. Persecution soon recommenced, Magian jealousy being stirred by Christian progress, and raged for four years (420-424, mainly under Bahram V.) with terrible severity. As usual, a Perso-Roman war coincided with the persecution, and the end of the one marked the end of the other also. With the return of peace another council was allowed, the catholicos Dad-Ishu presiding. This man had suffered much, both in the persecution and from the accusations of Christian enemies, and was most anxious to resign his office. There was, however, a strong feeling among Christians that their church must be markedly independent of "Western" Christianity (*i.e.* that of the Roman empire), as too much connexion spelt persecution. Thus they insisted that the catholicos should remain, and styled him also "patriarch," and specially forbade any appeal from him to "Western" bishops. The fact that Acacius of Amida, though actually the guest of the king at the time, was not at the council is another indication of their feelings. This declaration of independence is the first sign of the approaching schism, though the remainder of the catholicate of Dad-Ishu was peaceful, and the Nestorian controversy, at the time of its arising, was no more heard of in the East than the Arian controversy before it had been.

The Work of Bar-soma.—Another persecution fell on this much-tried church in 448, but otherwise we know little of its history till 480, when the Christological controversy reached it for the first time.

In the Roman empire at that period Chalcedon was past, and the Monophysite reaction that followed that council was at its height; the "Henoticon of Zeno" was the official confession, accepted by all the patriarchs of the empire with the exception of the Roman. The church in Persia, however, was emphatically "Dyophysite," and thus there was a theological force at work that hardened the independence already found necessary into actual separation.

The protagonist of the movement was Bar-soma of Nisibis, a very typical son of his nation; a quarrelsome and unscrupulous man, who yet had a real love both for his church and for learning. He was a favourite with the shah-in-shah, Piroz, who employed him as warden of the marches on the Romo-Persian frontier, and he was practically patriarch of the church. The real patriarch, Babowai, had just been put to death for supposedly treasonable correspondence with Rome, and Bar-soma had rather gone out of his way to secure that this prelate (his personal enemy) should not escape the consequences of his own imprudence. Bar-soma easily persuaded Piroz that it would be better that "his rayats" should have no connexion with the subjects of the Roman emperor, and under his influence a council was held at Bait Lapat, a "Dyophysite" (or perhaps Nestorian) confession published, and separation brought about. By another canon of this council marriage was expressly allowed to all ranks of the hierarchy.

Some say that the church was simply dragooned into heresy, but the mass of Christians seem to have at least acquiesced in the work of Bar-soma, and it must be remembered that they separated from a church that was Monophysite at the time. There was, moreover, a better side to the work of Bar-soma. He was a lover of learning, and when the imperial order brought the theological school at Edessa to an end (this had hitherto been the sole means of education open to sons of the "church of the East"), he took a statesman's advantage of the opportunity by founding at Nisibis a college that was a nursery of bishops to his church for 1,000 years.

Bar-soma's power ended with the death of Piroz (484), and Acacius became patriarch. His reign saw the breach with the "Westerns" healed more or less, as the council of Bait Lapat was repudiated (though the canon on episcopal marriage was allowed to stand) and another confession of faith was drawn up. This was not Nestorian, but was indefinite, designedly, and Acacius was received as orthodox during a visit to Constantinople, on condition of his anathematizing Bar-soma. As they were already at open feud on a minor matter, the patriarch readily agreed to this, but the memory of the schism was of evil omen for the future.

Mar Aba.—A period of confusion (490-540) followed. The whole country of Persia was disturbed by the communism preached by Mazdak, to which even the king, Kobad, was converted for a while. The strange movement was stamped out in blood, but it left indirect effects on the church, and Bar-soma also bequeathed them a bad tradition of quarrelsomeness. This culminated in an open schism in the patriarchate, lasting for 15 years, with open disorder in the whole church, a state of things that only terminated with the accession of Mar Aba to the patriarchate in 540.

Meantime, Monophysite supremacy in the Roman empire had ended with the accession of the emperor Justin in 518, and friendly relations between the church there and that in Persia had been resumed: the advantage had to be paid for by the latter, in that it implied a renewal of persecution.

Mar Aba, the greatest man in the series of patriarchs of the East, reformed the abuses in the church, going round from diocese to diocese with a "perambulatory synod," which judged every case on the spot with plenary authority—a precedent so excellent that it is surprising that it has never been followed. He was able to establish rules for the election of the patriarch which still hold good in theory, and founded schools and colleges (in particular, one at Seleucia), in addition to the one at Nisibis. His table of prohibited degrees in matrimony—a most necessary thing for Christians in a Zoroastrian land—is still the law of his church.

In his days the monastic life, which had wilted under Bar-soma and during the period of disorder, was revived, and was provided with a body of rules by Abraham of Kashkar, a pupil of Aba, while the friendship of the church in Persia with that in the empire led also (though dates are here rather uncertain) to the definite acceptance, by this "Nestorian" church, of the council of Chalcedon, which stands among the "Western synods" received by these "Easterns." This acceptance was certainly previous to 544.

Mar Aba's great work for his church was done in the teeth of great difficulties. He was a convert from Zoroastrianism, and as such was legally liable to be put to death, and therefore lived in daily peril from the Magians. The shah-in-shah, Chosroes I., would never allow his execution, but feared also to protect him efficiently, and for 7 of the 9 years of his tenure of office he was in prison, ruling his flock thence. Though he was released at last, and passed his last days in honour at court, there is no doubt that his sufferings hastened his death.

Position of the Church in the 6th Cent.—In the following half-century (550-600) there was no special incident. A series of patriarchs of the three stock eastern types (court favourite, respectable nonentity, and strict ascetic) ruled the church, and the services were arranged much in their present form. In particular the "Rogation of the Ninevites," still annually observed, was either instituted or remodelled by the patriarch Ezekiel, during an outbreak of plague.

The anomalous relation of the church in Persia with other parts of the Catholic church cannot be fitted into any defined theory. Several Christological confessions were issued by these so-called "Nestorians" which are certainly not unorthodox, and individual patriarchs were readily received to communion when they happened to visit Constantinople (*e.g.* Ishu-yahb, 585). Nevertheless, there was a growing estrangement, and a conviction on either side that the other was somehow wrong, which was strengthened as the church in Persia slowly realized that the man whom they called "the interpreter" *par excellence*, Theodore of Mopsuestia, had been condemned at Constantinople.

In Persia the church was a stationary *melet*, though beyond the frontier it was a missionary force among Arabs, Turks, and Chinese. It was numerous enough to make the king anxious not to offend it, the mercantile and agricultural classes being largely of the faith. On the other hand, the feudal seigneurs were very seldom of it, and soldiers practically never. In "the professions" doctors were generally Christian, and indeed are largely so to this day, while each faith had its own law and lawyers.

The clergy were usually married, but there was a growing feeling in favour of celibate bishops, though the law passed by Bar-soma was never repealed.

Monophysite Controversy.—The bulk of Persian Christians were Dyophysite in creed, but there was a Monophysite minority, organized under bishops (or a bishop) of their own, and including many monks. This body was recruited by the enormous "captivities" brought from Syria in 540 and 570. In 612 they were strong enough to make a daring and nearly successful attempt to capture the church hierarchy. The patriarchate was then vacant (Chosroes had been so annoyed by the substitution of another Gregory for the Gregory whom he had nominated to that office, that he had refused to allow any election when that man died in 608), and when petition was made for the granting of a patriarch, the Monophysites, whose interest at court was powerful, petitioned for the nomination of a man of their own. They had formidable supporters, for Shirin, the king's Christian wife, and Gabriel, his doctor, were both of that confession.

A deputation of Dyophysites came to court to endeavour to secure a patriarch of their own colour, and a most unedifying wrangle over the theological point followed, Chosroes sitting as umpire. Of course, neither side converted the other, but the occasion was important, for from it dates the employment of the Christological formula now used by this church, viz. "two Natures, two 'Qnumi,' and one Person in Christ," the repudiation of the term "Mother of God" as applied to the B.V.M., and the acceptance of the nickname "Nestorian" now given them by the Monophysites. Ultimately the Dyophysites saved themselves from the imposition of a Monophysite patriarch, at the cost of remaining without a leader till the death of Chosroes, and the Monophysites organized a hierarchy of their own.

During the long wars between Chosroes and Heraclius, and the anarchy that followed in Persia, the "Nestorian" church has naturally no recorded history, yet at their conclusion it was once more to have formal relations with the patriarchate and church of Constantinople.

Drift into Separation.—In the year 628 its patriarch, Ishu-yahb II., was sent as ambassador to Constantinople, and he was there asked to explain its faith, and was admitted as orthodox. He was, however, attacked on his return home, on suspicion of having made unlawful concessions, and not all the efforts of men like Khenana and Sahdona could shake the general conviction on each side that "those others" were somehow wrong. The two men named laboured to shew the essential identity, under a verbal difference, of the doctrines of the two churches, but the only visible result was the excommunication of both peacemakers.

Then the flood of Moslem conquest drifted the two churches apart, and the bulk of organized Monophysitism between them hid each from the other.

The separation of "Nestorians" from "orthodox" was a gradual process, commenced before 424, and hardly complete before 640. In that period, however, it was completed, and the "church of the East" commenced her marvellous medieval career in avowed schism from her sister of Constantinople. Whether her doctrine, then or at any time, was what the word "Nestorian" means to us, and what is the theological status of a church which accepts Nicaea, Constantinople, and Chalcedon, but rejects Ephesus, are separate and difficult questions. [MONOPHYSITISM; NESTORIUS (3).]

Authorities for the History of the Church.—*History of Mshikha-zca.* (ed. Mingana); *Acta Sanct. Syr.* (ed. Bedjan, 6 vols.); *Hist. de Jabalaha et de trois patriarches nestoriens* (Bedjan); *Synodicon Orientale* (ed. Chabot); Bar-hebraeus, *Chron. Eccles.* pt. ii.; John of Ephesus, *Eccl. Hist.* pt. iii. (Cureton); Amr and Sliba, *Liber Turris*; the *Guidi Chronicle* (ed. Noldeke); Zachariah of Mitylene (ed. Brooks); Socr., Soz., Theod., Evagr., *Eccles. Histories*; *Book of Governors* (Thomas of Marga, ed. Budge); Babai, *de Unione* (MS. only); Ishu-yahb III., *Letters* (ed. Duval); Tabari, *Gesch. der Sassaniden* (ed. Noldeke); Assemani, *Bibl. Orient.* iii.

Books and Pamphlets.—Labourt, *Christianisme dans la Perse*; Chabot, *Ecole de Nisibe; De S. Isaaci vita*; Duval, *Histoire d'Edesse;* Goussen, *Martyrius-Sahdona*; Hoffmann, *Aussuge aus Syrische Martyrer*; Bethune Baker, *Nestorius and his Teaching*; Wigram, *Doctrinal Position of Assyrian Church*; *Introd. to Hist. of Assyrian Church*; Rawlinson, *Seventh Oriental Empire*; Christiansen, *L'Empire des Sassanides.* [W.A.W.]

Nestorius (1), St. (*Nestor*), the first known bp. of Side in Pamphylia Prima (Le Quien, i. 997), a martyr in the Decian persecution, A.D. 250. He was arrested by the local Irenarch, required to sacrifice, and on refusing despatched in charge of two lictors to the court of the president Pollio, who tortured and then crucified him. The martyr's answer to the president's queries sufficiently indicate his theological position. Pollio said to him, "Are you willing to take part with us or with Christ?" To which Nestor replied, "Cum Christo meo et eram, et sum, et ero"; to which the president replied that as he was devoted to Jesus Who was crucified under Pontius Pilate, he should be crucified like his God. The Acts say his martyrdom was on the 5th day of the week at the third hour, Le Blant (*Actes des Martyrs*, p. 46) points out the accuracy of the details. [G.J.S.]

Nestorius (3) and **Nestorianism.** One of the most far-reaching controversies in the history of the church is connected with the name of Nestorius, who became patriarch of Constantinople in A.D. 428, in succession to Sisinnius. So protracted has it been that even to the present day Nestorian churches, as they are called, exist in Assyria and India, and their members are not in communion with those of the other Christian churches in the East. The history of the form of thought which produced such far-reaching results must be interesting to every student of theology. Nestorius himself was brought up in the cloister, and had, as Neander remarks, imbibed the tendencies to narrowness, partisanship, impatience, and ignorance of mankind which are not unfrequently found among those who have been educated apart from their fellows. He was brought from Antioch, we are told—a fact of which the significance will presently be seen. He appears to have been eloquent and sincere, and his austerity of life had won for him the admiration of man. Socrates, a specially well-informed contemporary, and a layman of judgment and fairness, speaks with some severity of his first steps after he became patriarch (*H. E.* vii. 29). He is described as addressing the emperor (Theodosius II.) immediately after his appointment, "before all the people," with the words, "Give me, O prince, a country purged of heretics, and I will give you heaven as a recompense. Assist me in destroying heretics, and I will assist you in vanquishing the Persians." Such language was more enthusiastic than wise. It was no doubt pleasing to the multitude, but (Socr. *l.c.*) it made a very bad impression on thoughtful hearers. "Before he had tasted of the waters of the city," the historian proceeds, using a proverbial phrase, he had flung himself headlong into acts of violence and persecution. On the fifth day after his consecration, he resolved to destroy the oratory in which the Arians were wont to celebrate their worship, and thereby he not only drove them to desperation, but, as Socrates adds, he alienated thinking men of his own communion. He next attacked the Quartodecimans and the Novatianists with equal violence, although neither sect was involved in heresy by its schism from the church, and the Novatianists had steadily supported the church in its controversy with the Arians. He then turned his attention to the Macedonians. [MACEDONIUS.] For his treatment of this sect there is more excuse. The bp. of Germa, on the Hellespont, had treated them with such severity that, driven to desperation, they had sent two assassins to murder him. For this rash act they were deprived of their churches in Constantinople and the neighbourhood. It was at least unwise to convert the members of four "denominations," as we should now call them, into bitter antagonists, and it was not very long before an occasion arose for them to display their hostility.

The development of theology in Syria had for some time taken a different direction from that which it had taken in Egypt, where the tendency had been to lay stress on the divine, and therefore mysterious, side of Christianity. But in Syria a school had arisen, of which Diodorus of Tarsus and the celebrated Theodore of Mopsuestia were the leaders, which devoted itself to the critical interpretation of Scripture, and favoured the application of logical investigation to the facts and doctrines of Christianity. These two tendencies were certain some day to come into collision, and when reinforced by the personal jealousy felt by successive patriarchs of Alexandria at the elevation in 381 of Constantinople, as New Rome, to the second place among the patriarchates, over the head of a church which could boast of St. Mark as its founder, there was plenty of material for a conflagration. Already premonitions of the approaching conflict between Alexandria and Constantinople had appeared in the successful intrigues of THEOPHILUS, patriarch of Alexandria, against the renowned JOHN CHRYSOSTOM, patriarch of Constantinople. The violence of Nestorius and his supporters set fire to the material already provided; the immediate occasion being the sermon of a presbyter named Anastasius, whom Nestorius had brought with him from Antioch, and in whom he reposed much confidence. Anastasius is said to have used the words (Socr. *H. E.* vii. 32), "Let no man call Mary *θεοτόκος*, for Mary was human, and it is impossible that God could be born from a human being." This utterance naturally caused amazement and distress, for the word *θεοτόκος* had been applied to the Virgin by authorities as high as Origen, Athanasius, and Eusebius of Caesarea, and it was insisted on with some vehemence by Gregory of Nazianzus. It is also found in the letter of Alexander of Alexandria to Alexander of Constantinople. [ARIUS.] Nestorius supported his protégé, and delivered several discourses, in which he maintained the thesis of his subordinate with ability and energy, and with some heat. He was promptly charged with having involved himself in the heresies of Photinus or Paul of Samosata. Socrates denies that this was the case. But he remarks on the unreasonable antipathy of Nestorius to a word to which orthodox churchmen were well accustomed. This antipathy may partly, perhaps, be explained by a dislike on the part of Nestorius to the tendency to undue honour to the Virgin which had already displayed itself. But it was still more due to the teaching of Theodore of Mopsuestia and his school, which had laid undue stress on the humanity of Christ, and had not shrunk from representing the inhabitation of the Man Christ Jesus by the Divine Logos as differing rather in degree than in kind from that by which God was pleased to dwell in the prophets and other holy men of old. If, they contended, there were any union of natures in Christ, it was not a personal union, but an ἕνωσις σχετική (an union of things diverse in a close relation). Such teaching had a dangerous tendency to humanitarianism, and to the division of Christ into two hypostases [ARIUS, FOLLOWERS OF], as well as implying the existence in Him of two separate and possibly antagonistic sources of will and action.

The ferment caused by these injudicious utterances spread far and wide, and soon reached Alexandria. Cyril, the patriarch, who had succeeded his uncle Theophilus, was by no means disinclined to lower the credit of a rival whose elevation he at once envied and despised. We must not suppose, however, that Cyril had no convictions of his own on the point, for, as Dorner very properly reminds us, he had already published his opinions on it. Not content, however, with assailing with rare theological ability the opinions of Nestorius, he condescended to less worthy expedients. Not only did he exaggerate and misrepresent the language of his antagonist, but he tried to involve him in charges of Apollinarianism [APOLLINARIS] and Pelagianism [PELAGIUS]. Theodore, from whom Nestorius had imbibed his theology, was in the most direct antagonism to Apollinaris, whose teaching, while insisting strongly on the Godhead of Christ, involved the denial of His Perfect Manhood. And the divines of all schools of thought in the East, in the opinion of the disciples of Augustine, were more or less tinged with Pelagianism. As Nestorius had shewn some kindness to Pelagians who had fled to him from the West, the accusation of Pelagianism suited Cyril's purpose.

Before entering into the history of the controversy, we must pause for a moment and endeavour to understand the questions involved, and the different aspects from which they were approached by the disputants. The Syrian school, as we have seen, approached these questions from the *human* side, and favoured inductive methods. The starting-point of Theodore was man, in the sphere of the visible and tangible. The starting-point of Cyril was God, in the sphere of the mysterious and unknown. The development (for of such a development Scripture unquestionably speaks) of the Manhood of Christ when inhabited by the Godhead seems to have been the prominent idea on the part of the Syrian school. It inquired whether the indwelling of the Godhead in Jesus Christ was one of Nature or simply of energy, and it undoubtedly leaned too much toward the assertion of a dual personality in Christ. The watchword (as Neander calls it) of the Alexandrians, on the other hand, was the ineffable and (to human reason) inconceivable nature of the inhabitation of the Man Christ Jesus by the Divine Logos. We must not forget that the Syrians, though not of course unacquainted with Greek, habitually thought in Syriac, and used a Syrian version of the Scriptures, which had been in existence in their churches in one form or another ever since the 2nd cent. The use of the term θεοτόκος had been approved by Theodore himself, under certain limitations, which makes the passionate protest of Nestorius against it the more unfortunate. Nestorius, unfortunately for himself, was not a clear thinker or reasoner, and was therefore no match for his antagonist Cyril. Great confusion, it should be remarked in passing, has been caused by the inaccurate translation of θεοτόκος into modern languages by the words *Mother of God.* Whether the soul of an infant is derived from its parents is an old and still debated question. But the term "mother" unquestionably involves in many minds the idea of *transmission of essence,* whereas the title θεοτόκος, as Theodoret does not fail to point out in his reply to Cyril's anathemas, simply means that she to whom it was applied was the medium through which a Divine Being was introduced into this world in human form. The controversy raised the question whether the term συνάφεια (*connexion* or *conjunction*) or ἕνωσις (union) were the better fitted to denote the nature of the relation between the Godhead and the Manhood in Christ. The Syrians inclined to the former, the Alexandrians to the latter. Some confusion of thought continued to exist about the use of the terms πρόσωπον and ὑπόστασις to signify what we in English express by the one inadequate word "person." These two Greek words [ARIUS, FOLLOWERS OF] were, from the council of Constantinople onward, usually understood to signify respectively the *appearance,* as regarded by one outside it, and the *inward* distinction, or, as Gregory of Nazianzus puts it, "speciality" (ἰδιότης), which distinguishes one individual of a *genus* or *species* from another. But when the word ὑπόστασις is applied to the conditions of Being in God, the caution of our own Hooker is very necessary (*Eccl. Pol.* V. lvi. 2), that the Divine Nature is *itself unique.* It seems pretty plain that even so clear a thinker as Cyril, in his defence of his anathemas as well as elsewhere, does not distinguish sufficiently between the use of the word ὑπόστασις at Nicaea, and the signification which had come to be attached to it in the first council of Constantinople. Nor should it be forgotten that though many modern divines are wont to represent Theodore of Mopsuestia as a dangerous heretic, he was rather, like Origen at an earlier period, a pioneer of theological inquiry [ARIUS], and that, like Origen, he lived and died in the communion of the church, though some of the propositions laid down by him were afterwards shewn to be erroneous. It may not be amiss to sum up these remarks on the question at issue in the words of Canon Bright, who certainly cannot be charged with undue tenderness for Nestorius, on the title θεοτόκος. "It challenged objection; it was open to misconstruction; it needed some theological insight to do it justice; it made the perception of the true issue difficult; it stimulated that 'cultus' which has now, in the Roman church, attained proportions so portentous."

History of the Controversy.—There was considerable ferment in Constantinople in consequence of the utterances of Nestorius and his followers, even before the intervention of Cyril. One Proclus, who had been appointed bp. of Cyzicus but had not been accepted by the church there, was residing in Constantinople, and raised a storm by inveighing not a little indecently, in the very presence of the patriarch, against the doctrines promulgated by him. Proclus was probably giving expression to real convictions, but was clearly not in a position which justified him in undertaking the task. Nestorius replied, and attacked the extravagant laudation of the Virgin by Proclus, describing it as derogatory to the honour of her Son. But, as was usual with him, he deprecated all noisy applause on the part of his hearers—therein displaying better taste than most of his contemporaries—and went on to declare that he did not object to the term θεοτόκος, provided Mary were not made into a goddess. The dispute grew warm. Placards were affixed to the walls of the churches in Constantinople, and sermons preached against the patriarch. The opportunity thus given was not one which Cyril was likely to neglect. Though a man of ability and a theologian far above the average, he was ambitious, violent, and unscrupulous. Socrates does not conceal his sense of Cyril's unfairness toward Nestorius, strongly as he animadverts on the lack of judgment and self-control displayed by the latter. Cyril wrote to the monks of Constantinople commenting severely on the action of Nestorius, and insisting strongly that the union of the Godhead and Manhood in Jesus Christ was a *real* union, and not a mere conjunction. When he learned that his letter was resented, he wrote one to Nestorius himself. He complained that the unfortunate language of Nestorius had reached Celestine of Rome, and was thus throwing the whole church into confusion. The affected moderation of his language did not deceive Nestorius, who defended himself with spirit and moderation, and maintained that χριστότοκος would be a more suitable appellation for the Virgin than θεοτόκος. Approached by an Alexandrian presbyter named Lampon, who came to Constantinople in the interests of peace, Nestorius professed himself much touched by Lampon's tone, and wrote to Cyril in a more friendly spirit. But it was too late. Cyril had already taken action against Nestorius, and when the latter suggested a council at Constantinople, took measures to undermine still further the influence of his antagonist. He wrote two treatises on the controversy, one addressed to the emperor and empress (Eudocia), and the other to Pulcheria and the other sisters of the emperor. Then he wrote to Celestine of Rome an unfair account of what had occurred. He contended that Nestorius had represented the Logos as *two* separate beings, knit closely together. Nestorius complained that Cyril garbled his quotations. He was, however, pronounced a heretic by two synods held at Rome and Alexandria (430). Whether Cyril acted as craftily as Neander supposes, or whether Nestorius maintained too lofty a tone in his letter to Celestine, and thus offended one who was anxious to secure his supremacy over the church of God, must be left undecided. Certain it is that the high-handed action of Celestine in requiring that Nestorius should at once readmit to communion the presbyters whom he had repelled from it, and that he himself should sign a written recantation within 12 days, was quite unprecedented in the history of the church. Another patriarch, John of Antioch, now appears on the scene. Cyril had endeavoured to intimidate him by representing that the whole West was united in condemnation of Nestorius, and John wished to act as a mediator. Cyril next issued 12 anathemas against the teaching of Nestorius. In one of these he seems to unite the flesh of Christ with the Logos, *according to His Person* (καθ' ὑπόστασιν), and in the 3rd he appears to speak of the union of the two hypostases in Him. Nestorius replied by 12 counter-anathemas. It is unfortunate for our full comprehension of the position that these are only to be found in a Latin translation by Marius Mercator, a layman from N. Africa, who was at Constantinople while the controversy was going on. But, as usual in theological controversy, each of the disputants replies rather to the inferences he himself draws from the propositions of his antagonist than to the propositions themselves. The famous Theodoret, bp. of Cyrus, now (430) came forward, at the request of John of Antioch, in defence of Nestorius. He laid his finger on the weak spot of Cyril's anathemas—his union of two hypostases in Christ; and condemned them as "foreign to Christianity." Cyril seems also to have contended that nothing could be unknown to the humanity of Christ which was known to Him as God. The doctrine, too, of the ἕνωσις φυσική (natural union) maintained by Cyril seemed perilously near to Monophysitism. On the other hand, it should not be forgotten that Nestorius publicly stated that he had no objection to the word θεοτόκος provided it was properly explained. The emperor at last resolved to call a council. Ephesus was chosen as the place of meeting (probably because of the excitement prevalent at Constantinople), and the meeting was fixed for Whitsuntide 431. The assembly was confined to the bishops of the more important sees (metropolitans, as they were now called), and the emperor sent a warning letter to Cyril, condemning his intemperate proceedings. Nestorius came at the appointed time, but fearing the violence of his adversary, requested a guard from the emperor. His request was granted. Cyril and his adherents were also present. But some 40 Syrian bishops were detained by floods, famine, and the riots consequent on the latter. Cyril, seizing the opportunity, and supported by Memnon, bp. of Ephesus, opened the synod, which consisted of some 200 metropolitans, and proceeded to condemn and depose Nestorius in the absence of the Syrian contingent. This sentence of deposition was affixed to the public buildings and proclaimed by the heralds. Meanwhile Cyril had contrived to remove from the emperor's mind the unfavourable impression his previous action had produced. Nestorius declined, though thrice summoned, to attend the synod in the absence of his Syrian supporters, and sent a complaint to the emperor of the illegality and unfairness of Cyril's proceedings, which was supported by ten bishops and the imperial commissioner. (Socrates, however, says that Nestorius attended one meeting, and left it after having expressed himself in somewhat unfortunate language.) Cyril pretended that the Syrian bishops had purposely stayed away. But this is neither probable in itself nor consistent with the subsequent conduct of the patriarch John.

When John and the Syrian bishops arrived, they, though only between 30 and 40 in number, held a counter-synod, which was ridiculed by Cyril and his party for its great inferiority in numbers. John, however, persisted, alleging that the rest of the bishops were simply creatures of Cyril and Memnon. John's party then excommunicated Cyril and Memnon, posted up their sentence and transmitted their report to the emperor. A letter had meanwhile arrived from Celestine in condemnation of Nestorius. This letter was read by Cyril to the bishops of his party, but Nestorius replied that it had only been obtained by gross perversions of his language. Cyril now resorted to other means of attaining his purpose. He endeavoured to gain over the emperor, a task which was only too easy. He contrived to bring the ladies of the court, including Pulcheria, over to his side. To attain this end, there is evidence extant—though Canon Bright has failed to notice it—(in a letter from Epiphanius, Cyril's archdeacon and syncellus, to the patriarch Maximian, see below), that he made a lavish use of money and presents of other kinds. He also stirred up the monks at Constantinople to tumult through an agent of his, one Dalmatius, who had immured himself in his cell for 48 years, and was in high repute for his ascetic practices. Dalmatius now represented himself as drawn from his retirement by a voice from heaven, in order to rescue the church from the peril of heresy. A torchlight procession to the emperor was organized. The excitement in Constantinople was general. The emperor was terrified at the furious riots which broke out, in which many persons were injured. So the influence of the court was now openly exerted in favour of Cyril, and the Oriental bishops began to waver. Nestorius himself lost heart. Even at the council he had gone so far as to say, "Let Mary be called θεοτόκος, and let all this tumult cease." He had throughout been less illiberal than his antagonists, and he was probably terrified at their violent and unscrupulous proceedings. He may also have discovered, when it was too late, that he had rushed into controversy without having been sufficiently sure of his ground. Therefore, although a deputation of 8 bishops from each side were sent to Constantinople, the result was a foregone conclusion. A compromise was arrived at. Cyril and Memnon were reinstated in their sees. John of Antioch signed a condemnation of Nestorius, while Cyril consented in 432 to sign an Antiochene formulary which had been submitted by Theodoret to the Syrian bishops at Ephesus and was afterwards transmitted to the emperor. It is worth noting that this formulary contains the ἕνωσις φυσική (see above), but guards it by a definite assertion of both the divinity and humanity of Christ. The sentence on Nestorius was carried out. He was deposed, and Maximian became patriarch in his stead, but soon died, and was succeeded by Proclus, the old antagonist of Nestorius. The controversy continued to rage. Rabbulas, bp. of Edessa, went so far as to attack Theodore of Mopsuestia, and raised a storm of opposition in the East by so doing. Cyril, writing to Acacius of Melitene (not to be confounded with the aged Acacius of Beroea), declared that though it was possible theoretically (ἐν ἐννοίαις) to conceive of the two natures in Christ as distinct, yet after their union in His Person they became but one nature. This doctrine, essentially Monophysite as it was, he did not scruple to attribute to his Syrian opponents in order to magnify the concessions he made to them (Neander, iv. p. 176). Meanwhile Theodoret still held out, though he offered to condemn those who denied the divinity of Christ, or divided Him into two Sons. And he implored John of Antioch and count (*comes*) Irenaeus, a friend of the emperor, to accept the word θεοτόκος. But he maintained that to condemn Nestorius would be unjust. Yet even he had become weary of the controversy, and was at last prevailed upon to exert himself in favour of a reconciliation. He had great difficulty in bringing over the Oriental bishops. So he went so far as to beseech Nestorius to yield for the sake of peace. It has been felt that the extent to which he carried his submission has left a stain on his otherwise high character. In his Commentary on the Psalms (written *c.* 433) he calls Nestorius δυσσέβης, and a worshipper of a foreign and new God, and classes his followers with Jews, Arians, and Eunomians; but he earnestly begged that the venerable age of Nestorius might be exempt from violence or cruelty, and besought the patriarch John to use his influence to prevent this; and [MONOPHYSITISM] he retrieved by his later conduct his reputation for courage and impartiality.

John, however, was not to be softened. He had thrown his influence on the side of the court, and he was determined to persevere in his policy. Nestorius was banished to a convent just outside the gates of Antioch, and Meletius of Mopsuestia, Alexander of Hierapolis, and Helladius of Tarsus, strong supporters of the school of Theodore, were involved in the fate of Nestorius. In 435 it was thought that Nestorius was nearer the patriarch of Antioch than was convenient, so his exile to Petra in Arabia was decreed, though he was actually taken to Egypt instead. An assault was made on his place of residence by a horde of Libyan barbarians, who carried him off. When released, he made his way to the Thebaid, and gave himself up to the prefect, begging for kindness and protection. This modest request was not granted. He was dragged about from place to place, with every sign of contempt and hatred. The historian Evagrius, who loses no opportunity of loading his memory by the use of opprobrious language and represents his fate as a judgment of God analogous to that which befel Arius, gives us a sketch of a second and most pathetic letter addressed by Nestorius to the prefect and known as his "Tragedy." In this he implores the protection of the Roman laws, and enlarges on the reproach which would fall on the Roman name if he received better treatment from barbarians than when seeking the protection of the Roman government. He gives a moving picture of the hardships to which, though "afflicted by disease and age," he had been subjected. But all was in vain. He obtained no mercy, and only death released him from his sufferings.

Though his enemies might remove him from this world, they could not so easily destroy his influence. The extent of his error had been much exaggerated. His opponents went ultimately to greater extremes than he had ever done, though it must be confessed that his utterances were often ill-considered, as when he denied without qualification that the Son could be said to have suffered. For the history of the immediate results of their victory see MONOPHYSITISM. Cyril, in his Ep. to Acacius of Melitene, had, before his death in 444, committed himself to the doctrine that the two natures (φύσεις) of Christ *became one* after the union had been effected. This doctrine, in the days of his successor, brought about a strong reaction in favour of the Syrian interpretation of the word θεοτόκος. Meanwhile the party of Nestorius was very rigorously treated by the emperor. In 435 laws were enacted ordaining that the Nestorians should be called Simonians (their own name for themselves was Chaldeans); that the writings of Nestorius should be burnt; that all bishops who defended his opinions should be deposed; punishments were decreed against any one who should copy, keep, or even read his writings or those of his supporters; and all meetings of Nestorians for public worship were rigorously proscribed.

The after-history of Nestorianism is extremely interesting, but cannot be treated in detail here. The rigorous measures above mentioned were fiercely resisted in Syria and Babylonia, and when Rabbulas sought to prohibit the reading of the works of Diodorus and Theodore, the Nestorian teachers crossed the border into Persia. Barsumas, bp. of Nisibis from 435 to 489, did much to spread Nestorianism in the far East, and his work received an additional impulse from the policy of the emperor Zeno, who persecuted Nestorians and Monophysites alike. [MONOPHYSITISM.] Thence Nestorianism spread to Chaldea, India, and even China. It has even been stated that there was a time when the disciples of Nestorius outnumbered the members of all the other communions in the Christian church. Of the progress of Nestorianism in China there can be no doubt, for the Jesuits found a monument there, recording the fact. Their statement has been disputed, but it is hardly likely that they would have pretended to have made a discovery which tended to glorify what they regarded as a deadly heresy. The Nestorian doctrines, however, in the extreme form they assumed when interpreted by their later exponents, did not contain the "seeds of eternity." The spread of Mohammedanism ultimately destroyed the once flourishing Nestorian churches outside the limits of the Roman empire, though the Arab caliphs, as distinguished from the Turks, shewed them some favour. At present only a few down-trodden communities in Assyria (to the assistance of which the Anglican church has lately sent a mission), and the so-called Christians of St. Thomas on the Malabar coast, remain to represent the church once dominant in the far East. The latter were harassed and all but destroyed in the 16th cent. by Portuguese Romanists, with the aid of the Inquisition; and the object of the Anglican mission to the struggling churches of Assyria—a purely educational one—has been very seriously hindered by the political protection promised, and often afforded, by Roman Catholic powers on the one hand, and by adherents of the Orthodox Russian church on the other. [NESTORIAN CHURCH.]

The revival of the persecution of the Nestorian churches still existing in the Eastern empire in the reign of Justinian (527-565) must be briefly mentioned. The empress Theodora favoured Monophysitism; the emperor inclined to the doctrines of Origen. The two parties, after having been in conflict for some years, agreed to put an end to their mutual hostility, and to turn their efforts against the remnant of the Nestorians. In 544 Justinian issued an edict against what were called the *Three Chapters*, a series of extracts from the writings of Theodore, Theodoret, and Ibas. This step led to a prolonged controversy, which in 547 brought Vigilius, bp. of Rome, to Constantinople. Justinian ordered him to take an oath condemning the Three Chapters. He consented to do this, but afterwards retracted his consent. In 551 the relations between Vigilius and the emperor had become so strained that the former, who had for some time been detained in Constantinople, was compelled to take sanctuary in a church. A council, known as the *fifth oecumenical council*, was summoned at Constantinople, in which the Three Chapters were condemned. Vigilius refused to submit to the decision on the grounds (1) that Theodore had died in full communion with the church, and (2) that the doctrines of Theodoret and Ibas had been approved by the council of Chalcedon. He afterwards yielded to pressure, submitted to the decrees of the council, and was released from captivity, but died on his way back to Rome. This was the last attack on Nestorianism on the part of members of the Christian church. As in the original controversy, a strong reaction followed, and Monotheletism, an offshoot of MONOPHYSITISM, was condemned at another council held at Constantinople, and Nestorianism henceforth ceased to attract the attention of the rulers of the Catholic church.

Bibliography.—Of contemporary writers the historians Socrates and Evagrius may be mentioned. The former is thoughtful, impartial, and generally accurate, and his *History* was published while Nestorius was still living. Evagrius published his *History* in the 12th year of the reign of the emperor

Maurice, *i.e.* in 594. He is painstaking and accurate, and a devout believer in the decisions both of Ephesus and Chalcedon. But his language is often violent, and he is credulous as regards the miraculous. Cyril and Theodoret, who were actively engaged in the controversy, have left abundant details of what took place; their own letters are especially valuable, and with the writings of Theodoret are pub. a collection of important letters from most of the principal persons concerned in it. Marius Mercator, who was at Constantinople when the conflict was at its height, has left an account of it in Latin. Of later authorities Mansi, Hardouin, and Hefele have handed down the proceedings of the council of Ephesus, and commented upon them. Assemani's learned work, pub. in the 18th cent., is a mine of information on Nestorianism. Neander and Dorner [ARIUS, FOLLOWERS OF] give full accounts of the struggle. Gieseler passes over the events more briefly. Mr. Percy Badger published a useful work on Nestorians and their ritual in 1852. Loof's *Nestoriana* (Halle, 1905) should also be consulted. Canon Bright's *Age of the Fathers* gives a most valuable account of the controversy, though he is somewhat inclined to favour Cyril. Mr. Bethune-Baker's recent work on the early heresies contains much useful information, imparted with great clearness and impartiality.

[Since these words were written, the Editor has called the attention of the writer to a work by Mr. Bethune-Baker, entitled *Nestorius and his Teaching*, pub. in 1908. It is strange that the discovery which it has made public has not elicited the enthusiasm which greeted the previous discoveries of the *Teaching of the Twelve Apostles* and the *Apology of Aristides*. It is nothing less than a resurrection of Nestorius from the dead to plead his cause before a fairer tribunal than that which pronounced upon him when living. A treatise has lately come to light called the *Bazaar* (or more properly *Emporium* or *Store*, *i.e.* a collection of merchandize) *of Heracleides*. This treatise appears to have been written in Greek, and translated into Syriac. It is this Syrian translation which has recently been recovered. The work is evidently that of the patriarch Nestorius himself, and its somewhat strange title is explained by the fact that all copies of the works of Nestorius were ordered to be seized and destroyed. The treatise has a peculiar interest for us, because it shews, as Mr. Bethune-Baker puts it, and as has been suggested in the above article, that "Nestorius was not a Nestorian." Thus the doctrinal decision reached at Ephesus is vindicated, while its personal application to the patriarch himself is shewn to be unfair. In his preface Mr. Bethune-Baker expresses the same respect for the decisions of the four great oecumenical councils which has been expressed by the writer in his summary of their general doctrinal bearing at the end of the art. MONOPHYSITISM—namely, that they were "more likely to give us a true theory of the relation between God and man than are the reflexions of any individual thinker or school of theologians." They do this because they "express the *communis sensus fidelicum*," and "their decisions need to be confirmed by subsequent acceptance by the church as a whole."] [J.J.L.]

Nicarete (Νικαρέτη), a lady of one of the noblest and richest families of Nicomedia, who devoted herself to perpetual virginity in connexion with the church of Constantinople. She was warmly attached to Chrysostom and was punished for her devotion to his cause by the confiscation of most of her property in the troubles that followed his expulsion. She was then advanced in life and had a large household dependent on her, but managed her lessened resources with such economy that she had enough for their wants and her own, and also to give largely to the poor. Skilled in the compounding of medicines, she often succeeded in curing where physicians failed. Her humility and self-distrust would never allow her to become a deaconess, and she declined the office of lady superior of the consecrated virgins when Chrysostom earnestly pressed it on her. She retired from Constantinople to avoid the persecution in 404 (Soz. *H. E.* viii. 23). [E.V.]

Nicetas (3) (*Niceta, Nicaeas, Niceas, Nicias*), bp. of Romaciana (Remesiana) in Dacia. Our knowledge of him is derived from the epistles and poems (Nos. 17 and 24) of Paulinus of Nola, whom he visited, A.D. 398 and 402. He was probably a native of Dacia. He evangelized the Scythae, Getae, Daci, Bessi, and Riphaei, but settled specially among the Daci, reducing the wild manners of the barbarians to meekness and honesty. He was noted for eloquence and learning, honoured by the Romans when he visited them, and specially beloved by Paulinus at Nola, but we cannot define the extent of his see or the dates of his episcopate. Boll. *Acta SS.* Jan. i. 365, and Jun. iv. 243; Tillem. *H. E.* x. 263 seq.; Fleury, *H. E.* xxi. c. 31; Ceill. *Aut. Sacr.* v. 458; viii. 84. For the latest view of the subject of this art. see Burn, *Niceta of Remesiana, his Life and Works* (Camb. Univ. Press). [G.T.S.]

Nicetius (3) (*Nicet, Nicesse*), St., 25th archbp. of Trèves, *c.* 527-566. In his day the bishop was already beginning to pass into the baron, and Nicetius was a territorial lord (Freeman, *Augusta Treverorum*, *Histor. Essays*, 3rd ser. p. 111). Our principal knowledge of him is from Gregory of Tours, who received his information from St. Aredius, an abbat of Limoges, Nicetius's disciple (*Vitae Patrum*, c. xvii.). At Trèves his position was a difficult one. The Franks around him were little else than barbarians, rioting in licence, and scarcely more than nominal converts to Christianity. Their respect Nicetius won by personal asceticism, an inflexible temper and fearless demeanour in the face of the strong, activity in good works, and uncompromising orthodoxy (*ib.*). He used excommunication freely against princes and nobles in cases of oppression or flagrant immorality (cf. Rettberg, *Kirchengeschichte Deutschlands*, i. 462-464). His orthodoxy is illustrated by two extant letters: one from him to Clodosinda, the wife of Alboin the Lombard, urging her to turn her husband to Catholicism; the other to the emperor Justinian, whose lapse in his latter days into a form of Eutychianism, Nicetius declares, is lamented by all Italy,

Africa, Spain, and Gaul (*Patr. Lat.* lxviii. 375-380; Hontheim, *ib.* 47-51). Nicetius set himself to restore the churches which had suffered in the storms of the previous generations and partly rebuilt the metropolitan church of Trèves (Venant. Fort. *Misc.* iii. 11, *Patr. Lat.* lxxxviii. 134). His alterations and additions are described by Wilmowsky, *Der Dom der Trier*, pp. 37 sqq., and Freeman, *ib.* p. 113. For his own defence he built a castle on a lofty hill overlooking the Mosel. The walls, with 30 towers, stretched down to the river banks, and the bishop's hall, with marble columns, occupied the highest point (Venant. Fort. iii. 12, *Patr. Lat. ib.* 135). It is the first recorded building of a class which later was greatly multiplied, but its site is unknown (Freeman, p. 112). For his architectural undertakings he summoned workmen from Italy (Rufus, *Ep.* Hontheim, *ib.* p. 37). He died *c.* 566, and was buried in the church of St. Maximin, where his tomb still is. Even in Gregory's time it was famous for its miracles (*de Glor. Conf.* 94; *Vitae Patr.* xvii.; *Gall. Christ.* xiii. 382). Nicetius also wrote two treatises called *de Vigiliis Servorum Dei* and *de Psalmodiae Bono*, slight works of a didactic character, to be found in the *Patr. Lat.* lxviii. 365-376, and, with the letters, discussed at some length by Ceillier, xi. 203-206. [S.A.B.]

Nicolaitanes. The mention of this name in the Apocalypse (see *Murray's Illus. B. D. s.v.*) has caused it to appear in almost all lists of heresies; but there is no trustworthy evidence of the continuance of a sect so called after the death of St. John. Irenaeus in writing his great work used a treatise against heresies by Justin Martyr; and that Justin's list began with Simon Magus and made no mention of Nicolaitanes may be conjectured from the order in which Irenaeus discusses the heresies, viz. Simon, Menander, Saturninus, Basilides, Carpocrates, Cerinthus, the Ebionites, the Nicolaitanes. So late a place is inconsistent with chronological order, and the most plausible explanation is that Irenaeus followed the order of an older list, and added the Nicolaitanes to it. About them he has nothing to say (I. xxvi. 3) but what he found in the Apocalypse; for the words "qui indiscrete vivunt," which alone have the appearance of an addition, seem only an inference from Rev. ii. 13, 14, and 20-22. In a later book (III. x. 6) Irenaeus incidentally mentions them as a branch of the Gnostics and seems to ascribe to them the whole body of Ophite doctrine. HIPPOLYTUS probably derived his view of them from Irenaeus. In his earlier treatise, as we gather from comparing the lists of Epiphanius, Philaster, and Pseudo-Tertullian, he brings them into an earlier, though still too late a place in his list, his order being Simon Menander, Saturninus, Basilides, Nicolaitanes; and he ascribes to them the tenets of a fully developed Ophite system. There is no sufficient evidence that the Ophites called themselves Nicolaitanes. In the later work of Hippolytus, Nicolaus the deacon is made the founder of the Gnostics; but the notice is short, and goes little beyond what is told in Irenaeus, bk. i. It is needless to notice the statements of later writers.

Stephen Gobar (cf. Phot. *Bibl.* 232) says that Hippolytus and Epiphanius make Nicolas the deacon of Acts vi. 5 answerable for the errors of the sect called after him; whereas Ignatius, Clement of Alexandria, Eusebius, and Theodoret condemn the sect, but impute none of the blame to Nicolas himself. [G.S.]

Nicolaus (1), bp. of Myra in Lycia at the time of Diocletian's persecution, and one of the most popular saints both in the East and West. His Acts, which may embody some historical elements, are filled with well-known legends and miracles. He is said to have been present at the council of Nice, where he waxed so indignant with Arius that he inflicted a box on the heretic's ear. Dean Stanley (*Eastern Church*, pp. 110, 132) represents Nicolaus as occupying the central place in all traditional pictures of the council. Tozer in his notes to Finlay's *Hist. of Greece*, t. i. p. 124, observes that Nicolaus has taken the place of Poseidon in Oriental Christianity. Thus, in the island of Eleüssa, a temple of Poseidon has been changed into the church of St. Nicolaus. In England 376 churches are dedicated to him. His feast-day was formerly connected in Salisbury Cathedral, Eton, and elsewhere with the curious ceremonial of choosing a boy-bishop, who presided till the following Innocents' Day over his fellow-choristers, arrayed in full episcopal attire (cf. *Antiq. of Cath. Church of Salisbury*, A.D. 1723, pp. 72-80, where the ritual of the feast is given). We can trace his fame back to the 6th cent., when Justinian built a church in his honour at Constantinople (Procop. *de Aedif.* i. 6). His relics were translated in the middle ages to Barri in Italy, whence he is often styled Nicolaus of Barri. His Acts are given at length in Surii, *Hist. Sanct.*, and his legends and treatment in art in Jameson's *Sacred Art*, t. ii. p. 450. The figure of St. Nicolaus is a leading one in the celebrated Blenheim Raphael in the National Gallery. [G.T.S.]

Nilus (3), a famous ascetic of Sinai, probably born in Galatia, as he speaks of St. Plato martyr of Ancyra as his countryman. He became prefect at Constantinople, married, and had two children, when he determined *c.* 390 to retire to Sinai with his son Theodulus. His epistles are very curious, detailing assaults by demons, and replying to various queries, doctrinal, disciplinary, and even political. Gaïnas, the Gothic general, discussed with him the Arian controversy, but without changing his opinions (*Epp.* lib. i. 70, 79, 114). Nilus boldly took the side of St. Chrysostom when banished from Constantinople in 404. The story of his ordination is a curious one. The Saracens invaded the desert of Sinai and captured some of the solitaries, including Nilus and Theodulus. They dismissed Nilus and the older men but retained the young men, intending to offer them next day as sacrifices to the Morning Star. They overslept themselves, however, and then, as the propitious time was past, sold Theodulus, who fell into the hands of a neighbouring bishop. There he was found by his father. The piety of both so struck the bishop that he compelled them to accept ordination. They returned to Sinai, and distinguished themselves by a yet severer piety. Nilus died *c.*

430. His writings throw much light on monasticism and Christian society generally at the end of 4th cent. *Epp.* 61 and 62, lib. iv., most interestingly illustrate the church life at that period. Olympiodorus, an eparch, desired to erect a church and to decorate it with images of saints in the sanctuary, together with hunting scenes, birds, and animals in mosaic, and numerous crosses in the nave and on the floor—a scheme of decoration which we find carried out some time later in the churches of Central Syria, depicted in De Vogüé's *Civil and Ecclesiastical Architecture of Syria.* Nilus condemns the mosaics as mere trifling and unworthy a manly Christian soul. He rejects numerous crosses in the nave, but orders the erection of one cross at the east end of the sanctuary, "Inasmuch as by the cross man was delivered from spiritual slavery, and hope has been shed on the nations." Good pictures from O. and N. T. meet with his approval. They serve as books for the unlearned; teach them Scripture history, and remind them of God's mercies. The church was to have numerous chapels. Each chapel may have a cross erected therein. *Ep.* 62 proves that his prohibition of mosaics only extended to hunting scenes and probably did not include the images of saints. It was written to exalt the fame of his favourite martyr, Plato of Ancyra, and conclusively proves that the invocation of saints was then practised in the East [cf. FIDENTIUS (2)]. Nilus did not approve of the extraordinary forms which monasticism was assuming. *Epp.* 114 and 115, lib. ii. are addressed to one Nicander, a Stylite, who must have set the fashion which St. Simeon followed. Nilus tells him his lofty position is due simply to pride, and shall find a fulfilment of the words "He that exalts himself shall be abased." In the second epistle he charges him with light and amorous conversation with women. Monastic discipline seems to have been then very relaxed, as the charges are repeated in his letters and works. We often find in them the peculiar practices of the monks or of the early church explained with mystical references. Cf. Fessler-Jungmann, *Inst. Patrol.* (1896), ii. 2, p. 108. [G.T.S.]

Ninian, British missionary bishop. The general facts of his life and work present comparatively few points for dispute, there being but one tradition, and that not materially departed from.

The primary authority is Bede (*H. E.* iii. 4), who, however, only incidentally alludes to St. Ninian in connexion with St. Columba, yet touches therein the chief points embodied in the later Life—his converting the southern Picts a long time before St. Columba's day, his being "de natione Brittonum," but instructed in the Christian faith and mysteries at Rome; his friendship with St. Martin of Tours, in whose honour he dedicated his episcopal see and church at Candida Casa in the province of the Bernicii, and his building the church there of stone "insolito Brittonibus more" (*M. H. B.* 176). This is repeated in the *Anglo-Saxon Chronicle* A.D. 565 (*ib.* 303). Ailred's *Vita S. Niniani* seems little more than an expansion of these details, but whether he, in the 12th cent., had authentic evidence of an earlier date to assist him we do not know, except that he specially refers to Bede's information and also to a "liber de vita et miraculis ejus, barbario [barbarice] scriptus," of the value of which we are ignorant. The chief Life is *Vita Niniani Pictorum Australium apostoli, auctore Ailredo Reivallensi,* first printed by Pinkerton (*Vit. Ant. SS.* 1 seq. ed. 1789) and reprinted with trans. and notes, by Bp. Forbes (*Historians of Scotland*, vol. v. 1874). (See also Hardy, *Descript. Cat.* i. 44 seq. 853; Bp. Forbes, *Lives of SS. Kent. and Nin.* Introd.; Grub, *Eccl. Hist. Scot.* i. c. 2 et al.; Skene, *Celt. Scot.* ii. 3, 444; Haddan and Stubbs, *Counc.* i. 14, 35; Pinkerton, *Enquiry,* ii. 263 seq.; Pryce, *Anc. Brit. Ch.* 104 seq.)

Ailred's Life is of the usual unhistoric character, fuller of moralizings than of facts, and having only one fixed point to suggest a date. St. Ninian was of royal birth and belonged to the valley of the Solway; his father was probably a regulus in the Cumbrian kingdom, and, being a Christian, had his son baptized. The youth soon manifested a desire to visit Rome, and appears to have reached it in the time of pope Damasus (A.D. 366-384), perhaps in 370. After devoting several years there to the Scriptures and holy learning, he was raised to the episcopate, A.D. 394, by the pope himself, probably Siricius (A.D. 385-399) and sent as bp. to the W. of Britain, where the Gospel was unknown, corrupted, or misrepresented by the teachers. Calling on St. Martin at Tours and receiving from him masons to build churches according to the Roman method, he returned to his native shores and built his church at Witerna, now Whithern in Wigtonshire, but whether near the site of the later abbey or on the island near the shore is uncertain. While building the church the news reached him of St. Martin's death (A.D. 397), in whose honour he dedicated it; this at the latest must have been in the spring of 398. We have no other landmark for ascertaining his dates. The chief field of his missionary labours was in the central district of the E. of Scotland among those barbarians who had defied the Roman power in the days of Agricola and who were separated from the Roman province of Valentia by the rampart of Antoninus; but the veneration attached to his name is shown by his dedications being found over all Scotland. (See Bp. Forbes, *Kals.* 424.)

His monastic school, known variously as Magnum Monasterium, Monasterium Rosnatense, Alba, and Candida Casa, was famous through Cumbria and Ireland, and was one of the chief seats of early Christian learning to which Welsh and Irish saints resorted, till both school and see were destroyed by the irruptions of the Britons and Saxons. The see was revived for a time in the 8th cent., under Saxon influence from York (Haddan and Stubbs, *Counc.* ii. pt. i. 7, 8, 56 seq.; Stubbs, *Reg. Sac. Ang.* 184 et al.), to be again restored in the 12th cent. by King David I. of Scotland. The date usually assigned for his death, though on no definite data, is Sept. 16, 432, and Bede (*H. E.* iii. c. 4) says he was buried in his church at Candida Casa, which in the middle ages became much frequented by pilgrims. [J.G.]

Noetus, a native of Smyrna according to

Hippolytus; of Ephesus according to Epiphanius (*Haer.* 57), probably by a mistake, as his narrative is in other respects wholly derived from Hippolytus. From Asia Minor also Praxeas, some years before, had imported into Rome the views which Noetus taught. Hippolytus traces the origin of the Patripassian heresy at Rome to Noetus, who in his opinion derived it from the philosophy of Heraclitus (*Refutation*, lib. ix. cc. 3-5, cf. x. 23). Noetus came to Rome, where he converted Epigonus and Cleomenes. He was summoned before the council of Roman presbyters, and interrogated about his doctrines. He denied at first that he had taught that "Christ was the Father, and that the Father was born and suffered and died," but his adherents increasing in number, he acknowledged before the same council, when summoned a second time, that he had taught the views attributed to him. "The blessed presbyters called him again before them and examined him. But he stood out against them, saying, 'What evil am I doing in glorifying one God?' And the presbyters replied to him, 'We too know in truth one God, we know Christ, we know that the Son suffered even as He suffered, and died even as He died, and rose again on the third day, and is at the right hand of the Father, and cometh to judge the living and the dead, and these things which we have learned we allege.' Then after examining him they expelled him from the church. And he was carried to such a pitch of pride, that he established a school." Cf. Routh's *Reliq. Sac.* t. iv. 243-248. As to his date, Hippolytus tells us "he lived not long ago," Lipsius and Salmon think this very treatise was used by Tertullian in his tract against Praxeas [HIPPOLYTUS ROMANUS], while Hilgenfeld and Harnack date Tertullian's work between A.D. 206 and 210. This would throw the treatise of Hippolytus back to *c.* 205. From its language and tone, we conclude that Noetus was then dead, a view which Epiphanius (*Haer.* 57, c. 1) expressly confirms, saying that he and his brother both died soon after their excommunication and were buried without Christian rites. The period of his teaching at Rome must then have been some few years previous to 205. But Hippolytus in his *Refutation of Heresies* gives us a farther note of time, telling us in ix. 2 that it was when Zephyrinus was managing the affairs of the church that the school of Noetus was firmly established at Rome and that Zephyrinus connived at its establishment through bribes. We cannot, however, fix the date of his excommunication and death more closely than *c.* 200. Hippolytus (x. 23) tells us that some Montanists adopted the views of Noetus. He seems to have written some works, from which Hippolytus often quotes. [G.T.S.]

Nomus, a leading personage at Constantinople in the latter years of Theodosius II., with whom he was all-powerful—*τὰ τῆς οἰκουμένης ἐν χερσὶν ἔχων πράγματα* (Labbe, *Concil.* iv. 407). Nomus filled in succession all the highest offices in the state. In 443 he was "magister officiorum" (*Cod. Theod.* Nov. p. 14, 1); consul in 445; patrician in 449, the year of the infamous "Latrocinium." He was the confidential friend of Chrysaphius the eunuch and shared with him the government of the emperor and the empire. Through them Dioscorus of Alexandria and the Eutychian doctrines he supported were brought into favour at court. Through Nomus the feeble Theodosius was induced to publish a decree in 448 confining Theodoret to his own diocese. The interesting series of letters, to the principal men of the empire, in which Theodoret, while observing the mandate, protested against its arbitrary character, contains several addressed to Nomus. With the death of Theodosius and the accession of Marcian and Pulcheria, Nomus's power sensibly waned. He took, however, a leading position as a high state official at the council of Chalcedon (Labbe, iv. 77, 475, etc.), where a libel or petition against him was presented by a nephew of Cyril, Athanasius by name, a presbyter of Alexandria, accusing him of violence and extortion which had reduced Athanasius and his relatives to beggary and caused his brother to die of distress (*ib.* 407-410). [E.V.]

Nonna (1), mother of Gregory Nazianzen; a lady of good birth, the child of Christian parents, Philtatius and Gorgonia, brought up in the practice of the Christian virtues, of which she was so admirable an example. Her son describes in glowing terms the holiness of her life and the beautiful conformity of all her actions to the highest standards of Christian excellence. To her example, aided by her prayers, he ascribes the conversion of his father from the strange medley of paganism and Christianity which formed the tenets of the Hypsistarian sect, to which by birth he belonged (Greg. Naz. *Or.* 11, 19; *Carm.* 1, 2). We know of two other children of the marriage, a sister named Gorgonia, probably older than Gregory, and a brother named Caesarius. Nonna's death probably occurred on Aug. 5 (on which day she is commemorated both by the Greek and Latin churches) in 374 (*Orat.* 19, p. 315; *Carm.* 1, p. 9). Tillem. *Mém. eccl.* t. ix. pp. 309-311, 317, 318, 322, 385, 397. [E.V.]

Nonnus (2) of Panopolis. The name is very common, being properly an Egyptian title equivalent to Saint. Consequently confusion has arisen between this writer and others of the same name. He has been identified, with some probability, with a Nonnus whose son is mentioned by Synesius (*Ep. ad Anastas.* 42, *ad Pyl.* 102); and, with very little probability, with the deacon Nonnus, secretary at the council of Chalcedon, A.D. 451; with Nonnus, the bp. of Edessa, elected at the synod of Ephesus, A.D. 449; and with Nonnus the commentator on Gregory Nazianzen (*vide* Bentley, *Phalaris*, ad in.).

Life.—He was a native of Panopolis in Egypt; cf. Eudoxia, *s.v.* Agathias, iv. p. 128; and an epigram in *Anth. Graeca*, i. p. 140. He is classed by Agathias among *οἱ νέοι ποιηταί*, and this, supported by a comparison of his poems with other late epic writers, makes it probable that he wrote at the end of the 4th and beginning of the 5th cents. A.D. Beyond this nothing is known for certain. His *Dionysiaca* shews frequently a knowledge of astronomy (cf. vi. 60; xxv.; xxxviii. 4), and a special interest in Berytus (xli.), Tyre (xl.), and Athens (xlvii.), but whether from a personal acquaintance with these towns is uncertain.

In iv. 250 the discoveries of Cadmus are traced to Egypt, but otherwise there is no reference to his native country. The whole tone of the *Dionysiaca*, with its delight in the drunken immoralities of Dionysus, makes it hard to believe the poem written by a Christian. Probably it was written early in life, and Nonnus converted to Christianity after it, and the paraphrase of St. John written after his conversion, possibly, as has been suggested, as a contrast to the *Dionysiaca*, portraying the life and apotheosis of one more worthy than Dionysus of the name of God. Possibly too, as has also been suggested, Nonnus may have been one of the Greek philosophers who accepted Christianity when the heathen temples were destroyed by decree of Theodosius (Socr. *H. E.* v. 16).

Works.—Of his literary position it is possible to speak with more certainty. He was the centre, if not the founder, of the literary Egyptian school, which gave to Greek epic poetry a new though short-lived brilliancy, and to which belonged Quintus of Smyrna, John of Gaza, Coluthus, Tryphiodorus, and Musaeus. This school revived the historical and mythological epic, treating it in a peculiar style of which Nonnus is the best representative. While frequently proclaiming himself an imitator of Homer, and shewing traces of the influence of Callimachus and later writers, he yet created new metrical rules, which gave an entirely new effect to the general rhythm of the poem—that of an easy but rather monotonous flow, always pleasant, but never rising or falling with the tone of the narrative. The style is very florid, marked by a luxuriance of epithets and original compounds (often of very arbitrary formation), elaborate periphrasis, and metaphors often piled together in hopeless confusion; and many unusual forms are invented.

The *Dionysiaca* attributed to Nonnus by Agathias (*u.s.*) is a history of the birth, conquests and apotheosis of Dionysus, spun out at great length. The poem has been regarded "as an allegory of the march of civilization across the ancient world"; but it would be simpler, and we hope truer, to describe it as "the gradual establishment of the cultivation of the vine and the power of the Wine-god."

The chief modern editions of the *Dionysiaca* are Graefe (1819-1826); Passow (1834); Le Comte de Marcellus, with interesting introduction, French trans. and notes, in Didot's *Bibl. Graeca* (1856); Köchly with *apparatus criticus* (1857), cf. Ouwarow (1817); Köhler, *Ueber die Dion. des Nonnus* (1853).

The *Paraphrase* (Μεταβολή) *of St. John's Gospel*, attributed to Nonnus by Eudocia (Viol. 311), is a fairly faithful paraphrase of the whole of the Gospel. The text of the Gospel that lies behind the paraphrase has been reproduced by R. Jannsen (*Texte und Untersuchungen, N. F.* viii. 4, 1903). The text is faithfully treated. The omissions, except when he has MSS. authority (*e.g.* v. 1, 4, vii. 53 sqq.), are rare (v. 1, 29, iv. 27, 41, 42, vi. 41, 53, viii. 38, xviii. 16, 18). The additions are chiefly those of poetical expansion. Homeric epithets form a strange medley with the Palestinian surroundings, and in many cases the illustrations are drawn out into insipid details (cf. iv. 26, vii. 21, xviii. 3, xx. 7). At other times we have interpretations suggested, in most of which he agrees with the Alexandrine tradition as represented by Cyril and Origen cf. i. 16, 24, 42 (Peter's name); vi. 71 (the motive of Judas); vii. 19 (the reference to the sixth commandment); viii. 40 (the hospitality of Abraham); xii. 6, 10; xviii. 15 (ἰχθυβόλου παρὰ τέχνης); xix. 7. In some he seems obviously wrong, *e.g.* ii. 12 (δυωδεκάριθμος); ii. 20, x. 12 (the reference to Solomon); vii. 28 (ὑψῶν); xi. 44, σουδάριον explained as a Syrian word; while in ii. 4, τί μοι γύναι ἠὲ καὶ αὐτῇ looks like an attempt to avoid a slight to her who is constantly called Θεοτόκος. He shews, too, a looseness in using theological terms (cf. i. 3, μύθος; 1, 50, xi. 27, λόγος) which, with the luxuriance of periphrasis, forms a striking contrast to the simplicity and accuracy of St. John. The chief modern editions are Passow (1834); Le Comte de Marcellus, with French trans. and notes (1860); A. Scheindler (1881), with text of the Gospel and *criticus apparatus*; Migne, vol. xliii. (with the notes of Heinsius and of Le Comte de Marcellus); Mansi, *Bibl. Patr.* vi. (ed. 1618), ix. (ed. 1677). See also a series of arts. in *Wiener Studien* for 1880-1881 and *Theolog. Literaturzeitung*, 1891, where the authorship is attributed to Apollinaris. [W.L.]

Novatianus and **Novatianism** (*Novatianus*, Cyprian, *Ep.* xliv.; Νοουάτος, Eus. *H. E.* vi. 43; Ναυάτος, Socr. *H. E.* iv. 28. Lardner (*Credibility*, c. 47, note) seeks to prove that Eusebius and the Greeks in general were correct in calling the Roman presbyter Novatus, not Novatianus. He attributes the origin of the latter name to Cyprian, who called the Roman presbyter Novatianus, as being a follower of his own rebellious priest, Novatus of Carthage. Novatian, the founder of Novatianism, is said by Philostorgius to have been a Phrygian by birth, a notion which may have originated in the popularity of his system in Phrygia and its neighbourhood (Lightfoot's *Colossians*, p. 98). He was, before his conversion, a philosopher, but of what sect we cannot certainly determine, though from a comparison of the language of Cyprian in *Ep.* lv. § 13, *ad Antonian.*, with the Novatianist system itself, we should be inclined to say the Stoic. The circumstances of his conversion and baptism are stated by pope Cornelius in his letter to Fabius of Antioch (Eus. *l.c.*), but we must accept his statements with much caution. His narration is evidently coloured by his feelings. The facts of the case appear to be these. He was converted after he had come to manhood, and received clinical baptism, but was never confirmed, which furnishes Cornelius with one of his principal accusations. He was, nevertheless, admitted to the clerical order. His talents, especially his eloquence, to which even Cyprian witnesses (*Ep.* lx. 3), rapidly brought him to the front, and he became the most influential presbyter of the Roman church. In this character, the see being vacant, he wrote *Ep.* xxx. to the Carthaginan church, touching the treatment of the lapsed, while the anonymous author of the treatise against Novatian, written A.D. 255 and included by Erasmus among Cyprian's works, describes him as "having been a precious vessel, an house of the Lord, who, as long as he was in the church, bewailed the faults of other men as his own, bore the burdens of his brethren as the apostle directs, and by his exhortations strengthened such as were weak in the faith." This testimony sufficiently disposes of the accusation of Cornelius that Novatian denied the faith in time of persecution, declaring himself "an admirer of a different philosophy." In 250 he approved of a moderate policy towards the lapsed, but later in the year changed his mind and took such extreme views that the martyr Moses, who probably suffered on the last day of 250, condemned them. In Mar. 251 Cornelius was consecrated bp. (Lipsius, *Chron. d. röm. Bisch.* p. 205). This roused the stricter party to action (Cyp. *Ep.* xlvi.). NOVATUS, the Carthaginian agitator, having meanwhile arrived at Rome, joined them and urged them to set up an opposition bishop. He made a journey into distant parts of Italy, and brought back 3 bishops who consecrated Novatian. After his consecration Novatian dispatched the usual epistles announcing it to the bishops of the chief sees, to Cyprian, Dionysius of Alexandria, Fabius of Antioch. Cyprian rejected his communion at once. Dionysius wrote exhorting him to retire from his schismatical position (Eus. *H. E.* vi. 45). Fabius, however, so inclined to his side that Dionysius addressed him a letter on the subject; and two bishops, Firmilianus of Cappadocia and Theoctistus of Palestine, wrote to Dionysius requesting his presence at the council of Antioch, to restrain tendencies in that direction (*ib.* 44, 46). In the latter part of 251 Novatian was formally excommunicated by a synod of 60 bishops at Rome. He then began to organize a distinct church, rebaptizing all who came over (Cyp. *Ep.* lxxiii. 2) and dispatching letters and emissaries to the most distant parts of the East and West (Socr. *H. E.* iv. 28). [CYPRIAN; NOVATUS.] His subsequent career is unknown, save that Socrates informs us that he suffered martyrdom under Valerian (*ib.*). He was a copious writer, as we learn from Jerome (*de Vir. Ill.* c. lxx.), who gives as his works, "*de Pascha, de Sabbato, de Circumcisione, de Sacerdote, de Oratione, de Instantia, de Attalo, de Cibis Judaicis,* et *de Trinitate,*" only the last two being now extant. (An ed. of *de Trin.* by W. Y. Fausset was pub. in 1909 in the *Camb. Patr. Texts.*) His work on Jewish meats was written at some place of retreat from persecution. The Jewish controversy seems to have been then very hot at Rome, and Novatian wrote to refute their contention about distinction of meats. Jerome describes his work on the Trinity as an epitome of Tertullian's, and as attributed by some to Cyprian (Hieron. *Apol. cont. Rufin.* lib. ii. *Opp.* t. iv. p. 415). It proves Novatian to have been a diligent student, as its arguments are identical with those of Justin Martyr in his *Dialog. cum Tryph.* c. cxxvii.; Tertull. *adv. Prax.* cc. xiv.-xxv.; Clem. Alex. *Strom.* ii. 16, v. 11, 12. He deals first with the absolute perfection of the Father, His invisibility, etc., then discusses the anthropomorphic expressions of the Scriptures, laying down that "such things were said about God indeed, but they are not to be imputed to God but to the people. It is not God Who is limited, but the perception of the people." In c. vii. he declares that even the terms Spirit, Light, Love, are only in an imperfect degree applicable to God. In cc. ix.-xxviii. he discusses the true doctrine of the Incarnation, explaining, like Clement and others, the theophanies of O.T. as manifestations of Christ, and refuting the doctrine of the Sabellians, or Artemonites, according to Neander (*H. E.* ii. 298), which had just then been developed. He ends by explaining the doctrine of the Holy Spirit, wherein he is thought by some to have fallen into error. He was quoted by the Macedonians of the next cent. as supporting their view (cf. Fabric. *Bibl. Graec.* xii. 565 and references noted there; Bull's *Def. of Nicene Creed,* ii. 476, Oxf. 1852; *Judg. of Cath. Ch.* pp. 9, 137, 291, Oxf. 1855). Lardner (*Credib.* c. 47, t. iii. p. 242) shews that Novatian did not accept *Hebrews* as Scripture, since he never quotes any texts out of it, though there were several which favoured his cause, notably Heb. vi. 4-8. His followers, however, in the next cent. did use them. Some have even thought Novatian to be the author of the *Refutation of all Heresies* (Bunsen, *Christ. and Mankind,* i. 480). A trans. of his works is in the vol. of Clark's *Ante-Nicene Lib.* which contains pt. ii. of St. Cyprian's writings (Edinb. 1869). Jackson's ed. is the best.

Novatianism.—The members of this sect called themselves Καθαροί (Eus. *H. E.* vi. 43). They were called by others Novatiani (Pacian. *Ep.* i. § 1).

Novatianism was the first great schism in the church on a pure question of discipline. In Montanism questions of discipline were involved as side issues, but did not constitute its essential difference. All sects previous to Novatianism had erred on the doctrine of the Trinity. The Novatianists alone were orthodox thereupon. The church therefore baptized even Montanists, but admitted Novatianists by imposition of hands (Conc. Laodic. can. vii. viii.; Hefele, *Councils,* ed. Clark, t. ii. 303, 332; Conc. CP. can. vii. in Hefele, *l.c.*; Pitra, *Jur. Eccles. Graec. Hist.* i. 430, 576).

The principles which Novatian formulated into a system, and to which he gave a name, existed and flourished long before him. The origin of the Novatianist schism must be sought in the struggle which, originating with the *Shepherd* of Hermas (Baur, *Church Hist.* trans. Menzies, 1879, t. ii. p. 50 note; cf. Ritschl, *Entstehung der Altkath. Kirche,* 2nd ed. p. 529), had been raging at Rome for 70 years, at first with the Montanists and the followers of Tertullian, and then between Hippolytus and Callistus. Every one of the distinctive principles of Novatianism will be found advocated by some or all of them (Baur, *l.c.* p. 270, note). The Montanists rejected the lapsed, and in fact all guilty of mortal sins, Tertullian rejected second marriages, as also did the strict discipline of the 2nd cent. (Ambr. *de Viduis,* c. ii.; Lumper, *Hist. SS. PP.* iii. 95; *de S. Athenag.*; Aug. *Ep.* ad Julian. *de Viduit.*). Hippolytus held, in a great degree, the same stern views. This identity in principle between Montanism and

Novatianism has been noted by many, both ancients and moderns, *e.g.* Epiph. *Haer.* 59; Hieron. *Opp.* Migne, *Patr. Lat.* t. i. 188, *Ep. ad Marcellam,* 457, *Ep. ad Oceanum*; t. vii. 697 *cont. Jovinian.* lib. ii.; Gieseler, *H. E.* t. i. pp. 213-215, 284, ed. Clark; Neander, *Anti-Gnostic,* t. ii. p. 362; Bunsen, *Christ. and Mankind,* t. i. 395, 428; Pressensé, *Life and Pract. of Early Ch.* lib. i. cc. 6, 7; Baur, *l.c.* pp. 124-126. With Donatism Novatianism is also allied, for the treatment of the lapsed underlay that schism too. Other points of similarity between the three may be noted. They all sprang up, or found their most enthusiastic supporters, in Africa. Each arose simultaneously with great persecutions. The two earliest, at least, proved their essential oneness, uniting their ranks in Phrygia in the 4th cent. Novatianism may be regarded as a conservative protest on behalf of the ancient discipline against the prevalent liberalism of the Roman church (Baur, *l.c.* p. 271). The sterner treatment of the lapsed naturally found favour with the more enthusiastic party, who usually give the tone to any religious society. Thus Eleutherus, bp. of Rome, in the latter part of 2nd cent. was inclined to take the Puritan view (Eus. *H. E.* lib. v. c. 3). Ozanam (*Hist. of Civilization in 5th Cent.* t. ii. p. 214, Eng. trans.) has noted an interesting proof of the prevalence of this view in Rome. Archaeologists have often been puzzled by the symbol of a Good Shepherd carrying a kid, not a lamb, on his shoulders, found in the cemetery of St. Callistus. Ozanam explains it as a reference by the excavators of the cemetery to the prevalent Montanist doctrine, which denied the possibility of a goat being brought back in this life. Novatianism thus fell upon ground prepared for it, and found in every quarter a body of ready adherents. But Novatian was the first to make the treatment of the lapsed the express ground of schism. In fact, many continued to hold the same view within the church during the next 150 years (cf. Hefele, *Councils,* t. i. p. 134, Clark's ed.; Innocent I. *Ep.* iii. *ad Exuperium,* in Mansi, iii. 1039). This fact accounts for the rapid spread of the sect. In Africa they established themselves in many cities within the course of the two years subsequent to Novatian's consecration in the spring of 251. [CYPRIAN.] In S. Gaul Marcian, bp. of Arles, joined them (Cyp. *Ep.* lxviii.; Greg. Turon. *Hist. Francor.* lib. i. in Migne, *Patr. Lat.* lxxi. 175). In the East they made great progress. Between A.D. 260 and the council of Nice we hear scarcely anything about them. The controversies about Sabellianism and Paul of Samosata, together with the rising tide of Arianism, occupied the church during the concluding years of the 3rd cent., while the peace it enjoyed prevented the question of the lapsed becoming a practical one. During this period, however, Novatianist doctrine became harder and sterner. Obliged to vindicate their position, they drew the reins tighter than Novatian had done. With him idolatry was the one crying sin which excluded from communion. During the long peace there was no temptation to this sin, therefore his followers were obliged to add all other deadly sins to the list (Socr. *H. E.* vii. 25; Ambr. *de Poenit.* lib. i. cc. 2, 3; Ceill. v. 466, 467). At the council of Nice we find them established far and wide, with a regular succession of bishops at the principal cities of the empire and of the highest reputation for piety. The monk Eutychian, one of their number, was a celebrated miracle-worker, reverenced by Constantine himself, who also endeavoured to lead one of their bishops, ACESIUS, to unite with the Catholics (Socr. *H. E.* i. 10, 13). During the 4th cent. we can trace their history much more clearly in the East than in the West, for Socrates gives such copious details as to lead some (Nicephorus, Baronius, and P. Labbaeus) to suspect that he was a member of the sect. In the East their fortunes were very varying. Under Constantine they were tolerated and even favoured (*Cod. Theod.* ed. Haenel, lib. xvi. tit. v. p. 1522). Under Constantius they were violently persecuted, together with the rest of the Homoousian party, by the patriarch Macedonius. Socrates (ii. 38) mentions several martyrs for the Catholic faith whom they then furnished, especially one Alexander, a Paphlagonian, to whose memory they built a church at Constantinople existing in his own day. Several of their churches, too, were destroyed at Constantinople and Cyzicus, but were restored by Julian upon his accession, and Agelius their bishop was banished. "But Macedonius consummated his wickedness in the following manner. Hearing there was a great number of the Novatian sect in the province of Paphlagonia, and especially at Mantinium, and perceiving that such a numerous body could not be driven from their homes by ecclesiastics alone, he caused, by the emperor's permission, four companies of soldiers to be sent into Paphlagonia that, through dread of the military, they might receive the Arian opinion. But those who inhabited Mantinium, animated to desperation by zeal for their religion, armed themselves with long reaping-hooks, hatchets, and whatever weapons came to hand, and went forth to meet the troops, on which, a conflict ensuing, many indeed of the Paphlagonians were slain, but nearly all the soldiers were destroyed." This persecution well-nigh brought about a union between the Catholics and the Novatianists, as the former frequented the churches of the latter party during the Arian supremacy. The Novatianists, however, as in Constantine's time, obstinately refused to unite with those whose church-theory was different from their own, though their faith was alike. Under Valens, seven years later, A.D. 366, they suffered another persecution and Agelius was again exiled. Under Theodosius their bp. at Constantinople, Agelius, appeared in conjunction with the orthodox patriarch Nectarius as joint defenders of the Homoousian doctrine at the synod of 383, on which account the emperor conferred on their churches equal privileges with those of the establishment (Socr. *H. E.* v. 10, 20). John Chrysostom's severe zeal for church discipline led him to persecute them. When visiting Ephesus to consecrate a bishop A.D. 401, he deprived them of their churches, an act to which many attributed John's subsequent misfortunes. An expression uttered by Chrysostom in reference to their peculiar views about sin after baptism, "Approach [the altar] though you may have repented a thousand times," led to a literary controversy between him and the learned and witty Sisinnius, Novatianist bp. of Constantinople (vi. 21, 22). About 374 a schism occurred in their ranks concerning the true time of Easter. Hitherto the Novatianists had strictly observed the Catholic rule. A few obscure Phrygian bishops, however, convened a synod at Pazum or Pazacoma, and agreed to celebrate the same day as that on which the Jews keep the Feast of Unleavened Bread. This canon was passed in the absence of Agelius of Constantinople, Maximus of Nice, and the bishops of Nicomedia and Cotyaeum, their leading men (iv. 28). Jewish influence was also at work, as Sozomen (vii. 18) tells us that a number of priests, converted by the Novatianists at Pazum during the reign of Valens, still retained their Jewish ideas about Easter. To this sect was given the name Protopaschitae (*Cod. Theod. u.s.* p. 1581, where severe penalties are denounced against them as worshippers of a different Christ because observing Easter otherwise than the orthodox). This question, when raised by a presbyter of Jewish birth named SABBATIUS, some 20 years later, caused a further schism among the Novatianists at Constantinople, under the episcopate of Marcian, A.D. 391; whence the name Sabbatiani. These finally coalesced with the Montanists, though we can trace their distinct existence till the middle of the 5th cent. (Socr. *H. E.* v. 21; Soz. *H. E.* vii. 16; *Cod. Theod. u.s.* pp. 1566, 1570, 1581.) Many particulars of the customs of the Eastern Novatianists and as to their reflex influence on the church as regards auricular confession are in Socr. *H. E.* v. 19, 22, who in c. 19 ascribes the original establishment of the office of penitentiary presbyter and secret confession to the Novatianist schism. [NECTARIUS (4).] The succession of Novatianist patriarchs of Constantinople during the 4th cent. was Acesius, Agelius, Marcianus, Sisinnius (Socr. *H. E.* v. 21, vi. 22; Soz. *H. E.* vii. 14). During the 5th cent. the Novatianists continued to flourish notwithstanding occasional troubles. In Constantinople their bishops during the first half of the cent. were Sisinnius, d. 412, Chrysanthus, d. 419, Paul, d. 438, and Marcian. They lived on amicable terms with the orthodox patriarch Atticus, who, remembering their fidelity under the Arian persecution, protected them from their enemies. Paul enjoyed the reputation of a miracle-worker, and died in the odour of universal sanctity, all sects and parties uniting in singing psalms at his funeral (Socr. *H. E.* vii. 46). In Alexandria, however, they were persecuted by Cyril, their bp. Theopemptus and their churches plundered; but they continued to exist in large numbers in that city till the 7th cent., when Eulogius, Catholic patriarch of Alexandria, wrote a treatise against them (Phot. *Cod.* 182, 208; Ceill. xi. 589). Even in Scythia their churches existed, as we find Marcus, a bp. from that country, present at the death of Paul, Novatianist bp. of Constantinople, July 21, 438. In Asia Minor they were as widely dispersed as the Catholics. In parts of it, indeed, the orthodox party seem for long to have been completely absorbed by those who took the Puritan view, *e.g.* Epiphanius tells us that there were no Catholics for 112 years in the city of Thyatira (*Haer.* li.; Lumper, *Hist. SS. PP.* viii. 259). They had established a regular parochial system. Thus (in Boeckh, *Corp. Gr. Inscriptt.* iv. 9268) we find at Laodicea in Lycaonia an inscription on a tombstone erected by one Aurelia Domna to her husband Paul, deacon of the holy church of the Novatianists, while even towards the end of the preceding century St. Basil, though hesitating on grounds similar to those of Cyprian to recognize their baptism, concludes in its favour on the express ground that it was for the advantage and profit of the populace that it should be received (Basil, *Ep.* clxxxviii. *ad Amphiloch.*; cf. R. T. Smith's *Basil the Great*, p. 119). After the close of the 5th cent. we find few notices of their history. Their protest about the lapsed became obsolete and their adherents fell away to the church or to sects like the Montanists. A formal notice of their existence in the East occurs in the 95th canon of the Trullan (Quinisext) council A.D. 692. In the West we have no such particular details of their history as in the East. Yet there is clear evidence of their widespread and long-continued influence. Already we have noted their extension into S. Gaul and Africa in their very earliest days. In Alexandria also we have noted its last historical manifestation. Between the middle of 3rd cent., when it arose, and the close of the 5th, we find repeated indications of its existence and power. Constantine's decree (*Cod. Theod.* XVI. v. 2, with Gothofred's comment), giving them a certain restricted liberty, was directed to Bassus, probably vicarius of Italy. Towards the close of the 4th cent. we find a regular succession of Novatianist bishops existing—doubtless from Novatian's time—at Rome, and held in such high repute for piety that the emperor Theodosius granted his life to the celebrated orator Symmachus on the prayer of the Novatianist pope Leontius, A.D. 388. Early in the 5th cent., however, pope Celestine persecuted them, deprived them of their churches, and compelled Rusticula their bishop to hold his meetings in private, an act which Socrates considers another proof of the overweening and unchristian insolence of the Roman see (*H. E.* vii. 11). In the Code several severe edicts were directed about the same time against the Novatianists (*Cod. Theod.* ed. Haenel, lib. xvi. tit. v. legg. 59, 65, cf. vi. 6). In S. Gaul, N. Italy, and Spain the sect seems to have taken as firm root as in Phrygia and central Asia Minor. Whether the original religious teaching of the people whose Christianity may have been imported from Africa but a short time before by MARCELLINUS, or the physical features, *e.g.* the mountainous character of these countries, may not have inclined them towards its stern discipline is a fair question. The treatises which Pacian of Barcelona and Ambrose of Milan felt necessary to direct against them are couched in language which proves the sect to have been then an aggressive one and a real danger to the church by the assertion of its superior sanctity and purity.

Ambrose evidently wrote in answer to some work lately produced by them (*de Poenit.* lib. ii. c. x.). The Separatist tendency begotten of Novatianism in this district and continued through Priscillianism, Adoptionism, and Claudius of Turin (Neander, *H. E.* t. vi. 119-130, ed. Bohn; cf. esp. note on p. 119) may be a point of contact between the Novatianists of primitive times and the Waldenses and Albigenses of the middle ages. Their wide spread in Africa in Augustine's time is attested by him, *cont. Gaudent.* in *Opp.* ed. Bened. (Paris), ix. 642, 794.

The principal extant controversial works against the sect beside those of Cyprian are the epistles of St. Pacian of Barcelona, the *de Poenitentia* of St. Ambrose, and the *Quaestiones in Nov. Testam.* No. cii. wrongly attributed to St. Augustine and found in the Parisian Ben. ed. t. iii. pars. ii. 2942-2958, assigned by the editor to Hilary the deacon who lived under pope Damasus. The work of Pacian contains many interesting historical notices of the sect. From it we find they refused to the Catholics the name of a church, calling them *Apostaticum, Capitolinum,* or *Synedrium,* and, on their own behalf, rejected the name Novatianists and styled themselves simply Christians (*Ep.* ii. § 3). The following were some of the texts relied on by them, to the consideration of which the writers on the Catholic side applied themselves: I. Sam. ii. 25; Matt. x. 33, xii. 31, xiii. 47-49; I. Cor. vi. 18; II. Tim. ii. 20; Heb. vi. 4-7; I. John v. 15. Novatianism in the tests which it used, its efforts after a perfectly pure communion, its crotchety interpretations of Scripture, and many other features, presents a striking parallel to many modern sects. In addition to authorities already quoted, see Ceillier, ii. 427, *et passim*; Walch, *Ketzerhist.* ii. 185; Natal. Alex. ed. Mansi, saec. iii. c. iii. art. iv.; Tillem. *Mém.*; Bingham, *Opp.* t. vi. 248, 570, viii. 233 (ed. Lond. 1840); Gieseler, *H. E.* i. 284 (ed. Clark); Neander, *H. E.* (ed. Bohn), i. 330-345. For an account of recent literature on the subject see Bardenhewer's *Patrology*, p. 220. [G.T.S.]

Novatus (1), presbyter of Carthage, seems to have been an original opponent of Cyprian's election, but is first mentioned by him in *Ep.* xiv. § 5, with three other presbyters—Donatus, Fortunatus, and Gordius—as having written about some question to Cyprian then in retirement. This was, doubtless, touching the request of the confessors, to have peace granted to certain of the lapsed which, in *Ep.* l., Cyprian refuses until he has consulted the presbyters and faithful laity. Cyprian reproves certain presbyters, evidently Novatus and his companions, who, "considering neither the fear of God nor the honour of the bishop," had already granted peace to the lapsed. In *Ep.* xliii., writing to the church of Carthage, he compares Novatus and his associates to the five chief commissioners entrusted with the conduct of the persecution, and, as it seems, intimates that they threatened to raise a riot upon his appearance from his place of retirement. In *Ep.* lii. 3 Cyprian, writing to Cornelius, gives a very bad character of Novatus. Cyprian's feelings may have here coloured his judgment, as such a bishop as he was could scarcely have tolerated such a bad man in the presbyterate. Cyprian describes Novatus as having made his follower Felicissimus a deacon, and then "at Rome committing greater and more grievous crimes. He who at Carthage made a deacon against the church, there made a bishop," *i.e.* that he brought about the ordination of both the deacon and bishop. *Ep.* xliii. 2 proves that Cyprian's wrath was, however, specially stirred by some anti-episcopal innovations of Novatus and his party. After the consecration of Novatian, Novatus was sent by him to organize his party in Africa (Cyp. *Ep.* l.). After this he disappears from sight. Cf. Dr. Pusey's note upon him, appended to Cyprian, *Ep.* lii. in Oxf. *Lib. of Fathers.* Milman, *Lat. Christ.* t. i. pp. 60-62 (ed. Lond. 1867). [G.T.S.]

O

Oceanus, a Roman of noble birth, connected with Fabiola and the Julian family; a friend of Jerome, Augustine, and Pammachius. He probably became known to Jerome during his stay in Rome in 383-385. He first appears as making a public protest against Carterius, a Spanish bp. who, having married before his baptism and lost his wife, had, as a Christian, married a second wife. Jerome points out that there is no law condemning such marriages and urges silence; *c.* 397. Either in 397 or 396 Oceanus, with Fabiola, visited Jerome at Bethlehem, whence they were driven by fear of Hunnish invasion. While there, he apparently met Rufinus, who, according to Jerome's insinuation (*adv. Ruf.* iii. 4), had an Origenistic document placed in Oceanus's room in Fabiola's house, hoping to identify him with that tendency. Rufinus having gone to Rome (397) and having published shortly afterwards his edition of Origen's Περὶ Ἀρχῶν, Oceanus and Pammachius watched his actions with critical eyes, and, on the appearance of the work, wrote to Jerome (Hieron. *Ep.* 83) asking him to deny the insinuation of Rufinus that he was only completing a work begun by Jerome, and to furnish them with a true translation of Origen's work. Oceanus, no doubt, took part in the subsequent proceedings which led to the condemnation of Origenism at Rome. On the death of Fabiola, *c.* 399, Jerome wrote to Oceanus her Epitaphium (*Ep.* 77), accompanied by his exposition, which had been intended for her, of the 42 resting-places of the Israelites in the desert. In 411 Oceanus, who had maintained his correspondence with Jerome, and possessed his books against Rufinus and other of his works, interested himself specially in the Pelagian controversy on the origin of souls. Jerome writes to Marcellinus and Anapsychius (*Ep.* 126) who had consulted him on this, referring them to Oceanus as one thoroughly "learned in the law of the Lord" and capable of instructing them. Augustine writes to Oceanus in 416 on the same subject, and on the reproof of St. Peter by St. Paul at Antioch. [W.H.F.]

Olympias (2), the younger, widow, a celebrated deaconess of the church of Constantinople, the most eminent of the band of holy and high-born women whom Chrysostom gathered round him. Her family was of high rank, but pagan. Her birth is placed by Tillemont *c.* 368. She was left at an early age the orphan heiress of an immense fortune. Happily for her, her uncle and guardian, Procopius, was a man of high character, an intimate friend and correspondent of Gregory Nazianzen. She was equally fortunate in her instructress, Theodosia, the sister of St. Amphilochius of Iconium, whom Gregory desired the young girl to set before her constantly as a pattern. During Gregory's residence at Constantinople, 379-381, he became much attached to the bright and beautiful maiden, then probably about 12 years old, calling her "his own Olympias," and delighted to be called "father" by her (Greg. Naz. *Ep.* 57; Cann. 57, pp. 132, 134). Olympias had many suitors. The one selected by her guardian, Procopius, was Nebridius, a young man of high rank and excellent character, whom she married in 384. There can be little doubt that her married life was not a happy one (Pallad. *Dial.* p. 164). In less than two years she was left a widow without children. She regarded this early bereavement as a declaration of the divine will that she was unsuited to the married life, and ought not again to be married. Theodosius desired her to wed Elpidius, a young Spanish kinsman of his. But Olympias steadily refusing to listen to his suit, Theodosius commissioned the prefect of the city to take the whole of her property into public custody until she attained her 30th year. The imperial orders were carried out with so much harshness that she was even forbidden to go to church for her devotions, or to enjoy the congenial society of the leading ecclesiastics. Theodosius soon restored to her the management of her estates (*ib.*), and thenceforward she devoted herself and her wealth entirely to the service of religion, practising the greatest austerities. Her whole time and strength were given to ministering to the wants of the poor and sick, and to the hospitable entertainment of bishops and other ecclesiastics visiting the imperial city, who never left her roof without large pecuniary aid, sometimes in the form of a farm or an estate, towards their religious works. Among these Palladius enumerates Amphilochius, Optimus, the two brothers of Basil, Gregory Nyssen (who dedicated to her the Commentary on a portion of the Song of Solomon, which he had written at her request, Greg. Nys. *in Cant.* t. i. p. 468), Peter, Epiphanius of Cyprus, and the three who subsequently became the unwearied persecutors of Chrysostom and even of Olympias herself, Acacius, Atticus, and Severianus. Her house was the common home of the clergy, and of the monks and virgins who swarmed from all parts of the Christian world to Constantinople. She was the victim of much imposition and her charity was grievously abused. Indeed, her liberality was so unrestricted and inconsiderate that Chrysostom interposed his authority to limit it, saying that her wealth was a trust from God which she was bound to use in the most prudent manner for the relief of the poor and destitute, not in making presents to the opulent and covetous (Soz. *H. E.* viii. 9). Olympias followed Chrysostom's advice, which brought upon her the ill-will of those who had enjoyed her lavish generosity.

When still under 30 years of age Olympias was appointed by Nectarius deaconess of the church of Constantinople. The courtly old prelate consulted her on ecclesiastical matters, in which he was a novice, and was guided by her advice (Pallad. p. 166; Soz. *H. E.* viii. 9). She retained this position under Chrysostom and became his chief counsellor and active agent in all works of piety and charity, not only in Constantinople, but in distant provinces of the church.

On the arrival of the Nitrian monks known as the Tall Brothers in Constantinople in 401, Olympias received them hospitably (Pallad. p. 153), careless of the indignant remonstrances of Theophilus (*ib.* p. 155). On Chrysostom's final expulsion from Constantinople, June 20, 404, Olympias was the chief of the band of courageous women who assembled in the baptistery of the church to take a last farewell of their deeply loved bishop and friend, and to receive his parting benediction and commands (*ib.* 89, 90). Suspicion of having caused the fire in the cathedral which immediately followed the departure of Chrysostom from its walls fell on Olympias and the other ladies. Olympias was brought before the prefect Optatus, who bluntly demanded why she had set the church on fire. He proposed that on condition of her entering into communion with Arsacius, as some other ladies had done, the investigation should be dropped and she freed from further annoyance. Olympias's proud spirit indignantly rejected the base compromise. A false charge had been publicly brought against her, of which her whole manner of life, which the prefect could not be ignorant of, was a sufficient refutation. The trouble brought on Olympias a severe and almost fatal illness. On recovering her health, in the spring of 405, she left Constantinople. Sozomen seems to speak of a voluntary retirement to Cyzicus. But the language of Chrysostom (*Ep.* 16, p. 603 c) leads us to believe that she was never allowed to remain long in one spot, her persecutors hoping that thus her spirit might be broken and she induced to yield. This hope being frustrated, Olympias was once again summoned before Optatus, who, on her renewed refusal to communicate with Arsacius, imposed a heavy fine of 200 pounds of gold (Soz. *H. E.* viii. 24; Pallad. p. 28). This was readily paid, and the news of Olympias's heroic disregard of all worldly losses and sufferings for truth's sake gave intense joy to Chrysostom in his banishment. He wrote congratulating her on her victory, calling upon her to glorify God Who had enabled her to acquire such great spiritual gain (Chrys. *Ep.* 16, p. 604 A). We know nothing very definitely of the remainder of her life. Our only trustworthy information is from Chrysostom's 17 letters to her, some of which are long religious tracts, the composition of which relieved the tedium of his exile and made him almost forget his miseries. We gather from them that Olympias was subject to frequent and severe attacks of sickness, and that the persecution of the party of Arsacius and Atticus was violent and unsparing. The compulsory dispersion of the society of young females of which she was head, and who, like her, had refused to hold communion with the intruding bishops, was a great sorrow to her (*ib.* 4, p. 577 A). But the dates of these letters are uncertain. The style in which she is addressed in this correspondence is "at once respectful, affectionate, and paternal" (Stephens, *S. Chrysostom*, p. 383), "but it exhibits a highly-wrought complimentary" tone, full of "bold and lavish praise" of her many signal virtues which is "too widely remote from the mind and taste of our own times to be fairly estimated by us." Chrysostom wrote for her consolation a special treatise on the theme that "No one is really injured except by himself" (t. iii. pp. 530-553); as well as one "to those who were offended by adversities" (*ib.* pp. 555-612). To both of these he refers in his 4th letter to her (*Ep.* 4, p. 576 C). The date of her death cannot be determined. She was living when Palladius pub. his *Dialogue* in 408, but not when the *Lausiac History* was pub. in 420. [E.V.]

Optatus (6), bp. of Milevis, or Mileum (Milah), in Numidia, 25 m. N.W. of Cirta (Shaw, *Trav.* p. 63), a vigorous opponent of the Donatists. He himself says that he wrote about 60 years, or rather more, after the persecution under Diocletian. St. Jerome speaks of him as having written during the reigns of Valentinian and Valens, A.D. 365-378. But in bk. ii. of his treatise Siricius is mentioned as bp. of Rome, "qui est noster socius." As Siricius did not succeed Damasus until 384, he may have outlived the period mentioned by St. Jerome and himself inserted these words later. The date of his death, however, is unknown. St. Augustine mentions him once in the same sentence as St. Ambrose, and elsewhere as a church-writer of high authority, even among Donatists. (*Opt. c. Don.* i. 13, ii. 3; Hieron. *Vir. Illustr.* c. 110, vol. ii. p. 706; Aug. *c. Don. ep.* (*de Unit. Eccl.*) 19, 50; *c. Parm.* i. 3, 5; *Brevic. Coll.* 20, 38; *Doctr. Christ.* ii. 40, 61; Baronius, *Ann.* vol. iv. p. 243; Morcelli, *Afr. Chr.* ii. 275; Dupin, *Optatus Praef.* 1.)

His treatise against the Donatists is in the form of a letter to Parmenian, Donatist bp. of Carthage, in six books, with a seventh of doubtful authenticity.

Bk. i. opens with a eulogy of peace, which he complains that the Donatists set at nought by reviling the Catholics. He adds some compliments to Parmenian, as the only one of his party with whom he can communicate freely, and regrets being compelled to do so by letter because they refuse to meet for conference. Five points put forward by Parmenian call for discussion, to which Optatus adds a sixth. (1) In accusing Catholics of "tradition," particulars ought to be specified of time and place. (2) The true church ought to be defined. (3) Which side was really responsible for calling in the aid of the soldiers. (4) What Parmenian means by "sinners" whose "oil and sacrifice" God rejects. (5) The question of baptism. (6) The riotous and rash acts of the Donatists. Optatus finds fault with Parmenian for his inconsiderate language about our Lord's baptism, to the effect that His flesh required to be "drowned in the flood" of Jordan to remove its impurity. If the baptism of Christ's body were intended to suffice for the baptism of each single person, there might be some truth in this, but we are baptized, in virtue not of the flesh of Christ, but of His name, and moreover we cannot believe that even His flesh contracted sin, for it was more pure than Jordan itself. The purpose of Optatus is to shew that it was not the church which cast off the Donatists, but they who separated from the church, following the example of Korah and his company. When they disclaim the right of princes to interfere in the affairs of the church they contradict their forefathers, who, in the matter of Caecilian, petitioned Constantine to grant them judges from Gaul instead of from Africa.

In bk. ii. Optatus discusses what the church, the dove and bride of Christ, is (Cant. vi. 9). Its holiness consists in the sacraments and is not to be measured by the pride of men. It is universal, not limited, as Parmenian would have it, to a corner of Africa, for if so where would be the promises of Pss. ii. 8, lxxii. 8? And the merits of the Saviour would be restricted, Pss. cxiii. 3, xcvi. 7. The church has five gifts: (1) The chair of Peter. (2) The angel inseparably attached to that chair, apparently the power of conferring spiritual gifts, which resides in the centre of episcopal unity. Parmenian must be aware that the episcopal chair was conferred from the beginning on Peter, the chief of the apostles, that unity might be preserved among the rest and no one apostle set up a rival. This chair, with whose exclusive claim for respect the little Donatist community can in no way compete, carries with it necessarily the "angel" ("ducit ad se angelum"), unless the Donatists have this gift enclosed for their own use in a narrow space, and excluding the seven angels of St. John (Rev. i.), with whom they have no communion; or if they possess one of these, let them send him to other churches: otherwise their case falls to the ground. (3) The holy spirit of adoption, which Donatists claim exclusively for themselves, applying to Catholics unjustly the words of our Lord about proselytism (Matt. xxiii. 15). (4) The fountain (probably faith) of which heretics cannot partake, and (5) its seal, "annulus" (probably baptism) (Cant. iv. 12). A want of clearness in the language of Optatus renders his meaning here somewhat doubtful. The Donatists add a sixth gift, the "umbilicus" of Cant. vii. 2, which they regard as the altar; but this, being an essential part of the body, cannot be a separate gift. These gifts belong to the church in Africa, from which the Donatists have cut themselves off, as also from the priesthood, which they seek by rebaptism to annul, though they do not rebaptize their own returned seceders. But these gifts belong to the bride, not the bride to them. They regard them as the generating power of the church instead of the essentials (viscera), viz. the sacraments, which derive their virtue from the Trinity. Parmenian truly compares the church to a garden, but it is God Who plants the trees therein, some of which Donatists seek to exclude. In offering the sacrifice to God in the Eucharist, they profess to offer for the one church, but by their rebaptism they really make two churches. Thanking Parmenian for his language about the church, which, however, he claims as applicable to the Catholic church alone, he challenges him to point out any act of persecution on its part. Constantine took pains to restore peace and suppress idolatry, but another emperor, who declared himself an apostate, when he restored idolatry allowed the Donatists to return, a permission for the acceptance of which they ought to blush. It was about this time that the outrages broke out in Africa [Felix (**185**); Urbanus], of which when Primosus complained, the Donatist council at Theneste took no notice. They compelled women under vows to disregard them and perform a period of penance, and deposed from his office Donatus bp. of Tysedis. Yet they speak of holiness as if Christ gave it without conditions, and take every opportunity of casting reproach on church ordinances, fulfiling the words of Ezek. xiii. 20.

In bk. iii., after going over some of the former ground, laying the blame of the schism on the Donatists, Optatus applies to them several passages of Scripture, esp. Pss. lxxxvii., cxlvii.; Isa. ii. 3, xxii. 1, 9.

In bk. iv., disclaiming all unfriendly feeling and appealing to the common possessions of both parties, Optatus charges them with infraction of unity by appointment of bishops, proselytism, forbidding social intercourse, and perversely applying to Catholics Scripture passages directed against obstinate heretics, as I. Cor. v. 11, II. John 10.

In bk. v. Optatus returns to the oft-repeated subject of rebaptism. The repetition of baptism, he says, is an insult to the Trinity, worse than the doctrines of Praxeas and the Patripassians. Three elements are requisite: (1) the Trinity, (2) the minister, (3) the faithful receiver; but of these the Donatists exalt the second above the other two. They use as a quotation words not found in Scripture, "How can a man give what he has not received?" (see I. Cor. iv. 7); but in baptism God alone is the giver of grace. As it is not the dyer who changes the colour of his wool, so neither does the minister of himself change the operation of baptism. Of two candidates for baptism, if one refused to renounce while the other consented, there can be no doubt which of them received baptism effectually. By rebaptizing, Donatists rob Christians of their marriage-garment, which suits all ages and conditions of life. The rebaptized will rise no doubt at the last day, but will rise naked, and the voice of the Master will be heard, "Friend, I once knew thee, and gave thee a marriage-garment. Who has despoiled thee of it? Into what trap, amongst what thieves hast thou fallen?"

In bk. vi. he repeats some previous charges, and adds others, how they destroyed altars, the "seats of Christ's Body and Blood," at which they themselves must have offered. They have broken up chalices and sold them to women and even to pagans, yet they quote Hagg. ii. 14; but even impurity of men does not profane the vessels of service (see Num. xvi. 37, 38).

Bk. vii., which is not mentioned by St. Jerome, but which may on good MS. grounds be ascribed to Optatus, is supplementary and answers a fresh Donatist complaint, that if they are the children of "traditors," as Optatus says, they ought to be let alone, and no attempt made to "reconcile" them; but, says Optatus, though their fathers deserved to be excluded, there is no reason why they should be so, for the church repels no baptized persons. Christ allows two sorts of seed to grow in His field, and no bishop has power to do what the apostles could not, viz. separate them. They might have refused to communicate with Peter because he denied his Lord, yet he retained the keys given him by Christ.

The work of Optatus is more important historically than doctrinally. As a theological treatise it is often loose and rambling, with frequent repetition; but it exposes with clearness and force the inconsistency of the Donatists, and of all who, like them, fix their attention exclusively on the ethical side of religion, estimated by an arbitrary standard of opinion, to the disregard of other conditions of the greatest importance in the constitution of a church. How perversely and inconsistently the Donatists applied this principle in the matter of rebaptism Optatus again and again demonstrates. That there was a doctrine of rebaptism in the African church, to which Cyprian had lent the weight of his authority, there can be no doubt; but with him it was directed against heretics, on the principle that the followers of Marcion, Praxeas, and the like, were in fact not truly Christians and thus their baptism was valueless. But Optatus is never weary of urging that though by their own act Donatists had incurred the charge of schism, the church did not regard them as heretics, and that they ought not to treat as heretical their brethren. Dupin's ed. (1702, fol.) is the groundwork of all subsequent editions. It has been reprinted in vol. xi. of Migne's *Patr. Lat.*, but the map is smaller and less clear than in Dupin's folio, and all documents previous to 362 are in vol. viii. of the *Patr. Lat.* An account of Optatus and his writings will be found in Ceillier, vol. v. The latest ed. is by Ziwsa (1893), in *Corpus Scr. Eccl. Lat.* xxvi. (Vienna). See Sparrow Simpson's *St. Aug. and Afr. Ch. Divisions* (1910), pp. 42 ff. [H.W.P.]

Origenes. *Sources.*—The main authority for the details of Origen's Life is Eusebius (*H. E.* vi.), who collected upwards of 100 letters of Origen (*ib.* 36). These, together with official documents (*ib.* 23, 33) and information from those acquainted with Origen (*ib.* 2, 33), formed the basis of his narrative. His account of the most critical period of Origen's life, his retirement from Alexandria, was given in bk. ii. of his *Apology*, which he composed with the help of Pamphilus (*ib.* 23). This unhappily has not been preserved.

Origen's own writings give but few details of his life. But the loss of his letters is irreparable. They would have given a fuller picture of the man, even if they gave little additional information on the outward circumstances of his life.

Of modern authorities, see Tillemont, *Mémoires*; Lardner, *Credibility*; Ceillier,

Auteurs sacrés; Lumper, *Hist. Patrum Theol. Critica*; Walch, *Gesch. d. Ketz.*; Du Pin, *Nouvelle bibliothèque des auteurs ecclés.*

His life and doctrine have been discussed, with special reference to his historical position in the development of Christian thought, by Guericke, *de Schola Alex. Catech.* (1825); Neander, *Kirch. Gesch.*; Thomasius, *Origenes* (1837); Redepenning, *Origenes* (1841-1846); Moehler, *Patrol.* (1840); Huber, *Philos d. Kirchenväter* (1859); Schaff, *Church Hist.* (1867); De Pressensé, *Hist. des trois premiers siècles* (1858-1877); Boehringer, *Kirchengesch. in Biogr. Klemens u. Origenes* (1869, 2te Aufl.).

Life.—Origen was probably born at Alexandria (Eus. *H. E.* vi. 1), but whether of Egyptian, Greek, or mixed descent is not known. The loose phrase of Porphyry, that he "was a Greek and reared in Greek studies" (*ib.* 19), is in itself of little value, but the name of his father (Leonides) points in the same direction. His mother's name has not been preserved. May she have been of Jewish descent? He is said to have learnt Hebrew so well that in singing the psalms "he vied with his mother" (Hieron. *Ep.* 39 [22], § 1).

Origen's full name was *Origenes Adamantius*. *Origenes* was the name of one contemporary philosopher of distinction, and occurs elsewhere. *Adamantius* has commonly been regarded as an epithet describing Origen's unconquerable endurance, or for the invincible force of his arguments. But the language of Eusebius (*H. E.* vi. 14) and of Jerome (*de Vir. Ill.* 54, "Origenes qui et Adamantius") shews that it was a second name, and not a mere adjunct. His father, Leonides, suffered martyrdom in the persecution of the 10th year of Severus (202), and Origen had not then completed his 17th year (Eus. *H. E.* vi. 2). He must have been born therefore A.D. 185-186, a date consistent with the statement (*ib.* vii. 1) that he died in his 69th year, in the reign of Gallus (A.D. 251-254). In Origen we have the first record of a Christian boyhood, and he was "great from the cradle." His education was superintended by his father, who especially directed him to the study of Scripture. The child's eager inquiries into the deeper meaning of the words he committed to memory caused perplexity to his father, who, while openly checking his son's premature curiosity, silently thanked God for the promise he gave for the future. Origen became the pupil of Pantaenus (after his return from India) and Clement, in whose school he met Alexander, afterwards bp. of Jerusalem (*ib.* vi. 14), with whom he then laid the foundation of that life-long friendship which supported him in his sorest trials.

When Leonides was thrown into prison, Origen wished to share his fate, but was hindered by his mother. He addressed a letter to his father—his first recorded writing, still extant in the time of Eusebius—in which he prayed him to allow no thought for his family to shake his resolution. This shews the position of influence which Origen already enjoyed in his family. Leonides was put to death and his property confiscated. Upon this the young Origen seems to have fulfilled the promise his words implied. Partly by the assistance of a pious and wealthy lady, and partly by teaching, he supported himself and (as may be concluded) his mother and brothers. Already he collected a library. At first he gave lessons in literature; but as the Christian school was without a teacher, all having been scattered by the persecution, he was induced to give instruction in the faith. Thus in his 18th year he was, at first informally, the head of the Christian school in Alexandria in a season of exceptional danger. He was so successful that Demetrius, bp. of Alexandria, soon definitely committed to him the office. The charge decided the tenor of his life. Origen henceforth devoted himself exclusively to the office of a Christian teacher, and to ensure his independence sold his collection of classical writers for an annuity of four oboli (sixpence) a day, on which he lived for many years, refusing the voluntary contributions his friends offered him (*ib.* 3). His position is a remarkable illustration of the freedom of the early church. He was a layman and yet recognized as a leading teacher. His work was not confined to any district. Numbers of men and women flocked to his lectures, attracted partly by his stern simplicity of life, which was a guarantee of his sincerity. For he resolved to fulfil without reserve the precepts of the Gospel. For many years he went barefoot, wore only a single robe (Matt. x. 10), and slept upon the ground. His food and sleep were rigorously limited (*ib.*). Nor did his unmeasured zeal stop here. In the same spirit of sacrifice he applied to himself literally the words of Matt. xix. 12, though wishing to conceal the act from most of his friends. Origen's own comment on the words of the Gospel which he had misunderstood is a most touching confession of his error (*in Matt.* t. xv. 1 ff.). But for the time the purpose of the act was accepted as its excuse.

For 12 or 13 years he was engaged in these happy and successful labours; and it was probably during this period that he formed and partly executed his plan of a comparative view of the LXX with other Greek versions of O.T. and with the original Hebrew text, though the work was slowly elaborated as fresh materials came to his hands (Eus. *H. E.* vi. 16). A short visit to Rome in the time of Zephyrinus, to see "the most ancient church of the Romans" (*ib.* 14), and an authoritative call to Arabia (*ib.* 19) alone seem to have interrupted his labours. Persecution tested the fruit of his teaching. He had the joy of seeing martyrs trained in his school; and his own escapes from the violence of the people were held to be due to the special protection of Providence (*ib.* 4, f. 3). During the same period he devoted himself with renewed vigour to the study of non-Christian thought, and attended the lectures of Ammonius Saccas (cf. Porphyry, *ap.* Eus. *H. E.* vi. 19; Theod. *Graec. Affect. Cur.* vi. p. 96). Heretics and Gentiles attended his lectures, and he felt bound to endeavour to understand their opinions thoroughly that he might the better correct them (cf. *c. Cels.* vi. 24). This excited ill-will, but he was able to defend himself, as he did in a letter written at a later time (*Ep.* ap. Eus. *H. E.* vi. 19), by the example of his predecessors and the support of his friends. His work grew beyond his strength, and Heraclas joined him in the catechetical school. Heraclas had been one of his first converts and scholars, and the brother of a martyr (Eus. *H. E.* vi. 3). He was a fellow-student with Origen under "his teacher of philosophy" (Ammonius Saccas); and when he afterwards became bp. of Alexandria he did not lay aside the dress or the reading of a philosopher (*ib.* 19).

At length, *c.* 215, a tumult of unusual violence (*ib.* 19; Clinton, *Fasti Romani*, i. 224 f.) forced Origen to withdraw from Egypt to Caesarea in Palestine. Here his reputation brought him into a prominence which occasioned his later troubles. His fellow-pupil Alexander bp. of Jerusalem, and Theoctistus (Theotecnus; Photius, *Cod.* 118) bp. of Caesarea, begged him to expound the Scriptures in the public services of the church, though he had not been ordained. Demetrius of Alexandria expressed strong disapprobation of a proceeding he described as unprecedented. Alexander and Theoctistus produced precedents. Demetrius replied by recalling Origen to Alexandria, and hastened his return by special envoys, deacons of the church (Eus. *H. E.* vi. 19). Origen's stay in Palestine was of some length, and it was probably during this time he made his famous visit to Mamaea, the mother of the emperor Alexander (*ib.* 21), herself a native of Syria.

Some time after his return to Alexandria (*c.* 219), Origen began his written expositions of Scripture, largely through the influence of Ambrose, whom he had rescued not long before from the heresy of Valentinus, or as Jerome says of Marcion (Hieron. *de Vir. Ill.* 56). Ambrose provided him with more than seven shorthand writers (ταχυγράφοι) to take down his comments and other scribes to make fair copies (Eus. *H. E.* vi. 23).

These literary occupations threw Origen's work in the catechetical school yet more upon Heraclas. At the same time the first parts of Origen's *Commentary on the Gospel of St. John* marked him out more decisively than before as a teacher in the church even more than in the school. But the exhibition of this new power was accompanied by other signs of a bold originality which might well startle those unfamiliar with the questionings of philosophy. The books *On First Principles*, which seem to have been written spontaneously, made an epoch in Christian speculation, as the *Comm. on St. John* did in Christian interpretation. Under such circumstances it is not surprising that Demetrius yielded, in the words of Eusebius, to the infirmity of human nature (*ib.* 8) and wished to check the boldness and influence of the layman. It became clear that Origen must seek elsewhere than in Alexandria free scope for his Scriptural studies. After he had laboured there for more than 25 years, the occasion came in an invitation to visit Achaia for the purpose, as it seems, of combating some false opinions which had arisen there (Hieron. *de Vir. Ill.* 54). The exact date is uncertain, but probably between 226 and 230. On the way Origen visited Caesarea, and sought counsel from his oldest friends as to his future course. No record remains of their deliberations, but Origen was ordained presbyter "by the bishops there" (Eus. *H. E.* vi. 23), Theoctistus of Caesarea and Alexander of Jerusalem (Hieron. *de Vir. Ill.* 54; Phot. *Cod.* 118). Origen then visited Ephesus (*Ep. Fragm.* ap. Ruf. *Apol.*, Delarue, i. p. 6), and stayed some time at Athens. During this stay he probably heard some of the teachers of philosophy there (Epiph. *Haer.* lxiv. 1). At length, having completed his mission, he returned to Alexandria, where he could not have been unprepared for the reception which awaited him from Demetrius. Demetrius had probably shewn clear unwillingness to admit him to the priesthood. At any rate, the fact that Origen received orders from Palestinian bishops without his consent might be construed as a direct challenge of his authority. Origen at once perceived that he must retire before the rising storm. The preface to bk. vi. of the *Comm. on St. John* shews how deeply he felt the severance of old ties and the hostility of former colleagues. In 231 he left Alexandria never to return; and his influence to the last is shewn by the fact that he "left the charge of the catechetical school" to his coadjutor Heraclas (Eus. *H. E.* vi. 26). It is difficult to trace the different stages in the condemnation which followed. Photius (*Cod.* 118), following the *Apology* of Pamphilus and Eusebius, gives the most intelligible and consistent account. According to him Demetrius, completely alienated from Origen by his ordination, collected a synod of "bishops and a few presbyters," which decided that Origen should not be allowed to stay or teach at Alexandria. Demetrius afterwards excommunicated Origen. Jerome describes with greater severity the spirit of Demetrius's proceedings, and adds that "he wrote on the subject to the whole world" (*de Vir. Ill.* 54) and obtained a judgment against Origen from Rome (*Ep.* 33 [29], § 4). So far the facts are tolerably clear, but in the absence of trustworthy evidence it is impossible to tell on what points the condemnation really turned. Demetrius unquestionably laid great stress on formal irregularities (Eus. *H. E.* vi. 8), and the sentence against him may have been based on these. Origen's opinions were probably displeasing to many, and no attempt was made to reverse the judgment after the death of Demetrius, which followed very shortly, and perhaps within three years, when Heraclas, the pupil and colleague of Origen, succeeded to the episcopate. Nor again was anything done by Dionysius, the successor of Heraclas, another devoted scholar of Origen, who still continued his intercourse with his former master (*ib.* 46). Whatever the grounds of Origen's condemnation, the judgment of the Egyptian synod was treated with absolute disregard by the bishops of Palestine, Arabia, Phoenicia, and Achaea (Hieron. *Ep.* 33), and Origen defended himself warmly (Hieron. *Apol. adv. Ruf.* ii. 18). He soon afterwards settled at Caesarea, which became for more than 20 years, up to his death, the centre of his labours. It had indeed not a few of the advantages of Alexandria, as a great seaport, the civil capital, and the ecclesiastical metropolis of its district.

Here Origen found ungrudging sympathy and help for his manifold labours. Alexander of Jerusalem and Theoctistus of Caesarea remained devoted to him; and Firmilian of Caesarea in Cappadocia was no less zealous in seeking his instruction (Eus. *H. E.* vi. 27; Hieron. *de Vir. Ill.* 54). Ambrose was with him to stimulate his literary efforts. He formed afresh something of a catechetical school, with a continual succession of distinguished students. He was unwearied in the public exposition of Scripture, which he explained popularly to mixed congregations in the church, to Christians and to catechumens (*Hom. in Ezech.* vi. 5), as a rule on Wednesdays and Fridays (Socr. *H. E.* v. 22), but often daily, and even oftener than once a day. His subjects were sometimes taken from the lessons (*Hom. in Num.* xv. 1; *in I. Sam.* ii. § 1), sometimes specially prescribed by an authoritative request (*Hom. in Ezech.* xiii. 1). His aim was the edification of the people generally (*Hom. in Lev.* vii. 1; *in Jud.* viii. 3); and not unfrequently he was constrained to speak, as he wrote, with some reserve, on the deeper mysteries of the faith (*Hom. in Num.* iv. 3; *in Lev.* xiii. 3; *in Ezech.* i. 3; *in Rom.* vii. 13, p. 147 L.; viii. 11, p. 272; cf. *Hom. in Jos.* xxiii. 4 *s.f.*; *in Gen.* xii. 1, 4).

These labours were interrupted by the persecution of Maximin (235-237). Ambrose and Protectetus, a presbyter of Caesarea, were among the victims. Origen addressed to them in prison his *Exhortation to Martyrdom.* He himself escaped (Eus. *H. E.* vi. 28). During part of the time of persecution he was apparently with Firmilian in Cappadocia, and is said to have there enjoyed the hospitality of a Christian lady Juliana, who had some books of Symmachus, the translator of O.T. (cf. Hieron. *l.c.*; Pallad. *Hist. Laus.* 147).

In 238, or perhaps 237, Origen was again at Caesarea, and Gregory (Thaumaturgus) delivered the *Farewell Address*, which is the most vivid picture left of the method and influence of the great Christian master. The scholar recounts, with touching devotion, the course along which he had been guided by the man to whom he felt he owed his spiritual life. He had come to Syria to study Roman law in the school of Berytus, but on his way met with Origen, and at once felt he had found in him the wisdom he was seeking. The day of that meeting was to him, in his own words, the dawn of a new being: his soul clave to the master whom he recognized and he surrendered himself gladly to his guidance. As Origen spoke, he kindled within the young advocate's breast a love for the Holy Word, and for himself the Word's herald. "This love," Gregory adds, "induced me to give up country and friends, the aims which I had proposed to myself, the study of law of which I was proud. I had but one passion, philosophy, and the godlike man who directed me in the pursuit of it" (c. 6).

Origen's first care, Gregory says, was to make the character of a pupil his special study. In this he followed the example of Clement (Clem. *Strom.* i. 1, 8, p. 320 P.). He ascertained, with delicate and patient attention, the capacities, faults, and tendencies of those he had to teach. Rank growths of opinion were cleared away; weaknesses were laid open; every effort was used to develop endurance, firmness, patience, thoroughness. "In true Socratic fashion he sometimes overthrew us by argument," Gregory writes, "if he saw us restive and starting out of the course. . . . The process was at first disagreeable to us and painful; but so he purified us . . . and . . . prepared us for the reception of the words of truth . . . by probing us and questioning us, and offering problems for our solution" (c. 7). Thus Origen taught his scholars to regard language as designed, not to furnish material for display, but to express truth with exact accuracy; and logic as powerful, not to secure a plausible success, but to test beliefs with the strictest rigour. Origen then led his pupils to the "lofty and divine and most lovely" study of external nature. He made geometry the sure and immovable foundation of his teaching, and rose step by step to the heights of heaven and the most sublime mysteries of the universe (c. 8). Gregory's language implies that Origen was himself a student of physics; as, in some degree, the true theologian must be. The lessons of others, he writes, or his own observation, enabled him to explain the connexion, the differences, the changes of the objects of sense. Such investigations served to shew man in his true relation to the world. A rational feeling for the vast grandeur of the external order, "the sacred economy of the universe," as Gregory calls it, was substituted for the ignorant and senseless wonder with which it is commonly regarded.

But physics were naturally treated by Origen as a preparation and not as an end. Moral science came next; and here he laid the greatest stress upon the method of experiment. His aim was not merely to analyse and to define and to classify feelings and motives, though he did this, but to form a character. For him ethics were a life, and not only a theory. The four cardinal virtues of Plato, practical wisdom, self-control, righteousness, courage, seemed to him to require for their maturing diligent introspection and culture. Herein he gave a commentary upon his teaching. His discipline lay even more in action than in precept. His own conduct was, in his scholar's minds, a more influential persuasive than his arguments.

So, Gregory continues, Origen was the first teacher who really led me to the pursuit of Greek philosophy, by bringing speculation into a vital union with practice. In him I saw the inspiring example of one at once wise and holy. The noble phrase of older masters gained a distinct meaning for the Christian disciple. In failure and weakness he was able to see that the end of all was "to become like to God with a pure mind, and to draw near to Him and to abide in Him" (c. 12).

Guarded and guided by this conviction, Origen encouraged his scholars in theology to look for help in all the works of human genius. They were to examine the writings of philosophers and poets of every nation, the atheists alone excepted, with faithful candour and wise catholicity. For them there was to be no sect, no party. In their arduous work they had ever at hand, in their master, a friend who knew their difficulties. If they were bewildered in the tangled mazes of conflicting opinions, he was ready to lead them with a firm hand; if in danger of being swallowed up in the quicksands of shifting error, he was near to lift them up to the sure resting-place he had himself found (c. 14).

The hierarchy of sciences was not completed till theology with her own proper gifts crowned the succession followed hitherto, logic, physic, ethics. Origen found in the Holy Scriptures and the teaching of the Spirit the final and absolute spring of Divine Truth. In this region Gregory felt his master's power to be supreme. Origen's sovereign command of the mysteries of "the oracles of God" gave him perfect boldness in dealing with all other writings. "Therefore," Gregory adds, "there was no subject forbidden to us, nothing hidden or inaccessible. We were allowed to become acquainted with every doctrine, barbarian or Greek, on things spiritual or civil, divine and human; traversing with all freedom, and investigating the whole circuit of knowledge, and satisfying ourselves with the full enjoyment of all the pleasures of the soul" (c. 15). Such was, Gregory tells us, Origen's method. He describes what he knew and what his hearers knew. There is no parallel to the picture in ancient times. With every allowance for the partiality of a pupil, the view it offers of a system of Christian training actually realized exhibits a type we cannot hope to surpass. The ideals of Christian education and of Christian philosophy were fashioned together. Under that comprehensive and loving discipline Gregory, already trained in heathen schools, first learnt, step by step, according to his own testimony, what the pursuit of philosophy truly was, and came to know the solemn duty of forming opinions not as the amusement of a moment, but as solid foundations of life-long work.

From Caesarea Origen visited different parts of Palestine: Jerusalem, Jericho, the valley of the Jordan (t. vi. *in Joh.* § 24); Sidon, where he made some stay (*Hom. in Josh.* xvi. § 2), partly at least to investigate "the footsteps of Jesus, and of His disciples, and of the prophets" (*in Joh. l.c.*). He also went again to Athens and continued there some time, being engaged on his Commentaries (Eus. *H. E.* vi. 32). In the first of two visits to Arabia he went to confer with Beryllus of Bostra, who had advanced false views on the Incarnation (*ib.* 33); in the second to meet some errors on the doctrine of the resurrection (*ib.* 37). In both cases he was specially invited and persuaded those whom he controverted to abandon their opinions.

His energy now rose to its full power. Till he was 60 (A.D. 246) he had forbidden his unwritten discourses to be taken down. Experience at length enabled him to withdraw the prohibition, and most of his homilies are due to reports made afterwards. The *Books against Celsus* and the *Commentaries on St. Matthew*, belonging to the same period, shew, in different directions, the maturity of his vigour. Thus his varied activity continued till the persecution of Decius in 250. The preceding reign of Philip had favoured the growth of Christianity; and there is no sufficient reason to question the fact of Origen's correspondence with the emperor and his wife Severa (*ib.* 36). Such intercourse marked Origen out for attack to Philip's conqueror and successor. His friend Alexander of Jerusalem died in prison. He himself suffered a variety of tortures, probably at Tyre—chains, the iron collar, and the rack; but his constancy baffled all the efforts of his enemies (*ib.* 39). He was threatened with the stake, and a report gained currency in later times that his sufferings were crowned by death (Phot. *Cod.* 118, p. 159). During this sharp trial his former pupil Dionysius, now bp. of Alexandria, addressed him a letter on martyrdom (Eus. *H. E.* vi. 46), shewing the old affection still alive, in spite of long separation. Origen described his sufferings and consolations in letters which Eusebius characterizes "as full of help to those who need encouragement" (*ib.* 39). The death of Decius (251, Clinton, *F.R.* i. 270), after a reign of two years, set Origen free. But his health was broken by his hardships. He died at Tyre in 253, "having completed seventy years save one" (Eus. *H. E.* vii. 1; Hieron. *Ep.* 65 *ad Pammach.*). He was buried there (William of Tyre, *c.* 1180, *Hist.* xiii. 1: "haec [Tyrus] et Origenis corpus occultat sicut oculata fide etiam hodie licet inspicere"), and his tomb was honoured as long as the city survived.

Of the later fortunes of his teaching it is enough to say here that his fate after death was like his fate during life: he continued to witness not in vain to noble truths. His influence was sufficiently proved by the persistent bitterness of his antagonists, and there are few sadder pages in church history than the record of the Origenistic controversies. But in spite of errors easy to condemn, his characteristic thoughts survived in the works of Hilary and Ambrose and Jerome, and in his own homilies, to stir later students in the West. His homilies had a very wide circulation in the middle ages in a Latin translation; and it would be interesting to trace their effect upon medieval commentators down to Erasmus, who wrote to Colet in 1504: "Origenis operum bonam partem evolvi; quo praeceptore mihi videor non-nullum fecisse operae pretium; aperit enim fontes quosdam et rationes indicat artis theologicae."

WRITINGS.—Epiphanius says (*Haer.* lxiv. 63) that in popular reports no less than 6,000 works were ascribed to Origen. Jerome denies this (*Ep.* lxxxii. 7) and brings down the number to a third (*adv. Ruf.* ii. c. 22; cf. c. 13). His works will be noticed in the following order: Exegetical, Dogmatical, Apologetic, Practical, Letters, Philocalia.

A. EXEGETICAL WRITINGS.—Epiphanius states that Origen undertook to comment on all the books of Scripture (*Haer.* lxiv. 3) and though his sole statement might be of very little value, independent and exact evidence goes far to confirm it.

His exegetical writings are of three kinds: detached *Notes* (Σχόλια, σημειώσεις, in the narrower sense, *excerpta*, *commaticum interpretandi genus*), *Homilies* addressed to popular audiences (Ὁμιλίαι, *Tractatus*), and complete and elaborate *Commentaries* (Τόμοι, σημειώσεις in the wider sense, *volumina*). Cf. Hieron. *in Ezech. Prol.*; *Praef. Comm. in Matt.*; Rufin. *Praef. in Num.*

i. THE PENTATEUCH. GENESIS.—Origen, according to Eusebius, wrote *twelve* books of Commentaries (Τόμοι) on Genesis, besides Homilies. Of these writings there remain: *Greek*: (1) On Gen. i. 2; *Fragm.* of *Tom.* iii. on Gen. i. 14; i. 16 f. (2) *Fragm.* of *Tom.* iii. (Eus. *H. E.* iii. 1); notes from Catenae; *Fragm.* of *Hom.* ii. (3) Additional notes. *Latin*: Seventeen *Homilies*, of which the last is imperfect, translated by Rufinus.

One of the fragments of the Commentary on Genesis contains a remarkable discussion of the theory of fate in connexion with Gen. i. 16; and in the scattered notes there are some characteristic remarks on the interpretation of the record of Creation. For Origen all Creation was "one act at once," presented to us in parts, in order to give the due conception of order (cf. Ps. cxlviii. 5). The Homilies deal mainly with the moral application of main subjects in the book. They contain little continuous exposition, but many striking thoughts. Among the passages of chief interest are the view of the Divine image and the Divine likeness as expressing man's endowment and man's end (i. §§ 12, 13), the symbolism of the ark (ii. §§ 4 ff.), the nature of the Divine voice (iii. § 2), the lesson of the opened wells (xiii. § 4), the poverty of the Divine priesthood (xvi. § 5).

EXODUS and LEVITICUS.—Of the Books, Homilies, and Notes he wrote on these books, no detailed account remains. (Cf. *in Rom.* ix. § 1, p. 283 L.; Ruf. *Apol.* ii. 20; Hieron. *Ep.* 33.) The following remain: EXODUS.—*Greek:* (1) On Ex. x. 27 (several fragments). (2) Notes from Catenae. Two short *fragments* of *Hom.* viii. (3) Additional notes. *Latin:* 13 *Homilies,* trans. by Rufinus.

The main fragment of the Commentary on Exodus (*Philoc.* 27 [26]) deals with interpretation of the "hardening of Pharaoh's heart" (Ex. x. 27), which Origen (to use modern language) finds in the action of moral laws, while Pharaoh resisted the divine teaching. The Homilies, like those on Genesis, were translated by Rufinus from the reports of Origen's sermons, which he supplemented with interpretative additions. Throughout Origen dwells upon the spiritual interpretation of the record. "Not one iota or one tittle is," in his opinion, "without mysteries" (*Hom.* i. 4). The literal history has a mystical and a moral meaning (*e.g. Hom.* i. 4 f., ii. 1, iii. 3, iv. 8, vii. 3, x. 4, xiii. 5). Some of the applications he makes are of great beauty, *e.g.* in regard to the popular complaints against religious life and the troubles which follow religious awakening (Ex. v. 4 ff., *Hom.* iii. 3); the difficulties of the heavenward pilgrimage (Ex. xiv. 2, *Hom.* v. 3); the believer as the tabernacle of God (*Hom.* ix. 4); turning to the Lord (Ex. xxxiv. 34, coll. II. Cor. iii. 16, *Hom.* xii. 2); the manifold offerings of different believers (Ex. xxxv. 5, *Hom.* xiii. 3).

LEVITICUS.—*Greek:* (1) *Fragm.* of *Hom.* 2 (5). (2) Notes from Catenae. (3) Additional notes. (4) A fragment (cf. *Hom. in Lev.* viii. 6), Mai, *Class. Auct.* t. x. p. 600. *Latin:* 16 *Homilies* (trans. by Rufinus).

In the interpretation of Leviticus Origen naturally dwells on the obvious moral and spiritual antitypes of the Mosaic ordinances. Not infrequently the use he makes of them is impressive and ingenious, *e.g.* his view of man's soul and body as the deposit which he owes to God (Lev. vi. 4, *Hom.* iv. 3); of the office of the Christian priest foreshadowed in that of the Jewish priest (Lev. vii. 28 ff., *Hom.* v. 12); of the priesthood of believers (Lev. viii. 7 ff., *Hom.* vi. 5; cf. *Hom.* ix. 9); of the Saviour's sorrow (Lev. x. 9, coll. Matt. xxvi. 9, *Hom.* vii. 2), of purification by fire (Lev. xvi. 12, *Hom.* ix. 7). Throughout Christ appears as the one Sacrifice for the world, and the one Priest (*Hom.* i. 2, iv. 8, v. 3, ix. 2, xii.), though elsewhere He is said to join with Himself apostles and martyrs (*Hom. in Num.* x. 2).

NUMBERS.—No mention is made of "Books" on Numbers. Of Notes and Homilies (cf. *Hom. in Jer.* xii. § 3) the following remain: *Greek:* (1) Notes from Catenae. Small *Fragment* of *Hom.* xiii. (2) Additional notes. *Latin:* 28 *Homilies,* trans. by Rufinus, which follow the whole course of the narrative.

One main idea is prominent throughout. The struggles of the Israelites on the way to Canaan are the image of the struggles of the Christian. The entrance on the Promised Land foreshadows the entrance on the heavenly realm (*Hom.* vii. 5). The future world will even, in Origen's judgment, offer differences of race and position corresponding to those of the tribes of Israel and the nations among whom they moved (*ib.* i. 3, ii. 1, xi. 5, xxviii. 4). The interpretation of the record of the stations (*ib.* xxvii.) is a very good example of the way he finds a meaning in the minutest details of the history. Of wider interest are his remarks on man's spiritual conflict (*ib.* vii. 6), the wounds of sin (*ib.* viii. 1), advance in wisdom (*ib.* xvii. 4), the festivals of heaven (*ib.* xxiii. 11), self-dedication (*ib.* xxiv. 2), and the stains of battle (*ib.* xxv. 6).

DEUTERONOMY.—Cassiodorus (*de Instit.* 1) mentions four Homilies of Origen on Deut. ("in quibus est minuta nimis et subtilis expositio"), and doubtless it was these (*oratiunculae*) Rufinus proposed to translate if his health had been restored. The scanty remains are: (1) Notes from Catenae. (2) Additional notes. One interesting note at least among (1) appears to be a fragment of a homily (*in Deut.* viii. 7).

It is probable (Hieron. *Ep.* 84, 7) that considerable fragments of Origen's comments on the Pentateuch are contained in Ambrose's treatise on the *Hexaemeron,* but the treatise has not yet been critically examined.

JOSHUA–II. KINGS.—Origen appears to have treated these historical books in homilies only, or perhaps in detached notes also. There remain of the several books: JOSHUA.—*Greek:* (1) *Fragm.* of *Hom.* xx. (2) Notes from Catenae. (3) Additional notes. *Latin:* 26 *Homilies,* trans. by Rufinus.

The homilies on Joshua, belonging to the latest period of Origen's life, perhaps offer the most attractive specimen of his popular interpretation. The parallel between the leader of the old church and the Leader of the new is drawn with great ingenuity and care. The spiritual interpretation of the conquest of Canaan, as an image of the Christian life, never flags. Fact after fact is made contributory to the fulness of the idea; and the reader is forced to acknowledge that the fortunes of Israel can at least speak to us with an intelligible voice. Rufinus himself may have felt the peculiar charm of the book, for he selected it for translation in answer to a general request of Chromatius to render something from Greek literature for the edification of the church. The homilies cover the whole narrative up to the settling of the land (c. xxii.).

Among passages of special interest are those on the help we gain from the old fathers (*ib.* iii. 1); the broad parallel between the Christian life and the history of the Exodus (*ib.* iv. 1); the Christian realizing Christ's victory (*ib.* vii. 2); growing wisdom (*ib.* xii. 2).

JUDGES.—*Greek:* (1) Notes from Catenae. (2) Additional notes. *Latin:* 9 *Homilies*, trans. by Rufinus.

RUTH.—*Greek:* A note on i. 4.

The Homilies on Judges are of much less interest than those on Joshua. A passage on martyrdom—the baptism of blood—is worthy of notice (*Hom.* vii. 2). In *Hom.* ix. 1 Origen seems to refer to the persecution of Maximin, which was but lately ended.

I. and II. SAMUEL, I. and II. KINGS (I.–IV. Kings). *Greek:* (1) *Hom.* on I. Sam. xxviii. (2) Notes from Catenae and Fragments. (3) Additional notes. *Latin:* Homily on I. Sam. i. 2 (*de Helchana et Fenenna*), delivered at Jerusalem (§ 1: nolite illud in nobis requirere quod in papa Alexandro habetis). The translator is not known. The remains of Origen's writings on the later historical books are very slight. The homily on the witch of Endor provoked violent attacks. In this Origen maintained, in accordance with much early Christian and Jewish opinion, that the soul of Samuel was truly called up from Hades. Among others Eustathius of Antioch assailed Origen in unmeasured terms.

THE HAGIOGRAPHA. JOB.—Origen composed many homilies on Job (Eustath. Antioch, *de Engastr.* 391), which were rendered freely into Latin by Hilary of Poictiers (Hier. *de Vir. Ill.* 100; *Ep. adv. Vigil.* 61, 2). The scattered Notes which remain are not sufficient to enable us to estimate their value. There remain: *Greek:* (1) Notes from Catenae. (2) Additional notes. *Latin:* Fragment quoted from a homily of Hilary by August. *Lib.* ii. *c. Jul.* § 27, and assumed to be translated from Origen.

THE PSALMS engaged Origen's attention before he left Alexandria. At that time he had written commentaries on Pss. i.-xxv. (Eus. *H. E.* vi. 24). He completed the book afterwards. Jerome expressly states that he "left an explanation of all the Psalms in many volumes" (*Ep.* cxii. §20); and his extant books contain numerous references to his commentaries on psalms (cf. Hier. *Ep.* xxxiv. § 1).

Besides these detailed commentaries, he illustrated the Psalter by short Notes ("a handbook": "enchiridion ille vocabat," Auct. ap. Hier. *Tom.* vii. *App.*), and by Homilies.

The Homilies which are preserved in Rufinus's Latin trans. belong to the latest period of Origen's life, *c.* 241-247 (*Hom.* 1 *in Ps.* xxxvi. § 2; *Hom.* 1 *in Ps.* xxxvii. § 1). They give a continuous practical interpretation of the 3 psalms (*v. inf.*), and are a very good example of this style of exposition. One passage on the permanent effects of actions on the doer may be specially noticed (*Hom.* ii. § 2). The Greek fragments preserved in the Catenae offer numerous close coincidences with the Latin Homilies, and no doubt represent the general sense of Origen's comments. Cf. *Comm. in Rom.* iv. § 1 ("cum de Psalmis per ordinem dictaremus"); *id.* § 11; *Hom. in Jer.* xv. 6. There remain: *Greek:* (1) *Fragments* from the Τόμοι and *Homilies.* (2) Additional fragments and notes from Catenae. (3) Additional notes. *Latin:* 9 *Homilies* on Pss. xxxvi. xxxvii. xxxviii. (trans. by Rufinus).

PROVERBS.—There remain: *Greek:* (1) Fragments. (2) Notes from Catenae. *Latin:* Fragments.

ECCLESIASTES.—Notes on iii. 3, 7, 16 f.

LAMENTATIONS.—Origen wrote commentaries on the Lamentations before 231, of which five books had come down to the time of Eusebius (*H. E.* vi. 24). The Greek notes are probably derived from these.

CANTICLES.—Jerome speaks of the work on Canticles with enthusiasm: "In his other books Origen," he says, "surpassed every one else, in this he surpassed himself" (*Prol. in Hom. in Cant.*). There remain: *Greek:* (1) *Fragments* of his early work. (2) Extracts by Procopius. *Latin:* Two *Homilies* (trans. by Jerome). Prologue and four books on Canticles, trans. by Rufinus.

THE PROPHETS. ISAIAH.—Origen interpreted Isaiah in each of the three forms which he used; in Books (τόμοι), in Notes, and in Homilies. Thirty books of his Commentaries remained when Eusebius wrote his *History* extending to c. xxx. 6 (Eus. *H. E.* vi. 32). Some of these had perished in the time of Jerome, who speaks of the work as abounding in allegories and interpretation of names (*Prol. in Lib.* v. *in Es*). There remain: *Latin:* Two fragments of the "Books." Nine *Homilies.* The Homilies were addressed to a popular audience, including catechumens, but they lack the ease of the latest discourses and follow no exact order. Subjects: The call of the prophet; The virgin's son; The seven women; The vision of God; The mission of the prophet; The prophet and his children. In a passage of characteristic excellence (*Hom.* vi. 4) Origen describes the "greater works" of Christ's disciples.

JEREMIAH.—Cassiodorus enumerates 45 homilies of Origen on Jeremiah "in Attic style" (*de Instit. Div. Litt.* § 3). They were written in a period of tranquillity, and therefore probably after the close of the persecution of Maximin, *c.* 245 (*Hom.* iv. 3). There remain: *Greek:* (1) 19 *Homilies* (with Jerome's version of 12). Fragment of *Hom.* xxxix. (2) Notes from Catenae. *Latin:* Two *Homilies*, trans. by Jerome.

The Homilies generally give a full interpretation of the text, accommodating the language of the prophet to the circumstances of the Christian church. But Origen's total want of historical feeling makes itself felt perhaps more in his treatment of this book than elsewhere, for the teaching of Jeremiah is practically unintelligible without a true sense of the tragic crisis in which he was placed. There are, however, many separate passages of the Homilies of considerable beauty, *e.g.* on the fruitful discipline of God (*Hom.* iii. 2), the ever-new birth of Christ (*ib.* ix. 4), the marks of sin (*ib.* xvi. 10). Cf. *Hom. in Josh.* xiii. § 3.

EZEKIEL.—There remain: *Greek:* (1) Fragments. (2) Notes from Catenae. *Latin:* 14 *Homilies.* The Homilies only cover a small portion of the book, and do not offer many features of interest. The passages on the responsibility of teachers (*Hom.* v. 5, vii. 3) are perhaps the most striking.

DANIEL.—Origen commented upon the histories of Susanna and of Bel (Dan. *Apocr.* xiii. xiv.) in bk. x. of his *Miscellanies* (Στρωματεῖς), and Jerome has preserved a brief abstract of his notes as an appendix to his commentary on Daniel (Delarue, i. 49 f.; Lommatzsch, xvii. 70 ff.).

THE MINOR PROPHETS.—Origen wrote extensive commentaries on the twelve minor prophets, of which 25 books remained in the time of Eusebius (*H. E.* vi. 36). The fragment on Hosea xii., preserved in the *Philocalia*, c. viii., is all that now remains. [Two books on Hos. (one on Ephraim); 2 on Joel; 6 on Amos; 1 on Jon.; 2 on Mic.; 2 on Nah.; 3 on Hab.; 2 on Zeph.; 1 on Hagg.; 2 on Zech. (principio); 2 on Mal.—H.C.].

WRITINGS ON THE NEW TESTAMENT.—Eusebius states that Origen wrote 25 Books (τόμοι) on St. Matthew (*H. E.* vi. 36). The commentaries seem to have been written *c.* 245-246. [25 Books; 25 Homilies.—H.C.]

Bk. x. gives a continuous exposition of Matt. xiii. 36-xiv. 15. The most interesting passages are where Origen discusses characteristically the types of spiritual sickness (c. 24) and the doubtful question as to "the brethren of the Lord" (c. 17). On internal grounds he favours the belief in the perpetual virginity of the mother of the Lord. In the account of Herod's banquet he has preserved definitely the fact that "the daughter of Herodias" bore the same name as her mother (c. 22), in accordance with the true reading in Mark vi. 22 (τῆς θυγατρὸς αὐτοῦ Ἡρῳδιάδος); but he strangely supposes that the power of life and death was taken away from Herod because he executed the Baptist (c. 21).

Bk. xi. (c. xiv. 15-xv. 32) contains several pieces of considerable interest on the discipline of temptation (c. 6), *Corban* (c. 9), the conception of things unclean (c. 12), the healing spirit in the Church (c. 18), and perhaps, above all, that on the Eucharist (c. 14), which is of primary importance for understanding Origen's view.

The most important passages in bk. xii., which gives the commentary on c. xvi. 1-xvii. 9, are those treating of the confession and blessing of St. Peter (cc. 10 ff.) and the Transfiguration (cc. 37 ff.). He regards St. Peter as the type of the true believer. All believers, as they are Christians, are Peters also (c. 11: παρώνυμοι πέτρας πάντες οἱ μιμηταὶ Χριστοῦ . . . Χριστοῦ μέλη ὄντες παρώνυμοι ἐχρημάτισαν Χριστιανοί, πέτρας δὲ πέτροι). His ignorance of the Hebrew idiom leads him, like other early commentators, to refer the "binding and loosing" to sins (c. 14).

Bk. xiii. (c. xvii. 10-xviii. 18) opens with an argument against transmigration, and contains an interesting discussion of the influence of planets upon men (c. 6). Other characteristic passages deal with the circumstances under which the Lord healed the sick (c. 3), the rule for avoiding offences (c. 24), and esp. the doctrine of guardian angels (cc. 26 f.).

Bk. xiv. (c. xviii. 19-xix. 11) contains a characteristic examination of the senses in which the "two or three" in Matt. xviii. 20 may be understood (cc. 1 ff.) and a discussion of points regarding marriage (cc. 16 ff.; 23 ff.).

Bk. xv. (xix. 12-xx. 16) has several pieces of more than usual interest: the investigation of the meaning of Matt. xix. 12 f. with (as it appears) clear reference to his own early error (c. 2); a fine passage on the goodness of God even in His chastisements (c. 11); and some remarkable interpretations of the five sendings of labourers to the vineyard (Matt. xx. 1 ff.), in one of which he likens St. Paul to one who had wrought as an apostle in one hour more perhaps than all those before him (c. 35).

Bk. xvi. (xx. 17-xxi. 22) gives some striking pictures of the darker side of Christian society, the growing pride of the hierarchy, the faults of church officers, the separation between clergy and laity (cc. 8, 22, 25). In discussing the healing of Bartimaeus Origen holds that a choice must be made between supposing that the three evangelists have related three incidents, if the literal record is to be maintained, or that they relate one and the same spiritual fact in different words (c. 12).

Bk. xvii. (xxi. 23-xxii. 33) contains interpretations of the parables of the two sons (c. 4), the vineyard (6 ff.), and the marriage feast (15 ff.), which are good examples of Origen's method; and his explanations of the questions of the Herodians (cc. 26 ff.) and the Sadducees (c. 33) are of interest.

The old Latin translation continues the commentary to Matt. xxvii. 63. Passages in it of chief interest are: the application of the woes (Matt. xxiii. 1 ff.), §§ 9-25; the legend of the death of Zachariah the father of the Baptist, § 25; the danger of false opinions, § 33; the gathering of the saints, § 51; the limitation of the knowledge of the Son (Matt. xxiv. 36), § 55; the administration of the revenues of the church, § 61; the duty of using all that is lent to us, § 66; the eternal fire, immaterial, § 72; the supposition of three anointings of the Lord's feet, § 77; the passover of the Jews and of the Lord, § 79; on the Body and Blood of Christ, § 85; the lesson of the Agony, § 91; tradition of the different appearance of the Lord to men of different powers of vision, § 100; the reading *Jesus Barabbas* to be rejected, § 121; tradition as to the grave of Adam on Calvary, § 126; on the darkness at the crucifixion, § 134.

ST. MARK.—A Latin commentary attributed to Victor of Antioch, pub. at Ingoldstadt in 1580, is said to contain quotations from Origen on cc. i. xiv. (Ceillier, p. 635). These, if the reference is correct, may have been taken from other parts of his writings. [15 Books; 39 Homilies.—H.C.]

ST. LUKE.—There remain: *Greek:* (1) Fragments. (2) Notes from a Venice MS. (xxviii.). (3) Additional notes, Mai, *Class. Auct.* t. x. pp. 474 ff. (4) Additional notes from *Cod. Coislin.* xxiii. *Latin:* 39 *Homilies.*

Origen wrote four Books on St. Luke (Hieron. *Prol. ad Hom.*) from which the detached notes were probably taken. The short Homilies on St. Luke, an early work of Origen, abound in characteristic thoughts. The most interesting passages are those dealing with the four canonical Gospels (*Hom.* 1), spiritual manifestations (*ib.* 3), the nobility and triumph of faith (*ib.* 7), spiritual growth (*ib.* 11), shepherds of churches and nations (*ib.* 12), spiritual and visible co-rulers of churches (*ib.* 13), infant baptism (*ib.* 14), second marriages (*ib.* 17), baptism by fire (*ib.* 24), man as the object of a spiritual conflict (*ib.* 35). Besides these homilies Origen wrote other homilies upon the Gospel which are now lost, but referred to *in Matt.* t. xiii. 29, xvi. 9; *in Joh.* t. xxxii. 2.

St. John.—[32 Books; some Notes.—H.C.] The remains of the Commentary on St. John are in many respects the most important of Origen's exegetical writings. There are left: Τόμοι i. ii. (iv. v. small fragments), vi. x. xiii. xix. (nearly entire), xx. xxviii. xxxii. These remains extend over the following portions of the Gospel: T. i. (John i. 1a), ii. (i. 1b-7a), vi. (i. 19-29), x. (ii. 12-25), xiii. (iv. 13-44), xix. (part) (viii. 19-24), xx. (viii. 37-52), xxviii. (xi. 39-57), xxxii. (xiii. 2-33). A revised text with critical intro. by A. E. Brooke has been pub. in 2 vols. by the Camb. Univ. Press.

The Commentary on St. John was undertaken at the request of Ambrose (*in Joh.* t. i. §§ 3, 6), and was "the first-fruits of his labours at Alexandria" (*ib.* § 4). It marks an epoch in theological literature and thought. Perhaps the earlier work of Heracleon may have suggested the idea, but Origen implies that the Gospel, by its essential character, claimed his first efforts as an interpreter.

Bk. i. deals mainly with the fundamental conceptions of "the Gospel" (§§ 1-15), "the beginning" (§§ 16-22), and "the Logos" (§§ 19-42). The Gospels are the first-fruits (ἀπαρχή) of the Scripture, the Gospel of St. John is the first-fruits of the Gospels (§ 6). As the Law had a shadow of the future, so too has the Gospel: spiritual truths underlie historical truths (§ 9). The Gospel in the widest sense is "for the whole world," not for our earth only, but for the universal system of the heavens and earth (§ 15). The discussion of the title Logos marks a critical stage in the history of Christian thought. In what sense, it is asked, is the Saviour called the Logos? It had come to be a common opinion "that Christ was as it were only a 'word' of God" (§ 23). To meet this view Origen refers to other titles, Light, Resurrection, Way, Truth, etc. (§§ 24-41), and by analogy comes to the conclusion that as we are illuminated by Christ as the Light, and quickened by Him as the Resurrection, so we are made divinely rational by Him as the Logos, *i.e.* Reason (§ 42). He thus preserves the personality of the Lord under the title of Logos, which expresses one aspect of His being and not His being itself (as a word); but recognizes that Christ may also be called the Logos (Word) of God as giving expression to His will.

In bk. ii. he continues his discussion of the meaning of the Logos, distinguishing, in a remarkable passage (§ 2), God and Reason taken absolutely (ὁ θεός, ὁ λόγος) from God and Reason used as predicates (θεός, λόγος). "The Father is the foundation of Deity, the Son of Reason" (§ 3). Afterwards he discusses the sense of the words "came into being through Him (δι' αὐτοῦ)," and the relation of the Holy Spirit to the Son (§ 6); and further, what "all things," and what that is which is called "nothing" (*i.e.* evil) which became without Him but is not (§ 7). The conceptions of life and light, of darkness and death, are then examined (§§ 11 ff.). In treating of the mission of John (§§ 24 ff.) Origen questions whether he may not have been an angel who sought to minister on earth to his Lord (§ 25); and characteristically remarks that he was "the voice" preceding "the Word" (§ 26). Perhaps it is not less characteristic that he blames those who, like Heracleon (t. vi. § 2), hold that John i. 16-18 are the words of the evangelist and not of the Baptist.

In bk. vi., after describing with calm dignity the circumstances which had interrupted his work, he examines in detail John i. 19-29. The question, *Art thou Elias?* leads to a remarkable discussion on the pre-existence of souls, and the entrance of the soul into the body, "a vast and difficult subject," which he reserves for special investigation (§ 7). The words of the Baptist (i. 26) give occasion for a minute comparison with the parallels in the other Gospels (§§ 16 ff.), in the course of which (§ 17) Origen strikingly contrasts the baptisms of John and Christ, and explains Christ's presence "in the midst of the Jews" (*v.* 26) of His universal presence as the Logos (§ 22). The mention of Bethany (*v.* 28) leads him to hastily adopt the correction "Bethabara" (§ 24), which he justifies by the frequent errors as to names in the LXX. His brief exposition of the title of Christ "as the Lamb of God" (§§ 35 ff.) is full of interest; and in connexion with this he notices the power of the blood of martyrs to overcome evil (§ 36).

Bk. x. deals with the history of the first cleansing of the temple and its immediate results (ii. 12-25). Origen thinks the discrepancy between the evangelists as to the sojourn at Capernaum (*v.* 12) is such that its solution can be found only in the spiritual sense (§ 2), to which every minute point contributes, though in itself outwardly trivial and unworthy of record (§§ 2 ff.). The phrase "the passover *of the Jews*" leads to an exposition of Christ as the true Passover (§§ 11 ff). The cleansing of the temple is shewn to have an abiding significance in life (§ 16); and Origen thinks that the sign Christ offered is fulfilled in the raising of the Christian church, built of living stones, out of trials and death, "after three days"—the first of present suffering, the second of the consummation, the third of the new order (§ 20).

Bk. xiii. is occupied with the interpretation of part of the history of the Samaritan woman and the healing of the nobleman's son (iv. 13-54). It is chiefly remarkable for the number of considerable quotations from Heracleon's Commentary it contains, more than twice as many as the other books. These still require careful collection and criticism. Lommatzsch failed to fulfil the promise of his preface (I. p. xiii.). Passages of interest in regard to Origen's own views and method are those on the relation of Christ's personal teaching to the Scriptures (§ 5), the five husbands as representing the senses (§ 9), the incorporeity of God (§ 25), the joy of the sower and reaper, and the continuity of work (§§ 46 f.), the unhonoured prophet (§ 54), spiritual dependence (§ 58), and the distinction between signs and wonders (§ 60).

Of bk. xix., which is imperfect at the beginning and end, a considerable fragment remains (viii. 19-25). The remarks on the treasury (John viii. 20) as the scene of the Lord's discourses (§ 2), and on the power of faith (§ 6), are characteristic.

Bk. xx. (viii. 37-53) has much that is of importance for Origen's opinions. It begins with an examination of some points in connexion with the pre-existence and character of souls; and, in a striking passage (§ 29), Origen illustrates the inspiration of evil passions. Other interesting passages treat of love as "the sun" in the life of Christians (§ 15); the ambiguities in the word "when" (§ 24); the need of help for spiritual sight (§ 26); and spiritual influences (§ 29).

The most remarkable passage in bk. xxviii. (John xi. 39-57) is perhaps that on the power of self-sacrifice among the Gentiles illustrating the vicarious sufferings of Christ (§ 14). Other remarks worthy of special notice are on the lifting up of the eyes (John xi. 41) (§ 4), the lesson of the death of Lazarus (§ 6), the duty of prudence in time of persecution (§ 18), and the passover of the Jews and of the Lord (§ 20).

Bk. xxxii. (John xiii. 2-33) treats of St. John's record of the Last Supper. Origen discusses the feet-washing at length, and says that it is not to be perpetuated literally (§§ 6 f.); he dwells on the growth of faith (§ 9), the difference of "soul" and "spirit" (§ 11), the character of Judas and moral deterioration (§ 12), and the sop given to Judas (§ 16).

Origen's Commentary is for us the beginning of a new type of literature. It has great faults of style, is diffusive, disproportioned, full of repetitions, obscure and heavy in form of expression, wholly deficient in historical insight, and continually passing into fantastic speculations. But it contains not a few "jewels five words long," abounds in noble thoughts and subtle criticisms, grapples with great difficulties, unfolds great ideas, and, above all, retains a firm hold on the human life of the Lord.

Acts.—[17 Homilies.—h.c.] *Greek:* (1) A single fragment from "the fourth homily on the Acts" is preserved in the *Philocalia.* (2) A few notes are given in Cramer's *Catena,* col. iii. 184, on Acts iv. 32, vii. 3, 53, xxi. 38.

Romans.—[15 Books.—h.c.] *Greek:* (1) Fragments from the first and ninth books contained in the *Philocalia.* (2) A number of important notes are contained in Cramer's *Catena,* t. iv. (1844), on the following passages: i. 1, 10; ii. 8, 16, 27; iii. 2, 4, 9, 13, 19, 21, 25, 27, 28, 30, 31; iv. 2. *Latin:* Ten books of Commentaries, translated and compressed from the *fifteen* books of Origen, by Rufinus, at the request of Heraclius.

The Commentary on Romans gives a continuous discussion of the text, often discursive, but still full of acute and noble conceptions. Origen's treatment of Rom. viii. as represented by Rufinus, is, on the whole, disappointing. It might have been expected to call out his highest powers of imagination and hope. His silence, no less than his rash conjectures as to the persons named in Rom. xvi., is a singular proof of the complete absence of any authoritative tradition as to the persons of the early Roman church. For the passage (x. 43) which refers to Marcion's mutilation of the epistle by removing the doxology (xvi. 25-27) and (though this is disputed) the last two chapters, see the papers by bp. Lightfoot and Dr. Hort in *Jour. of Philology,* 1869, ii. 264 ff.; 1871, iii. 51 ff., 193 ff.

I.-II. Corinthians.—[11 Homilies on II. Cor.—h.c.] *Greek:* Jerome mentions (*Ep. ad Pammach.* xlix. § 3) that Origen commented on this epistle at length; and Origen himself refers to what he had said on I. Cor. i. 2 (*Hom. in Luc.* xvii. *s.f.*). A very important collection of notes on I. Cor. is given in Cramer's *Catena,* vol. v. 1844. Some of the notes contain passages of considerable interest, as those on the vicarious death of Gentile heroes (I. Cor. i. 18; cf. *Hom. in Joh.* t. xxviii. § 14), the sovereignty of believers (I. Cor. iii. 21), evangelic "counsels" (vii. 25), the public teaching of women (xiv. 34, with reference to Montanism). Origen gives the outline of a creed (i. 9, 20), and touches on baptism (i. 14) and holy communion (vii. 5). He describes the Jewish search for leaven (v. 7); and supposes that many books of O.T. were lost at the Captivity (ii. 9).

Galatians.—[15 Books; 7 Homilies.—h.c.] Jerome, in the Prologue to his Commentary on Galatians, mentions that Origen wrote five Books on this epistle, as well as various Homilies and Notes (*tractatus et excerpta*), and that he interpreted it with brief annotations (*commatico sermone*) in his *Stromateis,* bk. x. (*Proem. in Comm. ad Gal.*; *Ep. ad August.* cxi. §§ 4, 6). Three fragments of the Commentary are contained in the Latin translation of Pamphilus's *Apology.*

Ephesians.—[3 Books.—h.c.] Origen's Commentary on the Ephesians may still be practically recovered. Jerome, in the *Prologue* to his own *Commentary,* says that "his readers should know that Origen wrote three books on the epistle, which he had partly followed." The extent of his debt could only be estimated by conjecture, till the publication of the Paris *Catena* (Cramer, 1842). This contains very large extracts from Origen's commentary, sometimes with his name and sometimes anonymous, and in nearly all cases Jerome has corresponding words or thoughts. A careful comparison of the Greek fragments with Jerome's Latin would make it possible to reconstruct a very large part of Origen's work. The corresponding notes on the description of the Christian warfare (vi. 11 ff.) well illustrate Jerome's mode of dealing with his archetype. Origen's comments are almost continuous. A fragment on Eph. v. 28 f., not found in the Greek notes, is preserved in the Latin trans. of the *Apology* of Pamphilus.

Philippians, Colossians, Titus, Philemon.—[1 Book on Philippians; 2 on Colossians; 1 on Titus; 1 on Philemon; 1 Homily on Titus.—H.C.] Short fragments from bk. iii. on Col. and the Comm. on Philemon, and more considerable fragments from Book on Titus (Tit. iii. 10, 11), are found in the trans. of Pamphilus's *Apology*. No Greek notes on these Epp. have been preserved.

I. THESSALONIANS. [3 Books; 2 Homilies. —H.C.] A considerable fragment from the third book of the Commentary on I. Thess. is preserved in Jerome's trans.: *Ep. ad Minerv. et Alex.* 9 (I. Thess. iv. 15-17).

HEBREWS.—[18 Homilies.—H.C.] Origen wrote Homilies and Commentaries on Hebrews. Two fragments of the Homilies are preserved by Eusebius (*H. E.* vi. 25), in which Origen gives his opinion on the composition of the epistle. Some inconsiderable fragments from the "Books" are found in the trans. of Pamphilus's *Apology*.

CATHOLIC EPISTLES.—The quotations from Origen, given in Cramer's *Catena* on the Catholic epistles, are apparently taken from other treatises, and not from commentaries on the books themselves: Jas. i. 4, 13; I. Pet. i. 4 (ἐκ τῆς ἑρμηνείας εἰς τὸ κατὰ πρόγνωσιν θεοῦ); I. John ii. 14 (ἐκ τοῦ ᾄσματος τῶν ᾀσμάτων T. A'.).

APOCALYPSE.—Origen purposed to comment upon the Apocalypse (*Comm. Ser. in Matt.* § 49), but it is uncertain whether he carried out his design.

B. DOGMATIC WRITINGS.—Origen's writings *On the Resurrection* were violently assailed by Methodius, and considered by Jerome to abound in errors (*Ep.* lxxxiv. 7). Probably they excited opposition by assailing the gross literalism of the popular view of the future life. The extant fragments are consistent with the true faith and express it with a wise caution, affirming the permanence through death of the whole man and not of the soul only. Thus Origen dwells rightly on St. Paul's image of the seed (*Fragm.* 2), maintains a perfect correspondence between the present and the future, and speaks very happily of the "ratio substantiae corporalis" as that which is permanent.

The book *On First Principles* is the most complete and characteristic expression of Origen's opinions. It was written while at Alexandria, when he was probably not much more than 30 years old and still a layman, but there is no reason to think that he modified, in any important respects, the views he unfolds in it. It was not written for simple believers but for scholars—for those who were familiar with the teaching of Gnosticism and Platonism; and with a view to questions which then first became urgent when men have risen to a wide view of nature and life. Non-Christian philosophers moved in a region of subtle abstractions, "ideas": Origen felt that Christianity converted these abstractions into realities, persons, facts of a complete life; and he strove to express what he felt in the modes of thought and language of his own age. He aimed at presenting the highest knowledge (γνῶσις) as an objective system. But in doing this he had no intention of fashioning two Christianities, a Christianity for the learned and a Christianity for the simple. The faith was one, one essentially and unalterably, but infinite in fullness, so that the trained eye could see its harmonies the most. Fresh wants made fresh truths visible. He who found much had nothing over: he who found little had no lack.

The book is the earliest attempt to form a system of Christian doctrine, or rather a philosophy of the Christian faith, and thus marks an epoch in Christian thought, but no change in the contents of the Christian creed. The elements of the dogmatic basis are assumed on the authority of the church. The author's object is, he says, to shew how they can be arranged as a whole, by the help either of the statements of Scripture or of the methods of exact reasoning. However strange or startling the teaching of Origen may seem to us, we must bear in mind that this is his own account of it. He takes for granted that all he brings forward is in harmony with received teaching. He professes to accept as final the same authorities as ourselves.

The treatise consists of four books. Digressions and repetitions interfere with the symmetry of the plan. But to speak generally, bk. i. deals with God and creation (religious statics); bks. ii. and iii. with creation and providence, man and redemption (religious dynamics); and bk. iv. with Holy Scripture. The first three books contain the exposition of a Christian philosophy, gathered round the three ideas of God, the world, and the rational soul, and the last gives the basis of it. Even in the repetitions (as on "the restoration of things") each successive treatment corresponds with a new point of sight.

In bk. i. Origen sets out the final elements of all religious philosophy, God, the world, rational creatures. After dwelling on the essential nature of God as incorporeal, invisible, incomprehensible, and on the characteristic relations of the Persons of the Holy Trinity to man, as the authors of being, and reason, and holiness, he gives a summary view of the end of human life, for the elements of a problem cannot be really understood until we have comprehended its scope. The end of life, then, according to Origen, is the progressive assimilation of man to God by the voluntary appropriation of His gifts. Gentile philosophers had proposed to themselves the idea of assimilation to God, but Origen adds the means. By the unceasing action of the Father, Son, and Holy Spirit towards us, renewed at each successive stage of our advance, we shall be able, he says, with difficulty perchance, at some future time, to look on the holy and blessed life; and when once we have been enabled to reach that, after many struggles, we ought so to continue in it that no weariness may take hold on us. Each fresh enjoyment of that bliss ought to deepen our desire for it; while we are ever receiving, with more ardent love and larger grasp, the Father and the Son and the Holy Spirit (i. 3, 8).

But it will be said that this condition of progress, effort, assimilation, involves the possibility of declension, indolence, the obliteration of the divine image. If man can go forward he can go backward. Origen accepts the consequence, and finds in it an explanation of the actual state of men and angels. The present position of each rational being corresponds, in his judgment, with the use he has made of the revelations and gifts of God. No beings were created immutable. Some by diligent obedience have been raised to the loftiest places in the celestial hierarchy; others by perverse self-will and rebellion have sunk to the condition of demons. Others occupy an intermediate place, and are capable of being raised again to their first state, and so upward, if they avail themselves of the helps provided by the love of God. "Of these," he adds, "I think, as far as I can form an opinion, that this order of the human race was formed, which in the future age, or in the ages which succeed, when there shall be a new heaven and a new earth, shall be restored to that unity which the Lord promises in His intercessory prayer. . . . Meanwhile, both in the ages which are seen and temporal, and in those which are not seen and eternal, all rational beings who have fallen are dealt with according to the order, the character, the measure of their deserts. Some in the first, others in the second, some, again, even in the last times, through greater and heavier sufferings, borne through many ages, reformed by sharper discipline, and restored . . . stage by stage . . . reach that which is invisible and eternal . . ." Only one kind of change is impossible. There is no such transmigration of souls as Plato pictured, after the fashion of the Hindoos, in the legend of Er the Armenian. No rational being can sink into the nature of a brute (i. 8, 4; cf. *c. Cels.* iv. 83).

The progress of this discussion is interrupted by one singular episode characteristic of the time. How, Origen asks, are we to regard the heavenly bodies—the sun and moon and stars? Are they the temporary abodes of souls which shall hereafter be released from them? Are they finally to be brought into the great unity, when "God shall be all in all"? The questions, he admits, are bold; but he answers both in the affirmative, on what he held to be the authority of Scripture (i. 7; cf. *c. Cels.* v. 10 f.).

In bk. ii. Origen pursues, at greater length, his view of the visible world, as a place of discipline and preparation. He follows out as a movement what he had before regarded as a condition. The endless variety in the situations of men, the inequality of their material and moral circumstances, their critical spiritual differences, all tend to shew, he argues, that the position of each has been determined in accordance with previous conduct. God, in His ineffable wisdom, has united all together with absolute justice, so that all these creatures most diverse in themselves, combine to work out His purpose, while "their very variety tends to the one end of perfection." All things were made for the sake of man and rational beings. Through man, therefore, this world, as God's work, becomes complete and perfect (cf. *c. Cels.* iv. 99). The individual is never isolated, though never irresponsible. At every moment he is acting and acted upon, adding something to the sum of the moral forces of the world, furnishing that out of which God is fulfilling His purpose. The difficulties of life, as Origen regards them, give scope for heroic effort and loving service. The fruits of a moral victory become more permanent as they are gained through harder toil. Obstacles and hindrances are incentives to exertion. Man's body is not a "prison," in the sense of a place of punishment only: it is a beneficent provision for discipline, furnishing such salutary restraints as are best fitted to further moral growth.

This view of the dependence of the present on the past—to use the forms of human speech—seemed to Origen to remove a difficulty which weighed heavily upon thoughtful men then as now. Very many said then that the sufferings and disparities of life, the contrasts of law and gospel, point to the action of rival spiritual powers, or to a Creator limited by something external to Himself (ii. 9, 5). Not so, was Origen's reply; they simply reveal that what we see is a fragment of a vast system in which we can only trace tendencies, consequences, signs, and rest upon the historic fact of the Incarnation. In this respect he ventured to regard the entire range of being as "one thought" answering to the absolutely perfect will of God, while "we that are but parts can see but part, now this, now that." This seems to be the true meaning of his famous assertion, that the power of God in creation was finite and not infinite. It would, that is, be inconsistent with our ideas of perfect order, and therefore with our idea of the Divine Being, that the sum of first existences should not form one whole. "God made all things in number and measure." The omnipotence of God is defined (as we are forced to conceive) by the absolute perfections of His nature. "He cannot deny Himself" (ii. 9, 1, iv. 35). It may be objected that our difficulties do not lie only in our present circumstances; the issues of the present, so far as we can see them, bring difficulties no less overwhelming; even if we allow this world to be a fit place of discipline for fallen beings capable of recovery, it is only too evident that the discipline does not always work amendment. Origen admits the fact, and draws the conclusion that other systems of penal purification and moral advance follow. World grows out of world, so to speak, till the consummation is reached. The nature, position, or constitution of the worlds to come he does not attempt to define. It is enough to believe that, from first to last, the will of Him Who is most righteous and most loving is fulfilled; and that each loftier region gained is the entrance to some still more glorious abode above, so that all being becomes, as it were, in the highest sense a journey of the saints from mansion to mansion up to the very throne of God. To make this view clear Origen follows out, in imagination, the normal course of the progressive training, purifying, and illumination of men in the future. He pictures them passing from sphere to sphere, and resting in each so as to receive such revelations of the providence of God as they can grasp; lower phenomena are successively explained to them, and higher phenomena are indicated. As they look backward old mysteries are illuminated; as they look forward unimagined mysteries stir their souls with divine desire. Everywhere their Lord is with them, and they advance from strength to strength through the perpetual supply of spiritual food. This food, he says, is the contemplation and understanding of God, according to its proper measure in each case, and as suits a nature which is made and created. And this measure—this due harmony and proportion between aim and power—it is right that every one should regard even now, who is beginning to see God, that is, to understand Him in purity of heart (ii. 11, 6 f.). But Origen goes on to shew that Scripture concentrates our attention upon the next scene, summed up in the words, resurrection, judgment, retribution. Nowhere is he more studiously anxious to keep to the teaching of the Word than in dealing with these cardinal ideas. For him the resurrection is not the reproduction of any particular organism, but the preservation of complete identity of person, an identity maintained under new conditions, which he presents under the apostolic figure of the growth of the plant from the seed: the seed is committed to the earth, perishes, and yet the vital power it contains gathers a new frame answering to its proper nature. Judgment is no limited and local act, but the unimpeded execution of the absolute divine law by which the man is made to feel what he is and what he has become and to bear the inexorable consequences of the revelation. Punishment is no vengeance, but the just severity of a righteous King, by which the soul is placed at least on the way to purification. Blessedness is no sensuous joy or indolent repose, but the opening vision of the divine glory, the growing insight into the mysteries of the fulfilment of the divine counsels.

In bk. iii. Origen discusses the moral basis of his system. This lies in the recognition of free will as the inalienable endowment of rational beings. But this free will does not carry with it the power of independent action, but only the power of receiving the help which is extended to each according to his capacity and needs and therefore justly implying responsibility for the consequences of action. Such free will offers a sufficient explanation, in Origen's judgment, for what we see and gives a stable foundation for what we hope. It places sin definitely within the man himself, not without him. It preserves the possibility of restoration, while it enforces the penalty of failure. "'God said,' so he writes, 'let us make man in our image after our likeness.' Then the sacred writer adds, 'and God made man: in the image of God made He him.' This therefore that he says, 'in the image of God made He him,' while he is silent as to the likeness, has no other meaning than this, that man received the dignity of the image at his first creation: while the perfection of the likeness is kept in the consummation (of all things); that is, that he should himself gain it by the efforts of his own endeavour, since the possibility of perfection had been given him at the first . . ." (iii. 6, 1). Such a doctrine, he shews, gives a deep solemnity to the moral conflicts of life. We cannot, even to the last, plead that we are the victims of circumstances or of evil spirits. The decision in each case rests with ourselves, yet so that all we have and are truly is the gift of God. Each soul obtains from the object of its love the power to fulfil His will. "It draws and takes to itself," he says in another place, "the Word of God in proportion to its capacity and faith. And when souls have drawn to themselves the Word of God, and have let Him penetrate their senses and their understandings, and have perceived the sweetness of His fragrance . . . filled with vigour and cheerfulness they speed after him" (*in Cant.* i.). Such a doctrine, so far from tending to Pelagianism, is the very refutation of it. It lays down that the essence of freedom is absolute self-surrender; that the power of right action is nothing but the power of God. Every act of man is the act of a free being, but not an exercise of freedom; if done without dependence upon God, it is done in despite of freedom, responsibly indeed, but under adverse constraint. The decision from moment to moment rests with us, but not the end. That is determined from the first, though the conduct of creatures can delay, through untold ages, the consummation of all things. The gift of being, once given, abides for ever. The rational creature is capable of change, of better and worse, but it can never cease to be. What mysteries lie behind; what is the nature of the spiritual body in which we shall be clothed; whether all that is finite shall be gathered up in some unspeakable way into the absolute,—that Origen holds is beyond our minds to conceive.

Bk. iv. deals with the dogmatic basis of Origen's system. For this to follow the moral basis is unusual and yet intelligible. It moves from the universal to the special; from the most abstract to the most concrete; from the heights of speculation to the rule of authority. "In investigating such great subjects as these," Origen writes, "we are not content with common ideas and the clear evidence of what we see, but we take testimonies to prove what we state, even those which are drawn from the Scriptures which we believe to be divine" (iv. 1). Therefore, in conclusion, he examines with a reverence, insight, humility, and grandeur of feeling never surpassed, the questions of the inspiration and interpretation of the Bible. The intellectual value of the work may best be characterized by one fact. A single sentence from it was quoted by Butler as containing the germ of his *Analogy*.

Before he left Alexandria Origen wrote ten books of *Miscellanies* (Στρωματεῖς: cf. Eus. *H.E.* vi. 18). In these he apparently discussed various topics in the light of ancient philosophy and Scripture (Hieron. *Ep. ad Magn.* lxx. 4). The three fragments which remain, in a Latin translation, give no sufficient idea of their contents. The first, from bk. vi., touches on the permissibility of deflection from literal truth, following out a remark of Plato (Hieron. *adv. Ruf.* i. § 18: cf. *Hom.* xix. *in Jer.* § 7; *Hom. in Lev.* iii. § 4). The second, from bk. x., contains brief notes on the history of Susanna and Bel (Dan. xiii. xiv.) added by Jerome to his Comm. on Dan. The third, also from bk. x., gives an interpretation of Gal. v. 13, which is referred to the spiritual understanding of the Scripture narratives (Hieron. *ad loc.*; cf. *in Jer.* iv. xxii. 24 ff.).

The *Letter to Julius Africanus on the History of Susanna* (Dan. xiii.) contains a reply to objections which Julius urged against the authenticity of the history of Susanna and offers a crucial and startling proof of Origen's deficiency in historical criticism. Africanus pointed out, from its plays upon words among other things, that the writing must have been Greek originally, and that it was not contained in the "Hebrew" Daniel. To these arguments Origen answers that he had indeed been unable (φίλη γὰρ ἡ ἀλήθεια) to find Hebrew equivalents to the paronomasias quoted, but that they may exist; and that the Jews had probably omitted the history to save the honour of their elders. It must be allowed that right lies with the aged Africanus, who could address Origen as "a son," and whose judgment was in the spirit of his own noble saying: "May such a principle never prevail in the church of Christ that falsehood is framed for His praise and glory" (*Fragm. ap.* Routh, *R. S.* ii. 230).

C. The Eight Books against Celsus.—The earlier apologists had been called upon to defend Christianity against the outbursts of popular prejudice, as a system compatible with civil and social order. Origen, in this work, entered a far wider field. It was his object to defend the faith against a comprehensive attack, conducted by critical, historical, and philosophical, as well as by political, arguments. He undertook the work very unwillingly, at the urgent request of Ambrose, but, once undertaken, he threw into it the whole energy of his genius. Celsus was a worthy opponent, and Origen allows him to state his case in his own words, and follows him step by step in the great controversy. At first Origen proposed to deal with the attack of Celsus in a general form; but after i. 27 he quotes the objections of Celsus, in the order of their occurrence, and deals with them one by one, so that it is possible to reconstruct the work of Celsus, in great part, from Origen's quotations. It would be difficult to overrate the importance both of attack and defence in the history of religious opinion in the 2nd and 3rd cents. The form of objections changes; but every essential type of objection to Christianity finds its representative in Celsus's statements, and Origen suggests in reply thoughts, often disguised in strange dresses, which may yet be fruitful. No outline can convey a true idea of the fullness and variety of the contents of the treatise. Speaking broadly, the work falls into three parts—the controversy on the history of Christianity (bks. i. ii.), the controversy on the general character and idea of Christianity (bks. iii.-v.), the controversy on the relations of Christianity to philosophy, popular religion, and national life (bks. vi.-viii.). There are necessarily many repetitions, but in the main this appears to represent the course of the argument. The lines were laid down by Celsus: Origen simply followed him.

After some introductory chapters (i. 1-27), dealing with a large number of miscellaneous objections to Christianity as illegal, secret, of barbarous origin, inspired by a demoniac power, an offshoot of Judaism, Origen meets Celsus's first serious attack, directed against the Christian interpretation of the gospel history. In this case Celsus places his arguments in the mouth of a Jew. The character, as Origen points out, is not consistently maintained, but the original conception is ingenious. A Jew might reasonably be supposed to be the best critic of a system which sprang from his own people. The chief aim of the objector is to shew that the miraculous narratives of the Gospels are untrustworthy, inconclusive in themselves, and that the details of the Lord's life, so far as they can be ascertained, furnish no adequate support to the Christian theory of His person. The criticism is wholly external and unsympathetic. Can we suppose, Celsus asks, that He Who was God would be afraid and flee to Egypt (i. 66)? could have had a body like other men (i. 69, ii. 36)? would have lived a sordid, wandering life, with a few mean followers (i. 62)? have borne insults without exacting vengeance (ii. 35)? have been met with incredulity (ii. 75)? have died upon the cross (ii. 68)? have shewn Himself only to friends if He rose again (ii. 63)? He repeats the Jewish story of the shameful birth of Christ, and of His education in Egypt, where Celsus supposes that He learned magical arts by which He imposed upon His countrymen. These illustrations sufficiently shew the fatal weakness of Celsus's position. He has no eye for the facts of the inner life. He makes no effort to apprehend the gospel offered in what Christ did and was, as a revelation of spiritual power; and Origen rises immeasurably superior to him in his vindication of the majesty of Christ's humiliation and sufferings (i. 29 ff.). He shews that Christ did "dawn as a sun" upon the world (ii. 30), when judged by a moral and not by an external standard (ii. 40); that He left His disciples the abiding power of doing "greater works" than He Himself did in His earthly life (ii. 48); that the actual energy of Christianity in regenerating men,* was a proof that He Who was its spring was more than man (ii. 79). In bk. iii. and following books Celsus appears in his own person. He first attacks Christianity as being, like Judaism, originally a revolutionary system, based upon an idle faith in legends no more credible than those of Greece (iii. 1-43); then he paints it in detail as a religion of threats and promises, appealing only to the ignorant and sinful, unworthy of wise men, and, in fact, not addressed to them, even excluding them (iii. 44-81). Here again Origen has an easy victory. He has no difficulty in shewing that no real parallel can be established between the Greek heroes (iii. 22), or, as Celsus suggested, Antinous (iii. 36 ff.) and Christ. On the other side he can reply with the power of a life-long experience, that while the message of the gospel is universal and divine in its universality, "education is a way to virtue," a help towards the knowledge of God (iii. 45, 49, 58, 74), contributory, but not essentially supreme. But he rightly insists on placing the issue as to its claims in the moral and not in the intellectual realm. Christians are the proof of their creed. They are visibly transformed in character: the ignorant are proved wise, sinners are made holy (iii. 51, 64, 78 ff.).

Bks. iv. and v. are in many respects the most interesting of all. In these Origen meets

* Seen, for example, in one like St. Paul, of whom Celsus took no notice (i. 63).

Celsus's attack upon that which is the central idea of Christianity, and indeed of Biblical revelation, the Coming of God. This necessarily includes the discussion of the Biblical view of man's relation to God and nature. The contentions of Celsus are that there can be no sufficient cause and no adequate end for "a coming of God" (iv. 1-28); that the account of God's dealings with men in the O.T. is obviously incredible (iv. 29-50); that nature is fixed, even as to the amount of evil (iv. 62); and that man is presumptuous in claiming a superiority over what he calls irrational animals (iv. 54-99). In especial he dwells on the irrationality of the belief of a coming of God to judgment (v. 1-24); and maintains that there is a divine order in the distribution of the world among different nations, in which the Jews have no prerogative (v. 25-50). On all grounds therefore, he concludes, the claims of Christianity to be a universal religion, based on the coming of God to earth, are absurd. In treating these arguments Origen had a more arduous work than hitherto. The time had not then come —probably it has not come yet—when such far-reaching objections could be completely met; and Origen was greatly embarrassed by his want of that historic sense which is essential to the apprehension of the order of the divine revelations. His treatment of the O.T. narratives is unsatisfactory; and it is remarkable that he does not apply his own views on the unity of the whole plan of being, as grasped by man, in partial explanation at least of the present mysteries of life. They underlie indeed all he says; and much that he urges in detail is of great weight, as his remarks upon the conception of a divine coming (iv. 5 ff., 13 f.), the rational dignity of man (iv. 13, 23 ff., 30), the anthropopathic language of Scripture (iv. 71 ff.), and on the resurrection (v. 16 ff.).

In the last three books Origen enters again upon surer ground. He examines Celsus's parallels to the teaching of Scripture on the knowledge of God and the kingdom of heaven, drawn from Gentile sources (vi. 1-23); and after a digression on a mystical diagnosis of some heretical sect, which Celsus had brought forward as a specimen of Christian teaching (vi. 24-40), he passes to the true teaching on Satan and the Son of God and creation (vi. 41-65), and unfolds more in detail the doctrine of a spiritual revelation through Christ (vi. 66-81). This leads to a vindication of the O.T. prophecies of Christ (vii. 1-17), the compatibility of the two dispensations (vii. 18-26), and the Christian idea of the future life (vii. 27-40). Celsus proposed to point Christians to some better way, but Origen shews that he has failed: the purity of Christians puts to shame the lives of other men (vii. 41-61).

The remainder of the treatise is occupied with arguments as to the relations of Christianity to popular worship and civil duties. Celsus urged that the "demons," the gods of polytheism, might justly claim some worship, as having been entrusted with certain offices in the world (vii. 62-viii. 32); that the circumstances of life demand reasonable conformity to the established worship, which includes what is true in the Christian faith (viii. 33-68); that civil obedience is paramount (viii. 69-75). Origen replies in detail; and specially he shews that the worship of one God is the essence of true worship (viii. 12 f.); that Christianity has a consistent certainty of belief, with which no strange opinions can be put into comparison (viii. 53 ff.); that Christians do, in the noblest sense, support the civil powers by their lives, by their prayers, by their organization (viii. 75).

The spirit of the arguments on both sides is essentially modern; in the mode of treatment much is characteristic of the age in which the writers lived. Two points of very different nature will especially strike the student. First, the peculiar stress which Origen, in common with other early writers, lays upon isolated passages of the prophets and the O.T. generally; secondly, the unquestioning belief which he, in common with Celsus, accords to the claims of magic and augury (i. 6, 67, iv. 92 f., vii. 67, viii. 58). But when every deduction has been made, it would not be easy to point to a discussion of the claims of Christianity more comprehensive or more rich in pregnant thought. Among early apologies it has no rival. The constant presence of a real antagonist gives unflagging vigour to the debate; and the conscious power of Origen lies in the appeal which he could make to the Christian life as the one unanswerable proof of the Christian faith (cf. *Praef.* 2; i. 27, 67).

There are many other passages of great interest and worthy of study apart from the context. Such are Origen's remarks on the spirit of controversy (vii. 46); the moral power of Christianity, its universality, and its fitness for man (ii. 64, iii. 28, 40, 54, 62, iv. 26, vii. 17, 35, 42, 59); foreknowledge (ii. 19 ff.); the anthropomorphism of Scripture (vi. 60 ff.); the beauty of the ideal hope of the Christian (iii. 81); the ideal of worship (viii. 17 f., vii. 44); the divisions of Christians (iii. 12 f., v. 61); spiritual fellowship (viii. 64); and future unity (viii. 72).

D. Practical Works.—Origen's essay *On Prayer* was addressed to Ambrose and Tatiana (φιλομαθέστατοι καὶ γνησιώτατοι ἐν θεοσεβείᾳ ἀδελφοί, c. 33), in answer to their inquiries as to the efficacy, manner, subject, and circumstances of prayer. No writing of Origen is more free from his characteristic faults or more full of beautiful thoughts. He examines first the meaning and use of εὐχή (§ 3), and the objections urged against the efficacy of prayer, that God foreknows the future, and that all things take place according to His will (§ 5). Divine foreknowledge does not, he points out, take away man's responsibility: the moral attitude of prayer is in itself a sufficient blessing upon it (§§ 6 ff.). Prayer establishes an active communion between Christ and the angels in heaven (§§ 10 f.); and the duty of prayer is enforced by the example of Christ and the saints (§§ 13 f.). Prayer must be addressed to God only, "our Father in heaven," and not to Christ the Son as apart from the Father, but to the Father through Him (§ 15).

The Exhortation to Martyrdom.—In the persecution of Maximin (235-237), Ambrose and Theoctetus, a presbyter of Caesarea, were thrown into prison. Origen addressed them in a book written from his heart: as a boy and as an old man he looked face to face on martyrdom. Their sufferings, he tells them, are a proof of their maturity (c. 1), and in some sense the price of future blessedness (2), for which man's earthly frame is unfitted (3 ff.). The denial of Christ, on the other hand, is the most grievous wrong to God (6 ff.). Believers are indeed pledged to endurance, which will be repaid with unspeakable joys (12 ff.). Moreover, they are encouraged in their trials by the thought of the unseen spiritual witnesses by whom they are surrounded in the season of their outward sufferings (18 ff.), and by the examples of those who have already triumphed (22 ff.). By martyrdom man can shew his gratitude to God (28 f.), and at the same time receive afresh the forgiveness of baptism, offering, as a true priest, the sacrifice of himself (30; cf. *Hom.* vii. *in Jud.* 2). So he conquers demons (32). The predictions of the Lord shew that he is not forgotten (34 ff.), but rather that through affliction is fulfilled for him some counsel of love (39 ff.), such as the union of the soul with God when freed from the distractions of life (47 ff.). Perhaps, too, the blood of martyrs may have gained others for the truth (50, τάχα τ τιμίῳ αἵματι τῶν μαρτύρων ἀγορασθήσονταί τινες: cf. *Hom. in Num.* x. 2; *c. Cels.* viii. 44).

E. Critical Writings. [Hexapla.]

F. Letters.—Eusebius, as already stated, had made a collection of more than 100 of Origen's letters (*H. E.* vi. 36, 2). Of these two only remain entire, those to Julius Africanus (already noticed) and Gregory of Neocaesarea, and of the remainder the fragments and notices are most meagre. In one fragment (Delarue, i. p. 3, from Suidas, *s.v.*) he gives a lively picture of the incessant labour which the zeal of Ambrose imposed upon him. Another fragment of great interest, preserved by Eusebius, contains a defence of his study of heathen philosophy (*H. E.* vi. 19). An important passage of a letter to friends at Alexandria, complaining of the misrepresentations of those who professed to recount controversies they had held with him, has been preserved in a Latin trans. by Jerome and Rufinus (Delarue, i. p. 5).

Gregory was as yet undecided as to his profession when the letter to him was written (*c.* 236-237: cf. pp. 101 f.). Origen expresses his earnest desire that his "son" will devote all his knowledge of general literature and the fruits of wide discipline to Christianity (c. 1). He illustrates this use of secular learning by the "spoiling of the Egyptians" (c. 2); and concludes his appeal by a striking exhortation to Gregory to study Scripture.

G. The Philocalia.—To this admirable collection of extracts from Origen's writings the preservation of many fragments of the Greek text is due. A revised text with critical intro. by Dr. J. A. Robinson is pub. by the Camb. Univ. Press. The collection was made, it appears, by Gregory of Nazianzus and Basil. The former sent it to Theodosius, bp. of Tyana, *c.* 382, with a letter (Greg. Naz. *Ep.* cxv.) in which he says: "That you may have some memorial from us, and at the same time from the holy Basil, we have sent you a small volume of the 'choice thoughts' of Origen (πυκτίον τῆς Ὠριγένους Φιλοκαλίας), containing extracts of passages serviceable for scholars (τοῖς φιλολόγοις). Be pleased to accept it, and to give us some proof of its usefulness with the aid of industry and the Spirit." The Philocalia is of great interest, not only from the intrinsic excellence of passages in it, but as shewing what Catholic saints held to be characteristic thoughts in Origen's teaching.

The book consists of xxvii. chaps., treating of the following subjects: (1) The Inspiration of divine Scripture. How Scripture should be read and understood. (2) That divine Scripture is closed and sealed. (3) Why the Inspired Books [of O.T.] are 22. (4) The solecism and poor style of Scripture. (5) What is "much-speaking," and what are "many books"; and that inspired Scripture is one Book. (6) That divine Scripture is one instrument of God, perfect and fitted (for its work). (7) The special character (τοῦ ἰδιώματος) of the persons of divine Scripture. (8) The duty of not endeavouring to correct the inaccurate (σολοικοειδῆ) phrases of Scripture and those not capable of being understood according to the letter, seeing that they contain deep propriety of thought for those who can understand. (9) What is the reason that divine Scripture often uses the same term in different significations, and (that) in the same place. (10) Passages in divine Scripture which seem to involve difficulties. (11) That we must seek the nourishment supplied by all inspired Scripture, and not turn from the passages (ῥητά) troubled by heretics with ill-advised difficulties (δυσφήμοις ἐπαπορήσεσιν), nor slight them, but make use of them also, being kept from the confusion which attaches to unbelief. (12) That he should not faint in the reading of divine Scripture who does not understand its dark riddles and parables. (13) When and to whom the lessons of philosophy are serviceable to the explanation of the sacred Scriptures, with Scripture testimony. (14) That it is most necessary for those who wish not to fail of the truth in understanding the divine Scriptures to know the logical principles or preparatory discipline (μαθήματα ἤτοι προπαιδεύματα) which apply to their use. (15) A reply to the Greek philosophers who disparage the poverty of the style of the divine Scriptures and maintain that the noble truths in Christianity have been better expressed among the Greeks. (16) Of those who malign Christianity on account of the heresies in the church. (17) A reply to those philosophers who say that it makes no difference if we call Him Who is God over all by the name Zeus, current among the Greeks, or by that used by Indians or Egyptians. (18) A reply to the Greek philosophers who profess universal knowledge, and blame the simple faith (τὸ ἀνεξέταστον τῆς πίστεως) of the mass of Christians, and charge them with preferring folly to wisdom in life; and who say that no wise or educated man has become a disciple of Jesus. (19) That our faith in the Lord has nothing in common with the irrational, superstitious faith of the Gentiles. . . . And in reply to those who say, How do we think that Jesus is God when He had a mortal body? (20) A reply to those who say that the whole world was made, not for man, but for irrational creatures . . . who live with less toil than men . . . and foreknow the future. Wherein is an argument against transmigration and on augury. (21) Of free will, with an explanation of the sayings of Scripture which seem to deny it. (22) What is the dispersion of the rational or human souls indicated under a veil in the building of the Tower, and the confusion of tongues. (23) On Fate, and the reconciliation of divine foreknowledge with human freedom; and how the stars do not determine the affairs of men, but only indicate them. (24) Of matter, that it is not uncreated (ἀγέννητος) or the cause of evil. (25) That the separation to a special work (Rom. i. 1) from foreknowledge does not destroy free will. (26) As to things good and evil. (27) On the phrase, "He hardened Pharaoh's heart."

View of Christian Life.—The picture of Christian life in Origen's writings is less complete and vivid than we might expect. It represents a society already sufficiently large, powerful, and wealthy to offer examples of popular vices. Origen contrasts the Christians of his own with those of an earlier time, and pronounces them unworthy to bear the name of "faithful" (*Hom. in Jer.* iv. 3; cf. *in Matt.* xvii. 24). Some Christians by birth were unduly proud of their descent (*in Matt.* xv. § 26). Others retained their devotion to pagan superstitions—astrology, auguries, necromancy (*in Josh.* v. 6, vii. 4; cf. *in Matt.* xiii. § 6) and secular amusements (*Hom. in Lev.* ix. 9, xi. 1). There were many spiritual "Gibeonites," men who gave liberal offerings to the churches but not their lives (*in Josh.* x. 1, 3). The attendance at church services was infrequent (*in Josh.* i. 7; *Hom. in Gen.* x. 1, 3). The worshippers were inattentive (*Hom. in Ex.* xiii. 2) and impatient (*Hom. in Jud.* vi. 1). Commercial dishonesty (*in Matt.* xv. 13) and hardness (*Sel. in Job.* p. 341 L) had to be reproved. Such faults call out the preacher's denunciations in all ages. An evil more characteristic of his age is the growing ambition of the clergy. High places in the hierarchy were sought by favour and by gifts (*Hom. in Num.* xxii. 4; cf. *in Matt.* xvi. 22; *Comm. Ser.* §§ 9, 10, 12). Prelates endeavoured to nominate their kinsmen as their successors (*ib.* xxii. 4); and shrank from boldly rebuking vice lest they should lose the favour of the people (*in Josh.* vii. 6), using the powers of discipline from passion rather than with judgment (*in Matt. Comm. Ser.* § 14), so that their conduct already caused open scandal (*Hom. in Num.* ii. 17). They too often forgot humility at their ordination (*Hom. in Ezech.* ix. 2). They despised the counsel of men of lower rank, "not to speak of that of a layman or a Gentile" (*Hom. in Ex.* xi. 6). Origen in particular denounces the pride of the leading men in the Christian society, which already exceeded that of Gentile tyrants, especially in the more important cities (*in Matt.* xvi. 8).

Traces still remained in his time of the miraculous endowments of the apostolic church, which he had himself seen (*c. Cels.* ii. 8, iii. 24; *in Joh.* t. xx. 28, ἴχνη καὶ λείμματα; cf. *c. Cels.* i. 2). Exorcism was habitually practised (*Hom. in Jos.* xxiv. 1). Demons were expelled, many cures wrought, future events foreseen by Christians through the help of the Spirit (*c. Cels.* i. 46; cf. i. 25, iii. 36, viii. 58); and he says that the "name of Jesus" was sometimes powerful against demons, even when named by bad men (*c. Cels.* i. 6; cf. v. 45). But this testimony must be taken in conjunction with the belief in magic which he shared with his contemporaries. He appeals unhesitatingly to the efficacy of incantations with the use of sacred names (*c. Cels.* i. 22, iv. 33 ff.; cf. *in Matt. Comm. Ser.* § 110), and otherwise according to secret rules (*c. Cels.* i. 24; *Hom. in Num.* xiii. 4; *in Jos.* xx. *fragm.* ap. *Philoc.* c. xii.).

Origen says little of the relations of Christians to other bodies in the state. The interpenetration of common life by paganism necessarily excluded believers from most public ceremonies and from much social intercourse. It also made them ill-disposed towards art, which was devoted to the old religion (*c. Cels.* iii. 56; *de Orat.* 17), and had not yet found any place in connexion with Christian worship (*c. Cels.* vii. 63 ff.). It is remarkable that while Origen was pre-eminently distinguished for his vindication of the claims of reason (*ib.* i. 13) and of Gentile philosophy, as being the ripest fruit of man's natural powers (cf. *Hom. in Gen.* xiv. 3; *in Ex.* xi. 6) and not their corruption (Tertullian), he still very rarely refers to the literature of secular wisdom in his general writings as ancillary to revelation. He even in some cases refers its origin to "the princes of this world" (*de Princ.* iii. 3, 2); and, in an interesting outline of the course of Gentile education, remarks that it may only accumulate a wealth of sins (*Hom.* iii. *in Ps.* xxxvi. 6). But his directions for dealing with unbelievers are marked by the truest courtesy (*Hom. in Ex.* iv. 9). In spite of his own courageous enthusiasm, he counselled prudence in times of persecution (*in Matt.* x. 23). Occasions for such self-restraint arose continually. For Origen notices the popular judgment, active from the time of Tertullian to that of Augustine, which referred "wars, famines, and pestilences" to the spread of the faith (*in Matt. Comm. Ser.* § 39); especially he dwells upon the animosity of the Jews, who "would rather see a criminal acquitted than convicted by the evidence of a Christian" (*ib.* § 16). Of the extension of Christianity he speaks in general terms, rhetorically rather than exactly. It was not preached among all the Ethiopians, especially "those beyond the river," or among the Chinese. "What," he continues, "shall we say of the Britons or Germans by the Ocean, Dacians, Sarmatians, Scythians, very many of whom have not yet heard the word?" (*ib.* § 39). But some inhabitants of Britain and Mauritania held the faith (*Hom. in Luc.* vi.). Christians generally declined public offices, not from lack of loyalty, but feeling that they could serve their country better through their own society (*c. Cels.* viii. 73, 75).

The church, according to Origen, is the whole body of believers animated by Christ, Who, as the Divine Logos, stirs each member, so that without Him it does nothing (*ib.* vi. 48). In the widest sense it has existed even from the Creation (*in Cant.* ii. p. 418 L.). Such a view, which makes the church coextensive with the existence of divine fellowship, carries with it the corollary, that "without the church there is no salvation" (*Hom. in Jos.* iii. 6). Origen, as has been seen, shewed practically his respect for the see of Rome, but he recognized no absolute supremacy in St. Peter (*in Matt.* xii. 11). He held indeed that he had a certain pre-eminence (*in Joh.* t. xxxii. 5) and that the church was founded on him (*Hom. in Ex.* v. 4), but every disciple of Christ, he affirms, holds in a true sense the same position (*Comm. in Matt.* xii. 10).

Origen lays great stress upon the importance of right belief (*in Matt.* t. xii. 23; *Comm. Ser. in Matt.* § 33; *de Orat.* 29). As a young man he refused every concession to a misbeliever in the house of his benefactress (Eus. *H. E.* vi. 2). In later years he laboured successfully to win back those who had fallen into error. But his sense of the infinite greatness of the truth made him tolerant (*c. Cels.* v. 63). Varieties of belief arose from the very vastness of its object (*ib.* iii. 12); and his discussion of the question, Who is a heretic? is full of interest (*Fragm. in Ep. ad Tit.*).

Casual notices in Origen's writings give a fairly complete view of the current religious observances. He speaks generally of stated times of daily prayer, "not less than three" (*de Orat.* 12), of the days they kept—"the Lord's days (cf. *Hom. in Ex.* vii. 5; *in Num.* xxiii. 4), Fridays, Easter, Pentecost" (*c. Cels.* viii. 22; cf. *Hom. in Is.* vi. § 2)—and of the Lenten, Wednesday, and Friday fasts (*Hom. in Lev.* x. 2). Some still added Jewish rites to the celebration of Easter (*Hom. in Jer.* xii. 13) and other traces remained of Judaizing practices (*ib.* x. § 2). Jewish converts, Origen says without reserve, "have not left their national law" (*c. Cels.* ii. 1, cf. § 3); though he lays down that Christ forbade His disciples to be circumcised (*ib.* i. 22; cf. v. 48). Christians, however, still abstained from "things strangled" (*ib.* viii. 30) and from meat offered to idols (*ib.* 24). Outward forms had already made progress; and the religion of some consisted in "bowing their head to priests, and in bringing offerings to adorn the altar of the church" (*Hom. in Jos.* x. 3).

Baptism was administered to infants, "in accordance with apostolic tradition" (*in Rom.* v. § 9, p. 397 L.; *Hom. in Lev.* viii. § 3; *in Luc.* xiv.), in the name of the Holy Trinity (*in Rom.* v. § 8, p. 383 L.; cf. *in Joh.* t. vi. 17), with the solemn renunciations "of the devil and of his pomps, works, and pleasures" (*Hom. in Num.* xii. 4). The unction (confirmation) does not appear to have been separated from it (*in Rom.* v. § 8, p. 381: "omnes baptizati in aquis istis visibilibus et in chrismate visibili"). The gift of the Holy Spirit comes only from Christ, and Origen held that it was given according to His righteous will: "Not all who are bathed in water are forthwith bathed in the Holy Spirit" (*Hom. in Num.* iii. 1). Cf. also *Sel. in Gen.* ii. 15; *Hom. in Luc.* xxi.; *de Princ.* i. 2; and for the two sacraments, *Hom. in Num.* vii. 2. Adult converts were divided into different classes and trained with great care (*c. Cels.* iii. 51).

Of the Holy Communion Origen speaks not infrequently, but with some reserve (*Hom. in Lev.* x. 10; *in Jos.* iv. 1). The passages which give his views most fully are *in Joh.* xxxii. § 16; *in Matt.* xi. § 14; *in Matt. Comm. Ser.* §§ 85 f.; *Hom. in Gen.* xvii. 8; *in Ex.* xiii. § 3; *in Lev.* ix. 10; *in Num.* xvi. 9. Cf. *c. Cels.* viii. 33, 57; *Hom. in Jud.* vi. 2; *Hom.* ii. *in Ps.* xxxvii. 6; *Sel. in Ps.* p. 365 L. The ruling thought of his interpretation is suggested by John vi.: "corpus Dei Verbi aut sanguis quid aliud esse potest nisi verbum quod nutrit et verbum quod laetificat?" (*in Matt. Comm. Ser.* § 85); "bibere autem dicimur sanguinem Christi non solum sacramentorum ritu sed et cum sermones ejus recipimus in quibus vita consistit, sicut et ipse dicit, *Verba quae locutus sum spiritus et vita est*" (*Hom. in Num.* xvi. § 9; cf. xxiii. § 6). The passage which is often quoted to shew "a presence of Christ in the sacrament *extra usum*," indicates nothing more than the reverence which naturally belongs to the consecrated elements ("consecratum munus," *Hom. in Ex.* xiii. 3). The kiss of peace was still given "at the time of the mysteries" (*in Cant.* i. p. 331 L.) "after prayers" (*in Rom.* x. § 33); and the love-feast (Ἀγάπη) was sufficiently notorious for Celsus to attack it (*c. Cels.* i. 1); but the practice of "feet-washing," if it ever prevailed, was now obsolete (*in Joh.* xxxii. § 7; *Hom. in Is.* vi. § 3). His use of Jas. v. 14, in *Hom. in Lev.* ii. 4, does not give any support, as has been affirmed, to the practice of extreme unction.

The treatise *On Prayer* gives a vivid picture of the mode and attitude of prayer. It was usual to turn to the east (*de Orat.* 31; *Hom. in Num.* v. § 1). Standing and kneeling are both recognized (*de Orat. l.c.*; *Hom. in Num.* xi. § 9; cf. *in Sam. Hom.* i. § 9). Forms of prayer were used (*Hom. in Jer.* xiv. § 14) and prayers made in the vernacular language of each country (*c. Cels.* viii. 31).

Origen frequently refers to confession as made to men and not to God only (*Hom. in Luc.* xvii.; *de Orat.* 28; *Hom.* ii. *in Ps.* xxxvii. § 6); and reckons penitence completed by such confession to a "priest of the Lord" as one of the modes for forgiveness of sins (*Hom.* ii. *in Lev.* § 4). He speaks of public confession (ἐξομολόγησις) to God as efficacious (*Hom.* i. *in Ps.* xxxvi. § 5), a form of penitence to be adopted after wise advice (*ib.* xxxvii. § 6); and he supposes that the efficacy of "the power of the keys" depends upon the character of those who exercise it (*in Matt.* t. xii. § 14). Discipline was enforced by exclusion from common prayer (*in Matt. Comm. Ser.* § 89); and for more serious offences penitence was admitted once only (*Hom. in Lev.* xv. § 2). Cf. also what is said on "sin unto death" (*ib.* xi. 2). Those who had offended grievously after baptism were looked upon as incapable of holding office (*c. Cels.* iii. 51).

The threefold ministry is treated as universally recognized; and Origen speaks of presbyters as priests, and deacons as Levites (*Hom. in Jer.* xii. 3). The people were to be present at the ordination of priests (*Hom. in Lev.* vii. 3) and he recognizes emphatically the priesthood of all Christians who "have been anointed with the sacred chrism" (*ib.* ix. 9; cf. *Hom. in Num.* v. 3; *in Jos.* vii. 2; cf. *Exh. ad Martyr.* 30). Widows are spoken of as having a definite place in the church organization (*Hom. in Is.* vi. § 3; *Hom. in Luc.* xvii.); yet not apparently combined in any order (*in Rom.* x. §§ 17, 20).

As yet no absolute rule existed as to the celibacy of the clergy. Origen himself was inclined to support it by his own judgment (*Hom. in Lev.* vi. § 6). "No bishop, however, or presbyter or deacon or widow could marry a second time" (*Hom. in Luc.* xvii.): such Origen held to be in a second class, not "of the church without spot" (*l.c.*; but cf. note on I. Cor. vii. 8). It was a sign of the difficulties of the time that some "rulers of the church" allowed a woman to marry again while her husband (presumably a Gentile who had abandoned her) was still living (*in Matt.* t. xiv. § 23). Origen's own example and feeling were strongly in favour of a strict and continent life (cf. *c. Cels.* vii. 48; *Hom. in Gen.* v. 4), while he condemns false asceticism (*in Matt. Comm. Ser.* § 10). He enforces the duty of systematic almsgiving (*ib.* § 61); and maintains that the law of offering the firstfruits to God, that is to the priests, is one of the Mosaic precepts which is of perpetual obligation (*Hom. in Num.* xi. 1; cf. *c. Cels.* viii. 34). Usury is forbidden (*Hom.* iii. *in Ps.* xxxvi. § 11). The rule as to food laid down in Acts xv. 29 was still observed (*in Rom.* ii. § 13, p. 128 L; *c. Cels.* viii. 30).

The reverence of Christian burial is noticed (*Hom. in Lev.* iii. § 3; *c. Cels.* viii. 30). Military service Origen thinks unlawful for Christians (*c. Cels.* v. 33, viii. 73), though he seems to admit exceptions (*ib.* iv. 82).

Origen as Critic and Interpreter.—Origen regarded the Bible as the source and rule of truth (*Hom. in Jer.* i. § 7). Christ is "the Truth," and they who are sure of this seek spiritual knowledge from His very words and teaching alone, given not only during His earthly presence, but through Moses and the prophets (*de Princ.* Praef. 1). The necessary points of doctrine were, Origen held, comprised by the apostles in a simple creed handed down by tradition (*ib.* ii.), but the fuller exhibition of the mysteries of the gospel was to be sought from the Scriptures. He made no sharp division between O. and N. T. They must be treated as one body, and we must be careful not to mar the unity of the spirit which exists throughout (*in Joh.* x. 13; cf. *de Princ.* ii. 4). The divinity of the O.T. is indeed first seen through Christ (*de Princ.* iv. 1, 6).

(1) *The Canon of Scripture.*—In fixing the contents of the collection of sacred books Origen shews some indecision. In regard to O.T. he found a serious difference between the Hebrew canon and the books commonly found in the Alexandrine Greek Bible. In his *Comm. on Ps.* i. he gives a list of the canonical books (αἱ ἐνδιάθηκοι βίβλοι) according to the tradition of the Hebrews, 22 in number (*ap.* Eus. *H. E.* vi. 25). In the enumeration the *Book of the Twelve* (minor) *Prophets* is omitted by the error of Eusebius or of his transcriber, for it is necessary to make up the number; and the "Letter" (*Baruch* vi.) is added to Jeremiah, because (apparently) it occupied that position in Origen's copy of the LXX., for there is no evidence that it was ever included in the Hebrew Bible. The *Books of the Maccabees*, which (*I. Macc.*) bore a Hebrew title, were not included (ἔξω τούτων ἐστί). But while Origen thus gives a primary place to the books of the Hebrew Canon, he expressly defends, in his letter to Africanus, the use of the additions found in the Alexandrine LXX. (cf. p. 122). He was unwilling to sacrifice anything sanctioned by custom and tending to edification. His own practice reflects this double view. He never, so far as we know, publicly expounded any apocryphal books of O.T., while he habitually quotes them as having authority, though he frequently notes that their authority was challenged. He quotes the *Book of Enoch* (*c. Cels.* v. 55; *de Princ.* iv. 35; *Hom. in Num.* xxviii. 2), the *Prayer of Joseph* (*in Joh.* ii. 25, εἴ τις προσίεται), the *Assumption of Moses* (*Hom. in Jos.* ii. 1), and the *Ascension of Isaiah* (*ib.*; *de Princ.* iii. 2, 1; cf. *in Matt.* t. x. 18); and it is probably to books of this class that his interesting remarks on "apocryphal" books in *Prol. in Cant.* p. 325 L. refer.

How far Origen was from any clear view of the history of O.T. may be inferred from the importance he assigns to the tradition of Ezra's restoration of their text from memory after the Babylonian captivity (*Sel. in Jer.* xi. p. 5 L.; *Sel. in Ps. id.* p. 371).

His testimony to the contents of N.T. is more decided. He notices the books which were generally acknowledged as possessing unquestionable authority: the *Four Gospels* [the *Acts* *], *I. Peter*, *I. John*, *thirteen Epistles of St. Paul*. To these he adds the *Apocalypse*, for he seems to have been unacquainted with its absence from the Syrian Canon (*ap.* Eus. *H. E.* vi. 25). In another passage, preserved only in the Latin trans. of Rufinus (*Hom. in Jer.* vii. 1), he enumerates all the books of the received N.T., without addition or omission, as the trumpets by which the walls of the spiritual Jericho are to be overthrown (*the Four Gospels*, *I.* and *II. Peter*, *James*, *Jude*, *the Epistles* and *Apocalypse of St. John*, the *Acts* by St. Luke, *fourteen Epistles of St. Paul*). This enumeration, though it cannot be received without reserve, may represent his popular teaching. In isolated notices he speaks of the disputed books as received by some but not by all (*Hebrews*; *ap.* Eus. *H. E.* vi. 25; *Ep. ad Afric.* § 9; *James*; *in Joh.* xix. 6; *II. Peter*; *Hom. in Lev.* iv. 4; *Jude*; *in Matt.* t. x. 17, xvii. 30); and he apparently limited doctrinal authority to the acknowledged books (*Comm. Ser. in Matt.* § 28).

Origen quotes frequently and with the greatest respect the *Shepherd* of Hermas (*e.g. de Princ.* i. 3, 3, iv. 11; *in Matt.* t. xiv. § 21; *in Rom.* x. 31, p. 437 L.).† He quotes or refers to the *Ep.* (i.) *of Clement*, "a disciple of the apostles" (*de Princ.* ii. 3, 6; *in Joh.* t. vi. 36; *Sel. in Ez.* viii. 3); "the *Catholic Ep. of Barnabas*" (*c. Cels.* i. 63; *de Princ.* iii. 2, 4; cf. *Comm. in Rom.* i. § 18), the *Gospel according to the Hebrews* (*in Joh.* t. ii. 6,

* Not specially mentioned, but Origen's usage is decisive as to the position he assigned to it. The tacit omission well illustrates the danger of trusting to negative evidence.

† The statement of Tarinus (*Philoc.* p. 683) that Origen wrote a commentary on the *Shepherd* is a false deduction from the word διηγούμεθα (*ib.* i. p. 22, 11).

ἐὰν προσίεταί τις; *Hom. in Jer.* xv. 4; *in Matt.* t. xv. 14, *Vet. int. Lat.*; cf. Hieron. *de Vir. Ill.* 2), the *Gospels* "*according to the Egyptians*," and "*according to the XII. Apostles*," "*according to Thomas*," and "*after Matthias*" (*Hom.* 1 *in Luc.*, "Ecclesia quatuor habet evangelia, haeresis plurima, e quibus . . .," the *Gospel according to Peter*, the *Book of James* (*in Matt.* x. 17, τοῦ ἐπιγεγραμμένου κατὰ Πέτρον εὐαγγελίου ἢ τῆς βίβλου Ἰακώβου), *Peter's Preaching* (*in Joh.* xiii. 17; *de Princ.* Praef. 8, *Petri doctrina*), the *Acts of Paul* (*in Joh.* xx. 12; *de Princ.* i. 2, 3), the *Clementines* (*Comm. Ser. in Matt.* § 77; *in Gen.* iii. § 14, αἱ περίοδοι), some form of the *Acts of Pilate* (*in Matt. Comm. Ser.* § 122), the *Testaments of the XII. Patriarchs* (*in Joh.* xv. 6), the *Teaching of the Apostles* (?) (*Hom. in Lev.* xi. 2).

Sayings attributed to the Lord are given *in Matt.* t. xiii. § 2, xvi. § 28 (*Sel. in Ps.* p. 432 L and *de Orat.* §§ 2, 14, 16; cf. Matt. vi. 33), xvii. § 31; *in Jos.* iv. 3. A few traditions are preserved: *in Matt. Comm. Ser.* § 126 (Adam buried on Calvary); *ib.* § 25 (death of the father of John Baptist); *c. Cels.* i. 51 (the cave and manger at Bethlehem); *ib.* vi. 75 (the appearance of Christ); *Hom. in Ezech.* i. 4 (the baptism of Christ in January).

Anonymous quotations occur, *Hom. in Luc.* xxxv.; *Comm. Ser. in Matt.* § 61; *Hom. in Ezech.* i. 5; *in Rom.* ix. § 2.

(2) *The Text.*—Origen had very little of the critical spirit, in the modern acceptation of the phrase. This is especially seen in his treatment of Biblical texts. His importance for textual criticism is that of a witness and not of a judge. He gives invaluable evidence as to what he found, but his few endeavours to determine what is right, in a conflict of authorities, are for the most part unsuccessful both in method and result. Generally, however, he makes no attempt to decide on the one right reading. He would accept all the conflicting readings as contributing to edification. Even his great labours on the Greek translations of O.T. were not directed rigorously to the definite end of determining the authentic text, but mainly to recording the extent and character of the variations. He then left his readers to use their own judgment.

This want of a definite critical aim is more decisively shewn in his treatment of N.T. Few variations are more remarkable than those in Heb. ii. 9: χάριτι θεοῦ and χωρὶς θεοῦ. Origen was acquainted with both, and apparently wholly undesirous to choose between them; both gave a good sense and that was a sufficient reason for using both (*in Joh.* t. i. 40: εἴτε δὲ χωρὶς θεοῦ . . . εἴτε χάριτι . . . *ib.* xxviii. 14: the Latin of *Comm. in Rom.* iii. § 8, v. § 7, *sine Deo*, is of no authority for Origen's judgment).

His importance as a witness to the true text of N.T. is, nevertheless, invaluable. Notwithstanding the late date and scantiness of the MSS. in which his Greek writings have been preserved, and the general untrustworthiness of the Latin translations in points of textual detail, it would be possible to determine a pure text of a great part of N.T. from his writings alone (cf. Griesbach, *Symb. Crit.* t. ii.). In some respects his want of a critical spirit makes his testimony of greater value than if he had followed consistently an independent judgment. He reproduces the characteristic readings which he found, and thus his testimony is carried back to an earlier date. At different times he used copies exhibiting different complexions of text; so that his writings reflect the variations faithfully. But great care is required in using the evidence which Origen's quotations furnish. He frequently quotes from memory; combines texts; and sometimes gives repeatedly a reading which he can hardly have found in any MS. (*e.g.* I. John iii. 8, γεγέννηται). Illustrations of this perplexing laxity occur in *Hom. in Jer.* i. 15 (Matt. iii. 12, xiii. 39); *ib.* iv. 2, v. 1 (Acts xiii. 26, 46); *ib.* iv. 4 (Luke xviii. 12); *ib.* v. 1 (Tit. iii. 5 f.).

(3) *Interpretation.*—Origen has been spoken of as the founder of a new form of literature in Biblical interpretation, and justly; though others, conspicuously Heracleon, preceded him in expositions of Scripture more or less continuous. Origen constantly refers to previous interpretors, esp. to Heracleon.

Origen's method of interpreting Scripture was a practical deduction from his view of the inspiration of Scripture. This he developed in the treatise *On First Principles*, bk. iv. He regarded every "jot and tittle" as having its proper work (*Hom. in Jer.* xxxix. fr. ep. *Philoc.* c. x.). All is precious; not even the least particle is void of force (*in Matt.* t. xvi. 12). Cf. *Ep. ad Greg.* § 3; *in Joh.* t. i. § 4. Minute details of order and number veil and yet suggest great thoughts (*e.g. Sel. in Pss.* xi. 370, 377 L). It follows that in interpretation there is need of great exactness and care (*in Gen.* t. iii. p. 46 L.; *Philoc.* xiv.) and scrupulous study of details (*in Joh.* xx. 29). Origen illustrates his principles by countless subtle observations of great interest. His skill in combining passages from different parts of Scripture in illustration of some particular phrase or detail is specially noticeable. Each term calls up far-reaching associations; and all Scripture is made to contribute to the fullness of the thought to be expressed.

Though Origen's critical knowledge of Hebrew was slight, he evidently learnt much from Hebrew interpreters and not unfrequently quotes Hebrew traditions and "Midrash." He gives also an interpretation of "Corban" (*in Matt.* t. xi. 9) and of "Iscariot" (*in Matt. Comm. Ser.* 78) from Jewish sources.

To obviate the moral and historical difficulties of O.T. he systematized the theory of a "spiritual sense," which was generally if vaguely admitted by the church (*de Princ.* 1, Praef. 8). There is, he taught, generally, a threefold meaning in the text of the Bible, literal (historical), moral, mystical, corresponding to the three elements in man's constitution, body, soul, and spirit (*de Princ.* iv. 11; *Hom. in Lev.* v. §§ 1, 5). Thus Scripture has a different force for different ages and different readers, according to their circumstances and capacities (*in Rom.* ii. § 14, p. 150 L.). But all find in it what they need.

This threefold sense is to be sought both in O. and N. T. The literal interpretation brings out the simple precept or fact; the moral meets the individual want of each believer; the mystical illuminates features in the whole work of Redemption (*Hom. in Lev.* i. §§ 4 f., ii. § 4; *de Princ.* iv. 12, 13, 22). There is then manifold instruction for all believers in the precise statement, the definition of practical duties, the revelation of the divine plan, which the teacher must endeavour to bring out in his examination of the text. Origen steadily kept this object in view.

It is easy to point out serious errors in detail in his interpretation of Scripture. On these there is no need to dwell. His main defect and the real source of his minor faults was his lack of true historic feeling. For him prophecy ceased to have any vital connexion with the trials and struggles of a people of God; and psalms (*e.g.* Ps. l.) were no longer the voice of a believer's deepest personal experience. In this Origen presents, though in a modified form, many of the characteristic defects of Rabbinic interpretation. He may have been directly influenced by the masters of Jewish exegesis. Just as they claimed for Abraham the complete fulfilment of the Law, and made the patriarchs perfect types of legal righteousness, Origen refused to see in the Pentateuch any signs of inferior religious knowledge or attainment. He deemed the patriarchs and prophets as wise by God's gifts as the apostles (*in Joh.* vi. 3); and the deepest mysteries of Christian revelation could be directly illustrated from their lives and words (*ib.* ii. 28), though sometimes he seems to feel the difficulties of this position (*ib.* xiii. 46; cf. *c. Cels.* vii. 4 ff.).

While this grave defect is distinctly acknowledged, it must be remembered that Origen had a special work to do, and did it. In his time powerful schools of Christian speculation disparaged the O.T. or rejected it. Christian masters had not yet been able to vindicate it from the Jews and for themselves. This task Origen accomplished. From his day the O.T. has been a part of our Christian heritage, and he fixed rightly the general spirit in which it is to be received. The O.T., he says, is always new to Christians who understand and expound it spiritually and in an evangelic sense, new not in time but in interpretation (*Hom. in Num.* ix. § 4; cf. *c. Cels.* ii. 4). If in pressing this he was led to exaggeration, the error may be pardoned in regard to the greatness of the service.

His method was fixed and consistent. He systematized what was before tentative and inconstant (cf. Redepenning, *de Princ.* pp. 56 f.). He laid down, once for all, broad outlines of interpretation; and mystical meanings were not arbitrarily devised to meet particular emergencies. The influence of his views is a sufficient testimony to their power. It is not too much to say that the medieval interpretation of Scripture in the West was inspired by Origen; and through secondary channels these medieval comments have passed into our own literature.

He was indeed right in principle. "He felt that there was something more than a mere form in the Bible; he felt that 'the words of God' must have an eternal significance, for all that comes into relation with God is eternal; he felt that there is a true development and a real growth in the elements of divine revelation, if not in divine communication, yet in human apprehension; he felt the power and the glory of the spirit of Scripture bursting forth from every part." No labour was too great to bestow upon the text in which priceless treasures were enshrined; no hope too lofty for the interpreter to cherish.

Origen as a Theologian.—Origen was essentially the theologian of an age of transition. His writings present principles, ruling ideas, tendencies, but are not fitted to supply materials for a system of formulated dogmas, after the type of later confessions. Every endeavour to arrange his opinions according to the schemes of the 16th cent. can only issue in a misunderstanding of their general scope and proportion. The whole structure of his treatise *On First Principles*, *e.g.*, presents a connected view of his intellectual apprehension of Christianity, widely different from medieval and modern expositions of the faith. Starting from a clear and deeply interesting exposition of what were acknowledged to be the doctrines held generally by the church, corresponding in the main with the Apostles' Creed (*de Princ.* Praef.), Origen endeavours to determine, by the help of Scripture and reason, subjects yet unexplored. But his inquiries and results cannot be judged fairly when taken out of their connexion with contemporary thought. The book contains very little technical teaching. It is silent as to the sacraments; it gives no theory of the atonement, no discussion of justification; yet deals with problems of thought and life which lie behind these subjects.

Origen found himself face to face with powerful schools which, within and without the church, maintained antagonistic views on man, the world, and God, in their extremest forms. There was the false realism, which found expression in Montanism; the false idealism, which spread widely in the many forms of Gnosticism. Here the Creator was degraded into a secondary place; there God Himself was lost in His works. Some represented men as inherently good or bad from their birth; others swept away moral distinctions of action. Origen sought to maintain two great truths: the unity of all creation, as answering to the thought of a Creator infinitely good and infinitely just; and the power of moral determination in rational beings. The treatment and apprehension of these truths are modified by the actual fact of sin. The power of moral determination has issued in present disorder; the divine unity of creation has to be realized hereafter.

(1) *Finite Beings, Creation, Man, Spirits.*—Origen endeavours to pass from the outward to the inward, from the temporal to the eternal. He thinks that we shall best realize the fact of creation, according to our present powers, by supposing a vast succession of orders, one springing out of another (*de Princ.* ii. 1, 3). The present order, which began and will end in time, must be one only in the succession of corresponding orders (*ib.* iii. 5, 3). "In the beginning," then, he writes, "when God created what He was pleased to create, that is rational natures, He had no other cause of creation beside Himself, that is His own goodness" (*ib.* ii. 9, 6; cf. iv. 35). This

creation answered to a definite thought, and therefore, Origen argues, was definite itself. God "could" not create or embrace in thought that which has no limit (*ib.* ii. *fragm. Gr.* 6; ii. 9, 1; iv. *fragm. Gr.* 4). The rational creatures He made were all originally equal, spiritual, free. But moral freedom, including personal self-determination, led to difference. Finite creatures, once made, either advanced, through imitation of God, or fell away, through neglect of Him (*ib.* ii. 9, 6).

Evil, it follows, is negative—the loss of good which was attainable, the shadow which marks the absence or rather the exclusion of light. But as God made creatures for an end, so He provided that they should, through whatever discipline of sorrow, attain it. He made matter also, which might serve as a fitting expression for their character, and become, in the most manifold form, a medium for their training. So it was that, by various declensions, "spirit" (πνεῦμα) lost its proper fire and was chilled into a "soul" (ψυχή), and "souls" were embodied in our earthly frames in this world of sense. Such an embodiment was a provision of divine wisdom which enabled them, in accord with the necessities of the fact, to move towards the accomplishment of their destiny (*ib.* i. 7, 4).

Under this aspect man is a microcosm. (*Hom. in Gen.* i. 11; *in Lev.* v. 2: *intellige te et alium mundum esse parvum et intra te esse solem, esse lunam, etiam stellas.*) He stands in the closest connexion with the seen and the unseen; and is himself the witness of the correspondences which exist between visible and invisible orders (*Hom. in Num.* xi. 4, xvii. 4, xxiv. 1, xxviii. 2; *Hom.* i. *in Ps.* xxxvii. 1; *in Joh.* t. xix. 5, xxiii. 4; *de Princ.* iv. *fragm. Gr.* p. 184 R.). He is made for the spiritual and cannot find rest elsewhere.

As a necessary consequence of his deep view of man's divine kinsmanship, Origen labours to give distinctness to the unseen world. He appears already to live and move in it. He finds there the realities of which the phenomena of earth are shadows (cf. *in Rom.* x. § 39). External objects, peoples, cities, are to him veils and symbols of invisible things; and not only is there the closest correspondence between the constitution of different orders of being, but also even now a continuation of unobserved intercourse between them (cf. *de Princ.* ii. 9, 3). Angels (*ib.* i. 8, iii. 2, *passim*) preside over the working of elemental forces, over plants and beasts (*in Num. Hom.* xiv. 2; *in Jer. Hom.* x. 6; *c. Cels.* viii. 31; *de Princ.* iii. 3, 3), and it is suggested that nature is affected by their moral condition (*in Ezech. Hom.* iv. 2). More particularly men were, in Origen's opinion, committed to the care of spiritual "rulers," and deeply influenced by changes in their feeling and character (*in Joh.* xiii. § 58; cf. *de Princ.* i. 8, 1). Thus he recognized guardian angels of cities, provinces and nations (*Hom. in Luc.* xii.; *de Princ.* iii. 3, 2), a belief which he supported habitually by the LXX version of Deut. xxxii. 8 (*in Matt.* t. xi. § 16; *in Luc. Hom.* xxxv.; *in Rom.* viii. § 8; *in Gen. Hom.* xvi. 2; *in Ex. Hom.* viii. 2; *in Ezech. Hom.* xiii. 1 f., etc.). Individual men also had their guardian angels (*in Matt.* t. xiii. 27; *in Luc. Hom.* xxxv.; *in Num. Hom.* xi. 4, xx. 3; *in Ezech. Hom.* i. 7; *in Jud.* vi. 2; *de Princ.* iii. 2, 4); and angels in the assemblies of Christians assisted the devotions of the faithful (*de Orat.* xxxi. p. 283 L.; *Hom. in Luc.* xxiii.; *c. Cels.* viii. 64). But while Origen recognizes most fully the reality and power of angelic ministration, he expressly condemns all angel-worship (*c. Cels.* v. 4, 11).

On the other hand, there are spiritual hosts of evil corresponding to the angelic forces and in conflict with them (*in Matt.* t. xvii. 2; *in Matt. Comm. Ser.* § 102; *Hom. in Jos.* xv. 5). He even speaks of a Trinity of evil (*in Matt.* xi. § 6, xii. § 20). An evil power strives with the good for the sway of individuals (*in Rom.* i. § 18); thus all life is made a struggle of unseen powers (*e.g.* notes on Ps. xxxvii.; *in Joh.* xx. §§ 29, 32; *Hom.* xx. *in Jos. Fragm.*).

One aspect of this belief had a constant and powerful influence on daily life. Origen, like most of his contemporaries, supposed that evil spiritual beings were the objects of heathen worship (*c. Cels.* vii. 5). There was, for him, a terrible reality in their agency. Within certain limits they could work so as to bind their servants to them.

Origen believed also that the dead, too, influenced the living. The actions of men on earth last, in their effects, after the actors have departed (*in Rom.* ii. 4, p. 80 L.). Disembodied (or unembodied) souls are not idle (*in Matt.* xv. 35). So the "soul" of Christ preached to "souls" (*c. Cels.* iii. 43); and the saints sympathize with man still struggling on earth with a sympathy larger than that of those who are clogged by conditions of mortality (*de Orat.* xi.; *in Matt.* t. xxvii. 30; *in Joh.* t. xiii. 57; iii. *in Cant.* 7).

Without extenuating the effects of man's sin, Origen maintained a lofty view of the nobility of his nature and destiny (*c. Cels.* iv. 25, 30); held that the world had been made by divine wisdom a fitting place for the purification of a being such as man (*de Princ.* ii. 1, 1; 2, 2; 3, 1; *c. Cels.* vi. 44; cf. *in Rom.* viii. 10, p. 261); and that everything has been so ordered by Providence from the first as to contribute to this end (*de Princ.* ii. 1, 2). Man can, if he will, read the lesson of his life: he has a spiritual faculty, by which he can form conclusions on spiritual things, even as he is made to form conclusions on impressions of sense. The body, so to speak, reflects the soul; the "outer man" expresses the "inner man" (*in Rom.* ii. 13, p. 142 L.). There is imposed upon us the duty of service (*in Matt. Comm. Ser.* § 66), and the offices are many (*in Joh.* t. x. 23), room being made even for the meanest (*Hom. in Num.* xiv. 2, p. 162 L.).

The visible creation thus bears, in all its parts, the impress of a divine purpose; and the Incarnation was the crowning of the creation, by which the purpose was made fully known, and provision made for its accomplishment (*de Princ.* iii. 5, 6).

(2) *The Incarnation. The Person of Christ. The Holy Trinity. The Work of Christ.*—On no subject is Origen more full or suggestive (*de Princ.* i. 2; ii. 6; iv. 31). No one perhaps has done so much to vindicate and harmonize the fullest acknowledgment of the perfect humanity of the Lord and of His perfect divinity in one Person. His famous image of

the "glowing iron" (*ib.* ii. 6, 6) made an epoch in Christology. Here and there his language is liable to misconception, or even proved erroneous by later investigations, but he laid down outlines of the faith, on the basis of Scripture, which remain unshaken. He maintained the true and perfect manhood of Christ, subject to the conditions of natural growth, against all forms of Docetism; and, on the other hand, the true and perfect divinity of the "God-Word" (θεὸς λόγος), so united with "the man Christ Jesus" through the human soul as to be one person, against all forms of Ebionism and Patripassionism (*ib.* ii. 6, 3).

His doctrine of the Incarnation of the God-Word rests in part upon his doctrine of the Godhead. "All," he held, "who are born again unto salvation have need of the Father, Son, and Holy Spirit, and would not obtain salvation unless the Trinity were entire" (*ib.* i. 3, 5). Hence he speaks of baptism as "the beginning and fountain of divine gifts to him who offers himself to the divinity of the power of the invocations of the adorable Trinity" (τῶν τῆς προσκυνητῆς τριάδος ἐπικλήσεων) (*in Joh.* vi. 17). But there is, in his judgment, a difference in the extent of the action of the Persons in the Holy Trinity. The Father, "holding all things together, reaches (φθάνει) to each being, imparting being to each from that which is His own, for He is absolutely (ὢν γὰρ ἔστιν). The Son is less than the Father (ἐλάττων παρὰ τ. π.), reaching only to rational beings, for He is second to the Father; and, further, the Holy Spirit is less (ἧττον), and extends (διικνούμενον) to the saints only. So that in this respect (κατὰ τοῦτο) the power of the Father is greater in comparison with (παρά) the Son and the Holy Spirit; and that of the Son more in comparison with the Holy Spirit; and, again, the power of the Holy Spirit more exceeding (διαφέρουσα μᾶλλον) in comparison with all other holy beings." To rightly understand this passage it is necessary to observe that Origen is not speaking of the essence of the Persons of the Godhead, but of their manifestation to creatures (cf. *de Princ.* i. 3, 7). Essentially the three Persons are of one Godhead, and eternal. The subordination which Origen teaches is not of essence but of person and office. His aim is to realize the Father as the one Fountain of Godhead, while vindicating true deity for the Son and the Holy Spirit. In this respect he worked out first the thought of "the eternal generation" of the Son, which was accepted from him by the Catholic church as the truest human expression of one side of the mystery of the essential Trinity.

The peculiar connexion which Origen recognizes between the Son (the God Word) and rational beings establishes (so to speak) the fitness of the Incarnation. The Son stood in a certain affinity with rational souls; and the human soul with which He was united in the Incarnation had alone remained absolutely pure, by the exercise of free choice, in its pre-existence (*ib.* ii. 6, 5). Through this union all human nature was capable of being glorified, without violating its characteristic limitations (cf. *c. Cels.* iii. 41 f.). The body of Christ was perfect no less than His soul (*ib.* i. 32 f.).

The work of Christ was, Origen emphatically maintained, for all men and for the whole of man (cf. *ib.* iii. 17; iv. 3 f.). It was therefore so revealed that it could be apprehended according to the several powers and wants of believers (*in Matt.* t. xii. 36, 41, xv. 241, xvii. 19; *c. Cels.* iv. 15, vi. 68; *in Joh.* ii. 12). Christ became, in a transcendent sense, "all things to all men" (*de Princ.* iv. 31; *in Joh.* t. xix. 1, xx. 28; cf. *c. Cels.* iii. 79).

Origen thus insists on the efficacy of Christ's work for the consummation of humanity and of the individual, as a victory over every power of evil. He dwells no less earnestly upon the value of the life and death of Christ as a vicarious sacrifice for sin. He seeks illustrations of the general idea of the power of vicarious sufferings in Gentile stories of self-sacrifice (*c. Cels.* i. 31), and extends it to the case of martyrs (*Exh. ad Mart.* c. 42; cf. *in Joh.* t. vi. 36; xxviii. 14). Though he does not attempt to explain how the sacrifice of Christ was efficacious, he frequently presents it as a ransom given to redeem man from Satan, to whom sin had made man a debtor. Christ, in His own person, freely paid the debt, by bearing the utmost punishment of sin, and so set man free, "giving His soul (ψυχή) as a ransom for him" (*in Matt.* t. xvi. 8; *in Rom.* ii. 13, p. 140 L.; *Comm. Ser. in Matt.* § 135). At other times he regards it as a propitiation for the divine remission of sins (*Hom. in Num.* xxiv. 1; *in Lev.* i. 3; cf. *c. Cels.* vii. 17).

Origen held that the death of Christ was of avail for heavenly beings, if not for the expiation of sin yet for advancement in blessedness (*Hom. in Lev.* i. 3, ii. 3; *in Rom.* v. *s.f.*, p. 409 L.; *ib.* i. 4; *Hom. in Luc.* x.). Thus in a true sense angels themselves were disciples of Christ (*in Matt.* t. xv. 7). At times indeed Origen speaks as if he supposed that the Word was actually manifested to other orders of being in a manner corresponding to their nature, even as He was revealed as soul to the souls in Hades (*Sel. in Ps.* iii. 5, xi. p. 420 L.). In this sense also he thinks that "He became all things to all," an angel to angels (*in Joh.* t. i. 34); and he does not shrink from allowing that His passion may be made available, perhaps in some other shape, in the spiritual world (*de Princ.* iv. *frag. Gr.* 2; cf. iv. 25, L.).

The work of the Holy Spirit, according to Origen, is fulfilled in believers. His office is specially to guide to the fuller truth, which is the inspiration of nobler life. Through Him revelation comes home to men. He lays open the deeper meanings of the word. Through Him, "Who proceeds from the Father," all things are sanctified (*de Princ.* iii. 5, 8). Through Him every divine gift, wrought by the Father and ministered by the Son, gains its individual efficiency (*in Joh.* t. ii. 6). Thus there is a unity in the divine operations, which tends to establish a unity in created beings. (For the doctrine of the Holy Spirit generally see *de Princ.* i. 3, iii. 7; *in Joh.* t. ii. 6.)

(3) *The Consummation of Being.*—These characteristic lines of speculation lead to Origen's view of the consummation of things. All human thought must fail in the endeavour to give distinctness to a conception which ought to embrace the ideas of perfect rest and perfect

life. Origen's opinions are further embarrassed by the constant confusion which arises from the intermingling of ideas which belong to the close of the present order (αἰών) and the close of all things. It is again impossible to see clearly how the inalienable freedom of rational beings, which originally led to the Fall, can be so disciplined as to bring them at last to perfect harmony. This, however, Origen holds; and though he is unable to realize the form of future purification, through which souls left unpurified by earthly existence will be cleansed hereafter, he clings to the belief that "the end must be like the beginning" (*de Princ.* i. 6, 2), a perfect unity in God. From this he excludes no rational creature. The evil spirits which fell have not lost that spirit by which they are akin to God, which in its essence is inaccessible to evil (*in Joh.* xxxii. 11, ἀνεπίδεκτον τῶν χειρόνων τὸ πνεῦμα τοῦ ἀνθρώπου), though it can be overgrown and overpowered (cf. *de Princ.* i. 8, 3). And, on the other hand, freedom remains even when perfect rest has been reached, and in this Origen appears to find the possibility of future declensions (*ib.* ii. 3, 3, *frag. Gr.* ii. 2). Whether matter, the medium through which rational freedom finds expression (*ib.* iv. 35), will at last cease to be, or be infinitely spiritualized, he leaves undetermined. The question is beyond man's powers (*ib.* i. 6, 4; ii. 2; ii. 3, 3; iii. 6, 1), though man cannot but ponder upon it (*ib.* i. 6, 1 f.; iii. 4, 5 *s.f.*). So he presents, in imaginary outlines, the picture of the soul's progress through various scenes of chastisement or illumination (*ib.* i. 6, 3; iii. 6, 6; iii. 5, 6 ff., and Redepenning's note), till he can rest in the thought of a restoration in which law and freedom, justice and love, are brought to a perfect harmony (cf. *de Orat.* § 27, p. 227 L.). This thought assists Origen in forming a theory of future punishments. All future punishments exactly answer to individual sinfulness (*in Matt. Comm. Ser.* § 16), and, like those on earth, are directed to the amendment of the sufferers (*c. Cels.* iv. 10; *Hom. in Ezech.* v. 1). Lighter offences can be chastised on earth; the heavier remain to be visited hereafter (*Hom. in Lev.* xiv. 4). In every case the uttermost farthing must be paid, though final deliverance is promised (*in Rom.* v. 2 f.). Origen looked forward to a fiery ordeal, through which men should pass in the world to come. Every one already baptized with water and Spirit would, he thought, if he needed cleansing, be baptized by the Lord Jesus in a river of fire, and so purified enter into paradise (*Hom. in Luc.* xxiv.). In this sense also he looked forward to a (spiritual) conflagration of the world, by which all beings in need of such discipline should be at once chastised and healed (*c. Cels.* v. 15; cf. iv. 13).

On the other hand, since the future state is the direct fruit of this, there are, so Origen held, varieties of blessedness in heaven (*in Rom.* iv. 12), corresponding to the life of saints (*ib.* ix. 3, p. 303), and foreshadowed by the divisions of Israel (*Hom. in Num.* i. 3; xxviii. 2; *Hom. in Jos.* xxv. 4). Speaking generally, the believer after death enters a state of fuller knowledge and loftier progress (*de Princ.* ii. 11, 6). The resurrection of the body completes the full transfiguration, without loss, of all that belongs to his true self; and he begins a nobler development of body and soul—moral, intellectual, spiritual—by which he is brought nearer to the throne of God (cf. *ib.* i. 3, 8; *in Matt. Comm. Ser.* § 51; *Hom.* i. *in Ps.* xxxviii. § 8). The relationships of earth come to an end (*in Matt.* t. xvii. 33: on this point Origen is not consistent). The visible ceases, and men enjoy the eternal, for which now they hope (*in Rom.* vii. 5). Thus human interest is removed from the present earth to its heavenly antitype. It is probably due to this peculiarity of his teaching that Origen nowhere dwells on the doctrine of Christ's return, which occupies a large place in most schemes of Christian belief. The coming of Christ in glory is treated as the spiritual revelation of His true nature (*de Princ.* iv. 25), though Origen says that he by no means rejects "the second presence (ἐπιδημία) of the Son of God more simply understood" (*in Matt.* t. xii. 30).

Characteristics.—It cannot be surprising that Origen failed to give a consistent and harmonious embodiment to his speculations. His writings represent an aspiration rather than a system, principles of research and hope rather than determined formulas; and his enthusiasm continually mars the proportion of his work. His theorizing needs the discipline of active life, without which there can be no real appreciation of history or of the historical development of truth. Yet even in regard to the practical apprehension of the divine education of the world it is only necessary to compare him on one side with Philo and on the other with Augustine, to feel how his grasp of the significance of the Incarnation gave him a sovereign power to understand the meaning and destiny of life.

While ready to fully acknowledge the claims of reason (cf. *Hom. in Luc.* i. p. 88 L.), Origen lays stress on the new data given by revelation to the solution of the problems of philosophy (*de Princ.* i. 5, 4). He points out repeatedly the insufficiency of reason, of the independent faculties of man, to attain that towards which it is turned. Reason enables man to recognize God when He makes Himself known, to receive a revelation from Him in virtue of his affinity with the Divine Word, but it does not enable the creature to derive from within the longed-for knowledge. The capacity for knowing God belongs to man as man, and not to man as a philosopher. Origen therefore acknowledges the nobility of Plato's saying that "it is a hard matter to find out the Maker and Father of the Universe, and impossible for one who has found Him to declare Him to all men." But he adds that Plato affirms too much and too little (*c. Cels.* vii. 43). As Christians "we declare that human nature is not in itself competent in any way to seek God and find Him purely without the help of Him Who is sought, of Him Who is found by those who confess after they have done all in their power that they have yet need of Him . . ." (cf. Clem. Al. *Cohort.* § 6).

In the endeavour to fashion a Philosophy of Christianity Origen did not practically recognize the limits and imperfection of the human mind which he constantly points out. His gravest errors are attempts to solve the insoluble. The question of the origin of the soul, *e.g.*, is still beset by the difficulties Origen sought to meet, but they are ignored. So too with regard to his speculations on an endless succession of worlds. Thought must break down soon in the attempt to co-ordinate the finite and the infinite. But with whatever errors in detail, Origen laid down the true lines on which the Christian apologist must defend the faith against Polytheism, Judaism, Gnosticism, Materialism. These forms of opinion, without the church and within, were living powers of threatening proportions in his age, and he vindicated the Gospel against them as the one absolute revelation, prepared through the discipline of Israel, historical in its form, spiritual in its destiny; and the principles which he affirmed and strove to illustrate have a present value. They are fitted to correct the Africanism which, since Augustine, has dominated Western theology; and they anticipate many difficulties which have become prominent in later times. In the face of existing controversies, it is invigorating to feel that, when as yet no necessity forced upon him the consideration of the problems now most frequently discussed, a Christian teacher, the master and friend of saints, taught the moral continuity and destination of all being, interpreted the sorrows and sadnesses of the world as part of a vast scheme of purificatory chastisement, found in Holy Scripture not the letter only but a living voice eloquent with spiritual mysteries, made the love of truth, in all its amplitude and depth, the right and end of rational beings, and reckoned the fuller insight into the mysteries of nature one of the joys of a future state.

Such thoughts bring Origen himself before us. Of the traits of his personal character little need be said. He bore unmerited sufferings without a murmur. He lived only to work. He combined in a signal degree sympathy with zeal. As a controversialist he sought to win his adversary, not simply to silence him (cf. Eus. *H. E.* vi. 33). He had the boldest confidence in the truth he held and the tenderest humility as to his own weakness (*in Joh.* t. xxxii. 18; *in Matt.* t. xvi. 13). When he ventures freely in the field of interpretations, he asks the support of the prayers of his hearers. His faith was catholic, and therefore he welcomed every kind of knowledge as tributary to its fullness. It was living, and therefore he knew that no age could seal any one expression of it as complete. This open-hearted trust kept unchilled to the last the passionate devotion of his youth. He was therefore enabled to leave to the church the conviction, attested by a life of martyrdom, that all things are its heritage because all things are Christ's.

Editions.—Through the labours of the great Benedictines of St. Maur the first two vols. of a complete edition of Origen (*Origenis opera omnia quae Graece vel Latine tantum extant et ejus nomine circumferuntur*) appeared at Paris in 1733, under the editorship of Charles Delarue, a priest of that society. Vol. iii. appeared at Paris in 1740, a few months after the death of the editor (Oct. 1739), who left, however, vol. iv. to the care of his nephew C. V. Delarue, who was not able to issue it till 1759. The service the two Delarues rendered was great; but their edition is very far from satisfying the requirements of scholarship. The collations of MSS. are fragmentary and even inaccurate; the text is only partially revised; the notes are inadequate. Later edd., particularly that of Lommatsch, have added little. This is the more to be regretted, as large additions have been, and are being, made to the Origenian fragments. These materials have been either wholly neglected or only partially used in the latest edd.; and practically nothing has been done to improve or illustrate the text. Migne's reprint of Delarue, in his *Patr. Gk.* t. xi.-xvii. (Paris, 1857), has the additions from Galland, most of those from Mai, and one fragment from Cramer as a supplement. An ed. of the *Philosophumena* (*e codice Parisino*), ed. by E. Miller, is pub. by the Clar. Press. A new ed. of Origen's works is now being pub. in the Berlin collection of early eccl. Gk. writers; Origen's *Werke*, i.-ii. von P. Koetshau (Leipz. 1899), vol. iii. ed. by Klostermann, and vol. iv. ed. by Preuschen (Berlin, 1903). A trans. of the *de Principiis*, the books *against Celsus* and the letters, with a life of Origen, is in 2 vols. of the *Ante-Nicene Lib. of the Fathers*. [W.]

Orosius, Paulus, was a native of Tarragona in Spain, as he himself says (*Hist.* vii. 22), though an expression in a letter of Avitus may be thought to connect him with Braga (*Ep. Aviti*, Aug. *Opp.* vol. vii. p. 806; Baronius, vol. v. p. 435, A.D. 415). When the Alani and Vandals were introduced into Spain, A.D. 409, Orosius, though his language is somewhat rhetorical, appears narrowly to have escaped their violence (*Hist.* iii. 20; v. 2; vii. 40). But a danger, more serious in his opinion, soon threatened to disturb the church in Spain, viz. the heresies of the Priscillianists and of the book by Origen, περὶ ἀρχῶν, lately translated by St. Jerome and brought from Jerusalem by Avitus, presbyter of Braga in Portugal, at the same time as a book by Victorinus was brought by another Avitus from Rome. Both books condemned the doctrines of Priscillian, but contained errors of their own. That by Victorinus attracted little notice, but Origen's was widely read, both in Spain and elsewhere; and Orosius, in his zeal against error, proceeded, not commissioned by the church of Spain but on his own account, to Africa, to consult St. Augustine as to how best to refute these heretical doctrines, A.D. 415. Augustine speaks of him as young in years, but a presbyter in rank, zealous, alert in intellect, ready of speech, and fitted to be useful in the work of the Lord. He gave a partial reply to this appeal in his treatise *contra Priscillianistas et Origenistas*, saying but little on the subject which forms its title. He referred Orosius to his books against Manicheism, and recommended him to go to Palestine, the seat of the errors in question, to consult St. Jerome. [Pelagius.] Orosius was kindly received by St. Jerome at Bethlehem; but being summoned by the clergy, he attended a synod at Jerusalem on July 28, in which he took his seat under the direction of John the bishop, and informed the assembly that Coelestius had been condemned by a council in Africa, A.D. 412 (Aug. *Epp.* 175, 176), and had abruptly departed from the country; that Augustine had written against Pelagius and had sent a letter to the clergy in Sicily, treating of this and other heretical questions, which letter Orosius read at the request of the members. He also quoted the judgment of St. Jerome on the Pelagian question, expressed in his letter to Ctesiphon and his Dialogue against the Pelagians (Hieron. vol. i. *Ep.* 133; vol. ii. p. 495). On Sept. 13, the feast of the dedication of the church of the Holy Sepulchre, Orosius, on offering to assist bp. John at the altar, was attacked by him as a blasphemer, a charge which Orosius refuted, saying that as he spoke only in Latin, John, who only spoke Greek, could not have understood him. At the council of 14 bishops at Diospolis (Lydda), Dec. 415, Orosius was not present (Aug. *de Gest. Pelag.* c. 16), but returned to Africa early in 416, bearing the supposed relics of St. Stephen, discovered the previous December, which at the request of Avitus he was to convey to the church of Braga in Portugal (Tillem. vol. xiii. 262.) About this time, on the request of Augustine, Orosius undertook his history, chiefly in order to confirm by historical facts the doctrine maintained by St. Augustine in his great work *de Civitate Dei*, on the 11th book of which he was then employed. These facts we gather from c. i., and from a passage in bk. v., where Orosius says that he wrote his history chiefly if not entirely in Africa. It could not have been begun earlier than 416, and must have been finished in 417, for it concludes with an account of the treaty made in 416 between Wallia, the Gothic king, and the emperor Honorius (Oros. *Hist.* v. 2, vii. 43; Clinton, *F. R.*). Orosius then proceeded towards Spain with the relics of St. Stephen. Being detained at Port Mahon in Minorca by accounts of the disturbed state of Spain through the Vandal occupation, he left his precious treasure there and returned to Africa, and nothing more is known of his history (*Ep.* Severi, Aug. *Opp.* vol. vii. *App.* Baronius, 418. 4). The work of Orosius is a historical treatise rather than a formal history, which indeed it does not pretend to be, though as it includes a portion of the subject belonging to Scripture and to Jewish affairs, its area covers wider space than any other ancient epitome. Besides the O. and N. T., he quotes Josephus, the church historians and writers, as Tertullian, Hegesippus, and Eusebius, besides the classic writers Tacitus, Suetonius, Sallust, Caesar, Cicero, and he was no doubt largely indebted to Livy. For Greek and Oriental history he made use of the works of Justin, or rather Trogus Pompeius, and Quintus Curtius; for Roman affairs, Eutropius, Florus, and Valerius Paterculus, together with others of inferior value, as Valerius Antias, Valerius Maximus, and Aurelius Victor. Written under the express sanction of St. Augustine, in a pleasing style and at convenient length, and recommended by church authorities as an orthodox Christian work, it became during the middle ages the standard text-book on the subject, and is quoted largely by Bede and other medieval writers. Orosius is for the last few years of his history a contemporary and so an original authority, and supplies some points on which existing writers are deficient (*e.g.* v. 18, p. 339, the death of Cato; vi. 3, 376, the acquittal of Catiline), but his work is disfigured by many mistakes, both as to facts and numbers, and by a faulty system of chronology. The general popularity it enjoyed as the one Christian history led to its translation into Anglo-Saxon by Alfred the Great, of which a portion was published by Elstob in 1690, and the whole, with an English version, in 1773, under the superintendence of D. Barrington and J. R. Foster. This was reprinted in 1853 in Bohn's *Antiquarian Library*, under Mr. B. Thorpe. The latest ed. of the *Hist.* and the *Lib. Apol.* is by Zangemeister in *Corp. Scr. Eccl. Lat.* v. (Vienna, 1882), and a smaller ed. by the same editor in the *Biblioth. Teubner.* (Leipz. 1889). [H.W.P.]

P

Pachomius (1), St., founder of the famous monasteries of Tabenna in Upper Egypt; one of the first to collect solitary ascetics together under a rule. Beyond a brief mention in Sozomen, who praises his gentleness and suavity (*H. E.* iii. 14), the materials for his biography are of questionable authenticity. Athanasius, during his visit to Rome, made the name Pachomius familiar to the church there through Marcella and others, to whom he held up Pachomius and his Tabennensian monks as a bright example (Hieron. *Ep.* 127, *ad Principium*). Rosweyd gives a narrative of his life in Latin, being a translation by Dionysius Exiguus, in the 6th cent., of a biography said to be written by a contemporary monk of Tabenna (*Vit. Patr.* in *Pat. Lat.* lxxiii. 227). If we may trust this writer, Pachomius was born of wealthy pagan parents in Lower Egypt, before the council of Nicaea. He served in his youth under Constantine in the campaign against Maxentius, which placed Constantine alone on the throne. The kindness shewn by Christians to him and his comrades in distress led him to become a Christian. He attached himself to a hermit, celebrated for his sanctity and austerities. He and Palaemon supported themselves by weaving the shaggy tunics (*cilicia*), the favourite dress of Egyptian monks. He became a monk, and many prodigies are related of his power over demons, and in resisting the craving for sleep and food (*Vit.* cc. 40, 44, 45, 47, 48, etc., ap. Rosw. *V. P.*). His reputation for holiness soon drew to him many who desired to embrace the monastic life, and without, apparently, collecting them into one monastery, he provided for their organization. The bishop of a neighbouring diocese sent for him to regulate the monks there. Pachomius seems also to have done some missionary work in his own neighbourhood. Athanasius, visiting Tabenna, was eagerly welcomed by Pachomius, who, in that zeal for orthodoxy which was a characteristic of monks generally, is said to have flung one of Origen's writings into the water, exclaiming that he would have cast it into the fire, but that it contained the name of God. He lived to a good old age (Niceph. *H. E.* ix. 14). The Bollandists (*Acta*

SS. 14 Mai. iii. 287) give the *Acta* of Pachomius by a nearly contemporary author, in a Latin trans. from the original Greek MSS., with notes and commentary by Papebroch. Pachomius died (*Acta*, § 77), aged 57, about the time Athanasius returned to his see under Constantius, *i.e.* A.D. 349, as computed by Papebroch. Miraeus (*Schol.* to Gennad. *Scr. Eccl.* c. 7) makes him flourish in 340; Trithemius in 390, under Valentinian and Theodosius. Sigebert (*Chron.* ann. 405) puts his death in 405 at the age of 110. Portus Veneris, now Porto Venere, a small town on the N.W. coast of Italy, near Spezia, claims that his body rests there. Cf. Amélineau, *Etude historique sur S. Pach.* (Cairo, 1887); also Grützmacher, *Pachomius und das Alteste Klosterleben* (Freiburg, 1896). [I.G.S.]

Palladius (7), bp. of Helenopolis, the trusted friend of Chrysostom, whose misfortunes he fully shared, was born *c.* 367, perhaps in Galatia. He embraced an ascetic life in his 20th year, *c.* 386. The ascetic career of Palladius can only be conjecturally traced from scattered notices in the *Lausiac History* (but see *infra*). He never remained long in one place, but sought the acquaintance of the leading solitaries and ascetics of his day to learn all that could be gathered of their manner of life and miraculous deeds. Tillemont thinks his earliest place of sojourn was with the abbat Elpidius of Cappadocia in the cavernous recesses of the mountains near Jericho (*Hist. Laus.* c. 106), and that he, *c.* 387, visited Bethlehem, where he received a very unfavourable impression of Jerome from the solitary Posidonius (*ib.* c. 78), and passing thence to Jerusalem formed the acquaintance of Melania the elder and Rufinus, the latter of whom he highly commends (*ib.* c. 5; c. 118). In 388 Palladius paid his first visit to Alexandria (*ib.* c. 1). Having visited several monasteries near Alexandria, and the famous Didymus, he retired (*c.* 390) to the Nitrian desert, whence, after a year, he plunged still deeper into the district known as the Cells, τὰ κελλία, where he mostly remained for 9 years (*ib.*). Here, for 3 years, he enjoyed the intercourse of Macarius the younger and subsequently of Evagrius of Pontus. Palladius appears during this period to have traversed the whole of Upper Egypt as far as Tabenna and Syene, and to have visited all its leading solitaries. Ill-health led him to return to the purer air of Palestine, whence he soon passed to Bithynia, where he was called to the episcopate (*ib.* c. 43). Palladius tells us neither when nor where he became bishop. If it is right to identify the author of the *Lausiac History* with the adherent of Chrysostom, his see was Helenopolis, formerly called Drepanum, in Bithynia. He was consecrated by Chrysostom, and the Origenistic opinions he was charged with having imbibed from Evagrius became a handle of accusation against his consecrator (Phot. *Cod.* 59, p. 57). This accusation of Origenism is brought against Palladius by Epiphanius (*Ep. ad Joann. Jerus.* Hieron., *Op.* i. col. 252, ed. Vallars.) and Jerome (*Proem. in Dial. adv. Pelagianos*), though Tillemont argues that this was another Palladius. Palladius was at the synod at Constantinople, May 400, at which Antoninus of Ephesus was accused by Eusebius, and he was one of three bishops deputed by Chrysostom to visit Asia and make a personal investigation into the charges (Pallad. *Dial.* pp. 131-133). When Chrysostom, at the opening of 401, resolved to go to Ephesus himself, Palladius was one of the bishops to accompany him (*ib.* p. 134).

Palladius was one of the first to suffer from the persecution which after 404 fell upon the adherents of Chrysostom. The magistrates having decreed that the house of any who harboured bishop, priest, or layman who communicated with Chrysostom should be confiscated, Palladius, with many other ecclesiastics, fled to Rome, arriving about the middle of 405, with a copy of the infamous decree which had driven him from Constantinople (*ib.* pp. 26, 27). The refugees were hospitably entertained by one Pinianus and his wife and by some noble ladies of Rome, a kindness which Palladius gratefully mentions (*Hist. Laus.* c. 121), and for which Chrysostom wrote letters of thanks from Cucusus. He was honourably received by pope Innocent, and his testimony gave the pope full knowledge of the transaction (Soz. *H. E.* viii. 26). On the departure of the Italian deputation sent by Honorius to his brother Arcadius, requesting that the whole matter should be subjected to a general council, Palladius and the other refugees accompanied them (Pallad. *Dial.* p. 31). On their arrival the whole party were forbidden to land at Constantinople. Palladius and his companions were shut up in separate chambers in the fortress of Athyre on the coast, and loaded with the utmost contumely, in the hope of breaking their spirit and compelling them to renounce communion with Chrysostom, and recognize Atticus (*ib.* p. 32). All threats and violence proving vain, the bishops were banished to distant and opposite quarters of the empire; Palladius to Syene, on the extreme border of Egypt (*ib.* pp. 194, 199). Tillemont considers that on the death of Theophilus in 412 Palladius was permitted to leave his place of exile, but not to return to his see. Between 412 and 420 Tillemont places his residence of four years near Antinoopolis in the Thebaid, of which district and its numerous ascetics the *Hist. Laus.* gives copious details (cc. 96-100; cc. 137, 138), as well as of the three years which the writer spent on the Mount of Olives with Innocent, the presbyter of the church there. During this time he may also have visited Mesopotamia, Syria, and the other portions of the eastern world which he speaks of having traversed. The peace of the church being re-established in 417, Palladius was perhaps restored to his see of Helenopolis. If so, he did not remain there long, for Socrates informs us that he was translated from that see to Aspuna in Galatia Prima (Socr. *H. E.* vii. 36). He had, however, ceased to be bp. of Aspuna in 431, when Eusebius attended the council of Ephesus as bp. of that see (Labbe, *Concil.* iii. 450). The *Historia Lausiaca* was composed *c.* 420. It is now, however, generally considered (*vide* works by Preuschen and Butler, *u.inf.*) that the author of this History is not to be identified with the bp. of Helenopolis, his contemporary. The work takes its name from one Lausus or Lauson, chief chamberlain in the imperial household, at whose request it was written and to whom it is dedicated. The writer describes Lausus as a very excellent person, employing his power for the glory of God and the good of the church, and devoting his leisure to self-improvement and study. Though the writer is credulous, his work is an honest and, except as regards supposed miraculous acts, trustworthy account of the mode of life of the solitaries of that age, and a faithful picture of the tone of religious thought then prevalent. It preserves many historical and biographical details which later writers have borrowed; Sozomen takes many anecdotes without acknowledgment. Socrates refers to Palladius as a leading authority on the lives of the solitaries, but is wrong in calling him a monk and stating that he lived soon after the death of Valens (*H. E.* iv. 23). The *Historia Lausiaca* was repeatedly printed in various Latin versions, from very early times, the first ed. appearing soon after the invention of printing. The latest and best authorities are E. Preuschen, *Palladius and Rufinus* (Giessen, 1897); C. Butler, *The Lausiac History of Palladius* (vol. i. critical intro. Camb. 1898; vol. ii. Gk. text with intro. and notes, 1904) in *Texts and Studies*; see also C. H. Turner, *The Lausiac Hist. of Pallad.* in *Jnl. of Theol. Stud.* 1905, vi. p. 321.

The question whether the *Dialogue with Theodore the Deacon* is correctly assigned to Palladius of Helenopolis has been much debated. It is essentially a literary composition, the characters and framework being alike fictitious. It was undoubtedly written by one who took an active part in the events he describes. No one corresponds so closely in all respects to the ideal presented by the narration as Palladius of Helenopolis, nor is there any really weighty objection to his authorship. For the closing days of Chrysostom's episcopate it is, with all its faults, simply priceless. Tillem. *Mém. Eccl.* t. xi. pp. 500-530, pp. 638-646; Cave, *Hist. Lit.* t. i. p. 376; Du Pin, *Auteurs eccl.* t. iii. p. 296; Cotelerius, *Eccl. Graec. Monum.* t. iii. p. 563. [E.V.]

Palladius (11), July 6, the first bp. sent to Ireland and the immediate predecessor of St. Patrick. Facts known about him are few, though legends are numerous. His birthplace is placed by some in England, by others in Gaul or Italy; some even make him a Greek (see Ussher, *Eccles. Britann. Antiq.* t. vi. c. xvi. of Elrington's ed.). His ecclesiastical position has also been disputed. He seems to have been an influential man in the earlier part of the 5th cent., as Prosper of Aquitaine, a contemporary, mentions him twice, affording the only real record of his life which we possess. Under 429 Prosper writes in his *Chronicle*: "By the instrumentality of the deacon Palladius, pope Celestinus sends Germanus, bp. of Auxerre, in his own stead, to displace the heretics and direct the Britons to the Catholic faith." Prosper's words under 431 are, "Ad Scotos in Christum credentes ordinatur a Papa Celestino Palladius et primus Episcopus mittitur." This mission of Palladius is referred to in the Book of Armagh, where Tirechan (*Analect. Boll.* t. ii. p. 67), or more probably some writer towards A.D. 900, calls him Patricius as his second name. Rev. J. F. Shearman, in his *Loco Patriciana*, p. 25 (Dubl. 1879), has discussed with vast resources of legendary lore the different localities in Wicklow and Kildare where Palladius is said to have preached and built churches, but his authorities have little historical value, being specially the *Four Masters* and Jocelyn. His work contains, however, much interesting matter for students of Irish ecclesiastical history and antiquities, its accuracy being guaranteed by his extensive knowledge of the localities. [G.T.S.]

Pammachius, a Roman senator of the Furian family (Hieron. *Ep.* lxvi. 6, ed. Vall.), cousin to Marcella (*ib.* xlix. 4), and said by Palladius (*Hist. Laus.* c. 122) to have been related to Melania. He was a friend of Jerome, Paulinus, and afterwards Augustine. He was a fellow-student of Jerome at Rome (*Ep.* xlviii. 1), but apparently not specially connected with church affairs in early life. During Jerome's stay in Rome in 382-385 they probably met, since in 385 Pammachius married Paulina, the daughter of Paula who went with Jerome to Palestine. Pammachius was learned, able, and eloquent (*Ep.* lxxvii. 1; xlix. 3). After his marriage, he seems to have occupied himself much with scriptural studies and church life. The controversy relating to Jovinian interested him, and he is thought to have been one of those who procured the condemnation of Jovinian from pope Siricius (Tillem. x. 568). But Jerome's books against Jovinian (pub. in 392) appeared to Pammachius to be too violent. He bought up the copies and wrote to Jerome asking him to moderate his language. Jerome refused, but thanked Pammachius for his interest, hailed him as a well-wisher and defender, and promised to keep him informed of his future writings (*Epp.* xlviii., xlix.). Thenceforth their intercourse was constant.

Pammachius is said by Jerome (xlix. 4) to have been designated for the sacerdotium at this time by the whole city of Rome and the pontiff. But he was never ordained. His growing convictions and those of his wife, the fact that all his children died at birth and that his wife died in childbirth (A.D. 397, see Hieron. *Ep.* lxvi., addressed to him 2 years later), led him to take monastic vows. He, however, still appeared among the senators in their purple in the dark dress of a monk (*ib.* lxvi. 6). He showed his change of life by munificent gifts and a great entertainment to the poor (Paulinus, *Ep.* xiii. 11; see also Pall. *Hist. Laus.* 122). With Fabiola he erected a hospital at Portus, which became world-famous (Hieron. *Ep.* lxvi. 11).

At the commencement of the Origenistic controversy, Jerome wrote (in 395) to Pammachius his letter *de Opt. Genere Interpretandi* (*Ep.* lvii. ed. Vall.). On Rufinus coming to Rome Pammachius, with Occanus and Marcella, watched his actions in Jerome's interest, and on his publication of a translation of Origen's Περὶ Ἀρχῶν wrote to Jerome to request a full translation of the work (*Epp.* lxxxiii., lxxxiv.). These friends also procured the condemnation of Origenism by pope Anastasius in 401, and to them Jerome's apology against Rufinus was addressed, and the book *cont. Joannem Hierosol.* During the Donatist schism in Africa Pammachius, who had property in that province, wrote to the people of Numidia, where the schism had begun, exhorting them to return to the unity of the church. This letter brought him into relations with Augustine, who wrote (in 401) to him (*Ep.* lviii.) congratulating him on an action likely to help in healing the schism, and desiring him to read the letter to his brother-senators, that they might do likewise. After this we hear of Pammachius only in connexion with the Bible-work of Jerome, who dedicated to him his commentaries on the Minor Prophets (406) and Daniel (407), and at his request undertook the commentaries on Is. and Ezek. (prefaces to Comm. on Am. Dan. Is. and Ezek.). Before the latter was finished, Pammachius had died in the siege of Rome by Alaric, A.D. 409. [W.H.F.]

Pamphilus (1), presbyter of Caesarea, the intimate friend (Hieron. *de Script. Eccl.* 75) and literary guide of Eusebius the church historian, who adopted his name as a surname, calling himself Εὐσέβιος Παμφίλου. Eusebius composed his friend's biography in three books. The work is entirely lost, and our only knowledge of this chief among the Biblical scholars of his age is derived from a few scattered notices in the existing writings of Eusebius, Jerome, and Photius. Pamphilus was a native of Phoenicia, and, if we accept the doubtful authority of Metaphrastes, born at Berytus, of a wealthy and honourable family. Having received his earlier education in his native city, he passed to Alexandria, where he devoted himself to theological studies under Pierius, the head of its catechetical school (Routh, *Rel. Sacr.* iii. 430; Phot. *Cod.* 118). Pamphilus afterwards settled at Caesarea, of which church he became a presbyter, probably during the episcopate of Agapius. Here he commenced the work of his life, hunting for books illustrative of Holy Scripture from all parts of the world. The library thus formed was subsequently repaired, after its injuries during the persecution of Diocletian, by Acacius and Euzoïus, the successors of Eusebius in the see of Caesarea (Hieron. *Ep.* xxxiv. vol. i. p. 155). Eusebius had catalogued it (*H. E.* vi. 32). It was especially rich in codices of the Scriptures, many transcribed or corrected by Pamphilus's own hand. In this Eusebius was a zealous coadjutor (Hieron. *de Script. Eccl.* c. 81). Jerome speaks of Palestinian manuscripts of the LXX current in the Syrian church, which, having been carefully prepared by Origen, were published by the two friends (Hieron. *Praef. in Paralip.; adv. Rufin.* ii. 27, t. ii. p. 522). Among other priceless literary treasures now lost was a copy of the so-called Hebrew text of the Gospel of St. Matthew (Hieron. *de Script. Eccl.* c. 3) and the *Tetrapla* and *Hexapla* of Origen in the original copy (Hieron. *in Tit.* iii. 9, t. vii. p. 734). In the catechetical school of Alexandria Pamphilus had conceived a most ardent admiration for Origen, with whose works he made it his special object to enrich his library, copying the greater part himself (Hieron. *de Script. Eccl.* c. 75). Jerome gloried in the possession of Origen's commentaries on the Minor Prophets in 25 volumes in Pamphilus's autograph. Pamphilus proved his affection for the memory and fame of Origen by devoting the last two years of his life to composing, in prison, with the assistance of Eusebius, an *Apology*, or *Defence* of Origen, addressed to the "Confessors condemned to the mines in Palestine." Five books were completed before his death, the sixth being added by Eusebius (Photius, *Cod.* 118). Photius gives a brief summary of the work, of which we have bk. i. alone in the inaccurate Latin version of Rufinus (Routh, *Rel. Sac.* iv. pp. 339, 392). What Pamphilus knew and had acquired he regarded as the common property of those who desired to share it. Eusebius describes him as ever ready to help all in need, either in the matters of the body, the mind, or the soul. The copies of the Scriptures he caused to be made by his students he distributed gratuitously, while he liberally supplied the temporal wants of those in distress (Eus. *de Martyr. Palaest.* c. 11; Hieron. *adv. Rufin.* i. 9, t. ii. p. 465).

In 307 Pamphilus was committed to prison by Urbanus, the persecuting governor of the city, and for two years was closely confined, cheered by the companionship of his second self, Eusebius (Hieron. *ad Pammach. et Ocean. Ep.* 84). Pamphilus sealed his life-long confession of his Master with his blood—"the centre of a brave company, among whom he shone out as the sun among the stars"—in 309, when Firmilianus had succeeded Urbanus as governor. The library he collected was destroyed when Caesarea was taken by the Arabs in the 7th cent. [E.V.]

Pancratius (1), (*St. Pancras*), martyr at Rome on the Via Aurelia, A.D. 304; a Phrygian by birth, but baptized at Rome by the pope himself. He suffered when only 14 years of age with his uncle Dionysius. His martyrdom was very celebrated in the early ages. His church still gives a title to a cardinal, and to a well-known parish church in London. Gregory of Tours (*de Glor. Martt.* i. 39) tells us that his tomb outside the walls of Rome was so sacred that the devil at once seized those who swore falsely before it. Gregory the Great mentions the martyr in his *Epp.* (iv. 18 and vi. 49), and in Homily (xxvii.) on St. John (Ceill. iii. 29; Tillem. *Mém.* v. 260; *AA. SS.* Boll. Mai. ii. 17; Ruinart. *AA. Sinc.* p. 407: *Mart. Rom. Vet.*, Usuard.). [G.T.S.]

Pantaenus, chief of the catechetical school of Alexandria, in the latter part of the 2nd cent. and perhaps the early years of the 3rd. Of his previous life little is known with certainty. We are not informed whether he was originally a Christian or became one by conversion. Our authorities agree, however, that he was trained in the Greek philosophy, and owed to this training much of his eminence as a teacher. Origen, in a passage preserved by Eusebius (*H. E.* vi. 19), names him as an example—the earliest, apparently, that he can adduce—of a Christian doctor who availed himself of his heathen learning. Eusebius tells us (*ib.* v. 10) that in his zeal for the faith he undertook the work of an evangelist in the East, and penetrated as far as India; where he found that St. Bartholomew had already preached the Word and had left there a copy of St. Matthew's Gospel in Hebrew characters, which was still treasured by the Christians there. Jerome (*de Vir. Ill.* 36) adds (but probably without authority) that Pantaenus brought this to Alexandria. He also represents that the people of India had heard his fame as a teacher and sent a deputation to solicit this mission. This is by no means incredible, considering the celebrity of Alexandria as a seat of learning. But Jerome raises a difficulty when he names Demetrius as the bishop by whom he was sent. For Eusebius places the accession of Demetrius to the patriarchate in the 10th year of Commodus (*H. E.* v. 22; cf. *Chron.*), A.D. 189; while he represents Pantaenus as head of the Alexandrian school in his 1st year (*H. E.* v. 9, 10) and distinctly conveys that this appointment was after his return from his Indian mission.

There is a like conflict of authority concerning the relation of Pantaenus to Clement of Alexandria. Eusebius (v. 11) unhesitatingly assumes that Pantaenus is the unnamed master whom Clement in his *Stromateis* (i. p. 322, Potter) places above all the great men by whose teaching he was profited, "last met, but first in power," in whom he "found rest." To this authority we may add that of Pamphilus, who was principal author of their joint *Apology for Origen*; for Photius (*Bibl.* cxviii.) states on the authority of that work (now lost) that Clement "was the hearer of Pantaenus and his successor in the school." This information Pamphilus no doubt had from his master Pierius, himself head of the same school, a follower of Origen and probably less than 50 years his junior. Maximus the Confessor (*Scholia in S. Greg. Naz.*) styles Pantaenus "the master" (καθηγητὴν) of Clement. But Philip of Side (*c.* 427) in his *Hist. Christiana*, as we learn from a fragment first pub. by Dodwell, made "Clement the disciple of Athenagoras, and Pantaenus of Clement." We unhesitatingly prefer the witness of Eusebius. Dodwell's attempts to discredit it are ineffectual. This contradiction, however, and the difficulty as to the chronology of Pantaenus, may be solved, or at least accounted for, if we suppose that Pantaenus was head of the school both before and after his sojourn in India, and Clement in his absence. Origen afterwards thus quitted and resumed the same office. If Pantaenus was the senior, Clement was the more brilliant; and at the close of the 2nd cent. it may well have seemed a question which was master and which disciple. This hypothesis agrees with the probable date of Clement's headship; and likewise with the note in the *Chronicon* of Eusebius, under year of Pertinax, or 2nd of Severus (*c.* 193), where we read that Clement was then in Alexandria, "a most excellent teacher (διδάσκαλος) and shining light (διέλαμπε) of Christian philosophy," and Pantaenus "was distinguished as an expositor of the Word of God." Thus also Alexander, bp. of Jerusalem (*ap.* Eus. *H. E.* vi. 14), in a letter to Origen, couples the names of Pantaenus and Clement (placing, however, Pantaenus first), as "fathers," and speaks of both as recently deceased. This letter shows, further, that this Alexander and the illustrious Origen himself were almost certainly pupils of Pantaenus.

We do not know the date of his death, but the *Chronicon* (*vid. sup.*) confirms Jerome in prolonging his activity into the reign of Severus (193-211), and not improbably, as Jerome states, he lived into the following reign—a statement repeated in the (later) Roman Martyrology. Photius is thus wrong in believing that Pantaenus was a hearer not only "of those who had seen the apostles" (which he may well have been), but also "of some of the apostles themselves." A man alive after 193 and not the senior of Clement by more than a generation could not possibly have been born so early as to have been a hearer even of St. John. Photius was probably misled by a too literal construction of Clement's statement (*Strom. u.s.*)—that his teachers "had received the true tradition of the blessed doctrine straight from the holy apostles Peter, James, John, and Paul."

Eusebius tells us that Pantaenus "interpreted the treasures of the divine dogmas"; Jerome, that he left "many commentaries on the Scriptures." Both however indicate that the church owed more to his spoken utterances than to his writings. The two extant fragments (see Routh, *Rel. Sac.* i. p. 378) appear to be relics of his oral teaching. One bears the character of a verbal reply to a question; it is preserved by Maximus the Confessor (*Scholia in S. Greg. Naz.*), who, in illustration of the teaching of Dionysius the Areopagite concerning the divine will, tells us that Pantaenus when asked by certain philosophers, "in what manner Christians suppose God to know things that are?" replied, "Neither by sense things sensible, nor by intellect things intelligible. For it is not possible that He Who is above the things that are, should apprehend the things that are according to the things that are. But we say that He knows the things that are, as acts of His own will (ὡς ἴδια θελήματα); and we give good reason for so saying; for if by act of His will He hath made all things (which reason will not gainsay), and if it is ever both pious and right to say that God knows His own will, and He of His will hath made each thing that hath come to be; therefore God knows the things that are as acts of His own will, inasmuch as He of His will hath made the things that are." The other, contained in the *Eclogae e Propheticis* appended to the works of Clement, is introduced by "Our Pantaenus used to say" (ἔλεγε), and lays down as a principle in interpreting prophecy that it "for the most part utters its sayings indefinitely [as to time], using the present sometimes for the future and sometimes for the past." Anastasius of Sinai (7th cent.), in his *Contemplations on the Hexaëmeron* (quoted by Routh, i. p. 15), twice cites Pantaenus as one authority for an interpretation according to which Christ and his church are foreshewn in the history of the creation of Paradise (I. p. 860; VII. *cont.* p. 893 in *Bibl. Max. PP.* t. ix. ed. Lyons, 1677), the true inference from these references apparently being that Pantaenus led the way in that method of spiritual or mystical interpretation of O.T., usually associated with his more famous followers, Clement and Origen.

Anastasius describes him as "priest of the church of the Alexandrians (τῆς Ἀλεξανδρέων ἱερεύς)"; which is noteworthy in the absence of all direct information concerning the time and place, or even the fact, of his ordination. That he was a priest may be inferred—not indeed from his headship of a school, for Origen was a layman, but—from the fact that he was sent by his bishop to evangelize India.

Besides authors quoted, see Baronius, *Ann.*, *s.a.* 183; Cave, *Primitive Fathers*, p. 185 (1677); *Hist. Lit.* t. i. p. 51 (1688); Du Pin, *Auteurs ecclés.* t. i. pt. i. p. 184; Lardner, *Credibility*, c. xxi.; Le Quien, *Oriens Chr.* t. ii. coll. 382, 391; Tillem. *Mém.* t. iii. p. 170. [J.GW].

Papa. [NESTORIAN CHURCH.]

Paphnutius (2), bp. in Upper Thebias, who suffered mutilation and banishment for the faith (Socr. *H. E.* i. 11; Theod. *H. E.* i. 7). At the council of Nicaea A.D. 325, he was much honoured as a confessor, specially by Constantine (Socr. *u.s.*), and earnestly opposed the enforcement of the law of clerical celibacy, on the ground of both principle and expediency, and prevailed (*ib.*). He closely adhered to the cause of St. Athanasius, and attended him at the council of Tyre, A.D. 335. Rufinus (*H. E.* i. 17), followed by Sozomen (*H. E.* ii. 25), tells a dramatic story of his there reproaching Maximus of Jerusalem for being in Arian company and explaining to him the exact position of affairs. Fleury, *H. E.* xv. c. 26; Ceill. *Aut. sacr.* iii. 420, 450; Boll. *Acta SS.* Sept. 11, iii. 778. [J.G.]

Paphnutius (5) (*Pafnutius*, *Pynuphius*, surnamed *Bubalus*, and *Cephala*), an anchoret and priest in the Scetic desert in Egypt. Cassian's words (*Coll.* iv. c. 1) regarding his promotion of abbat Daniel to the diaconate and priesthood have been held to prove that a presbyter had the power of ordaining, but Bingham (*Ant.* bk. ii. 3, 7) will not admit that Cassian is to be so understood. When Cassian visited him in 395, he was 90 years old, but hale and active (*Coll.* iii. c. 1). He seems to have fled twice from the Scetic into Syria for greater solitude and perfection (Cass. *de Coen. Inst.* iv. cc. 30, 31), and with some others had in 373 already found refuge at Diocaesarea in Palestine (Tillem. vi. 250, 251, ed. 1732). In the anthropomorphic controversy between Theophilus bp. of Alexandria and the monks of the Egyptian desert, Paphnutius took the side of the bishop and orthodoxy (Cass. *Coll.* x. c. 2); his attempt to convert the aged Serapion and his failure, till Photinus came, is very curious (*ib.* 3). [J.G.]

Papias (1), bp. of Hierapolis in Phrygia (Eus. *H. E.* iii. 36) in the first half of 2nd cent. Lightfoot says (*Coloss.* p. 48), "Papias, or (as it is very frequently written in inscriptions) Pappias, is a common Phrygian name. It is found several times at Hierapolis, not only in inscriptions (Boeckh, 3930, 3912 A, add.), but even on coins (Mionnet, iv. p. 301). This is explained by the fact that it was an epithet of the Hierapolitan Zeus (Boeckh, 3912 A, Παπίᾳ Διῒ σωτῆρι)." The date of Papias used to be regarded as determined by a notice in the *Paschal Chronicle*, which was thought to record his martyrdom at Pergamus under A.D. 163. But we have no ground for asserting that Papias lived so late as 163, and we shall see reason for at least placing his literary activity considerably earlier in the century.

His name is famous as the writer of a treatise in five books called *Expositions of Oracles of the Lord* (Λογίων Κυριακῶν ἐξηγήσεις), which title we shall discuss presently. The object of the book seems to have been to throw light on the Gospel history, especially by the help of oral traditions which Papias had collected from those who had met members of the apostolic circle. That Papias lived when it was still possible to meet such persons has given great importance to his testimony, though only some very few fragments of his work remain. Every word of these fragments has been rigidly scrutinized, and, what is less reasonable where so little is known, arguments have been built on the silence of Papias about sundry matters which it is supposed he ought to have mentioned and assumed that he did not. We give at length the first and most important of the fragments, a portion of the preface preserved by Eusebius (iii. 39), from which we can infer the object of the work and the resources which Papias claimed to have available. "And I will not scruple also to give for thee a place along with my interpretations to whatsoever at any time I well learned from the elders and well stored up in memory, guaranteeing its truth. For I did not, like the generality, take pleasure in those who have much to say, but in those who teach the truth; nor in those who relate their strange commandments, but in those who record such as were given from the Lord to the Faith and come from the Truth itself. And if ever any one came who had been a follower of the elders, I would inquire as to the discourses of the elders, what was said by Andrew, or what by Peter, or what by Philip, or what by Thomas or James, or what by John or Matthew or any other of the disciples of the Lord; and the things which Aristion and the elder John, the disciples of the Lord, say. For I did not think that I could get so much profit from the contents of books as from the utterances of a living and abiding voice."

The singular "for thee" in the opening words implies that the work of Papias was inscribed to some individual. The first sentence of the extract had evidently followed one in which the writer had spoken of the "interpretations" which appear to have been the main subject of his treatise, and for joining his traditions with which he conceives an apology necessary. Thus we see that Papias is not making a first attempt to write the life of our Lord or a history of the apostles, but assumes the previous existence of a written record. Papias enumerates the ultimate sources of his traditions in two classes: Andrew, Peter, and others, of whom he speaks in the past tense; Aristion and John the Elder, of whom he speaks in the present. As the passage is generally understood, Papias only claims a second-hand knowledge of what these had related, but had inquired from any who had conferred with elders, what Andrew, Peter, etc., *had* said, and what John and Aristion *were* saying; the last two being the only ones then surviving. But considering that there is a change of pronouns, we are disposed to think that there is an anacoluthon, and that his meaning, however ill expressed, was that he learned, by inquiry from others, things that Andrew, Peter, and others had said, and also stored up in his memory things which

Aristion and John said in his own hearing. Eusebius certainly understands Papias to claim to have been a hearer of this John and Aristion. The word "elders" is ordinarily used of men of a former generation, and would be most naturally understood here of men of the first generation of Christians, if it were not that in the second clause the title seems to be refused to Aristion, who is nevertheless described as a disciple (by which we must understand a personal disciple) of our Lord; and as those mentioned in the first group are all apostles, the word "elder," as Papias used it, may have included, besides antiquity, the idea of official dignity. As to whether the John mentioned with Aristion is different from John the apostle previously mentioned, see JOHANNES (**444**) PRESBYTER.

The fragment quoted enables us to fix within certain limits the date of Papias. He is evidently separated by a whole generation from the apostolic age; he describes himself as living when it was not exceptional to meet persons who had been hearers of the apostles, and (if we understand him rightly) he had met two who professed to have actually seen our Lord Himself. Eusebius tells that Philip the apostle (some suppose that he ought to have said Philip the deacon) came to reside at Hierapolis with his daughters; and that Papias, on the authority of these daughters, tells a story of Philip raising a man from the dead. Eusebius certainly understood Papias to describe himself as contemporary with those daughters and as having heard the story from them. If these were they whom St. Luke describes as prophesying at Caesarea in 58, and if they were young women then, they might have been still alive at Hierapolis between 100 and 110. But as Papias speaks of his inquiries in the past tense, a considerable time had probably elapsed before he published the results. On the whole, we shall not be far wrong in dating the work *c.* 130.

Papias evidently lived after the rise of Gnosticism and was not unaffected by the controversies occasioned by it. Strong asceticism was a feature of some of the earliest Gnostic sects; and their commandments, "Touch not, taste not, handle not," may well have been "the strange commandments" to which Papias refers. Lightfoot is probably right in thinking that the sarcasm in the phrase "those who have so very much to say" may have been aimed at the work on the Gospel by Basilides in 24 books, and some similar productions of the Gnostic schools of which the later book *Pistis Sophia* is a sample.

Of the traditions recorded by Papias, what has given rise to most discussion and has been the foundation of most theories is what he relates about the Gospels of SS. Matthew and Mark, which he is the first to mention by name. Concerning Mark he says, "This also the elder [John] said: Mark having become the interpreter of Peter wrote accurately everything that he remembered of the things that were either said or done by Christ; but however not in order. For he neither heard the Lord nor had been a follower of His; but afterwards, as I said, was a follower of Peter, who framed his teaching according to the needs [of his hearers], but not with the design of giving a connected account of the Lord's discourses [or oracles]. Thus Mark committed no error in thus writing down some things as he remembered them. For he took heed to one thing: not to omit any of the things he had heard, or to set down anything falsely therein." Concerning Matthew, all that remains of what Papias says is, "So then Matthew composed the oracles in Hebrew, and every one interpreted them as he could." For a long time no one doubted that Papias here spoke of our Gospels of SS. Matthew and Mark; and mainly on the authority of these passages was founded the general belief of the Fathers, that St. Matthew's Gospel had been originally written in Hebrew, and St. Mark's founded on the teaching of Peter. But some last-century critics contended that our present Gospels do not answer the descriptions given by Papias. There is a striking resemblance between the two as we have them at present; but Papias's description, it is said, would lead us to think of them as very different. St. Matthew's Gospel, according to Papias, was a Hebrew book, containing an account only of our Lord's discourses; for so Schleiermacher translates *τὰ λόγια*, which we have rendered "oracles." St. Mark, on the other hand, wrote in Greek and recorded the acts as well as the words of Christ. Again, St. Mark's Gospel, which in its present state has an arrangement as orderly as St. Matthew's, was, according to Papias, not written in order. The conclusion which has been drawn is, that Papias's testimony relates not to our Gospels of SS. Matthew and Mark, but to their unknown originals; and accordingly many constantly speak of "the original Matthew," the "Ur-Marcus," though there is no particle of evidence beyond what may be extracted from this passage of Papias that there ever was any Gospel by SS. Matthew or Mark different from those we have. Renan even undertakes to give an account of the process by which the two very distinct works known to Papias, St. Matthew's collection of discourses, and St. Mark's collection of anecdotes, came into their present similar forms. In the early times, every possessor of anything that purported to be a record of our Lord desired to have the story complete; and would write into the margin of his book matter he met elsewhere, and so the book of St. Mark's anecdotes was enriched by a number of traits from St. Matthew's "discourses" and *vice versa.*

If this theory were true, we should expect to find in early times a multitude of gospels differing in their order and selection of facts. Why we should have now exactly four versions of the story is hard to explain on this hypothesis. We should expect that, by such mutual assimilation, all would in the end have been reduced to a single gospel. The solitary fact to which Renan appeals in support of his theory in reality refutes it—the fact, *i.e.*, that the pericope of the adulteress (John vii. 53–viii. 11) is absent from some MSS. and differently placed in others. Such an instance is so unusual that critics have generally inferred that this pericope cannot be a genuine part of St. John's Gospel; but if Renan's theory were true, the phenomena present in a small degree in this case ought to be seen in a multitude of cases. There ought to be many parables and miracles of which we should be uncertain whether they were common to all the evangelists or special to one, and what place in that one they should occupy. Further, according to Renan's hypothesis, St. Mark's design was more comprehensive than St. Matthew's. St. Matthew only related our Lord's discourses; St. Mark, the "things said or done by Christ," *i.e.* both discourses and anecdotes. St. Mark's Gospel would thus differ from St. Matthew's by excess and St. Matthew's read like an abridgment of St. Mark's. Exactly the opposite is the case.

We count it a mere blunder to translate λόγια "discourses" as if it were the same as λόγους. In N.T. (Acts vii. 38; Rom. iii. 2; Heb. v. 12; I. Pet. iv. 11) the word has its classical meaning, "oracles," and is applied to the inspired utterances of God in O.T. Nor is there reason to think that when St. Paul, *e.g.*, says that to the Jews were committed the oracles of God, he confined this epithet to those parts of O.T. which contained divine sayings and refused it to those narrative parts from which he so often drew lessons (Rom. iv. 3; I. Cor. x. 1, xi. 8; Gal. iv. 21). Philo quotes as a λόγιον the narrative in Gen. iv. 15, "The Lord set a mark upon Cain," etc., and the words (Deut. x.), "The Lord God is his inheritance." Similarly the Apostolic Fathers. In Clement (I. Cor. 53) τὰ λόγια τοῦ θεοῦ is used as equivalent to τὰς ἱερὰς γραφάς. (See also c. 19, Polyc. *ad Phil.* 7.) As Papias's younger contemporary Justin Martyr tells us that the reading of the Gospels had in his time become part of Christian public worship, we may safely pronounce the silent substitution of one Gospel for another a thing inconceivable; and we conclude that, as we learn from Justin that the Gospels had been set on a level with the O.T. in the public reading of the church, so we know from Papias that the ordinary name τὰ λόγια for the O.T. books had in Christian use been extended to the Gospels which were called τὰ κυριακὰ λόγια, the "oracles of our Lord." There is no reason to imagine the work of Papias limited to an exposition of our Lord's discourses; we translate therefore its title Κυριακῶν λογίων ἐξηγήσεις, "Expositions of the Gospels."

The manner in which Papias speaks of St. Mark's Gospel quite agrees with the inspired authority, which the title, as we understand it, implies. Three times in this short fragment he attests St. Mark's perfect accuracy. "Mark wrote down accurately everything that he remembered." "Mark committed no error." "He made it his rule not to omit anything he had heard or to set down any false statement therein." Yet, for some reason, Papias was dissatisfied with St. Mark's arrangement and thought it necessary to apologize for it. No account of the passage is satisfactory which does not explain why, if Papias reverenced St. Mark so much, he was dissatisfied with his order. Here the hypothesis breaks down at once, that Papias only possessed two documents unlike in kind, the one a collection of discourses, the other of anecdotes. Respecting St. Mark's accuracy as he did, Papias would certainly have accepted his order unless he had some other document to which, in this respect, he attached more value, going over the same ground as St. Mark's but in a different order. If, then, Papias held that St. Mark's Gospel was not written in the right order, what, in his opinion, was the right order? Strauss considers and rejects three answers to this question, as being all irreconcilable at least with the supposition that the Gospel known to Papias as St. Mark's was that which we receive under the name: (1) that the right order was St. John's; (2) that it was St. Matthew's; (3) that Papias meant to deny to St. Mark the merit, not only of the right order, but of any orderly arrangement at all. Lightfoot defended (1) with great ability (*Contemp. Rev.* Oct. 1875, p. 848). But there remains another answer which we believe the true one—viz. that Papias regarded St. Luke's as the right order. The reason this solution has been generally set aside is that St. Luke's Gospel is not mentioned in any extant fragments of Papias, from which it has been assumed that he was unacquainted with Luke's writings. If we had the whole work of Papias the argument from his silence might be reasonable; but we have no right to assume his silence merely because Eusebius included no statement about St. Luke in the few brief extracts from Papias which he gives. Lightfoot has shewn (*Coloss.* p. 52) that Eusebius is not wont without some special reason to copy references made by his predecessors to undisputed books of the Canon. Hilgenfeld finds in the preface of Papias echoes of the preface to St. Luke's Gospel which induce him to believe that Papias knew that gospel. To us this argument does not carry conviction, but there is every appearance that Papias was acquainted with the Acts. In one fragment he mentions Justus Barsabas; in another he gives an account of the death of Judas Iscariot which seems plainly intended to reconcile the story in St. Matthew with that in the Acts. One extant fragment appears to have been part of a comment on our Lord's words preserved by St. Luke, "I beheld Satan as lightning fall from heaven."

But if Papias knew St. Luke's Gospel, his language with respect to St. Mark's is at once explained. St. Luke's preface declares his intention to write in order, γραψαι καθεξῆς; but his order is neither St. Mark's nor St. Matthew's. On this difference we conceive Papias undertook to throw light by his traditional anecdotes. His account is that Mark was but the interpreter of Peter, whose teaching he accurately reported; that Peter had not undertaken at any time to give an orderly account of our Lord's words and deeds, but had merely related some of them from time to time as the immediate needs suggested; that Mark therefore faithfully reported what he had heard, and if his order was not always accurate it was because it had been no part of his plan to aim at accuracy in this respect. With regard to St. Matthew's Gospel, his solution seems to be that the church had not then the Gospel as St. Matthew had written it; that the Greek Matthew was but an unauthorized translation from a Hebrew original which individuals had translated, each for himself as he could. Thus, so far from it being true that Papias did not use our present Gospels, we believe that he was the first to harmonize them, and to proclaim the principle that no apparent disagreement between them affects their substantial truth. Remembering the solicitude Papias here displays to clear the Gospels from all suspicion of error, and the recognition of inspired authority implied in the title λόγια, we cannot admit the inference which has been drawn from the last sentence of the fragment, that Papias attached little value to the Gospels as compared with the *viva voce* traditions he could himself attest; and we endorse Lightfoot's explanation, that it was the Gnostic apocryphal writings which Papias found useless in his attempts to illustrate the Gospel narrative accepted by the church.

As we have seen, the extant fragments of Papias do not mention the Gospels of SS. Luke or John by name. Eusebius says, however, that Papias uses testimonies from St. John's first epistle. There is therefore very strong presumption that Papias was acquainted with the Gospel, a presumption strengthened by the fact that the list of the apostles in the fragment of the preface contains names in the order in which they occur in St. John's Gospel, placing Andrew before Peter, and includes some, such as Thomas and Philip, who outside that Gospel have little prominence in the Gospel record, and that it gives to our Lord the Johannine title, the Truth. Irenaeus (v. 36) has preserved a fragment containing an express recognition of St. John's Gospel; and though Irenaeus only gives it as a saying of the elders, Lightfoot (*Contemp. Rev.*, *u.s.*) has given convincing reasons for thinking that Papias is his authority, a conclusion which Harnack accepts as highly probable. An argument prefixed to a Vatican (9th cent.) MS. of St. John's Gospel quotes a saying of Papias about that Gospel and speaks of Papias as having been John's amanuensis. On the latter statement, see Lightfoot, *u.s.* p. 854; but the evidence seems good enough to induce us to believe that the work of Papias contained some notices of St. John's Gospel which Eusebius has not thought it worth while to mention. Papias belonged to Asia Minor, where the Fourth Gospel according to all tradition was written, and where its authority was earliest recognized; and he is described by Irenaeus as a companion of Polycarp, of whose use of St. John's Gospel we cannot doubt. Eusebius does not mention that Papias used the Apocalypse; but we learn that he did from other trustworthy authorities, and on the subject of Chiliasm Papias held views most distasteful to Eusebius. We learn from Irenaeus (v. 33) that Papias, in his fourth book, told, on the authority of "the Elder" [John], how our Lord had said that "the days will come when there shall be vines having 10,000 stems, and on each stem 10,000 branches, and on each branch 10,000 shoots, and on each shoot 10,000 clusters, and in each cluster 10,000 grapes, and each grape when pressed shall give 25 measures of wine. And when any of the saints shall take hold of a cluster, another shall cry out, I am a better cluster, take me, and bless the Lord through me." The story tells of similar predictions concerning other productions of the earth, and relates how the traitor Judas expressed his unbelief and was rebuked by our Lord. The ultimate original of this story of Papias was a Jewish apocryphal book made known by Ceriani, *Monumenta Sac. et Profan.*, in 1866. See the Apocalypse of Baruch, c. 29, in Fritzsche, *Libri Apoc. Vet. Test.* p. 666. To this, and possibly other similar stories, Eusebius no doubt refers when he says that Papias had related certain strange parables and teachings of the Saviour and other things of a fabulous character. Amongst these Eusebius quotes the doctrine that after the resurrection the kingdom of Christ would be exhibited for a thousand years in a sensible form on this earth; and he considers that things spoken mystically by the apostles had wrongly been understood literally by Papias, who "was a man of very poor understanding as his writings shew." The common text of Eusebius elsewhere (iii. 26) calls him a very learned man, deeply versed in the Holy Scriptures; but the weight of evidence is against the genuineness of the clause containing this encomium, which probably expresses later church opinion.

Eusebius tells nothing as to Papias's use of St. Paul's Epistles, and, though the silence of Eusebius alone would not go far, Papias may have found no occasion to mention them in a work on the gospel history. In looking for traditions of our Lord's life, Papias would naturally inquire after the testimony of those who had seen Him in the flesh. The very gratuitous inference from the assumed fact that Papias does not quote St. Paul, that he must have been Ebionite and anti-Pauline, is negatived by the fact that, as Eusebius testifies, he used St. Peter's Epistle, a work the teaching of which, as all critics allow, is completely Pauline. If the silence of Eusebius as to the use by Papias of St. John's Gospel and St. Paul's Epistles affords any presumption, it is that Papias gave no indication that his opinion about the undisputed books differed from that which, in the time of Eusebius, was received as unquestioned truth. For Eusebius thought meanly of Papias and, if he had known him to have held wrong opinions about the Canon, would have been likely to have mentioned it in disparagement of his authority in support of Chiliasm.

Eusebius says that Papias tells a story of a woman accused before our Lord of many sins, a story also to be found in the Gospel according to the Hebrews. There is a reasonable probability that this story may be that of the woman taken in adultery, now found in the common text of St. John's Gospel. Eusebius does not say that Papias took this story from the Gospel according to the Hebrews, and the presumption is that Papias gave it as known to him by oral tradition and not from a written source. If so, Papias need have had no direct knowledge of the Gospel according to the Hebrews. Papias has a story about Justus Barsabas having taken a cup of poison without injury. If Papias's copy of St. Mark contained the disputed verses at the end, this story might appropriately have been told to illustrate the verse, "If they drink any deadly thing it shall not hurt them," a promise instances of the fulfilment of which are very rare, whether in history or legend. A story of the kind is told of the apostle John, but is probably later than Papias, or we should have been likely to have heard of it here.

Georgius Hamartolus quotes Papias as saying, in his second book, that the apostle John had been killed by the Jews. That there is some blunder is clear; but Lightfoot has made it very probable from comparison with a passage in Origen that a real saying of Papias is quoted, but with the omission of a line or two. Papias, in commenting on Matt. xx. 22, may very well have said, as does Origen, that John had been condemned by the Roman emperor to exile at Patmos and that James had been killed by the Jews.

In JOANNES PRESBYTER we quote several authorities (including Irenaeus) who speak of Papias as a disciple of John the Evangelist. He is called by Anastasius of Sinai ὁ πάνυ and ὁ πολύς, and passed in the church as an authority of the highest rank. Jerome (*Ep. ad Lucinium*, 71 Vallars.) contradicts a report that he had translated the writings of Papias and Polycarp, declaring that he had neither leisure nor ability for such a task. He does not, in his writings, shew any signs that he knew more of the work of Papias than he could have learned from Eusebius. The latest trace of the existence of the work of Papias is that an inventory, A.D. 1218, of the possessions of the cathedral of Nismes (Menard. *Hist. civil. ecclés. et littér. de la ville de Nismes*) contains the entry "Item inveni in claustro—librum Papie librum de verbis Domini." No trace of this MS. has been recovered. The fragments of Papias have been assembled in various collections, *e.g.* Grabe (*Spicilegium*), Galland and Routh (*Rel. Sac.*), but can best be read in Gebhardt and Harnack's *Apost. Fathers*, pt. ii.; a trans. is in the vol. of *Apost. Fathers* in *Ante-Nicene Lib.* (T. & T. Clark). Dissertations on Papias are very numerous; we may mention important articles in the *Theol. Studien und Kritiken* by Schleiermacher, 1832, Zahn, 1867, Steitz, 1868; an essay by Weiffenbach (Giessen, 1876), a reply by Leimbach (Gotha, 1878), and a rejoinder by Weiffenbach, *Jahrbuch f. prot. Theol.* 1877; Hilgenfeld in his *Journal*, 1875, 1877, 1879; Lightfoot, *Contemp. Rev.* 1867, 1875; Harnack, *Chronologie*.

Others of the name of Papias are—a martyr with Victorinus (Assemani, *Act. Mart. Or. et Occ.* ii. 60); a martyr with Onesimus at Rome, Feb. 16; a physician at Laodicea (Fabric. *Bibl. Gr.* vii. 154); and a grammarian Papias in the 11th cent., a note of whose on the Maries of the Gospel was published by Grabe among the fragments of Papias of Hierapolis and accepted as such until Lightfoot established the true authorship. [G.S.]

Papylus (*Papirius* or *Papyrius*, as Rufinus, and Ado after him, write), April 13. In 1881 Aubé brought some new facts to light respecting this martyr from the Greek MSS. in the *Bibliothèque Nationale*. Papylus is mentioned by Eusebius (*H. E.* iv. 15) at the end of his account of Polycarp's martyrdom. Ruinart (p. 27), in his preface to the Acts of Polycarp, says that according to Eusebius Papylus and his companions Carpus and Agathonice suffered about the same time as Polycarp. This is a mistake of the Bollandist Henschenius, arising out of the Latin version of Eusebius, which inserts the words "sub id tempus," which have no equivalent in the Greek original. The Acts of Papylus contained in Metaphrastes assign his martyrdom to the Decian persecution. These Acts, however, Aubé thinks utterly worthless. In the *Revue archéologique*, Dec. 1881, p. 350, he published a Greek MS. containing Acts which he thinks may be those seen by Eusebius. Aubé seems to agree in placing the martyrdom of Papylus in the Decian persecution. But Lightfoot points out (*Ignatius*, i. 625) that in the Acts mention is made of emperors in the plural, thence he infers that this rather points to the reign of M. Aurelius or of Severus. [G.T.S.]

Parmenianus, successor to Donatus the Great, who followed Majorinus as Donatist bp. of Carthage. Optatus calls him "peregrinus," *i.e.* probably not a native of Africa. Having adopted Donatist opinions, he succeeded Donatus *c.* 350, was banished A.D. 358, and returned under the decree of Julian A.D. 362 (Aug. *Retract.* ii. 17; Eus. *Chron.* ap. Hieron. *Opp.* vol. iii. p. 687). About this time, if not earlier, he published a work, not now extant, in five parts, in defence of Donatism, to which the treatise of Optatus is a reply. About 372 Tichonius, a Donatist, well versed in Scripture, becoming sensible of the narrow and exclusive views of the sect, wrote a book to condemn them, but without abandoning his party. Parmenian replied, condemning the doctrine of Tichonius as tending to connect the true church, that of the Donatists, with the corrupt one, the Catholic, especially its African branch. A council of 270 Donatist bishops was convened at Carthage, which sat for 75 days and at last resolved that "traditors," even if they refused rebaptism, should be admitted to communion (Aug. *Ep.* 93, 43).

The time of this council is not known. Parmenian died and was succeeded by Primian *c.* 392; but his book against Tichonius fell into the hands of St. Augustine, who, at the request of his friends, discussed it in a treatise in three books, *c.* 402-405 (Tillem. xiii. 128 and note 32). For a full account of the treatise, with a list of Scripture quotations, see Ribbek, *Donatus und Augustinus*, pp. 348-366. (See also Aug. *Retract.* ii. 17.) [H.W.P.]

Pascentius (1), steward or controller of imperial property in Africa, *comes domus regiae*, severe in the execution of his office, an Arian and a bitter opponent of the Catholic faith, very troublesome to the simple-minded and perhaps not very highly educated clergy of Carthage. (Possidius, *Vit. Aug.* c. 17; Böcking, *Not. Dign.* c. 11, vol. ii. p. 374·393.) He requested St. Augustine to confer with him at Carthage on the subject of religion, A.D. 406, but refused to allow written notes of the discussion to be made, and asserted that Augustine was afraid to declare his opinions. Augustine therefore wrote two letters in succession to give Pascentius an opportunity of reply. Augustine, compelled by his opponent's repeated evasions to declare his own belief, exhibits this in terms closely resembling the Athanasian Creed, its method of illustration, and sometimes its very words (Aug. *Ep.* 238, 239). Aug. *Opp.* vol. ii. *App.* pp. 1153-1162, ed. Migne; Tillem. *Mém.* vol.

xiii. 164, 165 and note 41; Ceill., vol. ix. pp. 185, 186, 194. [H.W.P.]

Paschasinus (2), bp. of Lilybaeum in Sicily, *c.* 440, when that country was devastated by Vandal raids (Leonis Magni, *Ep.* iii. c. i. Migne's ed., note *e*). Leo the Great, sending him pecuniary assistance, consulted him about the Paschal cycle (A.D. 443). He replies in favour of the Alexandrian computation against the Roman, but in an abject strain of deference to his patron. He relates in confirmation of his view a miracle which used to occur in the baptistery of an outlying church on the property of his see on the true Paschal Eve every year, the water rising miraculously in the font (*ib.* c. 3). In 451 he received another letter from Leo desiring him to make inquiries as to the Paschal cycle (*Ep.* lxxxviii. c. 4) and sending him the Tome to stir up his energies in the cause of orthodoxy. Immediately after he was sent as one of Leo's legates to the council of Chalcedon (*Ep.* lxxxix.) and presided on his behalf (Labbe, *Conc.* vol. iv. p. 580 E, etc. The phrase "synodo praesidens," however, does not occur in the Acta of the council, but only in the signatures of the prelates representing Rome.) [C.G.]

Paschasius (3), deacon of Rome, called by Gregory the Great in his *Dialogues*, bk. iv. c. 40, "a man of great sanctity." He was a firm supporter of the antipope Laurentius to his death, and his adhesion was a great source of strength to the opponents of Symmachus (cf. Baronius, ann. 498). There is extant a work of his in two books, *de Sancto Spiritu* (*Patr. Lat.* lxii. 9-40), which Gregory (*u.s.*) calls "libri rectissimi ac luculenti." The date of his death was *c.* 512. [G.W.D.]

Pastor (1). This name is connected with traditions of the Roman church, which, though accepted as historical by Baronius and other writers, including Cardinal Wiseman (*Fabiola*, p. 189), must be rejected as mythical. These traditions relate to the origin of two of the oldest of the Roman *tituli*, those of St. Pudentiana and St. Praxedis, which still give titles to cardinals, and the former of which claims to be the most ancient church in the world. The story is that Peter when at Rome dwelt in the house of the senator Pudens in the vicus Patricius, and there held divine service, his altar being then the only one at Rome. Pudens is evidently intended as the same who is mentioned II. Tim. iv. 21. His mother's name is said to have been Priscilla, and it is plainly intended to identify her with the lady who gave to an ancient cemetery at Rome its name. The story relates that Pudens, on the death of his wife, converted his house into a church and put it under the charge of the priest Pastor, from whom it was known us "titulus Pastoris." This *titulus* is named in more than one document, but in all the name may have been derived from the story. Thus in the Acts of Nemesius, pope Stephen is said to have held a baptism there (Baronius, A.D. 257, n. 23). Our story relates that the baptistery had been placed there by pope Pius I., who often exercised the episcopal functions in this church. Here the two daughters of Pudens, Pudentiana and Praxedis, having given all their goods to the poor, dedicated themselves to the service of God. This church, under the name of Ecclesia Pudentiana, is mentioned in an inscription of A.D. 384, and there are epitaphs of priests *tituli Pudentis* of A.D. 489 and 528 (de Rossi, *Bull.* 1867, n. 60; 1883, p. 107). The original authority for the story appears to be a letter purporting to be written by Pastor to Timothy (see Boll. *AA. SS.* May 19, iv. 299). He informs Timothy of the death of his brother Novatus, who, during his illness, had been visited by Praxedis, then the only surviving sisters. He obtains Timothy's consent to the application of the property of Novatus to religious uses according to the direction of Praxedis; and baths possessed by Novatus in the vicus Lateritius are converted into a second titulus, now known as of St. Praxedis. This titulus is mentioned in an epitaph of A.D. 491 (de Rossi, *Bull.* 1882, p. 65); and priests of both tituli sign in the Roman council of 499. On this letter are founded false letters of pope Pius I. to Justus of Vienna, given in Baronius (*Ann.* 166, i.), a forgery later than the Isodorian Decretals. Those who maintain the genuineness of the letter of Pastor are met by the chronological difficulty of connecting Pudens with both St. Paul and Pius I. It has been argued that such longevity is not impossible; and it has been suggested that Praxedis and Pudentiana were not granddaughters of Pudens. But the spuriousness of the whole story has been abundantly shown by Tillemont (ii. 286, 615). [G.S.]

Patricius (10) (*St. Patrick*), Mar. 17, the national apostle of Ireland, has been the subject of much controversy. His existence has been doubted, his name ascribed to 7 different persons at least, and the origin and authority of his mission warmly disputed.

I. *The Documents.*—The materials for St. Patrick's history which have a claim to be regarded as historical are, in the first place, the writings of the saint himself. We have two works ascribed to him, his Confession and his Epistle to Coroticus. Both seem genuine.

We have a copy of the Confession more than 1,000 years old preserved in the Book of Armagh, one of the great treasures of the library of Trinity College, Dublin. This copy professes, in the colophon appended to it, to have been taken from the autograph of dt. Patrick. "Thus far the volume which St. Patrick wrote with his own hand." Dr. Todd, in his Life of St. Patrick (p. 347), sums up the case for the Confession of St. Patrick: "It is altogether such an account of himself as a missionary of that age, circumstanced as St. Patrick was, might be expected to compose. Its Latinity is rude and archaic, it quotes the ante-Hieronymian Vulgate; and contains nothing inconsistent with the century in which it professes to have been written. If it be a forgery, it is not easy to imagine with what purpose it could have been forged." This strong testimony might have been made stronger and applies equally clearly to the Ep. to Coroticus. There are two lines of evidence which seem conclusive as to the early date. The one deals with the State Organization, the other with the Ecclesiastical Organization there alluded to and implied. They are both such as existed early in the 5th cent., and could scarcely be imagined afterwards.

To take the State Organization first. In the Ep. to Coroticus he describes himself thus: "Ingenuus fui secundum carnem, decurione patre nascor." We now know that decurions—who were not magistrates but town councillors rather, and members of the local senates—were found all over the Roman empire to its extremest bounds by the end of the 4th cent. Discoveries in Spain last century showed that decurions were established by the Romans in every little mining village, charged with the care of the games, the water supply, sanitary arrangements, education, and the local fortifications; while Hübner in the *Corp. Insc. Lat.* t. vii. num. 54 and 189, showed that decurions existed in Britain (cf. Marquardt and Mommsen, *Handbuch der römischen Alterthümer*, t. iv. pp. 501-516 and *Ephem. Epigraph.* t. ii. p. 137; t. iii. p. 103). This institution necessarily vanished amid the barbarian invasions of the 5th cent. Now, St. Patrick's writings imply the existence of decurions. Again, the Confession calls England Britanniae, using the plural, which is strictly accurate and in accordance with the technical usage of the Roman empire at the close of the 4th cent., which then divided Britain into five provinces, Britannia prima and secunda, Maxima Caesariensis, Flavia Caesariensis and Valentia, which were collectively called Britanniae (cf. Böcking's *Notitia Dig.* t. ii. c. iii. pp. 12-14). Further, the Ecclesiastical Organization implied is such as the years about A.D. 400 alone could supply. St. Patrick tells us in the opening words of his Confession that his father was Calpurnius, a deacon, his grandfather Potitus, a priest. A careful review of the councils and canons will shew that in Britain and N. Gaul there existed no prohibition of clerical marriage in the last quarter of the 4th cent. Exuperius, bp. of Toulouse, wrote in 404 to pope Innocent I. asking how to deal with married priests who had begotten children since their ordination. Innocent's reply, dated Feb. 20, 405, shews, first, that the prohibition of marriage was only a late innovation, as he refers to the decree of pope Siricius, not quite 20 years before (Mansi, iii. 670; Hefele, ii. 387, Clark's ed.); secondly, that Innocent permitted the clergy of Toulouse to live with their wives if they had contracted marriage in ignorance of papal legislation.

The aspect of the political horizon, and the consequent action of the church as depicted in these writings, correspond with their alleged age. In the Ep. to Coroticus Patrick says, "It is the custom of the Roman Gallic Christians to send holy men to the Franks and other nations with many thousand solidi, to redeem baptized captives." The term Roman was then used to express a citizen of the Roman empire wherever he dwelt; and the custom itself is one of the strongest evidences as to age. The writings of Zosimus, Salvian, and Sidonius Apollinaris prove the ravages of the Franks in Gaul about the middle of the 5th cent. Salvian mentions the rescue of a captive taken at Cologne in *Ep.* I. SEVERINUS, the apostle of Austria, a little later in the century, devoted his life to the same work in another neighbourhood, and introduced the payment of tithes for this special object. (See his Life in Pez. *Scriptores Rerum Austriacarum*, t. i., and in Pertz, *Monumenta.*) By the end of the 5th cent. the Franks had been converted, and Clovis was the one orthodox sovereign of Christendom, the ally and champion of Catholic bishops. The redemption of captives would be then no longer necessary. This passage could only have been written about the middle of the 5th cent. at the latest. These instances will show how capable St. Patrick's own writings are of standing the tests of historical criticism.

Next in importance stand the collection of Patrician documents contained in the Book of Armagh. The contents of the book are: 1st, Patrician documents, including the oldest copy of the Confession; 2nd, the N.T. in Latin; 3rd, the Life of St. Martin of Tours. The N.T. is remarkable as the only complete copy which has come down from the ancient Celtic church. "The collections," says Mr. Gilbert (*Nat. MSS. of Ireland*), "concerning St. Patrick in the first part of the Book of Armagh constitute the oldest writings now extant in connexion with him, and are also the most ancient specimens known of narrative composition in Irish and Hiberno-Latin." These documents are all now accessible in print, though a critical edition of them, and indeed of the whole Book of Armagh, is a desideratum in Celtic literature.

II. *Life and History.*—The story of St. Patrick's life may be derived from the primary authorities, his own writings and the Patrician documents which really belong to the 7th and 8th cents. He was born probably at Kilpatrick, near Dumbarton in Scotland. St. Patrick, in the *Confession*, names Bannavem Taberniae as the residence of his parents, a name which cannot now be identified. (Cf. archbp. Moran in *Dublin Rev.*, Apr. 1880, pp. 291-326.) He was carried captive into Antrim when 16 years old, in one of those raids which Roman writers like Ammianus Marcellinus and Irish Annalists like the *Four Masters* shew were so prevalent during the 2nd half of the 4th cent. He became the slave of Milchu, the king of Dalaradia, the commencement of whose reign the *Four Masters* assign to 388, so that the very earliest year for St. Patrick's birth would be 372. Dalaradia was the most powerful kingdom of N.E. Ireland. It extended from Newry, in the S. of co. Down, to the hill of Slemish, the most conspicuous mountain of central Antrim. In the 7th cent. traditions about his residence there were abundantly current in the locality, as indeed they are still. He lived near the village of Broughshane, 5 or 6 miles E. of Ballymena, where a townland, Ballyligpatrick, the town of the hollow of Patrick, probably commemorates the position of the farm where he fed Milchu's swine (cf. Dr. Reeves's *Antiq. of Down and Connor*, pp. 78, 83, 84, 334-348). After 7 years he escaped, went to Gaul and studied under Germanus of Auxerre. He remained for a very long period, some say 30, others 40 years, in Gaul, where he was ordained priest and bishop. He then returned to Ireland, visiting England on his way. He landed where the river Vartry flows into the sea at Wicklow, as Palladius had done before him. It was a very natural point for mariners in those days to make, though now a port diligently avoided by them. Wicklow head offers shelter along a coast singularly destitute of harbours of refuge. The Danes three centuries later learned its advantage, and founded a settlement there, whence the modern name of Wicklow. The nature of the harbour was attractive to navigators like Palladius and Patrick. Its strand and murrough, or common, extending some miles N. from the Vartry, offered special opportunities for dragging up the small ships then used. St. Patrick was received in a very hostile manner by the pagans of Wicklow on landing. A shower of stones greeted them, and knocked out the front teeth of one of his companions, St. Mantan, whence the Irish name of Wicklow, Killmantan, or Church of Mantan (Joyce's *Irish Names*, p. 103; Colgan, *AA. SS.* p. 451; Reeves's *Antiquities*, p. 378). St. Patrick then sailed N., compelled with true missionary spirit to seek first of all that locality where he had spent seven years of his youth and had learned the language and customs of the Irish. We can still trace his stopping-places. Dublin only existed in those days as a small village beside a ford or bridge of hurdles over the Liffey, serving as a crossing-place for the great S.E. road from Tara to Wicklow, a bridge, like those still found in the bogs of Ireland, composed of branches woven together, which serve to sustain very considerable weights. St. Patrick landed, according to Tirechan, at an island off the N. coast of co. Dublin, still called Inispatrick (in 7th cent. Insula Patricii), whence he sailed to the coast of co. Down, where his frail bark was stopped by the formidable race off the mouth of Strangford Lough. He sailed up this lough, which extends for miles into the heart of co. Down, and landed at the mouth of the Slaney, which flows into the upper waters of the Lough, within a few miles of the church of Saul, a spot successfully identified by Mr. J. W. Hanna in a paper on the "True Landing-place of St. Patrick in Ulster" (Downpatrick, 1858). There he made his first convert Dichu, the local chief, and founded his first church in a barn which Dichu gave him, whence the name Sabhall (Celtic for barn) or Saul, which has ever since continued to be a Christian place of worship (cf. Reeves, *Antiq.* pp. 40, 220). From Dichu he soon directed his steps towards Central Antrim and king Milchu's residence, where he had spent the days of his captivity. His fame had reached Milchu, whose Druids warned him that his former servant would triumph over him. So Milchu set fire to all his household goods and perished in their midst just as St. Patrick appeared. St. Patrick now (A.D. 433), determining to strike a blow at the very centre of Celtic paganism, directed his course towards Tara. He sailed to the mouth of the Boyne, where, as the Book of Armagh tells us, he laid up his boats, as to this day it is impossible for the smallest boats to sail up the Boyne between Drogheda and Navan. Patrick proceeded along the N. bank of the river to the hill of Slane, the loftiest elevation in the country, dominating the vast plain of Meath. The ancient Life in the Book of Armagh is here marked by touches of geographical exactness which guarantee its truth. Being determined to celebrate Easter on the hill of Slane, he, according to the custom of the early Christians, lit his Paschal fire on Easter Eve, a custom which we know from other sources was universal at that time (cf. Martene, *de Antiq. Ritib.* t. iii. lib. iv. c. 24, pp. 144, 145, and arts. on "Easter, Ceremonies of," and "Fire, Kindling of," in *D. C. A.*).

This fire was at once seen on Tara, where the king of Ireland, Laoghaire, was holding a convention of the chiefs of Ireland. The ritual of the convention demanded that no fire should be lit in his dominions on this night till the king's fire was lit on Tara. St. Patrick's act directly challenged the edict of the king, who proceeded to Slane to punish the bold aggressor. The narrative of the conflict between St. Patrick and king Laoghaire and his priests is marked by a series of miracles and legends, terminating, however, with the defeat of paganism and the baptism of great numbers of the Irish, including Laoghaire himself, who yielded a nominal adhesion to the truth. (See Mr. Petrie's great work on the Hill of Tara, where the subject has been exhaustively discussed.)

The Paschal controversy, about which Cummian wrote (A.D. 634), throws an interesting light upon the date of the introduction of Christianity into Ireland. The Irish have been accused of Quartodeciman practices as to Easter, which is quite a mistake. They simply adhered to the old Roman cycle, which was superseded in 463 by the Victorian cycle. ["Easter," in *D. C. A.* vol. i. p. 594.] The invasions of the barbarians then cut off the Celtic church from a knowledge of the more modern improvements in the calendar, which they afterwards resisted with a horror natural to simple people. The English surplice riots of bp. Blomfield's time shew how a much shorter tradition may raise a popular commotion. This fixes the introduction of Christianity into Ireland in the first half of 5th cent. The alleged connexion of the Irish church with Egypt and the East, as shewn in art, literature, architecture, episcopal and monastic arrangements, would afford material for an interesting article on the peculiarities of the Irish church. (See Butler's *Coptic Churches of Egypt*, Oxf. 1885.)

See Sir Samuel Fergusson's treatise on the *Patrician Documents* in the *Transactions of the Royal Irish Academy* (Dec. 1885), and Benjamin Robert's *Etude critique sur la vie de St. Patrice* (Paris, 1883), where a diligent use has been made of modern authorities, and, pp. 3-7, a convenient summary given of the literature. A cheap popular Life by E. J. Newell is pub. by S.P.C.K. in their *Fathers for Eng. Readers*, who also pub. the *Epp. and Hymns, including the poem of Secundinus in his praise*, in Eng. ed. by T. Olden. Cf. esp. *The Tripartite Life of Patrick*, with other documents, etc., by Whitley Stokes in Rolls Series, No. 89, 2 vols. (Lond. 1887); also W. Bright, *The Roman See in the Early Church*, pp. 367-385 (Lond. 1896). [G.T.S.]

Patroclus (2) (*St. Parre*), Jan. 21, a martyr supposed to have suffered under Aurelian, and commemorated by Greg. Turon. *Glor. Mart.* c. 64. His Acts are fully told by the Bollandists, *AA. SS* Jan. ii. 342-349. A curious story told by Gregory (*l.c.*) shews how his Acts originated. Patroclus had a chapel in Gaul served by a solitary priest. The populace despised this chapel because it possessed no Acts of his passion, and a traveller came to the priest one day and shewed him a book which proved to be the Acts of his own saint. The priest sat up all night copying them, and then returned the book to the traveller, who went his way. The priest at once shewed his bishop the Acts. The prelate was suspicious, taxed him with forgery, and, according to the stern discipline of the Gallic church, flogged him on the spot. An army, however, shortly afterwards invaded Italy, and brought back an identical copy of the Acts, thus proving the good faith of the priest. The people thereupon built a splendid church in honour of Patroclus. [G.T.S.]

Patroclus (3), bp. of Arles, between SS. Heros and Honoratus (A.D. 412-426). In 412 the people of Arles drove out Heros and elected Patroclus, a creature of Constantius (Prosper Aquit. *Chronicon*, Migne, *Patr. Lat.* li. 590). As bishop he is said to have sold ecclesiastical offices (Prosper Tyro, *Chronicon*, in Bouquet i. 638) and hoarded up stores of ill-gotten wealth (cf. the funeral sermon of Hilary of Arles upon St. Honoratus, c. vi. *Patr. Lat.* l. 1265). He seems, however, to have commended himself to pope Zosimus, who conferred upon him unprecedented privileges of jurisdiction, and his history illustrates the relations of the French dioceses. On the ground that Arles was the fountain-head of Gallic Christianity, the pope confirmed to the see all parishes it had ever held, whether within the province or not, and gave Patroclus exclusive rights of ordination over the independent provinces of Vienne, Narbonensis Prima, and Narbonensis Secunda, and deposed Proculus, bp. of Marseilles, for infringing these privileges by ordaining in his own diocese. On the ground of Patroclus's personal merits, the pope, in a letter addressed to all the Gallic bishops, forbade any cleric of whatever rank to visit Rome without first obtaining *literae formatae*, or letters of identification and recommendation, from the bp. of Arles. See the pope's correspondence from Mar. 22, 417, to Feb. 5, 418, which is chiefly occupied with Arles, *Epp.* i. v. vi. vii. x. xi. Migne, *Patr. Lat.* xx. 643, 665, 666, 668, 673, 674. These privileges were productive of great dissatisfaction in the neighbouring provinces and, in the matter of the jurisdiction, Zosimus's orders were virtually rescinded by his successor, Bonifacius I., who, in a letter written Feb. 9, 422, asserted the right of Hilary, bp. of Narbonne, to consecrate the bp. of Lodève in his province, as against Patroclus, who had usurped it (*Ep.* xii. *Patr. Lat.* xx. 772-774). In 425 Patroclus was ordered by Theodosius to assemble for discussion the Gallic bishops who professed the Pelagian and Celestian heresies, the emperor decreeing exile for such as should not recant within 20 days. Patroclus was murdered in 426 by a barbarian officer (*Chronicon, Patr. Lat.* li. 593-594). [S.A.B.]

Patrophilus (1) of Scythopolis, one of the original Arian party, took a leading part in all their principal acts and was one of the most relentless opponents of Athanasius, by whom he is designated as a πνευματόμαχος (*adv. Serap.* iv. 7, p. 360). He enjoyed considerable reputation for theological learning, and trained Eusebius of Emesa in the exposition of Scripture (Socr. *H. E.* ii. 9). When Arius, driven from Alexandria, took refuge in Palestine, Patrophilus was one of the Palestinian bishops who warmly espoused his cause, wrote in support of his teaching (Athan. *de Synod.* p. 886), and in A.D. 323 joined with Paulinus of Tyre and Eusebius of Caesarea in summoning a local synod, which granted Arius permission to hold private religious assemblies (Soz. *H. E.* i. 15). At Nicaea he was one of the 17 episcopal partisans of Arius, and united with them in drawing up a creed which was indignantly rejected by the council (Theod. *H. E.* i. 7). Embittered by defeat, he became one of the most relentless persecutors of Athanasius. In 330 he took part in the synod at Antioch by which Eustathius was deposed (*ib.* i. 21). At the synod of Tyre (A.D. 335) he was one of the most active in bringing about the condemnation of Athanasius (Labbe, ii. 436; Athan. *Apol. c. Arian.* cc. 73, 74, 77), and the same year he attended the abortive synod of the Dedication at Jerusalem (Socr. *H. E.* i. 31; Soz. *H. E.* ii. 26; Theod. *H. E.* i. 31). Passing thence to Constantinople at the empress's command, he denounced Athanasius as having threatened the imperial city with starvation by preventing the sailing of the Alexandrian corn-ships, and procured his banishment to Trèves (Socr. *H. E.* i. 35; Theod. *H. E.* i. 31; Theophan. p. 26; Athan. *Apol. c. Arian.* c. 87). In 341 he took part in the ambiguous council of Antioch, *in Encaeniis* (Soz. *H. E.* iii. 5). He was one of the ordainers of George, the violent heterodox intruder into the see of Alexandria in 353 (*ib.* iv. 8), and with his leader Acacius kept entirely aloof from Athanasius when Maximus of Jerusalem welcomed him on his return from banishment in 346, and before long contrived to establish Cyril in Maximus's place as their own nominee (Theophan. p. 34; Gwatkin, *Studies of Arianism*, p. 145). He was one of the few Eastern bishops who attended the council of Milan in 355 (his name appearing erroneously in the lists as Stratophilus), and he took part in the condemnation and deposition of Eusebius of Vercelli, on whose banishment to Scythopolis, Patrophilus, "his jailer," as Eusebius calls him, vented his annoyance by studied insults and ill-treatment (Eus. Vercell. *Ep.* apud Baronium *Annal.* 356, No. 93). According to Philostorgius (*H. E.* iv. 8-10) Patrophilus poisoned the mind of Constantius against Basil of Ancyra, who had at one time exercised unbounded influence over him, and was the proposer of the scheme of breaking up the proposed general council into two. When the Eastern division met at Seleucia, Sept. 27, 359, Patrophilus was a leading member of the shifty Acacian party pledged to the Homoiousion. Finding the majority of the synod against them, he and his party refused to take part in the later sessions, and at the fourth sitting, Oct. 1, he shared in the sentence of deposition passed on Acacius and his followers (Socr. *H. E.* ii. 40; Soz. *H. E.*

iv. 23). He immediately returned home, where he was kept informed by Acacius of the course events were taking in the synod held at Constantinople (Jan. 360), when Aetius and the Anomoeans were condemned, several leading semi-Arians deposed, the Ariminian creed imposed, and Eudoxius enthroned bp. of Constantinople (Socr. *H. E.* ii. 43). He died very soon afterwards, for his grave was desecrated during the temporary pagan reaction under Julian in 361, when his remains were scattered and his skull mockingly used as a lamp (Theoph. p. 40; Niceph. x. 13; *Chron. Pasch.* (ed. Ducange, 1688), p. 295; Tillem. *Mém. ecclés.* t. vi. vii.; Le Quien, *Or. Christ.* iii. 683). [E.V.]

Paula (2), a noble and wealthy Roman lady, who accompanied Jerome to Palestine in 385, and lived the rest of her life at Bethlehem, dying in 404. The chief facts of her life were given in Jerome's *Epitaphium* of her addressed to Eustochium (Hieron. *Ep.* 108, ed. Vall.). She was born in 347, and while quite young was married to the senator Toxotius, of the Julian family, which traced its descent from Aeneas. Through her mother Blaesilla she was connected with the Scipios and the Gracchi, through her father Rogatus with a Greek family, which traced its descent from Agamemnon. Her family was connected with the Aemilian gens, and her name taken from that of the illustrious Paulus. Jerome records these ancestral glories in her epitaph,

Scipio quam genuit, Pauli fudere parentes,
Gracchorum soboles, Agamemnonis inclyta proles.

She was possessed of great wealth, owning, amongst other properties, the town of Nicopolis or Actium. During her early married life, though always without reproach in her character, she lived in the usual luxury of Roman patricians. She gave birth to four daughters, BLAESILLA, who married, but lost her husband and died early in 384; PAULINA, wife of PAMMACHIUS; Julia, called EUSTOCHIUM, and Ruffina, who died early, probably in 386; and one son, called after his father Toxotius. After the birth of a son she appears to have adopted the practice of continency (Hieron. *Ep.* cviii. 4), but to have still lived with her husband, whose death (probably in 380) she deeply lamented. In 382, during the synod held at Rome (following on the council of Constantinople), she entertained the bps. Epiphanius of Salamis and Paulinus of Antioch, and by them her ascetic tendencies, already considerable, were heightened. Through them Jerome, who had come to Rome with them, became her friend. She imbibed through him her love for the study of Scripture, and, with her daughter Eustochium, attended his readings at the palace of Marcella. She gave vast sums to the poor, spending her own fortune and that of her children in charity. She assumed a coarse dress and a sordid appearance, and undertook all sorts of menial duties in the relief of distress. But her mind was set upon the monastic life and upon the country of the Eastern hermits. After the death of Blaesilla she determined to quit Rome, and, early in 385, disregarding the tears of her son Toxotius, then a child, who was left to the wardship of the praetor, and the entreaties of Ruffina, then a girl of marriageable age, who begged her mother to wait till she was married, she sailed for the East. After visiting Epiphanius in Cyprus, she rejoined Jerome and his friends at Antioch. With him she braved the winter's journey through Lebanon to Palestine [HIERONYMUS] and Egypt, from whence returning the whole party settled in Bethlehem in the autumn of 386.

Their life there is related under HIERONYMUS, and only personal details need here be given. Her letter to Marcella inviting her to come to Palestine (Hieron. *Ep.* 46) shows her enthusiastic delight in every sacred place and association in the Holy Land. Paula and Eustochium lived at first in a cottage till their convent and hospice (*diversorium*) were built. They then founded a monastery for men, and a convent of three degrees for women, who lived separately, though having the same dress, and met for the services. Paula's capacity of management, her patience and tact, are warmly praised by Jerome (*Ep.* cviii. c. 19). She is said by Palladius (*Hist. Laus.* 79) to have had the care of Jerome and to have found it a difficult task. Her scriptural studies, begun in Rome, were carried on earnestly at Bethlehem. She had (through her father's family) a good knowledge of Greek, and she learnt Hebrew to be able to repeat and sing the Psalms in the original (c. 26). She read constantly with Jerome, and they went through the whole Bible together (*ib.*). In his account of his writings in the catalogue (*de Vir. Ill.* 135) written in 392, Jerome says, "Epistolarum ad Paulam et Eustochium, quia quotidie scribuntur, incertus est numerus." She was remarkably teachable, and when doubts were suggested to her by Origenistic teachers, she was able at once, with Jerome's help, to put them aside. Her charities were so incessant that Jerome states that she left Eustochium with a great debt, which she could only trust the mercy of Christ would enable her to pay (c. 15). It is believed that Jerome, who had in vain counselled prudence and moderation (*ib.*), gave her pecuniary help in her later years. Her health was weak; her body slight; her mortifications, against many of which Jerome remonstrated and which gave occasion to some scandals, and her frequent illnesses had worn her away; and in her 57th year (404) she sank under a severe attack of illness. Jerome describes with deep feeling the scene at her death, the personal attention of her daughter to all her wants, the concern of the whole Christian community. The bishops of the surrounding cities were present. John of Jerusalem, who only four years before had been at strife with the convents of Bethlehem, was there. Her funeral was a kind of triumph, the whole church being gathered together to carry her to her resting-place in the centre of the cave of the Nativity. She is reckoned as a saint by the Roman church, her day, that of her death, being Jan. 26. [W.H.F.]

Paula (3), granddaughter of foregoing, daughter of Toxotius, and of Laeta the daughter of Albinus, a heathen and a priest. Laeta embraced Christianity and wrote to consult Jerome as to Paula's education, who replied in *Ep.* 107, written in 401. He desires that she should lead the ascetic life and prepare to consecrate herself to Christ in virginity; and begs that, if she could not carry out at Rome the system of instruction in scriptural knowledge which he prescribed, she might be sent to Bethlehem. She was probably sent there while still a child, though not till after her grandmother's death. Several of Jerome's commentaries are dedicated to her with her aunt Eustochium, and she is mentioned by both Jerome and Augustine in their correspondence in 416 (Hieron. *Epp.* 134, 143, both to Augustine). [W.H.F.]

Paulina (1), daughter of Paula the friend of Jerome, and wife of PAMMACHIUS. She married about the time when her mother and her sister Eustochium went with Jerome to Palestine in 385. Her children died at birth and she herself probably died in childbirth in 397. Her merits are described in consolatory letters to Pammachius from Jerome (*Ep.* 66, ed. Vall.) and Paulinus (*Ep.* 13, Migne's *Patr. Lat.* vol. 61). [W.H.F.]

Paulinianus, younger brother of Jerome. He was still young in 385 ("adolescens," Hieron. *c. Ruf.* iii. 22) when he left Rome with his brother and their friend Vincentius, and he was under 30 when ordained in 394 (Hieron. *adv. Joan. Hier.* § 8). He shared his brother's journeys in Palestine and settled with him in Bethlehem, where he probably remained to the end of his life. He was modest, only desiring to help his brother in the monastery. But Epiphanius, coming to Jerusalem in 394, and finding (or rather promoting) a schism between the monasteries of Bethlehem and bp. John of Jerusalem, took him to the monastery which he had founded at Ad, and there, against the protests and even resistance of Paulinian, ordained him priest. (See in Hieron. *Ep.* li. 1, ed. Vall. the trans. of Epiphanius's explanatory letter to John of Jerusalem.) Paulinian may perhaps have acted as presbyter in the monasteries for a time, but he felt it prudent during the vehement controversy which sprang up between Jerome and bp. John of Jerusalem to go to Epiphanius in Cyprus. Jerome declares (*contra Joannem* § 41) that his brother was in Cyprus. [W.H.F.]

Paulinus (3), bp. of Tyre and afterwards of Antioch, A.D. 328-329 (Clinton, *F. R.*). He was apparently a native of Antioch, and, according to his friend and panegyrist Eusebius (Eus. *in Marcell.* i. 4, p. 19), filled the office of bp. of Tyre with great splendour, and after the cessation of the persecution rebuilt with great magnificence the cathedral elaborately described by the historian in the inaugural oration delivered by him at its dedication (*ib. H. E.* x. 4). Paulinus was "claimed by the church of the Antiochenes as their own property," ὡς οἰκείου ἀγαθοῦ μεταποιηθῆναι, and chosen their bishop. According to Philostorgius, he only held his new dignity for half a year before his death (Philost. *H. E.* iii. 15). Paulinus, like his friend Eusebius of Caesarea, was an Arianizer, claimed by Arius in his letter to Eusebius of Nicomedia as one of his sympathizers (Theod. *H. E.* i. 5). Eusebius of Caesarea lavishes unstinting praise on his fellow-partisan, dedicates to him his *Ecclesiastical History* (Eus. *H. E.* x. 1), and speaks with great indignation of the unfounded charges brought against him by Marcellus, with the view of fixing on him the impious tenet that our blessed Lord is no more than a created being (*in Marcell. u.s.*). [E.V.]

Paulinus (4), St., 6th bp. of Trèves, between St. Maximinus and St. Bonosus, one of the foremost Gallic champions of orthodoxy against Arianism. He was probably consecrated in 349. In 351, at the council of Sirmium, Paulinus seems to have boldly championed the orthodox cause. The letter of condemnation of Athanasius tendered for his signature he scornfully rejected, exclaiming that he would sign the condemnation of Photinus and Marcellus, but not of Athanasius (Sulpicius Severus, *Hist. Sacr.* ii. 37, Migne, *Patr. Lat.* xx. 150). At the council of Arles in 353 Paulinus's fate was decided. The emperor Constantius there decreed the banishment of bishops who should refuse to subscribe the condemnation of Athanasius. Paulinus remained steadfast, and, after being condemned by the bishops, was driven into exile in Phrygia, to parts inhabited by heathen and heretics. This occurred in 353 or, at latest, in 354, not 356, as Jerome gives it. He died in 358 or 359. The church of his name outside the walls was one of the earliest at Trèves (Wilmowsky, *Der Dom zu Trier*, p. 11).

For his life see, further, the passages from the works of Athanasius collected, Boll. *Acta SS.* Aug. vi. 669 sqq.; Hilarius, *ad Const. Aug.* lib. i.; *Lib. contra Const. Imp.* 11; *Fragr.* Migne, *Patr. Lat.* x. 562, 588, 631. [S.A.B.]

Paulinus (5) (*Paulonas*), a priest and a disciple of Ephraem Syrus. Gennadius (*de Script. Eccl.* c. iii. in *Patr. Lat.* lviii. 1062) gives a short account of him, speaking of his great talent, knowledge of Scripture, and power as a preacher. After his master's death he "separated from the church, and wrote much against the faith," being of an ambitious temperament and eager for renown. [G.W.D.]

Paulinus (6), bp. of the Eustathian or old Catholic party at Antioch, 362-388, a man highly esteemed for piety. He was one of Eustathius's presbyters, and, subsequently to the death of Eustathius, was recognized as the head of the Eustathians, who, refusing to hold communion with Meletius, with whom they were doctrinally agreed, in consequence of his having been appointed and consecrated by Arians, remained some time without a bishop, holding their meetings for worship in a small church within the walls of Antioch, the use of which had been granted by the Arian bp. Evagrius, out of respect for Paulinus's high character. Lucifer of Calaris, on his way home from his banishment in Upper Egypt, A.D. 362, went straight to Antioch, where, finding it impossible to reconcile the two contending parties he took the fatal step of ordaining Paulinus bp. of the Eustathian Catholics. This rendered union impossible, and the church had to lament the consequent schism at Antioch for more than half a century. The controversy between the churches of the West and of Egypt which supported Paulinus, and that of the East which adhered to Meletius, was not finally healed till Alexander became bp. of Antioch, A.D. 413. For the history of this protracted schism see LUCIFERUS of Calaris; EUSTATHIUS (3) of Antioch; MELETIUS (3) of Antioch; EUSEBIUS (93) of Vercelli; FLAVIANUS (4). The death of Paulinus may be dated 388. [E.V.]

Paulinus (7), writer of the Life of St. Ambrose, a work which he says he undertook at the request of St. Augustine. He was well qualified for his task by his intimate acquaintance with St. Ambrose and attendance upon him in his last illness, and by information gathered from well-informed persons, especially his sister Marcellina. He seems to call himself the bishop's secretary (*notarius*) and he was certainly with him at his death (cc. 33, 35, 38, 42, 47). In his introduction he expresses his great anxiety to adhere strictly to the truth and to deliver what he has to say impartially, and this he appears to have done. After the death of St. Ambrose he went to Africa, where he was well received by the church, and distinguished himself by defending the memory of his friend and patron against an attack upon him by Muranus, bp. of Bollita. It was perhaps this which led to his acquaintance with St. Augustine, and his becoming the biographer of St. Ambrose. He took a prominent part in the proceedings of the council of Carthage, A.D. 412, against Celestius. Morcelli, *Afr. Chr.* iii. pp. 57, 80; Cave, *Hist. Lit.* i. p. 402; Ceillier, vol. vii. p. 533, viii. 549, ix. 453. [H.W.P.]

Paulinus (8), St., bp. of Nola, one of a patrician family of whom some had been Christians (Ausonius, *Ep.* xxiv. 103; Paulin. *Ep.* xl. Prudentius, Symm. i. 558, 560; Baronius, 394, 78, 79). They had property in Aquitania, and probably resided there habitually (Ambros. *Ep.* lviii. 1). His father was *praefectus praetorio* of Gaul, had large possessions in the province in which he lived, and was the founder of the town of Burgus (Bourg) on the Dordogne, and, as well as his wife, appears to have been a Christian.

I. *First Period* (353-394).—Besides Paulinus, his parents had an elder son and a daughter. He was probably born at Bordeaux, A.D. 353 or 354, and his tutor was Ausonius, who thought very highly of him as a pupil, regarded him with warm affection, and addressed to him many of his poetical epistles. The affection of Ausonius was fully returned by his pupil, who declares that he owed to him all the distinction he had attained.

Whatever merit his Latin compositions possess, he was by his own admission not strong in Greek, and in a letter to Rufinus, A.D. 408, regrets his inability to translate accurately an epistle of St. Clement (*Ep.* xlvi. 2). He entered early into public life, became a member of the senate, and filled the office of consul for part of the official year in the place of some one who had vacated it; in what year is not known, his name not appearing in the *Fasti*, but before 379 when Ausonius held the office and says that his pupil attained the dignity earlier than himself (Aus. *Ep.* xx. 4, xxv. 60). Paulinus has been supposed also to have been prefect of New Epirus, a supposition consistent with his own mention of frequent and laborious journeys by land and sea, but of which there is no direct evidence, though an edict of the joint emperors Valentinian, Valens, and Gratian undoubtedly exists, addressed to a prefect of that province of his name, A.D. 372. He certainly held a judicial office, for in one of his poems he expresses satisfaction at having condemned no one to death during his tenure of it. Lebrun conjectures that after his consulship he became *consularis* of Campania and resided at Nola (*Carm.* xxi. 396; Tillem. vol. xiv. p. 8). Possessed of easy fortune and enjoying the best society, he lived a life free from outward reproach, but one for which he afterwards found great fault with himself. His health was never good, and he suffered much from fatigue in his journeys (*Carm.* x. 134; xiii. 2, 10; *Ep.* v. 4). In the course of them he fell in with Victricius bp. of Rouen and Martin bp. of Tours at Vienne in Gaul, and ascribed to the latter the restoration of his sight, the loss of which was threatened, apparently by cataract (*Ep.* xviii. 9; Sulpic. Sev. *Vit. S. Mart.* xix. 3, ed. Halm.). He also regarded St. Ambrose with great veneration, calling him "father" (*Ep.* iii. 4). But his chief object of veneration was Felix of Nola, to whom he devoted himself specially when he visited Nola at about 26 or 27 years of age, A.D. 379 (*Carm.* xiii. 7, 9; xxi. 350, 381). About this time, but not later than 389, he and his brother received baptism at Bordeaux, from Delphinus, the bishop there (*Epp.* iii. 4; xx. 6; xxxv.; xxxvi.). Not long after he began to think of retiring from the world, and in 389 or 390 went to Spain, residing chiefly at Barcelona. During this time he married a Spanish lady of good fortune and irreproachable character, named Therasia, and a son was born to them, who died after a few days (Prudentius, *Peristeph.* v. 41, 44; Dexter, *Chron.* A.D. 296; *Carm.* v. 66; xxi. 400; xxxv. 599, 610). There seems good reason for placing the violent death of his brother about this time, when not only his brother's property was in danger of confiscation, but that of Paulinus himself and even his life (*Carm.* xxi. 414-427; Buse, vol. i. p. 157). It was perhaps partly due to these events that during his stay in Spain he was led to give up the senate and worldly business and refused to take any further interest in "profane" literature (*Ep.* iv. 2; xxii. 3; *Carm.* x. 304, 316). But he continued to write verses on sacred subjects to the end of his life. Determined to renounce the world, he parted with a large portion of his property and his wife's, spending some of the money in redeeming captives, releasing debtors, and the like. In compliance with a sudden popular demand, he was ordained priest, but without any especial cure of souls, by Lampius, bp. of Barcelona, on Christmas Day, 393 (*Epp.* i. 10; ii. 2; iii. 4). He appears to have been already well acquainted with some of the most eminent African clergy, Alypius, Augustine, Aurelius, and others. In a letter to St. Augustine he mentions his work against the Manicheans, *i.e.* probably his *de Doctrina Christiana*, together with the single volume *de Vera Religione*, in which Manichean doctrine is discussed (Aug. *Ep.* xxvii. 4). In the same letter Paulinus speaks of his own abandonment of the world, and requests Augustine to instruct and direct him.

II. *Second Period* (394-409).—In 394 he determined to retire to Nola, where he had property, including a house. On his way he saw St. Ambrose, probably at Florence, and in a letter to Sulpicius, whom he begs to visit him at Nola, he speaks of much jealousy being shewn him at Rome by pope Siricius and others of the clergy, probably on account of the unusual circumstances of his ordination; whereas at Nola, where not long after his arrival he had a serious illness, he was visited by nearly all the bishops of Campania, either in person or by deputy, by clergymen and some laymen, and received friendly letters from many African bishops who sent messengers to him. At Nola he entered with his wife at once upon the course of life he had marked out, and which he pursued as far as possible until his death, A.D. 431. SS. Ambrose, Augustine, and Jerome regarded the self-sacrifice of him and his wife with high respect and admiration (Ambros. *Ep.* lviii. 1-3; Hieron. *Epp.* lviii. 6; cxviii. 5). Augustine writes to him in terms of warm admiration and affection (Aug. *Ep.* xxvii.), and in a second letter announces his appointment as coadjutor to Valerius, bp. of Hippo, and urges Paulinus to visit him in Africa (Aug. *Ep.* xxxi.). St. Jerome exhorts him and Therasia to persevere in their self-denial, and praises highly his panegyric on the emperor Theodosius, a work which he himself mentions but which has perished (Hieron. *Ep.* lviii.; Paul. *Ep.* xxviii. 6; Gennadius, c. 48). In reply to Augustine and to letters of the African bishops, Paulinus writes to Augustine's friend Romanianus, congratulating the African church on the appointment of Augustine and hoping that his "trumpet" may sound forcibly in the ears of Romanianus's son Licentius, to whom also he addressed a letter ending:

Vive precor, sed vive Deo, nam vivere mundo
Mortis opus, vera est vivere vita Deo.

When Paulinus settled at Nola, the burial-place of Felix, called in the Martyrology of Bede *in Pincis* or *in Pineis*, about a mile from the town, had become the site of four churches (*basilicae*), one built by pope Damasus, and also a chapel. Probably none of these were of any great size. Paulinus added a fifth. The church whose dedication he mentions in *Ep.* 32 is described by him as having a triple apse (*trichorum, i.e.* τρίχωρον). (*Ep.* xxxii. 17; Isid. *Orig.* xv. 8, 7.) It was perhaps on the site of the one built by Damasus, and contained not only the tomb of Felix, but beneath the altar (*altaria*) remains of various saints and martyrs, including SS. John Bapt., Andrew, Luke, Thomas, and others of less note, including St. Nazarius, of whom some relics were sent to him by Ambrose (*Ep.* xxxii. 17; *Carm.* xxvii. 436, 439), but above all the precious fragment of the true cross, brought from Jerusalem by Melania and presented by her to Paulinus A.D. 398, and of which he sent a chip (*astula*) enclosed in a tube of gold to Sulpicius, as a special offering from Therasia and himself to Bassula, his friend's mother-in-law, to honour the churches built by him at Primuliacum (*Ep.* xxxi.). The pavement, walls, and columns of this apse were marble, and the vaulted roof, from which lamps were suspended by chains, was ceiled with mosaic representing the Trinity symbolically, and also the twelve apostles, with an inscription in verse describing the subjects represented. Of this mosaic some remains were visible in 1512. All the buildings, both churches and cloisters, were adorned with pictures representing Scripture subjects, in the older church from the N.T. and in the newer one from O.T., for the introduction of which Paulinus apologizes on the score of their utility in occupying the attention of the illiterate people who flocked to the grave of Felix in large numbers at all times, and sometimes spent whole nights there in the winter, watching and fasting, having brought torches with them. With these pictures Paulinus hoped to employ their minds and prevent them from excess in eating or drinking (*Carm.* xxvii. 552-598).

Paulinus also devoted much pains and cost to the erection of a new church at Fundi, a place endeared to him by early recollections and at which he possessed property. He enriched it with relics of martyrs and apostles, including St. Andrew, St. Luke, SS. Nazarius, Gervasius, and Protasius (*Ep.* xxxii. 17).

His own residence was a house he had formerly built or enlarged as an asylum for the poor. He added a second story for the use of himself, his associates, and his visitors, reserving the ground-floor for the poor, so that by their ascending prayers the buildings above might be strengthened (*Ep.* xxix. 13; *Carm.* xxi. 390). His mode of life was monastic in the fullest sense, and he calls his house a monastery (*Ep.* v. 15). The inmates dressed themselves in hair cloth with a rope girdle, cut their hair in a manner studiously unbecoming, were perhaps not careful as to personal cleanliness, observed strict rules of silence and fasting, even during Easter-tide did not eat until about 3 p.m., and used mostly a vegetable diet, lying down to sleep on the ground, wrapped only in a coarse cloak or patch-work blanket, and abridging the time usually devoted to sleep (*Epp.* xv. 4; xxii. 1, 2, 3, 6; xxix. i. 13; *Carm.* xxxv. 445-497).

He seldom, if ever, left Nola, except to visit Rome once a year to join in the festival of SS. Peter and Paul, on June 29, the day of their martyrdom ("beatorum apostolorum natalem") (*Epp.* xvii. 2; xviii. 1; xx. 2; xliii. 1; xlv. 1; *Carm.* xxi. 132-166; Aug. *Ep.* xcv. 6).

The event of all the year which was the chief interest for him and his little community at Nola was the festival of St. Felix, on Jan. 14. For many years he always composed a poem in honour of the day. In one of the earlier poems Paulinus tells how multitudes came from all parts of S. Italy, to be cured of their ailments or relieved of troubles, or to thank God for cures or relief already granted; how even Rome sent forth thousands on the Appian road, which became encumbered by the crowds of pilgrims, and how Nola, for a short time, became almost as populous as Rome (*Ep.* xiv.).

III. *Third Period* (A.D. *c.* 409-431).—Paulinus became bp. of Nola before the autumn of 410, when Alaric laid waste Campania, for St. Augustine speaks of him as being then bp. of Nola. Therasia's death perhaps took place in the latter part of 408, though Tillemont and Buse seem to place it a year or two later. The diocese of Paulinus was a small one, and appears, at any rate formerly, to have been notorious for drunkenness and immorality (*Ep.* xlix. 14; *Carm.* xix. 164-218). Without adopting all the glowing panegyric applied by Uranius to his behaviour as bishop, we may well believe that he shewed himself in this, as in other matters, a faithful, devout, humble, and munificent follower of his Master; and when Campania was laid waste by Alaric, A.D. 410, Paulinus devoted all he had to the relief of the sufferers and captives. The barbarian occupation did not last long, and from this time until his death, in 431, there are few events to record in the life of Paulinus. A letter from St. Augustine, probably in 417, seems to hint at a tendency on the part of Paulinus to adopt some, at least, of the erroneous doctrines of Pelagius, with whom he had been on friendly terms (Aug. *Ep.* 186 i. 1, and xii. 41). After the death of Zosimus, in Dec. 418, the appointment of his successor in the see of Rome becoming a matter of dispute, the emperor Honorius summoned a council of bishops at Ravenna, and afterwards at Spoletum, and invited Paulinus to attend, but he excused himself on the first occasion on the ground of ill-health and was probably prevented by the same cause from appearing on the second (Baronius, 419, 19, 20). After residing 36 years in retirement at Nola, a period devoted both by himself, and during her lifetime by his wife, to unsparing self-denial, religious observances, and works of piety and charity without stint, he died June 22, A.D. 431, aged 77 or 78. An account of his last illness and death has been left by Uranius in a letter addressed to Pacatus. "Three days before his death he was visited by two bishops, Symmachus (of Capua) and Acyndinus, by whose conversation he was much refreshed. He desired the sacred mysteries to be exhibited before his bed, so that the sacrifice having been offered in their company, he might commend his own soul to the Lord, and at the same time recall to their former peace those on whom, in the exercise of church discipline, he had pronounced sentence of exclusion from communion. When this was over, he called for his brothers, by whom the bystanders thought that he meant the bishops who were present; but he said that he called for Januarius bp. of Naples and Martin of Tours (both of them deceased), who, he said, had promised to be with him. He then raised his hands to heaven, and repeated Psalm cxx. [cxxi.], 'I will lift up mine eyes unto the hills,' etc. . . . Later in the day, as if the hour for vespers were come, he recited slowly, with outstretched hands, the words, 'I have prepared a lamp for my anointed,' Ps. cxxxi. 17 [cxxxii. 17]. At about the fourth hour of the night, while all were watching, the cell was shaken by an earthquake, which was felt nowhere else, and during this he expired." He was buried in the church of St. Felix, in Pincis, and his funeral was attended even by Jews and pagans (Uran. *de ob. S. Paul* ap. Migne, *Patr. Lat.* vol. liii.).

Writings.—He has left behind 51 letters and 36 poems. (*a*) *Prose.*—Of his letters, 13, some very long, are addressed to Sulpicius Severus, the first in 394, and the last in 403; 5 to Delphinus, bp. of Bordeaux, 6 to Amandus his successor, 4 to Augustine, 3 to Aper and Amanda, 2 to another Amandus and Sanctus, 2 to Rufinus, 2 to Victricius, 3 to persons unknown, and single letters to Alethius, Alypius, Desiderius, Eucherius and Gallus, Florentius, Jovius, Licentius, Macarius, Pammachius, Romanianus, Sebastianus, besides the account of the martyrdom of Genesius which is a sort of postscript to the letter to Eucherius and Gallus (*Ep.* 51). It does not appear that he ever saw Sulpicius after his visit to Spain, but the love of the two for each other never failed. His letters to Delphinus and Amandus exhibit his deep humility and cheerful humour, but are chiefly remarkable for the earnest request made to both, that they will offer their prayers on behalf of his deceased brother, of whom he speaks with great affection but with deep regret for his neglect in spiritual matters, hoping that by their prayers he may obtain some refreshment in the other world (*Epp.* xxxv.; xxxvi.). Of those to St. Augustine the third is chiefly occupied with remarks on the grief of Melania for the loss of her only son Publicola, and a reply to Augustine on the condition of the soul in celestial glory, which he thinks will be one of highly exalted powers and beauty resembling the condition of our Lord after His resurrection. He asks Augustine's opinion on the subject (*Ep.* xiv.). In the 4th letter Paulinus asks for Augustine's opinion as a doctor of Israel on various Scripture passages according to the Latin version. (1) Ps. xv. 3 [xvi. 4], "sanctis . . . multiplicatae sunt infirmitates eorum, postea acceleraverunt": who are meant by the "saints," and how are their infirmities multiplied? (2) Ps. xvi. 15, 16 [xvii. 14]: what is meant by "de absconditis tuis adimpletus est venter eorum," and "saturati sunt porcina," or, as he hears is read by some, "filiis." (3) Ps. lviii. 11 [lix. 11], "ne unquam obliviscantur legis tuae" (Vulg. "populi tui"): he cannot understand how knowledge of the law can be sufficient without faith in Christ. (4) Ps. lxvii. 23, 25 [lxviii. 21, 23], "Deus conquassabit capita inimicorum suorum, verticem capilli," etc.: the last expression he thinks void of sense; though he could understand "verticem capitis," who are the "dogs," v. 25, and what is the meaning of "ab ipso"? Some questions follow on passages in St. Paul's Epistles. (1) Eph. iv. 11: what are the special functions of each order named by St. Paul? what difference is there between "pastors" and "teachers"? (2) I. Tim. ii. 1, 2: what difference between "prayers" and "supplications," etc.? (3) Rom. xi. 28: how can the people of Israel be at the same time friends and enemies—why enemies for the sake of Christians, friends for that of the fathers? (4) Col. ii. 18, "nemo vos seducat in humilitate et religione angelorum." What angels does St. Paul mean?—if bad angels, how can there be any "humilitas" or "religio" connected with them? Paulinus thinks that heretics must be intended. (5) Col. ii. 18, 21. He asks Augustine to explain these two passages, which seem to contradict each other: what "shew of wisdom" ("ratio sapientiae") can there be in "will worship" ("superstitio"), and how can "neglect of the body" ("non parcendum corpori") agree with "satisfying of the flesh" ("saturitas carnis"), which seems contrary to St. Paul's own practice as mentioned I. Cor. ix. 27? He also asks Augustine to explain why our Lord was and was not recognized by the women and disciples on the Day of Resurrection, how He came to be known by the latter in the "breaking of bread"; what did He mean by bidding Mary not touch Him until after His ascension (John xx. 17)? He supposes He meant that He was to be touched by faith hereafter, though not then by the hand. Again what did Simeon mean by his words to the Virgin Mother (Luke ii. 34, 35)? What "sword" was to pierce her soul? Was it the word of God? and how could this cause the "thoughts of many hearts" to be "revealed"? These questions he doubts not that Augustine will be able to explain to him (*Ep.* l.). The letter of Paulinus to Pammachius is a very long one of condolence and exhortation on the loss of his wife Paulina, daughter of Paula, and sister of Eustochium. Feeling deeply for him in his loss, he nevertheless doubts whether he ought not to write more in thankfulness for the faith Pammachius has shewn in honouring her funeral, not with ostentatious pomp or gladiatorial shows, but with alms and good works, first presenting the sacred oblation to God and the pure libation ("sacras hostias et casta libamina") with commemoration of her whom he had lost, and then providing a meal for the poor of Rome in great numbers in the church of St. Peter, following in this the example or Scripture saints, Christ Himself, and the first Christians. Faith is a greater comfort than any words of his; by its means we can walk in Paradise with the souls of the departed. Relying on the truth of Scripture we cannot doubt the resurrection, his only doubt is as to his own claim to admission into the heavenly kingdom. Yet the door, he knows, is open to all, and the departed wife of his friend is a pledge to himself of the future in Christ (*Ep.* xiii.; see Hieron. *Ep.* lxvi.). The letters of Paulinus are generally clear and intelligible, pleasing as regards style, remarkable for humility of mind, an affectionate disposition, and a cheerful, playful humour, free from all moroseness or ascetic bitterness. Many of his remarks on Scripture and other subjects show good sense and sound judgment, and, though free from any pretension to learning, prove him an industrious student and careful inquirer into the sacred writings in the Latin version.

(*b*) *Verse.*—Paulinus wrote much in verse throughout his life, and sent many of his poems to his friends. Seventeen are more or less directly in praise of Felix, all of them dated Jan. 14, the day of his death, and consequently called Natalitia, though not by Paulinus himself. The 1st (*Carm.* xii.) was written in Spain, but when fully intending to retire to Nola, A.D. 394, the 2nd shortly after his arrival there (*ib.* xiii.). The 3rd describes the concourse from all parts to the tomb of Felix, and the power he manifested of casting out devils and curing diseases (*ib.* xiv. 21-43). The 15th and 16th relate the legend of FELIX. The 17th is a Sapphic ode to Nicetas, who was about to return to his see after his visit to Nola, A.D. 398 (*ib.* xvii.). He came a second time, A.D. 402, and his visit is mentioned with much satisfaction in the 27th poem. The 18th poem, 6th in honour of Felix, describes in hexameters the discovery of his tomb, mentions the five churches built around it, and how the country people came themselves and brought their animals to be cured of maladies by the saint's influence.

A poem of 730 lines describes how the relics of martyrs had been transferred to other places than those where they died, especially the more notable among them; how Nola was honoured and benefited by the grave of Felix; and how a thief who had stolen an ornament in the church containing a figure of the cross was discovered, partly by the agency of Felix, and partly by the miraculous operation of the sacred emblem (*ib.* xix.). The poem last in order is dedicated to a friend whom he calls Antonius, by which name he has been thought to denote Ausonius, and consists of a discourse of the insufficiency of the old mythological systems and of the advantages of the true faith he has adopted, whose doctrines on the Trinity, final judgment, and redemption through Christ he has described, and he invites his friend to consider the blessing of eternal life open to all who accept the offer (*ib.* xxxvi.).

As Bose remarks, the laws of versification and prosody were undergoing a great change in his day, and either of this or of intentional neglect of those laws, the verses of Paulinus afford abundant evidence. Nor can it be said truly that they shew much poetic power, though many are graceful and pleasing, especially his letters to Ausonius and his address to Nicetas. He wrote with facility and great pleasure to himself, and frequently wrote well, but his poems cannot justly claim a high rank as poetry. Ozanam, however, expresses a very favourable opinion of them (*Civilisation au cinquième siècle*, vol. ii. pp. 238-247). Of his amiable and affectionate disposition, love for his friends, profound humility, entire abnegation of self, earnest piety, and devotion to the service of God, sufficient evidence has been given. He was studiously orthodox on the Catholic doctrine of the Holy Trinity, which he states clearly on many occasions, but seems in one letter to favour the views of the semi-Pelagians (*Ep.* xxix. 7). He believed devoutly in the power and influence of departed saints, including their relics; his whole life from the time of his retirement to Nola may be said to turn upon this belief, which he carried, as the stories in his poems shew plainly, to the utmost bound of human credulity (Ampère, *Revue des deux mondes*, 1837, vol. xii. p. 66, and *Littérature chrétienne au cinquième siècle*, vol. i. p. 288).

The ed. of his works pub. by the abbé Migne, *Patr. Lat.* vol. lxi., contains the matter of most of the former edd. It is, however, in all matters of reference edited carelessly, and its index is exceedingly inaccurate. An account of Paulinus is given by Cave, *Hist. Litt.* i. p. 288; Dupin, *Hist. Eccl.* vol. iii.; Tillemont, vol. xiv.; and Ceillier, vol. viii. Dr. Gilly (*Vigilantius and his Times*, Lond. 1844) describes his mode of life, blaming greatly both it and his theology, though giving him full credit for his piety. In the *Revue des deux mondes* for 1878, vol. xxviii., is an art. by M. Gaston Boissier on a Life of Paulinus by the abbé Lagrange, pub. in 1877. Dr. Adolf Buse, professor at the Seminary of Cologne, has written a book in two vols., *Paulin und seine Zeit* (Regensburg, 1856), which answers fully to its title, containing all or nearly all known about him, and written with great care, moderation, and critical judgment. He avoids most of the legends, and shews that the use of bells in churches, an invention credited to him by tradition, is not due to him, nor even to the town of Nola. The latest ed. of his works is by Hartel (Vienna, 1894, 2 vols.) in the *Corpus Scr. Eccl. Lat.* xxix.-xxx.; see also Hartel, *Patristische Studien* (Vienna, 1895), v. vi. [H.W.P.]

Paulinus (12), son of a prefect (probably a vicarius) of Illyricum; born at Pella. His father soon afterwards went to Carthage as proconsul, and Paulinus was before long sent to Bordeaux to be brought up by his grandfather. In his 84th year (probably *c.* 460) he wrote a poem called "Eucharisticon Deo sub Ephemeridis meae textu," in which he returns thanks to God for his preservation and for many blessings throughout a long and rather eventful life. The poem throws some light on the history of his time, particularly on the movement of the northern nations. It has been erroneously attributed to St. Paulinus of Nola. It is in De la Bigne, *Bibl. Patr.* (App. col. 281, Paris, 1579), and was ed. by Daumius (Lips. 1686). *Hist. Litt. de la France,* ii. 363, where the events of his life are traced in some detail, from the account given in the poem itself; Alzog, *Handb. der Patrol.*; Ebert, *Gesch. der Chr. Lat. Lit.*; Cave, *Hist. Litt.* i. 290; Teuffel, vol. ii. Cf. also J. Rocafort, *De Paul Pell. vita et œuv.* (Bordeaux, 1890). [H.A.W.]

Paulinus (13) of Périgueux (*Petrocorius*), a poet of the 2nd half of the 5th cent., to whom properly belong certain works sometimes attributed to St. Paulinus of Nola, viz. *Vita Martini* in six books, a poem, "de Visitatione Nepotuli Sui," and a short poem composed as a dedicatory inscription for the basilica of St. Martin at Tours. Nothing can be clearly made out concerning his life or parentage, save the inference, from the name Petrocorius, that he was probably a native of Perigueux. The poem on St. Martin was probably written *c.* 470, certainly during the episcopate of Perpetuus of Tours (who presided at the council of Tours in 461), since it is dedicated to that bishop, and is partly based on a document drawn up by him. It is mainly a rather rough versification of the Life of St. Martin by Sulpicius Severus and of parts of the dialogues of the same writer; the last book is especially interesting, as representing a formal account by the bp. of Tours of the miracles wrought at his predecessor's tomb. The short dedication poem for the new basilica was written later, at the request of Perpetuus. The poem "de Visitatione Nepotuli Sui" records a miraculous cure of the author's grandson, by the joint agency, as he appears to consider, of St. Martin and Perpetuus.

His works are, under the name of St. Paulinus of Nola, in Migne, *Patr. Lat.* lxi. (Ebert, *Gesch. der Chr. Lat. Lit.* 385; Cave, *Hist. Litt.* i. 449; Teuffel, vol. ii.; Greg. Turon. *de Mir. B. Mart.*, and Ruinart's note in the Benedictine ed.) Cf. A. Huber, *Die poetische Bearbietung der Vita S. Mar. durch Paul von Périgueux* (Pamplon. 1901). [H.A.W.]

Paulinus (20), the first Christian missionary from Rome to Northumbria, and the bishop who begins the recognized succession in the archiepiscopal see of York.

He was sent from Rome by Gregory in 601, with Mellitus, Justus, and Rufinianus. They joined Augustine in Kent, and would take an active part in evangelizing that kingdom.

In 625 Edwin, king of Northumbria, wished to marry Ethelburga, daughter of Eadbald, king of Kent, who objected to a pagan son-in-law. A second embassy revealed Edwin's eagerness. He promised to allow the princess and her suite entire freedom in their religious worship, and even that he himself would adopt her faith, if his wise men should consider it right and just. Here was an opportunity for evangelizing Northumbria, and Eadbald sent his daughter. Paulinus accompanied the princess as her religious adviser, and, to add dignity and importance to his mission, Augustine consecrated him bishop before he set out, on July 21, 625.

At first, however, Paulinus found the king quiescent though respectful, and that the people paid no attention; while his own little party was in danger from the taint of heathenism. At the feast of Easter, 626, an attempt was made upon Edwin's life. That act probably accelerated the birth of Ethelburga's first child, a daughter, and Paulinus thanked God for the preservation of his master and mistress with such fervour that Edwin, touched at last, promised to become a Christian if he could be avenged upon those who had sent forth the assassin, and, to shew he was in earnest, permitted Paulinus to baptize the new-born princess, with eleven courtiers who chose to accompany her to the font.

Edwin obtained his revenge, but loitered over the fulfilment of his promise. Paulinus reminded the hesitating monarch of what had taken place twelve years before at Redwald's court. He laid his hand upon Edwin's head, and asked him if he remembered that sign and his pledge. Now was the time for its fulfilment. Whether Paulinus was the stranger himself, or had gathered from the queen, or some courtier, that Edwin had seen and heard all this in a dream, is a matter of doubt. A national gathering took place at Goodmanham, near York, to consider the subject, and resulted in the king, court, and many of the people becoming Christians.

Northumbria was now opened to the missionary work of Paulinus, and his time fully occupied. He made a convert of Blecca, the reeve of Lincoln, and through his means a church was erected on the summit of its hill in which Paulinus consecrated archbp. Honorius in 627. He is said soon after to have founded Southwell minster, and his appearance was described to Beda as he stood in the river baptizing convert after convert in king Edwin's presence.

Mark him, of shoulders curved, and stature tall,
Black hair, and vivid eyes, and meagre cheek.

At Donafeld, probably the modern Doncaster, amid the remains of the Roman camp, there was a Christian basilica with a stone altar, which may be ascribed to Paulinus. At Dewsbury was a stone cross with an inscription stating that he preached there; whilst at Whalley in Lancashire and near Easingwold, close to York, there were other crosses connected with his name. He is said to have baptized very many at Brafferton and Catterick. In Bernicia a streamlet called Pallinsburn in the N. of Northumberland retains the great preacher's name. He is said to have been occupied in instructing and baptizing for 36 consecutive days at Adgebrin or Yeavering. There would yet be very few churches, and these at first chiefly baptisteries on river banks. There the catechumens were taught, and thence went down with their instructor into the water below.

In 633, after six years of unceasing and successful exertion, the labours of Paulinus in the north came abruptly to a close. Edwin fell in battle at Hatfield, near Doncaster, and the disaster was so complete that the new-born Christianity of the north seemed utterly overwhelmed by the old idolatry. Paulinus thought that he owed his first duty to the widowed queen who had come with him into Northumbria, and he took her back, with her children and suite, to Kent. There he was made bp. of Rochester, which see had been vacant some time. In the autumn of 633 he received from the pope, who had not heard of the great disaster in the north, a pall designed for his use as archbp. of York. Whether or no, by virtue of the gift of this pall, he has a just claim to be considered an archbishop, he never went back to Northumbria. He is said to have been a benefactor to the monastery of Glastonbury, rebuilding the church and covering it with lead, and to have spent some time within its walls. He died Oct. 10, 644, and was buried in the chapter-house at Rochester, of which place he became the patron saint. Lanfranc translated his remains into a silver shrine, giving a cross to hang over it. Among the relics in York minster were a few of his bones and two teeth, but nothing else to commemorate his great work in the north, save an altar which bore his name and that of Chad conjoined.

His life has been carefully related in Dr. Bright's *Chapters of Early English Church History*, and in the *Lives of the Archbishops of York*, vol. i., for which see a full statement and sifting of the authorities. [J.R.]

Paulus (9) of Samosata, patriarch of Antioch, A.D. 260-270. A celebrated Monarchian heresiarch, "the Socinus of the 3rd century" (so Bp. Wordsworth), deposed and excommunicated for heretical teaching as to the divinity of our Blessed Lord, A.D. 269. His designation indicates that he was a native of Samosata, the royal city of Syria, where he may have become known to Zenobia, queen of Palmyra, through whom Cave and others ascribe his advancement to the highest post in the Syrian church. Dr Newman points out that the beginning of Paul's episcopate synchronizes with the commencement of the successes of Zenobia's husband Odenathus against Sapor (*Arians of the Fourth Cent.* p. 4, n. 6). Athanasius distinctly calls her Paul's patroness (Athan. *Hist. Ar.* c. 71).

Our only knowledge of his career and character is from the encyclical letter of the bishops and clergy who condemned him. The picture of him is most unfavourable there. He is described as haughty, ostentatious, vainglorious, worldly-minded, a lover of pomp and parade, avaricious, rapacious, self-indulgent and luxurious; as one whose manner of life laid him open to grave suspicions of immorality; and as a person originally of humble birth, who had adopted the ecclesiastical career as a lucrative speculation, and, by the abuse of its opportunities and the secular office obtained by favour of Zenobia, had amassed a large fortune. In public he affected the pomp and parade of a secular magistrate rather than the grave and modest bearing of a Christian bishop. He stalked through the forum surrounded by attendants, who made a way for him through a crowd of petitioners whose memorials he made a display of dispatching with the utmost celerity, dictating the replies without halting a moment. In his ecclesiastical assemblies he adopted an almost imperial dignity, sitting on a throne raised on a lofty tribunal (βῆμα), with a cabinet (σήκρητον) for private conferences screened from the public gaze. He is said to have suppressed the psalms which were sung to Christ as God, which had ever proved a great bulwark to the orthodox faith, as modern novelties not half a century old (cf. Caius *ap.* Routh, *Rel. Sacr.* ii. 129), and to have introduced others in praise of himself, which were sung in full church on Easter Day by a choir of women, causing the hearts of the faithful to shudder at the impious language which extolled Paul as an angel from heaven. By his flatteries and gifts, and by his unscrupulous use of his power, he induced neighbouring bishops and presbyters to adopt his form of teaching and other novelties. His private life is described in equally dark colours. He indulged freely in the pleasures of the table, and enjoyed the society of two beautiful young women, as spiritual sisters, "subintroductae," and encouraged other clergymen to follow his example, to the scandal of all and the moral ruin of many. Yet, disgraceful as his life was, he had put so many under obligations and intimidated others by threats and violence, so that it was very difficult to persuade any to witness against him (Eus. *H. E.* vii. 30).

However great the scandals attaching to Paul's administration of his episcopal office, it was his unsoundness in the faith which, chiefly by the untiring exertions of the venerable Dionysius of Alexandria, led to the assembling of the synods at Antioch, through which his name and character have chiefly become known to us. The first was held in 264, Firmilian of the Cappadocian Caesarea being the president. The second (the date is not precisely known) was also presided over by Firmilian, who, on his way to the third synod, in 269, was suddenly taken ill and died at Tarsus, the bishop of that city, Helenus, taking his place as president. In the first two synods Paul, by dialectical subtleness and crafty concealment of his real opinions (*ib.* vii. 29), escaped condemnation. The members of the second synod heard from all quarters that his teaching was unaltered, and that this could be easily proved if the opportunity were granted. A third synod, therefore, was convened at Antioch, towards the close of 269. The leading part was taken by Malchion, a presbyter of Antioch, at one time president of the school of rhetoric there. Athanasius says that 70 bishops were present (Athan. *de Synod.* vol. i. p. ii. p 605, ed. Patav.), Hilary says 80 (Hilar. *de Synod.* p. 1200). Malchion, as a skilled dialectician, was chosen by them to conduct the discussion. Paul's heresy being plainly proved, he was unanimously condemned, and the synod pronounced his deposition and excommunication, which they notified to Dionysius bp. of Rome, Maximus of Alexandria, and the other bishops of the church, in an encyclical letter, probably the work of Malchion, large portions of which are preserved by Eusebius (*H. E.* vii. 30). In it the assembled fathers announced that they had of their own authority appointed Domnus, the son of Paul's predecessor Demetrianus, to the vacant chair. The sentence of deposition was easier to pronounce than to carry out. Popular tumults were excited by Paul's partisans. Zenobia supported her favourite in his episcopal position, while the irregularity of Domnus's appointment alienated many of the orthodox. For two years Paul retained possession of the cathedral and of the bishop's residence attached to it, asserting his rights as the ruler of the church of Antioch. On the defeat of Zenobia by Aurelian towards the end of 372, the Catholic prelates represented to him what they termed Paul's "audacity." Aurelian relegated the decision to the bp. of Rome and the Italian prelates, decreeing that the residence should belong to the one they recognized by letters of communion (*ib.*). The Italian bishops promptly recognized Domnus, Paul was driven with the utmost ignominy from the temporalities of the church, and Domnus, despite his irregular appointment, generally accepted as patriarch (*ib.*; Cyril Alex. *Hom. de Virg. Deip.*; Routh, iii. 358).

The teaching of Paul of Samosata was a development of that of Artemon, with whose heresy it is uniformly identified by early writers. Like the Eastern heresiarch, Paul held the pure humanity of Christ, "He was not before Mary, but received from her the origin of His being" (Athan. *de Synod.* p. 919, c. iii. s. 10). His pre-existence was simply in the divine foreknowledge. He allowed no difference in kind between the indwelling of the Logos in Christ and in any human being, only one of degree, the Logos having dwelt and operated in Him after a higher manner than in any other man. This indwelling was not that of a person, but of a quality. There is no evidence that he denied the supernatural conception of Christ. Athanasius distinctly asserts that he taught Θεὸν ἐκ παρθένου, Θεὸν ἐκ Ναζαρὲτ ὀφθέντα (Athan. *de Salut. adv. Apoll.* t. i. p. 635); but he laid no particular stress upon it. His inferior Being was ἐκ παρθένου; his superior Being was penetrated by the Logos, Whose instrumentality by it was continually advancing itself towards God, until the "Jesus Christ from below" (κάτωθεν) became worthy of union with God (ἐκ προκοπῆς τεθεοποιῆσθαι). Therefore, although he called Christ God, it was not as God by His nature, but by progressive development. The Deity of Christ grew by gradual progress out of the humanity. He was convicted, according to Eusebius, of asserting that Christ was mere man deemed specially worthy of divine grace (Eus. *H. E.* vii. 27). He taught also that as the Logos is not a Person, so also the Holy Spirit is impersonal, a divine virtue belonging to the Father and distinct from Him only in conception.

It deserves special notice that Paul's misuse, "σωματικῶς et crasso sensu," of the term ὁμοούσιος, "consubstantial," which afterwards at Nicaea became the test word of orthodoxy, is stated to have led to its rejection by the Antiochene council (Athan. *de Synodis*, t. i. in pp. 917, 922). This is allowed by Athanasius, though with some hesitation, and only on the testimony of his semi-Arian opponents, as he said he had not seen the original documents (*ib.* pp. 918-920) by Hilary (*de Synod.* § 81, p. 509; § 86, p. 513) on the ground that it appeared that "per hanc unius essentiae nuncupationem solitarium atque unicum sibi esse Patrem et Filium praedicabat" (in which words he seems mistakenly to identify the teaching of Paul with that of Sabellius), and still more emphatically by Basil (*Ep.* 52 [30]).

Dr. Newman regards Paul of Samosata as "the founder of a school rather than of a sect" (*Arians*, p. 6). A body, called after him Paulianists, or Pauliani, or Samosatensians, existed in sufficient numbers at the time of the council of Nicaea for the enactment of a canon requiring their rebaptism and the reordination of their clergy on their return to the Catholic church, on the ground that orthodox formulas were used with a heterodox meaning (*Canon. Nic.* xix. Hefele, i. 43). The learned presbyter Lucian, who may be considered almost the parent of Arianism, was a friend and disciple of Paul, and, as being infected with his errors, was refused communion by each of the three bishops who succeeded the heresiarch. The many references to them in the writings of Athanasius show that for a considerable period after the Nicene council it was felt necessary for Catholics to controvert the Samosatene's errors, and for semi-Arians to disown complicity in them (Athan. *u.s.*). The Paulinians are mentioned by St. Augustine as still existing (Aug. *de Haer.* 44), though pope Innocent spoke of the heresy as a thing of the past in 414 (Labbe, ii. 1275), and when Theodoret wrote, *c.* 450, there did not exist the smallest remnant of the sect (*Haer.* ii. 11). Cf. Epiphan. *Haer.* 65; Tillem. *Mém. eccl.* t. iv. pp. 289-303. [E.V.]

Paulus (10) **II.**, patriarch of Antioch, A.D. 519-521 (Clinton, *F. R.*). On the expulsion of the Monophysite Severus by Justin, Paulus, a presbyter of Constantinople, warden of the hospice of Eubulus, was nominated by the emperor to the vacant see, and was canonically ordained at Antioch. He strictly attended to Justin's commands to enforce the decrees of Chalcedon, and by inserting in the diptychs the names of the orthodox bishops of that synod caused a schism in his church, many of the Antiochenes regarding the council with suspicion, as tending to Nestorianism. Clergy, laity, and resident foreigners joined in accusing him before the papal legates, who were at that time in Constantinople, of conduct unbecoming a bishop. They departed without coming to any conclusion, and the charge was repeated before Justin. Paulus, unable to clear himself, obtained leave of the emperor to retire from his bishopric, A.D. 521. He was succeeded by Euphrasius. Evagr. *H. E.* iv. 4; Theophan. p. 141; Joann. Malal. lib. xvii. p. 411; Eutych. ii. 152; *Ep. Justini*, Labbe, iv. 1555; Le Quien, *Or. Christ.* ii. 732. [E.V.]

Paulus (11), surnamed *The Black*, Jacobite patriarch of Antioch from about the middle of 6th cent. to 578, was a native of Alexandria (Assem. *B. O.* ii. 331) and, like most Egyptians, a Monophysite. Before he became bishop he maintained at Constantinople a successful public dispute in the patriarchal palace with the Tritheites Conon and Eugenius (*ib.* 329). Either Mennas or Eutychius must then have been patriarch. Paul was probably then syncellus to Theodosius, the Jacobite patriarch of Alexandria, who was in nominal exile at Constantinople, but exercising full authority over the Jacobite congregations there and in Egypt. Paul's connexion with Theodosius, and his success as a disputant, marked him out for the titular see of Antioch and the patriarchate of the whole Monophysite body, then beginning to be called Jacobites, and he was consecrated by Jacob Baradaeus himself who originated the name. We cannot feel sure that this was before 550. Paul appears in a list of celebrities flourishing in 571. All we hear of him afterwards is disastrous. The great persecution of the Monophysites by the patriarch John Scholasticus broke out at Constantinople, if the year is right, on Mar. 20, 571, and Paul was one of four bishops (another being PAULUS (13)) barbarously treated by him. He was induced to leave the monastery of the Acoemetae in Constantinople for the patriarch's palace, whither the three others were also brought, under pretence of conferring on the unity of the church. The four were kept in close custody, and cruelly used until they agreed to communicate with the persecutor on his promise to eject the synod of Chalcedon from the church (John of Eph. *H. E.* p. 42). They twice communicated with him, loudly anathematizing the obnoxious synod; but the patriarch put off his part of the compact with the excuse that he must first obtain the consent of the bp. of Rome. Thus they "fell into communion" with the deceitful "synodite," and on their loading him with reproaches the severity of their treatment was increased and they were thrown into prison in the monastery of Beth Abraham in Constantinople, where their sufferings continued. After a time Paul was allowed to escape, and made his way to Syria, where Jacob Baradaeus received him with great displeasure, but, after keeping him 3 years in suspense, restored him to communion, probably in 575. In 578 a new patriarch of Antioch, Peter of Callinicus, was appointed, and Paul withdrew into concealment at Constantinople, where he died in 582, as detailed by John of Ephesus. [C.H.]

Paulus (13), surnamed *of Asia*, Jacobite bp. of Aphrodisias and metropolitan of Caria in the reign of Justin II. We owe our knowledge of him to the *Ecclesiastical History* of John of Ephesus (Dr. R. Payne Smith's trans.). As his persecution by John Scholasticus, patriarch of Constantinople, marks a period in the history of the Monophysite body, it is important to fix its date, which in all probability was 571. The persecution fell chiefly on the numerous Monophysite monasteries, of both sexes, which had sprung up in and around Constantinople while the empress Theodora lived. These were burst into to admit the "synodite" clergy bearing the consecrated bread, of which the inmates were compelled to partake, though it was necessary in some cases to bind their hands and force it into their mouths. The chief difficulty was with the bishops, and Paul of Aphrodisias was singled out for the first example (p. 13). The historian describes him as an honest and simple-minded old man, dwelling quietly in his monastery in Caria, when the patriarch had him brought to Constantinople and imprisoned in his own palace, until, overcome by harsh treatment, he was compelled to receive the communion at his hands, besides signing an act of submission, which he was not allowed to read (given by the historian), to the effect that he accepted the decrees of Chalcedon and the jurisdiction of the patriarch of Constantinople. He was then sent back, but the "synodite" bp. of Aphrodisias had instructions to depose him from the episcopal office and consecrate him afresh to the see of the Carian Antioch, on the Meander, at the far east of the province and not very distant from Aphrodisias. All this was done, to the extreme grief and indignation of the venerable bishop, whom soon "death overtook, and his old age descended in affliction and misery to the grave" (p. 16). [C.H.]

Paulus (18) **I.**, 6th bp. of Constantinople, elected A.D. 336 (or 340), died after three exiles and two restorations *c.* 351, four or five years after the council of Sardica. He was a native of Thessalonica, a presbyter of Constantinople, and secretary to the aged bp. Alexander, his predecessor in the see. No sooner had Alexander breathed his last than the two parties came into open conflict. The orthodox party prevailed; Paulus was elected and consecrated by bishops who happened to be at Constantinople in the Church of Peace, close to what was afterwards the Great Church of St. Sophia.

The emperor Constantius had been away during these events. On his return he was angry at not having been consulted. He summoned a synod of Arian bishops, declared Paulus quite unfit for the bishopric, banished him, and translated Eusebius from Nicomedia to Constantinople. This is thought to have been in 338. Eusebius died in 341. Paulus was at once restored by the people to his see. But the Arians seized the occasion; Theognis of Nicaea, Theodorus of Heraclea, and other heterodox bishops, consecrated Macedonius in the church of St. Paul; and again the city became the prey of a civil war. The greatly exasperated emperor was at Antioch, and ordered Hermogenes, his general of cavalry, to see that Paulus was again expelled. The people would not hear of violence being done to their bishop; they rushed upon the house where the general was, set fire to it, killed him on the spot, tied a rope round his feet, pulled him out from the burning building, and dragged him in triumph round the city.

Constantius was not likely to pass over this rebellion against his authority. He rode on horseback at full speed to Constantinople, determined to make the people suffer heavily for their revolt. They met him, however, on their knees with tears and entreaties, and he contented himself with depriving them of half their allowance of corn, but ordered Paulus to be driven from the city.

Athanasius was then in exile from Alexandria, Marcellus from Ancyra, and Asclepas from Gaza; with them Paulus betook himself to Rome and consulted bp. Julius, who examined their cases severally, found them all staunch to the creed of Nicaea, admitted them to communion, espoused their cause, and wrote strongly to the bishops of the East. Athanasius and Paulus recovered their sees; the Eastern bishops replied to bp. Julius altogether declining to act on his advice.

Constantius was again at Antioch, and as resolute as ever against the choice of the people of Constantinople. Philippus, prefect of the East, was there, and was ordered to once more expel Paulus and to put Macedonius definitely in his place. Philippus was not ready to incur the risks and fate of Hermogenes; he said nothing about the imperial order. At a splendid public bath called Zeuxippus, adjoining a palace by the shore of the Hellespont, he asked the bishop to meet him, as if to discuss some public business. When he came, Philippus shewed him the emperor's letter, and ordered him to be quietly taken through the palace to the waterside, placed on board ship, and carried off to Thessalonica, his native town. He allowed him to visit Illyricum and the remoter provinces, but forbade him to set foot again in the East. Paulus was afterwards loaded with chains and taken to Singara in Mesopotamia, then to Emesa, and finally to Cucusus in Armenia, where he died. Socr. *H.E.* ii. 6, etc.; Soz. *H. E.* iii. 3, etc.; Athan. *Hist. Arian. ad Monach.* 275; Mansi, *Concil.* i. 1275. [W.M.S.]

Paulus (28) Edessenus, Monophysite bp. of Edessa; consecrated A.D. 510 in succession to Peter. In the first year of his episcopate he took part with Gamalinus, bp. of Perrha, against certain sectarians who refused the use of bread, water, and wine, except in the Eucharist. Justin, becoming emperor, undertook to force the decrees of Chalcedon on Severus of Antioch and his followers, and committed the task to Patricius, who came in due course to Edessa (Nov. 519), and ordered Paul either to subscribe the council or resign. Paul refused, and took sanctuary in his baptistery; whence he was dragged by Patricius and sentenced to be exiled to Seleucia. Justin, however, hoping to overcome the bishop's resistance, reinstated him after 44 days. But Paul still refused to submit, and was at length deposed and banished to Euchaita in Pontus, July 522. A later imperial order placed Asclepius in the see.

Paul translated, no doubt in his days of exile, the Greek hymns of Severus and other Monophysite writers, and arranged them so as to form a Syriac hymnal. A MS. of this collection as corrected by his famous successor Jacob—dated in the lifetime of that prelate (A.D. 675), and probably written by his hand—is in the Brit. Mus. (Add. MS. 17134). On the death of Asclepius (June 525), Paul "repented" (as the orthodox author of the *Chronicon Edessenum* states) and made submission to Justinian, then acting for Justin. From him he obtained a letter supporting the petition he addressed to Euphrasius, then patriarch, praying to be restored to his see. He was accordingly permitted to return to Edessa as bp. in Mar. 526. He survived this his third inauguration less than 8 months, dying on Oct. 30, less than a year before Justin died. The Jacobites, however, cannot have regarded him as a renegade, for he is commemorated in their calendar on Aug. 23, as "Mar Paulus, bp. of Edessa, Interpreter of Books," a title likewise given to Jacob of Edessa.

His hymnal consists of 365 hymns; 295 being by Severus, the rest by his contemporary John Bar-Aphtunaya, abbat of Kinnesrin, John Psaltes his successor there, and others. Though the trans. is no doubt mainly Paul's work, it includes a few hymns of obviously later date. Bp. Lightfoot (*Ignatius*, vol. i. p. 185) gives the hymns of this collection "On Ignatius" at length, with a trans. [J.GW.]

Paulus (30), bp. of Emesa, one of the most deservedly respected prelates of the period of the Nestorian controversy, the contemporary of Cyril and John of Antioch, the peacemaker between the patriarchs of Alexandria and Antioch after the disastrous close of the council of Ephesus, A.D. 431. He reached Ephesus together with John of Antioch and the other Oriental bishops, and joined in the deposition of Cyril and Memnon (Labbe, iii. 597) and in all the proceedings of the Oriental party. He was one of the eight Oriental deputies despatched to the emperor with plenipotentiary powers (*ib.* 724). His moderation in these difficult and delicate negotiations was condemned by the uncompromising Alexander of Hierapolis as proceeding from a mean desire for reconciliation at the cost of the truth (Baluz. *Concil. Nov. Collect.* 800). Paul was a sincere lover of peace, and above all things anxious to put an end to the disputes on points of faith, the mutual violence of which was a disgrace to the church, a scandal to the faithful, and a stumbling-block to unbelievers. He was a man of vast experience in ecclesiastical matters, an accomplished theologian, possessed of great tact and courtesy, and one who—for unblemished holiness as well as for his advanced age—enjoyed the confidence and reverence of both parties. Weary of conflict and anxious to obtain peace, John of Antioch despatched Paul as his ambassador to Alexandria to confer with Cyril on the terms of mutual concord, A.D. 432. Paul presented in his own name and John's a confession of faith originally drawn up by Theodoret. The formulary was accepted by Cyril as orthodox, and he exhibited a formulary of faith which Paul approved as consonant with the creed of the Orientals (Labbe, iii. 1090).

Paul was then received into communion by Cyril on exhibiting a written document acquiescing in the deposition of Nestorius, anathematizing his writings, and recognizing his successor Maximian (Cyrill. *Epp.* 32, 40, t. ii. pp. 100-102, 152). Paul was invited by Cyril to preach on the Sunday before Christmas Day and on Christmas Day itself. On the festival the chief church of the city was crowded, and Paul, having commenced with the "Gloria in excelsis Deo," passed on to Is. vii. 14, and concluded his exordium with words decisive of the whole controversy, "Mary the mother of God brings forth Emmanuel." The test title was received with loud acclamations by the congregation, "This is the true faith"; "This is the gift of God," which were repeated when he proceeded to enunciate the doctrine of "the combination of two perfect natures in the one Christ," with shouts of "Welcome, orthodox bishop, the worthy to the worthy" (Labbe, iii. 1095). Paul preached a third time the following Sunday, New Year's Day, 433, with equal acceptance. Portions of all these sermons are still extant (*ib.* 1091, 1095, 1097). To quicken John's delay in accepting the terms of peace proposed by Cyril, Paul accompanied Aristolaus and a deputation of two of Cyril's clergy to Antioch, to lay before John for his signature a document recognizing Nestorius's deposition and the anathematizing of his teaching. This, eventually, was signed by John, and brought back with great joy by Paul to Alexandria (*ib.* 1091). The happy reunion of the long-divided parties was published by Cyril, in the chief church of Alexandria, Apr. 23, 433. Cyril acknowledged the receipt of John's formulary in a well-known letter—conveyed to him by the aged peacemaker—commencing with the words of Ps. xcvi. 11: "*Laetentur caeli,*" etc., by which it was subsequently known (*ib.* 1106; Baluz. 786). The time of Paul's death is uncertain. Tillem. *Mém. eccl.* xiv. (index); Cave, *Hist. Lit.* i. 419; Coteler. *Mon. Eccl. Graec.* i. 48; Clinton, *Fast. Rom.* ii. 240; Migne, *Patr. Gk.* lxxvii. 1433; Hefele, *Hist. of Councils*, Clark's trans. iii. 127-137. [E.V.]

Paulus (73), St. (called *Thebaeus*; ὁ Θήβηθεν, Niceph.), Jan. 10; called by Jerome the founder of the monastic life ("auctor vitae monasticae," *Ep.* 22, *ad Eustoch*; "princeps vitae monasticae," *Vit. S. Pauli*, Prol.), and said to have been the first, in Egypt at least, to lead the life of a hermit, preceding even the celebrated Anthony (Rosweyd, *Vitae Patrum*, in *Patr. Lat.* lxxiii. 105 and notes). He lived in the desert of the Thebaid, whither he fled in youth from the terrors of the Decian persecution, and where he died, at an extraordinary age, hale and hearty to the last (Hieron. *Ep.* 21, *ad Paul. Concordiens.*). The palm-tree at the mouth of his cave supplied him with food and clothing (*Vita Pauli*, c. 6). The ravens are said to have brought him bread, and two lions dug his grave (*ib.* cc. 9, 13). Anthony is said to have paid him a visit shortly before his death, and ever afterwards to have worn his tunic of palm leaves on great festivals. Jerome adds (c. 13), with characteristic fervour, that such a garment, the legacy of so great a saint, was more glorious than the purple of a king. Niceph. Call. *H. E.* ix. 14; Boll. *Acta SS.* 10 Jan. i. 603; Butler, Jan. 15. [I.G.S.]

Paulus (110), sometimes called "the Silentiary," from his position as an officer of Justinian's court, wrote several epigrams preserved in the *Anthologia Palatina,* and some other works of minor importance; his poetical account of the buildings and dedication of the Great Church of Constantinople must, as the evidence of a contemporary, always be an important authority on the greatest effort of Byzantine church architecture. It is written in Homeric hexameters, with a dedication in iambic verse. Its vividness is much praised by Agathias, but, from his necessary avoidance of technical terms, it is not easy to follow his description of the building. Together with the ἔκφρασις τοῦ ἄμβωνος, it was edited by Graefe (Lips. 1822). Some assistance to its better understanding in relation to church architecture is given by Neale, *Hist. of Holy Eastern Church* (Intro.). [H.A.W.]

Pegasius (1), bp. of Troas *c.* 350-360. His name was found in a previously unknown letter of the emperor Julian, first published in *Hermes* (1875), pp. 257-266. This letter gives a very interesting description of a visit paid by Julian to Troy before he became emperor. It describes the graves of Hector and Achilles, and the temple of Minerva as being still honoured with sacrifices; while the bishop of the place Pegasius seems to have acted as custodian of the temple and of the images which were in their places and in good order. He had evidently discerned Julian's tendency to paganism. Julian, upon entering the temple, recognized traces of sacrifices, and asked if the people still sacrificed to the gods. The bishop defended the practice on the analogy of the honour paid by Christians to the martyrs. The bishop turned pagan on the accession of Julian, whose letter was written to plead his cause on the ground that such converts needed encouragement. This letter is of great interest in view of modern explorations of the site of Troy. Cf. Boissier's art. on Julian in *Revue des deux mondes*, July 1880, pp. 106-108. [G.T.S.]

Pelagia (3), surnamed *Margarita*, *Marina*, and *Peccatrix*, an actress of Antioch about the middle of 5th cent., celebrated for her repentance. Her history is discussed at length in the *AA. SS.* Boll. Oct. iv. 248-268, where she is distinguished from two other Pelagias of Antioch, and Pelagia of Tarsus, martyr under Diocletian. The story of our Pelagia has been told by Jacobus, a deacon and eyewitness of her conversion. Nonnus, bp. of Edessa and successor of Ibas in that see, was once preaching at Antioch when present at a synod of eight bishops. Pelagia was then the favourite actress and dancer of Antioch, whose inhabitants had poured riches upon her and surnamed her Margarita from the number of pearls she wore. She came into the church during the sermon, to the astonishment and horror of the other bishops. Nonnus had been an ascetic of the severe order of Pachomius of Tabenna, and he addressed Pelagia with such plainness and sternness touching her sins and the future judgments of God, that she at once repented, and with many tears desired baptism, which, after some delay, was granted, the chief deaconess of Antioch, Romana, acting as sponsor for her. She finally left Antioch for a cell on the Mount of Olives, where she lived as a monk in male attire, and died some three years afterwards from excessive austerities. Jacobus the deacon, recounting a visit he paid to her there, gives a very interesting description of an anchorite's cell, such as can still be seen in many places in Ireland. She was living as an enclosed anchorite, in a cell with a window as the only communication with the external world. Her whole history is full of interesting touches, describing the ancient ritual of baptism and other ecclesiastical usages. [G.T.S.]

Pelagianism and **Pelagius (2)**. The details of the early career of Pelagius, whose name is identified with the prominent subject of theological controversy of Latin Christendom in the 5th cent., are very imperfectly known from contemporary history. He is said by Augustine, Prosper, Gennadius, Orosius, and Mercator to have been a Briton. Jerome's words ("habet progeniem Scoticae gentis de Britannorum vicinia," Pref. lib. 3 in Hieron.) may imply that he was an Irishman, the Scoti being then settled in Ireland. His name undoubtedly looks like a Grecized version of some earlier name; but the tradition that the original name of the heresiarch was Morgan (Marigena, Πελάγιος), and that he came from Bangor in N. Wales, rests on late and untrustworthy authority. His birth probably occurred *c.* 370. Both Orosius and pope Zosimus speak of him as a layman. He came to Rome very early in the 5th cent. If Mercator's statement is accepted, that he imbibed his opinions from Rufinus the Syrian in the episcopate of Anastasius, we must fix his arrival in Rome not later than 401. His personal character at this period is spoken of with the utmost respect by his contemporaries. His great opponent St. Augustine describes him as being generally held to be a good and holy man, and of no mean proficiency as a Christian (*de Pecc. Mer.* iii. 1). Paulinus, bp. of Nola, who was much attached to him, esteemed him a special servant of God. Pelagius was actuated at Rome by a strong moral purpose, enforcing the necessity of a strict Christian morality as against a laxity of life content with external religious observances. To this period must be assigned his earliest 3 works: the first, in 3 books, on the Trinity; the second a collection of passages from Scripture, all bearing on Christian practice, called by Gennadius *Eulogiarum Liber*, by Augustine and Orosius *Testimoniorum Liber*; the third an exposition of the Epp. of St. Paul.

At Rome Pelagius became acquainted with Coelestius, whose name was so intimately associated with his in the subsequent controversy. Coelestius, originally an advocate, was led by Pelagius to a strict religious life, and very soon became an ardent disciple and a propagandist of his master's views. Despite the imputations of later opponents, it is evident that during his long residence at Rome Pelagius was animated by a sincere desire to be a moral reformer. The consciousness of the need of a pure and self-denying morality as an element in religion led him to lay exaggerated stress upon the native capacity of the free will of man, to form a wrong estimate of the actual moral condition of human nature, and to overlook or fatally undervalue the necessity of divine aid in effecting the restoration of man to righteousness. The first signs of his antagonism to the Augustinian theories, which were then developing and obtaining general acceptance in the Western church, are exhibited in an anecdote related by St. Augustine himself (*de Dono Persev.* c. 53). Pelagius was violently indignant on hearing a bishop quote with approbation the famous passage in the *Confessions of St. Augustine*, where he prays, "Give what Thou dost command, and command what Thou wilt." This language appeared to Pelagius to make man a mere puppet in the hands of his Creator. About the same time, apparently (A.D. 405), Pelagius wrote to Paulinus (Aug. *de Grat. Christi*, 38). The letter is not extant, but St. Augustine, who had read it, declared that it dwelt almost entirely upon the power and capacity of nature, only referring most cursorily to divine grace, and leaving it doubtful whether by grace Pelagius meant only the forgiveness of sins and the teaching and example of Christ, or that influence of the Spirit of God which corresponds to grace proper and is an inward inspiration. Pelagius remained at Rome till *c.* 409, when, as Alaric's invasion threatened the city, he withdrew with Coelestius to Sicily, and shortly after to Africa. He visited Hippo Regius, from which Augustine was then absent, and seems to have remained quiet at Hippo, but shortly afterwards repaired to Carthage, where he saw Augustine once or twice. Augustine was then deeply involved in the Donatist controversy, but learned that Pelagius and his friends had begun to advocate the opinion that infants were not baptized for the remission of sins, but for the sake of obtaining a higher sanctification through union with Christ. This novel doctrine appeared to Augustine to deny the teaching of the church, as it virtually involved the denial of any guilt of original sin which needed forgiveness. Augustine, pre-occupied with the Donatist errors and not ascribing much weight to the chief upholders of the new heresy, did not then write in defence of the doctrine assailed. Pelagius, after a short interval, sailed for Palestine, leaving Coelestius at Carthage. In Palestine he was introduced to Jerome in his monastery at Bethlehem. Coelestius at Carthage openly disseminated Pelagius's views, and on seeking ordination as a presbyter was accused of heresy before bp. Aurelius. A council was summoned at Carthage in 412. Augustine not being present, the accusation was conducted by Paulinus the deacon and biographer of Ambrose. The charges against Coelestius were that he taught that: (1) Adam was created liable to death, and would have died, whether he had sinned or not. (2) The sin of Adam hurt himself only, and not the human race. (3) Infants at their birth are in the same state as Adam before the fall. (4) Neither by the death nor the fall of Adam does the whole race of man die, nor by the resurrection of

Christ rise again. (5) The Law introduces men into the kingdom of heaven, just in the same way as the Gospel does. (6) Even before the coming of Christ there were some men sinless, *i.e.* men as a matter of fact without sin. (7) Infants, even though not baptized, have eternal life.

Coelestius endeavoured to explain away some of his assertions; but his explanations were judged evasive and his doctrines condemned as unscriptural and contrary to the Catholic faith. A sentence of excommunication was passed upon him and his followers. He shortly afterwards sailed to Ephesus. The prevalence of these opinions and the efforts made to diffuse them led Augustine to denounce them. In three or four sermons delivered at this time (170, 174, 175) he devoted himself to refuting the innovating doctrines, though he does not mention their chief upholders by name. His first written treatise on the controversy was called forth by a letter from his friend Marcellinus, who was troubled by daily assaults of Pelagian disputations. The work originally consisted of two books. The first established the positions that death in man was the penalty of sin, and not a mere condition of his natural constitution; that the whole offspring of Adam was affected by his sin, and that baptism of infants was for the remission of original sin, the guilt of which they bear from their birth. In the second book Augustine argued that the first man might have lived without sin by the grace of God and his own free will; that as a matter of fact no living man is wholly free from sin, for no man wills all that he ought to do, owing to his ignorance of what is right or his want of delight in doing it; that the only man absolutely without sin is Christ, the God-man and Mediator. Augustine added to this treatise as a third book a letter he wrote to Marcellinus when, a very few days after the compilation of the two books, he became acquainted with some fresh arguments against original sin advanced in the exposition of the Epistles of St. Paul by Pelagius, who, however, put the arguments in the mouth of another and did not avowedly express them as his own. In bks. i. and ii. Augustine never mentions Pelagius or Coelestius by name, possible hoping they might yet be won back to orthodoxy; in bk. iii., while arguing strongly against the views of the nature of original sin propounded by Pelagius, he speaks of Pelagius with marked respect, calling him a signally Christian man, a highly advanced Christian ("vir ille tam egregie Christianus," *de Pecc. Mer.* iii. 6; "non parvo provectu Christianus," *ib.* iii. 1).

Pelagianism continued to propagate and assert itself and found many upholders in Carthage. It claimed the authority of the Eastern churches, whose tendency had always been to lay stress on the power of the human will, and, boldly retorting the accusation of innovation, it declared that the views of Augustine and the dominant party in Africa were a departure from the old orthodoxy. This roused the indignation of Augustine. In a sermon preached June 27, 413, he dealt with infant baptism and refuted some new phases of Pelagian opinion. From it we learn that the Pelagians now taught that infants were baptized, not because they needed any remission of the guilt of original or actual sin, from which they were wholly free, but that they might enter the kingdom of God and thereby obtain salvation and eternal life. The critical passage in Rom. v. 12, "By one man sin entered into the world," they interpreted to mean that Adam sinned by an act of free choice and so caused all his descendants to sin by the imitation of his example. If, they scoffingly asked, men are born sinners from a sinful parent, why are not men born righteous from believing parents who have been justified by baptism? If Adam's sin hurt those who had not sinned, why, by parity of consequence, should not the death of Christ profit those who have not believed on Him? Towards the close of his sermon Augustine read to the congregation from the epistle of their martyred bishop St. Cyprian, written A.D. 255, a passage in which the judgment of the church of his day was emphatically pronounced that baptism was administered to infants for the remission of sin which they had contracted through their birth, and ended by making an earnest appeal to his opponents not to continue to maintain opinions which, being hostile to such a fundamental point of church doctrine and practice as infant baptism, must be disowned by the church as heretical. He entreated them, as friends, to see the error into which they were drifting and not to provoke a formal sentence of condemnation. About the same time he received a letter from Pelagius, who was still in Palestine, and replied in friendly and affectionate terms. This letter is preserved in Augustine's treatise *de Gestis Pelagii* (c. 52), where Augustine points out the unfair use which Pelagius endeavoured to make of it at the synod of Diospolis.

The condemnation of Pelagianism by the synod of Carthage deterred its more prominent upholders from the continued open assertion of its doctrines, but a quiet and secret circulation of them continued. Adherents increased so greatly that Augustine professed alarm as to where the evil might break out afresh (*Ep.* 157). Tidings of such a fresh outbreak came in 414 from Sicily, where one Hilary wrote to him that some Christians at Syracuse were asserting that man can be without sin and easily keep the commandments of God, if he will; that an unbaptized infant overtaken by death cannot possibly perish deservedly, as he is born without sin. Other opinions mentioned by Hilary as held by these Syracusans exhibit a fresh development of Pelagian thought, if they really originated from the same source. These were that a rich man cannot enter the kingdom of God unless he sell all he has, and that it cannot avail him to keep the commandments of God if he still retains and uses his riches. Such an assertion of the need of renouncing private property as a condition of religious life was probably an exaggeration of the real teaching of the monks, Pelagius, and Coelestius. Augustine elaborately replied to Hilary, repeating many of the arguments he had before employed. About the same time he learnt that two young men of good birth and liberal education, Timasius and James, had been induced by Pelagius to renounce the world and adopt the monastic life and had adopted many of the peculiar opinions of their master. They had, however, been powerfully impressed by the arguments of Augustine on the nature of Christian grace, and forwarded him a book of Pelagius, to which they requested a detailed answer. This Augustine gave in his treatise *de Naturâ et Gratiâ*. The book of Pelagius, if we may rely upon the fairness of Augustine's quotations, which there is no reason to distrust, advocated in the interests of morality the adequacy of human nature for good action. It affirmed it possible to live without sin by the grace or help of God. But the grace thus recognized was the natural endowment of free will, itself the gift of God, though sometimes the conception of it was enlarged so as to include the knowledge of right conveyed by the Law. Sin was pronounced avoidable if men were to be truly accounted responsible moral agents, and sin being rather a negation than a positive entity could not vitiate human nature. When man has actually sinned, he needs forgiveness. Nature was magnified, as if the admission of a subsequent corruption was derogatory to the goodness of the original creation. All the O.T. worthies who are described as having lived righteously were quoted as proofs of the possibility of living without sin. The continuance of controversy was obviously leading Pelagius to a more formal and systematic development of his theory.

The same tendency to systematization is seen in a document of definitions or arguments attributed to Coelestius, which was communicated to Augustine by two bishops, Eutropius and Paul, as having been circulated in the Sicilian church. A series of 16, or as some condense them 14, questions is designed to point out the difficulties of the Augustinian theory and to establish the contrary theory by one ever-recurring dilemma, that either man can live entirely free from sin, or the freedom of the human will and its consequent moral responsibility must be denied. Augustine replied to this early in 415, in his treatise *de Perfectione Justitiae Hominis*, addressed to Eutropius and Paul.

The scene of the controversy now changed from Africa to Palestine, where Pelagius had been resident for some years. In the beginning of 415 Paulus Orosius, a presbyter from Tarragona in Spain, came to Africa to consult Augustine as to certain questions, connected with Origenism and Priscillianism, which were rife in his native land. He had conceived an intense admiration for Augustine and became one of his most devoted disciples. Augustine describes him as quick in understanding, fluent in speech, and fervent in zeal. After giving him the instruction he required, he sent him to Jerome at Bethlehem, ostensibly to obtain further instruction, but really to watch the proceedings of Pelagius, and announce to the church in Palestine the steps taken in the African church to suppress the rising heresy. Orosius reached Palestine in June and spent a few weeks with Jerome, who was then writing his Dialogue against the Pelagians. He was invited to a synod at Jerusalem on July 28, and was asked what he could tell as to Pelagius and Coelestius. He gave an account of the formal condemnation of Coelestius by the council of Carthage in 412, and mentioned that Augustine was writing a treatise in answer to a work of Pelagius, and read a copy of the letter from Augustine to Hilary. Thereupon bp. John desired Pelagius himself to be sent for to have an opportunity of defending himself from any charges of unsound doctrine alleged. Pelagius was asked by the presbyters whether he had really taught the doctrines against which Augustine protested. He bluntly replied, "And who is Augustine to me?" This bold and contemptuous rejection of the name and authority of the great bishop whose influence was paramount in the West owing to his signal services in the Donatist controversy, roused the indignation of the presbyters, but, to the amazement of Orosius, the presiding bishop admitted Pelagius, layman and alleged heretic as he was, to a seat among the presbyters, and exclaimed, "I am Augustine here." He proceeded to hear charges against Pelagius. Orosius said that Pelagius, according to his own confession, had taught that man can be without sin and can easily keep the commandments of God, if he will. Pelagius acknowledged that he had used such language. Orosius claimed that such doctrine should be at once denounced as untenable on the authority of the recent council at Carthage, and of the writings of Augustine, and the judgment of their own venerated neighbour Jerome recently expressed in a letter to Ctesiphon. The bishop quoted the scriptural instances of Abraham, who was bidden "to walk before God and be perfect," and of Zacharias and Elizabeth, who were described as "walking in all the commandments and ordinances of the law blameless," as affording a *primâ facie* justification of Pelagius, and argued, If Pelagius said that man could fulfil the commands of God without the aid of God, his doctrine would be wicked and worthy of condemnation, but as he maintained that man could be free from sin not without the aid of God, to deny this position would be to deny the efficacy of divine grace. Orosius proceeded to anathematize the notion of such a denial of grace, and, seeing that John was unwilling to admit a charge of heresy against Pelagius, appealed to another tribunal. Declaring the heresy to be of Latin origin and most formidable in the Latin churches, he demanded that the whole question should be referred to pope Innocent, as the chief bishop of Latin Christianity. This compromise was accepted. The whole account of the proceedings of this synod at Jerusalem is derived from the *Apology* of Orosius, and must be received with some deductions, having regard to the fiery and intemperate invective which the impassioned Spaniard lavishes upon Pelagius and all his followers.

A renewed effort to quell Pelagianism, the result, Pelagius says, of the influence of Jerome and a small knot of ardent sympathizers at Bethlehem, was made towards the end of 415, when two deposed Western bishops, Heros of Arles and Lazarus of Aix, laid a formal accusation against Pelagius before a synod at Diospolis (the ancient Lydda), at which Eulogius, bp. of Caesarea and metropolitan, presided.

Fourteen bishops attended it—Eulogius, John, Ammonianus, Eutonius, two Porphyrys, Fidus, Zomnus, Zoboennus, Nymphidius, Chromatius, Jovinus, Eleutherius, and Clematius. The two accusers were absent from the hearing owing to the illness of one of them, but a document (*libellus*) was handed in containing the principal charges. Some of the propositions it attributed to Pelagius were capable of being explained in an orthodox sense, and he did so explain them. It was objected to him that he had said that no one could be without sin unless he had the knowledge of the law. He acknowledged that he had said this, but not in the sense his opponents attached to it; he intended by it that man is helped by the knowledge of the law to keep free from sin. The synod admitted that such teaching was not contrary to the mind of the church. It was charged again that he had affirmed that all men are governed by their own will. He explained that he intended by this to assert the responsibility of man's free will, which God aids in its choice of good; the man who sins is himself in fault as transgressing of his own free will. This too was pronounced in agreement with church teaching, for how could any one condemn the recognition of free will or deny its existence, when the possibility of God's aid to it was acknowledged? It was alleged that Pelagius had declared that in the day of judgment the wicked and sinners would not be spared, and it was inferred that he had intended thereby to imply that all sinners would meet eternal punishment, even those who had substantially belonged to Christ—it was probably implied that such teaching was a denial of the temporary purgatorial fire which was to purify the imperfectly righteous. Pelagius replied by quoting our Lord's words (Matt. xxv. 46), and declared that whoever believed otherwise was an Origenist. This satisfied the synod. It was alleged that he wrote that evil did not even enter the thought of the good Christian. He defended himself by saying that what he had actually said was that the Christian ought to study not even to think evil. The synod naturally saw no objection to this. It was alleged that he had disparaged the grace of N.T. by saying that the kingdom of heaven is promised even in O.T. It was supposed that by this he had proclaimed a doctrine that salvation could be obtained by the observance of the works of the Law. He explained it as a vindication of the divine authority of the O.T. dispensation, and its prophetic character. It was alleged that he had said that man can, if he will, be without sin, and that in writing a letter of commendation to a widow who had assumed the ascetic life, he used fulsome and adulatory language which glorified her unexampled piety as superlatively meritorious. He explained that though he might have admitted the abstract possibility of sinlessness in man, yet he had never maintained that there had existed any man who had remained sinless from infancy to old age, but that a man on his conversion might continue without sin by his own efforts and the grace of God, though still liable to temptation, and those who held an opposite opinion he begged leave to anathematize not as heretics but as fools. The bishops were satisfied with this acknowledgment that man by the help of God and by grace can be without sin. Other propositions alleged against him, such as those condemned by the synod of Carthage in 412, he declared were not his own, but made by Coelestius and others; yet he was willing freely to disavow them. It is hard to believe that in so doing Pelagius was not pronouncing condemnation on views he had himself on other occasions maintained. Finally, Pelagius professed his belief in the doctrine of the Holy Trinity and in all the teaching of the holy Catholic church, and the synod acknowledged him as a Catholic and in full communion with the church. Party feeling evidently ran very high. Jerome was regarded as a chief mover in the prosecution of Pelagius, and apparently by way of vengeance a violent and outrageous assault was made upon his monastery at Bethlehem, which was ascribed to some of the Pelagian party, with what justice it is not easy to ascertain. As Neander remarks, it is not likely that Pelagius had any share in the tumultuous proceedings, as in that case evidence of the outrage would doubtless have been laid before the Roman bp. Innocent in the subsequent proceedings. Jerome, suspecting the orthodoxy of many of its members, spoke of the synod of Diospolis as a "miserable synod." Augustine, in his treatise *de Gestis Pelagii*, written after he had received a full official record of the synod, argued that Pelagius had only escaped by a legal acquittal of little moral worth, obtained by evasive explanations and by his condemning the very dogmas he had before professed.

The controversy once more returned to the West. A synod of more than 69 bishops assembled at Carthage towards the close of 416. Orosius produced the accusations which had been presented against Pelagius by Heros and Lazarus. They recognized in them the same heretical opinions previously condemned at Carthage in 412, and determined to appeal to Innocent, bp. of Rome, on the great questions at issue. Granting that the synods of Jerusalem and Diospolis might have been justified in the acquittal of Pelagius on the ground of his explanations, evasions, and disclaimers of responsibility for some of the positions alleged, they called attention to the continued prevalence of doctrines which affirmed the sufficiency of nature for the avoidance of sin and fulfilment of the commandments of God (thus virtually superseding the need of divine grace), and which denied the necessity of baptism in the case of infants, as the way of obtaining deliverance from guilt and eternal salvation. A synod at Mileum in Numidia in 416, attended by 61 bishops, wrote a letter to Innocent to the same effect, and with these two synodical letters was sent a letter from Augustine and four brother-bishops, Aurelius, Alypius, Evodius, and Possidius, in which they sought to discount the acquittal of Pelagius in the East at Diospolis by saying that the result had only been obtained by the accused concealing his real sentiments and acknowledging the orthodox faith in ambiguous language, calculated to deceive the Eastern prelates, ignorant as they were of the full force of Latin words, and at the mercy of an interpreter. They demanded that Pelagius should be summoned to Rome and examined afresh, to see whether he acknowledged grace in the full scriptural sense. To enable the Roman bishop to judge dispassionately of the case they forwarded the book of Pelagius, on which Timasius and James had sought the judgment of Augustine, and the book (*de Naturâ et Gratiâ*) which Augustine had written in reply. They specially marked some passages in Pelagius, from which they thought Innocent must inevitably conclude that Pelagius allowed no other grace than the nature with which God had originally endowed man. Innocent answered this threefold appeal in three letters written Jan. 27, 417. He began each with a strong assertion of the supreme authority of his see and many expressions of satisfaction that the controversy had been referred to him for final decision. He expressed doubt whether the record of the proceedings at Diospolis he had received was authentic. The book of Pelagius he unhesitatingly pronounced blasphemous and dangerous, and gave his judgment that Pelagius, Coelestius, and all abettors of their views ought to be excommunicated.

Innocent died Mar. 12, 417, and was succeeded by Zosimus, whose name seems to indicate his Eastern origin. Coelestius left Ephesus, whither he had gone on his expulsion from Africa and obtained ordination as presbyter, and proceeded to Constantinople, whence, as he began disseminating his peculiar opinions, he was driven by its bishop, Atticus. He went at once to Rome to clear himself of the suspicions and charges urged against him. He laid before Zosimus a confession of his faith, which, after a minute and elaborate exposition of the chief articles of the Catholic faith, dealt with the controverted doctrines of grace. Treating them as really lying outside the articles of faith, he submitted himself to the judgment of the apostolic see, if in any way he had gone astray from scriptural truth. He professed his belief that infants ought to be baptized for the remission of sins in accordance with church practice, as the Lord had appointed that the kingdom of heaven could not be bestowed save upon the baptized. But he did not admit that infants derived sin by propagation ; sin is not born with man, but is his own act of choice. To impute evil to human nature antecedently to any exercise of the will he held injurious to the Creator, as making Him the author of evil. Zosimus held a synod in the basilica of St. Clement. He asked Coelestius whether he condemned all the errors ascribed to him. Coelestius answered that he condemned all that Innocent had condemned, and was ready to condemn all that the apostolic see deemed heretical. Zosimus declined to pronounce a definitive sentence, but deprived and excommunicated the bps. Heros and Lazarus, who had not appeared to substantiate the charges made against the Pelagians, and after an interval of two months wrote to Aurelius and other African bishops, censuring them for the premature condemnation of Coelestius. He refused to decide upon the merits of the case until the accusers appeared before him, whilst he informed the African bishops that he had admonished Coelestius and his followers to abstain from these nice and curious questions which did not tend to edification. After the despatch of this letter Zosimus received one from Praylius, the new bp. of Jerusalem, speaking favourably of Pelagius, and with it a letter from Pelagius and a confession of faith, which he had drawn up for Innocent, but which, reaching Rome after Innocent's death, were now delivered to his successor. This letter of Pelagius is lost, and known only by quotations in Augustine. The confession of faith is extant. Like that of Coelestius, it recapitulates the great articles of the Christian faith. In it he declared that he recognized free will in such a way as that man always needs the aid of God, and charged with error both those who say with the Manicheans that man cannot avoid sin, and those who assert with Jovinian that man cannot sin. He was willing to amend his statements if he had spoken incautiously, and to conform them to the judgment of the prelate "who held the faith and see of Peter." Zosimus had the letter and creed read in public assembly, and pronounced them thoroughly Catholic and free from ambiguity. He even spoke of the Pelagians as men of unimpeachable faith ("absolutae fidei") who had been wrongly defamed. He wrote afresh to Aurelius and the African bishops, upbraiding them vehemently for their readiness to condemn men without a proper opportunity of defence, strongly denouncing the personal character of Heros and Lazarus as rendering them untrustworthy witnesses, and gratefully acknowledging that Pelagius and his followers had never really been estranged from Catholic truth—a conclusion strikingly different from that of his immediate predecessor. Augustine generally passes over in silence this action of Zosimus, speaking of it as an instance of gentle dealing with the accused, and rather implying that Zosimus, with an amiable simplicity, had allowed himself to be deceived by the specious and subtle admissions of the heretics. The African bishops were not willing to accept without remonstrance this judgment in favour of opinions which long study had taught them to regard as inimical to the faith and destructive of all true spiritual life. Meeting at Carthage, they drew up a long letter to Zosimus, defending themselves from the charges of hastiness and uncharitableness, justifying the condemnation of Pelagianism pronounced by Innocent, and entreating Zosimus to inquire afresh into the doctrines of Coelestius. The subdeacon Marcellinus was the bearer of this letter. Zosimus replied in a letter, Mar. 21, 418, extolling extravagantly the dignity of his own position as the supreme judge of religious appeals, but declaring that he had not taken any further steps, hinting also at a possible reconsideration. On May 1, 418, a full council of the African church, composed of 214 (others say 224) bishops, held in the basilica of Faustus at Carthage, Aurelius presiding, was unwilling to wait for a theological determination from the see of Rome, but asserted its own independence and formulated nine canons anathematizing the principal Pelagian dogmas, some of them probably being a republication of canons passed at former minor councils. Anathemas were pronounced on the doctrine that infants derive no original sin from Adam which needs expiation in baptism, and that there is some middle place of happiness in the kingdom of heaven for infants who die unbaptized. A strong protest was made against the views that the grace of God by which we are justified through Jesus Christ avails only for the forgiveness of past sin and not for aid against the commission of sin, or that grace is only the revelation of the will of God and not an inspiring principle of righteousness, or that grace only enables us to do more easily what God commands. The two concluding canons point to a peculiar application of Pelagian doctrine, which was a curious anticipation of the teaching of some modern sectaries. They reject the idea that the petition in the Lord's Prayer, "Forgive us our sins," is inappropriate for Christian men and can only be regarded as a prayer for others, and that it can only be used as a fictitious expression of humility, not as a true confession of guilt.

Appeal was now made to the civil power. The emperors Honorius and Theodosius issued a decree banishing Pelagius and Coelestius from Rome, and pronouncing confiscation and banishment against all their followers. An imperial letter communicated this decree to the African bishops. Zosimus, whether in vacillation or in alarm at the strong force of dominant Catholic opinion now supported by the state, proceeded to investigate the subject afresh, and summoned Coelestius for fuller examination. Coelestius, seeing the inevitable result, withdrew from Rome. Zosimus thereupon issued a circular letter (*epistola tractoria*) confirming the decisions of the N. African church. He censured as contrary to the Catholic faith the tenets of Pelagius and Coelestius, particularly selecting for reprobation certain passages from Pelagius's Commentary on the Epistles of St. Paul, which since his former consideration of the case had been laid before him, and ordered all bishops acknowledging his authority to subscribe to the terms of his letter on pain of deprivation. This subscription was enforced through N. Africa under the protection of the imperial edict by Aurelius the bishop and president of the council at Carthage, and in Italy under the authority of the prefect. In Italy 18 bishops refused, and were immediately deprived. The ablest and most celebrated was Julian, bp. of Eclanum in Apulia, who entered into controversy with Augustine with much learning, critical power, and well-controlled temper. He complained, not without some justice, that the anti-Pelagian party sought to suppress their opponents by the strong hand of imperial authority rather than convince them by an appeal to reason. He charged the Roman bishop and clergy with a complete departure from their former convictions, and, complaining that subscription to the letter of Zosimus was being enforced on individual bishops in isolation and not at a deliberate synod, demanded further discussion in a fresh council, refusing to acknowledge the dogmatic authority of the N. African church. A letter commonly supposed to be written by him was circulated in Rome, the professed object of which was to shew the mischievous consequences of the dominant anti-Pelagian doctrine; and another letter, written in the name of the 18 deprived bishops of Italy to Rufus, bp. of Thessalonica, and remonstrating against their condemnation, was probably drawn up by Julian. The two letters reached Boniface, who at the end of the year succeeded Zosimus as bp. of Rome, and were communicated by him through Alypius to Augustine, who replied in his treatise *contra Duas Epistolas Pelagianorum*, addressed to Boniface, and subsequently pursued the argument against Julian, first in a treatise *contra Julianum* in six books, written in 421, and then in the closing years of his life in a work of which six books only were completed. Julian throughout his writings sought to cast a prejudice upon the Augustinian doctrine by raising forcible objections to its more unguarded assertions and exaggerations. He boldly challenged it as a revived form of Manicheism, implying that the early education of Augustine might still be moulding his doctrine. He objected that the Augustinian system denied the goodness of the original creation of God—represented marriage, although a divine institution, as necessarily evil—disparaged the righteousness of the O.T. saints—denied free will and its consequent moral responsibility—and nullified belief in the forgiveness of all sins at baptism. Augustine shewed that these were unfair deductions from his statements, maintaining that the original goodness of man's nature is not incompatible with the recognition of its corruption after Adam's fall, that the O.T. did not assert the sinlessness or freedom from temptation of the saints; that free will was so vitiated by the fall that it was powerless for righteousness without the prevenient and co-operating grace of God; and that even after the forgiveness conveyed in baptism there remained the sinful element of concupiscence. Augustine could confidently and successfully appeal to the popular consciousness of Christendom, as bearing witness to man's moral impotence and his need of redemption. The experience of the human heart was, after all, a better judge of such spiritual facts than the most subtle arguments of reason and conflicting interpretations of the meaning of N.T.

The tendency of Pelagianism to underrate the necessity of the divine redemption, and to disparage the dignity of the person of the Redeemer by denying His sinless humanity, is manifested in the case of Leporius, a monk and presbyter of S. Gaul who, coming into Africa, had been reclaimed from Pelagian views by Augustine. In recanting he acknowledged that he had taught that Jesus Christ as a mere man was liable to sin and temptation, but by His own efforts and exertions without divine aid had attained to perfect holiness. Jesus had not come into the world to redeem mankind from sin, but to set them an example of holy living (Cassian, *de Incarn.* i. 234; Gennad. *de Script. Eccles.* 59). Thus Leporius's peculiar anthropology coloured his theological conception of the God-Man. Annianus, a deacon of Celada, wrote at the same time in defence of Pelagian views, and, at the suggestion of Orontius, one of the deposed bishops, translated the homilies of John Chrysostom on St. Matthew in the interest, he alleged, of a high morality. He claimed Chrysostom as a powerful upholder of evangelical perfection, of the integrity of human nature against any Manichean notions of its essentially evil character, and of the free will which it was the glory of Christianity to recognize in opposition to pagan ideas of fate and necessity; and as giving co-ordinate prominence to grace and free will.

Pelagianism was not wholly extinguished even in Italy by the forcible measures adopted against it both by the civil and ecclesiastical authorities, for pope Leo, writing *c.* 444, desired the bp. of Aquileia not to receive into communion any in his province suspected of the heresy before they subscribed a formal renunciation. The letters of pope Gelasius also refer to occasional outbreaks of the heresy in Dalmatia and elsewhere towards the end of the 5th cent.

Pelagianism came under the formal condemnation of the Eastern church in an incidental way. Several deposed Pelagian bishops repaired to Constantinople, where they found Coelestius. Atticus, the patriarch, had refused to receive them, but his successor Nestorius gave them a patient hearing. He wrote to Coelestinus, bp. of Rome, for information about the reasons of their condemnation and the nature of their peculiar doctrines, but received no answer. When Nestorius himself fell into disgrace because of his own heresy about the person of Christ, he was disposed to sympathize with Coelestius and his followers as the objects of persecution by a dominant party. The East had apparently not specially discussed the Pelagian controversy; its leading rulers and writers recognized the co-operation of grace and free will without narrowly determining their limits. But the general council at Ephesus in 431 joined, under the influence of Cyril, in one condemnation the tenets of Nestorius and Coelestius, while refraining from specifying them. It pronounced sentence of deposition upon any metropolitan or cleric who had held or should hereafter hold their views.

The personal history of Pelagius after the condemnation of his views by Zosimus is obscure. He is said to have died in some small town in Palestine, being upwards of 70 years old. Coelestius similarly disappears after the council of Ephesus; the time and place of his death are unknown. Julian is said to have died *c.* 454 in an obscure town of Sicily, where he maintained himself by teaching. There is a story that in a time of famine he relieved the poor by parting with all he had. There is a tradition that in the 9th cent. the inscription was still visible on his tomb: "Here rests in peace Julian, a Catholic bishop."

A modified form of Pelagianism, called by later scholastic writers semi-Pelagianism, arose in the closing years of Augustine's life. Its advocates were spoken of at the time of its introduction as Massilienses, as they were connected with the church of Marseilles. Its originator was John CASSIAN, commonly called a Scythian but probably a native of Gaul. He had been brought up in a monastery at Bethlehem, and after living some time with the monks of Egypt, went to Marseilles, where he founded two monasteries, one for men and one for women. He differed widely from Pelagius, for he acknowledged that the whole human race was involved in the sin of Adam and could not be delivered but by the righteousness of the second Adam; that the wills of men are prevented by the grace of God, and that no man is sufficient of himself to begin or to complete any good work. But though he admitted that the first call to salvation sometimes comes to the unwilling and is the direct result of preventing grace, yet he held that ordinarily grace depends on the working of man's own will. Augustine, at the suggestion of two lay-friends, Prosper and Hilary, in two treatises, one on the predestination of the saints, the other on the gift of perseverance, defended the doctrines of an arbitrary election and of a will determined wholly by grace, but failed to satisfy the objections felt by the church of Marseilles, and the Gallic theologians continued after the death of Augustine to regard his predestinarian views as essentially fatalistic and injurious to moral progress. The monastery of Lerins was a principal centre of opposition to ultra-Augustinian views. At length the controversy was closed in the time of CAESARIUS, bp. of Arles, an ardent admirer of St. Augustine, at a council at Arausio (Orange) in July 529. Of its 25 canons the first two, in opposition to Pelagian doctrine, declare that by the sin of Adam not only his own soul but those of his descendants were injured. The next six expound the functions of grace, affirming that the initial act of faith is not from man but from God's grace, and that we cannot without grace think or choose any good thing pertaining to salvation. Others develop the doctrine on similar lines, but not one touches the disputed question of predestination. An address appended by the prelates to the canons repudiates indignantly the belief that any are predestined to evil and asserts that without any preceding merits God inspires men with faith and love, leads them to baptism, and after baptism helps them by the same grace to fulfil His will. Pope Boniface II., who had succeeded Felix, confirmed the decrees of this Gallican council in a letter written to Caesarius. The moderation and good sense of the fathers of Orange, and their earnest desire to avoid the extravagance either of extreme predestinarianism, which would annihilate the human will, or an arrogant self-trust, which would claim to be independent of divine grace, had their reward. Their decrees met with general acquiescence, and both Pelagianism and semi-Pelagianism ceased to be dominant forces in Western Christendom.

Semi-Pelagianism held man in his original state to have had certain physical, intellectual, and moral advantages which he no longer enjoys. In the beginning his body was not subject to death, he had extraordinary knowledge of external nature and apprehension of the moral law, and was sinless. The sin of the first man entailed physical death and a moral corruption which was propagated to his posterity. Freedom of will to do good was not lost, but greatly impaired. The imputation of original sin is removed in baptism, and baptism is essential to salvation. Man needs the aid of divine grace for the performance of good works and the attainment of salvation. The free will of man works in co-operation with divine grace. There is no such thing as an unconditional decree of God, but predestination to salvation or damnation depends upon the use which man makes of his freedom to good. Election is therefore conditional. The merit of man's salvation is, however, to be ascribed to God, because, without God's grace, man's efforts would be unavailing. Wiggers has forcibly observed that Augustinianism represented man as morally dead, semi-Pelagianism as morally sick, Pelagianism as morally sound.

The full theory of Augustinianism in all its strong asseverations of an unconditional election and a total corruption of human nature did not retain its hold on the theology of the Western church during the succeeding centuries, nor was it ever acknowledged in the Eastern church. Men like popes Leo I. and Gregory I., in the 5th and 6th cents., and Bede in the 8th, were Augustinian, but the general tendency of the West turned in another direction, while it sternly rejected Pelagianism proper. The famous history of the monk Gottschalk, in the latter part of the 9th cent., proves how distasteful unqualified predestinarianism had become, but this lies beyond the assigned limits of this Dictionary.

Pelagianism never developed into a schism by setting up any organization external to the Catholic church. It practised no distinctive rites, it accepted all the traditional ecclesiastical discipline. It freely retained the practice of infant baptism, though it formed a different opinion on the moral and spiritual significance of the act. It was a mode of thought which strove to win acceptance within the church, but which was successfully cast out. [AUGUSTINE, § 10.] Cf. Zunnier, *Pelagius in Irland* (Berlin, 1902). [W.I.]

Pelagius (8) I., bp. of Rome after Vigilius, in the reign of Justinian I., A.D. 555-560. A native, and deacon, of Rome, he had been appointed by pope AGAPETUS (A.D. 536) as his apocrisiarius at Constantinople. Under Vigilius he again held the same office, and joined with the patriarch Mennas in moving Justinian to issue his edict for the condemnation of Origenism. After this he returned to Rome, where he was one of the two deacons of Vigilius who applied to Ferrandus of Carthage for advice after the issue of the imperial edict "de Tribus Capitulis" (*c.* 544). Vigilius being summoned by the emperor to Constantinople in the matter of the Three Chapters, Pelagius remained as the archdeacon and chief ecclesiastic at Rome; and occupied this position when the Gothic king Totila (Dec. 546) entered Rome as a conqueror and went to pay his devotions in the church of St. Peter. There Pelagius, bearing the gospels, met him, and falling on his knees said. "Prince, spare thy people." The conqueror answered with a significant smile, "Hast thou now come to supplicate me, Pelagius?" "Yes," he replied, "inasmuch as the Lord has made me thy servant. But now withhold thy hand from these who have passed into servitude to thee." Moved by these entreaties, Totila forbade any further slaughter of the Romans. He also employed Pelagius, together with a layman Theodorus, in an embassy to Constantinople for concluding peace with the emperor, binding them with an oath to do their best in his behalf and to return without delay to Italy. They executed their commission and brought back Justinian's reply that Belisarius was in military command, and had authority to arrange matters (Procop. *de Bell. Goth.* L. 3).

Pope VIGILIUS having proceeded from Sicily on his voyage to Constantinople in the early part of 547, Pelagius joined him, and appears to have acted with him in his changing attitudes of submission or resistance to the emperor's will. He proceeded to Rome after the death of Vigilius at Syracuse, and was there consecrated pope, being supported by Narses, at that time in command of Rome, who acted under the emperor's orders. The appointment was not welcome to the Romans, and there was difficulty in getting prelates to consecrate him. The real cause of his unpopularity was his consenting to condemn the Three Chapters and to support the decisions of the Constantinopolitan council. A great part of the western church still, and for many years afterwards, resolutely rejected these decisions, and the chief recorded action of Pelagius as pope is his unavailing attempt to heal the consequent schism.

In Gaul Pelagius was accused of heresy. Consequently the Frank king Childebert sent to him an ambassador, by name Rufinus, requesting him to declare his acceptance of the tome of pope Leo, or to express his belief in his own words. He readily did both, asserting his entire agreement with Leo and with the four councils, and appending a long orthodox confession of faith. But he made no mention of the fifth council, or of the necessity of accepting its decrees. He praised the king for his zeal in the true faith, and expressed the hope that no false reports about himself might occasion any schism in Gaul (*Ep.* xvi. *ad Childebertum*; *Ep.* xv. *ad Sapaudum*). He showed anxiety to conciliate Sapaudus, bp. of Arles, fearing, we may suppose, the possible defection of the Gallican church from Rome. He sent him a short friendly letter (*Ep.* viii.), and afterwards the pall, and conferred on him the vicariate jurisdiction over the churches of Gaul which former popes had committed to metropolitans of Arles (*Epp.* xi. xii. xiii.). He speaks of "the eternal solidity of that firm rock on which Christ had founded His church from the rising to the setting of the sun, being maintained by the authority of his (*i.e.* Peter's) successors, acting in person, or through their vicars." And, as his predecessors had, by the grace of God, ruled the universal church of God, he commits to the bp. of Arles, after their example, and according to ancient custom, supreme and exclusive jurisdiction over Gaul, as vicar of the apostolic see. It cannot but strike readers of church history during the reign of Justinian I., and especially of the proceedings of the 5th council, how little the theory of universal spiritual dominion thus enunciated agreed with facts. Indeed Pelagius himself was really throughout his popedom acting as the creature of the emperor, who had defied and overruled the authority of the Roman see. [J.B—Y.]

Pelagius (9) II., bp. of Rome after Benedict I., under the emperors Tiberius, Constantine, and Mauricius, from Nov. 578 to Feb. 590. He was a native of Rome, the son of Winigild, and supposed from his father's name to have been of Gothic extraction. At the time of Benedict's death the Lombards, already the masters of a great part of N. Italy, were besieging Rome. Consequently the new pope was consecrated without the previous sanction of the emperor (required since the reign of Justinian). Partly, perhaps, to excuse this informality, as well as to solicit aid against the Lombards, the new pope, as soon as possible after his accession, sent a deputation to Tiberius, who had become sole emperor on the death of Justin II. in Oct. 578. It was doubtless now that Gregory, afterwards pope Gregory the Great, was first sent to Constantinople as apocrisiarius of the Roman see. On Oct. 4, 584, Pelagius sent him a letter to represent the lamentable condition of Italy and the imminent danger of Rome from the Lombard invasion; Longinus, the exarch at Ravenna, having been appealed to in vain. Gregory is directed to press on the emperor the urgent need of succour. He returned to Rome probably A.D. 585 (Joan. Diac. *ib.*).

The emperor Mauricius had engaged the Frank king, Childebert II., for a large pecuniary reward to invade Italy and drive out the Lombards. The invasion (probably A.D. 585) resulted in a treaty of peace between the Franks and Lombards (Greg. Turon. vi. 42; Paul. Diac. *de Gest. Longob.* iii. 17).

On the retirement of Childebert from Italy, it appears that Smaragdus exarch of Ravenna had also concluded a truce with the Lombards (*Epp.* Pelag. ii.; *Ep.* i. *ad Episcopos Istriae*). Pelagius took advantage of it to open negotiations with the bishops of Istria, who still remained out of communion with Rome in the matter of the Three Chapters. In the first of his three letters he implores them to consider the evil of schism, and return to the unity of the church. He is at pains to vindicate his own faith, and to declare his entire acceptance of the four great councils and of the tome of pope Leo, by way of shewing that his acceptance of the 5th council, and his consequent condemnation of the Three Chapters, involved no departure from the ancient faith. He does not insist on condemnation of the Three Chapters by the Istrian bishops themselves. He only begs them to return to communion with Rome, notwithstanding its condemnation of the same; and this in a supplicatory rather than imperious tone. In his second letter he declares himself deeply grieved by their unsatisfactory reply to his first, and by their reception of his emissaries. He quotes St. Augustine as to the necessity of all churches being united to apostolic sees, but further cites Cyprian *de Unitate Ecclesiae* (with interpolations that give the passages a meaning very different from their original one) in support of the peculiar authority of St. Peter's chair. Finally he calls upon the Istrians to send deputies to Rome for conference with himself, or at any rate to Ravenna for conference with a representative whom he would send; and mentions (significantly, as appears in the sequel) that he has written to the exarch Smaragdus on the subject. Another, called his third, letter to Elias and the Istrian bishops, is a treatise on the Three Chapters, composed for him by Gregory (*de Gest. Longob.* iii. 20). Appeals and arguments proving of no avail, Pelagius seems to have called on the civil power to persecute; for Smaragdus is recorded to have gone in person to Grado, to have seized Severus, who had succeeded Elias in the see, together with three other bishops, in the church, carried them to Ravenna, and forced them to communicate there with the bp. John. They were allowed after a year (Smaragdus being superseded by another exarch) to return to Grado, where neither people nor bishops would communicate with them till Severus had recanted in a synod of ten bishops his compliance at Ravenna (Paul. Diac. *ib.* iii. 27; cf. *Epp. S. Greg.* l. 1, *Ep.* 16).

Towards the end of the pontificate of Pelagius (probably A.D. 588), a council at Constantinople, apparently a large and influential one, and not confined to ecclesiastics, dealt with Gregory patriarch of Antioch, who being charged with crime, had appealed "ad imperatorem et concilium" (Evagr. *H.E.* vi. 7). This council is memorable as having called forth the first protest from Rome, renewed afterwards more notably by Gregory the Great, against the assumption by the patriarch of Constantinople of the title "oecumenical." The title itself was not a new one; as an honorary or complimentary one it had been occasionally given to other patriarchs; and Justinian had repeatedly designated the patriarch of Constantinople "the most holy and most blessed archbishop of this royal city, and oecumenical patriarch" (*Cod.* i. 7; *Novell.* iii. v. vi. vii. xvi. xlii.). Nor do we know of any previous objection, and at this council it may have been ostentatiously assumed by the then patriarch, John the Faster, and sanctioned by the council with reference to the case before it, in a way that seemed to recognize jurisdiction of the patriarchate of Constantinople over that of Antioch. In Nov. 589 a destructive inundation of the Tiber at Rome was followed by a plague, described as "Pestis inguinaria," of which Pelagius II. was one of the earliest victims, being attacked by it in the middle of Jan. 590 (Greg. Turon. l. x. c. 1). According to Anastasius he was buried on Feb. 8 in St. Peter's. [J.B—Y.]

Peregrinus (1), called *Proteus*, an apostate from Christianity and a Cynic philosopher of the 2nd cent., whose history has been satirically told by Lucian. That Lucian's work is not a romance is amply shown by the account of Peregrinus in Aulus Gellius, *Noct. Attic.* viii. 3, and xii. 11. Other writers, pagan and Christian alike, of the same age, mention him: *e.g.* Tatian, *Orat. adv. Graec.* c. 25; Athenagoras, *pro Christian.* c. 26, who tells us of his statue at Parium; Maximus Tyrius, *Diss.* iii.; Tertull. *ad Mart.* c. 4; and Eusebius in his *Chronicon* (ii. 178 seq. ed. Schöne); cf. also I. Sörgel, *Lucian's Stellung zum Christenthum*, (1875); Schiller's *Geschichte der Kaiserzeit*, p. 685; and Bernays' tract *Lucian u. die Kyniker* (Berlin, 1879). The story of Peregrinus is therefore a very valuable illustration of the life of the 2nd cent. He was born at Parium on the Hellespont, where he committed various crimes, including parricide. He escaped justice by transferring his property to the municipality and then passed over to Palestine, where he became a Christian, and, according to Lucian's account, a bishop or at least a presbyter. He was imprisoned for the faith, and Lucian's words are a valuable and truthful description of the conduct of the Christians towards confessors generally. Crowds attended at the prison and ministered to Peregrinus, bribing the gaolers to obtain admission. The "Teaching of the Twelve Apostles" takes elaborate precautions against wandering apostles and prophets, who desired only to make gain of the gospel. Such a false apostle was Peregrinus. His real character was, however, discovered, and he was excommunicated. He then became a Cynic philosopher, a sect which Lucian specially abhorred, and resided at Rome. He made use of the licence permitted them to abuse the emperor himself, but was speedily expelled by the prefect Urbis. He next passed into Greece, and there, to obtain a greater notoriety, burned himself alive at the Olympic games at the 236th Olympiad A.D. 165. Cf. Strabo, xv. i. 73; Dion Cassius, liv. 9; and Lightfoot *On Colossians*, p. 394. Dr. Lightfoot has elaborately discussed the relations between the stories of Peregrinus and St. Ignatius (*SS. Ignatius and Polycarp*, t. i. pp. 129, 133, 331, 450, ii. pp. 206, 213, 306, 356; cf. Salmon's *Introd. to the N.T.* pp. 522, 650). [LUCIAN.] [G.T.S.]

Perpetua (1), martyr. Her full name was Vibia Perpetua. She was well born, and had a father, mother, and two brothers living, one of whom was a catechumen. When 22 years old, married, and having lately borne a son, she was arrested. Her father repeatedly strove to induce her to recant. She and her fellow-martyrs were baptized after their arrest, possibly before their transference to the public prison (cf. Le Blant, *Actes des Mart.* v. 9, p. 48). They were attended in prison, according to the ancient discipline of the Carthaginian church, by the deacons Tertius and Pomponius (Cypr. *Ep.* 15 *ad Mart.*). Perpetua now had her first vision, indicative of her future passion. She saw a ladder reaching to heaven guarded by a dragon. Saturus mounted first and then Perpetua followed. They came to a large garden, where was a shepherd clad in white, feeding sheep, while thousands in white robes stood around. The shepherd gave Perpetua a piece of cheese, which she received "junctis manibus" and consumed, the attendants saying "Amen." Their trial came soon after. The procurator Hilarianus condemned the martyrs to the beasts. After her condemnation Perpetua saw a vision of her brother Dinocrates, who had died when 7 years old, in punishment, but after continuous prayer for him it was revealed to her that he was removed into a place of refreshment and peace. This vision is a clear proof that prayers for the dead were then used by that party in the church which claimed to adhere most closely to apostolic usages. Some, supposing Dinocrates unbaptized, have claimed it as sanctioning the view that the unbaptized dead are helped by prayer, a view which Augustine combated in *de Orig. Animae*, lib. i. c. 10, and lib. iii. c. 9, where he maintains that Dinocrates was in punishment for sins committed after baptism. The day before her passion Perpetua saw another vision, wherein she triumphed over an Egyptian, representing the devil, and was rewarded with a golden branch. When the hour of execution arrived the tribune attempted to array the men as priests of Saturn, the women as priestesses of Ceres, but yielded to the indignant protest of Perpetua. She suffered by the sword, after being tossed by an infuriated cow, but, like Blandina at Lyons in a like trial, was unconscious of any pain (cf. Dodwell's *Diss. in Iren.* ii. §§ 43, 46; Routh's *Rel. Sacr.* i. 360).

The precise year of the martyrdom is uncertain, the succession of African proconsuls being very imperfectly known. We know that they suffered in the year when Minucius Timinianus was proconsul. One circumstance would seem to fix the date as 202, or at farthest 203. There was as yet no general persecution of the Christians, such as soon after developed itself. The freedom enjoyed by the clergy and Christians in ministering to the martyrs is sufficient proof of this. Why, then, did they suffer? On Jan. 1, 202, Severus was at Antioch, where he appointed himself and Caracalla consuls for the ensuing year. During the month he proceeded by easy stages through Palestine to Egypt, exercising severities upon the Jews which, according to Renan, have left their mark on the Talmud (*Mission de Phénicie*, pp. 775, 776). He published an edict forbidding any fresh conversions from Paganism to Judaism or Christianity, while imposing no penalties on original Jews or Christians. Now all our martyrs were fresh converts, and as such seem to have suffered under this edict.

Some have maintained that Tertullian wrote the Acts of these martyrs. The style is in many places very similar to his. The documents themselves profess to have been written mainly by Perpetua and Saturus, and completed for publication by a third party, who cannot now be identified. Tertullian certainly knew the Acts, as he refers to the vision of Perpetua in *de Animâ*, c. 55.

All our MSS. are in Latin; yet Aubé (*Les Chrét. dans l'Emp. Rom.* p. 615) thinks they may have been originally written in Greek. One MS. represents Perpetua as speaking Greek to bp. Optatus in Paradise. The Acts contain very many Greek words in Latin characters, whence we may at least conclude that the martyrs were bi-lingual, and that Greek was then very current at Carthage. The Acts contain some interesting illustrations of ancient church customs. The kiss of peace is given (c. x.). The Trisagion is sung, and in Greek (c. xii.). In the language of the visions we can clearly see the influence of the Apocalypse (cf. specially c. xii.). The Acts were discovered and pub. by Lucas Holstenius in 17th cent. They are in Ruinart's *Acta Sincera*; *Acta SS.* Boll. Mart. i. p. 630; Munter, *Primord. Eccles. Afric.* p. 226; and trans. in Clark's Ante-Nicene Series, Cyprian's works, t. ii. p. 276. Aubé, *l.c.* p. 521, has pub. another version from a Parisian MS. The best ed. of all three texts is ed. by J. A. Robinson, *The Passion of St. Perpetua*, with intro., notes, and original Lat. text of the Scillitan martyrdom, in *Camb. Texts and Studies*, i. 2 (1901). [G.T.S.]

Perpetuus, St., 6th archbp. of Tours, between St. Eustochius and St. Volusianus, both of whom were his relatives, belonged to one of the great senatorial families of the Auvergne. He possessed considerable wealth (Greg. Tur. *Hist. Franc.* x. 31), was a student of sacred literature and a friend of the two poets Sidonius Apollinaris and Paulinus of Périgueux (Sid. Apoll. *Ep.* vii. 9; Paul. Petr. *de Vita S. Mart.* vi.; *Ep. ad Perpet.* Migne, *Patr. Lat.* lxi. 1064 sqq., 1071). Consecrated in 460 or 461, he presided in 461 over the council of Tours, convoked to check the worldliness and profligacy of the Gallic clergy (Mansi, vii. 943 sqq.). The council of Vannes, *c.* 465, over which apparently he also presided, had the same object (*ib.* 951 sqq.). His principal work was the construction of the great church of St. Martin at Tours. The one built by Briccius had become too small for the fame and miracles of the saint. Of the new one which replaced it at 550 paces from the city, and to which the saint's body was translated with great ceremony (*c.* July 4, 473), we have, owing to its being Gregory the historian's own church, full and interesting details and measurements. (See *Hist. Franc.* ii. 14; *de Mirac. S. Mart.* i. 6.) A good many other churches were built by Perpetuus, notably one in honour of St. Peter and St. Paul, which he constructed to receive the roof of St. Martin's old church, as it was of elegant workmanship. Perpetuus also bestowed much care on the services. Gregory recounts the fasts, vigils and regulations for divine service instituted by him for different seasons of the year and still observed in Gregory's own time (*Hist. Franc.* x. 31; cf. *Hist. Litt.* ii. 626-627; Ceillier, x. 438, 441). Perpetuus died in 490 or 491, after an episcopate of 30 years (*Hist. Franc.* ii. 26; x. 31), and, as he had asked in his will, was buried in the church he had built, at the feet of St. Martin (*Epitaphium* in Migne, *Patr. Lat.* lviii. 755, and elsewhere). [S.A.B.]

Petilianus, an eminent Donatist bishop, probably a native of Constantina or Cirta, chief town of Numidia, born of parents who were Catholics; but while still a catechumen carried off against his will by the Donatists, received by baptism into their community, and subsequently made, between 395 and 400, their bishop in Cirta. (Aug. *c. Lit. Petil.* ii. 104, 238; *Serm. ad pleb. Caesar. de Emerito*, 8.) He had practised as a lawyer with great success, so as to obtain the name of the Paraclete, the identity of which name with that of the Holy Spirit, if we may believe St. Augustine, was flattering to his vanity (*c. Lit. Petil.* iii. 16, 19). He took a prominent part in the Conference, A.D. 411, as one of the seven managers on the Donatist side, but after this we hear no more of him. (Aug. *Retract.* ii. 34; *c. Lit. Petil.* ii. 40, 95; iii. 57, 69; Optatus, *Opp. Mon. Vet. Don.* liii.) About 398 or 400, Augustine in a private letter invited some of the leaders of the Donatist sect in Cirta to discuss the questions at issue between them and the church, an invitation rejected by them with contempt. But when he was in the church of that place, together with Absentius (Alypius) and Fortunatus its Catholic bishop, a letter addressed by the Donatist bp. (Petilianus, but without a name) to his own clergy, proposing to cut off communion with the Catholic church, was put into Augustine's hands. This proposal seemed so monstrous as to make him doubt whether the letter could have proceeded from a man of Petilian's reputation, until he was assured that this was the case. Lest his silence should be misunderstood, he undertook at once to reply to it, though it was plainly imperfect and ought to be presented in a complete state. The writer accuses the Catholics of making necessary a repetition of baptism, because, he says, they pollute the souls of those whom they baptize. The validity of baptism in his view depends on the character of the giver, as the strength of a building depends on that of the foundation. He quotes Ecclus. xxxiv. 30 [25], applying to his own sect the words "wise men" (Matt. xxiii. 34), and interpreting the word "dead" to mean an ungodly person; he charges the Catholics with persecution and "tradition," and makes an insinuation about Manicheism. To these charges, Augustine replied in his first book against Petilian.

In his second book, for the benefit of the less acute among his brethren (*tardiores patres*) he takes one by one the charges of Petilian, whose letter had by that time been received in a complete state. The statements, 108 in number, including applications of Scripture passages, and an appeal to the Catholics, are answered by Augustine *seriatim*. The arguments used by Petilian come under two principal heads, but are much intermixed, and contain much coarse vituperation. (1) *The inefficacy of baptism by ungodly persons.* (2) *The iniquity of persecution.* In his reply Augustine shews, (1) *The true nature of baptism.* Those who fall away after baptism must return, not by rebaptism, but by repentance. (2) *As to persecution.* Augustine denies the charge, and retorts it upon his adversary, whose partisans, the Circumcellions and others, were guilty of persecution. (3) In near connexion with the last question comes that of *appeal to the civil power*; Augustine shews that the Donatists themselves appealed to Constantine, and took advantage of the patronage of Julian. (4) *Language of Scripture and of the church perverted.*

Of a second letter from Petilian only some passages quoted by Augustine are extant, but it appears from Augustine's reply to have contained no new arguments but much personal abuse (Possidius, *Indiculus*, iii.).

In close connexion with these letters is the treatise of St. Augustine on the Unity of the Church, written between the second and third of them, and intended to answer the question, "Where is the church?"

In the inquiry of 411 at Carthage Petilian took a leading part and was chiefly remarkable for ingenious quibbling and minute subtlety on technical details of procedure—using, in short, as Augustine said afterwards, every artifice in order to prevent real discussion; and on the third day losing his temper and insulting Augustine personally in a coarse and vulgar manner; appearing throughout as a pettifogging advocate, adroit but narrow, dishonest and suspicious of dishonesty in others; spinning out the time in matters of detail, taking every advantage he could, fair or unfair, and postponing, though with much ostentatious protest to the contrary, the real matters in dispute. See Sparrow Simpson, *St. Aug. and Afr. Ch. Divisions* (1910), pp. 64 ff. [H.W.P.]

Petronilla (1), saint and virgin. According to the legend related in the letter attributed to Marcellus, son of the prefect of the city, and incorporated in the apocryphal Acts of SS. Nereus and Achilleus, she was the daughter of St. Peter, was struck with palsy by her father and afterwards restored to health by him. Her great beauty led count Flaccus to fall in love with her and come with soldiers to take her by force as his wife. She rebuked him for coming with an armed band, and desired him, if he wished her as his wife, to send matrons and virgins on the third day to conduct her to his house. He agreed, and she passed the three days in prayer and fasting with her foster-sister Felicula, and on the third day died, after receiving the sacrament, and the women brought by Flaccus to escort her home celebrated her funeral. She was buried on the estate of Flavia Domitilla, on the road to Ardea, a mile and a half from Rome (*Acta SS.* May, iii. 10, 11, vii. 420-422).

The legend seems to have originated (see Lightfoot, *S. Clement*, 259-262) from the combination of two elements: (i) the Manichean apocryphal story mentioned by St. Augustine (*c. Adimantum*, xvii. *Op.* viii. in Migne, *Patr. Lat.* xlii. 161) that St. Peter by his prayers caused his daughter to be struck with palsy (the account in St. Augustine implies also her restoration to health by her father); (ii) the existence in the Christian cemetery of Flavia Domitilla of a sarcophagus inscribed with the words AURELIAE (or AUREAE) PETRONILLAE FILIAE DULCISSIMAE. Petronilla was assumed to be a diminutive of Petros; the inscription, it was imagined, had been engraved by the apostle himself. Later writers, *e.g.* Baronius, felt the supposition that St. Peter had a daughter to be a difficulty, and explained *filia* as a spiritual daughter, as St. Peter speaks of St. Mark as his son. Petronilla, however, is really derived from Petronius or Petro; and the founder of the Flavian family, the grandfather both of the emperor Vespasian and his brother, T. Flavius Sabinus, the head of that branch of the Flavii to which the supposed converts to Christianity belonged, was T. Flavius Petro of Reate. Petronilla therefore was probably one of the Aurelian gens. several of whom are shewn by the inscriptions discovered by De Rossi to have been buried in the same cemetery, and was by the mother's side a scion of the Flavian family, and therefore related to Flavia Domitilla, the owner of the land over the cemetery, and was probably, like her, a Christian convert.

Probably on account of her assumed relationship to St. Peter she was held in high veneration. Though the subterranean basilica constructed by pope Siricius between 391 and 395 contained the tombs of the martyrs SS. Nereus and Achilleus, it was in her honour it was dedicated, and there her body remained in its sarcophagus till in 757 it was translated by pope Paul I. to the Vatican and placed in what had been the mausoleum of the Christian emperors, close to St. Peter's (*Liber Pontificalis* in *Patr. Lat.* cxxviii. 1139).

Cav. de Rossi discovered and excavated the ancient basilica of St. Petronilla, determined the original positions of her sarcophagus and the tombs of SS. Nereus and Achilleus, and found a fresco, probably of the first half of the 4th cent. (*Bull.* 1875, 16), which represents St. Petronilla, designated in it a martyr, conducting one of her votaries to Paradise. A chamber was discovered (*Athenaeum*, Mar. 4, 1882) in these catacombs, its style of decoration, akin to the Pompeian, shewing its great antiquity. The inscription which had been over the door, written in characters of the Flavian era, is AMPLIATI, which suggests that this might be the tomb of the Ampliatus to whom St. Paul alludes (*Rom.* xvi. 8). An interesting account of these discoveries and a discussion of the legend of St. Petronilla and the history of her cultus is in Cav. de Rossi's papers (*Bullettino di Archeologia Christiana*, 1865, 46; 1874, 1, 68, 122; 1875, 1-77; 1878, 125-146; 1879, 1-20, 139-160; 1880, 169), and in vol. iv. of *Roma Sotterranea*. [F.D.]

Petrus (4) **I.**, St., archbp. of Alexandria, succeeded Theonas, A.D. 300. He had three years of tranquil administration, which he so used as to acquire the high reputation indicated by Eusebius, who calls him a wonderful teacher of the faith, and "an admirable specimen of a bishop, alike in the excellence of his conduct and his familiarity with Scripture" (Eus. viii. 13; ix. 6). Then came the Diocletian persecution, and in the early part of 306 Peter found it necessary to draw up conditions of reconciliation to the church, and of readmission to her privileges, for those who through weakness had compromised their fidelity. The date is determined by the first words of this set of 14 "canons" or regulations, "Since we are approaching the fourth Easter from the beginning of the persecution," *i.e.* reckoning from the Lent of 303. (This is overlooked in Mason's *Persecution of Diocletian*, p. 324, where these "canons" are assigned to 311.) The substance of these remarkable provisions (given at length in Routh's *Reliquiae Sacrae*, iv. 23 ff.) is as follows. (1) Those who did not give way until extreme tortures had overstrained their powers of endurance, and who had been for three years already "mourners" without being admitted to regular penance, might communicate after fasting 40 days more with special strictness. (2) Those who, as Peter phrases it, had endured only the "siege of imprisonment," not the "war of tortures," and therefore deserved less pity, yet gave themselves up to suffer some affliction for "the Name," although in prison they were much relieved by Christian alms, may be received after another year's penance. (3) Those who endured nothing at all, but lapsed under sheer terror, must do penance for four years. (4) is not, strictly speaking, a canon, but a lamentation over *lapsi* who had not repented

(Neale, i. 98). Peter cites the cursing of the fig-tree, with Is. lxvi. 24; lvii. 20. (5) Those who, to evade trial of their constancy, feigned epilepsy, promised conformity in writing, or put forward pagans to throw incense on the altar in their stead, must do penance for six months more, although some of them had already been received to communion by some of the steadfast confessors. (6) Some Christian masters compelled their Christian slaves to face the trial in their stead: such slaves must "shew the works of repentance" for a year. (7) But these masters who, by thus imperilling their slaves, shewed their disregard for apostolic exhortations (Eph. vi. 9; Col. iv. 1), must have their own repentance tested for three more years. (8) Those who, having lapsed, returned to the conflict, and endured imprisonment and tortures, are to be "joyfully received to communion, alike in the prayers and the reception of the Body and Blood, and oral exhortation." (9) Those who voluntarily exposed themselves to the trial are to be received to communion, because they did so for Christ's sake, although they forgot the import of "Lead us not into temptation, but deliver us," etc., and perhaps did not know that Christ Himself repeatedly withdrew from intended persecution, and even at last waited to be seized and given up; and that He bade His disciples flee from city to city (Matt. x. 23), that they might not enhance their enemies' guilt. Thus Stephen and James were arrested; so was Peter, who "was finally crucified in Rome"; so Paul, who was beheaded in the same city. (10) Hence, clerics who thus denounced themselves to the authorities, then lapsed, and afterwards returned to the conflict, must cease to officiate, but may communicate; if they had *not* lapsed, their rashness might be excused. (11) Persons who, in their zeal to encourage their fellow-Christians to win the prize of martyrdom, voluntarily avowed their own faith, were to be exempted from blame; cf. Eus. vi. 41, *fin.* Requests for prayer on behalf of those who gave way after imprisonment and torture ought to be granted: "no one could be the worse" for sympathizing with those who were overcome by the devil or by the entreaties of their kindred (cf. *Passio S. Perpet.* 3; *S. Iren. Sirm.* 3; Eus. viii. 9). (12) Those who paid for indemnity are not to be censured; they shewed their disregard for money; and Acts xvii. 9 is here quoted. (13) Nor should those be blamed who fled, abandoning their homes —as if they had left others to bear the brunt. Paul was constrained to leave Gaius and Aristarchus in the hands of the mob of Ephesus (Acts xix. 29, 30); Peter escaped from prison, and his guards died for it; the Innocents died in place of the Holy Child. (14) Imprisoned confessors in Libya and elsewhere had mentioned persons who had been compelled by sheer force to handle the sacrifices. These, like others whom tortures rendered utterly insensible, were to be regarded as confessors, for their will was steadfast throughout; and they might be placed in the ministry. These "canons" were ratified by the council in Trullo, c. 2, A.D. 692, and so became part of the law of the Eastern church. (Cf. Eus. *Mart. Pal.* 1; *Passio SS. Tarachi et Probi*, c. 8, in Ruinart, *Act. Sinc.* p. 467; C. Ancyr. c. 3.)

Very soon after these "canons" were drawn up the persecution was intensified by the pagan fanaticism of Maximin Daza. Peter felt it his duty to follow the precedents he had cited in his 8th canon and the example of his great predecessor Dionysius by "seeking for safety in flight" (Burton, *H. E.* ii. 441). Phileas, bp. of Thmuis, and three other bishops were imprisoned at Alexandria; and then, according to the Maffeian documents, Meletius, being himself at large, held ordinations in their dioceses without their sanction "or that of the archbishop," and without necessity (*Hist. Writings of St. Athanasius*, Oxf. 1881, Introd. p. xxxix). Peter, being informed of this lawless procedure, wrote to the faithful in Alexandria: "Since I have ascertained that Meletius, disregarding the letter of the martyred bishops, has entered my diocese, taken upon himself to excommunicate the presbyters who were acting under my authority . . . and shewn his craving for pre-eminence by ordaining certain persons in prison; take care not to communicate with him until I meet him in company with wise men, and see what it is that he has in mind. Farewell" (Routh, *Rel. Sac.* iv. 94).

Maximin, besides presiding over martyrdoms in Palestine (A.D. 306, 307, 308), practised other enormities at Alexandria (Eus. viii. 14; Burton, ii. 451). During Peter's retirement his habits had become more strictly ascetic. He continued to provide "in no hidden way" for the welfare of the church (Eus. vii. 32). The phrase οὐκ ἀφανῶς is significant, as it points to the well-understood system of communication whereby a bp. of Alexandria, although himself in hiding, could, as did Athanasius, make his hand felt throughout the churches which still owned him as their "father." Probably Peter's return to Alexandria, and the formal communication of the Meletians above mentioned, took place after a toleration-edict, which mortal agony wrung from Galerius in Apr. 311. This edict constrained Maximin to abate his persecuting energy; but he soon again harassed his Christian subjects, and encouraged zealous heathen municipalities to memorialize him "that no Christians might be allowed to dwell among them" (*ib.* ix. 2). Thus at the end of Oct. 311 "the Christians found themselves again in great peril" (Burton); and one of the first acts of Maximin's renewed persecution was to smite the shepherd of the flock at Alexandria. Peter was beheaded (Eus. vii. 32), "in the ninth year of the persecution" (311), by virtue of a "sudden" imperial order, "without any reason assigned" (ix. 6).

Johnson and Routh reckon as a "fifteenth" canon what is, in fact, a fragment of a work on the Paschal Festival. In it Petrus says it is usual to fast on Wednesday, because of the Jews "taking counsel for the betrayal of the Lord"; and on Friday, "because He then suffered for our sake." "For," he adds, "we keep the Lord's day as a day of gladness, because on it He rose again; and on it, according to tradition, we do not even kneel." The custom of standing at prayer on Sunday was again enforced by the Nicene council (c. 20;

Bright, *Notes on the Canons of the First Four Councils*, p. 73). [W.B.]

Petrus (5) II., archbp. of Alexandria, succeeded Athanasius in May 373. To promote the peaceful succession of an orthodox bishop, Athanasius, being requested to recommend one who could be elected by anticipation, named Peter, whom Gregory Nazianzen describes as honoured for his wisdom and grey hairs (*Orat.* 25. 12), "who had been a companion of his labours" (Theod. iv. 20), and, in Basil's phrase, his spiritual "nursling" (*Ep.* 133); and who, in conjunction with another presbyter, when they were passing through Italy to Egypt in 347, had accepted from the notorious Arian intriguers Valens and Ursacius a written attestation of their desire to be at peace with Athanasius, when his cause was for the time triumphant (Athan. *Hist. Ar.* 26). The clergy and magistrates assented to the nomination; the people in general applauded; the neighbouring bishops came together to attend the consecration, in which, according to a "fragment" of Alexandrian history, the dying archbp. took the principal part (cf. Theod. *l.c.*; and *Hist. Aceph.* ap. Athan.). Five days afterwards (May 2) Athanasius died, and Peter took possession of "the evangelical throne." But the Arians seized the opportunity for which they had been waiting, and employed, as in 340, the agency of a pagan prefect. Palladius, by means of bribes, assembled a "crowd of pagans and Jews" and beset that same church of Theonas within which Syrianus had all but seized Athanasius in 356. Peter was commanded to withdraw; he refused; the church doors were forced, and the brutal orgies described in Athanasius's Encyclical were repeated: a youth in female dress danced upon the altar; another sat naked on the throne, and delivered a mock sermon in praise of vice (cf. Peter *ap.* Theod. iv. 22 with Greg. Naz. *Orat. l.c.*). At this point Peter quitted the church; Socrates says that he was seized and imprisoned (iv. 21), but his own narrative points the other way. It proceeds to describe the intrusion of the Arian Lucius. Peter tells us that the pagans esteemed Lucius as the favourite of Serapis, because he denied the divinity of the Son; and dwells on the brave confessorship (1) of 19 priests and deacons whom Magnus, after vain attempts to make them Arianize, transported to the pagan city of Heliopolis in Phoenicia, sending also into penal servitude 23 monks and others who expressed their sympathy; (2) of 7 Egyptian bishops exiled to Diocaesarea, a city inhabited by Jews, while some other prelates were "handed over to the curia," their official immunity from onerous curial obligations being annulled in requital of their steadfastness in the faith. Damasus of Rome, hearing of this new persecution, sent a deacon with a letter of communion and consolation for Peter; the messenger was arrested, treated as a criminal, savagely beaten, and sent to the mines of Phenne. Peter adds that children were tortured, and intimates that some persons were actually put to death or died of cruel usage, and that, after the old usage in pagan persecutions, their remains were denied burial. The narrative illustrates at once the theology, ritual, and electoral customs of the Egyptian church. Peter puts into the mouth of the 19 confessors an argument, quite Athanasian in tone, from the eternity of the Divine Fatherhood (cf. Athan. *de Decr. Nic.* 12): like Athanasius, he there insists that God could never have existed without His "Wisdom" (cf. *Orat. c. Ar.* i. 14); disowns a materialistic conception of the γέννησις (cf. *de Decr. Nic.* 11; *Orat. c. Ar.* i. 21); quotes the Arian formula ἦν ὅτε οὐκ ἦν ("once the Son was not," cf. *Orat. c. Ar.* i. 5, etc.); and represents the Homoousion as summarizing the purport of many texts (cf. *de Decr. Nic.* 20).

Peter refers to the invocation of the Holy Spirit at the Eucharistic consecration, and intimates that monks used to precede a newly arrived bishop, chanting the Psalms. When describing the uncanonical intrusion of Lucius, he refers to the three elements of a proper episcopal election, as fixed by "the institutions of the church"—(1) the joint action of the assembled bishops of the province, (2) the vote (ψήφῳ) of "genuine" clergy, (3) the request of the people (αἰτήσει, the Latin *suffragium*, as Cyprian uses it, *Ep.* 55. 7, speaking of the same threefold process, "de clericorum testimonio, de plebis . . . *suffragio*, et de sacerdotum . . . collegio"; and for the "requests" of the people, sometimes urgently enforced, see Athan. *Apol. c. Ar.* 6). Peter remained for some time in concealment, whence he wrote his encyclical (Tillem. vi. 582); he afterwards went to Rome, and was received by Damasus, as Julius welcomed Athanasius in 340. He remained at Rome five years, gave information as to Egyptian monasticism (Hieron. *Ep.* cxxvii. 5), and was present, as bp. of Alexandria, at a council held by Damasus, probably in 377, for the condemnation of the Apollinarians. Timotheus, whom Apollinaris had sent to Rome, and Vitalis, bishop of the sect in Antioch, were included in the sentence pronounced against their master (cf. Soz. vi. 25 with Theod. v. 10); and Facundus of Hermiane, in his *Defence of the Three Articles*, quotes part of a letter addressed by Peter to the exiled Egyptian confessors at Diocaesarea. "I ask your advice," he writes, "under the trouble that has befallen me: what ought I to do, when Timotheus gives himself out for a bishop, that in this character he may with more boldness injure others and infringe the laws of the Fathers? For he chose to anathematize me, with the bps. Basil of Caesarea, Paulinus, Epiphanius, and Diodorus, and to communicate with Vitalis alone" (*Pro Defens. Trium. Capit.* iv. 2). Here Peter treats Paulinus, not Meletius, as the true bp. of Antioch, this being the Alexandrian view. His relations with Basil were very kindly; their common love and reverence for Athanasius drew them into a correspondence (Basil, *Ep.* 133, written in 373); and a letter of Basil's in 377 has an interest for the church-history of the time (*Ep.* 266). It appears that the Egyptian "confessors" had hastily received into their communion the gravely-suspected disciples of Marcellus of Ancyra. This had troubled Basil. Peter had heard of it, but not from Basil; and had remonstrated with his exiled subordinates. Moreover, Basil's enemy Dorotheus, visiting Rome to enlist Western sympathies in favour of Meletius as against Paulinus, met Peter in company with Damasus. Peter fired up at the name of Meletius, and exclaimed, "He is no better than an Arian." Dorotheus, angered in his turn, said something which offended Peter's dignity; and Peter wrote to Basil, complaining of this and of his silence in regard to the exile's conduct. Basil answers in effect: "As to the first point, I did not care to trouble you, and I trust it will come right by our winning over the Marcellians; as to the second, I am sorry that Dorotheus annoyed you, but you who have suffered under Arians ought to feel for Meletius as a fellow-sufferer, and I can assure you that he is quite orthodox."

Peter's exile ended in the spring of 378. The troubles of Valens with the Goths encouraged the prelates he had banished to act for themselves. Fortified by a letter of commendation from Damasus, Peter returned to Alexandria; the people forthwith expelled Lucius, who went to Constantinople; and Peter was thenceforth undisturbed in his see. Jerome taxes him with being too easy in receiving heretics into communion (*Chron.*); and in one celebrated affair of another kind, his facility brought him no small discredit. Early in 379 he had not only approved of the mission of Gregory of Nazianzus to act as a Catholic bishop in Constantinople, but had formally authorized it, had "honoured' Gregory "with the symbols of establishment" (*Carm. de Vita Sua*, 861), and thereby apparently claimed some supremacy over Constantinople (Neale, *Hist. Alex.* i. 206). Yet ere long he allowed himself to become the tool of the ambitious Maximus, who pretended to have been a confessor for orthodoxy, and thus perhaps reached Peter's weak side. He aimed at "securing the see of Constantinople; and Peter, contradicting himself in writing," as Gregory words it (*de Vita Sua*, 1015), commissioned some Egyptian prelates to go to Constantinople and consecrate Maximus. The scheme failed disgracefully: Maximus had to leave Constantinople, and after attempting in vain to propitiate Theodosius, went back to Alexandria and tried to intimidate Peter, "putting the old man into a difficulty" (*ib.* 1018), but was expelled by secular force. Peter reconciled himself to Gregory, who panegyrized him as "a Peter in virtue not less than in name, who was very near heaven, but remained in the flesh so far as to render his final assistance to the truth," etc. (*Orat.* 34. 3). Peter died Feb. 14, 380. In ignorance of this event, Theodosius, a fortnight afterwards, named him with Damasus as a standard of Catholic belief in the famous edict of Thessalonica (*Cod. Theod.* xvi. 1, 2; see Gibbon, iii. 363). He was succeeded by his brother Timotheus. [W.B.]

Petrus (6), surnamed *Mongus* (Stammerer), Monophysite patriarch of Alexandria, ordained deacon by Dioscorus, and said to have taken part in the outrages against Flavian at the Latrocinium (Mansi, vi. 1017). On the death of the Monophysite patriarch Timotheus Aelurus in 477, and in the absence of the orthodox Salofaciolus whom he had displaced, the Monophysites determined to place Peter in the see. The emperor Zeno, indignant at the boldness of the Monophysites (Neale, *Hist. Alex.* ii. 17), ejected Peter, and ordered his expulsion from Alexandria (Mansi, vii. 983-985). Accordingly, Peter was driven out of Egypt; John, surnamed Talaia, steward of the great church, was chosen patriarch, but neglected to announce his accession to Acacius, who, piqued by this omission, prevailed on Zeno to expel John, and to restore Peter on condition that he should support an attempt to promote doctrinal unity without enforcing the authority of the council of Chalcedon. Zeno ordered Talaia to be expelled from Alexandria and Peter Mongus enthroned after accepting the HENOTICON, or instrument of unity (A.D. 482). This was addressed to the bishops, clergy, monks, and laymen of the Alexandrian patriarchate; it recognized the creed of "the 318" at Nicaea as "confirmed by the 150" at Constantinople, the decisions of the council of Ephesus, together with the 12 articles of Cyril; it employed language as to Christ's consubstantiality with man which Cyril had adopted in his "reunion with the Easterns"; it rejected the opposite theories of a "division" and a "confusion" in the person of Christ, and included Eutyches as well as Nestorius in its anathema. Instead of renewing the explicit censure directed by Basiliscus in a previous circular against the council of Chalcedon, Zeno employed an ambiguous phrase, "We anathematize every one who thinks or ever has thought differently, either at Chalcedon or at any other synod," words which might be explained as pointed at those who were admitted to communion at Chalcedon after disclaiming Nestorianism, while, as their adversaries alleged, they were still Nestorians at heart. At the same time all recognition of that council was omitted (Evagr. iii. 14; Liberat. c. 18, and note thereon; Galland. *Bibl. Patr.* xii. 149). Peter was accordingly enthroned amid a great concourse, at Alexandria. His instructions were to unite all parties on the basis of the Henoticon. This, for the time, he effected at a public festival, when as patriarch he preached to the people, and caused it to be read (Evagr. iii. 13; Liberat. c. 18). In letters to Acacius, the patriarch of Constantinople, and pope Simplicius, he professed to accept the council of Chalcedon (Liberatus); and by playing the part of a time-server (*κόθορνος*, Evagr. iii. 17) disgusted the thorough-going Monophysite John, bp. of Zagylis in Libya, and various abbats and monks of Lower Egypt, who raised a tumult in the Caesarean basilica (Liberat. *u.s.*). Peter could not afford to quarrel with them, and probably thought himself secure enough to shew his hand. (See Valesius on Evagr. iii. 16.) He accordingly anathematized the council of Chalcedon and the Tome of pope Leo, substituted the names of Dioscorus and Timotheus Aelurus for those of Proterius and Timotheus Salofaciolus on his diptychs, and gratified his own vindictiveness by taking the body of Salofaciolus from its place among the buried patriarchs and "casting it outside the city" (Liberat.; cf. Felix. *ap.* Mansi, vii. 1076). This caused a great excitement; the earnest Catholics renounced Peter's communion; and tidings of this turn of events disturbed the mind of Acacius, who sent to Alexandria for an authentic account. Peter then surpassed himself in an evasive letter, which Evagrius has preserved. Acacius was glad to accept his explanations, as he could not afford to break with Mongus; but he had now to deal with the clear head and resolute will of pope Felix II. (or III.), the successor of Simplicius, who listened readily to the complaints of the exiled Talaia and other Egyptian bishops (Evagr. iii. 20) against Peter, and sent two bishops, Vitalis and Misenus, to Constantinople to denounce Peter and summon Acacius to defend himself before a council at Rome. The legates were partly coaxed and partly frightened into communicating with the resident agents of Peter at Constantinople, and brought back to Rome letters in which Zeno and Acacius assured Felix that Peter was an orthodox and meritorious prelate (Evagr. iii. 20; Mansi, vii. 1055, 1065, 1081). Their weakness was punished by deposition; and Felix, with his synod, proceeded not only to anathematize Peter as an "Eutychian" usurper, but even to excommunicate the bp. of Constantinople as his patron (July 28, 484). He then wrote again to Zeno, desiring him to "choose between the communion of Peter the apostle and that of Peter the Alexandrian" (Mansi, vii. 1066). Nothing daunted, Acacius broke off communion with Rome and upheld Peter to the last, although he must have felt his conduct highly embarrassing, for Peter again anathematized the proceedings of Chalcedon and the Tome of Leo, and those who would not accept the writings of Dioscorus and Timotheus Aelurus (Evagr. iii 22). He expelled certain orthodox bishops, and, from one named John, transferred the abbacy or hegumenate of Diolchos to his friend Ammon (Liberat.). These proceedings being reported to Zeno, he sent Cosmas to rebuke Peter and restore peace. Peter again modified his tone, and wrote to Acacius, as if acknowledging Chalcedon. This double-dealing, becoming known in Egypt, provoked some Monophysite clerics, monks, and laymen to disown him and to meet for worship apart, omitting his name in their diptychs (Liberat. 18), and these uncompromising dissentients became known as "Acephali" (Leontius, *de Sectis*, v. 2), and obtained as their bishop one Esaias from Palestine (Liberat.). When Fravitas, or Flavitas, succeeded Acacius in 489, he wrote to both Felix (Liberat. 18) and Peter (Evagr. iii. 23); but after four months he died, and was succeeded by Euphemius, who, on discovering Peter's real position in regard to the council of Chalcedon, indignantly broke off all relations with him (Evagr. iii. 23). A new strife between Constantinople and Alexandria was imminent, when Peter Mongus, respected by none, died at the end of Oct. 490 (Le Quien, ii. 422), leaving behind numerous works (Neale, ii. 24). [W.B.]

Petrus (10) (surnamed *Fullo*, "the Fuller"), intruding patriarch of Antioch, 471-488, a Monophysite, took his surname from his former trade as a fuller of cloth. Tillemont shews considerable skill in harmonizing various statements of his earlier life (*Empereurs*, t. vi. p. 404). He considers that Peter was originally a member of the convent of the Acoimetae, which he places in Bithynia on the Asiatic side of the Bosphorus, and being expelled thence for dissolute life and heretical doctrine, passed over to Constantinople, where he became a parasite to persons of distinction, by whom he was introduced to Zeno, the future emperor, the son-in-law of Leo, whose favour he secured, obtaining through him the chief place in the church of St. Bassa, at Chalcedon. Here his true character having speedily become known, he fled to Zeno, who was then setting out for Antioch as commander of the East. Arriving at Antioch A.D. 463, Peter's unbridled ambition soared to the patriarchal throne, then filled by Martyrius, and having gained the ear of the rabble, he adroitly availed himself of the powerful Apollinarian element among the citizens and the considerable number who favoured Eutychian doctrines, to excite suspicions against Martyrius as a concealed Nestorian, and thus caused his tumultuous expulsion and his own election to the throne. This was in 469 or 470 (Theod. Lect. p. 554; Labbe, iv. 1009, 1082). When established as patriarch, Peter at once declared himself openly against the council of Chalcedon, and added to the Trisagion the words "Who wast crucified for us," which he imposed as a test upon all in his patriarchate, anathematizing those who declined to accept it. According to the *Synodicon*, he summoned a council at Antioch to give synodical authority to this novel clause (Labbe, iv. 1009). The deposed Martyrius went to Constantinople to complain to the emperor Leo, by whom, through the influence of the patriarch Gennadius, he was courteously received; a council of bishops reported in his favour, and his restoration was decreed (Theod. Lect. p. 554; *Liberat.* c. 18, p. 122). But notwithstanding the imperial authority, Peter's personal influence, supported by the favour of Zeno, was so great in Antioch that Martyrius's position was rendered intolerable and, wearied by violence and contumely, he soon left Antioch, abandoning his throne again to the intruder. Leo was naturally indignant at this audacious disregard of his commands, of which he was apprised by Gennadius, and he despatched an imperial decree for the deposition of Peter and his banishment to the Oasis (Labbe, iv. 1082). According to Theodorus Lector, Peter fled, and Julian was unanimously elected bishop in his room, A.D. 471, holding the see until Peter's third restoration by Basiliscus in 475 (Theophan. p. 99; Theod. Lect. p. 533). During the interval Peter dwelt at Constantinople, in retirement in the monastery of the Acoimetae, his residence there being connived at on a pledge that he would not create further disturbances (Labbe, iv. 1009, 1082; Theophan. p. 104). During the short reign of the usurper Basiliscus (Oct. 475–June 477) the fortunes of Peter revived. Under the influence of his wife Basiliscus declared for the Monophysites, recalled Timothy Aelurus, patriarch of Alexandria, from exile, and by his persuasion issued an encyclical letter to the bishops calling them to anathematize the decrees of Chalcedon (Evagr. *H. E.* iii. 4). Peter gladly complied, and was rewarded by a third restoration to the see of Antioch, A.D. 476 (*ib.* 5). Julian was deposed, dying not long after. Peter on his restoration enforced the addition to the Trisagion, and behaved with great violence to the orthodox party, crushing all opposition by an appeal to the mob, whom he had secured by his unworthy arts, and who confirmed the patriarch's anathemas by plunder and bloodshed. Once established on the patriarchal throne, he was not slow to stretch its privileges to the widest extent, ordaining bishops and metropolitans for all Syria. The fall of Basiliscus, A.D. 477, involved the ruin of all who had supported him and been promoted by him. Peter was one of the first to fall. In 485 for the last time Peter was replaced on his throne by Zeno on his signing the Henoticon (Theophan. p. 115; Theod. Lect. p. 569; Labbe, iv. 1207; Evagr. *H. E.* iii. 16). He at once resumed his career of violence, expelling orthodox bishops who refused to sign the Henoticon and performing uncanonical ordinations, especially that of the notorious Xenaias (Philoxenus) to the see of Hierapolis (Theophan. p. 115). He was condemned and anathematized by a synod of 42 Western bishops at Rome A.D. 485, and separated from Christian communion (Labbe, iv. 1123-1127). He retained, however, the patriarchate at Antioch till his death, in 488, or according to Theophanes, 490 or 491. One of his latest acts was the unsuccessful revival of the claim of the see of Antioch to the obedience of Cyprus as part of the patriarchate. After long debate the council of Ephesus in 431 had declared the church of Cyprus autocephalous. Tillem. *Les Empereurs*, t. vi. pp. 404-407; *Mém. eccl.* t. xvi. *passim.*; Clinton, *F. R.* vol. ii. app. p. 553. [E.V.]

Petrus (12), bp. of Apamea, the metropolis of Syria Secunda, under Anastasius, *c.* 510; a Monophysite, a warm partisan of Severus the intruding patriarch of Antioch, the leader of the Acephali, and charged with sharing in the violent and sanguinary attempts to force the Monophysite creed on the reluctant Syrian church. Peter was accused of having taken forcible possession of his see, in violation of all ecclesiastical order, not having received canonical ordination either as monk or presbyter (Labbe, v. 120). The first formal complaint against him was made before count Eutychianus, governor of the province, by the clergy of Apamea, substantiated by their affidavits (*ib.* 219, 243). In these he is charged with declaring himself the enemy of the Chalcedonian decrees, erasing from the diptychs the names of orthodox bishops and fathers, and substituting those of Dioscorus, Timothy Aelurus, and other heresiarchs. Evidence is given of insulting language and overbearing conduct toward his clergy, acts of violence and grossness, and intercourse with females of loose character. He was accused with Severus of having hired a band of Jewish banditti, who slew, from an ambuscade, a body of 350 orthodox pilgrims and left their corpses by the roadside (*ib.* 119). Clergy were violently dragged from the altar by his emissaries and ruthlessly butchered if they refused to anathematize the Chalcedonian faith. On the accession of Justin, A.D. 518, the bishops of Syria Secunda laid their complaints against Peter and Severus before the council assembled at the imperial city, July 518, asking the emperor to deliver them from so intolerable a tyranny (*ib.* 215). Their prayer was granted; Peter was deposed and sentenced to exile as a Manichee—as the Monophysites were popularly designated (Theoph. p. 142). Nothing seems known of Peter between his banishment and reappearance at Constantinople with Severus, on the temporary revival of the fortunes of the Monophysites, through the influence of the empress Theodora. In 536 Mennas was appointed to the patriarchal chair, and lost no time in summoning a council to pronounce the condemnation of Monophysitism and its chief leaders, Peter and Severus being cut off from communion as men who had "voluntarily chosen the sin unto death," and "shown no signs of repentance and a better mind" (*ib.* 253). Justinian confirmed this sentence. Peter was forbidden to reside in or near Constantinople, or any other important city, commanded to live in complete retirement, and abstain from association with others lest he should poison them with his heresy (*ib.* 267). Nothing more is known of him. Letters to him from Severus exist among the Syriac MSS. of the Brit. Mus. (Wright, *Catal.* p. 559, No. 5, No. 20). Le Quien, *Or. Christ.* ii. 913; Fleury, *Hist. eccl.* livre xxxi., 40, 44; livre xxxii., 52, 54, 57. [E.V.]

Petrus (20), bp. of Edessa, succeeded Cyrus on his death, June 5, 498. During his episcopate Mesopotamia was ravaged by Cabades, king of Persia, in his endeavour to wrest the province from Anastasius. Of the horrors of this terrible time of war, pestilence, and famine, in which Edessa had a full share, being more than once besieged by Cabades, we have a moving account from a contemporary witness in the *Chronicle* of Joshua the Stylite. Peter signalized his entrance on the episcopate by several ritual reforms. He was the first to institute the feast of Palm Sunday in the church of Edessa, as well as the benediction of water on the eve of the Epiphany, and the consecration of chrism on Maundy Thursday, and he regulated the observance of other festivals (Jos. Stylit. c. 32). An earthquake occurring at Edessa A.D. 500, he instituted public processional litanies of the whole population (*ib.* 36). The same year, the city and province suffering grievously from famine, he visited Constantinople to petition Anastasius personally for a remission of taxes, but was only partially successful (*ib.* 39). The famine returning A.D. 505, Peter made a second application to the emperor, who received him with frowns and rebuked him for leaving his distressed flock at such a time, but, feeling the justice of the request, remitted the taxes for the whole province, sending the order without informing Peter (*ib.* 78). Peter died on Easter Eve, A.D. 510. Asseman. *Bibl. Orient.* t. i. pp. 268 ff., 279, 406 ff. [E.V.]

Petrus (28), patriarch of Jerusalem, A.D. 524-544 (Clinton, *F. R.*; Niceph. *Chron.* p. 410), born at Eleutheropolis, succeeded John II. (omitted by Evagr. *H. E.* iv. 37) in 524. He manifested the same reverence as his predecessors for the celebrated ascetic St. Sabas, and frequently visited him in the desert.

During his episcopate occurred the sanguinary insurrection against the Christians of the Samaritans, goaded to madness by the persecution of Justinian, offering only the alternative of baptism or rebellion (Gibbon, c. 48). Many Christians were reduced to beggary. Peter therefore begged St. Sabas to go to Constantinople and lay before Justinian a petition for the remission of the taxes. His mission was successful and he was received with much joy on his return by Peter and his flock (Cyrill. Scythop. *Vit. S. Sab.* No. 70-76). On the deposition of Anthimus, the Monophysite patriarch of Constantinople, by the single authority of pope Agapetus, then present on state business at the imperial city, and the appointment of Mennas as his successor, Agapetus issued a synodical letter dated Mar. 13, 536, announcing these facts, and calling on the Eastern church to rejoice that for the first time a patriarch of New Rome had been consecrated by the bp. of Old Rome, and, together with the errors of Anthimus, stating and denouncing those of Severus of Antioch, Peter of Apamea, and the monk Zoaras. On receiving this document Peter summoned a synod at Jerusalem and subscribed the condemnation, Sept. 19, 536, Agapetus having died on Apr. 21 (Labbe, v. 47, 275, 283). The rapid spread of Origenistic opinions in some monasteries of Palestine under the influence of Nonnus was vehemently opposed by other monastic bodies and caused serious troubles which Peter was unable to allay. The Origenists were supported by a powerful court party, headed by the abbats Domitian and Theodore Ascidas (Evagr. *H. E.* iv. 38). The dignity and authority of Peter, a decided enemy of Origenistic doctrines, being seriously weakened, he made concessions which compromised his position. His predecessor in the patriarchal chair, Ephraim, had issued a synodical letter condemning Origen, and the Origenistic party clamoured to have his name removed from the diptychs. Peter was convinced that Justinian had been hoodwinked by the powerful abbats and was ignorant of the real character of these doctrines. He therefore instructed two of his own abbats, Gelasius and Sophronius, to bring before him a formal complaint, setting forth the heresies of Origen in detail. This document he forwarded to Justinian, with a letter describing the disturbances created by the Origenistic monks and beseeching him to take measures to quell them. The emperor, flattered by this appeal at once to his ability as a theologian and his authority as a ruler, the petition being supported by a Roman deputation, headed by Pelagius, then at Constantinople on ecclesiastical business, granted the request and issued a decree condemning the heresies of Origen, and ordering that no one should hereafter be created bishop or abbat without first condemning him and other specified heretics. The emperor's edict was confirmed by a synod convened by Mennas, and was sent for signature to Peter and the other patriarchs, A.D. 541 (*Vit. S. Sab.* No. 84; Liberat. *Breviar.* c. 23; Labbe, v. 635; *Vit. S. Euthym.* p. 365). The object, however, was thwarted by the Origenist leaders subscribing the edict, thus sacrificing truth to self-interest. Theodore maintained his position at court and threatened Peter with deposition if he continued to refuse to receive back the expelled Origenistic monks (*Vit. S. Sab.* No. 85). To divert the emperor's attention an attack was craftily organized by Theodore Ascidas and others against writings of Theodore of Mopsuestia, Theodoret, and Ibas of Edessa, supposed to savour of Nestorianism. They had little difficulty, backed by the powerful influence of the empress Theodora, an avowed favourer of Monophysitism, in persuading the emperor to issue an edict condemning these writings, which, from the three points on which it specially dwells, obtained the name of "Edictum de Tribus Capitulis," or "The Three Chapters," by which the whole controversy became subsequently known. This edict being published on the sole authority of the emperor, without synodical authority, great stress was laid on its acceptance by the bishops, especially by the four Eastern patriarchs. No one of them, however, was disposed to sign a document which seemed to disparage the conclusions of Chalcedon. Mennas yielded first; Peter's signature was obtained after a longer struggle. On the first publication of the edict he solemnly declared, before a vast crowd of turbulent monks clamouring against its impiety, that whoever signed it would violate the decrees of Chalcedon. But Justinian's threats of deposition outweighed Peter's conscientious convictions, and, with the other equally reluctant patriarchs, he signed the document (Facundus, lib. iv. c. 4). He did not long survive this disgrace, and died, A.D. 544, after a 20 years' episcopate. Vict. Tunun. *ap.* Clinton, *F. R.* ii. 557; Fleury, *Hist. eccl.* livre 33; Neander, *Ch. Hist.* vol. iv. pp. 264 ff.; Le Quien, *Or. Christ.* vol. ii. 189 seq. [E.V.]

Petrus (35), first bp. of Parembolae in Palestine, *i.e.* of the military stations of the Saracens in Palestine. He was originally a Greek in the service of the Persians under Izdegird. The Christians being persecuted by the Magian party, Aspebetus, as Peter was then called, was commissioned to close the passes against the fugitives. Being sorry for the innocent victims of religious intolerance, he executed his duty remissly, and even assisted them in their flight. This being reported to Izdegird, Petrus in fear for his life deserted to the Romans with his son Terebo, his relatives, and all his property. Anatolius, then prefect of the East, gladly welcomed him, stationed him in Arabia, and put him in command over all the tributary Saracen tribes in those parts. Terebo, still a boy, had before his father's flight lost by paralysis the entire use of one side. After reaching Arabia the boy was warned in a dream to apply to Euthymius for cure. The application was successful, the boy recovered, and the grateful father, his brother-in-law Maris, and all his Saracen followers received baptism (Cyrill. Scythop. *Vit. S. Euthym.* cc. 18-24; Coteler. *Eccl. Graec. Monum.* ii. pp. 216-222). The new disciple devoted himself to a religious life; and the number of Arabian converts having become so large as to require a bishop of their own, he was recommended by Euthymius to Juvenal, bp. of Jerusalem, by whom, in defiance of the canonical rights of the old metropolitan chair of Caesarea, the new see was created, and Peter appointed its first bishop (*Vit. S. Euthym.* c. 39; Cotel. p. 231). Tillemont gives reasons for placing this event before 428 (*Mém. eccl.* xv. 196). Peter attended the council of Ephesus in 431. His name appears among those subscribing the deposition of Nestorius and the decrees of the council (Labbe, iii. 541, 692). Peter's death must be placed before 451, when his second successor John attended the council of Chalcedon, his immediate successor Auxolaus, a Eutychian, having had a very brief episcopate Le Quien, *Or. Christ.* iii. 767; Tillem. *Mém. eccl.* xiv. 378, 392, 432, 451; xv. 196, 203. [E.V.]

Petrus (41), bp. of Sebaste, the youngest brother of Basil the Great and Gregory Nyssen, and the last of the ten children of Basil the elder and Emmelia. His father died almost immediately after his birth, which must be placed before A.D. 349 (Greg. Nys. *de Vit. S. Macr.* ii. 185). His sister Macrina, more than 20 years his senior, adopted her infant brother as her special charge, proving herself, in Gregory Nyssen's words, "not only his sister, but his father, mother, tutor, and warder" (παιδαγωγός). When Macrina and her mother retired to their religious retreat on the banks of the Iris, Peter accompanied them, where, according to his brother, he proved all in all to them, working with them towards the angelical life. He shared the high physical and mental endowments of the family. His acquirements were very varied, and he had a natural gift for handicrafts, in which, without any direct instruction, he excelled as much as in intellectual pursuits (*ib.* 186). He assisted by manual labour to support his mother and sister, and the large crowds attracted in time of scarcity by their reputation for charity. For some years his brother Basil was his near neighbour on the other side of the Iris, where he had established a monastery for male ascetics, in the presidency of which Peter succeeded him when in 365 he was finally recalled to Caesarea by bp. Eusebius. He was ordained presbyter by Basil, *c.* 370 (*ib.* 187). He was present with Macrina at their mother's death-bed, A.D. 373, and was offered by her as her tenth to God (*ib.* 186). He continued to reside in his monastery till after Basil and Macrina died in 379. In 380 he was ordained bishop, probably of Sebaste in Lesser Armenia, on the death or deposition of Eustathius. That Peter was bp. of Sebaste is accepted without question by Tillemont (*Mém. eccl.* ix. 574). Nicephorus, however, a somewhat untrustworthy authority, is the first writer who names his see (*H. E.* xi. 19). Theodoret (*H.E.* v. 8) and Suidas (*sub voc.* Βασίλειος, i. 539) simply style him a bishop, without naming his diocese. He took part in the council of Constantinople, A.D. 381 (Theod. *u.s.*). Olympias, the deaconess, the friend of Chrysostom, entrusted large funds to him for distribution to the poor (Pallad. p. 166). Tillemont places his death between 391 and 394. The genius of Peter seems to have been rather practical than literary. Rufinus, instituting a comparison between the three brothers, says that the two younger combined equalled Basil; Gregory in word and doctrine, and Peter in the works of faith (Rufin. ii. 9). Theodoret remarks that, though Peter had not received such a training in classical literature as his brothers, τῆς θύραθεν παιδείας οὐ μετειληχὼς σὺν ἐκείνοις, he was equally conspicuous in the splendour of his life (*H. E.* iv. 30). But though undistinguished in theological literature himself, several of his brother Gregory's most important works were written at his instigation; *e.g.* as we learn from the proems, the two treatises supplementary to his brother Basil's *Hexaemeron*, the *Explicatio Apologetica* and the *de Hominis Opificio* (Greg. Nys. *Opp.* i. 1, 44). The latter treatise was sent to Peter as an Easter gift. Gregory's great doctrinal work against Eunomius was due to his brother's entreaties that he would employ his theological knowledge to refute that heretic, and disprove the charges brought by him against Basil (*ib.* ii. 265, 266). Gregory's original intention was to limit his refutation to the first of Eunomius's two books. But Peter wrote a letter to him, his only extant literary production (*ib.* 268), entreating him to strike with the zeal of a Phinehas both the heretical books with the same spiritual sword, which he knew so well how to wield. The language and style of this letter shew Peter as not intellectually inferior to the more celebrated members of his family (Tillem. *Mém. eccl.* ix. 572-580). [E.V.]

Petrus (64), a solitary commemorated by Theodoret in his *Religiosa Historia.* By birth a Galatian, he embraced a monastic life when 7 years old, and lived to the age of 99. After visiting the holy places at Jerusalem and Palestine, he settled at Antioch, living in an empty tomb on bread and water, and keeping a strict fast every other day. His companion and attendant, named Daniel, he had delivered from an evil spirit. Theodoret relates that his mother, when a beautiful young woman of 23, failing to obtain relief from a malady in her eye from any oculist, was induced by one of her female servants to apply to Peter. Going to him dressed richly and resplendent with gold ornaments and gems, the solitary upbraided her for presuming to attempt to improve on the handiwork of her Maker, and having thus cured her of the malady of vanity and love of dress, signed her eye with the cross and she was speedily healed. Other members of her household he cured in a similar manner. When, seven years after, she became the mother of Theodoret and was given up by the physicians, Peter, having been summoned, prayed over her with her attendants and she speedily revived. She was accustomed to bring her child once every week to receive the old man's blessing. Peter made the young Theodoret a present of half his linen girdle, which was believed to have the miraculous property of relieving pain and curing sickness. The amulet was frequently lent, till kept by one of its borrowers, and so lost to the family. Theod. *Hist. Rel.* c. ix.; Tillem. *Mém. eccl.* xv. 209-213. [E.V.]

Petrus (72), first abbat of the monastery of SS. Peter and Paul, commonly called St. Augustine's, Canterbury. He was probably one of the monks who accompanied Augustine on his first journey, and therefore probably a monk of the monastery of St. Andrew at Rome. He is first mentioned by Bede (*H. E.* i. 25) as joined with Laurentius in the mission which Augustine after his consecration sent to Rome to announce that the Gospel had been accepted by the English, and that he had been made bishop, and to put before the pope the questions which drew forth the famous "Responsiones Sancti Gregorii." He must have returned some time before the death of Augustine and been appointed or designated by him and Ethelbert as the future head of the monastery, which at his request Ethelbert was building outside the walls of Canterbury. The building was not finished when Augustine died, but Laurentius, his successor, consecrated the new church and Peter became the first abbat. If the Canterbury computation be accepted, and on such a point it may not be baseless, Peter must have perished in the winter of 606 or of 607 at the latest. There is a notice of him in Mabillon's *Acta SS. O.S.B.* saec. i. pt. i. p. 1; and the Bollandist Acts, Jan. t. i. pp. 335, 336.

See Gotselinus, *de Translatione Sti. Augustini*, ap. Mab. *Acta SS. O.S.B.* t. ix. p. 760; Elmham, ed. Hardwick, pp. 92-126; Thorn, cc. 1761, 1766; Hardy, *Catalogue of Materials*, etc. i. 206, 207; *Monasticon Angl.* i. 120. [S.]

Philaster (*Philastrius*), bp. of Brixia (Brescia), in the latter part of the 4th cent. His successor in the see, Gaudentius, used every year to preach a panegyrical sermon on the anniversary of his death (July 18). One of these (preached on the 14th anniversary) is extant, and from its vague laudatory statements we have to extract our scanty information concerning his life and work. We learn from it that he was not a native of Brescia. From what country he came we are not told; Spain or Africa has been conjectured. He is commended for zeal in the conversion of Jews and heathen, and in the confutation of heresies, especially of Arianism; and is said to have incurred stripes for the vehemence of his opposition to that then dominant sect. He travelled much; at Milan he withstood bp. Auxentius, the Arian predecessor of St. Ambrose; at Rome he was highly successful in his defence of orthodoxy. Finally he settled down at Brescia, where he is said to have been a model of all pastoral virtues.

The only details we have for dating his episcopate or the duration of his life are that he took part as bp. of Brescia in a council at Aquileia in 381 (see its proceedings in the works of Ambrose, ii. 802, or p. 935, Migne); and that he must have died before 397, the year of Ambrose's death, since that bishop interested himself in the appointment of his successor. St. Augustine mentions having seen Philaster at Milan in company with St. Ambrose; this was probably some time during 384-387. Possibly Philaster had been commended to the church of Brescia by Ambrose, who would know of his opposition to Auxentius. The notices of Philaster in ecclesiastical writers are collected in the Bollandist Life (*AA. SS.* July 18, vol. iv. p. 299).

He is now chiefly interesting as the author of a work on heresies, portions of which, having been copied by St. Augustine, became stock materials for haeresiologists. Augustine having been asked by Quodvultdeus to write a treatise on heresies, refers him in reply (*Ep.* 222) to the works of Epiphanius and Philastrius, the former of whom had enumerated 20 heresies before our Lord's coming and 60 since the ascension, the latter 28 before and 128 after. Augustine refuses to believe that Epiphanius, whom he accounts far the more learned of the two, could have been ignorant of any heresies known to Philaster, and explains the difference of enumeration as arising from the word heresy not being one of sharply defined application, thus leading one to count opinions as heresies which were not so reckoned by the other. As a matter of fact, Philaster, in his excessive eagerness to swell his list of heresies, has included many items which must be struck out unless we count every erroneous opinion as a heresy; and when he has completed his list of heretical sects called after their founders, he adds a long list of anonymous heresies, apparently setting down all the theological opinions with which he disagreed, and branding those who held them as heretics. Thus those are set down as heretics who imagined, as many excellent Fathers did, that the giants of Gen. vi. 2 were the offspring of angels (c. 108); thought that any uncertainty attached to the calculation of the number of the years since the creation of the world (c. 112); denied the plurality of heavens (c. 94) or asserted an infinity of worlds (c. 115), or imagined that there are fixed stars, being ignorant that the stars are brought every evening out of God's secret treasure-houses, and as soon as they have fulfilled their daily task are conducted back thither again by the angel who directs their course (c. 133). It is to be feared he regards those as heretics (c. 113) who call the days of the week by their heathen names, instead of the scriptural names first day, second day, etc.; and some of his transcribers have rebelled on being asked to write down those as heretics who believe (c. 154) that the ravens brought flesh as well as bread to Elijah, who surely would never have used animal food. But it is not true that all heresies enumerated by Philaster, but unnoticed by Epiphanius, are such as can be thus accounted for. When Augustine, at length yielding to his correspondent's request, wrote a short treatise on heresies, he first gives an abstract of the 60 post-Christian heresies discussed by Epiphanius, and then adds a list of 23 more from Philastrius, remarking that this author gives others also, but that he himself does not regard them as heresies.

The relation between Philaster and Epiphanius is important because of the theory of Lipsius, now generally accepted [see HIPPOLYTUS], that both writers drew from a common source, namely, the earlier treatise of Hippolytus against heresies. To establish this theory it is necessary to exclude the supposition of a direct use of Epiphanius by Philaster, which might seem the more obvious way of accounting for coincidences between the two.

It is chronologically possible for Philaster to have read the treatise of Epiphanius which appeared in 376 or 377. At what period of his life Philaster's work was written we cannot tell. The notes of time in it are confusing. He, or his transcriber, places his own date (c. 106) over 400 years after Christ, and (c. 112) about 430. In c. 83 he speaks of the Donatists, "qui Parmeniani nunc appellantur a Parmenione quodam qui eorum nuper successit erroribus et falsitati." Parmenianus became Donatist bp. of Carthage *c.* 368, and died in 391; and the "nuper" would lead us to think that Philaster wrote early in this episcopate. But the form Parmenio, if not a transcriber's error, seems to shew that Philaster knew little of African affairs. Lipsius suggests that Philaster mentions Praxeas and Hermogenes as African heretics (c. 54), because he got their names from Tertullian. Philaster's anonymous heresy (c. 84) seems plainly identified by Augustine (*Haer.* 70) with Priscillianism, the breaking out of which is dated in Prosper's *Chronicle* A.D. 379. But Philaster's silence as to the name Priscillian seems to indicate an earlier date.

However, the complete independence of his treatment shews that Philaster did not use the work of Epiphanius. Eager as he was to swell his list of heresies, he does not mention the Archontici, Severiani, Encratitae, Pepuziani, Adamiani, Bardesianistae, and others, with whom Epiphanius would have made him acquainted; and in the discussion of all heresies later than Hippolytus, which are common to Epiphanius and Philaster, the two agree neither in matter nor in order of arrangement. Hence Lipsius inferred that the agreements as to earlier heresies must be explained by the use of a common source. This also accounts for a striking common feature, viz. the enumeration by both of pre-Christian heresies. Hegesippus (see Eus. *H. E.* iv. 22) had spoken of seven Jewish sects (τῶν ἑπτὰ αἱρέσεων) and had given their names; and it would seem from the opening of the tract of Pseudo-Tertullian that Hippolytus began his treatise by declining to treat of Jewish heresies. His two successors then might easily have been tempted to improve on their original by including pre-Christian heresies.

Concerning the N.T. canon, Philaster states (c. 88) that it had been ordained by the apostles and their successors that nothing should be read in the Catholic church but the law, the prophets, the Gospels, the Acts of the Apostles, 13 Epistles of St. Paul, and the seven other epistles which are joined to the Acts of the Apostles. The omission of the Apocalypse and Hebrews seems intended only to exclude them from public church reading. In c. 60 he treats as heretical the denial that the Apocalypse is St. John's, and in c. 69 the denial that the Ep. to the Hebrews is St. Paul's. He accounts for difficulties as to the reception of the latter as arising from its speaking of our Lord as "made" (c. iii. 2), and from the apparent countenance given to Novatianism in vi. 4; x. 26. Consequently the public reading of this epistle is not universal: "[leguntur] tredecim epistolae ipsius, et ad Hebraeos interdum."

The first printed ed. of Philaster appeared at Basle in 1539; the most noteworthy subsequent edd. are by Fabricius in 1721, containing an improved text and a valuable commentary, and by Galeardus in 1738, giving from a Corbey MS. now in St. Petersburg chapters on six heresies, omitted in previous eds., but which are required to make the total of 156 mentioned by St. Augustine. This complete text has been reprinted by Oehler in his *Corpus Haeresiologum,* vol. i. The latest ed. is by F. Marx, in the *Corpus Script. Eccl. Lat.* (Vienna, 1898). See also Zahn, *Gesch. der N.T. Kanons* (1890), ii. 1, p. 233. [G.S.]

Philippus (1), of Tralles, asiarch at the time of the martyrdom of POLYCARP. The historic reality of this Philip has been confirmed by an inscription found at Olympia, and Lightfoot (*Ignatius,* i. 613) printed two new inscriptions relating to him, and also by means of his full name, Caius Julius Philippus, there given, has assigned to him three other previously known inscriptions. Philip is thus proved to have been a well-known man of great wealth and munificence. Lightfoot (*u.s.*) shews that the date of his tenure of office indicated by these inscriptions is quite reconcilable with the date, otherwise determined, of Polycarp's martyrdom, without need of recourse to the perfectly admissible supposition, that Philip held the office of asiarch more than once. Concerning the office, see Lightfoot, ii. 990, where it is shewn that the holder was "high-priest of the province of Asia" and his tenure of office to be probably four years. [G.S.]

Philippus (5), "the Arabian," emperor, a native of Bostra in Trachonitis and a man of low birth. Having been made pretorian prefect he supplanted the younger Gordian in the affections of the soldiers, and caused him to be deposed and put to death in Mar. 244. After making peace with Sapor the Persian king, he proceeded to Rome. In 248 the games to commemorate the thousandth anniversary of the foundation of Rome were celebrated with great splendour. In the summer of 249 Philip was defeated by Decius near Verona and slain. The authorities for his reign are most meagre and conflicting. The only thing that makes it important is the report that he was the first Christian emperor. The chief foundation for this is the narrative which Eusebius (*H. E.* vi. 34) gives without vouching for its truth, namely, that Philip being a Christian wished at Easter to join in the prayers with the congregation, but that on account of the many crimes he had committed the bishop of the place refused to admit him until he had confessed and taken his place among the penitents, and that he willingly obeyed. The name of the bishop is supplied by Leontius, bp. of Antioch *c.* 348 (quoted in *Chron. Pasch.* 270, in Migne, *Patr. Gk.* xcii. 668), who says it was St. Babylas of Antioch. We are also told that Origen wrote to Philip and the empress (Eus. *H. E.* vi. 36), but the letters are not preserved, nor do we know their contents. St. Jerome also (*Chronicon* and *de Vir. Ill.* 54) calls Philip the first of all Christian emperors, in which he is followed by Orosius; and Dionysius of Alexandria (Eus. *H. E.* vii. 10) speaks of emperors before Valerian who were reputed to be Christians, but does not mention names. Against this doubtful testimony must be set the following: (1) Constantine is called by

Eusebius (*Vit. Cons.* i. 3) the first Christian emperor. (2) No event, except his alleged penitence at Antioch, is recorded of Philip that implies he was a Christian. (3) He celebrated the millennial games with heathen rites. (4) He deified his predecessor, and was himself deified after death. (5) No heathen writer mentions that he was a Christian. (6) A year before Decius issued his edict against the Christians, and therefore while Philip was still reigning, a violent persecution had broken out at Alexandria (Eus. *H. E.* vi. 41), which would not have been allowed to go on had the emperor really been a Christian. It seems, therefore, safer to conclude with Clinton (*Fasti Rom.* ii. 51) that Philip was not a Christian. Is there, then, any foundation for the story of Philip and St Babylas? Philip may very possibly have been at Antioch at Easter, A.D. 244, on his return to Rome after Gordian's death, and perhaps feeling remorse for the way he had treated Gordian and believing that Babylas was able to purify him from his guilt, may have made some application to him, and this may be the origin of the story; but it seems impossible to say with any certainty what parts of it, if any, are genuine and what fictitious. Philip was the first emperor who tried to check the grosser forms of vice at Rome (Lampridius, *V. Heliogabali*, 31; *V. Severi*, 23), though his efforts were unsuccessful (Victor, *de Caesaribus*, c. 28). Zosimus, i. 18-22; *Vita Gordiani Tertii*, cc. 28-33; Tillem. *Mém. eccl.* iii. 262; Gibbon, cc. 7, 10, 16. [F.D.]

Philippus (6), bp. of Heraclea in Thrace and martyr in the Diocletian persecution *c.* 304 with Severus, a presbyter, and Hermes, a deacon. His Acts present one of the most vivid and minute pictures we possess of that persecution, and are often quoted by Le Blanc in his *Actes des Martyrs—e.g.* pp. 12, 41, 52, 54, etc., where many incidental marks of authenticity are pointed out. The various steps in the persecution can be clearly traced, the arrest of the clergy, the seizure and destruction of the sacred writings and vessels, and finally the torture and death of the martyrs. Philip was arrested and examined by a president Bassus, who then committed him to the free custody of one Pancratus (c. vii.). Bassus was soon succeeded by a certain Justinus, who was much more stern towards the Christians than his predecessor, whose wife was a Christian. After some time Justinus brought them to Adrianople, and there burned Philip and Hermes on the same day (Ruinart, *Acta Sincera*, p. 442). [G.T.S.]

Philippus (9), of Side, an ecclesiastical historian at the commencement of 5th cent., a native of the maritime town of Side in Pamphylia, the birthplace of Troilus the sophist, whose kinsman he was proud of reckoning himself. We find Philip at Constantinople enjoying the intimacy of Chrysostom, by whom he was admitted to the diaconate. Tillemont says that he was the imitator of Chrysostom's eloquence rather than of his virtues, and that the imitation was a very poor one. On the death of Atticus, A.D. 425, by whom he had been ordained presbyter, Philip was a candidate for the vacant see, and found a number of influential supporters (Socr. *H. E.* vii. 27). The preferring of Sisinnius caused him extreme mortification, which he exhibited in his *Christian History*, introducing a violent tirade against the character both of elected and electors, more particularly the lay supporters of Sisinnius. The bitterness and rashness of the charges are noticed by Socrates, who thought them undeserving mention in his history (*ib.* 26). Philip, when again a candidate, both after the death of Sisinnius, A.D. 428 and on the deposition of Nestorius in 431, had a considerable and energetic following (*ib.* vii. 29, 35), but was unsuccessful, and died a presbyter. His chief work, entitled *A Christian History*, was divided into 36 books and about a thousand chapters. It ranged from the creation to his own times. Except one or two fragments, the whole is lost. The descriptions of it given by Socrates (*ib.* 27) and Photius (*Cod.* 35) shew that its loss is not to be regretted on literary grounds. Socrates describes it as a medley of theorems in geometry, astronomy, arithmetic, and music, with descriptions of islands, mountains, and trees, and other matters of little moment. The chronological order of events was constantly disregarded. Photius's estimate is equally low: "diffuse; neither witty nor elegant; full of undigested learning, with very little bearing on history at all, still less on Christian history." A fragment relating to the school of Alexandria and the succession of the teachers has been printed by Dodwell at the close of his dissertations on Irenaeus (Oxf. 1689). Of this Neander writes: "The known untrustworthiness of this author; the discrepancy between his statements and other more authentic reports, and the suspicious condition in which the fragment has come down to us, render his details unworthy of confidence" (*Ch. Hist.* vol. ii. p. 460, Clark's trans.). Another considerable fragment is reported to exist in the Imperial Library at Vienna, entitled *de Christi Nativitate, et de Magis*, giving the acts of a disputation held in Persia concerning Christianity between certain Persians and Christians, at which Philip was himself present. Tillem. *Mém. eccl.* xii. 431; *Hist. des empereurs*, vi. 130; Cave, *Hist. Lat.* i. 395; Fabric. *Bibl. Graec.* vi. 112, lib. v. c. 4, § 28. [E.V.]

Philo (2), deacon. Among the proofs of the genuineness of the Ignatian letters [IGNATIUS] is the fact that we obtain a thoroughly consistent story on piecing together scattered notices about obscure persons. Thus two deacons are mentioned, Philo from Cilicia and Rheius Agathopus from Syria (*Philadelph.* ii., *Smyrn.* 10, 13). We find that these deacons had not started with Ignatius, but had followed afterwards, taking the same route; that at Philadelphia, where Ignatius himself had encountered heretical opposition, some had treated them also with contumely; that they had been too late to overtake the saint at Smyrna, but had been kindly entertained by the church there. Finally, they were with Ignatius at Troas, and from them doubtless he received the joyful news of the peace which the church of Syria had obtained since his departure. The clearness with which the whole story comes out from oblique inferences is evidence that we have here a true history (Lightfoot's *Ignatius*, i. 334, ii. 279).

It was no doubt the mention in the genuine epistles of this Philo from Cilicia that suggested to Pseudo-Ignatius to forge a letter in the name of the martyr to the church of Tarsus, and to specify that city as the place where Philo served as deacon. [G.S.]

Philogonius, bp. of Antioch, 22nd in succession, following Vitalis *c.* 319. He affords an example of a layman, a husband, and a father being raised at once, like Ambrose at Milan, to the episcopate of his city. He had been an advocate in the law courts, and gained universal esteem by his powerful advocacy of the poor and oppressed, "making the wronged stronger than the wronger." The few facts known of his history are gathered from a homily delivered at Antioch by Chrysostom on his *Natalitia* (Chrys. *Orat.* 71, t. v. p. 507, ed. Savile). Chrysostom comments upon the great difficulties (δυσκολίαι) Philogonius met with at the commencement of his episcopate from the persecution which had so recently ceased, and says that his highest eulogy is the pure and flourishing condition in which he left the church. The earliest ecclesiastical building in Antioch, "the mother of all the churches in the city," traditionally ascribed to apostolic times, the rebuilding of which had been begun by Vitalis, was finished by him (Theod. *H. E.* i. 3). He was denounced by Arius as one of his most determined opponents (*ib.* 5). He was succeeded by Paulinus, the Arianizing bp. of Tyre, *c.* 323. He is called Philonicus by Eutychius (p. 431), who assigns him 5 years of office (Tillem. *Mém. eccl.* t. vi. p. 194; Neale, *Patr. of Ant.* p. 84). [E.V.]

Philostorgius, a Cappadocian, born *c.* 368, and author of a church history extending from 300 to 425. The greater part has perished, but some fragments have been preserved by Photius. They were published by Godefrid at Geneva in 1642, and by Valesius, with a Latin trans. and notes, at Paris in 1673. An English trans. by Walford appeared in 1855. Photius regarded both author and book with worse than contempt. The style he allows to be sometimes elegant, though more frequently marked by stiffness, coldness, and obscurity. The contents he treats as unworthy of reliance, often beginning his extracts by denouncing the author as an "enemy of God," an "impious wretch," an "impudent liar." Even Gibbon, naturally inclined as he was to accept the statements of a heretic in preference to those of an orthodox theologian, is compelled to allow that "the credibility of Philostorgius is lessened, in the eyes of the orthodox, by his Arianism; and, in those of rational critics, by his passion, his prejudice, and his ignorance" (*Hist.* c. xxi.). Gibbon thinks that he appears to have obtained "some curious and authentic intelligence" (c. xxv.), yet was marked in making use of it by "cautious malice" (c. xxiii.). These unfavourable opinions are shared by Tillemont (*Hist.* vol. iv. p. 281), and, though with some just expressions as to what might have been the value of his history had it been preserved, by Jortin (*Eccl. Hist.* vol. ii. p. 122) and Schröckh (vol. i. p. 148). All existing evidence leads to the belief that the history of Philostorgius was less a fair statement of what he had seen and known than a panegyric upon the heretics of his time. [W.M.]

Philoxenus (4) (*Xenaias*), a conspicuous leader of the Monophysites at the beginning of 6th cent. He shares with Severus of Antioch, the true scientific head of the previously leaderless party of the Acephali, the reputation of having originated the Jacobite form of Monophysitism, which was long supreme in Egypt and is still adopted by the Copts. Our knowledge of Philoxenus comes almost exclusively from his theological opponents, against whom he was engaged in a determined and not very scrupulous warfare. Much that is stated to his discredit admits of reasonable doubt. Some stories we may absolutely reject. We know him as an acute dialectician, a subtle theologian, and a zealous and uncompromising champion of the unity of the nature of Christ against what he regarded as the heresy of the two natures, and as one to whose desire for a faithful rendering of N.T. the church is indebted for what is known as the "Philoxenian Syriac Version." We soon find him in Syria, where, having accepted the Henoticon and the Twelve Chapters of Cyril, he proved an active opponent of all Nestorianizers and a zealous propagator of Monophysite views in the country villages round Antioch. Calandio, the patriarch of Antioch, expelled him from his diocese. He was recalled by Peter the Fuller, who ordained him bp. of Hierapolis (Mabug) in place of the more orthodox Cyrus, *c.* 485. During Peter's turbulent rule Philoxenus actively supported his measures for suppressing the Nestorianizing section of the church and establishing Eutychian or Monophysite doctrines in his patriarchate and generally in the East. The accession in 498 of the vacillating Flavian to the throne of Antioch, and his change of front from opposition to support of Chalcedon, led Philoxenus to adopt a more active line of conduct (Evagr. *H. E.* iii. 31), pursuing Flavian with untiring animosity, endeavouring to force him to accept the Henoticon, on his refusal denouncing him as a concealed Nestorian, demanding that he should repudiate not only Nestorius but all who were regarded as sympathizing with him, Diodorus, Theodorus, Theodoret, and many others, repeatedly denouncing him to the emperor Anastasius, and at last accomplishing his deprivation and expulsion. [FLAVIANUS OF ANTIOCH.] In pursuance of his object Philoxenus more than once visited Constantinople. The first time was at the summons of Anastasius, A.D. 507. His arrival caused a great disturbance among the clergy, laity, and monastic bodies. To consult the peace of the city, the emperor was compelled to remove him secretly (Theophan. p. 128; Victor. Tunun. *sub. ann.* 499). Unable in any other way to secure the deposition of Flavian and his supporter Elias of Jerusalem, Philoxenus obtained from Anastasius an order for convening a synod ostensibly to define more exactly the points of faith, but really to remove the two obnoxious prelates. This synod of about 80 bishops met at Sidon early in 512, under the joint presidency of Philoxenus and Soterichus of the Cappadocian

Caesarea. Feeling ran so high and so much endangered the public peace that the synod was broken up by the emperor's command without pronouncing any sentence (Labbe, iv. 1413; Theophan. p. 131; *Vit. S. Sab.* ap. Coteler, *Mon. Eccl. Graec.* iii. 297 ff.). In the subsequent proceedings, when rival bodies of monks poured down from the mountain ranges into the streets of Antioch, and were joined by different parties among the citizens, converting the city into a scene of uproar and bloodshed (Evagr. *H. E.* iii. 32), Philoxenus was left practically master of the field. Flavian was banished, and the Monophysite Severus, the friend and associate of Philoxenus, was put in his place towards the close of 512 (*ib.* iii. 33). The triumph of Philoxenus, however, was but short. In 518 Anastasius was succeeded by the more orthodox Justin, who immediately on his accession, declaring himself an adherent of Chalcedon, restored the expelled orthodox bishops and banished the heterodox. Philoxenus is said to have been banished to Philippopolis in Thrace (Asseman. *Bibl. Orient.* ii. 19; Theophan. p. 141; *Chron. Edess.* 87), and thence to Gangra in Paphlagonia, where he died of suffocation by smoke (Bar-heb. ii. 56). He is commemorated by the Jacobites in their liturgy as a doctor and confessor.

The Syriac translation of N.T. known as the "Philoxenian Version," subsequently revised by Thomas of Harkel, in which form alone we possess it, was executed in 508 at his desire by his chorepiscopus Polycarp (Moses Agnellus, *ap.* Asseman. *Bibl. Orient.* ii. 83; *ib.* i. 408). It is extremely literal; "the Syriac idiom is constantly bent to suit the Greek, and everything is in some manner expressed in the Greek phrase and order" (Westcott in Smith's *D. B.* vol. iii. p. 1635 B).

Philoxenus and Severus were the authors of the dominant form of Monophysite doctrines which, while maintaining the unity of the natures of Christ, endeavoured to preserve a distinction between the divine and the human. This doctrine is laid down in eight propositions at variance with the tenets of the early Christians, whom he stigmatized as Phantasiasts. Christ was the Son of Man, *i.e.* Son of the yet unfallen man, and the Logos took the body and soul of man as they were before Adam's fall. The very personality of God the Word descended from heaven and became man in the womb of the Virgin, personally without conversion. Thus He became a man Who could be seen, felt, handled, and yet as God He continued to possess the spiritual, invisible, impalpable character essential to Deity. Neither the deity nor the humanity was absorbed one by the other, nor converted one into the other. Nor again was a third evolved by a combination of the two natures as by chemical transformation. They taught one nature constituted out of two, not simple but twofold, *μια φύσις σύνθετος*, or *μια φύσις διττή*. The one Person of the Incarnate Word was not a duality but a unity. The same Son Who was one before the Incarnation was equally one when united to the body. In all said, done, or suffered by Christ, there was only one and the same God the Word, Who became man, and took on Himself the condition of want and suffering, not naturally but voluntarily, for the accomplishment of man's redemption. It followed that God the Word suffered and died, and not merely a body distinct from or obedient to Him, or in which He dwelt, but with which He was not one. Their view as to the personal work of Christ is briefly summed up in the Theopaschite formula, "unus e Trinitate descendit de coelo, incarnatus est, crucifixus, mortuus, resurrexit, ascendit in caelum." Philoxenus held that "potuit non mori," not that "non potuit mori." It followed that he affirmed a single will in Christ. In the Eucharist he held that the living body of the living God was received, not anything belonging to a corruptible man like ourselves. He was decidedly opposed to all pictorial representations of Christ, as well as of all spiritual beings. No true honour, he said, was done to Christ by making pictures of Him, since His only acceptable worship was that in spirit and in truth. To depict the Holy Spirit as a dove was puerile, for it is said economically that He was seen in the likeness, not in the body, of a dove. It was contrary to reason to represent angels, purely spiritual beings, by human bodies. He acted up to these opinions and blotted out pictures of angels, removing out of sight those of Christ (Joann. Diaconus, *de Eccl. Hist.* ap. Labbe, vii. 369).

He was a very copious writer, and described by Assemani as one of the best and most elegant in the Syrian tongue (*Bibl. Orient.* i. 475; ii. 20). Assemani gives a catalogue of 23 of his works. To these may be added 13 homilies on Christian life and character (Wright, 764); 12 chapters against the holders of the Two Wills (*ib.* 730, 749); 10 against those who divided Christ (*ib.* 730). Evagr. *H. E.* iii. 31, 32; Theod. Lect. fragm. p. 569; Theophan. *Chronogr.* pp. 115, 128, 129, 131, 141; Labbe, iv. 1153, vii. 88, 368; Tillem. *Mém. eccl.* xvi. 677-681, 701-706; Neander, *H. E.* iv. 255, Clark's trans.; Gieseler, *H. E.* ii. 94; Schröckh, *Kirch. Geschich.* xviii. 526-538; Dorner, *Person of Christ,* div. ii. vol. i. pp. 133-135, Clark's trans. [E.V.]

Phocas, of Sinope, a celebrated martyr, of whom very little is actually known and whose real date is uncertain. Combefis places his martyrdom in the last years of Trajan, but Tillemont considers a later persecution, either that of Decius or that of Diocletian, more probable. Our sole knowledge of Phocas is from an oration in his honour by Asterius of Amasea. He states that Phocas was an honest and industrious gardener at Sinope, a convert to Christianity, and exceedingly hospitable to strangers. Being denounced as a Christian and sentenced to death, a party of soldiers was despatched to Sinope to carry the sentence into execution. Phocas hospitably entertained them, and on discovering their mission forbore to escape, as he might easily have done, and, on their asking him where they could find Phocas, made himself known to them and was at once decapitated. His trunk was buried in a grave he had dug for himself, over which a church was subsequently built. His relics were so fruitful in miracles that he obtained the name of Thaumaturgus. His body was transferred to

Constantinople with great magnificence in the time of Chrysostom, who delivered a homily on the occasion (*Hom.* 71, t. i. p. 775). A monastery was subsequently built on the spot, in which his relics were deposited, the abbats of which are often mentioned in early times (Du Cange, *Constant. Christ.* lib. iv. p. 133). Gregory Nazianzen mentions Phocas as a celebrated disciple of Christ (*Carm.* 52, t. ii. p. 122). That he was bp. of Sinope is a late invention. Some of his relics were said to be translated to the Apostles' Church at Vienne. He was the favourite saint of the Greek sailors, who were in the habit of making him a sharer at their meals, the portion set apart for him daily being purchased by some one, and the money put aside and distributed to the poor on their arrival at port. He is commemorated by the modern Greeks on two days, July 22 and Sept. 22. The former day may be that of his translation (Tillem. *Mém. eccl.* v. 581). [E.V.]

Photinus, a Galatian, educated by Marcellus of Ancyra and afterwards deacon and presbyter of his church, perhaps too (during the time when Marcellus, expelled from his own see, A.D. 336, was wandering about between Rome and Constantinople) transferred to the see of Sirmium. He made no secret of the doctrines he had imbibed from his master, and succeeded in obtaining a hearing for them. The Eusebians at Antioch, in their lengthiest formula, three years after the Encoenia, were the first to attack him, classing him with his preceptor. He was next attacked at Milan, then the imperial capital; by the same party soon after at Sardica (*D. C. A.* "Councils of Milan" and "Councils of Sirmium"); and two years later another and larger synod decreed his deposition. Moderns are not agreed where this synod met, but St. Hilary, beyond any reasonable doubt, fixes it at Sirmium (*Fragm.* ii. n. 21; cf. Larroque, *Diss.* i. *de Phot.* pp. 76 seq.), being the first of the councils held there, A.D. 349 (Larroque says 350). Constantius being absent when sentence was first passed on Photinus in his own city, the popularity he had gained there stood him in good stead, in spite of his avowed opinions, which Socrates tells us he would never disclaim. He remained in possession till 351, when a second council having assembled there by order of the emperor, then present in person, he was taken in hand by Basil, the successor of his master at Ancyra, and having been signally refuted by him in a formal dispute, was put out of his see forthwith. Hefele thinks he may have regained it under Julian for a short time, but was again turned out under Valentinian, to return no more; and dates his death A.D. 366 (*Counc.* ii. 199). For a collection of authorities on the chronological difficulties in connexion with his history, see a note to Hefele's *Councils* (Oxenham's trans. ii. 188-189). [E.S.FF.]

Photius, bp. of Tyre, and metropolitan, elected on the deposition of Irenaeus, Sept. 9, 448. He is unfavourably known for cowardly tergiversation in the case of IBAS of Edessa. Under the powerful influence of Uranius of Himera, he and his fellow-judges first acquitted Ibas at Tyre and Berytus, and the next year at the "Robber Synod" of Ephesus zealously joined in his condemnation (Martin, *Le Brigandage d'Ephèse*, pp. 118-120, 181). At the same synod he accused Acylinus, bp. of Byblos, of Nestorianism and with refusing to appear before him and Domnus, the real ground of offence being manifestly that he had been appointed by Irenaeus. On Photius's statement alone Acylinus was at once deposed. Photius at the same time undertook to clear Phoenicia of all clergy tainted with Nestorianism (Martin, *u.s.* p. 183; *Actes du brigandage*, pp. 86-89). With easy versatility Photius took his place among the orthodox prelates at Chalcedon, regularly voted on the right side, signed the decisions of the council, voted for the restoration of Theodoret to his bishopric, presented a résumé of the proceedings at Berytus favourable to Ibas, and signed the 28th canon conferring on Constantinople the same primacy, πρεσβεῖα, as that enjoyed by Rome (Labbe, iv. 79, 328, 373, 623, 635, 803). At the same time, after presenting a petition to Marcian (*ib.* 541), he obtained a settlement of the controversy between himself and Eustathius of Berytus as to metropolitical jurisdiction, in favour of the ancient rights of the see of Tyre, together with a reversal of Eustathius's act of deposition of the bishops ordained by Photius, within the district claimed by the former (*ib.* 542-546; *Canon. Chalc.* 29). Photius was no longer bp. of Tyre in 457, when Dorotheus replied to the encyclical of the emperor Leo. Labbe, iv. 921; Cave, *Hist. Lit.* i. 443; Ceillier, *Aut. eccl.* xiv. 271, etc.; Tillem. *Mém. eccl.* vol. xv. index; Fabric. *Bibl. Graec.* x. 678; Le Quien, *Or. Christ.* ii. 808). [E.V.]

Pierius (*Hierius*). An eminent presbyter of Alexandria, famous for voluntary poverty, philosophical knowledge, and public expositions of Holy Scripture. He ruled the catechetical school of Alexandria under bp. Theonas, A.D. 265, and afterwards lived at Rome. He wrote several treatises extant in St. Jerome's time, and some were known as late as that of Photius. One was a homily upon Hosea, which he recited on Easter Eve, wherein he notes that the people continued in church on Easter Eve till after midnight. Photius mentions a work on St. Luke's Gospel as part of a volume by him, divided into 12 books. From his eloquence he was called the younger Origen. Photius declares that he was orthodox about the Father and the Son, though using the words substance and nature to signify person. But his manner of speaking about the Holy Ghost was unorthodox, because he said that His glory was less than that of the Father and the Son. In the time of Epiphanius there was a church at Alexandria dedicated in his honour. Some have therefore thought that he suffered martyrdom in Diocletian's persecution. Eus. vii. 32; Hieron. *Vir. Ill.* c. 76; id. *Ep.* 70 al. 84, § 4, p. 429; id. *Praefat. in Osee*; Photius, *Cod.* 119; Niceph. Call. *H. E.* vi. 35; Du Pin, *H. E.* cent. iii.; Ceillier, ii. 462; Tillem. *Mém.* iv. 582. [G.T.S.]

Pinianus (2), the husband of Melania the younger. Palladius speaks of him as son of a prefect (*Vit. Patr.* 119). He and his wife entertained Palladius of Helenopolis when he came to Rome on Chrysostom's affairs (*Hist.*

Laus. 121). They left Rome in 408, when the siege by Alaric was impending. Melania the elder having died at Bethlehem, they inherited her vast estates. They were intent on doing good and are said to have liberated 8,000 slaves (*ib.* 119). After the sack of Rome in 410 they settled in Africa at Tagaste with bp. Alypius and desired to meet Augustine. He immediately wrote to welcome them (*Ep.* 124), but was unable to come to them, so they went with Alypius to Hippo. There the strange scene, so instructive as to the church life of the period, occurred, which is recounted by Augustine (*Ep.* 126). The clergy and people of Hippo, knowing their wealth, determined that they should, by the ordination of Pinianus, become attached to their church and city. A tumult was raised in the church, and though Augustine refused to ordain a man against his will, he was unable, or not firm enough, to resist the violence of the people, who extracted from Pinianus a promise that he would not leave Hippo nor be ordained in any other church. Next day, however, fearing further violence, he, with Melania and her mother Albina, returned to Tagaste. Some rather acrimonious correspondence ensued between them and Augustine (*Ep.* 125-128). Alypius considered that a promise extorted by violence was not valid, Augustine demanded that it should be fulfilled; and the controversy lasted until, by the rapacity of the rebel count Heraclian, Pinianus was robbed of his property, and the people of Hippo no longer cared to enforce the promise. Being now free, though poor, Pinianus, with his wife and mother-in-law, went to Egypt, saw the monasteries of the Thebaid, and thence to Palestine, settling at Bethlehem. On the appearance of the Pelagian controversy, their letters to Augustine induced him to write (A.D. 417) his book on grace and original sin. We only hear of Pinianus after this in a letter of Jerome in 419, in which he, Albina, and Melania, salute Augustine and Alypius. Hieron. *Ep.* cxliii. 2, ed. Vall.; Aug. *de Grat. Christi,* ii. and xxxii. [W.H.F.]

Pionius, martyr at Smyrna, in the Decian persecution, Mar. 12, 250. It was probably this Pionius who revived the *cultus* of POLYCARP in Smyrna, by recovering an ancient MS. martyrdom of that saint and fixing the day of commemoration in accordance with it.

When taken to prison, Pionius and his companions, Asclepiades and Sabina, found there already another Catholic presbyter, named Lemnus, and a Montanist woman named Macedonia. The divisions of the Christian community were now well known to their persecutors for in the examinations of the martyrs those who owned themselves Christians were always further interrogated as to what church or sect they belonged. The Acts give a long report of exhortations delivered by Pionius to his fellow-prisoners. With Pionius suffered a Marcionite presbyter Metrodorus, the stakes of both being turned to the east, Pionius on the right, Metrodorus on the left. The Acts are important on account of their undoubted antiquity. We only know them by a Latin translation, of which two types are extant—one which seems more faithfully to represent the original, published by Surius and reprinted by the Bollandists (Feb. 1); the other by Ruinart (*Acta Sincera,* p. 137). The common original was certainly read by Eusebius, who (*H. E.* iv. 15) gives a description of the Acts of Pionius which agrees too often with those extant for different Acts to be intended. Eusebius, however, represents Pionius as suffering at the same time as Polycarp, while the extant Acts place him a century later, a date attested by the *Paschal Chronicle,* which makes Pionius suffer in the Decian persecution, and confirmed by internal evidence. On the Life of Polycarp ascribed to Pionius, see POLYCARP. Cf. Zahn, *Forschungen zur Gesch. der N.T. Kanons,* iv. 271. [G.S.]

Pius I., bp. of Rome after Hyginus in the middle part of 2nd cent. The dates cannot be fixed with certainty, the traditions being contradictory. The Liberian Catalogue and the Felician both name Antoninus Pius (138-161) as the contemporary emperor, as does Eusebius (*H. E.* iv. 11). Lipsius (*Chronol der röm. Bischöf.*), after full discussion of the chronology, assigns from 139 to 154 as the earliest, and from 141 to 156 as the latest, tenable dates. The absence of distinct early records of the early Roman bishops is further shewn by the fact that both the Liberian and Felician Catalogues place Anicetus between Hyginus and Pius. So also Optatus (ii. 48) and Augustine (*Ep.* 53, *ordo novus*). But that the real order was Hyginus, Pius, Anicetus, may be considered certain from the authority of Hegesippus (quoted by Eus. *H. E.* iv. 22), who was at Rome himself in the time of Anicetus, and, when there, made out a succession of the Roman bishops. Irenaeus, who visited Rome in the time of Eleutherus, gives the same order (*adv. Haer.* iii. 3; cf. Eus. iv. 11; v. 24; Epiph. *adv. Haer.* xxvii. 6).

The episcopate of Pius is important for the introduction of Gnostic heresy into Rome. The heresiarchs Valentinus and Cerdo had come thither in the time of Hyginus and continued to teach there under Pius (Iren. i. 27, ii. 4; cf. Eus. *H. E.* iv. 11). Marcion of Pontus, who took up the teaching of Cerdo and developed from it his own peculiar system, arrived there after the death of Hyginus (Epiph. *Haer.* xlii. 1; cf. Eus. *H. E.* iv. 11).

Pius, according to the MURATORIAN FRAGMENT (*c.* 170) and the Liberian Catalogue, was brother to HERMAS, the writer of the *Shepherd.* Lipsius (*op. cit.*) considers this relationship established. Westcott (*Canon of N.T.* pt. i. c. 2) accepts it, and adduces internal evidence in the work of Hermas itself.

Those who maintain the view of the presbyterian constitution of the early Roman church, and of the earliest so-called bishops having been in fact only leading presbyters, to whom a distinct episcopal office was afterwards assigned by way of tracing the succession, would attribute the development of the later episcopal system to the age of Pius. Thus Lipsius speaks of him as the first bishop in the stricter sense ("Bischof im engeren Sinn"). He supposes both Hyginus and Pius to have presided over the college of presbyters, though only as *primi inter pares*, and the need of a recognized head of the church to resist Gnostic teachers to have led to the latter obtaining a position of authority which, after his time, became permanent. The advocates of this view adduce passages from the *Shepherd* of Hermas, in which messages are sent in rebuke of strifes for precedence among the Christians at Rome (*Vis.* iii. 9; *Mandat.* ix.; *Simil.* viii. 7). These strifes are assumed to denote the beginning of struggles for episcopal power in the supposed later sense. But there is no evidence in the passages of the strifes having anything to do with such struggles. [HERMAS.]

More cogent is the fact that, in the account given by Epiphanius of Marcion's arrival in Rome, he is represented as having applied for communion to the presbyters, without mention of the bishop. Those to whom he applied, and who gave judgment, are called "the seniors (πρεσβῦται), who, having been taught by the disciples of the apostles, still survived" (*adv. Haer.* xlii. 1); also "the presbyters (πρεσβύτεροι) of that time" (*ib.* c. 2); also ἐπιεικεῖς καὶ πανάγιοι πρεσβύτεροι καὶ διδάσκαλοι τῆς ἁγίας ἐκκλησίας. But these expressions do not disprove the existence of a presiding bishop, acting in and through his synod, who would himself be included in the designation πρεσβύτεροι. For it was not till some time after the apostolic period that the names ἐπίσκοπος and πρεσβύτερος were used distinctively to denote two orders of clergy. Even Irenaeus, though enumerating the bishops of Rome from the first as distinct from the general presbytery, still speaks of them as presbyters; using in one place (iii. 2, 2) the phrase "successiones presbyterorum," though in another (iii. 3, 1 and 2) "successiones episcoporum." Cf. iv. 26, 2, 3, 5; v. 20, 2; and *Ep. ad Victorem* (*ap.* Eus. v. 24); where the bishops before Soter are called πρεσβύτεροι οἱ προστάντες τῆς ἐκκλησίας. Tertullian also (*Apol.* c. 39) calls bishops and presbyters together *seniores*. Moreover, the omission by Epiphanius of any mention of a head of the Roman presbytery at the time of Marcion's visit may be due to a vacancy in the see. For it is said to be after the death of Hyginus, with no mention of Pius having succeeded. In such circumstances the college of presbyters would naturally entertain the case. Certainly very soon after the period before us, both Pius and his predecessors from the first were spoken of as having been bishops (however designated) in a distinctive sense, and Anicetus, the successor of Pius, appears historically as such on the occasion of Polycarp's visit to Rome (Iren. *ap.* Eus. *H. E.* v. 24).

Four letters and several decrees are assigned to Pius, of which the first two letters (to all the faithful and to the Italians) and the decrees are universally rejected as spurious. The two remaining letters, addressed to Justus, bp. of Vienne, are accepted as genuine by Baronius, Binius, and Bona, but have no real claims to authenticity. [J.B—Y.]

Placidia (1), empress. [GALLA.]

Poemen (1), (Ποιμήν, *Pastor*), a famous anchorite of Egypt. He retired very young into the monasteries of Scete *c.* 390, and continued there 70 years, dying *c.* 460. His Life occupies much space in Rosweyd's *Vitae Patrum*, v. 15, in *Patr. Lat.* t. lxxiii. and in Cotelerii *Monum. Eccl. Graec.* t. i. pp. 585-637. The anecdotes in the last-mentioned authority give the best idea of the man. He treated his aged mother with neglect, refusing to see her when she sought him. His solitary life destroyed all feelings of human nature. His story is concisely told in Ceillier, viii. 468-470, and Tillemont, *Mém.* xv. 147. [G.T.S.]

Polycarpus (1), bp. of Smyrna, one of the most prominent figures in the church of the 2nd cent. He owes this prominence less to intellectual ability, which does not appear to have been pre-eminent, than to the influence gained by a consistent and unusually long life. Born some 30 years before the end of the 1st cent., and raised to the episcopate apparently in early manhood, he held his office to the age of 86 or more. He claimed to have known at least one apostle and must in early life have met many who could tell things they had heard from actual disciples of our Lord. The younger generation, into which he lived on, naturally recognized him as a peculiarly trustworthy source of information concerning the first age of the church. During the later years of his life Gnostic speculation had become very active and many things unknown to the faith of ordinary Christians were put forth as derived by secret traditions from the apostles. Thus a high value was attached to the witness Polycarp could give as to the genuine tradition of apostolic doctrine, his testimony condemning as offensive novelties the figments of the heretical teachers. Irenaeus states (iii. 3) that on Polycarp's visit to Rome his testimony converted many disciples of Marcion and Valentinus. Polycarp crowned his other services to the church by a glorious martyrdom. When, at the extremity of human life, it seemed as if he could do no more for the church but continue his example of holiness, piety, and orthodoxy, a persecution broke out in which he, as the venerated head of the Christian community in Asia Minor, was specially marked out for attack. He gave a noble exhibition of calm courage, neither courting nor fearing martyrdom, sheltering himself by concealment while possible, and when no longer so, resolutely declaring in defiance of threats his unshaken love for the Master he had served so long. Such a death, following on such a life, made Polycarp's the most illustrious name of his generation in Christian annals.

Irenaeus states (III. iii. 4) that Polycarp had been instructed by apostles and conversed with many who had seen Christ, and had also been established "by apostles" as bishop in the church at Smyrna; and doubtless Tertullian (*de Praescrip.* 32) is right in understanding this to mean that he had been so established by St. John, whose activity in founding the episcopate of Asia Minor is spoken of also by Clem. Alex. in his well-known story of St. John and the robber (*Quis. div. Salv.* p. 959). The testimony of Irenaeus conclusively shews the current belief in Asia Minor during the old age of Polycarp, and it is certain that Polycarp was bp. of Smyrna at the time of the martyrdom of Ignatius, *i.e. c.* 110. Ignatius, journeying from Antioch to Rome, halted first at Smyrna, where, as at his other resting-places, the Christians flocked from all around to receive his counsels and bestow attentions on him. From the city where he next halted he wrote separate letters to the church of Smyrna and to Polycarp its bishop. A later stage was Philippi, and to the church there Polycarp wrote afterwards a letter still extant, sending them copies of the letters of Ignatius and inquiring for information about Ignatius, the detailed story of whose martyrdom appears not yet to have reached Smyrna.

The question as to the genuineness of the extant Ep. of Polycarp is very much mixed up with that of the genuineness of the Ignatian letters. The course of modern investigation has been decidedly favourable to the genuineness of the Ignatian letters [IGNATIUS], and the Ep. of Polycarp is guaranteed by external testimony of exceptional goodness. It is mentioned by Polycarp's disciple Irenaeus (III. iii. 4), and an important passage is quoted by Eusebius. Further, as Lightfoot has conclusively shown (*Contemp. Rev.* May 1875, p. 840), it is impossible that Polycarp's letter and those of Ignatius could have had any common authorship. Some of the topics on which the Ignatian letters lay most stress are absent from that of Polycarp; in particular, Polycarp's letter is silent about episcopacy, of which the Ignatian letters speak so much, and it has consequently been thought probable either that episcopacy had not yet been organized at Philippi, or that the office was then vacant. The forms of expression in the two letters are different; N.T. quotations, profuse in Polycarp's letter, are comparatively scanty in the Ignatian ones; and, most decisive of all, the Ignatian letters are characterized by great originality of thought and expression, while Polycarp's is but a commonplace echo of the apostolic epistles. When we compare Polycarp's letter with the extant remains of the age of Irenaeus, the superior antiquity of the former is evident, whether we attend to their use of N.T., their notices of ecclesiastical organization, their statements of theological doctrine, or observe the silence in Polycarp's letter on the questions which most interested the church towards the close of the 2nd cent. The question has been raised whether, admitting the genuineness of Polycarp's epistle as a whole, we may not reject as an interpolation c. xiii., which speaks of Ignatius. The extant MSS. of Polycarp's letter are derived from one in which the leaves containing the end of Polycarp's letter and the beginning of that of Barnabas were wanting, so that the end of Barnabas seemed the continuation of Polycarp's epistle. The concluding chapters of Polycarp are only known to us by a Latin translation. The hiatus, however, in the Greek text begins not at c. xiii. but at c. x.; and the part which speaks about Ignatius is exactly that for which we have the Greek text assured to us by the quotation of Eusebius. There is therefore absolutely no reason for rejecting c. xiii. unless on the supposition that the forgery of the Ignatian letters has been demonstrated.

Though Polycarp's epistle is remarkable for its copious use of N.T. language, there are no formal quotations, but it is mentioned that St. Paul had written to the church of Philippi, to which Polycarp's epistle is addressed. The language in which St. Paul's letters are spoken of, both here and in the epistles of Ignatius, decisively refutes the theory that there was opposition between the schools of John and Paul. It illustrates the small solicitude of Eusebius to produce testimony to the use of N.T. books undisputed in his time, that though he notices (iv. 14) Polycarp's use of I. Peter, he is silent as to this express mention of St. Paul's letters. Polycarp's Pauline quotations include distinct recognition of Eph. and I. and II. Tim., and other passages clearly shew a use of Rom., I. Cor., Gal., Phil., II. Thess. The employment of I. Peter is especially frequent. There is one unmistakable coincidence with Acts. The use of I. and II. John is probable. The report of our Lord's sayings agrees in substance with our Gospels, but may or may not have been directly taken from them. The coincidences with Clement's epistle are beyond what can fairly be considered accidental, and probably the celebrity gained by Clement's epistle set the example to bishops elsewhere of writing to foreign churches. Polycarp states, however, that his own letter had been invited by the church of Philippi. Some church use of Polycarp's epistle seems to have continued in Asia until Jerome's time; if we can lay stress on his rather obscure expression (*Catal.*) "epistolam quae usque hodie in conventu Asiae legitur." The chief difference between Clement's and Polycarp's letters is in the use of the O.T., which is perpetual in the former, very rare in the latter. There is coincidence with one passage in Tobit, two in Ps., and one in Is.; and certainly in one of the last 3 cases, possibly in all three, the adopted words are not taken directly from the O.T., but from N.T. This difference, however, is explained when we bear in mind that Clement had probably been brought up in Judaism, while Polycarp was born of Christian parents and familiar with the apostolic writings from his youth.

Our knowledge of Polycarp's life between the date of his letter and his martyrdom comes almost entirely from 3 notices by IRENAEUS. The first is in his letter to FLORINUS; the second in the treatise on Heresies (III. iii. 4); the third in the letter of Irenaeus to Victor, of which part is preserved by Eusebius (v. 24). Irenaeus, writing in advanced life, tells how vivid his recollections still were of having been a hearer of Polycarp, then an old man; how well he remembered where the aged bishop used to sit, his personal appearance, his ways of going out and coming in, and how frequently he used to relate his intercourse with John and others who had seen our Lord, and to repeat stories of our Lord's miracles and teaching, all in complete accord with the written record. The reminiscences of Irenaeus are in striking agreement with Polycarp's extant letter in their picture of his attitude towards heresy. He seems not to have had the qualifications for successfully conducting a controversial discussion with erroneous teachers, nor perhaps the capacity for feeling the difficulties which prompted their speculations; but he could not help strongly feeling how unlike these speculations were to the doctrines he had learned from apostles and their immediate disciples, and so met with indignant reprobation their attempt to supersede Christ's gospel by fictions of their own devising. Irenaeus tells how, when he heard their impiety, he would stop his ears and cry out, "O good God! for what times hast Thou kept me that I should endure such things!" and would even flee from the place where he was sitting or standing when he heard such words. In so behaving he claimed to act in the spirit of his master John, concerning whom he told that once when he went to take a bath in Ephesus and saw Cerinthus within, he rushed away without bathing, crying out, "Let us flee, lest the bath should fall in, for Cerinthus, the enemy of the truth, is within"; and when Marcion meeting Polycarp asked him, "Do you recognize us?" he answered, "I recognize thee as the first-born of Satan." This last phrase is found in the extant letter. He says, "Every one who doth not confess that Jesus Christ has come in the flesh is antichrist; and whosoever doth not confess the testimony of the Cross is of the devil; and whosoever perverteth the oracles of the Lord to his own lusts and saith that there is neither resurrection nor judgment, this man is a first-born of Satan." This coincidence has, not very reasonably, been taken as a note of spuriousness of the letter; the idea being that a writer under the name of Polycarp who employs a phrase traditionally known as Polycarp's betrays himself as a forger striving to gain acceptance for his production. It might rather have been supposed that a coincidence between two independent accounts of Polycarp's mode of speaking of heretics ought to increase the credibility of both. Irenaeus, who reports the anecdote, was acquainted with the letter, and, if we cannot accept both, it is more conceivable that his recollection may have coloured his version of the anecdote.

One of the latest incidents in Polycarp's active life was a journey which, near the close of his episcopate, he made to Rome, where Anicetus was then bishop. We are not told whether the cause of the journey was to settle points of difference between Roman and Asiatic practice; those existed, but did not interrupt their mutual accord. In particular Asiatic Quartodecimanism was at variance with Roman usage. We cannot say with certainty what kind of Easter observance was used at Rome in the time of Anicetus, for the language of Irenaeus implies that it was not then what it afterwards became; but the Asiatic observance of the 14th day was unknown in Rome, although Polycarp averred the practice of his church to have had the sanction of John and other apostles, and therefore to be what he could by no means consent to change. Anicetus was equally determined not to introduce into his church an innovation on the practice of his predecessors; but yet shewed his reverence for his aged visitor by "yielding to him the Eucharist in his church." This phrase seems capable of no other interpretation than that generally given to it, viz. that Anicetus permitted Polycarp to celebrate in his presence.

The story of the martyrdom of Polycarp is told in a letter still extant, purporting to be addressed by the church of Smyrna to the church sojourning (παροικούσῃ) in Philomelium (a town of Phrygia) and to all the παροικίαι of the holy Catholic Church in every place. This document was known to Eusebius, who transcribed the greater part in his *Eccl. Hist.* (iv. 15). A trans. of this and of Polycarp's Ep. appears in the vol. of *Apost. Fathers* in *Ante-Nicene Lib.* (T. & T. Clark). The occurrence of the phrase "Catholic Church" just quoted has been urged as a note of spuriousness; but not very reasonably, in the absence of evidence to make it even probable that the introduction of this phrase was later than the death of Polycarp. We know for certain that the phrase is very early. It is used in the Ignatian letters (*Smyrn.* 8), by Clem. Alex. (*Strom.* vii. 17), in the Muratorian Fragment, by Hippolytus (*Ref.* ix. 12) and Tertullian. Remembering the warfare waged by Polycarp against heresy, it is highly probable that in his lifetime the need had arisen for a name to distinguish the main Christian body from the various separatists. The whole narrative of the martyrdom bears so plainly the mark of an eye-witness, that to imagine, as Lipsius and Keim have done, some one capable of inventing it a century after the death of Polycarp, seems to require great critical credulity. With our acceptance of the martyrdom as authentic Hilgenfeld (*Zeitschrift*, 1874, p. 334) and Renan (*Eglise chrét.* 462) coincide. We see no good reason to doubt that the narrative was written, as it professes to be, within a year of the martyrdom, by members of the church where it occurred and who had actually witnessed it; and we believe it to have been written specially to invite members of other churches to attend the commemoration on the anniversary of the martyrdom. It is deeply tinged by a belief in the supernatural, but it is uncritical to cast doubts on the genuineness of a document on the assumption that Christians of the 2nd cent., under the strain of a great persecution, held the views of their 19th-cent. critics as to the possibility of receiving supernatural aid or consolation.

The story relates that Polycarp's martyrdom was the last act of a great persecution and took place on the occasion of games held at Smyrna, eleven others having suffered before him. These games were probably held in connection with the meeting of the Asiatic diet (τὸ κοινὸν τῆς Ἀσίας), which met in rotation in the principal cities of the province. If more information were available as to this rotation and as to the seasons when these meetings were held, we should probably be able to fix the date of Polycarp's martyrdom with more certainty. The proconsul came from Ephesus, the ordinary seat of government, to preside. It may have been to provide the necessary victims for the wild beast shows that the Christians were sought for (some were brought from Philadelphia) and required to swear by the fortune of the emperor and offer sacrifice. The proconsul appears to have discharged his unpleasant duty with the humanity ordinary among Roman magistrates, doing his best to persuade the accused to save themselves by compliance, and no doubt employing the tortures, of which the narrative gives a terrible account, as a merciful cruelty which might save him from proceeding to the last extremes. In one case his persuasion was successful. Quintus, a Phrygian by nation, who had presented himself voluntarily for martyrdom, on sight of the wild beasts lost courage and yielded to the proconsul's entreaties. The Christians learned from his case to condemn wanton courting of danger as contrary to the gospel teaching. The proconsul lavished similar entreaties on a youth named Germanicus, but the lad was resolute, and instead of shewing fear, provoked the wild beasts in order to gain a speedier release from his persecutors. The act may have been suggested by the language of Ignatius (*Rom.* v. 2); and certainly this language seems to have been present to the mind of the narrator. At sight of the bravery of Germanicus, a conviction seems to have seized the multitude that they should have rather chosen as their victim the teacher who had inspired the sufferers with their obstinacy. A cry was raised, "Away with the atheists! Let Polycarp be sought for!" Polycarp wished to remain at his post, but yielded to the solicitations of his people and retired for concealment to a country house, where he spent his time, as was his wont, in continual prayer for himself and his own people and for all the churches throughout the world. Three days before his apprehension he saw in a vision his pillow on fire, and at once interpreted the omen to his friends: "I must be burnt alive." The search for him being hot, he retired to another farm barely escaping his pursuers, who seized and tortured two slave boys, one of whom betrayed the new place of retreat. Late on a Friday night the noise of horses and armed men announced the pursuers at hand. There seemed still the possibility of escape, and he was urged to make the attempt, but he refused, saying "God's will be done." Coming down from the upper room where he had been lying down, he ordered meat and drink to be set before his captors and only begged an hour for uninterrupted prayer. This was granted; and for more than two hours he prayed, mentioning by name every one whom he had known, small or great, and praying for the Catholic church throughout the world. At length he was set on an ass and conducted to the city. Soon they met the irenarch Herod, the police magistrate under whose directions the arrest had been made, in whose name the Christians afterwards found one of several coincidences which they delighted to trace between the arrest of Polycarp and that of his Master. Herod, accompanied by his father Nicetes, took Polycarp to sit in his carriage, and both earnestly urged him to save his life: "Why, what harm was it to say Lord Caesar, and to sacrifice, and so on, and escape all danger?" Polycarp, at first silent, at last bluntly answered, "I will not do as you would have me." Annoyed at the old man's obstinacy, they thrust him out of the carriage so rudely that he scraped his shin, the marks no doubt being visible to his friends when he afterwards stripped for the stake. But at the time he took no notice of the hurt and walked on as if nothing had happened. At the racecourse, where the multitude was assembled, there was a prodigious uproar; but the Christians could distinguish a voice which cried, "Be strong, Polycarp, and play the man!" Under the protection of the tumult the speaker remained undiscovered; and the Christians believed it a voice from heaven. The proconsul pressed Polycarp to have pity on his old age: "Swear by the fortune of Caesar, say 'Away with the atheists!'" The martyr, sternly looking round on the assembled heathen, groaned, and looking up to heaven said, "Away with the atheists!" "Swear then, now," said the proconsul, "and I will let you go; revile Christ." Then Polycarp made the memorable answer, "Eighty and six years have I served Him, and He has never done me wrong; how, then, can I blaspheme my King and my Saviour!" The 86 years must clearly count from Polycarp's baptism; so that if we are not to ascribe to him an improbable length of life, we must infer that he was the child of Christian parents and had been baptized, if not in infancy, in very early childhood. The magistrate continuing to urge him, Polycarp cut matters short by plainly declaring himself a Christian and offering, if a day were assigned, to explain what Christianity was. "Obtain the consent of the people," answered the proconsul. "Nay," replied Polycarp, "I count it your due that I should offer my defence to you, because we have been taught to give due honour to the powers ordained of God; but as for these people, I owe no vindication to them." The proconsul then had recourse to threats, but finding them unavailing, ordered his crier thrice to proclaim in the midst of the stadium, "Polycarp has confessed himself a Christian." Then arose a furious outcry from heathen and Jews against this "father of the Christians," this teacher of Asia, this destroyer of the worship of the gods. Philip the asiarch, or president of the games, was called on to loose a lion on Polycarp, but refused, saying the wild beast shows were now over. Then with one voice the multitude demanded that Polycarp should be burnt alive; for his vision must needs be fulfilled. Rushing to the workshops and baths they collected wood and faggots; the Jews, as usual, taking the most active part. We have evidence of the activity of the Jews at Smyrna at an earlier period, Rev. ii. 9, and at a later in the story of the martyrdom of Pionius. When the pile was ready Polycarp proceeded to undress himself; and here the story has an autoptic touch, telling how the Christians marked the old man's embarrassment as he tried to take off his shoes, it having been many years since the reverence of his disciples had permitted him to perform that office for himself. When he had been bound (at his own request, not nailed) to the stake, and had offered up a final prayer, the pile was lit, but the flame bellied out under the wind like the sail of a ship, behind which the body could be seen, scorched but not consumed. The fumes seemed fragrant to the Christians, whether as the effect of imagination or because sweet-scented woods had been seized for the hasty structure. Seeing that the flame was dying out, an executioner was sent in to use the sword, when so much blood gushed forth that the flame was nearly extinguished.

The Christians were about to remove the body; but Nicetes, here further described as the brother of Alce, interfered and said, "If you give the body, the Christians will leave the Crucified One and worship him," an idea deeply shocking to the narrator of the story, who declares it was impossible for them to leave, for any other, Christ the Holy One Who died for the salvation of the world. Him, as the Son of God, they worshipped; martyrs they loved on account of the abundance of their zeal and love for Him. The Jews eagerly backing up Nicetes, the centurion had the body placed on the pyre and saw it completely consumed, so that it was only the bones, "more precious than jewels, more tried than gold," which the disciples could carry off to the place where they meant on the anniversary to commemorate the martyr's "birthday." The epistle closes with a doxology. Euarestus is named as the writer; Marcion [or Marcianus] as the bearer of the letter.

Then follows by way of appendix a note, stating that the martyrdom took place on the 2nd of the month Xanthicus, the 7th before the calends of March [there is a various reading May], on a great sabbath at the 8th hour; the arrest having been made by Herod; Philip of Tralles being chief priest, Statius Quadratus proconsul, and Jesus Christ King for ever. A second note states that these Acts were transcribed by Socrates (or Isocrates) of Corinth, from a copy made by Caius, a companion of Polycarp's disciple Irenaeus. A third note states that this again had been transcribed by Pionius from a copy much decayed by time, the success of his search for which was due to a revelation made by Polycarp himself, "as will be shewn in what follows," from which we infer that the martyrdom was followed by a Life of Polycarp.

The first chronological note may be accepted as, if not part of the original document, at least added by one of its first transcribers, and therefore deserving of high confidence. The name of the proconsul Statius Quadratus indicates best the date of the martyrdom. Eusebius in his chronicle had put it in the 6th year of Marcus Aurelius, *i.e.* A.D. 166. M. Waddington (*Mémoires de l'Académie des Inscriptions*, 1867, xxvi. 235) shewed that Eusebius's date was doubtful. Eusebius seems to have had no real knowledge of the date, and to have put it down somewhat at random, for he places Polycarp's martyrdom and the Lyons persecution under the same year, though the Lyons martyrdoms were as late as 177. At this time the ordinary interval between the consulship and proconsulate ranged between 12 and 16 years. Quadratus we know to have been consul A.D. 142. We are at once led to reject Eusebius's date as placing the inadmissible interval of 24 or 25 years between the consulship and proconsulate. Waddington made out a probable case for A.D. 155, and an additional argument appears decisive. The martyrdom is stated to have taken place on Sat. Feb. 23, and among the possible years 155 is the only one in which Feb. 23 so fell. The reading of this chronological date is not free from variations. The "great sabbath" would in Christian times be thought to mean the Sat. in Easter week, and as Easter could not occur in Feb. there was an obvious temptation to alter Mar. into May, but none to make the opposite change, and we have independent knowledge that Feb. 23 was the day on which the Eastern church celebrated the martyrdom. But we do not know why Feb. 23 should be a "great" sabbath. We believe the true explanation to be that the Latin date in this note is not of the same antiquity as the date by the Macedonian month. Probably Pionius, when he recovered the very ancient copy of the martyrdom, translated the date 2nd Xanthicus into one more widely intelligible and thus determined the date of subsequent commemorations. We accept, then, the 2nd Xanthicus as an original note of time faithfully preserved by a scribe who did not understand its meaning, because he interpreted according to the usage of his own day.

When we have abandoned the date Sat. Feb. 23 we lose one clue to fixing the exact date of the martyrdom, but we gain another. Since Nisan 2nd was Sat. the year must be one in which that lunar month commenced on a Friday. The only such years within the necessary limits were 155 and 159, and 155 again agrees best with the usual interval between consulship and proconsulate. The date Apr. 8, which A.D. 159 would require, is likely, moreover, to be too late. The chief difficulty raised by the date 155 is that if we adopt it the chronology of the Roman bishops obliges us to put Polycarp's visit in the last year of his life and the first of the episcopate of Anicetus.

For the literature connected with Polycarp see bp. Lightfoot's ed. of Ignatius and Polycarp. An ed. of Polycarp's remains by G. Jacobson is in *Patr. Apost.* (Clar. Press, 2 vols.). A small popular treatise on St. Polycarp by B. Jackson is pub. by S.P.C.K. Cf. also Zahn, *Forschungen*, iv. 249; Harnack, *Gesch. der Alt.-Chr. Lat.* 1897 (ii. 1, 334). [G.S.]

Polycarpus (5). Moyses of Aghel (*c.* 550), in a *Letter to Paphnutius* prefatory to his Syriac version of the *Glaphyra* of Cyril of Alexandria, prepares his readers to find variations from the Peshitto in Cyril's citations of Scripture after the Greek, by referring them to "the translation of the N.T. and of David into Syriac" from the Greek, which "the Chorepiscopus Polycarpus made for Xenaias [Philoxenus] of Mabug" (Assem. ii. p. 82; see also Dr. Ign. Guidi in *Rendiconti della R. Academia dei Lincei*, 1886, p. 397). Now we know from Gregory Bar-hebraeus (*Prooem. in Horr. Mystt.*) that, "after the Peshitto, the N.T. was more accurately translated again from the Greek at Mabug *in the days* of Philoxenus." The same facts are stated in a note purporting to be written by THOMAS OF HARKEL in 616, appended in slightly varying forms to many MSS. of the version of the N.T. known as the Harklensian, one of which (Assem. xi., now *Cod. Vat.* 268) is probably (Bernstein, *Das Heil. Evang. des Joh.* p. 2) of the 8th cent. In this MS., and others, the note gives also the date of this Philoxenian version, A.D. 508. In all of them it proceeds to describe the Harklensian version as based on this—in fact a revision of it; and the same description in more direct terms is given by Bar-hebraeus in two places in his *Chronicon*

Eccl. (i. 49, ii. 22; Assem. ii. pp. 334, 411). We may safely infer that this earlier version was made by the Polycarp named by Moyses (and by no other writer) at the instance of his bishop, Philoxenus, the great Monophysite leader (485-522). The aim of Philoxenus in having the version made was probably, as the remark of Moyses suggests, to enable Syriac-speaking Monophysites to read the Scriptures as they were read by those Greek Fathers whom he owned as authorities and by their Greek-speaking brethren within the Antiochene Patriarchate. It does not appear that the translation shewed, or was ever impugned as shewing, a doctrinal bias.

Of the Philoxenian N.T. as it was before Thomas of Harkel revised it, we only know with certainty the few small fragments of St. Paul recovered by Wiseman from the margin of his MS. of the Karkaphensian Syriac, and pub. by him in *Horae Syriacae* (p. 178, n. 11).

It seems highly probable that we have a considerable portion of this original Philoxenian, in the version of the four minor Catholic Epistles (II. Peter, II. and III. John, and Jude) not included in the Peshitto though printed with it in the Polyglotts and in most Syriac New Testaments—first published by Pococke (1630) from a MS. of no great age (Bodl. *Or.* 119). These four Epistles in the version in question are found also in a few Paris MSS. (see Zotenberg's *Catal.*), in one (formerly Wetstein's) at Amsterdam, in Lord Crawford's MS. in the Cambridge MS. (Oo. i. 1, 2), and in several MSS. in Brit. Mus.; one of which, Add. 14623 (7), written 823, is the oldest extant copy of this version. It is included also in the "Williams MS." of the N.T. Epistles, whence Prof. Hall issued it in photographic facsimile. This version is distinct from the Harklensian rendering of the same Epistles, which, however, though more servilely exact and grecised, is unmistakably founded on it. As then we have in this version the unmistakable basis of the Harklensian, and as the Harklensian is known to have been a revision of the Philoxenian, the identity of this version with the Philoxenian proper (as distinguished from the Philoxenian usually so-called, viz. the Harklensian revision) follows. We have then the materials for judging of Polycarp's merits as a translator, and we find reason to estimate them highly. The translation is in the main accurate and close without being servile. Dr. Scrivener (*Intro. to N.T.* p. 646, ed. 3) justly describes it as one which "well deserves careful study . . . of great interest and full of valuable readings," siding as it does frequently with the oldest Greek uncials. Here also we have material to determine the mutual relation between his work and Thomas's revision of it, and we conclude that the latter work is not (as has been taken for granted by many) a merely corrected re-issue of the earlier one, with merely linguistic alterations in the text and variants inserted on its margin; but is substantially a new version, proceeding on the lines of the former, but freely quitting them when the translator saw fit.

We are not informed what O.T. books were included in the work of Polycarp. Moyses mentions only his version of the Psalms, which is lost. But we have conclusive evidence that a Philoxenian Isaiah also existed; for a rendering of Is. ix. 6, differing from the Hexapla and from the Hebrew, but closely agreeing with a reading found in several MSS. of the LXX. (Holmes's 22, 36, 48, 51, 62, 90, 93, 106, 147, 233), is inserted on the margin of the Ambrosian Syro-Hexapla (8th cent.), and is there introduced as being "from the other text which was rendered into Syriac *by the care* of Philoxenus, bp. of Mabug," the word being the same as in the first citation (above) from the *Chron. Eccl.* of Bar-hebraeus. That the LXX. was in the hands of Syriac writers and translators before the time of Philoxenus is certain. Yet internal evidence conclusively proves that the Hebrew and not the LXX. is the main basis of the Peshitto Psalter. [J.GW.]

Polychronius (4), brother of Theodore of Mopsuestia and bp. of Apamea on the Orontes in Syria Secunda. He belonged to a wealthy family of position at Antioch, and the literary character of his remains indicates that his early education was liberal and many-sided. A Polychronius was among the correspondents of Libanius (*Epp.* 27, 207, 228, etc.), but that he was the same is more than doubtful. That our Polychronius fell more or less directly under the influence of Diodore seems certain. Polychronius was probably younger than Theodore; at any rate his consecration as bp. was some ten years the later. In the see of Apamea he must have followed Agapetus, who succeeded Marcellus A.D. 398 (Theod. *H. E.* v. 27; *Hist. Relig.* § 3). He was still bishop when his brother died, A.D. 428 (cf. Theod. *H. E.* v. 40). But within the next three years he had died or otherwise vacated the see, for in the records of the council of Ephesus Alexander is bp. of Apamea (Mansi, iv. 1235, 1270). Both Le Quien (*Oriens Christ.* ii. 911) and Gams (*Series Episc.* p. 436) strangely omit Polychronius from their lists of the bps. of Apamea. The testimony of Theodoret, however, is unequivocal, and is that of the contemporary bishop of a neighbouring see. The city of Apamea was raised by Theodosius II. to metropolitan rank (Joh. Malal. *Chronogr.* xiv.; Migne, *Patr. Gk.* xcvii. 543) and the see attained a corresponding dignity. In the history of the church, however, the name of Polychronius occupies a comparatively insignificant place. Our knowledge of him is drawn almost exclusively from the scanty encomiums of Theodoret re-echoed by Cassiodorus and Nicephorus. We must be content to learn that, as bishop, he was characterized by the excellence of his rule, grace of oratory, and conspicuous purity of life (Theod. *H. E.* v. 40; cf. Cassiod. *Hist. Tripart.* x. 34; Niceph. xiv. 30).

It has been generally assumed that the bp. of Apamea is identical with the recluse of the same name in Theodoret's *Religious History* (§ 24). But such evidence as we possess points in an opposite direction.

As a disciple of the school of Antioch, Polychronius would naturally apply himself to Biblical exegesis. No traces occur of any comments by him on N.T., but the catenae teem with *scholia* upon O.T. bearing his name. The following have been ascribed to him: (1)

Scholia on the Pentateuch in the catena of Nicephorus. (2) Prologue and fragments of a commentary on Job. (3) Scholia on the Proverbs. (4) A MS. exposition of Ecclesiastes, said to be preserved in several European libraries. (5) Scholia on the Canticles. (6) Scholia on Jeremiah. (7) An exposition of Ezekiel, cited by Joannes Damascenus (*De Imag.* iii.; Migne, *Patr. Gk.* xciv. 1380, Πολυχρονίου ἐκ τῆς εἰς τὸν Ἰεζεκιὴλ ἑρμηνείας). This work happily survives in an almost complete form, and has been published by Mai (*Nov. Patr. Bibl.* vii. p. 2, pp. 92 seq.). (8) A commentary on Daniel, quoted in 9th cent. by Nicephorus (Pitra, *Spic. Solesm.* i. p. 352).

Of these remains the scholia on Proverbs, Canticles, and Jeremiah are of more than doubtful genuineness. Those on Proverbs and Canticles are in some MSS. ascribed to "Polychronius the Deacon," and all these collections are characterized by a partiality for allegorical and mystical interpretations quite alien to the instincts of the Antiochenes.

The style of Polychronius has been described (Bardenhewer, *Polychronius*, p. 36) as clear and concise, contrasting favourably with the loose and complex manner of his brother Theodore, a criticism which agrees with the verdict of Theodoret (*supra*). As an expositor Polychronius follows the historico-grammatical method of his school, condemning expressly the Alexandrian tendency to convert history into allegory. "His manner of exposition is scholarly and serious, breathing at the same time an air of deep piety." So Mai, who points out the fulness of historical illustration in his commentary on Daniel. His comments are based (the book of Daniel excepted) on the LXX., but he calls in the aid of Symmachus and Theodotion; and the frequency of his references to the Hebrew, as well as the remarkable fragment on the "Obscurity of Scripture" among the extant fragments of his commentary on Job, shew some acquaintance with that language. With regard to the canon, Polychronius assumes an independent attitude. Against his brother he stoutly maintains the historical character of the narrative of Job, but discriminates between the Heb. Daniel and the Greek additions, refusing to comment upon the Song of the Three Children as not being in the original.

Of his doctrinal standpoint little can be learnt from his published remains. His temper was not controversial, and he has no place in the history of polemical theology—a circumstance which has saved him from the stigma of heterodoxy, but consigned his life and works to comparative obscurity. [H.B.S.]

Polycrates (1), bp. of Ephesus in the last decade of 2nd cent. When Victor of Rome sought to unify the practice of the whole Christian world in the matter of Easter celebration, he first asked for meetings of bishops in different places to report on the practice of their localities. This request was made in the name of his church, as we learn from the use of the plural in the reply of Polycrates. From every other place, as far as we can learn, the answer was that they celebrated the feast of our Lord's Resurrection on no other day than Sunday; but Polycrates, writing in the name of the bishops of Asia, declared that they had preserved untampered the tradition to celebrate only on the 14th day of the month, the day when the Jewish people put away their leaven. He appeals to the authority of the great luminaries which the Asian church could boast, and whose bodies lay among them, Philip, one of the twelve apostles, and his three daughters, John, who lay on our Lord's breast, a priest who wore the πέταλον, Polycarp of Smyrna, Thraseas of Eumenia, Sagaris, Papirius, Melito, all of whom had observed the 14th day, according to the Gospel, walking according to the rule of faith. Polycrates himself had followed the traditions of his kindred, seven of whom had been bishops before him, and had been confirmed in his view by his own study of the whole Scripture and by conference with brethren from all the world. Although his letter bore no signature but his own, he claims that it had received the assent of a great number of bishops (Eus. *H. E.* v. 24). For the sequel see IRENAEUS. [G.S.]

Pomponia Graecina, one of the earliest and most distinguished Roman converts. Tacitus (*Annals*, xiii. 32) tells us, referring to A.D. 57 or 58, that Pomponia Graecina, a distinguished lady, wife of the Plautius who returned from Britain with an ovation, was accused of some foreign superstition and handed over to her husband's judicial decision. Following ancient precedent, he heard his wife's cause in the presence of kinsfolk, involving, as it did, her legal status and character, and reported that she was innocent. She lived a long life of unbroken melancholy. After the murder of Julia, Drusus's daughter, by Messalina's treachery, for 40 years she wore only the attire of a mourner. For this, during Claudius's reign, she escaped unpunished, and it was afterwards counted a glory to her. This is the only notice of her in ancient literature. She came into prominence through De Rossi's discoveries in the catacomb of Callistus (*Roma Sotterranea*, ii. 360-364). De Rossi identified her with St. Lucina (cf. Aubé, *Hist. des perséc.* t. i. p. 180). Cf. for other notices Brownlow and Northcote's *Roma Sott.* t. i. pp. 82, 83, 278-282. De Rossi (*op. cit.* t. i. pp. 306-351) discusses the crypt and family of St. Lucina at great length (cf. also his *Bullettino di Archeol. Crist. passim*). [G.T.S.]

Pontianus (3), bp. of Rome from July (?) 21, 230, to Sept. 28, 235. These dates, given in the Liberian Catalogue, are probably correct, though later recensions of the Pontifical give them differently. The same record states that he was, with Hippolytus a presbyter, banished to Sardinia, which it describes as "nociva insula," implying possibly that he was sent to the mines there. His banishment doubtless took place under Maximinus, who succeeded Alexander after the assassination of the latter in May 235. The date, Sept. 28 235, was probably that of his deprivation only.

His only episcopal act of which anything needs to be said is his probable assent to the condemnation of Origen by Demetrius of Alexandria. Jerome (*Ep. ad Paulam*, xxix. in Benedict. ed.; *Ep.* xxxiii. in ed. Veron.) says of Origen: "For this toil what reward did he get? He is condemned by tne bp. Demetrius. Except the priests of Palestine

Arabia, Phoenicia, and Achaia, the world consents to his condemnation. Rome herself assembles a senate [meaning apparently a synod] against him." The condemnation of Origen by Demetrius being supposed (though not with certainty) to have been *c.* 231, the Roman bishop who assembled the synod was most probably Pontianus. Two spurious epistles are assigned to him. [J.B—Y.]

Pontitianus, a soldier, perhaps of the praetorian guard, an African by birth and a Christian, who indirectly contributed much towards the conversion of St. Augustine, who relates in his *Confessions* how one day, while he was at Milan with Alypius, Pontitianus came, as it seemed by accident, to visit his countrymen, and found on the table a book containing the writings of St. Paul, and having expressed some surprise, informed the friends that he was a Christian and constantly prayed to God both in public worship and at home. The conversation then turned upon Anthony the Egyptian monk, of whose history Pontitianus knew much more than they did. He told them how, when he was at Trèves, in attendance on the emperor, with three comrades he went to the public gardens. Having separated, two of them met again at the dwelling of a recluse, and found there an account of St. Anthony, which one read to the other until he was stirred to relinquish his military life and enlist in the service of God as a monk, and prevailed on his companion to join him. Pontitianus and the fourth member of the party coming up, the other two endeavoured to persuade them to follow their example, but without success. They returned to the palace while the disciples of St. Anthony remained behind. We hear no more of Pontitianus; for the sequel see AUGUSTINE (Aug. *Conf.* viii. 6, 7). [H.W.P.]

Pontius (2), Mar. 8, a deacon of Carthage. We know him only from his *Vita Cypriani*, prefixed to all editions of St. Cyprian's works. He was chosen by Cyprian to accompany him into exile to Curubis (cc. xi. and xii.; cf. Dodwell's *Dissertationes Cyprianicae*, iv. 21). The *Vita* is evidently an authentic record. Its style is rugged, and in places very obscure; yet presents all internal marks of truth and antiquity. It uses all the correct technical terms of Roman criminal law, and refers to all the usual forms observed in criminal trials. Jerome, in his *Liber de Vir. Ill.* c. 68, describes the *Vita* of Pontius as "egregium volumen vitae et passionis Cypriani." [G.T.S.]

Porphyrius (4), patriarch of Antioch, A.D. 404-413, succeeded Flavian (Socr. *H. E.* vii. 9), and is described in the dialogue which goes under the name of Palladius as a man of infamous character, who had disgraced the clerical profession by intimacy with the scum of the circus (Pallad. *Dial.* p. 143). Although his character was notorious, by his cleverness and adroit flattery he obtained considerable influence with the magistrates, and gained the confidence of some leading bishops of the province. Flavian's death having occurred almost contemporaneously with Chrysostom's exile, it became vitally important to the anti-Flavian cabal to have the vacant throne of Antioch filled with a man who would carry out their designs for the complete crushing of Flavian's adherents. Porphyry was chosen. To clear the field Constantius, the trusted friend of Chrysostom, whom the people of Antioch marked out as Flavian's successor, was accused at Constantinople as a disturber of the public peace. By his powerful influence with the party then dominant about the court, Porphyry obtained an imperial rescript banishing Constantius to the Oasis. Constantius anticipated this by fleeing to Cyprus (*ib.* 145). Porphyry then managed to get into his hands Cyriacus, Diophantus, and other presbyters of the orthodox party who were likely to be troublesome, and seized the opportunity of the Olympian festival at Antioch, when the population had poured forth to the spectacles of Daphne, to lock himself and his three consecrators, Acacius, Antiochus, and Severianus, whom he had kept hiding at his own house, with a few of the clergy, into the chief church, and to receive consecration at their hands. The indignant Antiochenes next morning attacked the house of Porphyry, seeking to burn it over his head. The influence of Porphyry secured the appointment of a savage officer as captain of the city guards, who by threats and violence drove the people to the church (*ib.* 147). Forewarned of his real character, pope Innocent received Porphyry's request for communion with silence (*ib.* 141). Porphyry was completely deserted by the chief clergy and all the ladies of rank of Antioch, who refused to approach his church and held their meetings clandestinely (*ib.* 149). In revenge Porphyry obtained a decree, issued by Arcadius Nov. 18, 404, sentencing all who refused communion with Arsacius, Theophilus, and Porphyry to be expelled from the churches, and instructing the governor of the province to forbid their holding meetings elsewhere (Soz. *H. E.* viii. 24; *Cod. Theod.* 16, t. iv. p. 103). His efforts to obtain the recognition of the Antiochenes proving fruitless, while Chrysostom's spiritual power in exile became the greater for all his efforts to crush it, Porphyry's exasperation drove him to take vengeance on Chrysostom. Through his machinations and those of Severianus, orders were issued for the removal of Chrysostom from Cucusus to Pityus, during the execution of which the aged saint's troubles ended by death (Pallad. *Dial.* p. 97). Porphyry's own death is placed by Clinton (*Fast. Rom.* ii. 552) in 413 (cf. Theod. *H. E.* iii. 5). He was succeeded by Alexander, by whom the long distracted church was united. It is a misfortune that the chief and almost only source for the character of Porphyry is the violent pamphlet of Palladius, whose warm partisanship for Chrysostom unduly blackens all his opponents, and refuses them a single redeeming virtue. That Porphyry was not altogether the monster this author represents may be concluded from the statement of the calm and amiable Theodoret, that he "left behind him" at Antioch "many memorials of his kindness and of his remarkable prudence" (Theod. *H. E.* v. 35), as well as by a still stronger testimony in his favour in Theodoret's letter to Dioscorus, when he calls him one "of blessed and holy memory, who was adorned both with a brilliant life and an acquaintance with divine doctrines"

(Theod. *Ep.* 83). Fragments of a letter addressed to Porphyry by Theophilus of Alexandria, recommending him to summon a synod, when some were seeking to revive the heresy of Paul of Samosata, are found in Labbe (*Concil.* p. 472). [E.V.]

Porphyrius (5), bp. of Gaza, A.D. 395-420. According to his biographer Mark, he was born at Thessalonica *c.* 352, of a good family. His parents were Christians, and took care to have him instructed in the Scriptures as well as in secular learning. When about 25 he retired to the desert of Scete in Egypt, which, at the end of 5 years, he left for Jerusalem, and passed another 5 years in a cavern near the Jordan. A painful disease, brought on by his austerities, compelled him to revisit Jerusalem, where he made the acquaintance of Mark, who became his devoted disciple and companion. By Porphyry's desire Mark visited Thessalonica, and turned the proceeds of Porphyry's share of his paternal property into money, the whole of which, on his return, Porphyry distributed to the poor and to various monasteries, supporting himself by manual labour. About his 40th year he reluctantly received ordination from John, bp. of Jerusalem, who committed to his guardianship the sacred relic of the True Cross. After a presbyterate of three years, in 395 on the death of Aeneas he with still greater reluctance became bp. of Gaza, being consecrated by John of Caesarea, who had sent for him on the pretext of consulting him on some scriptural difficulty. The people of Gaza were then almost all pagan, and the position of a zealous Christian bishop was one of no small difficulty and even danger. The cessation of a severe drought at the beginning of the 2nd year of his episcopate, Jan. 326, was attributed to his prayers and those of the Christians, and caused the conversion of a number of the inhabitants. This was succeeded by other conversions, arousing great exasperation among the heathen population, which vented itself in a severe persecution. Porphyry endured their ill-treatment with the utmost meekness. At the same time he despatched his deacon Mark and his minister Borocas to Constantinople, who, through the powerful advocacy of Chrysostom, obtained the emperor's order to destroy the idols and close the temples. This was carried out by an imperial commissioner, who, however, it was asserted, was bribed to spare the principal idol named Marnas, and to wink at the entrance of the worshippers into the temple by a secret passage. To these events Jerome refers in a letter to Laeta (Hieron. *Ep.* vii. p. 54). The idolaters still remained the dominant section, and were able to shut out Christians from all lucrative offices and to molest them in the enjoyment of their property. Porphyry took this so much to heart that he exhorted his metropolitan, John of Caesarea, to allow him to resign. John consoled him, and went with him to Constantinople to obtain an order for the demolition not of the idols alone, but of the temples themselves, arriving Jan. 7, 401. Chrysostom was then high in the empress Eudoxia's favour, and their suit was successful. The bishops reached Majuma, the port of Gaza, on May 1, and were followed in ten days by a commissioner named Cynegius, accompanied by the governor and a general officer with a large body of troops, by whom the imperial orders for the destruction of the temples were executed. In ten days the whole were burnt, and finally the magnificent temple of Marnas, and on the ground it occupied the foundations of a cruciform church were laid according to a plan furnished by Eudoxia, who also supplied the funds for its erection. The church was 5 years building, and was dedicated by Porphyry on Easter Day, 405 or 406, being called "Eudoxiana" after its foundress. Jerome refers to its erection (Hieron. *in Esaiam*, xvii. l. vii. t. v. p. 86). The heathen population, irritated at the destruction of their sacred buildings and at the spread of Christianity in Gaza, raised a tumult, in which several Christians were killed, and Porphyry himself barely escaped with his life. We may certainly identify him with one of the two bishops of his name who attended the anti-Pelagian synod at Diospolis in 415 (Aug. *in Julian.* lib. i. c. 15). He died Feb. 26, 419 or 420. He is said to have been indefatigable in instructing the people of Gaza in a simple and popular style, based entirely on Holy Scripture. Migne, *Patr. Lat.* xlv. pp. 1211 ff.; Ceillier, *Aut. eccl.* vi. 329; Tillem. *Mém. eccl.* x. pp. 703-716. [E.V.]

Possidius, bp. of Calama, a town of Numidia, S.W. of Hippo, between it and Cirta, but nearer Hippo (Aug. *c. Petil.* ii. 99; *Kalma*, Shaw, *Trav.* p. 64). His own account represents him as a convert from paganism, becoming on his conversion an inmate of the monastery at Hippo, probably *c.* 390. Thenceforward he lived in intimate friendship with St. Augustine until the latter's death in 430 (Possid. *Vita Aug. praef.* and cc. 12, 31). About 400 he became bp. of Calama. He seems to have established a monastery there, and, probably early in his episcopate, consulted Augustine on (*a*) the ornaments to be used by men and women, and especially earrings used as amulets; (*b*) the ordination of some one who had received Donatist baptism (Aug. *Epp.* 104, 4, and 245). In 401 or 402 a council was held at Carthage, at which Possidius was present, and challenged in vain Crispinus, Donatist bp. of Calama, to discuss publicly issues between the two parties. After this Possidius, though he modestly conceals his own name, while going to a place in his diocese called Figulina, was attacked by CRISPINUS, a presbyter, and narrowly escaped alive (Aug. *Ep.* 103; Possid. *Vit.* 12). In 407 he was one of a committee of seven appointed by Xanthippus, primate of Numidia, at the request of Maurentius, bp. of Tubursica, to decide a question, of whose nature we are not informed, but which was at issue between himself and the seniors of Nova Germania (Morcelli, *Afr. Chr.* iii. 34; Hardouin, *Conc.* ii. 922; Bruns, *Conc.* i. 185). In 408 Possidius was again in trouble and personal danger, in consequence of the disturbances at Calama described above. In 409, on June 14, a council was held at Carthage, and a deputation of four bishops, Florentinus, Possidius, Praesidius, and Benantus, was appointed to request the protection of the emperor against the Donatists. On this occasion Possidius conveyed a letter from Augustine to Paulinus of Nola, but nothing more is known as to the journey of the deputation or their interview, if any, with the emperor, who was then at Ravenna. In 410, however, an edict was issued by Honorius on or about the day on which Rome was taken by Alaric, viz. Aug. 26, to Heraclian, count of Africa, to restrain by penalties all enemies of the Christian faith, and another of a similar nature on Oct. 14, 410, to Marcellinus, the president of the conference in 411 (Aug. *Ep.* 95, i.; 105, i.; *Cod. Theod.* xvi. 5, 51, and ii. 3; Baron. 410, 48, 49). At the conference Possidius was one of the seven Catholic managers (*Coll. Carth. ap. Mon. Vet. Don.* liii. 1; ii. 29; iii. 29, 148, 168, ed. Oberthür). He was with Augustine at Hippo in 412 (Aug. *Ep.* 137, 20) and in 416 signed at the council of Mileum the letter sent to pope Innocent concerning the Pelagian heresy (Aug. *Ep.* 176). He also joined with Augustine, Aurelius, Alypius, and Evodius in a letter to the same on the same subject (*ib.* 181, 182, 183). He was at the meeting or council of bishops held at Caesarea on Sept. 29, 418. St. Augustine mentions that Possidius (*c.* 425) brought to Calama and placed in a memorial building there some relics of St. Stephen, by which many cures were wrought (*Civ. D.* xii. 8, 12, 20). When the Vandals invaded Africa, he took refuge in Hippo with other bishops, and there attended on St. Augustine in his last illness until his death, A.D. 430, in the third month of the siege. He has left a biographical sketch of Augustine, whose unbroken friendship he enjoyed for 40 years, being his faithful ally and devoted admirer. This sketch gives many particulars of great interest as to Augustine's mode of life, and a description, simple but deeply pathetic and impressive, of his last days and death. Though few men's lives are written in their own works more fully than that of Augustine, yet history and the church would have greatly missed the simple, modest, and trustworthy narrative, gathered in great measure from Augustine himself, which Possidius has left us. It was apparently published, not immediately after the death of Augustine, but before 439, as he speaks of Carthage and Cirta as still exempt from capture by the barbarians, and in Oct. 439 Carthage was taken by Genseric (Possid. c. 28; Clinton, *F. R.*). Possidius has also left a list of Augustine's works which, though very full and compiled with great care, does not pretend to be complete and of which some have not yet been discovered. It is given in the last vol. of Migne's ed. of Augustine's works. Prosper relates in his *Chronicle* that Possidius, together with Novatus, Severianus, and other bishops of less note, resisted the attempts of Genseric to establish Arian doctrine in Africa, and was driven with them from his see A.D. 437. Baron. 437, i.; Morcelli, *Afr. Chr.* iii. 140; Ceillier, ix. 564; Tillem. vol. xiii. 354. [H.W.P.]

Posthumianus (2), a friend of Sulpicius Severus of Gaul and Paulinus of Nola, was a native of Aquitania, and made at least two journeys to the East. After the first, when he made the acquaintance of Jerome at Bethlehem, he appears to have visited Campania to see Paulinus (S. Paulini, *Epp.* 16 in Migne. *Patr. Lat.* lxi. 227). He sailed from Narbonne in 401 or 402 on his second voyage, of which a full and interesting account is in bk. i. of the Dialogues of Sulpicius Severus (*Patr. Lat.* xx. 183), in which Posthumianus with Severus and Gallus are the speakers. In five days he reached Carthage, where he visited the tomb of St. Cyprian. Detained between Africa and Cyrene by bad weather, he landed to explore the country, which was inhabited by a very primitive tribe, who, however, were Christians, and was hospitably entertained by a priest. Alexandria was then convulsed by the quarrel between the patriarch Theophilus and the monks about the writings of Origen, and Posthumianus went on by land to Bethlehem, where he spent six months with Jerome, whom he praises highly both for virtue and learning. Posthumianus then returned to Alexandria, and thence went to the Thebaid, spending a year and seven months visiting its monasteries and hermitages. He penetrated into the Sinaitic peninsula, saw the Red Sea, and ascended Mount Sinai. After three years' absence he returned, taking 30 days from Alexandria to Marseilles. He may have been the priest of that name who was present at the death of Paulinus (Uranius, *Ep.* in *Patr. Lat.* liii. 861). [F.D.]

Potamiaena (June 28), one of the most celebrated martyrs at Alexandria in the persecution of Severus, being a virgin distinguished alike for her beauty, chastity, and courage. Eusebius (*H. E.* vi. 5) relates how she was cruelly tortured, and death finally inflicted by burning pitch poured slowly about her from feet to head. Her story is also given by Palladius (*Hist. Laus.* 3). [G.T.S.]

Pothinus (*Photinus*, Greg. Tur. *Fotinus*), martyr, first bp. of Lyons in the 2nd cent. Who consecrated him, and in what year, is unknown, though a desire to find an apostolic foundation has suggested to different writers the names of SS. Peter, John, and Polycarp. His name suggests that he was a Greek. Of his episcopate we have no record beyond the account of his martyrdom by pagans, with 47 others, contained in the letter of the Christians of Lyons and Vienne to the churches of Asia and Phrygia, which Eusebius preserves. Oppressed with infirmities and more than 90 years old, he was dragged by soldiers before the tribunal, where he comported himself with dignity. To the question of the president what the Christians' God might be, he replied, "If thou wert worthy, thou shouldst know." The blows and ill-usage of the crowd as he was carried back to prison caused his death two days later. His successor was St. Irenaeus. Eus. *H. E.* v. 1; Greg. Tur. *Hist. Franc.* i. 27; *Mirac.* lib. i.; *de Glor. Mart.* 49, 50 sqq.; *Gall. Christ.* iv. 4. [S.A.B.]

Praedestinatus. The author known by this name wrote an anonymous work, first pub. in 1643 from a MS. in the Cathedral Library of Rheims by Sirmond, who somewhat inappropriately gave it its title from those *against* whom it was directed, and several times reprinted, *e.g.* by Migne (*Patr. Lat.* liii.), and bk. i. by Oehler in his *Corpus Haeresiologicum*.

The author complains that men were passing themselves off as of the household of faith who really were most treacherous enemies of the church. These men taught that certain were by God's foreknowledge so predestined to death that neither Christ's passion nor baptism, faith, hope, nor charity could help them. They might fast, pray, and give alms, but nothing could avail them, because they had not been predestined to life. On the other hand, those who had received this predestination might neglect and despise all righteousness, yet the gate of life would be opened to them without knocking, while against others who knocked, nay shouted, for admission, it would remain firmly closed. A work by one of these heretics had lately fallen into the writer's hands, and it was necessary to drag it to light and completely refute it. This accordingly is done in the present treatise, consisting of three books. In bk. i. the author clears himself of all suspicion of sympathy with heresy of any kind by enumerating and reprobating the 90 heresies by which up to his time Christ's truth had been perverted, the last and worst being that of the Predestinarians. It determines limits for the date of the book that in this list the last but one is the Nestorian heresy. From this and the silence about Eutychianism we may infer that it was written between 431 and 449, just the period when the semi-Pelagian controversy was most active. The author professes that his heretical catalogue was epitomized from Hyginus, Polycrates, Africanus, Hesiodus, Epiphanius, and Philaster, who, he tells us, wrote against different heresies in this chronological order. It is remarkable that the first four of these confutations of heresy are not mentioned by any one else, but still more remarkable that the writer is silent as to his obligations to the tract on heresies which Augustine addressed to Quodvultdeus, although his list of 90 heresies agrees, article by article, with Augustine's list of 88, with the addition of the two later heresies, Nestorianism and Predestinarianism, while the substance of each article is manifestly taken from Augustine. These unfavourable suspicions of the writer's literary morality are confirmed as we proceed. It is the author's plan to mention with each heresy the name of the orthodox writer who refutes it. We are thus told of a number of personages whom no one else mentions—Diodorus of Crete who refuted the Secundians, Philo the Alogi, Theodotus of Pergamus the Colorbasians, Crato, a Syrian bishop, who refuted the Theodotians, Tranquillus the Noetians, Euphranon of Rhodes the Severians, and a host of others of whom we should expect to hear elsewhere if they were not imaginary personages. Moreover, when Praedestinatus ascribes the confutation to real persons his assertions are usually chronologically impossible. Thus he makes the apostle Thomas confute Saturninus, Barnabas in Cyprus the Carpocratians; he makes Alexander, who was bp. of Rome at the very beginning of the 2nd cent., write against Heracleon, who lived in the latter half of the century; the Tertullianists are condemned by Soter, who must have been dead 30 years before Tertullian separated from the church; the imaginary heresiologist, Hesiod of Corinth, is made to be the bishop who first opposed Arius, and in answer to whose prayers that heretic died. We have thus before us, not inaccurate history but unscrupulous and unskilful invention, and it can only be from want of acquaintance with his character as a writer that he is ever cited as an historical authority. [G.S.]

Praxeas, a somewhat mysterious heretic about whom various theories have been held. He was a Monarchian and Patripassian. Tertullian wrote a treatise against him and places his scene of activity first of all at Rome, but never mentions Noetus, Epigonus, Cleomenes, Sabellius or Callistus. On the other hand, Hippolytus, who denounces these in his controversial works for the very same tenets, never once mentions Praxeas as teaching at Rome or anywhere else. Some have regarded Praxeas as simply a nick-name. Thus De Rossi (*Bullet.* 1866, p. 70) identifies him with Epigonus, Hagemann (*Gesch. der röm. Kirche.* § 234) with Callistus. Döllinger however (*Hippol. u. Kallist.* § 198) and Lipsius (*Chronolog. der röm. Bisch.* § 175) maintain that Praxeas was a real person who first of all started the Monarchian and Patripassian heresy in Rome, but so long before the age of Hippolytus that his name and memory had faded in that city. They fix his period of activity in Rome during the earliest years of Victor, A.D. 189-198, or even the later years of his predecessor Eleutherus. This explanation, however, seems to ignore the fact that Hippolytus must have been a full-grown man all through Victor's episcopate, as he expressly asserts (*Refut.* ix. 6) that he and Callistus were about the same age. Praxeas remained but a short time in Rome, and the shortness of his stay offers a better explanation of Hippolytus's silence. He then proceeded to Carthage, where he disseminated his views. Tertullian (*adv. Prax.*) attacks the heresy under the name of Praxeas, the local teacher, but was really attacking Zephyrinus and Callistus. The facts of his life we gather from Tertullian's notices in c. 1. He was a confessor from Asia Minor, where he had been imprisoned for the faith. Asia Minor was then the seed-plot of Monarchian views. He came to Rome when the Montanist party had just gained over the pope. Praxeas converted the pope back to his own opinion, which was hostile to the Montanists. Most critics agree that the pope so converted by Praxeas was Eleutherus: cf. Bonwetsch's *Montanismus*, § 174; Hilgenfeld's *Ketzergeschichte*, p. 569. Dr. Salmon, however, maintains that it was Zephyrinus. [MONTANUS.] By this, says Tertullian, Praxeas did a twofold service for the devil at Rome, "he drove away prophecy and he introduced heresy. He put to flight the Paraclete and he crucified the Father." He then went to Carthage, where he induced some to adopt his opinions. Tertullian opposed him prior to 202, according to Hilgenfeld (*l.c.* p. 618), and converted Praxeas himself, who acknowledged his error in a document extant among the Catholic party when Tertullian wrote. Praxeas then seems to have disappeared from Carthage, while Tertullian joined the Montanists. The controversy some years later broke out afresh, spreading doubtless from Rome, and then Tertullian wrote his treatise, which he nominally addressed against Praxeas as the best known expositor of these views at Carthage, but really against the Patripassian system in general. Hilgenfeld (*l.c.* p. 619) dates this work *c.* 206; Harnack *c.* 210, *i.e.* about 25 years after the first arrival of Praxeas in Rome; while Dr. Salmon dates it after the death of Callistus in 222: so great is the uncertainty about the chronology of the movement. Harnack's article on "Monarchianismus" in t. x. of Herzog's *Real-Encyclopädie* contains a good exposition of the relation of Praxeas to the Patripassian movement; cf. Lipsius *Tertullian's Schrift wider Praxeas* in *Jahrb. für deutsche Theolog.* t. xiii. (1869) § 701-724. Among patristic writers the only ones who mention Praxeas are pseudo-Tertullian; August, *de Haer.* 41; Praedestinat. 41; and Gennad. *de Eccles. Dog.* 4. [G.T.S.]

Primasius, bp. of Adrumetum or Justinianopolis, in the Byzacene province of N. Africa. He flourished in the middle of 6th cent., and exercised considerable influence on the literary activity of the celebrated theological lawyer JUNILIUS, who dedicated to him his *Institutes*, which spread the views of Theodore of Mopsuestia in the West. Primasius first comes before us in a synod of his province in 541, the decrees of which are known only through Justinian's decrees confirming them, as given in Baronius, *Ann.* 541, n. 10-12. He was sent to Constantinople in connexion with the controversy on the Three Chapters *c.* 551. He assisted in the synod which pope Vigilius held against Theodore Ascidas and was still in Constantinople during the session of the fifth general council, but took no part in it, notwithstanding repeated solicitations (Mansi, ix. 199 seq.). He was one of 16 bishops who signed the Constitutum of pope Vigilius, May 14, 553. When, however, Vigilius accepted the decrees of the fifth council, Primasius signed them also. According to Victor Tunun. (Migne's *Patr. Lat.* t. lxviii. col. 959), other motives conspired to bring about this change. He was at first exiled to a convent, and then the death of Boethius primate of the Byzacene aroused his ambition to be his successor. He gained his point, but, returning home, his suffragans denounced him as guilty of sacrilege and robbery. He died soon afterwards. His writings (*ib.* pp. 407-936) embrace commentaries on St. Paul's Epp. and the Apocalypse; likewise a treatise (now lost), *de Haeresibus*, touching on some points which Augustine did not live to treat with sufficient fullness (Isid. Hispal. *Vir. Ill.* xxii. in *ib.* lxxxiii. 1095; Cave, i. 525; Tillem. xiii. 927, xvi. 21). Our Primasius is sometimes confounded with bp. Primasius of Carthage. The best account of Primasius of Adrumetum is in Kihn's *Theodor von Mopsuestia*, pp. 248-254, where a critical estimate is formed of the sources of his exegetical works. [CHILIASTS.] Cf. also Zahn, *Forschungen*, iv. 1-224 (1891). [G.T.S.]

Primianus, Donatist bp. of Carthage, successor to Parmenian, A.D. 392. Among many things charged against him by the Maximianists, they alleged that he admitted the Claudianists to communion and, when some of the seniors remonstrated with him, encouraged, if he did not even originate, a riotous attack upon them in a church in which some lost their lives. Further, that he was guilty of various acts of an arbitrary and violent kind, superseding bishops, excommunicating and condemning clergymen without sufficient cause, closing his church doors against the people and the imperial officers, and taking possession of buildings to which he had no right. (Aug. *En. in Ps.* 36, 20; *c. Cresc.* iv. 6, 7, and 7, 9, also 48, 58, and 50, 60; *Mon. Vet. Don.* xxxv. ed Oberthür.) At the proceedings before the civil magistrate, arising out of the decision of the council of Bagaia, Primian is said to have taunted his opponents with relying on imperial edicts, while his own party brought with them the Gospels only (Aug. *Post Coll.* xxxi. § 53). When the conference was proposed, he resisted it, remarking with scornful arrogance that "it was not fit that the sons of martyrs should confer with the brood of traditors" (*Carth. Coll.* iii. 116; Aug. *Brevic. Coll.* iii. 4, 4). As one of the seven managers at the conference, A.D. 411, on the Donatist side, he helped to delay the opening of the proceedings and to obstruct them during their progress, but showed no facility in debate (*Brevic. Coll.* ii. 30; *Carth. Coll.* i. 104). He passed a just sentence of condemnation on Cyprian, Donatist bp. of Tubursica, for an act of scandalous immorality (Aug. *c. Petil.* iii. 34, 40). See Dr. Sparrow Simpson, *St. Aug. and Afr. Ch. Divisions* (1910), p. 52. [H.W.P.]

Priscillianus and **Priscillianism.** The Priscillianists, whose doctrines were Manichean and Gnostic in character, were organized as a sect by their founder Priscillian. The spread of the heresy was not wide either in time or space. The sect sprang up and flourished in Spain during the last third of the 4th cent. in the reigns of the emperors Gratian and Maximus. After the synod of Saragossa, 381, it ramified into Aquitaine, but never took deep root beyond the Pyrenees. Where the heresy first appeared in Spain is unrecorded. There it spread through most provinces, especially in cities. The agitation at Cordova, Merida, Avila, Astorga, Saragossa, Toledo, Braga, sufficiently indicates its prevalence and popularity. The council of Bordeaux, 384, followed by the violent measures of Maximus, intensified for a while the enthusiasm of Priscillian's adherents. But in 390, at the synod of Toledo, many leading Priscillianists recanted and were admitted to church communion. The sect continued to diminish in number. Pope Leo I. exerted himself vigorously to repress it. It lingered in Spain till the middle of the 5th cent. After the council of Toledo, 447, and that at Braga in Galicia, 448, especially held against them, they disappear from history. Priscillianism became a remembrance and a suspicion.

Marcus, a native of Memphis in Egypt, introduced the Gnostic and Manichean heresies. Nothing is known of his life beyond his Egyptian origin, his coming to Spain, and his teaching. Two of his followers were Agape, a Spanish lady, and Helpidius, a rhetorician. Their convert was the layman Priscillian, whose place of birth or residence is unknown. He was of good family, wealthy, and well educated. He became at once an ardent proselyte; an apostle of the Oriental doctrines. His character is described by the contemporary historian Sulpicius Severus, in his *Sacred History* (ii. 46). Eloquent, learned, pious, sincere, austere, ardent, and zealous, Priscillian was well fitted to be the apostle and founder of a sect. Modifying and framing the Oriental doctrines into a system of his own, he soon became their able exponent and advocate. Attracting a large following, he organized them into a religious society. Many of the wealthy and noble, and a great number of the people, received his teaching. Some bishops, as well as clergy and laity, became his disciples. The Gnostic mysticism spread rapidly and widely in all Spain.

Among Priscillian's first and most devoted followers were two bishops, Instantius and Salvianus, in the S. of Spain. Adyginus, bp. of Cordova, was the first to oppose the rising sect. He reported the matter to Idatius, bp. of Emerita (Merida), and took counsel with him. Their conference led to an organized movement against the new errors. All S. Spain became agitated by the controversy. Idatius is blamed as too rough and violent. By intolerant severity he promoted rather than prevented the spread of the sect. Adyginus, dissatisfied with his colleague, became rather the protector of the Priscillianists and incurred thereby much reproach and odium. At length a synod was to be held at Caesar-Augusta (Saragossa) on the Ebro, a site sufficiently far north from the localities where the Priscillianists and the orthodox were in hostility to be neutral ground, and also having the advantage of nearness to Gaul. It was proposed to gather there the bishops of Spain and Aquitaine. The synod was held in 380. The Priscillianists did not venture to appear. In their absence their opinions were condemned. The four leaders, Instantius and Salvianus the bishops, Helpidius and Priscillian the laymen, were excommunicated. The bp. of Cordova fell under the lash of the leaders of the synod. He had received into terms of communion some of the heretics. The council anathematized all who shared or connived at the new errors of faith and practice. The task of promulgating the decrees and executing the ecclesiastical sentences was given to Ithacius, bp. of Sossuba. The important and lamentable result of the synod was the assumption by Ithacius of the leadership of the persecuting party.

A preconcerted counter-movement now began on the part of the Priscillianists. At the hands of Instantius and Salvianus, Priscillian received episcopal ordination. His see was Avila (Abila) on the Adaja, a tributary of the Douro, midway between Salamanca and Madrid (Hieron. *de Script. Eccl.*). This measure of defiance shewed the strength of his party. It led to further progress towards persecution. On behalf of the church authorities, Idacius and Ithacius applied to the secular government. Aid was brought against the heretics. Powers were asked for execution of the decree of the synod, and in 381 Gratian granted a rescript, excluding all heretics from the use of the churches and ordering them to be driven into exile. The Priscillianists were thus cut off from civil protection. Vigorous defensive measures were necessary to their very existence. An appeal was proposed by them to the two most eminent bishops of the West, Damasus of Rome and Ambrose of Milan. Their influence, it was hoped, might lead to a rescinding of the imperial decision. Instantius, Salvianus, and Priscillian went to Rome to clear themselves and their party in the papal court. On their way they penetrated into Interior Aquitaine, perhaps to try measures of conciliation among the bishops of that province, who had condemned them unseen and unknown at Saragossa. The seeds of the heresy were sown by them as they travelled. Elusa (Eluso) near Eauze, a town on the Gelise near Auch, is especially mentioned. All the church centres were, however, hostile to them. They were vigorously repulsed from Bordeaux (Burdegala), by the vigilance of bp. Delphinus. On their journey they were joined by many from Gaul whom they had infected with their errors. Euchrocia and her daughter Procula, amongst these, ministered of their substance to Priscillian and his colleagues. A promiscuous crowd of others, especially women, are mentioned. In consequence, injurious reports, probably calumnies, were vigorously circulated against Priscillian and his retinue.

On their arrival at Rome the Priscillianists were repulsed by pope Damasus. They retraced their steps to Milan, and found Ambrose, whose power and reputation were at their height, steadily opposed to them.

The Priscillianists put on a bold front and began aggressive measures against their assailants. The wealth of Priscillian and his followers was liberally employed. "The silver spears" were now in the hands of the partisans on both sides. Macedonius, the master of the offices (*magister officiorum*), was won over to the interests of Priscillian and his party. By his powerful influence a rescript from Gratian protecting them was obtained. The Priscillianists were to be restored to their churches and sees. Instantius and Priscillian, returning to Spain, regained their sees and churches. All things seemed turned in their favour. Idacius and Ithacius, though for the moment powerless, had not ceased to make a show of resistance. The Priscillianists charged them with causing divisions and disturbing the peace of the church, and Ithacius was compelled to fly. At Trèves resided the Caesar who ruled Gaul, Spain, and Britain. Ithacius escaped thither from Spain. Gregory, the prefect there, warmly espoused his cause and strove to bring the complaints of the orthodox bishops again before Gratian. The Priscillianists had, however, friends at court powerful enough to ward off the danger. The cause was taken out of the hands of Gregory and transferred to the court of Volventius the vicar of Spain.

An unlooked-for political change now came. The overthrow and assassination at Paris of the unpopular Gratian, the usurpation of the purple by Clemens Maximus, his proclamation as emperor by his soldiers in Britain, his triumphant entrance into Gaul, with the consequent official changes, destroyed all the bright hopes of the Priscillianists. The fortunes of their adversaries revived. On the arrival of Maximus at Trèves in 384 Ithacius brought a formal accusation with heavy charges against

Priscillian and his followers. Maximus, a Spaniard by birth, listened to the Spanish bishops and reversed the vacillating policy of Gratian, treating the matter not as one of ecclesiastical rivalry, but as one of morality and society. In his letter afterwards to Siricius, who succeeded Damasus in 384 in the see of Rome, he expressly dwells upon these points and glories in the part he had consequently taken against the heresy of Priscillian. Both parties were summoned to a synod at Bordeaux in 385. Instantius and Priscillian were the first to appear. Instantius was declared to have forfeited his bishopric. Priscillian resolved to forestall the expected hostile judgment and "appeal unto Caesar." No protest was made. The appeal was allowed. A purely spiritual offence was remitted for criminal trial to a secular tribunal. In due course both parties appeared before Maximus at Trèves.

At Trèves there was one at this crisis of the church whose prophetic insight saw the real significance of the issues at stake, Martin, bp. of Tours, whose influence was then at its height. Through his mediation between the contending parties, the trial of Priscillian was delayed, Maximus for a while yielding to his protests, even consenting to promise him that no life should be sacrificed. But at last St. Martin, at the call of other duties, was obliged to withdraw from Trèves. The emperor was now surrounded by other influences. By Idacius and Ithacius, ably supported by two bishops of a like stamp, Magnus and Rufus, powerful at court, Maximus was unremittingly urged to take severe measures.

The trial of the Priscillianists, once resolved upon, was soon brought about and they became a defenceless prey to their enemies. Their "appeal unto Caesar" was truly an appeal to a pitiless Nero. As a stroke of state policy nothing could be wiser in the eyes of the adherents of Maximus than their destruction. Both pagan and Christian authorities attribute mercenary motives to the emperor and state that the possessions of the rich Priscillian and of his followers excited his cupidity (Sulp. Sev. *Dialog.* iii. 9; *Panegyr. of Lat. Pac. Drep. on Theodosius*, *Panegyr. Vet.* xvi. 29). At the same time there could not be a more brilliant inauguration of the new reign than a vigorous assertion of orthodoxy on the lines of the now famous Theodosian decrees.

Priscillian and his chief followers were condemned to death by the imperial consistory at Trèves. Several others, after confiscation of their goods, were banished to the Scilly Isles, others into Gaul. Priscillian is recorded as the first of those who suffered death ("gladio perempti"). With him died two presbyters, lately become disciples, Felicissimus and Armenius, and Latronianus a poet and Euchrocia the rich and noble matron of Bordeaux. Instantius, deposed from his bishopric by the synod of Bordeaux, and Tiberianus were banished to the desolate Scilly Isles. Asarinus and Aurelius, two deacons, were executed. Tertullus, Potamius, and Johannes, as meaner followers who turned king's evidence, were temporarily banished within Gaul.

The immediate consequences were not reassuring to the persecuting party. At Trèves a violent strife arose between the bishops present on the merits of Priscillian's execution. Theognistes, a bishop of independent mind, boldly led the non-contents, refusing church communion to Ithacius and the others guilty of the judicial bloodshed. In Spain the Priscillianist enthusiasm was for a while intensified. The number of followers grew. The bodies of those who had suffered at Trèves were brought to Spain and their obsequies celebrated with great pomp. Priscillian, before revered as a saint, was now, says Sulpicius, worshipped as a martyr. Signs were not wanting, and terrified the orthodox, that the Priscillianist society aimed at shrouding themselves under the guise of a secret religious association.

Additional severities were proposed. Maximus resolved to send military tribunes to Spain with unlimited powers. They were to investigate charges of heresy, examine heretics, take life and property from the guilty. They were men little likely to temper justice with mercy. At this juncture Martin of Tours returned to Trèves. No efforts could induce him to be reconciled to the promoters and abettors of the late executions. The persuasion and threats of the emperor failing to move him, he was dismissed the imperial presence in anger. Tidings reached Martin that the tribunes had been really sent to Spain. He hurried to the palace, though it was night, and agreed to unite with the bishops in church fellowship. The emperor yielded to his importunity and Martin's firmness and zeal on the side of humanity were rewarded. The tribunes were recalled and the peninsula spared the horrors of a religious proscription.

The schism continued some time between those that approved and those that condemned the severities against Priscillian. For 15 years the contention was extreme, and the merits of the controversy long continued to be canvassed. The violent means had certainly not extinguished the heresy, which seemed even to take deeper root in Spain. In 400 at a council at Toledo many Priscillianists came over and were readmitted to Catholic communion. Amongst these was Dictinnius, a Priscillianist bishop, author of *The Scales* (Libra), wherein Priscillianist opinions were expounded and advocated. In 415 a Spanish presbyter, Orosius, wrote to Augustine concerning the sect. A long letter of Augustine is extant, written to Ceretius, a bishop, respecting the apocryphal Priscillianist Scriptures, especially a hymn attributed to Christ. Forty years later Turribius, bp. of Astorga, wrote in sorrow and perplexity to pope Leo I., asking advice for dealing with these insidious and dangerous adversaries. Two councils pursuant to Leo's recommendation were held: one at Toledo in 447, the other at Braga in Galicia in 448, where Priscillianism was condemned with the usual anathemas. A last contemporary mention of the Priscillianists comes in combination with the Arians, in the Acts of the council of Braga, in 563.

No ancient writer has given an accurate account of the Priscillianist doctrine. Our knowledge has to be gathered from the meagre accounts of their adversaries, the correspondence of eminent men of the time, the acts and canons of councils, the church histories, and a few verbal allusions in contemporary pagan writers. The Priscillianist system, already sufficiently dark and perplexed, has had new obscurity added by unstinted misrepresentation. The general outline may be made out of their opinions, fantastic allegories, daring cosmogonies, astrological fancies, combined with the severest asceticism. It is easier to compare the general resemblances of their doctrine to Cabalism, Syrian and Egyptian Gnosticism, Manicheism, Persian and Indian Orientalism, than to detect, analyse, and assign the differences.

There are no authentic extant records of the Priscillianist writers. A fragment of a letter of Priscillian himself has come down to us in quotation (Orosii *Common. in Aug. Op.*). There are allusions to a multitude of apocryphal scriptures which they used, thus differing from most heretical sects in accepting all apocryphal and canonical books as scripture, explaining and adapting them to their purpose in a mystical manner.

Our clearest account of their tenets is in the controversial correspondence slightly later than Priscillian, between Leo the Great and Turribius, bp. of Astorga. The latter summed up the doctrines in 16 articles. Leo replied in a lengthy epistle, commenting seriatim on each proposition (Leo, *Ep.* xv.).

(1) Their wild cosmical speculations were based on the bold Gnostic and Manichean conceptions of a primeval dualism. The two opposite realms of light and darkness, in eternal antagonism, were their basis.

(2) Their anti-materialism led them very far from the sublime simplicity of Scripture. Perplexed by the insoluble problem of the origin of sin, they indulged in most fantastic dreams and myths.

(3) The astrological fatalism which pope Leo condemned so sternly as subversive of all moral distinctions was a striking peculiarity (Leo, *Ep.* xv. 11-12). They believed the 12 signs of the Zodiac to have a mysterious supremacy over the members of the body.

(4) Their Christology is difficult to gather. If they held a Trinity at all, it was but a Trinity of names. Their adversaries accused them of Arianism and Sabellianism. Leo sharply criticizes their application and interpretation of the Scripture attributive of the Redeemer, "the Only-begotten."

(5) Their rigid asceticism resulted directly from their idea of the innate evil of matter. Marriage was proscribed; austerities of all sorts required.

(6) Their moral system plainly deserves the charge of dissimulation. Holding an esoteric and exoteric doctrine, they, with some other theosophic sects, affirmed falsehood allowable for a holy end; absolute veracity only binding between fellow-members. To the unenlightened they need not always and absolutely state the whole truth. This looseness of principle they supported by Scripture, distorting, *e.g.*, Eph. iv. 25 in support of their practice. It was a Priscillianist habit to affect to agree with the multitude, making allowance for what they considered their fleshly notions, and to conceal from them what they regarded them as incapable of comprehending (Dictinnius in *Libra*). In the agitation of controversy some church ecclesiastics were in favour of fighting the Priscillianists with their own weapons. Augustine's treatise *de Mendacio* was expressly written against such laxity. It is easy to see how such practice arose from their principles. We may illustrate it by their Gnostic ideas about Scripture. The Christian Scripture was to them an imperfect revelation. What the Jewish religion was to Christianity, that the Priscillianists considered Christianity was with regard to their own speculations. As the O.T. was full of types and shadows of Christianity, so the N.T. in their hands became a figurative and symbolical exposition and veil of Priscillianism. The outer form was for the ignorant and profane; the inner truth for the wise and initiated. The grace of faith was fitted only for the rude mass of men; to know was the vocation of the privileged, the spiritual, the elect. A step further led the Priscillianist to disregard moral distinctions and believe himself entitled to prevaricate, which often led to things still worse, in his dealings with the common herd (cf. Mansel, *Gnostic Heresies*, lect. xii. p. 196; ix. p. 135; Neander, *Ch. Hist.* ii. p. 26). See *Priscill. qua Supersunt, etc. accedit Orosii Commonitorum, etc.* (Vienna, 1889), in *Corpus Scr. Eccl. Lat.* xviii. [M.B.C.]

Priscus (11), St., 30th archbp. of Lyons, has been the subject of much controversy. Gregory of Tours, the historian, his contemporary, brings against him the gravest charges. According to the *Hist. Franc.* (iv. 36), he set himself, with his wife Susanna, to persecute and destroy those who had been the friends of his predecessor St. Nicetius, out of malice and jealousy, and never wearied of declaiming against his memory. The *Vitae Patrum* (viii. 5) also has an instance of his contempt for the same prelate, whose chaplain he is said to have been. On the other hand, he is numbered by the church among the saints. He was present at numerous councils, the 4th of Paris in 573, Châlons in 579, Mâcon in 581 or 583, 3rd of Lyons in 581, another at Lyons in 583, Valence in 584 or 585, and the 2nd of Mâcon in 585, at some of which he presided, and at the last was honoured in the preface with the dignified title, very rare in the West, of patriarcha (Mansi, ix. 949; Ceillier, xi. 896). For these and other reasons the Bollandists (*Acta SS.* Jun. vi. 120-127) refuse credence to Gregory's charges. [S.A.B.]

Privatus (2), once bp. of the important but shortlived city of Lambaesis in Numidia, the present *Tazzût* or *Tezzulot* (Momms.). He was condemned for heresy and *multa et gravia delicta*, by 90 bishops at a council under Donatus, bp. of Carthage (Cypr. *Ep.* 59, xiii.; 10), and apparently under the Roman bishopric of Fabian (A.D. 240, Morcelli). Apparently the council was held at Lambaesis, and afterwards Donatus and Fabian issued letters condemnatory of Privatus and his opinions.

In 250 Privatus visited Rome, and Cyprian, apprehensive of his influence, warned the clergy against him. They replied (*Ep.* xxxvi. 4) that they had already detected him in an attempt to obtain *litterae* (*communicatoriae*) from them fraudulently.

He presented himself (*vetus haereticus*) and desired to be heard on behalf of the party who took the lax view as to the *lapsi*, at the 2nd council Id. Mai., 252, and, on being rejected, consecrated Fortunatus pseudo-bishop (*Ep.* lix. 13), assisted by a pseudo-bishop, Felix, of his own consecration, and by Jovinus and Maximus, and a lapsed bishop, Repostus Suturnicensis. [E.W.B.]

Probus (4), Sextus Anicius Petronius (*Corp. Inscrip.* vi. 1, n. 1752), a member of one of the most illustrious families in Rome, consul with Gratian in A.D. 371, and four times pretorian prefect of Italy, Illyricum, the Gauls, and Africa. He had also been proconsul in Africa in 358 (*Cod. Theod.* xi. 36; xiii.). He was appointed pretorian prefect of Italy and Illyricum in 368 (Ammian. xxvii. 1). During his tenure of office he chose St. Ambrose, then a young advocate, as one of his council, and afterwards appointed him governor of Liguria and Aemilia with the rank of consular. On this occasion Probus uttered the words, afterwards considered prophetic, "Go, act not as a judge but as a bishop"; and many years later he sent one of his servants, who was possessed with a devil, to be healed by him (Paulinus, *Vita Ambr.* 5, 8, 21, in Migne, *Patr. Lat.* xiv. 28, 29, 34). Probus continued prefect of Italy until Valentinian died in 374. He appears as pretorian prefect of Italy in 380, and as pretorian prefect in 383-384 (*Cod. Theod.* vi. 28 ii.; xi. 13 i.; vi. 30 vi.). After the murder of Gratian in 383 he acted as regent to Valentinian II. in Italy, accompanying him and his mother Justina in their flight to Thessalonica on the invasion of Maximus in 387 (Socr. *H. E.* v. 11; Soz. *H. E.* vii. 13). He died before the end of 394 (Claudian. *in Prob. et Ol. Cons.* 31) at the age of nearly 60, after having received baptism (*Corp. Inscrip.* vi. 1, p. 389). It may be owing to his Christianity that Ammianus (xxvii. 11) paints him in such unfavourable colours, a remarkable contrast to the glowing panegyric of Claudian and Ausonius (*Ep.* 16). All agree as to his immense wealth and boundless liberality. His wife Anicia Faltonia Proba belonged to the Anician house, and their sons Probinus and Olybrius had the unique honour of being consuls together in 395. Six letters of Symmachus, who was his intimate friend (*Epp.* i. 56-61), are addressed to him (Tillem. *Emp.* v. 42, 72). [F.D.]

Prochorus (*Πρόχορος*), the name of one of the seven deacons in Acts vi. 5. Later tradition makes him one of the 70 disciples, and afterwards bp. of Nicomedia in Bithynia (cf. the list of the 70 in the so-called Dorotheus).

Under his name has been preserved an apocryphal *History of the Apostle John*, first published in the Greek text by Michael Neander in the appendix to the 3rd ed. of his Graeco-Latin version of Luther's Short Catechism, along with a Latin trans. by Sebastian Castalio (*Catechesis Martini Lutheri parva graeco-latina postremum recognita*, Basileae, 1567, pp. 526-663).

The narrative begins with the parting of the apostles and St. John's mission into Asia. In punishment for a first refusal to go by sea John suffers shipwreck, but arrives safely at Ephesus, accompanied by Prochoros his disciple. Here he takes service in a public bath; restores to life the owner's son, who has been slain by a demon, destroys the image of Diana (Artemis) and expels the demon which had harboured there; is banished himself, but soon returns to be again exiled to Patmos by command of the emperor. On the voyage thither he restores a drowned man to life, stills a tempest, and heals a sick guardsman. The greater part of the subsequent narrative is occupied with the wondrous deeds of the apostle in his banishment, his victorious encounters with demons and sorcerers, his refutation of a learned Jew in a public dispute, numerous miracles of healing and raising from the dead, and triumphant issues out of every conflict in which his persecuting enemies involve him. After a residence in Patmos of 15 years he has converted almost the whole island. Receiving permission to return to Ephesus, he first retires to a solitary place in the island (*κατάπαυσις*) and there dictates his gospel to Prochoros, and when finished leaves it behind as a memorial of his work in Patmos. He then goes by ship to Ephesus, and dwells there in the house of Domnus, whom he had formerly in his youth raised to life. After residing 26 years more at Ephesus he buries himself alive. Prochoros and six other disciples dig his grave, and when he has laid himself in it, cover him with earth. On the grave being subsequently reopened, the apostle has disappeared.

This writing of the alleged Prochoros is, in its main contents at least, in no way a recension of the old Gnostic Acts of John, but the independent work of some Catholic author. Though the writer makes some use of the Gnostic Acts, he can hardly have known them in their original text. Its purpose seems to be to supplement the Ephesian histories of the apostle which already existed in a Catholic recension by a detailed account of his deeds and adventures in Patmos. The author can have had no local interest in its composition. His notions of the situation, size, and general characteristics of the island, which he certainly never saw, are most extraordinary. In constructing his narrative he has made only partial use of older materials. By far the most of these narrations of the pretended Prochoros are free inventions of his own. None betray any leaning towards Gnosticism. The author shews no tendency to ascetic views except where he draws from older sources; and even in discourses attributed to the apostle the theological element is quite subordinate. He takes no notice of the Apocalypse, and, in opposition to the older tradition, places the composition of the gospel in Patmos. The account given of this is certainly not derived from the Gnostic Περίοδοι.

The date of composition cannot be later than the middle of 5th cent., since it is made use of, not only in the *Chronicon Paschale* (pp. 761, 470, ed. Bonn; cf. Zahn, pp. 162 sqq.), but also in the accounts of the apostles attributed to Dorotheus, Hippolytus, and others. The *terminus a quo* is the end of the 4th or beginning of the 5th cent., since, from that time onwards and not before, Catholic writers appear to have known the Gnostic histories of the apostles. With this, moreover, agrees the fact that the author can assume a universal diffusion of Christianity in Ephesus and the Aegean Archipelago. It is more difficult to determine the place of composition. The author is certainly not a native of Asia Minor, but rather perhaps of Antioch, or the coast region of Syria and Palestine. He is better acquainted with the topography of those parts than with the neighbourhood of Ephesus. Of his personal circumstances we can only say that he certainly was not a monk; perhaps he was a married cleric, possibly a layman. Cf. Zahn, *Acta Joannis* (Erlangen, 1880); Lipsius, *Die Apocryphen Apostelgeschichten*, i. 355-408. [R.A.L.]

Proclus (1) (*Proculus*), a Montanist teacher, and probably the introducer of Montanism into Rome at the very beginning of the 3rd cent. For the account given by Tertullian (*adv. Prax.* 1) of the apparently favourable reception the new prophesying at first met with at Rome, and its subsequent rejection, see MONTANISM. Proclus was publicly opposed by Caius, commonly called a Roman presbyter, and the record of their disputation, though now lost, was read by Eusebius, and is mentioned by several other writers. [CAIUS.] Pseudo-Tertullian states (*Haer.* 21) that the Montanists were divided into two sections by the Patripassian controversy, Proclus leading the section whose doctrine on that subject agreed with that of the church, and Aeschines the opposite section. This schism among the Montanists is mentioned also by Hippolytus (*Ref.* viii. 19).

We can scarcely be wrong in identifying Proclus the Montanist with the Proculus whom Tertullian in his tract against the Valentinians (c. 5) calls "Proculus noster, virginis senectae et Christianae eloquentiae dignitas." He there refers to him as one who, like Justin Martyr, Miltiades, and Irenaeus, successfully confuted heresy. He is also named as a leader of the Montanists by Pacian (*Ep. ad Sympron.*), and no doubt it is his name which is disguised as Patroclus in the MSS. of Theodoret (*Haer. Fab.* iii. 2). [G.S.]

Proclus (2), St., patriarch of Constantinople. The friend and disciple of Chrysostom, he became secretary to Atticus the patriarch, who ordained him deacon and priest. Sisinnius, the successor of Atticus, consecrated him bp. of Cyzicus, but the people there refused to receive him, and he remained at Constantinople. On the death of Sisinnius, the famous NESTORIUS succeeded, and early in 429, on a festival of the Virgin, Proclus preached the celebrated sermon on the Incarnation inserted in the beginning of the Acts of the council of Ephesus. When Maximianus died on Thur. before Easter, 434, Proclus was, by the permission of Theodosius, immediately enthroned by the bishops at Constantinople. His first care was the funeral of his predecessor, and he then sent both to Cyril and John of Antioch the usual synodical letters announcing his appointment, both of whom approved of it. In 436 the bishops of Armenia consulted him upon certain doctrines prevalent in their country and attributed to Theodore of Mopsuestia, asking for their condemnation. Proclus replied (437) in the celebrated letter known as the Tome of Proclus, which he sent to the Eastern bishops asking them to sign it and to join in condemning the doctrines arraigned by the Armenians. They approved of the letters, but from admiration of Theodore hesitated to condemn the doctrines attributed to him. Proclus replied that while he desired the extracts subjoined to his Tome to be condemned, he had not attributed them to Theodore or any individual, not desiring the condemnation of any person. A rescript from Theodosius procured by Proclus, declaring his wish that all should live in peace and that no imputation should be made against any one who died in communion with the church, appeased the storm. The whole affair shewed conspicuously the moderation and tact of Proclus. In 438 he transported to Constantinople from Comana, and interred with great honour in the church of the Apostles, the remains of his old master St. Chrysostom, and thereby reconciled to the church his adherents who had separated in consequence of his condemnation. In 439, at the request of a deputation from Caesarea in Cappadocia, he selected as their new bishop Thalassius, who was about to be appointed pretorian prefect of the East. In the time of Proclus the Trisagion came into use. The occasion is said to have been a time when violent earthquakes lasted for four months at Constantinople, so that the people were obliged to leave the city and encamp in the fields. Proclus died most probably in July 446. He appears to have been wise, moderate, and conciliatory, desirous, while strictly adhering to orthodoxy himself, to win over those who differed from him by persuasion rather than force.

His works (Migne, *Patr. Gk.* lxv. 651) consist of 20 sermons (some of doubtful authenticity), 5 more pub. by Card. Mai (*Spic. Rom.* iv. xliii. lxxviii.), of which 3 are preserved only in a Syriac version, the Greek being lost; 7 letters, along with several addressed to him by other persons; and a few fragments of other letters and sermons. Socr. *H. E.* vii. xxvi., and *passim*; Theophan. *sub an.* 430; Tillem. *Mém. eccl.* xiv. 704; *AA. SS.* Act. x. 639. [F.D.]

Procopius (8) **Gazaeus**, Christian sophist, *temp.* Justin and Justinian (518-565). Of his life we know only that he was the preceptor of Choricius the sophist. His fame rests on his Scripture commentaries. These, though diffuse, are but abridgements of the collections he had made (see his Prolog. to the commentary on Gen.); his profession of belief as to the nature of the Triune God, and the importance, authority, and interpretation of Scripture, is very satisfactory. His style is highly polished and concise. He must be distinguished from his contemporary sophist, PROCOPIUS (9) OF CAESAREA. His collected works are pub. by Migne, *Patr. Gk.* lxxxvii. in 3 parts, but his commentaries have also appeared separately. Of more doubtful authenticity and probably belonging to Procopius Caesarensis, though commonly attributed to P. Gazaeus is *Panegyricus in Imp. Anastasium* (Gk. and Lat.) in *Corp. Script. Hist. Byz.* (Bonnae, 1829), pp. 489 seq. and Migne *u.s.* pt. iii.; *Descriptio Basilicae Sanctae Sophiae* (Gk. and Lat.) Migne, *ib.*; and *Menodia in S. Sophiam terraemotu collapsum* (Gk. and Lat.) in Migne, *ib.* pt. ii. (Cellier, *Aut. Sacr.* xi. 176 seq.; Cave, *Hist. Lit.* i. 504; Fabricius, *Bibl. Graec.* vi. 258; vii. 535; viii. 375; ix. 447; L. Eisenhofer, *Procopius von Gaza*, Freiburg i/Br. 1897.) [J.G.]

Procopius (9) **of Caesarea**, Byzantine historian. Born at Caesarea in Palestine, he went during the reign of Anastasius to Constantinople, where he taught rhetoric and pleaded in the courts.

We meet him first *c.* 527, when he was sent by Justinian to accompany Belisarius, as secretary and privy councillor, in his expeditions against the Persians. In 533 he was with him in Africa, warring against the Vandals, and, after their subjection, was left behind to reduce the conquered into order. A mutiny of the soldiers drove him in 536 to Sicily, which Belisarius was then engaged in reducing, and he accompanied the latter into Italy in his campaign against the Goths. In 542 Procopius returned to Constantinople, where he seems to have remained to the end of his life, devoting himself mainly to writing a history of the expeditions, in which he had borne no unimportant part.

It is a question whether he was a Christian or a heathen. He speaks of the church of St. Sophia at Constantinople as the temple of the great Christ of God (*τὸ ἱερὸν τοῦ μεγάλου Χριστοῦ τοῦ Θεοῦ*, *de Bell. Vandal.* i. 6). He describes Jesus as the Son of God Who went about clothed with a human body, shewing that He was the Son of God both by His sinless life and His superhuman deeds (*de Bell. Pers.* ii. 12). Christians are in his eyes those who have right opinions respecting God (*de Bell. Vandal.* i. 21). The Virgin Mary is often mentioned under the name *θεοτόκος* (*e.g. de Aedif.* v. 7). The Hellenic religion is alluded to as impiety (*ib.* vi. 4). On the other hand, he often alludes alike to Christians and heretics as if he occupied a calm position superior to them both (*de Bell. Pers.* i. 18). The controversies of the church had done much to alienate him from doctrinal Christianity; and, though he does speak at times as if he had embraced some of its distinct tenets, it is hardly possible to think that he had done so in the sense of regarding them as an express revelation of divine truth to man.

His works consist of a history of the Persian war from 408 to 549; a history of the war with the Vandals in Africa from 395 to 545; a history of the Gothic wars in Italy from 487 to 574; a work *de Aedificiis Justiniani Imp.*; and a work entitled *Anecdota* or a secret history of Justinian, the empress Theodora, Belisarius, his wife Antonina, and others of the court. This last, intended for publication only after the author's death, is described by Cave in the strongest terms of reprobation, as written to shew the court of Justinian as no better than a *diabolorum lerna*, and as exhibiting such audacity, falsehood, calumny, and charges of unheard-of crimes, that it has been doubted whether Procopius really wrote it. (See Schröckh, vol. xvi. p. 168, etc.)

As to the value of the three works first mentioned there can be no doubt. Procopius had enjoyed most favourable opportunities of acquainting himself with the events he describes. Gibbon draws largely on the "sober testimony of Procopius," and also describes him as "the gravest historian of the times" (c. xxxviii.).

De Aedificiis is throughout a tribute to the glory of Justinian. It is devoted to a description of the great buildings, temples, forts, castles, bridges, monasteries, and structures of every description erected by Justinian in all the different parts of the Roman empire.

The works of Procopius may be consulted with advantage for information on such points as the condition of the nations and tribes of the Abasgi, Bruchi, Alani, Franks, Goths, Huns, Persians, Vandals; the wars of Belisarius, his character and life; geographical notices of towns, rivers, seas, mountains, and countries over a widespread area; the names of the bishops, and the ecclesiastical occurrences of his time, etc. The best ed. is that of Dindorf in the *Corpus Script. Hist. Byz.*, with the Latin trans. of Maltritus. [W.M.]

Proculus, Montanist. [PROCLUS.]

Proculus (7), bp. of Marseilles, at the council of Aquileia, A.D. 381, where he joined in condemning the errors of Palladius and Secundinianus (Ambros. *Ep.* viii. pp. 916 (786), 935 (802), 939 (805), ed. Migne). At the council of Turin, A.D. 399, or more probably 401, though Fleury places it as late as 404, Proculus claimed the primacy as metropolitan over the churches not only of his own province, but also of Nabonensis Secunda. The council, while ruling that the bishop of the civil metropolis of a province should be regarded as the metropolitan, sanctioned the claim of Proculus for his own life, in consideration of his age and high reputation (Bruns, *Conc.* ii. 114; Baron. vol. v. 397, 43; Fleury, *H. E.* xxi. 52). His high character is acknowledged by St. Jerome in his letter to Rusticus, A.D. 411 (*Ep.* 125, 20); but pope Zosimus seems to have had a strong feeling against him, and in 417 decreed that Patroclus, bp. of Arles from 412, was entitled to rank as metropolitan. Whether our Proculus was the Gallic bp. of that name to whom St. Augustine wrote in 427 is not quite clear. Tillem. vol. x. pp. 698, 699; Ceillier, vii. pp. 528-537. [H.W.P.]

Prodicus, a Gnostic teacher of 2nd cent., concerning whom trustworthy information is very scanty. He is not mentioned by the principal writers on heresies, Irenaeus, Hippolytus, Epiphanius, or Philaster. Tertullian twice mentions him (*Scorpiace* 15; *adv. Prax.* 3), both times in company with Valentinus, in such a way as to suggest that he regarded the two heretics as of the same school. In the first passage Prodicus and Valentinus are spoken of as teaching that Christ did not wish His disciples to confess Him publicly if that would expose their lives to danger; in the second they are described as introducing in opposition to the Creator, not a single rival god like Marcion, but a multiplicity of gods. Our only other trustworthy information about Prodicus is in three notices by Clement of Alexandria. The first (*Strom.* i. 15, p. 357) states that those who followed the heresy of Prodicus boasted of possessing secret books of Zoroaster. Apparently in Clement's time Prodicus was dead, but a sect founded by him still in existence. *Strom.* vii. 7, p. 854 states that his followers objected to the practice of prayer. Clement does not state their grounds of objection. The most characteristic notice of the sect is (*ib.* iii. 4, p. 525) that his followers who claim to be Gnostics (falsely so called) declare that they are by nature children of the first god, and privileged by their noble birth to live as they choose, being "lords of the sabbath," and "as king's children above the law"; and living "as they chose" meant living very licentiously.

For further information we have to come down to the 5th cent. to Theodoret (*Haer. Fab.* i. 6), who seems to have no knowledge of Prodicus except from Clement, whom he quotes, mixing up, however, some of the things which Clement says about other licentious Gnostic sects; *e.g.* it seems an unauthorized combination of Theodoret's to connect Prodicus with Carpocrates, and we may reject as equally arbitrary Theodoret's assertion that he founded the sect of the Adamites, of which Theodoret would have read in Epiphanius (*Haer.* 52). [G.S.]

Prosper (4), St., a native of Aquitaine, not certainly known to have been in holy orders; probably born *c.* 403. About 426-429 he removed to Marseilles, where he lived as a monk until 440. Some time between 420 and 427 John Cassian put forth in his *Collationes* a doctrine concerning grace and free will contrary to that taught by St. Augustine. This doctrine was taken up warmly by many monks at Marseilles, and both Prosper and Hilary (as to whom see further on), afraid lest a doctrine they believed erroneous should become prevalent among the monks, were thinking of writing to Augustine to request him to explain some of his statements. In the meantime came out Augustine's *Correptione et Gratia*, by which Prosper hoped all doubts would be settled. But those who thought differently only became more obstinate in their opposition. Although Prosper had never seen Augustine, he had written to him by Leontius, a deacon, and received a reply, but neither letter nor reply has survived. He now wrote again to him in 428, as also did Hilary, and his reply to these letters is contained in the consecutive treatises *de Praedestinatione Sanctorum* and *de Dono Perseverantiae*, written either in 428 or 429 (see Aug. *Epp.* 225, 226; and *Opp.* vol. x. pp. 947-1034, ed. Migne). [AUGUSTINE.] Augustine died A.D. 430, and the opponents of his doctrine in Gaul professing willingness to abide by the decision of the Roman pontiff, Hilary and Prosper went to Rome and brought back a letter from Celestine I. to the Gallic bishops, Venerius of Marseilles, Marinus, Leontius of Fréjus, Auxentius of Nice, Auxonius of Viviers, and Arcadius of Venice. In this he speaks of Hilary and Prosper as men "quorum circa Deum nostrum solicitudo laudanda est," and reproved, but without effect, the indiscretion and ill-informed zeal of their opponents (Coelest. *Ep.* xxi. 1, 2). To this letter are subjoined in some editions a series of so-called decisions of the apostolic see concerning grace and free will, which, however, cannot be regarded as authentic. When Leo I. returned from his mission into Gaul, A.D. 440, to be made pope, he persuaded Prosper to accompany him to Rome, and employed him as his secretary (*notarius*). Photius says that he confuted the Pelagians at Rome in the time of Leo, and a MS. of the monastery of Corbey adds, but without mention of authority, that he was sent by him on a similar errand into Campania to oppose Julian of Eclanum. Gennadius says that he was the real author of the epistle of Leo against Eutyches concerning the incarnation of Christ. The chronicle of Marcellinus shews him alive in 463. Fulgentius (*ad. Mon.* i. c. 30) speaks of him as "eruditus et sanctus"; Photius (*Biblioth.* 54) as one who was truly a man of God, but with no other title than Πρόσπειρός τις, who confuted the Pelagians in the time of Leo. Gennadius, no friend to him, speaks of him (*de Scr. Ecc.* 84) as "sermone scholasticus et assertionibus nervosus" (Butler, *Lives of Saints*, June 25; Ceillier, vol. x. p. 278). The letter of Prosper to Augustine describes the view taken at Marseilles and elsewhere concerning predestination. Those who adopted it, he says, believe that mankind has sinned in Adam, and that without God's grace there can be no salvation for any one. God offers salvation to all, so that they who attain faith and receive baptism are in the way of being saved. But before the creation of the world God foreknew who would believe and be saved, and predestined them to His kingdom, being called by grace and worthy of being chosen and of going out of life sound in faith. No man, therefore, need despair of salvation, but this selection on God's part makes human exertion needless either for recovery from sin or for progress in holiness. Thus a doctrine of fatal necessity is introduced. They also think that men can by their own merit, by praying, beseeching, knocking, attain that state of grace in which we are born anew unto Christ. Infants dying without baptism will be saved or not according as God foreknows what their conduct would have been if they had grown up. Christ died for the whole race of mankind, but some miss this salvation because they are known beforehand to have no inclination to receive it. They also deny that the merits of saints proceed from divine grace, and that the number of the elect can be either increased or diminished, and they assert that the only way in which a man is called either to repentance or to progress in holiness is by the exercise of his own free will. They thus place obedience before grace, and the first step towards salvation in him who is to be saved, not in Him Who saves. Great difficulties arise, Prosper says, in his attempts to convince the holders of these opinions of their errors, from his own want of ability and from the great and acknowledged sanctity of their lives, a remark which he probably intends especially of Cassian; and also from the elevation of some of them to the highest office in the church. He therefore begs Augustine to explain (*a*) how Christian faith can escape division through these disputes; (*b*) how free will can be independent of prevenient grace; (*c*) whether God's foreknowledge is absolute and complete; (*d*) whether foreknowledge depends in any way on human purpose, and whether there can be any good which does not proceed from God; (*e*) how those who despair of their own election can escape carelessness of life. He asks him to explain all this in a way consistent with God's previous ordinance of vessels of honour and dishonour. One of these men, Hilary, bp. of Arles, is known to Augustine as an admirer of his doctrine and as wishing to compare his own view with his by writing to him, but whether he will do so or not Prosper does not know (Aug. *Ep.* 225).

The letter of Prosper was accompanied or very soon followed by one on the same subject by Hilary, concerning whom three opinions have been held: (1) That he was the bp. of Arles mentioned by Prosper; (2) that he was a lay monk of Gaul; (3) that he was the Hilary who wrote to Augustine from Syracuse, A.D. 414. That he was a lay monk appears tolerably clear. Augustine replied in the *de Praed.* and *de Don. Persev.*, which are really consecutive volumes of one work.

About the same time Prosper wrote an answer on the same subject to a friend named Ruffinus or Rufinus, about whom nothing is known except that Prosper addresses him as *Sanctitas tua*, perhaps implying a member of a religious community. He wrote partly to vindicate himself from unfavourable reports as to his doctrine, partly to direct his attention to the writings of Augustine and clear them from the accusation of denying free will and setting up Manichean doctrine. The line of argument against Pelagian or semi-Pelagian views is much the same as in the letter to Augustine, but he also mentions the cases of Cornelius and Lydia as instances of persons who had been led by God's grace into the way of eternal life, and as not by any means favouring the Pelagian theory. Why all men are not saved is a mystery of God's, not explicable by human understanding, and of which we may be thankful to be ignorant (*Ep. ad Rufin.*; for a long account of which see Ceillier, vol. x. 279-284).

Prosper also wrote or compiled several works in prose and verse.

I. Verse.—The longest is the poem *de Ingratis*, a term by which he describes those who teach erroneous doctrine about grace, viz. the Pelagians and semi-Pelagians. It is explained clearly in v. 685:

> "Vos soli Ingrati, quos urit gratia, cujus
> Omne opus arbitrio vultis consistere vestro."

It consists of 1002 lines with a short elegiac preface, and is divided into four parts. A theological treatise in verse rather than a poem, it describes accurately the history of the Pelagian doctrine, whose author it calls "coluber Britannus," and mentions the treatment his opinions met at Rome, in the Eastern church and in Africa through the influence mainly of Augustine, "the light of the age." The manner in which the Roman church is spoken of is worthy of notice, v. 40:

> ". . . pestem subeuntem prima recidit
> Sedes Roma Petri, quae pastoralis honoris
> Facta caput mundo, quidquid non possidet armis
> Religione tenet.'

Though without any claim to high rank as poetry, and exhibiting, though in a less degree than does Paulinus, the degenerate standard of its age in language and versification, it treats its subject with well-sustained vigour and generally with clearness, and now and then expresses theological truths, though perhaps with severity, yet with remarkable force and terseness. Ampère condemns what he considers its violence, its hard, melancholy, and desponding tone, amounting sometimes "to a pale reflection of hell." He also points out a similarity in its sentiment to some works of Pascal and the Port-Royalists, which he contrasts unfavourably with the tone of Bossuet in his essay on the fear of God (*Hist. litt. de France*, vol. ii. c. 16, pp. 38-58).

There are other poems of an epigrammatic kind, generally regarded as genuine works of Prosper, though doubted by some editors. Two of them, doubted by Garnier, are addressed to a maligner (*obtrectatorem*) of St. Augustine. Another, entitled *Conjugis ad Uxorem*, is in some edd. of Paulinus's works, but is quoted by Bede in his treatise *de Arte Metrica* as the work of Prosper Tiro. It consists of 16 lines of Anacreontic metre, followed by 98 elegiac lines, describing the glory of the Christian life and having some passages of considerable force and beauty both of thought and expression. It was evidently composed during the confusion and disaster caused by the barbarian invasions, hence *c.* 407, but there is no evidence to shew that Prosper of Aquitaine was ever married, and if not besides the improbability arising from its date, the poem is not likely to be his composition.

II. Prose.—(1) *Responsiones pro Augustino ad Capitula Gallorum.* A statement under 15 heads of the objections of the Gallic bishops to the doctrines of St. Augustine on Predestination, with answers to each. (2) *Responsiones ad Capitula Objectionum Vincentianarum.* A similar work in 16 chapters. The objections express, in a manner harsh, revolting, and unfair, the possible results of predestinarian doctrine carried to its extreme point. (3) *Responsiones ad Excerpta Genuensium.*—Some clergymen of Genoa had misunderstood various passages from the two treatises of St. Augustine, *de Praedestinatione Sanctorum*, and *de Dono Perseverantiae*, and to them Prosper addresses a courteous explanation, quoting passages cited by them and adding his own replies, gathered in some cases from the words of Augustine, and in one case pointing out an egregious blunder made by them in quoting as his opinion words intended to express an opponent's objection. (4) *Contra Collatorem.* John Cassian had written a book entitled *Spiritual Conferences* (*Collationes*), 17 in number, in the 13th of which, entitled *de Protectione Dei*, he condemned severely Augustine's doctrine on predestination. This is defended by Prosper partly by arguments drawn from Scripture and the nature of the case, and partly by the authority of the churches of Rome, the East, and Africa. He warns his adversary of his near approach to the precipices of Pelagianism, and expresses the hope that his doctrine may be condemned by the present pontiff Sixtus (432-440), as it had been by those before him. The book must have been published between those dates. (5) *An Exposition of Pss. c. to cl.*, (omitting cvii. [cviii.]), taken substantially and often verbally, though much abridged, from St. Augustine's *Enarrationes in Psalmos*; not a mere servile curtailment, but a fair and judicious representation, executed with great skill, of the Augustinian work, together with some additions of Prosper's own, probably published *c.* 435. (6) *Book of Sentences taken from the Works of St. Augustine*, 392 in number, put together, probably, originally as a manual for his own use. They are very short, and are a sort of compendious index to the opinions of St. Augustine. Other works are assigned to Prosper, but on insufficient authority.

(6*a*) The *Chronicle*, probably the best known of the works of Prosper, is attributed to him without hesitation by Cassiodorus, Gennadius of Marseilles, Victorius, and Isidore, though Pithou and Garnier doubted it. It extends from the earliest age to the capture of Rome by the Vandals, A.D. 455, and consists of three parts: (1) To A.D. 326, founded, as it states, on that of Eusebius, and though much abridged, treating the subject with some independence. (2) From 326 to 378, which uses similarly Jerome's continuation of Eusebius, with both additions and omissions. (3) From 378 to 455. As might be expected, predominance is given to ecclesiastical events, especially such as concern the rise and fall of heretical doctrines. The *Chronicle* arose out of an endeavour to fix the date of Easter, for which purpose Prosper constructed a Paschal cycle now lost.

(*b*) *Chronicle of Tiro Prosper*. Besides the *Chronicle* just described, another much shorter and relating to the latest period only, bearing the name of Prosper, was edited by Pierre Pithou in 1588 from MSS. in the library of the monastery of St. Victor at Paris. It is difficult to believe that the two Chronicles could be by the same writer, or if they were, to understand why he published both, as must have been the case, about the same time. It is much more probable that Prosper of Aquitaine and Tiro Prosper, despite an apparently mistaken statement of Bede, were different persons.

The best ed. of Prosper's collected works, by Desprez and Desessarts (Paris, 1711), contains all the works rightly attributed to Prosper, together with others not belonging to him, and various pieces relating to the semi-Pelagian controversy. It is revised and reprinted in Migne's *Patr. Lat.* vol. li. See L. Valentin, *St. Prosper d'Aquitaine* (Paris, 1900). [H.W.P.]

Proterius, St., patriarch of Alexandria, was presbyter and church-steward under Dioscorus, and left in charge of the church when Dioscorus went to the council of Chalcedon. After Dioscorus was deposed by that council, the emperor Marcian ordered a new election to the see. The suffragan bishops, except 13 detained at Constantinople by a resolution of the council (Chalced. c. 30), were assembled in synod; and the chief laymen of Alexandria came as usual to express their mind and assent to the prelate's choice (cf. Liberat. *Breviar.* c. 14, and Evagr. ii. 5). There was great difficulty in reaching a conclusion; for the majority of the Alexandrian church people were profoundly aggrieved by the action of the council. In their eyes Dioscorus was still their rightful "pope," the representative of Cyril and of Athanasius. Ultimately, however, opposition to the imperial mandate was felt impracticable. It was resolved to elect, and then all favoured Proterius, who was consecrated and enthroned (A.D. 452); but the passions of the Dioscorian and anti-Dioscorian parties broke out at once into tumultuous dissension, which Evagrius likens to the surging of the sea. Proterius sending Leo the usual announcement of his elevation, Leo asked some definite assurance of his orthodoxy (Leo, *Ep.* 113, in Mar. 453), and received a letter which he regarded as "fully satisfactory," shewing Proterius to be a "sincere assertor of the Catholic dogma," inasmuch as he had cordially accepted the Tome (*Epp.* 127, 130). Thereupon (Mar. 454) he wrote again to Proterius, advising him to clear himself from all suspicion of Nestorianizing, by reading to his people certain passages from approved Fathers, and then shewing that the Tome did but hand on their tradition and guard the truth from perversions on either side. Leo took care, in thus addressing the "successor of St. Mark," to dwell on that evangelist's relation to St. Peter as of a disciple to a teacher; and he bespeaks the support of the Alexandrian see in this resistance to the unprincipled ambition of Constantinople, which in the 28th canon, so called, of Chalcedon had injured the "dignity" of the other great bishoprics (*Ep.* 129). Another question prolonged the correspondence. The Nicene Fathers were believed to have commissioned the Alexandrian bishops to ascertain and signify the right time for each coming Easter. Leo had consulted Cyril as to the Easter of 444; and he now, in 454, applied to Proterius, through the emperor, for his opinion as to the Easter of 455, which the Alexandrian Paschal table appeared to him to place too late (*Epp.* 121, 127). Proterius replied to Leo at some length (*Ep.* 133, Apr. 454) that Egypt and the East would keep Apr. 24 as Easter Day, and expressed his belief that all Christians everywhere would "observe one faith, one baptism, and one most sacred paschal solemnity."

Proterius had troubles with his own clergy. Not long after the council a priest named Timotheus and a deacon named Peter (nicknamed Mongus) refused to communicate with him, because in his diptychs he ignored Dioscorus and commemorated the council of Chalcedon. He summoned them to return to duty; they refused, and he pronounced in synod their deposition (Liberat. c. 15; *Brevic. Hist. Eutych.* or *Gesta in causa Acacii*, in Mansi, vii. 1062). Four or five bishops and a few monks appear to have actively supported them, and to have been included in their condemnation and in the imperial sentence of exile which followed (*Ep. Aegypt. Episc. ad Leonem Aug.* in Mansi, vii. 525). The monks in Egypt, as elsewhere, were generally attached to the Monophysite position, which they erroneously identified with the Cyrilline. They took for granted that the late council had been practically striking at Cyril through Dioscorus; and that Christ's single personality was at stake. Thus, besides those monks who had overtly taken part with Timotheus and Peter, others apparently had suspended communion with the archbishop; and Marcian had addressed them in gentle and persuasive terms, assuring them that the doctrine of "one Christ," symbolized by the term Theotokos, had been held sacrosanct at Chalcedon, and exhorting them therefore to join with the Catholic church of the orthodox, which was one (Mansi, vii. 481). But the schism, once begun, was not thus to be abated; the zealous seceders raised a cry, which has practically never died out, that the Egyptian adherents of the council of Chalcedon were a mere state-made church, upheld by the court against the convictions of the faithful. To this day the poor remnant of orthodoxy in Egypt bears a name which is a stigma, Melchites, or "adherents of the king." (Cf. Renaudot, *Hist. Patr. Alex.* p. 119; Neale, *Hist. Patr. Alex.* ii. 7. They both add that the orthodox accepted the term.) Even after Dioscorus died in exile Proterius was ignored and disclaimed, and knew that he was the object of a hatred that was biding its time, and "during the greater part of his pontificate," as Liberatus tells us, depended for safety on a military guard. At last, in Jan. 457, Marcian died, and the Monophysites thought they saw their opportunity. Some malcontent Egyptian bishops renewed their outcry against the council (Eulogius, in Phot. *Bibl.* 130, p. 283, ed. Bekk.); and Timotheus, returning to Alexandria, began those intrigues which won him his title of "the Cat." [TIMOTHEUS AELURUS.] The "dux" Dionysius being absent in Upper Egypt, Timotheus found it the easier to gather a disorderly following and obtain irregular consecration. Dionysius, returning, expelled Timotheus; and the latter's partisans in revenge rushed to the house of Proterius, and after besetting him for some time in the adjacent church of Quirinus, ran him through with a sword in its baptistery, and he died under many wounds with six of his clerics. His corpse was dragged by a cord across the central place called Tetrapylon, and then through nearly the whole city, with hideous cries, "Look at Proterius!" Beaten as if it could still suffer, torn limb from limb, and finally burnt, its ashes were "scattered to the winds." The day was Easter Day, Mar. 31, 457. See also Evagr. ii. 8; Le Quien, ii. 412; Neale, *Hist. Alex.* ii. 12. [W.B.]

Prudentius, Marcus (?) Aurelius Clemens, the chief Christian poet of early times, born A.D. 348 (Praef. 24, cf. *Apotheosis*, 449), somewhere in the N. of Spain, near the Pyrenees (*Peristeph.* vi. 146). His name, education, and career imply that he was of good family; he was educated in rhetoric and law, and his poems shew an exact knowledge of the Latin classical poets, especially Virgil, Ovid, Horace, and Juvenal; he seems to have known little Greek and no Hebrew. He speaks of his early life as stained with much sinfulness, but must have been held in high respect, for after practising as an advocate, he twice held an important civil office, and was at last raised to some high position at the emperor's court (cf. Kayser, p. 254 n.; Brockhaus, p. 16 n.; Faguet, p. 17). Late in life he received some deep religious impression, in consequence of which he gave up public life. Some expressions of his seem to imply that he joined a religious society (*Cath.* ii. 45; iii. 56; cf. *Psych.* 551-573). He has no longer any money to relieve the poor; the only offering he can make to God is his poetry (*Epil.* 10). To this and to prayer he devoted his life, seeking to spread among the educated classes a correct knowledge of Christianity, or, like a "Christian Pindar," to sing the triumphs of the martyrs on their festal days and so win them greater honour. At some period of great anxiety to himself he visited Rome; as he passed Imola he poured out his soul in prayer before the picture of St. Cassian in the church (*Perist.* x. 103, 104). At Rome his anxiety was increased by illness; and he implored the intercession of St. Hippolytus (xi. 127). His prayer was answered. At Rome he was deeply impressed with the memorials of the martyrs in the catacombs and churches (xi.) and composed his poem on the deaths of SS. Peter and Paul (xii.). There he probably became acquainted with the poems of pope Damasus, which influenced some of his own. Returning to Spain, he wrote his poems on St. Cassian (ix.) and St. Hippolytus, requesting his bishop to introduce the observance of the latter saint's festival into Spain (xi.). In 403 or 404 he wrote the second book *contra Symmachum*; and in 405 published an edition of his poems, with a preface shewing that all his extant works, except the *Dittochaeon* and perhaps the *Psychomachia*, were then written. Of his later life and death nothing is known.

His character, judging from his writings, was very lovable. He was a loyal Roman, proud of the empire, seeing in its past conquests and capacity for government a preparation for the kingdom of Christ, and looking for greater conquests under the banner of the cross (*Perist.* ii. 1-35, 413-484, x. *passim*; *c. Symm.* i. 415-505, ii. 577-771). He has a great fondness for art, wishing to keep even pagan statues if regarded only as ornaments (*c. Symm.* i. 505). He had an intellectual horror of heresy, though with a personal tenderness for heretics (*ib.* ii. *Pref.*). He was loyal to all church customs and ordinances, and had a strong appreciation of spiritual truth; see his lofty conception of the Nature of God (*Cath.* iv. 7-15; *Apoth.* 84-90; *Ham.* 27 seq.; *c. Symm.* i. 325; *Perist.* x. 310), of the True Temple (*Cath.* iv. 16-21; *c. Symm.* ii. 249; *Apoth.* 516), the True Worship (*Perist.* x. 341), the True Nobility of Birth (*ib.* 123), the True Riches (*ib.* ii. 203), the True Fast (*Cath.* vi. 201-220), the True Reward (*c. Symm.* ii. 750). He shews a pious tenderness of spirit (cf. *Apoth.* 393), kissing the sacred books (*ib.* 598) and the altar (*Perist.* ix. 100), and a deep personal humility which does not venture to contend with Symmachus (i. 609); which offers his verses to Christ, though they are but the "earthen vessel" (*Epil.* 29) of a "rustic poet" (*Perist.* ii. 574, x. 1); which has no merit in itself, but pleads for the intercession of the saints that he may be transferred from Christ's left hand to His right on the judgment day (*ib.* ii. 574, vi. 162, x. 1136), content if he be saved from the fires of hell and gently purified for the lowest place among the saved (*Ham.* 931). (Authorities—his own works, especially the Preface, and Gennadius, *de Vir. Ill.* c. 13).

Works.—His extant works are (*a*) lyrical, (*b*) apologetic or didactic, (*c*) allegorical; their most remarkable characteristic being their variety. All the poems have a considerable literary value; they are written on the whole in good classical Latin, with many new words needed for church purposes and with a touch of archaic forms and words characteristic of this period. The prosody is fairly correct. The lyrical poems shew great originality in the metres used, and are influenced both in form and phrase by Horace, Ambrose, and Damasus. The hexameter poems are much indebted to Virgil, and in a less degree to Lucretius and Juvencus. All shew great fluency, relieved by dramatic vividness (*e.g. Perist.* v.; *c. Symm.* ii. 654 sqq.), rhetorical vigour of description (*e.g. Apoth.* 450-503; *c. Symm.* i. 415), considerable power of satire (*Apoth.* 186-206; *Ham.* 246) and humour (*Perist.* ii. 169, 407, ix. 69, 82), and much epigrammatic terseness of expression; but he dwells on unpleasant details in the accounts of martyrdoms (*e.g. ib.* x. 901) and of the coarsenesses of heathen mythology (*Cath.* vii. 115 sqq.). They are full of typical adaptations of Bible history (*e.g.* prefaces to *Ham.*, *Psych.*, and i. ii. *Symm.*). In this way, and in the substance of their arguments, they have a theological value, as shewing the tone of thought common at the time. Their lack of originality of thought makes them even more valuable for this purpose. (For the substance of the theology v. Brockhaus, c. vii.) But perhaps their historical value is the greatest. They give considerable information about heathen antiquities, *e.g.* the kinds of torture in use (*Perist.* i. 42), methods of writing (*ib.* ix. 23), the corn supplies of Rome (*c. Symm.* ii. 920), the gladiatorial shows (*ib.* i. 384, ii. 1909), the religious rites (*ib.* i. ii. *passim*; *Perist.* x.), and still more about Christian antiquities: the luxury and avarice of the times (*Ham.* 246; *Apoth.* 183, 210, 450), the position of deacons and archdeacons at Rome (*Perist.* ii. 37, v. 29), the times and details of fasting (*Cath.* iii. 57, vii. viii. 9), the use of anointing (*ib.* vi. 125, ix. 98; *Apoth.* 357, 493; *Psych.* 360), the sign of the cross (*Cath.* vi. 129, ix. 84; *Apoth.* 493; *c. Symm.* ii. 712), lights in churches, especially on Easter Eve (*Cath.* v.), funeral rites (*ib.* x. 49), and the veneration for the saints (*Perist. passim.* esp. i. 10-21, ii. 530 sqq., x. *ad fin.*, xi. *ad in.* xii.). Especially do they illustrate the art of the time. We have mention of the Lateran church (*c. Symm.* i. 586), that of St. Laurence (*Perist.* xi. 216), of buildings over the tombs of SS. Peter and Paul (xii.) and of the catacombs (xi. 153) at Rome; of a church at Merida (iii. 191), and a baptistery apparently at Calahorra (viii.); of a picture of the martyrdom of St. Cassian in the church at Imola (ix.), of St. Hippolytus in the catacombs (xi. 123), and of St. Peter (xii. 38). The *Dittochaeon* consists of titles for pictures, and nearly all the symbols which he uses (the Dove, the Palm, the Good Shepherd, etc.), as well as the Bible scenes illustrating his poems, are found on gems or on the walls of the catacombs, so that he may have derived his use of them from thence (Brockhaus, c. ix.).

From the first his poems were held in great honour; they are quoted with high praise by Sidonius Apollinaris, Avitus, Leo, Isidore, Rabanus Maurus, Alcuin, etc. In the middle ages the *Psychomachia* and the *Cathemerinon* were special favourites, and the MSS. of them are very numerous. The best eds. of the poems are those of Areval, 1788 (reprinted in Migne, lix., lx.); Chamillard (in the Delphin classics, with useful index), 1687; Obbar, 1845; Dressel, 1860. The *Apotheosis* is separately printed in Hurter, *Patrum Opuscula Selecta*, xxxiii. Translations of selected poems were made by F. St. J. Thackeray (1890); a study of the text by E. O. Winstedt in *Class. Rev.* 1903; a metrical study by E. B. Lease (Baltimore, 1895); and an excellent monograph by Brockhaus, *A Prudentius ins einer Bedeutung für die Kirche seiner Zeit* (Leipz. 1872). We give a fuller account of each poem.

A. *Lyrical.* (*a*) *Cathemerinon* (*i.e.* καθημερίνων ὕμνων), described in the Pref. 37, 38; a collection of hymns for the hours of the day and for church seasons. Though necessarily too long for public worship, extracts were made at least as early as 9th cent., and are found frequently in the Mozarabic Liturgy (cf. v. vi. vii. ix. x.), and a few in the Roman and Salisbury breviaries; on Tues., Wed., Thurs. at Lauds (i. ii.), Compline at Christmas (ix.), Compline on Good Friday (vi.), Easter Eve (v.), Epiphany, the Holy Innocents, and the Transfiguration (xii.). (Daniel, i. 119, and Kayser, *Gesch. d. Kirchenhymnen*, 275-336.)

(*b*) *Peristephanon* (*i.e.* περὶ στεφάνων, *de Coronis Martyrum*), described in Pref. 42; a collection of 14 lyrical poems, all (except viii. which is an inscription for a baptistery) in honour of martyrs. The choice of the martyrs is inspired by circumstances of the poet's life; the details perhaps taken from existing Acta Martyrum. Half are connected with his own native church of Spain (i. ii. (?) iii.-vi. xiii.), the rest are saints whom he found specially honoured at Rome (ii. vii. x. (?) xi. xii.) or on his journey thither (ix.).

B. *Apologetic* (referred to in Pref. 39). (*a*) *Apotheosis*=ἀποθέωσις, perhaps *The Deification of Human Nature in Christ* (cf. Pref. 8, 9, and 176, 177; *c. Symm.* ii. 268). The writer deals with Patripassian, Sabellian, Ebionite, and Docetic errors on our Lord's Nature.

(*b*) *Hamartigenia* = ἁμαρτιγενεία. A treatise on the origin of sin; discussed in a polemical argument against Marcion. The poem falls into two parts. (1) 1-639. God is not the creator of Evil. The existence of good and evil does not justify Marcion's theory of two Gods, for unity is essential to our conception of God. (2) 640-931. God permits evil but does not sanction it. The whole object of the Incarnation was to save man from evil (640-669). The cause of evil is man's free will, but this was needed to secure moral goodness and his power of ruling creation. The thought is mainly based on Tertullian, *adv. Marcionem.* The language shews reminiscences of Vergil, Persius (384), and Juvenal (763). Like the other poems, it is full of O.T. illustrations, mystically applied (Pref. 409, 564, 723). The full description of hell and paradise, and also the graphic portraiture of Satan, are especially noteworthy as the earliest in Christian literature, and so probably of great influence upon later art and literature. Both Dante and Milton may indirectly be indebted to them.

(*c*) *Libri c. Symmachum* (described in Pref. 40, 41). In 384 Symmachus had presented a petition to Valentinian II. for the restitution of the altar of Victory in the senate-house, which had been removed by Gratian, and also of the incomes of the vestal virgins. Through the influence of St. Ambrose (*Epp.* 17, 18) this had been refused. In 392 the altar was restored by Eugenius; in 394 again removed by Theodosius. After his death the heathen party, encouraged by the invasion of the Goths, which they attributed to the neglect of heathenism, again attempted to have it restored by Arcadius and Honorius. Prudentius wrote these books to counteract their influence. The date of bk. ii. is fixed, as after the battle of Pollentia in A.D. 403, and before the abolition of the gladiatorial games, A.D. 404 (ii. 710, 1114). Bk. i. deals generally with the history and character of heathenism (cf. ii. 1-3). Bk. ii. also has a preface, with a prayer to Christ to help the poet as He once helped St. Peter on the water. The poet then deals in detail with the arguments of Symmachus. The poem is very interesting and of great historical value for the circumstances of the time and for the details of Roman mythology and religious rites. The prefaces consist of the typical use of Scripture, but there is no scope for it in the body of the books. They are full, however, of a sense of Rome's majesty, of vigorous description, and of high moral scorn. The language recalls Vergil (*passim*), Ovid, Juvenal, Horace, and Claudian (ii. 704). Plato is quoted in i. 30. The subject-matter is influenced in parts by Tertullian (i. 396) and Minucius Felix (i. 48), but mainly by St. Ambrose, whose arguments are at times reproduced almost verbally.

C. *Allegorical.—Psychomachia* = *Ψυχομαχία*, *De Compugnantia Animi* (Gennadius) (the Spiritual Combat). The Preface consists of a mystical application of Gen. xiv. As Abraham with his 318 servants freed Lot, was blessed by Melchizedek, then begat Isaac; so the Christian, with the aid of Christ's cross (*τιη*, 318=the cross (*τ*) of 'Ιησοῦς), frees his soul, wins Christ's blessing, and brings forth good works. The poem opens with a prayer to Christ to shew how the soul is aided in its conflict (1-20), which is then described.

D. The *Dittochaeon*, *διττόχαιον*, (?) *δίττος*, *ὀχή*, the double food, or double Testament, stands by itself, and can scarcely be called a poem. It comprises 49 sets of 4 verses on scenes from O. and N. T. They are dry and jejune, and chiefly interesting as apparently composed to describe a series of paintings. See Lanfranchi, *Aur Prud. Clem. Opp.* 1896, 1902, 2 vols. (Turin). [W.L.]

Pseudo-Chrysostomus. *Opus Imperfectum in Matthaeum.*—Among the works which have been ascribed to Chrysostom is a commentary on St. Matthew's Gospel. It is divided into 54 homilies; but this division does not proceed from the author, and (32, 132*) the work was one intended, not for oral delivery, but to be read by persons from whom the writer was absent. The work is defective, wanting from the middle of the 13th to the end of the 19th chapter, and breaking off at the end of the 25th. Hence its title, *Opus Imperfectum*, in distinction to the genuine series of Chrysostom's 90 homilies on St. Matthew, which have been preserved complete. It is quoted as Chrysostom's by Nicolas I. (*Respons. ad Bulg.* Mansi, xv. 403) and other popes; and in the middle ages was accepted without doubt as his. In the *Catena Aurea* of Thomas Aquinas it is largely employed; and Fabricius quotes Dionysius the Carthusian as saying that he would rather have this imperfect work perfect than be lord of all Paris. Yet the author, far from being Chrysostom or any other orthodox divine, was undoubtedly a bitter Arian. Much of its heresy was hidden from many of its readers by the expurgations of successive transcribers and editors, and some parts may have been so deeply tainted with heresy that only total excision would suffice. Some early critics, indeed, defended the genuineness of the expurgated form, contending that the passages found in some copies, where the doctrine of our Lord's equality with the Father is formally combated, had been but scribblings by an Arian in the margin of an orthodox writer, which through mistake had crept into the text. Some of the heretical passages can be cut out without injury to the context, but there remain many passages of undisputed genuineness in which the author unmistakably defines his position, and reveals himself as a member of a small persecuted sect which condemned the dominant church as heretical, and was in turn denounced as heretical by the state and as such visited with temporal penalties; and he marks the reign of Theodosius as the time when orthodoxy was overwhelmed and when what he calls the heresy of the Homoousians became triumphant (48, 199; 49, 20). It being clear that the author was not a member of the Catholic church, it is unreasonable to doubt the genuineness of the passages where he exhibits his Arianism, *e.g.* where he explains that our Lord called heretics "spinas et tribulos," because, foreseeing that heresy would prevail above all others, He called them "tribulos, quasi trinitatis professores et triangulam bajulantes impietatem." We must therefore regard the expurgation of the passages as probably due to their heterodoxy. It was not only the Arian passages which were expurgated. *E.g.* where the writer speaks (19, 93) of "offering the sacrifice of bread and wine," he is made to say "the sacrifice of Christ's body and blood"; and a passage is cut out altogether where he argues that if it be dangerous to transfer to private uses the consecrated vessels "which contain not the Lord's real body, but the mystery of His body," how much more to profane the vessels of our own body which God has prepared for His dwelling-place.

When the controversial passages had been expurgated, there was nothing to excite orthodox suspicions in our writer's language about our Lord's divinity. The Arians were not Unitarians, their doctrines, on the contrary, being open to the charge of Ditheism. Accordingly our writer uses very high language concerning our Lord, speaks of Him as "our great God and Saviour," as does also Maximinus, whose doctrine is in accurate accordance with that of the present work. His formula is "Deus genitus de ingenito Deo." Sometimes it is "unigenitus Deus" (*μονογενὴς θεός*). If in his controversial passages he is eager to argue that the Son, "to Whom all things were delivered by the Father," can neither be identical with the Father nor equal to Him, he is equally energetic in repelling the doctrine that He was mere man; and the heresy of the Homoousians is not more repro-

* In the references the first figure denotes the Homily; the second the Benedictine page.

bated than that of Photinus, who, in his recoil from Arian ditheism, completely separated the Saviour's manhood from the one supreme Divinity. The Third Person of the Trinity is comparatively seldom mentioned, but on this head the writer's doctrine is even more distinctly heretical. The Holy Spirit is evidently regarded as a third Being, as much inferior to the Son as the Son is to the Father (34, 146). This is the representation also of the *Ascension of Isaiah*, a work quoted in the present treatise.

Naturally a better side of Arianism is exhibited in this work than elsewhere, in the main not controversial but exegetical and practical, written when all court favour had long been lost, and when the sect met from the state with nothing but persecution. How much there was to recommend the book to a religious mind is evident from the fact that it passed so long as Chrysostom's. The work itself makes no claim to such authorship; the writer is evidently addressing persons who knew him, and to whom he had no motive for trying to pass himself off as other than he was. He had also written commentaries on St. Mark (49, 211) and St. Luke (1, 23; 9, 56). Fragments of ancient Arian homilies on St. Luke have been published by Mai (*Bib. Nov. Vet. Pat.* iii.), but they have no resemblance to this work. Many favourable extracts from this commentary could be given to justify the estimation in which it was so long held: *e.g.* the whole comment on the text "Seek and ye shall find" (Hom. 17). But possibly the book was commended to medieval readers less by its merits than by what most modern readers would count its faults, for, utterly unlike Chrysostom, this writer constantly follows the mystical and allegorical method commonly connected with Alexandria. In this style he shews remarkable ingenuity. *E.g.* the name Bathsheba, or, as he reads it, Bersabee, he finds in Hebrew denotes "seven wells." He deduces from Prov. v. 15 that "well" denotes "a wife." Bathsheba was the seventh wife the literal David; but we learn spiritually that Christ is the spouse of seven churches, for so the one church is designated on account of the seven Spirits by which it is sustained, and accordingly both Paul and John wrote to seven churches. This last remark may suggest the writer's acquaintance with the work of which the Muratorian Fragment is a part.

The writer shews a strong preference for the ascetic life. He remarks (24, 135) that when the disciples said "If the case of the man be so with his wife it is not good to marry," our Lord did not contradict them or say it was good to marry. He holds (1, 24), that conjugal union is bad and in itself a sin; and although on account of God's permission it ceases to be sin, yet it is not righteousness. In the beginning of the world men married sisters—a sin excusable at the time on account of the fewness of men. Afterwards this was forbidden, but a man was allowed to have more wives than one; then, as population increased, this too was forbidden, but a man was allowed to have one wife; "now that the world has grown old we know what is well-pleasing in God's sight, though on account of incontinent men we dare not say it." Some hard language concerning women will be found (24, 135). Yet to those who will not take his counsel he gives advice concerning the choosing and ruling of a wife. He regards the apostle's permission of a second marriage as but licence given on account of the hardness of men's hearts, a second marriage in itself being but "honesta fornicatio." This is quoted as Chrysostom's in the *Decretum* of Gratian (par. 2, caus. 31, quaest. 1, 9). The writer owns there was more continence in the dominant church than in his own sect, but is not any more disposed therefore to condone that church's heresy. A heretical sect is no more a church than an ape is a man. If you see a man who does not worship God in truth doing what seem to you good works, do not believe your eyes and say he is a man of good life, but believe God, Who says "An evil tree cannot bring forth good fruit." If you call him good you make Christ a liar; you only see the outside, God sees the heart. The works of a man who does not care to believe rightly can spring from no good motive, for it is better to believe rightly than to act rightly. Faith without works is dead, but still it is something; works without faith are nothing at all. The foolish virgins had the lamps of right faith, but not the oil of good works to burn in them; but what avails the oil of good works to Jews or heretics who have no lamps wherein to light it? He will not even own the baptism of heretics as valid.

It has been questioned whether the original language of this commentary were Greek or Latin, but it appears to us that it was certainly Latin. A translator may conceivably, indeed, have modified the language "Jesse latino sermone refrigerium appellatur" (p. 16), or "in graeco non dicit 'beati pauperes" sed 'beati egeni' vel 'beati mendici'" (9, 56). But there are other passages where the argument turns on the use of Latin, *e.g.* (53, 223) money passing from hand to hand—"usu ipso multiplicatur, unde dicitur usura ab usu," or (7, 53) where an explanation is suggested why, at the call of the apostles, Peter and his brother are described as "mittentes retia," John and his brother "retia componentes," "quia Petrus praedicavit evangelium et non composuit, sed Marcus ab eo praedicata composuit; Joannes autem et praedicavit evangelium et ipse composuit." The commentator, however, clearly uses Greek authorities. From such he must have derived his explanation (49, 205) why the commandments are ten—"secundum mysterium nominis Jesu Christi quod est in litera iota, id est perfectionis indicio" (see also 1, 23). He knew no Hebrew, though he lays great stress on the interpretation of Hebrew names, making use for this purpose of a glossary which we cannot identify with that used by any other writer. It must have been from the work of some Oriental writer that he came by the name of Varisuas as that of a heretic (48, 199), for Barjesus seems plainly intended. He does not use Jerome's Vulgate, but a previous translation. Thus (Matt. v. 22) he has "sine causa," which Jerome omits, and he anticipates bp. Butler in his observations as to the uses of anger—"Justa ira mater est disciplinae, ergo non solum peccant qui cum causa irascuntur sed e contra nisi irati fuerint peccant." In the Lord's Prayer he has "quotidianum," not "supersubstantialem." He has the doxology at the end; in this differing from the usage of Latin versions but agreeing with the *Apostolic Constitutions* (iii. 18), a work he highly valued. In the beatitudes he follows the received text in placing "Blessed are they that mourn" before "Blessed are the meek," contrary to Jerome and the bulk of the Latin versions. Both here, however, and in the case of the doxology, he agrees with the Codex Brixianus. He reads "neque filius" (Matt. xxiv. 36); he distinctly omits Luke xvii. 36 (50, 213).

Besides the Scriptures he uses the *Shepherd* of Hermas (33, 142), but acknowledges that it was not universally received; the Clementine *Recognitions* (20, 94; 50, 212; 51, 214), the *Apostolic Constitutions* or *Canons* as he calls them (13, 74; 53, 221). The first of these passages does not appear in our present text of the *Constitutions*; the second is from bk. viii., which Krabbe gives good reason for thinking an Arian addition to the previously known work. In the latter half of the 4th cent. the Arians appear to have made active use of literary forgery. In their interests was made the longer edition of the Ignatian epistles, which Zahn has conjecturally attributed to Acacius of Caesarea. Interpolations of Arian tendency were also made in the Clementine *Recognitions*. Our writer used Josephus. He had also, besides the *Ascension of Isaiah*, another O.T. apocryphal book (not the book of *Jubilees*), from which he learned the names of Cain and Abel's sisters, fuller details about the sacrifice of Isaac, was enabled to clear Judah from the guilt of incest in his union with Tamar, etc. He had further N.T. Apocrypha, which, though not absolutely authoritative, might, in his opinion, be read with pleasure. These related in full detail the story of the Magi, compendiously told by St. Matthew, telling how they had learned to expect the appearance of the star from a book preserved in their nation, called the book of Seth, and had in consequence for generations kept a systematic look-out for this star. Probably the same book told him that Joseph was not present when the angel appeared to Mary, and related how our Lord conferred His own baptism on John the Baptist. Directly or indirectly the writer was much indebted to Origen, and there may be traces of acquaintance with two or three other anti-Nicene fathers. His fanciful interpretations of Scripture, though including some few of what may be called patristical commonplaces, seem to be mostly original. With reference, however, to the question of authorship, it is important to determine whether his coincidences with St. Augustine are purely accidental. He is certainly no follower of Augustine. He has little in common with that father's comments on the same passages of St. Matthew, and differs in various details, *e.g.* (49, 205) he follows Origen's division of the Commandments, making "Honour thy father and mother" the fifth, and (p. 218) counting it as belonging to the first table; yet he appears to have been acquainted with Augustine's *Enarrationes* on the Psalms, as he has scarcely a quotation from the Psalms which does not shew some resemblance to Augustine's comment on the same passage; *e.g.* (4, 43) in Ps. viii. 4, "The heavens, the work of Thy fingers" mean the Holy Scriptures; (5, 37) on Ps. xc. 11, the remark "Portatur non quasi infirmus sed propter honorem potestatis" verbally agrees with Augustine's "Obsequium angelorum non ad infirmitatem domini pertinet sed ad illorum honorificentiam." There is a striking verbal similarity (7, 52) between the comment on "mittentes retia" and Augustine's remarks on that subject in Ps. lxiv. 4. The interpretation that the "mountains" to which Christians are to flee are the Holy Scriptures may have been suggested by Augustine in Ps. lxxv. 2; see also the sermon (46) "de Pastoribus."

Our author lays claim to no great antiquity. He says (52, 218) that the time since our Lord's ascension had been nearly as long as the life of an antediluvian patriarch. Accordingly Mill (*Praef.* N.T.) fixes his date A.D. 961. In favour of the late date there is the use of the medieval word "bladum" for corn, though we do not know the exact date when such words crept into popular language. But a very strong argument for an earlier date is that the author's studies appear all to have lain in Christian literature earlier than the middle of the 5th cent.; and that he appears to know nothing of any of the controversies in the Christian church after that date. Making all allowance for the narrowing influence of a small sect, we find it hard to believe that the type of Arianism which existed at the time specified could have been preserved in such complete purity two or three centuries later. Our author does not appear to have lived in an Arian kingdom outside the limits of the Roman empire. He draws illustrations (30, 130) from the relative powers of the offices praefectus, vicarius, consul; from the fact that a "solidus" which has not the "charagma Caesaris" is to be rejected as bad (38, 160). When he wrote, heathenism was not extinct, as appears from the end of Hom. 13 and from what he says (10, 13) as to the effect on the heathen of the good or bad conversation of Christians. All things considered, we are not disposed to date the work later than the middle of the 5th cent., which would allow it time to grow into such repute in an expurgated form as to pass for Chrysostom's with Nicolas I. If so early a date can be assigned to it, we have at once a claimant for its authorship in the Arian bp. Maximinus, who held a conference with St. Augustine. The *Opus Imperfectum* was written by an Arian bishop at a distance from his people, as Maximinus then was. The doctrine of the two writers is identical, and there are points of agreement in what Maximinus says as to the temporal penalties to which the expression of his opinions was liable, and as to the duty, notwithstanding, of confessing the truth before men. Maximinus, while in Africa, could hardly help making some acquaintance with the writings of St. Augustine, and might very conceivably adopt his exegesis of particular passages, though on the whole slightly regarding his authority. [G.S.]

Publius (3), a solitary, commemorated by Theodoret in his *Religiosa Historia*, c. v., born at Zeugma, on the Hellespont, of a family of senatorial rank. His person and mental endowments were equally remarkable. On his father's death he sold all he inherited from him, and distributing it to those in need, built for himself a small hut on high ground about 7 miles from his native town, where he passed the remainder of his days. He devoted his whole time to psalmody, reading the Scriptures, and prayer, together with the labour necessary for his maintenance and the entertainment of strangers, and latterly for the government of his brotherhood. His reputation for sanctity attracted many, whom he lodged in small huts near his own. He exercised a very strict oversight, imposing on them a very severe rule of abstinence and nightly prayer. After a while, on the advice of one of these fellow-ascetics, he erected a common house, or coenobium, that they might derive profit from their companions' virtues, and all be more immediately under his eye. At first all his fellow-coenobites were Greeks; but the native Syrians having expressed a desire to join the society, he built another house for them, and between the two erected a church common to both, where each might attend matins and evensong, singing alternately in their own language. This double coenobite establishment remained to Theodoret's time, who gives a record of its successive provosts. [E.V.]

Pulcheria (2), Sept. 10, daughter of the emperor Arcadius and sister and guardian of Theodosius II. She practically ruled the eastern empire for many years. For her secular history see *D. of G. and R. Biogr.* She was only two years older than her brother, whose education she superintended, having been born Jan. 19, 399. She was declared Augusta and empress July 4, 414, and at once entrusted with the management of affairs. She was learned and vigorous, could speak and write Latin and Greek, personally investigated the affairs of state, directed much attention to religion, and brought up her brother in the strictest orthodoxy (Soz. *H. E.* iv. 1). She was a correspondent of St. Cyril during the Nestorian controversy, and two letters are still extant from him written in 430, requesting her assistance (see Mansi, iv. 618-883). In 450 she had a long correspondence with pope Leo and his archdeacon Hilarius on the subject of Eutyches and the Monophysite heresy. We possess also an epistle of hers addressed to the Palestinian monks and another to one Bessa, abbess of a convent at Jerusalem, both in defence of the council of Chalcedon. Bishops and clergy from every part of the empire appealed to her and on every subject. Theodoret (*Ep.* 43) wrote in 445 about the taxation of his episcopal city of Cyrrhus; the clergy of Ephesus, in 448, concerning the episcopate of Bassianus. She had in early life taken a vow of virginity in conjunction with her sisters Arcadia and Marina. In 450 she was obliged to assume the government of the empire, and feeling herself incompetent for the task married Marcian, an eminent general. She reigned till her death, Feb. 18, 453. She convoked and assisted at the fourth general council of Chalcedon. Her devotion to the culture of relics was very great. She transported to Constantinople those of St. Chrysostom with great pomp in 438, and of the 40 martyrs of Sebaste in 446 (Soz. *H. E.* ix. 2). Ceillier (viii. 471, 533, x. 20, 67, 213-226) gives fully her religious history. Hefele's *Councils* (Clark's trans. t. iii.) gives details of her action against Nestorius and Eutyches. [G.T.S.]

Purpurius, bp. of Limata, or Liniata, some place in Numidia, a truculent ruffian, mentioned both by Optatus and Augustine as a sample of the leaders of the Donatists (Morcelli, *Afr. Chr.* i. 205). For some cause unknown he murdered his own nephews in the prison of Mileum, and when taxed with the crime threatened the same to any who stood in his way (Opt. i. 13; Aug. *Brevic. Coll.* iii. 15, 27; *c. Gaud.* i. 16, 17; *c. Cresc.* iii. 27, 30). This had taken place before the council of Cirta, A.D. 305. Purpurius was also dishonest, for of the money distributed by Lucilla in bribes (A.D. 311) his share amounted to 100 *folles.* At some time, perhaps soon after 313, when Christian worship was made legal and heathenism became unpopular, advantage appears to have been taken by some of the "baser sort" of Christians to plunder the heathen temples, and Purpurius carried off some cups from the temple of Serapis, probably of Carthage. This theft was brought to light at the inquiry held by Zenophilus, A.D. 320. But the result of the inquiry is unknown, as the MS. is imperfect (*Mon. Vet.* Don. iv. pp. 172, 173, ed. Oberthür). [H.W.P.]

Q

Quadratus (3), the author of an apology for the Christians, presented to the emperor Hadrian (*regn.* 117-138). Eusebius (*H. E.* iv. 3) says the work was still in circulation in his time and that he himself was acquainted with it. He quotes one sentence which proves, as he observes, the great antiquity of the work. Quadratus remarks that the Saviour's miracles were no transient wonders, but had abiding effects. Those who had been cured or raised from the dead did not disappear, but remained for a considerable time after the Saviour's departure, some even to the times of Quadratus himself. Accordingly Quadratus is called a disciple of the apostles by Eusebius in his *Chronicle*, under the 8th year of Hadrian according to the Armenian, the 10th according to the Latin.

St. Jerome twice (*de Vir. Ill.* 19; *Ep.* 70, *ad Magnum*) identifies the apologist with Quadratus, bp. of Athens, and states that the apology was presented when Hadrian visited Athens and was initiated in the Eleusinian mysteries. On chronological grounds we must reject this identification. For it is improbable that any one contemporary with subjects of our Lord's miracles should survive to 170. We may doubt also whether the apologist resided at Athens. A writer against the Montanists (*ap.* Eus. *H. E.* v. 17) contrasts the behaviour of the Montanist prophetesses with that of those recognized in the church as prophets, *e.g.* the daughters of Philip, Ammia, and Quadratus. Eusebius evidently understood the reference to be a Quadratus of whom he speaks (*H. E.* iii. 37) under the reign of Trajan, and who is apparently the apologist.

But since the author whom Eusebius quotes wrote in Asia Minor, it was probably there that Quadratus enjoyed the reputation of a prophet, as did the daughters of Philip in Hierapolis, and Ammia in Philadelphia.

His *Apology* seems to have survived until 6th cent., for several passages were quoted in controversy between the monk Andrew and EUSEBIUS (**86**) (Phot. *Cod.* 162). Cf. Zahn, *Forschungen* (1900), vi. 41; Harnack, *Gesch. der Alt.-Chr. Lit.* i. 95; ii. 1, 269-271. [G.S.]

R

Rabbûlas, bp. of Edessa, 412-435. Chief authorities: (1) a panegyric in Syriac, compiled soon after his death by a contemporary cleric, himself a native of Edessa, extant in a MS. of 6th cent., of which Bickell has furnished a German trans. in Thalhofer's *Ausgewählte Schriften der Kirchenväter* (vol. x. pp. 56-68); (2) the later and less trustworthy biography of Alexander, the founder of the Acoimetae. According to the panegyrist, Rabbûlas was born in Kenneschrin, known by the Greeks as Chalcis in Osrhoene, of rich and noble parentage. His father was a heathen priest, his mother a Christian. He received a liberal education, and was well versed in pagan literature. From his father he inherited a considerable fortune, and was chosen prefect of his native city. He was still a heathen and for a long time resisted his mother's entreaties to become a Christian. He took, however, a Christian wife. Various instrumentalities contributed to his conversion. The panegyrist attributes it to his intercourse with Eusebius of Chalcis and Acacius of Beroea, and to two remarkable miracles witnessed by him. The biographer of Alexander ascribes it to Alexander's influence and teaching. Both accounts probably are substantially true. On his conversion he went on pilgrimage to Jerusalem and was baptized in the Jordan, having previously renounced his property and manumitted his slaves. His wife, daughters, and all the females of his household embraced the religious life, and Rabbûlas retired to the monastery of St. Abraham at Chalcis. The see of Edessa being vacant in 412 by the death of Diogenes, Rabbûlas was appointed by a synod meeting at Antioch. Edessa was famous for its intellectual activity. Rabbûlas became the leading prelate of the Oriental church, regarded, according to the exaggerated language of the biographer of Alexander, as "the common master of Syria, Armenia, Persia, nay of the whole world." The panegyrist describes him as having steadily opposed the doctrines of Nestorius from the very first. The church of Edessa, with the East generally, followed the teaching of Diodore of Tarsus and Theodore of Mopsuestia, in which those doctrines were virtually contained, and Ibas, a presbyter of his church, who would have personal knowledge, says that Rabbûlas was no exception. By degrees, however, Rabbûlas veered round, and ended as the most uncompromising opponent of Theodore's teaching, using his utmost endeavours to bring about the suppression of his works. [IBAS.] (*Ep. ad Marium*, Labbe, iv. 666; Liberat. *Breviar.* c. 10, Labbe, v. 752.) His separation from Theodore's school of doctrine was strongly exhibited in the winter preceding the council of Ephesus, 430-431, in a letter to Andrew of Samosata, upbraiding him for having attacked Cyril, a fragment of which is printed by Overbeck among the Syriac documents in his ed. of Ephrem Syrus (Oxf. 1865). From Andrew's reply and from Theodorus Lector (lib. ii. p. 565) we learn that Rabbûlas's fiery zeal for orthodoxy had led him to anathematize Andrew before his congregation at Edessa; and according to the panegyrist, Rabbûlas, when visiting Constantinople, preached in the presence of Nestorius and denounced his doctrine. After this it is surprising to find Rabbûlas at the council of Ephesus, joining the Orientals in their opposition to Cyril. His signature appears to the letter to the clergy and laity of Hierapolis (Baluz. col. 705) and to that addressed to the deputies of the Orientals to Constantinople (*ib.* 725), in both of which the heretical nature of Cyril's teaching is asserted. From this vacillation Rabbûlas speedily recovered. A visit to Constantinople in the winter after the council, 431-432, enabled him to confer with Nestorius's successor, the wise and pious Maximian, and confirmed him in opposition to the Nestorian doctrine, which he returned to his diocese determined to eradicate. This was no easy task. The defenders of Nestorius claimed to be disciples of Diodore of Tarsus and Theodore of Mopsuestia, whose names were revered throughout the East. To denounce Nestorianism and accept Cyril's anathemas was to repudiate the theologians whom they had been taught to venerate as infallible guides. Rabbûlas saw clearly that the evil must be attacked at his source in the works of Diodore and Theodore. He called to his aid the strong will and unscrupulous pen of Cyril. We have a letter from Rabbûlas to Cyril (Labbe, v. 469), denouncing Theodore as the author of the heresy of Nestorius, which denied that Mary was truly the mother of God. Cyril, in his reply, of which a fragment is preserved (*ib.*), lauded Rabbûlas for his zeal in expelling the blasphemy of Nestorius, and indicated Theodore, though guarding himself from mentioning so revered a name, as "the Cilician," from whose root this impiety proceeded. The suppression of these writings, so fatal to his own system of doctrine, became a chief object with Cyril. An extension of the imperial decree was obtained which included "the sacrilegious books" of Diodore and Theodore under the condemnation previously passed on the writings of Nestorius (*ib.* v. 471, cf. iii. 1209). The letter of Ibas to Maris describes the violent conduct of Rabbûlas, ὁ πάντα τολμῶν, in publicly anathematizing Theodore and seeking out his works for destruction (*ib.* iv. 663). Rabbûlas's violence is also described in a letter of Andrew of Samosata to his metropolitan, Alexander of Hierapolis, shortly after Easter, 432, complaining that Rabbûlas was dealing with a high hand in Edessa, openly anathematizing Theodore's teaching of one nature in Christ, and excommunicating all who refused to accept the Cyrillian dogmas or who read Theodore's books, which he was everywhere committing to the flames. A synod summoned at Antioch by the patriarch John despatched letters to the bishops of Osrhoene desiring them, if the reports were true, to suspend communion with Rabbûlas (Baluz. xliv. col. 749). Meanwhile Rabbûlas was corresponding with Cyril on the terms of reconciliation between himself and the East; and the two prelates were agreed that nothing short of complete submission on the part of the Orientals and the withdrawal of the condemnation of Cyril's anathemas would satisfy them. A letter of Cyril to Rabbûlas (*ib.* cviii. col. 812) in 432 expresses the impossibility of his repudiating all he had written on the subject. The reconciliation was effected in the spring of 433. Andrew of Samosata, becoming convinced of Rabbûlas's orthodoxy by perusing his manifesto, at once left his diocese for Edessa to make reparation to his antagonist. Alexander's anger having been aroused, Andrew wrote to the oeconomi of Hierapolis to justify himself. He had not yet seen Rabbûlas, but he accepted communion with him and Cyril, and embraced the peace of the church (*ib.* ci. cvi. coll. 807-810).

Rabbûlas, also, with Acacius of Melitene, wrote to warn the Armenian bishops of the Nestorian heresy in the writings of Diodore and Theodore. In their perplexity they summoned a synod, and dispatched two presbyters to Proclus (who in Apr. 434 had succeeded Maximian as patriarch of Constantinople), entreating him to indicate which was the orthodox teaching. Proclus replied in his celebrated "Tome" on the Incarnation, wherein he condemned Theodore's opinions without naming him, a precaution counteracted by the officiousness of the bearers of the document (Liberat. *Breviar.* c. 10, *ap.* Labbe, v. 752; Garnerii *Praef. in Mar. Merc.* p. liii. ed. Par. 1673). The fiery Rabbûlas did not long survive this letter. His death is placed Aug. 7, 435, after an episcopate of 23 years.

Nearly all his few surviving works were printed by Overbeck in the original Syriac text, in his ed. of Ephrem Syrus (Oxf. 1865), pp. 210-248, 362-378. They include the scanty remains of the 640 letters which, according to his biographer, he wrote to the emperor, bishops, prefects, and monks. See also Bickell's *Ausgewählte Schriften*, pp. 153-271. [E.V.]

Radegundis, St., born in 519, queen of Clotaire I. and founder of the nunnery of Sainte-Croix, at Poictiers. Her father was a Thuringian prince named Bertharius. Her austerities were so incessant that it was commonly said the king had wedded a nun (Venant. Fort. *Acta S. Rad.* c. i.). Abhorring the married state from the first, she seems to have finally decided to escape from it upon her husband's treacherous murder of her brother. Withdrawing to Noyon on the pretext of some religious observance, her urgency overcame the hesitation of bp. Medardus to make her a deaconess. She then escaped from her husband's territory to the sanctuary of St. Martin of Tours, and thence to St. Hilary's at Poictiers. Here she founded her monastery within a mile or two of the city; finally, with the consent of Clotaire, clerks were sent to the East for wood of the true cross to sanctify it, and the rule of SS. Caesarius and Caesaria of Arles was adopted. Here the rest of her life was spent, first as abbess, then as simple nun under the rule of another. We have full information about the beginnings of this institution from the two Lives of Radegund, one by Venantius Fortunatus, her intimate friend (*Patr. Lat.* lxxii. 651), the other by one of her nuns called Baudonivia (*ib.* 663); and also from the fact that in Gregory's time, after Radegund's death, the attention of all France was drawn to the spot by the scandalous outbreak of a body of the nuns, headed by Chrodieldis, a natural daughter of king Charibert I. After a residence of about 37 years she died Aug. 13, 587, and was buried by Gregory of Tours (*de Glor. Conf.* c. cvi.). [S.A.B.]

Reccared (the uniform spelling in coins and inscriptions), younger son of LEOVIGILD by his first marriage. For his parentage and life till the death of his father see LEOVIGILD and HERMENIGILD. Between Apr. 12 and May 8, 586 (Hübner, *Insc. Hisp.* n. 155; Tejada y Ramiro, ii. 217), he succeeded his father without opposition, having been already associated with him in the kingdom. He first allied himself to his stepmother Goisvintha, the mother of Brunichild and grandmother of Childebert II. By her advice he sent ambassadors to Childebert and to his uncle GUNTRAMNUS (2), the Frankish king of Burgundy, proposing peace and a defensive alliance. The former alone were received.

Then followed the great event of Reccared's reign, his conversion from Arianism to Catholicism. We can only conjecture whether, as Dahn supposes, his motives were mainly political, or whether he yielded to the influence of the Catholic leaders such as Leander or Masona. In Jan. 587 he declared himself a Catholic, and, convening a synod of the Arian bishops, induced them and the mass of the Gothic and Suevic nations to follow his example. Some Arians did not submit quietly, and 587-589 saw several dangerous risings, headed by coalitions of Arian bishops and ambitious nobles. Perhaps, from the geographical situation, the most formidable was that of Septimania, headed by bp. Athaloc, who, from his ability, was considered a second Arius. Amongst the secular leaders of the insurrection the counts Granista and Wildigern are named. They appealed for aid to Guntram, whose desire for Septimania was stronger than his detestation of Arianism, and the dux Desiderius was sent with a Frankish army. Reccared's army defeated the insurgents and their allies with great slaughter, Desiderius himself being slain (Paul. Em. 19; J. Bicl.; Greg. T. ix. 15). The next conspiracy broke out in the West, headed by Sunna, the Arian bp. of Merida, and count Seggo. Claudius, the dux Lusitaniae, put down the rising, Sunna being banished to Mauritania and Seggo to Galicia. In the latter part of 588 a third conspiracy was headed by the Arian bp. Uldila and the queen dowager Goisvintha, but they were detected, and the former banished.

Reccared, after his conversion, had again sent to Guntram and Childebert in 587. The implacable Guntram refused his embassy, asking how could he believe those by whose machinations his niece Ingunthis had been imprisoned and banished and her husband slain? Childebert and his mother Brunichild accepted the present of 10,000 solidi, and were satisfied with Reccared's declarations that he was guiltless of the death of Ingunthis. In the spring of 589 Guntram, perhaps in concert with Goisvintha, made one more attempt on Septimania. It was defeated with great loss by the Goths under Claudius. The rest of his reign was peaceful, except for some expeditions against the Romans and Basques.

Third Council of Toledo.—This, the most important of all Spanish councils, assembled by the king's command in May, 589. On May 4 the king shortly declared his reasons for convening them, and the next three days were spent in prayer and fasting. Reccared's address, read to the assembly by a notary, contained an orthodox confession of belief. He declared that God had inspired him to lead the Goths back to the true faith, from which they had been led astray by false teachers. Not only the Goths but the Suevi, who by the fault of others had been led into heresy, he had brought back. These noble nations he offered to God by the hands of the bishops, whom he called on to complete the work. He then anathematized Arius and his doctrine, and declared his acceptance of Nice, Constantinople, Ephesus, Chalcedon, and all other councils that agreed with these, and pronounced an anathema on all who returned to Arianism after being received into the church by the chrism, or the laying on of hands; then followed the creeds of Nicaea and Constantinople and the definition of Chalcedon, and the *tomus* concluded with the signatures of Reccared and Baddo his queen. It was received with general acclamation. Its praises of Reccared, its numerous scriptural quotations, and the clearness with which the Catholic and Arian doctrines are defined shew that it was composed by a theologian, probably bp. Leander or abbat Eutropius, who had the chief management of the council (Jo. Bicl.). One of the Catholic bishops then called on the bishops, clergy, and Gothic nobles who had been converted to declare publicly their renunciation of Arianism and their acceptance of Catholicism. They replied that though they had done so already when with the king they had gone over to the church, they would comply. Then followed 23 anathemas directed against Arius and his doctrines, succeeded by the creeds of Nice and Constantinople and the definition of Chalcedon, the whole being subscribed by 8 Arian bishops with their clergy, and by all the Gothic nobles. The bishops were Ugnas of Barcelona, Ubiligisclus of Valencia, Murila of Palencia, Sunnila of Viseo, Gardingus of Tuy, Bechila of Lugo, Argiovitus of Oporto, and Froisclus of Tortosa. The names of at least six shew their Gothic descent. Five come from sees within the former Suevic kingdom, probably shewing that Leovigild, after his conquest, had displaced the Catholic by Arian bishops. Reccared then bid the council with his licence to draw up any requisite canons, particularly one directing the creed to be recited at the Holy Communion, that henceforward no one could plead ignorance as an excuse for misbelief. Then followed 23 canons with a confirmatory edict of the king. The 1st confirmed the decrees of previous councils and synodical letters of the popes; the 2nd directed the recitation of the creed of Constantinople at the communion; by the 5th the Arian bishops, priests, and deacons, who had been converted, were forbidden to live with their wives; the 7th directed the Scriptures should be read at a bishop's table during meals; by the 9th Arian churches were transferred to the bishops of their dioceses; the 13th forbade clerics to proceed against clerics before lay tribunals; the 14th forbade Jews to have Christian wives, concubines, or slaves, ordered the children of such unions to be baptized, and disqualified Jews from any office in which they might have to punish Christians—Christian slaves whom they had circumcised, or made to share in their rites, were *ipso facto* free; the 21st forbade civil authorities to lay burdens on clerics or the slaves of the church or clergy; the 22nd forbade wailing at funerals; the 23rd forbade celebrating saints' days with indecent dances and songs. The canons were subscribed first by the king, then by 5 of the 6 metropolitans, of whom Masona signed first; 62 bishops signed in person, 6 by proxy. All those of Tarraconensis and Septimania appeared personally or by proxy; in other provinces several were missing. The proceedings closed with a homily by Leander on the conversion of the Goths.

The information for the rest of Reccared's reign is most scanty. He is praised by Isidore for his peaceful government, clemency, and generosity. He restored various properties, both ecclesiastical and private, confiscated by his father, and founded many churches and monasteries. Gregory the Great, writing to Reccared in Aug. 599 (*Epp.* ix. 61, 121), extols him for embracing the true faith and inducing his people to do so, and for refusing the bribes offered by Jews to procure the repeal of a law against them. He sends him a piece of the true cross, some fragments of the chains of St. Peter, and some hairs of St. John Baptist. Reccared died at Toledo in 601, after reigning 15 years, having publicly confessed his sins. He was succeeded by his son Leova II., a youth of about 18. Dahn, *Könige der Germanen*, v.; Helfferich, *Entstehung und Geschichte des Westgothen-Rechts*; Gams, *Kirchengeschichte von Spanien*, ii. (2). [F.D.]

Remigius (2) (*Remi*), St., archbp. of Rheims and called the Apostle of the Franks (*c.* 457-530), holds an important position in Western history and is honoured as one of the 3 great patron-saints of France. His exact part in winning Clovis and his Franks to orthodox Christianity, and so probably deciding the belief of Western Europe, is not easy to define, since Gregory's account, written considerably later than the events, is plainly not to be trusted for details, and an earlier Life which apparently existed (see Greg. Tur. *Hist. Franc.* ii. 31) was lost before the 9th cent. Some think that Clovis was convinced by the exhortations of Remigius or Clotilda, or both, some that he saw his advantage in the partizanship of the orthodox clergy in his struggle with the Arian Burgundians and Visigoths. [CLOVIS.] At any rate, it was a happy event for orthodoxy that a man with force of character to impress a barbarian like

Clovis was stationed in the pathway of his conquests. Few details are known of Remigius's life. He was born *c.* 435, and consecrated in his 22nd year (*c.* 457). We first hear of his intercourse with Clovis in the campaign against Syagrius (*c.* 486). About 492 the king married the Catholic Clotilda, who proved a powerful ally for the bishop. The story of his baptism on Christmas Eve, 496, with his sisters Albofledis and the Arian Lanthechildis and more than 3,000 Franks, is well known. "Mitis depone colla, Sicamber, adora quod incendisti, incende quod adorasti," are the words put by Gregory into Remigius's mouth (*ib.* 27). His episcopate is said to have lasted 70 or more years, his death occurring *c.* 530. His literary remains are 4 letters (one, to 3 bishops, presents a curious picture of contemporary manners), a spurious will, and a few verses ascribed to him (*Patr. Lat.* lxv. 961-976; cf. *Hist. litt. de la France*, iii. 158 sqq.).

The references in Gregory of Tours (*Hist. Franc.* ii. 27, 31, viii. 21, ix. 14, x. 19; *Hist. Epit.* xvi.; *de Glor. Conf.* lxxix.), Sidonius Apollinaris (*Ep.* ix. 7), and Avitus (*Collat. Episc. sub init.*; *Patr. Lat.* lix. 387), comprise all that is historical about him. History and myth are mingled in the exhaustive notice of the Bollandists (Oct. 1, 59-187). [S.A.B.]

Rhodo (1), a Christian writer of the end of the 2nd cent., our knowledge of whom now exclusively depends on the account of his writings, and some extracts from them in Eusebius (*H. E.* v. 13). He was a native of Asia, converted to Christianity at Rome by Tatian, as he himself says in a treatise against Marcion addressed to Callistion. In it he tells of the sects into which the Marcionites split up after Marcion's death, and gives an interesting account of an oral controversy held by him with the Marcionite APELLES, then an old man. He mentions a book of "Problems" published by Tatian, intended to exhibit the obscurity of the Holy Scriptures, and promises to give the solutions; but Eusebius does not seem to have met with this work. He also wrote a treatise on the Hexaemeron. Through a lapse of memory Jerome (*de Vir. Ill.*) speaks of him as author of the anonymous treatise against the Montanists from which Eusebius makes extracts (*H. E.* v. 16). [G.S.]

Romanianus, a wealthy citizen of Tagaste, possessing there and at Carthage a house and other property. He shewed great kindness towards Augustine in his early life, which he did not fail in later days gratefully to acknowledge. In a passage of the second book against the heathen philosophers Augustine relates with pathetic simplicity how when he was but a boy and in poverty, arising no doubt from his father's "spirited" disregard of expense, he found in Romanianus a friend who provided him a home and pecuniary help in his studies at Carthage, and shewed him—what he valued more than these—friendship and kindly encouragement. After the death of Augustine's father in 371, Romanianus received him into his house at Tagaste as his honoured guest, and though, in a patriotic spirit, he tried to dissuade him from returning to Carthage, when he saw that his youthful ambition desired a wider range than his native town could afford, he supplied him with the necessary means. Nor, as Augustine mentions with special gratitude, was he offended at a neglect to write, but passed over it with considerate kindness (Aug. *Conf.* ii. 3, vi. 14; *c. Acad.* ii. 2; *Ep.* 27, 4). Romanianus had a son Licentius, who may have been a pupil under Augustine while he was teaching rhetoric at Carthage, but of this there is no evidence, though he undoubtedly was 10 or 12 years later at Milan. Romanianus appears to have had another son, Olympius, frequently mentioned in the various discourses composed by Augustine at Cassiciacum near Milan, who received baptism at the same time as Augustine, and who afterwards became bp. of Tagaste, of which place he was certainly a native, and of a rank in life agreeing entirely with that of Romanianus (Aug. *Conf.* vi. 7). Like Augustine himself, perhaps in some degree through his influence, Romanianus fell into the prevailing errors of Manicheism, which, however, he appears to have cast off, though without adopting as yet the true philosophy of the gospel, by the time when, as we gather from the description of Augustine, he visited him at Milan in 385. He had gone thither on important business, and entered with some warmth into the scheme of a life in common of 10 members. In 386, while Augustine was with his friends in the house of Verecundus at Cassiciacum, and meditating the great change of life which he made in 387, he composed 4 discourses, dedicating to Romanianus the one against the academic philosophers, entreating him to abandon their doctrines, and declaring his own intention to abide by the authority of Christ, "For," says he, "I find none more powerful than this" (*c. Acad.* i. 1; iii. 20; *Retract.* i. 1-4). Some time during the 3 years following the conversion of Augustine Romanianus became a Christian, thus drawing still closer the intimacy between Augustine and himself and his family. The same year Augustine addressed to Romanianus his book on true religion (*c. Acad.* ii. 3, 8; *de Ver. Rel.* 12; *Ep.* 27, 4; 31, 7). We find Augustine also writing, A.D. 395, to Licentius, entreating him in the most affectionate manner to shake off the bonds in which he was held by the world, to visit Paulinus at Nola and learn from him how this was to be accomplished (Aug. *Ep.* 26, 3). This letter he followed up by one to Paulinus, introducing to him Romanianus, the bearer of the letter, and commending Licentius to his attention (*Ep.* 27, 3, 4, 6). In 396 Paulinus wrote to Romanianus congratulating the church of Africa on the appointment of Augustine as coadjutor-bp. of Hippo, and expressing the hope that the trumpet of Augustine may sound in the ears of Licentius, to whom he wrote both in prose and in verse, exhorting him to devote himself to God (Paulin. *Epp.* vii. viii.). [H.W.P.]

Romanus (7), a solitary, born and brought up at Rhosus, who retired to a cell on the mountains near Antioch, where he lived to extreme old age, practising the utmost austerities. Theodoret describes him as conspicuous for simplicity and meekness, attracting to his cell by the beauty of his character large numbers, over whom he exercised a salutary influence (Theod. *Hist. Relig.* c. xi.). [E.V.]

Romanus (9), St., a celebrated hymn-writer of the Eastern church, who is said to have written more than 1,000 hymns, of the kind called κοντάκια, a form which he probably invented. It perhaps derives its somewhat disputed name from the legend as to its origin, found in the Synaxasion of St. Romanus's day (*Menaea*, Oct. 1), which says that the Blessed Virgin appeared to him, and commanded him to eat a roll (κοντάκιον) which she gave him, and that, obeying, he found himself endowed with the power of composing hymns. If he was the first who wrote κοντάκια, it is an argument in favour of placing him (as do Pitra and the Bollandists) in the reign of Anastasius I. (491-518) rather than of Anastasius II. (713-719). [H.A.W.]

Rufinus (3), *Tyrannius*, of Aquileia, the translator of Origen and Eusebius, the friend of Jerome and afterwards his adversary; a Latin ecclesiastical writer of some merit, and highly esteemed in his own time; born *c.* 345 at Concordia in N. Italy; baptized at Aquileia *c.* 371; lived in Egypt some 8 years and in Palestine about 18 (371-397); ordained at Jerusalem *c.* 390; in Italy, mostly at Aquileia, 397-408; died in Sicily, 410.

Sources.—The works of Rufinus himself, especially his *Apology* (otherwise *Invectives*), two books, against Jerome; Hieron. *Apology against Rufinus*, three books; Id. *Chronicle*, Ol. 289, An. 1, A.D. 378; Id. *Epp.* 3-5, 51, 57, 80-84, 97, 125, 133; Id. *Pref. to Comm. on Ezk.* and *Jer.* bk. i; Paulin. *Epp.* 28, 40, 46, 47; Aug. *Epp.* 63, 156; Pallad. *Hist. Laus.* 118; Gennad. *de Script. Eccl.* c. 17; Sid. Apoll. lib. iv. *Ep.* 3; Gelasius in *Concil. Rom.* (*Patr. Lat.* lix. col. 173).

Literature.—Rufinus's career has usually been treated as an appendage to that of Jerome. There is a full Life of Rufinus by Fontanini (Rome, 1742), reprinted by Migne in his ed. of Rufinus (*Patr. Lat.* xxi.)—minute and exhaustive in details and in fixing dates; a shorter account by Schoenemann, *Bibliotheca Historico-Literaria Patrum Lat.* (Lips. 1792), is also reprinted by Migne.

Works.—The genuine original works of Rufinus still extant are: *A Dissertation on the Falsification by Heretics of the Works of Origen*, prefixed to his trans. of Pamphilus's *Apology for Origen; A Commentary on the Benedictions of the Twelve Patriarchs* (Gen. xlix.); the Apology for himself against the attacks of Jerome, in two books; a shorter one addressed to pope Anastasius; two books of *Eccl. Hist.*, being a continuation of Eusebius; a History of the Egyptian Hermits; and an Exposition of the Creed. Besides these there are several prefaces to the translations from Greek authors, on which his chief labour was expended, and which include *The Monastic Rule of Basil*, and his 8 *Homilies*; the *Apology for Origen*, written by Pamphilus and Eusebius; Origen's Περὶ Ἀρχῶν and many of his commentaries; 10 works of Gregory Nazianzen; the Sentences of Sixtus or Xystus; the Sentences of Evagrius, and his book addressed to Virgins; the *Recognitions* of Clement; the 10 books of Eusebius's History; the Paschal Canon of Anatolius of Alexandria.

Early Life: Concordia and Aquileia.—His parents were probably Christians, since there is no trace of other than Christian associations in his writings. His mother did not die till his sojourn in Rome in 398 (Hieron. *Ep.* lxxxi. 1). He was not baptized till *c.* 371. That he made the acquaintance of Jerome in early life is shewn by his request to him when about to go into Gaul, *c.* 368, to copy out for him the works of Hilary upon the Psalms and upon the councils of the church (*Ep.* v. 2). Either before or about the time of the return of Jerome from Gaul, Rufinus had gone to Aquileia and embraced a monastic life ("in monasterio positus," Rufin. *Apol.* i. 4). There, about 30 years before he wrote his Apology against the attacks of his former friend, Rufinus was baptized (*ib.*) by Chromatius and his brother Eusebius (then respectively presbyter and deacon), and Jovinus the archdeacon, all of them ascetic friends, and all subsequently bishops. This must have been at the close of his stay at Aquileia ("Ille modo se lavit," Hieron. *Ep.* 4, A.D. 374).

Life in the East: Egypt.—We do not know how long the company of friends lived together at Aquileia, nor what caused its dissolution. But when the "subitus turbo" drove Jerome to the East, Rufinus left Italy in the company of Melania for Egypt and visited the monasteries of Nitria (Pallad. *Hist. Laus.* 118; Hieron. *Ep.* iii. 2), where Rufinus apparently intended to remain. But the church of Alexandria was then in a state of trouble. Athanasius died in 372, and his successor, the Arian Lucius, acting with the successive governors of Alexandria, came as a wolf among the sheep (Ruf. *H. E.* ii. 3; Socr. iv. 21-23; Soz. vi. 19). Rufinus himself was thrown into prison, and afterwards, with many other confessors, banished from Egypt (*H. E.* ii. 4; *Apol. ad Anastasium*, 2, "In carceribus, in exiliis"), but must have returned as soon as the stress of the persecution abated. In Egypt he saw and heard Didymus, who wrote for him a book on the questions suggested by the death of infants (Hieron. *Apol.* iii. 28), and whom he praises in his *Ecclesiastical History* (ii. 7). He also was a pupil of Theophilus, afterwards bp. of Alexandria (Hieron. *Apol.* iii. 18). He saw also the hermits, whose teaching he prized still more—Serapion and Menites and Paulus; Macarius the disciple of Anthony, and the other Macarius, Isidore, and Pambas. On their teachings he says he attended earnestly and frequently; and he afterwards described them in his *Historia Monachorum.* After 6 years he went to Jerusalem. Whether Melania had been with him in Egypt is not certain, though Palladius implies that he was her companion throughout. Certainly he now settled with her on the Mount of Olives. But it would seem that, "after a short interval," he returned to Egypt again for 2 years (*Apol.* ii. 22). Melania's settlement at Jerusalem is placed by Jerome in his *Chronicle* in 379, *i.e.* according to the present or Dionysian computation in 377. We may place Rufinus's final settlement there with her in 379. There is, however, some reason to believe they made one more journey to Egypt; for Palladius states, as a fact he had heard from Melania, that she had been present at the death of Pambas, which occurred after the accession of Theophilus in 385 (Fontanini, *Vita Rufini*, i. c. ii. § 7).

Palestine.—For 18 or 20 years, reckoning either from 377 or 379 to 397, Rufinus lived on the Mount of Olives. He was ordained either by Cyril or more probably by John (made bishop 385). He built cells at his own expense ("meis cellulis," *Apol.* ii. 8A) for monks, who occupied themselves in ascetic practices and learned pursuits. Palladius, who was at Jerusalem and Bethlehem for some time before he went to Egypt in 388, says of Rufinus: "He was a man of noble birth and manners, but very strong in following out his own independent resolutions. No one of the male sex was ever gentler, and he had the strength and calmness of one who seems to know everything"; and tells us that, in common with Melania, Rufinus exercised an unbounded hospitality, receiving and aiding with his own funds bishops and monks, virgins and matrons. "So," he says, "they passed their life, offending none, and helping almost the whole world." Jerome also, early in their stay at Jerusalem, spoke of Rufinus with highest praise, mentioning in his *Chronicle* (*sub ann.* 378) that "Bonosus of Italy, and Florentius and Rufinus at Jerusalem, are held in special estimation as monks"; and when he settled in Palestine in 386 had frequent literary intercourse with Rufinus and his monks. Rufinus records that Jerome was once his guest at the Mount of Olives (*ib.*); and Jerome acknowledges (*ib.* iii. 33) that, up to 393, he had been intimate with him.

In 394 Epiphanius, bp. of Salamis, came to Jerusalem, and in the dissension which arose between him and John, bp. of Jerusalem, Rufinus was the leader of the clergy who supported John, Jerome siding with Epiphanius, the consequence being an alienation between Jerome and Rufinus. This estrangement was but temporary. Jerome speaks frequently of their "reconciliatas amicitias" (*Ep.* lxxxi. 1; *Apol.* iii. 33). In 397, the year when Rufinus quitted Palestine, they met (probably with many friends on both sides) at a solemn communion service in the Church of the Resurrection, joined hands in renewal of friendship, and, on Rufinus's setting out for Italy with Melania, Jerome accompanied him some little way, perhaps as far as Joppa.

Italy, 397-409.—Melania returned to Italy in order to promote ascetic practices in her family. Rufinus, whom Paulinus speaks of as being to her "in spiritali viâ comitem," returned in her company. His mother was still living, and he wished to see his relations and Christian friends again (Hieron. lxxxi. 1; *Apol.* ii. 2). After a voyage of 20 days they arrived at Naples in the spring of 397. Thence they went to visit Paulinus at Nola, all the nobles of those parts and their retinues accompanying them in a kind of triumph (Paulin. *Ep.* xxix. 12). Melania, who was connected, probably, by ties of property with Campania, since Palladius speaks of her successors Pinianus and Melania living there (*Hist. Laus.* 119), after staying with Paulinus some time, went on to Rome, where her son Publicola and his wife Albina and her granddaughter Melania with her husband Pinianus were living. Rufinus went to the monastery of Pinetum near Terracina, of which his friend Ursacius or Urseius was the abbat, and there stayed probably for a year, from early spring 397 till after Lent 398.

He had brought many works of the Eastern church writers which were but little known in Italy; and his friends were eager to know their contents. Rufinus, having used Greek more than Latin for some 25 years, at first declared his incompetence (*Apol.* i. 11), but by degrees accepted the task of translation, which occupied almost all the rest of his life. He began with the Rule of Basil, which Urseius desired for the use of his monks. Next, probably, he translated the ***Recognitions*** of Clement. [CLEMENTINE LITERATURE.] Paulinus begged his assistance in the interpretation of the blessing upon Judah in Gen. xlix., and, some months later, of the rest of the blessings on the patriarchs. His reply is extant. Meanwhile he had a scholar named Macarius, who at Pinetum had been much exercised by speculations on Providence and Fate and in controversy with the many Mathematici (astrologists and necromancers) then in Italy. About the time Rufinus arrived he dreamed he saw a ship coming from the East to Italy which would bring him aid, and this he interpreted of Rufinus. He expected help from the speculative works of Origen, and besought Rufinus to translate some of them. Rufinus, though knowing from the recent controversy at Jerusalem that his orthodox reputation would be imperilled by the task, yet undertook it (*Apol.* i. 11; prefaces to bks. i. and iii. of the Περὶ Ἀρχῶν). He began, however, by translating the Apology for Origen written by the martyr Pamphilus in conjunction with Eusebius, adding a treatise on the corruption of Origen's works by heretics, and a profession of his own faith which he held in common with the churches of Aquileia and Jerusalem and the well-known bishops of those sees. Then he translated the Περὶ Ἀρχῶν itself, adding to the first two books, which he finished during Lent 398, a very memorable preface, in which he speaks of the odium excited by the name of Origen, but asserts his conviction that most of the passages which have given him the reputation of heresy were inserted or coloured by the heretics. He therefore felt at liberty to leave out or soften down many expressions which would offend orthodox persons, and also, where anything was obscure, to give a kind of explanatory paraphrase. He pointed out also that he was not the first translator of Origen, but that Jerome, whom he did not name but clearly indicated, and of whom he spoke in high praise, had in the time of Damasus translated many of Origen's works, and in the prefaces (especially that to the Song of Songs) had praised Origen beyond measure. Two questions gave rise to great controversy: First, was this reference to Jerome justifiable? Secondly, was Rufinus's dealing with the book itself legitimate? The reference to Jerome was hardly ingenuous. If the praises he bestows are not, as Jerome called them, "fictae laudes," they are certainly used for a purpose to which Jerome would not have given his sanction, and their use in view of the controversy at Jerusalem, without any allusion to Jerome's altered attitude towards Origen, was ungenerous and misleading. The second point is obscured by the loss of the chief part of the Greek of the Περὶ Ἀρχῶν, but we have enough upon which to form a judgment. Some passages, vouched for and translated by Jerome (*Ep.* cxxiv. 13), were, with much that leads up to them, omitted by Rufinus, who also carried the licence of paraphrasing difficult expressions to an extreme length. But the texts of Origen were somewhat uncertain; the standard of literary honesty was not then what is it now; and then Jerome himself had in his letter *de Opt. Gen. Interpretandi* (*Ep.* 57) sanctioned a mode of interpretation almost as loose as that of Rufinus. (See also his words to Vigilantius, *Ep.* lxi. 2, "Quae bona sunt transtuli, et mala vel amputavi vel correxi vel tacui. Per me Latini bona ejus habent et mala ignorant.") We may acquit Rufinus of more than a too eager desire, unchastened by any critical power, to make the greatest exponent of Oriental Christianity acceptable to Roman ears.

Rome.—The first two books Περὶ Ἀρχῶν, with the preface, were first published probably in the winter of 397-398; the other two, having been translated during Lent 398, were carried by Rufinus to Rome, whither Macarius had already gone, when he went to stay with Melania and her family. During his stay Apronianus, a noble Roman, was converted, partly through Rufinus, who addresses him as "mi fili." The friends of Melania were, no doubt, numerous. Pope Siricius also (elected in 385 when Jerome had himself aspired to the office) was favourable to Rufinus. But the expectations formed by Rufinus in his preface were realized at once. Many were astonished at the book of Origen, some finding even in Rufinus's version the heresies they connected with the name of Origen; some indignant that these heresies had been softened down. Jerome's friends at first were dubious. Eusebius of Cremona, who came to Rome from Bethlehem early in 398 (Hieron. *Ap.* iii. 24), lived at first on friendly terms with Rufinus and communicated with him (Ruf. *Apol.* i. 20). But Jerome's friends Pammachius, Oceanus, and Marcella resented the use made of their master's name and suspected Rufinus's sincerity. According to his account, Eusebius, or some one employed by him, stole the translation of the last two books of the Περὶ Ἀρχῶν, which were still unrevised, from his chamber, and in this imperfect state had them copied and circulated, adding in some cases words he had never written (*Ap.* i. 19; ii. 44). But, being in uncertainty as to the value of the translation, Pammachius and Oceanus sent the books and prefaces to Jerome at Bethlehem, who sat down at once, made a literal translation of the Περὶ Ἀρχῶν, and sent it to his friends with a letter (84) written to refute the insinuations through which, as he considered, Rufinus's preface had associated him with Origenism. He sent them also a letter (81) to Rufinus, protesting against his "fictae laudes," but refraining from any breach of friendship. When these documents arrived in Rome, affairs had changed. Rufinus had gone; pope Siricius had died (date in Fagius Nov. 29, 398); the new pope Anastasius was ready to listen to friends of Jerome; Rufinus the Syrian, Jerome's friend, had arrived in Rome (Hieron. *Ap.* iii. 24) and with Eusebius of Cremona had gone through the chief cities of Italy (Ruf. *Ap.* i. 21) pointing out all the heretical passages in Origen. Rufinus, a little before the death of pope Siricius, had obtained from him letters of recommendation ("literae formatae"), to which he appealed afterwards as shewing he was in communion with the Roman church (Hieron. *Ap.* iii. 21). At Milan he met Eusebius in the presence of the bishop, and confronted him when he read heretical passages from a copy of the Περὶ Ἀρχῶν received from Marcella and purporting to be Rufinus's work (Ruf. *Ap.* i. 19). He then went to Aquileia, where bp. Chromatius, who had baptized him 27 years before, received him.

Aquileia.—Here he soon heard that Jerome's translation of the Περὶ Ἀρχῶν, though intended only for Pammachius and his friends, had been published, and that Jerome's letter against him was in circulation. Of this letter he received a copy from Apronianus (*Apol.* i. 1); but Pammachius kept back the more friendly letter addressed to Rufinus himself. This act of treachery, which Jerome subsequently in his anger at Rufinus's Apology brought himself to defend (Hieron. *Apol.* iii. 28), caused Rufinus and Jerome to assail each other with fierce invectives. For that controversy and for the letters of pope Anastasius to Rufinus and John of Jerusalem, and Rufinus's letter of apology, see JEROME. We pass on to the last decade of Rufinus's life.

His friends at Aquileia were eager as those at Pinetum had been for a knowledge of the Christian writers of the East; and Rufinus's remaining years were almost entirely occupied with translation, though several of his original works belong also to this period. The translations have no great merit, but on the whole are accurate, with no need for omissions and paraphrases as in the Περὶ Ἀρχῶν. They were undertaken in no distinct order, but according to the request of friends. Rufinus wished to translate the Commentaries of Origen on the whole Heptateuch, and only Deuteronomy remained untranslated when he died. The Commentary on the Romans, however (see preface), and several others, besides other works, intervened.

The Exposition of the Creed is of importance, as a testimony to the variations in the creeds of the various churches (that of Aquileia having "Patrum *invisibilem et impassibilem,*" "in Spirit*u* Sanct*o,*" and "*hujus* carnis resurrectionem" as distinctive peculiarities), and from its intrinsic merits and as shewing the influence of Eastern theology, harmonized by a sound judgment, on Western theology.

The History is on a par with those of Socrates and Sozomen, exhibiting no conception of the real functions of history nor of the relative proportion of different classes of events, yet dealing honestly with the facts within the writer's view. It was trans. into Greek, and valued in the East, as his trans. of Eusebius, of which it is a continuation, was in the West (Gennad. *de Script. Eccl.* xvii.).

The History of the Egyptian monks presents many difficulties. It is distinctly attributed to Rufinus by Jerome (*Ep.* cxxxiii. 3), but not included in the list of his works given by Gennadius, who says that it was commonly attributed to Petronius, bp. of Bologna (Gennad. *op. cit.* xli.). The preface says it is written in response to repeated requests of the monks on the Mount of Olives. Fontanini (*Vita Rufini*, lib. ii. c. xii. § 4) grounds upon this with much reason the theory that Petronius, having been in the East, and having received the request of the Olivetan monks, but having himself, as Gennadius testifies, but little skill in composition, on his return to the West begged Rufinus to write the history. The adventures recorded would thus be those of Petronius, not of Rufinus. The *Historia Lausiaca* of Palladius is in many of its sections identical with the *Historia Monachorum*. It is, however, more probable that Palladius, who did not leave the solitary life in Egypt till 400, and wrote his History for Lausus at Constantinople apparently some time afterwards (he lived till 431), was indebted to Rufinus rather than the contrary.

Rufinus had not, like Jerome, any large range of literary knowledge, and his critical powers were defective. He quotes stories like that of the Phoenix (*de Symbolo*, 11) without any question. He had no doubt of the *Recognitions* being the work of Clement, and he translated the sayings of Xystus the Stoic philosopher, stating, without futher remark, that they were said to be those of Sixtus, the Roman bishop, thus laying himself open to Jerome's attack upon his credulity.

The *Apology* is well composed and more methodical than that of Jerome. Its reasoning is at least as powerful, though its resources of language and illustration are fewer. His efforts for peace and refusal to reply to Jerome's last invectives, though the temptation offered by a violent attack in answer to a peaceful letter was great, shews a high power of self-restraint and a consciousness of a secure position.

Last Years.—The years at Aquileia were uneventful. The letter of Anastasius which told him of the rumours against him at Rome and requested him to come there to clear himself, drew from him the *Apologia ad Anastasium*, a short document of self-defence not lacking in dignity. He enjoyed the friendship of Chromatius, at whose request he consented to cease his strife with Jerome, though Jerome, adjured by the same bishop, refused to do so (Hieron. *Apol.* iii. 2). He enjoyed the friendship of the bishops near him, Petronius of Bologna, Gaudentius of Brixia, Laurentius, perhaps of Concordia, for whom he wrote his work upon the Creed. Paulinus of Nola continued his friendship; and Augustine, in his severe reply to Jerome, who had sent him his work against Rufinus, treats the two men as equally esteemed, and writes: "I grieved, when I read your book, that such discord had arisen between persons so dear and so intimate, bound to all the churches by a bond of affection and of renown. Who will not in future mistrust his friend as one who may become his enemy when it has been possible for this lamentable result to come to pass between Jerome and Rufinus?" (Aug. *Ep.* 73 *ad Hieron.*).

Last Journey and Death.—Chromatius had died in 405, and Rufinus's thoughts turned again to Melania and to Palestine. He joined Melania in Rome in 408 or 409, Anastasius having been succeeded in 403 by Innocent, who had no prejudice against him. Owing to Alaric's invasion, they left Rome, with Albina, Pinianus, and Melania the younger (Pallad. *Hist. Laus.* 119), and resided in Campania and Sicily. Rufinus records that he was in the "coetus religiosus" of Pinianus on the Sicilian coast, witnessing the burning of Rhegium across the straits by the bands of Alaric, when he wrote the preface to the translation of Origen's Commentary on Numbers. Soon after writing this he died.

The cloud on the reputation of Rufinus due to Jerome's attacks has unduly depressed the general estimation of his character. In the list of books to be received in the church promulgated by pope Gelasius at the Roman council, in 494 (Migne's *Patr. Lat.* lix. col. 175), we read: "Rufinus, a religious man, wrote many books of use to the church, and many commentaries on the Scripture; but, since the most blessed Jerome infamed him in certain points, we take part with him (Jerome) in this and in all cases in which he has pronounced a condemnation." With this official judgment may be contrasted that of Gennadius in his list of ecclesiastical writers (c. 17): "Rufinus, the presbyter of Aquileia, was not the least among the teachers of the church, and in his translations from Greek to Latin shewed an elegant genius. He gave to the Latins a very large part of the library of Greek writers. . . . He also replied in two volumes to him who decried his works, shewing convincingly that he had exercised his powers through the insight given him by God and for the good of the church, and that it was through a spirit of rivalry that his adversary had employed his pen in defaming him." See *Ruf. Comm. in Symb. Apost.* ed. by Rev. C. Whitaker, Lat. text, notes, and trans. with a short hist. of Ruf. and his times (Bell). A trans. by Dean Fremantle of the works of Rufinus is in the *Lib. of Nicene and Post-Nicene Fathers.* [W.H.F.]

Rufinus (4), a Roman presbyter at the end of 4th cent.; an admirer of Jerome he espoused his cause in the Origenistic controversy and against Rufinus of Aquileia. Eusebius of Cremona, sent by Jerome to Rome in 398, reported the kindness of Rufinus, who wrote to Jerome to ask an explanation of the judgment of Solomon. This Jerome gives him, making the false and true mothers to be the Synagogue and the Church. Jerome speaks of him with gratitude and respect, hoping he may not only publicly defend him, but in private judge him favourably (*Ep.* 74, ed. Vall.). [W.H.F.]

Rufinus (5), a friend of Jerome; known as the Syrian, to distinguish him from (**3**) and (**4**), both his contemporaries. He was one of the company of Italians settled at Bethlehem with Jerome; and in 390 was sent by him to Rome and Milan in the cause of their friend Claudius, who was accused of a capital offence (Hieron. *Ep.* lxxxi. 2; *cont. Ruf.* iii. 24).

This Rufinus is doubtless the one mentioned by Celestius (Aug. *de Pecc. Orig.* c. 3) as having been known by him at the house of Pammachius at Rome and having asserted there that sin was not inherited. Marius Mercator says that it was this Rufinus who instilled into the mind of Pelagius the views known as Pelagian (Mar. Merc. *Lib. Subnotationum in Verba Juliani*, c. 2). [W.H.F.]

S

Sabas (2), a Gothic martyr under Athanaric, king of the Goths towards the end of 4th cent. His Acts seem genuine, and contain many interesting details of Gothic life in the lands bordering on the Danube. Thus village life, with its head men and communal responsibility, appears in c. ii. After various tortures he was drowned in the Musaeus, which flows into the Danube. The Acts are in the form of an epistle from the Gothic church to that of Cappadocia, whither Soranus, who was "dux Scythiae," had sent his relics (Ruinart. *Acta Sincera*, p. 670; *AA. SS.* Boll. Apr. ii. 88; Ceill. iv. 278; C. A. A. Scott, *Ulfilas, Apostle of the Goths*, 1885, p. 80). The topography of the region where he suffered is exhaustively treated in the *Sitzungsberichte der Wiener Akad.* 1881-1882, t. xcix. pp. 437-492, by Prof. Tomaschek, of Graz University. [G.T.S.]

Sabas (6), St., abbat in Palestine and founder of the laura of St. Sabas; born in 439, near Caesarea in Cappadocia. When 8 years old he entered a neighbouring monastery, and at 18 went a pilgrimage to the holy places at Jerusalem, where he entered the monastery of St. Passarion. At 30 he established himself as an anchorite in a cavern in the desert. Several persons joining him, he laid the foundations of his monastery on a rock on the Kidron river, where it still remains. (Cf. Murray's *Handbook for Syria*, p. 229.) He was ordained priest by Sallustius, patriarch of Constantinople, in 491. Several Armenians united themselves soon after to this community, which led to Sabas ordaining that the first part of Holy Communion should be said in Armenian, but the actual words of consecration in Greek. In 493 the monastery had increased so much that he built another at a short distance. He was sent as an ambassador to Constantinople in A.D. 511, by the patriarch ELIAS, to counteract the influence of Severus and the Monophysites with the emperor Anastasius; and again by Peter, patriarch of Jerusalem, in 531, to ask from the emperor remission of the taxes due by Palestine and help to rebuild the churches ruined by invasion. He died Dec. 5, 531, aged 91 years. His Life was written by Cyril of Scythopolis. [CYRILLUS (13).] Copious extracts from it are in Ceillier, xi. 274-277, and Fleury, *H. E.* lib. vii. §§ 30-32. The whole Life is in Coteler, *Monument.* t. iii. [G.T.S.]

Sabbatius (2), ordained by Marcianus as Novatianist bp. of Constantinople, seceded, before 380, from the main body of that sect, with two others, Theoctistes and Macarius, maintaining that Easter ought to be celebrated on the same day and in the same manner as by the Jews. He also complained that unworthy persons were admitted to the Novatianist communion, thus finding the same fault with the Novatianists that they did with the church. He became bishop of a small sect, called after him Sabbatiani, whose baptism was recognized in the 7th canon of the 2nd general council. Sozomen (*H. E.* vii. 18) gives a long account of his secession. [G.T.S.]

Sabellianism, the Eastern name for the movement designated Patripassianism in the West. It formed a portion of the great Monarchian movement, and can only be rightly understood in connexion therewith. We can trace its rise back to the age of Justin Martyr. In his *Apol.* i. § 63 he refers to those "who affirm that the Son is the Father," and condemns them—a condemnation which he repeats in his *Dialogue with Trypho*, § 128 (cf. Bull's *Defence of Nic. Creed*, t. i. 138, t. ii. 626; *Judgm. Cath. Ch.* iii. 198). The 2nd cent. was the age of Gnosticism, of which one of the essential principles was the emanation theory, which places a number of aeons, emanations from the Divine Being, intermediate between God and the Creation. The champions of Christian orthodoxy were led, in opposition, to insist strenuously upon the Divine Monarchy, God's sole, independent, and absolute existence and being. Thus we find Irenaeus writing a treatise περὶ μοναρχίας *c.* 190, addressed to a Roman presbyter, Florinus, who had fallen away to Gnosticism. Asian Gnosticism regarded the Son and the Holy Ghost as aeons or emanations (cf. Tertull. *cont. Prax.* c. 8). Christians had to shew that the existence of the Son and the Holy Ghost could be reconciled with the Divine Monarchy. Some therefore adopted the view which Dorner calls Ebionite Monarchianism, defending the Monarchy by denying the deity of Christ. Others identified the Persons of the Godhead with the Father, a theory which was called Sabellianism, though that name is not derived from the original inventor of this view. Sabellianism, in fact, was one of the mistakes men fell into while groping their way to the complete Christological conception. It was in the 2nd cent. an orthodox reaction against Gnosticism, as in the 4th cent. the Sabellianism of Marcellus of Ancyra was a reaction against Arianism. Tertullian expressly asserts, in the opening of his treatise against Praxeas, that this heresy had sprung out of a desire to maintain orthodoxy. The Roman church was one of the chief stages whereon the controversial struggle was waged. The visit of Origen to Rome, some time in 211-217, must have introduced him to the controversy, as abundant references to it and refutations of it are in his writings. The materials for tracing the development of Sabellian views during the 3rd cent. are very defective. Novatian on the Trinity (cc. 12, 18, 21, 22) treats it as an acknowledged heresy, using the same Scripture arguments as Justin Martyr in his *Dial. cum Tryph.* §§ 126-129. Novatian is the earliest author who distinctly calls this view the Sabellian heresy. The controversy next emerges into the full light of day in N. Africa *c.* 260. It permeated very largely the district of Pentapolis in Libya, under the leadership of two bishops of that district, Ammon and EUPHRANOR. Dionysius of Alexandria wrote against their teaching, whereupon he was accused of heresy to Dionysius of Rome. The documents bearing on the dispute between these two fathers are in Routh's *Rel. Sacr.* iii. 370-400; for a discussion of the controversy see DIONYSIUS (6). In 4th cent. it again burst forth when Marcellus of Ancyra, in opposing Arianism and the subordination theory of Origen, was led to deny any personal distinction between the First and Second Persons of the Trinity. Marcellus was probably only guilty of loose expressions, but his disciple Photinus worked out his system to its logical conclusions and boldly proclaimed Sabellian views. Eusebius of Caesarea wrote against Marcellus, and from the extracts in his two treatises, *cont. Marcell.* and *de Ecclesiast. Theolog.* we derive most of our information concerning Marcellus (cf. Epiph. *Haer.* lxxii.). Athanasius, Basil, Hilary, Chrysostom, all condemned Marcellus and his teaching. Basil's letters are a repertory of information about the controversy during the latter half of 4th cent. Basil first called Sabellius an African, solely, it would seem, because of the prevalence of Sabellianism in the Pentapolis, under Dionysius of Alexandria, when probably SABELLIUS himself was long dead. The interest in the controversy ceased by degrees as the great Nestorian and Eutychian discussions of the 5th cent. arose. Yet Sabellianism lingered in various quarters. Epiphanius (*Haer.* lxii.) says that in his time Sabellians were still numerous in Mesopotamia and Rome—a fact confirmed by an inscription discovered at Rome in 1742, which runs: "Qui et Filius diceris et Pater inveniris," evidently erected by Sabellian hands (Northcote's *Epitaph. of Catacombs*, p. 102). Augustine speaks of them, however, as practically extinct in Africa (cf. *Ep. ad Dioscorum*, cx.).

We add a brief exposition of this heresy. One section of the Monarchian party (see *supra*) guarded the Monarchy by denying any personal distinctions in the Godhead, and thus identifying the Father and the Son. But Christ is called the Son of God, and a son necessarily supposed a father distinct from himself (Tertul. *cont. Prax.* c. 10). They evaded this difficulty by distinguishing between the Logos and the Son of God. The Logos was itself eternally identical with God the Father. The Son of God did not exist till the Incarnation, when the Eternal Logos manifested its activity in the sphere of time in and through the man Christ Jesus. "In O.T.," says Sabellius, "no mention is made of the Son of God, but only of the Logos" (Athan. *Orat.* iv. § 23). The Sonship is a mere temporary matter, however (cf. Greg. Nys. *cont. Sabell.* in Mai's *Coll. Nov. Vett. Scriptt.* t. viii. pt. ii. p. 4), and when the work of man's salvation is completed the Logos will be withdrawn from the humanity of Christ into that personal union and identity with the Father which existed from eternity, while the humanity will be absorbed into the original Divine nature. All this was summed up in the distinction drawn between the λόγος ἐνδιάθετος and the λόγος προφορικός. Here Sabellianism merged into Pantheism. The ultimate end of all things, according to Sabellius, was the restoration of the Divine Unity; that God, as the absolute Μονάς, should be all in all. If, then, the absorption of Christ's humanity into the absolute Μονάς was necessary, much more the absorption of all inferior personal existences. Neander points out that this system presents many points of resemblance to the Alexandrian-Jewish theology. Epiphanius, indeed, expressly asserts (*Haer.* lxii. c. 2) that Sabellius derived his system from the apocryphal Gospel of the Egyptians, which stated that Christ had taught His disciples, as a great mystery, the identity of Father, Son, and Holy Ghost. This Gospel insisted upon the element of Sabellianism most akin to Pantheism, viz. that all contrarieties will be finally resolved into unity. Thus, according to it, Christ replied to the question of Salome when His kingdom should come, "When two shall be one, and the outer as the inner, and the male with the female; when there shall be no male and no female." Neander (*H. E.* t. ii. pp. 317-326, Bohn's ed.) gives the clearest exposition of this heresy and its connexion with kindred systems. [G.T.S.]

Sabellius, heretic, after whom the sect of the Sabellians was called (see preceding art.). The known facts of his history are but few. All 4th-cent. writers follow Basil in saying that he was born in Africa. The scene of Sabellius's activity was Rome, where we find him during the episcopate of pope Zephyrinus, A.D. 198-217. From the statement of Hippolytus, he was apparently undecided in his views when he came to Rome, or when he first began to put forward his views at Rome, for the silence of Hippolytus about his birthplace suggests that it may have been Rome. In *Refut.* ix. 6, Hippolytus says that Callistus perverted Sabellius to Monarchian views. Hippolytus argued with him and with Noetus and his followers (*ib.* iii.). Sabellius, convinced for a time, was again led astray by Callistus. In fact, during the episcopate of Zephyrinus, Callistus, Sabellius and the pope seem to have united in persistently opposing Hippolytus. Soon after his accession Callistus (A.D. 217) excommunicated Sabellius, wishing to gain, as Hippolytus puts it, a reputation for orthodoxy and to screen himself from the attacks of his persistent foe. Sabellius thereupon disappears from the scene. He seems to have written some works, to judge from apparent quotations by Athanasius in his 4th treatise against Arianism. [G.T.S.]

Sabina (1), Poppaea, empress, 2nd wife of Nero. Like certain members of the Flavian family, it is very highly probable, though not absolutely certain, that Poppaea was a Christian. She was almost certainly a Jewish proselyte, as the language of Josephus, θεοσεβὴς γὰρ ἦν (*Ant.* xx. 8, 11) almost implies. The fact that her body was embalmed and not burnt after the Roman custom (Tac. *Ann.* xvi. 6) has been urged to shew that she had embraced a foreign religion. Certainly at least twice (Jos. *l.c.*, and *Vita*, 3) she exerted her influence with Nero in favour of the Jews (see Lightfoot, *Philipp.* 5 note). It has even been conjectured that it was through her that the Christians and not Jews were selected as the victims to suffer for the burning of Rome. A romantic theory was put forward by M. Latour St. Ybars of a rivalry between the Jewish Poppaea and Acte the former mistress of Nero, who, on the strength of a passage in St. Chrysostom (*Hom. in Acta* xlvi. in Migne, *Patr. Gk.* lx. 325), is conjectured to have been a Christian. Schiller, *Gesch. d. röm. Kaiserreichs unter Nero*, 436 n., and Aubé, *Hist. des perséc.* 421 n. For the general history of Poppaea see Merivale, c. liii. [F.D.]

Sabinus (10), bp. of Heraclea in Thrace, and a leader of the party and sect of Macedonius. He was the author of a collection of the Acts of the councils of the church from the council of Nicaea to his own time, which was much used by Socrates in his *Eccl. Hist.*, who speaks of it as untrustworthy, because Sabinus was an unscrupulous partisan, and omitted, and even wilfully altered, facts and statements adverse to his views and interests (cf. Socr. *op. cit.* i. 8; ii. 15). Socrates shews how Sabinus tries to disparage the fathers of Nicaea in the face of the contrary evidence of Eusebius, and makes no mention whatever of Macedonius, lest he should have to describe his evil deeds. Baronius (*ad ann.* 325, xxxix., *ad ann.* 344, iii. etc.) speaks strongly of Sabinus's unscrupulous handling of history, calls him "homo mendacissimus," and suggests that Sozomen gives a garbled account of the election of Athanasius, "ex officina Sabini." Cave (*Hist. Lit.* i. 411) fixes the date at which Sabinus flourished as *c.* 425. [G.W.D.]

Salamanes (2), a solitary of Capersana, a village on the right bank of the Euphrates, who shut himself up in a cell on the opposite bank, having neither door nor window. Once a year he dug himself out, obtained food for the next year, and returned, having spoken with none. His diocesan, desiring to confer orders on so distinguished an ascetic, had the cell wall broken down and laid his hands upon him, Salamanes neither consenting nor dissenting. With equal passiveness he allowed himself to be transferred to another cell across the river by the inhabitants of the village, and to be taken back again by his former neighbours (Theod. *Hist. Relig.* c. xix.). [E.V.]

Salvianus (3), priest of Marseilles, a writer whose works illustrate most vividly the state of Gaul in 5th cent. The one external authority for his Life is Gennadius, *de Scriptt. Eccles.* c. 67, who gives a list of his writings. In 429 St. Hilary of Arles, in a sermon on St. Honoratus, describes him as "the most blessed man Salvianus the presbyter." His own expressions (*de Gub. Dei*, vi. 72) indicate that he was born in Gaul, probably at Trèves, the manners and customs of which place he knew intimately and reproves sharply. He, or at least some of his relations, resided at Cologne, occupying a respectable position in that city. When a young man he married Palladia, daughter of Hypatius, and had one daughter Auspiciola, after whose birth Salvianus and his wife adopted the monastic life. This greatly incensed Hypatius, who retired to a distant region, refusing any communication with them for 7 years. *Ep.* iv. is a very earnest appeal by Salvianus, his wife, and daughter, for a renewal of the love and friendship of Hypatius, with what success we are not told. Salvianus was in extreme old age when Gennadius wrote, and was held in the highest honour, being expressly termed "Episcoporum Magister," and regarded as the very type of a monk and a scholar. His writings are important from a social, political, and ecclesiastical point of view. In the *de Gub. Dei* he gives a lively picture of the social changes in the empire due to the iniquitous fiscal system in vogue. Thus lib. v. cc. 4-9 shew clearly the cause of brigandage, the origin of the serf system, and the evils of vast estates. In iv. 14 he refers to the crowds of Syrian merchants in all the cities of Gaul, a fact which the discovery of Syrian, Assyrian, and other Oriental inscriptions in France has amply confirmed (cf. Le Blant's *Ins. chrét. de la Gaule*, diss. Nos. 225, 557, and 613). He helps us to understand the interruption of intercourse between Roman and British Christianity in 5th and 6th cents. The empire was gradually surrounded by a ring fence of hostile states, all barbarous, and several of them heretical, which served as a retreat from the power, and a barrier to the religion, of Rome. For a cent. and a half the new kingdoms of the Franks and Burgundians afforded ample employment for Rome's missionary zeal without troubling with the regions beyond. The treatise against avarice is a laudation of the ascetic life and of almsgiving; he even in bk. i. seriously discusses whether a man should leave any property at all to his sons. Ceillier (x. 359) devotes a lengthened notice to Salvianus, with a full analysis of his writings.

The latest ed. of his works is that in the *Corp. Eccl. Scriptorum* of the Vienna Academy, t. viii. (Vindob. 1883), ed. by Fr. Pauly. [G.T.S.]

Salvina (*Silvina*), daughter of the Moorish chief Gildo, count of Africa. The Christian virtues which, according to Jerome and Chrysostom, distinguished the ladies of Gildo's family, were in strong contrast with brutal and savage vices which rendered his name detestable. While still a girl, Salvina was transferred by Theodosius to his own court, as a pledge of the loyalty of her father and of the province of Africa which he governed. She was brought up with the young members of the imperial family, and married *c.* 390 Nebridius, the son of the empress's sister, who had been educated with his cousins, the future emperors, Arcadius and Honorius. Nebridius, dying soon after, left her with a son, Nebridius, and a daughter (Hieron. *Ep.* ix.). She devoted herself to God's service, and, as her husband had done, protected the Oriental churches and ecclesiastics at the court of Arcadius. Her fame having spread to Palestine, Jerome, though a stranger, wrote her a letter—the arrogant tone of which might well have offended, if the coarseness had not shocked her. The young widow and her children then formed one household with her mother, Gildo's widow (he had died A.D. 398), and her paternal aunt at Constantinople (Hieron. *Ep.* 9; *de Serv. Virg.*; *Ep.* 11 *ad Geront. ad fin.*). Salvina's ardent piety speedily attached her to Chrysostom. She became one of his deaconesses, equalling Olympias and Pentadia in devotion to him. She remained with him to the last, and, together with the above-named and Procula, took a final farewell of him in the baptistery of the cathedral the night of his final expulsion (Pallad. p. 90). [E.V.]

Salvius (3), Donatist bp. of Membrasa (*Medjez el Bab*), one of the 12 ordainers of

Maximian. He is mentioned as one who practised rebaptism (Aug. *Parm.* iii. 22). Refusing to return to the party of Primian, he was displaced, and Restitutus appointed in his stead. Salvius believed that his opponents could not take advantage of the laws against heretics without implicating themselves in its operation (Aug. *c. Cresc.* iv. 57, 58, 60, 82; *Ep.* 108. 14; *En. Ps.* 57. 18; *Cod. Theodos.* xvi. 5, 22, 25, 26). The action appears to have been brought during the proconsulate of Herodes, A.D. 394, but not to have been decided until that of Seranus, A.D. 398. When the judgment was published, the people of Membresa, by whom Salvius, now an old man, was greatly beloved, appear to have supported him in opposition to the edict; but the people of Abitina, a neighbouring town, took upon themselves, without any official sanction, to execute it, and having attacked Salvius, maltreated him cruelly and ignominiously. Whether this attack caused the death of Salvius we know not, nor do we hear of him again, but his case is often quoted by Augustine when retorting on the Donatists their charge against the Catholics of persecution. [H.W.P.]

Salvius (5) (*Sauve*), St., bp. of Alby, an intimate friend of Gregory of Tours, who gives the story of his early life from his own lips. He had been an advocate, and had led an active and worldly life though unstained by the passions of youth. After his conversion he entered a monastery to embrace a new life of poverty, austerity, and worship. In time the monks made him abbat, but craving for still higher sanctity, he withdrew to a solitary cell, where, after a fever, he fell into a sort of trance, and was laid out for dead. While unconscious he was conducted by two angels to heaven, and shewn the glory of it, but not permitted to remain, as work still awaited him on earth. The account of this Dantesque vision, which Gregory calls God to witness he heard from the bishop's own lips, is interesting (*Hist. Franc.* vii. 1). The authenticity of this chapter has, however, been questioned (see Boll. *Acta SS.* Sept. iii. 575, 576). As bishop Salvius indignantly scouted the heretical and somewhat crude views on the Trinity which king Chilperic wished to force upon the church (*ib.* v. 45). He was at the council of Braine in 580, and while bidding farewell to Gregory there, he pointed to the king's palace and asked him if he saw aught above it. Gregory could see nothing but the upper story just built at Chilperic's command. Then Salvius, drawing a deep sigh, said: "Video ego evaginatum irae divinae gladium super domum hanc dependentem," and after 20 days the two sons of the king were no more (v. 51). When Mummolus carried off some of the flock of Salvius as prisoners, he followed and ransomed them at his own cost; and when Alby was almost depopulated by a plague that ravaged S. France, he refused to desert the city (vii. 1). He died *c.* 584, being succeeded by Desideratus (vii. 22). [S.A.B.]

Samson (1) (*Sampson*), Welsh saint, bp. of Dôl. His legend is obscured by the admixture of several traditions. The materials for his Life are of their kind very abundant.

Taking the Life in *Lib. Land.* as a type of the British tradition as distinguished from the Gallican, Samson was son of Amwn Ddu, prince of Armorica in the 5th cent. Born in Glamorganshire, educated by St. Illtyd at Llantwit Major, ordained deacon and priest by St. Dubricius, he became for three and a half years abbat of St. Peirio or Piro's monastery on an island near Llantwit; some say at Llantwit. Afterwards he lived in a desert near the Severn, was consecrated by St. Dubricius and others to the episcopate, though, according to the common Celtic custom, without reference to a specific see, and in course of time proceeded to Armorica, where he became the deliverer of the captive prince Judual, and died at Dôl (*Lib. Land.* 305). Thus far, and excluding the miraculous elements, the tradition is generally consistent and complete, though some Welsh traditions bring him back to die at Llantwit. To this are added several fictions, probably of the 12th cent., traceable to Geoffrey of Monmouth and to Girald. Cambr. The monumental inscribed stones to SS. Illtyd and Samson found in the churchyard of Llantwit Major cannot be of this early date; the Samson there mentioned must have lived in the 9th cent., and the lettering would agree with that date. Haddan and Stubbs, *Counc.* i. 626-628; Rees, *Welsh SS.* 181, 255). [J.G.]

Sarbelius (1) (*Sharbil*). Syriac Acts of Sarbelius and other Edessan martyrs are in Cureton's *Antiq. Mon. Syr.* (1864), and a Latin trans., with abundant illustrative matter, was pub. by Moesinger (Innsbruck, 1874). According to them, Sarbelius was chief priest of the idol-worship of Edessa. Trajan, in the 15th year of his reign (also described as the 3rd of Abgarus, the 7th king, and the 416th of the era of Alexander the Great), commanded the rulers of the provinces to see that sacrifices and libations were renewed and increased in every city, and to punish with torture those who refused to take part. Barsimaeus, the bp. of the Christians, accompanied by a priest and deacon, thereupon waited on Sarbelius and warned him of his responsibility in leading so many to worship gods made with hands. They briefly told him of the doctrine concerning our Lord's Incarnation and death, taught by Paluth, the disciple of Addai the apostle, and believed in by the earlier king Abgarus. Sarbelius was at once converted, baptized that night, and made his appearance next day clad in his baptismal robes. A great multitude, including some chief men of the city, were converted with him. The Acts then relate how the governor Licinius brought Sarbelius before him and commanded him to sacrifice. As each form of torture was tried without success, Licinius ordered a new and more severe one, 18 being described. Finally, Sarbelius was put to death with new tortures, being partially sawn asunder and then beheaded, his sister Barbea being martyred with him. There are separate Acts of Barsimaeus, evidently by the same hand. They relate how he, after the martyrdom of Sarbelius, was brought before the tribunal and similarly tortured. But a letter, ordering persecution to cease, arrived from Trajan, who had been convinced of the excellence of Christian morality and of the general agreement of their laws of conduct with the imperial laws.

These Edessan Acts acquired very considerable celebrity. Moesinger published an Armenian translation, and Sarbelius is commemorated in the Greek *Menaea* and the Latin Martyrologies under Jan. 29 and Oct. 15. There is also a Thathuel, commemorated Sept. 4, whose story is identical with that of Sarbelius. Moesinger argued that the extant Acts were written by a contemporary of Sarbelius and were historically trustworthy; but his arguments are too weak to deserve serious refutation. Two marks of fiction are obvious: the extravagant amount of tortures alleged, and the familiarity of Sarbelius with N.T., which would have been noteworthy in a Christian of long standing in A.D. 105, but is incredible in a newly-made convert. He is made to quote the Gospels several times, the Psalms, and Romans. We may ascribe the Acts to the latter part of 4th cent. They are probably later than Eusebius, who shews no knowledge of the story; but are largely employed in a sermon, printed by Moesinger, by James of Sarug (d. 522). There is a strong family likeness between the Acts of Sarbelius and those of Habibus, and of Samona and Guria, also given in Cureton's work. Since the latter martyrs are said to have suffered under Diocletian, the former Acts, which seem to have the same origin, are at least no earlier. [G.S.]

Saturninus (1). In the section of his work commencing I. 22 Irenaeus gives a list of heretics, apparently derived from Justin Martyr. The first two are the Samaritan heretics, Simon and Menander; the next, as having derived their doctrines from these, Saturninus and Basilides, who taught, the former in the Syrian Antioch, the latter in Egypt. Irenaeus says that Saturninus, like Menander, ascribed the ultimate origin of things to a Father unknown to all; and taught that this Father made angels, archangels, powers, authorities, but that the world and the things therein were made by a certain company of seven angels, in whom no doubt we are to recognize the rulers of the seven planetary spheres. He taught that man was the work of the same angels. They had seen a brilliant image (εἰκών) descend from the Supreme Power, and had striven to detain it, but in vain; for it immediately shot back again. So they encouraged each other: "Let us make man after the image and after the likeness" (κατ' εἰκόνα καὶ καθ' ὁμοίωσιν, Gen. i. 25). They made the man, but were too feeble to give him power to stand erect, and he lay on the ground wriggling like a worm (ὡς σκώληκος σκαρίζοντος) until the Upper Power, taking compassion on him because he had been made "in Its likeness," sent a spark of life which raised him and made him live. Saturninus taught that after man's death this spark runs back to its kindred, while the rest of man is resolved into the elements whence he was made.

The same creation myth is reported by Irenaeus (I. xxx. 5) to have been included in the system commonly known as Ophite; and literary dependence of the two stories is clear from the common use of the word σκαρίζω. But according to the Ophite story it is not the Supreme Power, but Ialdabaoth, the chief of the creative company, who bestows the breath of life; and these angels say, as in Genesis, "Let us make man after *our* image." We may count Saturninus as the originator of the myth, for the Ophite version has marks of less simplicity and originality.

Saturninus further taught that the God of the Jews was one of the seven creator angels. He and his company were in constant warfare with Satan and a company of evil angels. So, likewise, there were two distinct species of men, the bad ever aided by the demons in their conflicts with the good. Then the Supreme Father sent a Saviour to destroy the power of the God of the Jews and the other Archons; and to save those who had the spark of life in them—that is to say, the good. This Saviour had no human birth or human body, and was only a man in appearance.

Saturninus ascribed the Jewish prophecies, some to the creator angels and some to Satan. This is one of several points of coincidence between the reports given by Irenaeus of the teaching of Saturninus and of the Ophites. These do not ascribe any of the prophecies to Satan, but Irenaeus (§ 11) gives the scheme according to which they distributed them among the several angels. Saturninus does not appear to have left any writings. His sect is named by Justin Martyr (*Trypho*, 35) and by Hegesippus (Eus. *H. E.* iv. 22). No later heresiologist appears to know anything about him beyond what he learned from Irenaeus; and Irenaeus probably derived all his knowledge from Justin Martyr. [G.S.]

Saturninus (2) (*Sernin*), St., martyr, first bp. and patron of Toulouse. According to his *Acta*, published by Surius (Nov. 29) and by Ruinart after careful revision in his *Acta Sincera* (pp. 128-133), Saturninus came to Toulouse in the consulship of Decius and Gratius (A.D. 251), apparently from Rome (cf. Venant. Fort. *Misc.* ii. 12, Migne, *Patr. Lat.* lxxxviii. 101). Here his preaching so exasperated the people that they put him to a shocking death by binding him to a bull, which they infuriated by goads. There were two other traditions current in early times—one that Saturninus was sent into France by St. Clement at the end of the 1st cent., the other that his mission was from the apostles themselves. The former is in Gregory of Tours (*de Glor. Mart.* i. 48), and the latter is as old as Venantius Fortunatus, if the *Passio S. Dionysii* is rightly ascribed to him (Migne, *u.s.* 579), and appears in many other ancient sources (see Ceillier, ii. 111 n.). Sidonius Apollinaris celebrated his martyrdom in Sapphic stanzas (*Ep.* ix. 16). Venantius Fortunatus has some verses on the same event, the wonder-working virtues of his tomb (*Misc.* ii. 11, Migne, *u.s.* 99), and on the beautiful church built towards the close of 6th cent. by Launibodes on the spot where he was bound to the bull and which came to be known as du Taur or du Taureau (ii. 12, col. 100). [S.A.B.]

Saturninus (21), 8th bp. of Arles, a pillar of Arianism in the West. In the winter of 353 he presided at the council of Arles, which, in the presence of Constantius, condemned Athanasius and sentenced Paulinus of Trèves to deprivation and exile. About this time Hilary, bp. of Poictiers, appeared on the scene, and was henceforth in the West the champion of orthodoxy against Saturninus, Ursacius, Valens, and the emperor. In 356 Saturninus presided at the council of Béziers, which decreed the exile of Hilary; and it seems probable from allusions in Hilary's writings that he was also at the council of Rimini in 359, and was one of the legates dispatched thence to the emperor at Constantinople (Hil. *ad Const. Aug.* ii. 3; Migne, *Patr. Lat.* x. 565). This seems to have been the zenith of the bishop's fortune. Hilary, not long after, returned to Gaul; and Saturninus, still unbending in his opposition, was deprived of his see, and even excommunicated, as is thought, at the 1st council of Paris in 362. [S.A.B.]

Scapula, a proconsul of Africa, with whom Tertullian remonstrated for his persecution of the Christians; not because the Christians feared martyrdom, but solely because their love for their enemies made them desire to save them from the guilt of shedding innocent blood. Tertullian recounts the temporal calamities which had overtaken former persecutors of the Christians, and denounces the injustice of punishing men pure in life and loyal, and whose innocence the magistrates fully acknowledge by their evident unwillingness to proceed to extremities and by their exertions to induce the accused to withdraw their confession. If, as had been done in another province, the Christians of Carthage were to present themselves in a body before the proconsul's tribunal, the magistrate, he says, would find before him thousands of every age, sex, and rank, including many leading persons, and probably relations and intimates of his own friends, and might well shrink from severities which would decimate the city. The tract is later than the emperor Severus, of whom it speaks in the past tense.

The Scapula addressed was probably Scapula Tertullus, one of the ordinary consuls in 195. The usual interval between consulship and proconsulship was 15 to 20 years; this also would place the proconsulship not very long after Severus died on Feb. 9, 211. [G.S.]

Scillitan Martyrs, 12 martyrs at Carthage (one of them Felix) from the African town of Scillita. According to their *Acta*, one of the women, Donata, when they were called upon by the consul, Saturninus, to sacrifice, replied, "We render honour to Caesar as Caesar, but worship and prayers to God alone." On receiving their sentence they thanked God. It was Ruinart's theory that the Scillitan Martyrs suffered under Sept. Severus between 198 and 202. M. Léon Renier, an eminent French archaeologist, however, noticed that the first line of the received codices of the Acts of these martyrs gave the names of the consuls for the year of the martyrdom very variously, a fragment published by Mabillon (*Vet. Analect.* t. iv. p. 155) reading, "Praesidente bis Claudiano consule." He therefore suggested that the word "bis" ought to follow a proper name indicating a second consulship, and that the word "consule" ought to be replaced by "consulibus." Finding, moreover, in the *Fasti* the names Praesens II. and Condianus as consuls for 180, he proposed that the first line of our Acts should be read, "Praesente bis et Condiano Consulibus." Then in 1881 Usener, a Bonn professor, published a hitherto unknown text of these Acts from a Greek MS. in the *Bibl. Nat.* of Paris, dating from the end of 9th cent., and explicitly naming the very two consuls Renier suggested, Praesens II. and Condianus. There is no mention of Severus. It quite correctly speaks of one emperor, since Commodus on July 17, 180, was sole emperor. The proconsul of Africa is Saturninus. He continues the policy of the previous reign, which is not yet modified by the domestic influences which led Commodus to favour the Christians. In 177 persecution had raged at Lyons. It was now the turn of Africa. Usener regarded the Gk. text discovered by him as a translation from Latin. Aubé, viewing the Gk. text of Usener as an original document and the source of all the Latin texts, replied to Usener's arguments, pointing out that Greek was largely spoken at Carthage in the latter half of 2nd cent., and urging many critical considerations from a comparison of the Latin and Greek texts which seem to support his view. For a further discussion of the question see Aubé and Usener. To the Biblical critic these Acts in both shapes are interesting, as indicating the position held by St. Paul's Epp. in 180 in the N. African church. The proconsul asked the martyr Speratus what books they kept laid up in their bookcases? He replied, Our books, or, as the Latin version puts it, the four Gospels of our Lord Jesus Christ, and in addition the Epistles of Paul the holy man. *Etude sur un nouveau texte des Actes des Martyrs Scillitains* (Paris, 1881); cf. Lightfoot's *Ignatius*, t. i. p. 507. [G.T.S.]

Sebastianus (2), Jan. 20, military martyr at Rome under Diocletian. He was of Milan, where he commanded the first cohort. He confessed Christ, and was shot (apparently) to death with arrows in the camp. He was celebrated in the time of St. Ambrose (*Enarr. in Ps.* 118, No. 44), and is the favourite saint of Italian women, and regarded as the protector against the plague. His symbol is an arrow. [G.T.S.]

Secundinus (11), a poet, a contemporary and correspondent of Sidonius Apollinaris (*Ep.* v. 8) who apparently highly esteemed Secundinus as a writer of hexameter verse on minor subjects, such as royal hunting parties and marriages. Secundinus afterwards attempted satire, and Sidonius highly commends a composition in hendecasyllabic metre, urging him to continue this kind of composition. It appears (*Ep.* ii. 10) that some of his hexameters were inscribed upon the wall of the basilica built at Lyons by Patiens (bishop *c.* 451-491), and he may have been one of the many minor poets who flourished at Lyons in the latter half of 5th cent. [H.A.W.]

Secundus (1), Gnostic of 2nd cent., a disciple of Valentinus, and apparently one of the earliest of that teacher's successors, since he is the first of that school of whom Irenaeus gives an account (I. xi. 2). Irenaeus reports two things as peculiar in his teaching: (1) he divided the primary Ogdoad into two Tetrads, a right-hand and a left-hand one, the one being called light, the other darkness; (2) he did not allow the Sophia out of whose passions, according to the Valentinian theory, the material world took its origin to have been one of the 30 primary Aeons. The short notice in Irenaeus seems the ultimate source of all authentic information about Secundus. [G.S.]

Secundus (4), bp. of Tigisis, a fortified town of Numidia, in the neighbourhood of Lambese and Thamagada (Procop. *Vandal.* ii. 13). The persecution under Diocletian appears to have reached its height in Feb. 304, and on May 19 Paulus, bp. of Cirta, committed the act of "tradition" which partly gave rise to the proceedings in which Secundus became conspicuous. Paulus soon died, and some 11 or 12 bishops met at Cirta on Mar. 5 (according to Optatus May 8), 305, under the presidency of Secundus, as primate of Numidia, to appoint a successor. Although persecution had virtually ceased, the churches were not yet restored, and the assembly met in the house of Urbanus, where they ordained Silvanus. Optatus says that amid the uproar of mutual incrimination [DONATISM] Purpurius of Limata taxed Secundus with tradition, because, instead of leaving his post of duty before the inquisition, he remained until dismissed in safety, which would not have been the case unless he had purchased his safety by act of surrender. On this a murmur arose in the assembly, and Secundus, in alarm, accepted a method of escape suggested by his nephew Secundus the younger, that such questions as this of personal conduct ought to be left to the judgment of the Almighty, a judicious evasion received with acclamation by all (Opt. i. 14; Aug. *Ep.* 43. 6).

When, on the death of Mensurius, bp. of Carthage, A.D. 311, Caecilian was appointed to succeed him, Secundus was sent for in haste to preside at a meeting of 70 malcontents at Carthage, and their factious opposition resulted in the schismatic appointment of Majorinus (Opt i. 19; Aug. *Parm.* i. 5). The case was brought up afresh at the conference of 411. Tillem. vi. 5-14; Morcelli, *Afr. Chr.* ii. 194-207; Ribbek, *Aug. und Don.* pp. 52-57, 69; Sparrow Simpson, *St. Aug. and Afr. Ch. Divisions* (1910), p. 32. [H.W.P.]

Sedulius (1), a 5th-cent. poet, of whose life very few details are known. The only trustworthy information is given by his two letters to Macedonius, from which we learn that he devoted his early life, perhaps as a teacher of rhetoric, to heathen literature. Late in life he became converted to Christianity, or, if a Christian before, began to take a serious view of his duties. Thenceforward he devoted his talents to the service of Christ, living as a priest (cf. i. 7-9), in close intercourse with a small body of religious friends (pref.). He gives us a charming account of this group: Macedonius, the father and life of the whole; Ursinus, the reverent priest spending his life in the service of the King of Heaven; Laurence, the wise and gentle, who has spent all his money on the poor; Gallicanus, another priest, not learned, but a model of goodness and loyalty to church rule; Ursicinus, combining the wisdom of age with the brightness of youth; the deaconess Syncletica, of noble birth and nobler life, a worthy temple of God, purified by fasting, prayer, and charity, learned and liberal; and lastly Perpetua, the young pure matron, perpetual in fame and purity as in name. Sedulius, too, longed to devote his talent to God and to strengthen his own spiritual life by exhorting others. He yearned to tell the heathen of the wonders of the Gospel, and wrote the *Carmen Paschale* to invite then to share the Gospel feast. This was dedicated to Macedonius, and afterwards, at his request, was translated into prose (*Opus Paschale*). The works shew a character of much humility (cf. i. *ad fin.*), of tenderness of heart (v. 96), of warm gratitude (*Carm. Pasch.* pref.), and of keen susceptibility to criticism (*Opus Pasch.* pref.).

These are the only certain facts. Even his date is uncertain. He refers to St. Jerome as a well-known student, and his work is praised by a decree of pope Gelasius in 495 or 496. Syncletica may have been a sister of Eustathius, who lived early in 5th cent. Hence the date of Sedulius must be *c.* 450. A mass of information about him is in later writers, but much of it arises from a confusion with Sedulius the Scotchman. The best authenticated account makes him a native of Rome who studied philosophy in Italy, became an *antistes* (*i.e.* probably a presbyter) and wrote his book in Achaia. The internal evidence as to these details is very slight: his friends bear Latin names almost entirely; he is in the presence of educated idolaters and takes special pains to argue against sun-worship; but these indications are very vague. His works became popular very soon. They were edited by an editor of Vergil, T. Rufius Asterius (consul A.D. 494)—perhaps in consequence of the importance attached to them by the pope's decree. They are mentioned with praise by Venantius Fortunatus (viii. 1) and Theodulf of Arles; were commented on, perhaps by Remi of Auxerre (9th cent.), and frequently quoted and imitated by the writers of the middle ages. Areval quotes 16 MSS. dating from cents. vii. to xvi.; since then more than 40 editions have been printed, and special prominence was given to him by German writers last century.

(1) *Carmen Paschale,* "a poem in honour of Christ our Passover," consists of five books. Bk. i. is an introductory appeal to the heathen to give up idolatry and listen to the deeds of the true God. Bks. ii.-v. describe in full detail the miracles of the Gospel and the Lord's Prayer. In the earlier part the narratives of SS. Matthew and Luke are pieced together in chronological order. Throughout the ministry to the final entry into Jerusalem Sedulius follows St. Matthew, with a few insertions from SS. John and Luke; then adds a succession of miracles from SS. Mark and Luke, without regard to chronology (iv. 59-221), and the chief incidents of St. John's Gospel; from the entry into Jerusalem to the end he mainly follows St. John. As a rule the details of the scenes are given slightly and followed by frequent comment, sometimes dogmatical (*e.g.* on the Nature of the Trinity, i. 16-20, 281 sqq., ii. 171, the Fatherhood of God, ii. 234, the Priesthood of Christ, iv. 207, etc.), at other times pointing out the typical meaning of Scripture, both of O.T. (i. 102-109, 127, 142, 152, iii. 202, iv. 170) and N.T.; *e.g.* the number of the evangelists and of the apostles (Prol. to lib. ii.; iii. 172), the number and nature of the gifts of the Magi (ii. 95), the dove

(ii. 170), and all the details of the passion (v. 101, 169, 190, 243, 257, 275, 402). More often still they consist of moral warnings or of explanations of our Lord's teaching (cf. ii. 106, iii. 321, iv. 16, 163, etc.).

The style is rhetorical but pleasant, with considerable terseness and power of antithesis; and fairly correct in prosody, shewing considerable acquaintance with classical authors. The reference to Origen (*Opus Pasch.* pref.) and the play on Elias and ἥλιος (i. 170) imply some knowledge of Greek; of Latin authors he knew Terence, Juvenal, and specially Vergil, from whom he frequently borrows; possibly, too, the poem of Juvencus. There is a growing frequency in the use of leonine rhymes. For an analysis with a discussion of its sources and theology see Leimbach, *Ueber den Christlichen Dichter Sedulius* (Goslar, 1879).

(2) *Opus Paschale.*—This prose translation mainly follows the *Carmen* faithfully, but adds illustrations and fills up gaps. It is preceded by another interesting letter to Macedonius.

(3) *Elegia.*—An elegiac poem of 110 lines, corresponding in subject to the *Carm. Pasch.* It describes the effect of the Incarnation in contrast to the work of Adam, and Christ as the antitype of the types of O.T.

(4) *Hymn.*—"A solis ortus cardine." This may be called a lyrical expression of the *Carmen.* It is a call to praise Christ with a description of the chief facts of His birth, life, and death. It is an alphabetical hymn in iambic dimeters with four-lined strophes. It shews a growing tendency to rhyme and a careful attempt to avoid any conflict between accent and quantity. Two extracts have been widely used in church services, viz. A-G in Lauds for Christmas week; and H, I, L, N, which celebrate the adoration of the Magi, the baptism, and the miracle at Cana, on the feast of Epiphany. These sections are in Daniel Thes. i. p. 143, and with a full German commentary in Kayser, pp. 347-383.

(5) *Cento Virgilianus* "de Verbi Incarnatione" is sometimes ascribed to Sedulius (*e.g.* by Bähr), but is only found in one Corbey MS., and there only follows the other poems without being ascribed to Sedulius. It is in Martene, *Vett. Scr. Coll.* ix. p. 125.

The most available edd. are Migne, *Patr. Lat.* xix.; a text of the poetical works by J. Looshorn (Munich, 1879); of the *Carm. Pasch.* in Hurter's *Op. Selecta,* xxxiii.; and Huemer's ed. of the whole (Vienna, 1885). [W.L.]

Senochus (1), St., a presbyter of great reputation for sanctity near Tours; born *c.* 536 in a district near Poictiers called Theiphalia, which had been for many years settled by a Scythian or Tartar race, to which he belonged. He became a Christian, and in some ruined buildings by Tours built himself a cell, at a spot where an old oratory existed, in which St. Martin, according to tradition, had been wont to pray. St. Euphronius, then bp. of Tours, consecrated it afresh, and ordained Senoch a deacon. Here with a little company of three he practised the greatest austerities, but aspiring to higher sanctity, afterwards shut himself in a solitary cell. In 573 Gregory became bp. of Tours, and received a visit from him. Soon after Senoch went to see his kinsfolk in Poitou, and came back, according to Gregory, so puffed up with spiritual pride that the bishop had to reprove him. He consented, at Gregory's persuasion, to forego his absolute solitude, that the sick might be healed by his virtues. He died, aged about 40, *c.* 576. He had redeemed many from captivity or healed or fed them, and miracles were attributed to his corpse. Greg. Tur. *Hist. Franc.* v. 7; *Vitae Patrum,* c. xv.; *de Glor. Conf.* c. xxxv.; Boll. *Acta SS.* Oct. x. 764 sqq. [S.A.B.]

Senuti, an anchorite whose history was investigated by E. Revillout in a paper on the Blemmyes (*Mém. de l'Acad. des Inscr.* 1874, sér. 1, t. viii. p. 395), and still more elaborately in a series of articles in the *Revue de l'hist. des religions* (1883), Nos. 4 and 5. He was born about the middle of 4th cent. His father was a farmer in Egypt, and Senuti fed his sheep in boyhood. But it was an age when every enthusiast devoted himself to the monastic life. He attached himself to the monastery of Panopolis near Athrebi in Upper Egypt, where he soon attained such fame for sanctity and orthodoxy that Cyril would only set out for the council of Ephesus if he had the company of Senuti and Victor, archimandrite of Tabenna. Zoega, *Cat. MSS. Coptic Mus. Borg.* p. 29, gives us Cyril's account of this affair. Senuti's conduct at the council of Ephesus, as described by his disciple and successor Besa, fully justifies the charges of outrageous violence brought by the Nestorian party against their opponents. A lofty throne was in the centre of the hall with the four gospels on it. Nestorius entered with pomp, flung the gospels on the floor, and seated himself on the throne. This enraged Senuti, who, snatching up the book, hurled it against the breast of Nestorius with vigorous reproaches. Nestorius demanded who he was, and what brought him to the council, being "neither a bishop, nor an archimandrite, nor a provost, but merely a simple monk." "God sent me to the council," replied Senuti, "to confound thee and thy wickedness." Amid the plaudits of his adherents Cyril at once invested him with the rank and robe of an archimandrite. His career was now marked by miracle. He was wafted on a cloud to Egypt. His fame was everywhere established, and Roman commanders sought his assistance. Thus *c.* 450 the dux of Upper Egypt, Maximin, hurrying to repel a terrific invasion of the Blemmyes, before he would advance sought the presence of Senuti, who gave Maximin his girdle to wear whenever he joined battle. According to the Coptic MSS. Senuti followed Nestorius with bitter persecution to the last, even offering him personal violence when he lay dying in Egypt.

Senuti lived to be a heretic in the opposite extreme from Nestorius. After the council of Chalcedon he became a Monophysite and a violent partisan of the patriarch Dioscorus of Alexandria, dying under Timotheus Aelurus aged 118 years. [G.T.S.]

Serapion (1), bp. of Antioch, reckoned 8th in succession, A.D. 190-203 (Clinton), succeeding Maximin in the 11th year of Commodus (Eus. *H. E.* vi. 12; *Chron.*), was a theologian of considerable literary activity, the author of works of which Eusebius had no certain knowledge besides those enumerated by him. Of the latter Jerome gives an account (*de Script. Eccl.* c. 41) borrowed from Eusebius (*H. E.* v. 19; vi. 12). They are—(1) a letter to Caricus and Pontius against the Cataphrygian or Montanist heresy, containing a copy of a letter of Apollinaris of Hierapolis, and substantiated as to the facts by the signatures of several other bishops, including some of Thrace; (2) a treatise addressed to Domninus, who during the persecution of Severus had fallen away to the Jewish "will-worship"; and (3), the most important, directed against the Docetic gospel falsely attributed to St. Peter, addressed to some members of the church of Rhossus, who were being led away by it from the true faith. Serapion recalls the permission to read this apocryphal work given in ignorance of its true character and expresses his intention of speedily visiting the church to strengthen them in the true faith. Dr. Neale calls attention to the important evidence here furnished to "the power yet possessed by individual bishops of settling the canon of Scripture" (*Patriarch. of Antioch*, p. 36). Socrates refers to his writings, as an authority against Apollinarianism (*H. E.* iii. 7). Jerome mentions sundry letters in harmony with his life and character. Tillem. *Mém. eccl.* iii. 168, § 9; Cave, *Hist. Lit.* i. 86; Le Quien, *Or. Christ.* ii. 702. [E.V.]

Serapion (3), a penitent of Alexandria, who fell during the Decian persecution. Dionysius of Alexandria uses his case as an argument against the Novatianist schism, to which his correspondent, Fabius of Antioch, was inclined. Serapion lived a long life without blame, but had sacrificed at last. He often begged for admission to the church, but was refused. He was then taken sick, being three days without speech. When he awoke to consciousness he dispatched his grandson for a presbyter, who was sick and unable to come, but sent a portion of the consecrated Eucharist, telling the boy to moisten it and drop it into Serapion's mouth, who then died in peace. Reservation of the Sacrament must then have been practised in Alexandria. No argument, however, for communion in one kind can be drawn from this, as doubtless the bread had been dippedin the Eucharistic wine, according to Eastern fashion (see Bingham's *Antiq.* lib. xv. c. v.). Eus. *H. E.* vi. 44. [G.T.S.]

Serapion (9), surnamed *Scholasticus*, bp. of Thmuis in Egypt. He was a friend of St. Athanasius and St. Anthony of the desert, and occupied a position of some importance in 4th-cent. theological struggles. Anthony bequeathed one of his sheepskin cloaks to Serapion and the other to Athanasius (*Vita S. Anth. in Opp. S. Athan.*, Migne, *Patr. Lat.* t. xxvi. col. 971). Serapion's literary activity was considerable. St. Jerome (*Catal.* No. 99) mentions several of his writings, as his treatise *contra Manichaeos*, his *de Psalmorum Titulis* (now lost), and some epistles. His work against the Manicheans, described by Jerome as "Egregium librum," and noticed by Photius (*Cod.* 85), was for the first time printed in its original form by Brinkmann in 1894. It had previously been mixed up with a similar work by Titus of Bostra. In its restored form it is a valuable argument against Manicheism. Two letters by him were pub. by Cardinal Mai—one a consolatory letter to bp. Eudoxius, who had been tortured; the other censuring some monks of Alexandria. In *Texte und Untersuchungen* (Leipz. 1898) Wobbermin published a dogmatic letter "on the Father and the Son," and 30 liturgical prayers, the 1st and 15th of which are the work of Serapion. They have been reprinted, with valuable notes and discussions, by F. E. Brightman in the *Oxf. Journ. of Theol. Studies*, 1899-1910, under the title of *The Sacramentary of Serapion of Thmuis*, and an English trans., ed. by bp. Wordsworth of Salisbury, has been pub. by S.P.C.K. [G.T.S.]

Serapion (11), surnamed *Sindonites* from the linen or cotton clothing he always wore; an Egyptian monk in the time of Palladius. Though uneducated, he knew the Scriptures by heart. Some of his sayings are recorded in the *Verba Seniorum* (Rosweyd, *Vit. Pat.* lib. v libell. vi. § 12, libell. xi. 31), and in the *Apophthegmata Patrum* (Coteler. *Gr. Ecc. Monum.* i. 685, 686) there is an account of his visit to a lewd woman, whom he brought to repentance. His missionary zeal led him to travel, but in more than apostolic poverty, and he even sold his volume of the gospel to relieve a destitute person, a circumstance alluded to by Socrates (iv. 23), though without naming Serapion. Once he sold himself as a slave to a theatrical company, and once to a Manichean family, with a view to converting them from their errors. He visited Athens and Sparta. At Rome he met Domninus, a disciple of Origen (Pallad. *Laus Hist.* 83, 84; *Vit. Joan. Eleemos. c.* 22 in Rosweyd, lib. i.). He died, aged 60, *c.* 400, not at Rome as stated in the Latin version of the *Lausiac History*, but in the desert, as in Heraclides (*Paradis.* c. 24) and the Greek of Palladius. The Greeks honoured his memory on May 21, the *Menaea* erroneously calling him ὁ ἀπὸ Σειδόνος, belonging to Sidon. He may be the Serapion of Mar. 21 in the Latin Martyrologies (*vid. D. C. A.*), though the Roman Martyrology makes this one bp. of Thmuis. [C.H.]

Serapion (14), a solitary of Scete, and leader of the Anthropomorphites against the festal epistle of Theophilus, patriarch of Alexandria. The monks of Scete, with the one exception of Paphnutius, an abbat, rejected the orthodox view as to God's nature. Serapion, however, was converted by the efforts of Photinus, an Oriental deacon. Cassian tells us that an abbat Isaac explained to him in connexion with Serapion's conversion that the Anthropomorphite heresy was simply a relic of paganism. Pious men like Serapion had been so long accustomed to an image that without a material notion of God their prayers seemed objectless. Cassian, *Collat.* x. 16; Ceill. viii. 176. [G.T.S.]

Serapion (16), bp. of Heraclea, an Egyptian by birth, ordained deacon by Chrysostom (Socr. *H. E.* vi. 4), and by him made archdeacon of the church of Constantinople (Soz. *H. E.* viii. 9). His character as drawn by contemporary historians is most unfavourable. Presuming on his official power, he treated others with contempt and exhibited an intolerable arrogance (Socr. *H. E.* vi. 11;

Soz. *u.s.*). His unbounded influence over Chrysostom tended continually to widen the breach between the bishop and his clergy which the stern line of action originally adopted at Serapion's instance had opened early in his episcopate. Socrates records, as a characteristic speech, that Chrysostom, having vainly endeavoured to enforce his strict notions of discipline on his worldly and luxurious clergy, Serapion exclaimed in their hearing, "You will never be able to master these men, bishop, unless you drive them all with one rod" (Socr. *H. E.* vi. 4). Chrysostom mistakenly regarded Serapion's harshness as proof of his holy zeal (*ib.* vi. 17).

On Chrysostom's leaving Constantinople early in 401 to regulate the affairs of the church of Asia, he deputed SEVERIAN, bp. of Gabala, to act as his commissary, but the real management of the diocese and its clergy was left to Serapion. Severian was ambitious and devoid of a high sense of honour, and Serapion had soon to report, probably with exaggerations, that he was undermining Chrysostom's influence with the court and aristocracy, and seeking to outdo him as a preacher. Chrysostom hastened back to Constantinople, and Serapion greeted him with the astounding intelligence that Severian had denied the Incarnation. The grounds of this charge were the following: Serapion having ostentatiously refused to rise to pay Severian as he passed the accustomed homage of a deacon to a bishop, with the express intention, declared to the clergy around, of shewing "how much he despised the man." Severian, at this studied insult, indignantly exclaimed, "If Serapion dies a Christian, then Jesus Christ was not incarnate." Serapion repeated the latter clause alone, and delated Severian as a denier of the chief article of the Christian faith. The report was confirmed by bystanders and readily credited by Chrysostom, who expelled Severian from the city as a blasphemer (Soz. *H. E.* viii. 10; Socr. *H. E.* vi. 11). An account favourable to Serapion is found in a fragment (unwarrantably embodied in some Eng. translations of Socrates's *Hist.*) printed as an appendix to Socr. vi. 11. According to this, Serapion's act of disrespect was brought before a synod, which, on Serapion affirming on oath that he had not seen Severian pass, acquitted him of intentional rudeness, while Chrysostom, hoping to soothe Severian's ruffled feelings, suspended Serapion from his ecclesiastical functions for a short time. Severian, however, insisted on his deposition and excommunication. Chrysostom, annoyed at his pertinacity, quitted the synod, leaving the decision to the bishops, by whom his mild sentence was immediately confirmed. Chrysostom then broke off all intimacy with Severian and recommended him to return to his own diocese, which he had neglected too long. For the remainder of this unhappy transaction see SEVERIANUS (**2**). Chrysostom rewarded the supposed fidelity of Serapion by raising him to the priesthood, and returning from the brief expulsion which followed the synod of the Oak, gave Serapion the metropolitan see of Heraclea in Thrace (*ib.* 17). On Chrysostom's second and final banishment Serapion, taking refuge in a convent of Gothic monks known as the Marsi (Chrys. *Ep.* 14), was discovered, dragged from his hiding-place, brought before Chrysostom's enemies, deposed from his bishopric, banished to Egypt, and left at the mercy of the patriarch Theophilus (Pallad. p. 195; Soz. *H. E.* viii. 9). [E.V.]

Serenus (4), solitary in the Nitrian desert, who, when visited by Cassian, A.D. 395, discussed *de Animae Mobilitate et Spiritalibus Nequitiis* (*Coll.* vii.), and *de Principatibus seu Potestatibus* (*Coll.* viii. See Migne, *Patr. Lat.* t. xlix. 667 seq.). In the former he treats mostly of the nature of the soul, the rapid movement of the thoughts, the influence of evil spirits upon them, and the duty of fixing the desire on God. In the latter he declares the nature of evil spirits, their fall, subordination, and occupation. His Life, without details, is in *Vitae Patrum*, c. 50. Migne, *Patr. Lat.* t. lxxiii. 844 seq.; Ceill. *Aut. sacr.* viii. 170 seq.; Fleury, *H. E.* xx. c. 7. [J.G.]

Serenus (5), 10th bp. of Marseilles *c.* 595-600, known from the letters of Gregory the Great. To his good offices were commended St. Augustine on his mission to England in 596 (Greg. Magn. *Ep.* vi. 52; Migne, *Patr. Lat.* lxxvii. 836), and, three years later, the monks dispatched to help him (xi. 58, *Patr. Lat.* 1176). Two other letters from Gregory are preserved. Serenus in an excess of iconoclastic zeal had entered the churches of Marseilles and broken and cast forth the images. Gregory, commending his fervour against idolatry, reproved his violence, since the use of representations in a church was that the unlearned might read on the walls what they were unable to read in the Scriptures (ix. 105, *Patr. Lat.* 1027). Serenus, disregarding the warning and even affecting to believe the letter a forgery, received a severe rebuke and a reiteration of the pope's views (xi. 13, *Patr. Lat.* 1128, written Nov. 1, 600). *Gall. Christ.* i. 639; Ricard, *Evêques de Marseille*, 24, 25; *Vies des saints de Marseille, S. Serenus*, Bayle. [S.A.B.]

Sergius (2), a very celebrated military saint and martyr of the Eastern church. His Acts call him "Amicus Imperatoris." He and Bacchus were regarded as the patron saints of Syria. Sergius suffered at Sergiopolis, or Rasaphe, in Syria, early in the 4th cent. Their united fame soon became widespread. Le Bas and Waddington (*Voy. archéol.* t. iii. No. 2124) notice a church of E. Syria dedicated in their honour in 354 as the earliest case of such consecration to saints, and (*ib.* No. 1915) describe one dedicated in 512 to SS. Sergius, Bacchus, and Leontius, and offer reasons for regarding Leontius as a martyr under Hadrian when ruling Syria during the last years of Trajan. Theodora, wife of Justinian, presented a jewelled cross to a church of St. Sergius, which Persian invaders carried off. Chosroes, king of Persia, returned it to Gregory, patriarch of Antioch, in 593. (Cf. Evagr. *H. E.* iv. 28; vi. 21, where Chosroes is represented as a convert to the cult of Sergius.) The fame of Sergius and Bacchus spread to France, where Le Blant (*Christ. Lat. Inscrip. of France*, t. i. p. 305) notices a church at Chartres dedicated in their honour. Le Blant (*Actes des mart.* p. 77) notes the marks of genuineness in his Acts as told in *AA.SS. Boll.*; cf. Tillem. v. 491. [G.T.S.]

Sergius (12), the name of the two Monophysite priests persecuted with John of Ephesus at Constantinople. He relates the sufferings of the Sergii, one of whom was his syncellus, the other his disciple. While John was imprisoned in the penitentiary of the hospital of Eubulus the two priests were seized, and, as they would not yield, were publicly scourged and then imprisoned in a "diaconate," or hospital, attended by deacons and laymen, for 40 days. The syncellus was finally sent to the monastery of Beth-Rabula, where he was kindly treated, the monks there "having no love for the council of Chalcedon nor even proclaiming it in their worship" (John of Eph. *H. E.* p. 110, trans. Payne Smith). [C.H.]

Severianus (2), bp. of Gabala on the seaboard of Syria, *c.* 400; described by Gennadius (*Ill. Eccl. Scriptt.* c. 21) as "in Divinis Scripturis eruditus, et in Homiliis declamator admirabilis." He repaired to Constantinople, and was kindly received by Chrysostom, who often selected him to preach on important occasions. In spite of a rough provincial accent, he obtained considerable popularity with the people in general and with the emperor and empress, who often appointed him to preach (Gennad. *u.s.*). When early in 401 Chrysostom left Constantinople for the visitation of Asia Minor, he deputed his official authority to Severian as commissary, all real power being invested in his archdeacon Serapion. Severian, in Chrysostom's absence undermined his influence with the court, and fostered the dislike of the worldly and luxurious clergy of Constantinople, whom Chrysostom's severity had greatly alienated. His conduct was reported in the darkest colours to Chrysostom by his jealous and artful rival Serapion. For the events which compelled Severian to leave for his own diocese see SERAPION. Severian had barely crossed the Bosphorus when the imperious Eudoxia compelled Chrysostom to allow his return. But Chrysostom steadily refused to readmit the offender to friendly intercourse. The empress carried her infant son, the future emperor Theodosius, in her arms, into the church of the Apostles, and casting him in Chrysostom's lap, conjured him with solemn imprecations to be reconciled with Severian. Chrysostom consented, and exhorted his congregation to submit, as loyal subjects and good Christians, to the wishes of those in authority (*Homil. de recipiend. Severian.* t. iii. p. 422, ed. Migne). The request was acceded to with applause. Severian next day delivered a short rhetorical eulogy on the blessings of peace (*Sermo ipsius Severiani de Pace*, ib. p. 493). The hollowness of the reconciliation was soon proved. Severian joined in a plot, under the inspiration of the empress and the powerful female influence of the court, for Chrysostom's humiliation, which ultimately proved only too successful (Pallad. *Dial.* pp. 35, 48, 72). At the assembly of the Oak, Severian took a leading part (Pallad. p. 72; Phot. *Cod.* 59, p. 53), and on Chrysostom's deposition, mounted the pulpit and publicly expressed approbation of the act, which he said Chrysostom had well merited for his haughtiness alone. This "barefaced attempt to justify injustice" rendered the people furious, and they were only restrained from summary measures by Chrysostom's speedy recall. Severian and his brother-intriguers fled (Socr. *H. E.* vi. 16, 17; Soz. *H. E.* viii. 19; Pallad. *Dial.* p. 16). We find them at Constantinople seconding new designs for the destruction of Chrysostom set on foot by Eudoxia and the court party, and securing his final condemnation (Pallad. *Dial.* pp. 79, 88; Soz. *H. E.* viii. 22). Severian's malice did not cease with Chrysostom's expulsion. He is charged by Palladius with using his influence to obtain the removal of the aged invalid from Cucusus, where the climate had not proved so fatal as the malice of his enemies desired, to the more bleak and inaccessible town of Pityus (*Dial.* 97). Severian's death may be placed under Theodosius II. between 408 and 430.

Very few of his numerous writings are extant. Some homilies printed in Chrysostom's works have been attributed to him with more or less probability. The following are regarded on satisfactory grounds as his: *de Creatione Mundi, de Nativitate Christi, de Sigillis Librorum, de Serpente Aeneo, de Nativitate.* We may add *de Morte Innocentium*, and *de Cruce Homilia*, pub. by Combefis with some of Chrysostom's. Du Pin attributes to Severian, from internal evidence, a large number of homilies which pass under Chrysostom's name. Severian is said to have composed a large number of commentaries on Holy Scripture, the whole being lost except for fragments in the *Catenae.* Gennadius read with pleasure treatises of his on *Baptism* and the *Epiphany.* A work *contra Novatum* is quoted by Gelasius, *de Duabus Christi Naturis*; and one *contra Judaeos* by Cosmas Indicopleustes, vii. 292. According to Mabillon (*Mus. Ital.* i. pp. 13, 124), 88 homilies bearing his name exist in MS. in the Ambrosian library and others in the Coislinian. Fabr. *Bibl. Graec.* ix. 267; Cave, *Hist. Lit.* i. 375; Dupin, *H. E.* [E.V.]

Severinus (4), monk and apostle of Noricum (Austria) in the 5th cent. He was assisted by EUGIPPIUS, who afterwards presided over a monastery dedicated to his memory, and there wrote his Life *c.* 511, describing Severinus as coming from the East to preach in Pannonia and Noricum, about the time that Attila's death was followed by contests among his sons, which wrought havoc and destruction in these provinces. Severinus lived a life of the sternest asceticism in a small cell where he could barely stand erect. His Life is full of the wonders wrought and predictions uttered by him, but is important as illustrating the social life of the outlying provinces of the empire when the foundations of the modern European system were beginning to be laid. Thus c. vi. tells of the influence he exercised in introducing the payment of tithes. He was a most devoted missionary, reverenced by Roman and barbarian alike. Odoacer sought him out and desired his blessing when about to invade Italy. "Pursue," said the saint, "your design; proceed to Italy; you will soon cast away this coarse garment of skins, and your wealth will be adequate to your liberality of mind" (Gibbon, c. xxxvi.). Severinus died A.D. 482, near Vienna. His Life is in *AA. SS.* Boll. (Jan. 1, 483) and Pez,

Scriptt. Res Austr. I. 62. Herzog's *Encyclop.* has a very exhaustive article upon him. [G.T.S.]

Severus (1), L. Septimius, emperor, born at Leptis in Tripoli in Apr. 146. His family were of equestrian rank, and two of his uncles had been consuls. His early life at Rome was a mixture of study and dissipation, his talents attracting the attention of M. Aurelius, who conferred various offices upon him. In one capacity or another he held office in nearly all the western provinces. In 193 he was in command of Pannonia and Illyricum. When the news arrived of the murder of Pertinax and the sale of the empire to Didius Julianus, it aroused great indignation in the Pannonian army, and Severus, taking advantage of this feeling, got himself saluted emperor by them at Carnuntum in Apr. or May, and immediately marched on Rome. Julian was abandoned by the praetorians, and put to death by order of the senate on June 1 or 2. Severus left Rome after 30 days, to fight his most formidable rival Pescennius Niger, who had assumed the purple at Antioch a few days before himself, and overthrew him in 194. Albinus, who had assumed the title of emperor, was defeated and slain on Feb. 19, 197, in the plain of Trevoux near Lyons. In the autumn of 204 the secular games were celebrated with great magnificence for the last time. In 208 Severus set out for Britain, and marched through Caledonia to the extreme N., cutting down forests and making roads. He added a new rampart to the wall built by Hadrian from the Tyne to the Solway. He died at York on Feb. 4, 211. Of all emperors from Augustus to Diocletian, Severus was probably the man of greatest power. Crafty, ambitious, and unscrupulous, he allowed no considerations of humanity to stand in his way. Yet he did not delight in cruelty for its own sake, and any weakness on his part would have been fatal to himself and have plunged the Roman world again in the anarchy from which he had rescued it. Disorder and brigandage throughout the empire were put down with a firm hand. He was an adept in astrology and magic.

In the earlier part of his reign he favoured the Christians. He believed he had been cured of an illness by oil administered by a Christian named Proculus, whom till his death he maintained in the palace; and the nurse and some of the playmates of CARACALLA were Christians. No Christians took a prominent part on the side of Niger or Albinus, and it is even probable that those who tried to hold Byzantium for Niger ill-treated the Christians there during the siege. The number of councils held in the early years of Severus on the time of observing Easter proves that the church was then unmolested. The first change for the worse appears to have been at the emperor's entry into Rome, A.D. 197, after the defeat of Albinus. The Christians excited the fury of the mob by refusing to join in the rejoicings, an act they considered inconsistent with their religion. But Severus used his influence to protect Christian men and women of rank against the fury of the mob (*ad Scap.* 4). But in 202 he issued an edict forbidding future conversions to Judaism or Christianity (*Vita Severi*, 17). His motives are unknown. Probably, as a stern statesman of the old Roman school, he foresaw the peril to the national religion and the constitution of the state that lay in the active Christian propaganda, and though personally friendly to some among them, thought it time to check the further progress of the *religio illicita*.

Though the edict applied only to new converts, and catechumens were accordingly the greatest sufferers, yet there were numerous victims among the Christians of long standing. In the East, the Christians suffered most in Egypt, perhaps because the emperor had visited it immediately after the promulgation of his edict. So terrible was the outbreak that Judas, a Christian writer, made the 70 weeks of Daniel expire with the 10th year of Severus, and thought the advent of Antichrist at hand. Laetus the prefect and his successor Aquila were merciless enemies of the Christians, who were dragged from all parts of Egypt to their tribunal at Alexandria. Among the most notable martyrs was Leonidas, the father of Origen, who was only prevented by a stratagem of his mother from sharing his father's fate. By a strange inconsistency Origen was allowed to visit the martyrs in prison and to be present at their trial, and even to accompany them on their way to execution, apparently without being molested by the government, though several times in great danger from mob violence.

In Africa the persecution began with a violation of the cemeteries, and a bad harvest following, the rage of the people against the Christians increased (*ad Scap.* 3). [SCILLITAN MARTYRS.] In the spring of 203, under Hilarianus the procurator, who had assumed the government on the death of the proconsul, the famous group of martyrs among whom St. Perpetua was most conspicuous, suffered. Yet here again we find the same inconsistency as at Alexandria. Deacons were allowed to visit the imprisoned Christians, unmolested, to alleviate their sufferings, and even to procure their removal to a better part of the prison. In 205 or 206, under the milder government of Julius Asper, the persecution seems to have abated, after raging for 3 years (*de Pallio*, 2). Many Christians had sought refuge in flight, while others tried to escape by bribing the Roman officials, and in some cases the Christian community as a whole seems to have done so. These subterfuges were regarded with scorn and abhorrence by the more enthusiastic, but no trace is to be found of the Libellatici so notorious in later persecutions. The abatement seems to have continued till near the close of the reign, but in 210 and 211 the persecution broke out again in its sharpest form under the proconsul Scapula and extended to Mauritania. There the sword was the instrument of execution, whilst the cruel Scapula burnt his victims alive or flung them to the wild beasts of the amphitheatre.

Of persecution in other parts of the empire we have only a few isolated notices. The aged Irenaeus and his companions suffered at Lyons in this reign, but no details are preserved, and even the date is uncertain. In Syria, Asclepiades, afterwards bp. of Antioch, was a confessor (Eus. *H. E.* vi. 11). Cruel as it was, and severer than any previous one, the persecution under Severus had not the systematic character of those of Decius and Diocletian. Except Irenaeus, no bishops or prominent members seem to have been executed; many, like Tertullian and Origen, who might have been thought certain victims, were unmolested, and the resolution of the martyrs under their sufferings caused many conversions. Eus. *H. E.* vi. 1-12; Tillem. *Mém. eccl.* iii.; Görres, in *Jahrbücher für Protest. Theol.* 1878, 273; for Africa in particular, Tertullian, *Apologeticus*; *ad Martyres*; *ad Nationes*; *ad Scapulam*; *de Fuga*; *de Corona Militis*; Aubé, *Revue historique*, xi. 241. [F.D.]

Severus (2), Aurelius Alexander, emperor, born at Arca Caesarea in Syria, Oct. 1, 205 (Lampridius) or 208 (Herodian). For an account of his family see ELAGABALUS. Like him he was made in childhood a priest of the Sun at Emesa, and when his cousin became emperor he and his mother Julia Mammaea accompanied him to Rome. Mammaea took the utmost pains to educate her son and to preserve him uncontaminated by the monstrous excesses of his cousin. Created Caesar by the emperor in 221; on Feb. 1, 222 (Clinton), he became emperor on the death of Elagabalus and his mother Soaemis at the hands of the indignant soldiery. Being then at most not yet 17, the administration rested with his mother and grandmother Julia Mammaea and Julia Maesa, the latter of whom, till her death *c.* 225, enjoyed the greater power. Their chief minister or regent was the famous jurist Ulpian, whose appointment appears to have been due to Maesa's influence, though Mammaea afterwards acquiesced in it (Lamp. 50). He was assisted by a council of at least 70 members, 16 to 20 eminent jurists of whom formed a sort of inner cabinet (cf. Herodian, vi. i. with Lamp. 15); separate committees of this council administering different departments of the state.

The first step of the new administration was to reverse the acts of Elagabalus. The images of the gods he had collected at Rome from all parts of the empire were restored to their former shrines. His creatures were removed from offices obtained by disgraceful means. The senate, knights, tribes, and army were purged of the infamous persons appointed by Elagabalus, and the imperial establishment reduced as low as possible.

The praetorians and the army did not easily acquiesce in these reforms. Probably in order to check their mutinous spirit their prefects Flavianus and Chrestûs were put to death and Ulpian made sole prefect. From some trifling cause a riot broke out between the praetorians and the people, lasting for three days. The soldiers, getting the worst of it, set fire to the city and thus checked their assailants. They could not endure the firm rule of Ulpian. Several times he had to take refuge in the palace, and was saved with difficulty by the emperor from their fury. At last, probably in 228, he was killed by the soldiers in the presence of Alexander and his mother, who were only able by a stratagem to punish the ringleader. Throughout the empire the same insubordinate spirit prevailed. The troops in Mesopotamia mutinied and killed their commander, Flavius Heracleon. The historian Dion by his firm rule in Pannonia so excited the hatred of the praetorians that Alexander was driven to the humiliating expedient of requesting him not to come to Rome during his consulship.

This spirit of mutiny was the more dangerous as this reign witnessed the Persian revolt under Artaxerxes against the Parthians, which, after three great battles, in one of which the Parthian king Artabanus fell, completely broke the Parthian power, and by the most extraordinary revival in history re-established the kingdom of Darius in 226. As heir of the ancient monarchy he claimed all the Asiatic provinces of Rome. Such pretensions naturally produced a war. At the end of 231 or the beginning of 232 the emperor, accompanied by his mother, left Rome to fight the Persians, but returned without any decisive results to Europe, being summoned by news of the movements of the Germans on the Rhine and Danube. After a triumph at Rome on Sept. 25, 233 (Clinton), he proceeded to the Rhine frontier, where he was slain in his tent, and his mother with him, near Mayence, at the beginning of 235 (Clinton), by the mutinous soldiery.

Thus perished one of the most virtuous of the emperors. Apparently his only faults were an excessive deference to his mother and a certain want of energy. He was frugal, temperate, and chaste. He was fond of reading, preferring Greek to Latin authors. His favourite works were the *Republic* of Plato and the *de Officiis* and *de Republica* of Cicero. He was also fond of Vergil and Horace. He was acquainted with geometry, was able to paint, and could sing and play on various instruments. Though he attended the temples regularly and visited the Capitol every seventh day, and though he rebuilt and adorned the shrines of various deities, by a curious anticipation of Comtism, the objects of his peculiar veneration were not the gods of the various popular religions, but deified heroes and men. The private chapel in which he performed his devotions every morning contained no images of gods, but statues of canonized men, including the best of his predecessors, Alexander the Great, who might be called his patron saint, Orpheus, Apollonius of Tyana, Abraham, and Christ. In a smaller chapel were images of Achilles, Vergil (whom he used to call the Plato of poets), Cicero, and other great men. From his mother's intercourse with Origen (Eus. *H. E.* vi. 21) he would naturally have better means of learning the doctrines and practices of Christianity than any of his predecessors. It is said that he contemplated erecting a temple to Christ and placing Him among the gods. At any rate, though he did not give Christianity the status of a *religio licita*, the Christians during his reign enjoyed a *de facto* toleration. In the famous suit between the guild of cooks and the Christians for a piece of land, which according to tradition is the site of St. Maria in Trastevere, he decided in favour of the Christians on the broad ground that it was better God should be worshipped there under whatever form than that it should be given to the cooks. This decision implies a certain recognition of the right of the Christians as such to hold property, which is also implied by the life of CALLISTUS. Consistently with this, it is in the reign of Alexander that edifices set apart for Christian worship begin to appear—at any rate in some parts of the empire (cf. the letter of Firmilian to Cyprian (in Migne, *Patr. Lat.* iii. 1163) with Origen, *Hom.* 28 *on St. Matthew* (quoted in *contra Celsum*, viii. 755, in Migne, *Patr. Gk.* xi. 1539)). A form of the golden rule of Christian morality ("Do not do to another what you would not have done to yourself") was so admired by the emperor that he caused it to be inscribed on the palace and other buildings. A curious anecdote of Lampridius (44) shews the emperor's acquaintance with Christian usages and also the antiquity of the practice of publishing to the congregation the names of those who sought ordination. In imitation of this the emperor caused the names of persons he was about to appoint to be published beforehand, exhorting any who had charges against them to come with proofs.

Strange to say, in later tradition the emperor, whom all writers near his time represent as a friend, nay almost a convert, to Christianity, whose chapel contained an image of Christ and whose household was filled with Christians (Eus. *H. E.* vi. 28), appears as a cruel persecutor. It is said that pope Callistus with many companions, St. Caecilia and her comrades, pope Urban I., and many others suffered in his reign, and that he personally took part in their martyrdom. On the other hand, no Father of the 3rd, 4th, or 5th cents. knows anything of such a persecution, but on the contrary agree in representing his reign as a period of peace. Firmilian (*l.c.*) testifies that before the persecution of Maximin the church had enjoyed a long peace, and Sulpicius Severus (ii. 32 in *Patr. Lat.* xx. 447) includes the reign of Alexander in the long peace lasting from Septimius Severus to Decius, broken only by the persecution of Maximin. Against this can be set only the evidence of late authors, such as Bede, Ado, and Usuard and unauthentic Acts of martyrs. The most famous of the alleged martyrs of this reign, St. Caecilia and her companions, are placed by other accounts in the reigns of M. Aurelius or Diocletian. All are given up by Tillemont except Callistus. His chief ground for considering him a martyr is that in the *Depositio Martyrum*, written in 354 (in *Patr. Lat.* cxxvii. 123), a Callistus is mentioned as martyred on Oct. 14, the day on which the pope is commemorated. Lipsius (*Chronol. d. röm. Bischöfe*, 177) acutely conjectures that this notice refers, not to the martyrdom, but to the confession of Callistus before Fuscianus mentioned by Hippolytus, as up to the Decian persecution the word "martyr" was still used in the wider sense. We may therefore conclude that all these accounts of persecutions and martyrdoms, so inconsistent with the known character of the emperor and passed over in silence by all authors for more than two cents. afterwards, are fictions of a later date. [F.D.]

Severus (3) and Severians. [ENCRATITES.]

Severus (12) Sanctus (*Endelechius*). Perhaps identical with the rhetorician mentioned in the subscription of the *Cod. Flor.* of Apuleius, as teaching at Rome in 395. He is the author of a Christian idyll, in Asclepiad metre, upon the subject of a great cattle-plague; possibly that mentioned by St. Ambrose (*Comm. in Luc.* x. 10). This plague occurred *c.* 376, which fact, together with the date assigned for Endelechius's teaching, and the possibility that he was the correspondent of St. Paulinus of Nola (*Ep.* xxviii. 6), would fix the date of the poem at the end of the 4th or beginning of the 5th cent. The poem is entitled "de Mortibus Boum," and written with some taste and a good deal of vigour. It represents certain herdsmen—apparently Aquitanians—discussing their fortunes in the general affliction. One of them asserts that his herds have been protected by the sign of the Cross and by his own belief in Christ. The others resolve to adopt a religion which, according to his account, is at once profitable and easy. The poem has been often edited: first by Pithoeus (Paris, 1586). It is in Wernsdorf, *Poetae Lat. Min.* ii.; Migne, xix. Cave, *Hist. Litt.* i. 290; Ebert, *Gesch. der Chr.-Lat. Lit.*; Fabric. *Bibl. Graeca*, x. 626, 2nd ed.; Teuffel, vol. ii. [H.A.W.]

Severus (18), Sulpicius, ecclesiastical historian in Gaul, belonging to a noble family of Aquitaine, born after A.D. 353. He became an advocate and married a woman of consular rank and wealth, who did not long survive the marriage. While yet in the flower of his age, *c.* 392, caressed and praised by all and eminent in his profession (Paulinus, *Ep.* v., Migne, *Patr. Lat.* lxi. 169-170), he braved his father's anger and the flouts of worldly acquaintances (*ib.* i. col. 154), and retired from the world. Thenceforth with a few disciples and servants he led a life of ascetic seclusion and literary activity. Where he abode is not quite certain, but probably at Primuliacum, a village between Toulouse and Carcassonne, where he built two churches (*ib. Ep.* xxxii.). It was probably an estate of his wife or mother-in-law, his father apparently having disinherited him (cf. *Ep. ad Bassulam*). According to Gennadius he was a priest, but this has been questioned, and his tone towards the bishops and clergy, against whom he constantly inveighs as vain, luxurious, self-seeking, factious foes of Christianity and envious persecutors of his hero St. Martin, lends countenance to the doubt (*Hist. Sacr.* ii. 32; *Vita S. Martini*, 27; *Dial.* 1, 2, 9, 21, 24, 26). Later authors have believed him a monk, some of Marmoûtiers, Martin's foundation at Tours, others of Marseilles, whither he may have been driven by the Vandal invasion. This seems probable from c. i. of *Dial.* 1 (cf. also ii. 8). Gennadius asserts that in his old age he was deceived into Pelagianism, but recognizing the fault of loquacity, remained mute till his death, in order by penitential silence to correct the sin he had committed by much speaking. Others, from a passage in St. Jerome (*in Ezech.* c. xxxvi., Migne, *Patr. Lat.* xx. 85), have accused him of Millenarianism. At the Roman council held by pope Gelasius in 494 the *Dialogi*, under the name of *Opuscula Postumiani et Galli*, were certainly placed among the *libri apocryphi* (Mansi, viii. 151). The charge rested on *Dial.* ii. 14, where a strange theory as to the imminent appearance among men of Nero and Antichrist is put into the mouth of St. Martin. The chapter has been expunged in many Italian MSS. (Halm. *Sulpic. Sev. Praefatio*). Various years between 406 and 429 have been suggested for his death. The principal authorities for his Life are the short biography of Gennadius (*de Scriptt. Eccles.* xix., Migne, *Patr. Lat.* lviii. 1071), the letters of his friend Paulinus of Nola, with whom between 394 and 403 he constantly interchanged gifts and letters, though only one letter of Sulpicius, and that probably a forgery, survives (*Epp.* i. v. xi. xvii. xxii.-xxiv. xxvii.-xxxii., Migne, *Patr. Lat.* lxi. 153-330; Ceillier, vii. 55 sqq.), allusions in his own writings, esp. the *Vita S. Martini*, the *Epistolae*, and the *Dialogi*, and a panegyric by Paulinus of Périgueux (*de Vita S. Martini* lib. v. *Patr. Lat.* lxi. 1052). A modern and exhaustive notice is by Jacob Bernays, *Die Chronik des Sulp. Sev.* (Berlin, 1861).

His works consist of the *Historia Sacra* or *Chronica*, a Life of St. Martin of Tours, 3 letters, and 3 dialogues. An Eng. trans. is in Schaff and Wace's *Lib. of Post-Nicene Fathers.* The *Historia*, written *c.* 403, was an attempt to give a concise history of the world with dates from the creation to his own times, the consulship of Stilicho in 400. His sources are the LXX, the ancient Latin version of the Scriptures, the Chronicles of Eusebius, and the *Historici Ethnici*, as he calls the non-Christian authors (Herbert, *Notice*, p. 7). Bk. i. and part of ii. are occupied with universal history down to the birth of Christ. Then, omitting the period covered by the Gospels and Acts, he adds some details to Josephus's narrative of the siege of Jerusalem, recounts persecutions of the Christians under 9 emperors, and describes the Invention of the Cross by St. Helena, as he had heard it from Paulinus. His account of the Arian controversy (ii. 35-45) is inaccurate and of little value; but of more importance is that of the Priscillianist heresy, which had arisen in his time and with the details of which he was familiar.

The *Vita S. Martini*, the earliest of his writings, is very important as containing, with the Dialogues and 3 letters, practically everything that is authentic about that popular saint of Western Christendom. He tells us that, having long heard of the sanctity and miracles of Martin, he went to Tours to see him, asked him all the questions he could, and got information from eyewitnesses and those who knew (c. 25). This visit, probably *c.* 394, was followed by many others. The book was pub. during Martin's lifetime.

In the *Dialogi*, written *c.* 405, the interlocutors are his friend Postumianus, just back from a three years' stay in the East, Gallus, a disciple of St. Martin, now dead, and Sulpicius himself. Twenty-two chapters of *Dial.* i. contain interesting pictures of the controversy at Alexandria between archbp. Theophilus and the monks concerning Origen, St. Jerome at his church in Bethlehem, and the monks and hermits of the Thebaid. Postumianus asks about St. Martin, and bears witness to the enormous popularity of the Life in almost every country. Paulinus had introduced it at Rome, where the whole city had fought for it. All Carthage was reading it, the Alexandrians knew its contents almost better than the author, and it had penetrated into Egypt, Nitria, and the Thebaid. All were clamouring for those further wonders which Sulpicius had omitted (c. 23, cf. *Vita, prol.*) and with which the remainder of the Dialogues is almost entirely occupied.

The Epistles are also about St. Martin, the first giving the story of his death and burial. Seven more letters have been published under Sulpicius's name; several have been generally suspected (Ceillier, 119-120), but all are pronounced spurious by Halm (*Pref.* xi.-xiii.).

The best ed. of the collected works is that of C. Halm (*Sulpicii Severi Libri qui supersunt*, Vindob. 1866). His works have been several times translated into French, *e.g.* by M. Herbert (Paris, 1847).

Apart from the unique History of St. Martin (which, however, is the worst of his writings from a literary point of view), Sulpicius's chief title to fame rests on his beauty and purity of style, in respect of which he is pre-eminent, if not unique, among ecclesiastical authors, and well merits his appellation of the "Christian Sallust." He seems to have taken this historian as his model, but his writings shew familiarity with Vergil, Livy, Tacitus, and most classical authors. Perhaps his work is somewhat lacking in vigour, and not entirely free from the affectations and bad taste of his time. The credulity and superstition of the narrative had, as regards Martin's Miracles, evidently excited scepticism even among the Christians in Sulpicius's own time (see *Dial.* iii. 6). [MARTIN (1)]. For an estimate of Sulpicius's works see Ceill. viii. 121-122. [S.A.B.]

Severus (19), bp. of Mileum or Mileus, a native of the same place as Augustine, and a fellow-student, lifelong friend, and member of the same monastic community. Early in his episcopate, probably in 401, Augustine, Alypius, and Samsucius had to explain their conduct in the matter of Timotheus and to call on Severus to accept their explanation (Aug. *Epp.* 62, 63), but this temporary misunderstanding did not interrupt his friendship with Augustine, nor cause any ill-will on his part towards Timotheus (Aug. *En. Ps.* 95. 1; *de Civitate Dei*, xxi. 4). In a letter somewhat later, perhaps A.D. 406, addressed to Novatus, Augustine regrets being not often able to see his old friend, who wrote seldom, and then chiefly on business, not from want of goodwill but from necessity (Aug. *Ep.* 84). Severus exchanged letters and friendly messages with Paulinus of Nola (*ib.* 31. 9 and 32. 1), and *c.* 409 wrote to Augustine expressing his great delight in his writings, as leading him to greater love of God, and begging him to write in return (*Epp.* 109). Augustine replied, insisting that he himself was the debtor. Severus appears to have joined in the address to Innocentius concerning Pelagianism, A.D. 416 (Aug. *Epp.* 175, 176). He probably died *c.* 426. [H.W.P.]

Severus (22), bp. of Minorca, known by his encyclical letter referred to in the book *de Miraculis S. Stephani*, composed by order of Evodius of Uzalis (Migne, *Patr. Lat.* xx. 731). Orosius had deposited some recently discovered relics of St. Stephen in the church at Magona (Port Mahon), where there were a large number of Jews, one of whom, the rabbi

Theodorus, was *defensor civitatis*. The arrival of the relics caused great religious excitement among Minorcan Christians, which led to constant arguments between them and the Jews, ending in riots in which the synagogue was set on fire and burnt to the bare walls. The conversion of a great number of Jews, including Theodorus himself, followed. On the site of the destroyed synagogue the Jews erected a church. These events occurred in the last week of Jan. 418. Gams, *Kircheng. von Sp.* ii. (1) 406. [F.D.]

Severus (27), Monophysite patriarch of Antioch, A.D. 512-519, a native of Sozopolis in Pisidia, by birth and education a heathen, baptized in the martyry of Leontius at Tripolis (Evagr. *H. E.* iii. 33; Labbe, v. 40, 120).

He almost at once openly united himself with the Acephali, repudiating his own baptism and his baptizer, and even the Catholic church itself as infected with Nestorianism (Labbe, *u.s.*). On embracing Monophysite doctrines he entered a monastery apparently belonging to that sect between Gaza and its port Majuma. Here he met Peter the Iberian, a zealous Eutychian, who had been ordained bp. of Gaza by Theodosius, the Monophysite monk, during his usurpation of the see of Jerusalem (Evagr. *l.c.*). About this time Severus apparently joined a Eutychian brotherhood near Eleutheropolis under the archimandrite Mamas, who further confirmed him in his extreme Monophysitism (Liberat. *Brev.* c. xix.; Labbe, v. 762; Evagr. *l.c.*). Severus rejected the Henoticon of Zeno, applying to it contumelious epithets, such as κενωτικόν, "the annulling edict," and διαιρετικόν, "the disuniting edict" (Labbe, v. 121), and anathematized Peter Mongus, the Monophysite patriarch of Alexandria, for accepting it. We next hear of him in an Egyptian monastery, of which one Nephalius was abbat, who, having been formerly a Monophysite, had embraced the faith of Chalcedon. Nephalius with his monks expelled Severus and his partizans (Evagr. *l.c.*, cf. iii. 22). Severus is charged with having stirred up a fierce religious war among the excitable population of Alexandria, resulting in bloodshed and conflagrations (Labbe, v. 121). To escape the punishment of his turbulence he fled to Constantinople, supported by a band of 200 Monophysite monks (*ib.* iv. 1419). Anastasius, who had succeeded the emperor Zeno, the author of the Henoticon, in 491, was a declared favourer of the Eutychians, and by him Severus was received with honour. His advent was an unhappy one for the peace of Constantinople, where a sanguinary tumult was stirred up by rival bands of monks, orthodox and Monophysite, chanting in their respective churches the opposing forms of the "Trisagion." This tumult resulted, A.D. 511, in the humiliation of Anastasius, the temporary triumph of the patriarch Macedonius, and the depression of the Monophysite cause (Theophan, p. 132). Severus was eagerly dispatched by Anastasius to occupy the vacant throne of Antioch A.D. 511. He was ordained, or, in the words of his adversaries, "received the shadow of ordination" (Labbe, v. 40), and enthroned on the same day in his patriarchal city (*ib.* iv. 1414; Theod. Lect. ii. 31, pp. 563, 567; Theophan. p. 134), and that very day solemnly pronounced in his church an anathema on Chalcedon, and accepted the Henoticon he had previously repudiated. He caused the name of Peter Mongus to be inscribed in the diptychs; declared himself in communion with the Eutychian prelates, Timotheus of Constantinople and John Niciota of Alexandria; and received into communion Peter of Iberia and other leading members of the Acephali (Evagr. *H. E.* iii. 33; Labbe, iv. 1414, v. 121, 762; Theod. Lect. *l.c.*). Eutychianism seemed now triumphant throughout the Christian world. Proud of his patriarchal dignity and strong in the emperor's protection, Severus despatched letters to his brother-prelates, announcing his elevation and demanding communion. In these he anathematized Chalcedon and all who maintained the two natures. They met with a very varied reception. Many rejected them altogether, nevertheless Monophysitism was everywhere in the ascendant in the East, and Severus was deservedly regarded as its chief champion (Severus of Ashmunain *apud* Neale, *Patr. Alex.* ii. 27). Synodal letters were interchanged between John Niciota and Severus; the earliest examples of that intercommunication between the Jacobite sees of Alexandria and Antioch, which has been kept up to the present day (Neale, *l.c.*). The triumph of Severus was, however, short. His sanguinary tyranny over the patriarchate of Antioch did not survive his imperial patron. Anastasius was succeeded in 518 by Justin, who at once declared for the orthodox faith. The Monophysite prelates were everywhere replaced by orthodox successors. Severus was one of the first to fall. Irenaeus, the count of the East, was commissioned to arrest him. Severus, however, escaped, and in Sept. 518 sailed by night for Alexandria (Liberat. *Brev. l.c.*; Theophan. 141; Evagr. *H. E.* iv. 4). Paul was ordained in his room. Severus and his doctrines were anathematized in various councils. At Alexandria his reception by his fellow-religionists was enthusiastic. He was gladly welcomed by the patriarch Timotheus, and generally hailed as the champion of the orthodox faith against the corruptions of Nestorianism. His learning and argumentative power established his authority as "os omnium doctorum," and the day of his entrance into Egypt was long celebrated as a Jacobite festival (Neale, *u.s.* p. 30). Alexandria speedily became the resort of Monophysites of every shade of opinion, who formed too powerful a body for the emperor to molest. But fierce controversies sprang up among themselves on various subtle questions connected with Christ's nature and His human body. A vehement dispute arose between Severus and his fellow-exile Julian of Halicarnassus as to the corruptibility of our Lord's human body before His resurrection. Julian and his followers were styled "Aphthartodocetae" and "Phantasiastae," Severus and his adherents "Phthartolatrae" or "Corrupticolae," and "Ktistolatrae." The controversy was a warm and protracted one and no settlement was arrived at. The Jacobites, however, claim the victory for Severus (Renaudot, p. 129). After some years in Egypt spent in continual literary and polemical activity, Severus was unexpectedly summoned to Constantinople by Justin's successor Justinian, whose consort Theodora warmly favoured the Eutychian party. The emperor was utterly weary of the turmoil caused by the prolonged theological discussions. Severus, he was told, was the master of the Monophysite party. Unity could only be regained by his influence. At this period, A.D. 535, Anthimus had been recently appointed to the see of Constantinople by Theodora's influence. He was a concealed Eutychian, who on his accession threw off the orthodox mask and joined heartily with Severus and his associates, Peter of Apamea and Zoaras, in their endeavours to get Monophysitism recognized as the orthodox faith. This introduction of turbulent Monophysites threw the city into great disorder, and large numbers embraced their pernicious heresy (Labbe, v. 124). For the further progress of this audacious attempt to establish Monophysitism in the imperial city see JUSTINIANUS; AGAPETUS. Eventually, at the instance of pope Agapetus, who happened to visit Constantinople on political business at this time, the Monophysites Anthimus and Timotheus were deposed, and Severus again subjected to an anathema. The orthodox Mennas, succeeding Anthimus (Liberat. *Breviar.* c. xxi.; Labbe, v. 774), summoned a synod in May and June 536 to deal with the Monophysite question. Severus and his two companions were cast out "as wolves" from the true fold, and anathematized (Labbe, v. 253-255). The sentence was ratified by Justinian (*ib.* 265). The writings of Severus were proscribed; any one possessing them who failed to commit them to the flames was to lose his right hand (Evagr. *H. E.* iv. 11; Novell. Justinian. No. 42; Matt. Blastar. p. 59). Severus returned to Egypt, which he seems never again to have left. The date of his death is fixed variously in 538, 539, and 542. According to John of Ephesus, he died in the Egyptian desert (ed. Payne Smith, i. 78).

He was a very copious writer, but we possess little more than fragments. An account of them, so far as they can be identified, is given by Cave (*Hist. Lit.* vol. i. pp. 499 ff.) and Fabricius (*Bibl. Graec.* lib. v. c. 36, vol. x. pp. 614 ff., ed. Harless). A very large number exist only in Syriac, for which consult the catalogue of the Syriac MSS. in the Brit. Mus. by Prof. Wright.

Severus was successful in his great aim of uniting the Monophysites into one compact body with a definitely formulated creed. For notwithstanding the numerous subdivisions of the Monophysites, he was, in Dorner's words, "strictly speaking, the scientific leader of the most compact portion of the party," and regarded as such by the Monophysites and their opponents. He was the chief object of attack in the long and fierce contest with the orthodox, by whom he is always designated as the author and ringleader of the heresy. His opinions, however, were far from consistent, and his opponents apparently had much difficulty in arriving at a clear and definite view of them, and constantly asserted that he contradicted himself. This was partly forced upon him by the conciliatory position he aimed at. Hoping to embrace as many as possible of varying theological colour, he followed the traditional formulas of the church as closely as he could, while affixing his own sense upon them (Dorner, *Pers. of Christ,* div. ii. vol. i. p. 136, Clark's trans.). In 1904 the *Sixth Book of the Select Letters of Severus,* in the Syriac version of Athanasius of Nisibis, were ed. by G. E. W. Brooks (Lond.). For a full statement of his opinions see the great work of Dorner, and art. "Monophysiten" in Herzog's *Encyc.* [E.V.]

Severus (31), patriarch of Aquileia, succeeding Elias *c.* 586. Like his predecessors, he was a strenuous champion of the Three Chapters. Soon after his consecration the exarch Smaragdus seized him in his basilica at Grado, where the bishops of Aquileia had taken refuge, and carried him off to Ravenna with three other bishops—Severus of Trieste, John of Parenzo, and Videmius of Ceneda. There he was imprisoned a whole year and subjected to personal ill-treatment till he consented with those three suffragans, and two others, to communicate with John, archbp. of Ravenna. He was then allowed to return to Grado, but the people refused to communicate with him till he had acknowledged his fault in communicating with those who condemned the Three Chapters and had been received by a synod of ten bishops at Marano, *c.* 589 (Paulus Diac. *Hist. Lang.* iii. 26).

Gregory the Great, at the end of 590 or beginning of 591, wrote to him expressing his regret at his relapse into schism, and summoning him by the emperor's orders to Rome, with his followers, that a synod might decide the matter (*Epp.* i. ind. ix. 17 in Migne, *Patr. Lat.* lxxvii. 461). Three separate appeals were presented to the emperor Maurice, the third (and only one extant) being by the bishops of the continental part which was in the hands of the Lombards. In it the bishops urge the injustice of the pope, from whose communion they had separated, being judge in his own cause. They profess willingness, when peace is restored, to attend and accept the decisions of a free council at Constantinople, and point out that the clergy and people of the suffragans of Aquileia are so zealous for the Three Chapters that, if the patriarch is compelled to submit by force, when future vacancies occur among his suffragans the new bishops would be compelled to seek consecration from the bishops of Gaul, and the province of Aquileia would thus be broken up (Mansi, x. 463). Maurice accordingly directed the pope to leave Severus and his suffragans alone for the present. Gregory submitting, Severus maintained his position through Gregory's life, and died in 606 or 607 (Paulus Diac. iv. 33), after an episcopate of 21 years and a month. He bequeathed all his property to his cathedral at Grado (*Chr. Patr. Grad.* in *Script. Rer. Lang.* 394). [F.D.]

Sidonius (2) Apollinaris, St. His grandfather Apollinaris had been praefectus praetorio of Gaul under the rival emperor Constantine, A.D. 408 (Zos. vi. 4; Olympiodorus, *ap.* Phot. *Bibl.* p. 57, ed. Bekker), and was the first of the family to become a Christian. An epitaph written by his grandson for his tomb near Lyons speaks of him in the highest terms, especially on this account. His great-grandfather held a high official situation (Sid. *Ep.* iii. 12, i. 3); his father was a tribune and a notary or secretary under Honorius, and under Valentinian III. became praefectus praetorio of Aquitania I. A.D. 449 (*ib.* iii. 1, v. 9, viii. 6).

First Period, 431-471.—Sidonius was born Nov. 5, 431 or 432, probably at Lyons (*Carm.* xx. 1). He was apparently educated at that then famous seat of education, in the same school as his cousin Avitus. Soon after he was 20 years old he married Papianilla, only daughter of Flavius Eparchius Avitus, a native of Auvergne, who was praefectus praetorio at Arles from 439 to 443. Avitus, a soldier, diplomatist and lover of nature and literature, retired after 451 to his own house and patrimonial estate at Avitacum, near the modern Clermont (*ib.* vii. 230, 316, 339, 460, etc.). Avitus had two sons, Ecdicius and Agricola, with whom, after his marriage, Sidonius lived on most friendly and affectionate terms. He had a son Apollinaris and two daughters, Roscia and Severiana. A letter is extant, addressed to Apollinaris when almost 16 years old, commending his blameless behaviour, and warning him against the bad example and vicious society of some profligates at Lyons, where he was studying (*Ep.* iii. 13). There is also a letter to Agricola, mingling tender feeling with quiet humour, excusing himself from joining a fishing excursion as his daughter Severiana was alarmingly ill, on whose behalf, as well as his own, he begs Agricola's prayers. He expresses his firm trust in Christ as his best support (*Ep.* ii. 12). On the death of Maximus, Avitus was proclaimed emperor at Toulouse and at Beaucaire, A.D. 455, and was followed to Rome by his son-in-law, who pronounced on him a panegyric poem of 602 hexameter lines on Jan. 1, 456 (*Carm.* vii. 369-404, 510-572), and as a reward received the honour of a brazen statue in the basilica of Trajan, in a space between the two libraries. The reign of Avitus ended in 456. Majorian, who became emperor, crossed the Alps, defeated the Burgundian invaders, captured Lyons, imposing hard conditions and heavy taxes on the citizens, which he was induced to remit (Mar. 459) by a florid panegyric in 603 hexameters pronounced by Sidonius and some elegiac verses addressed to him and to his principal secretary Peter, a man ambitious of literary renown, whom Sidonius calls his Maecenas. Sidonius obtained also, perhaps somewhat later, the office of count of the Palace (*Ep.* i. 11; *Carm.* iii. iv. v. xiii.). In 460, when the emperor was holding his court at Arles, and had gathered round him the most eminent literary men of Gaul, Domnulus, Lampridius, and Severianus, Sidonius distinguished himself by an improvised poem in praise of a book by secretary Peter. From 461 to 465 Sidonius appears to have lived in retirement from public business, but fulfilling his part as a great landed proprietor at Avitacum of a possession into which he came in right of his wife on the death of Avitus, and which he describes enthusiastically, in a letter written in the style of Pliny to his friend Domitius. His description of the house and grounds is very pleasing and picturesque, its trees and underwood, its lake, fountains, and cascade.

Several letters to friends belong to this period, especially one to Eriphius, a citizen of Lyons, perhaps A.D. 461, describing a church gathering in commemoration of St. Justus at Lyons on Sept. 2, the procession before daybreak, the large congregation of both sexes, the psalms sung antiphonally by monks and clerks, the Eucharistic celebration, the great heat caused by the crowd and the number of lights, cooled after a time by the autumnal morning.

When Anthemius became emperor, A.D. 467, he sent for Sidonius to Rome, on business which the people of Auvergne deputed him to manage on their behalf. Under the favour of Christ, as he says, he undertook the mission, his expenses being provided by the imperial treasury. At Rome he stayed at the house of Paulus, a man of prefectorian rank, possessing literary and scientific ability, who persuaded him, as likely to promote his own interests, to celebrate the inauguration of Anthemius the new consul by a poem. The result was a panegyric in 548 hexameters. This was rewarded by the high office of prefect of the senate and of the city of Rome, of which he writes in a tone of gratified ambition to Philimatius. He remained at Rome until 469, and then retired to Gaul, residing partly at Lyons and partly at Avitacum. Towards the end of that year or the beginning of 470, the province of Lugdunensis I. was surrendered by Anthemius to the Burgundians as the price of their assistance against the Visigoths (Tillem. *Emp.* vi. p. 357). These barbarians Sidonius describes as less ferocious than other German races, but complains of their perverse ways, revolting and odious to those over whom they domineered. Of their ruler (tetrarches) Chilperic II., and his wife Agrippina, he speaks more favourably (*Ep.* v. 7; *Carm.* xii.). About this time a new church was erected at Lyons through the exertions of bp. Patiens, for whom Sidonius had the most affectionate reverence. He was present at the dedication, which he describes in hendecasyllables (*Ep.* ii. 10). At the request of bp. Perpetuus he wrote an elegiac inscription for the church of St. Martin at Tours, which Perpetuus had enlarged (*Ep.* iv. 18).

Second Period, 471-475.—Threatened by invasion and surrounded by enemies political and religious (for Euric, the Visigothic king, whose capital was Toulouse, was a zealous supporter of Arian doctrine and persecuted the Catholics with great severity), the people of Clermont, when their bishop, Eparchius, died, A.D. 471, united in a clamorous demand that Sidonius should succeed him. He was not in holy orders, but had shewn himself without ostentation a devout Christian, though a somewhat flexible and elastic politician. His ability was beyond question; as a man of letters he stood in the foremost rank; he held a high place, probably the highest, among the landed proprietors of his province, whose interests he was firm and patriotic in upholding, and had taken an active part more than once on behalf of its inhabitants, in which also he had been ably and zealously supported by his friends, of whom, both in military and civil affairs, Ecdicius, his wife's brother, held the chief place in the district (Greg. Tur. ii. 21). Fully aware of his own deficiencies, he accepted the office unwillingly, begging his friends, among them Fonteius bp. of Vaison, Euphronius bp. of Autun, Leontius bp. of Arles, and Lupus bp. of Troyes, who wrote to congratulate him on his appointment, to pray for him (*Epp.* v. 3; vi. 1, 3, 7; vii. 8, 9; ix. 2). From this time he gave up writing verses of a light kind, as ill-suited to his time of life and the gravity of his office (*Ep.* ix. 12). But at his friends' requests he criticized compositions and wrote hymns in honour of martyrs. With his wife Papianilla, though there is no doubt of his undiminished affection for her, he probably, as is assumed by Sirmond, Tillemont, and others, lived on terms not of connubial but of fraternal intimacy; no evidence of this appears from his own writings. That they continued to live together is plain from the story told by Gregory of Tours, that she found fault with him for parting with his plate to give to the poor (Greg. Tur. ii. 22). He became a diligent student of Scripture, though disclaiming earnestly any ability as a commentator, and also of ecclesiastical writers, as Augustine, Jerome, Origen, etc. (*Epp.* viii. 4; ix. 2).

From 471 until 474, when Auvergne was first attacked formally by the Visigoth, it is not easy to fix accurately all the dates of events or of letters.

After he came to the throne of Toulouse in 466 Euric lost no opportunity of increasing his dominions by aggression upon the Roman. During 473, or early in 474, the province of Berry fell to him, and he took advantage of the weakness of the Roman empire after the death of Anthemius to extend his dominion towards the Rhone and the Loire; Auvergne being now the only province remaining to the Romans W. of the Rhone and in constant danger of invasion. No formal attack, however, took place until the autumn of 474. At some time in 474, as it seems, Avitus, brother-in-law of Sidonius, endowed the see of Clermont with a farm called Cuticiacum (Cunhiae), not far from the city, and in the letter mentioning this Sidonius speaks also of the threatened invasion and of his confidence in Avitus in case of negotiation (*Ep.* iii. 1). Meanwhile, as the autumn advanced, the Visigoths entered the territory of Auvergne, and communication with distant places became more difficult. In preparations to resist the enemy Sidonius acted as a leader of the people, and was greatly assisted by his brother-in-law Ecdicius, who with a handful of cavalry attacked and defeated a large force of the enemy. They retired at the end of 474 or beginning of 475, but not so completely as to remove the apprehension of future attack or the necessity for watch to be kept on the walls during the snowy days and dark nights of winter (*Ep.* iii. 7). A brief truce with the Visigothic king appears to have been arranged early in 475, perhaps through the agency of Epiphanius, bp. of Pavia. During this temporary cessation of hostilities a report became current that Euric had invaded the Roman territory of Auvergne, and Sidonius summoned his people to join in acts of fasting and prayer conducted like the Rogations instituted, or rather revived and reorganized, some years previously by Mamertus, bp. of Vienne, and of which, in a letter to him, he recounts the history. He also begs the prayers of the bishop and his flock for the people of Auvergne, and as a claim upon their attention mentions the transfer to Vienne at some previous time of the remains of Ferreolus and the head of Julian, both of them martyrs and natives of Auvergne. He also wrote to his friend Aper, entreating him as a citizen of Clermont to leave his warm baths at Aquae Calidae and come to Clermont to take part in the solemn service (*Epp.* v. 14; vii. 1; Greg. Tur. *Hist. Fr.* ii. 11, *de Mirac.* ii. 1, 2; "Rogation Days," *D. C. A.* vol. ii. p. 1809; Baron. *ann.* 475, xii.-xxi.; Tillem. vol. xvi. pp. 247, 248). No actual invasion of Auvergne appears to have occurred, and negotiations, in which bps. Basilius of Aix, Faustus of Riez, Graecus of Marseilles, and Leontius of Arles, were among the acting counsellors, ultimately resulted in the surrender of Auvergne to the Visigoths. It was probably during these negotiations that Euric, a zealous partisan of the Arian heresy, whose hostility in this direction, Sidonius says, he feared more than his attacks on Roman fortifications, deprived of their sees, and in many cases put to death or banished, many bishops in the regions subject to him, allowing no successors to be appointed. Churches were overthrown, their sites overrun by animals, Christian discipline destroyed; and writing to Basilius, Sidonius implores him, as in touch with the political negotiators, to obtain permission for the exercise of episcopal ordination (*Ep.* vii. 6).

The surrender of Auvergne, marking as it did the utter prostration of Roman influence, was a heavy blow to Sidonius, and he wrote to Graecus, bp. of Marseilles, recounting the unswerving loyalty of the Auvergnians and their sufferings during the siege, and inveighing bitterly against the selfish policy which, to secure for a time only the districts in which the negotiators were interested, had handed over the faithful province of Auvergne for punishment to the enemy. The remonstrance was fruitless, and Auvergne passed to the Visigoth. It was placed under a governor named Victorius, with the title of Count, who appears at first to have behaved with real or affected moderation (Greg. Tur. *Hist. Fr.* ii. 20; Sid. *Ep.* vii. 17; Chaix, ii. 290).

Third Period, A.D. 475-489.—Sidonius was soon banished for a time to a fort named Livia, probably Capendu, about ten miles from Carcassonne on the road to Narbonne (*Epp.* viii. 3; ix. 3; Vaissette, *Hist. de Languedoc*, V. vol. i. p. 501). Some of the inconveniences he suffered there are described in his letters to Faustus, bp. of Riez, and to a friend, Leo, a native of Narbonne and of Roman origin, but filling a high office under Euric. They consisted chiefly in the annoyance caused by his neighbours, two quarrelsome drunken old Gothic women (*Ep.* viii. 3). Through Leo's influence he soon obtained release from confinement, but his return to Clermont was delayed by an enforced sojourn at Bordeaux, whither he went to seek from Euric authority for recovering the inheritance belonging to him in right of his mother-in-law. Two months passed before Euric would grant him an interview, nor do we know its result.

In no letter does he speak of opposition or personal ill-treatment, and the tone of his later letters is cheerful, and he appears from the last of them to have met with no hindrance in his episcopal duties except from weather. Gregory of Tours relates that, in the later years of his life, he was much annoyed by two priests, probably of Arian opinions, whose names he does not mention, but said by Chaix, though without citing any authority, to have been Honorius and Hermanchius. These men, Gregory says, succeeded in preventing him exercising his episcopal functions and even in reducing him to extreme poverty; but after the death of Honorius he was restored to his office, and being attacked by fever, desired to be carried into the church of St. Mary, and there, after speaking words of love to his people, and pointing out Aprunculus, bp. of Langres, as fit to be his successor, he died, though not, apparently, in the church, Aug. 489. He was buried in the chapel of St. Saturninus, in the centre of Clermont, beside his predecessor Eparchius, and an epitaph in hendecasyllabic verse by an unknown author was placed near his tomb with the date, "XII. Kal. Sept. Zenone imperatore." This has disappeared, but a copy is preserved in a MS. of the abbey of Cluny.

A gentleman of easy fortune living in the country, Sidonius entered eagerly into its employments and active amusements, but was also keenly sensible of the more refined and tranquil pleasures derived from natural objects. He exerted without scruple a lordly influence over his own dependants in the province, sometimes in a high-handed and peremptory manner, but usually with kindness and consideration. Affectionate and constant to his friends, he loved to give and receive hospitality, and some of his most agreeable letters describe such social gatherings. His eulogies were poured forth without stint or discrimination, alike on Avitus, Majorian, and Anthemius, and even Nepos did not fail to obtain a small share. He has compliments at fitting seasons, direct or indirect, for Euric and his wife. A poet laureate by nature, he must be regarded as a pliant politician, but he never forgot his duty as a patriotic citizen. Faithful to his countrymen, whether by birth as of Lyons, or of adoption as in Auvergne, he never failed to plead their cause, uphold their interests, denounce their oppressors, and stand by them against injustice or hostile invasion, nor need we wonder that his memory should be revered by them as that of a saint. Invested against his will, and without previous preparation, with the episcopate, he laboured hard to repair the deficiencies of which he was conscious. He shrank from no duty, personal trouble, or responsibility, and in times of extreme difficulty shewed courage, prudence, and discretion. His character and abilities commanded the respect and cordial affection of the best men of his time, as Basilius, Felix, Graecus, Lupus, Patiens, Principius, Remigius, as well as Leo and Arbogastes, and many others; and though he did not shrink from remonstrating gravely and even bitterly with some of them, especially Graecus, he does not appear to have forfeited their esteem and affection. A man of kindly disposition, he treated his slaves with kindness and took pains to induce others to do likewise. He was friendly to Jews, employed them, and recommended them to the good offices of his friends.

Literary Character.—Though he shewed himself a sincere and devout Christian, both before and after he became bishop, it is as a man of letters that he will always be best known, for, as it has been observed, his writings are the best-furnished storehouse we possess of information as to the domestic life, the manners and habits of public men, and in some points the public events of his period. Gifted with a fatal facility of composition, his longer poems are remarkable more for adroit handling of unpoetical material than for poetry in its true sense, and deserve to a great extent the contemptuous judgment of Gibbon. Yet some of the shorter compositions, especially those in hendecasyllabic metre, are more successful, and touch scenes and characters with a light and discerning hand. His letters, though often turgid and pedantic, defaced by an artificial phraseology and abounding in passages of great obscurity, often describe persons, objects, and transactions in a very lively and picturesque manner.

The ed. of his works by M. Eugène Baret (Paris, 1879) has an extremely valuable introduction, containing remarks on the times and state of society, and lists of grammatical forms, words, and phrases used by Sidonius, illustrating the transition state of the Latin language, and some peculiar to himself; also an attempt to settle the chronology of the letters, a task of great difficulty. The best ed. is by Lütjohann, in *Monum. Germ. Hist. Auct. Antiquiss.* (Berlin, 1887), viii., and a smaller ed. is by P. Mohr (Leipz. 1895). [H.W.P.]

Sigebert (1) I., king of the Austrasian Franks (561-575), son of Clotaire I. by Ingundis (Greg. Tur. *Hist. Franc.* iv. 1). Scarcely had the four brothers buried their father at Soissons when Chilperic the youngest began the civil wars which desolated France. Seizing the royal treasure at Braine, near Soissons, and purchasing the support of the Franks, he occupied Paris. His three half-brothers leagued together and compelled him to make a fair division. To Sigebert fell the kingdom which had belonged to Theodoric I., *i.e.* the country occupied by the Ripuarian Franks and a part of Champagne, with Rheims for his capital, which division was now beginning to be known as Austrasia (Greg. Tur. iv. 21, 22; *Hist. Epitom.* lv.; Marius Aventic. ann. 560). To Sigebert fell also, on the death of Charibert I., as far as can be gathered from later events (see Greg. Tur. ix. 20), a third share of the city of Paris, the coast of Provence with Avignon, the former possessions of Theodoric I., in Aquitaine, the N. part of Brie, Beauce, Touraine, and Poitou (Richter, *Annalen*, 68; Bonnell, *Anfänge des Karolingischen Hauses*, *Beilage*, pp. 206 sqq.; Fauriel, *Hist. de la Gaule Mérid.* ii. 175-177). About this time he married the famous Brunichild (Brunehaut), a daughter of Athanagild, the Visigothic king in Spain she having first renounced Arianism for orthodoxy (Greg. Tur. iv. 27; Venant. Fort. vi. 2, 3, Migne, *Patr. Lat.* lxxxviii. 204-209. For the character and accomplishments of this queen, who in later life became almost supreme in France, see also Fauriel, ii. 166 sqq.). The remainder of the reign was taken up with miserable civil wars between the brothers, in which Chilperic strove to capture parts of Sigebert's dominion; Tours and Poictiers, with their respective districts, being his principal object of attack. Two years running (A.D. 574-575) his armies overran those districts (Greg. Tur. iv. 46, 48). On the second occasion Gregory, after depicting the churches burnt and plundered, clergy killed, monasteries in ruins, and nuns outraged, uses these memorable words: "fuitque illo in tempore pejor in ecclesiis gemitus quam tempore persecutionis Diocletiani" (iv. 48. See too his outburst of indignation in c. 49). Sigebert recruited his forces with pagan Germans from beyond the Rhine (iv. 50, 51), and finally in 575, with the assistance of Guntram, carried his arms to Paris and Rouen, and while Chilperic was shut up in Tournay, was raised by his subjects on the shield and declared king in his place. At that very moment, however, he was struck down by assassins, probably emissaries of Fredegund (Greg. Tur. iv. 52; Marius Avent. *Chronicon.*; Venant. Fort. *Miscell.* ix. 2, Migne, *u.s.* 298 sqq.). He left a son of five years, Childebert II.

Sigebert was much the best of the sons of Clotaire. In happier circumstances he might have been a humane and enlightened king, but his misfortune was to reign at perhaps the darkest period of French history. His clemency towards Chilperic's son Theodebert, who had invaded his territory (Greg. Tur. iv. 23), his motives in seeking Brunichild's hand in marriage, as described by Gregory (iv. 27), and his intrepid attempts to restrain his barbarian trans-Rhenish allies from plundering (iv. 30), throw light upon his character. He was true to the orthodoxy of his race (iv. 27), and recalled St. Nicetius of Trèves from exile and appointed Gregory to Tours. [S.A.B.]

Sigismundus, St., martyr, 5th king of the Burgundians (516-524), brought up under the influence of Avitus, the orthodox archbp. of Vienne, who succeeded in winning him, with two of his children, from the Arianism of his nation and family (Avitus, *Epp.* 27, 29, Migne, *Patr. Lat.* lix. 243, 246; Agobardus, *adv. Leg. Gund.* xiii. *Patr. Lat.* civ. 124), and sought to lead his inclinations towards the Roman empire (see Mascou, *Annotation* ii., where the passages are collected, and Fauriel, *Hist. de la Gaule Mérid.* ii. 100). He married Ostrogotha, the daughter of Theodoric the Ostrogothic king of Italy (Jornandes in Bouquet, ii. 28). While his father was still living, Sigismund was invested with regal dignity and held his court at Geneva (Avit. *Epp.* 29, 30; Greg. Tur. *Epitom.* xxxiv.). In 515 he founded or (*Hist. litt. de la France*, iii. 89, 91) refounded the monastery of St. Maurice at Agaunum, where tradition placed the martyrdom of the Legio Thebaea (Marius Avent. *Chronicon, Patr. Lat.* lxxii. 796). In 516 he succeeded his father (Marius, *ib.*), and in 517 convened a council, under the presidency of Avitus, at Epaunum (supposed to be the present Iene on the Rhone; "Epaon," *D. C. A.*; *Hist. litt.* iii. 9). If the extent of his dominion may be inferred from the sees of the bishops present, Burgundy then included, besides the later duchy and county, Dauphiny and Savoy, the city and dominion of Lyons and the Valais, besides a part of the present Switzerland (Mascou, xi. 10, 31). In 523 Clodomir, Clotaire, and Childebert, three of the four sons of Clovis, stirred up by their mother the widowed Clotilda, invaded Burgundy. Sigismund was defeated and fled to St. Maurice, where he was betrayed by his own subjects to Clodomir and carried prisoner in the garb of a monk to Orleans. Shortly afterwards, with his wife and two children, he was murdered at the neighbouring village of Coulmiers, by being cast alive, as was said, into a well (Marius, *ib.*; Greg. Tur. iii. 6). His brother, Godemar, succeeded him as 6th and last king of the Burgundians.

Sigismund was well-intentioned but weak. He apparently yielded too much to the influence of Roman ideas and habits for the king of a barbarian people, neighboured on one side by the powerful Ostrogothic monarchy and on others by the fiercely aggressive Franks. His partisanship for the orthodox faith, while it harmed him with his subjects, was not thorough-going enough to win the clergy from their leaning towards the Franks (see Fauriel, ii. 100 sqq.). [S.A.B.]

Silvania. [SYLVIA.]

Silvanus (2), bp. of Gaza, a martyr in the persecution of Maximin, *c.* 305. He was a presbyter at its outbreak, and from the very beginning he endured many varied sufferings with the greatest fortitude. Not long before his martyrdom, which was one of the last in Palestine, he obtained the episcopate. Eusebius speaks with high admiration of his Christian endurance, saying that he was "reserved to the last to set the seal, as it were, to the conflict in Palestine" (Eus. *H. E.* viii. 7, 13). He was decapitated, according to the Roman martyrology, on May 4, 308. Theoph. p. 9; Le Quien, *Or. Christ.* iii. 605. [E.V.]

Silvanus (3), bp. of Emesa. In extreme old age, after 40 years' episcopate, he was thrown to the wild beasts in Diocletian's persecution. Eus. *H. E.* viii. 13; ix. 6; Theophan. p. 9; Le Quien, *Or. Christ.* ii. 837. [E.V.]

Silvanus (4), bp. of Cirta, subdeacon under Paulus, bp. of that see during the persecution under Diocletian, and, as well as he, guilty of "tradition." These facts were elicited at the inquiry under Zenophilus, A.D. 320, at which it was proved, by ample evidence, that Silvanus was guilty of this charge, and also that with others he had appropriated plate and ornaments from the heathen temple of Serapis; and after he became a bishop received as a bribe for ordaining Victor, a fuller, to be a presbyter, money which ought to have been given to the poor. After the inquiry he was banished for refusing to communicate with Ursacius and Zenophilus, at the time of the mission of Macarius, A.D. 348. Aug. *Petil.* i. 23, iii. 69, 70; *de Gest. Emer.* 5; *c. Cresc.* iii. 32, 33, 34, iv. 66; *de Unico Bapt.* 30. 31; Aug. *Ep.* 53. 4; *Mon. Vet. D.* pp. 178, 180, 182, ed. Oberthür; pp. 167-171, ed. Dupin. [H.W.P.]

Silvanus (6), bp. of Tarsus and metropolitan,

one of the most excellent of those semi-Arians whom Athanasius described as "brothers who mean what we mean, and differ only about the terms" (Ath. *de Synod.* 41). He succeeded Antonius in the reign of Constantius. He was one of the 22 Oriental bishops who, at the council of Sirmium, in 351, joined in the deposition of Photinus (Hilar. *Synod,* p. 129; *fragm.* i. p. 48). On the deposition and banishment of Cyril from Jerusalem, early in 358, Silvanus received him hospitably at Tarsus, despite the remonstrances of Acacius (Theod. *H. E.* ii. 22). That year he took part in the semi-Arian council of Ancyra (Labbe, ii. 790), and in 359 in that of Seleucia, at which he vociferously advocated (μέγα ἀνέκραγε) the acceptance of the Lucianic dedication creed of Antioch (Socr. *H. E.* ii. 39), the mere mention of which made the Acacian party leave the place of assembly as a protest. Silvanus was among the semi-Arian leaders who, first of the rival church parties, memorialized Julian on his arrival at Antioch after becoming emperor, requesting him to expel the Anomoeans and call a general council to restore peace to the church, and declaring their acceptance of the Nicene faith (Socr. *H. E.* iii. 25). In 366 he was, with Eustathius of Sebaste and Theophilus of Castabala, a deputy to Liberius. He returned with the letters of communion of Liberius and the Roman synod (Basil. *Ep.* 67 [50]). His death is placed by Tillemont in 373 (*Mém. eccl.* t. vi. p. 592; Le Quien, *Or. Christ.* ii. 872). [E.V.]

Silvanus (12), solitary of Sinai, a native of Palestine. "He founded at Geraris near the great torrent a very extensive establishment for holy men, over which the excellent Zachariah subsequently presided" (Soz. *H. E.* vi. 32). He trained his followers to industrial pursuits. A wandering ascetic seeing all the brethren working very diligently said to them, "Labour not for the meat which perisheth; Mary chose the better part." Silvanus overhearing this said, "Give a book to the brother and lead him to an empty cell." When the ninth hour came, no one came to call the stranger to eat. At last, wearied and hungry, he sought Silvanus, and said, "Father, the brethren have not eaten to-day." "Oh yes," replied the abbat, "they have eaten." "And why," said the other, "did you not send for me?" "Because," responded Silvanus, "thou art a spiritual man, and dost not require food; but we are carnal and wish to eat, and therefore are compelled to work. Thou, however, hast chosen the better part and continuest in study the whole day, nor art willing to consume carnal food." The stranger confessed his fault and was forgiven, Silvanus playfully saying, "Martha is evidently necessary to Mary." Cotelerius tells stories of his prolonged trances. On one occasion he awoke very sad because he had been in the eternal world and seen many monks going to hell and many secular persons to heaven (*Monument,* t. i. p. 679). [G.T.S.]

Silvanus (14), first known bp. of Calahorra. We know of him from 2 letters of Ascanius, bp. of Tarragona, and the bishops of his province to pope Hilary, and Hilary's reply dated Dec. 30, 465 (in Migne, *Patr. Lat.* lviii. 14). The first letter shows that Silvanus had, 7 or 8 years before, consecrated a bishop without any request from the places comprised in his see or the approval of Ascanius. The other bishops of the province were satisfied with admonishing him, and received the new bishop; but the see in question being again vacant Silvanus had lately repeated the act, with the aggravation that the priest consecrated belonged to the diocese of another bishop, and the other bishop at the instance of the bishops of Saragossa having refused to join, Silvanus had performed the consecration alone. In the second letter the bishops express their surprise at the pope's delay in answering. His reply was remarkably favourable, in consequence probably of letters from people of rank and property at Calahorra, Tarazona, and neighbouring towns, which alleged in excuse for Silvanus that his were not the only irregularities, bishops having been consecrated for other cities without the previous approval of the metropolitan. The pope in consideration of the troubled times granted an amnesty for the past, while enjoining strict observance of the canons for the future. As the first letter was written some time before Hilary's reply, Silvanus probably became bp. *c.* 455. *Esp. Sag.* xxxiii. 128; Gams, *Kirchg. von Sp.* ii. (1) 430. [F.D.]

Silverius, bp. of Rome during the reign of Justinian I. Agapetus having died at Constantinople when about to return to Italy (on April 22, according to Anastasius) in 536, Liberatus tells us (*Breviar.*) that on the news of his death reaching Rome, Silverius, a subdeacon and son of pope Hormisdas, was elected and ordained, doubtless in the same year. According to Anastasius (*Lib. Pontif. in Vit. Silverii*) the election of Silverius was forced upon the Romans by the Gothic king Theodatus, who then held the city, the presbyters assenting for the sake of unity. Silverius did not long enjoy his dignity. Belisarius, having got possession of Naples, entered Rome in the name of Justinian on Dec. 10, 536. Vitiges, the successor of Theodatus, commenced a siege of Rome, now in the possession of Belisarius, in Mar. 537. Belisarius, after entering Rome, is said in the *Hist. Miscell* (lib. 16 in Muratori, t. i. pp. 106, 107) to have been reproved and subjected to penance by Silverius for cruel treatment of the Neapolitans; whereas the contemporary historian Procopius (*Bell. Goth.* lib. i.) commends the peculiar humanity of Belisarius after the capture of Naples.

Vigilius, one of the deacons of Agapetus at Constantinople, had, on that pope's death there, been sent for by the empress Theodora and promised the popedom through the agency of Belisarius on condition of his disallowing, after his elevation, the council of Chalcedon, and supporting the Monophysites whom she favoured. Vigilius, on his arrival in Italy, found Belisarius at Naples, to whom he communicated the commands of Theodora (Liberatus, *Breviar.*). Belisarius having gained possession of Rome, Vigilius followed him there and measures were taken to carry out the wishes of the empress. Accusations were laid against Silverius of having been in communication with the Goths who were besieging

Rome, and having written to Vitiges offering to betray the city. Summoned before Belisarius, with whom was his wife Antonina, who was the spokeswoman and real agent in these proceedings, he was charged with the crime, and banished to Patara and then to Greece. The emperor, on hearing the facts, asserted himself, ordering his recall to Rome and investigation to be made. But the empress succeeded somehow in keeping her husband quiet. For, on the arrival of Silverius at Rome (as we are informed by Liberatus), Vigilius represented to Belisarius that he could not do what was required of him unless the deposed pope were delivered into his hands. He was thereupon given up to two dependants of Vigilius, under whose custody he was sent to Palmaria in the Tyrrhene sea (or Pontia, according to *Martyrol. Rom.* and Anastasius), where he died from famine, according to Liberatus and Anastasius. Procopius (*Hist. Arcan.*) speaks of one Eugenius, a servant of Antonina, as having been her instrument in bringing about his death, the expression used seeming to imply a death by violence. Allemann (note on *Hist. Arcan.*) argues that the account of Procopius, who was living at Rome at the time and likely to know the facts, is preferable; and attributes the implication of Vigilius to prejudice on the part of Liberatus.

Silverius died June 20 (xii. Kal. Jul. *al.* Jun. *Anastas.*), most probably A.D. 538, his deposition certainly occurring in 537. [J.B—Y.]

Silvester (1), bp. of Rome after Miltiades, Jan. 31, 314, to Dec. 31, 335. Though his time was important in church history, we have few genuine records of any personal action of his, but a great store of legend.

In his first year of episcopate Constantine the Great summoned the first council of Arles to reconsider the decision against the African Donatists of the synod held at Rome by his order in 313 under pope Miltiades. At the council of Arles Silvester was represented by two presbyters, Claudianus and Vitus, and two deacons, Eugenius and Cyriacus, whose names appear in his behalf fifth among the signatures. Whoever presided, the general conduct of the council seems to have been committed by the emperor to Chrestus, bp. of Syracuse (see a letter to him from Constantine preserved by Eusebius, *H. E.* x. 5). Certainly Silvester did not preside, nor did any representative in his place. Constantine, in making arrangements for the council, evidently takes no account of him, not even mentioning him in writing to Chrestus.

There is indeed a letter of the bishops of the Arles council to Silvester. It opens: "To the most beloved pope Silvester," and concludes in reference to the decrees: "We have thought it fit also that they should be especially made known *to all* through you, *who hold the greater dioceses.*" The phrase, "qui majores dioceses tenes," with the consequent desire expressed that the pope should promulgate the decrees, has been used in proof of the pope's then acknowledged patriarchal jurisdiction over the great dioceses (*i.e.* exarchates) of the western empire. For the word διοίκησις denoted the jurisdiction of a patriarch, larger than that of metropolitans, the word for a diocese in the modern sense being properly παροικία. But it is highly improbable that *diocese* was used ecclesiastically in this sense so early as 314. Hence Bingham contended (*Ant.* ix. i. 12, and ii. 2) that if the passage, "by all acknowledged to be a very corrupt one," be accepted, διοίκησις must be taken in the sense then generally expressed by παροικία; and he adduces instances of its use in this sense in canons of Carthaginian councils. But probably the whole epistle (note its general anachronism of tone) is a forgery intended to magnify the Roman see.

To the more memorable council of Nicaea in 325 Silvester was invited, but excusing himself on account of age, sent two presbyters, Vitus and Vincentius, as his representatives (Eus. *V. C.* iii. 7; Socr. *H. E.* i. 14; Sozs. *H. E.* i. 17; Theod. *H. E.* i. 6). The view that they presided in his name, or that (as Baronius maintains) Hosius of Cordova did so, is without foundation. In the subscriptions to the decrees Hosius signs first, but simply as bp. of Cordova, not as in any way representing Rome; after which come those of Vitus and Vincentius, who sign "pro venerabili viro papa et episcopo nostro, sancto Sylvestro, ita credentes sicut scriptum est." The earliest and indeed only authority for Hosius having presided in the pope's name is that of Gelasius of Cyzicus (end of 5th cent.), who says only that Hosius from Spain, "qui Silvestri episcopi maximae Romae locum obtinebat," together with the Roman presbyters Bito and Vincentius, was present (Gelas. *Hist. Concil. Nic.* l. ii. c. 5, in Labbe, vol. ii. p. 162). Equally groundless is the allegation first made by the 6th oecumenical council (680), that Silvester in concert with the emperor summoned the Nicene fathers. The gradual growth of this idea appears in the pontifical annals. The catalogue of popes called the Felician (A.D. 530) says only that the synod was held with his consent ("cum consensu ejus"); some later MSS. improve this phrase into "cum praecepto ejus." It is evident from all authentic documents that the synod of Nicaea, as that of Arles, was convened by the sole authority of the emperor, and that no peculiarly prominent position was accorded to the pope in either case.

But the most memorable fable about Silvester is that of the baptism of Constantine by him, and the celebrated "Donation." It is, though variously related, mainly as follows: The emperor, having before his conversion authorized cruel persecution of the Christians, was smitten with leprosy by divine judgment. He was advised to use a bath of infants' blood for cure. A great multitude of infants was accordingly collected for slaughter; but the emperor, moved by their cries and those of their mothers, desisted from his purpose. He was thereupon visited in night visions by SS. Peter and Paul, and directed to seek and recall Silvester from his exile in Soracte, who would shew him a pool by immersion in which he would be healed. He recalled the pope, was instructed by him in the faith, cured of his leprosy, and baptized. Moved by gratitude, he made over to the pope and his successors the temporal dominion of Rome, of the greatest part of Italy, and of other provinces, thinking it unfit that the place where the monarch of the whole church and the vicar of Christ resided should be subject to earthly sway. (See *Lib. Pontif. in Vit. Sylvestri*, and the Lections in *Fest. S. Sylvestri* in the Breviaries of the various uses). The earliest known authority for the whole story appears to be the *Acta Sylvestri* (see below).

The attribution of Constantine's conversion and baptism to Silvester is as legendary as the rest. His profession and patronage of Christianity were anterior to the time spoken of, and he was not actually baptized till long afterwards, at the close of his life. There is abundant testimony that he did not seek baptism, or even imposition of hands as a catechumen, till in a suburb of Nicomedia, as death drew near, he received both from Eusebius, the Arian bishop of that see. (Eus. *V. C.* iv. 61, 62; Theod. i. 32; Soz. ii. 34, iv. 18; Socr. i. 39; Phot. *Cod.* 127; Ambrose, *Serm. de obit. Theodos.*; Hieron. *Chron. an.* 2353; *Council of Rimini.*)

The *Acta S. Sylvestri*, which seem to have furnished the materials for most of the legends—including the banishment to Soracte, the leprosy of Constantine, his lustration by Silvester, and his Donation—are mentioned and approved as genuine in the *Decretum de Libris Recipiendis et non Recipiendis*, commonly attributed to pope Gelasius (492-496), but probably of a later date. They are quoted in the 8th cent. by pope Hadrian in a letter to Charlemagne, where the Donation is alluded to, and in another to the empress Irene and her son Constantine on the occasion of the 2nd Nicene council in 787. The original Acts have not been preserved. The extant editions of them, given in Latin by Surius (*Acta SS.* Dec. p. 368), and in Greek by Combefis (*Act.* p. 258), purport to be only compilations from an earlier document.

Silvester died on Dec. 31, 335, and was buried in the cemetery of St. Priscilla. [J.B—Y.]

Silvia. [GORDIANUS (7).]

Simeon (1), 2nd bp. of Jerusalem, succeeding James, the Lord's brother. According to the statement of Hegesippus preserved by Eusebius, Simeon was the son of Clopas "mentioned in Holy Scripture" (John xix. 25), the brother of Joseph, and therefore, legally, the uncle of our Lord, while Simeon himself—ὁ ἐκ τοῦ θείου τοῦ Κυρίου—was, legally, his cousin, ὄντα ἀνεψιὸν τοῦ Κυρίου, and of the royal line of David (Eus. *H. E.* iii. 11, 32; iv. 22). The language of Hegesippus (*H. E.* iv. 82) evidently distinguishes between the relationship of James and Simeon to our Lord. Dr. Mill, however, follows Burton (*H. E.* i. 290) in regarding Simeon as a brother of James and also of Jude, though perhaps by another mother (Mill, *Pantheistic Principles*, pp. 234, 253). Such an interpretation of Hegesippus's language is very unnatural and at variance with the statement of Epiphanius that Simeon was the cousin—ἀνεψιός—of James the Just (Epiph. *Haer.* lxxvii. c. 14, p. 1046; cf. Lightfoot, *Galatians*, p. 262). Bp. Lightfoot regards his age as "an exaggeration," and suggests that his being "a son of Cleopas mentioned in the Evangelical records" requires us to place his death earlier than the generally received date. According to Hegesippus, Simeon was unanimously chosen to fill the vacant see of Jerusalem on the violent death of James the Just, the date usually assigned for which being 62 or 63 (see Josephus, *Ant.* xx. 9. 1). Whether the appointment of Simeon immediately succeeded or was not made till the retirement of the Christian Jews to Pella cannot be determined. The former seems rather more probable. His retreat at Pella would save him from the inquisition after descendants of the royal line of David, made by Vespasian, according to Eusebius (*H. E.* iii. 12), as well as the later inquiry instituted by Domitian (*ib.* 19, 20). He must have returned with the Christians to Jerusalem when allowed to do so by the Roman authorities. Of his episcopate we know nothing. He was martyred in the reign of Trajan (ἐπὶ Τραϊανοῦ; Eus. *H. E.* iii. 32), but the exact date is uncertain. By a misinterpretation of the *Chronicon* of Eusebius, which seemed to assign his martyrdom with that of Ignatius to the 9th or 10th year of Trajan, Simeon's death has been assigned to 107 or 108. Bp. Lightfoot has shewn good reason for placing it earlier in Trajan's reign (Lightfoot, *Ignatius*, i. 21, 58-60, ii. 442-450). Hegesippus says that in his 121st year Simeon was accused before Atticus, then proconsul, by certain Jewish sectaries, first, that being of the line of David, he was a possible claimant of the throne of his royal ancestor, and secondly that he was a Christian. He was tortured for many days in succession, and bore his sufferings with a firmness which astonished all the beholders, especially Atticus himself, who marvelled at such endurance in one so advanced in age. Finally he was ordered to be crucified (Eus. *H. E.* iii. 32). [E.V.]

Simeon (12) Stylites, A.D. 388-460. Simeon was, according to Theodoret, originally an enclosed anchorite, and raised his cell to avoid the honours paid to him (cf. Reeves on church of St. Doulough, pp. 8-11, with Evagr. *H. E.* i. 21). The fashion rapidly spread even to the sects, as we learn from Joannes Moschus (*Prat. Spirit.* cxxix.; cf. Ceill. xi. 701) that the 6th-cent. Monophysites had pillar saints. Sometimes both parties had opposition Stylites in the same district. Evagrius tells us that Simeon's pillar was only three feet in circumference at the top, which would barely afford standing ground. Assemani has depicted Simeon's column in his Life of the saint with a railing or kind of wooden pulpit at the summit. Some such structure must have been there, not only to prevent his fall, but also for him to write the epistles he sent broadcast to emperors, bishops, and councils on all pressing questions. He was born at Sisan, a village on the borders of Cilicia and Syria, and when about 16 embraced the monastic life. From 413 to 423 Simeon dwelt in an enclosed cell near Antioch, where his austerities speedily attracted a number of followers, who formed a society called the Mandra. In 423 he built a low pillar, which he gradually raised, till in 430 it was 40 cubits high; there, with his neck manacled by an iron collar, he spent his last 30 years of life engaged in perpetual adoration, save when he was bestowing advice about mundane matters. His extraordinary life made a great impression; large numbers of Arabians, Armenians, and other pagans were converted by him, while emperors, bishops, and pilgrims from distant lands, even Spain and Britain, consulted him most reverently. An object of deepest reverence all through life, at the news of his approaching death great crowds assembled (July 459) round his pillar to receive his last words. On Aug. 29 he was seized with a mortal illness, and died Sept 2, 459. His body was transported with great pomp to Antioch, attended by bishops and clergy, and guarded by the troops under Ardabryius, commander of the forces of the East. The emperor Leo sent letters to the bp. of Antioch demanding it to be brought to Constantinople. The people of Antioch piteously reminded Leo, "Forasmuch as our city is without walls, for we have been visited in wrath by their fall, we brought hither the sacred body to be our wall and bulwark," and were permitted to retain it; but this did not avail to protect the city against capture by the Persians. Simeon wrote many epistles on current ecclesiastical matters: (1) one Evagrius mentions (*H.E.* i. 13), to the emperor Theodosius against restoring their synagogues to the Jews. It effectually incited the emperor to intolerant courses. He withdrew the concession and dismissed the official who advised it. (2) An epistle to Leo, on behalf of the council of Chalcedon, and against the ordination of Timotheus Aelurus (ii. 10). (3) Evagrius gives (*ib.*) extracts from one to Basil of Antioch on the same topic. (4) An epistle to the empress Eudocia on the same (Niceph. xv. 13), by which she was converted from Eutychian error. (5) Eulogius of Alexandria mentions his profession of the Catholic faith, which Cave conjectures to have been identical with (2) (cf. Phot. *Biblioth.* cod. 230). Besides these, there is extant a Latin version of a sermon, *de Morte Assidue Cogitanda*, which in the *Biblioth. Patr.* is usually ascribed to our Simeon. Lambecius, on the authority of a MS. in the imperial library at Vienna, ascribes it to Simeon of Mesopotamia (*Comm. de Biblioth.* Caesarea, vol. viii. lib. v. col. 198 D, ed. Kollar). Evagrius (i. 13) describes the appearance of Simeon's relics in his time, and also (i. 14) a visit he paid to the monastery and pillar of Simeon. The pillar was then enclosed in a church, which no woman was ever allowed to enter, and where supernatural manifestations were often seen. Count de Vogüé (*Syrie Centrale*, t. i. pp. 141-154, Paris, 1865-1877) describes fully the present state of the church, and shews Evagrius's minute accuracy. [G.T.S.]

Simon (1) Magus, the subject of many legends and much speculation. It is important to discriminate carefully what is told of him by the different primary authorities.

The Simon of the Acts of the Apostles.—Behind all stories concerning Simon lies what is related Acts viii. 9-24, where we see Simon as a magician who exercised sorcery in Samaria with such success that the people universally accepted his claim to be "some great one," and accounted him "that power of God which is called great." We are further told that he was so impressed by the miracles wrought by Philip, that he asked and obtained admission to Christian baptism; but that he subsequently betrayed the hollowness of his conversion by offering money to Peter to obtain the power of conferring the gift of the Holy Ghost. All subsequent accounts represent him as possessing magical power and coming personally into collision with Peter. The Acts say nothing as to his being a teacher of heretical doctrine; nor do they tell whether or not he broke off all connexion with the Christian society after his exposure by Peter.

The Simon of Justin Martyr.—When Justin Martyr wrote his *Apology* the Simonian sect appears to have been formidable, for he speaks four times of their founder Simon (*Apol.* i. 26, 56; ii. 15; *Dial.* 20), and undoubtedly identified him with the Simon of Acts. He states that he was a Samaritan, born at a village called Gitta; he describes him as a formidable magician, who came to Rome in the days of Claudius Caesar and made such an impression by his magical powers that he was honoured as a god, a statue being erected to him on the Tiber, between the two bridges, bearing the inscription "Simoni deo Sancto." Now in 1574 there was dug up in the place indicated by Justin, viz. the island in the Tiber, a marble fragment, apparently the base of a statue, bearing the inscription, "Semoni Sanco Deo Fidio," with the name of the dedicator (see Gruter, *Inscrip. Antiq.* i. p. 95, n. 5). The coincidence is too remarkable to admit of any satisfactory explanation other than that Justin imagined a statue really dedicated to a Sabine deity (Ovid. *Fasti*, vi. 214) to have been in honour of the heretic Simon.

Justin further states that almost all the Samaritans, and some even of other nations, worshipped Simon, and acknowledged him as "the first God" ("above all principality, power, and dominion," *Dial.* 120), and that they held that a woman named Helena, formerly a prostitute, who went about with him, was his "first conception" (*ἔννοια πρώτη*). In connexion with Simon, Justin speaks of another Samaritan heretic, MENANDER, and states that he (Justin) had published a treatise against heresies. When Irenaeus (*Haer.* i. 23) deals with Simon and Menander, his coincidences with Justin are too numerous and striking to leave any doubt that he here uses the work of Justin as his authority, and we get the following additional particulars: Simon claimed to be himself the highest power, that is to say, the Father who is over all; he taught that he was the same who among the Jews appeared as Son, in Samaria descended as Father, in other nations had walked as the Holy Spirit. He was content to be called by whatever name men chose to assign to him. Helen was a prostitute whom he had redeemed at Tyre and led about with him, saying that she was the first conception of his mind, the mother of all, by whom he had in the beginning conceived the making of angels and archangels. Knowing thus his will, she had leaped away from him, descended to the lower regions, and generated angels and powers by whom this world was made. But this "Ennoea" was detained in these lower regions by her offspring, and not suffered to return to the Father of whom they were ignorant. In this account of Simon there is a large portion common to almost all forms of Gnostic myths, together with something special to this form. They have in common the place in the work of creation assigned to the female principle, the conception of the Deity; the ignorance of the rulers of this lower world with regard to the Supreme Power; the descent of the female (*Sophia*) into the lower regions, and her inability to return. Special to the Simonian tale is the identification of Simon himself with the Supreme, and of his consort Helena with the female principle, together with the doctrine of transmigration of souls, necessary to give these identifications a chance of acceptance, it not being credible that the male and female Supreme principles should first appear in the world at so late a stage in history.

It is possible that Justin's Simon was not identical with the contemporary of the Apostles, the name Simon being very common, and the Simon of the Acts being a century older than Justin. Moreover, Justin's Simon could hardly have carried his doctrine of transmigration of souls to the point of pretending that it was he himself who had appeared as Jesus of Nazareth, unless he had been born after our Lord's death. Hence it is the writer's opinion that the Simon described by Justin was his elder only by a generation; that he was a Gnostic teacher who had gained some followers at Samaria; and that Justin rashly identified him with the magician of the Acts of the Apostles.

The section on Simon in the *Refutation of all Heresies*, by Hippolytus, divides itself into two parts; the larger portion is founded on a work ascribed to Simon called the μεγάλη ἀπόφασις, which we do not hear of through any other source than Hippolytus. But towards the close of the art. on Simon there is a section which can be explained on the supposition that Hippolytus is drawing directly from the source used by Irenaeus, viz. the anti-heretical treatise of Justin. In connexion with this section must be considered the treatment of Simon in the lost earlier treatise of Hippolytus, which may be conjecturally gathered from the use made of it by Philaster and Epiphanius. Between these two there are verbal coincidences which prove that they are drawing from a common source. When this common matter is compared with the section in the *Refutation*, it is clear that Hippolytus was that source.

But one thing common to them was apparently not taken from Hippolytus. Both speak of the death of Simon, but apart from the section which contains the matter common to them and Hippolytus, and here they have no verbal coincidences. Both, however, know the story which became the received account of his death, viz. that to give the emperor a crowning proof of his magical skill he attempted to fly through the air, and, through the efficacy of the apostle's prayers, the demons who bore him were compelled to let him go, whereupon he perished miserably.

We may conclude that the story known to Philaster and Epiphanius, though earlier than the end of the 4th cent. when they wrote, is of later origin than the beginning of the 3rd cent. when Hippolytus wrote. That Hippolytus did not find his account of Simon's death in Justin may be concluded from the place it occupies in his narrative, where it is in a kind of appendix to what is borrowed from Justin; and also because this form of the story is unknown to all other writers.

The Simon of the Clementines.—The Clementines, like Justin, identify Simon of Gitta with the Simon of *Acts*; but there is every reason to believe that they were merely following Justin. Justin has evidently direct knowledge of the Simonians, and regards them as formidable heretics; but in the Clementines the doctrines which Justin gives as Simonian have no prominence; and the introduction of Simon is merely a literary contrivance to bring in the theological discussions in which the author is interested.

The Simon of 19th Cent. Criticism.—The Clementine writings were produced in Rome early in 3rd cent. by members of the Elkesaite sect, one characteristic of which was hostility to Paul, whom they refused to recognize as an apostle. Baur first drew attention to this characteristic in the Clementines, and pointed out that in the disputations between Simon and Peter, some of the claims Simon is represented as making (*e.g.* that of having seen our Lord, though not in his lifetime, yet subsequently in vision) were really the claims of Paul; and urged that Peter's refutation of Simon was in some places intended as a polemic against Paul. The passages are found only in the Clementine *Homilies*, which may be regarded as one of the latest forms which these forgeries assumed. In the Clementine *Recognitions* there is abundance of anti-Paulism; but the idea does not appear to have occurred to the writer to dress up Paul under the mask of Simon. The idea started by Baur was pressed by his followers into the shape that, wherever in ancient documents Simon Magus is mentioned, Paul is meant. We are asked to believe that the Simon of Acts viii. was no real character, but only a presentation of Paul. Simon claimed to be the power of God which is called Great; and Paul calls his gospel the power of God (Rom. i. 16; I. Cor. i. 18), and claims that the power of Christ rested in himself (II. Cor. xii. 9), and that he lived by the power of God (xiii. 4). In Acts viii. the power of bestowing the Holy Ghost, which Philip does not appear to have exercised, is clearly represented as the special prerogative of the apostles. When, therefore, Simon offered money for the power of conferring the Holy Ghost, it was really to obtain the rank of apostle. We are therefore asked to detect here a covert account of the refusal of the elder apostles to admit Paul's claim to rank with them, backed though it was by a gift of money for the poor saints in Jerusalem. Peter tells him that he has no lot in the matter, *i.e.* no part in the lot of apostleship (see Acts i. 17, 25); that he is still in the "gall of bitterness and bond of iniquity"—*i.e.* full of bitter hatred against Peter (Gal. ii. 11) and not observant of the Mosaic Law. We are not to be surprised that St. Luke, Paulist though he was, should assert in his history this libel on his master. He knew the story to be current among the Jewish disciples, and wished to take the sting out of it by telling it in such a way as to represent Simon as a real person, distinct from Paul. So, having begun to speak of Paul in the beginning of c. viii., he interpolates the episode of Philip's adventures, and does not return to speak of Paul until his reader's attention has been drawn off, so as not to be likely to recognize Paul under the mask of Simon.

It is not necessary to spend much time in pulling to pieces speculations exhibiting so much ingenuity, but so wanting in common sense. If, by way of nickname, a public character is called by a name not his own, common sense tells us that that must be a name to which discreditable associations are already known to attach. If a revolutionary agitator is called Catiline, that is because the name of Catiline is already associated with reckless and treasonable designs. It would be silly to conclude from the modern use of the nickname that there never had been such a person as Catiline, and that the traditional story of him must be so interpreted as best to describe the modern character. Further, while obscure 3rd-cent. heretics, fearing the odium of assailing directly one held in veneration through the rest of the Christian world, might resort to disguise, Paul's opponents, in his lifetime, had no temptation to resort to oblique attacks: they could say what they pleased against Paul of Tarsus without needing to risk being unintelligible by speaking of Simon of Gitta.

Lipsius, whose account of his predecessors' speculations we have abridged from his art. "Simon," in Schenkel's *Bibel-Lexikon*, exercises his own ingenuity in dealing with the legendary history of Simon. The ingenuity which discovers Paul in the Simon of the Acts has, of course, a much easier task in finding him in the Simon of the legends. But since the history, as it has come down to us, leaves much to be desired as an intentional libel on Paul, we must modify the legends so as best to adapt them to this object, and must then believe we have thus recovered the original form of the legend. Thus, the *Homilies* represent the final disputation between Peter and Simon to have occurred at Laodicea; but we must believe that the original form laid it at Antioch, where took place the collision between Peter and Paul (Gal. ii.). The Clementines represent Simon as going voluntarily to Rome; but the original must surely have represented him as taken there as a prisoner by the Roman authorities, and so on. It is needless to examine minutely speculations vitiated by such methods of investigation. The chronological order is—the historical personage comes first; then legends arise about him; then the use made of his name. The proper order of investigation is, therefore, first to ascertain what is historical about Simon before discussing his legends. Now, it cannot reasonably be doubted that Simon of Gitta is an historical personage. The heretical sect which claimed him for its founder was regarded by Justin Martyr as most formidable; he speaks of it as predominant in Samaria and not unknown elsewhere; probably he had met members of it at Rome. Its existence is testified by Hegesippus (Eus. iv. 22); Celsus (Orig. *adv. Cels.* v. 62), who states that some of them were called Heleniani; and Clement of Alexandria (*Strom.* vii. 17), who states that one branch was called Eutychitae. It had become almost extinct in Origen's time, who doubts (*adv. Cels.* i. 57) whether there were then 30 Simonians in the world; but we need not doubt its existence in Justin's time, nor the fact that it claimed Simon of Gitta as its founder. Writings in his name were in circulation, *teste* the Clementine *Recognitions*, and Epiphanius as confirming Hippolytus. The Simon of Acts is also a real person. If we read Acts viii., which relates the preaching of Philip, in connexion with c. xxi., which tells of several days spent by Luke in Philip's house, we have the simple explanation of the insertion of the former chapter, that Luke gladly included in his history a narrative of the early preaching of the gospel communicated by an eye-witness. We need not ascribe to Luke any more recondite motive for relating the incident than that he believed it had occurred. There is no evidence that this Samaritan magician had obtained elsewhere any great notoriety; and there is every reason to think that all later writers derive their knowledge from the Acts of the Apostles. We have already said that we believe Justin mistaken in identifying Simon of the Acts with Simon of Gitta, whom we take to have been a 2nd-cent. Gnostic teacher; but this identification is followed in the Clementines. In any case, we see that the whole manufacture of the latter story is later than Simon of Gitta, if not, as we believe, later than Justin Martyr. The anti-Paulists, therefore, who dressed Paul in the disguise of Simon, are more than a century later than any opponents Paul had in his lifetime, who, if they wished to fix a nickname on the apostle, were not likely to go to the Acts of the Apostles to look for one. [G.S.]

Simplicianus, St., bp. of Milan next after St. Ambrose, a resident there between 350 and 360, and instrumental in converting Victorinus (Aug. *Conf.* viii. 2). Later perhaps than this he became intimate with St. Ambrose, whose father in the Christian faith he is called by Augustine. About 374, the year Ambrose was raised to the episcopate, Simplician appears to have settled at Milan (Tillem. vol. x. p. 398). He was held in deep reverence by St. Ambrose, who was often consulted by him, and speaks of his continual study of Holy Scripture (Aug. *Conf.* viii. 2; Ambr. *Epp.* 37. 2; 65. 1). Four reply-letters to him by St. Ambrose on points of Scripture are extant (Ambr. *Epp.* 37, 38, 61, 67).

Augustine, residing near Milan A.D. 386, became acquainted with Simplician, whose account of the conversion of Victorinus awakened an eager desire to follow his example (*Conf.* viii. 5), and the friendship lasted throughout Augustine's life. Simplician's appointment to the see of Milan, A.D. 397, is described by Paulinus in his Life of St. Ambrose (c. 46). He apparently died in 400, and was succeeded by Venerius. His inquiries elicited the treatise of Augustine, *de Diversis Quaes.*, concerning various passages in O. and N. T.

Tillem. x. 401; Ceill. iv. 325, vi. 7, ix. 6, 78, 249-254; Cave, *Hist. Litt.* vol. i. p. 299. [H.W.P.]

Simplicius (7), bp. of Rome after Hilarius, from Feb. 22, 468 (according to the conclusion of Pagi, *in Baron. ad ann.* 467, iv.), to Mar. 483. According to *Lib. Pontif.* he was a native of Tibur, the son of one Castinus. He witnessed, during his episcopate, the fall of the Western empire and the accession (A.D. 476) of Odoacer as king of Italy. This change, however politically important, does not seem to have affected at the time the pope or the church at Rome. The later emperors, Anthemius, Nepos, Augustulus, who reigned during the earlier years of Simplicius's popedom, being merely nominees of the Eastern emperor, had little power; and Odoacer, himself an Arian, did not interfere with church affairs.

The reigning emperors of the East were, first Leo I., the Thracian, called also "the Great," and after him Zeno, his son-in-law, who succeeded him A.D. 474, but whose reign was interrupted from 475 to 477 by the usurpation of Basiliscus. The contemporary bp. of Constantinople was Acacius (471-489). The most memorable incidents of the pontificate of Simplicius were his negotiations, and eventual breach, with this prelate and with the emperor Zeno who supported him—leading up to the long schism between the churches of the East and West, which ensued in the time of the following pope, FELIX III. (or II.). The difference arose on questions connected partly with the rival claims of the sees of Rome and Constantinople, partly with the Monophysite or Eutychian heresy.

The first occasion was the promulgation of an edict by the emperor Leo I., at the instance of Acacius, confirming the 28th canon of Chalcedon. This canon, said to have been passed unanimously by all present except the legates of pope Leo I., not only confirmed the 3rd canon of Constantinople, which had given to the bp. of new Rome (*i.e.* Constantinople) a primacy of honour (*i.e.* honorary rank) next after the bp. of old Rome, but further gave him authority to ordain the metropolitans of the Pontic, Asian, and Thracian dioceses, thus investing him with the powers as well as the rank of a patriarch, second only to the pope of Rome. Pope Leo had subsequently objected to this canon and never gave it his assent. He claimed that it was an infringement of the canons of Nice and entrenched on the rights of other patriarchs. It indicated a desire on the part of the bps. of Constantinople, then the real seat of empire, to rival and perhaps eventually to supersede the old primacy of Rome. At Rome the position maintained was that the authority of a see rested on its ecclesiastical origin, and that of Rome especially on its having been the see of St. Peter. The view at Constantinople was that the temporal pre-eminence of a city was a sufficient ground for ecclesiastical ascendancy. Hence the long struggle.

Acacius, by inducing the emperor to confirm the 28th canon of Chalcedon by a special edict, hoped to make it plain that the eminence and authority thereby assigned to his see were still maintained and had not been conceded to the remonstrances of pope Leo. The language used by the emperor in his edict—styling the church of Constantinople "the Mother of his Piety, and of all Christians, and of the orthodox faith"—confirms the supposition that an idea was even entertained of the new seat of empire superseding the old one in ecclesiastical prerogative as well as temporal rank. Simplicius naturally took alarm. He sent Probus, bp. of Canusium in Apulia, as his legate to Constantinople to remonstrate; but with what success we know not.

In the doctrinal controversies of the day between Rome and Constantinople, Simplicius appears to have been in accord with the emperor Leo, and for some time with Zeno, as well as with Acacius. The great patriarchal sees were, during the first years of his reign, occupied by orthodox prelates, who had the imperial support. Alexandria had been held by Timothy Salofaciolus since the Eutychian Timothy Aelurus had been banished by the emperor Leo I. in 460. At Antioch Julian, an orthodox patriarch, elected on the expulsion of Peter Fullo by Leo I., A.D. 471, was still in possession. But the usurpation of the empire by Basiliscus, A.D. 475, introduced immediate discord and disturbance. Basiliscus declared at once for Eutychianism, and promptly recalled Timothy Aelurus to Alexandria. Having taken possession of the see and driven Salofaciolus to flight, Aelurus repaired to Constantinople to procure the calling of a new general council to reverse the decisions of Chalcedon.

Certain clergy and monks of Constantinople sent a messenger with letters to represent this state of things to Simplicius at Rome. Simplicius promptly wrote to Basiliscus and Acacius. His letter to Basiliscus expresses horror at the doings of Aelurus, of whom he speaks in no measured language. The opportunity is not lost, in the course of the letter, of insinuating to the new emperor the peculiar spiritual authority of the Roman see: "The truths which have flowed pure from the fountain of the Scriptures cannot be disturbed by any arguments of cloudy subtilty. For there remains one and the same rule of apostolical doctrine in the successors of him to whom the Lord enjoined the care of the whole sheepfold—to whom He promised that the gates of hell should not prevail against him, and that what by Him should be bound on earth should not be loosed in heaven." And the pope conjures the emperor in the voice of St. Peter, the unworthy minister of whose see he is, not to allow impunity to the enemies of the ancient faith, and especially urges him to prevent, if possible, the assembling a council to review the decisions of Chalcedon.

Meanwhile Basiliscus at Constantinople, issuing an encyclic letter, repudiated and condemned the council of Chalcedon; required all, under pain of deposition, exile, and other punishments, to agree to this condemnation; and ordered the copies of pope Leo's letters and of the Acts of Chalcedon, wherever found, to be burnt. The document is given in full by Evagrius (iii. 4). Acacius refused to sign it. But in the compliant East elsewhere it was accepted generally. At Constantinople Acacius, supported by the clergy and monks, was resolute and successful in his resistance. Daniel Stylites, descending from his pillar, aided in rousing the populace; and Basiliscus had to leave the city for safety. The disaffection was taken advantage of by Zeno, who in 477 marched on Constantinople, and without further difficulty became again emperor of the East.

During these troubles under Basiliscus Simplicius seems to have had no opportunity of exercising influence; but as soon as he heard of the restitution of Zeno he wrote to that emperor, exhorting him to follow the steps of his predecessors Marcian and Leo, to allow no tampering with the decisions of Chalcedon, to drive all Eutychian bishops from the sees they had usurped, and especially to send Aelurus into solitude. To Acacius he wrote to the same effect. Zeno does not appear, however, to have taken any step against Peter Mongus. Possibly the emperor and his advisers were already disposed to the conciliatory policy towards the Eutychians which they afterwards maintained in spite of indignant protests from the pope. Simplicius complained, too, of the Eutychian leaders having been allowed to remain at Antioch, and attributed the troubles there to this cause.

The death of Timothy Salofaciolus at Alexandria in 482 gave rise to much more serious differences between Constantinople and Rome. Strained relations now resulted in decided conflict, ending in an open schism, which lasted 35 years, between Eastern and Western Christendom. John Talaias was elected canonically by a synod of the orthodox at Alexandria in the room of Salofaciolus. Simplicius received a notification of the election from the synod, and was about to express his assent, when he was startled by a letter from Zeno accusing Talaias of perjury, and intimating that Peter Mongus was the most proper person to succeed Salofaciolus. Simplicius at once (July 15, 482) addressed Acacius (who had not written himself), imploring him to do all he could to prevent it. The letter written to Zeno himself has not been preserved. Hearing nothing from Acacius, he wrote to him again in Nov., but still got no reply. So much appears from the extant letters of Simplicius (*Epp.* xvii. xviii. Labbe). [ACACIUS (7); JOANNES (11).]

Liberatus (c. 18) informs us that, driven from Alexandria, John Talaias appealed for support to Simplicius, who on his behalf wrote to Acacius, but received the reply that Acacius could not recognize Talaias, having received Peter Mongus into communion on the basis of the emperor's HENOTICON. Simplicius wrote to Acacius that he ought not to have received Peter into communion without the concurrence of the apostolic see; that a man condemned by a common decree could not be freed from the ban except by a common council; and that he must first accept unreservedly the council of Chalcedon and the Tome of pope Leo. Simplicius received no reply to this second letter, and died not long after, early in Mar. 483, according to Anastasius. [J.B—Y.]

Siricius, bp. of Rome after Damasus from late in Dec. 384, or early in Jan. 385, to Nov. 26 (?), 398. He followed the example of Damasus in maintaining the authority of the Roman see. When the prefecture of East Illyricum had been assigned (A.D. 379) to the Eastern division of the empire, Damasus had insisted on its being still subject to the spiritual authority of Rome, and had constituted Acholius, bp. of Thessalonica, and after him Anysius (who succeeded Acholius A.D. 383) his own vicars for the maintenance of such authority. Siricius, on his accession, renewed this vicariate jurisdiction to Anysius (Innoc. *Epp.* i., xiii.).

One of his earliest acts was to issue the first Papal Decretal that has any claim to genuineness, though he speaks in it of earlier *decreta* sent to the provinces by pope Liberius. It is dated Feb. 11, 385. Its genuineness is undisputed. It is plainly referred to by pope Innocent I. (*Ep.* vi. *ad Exsuperium*). Quesnel includes it without hesitation in his *Cod. Rom. cum Leone edit.* c. 29. Its occasion was a letter from Himerius, bp. of Tarragona in Spain, addressed to Damasus but received by Siricius, asking the pope's advice on matters of discipline and with regard to abuses prevalent in the Spanish church. Siricius, having taken counsel in a Roman synod, issued this decretal in reply, to be communicated by Himerius to all bishops of Spain and neighbouring provinces with a view to universal observance. The opportunity was taken of asserting in very decided terms the authority of the Roman see: "We bear the burdens of all who are heavy laden; nay, rather the blessed apostle Peter bears them in us, who, as we trust, in all things protects and guards us, the heirs of his administration." Among the rules thus promulgated for universal observance, one relates to the rebaptizing of Arians returning to the church, and another to clerical celibacy, which is insisted on. Thus what the oecumenical council had refused to require Siricius now, on the authority of the apostolic see, declared of general obligation. The rule laid down by him affected, however, only the higher clerical orders, not including subdeacons, to whom it was extended by Leo I. (*c.* 442. See *Epp.* xiv. 4; cxlvii. 3), in Sicily, by pope Gregory the Great (Greg. *Epp.* lib. i. Ind. ix., *Ep.* 42).

The zeal of Siricius against heresy appears in his correspondence with the usurper Maximus, who in 383 had obtained the imperial authority in Gaul. The pope wrote, exhorting him to support the Catholic faith and complaining of the recent ordination of one Agricius, who seems to have been suspected of heresy. Maximus, in his extant reply, declares his desire to maintain the true faith, undertakes to refer the case of Agricius to a synod of clergy, and takes credit for measures already in force against the Manicheans in Gaul, doubtless alluding to the Priscillianists, who were often called Manicheans. The pope was zealous against the Manicheans at Rome, where "he found Manicheans, whom he sent into exile, and provided that they should not communicate with the faithful, since it was not lawful to vex the Lord's body with a polluted mouth" (*Lib. Pontif. in Vita Siricii*). The reference seems to be to the alleged habit of the Manicheans to make a show of conformity by frequenting Catholic communion. It is added that even converts from them were to be sent into monasteries, and not admitted to communion till at the point of death.

Another class of heretics afterwards fell under the condemnation of Siricius. Jovinian, notorious through St. Jerome's vehement writings against him, having been expelled from Milan, had come to Rome and obtained a following there. His teaching came under the notice of two eminent laymen, Pammachius and Victorinus, who represented it to pope Siricius who assembled a synod of clergy at which Jovinian was excommunicated, together with his abettors, Auxentius, Genialis, Germinator, Felix, Frontinus, Martianus, Januarius, and Ingenius. These departed to Milan, whither Siricius sent three presbyters with a letter to the Milanese clergy, informing them of what had been done at Rome, and expressing confidence that they would pay regard to it. The letter is full of strong invective against Jovinian and his colleagues—"dogs such as never before had barked against the church's mysteries"—but contains no arguments. Siricius disclaims any disparagement of marriage, "at which," he says, "we assist with the veil," though he "venerates with greater honour virgins devoted to God, who are the fruit of marriages." The synodical reply from Milan is preserved among the epistles of St. Ambrose (*Ep.* xlii. ed. Bened.), who presided at the Milanese synod. He and his colleagues thank Siricius for his vigilance, concur with his strictures on Jovinian, supply the arguments which the pope's letter lacked, and declare that they had condemned those whom the pope condemned, according to his judgment. The introductory words of this epistle have been adduced in proof of the view then held of the pope's supreme authority. They are: "We recognize in the letter of your holiness the watchfulness of a good shepherd, diligently keeping the door committed to thee, and with pious solicitude guarding the sheepfold of Christ, worthy of being heard and followed by the sheep of the Lord." This language, though expressing recognition of the bp. of Rome as the representative of St. Peter, cannot be pressed as implying that he was the one doorkeeper of the whole church or an infallible authority in definitions of faith. On the contrary, the bishops at Milan endorsed his judgment, not as a matter of course or as being bound to do so, but on the merits of the case, setting forth their reasons. These proceedings apparently occurred in 390.

About the same time, or soon after, the Meletian schism at Antioch came under the notice of Siricius. His attitude to it is not certainly known. Some six months after the death of Damasus, whose highly valued secretary he had been, Jerome had left Rome for ever. In his bitterly expressed letter to Asilla, inveighing against his opponents and calumniators, he does not mention the new pope; but it may be concluded, if only from his silence, that he had lost the countenance he had enjoyed under Damasus. One expression suggests that he had been a little disappointed at not being made pope himself, and that coolness between him and Siricius may have arisen from this. Siricius and he were at one in their advocacy of virginity against Jovinian and in their general orthodoxy, but there seems to have been no intercourse between them, and, even in the course of the controversy against Jovinian, Siricius appears to have joined others at Rome in disapproving of Jerome's alleged disparagement of matrimony. Further, Rufinus, the once close friend of Jerome, having quarrelled with him in Palestine about Origenism but been temporarily reconciled, in 395 left Jerusalem for Rome. He was favourably received by Siricius, who gave him a commendatory letter on his departure, the quarrel with Jerome having recommenced with increased violence.

For his neglect of Jerome and patronage of Rufinus, Baronius disparages Siricius, even saying that his days were shortened by divine judgment (Baron. *ad ann.* 397; xxxii.). A further ground of complaint (*ad ann.* 394; xl.) is his supposed unworthy treatment of another ascetic saint, Paulinus of Nola, who says he was badly treated by the Roman clergy when passing through Rome (A.D. 395) on his way to Nola, and especially blames the pope (Paulin. *ad* Sulpic. Severum, *Ep.* i. *in nov. edit.* v.). For such reasons Baronius has excluded Siricius from the Roman Martyrology. Pagi (in Baron. *ad ann.* 398, I.) defends the pope against the animadversions of Baronius. Siricius died in 398. [J.B—Y.]

Sirmium, Stonemasons of. The Acts giving the history of the martyrdom of the five stonemasons of Sirmium have been known for centuries, being found in substance in Ado's Martyrology, but only last century was their relation to the history of Diocletian's period recognized. They were stonemasons belonging to Pannonia, engaged in the imperial quarries; one of them, Simplicius, was a pagan. They distinguished themselves by their genius and ability, and attracted the notice of Diocletian by the beauty of their carving. Simplicius was converted by his four companions, and baptized secretly by a bishop, Cyril of Antioch, who had been three years a slave in the quarries and had suffered many stripes for the faith. The pagans, jealous of their skill, accused them before Diocletian, who, however, continued to protect them. When, however, the emperor ordered them to make, among other statues, one of Aesculapius, the masons made all the others, but refused to carve that. The pagans thereupon procured an order for their execution. They were enclosed in lead coffins and flung into the Save. Their Acts then proceed to narrate the martyrdom of the saints called the Quatuor Coronati, whose liturgical history has been told at length in *D. C. A.* t. i. p. 461. Diocletian, coming to Rome, ordered all the troops to sacrifice to Aesculapius. Four soldiers, Carpophorus, Severus, Severianus, and Victorinus, refusing, were flogged to death, and their bodies buried by pope Melchiades and St. Sebastian on the Via Lavicana at the 3rd milestone from the city. These Acts are very valuable illustrations of the great persecution, but are full of difficulties. The whole story is in Mason's *Diocletian Persecution*, p. 259. Attention was first called to the Acts as illustrating Diocletian's period by Wattenbach in the *Sitzungsberichte der Wiener Akad.* Bd. x. (1853) S.

118-126. They were discussed in Büdinger, *Untersuch. zur röm. Kaisergesch.* ii. 262, iii. 321-338, with elaborate archaeological and chronological commentaries. [G.T.S.]

Sisinnius (7), a bishop of the Novatianists at Constantinople, succeeding on Marcian's death in Nov. 395 (Socr. *H. E.* v. 21; vi. 1; Soz. *H. E.* viii. 1). He published a treatise warmly controverting Chrysostom's impassioned language as to the efficacy of repentance and the restoration of penitents to communion, *de Poenitentia* (Socr. *H. E.* vi. 21). Chrysostom, taking umbrage at this and at his claim to exercise episcopal functions in Constantinople, threatened to stop his preaching. Sisinnius jocosely told him he would be much obliged to him for sparing him so much trouble, and thus disarmed his anger (*ib.* 22). Sisinnius enjoyed a great reputation for witty repartees. Several are collected by Socrates (*l.c.*), but do not give a very high idea of his powers. He is described as a man of great eloquence, enhanced by dignity of countenance and person, gracefulness of action, and by the tones of his voice. He had a considerable reputation for learning, being very familiar with philosophical writings as well as expositions of Scripture, and was well skilled in dialectics. Together with Theodotus of Antioch he composed a synodic letter against the Thessalians, in the name of the Novatianist bishops assembled at Constantinople for his consecration, addressed to Berinianus, Amphilochius, and other bishops of Pamphylia (Phot. *Cod.* lii. col. 40; Cave, *Hist. Lit.* i. 290). Though a bishop of a schismatic body, he was much esteemed by the orthodox bishops, especially by Atticus, and was the honoured friend of leading aristocrats of Constantinople. He kept a sumptuous table, though not exceeding the bounds of moderation himself. Sisinnius died the same year as Chrysostom, A.D. 407, and was succeeded by Chrysanthus (Socr. *H. E.* vii. 6; Cave, *u.s.*). [E.V.]

Sixtus I.—so called in the Liberian Catalogue by Optatus (l. 2) and Augustine (*Ep.* liii.); but *Xystus, Xistus*, or *Xestus*, in *Catal. Felic.*, Irenaeus (*adv. Haer.* iii. 3), Eusebius (*H. E.* iv. 4, 5, and *Chron.*), Epiphanius (*Haer.* 97, 6)—one of the early bps. of Rome, called the 6th after the apostles, and the successor of Alexander. All assign him an episcopate of about 10 years, and place him in the reign of Hadrian. *Catal. Liber.* dates his episcopate 117-126; Eusebius (*H. E.*) 119-128; his *Chronicle* 114-124. Lipsius (*Chronol. der röm. Bischöf.*) gives 124-126 as the possible limits for his death. The Felician Catalogue and the Martyrologies represent him as a martyr, and he is commemorated among the apostles and martyrs, after Linus, Cletus, Clemens, in the canon of the mass. But Telesphorus being the first bp. of Rome designated a martyr by Irenaeus, the claim to the title of Sixtus and other early bps. of Rome, to the great majority of whom it has been since assigned, is doubtful. [J.B—Y.]

Sixtus II. (*Xystus*), bp. of Rome after Stephen for about one year, martyred under Valerian Aug. 6, 258. A contemporary letter of St. Cyprian (*Ep.* 80) confirms this date as given in the Liberian Catalogue. Probably his accession was on Aug. 31, 257 (see Lipsius, *Chronol. der röm. Bischöf.*). His predecessor Stephen had been at issue with Cyprian of Carthage as to the rebaptism of heretics. Under Xystus, who was more conciliatory, though he upheld the Roman usage, peace was restored (Eus. *H. E.* vii. 5-7).

The circumstances of his martyrdom appear to have been as follows. The emperor Valerian had already, before the accession of Xystus, forbidden the resort of Christians to the cemeteries on pain of banishment. But in the middle of 258, when Valerian was arming for his Persian war, he sent a rescript to the senate of much severer import; ordering bishops, priests, and deacons to be summarily executed; senators and other persons of rank to be visited with loss of dignity and goods, and, on refusal to renounce Christianity, with death; matrons to be despoiled and exiled; and imperial officials (*Caesariani*) to be sent in chains to labour on the imperial domains (Cyp. *Ep.* 80). Xystus fell an early victim to this rescript. He was found by the soldiers seated on his episcopal chair, in the cemetery of Praetextatus on the Appian Way, surrounded by members of his flock. As these endeavoured to protect him, he thrust himself forward lest they should suffer in his stead, and was beheaded and several companions slain. His body was afterwards removed by the Christians to the usual burial-place of the bishops of that period, the neighbouring cemetery of Callistus. His two deacons, Agapetus and Felicissimus, with others, were buried in the cemetery where they fell. This account of the occurrence is gathered from Cyprian's contemporary letter to Successus (*Ep.* 80), and from the Damasine inscription in the papal crypt of the cemetery of Callistus, of which a few fragments have been found by De Rossi, and which originally began as follows:

> "Tempore quo gladius secuit pia viscera matris
> Hic positus rector coelestia dona docebam . . ."
> (Gruter, 1173, 13).

That these verses refer to Xystus, and not, as assumed in the Acts of St. Stephen, to his predecessor, is satisfactorily shewn by Lipsius (*op. cit.*). That he was buried there is expressly stated in the Liberian Catalogue of Martyrs, as well as by all later authorities; and the statement is confirmed by numerous *graffiti* on the walls of the crypt, in which his name is prominent. The line "Hic positus," etc., may refer to the *cathedra* on which he sat when found by the soldiers, which had been removed with his body to the papal crypt. That the cemetery of Praetextatus was the scene of his martyrdom ancient tradition bears witness, and in accordance with it an oratory was afterwards built on the spot, "coemeterium ubi decollatus est Xystus." The tradition is confirmed by representations of him and his chair in this cemetery, under one of which is the legend SVSTVS. [J.B—Y.]

Sixtus III., bp. of Rome (432-441) after Coelestinus, and the immediate predecessor of Leo the Great. Two notable heresies of his day were Pelagianism and Nestorianism. Before his accession he had taken part in both controversies. It appears from Augustine's letters to him when he was still a Roman presbyter under Zosimus, that the Pelagians had claimed him as being, with the pope, on their side; but that, when the pope was at length induced to condemn the heresy, he also had written to the African church expressing his concurrence with a vigour of language that fully satisfied Augustine, who also rejoices to have heard that he had been foremost in anathematizing Pelagianism in a large assembly at Rome (Aug. *Epp.* 191, *al.* 104, and 194, *al.* 105). Apparently Sixtus had, before his accession, also intervened in the Nestorian conflict, for in his letter to John of Antioch (*Ep.* ii.) he speaks of having once admonished Nestorius; and this must have been before the latter's final condemnation, and hence before the accession of Sixtus, who was evidently a man of mark and influence at Rome before becoming pope.

It seems, however, that the Nestorians as well as the Pelagians claimed Sixtus as once having favoured them; and he was reported to have taken in ill part the condemnation of Nestorius. These claims may have arisen from his having evinced a conciliatory spirit and a reluctance to condemn too hastily.

There are two extant epistles of his, written to Cyril and John of Antioch, expressing his great joy in their reconciliation; from one of which it further appears that he had written often previously to Maximian, the successor of Nestorius at Constantinople. A synod had been held at Rome on the occasion of his birthday, at which the joyful news of the reconciliation had been made known, and he was, when he wrote, expecting the speedy arrival of a deputation of clergy from John of Antioch. These two letters are given by Baronius (A.D. 433, xii. and xvii.); from a Vatican MS., which he speaks of as corrupt but trustworthy. (See also Labbe, *Concil. Eph.* iii. 1689, 1699.) The letter to John is quoted by Vincent of Lerins (*adv. Haer.*).

Two previous letters of Sixtus, conceived in a similar spirit, are given by Cotelerius from MSS. in the *Biblioth. Reg.* (Coteler. *Monum. Graec. Eccles.* vol. i. p. 42). One was to Cyril; the other was apparently an encyclic to him and the Easterns generally, sent by two bishops from the East, Hermogenes and Lampetius, who had been present at the pope's ordination. Both announced, as was usual, his accession to his see, and declared his communion with the Eastern churches. But in both, while he fully concurs in the condemnation of Nestorius by the council of Ephesus, he refers with regret to the dissent of John of Antioch and his adherents, whose reception into communion he desires and recommends, if they should come to a better mind, as he hopes they will.

Sixtus was no less vigilant than preceding popes in maintaining the jurisdiction of the Roman see over Illyricum, and that of the bp. of Thessalonica as the pope's vicar over the rest of the bishops there. Four letters of his (two written in 435, another in 437) on this subject were read in the Roman council held under Boniface II., A.D. 531. (See Labbe, vol. v., *Concil. Rom. III. sub Bonifac. II.*) In the fourth, addressed to all the bishops of Illyricum, he enjoins them to submit themselves to Anastasius of Thessalonica as, like his predecessor, vicar of the apostolic see, with authority to summon synods and adjudicate on all cases, except such as it might be necessary to refer to Rome. He bids them pay no regard to the decrees of "the oriental synod," except those on faith, which had his own approval. He probably refers to the council of Constantinople, which in its 3rd canon had given a primacy of honour after old Rome to Constantinople. On the strength of this the patriarchs of Constantinople had already assumed jurisdiction over the Thracian dioceses, though not till the council of Chalcedon (A.D. 451; can. xxviii.) was the express power of ordaining metropolitans in Illyricum formally given to them, despite the protest of pope Leo's legates.

Towards the end of his life Sixtus still concurred decidedly in the condemnation of Pelagianism. For we are told by Prosper (*Chron.*) that Julian, the eminent Pelagian, being deposed from the see of Eclanum in Campania, essayed in 439, by profession of penitence, to creep again into the communion of the church, but that Sixtus, under the advice of his deacon Leo, "allowed no opening to his pestiferous attempts." This Leo was the successor of Sixtus in the see of Rome, Leo the Great, who thus appears to have been his archdeacon and adviser.

Three works issued under the name of Sixtus (*de Divitiis, de Malis Doctoribus*, etc., and *de Castitate*) are apparently of Pelagian origin (see Baron. *ad ann.* 440, vi.), possibly put out in his name on the strength of the old report of his having once favoured Pelagianism.

Sixtus died A.D. 440, and was buried (according to Anastasius, *Lib. Pontif.*), "ad S. Laurentium via Tiburtini." He is commemorated as a confessor on Mar. 28: "Romae S. Sixti tertii, papae et confessoris" (*Martyrol. Roman*). Why he should be called a confessor is not obvious. The title may rest on a spurious letter to the bishops of the East, which complains of persecution.

In the *Lib. Pontif.* extraordinary activity in building, endowing, and decorating churches is attributed to him, and to the emperor Valentinian under his instigation. He is said to have built the basilicas of St. Maria Maggiore on the Esquiline (called *Ad Praesepe*), and of St. Laurence, and to have furnished both with great store of precious instruments and ornamentations. Pope Hadrian, in writing to Charlemagne (*Ep.* 3, c. 19) alludes to the former. [J.B—Y.]

Socrates (2), one of the most interesting and valuable historians of the early Christian age, was born at Constantinople, probably early in the reign of Theodosius the younger, A.D. 408. He tells us that he was educated there under Helladius and Ammonius, two heathen grammarians, who had fled from Alexandria to escape the emperor's displeasure. They had been guilty of many acts of cruel retaliation upon the Christians there, who had sought to overthrow the idols and temples (*H. E.* v. 16). Socrates studied rhetoric, assisted Troilus the rhetorician and sophist, and entered the legal profession, hence his name Scholasticus, the title for a lawyer. His life was spent at Constantinople, and hence he, in his history, occupies himself much with the affairs of that city. "No wonder," he says, "I write more fully of the famous acts done in this city (Constantinople), partly because I beheld most of them with my own eyes, partly because they are more famous and thought more worthy of remembrance than many other acts" (v. 23). Here we see the true spirit of the historian, and a worthy anxiety to be correct. How sincerely Socrates desired to be so is shewn by his use of similar expressions in the beginning of bk. vi., where he says he had a greater liking for the history of his own than of bygone times, because he had either seen it or learned it from eye-witnesses. A certain Theodorus, otherwise unknown, encouraged him to become a historian of the church. His object was to continue its history from where Eusebius had ended down to his own day. His work is divided into seven books, from Constantine's proclamation as emperor, A.D. 306 to 439, a period of 133, or, as he himself calls it, in round numbers, 140 years. Especially in bks. i. and ii. Rufinus appears to have exercised considerable influence. But at that point, the writings of Athanasius and the letters of other celebrated men coming into his hands, he found that Rufinus had been misinformed and had misled him on many points. His own statement seems to imply that he rewrote those books to have the satisfaction of knowing that he had set forth the history "in a most absolute and perfect manner" (ii. 1).

Of his own style Socrates, addressing Theodorus, says, "But I would have you know, before you read my books, that I have not curiously addicted myself unto a lofty style, neither unto a glorious show of gay sentences; for so peradventure, in running after words and phrases, I might have missed of my matter and failed of my purpose and intent. . . . Again, such a penning profiteth very little the vulgar and ignorant sort of people, who desire not so much the fine and elegant sort of phrase as the furtherance of their knowledge and the truth of the history. Wherefore, lest our story should halt of both sides, and displease the learned in that it doth not rival the artificial skill and profound knowledge of ancient writers, the unlearned in that their capacity cannot comprehend the substance of the matter by reason of the painted rhetoric and picked sentences, I have tied myself unto such a mean as that, though the handling be simple, yet the effect is soon found and quickly understood" (vi. pref.).

His matter was to be chiefly the affairs of the church, but not to the complete exclusion of "battles and bloody wars," for even in these there was something worthy to be recorded. He believed the narrative of such events would help to relieve the weariness which might overcome his readers if he dwelt only on the consideration of the bishops' affairs and their practices everywhere one against another. Above all, he had observed that the weal of church and state was so closely bound up together that the two were either out of joint at the same time, or that the misery of the one followed closely the misery of the other (v. pref.). It was the troubles of the church, too, that he desired chiefly to record. His idea was that, when peace prevailed, there was no matter for a historiographer (vii. 47).

One important qualification Socrates possessed for his task was that he was a layman. This in no degree hindered his capability of forming a correct judgment on theological controversies, for around these the main interest of lay as well as clerical Christians centred in his days and they were thoroughly understood by all educated Christian men; while his lay position and training unquestionably helped to raise him above the bitter animosities and persecuting spirit of his age, and led him to see the amount of hairsplitting in not a few of the current disputes. His recognition of good in those from whom he differed forms one of the most pleasing characteristics of his history. His impartiality has, indeed, exposed him to a charge of heresy. He saw, and ventured to own, some good in the Novatianists, and especially in several of their bishops, and he has been accordingly often charged with Novatianism. But his history shews little, if any, reason why we should doubt his orthodoxy. Like the most enlightened men of his age, he gave easy credence to miraculous stories, and there are many scattered throughout his pages quite as improbable and foolish as those found in the most superstitious writers of his time. Yet Socrates often displays a singular propriety of judgment, while his occasional reflections and digressions constitute one of the most interesting and instructive parts of his history. Thus his defence of the study by Christians of heathen writers may still be read with profit, and perhaps much more could not even now be added to his argument (iii. 14). His chapter on ceremonies, their place in the Christian system, the ground of their obligation, and their relation to the true word of the gospel, shews an enlargement and enlightenment of mind (v. 21). His whole history shews his keen eye for the mischief done by heated ecclesiastics, and for the unworthy motives that frequently swayed them (vi. 14).

For many other points the student will find his *History* valuable. It contains many original documents, *e.g.* decrees of councils and letters of emperors and bishops. It gives many important details as to the councils of Nicaea, Chalcedon, Antioch, Alexandria, Constantinople, Ephesus, etc.; the emperors of the time treated of; the most distinguished bishops, Basil of Caesarea, Gregory of Nazianzum, Ambrose, Athanasius, Chrysostom, Eusebius of Nicomedia, Cyril, etc.; the Egyptian monks and their miracles; Ulphilas, bp. of the Goths, and the famous Hypatia. It embraces some important statements on the independence of Rome claimed by the Eastern church and the encroachments of the Roman see upon the latter; on the beginnings of the secular power of the Roman church; and on the introduction of disciplinary arrangements. The progress of the gospel amongst the Goths, Saracens, and Persians, the persecutions of the Jews, and the progress of the Eastern controversy are treated at large.

A Greek and Latin ed., with notes, by Valesius, was pub. at Paris in 1668, repeated at Cambridge in 1720, and in Migne's *Patr. Gk.* (t. lxvii.) in 1859. In 1853 appeared the

Gk. and Lat. ed. of R. Hussey (Oxf. 3 vols. 8vo). An ed. with Eng. notes and intro. by W. Bright is pub. by the Clar. Press. There s an Eng. trans. by Meredith Hanmer, Prof. of Divinity, pub. in London by Field, 1619, and more recent ones pub. by Bagster in 1847, and in Schaff and Wace's *Post-Nicene Lib.*, and in *Bohn's Lib.* (Bell). [W.M.]

Sophronius (7), a learned Greek friend of Jerome, who was with him in 391-392, and is included in his catalogue of ecclesiastical writers. He had, while still young, composed a book on the glories of Bethlehem, and, just before the catalogue was written, a book on the destruction of the Serapeum, and had translated into Greek Jerome's letter to Eustochium on virginity, his Life of Hilarion, and his Latin version of the Psalms and Prophets. Jerome records that it was at Sophronius's instance that he wrote the last-named. Sophronius had, in dispute with a Jew, quoted from the Psalms, but the Jew said that the passages read differently in Hebrew. Sophronius therefore asked from Jerome a version direct from the Hebrew, which Jerome gave, though he knew that alterations from the received version would cause him some obloquy. The importance of these alterations led Sophronius to translate the versions into Greek. They were well received, and were read in many of the Eastern churches instead of the Septuagint. The translations have not come down to us; but a Greek version of the catalogue of ecclesiastical writers bears the name of Sophronius. It is not quite accurate, but appears to have been the version used by Photius. The presence of his name on this book probably gave rise toi ts insertion in some MSS. between the names of Jerome, who, however, does not appear to have adopted it. Hieron., *de Vir. Ill.* 134; *cont. Ruf.* ii. 24; Ceillier, vi. 278; and Vallarsi's pref. to Jerome, *de Vir. Ill.* [W.H.F.]

Sophronius (10), bp. of Tella or Constantina in Osrhoene, first cousin of Ibas, bp. of Edessa. He was present at the synod of Antioch which investigated the case of Athanasius of Perrha, in 445 (Labbe, iv. 728). At the "Robbers' Synod" of Ephesus in 449 (Evagr. *H. E.* 10) he was accused of practising sorcery and magical arts. He was also accused of Nestorian doctrine, and his case was reserved for the hearing of the orthodox metropolitan of Edessa, to be appointed in the place of Ibas. No further steps appear to have been taken, and at the council of Chalcedon he took his seat as bp. of Constantia (Labbe, iv. 81). His orthodoxy, however, was not beyond suspicion, and in the 8th session, after Theodoret had been compelled by the tumultuous assembly reluctantly to anathematize Nestorius, Sophronius was forced to follow his example, with the addition of Eutyches (Labbe, iv. 623). Theodoret wrote to him in favour of Cyprian, an African bp. driven from his see by the Vandals (Theod. *Ep.* 53). Assemani, *Bibl. Orient.* i. 202, 404; *Chron. Edess.*; Tillemont, *Mém. eccl.* xv. 258, 579, 686; Martin, *Le Pseudo-Synode d'Ephèse*, p. 184; Le Quien, *Or. Christ.* ii. 967. [E.V.]

Soter, bp. of Rome after Anicetus, in the reign of Marcus Aurelius, during 8 or 9 years. Lipsius (*Chronol. der röm. Bischöf.*) gives 166 or 167 and 174 or 175 as the probable dates of his accession and death. In his time the Aurelian persecution afflicted the church, though there is no evidence of Roman Christians having suffered under it. But they sympathized with those who did. Eusebius (*H. E.* iv. 23) quotes a letter from Dionysius, bp. of Corinth, to the Romans, acknowledging their accustomed benevolence to sufferers elsewhere, and the fatherly kindness of bp. Soter: "From the beginning it has been your custom to benefit all brethren in various ways, to send supplies to many churches in every city, thus relieving the poverty of those that need, and succouring the brethren who are in the mines. This ancient traditional custom of the Romans your blessed bp. Soter has not only continued, but also added to, in both supplying to the saints the transmitted bounty, and also, as an affectionate father towards his children, comforting those who resort to him with words of blessing."

The unknown author of a book called *Praedestinatus* (c. 26) states that Soter wrote a treatise against the Montanists. But the writer is generally so unworthy of credit that his testimony is of no value. [MONTANUS; PRAEDESTINATUS.]

As to the Easter dispute between Rome and the Asian Quartodecimans, it seems probable that Soter was the first bp. of Rome who was unwilling to tolerate the difference of usage. His immediate predecessor Anicetus had communicated with Polycarp when at Rome; but Victor, who succeeded Soter's successor Eleutherus, incurred the reproof of St. Irenaeus and others for desiring the general excommunication of the Asiatic churches on account of the dispute; and Irenaeus, in remonstrating with Victor, refers only to bps. of Rome before Soter, mentioning them by name, and ending his list with Anicetus, as having maintained communion with the Quartodecimans (Eus. *H. E.* v. 24). [J.B—Y.]

Sozomen, author of a well-known *Ecclesiastical History*, born *c.* 400. In his book Sozomen has some notices of his birth and of his bringing up (v. 15). His family belonged to Bethelia, a small town near Gaza in Palestine, where his grandfather had been one of the first to embrace Christianity. Thus Sozomen was nurtured amidst Christian influences. He tells us (*l.c.*) that his grandfather was endowed with great natural ability, which he consecrated especially to the study of the sacred Scriptures, that he was much beloved by the Christians of those parts, who looked to him for explanations of the word of God and the unloosing of its difficulties. Sozomen came to the writing of ecclesiastical history in no spirit of indifference. He believed in Christianity, and even in the more ascetic forms of it, with a genuine faith, "for I would neither," he says, "be considered ungracious, and willing to consign their virtue [that of the monks] to oblivion, nor yet be thought ignorant of their history; but I would wish to leave behind me such a record of their manner of life that others, led by their example, might attain to a blessed and happy end" (i. 1).

He was probably educated at first in Bethelia or Gaza, for some memories of his youth are connected with Gaza (vii. 28). Thence he seems to have gone to Berytus, a city of Phoenicia, to be trained in civil law at its famous school. His education finished, he proceeded to Constantinople, and there entered on his profession (ii. 3).

While thus engaged he formed the plan of his *Ecclesiastical History* (ii. 3), being attracted to the subject both by his own taste and the example of Eusebius. It appeared in 9 books, extending over the years 323-439, and was dedicated to Theodosius the Younger. It thus covers the same period as that of Socrates, and as both were written about the same time and have many resemblances, the question arises as to which was the original and which not unfrequently the copyist. Valesius, upon apparently good grounds, decides against Sozomen, although allowing that he often adds to and corrects his authority. Like Socrates, Sozomen is habitually trustworthy, and a conscientious and serious writer. In his account of the council of Nicaea, which may be taken as a favourable specimen of his work as a whole, he seems to have drawn from the best sources, to have proceeded with care, and to have made a sufficiently good choice among the apocryphal traditions and innumerable legends which in the 5th cent. obscured the reports of this great council (cf. De Broglie, iv. siècle, ii. 431). But he inserted in his history not a little that is trifling and superstitious. In style he is generally allowed to be superior, but in judgment inferior, to Socrates.

His *History* is especially valuable for its accounts of the monks, which, though by an admirer, are not therefore to be despised, or we should be equally entitled to set aside accounts by their detractors. It is impossible to read his repeated notices of the monastic institutions of his time or his long account of their manners and customs (i. 12), without feeling that here are statements as to the nature and influence of monasticism which cannot be set aside. He also gives not a few important particulars concerning both the events and men of the time covered by it, particularly of the council of Nicaea, the persecutions, the general progress of the gospel, the conversion of Constantine, the history of Julian, the illustrious Athanasius, and many bishops and martyrs of the age; and also a number of original documents.

The best ed., by Valesius, appeared at Paris in 1668, and was followed by one, with the notes of Valesius, at Cambridge, in 1720. The ed. of Hussey (Oxf. 1860) also deserves mention. An Eng. trans. in Bohn's *Eccl. Lib.* (1855) deserves high commendation; another was pub. by Baxter in 1847; and there is one in the *Lib. of Nicene and Post-Nicene Fathers*. [W.M.]

Spyridon, bp. of Trimithus in Cyprus, one of the most popularly celebrated of the bishops attending the council of Nicaea, although his name is not found in the list of signatures. He was the centre of many legendary stories which Socrates heard from his fellow-islanders (Socr. *H. E.* i. 12). Spyridon was married, with at least one daughter, Irene. He continued his occupation as a sheep farmer after, for his many virtues, he had been called to the episcopate. He is mentioned by Athanasius among the orthodox bishops at the council of Sardica (Athan. *Apol.* ii. p. 768). His body was first buried in his native island, then removed to Constantinople, and when the Turks captured the city it was transmitted to Corfu, where it is annually carried in procession round the capital as the patron saint of the Ionian isles (Stanley, *Eastern Church*, p. 126). His Life, written in iambics by his pupil, Triphyllius of Ledra, is spoken of by Suidas as "very profitable" (Suidas *sub voc.* Triphyllius, ii. 947). Rufin. 1, 3-5; Socr. *H. E.* i. 8, 12; Soz. *H. E.* i. 11; Niceph. *H. E.* viii. 15, 42; Tillemont, *Mém. eccl.* vi. 643, 679, vii. 242-246; Hefele, *Hist. of Councils*, vol. i. p. 284, Clark's trans.; Stanley, *op. cit.* pp. 124-126, 132). [E.V.]

Stagirus (*Stagirius*), a young friend of Chrysostom, of noble birth, who against his father's wishes embraced a monastic life, joining the brotherhood of which Chrysostom was a member, and continuing there after failure of health compelled Chrysostom's return to Antioch. The self-indulgent life Stagirus had led was a poor preparation for the austerities of monasticism, and he proved a very unsatisfactory monk. He found the nightly vigils intolerable, and reading hardly less distasteful. He spent his time in attending to a garden and orchard. He also manifested much pride of his high birth. His health broke down under the strain of so uncongenial a life. He became subject to convulsive attacks, which were then considered to indicate demoniacal possession. He employed all recognised means for expelling the evil spirit. He applied to persons of superior sanctity, often taking long journeys to obtain the aid of those who had the reputation of healing those afflicted with spiritual maladies, and visited the most celebrated martyrs' shrines, and prayed long and fervently both there and at home, but in vain, though his religious character sensibly improved. He rose at night and devoted much time to prayer and became meek and humble. Chrysostom's counsels to him are in the 3 books *ad Stagirium a daemone vexatum*, or *de Divina Providentia* (Socr. *H. E.* vi. 3). What the physical issue was we do not know. Nilus highly commends his piety, humility, and contrition, but uses language which indicates that his attacks did not entirely pass away (Nilus, *Epp.* lib. iii. 19). [E.V.]

Stephanus (1) **I.,** bp. of Rome, after Lucius, from May 12, 254, to Aug. 2, 257. These dates are arrived at by Lipsius (*Chron. der röm. Bischöf.*) after careful examination. Those given by the ancient catalogues are erroneous and conflicting. If Lucius died, as is supposed, on Mar. 5, 254, Stephen was appointed after a vacancy of 61 days.

At the time of his accession the persecution of the church, begun by Decius and renewed by Gallus, had ceased for a time under Valerian. The internal disputes as to the reception of the *lapsi*, which had given rise to the schism of NOVATIAN, still continued.

In the autumn of 254 a council was held at Carthage, the first during the episcopate of Stephen, on the matter of two Spanish bishops, Basilides and Martialis, deposed for compliance with idolatry. Basilides had been to Rome to represent his case to Stephen and procure reinstatement in his see; and Stephen had apparently supported him. The synodical letter of the council (drawn up, without doubt, by Cyprian) confirmed the deposition of the two prelates and the election of their successors, on the ground that compliance with idolatry incapacitated for resumption of clerical functions, though not for reception into the church through penance. The action of Stephen was put aside as of no account, though excused as due to the false representations of Basilides (Cyp. *Ep.* 67). A letter from Cyprian to Stephen himself, probably written soon after the council and in the same year, is further significant of the relations between Carthage and Rome. Stephen seems to have been determined to act independently in virtue of the supposed prerogatives of his see, while Cyprian shews himself equally determined to ignore such prerogatives. The subject of the letter is Marcian, bp. of Arles, who had adopted Novatianist views, and whose deposition Stephen is urged to bring about by letters to the province and people of Arles. The letter shews that Faustinus of Lyons had repeatedly written to Cyprian on the subject, having also, together with other bishops of the province, in vain solicited Stephen to take action. While allowing that it rested with the bp. of Rome to influence with effect the Gallic provinces, Cyprian is far from conceding him any prerogative beyond that of the general *collegium* of bishops, by whose concurrent action, according to his theory, the true faith and discipline of the Church Catholic was to be maintained. In praising the late bps. of Rome, Cornelius and Lucius, whose example he exhorts Stephen to follow, Cyprian seems to imply a doubt whether the latter was disposed to do his duty (*ib.* 68).

A new question of dispute, that of the rebaptism of heretics, led to an open rupture between Rome and Carthage, in which the Asian as well as the African churches sided with Cyprian against Rome. The question was raised whether the adherents of Novatian who had been baptized in schism should be rebaptized when reconciled to the church (*ib.* 69 *ad Magnum*). But it soon took the wider range of all cases of heretical or schismatical baptism. It had been long the practice in both Asia and Africa to rebaptize heretics, and the practice had been confirmed by synods, including the first Carthaginian synod under Agrippinus. Cyprian (*Ep.* 73, *ad Jubaianum*) does not trace the African custom further back than Agrippinus, but he insisted uncompromisingly on the necessity of rebaptism, and was supported by the whole African church. At Rome admission by imposition of hands only, without iteration of baptism, seems to have been the immemorial usage, the only alleged exception being what Hippolytus states (*Philosophum.* p. 291) about rebaptism having been practised in the time of Callistus. Stephen took a view opposite to that of Cyprian. Cyprian would baptize all schismatics, whether heretical in doctrine or no; Stephen would apparently rebaptize none, whatever their heresies or the form of their baptism (Cyp. *Ep.* 74).

The first council of Carthage on the subject, held in 255, issued a synodal letter supporting Cyprian's position. Cyprian then sent to Stephen a formal synodal letter, agreed on in a synod at Carthage, probably at Easter, 256, in which the necessity of baptizing heretics and of the exclusion from clerical functions of apostate clergy on their readmission into the church, is urged. But the tone of the letter is not dictatorial. Stephen may retain his own views if he will without breaking the bond of peace with his colleagues, every prelate being free to take his own line, and responsible to God (*Ep.* 72).

Stephen's reply, written, according to Cyprian, "unskilfully and inconsiderately," contained things "either proud, or irrelevant, or self-contradictory." Cyprian charges Stephen with "hard obstinacy," "presumption and contumacy," referring, by way of contrast, to St. Paul's admonition to Timothy, that a bishop should not be "litigious," but "mild and docile," and replying to the arguments advanced by Stephen. Stephen had so far apparently not broken off communion with those who differed from him (*Ep.* 74). Cyprian summoned a plenary council of African, Numidian, and Mauritanian bishops, numbering 87, with presbyters and deacons, in the presence of a large assembly of laity, which met on Sept. 1, 256. Cyprian and other bishops separately gave their opinions, unanimously asserting the decision of the previous synod. But Cyprian was careful, in his opening address, to repudiate any intention of judging others or breaking communion with them on the ground of disagreement. After this great council, probably towards the winter of 256, Firmilian, bp. of Neocaesarea, wrote his long letter to Cyprian, from which it appears that Stephen had by this time renounced communion with both the Asian and African churches, calling Cyprian a false Christ, a false apostle, a deceitful worker. The question has been raised whether Stephen's action was an excommunication of the Eastern and African churches, or only a threat. H. Valois and Baronius say the latter only; but Firmilian's language seems to imply more, and so Mosheim (*Comm. de Rebus Christian.* pp. 538 seq.) thinks. Routh and Lipsius also hold that excommunication was pronounced. Stephen claimed authority beyond other bishops as being St. Peter's successor, and took much amiss Cyprian's independent action; Cyprian, supported by all the African and Asian churches, utterly ignored any such superior authority; his well-known position being that, though Christ's separate commission to St. Peter had expressed the unity of the church, this commission was shared by all the apostles and transmitted to all bishops alike. Unity, according to his theory, was to be maintained, not by the supremacy of one bishop, but by the consentient action of all, allowing considerable differences of practice without breach of unity. Stephen seems to have taken the position, carried to its full extent by subsequent popes, of claiming a peculiar supremacy for the Roman see, and requiring uniformity as a condition of communion.

The arguments of Stephen were mainly these: "We have immemorial custom on our side, especially the tradition of St. Peter's see, which is above all others. We have also Scripture and reason on our side; St. Paul rejoiced at the preaching of the gospel, and recognized it, though preached out of envy and strife. There is but one baptism; to reiterate it is sacrilege, and its efficacy depends, not on the administrators, but on the institution of Christ; whoever, then, has been once baptized in the name of Christ, even by heretics, has been validly baptized, and may not be baptized again." Cyprian's answer was: "As to your custom, however old, it is a corrupt one, and not primitive; no custom can be set against truth, to get at which we must go back to the original fountain. Scripture is really altogether against you; those at whose preaching of the gospel St. Paul rejoiced were not schismatics, but members of the church acting from unworthy motives; he rebaptized those baptized only unto St. John's baptism, without acknowledgment of the Holy Ghost; he and the other apostles regarded schism and heresy as cutting men off from Christ; the Catholic Church is one, 'a closed garden, a fountain sealed'; outside it there is no grace, no salvation, consequently no baptism; people cannot confer grace if they have not got it; we do not reiterate baptism, for those whom we baptize have not previously been baptized at all; it is you that make two baptisms in allowing that of heretics as well as that of the church."

Stephen's martyrdom under Valerian is asserted in the Felician Catalogue, but not in the earlier Liberian Catalogue. [J.B—Y.]

Stephanus (12), bp. of Ephesus at the time of the "Robber Synod" and the 4th council of Chalcedon. The 11th session of that council (Oct. 29, 451) was wholly occupied with investigating a complaint brought by Bassianus, formerly bp. of Ephesus, against Stephen, who was in advanced age, having been then 50 years one of the clergy of Ephesus. Bassianus had been expelled by violence from the see *c.* 448, and succeeded by Stephen. Both were deprived of the see by decree of the synod, but allowed a pension of 200 gold pieces (Mansi, t. vii. 271-294; Hefele's *Councils*, t. iii. p. 371, Clark's trans.). The name of Stephen of Ephesus is attached to a MS. collection of sermons in the Vienna imperial library (Lambecii, *Comment.* iii. 66; Fabric. *Bib. Graec.* xii. 183, ed. Harles). [G.T.S.]

Stephanus (16) **1.**, patriarch of Antioch A.D. 478-480 (Clinton, *F. R.* ii. 536, 553). Stephen having sent a synodic letter to Acacius bp. of Constantinople acquainting him with the circumstances of his consecration, Acacius convened a synod, A.D. 478, by which the whole transaction was confirmed. The partisans of Peter the Fuller accused Stephen to Zeno of Nestorian heresy, and demanded to have his soundness in the faith investigated by a synod. Zeno yielded, and a synod was called for the Syrian Laodicea (Labbe, iv. 1152). The charge was declared groundless (Theophan. 108). Stephen's enemies, rendered furious by defeat, made an onslaught on the church of St. Barlaam in which he was celebrating the Eucharist, dragged him from the altar, tortured him to death, and threw his body into the Orontes (Evagr. *H. E.* iii. 10; Niceph. *H. E.* xv. 18). The emperor, indignant at the murder of his nominee, despatched a military force to punish the Eutychian party, at whose instigation the crime had been committed (*Simplicii Ep. xiv. ad Zenonem*, Labbe, iv. 1033; *Lib. Synod. ib.* 1152). According to some authorities it was Stephen's successor, another Stephen, who was thus murdered. Valesius, Seb. Binius, Tillemont (*Mém.* xvi. 315) and Le Quien (*Or. Christ.* ii. 726) take the view given above. [E.V.]

Stratonice, martyr at Cyzicum in Mysia with Seleucus her husband at the quinquennalia of Galerius during Diocletian's persecution. The wife of a leading magistrate of the town, she came to see a large number of Christians tortured. Their patience converted her and she converted her husband. Her father, Apollonius, after every effort to win her back to paganism had failed, became her most bitter accuser. Husband and wife were beheaded, and buried in one tomb over which Constantine built a church (Assemani, *Acta Mart. Orient.* t. ii. p. 65). The Acts offer many marks of authenticity. Cf. Le Blant, *Actes des Martyrs*, p. 224, etc.; *AA. SS.* Boll. Oct. xiii. pp. 893-916; Ceill. ii. 481-483. [G.T.S.]

Sylvia (*Silvania*), sister of Flavius Rufinus, consul in 392 and prefect of the East under Theodosius and Arcadius. A work written by her was discovered at Arezzo in 1885, bound up with an unpublished work of St. Hilary of Poictiers (*de Mysteriis*). It contained 2 hymns and an account of a journey in the East. M. Ch. Kohler gave an analysis of the text in *Bibl. de l'Ecole des Chartres*, and M. Gamurrini discussed its authorship in a paper before the Academy of Christian Archaeology at Rome (cf. *Revue Critique*, May 25, 1885, p. 419). It has since been shown by M. Fératin that the pilgrim author is Etheria, a Spanish nun, mentioned by the monk Valerius (Migne, *Patr. Lat.* lxxxvii. 421). It has been generally quoted, however, as the Peregrinatio Silviae. It is of the highest interest from its account of the services at Jerusalem at the time (*c.* 385). Important extracts from it are given in Duchesne's *Origines du Culte Chrétien*, of which a good trans. by Mrs. McClure has been pub. by S.P.C.K. Cf. also F. Cabrol, *Les Eglises de Jerusalem*; *la discipline et la liturgie au IVme Siècle, Etude sur la Peregrinatio Silviae.* [G.T.S. AND H.W.]

Symmachus (2), author of the Greek version of O.T., which in Origen's Hexapla and Tetrapla occupied the column next after that of Aquila and before those of the LXX and Theodotion. Eusebius speaks of Symmachus as a heretical Christian, while Epiphanius represents him merely as passing from the Samaritan sect to Judaism. The account of Eusebius is confirmed (1) by the name "Symmachians," which, as we know from the Ambrosiaster (*Prol. in Ep. ad Galat.*) and from Augustine (*cont. Cresc.* i. 31; *cont. Faust.* xix. 4), was applied even in the 4th cent. to the Pharisaic or "Nazarean" Ebionites; (2) by the fact that Eusebius could refer to a work of Symmachus as extant, in which he maintained the Ebionite heresy in the shape of an attack on St. Matthew's Gospel. This work, according to Eusebius (*H. E.* vi. 17; *Demonstr. Evang.* vii. 1), was stated by Origen to have been obtained by him, together with other interpretations on the Scriptures, from one Juliana, who had received them from Symmachus himself. A later writer, Palladius (*c.* 420), adds that this Juliana was a virgin who lived in Caesarea of Cappadocia, and gave refuge to Origen for two years during a persecution, adducing as his authority an entry which he found in Origen's own hand: "This book I found in the house of Juliana the virgin in Caesarea, when I was hiding there; who said that she had received it from Symmachus himself, the interpreter of the Jews" (*Hist. Laus.* 147). Heut (*Origeniana*, libb. I. iii. 2; III. iv. 2) is probably right in assigning the sojourn of Origen in this lady's house to the time of Maximin's persecutions (A.D. 238-241). Eusebius speaks of the version of Symmachus (vi. 16) as being, like those of Aquila and Theodotion, in common use in Origen's day, in contrast with the obscure "Fifth" and "Sixth" versions, which Origen brought to light; and Origen's extant remains shew that he knew and used Symmachus's version long before the time of Maximin (236-239).

Palladius, by his incidental statement, coming almost direct from Origen himself and resting on the testimony of a lady who had known Symmachus personally, powerfully confirms Eusebius, and makes it clear that Symmachus was a Christian (or "semi-Christian" as Jerome expresses it) of the Nazareo-Ebionite sect. Epiphanius's account is therefore to be rejected; and with it the theory of Geiger, who seeks to identify him with the Jew Symmachus, son of Joseph. The authority of Epiphanius has, however, been commonly accepted for placing the date of Symmachus under the reign of Severus (193-211)—*e.g.* by the compiler of the *Chronicon Paschale* (*s.a.* 202), Cave (*Hist. Lit. s.a.* 201), etc. The extract from Palladius roughly fixes limits for the possible date of Symmachus, by shewing that he was an elder contemporary of Juliana, who was contemporary with Origen, but that he had died before Origen's sojourn in her house.

Symmachus's object in his version seems to have been to imitate Aquila in following the Hebrew exclusively, but to avoid his barbarous diction and to commend his work to Greek readers by purity of style. Thus, his renderings are externally dissimilar to Aquila's, but (frequently) internally akin. Remarkable cases of identity of translation between these two versions occur, *e.g.* Dan. ix. 26, 27, which appears to have been borrowed by Symmachus verbally from Aquila. Of his other writings nothing is known. [J.GW.]

Symmachus (3) **Q. Aurelius,** the last eminent champion of paganism at Rome, son of L. Aurelius Avianus Symmachus, who was prefect of the city in 364, consul suffect and pretorian prefect in 376, and one of the envoys sent by Julian to Constantius (Ammian. xxi. 12, 24). He was educated at Bordeaux (*Epp.* ix. 88), where he and Ausonius became firm friends (Auson. *Id.* 11, in Migne, *Patr. Lat.* xix. 895; Symm. *Epp.* i. 13-43). After being questor and praetor, he became corrector of Lucania and Bruttium in 365 and proconsul of Africa in 373 (*Cod. Theod.* viii. tit. v. 25; xii. tit. i. 73). Being again in Gaul *c.* 369, he delivered his first panegyric on Valentinian as he witnessed the construction of his fortifications on the Rhine (*Laud. in Valent. Sen.* ii. 6). He was appointed prefect of the city at the end of 383 or the beginning of 384. He bore himself modestly in that office, which had been conferred on him unsolicited, declining the silver chariot which his predecessors had permission to use (*Epp.* x. 24, 40) and the title of "Magnificence" (*Epp.* iv. 42). In 382 he headed a deputation in the name of the majority of the senate, to the emperor Gratian, to request the replacement of the altar of Victory in the senate house and the restoration of their endowments to the vestals and the colleges of priests. The Christian senators, who, according to St. Ambrose, were really the majority, forwarded through pope Damasus a counter-petition, and by the influence of St. Ambrose the efforts of Symmachus were defeated, as again in 384, after Gratian's death (S. Ambr. *Epp.* 17, 18, 57, in *Patr. Lat.* xvi. 961, 972, 1175; Symm. *Epp.* x. 61). He probably took part in the missions for the same purpose sent by the senate by Theodosius after the fall of Maximus, and to Valentinian II. in 392 (S. Ambr. *Ep.* 57), and again suffered the same disappointment. In 393 the pagan party had a momentary triumph. Eugenius, at the instigation of Flavian and Arbogast, who had placed him on the throne, restored the altar of Victory and the endowments of the priests (Paulin. *Vita S. Amb.* in *Patr. Lat.* xvi. 30), but they were again abolished by Theodosius after the defeat of Eugenius and Arbogast. Symmachus appears to have made a final attempt in 403 or 404; at least such is the natural inference from the two books of Prudentius, *contra Symmachum*, written after Pollentia and consequently *c.* 404.

Though a champion of the pagan cause, Symmachus was on excellent terms with the Christian leaders. He was a friend of pope Damasus and apparently of St. Ambrose himself, whom Cardinal Mai considers to be the Ambrose to whom seven of his letters are addressed (*Epp.* iii. 31-37), of St. Ambrose's brother Satyrus (S. Ambr. *de Excessu Fratris*, i. 32, in *Patr. Lat.* xvi. 1300), and of Mallius Theodorus, to whom St. Augustine (*Retr.* i. 2, in *Patr. Lat.* xxxii. 588) dedicated one of his works. When prefect, he sent St. Augustine as a teacher of rhetoric to Milan (*Conf.* v. 19, in *Patr. Lat.* xxxii. 717), and was thus the unconscious instrument of his conversion. His Christian opponents always speak in high terms of his character and abilities. He was a member of the college of pontiffs, and as such exercised a strict supervision over the vestal virgins. In the case of one of the Alban vestals, who had broken her vow of chastity, he demanded the enforcement of the ancient penalty against her and her paramour (*Epp.* ix. 128, 129), and sternly refused the request of another to be released from her vows before her time of service ended (*Epp.* ix. 108).

The letters of Symmachus give a remarkable picture of the circumstances and life of a Roman noble just before the final break-up of the empire. His wealth, though not above that of an average senator (Olymp. *ap. Phot.*), was very great. He had a mansion on the Coelian near S. Stefano Rotondo and other houses in Rome (*Epp.* iii. 14), and numerous country residences, of which he mentions four suburban (*Epp.* i. 6, ii. 57, iii. 55, vi. 58) and several more remote (*Epp.* i. 1, 8, 10, ii. 60, iii. 50, iv. 44, vi. 66, 81, vii. 15, 35). He had property near Aquileia and in Samnium, Sicily, and Mauritania (*Epp.* iv. 68, vi. 11, ii. 30, vii. 66). The expenses of his son's praetorship, which he paid, amounted to 2,000 pounds of gold (Olymp. *u.s.*), and in many of his letters he asks his friends to send him rare wild beasts for the sports of his son's praetorship and questorship. Among other, seven Irish wolf-dogs are mentioned (*Epp.* ii. 77). In three of his letters he speaks of his advancing years (*Epp.* iv. 18, 32, viii. 48). He was certainly alive in 404.

His letters are reprinted in 10 books in *Patr. Lat.* xviii. Early in the 19th cent. Cardinal Mai discovered in the Ambrosian Library fragments of 9 speeches of Symmachus, which he published in 1815, and again in 1846. A new ed. of the *Relationes*, his official correspondence with emperors, was pub. in 1872 by W. Meyer. [F.D.]

Symmachus (9), bp. of Rome from Nov. 498, to July, 514, when Theodoric the Ostrogoth was king of Italy and Anastasius emperor in the East. For the circumstances of his election see LAURENTIUS (**10**).

The virulence of the two opposed parties is accounted for by the fact that they represented two opposite policies with regard to the then existing schism between the Western and Eastern churches. Laurentius was elected in the interests of the policy of concession to Constantinople and the East, which the previous pope, Anastasius II., had favoured; Symmachus for the maintenance of the unbending attitude taken by Felix III. when the schism first began.

Several extant letters of Symmachus refer to the rivalry between the Gallic sees of Arles and Vienne. [ZOSIMUS; LEO I.; HILARIUS (pope); HILARIUS ARELAT.] Anastasius II., the predecessor of Symmachus, had sanctioned some invasion, on the part of Vienne, of the jurisdiction assigned to Arles by Leo. After the accession of Symmachus, Eonus, then the primate of Arles, complained to him, apparently in 499, of Avitus of Vienne having, under such sanction, ordained bishops beyond his proper jurisdiction. The reply of Symmachus shews an evident readiness to impute blame to Anastasius (whose whole policy, with regard to the East, he had been elected to counteract), and is remarkable as a decided repudiation by a pope of the action of a predecessor. He lays down the principle that the ordinances of former popes ought not to be varied under any necessity, as those of Leo had been by Anastasius, and must be now maintained. He, however, requires both Eonus and Avitus to send full statements of their case to Rome; and in his letter to Avitus, while he repeats that the confusion introduced by Anastasius was not to be tolerated, he invites Avitus to state any reasons for some equitable dispensation under existing circumstances. It was not till 513 that we find the bp. of Arles finally confirmed in the rights accorded to his see by pope Leo; Caesarius having then succeeded Eonus. Symmachus then wrote to this effect to the bishops of Gaul, and in 514 to Caesarius, warning him to respect the ancient rights of other metropolitans and to report anything amiss in Gaul or Spain to Rome.

After the defeat of the party of Laurentius at Rome and the final settlement of Symmachus in the see, the emperor Anastasius, to whom the result would be peculiarly unwelcome, issued a manifesto against Symmachus, reproaching him with having been unlawfully elected, accusing him of Manichean heresy, and protesting against his presumption in having (as he said) excommunicated an emperor. Symmachus replied in a letter entitled "Apologetica adversus Anastasii imperatoris libellum famosum," and in strong and indignant language rebutted the charges against himself, and retorted that of heresy on the emperor; he accuses him of presuming on his temporal position to think to trample on St. Peter in the person of his vicar, and reminds him that spiritual dignity is, at least, on a par with that of an emperor; and he protests strongly against the violence used against the orthodox in the East. Anastasius was by no means awed or deterred by these papal fulminations, which had probably the opposite effect. He appears after this more than ever determined to support Eutychianism.

Some time during the episcopate of Symmachus Theodoric visited Rome. Cassiodorus gives an account of the visit, placing it under the consuls of A.D. 500; and that Theodoric remained at Ravenna while the case against the pope was pending may be gathered from the documents that refer to it. Himself an Arian, Theodoric evidently had no desire to intervene personally in the disputes of the Catholics, declaring it his sole desire that they should agree among themselves and order be restored at Rome.

Symmachus is said by Anastasius (*Lib. Pontif.*) to have built, restored, and enriched with ornaments many Roman churches, to have spent money in redeeming captives, to have furnished yearly money and clothing to exiled orthodox bishops, and to have ordered the "Gloria in excelsis" to be sung on all Sundays and Saints' days. [J.B—Y.]

Symphorianus (1), martyr, according to the MSS. of his Acts, under Aurelian, for which name Ruinart would substitute Aurelius, dating his passion *c.* 180. He was born in Autun, of noble parentage, and trained in Christianity from his childhood. Autun was devoted to the worship of Berecynthia; and the consular Heraclius, who governed there, anxious to convert the Christians by argument, entered into discussion with Symphorianus, who reviled his false deities. The judge used threats and tortures, and finally beheaded him outside the walls in the place of common execution. The Acts of this martyr have been evidently compiled out of very ancient documents. The judicial investigation is reported in the most exact and technical forms of Roman law. The questions proposed and the answers given are such as we find in the most genuine remains of antiquity. Yet there are also indications that they have been worked up into their present shape. The details of the worship of Cybele may be very usefully compared with those given in the passion of

St. Theodotus and the Seven Virgins of Ancyra. Celtic idolatry in Asia and in Gaul followed precisely the same ritual. Ruinart, *Acta Sincera*, pp. 67-73; Ceillier, i. 472; *AA. SS.* Boll. Aug. iv. 496-498. [G.T.S.]

Synesius (2), bp. of Ptolemais in the Libyan Pentapolis, early in 5th cent. A treatise by H. Druon, *Etudes sur la vie et les œuvres de Synesius* (Paris, 1859), gives valuable information respecting the chronological arrangement of Synesius's writings, especially the letters; another by Dr. Volkmann, *Synesius von Cyrene* (Berlin, 1869), is a well-written treatise, but not so elaborate.

Synesius of Cyrene witnessed the accomplishment of two great events on which the whole course of history for many centuries depended—the ruin of the Roman empire and the complete triumph of Christianity. He was born when the pagan world was mourning the untimely death of the last of the pagan emperors. He died amidst the horrors of the barbarian invasions, when the recent fall of Rome seemed to every portion of the Roman empire a sign of impending ruin.

He was born *c.* 365 at Cyrene, "a Greek city of ancient fame," but then already in decay, and superseded by Ptolemais as the capital of Pentapolis. He was of good family, inheriting an ample fortune, with considerable estates in the interior of the country. In his early years he served in the army and was passionately fond of field sports. Leaving the army, he commenced his studies at Alexandria, where Hypatia then lectured in philosophy. Through her he became attached to neo-Platonism.

But the great school of Alexandria was not then considered sufficient for any one who aimed at the reputation of a philosopher. To Athens, therefore, Synesius was driven by the remonstrances of his friends. But both with the city and its teachers he was profoundly disappointed. He returned to Pentapolis, determined to divide his time between country pursuits and literature, planting trees, breeding horses, training dogs for hunting, writing poetry, and studying philosophy. From this pleasant life he was called to plead the cause of his native city before the court of Constantinople, arriving there A.D. 397, and remaining 3 years. Through the friendship and influence of Aurelian, a distinguished statesman, the leader at that time of what may be called the patriotic party, Synesius was allowed to pronounce before the emperor Arcadius and his court an oration on the nature and duties of kingship. This oration is still extant, but the language is in parts so bold, the invective so personal, as to suggest a doubt whether it was actually delivered, at least in its present form.

Some of the evils which Synesius anticipated were soon realized. The Gothic leader Gainas revolted, and triumphed without difficulty over the effeminate court of Arcadius. Aurelian was sent into banishment, and his supporters in Constantinople exposed to considerable dangers. Synesius declared afterwards that he had only escaped the devices of his enemies through warnings sent him in dreams by God. In a few weeks the power of Gainas sank as rapidly as it had risen. Part of his army perished in a popular rising in Constantinople. The rest were destroyed by an army of Huns in the pay of the emperor. Aurelian returned to Constantinople, and for the remainder of Arcadius's reign had great influence at court. Through him Synesius obtained the boon he asked for Cyrene, and was able at length to quit the hateful city.

From his country retreat, and from the city of Cyrene, Synesius kept up a brisk correspondence with his friends in different parts of the world, especially at Alexandria and Constantinople. Some of his letters were to influential friends in behalf of persons in distress. Of the 156 letters still extant, 49 are to his brother Evoptius. They form a pleasant series, full of interesting details.

With the death of Theodosius the last hope of maintaining the grandeur of the Roman empire seemed suddenly to pass. Rome and Milan, Lyons and Arles, fell by turn before Goths and Vandals, leaving many records of suffering, but not one of a heroic struggle for life and liberty. The characteristics of the time are well illustrated by the letters of Synesius. The miseries of the empire did not spare the distant province of Pentapolis. The nomadic tribes of Libya took advantage of the weakness of the Roman government to sweep down upon the fertile land. Their inroads were at first merely predatory incursions. They seem to have begun not long after Synesius's return from Constantinople. At Cyrene, as elsewhere, there were no troops to oppose them. Synesius's spirits rose with the danger. "I at all events," he writes, "will see what manner of men these are who think they have a right to despise Romans. I will fight as one who is ready to die, and I know I shall survive. I am Laconian by descent, and I remember the letter of the rulers to Leonidas—'Let them fight as men who are ready to die, and they will not die.'" Here and there a few displayed the same courage. Things grew worse, till he wrote almost in despair this touching letter to Hypatia: "I am surrounded by the misfortunes of my country, and mourn for her as each day I see the enemy in arms, and men slaughtered like sheep. The air I breathe is tainted by putrefying corpses, and I expect as bad a fate myself, for who can be hopeful when the very sky is darkened by clouds of carnivorous birds? Still, I cling to my country. How can I do otherwise, I who am a Libyan, born in the country, and who have before my eyes the honoured tombs of my ancestors?" Shortly afterwards, owing to the arrival probably of a new general, the Ausurians were repulsed, and Synesius in 403 left for Alexandria, where he married and remained two years. Returning, he found Cerealis governor, under whose rule the predatory incursions of the barbarians became a regular invasion. "He is a man," wrote Synesius to an influential friend at Constantinople, "who sells himself cheaply, who is useless in war, and oppressive in peace." Obviously Synesius thought that, at least in Pentapolis, the country might have been easily protected against the barbarians if there had been any ability in the government or vigour in the people. He was probably right.

The Roman empire fell because so few of its citizens cared to do anything to preserve it.

It was but natural that men, even of strong patriotic feeling, like Synesius, should turn from the degradation of official life to live in thought among the glories of the heroic age of action in the pages of Homer, and the heroic age of thought in those of Plato. His philosophical studies did not meet with much encouragement among the people of Pentapolis. "I never hear in Libya the sound of philosophy, except the echo of my own voice. Yet if no one else is my witness, assuredly God is, for the mind of man is the seed of God, and I think the stars look down with favour on me as the only scientific observer of their movements visible to them in this vast continent." He pursued the study of astronomy, not only from his love for the beauties of nature, but as a valuable introduction to the highest branches of philosophy. To him, as to Plato, astronomy is "not only a very noble science, but a means of rising to something nobler still, a ready passage to the mysteries of theology." He had received instruction in it from Hypatia, his "most venerated teacher," at Alexandria. While at Constantinople he sent his friend Paeonius a planisphere, constructed in silver according to his own directions, with a letter giving a curious description of it. He mentions that Ptolemy, and the sacred college of his successors, had been contented with the planisphere on which Hipparchus had marked only the 16 largest stars by which the hours of the night were known, but he himself had marked on his all the stars down to the 6th degree of magnitude.

In philosophy Synesius is not entitled to rank as an independent thinker. He is simply an eclectic blending together the elements of his belief from widely different sources, without troubling to reduce them to a strictly harmonious system. He had neither depth nor precision of thought sufficient to win a high place in the history of philosophy. But he constantly speaks of his delight in philosophical studies, and always claims as his especial title of honour the name of a philosopher. If he had been asked which he considered the most philosophical of his writings, he would probably have answered his poems. For, from his point of view, poetry was inseparably connected with philosophy; for both are occupied with the highest problems of life; both look at the ideal side of things, and in the union of the two religion itself consists. The Homeric poems were valuable to him, not only for literary excellency, but as furnishing a rule of conduct. He quotes Homer as a Christian then quoted his Bible. He evidently regarded Homer as an authority in political, social, moral, and even religious questions. He was certainly well versed in the whole range of Greek literature. There is hardly a poet, historian, or philosopher of eminence not quoted or alluded to by him. In this, as in other respects, he faithfully represents one of the latest phases of thought in the Alexandrine school. The ascetic system of Plotinus and Porphyry had failed as an opposing force to the rising tide of Christianity. The theurgical rites and mysterious forms of magical incantation with which Iamblichus and others sought to prop up the falling creed had had but a limited success. Repeated laws of increasing severity had been passed to repress the magical arts, and many accused of practising them imprisoned and even executed. Besides, the very persons over whose credulity such pretensions could exercise any influence would in the 4th cent. naturally be much more attracted by the far more wonderful pretensions of the Christian hermits, and the countless tales of visions seen and miracles wrought by monks of Nitria and Scetis, which continually excited the wonder and stimulated the religion of the people of Alexandria. In supposed miracles, as in real austerities, no pagan philosopher was likely to rival Anthony or Ammon. Among the higher classes the great majority of thinking men, who were still unwilling to embrace Christianity, were chiefly influenced in the Eastern empire by their attachment to Greek literature, in the Western empire by their reverence, partly political, partly religious, for Rome itself, whose greatness seemed to them to depend on the maintenance of that system, partly political, partly religious, under which it had been acquired. The Greek mythology had lost its hold on their belief, but the poetry that mythology had inspired still retained its power over the imagination of educated men among the cities of the Eastern empire, which, however slightly Greek in origin, had become thoroughly Greek in language and in culture. Besides, the ideal of life presented in Greek literature was far more attractive to many minds than that presented by the popular teaching of Christianity, especially to those minds in which the intellectual were stronger than the moral impulses. Those who "still cared for grace and Hellenism," to use Synesius's expression, turned with increasing fondness from the intellectual degeneracy of their day to the masterpieces of former times, seeking to satisfy the universally felt craving for a definite religious creed, by taking from all the writers they admired the elements of a vague system, which they called a philosophy, but which depended far more upon poetical feelings than philosophical arguments.

Synesius's own poems are his most original works. Their literary merit is not of the highest order. His power lay not so much in the strength of imagination as in warmth of poetical feeling. The metres are unfortunately chosen and not sufficiently varied to escape monotony. The fatal facility of the short lines constantly led to a jingling repetition of the same cadences and turns of construction. Still, the ten hymns extant would be interesting, if only as specimens of a style of lyrical poetry, the meditative poetry partly philosophical and partly religious, which was hardly ever attempted in ancient Greece, though common enough in modern times. Their chief value, however, consists in the light thrown on the religious feelings and experiences of a man of deeply interesting character. Any one who wishes to know the religious aspect of neo-Platonism and the different phases of thought through which an able man of strong religious feelings could in the 5th cent. pass to Christianity, can hardly do better than study these hymns.

The God to Whom he thus offers the "unbloody sacrifice" of his prayers is at once One and Three—"one root, one source, a triple form." To attempt to explain the mystery of this Trinity would be the atheistic boldness of blinded men. The three persons of the Trinity, to use the Christian form of expression never employed by Synesius himself, are not as with Plotinus—Unity, Intelligence, Soul. Most frequently the Christian terms are used—Father, Spirit, Son—for the resemblance between the attributes assigned in neo-Platonic philosophy to the soul, the third God, the ruler of the world, and the attributes assigned by Christianity to the Son apparently led Synesius to place the Son third in his system of the Trinity. The Father is also called the Unity. The Spirit is nowhere called the Intelligence, but is often called the Will. The Son, Who emanates from the Father through the Spirit, is also called, with a curious combination of expressions, the Word, the Wisdom, and the Demiurgus. The stream of life and intelligence descends from the Father through the Son to the intellectual worlds, and from them to the visible world which is the image of the intellectual. To all in heaven and in the sky, and on the earth and beneath the earth, the Son imparts life and assigns duties. Nor is the Father, however mysterious in His nature, so "hidden in His glory" as to be inaccessible to sympathy for His children. In the efficacy of prayer and in the reality of spiritual communion with God Synesius firmly believed. "Give, O Lord, to be with me as my companion the holy angel of holy strength, the angel of divinely inspired prayer. May he be with me as my friend, the giver of good gifts, the keeper of my life, the keeper of my soul, the guardian of my prayers, the guardian of my actions. May he preserve my body pure from disease, may he preserve my spirit pure from pollution, may he bring to my soul oblivion of all passions." And again in the beautiful prayer of the soul for reunion with God: "Have pity, Lord, upon Thy daughter. I left Thee to become a servant upon earth, but instead of a servant I have become a slave. Matter has bound me in its magic spells. Yet still the clouded eye retains some little strength, its power is not altogether quenched. But the deep flood has poured over me and dimmed the God-discerning vision. Have pity, Father, on Thy suppliant child, who, often striving to ascend the upward paths of thought, falls back choked with desires, the offspring of seductive matter. Kindle for me, O Lord, the lights which lead the soul on high."

Synesius has nowhere expressly stated that he regarded matter not as created by God but as existing independently and necessarily evil, but this idea is most consistent with the language he generally employs. God is nowhere said to have created the world, but the Son is said to have framed the visible world as the form and image of the invisible. At all events the corruption of the soul in each individual is attributed to the seductive influence of matter, a view expressed at some length in his very curious treatise on Dreams. The soul, he says, descends from heaven in obedience to a law of Providence to perform its appointed service in the world. It then receives, as a loan, the imagination, figuratively called the boat or chariot by which the soul travels on its earthward voyage. In other words, it is the connecting link between mind and matter. It is something intermediate between the corporeal and incorporeal, and philosophy therefore has great difficulty in determining its real nature. It is the duty of the soul to purify and elevate the imagination. It is the constant aim of the daemon of matter to corrupt and degrade it.

The action of Providence in the government of the world is described by Synesius in his treatise written at Constantinople. All existence, he says, proceeds from God and has been assigned by Him to an infinite variety of beings, descending in regular gradations from God Himself, Who is pure existence, to matter, which, being in a state of constant flux, does not, properly speaking, admit of existence at all. The beings of the highest order are called gods, and they are divided into two classes, the first controlling the upper parts of the universe, the other ruling this earth. These gods find their chief happiness in contemplating the God Who is above them, but to preserve the earth from the evils which would soon result from the destructive activity of the earth-daemons they must interpose from time to time. This they do gladly, because thus they render their appointed service to the supreme Deity.

As regards a future state, Synesius says that philosophy teaches us that it is the result of the present life. With death the husk of matter, which we call the body, perishes, but the soul and the imagination remain.

He repeatedly protests against giving publicity to doctrines which are above the comprehension of men not thoroughly trained in philosophical studies. "Philosophy is one of the most ineffable of all ineffable subjects." He reproves his friend Herculian for talking of such with unphilosophical persons, and will not even discuss them in letters lest they fall into the hands of others. Proteus is the problem of the true philosopher eluding vulgar curiosity by concealing the divine under earthly forms, and only revealing it to the persistent efforts of heroic men. This desire for secrecy arose from a fear lest the highest truths should be corrupted and degraded by those unfit to receive them, a feeling by no means unknown in the Christian church at that time.* Lysis, the Pythagorean, quoted by Synesius with great approbation, says that "the publicity given to philosophy has caused many men to look with contempt upon the Gods." Doubtless enough is plainly stated for us to form a sufficiently accurate idea of Synesius's philosophical and religious views, but there are subjects—*e.g.* the nature of the Trinity, the connexion between the old mythology and philosophy, the reabsorption of the soul and of all intelligence and existence into

* So Theodoret (quoted by Bingham, vol. i. p. 35) says: "We speak of the divine mysteries in obscure language because of the uninitiated (the unbaptized), but when they are gone we instruct the initiated (baptized) plainly."

the Divinity, the nature and origin of matter, the nature and work of the imagination, the scientific arrangement and nomenclature of the virtues—on which we have not the last word of Hypatia's teaching.

We cannot say what means Synesius had of becoming acquainted with Christianity in his early years. No one living in any part of the Eastern empire at the close of the 4th cent. could fail to be brought into frequent contact with Christians. But throughout his works, written before he became a Christian himself, the same phenomenon appears which is so striking in Claudian's poems—the existence of Christianity is entirely ignored. In his speech addressed to Arcadius, though the greatest prominence is given to the religious idea of duty, there is no allusion to the principles of Christianity, even where such a reference would have given force to his arguments. The orator appears unconscious that he is addressing a Christian emperor. The deity to whom he appeals is the god of the Theist, "whose nature no man has ever yet found a name to represent." Still more striking is a passage in one of the hymns written immediately after his return from Constantinople: "To all Thy temples, Lord, built for Thy holy rites I went, and falling headlong as a suppliant bathed with my tears the pavement. That my journey might not be in vain, I prayed to all the gods Thy ministers, who rule the fertile plain of Thrace, and those who on the opposite continent protect the lands of Chalcedon, whom Thou hast crowned with angelic rays, Thy holy servants. They, the blessed ones, helped me in my prayers; they helped me to bear the burden of many troubles." Of course the temples of which he speaks were Christian churches. No pagan temples had been erected in Constantinople, and even in the other cities they had been closed some years by an edict of Theodosius. Yet it is perfectly certain that Synesius was not then a Christian. This picture of a pagan philosopher praying in a Christian church to the saints and angels of Christianity, while investing them with the attributes of the daemons of neo-Platonism, is no bad illustration of the almost unconscious manner in which the pagan world in becoming Christian was then paganizing Christianity. As eclectic in religion as in philosophy, Synesius took from Christianity whatever harmonized with the rest of his creed, often adapting the tenets he borrowed to make them accord with his philosophical ideas.

How his opinions were so far altered in the next four years that he became a Christian, we have, unhappily, but scanty means of knowing. In none of his letters is there the slightest trace of any mental struggle. The change was effected gradually, probably almost imperceptibly even to himself. He had never been really hostile to Christianity, and as the world gradually became more Christian he became more Christian too. Almost without a struggle the old pagan society had yielded, and was still yielding, to the tide which each year set more strongly in the direction of Christianity. With all the vigour he displayed, in great emergencies Synesius was not a man to stand long alone or to fight to the end a battle already lost. Some personal influences had also been brought to bear on him. He had known and highly respected Chrysostom at Constantinople, and afterwards come into contact with Theophilus the patriarch of Alexandria. His wife, to whom he was warmly attached and whom he married at Alexandria in 403, was a Christian, and in her he may have had an opportunity of remarking one of the noblest features of Christianity, the elevation it imparted to the female character by the prominence given to the feminine virtues in the character of Christ and therefore in the teaching of the church. But above all, when he returned to Pentapolis, in 404, to find his country desolated by barbarian invasion, he must have felt how little the highest form of neo-Platonism could meet the wants of such a troubled age. The philosophical and poetical creed was the religion of a prosperous man in peaceful times. When suffering and danger came, its support failed precisely where most needed. To enjoy that intellectual communion with God for which he craved with his whole heart, and on the possibility of which his whole system of belief depended, he needed above all things an untroubled mind. It was one of the points which had marked most strongly his separation from Christianity, that in his hymns he had always prayed at least as earnestly for freedom from anxieties as for freedom from sin. He had formed an ideal of life which could not be maintained in troubled times, and with it necessarily fell the beliefs with which it was intimately connected. The old creed told him that "the woe of earth weighs down the wings of the soul so that it cannot rise to heaven." The new religion taught him that cares and sorrows rightly borne, so far from hiding the divine light, reveal it in increased brightness. In former days, when he shrank into private life from "the polluting influence of business and the vicissitudes of fortune," he had probably considered the doctrine of the Incarnation as the greatest obstacle to his becoming a Christian, because it seemed to degrade the Deity by connecting it with the contamination of matter. Now, when he had left his seclusion to battle and suffer with his fellow-citizens, no doctrine of Christianity had such attraction for him as that which told of a God Who had resigned His glory to share the sufferings of His creatures and to be the Saviour of mankind. Formerly he had sought to purify his mind that it might ascend in thought to God; now he caught at the doctrine of the Holy Spirit descending into men's hearts to make them the temples of God. So the first hymn which marks the transition to Christianity begins with an invocation to Christ as the Son of the Holy Virgin, and ends with a prayer to Christ and to the Father to send down upon him the Holy Spirit "to refresh the wings of the soul, and to perfect the divine gifts." But though his prayers were now addressed to Christ, it is obvious that he had rather added certain Christian tenets to his old creed than adopted a new religion. The attributes of Christ are described in almost exactly the same terms as the attributes of the Son had been described in former hymns. The prayers for himself are almost identical. It is also curious to find that he still considered the Spirit the second person of the Trinity; to use his own illustration, "the Father is the root, the Son the branch, the Spirit intermediate between root and branch." Still, the decisive step had been taken by acknowledging Christ as the Saviour of mankind; after that the subsequent steps were natural and almost inevitable. He was baptized, probably about five years after his marriage. How far he then felt it necessary to give up the language and ideas of his old creed may be imagined from the following hymn, addressed to Christ: "Thou camest down to earth and didst sojourn among men and drive the deceiver, the serpent-fiend, from Thy Father's garden. Thou wentest down to Tartarus, where death held the countless races of mankind. The old man Hades feared Thee, the devouring dog (Cerberus) fled from the portal; but, having released the soul, of the righteous from suffering, Thou didst offer, with a holy worship, hymns of thanksgiving to the Father. As Thou wentest up on high the daemons, powers of the air, were affrighted. But Aether, wise parent of harmony, sang with joy to his seven-toned lyre a hymn of triumph. The morning star, day's harbinger, and the golden star of evening, the planet Venus, smiled on Thee. Before Thee went the horned moon, decked with fresh light, leading the gods of night. Beneath Thy feet Titan spread his flowing locks of light. He recognized the Son of God, the creative intelligence, the source of his own flames. But Thou didst fly on outstretched wings beyond the vaulted sky, alighting on the spheres of pure intelligence, where is the fountain of goodness, the heaven enveloped in silence. There time, deep-flowing and unwearied time, is not; there disease, the reckless and prolific offspring of matter, is not. But eternity, ever young and ever old, rules the abiding habitation of the gods."

While the old and new were thus strangely blended in his creed, an unexpected event changed the whole current of his life. In defiance of the law, which enacted that no one should hold the governorship of the province of which he was a native, Andronicus had been appointed governor of Pentapolis. A native of Berenice, of low origin, he had gained the office, Synesius says, by bribery. Against his appointment Synesius vigorously protested, in a letter to an influential friend at Constantinople: "Send us legitimate governors; men whom we do not know, and who do not know us; men who will not be biassed in their judgments by their private feelings. A governor is on his way to us who lately took a hostile part in politics here, and who will pursue his political differences on the judgment seat." When the ancient Romans were threatened with oppressive rulers, they chose the bravest of their fellow-citizens as tribunes to protect them. In the 5th cent. of the Christian era, under similar circumstances, the people of Ptolemais elected Synesius a bishop. They knew him as a man of high character and great abilities, universally liked and respected, but probably still more recommended to them by the vigour he had displayed in the recent siege. No one who has attentively studied his life and writings can doubt that he was sincere in his wish to decline the proffered honour. A frank statement of his feelings was made in a letter written to his brother Evoptius, then resident at Alexandria, and intended to be shewn to Theophilus: "I should be devoid of feeling if I were not deeply grateful to the people of Ptolemais who have thought me worthy of higher honours than I do myself. But what I must consider is not the greatness of the favour conferred, but the possibility of my accepting it. That a mere man should receive almost divine honours is indeed most pleasing, if he is worthy of them, but if he is far from being so, his acceptance of them gives but a poor hope for the future. This is no new fear, but one I have long felt, the fear lest I should gain honour among men by sinning against God. From my knowledge of myself I feel I am in every respect unworthy of the solemnity of the episcopal office.* . . . I now divide my time between amusements and study. When I am engaged in study, especially religious studies, I keep entirely to myself, in my amusements I am thoroughly sociable. But the bishop must be godly, and therefore like God have nothing to do with amusements, and a thousand eyes watch to see that he observes this duty. In religious matters, on the other hand, he cannot seclude himself, but must be thoroughly sociable, as he is both a teacher and preacher of the law. Single-handed, he has to do the work of everybody, or bear the blame of everybody. Surely then it needs a man of the strongest character to support such a burden of cares without allowing the mind to be overwhelmed, or the divine particle in the soul to be quenched, when he is distracted by such an infinite variety of employments." Again, there was the difficulty of his marriage. "God and the law, and the sacred hand of Theophilus, gave me my wife. I therefore declare openly to all and testify that I will not separate entirely from her, or visit her secretly like an adulterer. The one course would be contrary to piety, the other to law. I shall wish and pray to have a large number of virtuous children." Still more important in his opinion was the question of religious belief. "You know that philosophy is opposed to the opinions of the vulgar. I certainly shall not admit that the soul is posterior in existence to the body. I cannot assert that the world and all its parts will perish together. The resurrection which is so much talked about I consider something sacred and ineffable, and I am far from sharing the ideas of the multitude on the subject." He would indeed be content to keep silence in public on these abstruser points of theology, neither pretending to believe as the multitude, nor seeking to convince them of their errors, "for what has the multitude to do with philosophy? the truth of divine mysteries is

* ἱερεύς and the kindred terms are applied by Synesius after he became a Christian only to bishops; the term presbyter is always used of the second order of the Christian ministry. Before his conversion he uses ἱερεύς apparently of heathen priests, and on one occasion certainly of Christian presbyters. In one or two instances, however, ἱερεύς may be intended to include presbyters as well as bishops.

not a thing to be talked about. But if I am called to the episcopacy I do not think it right to pretend to hold opinions which I do not hold. I call God and man as witnesses to this. Truth is the property of God, before Whom I wish to be entirely blameless. Though fond of amusements—for from my childhood I have been accused of being mad after arms and horses—still I will consent to give them up—though I shall regret to see my darling dogs no longer allowed to hunt, and my bows moth-eaten! Still I will submit to this if it is God's will. And though I hate all cares and troubles I will endure these petty matters of business, as rendering my appointed service to God, grievous as it will be. But I will have no deceit about dogmas, nor shall there be variance between my thoughts and my tongue. . . . It shall never be said of me that I got myself consecrated without my opinions being known. But let Father Theophilus, dearly beloved by God, decide for me with full knowledge of the circumstances of the case, and let him tell me his opinions clearly."

For seven months at least the matter remained undecided. Synesius went to Alexandria to consult Theophilus, and popular feeling ran so high throughout the country that he felt if he declined the bishopric he could never return to his native land. The people also sent two envoys to Theophilus urging him to use all his influence to overcome Synesius's scruples. This Theophilus was sure to do, for, apart from the regard he may well have had for Synesius, it must have been a welcome triumph for him over his opponents at Alexandria that the most distinguished pupil of the Alexandrine school should be consecrated by him a Christian bishop, a visible sign to the people that even the noblest form of paganism was found insufficient by its noblest disciples. The religious difficulties were just those which might be expected in a pupil of the Alexandrine school, whether he derived his inspiration from Origen or from Hypatia. How far, and in what way, Theophilus, already so well known as a vigorous opponent of such views, succeeded in inducing Synesius to change them we have unfortunately no means of knowing. After all, these views were rather in opposition to the commonly received opinions among Christians than to any dogmatical teaching of the church. Even as regards the doctrine of the resurrection, Synesius would probably have had no difficulty in accepting the Greek form of the creed, the resurrection of the dead, though he could hardly have accepted the Latin form, the resurrection of the body, or the resurrection of the flesh. His amusements and his hunting seem to have been given up entirely. It has been assumed that he retained his wife, but there is no evidence whatever to shew that he did so. His own letter is a sufficient proof that a bishop was generally expected to separate from his wife, or, in the language of the day, to live with her as a sister, though it may be true, as Socrates asserts, that exceptions might easily have been found in the Eastern empire. The bishop, especially if occupying an important post, felt that by retaining his wife he lost caste among his people, and Synesius, in giving up so much in the hope of benefiting the people of Ptolemais, was hardly likely to pursue a course which must fatally damage his influence, even if his wife would have consented to a mode of life which must inevitably lower both herself and her husband in public estimation. Besides, Synesius never mentions his wife in any subsequent letter, and in one written only one year afterwards he speaks of his desolation in terms which make it almost incredible that his wife was living with him then. No child was born to him after he was elected bishop.

Yielding at last to the importunities and arguments of his friends, Synesius, in 410, wrote to the presbyters of the diocese of Ptolemais: "Since God has laid upon me not what I sought but what He willed, I pray that He Who has assigned me this life will guide me through the life He has assigned me."

He soon found that his fears had been more prophetic than his friends' hopes. When he returned, Ptolemais presented the appearance of a city taken by storm. Nothing was to be heard in the public places but the groans of men, the screams of women, and the cries of boys. New instruments of punishment had been introduced by Andronicus, racks and thumbscrews and machines for torturing the feet, the ears, the lips, the nose.

At first Synesius remonstrated; his remonstrances were treated with contempt. He reproved; his reproofs made the governor more furious. His house was beset with crowds demanding sympathy and protection. He could not move without seeing and hearing the sufferings of his people. To add to his grief "the dearest of his children died." With a heart wrung with anguish he turned for consolation to God. "But what was the greatest of my calamities, and what made life itself hopeless to me, I who had hitherto always been successful in prayer, now for the first time found that I prayed in vain." He had accepted the office of a bishop in times of difficulty without being sufficiently in sympathy with the prevailing spirit of the Christian church, and the consciousness of this increased his natural self-distrust. The calm serenity of thought, with which in happier years he had held communion with God, was gone. As he prayed, the calamities of his house and country rose up before him as a sign that he had, by his unworthiness, profaned the mysteries of God. The soul, distracted by conflicting feelings, grief and anger, shame and fear, could not rise above the earth. He prayed, and God was afar off. At first it seemed that he would sink in despair under these accumulated sorrows; there were even thoughts of suicide. He was roused by fresh tidings of Andronicus's excesses. Ever ready to assist others in their misfortunes, however great his own might be, he heard the people murmuring that they were forsaken by their bishop. Self-distrust gave way to indignation. Once roused he acted with vigour and judgment. He wrote to influential friends at Constantinople, detailing the cruelties of Andronicus, and earnestly pleading for his recall. Then, without waiting the result of his appeal to the authorities of the state, he proceeded to pronounce against the offender the judgment of the church by a formal act of excommunication.

Before this letter of excommunication was sent, Andronicus professed his penitence for his crimes, and entreated that the sentence against him might not be published—a strong proof of the power which the sentence of excommunication then exercised on men's minds. Synesius unwillingly yielded to his entreaties and to the representations of the other bishops of the province. Relieved from this momentary fear, Andronicus soon returned to his old cruelties, and the sentence of excommunication was definitely pronounced. A short time passed and Synesius wrote in triumph to Constantinople thanking his friends for procuring the dismissal of Andronicus. Another short interval, and Synesius was writing to the patriarch of Alexandria to implore his good offices for the fallen governor. "Justice has perished among men; formerly Andronicus acted unjustly, now he suffers unjustly." Freed for a time from these secular cares, Synesius could attend to other episcopal duties. In a long letter addressed to Theophilus he has given a very interesting account of a visitation tour, undertaken at Theophilus's request in the course of the same year, through a part of the country still exposed to the incursions of the barbarians, to the villages of Palaebisca and Hydrax on the confines of the Libyan desert. Near the village of Hydrax, on the summit of a precipitous hill, stood the ruins of an old castle, much desired by the people as a place of retreat in invasion. Their bishop Paul had obtained it for them by a surreptitious consecration, turning it into a church; but Synesius refused to sanction that, and insisted on a regular purchase.

The next subject which occupied his attention was one of the worst evils resulting from the misgovernment of the country. He found that even bishops were often accused by other bishops, not that justice should be done but to give the commanders of the armies opportunities for extorting money.

Then Synesius asked the patriarch's advice as to certain bishops who did not choose to have a fixed diocese, wandering to wherever they thought they would be best off.

The time during which he held his bishopric was so short, apparently only three years, and marked by so many public and private calamities, that we possess but few letters which throw much light upon his life. His principal correspondent at this period was Theophilus, whom he always addresses with a reverence and affection which may surprise those who have only known that prelate as the persecutor of Chrysostom, and which are the more important because Synesius, even in writing to Theophilus, professed his admiration for Chrysostom. Equally noticeable is the unqualified obedience which Synesius, though himself metropolitan of Pentapolis, cheerfully yielded to the "apostolic throne" of Alexandria. "It is at once my wish and my duty to consider whatever decree comes from that throne binding upon me," he writes to Theophilus. The unquestionable superiority of Alexandria to all the cities of E. Africa had given to the patriarch of Alexandria an authority over their bishops unsurpassed, even if it was rivalled, by the supremacy of Rome in that day over the bishoprics of Italy.

Of the bp. of Rome, and of the affairs of Rome, there is no mention in any of his letters —one of the many proofs his works afford of the greatness of the separation, in government and in feeling, between the Eastern and Western empires. Though thoroughly well versed in all the branches of Greek literature, he never alludes to any Latin author. It is almost impossible to resist the belief that he was ignorant of the Latin language. Still some notice of the crowning calamity, when Rome yielded to Alaric without a struggle, could hardly have failed to appear in his writings, had not the misfortunes of Pentapolis been so great as to absorb all his thoughts.

In the winter Synesius lost "the last comfort of his life, his little son." The blow was too much for the father already crushed by the cares of his office and the misery of his country. As death drew near his thoughts were curiously divided between the two objects to which in life he had given his faith. His last letter was addressed to Hypatia. His last poem was a prayer to Christ. The pagan philosopher retained to the end the reverence and affection of the Christian bishop. "You have been to me a mother, a sister, a teacher, and in all these relationships have done me good. Every title and sign of honour is your due. As for me, my bodily sickness comes from sickness of the mind. The recollection of the children who are gone is slowly killing me. Would to God I could either cease to live, or cease to think of my children's graves." In the hymn to Christ Synesius added an epilogue to the poems in which he had already recounted the drama of his soul. The actor who began so confident of success ended with a humble prayer for pardon. "O Christ, Son of God most high, have mercy on Thy servant, a miserable sinner, who wrote these hymns. Release me from the sins which have grown up in my heart, which are implanted in my polluted soul. O Saviour Jesus, grant that hereafter I may behold Thy divine glory." So in gloom and sadness, cheered by the Christian hope of the resurrection, closed the career of one who in his time had played many parts, who had been soldier, statesman, orator, poet, sophist, philosopher, bishop, and in all these characters had deserved admiration and love. A cheap popular Life of Synesius of Cyrene, by A. Gardner, is pub. by S.P.C.K. in their *Fathers for Eng. Readers*. [T.R.H.]

T

Tarachus, also called *Victor*, martyr, an Isaurian from Claudiopolis, and a soldier, who left the army on the outbreak of Diocletian's persecution. The Acts of Tarachus and his companions Probus and Andronicus are one of the most genuine pieces of Christian antiquity. They were first pub. by Baronius in his *Annals*, under A.D. 290, but from an imperfect MS. Ruinart brought out the most complete ed. in Greek and Latin from a comparison of several MSS. in the Colbertine Library. The martyrs were arrested A.D. 304 in Pompeiopolis, an episcopal city of Cilicia.

They were publicly examined and tortured at three principal cities—Tarsus, Mopsuestia, and Anazarbus, where they were put to death and their relics carefully preserved. The Acts are often quoted by Le Blant (*Les Actes des martyrs*) to illustrate his argument. Thus, p. 9, he notes the sale of copies of the Proconsular Acts by one of the officials for two hundred denarii. He also illustrates by them the judicial formularies, proconsular circuits, etc. (cf. pp. 27-29, 32, 63, 68, 72, 74, etc.). They suffered under a president Numerianus Maximus (Ruinart, *Acta Sinc.* 454-492). [G.T.S.]

Tatianus (1) the "Apologist," "born in the land of Assyria" (*Oratio*, c. xlii.), *i.e.* E. of the Tigris, in a land incorporated, under Trajan, with Mesopotamia and Armenia into one Roman province of Syria (Zahn, *Forsch. z. Gesch. d. N.T. lichen Kanons*; I. Theil, "Tatian's Diatessaron," p. 268). Of his parents, date of birth (*c.* 110, Zahn; *c.* 120, Funk), and early training, little or nothing is known. In Syria were Greek official representatives of Rome, merchants, and residents. Among such, stationed in the Assyrian district, may have been the parents of Tatian; persons perhaps of birth and wealth (cf. *Oratio*, c. xi.). The lad, Semitic as regards the land of his birth, but possibly Greek by parentage and name, was educated in the Greek teaching open to him (*Oratio*, c. xlii.). As he grew older his inquiring mind led him to a personal examination of the systems of his teachers (c. xxxv.). A peripatetic by disposition if not in philosophy, he "wandered over many lands, learning from no man," but with eyes open and ears unstopped, listening, observing, hearing, pondering, until he abandoned the learning that had made him a pessimist, and became a teacher of that "Word of God" which had taught him a holier faith and a happier life (cc. xxvi. xlii.). He notes that the simplicity of style of Holy Scripture first attracted and then converted him (c. xxix.). The "barbaric [*i.e.* Christian] writings," upon which he stumbled by chance, charmed him by their modest diction and easy naturalness. He soon discovered that these writings were older than the oldest remains of Greek literature, and in their prophecies and precepts diviner and truer than the oracles and practices of the most powerful gods or the purest philosophers.

Tatian's information about himself ceases with the autobiographical allusions and statements in the *Oratio*. According to Irenaeus (*adv. Haer.* i. c. 28; cf. Eus. *H. E.* iv. 29) he was a hearer (ἀκροατής) of Justin Martyr; and the *Oratio* indicates that he and the "most admirable" Justin were at Rome together, and were both exposed to the hostility of the Cynic Crescens (cc. xviii. xix.).

Tatian's Christian life, like that of Tertullian, divides into pre-heretical and heretical periods. So long as Justin was alive, says Irenaeus, he brought out no "blasphemy"; after his death it was different.

The testimony of his pupil Rhodon (Eus. *H. E.* v. 13) leaves the impression that Tatian for some time after Justin's death worked and taught at Rome, busying himself with his "book of questions" (προβλημάτων βιβλίον), dealing with what was "hidden and obscure in the sacred writings" (*i.e.* of O.T.).

The chronology of his literary career is more or less connected with the martyrdom of Justin *c.* 163-167. Many critics consider Justin's *Apology* and the *Oratio* to have been composed about the same time (cf. Zahn, p. 279; Harnack, *Texte u. Untersuch. z. Gesch. d. altchrist. Lit.* i. p. 196), *i.e.* A.D. 150-153. Others place the *Oratio* after the death of Justin (Lightfoot in *Contemp. Rev.* May, 1877; Hilgenfeld, *Ketzergeschichte*, p. 395; Funk, *Zur Chronol. Tatian's* in Tübingen *Theol. Quartalschrift* for 1883, p. 219, etc.). The difference in opinion turns very much upon the estimate formed of a passage in Eusebius (*H. E.* iv. 16). A similar want of unanimity prevails as to the place of composition of the *Oratio*. Harnack (pp. 198-199) argues from its language that it was not written at Rome, where Zahn (p. 280) places it.

A. *The Oratio*.—The *Oratio*, by which he is best known, belongs to that part of Tatian's the most interesting and difficult of the Greek apologetic writings. The title, Τατιανοῦ πρὸς Ἕλληνας, terse and abrupt, is characteristic of life which is reckoned orthodox. It is one of the treatise. Tatian did not care for style. Christianity was not, in his opinion, dependent upon it. It was absent from the Scriptures which had fascinated him; it belonged to the Greek culture he had left behind. Yet he at times shews himself no novice in the art he condemned. C. xi. is a noble piece of declamation; c. xix. a scathing denunciation of the false, passing into a grave appeal in behalf of the true. He can draw word-pictures, *e.g.* those of the actor (c. xxii.), the wealthy patron of the arena (*ib.*), and the Cynic philosopher (c. xxv.), which are as clever and life-like as those of Tertullian. The *Oratio* has two principal divisions introduced by a preface (cc. i.-iv.). Div. i. states the Christian doctrines and their intrinsic excellence and superiority to heathen opinions (cc. v.-xxx.); div. ii. demonstrates their superior antiquity (cc. xxxi.-xli.); the whole closes with a few words autobiographical in character (c. xlii.).

Tatian opens (c. i.) by deprecating as unreasonable the contemptuous animosity of the Greeks towards "Barbarians," and points out that there was no practice or custom current among them which they did not owe to "Barbarians." Oneirology, astrology, auguries from birds or sacrifices had come to them from external sources. To Babylonia they owed astronomy, to Persia magic, to Egypt geometry, to Phoenicia instruction by letters. Orpheus had taught them poetry, song, and initiation into the mysteries, the Tuscans sculpture, the Egyptians history, rustic Phrygians the harmony of the shepherd's pipe, Tyrrhenians the trumpet, the Cyclopes the smith's art, and Atossa, queen of the Persians, the method of joining letter-tablets (see Otto's note). They should not boast of their excellent diction when they imported into it "barbaric" expression and maintained no uniformity of pronunciation. Of Doric, Attic, Aeolian, Ionian, which was the real Greek? Further, let them not boast while they used rhetoric to subserve injustice and sycophancy, poetry to depict battles, the amours of gods, and the corruption of the soul.

C. v., one of the most important (doctrinally) and difficult in the *Oratio*, opens thus:

"In the beginning was God. We have been taught that the beginning is the power of the Logos. For the Lord of all, being Himself the substance (ὑπόστασις) of all, in so far that creation had not yet taken place, was alone; but in so far as He was Himself all power, and the substance of things visible and invisible, all things were with Him: (and thus) with Him by Logos-power (διὰ λογικῆς δυνάμεως), the very Logos Himself, Who was in Him, subsisted (ὑπέστησε). By the simple will of God the Logos springs forth, and not proceeding forth without cause (κατὰ κενοῦ), becomes the first-begotten work of the Father. Him we recognize as the beginning of the world. He was born by participation, not by scission (κατὰ μερισμὸν οὐ κατὰ ἀποκοπὴν); for He Who proceeds by scission is separated from the first, but He Who has proceeded by participation and has accepted a part in the administration of the world (τὸ . . , οἰκονομίας τὴν αἵρεσιν προσλαβόν), hath not rendered Him defective from Whom He was taken. Just as many fires are lighted from one torch, but the light of the first torch is not lessened through the kindling of the many, so the Logos coming forth from the power of the Father hath not made Him Who begat Him without Logos (ἄλογον)."

Tatian upholds the belief in the resurrection of the body at the end of all things. His argument is briefly: "There was a time when I did not exist: I was born and came into existence. There will be a time when (through death) I shall not exist; but again I shall exist, just as before I was not, but was afterwards born [cf. Tertull. *Apol.* xlviii.]. Let fire destroy my flesh, let me be drowned, or torn to pieces by wild beasts, I am laid up in the treasure-chambers of a wealthy Lord. God Who reigneth can, when He will, restore to its pristine state that which is visible to Him alone." In c. vii. Tatian returns to the Logos, that he may demonstrate His work as regards angels and men.

The thoughts of the better land and of God's revelation by the prophets lead Tatian to God's revelation of Himself in the Incarnation. That doctrine he treats in a manner likely to be admitted by a Greek, if very differently from the way (*e.g.*) Justin Martyr presented it to the Jews. We are not mad, he says (c. xxi.), nor do we utter idle tales when we say that God was made (γεγονέναι) in the form of man. The mythology of the Greeks was full of such appearances—an Athene taking the form of a Deiphobus, a Phoebus that of a herdsman, etc., etc. Further, what did so frequent an expression as the origin of the gods imply but that they were mortal? The difficulty attendant upon the heathen belief was not removed by the tendency to resolve all myths and gods into allegory. Metrodorus of Lampsacus, in his treatise on Homer, invited men to believe that the Hera or Athene or Zeus, to whom they consecrated enclosures and groves, were simply natural beings or elemental arrangements. That, argues Tatian, was to surrender their divinity; a surrender he freely endorses, for he will not admit any comparison between the Christian God and deities who "wallow in matter and mud."

Tatian (c. xxii.) lashes with ridicule the teaching offered to and accepted by the Greeks, the teaching of the theatre and arena. It might be urged that such places were frequented and delighted in by the uncultured only. Tatian therefore places the philosophers also at the bar of judgment, and his contempt for their teaching is only equalled by his ridicule of their appearance (c. xxv.). He denounces them as tuft-hunters and gluttons, to whom philosophy was simply a means of getting money. No two of them agreed. One followed the teaching of Plato, a disciple of Epicurus opposed him. The scholar of Democritus reviled the pupil of Aristotle. Why, protests Tatian, do you who are so inharmonious fight us Christians who are at least harmonious? "Your philosophers maintain that God has a body: I maintain that He is without a body; that the world shall be often consumed by fire, I once for all; that Minos and Rhadamanthus will be the judges of mankind, I God Himself (cf. c. vi.); that the soul alone is immortal, I the body together with the soul." We, he continues, do but follow the Logos of God, why do you hate us? We are not eaters of human flesh; the charge is false. It is among you that Pelops the beloved of Poseidon is made a banquet for the gods, that Saturn devours his own children, and Zeus swallows Metis.

After all, the philosophers do but make a boast of language taken from others (c. xxvi.), like the jackdaw strutting about in borrowed plumes. The reading of their books is like struggling through a labyrinth, the readers must be like the pierced cask of the Danaids. Why should they affirm that wisdom was with them only? The grammarians were at the bottom of all this folly; and philosophers who parcelled out wisdom to this and that system-maker knew not God and did but destroy each other. "Therefore," Tatian concludes scornfully, "you are all nothing—blind men talking with deaf; handling builder's tools but not knowing how to build; preaching but not practising; swaggering about in public but hiding your teaching in corners. We have left you because this is your character. We can have nothing more to do with your instructions. We follow the word of God."

Tatian then explains (c. xxix.) how he became a Christian. It was not through want of knowledge of what he was leaving. He had been initiated into the (Eleusinian) mysteries, and had made trial of every kind of religious worship. The result had sickened him. Among the Romans he had found the Latiarian Jupiter delighting in human gore, Diana Aricina similarly worshipped, and this or that demon systematically urging on to what was evil. He withdrew to seek by some means to discover the truth. "As," he says, "I was earnestly considering this I came across certain barbarian writings, older in point of antiquity than the doctrines of the Greeks, and far too divine to be marked by their errors. What persuaded me in these books was the simplicity of the language, the inartificial style of the writers, the noble explanation of creation, the predictions of the future, the excellence of the precepts, and the assertion of the government of all by One Being. My soul being thus taught of God I understand how the writings of the Gentiles lead to condemnation, but the sacred Scriptures to freedom from this world's slavery, liberating us from thousands of tyrants, and giving us, not indeed what we had not received, but what we had once received but had lost through error."

Tatian, with all the energy of a convert, loudly proclaimed the truth which satisfied him. He goes on to shew (cc. xxxi.-xli.) that the Christian religion was a "philosophy" far more ancient than that of the Greeks. He compares Homer and Moses, "the one the oldest of poets and historians, the other the founder of our barbarian wisdom." The comparison proves the Christian tenets older than those of the Greeks, and even than the invention of letters. After enumerating numerous variant opinions as to the date, parentage, and poetry of Homer, he remarks upon such discordant testimony as proving the history untrue; so different from the unanimity common among Christians. "We reject everything," he says, "which rests upon human opinion; we obey the commandments of God and follow the law of the Father of immortality. The rich among us follow philosophy, and our poor are taught gratuitously. We receive all who wish to be taught, aged women and striplings: every age is respected by us. . . . We do not test them by their looks, nor judge them by their outward appearance. In body they may be weak, but in mind they are strong. . . . What we do keep at a distance is licentiousness and falsehood." His mention of the women who received Christian instruction leads him to a digression in defence of them. The Gentiles scoffed, he says, at them, and alleged that the Christians talked nonsense among them. Tatian retorts (cc. xxxiii. xxxiv.) by pointing to the disgrace the Greeks cast upon themselves, not only by their unbecoming conduct to women generally, but by the statues they erected to courtesans and wanton poetesses. "All our women," bursts forth Tatian, "are chaste; and our maidens at their distaffs sing nobler songs about God than a Sappho." The Greeks should repudiate the lesson of immorality which their statues had immortalized and the foul practices inculcated by indecent writers, and turn to Christianity which enjoined truth and purity of thought and life. "I do not," says Tatian (c. xxxv.), "speak of these things as having merely heard about them. I have travelled much; I have studied your philosophy (*al.* rhetoric, cf. Eus. *H. E.* iv. 16, and Otto's note here), and your arts and inventions. At Rome I saw the multitude of statues you have collected there. And, as the result, I have turned from Roman boastfulness, Athenian exaggeration, ill-connected doctrines, to the barbaric Christian philosophy."

He now returns to the subject started in c. xxxi., after one word in deprecation of the sneer at himself: "Tatian, the man so superior to the Greeks, so superior to the numberless teachers of philosophy, has opened up a new vein of learning—the doctrines of the barbarians!" Whether Homer was contemporary with the Trojan war, or a soldier under Agamemnon, or even lived before the invention of letters, Moses yet lived long before either the building or taking of Troy. In proof of this, Tatian appeals to the Chaldeans, Phoenicians, and Egyptians. *E.g.* Berosus, the Babylonian historian, "a most competent authority," spoke of the wars of Nebuchadnezzar against the Phoenicians and Jews which happened 70 years before the Persian rule, and long after the age of Moses. Phoenician historians, such as Theodotus, Hypsicrates, and Mochus had referred to events connected with Hiram of Tyre, whose date was somewhere about the Trojan war. Both Solomon and Hiram lived long after Moses. The Egyptians were noted for the accuracy of their chronicles, and Ptolemy, the priest of Mendes, spoke of the departure of the Jews from Egypt as having taken place under the leadership of Moses under king Amosis. This king, according to him, lived in the time ot the Argive king, Inachus, after whose reign, dating 20 generations, the taking of Troy was reached. Therefore, if Moses was a contemporary of Inachus, he lived some 400 years before the Trojan war. It was not till after the time of Inachus that the most illustrious deeds of gods and men in Greece were committed to writing and became known. Such records, therefore, were far less ancient than the time of Moses. Tatian sums up (c. xl.) by affirming it self-evident that Moses was of far greater antiquity than the ancient heroes, wars, or gods (demons). Men ought, therefore, to believe the more ancient authority in preference to the Greeks, who had borrowed from Moses, as from a spring, without acknowledgment (*al.* unconsciously); and in many cases had perverted what they took. Moses was, moreover, older than all the writers before Homer, *e.g.* than Linus, the teacher of Hercules, who lived in the generation before the Trojan war, than Orpheus, who was a contemporary with Hercules, and than the wisest of the wise men of Greece, *e.g.* Minos—so famous for his wisdom, shrewdness, and legislative powers—who lived in the 11th generation after Inachus; Lycurgus, the Lacedemonian lawgiver, who was born long after the taking of Troy; Draco, Solon, Pythagoras, and those seven wise men, the oldest of whom lived about the 50th of those Olympiads which began about 400 years after the taking of Troy.

The treatise is a defence of Christianity rather than of Christians, and not so much a defence of doctrines as an answer or oration to those who sneered at them. He depicts Christianity as contrasting by its goodness, wisdom, and truth with the heathenism which revelled in vice, foolishness, and error. Unlike other apologists, there is little care to discuss Thyestean banquets (cf. c. xxv.), or refute want of patriotism (c. iv.) His weapons are weapons of offence rather than of defence. In Tatian "barbaric (*i.e.* Christian) philosophy" dares to carry the war into the enemy's camp, and scorn is turned upon the scorners. It is a typical specimen of the class to which the *Irrisio Gentilium Philosophorum* of HERMIAS also belongs.

The Opinions of Tatian.—(*a*) *God* (see c. iv.).—With Tatian, as with Justin, God, not contemplated as He is in His nature but as revealed in His works, is the starting-point of all Christian philosophy. Tatian's doctrine about the creation is in c. v. In the creation itself he recognizes two stages (c. ii.): (*α*) matter, shapeless and unformed, is put forth (προβεβλημένη) by God; and (*β*) the world, separated from this matter, is fashioned into what is full of beauty and order, though eventually to be dissolved by fire (*c.* xxv.).

(*b*) *The Logos* (see c. v.).—The relation between God (ὁ δεσπότης) and the Logos Who subsists in Him, *the* Hypostasis, is conceived from a different point of view, and set forth in different terms from those of Justin. With Tatian the Logos springs forth (προπηδᾷ) by the Will of God. The process of begetting, the relationships of Father and Son, and the worship due to the Son, are not brought forward. The inward communion between them which carries with it these truths is indeed expressed by the deep phrase σὺν αὐτῷ διὰ λογικῆς δυνάμεως αὐτὸς καὶ ὁ λόγος; but the outward exhibition of this communion—the "springing forth"—is suggestive of emanation rather than of begetting. The distinction between the λόγος ἐνδιάθετος and the λόγος προφορικός, so strongly expressed by the apologist Theophilus (ii. 10), is more than visible. Tatian, in fact, presents the Logos as the personification of an abstraction.

(*c*) *The Holy Spirit* is evidently with Tatian a distinct personal Being. He does not, as Justin (*Apol.* i. 60), speak directly of His share in the creation; he rather leads up to His work and office as "the Minister of the suffering God" (c. xiii.), when he would present its bearing upon the nature of man. Starting from the initial positions, "God is Spirit," and the Logos "a Spirit born of the Father," Tatian recognizes two varieties of Spirit: (*α*) "the spirit which pervades matter, inferior to (*β*) the more Divine Spirit" (c. iv.). To the Spirit is attributed prophetic powers. Abiding with the just and locked in the embrace of the soul (συμπλεκόμενον τῇ ψυχῇ), He proclaims to other souls by means of prophecies that which is concealed. He uses the Prophets as His organ (cf. c. xx.). This action Tatian has also attributed to "the Power of the Logos" (c. vii.). Perhaps, as with Justin, this title of the Logos, ἡ δύναμις, defines for Tatian the meaning of the πνεῦμα (cf. II. Cor. iii. 17). The Spirit is the Divine Power of the Logos.

(*d*) *Angelology and Demonology.*—Of good angels Tatian says nothing; but he speaks as strongly as Justin of evil angels, though he presents their work and ways in different language and (in some respects) from a different point of view. When expelled from heaven the fallen angels or demons lived with animals. Some of these they placed—the dog, the bear, the scorpion, etc.—in the heavens as objects of worship. Of demons, Tatian recognizes two classes. Receiving alike their constitution from matter, and possessing the spirit which comes from it, few only turned to what was purer, the many chose what was licentious and gluttonous (c. xii.); they became the very "effulgences of matter and wickedness" (c. xv.). Though material, none of the demons possess flesh; their structure is spiritual like that of fire or air (*ib.*).

(*e*) *Man.*—Tatian recognizes the three parts of body, soul, and spirit. At the fall man lost the spirit or highest nature, which had in it immortality (c. vii.). As the angels were cast down from heaven, so man was driven forth from earth, "yet not out of this earth, but from a more excellent order of things than exists here now." Tatian would seem to place Paradise above our earth; he describes it (c. xx.) as one of the better aeons unaffected by that change of seasons which is productive of various diseases, as partaking of a perfect temperature, as possessing endless day and light, and as unapproachable by mortals such as we are. Man, though deprived of the spirit, must aim at recovering his former state. Body and soul are left him. The soul is composite: it is the bond of the flesh; yet also that which encloses the soul is the flesh. The soul cannot appear without a body, nor can the flesh rise again without the soul.

Faith is a necessity for knowledge of divine things; ὁ πιστεύων ἐπιγνώσεται (c. xix.); faith and knowledge together help towards the victory over sin and death. Men, after the throwing away (ἀποβολήν) of immortality, have conquered death by the death which is through faith (cf. c. xi.: "Die to the world! Live to God!"); and through repentance a call has been granted to those who (according to God's word) are but a little lower than the angels (c. xv.). Through faith, and as the object of faith, Tatian proclaims that "God was born in the form of a man" (c. xxi.), and speaks of the Holy Spirit as the minister of the God Who hath suffered (τὸν διάκονον τοῦ πεπονθότος θεοῦ, c. xiii.). If he never mentions the names Jesus or Christ, it is because the facts of the Incarnation and Passion would commend themselves independently of names to Gentiles, to whom such facts were illustrated by their mythology (cf. Justin, *Apol.* i. 21). Faith animates the famous passage on the soul (c. xiii.), and especially in connexion with the resurrection. "We have faith in this doctrine," he exclaims (c. v.); but he does not rest his reasons on the resurrection of Christ (as St. Paul), but on an argument which may have suggested the more elaborate reasoning of Tertullian (*Apol.* c. xlviii.): There was a time when as man he was not; after a former state of nothingness he was born. Again, there would be a time when he would die; and again there would be a time when he should exist again. There was nothing of metempsychosis or transmigration of souls in his conception. Though the flesh were destroyed by fire or wild beasts, or dispersed through rivers or seas, "I," says Tatian, "am laid up in the storehouses of a wealthy Lord. God the King will, when He pleases, restore to its former state my substance which is visible to Himself alone" (c. vi.).

As regards free will, Tatian uses even more emphatic language than Justin (*e.g.* *Apol.* i. 43). He opposes the Scriptural (and Platonic) belief in free will to the fatalism of philosophers (cc. viii.-x.), and while he pours scorn upon their views, pens a touching appeal to them as men "not created to die" (see c. xi. end).

Christian Practice.—Though Tatian does not speak of his co-religionists as Christians, but accepts willingly the contemptuous expression "barbarians," it is the doctrines of Christ which alone have, in his opinion, raised them above a world deluded by the trickeries of frenzied demons (c. xii.), and wallowing in matter and mud (c. xxi.). Where the old nature has been laid aside, men have not only apprehended God (c. xi.), but through a knowledge of the True One have remodelled (*μεταῤῥυθμίζειν*) their lives (c. v.). Holy baptism and membership in the church did not enter into his argument. A passing allusion to the Holy Eucharist perhaps underlies his indignant protest against the frequent defamation that Christians indulged in Thyestean banquets (c. xxv.). He seems to prefer advancing the great help which the Scriptures had been to himself, and might be to his philosophical opponents. "Barbaric" though these Scriptures were, they were in the O.T. portion both older and more divine, more full of humility and of deep knowledge, more marked by excellence and unity than any writings claimed by the Greeks (c. xxix.). These "divine writings" made men "lovers of God" (c. xii.); and men thus God-taught were helped by them to break down the slavery in the world, and gain back what they had once received, but had lost through the deceit of their spiritual foes (c. xxix.).

The O.T. seems to have greatly attracted Tatian. It probably formed the basis of the lost work *προβλημάτων βιβλίον* mentioned by Rhodon; and in his attempt to collect and solve O.T. difficulties, Tatian was among the first, if not the first, of Christian commentators. The *Oratio* shews that he knew well the Gospels, Acts, and Pauline Epistles. If reference to O. and N. T. is more marked by allusion than by direct quotation, the cause is the well-known practice of the apologists, who usually abstain from such quotations when writing to Gentiles who would have allowed little authority to them. Tatian's references to St. John's Gospel are, however, both exceptional and indisputable, and testify to a widespread knowledge of that Gospel at the period in question. Independently of coincidences of exposition, three passages may be specified:

TATIAN.		ST. JOHN.	
Ch. iv.	πνεῦμα ὁ Θεός	Ch. iv. 24.	πνεῦμα ὁ Θεός.
Ch. xiii.	ἡ σκοτία τὸ φῶς οὐ καταλαμβάνει.	Ch. i. 5.	τὸ φῶς ἐν τῇ σκοτίᾳ φαίνει, καὶ ἡ σκοτία αὐτὸ οὐ κατέλαβεν.
Ch. xix.	πάντα ὑπ' αὐτοῦ καὶ χωρὶς αὐτοῦ γέγονεν οὐδὲ ἕν.	Ch. i. 3.	πάντα δι' αὐτοῦ ἐγένετο, καὶ χωρὶς αὐτοῦ ἐγένετο οὐδὲ ἕν. (*Westcott & Hort.*)

Of these the second is prefaced by *τὸ εἰρημένον*, the expression which in N.T. introduces the Scriptures (cf. Luke ii. 24; Acts ii. 16, xiii. 40; Rom. iv. 18). The third passage is punctuated by Tatian in the manner invariably followed by the early Christian writers (contrast the *textus receptus*, *οὐδὲ ἓν ὃ γέγονεν*). The coincidence is, as noted by Bp. Lightfoot, remarkable, for the words are extremely simple in themselves. Their order and adaptation give uniqueness to the expression.

B. *The Diatessaron.*—(1) *History.*—The history of the recovery of this work is sufficiently romantic. In the literature of the Western church there is no serviceable testimony to it till the middle of 6th cent.; in the Eastern church Eusebius († 339-340) is the only Greek writer of the first four cents. who gives any information about it. It was apparently (see *Codex Fuldensis*, ed. Ranke, 1868, ix. 1) mere chance which put into the hands of bp. Victor of Capua († 554) a Latin book of the Gospels without title or author's name, but evidently compiled from the four canonical books. This unknown work excited his interest; and searching in vain the Latin Christian literature of the past, he turned to the Greek, and found in Eusebius two notices of Harmonies. (*a*) In the letter to Carpianus the harmony of Ammonius of Alexandria (3rd cent.) was described. Its principle was that of comparison. The Gospel of St. Matthew was followed continuously, and the passages—and only those—from the other Gospels which tallied with the text of St. Matthew were referred to or inserted in the margin or in parallel columns. This excluded the greater part of St. John's Gospel and much of St. Luke's. The *Harmony* was for private use, not for the public service of the church. Whether or not the descriptive title given to it in Eusebius—*τὸ διὰ τεσσάρων εὐαγγέλιον*—was that of the church historian or of Ammonius remains undetermined. (*b*) In his Church History (iv. 29, 6), Eusebius refers to Tatian as having composed a "sort of connexion or compilation, I know not how, of the Gospels, and called it the *Diatessaron*" (*συνάφειάν τινα καὶ συναγωγὴν οὐκ οἶδ' ὅπως τῶν εὐαγγελίων συνθείς*. Cf. Bp. Lightfoot in *Contemp. Rev.* May 1877; Zahn, i. pp. 14, 15); and he adds that this work was current in his day. Its principle was amalgamation, not comparison. Victor came to the conclusion that his unknown work was substantially the *Diatessaron* of Tatian. This acute verdict—purged of some unimportant errors (see Lightfoot, *l.c.*; Zahn, i. pp. 2, 3)—has survived the difficulties which a comparison of the *Codex Fuldensis* with the *Diatessaron* at first presented.

A notice in the treatise on Heresies, written in 453 by Theodoret († 457-458), bp. of Cyrrhus on the Euphrates, is the first definite evidence to the *Diatessaron* after the time of Eusebius. The identification of it by Epiphanius (*Haer.* xlvi. 1) with the Gospel according to the Hebrews is an earlier testimony in point of date (Epiphanius † 403), but is connected with a blunder which, though capable of explanation, somewhat disqualifies the evidence. Testimony to the *Diatessaron* comes rather from the Syriac-speaking church of the East than from the Greek. Theodoret says of Tatian: "He composed the Gospel which is called *Diatessaron*, cutting out the genealogies and such other passages as shew the Lord to have been born of the seed of David after the flesh. This work was in use not only among persons belonging to his sect, but also among those who follow the apostolic doctrine, as they did not perceive the mischief of the composition, but used the book in all simplicity on account of its brevity. And I myself found more than 200 such copies held in respect in the churches in our parts. All these I collected and put away, and I replaced them by the Gospels of the four Evangelists" (i. 20. Cf. Lightfoot, *l.c.*; Zahn, i. p. 35). This passage indicates a considerable circulation of the *Diatessaron* in the bishop's diocese and neighbourhood. The language of that district was Syriac (Zahn, i. pp. 39-44); therefore the book to which Theodoret refers was in Syriac and not Greek. This simple fact helps to explain the language of Eusebius and the blunder of Epiphanius; and is itself illustrated by the fact that the commentary on the *Diatessaron* was composed not by a Greek writer, but by Ephrem the Syrian. Epiphanius's statement that Tatian on leaving Rome went into Mesopotamia, points to a visit to Edessa, the only place in the district where Christianity had secure footing (see Zahn, i. p. 282 and Excursus ii.) and a city famous for its schools. To the same Tatian rumour assigned the *Diatessaron* which some called "the Gospel according to the Hebrews." How did Epiphanius confound two works so essentially different? Zahn's explanation seems perfectly satisfactory. The report was current that there was a Syriac book of the Gospels, called a *Diatessaron*, used in the Syrian churches, *e.g.* those of the diocese of Cyrrhus. Further, it was reported that there was another book of the Gospels, written in a kindred dialect and used *e.g.* at Beroea, *i.e.* in the neighbourhood of Cyrrhus, by the half-heretical Nazareans. An outsider like Epiphanius might very easily confound them and even identify them (i. p. 25. See Wace, *Expositor* for 1882, p. 165). Eusebius had not actually seen Tatian's *Diatessaron*. His statement, "I know not how" Tatian composed it, shews that he had not personally examined it, doubtless because of non-acquaintance or non-familiarity with Syriac.

Theodoret's language implies, moreover, that the *Diatessaron* had been current in his diocese for a very long period; and this is confirmed by an examination of the commentary of Ephrem Syrus († 378). Dionysius bar Salibi, bp. of Amida in Armenia Major († 1171 Mösinger and Bickell, or 1207 Assemani and Lightfoot, see Zahn, i. p. 98, n. 4), states in the preface to his own commentary on St. Mark (quoted in Assemani, *Bibl. Or.* i. 57, ii. 159; see Mösinger, p. iii.; Zahn, i. pp. 44, 99) that Tatian, the pupil of Justin, made a selection from the four Gospels (*al.* Evangelists), which he wove together into one Gospel, and called a *Diatessaron, i.e.* Miscellanies. This writing St. Ephrem interpreted. Its opening words were, "In the beginning was the Word." An Armenian version (5th cent.) of Ephrem's Commentary was printed at Venice in 1836, but remained unserviceable until a MS. Latin and literal translation of the Armenian made by J. B. Aucher, one of the Mechitarist monks of that city, together with one of the Armenian codices, was placed in the hands of a Salzburg professor, Dr. G. Mösinger, who revised, corrected, and published the Latin text at Venice in 1876. Internal and external evidence (see Mösinger, pp. vi-x) combine in justifying the conclusion that in this Latin translation of the Commentary of Ephrem is contained substantially Tatian's *Diatessaron*, and that from it Tatian's text may be in a great measure recovered.

The bearing of Mösinger's translation upon the corresponding portion of the *Codex Fuldensis* may be briefly summarized. Dr. Wace (*Expositor* for 1881, pp. 128 seq.) may be said to have proved that Victor of Capua's *Harmony* preserved in that Codex is not only very closely allied with Tatian's *Diatessaron*, but exhibits substantially the document on which Ephrem commented with some occasional alterations of order and few additions; the difference being remembered that in Victor's *Evangelium* Tatian has been transferred into the Latin text of St. Jerome, whereas Ephrem commented upon him in a Syriac translation. The Mösinger text and the Codex proceed *pari passu*, and agree in order where that order is certainly remarkable. The very interesting fact is thus established, that Tatian's *Diatessaron* found acceptance in the West as well as the East, and was transferred rather than translated into a Western version. This is not surprising. Theodoret's statement as to its popularity in his diocese may well account for its existence in a Latin form a century later.

It remains to indicate the manner in which the Syriac *Diatessaron* passed into Latin form, such as is preserved in the *Codex Fuldensis* (Zahn, i. pp. 298-328). The interesting fact comes out that this took place without the use of any intermediary Greek *Diatessaron*. In language and form the Latin *Harmony* is based upon St. Jerome's version; and the differences between the Codex and Tatian—such as alterations in chronological order, expansions and abbreviations, coincidences and deviations—indicative as they are of dependence of the Codex upon Tatian, do not require the explanation which an intermediate Greek text would easily supply. The *Codex Fuldensis* must be dated between 383 (when Jerome put forward his revision of the translation of the Gospels) and 546 (when Victor of Capua wrote down the Latin *Harmony* preserved in the Codex); or, more approximately, *c.* 500 (Zahn, i. p. 310). Translations from Syriac into Greek existed in 4th cent. (Eus. *H. E.* i. 13, iv. 30), and the fact—with its consequence, a further translation from Greek into Latin—might be quoted in proof of a more early date than A.D. 500 for the *Codex Fuldensis*; but, independently of other reasons, the age of Victor of Capua has yielded proofs of direct translations from Syriac into Latin, which render appeals to a Greek *Diatessaron* unnecessary. Kihn (*Theodor von Mopsuestia und Junilius Africanus*; see Zahn, i. p. 311) has shewn that in the days of Victor of Capua, JUNILIUS, *Quaestor sacri palatii* at Constantinople (*c.* 545-552) sent to Primasius, bp. of Adrumetum, a Latin introduction to the Scriptures (*Instituta regularia divinae legis*) which was a free rendering of a work written (*c.* 533-544) by the Syrian Nestorian Paul, a pupil and teacher of the school of Nisibis.

(2) *Recovery of the Diatessaron.*—This is due to the energetic scholarship of Zahn. By the use principally of Ephrem's commentary (ed. Mösinger) and of the quotations in the

Homilies of Aphraates he has printed the text (i. pp. 113-219) in detail; comparing it throughout with the Syriac of Cureton (Sc.), the Peshito (P.), and frequently the Philoxenian text revised by Thomas of Harkel (Hl.), with the Greek MSS. ℵ, B, and D, and with Sabatier and Bianchini's editions of the MSS. of the Itala. Verse by verse the text is reconstructed and tabulated in sections. Each section is accompanied by an exhaustive critical and expository comment, and an index to all the passages incorporated in the *Harmony* enables the student to examine the evidence respecting any individual verse. These sections indicate the character of the *Harmony* and may be seen as given by Zahn, with the refs. to Ephrem omitted in favour of Eng. headings in Fuller's *Harmony of the Gospels* (S.P.C.K.). Zahn has pursued the subject further in his *Forschungen zur Geschichte des N.T. Kanons*, ii. 286-299, and his *Geschichte des N.T. Kanons*, (1888) i. 1, 369-429; (1892), ii. 2, 530-556.

(3) *The Theological Opinions of Tatian.*—Until the death of Justin Martyr he was considered orthodox; after that heterodox. The change can only be roughly sketched. In the *Oratio* are found traces of the three heretical views which Irenaeus attributed to him. (i) The allusion to Aeons above the heavens (c. xx.) may very well have led on to theories akin to those of Valentinus (Iren. *adv. Haer.* i. 28). (ii) The doctrine that the protoplast lost the image and likeness of God (cc. viii. xii. xv.) might lead to the denial of the salvation of Adam (*ib.* iii. 23, § 8). (iii) His allusion (c. xv.) to man as distinguished from the brute—implying by contrast points of resemblance between them—makes possible a transition to the severer views of denouncing marriage as defilement and fornication as did Marcion and Saturninus (Iren. c. xv.; Hieron. *Comm. l.c. in Ep. ad Gal.* vi.), and also the use of meats (Hieron. *adv. Jovin.* i. 3). Were the heretical writings in existence which Irenaeus affirmed that Tatian had written and he himself had read (Zahn, i. p. 281), we might be able to judge how far they justified Irenaeus in describing him as "elated, puffed up as if superior to other teachers, and forming his own type of doctrine," and to trace something of his erroneousness in the *Problems*, and other lost works, *e.g Concerning Perfection according to the Saviour*; and in the criticisms, paraphrases, or translations of some of St Paul's Epistles, which Eusebius (*H. E.* iv. 29) had heard of, and which Jerome described as repudiations of those apostolic writings (*Praef. in Comm. to Titus*, see Zahn, i. p. 6, n. 4). A few hints only are forthcoming on these points, and these filtered through unfriendly channels. But the general impression cannot be resisted. Tatian became first suspected and then denounced. He left Rome, possibly pausing at Alexandria to teach, among his pupils being Clement of Alexandria (cf. Lightfoot, p. 1133; Zahn, i. p. 12), and then proceeding to the East, to Mesopotamia (Epiphan. *Haer.* xlvi. 1. Correct his error in chronology by Lightfoot and Zahn, i. p. 282), there to live until his death. It is more than probable that on leaving Rome he carried the *Diatessaron* with him, unpublished. In the West he had become unacceptable. The language of Irenaeus *c.* 185—*i.e.* probably after Tatian's death—leaves no doubt upon this point. Men honoured and valued the *Oratio* (cf. *int. al.* Hilgenfeld, *Ketzergeschichte*, pp. 386, 387); but say nothing of the *Diatessaron.* In the Greek-speaking churches of the East the writer of the *Oratio* was not less valued (cf. Eus. *H. E.* iv. 29, v. 28), and they speak of the *Diatessaron*; but it is by report or at second-hand only. Ugly rumours circulated. Tatian, described broadly as "connexio omnium haereticorum" (Iren. *adv. Haer.* iii. 23), had become, in defiance of historical probability (Zahn, i. p. 288), an ENCRATITE, one whose tenets had spread into Asia Minor from Antioch, and who blossomed out at last into "Encratitarum acerrimus haeresiarches" (Hieron.). Had Irenaeus, Eusebius, or Jerome known the *Diatessaron*, would they not have examined it as they had examined Tatian's *Oratio* and other works? Would not the very compilation of a *Diatessaron* have been obnoxious to one who, like Irenaeus, counted the fourfold Gospels (neither more, nor less) an absolute necessity? But in the Syriac-speaking East he was unknown, or not followed by troublesome reflections upon his orthodoxy, and there the teacher who was eclectic rather than heterodox could produce and circulate that work, which commended itself to the "simplicity" of the churches around Edessa "on account of its brevity," till Theodoret enlightened them.

The date of his death is unknown, but if he left Rome *c.* 172 or 173 he would have been about 62 years of age, and, humanly speaking, with time before him to circulate the *Diatessaron* before he died.

Literature.—In the prolegomena (pp. xiii-xxix) to Otto's ed. of the *Oratio* will be found a description of the MSS., edd., etc., in existence (cf. also Harnack, *op. cit.* pp. 1-97; Donaldson, *History of Christian Literature and Doctrine*, iii. pp. 60-62). For other works besides those freely used and specified in this art. see Preuschen's art. *s.n.* in Herzog's *R. E.*3 The text of the *Diatessaron* ed. by J. White is pub. by Oxf. Univ. Press, and a trans. in *Ante-Nicene Lib.* [J.M.F.]

"Teaching of the Twelve Apostles." Bryennius discovered at Constantinople a MS. thus entitled in a vol. containing an unmutilated MS. text of the two Epp. ascribed to Clement, and pub. it at the close of 1883, no other copy being known to exist in MS. or print.

The MS. bears the heading "Teaching of the Twelve Apostles," followed by the fuller title "Teaching of the Lord by the Twelve Apostles to the Gentiles." That both titles belong to the original form appears probable from the phrase "the Twelve Apostles." The phrase διδαχὴ τῶν ἀποστόλων occurs in Acts ii. 42; and the earliest writers who have been supposed to speak of the work (Eusebius and Athanasius) do so merely under the name "Teaching of the Apostles"; the addition of "Twelve" being superfluous when the word "Apostle" had become limited to the Twelve. In the work itself "Apostle" is used in a very wide sense; so that if this really represents church usage when it was written, the title

"Teaching of the Apostles" would be quite vague without the addition "Twelve" (cf. Luke vi. 13; Rev. xxi. 14).

The title was only intended to describe the substance of the work, not to assert anything as to its direct authorship. Though called "Teaching (*Didaché*) of the Lord," our Lord is certainly not represented as the speaker; see such expressions as "concerning these things spake the Lord," "as the Lord ordered in His Gospel," "as ye have in the Gospel of our Lord." Neither is it written in the name of the twelve apostles; for the author uses the singular, addressing his disciple as "my child." Nor does the treatise contain any indication that the author of the whole claimed to be one of the apostles, or that the work is to be broken up into sections supposed to be spoken by successive apostles. In this respect it is favourably distinguished from a number of spurious works which claimed apostolic authorship in early times. But, as in the case of the Apostles' Creed, a title apparently originally only intended to assert conformity with apostolic teaching, came to be understood as an assertion of authorship, and later authorities undertook to specify the portions contributed by each apostle; and later works founded on the *Didaché* are divided into sections supposed to be contributed by individual apostles.

The work divides into two parts: the first, which we shall refer to as the "Two Ways," forming the first 6 chapters of Bryennius's ed., contains moral instruction; the second (cc. 7-15 Bryennius) deals with church ritual and discipline, a chapter (16) being added on our Lord's Second Coming. Several very early writers exhibit coincidences with pt. i., such as to prove that they borrowed from the *Didaché*, or the *Didaché* from them, or that both had a common source. With pt. ii. similar coincidences are much later and much more scanty. Part i. was intended for catechumens, or at least for use in their instruction, for part ii., which begins by treating of baptism, directs that candidates shall first have received the preceding teaching.

Contents.—The work begins by declaring that there are two ways: one of Life, the other of Death; phrases borrowed from Jer. xxi. 8, a passage itself derived from Deut. xxx. 19. It then describes first the Way of Life, which is summed up in two precepts: love God Who made thee; and love thy neighbour as thyself and do not to another what thou wouldest not have done to thyself.* Then follow several precepts from the Sermon on the Mount.

As c. i. is based on the Sermon on the Mount, so is c. ii. on the second table of the Decalogue. C. iii. instructs the disciple to flee not only from every evil, but from everything like it. C. iv. contains miscellaneous precepts. C. v. gives an enumeration of the sins which constitute the way of death. C. vi. is a short exhortation to abide in the foregoing teaching; but giving permission if the disciple cannot bear the whole yoke, especially as regards food, to be content with bearing as much as he can; provided always he abstains from things offered to idols. Here terminates the section addressed to the catechumen. Then follow (c. vii.) directions for the baptism of candidates who have received the preceding instruction. It is to be in the name of Father, Son, and Holy Spirit; in running water if it can be had; if not, in any water, even warm water. If sufficient water for immersion is not at hand, it will suffice to pour water three times on the head. Baptizer and baptized must fast beforehand; the baptized for a day or two: others, if possible, to join in the fast. This rule of fasting may be illustrated by the account given in the Clementines (*Hom.* iii. 11; *Recog.* vii. 36) of the baptism of Clement's mother. Peter directs that she shall fast one day previous to baptism.

C. viii. relates to fasting and prayer. The disciples must not fast "as the hypocrites," on the 2nd and 5th days of the week; but on the 4th and on the preparation day. Neither must they pray as the hypocrites, but as the Lord ordered in His Gospel. The Lord's Prayer is given in conformity with St. Matthew's text with but trifling variations, but adding the doxology "Thine is the power and the glory for ever." This prayer is to be used thrice daily. Chaps. ix. x. contain Eucharistic formulae. In the opening words "Concerning the thanksgiving, give thanks in this manner," we can scarcely avoid giving to the word εὐχαριστία the technical meaning it had as early as Ignatius (*Philad.* 4; *Smyrn.* 6, 8; *Eph.* 13; cf. Justin, *Apol.* 66). This interpretation is confirmed by a direction that of this "Eucharist" none but baptized persons should partake, since the Lord has said "Give not that which is holy unto the dogs." But the forms themselves are more like what we should expect in prayers before and after an ordinary meal than the Eucharist proper. There is no recital of the words of institution; no mention of the Body and Blood of our Lord, though both Ignatius and Justin Martyr so describe the consecrated food. The supposition that we have here private prayers to be said before and after reception is excluded by the direction that "prophets" should be permitted to offer thanks as they pleased, where it is plain that public thanksgiving is intended. The explanation seems to be that the celebration of the Eucharist still accompanied the Agape or Love Feast, and that we have here the thanksgivings before and after that meal. In the Clementines, which in several points manifest affinity with the *Didaché*, it is not merely the Eucharist from which the unbaptized are excluded. They can take no food of any kind at the same table with the initiated. An unbaptized person is the home of the demon, and until this demon has been driven out by baptism, no Christian can safely admit him to a common table (*Recog.* ii. 71; see also i. 19, vii. 36); and all

* This negative form is found in substance in Tob. iv. 15. It may be due to the influence of the *Didaché* that it is found appended in this form to the instructions to Gentiles in Acts xv. in D. and some cursive MSS., confirmed by Irenaeus or his translator (III. xii. 14) and Cyprian (*Test.* iii. 119). The precept is found in the same form in Theophilus (*ad Autol.* ii. 34); but the context does not furnish coincidences such as would prove the *Didaché* the source. Lampridius says (*Alex. Sev.* 51) that Alexander Severus was fond of quoting this precept, which he had learned either from some Jews or Christians.

through the Clementines the language in which the benediction of every meal is described is such as to make it uncertain whether a celebration of the Eucharist is meant. In the form in the *Didaché* we notice that: (1) the benediction of the cup precedes that of the bread (see Luke xxii. 17-19). (2) The broken bread has the technical name τὸ κλάσμα. (3) The thanksgiving for the cup runs: "We give thanks to Thee our Father, for the holy vine of Thy servant David which Thou hast made known to us through Thy servant Jesus." This expression the "vine of David" was known to Clement of Alexandria, who says of Christ (*Quis Dives Salv.* 29), "Who poured forth the wine, the blood of the vine of David, for our wounded souls." Elsewhere (*Paed.* i. 5), treating of Gen. xlix. "binding the colt to the vine," he interprets "the vine" of the Logos Who gives His blood, as the vine yields wine. (4) The benedictory prayer contains a petition that as the broken bread had been scattered on the mountains and had been brought together and made one, so might the church be collected together from the ends of the earth. (5) The thanksgiving prayer after reception is directed to be said "after being filled" (μετὰ τὸ ἐμπλησθῆναι), words answering better to the conclusion of an Agape than of a Eucharistic celebration (cf. *Recog.* i. 19).

Chaps. xi. xii. xiii. treat of the honour to be paid to Christian teachers, who are described as "apostles and prophets." This combination of terms reflects N.T. usage (I. Cor. xii. 28, 29; Eph. ii. 20, iii. 8, iv. 11). The word "apostle" in our document is not limited to the Twelve, but is used as our word "missionary." Every true apostle was a prophet, but only those prophets received the name apostle who were not fixed in one place, but accredited by churches on a mission to distant localities. This terminology is a proof of the antiquity of our document (see Lightfoot on the word Apostle, *Gal.* p. 92). The word was used by Jews to denote an envoy sent by the authorities at Jerusalem to Jews in foreign places, especially the envoy charged with the collection of the Temple tribute. Our document is solicitous to provide for the due entertainment of Christian missionaries, and yet to guard against the church's hospitality being traded on by impostors or lazy persons. Every apostle was to be received as the Lord; but if he wanted to prolong his stay beyond two days at most, he betrayed himself as a false prophet. Clearly the apostle is an envoy on his way to another place; for it could never have been intended to forbid a missionary to settle down in one spot for a longer period of preaching. The false apostle is said to betray himself if he asks for money or for a larger supply of travelling provisions than will provide for his next stage. There are commands in a similar spirit for the hospitable treatment of ordinary Christian strangers. If such a one wishes to settle among them, he must work at a handicraft or employ himself in some other way; but if he wants to eat the bread of idleness, he is one who makes merchandise of Christ (χριστέμπορός ἐστιν). The use of this word by Pseudo-Ignatius (*ad Trall.* 6, *ad Magn.* 9) agrees with the conclusion, drawn from other considerations, that the interpolator was acquainted with the *Didaché*.

There is a command in which commentators have found a difficulty, that a prophet speaking in the spirit must not be proved nor tested. "Every sin shall be forgiven, but not that." Yet there follow marks for discerning the false prophet from the true. The subsequent history of Montanism casts a clear light on the subject. The bishops attempted to test the Montanist prophetesses by applying to them the formulae of exorcism, to find whether it were possible to cast out an evil spirit who possessed them. This the Montanists naturally resisted as a frightful indignity. Such testing by exorcism is here manifestly forbidden, as involving, if applied to one really inspired by the Spirit of God, the risk of incurring the penalties denounced by our Lord, in words plainly here referred to, upon blasphemy against the Holy Ghost. That this precept of the *Didaché* was apparently not quoted in the Montanist disputes is one of many indications that our document had only a very limited circulation. Hilgenfeld's notion, that the *Didaché* is as late as Montanism, is condemned both by the whole character of the document and by its silence on the vital question in the Montanist controversy, whether true prophets lost their self-command when prophesying. To label every early document which speaks of prophesying Montanistic is to ignore the fact that prophetical gifts were recognized in the early church, and that Montanism was an unsuccessful local attempt to revive pretensions to them after they had generally ceased to be regarded as an ordinary feature of church life.* The *Didaché* gives a different way of discerning the false prophet from the true, viz. by his life and conversation. If he taught the truth but did not practise it, he was a false prophet. He might, when speaking in the spirit, command gifts to be bestowed on others; but if he asked anything for himself, or gave commands in the benefit of which he was to share, he was a false prophet. But a true prophet, settling in one place, deserves his maintenance. So also does a teacher, by which apparently is meant a preacher who does not speak in prophetic ecstasy. To the prophets are to be given the first-fruits of all produce; "for they are your high priests." If there are no prophets, the first-fruits are to go to the poor.

C. xiv. directs Christians to come together each Lord's Day to break bread and give thanks, having confessed their sins in order that their sacrifice may be pure. Those at variance must not pollute the sacrifice by coming without having been first reconciled. Our document then quotes Mal. i. 10, in which so many Fathers from Justin downwards (*Trypho*, 41, 116) have seen a prediction of the Eucharistic oblation. C. xv. begins: "Elect therefore to yourselves bishops and deacons." These are to receive the same honour as the prophets and teachers, as fulfilling a like ministration. In the preceding chapters where church officers are spoken of, mention

* In the Ep. of Ignatius, "the Prophets" means O.T. prophets, and there is no indication of an order of prophets then in the Christian church.

is made, as in I. Cor., only of apostles, prophets and teachers; and of these, apostles are only stranger visitors of the church, and prophets are men endowed with supernatural gifts of the Holy Ghost, who may or may not be found in any particular church. Bearing in mind the account given by Justin (*Apol.* i. 66) of the share taken by "the president" and the deacons in the Eucharistic celebration, we seem warranted in inferring from the "therefore" at the beginning of c. xv. that it was with a view to the conduct of the weekly stated service that bishops and deacons are described as appointed; and that, though gifted men were allowed to preach and teach in the church assemblies, the offering of the Eucharist was confined to these permanent officers. It is possible that the section on "bishops and deacons" may have been added later when the *Didaché* assumed its present form, the editor feeling it necessary that mention should be made of the recognized names of the officers of the church in his time.

C. xvi. is an exhortation to watch for our Lord's Second Coming, in order to be able to pass safely through the heavy trial that was immediately to precede it. This time of trial was to be signalized by the appearance of one who is called the "deceiver of the world" (κοσμοπλάνος), who should appear as God's Son and do signs and wonders, and into whose hands the earth should be delivered, so that under the trial many should be scandalized and be lost (cf. II. Thess. ii. 3, 4; Rev. xii. 9; Matt. xxiv. 21, 24, x. 22). But then shall appear the signs of the truth: first the sign of outspreading (ἐκπετάσεως) in heaven (a difficult phrase which need not here be discussed); then the trumpet's voice (Matt. xxiv. 31; I. Cor. xv. 52; I. Thess. iv. 16); thirdly the resurrection of the dead—not of all, but, as was said, the Lord shall come and all His saints with Him. Then shall the world see the Lord coming on the clouds of heaven.

External Attestation.—The sketch just given shews that our document bears marks of very high antiquity. We next ask what ancient writers expressly speak of the *Didaché*, or manifest acquaintance with it, earlier than the appearance in its present shape of the *Apostolic Constitutions*, the first half of bk. vii. of which contains an expansion of the *Didaché*. The forger of this book was plainly acquainted with the whole *Didaché*; for he goes through it from beginning to end, making changes and additions, the study of which throws interesting light on the development of church ritual during the interval between the two works. Harnack has given good reasons for thinking that the same forger manipulated the *Didaché* and the Ignatian letters, and that his work may have been as early as A.D. 350. Hence the *Didaché* was by then an ancient document, but one in such small circulation that it could be tampered with without much fear of detection.

It is necessary here to notice the tract professing to contain apostolic constitutions, published by Bickell in 1843 and described *D. C. A.* i. 123. This is quite independent of and earlier than the work commonly known as the *Apostolic Constitutions*. The two forms employ some common earlier documents, but there is no reason to think that the framer of either was acquainted with the other. Bickel calls this tract *Apostolische Kirchenordnung*, and to avoid confusion with the *Apostolic Constitutions*, we refer to it as the *Church Ordinances*. It had been translated into various languages, and is the foundation of Egyptian Canon Law. It has so much in common with Bryennius's *Didaché* that either the *Church Ordinances* certainly used the *Didaché* or both drew from a common source. In form they differ; for in the *Ordinances* the precepts are distributed among different apostles by name, the list being peculiar, Cephas appearing as distinct from Peter; he and Nathanael taking the place of James the Less and Matthias. In substance the two works closely coincide, but only in the section on the "Two Ways."

Writers earlier than the *Apostolic Constitutions* know of a work which professed to contain the teaching of the apostles, but concerning them we cannot say with certainty whether the work to which they witness is the same as ours. The list of direct witnesses is indeed much shorter than it must have been if the work had obtained any wide acceptance as containing really apostolic instruction. Earliest is Eusebius, who to his list of canonical Scriptures (*H. E.* iii. 25) adds a list of spurious books of the better sort, recognized by church writers, and to be distinguished from writings which heretics had forged in the names of apostles. Among these he enumerates next after the Ep. of Barnabas, "what are called the Teachings of the Apostles" (τῶν ἀποστόλων αἱ λεγόμεναι διδαχαί). Some years later Athanasius (*Ep. Fest.* 39) adds to his list of canonical Scriptures a list of non-canonical books useful in the catechetical instruction of converts, viz. the Wisdom of Solomon, the Wisdom of Sirach, Esther, Judith, Tobit, the so-called Teaching of the Apostles (διδαχὴ καλουμένη τῶν ἀποστόλων), and the Shepherd. The only obstacle to our supposing our *Didaché* to be here referred to is the Eucharistic formulae it contains, which Athanasius would scarcely place in the hands of the uninitiated, unless indeed he thought them so unlike the truth as to make no revelation of Christian mysteries. It will be observed that Eusebius uses the plural (διδαχαί), Athanasius the singular. Unmistakable coincidences with the *Didaché* have been pointed out in writings ascribed to Athanasius, but rejected as spurious in the Benedictine ed., though the genuineness of at least the second of these is still urged: viz. *de Virginitate* (Migne, p. 266), *Syntagma Doctrinae ad Monaches* (p. 835), and *Fides Nicena* (p. 1639). Among the spurious writings printed with those of Athanasius is a *Synopsis Sacrae Scripturae*, which, because of its coincidences with the *Stichometry* of Nicephorus, Credner has dated as late as 10th cent. The *Stichometry* doubtless preserves an ancient list, and there among the apocryphal books appended to the N.T. Canon we find the διδαχὴ ἀποστόλων. Those that precede it are heretical apocrypha; but those that follow, viz. the Epp. of Clement, Ignatius, Polycarp, and the Shepherd, are all orthodox. The number of στίχοι attributed to the *Didaché* is 200; whereas 1,400 are assigned to the Revelation of St. John. Calculations founded on stichometry are uncertain; so we cannot lay much stress on the fact that this appears to indicate a somewhat shorter work than Bryennius's διδαχή, which according to Harnack would make about 300 στίχοι. and on a rough estimate seems about a quarter the length of the Apocalypse. A list of 60 books of Scripture appended to a writing of Anastasius, patriarch of Antioch in the reign of Justinian, is in Westcott's *N.T. Canon*, p. 550. This gives as an appendix a list of apocryphal books; one being the *Travels* (περίοδοι) *and Teachings* (διδαχαί) *of the Apostles*. The absence of the *Didaché* from the list of the *Codex Claromontanus* agrees with other indications that this work possessed no authority in Africa. In one of the fragments, published by Pfaff, as from Irenaeus, we read: "Those who have followed the *Second Ordinances of the Apostles* (οἱ ταῖς δευτέραις τῶν ἀποστόλων διατάξεσι παρηκολουθηκότες) know that our Lord instituted a new offering in the New Covenant according to the saying of Malachi the prophet, 'From the rising of the sun to the going down, my name has been glorified in the Gentiles; and in every place incense is offered to my name and a pure offering.'" This passage is quoted in the *Didaché* with reference to the Eucharist; not, however, textually, as in the fragment, but very loosely. We can only say then that it is *possible* the *Didaché* may be the *Second Ordinances of the Apostles* referred to here. The fragment is probably ancient, but contains a citation of *Hebrews* as St. Paul's, which proves, as Zahn and others have remarked, that Irenaeus could not have been the author.

Western testimony to the *Didaché* is scanty, and rather indicates that any book which circulated in the West as the *Teaching of the Apostles* was not the same as Bryennius's *Didaché*. Rufinus (*Comm. in Symb. Apost.* 38) gives a list of canonical books which bears marks of derivation from that of Athanasius; but where the *Didaché* should come he has "qui appellatur Duae Viae vel Judicium Petri." This suggests that either the entire *Didaché*, or at least the first half, the "Two Ways," had been translated into Latin and circulated under the name of the *Judgment of Peter*, to whom, and not to the apostles generally, the authorship would seem to have been ascribed. The existence of a Latin "Two Ways" is independently proved by the discovery of a fragment by von Gebhardt, reprinted in his *Texte und Untersuchungen*, ii. 277. It is so short as to leave it undetermined whether the Latin version contained anything corresponding to what follows the "Two Ways" in Bryennius. Lactantius (*Div. Instit.* vi. 3, etc., and *Epit.* c. 59) gives an unmistakable expansion of the teaching of the "Two Ways," who must have used our Latin version, thus proving it older than A.D. 310.

The treatise *de Aleatoribus*, falsely ascribed to Cyprian, contains a quotation from *Doctrina Apostolorum* (Hartel, ii. 96) not found in the *Didaché*, though there is one passage (xiv. 2) which might have suggested the idea to the framer of the Latin. If we may ever rely on the argument from silence, we should gather from Tertullian's discussion on the "Stations" (*de Orat.* 19, *de Jejun.* 2, 10, 14) that he was unacquainted with our document. Thus, scanty though the Western notices are, they seem to prove that the *Didaché*, in Bryennius's form, never circulated in the West; that the Latin *Doctrina Apostolorum*, even as regards the section on the "Two Ways," was not a translation of Bryennius's *Didaché*, but contained a different manipulation of a probably common original; and that beyond the "Two Ways" there is no evidence that the Latin form had anything in common with the *Didaché*.

We now come to coincidences with the *Didaché* in works which do not mention it by name. Far the most important of these are found in the Ep. of Barnabas, in which, after the conclusion of the doctrinal teaching, the writer proposes to pass to another doctrine and discipline (γνῶσιν καὶ διδαχήν), and adds an appendix of moral instructions. This appendix agrees so completely in substance with the section on the "Two Ways" that a literary connexion between the two documents is indisputable. But there is great diversity of detail. The precepts in Barnabas are without any orderly arrangement, while the *Didaché* contains a systematic comment on the second table of the Decalogue. Bryennius differs from later critics and some earlier ones who consider it probable that Barnabas was the borrower. The whole character of the *Didaché* makes it unlikely that its author collected the precepts scattered in Barnabas's appendix, digested them into systematic order, and made a number of harmonious additions; while if in what Barnabas says about the "Two Ways" he is but reproducing an older document, his unsystematic way of quoting its precepts, just as they came to mind, is quite like his mode of dealing with O.T. We have still to inquire whether Barnabas borrowed from the *Didaché* or from a common source. Now a study of the *Didaché*, as compared with Jewish literature, shews very clearly its origin among men with Jewish training, and the work from which both borrowed may have been not only Jewish but pre-Christian. For Barnabas's letter is of so early a date that, if we suppose him to have copied an earlier Christian document, we bring that document into the apostolic age, which would give it all the authority that has been claimed for it. We must, then, in comparing Barnabas with the *Didaché*, distinguish carefully the specially Christian element from those parts which might have been written by a Jew unacquainted with Christianity. If Barnabas copied the *Didaché*, he would have naturally included the Christian element. If Barnabas and the *Didaché* independently copied an originally Jewish document, the Christian elements they might add would not be likely to be the same. In the section in Barnabas we are struck by the extreme meagreness of the Christian element. There is no mention of our Lord, scarcely any coincidence with N.T. language, very little that might not have been written by a Jew before our Lord's coming. In the *Didaché* coincidences with N.T. are extremely numerous, and it begins with a whole section embodying precepts from the Sermon on the Mount. This section is entirely absent from Barnabas. It is impossible to resist the conclusion that Barnabas did not know the *Didaché* in Bryennius's form. He has elsewhere coincidences with N.T., and had no motive for avoiding them. If a book before him contained a number of N.T. precepts he would never have studiously avoided these in using the work, nor have forgotten them even if he wrote from memory. The coincidences between the two works, therefore, must be explained by the use of a common document.

This conclusion is confirmed on taking into the comparison also the Latin "Two Ways," and the Egyptian *Church Ordinances*, both of which, like Barnabas, do not recognize the *Didaché* section founded on the Sermon on the Mount. Neither is this section recognized in Pseudo-Athanasius. The *Church Ordinances* exhibit signs of acquaintance with Barnabas; the Latin form does not. In the order of the precepts the *Ordinances* and the Latin both agree with the *Didaché* against Barnabas. The *Ordinances* differ from the Latin by excess, but scarcely at all otherwise. The same reasons that forbid us to think that Barnabas, if he had known the *Didaché*, would have left out its Christian element, prove the *Ordinances* and the Latin likewise independent of the *Didaché*. The phenomena are explained if we assume an original document in substantial agreement with the Latin, enlarged in the *Didaché* by additions from N.T., and afterwards independently enlarged by the framer of the *Church Ordinances*, who broke it up into sections supposed to be spoken by different apostles; while Barnabas worked up in his own way the materials he drew from the document. We cannot say positively whether this original proceeded beyond the "Two Ways." The Latin fragment breaks off too soon to give any information as to the length of the original: the *Church Ordinances* cease to present coincidences with the *Didaché* after the section on the "Two Ways"; but this may be because the directions for ritual and discipline had become out of date when the *Ordinances* were put together, the editor therefore designedly substituting what better agreed with the practice of his own age. The quotation by Pseudo-Cyprian leads us to think that the Latin *Doctrina Apostolorum* did go beyond the "Two Ways." No great weight can be attached to the length ascribed to the *Didaché* in the *Stichometry*, but this rather favours the idea that the document intended was longer than the "Two Ways," but shorter than the *Didaché* of Bryennius.

It remains to be mentioned that there is a coincidence between Barnabas and the *Didaché* outside the "Two Ways." The opening of the Ep. of Barnabas and the last or eschatological chapter of the *Didaché* both contain the warning that the disciples' faith would not profit them unless they remained stedfast in the last times. There is a good deal of difference in the wording of the warning, but not more than is usual in quotations by Barnabas. The supposition that Barnabas was acquainted with Bryennius's form of the *Didaché* has already been excluded; therefore either (1) the earlier form which Barnabas did use included an eschatological chapter containing this warning, or (2) the editor who changed the earlier form into that of Bryennius was acquainted with the Ep. of Barnabas. We prefer (2), on account of the reasons we shall presently give for thinking the document used by Barnabas to have been pre-Christian. If the editor of Bryennius's form knew Hermas, he might also have known Barnabas, with whom he has a second coincidence in a passage about almsgiving, which, as implying a knowledge of Acts and Romans, Barnabas was not likely to have found in his original. Possibly there is a third coincidence; for a plausible explanation of the difficult word ἐκπέτασις in c. xvi. is that it means the sign of the cross, being derived from Barnabas's interpretation of ἐξεπέτασα in Is. lxv. 2.

Hermas also presents coincidences with the *Didaché*, but it is not easy to say that there is literary obligation on either side, except in one case, viz. a coincidence between the second "commandment" of Hermas and the "Sermon on the Mount" section, which we have already seen reason to think belongs to a later form of the *Didaché*. In this case the original seems clearly that of Hermas. His instructions as to almsgiving are perfectly clear. The corresponding passage in the *Didaché* has many coincidences of language, but expresses the thought so awkwardly as to be scarce intelligible without the commentary of Hermas. It begins, "Blessed is he that giveth according to the commandment, for he is blameless: woe to him that receiveth." The words "for he is blameless," as they stand, are puzzling; for we should expect the "for" to introduce something stronger than merely an acquittal of blame. By comparison with Hermas we see that the case contemplated is that of giving to an undeserving person. Then the receiver deserves the woe; the giver obtains an acquittal. We conclude, then, without disputing the greater antiquity of the original *Didaché*, that the interpolator who brought the work to the form published by Bryennius was later than Hermas, and drew from him.

Clement of Alexandria was certainly acquainted with the *Didaché* in some form. He expressly quotes one sentence as Scripture (*Strom.* i. 20, p. 377), "My son, be not a liar, for lying leads to theft." This saying is not quoted by Barnabas; but the *Church Ordinances* attest that it belongs to the earlier form of the *Didaché*. Even the later form of the *Didaché* may well be considerably older than Clement; and he might easily have met with a copy during his travels in the East. He uses (*Quis Dives Salv.* 20) the phrase "vine of David," found in one of the benedictory prayers of the *Didaché*. He shews a knowledge (*Strom.* vii. 7, p. 854) of the Wednesday and Friday fasts (c. 12, p. 877), but does not seem to attribute to these institutions the authority which belongs to the name Scripture bestowed by him on the *Didaché*.

Origen was later than Clement and must have been well acquainted with the literature current in Egypt and Palestine; so that we might naturally expect him to be familiar with the *Didaché*. Yet no satisfactory proof of his knowledge of it has been produced.

Place of Composition.—The *Church Ordinances*, at the basis of which lies the *Didaché* in some form, are with good reason regarded as of Egyptian origin; Clement, one of the earliest to quote the *Didaché*, wrote in Egypt, and so very possibly did Barnabas. Hence, it was natural to think that the *Didaché* also is of Egyptian origin. But attention was called to the petition in the prayer of benediction of the bread, that as it had been scattered *on the mountains*, and collected together had become one, so the church might be collected together from the ends of the earth into the Lord's kingdom; and it was pointed out the words "on the mountains" could not have been written in Egypt; and, moreover, the proper inference from the use made of the *Didaché* in the *Church Ordinances* is that when the latter work was put together, the former was almost unknown in Egypt. There is nothing to contradict the inference suggested by the intensely Jewish character of the book, that it emanated from Christian Jews who, after the destruction of Jerusalem, had their chief settlements E. of Jordan.

Time of Composition.—The theory set forth is that the original, alike of Barnabas and of all the forms of the *Didaché*, was a Jewish manual for the instruction of proselytes. If Palestinian Christians had habitually used such a manual while still Jews, it would be natural for them to employ it, improved by the addition of some Christian elements, in the moral instruction of converts before admission into the church. The document, being a formula in constant practical use, would be added to and modified; and we seem to be able to trace three stages in its growth.

(1) Barnabas represents for us the original Jewish manual; probably quoting, not from any written document, but from his recollection of the instruction he had himself received or had been given to others. Barnabas's quotations do not proceed beyond the section on the "Two Ways," corresponding to cc. i.-iv. of the *Didaché*.

(2) In the *Church Ordinances* and in the Latin *Doctrina* we have the manual as it was modified for use in a Christian community. The Latin book may have been the first publication of this catechetical manual of Palestinian Christians, brought to the West by one himself instructed in it. It was probably called the *Teaching of the Apostles*, because the authorized formulary of a church founded by apostles and claiming to derive its institutions from them. We are without evidence whether this manual contained more than the "Two Ways," though it probably did. The only clue to the date of this publication is that the *Church Ordinances* contain that precept about almsgiving which we have already noted as the solitary instance of use of the N.T. in this section of Barnabas. Reasons have been already given for thinking that Barnabas was not here employing a Christian document, and we find it hard to believe that the phrases in which coincidences occur are older than N.T., so we seem forced to conclude that the first editors of the *Teaching of the Apostles* knew Barnabas. This would not be inconsistent with a date before the end of 1st cent.

(3) In the *Didaché* published by Bryennius we have the manual enlarged by further Christian additions; the precepts in the original manual being expanded, others added from N.T., and also some wholly new sections. Yet the whole character of the *Didaché*, and in particular the lively expectation of our Lord's Second Coming in c. xvi., disposes us to give it in its present form as early a date as we can; and since we place Hermas at the beginning of 2nd cent., we have no difficulty in dating the *Didaché* as early as A.D. 120.

Literature.—The publication of the *Didaché* by Bryennius produced an enormous crop of literature. The lists in Schaff's and in Harnack's editions may be supplemented by an article of Harnack's *Theol. Literaturz.* 1886, p. 271. Here we only mention, of editions, those by De Romestan (1884), Spence (1885), Schaff (1885 and 1886), Sabatier (1885), Hilgenfeld in a 2nd ed. of pt. iv. of his *Nov. Test. ext. Can.* (1884), and by Gebhardt and Harnack, *Texte und Untersuchungen*, vol. ii. (1884). Bp. Lightfoot's paper at the Church Congress of 1884, pub. in the *Expositor*, Jan. 1885; Zahn's discussions in his *Forschungen*, pt. iii. p. 278 (1884), and Taylor's Lectures at the Royal Institution, 1885, in which the *Didaché* is illustrated from Jewish literature. A new ed. with a fascimile (autotype) text and a commentary from the MS. of the Holy Sepulchre, Jerusalem, ed. by J. R. Harris, is pub. by Camb. Univ. Press, as is also an Eng. trans. from the Syriac by Dr. Margaret Gibson; while S.P.C.K. pub. an Eng. trans. with intro. and notes by Dr. C. Bigg. See also Bigg's *Notes on the Didaché* in *Journ. of Theol. Stud.*, July 1904. [G.S.]

Teilo, bp. of Llandaff and one of the principal saints of Wales, was son of Enlleu ap Hydwn Dwn and cousin to St. David. He was born near Tenby, and educated with St. David and other celebrated Welsh saints. He opened a school near Llandaff, called Bangor Deilo, and on account of his proficiency in the Scriptures is said to have received the name Elios or Eliud. His withdrawal to Armorica on the outbreak of the yellow plague in Wales is counted by Pryce (*Anc. Brit. Ch.* 163) one of the few incidents in his life which can be considered historical. In the *Chron. Series of the Bpp. of Llandaff* (*Lib. Landav.* by Rees, 623) he is said to have become bp. of Llandaff in 512, so that Rees (*Welsh SS.* 243) is probably safest in saying that his period in that see ended in its first stage with the appearance of the plague. [DUBRICIUS.]

Returning from Armorica after a stay, as is said, of 7 years and 7 months, he found St. David dead and the see of Menevia vacant. St. Teilo is said to have been elected to the vacant chair as archbp. of Menevia, but, preferring his old see, he consecrated Ishmael, one of St. David's earliest disciples, to be his suffragan at Menevia, raised others to the same rank in different parts of South Wales, while he himself removed to Llandaff, and, carrying with him the primacy, became archbp. with the title of the inferior see (Stubbs, *Reg.* 154, 156; Haddan and Stubbs, *Counc.* i. 115 seq.; Rees, *Welsh SS.* 174, 243 seq.; Pryce, *Anc. Br. Ch.* 158 seq.). The date of his death is variously fixed from 563 (*Lib.*

Land. 623) to 604 (Ussher). He is said to have died at a very advanced age.

The chief authority for his Life is *Vita S. Teliavi Episcopi a Magistro Galfrido Fratre Urbani Landavensis Ecclesiae Episcopi dicata*, belonging to 12th cent., and printed, with trans. and notes, in *Lib. Land.* by Rees, 92 seq., 332 seq. For MS. and other authorities see Hardy, Desc. Cat. i. pt. i. 130-132, pt. ii. 897, app.; Haddan and Stubbs, *Counc.* i. 146, app. C. 159. [J.G.]

Telesphorus (2), bp. of Rome, accounted the 7th from the apostles. According to Eusebius (*H. E.* iv. 5) he succeeded Xystus in the 12th year of Hadrian (A.D. 128), and suffered martyrdom in the 11th year of his episcopate and the 1st of the reign of Antoninus Pius (iv. 10). Lipsius (*Chron. der röm. Bischöf.*) considers his earliest probable dates to have been 124 to 135 or 126 to 137 as the latest. If so, Eusebius erred in placing his martyrdom in the reign of Antoninus Pius instead of Hadrian. For the fact of his martyrdom he alleges the authority of Irenaeus; the assertion of the date is his own. Telesphorus is remarkable as being the only one of the early Roman bishops, afterwards accounted martyrs, who appears on the early authority of Irenaeus as such (Iren. *Haer.* iii.; cf. Eus. *l.c.*). [J.B—Y.]

Tertullianus (1), Quintus Septimius Florens.

I. Life.—The earliest of the great Latin Fathers, their chief in fire and daring, and the first to create a technical Christian Latinity, is known almost entirely through his writings. It can only be conjectured that he was born between A.D. 150 and 160, and died between 220 and 240, with preference for the later dates. He was born at Carthage (Hieron. *Catal. Script. Eccl.* 53; cf. Tertull. *Apol.* c. ix.) of heathen parents (*de Poen.* c. i.; *Apol.* c. xviii. "de vestris sumus"), his father being a proconsular centurion (Hieron.). Tertullian received a good education (*Apol.* c. xiv.; *adv. Prax.* c. iii.). In after-life he recalled his school studies in Homer (*ad Nat.* i. c. x.); but poetry attracted him less than philosophy, history, science, and antiquarian lore. He spoke and composed in Greek, but his Greek writings are lost. He studied the systems of the philosophers if he mocked and hated the men (cf. *de Anima*, cc. i.-iii.). Possibly destined for state-official life, he was celebrated for his knowledge of Roman law (Eus. *H. E.* ii. 2), and the legal fence and juridical style of the advocate are observable throughout his apologetic and polemical writings.

He was probably attracted to Christianity by complex irresistible and converging forces: "Fiunt, non nascuntur Christiani" (*Apol.* c. xviii.). The constancy of the Christians in times of persecution staggered him. He knew men who began by denouncing such "obstinacy," and ended in embracing the belief which dictated it (*Apol.* c. l.; *ad Scap.* c. v.). Demons confessed the superiority of the new faith (*Apol.* c. xxiii.), and Tertullian, in common with his heathen and Christian contemporaries, was a profound believer in demons (cf. Réville, *La Religion à Rome sous les Sévères*, pp. 44, 46, 130 seq.). These facts led him to examine the faith which seemed to promise a foothold which no philosophical system furnished. It was illustrated by a life of holiness and humility—that of its Founder, the Just One—in contrast with which the life of the Cynic and the Stoic sickened him.

His conversion took place *c.* 192, in Carthage more probably than in Rome. Carthage was his home and usual dwelling-place (*de Pallio*, c. i.; *Apol.* c. ix.; *Scorpiace*, c. vi.; *de Resur. Carnis*, c. xlii.); Rome he had visited (*de Cultu Femin.* i. c. vii.), and he was well known there for his abilities (Eus. *l.c.*), but critics are by no means agreed whether he ever went there as a Christian (cf. Baron. *Annal. Eccl.* ii. 476, ed. Theiner). He was married but childless (cf. the two treatises *ad Uxorem*), and became a priest of the church. He probably exercised his presbyterate at Carthage and not at Rome.

In middle age (*c.* 119-203), says Jerome, Tertullian became a Montanist, his constitution and temperament predisposing him to a rigour opposed to the laxity prevalent at Rome, and so finding the austere doctrines and practices of Montanus perfectly congenial (Kaye, *Account of the Writings of Tertullian*,[3] p. 34). He became the head of the Montanist party in Africa—a party which existed till the 5th cent. under the name of "Tertullianists."

II. Times.—The golden age of the empire died with Marcus Aurelius (161-180); the age of iron began with his son Commodus (180-193). The golden age of the church began with that iron age of the empire (Aubé, *Les Chrétiens dans l'empire romain*, A.D. 180-249, pp. iii, 495-498). Expiring polytheism and ancient philosophy were confronted by a new philosophy and a nascent faith.

From one quarter only of the empire was the comparative peacefulness noticeable elsewhere absent. In Africa persecution, sharp, short, fitful, and frequent, marked the reign of Septimius Severus and the most active period of Tertullian's life. It is stamped in letters of blood upon his pages.

The church in Africa has no historian before Tertullian, though its foundation is placed, with much probability, at the end of cent. i. or the beginning of cent. ii. By the end of cent. ii. the Christians in Roman Africa were to be counted by thousands (cf. Aubé, p. 152) if not by millions (cf. *Apol.* c. xxxvii.; *ad Scapulam*, cc. ii. v.). They were fully organized and had their bishops, priests, deacons, places of assembly, and cemeteries. Immunity from the wholesale decimation which had befallen, by imperial command (cf. *Apol.* c. v.), other Christian bodies of the East and West, allowed in Africa growth and development, accelerated by occasional suffering and martyrdom. But the tempest broke upon the African church at last.

Facts connected with the persecutions can be followed in those writings of Tertullian which all critics place between A.D. 197 and 212, from the *ad Martyres* to the *ad Scapulam*.

The tract *ad Martyres* depicts men and women in prison, visited and relieved by the brethren, exhorted to unity, and prepared by fasting and prayer for the death which should be a victory for the church. Vigellius Saturninus was the first proconsul to draw the sword against Christians (*ad Scapulam*, c. iii.), and his date is not apparently earlier than 198 (see Aubé, p. 191, etc.). The martyrology of Africa had begun in 180. In a time of peace the Scillitan martyrs had died at Carthage (Görres, *Jahr. f. Prot. Theol.* 1884, pts. ii. iii.); but after that there is a blank till 198, when Namphamo was the new "archimartyr" of the church. A few months' respite followed. It was disturbed by an event which is with some plausibility alleged to have taken place at Carthage. A certain soldier refused the *donativum* of Severus and Caracalla, publicly declined the laurel crown accepted by his fellow-soldiers, and proclaimed himself a Christian. The incident is described in the *de Corona*; Tertullian, making it a test case, debated whether the Christian could accept military service. His advice, and the conduct founded upon it, infuriated the heathen. Under Hilarian (202-203) persecution broke out again. It took the special form of refusing the Christian dead their usual place of burial; the cry invaded the proconsul's tribune, "Areae non sint!" ("No cemeteries for the Christians!"). Just then the decree issued in 202 by Severus indirectly if not directly gave sanction to all measures of repression. It forbad proselytizing by either Jew or Christian. It was easy, were the African proconsul so minded, to read into this purely prohibitive measure a licence to persecute. The "fight of martyrdom and the baptism of blood" which ensued is perhaps to be traced in Tertullian's *de Fuga* and *Scorpiace* (between 202-212). These treatises are fiercely scornful against the flight once counselled when persecution raged. The *de Fuga* (c. v.) denounces, not less angrily, a growing practice—purchase of immunity. Of sterner mould and of more loving faith were the brothers Satyrus and Saturninus, the slaves Revocatus and Felicitas, and the nobly-born and nobly-wedded Perpetua. The Acts of their passion, by some (*e.g.* Bonwetsch and Salmon) attributed to Tertullian himself, have preserved a picture of the times—a reluctant proconsul, all-willing martyrs, and a scoffing crowd saluting their baptism of blood with the mocking cry, "Salvum lotum" (see the Acts in Migne's *Patr. Lat.* iii., and Aubé's collation, *op. cit.* pp. 221-224, 509, etc.).

Again there came a respite, and again must the character of the proconsul have been instrumental in securing it. Of Julius Asper (proconsul in 205 or 206) it is told that not only did he refuse to force a Christian to sacrifice who under the torture had lapsed from the faith, but publicly expressed regret to his assessors and the advocates at having to deal with such cases (*ad Scapulam,* c. iv.). For five or six years persecution was stayed, years of literary activity on the part of Tertullian. In 211, for some unknown reason, the religious war broke out afresh, and its cruel if brief progress is told in the *ad Scapulam.* Tertullian's last "Apology" is worthy of the Christian gladiator. Stroke upon stroke he deals his ponderous blows against the proconsul. "We battle with your cruelty," he cries; but his weapons are the "offensive" weapons which Christ had put in his hands—prayer for the persecutors, love for enemies (Matt. v. 44). God's judgments, he warns them, were abroad. Drought, fires, eclipses, declared His wrath; the miserable deaths of persecuting proconsuls betokened it. "This our sect shall never fail," is his triumphant shout. "Strike it down, it will rise the more. We recompense to no man evil for evil, but we warn you—Fight not against God!"

In 212 the blessing of peace rested again upon Africa and continued for some years.

III. Writings.—Tertullian's literary activity is by some confined to 197-212; by others, with far greater probability, it is extended to at least *c.* 223. A general chronological arrangement only is possible, the dates given being few and uncertain. The only work which supplies positive evidence of date is the first book *adv. Marcionem* (3rd ed.). In c. xv. Tertullian says he is writing in the 15th year of Severus, now considered to be A.D. 207 (Bonwetsch, *Die Schriften Tertullians nach der Zeit ihrer Abfassung,* p. 42). Tertullian was then a Montanist, but his pen had for some years been employed in behalf of the church.

Tertullian's writings represent him variously as layman, priest, and schismatic; and divide broadly into works written in the Catholic or Montanist periods of his life. The latter must further be subdivided into treatises in which Catholic or schismatic elements are respectively prominent. In character they are threefold: (*a*) Apologetic; (*b*) Dogmatic and polemical; (*c*) Moral and ascetic. The arrangements of Bp. Kaye and Bonwetsch have in the main suggested that which follows; though the dates attached are in almost all cases conjectural.

(1) Works written while still in the church: (*a*) Apologetic writings (*c.* 197-198): *ad Martyres; Apologeticum; de Testimonio Animae; ad Nationes,* i. ii; *adv. Judaeos.*

(*b*) Other works of this period, but of less certain date: *de Oratione; de Baptismo; de Poenitentia; de Spectaculis; de Cultu Feminarum,* i.; *de Idololatria; de Cultu Feminarum,* ii.; *de Patientia; ad Uxorem,* i. ii. (the last five *c.* 197-199); *de Praescriptione Haereticorum* (*c.* 199); *adv. Marcionem* i. (1st ed.), *c.* 200.

(2) Montanistic writings:—

(*a*) Defending the church and her teachings (*c.* 202-203): *de Corona; de Fuga in Persecutione; de Exhortatione Castitatis.*

(*b*) Defending the Paraclete and His discipline: *de Virginibus Velandis* (*c.* 203-204, a transition work); *adv. Marcion.* (2nd ed.; *c.* 206); *ib.* (3rd ed.; *c.* 207). Between 200-207 or later: *adv. Hermogenem; adv. Valentinianos; adv. Marcion.* (iv.); *de Carne Christi; de Resurrectione Carnis; adv. Marcion.* (v.). *De Pallio* and *de Anima* (*c.* 208-209); *Scorpiace* (*c.* 212; *al.* 203 or 204); *ad Scapulam* (*c.* 212). Three *c.* 217, *al.* 203-207: *de Monogamia; de Jejunio; de Pudicitia;* and *adv. Praxean* (*c.* 223, *al. c.* 208-209).

A. *Tertullian, Layman and Apologist.—Ad Martyres.*—Two thoughts (c. iii.) should animate the martyrs. (1) Christians were soldiers, "called to the military service of the living God" by a sacramental oath, to which they must be true. (2) They were Christian athletes whose prison was their training-school (*palaestra*), where "virtus duritia extruitur, mollitia vero destruitur." The words of Christ (Matt. xxvi. 41) should help them to subject the flesh to the spirit, the weaker to the stronger; the example of the heathens, Lucretia and Mucius, Heraclitus and Peregrinus, Dido and the wife of Hasdrubal, would teach them to count their sufferings trifling if, by enduring them, they might obtain a heavenly glory and a divine reward. In their own day many persons of birth, rank, and age had met their death at the hands of the emperor. Should Christians hesitate to suffer as much in the cause of God?

Apologeticum.—This Apology—the greatest of his works—was a cry for bare justice.

(1) A heading to c. i., "Quod religio Christiana damnanda non sit, nisi qualis sit prius intelligatur," sums up its protest: The rulers of Carthage were persecuting and condemning a "sect" which forthcoming evidence proved unworthy of condemnation. Their conduct was the reverse of that enjoined by the emperor Trajan—that Christians were not to be sought out; but if brought before Pliny were to be punished. Tertullian reminds the rulers (c. v.) that the laws against Christians had been enforced only by emperors whose memory men had learnt to execrate: *e.g.* Nero and Domitian. Not such as these was Tiberius (cf. Eus. *H. E.* ii. 2), in whose day Christ came into the world (cf. c. vii.), and who had desired the senate to admit Him among the Roman deities. Marcus Aurelius was a *protector*. Not even Hadrian, Vespasian, Pius, nor Verus had put into force the laws against Christians. The men who were demanding this were daily and contemptuously infringing laws of all kinds. In proof he draws a sad picture of luxury and immorality. The good old laws had gone which encouraged in women modesty and sobriety.

(2) Chaps. vii.-ix. What were the charges against the Christians? "We are called miscreants"—and the evidence was only rumour! "Fama malum, quo non aliud velocius ullum." It was, Tertullian retorts, the existence (secret or open) of evil practices among the heathen which explained their belief in similar deeds among Christians.

(3) Chaps. x.-xxvii. Tertullian faces the first of the two great charges, "sacrilege and treason." His "apology" as regards the former consists, briefly speaking, of (*a*) "demonstratio religionis eorum" (cc. x.-xvi. xxiv.-xxvii.) and of (*b*) "demonstratio religionis nostrae" (cc. xvii.-xxiii.), a most valuable *evidential* passage.

(*a*) You Christians, said the heathen, do not worship our gods. No, said Tertullian, and we won't, because we do not recognize them to be gods. They were nothing but men of long ago, whose merits should have plunged them into the depths of Tartarus. How much better would it have been if the *deus deificus* had waited and taken up to heaven in their place such men as Socrates, Aristides, Themistocles, and others. The images excite Tertullian's intense scorn, as "the homes of hawks and mice and spiders." Caustically does he describe the heathen treatment of their household gods. "You pledge them, sell them, change them. They wear out or get broken, and you turn your Saturn into a cooking-pot and your Minerva into a ladle! You put your national gods in a sale-catalogue; and the man who will sell you herbs in the herb-market will sell you gods at the Capitol. Or what could be more insulting than the company you give them? You worship Larentina, the prostitute, together with Juno or Ceres or Diana. You erect (at Rome) a statue to SIMON MAGUS and give him as inscription the title of *sanctus deus* (see Kaye's *Tertull.* p. 542, and Oehler's note here). You turn into a god a sodomite like Antinous" (see Kellner's note).

What then, it was asked, did Christians worship if not the gods? Tertullian answers, "Take in this first of all: they who are not worshippers of a lie are worshippers of truth." From this might be deduced the whole of the Christian religious belief. But before Tertullian proceeds to do this, he refutes some very false, but common, opinions about the Christians, *e.g.* the vulgar belief that the god of the Christians was an ass's head, that they worshipped the cross, or the sun. Lately a *bestiarius* (see Semler's and Kellner's notes) had exhibited a picture at Rome inscribed *Deus Christianorum* ονοκοιτης. The figure had the ears of an ass, one foot was hoofed, in his hand was a book, and he was dressed in a toga (see *D. C. A. s.n.* "Asinarii"). The name and the form only made us laugh, says Tertullian; and then he retorts: "But our opponents might well have worshipped such a biformed deity: for they have dog-headed and lion-headed gods, gods with horns, gods with wings, gods goat-limbed, fish-limbed, or serpent-limbed from the loins!"

(*b*) Tertullian turns from what Christianity was not to what it was, and the main lines of the evidences of Christianity in the 2nd cent. are still those of our own. These chapters (xvii.-xxiii.), so valuable in the history of religious belief, deserve the student's close attention. The eloquence, fervour, humility, and devoutness of the writer will be felt to be contagious. Irony and passion are comparatively absent. The section details (b_1) the nature and attributes of the Creator, (b_2) the mission of the prophets, men full of (*inundati*) the Holy Spirit, (b_3) the character of the Scriptures, and (b_4) the history of the Lord. Under b_3 Tertullian notes two things. These Scriptures were marked, first, by that *antiquity* which his opponents rightly valued. The most ancient heathen writings were far less ancient than those of Moses, the contemporary of the Argive Inachus, and (as some thought) 500 years older than Homer. Nay, the very last prophet was coeval with the first of the (heathen) philosophers, lawgivers, and historians. "Quod prius est, semen sit necesse est." Secondly, the Scriptures were marked by *majesty*. "Divinas probamus (*scripturas*), si dubitatur antiquas." This *internal* evidence was a proof of their antiquity, while the *external* and daily fulfilment of prophecy was a reason for expecting the verification of what was not yet fulfilled.

b_4 is in answer to the questions, Why did Jews and Christians differ? Did not these differences argue worship of different gods? Tertullian's reply (c. xxi.) is a history of the origin of the Christian sect and name, and an account of the Founder of Christianity, such as we have in the Gospels. His account is interspersed with most interesting statements, *e.g.* the Jewish inference from the humility of Christ that He was only man, and from His miraculous power that He was a magician, and not the Logos of God; the record of the darkening of the sun at the crucifixion preserved in the secret archives of the empire; the reason for the seclusion of the Lord after the resurrection, viz. "that the wicked should be freed from their error, and that faith destined for so glorious a reward should be established upon difficulty"; his own opinion that Caesars (such as Tiberius) would have believed in Christ, if they could have been Caesars and Christians at the same time; the sufferings of the disciples at the hands of the Jews; and at last, through Nero's cruelty, the sowing the seed of Christianity at Rome in their blood (cf. c. l.). He concludes: "Deum colimus per Christum." Count Him a mere man if you like. By Him and in Him God wishes to be known and worshipped.

One more point remained. Romans considered their position as masters of the world the reward of their religious devotion to their gods, and affirmed that they who paid their gods the most service flourished the most. Tertullian traverses this "assumption" in ironical terms, or meets it with positive denial.

(4) Chaps. xxviii.-xxxvi.—The charge *laesae augustioris majestatis* is now reached. The evil spirits stirred up the heathen to compel Christians to sacrifice *pro salute imperatoris*; and that compulsion was met by resistance not less determined. Ironically does Tertullian commend in the heathen the dread with which they regarded Caesar as more profound and reverential than that which they accorded to the Olympian Jupiter. Christians were counted *publici hostes*, because they would not pay to the emperor vain, lying, or unseemly honours; and because, as *verae religionis homines*, they kept the festival days not lasciviously, but as conscientious men. Truly if public joy was to be expressed by public shame, the Christians deserved condemnation.

(5) Chaps. xxxvii.-xlv.—This section, dealing with minor points of objection to the Christians, opens with an impassioned protest on behalf of men who, actuated by the principle "Idem sumus imperatoribus qui et vicinis nostris," never took vengeance for the wrongs done to them. Mob-law had attacked them with stones and fire, or with Bacchanalian fury had torn their dead from the graves to rend their bodies asunder. Had Christianity tolerated repaying evil with evil, what secret vengeance could have been wrought in a single night with a torch or two! Or, had they determined to act as open enemies, what numbers and resources would they have had! "We are but of yesterday," is Tertullian's proud boast (cf. c. i.), "and yet we have filled your cities, fortresses, towns, assemblies, camp, palace, senate, and forum: *sola vobis reliquimus templa*. Should we determine to separate from you and betake ourselves to some remote corner of the globe, your loss of so many citizens would cover you with shame. The solitude, silence, and stupor as of a dead world would fill you with fear. You would have to seek subjects to govern. Your enemies would be more numerous than your citizens. At present it is your Christian citizens who make your enemies so few." Tertullian therefore asks that Christians should be admitted "inter licitas factiones." The "sect" was incapable of any such acts as were dreaded in forbidden societies. If they had indeed their own occupations (*negotia*), why should that give offence? For what were the "negotia Christianae factionis"? (c. xxxix.). Tertullian's answer is a touching picture of the simple Christendom of his day. "We are a body linked together by a common religious profession, by unity of discipline, and by a common hope. We meet as a congregation and pray to God in united supplication. *Haec vis Deo grata est.* We pray for the emperors, their ministers, and those in authority, for the welfare of the world, for peaceful times, and for the delaying of the end (see c. xxxii.). We come together to listen to our Holy Scriptures (cf. Just. Mart. *Apol.* ii.); and by holy words we nourish faith, raise hope, stablish confidence, and strengthen discipline. Our presidents are elders of approved character, who have obtained this honour not by purchase but by desert. On the monthly day appointed each gives to the chest what he likes; the money is disbursed not in feasting and drinking, but in supporting and burying the poor, in providing for destitute orphan boys and girls, in supporting the aged, the infirm, and the shipwrecked, and in succouring those sent to the mines or incarcerated in prisons *ex causa Dei sectae*."

(6) Chaps. xlvi.-l.—Accusations had been met and the case of the Christian stated. What remained? One last perversion on the part of unbelief: "Christianity was no divine institution, but simply a kind of philosophy." The refutation of this closes the *Apology*. Tertullian, if frequently satirical, is at first grave and dignified, sober and patient, more than is his wont; but the smouldering fire bursts out at last; his last chapter is a climax of withering scorn and impassioned appeal.

Ad Nationes (i. ii.) is practically a short form of the *Apology*. It covers the same ground, uses the same arguments and largely the same language. But the *Apologv* was addressed to the rulers and magistrates of Carthage, this to the people. Its whole cast is consequently more popular, its arguments less prolonged, its illustrations less reserved (cf. I. cc. iv. viii. xvi.; II. c. xi.).

De Testimonio Animae was written very soon after the *Apology*, to which it refers (c. v.). Some have thought it the most original and acute of his works (see Neander, *Antignosticus*, p. 259). Many of his predecessors, says Tertullian (c. i.), had ransacked heathen literature to discover in it support of the Christian efforts to expel error and admit equity. The attempt was, in his opinion, a mistake and a failure. He would not repeat it. Neither would he adduce Christian writings when dealing with heathen, for nobody consulted them unless already a Christian. Therefore he turns to another and a new testimony, that of the soul. Apostrophizing it, he cries, "Thou art not, so far as I know, Christian. The soul is not born Christian [cf. *Apol.* xviii.], but becomes Christian. Yet Christians beg now for a testimony from thee, as from one outside them; a testimony against thine own that the heathen may blush for their hatred and mockery of us." The testimony of the soul to God is found in popular phrases indicative of knowledge and fear of God; then it is adjured to speak about immortality and the resurrection of the body (c. iv.; cf. *Apol.* xlviii.).

Adversus Judaeos.—The authenticity and integrity of the treatise, as usually printed, have both been disputed; the latter with justice, the former needlessly, and principally on account of the discredit attaching to the latter portion. Chaps. i.-viii. are certainly Tertullian's, written while still a churchman. The latter chapters are different, both in character and style. The treatise was occasioned by a dispute between a Christian and a heathen converted, not to Christianity but to Judaism. Practically, the question between them was the exclusion or not of Gentiles from the promises of God. But there was a preliminary question. Was any one expected, and if expected, had any one come, "novae legislator, sabbati spiritalis cultor, sacrificiorum aeternorum antistes, regni aeterni aeternus dominator," or was His advent still matter of hope? (c. vii.). The fulfilment of prophecy rightly understood was the answer. Tertullian does not need to prove that the Christ should come. Every Jew believed and hoped it. Is. xlv. 1 was sufficient proof of it. [He renders the passage differently from the present Hebrew text, and with one especially interesting variation, reading, "Thus saith the Lord God to my Christ the Lord (Κυρίῳ)," etc., instead of "to Cyrus Κύρῳ) His anointed," etc. So also in *adv. Prax.* cc. xi. xxviii.] In the then fulfilment of this prophecy he sees the proof that the Christ had come. Upon whom but upon Christ had the nations believed?—nations such as (*int. al.*) Moors, Spaniards, Gauls, Britons, "inhabiting places inaccessible to the Romans but subjugated to Christ" (in the same chapter he speaks of them as "shut up within the circuit of their own seas"), Germans and others, unknown to him, and too numerous to mention. Christ reigned everywhere, was adored everywhere: "omnibus aequalis, omnibus rex, omnibus judex, omnibus Deus et Dominus est."

B. *Tertullian the Priest.*—Tertullian had hitherto written as a layman. The writings now to be considered indicate more or less directly that he had become a priest (cf. *de Baptismo*, cc. xvii. xviii.). Persecution was for a time suspended. It is highly probable that about this time a synod of African bishops met at Carthage to discuss matters affecting the organization, discipline, and teaching of the church; and the occasion may have been used to ordain one who, as an "apologist," had proved himself so fearless a champion of the church. Questions concerning heretical baptism, and the attitude of the church towards the heretical sects, were very probably discussed, and Tertullian's lost treatise on heretical baptism was written in Greek to circulate the synod's decisions beyond the confines of the African church.

Other points, however, dealing with Christian life and ethics, came before him in his work in Carthage as a priest. The flock looked to their pastors for guidance: prayer, baptism, repentance, and the discipline connected with them; woman's dress and woman's life, married or unmarried; pleasures, amusements, how far lawful or unlawful,—all were matters upon which direction was desirable, and to all does Tertullian apply himself. Roughly divided, the treatises were practical and doctrinal, but the division must not be pressed too closely.

(1) *Practical Treatises.—De Oratione.* (*a*) Of the Lord's Prayer specifically (cc. i.-xi.); (*b*) of prayer generally—times, places, and customs (cc. xii.-end).

(*a*) As Christ was Spirit, Word, and Reason, so His prayer was formed of three parts: the word by which it was expressed, the spirit by which alone it had power, the reason by which it was appropriated (the reading is disputed); and the practice of prayer was recommended with three injunctions: that it should be offered up in secret, marked by modesty of faith," and distinguished by brevity. It was in very truth "breviarium totius evangelii." It is reckoned as containing seven clauses, the doxology not being given; and each clause is considered separately. The comments are reflections rather than interpretations; and if unequal and sometimes fanciful, they are very beautiful and can never be read without profit. His own summary (c. ix.) is a mine of spiritual thought. He approves of other prayers being used corresponding with the special circumstances of him who prays, but never to the omission of this, the regular and set form of prayer.

(*b*) Certain ceremonies, "empty" (*vacuae*) Tertullian calls them, but illustrative of many an interesting point of ritual and practice of the time, are next considered: Washing the hands before prayer; praying with the cloak taken off; sitting after prayer; the kiss of peace; the "Stations" (c. xix.; see Oehler's note); the dress of women, and veiling or non-veiling of virgins; kneeling in prayer; place and time of prayer; prayer when brethren met or parted; prayer and psalm. The closing chapter, dealing with the power and effect of prayer, is one of the gems of Tertullian's writings. "Never," he cries, "let us walk unarmed by prayer. Under the arms of prayer guard we the standard of our emperor; in prayer await we the angel's trump. Angels pray; every creature prays. 'Quid amplius? Etiam ipse Dominus oravit.'"

De Baptismo.—One Quintilla, "a viper of the Cainite heresy," had sought to destroy baptism. "What good could water do? Was it to be believed that a man could go down into the water, have a few words spoken over him, and rise again the gainer of eternity?" (see c. vi.). Quintilla was apparently a Gnostic, and the very simplicity of the means of grace repelled her. "Miratur simplicia quasi vana, magnifica quasi impossibilia." Her sneers had corrupted some; others were disturbed by such doubts as, Why was baptism necessary? Abraham was justified without it. The Christ Himself did not baptize. No mention was made in Scripture of the baptism of the apostles; St. Paul himself was bidden not to practise it.

Answers had to be given, lest catechumens should perish through lack of right instruction.

(*a*) The foundation for the sacrament (*religionem*) of baptism Tertullian finds in (cc. i.-ix.) the history of the creation. The hovering of the Spirit of God over the waters was typical of baptism; and water still, after invocation of God, furnished the sacrament of sanctification. Shortly but beautifully he describes the baptismal ceremonies (cf. *de Spect.* c. iv.), notes the types and figures of baptism in O.T., and the testimony to baptism in the life and passion of the Lord.

(*b*) Larger questions acquiescing in the necessity of baptism awaited consideration.

(i) *Heretical Baptism.*—Christians held firmly to a belief in one God, one Baptism, one Church. This unity was, as regards baptism, imperilled by heretical baptism. The *ademptio communicationis* (by some = deprivation of communion; by others = excommunication) stamped heretics as strangers. "We and they have not the same God, nor one [*i.e.* the same] Christ. Therefore we and they have not one [*i.e.* the same] baptism. What [baptism] they have, they have it not rightly, and therefore have not baptism at all." On these grounds he rejected heretical baptism. On the whole subject consult *Libr. of the Fath.* x. pp. 280 seq.

(ii) *Second Baptism.*—The belief and practice of the church Tertullian states thus: "We enter the font but once; our sins are washed away but once, because they ought not to be repeated." The Christian had, nevertheless, a second baptism, viz. the Baptism of Blood (cf. Luke xii. 50). Two baptisms had Christ sent forth from the wounds in His pierced side, that they who believed in His Blood might be washed with water, and that they who had been washed with water might also drink His Blood. This was that Baptism which stood in the place of the font when it had not been received, or restored it when lost (cf. *Scorp.* c. vii.).

(*c*) The remainder of the treatise deals with points of church practice and discipline as regards baptism (cc. xvii.-xx.). Laymen as well as clerics could administer it, but only if disciples and in cases of necessity. "Layman" was not taken to include women. Baptism was not to be administered rashly (cf. Matt. vii. 6). Tertullian, like the teachers of Alexandria, recommends delaying it in the case of children, till they had passed "the age of innocence," and in the case of the unwedded and widowed. The times most suitable for baptism were the Passover and Pentecost; but not to the exclusion of other opportunities. When about to receive baptism, candidates should prepare themselves by prayer, fasting, vigil, and confession of sins (cf. Matt. iii. 6); and after baptism they should rejoice rather than fast. Tertullian suggests to them a prayer: "When you rise from that holy font of your new birth and spread your hands for the first time in the house of your mother Church with your brethren, ask of the Father, ask of the Lord, special grace ["peculia gratiae"] and the divers gifts of the Holy Spirit ["distributiones charismatum"]. And, he adds with touching humility, "I pray you that when you ask, you remember in your prayers Tertullian the sinner."

De Poenitentia.—Repentance of sin before baptism (cc. i.-vi.). True repentance had its measure and its limit in the fear of God. God Himself initiated repentance, when He rescinded His sentence on Adam. He exhorted men to it by His Prophets; by St. John He pointed out its sign and seal in baptism. Its aim was the salvation of man through the abolition of sin. There was a tendency to say "God was satisfied with the devotion of heart and mind. Even if men did sin in act, they could do so without prejudice to their faith and fear." With an intensity of sarcasm Tertullian replies, "You shall be thrust down into hell without prejudice to your pardon." Such Antinomianism explained another frequent and lamentable practice. The Christians of the day most firmly believed in the washing away of sins in Holy Baptism, and in the necessity of true repentance as preparatory to the reception of it; but this led "novices" ("inter auditorum tirocinia") not to a willing and holy eagerness to receive baptism, but to a presumptuous and unholy spirit of delay, that they (the soldiers of the Cross) might steal the intervening time as a furlough ("commentum") for sinning rather than for learning not to sin. Tenderly and wisely does Tertullian plead with them. "If a man who has given himself to God is not to cease sinning till he be bound by baptism, I hardly know whether he will not feel, after baptism, more sorrow than joy."

De Spectaculis.—A period of temporary peace after persecution (cf. c. xxvii.) had fallen upon the church in Carthage. Spectacular shows and games were being given, possibly in commemoration of the victory of Severus over Albinus, and the grave question had to be faced—Should Christians attend them? The seal (*signaculum*) of baptism supplied *the* reason against attendance. All the preparations connected with the spectacles were based upon idolatry, and idolatry was renounced at the font. In cc. v.-xiii. Tertullian draws out in detail the origin of the spectacles, their titles, apparatus, localities, and arts; and the reader can realize to the very life the places and scenes he describes in impassioned but often one-sided invective. Everywhere in the circus were images and statues, chariots dedicated to gods, their thrones, crowns, and equipments. Religious rites preceded, intervened, and succeeded the games; guilds, priests, and attendants served the *conventus daemoniorum.* Consecrated to the sun, the solar temple rose in the midst, the solar effigy glittered on the summit. The chariots of the circus were dedicated to the gods, the charioteers wore the colours (white, red, green, and blue) of idolatry. The *designator* and the *haruspex* were two most befouled masters of the ceremonies connected with the funereal and sacrificial rites. The *theatrum* was the home of Venus and Bacchus; the performances there claimed their patronage. The very artistic gifts employed in producing the spectacles were the inspiration of demons, glozed over by a fallacious consecration. Men pleaded, "We cannot live without pleasure." Well, Christians had pleasures many and noble. What greater pleasure could be conceived than reconciliation to God and pardon of the many sins of a past life? What delight should exceed the trampling idolatry under foot, the expulsion of demons, acts of healing, a life unto God? These were the pleasures and spectacles of Christians, holy, perpetual, and free. In the Christian circus they might behold immodesty hurled down by chastity, perfidy slain by fidelity, cruelty bruised by mercy, wantonness overcome by modesty! These were the contests in which to gain the Christian crown. "Or do you wish to see the blood shed? Behold Christ's!" Then Tertullian closes his eyes to the spectacles of earth. There looms before him (c. xxx.) *the* spectacle close at hand of the Lord coming in His glory and triumph. He depicts angels exulting, saints rising from the dead, the kingdom of the just and the city of the New Jerusalem, the hell of the persecutor and scoffer; and there were spectacles even more glorious still. Man could not conceive them; but they were nobler than those of the circus, the amphitheatre, or the racecourse.

De Cultu Feminarum, i. and ii.—The luxury and extravagance of the women of the time is matter of notoriety. Tertullian and Clement of Alexandria do not express one whit more strongly than Seneca their ambition, cruelty, and licentiousness. Therefore, when women became Christians, and matronly and wifely virtues or virgin purity and modesty characterized them, it extorted the admiration of some and the impatient scorn of others. But luxury began to creep in and overrule the daughters of the church. Tertullian saw it, and the above works were among other efforts to recall Christian women to the Christian life.

De Idololatria is a protest against serving two masters—Christianity and heathenism. Many Christians had in adult age come over to Christianity from heathenism, and many Christian craftsmen gained their living by distinctly heathen trades, and would not or could not see that they were wrong. Many "servants of God" had official or professional engagements which brought them perpetually in contact with heathen customs, legal forms, sacrificial acts, and social courtesies. They drew sophistical distinctions between what they might write but not speak, or the image they might make but not worship. To Tertullian such contact and collusion, and therefore such professions and trades, were radically wrong. Heathenism in all its shapes was idolatry. Two professions connected with idolatry were especially obnoxious to him, (*a*) the astrologer (c. ix.), arguing that "astrology was the science of the stars which affirmed the Advent of Christ"; (*b*) the schoolmaster (*ludimagister*) and other professors of letters (c. x.), who had to teach the names, genealogies, honours of heathen gods, and keep their festivals from which they derived their income. On festival-days, in honour of emperors, victories, and the like, the doors of Christians were more decorated with lamps and laurels than those of the heathen (cf. *Apol.* c. xxxv.), men quoting Christ's command, "Render unto Caesar the things which are Caesar's" (Matt. xxii. 21). Private and social festivals stood on a different footing (c. xvi.), *e.g.* the natural ceremonies connected with the assumption of the *toga virilis*, espousals, nuptials, and the naming of children. It was a more important question (c. xvii.) what was to be the line of slaves or children who were believers, of officials in attendance upon their lords, patrons, or the chief magistrates when sacrificing? Tertullian answers all such questions in detail. From idolatry in act Tertullian passes to idolatry in word (c. xx.), forbidding ejaculations such as "By Hercules!" "By the god of truth" (*Medius-fidius*, see Andrews's Lex. s.n. *Fidius*). Lastly a yet subtler form of idolatry is considered (c. xxiii.). Christians borrowed money from the heathen, and by giving bonds in security avoided taking an oath. "Scripsi sed nihil dixi. Non negavi, quia non juravi." Indignantly does Tertullian protest against such sophistry: faults committed in mind were faults in deed (Matt. v. 28).

De Patientia, one of the most spiritual of Tertullian's compositions, is a sermon preached to himself quite as much as to others. His experience as a priest had taught him the need of patience every time he confronted pettiness not less than pride, frivolity not less than idolatry.

Ad Uxorem, i. and ii.—Among the questions discussed in, and disturbing, the Christian church at Carthage was that of second marriages. These were evidently numerous. Tertullian gave his advice in a treatise in two books addressed to his wife, which he hoped might be profitable to her and to any other woman "belonging to God." He does not go here beyond the position taken by St. Paul. If he evidently considered celibacy the higher state, though himself married, he does not forbid marriage. But second marriages were different, and he argues strongly against them.

(2) *Doctrinal Treatises.*—Three positions laid down by Tertullian (*de Praes. Haer.* cc. xxi. xxxii. xxxvi.), (*a*) apostolic doctrine, (*b*) episcopal succession from the apostles, (*c*) the apostolic canon of Scripture, were rocks on which the church was then firmly fixed.

(*a*) His *Regula Fidei* (cf. *de Praes. Haer.* c. xiii.; *de Virg. Vel.* c. i.; *adv. Prax.* c. ii.) is the form given by Irenaeus (*contr. Haer.* I c. x.; cf. the two in Denzinger's *Enchiridion*, pp. I, 2), expanded upon points which had come to the front during a lapse of about 30 years. But it had become something more than a mere *regula*; it had risen to a *doctrina*; and in the brotherhood of Carthage it was the *contesseratio* (cf. *de Praes. Haer.* cc. xx. xxxvi.) which reason and tradition united in approving. (*b*) The *regula* had come down to them through bishops "per successionem ab initio decurrentem" (cf. *ib.* c. xxxii.), and those bishops had received "cum successione charisma veritatis certum" (Iren. iv. c. xxvi. 2). The former fact gave historical value to the *regula*, the latter dogmatic credibility. The unworthy life of many a successor of the apostles (cf. *de Pudicitia*, c. i.) did not annul the validity of the doctrine. For (*c*) it was supported by the Scriptures. In the time of Irenaeus and Tertullian the Law and the Prophets, the Gospels and the Apostolic Epistles (cf. *de Praes. Haer.* c. xxxvi.)

formed an undisputed canon. Tertullian's nomenclature for the Bible (see Rönsch, *Das N. T. Tertullian's*, pp. 47-49) is alone sufficient record of the high value attached to the writings in the custody of "the one Holy Catholic Church." The sacred Scriptures contained the solution of every difficulty (cf. *de Idolotat.* c. iv. *et pass.*). It was the armoury of weapons offensive and defensive which the church permitted her children alone to use (cf. *de Praes.* c. xv., etc.), for she alone had taught them to use them aright. With such an equipment and in defence of "mother" church (*ad Mart.* c. i.; *de Orat.* c. ii. and *aliter*), Tertullian went forth to attack the "heresies" of men who, calling themselves Christians, yet abandoned the apostolic tradition for doctrines whose parentage he attributed to the devil, and whose precepts he scorned as derived from non-Christian religious systems and speculations, or as the offspring of self-willed wickedness.

De Praescriptione Haereticorum. — This treatise, with its title drawn from the language of jurisprudence, consists of (i), an introduction (cc. i.-xiv.), (ii) the main division of the work (cc. xv.-xl.). It is more than probable that it originated in the desire to emphasize the doctrinal stability of the African church in the face of some fresh tendency towards Gnosticism in general and the views of Marcion especially. (i) Persons of weak faith and character (c. iii.) were unsettled because some once accounted firm in the faith were passing over to heresy; and it was not sufficient simply to refer to Scripture, which the Gnostic teachers could apply as much as the orthodox. For the time Tertullian conceived no better way of meeting their difficulty than by positive injunction to refuse appeal to Scripture to their would-be seducers, to note the character of the heretics, and to surrender themselves entirely to the guidance of the church. The authority men advanced for their deviations from the faith was nothing less than the words of the Lord, "Seek, and ye shall find" (Matt. vii. 7). Tertullian argues that Christ's words could bear no such interpretation; they contained advice to search after definite truth and to rest content with it when found. There was safety only in the belief that "Christus instituit quod quaeri oportet, quod credi necesse est." Parables (Luke xi. 5, xv. 8, xviii. 2, 3) taught the same lesson—"finis est et quaerendi et pulsandi et petendi." Therefore Christians were to seek "in their own, from their own, and concerning their own; and only such questions as might be deliberated without prejudice to the rule of faith.

This mention of the *regula fidei* leads (c. xiii.) to the statement of it. This passage is therefore one of the most important in Tertullian's writings as an index to the articles of the Christian faith believed and accepted in his day (consult Pusey's notes *in loco*). This "rule" the Christians held to have been taught by Christ. Tertullian is quite willing (c. xiv.) that it should be examined, discussed, and explained to novices by some "doctor gratia scientiae donatus." But he gives a caution. It was not Biblical skill ("exercitatio scripturarum") but faith which saved (cf. Luke xviii. 42). Faith lay deposited in this "rule"; it had a law, and in the keeping of that law came salvation. "Cedat curiositas fidei, cedat gloria saluti."

(ii) Chaps. xv.-xl.—Heresy was sometimes defended on the ground that heretics used and argued from the Scriptures. But, answered Tertullian, their use of them was "audacious" and not to be admitted. None but they whose were the Scriptures had a right to use them. Tertullian adopts this position not from any distrust of his cause, but in accordance with apostolic injunctions (c. xvi.; cf. I. Tim. vi. 3, 4; Tit. iii. 10). Heretics did not deal fairly with the Scriptures; one passage they perverted, another they interpreted to suit their own purposes (cf. c. xxxviii.). A man might have a most admirable knowledge of the Scripture, but yet make no progress with heretical disputants. Everything he maintained they would deny, everything he denied they would maintain. As a result, the weak in faith, seeing neither side had decidedly the better in the discussion, would go away confirmed in uncertainty. Certain questions had therefore to be settled. Where was the true faith? Whose were the Scriptures? From whom, through whom, when, and to whom had been handed down the "disciplina qua fiunt Christiani"? It might be assumed that wherever the true Christian discipline and faith was, there would be also the true Scriptures, true exposition, and all true Christian traditions (c. xix.). In Christ, Tertullian finds Him Who first delivered the faith openly to the people or privately to His disciples, of whom He had chosen twelve "destinatos nationibus magistros." These twelve (St. Matthias having been chosen in the place of Judas) went forth and founded churches everywhere; and from them other churches derived then, and still derived, the tradition of faith and the seeds of doctrine. Hence their name of "apostolic churches." Though so many, they sprang from but one, the primitive church founded by the apostles. Thus all were primitive, all apostolic, all one; and this unity was proved by their peaceful inter-communion, by the title of brotherhood, and by the exercise of hospitality—all of which owed their basis and continuance to one and the same sacramental faith. From this was to be deduced the first rule (c. xxi.): None were to be received (cf. Matt. xi. 27) as preachers but those (apostles) whom the Lord Jesus Christ appointed and sent. A second rule was that what the apostles preached could only be proved by those churches which the apostles themselves founded, to which they preached, and to which they afterwards sent epistles. All doctrine therefore which agreed with these apostolic churches ("matricibus et originalibus fidei") was to be counted true, and firmly held as having been received by the church from the apostles, by the apostles from Christ, by Christ from God; and all doctrine must be pronounced false which contained anything contrary to the truth declared by the churches and apostles of Christ and of God. These rules Tertullian and his co-religionists affirmed to be held by the Holy Church to which they belonged: "Communicamus cum ecclesiis Apostolicis, quod nulla doctrina diversa. Hoc est testimonium veritatis."

Heretics advanced two "mad" objections to these rules: (*a*) The apostles did not know all things (c. xxii.). (*b*) Arguing from I. Tim. vi. 20 and II. Tim. i. 14, the apostles did not reveal everything to all men. Some doctrines they proclaimed openly and to all, others secretly and to a few (c. xxv.). Tertullian addressed himself to both these points.

C. *Tertullian and Montanism.*—About the end of 2nd cent. Montanism invaded Africa. Tertullian would seem to have embraced it wholeheartedly. It suited his temperament; it furnished the logical solutions to problems practical and theological which had been disturbing him. But his Montanism was not the Montanism of 172-177 or of Asia Minor; it had come to him through the purifying medium of distance and time. He knew or remembered nothing of the extravagances connected with the first deliverances of the "new prophets." Montanism was in truth to Tertullian little more than a name; development and restoration rather than novelty underlie the intention, and are stamped upon the thoughts, of every treatise which follows those hitherto considered. The practices Tertullian favoured and advocated, the doctrines he loved and enforced, had alike their roots in the existing practices and doctrines of the church. It is the manner in which he has insisted upon the one which has so much discredited it; it is the juridical fence with which he has driven home the other which has angered opponents. He defended his practice and teaching as necessary for his day. New fasts, protests against second marriages, a sterner accentuation of discipline, were conceived as absolutely necessary by the man who, beginning by tightening bonds which the church had wisely left relaxed, ended by the Pharisaic assumption that he and his were πνευματικοὶ and his opponents ψυχικοί. But if he drew his descriptive language from Gnostic codes, he burned in the spirit to depose Gnostic heresy. The merit he assigned to ecstasy, dream, vision, new prophecy, and special endowment by the Paraclete, were expansions of simpler but Scriptural teaching, with something of Pharisaic lordliness, but ever directed against the Sadduceeism, the materialism, the Patripassianism, and the Monarchianism of his day.

The career of Tertullian, his whole being and character, left him no choice when he had to make his decision. He was bound to side with the sterner party, and he did. If at first he retained his position in the church, that position before long became intolerable. The breach took place of which the *de Virg. Vel.* gives the ostensible cause; and the passion which animated the apologist in defence of the church was presently employed to revile, discard, and injure her. Few treatises are more painful to read than the *de Monogamia*, *de Jejunio*, and *de Pudicitia*. It is a relief to turn from them to the *adv. Praxean*. If the heart of the ascetic has been alienated from the church, he can still defend her faith with all his old loving energy, and, by his last existing writing, command respect from those whose affection he had lost.

(1) *Practical Treatises.*—*De Corona* is usually counted the first treatise which indicates traces of Montanism (cf. c. i.; Hauck places the *de Virg. Vel.* before it), and it was written after the *de Spectac.* (cf. c. vi.). Opinions were divided as to the soldier's conduct. Some blamed him as rash, as eager to die, some as bringing trouble on the Christian name about a mere matter of dress. Tertullian, with one word of laudation of the man—"solus scilicet fortis inter tot fratres commilitones, solus Christianus"—turns furiously upon his decriers.

De Fuga in Persecutione.—It may well have been that excitement threatening persecution was aroused against Christians by the conduct of the soldier specified in the *de Corona.* In Carthage (c. iii.) the question was anxiously debated, "May Christians flee from persecution or not?" The clergy answered "Yes," and set an example (c. xi.), which they probably defended by Christ's words (Matt. x. 23), and by the practice of a Polycarp and others. A few years before (*ad Uxor.* i. c. iii.) Tertullian himself had conceded that flight was "better" where the Christian was likely to deny the faith through the agony of torture; but now he thought differently. Montanistic severity had laid its spell upon him. His work deals with the two modes by which the timid and doubtful sought to evade persecution: (*a*) flight (cc. i.-xi.), and (*b*) bribery (cc. xii.-end).

De Exhortatione Castitatis.—Some years had elapsed since Tertullian had written *ad Uxorem,* deprecating for women a second marriage. The death of a friend's wife gave him an opportunity of urging upon men a like continence; and he did so in language declaratory of views far more exaggerated.

De Virginibus Velandis.—The veiling of virgins was a burning question among Christians at Carthage; and partisans in Carthage took sides according as they argued from what St. Paul (I. Cor. xi.) had said or had left to be inferred. Did his term "women" include virgins? Christian married women appeared veiled everywhere, in the church as well as the marketplace; their veil was the mark of their status. The Christian virgin did one of three things: she went everywhere unveiled, or veiled in the streets but unveiled in the church, or everywhere veiled. Of these the first was the oldest and local custom—it was the mark of the virgin and the practice of the majority. But a strong minority had adopted the last of the three practices. This Tertullian approved (cf. *de Orat.* cc. xx.-xxii.).

(2) *Doctrinal Works.*—The majority of these were written when Tertullian had become a Montanist. They present more or less the catch-words of the sect, and refer to the Paraclete and the new prophecy, if the doctrines inculcated and defended are those of the church Catholic. To be a Montanist was not with Tertullian to be a seceder from the church in points of faith, though the church found it necessary for the sake of her unity in life and doctrine to count him and his outside her.

Adv. Hermogenem.—For the nature of the opinions of this heretical teacher and of Tertullian's treatise against him see HERMOGENES.

The treatise contains two very beautiful passages, (*a*) the eulogy of wisdom (c. xviii.), and (*b*) the description of the development of cosmical order out of chaos (c. xxix.).

Adv. Valentinianos.—For a review of the opinions of this school ("frequentissimum plane collegium inter haereticos") see VALENTINUS. Tertullian's treatise does not so much discuss these opinions as state them; it is not so much a refutation as a satire, intended to provoke mirth (c. vi.). It claims no originality, but to be a faithful reflection of the teaching of Justin, Miltiades (cf. Eus. *H. E.* v. 17) Irenaeus, and Proculus.

De Carne Christi.—This is Tertullian's principal contribution to the Christological problem of the time: Was the flesh of Christ born of the Virgin and human in its nature (c. xxxv.)? In his *de Resurrectione Carnis* (c. ii.) he himself specifies the tenets he opposes here to be those of Marcion, Basilides, Valentinus, and Apelles. These "modern Sadducees" (c. i.; *de Praes. Haer.* c. xxxiii.) were apprehensive lest if they admitted the reality of Christ's flesh, they must also admit His resurrection in the flesh, and consequently the resurrection generally. It was necessary to discuss, therefore, His bodily substance. (i) (*a*) Marcion's views are examined (cc. ii.-v.); then (*b*) those of Apelles (cc. vi.-ix.); then (*c*) that of the Valentinians (cc. x.-xvi.). (ii) The second part of the treatise deals more especially with the single point—"Did Christ receive flesh from the Virgin" (cc. xvii.-end)?

The treatise fully responds to the intention of the writer. It examines the arguments employed and the Scriptures advanced (see esp. c. xviii.); and does so, on the whole, in a style moulded by the recollection that the subject was a grave and solemn one. There are bursts of irony (*e.g.* cc. ii. iv.); paradoxes (see c. v., perhaps the most famous of Tertullian's many paradoxes) and retorts; but the total result is a valuable contribution to the literature of the subject. His line of argument and his statement of the church's doctrine is that of Irenaeus. For a general view of the opinions attacked see APELLES, MARCION, and VALENTINUS.

De Resurrectione Carnis.—Tertullian wrote this (c. ii.) in fulfilment of the intention expressed in the *de Carne Christi* (c. xxv.), against those who allowed that the soul would rise again, but refused resurrection to the flesh on account of its worthlessness. It was a logical sequence to their fundamental position that the works of the Demiurge, or the god who created the world and was opposed to the supreme God, were marked by corruption and worthlessness, and that the flesh of man was consequently so also. Tertullian grants that his subject was invested with uncertainty; but it was too important to be passed over. The question affected the very Oneness of the Godhead. To deny the resurrection of the flesh would be to shake that doctrine, to vindicate the resurrection of the flesh would establish it. In contrast to the unseemly language (*spurciloquium*) of heathen and heretic, he will adopt a more honourable and modest style (cf. *de Anima*, c. xxxii.); and he has kept his word. There are few sentences which grate upon the ear, while there are many passages of considerable beauty and profound Christian faith.

Adv. Marcionem, bks. i.-v.—This work in its present form is assigned to the 15th year of Severus (bk. i. c. xv.) or *c.* 208; and comes to us as a work touched and retouched during many years (cf. i. c. xxii.). Tertullian had in other cases felt dissatisfaction with his writings of an earlier period, or altered his arguments to meet the ever-altering phases of false belief. Thus in the earlier work, *de Praes. Haer.* c. xix., he declines to allow appeal to the Scriptures in the discussion of heresy; in a later treatise, *de Resurr. Carnis*, c. iii., he demands of heretics that they should support their inquiries from Scripture alone (cf. *adv. Prax.* c. xi.). So now, his earliest edition of this treatise, if placed (conjecturally) *c.* 200, would have seemed to him very defective when writing *c.* 208. He had separated from his old friends, now branded as the "Psychics" (iv. c. xxii.), to find among the Montanists the true church (i. c. xxi.; iv. c. v.). To him "the new prophecy" was now the highest authority, the Paraclete the sole guide unto all truth. The doctrinal controversy between Tertullian and Marcion turned principally on questions of anthropology and Christology. All that Tertullian has to say upon it has been summed up under MARCION.

De Anima.—In the treatise *de Testimonio Animae* Tertullian had sought to prove that the soul of man bore natural testimony to the truth of the representations given in Holy Scripture of the unity, nature, and attributes of God, and of a future state. In the treatise *de Anima*, written some ten years or so later, he deals with the soul itself. Between these surviving treatises is to be placed one now lost, *de Censu Animae*, in which he had combated the opinion of Hermogenes that the origin of the soul was to be found in matter by the counter-opinion that it was formed by the *afflatus* of God (cf. *de Anima*, cc. i. iii. xi.; *adv. Marc.* ii. c. ix.). The attributes of the soul (*animae naturalia*) pointed, in his opinion, to propinquity to God and not to matter (cf. *de Anima*, c. xxii.), an opinion supported by the views of Plato, who had taught the *divinatio animae* (cf. *de Anima*, c. xxiv.). The discussion of its origin is followed by a general inquiry respecting the nature, powers, and destiny of the soul. An admirable analysis is that of Bp. Kaye (pp. 178-207; cf. also Neander, the careful analysis of Böhringer, and Hauck). In c. xxii. Tertullian gives his definition of the soul as deriving its origin from the breath of God (iv. xi.). The soul is immortal, corporeal (v.-viii.), and endowed with form (ix.); simple in its substance (x. xi.); possessing within itself the principle of intelligence (xii.); working in different ways or channels (xiii.-xv.); endued with free will; affected by external circumstances, and thus producing the infinite variety of disposition observable among mankind; rational (xvi.); supreme over man (xvii. xviii.); and possessing natural insight into futurity (xix.). The Gospels, in (*e.g.*) the history of the rich man in torment (Luke xvi. 23, 24), proved the corporeity of the soul (c. vii.; also a Stoic opinion), and medical science, "the sister of philosophy," in the volumes of a contemporary physician, Soranus (c. vi.), also attested this belief. The invisibility of the soul was no disproof of its corporeity; witness St. John, who, "when in the spirit," "beheld the souls of the martyrs" (Rev. vi. 9); witness also the testimony of "the sister so endowed with gifts of revelation" (c. ix.). This latter testimony is of interest as exhibiting Montanist religious observances. Revelations used to come to her in the church on the Lord's Day. While the solemn services were being performed, she used to fall into an "ecstasy in the spirit." In that state she conversed with angels, sometimes even with the Lord; she saw and heard mysteries (*sacramenta*); she read men's hearts; she prescribed remedies to the sick. Sometimes these visions took place when the Scriptures were being read, or when the Psalms were being chanted, or at the time of preaching or of prayer. On one occasion Tertullian thinks that he must have been preaching about the soul. The "sister" was rapt in spiritual ecstasy. After the people had been dismissed, she told him, as was her habit, what she had seen. "The soul was shewn to me in a bodily form. It seemed a spirit; not, however, an empty illusion, but one which could be grasped, 'tenera et lucida et aerii coloris, et forma per omnia humana.'" Such testimony was to the Montanist Tertullian all-conclusive.

The main purpose of cc. xxiii.-xxvii. is to prove that the souls of all mankind are derived from one common source, the soul of Adam. In cc. xxviii.-xxxv. Tertullian ridicules the conclusions necessitated by metempsychosis and metemsomatosis.

As a preliminary to the consideration of the manner in which the soul encounters death, Tertullian considers the subject of sleep—the image of death (cc. xlii.-end). He adopts by preference the Stoic definition of sleep as the temporary suspension of the activity of the senses ("resolutionem sensualis vigoris"), and limits the senses affected to those of the body; the soul, being immortal, neither requiring nor admitting a state of rest. While the body is asleep or dead, the soul is elsewhere.

Death, to which Tertullian now turns (c. l.), was to be the lot of all, let Epicurus and Menander say what they would. The voice of God (Gen. ii. 17) had declared death to be the death of nature. Independent of heathen examples of this truth, Tertullian finds one in the translation of Enoch and Elijah. Their death was deferred only; "they were reserved for a future death, that by their blood they might extinguish Antichrist" (Oehler refers to Rev. xi. 3). Where would the soul be when divested of the body (cc. liii.-lviii.)? Tertullian answers, In Hades; but his Hades is not that of Plato, nor his answer to the question that adopted by philosophers. To Hades, "a subterranean region," did Christ go (Matt. xii. 40; I. Pet. iii. 19); therefore Christians must keep at arms' length those who were too proud to believe that the souls of the faithful deserved to be placed in the lower regions. From Hades shall men remove to heaven at the day of judgment. But what would take place while the soul was in Hades? Would it sleep? No, Tertullian replies; souls do not sleep when men are alive. Full well the soul will know in Hades how to feel joy or sorrow even without the body. The "prison" of the Gospel (Matt. v. 25) was Hades, and "the uttermost farthing" the very smallest offence which had to be atoned there before the resurrection. Hence the soul must undergo in Hades some compensatory discipline without prejudice to the full accomplishment of the resurrection, when recompense would be paid to the flesh also. This conclusion Tertullian affirms to be one communicated by the Paraclete, and therefore accepted by all who admitted the force of His words from a knowledge of His promised gifts.

De Pallio.—This, a treatise intentionally extravagant, is a vindication of the philosopher's mantle (*pallium*) ridiculed by the people of Carthage. It might be called a juridical plea, couched in witty and forensic language, in an imaginary case of Pallium (see description *s.v.* in *D. C. A.*) *v.* Toga. Some have seen in Tertullian's assumption of the *pallium* an indication that he adopted it to show his separation from the church. The conjecture has nothing to prove or disprove it. The mantle had virtues of its own (cc. v. vi.). Did it not illustrate simplicity and capacity, economy and austerity, in protest against the follies and effeminacies, the gluttony and extravagance, the impurity and intemperance of the *togati*? "Grande pallii beneficium est." It was the garb not only of the philosopher, but also of those benefactors of the human race—the grammarian and the rhetorician, the sophist and the physician, the poet and the musician, the student of astronomy and the pupil of national history. In face of such facts, why mind the sneer, "The *pallium* ranked below the *toga* of the Roman knight," or the indignant question, "Shall I give up my *toga* for the *pallium*"? There was no indignity in the matter. "'Gaude pallium et exsulta!' Thou art honoured by a better philosophy from the time that thou didst become a Christian garment."

Scorpiace.—A defence of martyrdom stronger than is found in the Montanist works of his previous period, perhaps *c.* 211.

Ad Scapulam.—Probably at the beginning of the reign of Caracalla, A.D. 211, the African proconsula Scapula authorized the persecution to which this work refers. He was a fierce opponent of the Christians, and permitted his fanaticism to override his sense of justice (c. iv.). This treatise uses the arguments of the *Apology*, but with a change in tone. Tertullian's passion is still strong, but gravely and soberly expressed. There is the same appeal for justice, but defiance has given place to prayer, and hatred of the persecutor to love for the enemy. The treatise may fairly take rank among the best and most interesting of all which have been preserved. Scapula is told frankly that they who had joined the "sect" of Christians were prepared to accept its conditions. The persecutions of men ignorant of what they were doing did not alarm them or make them shrink from heathen "savagery." Against the charges usually brought against them (cf. c. ii.; *Apol.* cc. vii.-ix.) Scapula should set one plain fact—the behaviour of Christians. They formed the majority in every city, yet their conduct was always marked by silence and modesty. Their "discipline" enforced a patience which was divine; if they were known at all among men, it was for their reformation of the vices which once degraded them. Tertullian does not write to intimidate, but to warn—μὴ θεομαχεῖν. "Perform your duties as proconsul, but remember to be humane." If the Christians of Carthage should see fit to come to Scapula, how many swords and fires would he need for such multitudes of every sex, age, and rank! He would have to slaughter the leading persons of the city, and decimate the noble men and women of his own rank, friends and relations of his own circle. "Spare thyself, Scapula, if thou wilt not spare us. Spare Carthage, if thou wilt not spare thyself. Spare thy province, which the mere mention of thine intention has subjected to the threats and extortions of soldiers and of private foes [cf. *de Fuga*, cc. xii. xiii.]. As for us, we have no Master but God. Those whom you reckon your masters are but men, and must one day die. Our community shall never die. The more you pull it to the ground, the more it will be built up."

De Monogamia.—Some years passed, of peace from without but not from within; and a third time (*c.* 217) Tertullian returns to that question—marriage—which had occupied him in the *ad Uxorem* and *de Exhortatione Castitatis.* The third treatise is the bitterest. Tertullian now claims for his party that they and they alone were guided by the Paraclete. From Him they had received their teaching on monogamy. He had come to supersede the teaching of St. Paul by yet higher counsels of perfection. Much of Tertullian's argument—*e.g.* from Scripture—is repeated from his former treatises, and much of it is strained and conjectural, as he felt it would be said to be (c. ix.); but no one will dispute Tertullian's earnestness. Immorality was prevalent and contagious, and in monogamy—supposing celibacy and widowhood to be impossible—he saw a counteracting agency. Discipline and spirituality would be at least practicable to those who would rally round the standard of monogamy.

De Jejunio Adversus Psychicos (al. *de Jejuniis*).—Another great subject of difference between churchmen and Montanists had reference to fasts. Tertullian's paper is most distressing to read, scanty in argument, plentiful in abuse. Both sides indulged in unmeasured invective; both had lost their temper. The charges of luxury, gluttony, and immorality unhesitatingly and almost exultingly brought by Tertullian against church ecclesiastics and laymen are so gross as almost to refute themselves by their very exaggeration. They are more than the retort of a man infuriated by unjust accusations and meeting them by counter-charges. The ascetic has become a fanatic, and in his mad hatred besmirches and calumniates the church he had once so tenderly loved.

De Pudicitia.—This work has been placed before the *de Monogamia* and the *de Jejunio*, but internal and negative evidence, if slight, seems to assign it a place after them. An edict (c. i.) of the bp. of Rome (Zephyrinus, 202-218, or Callistus, 218-223) lashed Tertullian into fury, and completely dissolved the last links of union between him and the Psychics. The treatise is marked by intense bitterness from beginning to end.

Adversus Praxean.—For the history of Praxeas, the nature of his views and Tertullian's answer, see PRAXEAS.

Tertullian was the first who, in the controversy against the Monarchians, introduced prominently the doctrine of the Holy Spirit. Praxeas did not touch it. Hence the value of such chapters as viii. ix. xxv. xxx. He fully maintains the personality of the Third Person of the Trinity (cf. *ad Mart.* c. iii.) if his language is occasionally ambiguous (cf. c. xii., his comment on Gen. i. 26). He bases as usual his arguments on Scripture (cc. xxi. to end), and if not always free from his well-known tendency to read into them what he wants, the passages are as a rule well and wisely handled either in defence of the Catholic position or in refutation of that of Praxeas. He gives (c. xx.) the 3 texts especially valued by this teacher in support of his heresy (Is. xlv. 5; John x. 30, xiv. 9, 10), and refutes his views at length (cc. xxi.-xxiv.).

IV. SUMMARY.—The brief sketch here presented of these powerful writings will have indicated the investigation of many a doctrine and the record of contemporaneous practices heathen and Christian, as well as illustrated the mind, character, and style of their writer.

(*a*) *Tertullian and Heathenism.*—On its moral side, extravagance, luxury, immorality, and cruelty were to all external appearance as rampant in his day as ever. Tertullian knows heathenism only in its coarseness and repulsiveness. Yet a reformation was proceeding, religious in origin and intention, which must not be forgotten in any true estimate of the age. Tertullian lived when old pagan traditions and new tendencies were co-operating; when there had risen that religious movement which, owing its impulse to the eclecticism of a Julia Domna, passed through the stirring phases successively represented in the neo-Pythagoreanism of her *salon*, in the subordination by Elagabalus of every other cultus to that of the Oriental sun-god, and in the equalization by Alexander Severus of all worshipful beings in his common cultus of the heroes of humanity. That movement was the product of a real awakening.

The main centre of these changes and developments was Rome, but Tertullian's writings against heathenism prove that Carthage at least felt the effects of this great tidal wave of religiousness. They are as full of attack as of defence. He strikes at a vigorous paganism as much as he beats off the charges alleged against Christianity. Every page teems with allusions which reflect without effort the firm foothold acquired by all forms of heathen cultus. Ridicule of the worship of the ancient deities of Greece and Rome, of the cultus of the emperors, of the "genius," and of demons is found allied with contempt of the gods of Alexandria (Isis and Serapis), of Phrygia (the Magna Mater and Bellona), of Syro-Phoenicia (the Dea Syra), and of Carthage (the Juno Coelestis). The very fierceness of his invective and scorn against the polytheistic revival, the ridicule he pours upon *galli* and *flamines*, priests and priestesses, itinerant and mendicant propagators of this or that cultus, guilds, processions, festivals, evidences the success and popularity of heathenism. The *Apology* of Apuleius (end of 2nd cent.) is illustrated by the *Apology* of Tertullian, and the statements of Dio, Spartian, Herodian, Lampridius, etc., can be compared with those of our writer. Were those heathen works lost, it would be almost possible to reproduce from his pages, shorn of their extravagance, a picture of the religiousness of the age such as they have given.

(*b*) *Tertullian and Christianity*.—In passing from heathenism to Christianity, Tertullian believed himself to be passing from darkness to light and from corruption to purity. He embraced it with all the strength of a matured mind and life. All the more intelligible, therefore, is his vehement anger with any form of Christian precept and practice, whether at Rome or Carthage, which fell short of his ideal. The church was to him the Virgin and spotless Bride of the Ascended Lord, and her children—bishops, priests, and people—must worthily reflect her purity and faith. He would permit no shortcomings because he would admit no failure. A writer of the 4th cent. has left on record that the Africans as he knew them were "faithless and cunning. There might be some good people among them, but they were not many" (quoted in Mommsen, *The Provinces of the Roman Empire*, ii. p. 340). This estimate is reflected a century earlier in Tertullian's pages. It is a summary of his opinion of the spurious devotion which marked the Christian fop (*de Poenit.* c. xi.; cf. *de Cultu Fem.* ii. c. viii.), the would-be penitent (*de Poenit.* c. ix.), the rich Christian lady (*de Cultu Fem.* i. c. ix., ii. cc. v.-vii.; *de Virg. Vel.* c. xvii.), the fashionable virgin (*ib.* c. xii.; in contrast with her holy sister, c. xv.), the drugged and petted martyr (*de Jej.* c. xii., in contrast with the willing and happy martyr, *ad Martyres*, cc. i.-iii.); and it explains that final revulsion of mind which, spurning every kind of compromise, heaped indiscriminate abuse on what was best as well as what was worst in the life of the Christians of the church, and turned to find in asceticism and Montanism a seriousness and elevation impossible to him elsewhere. Paradoxical as it may seem, it was the same impulsive spirit which kept him staunch to the faith of that church whose discipline and ritual he abjured or carried with him to a schismatic body. Gnosticism was to Tertullian the embodiment of theological corruption, darkness, and falsehood, and he fought it with all his natural vehemence. His theology, if developed by Montanism, is in substance that which the church accepted, and accepts. The admiration felt for his writings by his countryman Cyprian (200-258), bp. of Carthage, should never be forgotten. Cyprian, says St. Jerome, never passed a day without reading a portion of Tertullian's works; he frequently asked for them with the words, "Da mihi magistrum"; and it is impossible to read Cyprian's existing treatises without seeing how largely the thoughts of Tertullian have been absorbed by him, if the language has been softened and deepened. In our own country Bp. Bull (*Defensio Fidei Nicenae*) and Pearson (*On the Creed*) have used many an argument which the Montanist of Africa had prepared for them, and Bp. Kaye's illustrations of the Articles of the Church of England from Tertullian's writings (pp. 246, etc.) concur in establishing the force of Möhler's description of his dogma as "so homelike" (*Patr.* i. p. 737). It is based on the teaching of Christ as handed down by apostles and apostolic men, and formulated in the "regula fidei una, sola, immobilis et irreformabilis" (cf. *de Praes. Haer.* cc. viii. ix.; *de Virg. Vel.* c. i.). Theology owes practically to him such words (*int. al.*) as *Trinitas, satisfactio, sacramentum, substantia, persona, liberum arbitrium*, transferred (some of them) from the Latin law courts to take their definite place in the language of Latin divinity (cf. the *index verborum* at the end of Oehler, vol. ii.).

(*c*) *Tertullian, the Man.*—Of no one, says Ebert, is Buffon's saying truer, "the style is the man," and the best illustration of his style he finds in the *Apology* (*Geschichte der Christlich-Lateinischen Literatur*, pp. 34-37). Tertullian cared nothing for form save as it best expressed his thought. He said right out from his heart what he had to say about friend or foe, without attempt to clothe his speech with the graceful charm of the Greek or the dignified periods of the Roman. Abrupt and impetuous, eloquent and stern, his sentences follow one another with the sweeping, rushing force of storm-waves. The very exceptions do but prove the rule. Such tender or beautiful passages as those which depict the life of Christ on earth (*de Pat.* c. iii.; *Apol.* c. xxi.; were these written with any acquaintance with the Life of the pagan Christ, Apollonius of Tyana, edited by Philostratus at the command of Julia Domna?), the power and effect of prayer (*de Orat.* c. xxix.), the virtues and portrait of patience (*de Pat.* c. xv.), contemporary civilization (*de Anima*, c. xxx.), the happy marriage (*ad Uxor.* ii. 8), and faith, the barque of the church (*de Idol.* c. xxiv.); or the impressive analogies of the resurrection he finds in nature (*re Resurr. Carnis*, c. xii.), and the illustrations of the Trinity (*adv. Prax.* c. viii.), come upon the reader as a surprise, as something so unlike one who is more in his recognized element when describing the place-hunter (*de Poenit.* c. xi.), the traitor (*Apol.* c. xxxv.), and the knowing Valentinian (*adv. Val.* end), or painting that ghastliest of his portraits, murder and idolatry crooning over adultery (*de Pud.* c. v.). His paradoxes are characteristic: To him the unity of heretics was schism (*de Praes. Haer.* c. xlii.); and heresy itself "tantum valeat quantum si non fuisset" (*ib.* c. i.). "God is great when little" (*adv. Marc.* ii. c. ii.); "Lie to be true" (*de Virg. Vel.* c. xvi.), contain thoughts only a shade less startling than the "Mortuus est Dei Filius; prorsus credibile est quia ineptum est; et sepultus resurrexit; certum est quia impossibile est" (*de Carne Christi*, c. v.), or the well-known "the blood of martyrs is the seed of the church" (*Apol.* c. i.). His right appreciation of the methods of Scripture exegesis (*de Pud.* c. ix.; cf. *de Res. Carn.* c. xxi.) is found side by side with such signal examples of perverse interpretation as those which disfigure the *de Jejunio* and *de Pudicitia*, or such fanciful expositions as his view of the cross (*adv. Marc.* iii. c. xviii.; cf. *adv. Jud.* cc. x. xiii.), St. Peter and the sword (*de Idol.* c. xix.), God's Voice to Adam (*adv. Marc.* ii. c. xxv.), and the phoenix (*de Res. Carn.* c. xiii.). Such paradoxes, contrasts, and contradictions are characteristic indications not so much of a want of comprehensiveness as of a determination to occupy himself with but one idea or one aspect of a great truth, and subjugate to that the wider bearings of the question. His great acuteness, power, eloquence, and causticity are concentrated for the time being upon a single principle; and whatever will illustrate it, prove it, and drive it home, is drawn into its service, often regardless of its fitness (see this drawn out in Pusey's pref. to *Libr. of the Fath.* vol. x.) Tertullian's style is strongly marked by the early training of his life: it is juridical in thought, language, and exposition—a fact which explains so much of its difficulty. The advocate is always present. His conduct of the contest between Christianity and heathenism is that of a law-court contest, God *v.* the devil; his conception of the contest between Montanist and Churchman is that of one who asserted and developed Christianity *v.* one who surrendered it or left it defective. Tertullian was often wrong, and the church has, with sorrow, so adjudged him; but the character of the man explains everything.

What that character was he has himself told: "Miserrimus ego, semper aeger caloribus impatientiae" (*de Pat.* c. i.). The sentence, caught up by Jerome, explained to him the man ("homo acris et vehementis ingenii"), as it explains his secession to Montanism and his intellectual and moral defects. Perverse in the sense of wrong-headed he often was in his narrow estimates, but he was never wrong-hearted. His life and work, full of the shades and contrasts of one who loved well and hated well, were after all a life and a work from which more has been gained than lost. If Hilary can regret that his "later error took away from the authority of what he had written," Vincentius can remind us that those writings were "thunderbolts"; they were hurled forth in defence of faith and practice. It will be to his earlier life or less polemical treatises that the reader will turn with Cyprian by preference, and in the perverse impatience of his later life see at once "the fire which kindles and the beacon which warns" (Pusey).

V. Literature.—Oehler's ed. of Tertullian is on the whole the best extant. A new and scientific ed. was commenced by Rufferscheid and Wissowa in the Vienna *Corpus Scr. Eccl. Lat.* xx. See a full list of recent litt. in Bardenhewer's *Patrology* (Freiburg im Br. 1908). Kaye is most serviceable in elucidating many points as to his life, era, teaching, and style. Translations into Eng. of some of his apologetic and practical treatises are in *Lib. of the Fathers*, vol. x., and of almost all his works in *Ante-Nicene Lib.* vols. ii. vii. xi. xviii.; but the translations are very unequal. Recent edd. are *de Praescrip. Haer.*, *ad Martyres*, and *ad Scapulam* in one vol. with intro. and notes, and *adv. Gentes*, both ed. by T. H. Bindley (Oxf. Univ. Press); *de Baptismo*, ed. with intro. and notes by J. M. Lupton (Camb. Univ. Press); *de Poen.* and *de Pud.* with French notes and intro. by Prof. de Labriolle (1906); and a reprint of the bp. of Bristol's illustrations of Ecclesiastical History from Tertullian's writings in the *A. and M. Theol. Libr.* (Griffith). [J.M.F.]

Thaddaeus. Eusebius (*Hist. Eccl.* i. 13) gives a story, which he says he found in the archives of Edessa, that after the ascension of our Lord, the apostle Judas Thomas sent Thaddaeus, one of the seventy disciples, to Edessa, to king Abgarus the Black, and that he cured the king of a serious illness, converted him with all his people to Christianity, and died at Edessa after many years of successful labours. The name of this apostle of the Edessenes is given by the Syrians as Addaeus (*Doctrina Addai*, ed. Phillips, p. 5, Eng. trans. 1876), and it is possible that Eusebius misread the name as Thaddaeus. Thaddaeus was at a later date confused with the apostle Judas Thaddaeus. The documents given by Eusebius contain a correspondence between Abgar and our Lord, which of course is spurious. Cf. R. A. Lipsius, *Die Edessenische Abgarsage kritisch untersucht* (Braunschweig, 1880), and in *D. C. B.* vol. iv.; also, by the same, *Die apokryphen Apostelgeschichten*, vol. ii. 2, 178-201, and Suppl. p. 105; also Texeront, *Les Origines de l'Eglise d'Edesse et la légende d'Abgar* (Paris, 1888). [H.W.]

Thaïs, St., a penitent courtesan of Egypt, converted *c.* 344 by Paphnutius of Sidon. Her story illustrates her age. Her fame reached to Paphnutius's monastery, whereupon he determined to make a great effort to convert her, though she was evidently a nominal Christian. He assumed a secular dress and put a single coin in his pocket, which he offered to Thaïs on arriving at her house. Recognizing his true character, she cast herself at his feet, destroyed all her precious dresses, and entered a female monastery, where Paphnutius shut her up in a cell, sealing the door, and leaving only a small window, through which to receive food. After 3 years she received absolution, and died 15 days after (*Vit. PP.* in Migne's *Patr. Lat.* lxxiii. 661). [G.T.S.]

Thecla (1), the heroine of a romantic story which from a very early date has had a strong hold on the imagination of the church, and which, though under the form in which it is now extant it can only be received as a fiction, has enough appearance of a foundation in fact to warrant us in treating of her as a real person. She was, as we read in the *Acts of Paul and Thecla*, a contemporary of St. Paul, a virgin of Iconium, daughter of a woman of rank (apparently a widow) named Theocleia, and affianced to Thamyris, a youth who was first among the nobles of that city. At the time when the narrative opens St. Paul is represented as being on his way to Iconium, after having been driven from Antioch of Pisidia; but whether his flight from Antioch, related in Acts xiii. 15, is meant, and consequently whether the ensuing events are to be taken as belonging to his first visit to Iconium, is not clear. One Onesiphorus of

Iconium, whose house adjoined that of Theocleia, hearing of his approach, went with his wife and sons to meet him, and recognizing him by a description he had received from Titus, invited him to his house with joy. Two persons named Demas and Hermogenes, who under a hypocritical guise of seeking instruction in the gospel had attached themselves to the apostle on his journey, were at their urgent request admitted along with him by Onesiphorus (though not without demur). In this house Paul began at once to preach "the word of God concerning temperance and the resurrection"; his discourse consisting of a series of beatitudes, in form like those of the Sermon on the Mount, but in substance taken up with the commendation of asceticism and celibacy. Thecla, sitting at a window in her mother's house, heard his words and became filled with passionate faith and zeal for virginity. Being restrained from satisfying her longing to see him and hear his doctrine face to face, she remained listening at her window, despite her mother's remonstrances. The tender entreaties of her betrothed Thamyris, whom Theocleia summoned, proved equally unavailing. The lover, thus repulsed, hurried into the street and watched the house where the stranger was preaching, whose eloquence had cast this deplorable spell over Thecla. Observing Demas and Hermogenes among those going in and out, he questioned them, invited them to a rich banquet at his house, and offered them money for information concerning the preacher. They disclaimed personal knowledge of Paul, but represented him as urging on the young abstinence from marriage, under the threat of forfeiting their part in the resurrection, which (they said) he promised to the celibate only; whereas the true resurrection (as they professed themselves ready to explain) was already past for those that have children in whom they live anew; and men rise again when they fully know the true God. They also advised him to bring Paul before Castelius the governor on the charge of teaching "the new doctrine of the Christians," which (they assured him) would ensure his execution. Accordingly, next morning Thamyris, with other magistrates, and a great multitude, repaired to the house of Onesiphorus, and dragged Paul before the tribunal of Castelius the "proconsul," accusing him merely of dissuading maidens from marriage; though Demas and Hermogenes were at hand prompting him, "Say that he is a Christian, and thus shalt thou procure his death." St. Paul, being called on by the governor for his defence, delivered a speech, not answering the specific charge of Thamyris, but declaring his gospel message and pleading his mission from God. The governor committed him to prison until it was convenient to hear him more attentively. Thecla made this imprisonment her opportunity. That very night, by bribing her mother's doorkeeper with her bracelets and the jailer with her silver mirror, she visited St. Paul's cell; and there, after a night spent at his feet in hearing his doctrine, was found next morning by her mother and lover. At their instance St. Paul was immediately dragged again before the governor, pursued by the multitude with the cry, "He is a sorcerer! Away with him!" Thecla was summoned likewise, and followed him exultingly to the tribunal. Castelius was at first disposed to listen favourably to Paul, as he declared the works of Christ; but afterwards, finding that Thecla would give no reply to his interrogations, but remained silent with her eyes fixed on Paul, and being wrought on by her mother, who demanded that her daughter should be burnt alive as an example to warn other women, he scourged Paul and cast him out of the city, and sentenced Thecla to the stake. When the pyre was ready, she mounted it undismayed. A deluge of hail and rain quenched the fire, the people fled, and Thecla escaped. Meantime St. Paul, with Onesiphorus and his family, on their way to Daphne, had taken refuge in a tomb, where he continued in prayer for Thecla, and sent one of the lads back to Iconium to sell his outer garment and buy bread. The youth met Thecla, who was seeking Paul, and brought her to the hiding-place. There they found Paul praying for her deliverance, and a scene of joyful thanksgiving ensued. The apostle with Thecla went on his way to Antioch. As they entered Antioch her beauty caught the eye of Alexander the Syriarch (this seems to prove that the city here meant is the capital of Syria), who sought to obtain possession of her by offering money to Paul. Baffled and enraged the Syriarch brought her before the Roman governor, who condemned her to be cast to wild beasts; committing her meanwhile to the care of Tryphaena, a widow lady (afterwards described as a queen, and kinswoman of the emperor), who, having lately lost her daughter Falconilla, found comfort in the charge of the condemned maiden, who converted her to Christ. After a series of marvellous escapes from the beasts, Thecla, interrogated by the governor, made profession of her faith: "I am a handmaid of the living God, and I believe in His Son in Whom He is well pleased; and therefore it is that none of the beasts hath touched me. . . . Whoso believeth not on Him shall not live for ever." Amid the jubilations of the women she was released. To rejoin St. Paul was her first thought, and hearing he was at Myra in Lycia, she disguised herself in man's attire and set out with a train of attendants, male and female. There she found him preaching the word. After relating to him in the house of Hermaeus (or Hermes) the wonderful story of her deliverances, she proceeded to Iconium, receiving from him the parting charge, "Go and teach (δίδασκε) the word of God." Arrived at Iconium, she first visited the house of Onesiphorus, and there prostrating herself on the spot where St. Paul had sat and taught, she thanked God and the Lord Jesus Christ for her conversion and preservation. There was no longer anything to fear from the importunities of Thamyris, who had died. She found her mother still living, and endeavoured, but apparently without success, to bring her to believe in the Lord. Finally, she departed to Seleucia, where she "enlightened many and died in peace." Thus the story ends in its oldest form, as preserved in ancient Syriac and

Latin versions; but the four extant Greek copies represent her as living an anchorite's life in a cave, on herbs and water, and they subjoin a marvellous account (certainly of more recent composition) of her latter years. She (according to three of these copies, A, B, and C) went to Rome to see St. Paul again, but was too late to find him alive. She died there soon after, aged 90, and was buried near his tomb 72 years after her martyrdom.

Though the story was undoubtedly written originally in Greek, the oldest Greek MS. is not earlier than 10th cent. But ample proofs of its high antiquity are forthcoming. The so-called *Decree* of Gelasius, *de Libris Recipiendis et non Recipiendis*, which is probably of the early years of the 7th cent., formally excluded (c. vi.) from the list of "scriptures received by the church" the "book which is called the *Acts of Paul and Thecla*." The Syriac version, extant in four MSS., one of 6th cent., contains internal evidence that the Greek text had been long in existence and frequently copied before the Syrian translator did his work. We have also an expanded *Life of Thecla*, composed before the middle of 5th cent. by Basil, bp. of Seleucia (in Isauria), professedly framed on the lines of a previous work then ancient. A comparison of our *Acts of Paul and Thecla* with this Life leaves no doubt that the former is the basis of the latter. These *Acts* (as we shall now call them") were thus "ancient" early in the 5th cent., and can hardly therefore be later than 300. In the 4th cent. Hilary (the Ambrosian) has several clear references to these *Acts* (*Comm.* on I. Tim. i. 20; II. Tim. i. 15, iv. 14; cf *Acts* 1: also on II. Tim ii. 18; cf. *Acts* 14); and even, as it seems, cites them in connexion with the last passage, as "alia Scriptura." Jerome, then or a few years later, mentions (*de Vir. Ill.* c. 7) but rejects a book called Περίοδοι Παύλου καὶ Θεκλης, which he says was discredited by startling marvels; probably Jerome is here inaccurately describing the book as we have it. The very early currency in Christendom of a written narrative of the life of Thecla is proved by the much earlier, more exact, and more authentic evidence of the writer whose authority Jerome here appeals to, Tertullian, in his treatise *de Baptismo* (c. 17), written *c.* 200. Tertullian refuses to admit the authority of certain writings falsely assuming the name of Paul, which some alleged in support of the claim of women to teach and baptize after "the example of Thecla"; for these (he says) were the production of a certain "presbyter of Asia," who was, on his own confession, proved to have composed them "through love of Paul" (as he said) and who for this fraud was degraded from the presbyterate. Jerome represents this degradation as occurring in St. John's time, which seems to be merely an addition of his own, and is inconsistent with our *Acts*, for they, in the age to which they prolong Thecla's life, imply that she survived St. John. Tertullian is our earliest witness that a story of Thecla existed; but whether the extant book of her *Acts* is identical with the Asian presbyter's production is a question. The balance of probability distinctly favours the identification. If so, it would be the oldest of the extant N.T. Apocrypha.

The story thus traced back, certainly as regards its substance and probably as regards its existing written form, to 2nd cent., was widely current in the church, East and West, thereafter. But though she is frequently mentioned by the Fathers, none of them, except Basil of Seleucia, cite our *Acts* or any written narrative. But of all the references to Thecla in ecclesiastical writers, not one (except that already noticed in Jerome) lies distinctly outside the range of the incidents which the *Acts* relate; so that a history of Thecla reconstructed out of the references to her in early Christian writers would be in fact an abridgment of these *Acts*, containing nearly all its chief points and adding nothing to them. Of these writers, the earliest seems to be Methodius, in his *Symposium Decem Virginum* (written *c.* 300; see Migne, *Patr. Gk.* xviii.). The incident of Thecla's sacrificing her ornaments to purchase access to Paul is turned to account by Chrysostom, "Thecla, for the sake of seeing Paul, gave her jewels; but thou, for the sake of seeing Christ, wilt not give an obolus" (*Hom.* 25 *in Acta App.* 4). Isidore of Pelusium (lib. i. *Ep.* 87) is apparently the first to style her by the glorious title, ever since appropriated to her, of protomartyr—that is, as Basil of Seleucia explains (p. 232), first among women as Stephen among men. Theodore of Mopsuestia is stated by Solomon of Bassora, a 13th-cent. Nestorian (cf. Assem. *B. O.* iii. p. 323), to have composed an oration on Thecla, in which it appears that her prayer for Falconilla was mentioned. Epiphanius (*Haer.* lxxviii. 16; lxxix. 5) praises her for sacrificing under St. Paul's teaching her prospects of prosperous marriage, and reckons her near to Elias, John the Baptist, and even the Virgin Mother. In the West her name is similarly joined with that of Agnes as a virgin worthy to rank with Mary herself, by Ambrose (*de Lapsu Virg.* p. 307); and by Sulpicius Severus (*c.* 400), who relates (*Dial.* ii. 13) how St. Martin of Tours was favoured with a vision, in which Mary, Agnes, and Thecla appeared and conversed with him (Migne, *Patr. Lat.* t. xx. col. 210). Ambrose likewise associates her with Mary the Lord's mother, and Miriam, Moses' sister (*Ep.* 63, *ad Vercell. Eccl.* t. ii. pt. 1, p. 1030); and here and in *de Virginibus* (ii. 19, p. 166) dwells on her deliverance from the wild beasts. Jerome in one of his *Epp.* (xxii. p. 125) also associates her with Mary and Miriam, promising that they shall welcome Eustochium, to whom he writes, into the virgin choir of heaven. And in his *Chronicle* (*s.a.* 377) he tells of one Melania, a Roman lady who by her sanctity earned the name of Thecla.

That the book as we have it is a fiction few will doubt; but it is a fair question whether it has been formed on a nucleus of fact; and if so, how far we can distinguish fact from fiction. The incidental reference to Thecla by Eusebius proves that he regarded her as a real person; and if Athanasius wrote her Life, he must be reckoned on the same side. Tertullian, even in rejecting her written history, raises no doubt as to her existence, as he certainly would if he had suspected her to be a creature of the Asian presbyter's imagination. Jerome, while still more emphatic in condemning the book, expressly names her as a virgin saint. It is hardly likely that if Thecla had not existed, her history and example could have so powerfully impressed themselves on the mind of Christendom for so many ages and been honoured by so many generations of the devout faithful, including some of the foremost intellects of the church. The monastery that marked her place of retreat and bore her name, which, as we learn from Gregory of Nazianzum (*Orat.* xxi. p. 399, t. i.; *Poemata Hist.* s. i. 11, p. 703, t. ii.), had made Seleucia a place of pilgrimage before he retired there (*c.* 375), is a further evidence of her reality, and also confirms the localization in that city of the traditions concerning her. It thus appears that our *Acts* probably grew out of a true tradition, handed down from the later apostolic age, of a maiden of Asia Minor who was converted to the Gospel and for its sake renounced all and braved death that she might remain a chaste virgin for Christ, and, having escaped martyrdom, lived and died in sanctity at Seleucia. The Asian presbyter whom Tertullian makes known to us, casting about for materials for a story in exaltation of virginity, would naturally choose for his hero St. Paul, as an unmarried apostle and the only N.T. writer from whom the doctrine of the superiority of the celibate over the married state could claim any support. The tradition which we have supposed current in the church, of a Christian who incurred the peril of martyrdom for virginity and ended her days as an anchorite near Seleucia, would supply his heroine and leading incidents. Her name was probably part of the traditional story; for an invented name would no doubt have been either a Scriptural one or one of obvious Christian significance. II. Tim. iii. 11 might suggest the scene, "at *Antioch*, at *Iconium*." Being of no critical turn, and writing for uncritical readers, the author would not inquire to what stage of St. Paul's course this Epistle belonged, or which Antioch was meant.

The history of Thecla, as we have it, whether this account of its origin be accepted or not, is not without literary merit. It has many touches of pathos, its incidents are striking and effectively told, and here and there the speeches (never of tedious length) rise nearly to the height of eloquence. Defective as we have seen it to be in structure, yet even here, as well as in interest of narrative, it compares advantageously with the clumsy dullness of the Clementine literature; its marvels, however startling, are less extravagant than those of the apocryphal Gospels and Acts; and on the whole it is distinctly above the level of the class of writings (most, if not all, of later date) to which it is usually referred. Its chief defect is the failure to realize and reproduce the spirit and personality of St. Paul. Schlau's opinion (p. 17), that the local knowledge displayed in the work is such as might naturally belong to a resident in Asia Minor, is not to be accepted without qualification. It might, on the contrary, be said that if the author had more carefully studied the canonical Acts with a view to local and chronological knowledge, he might have assigned the scene and date of his narrative with much more definiteness and accuracy. For instance, he seems uncertain how Lystra lay relatively to Iconium (cc. 1, 3), and his idea of the position and distance of Daphne seems equally indistinct (c. 23). So too in his records of Thecla's journeys he is content to name the starting-point and the terminus, never noting any place on the way. His knowledge of political geography is shewn to be lacking when he represents the chief magistrates of Iconium (c. 16) and Antioch (c. 33) as addressed by the title of proconsul (ἀνθύπατε), thus betraying that he supposed these cities to belong to proconsular provinces, whereas Iconium, though territorially included in Lycaonia, was in St. Paul's time extra-provincial, as the head of an independent tetrarchy (Pliny, *Nat. Hist.* v. 25), and Antioch was the capital of Syria, an imperial province governed by a propraetor. Even if we regard Iconium as of Lycaonia, and the Antioch meant to be the Pisidian, in neither city would so high an official as the proconsul of Asia be resident, as the *Acts* represent. The author, being of Asia—that is, of the Roman province—supposed a proconsul to be found at Iconium and at Antioch, because he had himself been accustomed to see a proconsul at Ephesus or Smyrna; and thus Tertullian's statement that he was of Asia (taken in that limited sense) is borne out, not by his exact knowledge, as Schlau supposed, but by his mistake. He has such knowledge of places and political arrangements, and only such, as would naturally belong to an untravelled ecclesiastic of the Roman province of Asia, possessing a familiar but far from critical or precise knowledge of N.T. in general and the book of Acts in particular. The contents of these *Acts* serve indirectly to confirm the authenticity of the canonical Acts by shewing how difficult—it may safely be said how impossible—it would be for a *falsarius*, even if writing at no great distance in place or time from the scene and date of his fictitious narrative, to avoid betraying himself by mistakes; and the history of the reception of his work proves that such attempt to palm off pseudo-apostolic documents for genuine was not difficult of exposure, nor passed over as a light offence. The Asian church of the 2nd cent. was quick to detect the pious fraud and severe in punishing it; and in her dealing with the case there is no trace of uncritical promptitude to receive whatever offered itself as apostolical, or of the lax morality that would accept as true whatever seemed edifying—such as some writers have imputed to the early generations of Christians. Dr. Lipsius, indeed, maintains (p. 460) that the work and its author were condemned, not because of the fraud attempted, but because of the Gnostic doctrine which he supposes it to have originally embodied. But this is mere conjecture; and, moreover, one which, while professedly based on Tertullian's authority, substitutes for his express statement an essentially different one. Tertullian, writing of a matter on which he was apparently well informed, and which was recent, is surely a competent witness; and his testimony is express, that the author of the *Acts* was deposed from the presbyterate, not because the teaching of his book was heretical, but because its narrative was an imposture.

Of edd. the best is Tischendorf's (in his *Acta Apost. Apocrypha*, p. 40; 1851). For Eng. translations see Hone's *Apocryphal N.T.* p. 83, and Clark's *Ante-Nicene Libr.* vol. xvi. p. 279. The principal authorities on which this article is based have been specified. To Dr. Schlau's work it is largely indebted for its materials, and in some cases for its conclusions. For further discussion of the story see Tillem. *Mém.* t. ii. p. 60 (2nd ed.); Spanheim, *Hist. Christiana*, i. 11; Ittig, *de Bibliothecis*, c. xx. p. 700; Ritschl, *Die Entstehung der altkath. Kirche* (2 Aufl.), pp. 292-294; Harnack, *Zeitschrift f. Kirchengesch.* ii. pp. 90-92; Ramsay, *Church in Roman Empire before* 170 (2nd ed. Lond. 1893), pp. 375-428; and by the same, *A Lost Chapter of Early Christian Hist.* (Acta Pauli et Theclae), in *Expositor*, 1902, pp. 278-295. [J.GW.]

Themistius. [AGNOËTAE.]

Theoctistus (2), bp. of Caesarea in Palestine, who on Origen's visit to Palestine received him at Caesarea and, like Alexander of Jerusalem, permitted him, though still a layman, to preach before him (Phot. *Cod.* 118). On the remonstrance of Origen's bishop, Demetrianus, he joined with Alexander in a letter defending their conduct (Eus. *H. E.* vi. 19). Later, *c.* 230, Theoctistus and Alexander ordained Origen (*ib.* vi. 8, 23). Theoctistus probably died when Xystus was bp. of Rome 257-259, and was succeeded by Domnus (*ib.* vii. 14). Clinton, *Fasti Romani*, i. 245, 271, 287, No. 83; Le Quien, *Or. Christ.* iii. 541. [E.V.]

Theoctistus (3) Psathyropola (Ψαθυροπώλης), or the cake-seller, the head of a sect among the Arians of Constantinople *c.* 390. His followers were called, from his occupation, Psathyr is. Led by a certain Marinus from Thrace, they maintained that the First Person of the Trinity was in a proper sense Father, and so to be styled before the Son existed; while their opponents, the followers of the Antiochene Dorotheus, maintained that He was only a Father after the existence of the Son. A large party of the Arian Goths, taught by their bp. Selena, adopted the Psathyrian view, which continued to divide the church of Constantinople for 35 years, till in the reign of Theodosius Junior a reconciliation was effected (Socr. *H. E.* v. 23). [G.T.S.]

Theodebert (1) I., king of the Franks (534-548), the most capable and ambitious of the Merovingian line after Clovis. For the extent of the kingdom inherited from his father in 533 see THEODORICUS I. It was increased in 534 by a portion of the now finally conquered Burgundy (Marius, *Chron.* ad ann. 534). In 538 an army of Theodebert's Burgundian subjects entered Italy with his connivance and helped the Goths to conquer Milan (Procop. *de Bell. Gotth.* ii. 12; Marius, *Chron.* ad ann.). In 539 Theodebert, invading Italy at the head of 100,000 Franks, overran a great part of Venetia, Liguria, and the Cottian Alps, till hunger and disease drove the remnant of his army back to France (Marius, ann. 539; Marcell. *Chron.* ann. 539; Procop. *u.s.* 25). Death cut short his ambitious projects in 548.

Theodebert was perhaps the best of the Merovingian kings. Marius calls him "the Great" (*Chron.* ad ann. 548); and according to Gregory of Tours, when he had come to the throne "he shewed himself governing with justice, honouring the priests, doing good to the churches, succouring the poor and distributing benefits charitably and liberally" (*Hist. Franc.* iii. 25, 36). Instances of his good qualities appear in his liberality to the churches of the Auvergne, which his father had plundered (iii. 25), and his generosity to the impoverished city of Verdun, at the suit of their bishop (iii. 34). See, too, Aimoin, ii. 25, and the letter of Aurelianus, archbp. of Arles, in Bouquet, iv. 63. [S.A.B.]

Theodelinda, queen of the Lombards, daughter of Garibald, king of the Bavarians, married to king Authari probably in 589. On Sept. 5, 590, Authari died (Greg. *Epp.* i. 17). Theodelinda, taking counsel with her wise men, chose in Nov. Agilulf, the duke of Turin, a kinsman of her late husband (Paul. Diac. iii. 55), who in the following May was accepted by all the Lombards as king in Milan. The Lombards, like the other Teutonic nations, except the Franks, had received Christianity under an Arian form, to which they still adhered. Further, nearly all who held the orthodox creed in the territories conquered by the Lombards were in schism from their refusal to accept the fifth general council which had condemned the Three Chapters. In this complication the position of Theodelinda was peculiar. By her influence king Agilulf became eventually a Catholic, though apparently not till after A.D. 603 (Greg. *Epp.* xi. 4; xiv. 12), gave munificently to the church, and restored the orthodox bishops to their positions (Paul. Diac. iv. 6). On the other hand, she continued to support the Three Chapters, threatened to withdraw from communion with Constantius, archbp. of Milan, and refused to accept the fifth council (Greg. *Epp.* iv. 2, 3, 4, 38, 39; cf. Columbanus, *Epp.* 5 in Migne, *Patr. Lat.* lxxx. 274). Gregory touches this difference most delicately, and was, notwithstanding, on most friendly terms with Theodelinda. Mainly by her influence Agilulf was induced to make peace (Paul. Diac. iv. 8; Greg. *Epp.* ix. 42, 43), and Gregory congratulated her upon the birth of her son Adaloald in 602, and sent him a cross containing a piece of the true cross and a lection from the gospels, and three rings to his sister Gundiperga. Theodelinda built and endowed the basilica of St. John Baptist at Monza. After the death of Agilulf in 616, Adaloald succeeded with Theodelinda as regent. The date of her death was probably before 626 (Paul. Diac. iv. 41). Her crown, the most ancient in existence except the Iron Crown, her fan, her comb, the golden hen and chickens she gave to the church, and the cross sent by Gregory, are still preserved in the treasury of the cathedral at Monza. [F.D.]

Theodora (10) I., empress, wife of Justinian I., daughter of Acacius, a bear-keeper at the amphitheatre at Constantinople, who died in the reign of Anastasius when she was 7 years old. When old enough, she appeared on the stage, as her elder sister had done. Though from the whole animus of his work and the absolute silence of all other writers we may infer that Procopius exaggerates, yet we may well believe that her life was an abandoned one, without believing all his scandalous stories. Reduced to great distress, she in appearance or reality changed her mode of life, and supported herself by spinning wool. Justinian, nephew of the reigning emperor Justin, married her, and succeeding his uncle in 527, caused her to be crowned as empress regnant, but not till 532 does she appear to have exercised a preponderating voice in public affairs. She died of cancer in June 548. Unlike her husband, she was an ardent Monophysite. Her influence was unbounded, her cruelty insatiable. She assumed an especial jurisdiction over the marriages of her subjects, giving the daughters of her former associates to men of high rank, and marrying noble ladies to the lowest of the people.

Her portrait in the mosaics at St. Vitale at Ravenna has been well engraved in Hodgkin's *Invaders of Italy*, vol. iii. 606.

Sources.—The three works of Procopius, esp. the *Anecdota*; Evagr. *H. E.* iv. 10, 11; Victor. Tunun. *Chron.*; Liberat. *Breviar.* 20-22; *Lib. Pont.*, *Vitae Silverii et Vigilii.*

Literature.—Gibbon, cc. 40-41; Dahn, *Prokopius von Cäsarea*; Hodgkin, *Invaders of Italy*, iii.-iv.; Prof. Bryce, in *Contemp. Rev.* Feb. 1885; M. Debidour, *Thesis* (pub. in 1877), who tries to make the best of Theodora. [F.D.]

Theodoretus (2), bp. of Cyrrhus, or Cyrus, in the province of Euphratensis, was born at Antioch probably *c.* 393 (Tillemont). His parents held a high position at Antioch. His maternal grandmother was a lady of landed property (*Relig. Hist.* p. 1191, vol. v. ed. Schulze, Halae, 1771). His writings indicate a well-trained and highly cultivated mind, enriched by complete familiarity with the best classical authors. But his chief study was given to the Holy Scriptures and the commentators upon them in several languages. He was master of Greek, Syriac, and Hebrew, but unacquainted with Latin. His chief theological teacher, to whom he never refers without deserved reverence and admiration, was Theodore of Mopsuestia, "the great commentator," as he was called, the luminary and pride of the Antiochene school, but one who undoubtedly prepared the way for the teaching of Nestorius by his desire to provide, in Dorner's words, "for a free moral development in the Saviour's manhood." Theodoret speaks also of Diodorus of Tarsus as his teacher, but this can only have been through his writings.

The parents of Theodoret were both dead when he was 23 years old. Being their sole heir, he immediately proceeded to distribute his inheritance among the poor (*Ep.* 113), taking up his abode in a monastery, one of two founded in a large village called Nicerte, 3 miles from Apamea, and about 75 from Antioch (*Ep.* 119).

After some 7 years in the Apamean monastery, he was drawn to assume the cares of the episcopate. Of the circumstances of his consecration we are entirely ignorant. The see was that of Cyrus, or more properly Cyrrhus, the chief city of a district of the province of Euphratensis, called after it Cyrrhestica, an extensive fertile plain between the spurs of the Amanus and the river Euphrates, intersected by mountain ranges. His diocese was 40 miles square, and contained 800 distinct parishes, each with its church. It was singularly rich in monastic houses for both sexes, some of them containing as many as 250 inmates, and it boasted of a large number of solitaries. All of these enjoyed Theodoret's unremitting and affectionate solicitude and frequent visits. Cyrrhus was equally fertile in heretics. The East has ever been the nursery of heresy. Lying, as it were, in a corner of the world, not reached by the public posts, isolated by the great river to the E. and the mountain chains to the W., peopled by half-leavened heathen, Christianity there assumed many strange forms, sometimes hardly recognizable caricatures of the truth. Eunomians, Arians, Marcionites, and others who still more wildly distorted the pure faith abounded. To the recovery of these Theodoret devoted his youthful ardour and still undiminished strength, at personal risk. "Often," he writes, "have I shed my blood; often have I been stoned; nay, brought down before my time to the very gates of death." Nor were his labours fruitless. Eight villages polluted by Marcionite errors, with their neighbouring hamlets comprising more than a thousand souls, one village filled with Eunomians, another with Arians, were brought back to the sound faith. He could boast with all honesty to pope Leo I. in 449 that by the help of his prayers not a single plant of tares was left among them, and that his whole flock had been delivered from heretical errors (*Epp.* 81, 113, 116, vol. vi. pp. 1141, 1190, 1197). He carried his campaign against error, which embraced Jews and heathen as well as misbelieving Christians, beyond his own diocese. He was unwearied in preaching, and his acquaintance with the Syrian vernacular enabled him to reach the poorest and most ignorant. His care for the temporal interests and material prosperity of his diocese was no less remarkable. The city of Cyrrhus, though the winter quarters of the tenth legion, could boast little dignity or architectural beauty. He calls it "a small and desolate city," with but "few inhabitants, and those poor," whose ugliness he had striven to redeem by costly buildings erected at his own expense (*Ep.* 183, p. 1231). From his own ecclesiastical revenues—which cannot have been small—he erected public porticos, two large bridges, and public baths, and, finding the city without any regular water-supply, constructed an aqueduct, and by a catchwater drain guarded the city against inundation from the marshes (*Epp.* 79, 81). These works attracted architects and engineers to the city, and afforded remunerative employment to many people, for whose benefit he secured the help of presbyters skilled in medical science (*Epp.* 114, 115). Finding that the severity of the state imposts caused many to throw up their farms, leaving the civil authorities to make good their deficiency, a liability they were seeking to avoid by flight, he wrote to the empress Pulcheria, entreating her to lighten so intolerable a burden (*Ep.* 43, p. 1102), as well as to the patrician Anatolius (*Ep.* 45, p. 1104). With considerable trouble he obtained from Palestine relics of prophets, apostles, and martyrs, for the greater glory of a church he had built (*Relig. Hist.* c. xxi. p. 1251 ; *Ep.* 66). So great was his zeal for orthodoxy that, having discovered in the churches of his diocese more than 200 copies of the *Diatessaron* of Tatian, which he regarded as tainted with heresy, he destroyed them all, and substituted the ordinary text of the four Gospels (*Haer. Fab.* lib. i. c. 20). His life as bishop differed as little as possible from that he had lived in his monastery. State and official routine were very distasteful to him, and he avoided them as far as possible, devoting himself to the spiritual side of his office (*Epp.* 16, 79, 81, 145).

The critical period in the life of Theodoret was in connexion with the Nestorian controversy, through which he is chiefly known to us. His personal share in it began towards the end of 430, with the receipt by John, the patriarch of Antioch, of the letters of Celestine and Cyril, relative to the condemnation of the doctrines of Nestorius obtained by the Western bishops in Aug. 429. The high-handed behaviour of the patriarchs of Rome and Alexandria towards the bp. of the new Rome, a personal friend of long standing to both of them, was no less offensive to Theodoret than to John. When these documents arrived, Theodoret was at Antioch with other bishops of the province. The admirable letter (see Labbe, iii. 390 seq. ; Baluz. col. 445, c. xxi.) despatched in the name of John and his suffragans to Nestorius, exhorting him to give up his objections to the term "Theotokos," seeing that its true sense was part of the Church's faith, and entreating him not to throw the whole of Christendom into confusion for the sake of a word, has been with great show of probability ascribed to the practised pen of Theodoret. The controversy was speedily rendered much fiercer by the publication of Cyril's celebrated twelve "Anathematisms" or "Articles." Designed to crush one form of heretical teaching as regards our Lord's personal nature, these "articles" (detached, against Cyril's intention, from the letter on which they were based) hardly escaped falling into the opposite error. The Godhead of Christ was asserted with such emphasis that to some readers His manhood might seem obscured. John was shocked at what he deemed the positive affinity to Apollinarian doctrine of some of these articles, and applied first to Andreas of Samosata and then to Theodoret to confute them. Theodoret readily replied to the anathematisms seriatim. So completely at variance with orthodoxy did he regard them, that in the letter to John (reckoned as *Ep.* 150) prefixed to his observations upon them, he expresses a suspicion that some "enemies of the truth" had been sheltering themselves under Cyril's name. For the nature of these documents and for the objections urged by Theodoret and his friends, which, with much that is illogical and inconsistent, contain much that is *prima facie* Nestorian see CYRILLUS. The documents were prior to the council of Ephesus and to the formal condemnation of Nestorius then passed. At that gathering Theodoret, accompanying his metropolitan, Alexander of Hierapolis, was among the earlier comers, anticipating the Oriental brethren, whose arrival he, with 68 bishops, vainly urged should be waited for before the council opened (Baluz. c. vii. 697-699). On the arrival of John and his Oriental brethren, Theodoret at once united himself to them, and gave his voice for the deposition and excommunication of Cyril, Memnon, and their adherents (Labbe, iii. 597-599). He took part also in the proceedings which ensued, when the "concilium" and the "conciliabulum" launched thunderbolts against each other, deposing and excommunicating. Theodoret was one of the Oriental commissioners to the emperor Theodosius II. at Constantinople, representing his metropolitan Alexander (*ib.* 728). The deputies not being allowed to enter Constantinople, audiences with the emperor were held at Chalcedon, Sept. 431. Theodoret's name appears in the letters and other documents passing between the Oriental party at Ephesus and their representatives in Chalcedon, in which much was said and written in a bitter spirit (Labbe, vol. iii. 724-746 ; Theod. ed. Schulze, vol. iv. pp. 1336-1354). Of the five sessions held at Chalcedon the proceedings of the first alone are recorded. We have also a few scanty fragments of speeches and homilies of Theodoret at this period, characterized by distressing acrimony (Theod. ed. Schulze, vol. v. pp. 104-109), and a letter of his to Alexander of Hierapolis, whom he was representing, informing him how matters were going on at Chalcedon, telling him of the popularity of the deputies with the people, who, in spite of the hostility of the clergy and monks by whom they had been repeatedly stoned, flocked to hear them, assembling in a large court surrounded with porticos, the churches being closed against them ; but Theodoret laments their ill-success with the emperor. Before the deputies finally left Chalcedon, the Orientals delivered addresses to the adherents of the deposed Nestorius who had crossed the Bosphorus from Constantinople. The first of these was by Theodoret. He and his companions, he said, were shut out from the royal city on account of their fidelity to Christ, but the Heavenly Jerusalem was still open to them. On their way home from Ephesus the Orientals, Theodoret among them, held a synod at Tarsus and renewed the sentence of deposition on Cyril in conjunction with the seven orthodox deputies to Theodosius II., which they published in a circular letter. They engaged also never to abandon Nestorius. Theodoret returned to his diocese, and devoted himself to composing a fresh work assailing the obnoxious anathematisms, entitled *Pentalogus*, from its division into five books. Only a few fragments remain. Other treatises he wrote then are lost. But we have, in a Latin version, a long letter addressed to the followers of Nestorius at Constantinople, declaring his adherence to the orthodox faith, although he had felt unable to acquiesce in the condemnation of Nestorius, not believing that the doctrines ascribed to him were actually held by him (Baluz. *Synod.* c. 40, 742). Cyril found it impossible to accept the terms proposed in Theodoret's articles. He explained his objections in a long letter to Acacius, which, however, opened a way for pacification by interpretations of some questionable points in his anathematisms which he refused to withdraw. This letter Theodoret regarded as orthodox, but irreconcilable with the anathematisms, which he still regarded as heretical. He was, however, precluded from accepting the terms of peace which John and others were increasingly inclined to acquiesce in, by the demand that he should anathematize the doctrine of Nestorius and Nestorius himself. To do this (Theodoret writes to his friend Andrew of Samosata) would be to anathematize godliness itself. He is ready to anathematize all who assert that Christ was mere man, or who divide Him into two Sons, or who deny His Godhead. But if they anathematized a man of whom they were not the judges, and his doctrine which they knew to be sound, *en bloc*, "indeterminate," they would act impiously (*ib.* 766, c. 61). At this epoch, as Hefele remarks (*Hist. of Councils*, vol. iii. p. 127, Eng. trans.), the Orientals were divided into two great parties: the peace-seeking majority, with John of Antioch and the venerable Acacius at their head, ready to meet Cyril half-way; the violent party of irreconcilables, with Alexander of Hierapolis as their leader, opposed to all reconciliation as treason to the truth; while a third or middle party was led by Theodoret and Andrew of Samosata, anxious for peace, but on terms of their own. Theodoret and his scanty band of adherents failed to secure the confidence of either of the two great parties. His inflexible metropolitan, Alexander, vehemently denounced as treason to the truth any approach to reconciliation with Cyril. Against this reproach and against the suspicion that he had given in to escape persecution or to secure a higher place Theodoret sought to defend himself (*ib.* c. 72, 775). Though still holding back from reconciliation with Cyril, he was virtually the means of bringing about the long-desired peace. The declaration of faith presented to Cyril by Paul of Emesa, as representing the belief of John, and accepted by Cyril, had been originally drawn up by Theodoret at Ephesus. The paragraphs directed against Cyril's twelve articles were slightly modified, but the main body was unaltered (Cyril. ed. Pusey, vi. 44; Baluz. c. 96, 97, 804; Tillem. *Mém. eccl.* xiv. 531; Hefele, *op. cit.* iii. 130 ff.). The reconciliation, however, was by no means acceptable to Theodoret. For it demanded acceptance of the deposition of Nestorius, the anathematizing of Nestorius's doctrines, and the giving up the four metropolitans of his party who had been deposed at Constantinople. Theodoret's protest was in vain. Theodosius insisted on the deposition and expulsion of all bishops who continued opposed to union. Finding his growing isolation more and more intolerable, Theodoret invited the chiefs of the fast-lessening band of his sympathizers, Alexander, Andrew, and others, to take counsel at Zeugma, in reference to the union with Cyril, which had been accepted by John and earnestly pressed upon them by the combined weight of the ecclesiastical and civil power. Alexander refused to attend the synod except on his own terms. The bishops who met, as Theodoret informed John (Baluz. c. 95, 662, 801), accepted the orthodoxy of Cyril's letter and regarded it as a recantation of his obnoxious twelve articles, but would not pronounce an anathema on Nestorius. John, now hopeless of peace otherwise, applied to the secular power. His method proved generally effectual. One by one the recalcitrant prelates yielded, except Alexander and some others. Theodoret was one of the last to yield. The coldness arising between him and John after John's reconciliation with Cyril had been much increased by John's uncanonical intrusion into the province of Alexander in the ordination of bishops. Theodoret, with the other bishops of the province, on this, withdrew from communion with him, and published a synodical letter charging him with ordaining unworthy persons (*ib.* 831, 850). Long and painful controversy ensued, only crushed at last by John's appealing to the imperial power. All eventually yielded to combined entreaties and menaces save Alexander and a small band of irreconcilables, who were banished from their sees. Theodoret was assailed on his tenderest side by harassing his diocese. The unhappy renewal of strife, concerning the doctrines of Diodorus and Theodoret, brought Theodoret and Cyril once more into collision. For the details of the conflict see CYRILLUS OF ALEXANDRIA; PROCLUS; RABBULAS; IBAS. The long and bitter controversy, in which both parties did and said many regrettable things, was closed by the death of Cyril, June 9 or 27, 444.

The succession of Dioscorus to Cyril's patriarchal throne led to fresh trials for Theodoret. Dioscorus was resolved to bring about Theodoret's overthrow, as Theodoret was one of the first to discern the nascent heresy of Eutyches, and directed the powers of a well-trained intellect and great theological learning to exposing it. The ear of the emperor was gained, and Theodoret was represented as a turbulent busybody, constantly at Antioch and other cities, taking part in councils and assemblies instead of attending to his diocese; a troublesome agitator, stirring up strife wherever he moved (*Ep.* 79, p. 1135, etc.). He was also accused on theological grounds. Dioscorus, who seems to have regarded himself as "the lawful inheritor of Cyril's guardianship of anti-Nestorian orthodoxy," wrote to Theodoret's patriarch, Domnus, who *c.* 442 had succeeded his uncle John in the see of Antioch, informing him that Theodoret was creating a crypto-Nestorian party, practically teaching Nestorianism under another name and striking at "the one Nature of the Incarnate." These accusations were accepted at court, and Dioscorus obtained an imperial edict (dated by Tillemont Mar. 30, 449) that as a disturber of the peace of the church Theodoret should keep to his own diocese. Theodoret submitted, leaving the city without bidding his friends farewell (*Ep.* 80, p. 1137).

From the "Latrocinium" or "Robbers' Synod," at Ephesus (449) [DIOSCORUS; EUTYCHES], Theodoret was excluded by an imperial edict of Mar. 4, unless summoned unanimously by the council itself (Labbe, iv. 100). Theodoret's condemnation was evidently the chief purpose in summoning this infamous synod. From his "internement" at Cyrrhus Theodoret calmly watched his enemies' proceedings. He had not long to wait for the confirmation of his worst fears. Dioscorus and his partisans, having by brutal violence obtained the acquittal of Eutyches and the deposition of Flavian, Ibas, Irenaeus, and other sympathizers with Theodoret, proceeded on the third session to deal with him. The indictment was formulated by a presbyter of Antioch named Pelagius, who, in language of the most atrocious violence, proceeded to demand of the council to take the sword of God and, as Samuel dealt with Agag, and Elijah with the priests of Baal, pitilessly destroy those who had introduced strange doctrines into the church. Those who adhered to the poisonous teachings of Nestorius deserved the flames. "Burn them!—burn them!" he cried. Pelagius was allowed to lay before the synod the proofs of his accusation, contained in "The Apology of Theodoret, bp. of Cyrrhus, in behalf of Diodorus and Theodorus, champions of God." The council exclaimed that they had heard enough to warrant the immediate deposition of Theodoret, as the emperor had already ordered. The unanimous sentence was that he should be deposed from the priesthood and deprived of even lay communion. His books were to be committed to the flames (*ib.* 125, 126, 129; *Le Brigandage*, pp. 193-195).

Dioscorus was now master of the whole Eastern church; "il règne partout." Theodoret knew that deposition was usually followed by exile, and prepared for the worst. He was allowed to retire to his monastery near Apamea (*Ep.* 119, p. 1202). An appeal to the West, forbidden him in person by Theodosius, was now prosecuted by letter, which, though addressed to Leo individually, was really meant for the bishops of the West assembled in the synod, to which he begs his cause may be submitted (*Mém. eccl.* xv. 294). "In this remarkable letter," writes Dr. Bright (*Hist. of Church*, p. 395), "he traces the primacy of Rome to her civil greatness, her soundness of faith, and her possession of the graves of the apostles Peter and Paul. He eulogizes the exact and comprehensive orthodoxy with which the Tome of Leo conveys the full mind of the Holy Spirit." He entreats Leo "to decide whether he ought to submit to the recent sentence. He awaits his decision. He will acquiesce in it, whatever it be, committing himself to the judgment of his God and Saviour." Theodosius continued to pay no heed to the remonstrances of Leo, asserting that everything had been decided at Ephesus with complete freedom and in accordance with the truth, and that the prelates there deposed merited their fate for innovations in the faith. The interposition of Pulcheria and of the Western princesses was employed in vain. On July 29, 450, Theodosius II. was killed by a fall from his horse, and the imperial dignity passed to the resolute hands of the orthodox Pulcheria and her soldier-husband Marcian. All was now changed. Eutychianism became the losing cause, and the orthodox sufferers were speedily recalled. Theodoret appears to have been mentioned by name in the edict of recall. The stigma of heterodoxy was speedily removed from him. There is no reason to doubt that he was one of the bishops who signed the Tome of Leo, prefixing a short résumé of his own faith regarding the Incarnation, and that on this Leo recognized him as a Catholic bishop (Tillem. xv. 304; Baron. 450, §§ 22-24). Though now at liberty to go where he pleased, Theodoret preferred to remain in his monastery (*Ep.* 146). His chief desire was to witness the complete triumph of truth, and to convince others of the purity of his own teaching. This desire he saw in part fulfilled. But for his complete satisfaction an oecumenical council was necessary, and to bring that about he laboured with all his might.

The council of Chalcedon met on Oct. 8, 451. Theodoret's entrance was the signal for outrageous violence on the part of the adherents of Dioscorus. The hall re-echoed with cries and counter-cries which interrupted all proceedings. Theodoret sat down "in the midst," not among his brother-bishops. He continued to attend the sessions of the council, but without voting, and taking no part in the deposition of Dioscorus. His own cause came on at the eighth session, Oct. 26. Although his orthodoxy had been acknowledged by Leo and his restoration required by the emperor, the anti-Nestorian section would not hear of his recognition as a bishop until he had in express terms anathematized Nestorius. This step he had repeatedly declared he would never take, and he now tried to satisfy the remonstrants with something short of it, but in vain. Wearied out, at last he yielded to their clamour and pronounced the test words, "Anathema to Nestorius, and to every one who denies that the Holy Virgin Mary is the mother of God, and who divides the one Son, the Only-begotten, into two Sons." The imperial commissioners now declared that all doubt had been removed and that Theodoret should now receive back his bishopric. The whole assembly raised the cry that Theodoret was worthy of his throne, and that the church must receive back her orthodox teacher. The leading bishops voted for his restoration, the rest signified their assent by acclamation, and the commissioners gave sentence that by the decree of the holy council Theodoret should receive again the church of Cyrrhus (Labbe, iv. 619-624).

But few years remained to Theodoret, and of these very little is known. It is not even certain whether he returned to his episcopal duties at Cyrrhus or remained in the quiet Apamean monastery, devoting himself to literary labours. Tillemont thinks that he probably did not live beyond 453. But if the statement of Gennadius (c. 89) be true, that his death took place under the emperor Leo, he must have lived till 457 or 458.

His writings may be divided roughly into: I. *Exegetical*, on the Scriptures of O. and N. T. II. *Controversial*, dealing with the anathematisms of Cyril, the Eutychian heresy, and, in a work written towards the end of his life, with heresies in general. III. *Theological*, including the *Graecarum affectionum Curatio*, *Orations on Divine Providence*, and sundry orations and lesser treatises. IV. *Historical*, and V. *Epistolary*.

I. *Exegetical.*—These include works on (1) the Octateuch, (2) the books of Sam., Kings, and Chron., (3) the Pss., (4) the Canticles, (5) the Major Prophets, (6) the Twelve Minor Prophets, (7) the Fourteen Epistles of St. Paul, including that to the Hebrews. The work on the Octateuch consists of answers to difficult points, for the most part characterized by the sound common-sense literalism of the Antiochene school, with but little tendency to allegory. He often, instead of his own opinion, cites that of his great masters Diodorus of Tarsus and Theodore of Mopsuestia, and Origen. In Leviticus and Numbers he naturally adopts more of the allegorical method, regarding the whole Levitical ritual and the moral ordinances as typical of the sacrificial and mediatorial work of Christ, and of the new law He came to inaugurate. The commentary on the Canticles was his earliest exegetical work. He controverts the opinion that this book contains the story of the earthly loves of Solomon either with Pharaoh's daughter or with Abishag, or that it is a political allegory, in which the bridegroom represents the monarch and the bride the people, and adopts the spiritual interpretation by which the bridegroom stands for Jesus Christ and the bride for the church. From one passage in the very interesting prologue we learn that Theodoret held the then current opinion, that the whole of the O.T. books having been burnt under Manasseh and other godless kings, or destroyed during the Captivity, Ezra was divinely inspired to rewrite them word for word on the return from the Captivity. He denounces the iniquity of the Jews, who had excluded Daniel from the prophets and placed his book among the Hagiographa, because no prophet had so clearly predicted the advent of Jesus Christ, and the very time of His appearance. The only portions of the N.T. commented on by him are the *Epistles of St. Paul*, including that to the Hebrews. Of these bp. Lightfoot writes, "His commentaries on St. Paul are superior to his other exegetical writings, and have been assigned the palm over all patristic expositions of Scripture. For appreciation, terseness, and good sense they are perhaps unsurpassed, and if the absence of faults were a just standard of merit, they would deserve the first place; but they have little claim to originality, and he who has read Chrysostom and Theodore of Mopsuestia will find scarcely anything in Theodoret which he has not seen before. It is right to add, however, that Theodoret himself modestly disclaims any such merit. In his preface he apologizes for attempting to interpret St. Paul after two such men who are 'luminaries of the world,' and he professes nothing more than to gather his stores 'from the blessed Fathers.'" (*Gal.* p. 220).

II. *Controversial.*—(1) *The Refutation of the Twelve Anathematisms of Cyril.* (2) *Eranistes* or *Polymorphus*, "a work of remarkable interest and of permanent value for theological students, to be read in connexion with the Tome of Leo and the definitions of Chalcedon" (Bright, *Later Treatises of Athanas.* p. 177). It consists of three dialogues between the "Mendicant" Ἐρανίστης who represents Eutychianism, and Theodoret himself as Ὀρθόδοξος. Their respective titles indicate the line adopted in each. These are Ἄτρεπτος, *Immutabilis*, Ἀσύγχυτος, *Inconfusus*, and Ἀπαθής, *Impatibilis*. (3) Αἱρετικῆς Κακομυθίας ἐπιτομή, *Haereticarum Fabularum Compendium*, a work directed against heresies in general, in five books. The *fourth* book, the most important as treating of matters with which he was more or less personally acquainted, begins with the heresies of Arius and Eunomius and comes down to those of Nestorius and Eutyches. His disgracefully violent language with regard to his former friend Nestorius—whom he stigmatizes as an instrument of Satan, a man who by his pride had plunged the church into disorders, and under the cloak of orthodoxy introduced the denial of the Divinity and of the Incarnation of the Only-begotten Son, and who at last met with the punishment he deserved, a sign of his future punishment—would warrant the charitable hope that this chapter has been erroneously ascribed to Theodoret. Of this, however, there is no evidence, and we are, though most reluctantly, compelled to accept it as his work, together with the equally atrocious letter to Sporacius on the Nestorian heresy. It is accepted by Photius (*Cod.* 56) and Leontius of Byzantius (art. 4, *de Sectis*) (cf. Neander, iv. p. 246, note, Ceillier, *Aut. ecclés.* x. 84).

III. *Theological.*—The chief is an apologetic treatise, intended to exhibit the confirmations of the truth of the Christian faith contained in the philosophical systems of the Gentiles, under the title Ἑλληνικῶν θεραπευτικὴ παθημάτων, *Graecarum Affectionum Curatio, seu Evangelicae Veritatis ex Gentilium Philosophia Cognitio*. It is in 12 discourses, and furnishes a very able and eloquent defence of Christianity against the ridicule and ignorant accusations of pagan philosophers, written probably before 437. It was followed by another of a similar character, in ten orations, on *Divine Providence*, regarded by the best critics as exhibiting Theodoret's literary power in its highest form, as regards the careful selection of thoughts, nobility of language, elegance and purity of style, and the force and sequence of his arguments (Ceillier, p. 88, § 10). To these may be added a *discourse on Charity*, περὶ θείας καὶ ἁγίας ἀγάπης (Schulze, 14, 1296 seq.) and some fragments of sermons, etc., given by Garnier (*Auctarium*, *ib.* t. v. pp. 71 seq.).

IV. *Historical.*—This class contains two works of very different character and of very different value: (1) the *Ecclesiastical History* and (2) the *Religious History*. (1) The former, in five books, was intended to form a continuation of that of Eusebius. It commences with the rise of Arianism under Constantius and closes with the death of Theodore of Mopsuestia, A.D. 429. From his opening words he has been thought to have had in view the histories of Socrates and Sozomen, and to have written to supply their omissions and correct their mistakes (Valesius). This is questioned by some, and must be regarded as doubtful. He gives more original documents than either of his brother-historians, but is very chary of dates, and writes generally without sufficient chronological exactness. Photius finds fault with his too great fondness for metaphor, while he praises his style as "clear, lofty, and free from redundancy" (*Cod.* 31). The history is learned and generally impartial, "though it is occasionally one-sided and runs off into a theological treatise." An Eng. trans. was pub. by Baxter in 1847. (2) The *Religious History*, φιλόθεος ἱστορία, is devoted to the lives of 30 celebrated hermits and ascetics, his contemporaries, and was written from personal knowledge and popular report before his *Ecclesiastical History*. It excites our wonder at what Dr. Newman calls the "easy credence, or as moderns would say large credulousness," which appears more astonishing as he had been brought up in the most matter-of-fact, prosaic, and critical school of ancient Christendom. "What," writes Dr. Newman, "made him drink in with such relish what we reject with such disgust? Was it that, at least, some miracles were brought home so absolutely to his sensible experience that he had no reason for doubting the others which came to him second-hand? This certainly will explain what to most of us is sure to seem the stupid credulity of so well-read, so intellectual an author" (*Hist. Sketches*, iii. 314). The whole subject presents a very curious intellectual problem.

V. *Epistolary.*—No portion of Theodoret's literary remains exceeds in interest and value the large collection of his letters. As throwing light on his personal history and character, and as helping us to understand the perplexed relations of the principal actors in that stormy period of theological strife and their various shades of theological opinion, their importance cannot be over-estimated. They give us a heightened esteem of Theodoret himself, his intellectual power, theological precision, warm-hearted affection, and Christian virtues. An Eng. trans. of this remarkable series of letters, arranged according to date and subject, is much to be desired.

The *Auctarium* of Garnier also contains the following: (1) *Prolegomena and Extracts of Commentaries on the Psalms*, probably derived from *Catenae*. (2) A *Short Extract from a Commentary on St. Luke*. (3) *Sermon on the Nativity of S. John Baptist*. (4) *Homily* spoken at Chalcedon in 431. (5) Fifteen additional *letters* of Theodoret. (6) Seven dialogues composed a little before the council of Ephesus, 2 each against *Anomoeans* and *Apollinarians*, and 3 against *Macedonians*. Their authorship is doubtful; they have been ascribed to Athanasius or Maximus, but Garnier claims them for Theodoret.

Editions.—There are 2 edd. of his complete works in Gk. and Lat.; the first in 4 vols. fol. (Paris, 1642), by the Jesuit Jac. Sirmond, to which a 5th vol. was added after Sirmond's death by his fellow-Jesuit, J. Garnier (Paris, 1684), containing an auctarium, comprising fragments of commentaries and sermons and some additional letters, together with Garnier's 5 learned but most one-sided dissertations on (1) the life, (2) the writings, (3) the faith of Theodoret, (4) on the fifth general council, and (5) the cause of Theodoret and the Orientals. This was succeeded by another ed. based on it, with additions and corrections by Lud. Schulze and J. A. Noesselt (Halae Sax. 1769-1774), in 5 vols. and in 10 parts. To this edition our references are made. The ed. of T. Gaisford is pub. by the Clarendon Press. There is a trans. of Theodoret's works in Bohn's Lib. (Bell), and by Blomfield Jackson in *Lib. of Post-Nicene Fathers*. Cf. N. Ghibokowski, *The Blessed Theodoret, bp. of Cyrus* (Moscow, 1890, 2 vols.); Harnack in *Theol. Literatur Zeitung* (1890), p. 502. [E.V.]

Theodoricus (1) **I.** (*Theodericus*), chosen king of the Visigoths on the death of Valia, A.D. 419. He was the real founder of the West Gothic kingdom. On his accession the Visigoths held nothing in Spain, but occupied in Gaul Aquitania Secunda, the region lying, roughly speaking, between the Loire and the Garonne, with some neighbouring cities, of which Toulouse, their capital, was the most important. This territory had been ceded to Valia as the price of the *foedus* with Rome. The history of Theodoric's reign consists of a series of endeavours to extend this territory when the Romans were otherwise occupied, with intervals of renewal of the *foedus*, the Goths, however, retaining what they had won. In the great battle of the Mauriac plains Theodoric, who was advanced in life, fell from his horse and was trampled to death by his own troops (A.D. 451). Salvian (*de Gub. Dei*, vii. 154) praises him for his piety, to which he attributes the defeat of the self-confident Litorius. Though, like the rest of his race, an Arian, he did not persecute the Catholics. Prosper and Idatius, *Chronica*; Jordanes, *Get.* 34-40; Isidorus, *Hist. Goth.*, *Hist. Suev.*, Dahn, *Die Könige der Germanen*, v. 71. [F.D.]

Theodoricus (3) (*Theodericus*), the Ostrogoth, king in Italy. The second is the spelling of all inscriptions (Mommsen, *Jordanes*, 144). He was the son of Thiudimer by his concubine Erelieva, and was born probably in 454. His father was the second brother of Valamir, king of the Ostrogoths, Vidimer being the third. The three lived in amity, occupying N. Pannonia, the part of the tribe under Thiudimer being settled near Lake Pelso at Theodoric's birth. He succeeded his father in 474 or 475, and assisted in 477 in Zeno's restoration. In 487 Zeno induced Theodoric to undertake an expedition to Italy for the purpose of overthrowing Odoacer. Theodoric willingly consented; his people, who in the course of their wanderings had mostly settled in Lower Moesia, Nova near Rustchuk being his capital, were discontented with their settlements; and in the autumn of 488 they started. It was not the march of an army, but the migration of a whole people. Their progress by Sirmium and Pannonia was slow, impeded by the winter weather and the opposition of the Gepidae and Sarmatians; not till the summer of 489 did they force their way through the Julian Alps into Italy. For the events of the war, terminated in Mar. 493 by Theodoric's complete victory, see *D. C. B.* (4 vols. 1900), art. "Odoacer." After Theodoric had shut up Odoacer in Ravenna in autumn 490, he sent Faustus, the chief of the senate, and Irenaeus (Gelasius, *Ep.* 8) to Zeno to ask his permission to assume the royal robes. Zeno died in Apr. 491, and, no answer having come from his successor Anastasius, on the fall of Ravenna the army proclaimed Theodoric king (*An. Val.* 53, 57). Already king of the Ostrogoths, he was thus recognized as king over his new conquests; but, like Odoacer, he assumed the title without any territorial definition such as "king of Italy." Gregory of Tours (iii. 31) indeed styles him "Rex Italiae," but this is merely a description, not a formal title; cf. the parallel of Odoacer and Victor Vitensis. This independent assumption was regarded at Constantinople as a usurpation, and not till 498 was a recognition grudgingly obtained by the embassy of the senator Festus, and the imperial ornaments returned which Odoacer had sent to Constantinople (*An. Val.* 64, Theodorus Lector, ii. 16, 17, in Migne, *Patr. Gk.* lxxxvi. 1, 189). Theodoric, while really independent, was ready to pay the emperor marks of respect, such as submitting for approval the name of the consul he nominated. But there was no real cordiality between the two. At Constantinople Theodoric was regarded merely as *de jure* the lieutenant of the emperor who had commissioned him to recover Italy, and the Byzantine claims were only kept in abeyance for a convenient opportunity.

His first care after the overthrow of Odoacer was to arrange the settlement of his followers in Italy. A third part of the lands was distributed to them. The Goths were very unequally distributed. In Calabria and Apulia there were none (Procop. i. 15); they began to appear in Samnium, and then increased to the N. and E., the settlements being thickest in the Aemilia and Venetia. The Goths were probably settled by families and tribes (*Var.* v. 27), and did not, like the Vandals, clear out and occupy the whole of a continuous province. Their dispersion among the previous inhabitants had many important consequences, the most important perhaps being the increase of the royal power, which was further strengthened by Theodoric uniting to his hereditary kingship the derelict prerogatives of the Western emperor. He governed the two nations—the Romans and the Goths—who lived side by side without intermingling, in a twofold capacity: the former as the successor of the emperor, the latter as the king of immemorial antiquity. The Roman forms of government were kept up; the senate met, and Theodoric submitted his appointments of patricians, consuls, etc., for their ratification. The Roman systems of taxation and administration were maintained. The Goths, like the Romans, had to pay taxes, but their special obligation was that of military service. Theodoric's care for his dominions is shewn by the multifarious subjects of the *Variarum*—*e.g.* drainage of marshes, regulations of the posting service, repairs of harbours, roads, and public buildings, such as Pompey's theatre and the cloacae at Rome, fortifications, searches for mines, etc. Under his firm rule Italy enjoyed 33 years of peace and prosperity such as she had not known for nearly a century, and was not to know again for generations.

The state of affairs in Gaul after 507 demanded Theodoric's interference. When his negotiations failed to prevent a breach between Clovis and his son-in-law Alaric, and when the rout and death of Alaric threatened that all Gaul, and perhaps Spain, would pass into the hands of the Franks, he felt compelled to interpose. The result was the preservation of Spain and the district of Narbonne or Septimania for the Visigoths, and the acquisition by Theodoric of a territory corresponding with the modern Provence, including Arles and Marseilles. He was thus placed in immediate communication with the Visigoths, among whose kings he is reckoned by Spanish historians as guardian of his infant grandson.

Though, like his countrymen, an Arian, Theodoric for most of his reign acted not only with impartiality but favour to the Catholics, some holding high offices under him. On his one recorded visit to Rome in 500, where he spent six months (*An. Val.*, Cassiod. *Chron.*), he gave magnificent presents to St. Peter's as if he had been a Catholic; he was on friendly terms with the most eminent bishops, such as EPIPHANIUS, whom he employed on an embassy to the Burgundians to obtain the release of the prisoners taken in their inroads into N. Italy during the war with Odoacer; and in his interference in the troubles following the disputed election of SYMMACHUS and LAURENTIUS he seems to have acted solely with a view to benefit the church. Nor did he object to the nullification by the synod, under Symmachus, of Odoacer's law against the alienation of ecclesiastical property, on the ground that it rested only on lay authority. He was careful also not to infringe on the privileges of the church, and extended his protection to the Jews.

During most of his reign the difficulties of his position were much lightened by the schism between the Eastern and Western churches. To the pope and the orthodox party a Eutychian emperor was as hateful as an Arian king. But when in 518 Anastasius was succeeded by Justin and the 37 years' schism was ended by the complete triumph of HORMISDAS, whose negotiations with the East had been conducted by Theodoric's permission (*Vita Hormisdae*), the obstacle to the desires of the orthodox Romans for reunion with the empire was removed. On the Eastern side the breach was widened by the persecution of heretics, commenced by Justin in 523. By the law of that year (*Cod.* i. v. 12), heretics were subjected to many civil and religious disabilities. The Goths serving in the army (*foederati*) were exempted from its provisions, but must, like the rest of their co-religionists, have felt the next measure, the seizure of all the churches belonging to heretics. Theodoric appears to have intended to occupy the churches of the Catholics and hand them over to the Arians as reprisals for the similar treatment they had experienced in the East, when he was seized with illness, and died Aug. 30, 526. He apparently never had a son. His only surviving daughter Amalasuintha he had given in marriage in 515 to Eutharic, a descendant of the Amals, whose consulship in 519 was celebrated with great magnificence at Rome. He died before Theodoric, leaving one son, Athalaric, whom his grandfather, shortly before his death, declared king, under the regency of his mother.

Theodoric was a great builder. He restored the aqueducts at Verona and Ravenna, built palaces at Verona and Ravenna, and baths there and at Pavia. But his greatest works are at Ravenna, his own mausoleum, with its marvellous dome, formed of one block of Istrian stone, and what is now St. Apollinare Nuovo, the church he built for his Arian fellow-worshippers, of which they retained possession till the time of bp. Agnellus (Agnellus, *Lib. Pont.* in *Rerum Script. Lang.* 334).

Almost our only source of information as to his internal administration is the *Variarum* of Cassiodorus (*vid.* Mr. Hodgkin's preface to this work). Of modern writings, Dahn's *Könige der Germanen*, ii.-iv. is the most valuable. Du Roure has published a Life of Theodoric, and there is a brilliant sketch in Gibbon, c. 39, of his rule in Italy. [F.D.]

Theodoricus (5) **I.** (*Thierry, Theuderich*), king of the Franks (511-533), one of the four sons of Clovis, by a concubine. He was considerably older than his three half-brothers, the sons of Clotilda, and had a grown-up son, Theodebert, when his father died (Greg. Tur. *Hist. Franc.* ii. 28, iii. 1) in 511. The four sons divided the kingdom, nominally into equal portions, but really Theodoric, owing probably to his greater age and capacity, obtained the largest portion. His capital was Metz, and his kingdom comprised the Ripuarian Frankish territory, Champagne, the eastern portion of Aquitaine and the old Salian Frankish possessions to the Kohlenwald (Richter, *Annalen*, p. 46). Fauriel says that besides Frankish Germany he had so much of Gaul as lies between the Rhine and the Meuse and, as his share of Aquitaine, the Auvergne with the Velai and Gévaudan, its dependencies, the Limousin in part or whole, and certain other cantons of less importance (*Hist. de la Gaule Mérid.* ii. 92). Theodoric died in 533. He was a strong and capable king, but to the ferocity and lawlessness of his race he added an unscrupulous cunning of his own (*ib.* iii. 7). His attitude towards the church seems to have been one of indifference, influenced neither by fear nor superstition. Orthodoxy had been so useful a political weapon to his father that the son was presumably a professing Christian, though he is not mentioned among the members of Clovis's family baptized by St. Remigius. He did not shrink from involving churches in his army's pillage and destruction in the Auvergne (iii. 12), and though he exalted St. Quintian, bp. of Clermont, it was not as a priest, but as a partisan who had suffered in his cause (iii. 2), while he bitterly persecuted Desiderius, bp. of Verdun (iii. 34). He has the credit of reducing to writing and amending the laws of the Franks, Alamanni, and Bavarians (Migne, *Patr. Lat.* lxxi. 1163). [S.A.B.]

Theodorus (6) **Askidas** (ὁ Ἀσκιδᾶς), archbp. of Caesarea in Cappadocia, the chief supporter of Origen's views in the first half of cent. vi. and the originator of the celebrated controversy concerning the "Three Chapters." The general history of his life belongs to that subject; we now give merely a brief outline. He was a monk of the convent of Nova Laura in Palestine, and made, *c.* 537, archbp. of Caesarea under Justinian. He supported the views of Origen when they were persecuted in Palestine. He secretly favoured Monophysite views, and, when Justinian condemned Origen, saw a chance of condemning the great authorities on the Nestorian side, Theodoret, Theodore, and Ibas. Working, therefore, through the empress Theodora, he persuaded Justinian to attempt to reconcile the Monophysite party; Justinian, at his suggestion, issuing his celebrated edict which gave rise to the great controversy concerning the Three Chapters. At the general council of Constantinople archbp. Theodore subscribed the condemnation of Origen on the one hand, and of Theodoret, Theodore, and Ibas on the other. He died probably *c.* 558 at Constantinople. The *Testimonium* of Theodore and of Cethegus the patrician concerning the contradictions of pope Vigilius about the Three Chapters is in Mansi, t. ix. col. 363 (Ceill. xi. 327, 865, 881; Hefele's *Councils*, § 258). [G.T.S.]

Theodorus (26), bp. of Mopsuestia; also known, from the place of his birth and presbyterate, as Theodore of Antioch, the most prominent representative of the middle Antiochene school of hermeneutics.

I. *Life and Work.*—Theodore was born at Antioch *c.* 350 (see Fritzsche, *de Th. M. V. et Scr.* pp. 1-4, for the chronology; cf. Kihn, *Theodor u. Junilius*, p. 39, n. 1). His father held an official position at Antioch, and the family was wealthy (Chrys. *ad Th. Laps.* ii. in Migne, *Patr. Gk.* xlvii. 209). Theodore's cousin, Paeanius, to whom several of Chrysostom's letters are addressed (*Epp.* 95, 193, 204, 220, in Migne, lii.), held an important post of civil government; his brother Polychronius became bp. of the metropolitan see of Apamea. Theodore first appears as the early companion and friend of Chrysostom, his fellow-townsman, his equal in rank, and but two or three years his senior in age. Together with their common friend Maximus, afterwards bp. of Isaurian Seleucia, Chrysostom and Theodore attended the lectures of the sophist Libanius (Socr. vi. 3; cf. Soz. viii. 1), then at Antioch in the zenith of his fame. We have the assurance of Sozomen that he enjoyed a philosophical education (*l.c.*). Chrysostom credits his friend with diligent study, but the luxurious life of polite Antioch seems to have received an equal share of his thoughts. When Chrysostom himself had been reclaimed from the pleasures of the world by the influence of Basil, he succeeded in winning Maximus and Theodore to the same mind. The three friends left Libanius and sought a retreat in the monastic school (ἀσκητήριον) of Carterius and Diodorus, to which Basil was already attached. Whether Theodore had been previously baptized is doubtful; Chrysostom, however, speaks of him shortly afterwards in terms which seem to imply his baptism (*ad Th. Laps.*). He gave himself to the new learning with characteristic energy. His days, as his friend testifies, were spent in reading, his nights in prayer; he fasted long, lay on the bare ground, and practised every form of ascetic self-discipline; he was full withal of light-hearted joy, as having found the service of Christ to be perfect freedom. His conversion was speedy, sincere, and marvellously complete, but was followed by a reaction which threatened an utter collapse of his new-found life. He had but just resigned himself to a celibate life when he was fascinated by a girl named Hermione (Chrys. *ib.* i., Migne, xlvii. p. 297), and contemplated marriage, at the same time returning to his former manner of life (Soz. viii. 2). His "fall" spread consternation through the little society. Many were the prayers offered and efforts made for his recovery. "Valerius, Florentius, Porphyrius, and many others," laboured to restore him; and the anxiety drew forth from Chrysostom the earliest of his literary compositions—two letters "to Theodore upon his fall." The second letter reveals at once the strength of Chrysostom's affection, and the greatness of the character in which at that early age (Theodore was not yet 20) he had already found so much to love. Theodore remained constant to his vows (Soz. *l.c.*), although the disappointment left traces in his after-life.

Chrysostom's connexion with Diodore was probably broken off in 374, when he plunged into a more complete monastic seclusion; Theodore's seems to have continued until the elevation of Diodore to the see of Tarsus A.D. 378. During this period doubtless the foundations were laid of Theodore's acquaintance with Holy Scripture and ecclesiastical doctrine, and he was imbued for life with the principles of scriptural interpretation which Diodore had inherited from an earlier generation of Antiochenes, and with the peculiar views of the Person of Christ into which the master had been led by his antagonism to Apollinarius. The latter years of this decade witnessed Theodore's first appearance as a writer. He began with a commentary on the Psalms, in which the method of Diodore was exaggerated, and which he lived to repent of (Facund. iii. 6, x. 1; *v. infra*, § III.). The orthodox at Antioch, it seems, resented the loss of the traditional Messianic interpretation, and, if we may trust Hesychius, Theodore was compelled to promise that he would commit his maiden work to the flames—an engagement he contrived to evade (Mansi, ix. 284).

Gennadius (*de Vir. Ill.* 12) represents Theodore as a presbyter of the church of Antioch; and from a letter of John of Antioch (Facund. ii. 2) we gather that 45 years elapsed between his ordination and his death. It seems, therefore, that he was ordained priest at Antioch A.D. 383, in his 33rd year, the ordaining bishop being doubtless Flavian, Diodore's old friend and fellow-labourer, whose "loving disciple" Theodore now became (John of Antioch, *ap.* Facund. *l.c.*). The epithet seems to imply that Theodore was an attached adherent of the Meletian party; but there is no evidence that he mixed himself up with the feuds which for some years after Flavian's consecration distracted the Catholics of Antioch. Theodore's great treatise on the Incarnation (Gennad. *l.c.*) belongs to this period, possibly also more than one of his commentaries on the O.T. As a preacher he seems to have now attained some eminence in the field of polemics (Facund. viii. 4). Theodore is said by Hesychius of Jerusalem (Mansi, ix. 248) to have left Antioch while yet a priest and betaken himself to Tarsus, until 392, when he was consecrated to the see of Mopsuestia, vacant by the death of Olympius, probably through the influence and by the hands of Diodore. Here he spent his remaining 36 years of life (Theodoret, *l.c.*).

Mopsuestia was a free town (Pliny) upon the Pyramus, between Tarsus and Issus, some 40 miles from either, and 12 from the sea. It belonged to Cilicia Secunda, of which the metropolitan see was Anazarbus. In the 4th cent. it was of some importance, famous for its bridge, thrown over the Pyramus by Constantine. It is now the insignificant town Mensis, or Messis (*D. of G. and R. Geogr.*).

Theodore's long episcopate was marked by no striking incidents. His letters, long known to the Nestorians of Syria as the *Book of Pearls*, are lost; his followers have left us few personal recollections. In 394 he attended a synod at Constantinople on a question which concerned the see of Bostra in the partiarchate of Antioch (Mansi, iii. 851; cf. Hefele, ii. 406). Theodore preached, probably on this occasion, before the emperor Theodosius I., who was then starting for his last journey to the West. The sermon made a deep impression, and Theodosius, who had sat at the feet of St. Ambrose and St. Gregory of Nazianzus, declared that he had never met with such a teacher (John of Antioch, *ap.* Facund. ii. 2). The younger Theodosius inherited his grandfather's respect for Theodore, and often wrote to him. Another glimpse of Theodore's episcopal life is supplied by a letter of Chrysostom to him from Cucusus (A.D. 404-407) (Chrys. *Ep.* 212, Migne, lii. 668). The exiled patriarch "can never forget the love of Theodore, so genuine and warm, so sincere and guileless, a love maintained from early years, and manifested but now." Chrysostom (*Ep.* 204) thanks him profoundly for frequent though ineffectual efforts to obtain his release. No titles of honour, no terms of affection, seem too strong to be lavished on his friend. Finally, he assures Theodore that, "exile as he is, he reaps no ordinary consolation from having such a treasure, such a mine of wealth within his heart, as the love of so vigilant and noble a soul." Higher testimony could not have been borne, or by a more competent judge; and so much was this felt by Theodore's enemies at the fifth council that they vainly made efforts to deny the identity of Chrysostom's correspondent with the bp. of Mopsuestia.

Notwithstanding his literary activity, Theodore worked zealously for the good of his diocese. The famous letter of Ibas (Mansi, vii. 247; Facund. vii. 7) testifies that he converted Mopsuestia to the truth, *i.e.* extinguished Arianism and other heresies there. Several of his works are doubtless monuments of these pastoral labours, *e.g.* the catechetical lectures, the ecthesis, and possibly the treatise on "Persian Magic." Yet his episcopal work was by no means simply that of a diocesan bishop. Everywhere he was regarded as "the herald of the truth and the doctor of the church"; "even distant churches received instruction from him." So boasts Ibas to Maris, and his letter was read without a dissentient voice at the council of Chalcedon (Facund. ii. 1 seq.). Theodore "expounded Scripture in all the churches of the East," says John of Antioch (*ib.* ii. 2) with Oriental hyperbole, and adds that in his lifetime Theodore was never arraigned by any of the orthodox. But in a letter to Nestorius (*ib.* x. 2) John begs him to retract, urging the example of Theodore, who, when in a sermon at Antioch he had said something which gave great and manifest offence, for the sake of peace and to avoid scandal, after a few days as publicly corrected himself. Leontius tells us (Migne, lxxxvi. 1363) that the cause of offence was a denial to the Blessed Virgin of the title *θεοτόκος*. So great was the storm that the people threatened to stone the preacher (Cyril. Alex. *Ep.* 69; Migne, lxxvii. 340). The heretical sects attacked by Theodore shewed their resentment in a way less overt, but perhaps more formidable. They tampered with his writings, hoping thus to involve him in heterodox statements (Facund. x. 1).

Theodore's last years were perplexed by a new controversy. When in 418 the Pelagian leaders were deposed and exiled from the West, they sought in the East the sympathy of the chief living representative of the school of Antioch. The fact is recorded by Marius Mercator, who makes the most of it (*Praef. ad Symb. Theod. Mop.* 72). With Theodore they probably remained till 422, when Julian returned to Italy. Julian's visit was doubtless the occasion upon which Theodore wrote his book *Against the Defenders of Original Sin.* Mercator charges Theodore with having turned against Julian as soon as the latter had left Mopsuestia, and anathematized him in a provincial synod (*op. cit.* 3). The synod can hardly be a fabrication, since Mercator was a contemporary writer; but it was very possibly convened, as Fritzsche suggests, without any special reference to the Pelagian question. If Theodore then read his ecthesis, the anathema with which that ends might have been represented outside the council as a synodical condemnation of the Pelagian chiefs. Mercator's words, in fact, point to this explanation.

A greater heresiarch than Julian visited Mopsuestia in the last year of Theodore's life. It is stated by Evagrius (*H. E.* i. 2; Migne, lxxxvi. 2425) that Nestorius, on his way from Antioch to Constantinople (A.D. 428), took counsel with Theodore and received from him the seeds of heresy which he shortly afterwards scattered with such disastrous results. Evagrius makes this statement on the authority of one Theodulus, a person otherwise unknown. We may safely reject it, so far as it derives the Christology of Nestorius from this single interview. The germ of the Nestorian doctrine was in the teaching of Diodore and in the earliest works of Theodore; it could not have been new to Nestorius, as a prominent teacher of the church of Antioch.

Towards the close of 428 (Theodoret, *H. E.* v. 39) Theodore died, worn out by 50 years (Facund. ii. 2) of literary and pastoral toil, at the age of 78, having been all his life engaged in controversy, and more than once in conflict with the popular notions of orthodoxy; yet he departed, as Facundus (ii. 1) triumphantly points out, in the peace of the church and at the height of a great reputation. The storm was gathering, but did not break till he was gone.

II. *Posthumous History.*—The popularity of Theodore was increased by his death. Meletius, his successor at Mopsuestia, protested that his life would have been in danger if he had uttered a word against his predecessor (Tillem. *Mém.* xii. p. 442). "We believe as Theodore believed; long live the faith of Theodore!" was a cry often heard in the churches of the East (Cyril. Alex. *Ep.* 69). "We had rather be burnt than condemn Theodore," was the reply of the bishops of Syria to the party eager for his condemnation (*Ep.* 72). The flame was fed by leading men who had been disciples of the Interpreter: by Theodoret, who regarded him as a "doctor of the universal church" (*H. E.* v. 39); by Ibas of Edessa, who in 433 wrote his famous letter to Maris in praise of Theodore; by John, who in 429 succeeded to the see of Antioch. Yet Theodore's ashes were scarcely cold when in other quarters men began to hold him up to obloquy. As early perhaps as 431 Marius Mercator denounced him as the real author of the Pelagian heresy (*Lib. subnot. in verba Juliani, praef*; Migne, *Patr. Lat.* xlviii. 110); and not long afterwards prefaced his translation of Theodore's ecthesis with a still more violent attack on him as the precursor of Nestorianism (*ib.* pp. 208, 1046, 1048). The council of Ephesus, however, while it condemned Nestorius by name, contented itself with condemning Theodore's creed without mentioning Theodore; and the Nestorian party consequently fell back upon the words of Theodore, and began to circulate them in several languages as affording the best available exposition of their views (Liberat. *Brev.* 10). This circumstance deepened the mistrust of the orthodox, and even in the East there were not wanting some who proceeded to condemn the teaching of Theodore. Hesychius of Jerusalem, about 435, attacked him in his *Ecclesiastical History*; Rabbûlas, bp. of Edessa, who at Ephesus had sided with John of Antioch, now publicly anathematized Theodore (Ibas, *Ep. ad Marin.*). Proclus demanded from the bishops of Syria a condemnation of certain propositions supposed to have been drawn from the writings of Theodore. Cyril, who had once spoken favourably of some of Theodore's works (Facund. viii. 6), now under the influence of Rabbûlas took a decided attitude of opposition; he wrote to the synod of Antioch (*Ep.* 67) that the opinions of Diodore, Theodore, and others of the same schools had "borne down with full sail upon the glory of Christ"; to the emperor (*Ep.* 71), that Diodore and Theodore were the parents of the blasphemy of Nestorius; to Proclus (*Ep.* 72), that had Theodore been still alive and openly approved of the teaching of Nestorius, he ought undoubtedly to have been anathematized; but as he was dead, it was enough to condemn the errors of his books, having regard to the terrible disturbances more extreme measures would excite in the East. He collected and answered a series of propositions gathered from the writings of Diodore and Theodore (Migne, xxvi. 1438 seq.), a work to which Theodoret replied shortly afterwards. The ferment then subsided for a time, but the disciples of Theodore, repulsed in the West, pushed their way from Eastern Syria to Persia. Ibas, who succeeded Rabbûlas in 435, restored the school of Edessa, and it continued to be a nursery of Theodore's theology till suppressed by Zeno, A.D. 489. At Nisibis Barsumas, a devoted adherent of the party, was bp. from 435 to 489. Upon the suppression of the school of Edessa, Nisibis became the seat of the Antiochene exegesis and theology. The Persian kings favoured a movement distasteful to the empire; and Persia was henceforth the headquarters of Nestorianism. Among the Nestorians of Persia the writings of Theodore were regarded as the standard both of doctrine and of interpretation, and the Persian church returned the censures of the orthodox by pronouncing an anathema on all who opposed or rejected them (cf. Assem. iii. i. 84; and for a full account of the spread of Theodore's opinions at Edessa and Nisibis see Kihn, *Theodor u. Junilius*, pp. 198-209, 333-336). At a later period the school of Nisibis reacted on the West, and the influence, though not the name, of Theodore appears in the *Instituta Regularia* of Junilius Africanus, and in the *de Institutione Divinarum Literarum* of Cassiodorus (Kihn, pp. 209 seq.).

The 6th cent. witnessed another and final outbreak of bitter hatred against Theodore, The fifth general council (553), under the influence of the emperor Justinian, pronounced the anathema which Theodosius II. had refused to sanction and which even Cyril shrank from uttering. This condemnation of Theodore and his two supporters shook the fabric of the Catholic church. This is not the place to enter upon the history of the "Three Chapters," but we may point out one result of Justinian's policy. The West, Africa especially, rebelled against a decree which seemed to set at nought the authority of the councils of Ephesus and Chalcedon, and also violated the sanctity of the dead. It was from no particular interest in Theodore's doctrine or method of interpretation that the African bishops espoused his cause. Bp. Pontian plainly told the emperor that he had asked them to condemn men of whose writings they knew nothing (Migne, *Patr. Lat.* lxvii. 997). But the stir about Theodore led to inquiry; his works, or portions of them, were translated and circulated in the West. It is almost certainly to this cause that we owe the preservation in a Latin dress of at least one-half of Theodore's commentaries on St. Paul. Published under the name of St. Ambrose, the work of Theodore passed from Africa into the monastic libraries of the West, was copied into the compilations of Rabanus Maurus and others, and in its fuller and its abridged form supplied the Middle Ages with an accepted interpretation of an important part of Holy Scripture. The name of Theodore, however, disappears almost entirely from Western church literature after the 6th cent. It was scarcely before the 19th cent. that justice was done by Western writers to the importance of the great Antiochene as a theologian, an expositor, and a precursor of later thought.

III. *Literary Remains.*—Facundus (x. 4) speaks of Theodore's "innumerable books"; John of Antioch, in a letter quoted by Facundus (ii. 2), describes his polemical works as alone numbering "decem millia" (*i.e.* μυρία), an exaggeration of course, but based on fact. A catalogue of such of his writings as were once extant in Syriac translations is given by Ebedjesu, Nestorian metropolitan of Soba, A.D. 1318 (J. S. Assem. *Bibl. Orient.* iii. i. pp. 30 seq.). These Syriac translations filled 41 tomes. Only one whole work remains.

(A) Exegetical Writings.—(i) *Old Testament.* (*a*) *Historical Books.*—A commentary on Genesis is cited by Cosmas Indicopleustes, John Philoponus, and Photius (*Cod.* 3, 8). Fragments of the Greek original survive in the catena of Nicephorus (Lips. 1772). Latin fragments are found in the Acts of the second council of Constantinople, and an important collection of Syriac fragments from the Nitrian MSS. of the British Museum was pub. by Dr. E. Sachau (*Th. Mops. Fragm. Syriaca,* Lips. 1869, pp. 1-21). Photius, criticizing the style of this work in words more or less applicable to all the remains of Theodore, notices the writer's opposition to the allegorical method of interpretation. Ebedjesu was struck by the care and elaboration bestowed upon the work. The catenae contain fragments attributed to Theodore upon the remaining books of the Pentateuch and of Joshua, Judges, Ruth, Samuel, and Kings (Mai, *Scr. Vet. Nov. Coll.* i. *praef.* p. xxi.). Theodore is stated by Leontius (Migne, *Patr. Gk.* lxxxvi. 1368) to have rejected the two books of Chronicles, and there is no trace of any comments upon them bearing his name.

(*b*) *Poetical Books.*—Theodore's commentary on Job was dedicated to St. Cyril of Alexandria. Of all his works it seems to have been the least worthy of this dedication. Only four fragments survive (Mansi, ix. pp. 223 seq.), but they are sufficient to justify the censure pronounced upon the work by the Fifth council. Theodore regards Job as an historical character, but considers him as traduced by the author of the book, whom he considers to have been a pagan Edomite.

The Psalms were the earliest field of Theodore's hermeneutical labours. The printed fragments, Greek and Latin, fill 25 columns in Migne. More recently attention has been called to a Syriac version (Baethgen), and new fragments of a Latin version and of the original Greek have been printed. That his first literary adventure was hasty and premature was frankly acknowledged by Theodore himself (Facund. *l.c.*). His zeal for the historical method of interpretation led him to deny the application to Christ of all but 3 or 4 of the Psalms usually regarded as Messianic.

No fragments have hitherto been discovered of the commentary of Ecclesiastes, which Ebedjesu counts among the Syriac translations. From the remains of the commentary on Job it appears that Theodore expressly denied the higher inspiration of both the sapiential books of Solomon. Of the Canticles he writes in terms of positive contempt (Mansi, ix. 225). He repudiates imputations of immodesty on it, but denies its spiritual character. It is merely the epithalamium of Pharaoh's daughter, a relic of Solomon's lighter poetry, affording an insight into his domestic life. For this reason, he adds, it had never been read in synagogue or church.

(*c*) *Prophetical Books.*—A commentary on the four greater prophets is in Ebedjesu's list;

but one or two inedited fragments alone remain. The commentary on the minor prophets has been preserved and published in its integrity by Mai (Rome, 1825-1832) and Wegnern. Its exegetical value is diminished by Theodore's absolute confidence in the LXX, excessive independence of earlier hermeneutical authorities, and reluctance to admit a Christological reference, as well as by his usual defects of style. It is, nevertheless, a considerable monument of his expository power, and the best illustration we possess of the Antiochene method of interpreting O.T. prophecy.

(ii) *N.T.* (*a*) *The Gospels.*—Ebedjesu recounts commentaries on SS. Matthew, Luke, and John. Fragments of these, with the remaining N.T. fragments, were collected and ed. by O. F. Fritzsche (Turici, 1847), and reprinted by Migne. The commentary on St. John exists in a Syriac version, and has been pub. by J. B. Chabot (Paris, 1897).

(*b*) *Acts and Catholic Epistles.*—One fragment only remains of the commentary on the Acts; we owe it to the zeal of Theodore's opponents at the Fifth council. Notwithstanding Mai (*l.c.* p. xxi), it is more than doubtful whether Theodore wrote upon the Catholic Epistles. With the rest of the Antiochians he probably followed the old Syrian canon in rejecting II. Peter and II. and III. John.

(*c*) *The Epistles of St. Paul.*—Ebedjesu distinctly states that Theodore wrote on all the Pauline epistles, including among them *Hebrews*. The commentary on Hebrews is cited by the Fifth council, Vigilius and Pelagius II.; that on Romans by Facundus (iii. 6). A fortunate discovery last century gave us a complete Latin version of the commentary on Galatians and the nine following epistles. The Latin, apparently the work of an African churchman of the time of the Fifth council, abounds in colloquial and semi-barbarous forms; the version is not always careful, and sometimes almost hopelessly corrupt. But it gives us the substance of Theodore's interpretation of St. Paul, and we have thus a typical commentary from his pen on a considerable portion of each Testament (pub. by Camb. Univ. Press, 1880-1882).

(B) Controversial Writings.—(*a*) Chief amongst these, and first in point of time, was the treatise, in 15 books, on the Incarnation. According to Gennadius (*de Vir. Ill.* 12) it was directed against the Apollinarians and Eunomians, and written while the author was yet a presbyter of Antioch, *i.e.* A.D. 382-392. Gennadius adds an outline of the contents. After a logical and scriptural demonstration of the truth and perfection of each of the natures in Christ, Theodore deals more at length with the Sacred Manhood. In bk. xiv. he approached the mystery of the Holy Trinity and the relation of the creature to the Divine Nature; in xv. the work was concluded, *teste* Gennadius, with an appeal to authority: "citatis etiam patrum traditionibus." Large fragments of this treatise have been collected from various quarters. None of the remains of Theodore throw such important light upon his Christology.

(*b*) *Books against Apollinarianism.*—Facundus (viii. 2) says that Theodore wrote several distinct treatises against Apollinarius. One, entitled *de Apollinario et ejus Haeresi*, was written, as Theodore states in the only surviving fragment, 30 years after the treatise on the Incarnation (Facund. x. 1). A number of important fragments preserved in the Constantinopolitan Acts and in the writings of Facundus, Justinian, Leontius, etc., are referred to bks. iii. and iv. "Against Apollinarius."

(*c*) Theodore wrote a separate polemic against Eunomius, and a single characteristic fragment has survived (Facund. ix. 3). The work professed to be a defence of St. Basil. In the original it reached the prodigious length of 25 (Phot. *Cod.* 4) or even of (*Cod.* 177) 28 books. Photius complains bitterly of the faults of style, and doubts the orthodoxy of the writer, but admits its clearness of argument and wealth of scriptural proof.

(*d*) Ebedjesu includes in his list "two tomes on the Holy Spirit"; probably a work directed against the heresy of the Pneumatomachi; but see Klener, *Symb. Liter.* p. 76.

(*e*) Three books on "Persian Magic." We learn from Photius that bk. i. was an exposure of the Zoroastrian system; bks. ii. and iii. contained a comprehensive sketch of the history and doctrines of Christianity, beginning with the Biblical account of the Creation. In this portion, especially in bk. iii., Theodore betrayed his "Nestorian" views, and even advanced the startling theory of a final restoration of all men. One cannot but regret the utter loss of so remarkable a volume, especially as it seems to have been written in the interests of Christian missions, an earnest of the missionary spirit which was afterwards so marked in the Nestorian church.

(*f*) According to Ebedjesu, Theodore wrote "two tomes against him who asserts that sin is inherent in human nature." The heading, as given in Marius Mercator, who published Latin excerpts from this book shortly after Theodore's death, is merely an *ex parte* description of its contents: "Contra S. Augustinum defendentem originale peccatum et Adam per transgressionem mortalem factum catholice disserentem." Mercator, a friend and disciple of St. Augustine, not unnaturally imagined Theodore's work to be directed against the great Western assailant of Pelagius; but Theodore seems actually to have selected Jerome as the representative of the principles he attacks. Such as they are, the remains of this book form our best guide to the anthropology of Theodore.

(C) Practical, Pastoral, and Liturgical Writings.—Ebedjesu mentions a treatise *On the Priesthood*, which seems to have been an extensive one, probably unfolding the doctrine of the Sacraments as based upon the doctrine of the Incarnation. It was written, Hesychius tells us, in Theodore's old age. A more popular treatment of the same subject seems to have been attempted in the Catechetical Lectures ("Catechismus," according to Marius Mercator; the Fifth council calls it "Allocutiones ad baptizandos," Facundus (ix. 3) less correctly, "Liber ad baptizatos"). The fragments, which are chiefly from bk. viii., refer almost exclusively to the doctrine of the Incarnation. A MS. of the whole in Syriac exists in the library of the American

College at Beyrout. Fritzsche thinks that to some copies at least of these lectures Theodore appended (1) an explanation of the creed of Nicaea, a fragment of which, preserved by the Fifth council, suggests that its object was to interpret the creed in harmony with the bishop's teaching upon the Person of Christ; and (2) the ecthesis afterwards produced at the Third council by the Philadelphian presbyter Charisius, and condemned, but without mention of the author's name (Mansi, iv. 1347 seq.). The document corresponds closely with Theodore's teaching, reveals his style in both its weakness and strength, and was attributed to him by his contemporary Mercator, who bases on it his attack upon Theodore's Christology. The ecthesis was probably composed in good faith, and intended to serve the interests of the Catholic doctrine.

Lastly, Leontius intimates that Theodore wrote a portion of a liturgy; "not content with drafting a new creed, he sought to impose upon the church a new Anaphora" (Migne, lxxxvi. 1367). A Syriac liturgy ascribed to "Mâr Teodorus the Interpreter" is still used by the Christians of Assyria for a third of the year, from Advent to Palm Sunday. The proanaphoral and post-communion portions are supplied by the older liturgy "of the Apostles" (so called), the *anaphora* only being peculiar. A Latin version of this *anaphora* is in Renaudot, pub. in English by Dr. Neale (*Hist. H. E. Ch.*) and Dr. Badger (*Eastern Ch. Assoc.*, occasional paper, xvii., Rivingtons, 1875). Internal evidence confirms the judgment of Dr. Neale, who regards it as a genuine work of Theodore.

IV. *Doctrine.*—We deal with the peculiarities of Theodore's teaching under: (A) Anthropology, (B) Christology, (C) Soteriology.

(A) His whole doctrinal system hinges, as Neander and Dorner rightly judged, upon his conception of man's relation to the Universe and to God. (1) The Universe (ὁ κόσμος=ἡ σύμπασα κτίσις) is an organic whole (ἓν σῶμα). consisting of elements partly visible and material, partly invisible and spiritual. Of this organism man is the predestined bond (φιλίας ἐνέχυρον, σύνδεσμος, συνάφεια, *copulatio*), and therefore made a composite creature, his body derived from material elements, his spiritual nature akin to pure spirits, the νοηταὶ φύσεις. He was also to be the image of God, *i.e.* His visible representative, and as such to receive the homage of all creation. Hence all things minister to him, and even angelic beings superintend the movements of the physical world for his benefit. Man is thus the crowning work of the Creator, and the proper medium of communication between the Creator and the creature. (2) In the history of all intelligent created life, Theodore distinguishes two stages (καταστάσεις), the first a state of flux, exposed to conflict, temptation, and mortality; the second immutable, and free from all the forms of moral and physical evil. From the beginning God purposed that the second of these conditions (ἡ μέλλουσα κατάστασις) should be revealed through the Incarnation of His Son. Man was created in the former state, his nature being from the first liable to dissolution. "Earth to earth"—the human body naturally returns to the element from which it was taken. (3) The fall therefore did not introduce mortality, but converted the liability into a fact. It was not said, "Ye shall become mortal," but "Ye shall die." As a matter of fact, "death came by sin"; and the dissolution of soul and body was followed by the still more serious dissolution of the bond which in the person of man had hitherto knit together the visible and invisible creations. The fall of the first man gave sin a foothold in the world. The same result followed in the case of each descendant of Adam who sinned; and since all sinned, death "passed upon all men, for that all sinned." (4) As our mortality was no after-thought with God, so neither was the sentence of death a vindictive punishment. The present life, with its vicissitudes and probationary trials, is a wholesome discipline, affording room for the exercise of free will and the attainment of goodness, which without our efforts would be destitute of moral worth. Although human nature is free, yet in its present condition of mortality and mutability it is insufficient to conquer the forces of evil and attain perfect virtue without supernatural aid. A new creation is needed to abolish sin and death.

(B) We are thus brought to Theodore's doctrine of the mission and Person of Christ. (1) The mission of Christ is primarily to restore the shattered unity of the κόσμος and gather up all things to Himself, by realizing in His Person the position of man as the visible Image of God and the head of the whole Creation; secondarily, to restore mankind by union with Himself as the Second Adam and the Head of the Church to a condition of perfect deliverance from sin and death. (2) To fulfil this mission it was necessary that God the Word should become perfect man. The perfection of His manhood required Him to possess a rational human soul, capable of exercising a real choice between good and evil, although persistently choosing good; and to attain the perfection of human experience it was necessary for Him to take human nature in its mutable state, to pass through a period of growth, and to enter into conflict not only with the Evil One, but with the passions of the human soul. (3) Though perfect man, the man Christ surpassed all other men. He was absolutely free from sin, and His life was a continual progress from one stage of virtue to another, a meritorious course of which the end was victory over death and an entrance into the immortal and immutable state. This sinlessness and ultimate perfection of the manhood of Christ was due (*a*) to His supernatural birth and subsequent baptism of the Spirit, which He received in a manner peculiar to Himself, *i.e.* in the fullness of His grace; but yet more (*b*) to His union with the Person of the Divine Word. This union he had indeed received as the reward of His foreseen sinlessness and virtue, for with Him, as with the rest of mankind, divine gifts depended upon the action of the human will. The union, however, necessarily reacted on the Man, with whom the Word was made one; the cooperation of the Indwelling Godhead rendered it morally impossible for him to fall into sin. (4) But after what manner did the Word unite

Himself to the Man whom He assumed? *A priori* there are three conceivable modes of divine indwelling: it might be essential, effectual, or moral (κατ' οὐσίαν, κατ' ἐνέργειαν, κατ' εὐδοκίαν). An essential indwelling of God is excluded by every adequate idea of His Nature. The indwelling of God in Christ and in the saints is *generically* the same, but there is an all-important *specific* difference, by which Theodore strives to retain the conception of a true incarnation of God. "I am not so mad," he says, "as to affirm that the indwelling of God in Christ is after the same manner as in the saints. He dwelt in Christ *as in a Son* (ὡς ἐν υἱῷ); I mean that He united the assumed man entirely to Himself and fitted him to partake with Him of all the honour of which the indwelling Person, Who is Son by nature, partakes." Further, the union of the Word with the man Christ differs from the divine indwelling in the saints in two other important particulars. It began with the first formation of the Sacred Manhood in the Virgin's womb ("a prima statim plasmatione . . . Creator . . . occulte eidem copulatus existens non aberat cum formaretur, non dividebatur cum nascebatur"). And once having taken effect, the union remains indissoluble (ἀχώριστον πρὸς τὴν θείαν φύσιν ἔχων τὴν συνάφειαν). So close was the union, so ineffable, that the Word and the man He assumed may be regarded and spoken of as One Person, even as man and wife are "no longer two but one flesh"; or as "the reasonable soul and flesh are one man." Hence in Scripture things are often predicated of one of the natures which belong to the other. Hence the question whether the Virgin is rightly called ἀνθρωποτόκος or θεοτόκος is an idle one; for she was both. She was the mother of the Man, but in that Man when she gave Him birth there was already the indwelling of God. On the other hand, every idea of the Incarnation which tends to a confusion of the natures is to be jealously excluded. When St. John says that "the Word was made flesh," we must understand him to speak only of what the Word apparently became; not that the flesh He took was unreal, but that He was not really transformed into flesh (τὸ 'ἐγένετο' . . . κατὰ τὸ δοκεῖν . . . οὐ γὰρ μετεποιήθη εἰς σάρκα). (5) There are not two Sons in Christ, for there are not two Christs; the unity of the Person must be as carefully preserved as the distinction of the Natures; the Man is Son only by virtue of His indissoluble union with the Divine Word; when we call Christ the Son of God, we think principally of Him Who is truly and essentially Son, but we include in our conception the man who is indissolubly One with Him, and therefore shares His honours and His Name.

(c) Lastly, what are the elements, conditions, and ultimate results of the restorative work which the Incarnate Son came to do? (1) Theodore placed the redemptive virtue of the death of Christ chiefly in this, that it was the transition of the Second Adam from the mutable state into the immutable, the necessary step to the resurrection-life, in which death and sin are finally abolished. (2) Baptism, which represents the death and resurrection of the Lord, unites us to the risen Christ by a participation of His Spirit, so that in it we pass as by a second birth into the sphere of the future life. (3) The regenerate occupy middle ground between the two worlds, living in the present yet belonging to the future, potentially sinless and immortal, actually liable to sin and death. It is their business, by the aid of the Holy Spirit, to mould their present lives into conformity with the life of the risen Christ, and the conditions of the future state. Living thus they are justified by faith, *i.e.* their faith enables them in some sort to anticipate their future sinlessness. (4) But actual and final justification can only be obtained at the resurrection. The Parousia is therefore the great hope of the church, as bringing with it the two great results of the Incarnation, the ἀναμαρτησία and the ἀφθαρσία of the Body of Christ. Nothing short of the final state of perfection which will be then inaugurated can exhaust the meaning of such terms as "redemption," "forgiveness of sins," and "salvation." (5) Although the Second Advent will bring these blessings only to those who have in some degree responded to their baptismal calling, and co-operated with the Spirit of Christ, Theodore is far from pronouncing the case of the unprepared to be hopeless. The punishments of the condemned will indeed be in their nature eternal, being such as belong to eternity and not to time; but both reason and Scripture shew that they will be remissible upon repentance. Where (he asks) would be the benefit of a resurrection to such persons if they were raised only to be punished without remedy or end? What would, then, be the meaning of such texts as Matt. v. 26, Luke xii. 47, 48? Moreover, Theodore's fundamental conception of the mission and Person of Christ compels him to believe that there will be a final restoration of all creation.

V. *Method of Interpretation.*—As a scholar and successor of Diodore (cf. Socr. vi. 3; Soz. viii. 2), Theodore inherited the Antiochene system of grammatical and historical interpretation, and denounced the licence of the Alexandrian allegorizers. The recovery of the commentary on Gal. iv. 24 shews that Theodore convinced himself that the allegorical method was essentially rationalistic, undermining the historical truth of the O.T. narrative. St. Paul's use of ἀλληγορία was different in kind, since it presupposed the facts of the history and employed them only by way of illustration. In his own interpretation of both the historical and prophetical Scriptures it was a first principle with Theodore to ascertain the intention of the writer, and to refuse a secondary and more subtle meaning when the words were capable of a literal and practical sense. But the application of this principle was checked by several considerations, such as (i) the usage (ἰδίωμα) of Scripture or of the individual writer; (ii) the guidance of the context; (iii) in the case of O.T. writers, the general purpose of the older covenant. The third point requires careful examination. (*a*) Theodore was deeply convinced of the propaedeutic character of O.T. He saw that the divine purpose which runs through the whole of its course culminates in the Incarnation and the Gospel of Christ. His commentary on the minor prophets appears to have been written to counteract the allegorists. The God of both Testaments, being one and the same, worked out His purpose with a single aim. Hence the events of O.T. were so ordered as to be typical of those which were to follow. Consequently the histories and prophecies of the older revelation are susceptible of an application to the facts and doctrines of the Gospel, to which they offer a divinely foreseen and instinctive parallel. The words of the Psalmists and Prophets are constantly Christological, because the events to which they relate find a perfect counterpart in Christ (*in Ps.* xvi. xxii.). Their language is often hyperbolical or metaphorical, if viewed in reference to its original object; exhausting itself only in the higher realities of the kingdom of heaven (*in Joel* ii. 28). (*b*) Excepting some few passages in which he recognizes direct prophecies of the Messiah and His times, Theodore holds that the language of O.T. is applied to Christ and the Christian dispensation only by way of accommodation. This accommodation is, however, amply justified by the fact that in the divine foreknowledge the earlier cycle of events was designed to be typical of the later. Thus Ps. xxii., Theodore says, is clearly a narrative of David's conflict with Absalom, yet rightly used by the Evangelist to portray the passion of Christ, in which the words found a complete, and even to some extent a literal, fulfilment. Again, the words of Joel ii. 28 cannot possibly have been a prediction of the coming of the Holy Ghost, since the O.T. writers knew nothing as yet of a personal Spirit of God; "I will pour out of my Spirit" meant only "I will extend to all the divine favour and protection." Yet St. Peter rightly quotes the prophecy as finding its accomplishment in the Pentecostal effusion; for its fulfilment to the Jews of the Restoration was a pledge and type of the descent of the Spirit upon the universal church. This view (so Theodore argues) at once secures for the prophecy a historical basis, and magnifies the Christian economy as that which converted into sober fact the highest imagery of the ancient Scriptures.

If Theodore's N.T. exegesis is less characteristic, it is certainly more satisfactory than his interpretation of the Hebrew prophecies. His mind and education were Greek; in expounding the O.T. he trusted entirely to the guidance of the LXX; in commenting on the Evangelists and St. Paul he found himself face to face with an original which he was competent to handle upon his own principles. In the remains of his commentaries of the Gospels we notice the precision with which he adheres to the letter of his author (*e.g.* on Matt. xxvi. 26), his readiness to press into the service of the interpreter minor words which are commonly overlooked (John xiii. 33, ἄρτι), his attention to the niceties of grammar (iii. 21) and punctuation (ix. 27), his keen discussion of doubtful readings (i. 3), his acuteness in seizing on the ἰδιώματα of Scripture (i. 14), and in bringing out the points of a parable or discourse (Mark iv. 26; John iii. 5, x. 1 seq., xv. 4, 26). Yet we note a want of spiritual insight (John xi. 21, ὁ δὲ λέγει κ.τ.λ.) and feeling (xi. 35), and detect an occasional departure from the author's own first principles under the pressure of theological prejudice (xx. 22, 28). The commentary on the Pauline Epistles seems on the whole worthy of its author's great name. It manifests in yet greater measure his care and precision, and, in addition, an honest and unceasing effort to trace the sequence of St. Paul's thought. Its principal fault is the continual introduction of theological disquisitions, which break the course of the interpretation and not seldom carry the reader into speculations entirely foreign to the mind of the Apostle. But even these digressions have their value as expositions of Antiochene theology and as shewing the process by which so acute an intellect as Theodore's could elicit that theology from the Epistles of St. Paul, or reconcile the two systems where they appear to be hopelessly at variance.

The worth of Theodore's contributions to the exegesis of Scripture has been very variously estimated. He is for ourselves the best exponent of Antiochene exegesis. Diodore has left too little to be representative; Chrysostom was a homilist rather than a scientific expositor; Theodoret is little else than a judicious compiler from Chrysostom and Theodore. Theodore is an independent writer, yet influenced more deeply than either Chrysostom or Theodoret by the Antiochene traditions. He had no audience to propitiate, no council to dread, and treads with the firmness of a man conscious that he represents a great principle and is fully convinced of its truth. His expositions, especially of N.T., possess intrinsic value of no common kind. Except when led astray by theological prepossessions, his firm grasp of the grammatical and historical method and a kind of instinctive power of arriving at the drift of his author's thought have enabled him often to anticipate the most recent conclusions of exegesis. Besides, however, being deterred by his unwieldy style, the reader misses the devotional and spiritual tone which recommends most Patristic commentaries. His abundant theological discussions and moral teachings do not compensate for this. Yet after every fair deduction on these and other grounds, we may still assign to Theodore a high rank among commentators proper, and a position in which he stands among ancient expositors of Scripture almost alone—that of an independent inquirer, provided with a true method of eliciting the sense of his author and considerable skill in the use of it.

Life and Writings.—O. F. Fritsche, *de Theod. Mops. Vita et Scriptis Commentatio Hist. Theologica* (Halae, 1836); J. L. Jacobi in *Deutsche Zeitschrift für Christl. Wissenschaft* (1854); F. J. A. Hort in the *Journal of Class. and Sacred Philology*, iv. (Camb. 1859); Bickell, *Conspect. Rei Syror. Liter.* (Monast. 1871); H. Kihn, *Theodor. v. Mops. u. Junilius Africanus* (Freiburg im Breisgau, 1880); F. Loofs, art. "Theodor. v. Mopsuestia" in Hauck-Herzog, *Realencyklopädie*, xix. (1907); O. Bardenhewer, *Patr.* pp. 301 ff.; F. Barthgen, "Du Psalmenkommentar d. Theodor. v. Mops in Syrichen Bearbeitung," in *Z. A. T. W.* v. (1889), "Sichenzahn Makkabäische Psalmen" in *Z. A. T. W.* vi. (1887); J. B. Chabot, *Commentarius Theod. Mops. in Evang. D.*

Johannis i. (*textus Syriacus*) (Paris, 1897); J. Lietzmann, *Der Psalmenkommentar, S.B.A.* (1902). For doctrine and method of interpretation see Neander, *Allgem. Geschichte,* II. iii.; Dorner, *Lehre v. der Person Christi,* II. i.; art. in *Ch. Quart. Rev.* Oct. 1875, entitled "Theodore and Modern Thought"; Prof. Sanday in *Expositor,* June 1880; A. Harnack, art. "Antiochenische Schule" in Hauck-Herzog, *Realencyklopädie,* i. (1896); *History of Dogmas* (Eng. trans.), iii. 279 ff., iv. 165 ff.; J. H. Soarsby, art. "Antiochene Theology" in Hastings, *Encyclopaedia of Religion and Ethics,* i. (1908); J. F. Bethune-Baker, *Early History of Christian Doctrine,* pp. 256 ff.; *Nestorius and his Teaching, passim* (1908). Migne's useful but uncritical ed. (vol. 66, 1864) of all the pub. works and fragments is in his *Patr. Gk.* In 1869 Dr. E. Sachau published the inedited Syriac fragments scattered through the Nitrian MSS. of Brit. Mus., with a reprint of the Theodorean matter already collected by P. de Lagarde in his *Analecta Syriaca* (Lips. 1858). The ancient Latin version of the commentaries on some of the Epp. of St. Paul, with a fresh collation of the Greek fragments, was issued by the Camb. Univ. Press in 1880-1882. A complete critical edition of all the literary remains of Theodore is still a desideratum. Cf. Zahn, *Das N.T. Theodors von Mops.* in *Neue Kirch. Zeitschr.* 1900, xi. pp. 788 f. [H.B.S.]

Theodorus (50), bp. of Tyana, a fellow-countryman and correspondent of Gregory Nazianzen. He was a native of Arianzus. Accompanying Gregory to Constantinople in 379, he shared in the ill-treatment received there from the Arian monks and rabble. He subsequently became bp. of Tyana, but not before 381. After Gregory returned to Arianzus many letters of friendship passed between him and Theodore. On the attempt of the Apollinarians to perpetuate the schism at Nazianzus, by appointing a bishop of their own, Gregory wrote very earnestly (A.D. 382) to Theodore, calling on him, as metropolitan, to appoint a bishop to replace him, as age and ill-health forbad his efficient superintendence of the church there (*Ep.* 88). After being compelled reluctantly to resume the care of Nazianzus, Gregory felt reason to complain of Theodore apparently siding with his enemies, and expressed his feelings with vehemence (*Ep.* 83). Their friendship, however, was not weakened, and on the completion, in 382, of the *Philocalia*—the collection of extracts from Origen made by him and Basil many years before—Gregory sent Theodore a copy as an Easter gift (*Ep.* 115 *al.* 87). Theodore was one of the bishops attending the council summoned against Chrysostom by Theophilus at the end of 403. Palladius describes him as a man of much wisdom and authority, who, when he discovered the malicious intention of Theophilus and his partisans, retired to his diocese soon after his arrival (Pallad. p. 23). The Theodorus to whom Chrysostom addressed his *Ep.* 112 has been identified with Theodore of Tyana by the second council of Constantinople (Labbe, v. 490). Tillemont decides (xi. 608) for Theodore of Mopsuestia. [E.V.]

Theodorus (53), priest and abbat of Tabenna in the Thebaid. Born A.D. 314, of noble parents in the Upper Thebaid, he forsook, at an early age, his worldly prospects, and found asylum with Palaemon the anchorite, and then in the monastery at Tabenna with Pachomius, under whom he became oeconomus. When Pachomius died Theodorus was offered the abbacy, but withdrew in favour of Orsisius, on whose retirement he succeeded, made many reforms, visited the subject monasteries, and founded 5 new ones at or near Ptolemais, Hermothis, Caius, Obi, and Bechre (Boll. *AA. SS.* Mai, iii. 327-328). During the lifetime of Pachomius Theodorus met St. Athanasius in the Thebaid, and is said to have announced to him the death of the emperor Julian, then occurring in Persia (Athan. *Opp.* ii. 695). St. Athanasius had a great regard for Theodorus, and bewailed his decease (*Epp. ad Orsisium* in *Patr. Gk.* xxvi. 978). St. Nilus (*de Orat.* c. 8) gives an anecdote of him. He died A.D. 367 (Tillem. *H. E.* vii. 225) or 368 (Boll. *u.s.* 291). Gennadius (*de Script. Eccl.* i. 8) calls him presbyter, and gives the substance of 3 epistles he is said to have addressed to other monasteries. Boll. *u.s.* 287-362, give the most elaborate account of Pachomius and Theodorus. Fabric. *Bibl. Graec.* ix. 318; Tillem. *H. E.* vii. 469 seq. 758 seq.; Cave, *Hist. Lit.* i. 208; Ceill. *Aut. Sacr.* iv. 233 seq. 391 [J.G.]

Theodorus (64) Lector, reader of the church of Constantinople. He composed in two books a tripartite history out of Socrates, Sozomen, and Theodoret, extant in MS. at Venice. It was copied by Leo Allatius, but not published. Valesius used his MS. in his edition of those authors. He also composed a history which extends from the last days of Theodosius the younger to the reign of the elder Justin, A.D. 518; some portions of which remain, and are in Migne's *Patr. Gk.* lxxxvi. col. 157-2280. They have been collected out of Nicephorus Callistus, John of Damascus, and the fifth action of the seventh general council. His history abounds with wonderful stories in defence of orthodoxy. He tells that Timotheus, bp. of Constantinople, A.D. 571, was the first to ordain the recitation of the Nicene Creed at all celebrations of the Holy Communion. It was previously only recited once a year, at the end of Lent. Evidently the Arian party must have been still strong at Constantinople in cent. vi. A question has been raised whether our Theodore did not live in cent. viii. rather than cent. vi. Combefis in his *Originum Rerumque Constant. Manip.* and Baudurius in his *Imper. Orient.* have given some quotations from a Theodorus Lector relating to the statues with which Constantinople was adorned, one containing an incident which proves the writer to have lived in the reign of Philip, 711-713 (Combef. p. 11; Baud. p. 88); but two men of the same name may have occupied the same office. Ceill. xi. 103-105; Fab. *Bibl. Graec.* [G.T.S.]

Theodorus (83) of Amasea, a young soldier who suffered in the persecution under Maximian and Galerius *c.* 306; surnamed "Tiro," a recruit. Our authorities are the *Encomium* of Gregory Nyssen (t. iii. pp. 578-586) and the less trustworthy Acts. He was of humble origin (Gregory says "a poor recruit") and a conscript. In winter quarters at Amasea the capital of Pontus, his refusal to join his comrades in sacrifice declared him a Christian. His trial was deferred some days to offer him time to recant. This interval he employed in firing the temple of the Mother of the Gods on the banks of the Iris in the midst of the city. The building and the statue of the deity were reduced to ashes. At the judgment-seat Theodore boldly acknowledged and gloried in the act. From prison, where he was visited at night by angels who filled the cell with light and song, he passed to death in a furnace. No fewer than three churches were dedicated in his honour at Constantinople (Du Cange, *Constantinop. Christ.* vol. iv. c. 6, Nos. 100-102). He had also a martyry at Jerusalem (Cyr. *Vit. S. Sab.* ap. Coteler. *Eccl. Gr. Mon.* iii. No. 78) and Damascus (Johan. Damasc. *de Sacr. Imag.* Or. iii.). The little circular church of San Teodoro, popularly known as St. Toto, at the base of the Palatine Hill in Rome, is well known. Zonaras, *Annal.* lib. xvii. c. 3, p. 213 (ed. Par. 1687); Credenus, *Hist. Compend.* pars. ii. p. 681 (ed. Par. 1647); Greg. Nyssen. *Oratio de Magno Martyre Theodoro*, t. iii. pp. 578-586 (ed. Par. 1638); Surius, Nov. 9, p. 231, § 7; Tillem. *Mém. eccl.* t. v. pp. 369-377, notes 732-735; Ruinart, *Acta Martyrum*, pp. 505-511. [E.V.]

Theodosius (2) **I.,** *the Great,* born A.D. 346 at Cauca, a Spanish town upon a small tributary of the Douro; died Jan. 17, 395. His father, an eminent general serving under Valentinian and Valens, was treacherously executed in 376. For the secular history of Theodosius see *D. of G. and R. Biogr.* We shall here set forth his ecclesiastical polity and his powerful influence on the fortunes of the church. His accession was the turning-point which secured the triumph of Trinitarian orthodoxy over the Arianism dominant in the East for at least the previous 40 years. Theodosius turned what seemed in many places an obscure and conquered sect into a triumphant church, whose orthodoxy, on this point at least, never afterwards wavered. In 378 the Roman empire was in great danger. Valens, the emperor of the East, had been defeated and put to death by the Goths on Aug. 9 in the fatal battle of Hadrianople, and the whole empire was depending on the young Gratian, then less than 20 years old. Gratian perceived that the crisis demanded the ablest general the empire possessed; he boldly summoned the deeply-injured Theodosius from his retirement, and invested him with the imperial purple, Jan. 19, 379, allotting him the government of the East with Illyricum in Europe. Theodosius fixed his residence at Thessalonica, skilfully selected as the headquarters of his operations against the Goths. Constantinople was just then the centre of the conflict between the Catholics and Arians. About July 379 Gregory of Nazianzus, coming there, assumed the care of its one orthodox church, the Arians having possession of the see and all the other churches. Meanwhile at Thessalonica, during the winter of 379-380, Theodosius had a severe illness which led to his baptism by Ascolius, the local bishop, a devoted adherent of the orthodox party. This was followed by his first edict about religion, issued at Thessalonica, Feb. 28, 380, and addressed to the people of Constantinople. It orders that the religion which St. Peter taught the Romans and which Damasus of Rome and Peter of Alexandria profess, should be believed by all nations; that Father, Son, and Holy Ghost should be equally adored; that the adherents of this doctrine should be called Catholic Christians, while all others were to be designated heretics, their places of assembly refused the name of churches, and their souls threatened with divine punishment.

On Nov. 24, 380, Theodosius made his formal entry into Constantinople, and at once took action against the unorthodox. He turned the Arian bp. Demophilus out of the churches, and personally installed Gregory in the great church. But he does not seem to have satisfied the orthodox zeal of Gregory, who in his *Carmen de Vita Sua*, 1279-1395, speaks very slightingly of him, finding fault with his toleration, and complaining that he made no attempt to heal the wounds and avenge the wrongs of the Catholics. Theodosius, however, soon improved under Gregory's tuition, direct or indirect. Gregory's tenure of the bishopric of Constantinople was only for 7 months. He retired about the end of June 381, yet continued to exercise a most active influence over the emperor through his successor Nectarius. Gregory in the East and Ambrose in the West must be largely credited with the intolerant ecclesiastical legislation of the Theodosian Code, lib. xvi. We may take the ecclesiastical legislation under two heads: (1) against heretics; (2) against pagans. Theodosius's first laws against heretics were issued immediately after the council of Constantinople, and rapidly increased in severity. In June or July, 381, he issued a law which must have been directly inspired by the council (*Cod. Theod.* lib. xvi. tit. v. leg. 6), prohibiting all assemblies of Arians, Photinians, and Eunomians, and ordering the surrender of all churches to the orthodox. A few weeks later two edicts (*ib.* tit. i. leg. 3, and tit. v. leg. 8) prohibited Arians, Eunomians, and Aetians from building churches to replace those taken from them. In law ix., Mar. 382, first appeared the word inquisitor in connexion with religious controversy, officers being appointed to detect and punish the Manicheans. Law xi. of July 383 prohibited any kind of heretical worship, while in Sept. law xii. prohibited heretical assemblies for worship, building of churches and ordinations of clergy, and confiscated to the fiscus places where they met. Evidently the heretics had many official supporters, and many magistrates were lax in proceeding against them, as stern penalties were threatened against such. Yet the heretics maintained their ground. So in Feb. 384, law xiii. was directed against the Eunomian, Macedonian, Arian, and Apollinarian clergy who had ventured back again and were concealed in Constantinople. The Apollinarians especially erected a regular church organization and established an episcopal succession. Gregory of Nazianzus, much troubled by the Apollinarian party, addressed *Ep.* 77 to the prefect, telling how they took advantage of his absence at the hot baths at Xanxaris to ordain a bishop at Nazianzus. He calls on the prefect to punish them for disobeying the edict, but requests a light penalty. His influence, too, seems to have caused the original issue of this edict of Feb. 384, for in *Orat.* 46, addressed to Nectarius, patriarch of Constantinople, he calls for it as necessary, and in his Ep. to Olympius praises it, apologizing for his own toleration which had led the heretics to act with increased boldness.

Nectarius, Ambrose, and Ascolius of Thessalonica, who baptized Theodosius, also urged persecution (cf. esp. *Ep.* x. of St. Ambrose, written in the name of the council of Aquileia, demanding the suppression by force of heretical assemblies and ordinations (Opp. Ambros. in Migne's *Patr. Lat.* xvi. 940)). In Mar. 388, when marching against the usurper Maximus, he issued for the East, and in June caused the younger Valentinian to issue for the West, a still more stringent edict, specially directed against the Apollinarians (*Cod. Theod.* xvi. tit. v. 14 and 15), and against clergy and laity alike. It banishes all Apollinarians, deposes and degrades their bishops, forbids new consecrations, and denies them all approach to the emperors. Even this does not seem to have satisfied his advisers or to have stopped the progress of heresy. The Eunomians were very troublesome at Constantinople, where Eunomius himself had long lived, and whence Theodosius had banished him. Theodosius, in May 389, issued a law rendering him and his followers incapable of making bequests and confiscating to the public treasury all bequests made to them.

Theodosius sought to suppress paganism also. The ruins of many temples, statues, and fountains may be traced to his legislation, which went far beyond that of his predecessor. *Cod. Theod.* xvi. tit. x. "de Paganis, Sacrificiis et Templis," enables us to trace accurately his progress. The policy of Constantine and his sons may be said to have abolished sacrifices as madness and essentially connected with immorality and crime, specially those celebrated at night, while at the same time protecting the temples. Constantius was the severest legislator in this respect. The temples were closed, but preserved as public monuments and caretakers appointed at the public expense. Had this policy continued, the world would have been now much richer in artistic treasures. It continued, with the short interval of Julian's reign, till the accession of Theodosius. Even he retained the appearance of it. He issued no decree for the destruction of the temples. But a new force, the monks, had now become a power throughout the East. They began the destruction in the very teeth of imperial edicts, trusting for protection to the influence of Ambrose, Nectarius, and other bishops with the emperor. In 382 Theodosius issued a rescript to Palladius, dux of the province of Osrhoene, which was marked by a wise and tolerant spirit. There was a magnificent temple in Edessa, useful for popular assemblies, festivals, elections, and other public meetings. Theodosius seems to have been specially anxious to use such temples for his provincial councils, a form of local government he largely developed and strengthened (cf. *Cod. Theod.* xii. tit. xii. legg. 12, 13). The local bp. Eulogius wished, however, to shut up the temple completely. He pleaded that the law was clear. All access to temples was long since forbidden, and this one was specially dangerous, being richly furnished with idols of rare beauty. The advocates of toleration for once gained the upper hand. All sacrifices were strictly forbidden, but the building was to be used for public purposes, and the statues retained as ornaments and public curiosities. Five years, however, elapsed. The emperor was taking sterner measures against Oriental paganism, and had just sent Cynegius as his deputy into Egypt and the East to see that his orders were strictly carried out; whereupon the monks, as Libanius expressly states, rose up and utterly destroyed the temple. The rage for destruction spread. The mob in another part of the same province, headed by the bishop, attacked and burned a Jewish synagogue and a Valentinian meeting-house. Theodosius was contemplating their punishment when Ambrose intervened, addressing a letter (*Ep.* xl.), which frightened the emperor from his purpose. He issued, however, a decree in 393 to the count of the East, prohibiting all interference with Judaism and specially forbidding attacks on their synagogues; but he significantly omitted all such protective measures as regards pagan temples. Destruction and confiscation raged on every side, and the destroyers found perfect impunity. The most notorious acts of destruction were in Egypt, and specially at Alexandria, as described by Socrates (*H. E.* v. 16, 17) when the celebrated Serapeum was destroyed. Socrates asserts, indeed, that this destruction took place at the imperial order, a special decree having been issued at the desire of the patriarch Theophilus, but of this there is no trace in the code. At Rome the same policy was pursued, either directly or indirectly, by Theodosius. In 382 Gratian issued an order abolishing the altar of Victory, as hitherto retained in the senate house, and the other traces of paganism which still remained. He confiscated the property of the vestal virgins, and probably seized their college. In 383 an effort to rescind this order was defeated by the vigorous action of pope Damasus. Symmachus renewed the attempt in 384 and appealed to the young emperor Valentinian. Ambrose, replying with extreme intolerance, warned Valentinian to consult Theodosius before complying with the senate's prayer. For this letter of Ambrose and the *Relatio* of Symmachus, see St. Ambros. *Ep.* Classis i. *Epp.* xvii., xviii. The protest of Ambrose was successful. The usurper Eugenius restored the pagan emblems and ritual, but Theodosius, on his victory, again abolished them, and adopted sterner measures against the vestal college.

Theodosius was a positive as well as a negative legislator. His legislation about the clergy and the internal state of the church was minute and far-reaching. He issued, in 386, a stringent edict for the observance of the Lord's Day, suspending all public business and branding as sacrilegious any one violating its sanctity (*Cod. Theod.* viii. tit. viii. leg. 3). Another edict, A.D. 389, prescribed among the annual holidays the 7 days before and after Easter (*ib.* ii. tit. viii. leg. 2), (cf. "Lord's

Day" in *D. C. A.* p. 1047), and another (*ib.* xvi. ii. 27) lays down most minute rules for deaconesses; while the previous law exempted guardians of churches and holy places from public duties. *Cod.* xi. xxxix. 10 exempted bishops and presbyters from torture when giving evidence, but left the inferior clergy subject to it. Theodosius was appealed to on all kinds of subjects by the bishops, and we find decrees dealing with all manner of topics. If, *e.g.*, religious controversy burst forth with special violence in Egypt or Antioch, the bishop applied for edicts imposing perpetual silence on the opposite factions (cf. *Cod.* xvi. iv. 2 and 3).

Theodosius was devout to superstition, passionate to an extreme. Two incidents, the insurrection of Antioch upon the destruction of the imperial statues, and the massacre of Thessalonica, illustrate his character in many respects. [AMBROSIUS; CHRYSOSTOM.] [G.T.S.]

Theodosius (3) II., emperor, born early in 401, the only son of the emperor Arcadius by EUDOXIA (2), had four sisters, Flaccilla, Pulcheria, Arcadia, and Marina. Pulcheria exercised a predominant influence over Theodosius throughout his life. He was appointed Augustus Jan. 402, and succeeded to the throne at the age of 7 on his father's death in 408. For the secular history of his reign see *D. of G. and R. Biogr.*; we deal here only with his actions and legislation so far as they bore on the history of the church. His reign was very long, covering the first half of 5th cent., and embracing the origin and rise of two great heresies, the Nestorian and Monophysite. His education was conducted by Pulcheria, who acted as Augusta and his guardian, from July 4, 414, when she was herself little more than 15 years old. Sozomen (ix. 1) tells us that she "superintended with extraordinary wisdom the transactions of the Roman government, concerted her measures well, and allowed no delay to take place in their execution. She was able to write and to converse with perfect accuracy in the Greek and Latin languages. She caused all affairs to be transacted in the name of her brother, and devoted great attention to furnishing him with such information as was suitable to his years. She employed masters to instruct him in horsemanship and the use of arms, in literature, and in science. He was also taught how to maintain a deportment befitting an emperor. . . . But she chiefly strove to imbue his mind with piety and the love of prayer; she taught him to frequent the church regularly, and to be zealous in contributing to the embellishment of houses of prayer. She inspired him with reverence for priests and other good men, and for those who in accordance with the law of Christianity had devoted themselves to philosophical asceticism." Socrates (vii. 22) tells us about his training that "such was his fortitude in undergoing hardships that he would courageously endure both heat and cold; fasting very frequently, especially on Wednesdays and Fridays, from an earnest endeavour to observe with accuracy all the prescribed forms of the Christian religion. His palace was so regulated that it differed little from a monastery; for he, together with his sisters, rose early in the morning and recited responsive hymns in praise of the Deity. By his training he learnt the Holy Scriptures by heart, and would often discourse with the bishops on scriptural subjects as if he had been an ecclesiastic of long standing. He was an indefatigable collector of the sacred books and of expositions written on them, while in clemency and humanity he far surpassed all others." Pope Leo I., in one of his letters to Theodosius, which is intended to be very laudatory (Mansi, v. 1341; cf. Socr. vii. 43), describes him as having "not only the heart of an emperor but also that of a priest." Theodosius delighted in that magnificent ceremonial which gathered round the cultus of relics. He brought the remains of John Chrysostom back to Constantinople, laid his face on the coffin, and entreated that his parents might be pardoned for having persecuted such a holy bishop. He assisted at the discovery and removal of the relics of the Forty Martyrs (Soz. ix. 2), and felt his reign honoured through the simultaneous discovery of the relics of the proto-martyr St. Stephen and Zechariah the prophet (ix. 16, 17). During the latter portion of his reign, terminated by a fall from his horse July 28, 450, his sister lost her power, a comparatively healthy influence, and Theodosius fell completely under the guidance of selfish and tyrannical eunuchs. Pulcheria had vigour and determination. Theodosius seems to have taken refuge from her sway by yielding himself completely to a rapid succession of favourites. He had 15 prime ministers in 25 years, the last of whom, the eunuch Chrysaphius, retained his power longest, A.D. 443-450. Under Theodosius II. paganism became in itself a disability. Some of the highest servants of the state towards the end of cent. iv. had been pagan; now by a law of Dec. 7, 416 (*Cod. Theod.* xvi. tit. x. 21), pagans were prohibited from entering the military and civil services or attaining any judicial office. This law was followed by 4 others within the next ten years, following closely upon the lines of Western legislation in the same direction as contained in the previous laws; law 25, for instance, passed at Constantinople Nov. 426, orders the cross, "signum venerandae crucis," to be placed on such temples as were allowed to remain intact, while the materials of those pulled down were to be used in repairing bridges, roads, aqueducts, etc. (*ib.* t. v. lib. xv. tit. 1, leg. 36). These measures seem to have produced an apparent uniformity, as Theodosius, in law 22 passed in 423, refers to the "pagans who remain, though we believe there are none such." The law, however, as yet protected them if they lived peaceably; thus law 24 forbids Christians making attacks on Jews and pagans living among them. Heretics scarcely came off so well. The Novatianists still, as throughout cent. iv., were specially favoured, though occasionally a law was aimed against their rebaptisms and unorthodox celebrations of Easter (lib. xvi. tit. vi. leg. 6, passed on Mar. 21, 413); but severe measures of exile, confiscation, and other penalties were dealt out against Montanists, Eunomians, etc., and their employment in the army or civil service was prohibited except apparently in the local militia (xvi. v. 58 and 61). Law 65 (tit. xvi.)

is the most sweeping passed in this reign. Nestorius was its author, and law 66 is a severe one against himself and his party. The Jews were protected, as hitherto, but certain restrictions were by degrees placed upon them. Their synagogues were not to be seized or destroyed, and if destroyed were to be restored, but no new ones were to be built (xvi. tit. viii. 25). They were forbidden to serve in the army, but permitted to be physicians and lawyers (lex 24). Their ecclesiastical and civil organization under their patriarchs was protected. The patriarchs, indeed, *c.* 415, seem to have advanced so far as to exercise jurisdiction over Christians and to force them to receive circumcision, while the Jewish people mocked the Christian religion and burned the cross (Socr. *H. E.* vii. 16). Under the influence of Nestorius, however, severer laws were enacted against Jews. In 429 we find one forbidding and confiscating the usual tribute to the patriarchs. This law with Gothofred's commentary is very important as regards the organization of Judaism in cent. v. (cf. the whole series of laws in lib. xvi. tit. viii. leg. 18-29). [G.T.S.]

Theodosius (20), a celebrated solitary of Syria contemporary with Theodoret, born at Antioch of a rich and noble family. Abandoning his worldly possessions, he dwelt in a hut in a forest on the mountain above the city of Rhosus, where he practised the severest self-discipline, loading his neck, loins, and wrists with heavy irons, and allowing his uncombed hair to grow to his feet. He speedily gathered a colony of ascetics, whom he taught industrial arts, as weaving sackcloth and haircloth, making mats, fans, and baskets, and cultivating, setting an example of laborious diligence, and carefully superintending every department. He was an object of reverence even to the Isaurian banditti, who on several predatory inroads left his monastic settlement uninjured, only requesting bread and his prayers. Fearing, however, that the Isaurians might carry him off for ransom, Theodosius was persuaded to remove to Antioch, settling near the Orontes and gathering about him many who desired to adopt an ascetic life, but not long surviving his removal (Theod. *Hist. Relig.* c. x.). [E.V.]

Theodosius (21), a fanatical Monophysite monk. Having been expelled from his monastery for some crime, he repaired to Alexandria, where he stirred up strife, was scourged, and paraded round the city on camelback as a seditious person (Evagr. *H. E.* ii. 5). He attended the council of Chalcedon in 451, apparently as one of the ruffianly followers of Barsumas. On the termination of the synod Theodosius hastened to Jerusalem, complaining that the council had betrayed the faith, and circulating a garbled translation of Leo's Tome (Leo Magn. *Ep.* 97 [83]). His protestations were credited by a large number of the monks and people, and having gained the ear of the empress dowager Eudocia, the former patroness of Eutyches, who had settled at Jerusalem, he so thoroughly poisoned the minds of the people of Jerusalem against JUVENAL as a traitor to the truth that they refused to receive him as their bishop on his return from Chalcedon, unless he would anathematize the doctrines he had so recently joined in declaring. On his refusal the malcontents attempted his assassination, and he barely escaped with his life to Constantinople. After Juvenal's flight Theodosius was ordained bp. of Jerusalem in the church of the Resurrection, and at once proceeded to ordain bishops for Palestine, chiefly for those cities whose bishops had not yet returned from Chalcedon. A reign of terror now began in Jerusalem. The public prisons were thrown open and the liberated criminals were employed to terrify by their violence those who refused communion with Theodosius. Those who refused to anathematize the council were pillaged and insulted in the most lawless manner. Finally, the emperor Marcian interposed, and issued orders to Dorotheus to apprehend Theodosius, who, however, managed to escape to the mountain fastnesses of Sinai (Labbe, iv. 879). What ultimately became of him is unknown. Evagr. *H. E.* ii. 5; Coteler. *Mon. Graec.* i. 415 seq.; Theophan. *Chron.* p. 92; Leo Magn. *Ep.* 126 [157]; Labbe, *Concil.* iv. 879 seq.; Niceph. *H. E.* xv. 9; Fleury, *H. E.* livre 38; Tillem. *Mém. eccl.* xv. 731 seq.; Le Quien, *Or. Christ.* iii. 164). [E.V.]

Theodotion, otherwise *Theodotus* (so Suidas *s.v.* κνίζων), author of the Greek version of the O.T. which followed, as those of Aquila and Symmachus preceded, that of the LXX in Origen's columnar arrangements of the versions. Of his personality even less is known than of either of the other two translators. The earliest author to mention him is Irenaeus, in a passage which, by reason of its higher antiquity and authority, must be our standard to test the accounts of later writers, who probably derived their accounts partly from it. Irenaeus (III. xxi. 1, p. 215), referring to the word "*virgin*" (παρθένος) in Is. vii. 14, affirms that the passage is to be read "not as certain of those who now venture to misinterpret the Scripture, 'Behold, the *damsel* (νεᾶνις) shall be with child and shall bear a son'; as Theodotion of Ephesus interpreted it and Aquila of Pontus, both Jewish proselytes; following whom the Ebionites pretend that he was begotten of Joseph." Eusebius cites this (*H. E.* v. 8), adding nothing to it.

In attempting to fix the time when Theodotion flourished, the one certain and tolerably determinate datum we possess is, that his version must have been made before the composition of the above treatise of Irenaeus—therefore before 180-189. A second but less available datum is the fact, admitted by all, that he came after Aquila. Thus we conclude that his work cannot have been so late as 189 or earlier than 130. Some consider that the expression of Irenaeus, "those who *are now venturing*" implies that Theodotion had then only just completed his translation; but this puts undue force on the words. The expression merely contrasts comparatively recent translations with the ancient and primary authority of the LXX. But direct evidence leads us to place Theodotion *c.* 180, and Symmachus from 15 to 30 years later—dates which agree well with the few known facts. Indirect evidence of an earlier date for

Theodotion has been claimed as found in the apparent use of his version in the *Trypho* of Justin Martyr, a work written not later than 164, perhaps some 20 years earlier. But the fallacious character of this evidence is shewn in *D. C. B.* (4-vol. ed. 1887).

Theodotion's work was not so much an independent translation as a revision of the LXX, with its insertions usually retained, but its omissions supplied from the Hebrew—probably with the help of Aquila's version. Theodotion's was the version Origen usually preferred to the other two for filling omissions of the LXX or *lacunae* in their text as he found it; and from it accordingly comes a large part of the ordinary Greek text of Jeremiah, and still more of that of Job. Thus in these books we have fuller materials for learning the character of his version than that of either of the others; and still more in his version of Daniel, which has come down to us entire, having since before Jerome's time (how long before we are not told) superseded that of the LXX so completely that the latter was lost for centuries, and is now extant only in a single Greek copy, the *Cod. Chisianus*, and in the Syro-Hexaplar translation contained in *Cod. Ambrosianus* (C. 313 *Inf.*). Any one who compares this version with Theodotion's which is usually printed in all ordinary editions of the Greek O.T. must agree with Jerome (*Praef. in Dan.*) that the church chose rightly in discarding the former and adopting the latter. Indeed, the greater part of this Chisian Daniel cannot be said to deserve the name of a translation at all. It deviates from the original in every possible way; transposes, expands, abridges, adds or omits, at pleasure. The latter chapters it so entirely rewrites that the predictions are perverted, sometimes even reversed, in scope. We learn from Jerome (*in Dan.* iv. 6, p. 646) that Origen himself ("in nono Stromatum volumine") abandoned this supposed LXX Daniel for Theodotion's. Indeed, all the citations of Daniel, some of them long and important passages, in Origen's extant works, agree almost verbatim with the text of Theodotion now current, and differ, sometimes materially, from that of the reputed LXX as derived from the Chisian MS. He seems, moreover, to have found the task of bringing its text to conform to the original by the aid of Theodotion's a hopeless one, as we may judge by his asterisks, obeli, and marginalia in the two MSS. referred to. Yet that this is the version which Origen placed as that of the LXX in the penultimate column of the Hexapla and Tetrapla is certain.

Theodotion, though not an independent translator, was by no means an "unlearned" one, as Montfaucon (*Praelimm. in Hexapla*) calls him. The chief, and apparently the only, ground for this is his practice of frequently transliterating words of his original. Dr. Field, however, has well shewn (*Prolegg. in Hexapla*, IV. iii.) that he guides himself mostly by definable rules—the words so dealt with being names of *animals* (as θεννὶν for σειρῆνες), *plants* (as ἀχὶ for βούτομον), *vestments* (as βαδδὶν for ποδήρης), or articles used in *worship* (as θεραφὶν for κενοτάφια or [Aq.] μορφώματα). In such cases, his chosing to transliterate, rather than adopt a conjectural Greek rendering from a former version or hazard a new guess of his own, indicates scrupulous caution, not ignorance. He proves at least that he diligently consulted the original, and often shews a wise discretion in forbearing to translate a word whose meaning cannot be determined, or for which the Greek language has no equivalent. As well might the English translators of 1611 be called "unlearned" for retaining such words as "teraphim," "Belial," or the revisers of 1881-1884 because they replace the "scapegoat" of A.V. by "Azazel," and for "hell" give "Sheol" in O.T. and "Hades" in N.T.

Theodotion's version included all the canonical books of O.T. except, probably, Lamentations. Of the apocryphal books, he is only known to have included Baruch and the additions to Daniel. [J.GW.]

Theodotus (4) of Byzantium. Eusebius (*H. E.* v. 27) has preserved extracts from a treatise directed against the heresy of Artemon, who taught that our Lord had been mere man. Theodoret (*Haer. Fab.* ii. 5) says that this treatise was called the *Little Labyrinth*; and the author was doubtless Caius of Rome, and its date the end of the first quarter of cent. iii. [HIPPOLYTUS ROMANUS.] These heretics claimed to hold the original doctrine of the church which, they alleged, had continued incorrupt till the episcopate of Victor, the truth being first perverted by his successor Zephyrinus (*c.* 199). Their antagonist replies that, on the contrary, it was in the episcopate of Victor that this God-denying heresy had been first introduced, that Theodotus the shoemaker (σκυτεύς) was the first to teach that our Lord was mere man, and he had been excommunicated for this by Victor, and had then founded an organized sect, with a bishop (Natalius) to whom they paid a salary. Its leading men in the time of Victor's successor were Asclepiades and another Theodotus, a banker. These two undertook to clear the text of N.T. of corruptions, but our authority describes what they called "corrected" copies as simply ruined, the two not even agreeing as to their corrections.

Our sole other primary authority for this Theodotus is Hippolytus. The section on Theodotus in the lost earlier work on heresies by Hippolytus may be partly recovered by a comparison of the corresponding articles in Pseudo-Tertullian, Epiphanius, and Philaster; and Epiphanius, whose treatment (*Haer.* 54) is the fullest, almost certainly drew his materials altogether from Hippolytus. There is an article on Theodotus in the later treatise of Hippolytus (*Ref.* vii. 35). The influence of Theodotus did not extend much beyond his own generation; later church writers appear to have only known him from the two nearly contemporary authorities we have named.

The place in which the article on Theodotus came in the lost work of Hippolytus exactly corresponds to the date assigned to him in the *Little Labyrinth*. He comes immediately after Blastus, whom we otherwise know to have caused schism in Victor's time by endeavouring to introduce the Quartodeciman usage in Rome. Hippolytus stated that Theodotus was a native of Byzantium, who denied Christ in time of persecution—a fact which accounted for his heresy, since he could thus maintain that he had only denied man, not God. Hippolytus reports that as to the Deity and the work of creation the doctrine of Theodotus was orthodox, but as to our Lord's person he agreed with Gnostic speculations, especially in distinguishing Jesus and Christ. The miraculous conception of Jesus he was willing to admit; but he held Him a man like others, though of the highest virtue and piety. He taught that at the baptism of Jesus, Christ descended on Him in the form of a dove, and that He was then able to work miracles, though He had never exhibited any before; but even so He was not God; though some of the sect were willing to acknowledge His right to the title after His resurrection.

Theodotus chiefly relied on texts of Scripture, specimens of which are given by Epiphanius (*Haer.* 54). He evidently acknowledged the authority of St. John's Gospel, for one of these texts was John viii. 40. He appealed to the prophecy, Deut. xviii. 15, of the prophet who was to be like unto Moses, and therefore man, and quoted also Is. liii. 3, Jer. xvii. 9 (LXX), and other texts in which our Lord is called man. [G.S.]

Theodotus (5) the banker, distinct from THEODOTUS (4), as asserted both in the *Little Labyrinth* and by Hippolytus. For the speculations which this Theodotus added to the heresy of (4) see MELCHIZEDEK. [G.S.]

Theodotus (9), May 18, martyr at Ancyra in Galatia in Diocletian's persecution. The narrative of his martyrdom is intermingled with that of the *Seven Virgins of Ancyra*. Theodotus was a devout dealer in provisions. THEOTECNUS, the apostate from Christianity, was sent with ample power to enforce conformity to the imperial edicts, and began by ordering all provisions sold in the market to be first presented to the gods. This would render them unfit for use in the Holy Communion. Theodotus supplied the Christians with bread and wine free from pollution. The persecution waxing hot, he was compelled to fly from Ancyra to a place, distant some 40 miles, where a cave, through which the Halys flowed, was a refuge for some fugitive Christians. The narrative shews us how quietly Christians in country districts pursued their occupations and enjoyed daily worship, while those in the cities were suffering tortures and death, and is most valuable as illustrating the general condition of the Christians in Asia Minor during the earlier years of Diocletian's persecution. In the cave Theodotus found certain brethren who had overturned the altar of Diana, and were being carried by their relations for judgment to the prefect when Theodotus had bribed the accusers to let them off. They were delighted to see their deliverer, and invited him to a meal, of which we have a graphic picture: the fugitives reclining on the abundant grass, surrounded with trees, wild fruit, and flowers, while grasshoppers, nightingales, and birds of every kind made music around. In this passage (§ 11) we find one of the few instances where an early Christian author seems capable of appreciating the beauty of nature. We then have a glimpse of the religious life of the time. Before he would eat, Theodotus sent some of their number to summon the presbyter from the neighbouring village of Malus to dine with them, pray with them before they started afresh on their journey, and ask a blessing on their food, for, says the Acts, "the saint never took food unless a presbyter blessed it." The presbyter, whose name was Fronto, or, according to the Bollandist Papebrochius, Phorto, was just leaving the church after the midday hour of prayer. The village dogs attacked the messengers, and the priest ran to drive them away, asked if they were Christians, and informed them that he had seen them in a vision the night before, bringing a precious treasure to him. They told him they had the most precious of treasures with them, the martyr Theodotus, to whom the presbyter at once departed. During the meal Theodotus suggested the spot as a fit place for a martyrium or receptacle for relics, and exhorted the priest to build one. When he said he possessed no relics, Theodotus gave him a ring off his finger in token that he would provide them. He then returned to Ancyra, which he found greatly disturbed by a violent persecution. [ANCYRA, SEVEN MARTYRS OF.] A writer in the *Rev. archéol.* (t. xxviii. p. 303) notes a passage in the Acts of these sufferers (§ 14) as a valuable illustration of the paganism of Galatia. Theodotus, having rescued the bodies of the nuns from the lake into which Theotecnus had cast them, prepared to suffer. He prayed with the brethren, and told them to give his relics to Fronto if he brought a ring as a token. Then he went to the tribunal, where the priests of Minerva were demanding his arrest as the leader of the Christian opposition. The Acts now offer some of the most striking illustrations used by Le Blant in his *Actes des Martyrs* (cf. pp. 25, 62, 78, 80). They illustrate every detail of Roman criminal procedure, especially the offer made to the martyrs of high promotion and imperial favour if they recanted. Theodotus was offered the high-priesthood of Apollo, now esteemed the greatest of all the gods, but in vain, till at last the president ordered him to be beheaded and his body burned. He was executed and his body placed on a pyre, when suddenly a bright light shone around it, so that no one dared approach. The president ordered it to be guarded all night, in the place of common execution, by soldiers whom he had just flogged for suffering the bodies of the nuns to be carried off. Fronto, who was a farmer, and kept a vineyard where he made wine, came to Ancyra to sell his wine, bringing the ring of Theodotus with him, and arriving at the place of execution just when night was falling and the gates of the city had been closed, found the guard erecting a hut of willow branches wherein to spend the night. The soldiers invited him to join them, which he did. Discovering what they were guarding, he made them drunk with his own wine and carried off the martyr's body, placing it in the spot Theodotus had marked as the site of a martyrium. The Acts purport to have been written by one Nilus, an eye-witness. They speak of the chapel erected to the memory of Theodotus, which could only have been done when peace was restored to the church. They are in Ruinart, *Acta Sinc.* p. 354, and translated into English as an appendix to Mason's *Persecution of Diocletian.* [G.T.S.]

Theodotus (11), bp. of Laodicea in Syria Prima, claimed as a zealous advocate of Arian doctrines by Arius in writing to Eusebius of Nicomedia (Theod. *H. E.* i. 5 ; v. 7). Eusebius gives him a high character for skill as a physician of both body and soul, remarkable for kindness, sympathy, sincerity, and zeal to help all who needed aid, reinstating the church in its prosperity which had suffered much by the cowardice of its last bishop, Stephen, who seems to have renounced the faith in the persecution of Diocletian (Eus. *H. E.* vii. 32). Theodotus was at the council of Nicaea in 325 (Labbe, ii. 51) ; before which he is coupled by Athanasius with the Eusebian party (Athan. *de Synod.* c. i. § 17, p. 886). On the visit of Eusebius of Nicomedia to Jerusalem in 330 or 331, ostensibly to see the newly built church, he formed one of the Arian cabal which, proceeding to Antioch, succeeded in deposing Eustathius (Theod. *H. E.* i. 21) and electing Eusebius of Caesarea in his room (Eus. *Vit. Const.* iii. 62). He also took part in the council of Tyre in 335 (Labbe, ii. 436) and of the Dedication at Antioch in 341 (*ib.* 560), and is mentioned by Athanasius as having been at Seleucia in 359 (Athan. *de Synod.* c. i. § 12, p. 880). The two Apollinarii, father and son, were excommunicated by Theodotus for being present at the recitation of a hymn in honour of Bacchus, composed by a sophist of Laodicea with whom he had interdicted an intercourse. He restored them on their repentance (Soz. *H. E.* vi. 25 ; Socr. *H. E.* ii. 46). Gelasius of Cyzicus (bk. iii. c. 3) gives a letter from the emperor Constantine to Theodotus, warning him to return to the orthodox faith (Labbe, ii. 284). It is quoted as genuine by Benignus of Heraclea at the fifth general council (*ib.* v. 481). According to Gams, Theodotus was bishop 30 years. [E.V.]

Theodotus (18), patriarch of Antioch, A.D. 420-429 (Clinton, *F. R.* ii. 552). He succeeded Alexander, under whom the long-standing schism at Antioch had been healed, and followed his lead in replacing the honoured name of Chrysostom on the diptychs of the church. He is described by Theodoret, at one time one of his presbyters, as "the pearl of temperance," "adorned with a splendid life and a knowledge of the divine dogmas" (Theod. *H. E.* v. 38 ; *Ep.* 83 *ad Dioscor.*). Joannes Moschus relates anecdotes illustrative of his meekness when treated rudely by his clergy, and his kindness on a journey in insisting on one of his presbyters exchanging his horse for the patriarch's litter (Mosch. *Prat. Spir.* c. 33). By his gentleness he brought back the Apollinarians to the church without rigidly insisting on their formal renouncement of their errors (Theod. *H. E.* v. 38). On the real character of Pelagius's teaching becoming known in the East and the consequent withdrawal of the testimony previously given by the synods of Jerusalem and Caesarea to his orthodoxy, Theodotus presided at the final synod held at Antioch (mentioned only by Mercator and Photius, in whose text Theophilus of Alexandria has by an evident error taken the place of Theodotus of Antioch) at which Pelagius was condemned and expelled from Jerusalem and the other holy sites, and he joined with Praylius of Jerusalem in the synodical letters to Rome, stating what had been done. The most probable date of this synod is that given by Hefele, A.D. 424 (Marius Mercator, ed. Garnier, Paris, 1673, *Commonitor.* c. 3, p. 14 ; *Dissert. de Synodis*, p. 207 ; Phot. *Cod.* 54). When in 424 Alexander, founder of the order of the Acoemetae, visited Antioch, Theodotus refused to receive him as being suspected of heretical views. His feeling was not shared by the Antiochenes, who, ever eager after novelty, deserted their own churches and crowded to listen to Alexander's fervid eloquence (Fleury, *H. E.* livre xxv. c. 27). Theodotus took part in the ordination of Sisinnius as patriarch of Constantinople, Feb. 426, and united in the synodical letter addressed by the bishops then assembled to the bishops of Pamphylia against the Massalian heresy (Socr. *H. E.* vii. 26 ; Phot. *Cod.* 52). He died in 429 (cf. Theodoret's *Ep. to Diosc.* and his *H. E.* v. 40). Tillem. t. xii. note 2, *Theod. Mops.* ; Theophan. *Chron.* p. 72 ; Le Quien, *Or. Christ.* ii. 720 ; Cave, *Hist. Lit.* i. 405. [E.V.]

Theognostus (1), a priest of Alexandria and a writer of about the middle of cent. iii., whom we only know from quotations in St. Athanasius and Photius. He composed a work called *Hypotyposes* in seven books, still extant when Photius wrote (*Cod.* 106). He used language in bk. ii. of very Arian sound, speaking of the Son as a creature, and in bk. iii. of the Holy Ghost in a style as little orthodox as that of Origen. In bk. v. he attributed bodies to angels and devils. In bks. vi. and vii. he discussed the doctrine of the Incarnation in a more orthodox manner than in bk. ii. Yet St. Athanasius regarded him as a useful witness against Arianism. Philip of Side says that he presided over the school of Alexandria after Pierius A.D. 282 (cf. Dodwell, *Dissert. in Irenaeum*, p. 488). The fragments of Theognostus are collected in Routh's *Reliq. Sac.* t. iii. 407-422, and trans. in *Ante-Nic. Lib.* Cf. Migne, *Patr. Gk.* t. x. col. 235-242 ; Ceill. ii. 450 ; Athan. *Ep.* 4 *ad Serap., de Decretis Nic. Syn.* [G.T.S.]

Theonas (1), 15th bp. of Alexandria (whom Eutychius absurdly calls *Neron*), succeeded Maximus in 282. His episcopate, says Neale (*Hist. Patr. Alex.* i. 86), was a time of much suffering to the Egyptians, owing to the revolt of Achilleus. Diocletian besieged Alexandria in 294 ; and after eight months' siege the city, "wasted by the sword and fire, implored the mercy of the conqueror, but experienced the full extent of his severity" in the form of "promiscuous slaughter" and sentences "of death or of exile" (Gibbon, ii. 76). Yet Theonas has left a very interesting and attractive picture of the relations which the emperor earlier in his reign maintained towards his Christian servants. Eusebius's testimony that those imperial domestics who held the faith (three of whom he afterwards names, Dorotheus, Gorgonius, and Peter) were allowed perfect freedom therein, and were even peculiarly valued by their master (viii. 1), is singularly illustrated by the "letter of Theonas the bp. to Lucian, *praepositus cubiculariorum* or high chamberlain," published in cent.

xvii. by D'Achery. It is obviously a translation from a Greek original, which no one will now hesitate to ascribe to Theonas of Alexandria. (See it in Routh's *Rel. Sac.* iii. 439, and an Eng. version in Mason's *Persecution of Diocletian*, p. 348, and see *ib.* p. 39). After some opening words on the duty of so using the peace which the church was then enjoying "by means of a kindly sovereign" that God might be glorified by genuinely Christian lives, Theonas urges Lucian to thank Him for a signal opportunity of thus promoting His cause by fidelity to "an emperor who was indeed not yet enrolled in the Christian ranks," but who might be favourably impressed in regard to Christianity by the loyalty of the Christians to whose care he had "entrusted his life." Thus it was a primary duty to avoid everything that was "base and unworthy, not to say flagitious," lest the name of Christ should thereby be blasphemed. The Christian chamberlains were not to take money for procuring audience, must be clear of all avarice, duplicity, and scurrility, acting in all things with modesty, courtesy, affability, and justice, must discharge their several duties in the fear of God, with love for their prince and with exact diligence, regarding all his orders which did not clash with God's as coming from God Himself, and taking care in their ministrations to put away all gloom or bad temper, and to refresh his weariness by a cheerful manner and glad obedience. [E.V.]

Theophilus (4), bp. of Antioch (Eus. *H. E.* iv. 20; Hieron. *Ep. ad Algas.* quaest. 6), succeeded Eros *c.* 171, and was succeeded by Maximin *c.* 183, according to Clinton (*Fasti Romani*), but the dates are only approximations. His death may probably be placed *c.* 183-185 (Lightfoot, *S. Ignatius*, vol. ii. p. 466). We gather from his writings that he was born a heathen, not far from the Tigris and Euphrates, and was led to embrace Christianity by studying the Holy Scriptures, especially the prophetical books (*ad Autol.* i. 14, ii. 24). He makes no reference to his office in his existing writings, nor is any other fact in his life recorded. Eusebius, however, speaks of the zeal which he and the other chief shepherds displayed in driving away the heretics who were attacking Christ's flock, with special mention of his work against Marcion (*H. E.* iv. 24). He was a fertile writer in different departments of Christian literature, polemics, exegetics, and apologetics. Dr. Sanday describes him as "one of the precursors of that group of writers who, from Irenaeus to Cyprian, not only break the obscurity which rests on the earliest history of the Christian church, but alike in the East and in the West carry it to the front in literary eminence, and distance all their heathen contemporaries" (*Studia Biblica*, p. 90). Eusebius and Jerome mention numerous works of Theophilus current in their time. They are (1) the existing *Apology* addressed to Autolycus; (2) a work against the heresy of Hermogenes; (3) against that of Marcion; (4) some catechetical writings; (5) Jerome also mentions having read some commentaries on the gospel and on Proverbs, which bore Theophilus's name, but which he regarded as inconsistent with the elegance and style of his other works.

The one undoubted extant work of Theophilus is his *Apologia ad Autolycum*, in three books. Its ostensible object is to convince a heathen friend, Autolycus, a man of great learning and an earnest seeker after truth, of the divine authority of the Christian religion, while at the same time he exhibits the falsehood and absurdity of paganism. His arguments, drawn almost entirely from O.T., with but very scanty reference to N.T., are largely chronological. He makes the truth of Christianity depend on his demonstration that the books of O.T. were long anterior to the writings of the Greeks and were divinely inspired. Whatever of truth the heathen authors contain he regards as borrowed from Moses and the prophets, who alone declare God's revelation to man. He contrasts the perfect consistency of the divine oracles, which he regards as a convincing proof of their inspiration, with the inconsistencies of heathen philosophers. He contrasts the account of the creation of the universe and of man, on which, together with the history contained in the earlier chapters of Genesis, he comments at great length but with singularly little intelligence, with the statements of Plato, "reputed the wisest of all the Greeks" (lib. iii. cc. 15, 16), of Aratus, who had the hardihood to assert that the earth was spherical (ii. 32, iii. 2), and other Greek writers on whom he pours contempt as mere ignorant retailers of stolen goods. He supplies a series of dates, beginning with Adam and ending with Marcus Aurelius, who had died shortly before he wrote, *i.e.* early in the reign of Commodus. He regards the Sibylline verses as authentic and inspired productions, quoting them largely as declaring the same truths with the prophets. The omission by the Greeks of all mention of O.T., from which they draw all their wisdom, is ascribed to a self-chosen blindness in refusing to recognize the only God and in persecuting the followers of Him Who is the only fountain of truth (iii. 30, *ad fin.*). He can recognize in them no aspirations after the divine life, no earnest gropings after truth, no gleams of the all-illumining light. The heathen religion was a mere worship of idols, bearing the names of dead men. Almost the only point in which he will allow the heathen writers to be in harmony with revealed truth is in the doctrine of retribution and punishment after death for sins committed in life (ii. 37, 38). The literary character of the *Apology* deserves commendation. The style is characterized by dignity and refinement. It is clear and forcible. The diction is pure and well chosen. Theophilus also displays wide and multifarious though superficial reading, and a familiar acquaintance with the most celebrated Greek writers. His quotations are numerous and varied. But Donaldson (*Hist. Christ. Lit.* iii. p. 69) remarks that he has committed many blunders, misquoting Plato several times (iii. 6, 16), ranking Zopyrus among the Greeks (iii. 26), and speaking of Pausanias as having only run a risk of starvation instead of being actually starved to death in the temple of Minerva (*ib.*). His critical powers were not above his age. He adopts Herodotus's derivation (ii. 52) of θεός from τίθημι, since

God set all things in order, comparing with it that of Plato (*Crat.* 397 C) from θέειν, because the Deity is ever in motion (*Apol.* i. 4). He asserts that Satan is called the dragon (δράκων) on account of his having revolted (ἀποδεδρακέναι) from God (ii. 28), and traces the Bacchanalian cry "Evoe" to the name of Eve as the first sinner (*ib.*). His physical theories are equally puerile. He ridicules those who maintain the spherical form of the earth (ii. 32) and asserts that it is a flat surface covered by the heavens as by a domical vault (ii. 13). His exegesis is based on allegories usually of the most arbitrary character. He makes no attempt to educe the real meaning of a passage, but seeks to find in it some recondite spiritual truth, a method which often betrays him into great absurdities. He discovers the reason of blood coagulating on the surface of the ground in the divine word to Cain (Gen. iv. 10-12), the earth struck with terror (φοβηθεῖσα ἡ γῆ) refusing to drink it in. Theophilus's testimony to the O.T. is copious. He quotes very largely from the books of Moses and to a smaller extent from the other historical books. His references are copious to Ps., Prov., Is., and Jer., and he quotes Ezek. Hos. and other minor prophets. His direct evidence respecting the canon of N.T. does not go much beyond a few precepts from the Sermon on the Mount (iii. 13, 14), a possible quotation from Luke xviii. 27 (ii. 13), and quotations from Rom., I. Cor., and I. Tim. More important is a distinct citation from the opening of St. John's Gospel (i. 1-3), mentioning the evangelist by name, as one of the inspired men (πνευματοφόροι) by whom the Holy Scriptures (αἱ ἅγιαι γραφαί) were written (ii. 22). The use of a metaphor found in II. Pet. i. 19 bears on the date of that epistle. According to Eusebius (*l.c.*), Theophilus quoted the Apocalypse in his work against Hermogenes; a very precarious allusion has been seen in ii. 28, cf. Rev. xii. 3, 7, etc. A full index of these and other possible references to O. and N. T. is given by Otto (*Corp. Apol. Christ.* ii. 353-355). Theophilus transcribes a considerable portion of Gen. i.-iii. with his own allegorizing comments upon the successive work of the creation week. The sun is the image of God; the moon of man, whose death and resurrection are prefigured by the monthly changes of that luminary. The first three days before the creation of the heavenly bodies are types of the Trinity—τύποι τῆς τρίαδος—the first place in Christian writings where the word is known to occur (lib. ii. c. 15)—*i.e.* "God, His Word and His Wisdom."

The silence regarding the *Apology* of Theophilus in the East is remarkable. We find the work nowhere mentioned or quoted by Greek writers before the time of Eusebius. Several passages in the works of Irenaeus shew an undoubted relationship to passages in one small section of the *Apology* (Iren. v. 23, 1; *Autol.* ii. 25 *init.*: Iren. iv. 38, 1, iii. 23, 6; *Autol.* ii. 25: Iren. iii. 23, 6; *Autol.* ii. 25, 26), but Harnack (p. 294) thinks it probable that the quotations, limited to two chapters, are not taken from the *Apology*, but from Theophilus's work against Marcion (cf. Möhler, *Patr.* p. 286; Otto, *Corp. Apol.* II. viii. p. 357; Donaldson, *Christ. Lit.* iii. 66). In the West there are certain references to the *Autolycus*, though not copious. It is quoted by Lactantius (*Div. Inst.* i. 23) under the title *Liber de Temporibus ad Autolycum.* There is a passage first cited by Maranus in Novatian (*de Trin.* c. 2) which shews great similarity to the language of Theophilus (*ad Autol.* i. 3). In the next cent. the book is mentioned by Gennadius (c. 34) as "tres libelli de fide." He found them attributed to Theophilus of Alexandria, but the disparity of style caused him to question the authorship. The notice of Theophilus by Jerome has been already referred to. Dodwell found internal evidence, in the reference to existing persecutions and a supposed reference to Origen and his followers, for assigning the work to a younger Theophilus who perished in the reign of Severus (*Dissert. ad Iren.* §§ 44, 50, pp. 170 ff. ed. 1689). His arguments have been carefully examined by Tillemont (*Mém. eccl.* iii. 612 notes), Cave (*Hist. Lit.* i. 70), Donaldson (*u.s.* ii. 65), and Harnack (*u.s.* p. 287), and the received authorship fully established. Cf. W. Sanday in *Stud. Bibl.* (Oxf. 1885), p. 89.

Editions.—Migne's *Patr. Gk.* (t. vi. col. 1023-1168), and a small ed. (Camb. 1852) by the Rev. W. G. Humphry. Otto's ed. in the *Corpus Apologet. Christ. Saec. Secund.* vol. ii. (Jena, 1861, 8vo) is by far the most complete and useful. English trans. by Belty (Oxf. 1722), Flower (Lond. 1860), and Marcus Dods (Clark's *Ante-Nicene Lib.*). [E.V.]

Theophilus (9), bp. of Alexandria, succeeding Timotheus in the last week of July 385. He had probably been a leading member of the Alexandrian clergy. Socrates states that Theophilus (probably two years later, Clinton, *Fast. Rom.* i. 522) obtained from Theodosius a commission to demolish the pagan temples of Alexandria (Socr. v. 16). Sozomen corrects this by saying that Theodosius granted to Theophilus, at his own request, the temple of Dionysus, on the site of which he proposed to build a church (vii. 15). Socrates says that Theophilus "cleared out the temple of Mithras, and exposed its bloody mysteries." Socrates adds that the foul symbols used in the worship of Serapis and other gods were, by the archbishop's order, carried through the *agora* as objects of contemptuous abhorrence. The votaries of Alexandrian idolatry arranged a tragically successful onslaught on the Christians and then took possession of the vast Serapeum, in the N.W. quarter of the city, which had been the popular sanctuary of Alexandrian paganism, and now became their stronghold of "furious despair" (*Orat. of Athan. against the Arians*, p. 5, ed. Oxf.). They made sallies from its precincts, captured several Christians, dragged them within, and inflicted torture or death on those who would not sacrifice. The general in command at Alexandria and the Augustal prefect summoned them to surrender, but in vain. Olympius, a philosopher, sustained their obstinate resolution until the arrival of an edict ordering the destruction of all the temples. Terrified by the shouts which proclaimed this mandate, the desperadoes abandoned the Serapeum; and Theophilus, with a great body of soldiers, exultant Christians, and astounded pagans, ascended the hundred steps leading up the mound, and penetrated into the faintly lighted sanctuary, from within which the Christians afterwards believed that Olympius, on the night before the evacuation, had heard a voice chanting "Alleluia" (Soz. vii. 15). There was the huge seated statue of Serapis, constructed of various metals, now dusky with age, and inlaid with various precious stones (Clem. Alex. *Cohort.* 48). The successor of Athanasius gazed on this visible concentration of the power of Egyptian idolatry, no doubt the symbol to many Alexandrians of the principle of life and of the powers that ruled the underworld. It was a supreme moment; at last the church had her foot on the neck of her foe. Mutterings of superstitious fear were heard; to draw near the image was to cause an earthquake. The archbishop turned to a soldier who held an axe, and bade him "strike hard." The man obeyed. A shriek of terror burst from many; another and another blow followed, the head was lopped off, and there ran out a troop of mice, which had "dwelt within the god of the Egyptians." Misgiving and alarm gave way to noisy triumph; the body of Serapis was broken up and burned; the head was made a public show. At Canopus, 14 miles from Alexandria, temples were immediately laid low. The images were melted down into cauldrons and other vessels required in the eleemosynary work of the Alexandrian church. The one exception was an image of an ape, which Theophilus set up in a public place "in perpetuam rei memoriam," to the vexation of the pagan grammarian Ammonius, who lived to teach the young Socrates at Constantinople, and used to complain seriously of the injustice thus done to "Greek religion" (Socr. v. 16). During the demolition of various temples there were found hollow statues of bronze and wood, set against the walls, but capable of being entered by the priests, who thus carried on their impostures, which Theophilus explained to his pagan fellow-citizens (Theod. v. 22). But when the Nile-gauge was removed from the Serapeum to the church, the pagans asked, Would not the god avenge himself by withholding the yearly inundation his power had been wont to effect? It was, in fact, delayed. Murmurs swelled into remonstrances; the state of the city was becoming dangerous; the prefect had to consult his sovereign. Theodosius's answer was: "If the Nile would not rise except by means of enchantments or sacrifices, let Egypt remain unwatered." Forthwith the river began to rise with vehemence; the fear was now of a flood (Soz. vii. 20). We know not the nature of those concessions to the pagans which, according to a letter from Atticus to Theophilus's nephew Cyril, Theophilus made at this time for the sake of peace (Cyril, *Epp.* p. 202), but they did not prevent a pagan like Eunapius from abusing him. To Eunapius the temple-breakers were impious men who "threw everything into confusion, boasted of having conquered the gods," enriched themselves by the plunder, "brought into the sacred places the so-called monks, men in form but swinish in life," deified the "bones and heads of worthless men who had been punished by the courts for their offences," and assigned to "bad slaves who had borne the marks of the lash the title of martyrs and intercessors with the gods."

In 391 or 392 Theophilus was named by the council of Capua as arbiter of the dispute between Flavian, as representing the Meletian succession to the see of Antioch, and Evagrius, whose claims, like those of his predecessor Paulinus, were upheld by the West. Theophilus undertook to examine the case with the aid of his suffragans. Evagrius soon died, but Flavian was not recognized by the West until Chrysostom primarily, and Theophilus secondarily, effected that result in 398 (Soz. viii. 3; cf. Tillem. x. 538).

In A.D. 394 we find Theophilus for the first time at Constantinople, at a council in the baptistery of the great church, on Sept. 29. He sat next to Nectarius of Constantinople, and there were present also Flavian, Gregory of Nyssa, and Theodore of Mopsuestia. Theophilus was in close relations with the solitaries of Egypt. In the *Sayings of the Fathers* he appears as inviting some of them to be present at the destruction of the temples, and again as visiting those of the famous Nitrian settlement, and penetrating to the more distant Scetis. Still more celebrated was his intimacy with four monks of Scetis, known as "the Tall Brothers." These years were the best in Theophilus's episcopate; and if it had lasted only ten years, he might have left the name, if not of a saint, at least of a good as well as an able and energetic prelate.

But in 395 the story of his life changes its character. He begins to justify the description afterwards given of him by an adversary: "Naturally impulsive, headlong, intensely contentious, insatiable in grasping at his objects, awaiting in his own case neither trial nor inquiry, impatient of opposition, determined to carry out his own resolves" (Pallad. *Dial.* p. 76). In 395, at the request of bp. John of Jerusalem, he sent his friend Isidore, said to have been an Origenist, as his envoy into Palestine, to abate the strife between John and Jerome. Isidore visited Jerome three times, but would not give him a letter which Theophilus had written him (*ib.* 39); and his so-called mediation only produced a soreness on Theophilus's part towards Jerome, whose letters for some time he ignored. At last he wrote, coldly exhorting Jerome to respect the authority of the bp. of Jerusalem, and again in 399 (according to Vallarsi), urging Jerome to come to terms with John.

Theophilus had been throwing his whole weight against the extreme literalism of the Anthropomorphists, a coarse reaction from the Alexandrian allegorism. A number of ill-informed and enthusiastic monks recoiled even from the ordinary explanation of those O.T. economies by which, as Epiphanius himself held, the divine manifestation had been adapted to the capacities of human nature (*Haer.* 70. 7; see also Aug. *Haer.* 50 and 76; Theodoret, iv. 10). They took the scriptural expressions "as to eyes, face, and hands of God, as they found them, without examination" (Soz. viii. 11). Hence, when Theophilus, in his Paschal Letter for 399, insisted peremptorily on the immateriality of the divine nature, a storm of wrathful zeal broke out among the solitaries; one of them, indeed, named Serapion, was candid enough to be convinced by argument, but the pain which ensued was such that when his brethren were engaged in their devotions, he exclaimed with tears, "They have taken away my God, and I know not whom to adore!" (Cassian, *Coll.* x. 3). Many others were of fiercer mood: was the "image of God" to be thus nullified? They hurried from their deserts to Alexandria and menaced the "pope" whom they had been wont to honour. "Impious man! thou deservest death!" He saw that they were not to be defied, but a smooth prevarication might disarm them. "In seeing you I see God's face!" It was enough: he had appeared to accept the imperilled phrase: they asked more calmly, "If you admit that God's face is like ours, anathematize the books of Origen; for some people contradict us on their authority. If you will not do this, be prepared for the treatment due to those who fight against God." Theophilus uttered the fateful words of compliance: "I will do what you think fit; do not be angry with me, for I object to Origen's books, and blame those who approve them." Here he was using "economy"; he stooped to propitiate the Anthropomorphists by using their phrase in a sense of his own and letting them think that he condemned Origen absolutely. About the end of 399 or beginning of 400 he held a synod at Alexandria, at which "Origenism" was condemned. He then wrote to Anastasius of Rome and Jerome, informing them of this. At the beginning of 401 he attacked Origenism in his Paschal Letter (Hieron. *Ep.* 96), a remarkable document which anticipates the Christology of his nephew and successor Cyril, while excluding all Apollinarian ideas. Theophilus traces to Origen the (Marcellian) notion that Christ's kingdom would have an end. He goes on to denounce Origenistic Universalism, and the notions that Christ would suffer again on behalf of the demons, and that after the resurrection human bodies would again be subject to dissolution. Fortified by an imperial edict forbidding all monks to read Origen (Anastasius, *ad Joan. Jerus.*), he ordered the neighbouring bishops to banish the chief Nitrian monks from their own mountains and from the farther desert. Some of the monks came to remonstrate with him. They probably disclaimed the special errors associated with the name of Origen, and urged that they ought not to be treated as heretics because they opposed the degrading literalism of the Anthropomorphists. Palladius represents him as glaring at them in a fury, throwing his scarf or *omophorion* over the neck of Ammonius, one of the Tall Brothers, and with a blow on the face drawing blood, and fiercely exclaiming, "You heretic, anathematize Origen!" (*Dial.* p. 54). Palladius adds that he induced five of the Nitrian monks ("men unworthy even to be doorkeepers"), whom he had promoted to ecclesiastical office, to sign accusations against three of their chief brethren, who were accordingly excommunicated in a council. At his request the Augustal prefect decreed their expulsion from Egypt; and Theophilus is said to have attacked the Nitrian settlement by night at the head of a force which was to execute this order. A wild scene, according to Palladius, ensued (*Dial.* p. 57). Against this account is to be set Theophilus's own statement in what is called the synodical letter to the bishops of Palestine and Cyprus (trans. by Jerome, *Ep.* 92), intended to be read by them when assembled for the Dedication Festival at Jerusalem in Sept. 401. Theophilus says that, having been memorialized by orthodox "fathers and presbyters," he went to Nitria with a great number of neighbouring bishops, and there, in presence of many fathers who come together from nearly the whole of Egypt, some of Origen's treatises were read, and the adherents of Origenism condemned. The Origenist monks were now going about in foreign provinces, "seeking whom to devour with their impiety"; their mad impetuosity must be restrained. Theophilus protests that he has done them no hurt and taken nothing wrongfully from them. It is clear that Theophilus did personally visit Nitria, and that its "Origenist monks" were put under ban, and driven forth, probably in the early summer of 401, and that their places were filled by others of whose "docility" Theophilus could rely.

The persecuted "Brothers" found a temporary refuge with many other fugitives (*Dial.* p. 160) at Scythopolis, on the slope of mount Gilboa. Some bishops of Palestine who shewed them countenance were peremptorily warned by Theophilus (*ib.* p. 58). Hunted from place to place, the Nitrians determined to seek redress at Constantinople. Here the current of the Origenistic controversy flows suddenly, and with momentous consequences, into the stream of Chrysostom's episcopate. Towards the close of 401 some 50 elderly men of the Nitrian party fell at his feet as suppliants (*ib.* p. 58). The bishop, moved to tears, asked who had accused them. "Sit down, father," they answered, "and provide some remedy for the harm that pope Theophilus has done us. If out of regard to him you will not act, we shall be obliged to apply to the emperor. But we beg you to induce Theophilus to let us live in our own country; for we have not offended against him or against the law of our Saviour." Chrysostom promised to do his best. "Meanwhile," he said, "until I have written to my brother Theophilus, keep silence about your affairs." He assigned them a lodging in the precincts of the church of Anastasia, and pious ladies contributed to their support. He wrote to Theophilus, "Oblige me as your son and brother" (alluding to his own consecration by Theophilus), "by being reconciled to these men." Theophilus saw his way to a blow, not only at the Origenists, but at Chrysostom, whom, according to Palladius, he had disliked from the first. He wrote to Epiphanius, urging him to get Origenism condemned by a synod of his suffragans in Cyprus. Epiphanius obtained from a synod of his insular church a decree forbidding the faithful of Cyprus to read Origen's works (A.D. 402). Meantime the "Brothers" had laid before the emperor Arcadius their charges against Theophilus, and requested the empress Eudoxia to promote a formal hearing of the case, and even to cause Theophilus to be brought to Constantinople to be tried by its bishop. Arcadius ordered Theophilus to be summoned. Theophilus delayed to obey the imperial citation. When at last he set forth, as he passed through Lycia he is said to have boasted that he was "going to court to depose John" (*ib.* p. 72). It was not a mere brag; he knew his own diplomatic ability, and that Chrysostom's unworldly strictness had alienated Eudoxia and some people of rank, and even not a few ecclesiastics. The great name of the see of Athanasius would also go for much, and the watchword of "No Origenism" for yet more. He felt that he could exchange the position of a defendant for that of a judge. Theophilus landed at Constantinople at midday on a Thursday in the latter part of June 403 (*ib.* p. 64). Not one of the clergy went to meet him or pay him the usual honour (Socr.). Chrysostom invited him to the episcopal residence (Chrys. *Ep.* i. to Innocent; Pallad. p. 12), but he ignored all friendly messages, would not enter the cathedral, and betook himself to lodgings without the city. The emperor now urged Chrysostom to sit as judge in the case; he refused, for he "knew" (so he says) "the laws of the Fathers, and had a respect for the man." Theophilus had no such scruples. Proceedings against Chrysostom were taken at the council of "the Oak," a suburb of Chalcedon, and a sentence of deposition passed. [CHRYSOSTOM.] Theophilus was afterwards pleased to take up the almost forgotten question of the Nitrian exiles. They were persuaded to ask their pope's forgiveness, and Theophilus restored them to his communion. Returning to Constantinople he boldly entered the cathedral with an armed following to enforce the installation of a successor to "John," but finding that he had undertaken too much, and that the people were resolutely loyal to Chrysostom, he went on board a vessel at midnight and fled with his followers (*Dial.* p. 16). It was high time, for, says Palladius drily, "the city was seeking to throw him into the sea" (*ib.* p. 75). Theophilus did not attack Chrysostom in his Paschal Letter for 404, but returned to the subject of Origenism as an error which deceived "simple and shallow" minds. He informed pope Innocent that he had deposed Chrysostom; and Innocent, disposed to censure his "hasty arrogance" in not communicating the grounds of the condemnation (*ib.* p. 9) wrote, "Brother Theophilus, we are in communion with you *and* with our brother John. . . . Again we write, and shall do so whenever you write to us, that unless that mock trial is followed by a proper one, it will be impossible for us to withdraw from communion with John."

Theophilus seems to have written a work of great length against Origenism (Gennadius, *de Vir. Ill.* 33), from which Cyril quotes in his treatise, *ad Arcadiam et Marinam* (P. Pusey's *Cyril*, vii. 166), in support of the "Personal Union," and Theodoret in his second dialogue on the distinction between Christ's soul and the Word. Theophilus affirmed that Origen had been condemned (not only by Demetrius, but) by Heraclas. Either in this work (as Tillemont thinks, xi. 497) or in another, he strove to shew that he had only seemed to agree with the Anthropomorphists, for "he shewed," says Gennadius, that, according to the faith, God was incorporeal, "neque ullis omnino membrorum lineamentis compositum." In 410 he consecrated the eccentric philosopher and sportsman SYNESIUS to the metropolitan see of Ptolemais, who thanked him warmly for his Paschal Letter of 411, and wished him a long and happy old age (Synes. *Ep.* 9). In another letter Synesius, after professing his readiness to "treat as a law whatever the throne of Alexandria might ordain," asks the archbishop what should be done in regard to the people of Palaebisca and Hydrax, who were most reluctant to be placed, as Theophilus intended, under a bishop of their own, and asked leave to remain under Paul, bp. of Erythrum, to which diocese these "villages" had always belonged, save while Siderius was their bishop. Theophilus had also asked him to reconcile the bps. of Erythrum and Dardanis to each other (*Ep.* 67).

Theophilus died "of lethargy" on Oct. 15, 412 (Socr. vii. 7), after an episcopate of 27 years and nearly 3 months. The moral of his life is the deterioration which too great power can produce in one whose zeal in the cause of religion, although genuine and active, is not combined with singleness of heart.

All his extant remains are collected in Gallandius (*Bibl. Patrum*, vol. vii. pp. 603 ff.); his "canons" in Beveridge (*Pand. Can.* ii. 170). The sense of these canons is given in Johnson's *Vade Mecum*, ii. 255. See also Zahn, *Forschungen*, ii. 234 ff. [W.B.]

Theophilus (13), a Christian who discussed Christianity with Simon, a Jew, in a treatise published by a Gallic writer named EVAGRIUS in 5th cent. The title as given by Gennadius (*de Vir. Ill.* c. 51) is *Altercatio Simonis Judaei et Theophili Christiani*. This work lay hid till Zacagni, the Vatican Librarian, noticed it in 1698 in his *Collect. Mon*, pp. 51, 53, 324. It was printed by Migne (*Patr. Lat.* t. xx. c. 1165) and by Gebhardt and Harnack (*Texte u. Untersuch. zur Gesch. der Altchrist. Lit.* Bd. i. Hft. 3; Leipz. 1883), with exhaustive notes and dissertations. It has an important bearing on the controversy during patristic times between the church and Judaism. The disputants discuss various arguments against the deity of Christ drawn from O.T., Theophilus making a very liberal use of the mystical method of exposition. The Jew begins by objecting that Christ cannot be God because in Deuteronomy it is said "There is no other God beside Me," and Isaiah says, "I am the first and the last, and beside Me there is no God." Theophilus then defends his position from the conduct of Abraham towards the angel whom he worshipped at the oak of Mamre and from the Psalms. He quotes Is. vii. 14, "Behold, a virgin shall conceive." Simon replies that the virgin was the daughter of Jerusalem, whom Isaiah represents as despising Shalmanezer, while the angel who smote the Assyrians is the fulfilment of the prophecy contained in the name Emmanuel, since he was for them indeed "Nobiscum Deus." Theophilus retorts that the virgin daughter of Jerusalem had brought forth no son. The difficulties of the Incarnation are then discussed, and Christ's descent from David maintained by Theophilus, who argues that conception by a virgin was no more difficult to God than bringing water out of a rock. Simon then raises the favourite difficulty of the Jews from 2nd cent. downwards, drawn from Deut. xxi. 23, "He that is hanged is accursed of God" [ARISTO PELLAEUS], which introduces the subject of Christ's passion, where Theophilus urges that Ps. xxii. describes all the circumstances of our Lord's sufferings. Harnack (*l.c.*) has a learned monograph on this, and discusses the Jewish controversy as it was maintained by the Fathers. He devotes 50 pages to stating the relation between the *Altercatio* and Tertullian's *Tract. adv. Jud.*, Cyprian's *Testimonia*, Lactantius's *Institutiones*, and Justin's *Dialogus cum Tryphone*, and skilfully uses the *Altercatio* to determine the nature and contents of the similar 2nd-cent. work, *Altercatio Jasonis et Papisci*, which he considers the groundwork of the 5th-cent. document. [G.T.S.]

Theophronius. [AGNOËTAE].

Theophylactus (1) Simocatta, an Egyptian by birth, related to Peter, who was viceroy of Egypt at the death of the emperor Maurice in 602. His *Oecumenical History*, or *Historiae Mauricii Tiberii Imperatoris*, is very important for Byzantine history at a critical period, just before the rise of Mahomet, and during the beginning of the struggles with the Turks and Slavs. For church history his historical writings are interesting, as giving a vivid picture of the rites, superstitions, and ideas of the close of cent. vi. They shew, *e.g.* that the emperor Maurice was in many points superior to his spiritual teachers. Thus in lib. i. c. 11 we have the story of a sorcerer named Paulinus, whom the patriarch of Constantinople brought before the emperor, pressing for his capital punishment. The emperor suggested that instruction, rather than punishment, was required. Many other points of interest occur, *e.g.* the frequent use of a miraculous image (ἀχειροποίητος) of our Lord (ii. 3; iii. 1); the conversion of Chosroes (v. 15), and of a woman of noble birth among the Magi of Babylon, named Golinducha, her escape, pilgrimage to Jerusalem, and life at Nisibis (v. 12); the continued existence of the Marcionists (viii. 9); the church in honour of St. Paul at Tarsus (viii. 13); the incredulity of the emperor about the liquefaction of the blood of St. Euphemia (viii. 14); his overthrow and murder by Phocas, and the miraculous announcement of it by his statues at Alexandria the same night (viii. 13). The History of Theophylact is included in the Bonn series of Byzantine historians, but the most complete and convenient ed. is by C. H. Fabrottus in Labbe's *Corpus Hist. Byzant.* (Paris, 1648). [G.T.S.]

Theosebas, a deacon of the Thirian (? Tyrian) church, ordained priest by bp. John of Jerusalem. Jerome takes this ordination as a justification of the ordination of his brother Paulinian by Epiphanius, bp. of Salamis. He describes Theosebas as an eloquent man, and believes John to have ordained him in order to employ him to speak against himself and his friends (Hieron. *Cont. Joan. Hierosol.* 41). [W.H.F.]

Theotimus (2), bp. and metropolitan of Tomi, the capital of Scythia Minor in Lower Moesia. By birth a Goth, he was educated in Greece, where he took the name by which he is known. Adopting strict asceticism for himself, he kept a liberal table for the savage Goths and Huns who visited Tomi as the great central market of the province, endeavouring by hospitality, gifts, and courteous treatment to prepare them to receive the Gospel. In some instances the seed was sown in good soil, and the Hunnish strangers returned to their distant homes as converts, eager to convert their fellow-barbarians. Theotimus is with much probability identified by Baronius (*sub ann.* 402) with the successful missionary to the Huns mentioned by St. Jerome. He was regarded by the Huns with superstitious reverence, and was styled by them "the God of the Romans." The long hair of a philosopher flowed over his episcopal attire. He was a frequent and much revered visitor at Constantinople. In 403, during the visit of Epiphanius of Salamis, he refused to affix his signature to the decree of the council of Cyprus condemning the teaching of Origen, denouncing the attempt to cast insult on a justly honoured name and to question the decisions of wise and good men before them. He supported his refusal by publicly reading passages from Origen. He was an author of some note. Jerome ascribes to him some treatises in the form of dialogues. Fragments of his are in John Damascene's *Parallel. Sacr.* (vol. ii. pp. 640, 675, 694, 785, Le Quien's ed.). The archimandrite Carosus at the council of Chalcedon boasted that he had been baptized by Theotimus and charged by him to keep the Nicene faith inviolate (Labbe, *Concil.* iv. 530). Socr. *H. E.* vi. 12; Soz. *H. E.* vii. 26, viii. 14; Tillem. *Mém. eccl.* xi. 190; Le Quien, *Or. Chist.* ii. 1217; Cave, *Hist. Lit.* i. 288. [E.V.]

Thomas (8) Edessenus appears in the Life of Mar Abas. The latter, originally Magian by religion, was converted to Christianity, learnt Syriac at Nisibis, and Greek at Edessa from Thomas a Jacobite, whom he afterwards took with him to Alexandria and there with his help translated the Scriptures (*or*, the books) from Greek into Syriac (Gregory Bar-hebr. *Chr. Eccl.* ii. 22, t. iii. col. 189). Amrus (*ap.* Assem. iii. 75) gives a similar history of their relations; but only ascribes to them the translation of the works of Theodore of Mopsuestia. He relates how they went to Constantinople, and finding their lives in peril in consequence of their refusal to "anathematize the Three Fathers," fled to Nisibis. There Mar Abas became a teacher, and an eloquent assailant of Zoroastrianism. Gregory says that he was at one time taught by John Grammaticus, the Tritheite; but the facts alleged by Amrus lead us to conclude that he lapsed early into Nestorianism. He was elected catholicus of the Chaldeans in 536, and persecuted by the Magians. Chosroes called on him to return to his original faith or to conform to Christian orthodoxy. Refusing to do either, he was exiled, and venturing to return to his see without the king's permission, was cast into prison, and died there, 552. Among his disciples Amrus (Assem. ii. 411) reckons "Thomas of Edessa," no doubt his former teacher drawn by him from the opposing sect into Nestorianism. Of their joint work, the version of Theodore's liturgy survives (Brit. Mus. 7181, Rich., R.-F. *Catal.* p. 59—see also Rénaudot, *Liturg. Or.* t. i. p. 616); and the liturgy of Nestorius (*ib.* p. 626), still in use in the Nestorian churches, is probably their version mentioned by Ebedjesu (*Catal.* Assem. iii. 36), who also says they translated the O.T. (*ib.* 75), and adds a list of the writings of Mar Abas. [J.GW.]

Thomas (9) Apameensis, bp. of Apamea, the metropolis of Syria Secunda; one of the bishops sent to invite pope Vigilius to the second council of Constantinople. He himself attended it. Two contemporary historians, Procopius and Evagrius (the latter praises Thomas as a "man most mighty in word and in deed"), record his tact and courage when a great peril threatened his city. In 540 Chosroes, at the head of his Persians, after burning Antioch, was reported to be marching on Apamea. The panic-stricken people entreated their bishop to strengthen them to meet their fate by displaying a piece of the true cross, a cubit in length, which was treasured in their church in a casket richly decorated with gold and gems, and usually shewn to the faithful but once a year. Thomas fixed a day for its exhibition, to which the people of the neighbouring towns also eagerly repaired; among them the parents of Evagrius, bringing with them the future historian, who vividly describes the crowds pressing to see, and seeking to kiss, the sacred wood. The bishop (as both narrators relate) took it out of the casket, and raising it up in both hands proceeded round the church, according to usage. "A flame of fire shining, but not consuming," around and above the relic, moved as he moved, lighting up the roof. This was repeated several times. The people greeted with joy this visible token of divine protection, and drew from it confident hopes of deliverance. As Chosroes approached, the bishop met him, and assured him that no resistance was contemplated by the citizens, on whose behalf he engaged that the king with a limited guard should be admitted within the gates. Chosroes accordingly, leaving his army in camp, entered with 200 men. In violation of a compact he had recently entered into with the emperor (to receive 5,000 pounds of gold paid down and 500 annually, and make no further demands), he exacted from the bishop more than 10,000 pounds of silver, and all the gold and silver ornaments in the church treasury. Thomas produced last of all the casket that enshrined the cross, and, shewing its contents to the king, said, "This alone is left; take the gold and gems—I grudge them not; only leave us the precious wood of salvation." The king granted his petition. Thomas conciliated Chosroes by assiduously courting his favour. It would be unfair to judge him hardly under circumstances of such great responsibility and peril, though he shews politic suppleness and tact rather than the higher virtues of a prelate and patriot. [J.GW.]

Tiberius (2) II., emperor of Constantinople, 578-582. For the secular history of his reign see *D. of G. and R. Biogr.* We shall confine ourselves to the religious history of the period, for which the church history of the Monophysite John of Ephesus (Dr. Payne Smith's trans.) afforded fresh material. Tiberius presented a striking example of toleration in an intolerant age. The patriarchs of Constantinople were ardent opponents of the Monophysites. The patriarch, John Scholasticus, soon after the emperor's accession to the position of Caesar (A.D. 574), called on him to persecute the Monophysites. The emperor, having extorted from the patriarch an acknowledgment of their Christian character, declared he would not become a Diocletian in persecuting such followers of Christ. Eutychius, restored after John in 577, again urged Tiberius in the same direction, and again Tiberius refused, whereupon Eutychius, of his own motion, set the laws against heresy in operation (cf. John of Ephesus, *H. E.* pp. 72, 201). On p. 207 John relates Tiberius's only act of persecution. He had hired an army of Goths (Arians) to fight against the Persians. They left their families at Constantinople, stipulating for the use of a church for Arian worship. Tiberius consulted the patriarch, whereupon interested parties roused the mob to hoot the emperor and accuse him of Arianism. To clear himself he permitted the mob to attack the houses of all heretics. A book concerning the nature of the resurrection, published by Eutychius, taught that the body would be impalpable like a pure spirit. Gregory, afterwards pope Gregory the Great, then a deacon and Roman apocrisiarius at the imperial court, at once detected heresy in the patriarch's teaching. The emperor, being appealed to, decided in favour of Gregory, while the patriarch was induced to burn the obnoxious book. John of Ephesus, p. 192, says that Tiberius substituted a cross on his coins for a female figure, like Venus, which Justin introduced. See also Evagr. *H. E.* v. 11-22; Paul Diac. *Hist. Miscell.* lib. xvii.; Theophan. *Chronogr.* i. 380-387; Baron. *Annal.* A.D. 582-585; Clinton's *Fasti*, p. 840. [G.T.S.]

Tiburtius. [CAECILIA.]

Tichonius (*Tychonius*), an African Donatist, whose personal history is very little known, but who was conspicuous in the Donatist controversy, chiefly because Augustine mentions him in his letters to Parmenian and elsewhere. He appears to have flourished between 380 and 420, but according to Tillemont his date may be as early as 370. He was apparently a layman with a strong turn for church matters, including theology, was well versed in Scripture, and though a Donatist, revolted from the exclusive views of the sect, and occupied a position intermediate, as Neander says, between it and the church (*Ch. Hist.* iii. 280, ed. Clark; cf. Dr. Sparrow Simpson, *St. Aug. and Afr. Ch. Divisions* [1910], p. 51). Early in his career, perhaps 370-373, he published a work maintaining the universality of the church, and that no misconduct of a portion can annul the promise of God or contaminate Christians elsewhere. Consequently Catholic Christians in Africa were not cut off from the church of Christ, but still in communion with it. He pointed out the arbitrary character of the Donatist test of holiness, summing it up in the epigrammatic phrase, "quod volumus sanctum est" (Aug. *c. Parm.* i. 1; ii. 13, 31; see also ii. 21, 40, and 22, 42; iii. 3, 17; *Ep.* 93, 43). In support of his argument he quoted the decision of a council at Carthage of 270 bishops, who, having debated for 75 days, concluded, as the words of Augustine seem to imply, that traditors ought to be invited to receive rebaptism, but if they declined to do so ought to be admitted to communion. He adds that down to the time of Macarius, A.D. 348, communion was not refused to Catholics by Donatists (Aug. *Ep.* 93, 43). Of this council no other record exists than the statement of Tichonius, who gives it no date. His book has perished, but is probably the same either as the one in three books mentioned by Gennadius under the title *Bellum Intestinum*, or the one entitled *Expositiones Diversarum Causarum*, unless these two titles refer to one book only, in which, says Gennadius, Tichonius mentions some ancient councils (*de Scr. Eccl.* 18). Though denounced strongly for his inconsistency by St. Augustine, he appears to have continued his allegiance to the Donatists (Aug. *de Doctr. Chr.* iii. 30; Gennad. *u.s.*), and while still belonging to them wrote another book entitled *The Seven Rules or Keys of Christian Life*, which was discussed by Augustine in his work *de Doctr. Christ.* iii. 30-42. Its main heads are: (1) The church is the Lord's body, indivisible from Him, so that in Scripture language applicable to Him is applied also to the church. (2) The two-fold Body of the Lord, *i.e.* the distinction between bad and good people in the church. (3) The promises and the law. (4) Genus and species. Readers must be careful not to ascribe to the one what belongs to the other, *e.g.* in explaining Ezek. xxxvi. 23, which must be compared with N.T. and the promise of baptism there contained. The "new land" is the church to be gathered from all nations, but not yet revealed. (5) Concerning Jewish expressions denoting time, as "three days and three nights," etc., and also such numbers as 7, 10, 12, etc. (6) Concerning what he calls Recapitulation. (7) The personality of Satan. Tichonius also wrote a commentary on the Revelation, which, Gennadius tells us, he interpreted entirely in a spiritual sense—that the human body is an abode of angels ("angelicam stationem corpus esse"); that the Millennium in a personal sense is doubtful, that there is only one resurrection in which human bodies of every sort and age will rise, and that of the two resurrections mentioned, one is to be understood of the growth of grace in the soul of man and in the church. The Seven Rules are printed at length in the *Bibl. Max. Patr.* (Lyons, 1677), vi. 49, and *Bibl. Patr.* Galland. (Venice, 1765), viii. 107. Prof. F. C. Burkitt pub. a critical ed. of them in the *Camb. Texts and Studies* (1894), iii. 1. [H.W.P.]

Timotheus (7) I., archbp. of Alexandria, unanimously elected, as Theodosius I. affirms (*Cod. Theod.* t. vi. p. 348; Tillem. vi. 621), on the death of his brother, Peter II., in the latter half of Feb. 381. He was an elderly man of high character, who had sat at the feet of Athanasius; and his distinguishing epithet of ἀκτήμων (Coteler. *Eccl. Gr. Mon.* i. 366) indicates that he had parted with all his property. The council of Constantinople met in May 381; he and his attendant suffragans arrived late, and did not contribute to the peace of the assembly (Greg. Naz. *Carm. de Vita Sua*, 1800 ff.). They were annoyed at finding Gregory of Nazianzus established in the see of Constantinople; their jealousy of the "Oriental" bishops who had "enthroned him" broke forth in angry debate. They assured Gregory that they had no objection to him personally; but they probably resented the disgrace of Maximus, who had attempted, by the aid of some Egyptian bishops, to possess himself of the see. Gregory was glad to take this opportunity of resigning it, and Timotheus perhaps presided over the council during the few days between this abdication and the appointment of Nectarius (Tillem. ix. 474). The third canon gave to the see of Constantinople the second rank throughout the church; Neale says that Timotheus "refused to allow" its "validity" (*Hist. Alex.* i. 209). The council of Aquileia alludes to some annoyance given to him and Paulinus of Antioch by those whose orthodoxy had previously been suspected (Ambr. *Ep.* 12); yet that he did not break off openly from the majority is proved by the law of July 30, 381, in which Theodosius names him as one of the centres of Catholic communion (Soz. vii. 9; cf. Tillem. ix. 720). His episcopate was brief and uneventful. Facundus transcribes a letter of his to Diodore of Tarsus, referring to Athanasius as having spoken highly of Diodore, and professing his own inability to do justice to his virtue and orthodox zeal (*Pro Defens. Tri. Capit.* iv. 2). Timotheus wrote an account of several eminent monks, which Sozomen used (vi. 29). His 18 "canonical answers" to requests by his clergy for direction are interesting, and became part of the church law of the East (see Beveridge, *Pand. Can.* ii. 165; Galland. vii. 345). He died on Sun., July 20, 385 (see Tillem. vi. 802), and was succeeded by Theophilus. [W.B.]

Timotheus (18), commonly called **Aelurus,** a Monophysite intruder into the see of Alexandria. He had been at first a monk, then a presbyter under Dioscorus, and soon after the deposition of the latter at the council of Chalcedon had come into collision with his successor PROTERIUS. Deposed from office and banished into Libya (Mansi, *Concil.* vii. 617), he awaited, as his opponents afterwards said, the death of the emperor Marcian (*ib.* 525, 532). When that occurred in Jan. 457, he returned to Alexandria, and practised the artifice which apparently procured him the epithet αἴλουρος, "cat." "Creeping" at night to the cells of certain ignorant monks, he called to each by name, and on being asked who he was, replied, "I am an angel, sent to warn you to break off communion with Proterius, and to choose Timotheus as bishop" (Theod. Lect. i. 1). Collecting a band of turbulent men, he took possession, in the latter part of Lent, of the great "Caesarean" church, and was there lawlessly consecrated by only *two* bishops, whom Proterius and the Egyptian synod had deposed, and who, like himself, had been sentenced to exile. Thus, without the countenance of a single legitimate prelate (see Mansi, vii. 585), "he enthroned himself," as 14 Egyptian bishops express it in their memorials to the emperor Leo I. and to Anatolius of Constantinople (*ib.* 526, 533), while the real archbishop was sitting in his palace among his clergy. He instantly proceeded to perform episcopal acts; but after thus playing the anti-patriarch for a few days, he was expelled by the "dux" Dionysius; and it was apparently in revenge that his adherents (*ib.* 526, 533) hunted Proterius into a baptistery and murdered him (Easter, 457). Thereupon Timotheus returned and acted as archbishop. He declared open war against the maintainers of "two natures" as being in effect Nestorianizers, and on this ground boldly broke off communion with Rome, Constantinople, and Antioch, denouncing bishops of the Alexandrian patriarchate who had accepted the formula of the council, and some of whom had held their sees before the accession of Cyril; he also sent to cities and monasteries a prohibition to communicate with such bishops or to recognize clerics ordained by them. The 14 prelates who supply our most authentic information on these events were forced by the storm thus raised to abandon their homes, travel to Constantinople, and present memorials to the emperor and archbishop. These are extant in Latin versions (*ib.* 524 ff.). Timotheus Aelurus sent some bishops and clerics to plead his cause with the emperor. We possess a fragment of their petition (*ib.* 536), to the effect that under their "most pious archbishop, the great city of the Alexandrians, with its churches and monasteries, was by God's favour enjoying complete peace," and that they and their archbishop held firmly to the Nicene Creed, refusing to admit any alterations in, or additions to, its text. The document, as we now have it, breaks off abruptly with the words, "for the church of the great city of the Alexandrians does not accept the council of Chalcedon"; but it appears from other evidence (Leo, *Ep.* 149; Mansi, vii. 522) that it went on to ask that the sanction given to that council might be recalled, and a new council summoned, asserting that the Alexandrian people, the civil dignitaries, the municipal functionaries, and the company of transporters of corn-freights, desired to retain Timotheus as their bishop. The emperor Leo refused the request of the emissaries of Timotheus for immediate action against the authority of the council of Chalcedon, which he had already constructively upheld by confirming the ecclesiastical acts of his predecessors (cf. pope Leo's *Ep.* 149 with Mansi, vii. 524), but yet deemed it expedient to send copies of both memorials to the bishops of Rome, Constantinople, Antioch, and Jerusalem, and to 55 other prelates and three leading monks (one of them being Symeon Stylites), requesting their opinion as to the case of Timotheus and as to the authority of the council (Evagr. ii. 9; Mansi, vii. 521). Of the prelates consulted, all but one, the inconstant Amphilochius of Side, accepted the council of Chalcedon (Evagr. ii. 10), and all condemned Timotheus in more or less energetic terms, although some with "a salvo, if the statements of the exiles were true" (Mansi, vii. 537 ff.). In the early summer of 460 Leo I. sent orders to Stilas, the "dux" commanding at Alexandria, to expel Timotheus from the church, and to promote the election of an orthodox bishop (Liberat. *Brev.* 15). "The Cat" was then ejected, but shewed his wonted acuteness by obtaining permission to come to Constantinople and pretend that he had adopted the Chalcedonian doctrine, as if heterodoxy had been his only fault, and so on becoming orthodox he might hope to retain his see. Pope Leo wrote, on June 17, 460, to the emperor Leo and to Gennadius, the new patriarch of Constantinople, urging that Timotheus, even supposing his conversion sincere, was disqualified by having "invaded so great a see during the lifetime of its bishop" (*Epp.* 169, 170). Accordingly Timotheus was a second time exiled with his brother Anatolius—first to Gangra and then, on his causing fresh disturbances, to a village on the shore of the Chersonesus which Eutychius calls Marsuphia (cf. Evagr. ii. 11; Liberat. *Brev.* 16; Theophan. *Chronogr.* i. 186; Eutychius, ii. 103); and during 16 years the church over which he had tyrannized was at peace under the rule of his namesake, Timotheus, called Salofaciolus. But when the next emperor, Zeno, fled from the usurper Basiliscus, towards the close of 475, a new scene opened for Aelurus. He was summoned to Constantinople, where his admirers greeted him with "Blessed is he that cometh in the name of the Lord!" (Simplicius, in Mansi, vii. 976). The patriarch Acacius closed the churches against him, but he held services in private houses (Mansi, *l.c.*). Basiliscus recognized him as rightful bp. of Alexandria, and by his advice put forth a circular to the episcopate, condemning "the innovation in the faith which was made at Chalcedon" (Evagr. iii. 4). But when the Eutychians of Constantinople, deeming his arrival a godsend, hastened to pay court to him, he disappointed them by declaring that he for his part accepted the statement which Cyril had in effect adopted at his reunion with John of Antioch, that "the Incarnate Word was consubstantial with us, according to the flesh" (*ib.* 5). On his way home he visited Ephesus, and gratified its clergy and laity by declaring their church (the fifth in Christendom in point of dignity) to be free from that subjection to Constantinople which had been imposed on it by the 28th canon of Chalcedon (*ib.* 6). When he reached Alexandria, the kindly and popular Salofaciolus was allowed to retire to his monastery at the suburb called Canopus. Aelurus did not long survive, dying probably in the autumn of 477 (Neale, *Hist. Alex.* ii. 17). [W.B.]

Timotheus (19), commonly called **Salofaciolus,** patriarch of Alexandria, elected after the expulsion of Timotheus Aelurus, at the beginning of Aug. 460. He was attached to the Chalcedonian dogma, and may be identified with the "Timotheus, presbyter, and a steward of the Alexandrian church," who signed the memorial which the persecuted Catholic bishops presented to the emperor Leo in 457 (Mansi, *Concil.* vii. 530). His name Salofaciolus, or Salafaciolus, appears to be made up of a Coptic and a Latin word, and to signify "wearer of a white head-gear or cap" (Du Fresne, *Gloss. Med. et Infim. Graecit.* ii. 1659). After his consecration he sent a letter to pope Leo, who replied in terms of warm congratulation, and urged the newly appointed "Catholic bishop of the Alexandrian church" to root out all remains of Nestorian as well as of Eutychian error (*Ep.* 171, Aug. 18, 460). Ten orthodox Egyptian bishops had also written to Leo that the election had been unstained by "canvassing, sedition, or unfairness of any kind," and that Timotheus was approved as worthy of so eminent a bishopric for purity of character and integrity of faith (*Ep.* 173). "In his episcopal administration," says Liberatus, "he was exceedingly gentle, so that even those who were of his communion complained of him to the emperor for being too remiss and easy-going towards heretics, in consequence of which the emperor wrote to him not to allow the heretics to hold assemblies or to administer baptism; but he continued to treat them gently, and while he thus discharged his office the Alexandrians loved him, and cried aloud to him in the streets and in the churches, 'Even if we do not communicate with thee, yet we love thee.'" This gentleness became weakness when, in the hope of conciliating the Monophysites, he reinserted the name of Dioscorus in his church diptychs (Mansi, vii. 983), and so gave occasion for the blundering Eutychius to rank him with the other Timotheus as a "Jacobite" (*Ann.* ii. 103). When Timotheus Aelurus returned in 476 and took possession of the archbishopric, Salofaciolus was allowed to reside in the monastery of the monks of Tabennesus, situated in a suburb of Alexandria called Canopus (see Le Quien, *Or. Christ.* ii. 415). He remained there when Aelurus died, fearing to cause a "tumult" if he shewed himself in the city; whereupon the Monophysites took the opportunity of electing and enthroning Peter Mongus, who had been archdeacon under Aelurus; but the Augustal prefect Anthemius, acting on a mandate from Zeno, expelled Peter from the church, and reinstated Timotheus Salofaciolus (Evagr. ii. 11). This step was followed up by rigorous edicts, intended to overawe the numerous clerics, monks, and laymen who refused to communicate with the restored patriarch (*Brev. Hist. Eutych.* in Mansi, vii. 1063). Peter Mongus was lurking in corners of Alexandria, "plotting against the church"; the patriarch wrote to Zeno and Simplicius, begging that he might be removed to a distance (Liberat. *Brev.* 16; Mansi, *l.c.*). Simplicius pressed the point in letters to Acacius; but Zeno could not be induced to take this step against Peter, and probably Acacius was at least lukewarm in the cause. At last, according to the *Breviculus*, Timotheus sent John Talaia again to Constantinople, and obtained a promise that he should have a Catholic successor. Soon afterwards he "died undisturbed" (Liberat.), about midsummer 482, as we learn from letters of Simplicius dated July 15, 482 (Mansi, vii. 991). [W.B.]

Timotheus (24), patriarch of Constantinople, appointed in 511 by the emperor Anastasius the day after the deposition of MACEDONIUS (3). He had been priest and keeper of the ornaments of the cathedral, and was a man of bad character. He apparently adopted the Monophysite doctrines from ambition, not conviction. Two liturgical innovations are attributed to him, the prayers on Good Friday at the church of the Virgin, and the recital of the Nicene Creed at every service, though the last is also ascribed to Peter the Fuller. He sent circular letters to all the bishops, which he requested them to subscribe, and also to assent to the deposition of Macedonius. Some assented, others refused, while others again subscribed the letters but refused to assent to the deposition of Macedonius. The extreme Monophysites, headed by John Niciota, patriarch of Alexandria, whose name he had inserted in the diptychs, at first stood aloof from him, because, though he accepted the Henoticon, he did not reject the council of Chalcedon, and for the same reason Flavian II. of Antioch and Elias of Jerusalem at first communicated with him. With SEVERUS of Antioch he afterwards assembled a synod which condemned that council, on which Severus communicated with him. Timothy sent the decrees of his synod to Jerusalem, where ELIAS refused to receive them. Timothy then incited Anastasius to depose him (Liberat. 18, 19; Mansi, viii. 375). He also induced the emperor to persecute the clergy, monks, and laity who adhered to Macedonius, many of whom were banished to the Oasis in the Thebaid. His emissaries to Alexandria anathematized from the pulpit the council of Chalcedon. Within a year of his accession Timotheus directed that the *Ter Sanctus* should be recited with the Monophysite addition of "Who wast crucified for us." On Nov. 4 and 5 this caused disturbances in two churches, in which many were slain, and the next day a terrible riot broke out which nearly caused the deposition of Anastasius. Timothy died Apr. 5, 517. Vict. Tun. *Chron.*; Marcell. *Chron.*; Theod. Lect. ii. 28, 29, 30, 32, 33; Evagr. iii. 33; Theophanes; Tillem. *Mém. eccl.* xvi. 691, 698, 728. [F.D.]

Titus, emperor. [VESPASIANUS.]

Titus (2), bp. of Bostra in Arabia Auranitis, *c.* 362-371, of very high repute for learning and eloquence. He is named by Jerome among the many distinguished Christian writers of great secular erudition and knowledge of Holy Scripture (Hieron. *Ep.* 70 [84]). Jerome mentions his works, dwelling especially on three written against the Manicheans (Hieron. *de Vir. Ill.* c. 102). He is also enumerated by Sozomen (*H. E.* iii. 14, *ad fin.*) with Eusebius of Emesa, Basil of Ancyra, Cyril of Jerusalem, and others, as writers of the highest celebrity, whose learning is proved by the many remarkable writings they left. The appearance of Titus in such company, and his being distinctly reckoned among the Acacians by Socrates (*H. E.* iii. 25), makes his orthodoxy doubtful. He is chiefly known to us from the attempt made by the emperor Julian to induce the citizens of Bostra to expel him as a calumniator of their city. The pagan inhabitants made the authoritative revival of their cult by Julian the signal for organized attacks on their Christian fellow-citizens. The Christians retaliated. Julian, choosing to assume that the Christians were responsible for these disturbances, threatened to call Titus and the city clergy to judicial account if any fresh outbreak occurred (Soz. *H. E.* v. 15). Titus replied that though the Christian population exceeded the heathen in numbers, in obedience to his admonitions they had remained quiet under severe provocations, and there was no fear of the peace of the city being disturbed by them (*ib.*). Julian then issued a rescript to the citizens of Bostra, Aug. 1, 362, charging Titus with calumniating them by his representations that they only abstained from violence in obedience to his monitions, and calling upon them to drive him out of their city as a public enemy (Julian Imp. *Ep.* 52, p. 437). The death of Julian found Titus still bp. of Bostra (Rendell, *Emperor Julian*, pp. 188, 222). On the accession of Jovian, Titus is enumerated by Socrates (*H. E.* iii. 25) as a member of the Acacian party. According to Jerome, he died in the reign of Valens, *c.* 370. Of his works (Soz. *H. E.* iii. 14) we have only very scanty remains. Of that against the Manichees in four books ("fortes libros," *l.c.*) commended by Jerome and referred to by Epiphanius (*Haer.* lxvi. c. 21) and Theodoret (*Haer. Fab.* lib. i. c. 26), three books exist in MS. in the library of the Johanneum at Hamburg. Tillem. *Mém. eccl.* vii. 385; Ceill. *Aut. eccl.* vi. 43 ff.; Cave, *Hist. Lit.* i. 228; Migne, *Patr. Gk.* xviii. 1069 ff.; Fabr. *Bibl. Graec.* vi. 748, viii. 684, ix. 320; Clinton, *Fasti Rom.* No. 141. [E.V.]

Trajanus (1), **M. Ulpius (Nerva),** emperor, belonged to a family of Italian origin settled in the colony of Italica in Baetica. He was born on Sept. 18, probably in A.D. 53, and passed his early life in the army under his father, a distinguished officer who had risen to the consulship. In Oct. 97, being then in command of the army of Lower Germany, he was adopted by Nerva, with whom, till his death on Jan. 27, he reigned jointly, and then became sole emperor. He remained on the Rhine, placing that frontier in a state of defence, till in the latter half of 99 he made his entrance into Rome, being received with the greatest joy. He died at Selinus in Cilicia, probably *c.* Aug. 7 or 8, 117.

For us the interest of his life centres in the famous rescript, addressed to his friend Pliny in reply to his letter detailing his procedure towards the Christians in Bithynia. Pliny had arrived in his province immediately before Sept. 18, 110, or more probably 111 (Mommsen, *Hermes*, 1869, 59), and the letter was probably written in the year after his arrival. The rescript is one of a series of replies to inquiries on the most various subjects—police, baths, sewerage, precautions against fires, water supply, public buildings, etc.—and neither Pliny nor Trajan seems to have considered the subject one of special importance. Pliny's letter is the earliest heathen account of the services and behaviour of the Christians, and Trajan's reply is the earliest piece of legislation about Christianity that we possess.

After stating that, having never been present at trials of Christians, he was ignorant of the precise nature of the crime and the usual punishment, and also how far it was the practice to pursue the inquiry, Pliny asks the emperor whether any distinction should be made on the ground of age; whether those who abjured Christianity should be pardoned, or a man who had embraced Christianity gain by renouncing it; whether the mere name apart from any crime or the crimes associated with the name should be punished? Provisionally he had taken the following course in the case of those charged before him with being Christians. "I demanded," he says, "of the accused themselves if they were Christians, and if they admitted it, I repeated the question a second and a third time, threatening them with punishment; if they persisted, I ordered them to be led to execution. For I felt convinced that, whatever it might be they confessed they were, at any rate their unyielding obstinacy deserved punishment. Some others, who were Roman citizens, I decided should be sent to Rome for trial. In the course of the proceedings, as is generally the case, the number of persons involved increased and several varieties appeared. An anonymous document was presented to me which contained the names of many. Those who denied that they were or ever had been Christians I thought should be released when they had, after my example, invoked the gods and offered incense and wine to your image, which I had ordered to be brought for the purpose along with those of the gods, and had also blasphemed Christ, none of which things, it is said, can those who are really Christians be compelled to do. Others, who were accused by an informer, first said they were Christians and then denied it, saying that they had been, but had ceased to be, some three years, some several, and one twenty years ago. All adored your image and those of the gods, and blasphemed Christ. They declared that all the wrong they had committed, wittingly or unwittingly, was this, that they had been accustomed on a fixed day to meet before dawn and sing antiphonally a hymn to Christ as a god, and bind themselves by a solemn pledge [*sacramento*] not to commit any enormity, but to abstain from theft, brigandage, and adultery, to keep their word, and not to refuse to restore what had been entrusted to their charge if demanded. After these ceremonies they used to disperse and assemble again to share a common meal of innocent food, and even this they had given up after I had issued the edict by which, according to your instructions, I prohibited secret societies [*hetaeriae*]. I therefore considered it the more necessary, in order to ascertain what truth there was in this account, to examine two slave-girls, who were called deaconesses [*ministrae*], and even to use torture. I found nothing except a perverted and unbounded superstition. I therefore have adjourned the investigation and hastened to consult you, for I thought the matter was worth consulting you about, especially on account of the numbers who are involved. For many of every age and rank, and of both sexes, are already and will be summoned to stand their trial. For this superstition has infected not only the towns, but also the villages and country; yet it apparently can be checked and corrected. At any rate it is certainly the case that the temples which were almost deserted begin to be frequented, the sacred ceremonies which had long been interrupted to be resumed, and there is a sale for fodder for the victims ["pastumque venire victimarum," so Lightfoot], for which previously hardly a buyer was to be found. From this one can easily conclude what a number of people may be reformed, if they are given a chance of repentance." Trajan replied with the following rescript: "You have followed the right course, my dear Secundus, in investigating the cases of those denounced to you as Christians, for no fixed rule can be laid down for universal adoption. Search is not to be made for them; if they are accused and convicted they are to be punished, yet with the proviso that if a man denies he is a Christian and gives tangible proof of it by adoring our gods, he shall by his repentance obtain pardon, however strong the suspicion against him may be. But no notice should be taken of anonymous accusations in any kind of proceeding. For they are of most evil precedent and are inconsistent with our times" (*Plini et Trajani Epp.* 96, 97).

Besides the interesting information thus afforded on the belief and practice of the early Christians (hints are apparently given of the existence of some formula of prayer, of the Eucharist and Agape), what light does it throw on the legal position of the Christians? That trials of Christians had to Pliny's knowledge already taken place appears by it, and the allusion cannot be to the Neronian persecution when he was scarcely three years old, and hardly can be to that which was commenced and almost immediately discontinued by Domitian, assuming that the objects of it were Christians and not Jews. Pliny's language points rather to proceedings of a regular kind against Christians. On the other hand, the fact that a man who had attained distinction at the bar, and who had held all the high offices of state, had never witnessed a trial of this kind, proves that they were rare. Again, no statutory enactments as to Christianity existed, or Trajan would have referred to them in his rescript according to his usual custom, when *senatus consulta* or edicts of preceding emperors bore on the subject on which he is writing (cf. lxvi. and lxxiii.). Pliny's action was therefore based on the fact that Christianity was a *religio illicita*, its professors members of a *collegium illicitum*, at what might be termed the Roman common law. While Christians were regarded by the Roman government as a mere variety of Jews, they shared in the toleration enjoyed by Judaism as a *religio licita*. When the separation between the two religions became apparent to Roman eyes, Christianity lost this shelter and its professors fell under the ban that extended to all unlawful associations. The exact time when the Romans became aware of the distinction has been the subject of much controversy; at any rate, it had become apparent by the end of the 1st cent. Nero does not appear to have issued any edicts against Christians in general, and if Christianity, either apart from or along with Judaism, suffered under Domitian (Dion, lxvii. 14), all the measures on the subject were repealed by Nerva on his accession (*ib.* lxviii. 1).

What, then, was the effect of Trajan's rescript? Formally it made the position of the Christians worse. It confirmed, by a positive enactment, the view Pliny had taken of their status at common law. Practically, however, the qualifications that they were not to be sought for, and anonymous accusations ignored—qualifications due to Trajan's abhorrence of delation in all its forms (cf. Juv. iv. 87; Tac. *Ann.* iv. 30; Pliny, *Pan.* 34, 35), and from which it was his especial pride to be free—must frequently have been a boon to the Christians. This secondary bearing of the rescript was first insisted on by Tertullian (*e.g. Apol.* c. 5, in Migne, *Patr. Lat.* i. 276) and the primary thrown into the background. From Tertullian this view of the rescript passed to Eusebius and from him to other Christian writers, till at last it came to be taken as an edict of toleration terminating a general persecution (Sulp. Sev. ii. 31; Orosius, vii. 12, in *Patr. Lat.* xx. 146, xxxi. 1091), a theory excluded by the words of the rescript itself, "That no fixed rule could be laid down for the whole empire." It was not from favour to the Christians that these limitations were introduced, and Trajan's chief objection to them was his dread of secret societies, which were especially prevalent in Bithynia (*Epp.* xxxiv. xciii. cxvii.).

Overbeck (*Studien zur Geschichte der Alten Kirche*) maintained that the rescript was the law that regulated the position of the Christians till the beginning of the persecution of Severus in 202, and that from Tertullian downwards a thoroughly mistaken view of it had been taken. He asserts that during this period it regulated the practice of the emperors, and that they did not deviate from it either in favour of the Christians or against them. He supports his position by pointing out that Justin Martyr under Antoninus Pius, Athenagoras under M. Aurelius, and Tertullian under Severus (*Apol. I.* 4, *Legatio pro Christ.* 1 and 2, in *Patr. Gk.* vi. 333, 892-893, and *Apol.* 1-4, in *Patr. Lat.* i. 259-289), all agree in stating that the mere name of Christian was punishable. The trials of Ptolemy and Lucius before the prefect of the city are conducted precisely in the manner laid down by the rescript (Justin, *Apol. II.* in *Patr. Gk.* vi. 445). M. Aurelius, on the occasion of the persecution of Lyons, issues a rescript following the same rule, that those who abjured Christianity should be released, those who refused should be executed (Eus. *H. E.* v. 1). Overbeck, therefore, rejects not only the protection edicts ascribed to M. Aurelius and Antoninus Pius, which are now generally considered to be forgeries, but also, following Keim, argues (134-148) for the spuriousness of Hadrian's letter to Minucius Fundanus, which has usually been thought to be genuine, and which is not really inconsistent with Trajan's rescript.

The only martyrs known by name as having suffered under Trajan are the bishops Symeon of Jerusalem and IGNATIUS of Antioch.

For Trajan's relations with the Christians consult also Eusebius (*H. E.* iii. 32, 33, 36), Tillemont, *Mém. eccl.* (ii. 167-212), and Gibbon (c. 16). The ancient authorities for his reign are singularly meagre, and the dates, and even the order of many important events, have been determined only by the evidence of inscriptions and coins. [F.D.]

Trophimus (1) (Cyp. *Ep.* 55, 11), an Italian bishop (*sacerdotii*) who with all his flock offered incense in the Decian persecution. He was restored to lay-communion by Cornelius, bp.

of Rome. It is not denied that his people's attachment to him, and the assurance that they would follow his return, eased the reception of Trophimus. The Novatianists forwarded to Africa the misstatement that Cornelius had restored him to his episcopal orders, and so shook the confidence of some in him; but Cyprian of his own knowledge denies the statement. It is improbable that a lapsed bishop would be obliged or allowed to do public penance. The expression that Trophimus with "penance *of entreaty* confessed his own fault" is itself against it, and although it is said that he made "satisfaction," it is presently added that "the return of the brethren made satisfaction for him." The restoration seems to have been made at the Roman council of June (or July) A.D. 251, from the words (*Ep.* 55, ix. [6], H. 11), "Tractatu cum collegis plurimis habito susceptus est." Ritschl (*Cyprian von Karthago*, p. 79) calls Trophimus a "sacrificatus," though the case of the sacrificati is treated separately in the next section of *Ep.* 55, and the words "Trofimo et turificatis" do not make it certain that he was even a "Turificatus." [E.W.B.]

Trophimus (3), St., 1st bp. of Arles, a subject of eager controversy. According to the tradition of the see, he was the disciple of St. Paul mentioned in Acts and II. Tim., and was sent forth as a missionary to Arles by St. Peter or St. Paul, or both. As early as 417 pope Zosimus, in a letter to the bishops of Gaul, speaking of the city of Arles, says, "Ad quam primum ex hâc sede Trophimus summus antistes, ex cujus fonte totae Galliae fidei rivulos acceperunt, directus est" (*Ep.* 1, *Patr. Lat.* xx. 645); and in the same pope's letter to Hilary, bp. of Narbonne, Trophimus was "quondam ad Arelatensem urbem ab apostolica sede transmissus" (*Ep.* 6, *Patr. Lat. ib.* 667). Again, the 19 bishops of the province of Arles, writing to pope Leo about the middle of 5th cent., assert that it is known to all Gaul and to the church of Rome "prima intra Gallias Arelatensis civitas missum a beatissimo Petro apostolo sanctum Trophimum habere meruit sacerdotem, et exinde aliis paulatim regionibus Galliarum bonum fidei et religionis infusum" (*Patr. Lat.* liv. 1880), though it should be mentioned that the genuineness of this letter has been questioned. So, too, Ado, in his *Martyrologium* (Dec. 29) and *Chronicon*. On the other hand, Gregory of Tours, apparently quoting from the *Acta* of St. Saturninus, says in effect that Trophimus arrived in Gaul with the first bishops of Tours, Paris, and other cities in the consulate of Decius and Gratus, *i.e.* after the middle of 3rd cent.; and in a very old catalogue of the archbishops published by Mabillon, *Vetera Analecta*, p. 220 (Paris, 1723), he is preceded by Dionysius, as though he were the second bishop. The question, to which some bitterness has been imparted as being closely connected with the hotly resented claims of the early archbps. of Arles to a sort of primacy in Gaul, is elaborately discussed by Trichaud (*Hist. de l'Eglise d'Arles*, i. 21-143). The cathedral church at Arles was dedicated to Trophimus, with St. Stephen (*Gall. Christ.* i. 519). [S.A.B.]

U

Ulfilas (*Urphilas* in Philostorgius), the apostle of the Goths in the 4th cent. His career is involved in much obscurity. The 5th-cent. church historians were our only source until Waitz, in 1840, discovered a MS. of the Louvre, containing an independent account, written by one of Ulfilas's own pupils, Auxentius, Arian bp. of Silistria, who is thus an original witness. This MS. gives details which shed light on the obscurity. From these two sources we learn that he was born early in 4th cent., probably in 311. He was consecrated bishop when 30 years of age, possibly by Eusebius of Nicomedia, at the council of the Dedication, held at Antioch 341. In 380 he went to Constantinople, and died there the same year or early in 381. The circumstances of his life raise the question of the origin of Gothic Christianity. Philostorgius tells us that, under Valerian and Gallienus in the second half of cent. iii., the Goths from N. of the Danube invaded the Roman territory, laid waste the province of Moesia as far as the Black Sea, crossed into Asia and ravaged Cappadocia and Galatia, whence they took a vast number of captives, including many Christian ecclesiastics. "These pious captives, by their intercourse with the barbarians, brought over large numbers to the true faith, and persuaded them to embrace the Christian religion in place of heathen superstitions. Of the number of these captives were the ancestors of Urphilas himself, who were of Cappadocian descent, deriving their origin from a village called Sadagolthina, near the city of Parnassus" (Philost. *H. E.* ii. 5). The Goths carried back these Christian captives into Dacia, where they were settled, and where considerable numbers embraced Christianity through their instrumentality. Ulfilas, the child of one of these Christian captives, was trained in Christian principles. Socrates asserts that he was a disciple of a bishop, Theophilus, who was present at Nicaea and subscribed its creed. He was at first a reader in the church. The king of the Goths then sent him to Constantinople as ambassador to the emperor, *c.* 340, when he was consecrated bishop. He returned to Dacia, laboured there for 7 years, and then migrated into Moesia, driven from his original home by a persecution, probably between 347 and 350. About that period he produced his great literary work, inventing the Gothic character and translating "all the books of Scripture with the exception of the Books of Kings, which he omitted because they are a mere narrative of military exploits, and the Gothic tribes, being especially fond of war, were in more need of restraints to check their military passions than of spurs to urge them on to deeds of war" (Philost. *l.c.*). We next hear of him as present at the synod of Constantinople A.D. 360, when the Acacian party triumphed and issued a creed taking a middle view between those of the orthodox and Arian parties. This was the creed of the Homoean sect, headed by Acacius in the East and Ursacius and Valens in the West. It is important to note its exact words, as it defines the position of Ulfilas. The material part runs thus: "We do not despise the Antiochian formula of the synod *in Encoeniis*, but because the terms Ὁμοούσιος and Ὁμοιούσιος occasion much confusion, and because some have recently set up the ἀνόμοιος, we therefore reject ὁμοούσιος and ὁμοιούσιος as contrary to the Holy Scriptures; the ἀνόμοιος, however, we anathematize, and acknowledge that the Son is similar to the Father in accordance with the words of the apostle, who calls Him the image of the invisible God. We believe in our Lord Jesus Christ, His Son, Who was begotten by Him before all ages without change, the only-begotten God, Logos from God, Light, Life, Truth, and Wisdom. . . . And whoever declares anything else outside this faith has no part in the Catholic church" (see Hefele, ii. 265, Clark's ed.; and Gwatkin's *Studies of Arianism*, pp. 180-182). The subsequent history of Ulfilas is involved in much obscurity. Sozomen (vi. 37) intimates that Ulfilas and his converts suffered much at the hands of Athanaric, a lively picture of whose persecution, A.D. 372-375, will be found in the Acts of St. Sabas (Ruinart's *Acta Sincera*, p. 670) and of St. Nicetas, Sept. 15 (cf. *AA. SS.* Boll. Sept.), both of which documents are full of most interesting details concerning the life and manners of the Goths. Mr. C. A. Scott, of Cambridge, published an interesting and full monograph on Ulfilas, in which he discusses his history and that of Gothic Christianity during this period. Arianism seems to have specially flourished during the first half of cent. iv. in the provinces along the Danube. VALENS and URSACIUS, who lived there, were the leaders of Western Arianism, and Sulpicius Severus expressly asserts (*Chron.* ii. 38) that almost all the bishops of the two Pannonias were Arians. This would sufficiently account for the Arianism of the Goths who were just then accepting Christianity. The literary fame of Ulfilas is connected with his Gothic translation of the Bible, the one great monument of that language now extant. It does not exist in a complete shape. The fragments extant are contained in (1) the *Codex Argenteus*, now at Upsala; (2) the *Codex Carolinus*; and (3) the Ambrosian fragments published by Mai. A complete bibliography of these fragments, as known till 1840, will be found in Ceillier (iv. 346), and a complete ed. in Migne (*Patr. Lat.* t. xviii.) with a Life, Gothic grammar, and glossaries. Scott (*Ulfilas, the Apostle of the Goths*, 1885) gathered together the literature after 1840, and gave a long account of the MS. of Waitz. He also discussed (p. 137) some fragments attributed to Ulfilas. The best German works on the life of Ulfilas are those of Waitz (1840), Krafft (1860), and Bessel (1860). Works on the Gothic Bible are by E. Bernhardt (Halle, 1875) and Stamm (Paderborn, 1878); Bosworth's *Gothic and Anglo-Saxon Gospels* (1874); Skeat, *Gospel of St. Mark in Gothic* (Oxf. 1883); *An Introduction, Phonological, Morphological, Syntactic, to the Gothic of Ulfilas*, by T. Le Marchant Douse (1886). The chief ancient sources for the life of Ulfilas are Philostorgius, *H. E.* ii. 5; Socr. ii. 41, iv. 33; Soz. vi. 37; Theod. iv. 37. [G.T.S.]

Urbanus (1), bp. of Rome under the emperor Alexander Severus, from 223 (or 222) to 230. The Liberian Catalogue gives 8 years 11 months and 11 days as the length of his episcopate. Nothing certain is known of his life. The *Acta S. Urbani* cannot be relied on.

The discovery by De Rossi in the papal crypt of the cemetery of St. Callistus of a broken stone (apparently once the *mensa* of an altar-tomb), bearing the imperfect inscription OVRBANOC E . . . has raised an interest in the question of his burial-place and alleged connexion with St. Caecilia. Lipsius inclines to the view that the Urban of the papal crypt was some other Urban, not necessarily a bishop, since the letter E after his name might have begun some other expression than ἐπίσκοπος, *e.g.* ἐν εἰρήνῃ. De Rossi, however, thinks that the slab in the papal crypt must have been that of the pope, who was actually buried there; and he attributes the contrary tradition to a confusion between him and the earlier Urban, whom he supposes to have been contemporary with St. Caecilia and buried in the cemetery of Praetextatus. [J.B—Y.]

Urbanus (6), bp. of Sicca Veneria, a town of proconsular Africa (Kaff) 22 miles from Musti (Ant. *Itin.* xli. 4; Shaw, *Trav.* p. 95; Aug. *Ep.* 229). Apparently a member of Augustine's monastic society at Hippo (Aug. *Ep.* 139. 34), he had occasion to remove from his office for grave misconduct a presbyter named Apiarius. Apiarius appealed to Zosimus, bp. of Rome, who ordered his restoration. In a council which met May 1, 418, the African bishops decreed that no priest, deacon, or inferior clerk should prosecute any appeal beyond sea. Zosimus then sent a commission to Africa, headed by Faustinus, bp. of Potenza, with instructions as to four points they were to impress on the African bishops: (1) That appeals from bishops of other churches should be made to Rome. (2) That bishops should not cross the sea unnecessarily (*importune*) to visit the seat of government (*comitatum*). (3) About settling through neighbouring bishops matters relating to priests and deacons excommunicated by their own bishops. Zosimus quotes a decree purporting to be one of the council of Nicaea, enjoining appeal to the bp. of Rome in case of bishops degraded by the bishops of their own province. (4) About excommunicating Urbanus, or at least summoning him to Rome unless he revoked his decision against Apiarius. This was in the latter part of 418. The African bishops were willing to accept provisionally the first and third propositions, until the canons of Nicaea, on which they were said to be founded, should be examined, for they were not aware of the existence among them of such rules. But at the end of 418 Zosimus was succeeded by Boniface, and no further action was taken until May 419, when 217 bishops met in council at Carthage (Hardouin, *Conc.* vol. i. p. 934; Bruns, *Conc.* i. 156, 157 D). Faustinus and his colleagues attended, and stated the conditions proposed by Zosimus. The bishops insisted on seeing them in writing, and the documents were accordingly then produced and read. On this Alypius, bp. of Tagaste, remarked that the decree referred to as one of Nicaea and quoted by Zosimus did not appear in the Greek copies with which the African bishops were acquainted. He proposed that reference should be made by themselves and by Boniface to the bishops of Constantinople, Alexandria, and Antioch, to obtain information as to its genuineness. Pending these consultations, the council determined that Apiarius should be allowed, under a circular letter, to exercise his office in any place except Sicca. No mention is made of any action taken in this matter by Boniface, who died A.D. 422, and was succeeded by Celestine I.; but in 426 the question was revived by further misconduct on the part of Apiarius at Tahraca, and, when removed from his office by the African bishops, he again appealed to Rome. At a council summoned for the purpose Faustinus appealed again and behaved with great insolence, demanding on the part of the Roman pontiff that Apiarius should be restored. The bishops refused. A strenuous dispute lasted 3 days, and was ended by Apiarius confessing his guilt. The assembled bishops took the opportunity of requesting the bp. of Rome to be less easy in receiving appeals, and not to admit to communion persons excommunicated by them; all appeals ought to be terminated in the province in which they begin, or in a general council. Rohrbacher says some good theologians thought the whole history of Apiarius a forgery (*Hist. de l'Eglise*, vol. iv. pp. 348-371). [H.W.P.]

Ursacius (1), bp. of Singidunum (Belgrade). He and Valens, bp. of Mursa, appear at every synod and council from 330 till *c.* 370, as leaders of the Arian party both in the East and West. They seem to have imbibed their Arian views from Arius himself during the period of his exile into Illyricum immediately after the council of Nicaea. They are described by Athanasius (*ad Episc. Aegypt.* 7, p. 218) as the disciples of Arius. This could scarcely have been at Alexandria, but they may easily have come in contact with him during his exile, which seems to have been very fruitful in spreading his views, as almost all the bishops of the Danubian provinces, together with Ulfilas and the Gothic converts, appear as Arians immediately afterwards (cf. Sulp. Sever. *Chron.* ii. 38). Ursacius must have been born, at latest, *c.* 300, as we find him a bishop, actively engaged in conspiracy against Athanasius, when Arius was recalled, *c.* 332. From Socrates we gather the leading events of his life. In *H. E.* i. 27 we find him united with Eusebius of Nicomedia, Theognis of Nicaea, Maris of Chalcedon, and Valens, in getting up a case against Athanasius and fabricating the scandalous charges of theft, sacrilege, and murder, investigated at the council of Tyre in 335, Ursacius and Valens being present there. They must have been very active and influential members of the party even at that early period, for they were sent to Egypt, as deputies of the synod, to investigate the charge on the spot, notwithstanding the protests of Athanasius (*l.c.* i. 31). In 342 they assisted at Constantinople at the consecration of Macedonius as patriarch. Upon the triumph of Athanasius in 346 they made their peace with Julius, bp. of Rome, accepted the Nicene formula, and wrote to Athanasius, professing their readiness to hold communion with him. At the synod of Sirmium in 359 they were again active members of the Homoean party, who drew up the Dated Creed, May 22, 359. They duly presented this creed to the council of Ariminum a few weeks later, which promptly rejected it, deposing Ursacius and Valens from their sees, "as well for their present conspiracy to introduce heresy, as for the confusion they had caused in all the churches by their repeated changes of faith." Ursacius and Valens at once sought the emperor's presence and gained him over to their side. The council also sent a long epistle to the emperor, which Socrates (ii. 37) inserts. The emperor refused to see the deputies of the council, and sent them to wait his leisure at Hadrianople first, and then at Nice in Thrace; where Ursacius and Valens induced these same deputies to sign, on Oct. 10, 359, a revised version of the creed, which the council had rejected. Socrates tells us that Nice in Thrace was chosen in order that it might impress the ignorant, who would confound it with Nicaea in Bithynia, where the orthodox symbol had been framed. Cf. Soz. *H. E.* iv. 19; Hieron. *adv. Lucif.* p. 189; Sulp. Sev. *Chron.* ii. 44; and Gwatkin's *Studies of Arianism*, pp. 157-178, for the history of this period. Ursacius and Valens seem to have remained influential with the court till the end of life, for the last notice of either of them in history tells how Valens obtained the recall of the Arian Eunomius from exile in 367 (Philostorg. *H. E.* ix. 8). The writings of Athanasius and Hilary frequently mention them. Gwatkin's *Studies* is very full of information, and Hefele's *Councils* (t. ii. Clark's trans. *s.nn.*) gives abundant references to the synods in which they took part; see also Tillem. *Mém.* vi. [G.T.S.]

Ursinus (2) (*Ursicinus*), antipope, elected after the death of Liberius in Sept. 366, in opposition to DAMASUS. For the conflicts during the life of Liberius between his adherents and those of Felix, who had been intruded into the see by the emperor Constantius, see LIBERIUS (4) and FELIX (2); Damasus being set up by the party of Felix, Ursinus by that of Liberius. Conflicting evidence exists as to the circumstances. St. Jerome (*Chron.*), Rufinus (ii. 10), and Socrates (iv. 24), agree that Damasus was elected first, and lay the blame on Ursinus, who after this election is said to have got hold with his followers of the church of Sicinus (or Sicininus), and to have been ordained. Sozomen (vi. 22) and Nicephorus (xi. 30) give similar accounts. A council at Rome twelve years afterwards, and an influential one at Aquileia, A.D. 381, in which St. Ambrose took a prominent part, both declared Ursinus to be a usurper, and addressed letters to the emperors Gratian and Valentinian against him (*Epist. Concil. Roman.* ad *Grat. et Valentin.*, Labbe, t. ii. p. 1187; *Ep. I. Conc. Aquil.* ad *Grat. Imp. ib.* p. 1183). St. Ambrose (*Ep.* 11) speaks of Damasus having been elected by the judgment of God. The emperors also, and the civil authorities at Rome, throughout the contest supported Damasus as the lawful pope.

But a different account is given by Marcellinus and Faustinus, two Luciferian priests, who, being expelled from Rome under Damasus, presented a petition (*Libellus Precum*) to the emperors Valentinian, Theodosius, and Arcadius (*c.* 383). They had been supporters of Ursinus, and in the preface to their petition assert that he was elected before Damasus by the people who had been in communion with Liberius in the church of Julius beyond the Tiber, and was ordained by Paul, bp. of Tivoli; and that Damasus had subsequently, with a mob of charioteers and other low fellows, broken into the church of Julius, massacred many persons there, and after seven days had, with his bribed followers, got possession of the Lateran Basilica, and been there ordained. The balance of evidence appears decidedly in favour of Damasus, the only witnesses against him, the two Luciferian presbyters, being partisans whose veracity we have no means of testing. After the two elections all accounts agree that the rival parties disturbed Rome by continual conflicts, in which lives were lost. At length Juventius, the praefectus urbi, and Julianus, the praefectus annonae, concurred in banishing Ursinus, but the disturbances continued. Ammianus Marcellinus, the historian, throws light on the Roman church at this time from the point of view of an intelligent and impartial heathen. "The ardour of Damasus and Ursinus to seize the episcopal seat surpassed the ordinary measure of human ambition. They contended with the rage of party; the quarrel was maintained by the wounds and death of their followers, the prefect . . . being constrained by superior violence to retire into the suburbs. Damasus prevailed: . . . 137 dead bodies were found in the basilica of Sicininus, where the Christians hold their religious assemblies; and it was long before the angry minds of the people resumed their accustomed tranquillity. When I consider the splendour of the capital, I am not astonished that so valuable a prize should inflame the desires of ambitious men and produce the fiercest contests. The successful candidate is secure that he will be enriched by the offerings of matrons; that as soon as his dress is composed with becoming care and elegance, he may proceed in his chariot through the streets of Rome; and that the sumptuousness of the imperial table will not equal the profuse and delicate entertainment provided by the taste and at the expense of the Roman pontiffs. How much more rationally would those pontiffs consult their true happiness if, instead of alleging the greatness of the city as an excuse for their manners, they would imitate the exemplary life of some provincial bishops, whose temperance and sobriety, mean apparel and downcast looks, recommended their pure and modest virtue to the Deity and His true worshippers!" (Ammian. 27, 3, Gibbon's trans. c. xxv.).

In 367 the emperor Valentinian permitted those who had been banished to return, but threatened severe punishment in case of renewed disturbance. (Baronius, *ad ann.* 368, ii., iii. iv., gives extracts from these rescripts.) Ursinus returned, and is said to have been received by his followers on Sept. 15, 367, with great joy (*Lib. Precum*), but was again banished by order of the emperor (Nov. 16), with seven of his adherents, into Gaul. Yet peace was not at once restored. His followers continued to assemble in cemeteries, and got possession of the church of St. Agnes without the walls. Thence they were dislodged; Marcellinus and Faustinus say by Damasus himself with his satellites, and with great slaughter. We may doubt the pope's personal complicity. After this the prefect Praetextatus banished more of the party, and the two presbyters allege cruel persecution, having been themselves among the sufferers. Rescripts of the emperors Valentinian, Valens, and Gratian (A.D. 371) again release Ursinus and his friends from their confinement in Gaul, allowing them to live at large, but away from Rome and the suburbicarian regions (Baron. *ad ann.* 371, i. ii. iii.). A Roman council (A.D. 378) addressed a letter to the emperors Gratian and Valentinian II., representing that Ursinus and his followers continued their machinations secretly (Labbe, t. ii. pp. 1187-1192).

After this we find Ursinus at Milan, where he is said to have joined the Arian party, who promised him their support (Ambrose, *Ep.* 4). But St. Ambrose, bp. of Milan, having informed the emperor Gratian of what was going on, the latter banished Ursinus from Italy, and confined him to Cologne (*Ep. I. Conc. Aquil. u.s.*). No more is heard of Ursinus till after the death of Damasus (Dec. 384), when he opposed Siricius, who, having been a supporter of Damasus against him, was elected with the general consent of the Roman people. Ursinus appears not to have then had sufficient support in Rome to cause conflict and disturbance. [J.B—Y.]

Ursula, a famous British virgin and martyr, celebrated as having suffered with 11,000 other virgins at Cologne. Her notice in the Roman Martyrology is simple: "At Cologne, the natal day of SS. Ursula and her companions, who, being slain by the Huns for their Christianity and their virginal constancy, terminated their life by martyrdom. Very many of their bodies were discovered at Cologne." On this foundation the new Bollandists have raised a prodigious edifice of 230 folio pages, where they discuss (*AA. SS.* Boll. Oct. t. ix. pp. 73-303) every conceivable fact, topic, or hypothesis concerning these problematical martyrs. Their story, which is purely medieval, is briefly this. Ursula, the daughter of Dionoc, king of Cornwall, was sent by him with her numerous companions to Conan, a British prince, who had followed the tyrant Maximus into Gaul, *c.* 383. They were somehow carried up the Rhine to Cologne by mistake, where the Huns murdered them all. The enormous number of her companions has been explained as a mistake of the early copyists, who found some such entry as "Ursula et xi. M. V.", which, taking M. for millia, not for martyrs, they read Ursula and 11,000 virgins instead of 11 martyr virgins. Such mistakes frequently occurred in the ancient martyrologies. [MAXIMUS (2).] [G.T.S.]

V

Valens (4), Arian bp. of Mursa in Pannonia, and together with URSACIUS the leading Western opponent of Athanasius. He must have been born *c.* 300, as we find him a most influential bishop from A.D. 332 (cf. Socr. *H. E.* i. 27). The activity and influence of Valens was confined to the East. The West was always hostile to him, and frequently excommunicated him, the last occasion being at a council held at Rome in 369. He probably died some time prior to 375. [G.T.S.]

Valens (5), emperor, A.D. 364-378, the brother of Valentinian I. and born *c.* 328. By his wife, Albia Dominica, he had a son, Galates, and two daughters, Anastasia and Carosa. Made emperor of the East in Mar. 364, he immediately displayed sympathy with Arian doctrines, and was actively hostile to the Athanasian party. For his secular history see *D. of G. and R. Biogr.* He was baptized in 368 by the Arian Eudoxius, patriarch of Constantinople. In 370 he is credited by all the historians (Socr. iv. 16; Soz. vi. 14; Theod. iv. 24) with an act of atrocious cruelty. Eighty ecclesiastics, led by Urbanus, Theodorus, and Mendemus, were sent by the orthodox party of Constantinople to protest against the conduct of the Arians there. Valens is said to have sent them all to sea, ordering the sailors to set fire to the ship and then to abandon it. They all perished off the coast of Bithynia, and are celebrated as martyrs on Sept. 5 (*Mart. Rom.*). In 371 he made a tour through his Asiatic province. At Caesarea in Cappadocia he came into conflict with St. Basil, whose letters (Migne, *Patr. Gk.* t. xxxii.) afford a very lively picture of the persecution of Valens. He proposed to send St. Basil into exile. Just then his only son fell sick. Valens had recourse to the saint, who promised to heal him if he received orthodox baptism. The Arians were, however, allowed to baptize the young prince, who thereupon died. Basil and the orthodox attributed his death to the judgment of heaven on the imperial obstinacy. In 374 Valens raised a persecution against the neo-Platonic philosophers, and put to death several of their leaders, among them MAXIMUS (25) of Ephesus, the tutor and friend of the emperor Julian, Hilarius, Simonides, and Andronicus. His anger was excited at this period against magical practices by a conspiracy at Antioch (Socr. *H. E.* iv. 19; Soz. vi. 35) for securing the succession of Theodorus, one of the principal court officials. Numerous acts of persecution at Edessa, Antioch, Alexandria, and Constantinople are attributed to Valens, in all of which MODESTUS, the pretorian prefect, was his most active agent, save in Egypt, where Lucius, the Arian successor of Athanasius, endeavoured in vain to terrify the monks into conformity. The last year of Valens's life was marked by a striking manifestation of monkish courage. In 378 he was leaving Constantinople for his fatal struggle with the Goths at Adrianople. As he rode out of the city an anchorite, Isaac, who lived there, met the emperor and boldly predicted his death. The emperor ordered his imprisonment till his return, when he would punish him—a threat at which the monk laughed. See Clinton's *Fasti*, i. 476, ii. 119, for the chronology of Valens. Tillemont's *Emp.* (t. v.) and De Broglie's *L'Eglise et l'Empire Romain* (t. v.) give good accounts of the career and violence of Valens. [G.T.S.]

Valentinianus (1) **I.**, emperor A.D. 364-375, a native of Cibalis in Pannonia. Having served in the army with distinction, he was captain of the guards during the reign of Julian, when he boldly confessed Christ. Theodoret tells us (*H. E.* iii. 16) that when Julian was one day entering the temple of Fortune with great pomp, Valentinian was marching in the procession before him. Two priests were at the gate to sprinkle all who entered with lustral water. Some fell upon Valentinian's robe, whereupon, crying out that he was defiled, not purified, he struck the priest and banished him to a desert fortress. When Jovian died, Valentinian was elected, Feb. 26, 364, and reigned till his death, Nov. 17, 375. For an account of his civil history see *D. of G. and R. Biogr.* He presents the rare phenomenon of an emperor who, sincerely attached to orthodoxy, was yet tolerant of the Arians and other heretical sects. He published an edict at the very beginning of his reign, giving complete toleration in religious opinion. To this fact we have the most opposite testimonies. The emperor refers to it in *Cod. Theod.* ix. 16. 9, in a law directed against the practices of the haruspices. Ammianus Marcellinus (xxx. 9) praises him for it, and St. Ambrose, in his oration *de Obitu Valent. Junioris*, implicitly censures him (cf. Hilar. Pictav. *Cont. Auxent. Opp.* t. iii. p. 64). His toleration did not, however, extend to practices. Thus in Sept. 364 he issued a law (*Cod. Theod.* ix. 16. 7) prohibiting nocturnal sacrifices and magical incantations, and further enforced it by legg. viii. and ix. of the same title. These edicts seem to have been issued more from a moral and social than religious point of view. They were directed against immorality, not paganism, as is evident from the fact, which Ambrose (*l.c.*) laments, that he tolerated the public profession and practices of paganism in the Roman senate-house. One circumstance demonstrates his tolerance towards the followers of the ancient religion. There is not a single edict in the Theodosian code, lib. xvi. tit. x.—the celebrated title *de Paganis*, which is filled with persecuting laws—dating from any year between 356 and 381; while the same remark will also apply with one exception to the titles *de Haeretici* and *de Judaeis*, lib. xvi. tit. v. and viii. The one exception is the Manichean heresy, which he strictly prohibited by a law of 372 (*Cod. Theod.* xvi. v. 3), ordering the punishment of their teachers and the confiscation of the houses where they instructed their pupils in Rome; for Manicheism seems at that time to have assumed the character of a philosophy rather than of a religion. That this tolerant spirit of the emperor was helpful to true religion appears from the fact that, under Valentinian heathenism began first to be called the peasant's religion ("religio paganorum"), a name first so applied in a law of 368 (*ib.* xvi. ii. 18). Valentinian legislated also for the clergy (*ib.* xv. ii. 17-22), restraining the tendency of rich men to take holy orders to escape civil duties (legg. 17, 18, 19); and rendering illegal the bequests to clergy and monks from widows and virgins by a celebrated law (leg. 20) addressed in 370 to Damasus, bp. of Rome, under the description "De Vita,

Honestate, Conversatione Ecclesiasticorum et Continentium," which was the model for much subsequent legislation. (Cf. the commentary of Godefroy, *Theod. Cod.* t. vi. p. 54, where all contemporary notices of this law are collected.) The legislative activity of Valentinian in every direction was very great, as shewn by the Theodosian Code.

Other modern authorities are Clinton's *Fasti*, i. 460, and appendix, pp. 110-119, where is an exhaustive statement of all his legislation, together with notices of medals, coins, etc., bearing on his reign, and De Broglie's *L'Eglise et l'Empire Romain*, pt. iii. c. i. [G.T.S.]

Valentinianus (2) II., emperor, A.D. 375-392, son of Valentinian I. and of Justina, his second wife. For his secular life see *D. of G. and R. Biogr.* His name is celebrated in church history in connexion with two matters: (1) An attempt in 384 by the Roman Senate to restore the altar of Victory and the pagan rites connected with the Senate. We possess the document *Relatio Symmachi Urbis Praefecti* on the one side and the Epp. xvii. and xviii. of St. Ambrose to Valentinian on the other (cf. St. Ambr. opp. Migne, *Patr. Lat.* t. xvi. col. 962-982). St. Ambrose carried the day, and the senatorial petition was rejected, as again in 391 (see Tillem. *Emp.* v. 244, 300, 349). (2) The other matter concerned the necessity of baptism. Valentinian died at Vienne in Gaul, being then about 20, and only a catechumen. Being anxious to receive baptism, he sent for St. Ambrose to baptize him. Before the sacrament could be administered, he was found dead. St. Ambrose's treatise, *de Obitu Valentiniani Consolatio*, §§ 51-56, shews how Ambrose rose superior to any hard mechanical view of the sacraments and recognized the sincere will and desire as equivalent to the deed (cf. Tillem. *Emp.* v. 356; De Broglie, *L'Eglise et l'Empire*, pt. iii. cc. v. and viii.). At one time Valentinian was inclined to support the Arian party at Milan, influenced by his mother Justina, who was bitterly hostile to St. Ambrose. Sozomen (*H. E.* vii. 13), followed by Ceillier (v. 386), represents Valentinian and the empress as persecuting St. Ambrose and the Catholics of Milan in 386, referring to *Cod. Theod.* lib. xvi. tit. i. leg. 4. [AMBROSIUS; JUSTINA.] [G.T.S.]

Valentinianus (3) III., emperor, 425-455, the son of Constantius III. by Galla Placidia, daughter of Theodosius the Great and consequently great-grandson of Valentinian I. For his civil history see *D. of G. and R. Biogr.* His reign was signalized by several laws bearing on church matters. At its very beginning (July 17, 425) there was issued at Aquileia in his name a decree (*Cod. Theod.* lib. xvi. tit. v. l. 62), expelling all heretics and schismatics from Rome. A special provision ordered the adherents of Eulalius, elected anti-pope in 419, to be removed to the 100th milestone from the city. This law has been illustrated at great length by Gothofred, t. vi. 204. Identical laws (tit. v. ll. 63, 64) were issued for the other cities of Italy and for Africa in 425, and also edicts (lib. xvi. tit. ii. ll. 46 and 47) renewing clerical privileges and reserving clerical offenders to the tribunal of the bishops alone, a rule which he abrogated later. In tit. vii. of the same bk. is a law against apostates dated Ravenna Apr. 7, 426, depriving them of all testamentary power. On the next day a law was enacted (tit. viii. l. 28) preventing Jews from disinheriting their children who became Christians. The most interesting portion of his ecclesiastical legislation is in his Novels embodied in Ritter's appendix to Gothofred's great work (Lip. 1743, t. vi. pt. ii. pp. 105-133). Thus tit. ii. p. 106, A.D. 445, treats of the Manicheans and gives particulars as to the action of pope Leo the Great against them; tit. v. p. 111, A.D. 447, of the violations of sepulchres, with severe penalties against such crimes, of which the clergy themselves were frequently guilty. Tit. xii. p. 127, A.D. 452, his most celebrated law, is an anticipation of medieval legislation; it withdraws the clergy from the episcopal courts and subjects them to lay judges. Baronius (*Annals*, A.D. 451) heartily abuses Valentinian for this law, and considers Attila's invasion a direct and immediate expression of Heaven's anger. [G.T.S.]

Valentinus (1) (Οὐαλεντῖνος), founder of one of the Gnostic sects which originated in the first half of 2nd cent.

I. *Biography.*—According to the tradition of the Valentinian school witnessed to by Clemens Alexandrinus (*Strom.* vii. 17, 106, p. 898, Potter), Valentinus had been a disciple of Theodas, who himself, it is very improbably said, knew St. Paul. Valentinus cannot have begun to disseminate his Gnostic doctrines till towards the end of the reign of Hadrian (117-138). Before this he is said to have been a Catholic Christian. It must have been, therefore, at most only shortly before his appearance as the head of a Gnostic sect that Valentinus became a hearer of Theodas and received, as he said, his doctrines from him. The Gnostics were fond of claiming for their secret doctrines apostolic tradition and tracing them back to disciples of the apostles. To this otherwise unknown Theodas the Valentinians appealed as an authority in much the same way as Basilides was said to have been a disciple of Glaucias, and he, in turn, an "interpreter of Peter."

Irenaeus (i. 11, 1) speaks of Valentinus as the first who transformed the doctrines of the Gnostic "Heresy" to a peculiar doctrinal system of his own (εἰς ἴδιον χαρακτῆρα διδασκαλείου). By the expression γνωστικὴ αἵρεσις we understand a party which called themselves "Gnostics," whom we may recognize in the so-called Ophites, described by Irenaeus (i. 30), when he remarks that the Valentinian school originated from those unnamed heretics as from the many-headed Lernean Hydra (i. 30, 15). Concerning the home and locality of these so-called "Gnostics" Irenaeus tells us nothing. But we know from other sources that those Ophite parties to whom he refers had their homes both in Egypt and Syria.

Concerning the fatherland of Valentinus himself Epiphanius is the first to give accurate information, which, however, he derived simply, it appears, from oral tradition (Epiph. *Haer.* xxxi. 2). According to this his native home was on the coast of Egypt, and he received instruction in Greek literature and science at Alexandria. Epiphanius, who makes him begin to teach in Egypt, relates further that he also went to Rome, and appeared as a religious teacher there, but that, both in Egypt and at Rome, he was regarded as orthodox, and first made shipwreck of faith in Cyprus and began to disseminate heretical opinions. But this statement rests merely on a combination of different accounts. According to Irenaeus, Valentinus "flourished" at Rome in the times of Pius and Anicetus. Epiphanius, on the other hand, read (as we learn from Philaster, *Haer.* 38) in the σύνταγμα of Hippolytus, that Valentinus stood once in the communion of the church, but being drawn by overweening pride into apostasy had, during his residence in Cyprus, propounded his heretical doctrine. But we cannot doubt that when Irenaeus speaks of Valentinus's flourishing at Rome during the times of Pius and Anicetus, he refers to the fact that his chief activity as a religious teacher was then displayed, and that under Anicetus he stood at the head of his own Gnostic school. With this there is no difficulty in reconciling Tertullian's statement, that Valentinus no more than Marcion separated himself from the Church on his arrival at Rome (*Praescript. Haeret.* 36). For the Gnostics, for the very sake of disseminating their doctrines the more freely, made a great point of remaining in the Catholic church, and made use for that end of a twofold mode of teaching, one exoteric for the simpler sort of believers, the other esoteric for the initiated, as is shewn in the fragments which have come down to us, the most part of which purposely keep the peculiarly Gnostic doctrines in the background.

We may, then, conclude that Valentinus, towards the end of Hadrian's reign (*c.* 130), appeared as a teacher in Egypt and in Cyprus, and early in the reign of Antoninus Pius he came to Rome, and during the long reign of Antoninus was a teacher there. He had probably developed and secretly prepared his theological system before he came to Rome, whither he doubtless removed for the same motive as led other leaders of sects, *e.g.* Cerdon and Marcion, to go to Rome—the hope to find a wider field for his activity as a teacher. From a similar motive he attached himself at first to the communion of the Catholic church.

II. *History of the Sect.*—Valentinus had numerous adherents. They divided themselves, we are told, into two schools—the anatolic or oriental, and the Italian school (Pseud-Orig. *Philosoph.* vi. 35, p. 195, Miller, cf. Tertullian, *adv. Valentinian.* c. 11, and the title prefixed to the excerpts of Clemens Ἐκ τοῦ Θεοδότου καὶ τῆς Ἀνατολικῆς καλουμένης διδασκαλίας). The former of these schools was spread through Egypt and Syria, the latter in Rome, Italy, and S. Gaul. Among his disciples, Secundus appears to have been one of the earliest. Tertullian (*adv. Valentinian.* 4) and the epitomators of Hippolytus mention him after Ptolemaeus (Pseudo-Tertull. *Haer.* 13; Philast. *Haer.* 40); the older work, on the other hand, excerpted by Irenaeus is apparently correct in naming him first as Valentinus's earliest disciple (*Haer.* i. 11, 2). Then follows, in the same original work as quoted by Irenaeus (*Haer.* i. 11, 3), another illustrious teacher (ἄλλος ἐπιφανὴς διδάσκαλος), of whom a misunderstanding of later heresiologists has made a Valentinian leader, named Epiphanes; who this illustrious teacher was is matter of dispute. The more probable conjecture is with Neander (*Gnostische Systeme*, p. 169) and Salmon to suppose it was MARCUS (17), whose first Tetrad exactly corresponds to that of this unnamed teacher (cf. *Haer.* i. 15, 1, καθ' ἃ προείρηται). Marcus himself will, in any case, be among the earliest of Valentinus's disciples (Lipsius, *Quellen der ältesten Ketzergesch.* p. 33). His labours in Asia were probably contemporaneous with Valentinus's residence and activity at Rome, and there a "godly elder and herald of the truth," whom Irenaeus quotes from as an older authority, made him the subject of metrical objurgation as the "forerunner of anti-Christian malice" (Iren. *Haer.* i. 15, 6).

PTOLEMAEUS, on the other hand, was a contemporary of Irenaeus himself, and one of the leaders of the Italian school (Iren. *Haer. Praef.* 2, Pseud-Orig. *Philos.* vi. 35), whom Hippolytus in the *Syntagina*, and probably on the basis of an arbitrary combination of Iren. i. 8, 5 with 11, 2, puts at the head of all other disciples of Valentinus. HERACLEON was still younger than Ptolemaeus, and the second head of the Italian school. His doctrinal system appears to be that mainly kept in view in the *Philosophumena* (cf. vi. 29, 35). Irenaeus names him as it were in passing (*Haer.* ii. 4, 1), while Tertullian designates his relation to his predecessors with the words, Valentinus shewed the way, Ptolemaeus walked along it, Heracleon struck out some side paths (*adv. Valentinian.* 4). He makes also the like remark concerning Secundus and Marcus. Clemens speaks of Heracleon (*c.* 193) as the most distinguished among the disciples of Valentinus (*Strom.* iv. 9, 73, p. 595), meaning, of course, among those of his own time. Origen's statement, therefore, that he had a personal acquaintance with Valentinus (Origen, *in Joann.* t. ii. 8) is to be received with caution. In part contemporaneously with him appear to have worked the heads of the anatolic (oriental) school Axionikos and Bardesanes (Ἀρδησιάνης, *Philos.* vi. 35), who both lived into the first decennia of cent. iii.

Axionikos was still working at Antioch when Tertullian composed his book against the Valentinians, therefore *c.* 218 (Tertull. *l.c.*). We cannot here discuss how far the celebrated Edessene Gnostic BARDESANES (*ob.* 223) is rightly accounted a Valentinian. Tertullian indicates Axionikos as the only one who in his day still represented the original teaching of Valentinus. Theotimus, therefore, who is previously mentioned by Tertullian, and seems to have occupied himself much with the "Figures of the Law," was, it appears, an older teacher. The same was also probably the case with Alexander, the Valentinian whose syllogisms Tertullian had in his hands (*de Carne Christi* cc. 16 sqq.).

Concerning the later history of the Valentinian sect we have but meagre information. Tertullian, writing *c.* 218, speaks of the Valentinians in his book against them as the "frequentissimum collegium inter haereticos." This is confirmed by what is told us of the local extension of the sect. From Egypt it seems to have spread to Syria, Asia Minor, and to Rome. Its division into an oriental and an Italian school shews that it had adherents even after the death of its founder, in both the East (Egypt, Syria, Mesopotamia) and West (specially at Rome). In Asia Minor the doctrine appears to have been mainly disseminated by Marcus, who was so vigorously attacked (*c.* 150) by the "godly elder," quoted by Irenaeus (*Haer.* i. 15, 6). Disciples of Marcus were found by Irenaeus in the Rhone districts (*Haer.* i. 13, 7), where also he appears to have met with adherents of Ptolemaeus (*Haer. Praef.* 2). In Rome, *c.* 223, an important work of the Italian school came into the hands of the writer of the *Philosophumena*, who speaks of both schools as being in existence in his time (*Philos.* vi. 35, p. 195). Tertullian also mentions the *duae scholae* and *duae cathedrae* of the party in his time (*adv. Valent.* 11). Remains of the sect were still found in Egypt in the time of Epiphanius (*Haer.* xxxi. 7). Theodoret, on the other hand (*H. f. Praef.*), can only speak of the Valentinians as of other Gnostic sects (whom he deals with in his first book) as belonging to the past—παλαιὰς αἱρέσεις—of whom he possesses a mere historical knowledge.

III. *Writings.*—The fragments of the writings of Valentinus have been collected by Grabe (*Spicilegium*, ii. 45-48), and more completely by Hilgenfeld (*Ketzergeschichte*, pp. 93-207). They consist of fragments of letters and homilies preserved by Clemens Alexandrinus (*Strom.* ii. 8, 36, p. 448; ii. 20, 114, pp. 488 seq.; iii. 7, 59, p. 538; iv. 13, 91, p. 603; vi. 6, 52, p. 767), and of two pieces contained in the *Philosophumena*, the narrative of a vision (ὅραμα) seen by Valentinus (*Philos.* vi. 42, p. 203), and the fragment of a psalm composed by him (*Philos.* vi. 37, pp. 197 seq.). Psalms of Valentinus's authorship are mentioned by Tertullian (*de Carne Christi*, 17, 20).

Remains of the writings of the school of Valentinus are more abundant. Beside the numerous fragments and quotations in Irenaeus and the *Philosophumena*, and in the excerpts from Theodotus, and the anatolic school, which seem yet to need a closer investigation, we may mention: the letter of Ptolemaeus to Flora (*ap.* Epiphan. *Haer.* xxxiii. 3-7), numerous fragments from the commentaries (ὑπομνήματα) of Heracleon on St. Luke (*ap.* Clem. Alex. *Strom.* iv. 9, 73 seq., pp. 595 seq.; excerpt. ex prophet. § 25, p. 995), and on St. John (ap. Origen *in Joann.* passim), collected by Grabe (*Spicil.* i. 80-117) and Hilgenfeld (*Ketzergeschichte*, 472-498); lastly, a rather large piece out of an otherwise unknown Valentinian writing preserved by Epiphanius (*Haer.* xxxi. 5 and 6).

IV. *Accounts given by the Fathers.*—Statements concerning Valentinus and his school are very numerous, but many are so contradictory that it is difficult to distinguish the original doctrine of Valentinus from later developments. Even in his day Tertullian made the complaint (*adv. Valentinian.* 4), "Ita nunquam jam Valentinus, et tamen Valentiniani, qui per Valentinum." Among those who before him had controverted the Valentinians, Tertullian enumerates (*ib.* 5): Justin Martyr, Miltiades, Irenaeus, and the Montanist Proculus. Of the writings of these four on this subject one only has been preserved, the great work of Irenaeus in five books, entitled Ἔλεγχος καὶ ἀνατροπὴ τῆς ψευδωνύμου γνώσεως, which has come down to us in great part only in the ancient Latin version. This work was written (see iii. 3, 3) in the time of the Roman bp. Eleutherus, *c.* 180-185. The greater part of bk. i., which Epiphanius has preserved to us almost completely, deals exclusively with the Valentinians, and the refutations in the following books are principally concerned with them.

The sources which Irenaeus used are of sufficient variety. In the preface to bk. i. (c. 2) he refers to the writings of those who call themselves disciples of Valentinus, adding that he had met some of them himself and heard their opinions from their own mouths. Immediately afterwards he indicates that the contemporary Valentinians, whose doctrine he promises to describe, are those of the school of Ptolemaeus. In bk. i. (c. 8, 5) he introduces into a detailed description of the Valentinian method of interpreting Scripture a large fragment which undertakes to prove the truth of the higher Ogdoad of the Valentinian Pleroma from the prologue of the Gospel of St. John. The concluding notice (found only in the Latin text) expressly ascribes the authorship of this fragment to Ptolemaeus. Irenaeus likewise obtained his information as to the doctrine and practices of the Marcosians partly from a written source, partly from oral communications. We can hardly assume that Marcus was still alive when Irenaeus wrote, but it is not unlikely that adherents of Marcus may have appeared then in the Rhone districts. The section which specially treats of Marcus (i. 12-15) is apparently from a written source; but what he brings to light for the first time (cc. 16-18) concerning the mysteries celebrated by the Marcosians is from oral information.

Next in importance to the statements of Irenaeus, as a source of information concerning Valentinus and his school, are the fragments preserved among the works of Clemens Alexandrinus, and entitled Ἐκ τῶν Θεοδότου καὶ τῆς ἀνατολικῆς καλουμένης διδασκαλίας ἐπιτομαί. The text has come down to us in a somewhat forlorn condition. The best ed. is Bunsen's, in *Analecta Antinicaena*, vol. i. (Lond. 1854), pp. 205-278. The general character of these excerpts is similar to others in other writings of Clemens Alexandrinus, and does not justify the assumption that their present abrupt fragmentary form proceeded from Clemens himself.

Very little is obtainable from the *Syntagma* of Hippolytus, preserved in the excerpts of Pseudo-Tertullian (*Haer.* 12) and by Philaster (*Haer* 38), as also partly by Epiphanius (*Haer.* xxxi. 8; cf. *Quellen d. ält. Ketzergesch.* p. 166). Hippolytus combined Irenaeus (cc. 1-7) with some authority belonging to the older anatolic system.

Pseud-Origines, now almost universally assumed to be HIPPOLYTUS, gives us in the *Philosophumena* (the larger Ἔλεγχος κατὰ πασῶν αἱρέσεων) a quite peculiar account of the Valentinian system, one more uniform and synoptical than that of Irenaeus. The original authority on which this description is based cannot have been the same as that in the *Syntagma* which belonged to the anatolic school, the former being a product of the Western or Italian. The doctrinal system reproduced by Pseud-Origines is in general akin to the Ptolemaic presented by Irenaeus. But his original authority is entirely independent of the sources used by Irenaeus.

Tertullian's tractate *adversus Valentinianos* is not an independent authority. Apart from a few personal notices concerning him and his disciples which he may have taken from the lost work of Proculus (c. 4, cf. c. 11), his whole account is a paraphrase of Irenaeus, whom he follows almost word for word, and more or less faithfully from c. 7 onwards.

Epiphanius (*Haer.* xxxi. 9-32) has incorporated the whole long section of Irenaeus (i. 1-10) in his *Panarion. Haer.* xxxii. and xxxiv. (Secundus, Marcus) are simply taken from Irenaeus. He follows Irenaeus also in his somewhat arbitrary way in what he says about Ptolemaeus, Colarbasus, Heracleon (*Haer.* xxxiii. xxxv. xxxvi.). On the other hand, *Haer.* xxxi. 7, 8, is taken from the *Syntagma* of Hippolytus; *Haer.* xxxiii. 3-7 contains the important letter of PTOLEMAEUS to Flora. *Haer.* xxxi. 5 and 6 gives a fragment of an unknown Valentinian writing, from which the statements in c. 2 are partly derived. This writing, with its barbarous names for the Aeons and its mixture of Valentinian and Basilidian doctrines, shows anatolic Valentinianism as already degenerate.

Later heresiologists, *e.g.* Theodoret, who (*Haer. Fab.* i. 7-9) follows Irenaeus and Epiphanius, are not independent authorities.

V. *The System.*—A review of the accounts given by the Fathers confirms the judgment that, with the means at our command, it is very difficult to distinguish between the original doctrine of Valentinus and the later developments made by his disciples. A description of his system must start from the *Fragments*, the authenticity of which (apart from the so-called ὅρος Οὐαλεντίνου in *Dial. de Recta Fide*) is unquestioned. But from the nature of these fragments we cannot expect to reconstruct the whole system out of them. From an abundant literature a few relics only have been preserved. Moreover, the kinds of literature to which these fragments belong —letters, homilies, hymns—shew us only the outer side of the system, while its secret Gnostic doctrine is passed over and concealed, or only indicated in the obscurest manner. The modes of expression in these fragments are brought as near as possible to those in ordinary church use. We see therein the evident desire and effort of Valentinus to remain in the fellowship of the Catholic church. Of specific Gnostic doctrines two only appear in their genuine undisguised shape, that of the celestial origin of the spiritual man (the Pneumaticos), and that of the Demiurge; for the docetic Christology was not then, as is clear from Clemens Alexandrinus, exclusively peculiar to the Gnostics. All the more emphatically is the anthropological and ethical side of the system insisted on in these fragments.

As the world is an image of the living Aeon (τοῦ ζῶντος αἰῶνος), so is man an image of the pre-existent man of the ἄνθρωπος προών. Valentinus, according to Clemens Alexandrinus (*Valentini Homil.* ap. *Clem. Strom.* iv. 13, 92), spoke of the Sophia as an artist (ζωγράφος) making this visible lower world a picture of the glorious Archetype, but the hearer or reader would as readily understand the heavenly Wisdom of the Book of Proverbs to be meant by this Sophia as the 12th and fallen Aeon. Under her (according to Valentinus) stand the world-creative angels, whose head is the Demiurge. Her formation (πλάσμα) is Adam created in the name of the Ἄνθρωπος προών. In him thus made a higher power puts the seed of the heavenly pneumatic essence (σπέρμα τῆς ἄνωθεν οὐσίας). Thus furnished with higher insight, Adam excites the fears of the angels; for even as κοσμικοὶ ἄνθρωποι are seized with fear of the images made by their own hands to bear the name of God, *i.e.* the idols, so these angels cause the images they have made to disappear (*Ep. ad Amicos* ap. *Clem. Alex. Strom.* ii. 8, 36). The pneumatic seed (πνεῦμα διαφέρον or γένος διαφέρον) nevertheless remains in the world, as a race by nature capable of being saved (φύσει σωζόμενον γένος), and which has come down from a higher sphere in order to put an end to the reign of death. Death originates from the Demiurge, to whom the word (Ex. xxxiii. 20) refers that no one can see the face of God without dying. The members of the pneumatic church are from the first immortal, and children of eternal life. They have only assumed mortality in order to overcome death in themselves and by themselves. They shall dissolve the world without themselves suffering dissolution, and be lords over the creation and over all transitory things (*Valent. Hom.* ap. *Clem. Strom.* iv. 13, 91 seq.). But without the help of the only good Father the heart even of the spiritual man (the pneumaticos) cannot be cleansed from the many evil spirits which make their abode in him, and each accomplishes his own desire. But when the only good Father visits the soul, it is hallowed and enlightened, and is called blessed because one day it shall see God. This cleansing and illumination is a consequence of the revelation of the Son (*ib.* ii. 20, 114).

We learn from the fragments only (*Valent. Ep. ad Agathopoda* ap. *Clem. Strom.* iv. 7, 59) that Jesus, by steadfastness and abstinence, earned for Himself Deity, and by virtue of His abstinence did not even suffer to be corrupted the food which He received (*i.e.* it did not undergo the natural process of digestion), because He Himself was not subject to corruption. It must remain undetermined how Valentinus defined the relation of Jesus to the υἱός. If the text of the passage quoted above be sound, Jesus put Himself in possession of Godhead by His own abstinence, a notion we should expect in Ebionite rather than in Gnostic circles. But the true reading may be εἰκάζετο (not εἰργάζετο), and in that case the meaning will be that by an extraordinary asceticism Jesus avoided every kind of material pollution, and so became Himself the image of the incorruptible and imperishable Godhead. At any rate, this fragment does not tell us whether, according to the teaching of Valentinus, the body of Jesus was pneumatic or psychical. According to another fragment attributed to Valentinus, and preserved by Eulogius of Alexandria (ap. Photium, *Bibl. Cod.* 230), he appears to have treated with ridicule the opinion of the "Galileans" that Christ had two natures, and to have maintained that He had but one nature composed of the visible and the invisible. Hilgenfeld (*l.c.* pp. 302 seq.) supposes the Valentinus of this fragment to be the Gnostic, while others take him to have been the Apollinarian. But we have no other instance of any Gnostic giving to Catholic Christians (as did the emperor Julian later) the epithet "Galilean." Further, although Tertullian (*adv. Prax.* 29) and Origen (*de Princip.* i. 2, 1) may have spoken of two natures or two substances in Christ, we can hardly imagine Valentinus pronouncing a doctrine ridiculous, and yet it finding acceptance in his school. For we find the Occidental Valentinians actually teaching in very similar terms, that Soter, the common product of the whole Pleroma, united himself with the Christus of the Demiurge the Man Jesus. Could we otherwise assume that the fragment is genuine, it would serve to prove that the doctrine of the Oriental school concerning the pneumatic body of Christ was in fact the original teaching of Valentinus. How Valentinus thought concerning the origin of matter and of evil cannot be made out from existing fragments. When, however, we find him designating the Demiurge as author of death, we can hardly suppose that he derived the transitory nature and other imperfections of the terrestrial universe from an originally evil material substance. The view, moreover, which underlies the psalm of Valentinus, of which the *Philosophumena* have preserved a fragment (*Philos.* vi. 37, pp. 197 seq.) is decidedly monastic. He there sees in the spirit how "all things are hanging (κρεμάμενα) and are upborne (ὀχούμενα), the flesh hanging on the soul, the soul upborne by the air, the air hanging on the aether, from Bythos fruits produced and from the womb the child." An interpretation of these sayings current in the Valentinian school is appended. According to this interpretation, flesh is the ὕλη which depends upon the soul (the psychical nature) of the Demiurge. Again the Demiurge hangs from the spirit which is outside the Pleroma, *i.e.* the Sophia in the kingdom of the Midst, the Sophia from Horus and from the Pleroma, and finally the world of Aeons in the Pleroma from the abyss, *i.e.* their Father. If this interpretation be, as we may assume, correct, Valentinus must have conceived the whole universe as forming a grand scale of being, beginning with the abysmal ground of all spiritual life, and thence descending lower and lower down to matter. The whole scale then is a descent from the perfect to ever more and more imperfect images; according to the principle expressly laid down by Valentinus, that the cosmos is as inferior to the living Aeon as the image is inferior to the living countenance (ap. *Clem. Strom.* iv. 13, 92). This view of the nature of the universe exhibits a much nearer relationship to Platonic philosophy than to the Oriental dualism which underlay the older Gnostic systems; and Hippolytus is therefore completely right, when dealing with the psalm of Valentinus, to speak of *Platonizing* Gnostics (*Philos.* vi. 37, p. 197).

The fragments do not give us any detailed acquaintance with the doctrine of Valentinus concerning the Aeons. The Πατήρ or Βυθός stands at their head; but what place in the Valentinian Pleroma was assigned to the Ἄνθρωπος προών in whose name Adam was created, is difficult to determine.

Of a two-fold Sophia, a higher and a lower, we read nothing. Sophia is the artist (ζωγράφος) who forms the world after the archetype of the living Aeon, in order to be honoured by his name. The world as formed obtains credit and stability through the invisible nature of God (*Strom.* iv. 13, 92).

To what authority Valentinus made appeal as the source of his doctrine cannot be made out from the fragments. From the *Homily to the Friends* Clemens Alexandrinus has preserved a sentence which defines "many of the things written in the public books" (δημοσίοις βίβλοις: he means doubtless the writings of the O.T.) as "found written in the church of God"—"for," he adds, "those things which are common" (*i.e.* not *merely* found in books—read, with Heinrici κοινά instead of κενά) "are words from the heart"; and proceeds, "The law written in the heart is the People of the Beloved One, both loved and loving" (Grabe was wrong in proposing to emend λαός into λόγος). The meaning is that this "People" is in virtue of the inward revelation of the Logos a law unto itself (cf. Rom. ii. 14). But this inward revelation has reference only to "that which is common" (τὰ κοινά), *i.e.* to the universal ethical truths written in the heart which "the church of God" needs not first to learn from "the public books." But this passage tells us nothing about the sources whence Valentinus derived his Gnosis. For these we must go back to the statement of Clemens (*Strom.* vii. 17, 106), according to which the Valentinians spoke of their leader as having learned of a certain Theodas, a disciple of St. Paul. But the actual statement of Irenaeus is more to be depended on, that Valentinus was the first who transformed the old doctrines of "the Gnostics" into a system of his own (*Haer.* i. 11, 1; cf. Tert. *adv. Valentinian.* 4). The fragments, moreover, give a series of points of contact with the opinions of these older "Gnostics." We may therefore regard as an axiom to be adhered to in our investigations that of any two Valentinian doctrines, that is the older and more original which approaches more closely to the older and vulgar Gnosis (Iren. i. 30). Yet the system of Valentinus had a peculiar character of its own. He was the first to breathe a really philosophic spirit into the old vulgar Gnosis, by making use of Plato's world of thought to infuse a deeper meaning into the old Gnostic myths. Baur, therefore, was quite right in emphasizing the Platonism of Valentinus (*Christliche Gnosis*, pp. 124 seq.), to which the *Philosophumena* had already called attention (*Philos.* vi. 21 sqq.).

Irenaeus completes the information afforded

by the fragments concerning Valentinus's doctrine of the Aeons. At the head of them stands a δυὰς ἀνονόμαστος, the Ἄρρητος (called also Βυθός and Πατὴρ ἀγέννητος) and his σύζυγος the Σιγή. From this Dyad proceeds a second Dyad, Πατήρ and Ἀλήθεια, which with the first Dyad forms the highest Tetrad. From this Tetrad a second Tetrad proceeds—Λόγος and Ζωή. Ἄνθρωπος and Ἐκκλησία, and these complete the First Ogdoad. From Λόγος and Ζωή proceed a Decad, from Ἄνθρωπος and Ἐκκλησία a Dodecad of Aeons. In this the number 30 of Aeons forming the Pleroma is completed. The names of the Aeons composing the Decad and the Dodecad are not given. We may, however, venture to assume that the names elsewhere given by Irenaeus (i. 1, 2), and literally repeated by Pseud-Origenes (*Philos.* vi. 30), and then again by Epiphanius (xxxi. 6) with some differences of detail, in his much later account, did really originate from Valentinus himself. They are as follows: From Λόγος and Ζωή proceed Βύθιος and Μίξις, Ἀγήρατος and Ἕνωσις, Αὐτοφυής and Ἡδονή, Ἀκίνητος and Σύγκρασις, Μονογενής and Μακαρία. From Ἄνθρωπος and Ἐκκλησία proceed: Παράκλητος and Πίστις, Πατρικός and Ἐλπίς, Μητρικός and Ἀγάπη, Ἀείνους and Σύνεσις, Ἐκκλησιαστικός and Μακαριότης, Θελητός and Σοφία. However arbitrary this name-giving may seem, it is evident that the first four masculine Aeons repeat the notion of the First Principle, and the first four feminine the notion of his syzygy, in various forms of expression. The names Μονογενής and Νοῦς (here Ἀείνους) meet us again among the Valentinians of Irenaeus as expressions for the second Masculine Principle, and Παράκλητος as that for the common product of all the Aeons—the Soter. Πατρικός, Μητρικός, Ἐκκλησιαστικός are names simply expressing that the Aeons which bear them are derived from the higher powers within the Pleroma. The feminine names Μακαρία, Πίστις, Ἐλπίς, Ἀγάπη, Σύνεσις, Σοφία, describe generally the perfection of the Pleroma by means of Predicates borrowed from the characteristics of the perfect Pneumaticos. So that all these inferior Aeon names are but a further and more detailed expression of the thought contained in the names of the first and second Tetrad. The first Tetrad expresses the essence of the Upper Pleroma in itself, the second Tetrad divided into two pairs of Aeons expresses its revelation to the Pneumatici and the Pneumatic World.

The last of the 30 Aeons, the Sophia or Μήτηρ, falls out of the Pleroma. In her remembrance of the better world she gives birth to Christus with a shadow (μετὰ σκιᾶς τινος), Christus, being of masculine nature, cuts away the shadow from himself and hastens back into the Pleroma. The mother, on the other hand, being left behind and alone with the shadow, and emptied of the pneumatic substance, gives birth to another Son the Demiurge, called also Παντοκράτωρ, and at the same time with him a sinistrous archon (the Κοσμοκράτωρ). So then from these two elements, "the right and the left," the psychical and the hylical, proceeds this lower world. This the original doctrine of Valentinus appears to have had in common with that of the Ophites (Iren. i. 30), that both doctrines knew of only one Sophia, and that for the Ophites also Christus leaves the Sophia behind and escapes himself into the upper realm of light.

The notion of a fall of the last of the Aeons from the Pleroma, and the consequent formation of this lower world as the fruit of that fall, is new and peculiar to Valentinus in his reconstruction of the older Gnosticism. He set his Platonic Monism in the place of the Oriental Dualism. The Platonic thought of the soul's fall and longing after the lost world of light he combined with the other Platonic thought of the things of this lower world being types and images of heavenly Archetypes, and so obtained a new solution of the old problems of the world's creation and the origin of evil.

The statements of Irenaeus concerning his teaching are, alas! too fragmentary and too uncertain to supply a complete view of the system of Valentinus. But the excerpts in Clemens Alex. taken from Theodotos and the anatolic school contain a doctrine in §§ 1-42, which at any rate stands much nearer to the views of Valentinus than the detailed account of Ptolemaic doctrines which Irenaeus gives in i. 1-8. We have in these excerpts a somewhat complete whole, differing in some important respects from the doctrinal system of the Italic school, and agreeing with that of Valentinus in that it knows of only one Sophia, whose offspring Christus, leaving his mother, enters the Pleroma, and sends down Jesus for the redemption of the forsaken One.

The doctrine of the Aeons stands as much behind the anthropological and ethical problems in these excerpts as it does in the fragments. We find something about the Pleroma in an interpretation of the prologue of St. John's Gospel (*Excerpt.* §§ 6, 7). By the ἀρχή of St. John i. 1, in which the Logos "was," we must understand the Μονογενής "Who is also called God" (the reading ὁ μονογενὴς θεός John i. 18 being followed). "The Logos was ἐν ἀρχῇ" means that He was in the Monogenes, in the Νοῦς and the Ἀλήθεια —the reference being to the syzygy of Λόγος and Ζωή which is said to have proceeded from Νοῦς and Ἀλήθεια. The Logos is called God because He is in God, in the Νοῦς. But when it is said ὃ γέγονεν ἐν αὐτῷ ζωὴ ἦν, the reference is to the Ζωή as σύζυγος of the Logos. The Unknown Father (πατὴρ ἄγνωστος) willed to be known to the Aeons. On knowing Himself through His own Ἐνθύμησις, which was indeed the spirit of knowledge (πνεῦμα γνώσεως), He, by knowledge, made to emanate the Monogenes. The Monogenes having emanated from the Gnosis, *i.e.* the Enthymesis of the Father, is in Himself Gnosis, *i.e.* Son, for it is through the *Son* that the Father is *known*. The πνεῦμα ἀγάπης mingles itself with the πνεῦμα γνώσεως as the Father with the Son (*i.e.* the Monogenes or Νοῦς) and the Enthymesis with Ἀλήθεια, proceeding from the Aletheia as the Gnosis proceeds from the Enthymesis. The μονογενὴς υἱός, Who abides in the bosom of the Father, emanates from the Father's bosom and thereby declares (ἐξηγεῖται) the Enthymesis through Gnosis to the Aeons. Having become visible on earth, He is no longer called by the apostle Monogenes (simply), but ὡς μονογενής. For though remaining in Himself one and the same, He is in the creation called πρωτότοκος, and in the Pleroma Μονογενής, and appears in each locality as He can be comprehended there.

The preceding survey shews that in the first 42 paragraphs or sections of Clemens's fragments from Theodotus we really have a well-connected and consistent doctrinal system. The scattered notices in §§ 1-28 fit tolerably well into the dogmatic whole, and doubtless we have here an account of the so-called anatolic school, and in substance the oldest form of the Valentinian system.

The historical development of the Valentinian doctrine can be traced with only approximate certainty and imperfectly. The roots of the system are to be found in the old vulgar Gnosis. For even if the original dualistic foundation is repressed and concealed by a Platonizing pantheism, it still gives evident tokens of its continued existence in the background. The ὕλη and "dark waters" into which the Ophitic Sophia sinks down (Iren. i. 30, 3) are here changed into the κένωμα or ὑστέρημα, which in antithesis to the πλήρωμα is simply an equivalent for the Platonic μὴ ὄν.

The notion of a psychical Christus who passes through Mary as water through a conduit (Iren. vii. 2) is to be found everywhere in the Italic school (*Philos*. vi. 35, pp. 194 seq.).

The centre of gravity of the whole system lies undoubtedly in its speculative interests. The names alone of the 30 Aeons are a proof of this. It deserves notice that the designations Νοῦς and Μονογενής applied to the first masculine principle emanating from the supreme Father do not seem to have been used by Valentinus himself. It was called simply Πατήρ or Ἄνθρωπος (υἱὸς ἀνθρώπου). It is a genuinely speculative feature that the knowledge of the Father through the Son is derived from a union of the Spirit of Love with the Spirit of Knowledge.

Since the doctrine of Valentinus concerning the Aeons originated in the cosmogonic and astral powers of the old Syrian Gnosis, one cannot doubt that the Aeons were originally thought of as mythological personages and not as personified notions, although Tertullian (*adv. Valentin.* 4) would refer the former view to Ptolemaeus, and not Valentinus, as its first author.

A yet more widely different conception of the Valentinian doctrine of Aeons is found in the fragment given by Epiphanius (xxxi. 5-6). Here, too, the speculative interest is manifest in the endeavour to follow up in detail the process of the emanation of individual Aeons within the Pleroma from the Αὐτοπάτωρ. But the whole description, bathed as it is in sensuous warmth, with its peculiar plays with numbers and its barbarous names for individual Aeons, appears to be merely a degenerate Marcosian form of Gnosis.

Finally, we have a quite peculiar transformation of the Valentinian system in the doctrine of the so-called Docetae, as preserved in the *Philosophumena* (viii. 8-11). From the πρῶτος θεός, who is small as the seed of a fig-tree but infinite in power, proceed first of all three Aeons, which by the perfect number ten enlarge themselves to thirty Aeons; from these proceed innumerable other bisexual Aeons, and from these an infinite multiplicity of Ideas, of which those of the third Aeon are expressed and shapen in the lower world of darkness as φωτειναὶ χαρακτῆρες.

The Platonic foundation of the Valentinian system is very perceptible in this its last offshoot, though mixed up in a peculiar way with Oriental Dualism. At the same time these Docetae endeavour to reduce the metaphysical distinctions which they maintain to merely gradual ones. No part of Christendom therefore is entirely excluded from the knowledge of the Redeemer, and participation in His Redemption: all, even those of the lower grades of the spirit-world, participate at least ἐκ μέρους in the Truth. The way in which all, and each according to his measure, attain knowledge of the truth, is, as in the doctrine of the church, *Faith*. Since the Redeemer's advent—so we read expressly—"Faith is announced for the forgiveness of sins."

Beside working out philosophical problems, the disciples of Valentinus were much occupied with seeking traces of their Master's doctrine in Holy Scripture. The excerpts of Clemens and abundant notices in Irenaeus tell of an allegorical method of scriptural exposition pursued with great zeal in the Valentinian schools, not limited to the Gospels or the Pauline Epistles, but extending to the O.T., and attaching special significance to the history of creation in Genesis. Valentinian expositors shew a special preference for St. John's Gospel, and above all for its prologue. Some allegorical expositions have been preserved belonging to the anatolic school (*Exc. ex Theod.* §§ 6, 7) and others derived from Ptolemaeus (Iren. i. 8, 5). But before all we must make mention of the labours of Heracleon, of which Origen has preserved numerous specimens. From Heracleon proceeded the first known commentary on St. John's Gospel.

VI. *Literature.*—Valentinus occupies a distinguished place in all works on Gnosticism, *e.g.* in Neander, Baur, Matter, Lipsius, Möhler (*Geschichte der Kosmologie in der Christlichen Kirche*), Mansel (*The Gnostic Heresies of the First and Second Centuries*—a posthumous work, ed. by Bp. Lightfoot), and in the Prolegomena of Harvey's ed. of Irenaeus. The best monograph is by Heinrici (*Die Valentinianische Gnosis und die Heilige Schrift*, Berlin, 1851), with which cf. the review by Lipsius (*Protestantische Kirchenzeitung*, 1873, pp. 174-186). [HERACLEON; MARCUS (17).] [R.A.L.]

Valerianus (1), **C. Publius Licinius,** emperor. A.D. 253-260. Before the close of 253 Valerian was proclaimed emperor by the legions of Rhaetia and Noricum, and he associated his son Gallienus with him in that dignity.

Their reigns were the most disastrous period in the history of Rome until that of Honorius. The empire seemed on the verge of dissolution. Every frontier was menaced by barbarian attacks, and even the interior provinces were invaded and ravaged. A German host entered Italy itself, and penetrated to Ravenna. The Franks, now first appearing under this name, assailed the Rhine frontier. The

Goths and their kindred tribes poured across the Danube into Illyricum and Macedonia. The Persians took Nisibis, and, penetrating into Syria, captured Antioch (? A.D. 255). Worse even than all these wars was the great plague which had begun in the reign of Decius and which raged for 15 years (Zon. xii. 21).

To these calamities was added the most terrible persecution the church had yet experienced. In the early part of his reign Valerian was exceedingly favourable to the Christians, and his palace was filled with them. But in 257 a terrible change took place. Valerian fell more and more under the influence of the pretorian prefect Macrianus, an Egyptian, chief of the "magi" of that country. Under his influence Valerian ordered those who did not belong to the religion of Rome at least to render outward signs of conformity to it under pain of exile. By the same edict, Christians were forbidden, under pain of death, to assemble for worship or enter their cemeteries. The cases of St. Cyprian (*Acta Procons.* c. 1, in Migne, *Patr. Lat.* iii. 1499) and St. Dionysius of Alexandria (Eus. *H. E.* vii. 11) shew how uniform the procedure was under this edict. St. Cyprian was apparently the first to suffer in Africa, and the date of his exile (Aug. 257) shews when the persecution began. His sentence was simple banishment, but a great number of African bishops, priests, deacons, and some of the laity, were sent to the mines and endured great hardships (Cypr. *Epp.* 77-80 in *Patr. Lat.* iv. 414).

This edict was followed in 258 by a rescript of tremendous severity from Valerian, who, in the interval, had probably set out to the East to take command against the Persians. (Early in the year he had held a council of war at Byzantium [Vopiscus, *Vit. Aureliani*, 13].) The punishment for the clergy of every grade was death. Apparently even recantation was unavailing. Senators, *viri egregii*, and knights were punished with degradation and confiscation of property, and with death if they refused to recant. Noble ladies were to forfeit their property and be exiled. Members of the imperial household suffered a similar forfeiture, and were to be sent in chains to work on the imperial possessions. It is remarkable that mention is only made of the clergy and the higher classes of the laity. The emperor's policy was apparently to strike at the leaders. The first victim of this rescript was pope Xystus, put to death on Aug. 6 as he sat in his episcopal chair. Four of his deacons suffered with him. This was the beginning of a violent persecution at Rome (Cypr. *Ep.* 82) in which four days later the famous St. Lawrence followed his master. Cyprian was beheaded on Sept. 14. Both in Rome and Africa a great number of Christians suffered. The best proof of the violence of the persecution is the long vacancies (about 11 months) of the sees of Rome and Carthage. In Spain Fructuosus, bp. of Tarragona, with two deacons, was burnt alive in the amphitheatre (Jan. 21, 259). In Palestine the names of three martyrs are preserved by Eusebius (*H. E.* vii. 12). They came before the governor and declared themselves Christians. A woman who was a follower of Marcion shared their fate.

But the reign of Valerian was not destined to be of long duration. Dionysius regards his persecution as lasting the 42 months mentioned in the Apocalypse. His campaign against Sapor, king of Persia, the scene of which was the neighbourhood of Edessa, was disastrous. He was taken prisoner late in 260. How long he lived in captivity is unknown. Gallienus, immediately after his father's captivity, stopped the persecution, but it probably lasted in the East till the fall of Macrianus, who had assumed the purple in 262. Zos. i. 28-36; Zon. xii. 22, 23; Bernhardt, *Geschichte Roms von Valerian*; Tillem. *Emp.* iii., *Mém. eccl.* iv. 1; Victor, *de Caes.* 32; *Epit.* 32; the Life of Valerian in the Augustan history; Gibbon, cc. 10, 16). [F.D.]

Valerianus, martyr. [CAECILIA.]

Valerius (6), bp. of Hippo Regius, predecessor of Augustine, whom he had admitted to the priesthood at the earnest desire of the people, against Augustine's wish, expressed in a letter to Valerius, but in answer, as Valerius thought, to his own prayers (Aug. *Ep.* 21; Possidius, *Vit. Aug.* 4, 5). Contrary to African, but in accordance with Eastern, usage, Valerius caused Augustine to preach in his presence when he himself became unable to do so. When Valerius felt his own infirmities increase, he obtained the consent of the other bishops, but at first not that of Megalius of Calama, primate of Numidia, to ordain Augustine as coadjutor to himself, contrary to the usual practice of the church and to the express wish of Augustine, who refused on this ground to accept the office, though, as he said afterwards, he was not then aware of the canon of the council of Nicaea, forbidding two bishops in the same place. (Conc. Nic. *can.* 8, Bruns, *Conc.* p. 16; Aug. *c. Petil.* iii. 16, § 19, *c. Cresc.* iv. 64, § 79; *Brevic. Coll.* iii. 7, § 9). His objection was overruled by the earnest desire of all concerned, and by similar instances in Africa and elsewhere (Aug. *Epp.* 31, 4; 213, 4). Valerius, better acquainted with Greek than with Latin, was rejoiced to have one so able as Augustine to teach and preach in the Latin language. He is spoken of in the highest terms by Augustine, Possidius, and Paulinus of Nola (Aug. *Epp.* 31, 4; 32; Possid. *Vit. Aug.* 5; Paulinus, *Ep.* 5). After Augustine's appointment, Valerius gave him a piece of land for his monastery (Aug. *Serm.* 355, 1, 2). He died A.D. 396 (Aug. *Ep.* 33, 4). Proculeianus was bp. of the Donatists at Hippo during his lifetime (Aug. *Ep.* 33). [H.W.P.]

Verecundus (2), d. 552, bp. of the Civitas Juncensis in Byzacena. He was summoned to Constantinople in 549, touching the question of the "Three Chapters." He died at Chalcedon the year before the second council of Constantinople. In the controversy on the "Three Chapters" he seems to have acted until his death with Virgilius, defending the works in question, and joining with Virgilius in his censure on Theodore of Caesarea and Menas of Constantinople. He is probably the presbyter Verecundus who composed a commentary on the ecclesiastical canticles, comprehending the songs of Miriam, Moses (from Deut.), Azariah, Hezekiah, Habakkuk, and Deborah, the prayer of Manasseh, and the thanksgiving of Jonah. The commentary is printed in vol. iv. of the *Spicilegium Solesmense*, with other works attributed to Verecendus. It shews some philosophical learning and historical knowledge, and some illustrations are drawn from his own experience. His manner of referring to the Vandal persecution in Africa and the unsettled state of affairs seems to fix its date before 534, when the persecution ended. The poems attributed to him, and also published in the *Spicilegium*, are (1) "Exhortatio Poenitendi," (2) "de Satisfactione Poenitentiae," (3) "Crisias."

The spirit of the first two poems is alike: both express a strong sense of the need of repentance and an earnest anticipation of the Judgment. The poems are hortatory rather than penitential. The third poem, concerning the signs of the Judgment, is probably not by the same hand. It has much more artificiality and much less earnestness.

A *Breviarium Concilii Chalcedonensis*, drawn up so as to favour the supporters of the "Three Chapters," is attributed to Verecundus. It is very possibly his, but may have been composed by a more extreme partisan and issued under his name by one who regarded him as a confessor and wished to obtain the influence of his reputation. Pitra prints this also in the *Spicilegium*. [H.A.W.]

Veronica (*Haemorrhoissa, ἡ αἱμοῤῥοοῦσα*), the woman cured of a bloody issue (Matt. ix. 20). Eusebius (*H. E.* vii. 18) relates that she was a native of Caesarea Philippi, and adds that "at the gates of her house, on an elevated stone, stands a brazen image of a woman on a bended knee, with her hands stretched out before her, like one entreating. Opposite to this there is another image of a man erect, of the same materials, decently clad in a mantle, and stretching out his hand to the woman. Before her feet, and on the same pedestal, there is a strange plant growing which, rising as high as the hem of the brazen garment, is a kind of antidote to all kinds of diseases. This statue, they say, is a statue of Jesus Christ, and it has remained even until our times, so that we ourselves saw it whilst tarrying in that city. Nor is it to be wondered at that those of the Gentiles who were anciently benefited by our Saviour should have done these things. Since we have also seen representations of the apostles Peter and Paul and of Christ Himself still preserved in paintings, it is probable that, according to a practice among the Gentiles, the ancients were accustomed to pay this kind of honour indiscriminately to those who were as saviours or deliverers to them." Legendary tradition about Veronica flourished during and after 4th cent. Macarius Magnesius says she was princess of Edessa, and that her name was Veronica or Berenice (Macarii Magnet. ed. Blondel, Paris, 1876; Tillem. *Mém.* i. 20; *Hist. des emp.* iv. 308), following whom Baronius (*Annal.* xxxi. 75) makes her rich and noble. A late tradition represents her as a niece of king Herod and as offering her veil, or a napkin, as a *sudarium* to the suffering Christ on the Way of the Cross, Whose pictured features were thus impressed upon the linen. This tradition has found no acceptance since the 11th cent.; the "veronicas" often shewn, and accredited with miraculous powers of healing, are face-cloths from the catacombs on which Christian reverence and affection have painted the features of the Saviour (see Wyke Bayliss, *Rex Regum*, 1905), and the legend has arisen from the finding of these; the name of the saint being clearly formed from the description of such a face-cloth as a *vera icon*. *The Gospel of Nicodemus* introduces her as one of the witnesses on behalf of Christ at His trial by Pilate; (Thilo, *Cod. Apocryph. N.T.* p. 560; *Acta SS.* Bol. Jul. iii. 273-279). [G.T.S. AND ED.]

Vespasianus, Titus Flavius, emperor July 1, 69, to June 24, 79, and his son **Titus**, emperor June 24, 79, to Sept. 13, 81. As a great part of the imperial power was exercised by Titus during his father's reign, of which his own short reign may be regarded as the continuation, it seems convenient to treat them together. The influences of these princes on Christianity was wholly indirect. The destruction of Jerusalem and the temple tended to hasten the complete separation of Judaism and Christianity. This distinction, however, had not as yet become apparent to the Roman authorities, and as far as they had any knowledge of the existence of Christians, they regarded them as merely a Jewish sect. A long and almost unbroken chain of Christian authorities bear witness to the favourable condition of Christianity under these emperors. Melito of Sardis, writing in the reign of M. Aurelius (Eus. *H. E.* iv. 26), knows of no imperial persecutors except Nero and Domitian. Tertullian (*Apol.* 5) expressly denies that Vespasian was a persecutor. Lactantius (*Mortes* 2, 3) knows of no persecution between Nero and Domitian. Eusebius (*H. E.* iii. 17) expressly asserts that Vespasian did no harm to the Christians. Hilary of Poictiers, writing after 360, is the first to make any charge of persecution against Vespasian. In a rhetorical passage (*contra Arianos*, 3, in Migne, *Patr. Lat.* x. 611), contrary to all previous Christian testimony, he couples Vespasian with Nero and Decius. Sulpicius Severus (*H. E.* ii. 30 in *Patr. Lat.* xx. 146), in a passage whose style suggests it was borrowed from one of the lost books of Tacitus, states that the motive of Titus in destroying the temple was to abolish not only Judaism but Christianity, but he does not mention any hostile act on the part of Vespasian or his son against the Christians.

We may consider that the reigns of these first two Flavian emperors were a period of tranquillity for the church. For their relation to the church see Tillemont, *Mém. eccl.* ii. 102, 152, 555; Aubé, *Hist. des persec.* c. 4; Görres, *Zeitsch. für wissent. Theol.* xxi. 492. M. Double (*L'Empereur Titus*) ingeniously that maintains, contrary to the usual opinion, he was a monster of wickedness. [F.D.]

Vettius Epagathus. In the early persecutions the Christians felt it to be a gross injustice that a man should be put to death merely because he acknowledged himself to be a Christian, and without any investigation whether there was anything contrary to morality or piety in the Christian doctrines or practices. It not unfrequently happened [LUCIUS] that a bystander at a trial would press on the judge the necessity of such an investigation, whereupon the magistrate would say, I think you must be a Christian also yourself, and on the advocate's confessing that he was, would send him to share the fate of those whom he had attempted to defend. This befell Vettius Epagathus, a distinguished Christian citizen of Lyons in the persecution of A.D. 177. He came forward as the advocate of the Christians first apprehended, and in consequence was himself "taken up unto the lot of the martyrs." The word "martyr," as at first used, did not necessarily imply that he who bore witness for Christ sealed his testimony by death; and Renan (*Marc Aurèle*, p. 307) is of opinion that Vettius had "only the merits of martyrdom without the reality," since no mention is made of Vettius in the subsequent narration of the sufferings of Christians tortured in the amphitheatre, and, what Renan thinks decisive, the epistle of the churches says of Vettius that "he was *and is* a genuine disciple of Christ, following the Lamb whithersoever he goeth." But the addition "following the Lamb, etc." indicates that the "is" does not refer to the life of Vettius in this world, but rather to that which he enjoyed in company with Christ. Vettius was probably a Roman citizen, and as such was simply beheaded instead of undergoing the tortures of the amphitheatre. [G.S.]

Victor (1), bp. of Rome after Eleutherus, in the reigns of Commodus and Severus. The Eusebian *Chronicle* assigns him 12 years, ending 198 or 199; Eusebius (*H. E.* v. 28) 10 years, and says that Zephyrinus succeeded him about the 9th year of Severus, *i.e.* A.D. 202. Lipsius (*Chron. der röm. Bischöf.*) supposes his episcopate to have been from 189 to 198 or 199. Soon probably after his accession he excommunicated Theodotus of Byzantium (ὁ σκυτεύς), who had come to Rome, and taught that Christ was a mere man (Eus. *H. E.* v. 28; cf. Epiphan. *Haeres.* liv. 1). Eusebius is quoting from an opponent of the sect of Artemon, who afterwards under pope Zephyrinus maintained a similar heresy. It appears from the quotation that the Artemonites alleged all the bps. of Rome before Zephyrinus to have held the same views with themselves; and the allegation is refuted by the fact of Victor, the predecessor of Zephyrinus, having excommunicated Theodotus, "the founder and father of the God-denying apostasy." Montanism also was rife in Asia Minor during the reign of Victor, who is supposed by some of have been the bp. of Rome alluded to by Tertullian (*adv. Prax.* c. 1) as having issued letters of peace in favour of its upholders, though afterwards persuaded by Praxeas to revoke his approval. But others think it more probable that Eleutherus was referred to. See, however, MONTANUS.

Victor's most memorable action was with regard to the Asians on the Easter question. They still persisted in the Quartodeciman usage, pleading the authority of St. John for keeping their *Pasch* on the 14th of Nisan, on whatever day of the week it fell. So far intercommunion between them and the church of Rome had not been broken on this account. In the time of Victor the usage of the Asians (in which, according to Eusebius, they stood alone among all the churches of Christendom) attracted general attention. Synods were held on the subject in various parts—in Palestine under Theophilus of Caesarea and Narcissus of Jerusalem, in Pontus under Palmas, in Gaul under Irenaeus, in Corinth under its bishop, Bachillus, at Osrhoene in Mesopotamia, and elsewhere, by all of which synodical letters were issued, unanimous in disapproval of the Asian custom, and in declaring that "on the Lord's Day only the mystery of the resurrection of the Lord from the dead was accomplished, and that on that day only we keep the close of the paschal fast" (Eus. *H. E.* v. 23). But the general feeling was that the retention of their own tradition by the Asians was no sufficient ground for breaking off communion with them. Victor alone was intolerant of difference. He had issued a letter in behalf of the Roman church to the like effect with those of the synods held elsewhere. From a reply to it we may conclude it to have been peremptory in its requirement of compliance. This reply was from Polycrates, bp. of Ephesus, as head of the Asian churches, who, at Victor's desire, had convened an assembly of bishops which concurred with Polycrates in his rejoinder. He resolutely upholds the Asian tradition, supporting it by the authority of Philip the apostle, who, with his two aged virgin daughters, was buried at Hierapolis; of another saintly daughter of his who lay at Ephesus; of St. John, also at rest at Ephesus; of Polycarp of Smyrna, bishop and martyr; of Thraseas of Eumenia, also bishop and martyr, who slept at Smyrna. After naming others who had kept the 14th day according to the Gospel, he speaks of seven of his own kinsmen, all bishops, who had maintained the same usage. He adds, "I therefore, having been for 65 years in the Lord, and having conferred with the brethren from the whole world, and having perused all the Holy Scripture, am not scared with those who are panic-stricken. For those who are greater than I have said, 'It is right to obey God rather than men.'" After receiving this reply Victor endeavoured to induce the church at large to excommunicate the Asians, but failed. Whether he himself, notwithstanding, renounced communion with them on the part of the Roman church is not clear from the language of Eusebius. Socrates (*H. E.* v. 22) says he did; and this is probable. Jerome (*de Vir. Ill.* c. 35) speaks only of his desire to have them generally condemned. Evidently the judgment of the bp. of Rome did not in that age carry any irresistible weight with other churches, for Eusebius expressly tells us that "these things did not please all the bishops," and that they wrote "sharply assailing Victor." He cites a letter sent on the occasion to Victor by Irenaeus, who, though holding with him on the question at issue, exhorted him in the name of a synod of the church of Gaul "that he should not cut off whole churches of God for preserving the tradition of an ancient custom." Lastly, he cites "the elders before Soter," chiefs of the Roman church, who had been at peace with those from other dioceses differing from them in the matter at issue; and especially Anicetus, who, though unable to persuade the blessed Polycarp to give up the custom which, "with John the disciple of our Lord, and the other apostles with whom John lived," he had always observed, and though himself not persuaded to renounce the custom of the elders in his own church, had still honourably accorded the Eucharist in the church to Polycarp, and parted from him in peace (Eus. *H. E.* v. 24). Jerome (*u.s.*) alludes to several letters written by Irenaeus to the same purpose. The Quartodecimans seem to have maintained their usage till the council of Nicaea, which enjoined its discontinuance. The intolerance of Victor evidently neither won general approval nor effected his intended purpose. Victor is mentioned by St. Jerome (*op. cit.* c. 34) as a writer of a treatise on the Easter question and other works. [J.B—Y.]

Victor (39) (*Victorius, Victorinus*), **Claudius Marius,** the author of three books in hexameter verse, containing the narrative of Genesis down to the destruction of the cities of the Plain; author also of a letter to "Salmon," or Solomon, an abbat, in hexameter verse, on the corrupt manners of his time. He is probably the Victorius, or Victorinus, mentioned by Gennadius (*de Vir. Ill.* 60) as a rhetorician of Marseilles, who died "Theodosio et Valentiano regnantibus" (*i.e.* 425-450), and who addressed to his son Aetherius a commentary on Genesis. Gennadius says "a principio libri *usque ad obitum patriarchae Abrahae* tres diversos edidit libros." This does not accurately describe the work we have under the name of Cl. M. Victor. But there is a diversity of reading in the passage of Gennadius. In Erasmus's ed. of St. Jerome the passage stands "*quatuor versuum* edidit libros." If this be the right reading, it seems almost certain that the three books we have of Cl. M. Victor, ending as they now do at a point which seems to call for some explanation, are the first three books of those mentioned by Gennadius, and that a fourth book, now lost, carried on the narrative to Abraham's death, where a natural halting-place for the work is presented. The three books correspond very well with what Gennadius says of the work of Victorius; they are written in a pious and Christian spirit, but without depth or great force of treatment. They are, mainly, a paraphrase in verse of part of Genesis with but few reflections; the narrative, with one or two exceptions, keeping closely to that of Scripture. The most notable variation is the introduction of a prayer by Adam on his expulsion from Paradise, which is followed by a strange episode. The serpent is discerned by Eve, who urges Adam to take vengeance on him. In assailing him with stones, a spark is struck from a flint, which sets fire to the wood in which Adam and Eve had taken shelter, and they are threatened with destruction. This mishap is the means of revealing to them metals, forced from the ground by the heat, and of preparing the earth, by the action of the fire, for the production of corn. The style of the poem and its language are in no way remarkable; its versification is generally tolerable, but there are instances of wrong quantities of syllables. The Ep. to Salomon is a poem of about 100 hexameters, and more original, though not of special interest. Both are in De la Bigne's *Bibl. Patr.* viii. 278, and Appendix; and in Maittaires' *Corpus Poetarum Lat.* ii. 1567. [H.A.W.]

Victor (44) **Vitensis,** a N. African bishop and writer. The known facts of his life are very few. He was called Vitensis either after his see or after his birthplace. He seems to have been numbered amongst the clergy of Carthage *c.* 455. His *Hist. Persecutionis Provinciae Africanae* is very interesting, as he appears to have been with safety an eyewitness of the Vandal persecution for more than 30 years. He was actively employed by Eugenius, metropolitan of Carthage, in 483. Early in that year Hunneric banished 4,966 bishops and clergy of every rank. Victor was used by Eugenius to look after the more aged and infirm of the bishops. The *History* gives us a view of the religion of the Vandals. It also relates many particulars about Carthage, its churches, their names and dedications, as those of Perpetua and Felicitas, of Celerina and the Scillitans (i. 3). It shews the persistence of paganism at Carthage, and mentions the temples of Memory and of Coelestis as existing till the Vandals levelled them after their capture of Carthage. This temple of Coelestis existed in the time of Augustine, who describes in his *de Civ. Dei*, lib. ii. cc. 4, 26 (cf. Tertull. *Apol.* c. 24) the impure rites there performed. Its site was elaborately discussed by M. A. Castan in a Mém. in the *Comptes rendus de l'Acad. des Inscript.* t. xiii. (1885), pp. 118-132, where all the references to its cult were collected out of classical and patristic sources. Victor's *History* contains glimpses of N. African ritual. In lib. ii. 17 we have an account of the healing of the blind man Felix by Eugenius, bp. of Carthage. The ritual of the feast of Epiphany is described, while there are frequent references to the singing of hymns or psalms at funerals. In *Hist.* lib. v. 6, we read that the inhabitants of Tipasa refused to hold communion with the Arian bishop. Hunneric sent a military count, who collected them all into the forum and cut out their tongues by the roots, notwithstanding which they all retained the power of speech. This remarkable fact has been discussed by Gibbon, c. xxxvii., by Middleton in his *Free Inquiry*, pp. 313-316, and by many others. The *History* of Victor is usually divided into five books. Bk. i. narrates the persecution of Genseric, from the conquest of Africa by the Vandals in 429 till Genseric's death in 477. Bks. ii. iv. and v. deal with the persecution of Hunneric, A.D. 477-484; while bk. iii. contains the confession of faith drawn up by Eugenius of Carthage and presented to Hunneric at the conference of 484 (cf. Gennadius, *de Vir. Ill.* No. 97). In the Confession (lib. iii. 11) the celebrated text I. John v. 7, concerning the three heavenly witnesses, first appears. (See on this point Porson's letter to Travis, and Gibbon's notes on c. xxxvii.). The life and works of Victor have been the subject of much modern German criticism, which has not, however, added a great deal to our knowledge. Ebert's *Literatur des Mittelalters im Abendlande* (Leipz. 1874), t. i. 433-436, fixes the composition of the *History* at *c.* 486. In A. Schaefer's *Historische Untersuchungen* (Bonn, 1882), Aug. Auler (pp. 253-275) maintains, with much learning and acuteness, that Victor was born in Vita, that his see is unknown, that he was consecrated bishop after the persecution, and wrote his *History* before 487, and that this *History* is a piece of tendency-writing and untrustworthy. He cannot recognize in the action of Genseric against the Catholic party anything but a legitimate measure of state repression. The best of the older editions of the *History* is that of Ruinart, reprinted with its elaborate dissertations in Migne's *Patr. Lat.* lviii. Michael Petschenig, in the Vienna *Corpus Scriptt. Ecclesiast. Lat.* t. vii. (Vindob. 1881) abandons the old division of the text, dating from Chifflet in 17th cent., and divides it into three books. In all the editions will be found the *Notitia Prov. et Civit. Africae*, a valuable document for the geography and ecclesiastical arrangements of N. Africa. Ceill. (x. 448-465) gives a full analysis of Victor's *History*. It was translated into French in 1563 and 1664, into English in 1605. [G.T.S.]

Victor (47), bp. of Capua, apart from his writings is known only by his epitaph, which states that he died in Apr. 554, after an episcopate of about 13 years from Feb. 541 (Ughelli, vi. 306).

Writings.—I. He is best known from his connexion with the *Codex Fuldensis* (F), after the *C. Amiatinus* the most ancient and valuable MS. of the Vulgate, transcribed by his direction and afterwards corrected by him. The MS. is remarkable for containing the Gospels in the form of a Harmony. In his preface he relates that a MS. without a title had come into his hands containing a single Gospel composed of the four. Inquiring into its authorship, he concludes, though with some doubt, that it was identical with the works of Tatianus (T), which by a blunder he calls *Diapente* instead of *Diatessaron.* So little was known till 1876 of the *Diatessaron* that it was generally supposed that Victor was mistaken. It was known that the *Diatessaron* began with John i. 1, whereas F begins with the preface from Luke. But Mösinger's ed. in 1876 of Aucher's Latin trans. of the Armenian version of Ephraim Syrus's Commentary on the *Diatessaron* (E), followed by Zahn's *Forschungen zur Geschichte des Neutestamentlichen Kanons*, i. (Z), made known the contents and arrangements of the *Diatessaron* sufficiently to show that the archetype of F was formed by taking T and substituting for each Syriac fragment in Tatian's mosaic the corresponding fragment from the Vulgate, the adapter occasionally altering the order and inserting passages missing in T. The discrepancies between the index and text in F shew that it underwent further changes after assuming a Latin shape, but it is impossible to say how far the differences between it and T proceed from such subsequent alterations or are due to the original adapter. The date of the adaptation is uncertain, the limits being 383, the date of the Vulgate being brought out, and 545, the date of F. The discrepancies between index and text demand a date considerably before the latter limit, but it must have been made after the Vulgate had become well known and popular, which was not till long after it appeared. The most probable date, therefore, seems to be midway between the limits, or the second half of 5th cent., say *c*, 470. The notices in Gennadius (*de Vir. Ill.*). who wrote during this period, collected by Zahn (312, 313), shew that either the author was a Syriac scholar or was acquainted with one; pilgrimages from the West to Egypt and Palestine were then frequent. To substitute in Tatian's mosaic the proper fragments of the Vulgate would require a much less thorough knowledge of Syriac than an independent translation would imply.

F also contains the rest of the N.T. with the Ep. to the Laodiceans in the order: Pauline Epistles (Phil. being followed by I. and II. Thess., Col., Laodiceans, I. and II. Tim., Tit., Philemon, and Heb.), the Acts, the seven Catholic Epistles and the Apocalypse, the whole concluding with the verses of pope Damasus on St. Paul. To each book, except the Laodiceans, is prefixed a *brevis* or table of headings, and to each Pauline Epistle except Hebrews, and to the Acts and the Apocalypse, a short preface. To the Pauline Epistles are also prefixed a table of lessons from them, a general preface or argument of them, a long special argument of the Romans, and a concordance of the Epistles giving references to the various passages treating of each particular doctrine. To the Acts is prefixed an account of the burial-places of the Apostles. There is a short general preface to the seven Catholic Epistles, and also the remarkable preface purporting to be St. Jerome's, which contains the accusation, referred to by Westcott and Hort (*G. T. ii. Notes on Select Readings*, 105), against the Latin translators of omitting the "Patris Filii et Spiritus testimonium" in I. John v. 7, 8, while the text itself is free from the interpolation. Besides this there are other places where, as in the Gospel, the text and supplementary matter no longer correspond exactly, shewing that changes have occurred since the former was composed. *E.g.* the General Argument to the Pauline Epistles reckons but 14 in all, including the Hebrews, and therefore excluding that to the Laodiceans, though it stands in the text. Again, the preface to the Colossians, "Colossenses et hii sicut Laodicienses sunt Asiani," must have been written when the Laodiceans preceded the Colossians, but the transposition may be due to Victor himself.

The whole MS. was carefully revised and corrected by Victor, in whose hand are three notes, one at the end of the Acts and two at the end of the Apocalypse, respectively recording that he had finished reading the MS. on May 2, 546, Apr. 19, 546, and a second time on Apr. 12, 547. In the same hand are occasional glosses, the most remarkable being the explanation of the number of the beast in the Revelation as Teitan. The MS. was ed. in 1868 by E. Ranke, whose preface fully describes it and its history; the Harmony only is in Migne (*Patr. Lat.* lxviii. 255).

II. Victor was the author of several commentaries on the O. and N. T., partly consisting of extracts from various fathers, partly original. Pitra (*Spicil. Sol.* i.) has edited fragments of some on O.T., contained in an *Expositio in Heptateuchum* by Joannes Diaconus. Another work is the *Reticulus*, or *On Noah's Ark* (p. 287), containing an extraordinary calculation to shew that its dimensions typify the number of years in the life of our Lord. On N.T. Victor wrote a commentary, 11 fragments of which, preserved in the *Collections* of Smaragdus, are collected by Pitra (*Patr. Lat.* cii. 1124), according to whom a St. Germain MS. of Rabanus Maurus's *Commentary on St. Matthew* marks numerous passages as derived from Victor. Fragments of *Capitula de Resurrectione Domini* are given in *Spicil. Sol.* i. (liv. lix. lxii. lxiv.), in which Victor touches on the difficulties in the genealogy in St. Matthew and on the discrepancy between St. Mark and St. John as to the hour of the Crucifixion. Of the last he gives the explanation of Eusebius in *Quaestiones ad Marinum*, and also one of his own.

III. Victor's most celebrated work was that on the Paschal Cycle mentioned by several chroniclers and praised by Bede (*de Rat. Tempa.* 51), whose two extracts are in *Patr. Lat.* lxviii. 1097, xc. 502. The rest was supposed to be lost till considerable extracts from it contained in the *Catena* of Joannes Diaconus were pub. in *Spicil. Sol.* (i. 296). It was written *c.* 550, to controvert the Paschal Cycle of VICTORIUS (2), according to which Easter Day would have fallen that year on Apr. 17, while Victor considered Apr. 24 the correct day in accordance with the Alexandrine computation which he defends. [F.D.]

Victor (48) Tununensis, an African bishop and chronicler. He was a zealous supporter of the "Three Chapters," enduring much persecution after 556 and till his death *c.* 567, both in his own province and in Egypt. Of his *Chronicle*, from the creation to A.D. 566, only the portion 444-566 remains, dealing almost exclusively with the history of the Eutychian heresy and the controversy about the "Three Chapters." It also gives details about the Vandal persecution, the memory of which must have been still fresh in his youth, and various stories telling against Arianism. The *Chronicle* is very useful for illustrations of the social and religious life of cent. vi. It is printed in Migne's *Patr. Lat.* t. lxviii. with Galland's preface. Cf. Isid. *de Vir. Ill.* c. 38; Cave's *Hist. Lit.* i. 415. A treatise *On Penitence,* included among the works of St. Ambrose, is attributed to Victor; Ceill. v. 512, x. 469, xi. 302. [G.T.S.]

Victorinus (4), St., of Pettau, bishop and martyr. He was apparently a Greek by birth, and (according to the repeated statement of Cassiodorus) a rhetorician before he became bp. of Pettau (Petavio) in Upper Pannonia. He is believed to have suffered martyrdom in Diocletian's persecution. St. Jerome (our chief authority concerning him) mentions him several times, and with respect even where his criticisms are adverse. He enumerates among his works (*Catal. Script. Eccl.* 74) commentaries on Gen., Ex., Lev., Is., Ezek., Hab., Eccles., Cant., Matt., and Rev., besides a treatise "adversus omnes haereses." Jerome occasionally cites the opinion of Victorinus (*in Eccles.* iv. 13; *in Ezech.* xxvi. and elsewhere), but considered him to have been affected by the opinions of the Chiliasts or Millenarians (see *Catal. Script.* 18, and *in Ezech. l.c.*). He also states that he borrowed extensively from Origen. In consequence, perhaps, of his Millennarian tendencies, or of his relations to Origen, his works were classed as "apocrypha" in the *Decretum de Libris Recipiendis*, which Baronius (*ad ann.* 303) erroneously refers to a synod held under Gelasius. Little or nothing is left—nothing, indeed, which can be said to be his with any certainty. Poems are attributed to him with no authority better than that of Bede; while the two lines Bede quotes as his were clearly written by some one with a tolerable knowledge of Latin. [H.A.W.]

Victorinus (6), called *Caius Marius* (Hieron. *Comm. on Gal. Proleg.*) and also *Marius Fabius* (see Suringar, *Hist. Scholiast. Lat.* p. 153, note); known also as *Afer*, from the country of his birth. He is to be distinguished from two Christian writers called Victorinus mentioned by Gennadius (*de Scriptor. Eccl.* cc. 60 and 88), and from Victorinus of Pettau, the commentator on the Apocalypse. He was a celebrated man of letters and rhetorician in Rome in the middle of 4th cent.

His conversion is the subject of the well-known narrative in St. Augustine's *Confessions* (bk. viii. cc. 2-5). In extreme old age zealous study of Scripture and Christian literature convinced him of the truth of Christianity. He told Simplician, afterwards bp. of Milan, that he was a Christian, and when Simplician refused to regard him as such till he saw him "in the church," asked him in banter "whether walls, then, make Christians?"—a characteristic question from one disposed to regard Christianity rather as another school of philosophy than as a social organization. The fear of his friends, however, which kept him from making profession of his faith, was removed by further meditation, and after being enrolled as a catechumen for a short time, he was baptized, and by his own deliberate choice made his preliminary profession of faith with the utmost publicity. St. Augustine gives us a vivid account of the excitement and joy his conversion caused in Christian circles at Rome. This was at least before the end of the reign of Constantius, A.D. 361; but he continued to teach rhetoric in Rome till 362, when Julian's edict forbad Christians to be public teachers (Aug. *Conf. l.c.*). Then, "choosing rather to give over the wordy school than God's Word," he withdrew, and as St. Jerome emphasizes his great age before conversion, it is not surprising that we hear no more of him. He lived, however, long enough to write a number of Christian treatises and commentaries, and it is possible that Jerome alludes to him as alive on the outbreak of the disputes connected with the name of Jovinian in 382. (See *Proleg.* to Victorinus in Migne's *Patr. Lat.* vol. viii. p. 994 for question of reading.)

The following is a list of his Christian writings: (1) The anti-Arian treatise, *de Generatione Verbi Divini*, in reply to the *de Generatione Divina* by Candidus the Arian. (2) The long work *adversus Arium*, elicited by Candidus's brief rejoinder to the former treatise. Bk. ii. must have been written not later than 361 (see c. 9), bk. i. *c.* 365 (see c. 28). (3) The *de ὁμοουσίῳ Recipiendo*, a summary of (2). (4) Three *Hymns*, mainly consisting of formulas and prayers intended to elucidate the relations of the Trinity. (5) Commentaries on Gal., Phil., and Eph. Though lacking continuous merit (see Lightfoot, *Gal.* p. 227), these are probably the first Latin commentaries on St. Paul's Epistles (see Hieron. *Comm. in Gal. Proleg.*). (6) An anti-Manichean treatise, with reasonable certainty ascribed to him (Migne, *Proleg.* § 3), *ad Justinum Manichaeum*, is the earliest extant treatise against the Manicheans, and insists with considerable insight on the inconsistencies of their dualism. (7) A very strange little treatise, *de Verbis Scripturae "Factum est vespere et mane dies unus."* For an Eng. trans. of the fragments see *Ante-Nicene Lib.*

Besides these we may notice the *de Physicis*, ascribed to him by Cardinal Mai (see his remarks in Migne prefixed to the treatise, p. 1295). It is an ably written treatise on the Creation, Fall, and Recovery of Man. But the style does not suggest the authorship of Victorinus, and the character of the quotations from N.T. seems to argue a different author.

We have some allusions in his extant works to others which have perished, *e.g.* on Eph. iv. 10 (lib. ii. *init.*) there is an allusion to a commentary on Cor. Cardinal Mai refers to a commentary on Leviticus by Victorinus extant in the Vatican (see Ceillier, *Auteurs sacrés*, vol. iv. p. 328, note 2).

All these writings of Victorinus (except the commentaries, which approach more nearly to lucidity) are very astonishingly obscure for one of Victorinus's reputation as a rhetorician. This, together with the recondite nature of the theological subjects he treats, the extremely corrupt condition of the text as hitherto edited, the barbarous mixture of Greek and bad Latin in which he often writes, and his prolixity and repetitions, have caused him to be ignored more than his substantial merits deserve. There is one notable exception to the usual severe judgments on his style and matter. Thomassin, whose theological judgment is weighty, speaks of him as "inferior to none in the profundity of his insight into the inmost mysteries" of the Divine Being, and the relation of the Persons of the Trinity to one another (*de Incarn. Verbi*, bk. ii. c. i. § 6). This judgment will put us on the right lines for estimating his position and powers. He has no special merits as a commentator, nor the capacities of a dogmatic theologian in the ordinary sense. He does not manipulate skilfully the stock anti-Arian arguments. He combats, generally as badly as possible, the objection to the ὁμοούσιος as an unscriptural term (*adv. Ar.* i. 30, p. 1063 B, C *; and ii. 8, 9, pp. 1094-1095). He has none of the controversial power and vividness of Athanasius or Augustine. Almost all his importance lies in his metaphysical and speculative capacities, and in his belief in the power of the intellect to give a rational presentation of the Trinitarian Creed, etc. He does, indeed, feel the danger of such speculation. "It is madness," he says (*adv. Justin.* 2, 1000 C), "to suppose that while we are almost unknown to ourselves, we should have either the capacity or the leave to investigate what lies beyond ourselves and the world." He rebukes Candidus for writing about God "tam audenter," and not keeping to Scripture. "Magnam tuam intelligentiam quis fascinavit?" he asks. "De Deo dicere, supra hominem audacia est" (*de Gen.* i. p. 1019 C, D). He ends his own first answer to Candidus with a striking prayer to God to forgive his sin involved in writing about God (*de Gen.*, *ad fin.*). But the "fascination" of such subjects he feels to the full, and, on the whole, he is sure that they are within the power of the illuminated Christian intellect. "Lift up thyself, my spirit!" he cries, "and recognize that to understand God is difficult, but not beyond hope" (*adv. Ar.* iii. 6, 1102 D).

* References are to vol. viii. of Migne's *Patr.* Gk.

The special character of his theology may be further explained by two epithets. (1) Though post-Nicene in date, it is *ante-Nicene* in character. The doctrine of the subordination of the Son is emphasized by him, and this very subordination doctrine is used against Arianism without the least suspicion of its being itself open to the charge of any Arianizing tendency. He sees, as boldly as the earlier theologians, anticipations of the Incarnation in the Theophanies of O.T. (*adv. Ar.* iv. 32, 1136 C). He retains the ante-Nicene interpretations of crucial texts—"My Father is greater than I" (John xiv. 28), etc. "What has come into being in Him was life" (John i. 3). He keeps the functions of the Incarnate in the closest possible relation to the cosmic function of the pre-Incarnate Word.

(2) His theology is *neo-Platonist* in tone. Here is the special interest attaching to Victorinus's works. He had grown old in the neo-Platonist schools before his conversion. When converted, he applied many principles of the Plotinian philosophy to the elucidation of the Christian mysteries. His importance in this respect has been entirely overlooked in the history of theology. He preceded the Pseudo-Dionysius. He anticipated a great deal in Scotus Erigena. If sometimes more neo-Platonist than Christian, this is no doubt due in part to the great age he had attained before studying Christian theology.

We deal with, I. his theological system; II. its relation to neo-Platonism; III. further points in his theology which demand notice; IV. his importance in relation to ante-Hieronymian versions of the Latin Bible.

I. The following is a summary of his mode of conceiving the relations of the Trinity and the processes of creation and redemption.

Candidus had objected to the orthodox doctrine that in asserting *generation* in God, it asserted *change* ("omnis generatio per mutationem est"), and thus contradicted the essential idea of God; and further that the idea of a "genitus Deus ex prae-existente substantia" is in contradiction to the "simplicity" of the Divine substance. Dwelling on ideas such as these of the Divine immutability and simplicity, he believed himself, in fighting against the Catholic doctrine, to be contending for the dignity of God, "the infinite, the incomprehensible, the unknowable, the invisible, the unchangeable" (Candidi Arian. *Lib. de Gen. Div.* 1-3; Migne, *Patr. Lat.* viii. 1015). Victorinus's reply is central and final. Your transcendent and immutable God is so conceived that He can come into no possible relation to anything beyond Himself. To become a creator at a certain moment in time—to act in creation as much involves *change* as the act of generation. If you admit, as you must, that God can create without change, you must admit equally that He can generate. You have admitted a "motus" which is not "mutatio" (*de Gen.* 30, 1035, A, B). But this proceeding forth of God in the action of creation is only not a "change" in the Divine Essence, because it has its origin and ground there. It has been the eternal being of God to proceed forth, to move, to live. This eternal motion, eternal transition in God, it is, that we, speaking in the necessarily inadequate terms of human discourse, call the "eternal generation of the Son" (*de Gen.* I, 1019 D; *de Gen.* 29, 1034 B; *adv. Arium*, i. 43, 1074 A, B. The "esse" of God is equivalent to "moveri," "et moveri ipsum quod est esse"). This "generatio" is expressed as the eternal utterance of the Divine Will, moving eternally into actuality; the will of God not for one instant failing of its absolutely self-adequate effect. "Every act of will is the progeny of that which wills." Thus of the Father's will, the Word or Son is the summary or universal effect.

As the Son is thus conceived of as the eternal object of the Divine will, so He is the eternal and adequate object of Divine self-knowledge. As the Father eternally wills, so He eternally knows Himself in the Son. The Divine knowledge, like the Divine will, must have its adequate object. God knows Himself in the Son; for the Son is the expression of His own being. The Son is thus the "forma" of God and His limitation. This thought constantly recurs. It is not that God is limited from outside, but that the infinite and the indeterminate in expressing Himself limits or conditions Himself. He knows Himself in the Logos or determinate, definite Utterance; and thus the unconditioned, the absolute, the Father, limits or conditions Himself in that eternal utterance by which He knows Himself. Knowledge is thus conceived of as limitation or form; it is an eternal abiding relation of subject and object. Once for all the Father knows Himself as what He is in the Son.

It is only stating this same principle in broader terms to say that the Son is to the Father as effect to cause (*adv. Arium*, iv. 3, 1115 A), that is to say, He is the revelation of all the Father is. What the Father *is*, the Son *expresses, exhibits, manifests*. As outward intelligence and life express our inner being, so the Father, the inner Being, is expressed in the Son. The Father is the *esse*, the *vivens*, the Son the *vita*, the actualized life (i. 32, 42). Substance can only be known by its manifestations in life (iii. 11, 1107 B). The Father is the "motio," the Son the "motus." What the Father is inwardly ("in abscondito") the Son is outwardly ("foris").

The passages in which the distinction between the ἐνδιάθετος and the προφορικὸς Λόγος are implied are not many nor emphatic in Victorinus, as, *e.g.*, in Tertullian. The Son is eternally Son and self-subsistent. That "effulgentia" "Filietas" is out of all time, absolute (i. 27, 1060 D). "Catholica disciplina dicit et semper fuisse Patrem et semper Filium" (*in Phil.* 1210 A). Yet Victorinus admits a sense in which he may be called "maxime filius" in Humanity (1061 A), and speaks of Him as getting the name of Son, the "Name above every Name," only in His Incarnate exaltation (1210 C, D, "ita ut tantum nomen accesserit, res eadem fuerit"). His thought expresses itself thus naturally in the doctrine of the generation of the Son and His co-essential equality with the Father. But it does not so easily adapt itself to formulae which express the Being, Procession, and Substantiality of the Holy Ghost. He intends to be perfectly orthodox. He accepts the faith, even though he finds it difficult to formulate. He teaches emphatically that the Holy Ghost proceeds "from the Father *and* the Son." He is subsequent in order to the Son. But as "Spirit of the Father" there is a sense in which He precedes the Son; that is, as that which God is—Spirit—He is that in which the Father begets the Son. He conveys the Father's Life to the Son.

The distinction of Son and Spirit is carefully maintained, but yet the essential duality which is in God—the distinction of that which is from that which proceeds forth—the distinction expressed in all the antitheses referred to above, is clearer to Victorinus than the Trinity of relations. The Son and the Spirit seem to him more utterly one than the Father and the Son. They are "existentiae duae," but they proceed forth "in uno motu" and that "motus" *is* the Son; so that the Spirit is, as it were, contained in the Son (*adv. Ar.* iii. 8, 1105 A). Thus Victorinus sometimes speaks as if the Spirit were the Son in another aspect (he even says "idem ipse et Christus et Spiritus Sanctus," see *ib.* iii. 18, 1113 D and i. 59, 1085 B). He has also a subtle mode of speaking of the Spirit as the "Λόγος in occulto," and Christ Incarnate as the "Λόγος in manifesto"; Logos and Spiritus being used interchangeably *; or again Christ is the "Spiritus apertus," the Spirit the "Spiritus occultus" (iii. 14, 1109 B, C). Again, the Spirit is the "interior Christi virtus" (iv. 17, 1125 C) in Whom Christ is present (1109 C). The confusion seems to spring from the use of "Spiritus" as meaning the Divine nature. But in intention and generally the two persons are kept distinct. If Christ is the "vox," the Spirit is the "vox vocis" (iii. 16, 1111 C, i. 13, 1048 A), or again, as the Son is Life the Spirit is Knowledge ("vivere quidem Christus, intelligere Spiritus," i. 13, 1048 B), or again the relations of the Trinity are expressed in formulas such as these: "visio, videre, discernere"; "esse, vivere, intelligere," expressing three stages of a great act (iii. 4, 5; the latter chapter should be studied). Victorinus is the first theologian to speak of the Spirit as the principle of unity in the Godhead, the bond or "copula" of the eternal Trinity, completing the perfect circle of the Divine Being, the return of God upon Himself (i. 60, 1085 C, D, "sphaera," "circularis motus").

* So the words "genitus," "procedens," are not kept strictly to the second and third Persons of the Trinity respectively. The Spirit is said once (*adv. Ar.* iv. 33, 1138 A) to be "genitus," and the "processio" of the Son is frequently spoken of, *e.g.* i. 27, 1060 D; i. 14, 1048 B.

We pass on to his conception of the relation of God to Creation. All things are conceived as pre-existing in God—potentially in the Father, actually in essence in the Son. In Him dwells all the fullness bodily, that is (according to V.) in the Eternal Word dwells all existence substantially—οὐσιακῶς. Whatever came into being subsequently in time, in Him was eternally Life. Thus the Λόγος is the "Λόγος of all things"—the universal Logos—the seed of all things, even in His Eternal Being, containing all things in Himself in archetypal reality. (*Adv. Ar.* i. 25, 1059 A; ii. 3, 1091 B; iii. 3, 1100 C, and iv. 4, 1116 C, where the Word is almost identified with the Platonic "ideas"; at least, He contains the ideas in Himself, as "species" or "potentiae principales.") It follows that the Son is very mainly considered as existing with a view to Creation. He exists as the "Λόγος of all that is" with a view to the being of whatever is ("ad id quod est esse iis quae sunt"). It is His essence to move, as it is the Father's to repose. The "motus" in virtue of which He is, is still pressing outward, so to speak, from the "fontana vita" of the Father.

All this is somewhat neo-Platonic in tone. What follows is almost pure and undiluted neo-Platonism, *e.g.* his description of the process of Creation, as a drawing out of the plenitude of God into a chain or gradation of existences. He adopts the neo-Platonic conception of "anima" as something capable of spiritualization, but not yet "spirit"—intermediate between spirit and matter. He follows neo-Platonism in his conception of the "return of all things" into God (*adv. Ar.* iii. 1, 1098 B; iv. 11, 1121 A, B; *de Gen.* 10, 1026 A, B; *adv. Ar.* iii. 3, 1100 C; Hymn 1, 1141 A; *in Eph.* i. 4, 1239 B, C). He is simply neo-Platonic in his conception of matter and the material world. "Matter" has no existence independent of God; in itself it is "non-existent"—an abstraction. Man is regarded as a mixed being, a spiritual "anima" (see *in Eph.* 1, 4, 1239 C) merged in the corruption of matter. He calls the human race "animae seminatae saeclis" corrupted by the material darkness in which they are merged (Hymn 1, 1142 A; *adv. Ar.* i. 26, 1060 A; i. 62, 1087 B). Misled by this ineradicable misconception of material life, he thinks in a Platonic and non-Christian spirit of men as existing in an unfallen condition, in a pre-mundane state of being, and being born into the corruption of material life at their natural birth. Moral evil, from this point of view, must be physical and necessary.

The other main effect of Platonism upon Victorinus's anthropology is to produce a profound and unmitigated Predestinarianism. His ideology leads him (in his *Comm. in Eph.* at least) to assert not only the pre-existence of the absolute "anima" in the Eternal Word, but the pre-existence of all particular souls. All the history of the soul in its descent into matter, and its recovery therefrom through the Incarnate Christ, is only the development of the idea of the soul which pre-existed eternally, individually, and substantially in the Mind and Will of God. (1245 C, 1243 C, 1238 C, 1239 B, 1242 B. What exists in God's thought must exist substantially.)

But these Platonizing elements in his teaching do not occupy all the ground. They lie side by side with the stock conceptions of Christian truth, no less emphasized sometimes than the Platonic views. Thus the common view of sin and responsibility and the origin of evil in the corrupt choice of the free will is emphasized several times (*e.g. ad Justin. Man.* 16, 1008 B), and it would seem that, much as the mode of conceiving Redemption which Victorinus adopts would lead to Universalism, he is not a Universalist. (*In Eph.* 1281 A, B; cf. 1282 C, D; 1286 B, C. On Universalism, see *in Phil.* 1221 B, "universos, *sed qui sequerentur*"; *in Eph.* 1245 B, "non omnia restaurantur sed quae in Christo sunt"; cf. 1274 C, "quae salvari possent." This interprets such passages as 1252 C.)

Again, though on one occasion the view given of the Incarnation is vitiated by the notion of the essential corruption of matter (*adv. Ar.* i. 58, 1084 C), in general his Incarnation teaching is strikingly sound and repudiates by anticipation a good deal of 5th-cent. heresy. God the Son enters into conditions of real humanity. He takes human nature whole and complete into the unity of a single Person (it is an "acceptio carnis," not a proper "generation" of a person), and He lives, God in Manhood ("*Deus in homine*" [homo = manhood] *adv. Ar.* i. 14, 1048 D; i. 45, 1075 B; *in Phil.* 1208 C, 1224 C.; he, however, uses an Adoptionist phrase, *adv. Ar.* i. 10, 1045 C.) The humanity which He takes is emphasized as universal ("universalis caro, universalis anima; in isto omnia universalia erant," iii. 3, 1101 A). Thus the passion in which He suffers for man's redemption is universal, because He suffers as representative of the race He is to re-create (*in Phil.* 1196 D, 1221 B, and *adv. Ar. l.c.*). The effect of Christ taking humanity is to make the whole of that which He assumed—soul and flesh—vital with new capacities of life. The "Word made flesh" makes the flesh He took to be life in Him Who is the Life ("omne quod Christus est vita aeterna est," etc., iv. 7, 1118 A; cf. language about Eucharist below); and in this humanity—spirit, soul, and body—which Christ took, He is glorified and exalted (iv. 7, 1118 B; cf. *in Eph.* 1259 B, "aeterna caro," "corporalis majestas"). Through it He lives in His people, so that they become what He is, through Him. They become part of the Christ. The church is Christ (*in Gal.* 1173 C, D; cf. 1184 B), and we are to be glorified, body and soul, in Christ (*in Phil.* 1226 A, B, 1227 A; cf. *in Eph.* 1255 B, "resurrectio Christi, resurrectio nostra").

Victorinus uses suggestive language about the sacraments and ministry of the church in relation to the communication to us of the life of Christ, *e.g.* (on baptism) *in Gal.* iii. 27; 1173 B and 1184 B; *in Eph.* v. 25, 1287 C; (on the Eucharist) *adv. Ar.* ii. 8, 1094 C ("quod accipimus Corpus Christi est, ipse autem Christus, vita est . . . divitiae in Christo *corporaliter* habitant"; cf. *adv. Ar.* i. 30, 1063 B, "Corpus ipsius Vita est, Corpus autem Panis." "Panis ἐπιούσιος," in the Lord's Prayer, is interpreted as "panis ex ipsa aut in ipsa Substantia, hoc est vitae panis," and referred to the Eucharist, and, in the same way, "populus περιούσιος" is given an Eucharistic reference, as meaning "populus circa Tuam Substantiam veniens." See quotation from old African Liturgy, p. 25; and (on ministry) *in Eph.* iv. 12, 1275 c.

II. It is necessary further to explain in what general relation Victorinus's teaching stands to the neo-Platonic system, since his chief claim upon our attention is that he was the first systematically to convert the results of that system to the uses of Christian theology and that he developed in one or two cases as against Arianism the really higher philosophical truth latent in Catholic doctrines.

The idea of a being or beings mediating between the supreme God and the lower world was common to almost all the later schools of ancient philosophy (see Zeller, pp. 219, 220). Eusebius of Caesarea had already seen in this a common ground for philosophers and Christians. (See Gwatkin's *Studies of Arianism*, p. 22. Cf. Athan. *de Incarn.* c. xli.) It appeared in Plotinus's theory of the νοῦς and anima, which with the One, the God, make up what is called "the neo-Platonic Trinity." Now, a good deal of Victorinus's language, in which he seeks to express the relation of the Λόγος to the Father, is based on Plotinus's language about the relation of the νοῦς to the One. But as a Christian, Victorinus is able to fill the neo-Platonic formulas with the powers of a new life. Again, Victorinus's formula for the Trinity, the "status, progressio, regressus," is the reflex of a neo-Platonic idea—an idea first definitely formulated by Proclus but implied by Plotinus—the idea of all progress and development of life involving (1) the immanence of the caused in that which causes it, (2) the issuing of the caused out of that which causes it, (3) the return of the caused into that which causes it. This threefold relation of immanence, progress, return, the neo-Platonist regarded as essential to the development and unity of life both in general and in detail (Zeller, pp. 787-789). This conception in its earlier stage Victorinus, whether consciously or not, adopts, and what new force it gains when it is seen to find its highest expression in the very life of God Himself! This threefold relation is seen to be the very being of God. The Son is eternally abiding in the Father, eternally proceeding from the Father in His eternal Generation, and eternally pouring back into the bosom of the Father that which He receives, in that Holy Ghost Who is Himself the life of Father and Son, the love and bond of the Holy Trinity.

It is in describing the relation of the Λόγος to the world, in His function as Creator, that, as we have seen, Victorinus allows himself to be too entirely moulded by neo-Platonic ideas. His "development of the plenitude" (Gwatkin, p. 20), his pre-existing "anima" and "animae," his corporeal demons, his matter the seat of corruption—all these have their source in the Plotinian system, and are only very imperfectly adapted to Christianity (see Zeller, pp. 545-557, 570-575). We may wonder that he did not use even more emphatically an element of right-minded inconsistency in neo-Platonism and with that system emphasize the freedom of the will (Zeller, pp. 585-587).

This brief account will help us to recognize the "divine preparation" for Christianity involved in the independent growth of the neo-Platonic system—so many philosophic ideas needed for the intellectual presentation of Christianity being made ready to hand—and shows Victorinus as a pioneer in claiming for Christianity the products of philosophy, a pioneer whose name has well-nigh passed into undeserved oblivion.

III. A few other characteristic points in Victorinus's teaching still deserve notice. He is an intensely ardent follower of St. Paul, devoted to St. Paul's strenuous assertion of justification by faith. Indeed, he uses very strongly solifidian language and (by anticipation) very strongly anti-Pelagian language. This element in his teaching is most remarkably emphatic in his commentaries, *e.g. in Gal.* iii. 22, 1172; *in Phil.* iii. 9, 1219 C, D. This solifidian tendency led him, like Luther, to a disparagement of St. James and a somewhat minimizing tone as regards the efficacy of good works. (See some very remarkable passages in *Comm. in Gal.* i. 19, 1155 B, C, 1156 A, B, cf. 1161 B, 1162 D.)

It is worth while calling attention to the evidence, suggested by a good deal of Victorinus's theology, of a closer connexion than has been yet noticed between him and St. Augustine. His strong insistence in his Trinitarian theology on the double Procession of the Holy Spirit—his conception of the Holy Spirit as the "Bond" of the Blessed Trinity—his emphasis on the unity of Christ and His church—his strong predestinarianism—his vehement assertion of the doctrines of grace—his assertion of the priority of faith to intelligence (p. 16, note n),—all reappear in St. Augustine, and it may be that the (hitherto unsuspected) influence of the writings of the old philosopher whose conversion stirred him so deeply was a determining force upon the theology of St. Augustine.*

IV. A word must be said on the Latin text of the Bible used by Victorinus. No adequate use seems yet to have been made of the very large bulk of quotation in his writings.

Sabatier (*Bibl. Sacr. Lat. Versiones Antiq.* t. iii. Remis 1749) occasionally refers to him, but omits some of his most remarkable quotations, and wrote before Mai's publication of the commentaries, etc. Some quotations, not noticed by Sabatier, may be given:

St. John i. 1 is quoted as "Λόγος erat *circa* Deum," and it is added, "Romani *apud* Deum dicunt," *Libri de Gen.* 20, 1030 c. Elsewhere he uses "circa Deum" and "ad Deum" (*adv. Ar.* 1, 3). These do not seem to be merely his own renderings. ("Ad Deum" is noticed by Sabatier.) In Phil. ii. 30 (p. 1216) "exponens in incertum animam suam" is a better

* There are one or two contributions to the history of heresies, made by Victorinus, which are worth noticing. *In Gal.* i. 19, we have an account of a Judaizing or Ebionite sect called the "Symmachians" (see pp. 1155 B and 1162 D). They made a point of the apostolate of James, the Lord's brother. See also for heresies in regard to Christ's person an interesting passage, *adv. Ar.* i. 45, 1075 B, C; cf. i. 28, 1061 B, C. He calls the definition of Nicaea "a wall and a defence" (ii. 9, 1095 D). We notice also that he probably is the first to use "paganus" for the heathen (*de Recip.* ὁμοουσίῳ, i.; *in Gal.* 1158 C). For the origin of the term *godfather* see *in Gal.* 1184 B.

rendering than the Vulgate "tradens" and the St. Germain "parabolatus de anima sua." *Ib.* iii. 20 (p. 1225) he uses "Salutaris" for *Saviour*, a term not found in other authorities in this place (cf. Rönsch, *Itala und Vulgata*, p. 100, 1875). *Ib.* iv. 3 (p. 1228) "unijuge" is a remarkable rendering of σύνζυγε. *Ib.* iv. 6, 7 (p. 1229) reads: "Nihil ad sollicitudinem redigatis, sed in omni precatione et oratione cum bona gratia petitiones vestrae innotescant apud Deum. Et pax Dei quae habet omnem intellectum custodiat corda vestra, item corpora vestra in Jesu Christo." St. Luke ii. 14: "Pax in terra *hominibus boni decreti*" (p. 1306). These words, from the *de Physicis*, conclude a long quotation thoroughly independent of any known version. Eph. iv. 14 (πρὸς τὴν μεθοδείαν τῆς πλανῆς), "ad *remedium* erroris" (p. 1276 B), a reading found also in other authorities. *Ib.* vi. 14, "et *omnibus effectis* stare," supports the correct reading of Jerome's text, "et *omnibus perfectis* stare." Tit. ii. 14: besides the version "populum abundantem" (p. 1094 D), a remarkable rendering of the word περιούσιον is given as occurring in a Eucharistic office ("the prayer of the oblation") to which he more than once refers (see *adv. Ar.* I, 30, 1063 B, and ii. 7, 1094 D). It is as follows: "Munda tibi populum *circumvitalem* emulatorem bonorum operum, *circa tuam substantiam venientem*" (p. 1063 B). [C.G.]

Victorius (2) of Aquitaine. During the pontificate of Leo the Great in 444 and 453 differences arose between the Western churches headed by Rome, and the Eastern headed by Alexandria as to the correct day for celebrating Easter. Pope LEO yielded on both occasions, but to avoid such disputes in future, directed his archdeacon HILARIUS, who succeeded him, to investigate the question. Hilary referred it to his friend Victorius, who in 457 drew up a cycle to determine the date of Easter in past and future years.

The cycle of 532 years, consisting of 28 Metonic (28 × 19) or rather 7 Calippic (7 × 76) cycles, was adopted or independently discovered by Victorius. He began it with the year of the crucifixion, which he placed on Mar. 26, in the consulship of the two Gemini. As the year in which he composed his cycle, the consulship of Constantinus and Rufus, which corresponds with A.D. 457, was the 430th of his cycle, its first year corresponded with A.D. 28. He made his earliest Easter limit Mar. 22, the same as the Alexandrians; his latest Apr. 24, while theirs was the 25th.

The cycle of Victorius was widely, though not universally, accepted in the West, and especially in Gaul. In 527, however, DIONYSIUS published a new period of the Cyrillian 95-year cycle, which would terminate in 531; and VICTOR of Capua, *c.* 550, wrote against Victorius's cycle and in favour of the Alexandrian method of computation. Victorius's cycle seems thereafter to have become disused in Italy, but lingered much later in parts of Gaul. It has been edited with elaborate dissertations by Bucherius, *de Doctrina Temporum*, where all notices of Victorius are collected. The only additional information they give is Gennadius's statement (*de Vir. Ill.* 88) that he was a native of Aquitaine. As Hilary calls him "Dilectissimus et honorabilis sanctus frater," he was probably in orders. A full account of his cycle is given by Ideler (*Handbuch d. Chronol.* ii. 275-285), who points out that what Dionysius did was to continue the 95-year cycle, and that there is no evidence that he did anything to the Victorian cycle. The fact that his continuation of the Cyrillian cycle began in 532, which would be the first year of a new period of the Victorian cycle if the latter commenced with the year of Christ's birth, probably suggested the notion that he had thus altered the beginning of the Victorian cycle, and started a new period of it from 532. Victorius is by later writers sometimes called Victorinus and Victor, the last mistake leading to confusion with Victor of Capua. [F.D.]

Victricius, St., 8th archbp. of Rouen, friend of St. Martin of Tours (Sulpic. Sev. *Dial.* iii. 2; Boll. *Acta SS.* Aug. ii. 194) and St. Paulinus of Nola, to whose letters we owe some details of his life. He became bp. of Rouen before 390, and occupied himself with the conversion of the heathen Morini and Nervii in Flanders and Brabant. He was summoned in 394 or 395 to Britain to assist the bishops there in re-establishing peace, probably in their contest with Pelagianism (Victricius, *Lib. de Laude SS.*, Migne, *Patr. Lat.* xx. 443). An accusation of heresy, as it seems (cf. Ceillier, viii. 76), brought him to Rome at the close of 403 to defend himself before the pope (Paulinus, *Ep.* xxxvii. [36], Migne, *Patr. Lat.* lxi. 353). While there he received, in answer to a request for information, the famous letter of Innocent I. called the *Liber Regularum*, treating of various heads of ecclesiastical practice and discipline (*Patr. Lat.* lvi. 519). [INNOCENTIUS.] The church at Rouen flourished under his care. The relics he obtained, the musical services he instituted, and the devotion—under his guidance—of the virgins and widows, caused the city, hitherto unknown, to be spoken of with reverence in distant lands, and counted among cities famed for their sacred spots (Paulinus, *Ep.* xviii. § 5, *Patr. Lat.* col. 239). In 409 he was apparently dead (*Ep.* xlviii. col. 398). (Migne, *Patr. Lat.* xx. 437, 438; *Hist. Litt.* ii. 752-754; Le Brun in Boll. *Acta SS. u.s.*; *Gall. Christ.* xi. 7.)

An extant treatise or sermon called the *Liber de Laude Sanctorum*, composed on the occasion of the receipt of some relics from St. Ambrose of Milan, was formerly ascribed to St. Germanus of Auxerre (*Hist. Litt.* ii. 261, 750), but the discovery of a MS. at St. Gall, in the 18th cent., made it clear that it belonged to Victricius (see *Praefatio* of the abbé Lebeuf in Migne, *Patr. Lat.* xx. 437-442). It gives a few details of the condition of the church at Rouen. Paulinus had perhaps read this document (*Ep.* xviii.). [S.A.B.]

Victurinus (1) (*Victor*), St., bp. of Grenoble, a correspondent of St. Avitus, of Vienne. Whether churches and church furniture which heretics had made use of could again, by virtue of a fresh consecration, be made serviceable for the orthodox, to which Avitus replies in the negative (Avitus, *Ep.* vi.), and as to the penalties to be inflicted in the case of marriage with a deceased wife's sister, which were very severe (*Epp.* xiv. xv. xvi.), are points on which he consulted the archbishop. He is among the bishops present at the council of Agaunum, in 515, if it is to be accepted as genuine, and also at Epaon and Lyons in 517. [S.A.B.]

Vigilantius (1), a presbyter of Comminges and Barcelona, known by his protests against superstitious practices in the church. He was born *c.* 370 at Calagurris, near Comminges (Convenae), a station on the great Roman road from Aquitaine to Spain (*Itiner. Antonin.* quoted in Gilly's *Vigilant.* p. 128). His father probably kept the *statio* or place of refreshment there; and Vigilantius was apparently brought up as an inn-keeper and wine-seller ("Iste Caupo Calagurritanus," Hieron. *cont. Vig.* 1), but had from the first an inclination to learning. Sulpicius Severus, who had estates in these parts, took him into his service, and probably baptized him. It is certain that in 395 he was sent with letters from Sulpicius to Paulinus, then recently settled at Nola (Paul. *Ep.* i. 11), by whom he was treated as a friend. Paulinus speaks of hm as "Vigilantius noster" (*Ep.* v. 11), and reports the care with which he had watched him during illness, refusing to let him depart till well. On his return to Severus, then living at Elusa in Gaul, he was ordained; and, having a desire for learning and a wish to visit Jerusalem, set forth by way of Nola. His father, it seems, had died, since he was wealthy enough to have many notaries in his employ (Hieron. *Ep.* lxi. 4), and he was the proprietor of the inn at Convenae (*ib.* lxi. 3; *cont. Vig.* i.). Paulinus gave him a very honourable introduction to Jerome (Hieron. *Ep.* lxi. 3), then living at Bethlehem, where he was received with great respect (lviii. 11). He remained there a considerable time, staying partly with Jerome, but partly, it is supposed, with others, possibly with Rufinus (Hieron. *Apol.* iii. 11). The schism between the monasteries of Bethlehem and the bp. of Jerusalem was at its height; and probably in connexion with this Vigilantius had his first disagreement with Jerome (Hieron. *Ep.* lxi. 1; *Apol.* iii. 19). Origenism, which had caused the schism, and with which Vigilantius afterwards connected Jerome's name, was, no doubt, the subject of this disagreement. But Vigilantius was brought to confess himself in the wrong and to ask pardon (Hieron. *Ep.* lxi. end). He was an inmate of Jerome's monastery on the occasion of a tremendous storm with earthquake and eclipse (*cont. Vig.* ii.). He was for a time favourably impressed by what he saw at Bethlehem, and on one occasion, when Jerome was preaching upon the reality of the body at the resurrection, sprang up, and with applause of hands and feet saluted Jerome as champion of orthodoxy (*Ep.* lxi. 3). But the extremes of asceticism, the corruption produced by indiscriminate almsgiving, and the violence, perhaps the insincerity, of Jerome's dealing with the question of Origen [HIERONYMUS, § *Origenism*] produced a reaction against Jerome. Vigilantius begged to be dismissed, and left in great haste (*Ep.* cix. 2) without giving any reason. He bore Jerome's reply to Paulinus at Nola (*Ep.* lxi. 11); but his journey home was first by Egypt (*ib.* 1; *cont. Ruf.* iii. 12), "by Hadria and the Cottian Alps" (Hieron. *Ep.* cix. 12). He landed probably at Naples, and, after visiting Nola, went home by the land route, staying a considerable time at various places. His account of what he had seen in the East, which was related to Jerome either by report or by some writing of Vigilantius to or about Jerome, provoked a reply (*Ep.* lxi.), wherein Jerome shews a jealous sensitiveness for his own orthodox reputation, and treats him with contempt, declaring that he had never understood the points in dispute (lxi. 1). On his return to Gaul, Vigilantius settled in his native country.

His work against superstitious practices was written *c.* 403. We may presume that his intercourse with Severus, Paulinus, and Jerome furnished the principal motives and materials for it. Similar practices no doubt arising in a grosser form in his own neighbourhood among a population emerging from heathenism provoked his protest against the introduction of heathen ceremonial into Christian worship. The work is only known to us through the writings of Jerome, of whose unscrupulousness and violence in controversy we have many proofs. Nothing of the kind appears in the quotations from the book of Vigilantius, which, considering the extreme difficulty of his position in the rising flood of superstition, we must presume to have been a serious and faithful protest. It was not written hastily, under provocation, such as he may have felt in leaving Bethlehem, but after the lapse of six or seven years. His own bishop (Hieron. *Ep.* cix. 2) and others in his neighbourhood (*cont. Vig.* ii.) approved his action, and he was apparently appointed after the controversy to a church in the diocese of Barcelona (Gennad. *ut infra*).

The points against which he argues are four: (1) The superstitious reverence paid to the remains of holy men, which were carried round in the church assemblies in gold vessels or silken wrappings to be kissed, and the prayers in which their intercession was asked; (2) the late and frequent watchings at the basilicas of the martyrs, from which scandals constantly arose, the burning of numerous tapers, which was a heathen practice, the stress laid on the miracles performed at the shrines, which, Vigilantius maintained, were of use only to unbelievers; (3) the sending of alms to Jerusalem, which might better have been given to the poor in each diocese, and generally the monkish habit of divesting oneself of possessions which should be administered as a trust by the possessor; and (4) the special virtue attributed to the unmarried state. Vigilantius held that for the clergy to be married was an advantage to the church; and he looked upon the solitary life as a cowardly forsaking of responsibility.

The bishop of the diocese (possibly Exuperius of Toulouse, known to have had communications with pope Innocent about this time on points of discipline) strongly favoured the views of Vigilantius, and they began to spread widely in S. Gaul. The clergy who were fostering the practices impugned by him found their people imbibing his opinions, and two of them, Desiderius and Riparius, wrote to Jerome, representing the opinions of Vigilantius and asking for his advice. Jerome answered Riparius at once (*Ep.* 109, ed. Vall.), expressing chagrin and indignation but without sober argument. He declares that no adoration was paid to martyrs, but that their relics were honoured as a means of worshipping God. He expresses wonder that the bishop of the diocese should acquiesce in Vigilantius's madness. It was a case for such dealing as that of Peter with Ananias and Sapphira. He offered to answer more fully if the work of Vigilantius were sent him. This offer was accepted. Through their friend Sisinnius, Riparius and Desiderius sent the book in the latter part of 406 (*Pref. to Comm. on Zach.*). Jerome gave little attention to it at first, but finding Sisinnius obliged to leave Bethlehem in haste, sat down, and in one night wrote his treatise *contra Vigilantium*. This treatise has less of reason and more of mere abuse than any which he wrote. He throughout imputes to his adversary extreme views, which it may certainly be assumed he did not hold.

What effect was produced by this philippic is unknown. Possibly Exuperius, if Vigilantius was in his diocese, by degrees changed towards him, and that it was on this account that Vigilantius passed into the diocese of Barcelona, where Gennadius places him. Jerome in his *Apology* (iii. 19) expressly repels the imputation of having asserted that the character of Vigilantius had been stained by communion with heretics. But the official leaders of the church came to reckon as enemies those whom Jerome had so treated, and Vigilantius was by degrees ranked among heretics. The judgment of Gennadius (*de Sc. Eccl.* 35) is: "Vigilantius the presbyter, a Gaul by birth, held a church in the Spanish diocese of Barcelona. He wrote with a certain zeal for religion; but was led astray by the praise of men, and presumed beyond his strength; and being a man of elegant speech but not trained in discerning the sense of the Scriptures, interpreted in a perverse manner the second vision of Daniel, and put forth other works of no value, which must be placed in the catalogue of heretical writings. He was answered by the blessed presbyter Jerome." This judgment lasted long. In 1844 Dr. Gilly, canon of Durham, published a work on *Vigilantius and his Times* (Seeley), bringing together all the known facts, and shewing the true significance of his protest by describing the life of Severus, Paulinus, and Jerome from their own writings. [W.H.F.]

Vigilius (4) Thapsensis, an African bishop mentioned in the *Notitia* published at the end of the *Historia* of Victor Vitensis, was present at the conference convened by the Vandal Hunneric in 484. He belonged to the Byzacene province, and was banished by the Vandal king. He seems to have fled to Constantinople, where he wrote against Eutychianism and Arianism. He published one work alone under his own name, viz. his five books against Eutyches, stating very clearly the usual arguments against the Eutychian system. An extremely good and copious analysis of it is in Ceillier (x. 472-485). It is an interesting specimen of 5th and 6th cent. controversy, and shews the evolution of thought among the Eutychians who in his day had not completed or thought out their system. They had not fixed, *e.g.*, on a date for the disappearance of Christ's human nature. A cent. or so later they determined upon the resurrection as the time when the human nature was swallowed up in the divine. Vigilius refers to this in bk. i. as a view taught by some, not by all. In bk. iv. he discusses the Tome of St. Leo and the orthodoxy of the decrees of Chalcedon, and has some remarks, important for liturgiology, on the form of the creed used at Rome ("Creed," *D. C. B.* 4-vol. ed.). He defends St. Leo on the ground that he quoted the creed used in the Romish church from apostolic times. Vigilius wrote several works under various distinguished names. Thus Chifflet, whose is the best edition (Dijon, 1664) of his writings, attributes to him a dialogue in 12 books on the *Trinity*, printed among the works of St. Athanasius, a treatise against an Arian called Varimadus published under the name of Idacius Clarus, a book against Felicianus the Arian under that of St. Augustine; and two conferences, in which he represents Athanasius as disputing against Arius before a judge named Probus, who of course gives sentence against Arius. These conferences he published in two editions, one in two books, where Athanasius and Arius alone appear; another in three books, in which Sabellius and Photinus are introduced. His authorship of these conferences is absolutely certain, because in his *contra Eutych.* (bk. v. p. 58) he speaks of his argument "in eis libris quos adversus Sabellium, Photinum et Arianum sub nomine Athanasii, conscripsimus." Chifflet also ascribes to him a treatise against Palladius, an Arian bishop, printed among the works of St. Ambrose and of Gregory Nazianzen, and also the Acts of the council of Aquileia found among the *Epp.* of St. Ambrose. The Athanasian Creed has also been attributed to him, chiefly because both in the creed and in his treatise against Eutyches the union of two natures in man is brought forward as an explanation of the union of two natures in the one person of Jesus Christ. Chifflet's edition and elaborate commentary, which includes the works of Victor Vitensis, is reprinted by Migne, *Patr. Lat.* t. lxii. [G.T.S.]

Vigilius (5), bp. of Rome, intruded into the see in the room of Silverius, A.D. 537, by Belisarius, by order of the empress Theodora. By birth a Roman of good position, he had accompanied AGAPETUS as one of his deacons when that pope went to Constantinople A.D. 536 and procured from Justinian the deposition of the Monophysite patriarch Anthimus, and the appointment of Mennas in his room. The Monophysite party (then called commonly the ACEPHALI), who continued to reject the council of Chalcedon, had a resolute supporter in the empress Theodora. Agapetus dying April, 536, when about to depart for Rome, she sent for Vigilius and promised him an order to Belisarius to get him ordained pope if he would secretly undertake to disallow the council of Chalcedon. Vigilius (says Liberatus) willingly complied, and proceeded to Rome, but found SILVERIUS already ordained.

Vigilius having been thus ordained in 537 (on Nov. 22, according to the conclusion of Pagi; on Mar. 25, according to that of Mansi), and the death of Silverius having been certainly not earlier than June 20, 538, for at least seven months his position was that of an unlawful antipope, his predecessor never having been canonically deposed. However, as pope he was accepted, the deposition of bishops and the ordination of others in their room under imperial dictation being at that time, however irregular, common enough elsewhere; and the ancients seem to have dated his episcopate from his intrusion.

Through Antonina, the wife of Belisarius and the real agent of the empress throughout, Vigilius sent without delay letters to Anthimus, Theodosius, and Severus, in fulfilment of his secret promise, expressing his entire agreement with them in matters of faith, but charging them to keep his avowal in the dark, that he might more easily accomplish what he had undertaken. He added a confession of his own faith, condemning the Tome of pope Leo (in which the orthodox doctrine of two Natures in Christ was enunciated), and anathematizing Paul of Samosata, Diodorus of Tarsus, Theodore of Mopsuestia, Theodoret, and all who agreed with them. Binius and Baronius, jealous for the credit of the Roman see, argue that this letter was forged by the Monophysite party. But no valid ground has been adduced for suspecting it. It is given by Liberatus and Victor Tununensis; and Facundus (*c. Mocianum*), like them a contemporary, seemingly alludes to it. Pagi (Baron. *ad ann.* 538) refutes all the arguments of Baronius, while alleging that the Roman see was not compromised, since Vigilius was not the true pope when he wrote.

Justinian was evidently kept in the dark about these secret proceedings, since, after the death of Silverius, he wrote to Vigilius, sending a confession of his own faith and recognizing him as pope without any suspicion of his orthodoxy. In his reply, dated 540, Vigilius declares himself altogether orthodox, accepts the Tome of Leo and the council of Chalcedon, and condemns by name all abettors of the Eutychian heresy.

In 541 began at Constantinople the new theological disputes which led to the 2nd council of Constantinople (called the 5th oecumenical), in the course of which Vigilius came in conflict with the emperor. Peter, the patriarch of Jerusalem, who was opposed to the Origenists, sent two abbats to Constantinople, with a letter to the emperor, and extracts from Origen's writings, complaining of the commotions excited by the Origenistic party and praying for their condemnation (*Vit. S. Sabae*). The emperor, readily acceding, issued a long edict, addressed to the patriarch Mennas, setting forth and confuting the heresies attributed to Origen; commanding the patriarch to assemble the bishops and abbats then at Constantinople for the purpose of anathematizing him, his doctrine, and his followers, and to suffer no bishop or abbat to be thenceforth appointed except on condition of doing the same. There seems to have been no resistance to this imperial command.

Justinian was engaged, we are told, after his condemnation of Origen, in composing a treatise on the Incarnation in defence of the council of Chalcedon and in refutation of the Eutychians. But there were two Origenistic abbats from Palestine, resident at his court, in great credit with him, Theodore of Ascidas and Domitian, who suggested that he might better serve the cause of orthodoxy by procuring a condemnation of certain writers accused of Nestorianism but acquitted by the council of Chalcedon, viz. Theodore of Mopsuestia, Theodoret of Cyrus, and Ibas, the alleged author of a letter to Maris. It was represented to the emperor that, if these were now authoritatively condemned and the council of Chalcedon freed from the imputation of having approved their errors, the Acephali would no longer refuse to accept that council. The emperor, who warmly desired this reconciliation, readily fell into the snare. The writings thus prepared for condemnation are known as the "Three Chapters" ("Tria Capitula"). The imperial edict against them (περὶ τριῶν κεφαλαίων), issued probably *c.* 544, anathematized their deceased authors and all defenders of them, with a saving clause to guard against any inculpation of the council of Chalcedon. But the edict was regarded as disparaging its authority. Mennas, at first refusing, at length gave his acquiescence in writing. The three other patriarchs of the East also yielded to threats of deposition, as did the rest of the Eastern bishops, except a few who were deposed and banished. In the West, less accustomed to imperial despotism, there was more difficulty. Vigilius, from his antecedents, might have been expected to obey, but shewed considerable independence of spirit, being probably influenced by the prevailing feeling at Rome and in the West generally. He refused his assent to the emperor's edict, and being thereupon summoned peremptorily to Constantinople, unwillingly obeyed.

He sailed first to Sicily, where he was joined by Datius, bp. of Milan, a resolute opponent of the condemnation of the Three Chapters. Arrived at Constantinople (A.D. 547), he persevered for a time in the same attitude, but before long gave a secret promise to condemn the Chapters (Facund. *c. Moc.*), and presided over a synod with the hope of inducing it to do what the emperor required. Meeting opposition there, especially from bp. Facundus of Ermiana, who requested leave to argue the question (Facundus himself tells the story), he suspended the proceedings, requiring the bishops separately to send him their opinions in writing. Seventy bishops were thus induced to declare for the condemnation of the Chapters, including many who had previously refused. Vigilius, supported by these 70 signatories, issued the document known as his *Judicatum*, addressed to Mennas, on Easter Eve, 548 (*Ep.* Vigilii, *ad Rustianum et Sebastianum*), condemning the Chapters, though disavowing any disparagement of Chalcedon. The *Judicatum* provoked serious opposition. At Constantinople Facundus continued resolute, protesting against bishops who betrayed their trust to win favour with princes. Vigilius's own deacons, Rusticus and Sebastianus, declared against him, but were deposed and excommunicated. The bishops of Illyricum condemned the *Judicatum* in synod; those of N. Africa did the same, and even formally excommunicated Vigilius (Vict. Tunun. *ad ann.* 549, 550). Alarmed by these consequences, Vigilius now recalled his *Judicatum*, and seems to have represented to the Westerns that he had issued it unwillingly. Facundus attributes his whole action to desire of court favour and position, as his earlier secret promise to Theodora had been due to ambition. Vigilius could not now undo what he had done, for the *Judicatum* was known far and wide. If any further proof were needed of his double dealing we should have a signal one in the fact (if it be one) that, even while thus trying to persuade the Westerns that he was on their side, he was induced by the emperor to take a secret oath before him to do all he could to bring about the condemnation of the Three Chapters. The oath, dated the 23rd year of Justinian, is given among the Acts of the 7th session of the 5th council (Labbe, vol. vi. p. 194). There seems to be no sufficient reason to doubt its genuineness. In it he swore to unite with the emperor to the utmost of his power to cause the Chapters to be condemned and anathematized, and to take no measures or counsels with any one in their favour against the emperor's will. The result of his crooked policy was that neither party trusted him.

In the year in which the *Judicatum* was issued Theodora died; but the emperor continued resolute in carrying out his project for the condemnation of the Three Chapters by full ecclesiastical authority. Vigilius, hampered by the repudiation of his *Judicatum* in the West and by his own secret understanding with the emperor, would gladly have left the scene of action. But his presence was still required at Constantinople by the emperor. The plan he now adopted was to persuade the emperor to summon the bishops, both of the East and West (including especially those of Africa and Illyricum who had shewn themselves so strongly opposed to the *Judicatum*), to a council at Constantinople, and meanwhile to take no further steps. Justinian acted on his advice; but though the obsequious Easterns obeyed the summons, very few of the Westerns came—a small number from Italy, two from Illyricum, but none from Africa. Justinian would have had Vigilius proceed at once with such bishops as were in Constantinople. Vigilius, with considerable spirit, refused. Thereupon the emperor issued a new edict against the Chapters, which he caused to be posted in the churches. Vigilius protested against this as a violation of their agreement, called an assembly of bishops in the palace of Placidia where he lodged, conjured them to use their efforts to procure a revocation of the edict till the episcopate of the West should have an opportunity of pronouncing its opinion, and in virtue of the authority of the apostolic see declared all excommunicated who should meanwhile sign or receive it. Justinian sent the praetor whose office it was to apprehend common malefactors, with an armed band, to seize the pope in his place of refuge. Vigilius escaped to Chalcedon, and there sought sanctuary in the church of St. Euphemia two days before Christmas, 551. No attempt was made to violate this sanctuary. The pope was able from it to dictate terms on which he would take part in the forthcoming council. The emperor, anxious to secure his concurrence at the council, at length acceded to his conditions, and revoked the edict.

Vigilius returned to Constantinople towards the end of 552, after nearly a year in St. Euphemia. Justinian summoned the council to meet on May 5, 553. The Easterns met, in number 165, under the presidency of Eutychius, who had succeeded on the death of Mennas. Vigilius and the Westerns kept aloof, assembling by themselves in the Placidian palace, and prepared a very lengthy document, known as his *Constitutum ad Imperatoren*, addressed to the emperor. It refutes extracts that had been made from the works of Theodorus of Mopsuestia, and condemns the views expressed as heretical, but proceeds to protest against the condemnation of Theodorus himself as a heretic after his death, since he had not been so condemned when alive and had died in communion with the church; and also against any such condemnation of Theodoret or of the letter of Ibas, both having been acquitted of heresy by the council of Chalcedon. This *Constitutum*, dated May 14, 553, was signed also by 16 Western bishops. It does not appear that the emperor transmitted it to the council; but he handed in, on May 26, a statement of how Vigilius had once himself condemned the Chapters, had pledged himself to do so by word, writing, and solemn oath, and had been invited to the council and refused to come. Anathemas were pronounced against Theodorus of Mopsuestia and his writings, against the inculpated writings, but not the persons, of Theodoret and Ibas; and all who should continue to defend the condemned writings were, if ecclesiastics, to be deprived, if monks or laymen, excommunicated.

Vigilius soon changed sides once more, assenting to the decrees of the council, and thus giving them at length the sanction of the Roman see. That he did this is indisputable, and according to Evagrius (lib. iv. c. 34) in writing, ἐγγράφως; nor does there seem valid reason to doubt the genuineness of the two written documents in which his recantation is declared. The first of these is a letter to the patriarch Eutychius, dated Dec. 8, 553, *i.e.* six months after the conclusion of the council. The other document (dated Feb. 23, 554) is entitled "Constitutum Vigilii pro damnatione Trium Capitulorum" (given in Labbe, vol. vi. p. 239). It expresses entire agreement with the decisions of the council, and ends with the same declaration, word for word, as the letter to Eutychius.

Justinian, having thus attained his end, Vigilius was allowed to leave Constantinople for Rome, after a compelled absence of 7 years, the emperor giving him certain grants, privileges, and exemptions for the people of Rome and Italy (Baron. *ad ann.* 554, ix. x. xi. xii.). But he died on his way at Syracuse towards the end of 554 or early in 555. His body was conveyed to Rome and buried in the church of St. Marcellus on the Salarian Way.

He was evidently a man with no firmness of character or principle. The attempts of Baronius to vindicate his conduct after he had become lawful pope, though allowing him to have been a poor creature before, are pitiably unavailing. To his final submission to Justinian's will is due the important fact that the Fifth council, the origin, purpose, and conduct of which had so little to commend them, came at last to be universally accepted, in the West as well as the East, though not without prolonged resistance in some parts of the West, as oecumenical and authoritative. For, though its anathemas against the dead and their writings were passed under imperial dictation in defiance of the pope and of the Western church, Vigilius's eventual approval of them was endorsed by his successors.

There is no lack of contemporary authority for the history given above—viz. the *Breviarium* of Liberatus, archdeacon of Carthage; the *Eccl. Hist.* of Evagrius; the *Chronicon* of Victor, bp. of Tununum; the *Pro Defensione Trium Capitulorum,* and the *Liber contra Mocianum* of Facundus, bp. of Ermiana; and the *Hist. Bell. Goth.* and the *Anecdota,* or *Hist. Arcana,* of Procopius. The writings of Facundus are peculiarly valuable in giving an insight into the state of parties, and the course of events in which he was himself implicated, having been, with Victor Tununensis, a prominent opponent at Constantinople of the condemnation of the Three Chapters. We have also the letters written by Vigilius, of great historical value, and the Acts of the Fifth council, with contemporary documents preserved among them. [J.B—Y.]

Vincentius (8), presbyter of Constantinople, intimately attached to Jerome, through whose writings we hear of him throughout the last 20 years of 4th cent. Jerome became acquainted with him when he came to Constantinople in 380, from which time Vincentius shared his interests and pursuits. To him, with Gallienus, Jerome dedicated his translation of Eusebius's *Chronicle* in 382 (Hieron. *cont. Joan. Hieros.* c. 41). We may therefore suppose he was ordained early in 382. But he never fulfilled the office of presbyter. That he knew Greek and Latin and was interested in general history is shewn by Jerome's preface to the *Chronicle* of Eusebius. He shared Jerome's admiration of Origen, then at its height, and asked Jerome to translate all his works into Latin. In 382 he accompanied Jerome to Rome, but without intending to stay there. We do not hear of him during Jerome's stay, but they left Rome together in 385 and settled at Bethlehem (*cont. Ruf.* iii. 22). He shared Jerome's studies and his asceticism and controversial antipathies. He was severe in his judgment upon Vigilantius (Hieron. *Ep.* lxi. 3, A.D. 396), and co-operated eagerly in the subsequent condemnation of Origenism. In 396 or 397 he went to Rome, for what cause is unknown (*cont. Ruf.* iii. 24). No doubt he took part in the proceedings against Origenism, in which Eusebius of Cremona and Jerome's Roman friends were actively engaged. On his return to Bethlehem in 400 he was full of the subject. All Rome and Italy, he reported, had been delivered; and his praise of Theophilus of Alexandria as having by his letter to the pope Anastasius procured this deliverance is communicated to that prelate in Jerome's letter (*Ep.* 88, ed. Vall.) to him, the last mention of Vincentius which we have. [W.H.F.]

Vincentius (11) **Lirinensis** (*Vincent of Lerins*), St., a distinguished presbyter of Gaul in 5th cent. Date of birth uncertain; must have died in or before A.D. 450.

Authorities.—Gennadius, *Vivorum Illustrium Catalogus* (c. 64). References to himself and to his times in his chief (most probably his sole) work, the *Commonitorium.*

Life.—Concerning the events of Vincent's life we are almost entirely ignorant. He was a native of Gaul, possibly brother of St. Loup, bp. of Troyes [LUPUS (2)], involved in the turmoils of worldly life before his retirement into a monastery near a small town, remote from the stir of cities. This was that of Lerins (*Lerinum*), situated in the island of that name near Antibes, now known as *L'Ile de St. Honorat,* from the founder of this celebrated institution. Here he wrote *adversus Profanas Omnium Novitates Haereticorum Commonitorium,* almost 3 years (as he tells us in c. 42) after the council of Ephesus, *i.e.* in 434.

Writings.—The only one *universally* admitted to be the genuine and authentic pro duction of Vincent is briefly known as *Commonitorium.* In the form in which we have it it extends, even in a 12mo ed., to only 150 pages, and consists of 42 short chapters. *Peregrinus* (as Vincent called himself) begins by stating that he thought it might be useful and in accordance with scriptural precepts (Deut. xxxii. 7; Prov. xxii. 17, iii. 1) to write down certain principles which he had received from holy Fathers. His tests to discern the truth of the Catholic faith from heresy will be sought first in *the authority of the divine law,* and next in *the tradition of the Catholic church.* The second source of information would not be needed had not all the leading heretics claimed the support of Holy Scripture (cc. i. ii.). We must hold that which has been believed everywhere, always, by all ("quod ubique, quod semper, quod ab omnibus creditum est"); in other words, we must follow *Universitatem, Antiquitatem, Consensionem*; understanding by the last the agreement of all, or almost all, bishops and doctors (c. ii.). A small portion of the church dissenting from the rest must be cut off like an unsound limb; nay, even a large portion if it does not abide by antiquity. Illustrations are afforded negatively by Donatism and Arianism; positively by the teaching of St. Ambrose and other eminent confessors (cc. iv.-viii.). Antiquity was on the side of pope Stephen, bp. of the apostolic see, and against the excellent Agrippinus, bp. of Carthage, who desired to rebaptize heretics. True, the rebaptizers claim the sanction of the holy Cyprian; but to do so is behaving like Ham towards Noah, for on this point that pious martyr erred (cc. ix.-xi.). Apostolic warrant for what has been advanced may be found in St. Paul's writings, *e.g.* in Tim. and Tit. (*passim*), Rom. xv. 17, and Gal. i. 7-10. Those who would make accretions to the faith stand thereby condemned for all time. The Pelagians are such (cc. xii.-xiv.). Valentinus, Photinus, Apollinaris, and others are similarly condemned by the warnings of Moses (Deut. xiii. 1-11). Even good gifts, such as those of Nestorius, or useful labours like those of Apollinaris against Porphyry, cannot be pleaded against their novelties (cc. xv. xvi.). He explains with some minuteness wherein consisted the heresies of Photinus, Apollinaris, and Nestorius, and the true doctrine of the church as opposed to them (cc. xvii.-xxii.).

The danger of ignoring the principles here laid down, more especially the test of antiquity, is painfully exhibited in the case of Origen, whose acute, profound, and brilliant genius (fully recognized by imperial disciples and the church at large) has not saved his writings from becoming a source of temptation; though it is just possible, as some think, that they may have been tampered with (c. xxii.). A very similar judgment must be passed upon Tertullian, of whom Hilary (of Poictiers) too truly said that "by his errors he had diminished the authority due to his approved writings" (c. xxiv.). The true and genuine Catholic is he who loves Christ's body, the Church; who puts God's truth before all things, before any individual authority, affection, genius, eloquence, or philosophy. Many who fall short of this standard, when not slain, are yet sadly stunted in their spiritual growth (c. xxv.). Additions to the faith or detractions from it are alike condemned by Holy Scripture, especially by St. Paul (I. Tim. vi.). The deposit is the talent of the Catholic faith, which the man of God must, like a spiritual Bezaleel, adorn, arrange, and display to others, but not injure by novelties (cc. xxvi. xxvii.). Certainly there is to be progress ("profectus religionis"), but it must resemble the growth of the infant into manhood and maturity—a growth which preserves identity. The dogmas of the heavenly philosophy may by the operation of time be smoothed and polished, and gain, by greater fullness of evidence, light and elucidation ("distinctionem"), but they must retain integrity and all essential characteristics (cc. xxviii.-xxx.). Such has been the church's task in the decrees of councils, which have simply aimed at adding clearness, vigour, and zeal to what was believed, taught, and practised already (cc. xxx.-xxxii.). St. John, in his 2nd epistle, is as emphatic as St. Paul against the teacher of false doctrine. Such an one cannot be encouraged without a virtual rejection of saints, confessors, and martyrs—a rejection, in short, of the holy church throughout the world. Pelagius (with his disciple Coelestius), Arius, Sabellius, Novatian, Simon Magus, were all introducers of novelties (cc. xxxiii. xxxiv.). The heretics use the Scriptures, but only in the way in which bitter potions are disguised for children by a previous taste of honey, or poisons labelled as healing medicines. The Saviour warned us against such perils by His words concerning wolves in sheep's clothing. We must attend to His subsequent advice, *by their fruits ye shall know them.* His apostle bids us beware of false apostles (II. Cor. xi. 13-15), the imitators of Satan, who transform themselves into angels of light. Their employment of Scripture resembles that of Satan in the temptation of our Lord. They presume, in the teeth of the teaching of the church, to claim a special illumination for their own small conventicle (cc. xxxv.-xxxvii.). Catholics must apply to the interpretation of Scripture the tests of universality, antiquity, and consent. Where they can, let them adduce the decrees of general councils; failing those, the consistent rulings of great doctors. This does not apply to small questions, but only to whatsoever affects the rule of faith. Inveterate heresies can generally be met by Holy Scripture alone, or by clear decisions of oecumenical councils. New ones often present at first greater difficulty, and we must be careful to cite those Fathers only who lived and died in the faith. What all or the majority clearly and perseveringly received, held, and taught, let that be held as undoubted, certain, and ratified. But any merely private opinion, even of a saint or martyr, must be put aside. This again agrees with St. Paul (I. Cor. i. 10, xii. 27, 28, xiv. 33, 36; Eph. iv. 11). That Pelagian writer Julian neglected these cautions, and broke away from the sentiments of his colleagues (cc. xxxviii.-xl.).

Bk. ii., as Gennadius informs us, was mostly lost, having been stolen from its author, who gives a recapitulation of its substance, which occupies 3 additional chapters. The first of these (c. xli.) simply re-states the main proposition of the earlier book. The author then, to shew that his view is no offspring of private presumption, adduces the example of the council of Ephesus, held nearly 3 years before the time of writing, in the consulship of Bassus and Antiochus. Great pains were taken to avoid an unfortunate issue, such as that of the council of Rimini (*Concil. Ariminense*); and the testimonies of martyrs, confessors, and orthodox doctors were considered by an assemblage of nearly 200 bishops to prove Nestorius an irreligious impugner of Catholic truth, and Cyril to be in accordance with it. Amongst the saintly doctors present in person, or whose works were cited as authoritative, were Peter of Alexandria, Athanasius, Theophilus, Cyril, Gregory Nazianzen, Basil and his excellent brother Gregory of Nyssa. The West was represented by letters of Felix and of Julius, bps. of Rome; the South by the evidence of Cyprian of Carthage; the North by that of Ambrose of Milan. The whole of the bishops, for the most part metropolitans, acted upon the principles maintained in this treatise and censured Nestorius for his unhallowed presumption—that he was the first and only man who rightly understood the Scriptures (xli.).

One element must be added, lest to all this weight anything seem lacking, namely, the authority of the apostolic see, which was illustrated by the twofold testimony of the reigning pope, SIXTUS III., and of his predecessor Coelestine. It was on the principles herein set forth that pope Sixtus condemned Nestorius; and Coelestine wrote in the same spirit to certain priests in Gaul who were fostering novelties. It is, in fact, an acceptance of the warning of St. Paul to Timothy to keep *the deposit* (I. Tim. vi. 20, R.V. marg.) and to the Galatians, that he would be *anathema* who should preach to them any other gospel (Gal. i. 8). Justly upon these grounds are Pelagius and Coelestius as well as Nestorius condemned * (xlii.).

* It must be owned that there is a certain amount of difficulty, one may almost say mystery, connected with these last two chapters. In the first place, they

It may safely be asserted that few theological books of such modest bulk, published within our period, have attracted so large a share of attention. It has been included in all the best known collections of the Fathers (*e.g.* in the *Maxima Bibliotheca Patrum*, Lugduni, A.D. 1677; and in that of Migne), repeatedly published separately in many lands, and not unfrequently translated. A Scottish trans., dedicated to Mary Queen of Scots, was issued by Knox's opponent, Ninian Winzeit, at Antwerp, in 1563 *; an Engl. one in Schaff and Wace's *Post-Nicene Lib.* by Dr. Heurtley, and another by Rev. W. B. Flower (Lond. 1866).

The *Commonitorium* has gathered around itself a literature. How far its leading principles have been accepted, either explicitly or implicitly, in the past; how far they made a line of demarcation between those who accepted or rejected the Reformation; to what extent they are available in the controversies between the various Christian communions, or in the contest between Christianity and unbelief—these questions have all been keenly discussed. To review these controversies would far exceed our limits, but it seems right to call attention to one or two features of the debate which have not received elsewhere the notice which they deserve.

That the *Commonitorium* lays down a broad line of demarcation between the Protestant and the Roman churches is an obvious overstatement. The Magdeburg Centuriators distinctly pronounced in its favour as a work of learning and acuteness; as a book which revealed and forcibly assailed the frauds of heretics, supplied a remedy and antidote against their poisons, set forth a weighty doctrine and displayed a knowledge of antiquity with skill and clearness in its treatment of Holy Scripture. The praise given by Casaubon to the principles of the English Reformation, the challenge of Jewel, and a large consensus of 17th-cent. divines, all rest, more or less explicitly, upon the famous dictum of Vincent—which, indeed, derives considerable support from certain portions of the Prayer-Book, Articles, and Canons.

It is, of course, equally true that Roman Catholic divines, especially at the epoch of the Reformation and long after, also professed to take their stand upon the principles asserted in the *Commonitorium*. There is no reason to doubt their sincerity in so acting. They introduce a new element into the discussion—namely, the authority claimed for the Roman see. The author appears to assume that this authority will always be manifested on the side of his great maxim of the "quod semper, quod ubique, quad ab omnibus," and makes no provision for the possibility of a divergence between the teaching of Rome and that of antiquity. Secondly, while the language concerning Nestorius and his opponent Cyril is clear and emphatic, there does seem to be a certain degree of reticence about some of the opponents of Augustine, *e.g.* Julian. The name of Augustine is not even mentioned, and though this is equally true of Jerome and Chrysostom, there was no special reason to introduce their names, while the repeated mention of Pelagius would have rendered the introduction of that of his chief opponent only natural.

* "A richt goldin buke writtin in Latin about xi c ȝeris [years] passit and neulie translated in Scottis be Niniane Winzet a catholik Preist." (Original title.)

were not in a position to judge the evidence on behalf of this and that portion of medieval doctrine and practice, and they appealed with confidence to such stores of learning as lay open to them. A day came when this confidence was rudely shaken. The Benedictine editions of the works of the Fathers appeared, with honest and discriminating criticism applied to their writings. Not only was it seen that a considerable portion of their works, long accepted as genuine and authentic, was in reality spurious, but also that while distinctively Roman tenets and practices received much support from the sermons and treatises relegated into the appendix of each volume, the case was widely different when reference was made to genuine Patristic remains. A new school of Roman Catholic divines arose, of whom Father Petau (Petavius) may perhaps be considered the earliest, as he is certainly among the greatest. The process of development in the church of Rome has widened the breach between her teaching and the principles of Vincent of Lerins. The church which set forth the doctrine of the Immaculate Conception of the Virgin Mother, not merely as a lawful opinion but as a dogma, has broken with the maxim, "Quod semper, quod ubique, quod ab omnibus." A new ed. for academical use was ed. by Jülicher, *Sammlung . . . Quellenschrifter* (Freiburg i. Br. 1895). [J.G.C.]

Vitalius (*Vitalis*), bp. of the Apollinarian congregation at Antioch. Vitalius was a man of high character, brought up in the orthodox faith at Antioch, and ordained presbyter by Meletius (Theod. *H. E.* v. 4; Soz. *H. E.* vi. 25). Jealousy of his fellow-presbyter Flavian caused a breach between him and his bishop, deprived of whose guidance Vitalius fell under the influence of Apollinaris and embraced his theological system. Tidings of his unsoundness having reached Rome, Vitalius made a journey thither in 375 to clear himself before pope Damasus, and to be received by him into communion. By the use of equivocal terms he convinced Damasus of his orthodoxy. Damasus did not, however, receive him into communion, but sent Vitalius back to Antioch with a letter to Paulinus, whom, during the Meletian schism, Rome and the West recognized as the orthodox and canonical bishop of that see, remitting the whole matter to his decision. Shortly after Vitalius had left Rome Damasus despatched a second letter to Paulinus, containing a profession of faith, which, without naming Apollinaris, condemned his doctrines, desiring Paulinus to require signature to it as the terms of admission to communion (Labbe, ii. 900 seq.; Theod. *H. E.* v. 11). Vitalius refused, and the breach between him and Paulinus became complete. Apollinaris ordained Vitalius bishop of his schismatical church, his holiness of life and pastoral zeal gathering a large number of followers, the successors of whom were still at Antioch under the name of Vitalians when Sozomen wrote (Soz. *H. E.* vi. 25). The unsoundness of Vitalius on the point on which Apollinaris diverged from the orthodox faith did not prevent his receiving much esteem and affection from leaders on the orthodox side, with whom, this one point excepted, he completely agreed. It must have been very shortly after Vitalius's return to Antioch that Epiphanius, urged thereto by Basil (Bas. *Ep.* 258 [325]), visited Antioch to try to heal the differences then rending that church. There he met "Vitalius the bishop," of whom he speaks in the highest terms. He earnestly besought him to reunite himself to the Catholic church. Finding that the misunderstanding was chiefly a personal one between him and Paulinus, each charging the other with unsoundness in the faith, Epiphanius invited both to a conference. At first Vitalius's language appeared perfectly orthodox. He acknowledged as fully as Paulinus that Christ was perfect man with a human body and soul (ψυχή); but when pressed as to whether He also had a human mind (νοῦς), he said that His divinity was to Him in its place. Neither party could persuade the other, and Epiphanius had to give up the hopeless attempt (Epiph. lxxvii. cc. 20-23). [DIMOERITAE.] The schism of Vitalius added a third or, counting the Arians, a fourth church at Antioch, each denouncing the others. Meletius, Paulinus, and Vitalius each claimed to be the orthodox bishop. The perplexity created is graphically described by Jerome to pope Damasus (Hieron. *Epp.* 57, 58). Tillem. *Mém. eccl.* vii. 617-622; Dorner, *Person of Christ*, div. I, vol. ii. pp. 386 ff., Clark's trans. [E.V].

Vitus (1) (*Guy*), St., a youthful martyr in Diocletian's persecution; the son of a pagan gentleman in Sicily, but secretly trained in Christianity by his nurse Crescentia and her husband Modestus. After the boy had encountered much cruel suffering, they succeeded in carrying him over to Italy, where all three fell victims, either in Lucania or at Rome (Boll. *Acta SS.* 15 Jun. iii. 491, ed. 1867). He is invoked against sudden death and hydrophobia (*ib.* App. p. 21 *), and against prolonged sleep and the complaint known as the chorea or dance of St. Vitus (Guérin, *Les Pet. Boll.* vii. 30). He is also, says Guérin, the patron of comedians and dancers. Two German medical writers, Gregory Horst and John Juncker, of the 17th and 18th cents. respectively, relate how the malady came to take his name (see Rees's *Encyclopedia*, *s.v.* "Chorea"). There sprang up, they say, in Germany in the 17th cent., a superstitious belief that by presenting gifts to the image of St. Vitus, and dancing before it day and night on his festival, people ensured themselves good health through the year. The saint's two chapels at Ulm and Ravensberg became more especially noted for the annual resort of these dancing fanatics. [C.H.]

Volusianus (1), **C. Vibius Afinius Gallus Veldumnianus,** joint emperor with his father Gallus, A.D. 251-254. At the end of 251 Gallus was proclaimed emperor after the defeat and death of Decius, which he is said to have caused by his treachery. He associated Volusian with himself in the empire, and, after making peace with the Goths on the shameful terms of allowing them to keep their prisoners and paying them tribute, the emperors proceeded to Rome. Their short reign was marked by the dreadful pestilence which began in Ethiopia and spread over the whole Roman world, and in which Hostilianus, the son of Decius, who had been associated with the Galli in the empire, died. Their numerous medals, bearing representations of Apollo and Juno, the deities of the sun and the air (Eckhel, vii. 357), support the statement of St. Cyprian (*Ep.* 55 in Migne, *Patr. Lat.* iii. 805), that they issued an edict, ordering sacrifices to be offered everywhere to appease the wrath of the gods. By refusing to obey the Christians aroused the hatred of the populace. In Africa the cry of "Cyprianum ad leonem" was again raised, and the outbreak of a persecution worse than that of Decius was daily feared (*Ep.* 54 in *ib.* 855, 861). Fortunately these fears were not realized. The only overt acts of persecution we certainly know of were confined to Rome. The outbreak was sudden (*Ep.* 58 in *ib.* 274), and Cornelius, bp. of Rome, was specially singled out for attack. His flock rallied bravely round him, and some who had fallen away in the Decian persecution distinguished themselves by their firmness (*Ep.* 37 in *ib.* 832). He with some of them was banished to Centum Cellae, where he died, probably a natural death, June 253 (see Lipsius, *Chron. der röm. Bisch.* 207). His successor Lucius was apparently elected in exile but soon allowed to return, the persecution ceasing, probably owing to the outbreak of civil war. There is no clear proof of any severer punishment than exile in this persecution. This is the worst mentioned by the contemporary St. Cyprian and St. Dionysius of Alexandria (in Eus. *H. E.* vii. 1). In the summer of 253 Aemilianus was proclaimed emperor by his soldiers, and *c.* Feb. 254 Gallus and Volusianus were murdered by their troops at Torni (Zos. i. 23-28; Zon. xii. 21). [F.D.]

X

Xystus. [SIXTUS II.]

Z

Zeno (16), emperor of the East A.D. 474-491, is famous in church history for the publication of the HENOTICON and for his active part in the prolonged disputes about Timotheus Aelurus, Timotheus Salofaciolus, Peter Mongus, and Peter the Fuller. Pope SIMPLICIUS and ACACIUS used him very effectually against their opponents. For a full analysis of the letters of popes Simplicius and Felix III. to him see Ceillier, t. x. pp. 410-420. [G.T.S.]

Zephyrinus, bp. of Rome after Victor, under the emperors Septimius Severus and Caracalla. Lipsius concludes his episcopate to have been either 18 or 19 years, from 198 or 199 to 217. His reign was marked by serious disturbance at Rome owing to doctrinal controversies and consequent schism. Zephyrinus seems to have been of no sufficient mark to take a personal lead, but to have been under the guidance of Callistus, a man of more practical ability who succeeded him as pope. This Callistus and his learned opponent Hippolytus appear to have been the leading spirits of the time at Rome.

The two notable heresies of the time were Montanism and Monarchianism. The see of Rome, when occupied by Zephyrinus, declared against Montanism (Eus. *H. E.* ii. 25; iii. 28, 31; vi. 20). [CAIUS.] Thus Zephrinus, though no action of his in the matter is recorded, may certainly be concluded to have been no favourer of the Montanists. But neither he nor Callistus, who succeeded him, is free from the imputation of having countenanced one school of the Monarchians, that which Praxeas had introduced into Rome. Montanism and Monarchianism represented two opposite tendencies. The former was the product of emotional enthusiasm, the latter of intellectual speculation grounded on the difficulty of comprehending the mystery of the Godhead in Christ. Those called by the general name of Monarchians, though differing widely in their views, agreed in denying a divine personality in Christ distinct from that of the Father, being jealous for the Unity, and what was called the *Monarchy* of God. One school was also called Patripassian, because its position was held to imply that in the sufferings of Christ the Father suffered. "They taught that the one Godhead, not one Person thereof only, had become incarnate, the terms Father and Son with them denoting only the distinction between God in His Eternal Being, and God as manifested in Christ. Such views were obviously inconsistent with orthodox Trinitarian doctrine, and their outcome was the Sabellian heresy. Praxeas appears to have been the first to introduce this form of heresy at Rome, and, if Tertullian is to be believed, the popes of the time supported Praxeas and his doctrine rather than otherwise. In addition to this testimony of Tertullian (whose treatise against Praxeas, written in the time of Zephyrinus, has been supposed, not without reason, to have been directed against the reigning pope as much as against the original heresiarch) we have that of the *Refutation of all Heresies*, attributed to HIPPOLYTUS, a learned writer of great note in his day, whose real ecclesiastical position is still open to discussion. He probably was bishop over a community at Rome which claimed to be the true church, out of communion with the pope, after the accession of Callistus, and possibly also under Zephyrinus.

Callistus, in the time of pope Victor, had been residing under suspicion at Antium. Zephyrinus, the successor of Victor, seems to have had no misgivings about him, recalled him to Rome, gave him some position of authority over the clergy, and "set him over the cemetery." Zephyrinus is described as an unlearned and ignorant man, entirely managed by Callistus, who induced him, for his own purposes, to declare generally for, but sometimes against, the Patripassians. The picture of the Roman church during the episcopate of Zephyrinus, as given in the *Refutation* of Hippolytus, discloses a state of discord and disruption not recorded by the historians. The picture, indeed, may be somewhat overcoloured under the influence of *odium theologicum*, and Callistus may not be the unprincipled adventurer, or Zephyrinus altogether the greedy and ignorant tool, that the writer describes. Dr. Döllinger (*Hippolyt. und Callist.*), who attributes the whole work to Hippolytus, takes this view. He defends Callistus against the libel on his character, which, however, he allows may have had some ground, but acquits Hippolytus of wilful misrepresentation, supposing him to have been partly misled by false reports and partly by prejudice, being himself a strict maintainer of ancient discipline, while Callistus was a liberal. It is difficult, however, to acquit the writer of deliberate and malignant slander unless the picture given of the popes was mainly a true one. There remains the idea of Dr. Newman, that "the libellous matter" in the *Elenchus* of Hippolytus was not his; but for this there is no foundation beyond the supposed difficulty of believing it so. If Hippolytus wrote it, it is to be remembered that he was undoubtedly a divine of greater learning and repute than his rivals, and that he seems to have left a name without reproach behind him. All three (like some others who were bitterly at variance during life) are now together in the Calendar of Saints.

Zephyrinus is further accused of undue laxity in matters of discipline. Our informant, Tertullian, writing in his time, speaks indignantly of a papal edict allowing admission of adulterers, after penance, to communion.

There was yet another school of Monarchians at Rome in the time of Zephyrinus, adding to the discord. Its teacher, Theodotus the banker, who held that Christ, though conceived by the Holy Ghost, was a mere man, and even inferior to Melchizedek, had his sect apart and out of communion with the church (Eus. *H. E.* v. 28; Tertull. *de Praescript.*). Eusebius (*l.c.*), quoting from an unnamed writer of the time, tells a story of Natalius, a confessor for the faith, having been persuaded by Theodotus and his colleague Asclepiodotus to be made bishop of their sect, of his having subsequently thrown himself in sackcloth and ashes with many tears at the feet of Zephyrinus, and been thereupon received into communion. Another of the same school, Artemon or Artemas, taught at Rome under Zephyrinus, and apart from his communion. He alleged that his own doctrine was that which the apostles had handed down, and which had been accepted by the Roman see till pope Victor's time, Zephyrinus having been the first to falsify the ancient creed. To this bold assertion his opponents replied that the fact of Victor having excommunicated Theodotus the currier, who was "the leader and father of this God-denying apostasy," was proof that Artemon's doctrine had not been formerly that of the Roman church (Eus. *H. E.* v. 28; cf. Epiphan. *Haer.* lxv. 1, 4; Theodoret, *Haer. Fab.* ii. 4; Phot. *Biblioth.* 48). During this episcopate the emperor Severus, A.D. 202, issued an edict which forbade any person to become a Jew or a Christian (Aelii Spartiani *Severus*, c. 17), which was probably interpreted so as to include existing converts; for in some parts it was followed by severe persecution, though there is no evidence that Zephyrinus or the Christians at Rome were then molested.

Some time during this episcopate Origen paid a short visit to Rome (Eus. *H. E.* vi. 14).

Zephyrinus is said (*Catal. Felic.*) to have

been buried "in cimiterio suo juxta cimiterium via Appia"—*i.e.* apparently not in "the cemetery" itself, over which Callistus had been set (*supra*), but in one of his own adjoining it. Lipsius supposes that the cemetery here meant was one which Zephyrinus had acquired, and that, Callistus having greatly added to it, the larger extension was afterwards called "the cemetery."

Zephyrinus is said in *Catal. Felic.* to have ordered that no cleric of any order should be ordained except in the presence of the clergy and faithful laity, and to have made a constitution, the purport of which, as it stands now in the texts of *Cat. Fel.*, it is not easy to understand, but which is given in the *Lib. Pontif.* (*Vit. S. Zephyr.*) as meaning that "the ministers should carry patens of glass in the church before the priests when the bishop celebrated masses, and that the priests should stand in attendance while masses were thus celebrated." There is other conclusive evidence that anciently, and to a date considerably later than that of Zephyrinus, glass patens as well as chalices were in use (see Labbe, p. 619—*nota* Binii (c.) *in Vit. Zephyr.*).

Together with most of the early popes, St. Zephyrinus is commemorated as a martyr; "Aug. 26. Romae S. Zephyrinus Papae et martyris" (*Martyr. Rom.*). There is no ground for supposing him to have been one. Two spurious epistles have been assigned to him (see Labbe). [J.B—Y.]

Zoaras (2), a turbulent Monophysite Syrian monk, a zealous adherent of Severus, associated with him and Peter of Apamea in the petitions of the orthodox clergy of Syria to the council of Constantinople under Mennas, A.D. 536, as leaders of the Monophysite heresy, and condemned with them by the synod. He became a Stylite. On being driven after several years from his pillar by the orthodox party (the "Synodites"), he started for Constantinople with ten of his monks to complain to Justinian, who hastily summoned a synod to give him audience. Zoaras uncompromisingly denounced "the accursed council of Chalcedon." This greatly irritated Justinian, who rebuked him for his presumption. Zoaras in no measured terms denounced the emperor for his support of heresy. A monastery in the suburb of Sykas was assigned as a residence to him and his followers by the emperor, where he lived quietly, exercising great liberality. The embassage of Agapetus, patriarch of Rome, with whom Zoaras held a very stormy encounter which resulted in the deposition of the patriarch Anthimus as a concealed Monophysite and the appointment of Mennas, A.D. 536, caused an outbreak of orthodox fury against Zoaras and his followers. In the various "libelli" presented to the synod under Mennas he and his heresy are denounced in no measured terms. He is described as a leader of the Acephali (Labbe, v. 108). He had been already condemned and excommunicated by Anthimus's predecessor Epiphanius (*ib.* 251). Mennas and his synod repeated the condemnation, and Justinian banished Zoaras from Constantinople and its vicinity, and from all the chief cities of the empire, charging him to live in solitude. According to the biography in Land, however, Justinian assigned him a monastery in Thrace, named Dokos, 30 miles away. Here Theodorus, the Monophysite patriarch of Alexandria, was living and propagating his doctrines. The length of Zoaras's residence here is uncertain. After a time he left Thrace, and after some years died, leaving as his successor his disciple the presbyter Ananias. Assem. *Bibl. Or.* ii. 58, 235; Land, *Anecdot. Syr.* ii. 12-22; Bar-heb. *Chron. Eccl.* ed. Abbeloos, i. pp. 206-208; Labbe, v. 108, 254, 267. [E.V.]

Zosimus (4), bp. of Rome after Innocent I., from Mar. 18, 417, to Dec. 25, 418, under Honorius as the Western and Theodosius II. as the Eastern emperor.

COELESTIUS, having been expelled from Constantinople by the patriarch Atticus, went to Rome, A.D. 417, hoping for the support of Zosimus, who had newly succeeded to the Roman see. Atticus had written letters about Coelestius to Asia, Carthage, and Thessalonica, but not to Rome; the churches of Rome and Constantinople not being then in full communion, owing to the name of John Chrysostom not having been restored to the diptychs of the latter church. On the other hand, Zosimus had before him, when Coelestius appealed to him, letters addressed by Pelagius to pope Innocent, but not received by him before his death. These letters had by no means satisfied St. Augustine (*de Pecc. Orig.* c. 17, 21; *De Grat.* x. 30, 31); but being expressed so as to evade the main points at issue, they may have seemed a sufficient exculpation to the pope, less sharpsighted than Augustine in detecting heresy, and apparently less ready to find fault with it in this case. Thus Zosimus was disposed to receive Coelestius with favour, while the independent action of the African bishops in the time of Innocent may have further inclined him to give the condemned persons a chance of clearing themselves. Coelestius appeared before him in the church of St. Clement, presented his defence, and was questioned as to whether he spoke sincerely and assented to what pope Innocent had written to the African bishops against the heresies imputed to him and Pelagius. This, Augustine tells us, he did, but refused to condemn the alleged errors imputed to him in the *libellus* of Paulinus (his original accuser at Carthage, A.D. 412), which had been sent to Rome. He further, according to Augustine, desired the pope's correction of any error of which he might through ignorance have been guilty (Aug. *de Pecc. Orig.* c. 607). Zosimus thereupon took up his cause, as that of one unfairly and improperly condemned. He wrote to this effect to Aurelius and the African bishops, desiring them either to send persons to Rome to convict the accused of heresy or to hold him innocent, and inveighing against the two Gallican bishops, Heros and Lazarus, who had been the accusers of Coelestius. Zosimus wrote a second time to Aurelius and the Africans, having meanwhile received a letter in favour of Pelagius from Praylius, bp. of Jerusalem, and others from Pelagius himself. These last had entirely satisfied him of the writer's orthodoxy; they had been publicly read at Rome, and received (says Zosimus) with universal joy; and Zosimus wrote again to Carthage, declaring Pelagius and Coelestius to have fully vindicated themselves against the calumnious accusations of those "whirlwinds and storms of the church," Heros and Lazarus; to have been condemned by unjust judges; and to be still in the church's communion. He sent with his letter copies of those which he had received from Pelagius.

By the same messenger Zosimus summoned Paulinus, the original accuser of Coelestius, to Rome. Coelestius had retorted on Paulinus the charge of heresy, and neither the latter nor any other accusers had come to Rome to prove their charges, and now Paulinus respectfully refused to go, saying there was no need. He assumes in his extant reply that the pope's verdict had already been on his side, in that Coelestius had been called upon at Rome, however in vain, to condemn the heresies which he, Paulinus, had charged him with. Aurelius also, and the other African bishops, remained resolute. Several letters, no longer extant, appear to have passed between them and Zosimus, alluded to by Augustine (*contra Duas Ep. Pelag.* lib. ii. c. 3), and by Zosimus himself. Early in 418 they held a council of 214 bishops at Carthage, which confirmed their condemnation of Pelagius and Coelestius, and declared, with regard to Rome, that they must hold the verdict of Innocent against the heresiarchs to be still in force, unless the latter should recant. The decrees of this council were sent to Zosimus; and he, in his extant reply, dated Mar. 21, 418, begins by a lengthy assertion of the authority of the Roman see inherited from St. Peter, which was such, he says, that none might dare to dispute its judgment. Still, he declares himself willing to consult his brethren, though not as being ignorant of what ought to be done or requiring their concurrence.

Zosimus is further memorable for his adjudication on the question of the jurisdiction of the see of Arles in Gaul, when some of the Gallic bishops were as little ready as the Africans to submit to his authority. Patroclus had been elected and ordained metropolitan of Arles, A.D. 412, on the expulsion by the people of the former metropolitan, Heros—the Gallican bishop, above named, who subsequently, with Lazarus, accused Pelagius of heresy in Palestine and Africa. There had been a long rivalry and struggle for jurisdiction between the two ancient sees of Arles and Vienne. A recent synod at Turin had decided against the claim of Arles to general jurisdiction over other provinces. Consequently other metropolitans—Simplicius of Vienne, Hilarius of Narbonne, and Proculus of Marseilles—had claimed the right of ordaining bishops in their respective provinces; and, notably, Proculus, acting on powers assigned him by the Turin synod as metropolitan of Narbonensis Secunda, had ordained Lazarus (the friend and associate of Heros) to the see of Aquae Sextiae (Aix). Patroclus appealed to Zosimus (A.D. 417), who at once wrote to the bishops of Gaul, to the Spanish bishops, and to Aurelius of Carthage and the rest of the African bishops, asserting the authority of the bishop of Arles over the provinces of Vienne and Narbonensis Prima and Secunda, and declaring all who should ordain bishops, or be ordained, within those provinces without his concurrence, to be degraded from the priesthood. He required that ecclesiastics of all orders from any part of Gaul whatever, proceeding to Rome, or to any other part of the world, should not be received without letters commendatory (*firmatae*) from the metropolitan of Arles. This last privilege he rests, not on ancient right, but on the personal merits of Patroclus. The jurisdiction of Arles over the above-named provinces he rests on ancient right, derived from Trophimus having been sent from Rome as first bishop of the see, and all Gaul having received the stream of faith from that fountain. Gregory of Tours (*Hist. Franc.* i. 28), referring to *Passio S. Saturnini Episc. Tolos.*, speaks of seven missionary bishops, including Trophimus, who founded the see of Arles, having been sent from Rome to Gaul, "Decio et Grato consulibus," *i.e.* A.D. 250. But the see of Arles must have existed before then, since it appears from Cyprian (*Ep.* vi. 7) that in 254 Marcion had long been bishop of it. Possibly some Trophimus of an earlier date had been sent from Rome to Arles; but if so, nothing is known about him.

Zosimus wrote also to the bishops of the provinces Viennensis and Narbonensis Secunda, disallowing the independent authority conceded to the metropolitans of those provinces by the Turin synod; to Hilarius of Narbonne, the metropolitan of Narbonensis Prima, forbidding him to ordain bishops independently of Arles, declaring all whom he should so ordain excommunicate, and threatening him with the same sentence; and also to Patroclus, confirming to him the alleged ancient rights of his see, together with the privilege, above mentioned, of alone giving *firmatae* to ecclesiastics from all parts of Gaul. Simplicius of Vienne so far deferred to the pope's authority as to send a legate to him; and Zosimus, writing to him on Oct. 1, 417, allowed him, for the sake of peace, to go on for the present ordaining bishops in the neighbouring cities of the province in accordance with the order of the Turin synod. No such deference to Rome was shewn by Proculus of Marseilles, who continued to ordain, though the pope had pronounced his deposition. Tumults ensued at Marseilles, where there seem to have been two parties. Consequently in 418 Zosimus wrote to the clergy and people there, warning them to oppose the attempts of Proculus, and to submit to Patroclus; and to Patroclus himself, enjoining him to assert his authority. Notwithstanding this, Proculus maintained his position as bp. of Marseilles and metropolitan of Narbonensis Secunda. The jurisdiction of Arles was long a bone of contention in Gaul. Zosimus died soon after writing the letters last mentioned, and was buried, according to the *Lib. Pontif.*, on Dec. 26, "via Tiburtina juxta corpus beati Laurentii martyris."

The main authorities for his life are his own letters and other documents to be found in Baronius and Labbe, the works of Augustine, and Prosper (*Chron.*). [J.B—Y.]

Zosimus (5), a Byzantine historian worthy of particular attention, not only for his general merits as an historian, but because, as a heathen bitterly opposed to Christianity, he gives the heathen view of the causes of the decline and fall of the Roman empire. There is considerable uncertainty as to when he flourished. The middle of the 5th cent. is a probable date. Zosimus was not a polytheist, for in one passage at least of his history, when referring to an oracle which had predicted the greatness of Old Byzantium, he speaks of the Deity in highly worthy terms (ii. 37). He paid honour, however, to the heathen religious rites, as having come down from former generations (v. 23), complaining of the attempts of various emperors to extinguish them (ii. 29; iv. 59), lamenting that the oracles of the gods were no longer listened to (i. 57), and finding in the abandonment of the old religion one main cause of the decline of the empire (iv. 59). He ridicules Christianity as an unreasonable conglomerate, *ἄλογος συγκατάθεσις* (iv. 59), sneers at Christian soldiers as only able to pray (iii. 2; iv. 23), and welcomes any opportunity of giving the most false representations of the Christian faith (ii. 29; iv. 59). An historian of such a spirit can hardly be relied on for an account of the events of a time when the old superstitions he venerated were compelled to yield to the advancing power of a religion he abhorred; and even his admirers are constrained to admit that he is not to be trusted where his religious prejudices come into play. Reitemeier, who defends him on the whole, allows that he was too partial to the heathen, too unjust to Christians (*Disquis.* p. 26); and Gibbon speaks of his "passion and prejudice," "ignorant and malicious suggestions," and "malcontent insinuations" (cc. xvii., xx.). His accounts of the conversion of Constantine, and of the character of Theodosius (ii. 29; iv. 26-33) suffer from this prejudice. To the former, as well as to many other of his most scandalous charges against that emperor, Evagrius replied in fierce language, addressing him as a "wicked spirit and fiend of hell" (iii. 41); and for the latter he has been condemned by Gibbon in hardly less emphatic language (c. xxvii.). De Broglie refers, for a full refutation of the story regarding the conversion of Constantine, to the *Mém. de l'Acad. des Inscrip.* 49, p. 470, etc.

The inference must not, however, be hastily drawn that Zosimus is an historian unworthy of our regard. On the contrary, he may be justly described as one of the best historians of these early centuries. Even his views on church matters are highly interesting, as shewing how they were regarded by the more intelligent heathen; nor are they always wanting in truth. In estimating, too, his value as an historian, it must be remembered that he treats more largely of civil affairs than others had done, and we owe to him many facts connected with the condition of the military, their degeneracy, exactions, and dissoluteness, which contributed in no slight degree to the fall of the empire.

There seems indeed no sufficient ground to ascribe intentional bad faith to his history. That he was mistaken in many of his conclusions, and especially in those relating to the influence of Christianity, is unquestionable. That he occasionally gave too easy credence to unfounded statements is not less so; but it has never been proved that he wilfully perverted facts to establish any theory.

He was not in all respects an original historian. His *History* closes with A.D. 410. Either he had been hindered by death from prosecuting it further or some portions have been lost. He is thus occupied throughout with events before his own day, and in relating these he seems rather to epitomize works of predecessors than to write original narrative. Reitemeier finds that in the first part of his *History* he followed the *Synopsis* of Denippus, in the middle and larger part the *Chronicon* of Eunapius, and in the last part the *Silva* of Olympiodorus (*Disquis.* p. 35). Photius charges him with extensive copying of Eunapius (cf. Fabric. vi. p. 232, note). It seems to have been his admiration of Polybius that led him to write. That historian had described the rise of the Roman empire, and Zosimus, beholding everywhere around him its majestic ruins, would describe its fall. Nor will he merely describe the phenomena: he proposes also to investigate their causes. He begins, accordingly, with the reign of Augustus, and, passing hastily over the time till the accession of Constantine, he occupies himself mainly with the reigns of that emperor and his successors. He sets forth as the causes of the fall of the Roman empire: the change of government to its imperial form (i. 5); the removal of the soldiery into cities where they were debased by luxury and vice (ii. 34); the iniquitous exactions of successive emperors (ii. 38; iv. 28, 29, 41; v. 12); above all, the casting aside of the old religion, and the neglect of the responses of the oracles (i. 57). There can be little doubt that he regarded this last as the most important, so frequently does he allude to it (ii. 7; iv. 37, 59; v. 38, etc.). He expresses what was often thought and said at the time, and to the view thus taken we owe, in no small degree, St. Augustine's immortal work, *de Civitate Dei.*

The style of the *History* of Zosimus has been praised by Photius as concise, perspicuous, pure, and, though not adorned by many figures, yet not devoid of sweetness (*Cod.* 98). (Cf. Heyne, *Corp. Ser. H. B.*, *Zosimus*, p. 16.) These commendations are deserved. Zosimus is generally free from the ambitious periods of most historians of his age. His narrative is circumstantial, but clear; his language well chosen, and often very nervous and antithetical. He was not free from superstition; and the fact that an historian, generally so calm and so far removed from the credulity of his day, should have put his faith in oracles and recorded without hesitation appearances of Minerva and Achilles to Alaric, and various other miracles (see them in Fabric. vi. p. 610), shews how deep-seated such ideas were in the minds of his contemporaries, and may help to prove that the Christian belief in visions and miracles then prevailing was not inconsistent with sobriety of judgment and sound principles of criticism in other matters.

The *History* of Zosimus may be consulted for the lives and actions of the emperors between Augustus and A.D. 410, more especially for those of Constantine, Constantius, Theodosius the elder, Honorius, and Arcadius;

for accounts of the Huns, Alamanni, Scythians, Goths, and minor barbarous tribes; the war in Africa in the time of Honorius, the campaign of Alaric in Italy, and the taking of Rome; for the right of asylum in Christian churches, and the changes introduced into the army; for an important description of Byzantium, old and new, and of Britain; and finally, for an account of the secular games to which, celebrated only once in 110 years, the people were summoned with the stirring yet solemn cry, "Quos nec spectavit quisquam nec spectaturus est." Some of the ancient oracles are preserved by him.

The best ed. is by Reitemeier, in Gk. and Lat., with Heyne's notes (Leipz. 1784); Bekker's ed. (Bonn, 1837) has Reitemeier's notes. [W.M.]